Encyclopædia
of
Religion and Ethics

Encyclopædia of Religion and Ethics

EDITED BY

JAMES HASTINGS

WITH THE ASSISTANCE OF

JOHN A. SELBIE

AND OTHER SCHOLARS

VOLUME I

A—ART

T&T CLARK
EDINBURGH

T&T CLARK LTD
59 GEORGE STREET
EDINBURGH EH2 2LQ
SCOTLAND

Edition Completed and Corrected Editions 1926–1976
Reprinted 1994

ISBN 0 567 06501 4

British Library Cataloguing-in-Publication Data
A catalogue record for this book is available from the British Library

Printed and bound in Great Britain by Antony Rowe Ltd, Wiltshire

PREFACE

THERE is at the present time an unusual demand for works of reference. It may be due partly to a higher general standard of education, increasing the number of readers, and compelling teachers, whether they are writers or speakers, to 'verify their references.' But it may be due also to the great increase of knowledge in our time. We must possess ourselves of dictionaries and encyclopædias, because it is not possible otherwise to have at our command the vast stores of learning which have accumulated.

But the enormous increase of knowledge in our time has not only created a demand for general works of reference; it has also made known the necessity for dictionaries or encyclopædias of a more special character. Musicians have found the need of a Dictionary of Music, painters of Painting, engineers of Engineering, and they have had their wants supplied. The present work is an attempt to meet the necessity for an Encyclopædia of Religion and Ethics.

Scope of the Encyclopædia.

The words 'Religion' and 'Ethics' are both used in their most comprehensive meaning, as the contents of this volume will show. The Encyclopædia will contain articles on all the Religions of the world and on all the great systems of Ethics. It will aim, further, at containing articles on every religious belief or custom, and on every ethical movement, every philosophical idea, every moral practice. Such persons and places as are famous in the history of religion and morals will be included. The Encyclopædia will thus embrace the whole range of Theology and Philosophy, together with the relevant portions of Anthropology, Mythology, Folklore, Biology, Psychology, Economics, and Sociology. It is a wide field, but its limits are clearly defined. Only once or twice throughout the course of this volume has the question been raised whether a particular topic should be included or not.

Subjects and Authors.

Very great care has been taken to make the list of subjects complete, and to assign each subject to the right author. If mistakes have been made they will be pointed out by readers and reviewers; and the Editor will welcome every suggestion that is offered towards the improvement of the succeeding volumes. In order to avoid overlapping, and yet to have every topic treated with sufficient fulness, the method has occasionally been adopted of describing a subject comprehensively in one general article, and then taking one or more particular topics embraced by the general article and dealing with them separately and more fully. Thus there will be a general sketch of the Socialistic Communities of America, out of which the Amana Community has been selected to be separately and fully described. Again, there are articles on Aphrodisia and Apollonia in addition to the general article on Greek Festivals; and in the second volume there will be an article on the Arval Brothers, while the Roman Priesthood will be treated comprehensively afterwards.

It is not necessary to draw attention here to the series of comparative articles on such topics as Adoption, Adultery, Ages of the World, Altar, Ancestor-Worship, Anointing, Architecture, and Art.

The important subject of cross-references is referred to on another page.

Editors and Assistants.

How can due acknowledgment be made to all those who have been counsellors and colleagues, and have assisted so willingly to make the Encyclopædia of Religion and Ethics an authoritative work of reference throughout the whole of its great and difficult field of study? Professor A. S. Geden, Dr. Louis H. Gray, and Professor D. B. Macdonald have worked over every article from the beginning. Next to them must come Principal Iverach, Canon J. A. MacCulloch, Mr. Crooke, Professor Rhys Davids, Dr. Grierson, and Sir C. J. Lyall. Then follow Professor Wenley, Dr. J. G. Frazer, Mr. Sidney Hartland, Dr. Keane, Mr. W. H. Holmes, Mr. J. Mooney, Mr. E. E. Sikes, Professor Riess, Professor Poussin, Professor Anesaki, Dr. Aston, Mr. Cornaby, Professor Macdonell, Professor Lloyd, Mr. Nutt, Mr. Watson, Mr. Gait, Principal Fairbairn, Professor Jacobi, Professor Takakusu, Professor Bonet-Maury, Colonel Sir R. C. Temple, Bart., Professor Nöldeke, Dr. Moulton, Dr. Macpherson, Baron Friedrich von Hügel, Professor Lawlor, Professor Schaff, Abbot E. C. Butler, Professor Sanday, Professor Hillebrandt, Professor Seth, Professor Sorley, Professor Woodhouse, Principal Stewart, Professor Swete, and Colonel Waddell. These all have suggested authors, read manuscripts, corrected proofs, or in some other way taken a helpful interest in the work. And the list could be doubled without exhausting their number.

Acknowledgment is due also to the Right Hon. the Secretary of State for India and the Librarian of the India Office; to Sir A. H. L. Fraser, K.C.S.I., LL.D., Lieutenant-Governor of Bengal; to the Right Hon. Sir Wilfrid Laurier, G.C.M.G., Premier of Canada; and to the Chief of the Bureau of Ethnology of the Smithsonian Institution, Washington, for the use of valuable books.

After six years' exacting labour this first volume goes forth in the earnest hope that it will be found worthy of a place among the rapidly increasing number of books devoted to the study of Religion and Ethics, and that it will help forward that study along the right lines. The work will consist of about ten volumes.

AUTHORS OF ARTICLES IN THIS VOLUME

ABRAHAMS (ISRAEL), M.A. (Lond. and Camb.).
Reader in Talmudic and Rabbinic Literature in the University of Cambridge; formerly Senior Tutor in the Jews' College, London.
Abravanel, Acosta, Adultery (Jewish), **Architecture** (Jewish), **Art** (Jewish).

ACHELIS (HANS), D.Theol., D.Phil.
Professor der Theologie, Halle (a. Saale).
Agapetæ.

ADLER (E. N.), M.A., M.R.A.S.
Member of the Council of the Jewish Historical Society; Corresponding Member of the Royal Academy of History of Spain and of the Jewish Historical Society of America; author of *Jews in Many Lands*.
Ages of the World (Jewish), **Akiba ben Joseph.**

ALEXANDER (HARTLEY BURR), Ph.D.
Professor of Philosophy in the University of Nebraska; Member of the American Philosophical Association.
Aboulia.

ANANIKIAN (MARDIROS H.), B.D., S.T.M.
Assistant Librarian and Instructor in Oriental Languages in Hartford Theological Seminary.
Armenia (Zoroastrian).

APACHE (ANTONIO).
Of the Fields Columbian Museum, Chicago.
Apaches.

ARSDALE (FRANK DAWES VAN), Newark, New Jersey.
Angel Dancers.

ASTON (WILLIAM GEORGE), M.A., D.Lit., C.M.G.
Formerly Japanese Secretary of H.M. Legation, Tokyo; author of *History of Japanese Literature*, *Shinto*.
Abandonment and Exposure (Japanese), **Adoption** (Japanese), **Altar** (Japanese), **Architecture** (Shinto), **Art** (Shinto).

BAILLIE (JAMES BLACK), M.A. (Edin. and Camb.), D.Phil. (Edin.).
Professor of Moral Philosophy in the University of Aberdeen.
Absolute, Absolutism.

BALDWIN (JAMES MARK), M.A., Ph.D., D.Sc., LL.D.
Professor of Philosophy and Psychology in Johns Hopkins University; author of *Handbook of Psychology*, *Thought and Things*; editor of the *Dictionary of Philosophy and Psychology*.
Accommodation, Affection, Alter.

BARKER (HENRY), M.A.
Lecturer in Moral Philosophy in the University of Edinburgh.
Act, Action.

BARNS (Rev. THOMAS), M.A.
Vicar of Hilderstone, Staffordshire.
Abbot of Unreason, Alchemy (European), **All Fools' Day.**

BARTON (GEORGE AARON), A.M., Ph.D.
Professor of Biblical Literature and Semitic Languages in Bryn Mawr College; author of *A Sketch of Semitic Origins*.
Altar (Semitic).

BATCHELOR (Rev. John).
Of the Church Missionary College, C.M.S. Mission, Sapporo, Hokkaido, Japan; author of *The Ainu and their Folklore*.
Ainus.

BENNETT (Rev. WILLIAM HENRY), M.A. (Lond.), D.D. (Aber.), Litt.D. (Camb.).
Sometime Fellow of St. John's College, Cambridge; Professor of Old Testament Exegesis, Hackney College and New College, London; author of *The Post-Exilic Prophets*.
Adam.

BERCHEM (MAX VAN), D.Phil.
Correspondant de l'Institut de France.
Architecture (Muhammadan in Syria and Egypt).

BETHE (ERICH), D.Phil.
Professor der Klass. Philologie an der Universität zu Leipzig; Geheimer Hofrat.
Agraulids, Amphiaraus.

BEVERIDGE (HENRY), B.C.S. (retired).
Akbar.

BLAKISTON (Rev. HERBERT EDWARD DOUGLAS), D.D.
President of Trinity College, Oxford.
Æschylus.

BONET-MAURY (AMY-GASTON), Knight of Legion of Honour, D.D. (Paris, Glas., Aber.), LL.D. (St. And.).
Professeur honoraire de l'Université de Paris; Professeur titulaire à la Faculté libre de Théologie protestante de Paris; Membre correspondant de l'Institut de France.
Ages of the World (Christian).

BOUSSET (WILHELM), D.Theol.
Professor der Neutest. Exegese an der Universität zu Göttingen; author of *Antichrist*, *Religion des Judentums im NT Zeitalter*.
Antichrist.

BOX (Rev. GEORGE HERBERT), M.A.
Formerly Scholar of St. John's College, Oxford; sometime Hebrew Master at Merchant Taylors' School, London; Incumbent of Linton; joint author of *The Religion and Worship of the Synagogue*; Lecturer (1908–1909) in the Faculty of Theology, Oxford.
Adoption (Semitic).

BRABROOK (Sir EDWARD), C.B.
Of Lincoln's Inn Barrister-at-Law; Vice-President S.A., R.S.L., R.S.S., and R.A.I.; President of the Sociological Society and Child Study Society; Past President of the Economic and Anthropological Sections, British Association; Treasurer of the Royal Asiatic Institute; formerly Chief Registrar of Friendly Societies.
Arbitration.

BROWN (GERARD BALDWIN), M.A. (Oxon.).
Sometime Fellow of Brasenose College, Oxford; Professor of Fine Art in the University of Edinburgh; author of *The Fine Arts*.
Art (Celtic, Christian).

BURN (Rev. A. E.), M.A., D.D.
Rector and Rural Dean of Handsworth; Prebendary of Lichfield; Examining Chaplain to the Bishop of Lichfield; author of *An Introduction to the Creeds*.
Adoptianism.

BURNET (JOHN), M.A. (Oxon.), LL.D. (Edin.).
Professor of Greek in the United College of St. Salvator and St. Leonard, St. Andrews; late Fellow of Merton College, Oxford.
Academy.

CABATON (ANTOINE).
Professeur à l'École des Langues orientales vivantes, Paris; Ancien Membre de l'École Française de l'Extrême-Orient.
Annam.

CANNEY (MAURICE A.), M.A. (Oxon.).
Formerly Hebrew Master at Merchant Taylors' School, London.
Apollonius of Tyana.

CARRA DE VAUX (BON BERNARD).
Professeur à l'École libre des Hautes Études; Membre du Conseil de la Société Asiatique de Paris.
Abd Al-Qadir Al-Jilani, Alchemy (Muhammadan).

CARTER (JESSE BENEDICT), Ph.D. (Halle).
Director of the American School of Classical Studies in Rome.
Ancestor-Worship and Cult of the Dead (Roman).

CHADWICK (HECTOR MUNRO), M.A.
Fellow and Librarian of Clare College, Cambridge; author of *The Cult of Othin*.
Ancestor-Worship and Cult of the Dead (Teutonic).

CHAMBERLAIN (ALEXANDER FRANCIS), M.A. (Toronto), Ph.D. (Clark).
Assistant Professor of Anthropology, Clark University; Hon. Member of the American Folklore Society, of the American Anthropological Association, etc.; editor of the *Journal of American Folklore* (1900–1908); author of *The Child: A Study in the Evolution of Man*.
Aleuts.

CHAPMAN (Rev. JOHN), O.S.B.
Of Erdington Abbey.
Abbot (Christian).

CLARK (ARCHIBALD BROWN), M.A., F.S.S.
Lecturer on Economics in the University of Edinburgh.
Ability, Accumulation.

CLODD (EDWARD).
Corresponding Member of the Société d'Anthropologie de Paris, and Vice-President of the Folklore Society.
Abiogenesis.

COBB (Rev. W. F.), D.D.
Rector of the Church of St. Ethelburga the Virgin, London, E.C.
Abuse and Abusive Language.

COCKERELL (SYDNEY C.).
Director of the Fitzwilliam Museum, Cambridge.
Art in MSS (Christian).

COE (GEORGE ALBERT), Ph.D.
John Evans Professor of Moral and Intellectual Philosophy in Northwestern University; author of *The Spiritual Life: Studies in the Science of Religion, The Religion of a Mature Mind*.
Adolescence.

COOK (STANLEY ARTHUR), M.A.
Ex-Fellow and Lecturer in Hebrew and Syriac in Gonville and Caius College, Cambridge; author of *The Laws of Moses and the Code of Hammurabi*.
Adultery (Semitic).

COWAN (Rev. HENRY), M.A., D.D.
Professor of Church History in the University of Aberdeen; author of *Landmarks of Church History, Influence of the Scottish Church in Christendom* (Baird Lecture for 1895), and *John Knox* in Putnam's 'Heroes of the Reformation.'
Action Sermon.

CRAFER (Rev. THOMAS WILFRID), B.D.
Chaplain and Lecturer in Classics and Theology in Downing College, Director of Theological Studies at Fitzwilliam Hall, and Vicar of All Saints', Cambridge.
Apologetics.

CRAWLEY (Rev. ARTHUR ERNEST), M.A. (Camb.).
Headmaster of Derby School; Fellow of the Royal Anthropological Institute and the Sociological Society; author of *The Mystic Rose, The Tree of Life*.
Anointing (Introduction, Hindu).

CREIGHTON (JAMES EDWIN), B.A., Ph.D., LL.D.
Sage Professor of Logic and Metaphysics in Cornell University; editor of the *Philosophical Review*.
Abstraction.

CROOKE (WILLIAM), B.A.
Ex-Scholar of Trinity College, Dublin; Fellow of the Royal Anthropological Institute; Member of the Folklore and Hellenic Societies; late of the Bengal Civil Service.
Abor, Abu, Agaria, Aghori, Agra, Aheria, Ahir, Ahmadabad, Ajanta, Ajmer, Alaknanda, Allahabad, Amarkantak, Amarnath, Amber, Ancestor-Worship and Cult of the Dead (Introduction, Indian), **Arakh.**

CUMONT (FRANZ), D.Phil., LL.D. (Aber.)
Professeur à l'Université de Gand; Conservateur aux Musées royaux de Bruxelles; Correspondant de l'Académie Royale de Belgique et de l'Académie des Inscriptions de Paris; auteur de *Textes et monuments figurés relatifs aux mystères de Mithra*.
Anahita, Architecture (Mithraic), **Art** (Mithraic).

D'ALVIELLA (COUNT GOBLET), Ph.D., LL.D. (Glas. and Aber.).
Member and Secretary of the Belgian Senate; Professor at the University of Brussels; Commander of the Order of Léopold; author of *The Migration of Symbols.*
Animism.

DAVIDS (T. W. RHYS), LL.D., Ph.D.
Professor of Comparative Religion, Manchester; President of the Pāli Text Society; Fellow of the British Academy.
Abhayagiri, Adam's Peak, Adultery (Buddhist), **Agama, Ahimsa, Anagata Vamsa, Ananda, Anguttara Nikaya, Anuradhapura, Apadana, Arhat.**

DAVIDS (Mrs. RHYS), M.A., Manchester.
Abhidhamma.

DAVIDSON (JOHN), M.A., D.Sc.
Formerly Professor of Political Economy in the University of New Brunswick.
Adulteration.

DAVIDSON (WILLIAM LESLIE), M.A., LL.D.
Professor of Logic and Metaphysics in the University of Aberdeen; President of the Aberdeen Philosophical Society; author of *The Logic of Definition, Theism as Grounded in Human Nature, The Stoic Creed.*
Anger (Psychological and Ethical), **Appetite** (Psychological).

DILL (SAMUEL), M.A. (Oxon.), Litt.D. (Dublin), LL.D. (Edin. and St. And.).
Professor of Greek in Queen's College, Belfast; Hon. Fellow and sometime Fellow and Tutor of Corpus Christi College, Oxford; author of *Roman Society in the Last Century of the Western Empire, Roman Society from Nero to Marcus Aurelius.*
Alexander of Abonoteichos.

DOTTIN (GEORGES), Docteur ès Lettres.
Professeur de langue et littérature celtique à l'Université de Rennes.
Architecture (Celtic).

DUCKWORTH (W. LAURENCE H.), M.A., M.D., Sc.D.
Fellow of Jesus College, Cambridge; University Lecturer in Physical Anthropology; Senior Demonstrator of Anatomy.
Abnormalities (Biological).

DUKES (Rev. EDWIN J.).
Minister of St. Paul's Chapel, Kentish Town, London; formerly London Society Missionary in China; author of *Everyday Life in China.*
Agapemone.

DUTT (ROMESH C.), C.I.E.
Member of the Indian Civil Service (retired); Barrister-at-Law, Middle Temple; Fellow of the Royal Society of Literature for Great Britain and Ireland; Member of the Royal Asiatic Society; late Revenue Minister of Baroda State.
Adam's Bridge.

EDWARDS (EDWARD), B.A. (Wales and Cantab.), M.R.A.S.
Assistant in the Department of Oriental Printed Books and Manuscripts in the British Museum.
Altar (Persian).

EHRENREICH (PAUL), Dr. Med. and Phil.
Privatdozent an der Kgl. Universität, Berlin.
America (South).

FAIRBANKS (Rev. ARTHUR), Ph.D. (Freiburg i. B.).
Professor of Greek Archæology in the State University of Iowa, 1900–1906; in the University of Michigan, 1906–1907; Director of the Museum of Fine Arts, Boston, 1907.
Amazons.

FICK (Dr. RICHARD).
Oberbibliothekar an der königlichen Bibliothek, Berlin.
Adultery (Hindu).

FINDLAY (Rev. ADAM FYFE), M.A.
Minister of Erskine United Free Church, Arbroath.
Amusements.

FOAKES-JACKSON (FREDERICK JOHN), D.D.
Fellow of Jesus College, Cambridge, and Hon. Canon of Peterborough Cathedral; author of *The History of the Christian Church to A.D. 337, A Bible History of the Hebrews.*
Apostasy (Jewish and Christian), **Arianism.**

FOLEY (Rev. WILLIAM MALCOLM), B.D.
Rector of Tralee, Co. Kerry; Canon of St. Mary's Cathedral, Limerick; Examining Chaplain to the Bishop of Limerick; formerly Donnellan Lecturer (1892–93) in the University of Dublin.
Adultery (Christian).

FORTESCUE (Rev. ADRIAN), D.D. (Munich), Ph.D. (Vienna).
Roman Catholic Priest at Letchworth.
Apollinarism.

FRANKS (Rev. ROBERT SLEIGHTHOLME), M.A., B.Litt.
Theological Lecturer at the Friends' Settlement for Religious and Social Study, Woodbrooke, Birmingham.
Acceptilation, Adelard.

FULTON (Rev. W. WYLIE), B.D.
Minister of Battlefield Church, Glasgow.
Abraham-men.

GARDNER (ERNEST ARTHUR), M.A.
Yates Professor of Archæology in the University of London; late Director of the British School at Athens.
Ægis, Altar (Greek, Roman), **Art** (Greek and Roman).

GARVIE (Rev. ALFRED ERNEST), M.A. (Oxon.), D.D. (Glas.).
Principal of New College, London; author of *The Ritschlian Theology.*
Agnosticism.

GASKELL (CATHERINE JULIA).
Cambridge University Classical Tripos, Part I. (Class II.) and Part II. (Class I.).
Altar (Teutonic), **Art and Architecture** (Teutonic).

GEDEN (Rev. ALFRED S.), M.A., (Oxon.), D.D. (Aber.).
Professor of Old Testament Languages and Literature and of Comparative Religion at the Wesleyan College, Richmond; Honorary Life Governor of the British and Foreign Bible Society; author of *Studies in Comparative Religion, Studies in Eastern Religions.*
Aiyanar, Aranyakas.

GEFFCKEN (Dr. Johannes).
Ordentlicher Professor der Klass. Philologie an der Universität zu Rostock.
Allegory and Allegorical Interpretation.

GILES (PETER), M.A., LL.D. (Aber.).
Fellow and Lecturer of Emmanuel College, Cambridge; University Reader in Comparative Philology; author of *A Short Manual of Comparative Philology.*
Abandonment and Exposure (General), **Agriculture.**

GRAY (B. KIRKMAN).
Author of *A History of English Philanthropy.*
Agitation.

GRAY (LOUIS HERBERT), Ph.D.
Sometime Member of the Editorial Staff of the *New International Encyclopedia, Orientalische Bibliographie*, etc.
Abandonment and Exposure (American, Persian), **Abipones, Achæmenians, Afghanistan, Ages of the World** (Primitive), **Altar** (Introduction, African, American, Celtic, Polynesian), **Ancestor-Worship and Cult of the Dead** (Celtic, Polynesian, Tasmanian), **Architecture** (American), **Art** (American).

GRIERSON (GEORGE ABRAHAM), C.I.E., Ph.D. (Halle), D.Litt. (Dublin), I.C.S. (retired).
Hon. Member of the Asiatic Society of Bengal, of the Nāgarī Prachārinī Sabhā of Benares, and of the American Oriental Society; Foreign Associate Member of the Société Asiatique de Paris; Corresponding Member of the Königliche Gesellschaft der Wissenschaften zu Göttingen; Vice-President of the Royal Asiatic Society; Superintendent of the Linguistic Survey of India.
Alakhnamis.

GRIFFITH (FRANCIS LLEWELLYN), M.A., F.S.A.
Reader in Egyptology in the University of Oxford; editor of the Archæological Survey and the Archæological Reports of the Egypt Exploration Fund; Corresponding Member of the Royal Academy of Sciences at Berlin; Fellow of the Imperial German Archæological Institute; Foreign Associate of the Société Asiatique.
Adultery (Egyptian), **Ages of the World** (Egyptian), **Altar** (Egyptian).

DE GROOT (J. J. M.), D.Phil.
Professor of Chinese Language and Archæology in the University of Leiden; author of *The Religious Systems of China.*
Adoption (Chinese).

GURDON (Major P. R. T.), Indian Army.
Officiating Commissioner Assam Valley Districts; Hon. Director of Ethnography, Assam.
Ahoms.

HADDON (ALFRED CORT), M.A., Sc.D. (Cantab.), F.R.S., F.R.A.I.
University Lecturer in Ethnology, Cambridge and London; President of the Anthropological Section of the British Association in 1902; author of *Evolution in Art.*
Art (Primitive and Savage).

HAGAR (STANSBURY), B.A., LL.B.
Counselor at Law; Fellow of the American Association for the Advancement of Science, and the American Anthropological Association; Director of the Explorers' Club of New York; Executive Officer of the Departments of Ethnology and Astronomy in the Brooklyn Institute of Arts and Sciences.
Ancestor-Worship and Cult of the Dead (American).

HALL (FREDERICK WILLIAM), M.A.
Fellow and Tutor of St. John's College, Oxford.
Adultery (Greek, Roman).

HALL (H. R.), M.A., F.R.G.S.
Assistant in the Department of Egyptian and Assyrian Antiquities in the British Museum.
Ancestor-Worship and Cult of the Dead (Egyptian).

HARTLAND (EDWIN SIDNEY), F.S.A.
President of the Folklore Society, 1899; President of the Anthropological Section of the British Association, 1906; author of *The Legend of Perseus.*
Adoption (among lower races).

HEALD (Rev. J. M.).
Formerly Scholar of Trinity College, Cambridge, and Rector of Litcham in Norfolk.
Aquinas.

HIBBEN (JOHN GRIER), Ph.D., LL.D.
Stuart Professor of Logic in Princeton University; author of *Inductive Logic, The Problems of Philosophy.*
Accidentalism.

HIRN (YRJÖ), D.Phil.
Dozent in Ästhetik und neuere Literatur an der Universität Helsingfors, Finland.
Art (Origins).

HOERNLE (A. F. RUDOLF), C.I.E., Ph.D. (Tübingen), Hon. M.A. (Oxon.).
Late of the Indian Educational Service and Principal of the Calcutta Madrasah.
Ajivikas.

HOGARTH (DAVID GEORGE), M.A., F.S.A., F.R.G.S.
Fellow of Magdalen College, Oxford; Fellow of the British Academy; editor of *Authority and Archæology.*
Ægean Religion.

HOLBORN (J. B. STOUGHTON), M.A. (Oxon.), F.R.G.S.
University Extension Lecturer in Art and Literature to the Universities of Oxford, Cambridge, and London.
Architecture (Ægean, Christian, Greek, Roman).

HORN (EDWARD TRAILL), D.D., LL.D.
Pastor of Trinity Lutheran Church at Reading, Pennsylvania.
Adiaphorism, Arcani Disciplina.

HYAMSON (ALBERT MONTEFIORE).
Vice-President of the Union of Jewish Literary Societies; author of *A History of the Jews in England.*
Anglo-Israelism.

HYSLOP (JAMES HERVEY), Ph.D., LL.D.
Secretary of the American Society for Psychical Research; formerly Professor of Logic and Ethics in Columbia University.
Affirmation, Antipathy.

INGE (Rev. WILLIAM RALPH), D.D.
Lady Margaret Professor of Divinity in the University of Cambridge; author of *Faith and Knowledge.*
Alexandrian Theology.

IRONS (DAVID), M.A. (St. And.), Ph.D. (Cornell).
Formerly Associate-Professor of Bryn Mawr College; author of *The Psychology of Ethics.*
Admiration.

ITO (CHIUTA).
Professor in the University of Tokyo, Japan.
Architecture (Chinese).

IVERACH (Rev. JAMES), M.A., D.D.
Principal and Professor of New Testament Language and Literature in the United Free Church College, Aberdeen.
Altruism.

JACKSON (A. V. WILLIAMS), Litt.D., Ph.D., LL.D.
Professor of Indo-Iranian Languages in Columbia University, New York.
Afghanistan, Ahriman, Amesha Spentas, Architecture (Persian), **Art** (Persian).

JACKSON (HENRY), Litt.D. (Camb.), Hon. LL.D. (Aber. and Glas.).
Of the Order of Merit; Regius Professor of Greek in the University of Cambridge; Fellow of Trinity College, Cambridge, of Winchester College, and of the British Academy; Foreign Honorary Member of the American Academy of Arts and Sciences.
Aristotle.

JACOBI (HERMANN), Ph.D.
Professor der Sanskr. u. vergleich. Wissensch. an der Universität zu Bonn; Geheimer Regierungsrat.
Agastya, Ages of the World (Indian).

JASTROW (MORRIS, jun.), Ph.D. (Leipzig).
Professor of Semitic Languages and Librarian of the University of Pennsylvania.
Anointing (Semitic).

JEREMIAS (Lic. Dr. ALFRED).
Pfarrer der Lutherkirche und Privatdozent an der Universität zu Leipzig.
Ages of the World (Babylonian).

JEVONS (FRANK BYRON), M.A., Litt.D., F.R.E.S.
Principal of Bishop Hatfield's Hall, and Sub-Warden of the University of Durham.
Anthropomorphism.

JOLLY (JULIUS), Ph.D. (Munich), Hon. M.D. (Göttingen), Hon. D.Litt. (Oxford).
Hon. Member R.A.S. (London); Corresponding Member of the R. Bavarian Academy of Science, Munich, and of the K. Gesellschaft der Wissenschaften, Göttingen; Ord. Professor of Sanskrit and Comparative Philology and Director of the Linguistic Seminary in the University of Würzburg; formerly Tagore Professor of Law in the University of Calcutta.
Abandonment and Exposure (Hindu), **Adoption** (Hindu), **Altar** (Hindu).

JOYCE (GILBERT CUNNINGHAM), M.A., B.D.
Warden of St. Deiniol's Library, Hawarden.
Analogy, Annihilation.

JUYNBOLL (TH. W.), Dr. juris. et phil.
Adjutor interpretis: 'Legati Warneriani,' Leiden.
Adoption (Muhammadan), **Adultery** (Muh.), **Apostasy** (Muh.).

KALWEIT (PAUL), Lic. der Theol., D.Phil.
Director des evangelischen Predigerseminars in Naumburg a. Queis, und Pfarrer.
A Priori.

KARO (GEORG), D.Phil.
Secretary of the German Archæological Institute, Athens.
Architecture and Art (Etruscan and Early Italian).

KEANE (AUGUSTUS HENRY), LL.D., F.R.G.S., F.R.A.I.
Late Vice-President of the Anthropological Institute; late Professor of Hindustani in University College, London; Hon. Member of the Paris, Florence, Rome, and Washington Anthropological Societies; Hon. Member of the Virginia Historic Society, and Polynesian Society; author of *Ethnology, Man Past and Present.*
Aborigines, Africa, Air and Gods of the Air, America.

KENNETT (Rev. ROBERT HATCH), B.D.
Regius Professor of Hebrew in the University of Cambridge; Canon of Ely; Fellow and Chaplain of Queens' College, Cambridge; Examining Chaplain to the Bishop of Ely.
Ark.

KILPATRICK (Rev. THOMAS B.), M.A., B.D., D.D.
Professor of Systematic Theology in Knox College, Toronto; author of the articles 'Conscience' and 'Philosophy' in the *Dictionary of the Bible*, and of 'Character of Christ' and 'Incarnation' in the *Dictionary of Christ and the Gospels.*
Anger (Wrath) of God.

KROHN (KAARLE LEOPOLD), D.Phil.
Professor der finnischen und vergleichenden Folk-Lore an der Universität zu Helsingfors.
Ancestor-Worship and Cult of the Dead (Ugro-Finnic).

KROLL (Dr. WILHELM), D.Phil.
Professor der Klass. Philologie an der Universität zu Münster.
Apathy.

LEGER (LOUIS).
Membre de l'Institut de France; Professeur au Collège de France; Professeur honoraire à l'École des langues orientales.
Altar (Slavonic), **Ancestor-Worship and Cult of the Dead** (Slavonic), **Architecture and Art** (Slavonic).

LEHMANN (EDVARD), D.Phil.
Docent i religionshistorie v. Universitetet i København.
Ancestor-Worship and Cult of the Dead (Iranian).

LÉVI (SYLVAIN).
Professeur au Collège de France; Directeur d'Études à l'École des Hautes Études.
Abhidharma Kosa Vyakhya.

LIDZBARSKI (MARK), Ph.D.
Ord. Professor der Semit. Philologie an der Universität zu Greifswald.
Ahiqar.

LINDSAY (THOMAS MARTIN), D.D., LL.D.
Principal of the United Free Church College, Glasgow, and Professor of Church History; author of *The History of the Reformation* in the 'International Theological Library.'
Amyraldism.

LITTMANN (ENNO), Ph.D.
Professor der Semit. Philologie an der Universität zu Strassburg.
Abyssinia.

MACCULLOCH (JOHN ARNOTT).
Rector of St. Columba's, Portree, Isle of Skye; Canon of the Cathedral of the Holy Spirit, Cumbrae; author of *Comparative Theology, Religion: its Origin and Forms, The Childhood of Fiction.*
Adultery (Primitive and Savage), **Agaos, Art** (Note on Painting).

MACDONALD (DUNCAN B.), M.A., B.D.
Sometime Scholar and Fellow of the University of Glasgow; Professor of Semitic Languages in Hartford Theological Seminary; Haskell Lecturer on Comparative Religion in the University of Chicago, 1906; Lamson Lecturer on Muhammadanism in Hartford Seminary, 1908–1909.
Allah.

MCGIFFERT (ARTHUR CUSHMAN), Ph.D., D.D.
Washburn Professor of Church History in Union Theological Seminary, New York; author of the *History of Christianity in the Apostolic Age* (I. T. L.).
Apostolic Age.

MCGLOTHLIN (WILLIAM JOSEPH), Ph.D., D.D.
Professor of Church History in the Southern Baptist Theological Seminary, Louisville.
Anabaptism.

MCINTYRE (JAMES LEWIS), M.A. (Edin. and Oxon.), D.Sc. (Edin.).
Anderson Lecturer in Comparative Psychology to the University of Aberdeen; formerly Examiner in Philosophy to the University of Edinburgh; author of *Giordano Bruno* (1903).
Activity (Psychological and Ethical), **Apperception.**

MACKICHAN (Rev. D.), M.A., D.D., LL.D.
Principal of Wilson College and Vice-Chancellor of the University of Bombay.
Advaita.

MACKINTOSH (HUGH ROSS), M.A., D.Phil., D.D. (Edin.).
Professor of Systematic Theology in the New College, Edinburgh.
Note on **Ages of the World** (N.T.).

MACLAGAN (EDWARD DOUGLAS), M.A.
Of the Indian Civil Service, Simla; Chief Secretary to the Government of the Panjab, India.
Amritsar.

MACLEAN (Right Rev. ARTHUR JOHN), D.D. (Camb.), Hon. D.D. (Glas.).
Bishop of Moray, Ross, and Caithness.
Abrenuntio, Agape.

MACLER (FRÉDÉRIC).
Ancien Attaché à la Bibliothèque Nationale; Laureat de l'Institut; Professeur chargé du cours d'Arménien á l'École des Langues orientales vivantes.
Armenia (Christian).

MACPHERSON (JOHN), M.D., F.R.C.P.E.
Commissioner in Lunacy for Scotland.
Abnormalities (Psychological).

MARGOLIOUTH (Rev. GEORGE), M.A. (Cantab.).
Senior Assistant in the Department of Ancient Printed Books and MSS in the British Museum.
Ancestor-Worship and Cult of the Dead (Babylonian, Hebrew, Jewish).

MARKHAM (Sir CLEMENTS), K.C.B., D.Sc. (Camb.), F.R.C., F.S.A., V.P.R.G.S.
President of the Hakluyt Society.
Andeans.

MARSHALL (JOHN TURNER), M.A., D.D.
Principal of Manchester Baptist College; Lecturer in History of Christian Doctrine in Manchester University.
Adoration (Biblical).

MILLS (LAWRENCE HEPWORTH), D.D. (N.Y.), Hon. M.A. (Oxon.).
Professor of Zend Philology in the University of Oxford.
Ahuna Vairya.

MODI (SHAMS-UL-ULMA JIVANJI JAMSHEDJI), B.A.
Fellow of the University of Bombay; Officier d'Académie (1898); Officier de l'Instruction Publique (1902); Vice-President of the Bombay Branch of the Royal Asiatic Society.
Adultery (Parsi).

MORRISON (WILLIAM DOUGLAS), LL.D.
Rector of St. Marylebone, London; author of *The Jews under the Roman Empire, Crime and its Causes.*
Abduction, Abetment, Admonition.

MOSS (Rev. RICHARD WADDY), D.D.
Professor of Systematic Theology in Didsbury College, Manchester.
Alexander the Great.

MULLINGER (J. BASS), M.A. (Camb.).
University Lecturer in History; formerly Lecturer and Librarian of St. John's College, Cambridge.
Albigenses.

MUNRO (ROBERT), M.A., M.D., LL.D.
Vice-President of the Royal Society of Edinburgh; Hon. Vice-President of the Royal Archæological Institute of Great Britain and Ireland; Hon. Member of the Royal Irish Academy, and of numerous Foreign Societies; author of *The Lake-Dwellings in Europe.*
Anthropology.

MURRAY (JOHN CLARK), LL.D. (Glas.), F.R.S.C.
Emeritus Professor of Philosophy in McGill University, Montreal.
Agnoiology, Amiability.

MYRES (JOHN L.), M.A., F.S.A., F.R.G.S.
Gladstone Professor of Greek, and Lecturer in Ancient Geography in the University of Liverpool; formerly student of Christ Church, Oxford, and Lecturer in Archæology in the University of Oxford.
Archæology.

NEWMAN (ALBERT HENRY), D.D., LL.D., Litt.D.
Professor of Church History in Baylor University; author of *A History of the Baptist Churches in the United States, A Manual of Church History.*
Æons.

NICHOLSON (REYNOLDS ALLEYNE), M.A.
Lecturer in Persian in the University of Cambridge; sometime Fellow of Trinity College.
Abd ar-Razzaq.

NÖLDEKE (THEODOR), Ph.D., LL.D. (Edin.).
Professor emeritus an der Kaiser-Wilhelms-Universität zu Strassburg.
Arabs (Ancient).

OESTERLEY (Rev. W. O. E.), D.D. (Cantab.).
Organizing Secretary to the Parochial Missions to the Jews at Home and Abroad; Lecturer to the Palestine Exploration Fund; joint-author of *The Religion and Worship of the Synagogue.*
A and Ω, Adoration (Post-Biblical).

OWEN (MARY ALICIA).
President of the Missouri Folklore Society; Councillor of the American Folklore Society; admitted to Tribal Membership with the Indians, 1892.
Algonquins (Prairie Tribes).

PASS (H. LEONARD), M.A.
Formerly Scholar and Hutchinson Student of St. John's College, Cambridge; Tyrwhitt Scholar, 1902; 'Recognized Lecturer' in Theology in the University of Cambridge.
Altar (Christian), **Am Ha-Ares.**

PATON (Rev. LEWIS BAYLES), Ph.D., D.D.
Nettleton Professor of Old Testament Exegesis and Criticism, and Instructor in Assyrian in the Hartford Theological Seminary; late Director of the American School of Archæology in Jerusalem.
Ammi, Ammonites.

PATRICK (MARY MILLS), A.M. (Jena), Ph.D. (Berne).
President of the American College for Girls at Constantinople.
Anaxagoras.

PEARSON (A. C.), M.A.
Late Scholar of Christ's College, Cambridge.
Achelous, Achilles, Æther.

PETRIE (WILLIAM MATTHEW FLINDERS), D.C.L. (Oxon.), LL.D. (Edin., Aber.), Litt.D. (Camb.), Ph.D. (Strassburg).
Fellow of the Royal Society and of the British Academy; Edwards Professor of Egyptology in the University of London.
Architecture (Egyptian), **Art** (Egyptian).

PINCHES (THEOPHILUS GOLDRIDGE), LL.D. (Glas.), M.R.A.S.
Lecturer in Assyrian at University College, London, and at the Institute of Archæology, Liverpool; Hon. Member of the Société Asiatique.
Architecture (Assyro-Babylonian, Phœnician), **Art** (Assyro-Babylonian, Phœnician).

PLATT (Rev. FREDERIC), M.A., B.D.
Tutor in Old Testament Languages and Literature, and in Philosophy, in the Wesleyan College, Didsbury, Manchester.
Arminianism.

POUSSIN (LOUIS DE LA VALLÉE), Docteur en philosophie et lettres (Liège), en langues orientales (Louvain).
Professeur de sanscrit à l'université de Gand; Co-directeur du Muséon; Membre de R.A.S. et de la Société Asiatique.
Adibuddha, Ages of the World (Buddhist), **Agnosticism** (Buddhist).

PRINCE (J. DYNELEY), B.A., Ph.D.
Professor of Semitic Languages in Columbia University, N.Y.; Member of the New Jersey Legislature; Advisory Commissioner on Crime and Dependency for New Jersey Legislative Committee on Education.
Algonquins (Eastern).

REVON (MICHEL), LL.D., D.Lit.
Late Professor of Law in the Imperial University of Tokyo and Legal Adviser to the Japanese Government; Professor of History of the Civilization of the Far East in the University of Paris; author of *Le Shinntoïsme.*
Ancestor-Worship and Cult of the Dead (Japanese).

RIESS (ERNST), M.A., Ph.D.
Assistant Professor of Latin in the University of New York.
Alchemy (Greek and Roman).

ROBERTSON (CHARLES DONALD), M.A.
Fellow of Trinity College, Cambridge.
Ambition.

ROSE (H. A.), I.C.S.
Superintendent of Ethnography, Panjab, India.
Abandonment and Exposure (Hindu), **Akalis.**

ROSS (G. R. T.), M.A., D.Phil.
Lecturer in Philosophy and Education in Hartley University College, Southampton; author of *Aristotle's De Sensu and De Memoria.*
Accidents, Arbitrariness.

SALADIN (HENRI).
Architecte du Gouvernement, chargé de Missions Archéologiques en Tunisie; Membre de la Commission archéologique de l'Afrique du Nord au Ministère de l'Instruction Publique de France.
Architecture (Muhammadan).

SAYCE (ARCHIBALD HENRY), Hon. D.Litt. (Oxon.), LL.D. (Dublin), Hon. D.D. (Edin. and Aber.).
Fellow of Queen's College and Professor of Assyriology in the University of Oxford; President of the Society of Biblical Archæology.
Armenia (Early Vannic).

SCOTT (ERNEST FINDLAY), M.A. (Glas.), B.A. (Oxon.).
Professor of Church History in Queen's University, Kingston, Canada.
Æons.

SHAMBAUGH (BERTHA MAUD HORACK).
Author of *Amana: The Community of True Inspiration.*
Amana Society.

SIMPSON (Sir ALEXANDER RUSSELL), M.D., D.Sc., LL.D.
Emeritus Professor of Midwifery and Diseases of Women and Children, and formerly Dean of the Faculty of Medicine in the University of Edinburgh.
Anæsthesia.

SIMPSON (ANDREW FINDLATER), M.A.
Professor of New Testament Exegesis and Criticism in the Congregational Theological Hall, Edinburgh.
Acceptance, Access.

SIMPSON (JAMES GILLILAND), M.A.
Lecturer of Leeds Parish Church; Principal of the Clergy School; Examining Chaplain to the Bishop of Argyll and the Isles.
Apostolic Succession.

SMITH (KIRBY FLOWER), Ph.D. (Johns Hopkins).
Professor of Latin in the Johns Hopkins University.
Ages of the World (Greek).

SMITH (VINCENT ARTHUR), M.A.
Of the Indian Civil Service (retired); author of *Asoka* in 'Rulers of India.'
Amaravati, Architecture (Hindu), **Art** (Hindu).

SÖDERBLOM (Rev. NATHAN), D.D. (Paris).
Élève diplômé de l'École des Hautes Études; Ord. Professor of the University of Upsala; Member of the Chapter of Upsala; Prebendary of Holy Trinity in Upsala.
Ages of the World (Zoroastr.), **Ardashir I.**

SRAWLEY (Rev. JAMES HERBERT), D.D.
Tutor and Theological Lecturer in Selwyn College, Cambridge; Examining Chaplain to the Bishop of Lichfield.
Antiochene Theology.

STAWELL (FLORENCE MELIAN).
Certificated Student of Newnham College, Cambridge (Classical Tripos, 1892, Part I. Class I. Div. I.); sometime Lecturer in Classics at Newnham College.
Abasement, Adoration.

STERRETT (Rev. J. MACBRIDE), D.D.
Professor of Philosophy in the George Washington University, Washington.
Antinomianism, Antinomies.

STOKES (GEORGE J.), M.A. (T.C.D.).
Of Lincoln's Inn, Barrister-at-Law; Professor of Mental and Social Science in Queen's College, Cork.
Accident, Ætiology.

STRACK (HERMANN L.), Ph.D., D.D.
Professor der Theologie an der Universität zu Berlin.
Anti-Semitism.

STRONG (Very Rev. THOMAS BANKS), D.D.
Dean of Christ Church, Oxford; author of *A Manual of Theology*; Bampton Lecturer in 1896.
Absolution.

STRZYGOWSKI (HOFRAT Dr. JOSEF).
Professor der Kunstgeschichte an der Universität zu Graz.
Art (Muhammadan).

TASKER (Rev. JOHN G.), D.D.
Professor of Theology in the Wesleyan College, Handsworth, Birmingham.
Abandonment, Advocate.

TAYLOR (Rev. CHARLES), D.D., Hon. LL.D. (Harvard).
Master of St. John's College, Cambridge; Vice-Chancellor of the University, 1887–1888.
Accidie, Acrostic.

TAYLOR (Rev. JOHN), D.Lit., M.A., B.D.
Vicar and Rural Dean of Winchcombe, Gloucs.
Abyss.

TAYLOR (Rev. ROBERT BRUCE), M.A.
Examiner in Economics to the University of Glasgow.
Anarchism.

TEMPLE (Lt.-Col. Sir RICHARD), Bart., C.I.E.
Hon. Fellow of Trinity Hall, Cambridge; late of the Indian Army; Chief Commissioner Andaman and Nicobar Islands, 1894.
Andamans.

THOMAS (FREDERICK WILLIAM), M.A.
Librarian of the India Office; late Fellow of Trinity College, Cambridge.
Abhiseka.

THOMAS (NORTHCOTE WHITRIDGE).
Élève diplômé de l'École pratique des Hautes Études; Corresponding Member of the Société d'Anthropologie de Paris; Member of Council of the Folklore Society; author of *Thought Transference, Kinship Organization and Group Marriage in Australia.*
Alcheringa, Animals.

THOMSON (BASIL HOME).
Barrister-at-Law; formerly Acting Native Commissioner in Fiji.
Ancestor-Worship and Cult of the Dead (Fijian).

THOMSON (J. ARTHUR), M.A.
Regius Professor of Natural History in the University of Aberdeen; author of *The Study of Animal Life, The Science of Life, Outlines of Zoology, Heredity.*
Abiogenesis, Adaptation, Age.

VIDYABHUSANA (SATIS CHANDRA), M.A., Ph.D., M.R.A.S.
Professor of Sanskrit and Pali and Indian Philosophy in the Presidency College, Calcutta; Joint Secretary of the Buddhist Text Society of India.
Absolute (Vedanta and Buddhist).

WADDELL (L. AUSTINE), C.B., C.I.E., LL.D., F.L.S., F.R.A.I., Lt.-Colonel, I.M.S.
Professor of Tibetan in University College, London; author of *The Buddhism of Tibet, Lhasa and its Mysteries.*
Abbot (Tibetan), Amitayus.

WALSHE (Rev. W. GILBERT), B.A.
Recording Secretary of the Society for the Diffusion of Christian and General Knowledge among the Chinese, Shanghai.
Altar (Chinese).

WENLEY (ROBERT MARK), D.Phil., Sc.D., Litt.D., LL.D.
Professor of Philosophy in the University of Michigan; author of *Contemporary Theology and Theism.*
Acosmism.

WHIBLEY (LEONARD), M.A.
Fellow of Pembroke College, Cambridge; University Lecturer in Ancient History.
Amphictyony.

WHYTE (J. MACKIE), M.A., M.D. (Edin.), M.R.C.S. (Eng.).
Physician to the Dundee Royal Infirmary; Lecturer on Clinical Medicine in St. Andrews University.
Alcohol.

WILDE (NORMAN), Ph.D.
Professor of Philosophy and Psychology in the University of Minnesota.
Æstheticism.

WOODHOUSE (WILLIAM J.), M.A.
Professor of Greek in the University of Sydney, New South Wales.
Adoption (Greek, Roman), Amnesty, Aphrodisia, Apollonia.

WOODS (Rev. FRANCIS HENRY), M.A., B.D.
Rector of Bainton, Yorkshire; late Fellow and Theological Lecturer of St. John's College, Oxford.
Antediluvians.

WORKMAN (Rev. HERBERT B.), D.Lit.
Principal of the Westminster Training College.
Abelard, Ambrose of Milan, Anselm of Canterbury.

DE WULF (MAURICE), Docteur en droit, Docteur en philosophie et lettres.
Professeur de Logique, de Critériologie, d'Histoire de la Philosophie à l'Université de Louvain; Membre de l'Académie royale de Belgique, et du Conseil d'administration de la Bibliothèque royale de Belgique; Secrétaire de Rédaction de la Revue Néo-Scolastique.
Æsthetics.

CROSS-REFERENCES

In addition to the cross-references throughout the volume, to which great attention has been paid, for the subject is one of the utmost importance, the following list should be consulted. It contains topics which have been considered as belonging to the Encyclopædia, but which will be treated more conveniently under other titles. The list does not include the Indian castes or the names of the minor gods.

Topic.	Probable Title of Article.
Aalu	State after Death (Egyp.).
Aaron	Old Testament.
Ab (month)	Calendar.
Abaddon	Abyss, Sheol.
Abarbanel	Abravanel.
Ab bet din	Worship (Jew.).
Abbey	Monasticism.
Abd al-Wahhab	Wahhab.
Abdhuts	Atits.
Abel	Old Testament.
Abelites, Abelonites	Sects (Chr.).
Abenakis	Algonquins (E.).
Aben Ezra	Ibn Ezra.
Abjuration	Abrenuntio.
Ablution	Bathing, Purification.
Abnegation	Asceticism.
Aboda	Day of Atonement.
Abolitionism	Slavery.
Abomination	Tabu.
Abracadabra	Gnosticism.
Abraham	Old Testament.
Abraham (Apoc.)	Bible, Literature.
Abraham of Avila	Pseudo-Messiahs.
Abrahamites	Paulicians.
Abrasax, Abraxas	Basilidians.
Abrogation	Law.
Absent-mindedness	Concentration.
Absolute Idealism	Transcendentalism.
Absorption	Concentration, Samadhi.
Abstinentism	Priscillianism.
Abstract Notions	Aryans, Personification.
Abubacer	Ibn Tofail.
Abu Bakr	Muhammadanism.
Abu-l-ʻAla al-Maʻarri	Maʻarri.
Abulia	Aboulia.
Acacians	Arianism.
Accaophori	Sects (Chr.).
Accessory	Crime.
Accusation	Informers.
Acephali	Monophysitism.
Achara	Custom (Hindu).
Acheron	Greek Religion.
Acœmetism	Monasticism.
Acolyte	Ministry (Chr.).
Acquirements	Adaptation, Heredity.
Acquisitiveness	Desire.
Actors	Stage.
Acts of the Apostles	Bible.
Acts of the Martyrs, Saints	Martyrs, Saints.
Actuality	Potentiality.
Acuanites	Manichæism.
Adamites	Sects (Chr.).
Adam Kadmon	Gnosticism.
Adecerditæ	Descent to Hades.
Adelophagi	Sects (Chr.).
Adelphians	Euchites.
Adessenarians	Sects (Chr.).
Adevism	Atheism.
Adhvaryu	Priesthood (Hindu).
Adi Granth	Granth.
Adi Samaj	Brahmo-Samaj.
Aditi, Adityas	Vedic Religion.
Adjuration	Oath.
Adonis	Tammuz.
Adrianists	Sects (Chr.).
Adrumetians	Sects (Chr.).
Advent	Calendar (Chr.), Eschatology.
Adventism	Chiliasm.
Adversity	Suffering.
Æneas	Heroes.
Æolus	Wind, Wind-gods.
Æquiprobabilism	Equiprobabilism.
Aërians	Sects (Chr.).
Aerolites	Prodigies and Portents.
Æsculapius	Health.
Aëtians	Sects (Chr.).
Affinity	Blood-relationship.
Affliction	Suffering.
Affusion	Baptism.
Afrits	Spirits.
Agamemnon	Heroes.
Aganippe	Wells.
Agathodæmon	Spirits.
Agionites	Sects (Chr.).
Agnation	Marriage.
Agnayi, Agni	Vedic Religion.
Agnihotri	Brahman, Priest.
Agnoëtism	Monophysitism.
Agonia	Festivals.
Agonyclites	Sects (Chr.).
Agows	Agaos.
Agynians	Manichæism.
Ahmad ibn Hanbal	Ibn Hanbal.
Ahmadiya	Sects (Muh.).
Aitareya	Upanishads.
Aitkenites	Sects (Chr.).
Ajiva	Jains.
Akals	Druses.
Akas, Akas-Mukhis	Assam.
Akkad	Sumero-Akkadians.
Alakhgirs	Alakhnamis.
Alastor	Spirits.

Topic.	Probable Title of Article.
Albertus Magnus	Scholasticism.
Alexians	Sects (Chr.).
Algeria	Berbers.
Al Ghazali	Ghazali.
Alienation	Sin.
Allat	Arabs.
Allenites	Sects (Chr.).
All-Father	God.
Alligator	Crocodile (under Animals).
Almaricians	Brothers of the Free Spirit.
Almohads, Almoravids	Sects (Muh.).
Alogi	Logos.
Aloneness	Solity.
Alpha and Omega	A and Ω.
Alphabet	Writing.
Alphadelphia Phallanx	Communistic Societies.
Alphitomancy	Divination.
Alroy	Pseudo-Messiahs.
Altruists	Communistic Societies.
Amairgen	Transmigration.
Amalricians	Brothers of the Free Spirit.
Amazulu	Bantus.
Ambrosians	Sects (Chr.).
Amen, Amon	Egyptians.
Amenhotep	Egyptians.
Amerinds	America.
Amitabha	Adibuddha.
Ammonians	Neo-Platonism.
Amoraim	Judaism.
Amorites	Canaanites.
Amrita	Vedic Religion.
Amsdorfians	Sects (Chr.).
Amshaspand	Amesha Spentas.
Ananites	Karaites.
Anathema	Cursing.
Anchorite	Asceticism.
Angamis	Nagas.
Angirases	Vedic Religion.
Anglo-Saxons	Teutons.
Aniconism	Images.
Anomœans	Arianism.
Ansab	Pillars.
Ansarians	Nosairis.
Ant	Animals.
Anthesteria	Festivals.
Anthropomorphites	Sects (Chr.).
Anthropophagy	Cannibalism.
Anti-burghers	Presbyterians.
Anti-clericalism	Clericalism.
Antidicomarianites	Sects (Chr.).
Antisthenes	Cynics.
Anti-trinitarians	Unitarianism.
Anubis	Egyptians.
Aos	Nagas.
Apam napat	Vedic Religion.
Aparimitayus	Amitayus.
Apaturia	Festivals.
Ape	Monkey (under Animals).
Apelleians, Apellianists	Sects (Chr.).
Apepi	Egyptians.
Aphthartodocetism	Monophysitism.
Apis	Egyptians.
Apologists	Apologetics.
A Posteriori	A Priori.
Apostle	Christianity.
Apostolicals	Sects (Chr.).
Apostolic Fathers	Patristics.
April Fool	All Fools' Day.
Apsarases	Vedic Religion.
Arabi	Muhiyy'ddin ibn Arabi.
Archontics	Sects (Chr.).
Ares	Greek Religion.
Argei	Puppets.
Argonauts	Heroes.
Aristippus	Cyrenaicism.
Armorican Lit.	Literature (Celtic).
Arnoldists	Sects (Chr.).
Arrephoria	Festivals.
Arrogance	Pride.
Arson	Crime.

SCHEME OF TRANSLITERATION

I. HEBREW

CONSONANTS

'	א	l	ל
b, bh	ב	m	מ
g, gh	ג	n	נ
d, dh	ד	s	ס
h	ה	'	ע
v, w	ו	p, ph	פ
z	ז	ṣ	צ
ḥ or ch	ח	q or ḳ	ק
ṭ	ט	r	ר
y or j	י	ś, sh	שׂ שׁ
k, kh	כ	t, th	ת

VOWELS

Short.		Long and Diphthongal.		Sh^e^vas.		
a	◌ַ	ā	◌ָ	ă	◌ֲ	Composite sh^e^vas.
e	◌ֶ	ē, ê	◌ֵ, ◌ֵי	ĕ	◌ֱ	
i	◌ִ	î	◌ִ, ◌ִי	ŏ	◌ֳ	
o	◌ָ	ō, ô	◌ֹ, וֹ	ᵉ	◌ְ	(simple sh^e^va).
u	◌ֻ	û	◌ֻ, וּ			

II. ARABIC

CONSONANTS

'	أ	ḍ	ض
b	ب	ṭ	ط
t	ت	ẓ	ظ
th	ث	'	ع
j	ج	gh	غ
ḥ	ح	f	ف
ḫ	خ	q	ق
d	د	k	ك
dh	ذ	l	ل
r	ر	m	م
z	ز	n	ن
s	س	h	ه
sh	ش	v, w	و
ṣ	ص	y	ي

II. ARABIC—*continued*

VOWELS

Short.		Long.		Diphthong.	
a	ـَ	ā	ـَا	ai	ـَیْ
i	ـِ	ī	ـِی	au	ـَوْ
u	ـُ	ū	ـُو		

III. PERSIAN AND HINDUSTANI[1]

The following in addition to the Arabic transliteration above

p	پ	z̲	ذ
t̤	ٹ	ṛ	ڑ
s̤	ث	zh	ژ
ch	چ	z̤	ض
d̤	ڈ	g	گ

[1] The diacritical marks in this scheme are sometimes omitted in transliteration when absolute accuracy is not required, the pronunciation of s̤ being the same as that of s, while z, z̲, z̤, are all pronounced alike.

IV. SANSKRIT

CONSONANTS

Gutturals—k, kh ; g, gh ; ṅ (=ng in finger).
Palatals—ch (=ch in church), chh ; j, jh ; ñ (=n in onion).
Cerebrals—ṭ, ṭh ; ḍ, ḍh ; ṇ (a sound peculiar to India).
Dentals—t, th ; d, dh ; n (=n in not).
Labials—p, ph ; b, bh ; m.
Semi-vowels—y ; r ; l ; v.
Sibilants—ś or sh ; ṣ or sh ; s.
Aspirate—h.
anunāsika (ँ) ; anusvāra, ṁ ; visarga, ḥ ; avagraha (ʼ).

VOWELS

Simple.				Diphthongal.	
a	ā	or	â	e	āi
i	ī	or	î	o	āu
u	ū	or	û		
ṛ	ṝ				
ḷ					

LISTS OF ABBREVIATIONS

I. General

A.H. = Anno Hijrae (A.D. 622).
Ak. = Akkadian.
Alex. = Alexandrian.
Amer. = American.
Apoc. = Apocalypse, Apocalyptic.
Apocr. = Apocrypha.
Aq. = Aquila.
Arab. = Arabic.
Aram. = Aramaic.
Arm. = Armenian.
Ary. = Aryan.
As. = Asiatic.
Assyr. = Assyrian.
AT = Altes Testament.
AV = Authorized Version.
AVm = Authorized Version margin.
A.Y. = Anno Yazdigird (A.D. 639).
Bab. = Babylonian.
c. = *circa*, about.
Can. = Canaanite.
cf. = compare.
ct. = contrast.
D = Deuteronomist.
E = Elohist.
edd. = editions or editors.
Egyp. = Egyptian.
Eng. = English.
Eth. = Ethiopic.
EV = English Version.
f. = and following verse or page: as Ac $10^{34f.}$
ff. = and following verses or pages: as Mt $11^{28ff.}$
Fr. = French.
Germ. = German.
Gr. = Greek.
H = Law of Holiness.
Heb. = Hebrew.
Hel. = Hellenistic.
Hex. = Hexateuch.
Himy. = Himyaritic.
Ir. = Irish.
Iran. = Iranian.
Isr. = Israelite.
J = Jahwist.
J″ = Jehovah.
Jerus. = Jerusalem.
Jos. = Josephus.
LXX = Septuagint.
Min. = Minæan.
MSS = Manuscripts.
MT = Massoretic Text.
n. = note.
NT = New Testament.
Onk. = Onkelos.
OT = Old Testament.
P = Priestly Narrative.
Pal. = Palestine, Palestinian.
Pent. = Pentateuch.
Pers. = Persian.
Phil. = Philistine.
Phœn. = Phœnician.
Pr. Bk. = Prayer Book.
R = Redactor.
Rom. = Roman.
RV = Revised Version.
RVm = Revised Version margin.
Sab. = Sabæan.
Sam. = Samaritan.
Sem. = Semitic.
Sept. = Septuagint.
Sin. = Sinaitic.
Skr. = Sanskrit.
Symm. = Symmachus.
Syr. = Syriac.
t. (following a number) = times.
Talm. = Talmud.
Targ. = Targum.
Theod. = Theodotion.
TR = Textus Receptus.
tr. = translated or translation.
VSS = Versions.
Vulg. = Vulgate.
WH = Westcott and Hort's text.

II. Books of the Bible

Old Testament.

Gn = Genesis.
Ex = Exodus.
Lv = Leviticus.
Nu = Numbers.
Dt = Deuteronomy.
Jos = Joshua.
Jg = Judges.
Ru = Ruth.
1 S, 2 S = 1 and 2 Samuel.
1 K, 2 K = 1 and 2 Kings.
1 Ch, 2 Ch = 1 and 2 Chronicles.
Ezr = Ezra.
Neh = Nehemiah.
Est = Esther.
Job.
Ps = Psalms.
Pr = Proverbs.
Ec = Ecclesiastes.
Ca = Canticles.
Is = Isaiah.
Jer = Jeremiah.
La = Lamentations.
Ezk = Ezekiel.
Dn = Daniel.
Hos = Hosea.
Jl = Joel.
Am = Amos.
Ob = Obadiah.
Jon = Jonah.
Mic = Micah.
Nah = Nahum.
Hab = Habakkuk.
Zeph = Zephaniah.
Hag = Haggai.
Zec = Zechariah.
Mal = Malachi.

Apocrypha.

1 Es, 2 Es = 1 and 2 Esdras.
To = Tobit.
Jth = Judith.
Ad. Est = Additions to Esther.
Wis = Wisdom.
Sir = Sirach or Ecclesiasticus.
Bar = Baruch.
Three = Song of the Three Children.
Sus = Susanna.
Bel = Bel and the Dragon.
Pr. Man = Prayer of Manasses.
1 Mac, 2 Mac = 1 and 2 Maccabees.

New Testament.

Mt = Matthew.
Mk = Mark.
Lk = Luke.
Jn = John.
Ac = Acts.
Ro = Romans.
1 Co, 2 Co = 1 and 2 Corinthians.
Gal = Galatians.
Eph = Ephesians.
Ph = Philippians.
Col = Colossians.
1 Th, 2 Th = 1 and 2 Thessalonians.
1 Ti, 2 Ti = 1 and 2 Timothy.
Tit = Titus.
Philem = Philemon.
He = Hebrews.
Ja = James.
1 P, 2 P = 1 and 2 Peter.
1 Jn, 2 Jn, 3 Jn = 1, 2, and 3 John.
Jude.
Rev = Revelation.

III. For the Literature

1. The following authors' names, when unaccompanied by the title of a book, stand for the works in the list below.

Baethgen = *Beiträge zur sem. Religionsgesch.*, 1888.
Baldwin = *Dict. of Philosophy and Psychology*, 3 vols. 1901–1905.
Barth = *Nominalbildung in den sem. Sprachen*, 2 vols. 1889, 1891 (2nd ed. 1894).
Benzinger = *Heb. Archäologie*, 1894.
Brockelmann = *Gesch. d. arab. Litteratur*, 2 vols. 1899–1902.
Bruns-Sachau = *Syr.-Röm. Rechtsbuch aus dem fünften Jahrhundert*, 1880.
Budge = *Gods of the Egyptians*, 2 vols. 1903.
De la Saussaye = *Lehrbuch der Religionsgesch.*[3], 1905.
Deussen = *Die Philos. d. Upanishads*, 1899 [Eng. tr., Edin. 1906].
Doughty = *Arabia Deserta*, 2 vols. 1888.
Grimm = *Deutsche Mythologie*[4], 3 vols. 1875–1878, Eng. tr. *Teutonic Mythology*, 4 vols. 1882–1888.
Hamburger = *Realencyclopädie für Bibel u. Talmud*, i. 1870 ([2]1892), ii. 1883, suppl. 1886, 1891 f., 1897.
Holder = *Altceltischer Sprachschatz*, 1891 ff.
Holtzmann-Zöpffel = *Lexicon f. Theol. u. Kirchenwesen*[2], 1895.
Howitt = *Native Tribes of S. E. Australia*, 1904.
Jastrow = *Die Religion Bab. u. Assyriens*, 2 vols. 1905– .
Jubainville = *Cours de Litt. Celtique*, i.–xii., 1883 ff.
Lagrange = *Études sur les religions Sémitiques*[2], 1904.
Lane = *An Arabic English Dictionary*, 1863 ff.
Lang = *Myth, Ritual and Religion*[2], 2 vols. 1899.
Lepsius = *Denkmäler aus Ægypten u. Æthiopien*, 1849–1860.
Lichtenberger = *Encyc. des sciences religieuses*, 1876.
Lidzbarski = *Handbuch der nordsem. Epigraphik et Ephemeris*, 1898.
McCurdy = *History, Prophecy, and the Monuments*, 2 vols. 1894–1896.
Muir = *Sanskrit Texts*, 1858–1872.
Muss-Arnolt = *A Concise Dict. of the Assyrian Language*, 1894 ff.
Nowack = *Lehrbuch d. Heb. Archäologie*, 2 vols. 1894.
Pauly-Wissowa = *Realencyc. der classischen Altertumswissenschaft*, 1894.
Perrot-Chipiez = *Hist. de l'Art dans l'Antiquité*, 1881 ff.
Preller = *Römische Mythologie*, 1858.
Réville = *Religion des peuples non-civilisés*, 1883.
Riehm = *Handwörterbuch d. bibl. Altertums*[2], 1893–1894.
Robinson = *Biblical Researches in Palestine*[2], 1856.
Roscher = *Lex. d. Gr. u. Röm. Mythologie*, 1884.
Schenkel = *Bibel-Lexicon*, 5 vols. 1869–1875.
Schürer = *GJV*[3], 3 vols. 1898–1901 [*HJP*, 5 vols. 1890 ff.].
Schwally = *Leben nach dem Tode*, 1892.
Siegfried-Stade = *Heb. Wörterbuch zum AT*, 1893.
Smend = *Lehrbuch der alttest. Religionsgesch.*[2], 1899.
Smith (G. A.) = *Historical Geography of the Holy Land*[4], 1896.
Smith (W. R.) = *Religion of the Semites*[2], 1894.
Spencer (Herbert) = *Principles of Sociology*[3], 1885–1896.
Spencer-Gillen[a] = *Native Tribes of Central Australia*.
Spencer-Gillen[b] = *Northern Tribes of Central Australia*, 1904.
Swete = *The OT in Greek*, 3 vols. 1893 ff.
Tylor (E. B.) = *Primitive Culture*[3], 1891.
Ueberweg = *Hist. of Philosophy*, Eng. tr., 2 vols. 1872–1874.
Weber = *Jüdische Theologie auf Grund des Talmud u. verwandten Schriften*[2], 1897.
Wiedemann = *Die Religion der alten Ægypter*, 1890 [Eng. tr., revised, 'Religion of the Egyptians,' 1897].
Wilkinson = *Manners and Customs of the Ancient Egyptians*, 3 vols. 1878.
Zunz = *Die gottesdienstlichen Vorträge der Juden*[2], 1892.

2. Periodicals, Dictionaries, Encyclopædias, and other standard works frequently cited.

AA = Archiv für Anthropologie.
AAOJ = American Antiquarian and Oriental Journal.
ABAW = Abhandlungen d. Berliner Akad. d. Wissenschaften.
AE = Archiv für Ethnographie.
AEGL = Assyr. and Eng. Glossary (Johns Hopkins University).
AGG = Abhandlungen d. Göttinger Gesellschaft der Wissenschaften.
AGPh = Archiv f. Geschichte der Philosophie.
AHR = American Historical Review.
AHT = Ancient Hebrew Tradition (Hommel).
AJPh = American Journal of Philosophy.
AJPs = American Journal of Psychology.
AJSL = American Journal of Semitic Languages and Literature.
AJTh = American Journal of Theology.
AMG = Annales du Musée Guimet.
APES = American Palestine Exploration Society.
APF = Archiv f. Papyrusforschung.
AR = Anthropological Review.
ARW = Archiv für Religionswissenschaft.
AS = Acta Sanctorum (Bollandus).
ASG = Abhandlungen der Sächsischen Gesellschaft der Wissenschaften.
ASoc = L'Année Sociologique.
ASWI = Archæological Survey of W. India.
AZ = Allgemeine Zeitung.
BAG = Beiträge zur alten Geschichte.
BASS = Beiträge zur Assyriologie u. sem. Sprachwissenschaft (edd. Delitzsch and Haupt).
BCH = Bulletin de Correspondance Hellénique.
BE = Bureau of Ethnology.
BG = Bombay Gazetteer.
BJ = Bellum Judaicum (Josephus).
BL = Bampton Lectures.
BLE = Bulletin de Littérature Ecclésiastique.
BOR = Bab. and Oriental Record.
BS = Bibliotheca Sacra.
BSA = Annual of the British School at Athens.
BSAA = Bulletin de la Société archéologique à Alexandrie.
BSAL = Bulletin de la Soc. d'Anthropologie de Lyon.
BSAP = Bulletin de la Soc. d'Anthropologie, etc., Paris.
BSG = Bulletin de la Soc. de Géographie.
BW = Biblical World.
BZ = Biblische Zeitschrift.
CAIBL = Comptes rendus de l'Academie des Inscriptions et Belles Lettres.
CBTS = Calcutta Buddhist Text Society.
CF = Childhood of Fiction (MacCulloch).
CGS = Cults of the Greek States (Farnell).
CIA = Corpus Inscrip. Atticarum.
CIG = Corpus Inscrip. Græcarum.
CIL = Corpus Inscrip. Latinarum.

CIS=Corpus Inscrip. Semiticarum.
COT=Cuneiform Inscriptions and the OT [Eng. tr. of *KAT*²; see below].
CR=Contemporary Review.
CeR=Celtic Review.
ClR=Classical Review.
CQR=Church Quarterly Review.
CSEL=*Corpus Script. Eccles. Latinorum.*
DACL = Dict. d'Archéologie Chrétienne et de Liturgie (Cabrol).
DB=Dictionary of the Bible.
DCA = Dict. of Christian Antiquities (Smith-Cheetham).
DCB=Dict. of Christian Biography (Smith-Wace).
DCG=Dictionary of Christ and the Gospels.
DI=Dict. of Islam (Hughes).
DPhP=Dictionary of Philosophy and Psychology.
DWAW=Denkschriften der Wiener Akad. der Wissenschaften.
EBi=Encyclopædia Biblica.
EBr=Encyclopædia Britannica.
EEFM=Egyp. Explor. Fund Memoirs.
Exp=Expositor.
ExpT=Expository Times.
FHG=Fragmenta Historicorum Græcorum, coll. C. Müller (Paris, 1885).
FL=Folklore.
FLJ=Folklore Journal.
FLR=Folklore Record.
GA=Gazette Archéologique.
*GB*²=Golden Bough² (Frazer).
GGA=Göttingische Gelehrte Anzeigen.
GGN=Göttingische Gelehrte Nachrichten (Nachrichten der königl. Gesellschaft der Wissenschaften zu Göttingen).
GIAP=Grundriss d. Indo-Arischen Philologie.
GIrP=Grundriss d. Iranischen Philologie.
GJV=Geschichte des Jüdischen Volkes.
GVI=Geschichte des Volkes Israel.
HE=Historia Ecclesiastica.
HGHL=Historical Geography of the Holy Land (G. A. Smith).
HI=History of Israel.
HJ=Hibbert Journal.
HJP=History of the Jewish People.
HN=Historia Naturalia (Pliny).
HWB=Handwörterbuch.
IA=Indian Antiquary.
ICC=International Critical Commentary.
ICR=Indian Census Report (1901).
IGA=Inscrip. Græcæ Antiquissimæ.
IGI=Imperial Gazetteer of India² (1885).
IJE=International Journal of Ethics.
ITL=International Theological Library.
JA=Journal Asiatique.
JAFL=Journal of American Folklore.
JAI=Journal of the Anthropological Institute.
JAOS=Journal of the American Oriental Society.
JASB=Journal of the Anthropological Society of Bombay.
JBL=Journal of Biblical Literature.
JBTS=Journal of the Buddhist Text Society.
JD=Journal des Débats.
JDTh=Jahrbücher f. deutsche Theologie.
JE=Jewish Encyclopedia.
JGOS=Journal of the German Oriental Society.
JHC=Johns Hopkins University Circulars.
JHS=Journal of Hellenic Studies.
JLZ=Jenäer Litteraturzeitung.
JPh=Journal of Philology.
JPTh=Jahrbücher f. protest. Theologie.
JPTS=Journal of the Pāli Text Society.
JQR=Jewish Quarterly Review.
JRAS=Journal of the Royal Asiatic Society.
JRASBe=Journal of the Royal Asiatic Society, Bengal branch.
JRASBo=Journal of the Royal Asiatic Society, Bombay branch.
JRASJ=Journal of the Royal Asiatic Soc., Japan.
JRGS=Journal of the Royal Geographical Society.
JThSt=Journal of Theological Studies.
*KAT*²=Die Keilinschriften und das AT (Schrader), 1883.
*KAT*³=Zimmern-Winckler's ed. of the preceding [really a totally distinct work], 1903.
KB or *KIB*=Keilinschriftliche Bibliothek (Schrader), 1889 ff.
KGF=Keilinschriften und die Geschictsforschung, 1878.
LCBl=Literarisches Centralblatt.
LOPh=Literaturblatt f. Oriental. Philologie.
LOT=Introduction to Literature of OT (Driver).
LP=Legend of Perseus (Hartland).
LSSt=Leipziger sem. Studien.
M=Mélusine.
MAIBL=Mémoires de l'Acad. des Inscriptions et Bulletins.
MBAW = Monatsbericht d. Berliner Akad. d. Wissenschaften.
MGH=Monumenta Germaniæ Historica (Pertz).
MGWJ=Monatsbericht f. Geschichte u. Wissenschaft des Judentums.
MNDPV = Mittheilungen u. Nachrichten des deutschen Palästina-Vereins.
MR=Methodist Review.
MWJ = Magazin für die Wissenschaft des Judentums.
NBAC=Nuovo Bulletino di Archeologia Cristiana.
NC=Nineteenth Century.
NHWB=Neuhebräisches Wörterbuch.
NINQ=North Indian Notes and Queries.
NKZ=Neue kirchliche Zeitschrift.
NQ=Notes and Queries.
NR=Native Races of the Pacific States (Bancroft).
NTZG=Neutestamentliche Zeitgeschichte.
OLZ=Orientalische Litteraturzeitung.
OS=Onomastica Sacra.
OTJC=Old Testament in the Jewish Church.
OTP=Oriental Translation Fund Publications.
PAOS=Proceedings of American Oriental Society.
PASB=Proceedings of the Anthropological Society of Bombay.
PB=Polychrome Bible (English).
PBE=Publications of the Bureau of Ethnology.
PEFM=Palestine Exploration Fund Memoirs.
PEFSt = Palestine Exploration Fund Quarterly Statement.
PG=Patrologia Græca (Migne).
PJB=Preussische Jahrbücher.
PL=Patrologia Latina (Migne).
PNQ=Punjab Notes and Queries.
PR=Popular Religion and Folklore of N. India (Crooke).
*PRE*³=Prot. Realencyclopädie (Herzog-Hauck).
PRR=Presbyterian and Reformed Review.
PRSE=Proceedings Royal Soc. of Edinburgh.
PSBA=Proceedings of the Society of Biblical Archæology.
PTS=Pāli Text Society.
RA=Revue Archéologique.
RAnth=Revue d'Anthropologie.
RAS=Royal Asiatic Society.
RAssyr=Revue d'Assyriologie.
RB=Revue Biblique.
RBEW=Reports of the Bureau of Ethnology (Washington).
RC=Revue Critique.
RCel=Revue Celtique.
RCh=Revue Chrétienne.
RDM=Revue des Deux-Mondes.
RE=Realencyclopädie.
REg=Revue Égyptologique.
REJ=Revue des Études Juives.
REth=Revue d'Ethnographie.
RHLR=Revue d'Histoire et de Littérature Religieuses.

RHR=Revue de l'Histoire des Religions.
RN=Revue Numismatique.
RP=Records of the Past.
RPh=Revue Philosophique.
RQ=Römische Quartalschrift.
RS = Revue sémitique d'Epigraphie et d'Hist. ancienne.
RSA=Recueil de la Soc. archéologique.
RSI=Reports of the Smithsonian Institution.
RTAP=Recueil de Travaux rélatifs à l'Archéologie et à la Philologie.
RTP=Revue des traditions populaires.
RThPh=Revue de Théologie et de Philosophie.
RTr=Recueil de Travaux.
SBAW=Sitzungsberichte der Berliner Akad. d. Wissenschaften.
SBE=Sacred Books of the East.
SBOT=Sacred Books of the OT (Hebrew).
SK=Studien u. Kritiken.
SSGW=Sitzungsberichte d. Kgl. Sächs. Gesellsch. d. Wissenschaften.
SWAW=Sitzungsberichte d. Wiener Akad. d. Wissenschaften.
TAPA = Transactions of American Philological Association.
TASJ=Transactions of the Asiatic Society of Japan.
TES=Transactions of Ethnological Society.
ThLZ=Theologische Litteraturzeitung.
ThT=Theol. Tijdschrift.
TRHS=Transactions of Royal Historical Society.
TRSE=Transactions of Royal Society of Edinburgh.
TS=Texts and Studies.
TSBA=Transactions of the Society of Biblical Archæology.
TU=Texte u. Untersuchungen.
WAI=Western Asiatic Inscriptions.
WZKM=Wiener Zeitschrift f. Kunde des Morgenlandes.
ZA=Zeitschrift für Assyriologie.
ZÄ=Zeitschrift für ägyp. Sprache u. Altertumswissenschaft.
ZATW = Zeitschrift für die alttest. Wissenschaft.
ZCK=Zeitschrift für christliche Kunst.
ZDA=Zeitschrift für deutsches Altertum.
ZDMG = Zeitschrift der deutschen morgenländischen Gesellschaft.
ZDPV = Zeitschrift des deutschen Palästina-Vereins.
ZE=Zeitschrift für Ethnologie.
ZKF=Zeitschrift für Keilschriftforschung.
ZKT=Zeitschrift für kathol. Theologie.
ZKWL=Zeitschrift für kirchl. Wissenschaft u. kirchl. Leben.
ZM=Zeitschrift für die Mythologie.
ZNTW= Zeitschrift für die neutest. Wissenschaft.
ZPhP=Zeitschrift für Philosophie und Pädagogik.
ZTK=Zeitschrift für Theologie u. Kirche.
ZVK=Zeitschrift für Volkskunde.
ZVRW = Zeitschrift für vergleichende Rechtswissenschaft.
ZWT=Zeitschrift für wissenschaftliche Theologie.

[A small superior number designates the particular edition of the work referred to, as *KAT*², *LOT*⁶, etc.]

ENCYCLOPÆDIA OF RELIGION AND ETHICS

A

A AND Ω.—1. The meaning of this phrase is expressed in Rev 21^6 22^{13} as 'the beginning and the end' (ἡ ἀρχὴ καὶ τὸ τέλος). The conception is to be traced to such passages as Is 41^4 44^6 48^{12}. And it would appear that the thought was taken from the Hebrew rather than from the Septuagint, for in the former each of the three passages expresses finality (אַחֲרוֹן), which is in accordance with Rev 21^6 22^{13}; while in the Septuagint the Greek equivalent, though differing in each case, emphasizes the idea of something further (τὰ ἐπερχόμενα, μετὰ ταῦτα, εἰς τὸν αἰῶνα). The point, though a small one, is significant, as it affords a piece of subsidiary evidence for a Hebrew original of the Apocalypse (see below).

2. The origin of the phrase is to be sought in pre-Christian times. Among the Jews, the first and last letters of the Hebrew alphabet, א ת, were used to express totality; thus in *Yalkut Rubeni*, fol. 3. 2, where the words of Gn 1^1 'the heavens' (את השמים) are commented upon, it is said that את, which includes all the letters, implies that all the heavens are meant, their beginning and their end; again, it is said that Adam sinned from א to ת, meaning that he was guilty of every sin; or, once more, Abraham kept the Torah from א to ת, *i.e.* he kept the whole Law.* There is a well-known Rabbinical saying, 'The seal of God is *'Emeth'* (אֱמֶת='truth'); and in Jerus. *Sanh.* i. 18*a*, *'Emeth* is said to be the name of God, who includes all things: the beginning (א), the middle (מ is approximately the middle letter of the Hebrew alphabet), and the end (ת). אמת might then well correspond to the ὁ ὢν, ὁ ἦν, ὁ ἐρχόμενος, 'who is, who was, who is to come,' of Rev 1^8. Logically, indeed, the order should be ὁ ἦν, etc.; but to a Hebrew (as the original writer of the book must have been) ὁ ὢν, as being equivalent to יהוה (Jahweh), would probably on that account come first. The Hebrew את, being a well-known formula expressive of entirety, may therefore have been the prototype of AΩ. It is, however, necessary to state that the phrase 'א and ת' is never (in pre-Christian times) used of God in the way that AΩ is; it is once used of the Shekinah in the Talmud,* but as applied to God it occurs first in the Peshiṭta, which in each case renders A and Ω by ܐܠܦ ܘܬܘ.

3. It is noticeable that wherever the expression occurs in the Apocalypse it is written τὸ Ἄλφα καὶ τὸ Ὦ, *i.e.* the first letter is written out in full, while the second is represented only by its sign; there must have been some reason for this, and possibly it is to be accounted for in the following way. It is generally held that parts of the Apocalypse were originally written in Hebrew; in this case the form of the expression would be אלף ותו. Now, the Hebrew characters, as used in the 1st cent., might well have appeared to the Greek translator as representing the *'Aleph* written in full, and *the Tau as the letter Omega*. Thus, in 1st cent. script: אלף ותו; the similarity in both languages of the written first letter might have suggested that the second one was intended for an *Omega*. The phrase was thus imitated direct from the Hebrew manner of writing the equivalent expression. This would also account for the fact that in the vast majority of instances (certainly in *all* the earliest) the *symbol* was written Aω, *i.e.* an uncial Alpha and a cursive Omega.

4. *Use of the symbol in the Christian Church.*—A great variety of objects have been found with this symbol inscribed upon them; it figures on tombstones, as well as on other monuments, on mosaics, frescoes, and bricks, also on vases, cups, lamps, and on rings; it appears also on coins, its earliest occurrence on these being of the time of Constans and Constantius, the sons of Constantine the Great.† These all belong to different ages and different countries; in its earliest known form (Rome, A.D. 295)‡ it appears as 'ω et A,' but this is exceptional, and is perhaps of Gnostic origin. The symbol in its usual form is found on objects

* See also *Yalk. Rub.* fol. 17. 4, fol. 48. 4, quoted in Schoettgen's *Horæ Hebraicæ et Talmudicæ*, i. pp. 1086, 1087, and *Yoma* 69*b*, *Sanh.* 64*a*, Jerus. *Yeb.* xii. 13*a*, Jerus. *Sanh.* i. 18*a*, quoted in *JE* i. pp. 438, 439; also *Sanh.* 55*a*.

* 'Particula את quoque est nomen Schechinæ, q.d. Ezech. 1^{28} Et audivi את vocem loquentem mecum' (Schoettgen, *op. cit.* p. 1086). It is interesting to note that אַחֲרוֹן ('the last') is, in Midrashic literature, used as a name of the Messiah, and is identified with the גּוֹאֵל ('Redeemer') of Job 19^{25}.

† See Cabrol's *DACL*, art. 'AΩ.'

‡ Cf. *PRE* [3], art. 'A und Ω.'

belonging to the 3rd cent. in Rome and N. Africa; on objects belonging to the 4th cent. it has been found in Asia Minor, Sicily, Upper and Lower Italy, and Gaul; by the beginning of the Middle Ages it must have become known in most of the countries of Central Europe.

The combinations in which the symbol is found are very varied,* the most frequent being the following: with a cross, with a cross and the Christ-monogram (A ☧ ω), surrounded by a wreath (symbolic of the victory over death), within a circle (symbolic of eternity), in combination with a triangle (the symbol of the Trinity). It will be seen, therefore, that, generally speaking, the letters are combined with figures which have reference to Christ, not to the other Persons of the Trinity (but see below); so that they were clearly used as inculcating the doctrine of Christ's Divinity; for this reason the letters, in this form, were avoided, as far as our knowledge goes, by the Arians.

Among the Gnostics the symbol was used for figure-jugglery and for mysterious doctrines of various kinds; *e.g.*, when written backwards, Ω and A have the numerical value 801, which is likewise the sum of the letters of the word *περιστερά* ('dove'); therefore, they taught, Christ called Himself A and Ω because the Holy Spirit came down upon Him at His baptism in the form of a dove.† This is doubtless the reason why Aω is found in combination with a dove; not infrequently two doves figure, one on either side of the letters. Examples of this are the two little golden boxes, found in Vatican graves, which have inscribed on them the device A ☧ ω and a dove (5th cent.).‡ The like device is seen on a silver *capsella*, found at Trêves, belonging to the 4th or 5th cent.; indeed, this combination would almost appear to have been the normal form of the symbol in Trêves, judging by the frequency of its occurrence there.§

5. There is one other point that is worth alluding to. In the Apocalypse A and Ω is explained as signifying *ἡ ἀρχὴ καὶ τὸ τέλος*, 'the beginning and the end' (21^{6}). This is the simplest, and no doubt the earliest, form of explanation; in 22^{13} the same form is preceded by a parallel one, 'the first and the last' (*ὁ πρῶτος καὶ ὁ ἔσχατος, ἡ ἀρχὴ καὶ τὸ τέλος*); these two forms of explanation agree closely with the OT prototype, as seen in Is 44^{6} 48^{12}; the explanatory clause given in Rev 1^{8} (*ὁ ὢν καὶ ὁ ἦν καὶ ὁ ἐρχόμενος, ὁ παντοκράτωρ*) is unquestionably a developed, and therefore a later, form. The title with its explanatory clause is applied to Christ, as indicating His eternal Being. Now, it must strike one at first sight as strange that a title should be used for this purpose which contains the idea of finality, the very reverse of eternal being.‖ But on a closer examination of the passages 21^{1-7} 22^{10-15} it appears that the 'end' is to be the herald of a new *beginning*. We have here, that is to say, the echo of the eschatological belief that the 'last times' shall be parallel to the 'beginning.' This idea is brought out with great clearness in a passage cited (from some unknown work) in Ep. Barn. 6^{13} 'Behold, I make the last things as the first' (*ἰδοὺ ποιῶ τὰ ἔσχατα ὡς τὰ πρῶτα*). He, the Alpha and the Omega, the First and the Last, makes the last things as the first.* Thus, so far from Ω denoting 'the last' or 'the end' in the usual sense of the words, it really implies the beginning of a new era. From this point of view one can well understand the frequency of the symbol AΩ on tombstones; for, when experience had proved that the belief in Christ's imminent *Parousia* was a mistaken one, the hopes of Christians would naturally be transferred to the life beyond the grave.

* See the exhaustive list of symbols in Cabrol, *op. cit.* i. pp. 7–23.

† Irenæus, *adv. Hær.* I. xiv. 6, xv. 1, quoted in *PRE*³. In the Egyptian Museum in Berlin there can be seen, on both papyrus and parchment leaves, magical formulæ in combination with AΩ and a cross; they were most probably worn as amulets.

‡ *Bullett. crist.* 1872, 12 ff., t. 2. 2, 3.

§ See the fine plates in F. X. Kraus, *Die christlichen Inschr. der Rheinlande*, i. (Nachtrag); in one case a horse takes the place of the dove; is this an instance of syncretism?

‖ The later form of explanation (1^{8}) was perhaps due to this.

LITERATURE.—Schoettgen, *Hor. Heb. et Talmud.* (1733–42); N. Müller, art. 'AΩ' in *PRE*³; F. X. Kraus, *Die christlichen Inschriften der Rheinlande* (1890, 1894); Cabrol, art. 'AΩ' in *DACL* (1903 . . .); art. 'Alpha and Omega' in Hastings' *DB* and *DCG*, and in *JE*; *CIL* xiv.

W. O. E. OESTERLEY.

ABANDONMENT.—In considering the ethical and religious uses of this word, we have to remember that abandonment has an active, a reflexive, and a passive meaning. It may signify (1) the action of abandoning; (2) self-abandonment, defined by Murray as 'the surrender of oneself to an influence'; (3) the condition of being abandoned.

1. The abandonment of infants, sick persons, and aged parents, now rightly condemned as immoral, was not always prompted by motives of inhumanity. Westermarck (*The Origin and Development of the Moral Ideas*, 1906, vol. i. ch. xvii.) has accumulated a mass of evidence which proves that practices regarded by us as atrocious, are 'largely explained by the pitiful condition of the invalid, the hardships of a wandering life, and the superstitious opinions of ignorant men.' Amongst the testimonies cited, especially important are those which show that 'the most common motive for abandoning or destroying sick people seems to be fear of infection, or of demoniacal possession, which is regarded as the cause of various diseases.' Abandonment often meant death, but not always; exposed infants were sometimes adopted into families, but they were also sometimes saved for a life of infamy. Justin Martyr, in his *First Apology*, charges (ch. xxix.) those who abandon children with the crime of murder, if the waifs 'be not picked up, but die'; he also dwells (ch. xxvii.) on the wickedness of exposing children to the peril of being kept alive for immoral purposes. See following articles.

2. There may be an abandonment of self to influences good or bad, holy or unholy. Our language testifies against us when, without saying whether there has been surrender to virtue or to vice, we describe a profligate as an abandoned youth, or a harlot as an abandoned woman. Stanhope (*Paraph.* xi. 476) calls Judas 'an abandoned disciple,' not because Jesus had abandoned him, but because the betrayer had surrendered himself to the evil one.

The Mystics understood by abandonment the complete surrender of the soul to the influences of the Divine Spirit, its entire absorption in the contemplation of the Divine glory, and its absolute devotion to the Divine will. In the dialogue narrated by Doctor Eckhart (Vaughan, *Hours with the Mystics*, bk. vi. ch. i.), a learned man asks a beggar, 'Where hast thou found God?' and the answer is, 'Where I abandoned all creatures.' To the scholar's greeting, 'God give thee good morrow,' the poor man's response is, 'I never had an ill morrow.' Whereupon the scholar says, 'But if God were to cast thee into hell, what wouldst thou do then?' The beggar's reply closes with the words, 'I would sooner be in hell and have God, than in heaven and not have Him.' Doctor Eckhart's comment is, 'Then understood this Master that true Abandonment, with utter Abasement, was the nearest way to God.'

3. When abandonment means 'the condition of being abandoned,' the reference is usually to the

* Cf. Gunkel, *Schöpfung und Chaos in Urzeit und Endzeit*, p. 369.

absence of any consciousness of the Divine presence, such as finds expression in the Psalmist's cry, reiterated by Christ upon the cross, 'My God, my God, why hast thou forsaken me?' (Ps 22[1], Mt 27[46]). But the condition of one who is abandoned by his friends also involves moral issues, as, *e.g.*, the degree in which he is himself to blame for his isolation. Martensen treats the subject luminously (*Christian Ethics*, vol. i. [Individual] p. 358 ff.) in the chapter which assigns to domestic happiness and friendship a high place among 'the relative goods of life.' But in proportion to the pleasure, of which our friends may be the legitimate sources, is the pain occasioned, when by those friends 'we are morally abandoned . . . because we, in their consciousness, in their love, as it were, die, and are buried; or, what is the same thing, because we are changed in their idea, and become other than we were before, although in reality we are still the same. Such an abandonment is, in many cases, not without guilt on our side; and, had we a richer measure of love, we would in no case so easily feel ourselves lonely and forsaken.'

The foregoing considerations cast light upon questions involved in the experience of devout souls whose complaint is 'Jehovah hath forsaken me, and the Lord hath forgotten me' (Is 49[14]).* On the one hand, expression is repeatedly given in the OT to the truth which lies at the foundation of the Hebrew religion: 'The Lord will not forsake his people for his great name's sake' (1 S 12[22], cf. Dt 31[6], Ps 9[10] 37[28], Is 41[17] 42[16]). Broad-based on the history of God's dealings with Israel was the 'strength and comfort' which 'fell with weight' upon John Bunyan's spirit, as he took courage from the noble words of Sir 2[10] 'Look at the generations of old and see; did ever any trust in the Lord, and was confounded? or did any abide in his fear, and was forsaken?' (*Grace Abounding*, § 62 ff.). On the other hand, the OT recognizes that God's promise is conditional. The message of God's Spirit through the prophets is, 'If ye forsake him, he will forsake you' (2 Ch 15[2], cf. 24[20]). But this forsaking is not to be understood as implying that God would cast off His people for ever (Ps 94[14], Jer 33[24ff.]); even when He seems to have abandoned 'the sheep of his pasture,' a voice is raised beseeching Him to 'have respect unto the covenant' (Ps 74[1. 20]). The question, 'Will the Lord cast off from age to age?' passes into the more hopeful cry, 'Will he not once again show favour?' (Ps 77[7], cf. Is 54[7]).

The biographies of devout believers bear witness, however, to a sense of abandonment by some who can reproach themselves neither on account of their departing from God, nor on account of their doubting His faithfulness. Martensen (*op. cit.* p. 391 ff.) describes this condition as one in which 'the individual is, in a relative sense, left to himself.' In the religious life he distinguishes two states of holiness: one in which 'the blessing of the Divine grace is perceptibly revealed,' and another in which 'grace, as it were, retires and remains hidden.' The latter state is one of 'inward drought and abandonment,' and may be the result of bodily indisposition or mental weariness. At such times 'we should hold to God's word, whose truth and grace are independent of our changing moods and feelings; and remain confident that even in states of deepest abandonment God the Lord is with us, although with veiled face.'

A sense of abandonment by the Father was the experience of Christ during the darkness that shrouded Calvary; to this fact witness is borne in the earliest Gospel, for St. Mark records none of the Seven Sayings from the Cross save this: 'My God, my God, why hast thou forsaken me?' (Mk 15[34], Mt 27[46]). Professor Schmiedel accepts this as one of the five 'absolutely credible passages' in the Gospels concerning Christ (*EBi*, vol. ii. col. 1881). Bengel (*Com. in loc.*) lays stress on the preterite tense of ἐγκατέλιπες, and renders, 'why didst thou forsake me?' In his view, 'at that very instant the dereliction came to an end. . . . In the deepest moment of dereliction He was silent.' This suggestion need not be pressed; the cry itself testifies to an actual feeling of abandonment by Him whose spirit never lost its faith in God. The mystery it expresses is unrelieved unless He who uttered it was the sinless Saviour, who in His infinite love was bearing 'our sins in his body upon the tree' (1 P 2[24]). In a lucid exposition of this Word from the Cross, W. L. Walker says: 'Our Lord felt Himself in this supreme moment forsaken, even by His Father. . . . We here see Christ suffering that which is the last consequence of sin—the sense of separation from God. . . . It is in entire keeping with, and indeed appears as the natural culmination of, His thought of giving His life as "a ransom for many," as a sacrifice for sin, or "a guilt-offering"' (*The Cross and the Kingdom* [1902], p. 138 f.). [See art. 'Dereliction' in Hastings' *DCG*].

J. G. TASKER.

ABANDONMENT AND EXPOSURE.

THE most helpless of mankind are those who have just begun life, and those who, through old age or infirmity, are about to leave it. Unable to provide for their own needs, they are entirely dependent upon the love or the compassion of others. Individual cases of neglect of infancy and age are not unknown in any country, but in some cases this neglect passes beyond an individual idiosyncrasy and becomes a national custom. When this neglect of children takes the form of removing them from the mother's habitation and leaving them unprotected to perish by starvation, the elements, or wild beasts, or to be rescued by the chance passer-by, it is called *Exposure.* The similar treatment of the aged and infirm is called *Abandonment.*

I. Exposure. — For the exposure of children there are several causes, which require to be treated independently. In different countries different causes often bring about the same result.

(1) In most countries the commonest cause of the exposure of infants is *shame*, the child being the offspring either of an unmarried woman or of a union not recognized as regular by the customs of her country. Less frequently, the shame may be occasioned by some malformation of the infant itself, the parents regarding it as a reproach to them to be associated with a monster. In the legends of most countries great heroes are often represented as having been exposed to conceal the shame of their mothers. The exposure may be the act of the mother herself, as in the case of Evadne exposing Iamos (Pindar, *Olympian.* vi. 44 ff.; cf. the exposure of Ion in Euripides' *Ion*, 18 ff.), or it may be ordered or executed by the parents of the mother. Acrisius, in the fragment of Simonides, sends Danae and Perseus together adrift; in Roman legend, Romulus and Remus, the twin children of Rhea Sylvia, are exposed by the orders of the cruel uncle, Amulius (Livy, i. 4). In cases of this kind children are exposed without regard to sex.

(2) Children are exposed from *fear that the means of subsistence will not be sufficient to maintain a larger population.* Here exposure is often only

* The words 'abandon' and 'abandonment' are not found in the EV, but the essential thought is expressed in such passages as are quoted above.

one of many methods of infanticide. The populations among which it is most common are those which live by hunting or as nomad herdsmen. Thus, amongst the native tribes of South-East Australia it is usual to kill infants by starvation, first by depriving them of food in the camp, and, when they become peevish, removing them to a distance and leaving them to die. The death, however, is assigned to *muparn* (magic) (Howitt, *Native Tribes of S. E. Australia*, p. 748). In the South Sea Islands the same end is achieved by drowning or burying alive (Turner, *Samoa*, pp. 286, 333). The Koniagas, a tribe of Eskimos, abandon girls in the wilderness after stuffing grass into their mouths (Bancroft, *Native Races of the Pacific States of America*, i. p. 81, cf. pp. 131, 566, etc., and see foll. art.). Amongst the Arabs before Muhammad the same system prevailed, and is referred to frequently in the Qur'ān as a practice to be forbidden. Here sons were preserved, but daughters were usually buried alive. 'They attribute daughters unto God (far be it from Him!); but unto themselves children of the sex which they desire. And when any of them is told the news of the birth of a female, his face becometh black, and he is deeply afflicted . . . considering within himself whether he shall keep it with disgrace, or whether he shall bury it in the dust. Do they not make an ill judgment?' (Qur'ān, *Sur.* xvi. 59. 60; cf. also *Sur.* vi. 43. 81; Robertson Smith, *Kinship and Marriage in Early Arabia*, ch. iv. and especially note C). In tribes of this kind the carrying about of the weak and helpless causes great difficulty; hence many nomad tribes abandon the old as well as expose the young. Where such practices prevail, if the religion of the tribe includes ancestor-worship, daughters only will be exposed. In the patriarchal system only a son can properly present the sacrifice to the dead ancestors. On the other hand, where wives are purchased, a large family of daughters is a profitable possession, and naturally they will not be exposed. Hence in Homeric Greece, where girls are described as παρθένοι ἀλφεσίβοιαι, 'maidens that win cattle,' because cattle were, at any rate originally, the bride-price, it was only boys that were exposed. The only exceptions are cases like the Arcadian Atalanta, who was exposed by the orders of her father Iasios, because he was disappointed that she was not a boy.* In Sarawak it is considered specially fortunate to have a large family of girls, because the successful suitors for the daughters come to live in their parents' house and work on their sugar plantations, while sons expect their parents to help them with the wedding portion, and leave them in order to work for their father-in-law (H. Ling Roth, *Sarawak*, p. 125). Exposure in Sarawak, presumably of male children, is practised by hanging them up in a basket on a tree (*op. cit.* p. 101, note).

(3) Exposure *for other economic reasons.* Amongst those reasons which prevail especially among agricultural populations, perhaps the chief is the serious drain upon family resources in providing dowries for a large number of daughters. In modern India, exposure and other methods of infanticide have on this account been widely employed to reduce the number of daughters. Although the British Government has made every effort to stop the practice, it is doubtful if it has entirely succeeded (H. H. Risley, *Census of India*, 1901, vol. i. p. 115 f.). Exposure of female infants is common in most parts of the East, nowhere more so than in China, where the foundling hospital is a regular institution. The practice was very prevalent at Rome, where, after the Second Punic War, it was considered unnecessary to have a *praenomen* for the daughters of the family, as generally only one, or at most two, were reared. Full discretion in this matter lay with the father, who took up (*sustulit*) the newborn child laid at his feet, if he wished it reared. If he did not, it was exposed. According to Dionysius of Halicarnassus (ii. 15), a law of Romulus forbade the exposing of sons or of the eldest daughter. If five neighbours gave their consent after viewing the child, any infant might be exposed. Otherwise exposure made the father liable to various pains and penalties, including the loss of half his property. In historical times this law had apparently fallen into desuetude. A similar practice prevailed amongst the ancient Germans. If the father did not take up the newborn babe from the floor, it was not reared. When once its lips had been smeared with honey or milk, however, it could not be exposed. By tasting of the family food, it became a member of the family. Even so, in Greek legend, Aristaeus becomes a god by having nectar and ambrosia dropped upon his lips by deities (Pindar, *Pythian.* ix. 68). The exposure was carried out by placing the child under a tree or committing it to the waves in a rude boat (Grimm, *Rechtsalterthümer*, p. 456; Gummere, *Germanic Origins*, p. 188 ff.). In a much more remote antiquity the same practice prevailed among the Hindus. In the Yajur Veda mention is made of exposing female children and of lifting up a son * (Zimmer, *Altindisches Leben*, p. 319 f.). Among most tribes, however primitive, even amongst the natives of Australia, it is the father that decides whether a child is to be reared or not, though he is not infrequently beguiled by the mother (Lumholtz, *Among Cannibals*, p. 272).

(4) *Superstitious reasons* may be of various kinds: an oracle, as in the case of Œdipus, that the child will be dangerous to his sire; a dream, either of the mother, as in the case of Paris, whose mother dreamt that she had been delivered of a firebrand which consumed Troy; or of some other relative, as in the case of Cyrus, founder of the Persian Empire, who was exposed by the orders of his maternal grandfather, Astyages, because Astyages dreamt that his daughter gave birth to a deluge which flooded, and afterwards to a vine which overshadowed, all Asia (Herod. i. 107–108). In modern India, till recently, a child was exposed if it happened to be born on a certain day which the professional astrologer declared to be unlucky (Dubois and Beauchamp, *Hindu Manners*[3], p. 606). In many countries twins are looked upon as ill-omened. Even where, as in Uganda, the birth of twins is regarded as lucky, it is considered 'rather a tempting of providence' (Sir H. H. Johnston, *Uganda Protectorate*, p. 878). Even in mediæval Scotland it was considered impossible that the mother of twins should have been faithful to her husband, for two children implied two fathers. Exposure is sometimes employed in order to avert continuous misfortune. In the Kavirondo country and amongst the Nilotic negroes, a woman who has already lost several children leaves the next child on the road at dawn. Presently it is brought back by a friendly neighbour, who is regarded and looked on henceforth as the child's foster-mother (*Uganda Protectorate*, pp. 748, 793). The exposure of emaciated children for a night on a stone altar, which is still practised, though now only surreptitiously, amongst the Greeks of the island of Melos (Bent, *Cyclades*, p. 64), is a survival of the ancient ἐγκοίμησις in a temple to be cured by the god.

(5) *Care of the race character.* The best known example of this is the practice of Sparta, where children regarded as physically unfit were ex-

* The evidence for this, however, is late; Aelian, *Varia Historia*, xiii. 1.

* But see Jolly, below, p. 6 f.

posed in a ravine called Apothetæ near Mt. Taygetus after they had been examined and rejected by the elders of the tribe (φυλή) (Plutarch, *Lycurgus*, c. 16). A similar procedure is recommended by Plato in the *Republic* (461 C and elsewhere; see Appendix IV. to bk. v. in Adam's edition). In a State like Sparta, where, as Aristotle remarks, all its neighbours were enemies (Aristotle, *Politics*, ii. 9. 3), and where the Spartans proper were only a small governing caste amid a hostile population, the need for such a regulation is obvious. But in a less stringent measure the regulation no doubt existed in other States. At Athens, if the father did not celebrate the *amphidromia* for his child, it was not reared. No State save Thebes, and this apparently only at a late date, forbade exposure (Aelian, *Varia Historia*, ii. 7). The child was to be taken to the authorities, who disposed of it to a person willing to undertake to bring it up as a slave, and recoup himself for his outlay by the child's services when it grew up.

(6) *Luxury and selfishness.* Although luxury is supposed to characterize only States which are highly civilized, selfishness can be found in all lands. Among the native Australians, where the children are often nursed for several years, it is inconvenient for the mother to have a younger child on her hands. Such a child is either killed immediately after birth or left behind when the camp is changed (Spencer and Gillen, *Native Tribes of Central Australia*, 1899, p. 51; Howitt, *The Native Tribes of South-East Australia*, 1904, p. 750). In many countries, ancient and modern, an improvement in the standard of living is accompanied by a disinclination to rear children. From the 4th cent. B.C. onwards, this was conspicuous in Greece, and in Rome it formed a theme of discussion for philosophers and satirists. How common the practice of exposure was, may be gathered from the frequency with which the heroines of the New Comedy, who come before us in the Latin versions of Plautus and Terence, are represented as having been exposed. They are, of course, recognized at the critical moment by the trinkets (*crepundia*) which were attached to the exposed infant. Under the Roman Empire, Musonius Rufus (p. 77, Hense) discusses whether all the children born should be reared; and Pliny (*Epp.* x. 74 f.) consults the emperor Trajan as to the legal position of the exposed children reared by others (θρεπτοί) in his province of Bithynia. As the Roman comedy shows, the persons who thus reared exposed children were not moved by philanthropy; their aim was to make them slaves or courtezans (cf. *e.g.* Terence, *Heautontimorumenos*, 640; Plautus, *Cistellaria*, ii. 3. 543–630). Only when a child was exposed for superstitious reasons which made its death desirable, was it exposed where it was not likely to be found. As the Athenians exposed children in a pot (χυτρίζειν, ἐγχυτρίζειν), and as first-fruits were offered to the household gods in pots, it has been suggested that putting a child in a pot was a way of entrusting it to the gods. This is possible, but there is at present no sufficient evidence to prove it.

Besides these categories, exposure may be due, in isolated cases, to other causes, *e.g.* domestic persecution. This led to the expulsion of Hagar and her child from the family of Abraham, and her temporary abandonment of Ishmael (Gn 21[15ff.]). Temporary national persecution also may lead to exposure, as in the case of Moses (Ex 2[3ff.]). But neither is an example of a practice pursued by a nation in ordinary circumstances.

LITERATURE.—Besides the works referred to in the text, there is an article upon exposure amongst the Indo-Germanic peoples in Schrader's *Reallexicon der idg. Altertumskunde* (*s.v.* 'Aussetzung'), and a very full article in Daremberg-Saglio's *Dict. des Antiquités grecques et romaines* (*s.v.* 'Expositio'). For general treatment of the subject see Platz, *Gesch. des Verbrechens der Aussetzung* (Stuttgart, 1876 [mostly modern legal procedure]), and Lallemand, *Hist. des enfants abandonnés et délaissés* (Paris, 1885). See also Westermarck, *History of Human Marriage* (1891), pp. 311–314; Ploss, *Das Kind*[2] (1884), vol. ii. pp. 243–275.

2. **Abandonment.**—Abandonment of the aged seems to arise simply from dread of the food supply running short, or the difficulty amongst nomad peoples of carrying about with them those who are no longer able to share in the work of the tribe or to shift for themselves. The practice, however, does not prevail amongst all wandering tribes. Among the native Australians the aged and infirm are treated with special kindness and provided with a share of the food (Spencer and Gillen, *Native Tribes of Central Australia*, 1899, p. 51). On the other hand, the natives of South Africa in their primitive state abandoned the old. 'I have seen,' says Moffat (*Missionary Labours and Scenes in Southern Africa*, 1842, p. 132), 'a small circle of stakes fastened in the ground, within which were still lying the bones of a parent bleached in the sun, who had been thus abandoned.' Amongst the American Indians of the Pacific coast the old are generally neglected, and when helpless are abandoned (Bancroft, *Native Races of the Pacific States of America*, i. pp. 120, 131, 205, 390, and elsewhere). Among many tribes the duty of looking after the old belongs only to their own descendants. Hence the members of such tribes pray for large families, in order that when old they may have some one to support them (H. Ling Roth, *Benin*, p. 47). In the Qur'ān, Muhammad combines the injunction to be kind to parents with a warning not to kill the children (*Sur.* vi. 150). Amongst the Indo-Germanic peoples, abandonment of the old is mentioned in the Vedas (Rig Veda, viii. 51. 52 [1020]; Atharva Veda, xviii. 2. 34; Zimmer, *Altindisches Leben*, p. 327 ff.). In ancient Persia and Armenia, cripples were left to shift for themselves; and Strabo, who is supported by other authorities, tells us that the Bactrians left the old and infirm to be eaten by dogs; and the Avesta itself recognizes the practice of setting a portion of food by such persons and leaving them to die (Strabo, xi. 11. 3; Vendīdād, iii. 18 [in this case a person ceremonially impure is thus shut up for life]; Spiegel, *Eranische Altertumskunde*, iii. p. 682). The Caspians allowed those over seventy to die of hunger, and exposed their bodies in the desert to wild animals (Strabo, xi. 11. 3). Still more gruesome stories are told by Herodotus (i. 216, iii. 99, iv. 26) of the Massagetæ, of the Padæi (an Indian tribe), and of the Issedones. Even among the Greeks the removal of the old was not unknown. Most remarkable was the law of Ceos, which prevented 'him who was unable to live well from living ill.' By it all over sixty years of age were poisoned with hemlock (Strabo, x. 5–6). Amongst the Romans, sexagenarians are supposed to have been in early days cast over a bridge (the *pons sublicius*) into the Tiber ('Sexagenarii de ponte,' cf. Cicero, *pro Roscio Amerino*, § 100). The northern nations were equally cruel (Gummere, *Germanic Origins*, p. 203). When, however, such a custom prevails in a nation from time immemorial, its action is looked upon as natural, and is borne with resignation. And even in Britain, till recent times, seventy was regarded as extreme old age, and few reached it. In the New Hebrides, Turner found that the aged were buried alive at their own request (*Samoa*, p. 335), and it was considered a disgrace to their family if they were not. Not infrequently persons in delirium or very ill are abandoned by their relatives (H. Ling Roth, *Sarawak*, i. p. 311), no doubt because they are supposed to be under

the influence of an evil power, generally a ghost (Codrington, *The Melanesians*, p. 194).

LITERATURE. — For the Indo-Germanic peoples a general account is given in Schrader's *Reallexicon der idg. Altertumskunde*, s.v. 'Alte Leute.' See also G. H. Jones, *Dawn of Europ. Civilization* (1903), 168 ff.; E. Westermarck, *Origin and Development of the Moral Ideas*, i. (1906) 386 ff.; L. T. Hobhouse, *Morals in Evolution* (1906), i. 349.

P. GILES.

ABANDONMENT AND EXPOSURE (American). — **1.** The practice of infant-exposure was widespread throughout **North America**. The usual motive, especially in the North, was the lack of food, and the consequent difficulty of supporting a family. This practice is recorded among the Eskimos of Smith Sound in the extreme north-east of the American continent, where all children above the number of two are either strangled or exposed to die of hunger or cold, without regard to sex. Infanticide, both before and after birth, which is but another form of exposure, is also common, as when the women of the Kutchins, an Athapascan tribe, kill their female children to save them from the misery which their mothers must endure (Ploss, *Das Kind*, ii. 251, 252). Among the Koniagas, a tribe of the Pacific coast, boys were highly prized, but girls were often taken to the wilderness, where their mouths were stuffed with grass, and they were left to perish. Certain Columbian tribes usually treated both children and the aged with kindness, yet abandoned and even killed them in time of dire need, while exposure was not uncommon among the Yulan tribe of Cochimis in New Mexico (Bancroft, *Native Races of the Pacific States*, San Francisco, 1883, i. 81, 279, 566). That this practice is by no means modern, is shown by the fact that the Indians of Acadia in the 17th cent. frequently abandoned their children for lack of time to take care of them, and in Quebec orphans were often exposed. An interesting case is also recorded of a Huron mother who regarded the circumstances associated with her unborn child as uncanny, and therefore procured an abortion. The fœtus proved, however, to be viable and later she took it back, although it grew up to be a 'medicine-man' (*Jesuit Relations and Allied Documents*, i. 256, ix. 28, xiii. 106).

Abandonment of the sick and the aged, sparing neither sex, rank, nor kinship, seems to have been common among the American Indians of all times and localities. In Acadia (New France), those who were exhausted with age or protracted illness were frequently killed, this act being deemed, as it doubtless was in many instances, a kindness. Old men were abandoned to die, especially when sick; but if they did not expire within three days, they were killed by sucking blood from incisions made in the abdomen, and then dashing quantities of cold water on the navel. During this process and at the first desertion the victims wrapped themselves in their mantles and formally chanted the death-hymn. Among the Hurons and Iroquois the sick were left to their fate, and in the latter tribe even husband and wife deserted each other in an illness deemed mortal. Old women were abandoned among the Hurons, and the Abenakis deserted their medicine-men with equal readiness. The custom of abandoning the sick is said to have been especially common among the Algonquins. Not only the old but the young were deserted in time of serious illness, whether the sick were boys or girls. Such desertions were practised with special frequency in time of sudden alarm or removal, although they were also common for the simple reason that the old and sick were deemed a burden, and the *Jesuit Relations* (63 vols., Cincinnati, 1896–1901) abound in pathetic instances (i. 211, 258, 274, ii. 14, 18, 250, iii. 122, iv. 198, v. 102, 140–142, vii. 280, xiv. 72, 152, xv. 134, xviii. 136, xix. 100, xxiv. 42, xxix. 84, xxx. 134, xxxi. 196, etc.). As late as the 19th cent. the Utes abandoned the old and sick when they became encumbrances, while aged parents were murdered in most cold-blooded fashion among the Californian Gallinomeros; and in Lower California the aged sick were abandoned, being killed if they survived their desertion too long (Bancroft, *op. cit.* i. 83, 390, 437, 568).

2. In **South America**, in like manner, the exposure of infants was and is extremely common. Among the Salivas and the Manaos, malformed children are put to death, since their deformity is supposed to be the work of a demon. Guaycuran women under the age of thirty killed the majority of their children, thus seeking to retain the good will of their husbands, who were denied all marital relations during the long period of suckling, and consequently frequently married other wives. The Abipones put to death all but two children in a family, though girls were given preference over boys, since wooers paid large sums for brides, while sons, for this very reason, were a heavy expense to their parents. In Patagonia the parents decided whether to adopt their children or not; and if the resolve was adverse, the infant was either strangled or exposed to the dogs. (See Ploss, *op. cit.* ii. 252–253). The women of the Amazon tribes frequently procure abortion rather than endure the pangs of childbirth (von den Steinen, *Unter den Naturvölkern Zentral-Brasiliens*, Berlin, 1894, pp. 334, 503); and among the Indians of the Paraguayan Chaco fully half the children born are put to death, especially if they are deformed or posthumous, or if their fathers or mothers die about the time the offspring in question are born; while girls, if born before boys, are invariably killed (W. B. Grubb, *Among the Indians of Paraguayan Chaco*, London, 1904, p. 64). The same tribes abandon the sick or bury them alive, the invalid frequently hastening his own end by refusing food (*ib.* p. 41). Abandonment probably prevails more generally in South America, however, than the relatively scanty data would seem to imply.

LOUIS H. GRAY.

ABANDONMENT AND EXPOSURE (Hindu).—The ancient Sanskrit literature of India appears to have preserved some remnants of the time when the *patria potestas* gave the father a right to abandon and expose his children, especially *daughters*. Thus it is stated in the lawbook of *Vasiṣṭha* (xv. 2), that 'the father and the mother have power to give, to sell, and to abandon their son.' More ambiguous is a text in the Yajur Veda, to the effect that 'they put aside a girl immediately after her birth.' It is by no means certain that this 'putting aside' of a daughter is an equivalent for exposing her, as was supposed by some writers. Others explain the term as referring to the delivery of a girl to her nurse or attendant (see Zimmer, *Altindisches Leben*, p. 328; Böhtlingk's art. 'Pflegten die Inder Töchter auszusetzen?,' in *JGOS* xliv. 494 ff.; also Schrader, *Reallexicon*, p. 53). It is true that female infanticide has been a common practice with some castes up to very recent times, and the barbarous custom of widow-burning (*satī*) would seem to show that sentiment could not have stood in the way if it was thought expedient to do away with female children as soon as born. As regards the desertion of *sons*, there are, particularly, the law-texts referring to the rights and position of the *apaviddha*, or son cast off, one of the twelve species of sons that are enumerated and described by Indian legislators. Thus in the Code of Manu (ix. 171), the *apaviddha* is described as one deserted by his parents or by either of them. The old commentator (Medhātithi) adds that the reason of the desertion may be either extreme distress of the parents, or the committing of some fault on the part of the boy. If some one else takes pity on the helpless child and brings him up, he is reckoned as his adopted child, though taking a rather low rank in the series of secondary sons. The *pālak-putra* or foster son of the present day may perhaps be viewed as a relic of the ancient usage. On the other hand, there seems to have been a strong feeling against abandoning sons or other relatives without a just cause. *Yājñavalkya* (ii. 237) says: 'Whoever, being father and son, sister and brother, husband and wife, preceptor and pupil, abandon each other when not degraded (put out of caste), shall be fined 100 paṇas.' Analogous rules are laid down by Viṣṇu, v. 113, and Manu, viii. 389. The practice of buying or selling children is specially reprobated (see Āpastamba, ii. 13. 11). The desertion or repudiation of a *wife* is frequently referred to in the lawbooks as a punishment for misconduct on her part, but it appears that in most cases she was not to be deprived of a bare maintenance. In a modern text, the repudiation of a wife for any offence short of adultery is characterized as a practice no longer fit for the present (or Kali) age. The higher Hindu castes of the present day do not admit divorce or repudiation except for very stringent reasons, if at all; but it is common enough among the lower castes, especially those of Dravidian origin, where the marriage tie is very loose. For the supposed abandonment and exposure of *old people*, Sanskrit literature seems to contain no other evidence than a text of the Atharva Veda (xviii. 2. 34), in which the spirits of exposed ancestors are invoked side by side with those buried or burnt. However, the term 'exposed' (*uddhita*) is ambiguous, and may refer either to dead bodies exposed on the summits of hills or to those on trees, according to Persian fashion. Exposure of old people, in a certain way, may be found in the barbarous custom, suppressed by the British Government, of taking persons supposed to be dying to the banks of the Ganges and immersing them in water.

LITERATURE.—Jolly, *Recht u. Sitte*, Strassburg, 1896; Zimmer, *Altindisches Leben*, Berlin, 1879; Oldenberg, *Die Religion des Veda*, Berlin, 1894; *Census of India* 1901, *General Report*, Calcutta, 1903.

J. JOLLY.

There is statistical evidence * that in the Panjab female infant life is still culpably neglected in comparison with male; and that, using the term in a wide sense, female infanticide still prevails in that part of India on a large scale, chiefly among the Jaṭs, and, despite the prohibition of the Sikh teachers, especially among those of that caste who profess Sikhism. H. A. ROSE.

ABANDONMENT AND EXPOSURE (Japanese).—There is no evidence of the existence in Japan of the custom of abandoning the aged. Isolated cases of the practice of exposure of infants occur in Japan, as in other countries, but it has never approached recognition as a general custom. From the myth of the god Hiruko (leech-child), it may be inferred that the abandonment of deformed infants was not uncommon in the earliest times. The *Nihongi* tells us that when this god had completed his third year he was still unable to walk. His parents therefore placed him in the rock-camphor-boat of heaven and sent him adrift. We may compare the stories of Moses and Sargon.

W. G. ASTON.

ABANDONMENT AND EXPOSURE (Persian).—The data concerning the exposure of infants in Persia are scanty. According to the Avesta (*Vendīdād*, ii. 29), all deformities were regarded as the work of the Evil One. It is not impossible, therefore, that deformed children and viable monsters were exposed with more or less frequency; and this is expressly stated to have been the case with Zal, who was exposed by order of his father Sam, because he was born with white hair, which distinctly marked him, in his parent's eyes, as the offspring of Ahriman (*Shah-Namah*, ed. Vullers-Landauer, pp. 131–135). There is, on the other hand, no reason to suppose that such exposure was the rule. Cyrus the Great, in like manner, according to Herod. i. 107 f., was by his grandfather exposed and ordered to be killed because of a dream which prophesied that the infant would be the future lord of Asia. Nor can it be inferred, from the marked preference given in the Avesta to sons rather than daughters (Geiger, *Ostiran. Kultur*, pp. 234, 235), that the latter were exposed, the entire spirit of Zoroastrianism making such a conclusion most improbable. Even in the case of an illegitimate child, it was regarded as a heinous offence to procure an abortion (*Vendīdād*, xv. 5–16). On the contrary, the prospective mother of an illegitimate child must be carefully protected by the man responsible for her condition, lest some harm might come to the fœtus. This undoubtedly implies that, despite sporadic instances of exposure, the desertion of infants was abhorrent to the noblest minds of Persia. The Pahlavi *Shayast la-Shayast*, dating perhaps from the 7th cent., states that the father of children by a concubine 'shall accept all those who are male as sons; but those who are female are no advantage' (xii. 14). This does not, however, imply that female bastards were exposed. In the book of Arda-Viraf the failure of a father to acknowledge his illegitimate offspring condemned them to a piteous life in hell, while at the feet of such a parent 'several children fell, and ever screamed; and demons, just like dogs, ever fell upon and tore him.' The punishments of hell also awaited the mother who destroyed her infant and threw away its corpse, or left it crying for cold and hunger; while those who, in their greed for wealth, withheld their milk from their own infants that they might act as wet-nurses to the offspring of others, likewise suffered punishment in the future life (ed. Haug and West, xlii–xliv, lix, lxxxvii, xciv). LOUIS H. GRAY.

* Punjab Census Reports, 1881, 1891, 1901; also Sanitary Commissioner's Reports for the Punjab, 1905 § 22, 1904 § 20, 1901 § 14, 1897 § 20, and earlier Reports.

ABASEMENT.—Abasement in religious experience is closely connected with Adoration and Humility (see these articles). It appears to be essentially relative, and the essence of it to lie in a recognition of the comparative worthlessness of the self in the presence of a superior. In those religions which give great room to prayer and to the sense of God, abasement has always been an important element; its influence is marked in the Hebrew (see, for instance, the penitential psalms), and in all forms of the Christian, *e.g.* in St. Paul's determination to know nothing but Christ crucified (1 Co 2[2]), in Luther's conviction that the soul was weak though Christ was strong (letter to Pope Leo X. concerning Christian liberty), in Thomas à Kempis' warning never to esteem oneself as anything because of any good works (*de Imit. Chr.* bk. iii. ch. 4), in Wesley's demand that the sinner should first and foremost empty himself of his own righteousness in order to trust only in the blood of the Redeemer (*Journal*, 8th Sept. 1746).

Extravagances have been common, and in modern times there has been a great reaction. Ibsen, Nietzsche, Walt Whitman, preach in different ways the need of man's 'pride in himself.' A strong common-sense expression of this feeling is given by Jowett:

'The abasement of the individual before the Divine Being is really a sort of Pantheism, so far that in the moral world God is everything and man nothing. But man thus abased before God is no proper or rational worshipper of Him. There is a want of proportion in this sort of religion. God who is everything is not really so much as if He allowed the most exalted free agencies to exist side by side with Him' (*Life of Jowett*, by Abbott and Campbell, vol. ii. p. 151. London: Murray, 1897).

But this should not blind us to the fact that prayer and the religions of prayer seem bound up with the belief that man *depends on* God, and does not merely exist *side by side* with Him. Now, in the last analysis, humility and the abasement that is its intenser form appear as a reflexion in conduct and emotion of this belief. The sense that man does no good thing of himself alone, but always as flinging himself on the Eternal Love, is, in especial, a leading characteristic of Christianity. The repentant Publican is set above the moral Pharisee precisely because he would not attempt to justify himself (Lk $18^{9.14}$).

Even those religions—those systems of aspiration and effort—which do not recognize this kind of dependence, would still find room for some abasement in the recognition of the gap between what the individual is and what he wishes to be. But, from their point of view, why should not a man pride himself on such good as he has already attained? Yet to the religious consciousness of many the presence of this pride would appear to vitiate it all. The theoretic justification for this must lie in the conviction that man does depend for his goodness on something greater than himself. To a certain extent, no doubt, this might be found in the good elements of the order that has produced and surrounds the individual. But the Christian hatred of self-complacency seems to go further still, and to imply a belief that in the very assimilation by the individual of these good elements another power than himself is active.

It would be idle to deny the difficulties in this conception, or to pretend that they have ever yet been solved. The paradox of St. Paul—'Work out your own salvation . . . for it is God that worketh in you both to will and to work' (Ph $2^{12.13}$)—has remained a paradox even for those who maintain it. But conviction of some truth in the paradox is, at bottom, the same as the conviction of Ruskin that, if the Greeks were great at Thermopylæ, greater still were the Hebrews at the Red Sea, trusting not in the resolution they had taken, but in the hand they held (see *Modern Painters*, Part III. § i. ch. 7). F. M. Stawell.

ABBOT (Christian).—'Abbot,' in Latin *abba* or *abbas* (Old Eng. by-form 12th to 17th cent. *abbat*), from the Syriac ܐܒܐ, meaning 'father' (cf. Mk 14^{36}, Ro 8^{15}, Gal 4^{6}), was used in the earliest religious communities for the older or more venerated monks (cf. Jerome *in Gal.* 4^{6} and *in Matt.* 23^{9}, vol. vii. 451, 185, and the *Collationes* of Cassian, *passim*). The superior was not called abbot, but προεστώς, ἀρχιμανδρίτης or ἡγούμενος, and in the West *præpositus* (Cassian, etc.). The prevailing Byzantine term was ἡγούμενος (translit. *igumenus* in Latin), while an archimandrite was often a superior kind of abbot, and this title was also given to various ecclesiastical functionaries (see *Dict. d'Arch. Chrét. et de Lit. s.v.* 'Archimandrite,' 1906). In the East ἄββας appears as a tr. from the Latin, or as an honorific title, *e.g.* in the Acts of St. Maximus Conf. in the 7th century. In the West, however, *abbas* must have become the regular title of the superior of a monastery during the 5th cent., since this sense is taken for granted by St. Benedict in the first half of the 6th cent., and from that period this usage became universal. St. Benedict assumes that *præpositus* will be understood of the second in command, who was later always called prior, even by Benedictines. The name *abbas* is also applied, it seems, by Gregory of Tours to what we should call a rector with many curates, and it was extended in Merovingian times to chaplains of the king, the army, etc. (*abbas curiæ, palatinus, castrensis*, etc.). A layman holding an abbey *in commendam* in the 9th or 10th cent. was called *abbacomes* or *abbas miles*. When considerable dignity had come to attach to the name, the heads of smaller communities were called priors. The Camaldolese branch of Benedictines called their superior *major*, and neither the Carthusians nor any of the orders of friars which arose in the 13th cent., nor any subsequent religious congregation, have ever taken up the title of abbot, though 'abbess' was retained in the second order of Franciscans (Poor Clares). At the present day the Benedictines (black monks), with their branches, the Cistercians, reformed and unreformed, and the black and white canons regular (canons reg. of the Lateran and Premonstratensians) are governed by abbots.

The first mention of an abbess (*abbatissa*) is said to be in an inscription set up by an Abbess Serena at St. Agnes *extra muros* in 514.

Some heads of congregations have the title abbot general, archabbot, abbot president. The Abbot of Montecassino has the honorific title of archabbot, and in the Middle Ages, when head of a congregation, was called *Abbas Abbatum*. A new title, *Abbas Primas*, was given in 1893 to the Abbot of St. Anselmo, Rome (built by Leo XIII.), as president of the new union of all black Benedictines.

The government of an abbot or an abbess is strictly monarchical. Before St. Benedict (*c.* 530) the abbot was the living rule, guided, if he chose, by the traditions of the Fathers of the desert, by the rules of Pachomius, or Basil, or Augustine, or by the customs of Lerins or Marmoutier. From St. Benedict's time (whose Rule was propagated in Italy by Gregory the Great, and became approximately universal soon afterwards) the abbot's government is constitutional, for he is bound by the Rule (*Regula*, cap. 64), which was gradually supplemented by decrees of popes, and of councils, and by regulations like those in England of Lanfranc. When branch congregations were formed (as Cluniacs, Cistercians, Camaldolese, etc.) of many monasteries, or congregations of black monks (as those of Bursfeld, St. Justina, etc.), the Rule was supplemented by *constitutiones* or commentaries on portions of the Rule, and by the regulations enforced by visitors or general chapters. All this applies also *mutatis mutandis* to the government of the canons regular. But the supremacy of the abbot was never seriously weakened, and the monarchical character of abbatial government is the distinguishing feature of the older orders as compared with the later friars, clerks regular, brothers, etc.

As it gradually became customary for many monks to be clerics, it also became the rule for abbots to be priests—in the East from the 5th cent., in the West from about the 7th. A council under Eugenius II. at Rome in 826 made this obligatory (Mansi, *Conc.* xiv. 1007). It seems that by *ordinatio abbatis* St. Benedict meant the 'appointment,' not the 'ordination,' *i.e.* 'blessing' of an abbot. St. Gregory the Great speaks of a bishop 'ordaining' an abbot (*Ep.* ix. 91), and also of the decision as to the ordination of an abbot being made by the abbot of another monastery (*Ep.* xi. 48). The latter had changed his mind and appointed another man in the afternoon of the same day. Gregory orders him to invite a bishop to 'ordain' the monk first designated during the celebration of Mass. St. Theodore of Canterbury orders that an abbot shall be 'ordained' by a bishop, who must sing the Mass, in the presence of two or three of the abbot's (not the bishop's) brethren, *et donet ei baculum et pedules*. This is the earliest form of the abbatial blessing. The Pontifical of Egbert of York (732–766) gives a *consecratio Abbatis vel Abbatissæ*. There are now two forms provided in the Roman Pontifical for the blessing of an abbot, one for an *Abbas simplex*, the other for a mitred abbot. The former appears to be no longer used. The latter is largely modelled on the order of consecration of a bishop, and the officiating bishop is assisted by two mitred abbots.

The blessing of an abbess is permitted to a priest by Theodore.

The form in the Pontifical is simple, but many abbesses have had, and still have, the privilege of being invested with ring and crozier. When temporary abbots were introduced in the 15th cent., the blessing was dispensed with, but Benedict XIV. severely censured the omission to obtain the blessing on the part of abbots elected for life.

At an early date abbots took an important place in ecclesiastical affairs. In the 5th cent. we find 23 abbots signing the condemnation of Eutyches at the council held by Flavian of Constantinople in 448, and these were probably regular members of the patriarch's *σύνοδος ἐνδημοῦσα*. In Spain and Gaul they appear at councils to represent absent bishops, but in 653 ten abbots are found sitting in their own right at a council of Toledo, and they sign before the representatives of absent bishops (Mansi, x. 1222). It became the custom throughout the Middle Ages for abbots to attend councils. At the Vatican Council of 1869 only those abbots who were heads of congregations were invited, naturally without a vote.

Abbots, being the administrators of the temporal goods of their monastery, attained considerable worldly importance. They were often envoys of monarchs and of popes. They sat in Parliaments, ranking in England next after barons. Like barons, the abbots were originally called to Parliament at the good pleasure of the king, but by custom a certain number gained the right of sitting. On the last occasion when the abbots as a body sat in Parliament (28th June 1539), 17 were present. In the first Parliament of Elizabeth, however, Abbot Fecknam of Westminster had a seat and vote, since that abbey had been restored to all its privileges under Queen Mary.

The worldly grandeur assumed by abbots has been frequently censured,—for instance, by St. Bernard. In England their position as great landowners and peers of Parliament necessitated considerable state. The sons of the nobility were sent to be brought up under their care. Monasteries were hotels, and all guests of gentle birth were entertained in the abbot's hall. The Abbot of Glastonbury administered a revenue larger than that of the Archbishop of Canterbury. The Abbot of Bury St. Edmunds had a mint of his own. Yet such a position was not incompatible with personal sanctity, as may be seen in the case of Richard Whiting (Gasquet, *The Last Abbot of Glastonbury*, 1895, p. 56 f.). This external state of abbots lasted in Austria into the 19th cent., and to some extent is still to be seen.

Exemption of abbots from episcopal control became the rule only when they were joined together in congregations, but it was often granted as an exceptional privilege, and early traces of it are found. A council held at Arles, *c.* 455, exempted Faustus of Lerins from the Bishop of Fréjus, so far as the government of his abbey was concerned (Mansi, vii. 907; Duchesne, *Fastes épisc.* i. 124). Westminster is said to have received the privilege from John XIII. (*c.* 970). Some of the greatest English monasteries were never exempt, as Glastonbury, and only five Benedictine houses had the privilege at the Reformation, apart from the Cluniacs, Cistercians, etc. Christ Church, Oxford, still retains its papal exemption from the bishop. Grants of *Pontificalia*, or episcopal ornaments, mitre, ring, gloves, sandals, were made by the pope to the principal abbots (*e.g.* to Westminster in 1276, to the Prior of the Cathedral Abbey of Ely in 1413). These privileges eventually became general, but were limited by a decree of Alexander VII. in 1659. Since then further privileges have been granted or confirmed. In some cases a number of parishes are subject to an abbot, who acts as their bishop, as at Montecassino, Cava, etc. The small diocese once administered by the Abbot of Westminster is still under the dean and chapter, and is independent of the Bishop of London. In the case of such abbots, who are called *Abbates nullius dioeceseos*, permission is usually given to administer confirmation. Since the monastic state was anciently equivalent to the clerical, and the monastic tonsure to the clerical tonsure, it became the custom to allow abbots to confer tonsure and minor orders on their own subjects, and this is still in force. The Second Council of Nicæa (787) permitted *hegumeni* to ordain *lectores* for their monasteries. Abbots were sometimes also allowed to give the subdiaconate, but this is obsolete. The supposed permission of Innocent VIII. to Cistercian abbots to confer the diaconate is too much opposed to the theological opinions of the period to be probably authentic.

The elections of abbots by their monks were often interfered with by the civil power. St. Benedict permits neighbouring bishops or laymen to interfere if a bad man is elected. Charles Martel gave abbeys to his officers; even Charlemagne disposed of them at will. The king's *congé d'élire* had to be obtained for an election in England. In France and elsewhere abbacies came to be in the royal gift. The habit of giving abbacies to seculars *in commendam* in the 8th to 10th cents. unhappily revived in the 15th to 18th. The goods of the community were usually already divided with the abbot, and the latter had a fine house in which to receive guests. When these were in the hands of seculars, the monasteries were greatly impoverished, and suffered much in regularity. The congregation of St. Justina of Padua (afterwards called the Cassinese) introduced abbots elected for a short period in order to avoid the granting away of abbacies. Other congregations followed. The famous French congregations of St. Maur and of St. Vannes and St. Hidulphe preferred to be governed by priors appointed by the general chapter for the same reason. When it had become the rule for all ecclesiastics of good family to possess at least one abbey *in commendam*, it became customary to presume this in all ecclesiastics, and to address them as Monsieur l'abbé. Hence in France, and to some extent in Italy, even youths in seminaries, not yet in minor orders or even tonsured, are regularly addressed by this title, which in the Middle Ages had been considered too dignified for even the generals of the Carthusians or the Friars.*

LITERATURE.—See further under MONASTICISM. For Canon Law, Ferraris, *Bibliotheca*, *s.v.* 'Abbas,' 'Abbatissa,' and the collections of decrees.

JOHN CHAPMAN.

ABBOT (Tibetan).†—The head of the monastery in Tibet is called 'teacher' or *k'an-po* (the literal equivalent of the Sanskrit *upādhyāya*). He is superior to the ordinary monastic teacher or professor (*lob-pön*), and is credited with being endowed, by direct transmission from saints, with the three prerogatives for consecration, namely, spiritual power (*ḍbang*), thorough knowledge of the precepts (*lung*), and capability of expounding the same (*k'rid*), which confer on him the authority to empower others. He has under him all the common monks, scholars, and novices, and is strictly the only one entitled to be called a Lama. The lady superior of a convent bears the corresponding title of *k'an-mo*; the most celebrated of these is the 'Thunderbolt Sow,' a Tibetan Circe residing at Samding on the inland sea of Yamdok.

LITERATURE.—H. A. Jäschke, *Tibetan-English Dictionary*, 1882, p. 53; W. W. Rockhill, *Journey through Mongolia and Tibet*, 1894, p. 359; L. A. Waddell, *Buddhism of Tibet*, 1895, p. 172, and *Lhasa and its Mysteries*, 1905, pp. 219, 226, 403.

L. A. WADDELL.

ABBOT OF UNREASON.—This title was given in Scotland to one of the mimic dignitaries who presided over the Christmas revels. In England he had the title of Abbot or **Lord of Misrule**. In France the Abbé de Liesse held the same office. The Abbé de Liesse was the chief of a confraternity established at Lille. He was appointed by the magistrates and the people. He wore a cross of silver-gilt in his hat, and was accompanied by the officers of his mimic household. A banner of rich silk was carried before him, and his duty was to preside at the games which were celebrated at Arras and the neighbouring cities at the carnival. Ducange in his *Glossarium* says he also bore the titles of *Rex Stultorum* and *Facetiarum Princeps.*

* It may be noted here that for centuries in Ireland the abbots had all ecclesiastical power in their hands; the Church was organized not by dioceses but by tribes, and the bishop was in reality a subject of the abbot.

† The 'Abbot' in Buddhism generally will be described under MONASTICISM (Bud.), and the Muhammadan Abbot under MUHAMMADANISM.

At Rouen and Evreux the leader of the frolics was called *Abbas Conardorum.* Another title was *Abbas Juvenum.* In certain cathedral chapters in France he was called *l'Abbé des Foux.* He was the monastic representative of the **Boy Bishop**, or *Episcopus Puerorum,* whose office is recognized in the service 'in die Sanctorum Innocentium' in the Sarum *Processionale* of 1555. In some cathedral churches he was styled *Episcopus* or *Archiepiscopus Fatuorum.* In churches exempt from diocesan jurisdiction he had the exalted title *Papa Fatuorum.*

In every case these mimic dignitaries represented the highest authority in the Church. They masqueraded in the vestments of the clergy, and exercised for the time being some of the functions of the higher clergy. The clergy themselves gave their sanction to the mimic rites: 'Deinde episcopus puerorum conversus ad clerum elevet brachium suum dicens hanc benedictionem: Crucis signo vos consigno' (*Sarum Process.* fol. xiv). In the York Inventory of 1530 a little mitre and a ring are mentioned, evidently for the *Episcopus Puerorum.*

These titles are all closely connected with the **Feast of Fools**, the *Festum Fatuorum,* in the mediæval Church. There is little doubt that their privileges go back to much earlier times. The standard authority for the whole subject is the treatise *Mémoires pour servir à l'histoire de la Fête des Foux,* by M. du Tilliot, published at Lausanne and Geneva, 1741. Du Tilliot, with good reason, traces them back to the Saturnalia, the *Libertas Decembris* of which Horace (*Sat.* II. vii. 5 f.) speaks when he bids his slave Davus exercise his annual privilege of masquerading as master:

> 'Age, libertate Decembri,
> Quando ita majores voluerunt, utere, narra.'

Du Tilliot says:

> 'Car comme dans les Saturnales, les Valets faisoient les fonctions de leurs Maîtres, de même dans la Fête des Foux les jeunes Clercs et les autres Ministres inférieurs de l'Eglise officioient publiquement et solennement, pendant certains jours consacrés à honorer les Mystères du Christianisme.'

The policy of the early Church was to divert the people from their pagan customs by consecrating them, as far as possible, to Christian use. The month of December was dedicated to Saturn. The Saturnalia were originally held on Dec. 17. Augustus extended the holiday to three days, Dec. 17–19. Martial (*ob.* 101) speaks of it as lasting five days. Lucian, in the 2nd cent., says it lasted a week, and that mimic kings were chosen. Duchesne (*Origines,* p. 265) allows that the Mithraic festival of *Natalis Invicti,* on Dec. 25, may have had some influence in fixing the date of Christmas in the Western Church. He hesitates as to the Saturnalia. Yet the Christianized festivities of the Saturnalia were probably slowly transferred to the Christmas season by the appointment of the Advent fast. A relic of this still lingers on in North Staffordshire, where the farm-servants' annual holiday extends from Christmas to New Year.

The Boy Bishop (*Episcopus Puerorum*) was elected on St. Nicholas' Day, Dec. 6, and his authority lasted till Childermas, or Holy Innocents' Day. Edward I., in 1299, permitted him to say vespers in the royal presence on Dec. 7. The **Santa Claus** of to-day still keeps alive the tradition of the Boy Bishop and the Abbot of Unreason.

The concessions of the early Church did not succeed in checking the abuses which had been associated with the Saturnalia. The 'Liberty of December' extended to New Year and Epiphany, covering the whole of the Christmas festival. The 'Misrule' called forth constant protests. Pseudo-Aug. (*Serm.* 265) condemns the dances, which afterwards became a recognized feature of the Feast of Fools: 'Isti enim infelices et miseri homines, qui balationes et saltationes ante ipsas basilicas Sanctorum exercere nec metuunt nec erubescunt, etsi Christiani ad Ecclesiam venerint, Pagani de Ecclesia revertuntur.' The sermon has been ascribed to Cæsarius of Arles (*ob.* 547). The description of the Feast of Fools at Antiles in 1644, quoted by du Tilliot from a contemporary letter to Gassendi, shows that the custom was too deeply rooted in the same district to yield to the censures of the Church. The excesses connected with the Calends Brumalia and other festivals were condemned in Can. lxii. of the Council in Trullo in 692. The mimic pageantry of bishop and abbot was specially censured in Sessio xxi. of the Council of Basel in 1435:

> 'Turpem etiam illum abusum in quibusdam frequentatum ecclesiis quo certis anni celebritatibus nonnulli cum mitra, baculo, ac vestibus pontificalibus more episcoporum benedicunt. Alii ut reges ac duces induti, quod festum fatuorum vel Innocentium vel puerorum in quibusdam regionibus nuncupatur, ut alii larvales et theatrales jocos.'

Tilliot also mentions the condemnation of these abuses by the Council of Rouen in 1435, Soissons in 1455, Sens in 1485, Paris in 1528, and Cologne in 1536. In England they were abolished by proclamation of Henry VIII., July 22, 1542, though restored by Mary in 1554.

In Scotland the annual burlesque presided over by the Abbot of Unreason was suppressed in 1555. The guisers, who in Scotland play the part of the mummers in the Christmas revels in England, wear mitre-shaped caps of brown paper, which are derived either from the Boy Bishops or from the Abbots of Unreason. In fiction, Sir Walter Scott has left a vivid picture of the 'right reverend Abbot of Unreason' in the *Abbot.*

LITERATURE.—Du Tilliot, *Mémoires*; Ducange, *Glossarium*; *Sarum Processionale,* 1555; Sir W. Scott, *The Abbot,* with historical note; Chambers, *Book of Days*; Jamieson, *Scottish Dict.*; *Dict. Larousse.*

THOMAS BARNS.

'ABD AL-QĀDIR AL-JĪLĀNĪ.—I. *Life.*—

Sīdī 'Abd al-Qādir al-Jīlānī, one of the greatest religious personalities of Islām, ascetic, wonder-worker, teacher, and founder of a brotherhood, was born in 471 A.H. [1078 A.D.]. The Muslims make him a *sharīf* of the blood of the Prophet and a descendant of 'Ali; but this claim has little likelihood, for he was probably of Persian origin. His complete name reads Muḥyī ad-Dīn 'Abd al-Qādir, son of Abū Ṣāliḥ, son of Jenki-Dost al-Jīlī or Jīlānī. Jenki-Dost is a Persian name. Historians, such as Abū-l-Maḥāsin (ed. Juynboll, i. p. 698), tell us that his national name (Jīlānī, 'the Jīlānite') came to him not from the Persian province Jīlān, but from Jīl, a locality near Baghdad. Various legends, however, call him 'the 'Ajamī,' *i.e.* the Persian. He came to Baghdad in 488 to study Ḥanbalite law. He learnt the Qur'ān from Abū Sa'īd al-Mubārak al-Muḥarrimī, and polite literature from Abū Zakarya Yaḥyā of Tabrīz. His master in asceticism was Hammād ad-Dabbās; he spent long years in the deserts and among the ruins around Baghdad, leading a hermit's life. In 521 he felt himself called back into the world, and returned to Baghdad, where the Qāḍī, Abū Sa'īd al-Muḥarrimī, gave him charge of the school which he had been directing in Bāb el-Azaj (Le Strange, *Baghdad,* Map viii. No. 29, and p. 296 ff.). His teaching met with very great success; the school had to be enlarged time after time; it was finally completed in 528, and took the name of Sīdī Jīlānī. He spoke there three times a week—twice in the school, on law, and once in his oratory, on mysticism. He drew many hearers from all parts of Mesopotamia, Persia, and even Egypt. It is affirmed that he converted Jews and Christians. He gave legal decisions, which became authoritative among both the Ḥanbalites and the Shāfi'ites. Among his hearers might be mentioned the jurisconsult Muwaffaq ad-Dīn ibn Qudāma al-Maqdisī and the famous mystic Shihāb ad-Dīn as-Suhrawardī. He married and had many children—thirteen, according to a tradition reported by Depont and Coppolani (p. 298); forty-nine, of whom twenty-seven were sons, according to another tradition, which seems to be legendary. Many of his children went, during his lifetime, to preach his doctrine in Egypt, Arabia, Turkestan, and India. He died at Baghdad on the 8th of the month of Rabī' ii., 561 A.H. [1166 A.D.].

2. *Legend.*—Besides the above facts, the numerous traditions which have been preserved concerning 'Abd al-Qādir are for the most part of a legendary character. They deal with his austerities, his visions, and his miracles. Among them are the following:—His mother bore him when she was sixty years old. As a nursling he declined to take the breast in the month of Ramaḍān. When he came to Baghdad to study, the prophet Ḥidr appeared to him and prevented him from entering the city; he remained seven years before the walls, practising asceticism and living on herbs. When he withdrew into the deserts around Baghdad, he was visited by the same prophet Ḥidr, and was fed miraculously. He also received cakes, herbs, and water from the heavens, on his pilgrimage to Mecca. In the desert he was tormented by Satan, who appeared to him under various forms. From time to time he fixed his abode in the ruins of Aiwān Kisrā, the famous palace of Chosroës (Le Strange, *Eastern Caliphate*, p. 34). One tradition makes him spend eleven years in a tower which ever since bears the name of *Burj al-'Ajamī*, 'the tower of the Persian.' One day Satan tried to seduce him by a false vision. While he stood on the seashore with a great thirst, a cloud sailed towards him from which fell a kind of dew. He quenched his thirst with this dew, and then a great light appeared, and a form, and he heard a voice saying to him, 'I allow thee that which is forbidden.' 'May God preserve us from Satan, the accursed one,' replied the ascetic. At once the light gave place to darkness, and the form became smoke. He was asked later how he had recognized the deceitfulness of this vision. He answered: 'By the fact that God does not advise to do shameful things.' While he taught, he was often seen lifted up from the ground; he would walk a few paces through the air and then return to his pulpit. Once, as he was speaking in the Niẓāmīya school, a Jinnī appeared in the form of a snake, which wound itself around his body and exchanged a few words with him. One year the river Tigris rose high, and the inhabitants of Baghdad, fearing their city would be flooded, came to implore the protection of the wonder-worker. Al-Jīlānī advanced to the bank of the river, planted his stick in the ground, saying, 'Thus far.' From that moment the waters decreased. Many of these legends have a close resemblance to those of Christian hagiography.

3. *Works.*—Many works, mystical treatises, collections of prayers and sermons, are ascribed to him. Brockelmann (*Arab. Litt.* i. 435 f.) mentions twenty-four titles of his books still existing in MS. in the libraries of Europe. The two most important are:—*Al-ghunya liṭālib ṭarīq al-ḥaqq*, 'Sufficiency for the seeker of the way of truth,' and the *Futūḥ al-ghaib*, 'The conquests of the mystery.' The latter work contains his mystical teaching, collected by his son 'Abd ar-Razzāq. It was printed in Persian at Lucknow in 1880; in Arabic at Cairo in 1303 A.H. A collection of sermons (*Ḥuṭab*) and of 'Sessions' (*Majālis*) was printed at Cairo in 1302, a *ḥizb* at Alexandria in 1304. In the language of the dervish orders, a *ḥizb* is a kind of service composed in great part of passages from the Qur'ān. Le Châtelier (*Confr. Musul. du Hédjaz*, p. 23, n. 1) cites also a collection of prayers named in Turkish *Evrādi Sherīfeh*, printed at Constantinople in 1869 A.D. A *wird* (plu. *aurād*; Turk. *evrād*) is a short invocation. His remaining works include exhortations, prayers, a treatise on the Divine names, mystical poems, one of which is on the author's being lifted up into the higher spheres. Ibn Taimīya commented on some of his maxims.

4. *Teaching.*—His teaching may be gathered from the above-mentioned works (cf. also the *Lawāqiḥ al-anwār* of ash-Sha'rānī, ed. of Cairo, 1316, i. pp. 100–105) and from the tradition of his order. It is that of orthodox Muslim mysticism. One cannot fail to recognize a certain Christian influence in it, especially in the importance given to the virtues of charity, humility, meekness, in his precept of obedience to the spiritual director, and in the aim held before an ascetic, which is spiritual death and the entire self-surrender of the soul to God. Al-Jīlānī's respect for Jesus was very great, and the tradition of this respect is still kept in his order. His love of poverty recalls that of St. Francis of Assisi. In all parts of the Muslim world the poor put themselves under his protection, and ask for alms in his name. His mystical teaching is expounded in his book, *Futūḥ al-ghaib.* Among the titles of its 78 chapters, the following are characteristic:—Spiritual death; unconsciousness of created things; the banishment of cares from the heart; drawing near unto God; unveiling and vision; the soul and its states; self-surrender to God; fear and hope; how to reach God through the medium of a spiritual director; poverty. The book contains expressions that are altogether Christian. Commending the excellence of becoming dead to created things and to one's own will, the author says, 'The sign that you have died to your lusts is that you are like a child in the arms of its mother; the sign that you have died to your own will is that you wish nothing but the will of God.' Exhorting the soul to search after God, he hits upon an expression of St. Augustine: 'Rise and hasten to fly unto Him.' A little further on, he appropriates the famous comparison of the corpse: 'Be in the hands of God like a dead body in the hands of the washer.' The effect of this self-surrender of the soul is spiritual clear-mindedness and joy.

It is a custom in Muslim mysticism to ascribe the essence of the teaching of the founder of an order to some anterior personages, by means of a chain of intermediaries who go as far back even as Muhammad. Among the predecessors, thus cited, of al-Jīlānī should be named the famous ascetic Abū-l-Qāsim al-Junaid (died A.H. 268).

Certain traditions attribute to our mystic, especially while on his deathbed, some very proud words which contrast with what we have just said about his feelings and his doctrine. They are thus reported by al-Biqā'ī (Goldziher, *Muh. Stud.* ii. p. 289): 'The sun greets me before he rises; the year greets me before it begins, and it unveils to me all things that shall happen in its course . . . I plunge into the sea of God's knowledge, and I have seen Him with my eyes. I am the living evidence of God's existence . . .' Similar sayings are ascribed to many of the great mystics of Islām. It is probable that they are the work of enthusiastic disciples, and that they express only the close union of the mystic with God in a symbolic fashion.

5. *Order.*—The order, or brotherhood, founded by 'Abd al-Qādir al-Jīlānī bears the name al-Qādirīya. It has great importance in Islām. After the death of the founder it was led by his sons and then by their descendants. The majority of his sons became disciples of their father, ascetics, missionaries, and men of learning like him. The eldest was 'Abd ar-Razzāq (A.H. 528–603), the youngest Yaḥya (550–600). It was 'Abd ar-Razzāq

who succeeded his father in the leadership of the order, and who built over the tomb of the founder the mosque with seven gilt domes, once celebrated by historians and poets, but to-day lying in ruins (Le Strange, *Baghdad*, p. 348 f.). Along with the order the posterity of al-Jīlānī's children have spread all over the Muslim world. Branches of this family can be found especially in Baghdad, Cairo, Ḥamāh, and Yā'ū in the district of Aleppo. A Western tradition claims that one son of al-Jīlānī, 'Abd al-'Azīz (532–602), emigrated to Fez; but this is contradicted by another tradition (*Qalā'id al-jawāhir*, p. 54), according to which 'Abd al-'Azīz emigrated only to the province of Jibāl. Baghdad has remained the moral centre of the order. But the jurisdiction of the mother-house does not extend beyond Mesopotamia, Syria, and Turkey. In the other Muslim countries the brotherhood went through a process of disintegration, and the congregations have ceased to be subordinate to the mother-house. The monastery (*zāwiya*) of Baghdad was destroyed by Shah Ismail, and restored by Sultan Sulaiman.

The branches of the brotherhood reach out as far as the Farther East, into the Dutch East Indies and Chinese Yunnan. In India there are many kinds of Qādirīyas. The Qādirīya Akbarīya, the best-known, founded at the end of the 6th cent. A.H. by Shaiḫ al-Akbar Muḥyī ad-Dīn ibn al-'Arabī al-Kātimī, forms a distinct order; the *Bī Nawā* are begging *faqīrs*, recruited from the inferior castes of Muslims, and connected with the Qādirīya. In Arabia the brotherhood is powerful. It possesses important *zāwiyas* in Jiddah and Medina, and has thirty *muqaddims* (prefects of congregations) in Mecca. In Constantinople it owns forty houses (*takyas*). It is widespread in Egypt, at Cairo, all along the Nile Valley; and its missions have advanced as far as Khartum, Kordofan, Darfur, Wadai, Bornu, and Sokoto. There are *zāwiyas* at Tripoli and Ghadames. In Algeria and Morocco the order consists of various decentralized congregations whose membership reaches a high figure. 24,000 are reckoned in Algeria (Depont and Coppolani), and in the province of Oran alone two hundred chapels (*qubbas*), under the name of Sīdī al-Jīlānī, are to be found (Rinn). The brotherhood makes great efforts to convert the Berbers to Islām.

The *dhikr* of the order is nothing but the Muslim confession of faith: *la ilāh illā-llāh*, 'There is no God but Allah.' But according to a usage, probably instituted by al-Jīlānī himself, these words are not always pronounced entirely. During the prayer in common, which is accompanied by motions of the head and of the body, and in which the dervishes endeavour to attain a state of ecstatic excitement, after having already pronounced the whole formula, they say only *Allah, Allah!* and finally, when the rhythm becomes more rapid, they pronounce nothing but *hū, hī, hā*, the sound being sustained until loss of breath.

Many orders or brotherhoods have separated themselves from the Qādirite order. The most famous, besides the above-mentioned Akbarīyas of India, are the Rifā'iyas, commonly called the 'Howling Dervishes,' founded by Aḥmad ar-Rifā'a (died A.H. 570), a nephew of al-Jīlānī; the Badawīyas, an Egyptian order, and the 'Īsawīyas. The other orders are those of the Bakkā'īyas, Jabāwīyas, Jishtīyas, Baiyūmīyas, Dasūqīyas, Maulanīyas, 'Arūsīya-Salāmīyas, Bū-'Alīyas, 'Ammārīyas (cf. MUHAMMADANISM, § viii.).

LITERATURE.—(1) *ORIENTAL*: *Bahja al-asrār*, by 'Ali b. Yūsuf ash-Shatnūfī (A.H. 647–713), Cairo, 1304; *Qalā'id al-jawāhir fi manāqib ash-Shaiḫ 'Abd al-Qādir*, by Muhammad b. Yaḥya at-Tādifī (died A.H. 963), Cairo, 1303. These two are the most important. Brockelmann (*Arab. Litt.* i. p. 435) mentions three other biographies still in MS. Colas translated a MS by Shaiḫ as-Sanūsī, used also by Rinn. Rinn mentions also the *Anwār an-nāẓir*, by 'Abd allah al-Bakrī aṣ-Ṣaddīqī, and the *Nuzha an-nāẓir*, by 'Abd al-Latīf al-Hāshimī. Cl. Huart (*Litt. Arab.* pp. 344, 368) mentions that 'Afīf ad-Dīn al-Yāfi'ī (died 1367 A.D.) and Shihāb ad-Dīn al-Qastallānī (died 1517 A.D.) collected a number of interesting stories relating to Sidi Jīlānī. The *Natīja at-taḥqīq*, by Muhammad ad-Dilā'ī, lithographed at Fez, A.H. 1309, is translated by T. H. Weir in *JRAS*, 1903, p. 155 ff. His *Life* by Dhahabī is printed, trans., and commented on by D. S. Margoliouth in *JRAS*, 1907, p. 267 ff.

On the mystics generally see the *Nafaḥāt* of Jāmī, Calcutta, A.D. 1859; the *Wafayāt* of Ibn Ḥallikān, Bulaq, 2 vols., A.H. 1299 (Eng. trans., Paris, 1843–1871); a recent Turkish work on the origin of the principal Muslim orders and their doctrines is *Mir'āt al-Maqāṣid fi daf'i-l-mafāsid*, by Ahmed Rifā'āt Effendi, Constantinople, n.d.

(2) *WESTERN*: Rinn, *Marabouts et Khouan*, Algiers, 1884; Depont-Coppolani, *Les confréries religieuses musulmanes*, published under the auspices of M. Jules Cambon, Algiers, 1897; Le Châtelier, *Les confréries musulmanes du Hédjaz*, Paris, 1887; Carra de Vaux, *Gazali*, Paris, Alcan, 1902; Brockelmann, *Gesch. der Arab. Litt.*, Berlin, 1897. Among older publications, Général de Neveu, *Les Khouans*, 1845; Mercier, 'Études sur la confrérie des Khouan de Sidi Abd el-Kader el-Djilani,' *RSA de Constantine*, iii [1869].

BON CARRA DE VAUX.

'ABD AR-RAZZĀQ.—I. *Life.*—The well-known Ṣūfī, Kamāl ad-Dīn 'Abd ar-Razzāq Abū 'l-Ghanā'im ibn Jamāl ad-Dīn al-Qāshānī (Kāshānī, Kāshī), was a native of Qāshān (Kāshān), a considerable town in the Jibāl province of Persia, situated about half-way between Teherān and Iṣfahān. The year of his birth is not recorded, but Ḥājjī Ḥalīfa (iv. p. 427) gives as the date of his death A.H. 730 = A.D. 1329–30. Elsewhere he gives A.H. 887 = A.D. 1482–83; but this is manifestly an error due to confusion with the historian Kamāl ad-Dīn 'Abd ar-Razzāq of Samarcand. The former date is confirmed by the following anecdote (Jāmī, *Nafahāt al-uns*, Calcutta, 1859, p. 557). On one occasion 'Abd ar-Razzāq was accompanying the Emīr Iqbāl Sīstānī on the road to Sulṭānīya, and asked him in the course of conversation what his shaiḫ—meaning Aḥmad ibn Muṣṭafā Rukn ad-Dīn 'Alā' ad-Daula of Simnān—thought of the celebrated Ṣūfī Muḥyī ad-Dīn Ibn 'Arabī. The Emīr replied that Rukn ad-Dīn regarded him as a master of mystical science, but believed him to be mistaken in his pantheistic doctrine touching the unity of the Divine substance; whereupon 'Abd ar-Razzāq retorted that the doctrine in question was the foundation of Ibn 'Arabī's philosophy, that it was the most excellent he had ever heard, and that it was held by all the saints and prophets. These remarks were communicated by the Emīr Iqbāl to his shaiḫ, Rukn ad-Dīn, who stigmatized Ibn 'Arabī's doctrine as abominable and far worse than avowed materialism. Jāmī has preserved the correspondence which ensued between 'Abd ar-Razzāq and his adversary (*Nafaḥāt*, pp. 558–568).

This dispute enables us to fix the epoch at which 'Abd ar-Razzāq flourished, since the shaiḫ Rukn ad-Dīn, his contemporary, was charged with a political mission to the court of Abū Sa'īd, son of Uljaitu, the Mongol sovereign of Persia (A.D. 1316–1335), and we know, moreover, that he composed one of his works, entitled the '*Urwa*, in 1321 (*JA* for 1873, p. 133). This book was read by 'Abd ar-Razzāq, who addressed to the author a letter on the subject (Nūr Allāh of Shustar in the *Majālis al-mu'minīn*, *ib.* p. 135, also British Museum MSS add. No. 26,716, fol. 331 vo. and No. 23,541, fol. 364 vo.). This letter, with the answer of Rukn ad-Dīn, is extant in the library of Trinity College, Cambridge (*Catalogue of the Arabic, Persian, and Turkish Manuscripts in the Library of Trinity College*, by E. H. Palmer, p. 116). Consequently there can be little doubt that the closing years of 'Abd ar-Razzāq's life fall within the reign of Abū Sa'īd, and he may well have died, according to the earlier date mentioned by Ḥajjī Ḥalīfa, in A.H. 730 = A.D. 1329–30.

Concerning the outward events of his life we

possess scarcely any information. Jāmī states (*Nafaḥāt*, p. 557) that he was a disciple of shaiḫ Nūr ad-Dīn 'Abd aṣ-Ṣamad of Naṭanz, through whom, as appears from the articles on that shaiḫ and his teacher, shaiḫ Najīb ad-Dīn 'Alī ibn Buzghush (*Nafaḥāt*, pp. 554 f., 546 ff.), he traced his spiritual descent to the illustrious ṣūfīs Shihāb ad-Dīn 'Umar as-Suhrawardī and Muḥyī ad-Dīn ibn 'Arabī. It is related by Yāfi'ī (*Rauḍ ar-rayāḥīn*, 106th anecdote: p. 65 of ed. of Cairo, 1315) that one day while 'Abd ar-Razzāq was discoursing in the mosque at Medīna, a dervish among his audience withdrew into a corner and gave himself up to meditation. On being asked why he did not listen like the rest, he answered: 'They are hearing the servant (*'abd*) of the Provider (*ar-Razzāq*),* but I am hearing the Provider, not His servant.'

2. *Writings.*—The most famous work of 'Abd ar-Razzāq is his dictionary of the technical terms of the ṣūfīs, *Iṣṭilāḥāt aṣ-Ṣūfīya*. It is divided into two parts, the first on the technical expressions (*muṣṭalaḥāt*), and the second on the so-called 'stations' (*maqāmāt*). 'Abd ar-Razzāq states in his preface that he composed it for the instruction of his friends who, not being ṣūfīs, could not understand the technical terms which he had employed in some of his other works. The *Iṣṭilāḥāt* was largely utilized by Saiyid 'Alī al-Jurjānī, the author of the *Ta'rīfāt* or 'Definitions,' a well-known treatise of the same kind, and the first part has been edited by Sprenger (Calcutta, 1845). The *Laṭā'if al-i'lām fī ishārāti ahl al-ilhām*, of which Tholuck has made use, is also devoted to explaining the peculiar Ṣūfīistic terminology. Some account will be given below of the *Risālat fī 'l-qaḍā wa 'l-qadar* or 'Tract on Predestination and Free-will,' which has been published, analyzed, and translated by Guyard. 'Abd ar-Razzāq wrote several books of less importance, such as his allegorical interpretation of the 38th chapter of the Qur'ān (*Ta'wīlāt al-Qur'ān*) and his commentaries on the *Fuṣūṣ al-hikam* of Ibn 'Arabī, on the *Tā'iyat al-kubrā* of Ibn al-Fāriḍ, and on the *Manāzil as-sā'irīn* of 'Abdullāh al-Anṣārī.

3. *Doctrine.*—Like the later ṣūfīs generally, 'Abd ar-Razzāq finds a basis for his system in the Neo-Platonic philosophy as expounded to the Muslims by Fārābī, Ibn Sīnā (Avicenna), and Ghazālī. He is a thoroughgoing pantheist, in the sense that he considers the whole universe, spiritual and material, to be an emanation from God. From the Absolute Being, who alone exists, and who is known solely to Himself, there radiates a spiritual substance, the Primal Intelligence (*al-'Aql al-Awwal*) or Universal Reason, which answers to the νοῦς of Plotinus and the λόγος of Philo. This substance contains the types or ideas of all existing things, and by a further process of emanation these types descend into the world of the Universal Soul, the Plotinian ψυχή, where they become individualized and are transmitted to the material world. Here begins an upward movement by which all individual souls are drawn back to the Primal Intelligence and ultimately reabsorbed. 'Abd ar-Razzāq distinguishes three classes of mankind: the slaves of passion (*ahli nafs*) and sense, who are ignorant of God and of His attributes, and say, 'The Qur'ān is the word of Muhammad,' but are saved from hell if they have faith; secondly, the men of intellect (*ahli qalb*), who attain to the knowledge of the Divine attributes by means of reflexion and argument; and, thirdly, the spiritualists (*ahli rūḥ*), who pierce through the veil of plurality into the presence of the eternal Oneness and contemplate God as He really is (*Nafaḥāt*, p. 559 f.).

Much of this doctrine is not peculiar to 'Abd ar-Razzāq, but belongs to the philosophical school of Ṣūfīism. His originality lies in the fact that he combined his pantheistic principles with an assertion of moral freedom which at first sight appears to be incompatible with them. His theory on this subject is set forth in the *Risālat fī 'l-qaḍā wa 'l-qadar* (see Guyard's article in *JA* VII. i. p. 125 ff.), and may be summarized as follows: Everything that exists in the terrestrial world is the manifestation of some universal type prefigured in the world of decree (*qaḍā*), *i.e.* in the Primal Intelligence, and undergoes a process of creation, development, and destruction which is predetermined in every particular. How then, we may ask, is it possible for men to have any power over actions emanating from a Divine source, and governed by immutable laws? What is the use of commands and prohibitions, of rewards and punishments, if there is no liberty to choose good or reject evil? 'Abd ar-Razzāq, diverging at this point from Ibn 'Arabī, solves the difficulty by declaring that all actions are the result of direct or indirect causes, themselves predetermined, one of which is Free-will itself. In other words, it is foreknown to God and inevitably decreed that every human act shall be produced by the united operation of certain causes, at a certain time, in a certain place, and in a certain form; but it is also decreed, no less inevitably, that the agent shall exercise his free choice (*iḫtiyār*) in the production of the act. Therefore every act is at once fatal and free. The Qadarites (Mu'tazilites), who maintain that men are the authors of their own actions, regard only the proximate causes; while the Jabarites, who hold that all actions are created by God, regard only the remote causes (cf. MUHAMMADANISM, § ii.). Both parties see but half the truth, which, as Ja'far Ṣādiq remarked, is neither absolute fatalism nor absolute liberty, but something between those two extremes. Hence the utility of religion and morals, whereby men are incited to good actions and deterred from evil. The Prophet said of Abū Huraira: 'The pen which has written his destiny is dry,' meaning that what should happen was already fixed; but to the question, 'Why then do aught?' he replied: 'Nay, do it; every one of you has received the capacity of doing that for which he was created.' 'Abd ar-Razzāq next proceeds to deal with the objection that, if our acts are determined in advance and produced, though willingly, by us, we should all have an equal share of good and evil. He argues that the injustice is only apparent, as, for example, in the story of Moses and Ḫiḍr (Qur. xviii. 59 ff.), and that 'whatever is, is right'; for if God could have created a better world, He would have done so. Moreover, the distinction of good and evil is essential to the perfection of the Divine scheme, which demands all possible varieties of aptitude, disposition, and endowment. If the beggar were a sultan, and if the ignorant knave were wise and virtuous, the harmony of the universe would be destroyed. None is responsible for his natural deficiencies—God pardons an ugly man for not resembling Joseph, the Muslim example of masculine beauty, or a wicked man for not behaving like Muhammad; but those are justly condemned who follow their evil bent in defiance of the promptings of reason and religion. As regards the future life, all shall receive such retribution as they deserve, and shall enjoy that degree of felicity of which each is capable according to his spiritual rank. 'Abd ar-Razzāq affirms that the wicked shall not suffer eternal punishment, though he adds the saving clause, 'unless God will otherwise.'

LITERATURE.—See, in addition to the references in the article, Tholuck, *Die speculative Trinitätslehre des späteren Orients*, Berlin, 1826, pp. 13 ff., 28 ff. [extracts from the *Laṭā'if al-i'lām*, with German translation: see Dozy's *Catalogue of the Oriental MSS in the Library of the University of Leyden*, vol. i. pp.

* *Ar-Razzāq*, 'the Provider,' is one of the names of Allāh.

86–87]. Von Hammer published an analysis of the second part of the *Iṣṭilāḥāt aṣ-Ṣūfiya* in the *Jahrbücher der Literatur*, vol. lxxxii. p. 68. See also art. on 'Abd al-Razzāḳ by D. B. Macdonald in *Moh. Encyc.* REYNOLD A. NICHOLSON.

ABDUCTION.—In English law abduction is a term usually, though not exclusively, applied to the taking away or detention of a girl under twenty-one years of age against the will of her parents or guardians; or the taking away and detention by force of a woman of any age with intent to marry or carnally know her, or to cause her to be married or carnally known (*Criminal Law Amendment Act*, 1885). The penalty for such an offence may be either a period of penal servitude not exceeding fourteen years, or a period of imprisonment not exceeding two years. Crimes of this kind are now comparatively rare: in England the number tried at Sessions and Assizes during the ten years ending 1904 amounted only to an annual average of thirteen (*Criminal Statistics*, 1904, p. 29).

It is to be noted that abduction, which is now regarded as a serious crime among all civilized communities, is probably a survival of one of the most primitive forms of marriage, namely, marriage by capture. This primitive form of marriage relationship still prevails among some uncivilized peoples in various parts of the world; it is, in fact, a customary form in which marriage is contracted, and even among communities which have reached a certain stage of culture, as, for instance, the South Slavonians, marriage by abduction was in full force at the beginning of the 19th century. Our Teutonic and Scandinavian ancestors regularly resorted to the forcible abduction of women for wives, and war was often carried on among them for the purpose of capturing wives. The same custom prevailed in the early stages of Greek life, and the Romans of the heroic age were often obliged to resort to surprise and force to secure wives for the community.

Distinct traces of the same custom are to be found in Old Testament literature. The tradition is handed down in the Book of Judges that the men of the tribe of Benjamin were supplied with wives from the virgins who had been captured as the result of a war upon the inhabitants of Jabesh-Gilead (Jg 21[12]); and when these did not suffice, the sons of Benjamin in their search for wives made a raid upon the daughters of Shiloh, when they were celebrating an annual religious festival, and carried them off (v.[19ff.]) when they came out to dance.

Among some races abduction was the ordinary legal method of procuring a wife, and the parents of the abducted woman were liable to punishment if they attempted to get back their daughter. Among other races abduction led to blood feuds, and it is possible, as Herbert Spencer suggests, that the fear of vengeance led to the offer of compensation by the abductor, and prepared the way for the more advanced matrimonial custom of marriage by purchase. After the decay of marriage by capture, many traces of it still remained in marriage customs and ceremonies. In some cases the bridegroom is expected to go through the form of carrying off the bride by stratagem or force; in other cases the bride conceals herself in a hiding-place, and has to be discovered by her future husband; in some marriage ceremonies it is considered a point of honour with the bride to resist and struggle, no matter how willing she may be to enter into the marriage compact. With the advance of civilization, and more especially in those forms of society where marriage became a matter of mutual consent, and in this way assumed an ethical character, abduction, from being a tolerated custom, descended to the position of a crime. In Chinese legislation abduction is a capital offence, and a marriage taking place as the result of it is null and void. The code of Justinian also nullifies a marriage of this kind. The Church, although condemning the perpetrator of abduction to severe spiritual pains and penalties, refrained till the 9th cent. from regarding the marriage as invalid, but at that period ecclesiastical law was brought into conformity with the jurisprudence of Justinian. Innocent III., however, made the legality of the marriage dependent on the consent of the abducted woman, and the Council of Trent adopted a somewhat similar principle. It declared that, so long as the woman was in the power of the abductor and unable to exercise the freedom of her will, abduction was an *impedimentum*, but if she regained her liberty and freely became a consenting party, the marriage ceased to be invalid. The abductor incurred the penalty of excommunication. The growth of the ethical conception of marriage as a matter of free will and mutual consent on the part of persons who have arrived at the age of maturity, necessarily led to the reprobation of abduction as an act of force or fraud, and involved the enactment of the pains and penalties which are now attached to it by the criminal jurisprudence of civilized peoples. See also MARRIAGE, WOMAN.

LITERATURE.—J. F. M'Lennan, *Primitive Marriage* (1865); H. Spencer, *Principles of Sociology*, vol. i. (1877); Edward Westermarck, *History of Human Marriage* (1891); A. E. Crawley, *The Mystic Rose* (1902); A. H. Post, *Grundriss der ethnologischen Jurisprudenz* (1894); C. H. Letourneau, *Condition de la Femme dans les diverses races et civilisations* (1903); L. T. Hobhouse, *Morals in Evolution* (1906). W. D. MORRISON.

ABELARD.—**I. Life.**—Master Peter, surnamed *Abailard*,* the commanding figure in the intellectual movements of the 12th cent., was born at Le Pallet (*Palatium*) † in Brittany, a castle 11 miles S.E. from Nantes, about the year 1079. His parents were nobles, whose piety led them in later life to enter the monastic life. Abelard, though the eldest son, renounced his claims, that he might the better devote himself to learning. 'I prefer,' he said, 'the strife of disputation to the trophies of war.' After studying for a while under the extreme nominalist Roscelin, probably at Locminé near Vannes, and trying, though without avail, to learn mathematics under Theodoric of Chartres (Poole, *op. cit.* 365, 115), Abelard was at last attracted to the Notre Dame of Paris by the fame of its master, William of Champeaux, whose crude realism soon provoked Abelard, though not yet twenty, to open combat. The duel, protracted through years, resulted at length in the overthrow of the older man's reputation, and the installation for a while of Abelard as an independent master. When expelled from the Notre Dame by the cathedral authorities, at the instigation of William, Abelard took refuge first at Melun, afterwards at Corbeil, and finally at St. Geneviève, at that time outside the city and free from the jurisdiction of the cathedral. This abbey of secular canons of somewhat lax life thus became the headquarters of philosophic teaching at Paris, round which gathered in the next generation the famous University (Rashdall, *Univ. in M. A.* i. ch. 5).

The next encounter of Abelard with authority was even more revolutionary. Desirous of attaining distinction not merely, as hitherto, in dialectics, but also in theology, perhaps under the influence of the religious revival which led his mother Lucia, whom he visited at this time, to withdraw

* This spelling would seem more nearly to correspond to the original form (see Poole, *op. cit.* 137 n.). For its proposed derivations see Ducange, *s.v.* 'baiare' (cf. Poole, *op. cit.* 364), and the pun on the Fr. *abeille* below. Cf. also Rémusat, *op. cit.* i. 14 n.

† Hence the name by which he was called, *Peripateticus Palatinus* (John of Salisbury, *Metal.* ii. 10).

into a nunnery, Abelard, at the age of thirty-four, put himself under the most famous theologian of the day, Anselm of Laon (*c.* 1113, Deutsch, *op. cit.* 30 n.). The venture, whether due to religious impulse or to ambition, was not a success. A few lectures convinced Abelard that he would find little fruit 'on this barren fig-tree.'

'Anselm,' continues Abelard, 'was that sort of man that if any one went to him in uncertainty, he returned more uncertain still. He was wonderful to hear, but at once failed if you questioned him. He kindled a fire not to give light, but to fill the house with smoke' (*Hist. Cal.* c. 3).

Abelard soon shocked his fellow-students by expressing the opinion that educated men should be able to study the Scriptures for themselves with the help of the 'glosses' alone. (As a matter of fact, the 'gloss' in universal use was his tutor Anselm's amended form of the *Glossa Ordinaria* of Walafrid Strabo († 849) [Poole, *op. cit.* 135 n.]). In proof of his view, he gave, at their request, a series of lectures on *Ezekiel*. Such was his success, if we may accept his own statement, that it was only by expelling him from Laon as an unauthorized teacher, as in theology he certainly was, that the authorities were able to check the rush to his class-room. 'Anselm,' says Abelard, in a characteristic sentence, 'had the impudence to suppress me' (*Hist. Cal.* cc. 3, 4).

On his return to Paris, Abelard resumed his lectures, though whether in the cathedral or in St. Geneviève is uncertain. Scholars from every land (Fulk of Deuil, *Ep. ad Abælardum* in Migne, *PL* clxxviii. 371, gives an interesting catalogue) hastened to sit at the feet of this wonder of the age—philosopher, poet, musician, and theologian in one. The Church smiled on his success, and appointed him, though not yet a sub-deacon, a canon of Notre Dame (Poole, *op. cit.* 145 n.; Rémusat, i. 39 n.). Abelard had reached the zenith of his fame. Henceforth the story of his life is one of 'calamity,' not the least element in which was his own moral downfall, the conscious deliberateness of which, however, in our judgment, he characteristically exaggerates in his later reminiscences (*Hist. Cal.* c. 6; cf. Rémusat, i. 49, as against Cotter Morison, *St. Bernard*, 263). Into the romance of his connexion with Heloise (Heloïssa = Louise) we need not enter. The repetition of this well-known story distracts attention from the real greatness of Abelard in the history of thought. In spite of the protests of Heloise that 'Abelard was created for mankind, and should not be sacrificed for the sake of a single woman,' Abelard privately married the woman he had seduced, and, when the secret was out, removed her to the convent of Argenteuil, the discipline of which was very lax. In Abelard's opinion, as reported for us by one of his students, marriage was lawful for such of the clergy as had not been ordained priests (*Sententiæ*, c. xxxi.; cf. Poole, 147 n.). We draw a veil over the story of the revenge of Fulbert, his wife's uncle. Abelard in an agony of soul and body fled to St. Denys, while Heloise, on his demand, tried to transfer her passions to more spiritual objects, and took the veil at Argenteuil, chanting, as she did so, a verse out of Lucan's *Pharsalia* (c. 1119). Their boy, to whom the parents had given the curious name of Astrolabe, was left with Abelard's sister, Denys (*Hist. Cal.* c. 8. For his career see Rémusat, i. 269).

Abelard found the abbey of St. Denys worldly and dissolute. He retired in disgust to a cell of the house in Champagne, the exact location of which is a little uncertain (*Recueil*, xiv. 290 n.; Rémusat, *op. cit.* i. 73 n.; Poole, *op. cit.* 156 n.), and opened a school of theology. Very soon the throng of his students made it difficult to procure either food or shelter. His lectures were as daring as they were brilliant. In his *Tractatus de Unitate et Trinitate Divina*, a work recently discovered and edited by Dr. Stölzle (Freiburg, 1891), and afterwards recast into his *Theologia Christiana*, he discussed the great mystery. His line of thought may be gathered from his position: a doctrine is not believed merely because God has said it; but because we are convinced by reason that it is so (cf. *Int. ad Theol.* ii. 18). We need not wonder that he was summoned by the legate, Cardinal Cuno of Preneste, to answer for his teaching before a Synod at Soissons (1121) at the instance, curiously, of his first master, the aged Roscelin (on this see Rémusat, i. 81 n.), and of two rival masters of theology, Alberic of Rheims and Lotulf of Novara, the leading spirits in his former expulsion from Laon. The charge against him of Sabellianism seems to have had little justification (Rashdall, i. 53; Deutsch, 265). In reality the chief cause of offence lay in his appeal to reason. According to Abelard, the Synod, without either reading or inquiring, in spite also of the efforts of bp. Geoffrey of Chartres to secure an adjournment, 'compelled me to burn the book with my own hands. So it was burnt amid general silence.' He was not allowed to justify his orthodoxy. A copy was handed to him of the Athanasian Creed, 'the which I read amid sobs and tears as well as I might.' He was then sent to St. Medard, a convent near Soissons, which had acquired the reputation of a penitentiary through the stern discipline of its abbot Geoffrey and his frequent use of the whip (*Hist. Cal.* cc. 9, 10). 'Good Jesus,' cried Abelard in his distress, 'where wert Thou?' There he suffered much from the zeal of its prior, the rude but canonized Goswin (*Recueil des historiens des Gaules*, xiv. 445), who had previously come into conflict with him at St. Geneviève, 'as David with Goliath' (*ib.* 442). (The student should note that the records of the Synod of Soissons have been lost. We are dependent on Abelard, Otto of Freising, and St. Bernard).

Abelard was soon permitted to return to St. Denys. There his love for truth overwhelmed him in a new calamity. He had been led by Bede (*Expos. in Acts*, xvii. 34) to doubt whether the foundation was indeed due, as the monks proclaimed, to Dionysius the Areopagite. Characteristically Abelard 'showed the passage in a joke to some of the monks.' Alarmed by their threats of handing him over to the king, the patron of the abbey, Abelard fled by night to St. Ayoul's, a priory near Provins in Champagne. Efforts were made to secure his return, if necessary by force. He himself became willing to explain away the authority of Bede (Deutsch, *op. cit.* 38, for a defence of Abelard). Fortunately at this stage abbot Adam of St. Denys died (Feb. 19, 1122). He was succeeded by the famous Suger (1081–1152), at that time not the saint and reformer he became later through the influence of St. Bernard (1127), but one of the king's trusted ministers. At the instance of certain courtiers, Suger gave permission to Abelard to seek any refuge he liked, provided he did not become the subject of any other monastery. Abelard thus became a hermit, or unattached member of the house. But his eager pupils soon found out his retreat. His hut of wattles and stubble 'in a solitude abandoned to wild beasts and robbers' on the Ardusson, near Troyes, became the crowded monastery of the Paraclete. 'The whole world,' wrote Abelard, 'is gone out after me. By their persecutions they have prevailed nothing.' Nor was his monastery one to escape suspicion. It was rather a school of philosophers, where disputations took the place of constant devotions, where there were neither vows nor rigid rules. The very title of Paraclete, 'the Comforter' of his sad life, was an innovation; 'dedications should be either to the Trinity, or to the Son alone' (*Hist. Cal.* c. 11). That Abelard maintained strict order among his flock is shown, however, by a curious surviving fragment of verse (Rémusat, i. 111).

In 1125, Abelard was invited to be the abbot of the lonely monastery of St. Gildas de Rhuys, near Vannes, the oldest monastery in his native Brittany. Abelard accepted, either urged by his fears of further councils (for Clairvaux, the monastery of the ever vigilant St. Bernard, was at no great distance from Paraclete; while he dreaded also an attack from Norbert of Magdeburg, the founder of the Premonstratensians), or in one of his frequent moods. 'God knows,' he writes, 'that at times I fell into such despair that I proposed to myself to go off and live the life of a Christian among the enemies of Christ.' His life there for the next six, or possibly eight, years (Poole, 158 n.), was one of almost unrelieved misery. The abbey was poor in resources, shameless in its depravity; the monks unscrupulous in their determination to get rid of any reformer. They tried to poison Abelard, first in his food, then in the cup of the Eucharist. After several abortive attempts, Abelard succeeded in flight. But Paraclete was no longer open to him. In 1129 he had formally handed it over—with the added sanction (Nov. 28, 1131) of a Bull, which he had obtained from Pope Innocent II. on his stay at Morigny, near Etampes (*Recueil*, xii. 80)—to Heloise 'the prioress, and the other sisters in the oratory of the Holy Trinity.' Heloise had been expelled from Argenteuil in 1128 (*Recueil*, xii. 215) by the mingled rapacity and reforming zeal of Suger, who had made good at Rome the claims of St. Denys to the convent.

The movements of Abelard for the next three or four years are a little uncertain, the more so as he seems to have maintained the rank and title of abbot of St. Gildas. Probably he lived near Paraclete, engaged in collecting and publishing his writings, including his *Historia Calamitatum*, and in resolving for Heloise the various problems which arose in the establishment of Paraclete as a nunnery. To this period belongs also his famous correspondence with Heloise. To pass from these impassioned letters to the scholastic trifling of many of the *Problemata Heloissæ* is chiefly of interest as a study in repression. He resumed also his teaching at St. Geneviève, though perhaps fitfully. From the enthusiastic description of John of Salisbury in 1136 we learn that the master had lost none of his power (*Metalogicus*, ii. 10, 'contuli me ad peripateticum palatinum'). But for this mention, Abelard's history at this time would be almost a blank. We know, however, that about this date Arnold of Brescia attached himself to Abelard.

When next Abelard appears before us, he is at fatal theological strife with St. Bernard, whom he had first met at Morigny when in quest of the papal grant of the Paraclete (Jan. 20th, 1131). The differences of the two men were fundamental, of the kind that no argument or personal intercourse can remove. That Bernard was a realist goes without saying. Realism in those days was almost identical with orthodoxy. But this was not the difference. The two were representatives of opposing forces. Abelard summed up in himself the spirit of a premature revolt against unreasoning authority. Bernard, the last of the Fathers, was the supreme representative to the age of all that was best in the old faith: a reformer in morals and life, a rigid conservative in creed and ritual. Abelard, profoundly religious in his way, was the representative of a creed full of dry light and clear of cant, but destitute of spiritual warmth; and which had shown, both at St. Denys and St. Gildas, little power in turning men from their sins to the higher life. With all his narrowness of intellectual vision compared with Abelard, put St. Bernard down at St. Gildas, and that abode of loose livers would have felt at once the purifying power of his zeal. Bernard's was that baptism with fire which not only cleanses but warms; but of this the cold, subtle, intellectual religion of Abelard knew little or nothing. To Bernard—

'Faith is not an opinion but a certitude. "The substance of things hoped for," says the Apostle, not the phantasies of empty conjecture. You hear, the substance. You may not dispute on the faith as you please, you may not wander here and there through the wastes of opinion, the byways of error. By the name "substance" something certain and fixed is placed before you; you are enclosed within boundaries, you are restrained within unchanging limits' (*Tractatus de erroribus Abœlardi*, iv. 9).

Abelard, on the contrary, argued that reason was of God, and had, as philosophy showed, found God. He argued that 'he that is hasty to trust is light-minded' (Sir 19[4]). Conflict between the two was inevitable; it had already broken out. In one of his letters, Bernard inveighs with his customary rhetoric against 'Peter Abelard disputing with boys, conversing with women . . . who does not approach alone, as Moses did, towards the darkness in which God was, but advances attended by a crowd of disciples' (Bernard, *Ep.* cccxxxii.). On his part, Abelard had attacked the saint for preferring the usual form of the Lord's Prayer to that in use at Paraclete (τὸν ἄρτον τὸν ἐπιούσιον, which Abelard translates *supersubstantialem*; see Abelard, *Ep.* x. in Migne, *op. cit.* col. 337). Nor would the attachment to Abelard of his former pupil, the daring revolutionary Arnold of Brescia, tend to lessen the suspicions against him.

The two representatives of systems whose conflict from the nature of things is as inevitable as it is unending, were now to meet in fierce combat at Sens, in the province of whose archbishop both Paris and Clairvaux lay. The challenge seems to have come from Abelard; for we may dismiss as fiction the statement of Bernard's biographer, Geoffrey of Auxerre, that Bernard privately visited Abelard and secured his repentance (*Recueil*, xiv. 370). Abelard felt the need of publicly clearing himself from the charges of heterodoxy brought against him by William of St. Thierry in collusion, as some think, with Bernard himself (Bernard, *Ep.* cccxxvii.). In this challenge Abelard once more shows that neither misfortune nor years had taught him wisdom. 'He entered the lists against authority where authority was supreme—in a general council. At issue with the deep devotional spirit of the age, he chose his time when all minds were excited by the most solemn action of devotion—the Crusade: he appealed to reason when reason was least likely to be heard' (Milman, *Latin Christianity*, iv. 355). His one advantage would appear to have been that Henry le Sanglier, the archbishop of Sens, had a grudge against Bernard (Rémusat, i. 210–211). Perhaps for this reason Bernard at first was unwilling to come to the duel. Such contests, he pleaded, were vain; the verities of faith could not be submitted to their decision (*Ep.* clxxxix. 4). At length Bernard yielded to the representations of his friends and the summons of his metropolitan, and set out for Sens, Whitsuntide 1141 (for date, not 1140 as Poole, Rémusat, see Deutsch, *Die Synode v. Sens*, Berlin, 1880). Hardly had the council opened (June 4), and Bernard demanded the recital of Abelard's heresies, than Abelard, whether from characteristic irresolution, fear of the people of Sens, loss of nerve, or revulsion of feeling, appealed from the very tribunal he had chosen to the judgment of the Pope, and left the assembly to mumble out over its wine-cups its *condemnamus*, already decided upon, it seems, on the previous day (Berengar of Poictiers, *Apologeticus pro Magistro* in Migne, *PL* clxxviii. col. 1857 ff.; to be read with caution). The folly of Abelard's appeal is shown by the haste with which (July 16, 1141) Pope Innocent II. ratified the sentence of Sens, largely as the result of the invectives of Bernard against 'the French bee' (*abeille*) and 'Goliath's weapon-bearer, Arnold of Brescia' (*Epp.* clxxxviii., cxcii., cxciii., cccxxxi.–cccxxxvi., cccxxxviii., Poole, 166 n.), who seems, in fact, to have appealed to the Pope, even before the condemnation of Abelard—a matter scarcely to the credit of Bernard (Rémusat, i. 223. For the condemnation see Migne, *PL* clxxix. cols. 515–517. The records of Sens have not been preserved).

Abelard had appealed unto Cæsar, but it was before a different tribunal that he was to stand. After lingering some days in Paris, he set off for Rome, but on his way old age came upon him suddenly; so in the monastery of Clugny, 'renouncing the tumult of schools and lectures, he awaited the end.' Through the efforts of the abbot, Peter the Venerable, Abelard was reconciled to St. Bernard (see possibly his *confessio*, Migne, *op. cit.* 105). His increasing weakness led to his removal to the dependent priory of St. Marcel at Chalons-sur-Sâone. There, in the spring of 1142 (April 21), as the abbot wrote to 'his dear sister,' the sorrowing Heloise:—

'The advent of the Divine Visitor found him not sleeping, as it does many, but on the watch. . . . A long letter would not unfold the humility and devotion of his conversation while among us. If I mistake not, I never remember to have seen one so humble in manners and habit. Thus Master Peter finished his days, and he who throughout the world was famed for his knowledge persevered in meekness and humility, and, as we may believe, passed to the Lord' (Peter the Venerable, *Ep. ad Heloissam*, Migne, *PL* clxxix. col. 347 ff.).

His body was secretly conveyed by Peter to the Paraclete, and buried in the crypt of the church. Heloise survived his death 21 years, and was buried near him; not, however, until Nov. 6, 1817, did they rest together in Père Lachaise ('ἀεὶ συμπεπλεγμένοι,' Rémusat, i. 268).

2. Influence.—Abelard was no heretic, nor was his a deathbed repentance. He always maintained that he was the devoted son of the Church. He was, in the verdict of Peter the Venerable, 'ever to be named with honour as the servant of Christ, and verily Christ's philosopher' (Petrus Ven. *ut supra*). In his last letter to Heloise, Abelard had pleaded: 'I would not be an Aristotle if this should keep me away from Christ' (Migne, *PL* clxxviii. col. 375). He owes his importance not to his heresies, but to his demand for reverent, though thorough, inquiry into matters of religion. Modern Catholics have no hesitation in saying that both the Synods, Soissons and Sens, were conspicuous for zea' ather than knowledge. It is well known also that the work of his disciple, the famous *Sentences* of Peter Lombard, a work that is largely the *Sic et Non* in a more reverent form, became the accredited textbook in theology, the very canon of orthodoxy of the later Middle Ages, though many of its views were those for which Abelard had been condemned. But we need not marvel at the misfortunes of Abelard. In part they were the results of an ill-balanced judgment, always in extremes, in part the necessary outcome of his real greatness.

For Abelard was so great intellectually, so completely in advance of his age, both in the extent of his knowledge and the width of his outlook, that his positions were bound to seem heterodox to a generation that leaned wholly on the past. Abelard, in fact, belonged to the future. The very spirit of Protestantism is contained in his declaration that the 'doctors of the Church should be read not with the necessity to believe, but with liberty to judge' (*Sic et Non*, prol. in Migne, *op. cit.* p. 1347). We seem transported to the 20th cent. when Abelard claims that the interpretation of Scripture may err or the text be faulty (*l.c.*). In the preface to his *Sic et Non*—a collection of contradictory opinions from the Fathers on all the leading disputes of theology, the prologue of which was probably written not later than 1121 (Deutsch, 462)—he lays down a defence of all criticism: 'By doubting we are led to inquire, by inquiry we perceive the truth.' Of those who argue that we must not reason on matters of faith, Abelard asks:

'How, then, is the faith of any people, however false, to be refuted, though it may have arrived at such a pitch of blindness as to confess some idol to be the creator both of heaven and earth? As, according to your own admission, you cannot reason upon matters of faith, you have no right to attack others upon a matter with regard to which you think you ought yourself to be unassailed' (*Introd. Theol.* ii. c. 3, Migne, *op. cit.* col. 1050).

The dilemma of unreasoning pietism has never been better exposed.

The circumstances of the times flung Abelard into conflict with Bernard. Intellectually, the only foeman worthy of his steel would have been Anselm of Canterbury. At first sight there seems to be between these two philosophers an impassable abyss, unconsciously summed up by Anselm in the preface to his *Cur Deus Homo*. Some men seek for reasons because they do not believe; we seek for them because we do believe! 'This is my belief, that, if I believe not, neither shall I understand' (*credo ut intelligam*). The rule of Abelard is the exact opposite. He argues that men believe not because of authority but because of conviction. Doubt is his starting-point, reason his guide to certitude. But a deeper study reveals that the differences between the two may be exaggerated, as in Abelard's own generation they certainly were. Abelard owns that the highest truths of theology stand above the proof of our understanding; they can only be hinted at by analogies, as, for instance, his favourite analogy of the seal and the Trinity. But through knowledge faith is made perfect (Deutsch, *op. cit.* 96 ff., 433 ff.). Anselm was no less anxious to satisfy reason than Abelard, only he wanted to make sure of its limits before he began. Thus the difference between the two great thinkers was one rather of order of thought than real divergence. If the chronological order be regarded, Anselm is right; if the logical, Abelard. In the order of experience faith precedes reason; in the maturer life reason leads up to faith (see some excellent remarks in Fairbairn, *Christ in Mod. Theol.* 120 ff., on the contrast; cf. also Deutsch, *op. cit.* 172). It is in the clear perception of this last that the true greatness of Abelard lies. But, like Bacon, he had to leave his name and memory to the next age, that age which he had done more than any man to usher in. The school in which he taught developed within a generation into the greatest university of Europe, largely through his influence. With Abelard also closes the first period of Scholasticism. In the next generation James of Venice translated the works of Aristotle, hitherto for the most part unknown, into Latin. Henceforth the 'New Logic,' the basis of which in many ways was the same as that which led Abelard in his protests, dominated Europe. In the place of St. Bernard we have Aristotle as the all but canonized leader of the Church.

In nothing is Abelard's influence more visible than in his scholars. Of his pupils, twenty-five, it is said, became cardinals, including Pope Alexander III., and more than fifty were bishops. Through Peter Lombard's *Sentences*, founded on the model of Abelard's *Sic et Non*, Abelard swayed and moulded the theology of the next three hundred years. As Abelard was the incarnation of the new spirit claiming for itself the freedom of thought, so in his pupil Arnold of Brescia we find the leader in the new claim for freedom of will in an ideal Christian republic. Another pupil, William of Conches, made a firm though ineffectual protest against the growing neglect of literature (John of Salisbury, *Metal.* i. 24 in Migne, *PL* clxxviii. col. 856).

Of particular doctrines which illustrate Abelard's influence or drift, we select the following as of special theological interest :—

(*a*) *Inspiration.*—He limits inspiration to matters concerning 'faith, hope, charity, and the sacraments.' The rest is largely 'for the adornment or enlargement of the Church' (see his Prol. in *Ep. Rom.*, Migne, *op. cit.* 785). Even 'prophets and apostles may err' (Prol. in *Sic et Non*, Migne, *op. cit.* 1345), while a place must be found in the evolution of life and doctrine for revelation given to the heathen philosophers, especially Plato (*Theol. Christ.* lib. ii. *passim*, e.g. Migne, *op. cit.* 1179. Cf. *Epit. Theol. Christ.* c. 11).

(*b*) *The humanity of Christ.*—This he claims to be essentially real. He goes so far even as to claim that it includes 'humanæ infirmitatis veros defectus' (*Epit. Theol. Christ.* c. 25). In his emphasis on the real humanity of Jesus, Abelard is a complete contrast to his age.

(*c*) He claimed that *sin lies in the intention*, the consent of the will to an action which is not of itself evil. Virtue cannot be attained except by conflict. Ignorance in the case of the unenlightened does not constitute sin, and the Jews who ignorantly crucified Jesus must be judged accordingly. (Abelard's doctrine of sin may be best gathered from his *Scito te ipsum*, esp. cc. 2, 3, 13. Its very title shows the emphasis he places on self-knowledge or intention). Original sin is thus the penal consequence of sin and not sin itself. 'It is inconceivable that God should damn a man for the sin of his parents' (*Ep. Rom.*, Migne, *op. cit.* 866 ff.).

(*d*) From this it is an easy transition to Abelard's *moral theory of the Atonement*—Christ's creating within us by His passion a love which itself delivers from sin (*Exp. Ep. Rom.* in Migne, *op. cit.* 836, 859). He rejects totally any theory that makes the Atonement a redemption from the right of the devil (*Epit. Theol. Christ.* c. 23).

Abelard's influence in the field of Logic was very great, amounting almost to a revolution. He struck out a theory which to-day we should call Conceptualism, midway between the Nominalism of Roscelin and the crude Realism of William of Champeaux. He held that we arrive at the general from the particular by an effort of thought. Thus he allowed the reality of the individual, and the reality also of the universals, in so far, that is, as they were the necessary creations of the intellect. Abelard thus returned to the position of Aristotle, probably without any direct knowledge of Aristotle's arguments (Poole, 142 n.). Hence the reputation of Abelard in dialectics in the following centuries, when Aristotle had become dominant. (For a full discussion see Rémusat, vol. ii., or von Prantl, or Ueberweg, i. 392 f.).

Abelard's versatility was very great. In dialectics and theology he was the master without a rival; he also lectured on the great classical law-texts (Rashdall, i. 63 n.). His vernacular songs have perished; the religious hymns (in Migne, 1759 ff.) give little indication of the great power that he exercised in this matter. As a humanist, his qualifications, as also in the case of Heloise, have been exaggerated. His knowledge of Latin literature was considerable, of Greek slight, and of Hebrew nil (Rémusat, i. 30; Deutsch, 58 ff.). Of all mathematics he professes his complete ignorance. His citations from the Fathers are extensive (Deutsch, 69 ff.), as the reader may see for himself by turning over the pages of *Sic et Non*, though many no doubt are second-hand. His eloquence, wit, and charm of manner, added to a culture that covered almost the whole range of knowledge as then conceived, were acknowledged by his enemies. To this we have the witness of his epitaph :—

'Est satis in titulo : Petrus hic jacet Abaillardus
Huic soli patuit scibile quidquid erat'

(Poole, 145 n.; for different and inferior reading, Migne, 103; Rémusat, i. 259 n.).

But the truest estimate of Abelard's greatness is that unconsciously given by William of St. Thierry in his invective against him in 1139 :—

'His books pass the seas, cross the Alps. His new notions and dogmas about the faith are carried through kingdom and province; they are preached before many and publicly defended, insomuch that they are reported even to have influence at the court of Rome' (*Op. Bernard*, Ep. cccxxvi.).

Abelard's spirit lived in the victories and movements of later thought.

LITERATURE.—*A.* The chief source for the life of Abelard will be found in his autobiography, the *Historia Calamitatum.* In addition, we have stray references in Otto of Freising's *de Gestis Frederici* (ed. Pertz, v. 20), esp. i. cc. 47–48, with reference to the Synods of Soissons and Sens; John of Salisbury, *Metalogicus* (in Migne, *PL* v. 199, or Bouquet, *Recueil*, xiv.), and, of course, the *Letters* of St. Bernard. We may add the *Vita b. Goswini* (in Bouquet or Brial, *Recueil des Hist. des Gaules*, xiv.), and Suger's *de rebus in admin. sua gestis* (in Duchesne's *Script. Franc.* iv.). Of modern Lives the best sketch in English is by R. L. Poole in his *Illust. of Hist. of Med. Thought* (1884); Abelard's connexion with the University is judiciously dealt with by Rashdall, *Univ. in M. A.* (1895) i. ch. 1; Compayré's *Abelard and the Origin of Universities* (1893) is altogether misnamed; M'Cabe's *Peter Abélard* (1901) is the work of a partisan; the chapter in Cotter Morison's *St. Bernard* (many eds.) is not altogether satisfactory. In French we have the admirable *Abélard*, 2 vols. (Paris, 1845), of Charles de Rémusat. In German: Deutsch, *Peter Abälard* (Leipzig, 1883), has given us a thorough criticism of Abelard's theology which may be compared by the student with that in Rémusat. Deutsch has added much to our knowledge of Abelard's closing years by his *Die Synode von Sens* (Berlin, 1880). Adolf Hausrath's *Peter Abälard* (Leipzig, 1893) is concise yet full. For the philosophy of Abelard, in addition to the exhaustive discussion in Rémusat, we have Reuter, *Gesch. der relig. Entklärung* (2 vols. 1875–1877); Hauréau, *Hist. de la Philosophie scolastique* (Paris, 1872); and, more especially for his Logic, von Prantl, *Gesch. d. Logik im Abendlande* (4 vols., Leipzig, 1855–1870).

B. Of the works of Abelard we have the following editions: Migne, *PL* v. clxxviii. (1855), but without the *Tractatus de Unitate et Trinitate*, first published by Stölzle (Freiburg, 1891). On p. 375 of Migne's edition there is an amazing suppression of 'what would shock Catholic ears.' Migne's edition contains the *Sic et Non* first edited in full by Henke and Lindenkohl (Marburg, 1851), as also all the works of Abelard, for the first editing of which we are indebted to Victor Cousin; *Ouvrages inédits d'Abélard* (Paris, 1836), and the later *Petri Abœlardi Opera*, ed. V. Cousin, C. Jourdain, and E. Despois (Paris, 1849). Cousin's contributions to our knowledge of Abelard are very great.

H. B. WORKMAN.

ABETMENT.—In its most general sense 'abetment' means encouragement, countenance, aid; but the word is now used almost entirely in a bad sense as encouragement, counsel, and instigation to commit an offence against the law. When any one 'directly or indirectly counsels, procures, or commands any person to commit any felony or piracy which is committed in consequence of such counselling, procuring, or commandment,' he is described in English law as an accessory before the fact (cf. Stephen, *Digest of the Criminal Law*). In most criminal codes an abettor or accessory is usually described as a person who has in some manner led to, or facilitated the execution of, an offence by rendering material or intellectual assistance. Without being present at the actual perpetration of a crime or an injustice, a man may be useful to the perpetrator of it by assisting him to plan it, or by placing information before him which will facilitate the offence or enable him to escape. Or abetment may take the form of rendering material assistance to the principal agent, such as procuring for him the instruments or physical means by which he is enabled or assisted to commit an offence.

In China, complicity of a purely moral character is punished with the same severity as if the accomplice were the actual agent, and an offender found guilty of counselling the perpetration of murder receives the same punishment (namely, decapitation) as if he had committed it. (Cf. Letourneau, *L'Evolution juridique*, p. 169). In Roman law, in ancient German law, in old French law, and in

English and American law, no distinction is made, in cases of serious crime, between an accessory and a principal. 'Each in English law may be indicted, tried, convicted, and punished as if he alone and independently' (Stephen) had committed the offence (cf. Post, *Ethnologische Jurisprudenz*, 1894, ii. 296 f.). In ancient Jewish law, any one inciting or seducing the people to commit idolatry was ordered to be stoned to death (Dt 13^{6-11}). Idolatry was regarded as an act of supreme treason against the theocracy, and every sort of incitement to commit it was visited with the severest penalties. In primitive penal law, abetment does not appear to have been a punishable offence (Post), and in Talmudic jurisprudence no cognizance is taken of incitement by thoughts or words (*JE*, i. p. 54).

In recent years, certain Italian jurists (*e.g.* Sighele, *Teoria positiva della complicita*, Torina, 1894) have contended that no distinction should be made between accessories and principals, on the ground that a crime committed by persons acting in concert is more dangerous in character than a crime committed by a single individual, and that men united for the common purpose of committing a crime ought to share the responsibility for it in common. Habitual offenders, it is contended, frequently act together; it is often a mere accident which of them shall be the actual perpetrator; therefore all of them ought to be held equally responsible. The supreme object of the law should be to strike at the association, and not merely at the individuals of which it is composed. It is the association that is the danger. W. D. MORRISON.

ABHAYAGIRI.—Name of a celebrated monastery at Anurādhapura, the ancient capital of Ceylon. *Giri* means 'mountain,' and *Abhaya* was one of the names of king Vaṭṭa Gamini, who erected the monastery close to the *stūpa*, or solid dome-like structure built over supposed relics of the Buddha. It was this *stūpa* that was called a mountain or hill, and the simile was not extravagant, as the *stūpa* was nearly the height of St. Paul's, and its ruins are still one of the sights of Anurādhapura.

There was considerable rivalry from the outset between the monks at this establishment and those at the much older Mahā Vihāra (the Great Minster), founded 217 years earlier. The rivalry was mainly personal, but developed into differences of doctrinal opinion. Of the nature of these latter we have no exact information, and they were probably not of much importance. On one occasion, in the reign of Mahāsena (A.D. 275–302), the Great Minster was abolished, and its materials removed to the Abhayagiri. But the former was soon afterwards restored to its previous position, and throughout the long history of Ceylon maintained its pre-eminence.

LITERATURE.—H. W. Cave, *Ruined Cities of Ceylon*, London, 1900, pp. 91–93, with plates. T. W. RHYS DAVIDS.

ABHIDHAMMA.—The title of the third (and last) group, or *piṭaka*, of the Buddhist canonical books; a name also for the specific way in which the Dhamma (doctrine) is set forth in those books. It is in that specific treatment, and not in any distinctive subject-matter, that the real use and significance of these books for early Buddhism are to be found. A myth grew up among 19th cent. Indologists, that the Abhidhamma *piṭaka* was the repository of Buddhist metaphysic. Acquaintance with the contents of the *piṭaka* has dispelled this notion. There is, no doubt, an abstruse and abstract suggestiveness in the titles and opening sentences of the books and their divisions, giving a fictitious suggestion of originality and profundity. But, besides this, there is an ancient tradition of superior erudition and higher standing attaching to those of the Buddhist order who were Abhidhammikas, or experts in Abhidhamma. Thus, in the Mihintale rock inscription, dating from about the commencement of our Middle Ages, tithes from 12 villages or farms are allotted to the cave-recluses there who were Abhidhammikas, as against tithes from 7 and 5 respectively allotted to experts in Suttanta and Vinaya (that is, in the Doctrine and in the Rules of the Order). And whereas mastery of these two was held to establish the expert in *sīla* and *samādhi* respectively (that is, in conduct and meditation), knowledge of Abhidhamma involved the development of *paññā*,—constructive imagination and comprehension,—which ranked among the highest virtues. Once more, in the ancient book translated as *The Questions of King Milinda*, the acquisition by the youthful genius Nāgasena of the contents of the Abhidhamma is acclaimed with wonder and delight in earth and heaven, while his rapid attainment of the remaining *piṭakas* excites no such commotion. Finally, the title itself may have helped to mislead Western, and even Eastern notions. *Abhi* can mean *sur*, *super*, and hence suggests an analogy with Aristotle's *Physics* and *Metaphysics*. Buddhaghosa himself, in explaining the title, gives *ati* ('beyond,' 'above,' 'to excess') as the equivalent of the prefix, inasmuch as Abhidhamma goes beyond the Dhamma, and is distinct from it. But he proceeds to explain that this distinction is due, not to any superior profundity of method, or nature of subject-matter, but to the more detailed analysis given to points of doctrine in the Abhidhamma as compared with the Suttanta methods. There was a legend in his day that the Abhidhamma was first uttered by the Buddha in the Tāvatimsa heaven, whither he had transported himself to preach the Dhamma to his deified mother and hosts of devas. It is not consonant with the Buddhist standpoint, that such an audience should be held capable of benefiting by disquisitions on philosophical problems which had been withheld from the stronger intellects of the Buddha's chief disciples, whom he instructs in the Suttanta. In fact, the legend sprang probably from the orthodox anxiety to invest with a sanction, not inferior to that of the two earlier *piṭakas*, a series of compilations which are manifestly of later date, and the work of elaborating scholiasts.

Let it, then, be clearly understood that our present knowledge of such philosophy as is revealed in the Buddhist Pāli canon would be practically undiminished if the whole of the Abhidhamma *piṭaka* were non-existent. That philosophy is all to be found in the Sutta *piṭaka*. The Abhidhammika may nevertheless be held to have surpassed his Suttantika *confrère* in two ways. It should always be remembered (and the usually wearisome form of the Abhidhamma books never lets the reader forget it) that the canon was compiled, and for generations learnt, as an unwritten composition. In the first two *piṭakas* the memory is aided by episodes giving occasion for the utterance of rule, doctrine, or discussion, and also by frequent verse. The Abhidhamma gives no such aids. It helps only by catechism; in its last and longest books, not even by that. Hence the call for sustained reconstructive and reproductive effort must have been more severe. And, further, since the work is mainly a recount, with analysis and elaborations and comment, of Suttanta doctrines, to know one's Abhidhamma might be said to involve a knowledge of the gist of the Sutta *piṭaka*.

The burden, then, of Abhidhamma is not any positive contribution to the philosophy of early Buddhism, but analytic and logical and methodological elaboration of what is already given. As such it might have almost equalled, in value to the world, the contents of the discourses. As a fact it is the *reductio ad absurdum* of formalism. It is impossible to estimate the extent to which the exaggeration of the Indian temperament and the temperance of the Greek temperament were due to the absence and presence respectively, during the florescence of each, of the written book. Nowhere as in India do we find imagination so elastic and exuberant, running riot through time, space, and the infinite; and nowhere else is seen such determined effort to curb and regulate it. Abhidhamma training was one of the most noteworthy forms of this effort. It was specially calculated (according to Buddhaghosa, *Atthasālinī*, p. 24) to check those excesses over the normal mind (*dhammachitta*) which, in the Buddha's words, tended to loss of balance, craziness, and insanity. The chief methods of that training were: first, the definition and determination of all names or terms entering into the Buddhist scheme of culture; secondly, the enunciation of all doctrines, theoretical and practical, as formulas, with co-ordination of all such as were logically interrelated; and finally, practice in reducing all possible heterodox positions to an absurdity—a method which is confined to the somewhat later fifth book, the *Kathāvatthu*. Even in these lofty aims, however, the want of restraint, helped by the cumbrousness of purely mnemonic compilation, tends to defeat the very objects sought. The logic of definition is not the same as we have inherited, and the propositions yield strings of alternatives that have often little or no relation to facts.

Of the seven books of the Abhidhamma *piṭaka*, the first five have been published by the Pāli Text Society, viz. *Dhammasaṅgaṇi*, *Vibhaṅga*, *Dhātu-kathā*, *Puggala-paññatti* and *Kathāvatthu*; the sixth, or *Yamaka*, is not yet edited; the seventh, the *Paṭṭhāna*, is [1907] in the press. The first book has been translated by the present writer under the title, *A Buddhist Manual of Psychological Ethics*, London, 1900. Besides these seven, there still survive, in Chinese or Tibetan translations, other seven books, which form the Abhidhamma literature of the Sarvāstivādins—a school which split off from the original nucleus of Buddhist culture. A very full index to the contents of these seven is given by Professor Takakusu in *JPTS*, 1905. But the books themselves have not as yet been edited or translated. Their date also is not yet settled, but they are certainly earlier than the Christian era. These works form the basis of the celebrated, but as yet undiscovered, *Abhidharma-kośa*, or Dictionary of Abhidhamma, written in Sanskrit, as well as that of its Commentaries, and other cognate works, some of which survive in Sanskrit and others in Chinese or Tibetan versions, and which carried on the development of Abhidhamma down to the 2nd or 3rd cent. A.D. Professor Bunyiu Nanjio, in his catalogue of Chinese Buddhist literature (Oxford, 1883), gives the titles of no fewer than thirty-seven of these works still extant. In the later developments of Buddhism in India, notably in the so-called 'Great Vehicle,' the use of the term *Abhidhamma* gradually died out. But in other Buddhist countries, where Pāli has remained the literary language, books on Abhidhamma have continued to be written down to the present day, the best known being the *Abhidhammatthasangaha*, published in 1884 by the Pāli Text Society.

C. RHYS DAVIDS.

ABHIDHARMA KOŚA VYĀKHYĀ.—One of the most important Buddhist texts preserved in Nepal. It is a commentary, written by a scholar named Yaśomitra, on a classical account of Buddhist metaphysics: *Abhidharma-kośa*, 'the treasure of Abhidharma.' The Sanskrit original of the Kośa seems to be irrevocably lost; but there still exist Chinese and Tibetan versions, of which the Chinese are the oldest. The earliest of these is the work of a Hindu monk, Paramārtha, dated A.D. 563–567; the second, being a revised translation, was made by Hiuen-tsiang, the celebrated pilgrim, A.D. 651–654. The author of the Kośa is Vasubandhu, one of the most illustrious doctors of the Buddhist Church, who flourished about the end of the 5th cent. A.D.

The Kośa itself consists of two parts: (1) a summary account of the doctrine in 602 verses (*kārikās*); (2) an illustrative commentary (*vṛtti*) on these verses. The subject-matter is discussed in eight sections, viz.: the first principles (*dhātus*), the senses (*indriyas*), the worlds (*lokas*), the inclinations (*anuśayas*), the saint (*ārya pudgala*), the science (*jñāna*), the trance (*samādhi*), the individuality (*pudgala*). Vasubandhu belongs to the school of the Sarvāstivādins, who affirm the existence of all things,—a school of the Hīnayāna, or 'Little Vehicle.' The Kośa has nevertheless been admitted as an authority by all schools of Buddhism; the author of the Vyākhyā, Yaśomitra, is a Sautrāntika, and Chinese and Japanese Mahāyānists have always employed it as a text-book. A huge literature of notes and glosses on the Kośa has grown up. In India, before Yaśomitra, Sthiramati, Guṇamati, and Vasumitra wrote commentaries on it, which still exist in Tibetan versions. In China, two pupils of Hiuen-tsiang, Fu-koang and Fa-pao, compiled the lectures and explanations given by their master. It would be easy to-day to fill a whole library with the Kośa literature. That the work achieved so great popularity is due to the rare merits of the author. Familiar with the pedantic intricacies of each school, Vasubandhu elucidates them by the strength of his genius; he brings order, clearness, precision, and cohesion into the whole, combining in a harmonious synthesis the tenets sanctioned by general consent of Buddhists.

SYLVAIN LÉVI.

ABHIṢEKA (literally 'pouring upon' [from *abhi*+*sich*]).—A compound which, without definite ceremonial implications, occurs several times in the Atharva Veda, but not in the Rig or the Sāma. In the White Yajur Veda, and in the three Saṁhitās of the Black Yajur Veda, as well as in several Brāhmaṇas and the *śrauta* ritual of all the four Vedas, we find *abhiṣechanīya* as the name of a rite included in the *rājasūya*, and the last book of the Aitareya Brāhmaṇa has *abhiṣeka* itself for its main topic.

The ceremonial sprinkling, anointing, or baptizing of persons and things is a usage of such antiquity and universality, that its origin and significance could not methodically be made the subject of an inquiry confined to India (see artt. on ANOINTING). If the earliest anointing was with blood, and the object of it to confer vigour, the evidence for the former truth must be sought outside India; and although an invigorating power is in fact ascribed (*e.g.* Satapatha Brāhmaṇa, v. 4. 2. 2) to the rite, the Brāhmanical theologians were quite capable of arriving at such a conclusion without the help of an old tradition.

We may (A) begin by a statement of the actual employment of such a ceremony, so far as it is known to us from narrative sources, and then (B) append an account of the Brāhmanical prescriptions in connexion with *abhiṣeka*, *vājapeya*, and *rājasūya* ceremonies, and the ritual appertaining to them.

A. 1. Subjects of the ceremony.—The persons who underwent the rite of *abhiṣeka* were in the first place *emperors*. The Aitareya Brāhmaṇa (viii. 15) states as the object of the rite the attainment of paramount power, which it names with a great amplitude of synonyms, and it annexes a list of the famous rulers of former times who had been so distinguished (viii. 21–23). In the Mahābhārata we have two *abhiṣekas* of Yudhiṣṭhira: the first (Sabhā Parvan, cc. 33, 45, esp. 45) is preceded by victorious expeditions in all directions and celebrated as part of a *rājasūya* in the presence of subordinate kings, while the second (Śānti Parvan, c. 40) follows the conclusion of the great war. The Buddhist emperor Aśoka was not crowned until four years of conquest had followed his accession (Mahawanso, Turnour, p. 22), and in the case of

Harṣa Sīlāditya of Ujjain there was a similar postponement (Hiuen-tsiang, *Si-Yu-Ki*, tr. Beal, i. pp. 212–213). An imperial *abhiṣeka* occurs also in Kālidāsa's Raghuvaṁśa, sarga ii., and the inauguration of Naravāhanadatta in the different versions of the Bṛhatkathā (Kṣemendra, xvii. ; Somadeva, xv. 110, esp. v. 89) is that of an emperor; cf. also *Epigraphia Indica*, ii. 4; v. 16.

We have less testimony for the practice in the case of ordinary *mahārājas* or *kings*. But no doubt it would be usual with these also, so long as they retained any measure of independence. For, in the first place, the line between kings and emperors would be very hard to draw, and the Aitareya Brāhmaṇa (viii. 14) plainly contemplates also the *abhiṣeka* of mere kings. Secondly, the Kauśika Sūtra of the Atharva Veda (xvii. 11–13, *ap.* Weber, 'Ueber den Râjasûya,' p. 141) distinguishes the *abhiṣeka* of a simple king (*ekarāja*) from that of a higher (*varṣīyas*). The Mahābhārata (Śānti Parvan, v. 2496, *ap.* Goldstücker, *s.v.* 'abhiṣeka,' p. 280) speaks of the *abhiṣechana* of a king as the most essential matter for any country. The father of Harṣa Śīlāditya, Pratāpaśīla, underwent the rite of *abhiṣeka*, although he was no universal emperor (Harṣa-Charita, ed. Bombay, 1892, p. 132, ll. 9, 10). See also Jātaka, Nos. 456 and 458; Jacobi, *Erzählungen aus dem Mahārāṣṭrī*, p. 26, l. 5, ll. 13 ff.; the various Rājyābhiṣekapaddhatis and prayogas, and esp. Bhaṭṭa Nīlakaṇṭha's Nītimayūkha, where a full ritual is given (*sub init.*).

We may mention here that the Atharva Veda includes a coronation (*rājasūya*) hymn (iv. 8).

The anointing of an *heir-apparent* (*yuvarāja*) by his father is supported by several examples from the Epics (Goldstücker, *op. cit.* p. 282), to which we may add the references in the Harṣa-Charita, c. vi. (ed. Bombay, 1892, p. 223, ll. 12, 13), the Bṛhatkathā (Kṣemendra, vii. 23. 559; Somadeva, vi. 34, 107 ff.), *Epigraphia Indica*, iv. p. 120, l. 2, and Kalpasūtra (ed. Jacobi), p. 74, § 211.

The case of Rāma in the Rāmāyaṇa, of which the Ayodhyā-kāṇḍa (cc. 1–17, with Yuddha-kāṇḍa, c. 112) supplies the fullest account of the state and circumstance of a royal inauguration, is peculiar in two respects—the inauguration was initiated as a *yauvarājyābhiṣeka*, though completed after Rāma's final accession, and it was an example of the *puṣyābhiṣeka*, which we find fully described in three texts, namely, Atharva Veda Pariśiṣṭa, No. 4, the Bṛhatsaṁhitā of Varāhamihira, c. 48, and the Kālikā Purāṇa, c. 89. The special feature of this rite was that it took place at the conjunction of the moon with the asterism *puṣya* (December-January), at which time, we are informed, Indra originally conquered the demons (Rām. ii. 14. 46), while, according to the Buddhists, both the anointing of an heir-apparent and the *abhiniṣkramaṇa* (cf. the Jaina *nekkhamābhiṣeka* in Bhagavatī, ix. 33, p. 819, a ref. due to Prof. Leumann) of a Bodhisattva befall at the same hour (Mahāvastu, vol. ii. p. 158, ll. 2–4). This date is many times cited in the passages from the Rāmāyaṇa (*e.g.* ii. 2. 10, 3. 39, 4. 20, 14. 46, vi. 112. 56, 70), which also mentions a specially adorned chariot (*puṣyaratha*), described by Hemādri, i. 283, 284 (cf. Siśupālavadha, iii. 22, and *Epigr. Ind.* iii. 71), and no doubt identical with the *phussaratha* of the Jātaka (Nos. 378, 445). The ceremony *puṣyābhiṣeka* or *puṣyasnāna*, as described in the Kālikā Purāṇa and Bṛhatsaṁhitā, presents some very interesting features,—it is by no means confined to the inauguration of sovereignty,—and would probably repay anthropological investigation.

Anointing was also practised in the case of certain *ministers of state*. The Harṣa-Charita speaks of 'anointed counsellors of royal rank' (*mūrdhābhiṣiktā amātyā rājānaḥ*, p. 193, ll. 13, 14); and for the *purohita*, or state priest, there was a special ceremony called *bṛhaspatisava* connected, though somewhat indefinitely, with the *vājapeya* (Eggeling, *Śatapatha Brāhmaṇa*, iii. p. xxv). The account of the *purohita*, which in the Aitareya Brāhmaṇa viii. 24 ff., and Kauśika Sutra xvii. 30 ff., immediately follows *abhiṣeka*, seems not to include a mention of sprinkling. As regards the *senāpati*, or commander-in-chief, Goldstücker has given (*op. cit.* p. 285) quotations from the Mahābhārata (Śalya Parvan, adhy. 46) and elsewhere. From Jaina sources we may cite the case occurring in Prof. Jacobi's *Erzählungen aus dem Mahārāṣṭrī*, p. 17, l. 29.

The anointing of *images* at the time of their inauguration (*pratiṣṭhā*), on occasion of festivals or of distress, or regularly, is a custom still prevalent among the Hindus in India and the Buddhists in Nepal. Rules for it are given in many manuals (Pūjāvidhi's and Pratiṣṭhāvidhi's); an earlier allusion to it may be cited from the Harṣa-Charita (ed. Bombay, 1892, p. 171, l. 2). The fluid mentioned in this case is milk; but a variety of other substances, including water of various kinds, cow-dung, earth from an anthill, etc. etc., are named by the authorities whom Goldstücker quotes.

Finally, the name *abhiṣekabhūmi* is given by the Buddhists to the last of their ten *bhūmis* or stages of perfection (Mahāvastu, i. 124. 20). And further, the word *abhiṣeka* was applied to any ceremonial bathing, such as has always been, and still is, practised by Hindus at sacred fords, tanks, etc. etc. For *abhiṣeka* of neophytes, see Agnipurāṇa, c. 90, Poussin, *Études*, 208 ff., and Rājendralāla Mitra, *Notices of Sanskrit MSS*, No. 1536; of barren women, etc., Hemādri, *Vratakhāṇḍa*.

2. Ritual and occasion of the ceremony.—This is not the place for enlarging on the varying details of the inauguration ceremony as described in the Sanskrit literature. The reader will find in Goldstücker's Dictionary, *s.v.* 'Abhiṣeka,' ample material, extracted from the Mahābhārata (Śānti Parvan, c. 40), Rāmāyaṇa, Agni-Purāṇa (c. 209), and Mānasāra. Although in these works the special priestly aspect of the ceremony is but little developed, Goldstücker finds (p. 280) that the details as given in the Mahābhārata and Rāmāyaṇa show 'that the vaidik ceremony had undergone various modifications at the time of their composition,' while (p. 282) 'the inauguration ceremony at the Paurāṇic period has but little affinity with the vaidik rite; it is a series of proceedings which are founded on late superstitions, and reflect scarcely any of the ideas which are the groundwork of the ceremony of the *Aitareya Brāhmaṇa*.' Such changes are, of course, far from unnatural; but there may also have been special causes at work, such as the neglect of the old *śrauta* ritual, or the necessity of providing new forms for rulers who were without title to *kṣatriya* rites.

The general features of the ceremony seem to be as follows: Prior to the rite (*e.g.* on the previous day) the king undergoes a purification, consisting of a bath, etc., no doubt analogous to the Vedic *dīkṣā*. Essentials* are—(1) appointment of the various ministers of state either before or in the course of the inauguration; (2) choice of the other royal *ratnas*, a queen, an elephant, a white horse, a white bull, a white umbrella, a white chowrie or two, etc.; (3) a throne (*bhadrāsana, siṁhāsana, bhadrapīṭha, paramāsana*) made of gold and covered with a tiger-skin; (4) one or several

* See Rāmāyaṇa, ii. 15. 4–12; Kṣemendra, xvii. 38 ff.; Somadeva, xv. 110. 62 ff.; Jacobi, *op. cit.* p. 26, ll. 13 ff.; Śānti Parvan, c. 40.

golden vessels (or one of them golden), filled with water of various special kinds, honey, milk, clarified butter, *udumbara* shoots, and other very miscellaneous ingredients. In the actual ceremony the king is seated with his queen on the throne, surrounded by his chiefs, and he is sprinkled not only by the *purohit*, but also by other priests, by the ministers and relatives, and by the citizens. In the Mahābhārata, Kṛṣṇa is the first to sprinkle Yudhiṣṭhira, representing perhaps the *rājakartṛ* mentioned in the Aitareya Brāhmaṇa. The rite is performed with prayer to Indra, or after the manner of Indra's inauguration as king of the gods. After the consecration, the king makes presents (cf. Harṣa-Charita, ed. Bombay, 1892, c. iii. p. 132, ll. 9, 10), and, of course, the officiating Brāhmans receive their *dakṣiṇās*. According to the Agni Purāṇa and the Mānasāra, the king concludes by riding *pradakṣiṇa*-wise round his city. The liberation of prisoners mentioned by the Agni Purāṇa is an incident known in other connexions (*e.g.* the birth of a prince, Harṣa-Charita, c. iv. p. 142, ll. 18, 19).

3. Time chosen for the ceremony and substances employed.—In the case of the recorded *abhiṣeka*, the temporal restrictions seem to have been, except as explained above, merely such as were necessary in order to ensure auspicious conjunctions: for details see Goldstücker, *op. cit.* p. 285. For the *rājasūya* and *vājapeya* there were, as we shall see, fixed periods in the year.

The substances, which varied in the different ceremonies, are mentioned under the several heads (*vid. supra* and *infra*). Water, milk, curds, and honey generally recur.

B. 1. Turning now to the sacred literature, we find that only one Vedic work gives rules for a royal consecration as such. This is the Aitareya Brāhmaṇa, where we find distinguished two forms of *abhiṣeka*, namely, *punarabhiṣeka* (viii. 5–11) and *aindra mahābhiṣeka* (viii. 12–20). As the former, which takes place after a sacrifice, has apparently no relation to the installation of a sovereign and refers probably to the *rājasūya*, we may reserve it for consideration in that connexion.

The *aindra mahābhiṣeka* is so named because it follows the rites whereby Indra was consecrated king of the gods,—we have already seen that the coronation ceremony continued in later times to be associated with Indra. Thereby a priest who wishes universal victory and paramountcy for his king is to consecrate a *kṣatriya* who is ambitious of those objects (*ahaṁ sarvā jitīr jayeyam ahaṁ sarvāṅl lokān vindeyam ahaṁ sarveṣāṁ rājñāṁ śraiṣṭhyam atiṣṭhām paramatām gacheyaṁ sāmrājyam bhaujyaṁ svārājyaṁ vairājyam pārameṣṭhyaṁ rājyam māhārājyam ādhipatyam ahaṁ samantaparyāyī syāṁ sārvabhaumaḥ sārvāyuṣa āntād ā parārdhāt pṛthivyai samudraparyantāyā ekarāṭ*). The requirements for the ceremony are: (1) vessels of *nyagrodha* (*ficus indica*), *udumbara* (*ficus glomerata*), *aśvattha* (*ficus religiosa*), and *plakṣa* (*ficus infectoria*) wood—to be used, no doubt, as in the *rājasūya* (see below); (2) blades of rice of two kinds, *priyaṅgu* (*panicum*), and barley—to be put in the consecration liquids; (3) a throne-seat (*āsandī*) of *udumbara* wood (mentioned also in the Jātaka, No. 283), a cup (or ladle), and a branch of the same; (4) for the consecration fluid—curds, honey, butter, and water of a sunshine shower. After a mantra addressed to the throne-seat, the king is made to mount it, and then proclaimed aloud by the king-makers (*rājakartāraḥ*). The priest then recites a mantra referring to Varuṇa as *samrāj*, etc., and sprinkles the seated king by pouring the fluid through the interposed *udumbara* branch and a golden *pavitra* (plate) over his head. After receiving a gift from him, he hands to him a vessel of *surā* (spirit) to drink, identifying the *surā* with *soma*.

Any comments upon this ceremony, which is preceded by an oath of life-long fealty on the part of the king towards the priest, may be reserved for the end of this article. After the description of it, there follows in the Brāhmaṇa a list of all the famous kings of old who had been consecrated thereby, together with the names of the consecrating priests. These names may be cited here:—

1. Janamejaya Pārikṣita, consecrated by Tura Kāvaṣeya;
2. Śāryāta Mānava, consecrated by Chyavana Bhārgava;
3. Śatānīka Sātrājita, consecrated by Somaśuṣman Vājaratnāyana;
4. Āmbāṣṭya, consecrated by Parvata and Nārada;
5. Yudhāṁśrauṣṭi Augrasainya, consecrated by Parvata and Nārada;
6. Viśvakarman Bhauvana, consecrated by Kaśyapa;
7. Sudāsa Paijavana, consecrated by Vasiṣṭha;
8. Marutta Āvikṣita, consecrated by Saṁvarta Āṅgirasa;
9. Aṅga, consecrated by Udamaya Ātreya;
10. Bharata Dauḥṣanti, consecrated by Dīrghatamas Māmateya.

The following were victorious by mere knowledge of the rite:—

11. Durmukha Pāñchāla, having learned it from Bṛhaduktha;
12. Atyarāti Jānantapi (though not a king), having learned it from Vasiṣṭha Sātahavya.

For other lists see Goldstücker, *op. cit.* p. 279.

2. Before dealing with the *rājasūya* proper, we may conveniently take into consideration the other ceremony described in the Aitareya Brāhmana (viii. 5–11), the *punarabhiṣeka*, which, though widely differing in procedure, is of an analogous character, as it presents the rite of *abhiṣeka* in a ritual routine disconnected from the actual accession of a king. It is not, however, as in the *rājasūya*, imbedded in a composite series of rituals, but placed at the end of a sacrifice.

The name *punarabhiṣeka* implies that the person concerned was an already crowned king, and the object of the rite was probably to reinforce his vigour as such. Thus, it is stated that the royal power is quickened by it (*sūyate ha vā asya kṣatraṁ yo dīkṣate kṣatriyaḥ san*—an expression perhaps implying a knowledge of the word *rājasūya*), and the various substances used are said to restore to the king various powers (*brahmakṣatre ūrg annādyam apām oṣadhīnāṁ raso brahmavarchasam irā puṣṭiḥ prajātiḥ*) which through the sacrifice had passed out of him (§§ 7, 8). It is with this object that the god Savitṛ is invoked in the mantra *devasya tvā savituḥ prasave, etc.* (§ 7), which recurs in the *aindra mahābhiṣeka* and the *rājasūya*.

The actual rites are very similar to those of the *aindra mahābhiṣeka*. The apparatus consists of: (1) a seat of *udumbara* wood with a covering of tiger-skin, (2) a cup and branch of *udumbara* wood, (3) a consecration fluid of curds, honey, butter, and water of a sunshine shower, with grass, sprouts, *surā*, and *dūrvā*-grass. The sacrificial space (*vedi*) is marked out with a *sphya* (wooden sword), and the seat is placed half within and half without the same. Sitting behind the seat with his right knee bent to the ground, the king takes hold of it with both hands and invites the gods to ascend it, in order that he may after them ascend it 'for royalty, paramountcy, etc. etc.' He then ascends, and the priest, having blessed the consecration fluid, sprinkles him through the interposed *udumbara* branch, and hands to him the cup of *surā*, from which he drinks; then he offers the remains to a friend. He descends from the throne, placing his feet on the *udumbara* branch, and, sitting with his face eastward, utters thrice the words *namo brahmaṇe*. He then presents a gift to the priest, expressing a wish for victory, rises and places fuel upon the fire, and with fuel in his hand takes three steps in a north-easterly direction, *i.e.* towards the region of Indra, the invincible (*aparājita*) region, to signify his desire for security (*yogakṣema*) and freedom from defeat. Lastly, he goes home and sits behind his house, while the priest offers in a certain order oblations from the *surā*-cup and pronounces a prayer for progeny of oxen, horses, and men.

3. The *rājasūya* is an elaborate ritual prescribed for a kṣatriya king desirous of paramountcy. It is brought into connexion with Varuṇa, the first emperor, and after him named *Varuṇasava*. Like the *punarabhiṣeka*, it was applicable to an already consecrated king, although very likely the two ceremonies may have been susceptible of combination. The essential difference between the two is that *abhiṣeka* was a necessary act of State, including priestly rites, while the *rājasūya* was an optional religious rite, undertaken with a certain object, and including a ceremony of consecration. In Sanskrit inscriptions the kings sometimes glory in having performed the rite, which they mention in connexion with the *vājapeya, aśvamedha*, etc. (*Epigraphia Indica*, iv. p. 196, l. 3).

Weber holds ('Über den Râjasûya,' pp. 1–6) that the *rājasūya*, like the *vājapeya*, was originally a simpler popular institution, which subsequently found admission, with many elaborations, into the *śrauta* ritual, and Hillebrandt (*Vedische Opfer und Zauber*, pp. 141 and 144) agrees with him. On the analogy of the *devasūhaviṣ* we may explain the word as meaning 'the *rājasū* ceremony (the word *rājasū* occurring in the ritual, see Weber, p. 37), and conclude, in accordance with primitive notions, that the inherent vigour of a king needed from time to time *a reinforcement* (see above, under *punarabhiṣeka*). In that case the earliest *rājasūya* may have been a regularly repeated (*e.g.* annual), or an occasional quickening rite undergone by kings.

The actual *rājasūya* consists of seven rites (*pavitra* or *abhyārohaṇīya, abhiṣechanīya, daśapeya, keśavapanīya, vyuṣṭi, dvirātra, kṣatradhṛti*), to which some authorities add (after *daśapeya* or after *kṣatradhṛti*\ an eighth (*sautrāmaṇī*). Concerning the *pavitra* we need only say that it must be taken to cover the preparatory and purificatory ceremonies, beginning in the month Phālguna (Feb.-March), and extending over a whole year. It is stated that according to the Mānavas the rite took place in autumn. The *keśavapanīya* is the formal cutting of the king's hair, which remains unshorn for a whole year after the *abhiṣechanīya*, and the *vyuṣṭi*, etc., need not detain us. Of interest here are only the *abhiṣechanīya* with its preceding *ratnahavīṁṣi* and the *daśapeya*. With the first day of the month Phālguna in the second year commence certain introductory rites (*śunāsīrīya, pañchavatīya, indraturīya, apāmārgahoma, triṣaṁyukta ratnahavīṁṣi*), of which the last and most important is a series of sacrifices on 12 successive days in the houses of the king's *ratnas* (see above), who are variously enumerated. The *abhiṣechanīya*, commencing on the first day of the month Chaitra (March-April), occupies five days. After the completion of eight *devasūhavīṁṣi* comes the proclamation of the king by the priest, who, grasping his right arm, pronounces a mantra referring to Savitṛ, Agni, Bṛhaspati, Soma, Indra, Varuṇa, etc., and stating the name of the king, his father and mother, and his kingdom. Next are provided for the sprinkling 17 fluids, namely, 13 forms of water, together with honey, embryonic water of a calving cow, milk, and clarified butter, each in a separate vessel of *udumbara* wood, and having sun-motes mixed with them. These are then transferred into a single *udumbara* vessel, which, together with four other vessels, of *palāśa* (*Butea frondosa*), *udumbara, nyagrodha*, and *aśvattha*, is set down before one of the altars. Next day a tiger-skin is placed in front of the four vessels, into which the consecration liquid is poured: the king is specially arrayed for the ceremony and armed with bow and arrows, then announced to gods and people: to avert evil, a piece of copper is put into the mouth of an eunuch standing by. After taking a step towards each of the four points of the compass and also upwards (to signify universal dominion), the king kicks away from the tiger-skin a piece of lead; as he stands on the skin, a gold plate is put under his foot, and another, with 9 or 100 holes, upon his head, and he is made to hold forth his arms facing eastward, while with the four vessels severally he is anointed by the purohita or adhvaryu, a kinsman (brother), a friendly kṣatriya, and a vaiśya. At this point (according to one account) is related to him the story of Śunaḥśepa (a reminiscence of human sacrifice). He then rubs himself with the consecration fluid, after which he takes three steps (reminiscent of Viṣṇu's *trivikrama*) upon the tiger-skin. The remnant of the liquid, poured into the *palāśa* cup, he hands to his dearest son. The latter holds on behind to the adhvaryu, who pours the remnant upon the sacrificial fire, mentioning, and once intentionally confusing, the name of the king and his son. There follow: (1) a symbolical seizure of a cow, one of a hundred, belonging to one of the king's relatives, the king driving against them in a war-chariot and ultimately returning to the sacrifical edifice, where, after assuming shoes of pig-skin, he dismounts; (2) enthroning of the king upon a seat of *khadira* (acacia catechu) wood, placed upon the tiger-skin; (3) beating of the king (who holds five dice) by the piiests with sticks, in order to expel his sins, after which he is proclaimed as *Brahman, Savitṛ, Indra*, and *Rudra*; (4) a symbolical game with dice, in which the king, his brother, his *sūta* (panegyrist or marshal) or *sthapati* ('police magistrate,' according to Weber), a *grāmaṇī* (village-headman), and a relative take part; (5) various minor ceremonies. On the seventh day of Chaitra takes place the *daśapeya*, a ceremony in which 100 persons, including the king, drink in groups of 10 out of 10 cups: a genealogical test is implied, the qualification being that each must be able to cite 10 generations of soma-drinking ancestors. A year later come the *keśavapanīya*, etc.

The above account of the *rājasūya* is taken chiefly from Eggeling's tr. of the *Śatapatha Brāhmaṇa* and Weber's translation and exposition of the *Kātyāyana Śrauta-sūtra* ('Über den Rājasūya'), which, as representing the part of the operant priests, is naturally the fullest Sanskrit authority. The *śrauta* ritual of the other Vedas, also cited by Prof. Weber, agrees in the main. The *punarabhiṣeka* of the Aitareya Brāhmaṇa, though it has many common features, is distinctly simpler. But it does not follow that the additional matter of the *rājasūya* is necessarily of later origin: that there were various forms of the rite appears from the Āśvalāyana Śrauta-sūtra, which employs a plural—*atha rājasūyāḥ*, ix. 3. 3. 1. Weber, who has elaborately discussed the various incidents, regards the references to Varuṇa and Savitṛ as, from the point of view of Indian religion, remnants of antiquity. Similarly ancient must be the mimic freebooting expedition, game of dice, and *daśapeya*. A general anthropological interest attaches to (1) the association of the king with the *udumbara* tree and with the rain-water, (2) the notion of quickening the royal energy by means of the rite, (3) the reminiscence of human sacrifice in the legend of Śunaḥśepa, which, in connexion with *punarabhiṣeka*, is also related in the Aitareya Brāhmaṇa and the Sāṅkhāyana Śrauta-sūtra.

4. The *vājapeya*, which is mentioned in the Atharva Veda (xi. 7. 7) and the Aitareya Brāhmaṇa (iii. 41. 1), and fully described in the *śrauta* ritual of all the Vedas, also includes a form of consecration. At the outset it presents us with a difficulty as to the object with which it was to be celebrated. The Āśvalāyana Śrauta-sūtra (ix. 9. 1) prescribes it for 'one desiring supremacy' (*ādhipatyakāma*); the Sāṅkhāyana gives, instead, 'one desiring abundance of food' (*annādya*), explaining

the word *vājapeya* as meaning 'food and drink'; the Lāṭyāyana requires it for 'one promoted by brāhmans and kings' (*yām brāhmaṇā rājānaś cha puraskurvīran sa vājapeyena yajeta*), and forbids those who have celebrated it to rise before, salute, etc., those who have not; the ritual of the White Yajur Veda states that whoso sacrifices with the *vājapeya* wins Prajāpati, and so wins everything. According to Āśvalāyana (ix. 9. 19), it is reserved for kings and brāhmans; Śāṅkhāyana (xvi. 17. 1–4) allows it to the three highest castes, the *bṛhaspatisava* following in the case of a brāhman; Lāṭyāyana (viii. 11. 12) mentions a view that it might be preceded and followed by the *bṛhaspatisava*; while Kātyāyana (xiv. 1. 1), confining it to kṣatriya and vaiśya, orders it to be both preceded and followed by the *bṛhaspatisava*. According to the Śatapatha Brāhmaṇa (v. 1. 1), the rite originated with Indra and Bṛhaspati, who, both by the aid of Savitṛ, 'won Prajāpati.' The rank of the rite also is variously estimated: Āśvalāyana (ix. 9. 19) would make it a preliminary to the *rājasūya* (for a king) or *bṛhaspatisava* (for a priest), while the White Yajur definitely forbids the *rājasūya* to follow, explaining that the latter is inferior, as the effect is to constitute a king, while by the *vājapeya* an emperor is constituted.

The most reasonable solution seems to be that of Eggeling and Hillebrandt, that the *vājapeya* was originally general for all the ranks, which severally had more special rites, the *rājasūya*, *bṛhaspatisava*, *sthapatisava*, *grāmaṇīsava*, etc. etc. The features of the *vājapeya* itself seem to point to the conclusion of Weber that it was originally a popular celebration of victory or promotion.

The most prominent of these features are (1) *āji*, a mimic race; (2) *roha*, mounting a post; and (3) the recurrence of the number 17.

The *vājapeya* takes place in autumn. There are preliminary *dīkṣā*, soma-purchase, etc., 17 cups of soma and 17 of surā being provided; and the gifts to the priest include 1700 cows, etc., 17 slave-women, 17 elephants, and so on. At the midday ceremony on the final day a racing-car is rolled into the sacrificial area, and to it are yoked four horses, which receive a specially prepared food. Sixteen other cars are arranged outside. Seventeen drums are beaten, the course is marked off by 17 arrow-shots, and an *udumbara* branch serves as goal. The race takes place and the sacrificer wins: the horses of all the cars are fed and, with the cars, presented to the priests. After certain libations, the wife of the sacrificer is brought in and specially dressed. A ladder is placed against the sacrificial post, and the sacrificer, after calling to his wife, 'Come, wife, ascend we to the sky,' mounts until his head overtops the post: he looks forth in all directions, salutes the earth, and descends, alighting on a gold plate placed upon the ground or upon a goat-skin. A subordinate priest covers a seat of *udumbara* wood with a goat-skin, and, taking his arm, seats him thereupon, saying, 'This is thy kingdom.' A mixture of water and milk having been prepared in an *udumbara* vessel and poured in libations, the offerer is sprinkled with the remainder, and thrice proclaimed with the words, 'This man is Samrāj.' There follow 17 mantras of victory (*ujjiti*).

LITERATURE.—For anointing and consecration in general: artt. ANOINTING below; cf. also Frazer, *Lectures on the Early History of Kingship*, London, 1906.

For *abhiṣeka*: *Aitareya Brāhmaṇa*, viii. 5 ff.; *Mahābhārata Sabhā Parvan*, cc. 33–45, and *Śānti Parvan*, c. 40; *Rāmāyaṇa Ayodhyākāṇḍa*, cc. 1–15, and *Yuddhakāṇḍa*, c. 112; *Agni Purāṇa*, *adhyāya* 209; *Nītimayūkha* and other works cited above, pp. 1544–1546; Goldstücker, *Dict. Sanskrit and English*, Berlin and London, 1856, *s.v.*; Rājendralāla Mitra, *Indo-Aryans*, ii. pp. 1–48; Weber, 'Über den Rājasūya' (*ABAW*, 1893), pp. 114–118.

For the *rājasūya*: *Vājasaneyi Saṁhitā* (ix. 35–x. 34), *Kāṭhaka-S.* (xv. 1–13), *Maitrāyaṇi-S.* (ii. 6. 1–13, iv. 3. 1–4. 10), *Taittirīya-S.* (i. 8. 1–21), *Śatapatha Brāhmaṇa* (v. 2. 2–5. 5), *Taittirīya Br.* (i. 6. 1–8. 10), *Tāṇḍya Br.* (xviii. 8–11); the *Śrauta-Sūtras* of *Āśvalāyana* (ix. 3. 3 ff.), *Śāṅkhāyana* (xv. 12–27, xvi. 18), *Lāṭyāyana* (ix. 1–3), *Kātyāyana* (xv. 1–10), *Āpastamba* (xviii.); the *Vaitāna Sūtra* (xxxvi. 1–13), *Kauśika-Sūtra* (xvii.); various *paddhatis* and *prayogas*; Weber, *op. cit.* pp. 1–158; Eggeling's tr. of the *Śatapatha Brāhmaṇa*, vol. iii. pp. xxvi, 42–142; Hillebrandt, *Vedische Opfer und Zauber*, pp. 143–147; Rājendralāla Mitra, *op. cit.*

For the *vājapeya*: *Vājasaneyi-S.* (ix. 1–34), *Kāṭhaka-S.* (xiii. 14–xiv. 10), *Maitrāyaṇī-S.* (i. 11. 1–10), *Taittirīya-S.* (i. 7. 7–12), *Śatapatha Br.* (v. 1. 1–2 2), *Taittirīya Br.* (i. 3. 2–9), *Tāṇḍya Br.* (xviii. 6–7); *Āśvalāyana Ś.S.* (ix. 9), *Śāṅkhāyana Ś.S.* (xv. 1 and xvi. 17), *Lāṭyāyana Ś.S.* (viii. 11 and 12 and v. 12. 8–25), *Kātyāyana Ś.S.* (xiv. 1 ff.), *Āpastamba Ś.S.* (xviii. 1–7); *Vaitāna S.* (xxvii.); various *paddhatis* and *prayogas*; Weber, 'Über den Vājapeya' (*SBAW*, 1892, pp. 765–813); Eggeling, *op. cit.* pp. 1–41; Hillebrandt, *op. cit.* pp. 141–143.

F. W. THOMAS.

ABILITY.—Ability (Lat. *habilitat-em, habilis*) in its historical usage has two meanings. **1.** It signifies material power, wealth, estate, or resources. In this sense it occurs in both the OT and the NT: *e.g.* 'They gave after their *ability* unto the treasure of the work' (Ezr 2[69]); 'Then the disciples, every man according to his *ability*, determined to send relief' (Ac 11[29]). Similarly, Shakespeare has—

> 'Out of my lean and low *ability*
> I'll lend you something' (*Twelfth Night*, III. iv. 351).

In the same sense, the term is used in 16th cent. Poor Law statutes. Thus, by the Act of 1555 the town magistrates, in making orders for the relief of an overburdened parish by its wealthier neighbouring parishes, are directed to 'consider the estate and *ability* of every parish.' The Act of 1601, too, provides for the taxation of every inhabitant of the parish 'according to the *ability* of the parish'—'ability' being interpreted to mean property. Later on, however, 'ability' or faculty came to be measured not by property, but by income or revenue. This is the measure adopted in Adam Smith's celebrated maxim: 'The subjects of every State ought to contribute towards the support of the Government, as nearly as possible, in proportion to their respective *abilities*; that is, in proportion to the revenue which they respectively enjoy under the protection of the State' (*Wealth of Nations*, bk. v. ch. ii. pt. 2). And since Adam Smith's day, the adoption of the utilitarian ideal of 'equality of sacrifice,' and the application of the 'law of diminishing utility'—that the more wealth, *ceteris paribus*, a person has, the less, beyond a certain point, is the utility to him of successive equal increments, and, consequently, the less the disutility of the decrements caused by taxation—have led to income being accepted as the criterion of ability, for the purpose of taxation, subject only to exemptions and abatements at the one extreme, and progressive or graduated taxation at the other (cf. J. S. Mill, *Principles of Political Economy*, bk. v. ch. ii. §§ 2, 3; E. R. A. Seligman, *Progressive Taxation*). But, apart from this *quasi*-technical use of the term in Economics, in which 'to give,' 'to contribute,' or 'to pay' is understood, the use of 'ability' in the sense of wealth is obsolete, the latest literary instance being probably that in Goldsmith's *Vicar of Wakefield*, ch. xiv.: 'A draft upon my neighbour was to me the same as money; for I was sufficiently convinced of his *ability*.'

2. It signifies personal power, cleverness, physical or mental, and sometimes a special power of the mind, a faculty (usually, however, in the plural). This usage is also found in both the OT and the NT: 'such as had *ability* in them' (Dn 1[4]); 'If any man minister, let him do it as of the *ability* which God giveth' (1 P 4[11]). So with Shakespeare:

> 'Though it be fit that Cassio have his place,
> For, sure, he fills it up with great *ability*' (*Oth.* III. iii. 247).

Again—

> 'Your abilities are too infant-like for doing much alone' (*Cor.* II. i. 35).

The use of 'ability' as denoting physical strength is now obsolete, save in Scotland; and, in its use with reference to mental power, 'ability' denotes active power, as distinct from 'capacity,' which signifies rather latent power or resources. In general, also, natural ability is to be contrasted with acquired skill. 'For natural abilities are like natural plants that need pruning by study' (Bacon, *Essays*: 'Of Studies'). The distinction is important in Economics, in which natural ability is regarded as yielding an income of the nature of rent, while acquired skill yields profits. Again, general ability, natural or acquired, is often contrasted with specialized technical skill. With the growing complexity of industry and the increasing use of machinery, general ability, which is easily transferable from one trade to another, is yearly becoming a relatively more important factor in industrial skill (cf. A. Marshall, *Principles of Economics*[4], 1898, pp. 284-291, 331-342, 657).

In Theology, the terms 'ability' and 'inability' refer to man's power, or want of power, to do the will of God. 'Man by his fall into a state of sin hath wholly lost all *ability* of will to any spiritual good accompanying salvation' (*Westminster Confession*). Here the opposition is to be noted between the doctrine of 'original ability,' as based on the Scriptures, and the 'plenary ability' of the Pelagians, the 'gracious ability' of the Arminians, and the 'natural ability' of the New School (or Edwardian) theologians (cf. A. H. Strong, *Systematic Theology*, 1886, pp. 342-345).

ARCH. B. CLARK.

ABIOGENESIS (I.).—*Abiogenesis* (from Gr. ἄβιος, 'without life,' and γένεσις, 'birth') is the theory of the origin of living from not-living matter. It is more commonly known as the theory of 'spontaneous generation.' So far as the beginnings of life on the earth are concerned, the doctrine of abiogenesis is generally accepted by biologists. For, in its passage from the nebulous to the more or less solid state, our globe reached a temperature and general conditions which made possible the evolution of the organic from the inorganic. Life, as Buffon was among the first to suggest, probably originated in the polar regions, these being the earliest to cool. The inter-relation between living and lifeless matter is a fundamental canon of the theory of Evolution, which recognizes no break in continuity, and which also recognizes the ultimate mystery investing all phenomena, whether these be defined in terms of mind or of matter. 'All our philosophy, all our poetry, all our science, all our art—Plato, Shakespeare, Newton, and Raphael—are potential in the fires of the sun,' says Tyndall; and Huxley, while holding abiogenesis to be unproved, added that 'if it were given him to look beyond the abyss of geologically recorded time to the still more remote period when the earth was passing through physical and chemical conditions which it can no more see again than a man can recall his infancy, he should expect to be a witness of the evolution of living protoplasm from not-living matter' (*Coll. Essays*, viii. p. 256). Hence, both physicist and biologist reject the theory of 'Vitalism,' or the existence of a vital principle or energy distinct in kind from other cosmic energies. The problem of abiogenesis is therefore narrowed to this—Given the origin of life from the not-living, do the conditions which resulted in that still prevail, or have they so far passed away that life is now derived only from pre-existing life?—as the phrase has it, *Omne vivum ex vivo*.

Belief in spontaneous generation was unchallenged for above 2000 years. It was on the Ionian seaboard that speculation arose about origins and laws governing phenomena, hence scepticism as to the validity of old cosmogonies and legends. Anaximander (B.C. 610-547), the friend and pupil of Thales, appears to have been the earliest to speak of life as a product of 'the moist element as it was evaporated by the sun.' Aristotle (B.C. 384-322) accepted abiogenesis with limitations, applying it to parasites, certain invertebrates, and a few vertebrates, as eels (the mode of generation of which was, until recent times, a mystery), but not to animals in which sexual organs are apparent. Lucretius (*c.* B.C. 95-51) speaks of 'many living creatures, even now, springing out of the earth and taking form by the rains and the heat of the sun' (*de Rerum Natura*, v. 795, 796).

It was not until the latter half of the 17th cent., nearly fifty years after Harvey's discovery of the circulation of the blood, that the doctrine of spontaneous generation was assailed, and that by the only effective weapon—experiments. These were started by an Italian scholar-naturalist, Francesco Redi (1626-1698), and, like other methods which have led to momentous results, were simplicity itself. Observing how rapidly dead flesh, exposed to the air, swarmed with maggots, he put some pieces of meat into a jar which he covered with fine gauze, leaving other pieces exposed. In the one case no maggots appeared, while, in the other, they were as numerous as usual. The inevitable conclusion was that the maggots were hatched from eggs deposited by blowflies on the dead stuff. A temporary reaction against Redi's conclusions was brought about by Needham (1713-1781) and Buffon (1707-1788), who adduced the case of animalcules which, after a certain lapse of time, appeared in infusions boiled and hermetically sealed. But Spallanzani (1729-1799) showed that the air had not been wholly excluded from the infusions, the animalcules in which, by reason of inadequate heating, remained undestroyed. The discovery of oxygen (by Priestley, in 1776), the presence of which is essential to life, compelled the repetition of experiments 'under conditions which would make sure that neither the oxygen of the air nor the composition of the organic matter was altered in such a manner as to interfere with the existence of life.' Schultze and Schwann (1836-1837), after boiling the infusions, and supplying air passed through red-hot tubes, the properties of its oxygen being unaffected thereby, although organic matter in it would be destroyed, found no animalcules, which, however, were present in the infusions not supplied with purified air. There followed other experiments, carried on by Cagniard de la Tour, the illustrious Helmholtz, and others, which differed from the foregoing only in completeness of detail, and, therefore, do not need recapitulation in this summary. Each in turn was more effective in destroying whatever agents were essential to the reproduction of life in the infusions. Thus were laid slowly, but surely and abidingly, the foundations of the bacteria or germ theory which has revolutionized old theories of diseases and old methods of attacking them. As recently as 1859, Pouchet reported that he had effected the generation of microscopic animals from inorganic substances. This prompted Pasteur and Tyndall to demonstrate, with a precision hitherto unapproached, that, despite the ubiquity of microbes, their activity and reproduction are rendered impossible where sterilization is effectively performed.

Thirty years ago, Dr. Bastian published a series of volumes embodying results of experiments which, he contends, support abiogenesis. In 1904, M. Dubois, of Lyons, reported the production of living germs in a sterilized medium under the agency of radium, and in 1905 the question was reopened by Mr. Butler Burke, of the Cavendish laboratory, Cambridge, who stated that, as the result of experiments made with radium bromide (which appears to have a destructive effect on micro-organisms) and sterilized beef-gelatine in sealed tubes subjected to a temperature above the boiling point of water, there had appeared minute 'cultures' or growths of globe-shaped bodies, which, on reaching a given stage, subdivided. Mr. Butler Burke inclines to the conclusion that they are organisms on the border lines between microbes and crystals, and, provisionally, he names them 'radiobes.' But their organic character is not established to the satisfaction of competent authorities. The fundamental identity of the living and the not-living being admitted (proof of advance thereto being furnished by the production of organic compounds from inorganic matter in our chemical laboratories), there is no warrant for the contention that abiogenesis is impossible in the present or the future. All that can be said is that the experiments which appear to favour the theory do not wholly exclude doubt as to complete sterilization, and consequent exclusion or destruction, of life-producing germs.

It is the demonstration of the universality of these micro-organisms in their innumerable myriads that has given impetus to antiseptic and prophylactic methods whereby unspeakable benefits have accrued to man and the lower animals. Louis Pasteur—warrior in the noblest of campaigns—was the benefactor not only of France, but of the world, in his application of remedies for diseases in plants and animals which threatened large industries with extinction. In the case of chicken cholera, he reduced the death-rate from ten per cent. to one per cent.; in that of anthrax or woolcomber's disease, which had killed off millions of cattle, the economic gain has been enormous; while perhaps his greatest victory was won in the treatment of those dread evils, rabies and hydrophobia. Lord Lister has acknowledged that Pasteur's germ-theory of putrefaction furnished him 'with the principle upon which alone the antiseptic system can be carried on.' Armed with antitoxins, the physician battles successfully with human ills, and one by one reduces the number of diseases hitherto ranked as inevitable and incurable. See also next art. and BIOGENESIS.

LITERATURE.—Redi, *Esperienze intorno alla Generazione degl' Insetti* (1668); Huxley, 'Biogenesis and Abiogenesis' (1870), *Collected Essays*, vol. viii.; Bastian, *The Modes of Origin of Lowest Organisms* (1871), *The Beginnings of Life* (1872), *The Nature and Origin of Living Matter* (1905); Butschli, *Investigations on Protoplasm* (1894); J. A. Thomson, *The Science of Life* (1899), ch. viii.; René Vallery-Radot, *The Life of Pasteur*, 2 vols. (1901); Chunder Bose, *Response in the Living and Non-Living* (1902); Meldola, *The Chemical Synthesis of Vital Products* (1904); J. Butler Burke, 'The Origin of Life,' *Fortnightly Review*, Sept. 1905.

EDWARD CLODD.

ABIOGENESIS (II.).—During the early phases of the earth's existence, before it cooled and consolidated, the conditions were such that no living creature like any we now know could have then lived there. At an uncertain but inconceivably distant date, after the earth became fit to be a home of organic life, living creatures somehow appeared.

(*a*) Preyer and others have suggested that germs of life, confessedly unlike any we now know, may have existed from the beginning even in nebulous masses, and that the origin of life is as futile a question as the origin of motion. It was not, indeed, the protoplasm we know that was encradled in the fire-mist; it was a kind of movement, a particular dance of corpuscles, different in its measures from inorganic dances. But there does not seem much utility in discussing a hypothetical kind of organism which could live in nebulæ; our conception of organic life must be based on the organisms we know. It is interesting, however, to note that Preyer strongly opposed the view that organic substance could arise or could have arisen from inorganic substance, the living from the not-living; the reverse supposition seemed to him more tenable.

(*b*) As far back as 1865, H. E. Richter started the idea that germs of life are continually being thrown off from the heavenly bodies, and that some of these found lodgment on the earth when it was ready for them. He also could not think of life beginning; his dictum was, 'Omne vivum ab æternitate e cellula.' To Helmholtz (1884) and to Sir William Thomson (Lord Kelvin) the same idea occurred, that germs of life may have come to the earth embosomed in meteorites. 'I cannot contend,' Helmholtz said, 'against one who would regard this hypothesis as highly or wholly improbable. But it appears to me to be a wholly correct scientific procedure, when all our endeavours to produce organisms out of lifeless substance are thwarted, to question whether, after all, life has ever arisen, whether it may not be even as old as matter, and whether its germs, passed from one world to another, may not have developed where they found favourable soil. . . . The true alternative is evident: organic life has either begun to exist at some one time, or has existed from eternity.' On the other hand, we may note that the word 'eternal' is somewhat irrelevant in scientific discourse, that the notion of such complex substances as proteids (essentially involved in every organism we know) being primitive is quite against the tenor of modern theories of inorganic evolution; and that, though we cannot deny the *possibility*, it is difficult to conceive of anything like the protoplasm we know surviving transport in a meteorite through the intense cold in space and through intense heat when passing through our atmosphere. The milder form of the hypothesis associated with the name of Lord Kelvin was simply one of transport; he wisely said nothing about 'eternal cells' or any such thing; he simply shifted the responsibility for the problem of the origin of living organisms off the shoulders of our planet.

So far, then, the suggestions are (*a*) that the physical basis of life is as old as the cosmos, and (*b*) that germs of organisms may have come from elsewhere to our earth. Apart from an abandonment of the problem as scientifically insoluble,—apart, that is to say, from the view that living creatures began to be in some way which we cannot hope to formulate in terms of the scientific 'universe of discourse,'—there is but one other possible view, namely, that what we call living evolved in Nature's laboratory from what we call not-living—a view to which the whole trend of evolutionist thinking attracts us. There are few living biologists who doubt the present universality of the induction from all sufficiently careful experiment and observation—*omne vivum e vivo*; Dr. Bastian is practically alone in believing that creatures like Infusorians and Amœbæ (highly complex individualities in their own way) can now arise from not-living material; but it is quite another thing to say that abiogenesis may not have occurred in the past or may not occur in the future.

But though many thoughtful biologists, such as Huxley and Spencer, Nägeli and Haeckel, have accepted the hypothesis that living organisms of a very simple sort were originally evolved from not-living material, they have done so rather in their faith in a continuous natural evolution than from any apprehension of the possible sequences which might lead up to such a remarkable result. The hypothesis of abiogenesis may be suggested on *a priori* grounds, but few have ventured to offer any concrete indication of how the process might conceivably come about. To postulate abiogenesis as if it were a matter of course, seems to betray an extraordinarily easy-going scientific mood.

One of the few concrete suggestions is due to the physiologist Pflüger (1875), whose views are clearly summarized in Verworn's *General Physiology* (translation). Pflüger suggested that it is the cyanogen radical (CN) that gives the 'living' proteid molecule its characteristic properties of self-decomposition and reconstruction. He indicated the similarities between cyanic acid (HCNO) —a product of the oxidation of cyanogen—and proteid material, which is admitted to be an essential part, at least, of all living matter. 'This similarity is so great,' he said, 'that I might term cyanic acid a half-living molecule.' As cyanogen and its compounds arise in an incandescent heat when the necessary nitrogenous compounds are present, they may have been formed when the earth was still an incandescent ball. 'If now we consider the immeasurably long time during which the cooling of the earth's surface dragged itself slowly along, cyanogen and the compounds that contain cyanogen- and hydrocarbon- substances had time and opportunity to indulge extensively in their great tendency towards transformation and polymerization, and to pass over with the aid of oxygen, and later of water and salts, into that self-destructive proteid, living matter.' Verworn adopts and elaborates this suggestion. Compounds of cyanogen were formed while the earth was still incandescent; with their property of ready decomposition they were forced into correlation with various other carbon compounds likewise due to the great heat; when water was precipitated as liquid upon the earth, these compounds entered into chemical relations with the water and its dissolved salts and gases, and thus originated extremely labile, very simple, undifferentiated living substance.

Professor E. Ray Lankester, in his art. 'Protozoa' in the *Encyc. Brit.*[9], makes the suggestion, 'that a vast amount of albuminoids and other such compounds had been brought into existence by those processes which culminated in the development of the first protoplasm, and it seems therefore likely enough that the first protoplasm fed upon these antecedent steps in its own evolution.'

Dr. H. Charlton Bastian suggests, in regard to the *first* origin of living matter upon the earth, that the nitrate of ammonia which is known to be produced in the air during thunderstorms, and is discovered in the thunder-shower, may have played an important part in the mixture of ingredients from which the hypothetical natural synthesis of living matter was effected. Mr. J. Butler Burke postulates original vital units or 'bio-elements,' which 'may have existed throughout the universe for an almost indefinite time,' which are probably 'elements possessing many of the chemical properties of carbon and the radio-active properties of the more unstable elements,' and which, by interacting on otherwise present carbon-compounds, probably gave rise to cellular life as we know it to-day.

It must be admitted that, in spite of these and other concrete suggestions, we are still far from being able to imagine how living matter could arise from not-living matter. In postulating possible processes which may have occurred long ago in Nature's laboratory, it seems desirable that we should be able to back these up with evidence of analogous processes now occurring in Nature,—the usual mode of argument in evolutionist discourse,—but these analogues are not forthcoming at present. It is usual to refer to the achievements of the synthetic chemist, who can now manufacture artificially such natural organic products as urea, alcohol, grape sugar, indigo, oxalic acid, tartaric acid, salicylic acid, and caffeine. But three facts should be borne in mind: (1) the directive agency of the intelligent chemist is an essential factor in these syntheses; (2) no one supposes that a living organism makes its organic compounds in the way in which many of these can be made in the chemical laboratory; and (3) no one has yet come near the artificial synthesis of proteids, which are the most characteristic substances in living matter.

We are in the habit of comparing what man can do in the way of evolving domesticated animals and cultivated plants with what we believe Nature has done in the distant past. Why, then, should we not argue from what the intelligent chemist can do in the way of evolving carbon compounds to what Nature may have done before there was anything animate? There is this difference, among others, in the two cases, that in the former we can actually observe the process of Natural Selection which in Nature takes the place of the breeder, while we are at a loss to suggest what in Nature's as yet very hypothetical laboratory of chemical synthesis could take the place of the directive chemist.

Thus Professor F. R. Japp, following Pasteur, pointed out in a memorable British Association address that natural organic compounds are 'optically active' (a characteristic property which cannot be here discussed), that artificially prepared organic compounds are primarily 'optically inactive,' that by a selective process the intelligent operator can obtain the former from the latter, *but* . . . it is difficult to conceive of any mechanism in nature which could effect this. 'No fortuitous concourse of atoms, even with all eternity for them to clash and combine in, could compass this feat of the formation of the first optically active organic compound.' 'The chance synthesis of the simplest optically active compound from inorganic materials is absolutely inconceivable.'

Not content, however, with indicating the difficulty which the believer in abiogenesis has here to face, Professor Japp went on to say—perhaps, in so doing, leaving the rigidly scientific position: 'I see no escape from the conclusion that, at the moment when life first arose, a directive force came into play—a force of precisely the same character as that which enables the intelligent operator, by the exercise of his will, to select out one crystallized enantiomorph and reject its asymmetric opposite.' After prolonged discussion, and in view of various suggestions of *possible* origins, he wrote: 'Although I no longer venture to speak of the *inconceivability* of any mechanical explanation of the production of *single optically active compounds asymmetric always in the same sense*, I am as convinced as ever of the *enormous improbability* of any such production under chance conditions.'

Apart, then, from the fact that the synthesis of proteids seems still far off, apart also from the fact that there is a great gap between a drop of proteid and the simplest organism, we have perhaps said enough to show that the hypothesis of abiogenesis is not to be held with an easy mind, attracted as we may be to it by the general evolutionist argument.

In thinking over this difficult question, there are two cautions which should be borne in mind. We must not exaggerate the apartness of the animate from the inanimate, nor must we depreciate it. On the one hand, we must recognize that modern progress in chemistry and physics has given us a much more vital conception of what has been libelled as 'dead matter'; we must not belittle the powers of growth and regrowth which we observe in crystals, the series of form-changes through which many inorganic things, even drops of water, may pass; the behaviour of ferments; the intricate internal activity of even the dust. When we consider, too, such phenomena as 'latent life' and 'local life,' and the relatively great simplicity of many forms and kinds of life, we do not find it altogether easy to discover absolute, universal, and invariable criteria to distinguish between animate and inanimate systems, or between the quick and the dead. To some extent, also, the artificial synthesis of complex organic compounds, and the ingenious construction of 'artificial cells' which closely mimic the structure of living cells, though no one supposes that they are in the faintest degree 'alive,' serve to lessen the gap which seems at first so wide.

On the other hand, it is the verdict of common sense and exact science alike that living creatures stand apart from inanimate systems. The living creature feeds and grows; it undergoes ceaseless change or metabolism, and passes through a cycle of changes, yet has a marvellous power of retaining its integrity; it is not merely a self-stoking, self-repairing engine, but a self-reproducing engine; it has a self-regulative development; it gives effective response to external stimuli; it profits by experience; it co-ordinates its activities into unified behaviour, it may be into intelligent deeds and rational conduct; even in very simple animals (Infusorians) there are hints of mind. Allowing for the gradual realization of potentialities in the course of evolution, we cannot but feel that if the living emerged from the not-living then our respect for not-living matter must be greatly enhanced. As a matter of fact, however, we cannot at present re-describe any vital behaviour in terms of physical and chemical categories, and the secret of the organism has to be admitted as such whether we advance to a vitalistic statement of it or not.

Finally, let us suppose that some bold experimenter in the border-land between chemistry and biology, a man like Prof. Jacques Loeb of Chicago, succeeded this year or next year in making, not merely a corpuscle of proteid, but a little living thing, by some ingenious synthesis. What then?

(*a*) It is quite likely that the steps leading to this hypothetical achievement might be as unlike those which, on the hypothesis of abiogenesis, once occurred in Nature's laboratory, as the artificial synthesis of, say, oxalic acid is unlike what takes place in the sorrel in the wood. (*b*) At present we cannot assert that the laws of the movements of organic corpuscles can be deduced from the laws of motion of not-living corpuscles,—continuous as we may believe cosmic evolution to have been,—and the artificial production of a living creature would not enable us to make this assertion. What simplification of descriptive formulæ the future has in store for us no one can predict. We may have to simplify the conceptual formulæ which we use in describing animate behaviour, and we may have to modify the conceptual formulæ which we use in describing inanimate sequences, but at present the two sets of formulæ remain distinct, and they would so remain even if a little living creature were manufactured to-morrow. (*c*) If we discovered a method of artificially producing an organism, as Loeb has discovered a method of inducing an egg to develop without fertilization, it would render the hypothesis of abiogenesis more credible. We would then *know*, what no naturalist at present knows, however strongly he may believe it, that what we call not-living has in it the potentiality of giving origin to what we call living. But the hypothetical discovery would in no way affect the dignity and value of living creatures, or of our own life. (*d*) If it came about that we were able to bring materials and energies together in such a way that living creatures of a simple sort resulted, we should still have to remember that we had acted as directive agents in the synthesis. (*e*) Finally, if the experiment succeeded, we should not have arrived at any *explanation* of life. We should be able to say that, given certain antecedent conditions, certain consequences ensue, but we should still be unable to answer the question *how* or *why*. We should have a genetic description of an occurrence, but no explanation of it. For that is what science never supplies.

In conclusion, to quote Principal Lloyd Morgan, 'Those who would concentrate the mystery of existence on the pin-point of the genesis of protoplasm, do violence alike to philosophy and to religion. Those who would single out from among the multitudinous differentiations of an evolving universe this alone for special interposition, would seem to do little honour to the Divinity they profess to serve. Theodore Parker gave expression to a broader and more reverent theology when he said: "The universe, broad and deep and high, is a handful of dust which God enchants. He is the mysterious magic which possesses,"—not protoplasm merely, but—"the world."'

LITERATURE.—H. Charlton Bastian, *Studies on Heterogenesis*, London, 1903, and *Nature and Origin of Living Matter*, London, 1905; J. Butler Burke, *The Origin of Life*, London, 1906; T. H. Huxley, *The Physical Basis of Life*, 1868; F. R. Japp, Presidential Address, Chemical Section, British Association, 1898; Karl Pearson, *The Grammar of Science*[2], London, 1900, ch. ix.; Herbert Spencer, *The Principles of Biology*, revised ed. (1898) vol. i. Appendix D; J. Arthur Thomson, *The Science of Life*, Glasgow, 1899; Max Verworn, *General Physiology*, tr. by F. S. Lee, London, 1899.

J. ARTHUR THOMSON.

ABIPONES.—A tribe of South American Indians, of Guaycuran stock, who formerly roved from the head waters of the Rio Grande in Bolivia to the Vermejo in Argentina, although their central habitat was the Gran Chaco, west of the Paraguay River, in Northern Argentina and Paraguay. About 1780 the tribe numbered some 5000, but it is now supposed to be extinct, like the kindred Caduves, Payaguas, Lenguas, and their own destroyers, the Mocovis (J. Deniker, *Races of Man*, London, 1901, pp. 572–573). Practically the only information concerning them is that given by Martin Dobrizhoffer, a Jesuit missionary who resided among them for seven years. They are described as tall and well formed, while in their habits they were nomads and hunters. They were well clad, and were fond of adornment and of painting themselves. Both sexes were tattooed by pricking the skin with thorns and smearing the bleeding wound with fresh ashes, thus leaving an indelible black outline. The males were tattooed with a cross on the forehead, and the women with the cross, as well as an ornamental design, on the face, breast, and arms. This operation was performed at the age of puberty, and was designed to render a girl sufficiently attractive to win a husband, and also to test her courage. Males above the age of seven wore labrets, the most esteemed being of brass or (for the chiefs) of a sort of gum. These adornments came down to the breast; and both sexes distended the lobes of the ears until they almost reached the shoulder. Dobrizhoffer ascribes to them an ethical system of singular attractiveness. Their chastity was remarkable, and they observed the uttermost decorum and modesty in clothing, deportment, and conversation. Their courtesy was invariable; captives were treated with all kindness, and the torture of prisoners was unknown, although for trophies they cut off the heads or skinned the faces of those slain in war. Annual feasts in honour of victories were celebrated with merrymaking and with copious indulgence in wine made of *alfaroba* or honey, the only vice of the Abipones being intoxication. In temperament they were somewhat phlegmatic, not being reckless in war, despite their undoubted bravery.

Their superb physique was due, in great measure, to the fact that consanguineous marriages were forbidden, and that early sexual excess was said to be unknown, while men did not marry under the age of thirty, or women under twenty. At the birth of a child the father practised the couvade (*q.v.*). Infanticide and abortion were common, each woman killing all her children but two. The custom of infanticide was increased by the suckling of infants for three years, during which time the husband was denied all marital rights, and consequently often married again—marriage being terminable at his will. On the other hand, polygamy was rare, and even when practised the wives were not required to live together lest they should become jealous. Fidelity in marriage was almost invariable. A curious deviation from the ordinary usage of infanticide is found in the fact that girls were killed less often than boys, since parents received large sums for giving their daughters in marriage, while sons were required to pay heavy dowries to the parents of their brides.

In their religion, Dobrizhoffer states that the Abipones had little taste for meditation, speculation, or reasoning, although they were cunning imitators. According to him, they had no word for God, but reverenced an 'evil spirit' (who seems, however, to have had no qualities essentially evil). This deity was called Aharaigichi or Queevet, and also 'grandfather' (Groaperike), and it was he who gave the Abipones valour and the Spaniards riches. Aharaigichi was represented by the Pleiades. When this constellation disappeared from the horizon, the Abipones thought him sick and in danger of extinction; so they celebrated the rising of the Pleiades in May by feasting, dancing, and singing. The cult was maintained by priests (*keebet*), to whom Aharaigichi had given supernatural power. These 'jugglers,' as the good Jesuit calls them, were much feared, since when angry they could transform themselves into invisible and invulnerable tigers. To the malice of the *keebet* was ascribed death, and the Abipones quaintly said that were it not for the *keebet* and the Spaniards, they would never die. Thunder and lightning were supposed to be obsequies of a dead *keebet*, and bones and other relics of these medicine-men were carried by the Abipones in their wanderings. In addition to thunder and lightning, comets and eclipses of the sun and of the moon were objects of terror. Besides the *keebet*, old women, who gathered in bands to perform secret rites with wailing and discordant drumming, were dreaded, especially as they were able to conjure up the dead.

Immediately after death, the heart and tongue of the deceased were boiled and given to a dog to eat, in order that the *keebet* who had caused the dissolution might himself perish. Relatives and friends shaved their heads in sign of mourning, and the women wailed for nine days and nights, the nocturnal lamentations being restricted to those who were specially invited for the purpose. A woman might also wail whenever she remembered a dead ancestor, whereupon all others of her sex who heard her were expected to unite with her in howling lugubriously. All mention of the name of the dead was avoided; his house was destroyed, and his relatives and friends changed their names. The soul was believed to survive the body, although the Abipones had no clear idea of its fate. The ghosts of the dead, however, were the objects of intense dread, and were supposed to enter into small ducks called *ruililie*, which fly in flocks by night, and have a doleful hissing note. On the grave were placed, for the use of the dead, a water-pot, a garment, weapons, and the bodies of his horses and cattle which had been killed at the time of his death. The graves of ancestors were venerated,—thus clearly implying the existence of ancestor-worship,—and their bones were often repeatedly exhumed by the Abipones in the course of their wanderings, and carried from place to place, until they could finally be buried in the family burial-ground which contained the bodies of their kin.

LITERATURE.—M. Dobrizhoffer's *Historia de Abiponibus, equestri bellicosaque Paraguariæ natione* (3 vols., Vienna, 1784; English translation: *Account of the Abipones, an Equestrian People of Paraguay*, by Sara Coleridge, 3 vols., London, 1822).

LOUIS H. GRAY.

ABNORMALITIES (Biological).—In biology, the term 'abnormality' is used in a comprehensive sense to describe forms of life, or parts or structures thereof, differing in appearance or constitution from such of their fellows as are shown by statistics to be so closely similar that for general purposes they may be regarded as identical, or, in other words, normal. It is now acknowledged that all organisms are variable, and that, while we tacitly ignore the smaller degrees of variation from the mean,* yet we do recognize the variations of higher degree, and these we call abnormalities. Once again, abnormalities may be defined as the more aberrant of the variations to which every organism, and every structure, is liable or subject. The most extreme cases of abnormality will be described separately as 'monsters' (cf. art. MONSTERS), though it must be remembered that no true line of distinction exists, and that, as has just been stated, they are really the extreme instances of abnormalities.

With the exclusion of monsters, the field of our subject is somewhat narrowed. It remains to review briefly the classes of these aberrant forms, and to indicate the importance of their study in biology. Abnormalities may be classified in various ways. One of the most comprehensive schemes is that proposed by Professor Macalister in his *Boyle Lecture* (1894). It includes nine categories or classes, viz.: the abnormalities of (1) quantity, (2) material, (3) repetition, (4) cohesion, (5) alternation, (6) position, (7) series, (8) inheritance, (9) new formation. For present purposes it is, however, most convenient to review briefly (1) the origin of abnormalities, and (2) their transmission from parent to offspring.

1. Origin of abnormalities.—In some cases an origin can be discerned and a cause assigned. Thus (*a*) interference with the normal course of development is evidently the determining cause in certain instances. A typical example met with in medical practice is the individual in whom the development of the partitions within the heart has been affected. In such instances the blood is not properly aerated, and the patient has a 'cyanotic' aspect, *i.e.* he looks blue and cold. The study of the developmental history of animals has shown that any interference can produce more profound and extensive changes when acting in the earlier stages of growth than in the later period. And progress in embryological science has shown how some of the observed effects may be produced. Thus in the higher animals, for instance, an aberration of growth can be referred to defects in the body of the embryo itself, though in other cases the membranes immediately surrounding the embryo or the adjacent maternal tissues are capable, if themselves imperfect, of reacting on the embryo so as to modify its form. The effect may seem to be produced either directly or

* In a fuller discussion of this part of the subject, attention would have to be directed to the difference between what are termed respectively the 'mean' and the 'mode' of any series.

mechanically, or yet again, the result may be due to an indirect cause in turn determined by interference with nutrition. Again, (*b*) the nutrition, and the quantity and quality of the food, are alone capable, if altered, of leading to deviations from the ordinary course of events, sufficiently marked to come within the definition of abnormality. Cases of hypertrophy, overgrowth, or gigantism fall under this heading. (*c*) In other cases, no such obvious interference can be detected or held accountable. And among these, even if those examples are eliminated in which by analogy there is a fair show of reason for believing that they fall under heading (*a*) or (*b*) as above (though the acting cause is not quite so clear), there is a remnant of instances in which it does not seem justifiable to invoke causes of this kind. Pending the discovery of a more intelligible explanation, the only course open to biologists in such cases is to recognize in living matter an inherent power, or capability, of producing abnormalities, or, as they are sometimes termed, 'sports.'

2. Transmission from parent to offspring.—The transmission of abnormalities from parent to offspring is inconstant and uncertain. The study of this question is inseparably connected with that of the transmission of those more constant features which distinguish the normal individual. The discussion of this problem is beyond the scope of this article, and it will suffice to state that abnormalities can even be classified according as they are constantly transmitted, or not so constantly transmitted, from parent to offspring. It is thus possible to distinguish the former, or constantly transmitted varieties, now termed 'mutations,' from the latter, not so constantly transmitted, now called 'fluctuations.' The importance of this distinction depends on the relation of this subject to the problem of the origin of the species met with in organic nature. In nature the occurrence of abnormalities, and the difference (just remarked) concerning their transmissibility, are facts of observation concerning which there is nothing speculative. But, granted the production of abnormalities, and the greater capability for propagation of some (through inheritance), with, at the same time, the lesser tendency to persistence shown by others, the ground is cleared for the erection of a theory of the origin of organic species through transformation. This seems to depend further upon the postulate that certain kinds of abnormality confer upon the individual exhibiting them an advantage not shared by his congeners. Hence, were the advantage to be maintained, the abnormal stock might in time outnumber the original stock. But the latter would then no longer be the normal stock, for by definition the normal must be in a majority, so that the type of the organism would have changed. Such a process, if it occurred on a large scale, would lead to the production of forms so different from their ancestors that they might well be classified as new species. It is not proposed to embark upon an examination of this position here, the main object in view being to draw attention to the importance of the study of abnormalities in biology.

LITERATURE (selected works in chronological order).—Darwin, *Origin of Species*, etc., 1859; Mendel, *Experiments in Plant Hybridisation*, 1865 (tr. by Bateson in Mendel's *Principles of Heredity*, 1902); Darwin, *Variations of Animals and Plants under Domestication*, 1867; Bateson, *Materials for the Study of Variation*, 1894; De Vries, *Species and Varieties, their origin by Mutation*, 1905; Punnett, *Mendelism*, 1907; Lock, *Recent Progress in the Study of Variation, Heredity, and Evolution*, 1906.

W. L. H. DUCKWORTH.

ABNORMALITIES (Psychological).—Human abnormalities, psychologically considered, are included within the great class of mental affections which owe their origin to arrested development of the brain. The development of the brain may be arrested, as the result of congenital malformation, or from the effect of disease in the earlier periods of existence. As a rule, it is by no means easy to differentiate congenital defect from that arising from interference with the natural course of development immediately before or after birth, but there is reason to believe that congenital malformation accounts for much the larger number of cases of feeble-mindedness.

Congenital mental defect is wholly or in part correlated with the development of the physical organization, especially with that of the nervous system; and it is rare to meet with imperfect congenital structure of the nervous system in the absence of other imperfections of the body. These imperfections of the body are technically known as physical stigmata. They are the outward signs of the nervous imperfections. It is acknowledged on all hands that the more grave the mental defect, the more numerous and the more grave are the physical malformations. Thus, as we pass up the scale from monsters to idiots, imbeciles, and the higher class of the latter, we find a gradually diminishing number of bodily malformations, quantitatively and qualitatively, until they disappear altogether and we emerge upon the apparently normal plane of the race so far as regards mental functions and bodily structure.

Besides the physical stigmata, there are certain well recognized mental stigmata, such as epilepsy, hysteria, alcoholism, chorea, and the various tics and obsessions which are the outward manifestations of underlying defects in the nervous system, especially in the brain. Although we know that every functional peculiarity must have an underlying organic basis, we are still very far from a knowledge of the intimate correlation between structure and function. The most important attempt to correlate mental power with the structure of the cortex cerebri has been made by Dr. J. S. Bolton, writing in Motts' *Archives of Neurology* for 1903. His observations, as yet unconfirmed, show that the pyramidal layer (second layer) of nerve cells in the pre-frontal cortex varies inversely in depth with the degree of amentia or dementia present in each case. This is the only layer that appreciably varies in depth in normal brains; the degree of its development in normal infants and in congenital aments (idiots) varies directly with the mental endowment of the individual, and the degree of its retrogression in demented patients varies directly with the amount of existing dementia.

Idiocy and imbecility are abnormalities connected by gradation with the more pronounced class of human monsters which are either non-viable or, owing to defective organization, unable to survive for any considerable time after birth. As the non-viable monsters and those which, owing to imperfect development, are unable to live through infancy, are all mindless, a description of them does not fall under the scope of the present article.

The present divisions of congenital mental abnormalities are (1) Idiocy, (2) Intellectual Imbecility, and (3) Moral Imbecility. It must be borne in mind that the following descriptions refer to types only, and that the forms of the various classes referred to merge into one another insensibly without any fast dividing differences.

1. Idiocy.—For clinical purposes and convenience of description, idiocy is frequently subdivided into (*a*) complete idiocy, and (*b*) ordinary idiocy.

(*a*) *Complete Idiocy.*—The greater number of the members of this group manifest scarcely any signs of psychical life. Their intelligence is of a very low order, and all the ordinary mental faculties are practically absent. There remains at the most a species of local memory, applicable to simple habitual wants, and to the requirements of the moment. There is no will-power and no faculty of initiative. They have no command of articulate language, but some of them are able to make their few desires known by signs, cries, or sounds understood only by those in immediate attendance upon them. The presence of the ordinary instincts and sentiments is not revealed by such cases. Many of them do not appear even to be conscious of their own existence, much less of the ordinary feelings of pleasure, pain, fear, or love. In the great majority of instances the sexual instinct is absent. The only instinct they exhibit is that of hunger, and it is expressed only when food is presented before them.

On the physical side, the facial expression is marked by the most complete hebetude, relieved only by the occasional appearance of passing emotions of a superficial and vague kind. The general impression left upon the observer of one of these faces is one of a peculiar mingling of youth and old age. The form of the head is very variable, being microcephalic or macrocephalic, and the size of the face is generally disproportionate to that of the head, being in the former case too large and in the latter too small. The lips are thick, the tongue has a swollen appearance, and the saliva constantly overflows. The skin has an earthy colour, and is covered with an oily secretion which gives off an offensive odour. Most of these idiots are unable to walk, and when they can do so, the gait is tottering and uncertain, and all the muscular movements are in-coordinate and ungainly. Among the disorders of motility to which they are subject may be mentioned: general and local spasms, chorea, and epileptic convulsions; while contractures of the limbs, hemiplegia, and local paralyses are very common. They exhibit in abundance the ordinary stigmata of degeneration, such as cleft palate, hare-lip, disordered and irregular dentition, and dwarfism.

(*b*) *Ordinary Idiocy.*—Idiots of this class are, as a rule, fairly conversant with their immediate surroundings. Although they may know their own names and respond when addressed, their command of language is extremely limited; they are able to pronounce only a few words, or at most a few phrases, the correct significance of which they understand. They make particular use of interjections and nouns in conversation. It is impossible to train them either to read or write beyond the simplest words. Some of them show an aptitude for drawing imperfect resemblances of natural objects; but they are unable to count beyond certain limited figures, and arithmetic is entirely beyond their power. A great many idiots possess the faculty of imitation very strongly, but in most of them the imitative art is imperfect and grotesque. Many of them manifest affection to those with whom they live and who treat them kindly, but this feeling bears a stronger affinity to dog-like attachment than to the more reasoned human instinct of friendship. In short, their sentiments are usually confined to a crude appreciation of pleasure and pain, expressed emotionally in an unrestrained barbaric manner. They are, however, capable of a certain amount of training and discipline, as regards external behaviour. Thus, if properly trained, they may learn to dress themselves more or less tidily, to eat inoffensively, and to control their animal impulses; but if for any reason supervision is for long relaxed, they are apt to become degraded and repulsive in their habits.

In this class, as in the former, the body is stunted, and most of the individuals are ungainly and ugly in appearance. A great variety of physical stigmata and malformations are manifested by the subjects. In addition to microcephalism and macrocephalism, the shape of the head may be altered in one or other of the following ways,—namely, flattening of the cranial vertex or occiput, low or swiftly receding forehead, asymmetry of opposite sides of the head or face, prognathism and extreme vaulting, flattening, or asymmetry of the palate. The teeth are liable to numerous malformations; the second dentition may fail altogether, or, if it does occur, the teeth are badly formed and carious. In the eyes, strabismus, astigmatism, and anomalous pigmentation are frequent; in some cases the distance between the eyes is narrowed, while in others, as in the Mongolian type of idiot, they present the true Oriental appearance, being set far apart and almond-shaped. Idiots are subject to various disorders of the gastro-intestinal tract, especially to inflammatory conditions of the mucous membranes. The skin is usually pigmented and unhealthy-looking, and gives off an offensive odour.

About 25 per cent. of all idiots are subject to epilepsy. Most of them exhibit a tendency to instinctive impulses, irritability of temper, and occasionally to maniacal excitement. The physical resistance to disease of all kinds is extremely low, and tuberculosis is one of the most frequent causes of death. Few of them live longer than thirty years; in complete idiocy the duration of life is very much shorter.

2. Intellectual Imbecility.—It is often impossible to detect in early childhood any outstanding difference between imbeciles and normal children. In many instances it is only when education begins to be communicated that a radical difference shows itself in the greater inaptness of the feeble-minded to assimilate ordinary elementary instruction. As imbeciles approach the age of puberty, their mental defects become more apparent; besides being slow of apprehension and dull-witted, they are deficient in ordinary interest, in judgment, and in common-sense. Listlessness, inattention, and a tendency to become absorbed in subjective thought—commonly called 'day-dreaming'—are frequent symptoms of their intellectual feebleness, in addition to the symptoms which result from imperfect cerebral development. In a certain sense it may be said of them that they do not grow old with their years, and when they approach adolescence they do so without any appreciable increase of responsibility. They remain childish, easily satisfied with trifles, and display an interest and curiosity in things which have long ceased to interest people of the same age. The sexual instinct is early developed, and often manifests itself as an exaggeration or perversion of the normal condition. Mental conceptions, the association of ideas, and power of initiative are slow and difficult. Within their somewhat limited sphere of reasoning, which never passes into abstruse consideration, they think and act in a normally logical manner; yet they lamentably fail either in foreseeing the consequences of their actions or in understanding the more complicated actions of their normal fellow-creatures. The moral aberrations are as pronounced as the intellectual. Imbeciles are prone to be egotistic, vain, and sensitively proud. Family ties are apt to be loosely felt; the ordinary affection for relatives is generally feeble, and, although they may be capable of forming strong attachments to individuals, such feelings rapidly yield after short periods of separation. Religious and altruistic ideas as well as moral discrimination are not, as a rule, based upon conviction so much as upon habit and the discipline exercised by other people. Most imbeciles are untruthful and unreliable, more especially in small matters such as the appropriation of trifling articles, the property of other people. They are often irritable, and are subject to outbursts of rage or excitement, for inadequate reasons. Many imbeciles are able to earn a somewhat precarious livelihood by ordinary manual labour, or by working at some trade which they may have learned indifferently well, but the technique of which they are able to execute only imperfectly. Whatever work they do requires the active supervision and guidance of others. Their artistic sense is rarely developed to an exceptional degree, although a few of them are musical; while others exhibit an extraordinary memory for detail, or arithmetical powers wholly disproportionate to their general mental development.

Imbeciles are subject to attacks of mental excitement or depression, which have a tendency to recur periodically. It is during these attacks, especially of excitement, that they are prone to commit criminal or morbidly impulsive acts. A considerable proportion of them are afflicted with epilepsy.

The physical characteristics of imbecility are neither numerous nor important. The subjects are usually well developed, and their outward conformation differs but slightly from that of normal individuals. The facial expression, however, usually indicates a want of mental power; and certain speech-defects, such as lisping, stammering, and imperfect pronunciation, are common, to which may be added a tendency to misapply the meaning of certain words, and to misunderstand the grammatical use of certain parts of speech, such as adverbs and the infinitive mood of verbs. The physical resistance is lowered, and the activity of the various bodily functions is much less vigorous than in normal individuals. Hence it is that imbeciles succumb more easily to bodily diseases, especially such as are of infectious origin, and that a considerable number of them die of phthisis.

3. Moral Imbecility.—Whether or not congenital moral defect can exist independently of intellectual defect is a disputed question. We have already seen that moral defect is a concomitant of congenital intellectual weakness; but there undoubtedly occur cases of moral non-development in which the intellectual faculties are as vigorous as, or even surpass, those of ordinary individuals. We are therefore compelled to admit that congenital perversion of the moral nature may exist without any apparent intellectual defect. But a closer observation of such cases shows not only that they are non-moral in one or more particulars, but that they also exhibit eccentricities of conduct or singular and absurd habits, or the tendency to perform the common actions of life in an unconventional manner. Moreover, a prolonged observation of such persons reveals a liability in them to various forms of intellectual perversions, such as unfounded suspicions, gross superstitions, obsessions, delusions, hallucinations, and even confirmed insanity.

In the more pronounced forms of moral imbecility without apparent intellectual defect we find a wayward and impracticable temper, an absence of social instincts and of normal affection, which may even express itself as a positive aversion to relatives and friends. Such persons are incapable of realizing the value of truth, and become so notorious in this respect among the people who know them, that their statements on the most ordinary matters of fact are never believed. They steal systematically without shame, the only restraint being the fear of being found out. Perhaps their most prominent characteristic is their cruelty. It is not so much that they are ruthless in the pursuit of objects which they desire, as that they go out of their way to inflict pain presumably for the pleasure of witnessing suffering. They are, however, apt to be extremely resentful of injury to themselves, and seldom forget to avenge an insult. They are also vain, proud, and supercilious. They yield to the worst impulses of their lower nature without any evident desire to resist them, and they never express sincere contrition for any action. As might be expected, they cause endless grief and anxiety to their relatives, and their lives are lamentable failures from the point of view of worldly success. Their intellectual faculties, often very acute, are exercised in the gratification of their selfish desires or in the justification of their conduct, rather than in the pursuit of any continuous honest endeavours. As a rule, their affinity for evil courses leads them to indulgence in habits which tend to accelerate their degeneration and to terminate life prematurely.

In the case of children and young adolescents it is unwise to pass too hasty a judgment, for it may happen that the moral sense is not absent but only tardily manifested. In such cases the children may be bright, intelligent, quickly receptive, often emotionally impressionable,—perhaps to a morbid degree,—but lacking in the very elements of moral perception. Many of these individuals, as they approach adult life, begin to change radically in their moral nature, and some of them have even attained to saintliness and canonization.

There are, finally, many persons who never attain to the average moral sense, and whom no appeal based on moral grounds can touch, yet who are possessed of such clear reasoning powers and self-control, that they successfully conceal their non-morality by a rigid observance of the conventions of their fellow-men.

Pathology.—In congenital mental defect, especially in its more pronounced forms, such as idiocy, the brain convolutions present a simple arrangement suggestive of a tendency to revert to the type of the higher mammalia; thus they may either present few secondary folds, or be small, slender, and curling (*microgyri*). Arrested development of certain convolutions is frequently observed, especially in the frontal and parietal regions, which gives to the brain a peculiar and irregular appearance.

The size of the cerebrum relative to that of the cerebellum may be deficient, so that the latter is not covered over by the occipital lobes, as is the case in the carnivora and higher herbivora. Parts of the brain, most frequently the *corpus callosum*, may be absent, and many inequalities in the development of the two hemispheres have been recorded.

In the second and third layers of the cortex of the ape and in a similar situation in the cortex of the pig, Bevan Lewis (*Text Book of Mental Diseases*, 1899, p. 70) describes a perfectly globose cell, with a single delicate apex process and two or more, extremely delicate basal processes without any angular projection from the rounded contour of the cell. These cells occur in man only in cases of idiocy and imbecility. Hammarberg (quoted by Ireland, *Mental Affections of Children*) found the pyramidal cells fewer in number than in normal man. This confirms to a certain extent the observations of Bolton, referred to at the commencement of this article. If only small portions of the brain presented this paucity of cell development, while the remaining portions were normal, though having fewer cells than usual, the individual was, according to Hammarberg, not idiotic, but imbecile or weak-minded. Where the cells were not only abnormal in shape, but also, generally, very few in number, the idiocy was profound; where the cells were more numerous, though at places globose, badly developed or degenerate, there was more intellectual development, though the individual was still idiotic. Concomitant with these arrests in the development of nerve cells there is a corresponding diminution in cell processes, and consequently in the number of the nerve fibres of the cortex. We thus see that the essential pathological condition in idiocy and imbecility is an arrest in the development of the cortical neurous, and that the degree of mental weakness depends upon the extent of the imperfect development of these elements.

JOHN MACPHERSON.

ABOR, ABOR-MIRI.—A title applied to a group of hill tribes of the Mongolian type, on the N. frontier of the Indian province of Assam.

The word *Abar* or *Abor* seems to mean 'barbarous' or 'independent.' The Miris, according to Dalton (p. 22), are so called because they acted as mediators between the Assamese and the more isolated Abors; and he suggests (p. 29) that the word is identical with the *miria* or *milia* of Orissa, which, according to him, has originated the title applied to the Meriah victim by the Kandhs (which see). But this is more than doubtful; and Dr. Grierson, to whom the question was recently referred, with more probability suggests that the word is *Mi-ri*, of which the first syllable in Tibetan means 'man,' and the whole compound may possibly mean 'nobleman' or 'gentleman.'

The Abors or Abars occupy a tract of country on both banks of the Dihang river, which is the upper course of the Brahmaputra. To the W. of this is the Miri country. Most of the Abors live outside British territory, within the Tibetan border, only 321 being recorded as British subjects at the Census of 1901. Of these, 53 were described as Hindus, 7 as Buddhists, and the remaining 261 as Animists. Of the Miris, 46,720 persons were enumerated within British territory at the same Census, of whom about half represented themselves as Hindu and half as Animist. They seem, like the tribes which occupy the hills on both sides of this group, the Mishmis (wh. see) to the E. and the Daphlas (wh. see) to the W., to be little affected by either Hinduism or Buddhism, and to be in the main Animists. Dalton (p. 25) states that when their children are lost, probably being kidnapped by the Mishmis, the Abors attribute their disappearance to the wood-spirits, in whom they firmly believe, and to each of whom some particular department in the destiny of man is assigned. Each disease has a spirit of its own, and, as they have no medicine for the sick, the only remedy is a sacrifice to the spirit to whom the illness is attributed. The favourite haunt of these spirits is a mountain called *Rigam*, which is held in awe by them. No one can return from it, hence its mysteries have never been disclosed. They acknowledge and adore one Supreme Being as the father of all, and have some vague belief in a future state; but their ideas on the subject are ill-defined, and Dalton, who heard them speak of a Judge of the Dead under the name of *Jam*, who is clearly the Hindu *Yama*, reasonably inferred that much of this belief had been borrowed from Hindu sources. Needham (*Assam Census*, 1901, i. 48) adds that the chief of the malignant spirits whom it is the main object of their religion to propitiate, is called *Apom* or *Epom*, and his younger brother *Pomsa*, both of whom inhabit the rubber tree, and must be propitiated in times of sickness. *Urom* is another malignant spirit who resides in unclean places, attacks people after dark, and causes stomachic pains and headaches. He is generally propitiated with an offering of some dry bones and spirits. *Kilū Delē*, who represent the male and female earth spirits of the Dravidians (which see), live underground, and destroy crops and other field produce. A sacrifice of two cooked fowls, rice, and other delicacies must be offered to them under the farm granary. *Nipong* is an evil spirit to whose malignity all female diseases are attributed, and he attacks men also with hæmorrhage and colic, which cause the sufferer to roll about like a woman in travail. He is said to live in plantain groves or amongst stinging nettles, on the seeds of which it is believed that he exists. Dalton notices one peculiarity in their sacrifices, that, when an animal is offered to the spirits, no one is allowed to have a share of the meat except the old and infirm, who may be regarded as being provided for in this way. They have no hereditary priesthood, but there are certain persons called *deodārs* who gain the position of soothsayers, from their superior knowledge of the science of omens. These officials practise divination by observing the entrails of birds and the liver of a pig.

One of these men informed Dalton that the whole human race is descended from a single mother, who had two sons, the elder a bold hunter, the younger a clever craftsman and his mother's favourite. She migrated to the W., taking her younger son with her and all the household utensils, arms, and implements. The people of the land who remained behind thus lost all knowledge of arts and handicrafts, and from them sprang the present Abors. The Western nations, including the English, are descended from the younger son.

The beliefs of the hill Miris closely resemble those of the Abors. But those who have migrated to the Assam plains have, to a large extent, abandoned the more savage beliefs of their wilder kinsmen. They have now come under the influence of the Order of Gusāins (wh. see) or of Brāhman priests, who have induced them to adopt, in some degree, the ordinary Hindu beliefs, but they have failed to wean them from their impure manner of living, such as the eating of fowls, pork, and beef, the use of intoxicating liquor, and the neglect of caste rules in the preparation of their food—all gross offences in the eyes of the Hindu, and much more dangerous than any heretical belief. Allen records that some Miris asserted that they believed in a future life, but they were careful to add that they had never heard of a dead man who returned to this earth. Their belief in the survival of the spirit is shown by the care taken that the dead shall be buried as if equipped for a long journey—with food, cooking utensils, arms, and ornaments suitable to his position in life, so that his rank may be made manifest to the Judge of the Dead. They also attach great importance to the burial of the corpse near the graves of its ancestors, and if a man of rank dies in the plains of a disease not regarded as contagious, they take pains to send his body to the family cemetery in the hills.

LITERATURE.—Dalton, *Descriptive Ethnology of Bengal*, 21 ff.; *JASB* xiv. 426 ff.; Gait, *Census Report Assam*, 1891, i. 221 f.; Allen, *ib.* 1901, i. 47 f.; Peal, *JASB* xli. 27; Hodgson, *ib.* xviii. pt. ii. 967; Robinson, *ib.* xviii. pt. i. 230.

W. CROOKE.

ABORIGINES.—In the article ETHNOLOGY it is pointed out that the four main divisions of mankind 'have not remained stationary in their respective original homes, but have been subject to great fluctuations during historic times.' But no rigid parting-line can be drawn between the historic and the prehistoric ages, which everywhere tend to merge imperceptibly one in the other. Hence the remark may confidently be extended to all times since early man first began those migratory movements by which he has replenished the earth. We know, for instance, that, during the Stone Ages, Europe was occupied by both long-headed and short-headed races, and Señor F. Outes has now shown that the same two types had already reached Austral-America in Pleistocene times (*La Edad de la Piedra en Patagonia*, 1905). It follows that the two primary divisions recognized by anthropologists have been intimately associated together for countless generations, and consequently that there are no more any pure stocks, except perhaps a few isolated groups, still surviving in some remote and hitherto inaccessible corners of the world, such as the Andamanese Islanders, the recently-discovered Toálas of Celebes, and the Fijian Kai-Colos.

The term 'Aborigines' is therefore generally to be taken in a purely relative sense, and the claim often made by them to be regarded as true autochthones must be unhesitatingly rejected. They are normally 'mestizos,' in whom the physical and psychic characters of two or more races are intermingled in varying proportions. But the psychic character of primitive peoples finds its chief expression in their religious concepts, since their whole conduct is almost exclusively controlled by their views regarding the unseen world. Put in this way, the statement that their religious systems have been influenced by foreign contact follows of itself, and the inference that, as there are no longer any unmixed races, so there are no longer any unmixed religions, becomes almost a truism. The inference is certainly not quite obvious at first sight, although the analogous somatic mixtures, as between whites and blacks, are often self-evident. But that is only because mental are necessarily more subtle and elusive than material phenomena. The savage may hide his inmost thoughts regarding the supernatural, as he often does to casual visitors; but he cannot hide the constituent elements of his outward form from the searching eye of intelligent observers.

1. Thus the main physical features of the *Australian* aborigines have long been determined, while the source of many of their religious ideas is still the subject of heated discussions between the Spencers, Gillens, Langs, Frazers, and other serious students of primitive psychologies. The Narrinyeri people of South-East Australia have a 'god' or mythical being, Nurunderi, who dwells in a shadowy Elysium in the far west; and to reach this abode of bliss the souls of the dead have to pass under the sea and over a fiery pit, into which the wicked fall while the good escape. But such abodes of bliss and misery form no part of the genuine beliefs of the natives, who do not distinguish between morally good and wicked people; and careful inquiry has now shown that these are merely distorted reminiscences of the heaven and hell preached to the Narrinyeri tribe by the early missionaries.

The same god Nurunderi (Ngurundere) plays a great part in the myths of the kindred Tanganarin people of the Lower Murray River, and also affords a curious illustration of the way in which the Biblical stories get perverted in the minds of the natives.

This great King of Wyir (Heaven) had two wives, who caught a large and a small fish, keeping the first for themselves and giving him the little one. Discovering the fraud, he was very angry, and said, 'You shall die for this, and all Tanganarin shall die; and there shall be fighting and sickness, and evil spirits until then.' Ngurundere had created and done everything for them, giving them knowledge and skill in hunting, fishing, and fighting. But after the sentence of death for the trick played upon him by his wives, he took away their knowledge and power, left them, and ascended into heaven. Then they became ignorant and blind, and lived like the beasts of the field for a long time, till of a virgin was born a good and wise man named Wyungare. He gave them back their lost wisdom and power, and taught them sorcery; and when he had regenerated all the tribe, he was taken up to heaven by Ngurundere, and now reigns there as second King. And when a Tanganarin dies, Wyungare takes his spirit up to heaven, and gets him a good hunting-ground in that place, through his influence with Ngurundere. This might be called the Australian version of the doctrines of the Fall and the Atonement.

The native account of the Creation of the first man is more detailed than that of Scripture. The people of the present Melbourne district say that Punjil, Creator of all things, made two male blacks by cutting three large strips of bark with his big knife, and on one of them kneading a quantity of clay to the required consistency. Then he carried some of the dough to another of the strips, and began to mould it into a man, beginning at the feet and working upwards to the head. This he repeated on the third strip; and being well pleased with his work, he danced round about the two figures. He next made some hair out of stringy bark, curled for one man and straight for the other; and, being again pleased with his work, once more danced round about them. After smoothing their bodies with his hands, he lay upon them and blew hard into their mouths and nostrils until they stirred, when he danced round them a third time. He then made them speak and walk about, and they were finished.

The Dieris tell it differently. In the beginning Mûra-Mûra, the Good Spirit, made a number of small black lizards, and being pleased with them, promised them power over all creeping things. He divided their feet into toes and fingers, and with his forefinger added nose, eyes, mouth, and ears. Then he stood one on end, but it toppled over; so he cut off its tail, after which the lizard walked erect like a man. He did the same with another, which happened to be a female, and so the race was perpetuated. After a time mankind became very numerous and wicked, whereat Punjil, being angry, raised storms and fierce winds, which shook the big trees on the hill-tops. And Punjil went about with his big knife, cutting this way and that way, and men, women, and children he cut into very little pieces. But the pieces were alive, and wriggled about like worms, whereupon great gales came, and blew them about like snowflakes. They were wafted into the clouds, and by the clouds borne hither and thither all over the earth, and thus was mankind dispersed. But the good men and women were carried upwards and became stars, which still shine in the heavens.

Death came in this way. The first pair were told not to go near a certain tree, in which lived a bat which was not to be disturbed. But one day the women were getting fuel, and were tempted to go near the tree. Thereupon the bat flew away, and so death came into the world.

It should be noted that all these Creation myths have been gathered from tribes which have long been in association with the whites, and probably derived the substance and the moral tendency from the missionaries. The local colouring would gradually be supplied as the stories passed from tribe to tribe.

2. Similar Biblical legends are widespread among the *Masai* of East Africa, and here the parallelisms are so striking that Captain Merker can account for them only by supposing that the Masai nomads are a Semitic people who dwelt originally with the kindred Israelites in North Arabia, whence they migrated some 6000 or 7000 years ago to their present domain east of Lake Victoria Nyanza. Surprising coincidences are pointed out between the traditions, myths, legends, and religious observances of the two nations. The Masai *el-Eberet* is equated with *Eber* (Gn 10[21]); *Hau*, 'Great,' with *Jahweh*; *Nabe* with *Abel*; *Narabā* with *Abraham*; and it is shown that the Masai have also their ten commandments, the first of which is: 'There is one only God; heretofore you called Him *E'magelani*, "Almighty"; henceforth you shall call Him *Ngai*'; just as in Ex 6[3] *Shaddai* is replaced by *Jahweh*. Here we have unquestionably many Jewish religious notions superimposed on the primitive Masai animism. These were not, however, brought from Arabia thousands of years ago, but are obviously due to contact with the Judaizing Falashas of the neighbouring Abyssinian uplands (cf. M. Merker, *Die Masai*, Berlin, 1904).

3. In *Senaar* there is a curious intermingling of Muslim and animistic beliefs, which corresponds completely with the Negro and Semitic interminglings of its Funj inhabitants. These pass for fairly good Muhammadans; practise circumcision, make the pilgrimage to Mecca, have zealous faqīrs and dervishes (who act as teachers and scribes in the towns), and conform to most of the other Qur'ānic precepts. Yet beneath this thin Muslim veneer these Negroid natives are still sheer pagans, firmly believing in the gross superstitions which are associated with the wer-wolf notions referred to in art. ETHNOLOGY. Their much-dreaded *sāḥirs* (magicians) are credited with the power of transforming themselves at night into hyænas and hippopotami, which roam about seeking to destroy their enemies, and inflict injuries even on the most devout Musalmāns. The *marafils*, as the metamorphized human hyænas are called, hold unhallowed cannibal feasts in the recesses of the woodlands, indicating their presence by their terrible howlings, just as wayfarers were stricken with awe by the midnight roar of the transformed human jaguars amongst the Aztecs of pre-Columbian times. In the daytime the *marafils* again

assume their human form, but are still dangerous, since a glance from their evil eye suffices to wither the limbs, the heart, or the entrails of their victims, who thus perish in the most horrible torments. To counteract these dire machinations, the scribes write passages of the Qur'ān on slips of paper, which are then burnt, and the smoke inhaled by those who suppose themselves threatened by the hostile *sāḥirs*. It would be difficult to imagine a more complete fusion of higher and lower religious forms than this inhaling of Qur'ānic texts against evil influences opposed to Qur'ānic teachings (see E. Marno, *Reisen im Gebiete des blauen u. weissen Nil*, 1874).

Featherman aptly remarks that 'Muhammadanism, introduced by the Arabs, has been adopted by some of the Nigritian nationalities of higher mental capacities, but they are Muhammadans *in their own way*. Christianity has also made some converts in isolated localities, but they are Christians *only in name*' (*Social History*, etc., i. p. 12). In some places, as in the West Sudan, the primitive pagan substratum has been partly overlaid by both of these higher religions, with the curious result that, for instance, some of the Senegal Wolofs have charms with texts from the Qur'ān which they cannot read, while others have medals and scapulars of the 'Seven Dolours,' or of the Trinity, which they cannot understand. Other violent contrasts are seen in the lofty conception of *Takhar*, 'god of justice,' associated amongst the neighbouring Serers with lowly household gods, such as the lizard, for whom the daily milk-bowl is set apart. Here again the fusion of higher and lower ideals is obvious enough, and so it is throughout Negroland, wherever the seething masses of heathendom have been touched by higher influences.

4. Turning to *India*, in this fathomless ocean of heterogeneous elements we are at once confronted with perhaps the saddest tragedy ever witnessed anywhere in the whole history of human development. Here are seen, not so much gross anthropomorphic systems leavened by contact with superior ideals, as the very reverse process of these ideals being themselves gradually contaminated and utterly debased by submersion in the great flood of aboriginal heathendom. The present writer has elsewhere shown (*East and West*, April 1905) that the whole of the peninsula, from the Himālayas to Ceylon, was occupied by these aborigines — Kolarians and Dravidians — ages before the advent of the tribes of Aryan (Sanskritic) speech, who may have reached the Panjāb from the north-west, some 5000 or at most 6000 years ago. It is clear from the Vedic texts (see VEDAS) that these proto-Aryans drew their inspiration from above; that their deities—Varuṇa, Indra, Agni, Sūrya, Dyaus, the Maruts—were all personifications of the forces of the upper regions, and were looked upon in the main as beneficent beings, who associated almost on a familiar footing with their votaries, from whom they accepted mild offerings of soma and the fruits of the earth, without exacting any gross or cruel sacrifices. On the other hand, the Dravido-Kolarian aborigines drew, and for the most part still draw, their inspiration from below, and their chthonic gods were really demons, ever hostile to mortals, and to be appeased by sanguinary rites and the sacrifice of everything most prized by the living. But, as the Vedic Aryans ranged farther and farther into the Indo-Gangetic plains, there took place those inevitable religious and racial intermixtures which resulted in the present Hindu populations and in the degraded forms of religion which collectively we call Brāhmanism or Hinduism. Over this monstrous system the triumphant Aryans spread the prestige of their language and general culture; but in the struggle they forfeited their heaven-born pantheon, which was replaced by the chthonic gods of the aborigines. As *Græcia capta ferum victorem cepit*, so here the Vedic Sun-god and Sky-god, Rain-god and Wind-gods were vanquished by the Dravido-Kolarian Viṣṇu, the Preserver, Mahādeva (Śiva, the Destroyer, with his wife Durgā or Kālī), Birmha Devī (the Fire Goddess), the gross symbolism typified by the *liṅga* and the rest. However disguised by a Sanskrit nomenclature, the true parentage of these entities is clearly seen, for instance, in the Śiva of the later Hindu triad, who is evolved out of the later Vedic Rudra, the Roarer or Storm-god, who guides and controls the destroying cyclone.

Thus was constituted the present Hindu system, in which, as we now see, the higher forms have been not merely influenced or modified by, but almost completely submerged in, the lower. Since the expulsion of Buddhism, which had prevailed for about 1000 years (B.C. 250 to A.D. 750), this exceptional process has again been reversed, and during the last 2000 years Brāhmanism has spread over the whole peninsula, absorbing or driving to the uplands all the primitive beliefs, and even attacking them in their last retreats in the Vindhyan range and the extreme southern highlands. Hence it is that even in these less accessible tracts unalloyed primitive forms are gradually disappearing. Still, enough remains to enable us to discriminate between the original Dravido-Kolarian and the intruding Hindu elements. Thus Mr. A. Krishna Iyer writes that the Malayars of Cochin 'are pure animists, but, owing to their association with the low-caste men of the plains and their attendance at the neighbouring village festivals, they have been imbibing the higher forms of worship.' Of their six gods two are demoniacal (chthonic), and four are merely different names for the Hindu Kālī, who was originally borrowed by the Hindus from the natives. From the higher castes are also taken Bhagavatī Bhadrakālī and Nagasāmī, who have penetrated into the neighbouring Kollencode forests, and are there worshipped with semi-Hindu rites, jointly with Muniappan and the other demon-gods, for all these aborigines are still everywhere at heart devil-worshippers. But these demons themselves, as well as all preternatural beings, are really human like the suppliants, only invisible and more potent. Hence 'they are held in fear and pious reverence, and their favour can be sought by sacrifice alone' (Iyer, MS. notes). Much the same account is given of the Eravallers of the Chittur forests, who also include Kālī amongst their demoniacal gods, and seek her protection with like offerings.

Amongst the Bhils, Kols, Gonds, and other *Pahārias* of the Vindhyan uplands, great respect is paid to Mahādeva, to whom have been consecrated the Mahādeo heights east of the Satpuras. He is even confounded with the chthonic Tiger-god, and associated with Bhīma, Arjuna, and other heroes or demi-gods of the Mahābhārata epic. Yet these almost Hinduized hillmen offered till lately human sacrifices to the various members of their limitless pantheon, which includes sun, moon, rocks, trees, torrents, the passing winds, and especially the departed spirits who return in the form of nightmare, sit on the chest, squeeze the throat, and suck the blood, like the vampires of the popular Slav legend (see ETHNOLOGY). So intermingled are the higher and lower forms throughout Gondwāna and the Southern highlands, that the Census agents are often puzzled how to return certain ethnic groups, whether as outcaste Hindus or Hinduized outcastes.

5. But this new field of research is boundless, and we must hasten through Indo-China, where

the superficial Buddhism is everywhere intimately associated with the never-dying animism, eastwards to the *Malay* lands, where analogous associations crop out everywhere between Islām and the still rampant heathenism of Borneo, Celebes, Gilolo, and Mindanao. Much light has recently been thrown on this religious syncretism in Celebes by the brothers F. and P. Sarasin, in whose *Reisen* (Berlin, 1905) the reader will find much instructive matter. The prevalent relations in the hitherto almost absolutely unknown island of Mindanao have also been revealed by N. M. Saleeby in his *Studies in Moro History, Law, and Religion*, vol. iv. of the Philippine Ethnological Survey Publications (Manila, 1905). Here the 'authentic' genealogies of the Moro (Muhammadan) dynastic families are interwoven with curious pagan elements, and we read of orthodox Sultans descended from unions not only with houris sent down from heaven, but also with a native princess found inside a bamboo stalk. This occurred at the time Tabunaway and Mamālu were cutting bamboo to build their fish corral. When the last tree was felled, out came a child who was called Putri Tunīna, and whose little finger was wounded, the *bolo* having cut through the bamboo, and from her sprang Mālang-sā-Ingud, third *datu* (king) of the Bwayan dynasty. The Mindanao Muslims have also assimilated some of the pagan folk-lore, and firmly believe in the Balbal vampire, a huge night bird, whose screech is supposed to be distinctly heard after sunset. It is really 'a human being who transforms at night into an evil spirit which devours dead people,' in this differing from other vampires, which come out of the dead and prey on the living. But so detested is the creature, that in the local Muhammadan code, here published in full, anyone calling another *balbal* is fined one slave or his value (p. 68). Thus in Mindanao it is again the higher Muslim system that is affected by the lower ideals of the aborigines, many of whom have withdrawn to the uplands of the interior, where interesting discoveries await future explorers in primitive psychologies.

6. Once more the balance is redressed in *Oceania*, where the more civilized Eastern Polynesians have inoculated the Western Melanesian cannibal head-hunters with their *mana* and other subtle religious essences. But in the process modifications naturally take place, and the Maori or Samoan *mana* is not, perhaps, quite the same thing as that of the New Hebrides savages. The Maori *mana*, brought from Hawaiki (Samoa?) to New Zealand by the kaka bird, is not easily distinguished from the forest, the human, and the other local *mauri*, and is generally defined as 'power, authority, influence, prestige' (A. Hamilton, *Maori Art*, p. 396). But the Melanesian *mana* is more spiritual, analogous to the Augustinian 'grace,' without which no works avail, but with which all things superhuman can be achieved. Thus a person may have *mana*, but is not himself *mana*,—a force which 'is present in the atmosphere of life, attaches itself to persons and to things, and is manifested by results which can only be ascribed to its operation'; and again: 'a force altogether distinct from physical power, which acts in all kinds of ways for good and evil, and which it is of the greatest advantage to possess or control' (Codrington, *The Melanesians*, pp. 118–119). But however homologous with, or divergent from, the Maori *mana*, this impersonal essence permeates the whole religious thought of the Melanesians, whose religion 'consists, in fact, in getting this *mana* for oneself, or getting it used for one's benefit—all religion, that is, as far as religious practices go, prayers and sacrifices' (*ib.*). And as the principle is admittedly derived from the more highly cultured Polynesians, we have here again a primitive system influenced, and, in this instance, somewhat elevated, by a more advanced line of thought. How primitive in other respects is the Melanesian system, may be seen from the belief current in the Banks' Islands that people may become *talamaur*, a kind of vampire which prowls about at night, and, like the Mindanao *balbal*, devours the bodies of the dead. In this and several other Melanesian groups lycanthropy also (see ETHNOLOGY) is widely prevalent, only here the non-existent wolf is replaced by sharks, owls, eagles, and blow-flies. These last are perhaps the most dreaded, since magicians assuming such minute forms can buzz about, penetrate unseen into the houses, and torment their victims with impunity. How such childish notions can persist side by side with the subtleties of the *mana* doctrine is a psychological puzzle awaiting solution.

7. Perhaps even more inexplicable is the pure animism of the crudest type still everywhere surviving amongst the cool-headed and practical *Chinese*, beneath, or rather almost above, several layers of higher forms, such as ancestor-worship, Buddhism, Taoism, and the common-sense ethical teachings of Confucius. It is impossible here to dwell on these different systems which are elsewhere fully described (see art. CHINA [RELIGION OF]). It will suffice for our purpose to point out that in China the various religions, or so-called religions, are, so to say, stratified or superimposed one on the other rather than intermingled, as mostly elsewhere. Hence the curious phenomenon that the Government recognizes three official religions,—Buddhism, Taoism, and Confucianism,—to all of which, in virtue of his position, the Emperor himself belongs, and whose observances he scrupulously fulfils, while millions of his subjects simultaneously profess these, and perhaps others, without any sense of incongruity. The several beliefs do not contradict each other, but lie peacefully side by side; and the devout Buddhist, after duly burning his tapers and incense to the innumerable idols of the joss-house, proceeds as an incurable Animist to take active measures to baffle the *Feng-shui* (evil spirits) by effacing the straight lines affected by them, and to encourage the *Fung-shui* (good spirits) by developing the curves along which they prefer to travel.

8. Coming *westwards*, we find the early and the late again amalgamated, and indeed so inextricably that only in recent years have folk-lorists and classical students begun to distinguish between the coarse chthonic gods of the Pelasgians and the bright Aryan deities of the Hellenes, which have so long been merged together in the Greek mythologies, as typified, for instance, by the marriage of the Uranian Aphrodite with the hirsute and deformed cave-dwelling Hephæstus. But the fusion of the pre-Aryan Pelasgians with the proto-Aryan Hellenes was a slow process, lasting for many generations, as is evident from the different social and religious institutions prevailing in various parts of Greece during the early historic period. Thus, of fetishism we find no trace in Homer, who represents the Achæan (Hellenic) side, whereas fetish worship long persisted in Arcadia, Attica, and other distinctly Pelasgic lands. So also with totemism and the dark Poseidon of the Pelasgians, who was finally eclipsed by the fair Apollo, Zeus, and the other Aryan gods of the Achaioi. After, or perhaps during, the fusion, other religious contacts took place, as shown by the Greek Adonis borrowed with *another* Aphrodite (Astarte) from the Semites. The conflicting accounts of these and other deities are but the results of the unconscious efforts of the ancient folk-lorists to harmonize the various legends of originally distinct personalities, and are themselves a clear indication of the higher Aryan and Semitic influences brought to bear on the primitive religion of the Pelasgian aborigines. But these influences must not be pushed too far, as when Eduard Glaser imports the Vedic *Dyaus* into Greece (Zeus) and Italy (Jove), as well as into Israel (Jahweh). It is clear from the compound forms *Dyauspiter*, (Vedic Sanskrit), Ζεῦ πάτερ (Gr.), *Juvepatre*, *Jupater* (Umbrian), *Diespiter*, *Jupiter* (Latin), that this personification of the bright sky had already found expression in the Aryan mother-tongue, and was consequently a common inheritance of all the proto-Aryans who, after the dispersion, brought it *independently* into their Indian, Hellenic, and Italic settlements. Thus we have here no reciprocal influence of Aryans upon Aryans; but as to the same root belong the Avestan *daēva*, the Lithuanian and Lettic *Dēvas*, *Dēws*, 'God,' and other Western variants, it follows that the pantheons of the Iranian and European aborigines were enlarged and otherwise modified in remote prehistoric times by their proto-Aryan conquerors. What other early interminglings of religious systems may have taken place, as between Aryans and Ligurians in Italy, or Aryans (Celts) and Iberians in Spain, Gaul, and the British Isles, is a subject of too speculative a nature to be here discussed. One point, however, seems fairly well established, that the Semitic Phœnicians reached the far west with their Baal, who was adopted as one of their chief deities by the Ibero-Celtic peoples of Britain and Ireland. The expressions *Bal mhaith art*, 'may Baal prosper thee,' and *Bal Dhia dhuit*, 'God Baal be with thee,' were not so many years ago still addressed to strangers on the banks of the Suir in Tipperary (see J. Bonwick, *Irish Druids and Old Irish Religions*; H. O'Brien, *Phœnician Ireland*; D'Arbois de Jubainville, *Cours de Littérature Celtique*).

9. In *the New World*, effectively cut off from the Old most probably since Neolithic times, the interchanges of cultures and religious notions can have been only between the American aborigines themselves. But here also there were very great local developments, in virtue of which some, such as the Aztecs, Mayas, Zapotecs, Chibchas, Peruvians, and Aymaras reached a relatively high degree of civilization, while most of the others lagged behind, and are still at the barbaric or even pure savage state. These last have, till recently, stood for the most part aloof from all extraneous contacts, so that many, such as the Mexican Seris, the Caribs and Arawaks of British Guiana, the Brazilian Botocudos, and the Fuegian Yahgans, afford excellent object-lessons for the study of the earliest types of unmodified religious thought, but for that very reason do not come within the scope of the present inquiry. Thus, in America, the mutual influences are confined mainly to the more advanced cultural peoples, amongst whom interminglings appear to have been more the rule than the exception. Apart from the much discussed subject of the long-extinct Toltecs, it may be stated in a general way that the two great Aztec and Maya cultures betray undoubted proofs of endless borrowings, especially in matters associated with astrology, divination, and religious observances. Who were the givers and who the recipients may still be a moot point, but the contacts are not open to question.

E. Förstemann, who takes the Maya side against Seler and others, holds that 'the Aztecs adopted many things which they learned from the Mayas, especially their deities, whose names they simply translated. The translation of Kukulcan into Quetzalcoatl is a very typical case, for *kuk* and *quetzal* designate the bird *Trogon resplendens*, and *can* and *coatl* mean the snake. The Aztecs first came in contact with the higher civilization not very long before the arrival of the Spaniards, so that they did not have time to establish their supremacy and so absorb the Mayas, but, on the contrary, were absorbed by them' (*Mexican and Central American Antiquities*, Washington, 1904, p. 542). It is also shown that the *tonalamatls* which were common to all Central American cultured peoples, and were not calendars, but horoscopes covering a period of 260 days, the period of gestation, originated with the Mayas, and were slavishly copied by the Aztecs (*ib.* p. 527; see also Keane's Eng. ed. of Seler's *Elucidation of the Aubin Tonalamatl*, 1901).

Dealing with the wall-paintings of Mitla in the Zapotec domain (the present State of Oaxaca), Professor Seler shows that this cultured nation drew many of its religious inspirations from the neighbouring Aztecs. 'The conclusion seems inevitable that the cosmogonic representations referring to Quetzalcoatl, as well as the Olympus with its many personages occurring in the picture-writings, were not strictly national, did not have their roots in the Zapotec country, but represented *a superimposed culture* which owes its origin to the influence of Nahua tribes dating back to prehistoric times' (*Wandmalereien von Mitla*, Berlin, 1895).

On the other hand, the views advanced by the late Mr. Leland in *The Algonquin Legends of New England* regarding the old Norse origin of the north-eastern Indian mythology cannot be upheld. But although they are now shown to be untenable, later European influences have been at work, and Mr. Andrew Lang has found clear traces of Irish, French, and a few Anglo-American strains in many of the Passamaquoddy legends. Still, Prof. J. D. Prince, of Columbia University, holds that what is genuinely native 'stands forth with unmistakable distinctness in some of the Kulóskap tales,' that is, the witchcraft and other stories recorded in *Kulóskap the Master*, the joint work of himself and Mr. Leland. A. H. KEANE.

ABORTION.—See FETICIDE.

ABOULIA.—A mental disorder characterized by loss of volitional control over action or thought. There are three general types of *aboulia*. (1) In the purely ideational field it may occur as a result of the loss of inhibitive powers or of control of attention. In such cases, when a motive or impulse appears in consciousness with a preponderating force, there is an ill-balanced tendency to immediate action. The suggestion is without natural check, and rash and inconsiderate execution of it follows. The limiting cases of such disorder (sometimes termed *hyperboulia*) are to be found in the obsessions of fixed ideas, in hypnotic suggestion, etc., where the force of the suggested idea is so strong that there is no consciousness of competitive motor impulse (and hence none of volition). (2) Distinguished from this, but still in the ideational field, is *aboulia* which takes the form of extreme hesitancy. Where a series of ideas or impulses is presented to consciousness as alternatives, —that is, with equal or nearly equal suggestive power,—the loss of ability to inhibit prevents selection, and irresolution and failure to act at all are the result. It is probable that conduct which is often interpreted as extreme scrupulousness, or conscientiousness in affairs of no real moral moment, taking the form of indecision, is merely a manifestation of this type of *aboulia*. (3) *Aboulia* due to ideomotor derangement should be sharply discriminated from the preceding. It is due not to failure to make rational choice, but to inability to execute the choice made. Its psychical form is failure of the kinæsthetic equivalent, or motor image adequate to action, and its physiological basis is probably lesion or loss of tone in the association tracts. It shows itself in a sort of muscular stammering, repeated efforts being required to perform some ordinarily easy action. *Aboulia* is a characteristic neurasthenic condition, appearing in connexion with multiple personality, automatism, etc. It is the natural pre-condition of excessive susceptibility to suggestion.

LITERATURE.—Ribot, *Les maladies de la volonté*[2] (1883); Janet, *Névroses et des idées fixes* (1898); Duprat, *Morals* (1903); Jastrow, *The Subconscious* (1906). H. B. ALEXANDER.

ABRAHAM-MEN.—A class of sturdy beggars, who feigned to have been mad, and to have been kept in Bedlam for a term of years. 'Bedlam'—a lunatic asylum or madhouse—is a contraction for *Bethlehem*, the name of a religious house in London, founded as a priory in 1247, and in 1547 converted into a hospital for lunatics. Originally 'Abraham man' or 'Abraham cove' denoted an inmate of the lunacy ward under the patronage of the patriarch Abraham. On discharge from hospital he wore a badge for identification, and was formally permitted to roam the country as a 'Tom o' Bedlam' and solicit alms.

This character was personated by vagabonds and sturdy rogues, who wandered over England in a disorderly manner, feigning lunacy and preying upon the charitable. Hence the slang phrase, 'to sham Abraham.' Where begging failed they did not hesitate to live by pilfering, and, when detected in any depredation, they would plead the immunities and privileges of a Bedlamite. The character is common in Shakespeare's time, and seems to have survived till the period of the Civil Wars.

For a specimen of the language and demeanour of the Abraham-men, see speech of Edgar in *King Lear*, Act ii. sc. 3; for synonyms, Beaumont and Fletcher's *Beggar's Bush*, ii. sc. 1:—

'And these, what name or title e'er they bear,
Jackman, or Patrico, Cranke, or Clapper-dudgeon,
Fraier, or *Abram-man*, I speak to all.'

Cf. Awdeley's *Fraternitye of Vacabondes*, 1565: 'An Abraham man is he that walketh bare-armed and bare-legged, and fayneth himself mad, and carryeth a pack of wool, or a stycke with baken on it, or such lyke toy, and nameth himself "Poor Tom"' (ed. Early Eng. Text Soc. p. 3). See also Dekker's *Belman of London*, 1608: 'Of all the mad rascalls the Abraham man is the most phantastick. . . . The fellow that sat half naked (at table to-day) is the best Abraham man that ever came into my house, the notablest villain: he swears he hath been in Bedlam, and will talk frantickly of purpose: you see pinnes stuck in sundry places of his naked flesh, especially in his arms . . . onely to make you believe he is out of his wits: he calls himself by the name of Poore Tom. . . . Of these Abraham men some be exceeding merry, and doe nothing but sing songs: some will dance: other will doe nothing but laugh or weep: other are dogged and so sullen both in look and speech, that, spying but small company in a house, they boldly and bluntly enter, compelling the servants through fear to give them what they demand, which is commonly bacon or something that will yield ready money.'

The great authority is Harman's *Caueat, or Warening for Common Corsetors*, 2nd ed., 1567.

W. W. FULTON.

ABRAVANEL (or ABARBANEL), Isaac (1437–1508).—Statesman and author, Don Isaac Abravanel shared in the general expulsion of the Jews from Spain in 1492. He had been in the service of King Alfonso V. of Portugal and Queen Isabella of Castile, and after his banishment acted as finance minister in the states of Naples and Venice. His fame now rests chiefly on his Commentaries on the Bible. He wrote on the Pentateuch, the Historical Books, and the Prophets, but not on the Hagiographa. Among the characteristics of his Commentaries, mention must be made first of his general prefaces to the various books. In this respect he deserves to be considered 'a pioneer of the modern science of Bible propædeutics' (Ginzberg). In addition, his Commentaries are remarkable for the use made of the knowledge of the world which the author had acquired in the vicissitudes of his public career. He thus takes account, in his exegesis of the Biblical histories, of political conditions and social life, and attempts to explain the Bible from the standpoint of its actual contemporaries. In this respect, too, Abravanel was an innovator, for he anticipated the modern principle which relies not solely on literary exegesis, but calls into play all available historical and archæological materials. Again, Abravanel makes free use of Christian Commentaries; he quotes Jerome, Augustine, Nicholas of Lyra, Paul of Burgos, and others. Thus he deserves credit for perceiving that there is room for an unsectarian exegesis—for an exegesis which shall attempt to explain Scripture without theological prejudice.

In all these points Abravanel's services were appreciated by Christians as well as Jews. 'No less than thirty Christian writers of this period—among them men of eminence, like the younger Buxtorf, Buddeus, Carpzov, and others—occupied themselves with the close study of Abravanel's exegetical writings, which they condensed and translated, and thus introduced to the world of Christian scholarship' (Ginzberg). Certainly Abravanel gains by compression, for his works are very prolix. They were often written in great haste. Thus his long Commentaries on Joshua, Judges, and Samuel occupied him only six months. Yet these Commentaries include some of his very best work.

The philosophical works of Abravanel are of less importance than the exegetical. His *Rōsh Amānāh* ('Pinnacle of Faith') is a treatise which aims at dissociating Jewish theology from philosophy; he upheld, against Maimonides, the view of miraculous inspiration. His Messianic books were very popular, and were often reprinted. In these he disputes alike the views of Christian and of Jewish rationalists. His *Yeshuoth Meshicho* ('Salvation of His Anointed') is a clear and full account of the Rabbinic doctrines concerning the Messiah. Abravanel himself claimed descent from the royal house of David.

LITERATURE.—Graetz, *History of the Jews*, Eng. tr., vol. iv. ch. xi.; M. H. Friedländer, *Chachme ha-Dorot* (1880), 136–150; L. Ginzberg in *Jewish Encyc.* vol. i. (1901) pp. 126–128 (where an alphab. list of A.'s works will be found); I. Abrahams, *A Short History of Jewish Literature* (1906), ch. xxi.; S. Schechter, *Studies in Judaism* (1896), ch. on 'The Dogmas of Judaism.'

I. ABRAHAMS.

ABRENUNTIO.—The renunciation of the devil at baptism is a custom which goes back certainly to the 2nd century. At first, as we see from the Patristic references, the renunciation was thought of as intellectual as well as moral, as a repudiation of heathenism with its teachings as well as with its vices and abuses; while later, after the triumph of Christianity (and so at the present day), the renunciation is thought of almost entirely as moral, as a promise to lead a good life.

The custom of interrogating the candidates to see whether they really gave up heathenism and believed in Jesus Christ probably goes back to Apostolic times; it would be a necessary precaution which could scarcely be dispensed with. Perhaps the earliest certain reference to it is the gloss of Ac 8^{37} AV, the confession of faith by the Ethiopian eunuch, which, though probably no part of the original text, is found in Irenæus and Cyprian, and must therefore reflect the usage of at least the 2nd century. It is quite probable, however, that the 'interrogation (*ἐπερώτημα*, not *ἐπερώτησις*) of a good conscience' in 1 P 3^{21} refers to the practice in question.

For our present purpose it is more important to know how the early Church interpreted 1 P 3^{21} than how it was intended by its writer; but as to the early interpretation we have no evidence. The commentators vary in their views. Almost all take *εἰς θεόν* with *συνειδήσεως ἀγαθῆς ἐπερώτημα*, and so the Peshiṭta ('not washing away . . . but confessing God with a clear conscience') and the Vulgate ('conscientiæ bonæ interrogatio in Deum'); some, like Alford, denying any reference to the baptismal interrogations, and rendering 'inquiry of a good conscience after God' (so RVm; cf. 2 S 11^7),—but if so, one would expect *ἐπερώτησις*; and others taking *ἐπερώτημα* to be the baptismal questions, as Œcumenius (11th cent.?), Hooker (*Eccles. Pol.* v. 63), Estius (*Com. in loc.*), de Wette, and others. Dr. Bigg (*ICC, in loc.*) also upholds the reference to the baptismal questions, but gives a strong argument for taking *εἰς θεόν* with *σώζει*, as corresponding to *εἰς ἣν διεσώθησαν*, just as *δι' ἀναστάσεως* corresponds to *δι' ὕδατος*. The translation in that case would be: '. . . the ark into which few . . . were brought safely through water, which also after a true likeness doth now bring you safely to God, even baptism (not the putting away of the filth of the flesh, but the interrogation of a good conscience), through the resurrection of Jesus Christ.'

Turning to the Patristic evidence, we may notice that Justin Martyr speaks (*Apol.* i. 61) of those who are being prepared for baptism 'promising to be able to live according [to the truth].' The first witness for renunciations, however, is Tertullian. He says (*de Spect.* 4):—

'When entering the water, we make profession of the Christian faith in the words of its rule, we bear public testimony that we have renounced the devil, his pomp, and his angels. Well, is it not in connexion with idolatry, above all, that you have the devil with his pomp and his angels? . . . Our renunciatory testimony in the laver of baptism has reference to the shows, which through their idolatry have been given over to the devil and his pomp and his angels.'

Elsewhere (*de Idol.* 6) he says that idol-making is prohibited to Christians by the very fact of their baptism. 'For how have we renounced the devil and his angels if we make them?' In *de Cor.* 3, after describing the act of disowning 'the devil and his pomp and his angels,' he says: 'Hereupon we are thrice immersed, making a somewhat ampler pledge than the Lord has appointed in the Gospel.' So in the *Canons of Hippolytus*, which probably represent Roman or Alexandrian usage early in the 3rd cent., the candidate for baptism turns to the West and says: 'I renounce thee, Satan, with all thy pomp.' He is then anointed by the presbyter, and before being baptized turns to the East and says: 'I believe and bow myself in thy presence and in the presence of all thy pomp, O Father, Son, and Holy Ghost' [for the meaning of 'pomp' see below]. Other 3rd cent. writers mention the interrogations, but not the renunciations in particular. Cyprian (*Ep.* lxix. 2, [Oxford ed., lxx.] *ad Januarium*) gives the interrogations thus: 'Dost thou believe in eternal life and remission of sins in the holy Church?' So Firmillian (Cyprian, *Ep.* lxxiv. 10, [Oxford, lxxv.]) speaks of a prophetess in Cappadocia, 22 years before, who had baptized many, 'making use of the usual and lawful words of interrogation.' And Dionysius of Alexandria, writing to Pope Xystus (*ap.* Euseb. *HE* vii. 9), speaks of the questions and answers (τῶν ἐπερωτήσεων καὶ τῶν ἀποκρίσεων ὑπακούσας). It is clear, then, that in the 3rd and probably in the 2nd cent. the candidates made an act of submission to God at baptism as well as a renunciation of the devil.

The same thing is also evident in the 4th century. The act of submission might be the recital of a creed ('redditio symboli'), which had been taught to the candidates during their catechumenate ('traditio symboli'); or it might be a simple formula, or both the formula and the creed. In Cyril of Jerusalem (*Cat. Lect.* xix. 2–9) we read of the candidate first facing West, because 'the West is the region of sensible darkness,' and Satan, 'being darkness, has his dominion also in darkness,' whereas the East is 'the place of light.' He says, stretching out his hand: 'I renounce thee, Satan, and all thy works, and all thy[*] pomp, and all thy service (*or* worship, λατρείαν).' The word 'pomp' is explained as being the shows, horse races, hunting, and all such vanity; the word 'service' as idolatry, prayer in idol temples, etc. Then the candidate faces East and says: 'I believe in the Father, and in the Son, and in the Holy Ghost, and in one baptism of repentance,' and is anointed and baptized. The renunciation and submission are pronounced in the outer chamber; the anointing and baptism follow in the baptistery, where the candidate is again asked whether he believes in the name of the Father, and of the Son, and of the Holy Ghost (xx. 4). It does not appear that at Jerusalem in Cyril's time the Creed was recited *at baptism.* Of the 4th cent. *Church Orders* we may first cite the Egyptian and Ethiopic *Orders*, which are almost alike. The candidate says: 'I renounce thee, Satan, and all thy service and all thy works' (Ethiopic: 'all thy angels and all thy unclean works'); he is then anointed, and a long

[*] Cyril has 'his' here, probably by error.

creed takes the place of the formula of submission. Turning to the West and East is not mentioned in these two *Church Orders.* In the corresponding part of the *Verona Latin Fragments of the Didascalia* (ed. Hauler) there is a lacuna. In the *Testament of our Lord* (ii. 8) the candidate turns to the West and says: 'I renounce thee, Satan, and all thy service (lit. 'military service'), and thy shows (lit. 'theatres'), and thy pleasures, and all thy works.' After being anointed, he turns to the East and says: 'I submit to thee, Father, Son, and Holy Ghost,' etc.[*] In the *Apostolic Constitutions* the form is somewhat different (vii. 41). The renunciation is: 'I renounce (ἀποτάσσομαι) Satan, and his works, and his pomps, and his worships, and his angels, and his inventions, and all things that are under him.' This is immediately followed by the act of submission: 'I associate myself (συντάσσομαι) with Christ, and believe and am baptized into one unbegotten Being,' etc. (a long creed); then come the anointing and baptism. Turning to the West and East is not mentioned; but later, after confirmation, the neophyte is directed to 'pray towards the East' (vii. 44). We have some confirmatory evidence from other 4th cent. writers. St. Basil (*de Spir. Sancto*, xi. [27]) says: '[Apostates] have set at naught their own confessions . . . belief in the Father, and in the Son, and in the Holy Ghost, when they renounced the devil and his angels, and uttered those saving words.' The *Pilgrimage of Silvia* (or *of Etheria*) does not mention the renunciation, but says that the 'redditio symboli' was made publicly. Pseudo-Ambrose in *de Sacramentis* (ii. 7, *c.* 400 A.D.?) also does not mention the renunciation, but gives the interrogations at the time of the trine immersion: 'Dost thou believe in God the Father Almighty?'—'Dost thou believe also in our Lord Jesus Christ and in His cross?'—'Dost thou believe in the Holy Ghost?'

When the candidates were too young to make the answers to the interrogations and to say the renunciations themselves, this was done for them by the sponsor, or the parents, or a relation (*Canons of Hippolytus*, 113; *Egyptian Church Order*, § 46; *Testament of our Lord*, ii. 8; for sponsors see also Tertullian, *de Bapt.* 18, and the allusion to them—'inde suscepti'—in *de Cor.* 3).

The custom of renouncing the devil has persistently remained. Duchesne (*Origines du culte chrétien*, Eng. tr. ['*Christian Worship*'] p. 304), gives the form long in use at Rome. At the seventh and last scrutiny, after the 'Effeta' and anointing on the breast and back, the candidate was asked: 'Dost thou renounce Satan?'—'And all his works?'—'And all his pomps?' To each question he answered, 'I renounce (*abrenuntio*).' The candidate recited the Creed publicly, but in the 8th cent. the priest recited it for him.

In the Gallican use, the candidate, facing West, was asked: 'Dost thou renounce Satan, the pomps of the world and its pleasures?' The candidate replied, entered the font, and answered a threefold interrogatory on the faith with 'I believe,' and was baptized (*Missale Gallicanum*, see Duchesne, *op. cit.* p. 324).

In the *Sarum Manual* the renunciations were as at Rome (see above); after the anointing the priest asks the candidate a threefold interrogatory which is a short form of the Apostles' Creed, to each part of which he answers 'I believe,' and the baptism follows (Maskell, *Monumenta*[1], i. 22 f.).

The custom in the Eastern Churches is much the same as in the West. In the Orthodox Eastern Church the renunciations come in the 'Office for

[*] In the *Testament*, the *Verona Fragments*, and in the *Canons of Hippolytus*, a form of the Apostles' Creed is put before the candidates in the shape of three questions at the act of baptism.

Making a Catechumen,' which is separate from the baptismal service. The candidate, or (if he be a 'barbarian or a child') his sponsor, is asked thrice: 'Dost thou renounce Satan, and all his works, and all his angels, and all his service, and all his pomp?' and answers: 'I renounce.' He is thrice asked: 'Hast thou renounced Satan?' and answers: 'I have renounced,' and is bidden to blow upon him and spit upon him. Then he is thrice asked: 'Dost thou join Christ?' The Nicene Creed follows here, and after some repetition of the same question the candidate says: 'I bow myself to the Father, and to the Son, and to the Holy Ghost, to the consubstantial and undivided Trinity' (Shann, *Book of Needs*, p. 19; Littledale, *Offices of the H. E. Church*, p. 134). In the Armenian baptismal rite the catechumen says: 'We (*sic*) renounce thee, Satan, and all thy deceitfulness, and thy wiles, and thy service, and thy paths, and thy angels.' He is asked, with some repetition, if he believes in the Holy Trinity, and the Nicene Creed is said in full (Conybeare-Maclean, *Rituale Armenorum*, p. 92; Denzinger, *Ritus Orientalium*, i. 385, also p. 392, where there is a longer profession of belief). The Coptic and Ethiopic customs are almost the same (Denzinger, i. 198, 223; see a shorter form at p. 234, where the renunciation is explained as a purely moral one, without reference to heathenism). For the Jacobite Syrians see Denzinger, i. 273, 321 (the latter is the 'rite of St. Basil'). In the 6th cent. James of Edessa describes the catechumens as renouncing 'Satan and all that belong to him,' and as professing their belief (*ib.* i. 279); and Severus of Antioch gives the form as, 'I renounce Satan, and all his angels, and all his works, and all his worship,' followed by an act of submission (*ib.* p. 304). For the Maronites see Denzinger, i. 340, 354. In all these rites the turning to the West and East is emphasized, and the acts of renunciation and of submission are recorded.

Meaning of 'pomp.'—The word πομπή (from πέμπω) means properly 'a sending under an escort,' and so 'a company,' and then 'a solemn procession' (Liddell and Scott). It was taken into Latin (*pompa*) as meaning 'a procession,' and so (*a*) 'a train' or 'suite,' and (*b*) 'parade,' 'display.' Both these last meanings are found in the formulas of renunciation. In Tertullian and the *Canons of Hippolytus* the meaning is apparently neutral, 'a retinue'; it is used in the *Canons* in a good sense, 'the pomp (*i.e.* retinue) of God' (see above). But from the 4th cent. the bad sense of the word, 'display,' 'pride,' comes to the front, as in Cyril of Jerusalem and the later *Church Orders*; the plural is often used with this meaning to this day in the phrase 'pomps and vanities of this wicked world' of the Book of Common Prayer. A late Latin usage of *pompa* is recorded by Ducange; it was used for a kind of cake given on Christmas Eve by sponsors to their godchildren until they grew up, apparently (says Ducange, *s.v.*) to remind them of their having renounced the pomps of the devil.

Thus we see a most persistent survival of a formula which dates back at least to the 2nd century. The case is exactly parallel with the survival of the *Sursum Corda* in the Eucharistic Liturgy. There is, however, one exception to the universal use of the Renunciation. The Nestorians or Eastern Syrians appear not to have it. Their baptismal service is drawn up in a form closely resembling the Eucharistic Liturgy, with lections, creed, *Sursum Corda*, invocation, etc., and presents many unique features. The Renunciation among the Nestorians probably formed part of a separate office (as in many other Churches), and this office has now perished and the Renunciation with it. But the Nicene Creed, recited in the baptismal service on the analogy of the Liturgy, serves the purpose of a profession of faith.

A. J. MACLEAN.

ABSOLUTE.—1. Meaning of the term.—The term 'absolute' (*absolutum* = 'unrestricted,' 'set free,' and hence what can subsist by itself in that condition, what is complete as it stands) is used either as an adjective or as a substantive, and, in either case, takes on a variety of allied but distinct meanings. It seems probable that the adjectival use is grammatically prior. One of the first writers to use the term is Cicero, who (in *de Finibus*) employs it to describe a characteristic of the blessed life, and also a form of necessity. As an adjective it may be predicated of any substantive which has or can have the qualification of subsisting by itself. This qualification may be given either negatively, in the form of the absence of all relation of dependence on anything else; or positively, when stress is laid on its internal coherence and self-sufficiency. We find it employed not merely in philosophy, but in science and in everyday experience. Characteristic uses in science are, *e.g.*, 'absolute temperature,' 'absolute alcohol,' 'absolute position,' or again 'absolute space.' In common thought it is found in the expressions 'absolute fact,' 'absolutely false.' As a substantive it is primarily a philosophical term, and is in general used to designate the basis or fundamental principle of all reality, that which in some sense is or contains all the variety that exists. It is with the philosophical use of the term that we are mainly concerned here; but it will be of service to introduce the discussion of its philosophical significance by a general analysis of its various meanings.

The meaning of the term may be brought out negatively or positively, or both. Sometimes one is emphasized, sometimes another, as circumstances require. This is possible, because the term has, even etymologically, a negative nuance, and a negative qualification implies a positive ground. In general, it seems safe to say that the negative aspect is the more prominent. That is 'absolute' which does not require for its existence, or for its meaning, that supplementary facts or factors should be brought into consideration. And any one using the term will in general be satisfied to take it as simply equivalent to 'without qualification,' *i.e.* without positive relation to something which lies beyond what is described or stated, and limits or restricts its meaning. In such a case, what is spoken of as 'absolute' can appear in a variety of settings, and yet be unaffected by the process. This is always implied when the negative character is emphasized. What is absolute is not merely so at a given time and in given circumstances; but, however it is shifted about, it will remain permanently what it is, it will preserve its content, and defy internal alteration by external associations. 'Absolute' here means simply *out* of relation. An example is the expression 'absolute freedom,' as employed, *e.g.*, by indeterminists. Sometimes this is true only up to a certain point; sometimes it is held to be true indefinitely. Thus, when it is said that such and such is an 'absolute fact' or is 'absolutely true,' it is not always implied that, no matter where the 'fact' is placed, it will remain unaltered, but that within a certain range of reality or range of truth it will defy alteration. It is clear that something particular may be, in this sense, quite legitimately spoken of as an 'absolute fact': *e.g.* 'the accident is an absolute fact,' *i.e.* something that has an independent place of its own in a certain range of history, no matter whether we look at it in association with other particular events or not. Of course, when we go beyond a certain range, and put this 'accident' in a wide and comprehensive system, its individual independence will disappear, and we shall then in general speak of it, not as an 'absolute fact,' but as one whose nature and meaning are constituted by other related elements. There are, however, aspects or factors of experience to which the adjective 'absolute' could and would be applied indefinitely. When we speak, for example, of an Absolute Being, Absolute Reality, here it is implied that no amount of change of relation whatsoever will alter its permanent independence. In the long run, as we shall see, this is the only consistent form in which the term can be used, and is indeed the basis for all other uses of it. But, when describing common usage, it is desirable to indicate other ways in which the term is employed.

This independence of alteration by external association, to which we have referred, already contains within its negative expression the positive character which the term 'absolute' also possesses, and which in certain cases is more particularly emphasized. By 'absolute' is then meant that quality in virtue of which an object can stand by itself, has an internal constitution of its own, is controlled and determined from within by its very nature. This positive character is really the ground of that negative meaning above described; and the latter is in strictness inseparable from the other. But for certain purposes it is of importance to lay special stress on the positive character *per se*. In this case, the term 'absolute' refers to what is included rather than to what is excluded; to the inner nature of the object so qualified rather than to its possible relation to other objects; to its individual constitution rather than to its connexion with other individuals. Examples of this use would be such expressions as an 'absolute system,' an 'absolute unit,' 'absolute equality.' This positive significance may be taken in specifically different senses. It may refer simply to what, in virtue of the internal constitution of the object, can stand by itself or hold good; and we may know its internal constitution so completely as to justify us in applying the term 'absolute' to it. This is one meaning of the expression, 'Such and such is an absolute possibility,' or 'absolutely possible.' Its contents, the predicates we can apply to the object, are internally consistent. This is the least we can say of anything which we can think—its lowest claim to be something *per se*. This is 'absolute' as opposed to 'relative.' On the other hand, we may mean that the object maintains its being, not in spite of relation to all other things, but *in* every possible relation to other objects in which it may stand. We may compare it with other objects as we please, may subject it to any condition, and find its meaning unaffected. This is 'absolute' as opposed to 'comparative.' The expression 'absolutely possible,' in this sense, is the utmost we can say of anything when taken by itself. Other examples of this sense are: the 'absolute impenetrability' of matter; 'absolute dominion' over individuals in a society; 'absolute simplicity' of physical elements; an 'absolute subject,' *i.e.* a subject which, in every possible sphere, remains a subject, and cannot be a predicate of anything. Sometimes, indeed, we may use the term to cover simultaneously both of the forms of its positive meaning. But in general they would not be true together; for while, *e.g.*, the least we could say of anything can also be said of it if we first state the most we can say of it, the reverse of this would not be true. The expression, an 'Absolute Being,' taken positively, is a case in point. Another, and an important positive use of the term, is when it is employed to designate not what has being simply by itself, or what maintains its being in every possible relation, but what is the ultimate ground of all possible relations. This is the meaning often attached to the expression 'Absolute Reality.' The use of the term 'Absolute Space' to signify that which is the ground of the possibility of all determinate spatial relations, of phenomena appearing in spatial form, is another example. Here 'absolute' is nearly equivalent to 'ultimate,' or the logical prius. The object in question here *contains* all relations, and is absolute in that sense. In the other positive senses an object was absolute either as existing by itself in spite of relation, or as subsisting throughout all relation.

The foregoing analysis of the negative and positive significance of the term has already, no doubt, indicated that neither sense alone is really adequate as a complete expression of its meaning. Each is in strictness one-sided. Indeed, each implies the other, and is more or less consciously present when, for certain purposes, stress is laid on one side rather than another. It is clear that 'absolute,' in the sense of 'out of relation,' 'without qualification,' is predicable of a particular object only *in virtue of* relation. A negative relation is still a relation, and a relation cannot exist unless both terms constituting it are affected and involved. Strictly, 'absolute' is never meant to convey that the object is really outside all relation; but either that the effect of the relation may be ignored or that the object has so secure a place in a general system, that the whole system stands and falls with its individual subsistence. Thus, when a particular statement is said to be 'absolutely true,' we shall find that one or other of these assumptions is made. But it is evident that 'absolute' in this sense really implies relations which are merely unexpressed. In short, since 'absolute,' negatively considered, means simply *without* the qualifications which specific relations would bring, these qualifications, and therefore these relations, must be *there* to give it its meaning. Relation thus enters into the constitution of the term in its negative aspect; and, with it, the positive content which the term related must possess to enter into a relation at all. In the limiting case, when by hypothesis there is no other term with which to constitute a relation, the positive aspect explicitly coincides completely with the negative. This is found when we speak of the 'absolute whole.'

Similarly, when we take the positive meaning by itself and apply it to a specific object, it contains, as part of its significance, a reference to other objects. An object cannot be conceived as something *in itself* without *ipso facto* implying a distinction from other things. What it is in itself logically implies others from which it is at least abstracted in order to be by itself. This is still more obvious when, as in the case, *e.g.*, of 'absolute simplicity' above mentioned, it is what it 'absolutely' is only through relation to other things. The same is true again when it is the 'ultimate ground' of other things. In the limiting case the positive explicitly coincides with its negative, when the reality contains all possible otherness, and is in itself, not through others, but through itself.

If, then, the negative meaning in this way implies the positive and *vice versâ*, we seem forced to the conclusion that what is really involved in either use of the term is the whole which contains both aspects, and that this alone is truly absolute. For, between them, positive and negative in strictness exhaust all that is to be said. When we predicate the term 'absolute' positively or negatively, it is implied that there is no restriction as to what is excluded or included. Absolute in the sense of, *e.g.*, without qualification, is in principle unrestricted in its range of negations. If, therefore, the positive, fully understood, involves the entirety of what is negated and conversely, this means that it is a whole, and one and the same whole, that is implied in every use of the term 'absolute.' This whole, then, is what the use of the term 'absolute' in any given case refers to, and this alone is absolute. If this is not admitted, we are bound to conclude that the predicate 'absolute' is in every case through and through affected by relativity. But a relative absolute is a contradiction in terms; and if this is meant, we must give up the use of the term altogether, except as a way of being emphatic. Otherwise we must accept the view that in every strict use of the term it is logically a single whole that is involved, and that this is alone absolute.

The above analysis certainly compels us to accept this interpretation. If we admit it, we can at once give a logically valid meaning to the use of the term in its positive form and in its negative form. For in either case it means that the object so qualified has a necessary place in the one whole, and that without it also the whole would not be what it is. Or, in other words, the whole and the parts stand together. The predication of the term 'absolute' of any specific part is thus merely our way of affirming our conviction of its necessary place in the one totality, the one systematic unity. The whole being the absolute, each part, of whose place in it we are assured, can be 'absolutized.' And this is done by us in a negative or a positive way according to circumstances. If we apply this interpretation to any current use of the term, we shall find that it gives an intelligible and justifiable meaning to the idea we have in mind. The denial of this view involves the denial of all absoluteness in experience. This is the position of those who maintain the doctrine of thoroughgoing *Relativity*.

2. Philosophical application of the term.—So far we have merely considered the various uses of the term, and have not considered the application of the conception of absoluteness to specific philosophical problems. There are two such problems which are historically important and philosophically fundamental: (1) the problem of absoluteness in human knowledge, which raises in part the question of the 'relativity of knowledge'; (2) the problem of the Absolute in metaphysics. We must deal with each of these separately, so far as they can be separated.

I. *ABSOLUTE AS APPLIED TO HUMAN KNOWLEDGE.*—There are two distinct ways in which the term 'absolute' may be applied to human knowledge. Both start from the position that in all knowledge we aim at an ideal, and that the consummation of our knowledge would be the explicit articulation of that ideal in systematic form. The term 'ideal,' however, may or may not be used, and may be variously interpreted.

(*a*) We may call it 'complete' truth, and regard this as the complete 'agreement' of our thoughts with the 'nature of things.' If we attempt to express with systematic fulness what this ideal as such contains, to give in some sense the whole truth, the knowledge so supplied would be spoken of as 'absolute' knowledge. In general it is also implied that in such a case we are at the point of view of the whole ideal as such; that we do not rise to it gradually and give the content of the ideal at the end of our journey, so to speak, but rather that we *start* our exposition of what the ideal contains by occupying at the outset the position of an absolute knowing mind. We interpret the ideal as an objective system of truth in virtue of our taking up an objective or trans-individualistic attitude, where all the perspective of specific individual minds is eliminated. This point of view is essential, because an ideal of knowledge in this sense involves the disappearance of finite qualifications and reservations.

This conception of absolute knowledge may be regarded in two ways. (*α*) It has been taken to mean an exposition of the general elements constituting the supreme or whole truth, a systematic development of the fundamental conceptions or principles involved in, and making possible, the different forms of knowledge. Spinoza's *Ethics* or Hegel's *Logic* would be an illustration of absolute knowledge in this sense. (*β*) It has also been taken to mean an exposition of the whole truth both in its general content and in its particular details—a system, in fact, not simply of principles, but of conceptions *with* their details in all their manifold form. Absolute knowledge in this sense has generally been considered impossible of achievement, and certainly there is no historical example of a single system which claims to give so much. These two senses of the term 'absolute knowledge' may be conveniently characterized in the language of a recent philosophical work (Laurie's *Synthetica*) as, respectively, knowledge which gives a 'synthesis of the absolute,' and knowledge which gives an 'absolute synthesis.'

(*b*) Another use of the term as applied to knowledge is found when we speak of knowledge in a given case being 'absolute knowledge,' or conveying 'absolute truth.' This need not refer directly or even at all to any absolute system of knowledge. It can be applied to any case where, as we sometimes say, we are 'absolutely certain,' or where the judgment does not contradict itself or any other judgment. From this point of view, many or most of the judgments making up our knowledge can be spoken of as absolute, whether the knowledge be given in the form of a scientific statement, like 'two and two are four'; or even in the case of a judgment of perception: 'this paper is white.' The latter may be said to be as 'absolutely true,' to convey as absolute knowledge of this specific area of perceptive experience, as the former type of judgment. Indeed, the assertion of any ultimate fact, from this point of view, becomes an 'absolute truth,' a case of 'absolute knowledge'; and all the steps in the attainment of the complete truth, the complete systematic ideal of knowledge, are at least capable of being characterized in this way, whether we ever attain to the complete system or not. Hence the term can be applied in this second sense to knowledge without any implication of the possibility of 'absolute knowledge' in the first sense. Indeed, it may be denied in the latter sense, and asserted only in the former.

In considering the question as to the validity of the idea of absolute knowledge, we have to bear in mind this difference in the use and application of the term. It may, no doubt, be said with some truth that absolute in the second sense really implies in the long run the admission of absolute in the first sense. But, at any rate, that is not explicitly maintained, and can even be fairly denied. This comes out in the controversy between 'absolute' and 'relative' truth. It is often held that all our knowledge is relative to us, and *therefore* absolute knowledge is impossible to man. By this is meant that the attainment of an 'absolute system of truth' is impossible, and not that our knowledge, 'so far as it goes,' is not absolutely true. Thus relativity of knowledge may be maintained along with the assertion that we do possess absolutely valid knowledge. This is in general the position of the narrowly scientific mind. Relativity may, indeed, also be asserted of all forms of our knowledge. In this case absolute knowledge is denied in *both* senses of the term. Relativity, then, logically leads either to pure scepticism or to individualistic anthropomorphism. It is thus important, in discussing the 'relativity' of knowledge, to determine both what kind of relativity is asserted and with what kind of absoluteness it stands in contrast. Nothing but confusion can result, *e.g.*, when defending relativity in opposition to absoluteness of knowledge, if one disputant is using 'absolute' in the first sense and the other in the second.

Justification of (*a*).—The argument in defence of absolute knowledge, in the sense of a complete system of the fundamental conceptions constituting the ideal of knowledge, rests on the simple proposition that knowledge as such can be an object of knowledge. When knowledge is itself an object of consideration, all that it implies must be offered up without reserve for critical analysis. If this cannot be done, the discussion of knowledge as such is futile; for to assert at the outset that we can know only a part of an object which we set out to know, is to check our knowledge in advance by the hand of scepticism. We should never attempt to know any object if we consciously assumed as a fact that in its entirety it could not be known. The edge would be taken off the seriousness of the problem at once, and neither common sense nor the scientific mood would sanction the effort. But, indeed, it would require an interpretation of knowledge to prove such an assumption to be valid: and hence this hypothesis may be dismissed as logically impossible, because self-contradictory. But if knowledge as such can be an object of knowledge, it must have the rounded completeness of a determinate object to justify the attempt. That completeness lies in the ideal unity of knowledge and nowhere else. This ideal, therefore, must be capable of analysis, of criticism, and, because a unity, of systematic expression. It may very well be that we are incapable of exhausting its content in all its manifold detail. For the limitation of our command over the particulars of our experience is one form in which finitude of intelligence appears. There still remain, however, the ground principles which constitute the general or typical forms in which the unity of knowledge is specifically realized. These we may grasp and systematically arrange. They may be as general, and as numerous, or as few, as the growth of the various sciences and the advancement of human intellectual activity determine. But, as such, they are an expression in every case of the general forms in which this ultimate unity is realized. To state in some connected way, therefore, the constituent general conceptions which the ideal unity of knowledge contains, is always a possible achievement. That ideal unity is at once the logically implied beginning and the final end of all knowledge in its various forms. The knowledge of it is the self-knowledge of knowledge; and that is absolute knowledge in both the negative and positive senses of the term 'absolute.' This kind of knowledge may, of course, be supplied in different ways, and with different degrees of success. These must always vary with the variation which is at once the privilege and the limitation of the individual thinker. But such peculiarities do not concern the question as to the *possibility* of truly achieving the result. What relation exists between the various forms which absolute knowledge in this sense has historically assumed, is a further question, which lies beyond that of the justification of its possibility.

Justification of (*b*).—The position that knowledge may be absolute without being at the same time a finished system, or without at least waiting till a finished system is obtained, rests on different grounds. It is maintained that every true judgment is absolute as knowledge, just as it stands. An isolated judgment is absolutely valid without any other judgment being implied to guarantee or ratify its truth. The addition of other judgments may or may not modify its truth, but it will only be in so far as it is *not* true that it is capable of supplementation. And, even at the worst, this will always leave what truth it does contain unaffected. It is maintained that this does not involve relativity in the sense of scepticism or individualism; for there is a distinction between a judgment which stands in a relation and judgment which is relatively valid. The first may, in virtue of the internal coherence of its content, hold a necessary and unalterable place in a series, or in a whole, from which it is inseparable; in the second, the content is incompletely determined, and therefore the judgment is only approximately coherent: its stability is liable to be disturbed by external agencies. The first may well be described as absolute, since, on the one hand, such judgments are not subject to alteration, but only to supplementation; and, on the other, it is out of such judgments that any system, even one claiming to be the complete ideal, has to be built up, if there is to be a system at all. Such judgments do not require to wait for the complete system to be evolved before claiming to be absolute, and hence, it is held, they possess that character whether or not the system be ever arrived at. A type of these judgments is found in mathematical truth; but, indeed, any scientific judgment tends to claim this attribute. That such judgments may be absolute *per se*, can also be justified by pointing out that, even if it be a system that makes them in the long run absolutely true by giving them a place in the absolute system, then each is absolutely valid at least by means of it, and may therefore legitimately be spoken of as an absolute judgment. A system must be a system of different parts, and the character of the whole is present in each part. This, however, would not justify the claim to regard each as absolute independently of a system. For it seems clearly paradoxical to maintain that a judgment can be absolute both because of its place in a system and yet *in spite of* that system. It is only in the case of certain judgments that the attribute can be applied. And it will be found that only when a judgment has an individuality of its own does it possess that completeness and internal coherence which justify the use of the term 'absolute.' Individuality, however, is precisely the characteristic of system, whether the range of the system be all-comprehensive or not. Moreover, it is impossible to state a judgment which is definite and restricted in meaning without at the same time by implication excluding from its content other equally definite judgments. What it does *not* say determines its meaning as well as what it does affirm. To be, therefore, completely true, it involves and is maintained by a wider whole than it *explicitly* asserts.

II. *The Absolute in Metaphysics*.—This must be treated apart from the question just considered. The term is applied in metaphysics to the whole of 'Reality,' and whether or not it is true that knowledge contains or covers all Reality, certainly it is true that Reality as a whole includes knowledge.

Hitherto the term has been discussed mainly as an attribute of a subject. In metaphysics it is used as a subject of all possible predication, and therefore itself incapable of being a predicate. The transition to the substantive use of the term is fairly obvious. It consists simply in transforming a supreme quality into the name for the supreme subject of all qualities, much as is done in the case of 'cause'; for example, when we speak of the 'first cause.' When we use the term 'absolute' in this connexion, we have in mind primarily the general ideas of 'all-containing,' 'ultimate,' in the sense of logical prius, the 'one ground of all finitude,' and such like,—all of them, in the long run, implying that the Reality so described combines in itself those positive and negative characteristics above mentioned. The Absolute so understood may be said to be the vaguest of terms, and little better than meaningless. But that criticism is over hasty, since it is the aim of a metaphysical theory to determine what the full meaning of the term is; and obviously that meaning cannot be given in the mere description of the signification of a word, which can in point of fact be used by a great variety of theories. Indeed, to regard the term as wholly and essentially indeterminate, is legitimately possible only as the result of a theory.

When the Absolute, then, is said to be the object-matter of metaphysics, we have to understand the term as the designation of the one all-inclusive uniting principle of whatever experience contains. From the point of view of metaphysical knowledge it is, at least to begin with, little or nothing more than the existential counterpart of the unity of experience, which such knowledge postulates as a precondition of its progress, and the elucidation of which constitutes the achievement of the aim and ideal of metaphysics. It is therefore at the outset quite colourless; any more definite specification of its nature is possible only in virtue of a metaphysical theory. Thus for metaphysics it is simply a problem, and not an assumption, whether the Absolute is 'personal' or a 'cause,' or 'real' or an 'appearance,' or all or none of these. Only metaphysical inquiry can determine legitimately how far the Absolute contains any of these features, and which of them, if any, it is primarily. It is evident that this must be so, when we reflect that if it were not true, the mere meaning of the Absolute would give a solution to all metaphysical questions. Certainly we sometimes find more, and sometimes less, imported into the idea. But if this is done *before* the inquiry, we must regard the fact as merely a peculiarity of the thinker, which does not affect the principle here laid down; while, if it is done at the *end* of the inquiry, that is quite legitimate, a necessary result, indeed, of having a theory at all.

If we bear this in mind, we can see at once the distinction between the metaphysical conception of the Absolute and the religious idea of God. The latter always involves personality—at least, spirituality in some form or other; the former does not. Both name the whole, and the same whole. But whereas religion is bound to do it by a certain category, to satisfy certain human needs, metaphysics is not committed to any category at all. It may well be that the legitimate conclusion of metaphysics satisfies the demands of the religious consciousness. But it may not. Hence the possibility of conflict between the two, which we find historically as a fact. In the long run, the term 'God' in religion and 'the Absolute' in metaphysics must, if the religious mood is valid, be the same in meaning; if not, one of them will inevitably condemn the claims of the other, for both seek to express the same whole. But it has to be borne in mind at the outset, that while the God of religion must be the Absolute, the Absolute of metaphysics may or may not be conceived of as the God that will satisfy the religious mind: that will depend entirely on how the Absolute is interpreted by metaphysics.

The metaphysical problem, then, regarding the Absolute, resolves itself into the question how to conceive the nature of the principle which is at once single and realized in the manifold ways that make up experience. The problem is one of interpretation, not of discovery; for it is assumed that knowledge by which we conceive and think the nature of the Absolute itself falls within its compass. To try to demonstrate the actual existence of the Absolute, which a process of discovery seeks to do, is thus logically absurd. At the same time, since the knowledge, which interprets, falls by hypothesis within the one-all, the relatively subordinate question, regarding the relation between our knowledge and the whole which contains it, may well press for solution before the interpretation of the whole in the strict sense is given. Thus, in general, the metaphysical problem is found to have two parts—(1) The relation of our knowledge to the Absolute; (2) the nature of the principle constituting the Absolute.

(1) *Relation of knowledge to Absolute Reality.*—On this point different views have been held. We must be content here to indicate the source of these differences.

(*a*) In the first place, it is held that, because our knowledge falls within the whole, is a factor or process in it, and works by its own peculiar conditions, it is not merely unequal to grasping the whole, but that it is logically meaningless to attempt the task. We can think it possible only by making the Absolute a part with which our knowledge, as another part, stands in relation. But the Absolute, being the whole, cannot logically be treated as a part in any sense. Or the same position is maintained when it is said that the unity of the whole cannot be itself an object for the subject thinking or knowing. The distinction between subject and object is fundamental for knowledge, and the object must in some sense be 'given' to the subject before it can be known. But a whole which *includes* by hypothesis the subject cannot be presented or given in this way. Therefore the Absolute cannot be known consistently with the nature and naming of knowledge. And since here is no other way of knowing than by way of a relation between subject and object, the attempt to know the Absolute in any sense is logically impossible.

The issue here is what may be called metaphysical agnosticism resting on the basis of epistemological 'criticism.' A recent representative of this view is Adamson (see *Development of Modern Philosophy and other Lectures*). It admits only empiricism or 'naturalism' and epistemology within the range of positive human knowledge. The line of argument against this position would be—(1) That the distinction and relation of subject and object must itself imply in some sense a unity between them, which is not simply imagined as *outside* the two terms, but is constitutive of this connexion, and necessary to it; (2) that the apprehension of this unity cannot logically be denied, asserted, or criticised by reference to the relational process which this unity constitutes; (3) that the unity is, from our point of view, an ideal; and an ideal in the nature of the case cannot be *given or presented* as a fact, either at the beginning of experience as such, or even at the end as such: for it determines and embraces the entire content from first to last, and must therefore be grasped in that sense.

(*b*) Another view of the relation of knowledge to an Absolute which contains it, is that which regards the subject-mind and its processes, among which falls knowledge, as forming an ultimate element in the unity of the whole. The other element, in itself generically distinct from the former, may be described as the object world of 'nature' and natural processes. These two between them exhaust the content of the Absolute so far as our experience is concerned. The Absolute *per se* is not one any more than the other; it is both, but may be either one or other. In any case it is known only in and through these aspects or appearances; but it still has a nature of its own behind the appearances, its being *per se*. Our knowledge belongs to and has to do with the sphere of appearances only. There is no ground for supposing it adequate to what the Ultimate Reality is *per se*; on the contrary, its origin and its processes necessarily confine it to the phenomenal. Still, the absence of knowledge does not involve an entirely negative attitude to the Absolute. The mere fact that knowledge belongs to the sphere of appearance points the way towards, or indicates the need for, the actual existence of an attitude distinct from knowledge, and one which can be concerned with the Absolute *per se*. We may call this attitude belief, or mystical intuition, or what not, so long as we bear in mind that its purport is to deal with this Ultimate Reality. Hence, while from the point of view of reflexion or knowledge in its various forms, scientific or otherwise, there is no approach to the Absolute, there is a way open in another direction, and this may constitute a specific mood of our lives, the mood, *e.g.*, of religion.

This is the point of view of metaphysical agnosticism, which appeals for its justification to the anthropomorphic character of knowledge, and rests, on the one hand, upon a psychological analysis of knowledge, and, on the other, upon the necessary limitations of scientific reflexion by which alone knowledge is to be had. One of its best-known representatives in recent times is Spencer (see his *First Principles*). The argument against this view takes the form of showing (1) the radical contradiction in the twofold-aspect conception of an Ultimate Reality, in the idea of appearances *per se*, which leave the noumenal reality unrevealed, *i.e.* appearances of what does *not* appear; (2) that the Absolute is so far known in that it is *conceived* to have certain characteristics, and at least to be related to its appearances in a certain way; (3) that the psychological history of knowledge, and even the essential anthropomorphism of knowledge, do not necessarily prove either that Spirit may not express the Ultimate Reality more truly than Force, or that Spirit and Force have equal value as forms of the Absolute.

(*c*) A third view of the relation of knowledge to the Absolute finds a typical expression in the interpretation developed by Bradley in his *Appearance and Reality*. Basing his conception of knowledge partly on psychological, partly on logical and epistemological considerations, he insists that knowledge strictly understood is relational in character. It requires for its operation something given, an existential fact over against thought or the ideal process. This antithesis and duality of the terms in the process of knowledge both creates and limits the range of the value in experience of the function of reflective knowledge. It can, for example, never exhaust the given, the 'that,' without *ipso facto* destroying the very condition of its own operation and so disappearing. If it had the 'that' within itself, the operation would be both unnecessary and impossible. Since this falls without itself, there always remains, so far as reflective knowledge is concerned, a surd in our experience. The distinction between knowledge and the real never passes into an existential continuity of content. 'Knowledge is unequal to the real': it is relational, is not inherently self-complete, is not self-sufficient; it is an 'appearance' of the Absolute. Hence by reflective knowledge the Absolute cannot be expressed. But just as psychologically there is an infra-relational level of feeling-experience out of which knowledge arises, by the development of the distinction of the 'what' from the 'that,' so there is a supra-relational level of experience which transcends knowledge. This supra-relational level is akin or analogous to the infra-relational level, in that positively there is in both a direct continuity of experience, and negatively both are realized apart from the distinctions which characterize relational thought. But, while the former has the character of mere feeling, the latter consists rather of mystical insight or intuition. At this highest level the apprehension of the Absolute as such is possible and is attained. It does not abolish the distinctions determined by the procedure of relational thought; it retains them, not, however, as distinctions, but as elements or constituents in the unique acts which characterize the intuitive apprehension of the whole as such. Hence, while the Absolute is thus beyond knowledge, it is not beyond conscious experience at its highest level. It gives us the Absolute with and in its appearances, and not apart from them.

The general objection to this view of the relation of knowledge to the Absolute is its emphasis on the discontinuity between relational and supra-relational 'thought.' It seems to refuse with one hand what it gives with the other. A supra-relational thought transcending the conditions of that critical reflexion which works by distinctions, lays itself open to the attack of sceptical negation by its very attempt to transcend it. Either it is justified or it is not. In the former case it cannot adopt the methods of systematic reflexion to defend its position; in the second, there is nothing to distinguish its attitude from caprice and mere dogmatic assertion. Moreover, even the apprehension of the 'higher unity' must prove itself coherent. But a coherent whole is a whole of parts distinct from one another and claiming recognition as distinct. The privileges of mere mysticism are inseparable from the dangers of pure individualism. From mysticism, as the professed negation of knowledge, the transition is easy to sheer scepticism, which makes the same profession.

(2) *The nature of the Absolute.*—The metaphysical interpretation of the Absolute is determined in the long run by the emphasis laid on the essential factors involved in the problem of construing its meaning. The factors are: subject in relation to object within a unity which holds those ultimate elements in their relation, whatever that relation be. The problem is to determine this unity *with* the elements which stand thus related. We shall merely indicate the different interpretations given, without developing those interpretations into any detailed system. The systems in all their detail constitute the various metaphysical theories which make up the history of philosophy.

(*a*) We may take our stand on the subject with its activity and processes, and from this basis show that the object-world falls within the range of the subject's activity, which by implication, therefore, also contains all that constitutes the unity in virtue of which object and subject are bound up together. We may accomplish this result in various ways, but the essential principle is the same. (*a*) We may so resolve the object into the being of the subject as to destroy even the semblance of distinction, and certainly all the opposition they may *prima facie* present. This is the position adopted by pure *Solipsism*. (*β*) We may again seek to secure to the object its claim to be distinctive, but may endeavour to show that the ground of that distinctiveness which it possesses, falls within the scope of the activity of the subject and is determined altogether by the action of the subject. This is the position of *Subjective Idealism*. It may take two forms. (*aa*) We may regard the objectivity of the object as a *fact*, and resolve its characteristic nature into ideal elements in the subject's life. This has been done primarily in the case of the external world revealed to 'outer' perception, which presents a peculiarly stubborn problem to Subjective Idealism. The historical representative of this form of Subjective Idealism is Berkeley. (*ββ*) On the other hand, we may regard the objectivity as a *result*, and 'deduce' it from an ultimate act of spontaneity on the part of the subject. Objectivity is here conceived in a much wider sense than that involved in the case of the external world. It embraces all forms of objectivity, that of other selves, and society, as well as the 'outer world' found by perception. The last, in fact, is merely a particular realization of a more fundamental objectivity which we meet with primarily in the social order of 'free wills.' This more thorough-going and more comprehensive expression of Subjective Idealism is found in Fichte.

(*b*) Again, we may start from the basis of the object as such, and resolve the subject's life, and with that the unity containing subject and object, into the forms and processes of the object-world. Everything will here depend on what constituents of the object-world are regarded as ultimate and primary. This will determine the form assumed by the interpretation. The strongest case historically has been made for the theory which takes physical matter and physical energy as the fundamental elements with which we have to deal. The developed expression of this view takes the form of what is called variously *Materialism*, *Naturalism*, or *Physical Realism*.

(*c*) Once more, we may start explicitly by laying primary stress neither on the subject nor on the object, but on their unity as such. This may take different forms. (*α*) We may take subject and object to be, from the point of view of the unity, of equal significance in its constitution. The unity being neither specially, is *as such* equally indifferent to each. But since these, nevertheless, are all it does contain, it is *per se* indeterminate; it is the indifferent neutrum in which both merely subsist. So far as any interpretation of it is to be given, we can express its nature either from the side of the object or from the side of the subject. Either point of view is equally valid, since a neutral unity, which is indifferently one factor as much as the other, is equally both. It must be expressible in either way, for, if it were neither, it would be nothing. This is in the main the position of Schelling.

(*β*) Again, we may start from the unity and develop an interpretation of it by taking the unity to be one factor *more than* the other. In this case there is for the unity an inequality of value between the two elements which constitute it. It is therefore not one as much as the other, and is not indifferent to either. It is one more than the other. It is thus not a colourless neutrum, but a concrete whole, of which each is a distinct mode or level of realization. It is not interpretable in two forms, distinct or even separate from one another, as in the former case; but in one form, and that form is adequate and complete as an expression of the entire concrete unity. From this point of view it is clear that there may be two ways of stating its meaning, according as we take the object side to be primary, or the subject side. Either view will present the whole concretely; but will interpret it in a different manner, and the dominant principle or category for determining the whole will be different. Starting from the object side, we will look on the whole as determinable by objective categories, and the kind of connexion amongst the parts of the whole will have the character which objective categories require. The supreme form of objectivity is what we call the order of 'Nature'; the supreme objective category that of 'Substance'; and the primary form of connexion among the parts will be that of relation by external necessity. The unity will thus be conceived of as nature in its totality, as working by natural processes of connexion, physical and spatial—*natura naturans.* The various elements constituting it will be the realization of this supreme unity in its phenomenal character, as a product in natural form of natural activity—*natura naturata.* The subject world will be a mode of this realization—one way in which Nature is phenomenalized or made determinate. But Nature as such is, in its very meaning, a resolution of differences into a single continuous identity, the identity of the one substance, the one 'nature.' Relatively to this all else is accident, an essentially negative moment, not a permanent expression. All explicit specific determination is implicit universal negation. There are no differences of degree in the contents; all are on the same footing *relatively* to the *whole*, and therefore relatively to one another. There are merely different modes of manifesting the one and only Reality. *Inter se*, these modes are generically distinct, and hence, in their modal manifestation of the one Reality, are merely side by side, parallel to one another, converging only at infinity, where they disappear or coincide. The external necessity, connecting the parts in each mode and the modes in the whole, involves, and is merely a finite expression of, this essential continuity into which they are dissipated. This interpretation of the Absolute finds its great historical representative in Spinoza.

(*γ*) But we may also conceive the problem in the same concrete way, and take the subject factor as primary, and the object reality as subsidiary. Here we shall proceed by another principle, by another category, and by another method of connecting the elements involved. We lay stress, not on the impersonal attitude towards objectivity, which characterizes the physical and mathematical consideration of the object-world, and which dissipates the subject-life into its processes, but on the personal attitude, which is found in its highest expressions in morality and religion. In these the object-world, so far from being primary, is subsidiary to personal or spiritual ends. We shall therefore take the principle to be, not Nature, but Spirit. The ultimate category will be not 'Substance,' but 'Subject.' The essential method of establishing connexion with the whole will be not external necessity, but internal necessity, the necessity of ideals and purposes, the necessity which is Freedom. The process of connecting the factors inside the unity of the whole will be that which, accepting the ethical and religious insistence on the subordination of the object-world, shows the latter to be in its essence an imperfect realization of the nature of Spirit, and shows Spirit therefore as at once arising out of, rising above, realizing and so retaining the true significance of Nature. This will be done by showing the content of the whole in its different moments to be simply the logically necessary evolution of the one final principle; which would not be itself unless it manifested itself in varying degrees of completeness of expression. These degrees form distinct and seemingly separate areas of reality to finite experience, but to the one supreme Reality they are merely stages in the realization of its single and self-complete spiritual existence. Such an interpretation, expressed essentially in the same general form by Plato, Aristotle, and Leibniz, finds its most impressive historical representative in Hegel.

These various ways of construing the meaning of the Absolute have doubtless each its value and place in the history of man's higher spiritual life, and amongst them seem to exhaust the possible interpretations of the supreme unity of experience. It would be out of place here to try to consider their respective merits, since we are not concerned to give a metaphysical theory of the Absolute, but to indicate what theories have been propounded.

LITERATURE.—The literature on the Absolute is almost co-extensive with the history of philosophical speculation.

I. *THE TERM 'ABSOLUTE.'*—A discussion of the meaning of the term, and of the relation of the Absolute to knowledge, will be found in Hamilton's *Discussions on Philosophy and Literature*; see also Laurie's *Synthetica*, vol. ii. p. 392 ff.

II. *'ABSOLUTE' AS A PHILOSOPHICAL PRINCIPLE.*—(*a*) DISCUSSIONS.—Bosanquet, 'Time and the Absolute' in *Proc. of Aristot. Society*, 1896; Braun, 'La Logique de l'Absolu' in *Revue Philosophique*, xxiv. [1887]; Haldar, 'The Conception of the Absolute' in *Philos. Review*, viii. [1899]; James, 'Absolutism and Empiricism' in *Mind*, O. S. ix. [1884]; Joachim, 'Absolute and Relative Truth,' *ib.*, Jan. 1905; Logan, 'The Absolute as Ethical Postulate' in *Philos. Review*, viii. [1899]; Powell, 'The Absolute and the Relative' in *Science*, iii. [1896]; Renouvier, 'Les Catégories de la raison et la métaphysique de l'Absolu' in *L'année philosophique*, vii. [1897]; Rogers, 'The Absolute of Hegelianism' in *Mind*, N. S. ix. [1900]; Russell, A., on 'The Absolute' in *CR* xvii. [1871]; Schwarz, 'Die verschied. Fassung d. Substantialität d. Absoluten' in *Ztschr. f. Philos. u. phil. Krit.* xxiii. [1853]; Vaihinger, 'Der Begriff d. Absoluten mit Rücksicht auf Spencer,' *ib.* xxiii. [1853]; Watson, 'The Absolute and the Time Process' in *Philos. Rev.* iv. [1895].

(*b*) INTERPRETATIONS.—Aristotle, *Metaphys.*; Bradley, *Appearance and Reality*; Fichte, *Wissenschaftslehre*; Hegel, *Encyclopädie*; Plato, *Timæus*, *Republic*; Royce, *World and the Individual*; Schelling, *Transcendental Idealismus*, *Naturphilosophie*; H. Spencer, *First Principles*; Spinoza, *Ethics*. For further literature see Baldwin, *DPhP* iii. pt. ii. 597.

J. B. BAILLIE.

ABSOLUTE (Vedāntic and Buddhistic).—In India a broad conception of the Absolute is first met with in the Upaniṣads, compiled about B.C. 500. There Brahma, the All-pervading Being, is described as the One Reality, or the Absolute, who is self-supporting and self-existent.

'He has no hands or legs, but He can catch and move; He has no eyes, but He can see, has no ears but can hear; He knows all, but there is none who knows Him; He is called the Good and Great Being. Upon Him the sun cannot shine, nor the moon nor the stars; the lightning cannot flash on Him, how can the fire? They all reflect His radiant light, and through His light they are illumined.' *

Since B.C. 500 the doctrine of the Absolute has been considerably developed in the Vedānta and Buddhist systems of philosophy. In the Brahma-sūtra, the first work of the Vedānta philosophy composed before the Christian era, Brahma is spoken of as the pure 'Being' who, associated with the principle of illusion (*māyā*), is enabled to project the appearance of the world, just as a magician is enabled to produce illusory appearances of animate and inanimate beings.† When the veil of illusion is withdrawn, the phenomenal world vanishes, and Brahma asserts himself in his true nature, which is nothing but the Self-existent Absolute Being. In the Vedānta philosophy the doctrine of the Absolute is styled monism (*advaita-vāda*). It underwent further developments at the hands of Śaṅkarāchārya (A.D. 785), Rāmānuja (12th cent. A.D.), Madhvāchārya (13th cent. A.D.), Vallabhāchārya (A.D. 1479), and others.

But the philosopher who most firmly grasped the doctrine of the Absolute was Buddha-Śākya-Siṁha, the eminent founder of Buddhism, who flourished about B.C. 500. In the Sutta and Abhidhamma *piṭakas* of the Pāli Scriptures, supposed to have been delivered by Buddha himself, the doctrine of the Absolute is designated as the philosophy of the Void (*śūnya-vāda*) or the Middle Path (*majjhimā paṭipadā*), according to which the world is neither real nor unreal, nor both, nor neither.‡ In the Sanskrit works of the Mahāyāna Buddhists, such as in the Mādhyamika-Sūtra (of Nāgārjuna, about A.D. 200), Laṅkāvatāra-Sūtra (about A.D. 400), Lalitavistara (about A.D. 100), Prajñāpāramitā (about A.D. 200), etc., the doctrine has been further developed, and has often been styled the 'phenomenal doctrine' (*nairātmavāda*) or the 'perfection of wisdom' (*prajñāpāramitā*).§

In order to understand the Buddhist doctrine of the Absolute, we may suppose that Indian philosophers are mainly divided * into three classes: (1) Realists (*āstika*), (2) Nihilists (*nāstika*), and (3) Absolutists (*advayavādin*). Some sections of the Chārvākas, who maintain that the world is not permanent, not real, and not existent,—that is, who emphasize the negative aspect of the world,—are designated Nihilists or Negativists. The propounders of the six orthodox systems of Hindu philosophy, viz. the Sāṅkhya, Yoga, Nyāya, Vaiśeṣika, Mīmāṁsā, and Vedānta, who maintain that the world is somehow permanent, real, and existent,—that is, who emphasize the positive aspect of the world,—are designated the Realists. According to them, there is at least one reality on which the fabric of the world stands. Thus the Nyāya and Vaiśeṣika hold that the material atoms, sky, space, and time, are the permanent entities in the external world, while the souls are the eternal realities in the internal world. The Sāṅkhya and Yoga maintain that nature (*prakṛti*) is the permanent reality in the external world, while the souls (*puruṣa*) are the eternal realities in the internal world. The Vedānta school affirms that Brahma, the All-pervading Being, is the one eternal reality in the external as well as in the internal world. So we find that the various branches of the Realistic philosophy, in spite of their mutual differences in other respects, agree in maintaining that there is at least one permanent reality on which the whole world hinges.

The Buddhists, who maintain † that the world is neither real nor unreal, that it is neither an existence nor a non-existence, but transcends both,—that is, who emphasize neither the negative nor the positive aspect of the world, but go beyond both,—are designated the Transcendentalists, Absolutists, Phenomenalists, Voidists, Agnostics, or the Followers of the Middle Path.

The world, according to the Buddhists,‡ is an aggregate of conditions or relations. Things come into existence in virtue of these relations or conditions. There are infinite kinds of relation, such as the relation of substance and quality, part and whole, cause and effect, etc. Taking the relation of substance and quality, we find that the substance exists only in relation to its qualities, and the latter exist only in relation to the former. Take, for instance, a table. It has a certain weight, colour, taste, smell, size. The table exists only as the repository of these qualities, and the latter exist only as inherent in the former. We cannot conceive a table which has no size, weight, colour, etc., nor can we think of size, weight, etc., apart from the table in which they inhere. Arguing in this way, we find that the parts exist only in relation to the whole, and the whole exists only in relation to the parts. So the eye exists in relation to the colour, and the colour exists only in relation to the eye. Similarly, the fire exists in relation to the fuel, and the fuel exists in relation to the fire. Proceeding in this way, we find that the whole world is resolvable into infinite kinds of relation or condition. The relations or conditions themselves are dependent upon one another. The very notions of 'existence' and 'non-existence' are interdependent, for the one is possible only in relation to the other.

Origination and cessation, persistence and discontinuance, unity and plurality, coming and going—these are the eight principal relative conceptions which are the fundamental faults of ignorant minds, from which most of our prejudices and wrong judgments arise. People think that the law of coming and going actually operates in the world, that there are in reality persistence and

* Śvetāsvatara-Upaniṣad and Kaṭhopaniṣad.
† Thibaut, Introd. to *Vedanta Sūtra*, i. p. xxv (*SBE*).
‡ Cf. *Sarva-darśana-saṅgraha*², Cowell and Gough's tr., 22 f.
§ *Laṅkāvatāra-sūtra*, p. 1; *Aṣṭa-sāhasrikā Prajñā-pāramita*, p. 1.

* *Mādhyamikā-vritti.*
† *Ib.* ch. xv.
‡ *Ib.* ch. i. (Cf. also Vidyabhusana in *JBTS* iii. pt. 3).

discontinuance of things, that things do really undergo the states of origination and cessation, and that things are really capable of being counted as one or many; but they are wholly unconscious of the fact that all those ideas are limited, relative, conditional, and therefore not the truth, but merely the production of our imperfect subjective state. There nestles in those ideas the principle of misery, and as the people cling to them, their life is a perpetual prey to the changing feelings of exultation and mortification.

The world is nothing but an aggregate of conditions.* Now, the conditions themselves are not self-existent, but are dependent upon one another. Those which do not possess self-existence are not real, but merely illusory. Therefore the whole world, as an aggregate of conditions, is a mere illusion. To look upon the world as real is mere folly on our part.

Where conditionality is, there is no truth; truth and conditionality are incompatible. Therefore, to attain to truth, conditionality must be completely cast aside. The eight conditional notions mentioned before must be thoroughly removed, and we should try to see the world as freed from all conditions. When our subjective mind is purified from the taint of conditionality, our ignorance will vanish away and the serene moonlight of 'Such-ness' or 'Transcendental Reality,' otherwise known as the 'Absolute,' will illumine us.

Here questions may be raised as to whether there is actually anything called 'Such-ness,' 'Transcendental Reality,' or the 'Absolute.' In answer to these questions, the Buddhists have said † that 'is' and 'is not'—that is, 'Being' and 'Non-being' or existence and non-existence—are conditional terms. The Transcendental Reality or the Absolute, which lies beyond all conditions, cannot be expressed in terms of 'is' and 'is not.' The Absolute lies beyond both 'Being' and 'Non-being.' It is, in fact, the unification or harmonization of the two. As the Absolute cannot be cognized in terms of our notions of the sense, understanding, or reason, we must be satisfied with describing it in our imperfect language as 'Unnameable' and 'Unknowable' (*avāchya* and *avijñaptika*).

The Nihilists, we have found, say ‡ that there is no permanent reality underlying the world. The Realists, on the other hand, affirm that there is at least one eternal Reality from which the world has emanated. The Buddhists, who abhor all sophisms, say that the Nihilists and Realists are holders of extreme views. The philosophy of 'is' or Being and the philosophy of 'is not' or Non-being are equally false. As the Buddhists avoid the philosophy of 'Being' as well as 'Non-being,' and choose a middle path, their ethical doctrine is often called the Middle Path Doctrine.

The Middle Path is to be understood from four standpoints: (1) the Middle Path in contradistinction to one-sidedness, (2) the Middle Path as the abnegation of one-sidedness, (3) the Middle Path in the sense of the absolute truth, and (4) the Middle Path as unity in plurality.§

The philosophy of Being held by the Realists and the philosophy of Non-being held by the Nihilists are both of them one-sided and therefore imperfect, because neither the Being nor the Non-being is possible, independently of the other. The doctrine of the Middle Path stands free from one-sidedness, as it repudiates and avoids the two extremes of Being and Non-being. This is the first aspect of the doctrine.

A Middle Path reveals itself when the two extremes are completely out of sight; in other words, the harmonization or unification of them leads to the perfect solution of existence. Neither the philosophy of Being nor the philosophy of Non-being should be adhered to. They condition each other, and anything conditional means imperfection, so the transcending of one-sidedness constitutes the second aspect of the Middle Path.

But when we forget that the doctrine of the Middle Path is intended for the removal of the intellectual prejudices, and cling to or assert the view that there is something called Middle Path beyond or between the two extremes of Being and Non-being, we commit the fault of one-sidedness over again, by creating a third statement in opposition to the two. As long as the truth is absolute and discards all limitations, clinging even to the Middle Path is against it. Thus we must avoid not only the two extremes but also the middle, and it should not be forgotten that the phrase 'Middle Path' has, from the deficiency of our language, been provisionally adopted to express the human conception of the highest truth.

The final aspect of the Middle Path is that it does not lie beyond the plurality of existence, but is in it underlying all. The antithesis of Being and Non-being is made possible only through the conception of the Middle Path, which is the unifying principle of the world. Remove this principle and the world will fall to pieces, and the particulars will cease to be. The Middle Path doctrine does not deny the existence of the world as it appears to us; it condemns, on the contrary, the doctrine which clings to the conception of Absolute Nothing. What the doctrine most emphatically maintains is that the world must be conceived in its totality—in its oneness, that is, from the standpoint of the Middle Path.

Nirvāna, according to the Vedāntists, is the absorption of the self into the Absolute. The Absolute, we have found, is something which is free from all contradictions, and which cannot be expressed in terms of 'is' and 'is not.' As soon as one reaches the Absolute, conditionality vanishes. This state is called Nirvāna. It is the harmonization of all contradictions. In this state, unity is harmonized with plurality, origination and cessation are accomplished in one and the same way, persistence is unified with discontinuance, and one and the same law operates in the acts of coming and going. It is, in fact, an unconditional condition in which Being and Non-being are unified. All conditionality having disappeared, our veil of ignorance is withdrawn. The fabric of the world, including that of the self, breaks up, leaving us to be identified with the Infinite, the Eternal, the Uncreated, the Unconditioned, the Formless, the Void. This is the state of Nirvāna. The finite mind altogether fails to comprehend this state, and no language can give adequate expression to it.

LITERATURE.—The Pāli works of the *Sutta-piṭaka* and *Abhidhamma-piṭaka* published by the London Pāli Text Society; *Mādhyamika-sūtra*, *Laṅkāvatāra-sūtra*, and the Journal, etc., published by the Buddhist Text Society of Calcutta; *Lalitavistara* (ed. by Rājendralāl Mitra in *Bibl. Indica*, 1853–1877 [French tr. by E. Foucaux, *AMG* xix. 1892]), *Aṣṭa-sāhasrikā Prajñā-pāramitā* (ed. Max Müller and B. Nanjio in *Anec. Oxon.*, Aryan ser., i. 3, Oxf. 1884 [and tr. in *SBE* xlix., Oxf. 1894]), etc., published by the Asiatic Society of Bengal; *Vedānta-sūtra*, translated by Dr. Thibaut in *SBE*; Max Müller, *Six Systems of Indian Philosophy*; P. Deussen, *System des Vedanta*², Leipzig, 1906; *Philosophie der Upanishads*, Leipzig, 1899, pp. 150 f., 347 ff. [Eng. tr., Edin. T. & T. Clark, 1906]; *Sechzig Upanishads des Veda*, Leipzig, 1897, p. 342 and *passim*; F. Max Müller, *Upanishads*, tr. in *SBE*, vols. i. and xv. *passim*; *Sarva-darśana-saṅgraha*, tr. Cowell and Gough, 2nd ed., London, 1894, p. 12 ff., *Bauddha System*; T. W. Rhys Davids, *Dialogues of the Buddha*, London, 1899, pp. 39 f., 44 ff., 187 ff.

SATIS CHANDRA VIDYABHUSANA.

* *Mādhyamikā-vritti*, ch. i.

† *Lalitavistara* (Rājendralāl's ed., Calcutta, p. 510; *Samādhirāja-sūtra* (*CBTS*), p. 30.

‡ *Mādhyamikā-vritti* (*CBTS* ed.), p. 41, etc.

§ J. Suzuki in *JBTS*, vol. vi. pt. 4.

ABSOLUTION (religious and ethical value of).—**1.** The idea of Absolution, as it appears in the Christian Church, is closely connected with two other ideas—the idea of sin, and the idea of the Church as a society. It is maintained, and may be true, that many of the practices and associations connected with Absolution took their origin in a state of mind to which ceremonial uncleanness seemed the thing most to be dreaded; but this fact, if it be a fact, does not affect the Christian view of Absolution. To the Christian mind, absolution is required when sin has been committed; *i.e.*, when some deliberate and voluntary defiance has been given to a moral law, which expresses the will of God, and the breach of which tends to separation from God. A soul, when it has sinned, requires to be forgiven; otherwise it remains in a permanent condition of alienation from God; and the authoritative declaration of its freedom from guilt, and reconciliation with God, is its absolution.

2. It is important that this should not be confused with the consciousness in the sinner that his sin is forgiven. The declaration of his freedom, however conveyed, may fail to carry conviction to his mind; or, again, he may have the strongest possible sense of forgiven sin without any decisive declaration of absolution at all. In other words, authoritative absolution and consciousness of forgiveness do not necessarily coexist: they may do so, but it is not necessary that they should.

3. It is obvious that, so far, we have considered only the relation of the individual soul and God. We have imagined the soul standing, as it were, alone in the world before the eyes of God, and receiving from Him the declaration of absolution. We have abstracted altogether this one relation from all its concomitants, the nature of sin, the ground of forgiveness, and the like. But it is plain that this abstract isolation is not the normal condition of any human soul. Every soul has an environment, which it affects, and by which it is affected; and no question of guilt or innocence, forgiveness or condemnation, is limited to the individual by himself. This truth, which goes far back into the history of man's ideas about himself, is emphatically presented in the Bible. Thus Ps 51, which gives expression most poignantly to the sense of personal guilt, also represents the sinner as born in a sinful environment: and again, Isaiah (6^{5}) is conscious not only that he is a man of unclean lips, but that he dwells among a people of unclean lips. Not only is sin a personal act of rebellion, but it produces a sinful atmosphere, a condition of alienation from God. In like manner, the absolution or declaration of freedom from sin cannot concern the individual alone: it must have an eye also to the society in which he lives and to his relations towards it.

4. We are not here concerned with the nature or process of forgiveness, or even with the conditions of it as regards God. The idea of Absolution brings forward only the place of sin and forgiveness in the Christian Society. It is not hard to illustrate this from the NT. We may notice, at once, the following points:—(1) It can scarcely be questioned that the Christian Society set out with an ethical purpose. Admission to it was by repentance, and by submitting to the rite which figured forth the remission of sins; and those who had become members of it were expected to lead a new life, abstaining from the sins which beset them in their 'former conversation.' It is but the corollary of this to say that sin after baptism involved a breach of the principle upon which the society was founded, no less than an outrage upon the Divine Law. All sin is lawlessness, the breach of some commandment enacted by God; and sin within the Church is more than this: it is a wilful disloyalty to the gifts which come through union with Christ, and, if carried on persistently, may place a man outside the reach of the sacrifice for sin (He 6^{4-6} $10^{26.\ 27.\ 39}$). (2) It is not less plain that the existence of post-baptismal sin forced a problem upon the attention of the Church with which its representatives were not slow to deal. In doing so, they doubtless rested for their authority upon words of Christ, such as we find in Mt $18^{18.\ 19}$ or Jn 20^{23}. The Epistles of St. Paul give instances of directions on disciplinary matters (1 Th 5^{14}, Ro 16^{17-20}, 1 Ti 4^{11-16}, and the like). St. Paul clearly contemplates the action of the Society in repressing evil, and even excluding evil-doers. But, of course, the clearest and most fully described case is that of the incestuous man at Corinth (1 Co 5). Here we find that the Corinthian Church had at first shown laxity in leaving the sin unrebuked. St. Paul, in the most solemn way, announces his decision in the matter (1 Co 5^{3-5}); the Corinthians clearly give effect to it in some way not recorded; and St. Paul (2 Co 2^{5-11}) exhorts them to comfort and restore the offender on his submission. The language used by St. Paul is not free from ambiguity. Though absent, he claims to act as if present at Corinth in association with the Church as a whole. And his judgment is to deliver 'such a one unto Satan for the destruction of the flesh, that the spirit may be saved in the day of the Lord' (1 Co 5^{5}) It is not clear what exactly is meant by this delivery to Satan, either here or in 1 Ti 1^{20}; but in both cases it seems to have been intended for discipline—for reformation with a view to restoration, not a final severance from the Society. Though, therefore, we cannot give any detailed description of the disciplinary measures of St. Paul, it is perfectly clear that he claimed to exercise such powers, that in so doing he assumed the co-operation of the Church, and that he regarded his judgments as valid: they are not merely strong expressions of reprobation, but judgments which will have consequences.

5. It has been necessary to approach the subject of Absolution indirectly as a special case of the exercise of discipline, because there is no direct discussion of it in Scripture, and the actual word never occurs. We do find, however, cases in which the Society exercises functions of discipline, such as those above alluded to, and these, when they take the form of a declaration of freedom from sin, correspond with the idea of Absolution. With these in view, it becomes necessary now to ask, what indications there are, if any, as to its meaning and validity. In answer to this we think that the following points may be safely asserted:

(1) The acts of the Society in discipline, and so in the exercise of Absolution, are spiritual acts, and have validity in the spiritual world. So much as this appears to follow from such words as Mt 18^{18-20} and Jn 20^{23}: what is bound on earth is bound in heaven: whosesoever sins the Society remits or retains, they are remitted or retained. It is true that the overt indication in the world of this disciplinary power consists merely of the confirmation or the withdrawal of the privilege to use the advantages of membership of the Society, to participate in the sacraments and so forth. But the functions of the Society cannot be limited to this. It is a spiritual society formed of persons held, in Christ, in certain close spiritual relations: not a loose aggregate of people individually in union with Christ, and casually connected in an outward society in the world. Such a division of the inward and outward relations of men in Christ is not Scriptural: the Church is a spiritual society of which the acts take place in the spiritual world: they have effect upon occasion in the world of sense, because they are already spiritually valid, not *vice versa*.

(2) The view of sin which makes the whole conception of Absolution possible is ethical and not legal. That is, the Church considers as requiring Absolution not merely overt acts which carry legal consequences in the State, but inward conditions, of which there is nothing more to be said than that they imply a tendency to rebellion against God. The State, like the Church, condemns thieves and murderers, because they are detrimental to its interests: the Church condemns also those who walk disorderly, who are proud, or impure in heart. If it were merely a casual aggregate of persons on its outward and social side, it could have no more concern with these things than the State: it claims that inward sins of the heart must be put away before the man can enjoy its privileges, because it is a spiritual society acting in the spiritual world.

(3) The exercise of discipline upon such conditions as these depends upon the voluntary acquiescence of the members of the Society. The Church is, no doubt, at liberty to say that it will not grant membership except upon condition of such acquiescence, and will punish any disloyalty to the principle. But it must trust ultimately to the voluntary submission of its members to the rule. The mode in which the rule is administered may vary widely from time to time: it is carried out by a general formula of confession and absolution, by a private particular confession to, and absolution by, an accredited minister, or by open individual confession and absolution in the public service of the Church. But the Church cannot, so long as it claims to be a spiritual society, disclaim or relinquish responsibility for the spiritual condition of its members.

It lies outside the scope of this article to consider the various casuistical questions which have arisen in the course of history over this matter. We will only add here the following remarks: (1) It in no way conflicts with the view here adopted that absolution may be, and has been, fraudulently administered. The whole problem of the visible Church is, and has always been, to make the outward order correspond with the spiritual reality it expresses: and it has always been impeded by sin. The individual who seeks absolution without penitence, or the priest who fraudulently declares him absolved, commits a great sin: just as Ananias and Sapphira or Simon Magus committed a great sin. But the fact that insincere penitence or fraudulent absolution has occurred in the Church no more disturbs its general character and principles, than did the fraud of Ananias and Sapphira or the base motive of Simon Magus. The action of St. Peter on the two occasions shows the place of such disorders in the outward history of the Church.

(2) It is impossible to deny that the gravest evils have come from the misuse of the disciplinary power of the Church, especially of one particular mode of administering it: and the existence of these has brought the whole subject into disrepute. At the same time, it is difficult to read the Epistles of St. Paul, especially those chapters in which he lets us see into the internal conditions of the early Societies of Christians, without feeling how largely the Church depended for its advance upon a strong discipline, fearlessly exercised over its members. The case at Corinth, to which we have already referred, was, we may hope, exceptional. Yet a very serious situation would clearly have arisen if it had not been for St. Paul's action. The sin was one which public opinion among the pagans condemned (1 Co 5[1]), but the machinery of the Church, as it was, provided apparently no means of dealing drastically with it: St. Paul's strong denunciation was required to rouse the Corinthians to the necessary severity. It is easy to see from this, and the impression is continually confirmed by early Church history, that a weak discipline implies a feeble consciousness of the Church's moral standard, and allows the existence within its pale of a variety of lower and more worldly ideals beside its own. It would be difficult to deny that the almost total absence of discipline of any kind in modern Christian communities bears a similar implication.

LITERATURE.—See under CONFESSION and PENITENCE.

THOMAS B. STRONG.

ABSOLUTISM.—(*a*) *In philosophical speculation*: a method of interpreting reality which starts from the point of view of, and constructs a system by direct reference to, the complete unity of the whole. This self-contained unity is in metaphysics named the Absolute (q.v.). (*b*) *In æsthetics*: a view of the nature of Beauty which regards the quality of the beautiful as a constitutive character of the object as such, and in itself, independently of the judgments or emotions of the subject. This is 'æsthetic absolutism.' (*c*) *In politics*: a form of political government from, or by means of, a single supreme source of authority concentrated in the will of a specific individual, and executing its demands from itself and for itself, with or without the consent of the will of the community. It is in the main identical with Despotism (see GOVERNMENT).

J. B. BAILLIE.

ABSTINENCE.—See ASCETICISM.

ABSTRACTION (*abs-trahere*, 'to draw off *or* separate') is the separation or detachment of one part or element in a total experience from the whole to which it belongs. To abstract is thus to isolate any portion of the content of experience from its setting, and to consider it for the time being as it is in itself, 'loose and separate' from the structural and functional relations which belong to it in the concrete conscious life. Psychologically, Abstraction is the necessary condition and accompaniment of Attention (which see). To attend to one object of experience implies the withdrawal of attention from other objects.

Professor James (*Princ. of Psychology*, i. 403) says: Attention 'is the taking possession by the mind, in clear and vivid form, of one out of what seem several simultaneously possible objects or trains of thought. Focalization, concentration, of consciousness is of its essence. It implies withdrawal from some things in order to deal effectively with others.' Similarly, Sir William Hamilton (*Logic*, Lect. vii.) writes: 'The result of Attention, by concentrating the mind upon certain qualities, is thus to withdraw or abstract it from all else. In technical language, we are said *to prescind* the phenomena we exclusively consider. *To prescind, to attend*, and *to abstract* are merely different but correlative names for the same process; and the first two are nearly convertible. When we are said to prescind a quality, we are supposed to attend to that quality exclusively; and when we abstract, we are properly said *to abstract from*, that is, to throw other attributes out of account. I may observe that the term *abstraction* is very often abusively employed. By Abstraction we are frequently said to attend exclusively to certain phenomena—those, to wit, which we abstract; whereas the term *abstraction* is properly applied to the qualities which we abstract from; and by abstracting from some we are enabled to consider others more attentively. Attention and Abstraction are only the same process viewed in different relations. They are, as it were, the positive and negative poles of the same act.'

In spite of Hamilton's protest against using the term 'abstraction' as applying to the elements to which we attend,—a protest previously made by Kant (*Logik*, § 6),—the usage has persisted. As we shall presently notice, abstraction plays a part in the formation of concepts or general ideas. It is usually said that by abstraction the identical or similar elements or attributes in a number of different objects are singled out and combined into a general concept. Thus by abstracting from the objects denoted by man, horse, bird, fish, etc., the common property or identity of structure, we form the concept of 'vertebrate.' Without now raising the question whether concepts are formed solely by abstraction, we may notice that the essential element in abstraction is not the omission of the characteristics which are unlike, but the focussing of consciousness on what is similar in the different cases. This Kant himself admits, and in applying the term 'abstraction' to the process of separating out the common elements, the usage of logic agrees with that of grammar and of ordinary life.

It is essential in considering the nature of abstraction, to distinguish carefully the psychological from the logical discussion of the subject. We may describe abstraction psychologically as a process of isolation, closely correlated with active attention, and go on to exhibit its various forms and characteristics in terms of the structural mechanism of the conscious elements. From the logical point of view, however, abstraction has to be considered as playing a part in knowledge. Here we have to deal, not with its psychological form or structure, but with its function or purpose in the development of the intellectual life. This distinction of standpoint does much to clear away the difficulties and confusions which attended the older discussions of the subject. For example, it puts in a new light the point at issue between Locke and Berkeley regarding the existence of abstract general ideas. It is possible to grant Berkeley's contention that abstract ideas must exist psychologically as particulars in individual form, and at the same time to maintain that as functions of the knowledge-process, *i.e.* as logical ideas, they necessarily transcend their individual mode of existence and are real universals.

The question then arises as to the relation of the knowledge-process to the ideas viewed as psychical content. Can the psychological states of consciousness be regarded as the original form from which the logical idea is derived by abstraction? This has been very commonly maintained. Mr. F. H. Bradley tells us that a logical meaning 'consists of a part of the content (original or acquired) cut off, fixed by the mind, and considered apart from the existence of the sign.' The whole trend of modern logic (including Mr. Bradley's own work) shows conclusively, however, that it is impossible to begin with 'mental states' and pass by way of abstraction to logical ideas. The view of the cognitive side of consciousness, as at first made up of particular images or ideas, is now acknowledged to be a fiction. And similarly we must reject the *quasi*-mechanical account of the formation of general ideas which is based on this fiction, according to which we are said first to abstract the common element from the particular images and then proceed further to generalize it, thus in some mysterious way transforming it into a logical idea. But we cannot derive knowledge from an anoetic process, and therefore must postulate that consciousness is from its first beginnings a process of interpretation and generalization. It starts from a content that is a vague presentation continuum, lacking both differentiation and integration, and, as such, not yet either particular or universal. It is the work of intelligence to transform this into a coherent system of parts. Now it must constantly be borne in mind that it is within this total knowledge-process, and as contributory to it, that abstraction finds its function and justification. It is not the end or essence of thinking, but a process or method which thought uses in the accomplishment of its own ends. The purpose which it fulfils is closely related to that of Analysis, though the specific method of abstraction has its own differentia. 'The reflective idea which guides it,' says Bosanquet, 'is the equivalent in general knowledge of the mathematical axiom that if equals be taken from equals the remainders are equal.' But, as within any real whole the withdrawal of one part never leaves the other parts unaffected, the guiding idea of abstraction is only provisional. 'It amounts to no more than this, that within known wholes known changes may appear to leave remainders known *as unchanged*' (*Logic*, ii. 22 f.).

Abstraction as a specific process is thus only a provisional expedient; and, unless corrected by a more adequate conception of the nature of the whole, it is likely in most fields to lead to error. But thinking proceeds both by concretion and abstraction, and these two moments are never entirely distinct and separate. Aristotle, and the formal logicians following him, have seemed to oppose Abstraction (ἀφαίρεσις) and Determination (πρόσθεσις). When, however, we emphasize the unity of the intellectual process within which both these functions operate, we see that the opposition can never be more than relative. Abstraction and Determination, like Analysis and Synthesis (within which they may be said to be included), imply each other as complementary moments of real thinking. The goal which thought seeks is not to be gained by passing to the highest abstraction; for this is the emptiest of all thoughts. Nor can it be reached by the determination of a plurality of particulars. But the methods of abstraction and determination must unite in defining experience in terms of a concrete universal. It is against the abuse of abstraction, against making isolation and mutilation the final goal of thinking, and thus neglecting the organic wholeness and unity of things, that Hegel's criticism is chiefly directed. The process of abstraction is for him never an end in itself, but only a means in the progress towards greater unity and concreteness.

LITERATURE.—B. Maennel, *Ueber Abstraktion* (1890); A. Meinong, *Vierteljahrschr. f. wissen. Phil.* (1888) 329 ff., and *ZP* xxiv. 34 ff.; Bosanquet, *Logic*, 1898, ii. 21 ff.; J. Ward, *Naturalism and Agnosticism*[2] (1903), i. 255 ff.; Baldwin, *DPhP*, *s.v.*, and the literature under ATTENTION, PSYCHOLOGY.

J. E. CREIGHTON.

ĀBŪ (Mount).—A famous mountain and place of Hindu and Jain pilgrimage, rising like an island out of the great plain of Rājputāna, in the native State of Sirohi. The name is derived from its Skr. title *Arbuda*, 'a serpent,' 'a long round mass,' perhaps from the root *arb*, 'to go,' 'to hurt,' probably with reference to its form. Its summit, *Guru Śikhara*, 'Peak of the Teacher,' rises to a height of 5,653 feet above the level of the sea.

'It is hardly to be wondered at,' writes Fergusson (*History of Indian and Eastern Architecture*, ed. 1899, p. 234), 'that Mount Ābū was early fixed upon by the Hindus and Jains as one of their sacred spots. Rising from the desert as abruptly as an island from the ocean, it presents on every side inaccessible scarps 5000 ft. or 6000 ft. high, and the summit can be approached only by ravines cut into its sides. When the summit is reached, it opens out into one of the loveliest valleys imaginable, 6 or 7 miles long by 2 or 3 miles in width, cut up everywhere by granite rocks of the most fantastic shapes, and the spaces between covered with trees and luxuriant vegetation. The little Nucki Talao [properly Nakhī Talāo, as it was supposed to have been excavated by the nails (Skr. *nakha*) of the gods] is one of the loveliest gems of its class in India, and it is near to it, at Dilwarra, that the Jains selected a place for their Tirth [Skr. *tīrtha*] or sacred place of rendezvous. It cannot, however, be said that it has been a favourite place of worship in modern times. Its distance and inaccessibility are probably the causes of this, and it consequently cannot rival Palitāna or Girnār in the extent of its buildings.'

Tod styles Mount Ābū 'the Olympus of India,' because in olden times it was reputed to be the favourite residence of the gods, and was believed to be the scene of two famous events in Hindu mythology. Here the *munis* (or sages), of whom Vasiṣṭha, a worshipper of Śiva, was the leader, practised austerities, living on milk and the fruits of the earth. There was then no mountain, but only a cleft in the plain, into which the cow that supplied the wants of the sage fell, and was miraculously floated out by a rise of water from beneath. To prevent the recurrence of such an accident, the sage prayed to Śiva, then enthroned on the Kailāsa peak of the Himālaya. He called on the sons of Himāchal, the deified mountain range, to relieve the saint. The youngest son of Himāchal volunteered to exile himself, and, mounted on the serpent Takshaka, he journeyed to the holy land. At the behest of the sage he leaped into the cleft, embraced, as he fell, by the serpent god. Within the cleft the snake writhed so violently that Vasiṣṭha appealed again to Śiva, who from the depths of Pātāla, the nether-world, raised his toe until it appeared at the top of the mountain, which was thus formed by the god. Hence, under the title of *Achala Īśvara*, 'Immovable Lord,' Śiva has become the patron deity of the hill. But in accordance with the eclectic spirit of Hinduism, this does not prevent the place from becoming a site sacred both to Vaiṣṇavas and Jains. The second legend tells of the creation of the *Agnikula*, or 'fire-born' septs of the Rājputs. The *Daityas*, or demons, it is said, disturbed the performance of the rites of Siva on the hill. Viśvāmitra, another sage, appealed to the gods, who proceeded to the spot, and out of the *Agnikuṇḍa*, or fire-pit, in which the fire-sacrifice was performed, created the four *Agnikula*, or 'fire-born' septs—Chauhān, Parihāra, Solanki, and Pramāra, who destroyed the Daityas, and restored the cult of Śiva. Both these legends seem to indicate some early conflict of rival cults, the nature of which is unknown.

The chief Hindu religious sites are, first, the crowning peak of Guru Sikhara, where in a cavern are to be seen the footprints of the saint Dātuvrija, presided over by some dissolute-looking Gaṇapati priests, and those of Rāmānanda, the great apostle of the Vaiṣṇava cultus. At the temple of Achala Īśvara, which is now, according to Cousens, in a state of deplorable decay and neglect, is shown the toe-nail of Śiva in a cleft of the rock. His female counterpart is worshipped as Adharā Devī and Arbuda Mātā, the Mother-goddess of the hill. The sage Vasiṣṭha is honoured at a shrine called *Bastonjī*, or *Gaumukha*, 'Cow-mouth,' where a fountain falls from a spout shaped like a cow's head. To the W. of this is the shrine of the saint Gotamjī, or Gautama Ṛishi, containing two images, one of Viṣṇu and the other of a female beside a male bearded figure. The temples at Devāngan, 'Court of the Gods,' have not been fully described, if they have ever been visited, by an European, the approach being over rugged, dangerous rocks. The largest is dedicated to Viṣṇu, and close to it is Narasiṁha, the fourth Avatāra, or incarnation of the god, said to be one of the finest images on the hill.

Of the Jain temples at Delvāda or Devalvāda, 'place of temples,' two are described by Fergusson as 'unrivalled for certain qualities by any temples in India.' The first was built by Vimala, a merchant Jain prince, about A.D. 1032, two years after the death of that arch-raider Mahmūd of Ghazni, who desecrated the older temples. It is dedicated to Ṛishabhadeva, the first Jaina *arhat*, or saint. The original image was destroyed by the Musalmāns, and that now in the temple is the second or perhaps the third in succession. The second great temple was built by the brothers Tejapāla and Vastupāla between A.D. 1197 and 1247. It is in honour of the 23rd *arhat*, Pārśvanātha, the only one in the series readily identifiable by the many-headed serpent's hood which rises above him. Both these temples are built of white marble, though no quarry of this material is known to exist within 300 miles of the spot, and the stone could have been conveyed up the rugged slopes of the hill only by incredible exertions and at enormous cost. Both these remarkable buildings have been fully described by Fergusson, whose account is supplemented and in part corrected by that of Cousens.

Ābū was once the haunt of a colony of those loathsome ascetics, the Aghorīs, but they have long since disappeared.

LITERATURE.—Tod, *Annals of Rajasthān*, Calcutta reprint, i. 96 ff., *Travels in W. India*, 101 ff.; Fergusson, *Picturesque Illustrations of Architecture in Hindostan*, 39 f., *Hist. of Indian and Eastern Architecture*, ed. 1899, 234 ff.; Cousens, *Progress Report, Arch. Survey of W. India*, for 1901, p. 2 ff.; Rowland, *Indian Antiquary*, ii. 249 ff. In the editor's note to the last article, some of the Ābū inscriptions are given as a supplement to those recorded by H. H. Wilson, *Asiatic Researches*, xvi. 284 ff. The place has been well described by Major C. A. Baylay in *Rājputāna Gazetteer* (1880), iii. 129 ff., to which this article is largely indebted.

W. CROOKE.

ABUSE, ABUSIVE LANGUAGE

ABUSE, ABUSIVE LANGUAGE (Gr. λοιδορεῖν; Lat. *contumeliâ afficere, conviciari*; Ger. *schimpfen, lästern*; Fr. *maudire*).—Abuse in general denotes an evil use of a thing caused by excess or injustice; in law it denotes 'to injure, diminish in value or wear away by using improperly.' Examples of such abuse are signified in the phrases 'abuse of authority,' 'abuse of confidence,' 'abuse of privilege,' 'abuse of legal process,' in all of which the *use* is assumed as determined by corrective justice, and its opposite, the *abuse*, is a departure, either in the way of defect or excess, from the mean laid down by corrective justice. In this article we are concerned, however, only with a narrower signification of the term 'abuse,' viz. that which deals with the improper use of language, and yet more narrowly with such an improper use as tends to the injury or harm of another human being. Abuse in this narrower and colloquial sense, then, denotes all that class of injuries which are inflicted on others by the means of language, under the sway of passion or any other motive opposed to the principle of justice, or of love, or of both. It ranges from blasphemy at the one end to the 'jesting which is not convenient' at the other, and varies according to the spirit which produces it or the means adopted for its manifestation. It is usefully classed by Aquinas under the heads of contumely (*contumelia*), detraction (*detractio*), backbiting (*susurrus*), ridicule (*derisio*), and cursing (*maledictio*).

1. **Contumely** is an injury inflicted in words, whereby there is denied to a man some good quality on account of which he is held in honour, or whereby some concealed fact to his discredit is unnecessarily and uncharitably made public. If, for example, it is said of a man that he is blind, this is abuse indeed, but of less gravity than if he were charged with being a thief. Another and more venial form of abuse is to reflect needlessly on a man's defect, as, *e.g.*, that he is of lowly birth, or that he has been badly educated, or that he spent a wild and profligate youth, such things being said in order to deprive the person of whom they are said of some honour he has won for himself by virtuous conduct or public service. Such language is to be placed under the general head of *contumely*, as a form of abusive language which has its root in anger and has pride for its foster-mother. It is a kind of revenge, and is indeed the readiest and easiest form in which revengeful feelings find expression.

2. **Detraction** differs from contumely both in its object and in its source. It does not seek so much to rob a man of his honour as to blacken his reputation, and it springs from envy rather than from anger. It effects its purpose (1) directly by bringing a false charge, by exaggerating a fault, by revealing a hidden defect, or by imputing an evil motive; and (2) indirectly by denying, concealing, or minimizing what is meritorious. 'He that filches from me my good name robs me of that which not enriches him, and makes me poor indeed.' The words used may not be contumelious—in the case of Iago they included both contumely and detraction—but they are abuse, and abuse of the worst kind.

3. **Backbiting**, whispering, or innuendo is another form of abusive language which has for its object the separating of friends. The detractor abuses language by saying what is evil about his neighbour *simpliciter*; the whisperer injures him *secundum quid*, viz. by saying of a man what will alienate his friend. 'Sin against our neighbour is so much the greater as the greater loss is inflicted, and the loss is the greater as the good taken away is greater. But the loss of a friend is a great loss, and therefore the whisperer is a great sinner.'

4. **Ridicule**, when apart from love, is a further abuse of language. The three forms of abuse mentioned above tend to deprive a man of some external good, such as honour, reputation, or friends. Derision, however, goes to deprive a man of his inward peace, the testimony of a good conscience. It is to be classed with contumely, de-

traction, and whispering as abusive language, but it differs from them in its end. It holds a man up to scorn for some evil in him or some defect, and springs from contempt for him,—a contempt which is rooted in pride and finds enjoyment in the contrast between the person who is ridiculed and the ridiculer. It is this special form of abusive language which is condemned by Jesus Christ in the sayings (Mt 5[22]) in which He forbids contempt for a man's intellectual qualities (expressed by *raca*), or for his moral qualities (expressed by *moreh*).

5. Cursing is abusive language whereby evil is pronounced against a man in the imperative or the optative mood. Words which inflict deserved punishment (as in the case of Gehazi, 2 K 5[27]), or state a fact (as in the case of Adam and Eve, Gn 3[16ff.]), or express abhorrence of evil in itself (as David and the mountains of Gilboa, 2 S 1[21]), or are used symbolically ('*Dominus maledixit ficulneum in significationem Judææ*'), do not come under this definition, and are not, therefore, of the nature of abusive language. To curse is 'to pronounce against anyone, in the name of religion, or under the impulse of some violent movement of the soul, words of reprobation or of condemnation.' God's name is either explicitly used, or lies implicit in the current forms, especially those in use among the more uncultured classes. To this it seems necessary to add that in these classes sexual processes or aberrations are largely drawn on for the purpose of supplying the vocabulary of abuse, a fact which serves the purpose of demonstrating incidentally the close connexion between sensual indulgence and contempt or hatred or scorn of our fellows. The peevishness which finds expression in abusive language directed against others is at bottom a deep-seated discontent with self.

The subject of blasphemy (q.v.) is beyond the scope of this article, and the only remark to be made here about it is that cursing any creature as a creature comes under that head.

Abusive language, when it is used in the hearing of several persons in a public place (even when the name of God is not uttered, but words importing an imprecation of future Divine vengeance only), may constitute profane swearing, and is a nuisance at common law. Blasphemy and profane swearing differ at law only in this, that blasphemy is a word of larger meaning.

LITERATURE.—Thomas Aquinas, *Summa*, II. ii. 13 and 72–76; Aristotle, *Eth. Nikom.* viii. 9; Grimm, *Deutsches Wörterbuch*, *s.v.* 'Schimpfen'; Migne, *Encyc.* tom. xxxii. col. 263 ff.; *American and English Encyc. of Law*, *s.v.* 'Abuse'; Profane Oaths Act, 1745; Stephen, *Com. on the Laws of England*, iv. 193–194; Town Police Clauses Act, 1847, § 28.

W. F. COBB.

ABYSS (ἄβυσσος).—The Greek word, of which our 'abyss' is a transliteration, occurs in the classics as an adjective signifying 'bottomless,' 'boundless.' It is composed of the intensive ἀ, and βυσσός = βυθός, 'depth.' In the LXX it represents *tĕhōm* (תְּהוֹם) and *ṣûlāh* (צוּלָה). Most of the passages in the Bible where it is employed belong to the poetical books, and are of late date. Seeing also that the Pentateuch was the first part of the Bible to be turned into Greek, we must regard Gn 1[2] as the earliest instance of its use, so far as our investigation is concerned. What, then, is the meaning of *tĕhōm* (תְּהוֹם), the word for which it stands? The answer must be sought outside the limits of our extant Heb. literature. Dillmann and others have, indeed, been inclined to derive it from *hūm* (הוּם), 'to roar *or* rage'; but it is so obviously cognate with the *Tiāmat* of Bab. cosmogony that we must look on the *t* as part of the root. Jensen's suggestion (adopted in *KAT*[3] 492) is that the root is *tāham* (תָּהַם), 'to stink.' The *Oxf. Heb. Lex.* argues that תהם is probably the root, 'in view of As. *tiâmtu*, *tāmtu*.' In any case, *Tĕhōm*, like *Tiāmat*, was a proper noun, 'Deep,' not 'the deep.' Frequent as are its appearances in the OT, it is almost invariably without the article. Turning now to that Babylonian conception, of which the Heb., if a derivative,* is a greatly modified one, we find that *Tiāmat* was the dark and watery chaos, the primeval undifferentiated matter, out of which gods and men, heaven and earth sprang. Berosus (*c.* 275 B.C.) conveys the idea (τὸ πᾶν σκότος καὶ ὕδωρ), and Wis 11[17] has the same in view (ὕλη ἄμορφος). Such a chaos is postulated in the myths of Egyptians, Phœnicians, Indians, and Greeks. Hesiod, *e.g.*, *Theog.* 115, asserts: ἤτοι μὲν πρώτιστα χάος γένετ' κ.τ.λ. The well-known Bab. legend opens thus:

> 'When on high the heavens were unnamed,
> Beneath, the earth bore not a name;
> The primeval ocean (*apsû rêstû*) was their producer;
> Mummu Tiamtu was she who begat the whole of them.
> Their waters in one united themselves, and
> The plains were not outlined, marshes were not to be seen.'
> (Pinches, *Old Test.* etc., p. 16).

There is a substantially correct reproduction of this legend in the Syrian writer Damascius (6th cent. A.D.), who states that the Babylonians believed in two principles of the universe, Tauthé and Apason, the latter being Tauthé's husband. Apason, here, is evidently the same as *Apsû* (= the waters under, around, and above the earth, especially the sweet waters in contrast to Tiāmat, the salt), whilst Tauthé (Berosus, Θαμτέ) is *Tiāmat*. The latter also sometimes bears the name *Bahu* (the בֹּהוּ *bōhû* = 'emptiness,' of Gn 1[2], LXX ἀκατασκεύαστος), the Phœnician *Baau*, mother of the first men. Here we have the origin of the Heb. idea of the abyss. Gunkel (*Schöpf. u. Chaos*, 15) has pointed out that such a picture of the primal state of the universe would naturally present itself in a land like Babylonia, where the winter rains pour down from heaven and, uniting with the streams and rivers, turn all things into chaos: only when spring returns do land and water take their separate places. This idea reached the Hebrews through the medium of Phœnicians and Canaanites, and was reinforced by a similar Egyptian idea of a boundless primeval water (*Nun*), which filled the universe and contained the germ of all existence. We may therefore say, with Trevisa (1398): 'The primordiall and fyrste matere in the begynnynge of the worlde not dystinguyd by certayn fourme is called Abyssus.' In it were the potencies of the life that would hereafter appear.† The process, according to the Bab. theory, was one of evolution; according to Gn 1, it was determined wholly by the creative fiat of God.

The memory of the original abyss was kept up by the 'seas' and 'abysses' which were common in the temples of Babylonia. Urninā of Lagas (*c.* 4000 B.C.) set up a greater and a smaller *apsû* (Gunkel, pp. 28, 153). Argum (*c.* 17th cent. B.C.) placed a *tamtu*, or sea, in Marduk's shrine. 'This was, no doubt, a large basin or "laver," similar to the brazen sea of Solomon's temple which stood upon twelve oxen' (King, *Bab. Rel.* (1899) p. 109).

The recalcitrancy of matter and the struggle of darkness against light are portrayed in the myth of *Tiāmat*, as a dragon-like monster, fighting with Marduk, but slain by him. Out of one half of her body he constructed a vault (the earth), the two ends of which rest on the ocean (*apsû*). A similar picture of the position of the earth is present to the Heb. poet's mind when he declares that

* A. Jermias declares (*Das AT im Lichte des Alten Orients*) that borrowing on either side, or direct dependence, is not to be thought of.

† Didron (*Christian Iconog.* ii. 127) copies a miniature from a 10th cent. MS—a small, conical mound, divided into stages by spiral bands. The lowest zone contains birds, the next fishes, then vegetation, finally a human head issues from the summit. By the side is written 'Abissus.'

Jahweh has 'founded it upon seas and established it upon floods' (Ps 24^{2}). The disc of the earth rests on the all-surrounding ocean, and the 'waters under the earth' are called *tĕhōm* or *tĕhōm rabbā*, 'abyss,' 'great abyss' (Gn 7^{11} 8^{2}, Dt 8^{7} 33^{13}, Am 7^{4}, Pr 3^{20} 8^{24}), whose fountains are broken up at the Flood, from which well up the sources that fertilize the land and (Ezk 31^{4}) refresh the trees. It is in this sense that Clem. Rom. (I. xx.) speaks of the inscrutable depths of the abysses (*ἀβύσσων τε ἀνεξιχνίαστα*). Trevisa also says: 'Abyssus is depnesse of water vnseen, and therof come and springe welles and ryuers.'

Tĕhōm or 'Abyss' is a frequent designation of the oceans and seas, without any reference to their being 'under the earth.' And although there is no trace of the refractoriness of matter in the narrative of Gn 1, this comes out strongly in many references to the sea (Is 50^{2} 51^{10}, Jer 5^{22}, Ps 77^{16} 104^{6-9} 106^{9} 107^{24} 135^{6} 148^{7}, Pr 8^{29}, Job 7^{12} 26^{12} $38^{8ff.}$, Sir 43^{23}, Pr. Man 3, En 60^{7-9}, Rev 21^{1}).

The question has been raised whether the תְּהֹמוֹת of Ps 71^{20} should not be corrected to תַּחְתִּיּוֹת (cf. Ps 63^{10} 139^{15}, Is 44^{23}). However that may be, the LXX has 'abysses' (*ἄβυσσοι*), which word, either in the sing. or the plur., became one of the names for Hades. In the verse in question it points to the profound depths of the invisible world, from which the persecuted are to be brought back again. The Bab. scheme of the universe also locates the abode of the dead in the heart of the earth, making the entrance thereto lie in the extreme west (*KAT*[3] 636), designating it 'the country whence none return,' dividing it into seven zones, corresponding to the seven planetary spheres (Lenormant, *Chald. Magic*, 165, 169); cf. Mt 12^{40}, Ph 2^{10}. Enoch (17^{6}) sees in the west the great streams and the great flood, and enters into the great darkness [of Hades], into which all flesh comes. In the only classical passage where *ἄβυσσος* is a noun, it is employed for Hades (Diog. Laert. *Epig.* iv. 27, *χοὔτω κατῆλθες εἰς μέλαιναν Πλουτέως ἄβυσσον*).

To take yet another step is easy. מְצוּלָה יָם (Job 41^{23}) is represented in the LXX by *τὸν δὲ τάρταρον τῆς ἀβύσσου*. This is a free translation by an Alexandrian Hellenist, who knew his classics (Swete, *Introd. to OT in Greek*, pp. 256, 318), and remembered that Tartarus was a prison, a murky pit, into which Zeus threatens to cast any god who may venture to oppose him (*Il.* viii. 11–16), as far beneath Hades as this is below the earth (cf. *Τάρταρά τ' ἠνεμόεντα μυχῷ χθονὸς εὐρυοδείης*, Hes. *Theog.* 120). Now at Job 38^{16} *Sheol* is at the bottom of the sea, and we here (41^{23} LXX) find hell in the same locality, for the sea-monster Leviathan considers the Tartarus of the abyss his captive. The Book of Enoch often speaks of the abyss as a place of punishment. The traveller reaches a deep abyss, in which are lofty pillars of fire, some of them prostrate (18^{11-16}). Here is the prison of the rebellious angels; he sees a place with a cleft or chasm (*διακοπή*) running down into the abyss. Uriel informs him that the angels are imprisoned there for ever (21^{7-11}); judgment began with the stars, which were found guilty and cast into an abyss full of fire (90^{24}). English writers have freely used the word as an equivalent for 'hell.' Lydgate (1413) says: 'This pytte is the chyef and the manoyr of helle that is clepid Abissus.'

We pass to the NT. The abyss is the ordinary abode of demons who, having been permitted to take temporary possession of a man, now deprecate being remanded to their own place, because their power of doing mischief is thus terminated (Lk 8^{31}); it is Hades, where the spirits of the departed dwell, where Christ spent the interval between death and resurrection (Ro 10^{7}). 'Ipsa anima fuit in abysso' (Ambrose). The impression conveyed by St. Paul's language is of the vastness of that realm, as of one that we should vainly attempt to explore. The abyss communicates with our earth by a pit or shaft (*φρέαρ*), Rev 9^{1-11}, with which the *διακοπή* of En 21^{7} should be compared. According to the Tractate *Sukkah* of the Talmud, the mouth of this pit is under the foundations of the temple, and can be closed by magical formulæ: 'Qua hora David fodiebat fundamenta templi, exundavit abyssus mundum submersurus. Dixit David: Estne hic, qui sciat, an liceat testæ inscribere nomen ineffabile, et projiciemus illam in abyssum, ut quiescat?' (Bousset, *Die Offenbarung Johannis*, p. 251). When the *φρέαρ* of Rev 9 is opened, there issue from it poisonous, stinging locusts, which cause exquisite anguish to men. Over them is a king, 'the angel of the abyss,' whose Greek name, *Apollyon*, represents pretty accurately his Heb. title *Abaddon*. This is a different point of view from that of En 20^{1}, where *Uriel* is designated the holy angel who presides over both the angelic host and Tartarus. At Pr 15^{11} 27^{20} etc., Abaddon is parallel to Sheol, and the Rabbis make it a name of the lowest pit of hell. The abyss, then, in the present passage, as in Lk 8^{31}, is the abode of the ministers of torment, from which they go forth to do hurt. In the Bab. documents, demons and spirits of disease proceed from hell:

> 'They, the productions of the infernal regions,
> On high they bring trouble, and below they bring confusion.'
> (Lenormant, *Chald. Magic*, p. 30).

The Rabbis, too, represent Sammael and his angels as emerging thence (Eisenmenger, *Entdeckt. Jud.* ii. 336 f.). The abyss of Rev 11^{7} 17^{8} is put in the same light: a beast which occasions calamities to the saints arises out of it. The dragon, 'that old serpent, which is the devil, and Satan,' is shut up therein, and its mouth is sealed for a thousand years (20^{3}). The language in which this is set forth should be compared with Prayer of Manasses 3:

> *ὁ πεδήσας τὴν θάλασσαν τῷ λόγῳ τοῦ*
> *προστάγματος αὐτοῦ,*
> *ὁ κλείσας τὴν ἄβυσσον καὶ σφραγισάμενος*
> *αὐτὴν τῷ φοβερῷ καὶ ἐνδόξῳ ὀνόματί σου.*

In the *Rituale Romanum*, part of the formula of Exorcism runs: 'Cede Ergo Deo + qui te, et malitiam tuam in pharaone, et in exercitu ejus per Moysen servum suum in abyssum demersit': with this cf. Jubilees 48^{14}.

The Gnostics, as might have been expected, made an altogether different use of the idea of the abyss. Their special name for it was *Βυθός*, *Bythus*, and by this they meant the Divine first principle, the fountain of all existence, the infinite, unfathomable, inscrutable abyss of Deity:

> 'A vast, unfathomable sea,
> Where all our thoughts are drowned.'

Λέγουσι γάρ τινα εἶναι ἐν ἀοράτοις καὶ ἀκατονομάστοις ὑψώμασι τέλειον Αἰῶνα προόντα· τοῦτον δὲ καὶ [προαρχὴν καὶ] προπατόρα καὶ βυθὸν καλοῦσιν (Iren. *adv. Hær.* i. 1: 'For they say that in the invisible and nameless heights there is a certain perfect, pre-existing Æon. And they call him [first principle and] progenitor and Bythus'). Hippolytus (vi. 37) bears the same testimony: speaking of Valentinus, he says: *ὑπεστήσατο τὸν πάντων βασιλέα ὃν ἔφη Πλάτων, οὗτος πατέρα καὶ βυθὸν καὶ [προαρχὴν ?] τῶν ὅλων αἰώνων* ('He whom Plato spoke of as King of all, this man postulated as father and Bythus and first principle [?] of all the æons'). The Valentinians held that by a process of self-limitation the *Bythus* evolved a series of pairs of æons, male and female, any pair of which may be called the *pleroma*, the latter name being also given to the whole series taken together, which then stands to the *Bythus* in the feminine relation, as *Tiāmat* did to *Apsū*. But Gnosticism never formed a homogeneous body of opinion. There were, as Hippolytus warns us, many varying opinions concerning the *Bythus* itself. According to some thinkers, he was outside the *pleroma*: others held him to be within it, but separated from the rest by *Horus* (Ὅρος), a personified boundary (Lightfoot, *Coloss.* p. 332). There were some who actually deposed him from his place at the head of the series, and made him follow the first ogdoad. Some thought of him as unwedded, and neither male nor female; whilst others again gave him *Sigē* as his consort, or the two powers Thought and Will (Hippol. *loc. cit.*). The relation of Gnostic speculation on the *Bythus* to later philosophical thought is perhaps sufficiently indicated in one sentence of Irenæus, *ap.* Epiphan. xxxii. 7: *Οἱ μὲν γὰρ αὐτὸν ἄζυγον λέγουσιν, μήτε ἄρρενα, μήτε θήλειαν, μήτε ὅλως ὄντα τι.* ('For some say that he is unwedded and is neither male nor female, nor, in fact, anything at all'). He was exalted above all contrarieties—the Absolute, identical with Nothing, the Being of whom even existence might not be predicated. No wonder that the Mystics took up both the thought and the term: 'I saw and knew the being of all things, the Byss and the Abyss, and the eternal generation of the Holy Trinity, the descent and original of the world and of all creatures through the Divine wisdom' (Jacob Behmen, quoted by James, *Varieties of Rel. Experience*, p. 411).

LITERATURE.—In addition to the works mentioned above, see Jensen, *Kosmogonie der Babylonier*; Sayce, *Hibbert Lectures*, 1887; Smythe Palmer, *Tĕhōm and Tiāmat*, 1897, and art. in *Guardian*, Feb. 6, 1907; Driver on *Genesis*, 1904; Neander, *Hist. of the Christian Church*, vol. ii. (for the Gnostics); *New English Dictionary* (for the words 'Abime,' 'Abysme,' 'Abyss' in Eng. literature).

JOHN TAYLOR.

ABYSSINIA.—The peoples of Abyssinia belong to three distinct races, viz. the African aborigines, the Hamitic (Cushitic) tribes, and the Semitic immigrants.

(*a*) The *African aborigines* are now found only in the western and north-western part of Abyssinia; they are called by the other Abyssinians *Shangalā* or *Shanqelā*. Originally the name of a certain tribe, this has come to be a generic term for all non-Semitic or non-Hamitic people of probably negro origin. The largest aggregation of these Abyssinian 'negroes' are the Kunamas or Bāzēns, and the Bāriās, whose languages also are entirely different from those of the Cushites and the Semites. They inhabit the country around the Takkazē and the Gash Rivers, mostly in the present Italian Colonia Eritrea. The Christian Abyssinians call them sometimes by the derogatory term 'mouse-eaters'; *bāriā* in Amharic means also 'slave,' because these aborigines are taken as slaves all over Abyssinia. This part of the population is, to a large extent, pagan; others, like the Bāriās, have become Muhammadans; some of them, especially the slaves among the Christians, have adopted the Christian faith.

(*b*) The *Hamitic* or *Cushitic* tribes form the stock of the population of Abyssinia. They immigrated into that country at some remote period of which we have no record. There is scarcely a part of Abyssinia where the Semites, who imposed their language almost everywhere, did not intermingle with them. In the south the Semitic blood was almost absorbed by the Hamitic; in the north the Hamitic tribes seem to have been kept a little more separate. The main tribes of the Cushites or Abyssinian Hamites are the Somalis and the Gallas in Southern Abyssinia; the 'Afar (called by the Arabs *Danakil*, perhaps of Arab origin, but speaking a Cushitic language) in the east; the Agaos (with several subdivisions) all over the centre; the Sahos in the north-east, the Bogos (also called Bilin after the name of their language, of Agao origin), finally, the Beḍawīn in the north, who extend into the Egyptian Sudan. The Gallas, or Oromos, are very numerous, and are divided into many tribes, some of which extend as far as the equatorial lakes. Their language is a Hamitic one, and the Abyssinians make a distinction between them and the Shangalās. Since, however, many Gallas whom the writer has seen (in Northern Abyssinia) have pronounced negroid features, it may be that a part of this nation is of negro origin and has adopted a Hamitic language. Similar cases occur very frequently, as, for instance, with the Celts in Bavaria, who speak German, and the negroes in the United States of America, who have adopted the English language. The Gallas are partly pagan, partly Muhammadan. Some of them became Christians, but the wholesale baptism of Galla people by King Theodore I. (1855–1868) met with little success. The Somalis and the 'Afar are practically Muhammadan; the Sahos and the Beḍawīn are Muhammadan; the Bogos partly Christian, partly Muhammadan.

(*c*) The *Semitic* population of Abyssinia is strongest in the north, *i.e.* in the region of the ancient kingdom of Aksum. There is no doubt that these Semites came to Abyssinia from Arabia. The bulk of them may have come within the last cents. B.C., but the Semitic immigration never stopped. It was rather, as Renan has said, a 'gradual infiltration,' and even in our days an Arab tribe, the Rashāida, has crossed to the other side of the Red Sea and is beginning to be nationalized in Africa; they still speak Arabic, but have commenced to use the Tigrē language as well. The Semites have been, beyond doubt, the civilizers of, or at least the bearers of some civilization to, Abyssinia. They founded an empire, they built temples, palaces, and entire cities, as well as dams and reservoirs; they originated and carried on the only literature that Abyssinia ever had. When they came they were, of course, pagan, but after some centuries they became Christian; and, whatever their Christianity is, or may have been, it has always tended to a higher state of morals and religion than that which native Africa, south of Egypt and the other countries along the north shore, has ever been capable of producing. The Semitic language which was first written (after the Sabæan) is the Ethiopic or Ge'ez. A few pagan and Christian inscriptions and almost the entire Christian literature are committed to writing in this language, which must have died out before the 10th cent. A.D. At present there are three main Semitic languages in Abyssinia: Amharic, Tigriña, and Tigrē. Amharic is the language of the south and the centre; Tigriña that of the region of the old Aksumitic kingdom; Tigrē is spoken by the half-nomadic tribes of the north, and has been adopted by many of the Hamites of that region. The majority of those who speak Amharic and Tigriña are Christians; Tigriña is often called *zärävā kheshtān* (in Tña) or *hīgā kestān* (in Tē), *i.e.* the language of the Christians. The Tigrē tribes are now mostly Muhammadans, but about half of the Mänsa' tribe have retained Christianity.

We have therefore, in speaking of the religions of Abyssinia, to deal with Paganism, Islām, and Christianity. Paganism is at the bottom of all of them, and even the religious ideas of the common people in Christian and Muhammadan districts are more like pagan superstitions than like the ideas of the founder of Christianity or of the prophet of Islām. We may here dispense entirely with official Islām or Christianity. It will suffice to record the following facts: Islām in Abyssinia is Sunnite, the Muhammadans living in Christian surroundings are called Djabartī, the people who do missionary work there at present are mostly of the Senūsī order. The Confession of the Christian Church of Abyssinia is that of Jacobus Baradæus,—in other words, the Abyssinians are Monophysites. A few remarks on the history of Christianity in this country will be found below.

Still another religion exists in Abyssinia,—the country of many races, languages, and religions, —viz. *Judaism.* There are a number of Jewish communities, mainly in the region between Aksum and Gondar. They are called **Falashas,** and they speak an Agao dialect; their books are in Ge'ez. Their origin is altogether unknown to us. According to Abyssinian tradition, the Queen of Sheba, who was a princess of Aksum, was at Jerusalem instructed in the Jewish religion by Solomon and then introduced it into her own country. This is, of course, legendary, for the oldest inscriptions prove—if we need any proof—that the official religion of the Aksumitic kingdom, before it became Christian, was pagan. But this curious legend seems to reflect some historical events of which no other records have come down to our time. For a number of OT practices and ideas are integral parts of Abyssinian Christianity, and, what is more significant, the Aramaic loan-words in Ge'ez, mostly denoting religious ideas and objects, are probably of Jewish-Aramæan, not of Christian-Aramæan, origin.

I. *PAGAN ABYSSINIA.*—1. PAGAN RELIGION OF THE AFRICAN ABORIGINES.—As far as we know the religion of the Kunamas, it may be characterized as animistic or as ancestor-worship. For the spirits or the souls of their forefathers play the most important rôle in their religious life. Above all spirits there is the unknown Great Spirit, with whom man comes little into contact. This idea of one mysterious, almighty, supernatural being seems to pervade almost all pagan religions. The Great Spirit is far away, the other spirits are near, and are in a way mediators between mankind and the Great Spirit. He it is that gives rain, the most important and vital thing for the agricultural Kunamas, and he is probably the god of heaven, just as Wāq is among the Gallas (see below). To him only the chief of the tribe may sacrifice. At the beginning of the ploughing season the chief has a revelation bidding him immolate a red goat and a white sheep, and in return promising abundance of rain. The animals are killed, the blood is sprinkled on the ground, and the chief says: 'Behold, thou hast the blood that we have offered; now give us rain.' After that, the chief and priest eat the meat in communion with the spirits, whereupon mankind and spirit world are reconciled and friendly.

It is only upon important occasions that the priest or chief enters into action: the religious affairs of everyday life are in the hands of sorcerers and witches, *i.e.* men and women who are believed to have communication with the spirits, or even to be possessed by them. Sorcerers and witches are in contact with, or in the service of, either good or evil spirits. The latter form no separate caste; certain persons are believed to be poisoners or to have the evil eye. Against their power the people take refuge, or protect themselves by using a branch of the 'ghost-tree.' Naturally, members of the sorcerers' caste sometimes make ill use of their power,—and then the same remedies are used against them; but generally their work is that of prophesying, healing, and doing other miracles; in general, mediating between the people and the spirits.

The sorcerers wear women's clothes, decorate themselves with necklaces, bracelets, anklets, rings, beads, and pearls of many colours. They receive revelations from the spirits about diseases, ordinary perils, and the like, and they remedy them—or not—in return for high payment. The witches do their duty only at a certain period, viz. the harvest time. Then the people wish to 'greet' their ancestors and to give them mead. These demoniac women all of a sudden are possessed by the spirits, fall to the ground in a state of ecstasy, and begin to speak and sing in foreign tongues. After that, they put on their trinkets, and the people 'greet' their ancestors and pour mead for them. When all have done so, a special sacrifice is offered to free the women from their possessors, and every one returns to his usual life.

Remedies against the influence of malevolent spirits are incantations and the twigs of the ghost-tree. The spirits and the tree have the same name, and in this identity of name lies the power of the latter. For instance, at the time of childbirth twigs of this tree are placed crosswise over the door of the house to protect the child. The first night after someone has died, all the spirits visit the house of the dead and drink mead: the living sit outside, with the magic twigs around the neck or the arms. Again, the next day, when a libation is offered at the grave, they protect themselves in the same way. Other trees or bushes are used to protect the cattle or the crops. The spirits of the ancestors rule and regulate the entire life of these people. They have established the laws of social and political life; in other words, these laws are based on tradition and custom. For this reason the spirits watch over the laws and punish transgressions,—above all, the omission of taking blood-vengeance.

2. PAGAN RELIGION OF THE HAMITES.—The pagan religion of the Hamitic tribes of Abyssinia does not seem to differ essentially from that of the aborigines. According to our sources, however, it appears that the Gallas, who nowadays are practically the only pagan Hamites in Abyssinia, have outgrown the stage of crude animism, and have developed a sort of polytheism with one highest god, and that with them, partly at least, true religiosity has taken the place of torpid fear and awe. That highest god is called *Wāq* (or Wāqayo), and many say he is their only god. This being seems to be 'deity' or *numen* in general, in a way to be compared, therefore, with the Semitic אֵל. The noun *wāq* originally means 'heaven,' and thus the god Wāq is also named *Gurača*—a word which, as an adjective, denotes 'dark-blue,' and as a substantive 'heaven' or 'sky.' Wāq is the god of heaven, but he is omnipresent; he is everywhere in nature; he lives on mountain peaks, in high trees, near springs, in rivers, and in caves. In all these places he is worshipped with sacrifices and prayers. There are various kinds of offerings, but it seems most natural to assume that the communion between men and their god is the main idea of these offerings. This communion is effected by (*a*) the blood covenant; (*b*) the sacrificial meal. The blood is, on the one hand, poured out for the deity; on the other hand, it is smeared on the doorposts and on the foreheads of the offerers (in a line or crosswise), or sprinkled on them. The sacrificial meal is shared by deity and men: for a part is burned, the rest is eaten by men. The sacrificial animals are cattle and sheep; we even hear of 'expiatory cows.' There is also a recollection of human sacrifices among the people. The libations consist of milk and mead. All sacrifices are offered by the *pater familias,*—the head of the family,—who is at the same time their priest. On special occasions the chief of the tribe takes his place. After the animal is killed, the *ogēsa,*—'the wise man,'—the *haruspex,* comes in order to inspect the entrails and to interpret the omen. These 'wise men' form a kind of sacerdotal caste, and officiate at all important political affairs; they also interpret the flight of birds; they are *haru-*

spices and *augures* at the same time. Of course, they consider themselves much better than the ordinary sorcerers. There seem to be certain sects among them, *e.g.* the sect of Abba Muda, who lives in a mysterious cave with a serpent to which offerings are made. When the members of this sect make pilgrimages to the famous cave, they wear women's clothes, let their hair grow, and perform some well-known religious duties. An example of a Galla prayer is the following: 'Thou hast made the corn to grow, and shown it to our eyes; the hungry man beholdeth it and is consoled. When the corn is ripening, thou sendest caterpillars and locusts into it, locusts and pigeons. Everything cometh from thee, thou allowest it to happen: why thou doest this, thou knowest.'

Besides Wāq, there is a host of lesser deities, who fall into two groups, viz. the 'good spirits,' named *ayāna*, and the 'evil spirits,' named *jinnī*. The *ayāna* live in all places where Wāq lives, especially in rivers; but they also comprise the house-gods (*penates*) and the souls of the ancestors (*manes*). Even in a newly built house there is an *ayāna*, and crumbs are thrown on the floor for him when the people first enter the house. Individual members of this class of gods are *Kilēsa*, the god of war and of the winds; and *Atēte*, the goddess who protects women, like the Greek Eileithyia. It seems that even the personified Sabbath, called Sambata, is known as a goddess to the pagan Gallas, who must have borrowed her worship from the Falashas. Among the 'evil spirits' the *buda*, or the devil of the evil eye, is the most feared. It is well known that this superstition, so common over all Southern and Eastern countries, is particularly deep-rooted in Abyssinia. Other evil demons seem to be the monsters *banda* and *bulgu*. The former is the wolf, a demoniac animal among various peoples; the latter is explained as 'man-eater.' A special caste of sorcerers has to do with these evil spirits. Among them there are different degrees and specialists, some of whom predict the future, others cure diseases by driving out the devils, and others know the art of making good weather and of producing rain.

Sacred animals are, among others, the hyæna, the snake, the crocodile, and the owl. The hyænas eat the dead, and thus the souls enter their bodies; hence the spirits who are in the hyænas enter living men, and men—especially blacksmiths, who know magic art—change into hyænas. The snake is worshipped by almost all primitive peoples. The crocodile is sacred because it lives in the sacred rivers. Again, a certain owl is believed to be the bird of the dead; these owls are the souls of people who died unavenged. Life after death is, according to the belief of the pagan Gallas, a shadow-like existence in a sort of Hades or Sheol, called *ekerā* (taken from the Arabic *al-āḫira*, 'the other,' *scil.* world, but adapted to Galla ideas).

3. Pagan religion of the Semites.—What we know about the religion of the Semitic conquerors of Abyssinia is very little indeed—scarcely anything more than a few names. Our sources are the ancient inscriptions and native tradition. According to the famous Greek inscription copied at Adulis by Kosmas Indikopleustes, the king of Aksum, who had this inscription written (1st cent. A.D.), sacrificed *τῷ Διὶ καὶ τῷ Ἄρει καὶ τῷ Ποσειδῶνι* and erected a throne in honour of his god Ἄρης. The next earliest document is that of King Aizanas, who reigned about A.D. 350. This inscription is carved in Greek, Sabæan, and Old Ethiopic. The Greek part speaks only of the god Ἄρης, the Sabæan of Maḥrem, 'Astar and Beḥēr, the Old Ethiopic of Maḥrem, 'Astar and Medr. A Greek fragment from Abbā Pantaleon, a Christian shrine near Aksum, built over an ancient Sabæan sanctuary, mentions the Ἄρης ἀνίκητος of Aksum. But in only one case are all these gods found together, viz. in the first inscription of (Tā)zānā, written perhaps about A.D. 450. There the throne is dedicated to 'Astar, Beḥēr, and Medr; and thanks are rendered to Maḥrem, the god 'who begat the king.' From this it appears that the Semites who came from South Arabia to found the Aksumitic empire worshipped the ancient triad of Heaven, Sea, and Earth. 'Astar in Tigrē means 'heaven,' and Atar-Samain (Atar, *i.e.* 'Astar in Aramaic, of the heavens) as well as Ištar bēlit šamā (Ishtar Lady of the Heavens) are known in Semitic mythology. Thus 'Astar is the Aksumitic god of heaven translated into Greek by Zeus. *Medr* is the Ethiopic word for 'earth,' and here it must necessarily mean the god (or goddess) of the earth. Now, if the Adulitan inscription mentions Poseidon together with Zeus, the conclusion is unavoidable that Beḥēr is the god of the sea, in spite of the fact that the Ethiopic word *beḥēr* means 'land,' and is even used in this sense in our inscriptions. We must connect it with the word *baḥr* ('sea'), and assume that, being a proper name, it retained its ancient meaning even after the common noun corresponding to it had received a different meaning of its own. Besides this triad, Ares-Maḥrem, the tribal or ancestral god of the kings of Aksum, was worshipped. Since they fought many wars to establish their empire and to protect their dominions, it was most natural that they should identify Maḥrem with Ares, the war-god. From the inscription of (Tā)zānā it seems that bulls and captives were sacrificed to this god. From other texts it appears that 'thrones' and statues were erected to him and the other gods. [Drawings and photographs of the thrones will be found in the publications of the German Expedition to Aksum].

In a way Maḥrem-Ares may be connected with the native tradition. For the Abyssinians tell that before their ancestors adopted King Solomon's religion they worshipped a dragon, and that this dragon was their king. According to Greek mythology, Ares begat, in a cave near Thebes, a dragon, his own image. It is therefore not impossible that a similar association existed between Maḥrem-Ares and the dragon, but of this no record has come down to us thus far. (A study of the Abyssinian dragon legends was published in the writer's *Bibliotheca Abessinica*, i. pp. 17-31).

Another hint with regard to the cult of the ancient Aksumites may be taken from the great monuments of Aksum. Hitherto they have been called 'obelisks,' but they should rather be termed 'stelæ,'—stelæ, it is true, of huge dimensions, as may be seen from the illustrations in the late Mr. Bent's book, *The Sacred City of the Ethiopians*, and in the publications of the German Expedition. The stele is an integral part of a South Semitic tomb, and there is a certain mysterious connexion between the stone and the personality of the dead, for the stele is called *nephesh* ('soul'). If, then, at Aksum we find a large number of such stelæ, and among them huge highly decorated monoliths, ranging in height from 15 to 33 metres, and in front of them, or rather around them, large slabs representing, in all likelihood, altars, we may conclude, with a certain degree of probability, that these monuments served for 'ancestor-worship,' that form of religion which, as we have seen, is at the bottom of the pagan religions of Abyssinia.

II. *Christian Abyssinia.*—Christianity became the religion of the Aksumitic empire about A.D. 450. The king (Tā)zānā was the Constantine of Abyssinia; for in his first inscription he is pagan, in the second he is Christian. In the latter he speaks of only one god, the 'Lord of Heaven,' or the 'Lord of the Land' ('*egzī'a beḥēr*,—in Ethiopic the word for the Christian God), who enthroned him and gave him victory over his enemies. But in the king's own mind this 'Lord of Heaven' was probably not very different from 'Astar. We have no contemporaneous records of the first appearance of Christianity in Abyssinia, nor do we know whether the Jewish communities were older, or whether they had anything to do with preparing Abyssinia for the Christian faith. However this may be, the Christian kings soon regarded themselves as the protectors of the new faith, and when the Christians in South Arabia were persecuted by a king who had adopted Judaism, a king of Aksum fought against the latter, although his main object was probably to aggrandize his empire. South Arabia had been partly Christianized by Syrian missionaries, and it is most likely that Abyssinia, too, received its Christian religion from Syria. The first missionaries are said to have been Ædesius and Frumentius from Antioch, and the 'nine saints,' who about A.D. 500 strengthened Christianity, probably came from Syria. They may even have influenced the style of church architecture, since basilical plans are to be recognized in some of the most ancient churches of Abyssinia. The ancient shrines were now changed into Christian sanctuaries, the high places were dedicated to saints, and the sacred sycamore trees to the Virgin Mary. Within the first centuries of its history in Abyssinia, Christianity probably did not spread beyond the borders of the kingdom of Aksum, and it scarcely reached as far south as the Ṭānā Lake. In the 7th or 8th cent. great political changes must have taken place; but the history of Abyssinia, from about 650 until 1270, is shrouded in darkness. During this time many wars must have been fought between Christians and pagans, and also between Christians and Muhammadans. The outcome was that political conquest and missionary activity spread far to the south, and that the centre of the empire was transferred to the southern provinces. Abyssinian legendary history tells of many miracles performed by the saints who converted the pagan Hamites and negroes. Among them Takla Hāimānōt (Plant of Faith), and Gabra Manfas Qeddūs (Servant of the Holy Ghost), were the most famous and popular. Meanwhile Abyssinia had been cut off from South Arabia, which had become Muhammadan, and had sought and found close contact with the Coptic Church of Egypt. In the Abyssinian empire itself Christianity has been the official religion ever since, and many conquered tribes have been forced to be baptized. But outside of these limits Islām made rapid progress, and at present the Christians are surrounded by Muhammadans on all sides. Many Muhammadans even live among the Christians, although the building of mosques is not allowed. The country has seen many internal quarrels concerning dogmas or ecclesiastical and secular power, and has also witnessed repeated struggles against Roman Catholicism (about 1550–1635). The greatest dangers that the Church experienced were the wars waged by Muḥammad Grāñ, the Muhammadan conqueror who overran Abyssinia from 1525 to 1540. From these perils Abyssinian Christianity was finally saved by the Portuguese.

The Christian religion of Abyssinia became more and more degenerate, the more it was shut off from the rest of the civilized world, and the more the Semitic element was absorbed by other races. From time to time a king or a patriarch who was more enlightened and energetic than his fellow-countrymen tried to introduce reforms; but although they did their best, it was not very much. An altogether exceptional case is that of the monk Zar'a-Ya'qōb (1599–1692), who evolved a rationalistic system of religious philosophy (pub. and tr. by the present writer under the title *Philosophi Abessini*, Paris and Leipzig, 1904).

In conclusion, it may be stated that at present there are three main divisions in the Ethiopian Church. These are: (*a*) those who profess *ya-segā lej* ('son of the flesh'), *i.e.* that Jesus was in the flesh Son of Mary only, not of God, and that the Divine nature was later infused into Him by God, but do not admit Christ's Divinity as a man; (*b*) the followers of the *qeb'at* ('unction'), who profess that Christ, when He was anointed with the Holy Ghost in the Jordan after His baptism, became a participant of Divinity, even as man; (*c*) the true Monophysites or followers of the *tawāhedō* (unity) doctrine.

Possible Jewish traces in Abyssinian Christianity.—As has been said above, there seems to be some connexion between Judaism and Christianity in Abyssinia. The Aramaic words in Ethiopic denoting religious ideas were apparently taken from the Jewish Aramaic rather than from the Christian Syriac. Besides this, there are traces that may indicate a Jewish influence, unless they be regarded as general Semitic, or more specially Sabæan. These are chiefly (*a*) the observance of the Sabbath ('Sanbat' has even been personified, and is considered a female saint. In a church at Adua, the picture of a woman with a halo, soaring in the sky over a crescent, with an angel on either side, was by some declared to be 'Sanbat,' whereas others asserted that this was the picture of the assumption of Mary); (*b*) the distinction between clean and unclean animals, in the main following the OT; (*c*) the idea of ritual uncleanness of persons who have had sexual intercourse (even if legitimate) during the day, or of women during menstruation; (*d*) the duty of a man to marry his deceased brother's wife, if this brother dies without a son. Among the Christians a man who has his own and his brother's wife is not considered or treated as a bigamist. On the other hand, the practice of circumcision is general, being Semitic and Hamitic (even the girls are circumcised and infibulated), and the sacred dance may just as well be pagan as Jewish. With regard to images, the Ethiopian Church allows painted pictures, but no graven images.

Pagan traces in Abyssinian Christianity and Islām.—The excessive and unbounded cult of the Virgin Mary, which even the Muhammadans share to some extent, must in a way reflect the cult of a deposed pagan goddess. Mary lives on high mountains, at springs, and in the sycamore trees, which in ancient Egypt were sacred to Hathor. Who the pagan prototype of Mary was we cannot determine; she may have been Allāt of the Arabs, or 'Earth Mother,' scarcely Ishtar, the 'Lady of Heaven,' since 'Astar was a male deity in ancient Abyssinia. Furthermore, there is a large number of saints who have performed, and still perform, miracles of all sorts; one of them, the famous Gabra Manfas Qeddūs (see above), commonly called Gāber, even opposed successfully the will of God. Again, the Christians and Muhammadans believe in a host of evil spirits in the same way as the pagans do. These spirits live in dark places or near the cemeteries; they gather around the doors or haunt barren spots where no grass grows (like the elves in Northern Germany), or, finally, they possess animals, like the hyæna, the wolf, and the snake, and especially human beings. The devil that usually enters into people and makes them mad or sick is called *Waddegennī* (demon's son) among the Tigrē, and *Tegertī* (probably of African origin) in Tigriña. Then there is the famous Abyssinian Lilith, called *Werzelyā*, the demoness who makes a business of killing little children, etc. These spirits are driven out by burning the root (or a branch) of the ghost-tree. They are 'smoked out,' or they are exorcised by incantations. Magic prayers, written on scrolls or small booklets, and carried in little leather cases around the neck or the arms, are exceedingly common in Abyssinia. They deal with all possible dangers, and are good not only against many different diseases caused by the demons, but also against snakes, leopards, hyænas, drought, hail, locusts, and the like. Even the animal world has to suffer from devils in its midst, for the *debbī* or *dübbᵘⁱī*, described as somewhat smaller than a dog, drives every other animal away wherever it goes.

It deserves to be mentioned also that among the Tigrē tribes, tales about the doings of certain stars—star-myths, so to speak—are to be found which may possibly reflect ancient star-worship. The remnants of moon-worship among the same people are more pronounced.

A very conspicuous remnant of paganism is the idea of a nether world, where the shades live until the Day of Judgment. The shades or 'people of below' (*sab taḥat* in Tigrē) often appear to the living in dreams, or they punish a man by beating him, if he does not fulfil his duty of blood-vengeance, or is niggardly enough not to offer the proper sacrifices to the dead. The souls of those who die unavenged or before they have attained their desires, are changed into a kind of owl (*gān* in Tigrē), and howl and screech until they are avenged, or until some descendant or relative carries out their designs.

LITERATURE.—Nilsson in *Varde Ljus* (*Nordisk Missions Kalender*) for 1905, pp. 159–164; Paulitschke, *Ethnographie Nordost-Afrikas*, also *Harar*; Cecchi, *Da Zejla alle frontiere del Caffa*; Dillmann, 'Über die Anfänge des Axumitischen Reiches' (*ABAW*, 1878), also 'Zur Gesch. des Axumit. Reiches im vierten bis sechsten Jahrhundert' (*ib.* 1880); Müller, 'Epigraphische Denkmäler aus Abessinien' (*ABAW*, 1894); Basset, *Les Apocryphes Éthiopiens*; Littmann, 'The Princeton Ethiopic Magic Scroll' (*Princeton University Bulletin*, 1903–1904), also 'Arde'et, the Magic Book of the Disciples' (*JAOS*, 1904). Other material will be found in the Publications of the German Expedition to Aksum (preliminary report in *ABAW*, 1906), edited by the present writer, and in the Publications of the Princeton University Expedition to Abyssinia, by the same.

E. LITTMANN.

ACADEMY, ACADEMICS.—The Academy (Ἀκαδήμεια, older form Ἑκαδήμεια, later Ἀκαδημία), so called from the local hero Akademos or Hekademos, was one of the three great gymnasia outside the walls of Athens, the others being the Lyceum and the Cynosarges. It was situated less than a mile from the Dipylon Gate, off the road which ran N.W. through the outer Ceramicus, among the olive groves below Colonus Hippius. As a gymnasium it already existed in the time of the Pisistratids, but it was Cimon that laid it out as a public park with shady avenues of plane trees (Plut. *Cim.* 13). Here was the precinct of Athena with the twelve sacred olives (μορίαι), and the ancient pedestal (ἀρχαία βάσις) with representations of Herakles and Prometheus, which formed the starting-point of the torch-race at the Lampadēdromia (Apollodorus *ap.* schol. Soph. *Œd. Col.* 57). This last worship gave rise to several features of the Prometheus myth.

It was in the Academy that Plato founded the first Athenian philosophical school, the idea being doubtless suggested to him by the Pythagorean societies, such as those of Thebes and Phlius (cf. the *Phædo*), and possibly by that of his friend Euclides at Megara. The school possessed a shrine of the Muses (μουσεῖον), at which votive statues (ἀναθήματα) were dedicated (Diog. Laert. iii. 25, iv. 1, 19), and Antigonus of Carystus (*ap.* Athen. xii. 547 f., 548a) spoke of a 'sacrificer' (ἱεροποιός) and an 'attendant of the Muses' (Μουσῶν ἐπιμελητής) as officials of the school. He also spoke of the monthly common meals (συσσίτια) as religious acts (ἵνα φαίνωνται τὸ θεῖον τιμῶντες). From all this it has been inferred by Wilamowitz-Moellendorff (*Philol. Unters.* iv. 263 ff.) that the legal status of the Academy was that of a religious association (θίασος). That, indeed, was the only form which a corporation could take at Athens, and it was of great importance that membership of such associations was open to others than Athenian citizens.

The original property of the society was a house and garden, in which Plato and most of his successors lived. It is not quite certain whether the place of teaching was here or in the actual gymnasium; for the name 'Academy' is given to both. A semicircular marble bench (*exedra*, *sessio*) still existed in Cicero's days, which was at least as old as the scholarchate of Polemo (Cic. *de Fin.* v. 2, 4). It is not certain whether the scholarchs (σχόλαρχοι) were elected or selected by their predecessors. The official title seems to have been *diadochus* (διάδοχος, 'successor'). After the siege of Athens by Sulla (86 B.C.), the suburbs became unhealthy, and the school was moved into the town; but the house and garden remained in its possession to the end.

From an early date it was customary to distinguish the Old and the New Academy, though Philo (see below) objected to this (Cic. *Acad.* i. 13). The Old Academy includes the immediate followers of Plato, the New begins with Arcesilas, who introduced the sceptical doctrine for which the school was best known from the 3rd to the 1st cent. B.C. Later writers speak of three Academies, beginning the Middle with Arcesilas and the New with Carneades. Others added a fourth consisting of Philo and his followers, and a fifth consisting of Antiochus and his (Sext. *Pyrrh.* i. 220). All these divisions only mark stages in a continuous history.

1. The 'Old Academy' carried on the discussion of the problems which Plato had raised in his oral teaching. In the main, these were mathematical, and concerned with the distinction between continuous and discrete quantity. The former Plato calls in the *Philebus* the 'unlimited' (ἄπειρον), but we know from Aristotle that in his oral teaching it was called 'the great-and-small' (τὸ μέγα καὶ μικρόν). The problem was to show how discrete or 'ideal' numbers (εἰδητικοὶ ἀριθμοί) could arise from this, and similarly how 'magnitudes' (μεγέθη) could arise from continuous and infinitely divisible space by the introduction of limit (τὸ πέρας). If once we get to magnitudes, it may be possible to give at least a tentative mathematical construction of the 'elements,' and even of the things of sense.

The true glory of the Old Academy is the impulse which it gave to mathematical science by the study of these problems. Solid geometry, trigonometry, and conic sections all took their rise from this source, and the new conception of continuous quantity led to the solution of many old difficulties. Eudoxus of Cnidus and Heraclides Ponticus, both members of the Academy in Plato's time, attacked the problem of the solar system with extraordinary boldness, and prepared the way for the great discovery of the sun's central position by Aristarchus of Samos (*c.* 150 B.C.) It is unfortunate that most of our knowledge of the Old Academy comes from Aristotle, who was not in sympathy with the mathematical movement of his time.

Plato was succeeded by his nephew **Speusippus** (scholarch 347–339 B.C.). Xenocrates and Aristotle at once left Athens, the former returning later to succeed Speusippus, the latter to found a rival society.

Speusippus regarded number as arising from the union of unity (τὸ ἕν) and plurality (τὸ πλῆθος), but he made no attempt to derive magnitudes and other forms of reality (οὐσίαι) from numbers. He explained them instead as parallel series formed on the analogy of number. Magnitudes, for instance, arose from the union of 'something like unity' (the point) with 'something like' plurality, and so on with souls and sensible things (Arist. *Met.* 1028*b*, 9 ff., 1075*b*, 37 ff., 1085*a*, 31 ff., 1090*b*, 13 ff.). His most characteristic doctrine, however, was his denial of the identity of the Good and the One. The Good was not 'in the beginning' (ἐν ἀρχῇ), but reveals itself (ἐμφαίνεται) in the process of development. As in the case of plants and animals, it is only in the 'full-grown' (τὸ τέλειον) that we see the Good (Arist. *Met.* 1072*b*, 30 ff., 1091*b*, 14 ff.). Speusippus is thus the originator of the 'teleological' (derived from τέλειον, 'full-grown') or evolutionary view of the world, and this explains the fact that he wrote chiefly on biological subjects. We know from the quotations of Athenæus that in his ten books of 'Similars' (Ὅμοια) he discussed shellfish and mushrooms. It is in accordance, too, with this evolutionary standpoint that he regarded sense-perception as rudimentary science (ἐπιστημονικὴ αἴσθησις), and that he defined happiness (εὐδαιμονία) as the 'full-grown state' (ἕξις τελεία) of those in a natural condition (ἐν τοῖς κατὰ φύσιν ἔχουσιν). It was not pleasure; for pleasure and pain were two evils, opposed to one another, and also to the middle state of 'imperturbability' (ἀοχλησία), which is the happiness aimed at by good men (Clem. *Strom.* ii. 21).

Xenocrates of Chalcedon (scholarch 339–314 B.C.) spoke of the limit and the unlimited as the 'unit' (μονάς) and the 'indeterminate dyad' (ἀόριστος δυάς), and he reverted to the strictly Platonic view of the 'ideal numbers' (εἰδητικοὶ ἀριθμοί). It is characteristic of him that he was fond of religious language, calling the unit the Father, and the dyad the Mother, of the gods. The heaven of the fixed stars was also a god, and so were the planets. When we come to the 'sublunary' (ὑποσέληνος) sphere, however, we find 'demons' (δαίμονες)—beings who, like Eros in the *Symposium*, are intermediate between gods and men. The souls of men were also 'demons' (Arist. *Top.* 112*a*, 37), though the scientific definition of a soul was 'a self-moving number.' This theory of 'demons' had, of course, an enormous influence upon later theology, both Platonist and Christian, and marks Xenocrates as the originator of the 'emanationist' view of the world, as opposed to the 'evolutionary' view of Speusippus. It is important to notice, however, that he was quite conscious of the allegorical character of this doctrine. He asserted that his account of the creation was only a device intended to make his theory clear for purposes of instruction. Really, the creation of the world was eternal or timeless, a view which, he maintained, had also been that of Plato (Plut. *An. Procr.* 3).

Like Speusippus, Xenocrates was inclined to attach much value to rudimentary forms of knowledge. He distinguished φρόνησις as the wisdom possible to man from σοφία or complete knowledge, and he thought that even irrational animals might have the idea of God and immortality. In his ethics he was less ascetic than Speusippus, and attached importance to the possession of the power which ministers to goodness (ὑπηρετικὴ δύναμις), that is, to 'external goods' (Clem. *Strom.* ii. 22, v. 13).

The next two scholarchs, **Polemo** and **Crates**, seem to have busied themselves almost entirely with popular ethics. The most distinguished member of the Academy in their time was Crantor, who wrote a much admired treatise on mourning (Περὶ πένθους). He was a disciple of Xenocrates, but died before Crates, and was never scholarch.

2. The 'New Academy' ('Middle Academy' according to those who reckon the New from Carneades) begins with **Arcesilas** (scholarch 270?–241 B.C.), who made use of the weapons provided by scepticism to combat the Stoic theory of 'comprehension' (κατάληψις) as a criterion of truth intermediate between knowledge (ἐπιστήμη) and belief (δόξα). As he appears to have left no writings, we cannot tell how far his scepticism really went, though Cicero certainly states that he denied the possibility of knowledge (*Acad.* i. 44). On the other hand, Sextus Empiricus says that his Pyrrhonism was merely apparent, and that he taught Platonic dogmatism to the inner circle of his disciples, quoting in support of this a verse of his contemporary Ariston of Chios, describing him as a sort of Chimæra, 'Plato in front, Pyrrho behind, and Diodorus in the middle.' In any case, we must remember that Plato himself had denied the possibility of knowledge as regards the world of sense, and it was quite natural that this side of his teaching should become the most prominent in an age of dogmatic materialism. The next scholarch, Lacydes (241–215 B.C.), continued the tradition of Arcesilas. Of his successors, Telecles, Euander, and Hegesinus, we know nothing.

The most distinguished head of the New Academy was **Carneades** of Cyrene (214–129 B.C.), who threw himself whole-heartedly into the attack on Stoicism as represented by Chrysippus. In 156 B.C. he came to Rome as ambassador, with the Stoic Diogenes and the Peripatetic Critolaus, and astonished the Romans by his power of arguing both for and against justice and the like (*in utramque partem disputare*). Like Arcesilas, he wrote nothing, but his arguments were preserved by his successor Clitomachus. They were directed against all theories which admitted a 'criterion' of truth; but, on the other hand, he himself set up three criteria of probability as necessary for practical life and the pursuit of happiness. In ordinary matters we take 'probable impression' (πιθανὴ φαντασία) as our criterion; in important matters the impression must also be 'incapable of distortion' by other impressions (ἀπερίσπαστος), while in those which pertain to our happiness, it must also be 'tested and approved' (διεξωδευμένη). The Stoic doctrine of 'assent' (συγκατάθεσις) to a 'comprehending impression' (καταληπτικὴ φαντασία) can yield no more than this.

Carneades died in his eighty-fifth year (129 B.C.), and was succeeded by **Clitomachus** of Carthage, who was succeeded by **Philo** of Larissa. During the Mithridatic war (88 B.C.), Philo took refuge at Rome, where he had Cicero as an enthusiastic student. Sextus tells us distinctly (*Pyrrh.* i. 235) that he held things were in their own nature 'comprehendible' (καταληπτά), though 'incomprehendible' (ἀκατάληπτα) so far as the Stoic criterion went. His disciple **Antiochus** of Ascalon broke with the tradition of Carneades altogether, and even with the teaching of Philo, whom he succeeded. He held that all Stoic doctrines were to be found in Plato, and that the differences of the Peripatetics and Stoics from the Academy were merely verbal. Cicero heard him at Athens in 79 B.C., and it was on his teaching that he based his own Academic eclecticism.

After Antiochus the history of the Academy is a blank for many generations. Neoplatonism did not originate within it, and was not introduced into it till the 5th cent. A.D. by **Plutarch** of Athens († c. 430 A.D.). His successor **Proclus** is an important figure in the history of philosophy and religion, but he does not concern us here. The school produced in its last days some distinguished commentators on Plato and Aristotle, notably **Simplicius** the Cilician and **Damascius** the Syrian. Damascius was the last scholarch; for, in 529 A.D., Justinian closed the school and confiscated its revenues, amounting to 1000 gold pieces, of which Plato's garden brought in only three. Damascius, with Simplicius and some others, took refuge at the court of Chosroës, king of Persia, who was supposed to be devoted to philosophy. They were disappointed in him, however, and returned on the conclusion of peace, when Chosroës made it a condition that they should not be molested in their religious faith and observances (Agath. *Hist.* ii. 30). Simplicius speaks with excusable bitterness of Christian theology; but the best of Platonism, as then understood, had already been absorbed by that very theology, and the work of the Academy was done, at least for the time. When Justinian closed it, it had lasted over nine hundred years.

LITERATURE (in addition to the histories of philosophy).—On the topography, see Wachsmuth, *Stadt Athen.* i. 255 ff., 270 f., 590 f.; on the organization, *Academicorum philosophorum index Herculanensis*, ed. Bücheler (Greifswald, 1869–1870); Wilamowitz-Moellendorff, *Philol. Unters.* iv. 263 ff. For Speusippus, see Ravaisson, *Speusippi de primis rerum principiis* (Paris, 1838); for Xenocrates, Heinze, *Xenokrates* (Leipzig, 1892); for New Academy, Hirzel, *Untersuchungen zu Ciceros philosophischen Schriften*, Leipzig, 1877–1883.

JOHN BURNET.

ACCEPTANCE.—'Acceptance,' as a Scriptural and theological term, may be said to denote a state of favour in the sight of God which men may enjoy when they fulfil the conditions upon which such favour depends. The gracious purpose of God which the mission of His Son fully reveals, has in view the establishing of a state of reconciliation in which men may find abiding acceptance for themselves and their service, and share in all the benefits of redemption. But the idea of acceptance, as presented in Scripture, does not depend either upon redemption actually accomplished, or upon any prescribed measure of knowledge or of character. It is everywhere taken for granted that the way to the Divine favour has always been open, and that it may be secured everywhere by a true heart and an obedient spirit, in which there is always the pledge that all available means will be used to attain to a life well-pleasing to God. There can be no barrier to forgiveness and acceptance but in the sin and unbelief of men.

Yet the actual conditions in which this state is reached in Scripture cover a wide field of experience, and belong to all stages of revelation, and are described in various terms which give prominence to different aspects of the conception. A cursory glance at the numerous instances in which the persons or the conduct of men are spoken of as finding acceptance with God, will show that this favour has been open to men in all ages and in all conditions of human life. Yet there are special means calculated to secure it which revelation seeks to make known, along with the objective grounds upon which, in the economy of redemption, it is established and guaranteed to men. The full knowledge of these was not possible before Christian times, yet it is clear that God has always and everywhere been gracious and friendly in His relations with men. Nowhere is it taught that He is by nature hostile, as heathen gods were often supposed to be, or that His favour can be procured by costly gifts or sacrifices. On the contrary, the gift and sacrifice of His Son are the highest proof of His love that could be given (Jn 3^{16}, Ro 5^{8}).

(1) There is the wide sphere of religious experience which the worship of God by sacrifice may be said to cover; of which Gn 8^{21} may be taken as a type. Of Noah's sacrifice it is said: 'The Lord smelled a sweet savour; and the Lord said in his heart, I will not again curse the ground any more for man's sake.' This language shows the favour with which this sacrifice was regarded, and the effect it had upon the future course of the world. It was an act which consecrated a new world. Similar phraseology is frequently used, both of the purpose which sacrifice had in view, and of the result which it effected in procuring favour for the worshipper. Whether all worship in the earlier ages was expressed by sacrifice or not, it is obvious that sacrifice constituted the central and essential feature of it, and genuine piety would naturally seek satisfaction in the faithful observance of all prescribed forms. This tendency exposed the worshipper to the danger of externalism and mere work-righteousness. The religious consciousness in its OT form was based on the thought that sacrifice was the appropriate form for acknowledging God and mediating His favour. In the different kinds of offerings and in a ritual appropriate to each, the Law provided for a wide variety of religious need; and in the faithful observance of what the Law had prescribed, the true Israelite could assure himself of acceptance in the presence of Jahweh.

(2) To what extent the character of the worshipper was an essential element in acts of sacrifice in early times, it is not easy to determine. It is not likely that the religious acts even of primitive men would stand out of all relation to their habitual life. With the advance of culture, however, increased importance would come to be attached to the spirit of worship as contrasted with the form. And once it became clear that the two might be not only different but even opposed, as was manifest in the time of the Prophets, then the call would begin to be made for mercy and not sacrifice, for righteousness in life and conduct rather than multitudes of sacrifices. Yet the maxim that obedience is better than sacrifice (1 S 15^{22}, Is $1^{11ff.}$, Mic 6^{8}) was not new in the time of Isaiah. It was an element in the regulation of worship from the first, and its importance increased with a deepening sense of the inner character of religion; especially when it began to be felt that the outward forms of worship were subject to change. The movement to restrict worship by sacrifice to one central sanctuary, whenever or however it originated, is a sure sign of the decadence of the old belief, and shows that sacrifice was unsuitable as a general and universal medium of worship. That the Prophets were against all sacrifices, wherever they might be offered, cannot be made out. Yet the old corruptions of the high places, which had invaded the Temple in their day, gave point to their loud rebukes and increased the longing for a new and better time. It cannot be said, however, that the Prophets taught indifference to sacrifice as such. In any case, the worth of the latter as a religious act was always dependent upon the moral state of the worshipper, and this circumstance explains their insistence upon moral conditions, upon 'clean hands and a pure heart' as necessary to acceptance with God.

(3) The broad principle of acceptance in its widest universality may be inferred from the spiritual nature of God, as in Christ's words to the woman of Samaria (Jn 4^{24} 'God is spirit, and they that worship him must worship in spirit and in truth'). It is well expressed by St. Peter in the case of Cornelius (Ac $10^{34.35}$ 'Of a truth I perceive that God is no respecter of persons: but in every nation he that feareth him, and worketh righteousness, is accepted with him').

(4) But, while the broad principle of acceptance is contained implicitly in the revealed character of God, and was boldly proclaimed by the Prophets, it is never realized as a living experience except in the life of faith and obedience, in the life which, based on the redeeming work of Christ, seeks for and accepts all available helps both to know and to do the will of God.

LITERATURE.—Harnack, *Hist. of Dogma*, vi. (Eng. tr. 1899) pp. 196 f., 308 ff.; Morris, *Theology of the Westminster Symbols* (1900), p. 442 f.; A. Stewart in Hastings' *DB*; E. B. Pollard in *DCG*. See also ACCEPTILATION, ACCESS, ATONEMENT, FORGIVENESS, JUSTIFICATION.

A. F. SIMPSON.

ACCEPTILATION is a term which, like many others, has passed from Roman law to Christian theology. According to its derivation, *acceptilatio* means 'a reckoning as received,' *acceptum* being the proper name for the credit side of the ledger. In Roman law, however, the term had a special technical use. It meant the discharge of an obligation by the use of a solemn and prescribed form of words, in which the debtor asked the creditor if he had received payment, and the creditor replied that he had—no real payment, however, having taken place. Gaius consequently says that acceptilation resembles an imaginary payment. This method of discharge was properly applicable only to obligations contracted verbally by stipulation, *i.e.* by the use of a similar solemn form of words, in which the creditor asked the debtor to own his debt, and the debtor did so. Obligations contracted in other ways could, however, be transformed into verbal obligations by the use of a special stipulation invented for the purpose, named the Aquilian, and could thus be made terminable by acceptilation. See Gaius, *Inst.* iii. 169; Justinian, *Inst.* iii. 29. 1 and 2, *Digest.* 'de Acceptilatione,' xlvi. 4.

In Christian theology, the term 'acceptilation' is commonly used in a loose sense to denote the principle of that theory of the Atonement, in which the merit of Christ's work is regarded as depending simply on the Divine acceptance, and not on its own intrinsic worth. This theory was taught by Duns Scotus, who says that 'every created offering is worth what God accepts it at, and no more,' and further, that Christ's human merit was in itself strictly limited, but God in His good pleasure accepted it as sufficient for our salvation (Com. *in Sent.* lib. iii. dest. 19). Fisher accordingly says of Duns Scotus: 'He holds to what is termed the theory of "acceptilation." The Saviour's work becomes an equivalent (for the debt of sin) simply because God graciously wills to accept it as such' (*Hist. of the Chr. Church*, 1894, p. 222). Ritschl has sharply criticised the description of the doctrine of Duns as one of acceptilation. He says: 'It is incredible, but it is a fact that the expression "acceptilatio" is used almost universally as equivalent to "acceptatio," as though it presupposed a verb *acceptilare*. For instance, Schneckenburger (*Lehrbegriffe der kl. prot. Kirchenparteien*, p. 18) speaks of the acceptilation of the merit of Christ in Duns Scotus' (*Rechtfertigung und Versöhnung*[3], i. p. 328, note). The theory of Duns Scotus is certainly not very suitably spoken of as one of acceptilation. In the solution of an obligation by acceptilation there is no payment at all; whereas, in the theory of Duns there is a payment, though it is accepted beyond its intrinsic value. But the usage of applying the name 'acceptilation' to Duns's theory is probably too confirmed to be done away with. It is to be understood, then, that the term is used only loosely. The danger of such usage is, however, shown by the fact that Shedd (*Hist. of Christ. Doct.* 1862, vol. ii. p. 348) not merely states that Duns Scotus taught a doctrine of acceptilation, but actually speaks of him as having transferred the term 'acceptilatio' to the doctrine of Christ's satisfaction—a statement which is historically quite inaccurate.

The confusion which has gathered round the term does not, however, end here. It has been used even more indefensibly than in the case of Duns Scotus to describe the doctrine of the Atonement taught by Socinus. The only excuse for this is that Socinus states his preference for the view of Duns Scotus just described, in contrast to the orthodox Protestant view according to which the death of Christ was a strict satisfaction for sin ('de Jesu Christo Servatore,' Pars Tertia, cap. vi. in *Bibliotheca Fratrum Polonorum*, 1656). His positive teaching is, however, quite different. 'Jesus Christ is our Saviour because He announced to us the way of life eternal, confirmed it (by His miracles and His death), and showed clearly in His own Person, both by the example of His life and by His resurrection from the dead, that He would give us life eternal, if we put faith in Him' (Pars Prima, cap. i.; cf. cap. iii.). Grotius, however, accuses Socinus of applying the legal word 'acceptilation' to the remission of sins, which God grants us, and then waxes eloquent upon the fallacies involved in such usage (*Defensio Fidei Catholicæ de Satisfactione Christi*, cap. iii. Oxon. 1637). The only explanation of the language of Grotius seems to be that he had misread or misunderstood a passage in Socinus, where he criticises Beza for using the word 'acceptilation' in explaining St. Paul's doctrine of imputation ('de Jesu Christo Servatore,' Pars Quarta, cap. ii.). The Socinian theologian Crell points out the mistake in his 'Responsio ad Grotium' (ad cap. iii. in *Bibliotheca Fratrum Polonorum*, 1656); it is he who tells us that it was Beza whom Socinus had in view. Crell, however, did not succeed in preventing the general impression that Socinus taught a doctrine of acceptilation. We still find Turretin saying (*de Satisfactionis Christi Necessitate*, Disp. xx. cap. x.): 'We admit no Socinian acceptilation'; though his Disputations on the Satisfaction of Christ did not appear till 1666 (enlarged edition, 1687; see Turretin's *Works*, Edin. 1848, vol. i. p. xlii).

ROBERT S. FRANKS.

ACCESS.—'Access' is the term used in the NT to denote the privilege and right of approach to God which men have through Jesus Christ. The term occurs in three places (Ro 5^2, Eph 2^{18} and 3^{12}), and in each of these as the tr. of προσαγωγή. The importance of the conception may be inferred from the circumstance that the article accompanies the term in two of these instances, indicating that the thing spoken of has an acknowledged and familiar place in Christian faith. In classical literature the transitive use of προσαγωγή is by far the more common; and several commentators of note maintain that it should be so read in the texts cited. It would thus = 'introduction,' and, so taken, the term will have a narrower meaning than that associated with 'access.' The usage of courts in which access to kings was obtained through a προσαγωγεύς or *sequester*, if taken to explain our 'introduction' to the Father, does certainly suggest something less than seems implied in the above given texts.

It is quite true that the word is often used both of persons and things in the sense of *leading up* to or towards, and this much at least Christ accomplishes for us in bringing us to God. Yet the introduction which we have in Him implies not a passing event or incident at the beginning of the Christian life, but something which is always valid, and which establishes and secures for us an open way of approach together with all the privileges of children of God. Even if we hold strictly to the transitive meaning of the term, we must so explain it as to imply the further blessings and privileges which introduction brings and secures; and this Meyer readily does. This consideration has doubtless inclined most commentators to favour the intransitive sense of the word and to render it by 'access.' This use of προσαγωγή, though rare, is not without support (see Plutarch, *Æmil. P.* 13; Polyb. x. 1. 6). Most of the versions take this view; the RV adhering to 'access' of the AV; and the same view appears in some of the older English versions. Tindale has 'a way in through faith,' 'an open way in'; Cranmer and the Genevan, 'an entrance,' 'an open way in.' The Rheims version, like the RV, adheres to 'access.' Luther and various German versions render by *Zugang*, similar in meaning to 'access'; and this term is now consecrated by long usage in English, and could not easily be supplanted by another.

Though the passive aspect of the conception is more prominent in 'access,' as the active is in προσαγωγή, there is in the associations of the word a blending of the two which must be kept in mind in order to realize the full force of the Apostle's use of it. The essential points in the conception are obvious in the three texts where the word stands.

(1) In Ro 5^2 it is used of the entrance upon, or the introduction to, the state of grace, or the Christian state, which in the context is described as that of justification, of acceptance and peace. This state is a new relation to God which is established and constituted by the Redeemer's gracious and atoning sacrifice, the benefits of which are immediately secured by faith. These benefits embrace the whole content of the Christian salvation—justification, acceptance, all the privileges of Divine sonship, with the hope of coming glory.

Our access to this state has been established through the incarnation and death of the Son of God, who bears away the sins of men and gives them power to become sons of God. It is not merely an open way; it is an actual leading of men into this blessed state by One who takes them in hand and conducts them into the blessedness and peace of the Divine kingdom.

(2) In Eph 2[18] it is clear that much more is meant than the open way to God. It is an actual and effectual introduction of a personal kind which begins a state of friendship and fellowship by means of the indwelling spirit common to all believers. In the former text the Christian state as a whole is in view, as that to which Christ introduces us; here we are shown the still higher sphere of Divine fellowship, of filial privilege and power which Christ opens up to us, and into which He conducts us. Jew and Gentile have their *access* to the Father through the Son by one Spirit. All outward differences which separate and divide men fall away in presence of the higher unity which is produced by the life of God mediated by Christ and the Spirit of Christ.

(3) In Eph 3[12] *access* is viewed as a standing condition of the life of faith, a state of exalted confidence, boldness, and freedom which faith in Christ ever sustains and renews. It secures all the possibilities of a free and joyous fellowship, and provides the power by which the energies and needs of the higher life may be sustained and filled. The filial spirit is nourished and enlarged from the fulness of the Divine life and love.

The idea of access to God through Christ differs in many respects from that access which must be open to man as a spiritual being. This latter is never denied but rather taken for granted in Scripture. Compared with the former, however, it can never come into competition with it, or supply its place. In the light about God which Christianity reveals, it soon becomes clear that none but Christ can lead us to Him. The Father whom the Son reveals can never be known or approached through any save the Son. The incarnation and mission of the Son, accepted and believed, must henceforth determine the character of our access to God. This St. Paul has very clearly perceived, and he has brought the thought to clear formal expression. It appears in various parts of the NT: in the Fourth Gospel as a general principle of Christianity (Jn 14[6]), in Hebrews and 1 Peter in closer relation to St. Paul. As a broad principle, we readily see that we cannot have real access to God except amid the conditions which Christianity has established, both as to the character of God and the way of acceptable service and worship. Yet it is important to keep in mind that the NT ascribes our access specifically to the great sacrifice which removes the barrier of sin and establishes peace and friendship between God and men (He 10[19. 20], 1 P 3[18]).

A use of the word 'access,' different from, but related to that given above, is found in some liturgical writers, by whom the term is employed to characterize and describe certain prayers in the old Liturgies and in the Roman service of the Mass. It is applied to one of the prayers offered by the officiating priest in approaching the altar at the commencement of the service, and also to brief prayers for people and priest which immediately precede the act of communion. In some editions these prayers are noted in the margin as 'Prayer of Access' or 'Prayer of humble Access.' The prayers in question express generally deep humility in presence of the Divine greatness, and ask for the necessary preparation. It is to be noted, however, that the term does not stand in the text of the Liturgies, either in the prayers or in the rubrics which direct the order of the service. It is a word of the editors and commentators, and one has difficulty in discovering the special aptness of the term with reference to the prayers which are so described, there being many others of the same character throughout the service. The explanation probably is that the approach of the priest to the altar at the commencement, and the nearing of the worshippers to the Divine presence in the consecrated and now transformed elements, are the two points in which access to Deity now present in the great Sacrament begins and culminates. In this sense the term is apt enough, as it expresses the view of the Supper which is already latent in the old Liturgies and is seen fully developed in the Roman Missal. (See Hammond's *Liturgies Eastern and Western*, Clarendon Press, 1878).

LITERATURE.—J. O. F. Murray in Hastings' *DB* i. 22; D. A. Mackinnon in *DCG* i. 12; the Comm., esp. B. F. Westcott on *Hebrews* and J. A. Robinson on *Ephesians*; *Expos.* IV. [1890] ii. 131, II. [1882] iv. 321; W. Robertson Nicoll, *The Church's One Foundation* [1901], 43; J. G. Tasker, *Spiritual Religion* (Fernley Lect. 1901), pp. 102, 123; W. P. Du Bose, *The Gospel acc. to St. Paul* (1907), 143.

A. F. SIMPSON.

ACCIDENT (*accidens*, *συμβεβηκός*).—**1.** *One of the five Predicables* (*accidens prœdicabile*).—According to Mill, under *accidens* 'are included all attributes of a thing which are neither involved in the signification of the name, nor have, so far as we know, any necessary connexion with attributes which are so involved' (*Logic*, vol. i. p. 149). This, allowing for the Nominalist standpoint of Mill, is the same view as that contained in Aldrich's definition, 'that which is predicated as contingently joined to the essence,' as contrasted with *proprium* which is predicated as necessarily joined. Some such definition or its equivalent is given by most writers on Logic, and is, according to Mansel, (*Aldrich*, 4th ed. p. 25), found in Albertus Magnus (*de Prœdicat.* Tract ii. cap. 1).

The view taken by Aristotle is different. The attribute of a triangle, that its three angles are equal to two right angles, which on the ordinary view would be a *proprium*, is by him regarded as an accident (*Metaphys.* iv. 30). The distinction between property and accident in Aristotle turns on the convertibility or non-convertibility of the attribute. It is essential to the Aristotelian property (*ἴδιον*) that it should be present in certain objects and in them alone. If present in other objects, it is either identical with the genus, or it is not. If not, it is an accident. The test of an accident is that it is common to heterogeneous things. Aristotle at the same time recognizes that that which, simply considered, is an accident may become in a certain relation and at a certain time a property. He gives two definitions of 'accident': (1) 'that which is neither definition nor property nor genus, but is in the thing'; (2) 'that which is able to be in and not to be in one and the same individual' (*Top.* i. 5). Porphyry gives a third definition: 'that which is present and absent without destruction of the subject' (*Isagoge*, v.).

Aristotle recognizes two classes of 'accidents': those which are necessarily connected with the essence and deducible from it (*συμβεβηκὸς καθ' αὑτό*); and those which are not (cf. Ueberweg, *Hist. of Philos.*, Eng. tr. vol. i. p. 155, and Grote's *Aristotle*, vol. i. p. 142 note). Sanderson in his *Logic* (*Works*, vol. vi. p. 10) distinguishes separable and inseparable accident thus: Separable—that which can be actually separated from its subject, as cold from water; Inseparable—that which cannot be separated except in the intellect, as wetness from water. Aldrich gives a similar distinction. Mansel and most logicians define the inseparable accidents of a class as those accidents which, though not connected with the essence either by way of cause or consequence, are as a matter of fact found in all the members of the class; the separable accidents as those found in some members of the class and not in others. The inseparable accidents of an individual are those which can be predicated of their subject at all times; the separable only at certain times.

2. *Accident, Fallacy of.*—This fallacy is generally considered as arising when we infer that whatever agrees with a thing considered simply in itself agrees with the same thing when qualified by some accident. Aristotle's view of the fallacy was different. He defines it as arising 'when it is held that anything belongs in a similar way to a subject and to the accident of that subject.' This definition does not mean merely that the attribute is assumed to exist along with both subject and accident, but that the mode of attachment is the same (*Soph. Elench.* v.). The condition of valid reasoning which Aristotle here lays down, is precisely the same as Herbert Spencer (*Psychology*, vol. ii. ch. v.) has in view when he speaks of 'connature.' Aristotle regards the nine categories which follow substance as accidents, and the classification itself may be regarded as a classification of 'connatures.'

3. *Accident in relation to substance.*—Sir W. Hamilton (*Lectures*, vol. i. p. 150) says 'accident' is employed in reference to a substance as existing; the terms 'phenomenon,' 'appearance' in reference to it as known. The Scholastics distinguished 'accident' in this sense as *accidens prædicamentale* or categorical accident from *accidens prædicabile* or logical accident (Aquinas, *Summ. Theol.* i. q. 77, a. 1–5). The former is the wider term. 'Accident' in this sense is defined as *ens entis*, or *ens in alio*, substance being *ens per se*. Thomas Aquinas (*ib.* iii. q. 77, a. 1) says the proper definition is not actual inherence in a subject, but aptitude to inhere. The chief reason of this definition is that in the doctrine of Transubstantiation the accidents of bread and wine remain when the substance is changed. The substance of the body and blood cannot be affected by the accidents, therefore these must be capable of existing apart from their substance, being supported by Divine power. This has led to a distinction of three kinds of accidents: (1) *metaphysical*, accident which, although we may conceive the substance without it, is nevertheless identified with it. There is a *distinctio rationis ratiocinatæ* between them. Opposed to this is physical accident, which, if different from the substance itself as thing or entity, is (2) *absolute* or real, as quantity, motion. If it signifies merely a state of being, as to sit or stand, it is (3) a *modal* accident. It is for the absolute accidents that the capacity of being miraculously sustained in the Eucharist is claimed (Zigliara, *Summa Philos.* i. 441; Pesch, *Institutiones Logicales*, Pars II. vol. ii. p. 281). Aquinas maintained the real distinction of absolute accidents from the substance of both mind and matter. (For list of opponents with regard to mental faculties, see Sir W. Hamilton, *Lectures*, ii. pp. 5–8. The question is still disputed by Roman Catholic theologians). Leibnitz supported the view of Aquinas (*System of Theology*, tr. by Russell, pp. 112–114; *Opera Philosophica*, ed. Erdmann, pp. 680, 686, etc.). He distinguishes mass as an absolute accident from substance (*System of Theology*, p. 115).

Accidents, according to Locke, are qualities which are capable of producing simple ideas in us (*Essay*, bk. ii. ch. xxiii.).

According to Kant, accidents are the determinations of a substance which are nothing else than its particular modes to exist; or the mode in which the existence of a substance is positively determined (*Werke*, ed. Rosenkrantz, vol. ii. p. 160).

In Hegel, accidents are the determinations which unconditioned Being has in so far as it has immediate existence (*Philosoph. Propädeutik*, p. 105).

4. *'Accident' in the sense of that which happens by chance*, is defined by Aristotle as that which occurs neither always, nor from necessity, nor for the most part (*Metaph.* x. (xi.) 8). Elsewhere (*Metaph.* iv. (v.) 30) he gives, as illustration, finding a treasure when digging a hole for a plant.

LITERATURE. — Aristotle, *Organon*, *Metaphysics*; Petrus Hispanus, *Summulæ Logicales*, with exposition of Versorius; Thomas Aquinas, *Summa Theologica*; Sanderson, *Logic* (*Works*, vol. vi.); Hamilton, *Lectures on Metaphysics*; Mansel, *Aldrich's 'Artis Logicæ Rudimenta'*; J. S. Mill, *Logic*; Schouppe, *Elem. Theol. Dogmaticæ*.

G. J. STOKES.

ACCIDENTALISM.—The theory that events may happen without a cause. This is a view of the world which characterizes a pre-scientific period of thought. With the rise of the scientific method and spirit all events come to be regarded as connected in a causal manner, and no single event whatsoever is conceived as possibly falling without the closed circle of cause and effect relations. Chance or accident, therefore, is not to be considered as opposed to the idea of causation, so that it could be possible to say, 'This event happened by chance, but that event was evidently the effect of some cause.' There is no such antithesis, for every event is caused. The accidental event is merely one whose cause is so complex that it cannot be determined, and, therefore, it affords no basis for any exact prediction of the re-occurrence of the event in question. It becomes a matter of treatment according to the theory of probability. Chance, in the theory of probability, means always a complex combination of possible causal relations, whose interaction sometimes produces a certain event, and sometimes fails to produce it. The interacting causes may co-operate and reinforce, and, again, may oppose and neutralize one another, and therefore the resulting combinations are not predictable. This is the scientific view of chance, which is not free in any sense of the law of causation.

In the early Greek philosophy the idea of a certain kind of accidentalism in the world of events was a very persistent one. It appears in Plato, and even in Aristotle; and it was not until the Stoics emphasized the scientific view of the universe that the unscientific nature of accidentalism became fully recognized. Aristotle held that single events may be referred to universal laws of cause and effect, but he did not commit himself to this conception wholly without reservation. He ascribes events to a causal order 'for the most part' (ἐπὶ τὸ πολύ), and insists upon the contingent in nature, that which is without cause and without law (*Met.* 1065*a*, 4). Plato finds a place for chance in the economy of the universe. 'God governs all things, and chance and opportunity co-operate with Him in the government of human affairs' (*Laws*, iv. 709). And yet among the Greeks there was an instinctive shrinking from the idea of chance as the antithesis of cause and law. The Fates were, after all, the daughters of Necessity. Of them Plato remarks: 'Lachesis or the giver of lots is the first of them, and Clotho or the spinner is the second of them, and Atropos or the unchanging one is the third of them; and she is the preserver of the things of which we have spoken, and which have been compared in a figure to things woven by fire, they both (*i.e.* Atropos and the fire) producing the quality of unchangeableness' (*Laws*, xii. 960). This quality of unchangeableness is opposed alike to the caprice or whim of a goddess, and to the chance control of the destinies of man.

Moreover, accidentalism in the field of ethics appears in the theory of indeterminism. Epicurus, for instance, regards the uncaused will of man as analogous to the accidental deviation of atoms from the direct line of their fall. The uncaused event and the uncaused will both present the same general characteristics and the same difficulties also.

JOHN GRIER HIBBEN.

ACCIDENTS (from the theological point of view). — Accidents, to a teleological theology, must be not merely what they are to logic, viz. occurrences which do not fall under a general law of nature. The laws of nature are, from the teleological point of view, rules expressing the purposes of a conscious Being, and accidents will be occurrences not conforming to such purposes.

The theologian who adopts the theory that contingency in the natural world is an illusion due to our ignorance of general causes, must hold that there is no event not in conformity with Divine design; the very illusion of contingency must itself be the result of purpose. The difficulties that attend this subject are the same as surround the problem of Evil (wh. see). Practically, the belief that there are real influences in the world thwarting the Divine design is an incitement towards activity; the opposite doctrine—that accidents are, after all, part of the Divine purpose, gives consolation in failure. On the whole, Christian theology tends to maintain that the solution of such difficulties falls outside the province of reason, and does not attempt such a synthesis of contradictory opinions as constitutes the Hegelian treatment of the contingent. G. R. T. Ross.

ACCIDENTS (Injurious).—Accidents, in the general sense of the term as popularly employed, may be defined as unforeseen occurrences in human experience. Obviously the accidental character of events will thus be relative to the knowledge and reasoning power of different individuals. In order to mitigate the consequences of *injurious* accidents, the method of insurance (wh. see) is the most effective. By this means the consequences of an injurious accident, in so far as they can be expressed in terms of money, may be entirely deprived of their momentary and future effect by a previous economy, much less in most cases than would be necessary to equalize, as a sum of payments, the damage sustained. Not only so, but the diffusion of the evil results of contingency over a lengthened period, and their transference to a corporation, prevent them from having that cumulative effect which may lead to further disaster of new and increasing nature.

Injurious accidents may lead to legal action, wherever the occurrences so styled are the result of the agency of at least one individual other than the sufferer, and that other agency can be distinguished from society in general.

(*a*) In the first class of such suits—actions for damages at common law—the first plea to be established by the prosecutor is substantially the proposition that the occurrence, which relatively to him was accidental, was not so to the defender, but fell within the scope of the latter's knowledge and foresight. But there are numerous circumstances which might neutralize the effect even of the establishment of such a contention.

(*b*) Claims for compensation may be brought in cases where the injurious accident occurs in an enterprise concerning which there was a previous contract or agreement between the litigating parties. In numerous classes of such joint enterprise the extent to which the risk of accident is borne by either party is laid down by law. For each species of relation a different rule may obtain. Thus in British law the liability for damage to goods entrusted to their care differs in the cases of warehousemen and of common carriers. The relation involving joint enterprise to which Parliamentary enactment has most recently extended delimitation of the risk of the contracting parties, is that of employer and employed. In consequence of the Workmen's Compensation Acts of 1897, 1900, and 1906, in a great number of industries, and not merely in those involving an unusual amount of danger to workers, the employer now bears the risk of injury to his workmen. Every workman may claim compensation from his employer for injury through accident, unless the accident be caused by his own serious and wilful misconduct. The result of these enactments is practically to make the employer bear the cost of the insurance of his employees against accident. It is only to be expected, however, that, though the immediate consequence will be a diminution of the revenue of employers, in time the expense of this system will fall partly upon the workmen, in the shape of a diminution or absence of increase in wages.

LITERATURE.—Willis, *Workmen's Compensation Acts, 1897 and 1900*, 8th ed. pp. 1–7; Baylis, *Workmen's Comp. Acts*[7] (1906); Emery, *Handbook to Workmen's Comp. Act, 1906*.

G. R. T. Ross.

ACCIDIE.—The obsolete 'accidie,' from ἀκηδία, *incuria, torpor* (Hippocr.), through med. Lat. *accidia* (as if from *accidere*), was once current as the name of a quality related on one side to sloth, which has superseded it in some lists of the principal vices. Chaucer in the *Parson's Tale*, dilating upon the 'Seven Mortal Sins,' *Superbia, Invidia, Ira, Accidia, Avaritia, Gula, Luxuria*, writes of the fourth: 'Agayns this roten-herted sinne of Accidie and Slouthe sholde men exercise hem-self to doon gode werkes, and manly and vertuously cacchen corage well to doon' (Skeat, *Student's Chaucer*, p. 700). In Dante see *accidia* and adj. *accidioso* (*Purg.* xviii. 132; *Inf.* vii. 123). The Patristic uses of ἀκηδία rest upon the Old Testament. The earliest of them is not noticed by the authorities mentioned below. The correct Latin form is *acedia*. Bp. Hall is quoted for 'acedy' (1623).

Ἀκηδία, ἀκηδιᾶν are found as below in the LXX: the renderings in brackets are from the Vulgate. (1) Ps 118^{28} ἐνύσταξεν ἡ ψυχή μου ἀπὸ ἀκηδίας (*præ tædio*). (2) Is 61^{3} ἀντὶ πνεύματος ἀκηδίας (*mœroris*). (3) Sir 29^{5} ἀποδώσει λόγους ἀκηδίας (*tædii*). (4) Ps 60^{3} ἐν τῷ ἀκηδιάσαι τὴν καρδίαν μου (*dum anxiaretur*). (5) Ps 101^{1} Προσευχὴ τῷ πτωχῷ ὅταν ἀκηδιάσῃ (*cum anxius fuerit*). (6) Ps 142^{4} καὶ ἠκηδίασεν ἐπ' ἐμὲ τὸ πνεῦμά μου (*anxiatus est*). (7) Dn 7^{15} LXX, ἀκηδιάσας ἐγὼ Δανιήλ, Theod. ἔφριξεν (*horruit*). (8) Bar 3^{1} ψυχὴ ἐν στενοῖς καὶ πνεῦμα ἀκηδιῶν (*anxius*) [Schleusner, *s.v.* ἀκηδία, *anxietatum*]. (9) Sir 6^{25} μὴ προσοχθίσῃς (*ne acedieris*). (10) Sir 22^{13} καὶ οὐ μὴ ἀκηδιάσῃς (*non acediaberis*).

The phrase 'spirit of acedy' is from (2) above; Antioch. *Hom.* 26 alludes also to (1), (4), (6), (8); and (9), (10) in the Latin are cited by Alardus Gazæus on Cassian.

In *Vis.* iii. of *Hermæ Pastor* it is explained that the Church appeared first as old, 'because your spirit was aged and already faded and powerless from your ailings and doubts. For as the aged, having no hope any more to renew their youth, expect nothing but their last sleep; so ye, being weakened by worldly affairs, yielded yourselves up to *acedies* (τὰς ἀκηδίας), and cast not your cares upon the Lord, but your spirit was broken, and ye were worn out with your griefs (λύπαις).' Thus acedy is associated with sadness (λύπη), one of the four *plus* eight principal vices in *Sim.* ix. 15; which is *more wicked than all the spirits*, and destroys the power of prayer (*Mand.* v., x.). The parable of the Unclean Spirit which takes to it *seven other spirits more wicked than itself* (Mt 12^{45}, Lk 11^{26}) serves as a proof-text for the number *eight* (afterwards *seven*) of the *principalia vitia*. Nilus of Sinai calls them the 'Eight Spirits of Wickedness' (Zöckler, *op. cit. inf.* p. 65).

In Cassian's *Collat.* v. 'De octo principalibus Vitiis,' which embodies the teaching of Serapion, the eight vices are said to be *Gastrimargia, Fornicatio, Philargyria, Ira, Tristitia, Acedia* sive tædium cordis, *Cenodoxia, Superbia*. They are referred to in Lk $11^{24ff.}$, and they correspond to the like number of nations hostile to Israel. Why eight vices, when Moses enumerates only seven such nations? (Dt 7^{1}). Egypt, corresponding to the first vice (Nu 11^{5}), makes up the number: the land of Egypt was to be forsaken, and the lands of the seven taken. Acedy, the besetting sin of the monk, was of two kinds: it sent him to sleep in his cell, or drove him out of it. The same vices attack all men, but not all in the same manner and order. This remark foreshadows the disagreement of later moralists in their accounts of the vices, which are all more or less subjective.

Cassian, in *Cœnob. Inst.* x. 'De Spiritu Acediæ' (cf. Evagr. *ap.* Zöckler; Antioch. *Hom.* 26), details the effects of acedy, beginning: 'Sextum nobis certamen est quod Græci ἀκηδίαν vocant, quam nos tædium sive anxietatem cordis possumus nuncupare.' It is akin to *Tristitia*; is most felt by recluses; and attacks chiefly about the sixth hour, so that it has been called the 'midday demon' (Ps 90[6]). Then, heated and famished, the monk is as if wearied by long travel or toil, or as if he had fasted two or three days. Impatient for the repast, he leaves his cell again and again to look at the sun, which seems to 'hasten too slowly to its setting.' Through 'not-caring' he is remiss at his tasks, and finds it a weariness even to listen to the voice of the reader. Solitude impels him to gad about visiting the brethren or the sick. Discontented with his surroundings, he vainly imagines that he would do better in some distant monastery.

To replace the complex acedy by sadness or sloth is to evade a difficulty. In Serapion's octad it is distinct from *Tristitia* and different from mere *pigritia*. Briefly, it was the state of mind of a monk who had mistaken his vocation: the natural effect in him of the 'religious' life, with its fastings from food and 'from the world.'

LITERATURE.—*Oxford New English Dictionary*, *s.v.*; *Encyc. Brit.*[9] art. 'Ethics' (by H. Sidgwick); E. Moore, *Studies in Dante*, ser. 2 (1899); O. Zöckler, *Die Tugendlehre des Christentums* (1904); F. Paget, *Spirit of Discipline* (1891), 1; C. J. Vaughan, *Authorized or Revised?* (1882), 115; T. B. Strong, *Christian Ethics* (1896), 231, 255, 263 f.; J. O. Hannay, *Christian Monasticism* (1903), 153 ff.; Sir J. T. Coleridge's *Memoir*, 66, 68; J. S. Carroll, *Prisoners of Hope* (1906), 224 ff.

C. TAYLOR.

ACCOMMODATION (in Biology and Psychology).—The process of organic or psychological adjustment understood in an individual and functional sense. The concept of accommodation has arisen in the group of genetic sciences by a process of growing specialization of problems. The old problem of 'adaptation' (*q.v.*) was one concerned with the adjustments of organisms to their environment, understood in a very static or agenetic way. Each adaptation was looked upon largely as a definite structural arrangement whereby the organism responded effectively to the conditions of the world. The theory of evolution, and with it that of individual development, has made necessary a more functional statement of the whole series of problems involved in the notion of adaptation. The description of the 'organs' involved and the 'ends' they serve—as in the case of the eye—has given place to the functional problem of the reactions and evolving functions through which the organ has come to be part of the endowment of the organism. This has given rise to a distinction between 'adaptation' proper and 'accommodation.' Adaptation is, by the terms of this distinction, restricted to the congenital adjustments for which the organism inherits structures adequate and fit; accommodation is applied to the adjustments which the organism, in the lifetime of the individual, achieves and perfects. Instinct in the animals is, in many cases, an adaptation; the adjustments of the senses to their appropriate stimulations are likewise adaptations: such processes, on the contrary, as modifications of instinct to meet special conditions, the special reactions learned by the individual, such as handwriting, together with the functional effects of conditions in the environment upon the organism, are accommodations.

The importance of the problem of accommodation is seen in Biology in all cases in which the endeavour is made to interpret the influence of individual behaviour and individual modification upon the organism and upon the next and following generations. As early as the work of Lamarck, this factor was made very prominent in evolution theory, in the Lamarckian hypothesis that the results of accommodation—of 'use and disuse'—were inherited. This was also maintained by Darwin, as subsidiary to his main principle of Natural Selection. Weismann and the neo-Darwinians reject this direct influence of the accommodation factor; they deny its hereditary transmission, but still admit its importance as a constant process in successive generations of essential learning, whereby the individuals of each generation grow up to be competent and fertile—this position being that known as 'Intra-Selection' (Weismann). A more recent theory, called by the present writer 'Organic Selection,' discovers the importance of accommodations in *directing* the line of evolution. It is pointed out that, even though the modifications due to accommodation are not inherited, they still so effectively aid and protect individuals against the action of natural selection, that certain lines of adaptations and correlated characters are preserved and accumulated rather than others. The trend of evolution is thus in the lines marked out in advance by accommodations, natural selection following up and clinching the results first secured by accommodation.

The effects of accommodation on the structure of the organism are technically known as 'modifications'; they are contrasted with 'variations,' which are differences of structure of the 'adaptive' and congenital sort. Individuals are born different by variation; they become different during their lives by modification.

In Psychology the theory of accommodation is of even greater importance. The remarkable range and importance of the learning processes are never made matter of question. The problem of accommodation becomes therefore in Psychology—as also in Biology—that of the possibility of learning anything new. Thus stated, the fact of accommodation is set over against that of 'habit.' If we call all those functions, of whatever sort, that the individual is already able to perform, his 'habits,' it then becomes necessary to explain the process by which habit is modified, cancelled, and added to: this is accommodation.

The present solutions of this problem are in line with the requirements of genetic science as science of function. It is no longer considered possible that an individual may simply, by an act of will, do a thing that he has not learned to do; only certain fixed instincts work in that way, and that because they are fixed as habits by the gift of heredity. No muscular combination is possible, even when it involves the voluntary muscles—as, for example, those for moving the ear in man—that has not been learned, and the process of learning is a slow and effortful one. The theory most current, and having the greater weight because held by both biologists and psychologists, is that known as 'theory of excess discharge,' of 'trial and error,' or of 'persistent imitation,' etc. In effect it considers any act of accommodation or learning as due to the excessive and varied exercise of habits already formed, the element of learning arising from the modifications that come through the happy hits, the successful imitations, the pleasurable results, etc., of the muscular or other combinations thus set in movement. The writer has illustrated this in many ways, treating of the acquisition of handwriting as a typical case in *Mental Development in the Child and the Race* (1895). Spencer and Bain worked out a similar conception. In Biology, the movements of unicellular organisms, as well as the accommodations of grosser function in higher animals, are being fruitfully interpreted in accordance with this view (see Ll. Morgan, *Animal Behaviour*; Jennings, *Behaviour of the Lower Organisms*).

In the higher reaches of psychic function, the analogous problem is that of 'Selective Thinking,' together with the theory of adjustment to various non-physical environments. There is the social life, to which each individual must be accommodated; there is the environment of truth, to which all our processes of thinking selectively must conform. All this carries the problem of accommodation up into the realms of Social Psychology, Ethics, and Theory of Knowledge.

LITERATURE.—Besides the works cited in the text, see the general discussions of evolution, such as Conn, *Method of Evolution* (1901); Gulick, *Evolution Racial and Habitudinal* (1905); Headley, *Problems of Evolution* (1901). On Organic Selection see Lloyd Morgan, *Habit and Instinct* (1896); and Baldwin, *Development and Evolution* (1903), and *Dictionary of Philosophy and Psychology*, where lists of selected works are given under artt. 'Accommodation,' 'Adaptation,' 'Evolution,' etc.

J. MARK BALDWIN.

ACCUMULATION.—'Accumulation' (Lat. *ad* 'to,' *cumulus* 'a heap') signifies (1) a heap, mass, or pile; (2) the process of growing into a heap, *e.g.* the growth of a debt, or of a deposit at the bank, through the continuous addition of interest to principal; (3) the action of heaping, piling or storing up, amassing, as in the case—important from the standpoint of the present article—of the growth of capital.

The accumulation of capital is the result of saving. This, however, does not necessarily imply abstinence, privation, or sacrifice, in the ordinary sense. Saving on the part of the great capitalist involves no personal abstinence from immediate consumption, no sacrifice of present gratifications. His immediate expenditure is limited only by his tastes. Often the pleasure of accumulation is greater than that of careless extravagance, and at times the dominant idea is the increase of wealth for the sake of power. 'Abstinence here means abstinence from senseless waste; it is a negative not a positive merit' (E. R. A. Seligman, *Principles of Economics*, p. 320). This much must be conceded to Karl Marx and his followers. Hence the neutral term 'waiting' has been suggested as a substitute for 'abstinence.'

In the case of smaller incomes the subordination of present to future utility often involves real sacrifice, forbearance, prudence, forethought. But even here it must be borne in mind that anything that increases the productive power of labour so far increases the amount which can be saved. 'To increase capital there is another way besides consuming less, namely, to produce more' (J. S. Mill, *Principles of Political Economy*, Bk. I. ch. v. § 4). Thus, in general, all that we can say is that saving implies an excess of production over consumption—a favourable state of that balance 'which, according as it happens to be either favourable or unfavourable, necessarily occasions the prosperity or decay of every nation' (Adam Smith, *Wealth of Nations*, Bk. IV. ch. iii.).

To say that capital is the result of saving does not mean that it is not consumed. Saving is not hoarding. All capital is consumed. It fulfils its primary function—the satisfaction of future needs—only in being consumed, that is, used; but it is not immediately consumed by the person who saves it. Saving thus simply implies that productive power is directed to the satisfaction of prospective or future needs. In general, this is done through saving 'money,' not, however, as a hoard, but as giving, through the banking system, the power of directing national industry into particular channels. In this way, saving gives an increase in the productive power, and consequently in the consuming power of the society (see Nicholson, *Principles of Political Economy*, Bk. I. ch. xii. § 4).

In this connexion, Mill points out the erroneous nature of the popular idea that the greater part of a nation's capital has been inherited from the distant past in which it was accumulated, and that no part was produced in any given year save that year's addition to the total amount. The fact, he says, is far otherwise. 'The greater part in value of the wealth now existing in England has been produced by human hands within the last twelve months.' The growth of capital is similar in many respects to the growth of population. Each is kept in existence, and increases from age to age, not by preservation but by perpetual consumption and reproduction. It is only the value of the capital that remains and grows; the things themselves are ever changing (see Mill, *Principles*, Bk. I. ch. v. § 6).

This consideration helps us to understand the, at first sight, amazing rapidity with which countries often recover from the effects of a devastating war. The material capital destroyed or removed would, for the most part, have required reproduction in any case; while the land and its *quasi*-permanent improvements subsist. So long, therefore, as the country has not been depopulated, and the necessaries of a working life remain, the character and skill of the people being unchanged, there are all the essential conditions of a speedy recovery (*ib.* Bk. I. ch. v. § 7).

Here the relatively greater importance of what is known as *personal* or *immaterial*—*i.e.* mental and moral—capital, as compared with material capital, is apparent. It is indeed this immaterial capital that constitutes our great inheritance from the past. 'The present state of the nations,' says List, the German protectionist, 'is the result of the accumulation of all discoveries, inventions, improvements, perfections, and exertions of all generations that have lived before us; they form the mental capital of the present human race' (*National System of Political Economy*, Eng. tr. p. 140). The economic condition of a country depends far more on the mental and moral qualities of its inhabitants than on their accumulation of dead material capital.

It is thus with reason that Adam Smith includes the acquired skill of the people in the fixed capital of the nation. 'The improved dexterity of a workman may be considered in the same light as a machine or instrument of trade which facilitates and abridges labour, and which, though it costs a certain expense, repays that expense with a profit' (*W. of N.*, Bk. II. ch. i.). The successors of Adam Smith, however, lacked his comprehensive grasp of the realities of industrial life; and much of the popular antipathy to the teaching of the English economists of the early part of the 19th cent.—the followers of Ricardo—may be traced to their use of narrow and faulty abstractions, and in particular to their intensely materialistic conception of capital, which ignored altogether the skill of the worker. The force of attention was thus misdirected. Regard was had to the quantity rather than to the quality of labour, and consequently the influence of efficiency on wages was overlooked. Every proposed reform, *e.g.* the Factory Acts, was judged by reference to its probable immediate effect on the accumulation of dead material wealth. It was not seen that the capital of a country may be as profitably invested in the physical, mental, and moral training of its inhabitants as in the accumulation of dead material wealth in the shape of machinery, factory buildings, and the like.

To take but one other example of immaterial capital, and that a characteristic product of the mental and moral qualities of the people of these islands, the British money market—that marvellous banking and credit organization through which the capital of the country finds its way into the hands of those who can turn it to the most productive purposes—has been described by Bagehot as 'the greatest combination of economical power and economical delicacy that the world has ever seen' (see *Lombard Street*, ch. i.).

Some idea of the relative importance of immaterial capital is given by Professor Nicholson, who estimates the 'living capital' of the United Kingdom as worth about five times the value of its dead material capital (see *Strikes and Social Problems*, pp. 97–116). Enough has been said to show that, for an explanation of the rise and fall of nations, we should look to the growth and decay of their immaterial rather than their material capital.

To return to material capital, the state of the balance of production and consumption, or, in other words, the accumulation of capital—which in a modern industrial society, with its vast and increasing variety of forms and substitutes, is necessarily measured in terms of money—depends on causes which naturally fall into two groups, those, namely, which determine the amount of the fund from which saving can be made, or, in other words, the *power to save*, and those which determine the strength of the dispositions which prompt to saving, or, in brief, the *will to save*.

1. **The power to save** is necessarily limited to the amount of the national dividend or real net produce of the society, *i.e.* the surplus of the annual produce over what is required to supply the efficiency-necessaries of the producers, including those engaged in replacing raw material, repairing the auxiliary capital (*e.g.* machinery, buildings, etc.), and keeping up the consumption capital (*e.g.* dwelling houses, museums, etc.). The amount of this national dividend depends on (*a*) the *natural resources* of the country, (*b*) the *state of the arts of production* in the widest sense, including not only the means of communication and transport, but also the machinery of exchange; for under the modern system of division of labour production involves exchange, and thus the state of the credit institutions must also be considered.

The causes embraced under these two heads together determine the amount produced within the country. But the amount of the national dividend is further affected by (*c*) the *state of foreign trade*, which determines the amount of imports obtained in return for exports. (*d*) The *amount taken by Government for public purposes*, whether in the form of taxes or burdens like conscription, must also be considered (see Nicholson, *Elements of Political Economy*, p. 86).

These causes determine the annual national dividend or maximum which can be saved. But the amount annually added to capital always falls short, and generally far short, of this, depending as it does on the *will to save*.

2. **The will to save** is the resultant of a complexity of causes, amongst the most important of which are: (*a*) *Security*. To induce saving there must be some reasonable expectation that the owner will be allowed to enjoy the fruits of his saving. This involves protection *by* the Government against force and fraud, which includes the enforcement of freely made contracts; and protection *against* the Government, *e.g.* against oppressive and, above all, arbitrary taxation (see Mill, *Principles*, Bk. I. ch. vii. § 6; Nicholson, *Principles*, Bk. I. ch. xii. § 3). The importance of security in both these forms finds abundant illustration in the history of all nations and ages. Compare, for example, Egypt or India under British rule with Armenia or Macedonia under the dominion of the Turk, or the present state of Russia under the government of the Czar. The British credit system, already referred to, is the outcome of security and good government, just as the hoarding so prevalent in the East is the natural fruit of the uncertainty so often associated with Oriental systems of taxation and government. Even in India the influence of the *pax Britannica* has not yet sufficed to eradicate from the native mind the traditional tendency to hoard, engendered by centuries of turbulence and insecurity.

There must also be a sense of security against the violence of the powers of nature. In balancing the advantages of present and future utilities the uncertainty of the future is an important factor. Where a country has an unhealthy climate, and is liable to plagues, or is subject to earthquakes, volcanic eruptions, tornadoes, or other physical disasters, the consequent uncertainty of life does, so far, tend to check accumulation by lessening the will to save, apart altogether from the influence of such disasters on the power to save. On the occasion of great plagues, popular practice follows the maxim of pagan philosophy: 'Let us eat, drink, and be merry, for to-morrow we die.'

(*b*) The effect of *the rate of interest* on saving is somewhat complex. A high rate, security being unchanged, affords a greater reward for saving, and thus, so far, a greater inducement to save. But the higher the rate of interest the lower, *ceteris paribus*, the rate of wages; and thus a high rate may react on the efficiency of labour and may check enterprise, and thus lessen the power to save. At the same time, those who merely wish to obtain a certain annuity need save less if the rate of interest is high. In general, however, a fall in the rate of interest will tend to check accumulation. But some accumulation would go on even if the rate of interest became negative (see Nicholson, *Principles*, Bk. I. ch. xii. § 3; Marshall, *Principles of Economics*, Bk. IV. ch. vii. §§ 8, 9).

(*c*) The accumulation of capital is affected also by the existing *facilities for investment*. The multiplication of branch banks in Scotland has undoubtedly contributed to increase both the power and the will to save. The more recent extension of savings banks and the growth of joint stock companies with limited liability have also greatly stimulated saving throughout the community.

(*d*) *The distribution of national wealth* amongst the different economic classes has likewise a certain influence on accumulation. When the bulk of the wealth of England was in the hands of the feudal landowners, extravagance prevailed, as explained by Adam Smith (*W. of N.* Bk. III. ch. iv.), and it is only after the revolution of 1688 that, with the rise of the mercantile class, we find a rapid accumulation of wealth. Similarly in France the contrast is striking between the extravagance of the *ancien régime* and the thrift of the peasantry in modern times. Amongst the latter the effective desire of accumulation appears to be excessive. The living or immaterial capital is sacrificed to the dead. 'In England,' says Lady Verney, 'thrift appears to be a great virtue. Here one hates the very mention of it. . . . The sordid, unclean, hideous existence which is the result of all this saving and self-denial, the repulsive absence of any ideal but that of *cacher de petits sous dans de grands bas* as object for life, is incredible if it is not seen and studied' (*Peasant Properties*, p. 151).

(*e*) The *effective desire of accumulation* is compounded of many elements, intellectual and moral, including the development of the 'telescopic faculty' (Marshall), the growth of the family affections, the hope of rising in the world, and the social and other advantages attendant on the possession of wealth. The strength of this desire may be weak from intellectual deficiency. The wants of the present are vividly realized, those of the future are but dimly imagined. There is frequent lack of the power of imagination necessary to the proper appreciation of the importance of future benefits, as in the case, mentioned by Dr. Rae, of the Indians on the banks of the St. Lawrence, who, when a speedy result was to be obtained, would toil even more assiduously than the white man, but would undertake no work for which the return was at all remote (see Rae, *The Sociological Theory of Capital* [ed. Mixter, pp. 71–73]; also Mill, *Principles*, Bk. I. ch. xi. § 3). As we go lower in the scale, this weakness becomes more pronounced. The Australian native, in respect of foresight in providing for the future, is inferior to many of the lower animals (see Letourneau, *Property*, Eng. tr. p. 30).

Often, however, the effective desire of accumulation is weak, not so much from intellectual as from moral deficiency. Even in the most highly civilized nations, there are too many instances of men of the most vivid imagination—men who are in no way defective in the telescopic faculty—who yet, through lack of will power, interest in others, family affection or sense of independence, are unable to resist the temptations of the present sufficiently to provide for the clearly foreseen needs of the future, or unwilling to make any provision for the welfare of wife and children or for their own independence in old age or disablement. Amongst the unskilled labour class in this country the average degree of providence and self-restraint is not much above that of uncivilized man. It is this that constitutes the chief difficulty of the problem of unemployment. But amongst the professional, manufacturing, trading, and skilled artizan classes, on the other hand, the effective desire of accumulation is strong. The vastness of the sums yearly paid as premiums to life insurance companies—only one form of saving—affords sufficient proof of this.

The movement of progressive societies from status to contract, emphasized by Sir Henry Maine (*Ancient Law*, p. 170), accompanied and promoted, as it has been, by the extension of money payments in place of services and payments in kind, has greatly contributed to the accumulation of capital. The introduction of a money economy made it possible for a person to store up capital which would yield him an income in money, and was therefore capable of being turned to the satisfaction of any want whatever. At the same time, the displacement of a state of things in which a man's position in society is fixed at his birth according to the rigid rule of caste, by a state in which he makes his own position in society by contract with his fellow-men, has enormously increased the inducement to save, by affording full scope for that hope of raising oneself and one's family in the social scale, than which there are few stronger incentives to energy, enterprise, and the accumulation of wealth. 'The principle which prompts to save,' says Adam Smith, 'is the desire of bettering our condition, a desire which, though generally calm and dispassionate, comes with us from the womb, and never leaves us till we go into the grave' (*W. of N.* Bk. II. ch. iii.).

Mill asserts that to get out of one rank in society into the next above it is the great aim of English middle-class life, and that to this end it is necessary to save enough to admit of retiring from business, and living on the interest of capital (*Principles*, Bk. I. ch. xi. § 4). In America, on the other hand, success in business itself is often the dominant idea. Many of the most successful business men in the United States seem to be wholly absorbed in the acquisition and accumulation of capital, simply and solely as a necessary condition of pre-eminence in the world of business. They know no other goal. In some cases, indeed, the means is mistaken for the end, and the mere accumulation of wealth becomes the mainspring of life; or it may be that the habit of accumulating, acquired in time of need, maintains its sway when the need has passed.

But though the effective desire of accumulation is thus sometimes in excess of what reason would justify, there is much more danger in the other extreme. Nations may be ruined by extravagance, never by parsimony.

The popular idea of the social effects of extravagant expenditure is based on reasoning the fallacious nature of which has often been exposed. Saving is identified with selfish hoarding, while the spendthrift is regarded as benefiting all around him. It is admitted that he may be ruining himself and his family, but it is not generally recognized that he is almost equally the enemy of society. The lavish outlay of the spendthrift makes money circulate, and increases the profits and wages of wine-merchants, tailors, domestic servants, and others. That is *what we see.* What we *do not* so readily *see* is that, had the money not been thus squandered, the capital which it represents would not have lain idle, but would have found its way, through the medium of our banking organization, into the hands of some manufacturer or shipbuilder, say, to be employed by him in productive industry. The spendthrift, then, does not benefit trade, or give employment to labour; he simply alters the direction of the employment of capital, and he renders the nation poorer by the amount of the wealth he thus wastefully consumes. The saving person, on the other hand, creates a fund which, in its consumption, affords an equal employment for labour, and yet is continually renewed (see Mill, *Principles*, Bk. I. ch. v. §§ 3, 5). Economy, in short, enriches, while extravagance impoverishes, the individual and the nation.

And in this, as in most other cases, good economy is good morality. The accumulation of wealth implies, in the normal case, forethought, self-restraint, energy, and enterprise on the part of the individual, and it is an essential condition of his economic freedom. For the nation, it is an essential prerequisite of the highest civilization. It means increased scope for Division of Labour. 'As the accumulation of stock must, in the nature of things, be previous to the division of labour, so labour can be more and more subdivided in proportion only as stock is previously more and more accumulated' (Adam Smith, *W. of N.*, Bk. II. Introd.). It thus means increase in man's power over nature, with consequent economy of human effort in the satisfaction of the primary needs, and increased leisure for the culture of Art and Science and Literature. Nations, like men, may grow rich without culture, but the highest civilization is impossible in the absence of a sound economic basis of accumulated capital.

ARCH. B. CLARK.

ACHÆMENIANS.—A dynasty which ruled in Persia from B.C. 558 to 330, and whose religion is important for the study of the development of Zoroastrianism. The monarchs of the line were as follows: Cyrus the Great (558–530), Cambyses (530–522), Darius I. (522–486), Xerxes I. (486–465), Artaxerxes I. (465–424), Xerxes II. (424), Sogdianus (424), Darius II. (424–404), Artaxerxes II. (404–358), Artaxerxes III. (358–337), and Darius III. (337–330). The scanty data concerning their religion are contained in classical writings, in inscriptions in Babylonian, Egyptian, and Greek, and above all in their own inscriptions, which were written in Old Persian, with Babylonian and New Elamitic translations. The only kings of this dynasty who come into consideration here are Cyrus, Cambyses, Darius I., Xerxes I., and Artaxerxes II. and III.

1. Cyrus the Great.—The material for a knowledge of the religion of this monarch is restricted to the *Cyropædia* of Xenophon, the OT, and the Babylonian inscriptions. The *Cyropædia*, as is well known, is a historical romance, and its statements, therefore, can be accepted only with caution, unless they can be controlled by the Avesta or other sources. On the other hand, it must be borne in mind that Xenophon had exceptional opportunities for observing the Achæmenian religion, through his long association with Cyrus the Younger, so that under his apparent Hellenic veneer there may lurk some true elements of Achæmenian belief. In this romance Cyrus is repeatedly represented as offering sacrifices, and it is noteworthy that he invokes the assistance of the magi (iv. 5. 14, vi. 5. 57, viii. 1. 23). The deities to whom he rendered sacrifice appear under the Greek nomenclature of Zeus, Helios, Ge, and Hestia (i. 6. 1, iii. 3. 22, viii. 7. 3), and in addition to them he worshipped 'the other gods' or 'all the gods' (the latter phrase is interesting as being a striking, though doubtless accidental, parallel with a phrase of similar meaning in the Old Persian inscriptions of Darius) and the tutelary divinities (ἥρωες) of Assyria, Syria, Media, and Persia. With this list must be compared the statement of Herodotus (i. 131) and of Strabo (xv. 3. 13) that the Persians worshipped the sun, the moon, earth, fire, water, the winds, Aphrodite, and, above all, the sky, which they called Zeus. It thus becomes evident that the worship ascribed to Cyrus by Xenophon was a nature-worship closely akin to the Iranian cult which finds its revival in the so-called Younger Avesta. The deities honoured by him were doubtless identical with Ahura Mazda, Mithra, Ataš (the sacred fire), and Anahita (apparently identified with the earth as being a goddess of fertility). The identification of Hestia with the sacred fire receives its confirmation in the rôle ascribed to fire in the sacrifice recounted in *Cyrop.* viii. 3. 12, but the equation of Ge with Anahita is more doubtful. This goddess is represented by the Aphrodite of Strabo, and the divine personification of earth in Iranian mythology was Spenta Armaiti (Gray, *ARW* vii. 364–370). If, however, the identification here proposed be accepted, it finds a striking parallel in the collocation of Ahura Mazda, Mithra, and Anahita in the Old Persian inscription of Artaxerxes II. The tutelary divinities whom Cyrus is represented as worshipping are none other than the *fravashis*, who were originally the ghosts of the dead, yet who later came to be protecting godlings, and are thus invoked in *Yasna*, xxiii. 1: 'I invoke to worship those *fravashis* who aforetime were of the houses, and of the villages, and of the districts, and of the lands; who sustain the heaven, who sustain the water, who sustain the earth, who sustain the kine, who sustain children in the wombs to be conceived that they die not.' In the instructions of the dying Cyrus concerning the disposal of his body, on the other hand (*Cyrop.* viii. 7. 25), he departed widely from Zoroastrian usage when he requested that he be buried in earth, a request whose accuracy is confirmed by the elaborate description of his tomb as given by Strabo (xv. 3. 7), which agrees strikingly with the so-called Tomb of Cyrus at Pasargadæ. It may be noted in this connexion that the Achæmenian kings were entombed in rock sepulchres, as is evidenced by their tombs at Persepolis and elsewhere; while Herodotus (i. 140) states that the Persians, after exposing the corpse to birds or dogs, coated it with wax and placed it in the ground. It would seem, therefore, that the data of Xenophon concerning the founder of the Achæmenian dynasty are not so valueless as is sometimes supposed. They agree remarkably with the statements of the Younger Avesta, which, despite its comparatively late date, doubtless represents in its main outlines the religion of the Iranians before the reform associated with the name of Zoroaster.

Turning to the Babylonian inscriptions of Cyrus, we find that the religion of Cyrus is mentioned in the two texts of the Nabuna'id-Cyrus Chronicle and the Cylinder Inscription. In both Cyrus declares that Nabuna'id, the last native sovereign of Babylon, had brought the gods of Sumer and Akkad from their own temples to his capital, while he, on the other hand, as the chosen of Marduk, restored them to their homes. The view has been advanced that Marduk and his son Nabu, who are mentioned in close association in both these inscriptions, were regarded by Cyrus merely as other names for Ahura Mazda and his son Ataš (the sacred fire). This theory seems, on the whole, scarcely tenable; and a general consideration of the character of the Achæmenian, so far as it can be traced, leads to the interpretation that he acted as a clever politician, and not as a religious leader. Nor can the famous passage in Is 44^{28}–45^{4} be construed as casting any real light on the religion of Cyrus. Though the Persian king is addressed as 'the shepherd of Jahweh,' as His 'anointed,' before whom all nations should be subdued, and as the one whom Jahweh had called and in whom He took delight, this implies nothing more than a recognition of the close sympathy existing between Israel and Persia, and the conviction that the conqueror of Babylon would free the Jews from their exile. It is, in other words, the eulogy of the enthusiastic and hopeful prophet in honour of the politic victor.

Of these three sources, the Greek, even making all allowances for possible inaccuracies, seems to be the most reliable. The most that can be said, in the light of the data now available, is that the religion of Cyrus approximated closely to that contained in the Younger Avesta. There is no evidence whatever to show that he was a Zoroastrian.

2. Cambyses.—The religious records concerning this monarch are extremely scanty. Herodotus (iii. 16) mentions his impiety in burning the corpse of Amasis, 'since the Persians regard fire as a god . . ., saying that it is not right to give the corpse of a man to a god.' Both in Persia and in the home of the Avesta the defilement of the fire by contact with dead matter was regarded as a most grievous sin (cf. *Vendīdād*, vi. 73–81). The only other document which throws light on the religion of Cambyses is an Egyptian text on a naophoric statue in the Vatican. According to this inscription, the strangers had intruded within the precincts of the goddess Neit at Sais and had placed various obstructions there. In answer to a petition received by him, Cambyses commanded that the fane be purified and that its worship be restored. He himself then went to Sais, restored all offerings to the goddess and also to Osiris, while he likewise 'worshipped before the holiness of Neit with much devotion, as all the kings had done; he made great offering of all good things to Neit, the great, the divine mother, and to all the gods who dwell in Sais, as all the pious kings had done' (Petrie, *History of Egypt*, 1905, iii. 361, 362). Though Cambyses was, as is universally acknowledged, a madman, his policy with regard to this temple was thoroughly in accord with that pursued by Cyrus before him and Darius after him. His stabbing of the Apis bull, on the other hand, was the act of a maniac's cruelty, and was not inspired by any devotion to religious tenets of his own.

3. **Darius I.**—The chief source for a study of the religion of this monarch is furnished by his inscriptions in Old Persian, with their Babylonian and New Elamitic versions. The texts are found at Behistun, Persepolis, Naqš-i-Rustam, Elvand, Susa, Kirman, and Suez. In his inscriptions the king constantly ascribes the source of his authority to the 'grace of Ahura Mazda,' declaring: 'Auramazda brought me the kingdom; Auramazda bore me aid until this kingdom was held; by the grace of Auramazda I hold this kingdom' (Bh. i. 24–26). All evil in the realm is regarded as due to the malignant influence of the 'Lie' (*drauga*), which is to be compared with the *druǰ* of the Avesta. The 'Lie' was the cause of rebellion, while the power of Darius was due, in his opinion, largely to the fact that he had not been a 'liar.' The 'Lie' is thus closely parallel with the Aṅra Mainyu of the Avesta, and it is not impossible that it is a euphemistic term for the arch-fiend, thus accounting for the omission of all mention of Aṅra Mainyu in the Old Persian inscriptions. The fact that the Pahlavi translation of *Yasna*, xxx. 10, identifies the *druǰ* with Ahriman cannot, however, be cited in support of this hypothesis. Ahura Mazda is frequently described in the texts of the Achæmenian kings as 'a great god who created this earth, who created yon heaven, who created man, who created peace for man, who made Darius [or, Xerxes, Artaxerxes] king, the one king of many, the one ruler of many.' This passage is very similar to the Gāthā Avesta *Yasna*, xxxvii. 1: 'Here praise we Ahura Mazda, who created both kine and holiness, and created waters, created both good trees and light, both the earth and all good things.' This is but one of a number of parallels between the Old Persian texts and the Avesta which might be cited (cf. Windischmann, *Zoroastr. Studien*, 121–125); yet, on the other hand, an equal mass of coincidences exists between the Achæmenian inscriptions and the Assyr.-Bab. records (cf. Gray, *AJSL* xvii. 151–159).

It has been suggested that Ahura Mazda was regarded, in a sense, as the author of evil as well as of good, since Darius says (Bh. iv. 57–59): 'If thou hidest this tablet, (and) tellest it not to the people, may Auramazda be thy slayer, (and) may thy family be not.' This is not, however, altogether certain, for Ahura Mazda, as the god of the king, might fairly be invoked to destroy his enemies, such an act scarcely being regarded as evil. On the other hand, the only direct allusion to Ahriman in connexion with an Achæmenian monarch is found in Plutarch's Life of Themistocles, iii., where Xerxes prays that Ἀριμάνιος may always give the Greeks the mad impulse to drive their best men from them. Yet one can hardly give much weight to an isolated statement of a late and somewhat rhetorical author, especially as he was well acquainted with orthodox Zoroastrianism (see his *de Iside et Osiride*, xlvi.).

The course which the upright man should pursue is termed 'the right path' *paθim* (*tyām rāstām*), an idea which recurs not only in the Avesta (*Yasna*, lxxii. 11; *Yašt*, x. 3, 86; *Vendīdād*, iv. 43), but also in the OT, the Veda, and especially in Buddhism. In this spirit Darius declares, in a much-disputed passage, that 'I walked according to rectitude' (*upariy arštām upariyāyam*, Bh. iv. 64; for the establishment of this text see Jackson, *JAOS* xxiv. 90–92), the Arštā here mentioned being doubtless identical with the Arštāt of the Younger Avesta, 'who furthereth creatures, prospereth creatures, giveth health unto creatures' (*Yašt*, xi. 16). If these two beneficent powers are represented both in Old Persian and in the Avesta, the two sources agree in their view of the demon of drought, for the Dušiyārā against whom Darius invokes the protection of Ahura Mazda is to be identified with the Dužyāiryā, for whose destruction, according to the Younger Avesta (*Yašt*, viii. 50–56), Tištrya, the Dog-Star, was especially created by Ormazd (note also the mention of the 'horde,' Old Persian *hainā*, Avesta *haēnā*, in both texts in close association with 'drought').

It is thus evident that the Old Persian inscriptions of Darius represent him as a worshipper of Ahura Mazda and as filled with abhorrence of the 'Lie.' One beneficent godling (Arštā) and one maleficent fiend (Dušiyārā) are mentioned under the same names in the Younger Avesta. The stylistic parallels which may undoubtedly be traced between the Achæmenian texts and the Avesta, on the other hand, are counterbalanced by the Assyr.-Bab. inscriptions from which Darius and his successors manifestly drew. His policy towards other faiths than his own was that of Cyrus. In his reconstruction of the kingdom on his accession, he states that he 'restored the places of worship which Gaumata had digged down' (Bh. i. 64). He thus appears as an opponent of rigid Magian orthodoxy, for the 'places of worship' (*āyadanā*) are shown by the Bab. version to have been 'houses of the gods' (*bītāti ša ilāni*). That these were fire temples, like the Magian structures described by Strabo (733) as existing in Cappadocia, seems less probable than that they were temples of the gods of non-Persian peoples.

This view receives confirmation from a Greek and an Egyptian inscription of Darius. In the former text, found in 1886 at Deirmenjik (ed. Cousin and Deschamps, *BCH* xiii.), the king reproves his subject Gadates, who had sought to efface all traces of the royal attitude towards the gods, which, Darius expressly states, had been that of his predecessors, and who had exacted a tax from the priests of 'Apollo.' Who 'Apollo' was is doubtful. Cousin and Deschamps, somewhat strangely, identify him with Ātarš (the sacred fire), who appears in Greek, as noted above, under the name of Hestia. He is probably, however, the Greek divinity Apollo, who in times past had given a favourable oracle to Cyrus, perhaps during his Lycian campaign, and who was consequently honoured by the Achæmenian dynasty. At all events, the inscription is non-Zoroastrian in tone.

Still more polytheistic is the stele of Darius at Tell el-Maskhutah (ed. Golénischeff, *RTAP* xiii. 106–107), which contains the following words: '(Darius) born of Neit, the lady of Neit, the lady of Sais, image of the god Ra who hath put him on his throne to accomplish what he hath begun . . . (master) of all the sphere of the solar disc. When he (Darius) was in the womb (of his mother) and had not yet appeared upon earth, she (the goddess Neit) recognized him as her son . . . she hath (extended) her arm to him with the bow before her to overthrow for ever his enemies, as she had done for her own son, the god Ra. He is strong . . . (he hath destroyed) his enemies in all lands, king of Upper and Lower Egypt, Darius who liveth for ever, the great, the prince of princes . . . (the son) of Hystaspes, the Achæmenian, the mighty. He is her son (of the goddess Neit), powerful and wise to enlarge his boundaries.'

Devout and noble though his inscriptions show him to be, Darius seems to have been by no means a strict monotheist. This statement is borne out by the old Persian texts themselves, which show that he felt merely that Ahura Mazda was, as he himself says, 'the greatest of gods.' A Persepolitan inscription thrice contains the words *hadā viθaibiš bagaibiš*, which were formerly rendered 'with the clan-gods,' but which are now regarded as meaning 'with all the gods.' This interpretation is confirmed by the Bab. *itti ilāni gabbi* and the New Elamitic *annap marpepta-itaka* ('with all the gods') in texts of closely similar content and phraseology. The plural of *baγa* ('god') occurs in the Avesta only in *Yašt*, x. 141, which states that Mithra 'is the wisest of gods,' but its Pahlavi form occurs at least thrice, an undoubtedly Zoroastrian passage (*Dēnkarṭ*, viii. 15. 1) being especially interesting in this connexion, since it speaks of the 'worship of Auharmazd, the highest of divinities.' This phrase is strikingly similar to passages in the inscriptions of Darius and Xerxes which describe Ahura Mazda as 'the greatest of gods.' That such a phrase is not necessarily polytheistic is clear from such passages of the OT as Ps 82[1] 95[3] and 97[9]. In the New Elamitic version, however, occurs the statement, which may be significant, that Ahura Mazda was 'the god of the Aryans.' If stress may be laid on this (a fact which is by no means certain), it may serve as a partial explanation of the policy pursued by the Achæmenians with regard to the gods of the Babylonians, Egyptians, and Greeks. This view of Ahura Mazda as a national deity in the eyes of the Persian kings may readily be paralleled from other Oriental nations of antiquity. It may also explain the collocation of Ahura Mazda 'with all the gods,' of whom he was the greatest. In the light of this, the epithet πατρῷος, applied by Cyrus, according to Xenophon, to Zeus (Ahura Mazda) and Hestia (Ataršs, the sacred fire), possibly likewise becomes explicable (cf., however, the same epithet given by Greek poets to Æther, Apollo, Hekate, Hermes, and Zeus; see Bruchmann, *Epitheta Deorum quæ apud Poetas Græcos leguntur*, Leipzig, 1893). Under any explanation it is a far cry from the nationalistic Ahura Mazda of the politic Achæmenians to the god of the Avesta, who brooks no rivals and urges his follower to 'convert all men living' (*Yasna*, xxxi. 3).

4. Xerxes I.—The chief source for a knowledge of the religion of Xerxes I. is Herodotus, who states (vii. 43, 53, 54) that this king, when he arrived at the Hellespont in his expedition against Greece, sacrificed a thousand oxen to 'Athene of Ilium,' and also made a libation to the sun, and gave an offering to the sea. 'Athene of Ilium' seems to be the Persian Anahita, who is mentioned in the inscriptions of Artaxerxes II., and to whom were offered, according to the Younger Avesta (*Yašt*, v.), 'a hundred stallions, a thousand bulls, and ten thousand sheep.' The correspondence in the number of oxen offered in both accounts is surely noteworthy. The homage to the sun (Mithra) and the waters is too well known to require further elucidation (cf. Strabo, xv. 3. 13). If Herodotus may be believed, moreover, Xerxes sacrificed at a place called Nine Roads nine Greek boys and nine Greek girls, and he adds (vii. 114) that it was customary for the Persians to offer victims by burying them alive. In view of the fact that this custom is mentioned nowhere else, and of the defilement of the sacred element earth which it would cause, the statement of the Greek historian seems too improbable to be accepted as authentic. A passage of much interest, however, is that in which Herodotus says (vii. 40) that Xerxes was accompanied in his march by the 'sacred chariot of Zeus,' which was drawn by eight white horses, whose driver went on foot, 'for no man mounteth on this throne' (cf. Quintus Curtius, iii. 8–12). This 'chariot of Zeus' was, it may be conjectured, none other than the shrine in which dwelt Ahura Mazda, the national deity, who thus escorted the king to victory quite as Jahweh did in His ark carried by the Israelites.

5, 6. Artaxerxes II. and III.—The brief texts of Artaxerxes II. and III. are interesting solely as adding the names of Mithra and Anahita to that of Ahura Mazda. That this was a real innovation seems far from probable, in the light of the religion ascribed by the allusions in the classics to Cyrus and Xerxes. It is noteworthy, in this connexion, that Plutarch, who was by no means unacquainted with true Zoroastrianism, confirms the testimony of the inscriptions. In his Life of Artaxerxes II. he mentions the king's worship of Anahita, his oaths in the name of Mithra, as well as his coronation in a temple of 'Minerva' (a deity of uncertain identification).

The Achæmenians are curiously, and perhaps significantly, ignored in the Middle Persian writings. The theory has been advanced that Artaxerxes I. Longimanus is mentioned in the Pahlavi texts under the name of 'Ardashir the Kayan, whom they call Vohuman, son of Spend-dad,' who, according to *Bahman Yašt*, ii. 17, 'separates the demons from men, scatters them about, and makes the religion current in the whole world.' This hypothesis lacks all foundation. The Zoroastrian Artaxerxes was the son of Spend-dad; the Achæmenian was the son of Xerxes; al-Bīrūnī rightly distinguishes between them, and the identification of the two in the *Shāh-Nāmah* and other sources is properly regarded as contrary to history, since it is due to the accidental coincidence that the grandfather of each was named Darius. Again, according to the *Dēnkarṭ* (iv. 23), 'Darai, son of Darai, ordered the preservation of two written copies of the whole Avesta and Zand.' This Darius, who was the son of Darius, is identified with the Achæmenian Darius III. Codomanus, who was the son of Arsanes. Al-Bīrūnī once more carefully distinguishes between the two, and it is not unlikely that he is right in so doing (cf. Nöldeke in Geiger-Kuhn's *Grundriss der iran. Philologie*, ii. 141), even though other Oriental sources identify the two. At all events, the equation is too doubtful, with the data now available, to serve as a basis for any hypothesis, either for or against the Zoroastrianism of the Achæmenians.

In this connexion, however, mention may be made of the very plausible hypothesis of the Parsi scholar Desai, who supposes (*Cama Memorial Volume*, Bombay, 1900, 37) that this Darius and his immediate predecessors were transferred from the one dynasty to the other by the Pahlavi writers 'in their attempt to palm off some of the last kings of the Achæmenian house mentioned above, as the last Kayanian monarchs, the successors of king Gushtasp.' If this may be accepted (and it is by no means improbable), it would readily follow as a matter of course that the undoubted Zoroastrianism of the dynasty of Vishtaspa should be attributed to the added kings, whatever their own faith may have been. The lack of agreement between the monarchs recorded in the Pahlavi texts and the dynasty of the Achæmenians must, however, be taken into account in any attempt to solve this problem.

In the light of what has been said, it would appear that the Achæmenians were pre-eminently worshippers of Ahura Mazda, though they did not refuse to recognize other Iranian deities, such as the sun, the fire, and the waters, or even hesitate to honour the divinities of other countries, rebuild their temples, and restore their cult. Ahura Mazda was to them a purely national god, surrounded by subordinate deities who were clearly nature-divinities. Numerous parallels may be drawn, both in concept and in phraseology, between the Old Persian inscriptions and the Avesta, although it is most significant that these coincidences are with the Younger Avesta, with its probable recrudescence of the pre-Zoroastrian nature-cult, rather than with the Gāthās; and it must also be remembered that equally striking analogues exist between the Old Persian and the Assyr.-Bab. texts. The Old Persian inscriptions must be supplemented by all available sources, whether in Greek, Egyptian, Babylonian, or New Elamitic. From a careful study of all these documents, it becomes clear that the only conclusion which can safely be reached concerning the religion of the kings of this dynasty is that they were Mazdayasnians, not Zoroastrians.

LITERATURE.—Spiegel, *Altpers. Keilinschriften*[2] (Leipzig, 1881); Weissbach-Bang, *Altpers. Keilinschriften* (Leipzig, 1893); Bezold, *Achämenideninschriften* (Leipzig, 1882); Weissbach, *Achämenideninschriften zweiter Art* (Leipzig, 1890), also, 'Die altpers. Inschriften' in Geiger-Kuhn's *Grundriss der iran. Philologie*, ii. (Strassburg, 1904); Schrader, *KIB* iii. pt. 2 (Berlin, 1890); Brugsch, *Thesaurus inscrip. Egyp.* (Leipzig, 1883–1891); Brisson, *De regio Persarum principatu* (ed. Lederlin, Strassburg, 1710); Kleuker, *Anhang zum Zend-Avesta*, iii. pt. 3 (Leipzig, 1783); Rapp, 'Relig. u. Sitte der Perser und übrigen Iranier nach den griech. und röm. Quellen,' in *ZDMG* xix., xx. (Eng. tr. by Cama, Bombay, 1876–1879); Justi, *Iran. Namenbuch* (Marburg, 1895); Jackson, 'Iran. Religion' in Geiger-Kuhn, *op. cit.*; Lehmann, 'Die Perser' in Chantepie de la Saussaye's *Lehrbuch der Religionsgeschichte*[3] (Freiburg, 1905); Jackson, *Zoroaster, the Prophet of Ancient Iran* (New York, 1899); Spiegel, *Eran. Alterthumskunde*, ii. (Leipzig, 1873); Rawlinson, *Fifth Great Oriental Monarchy* (London, 1862); Justi, 'Gesch. Irans bis zum Ausgang der Sāsāniden,' in Geiger-Kuhn, *op. cit.*; Meyer, *Geschichte des Alterthums*, iii. (Stuttgart, 1901); de Harlez, *Avesta, livre sacré du Zoroastrianisme* (Paris, 1881); Darmesteter, *Le*

Zend-Avesta, iii. (Paris, 1893); Windischmann, *Zoroastr. Studien* (Berlin, 1863); Stave, *Einfluss des Parsismus auf das Judenthum* (Haarlem, 1898); Tiele, *Gesch. van den Godsdienst in de Oudheid* (Amsterdam, 1901), also *Kompendium der Religionsgeschichte*³ (Breslau, 1903); Orelli, *Allgemeine Religionsgeschichte* (Bonn, 1899); Röth, *Gesch. unserer abendländ. Philosophie*², i. (Mannheim, 1862); Cheyne, *Origin and Religious Contents of the Psalter* (London, 1891); Modi, *Glimpse into the Work of the B.B.R.A. Society during the Last 100 Years, from a Parsee Point of View* (Bombay, 1905); Mills, *Zarathushtra, the Achæmenids, and Israel.* For additional bibliographical references to briefer articles, see Jackson, *Iran. Religion*, and *JAOS* xxi.

LOUIS H. GRAY.

ACHELOUS.—The name of the greatest river in Greece. Flowing from the watershed of Pindus in a southerly direction, it forms in its lower waters the boundary-line between Ætolia and Acarnania before falling into the Ionian Sea. The river-god who presided over it was reputed the son of Oceanus and Tethys (Hes. *Theog.* 340); he was the eldest of 3000 brothers and supreme amongst them, in power second only to Oceanus himself (Acusilaus fr. 11*a*, *Fragm. Hist. Gr.* i. 101). Other legends, after the manner of Euhemerus, represent him as a man in consequence of whose sorrows the river first gushed forth as a divine solace (see, *e.g.*, Prop. ii. 25, 33). Tradition regarded him as the king of streams, from whom are derived the waters of all other rivers (Zenodotus on Hom. *Il.* xxi. 195), and as such he was worshipped throughout the Greek world, from Athens and Oropus as far as Rhodes and Metapontum. Thus it is not surprising that smaller streams besides the Ætolian river bore his name—in Thessaly, Achæa, Arcadia, and elsewhere. Further, we find the word Achelous generalized in the sense of water (Eur. *Bacch.* 625, etc.); this occurs especially in the ceremonial phraseology of sacrifices and oaths—proving that the identification is not a poetical refinement, but the survival of an old religious formula (Ephorus fr. 27; *Fragm. Hist. Gr.* i. 239). Again, Achelous is the father of a numerous progeny of water-nymphs, such as Peirene, Castalia, and Dirce, the guardian spirits of local Hellenic streams. The appropriateness is less obvious when the Sirens appear as his daughters (Pausan. ix. 34, 2): perhaps they are so viewed in their aspect as the windless calm of the southern sea in summer (cf. *Od.* xii. 168). For it has been held that Achelous was not only a river-god, but, as signifying water in general, also the lord of the sea (Wilamowitz-Moellendorff, Eur. *Herakles*², i. p. 23). His most famous appearance in mythical story is as the suitor of Deianeira, who was vanquished by Herakles after a fierce struggle. Like Proteus, he possessed the power of metamorphosis, and in this battle he assumed the form of a wild bull (Soph. *Trach.* 9 ff., 507 ff.). In the course of the fight, one of his horns was broken off by Herakles, and, according to one account, he ransomed it from his conqueror by giving in exchange for it the horn of Amaltheia or cornucopia (Apollod. *Bibl.* II. 7, 5). The ancients gave a rationalistic explanation of the story: Herakles represents the growing power of civilization, which reclaimed the marsh-land for agriculture by damming and diverting the wild exuberance of the river (Strabo, x. p. 458). It seems rather as if Achelous was a name consecrated in primitive ritual to express the principle of moisture as the source of life and growth. Further, since to a nation of cowherds the bull is typical of generative power, the fostering river-god was worshipped in bull form. Whatever be the explanation, it should not be forgotten that the bull shape is common to all river-gods and is not limited to Achelous (cf. Eur. *Ion* 1261). A symbolical connexion between the two aspects of divinity was found in the horn of plenty, which, as we have seen, was mythically associated with Achelous.

In art, Achelous is represented either as an old man with horns, as a sea-serpent with human head and arms and bull's horns, or as a bull with human face and long dripping beard.

The etymology of the word is unknown, and inferences based merely upon conjectural explanations of it should be unhesitatingly rejected.

LITERATURE.—Artt. by G. Wenzel in Pauly-Wissowa, and by H. W. Stoll in Roscher; O. Gruppe, *Griech. Mythol. u. Religionsgesch.* (1897) pp. 343, 828, etc.; Jane E. Harrison, *Prolegomena to the Study of Greek Religion* (1903), p. 435; J. G. Frazer, *Pausanias*, ii. p. 527.

A. C. PEARSON.

ACHILLES was extensively worshipped throughout the Hellenic world. Numerous guesses have been made at the derivation of his name both in ancient and in modern times, but the etymology remains quite uncertain. Nor does it appear possible to attribute to him with confidence any exclusively naturalistic significance, though he has been claimed as a river-god, as a god of light, and even as a moon-god; for us, he is merely the chief of the heroic figures of Greek myth who were deified by later generations as transcending the normal powers of humanity. Nevertheless, there are certain prominent features in his worship which claim recognition.

He appears most conspicuously as a sea-god, whose temple was placed on promontories or navigable coasts, and whose help as a pilot would secure a safe anchorage, or, in time of stress, would assuage the violence of the storm. The contrary winds, with which his spirit visited the Greeks after the capture of Troy, ceased when Polyxena had been sacrificed (Eur. *Hec.* 109, 1267). In this capacity his name was perpetuated, and honours were paid to him at harbours, as at Tainaron and Skyros. The popularity of his worship amongst the Greek settlers in Asia Minor accords with this; at Miletus a spring was called by his name, and in his temple at Sigeum in the Troad offerings were made to him as a hero. But the most significant testimony to the high estimation in which he was held is the extension of his cult to the shores of the Euxine, where he was honoured as Pontarches (*CIG* ii. p. 87 n. 2076). To this neighbourhood it seems to have been carried by the earliest Greek navigators in their adventurous voyages of discovery. His chief temple in this region was situated at Olbia on the mouth of the Hypanis, where a college of priests was devoted to his service (Dio Chrys. xxxvi. 80 ff.); facing the narrowest part of the Cimmerian Bosporus a village settlement had grown up round another of his precincts (Strabo, xi. p. 494). The most interesting and celebrated of his local cults was connected with the lonely shrine in the uninhabited island of Leuke (or Achilles Island, sometimes confused with Ἀχίλλειος δρόμος, which Strabo places at the mouth of the Borysthenes), opposite to the mouth of the Danube (Eur. *Andr.* 1260; Pind. *Nem.* iv. 48). Here the only ministrants were the sea-birds, and though navigators, for whom the temple served as a beacon, might land to sacrifice, they were obliged to leave at sunset. Here also Helen and Achilles were believed to consort together; for sounds of high revelry and the noise of armed men were heard by night, proceeding from the sanctuary, and filling with awe and amazement those who had been rash enough to anchor near (Philostr. *Her.* xx. 32–40).

In another aspect, Achilles was recognized as a god of healing (Gruppe, see below). This is inferred from the association of his worship with that of Asklepios, from the healing properties of his spear, from his connexion with healing-goddesses such as Medea and Iphigenia, from his detection of the magician and thief Pharmakos, and from his victory over the Amazons. There are also distinct traces of his beneficent power in cases of ceremonial purification: the clearest is to be found in the story of Poimandros, who successfully obtained his help when suffering from the pollution of accidental homicide (Plut. *Quæst. Gr.* 37, p. 299 C–E).

LITERATURE.—Artt. by C. Fleischer in Roscher, and by J. Escher in Pauly-Wissowa; O. Gruppe, *Griech. Mythol. u. Religionsgesch.* (1897) § 223, pp. 616–618; J. B. Bury in *ClR* xiii. (1899) p. 307.

A. C. PEARSON.

ACOSMISM (Gr. α privative, and κόσμος, 'the universe,' in the sense of an ordered or arranged whole).—This term belongs primarily to the field of Ontology, *i.e.* the theory of the ultimate nature of Being and Reality; but it has ethical bearings also. Allowing for several possible differences of theoretical interpretation, the doctrine of Acosmism implies that the universe, as known to human experience, possesses no reality in itself, but is dependent upon, or is a manifestation of, an underlying real being. In a word, the universe must be viewed as a semblance. In the history of modern thought the classical example of the doctrine may be described as the metaphysical parallel to Hume's psychological scepticism. For Hume, *Cogito, ergo videor esse.* And just as he thus fixes illusion upon the experience of the individual man, so the acosmist holds the universe as a whole to be illusory. This conclusion, while defensible, as in Spinoza's case, from the standpoint of the historical and speculative conditions of the time, may be controverted on the strictly theoretical side. For it is obvious that the reality constituting the substratum of the universe must be regarded as *the* real; it is no less obvious, however, that the only reality attributable to it must be derived, as concerns human experience, from the universe already declared to be illusory. For example, Spinoza's Absolute Substance—the reality underlying the universe—is known to man in the two 'attributes' Thought and Extension. These in turn differentiate themselves into 'modes,' each mode of Thought being the correspondent of a mode of Extension. God is, therefore, at once the 'Thing' which thinks and the 'Thing' which is extended. Hence (as the conditions of his age prevented him from seeing fully) any attribute of God, whether known to man or not, is a *method* of perceiving substance. 'By attribute I understand what intellect perceives of substance as constituting its essence' (cf. *Ethics*, ii. 21, Schol.). Between this conclusion and Hegelian idealism there may be, doubtless, a distinction, but without fundamental difference. And the reason lies open. Only from human experience can Spinoza, or any one, derive reality and meaning to inject into the so-called substratum or 'Unknowable.' In other words, either the reality underlying the cosmos is nothing, or it achieves reality just to the extent to which it may be viewed as an effective component of human experience.

One need not do more than indicate the importance of this as bearing upon theological problems, especially those raised by the religions of India; or upon ethical questions, particularly those connected with Quietism (wh. see).

The *feeling* of the overwhelming nature of the Ultimate Being tends naturally to Acosmism; so, too, does undue emphasis upon the transcendence of Deity. In both cases, however, the conclusion follows usually from a more or less vague ethical attitude, rather than from metaphysical analysis and logical argument.

LITERATURE.—G. B. Jäsche, *Der Pantheismus nach seinen verschiedenen Hauptformen* (1826–32), vol. iii.; Dorner, *Syst. of Chr. Doct.* (Eng. tr.) vol. i. 340 f., vol. ii. 247 f.; F. Paulsen, *Einleitung in d. Philosophie*, 239 f.; F. C. S. Schiller, *Riddles of the Sphinx*, ch. x.; A. E. Taylor, *Elements of Metaphysics*, 101 f.; Hegel, *Encyclopædia*, § 50 ('Logic of Hegel,' tr. W. Wallace, 102 f., 2nd ed. 1894); H. L. Mansel, *Prolegomena Logica*[2] (1860), 298; J. Martineau, *Essays* (1890), vol. ii. 223; R. A. Duff, *Spinoza's Political and Ethical Philosophy* (1903), ch. v.; R. Flint, *Anti-Theistic Theories* (1879), 409 f.; G. H. Lewes, *Hist. of Philosophy*, vol. ii. 176 (ed. of 1867); the *Histories of Modern Philosophy* (under 'Spinoza') of J. E. Erdmann (Eng. tr.), Kuno Fischer (German only), W. Windelband (Eng. tr.), H. Höffding (Eng. tr.); *Mind* (O. S.), vol. iii. 203 f., *ib.* (N. S.) vol. v. 151 f.; P. Deussen, *The Philosophy of the Upanishads* (Eng. tr. 1906), 38–50, 226 f. See PANTHEISM.

R. M. WENLEY.

ACOSTA.—Uriel (or, as he was originally named, Gabriel) da Costa is an interesting but overrated personality. Interest in his career is due mainly to the similarity between his life and that of another Amsterdam Jew of the same period —Spinoza. It may even be said that the harsh treatment which the latter received from the Jewish community was the result of the vagaries of Acosta; but there was no real parallel between the two men. Acosta did not possess the strength or originality of character which enables a religious thinker to stand alone, yet he was gifted with enough independence to render it impossible for him to submit to the restraint of authority. Acosta was born about 1590 at Oporto, of a Marano family, *i.e.* a family of Jewish origin forced to conform to Roman Catholicism. Carefully educated in the new faith, he had every prospect of advancement; but, as he tells us, his studies of the OT left him dissatisfied with Catholicism. Determined to resume Judaism, Acosta with other members of his family contrived to escape to Amsterdam in 1617. Here he lived openly as a Jew; but, as was to be expected, he found Judaism less ideally perfect than he had dreamed. He soon came into conflict with the Synagogue as he had done with the Church, was excommunicated, recanted, again defied the authorities, was again excommunicated, and finally submitted to a public and degrading penance in the Synagogue, shortly after which he shot himself. This was probably in 1647; Spinoza was a boy of fifteen at the time.

Gutzkow, author of the well-known drama on the subject, represents Uriel Acosta as a youth at the time of his suicide: he was certainly over 50; and if the dates given above be correct (as is most probable), he was nearer 60. Thus we are not dealing with a persecuted youth, but with a man of advanced years, who deserves sympathy rather for what he was than for what he endured. His brief autobiography, written just before his death, is indeed a pathetic document. He called it *Exemplar humanæ vitæ*; it was published in Latin by Philip Limborch on pp. 346–354 of his *de Veritate Religionis Christianæ* (Gouda, 1687, since reprinted), and in a German translation by H. Jellinek in *Acostas Leben und Lehre* (Zerbst, 1874). In this autobiography he tells us most of what we know of his career. He abjures both Christianity and Judaism, expressing himself with peculiar bitterness against the latter, whose teachers he repeatedly terms Pharisees. The only authority that he admits is the 'lex naturæ,' thus placing himself among the Deists. Nature, he says, teaches all human virtue and fraternity, while revealed religion produces strife. He speaks sympathetically of Jesus. Strangely enough, he finds all necessary rules for conduct in the Noachian laws formulated by the Talmudists: these were seven in number; and though the details differ in different Rabbinic sources, they include belief in God, the avoidance of adultery, murder, and robbery. These Acosta considers to be 'laws of nature.'

As a contributor to religious thought, Acosta was not original. But he belongs to the direct line of rationalists who were subsequently to attain to so much significance in religious history. He lived in an age when tolerance was little understood even in free Amsterdam, and though his troubles were mainly self-inflicted, he must always enjoy the sympathy of those who condemn the attempt of public authority to regulate belief and compel conformity. As a champion of freedom,

Acosta must be honoured, but his championship was fantastic rather than robust.

LITERATURE.—Whiston, *The Remarkable Life of Uriel Acosta, an Eminent Freethinker* (1740); *Uriel Acosta's Selbstbiographie* (1847); I. da Costa, *Israel en de Volke* (1849); H. Jellinek, *Acosta's Leben und Lehre* (1874); F. de Sola Mendes in *JE* i. 167 (1901).

I. ABRAHAMS.

ACROSTIC.—An *acrostic(h)* is etymologically an extremity of a line or verse, lit. 'row' (*στίχος*). *Apost. Const.* ii. 57 prescribes an antiphonal chanting of psalms in which a single voice begins the verses, and the congregation sing *the acrostics* (τὰ ἀκροστίχια). Epiphanius (*Migne*, xlii. 365) calls the numeral *iota* the 'acrostic' (ἀκροστιχίς) of the name Jesus. But an acrostic is usually a poem in which the initials of lines or sections spell a word or words or an alphabet. An abecedary acrostic is sometimes called simply an alphabet.

1. Bickell and others find fifteen complete alphabets or remains of them in the Heb. OT and Sirach, viz. in the following Psalms or chapters: (1–8) Pss 9–10. 25. 34. 37. 111. 112. 119. 145; (9) Pr 31; (10–13) La 1. 2. 3. 4; (14) Nah 1–2; (15) Sir 51.*

(1) Pss 9–10 (LXX 9).—Remains of an alphabet spelt by the first letters of alternate verses (Ps 9$^{2.4.6}$ . . . 10 . . . $^{14.15.17}$). With פיהו and עיניו from 10$^{7.8}$ as initial words we should have פ before ע, as in other cases noted below. The order צפעס brings somewhat similar letters together.

(2) Ps 25.—An alphabet *minus* ק, with a letter from each verse, except that the ו is included in the ה verse. To restore the ק, begin v.^{18} with 'Arise' (Ps 10^{12}). An appended פדה כו' makes up the number of the verses to the alphabetic twenty-two. 'Carmina *alphabetizantia*,' like Ps 33, La 5, etc., are such as have that number of verses or sections, but are not alphabets (Bickell).

(3) Ps 34.—An alphabet like (2), the added verse beginning פודה. EV and LXX have in v.^{18} '*The righteous* cry (*or* cried),' for Heb. צעקו. But with פ before ע (vv.$^{17.16}$) there would be no need to repeat 'The righteous.'

(4) Ps 37.—An alphabet *minus* ע, formed like (1). To complete it, read in v.^{28} (עוילים) לעולם נשמדו with *daleth* for *resh*, the word in brackets for LXX A ἄνομοι. In v.^{39} ותשועת *minus* ו gives the ת.

(5. 6) Pss 111. 112.—Alphabets with their letters from the halves of the verses, of which three at the end are numbered as two ($^{9.10}$).

(7) Ps 119.—Known as א"ב רבתא, 'the great alphabet' (Buxtorf, *Lex. s.* √ אלף). Eight verses begin with *aleph*, eight with *beth*, and so on. The names of the letters are given in the English Bible, but not in the LXX. Note, however, that the Psalm is missing in B; and see the variants from the Psalters R and T (Swete).

(8) Ps 145.—An alphabet *minus* נ, with a letter from each verse, one beginning נאמן יהוה (LXX πιστὸς K.) having fallen out before סומך יהוה כו' (v.^{14}).

(9) Pr 31$^{10-31}$.—An alphabet with a letter from each verse; but in LXX B the פ verse precedes the ע verse.

(10) La 1.—An alphabet like (9), with the letters in the usual order. The LXX gives their names, some of them in B in strange forms. With Τιαδή for צ cf. Aquila's Greek for 'Sion' in Ps 102$^{17.22}$ (*Cairo Geniz. Palimpsests*, p. 81).

(11. 12. 13) La 2$^{1-22}$ 3$^{1-66}$ 4$^{1-22}$.—Three alphabets, of which every verse gives a letter, that in (12) being of the form AAA, BBB, etc. Heb. פ before ע; but in the LXX, which here also names the letters, B gives Ἄιν and Φή wrongly as titles of the *pe* and *ayin* verses.

(14) Nah 1 f.—On the supposed traces here of an alphabet arranged 'exquisito artificio,' see Bickell's *Carm. V.T.*, and art. 'Nahum' in Hastings' *DB* and in *EBi*.

(15) Sir 51$^{13-29}$.—From the Versions, before the discovery of the Cairene Hebrew, Bickell saw that Ben Sira's poem on Wisdom was an alphabet, but he did not satisfactorily determine all the letters. In the LXX B (ed. Swete) supplies materials for the beginnings of all but the *yod* verse in their right order. In v.^{18} begin וזממתי (διενοήθην); in v.^{19} מפחתי (ἐξεπέτασα); and supply the *yod* line from the Hebrew. The other letters may then be found without difficulty. Comparing (2) and (3), Bickell retranslated v.^{30} as an added *pe* line, but in the Heb. it begins rightly or wrongly with *mem*.

2. Evidently the alphabeticism of a composition is not without critical importance: it enables us in places to detect and emend errors, or to supply deficiencies. Sometimes at least it connotes completeness, as in Pr 31$^{10-31}$, where the praises of the virtuous woman exhaust the alphabet. In the NT compare 'I am the ALPHA and the O.'

3. Alphabets and other acrostics are found in Jewish Prayer Books and secular writings. Famous names were shortened acrostically, as in RaMBaM for Rabbi Moses Maimonides (ben Maim.). A name given by acrostic verses may settle a question of authorship, as in the case of R. Jacob Ben Shimshon's commentary on *Aboth*, often found ascribed to a better known writer. The mistake may have arisen partly from his name having been written ר"יש for *Rabbi Jacob Shimshoni*, and then read רש"י *Rashi*.

4. Syriac acrostics abound in Service Books and other early writings. Aphraates prefixed the letters of the alphabet to his twenty-two *Homilies*. Ephraim wrote alphabetic hymns, two of which may be seen transliterated at the end of Bickell's *Carm. V.T.*

5. That acrostics were used in oracles is thought to be indicated by their occurrence in the pretended oracles of the Sibyl. These make the name Ἀδάμ an acrostic of east, west, north, south in the line Ἀντολίην τε Δύσιν τε Μεσημβρίην τε καὶ Ἄρκτον (iii. 26, viii. 321; cf. ii. 195, xi. 3). Romulus and Remus are alluded to by the word ἑκατόν (xi. 114), the Greek R standing for *a hundred*. The initials of the lines viii. 217–250 give the Greek for 'Jesus Christ God's Son Saviour Cross,' whence, without *Cross*, as an acrostic of an acrostic, comes ΙΧΘΥΣ, 'fish,' a mystic name of Christ (Aug. *Civ. Dei*, xviii. 23).

6. Otfried's metrical rendering of a form of the *Diatessaron* into Old High German (9th cent.) is preceded by the acrostics, 'Ludovico (Luthovvico) Orientalium Regnorum Regi sit Salus æterna,' 'Salomoni Episcopo *Otfridus*,' and followed by a longer one to the effect, '*Otfr. W.* monachus H. et W. Sancti Galli monast. monachis.' Thus again acrostics testify to authorship.

7. Professor H. A. Giles, of Cambridge, informs the writer that 'the Chinese have several forms of the acrostic. The simplest is that in which the hidden sentence is revealed by taking the first word in each line of a short poem. This form is often still further elaborated by using, not the actual words required to make sense, but homophones of a more or less misleading character; Anglicé, "*Boughs* are made," etc., where *Bows* is required for the sense. Other kinds of acrostic are produced by the dissection of words, to which the Chinese script readily lends itself, much as we form charades.'

LITERATURE.—Gustav Bickell, *Carmina Vet. Test. Metrice* (1882), and art. 'Ein alphabetisches Lied Jesus Sirachs' (1882) in *ZKT*; art. 'Acrostic' in Oxford *New Eng. Dict.*; I. Abrahams, art. 'Acrostics' in *JE*; Lagarde, *Symmicta*, i. 107 (1877); Bingham, *Works*, Bk. XIV. i. 12 (vol. v. 17, Oxford, 1855); Driver, *LOT*, ch. vii.; Karl Krumbacher, *Gesch. der Byzant. Litteratur*, § 287 (1897), and Index, *s.vv.* 'Akrostichis,' 'Alphabete'; *Orac. Sibyll.* ed. Rzach (1891), Geffcken (1902); *JPh*, No. lix. art. 'The Alphabet of Ben Sira' (1906); Appendix (1900) to C. Taylor's *Sayings of the Jewish Fathers*, p. 93 f.; *Otfrids von Weissenburg Evangelienbuch*, ed. Johann Kelle, vol. i. (1856), see, after the Introduction, pp. 3 f., 12 f., 389–394; Wilhelm Braune, *Althochdeutsches Lesebuch*⁴ (1897), pp. 40 f., 82–88, 167, 176 f.

C. TAYLOR.

ACT, ACTION.—The English word 'action' is used very widely. We speak of the 'action' of one body upon another as readily as of a man's action, and we have no word like the Greek πρᾶξις or the German *Handlung*, *das Handeln*, to designate human agency as such, both in general and in the particular instance. In the word 'conduct' we have a general term for human action as such, when we speak of it in a more or less comprehensive way, but in speaking of the particular instance

* Some find the names *Pedahel*, *Pedaiah*, *Simon* in Pss 25^{22} 34^{23} 110$^{1-4}$. *Pesikt. Rab.* detects *Moses* in Ps 92^{1}, and so from Ps. 96^{11} we may spell out יהוה יהו. The Midrash knows also of Greek ἀλφαβητάρια.

we must have recourse to the words 'act' and 'action.' Hence, when we wish to designate the agency of man in its peculiar character, we must prefix the epithet. The peculiar character of human action, as the phrase is ordinarily used to mark the distinction from any sort of physical action, is that the former is an expression of consciousness. But in making this broad distinction we must notice, first, that it applies equally to all animal action as distinguished from physical and merely physiological action; and, second, in the discussion of human action the phrase is often used more widely to include unconscious actions exhibited by the human organism. The fact is, of course, that the human organism exhibits all grades of action, physical, animal, and human in the strictest sense. The only physical actions of the organism, however, which concern us in relation to our study of conscious actions, are those which are like the latter in depending directly upon the nervous system, but unlike them in not expressing consciousness, whether in the form of feeling or purpose. Of such actions of the nervous system, not expressive of consciousness, two grades are distinguished: the simple Reflex action, and the more complex Instinctive action in which a number of movements are co-ordinated in the production of a single result—though it should be observed that the range of true instincts is very limited in the case of man. When we say that these actions are not expressive of consciousness, we do not necessarily imply that they have no conscious accompaniments, but only that the nature of the action is not determined by these conscious accompaniments even when present. The reflex action of sneezing is not determined by the sensations which accompany it. And similarly, though an instinctive action may be accompanied by sensation and feeling, the purposive character which it displays is not due to conscious forethought.

Of human actions, in the stricter sense, which are expressive of consciousness—or which, to use the technical term of psychology, are 'conations'—the most obvious type is the purposed action, in which the performance of the action is preceded by an idea of the thing to be done. But it is evident that such purposed action cannot be psychologically primitive, since those ideas or images of movements to be executed, which are implied in purposed action, could have been formed only after previous experience of the same movements brought about in some other way. Consequently, either we must fall back upon reflex actions for a beginning, or we must hold that, in the most primitive phase of conation, a change of sense-perception, or the feeling which accompanies it, finds immediate expression in movement. To the former course, which is apt to be favoured by physiologists, there is the objection that reflexes, even though they may be primitive for the individual in the sense of being inherited nervous arrangements, must have been developed at some time in the experience of the race. In our present experience of the formation of a habit, we can trace the degradation of conative action into action that resembles the reflex type. And unless we are prepared to assume that our inherited reflexes were originally formed by some similar process of degradation, the beginnings of action are left psychologically inexplicable. From the psychological point of view, then, we must prefer the other course, and regard as the original type of action that in which a change of sense-perception or feeling finds immediate expression in movement (cf. Ward's art. 'Psychology' in *EBr*, vol. xx. pp. 42–43). And this view will appear all the more plausible if we remember two points. First, such 'impulsive' action, as we call it—the terminology of the subject is very confused—although as a rule definite enough in the adult (*e.g.* in warding off a blow), is to be conceived as having been originally vague, diffused, and uncertain, as the movements of an infant are in comparison with those of an adult. Second, it is now recognized, and has been shown experimentally, that all mental states have this impulsive quality, this tendency to affect movement, although in our present experience these motor effects are to a great extent either quite inappreciable or else inhibited (cf. James, *Principles of Psychology* [1890], ii. ch. xxiii.). And the difficulty of a psychological theory of action is thus greatly diminished when we see that action does not begin with particular and isolated definite movements, but that these, whether they be inherited reflexes or acquired impulses, must have been developed by the progressive restriction or specialization of movement that was originally more diffused.

Although it is with purposed rather than impulsive action that the moralist is mainly concerned, it seems a mistake to confine the epithet 'voluntary' to the former, and the practice of those psychologists is rather to be followed who tend to apply the epithet widely to all action that is expressive of consciousness. There are, of course, objections to such a usage. We use the noun 'will' in a much narrower sense. And the term 'voluntary' no doubt seems paradoxical as applied to the simpler expressive movements which are hardly to be distinguished from mechanical reactions. But we have to remember that the impulsive actions of the adult are usually of a higher type. The hasty words of an angry man may burst from him without any previous distinct idea of what he is going to say, and yet there accompanies his utterance a consciousness of its meaning, in virtue of which we hold him responsible for what he has said. The more definite and significant an impulse is, the more it must be regarded as an expression of character. One man will say things in anger which would be impossible to another however enraged. And the very fact that he permits himself to go on, that he is not brought to a halt by the consciousness of what he is saying, shows a basis for the impulse in the man's general character which forbids us to regard the outburst, however devoid of previous purpose, as simply involuntary. What we must rather say, then, is that all impulsive action is also in a broad sense voluntary action, but that voluntariness has many degrees, and that, the lower down we go in the scale, the less possible it becomes to distinguish voluntary from involuntary action in character.

Before proceeding to the consideration of purposed action, we may refer very briefly to a general conception of human action, which, if true, would profoundly modify the significance to be attached to the element of conscious foresight in man's life. It is a conception which is apt to find a ready acceptance with those who look upon human conduct from the point of view of biological evolution, or, again, from the point of view, not very dissimilar, of a philosophy like Schopenhauer's or v. Hartmann's, which sees in blind will the ultimate principle of all existence. Human action, it is sometimes argued, is not really determined by the transient desires, the petty motives and calculations of interest, of which an introspective psychology makes so much. All this constant fluctuation and transition from one object of desire to another is only so much surface play. The true forces lie far deeper, in the strong instinctive tendencies of man's nature. It is these that have the real shaping of his life, these that use for their own hidden ends all the superficial activity of desire and feeling and calculating intellect, to which the reflexion of the individual naturally but mistakenly attributes the direction of his life. Now, such a conception of human life may have an appearance of profundity, but it conveys no real insight. It does not aid, on the contrary it obstructs, the work of scientific analysis and explanation. To appeal to instinctive tendencies is only to involve ourselves in empty mystery, unless we can definitely characterize these tendencies, and show how they operate, and why they manifest themselves in just such ways as they do. Yet for such concrete analysis we must, of course, return to the very surface processes of consciousness which we had affected to despise, and must seek in their definite modes of interconnexion, and not in the vague and mysterious depths of instinctive tendencies, the definite explanation of the course of human life.

When these two conditions are fulfilled, first, that definite movements have begun to emerge from the earlier stage of diffused movement—an emergence which may be greatly facilitated by the existence of inherited nervous co-ordinations; and, second, that images have begun to be formed, then the higher stage of purposed action becomes possible, in which the idea or image of a movement to be executed precedes and directs its actual execution. The idea of movement may be prompted by a present object (with whose attainment or avoidance the movement must, of course, have been already associated), and, as so prompting, the object is an object of desire or aversion. But the range and significance of desire are vastly widened when not merely present objects, but objects that are themselves represented only in idea or imagination, are sufficient to prompt ideas of movement. For the agent is thereby delivered from his former bondage to the immediate present, and is enabled both to modify his present situation by the aid of ideas derived from his past experience, and to anticipate the future by present preparation. With the development of such desire-prompted action there is bound to emerge the situation described as a conflict of desires, with its need for a voluntary decision between them. This decision has often been represented by psychologists and moralists of the Associationist school as brought about in a *quasi*-mechanical way: it is the strongest desire that prevails, and the conflict is simply a conflict of opposed intensities. Now it is true that, as in the case of impulse, so here, if we take desires of a very simple kind, the epithet 'voluntary' seems hardly to mark any essential peculiarity of the process so described. The voluntary decision between two desires of a very simple kind, depending as it does merely on their relative strength, seems hardly to be distinguished in character (save for the fact that the process goes on in consciousness) from the mechanical result of a conflict between two forces. But here, too, we must remember that the simplest type of choice, say the choice of a child between an apple and an orange, is not really representative of the more important choices which the adult has constantly to make. And it is just in proportion as the 'conflicting' desires are not simple or low-grade, but complex and significant, that the choice becomes an expression of character, and becomes therefore in a fuller degree voluntary. Now, the more complex and significant the desires are, the less is it possible to picture their 'conflict' as a mere collision between two forces of different intensities. The man who has to decide whether he will continue in his present accustomed vocation or accept a new career that has opened out for him, is not simply distracted between a love of ease and a love of gain. He is deciding ultimately between two complex schemes of life, and to represent such a decision in terms of a simple quantitative difference would be a caricature. The factors which do admit of quantitative measurement in money value may even be the least influential of all.

It is evident, of course, that in an example like this we have gone far beyond the range of the desires that merely reproduce past experience in imagery. We are at a level at which conceptual thinking has long been at work upon the materials which memory supplies, a level at which the agent habitually thinks in terms of generalized purposes, to which he refers, and by which he guides, his particular actions. The desires of the adult are nearly always more or less significant. That is to say, the desired object is desired not merely for its own sake, but because it fits in with some wider purpose. And the more intelligent and thoughtful the agent is, the more his desires and purposes will be organized in this way, and rendered subservient to the scheme or type of life in which he sees the completest realization of his powers.

We must indicate the psychological processes involved in this higher development of conation and action. One practical relation that must soon be forced upon the attention of an agent trying to bring about an ideally represented state of things, is that of means and end. With the fuller recognition of this relationship among objects comes the process of deliberation, in which the agent seeks to discover the means of attaining an end, or to determine which of two or more ways of attaining it is the best. In Aristotle's classical analysis of the deliberative process (*Nic. Ethics*, III. iii.), choice is expressly characterized as choice of the means. Such a view of choice will not, however, apply to all cases without straining. For, although in every choice between two objects or courses of action some end or criterion is implicitly assumed, there is an obvious difference between the case in which the end or criterion is explicit from the start of the deliberative process, and the case in which it emerges only as a balance of advantage at the end. And we must further recognize the possibility, of which Aristotle takes no account, that even where we start with a certain end explicitly before us, our deliberation may, by bringing out other elements of significance in our end which we had not before fully appreciated, cause us to modify or abandon it altogether. In short, the more important the matter for decision is, the more does the choice tend to express, not an isolated desire for a particular end, but the whole character of the agent, or, what is the same thing, his ultimate and all-inclusive desire for the kind of life which is to him best. And the more strenuously a man lives, the more will the unity of his character tend to work itself out in even the simpler actions of his daily life.

It is for choices of a more or less deliberate kind that the term 'will' is often reserved in psychological and ethical discussions. But we must not suppose that the new term denotes a new faculty or energy of mind. The expression 'fiat of will' often used in this connexion is very misleading. The man who seriously sets himself to deliberate must mean to come to a decision. He starts, that is to say, with some sort of decision already vaguely outlined in the shape of possible alternatives, and the only function of deliberation is to eliminate what is doubtful and make the proper course of action clear. This being done, nothing more is needed: if the man was impatient to act, the obstacles in his way have now been removed, and he will act at once. The general purpose of acting was present all through, and by means of the deliberative process this general purpose takes shape in a definite volition. A fiat of will, additional and subsequent to the phase of conation in which the deliberative process was complete, would be otiose if it merely gave its consent, and wholly arbitrary if it withheld it. For, if any reason remained for withholding consent, the deliberation could not have been complete, and it is only a sense of such incompleteness that could make the agent hesitate and hold himself back from action. Thus, if we are to give this notion of a fiat of will any meaning at all, we must regard it as merely emphasizing the last or finally decisive element in the deliberative process itself, the thought that clinches the slowly forming decision and issues at once in action.

In our consideration of the development of conation in the individual, we have so far been abstracting from those aspects of the individual's action which depend upon the essentially social character of human life. In point of fact, however, the actions of the individual for the most part do either explicitly contain or not remotely imply a reference to other persons, and to their agency in relation to himself as well as to his own agency in relation to them. And this social factor in individual action manifests itself not merely in the social content of the action, but in the definite control which social influences exert over the will of the agent. The child is no sooner able to understand a particular prohibition or command, than he begins to experience this social control, which in varying forms is to continue all through his life. At first it comes to him from without as a constraint upon his desires, but more and more it tends to become an internal factor in his own will and character, and so not more society's law than that of his own nature. At first it comes to him in the form of particular injunctions to refrain from particular objects or to do particular acts, and his obedience is an obedience given merely to particular persons, but more and more it tends to take the generalized and impersonal form of rules of action to be obeyed merely as such. These rules become concrete, of course, only in the personal claims and expectations which they warrant, but their control reaches out beyond every particular case, and pervades the whole practical thinking of the individual. Hence the important consequence that action constantly expresses, not a consideration of means and ends at all, but a simple obedience to rule, and that, even where it does express a consideration of means and ends, this consideration itself is controlled through and through by the habitual regard which we pay to social rules in all our practical thinking.

To complete our sketch, we may ask as a final question, how far we can bring the whole development of conation and action under a single formula. Various attempts have been made to find an explanatory formula applicable to action at all stages. Many psychologists and moralists have sought such a formula in the connexion of action with feeling, *i.e.* with pleasure and pain. This connexion has been asserted in two forms which it is important to distinguish clearly from each other. On the one hand, it may be held that feeling is the efficient cause of action. This doctrine is applied over the whole range of human action, and means that between various impulses, desires, or aims, that one will always tend to be realized which gives the greatest present pleasure or relieves the greatest present uneasiness. And we must, of course, observe that present pleasure or uneasiness may be caused not merely by present events and objects, but also by the mere images or thoughts of distant events and possibilities. On the other hand, it may be held that feeling is the end or final cause of action. This doctrine (technically known as Psychological Hedonism) is obviously narrower in range, since it applies only to purposed and not to impulsive action. It means that of various possible courses of action represented before the mind, that one will always be chosen which promises most future pleasure or least future pain, pleasure being thus regarded as the only real object of desire. This doctrine is now almost universally abandoned in psychology and ethics. For it is quite evident that there is a great deal of purposed action, at all levels of conduct, which is not determined by calculations of future pleasure and pain at all. The hungry man seeks food not for the pleasure of eating, but for the mere satisfaction of his hunger. The honest man desires to pay his just debts not for the pleasure of having been honest, but merely because he is honest and wants to remain so. The other form of doctrine, according to which we do what continues present pleasure or relieves present uneasiness, is more plausible (cf. the change of view in the chapter on 'The Idea of Power' in Locke's *Essay*, Fraser's ed. vol. i. p. 332). Nevertheless it is open to objection on grounds both of fact and of principle. The objections of fact are: (1) that action often goes on for a considerable stretch in a practically neutral state of feeling, (2) that we may persist in painful actions in spite of their painfulness. Now we may, of course, to save our theory, attribute this persistence to the greater uneasiness experienced on stopping. But such uneasiness would seem itself to imply a direct interest of corresponding strength in the object of our action, and it is surely simpler, therefore, to refer the persistence to this interest directly. Moreover, as a matter of principle, it seems impossible to explain in terms of merely quantitative variations of feeling the definite forms which action takes. What we have to explain is not simply varying degrees of one fundamental type of action, but many actions of widely different types, and the particularity of the action can be explained only by the particularity of the interest which it expresses. There is thus a good deal to be said for a view which seems to be finding increasing favour with recent psychologists (*e.g.* Stout, *Analytic Psychology* (1896), i. 224 ff.; Titchener, *Outline of Psychology*[3] (1898), § 38), viz., that pleasure and pain, agreeableness and uneasiness, are not so much factors in the causation of activity as the feeling-tone which accompanies and reflects its varying fortunes.

Another well-known formula for purposed action affirms that in all choice the object or course of action chosen is conceived as realizing what is there and then the agent's good (so, *e.g.*, Green in his *Prolegomena to Ethics*). The same meaning is negatively expressed in the Socratic maxim, that no one willingly chooses what is evil; and this famous paradox, when rightly interpreted, only says what cannot well be denied, that a man's actions, not his professions, are the test and index of his real convictions. The formula, as it stands, however, is not sufficiently comprehensive, for many actions are done without any *explicit* reference to the agent's personal good at all, *e.g.* assistance given to a person in distress from the mere pity felt on seeing it.

The defect of such formulæ is apt to be that they are framed with a too exclusive regard for special types of action. If we want a formula which applies to all human action, we must fall back on the more generalized conception used above, and say that all human action is as such expressive of consciousness, and that in proportion as the immediate consciousness expressed, be it impulse, desire, or general aim, is intelligent and significant, in the same proportion is the action voluntary and expressive of character.

LITERATURE.—In the text-books of psychology the various phases of conation or action are apt to be treated in detached sections. For a comprehensive and continuous account, see Sully, *Human Mind* (1892), vol. ii. H. BARKER.

ACTION SERMON.—The designation given by Presbyterians in Scotland, and where Scottish communities exist, to the sermon which immediately precedes the celebration of the Lord's Supper.* The name is derived directly from John Knox's *Book of Common Order*† and from the Westminster *Directory for the Public Worship of God*.‡ In both these works the celebration of the Holy Communion is described as 'the Action.' The use of the phrase in the earlier document may be traced partly (1) to the Liturgy of Calvin, which was largely the basis of the *Book of Common Order*, and in which the section entitled 'Mode of celebrating the Lord's Supper' contains this rubric: 'The ministers distribute the bread and the cup to the people . . . finally, *on use d'action de grâce*';§ (2) to the pre-Reformation use of the word *actio* to denote what was regarded as the essential part of the Eucharist, the Sacrifice of the Mass, wherein 'Sacramenta conficiuntur Dominica.'‖ Knox, of course, and those who followed him, while retaining the word 'Action,' used it with a different signification, applying it to the celebration as a whole, or to the sanctification and distribution of the sacred symbols, without reference to any 'sacrifice.' While Calvin's 'action de grâce' was probably the chief cause (although indirectly) of the term 'Action Sermon' being *introduced* in Scotland, the long and popular *retention* of this term is due, doubtless, to the broader application of the word 'action' to the entire sacramental celebration; for the designation 'Eucharist' (Thanksgiving) has never been widespread among Scottish Presbyterians.

The employment of the phrase 'Action Sermon,' while still frequent, has within living memory declined, owing (1) to the somewhat diminished *relative* importance now attached to the pre-Communion sermon, as compared with the devotional parts of the pre-Communion service; (2) to the prevalence in towns of additional Communion services (in the afternoon and evening), which are not immediately preceded by any sermon.

LITERATURE (in addition to works quoted).—Du Cange, *Glossarium*; Jamieson, *Scottish Dictionary*, *s.v.*

HENRY COWAN.

ACTIVITY (Psychological and Ethical).—No definition can be given of Activity which does not involve the term itself in some concealed or overt form; we can only (1) indicate the wider class of things or events to which it belongs; (2) describe the general conditions of its genesis or occurrence, and the general nature of its expressions or consequences; (3) distinguish one form of activity from another, as bodily from mental; and (4) describe the conditions of our knowledge of that form with which we are concerned.

I. (*a*) Activity belongs, within the world of existence, to the class not of things and qualities, or substances and attributes, but of events, processes, or changes: an activity has a beginning and an end; it occurs in time, it has prior conditions and subsequent consequences, and does not occur independently; a pure activity, in the sense of one which expresses itself without conditions and is not subject to time, is therefore a contradiction in terms. On the other hand, a process is always relative to a thing or things, a substance or substances, *in* or *to* which it takes place; all change implies something relatively permanent, as Kant pointed out, as a condition not only of its being known, but also of its existence. The activity of a fragment of radium must be referred either to the visible substance itself, or to the physical atoms (however conceived) the interaction of which gives rise to the observed effects. These, in the last resort, are the permanent entities in which the activity inheres. The activity does not occur, however, except under conditions, viz. the presence of other similar or opposite particles, or the like. So mental activity, being a process, is inherent in a substance,—either in the organism as a whole, the union of mind and body, or in the soul or mind as a reality independent (relatively at least) of the body. But neither thinking, nor willing, nor attending, nor any other form of mental activity, occurs without conditions which call it forth, and to which its expression is subject; and these conditions may be either mental or bodily, or both. Activity is not merely a more general 'faculty' in which the other faculties—sensation, memory, imagination, and the rest—are contained (Stout, *Manual of Psychology*, bk. i. ch. 3). The only faculty which really exists in the psychical world is the soul itself, or the individual, as a complex resultant of congenital dispositions and consolidated experiences. On the other hand, processes may be more or less complex, and the problem of mental activity involves the question (5) whether there is any ultimate or fundamental or simple form of activity to which the others may be reduced.

(*b*) What distinguishes an activity from any other kind of process or change? In actual practice we apply the term (i.) to persistent or repeated process; (ii.) to a process of which the conditions are wholly or partially *within* the subject of the activity; (iii.) to a process which is transmitted from the active being to others.

(i.) The term may be applied to light, heat, gases, etc., because their action, under given conditions, is continuous; they represent not stores which can at any time be tapped, but supplies which are always running; special conditions only increase or decrease the available flow. In the same way, mental activity is, during waking life, a process which is always going on; it may take different forms and different expressions, but whatever description we apply to it must apply to every phase of waking consciousness. According to some, mental activity is continuous not only during wakefulness, but during life. Sir Arthur Mitchell (*Dreaming, Laughing, and Blushing*, 1905, p. 44, etc.), for example, is of opinion that there 'is no such thing as dreamless sleep'; 'that thinking is involuntary—to the extent at least that we cannot cease to think under any order of the will'; that 'thinking never ceases during life, and is essential to the continuance of life.' And the same conception is to be found in Leibniz, *Monadology*: the function of the monad is to represent or mirror the universe in all its changes, therefore each monad must be continuously having perceptions, although not always conscious perceptions. In another view, the activity of the individual is the outflow of an energy of which the sum is constantly increasing or decreasing, sleep representing the period of maximum recuperation and minimum activity. For this sum of energy the mind is dependent wholly upon the body; it itself determines only the form of the

* Two notable examples of the designation being used may be quoted. (1) In 1674, during the persecution of the Covenanters, John Welsh, great-grandson of John Knox, is stated to have 'preached the Action Sermon' at a conventicle held near the bank of the Whitadder, in Teviotdale (see Blackadder's contemporary *Memoirs*, p. 205). (2) In the diary of Edward Irving for 1825, the entry occurs, 'I addressed myself to write my Action Sermon' (see Mrs. Oliphant's *Life of Edward Irving*, vol. i. p. 368).

† Chapter on the 'Manner of the Administration of the Lord's Supper.'

‡ Chapter entitled 'Of the Celebration of the Communion.'

§ *Corpus Reformatorum*, vol. xxxiii. p. 199; cf. Iren. *adv. Hær.* IV. xviii. 4, 'panem in quo gratiæ actæ sint.'

‖ Walafrid Strabo, *de Rerum Eccles. Exordiis*, c. 22. *Agere* is used even in classical Latin to denote a sacrificial act (Ovid, *Fasti*, i. l. 322). Honorius of Autun (*Opera*, i. 103) and others derive the sacramental use of *actio* (with less probability) from its employment in legal processes: 'Actio dicitur quod causa populi cum Deo agitur.'

activity or the expression of activity, and the amount to be put forth at any moment (Fechner, *Psychophysik*, 1860; Höfler, *Psychische Arbeit*, 1895). The activity is continuous because of the constant shocks which the equilibrium of the organism receives from the play of the environing forces. It may be doubted, however, whether the term 'activity' would be applied, *e.g.*, to the movement of a body according to the law of inertia, as Dr. Stout suggests (a body tending to continue its motion with the same velocity in the same direction) (*Analytic Psychology*, i. 146; but cf. 148). Such a body would be described as active only when it impinges upon another body and transmits its own motion, wholly or partially, to the latter. The 'activity' in the continuous movement of the first body would be referred rather to the initial impulse of that force which sent it on its way.

(ii.) The second criterion is that as to the conditions of activity being within the active body. From this point of view, a body is active so far forth as its changes are determined from within itself. Thus Condillac wrote of his statue: 'It is active when it recalls a sensation, because it has *in itself* the cause of the recall, viz. memory. It is passive at the moment when it experiences a sensation; for the cause which produces the latter is outside of it (the statue), *i.e.* in the odoriferous bodies which act upon its organ.'* (At this stage the statue was supposed to have only one sense—that of smell). Substantially, Condillac's statement, that 'a being is active or passive according as the cause of the effect produced is in it or without it,' would be accepted to-day. The difficulty would be (1) to determine what *is* the cause of a given change, and (2) to determine whether the discovered cause is within or without the active being. If, for example, we refer all actions of the body to purely physical causes,—brain and nerve processes and the rest,—and regard the soul or consciousness as a mere spectator or accompanist of these central processes, without causal efficacy, then there is no such thing as mental activity, but only mental passivity.† The mind would not determine even its own changes, and so be active with respect to them, for the conscious change is always a by-product of certain physical changes. Of theories with regard to the relation of mind and body, neither automatism nor psychophysical parallelism is consistent with the existence of mental activity; the latter is compatible only with spiritualism on the one hand, the interaction theory on the other. The second difficulty—that of determining what is and what is not *in* the active being—may be illustrated from the controversy as to the existence of mental or psychical dispositions, or tendencies towards action, as opposed to merely physical dispositions, *i.e.* special arrangements or structures of the brain. Probably nine-tenths of the conditions of any mental act—an act of seeing, for example, or of hearing; an act of imagination or memory, or volition—lie beyond consciousness, or below the threshold of distinct consciousness. Our visual perception at any moment is determined largely by our own experience in the past and the general direction of our interests: the purely sense element,—what is *given*,—the affection of the retina, or the feeling of the ocular movements, is infinitesimal as a contribution to the resultant perception. Yet the latter appears instantaneously and as a single act. Are the submerged factors wholly physical—the excitation of special cortical arrangements which in their turn are the direct product of past experience, or are there also mental tendencies actually present, although out of distinct consciousness, and which are re-excited by the given sensation? (Stout, *Manual of Psychology*, bk. i. ch. 2, and *Analytic Psychology*, ch. 2). The analysis of a complex tone into its partials is given as an instance:

'Dr. Lipps holds that the unanalyzed note is a simple experience. The new tones which analysis discovers are, according to him, not in any sense precontained in the original presentation. The analysis itself brings them into existence, not only as distinguished differences, but as felt differences. According to him, what is analyzed is not an actual experience, but an unconsciously complex mental disposition corresponding to a complex physiological modification of the brain substance' (*Analytic Psychology*, vol. i. p. 61).

The value of the argument here is to show that our idea of mental activity will differ according as we interpret the disposition or tendencies from which acts of perception, of memory, of association flow as psychical or physiological, or both; if they are physiological merely, as many hold, then, not being *in* the mind, they cannot be regarded as internal causes of mental changes or effects, and therefore the mind is not active so far as their effects are concerned.

(iii.) The third characteristic is much more controversial than either of the others. A being is active, in popular speech, only so far as the effects or consequences of changes in it are transmitted to other beings; in other words, activity is *transient* causality, not *immanent*. In a body moving under the law of inertia, it may be said that the cause of its motion, in a given direction, with a given velocity, at any one moment, is its motion in the same direction and with the same velocity at the previous moment (Stout, *Analytic Psychology*, i. p. 146). Hence its motion at any moment is self-determined, *i.e.* both cause and effect are within the same being. And, according to many, mental activity exists only when there is self-determination in this full sense. It may be questioned, however, whether immanent activity in this sense ever falls within the scope of human experience: the continuance of a body under the law of inertia is not activity; it is absolute passivity, the movement *as a whole* being the effect of the original impulse. In mental activity, again, we never find that all the intermediate factors, in a case of self-determination, are within the mind. The volition to recall a name, for example, works itself out only when the necessary physiological substratum is present and uninjured. Even the moral resolution must make use of similar physical aids. It does not appear, then, that immanent activity, so far as our experience goes, is ever anything but indirect: the mind does not act upon itself, except by exciting physiological processes, to which presentations correspond. This conclusion may seem to render introspection, internal perception, or self-observation an impossibility, since knowledge is a form of action. Comte's arguments against introspection are indeed irrefutable, so far as pure introspection is concerned (cf. Miss Martineau's edition of the *Positive Philosophy*, vol. i. pp. 9, 81); but introspection on the basis of experiment is free from these objections, and is, in fact, the first method not of psychology alone, but of all science (Wundt, *Philos. Stud.* iv. 1886). This introspection is merely the analysis of presentations, whether primary (sensations) or secondary (memories, etc.), through repeating the conditions of the experience itself which has given the presentation: introspection is thus in no sense a turning of the mind upon itself, it is not a different process from external perception, it is only *a more accurate* and detailed perception, so as

* Condillac, *Traité des Sensations*, ch. ii. § 11. The note may be added here: 'There is in us a principle of our actions which we feel, but which we cannot define: it is called force. We are active alike in respect of all that this force produces in us and outside of us. We are active, for example, when we reflect, or when we cause a body to move. By analogy we suppose, in all bodies which cause change, a force of which we know still less, and we are passive with regard to the impressions they make upon us. Thus a being is active or passive according as the cause of the effect produced is in it or without it' (*ib.* note *a*).

† See Huxley's essay on 'Animal Automatism' (*Coll. Essays*, 1893).

to bring out elements not previously or directly experienced. Introspection is thus, as a form of mental activity, indirectly immanent; directly, it is an interaction between the mental and the physical. The first effect of the action is a change in the physiological process (see below); this in turn reacts upon the mind, and a new and modified presentation results. All activity is of this type,—a moving body would be described as active only when it effects a change in another body: no doubt, in such a case, the original body suffers a change, but *this* change is not that in which the activity is thought to result, or which is referred to the activity. In itself activity is essentially transitive. This does not exclude, of course, the possibility that the highest forms of activity are those which are indirectly immanent, *i.e.* in which the outcome of the activity is a change in the subject itself or self-determination.

2. *The general conditions of mental activity* are partly physical and partly psychical. Among the former must obviously be included the nature of the cortical systems present, their degree of nutrition, and the like. Among the latter fall all presentations and feelings. The mind is wholly passive, so far as its direct presentations are concerned: it may select among them, give prominence to some and reject others, but their immediate condition is always a cortical process. What is true of presentations is true also of feelings and emotions: a feeling represents on the subjective side the attitude of the individual as a whole in a given situation, while a presentation is representative of changes in his environment, directly or indirectly affecting him. In both, the mind itself is passively affected, but each may be stimulative or directive of its activity. Feeling especially has been throughout mental evolution the stimulant of activity, becoming deeper or more intense or more persistent as the presentational side of mental life received greater expansion and greater differentiation. The activity itself has no presentational or feeling-side. Although an element, it is not one of which the subject himself can be directly aware. The immediate *effects* of mental activity, on the other hand, are cortical changes and bodily movements, in primitive life diffuse, indefinite, uncoordinated; later, as experience moulds the organism, becoming definite, coordinated, and centralized. It is only through these bodily changes that mental activity produces changes in the mind itself, effecting there the recall of past impressions, or the building up of new and creative mental syntheses. The formation of a moral character, for example, is impossible without the constant practice of moral actions. These outward actions are reflected in the physical organization, and thereby the mental organization as a whole is modified in accordance with them. Without action, a character cannot be formed; nor, being formed, can it be maintained.

3. *The contrast between bodily and mental activity* has been already discussed in what has been said above. We have assumed that body acts upon mind, giving rise to presentations, and mind upon body, producing bodily movements, which in their turn may lead to changes in the cortical system, and thus indirectly to changes in the presentational field. Whether there is any real causation in the one case or the other is a metaphysical question on which we do not touch.

4. It will follow that *mental activity cannot be directly apprehended either through feeling or in any other way.* All that is apprehended is the sequence of conditions and of effects, so far as the latter are represented in consciousness. There is no more ground for assuming a primitive *consciousness* of activity as the basis of the *conception* of activity than there is for assuming such in any other case of symbolic knowledge,—for example, that of chemical affinity. There are, of course, primitive experiences on which these conceptions are based, but the conceptions are built upon them, not drawn out of them. The most complete description of the phenomena on which our knowledge of mental activity is founded is that of Wundt: 'If we try to find for the "striving" in the will-process itself a substrate corresponding in some degree to this expression, we always come to certain feelings, belonging principally to the class of strain and excitement feelings, and which may most fittingly be called feelings of activity' (*Physiolog. Psychologie*, iii. 249). These 'mediate the consciousness of activity, which is known to all from self-observation, and which, under whatsoever circumstances we find it, whether accompanying an external action, or an act of attention directed upon the contents of consciousness themselves, appears of a uniform nature' (*ib.* 252). It may be defined as a total-feeling, composed of partial feelings of tension and excitement, following a regular course from beginning to end, the completion being the sudden conversion of one of the partial feelings (that of strain or tension) into its contrast-feeling (*ib.* 253). They accompany every form of mental activity from the simplest upwards. Thus experiments have shown that an impression requires a certain time in order to penetrate to the focus of consciousness—its 'apperception,' in Wundt's terminology. During this time we always find, according to him, the above-mentioned feeling of activity. It is the more vivid the more the mental vision is concentrated, and continues until the idea has reached perfect clearness of consciousness. It is more distinct, however, in the state of active thought or tension towards some expected impression or idea. In such a case there are always certain sensation-elements accompanying or entering into it,—those of the muscular strain of accommodation of the sense-organ in attention, which Fechner has described (*ib.* 337; cf. Fechner, *Psychophysik* [2nd ed. 1889], ii. p. 475). There is no such thing as an abstract activity, always the same, but turned, like a searchlight, in different directions, of which, moreover, we are directly aware. What is always the same and is always found, in every case of volition or mental activity, is just the peculiar complex of feelings and sensations referred to. The feeling as a whole is a direct contrast to that which we have when an external impression, or a memory-image, arises, which does not harmonize with or correspond to the *present* disposition of the attention, but suddenly compels it into a direction opposed to that of its activity up to that moment; this feeling is the feeling of passivity. Each as a whole is simple and indefinable, but each belongs, at the same time, to several of the general classes of feeling, of which Wundt recognizes six (*ib.* 332). It is clear that for Wundt, as for others, the activity itself, the inward act, is not directly cognized at all; the complex of feelings is merely an index or sign by which we infer the activity to be taking place. With Dr. Ward this is still more definitely stated.

'There is, as Berkeley long ago urged, no resemblance between activity and an idea; nor is it easy to see anything common to pure feeling and an idea, unless it is that both possess intensity. —Instead, then, of the one *summum genus* state of mind or consciousness, with its three coordinate subdivisions,—cognition, emotion, conation,—our analysis seems to lead us to recognize three distinct and irreducible facts,—attention, feelings, and objects or presentations,—as together in a certain connexion, constituting one concrete state of mind or *psychosis*' (*Encyc. Brit.* art. 'Psychology' [1886], p. 44a).

Neither activity (attention) nor feeling can accordingly be presented to the mind; we know them only by their presentational conditions, accompaniments, or effects.

'Our activity as such is not presented at all: we are, being active; and further than this psychological analysis will not go. There are two ways in which this activity is manifested, the receptive or passive, and the motor or active in the stricter sense; and our experience of these we project in predicating the causal relation. But two halves do not make a whole; so we have no complete experience of effectuation, for the simple reason that we cannot be two things at once' (*ib.* 83[a]).

Activity and feeling are present in all states of consciousness, they show no differentiation of parts, possess therefore no marks of individuality by which they may enter into association with other activities, feelings, or presentations: and as they cannot enter into associations, so they cannot be reproduced or recalled in any sense analogous to that in which presentations are recalled (*ib.* 44[b]). It might perhaps be said that, on Dr. Ward's view, activity is a simple unanalyzable phase of experience, but can never be an object or *content* of experience. Professor James has argued with great force against the conception that there is any peculiar consciousness of activity, more especially in the form of a *feeling of innervation* as it has been called—the feeling of the current of outgoing energy, in volition or attention or other active states,—which is defended by writers otherwise so diverse as Bain, Helmholtz, and Wundt (*Principles of Psychology*, ii. 492 ff.; cf. i. 299 f.). What is *in the mind* in ordinary volition before the act takes place is simply a kinæsthetic idea of what the act is to be—'a mental conception, made up of memory images' of the muscular sensations defining which special act it is. All our ideas of movement, including those of the effort which it requires, as well as those of its direction, its extent, its strength, and its velocity, 'are images of peripheral sensations, either "remote," or resident in the moving parts, or in other parts which sympathetically act with them in consequence of the diffuse "wave"' (*ib.* 494). Wundt himself, as James points out, has come to admit that there are no differences of quality in these feelings of innervation, but only of degree of intensity. 'They are used by the mind as guides, not of *which* movement, but of *how strong* a movement it is making, or shall make. But does not this virtually surrender their existence altogether?' (*ib.* 500). The fundamental form of mental activity, according to James, is attention, and the fact of attention is known partly through changes undergone by the idea to which we attend, and partly by muscular sensations, in the head and elsewhere, which accompany the strain of accommodation, sensory and mental. Dr. Stout has rightly pointed out that James here separates activity from the process which is active, and makes it consist in another collateral process. It 'is like identifying the velocity of a moving body with the motion of some other body' (*Anal. Psychol.* i. p. 163). James does not, however, identify the activity with the sensations by which we become aware of it; they are indexes of something which directly we cannot know. By Dr. Stout himself this is precisely what is denied: an idea must be based upon some direct experience or sentience—'The thought of succession in time must be based on the direct experience of time-transience, as the thought of red colour is based on the corresponding sensation.' 'The cardinal antithesis between mental activity and passivity is not merely a group of relations ideally cognized by the reflective intelligence. Mental activity exists in being felt.' It may readily be admitted that change or transition is given as a direct experience; but an activity is much more than a transition. It involves (1) direction or tendency of the transition towards an end, and (2) some feeling or knowledge of *effectuation* in the successive phases of the realization of the end. It is impossible to see how either a tendency towards an end, or the effectiveness of a process in furthering the tendency, can be a direct experience or feeling of the mind. Causality cannot 'exist in being felt,' and causality is an essential feature of activity. We conclude, then, (1) that there is no direct consciousness of activity; (2) that the conception of activity is a symbolic knowledge, founded on certain complex groups of feelings and presentations, in which similar elements and arrangements of elements constantly recur.

5. *What is the simplest or primary form of mental activity?* At least three possible answers may be given: (1) Effectuation of physical change, (2) Attention, (3) Apperception. The first identifies activity with conation simply, of which the lowest form is impulse to movement; the second reduces the mental element in conation to the movement of the attention; the third, to the play of apperception. In the first, which is that adopted above, mental activity is self-determination only in an indirect way; the mind cannot act immediately upon itself; it can produce a desired change only by subjecting itself to certain physical conditions or circumstances through which the change may be effected. The question of Liberty and Determinism does not turn in the least upon this of the relation of mental activity to bodily. As has been said, 'Whatever be our opinion about our liberty or our determinism, we accord to the different moments of our mental life a decisive influence upon the nature of the following moments. We consider our actual modifications as acting upon our future modifications.' Even those who feel themselves subject to an inflexible necessity do so not because their will is without efficacy, but, 'on the contrary, because the efficacy of every idea, every feeling, every volition is such that it does not leave the smallest place to contingence' (van Biéma, *Revue de Métaphys. et Morale*, 1900, p. 286). But an idea has efficacy not in itself, but only in so far as it excites feeling, and thereby stimulates activity or striving. Both Dr. Ward and Professor James, from different points of view, regard *attention* as the primary and fundamental phase of mental activity. 'The effort of attention is thus the essential phenomenon of will' (James, ii. p. 562); but 'this *volitional* effort pure and simple must be carefully distinguished from the muscular effort with which it is usually confounded. The latter consists of all those peripheral feelings to which a muscular "exertion" may give rise.' The attention is kept strained upon an object of thought which is out of harmony with the prevailing drift of thought, 'until at last it grows so as to maintain itself before the mind with ease. This strain of the attention is the fundamental act of will. And the will's work is in most cases practically ended when the bare presence to our thought of the naturally unwelcome object has been secured. For the mysterious tie between the thought and the motor centres next comes into play, and, in a way which we cannot even guess at, the obedience of the bodily organs follows as a matter of course' (*ib.* p. 564). 'Consciousness (or the neural process which goes with it) is in its very nature impulsive' (*ib.* p. 535). Now, it is in precisely this impulsiveness, this transition from thought to bodily action, that we have sought the primitive or essential form of the activity of mind. The retaining or strengthening of an idea in attention is only an instance of it. Attention is not a pure activity which can be called now to one idea, now to another: it is the interaction between the mind and its presentations, the degree and form of attention being proportional to the mental organization; and the effect of attention is never directly upon the idea, the content of consciousness itself, but upon the motor centres by which the physiological process underlying the idea is strengthened or heightened, and thus the idea itself brought indirectly into clearer consciousness. As Volkmann has

said, 'The willing to hold a presentation fast is not the willing of the presentation itself—and cannot therefore be directed immediately upon the presentation, but must take the roundabout way through renewing the stimulus or keeping up the activity of auxiliary (*i.e.* associated) ideas' (Volkmann, *Lehrbuch der Psychologie*[4] [1894], ii. p. 205). With Wundt, the elementary process is 'the apperception of a psychic content' (*l.c.* iii. 307), or the bringing of a presentation into the *focus* of consciousness. Consciousness and will belong together from the beginning onwards, and external action as a volition-process differs from the internal action of apperception only in its consequences, not in its immediate psychological nature. Considered as a phenomenon of consciousness, the former consists in nothing but 'the apperception of an idea of movement' (*ib.*; on Wundt's 'Theory of Apperception' see Villa, *Contemporary Psychology*, p. 211 ff.). If we analyze this process of apperception, we find there are three steps: (i.) the idea is perceived or enters consciousness; (ii.) it acts as a motive or stimulus, through the feelings connected with it, upon the internal will; (iii.) the will reacts upon it, and it is 'apperceived.' The sole effect of the will upon the ideas is to raise them into the focus of consciousness: all that follows springs from the mechanism of the ideas themselves. Volkmann objects to the theory that it implies a will hanging above the ideas, and striking in among them, but which in itself is wholly inert,—a will which wills nothing, but must wait for stimulation from without (*l.c.* p. 194). The latter objection holds only if we suppose that perception precedes apperception in time, as Wundt indeed assumes: it fails if we regard the analysis as that of a single process into constituents which can be held apart only by abstraction, but which have no separate conscious existence. The former objection is, however, conclusive: a will which acts upon our ideas and affects them directly is non-existent. We conclude that attention and apperception are alike modes of the more fundamental form of mental activity which consists in the response of the mind to a presentation, through feeling, by effecting some bodily change.

6. *The essence of moral activity* is to be found in that form of mental activity in which an idea is retained before the mind, in spite of its incongruity with tendencies or dispositions already present. In such cases there is a choice or selection of one idea among several possible ones, for realization: to realize an idea is to give it bodily form, or *real* existence—in other words, to carry out the actions which the idea involves. But it is only when an idea is sufficiently strengthened (centrally or peripherally) that it acquires this impulsive force. 'Consent to the idea's undivided presence, this is effort's sole achievement. Its only function is to get this feeling of consent into the mind. And for this there is but one way'—*i.e.* to keep it steadily before the mind until it *fills* the mind—'To sustain a representation, to think, is, in short, the only moral act, for the impulsive and the obstructed, for sane and lunatic alike' (James). The consent of which James writes is a somewhat mythological process—it is a *fiat* of the mind, a resolve that the act shall ensue (*l.c.* pp. 501, 567 ff.), 'a subjective experience *sui generis* which we can designate but not define.' Perhaps an ultimate analysis would show it to be not an apparently unmotived act of the mind, but a function of the ideas themselves in their relation to the mind as an organized system of dispositions and tendencies. The ethical or metaphysical problem of freewill or determinism belongs elsewhere; for psychology the problem does not exist.

7. *Historical.*—The first philosophical treatment of mental activity occurs in Plato's theory of Ideas. The Ideas, as the ultimate and only realities, have movement and life, soul and intelligence. The finite soul has both a transient and an immanent causality, the former as the cause of the motion and life of its body, the latter through its faculty of knowing, by which it participates in the life of the Ideas and assimilates their active power. Passivity of mind consists in the affecting of the mind by the body, through its senses; passivity thus comes to mean imperfect, inaccurate, confused and inadequate knowledge. The soul is most active when detached from the body, and in the ecstatic union with the infinite and eternal Idea of the Good.

'The soul reasons best when disturbed by none of the senses, whether hearing or sight, or pain or pleasure: when she has dismissed the body and released herself as far as possible from all intercourse or contact with it, and thus, living alone with herself so far as possible, strives after real truth' (*Sophistes*, 248 A ff., *Republic*, vii. 532 ff., *Phædo*, 65; cf. Zeller, *Phil. der Griechen*, ii. p. 436).

The dualism of soul and body is already partly overcome in Aristotle: it is not the soul in man that thinks or learns of itself, but man thinks through the soul; *i.e.* the man is an organic whole. On the other hand, the dualism returns within Reason or Intelligence, which is of two kinds, passive and active. All human knowledge depends upon experience, and rational truths are merely the highest inductive generalizations from experience; the mind is passive in the double sense: (1) that it is dependent upon the body for its material, and even the forms into which the material is moulded, through successive impressions; (2) that the separate phases of consciousness are transitory and fleeting. On the other hand, the possibility of these empirical generalizations implies the co-operation of an Active or Creative Intelligence which gives the ideas their reality, as eternal, imperishable existences. This Active Reason is separate from the body, as from all matter, whereas the Passive Reason is merely the essence or form of the body itself: the Passive Reason perishes with the body, the Active Reason is the eternal element in man (*de Anima*, iii. Cf. Siebeck, *Gesch. der Psychologie*, i. 2, pp. 64 f., 72). The difficulties of the theory are: (1) that the Active Reason appears to be simply identical with the Divine Consciousness itself, by which the finite mind is passively affected, so that there is no real activity of the finite consciousness; (2) that from another point of view the Active Reason as a *separate* principle means simply Truth, as an ideal system of knowledge, of which our every thought is a partial realization. It has validity, not real existence. Aristotle's theory suggested, however, that the mind is *active*, the human understanding at work, in *all* knowledge, from sense-experience onwards. This conclusion was brought out first by Alexander of Aphrodisias —2nd cent. A.D.—(*ib.* p. 202). In Plotinus also (3rd cent.) consciousness is not merely the passive spectator of its own experiences, but a synthetic activity, grasping together, holding together and moulding the impressions it receives (*ib.* pp. 333, 337). Throughout the Mediæval Period controversy as to mental activity resolved itself mainly into the relation of soul to body, or the problem of the relation of the finite to the Divine mind. In Avicenna (A.D. 980–1038) the intelligence is wholly unattached to any bodily organ, and its objects are wholly distinct from those of sense; on the other hand, he distinguishes, with Aristotle, between an active and a passive principle within the intelligence itself. The latter is only in the individual soul and perishes with it; the former is distinct and separate from the individual soul, is universal, one and the same in all, and it alone is immortal (Stöckl, *Gesch. d. Philosophie des Mittelalters*, II. i. § 12).

The question of ethical activity in its modern form first emerges in Averroës (A.D. 1126–1198). He distinguishes between beings which are active, *i.e.* act upon other beings, by *nature*, and those of which the activity is conditional upon *desire*. 'The powers of the former are determined to one thing, and must, when the corresponding conditions are given, necessarily enter into the act. The latter—beings which act from desire or choice—do not enter into activity necessarily, when a fitting object is presented, but are in themselves indifferent to the object, and may desire or choose the one or the other,' *i.e.* their choice is an activity acceding to the object and independent of it (*ib.* § 21). Some of the Muslim dogmatists denied that any source of activity exists in man or in any other finite being: all movement and activity in the created world depends directly and solely upon an external cause—*viz.* God. That definite events appear to follow upon definite causes is due to the fact that God observes the *habit* of allowing it so. Each process is an accident, momentarily created by God, according to the custom He has prescribed to Himself. Man does not really will or act, God creates in him the volition and the act; man is thus wholly passive, the blind instrument of God's will. His activity is an illusion. These ideas return in Geulincx and the Occasionalists. The doctrine of the soul as a substance, and therefore a *source of activity*, was upheld by Albertus Magnus (13th cent.) and Thomas Aquinas (*ib.*), and prevailed, along with a side current of scepticism, until Descartes (1596–1650). In his metaphysical theory Descartes makes mind the diametrical opposite of body; the former alone is active or free, the body a pure automaton: the soul is nothing that is not spiritual, unextended, immaterial; no intercourse, therefore, is possible between soul and body, except by the Divine interference. The soul produces its sensations from itself, *on occasion of*, but not through, the bodily excitations. In his Psychology, however, as Weber has pointed out (Weber, *Hist. of Philosophy*, tr. Thilly, p. 316; cf. Descartes, *Traité des Passions*, *Traité de l'Homme*), Descartes entirely contradicts these principles and speaks of the soul as united to the body, and as acting upon it and acted upon by it in its turn. In both Spinoza and Leibniz the special activity of the soul is knowledge; it is passive just in so far as its ideas or perceptions are inadequate or confused. With Malebranche, as later with Schopenhauer, but from a totally different standpoint, the centre of activity is transferred to the *will*—the mind in relation to the outward world. In the English Psychologists it is jointly placed in the will and in the inward power of combining, synthesizing, and transforming the ideas. In modern psychology, as we have tried to show above, the tendency has been to reduce one of these different forms of mental activity to the other.

LITERATURE.—The following are some of the more important references, in addition to those mentioned in the text:
1879: **W. James**, 'Are We Automata?' in *Mind*, iv.; **Chr. Sigwart**, *Der Begriff des Wollens*, u.s.w., Tübingen.
1880: **W. James**, 'The Feeling of Effort' in *Mind*, v.; **Laas**, 'Die Causalität des Ich' in *Viertelj. f. wiss. Phil.* iv.
1888: **H. Münsterberg**, *Die Willenshandlung*, Freiburg i. B.
1889: **Alf. Fouillée**, 'Le sentiment de l'effort et la conscience de l'action' in *Rev. Philos.* xxviii.; **E. Montgomery**, 'Mental Activity' in *Mind*, xiv.; **Fr. Paulham**, *L'Activité mentale et les éléments de l'esprit*, Paris; **A. Bertrand**, *La Psychologie de l'effort*, Paris.
1890: **Th. Lipps**, 'Zur Psychologie der Causalität' in *Zeit. für Psychol.* i.
1891: **H. Höffding**, 'Psychische und physische Activität' in *Viertelj. f. wiss. Phil.* xv.; **A. D. Waller**, 'The Sense of Effort' in *Brain*, xiv.
1894: **Dewey**, 'The Ego as Cause' in *Philos. Rev.* iii.; **W. Wundt**, 'Ueber psychische Kausalität,' u.s.w., in *Phil. Stud.* x.; **Höfler**, 'Psychische Arbeit' in *Zeit. f. Psychol.* viii.
1895: **A. F. Shand**, 'Attention and Will' in *Mind*, xx.
1897: **Dewey**, 'Psychology of Effort' in *Philos. Rev.* vi.
1898: **N. J. Grot**, 'Die Begriffe der Seele und der psychischen Energie in der Psychologie' in *Arch. Syst. Phil.* iv.
1899: **G. F. Stout**, *Manual of Psychology*; **J. Ward**, *Naturalism and Agnosticism*, 2 vols.
1900–1: **J. Royce**, *The World and the Individual*, 2 vols.
1901: **Lipps**, 'Psychische Vorgänge und psychische Causalität' in *Zeit. f. Psychol.* xxv.; **Loveday**, 'Theories of Mental Activity' in *Mind*, N.S. x.
1902: **F. H. Bradley**, 'The Definition of Will' in *Mind*, N.S. xi.; **H. Bergson**, 'L'Effort intellectuel' in *Rev. Philos.* liii.
1903: **C. A. Strong**, *Why the Mind has a Body*, N.Y.
1905: **W. James**, 'Experience of Activity' in *Psych. Rev.* xii.
1907: **G. F. Stout**, 'The Nature of Conation and Mental Activity' in *Brit. Journ. of Psych.*, vol. ii. pt. 1.

J. L. M'INTYRE.

ADAM.—1. The name.—The Heb. אָדָם (*'ādhām*) is properly a common noun denoting 'mankind' or 'human being,' *homo* as distinguished from *vir*. In Gn 1[26-28] (P), *'ādhām* = 'mankind'; in 2[4]–4[26] we have *hā-'ādhām* = 'the man,' *i.e.* the first man;* in 5[1-5] it is used as a proper name. The etymology of 'Adam' is uncertain; Gn 2[7] 'Jahweh Elohim formed man (*'ādhām*) of the dust of the ground' (*'ădhāmāh*) is not to be taken as a scientific derivation. The usual words for 'man' in the Semitic languages generally are not cognate with *'ādhām*. 'Adam' has been connected with an Assyr. *adum* 'child,' 'one made,' 'created'; with the Heb. root *'dm* 'red,' the name having originated in a ruddy race; Dillmann on Gn 1. 2 suggests a connexion with an Eth. root = 'pleasant,' 'well-formed,' or an Arab. root = 'to attach oneself,' and so = 'gregarious,' 'sociable.' Any connexion with *Adapa*, the hero of a Babylonian myth, is most improbable.

2. Adam in the OT.—The only references to Adam are in Gn 1–5, and in the dependent passage 1 Ch 1[1]. The common noun *'ādhām* is misread as the name in AV of Dt 32[8] and Job 31[33]; RV corrects Dt. but retains Adam in the text of Job, putting the correction 'after the manner of men' for 'like Adam' in the margin. In view of the OT habit of playing upon words, there may be a secondary reference to Adam in Job and possibly elsewhere; but as 'man' or 'mankind' gives a satisfactory sense, there is not sufficient ground for recognizing a secondary meaning.

In the Priestly narrative (P) of Creation (Gn 1[1]–2[4a]) Elohim creates 'mankind' (*'ādhām*) in His own image, in two sexes, makes man supreme over all living creatures, bids him multiply, and gives him the fruits and grains for food. He blesses man. But whereas it is said separately of each of the other groups of creatures, 'God saw that it was good,' there is no such separate utterance concerning man; he is simply included in the general statement, 'God saw everything that he had made, and, behold, it was very good.' In 5[1-5] Adam is the ancestor of the human race; when he is 130 years old he begets Seth 'in his own likeness, after his image.' Afterwards Adam begat other children, and died at the age of 930.

In the Prophetic (J) narrative (Gn 2[4b]–4[26]) Jahweh Elohim moulds 'the man' out of dust, gives him life by breathing into his nostrils the breath of life, and places him in Eden to dress and keep it. Jahweh Elohim also makes the animals out of the soil (*'ădhāmāh*) in order that 'the man' may find a helpmeet; 'the man' names them but finds no suitable helpmeet, and at last Jahweh Elohim builds up a woman out of a rib taken from 'the man' while he slept: the woman proves a suitable helpmeet. Jahweh Elohim had forbidden 'the man' to eat of the fruit of a certain 'tree of the knowledge of good and evil' planted in the midst of Eden; but, tempted by the serpent, the woman ate of the forbidden fruit, and also persuaded the

* RV has 'Adam' as proper name in three passages, following MT; but in two (3[17. 21]) the pointing should be slightly altered, and in the third (4[25]) the article should probably be inserted, changing it in each case to 'the man.'

man to eat. Thereupon Jahweh Elohim drove them out of Eden, and men became subject to death. After the expulsion the man and the woman became parents of three sons; one of these, Abel, was murdered by his brother Cain; while the other two, Cain and Seth, became the progenitors of the human race.

These two narratives differ markedly in form; the Prophetic narrative is frankly anthropomorphic, but the Priestly narrative minimizes the anthropomorphic element. Both are adapted from ancient Semitic traditions;* but here again in Gn 1 the mythological element is reduced to language and framework, and is altogether subordinated to the teaching of revelation; whereas in Gn 2–4 the author is evidently glad to retain a picturesque story for its own sake as well as for the sake of its moral. In other words, he uses an ancient tradition as a parable, and we have no right to extract theology from all the details.

The two narratives agree in their pure monotheism, in representing man as the immediate creation of God, without intervention of angels, æons, or other intermediate supernatural beings; in representing him as a creation of God, and not as born of God by any *quasi*-material process; and in representing the human race as descended from a single pair. They are also substantially at one in other points: man is Godlike; in the Priestly narrative he is made 'in the image and likeness' of God, and passes that 'image and likeness' on to his descendants (Gn $1^{26f.}$ $5^{1ff.}$, cf. below); in the Prophetic narrative man's life is the breath of God (Gn 2); in the Priestly narrative man is given the dominion over all other creatures; in the Prophetic narrative the animals are specially formed for the service of man, and receive their names from him.

It is characteristic of the Priestly narrative that its express moral is found in two points of ritual: man is to be vegetarian, and to observe the Sabbath. The Prophetic narrative, on the other hand, is concerned with the moral life: the marriage tie is to be permanently binding, and marriage is spoken of in terms which imply a preference for monogamy. Man is under a Divine law; God has provided for his welfare, and ordained his abode, his work, his food. There is moral retribution; the disobedience of the man and the woman, wrongdoing, murder on the part of Cain, are punished; but even while Jahweh Elohim punishes, He still cares for men; He clothes the man and the woman, and protects Cain from being put to death.

Passing to other features of the Prophetic narrative, we note the inferior position of woman, corresponding to her status in the East, suggested by her formation after man, from his body, and for his service; she is also the instrument of his ruin. Again, man enjoys immediate fellowship with God; and this is not terminated by the expulsion from Eden, for Jahweh converses in the same fashion with Cain as He does with Adam; and the dwelling-place of the first family *outside* Eden is still thought of as being in the special presence of God. When Cain leaves this dwelling-place, he goes 'out from the presence of Jahweh' and feels that he will 'be hidden from his face' (Gn $4^{14.\,16}$).

The original sin of man, the fatal source of all his misery, was inordinate desire, indulged in contrary to the Divine prohibition. This desire is comprehensive. It is sensual: the woman sees that the tree is 'good for food'; it is æsthetic: 'it was a delight to the eyes.' The desire is also intellectual: the tree is 'the tree of the knowledge of good and evil'; the serpent promises that by eating it 'their eyes shall be opened . . . to know good and evil,' and the woman sees that the tree is 'to be desired to make one wise.'* But the desire for 'the knowledge of good and evil' is not merely intellectual, it is also a desire for a deeper, more varied, more exciting experience of life, a desire to 'see life,' to use popular language. And as the serpent promises that by eating they shall become 'like gods,' this desire included ambition. In other words, the first sin consisted in defying God by giving the reins to the various impulses which make for culture and civilization. Similarly, in Gn 4^{16-24} progress in civilization is due to the evil race of Cain.

* As far as the Fall and Cain and Abel are concerned, only uncertain hints of such stories have yet been discovered in the inscriptions of Western Asia; but the character of Gn 3–4 shows that the author is adapting ancient tradition.

The author of the source which the Prophetic narrator follows regards the life of man as accursed, a life of sordid toil, poorly rewarded, embarrassed by shame arising out of the sexual conditions of human existence, burdened for woman by the pain of travail and by her subjection to her husband. These evils are the punishment of the first sin, the consequences of the unholy appetite for luxury and culture, knowledge and power. Smend (*Alttest. Rel.-Gesch.* 121 f.) has pointed out that this conception of life does not control the patriarchal stories or the other portions of the Prophetic narrative; hence the author must have taken it over from older tradition, and it does not represent his formal and complete judgment on life, though he retains it as expressing one side of the truth.

Similarly, there are other theological implications which might be discerned by pressing details; but such implications are no part of the teaching which the Prophetic narrator intended to enforce; such details also are merely retained from ancient tradition; *e.g.* the feud between man and the serpent is retained as corresponding to the facts of life, but in the original story it was probably a reminiscence of the contest between Marduk and the primeval Dragon.

Again, the story serves to explain the miserable estate of man and the sense of alienation from God; but it does not profess to explain the origin of evil or of sin. It is indeed implied that sin did not originate in man or from man, but was due to suggestion from outside.

Obviously we are not intended to deduce doctrines by combining features of the two narratives, otherwise we should be confronted by the difficulty that the serpent would be included amongst the creatures whom God pronounced 'very good.'

In the Priestly narrative the fact of sin is not mentioned till the time just before the Flood, when we are told that the earth was corrupt and full of violence (Gn 6^{11}); no account is given of the origin of this corruption. It is noteworthy that we are told that Adam transmitted the Divine likeness to Seth (cf. 5^1 and vv.$^{2-4}$); but no such statement is made as to Adam's other children. Possibly the Divine likeness was a birthright transmitted from eldest son to eldest son, till it reached Noah, but not possessed by other men, hence their corruption; or again this likeness may have been shared by the descendants of Seth, but not possessed by other races. The Book of Chronicles simply traces the genealogy of Israel from Adam.

3. Adam in the Apocrypha and later Jewish literature.—As the first man, Adam occupies a prominent place in theology and tradition. An immense body of tradition gathered round the brief Scripture narratives. The notices of Adam in the Apocrypha, however, are for the most part mere references to the accounts in Genesis. Thus 2 Es 3^{4-10} is a summary of these accounts, followed in v.^{21} by the comment, 'For the first Adam, bear-

* Not as in RVm 'desirable to look upon,' cf. Dillmann.

ing a wicked heart, transgressed, and was overcome; and not he only, but all they also that are born of him.' The author does not explain how the immediate creation of God came to have a 'wicked heart'; but perhaps the term is used proleptically—a heart that became wicked through the Fall. Again, 6^{54-56} refers to Adam as the ancestor of the human race (cf. also $7^{11.70}$); and in 7^{46-56} Esdras laments the sin and punishment which Adam has brought on mankind.*

It is remarkable that when Jesus ben Sirach sets out to 'praise famous men' (Sir 44–50), he passes over Adam and begins with Enoch; then he reviews the series of OT heroes, concluding with Nehemiah, and then (49^{14-16}) reverts to Enoch and Joseph, and at last by way of Shem and Seth arrives at Adam: 'Above every living thing in the creation is Adam.'

The position of Sir 49^{14-16} suggests that this paragraph was either an afterthought of Ben Sira, or an addition by a later writer who had noticed the absence of Adam and others. Perhaps Ben Sira felt that the Fall rendered Adam unfit to figure in a list of ancient worthies.

Adam plays a considerable part in the other Apocalyptic literature. In the *Book of the Secrets of Enoch* ($30^{8ff.}$),† for instance, Adam is made of seven substances: his flesh from the earth, his blood from the dew, his eyes from the sun, his bones from the stones, his veins and hair from the grass, his thoughts from the swiftness of the angels and from the clouds, his spirit from the Spirit of God and from the wind. He is 'like a second angel,' endowed with the Divine Wisdom. His name Adam was constructed from the initials of the [Greek] names of the four quarters of the earth: *Anatole* (E.), *Dusis* (W.), *Arktos* (N.), *Mesembria* (S.). He fell through ignorance, because he did not understand his own nature.

We read of a Jewish *Book of Adam*,‡ but it is not now extant.

The other branch of later Jewish literature, Talmud, Midrashim, etc., embellishes the Scripture narrative with a variety of fanciful legends. In the famous *Baraitha* of the Talmud on the origin of the books of the OT, Adam is one of the ten elders who contributed to the Psalter. Ibn Ezra explains the birth of children to Adam by suggesting that when he found that the permanent continuance of the race in his own person would be prevented by death, he provided for its continuance by begetting children. Rabbinical traditions also state that the tree of knowledge was a fig-tree, that Eve gave the fruit to the animals, etc. etc.§ Philo expounds and allegorizes the Biblical narratives in *de Opificio Mundi, Sacrarum Legum Allegoriæ de Cherubim*; pointing out, for instance, that the statement that man was made in the image of God must not be understood in a material sense; it means that the mind in man corresponds to God in the cosmos (*de Opif.* 23); and the narrative of the Fall is an allegory of the disastrous consequences of lust (*ib.* 57, 58).

Josephus (*Ant.* I. i. 2) merely puts the Biblical narrative into what he conceived to be a better literary form, expanding, for instance, the few words of Jahweh Elohim into a speech. It is noteworthy, however, that he speaks in his preface of some of the Mosaic narratives as being allegorical.

The Jewish development of this subject reaches its climax in the mediæval mysticism called the Qabbālā, where the Sephīroth, or emanations by which God creates, are grouped sometimes as the tree of life and sometimes as Adam Qadmon, the primeval man.

* 2 Esdras (so Eng. Apocrypha; Vulg. 4 Esdras) is the work of a Palestinian Jew, A.D. 81–96, with Christian interpolations.

† Morfill and Charles attribute the work to a Hellenistic Jew (A.D. 1–50).

‡ See Hastings' *DB*, i. 37, art. 'Adam, Books of.'

§ Hershon, *Rabbinical Commentary on Genesis.*

4. Adam in the NT.—Adam is mentioned in Lk 3^{38} as the ancestor of Jesus, thus emphasizing the Incarnation, the reality of our Lord's humanity. In 1 Ti $2^{13.14}$ the authority of the husband over the wife is deduced from the fact that Adam was 'first formed'; and that it was Eve, not Adam, who was deceived by the serpent. The idea that Adam was not deceived probably rests on some Rabbinical exegesis, *e.g.* the suggestion that Adam did not know that the apple Eve gave him came from the tree of life. Jude [14] has the casual reference, 'Enoch also, the seventh from Adam.' Also, 1 Co 11^{2-16} supports the current etiquette as to the way in which women wore their hair, and as to their wearing veils, by the fact that the first woman was created from the man, and for the sake of the man, and not *vice versa*.

But the most important NT passages are Ro 5^{12-21} and 1 Co $15^{20-22.45-49}$, which state a parallel and a contrast between Adam and Christ. To a certain extent, Adam and Christ stand in the same relation to the human race; in each case the nature and work of the individual affects the whole race; Adam 'is a figure of him that was to come' (Ro 5^{14}). But while the one man Adam's one sin introduces sin and guilt and death, the one Christ's one act of righteousness justifies the guilty, restores them to righteousness, and enables them to reign in life. This 'one act of righteousness' is also spoken of as 'the obedience of the one'; the general tenor of St. Paul's teaching identifies this 'act' with the death of Christ (Ro 5^{12-21}, 1 Co 15^{20-22}). St. Paul does not make it clear how, or in what sense, Adam's sin became the cause of sin, guilt, and death to his posterity. The statement of Ro 5^{14}, that 'death reigned from Adam until Moses, even over them that had not sinned after the likeness of Adam's transgression,' suggests that men were involved in the guilt and punishment of Adam apart from their own sins.

1 Co 15^{26-49} is not *prima facie* quite consistent with Romans; and there is nothing to show that St. Paul had correlated the two sets of ideas. In Corinthians, mankind inherits from Adam limitations; and Christ enables mankind to transcend these limitations. 'The first man is of the earth, earthy,' merely a living 'soul' (ψυχή); and such were his descendants until Christ came. 'The last man,' 'the second man from heaven,' was 'a life-giving spirit' (πνεῦμα), and apparently communicates this *pneuma* to Christians, who are 'heavenly' like their Master, and bear His image. In other words, by the Incarnation human nature was raised to a higher plane. But again it is doubtful how far St. Paul would have been prepared to affirm all that his words imply.* The idea of a higher and a lower Adam, of a heavenly and an earthy or earthly man, is found in Philo, in some of the Gnostic systems,† and in the Qabbālā.‡

5. Adam in Christian literature.—The Patristic commentaries on the stories of the Creation and the Fall largely follow Jewish precedents; they often allegorize and ornament the narrative by legendary additions; while the Gnostic cosmologies anticipate and pave the way for the mysticism of the Qabbālā. Adam becomes a Gnostic Æon.§ The Ophites speak of 'the spiritual seed or ὁ ἔσω ἄνθρωπος as an efflux ἀπὸ τοῦ ἀρχανθρώπου ἄνωθεν Ἀδαμάντος,'‖ Greek equivalents of the Adam Qadmon or Adam Elyon which figure in the Qabbālā.

* Franz Delitzsch, in his *Brief an die Römer in das Hebräische übersetzt und aus Talmud und Midrasch erläutert*, quotes from Martini a passage from *Sifrê* (an early Midrash) which contrasts the effects of Adam's sin with those of the vicarious sufferings of the Messiah.

† Harvey's *Irenæus*, i. 134 n. 2.

‡ *Dict. of Christ. Biogr.*, art. 'Cabbalah' by Ginsburg. Philo (*Leg. Allegor.* i. 16) speaks of a higher and a lower man introduced into Paradise; the lower is expelled, the higher remains.

§ Harvey's *Irenæus*, i. 224, n. 1. ‖ Harvey, i. 134, n. 2.

To derive these Gnostic ideas from the Qabbālā is an anachronism; both are developments from Rabbinical mysticism. Mediæval and Protestant divines, especially Calvin following Augustine, develop the doctrine of Original Sin from St. Paul's teaching. Thus Calvin:* 'He (Adam) not only was himself punished . . . but he involved his posterity also. . . . The orthodox, therefore, and more especially Augustine, laboured to show that we are not corrupted by acquired wickedness, but bring an innate corruption from the very womb. It was the greatest impudence to deny this.' †

6. Adam in Islām.—The Muhammadans accept the Christian Scripture subject to the necessary correction and interpretation; they have also borrowed many of the Jewish legends. Adam, therefore, is an important person in their religious system; and they have adorned his story with legends of their own. For instance, on the site of the Ka'ba at Mecca, Adam, after his expulsion from Eden, first worshipped God in a tent sent down from heaven for the purpose; and Eve's tomb may be seen near Mecca; it shows the outlines of a body 173 ft. by 12 ft.; the head is buried elsewhere.‡

LITERATURE.—Comm. on the Biblical passages; Handbooks of OT and NT Theology and of Dogmatics on the doctrines of Man, Creation, and Original Sin; H. G. Smith, 'Adam in the RV,' in *AJTh*, vi. (1902), 758; G. F. Moore, 'The Last Adam,' in *JBL*, xvi. (1897), 158; J. Denney, 'Adam and Christ in St. Paul,' in *Exp.* 6th ser. ix. (1904), 147; Hastings' *DB*, artt. 'Adam,' 'Adam in the NT,' and 'Adam, Books of'; *JE*, artt. 'Adam,' 'Adam, Book of,' 'Adam Ḳadmon.'

W. H. BENNETT.

ADAM'S BRIDGE, or *Rāmasetu*='Rāma's causeway.'—A chain of sandbanks over 30 miles in length, extending from the island of Rāmesvaram off the Indian coast, to the island of Manar off the coast of Ceylon. These sandbanks—some dry and others a few feet under the surface of the water—seem to connect India with Ceylon; and this fact has given rise to the tradition that they are portions of a causeway which was constructed by Rāma, the hero of the ancient Indian Epic called the *Rāmāyaṇa*.

The story of the Epic is well known. Rāma, the prince of Ayodhya or Oudh, was banished by the king, his father, for fourteen years, and came and lived in a forest near the sources of the Godāvarī, accompanied by his wife Sītā and his younger brother Lakṣmaṇa. During the absence of the two brothers from their cottage, Sītā was taken away by Rāvaṇa, king of Ceylon. After long search Rāma got news of Sītā, and determined to cross over from India to Ceylon with a vast army of monkeys and bears to recover her. It was for this purpose that the causeway across the ocean is said to have been constructed. Rāma crossed over with the army, defeated and killed Rāvaṇa, recovered his wife, and returned to Oudh. The period of exile had expired; Rāma's father was dead; and Rāma ascended the throne.

The building of the causeway across the ocean is described at great length in the epic poem. And after Rāma had killed his foe and recovered his wife, he is described as sailing through the sky in an aërial car—all the way from Ceylon to Oudh. The whole of India was spread below; and few passages in the epic are more striking than the bold attempt to describe the vast continent as seen from the car. It was then that Rāma pointed out to his wife, who was seated by him in the car, the great causeway he had constructed across the ocean.

'See, my love, round Ceylon's island
How the ocean billows roar,
Hiding pearls in caves of coral,
Strewing shells upon the shore,
And the causeway far-extending,—
Monument of Rāma's fame,—
Rāmasetu unto ages
Shall our deathless deed proclaim!'

The Hindus regard Rāma as an incarnation of Viṣṇu, the second of the Hindu Trinity—the god who preserves and supports the universe. The island of Rāmesvaram, from which Rāma is supposed to have crossed to Ceylon over the causeway built by him, is therefore a sacred place of pilgrimage, visited by thousands of pious Hindus every year from all parts of India. The famous temple of Rāmesvaram, with its pillared corridors, 700 feet long, is perhaps the finest specimen of Dravidian architecture in India.

LITERATURE.—*Rāmāyaṇa* (Griffith's tr. and Romesh Dutt's condensed tr.). For an account of the temple of Rāmesvaram, see Fergusson, *Indian and Eastern Architecture*.

ROMESH DUTT.

ADAM'S PEAK.—This is the English name, adopted from the Portuguese, of a lofty mountain in Ceylon, called in Sinhalese *Samanala*, and in Pāli *Samanta-kūṭa* or *Sumana-kūṭa*. It rises directly from the plains, at the extreme south-west corner of the central mountainous district, to a height of 7420 feet. The panorama from the summit is one of the grandest in the world, as few other mountains, though surpassing it in altitude, present the same unobstructed view over land and sea. But the peak is best known as a place of pilgrimage to the depression in the rock at its summit, which is supposed to resemble a man's footprint, and is explained by pilgrims of different religions in different ways. It is a most remarkable, and probably unique, sight to see a group of pilgrims gazing solemnly at the depression, each one quite undisturbed in his faith by the knowledge that the pilgrim next to him holds a divergent view—the Buddhist thinking it to be the footprint of the Buddha, the Śaivite regarding it as the footprint of Śiva, the Christian holding it to be the footprint of St. Thomas, or perhaps admitting the conflicting claims of the eunuch of Queen Candace, and the Muhammadan thinking he beholds the footprint of Adam. The origin of these curious beliefs is at present obscure. None of them can be traced back to its real source, and even in the case of the Buddhist belief, about which we know most, we are left to conjecture in the last, or first, steps.

The earliest mention of the Buddhist belief is in the *Samanta Pāsādikā*, a commentary on the Buddhist Canon Law written by Buddhaghosa in the first quarter of the 5th cent. A.D. This work has not yet been published, but the passage is quoted in full, in the original Pāli, by Skeen (pp. 50, 51). It runs as follows: 'The Exalted One, in the eighth year after (his attainment of) Wisdom, came attended by five hundred Bhikshus on the invitation of Maniakkha, king of the Nāgas, to Ceylon; took the meal (to which he had been invited), seated the while in the Ratana Maṇḍapa (Gem Pavilion) put up on the spot where the Kalyāni Dāgaba (afterwards) stood, and making his footprint visible on Samanta Kūṭa, went back (to India).' Seeing that Adam's Peak is a hundred miles away from the Kalyāni Dāgaba, the clause about Adam's Peak seems abrupt, and looks as if it had been inserted into an older story written originally without it. But it is good evidence that the belief in the Adam's Peak legend was current at Anurādhapura when the passage quoted was written there about A.D. 425. The whole context of the passage is known to have been drawn from a history of Ceylon in Sinhalese prose with mnemonic verses in Pāli.* Those verses were collected in the still extant work, the *Dīpavaṁsa*, written probably in the previous century. That work (ii. 52–69) gives the account of the Buddha's visit to Maniakkha. It mentions nothing about Adam's Peak. Ought we to conclude that the legend arose between the dates of the two works? Probably not. The argument *ex silentio* is always weak; and in another passage of the *Samanta Pāsādikā*, where this visit of the Buddha is mentioned,† nothing is said about Adam's Peak. Neither can it be an interpolation; for in the *Mahāvaṁsa* (1. 76, p. 7), written about half a century later,‡ also at Anu-

* *Institutes*, Bk. II. ch. i. § 5.

† For Christian Apocrypha connected with Adam cf. Hastings' *DB* i. 37 f. For the legend (as old as Origen) that Adam was buried on Golgotha, see Wilson, *Golgotha and the Holy Sepulchre*, 1906, p. 2 ff.

‡ Hadji Khan and Sparrow, *With the Pilgrims to Mecca*, 105, 106.

* Geiger, *Mahāvaṁsa und Dīpavaṁsa* (Leipzig, 1905), p. 78.

† Printed in Oldenberg, *Vinaya Piṭaka*, vol. iii. p. 332.

‡ Sir E. Tennent, *Ceylon*, ii. 133, dates it 'prior to B.C. 301'!

rādhapura and also on the basis of the lost Sinhalese history, the Adam's Peak legend is referred to in almost identical words and in the same abrupt manner. If, then, the few words about Adam's Peak and the footprint have been inserted in a previous story, they must have been so inserted already in the lost Sinhalese *Mahāvaṁsa*. It seems curious that we hear no more of the legend, or of pilgrimages to the footprint, for many hundred years. Then in the continuation of the *Mahāvaṁsa* (ch. 64, line 30) the footprint is curtly mentioned in a list of sacred objects; and again (ch. 80, line 24), King Kitti Nissaṅka, A.D. 1187–1196, is said to have made a pilgrimage to Samanta-kūṭa. But as much of the literature of the intervening period has been destroyed, and as what survives is still buried in MS., this should not be deemed so surprising as it looks at first sight. It should perhaps be added that the local tradition, which the present writer heard when a magistrate in the adjoining district of Sītāwaka, was that the footprint was discovered by King Walagam Bāhu (B.C. 88–76) during his exile in the southern mountains in the early years of his reign. But we have found no literary record of this. It remains to say with regard to the Pāli evidence, that there is a poem called the *Samanta-kūṭa-vaṇṇanā*, written at an uncertain date, and probably by an author Wideha (who also wrote a popular collection of stories in Pāli, and an elementary grammar in Sinhalese), who seems more careful of little correctnesses and little elegances than of more important matters.* This work contributes nothing of value to the present question.

Fa Hian, who visited Ceylon about A.D. 412, mentions the footprint; and Sir Emerson Tennent (*Ceylon*, i. pp. 584–586) gives, on the very excellent authority of the late Mr. Wylie, quotations from three mediæval Chinese geographers who speak reverentially of the sacred footmark impressed on Adam's Peak *by the first man*, who bears, in their mythology, the name of Pawn-ku. It would seem probable that these geographers may have derived this idea from the Muhammadans. For there were large settlements of Arabs, or at least Muhammadans, in China, before they wrote; the Arab traders were rightly regarded as good authorities in matters relating to foreign countries, and they had already the idea of connecting the footprint with Adam. This idea has been traced back in Arab writers to the middle of the 9th cent.,† and occurs frequently afterwards. Ibn Batūta, for instance, who saw the footprint of Moses at Damascus, gives a long account of his visit to the footprint of Adam on Adam's Peak. Whence did they derive the belief? Sir Emerson Tennent (vol. i. p. 135) is confident that it must have been from Gnostic Christians.

His combination is, shortly, as follows. It is well known that the Muslims regard Adam in a peculiarly mystic way, not only as the greatest of all patriarchs and prophets, but as the first vice-regent of God. This idea is neither Arabian nor Jewish; but the Gnostics, with whom the early Muhammadans were in close contact, rank Adam as the third emanation of God, and assign him a singular pre-eminence as Jeu, the primal man. Now they also say, as recorded in the *Pistis Sophia*,‡ that God appointed a certain spirit as guardian of his footprint; and in Philo Judæus, in his pretended abstract of Sanchoniathon, there is also reference to the footstep of Bauth (? Buddha) visible in Ceylon. So far Sir Emerson Tennent; and we will only say that now, when so much more is known of the *Pistis Sophia* and Philo Judæus, it is desirable that these curious coincidences should be examined by a competent scholar.

The evidence as to the Śaivite belief is much later. Ibn Batūta (*circa* 1340) mentions that four Jogis who went with him to the Peak had been wont yearly to make pilgrimage to it; and the *Pærakum Bā Sirita* (Parakkama Bāhu Charita), which is about a century later, mentions a Brahman returning from a pilgrimage to Samanala, the Sinhalese name of the Peak. But neither of these authorities says that the footprint was Śiva's; and indeed the latter says that the deity of the spot was Sumana. But in the Mahāvaṁsa (ch. 93ff.) it is stated that King Rāja Siṁha of Sītāwaka (A.D. 1581–1592) granted the revenues of the Peak to certain Śaivite ascetics. Rāja Siṁha had slain his father with his own hand; the Bhikshus had declared they would not absolve him of the crime; the ascetics said they could; so he smeared his body with ashes and adopted their faith, that of Śiva. The *sanna* or grant, issued by King Kīrti Śrī of Kandy in 1751, making a renewed grant to the Buddhist Bhikshu at the Peak, calls these Śaivite faqīrs Āṇḍiyas.* Possibly the Śaivite tradition may date from this event. But it may also be somewhat older. In the *Thatchana Kailāsa Mānmiyam*, a Tamil legendary work on Trinkomali, it is said that rivers flow from the Peak out of Śiva's foot there. The date of this little work is unknown, and the present writer has seen only the extract given by Skeen (p. 295).

Whatever opinion they hold about the footprint, both Tamils and Sinhalese consider the deity of the place to be Saman Dewiyo, as he is called in Sinhalese, or Sumana (also Samanta) as he is called in Pāli. His shrine still stands on the topmost peak just beneath the pavilion over the footprint, and his image has been reproduced by Skeen (p. 258). Skeen also gives (p. 206) a ground plan and woodcut of the buildings on the Peak in 1880; Tennent (ii. 140) gives a ground plan and woodcut of them as they appeared in 1858; and Dr. Rost, in the *Journal of the Royal Asiatic Society*, 1903, p. 656, gives two woodcuts, one of the upper pavilion and one of the footmark. On the little rock plateau at the top of the mountain—it is only about 50 by 30 ft.—there is the boulder on the top of which is the footprint covered by a pavilion, the shrine of Saman Dewiyo, a shrine containing a small image of the Buddha recently erected, and a hut of wood and plaster work occupied by Buddhist Bhikshus. The four who were there when Rost visited the Peak told him that they had not been down from the mountain for four years. They complained of the cold, but said that otherwise they were quite contented, and had much time for study, and showed him their palm-leaf books. Rost says that the depression in the rock is now 5½ ft. long by 2¾ ft. broad, and that the heel of the footprint is well preserved, but the toes are not visible, being covered by the wall of the pavilion.

LITERATURE.—Tennent and Rost as cited above, and William Skeen, *Adam's Peak*, Colombo, 1880.

T. W. RHYS DAVIDS.

ADAPTATION.—Almost every detail of inherited structure and congenital behaviour shows fit adjustment to the needs and conditions of life, and may be spoken of as an adaptation. Wherever we look throughout the wide world of animate nature, we find illustrations of particular fitness to particular conditions. The size, the shape, the colour of an organism, the structure of parts in relation to their use and in their relations to other parts, the everyday behaviour and the only occasional activities, *e.g.* those concerned with reproduction,—almost every detail of structure and function is *adaptive*. The term may be used simply as a descriptive adjective, implying that the structure or function in question is fit, effective, well-adjusted, making for the preservation or well-being of the individual or of the species; but in biological usage it has also a theoretical implication, that the detail in question—if it be more than an individual accommodation, more than an individually acquired modification—is *the result of a process of evolution*. It was not always as it is now, it has a history behind it, it is a product of the factors of evolution, whatever these may be (see EVOLUTION).

The structure of a long bone in a mammal is adapted to give the utmost firmness with the minimum expenditure of material; the unique pollen-basket on the hind legs of worker-bees is adapted to stow away the pollen; the colours and patterns on the wings of leaf-insects are adapted to harmonize with the

* James D'Alwis, *Sidat Saṅgarawa*, p. clxxxiii., puts him in the 14th cent.; Wijesinhe, *Sinhalese Manuscripts in the British Museum*, p. xvii., in the 13th century. This may be the same as the *Sumana-kūṭa-vaṇṇanā* assigned at p. 72 of the *Gandha Vaṁsa* (*JPTS*, 1886) to Vācissara, who belongs to the 12th cent. A.D.

† Reinaud, *Voyages Arabes et Persans dans le ixme siècle*, vol. i. p. 5 f. It is also found in Tabarī.

‡ Schwartze's translation, p. 221.

* A full translation of the *Sanna* is given by Skeen. See p. 299.

foliage on which they settle; the parts of flowers are often adapted to ensure that the insect-visitors are dusted with pollen, and thus to secure cross-fertilization; the leaf of the Venus Fly-Trap is adapted to attract, capture, and digest flies; the peacock is adapted to captivate the pea-hen; the mother mammal is adapted for the prolonged pre-natal life of the young; the so-called 'egg-tooth' at the end of a young bird's bill is adapted to the single operation of breaking the egg-shell, —and so on throughout the whole of the animate world. It is indeed a mistake to dwell upon signal instances of adaptations, since (apart from degenerative changes in old age, morbid processes, perverted instincts, rudimentary or vestigial structures, and certain 'indifferent' characters which are not known to have any vital significance) almost every detail of structure and function may be regarded as adaptive.

To gain a clearer idea of what is one of the most difficult and fundamental problems of biology, it may be useful to consider briefly—(1) effectiveness of response; (2) plasticity; (3) modifiability, which lead on to the conception of adaptiveness.

1. Effectiveness of response.—One of the characteristics of organisms, as contrasted with inanimate systems, is their power of *effective response* to environmental stimuli. The barrel of gunpowder can respond to the external stimulus of a spark, but it responds self-destructively; the living creature's responses tend to self-preservation or to species-preservation. A piece of iron reacts to the atmosphere in rusting, it becomes an oxide of iron and ceases to be what it was; a living organism also reacts to the atmosphere, every muscular movement involves a rapid oxidation, but in spite of this and many another change the organism retains its integrity for a more or less prolonged period. Its reactions are effective. Not that the organism can respond successfully to all stimuli, *e.g.* to a strong current of electricity, for it is not able to live anywhere or anyhow, but only within certain environmental limits which we call the essential conditions of its life. We cannot account for this primary and fundamental power of effective response; it is part of our conception of life. In some degree it must have been possessed by the first and simplest organisms, though it has doubtless been improved upon in the course of evolution. Without wresting words, it cannot be said that inanimate systems ever exhibit effectiveness of response. A river carves through a soft rock and circles round a hard one, a glacier circumvents a crag, a crystal may mend itself, but it cannot be said that there is any advantage to river, glacier, or crystal in the way it behaves. The biological concept is plainly irrelevant. The nearest analogues, perhaps, to organic effectiveness of response are to be found in automatically regulated machines, but the analogy is little more than a pleasing conceit, since the machine is a materialization of human ingenuity and without any intrinsic autonomy.

2. Plasticity.—But in addition to the primary inherent power of effective response, we must also recognize that living creatures are in different degrees plastic. That is to say, they can adjust their reactions to novel conditions, or they can, as we seem bound to say, 'try' first one mode of reaction and then another, finally persisting in that which is most effective. Thus, Dallinger was able to accustom certain Monads to thrive at an extraordinarily high temperature; thus Jennings reports that the behaviour of certain Infusorians may be compared to a pursuance of 'the method of trial and error'; thus some marine fishes are plastic enough to live for days in fresh water. How much of this plasticity is primary or inherent in the very nature of living matter, how much of it is secondary and wrought out by Natural Selection in the course of ages, must remain in great measure a matter of opinion. Each case must be judged on its own merits. It is certain that many unicellular organisms are very plastic, and it seems reasonable to suppose that, as differentiation increased, restrictions were placed on the primary plasticity, while a more specialized secondary plasticity was gained in many cases, where organisms lived in environments liable to frequent vicissitudes. It is convenient to use the term '*accommodation*' for the frequently occurring functional adjustments which many organisms are able to make to new conditions. When a muscle becomes stronger if exercised beyond its wont, we may speak of this temporary individual acquisition as a functional accommodation. See ACCOMMODATION.

3. Modifiability.—Advancing a third step, we recognize as a fact of life that organisms often exhibit great *modifiability*. That is to say, in the course of their individual life they are liable to be so impressed by changes in surrounding influences and by changes in function, that, as a direct consequence, modifications of bodily structure or habit are acquired. 'Modifications' may be defined as structural changes in the body of an individual organism, directly induced by changes in function or in environment, which transcend the limit of organic elasticity and persist after the inducing conditions have ceased to operate. They are often inconveniently called 'acquired characters.' Thus a man's skin may be so thoroughly 'tanned' by the sun during half a lifetime in the tropics, that it never becomes pale again, even after migration to a far from sunny clime. It is a permanent modification, as distinguished (*a*) from a temporary adjustment, and (*b*) from congenital swarthiness.

It is admitted by all that both temporary adjustments and more permanent modifications may make for survival or for an increase of well-being that favours survival in the long run. But they may also be indifferent (as far as we can see), or they may even be injurious to the organism as a whole, *e.g.* when an important organ, in response to inadequate nutrition or stimulus, is arrested at a certain stage in its development. In themselves, however, they seem always in the direction of at least local effectiveness. It is difficult to bring forward any instance where the reaction is in itself in the wrong direction. It may spell degeneration, when judged by the normal level attained in other members of the species or in antecedent species, but the degeneration is in itself an effective response to the conditions thereof. A growing organ which does not receive adequate nutrition and the appropriate liberating stimuli, may stop growing; but while this *may be* injurious to the organism as a whole, it may be actually beneficial, and in any case it is the most effective response the organ as such could give. The change-provoking stimuli may imply conditions with which the organism cannot possibly cope, but the parts primarily affected may be said to do their best within the limits of their modifiability. Even a pathological process like inflammation, set up in response to intrusive microbes, is an effective reaction, and sometimes a life-saving one.

When a mammal taken to a colder climate acquires a thicker coat of hair, when a plant similarly treated acquires a thicker epidermis, when an area of skin much pressed upon becomes hard and callous, when a shoemaker in the course of his trade develops certain skeletal peculiarities, —and hundreds of examples might be given,—we call the results *adaptive modifications*. The changes are effective, useful, fit,—they may even make for the preservation of the individual, when the struggle for existence is keen. And yet these adjustments are not what are usually meant by 'adaptations.' For this term (used to denote a result, not a process) is most conveniently restricted to racial adjustments, that is, to characters which are inborn, not acquired; which are expressions of the natural inheritance, not individual gains. It goes without saying that though these adaptations are potentially implicit in the germinal material — in the fertilized ovum—they cannot be expressed without appropriate 'nurture'; that is a condition of all development. But they are theoretically—however difficult the distinction may be in practice—quite different from acquired adaptive modifications, which are not innate though the potentiality of their occurrence necessarily is. According to the Lamarckian hypothesis, adaptations are due to the cumulative inheritance of individually acquired modifications; but as satisfactory evidence of the hereditary transmission of any modification as such or in any representative degree is, to say the least, far to seek, and as it is difficult to conceive of any mechanism whereby such transmission could come about (see HEREDITY), some other origin of adaptations must be sought for.

4. **Origin of adaptations.**—Within the limits of a short article it is impossible to discuss adequately a problem so difficult as that of the origin of adaptations. Like the correlated, but really distinct problem of the origin of species, it is one of the fundamental — still imperfectly answered — questions which the interpreter of animate nature has to face. We cannot do more than indicate the general tenor of the suggestions which evolutionists have offered.

(*a*) According to the Lamarckian theory, racial adaptations are due to the cumulative inheritance of individual adaptive modifications. But there is a lack of evidence in support of this interpretation, plausible as it seems; it is difficult to conceive of any internal mechanism whereby a change acquired by a part of the body can affect the germinal material in a manner so precise and representative that the offspring shows a corresponding change in the same direction. Moreover, there are many known cases where any such transmission of modifications certainly does *not* occur.

(*b*) The general Darwinian theory is that adaptations are due to the selection of those inborn and heritable variations which, by making their possessors better adapted to the conditions of their life, have some survival value. It is a fact of observation that in many groups of organisms the individuals fluctuate continually in various directions. These fluctuating variations appear as if they followed the law of chance. It is also a fact of observation that some of these variations increase the survival value of their possessors. It is inferred that the cumulative inheritance of these favourable variations, fostered by selection in any of its numerous forms, and helped by the elimination—gradual or sudden—of forms lacking the variations in the fit direction, or having others relatively unfit, may lead to the establishment of new adaptations. The greatest difficulty in this argument is to account for the origin of the fit variations, and this has to be met by the accumulation of observational and experimental data bearing on the origin and nature of variations. It is also necessary to accumulate more facts showing that selective processes — acting directively on fluctuating variations—do really bring about the results ascribed to them. To many, furthermore, it appears that more emphasis should be laid upon the power that many animals have of actively seeking out environments for which the variations they possess are adapted. Here, too, it is necessary to refer to the probable importance of some of the many forms of *Isolation*.

(*c*) The work of recent years—notably that of Bateson and De Vries—has made it plain that, besides the continually occurring 'fluctuating variations,' there are 'discontinuous variations' or 'mutations,' where a new character or group of characters not only appears suddenly, but may come to stay from generation to generation. It cannot be said that we understand the origin of these mutations, in some of which the organism in many of its parts seems suddenly to pass from one position of organic equilibrium to another; but that they do occur is indubitable, and their marked heritability is also certain. Mendel has given at once a demonstration and a rationale of the fact that certain mutations, when once they have arisen, are not likely to be swamped, but are likely to persist, unless, of course, selection is against them. In horticulture, in particular, artificial selection has operated in great part on mutations. If this interpretation be confirmed and extended, it will not be necessary to lay such a heavy burden on the shoulders of selection. But more facts are urgently needed, and how and under what conditions mutations—whether adaptive or non-adaptive—occur, remains an unsolved problem.

(*d*) In his theory of Germinal Selection, Weismann has elaborated an attractive subsidiary hypothesis. Supposing that the germinal material consists of a complex—a multiplicate—of organ-determining particles (the determinants), he postulates a struggle going on within the arcana of the germ-plasm. Supposing limitations of nutrition within the germ, he pictures an intra-germinal struggle in which the weaker determinants corresponding to any given part will get less food and will become weaker, while the stronger determinants corresponding to the same part will feed better and become stronger. Thus the theory suggests a hypothetical internal selection which will abet the ordinary external selection of individual organisms, and it makes the rise, if not the origin, of adaptations more intelligible. Or, to put it in another way, the theory suggests a possible mechanism by which the survival of any form with a favourable variation may influence the subsequent variational direction of that form. The determinants are supposed to be variable—everything living is; for each character separately heritable there are in the germ multiple determinants (paternal, maternal, grand-parental, ancestral): these are not all of equal strength; there is a germinal struggle and selection, the strongest asserts itself in development, and the resulting determinate corresponds in character to the victorious determinant. If the character of the resulting determinate is of survival value, those organisms which have that character tend to survive, and their progeny will tend to keep up the same strain. But while the external selection is proceeding, it is being continually backed up by the germinal selection. Thus nothing succeeds like success.

(*e*) Various evolutionists—Professors Mark Baldwin, H. F. Osborn, and C. Lloyd Morgan—have suggested that although individual adaptive modifications may not be transmissible, they may have indirect importance in evolution, by serving as life-preserving screens until coincident inborn or germinal variations in the same direction have time to develop. As Lloyd Morgan puts it—(1) 'Where adaptive variation v is similar in direction to individual modification m, the organism has an added chance of survival from the coincidence $m+v$; (2) where the variation is antagonistic in direction to the modification, there is a diminished chance of survival from the opposition $m-v$; hence (3) coincident variations will be fostered while opposing variations will be eliminated.' As Groos expresses it, in reference to some instinctive activities—Imitation may keep 'a species afloat until Natural Selection can substitute the lifeboat heredity for the life-preserver tradition.' As Mark

Baldwin states it, the theory is 'that individual modifications or accommodations may supplement, protect, or screen organic characters and keep them alive until useful congenital variations arise and survive by natural selection.'

Finally, in thinking over this difficult problem of adaptations, we must remember the importance of the active organism itself. As Professor James Ward has well pointed out, it may seek out and even in part make its environment; it is not only selected, it selects; it acts as well as reacts. And although the details and finesse of this may have been elaborated in the course of selection, the primary potentiality of it is an essential part of the secret of that kind of activity which we call Life.

LITERATURE.—J. Mark Baldwin, *Development and Evolution*, New York, 1902; W. K. Brooks, *The Foundations of Zoology*, New York, 1899; C. Lloyd Morgan, *Animal Behaviour*, London, 1900, *Habit and Instinct*, London, 1896, *The Interpretation of Nature*, London, 1905; T. H. Morgan, *Evolution and Adaptation*, New York, 1903; H. Münsterberg, *Die Lehre von der natürlichen Anpassung*, Leipzig, 1885; R. Otto, *Naturalistische und religiöse Weltansicht*, Tübingen, 1904 (Eng. tr. London, 1906); Herbert Spencer, *Principles of Biology*, revised ed. 1898, Part II. ch. v.; A. Weismann, *The Evolution Theory*, 2 vols. (Eng. tr. London, 1904).

J. ARTHUR THOMSON.

ADELARD.—Adelard of Bath (*Philosophus Anglorum*) occupies a distinctive position among the schoolmen of the 12th cent., as a chief representative of the philosophic doctrine of 'Indifference.' This was one of the mediating theories in the great mediæval conflict as to the nature of universal conceptions (genera and species) and their relation to the individuals comprehended under them. It lies between the extreme Realism on the one hand, which attached substantiality only to the universals, and the extreme Nominalism on the other, according to which generic conceptions were mere names, while reality belonged only to the individuals. It tends, however, to the side of Nominalism, inasmuch as it gives up the substantiality of universals, and makes the universal to consist of the non-different elements (*indifferentia*) in the separate individuals, which alone subsist substantially. Everything depends on the point of view from which the individuals are regarded: according as attention is fixed on their differences or their non-differences, they remain individuals or become for us the species and the genus. Thus Plato as Plato is an individual, as a man the species, as an animal the subordinate genus, as a substance the most universal genus.

This doctrine of Indifference was probably first stated in Adelard's treatise *de Eodem et Diverso*, composed between 1105 and 1116. [It has recently been edited by H. Willner in *Beitr. z. Gesch. d. Philos. des Mittelalters*, ed. by Cl. Bäumker and G. v. Hertling, Münster, 1903.] Adelard seeks to reconcile Plato and Aristotle, and says:

> 'Since that which we see is at once genus and species and individual, Aristotle rightly insisted that the universals do not exist except in the things of sense. But since those universals, so far as they are called genera and species, cannot be perceived by any one in their purity without the admixture of imagination, Plato maintained that they existed and could be beheld beyond the things of sense, to wit, in the Divine mind. Thus these men, though in words they seem opposed, yet held in reality the same opinion.'

The doctrine of Indifference was also represented by Walter of Mortagne (died as bp. of Laon, 1174), whom some indeed have regarded as its originator, while others again have traced it to a supposed late view of William of Champeaux.

Besides the above-mentioned tractate, Adelard wrote also *Quæstiones Naturales*. He had travelled widely and acquired great physical learning, especially from the Arabs, out of whose language he translated Euclid. He teaches that the knowledge of the laws of nature should be united with the recognition of their dependence on God's will. He says: 'It is the will of the Creator that herbs should grow from the earth, but this will is not without reason.' Mere authority he compares to a halter, and desiderates that reason should decide between the true and the false.

LITERATURE.—Art. 'Scholasticism' in *EBr*[9] xxi.; Erdmann, *Grundriss der Gesch. d. Philos.*[4] [Eng. tr. 1890] i. § 160; Windelband, *Lehrbuch der Gesch. d. Philos.*[3] (1893) § 23; Ueberweg-Heinze, *Grundriss der Gesch. d. Philos.*[9] (1894–8) ii. § 25, which see for a fuller bibliography.

R. S. FRANKS.

ADIAPHORISM.—Three meanings of this word are given in the dictionaries: (1) the theory that some *actions* are indifferent, *i.e.* neither bad nor good, not being either commanded or forbidden by God, either directly or indirectly; so that they may be done or omitted without fault; (2) the theory that certain *rites or ceremonies*, not having been either commanded or forbidden by God, may freely be used or omitted without fault; (3) the theory that *certain doctrines of the Church*, though taught in the word of God, are of such minor importance, that they may be disbelieved without injury to the foundation of faith. (Although this use of the word can be found in good authors, it is a question whether it is accurate).

1. Actions.—Very early in the history of the Christian Church the gospel began to be conceived as a *new law*. Perhaps the wider meaning of the word 'law' had something to do with this. But it was to be expected that those who had grown up under a system of rigid prescription, not only of rites and ceremonies, but also of domestic observances and the details of personal conduct,—a prescription, moreover, that had Divine authority,—should be unable to conceive any other method of moral life. It is not strange, therefore, that St. James (1[25]) speaks of the gospel as 'the perfect law of liberty.' The early converts to the gospel had been heathen; the customs in which they had been bred were abhorrent to a Jew; they were corrupting; and therefore those new-made Christians had to be taught and drilled in the first principles of morality. In the Early Church, before the books of the NT had been written and for many years afterwards, the OT was the word of God read in their assemblies for worship; and its prescriptions for conduct, its rules of common life, and its religious institutions became authoritative. It seems likely that a legalistic conception of Christianity must always preponderate in a community recently won from heathenism. Such converts remain under tutelage, and discipline must be rigidly exercised, until the fundamental principles of right living are wrought into their conscience.

Marcion urged the rejection of the OT Law. As the Church began to spread through all classes of men, and to have part in the whole of their daily life, it began insensibly to accommodate its ascetic rules to the necessities of the case. Gradually there grew up a distinction between a law of morals incumbent upon all men and a higher rule of life voluntarily assumed, but when once assumed, of lasting obligation, and by the observance of which a man might earn a higher reward than was due to the simple observance of the commandments of God (*consilia evangelica*), and might even deserve enough of God to be able to transfer some of his merit to others (*opera supererogativa*). An ascetic life was looked upon as holier than the observance of the duties of one's calling in the world. To the commandments of God were added the commandments of the Church.

The Reformation assailed this notion of an esoteric and artificial righteousness. The moral injunctions of Jesus and His holy example are for all alike. The works of our calling are the sphere in which to serve God. No one can fulfil the law of God, much less can any one exceed it. All are dependent upon God's mercy; and, forgiven for Christ's sake, depending upon that grace and thankful for it, are to go forth to the performance of daily duty, pleasing Him by childlike faith, not by the excellence of what they do.

It has been charged that the immediate result of the Reformation was a deterioration of morals, especially in regions where the Lutheran doctrine was taught, no efficient external discipline being at hand to take the place of the ecclesiastical rules and jurisdiction of the older time (see Döllinger, *Reformation*). A more successful effort was made under Calvin to introduce in Geneva a complete censorship of morals. The Puritans of England revived the conception of the gospel as a law. The Pietistic movement in Germany forbade as inconsistent with the Christian name all mere enjoyment and all the merely artistic activities of life. To do everything to the glory of God forbade all play. There was a revival of asceticism, which was taken up by the early Methodists in England (see Ritschl, *Geschichte des Pietismus*, 3 vols., 1880–6). In our own day there are many sects, notably the Second Adventists, who regard the OT Law as still in force in all its regulations, even concerning meat and drink.

To appreciate the answer which Christ gave to this question, we must bear in mind that the Pharisaism which He refuted endeavoured to secure the law of God by 'putting a fence around the Law,' consisting of inferential and artificial rules of life. Those who vigorously observed these the Pharisees accounted meritorious; and they put such stress on these comments and additions that by them they made the law of God of no effect. Our Lord rebuked the substitution of a human law for the simple law of God, and also the exaltation of human rules of life to the same sanctity as belonged to the revealed law. He required the inward service of the heart. Jesus was not an ascetic in the usual meaning of that word. He accepted invitations to the table (Lk 7^{36}), He honoured a wedding-feast (Jn $2^{1ff.}$), He spoke sympathetically of the children playing in the streets (Lk 7^{32}), He commended Mary's sacrifice of precious ointment (Mt $26^{6ff.}$, Jn $12^{2ff.}$), He submitted to be called a wine-bibber and a glutton (Mt 11^{19}). Neither was St. Paul an ascetic. It is evident that he did not consider it essential to his personal salvation to make distinctions of meats (Ro $14^{2.6.14}$, 1 Co 8^{4}, 1 Ti $4^{4.5}$), to forego the use of wine (1 Ti 5^{23}), to raise anxious questions about the material of entertainments (1 Co 10^{27}), or to avoid social pleasures (*ibid.*); and he could look upon and talk about the games of Greece with no word of abhorrence or disapproval (1 Co 9^{24-27}). In writing to Timothy (1 Ti 4^{3-5}) he foretold those errorists who would 'forbid to marry, and command to abstain from meats, which God created to be received with thanksgiving by them which believe and know the truth. For every creature of God is good, and nothing is to be refused, if it be received with thanksgiving: for it is sanctified through the word of God and prayer.' 'Meat will not commend us to God,' he says (1 Co 8^{8}); 'neither, if we eat not, are we the worse; nor, if we eat, are we the better' (see also 1 Co $7^{26.38}$, and cf. He 5^{14}). It is evident that a sphere is left for Christian freedom, in which a man may, nay must, use his own judgment, and in reference to which good men may differ, and no man may condemn his brother. Here we have the justification of what are described as merely æsthetic activities of human life, in which the natural delight of man in simple enjoyment has place, and where the law of beauty is supreme rather than the law of duty. No doubt St. Paul would have barred these out, because of 'the present distress' (1 Co 7^{26}); but his 'opinion' in contradistinction from 'the commandment of the Lord' allows them, though with the important qualifications we have yet to allude to. They derive a sanction from the constitution of man. Under this category we put the drama, music, art, all recreation. We therefore assert that there is a sphere for the freedom of a Christian. He is not under a positive law which extends to every corner of his life. He does not move in the sphere of a moral necessity. He must exercise judgment and choice. He must abound more and more in knowledge and all discernment, and prove the things that differ (Ph $1^{9f.}$). It is wrong for him to hinder and lame his conscience either by the cultivation of rigid unreasoning habits or by the adoption of a formal law (Frank, *Theologie der Concordienformel*, IV. x. 16 ff.).

But Christian freedom has its limits. These limits are external and internal. Our liberty may not 'become a stumblingblock to the weak, sinning against the brethren, wounding their conscience when it is weak' (1 Co 8^{9-12}). Some things that are lawful edify not (10^{23}); they contribute nothing (6^{12}). We are not to live in the moment, wasting the material of everlasting life (7^{30}). 'All things are lawful for me, but I will not be brought under the power of any' (6^{12}, Gal 5^{13}). To watchfulness on his own account the Christian must add a watchful love of his fellow-man.

LITERATURE.—See besides works quoted, writers on Christian Ethics, such as Harless, Wuttke, Martensen, Luthardt, *Gesch. der Christl. Ethik*; Gottschick in *PRE*^{3}, and Kübel in *PRE*^{2}.

2. Rites and ceremonies.—If we take up the second definition of our subject, we find that the same causes led the Early Church to believe that its rites and ceremonies had been commanded by God. The ceremonial laws of the OT doubtless do reveal the essential principles of the worship of God. These principles were enshrined in forms suitable to primitive times and prophetic of the realities by which the redemption of mankind was accomplished by our Lord Jesus Christ. But the OT, applied to forms of worship by way of illustration and explanation, became normative; so that gradually the Church came to have a priesthood, altars, and sacrifices of its own, with vestments and a ritual, and feasts and days; the observance of which was regarded as essential to the validity of its sacraments, and therefore to salvation, and the neglect of which was as deadly as a violation of the Decalogue. This view persists in parts of the Christian Church, and is invoked for the defence of existing institutions and privileges.

The Reformers acknowledged that the Church had a right to institute rites and ceremonies, and even ascribed to the Church the hallowing of the first day of the week instead of the seventh; but they denied that the Church had a right to claim for its institutions the unchangeableness and sanctity of the institutions and commandments of God. Christ left few ordinances—His Word, the two Sacraments, a ministry of the Word and Sacraments, His assured presence with the assembly of His people, the Lord's Prayer, these are all—and for the rest the Church was left to develop its forms of government and its forms of worship to suit the times and places in which it might be found. But what do we mean by 'the Church' in this statement? The clergy only? Or those who have attained to a headship of the clergy? Or, in countries where the State controls the Church, the ministry of worship? Or duly authorized Councils? Or representatives chosen by clergy and laity, expressing their preference by the vote of a majority? None of these. The judgment of the Church may finally decide a matter which has been approved with the concurrence of all these. A rite that once was significant and edifying may fall out of use, or may become harmful in the lapse of time and under changing circumstances. All rites and ceremonies instituted by men are subject to the judgment of Christian conscience enlightened by the word of God.

In the Silver Age of the Reformation a warm controversy among Lutheran theologians was precipitated by the attempt of Charles V. to compromise the differences between the Evangelical Churches and the Roman Church, in the *Augsburg Interim* of 1548. The controversy raged about the permissibility of a vague formula which might be interpreted in two ways, and the revival of usages which the one side had rejected because they served error, and the other regarded as sacred and necessary. Flacius was the protagonist on the one side; Melanchthon was the target. The matter and the true position cannot be set forth more clearly than is done in the *Formula of Concord*, 1580.

'For the settlement of this controversy, we believe, teach, and confess, with one consent, that ceremonies or ecclesiastical rites (which had been neither commanded nor forbidden by the Word of God, but instituted only for the sake of decency and order) are not of themselves Divine Worship or any part of it. For it is written (Mt 15[9]): "*In vain do they worship me, teaching for doctrines the commandments of men.*"'

'The Churches of God everywhere throughout the world, and at any time, have the right to change such ceremonies according to the occasion, in whatever way it may seem to the Church most serviceable for its edification.'

'But in so doing all levity should be avoided and all offence, and especially should care be taken to spare those weak in faith (1 Co 8[9], Ro 14[13]).'

'In times of persecution, when a clear and steadfast confession is required of us, we ought not to yield to the enemies of the Gospel in things indifferent. For the Apostle says (Gal 5[1]): "*Stand therefore in the liberty wherewith Christ hath made us free, and be not entangled again with the yoke of bondage*"; and (2 Co 6[14]): "*Be not unequally yoked together with unbelievers. For what fellowship is there between light and darkness?*" etc.; also (Gal 2[5]): "*To whom we gave place by subjection, no, not for an hour; that the truth of the gospel might continue with you.*" For in such a state of things the dispute no longer is about things indifferent, but concerning the truth of the Gospel and the preservation and protection of Christian liberty, and how to prevent open idolatry; and the protection of those who are weak in faith against offence. In matters of this sort we ought not to yield anything to our adversaries, but it is our duty to give a faithful and sincere confession, and patiently to bear whatever the Lord may lay upon us and may permit the enemies of His Word to do to us.'

'No Church ought to condemn another because that Church observes more or fewer of outward ceremonies which the Lord did not institute, if only there be between them consent in all articles of Doctrine and in the right use of the Sacraments. Well and truly was it said of old: "*Disagreement as to fasting does not dissolve agreement in faith.*"'

'We repudiate and condemn these false teachings, as contrary to the Word of God, viz.: that human traditions and constitutions in matters ecclesiastical are to be considered by themselves a Worship of God or a part of such worship; that such ceremonies and constitutions should be forced upon the Church of God as necessary, against the Christian liberty which the Church of Christ has with reference to outward things of this sort; that in time of persecution, when a clear confession is required, the enemies of the Gospel may be placated by the observance of things of this sort that are in themselves indifferent, and that it is permitted to agree and consent with them—a thing detrimental to heavenly truth; that outward ceremonies, because they are indifferent, should not be observed, as if the Church of God were not free in Christian liberty to use this or that ceremony which it may deem useful for edification.' (See Planck, *Gesch. des Prot. Lehrbegriffs*, iv.; Jacobs, *Book of Concord*, ii.; Bieck, *Das Dreyfache Interim*).

There remains the question whether each person has a right to change the ordinances of the Church according to his own judgment and taste, observing such as he pleases, and omitting those of which he disapproves. Inasmuch as these rites and ceremonies are things indifferent, he should conform to the custom of the Church, lest he be disorderly (2 Th 3[6. 11], 1 Co 11[16]). Again, it may be asked by what test a rite or ceremony handed down in the Church is to be estimated. The *Augsburg Confession* teaches (Art. vii.) that rites should be observed that contribute to unity and good order, and the *Apology for the Confession* (iv. 33), 'that the Church of God of every place and every time has power, according to circumstances, to change such ceremonies *in such manner as may be most useful and edifying to the Church of God.*'

A further question may be raised, as to the authority of good taste, of æsthetic canons, in regard to the forms and accessories of Christian worship. In this matter, without doubt, edification is of more value than artistic merit, and all must yield to the instinct of Christian love.

3. Doctrines.—In order to answer the question suggested by the third definition, the distinction between a 'dogma,' a 'doctrine,' and 'the faith' must be clearly apprehended. *Dogmas* result from an analysis of the faith, and the word is properly restricted to those statements of Christian truth which have been finally declared by the authorities of the Church and accepted by the Church in its Confessions. A dogma is always subject to examination and challenge. Not even a Council of the Universal Church is infallible. Even the Œcumenical Creeds must justify themselves to the Christian consciousness by their evident agreement with the word of God. *Doctrine* is an explanation and elaboration of the faith which has not yet crystallized into dogma. *The Faith* is the gospel—the 'faith once delivered to the saints' (Jude [3]).

Dogmas can be understood either in the original sense in which they were approved and confessed by the Church, or in the sense in which they are apprehended by any age. It is conceivable that a student may discover a deflection of popular and universal faith from the idea which the original authors of a Confessional formula meant to set forth in it. Every dogma must be understood in relation to the entirety of the faith. Each age gives especial attention to different aspects of the faith. The 'spirit of the age,' its conception of human duties and human rights, its philosophical notions, colour its explanations of Divine truth and cause the emphasis laid upon different aspects of it to vary. From its own standpoint every age and clime develops first doctrine, then dogma. That, finally, is recognized as Christian dogma *quod semper, quod ubique, quod ab omnibus creditur. Securus judicat orbis terrarum.*

EDWARD T. HORN.

ĀDIBUDDHA (the theistic system of Nepāl, including its Buddhist antecedents, Dhyānibuddhas, etc.).—*Introduction.*—Abel Rémusat stated in 1831 that 'the learned of Europe were indebted to Mr. Hodgson for the name of Ādibuddha.'* And it might almost be said with truth still that nowhere else do we find such a systematic and complete account of the theory of the theistic Buddhists of Nepāl (*Aiśvarikas*) † as Hodgson has given in his *Essays*.

Unitarian and theistic Buddhism, after having aroused keen interest,‡ fell later into neglect, when attention was drawn to primitive or ancient Buddhism, especially by the works of Spence Hardy and Burnouf. The result of the iconographic discoveries and the Tibetan studies of the last few years seems to have been to bring it again into greater prominence. It is well worth examining, because, although more 'Alexandrian' than Buddhist, Buddhist in fact only in name and in so far as it employs Buddhist terminology, it nevertheless is, as it were, the consummation of the philosophical, mystical, and mythological speculations of the Great Vehicle, and differs from several other systems, widespread in the Buddhist world, only by its markedly 'theistic' colouring. The system of the *Aiśvarikas* is, in effect, merely the half-*naiyāyika* (*i.e.* theistic), half-*Śaivite* (*i.e.* pantheistic) interpretation of the ontological and religious speculation of the Great Vehicle in the last

* See Hodgson, *Essays*, p. 110.
† From *Īśvara*, the personal and supreme god. (See THEISM).
‡ See Schmidt, *Grundlehre*; Burnouf, *Introduction*.

stage of its development. It differs from it sufficiently clearly, however, to justify Burnouf in recognizing in the system of the *Ādibuddha* a new kind of Buddhism — a third (or a fourth) Buddhism *; and, in order to give the reader a just appreciation of the significance of this new interpretation of Buddhism, before unheard of, it will suffice to state that the old formula, 'Of all that proceeds from causes the Tathāgata has explained the cause,' was transformed into, 'Of all that proceeds from causes the Tathāgata *is* the cause.' †

A further characteristic of the *Aiśvarikas* of Hodgson, in which they stand apart from Hindu or Nepalese thought, is the absence from their theology of every feminine, tantric, and magical element. It is well known that Hodgson had recourse for his information to native scholars, whom he ceremoniously styles 'living oracles,' and who, in support of their statements, supplied him with fragments of texts, which were not all authentic. These mutilated testimonies, this tradition arranged with a view to meet questions conceived in an altogether European spirit, are, as far as the absence of the above-mentioned element is concerned, confirmed by the Svayambhūpurāṇa, which is not very tantric. We do not, however, believe that, even apart from the wide and comprehensive nature of its mythology, Nepalese theism has in reality ever been quite free from intermixture of Saivite thought.

Plan and division.—As the problem has not been examined in its entirety for a long time, and as much light has been thrown upon it by recent research, we propose to state it here, as completely as possible, from the doctrinal point of view, of course; for we shall willingly dispense with legendary, iconographic, and ritual details.‡

The interest of *Ādibuddha* systems (for there are at least two of them) lies chiefly in their relation to genuine Buddhism and to Hinduism. It will be most convenient (I.) to give a brief account of those Ādibuddha systems which are more or less well known, and (II.) to inquire into their antecedents, often obscure and problematic, beginning with the sources, so that we may be able in this way (III.) to 'locate' the systems in question, doctrinally and historically, and to present a more accurate appreciation of them.

As most of these antecedents will demand separate treatment (see AVALOKITEŚVARA, LOTUS OF THE TRUE LAW, MAHĀYĀNA, MAÑJUŚRĪ), a brief reference will here suffice. We shall confine ourselves to Buddhist ground, for, although this long elaboration of the elements of the Buddhist systems of Ādibuddha may be inexplicable without Hinduism, it will be sufficient to note, in passing, the points of contact.

I. *ĀDIBUDDHA SYSTEMS.*—**1.** *Aiśvarika system* (Hodgson's sources). — There is an *Ādibuddha* or *Paramādibuddha* (Tib. *daṅ-poi saṅs-rgyas, mchog-gi daṅ-poi* . . ., § *thog-mai* . . . ‖), *i.e.* first Buddha, primary Buddha, Buddha from the beginning, Buddha unoriginated. ¶ He exists by himself, and in fact is called *Svayambhū*,** like Brahmā, and is worshipped under this name in his great temple at Kāṭhmaṇḍu.* He has never been seen; † he is in *nirvāṇa*. Nevertheless, he is 'pure light'; he issues from the 'void' (*śūnyatā*); and his names are innumerable. It is said that prayers are not addressed to him; yet he is worshipped in his temple. He dwells in the *Akaniṣṭhabhavana*, that is, in the upper region of the world of forms,‡ symbolized by the apex of the *chaitya*, as if it had been forgotten that in the Buddhist cosmology there are numerous formless heavens. § He has, besides, like every divinity, a *maṇḍala*, ‖ or mystic circle, for conjuratory or mystical purposes.

By five acts of his contemplative power (*dhyāna*), the Ādibuddha or Mahābuddha creates five Buddhas called Buddhas of contemplation or *Dhyānibuddhas*.¶ They are Vairochana, Akṣobhya, Ratnasambhava, Amitābha, and Amoghasiddha.** These are in the world of becoming (*pravṛtti*). Prayers are not addressed to them (so Hodgson); but they have temples called *chaityas*, like those of Ādibuddha. By the twofold power of knowledge and contemplation, to which they owe their existence, they give birth to 'Bodhisattvas of contemplation,' *dhyānibodhisattvas*,†† viz., Samantabhadra, Vajrapāṇi, Ratnapāṇi, Avalokita or Padmapāṇi, and Viśvapāṇi respectively. These are the actual creators of the physical universe, but the worlds which they produce are perishable, and three of these creations have already ceased to exist. That of which we form a part is the fourth, *i.e.* it is the work of Avalokiteśvara, the fourth Bodhisattva, the 'Providence' of the present; and has as its special Buddha, 'protector' and 'conqueror' (*nātha, jina*) Amitābha, who is enthroned in the midst of his elect. For its instructor it has had Śākyamuni, the fourth human Buddha. There are five human Buddhas (*mānuṣibuddhas*),‡‡ who correspond to the

* *Introduction*, p. 581.

† For the ancient formula see Kern, *Manual*, pp. 25, 49; Hodgson, *Essays*, p. 111.

‡ See NEPĀL, LĀMAISM, ICONOGRAPHY (BUDDHIST).

§ Csoma's and Grünwedel's sources (Mongol. *Angh'an burh'an*).

‖ Waddell's sources.

¶ Urbuddha (Lassen, *Ind. Alt.*[2] ii. 1103), Buddha of the Buddhas (Wass. p. 134); ādibuddha = ādau buddha (Nāmasaṅgīti, 100), or = anādibuddha. He appears at the beginning of time (at the commencement of the *Kalpa*), the crystal jewel in the lotus (*maṇi* . . . *padme*). Ādinātha = Ādibuddha; it is also the name of a more or less historical (?) personage (Wilson, i. 214; see AVALOKITEŚVARA, note *ad fin.*).

** Svayambhūlokanātha, 'self-existing protector of the world,' also Sambhū (a name of Śiva), and Ādinātha, 'first protector.' See a beautiful hymn addressed to him, Svayambhūpurāṇa, p. 56. The term Svayambhū has been from ancient times an epithet of Buddhas, because Buddhas have obtained Buddhahood without any external help, and also because Buddhahood is uncaused. Even in late texts we find Svayambhū explained as follows: *svayambhavati svayambhūr bhāvanābalād bhavatīty arthaḥ* (Nāmasaṅgīti, 10); *svayambhūḥ sarvavikalparahitatvāt* (*ib.* 60). See Aṣṭasāhasrikā prajñāpāramitā, 2 ff., 10; *tathāgatatvam buddhatvaṁ svayambhūtvaṁ sarvajñatvam*.

* The temple is described in Fergusson, *Hist. of Ind. Arch.* fig. 170; Wright, *Hist. of Nepāl*; Bendall and S. Lévi, *Népal*. It is represented in the miniatures of MSS of the 11th cent. (Foucher, *Icon. Bouddhique*, i.). Köppen (ii. p. 367) recalls the fact that, according to Kirkpatrick (*An Account*, p. 148), the Great Lāma for a long time maintained relations with the temple.

† The Ādibuddha is sometimes called *Viśvarūpa*, 'who takes every form,' and is so represented (Hodgson, *Essays*, 83; Foucher, *Catalogue*, pp. 12, 13).

‡ The world to which those saints ascend, who, being comparatively little advanced, must wait many centuries before attaining to *nirvāṇa*, although they are not on that account condemned to a new earthly existence; they are the fifth class of the *Anāgāmins*, according to the Little Vehicle.

§ It is not clear that the Ādibuddha of the Nepalese extends his reign beyond the present *Kalpa* (Age of the World). He is father of five Buddhas only. It seems to be forgotten that there are millions of Kalpas and millions of Buddhas.

‖ That is a *nakṣatramaṇḍala*, a 'constellation circle.' Recalling the triad, Buddha, Dharma, Saṅghamaṇḍala (*Svayambhūpurāṇa*), Ādibuddha is *triratnamūrti*, 'the three gems embodied.'

¶ The present writer has never, in any Sanskrit or Tibetan text, met with the expression 'dhyānibuddha.' The five Buddhas are called the 'five Jinas' or the 'five Buddhas' in the Sanskrit texts as well as in Tibet, in Cambodia, and in Java. He is inclined to believe that we have to do here either with an invention due to Hodgson's pandits or with a very late source. As the St. Petersburg Dictionary observes, *Dhyānibuddha*, if rightly contrasted with *Mānuṣibuddha* (human Buddha, cf. *mānuṣikanyā*) ought to mean 'Buddha born of meditation [of Ādibuddha]' and not 'meditating Buddha' = Dhyānin-buddha = dhyānibuddha. We know of Jñānabuddhas, Jñānabodhisattvas (*ye-śes saṅs-rgyas, ye-śes byaṅ-chub-sems-dpa*), who cannot be distinguished from the Vajrabuddhas. They correspond to the five jñānas or mystic sciences. These are the five so-called Dhyānibuddhas, regarded from the tantric point of view (*jñānam bhagam iti smṛtam*).

** Sometimes a sixth, Vajrasattva, who creates (or causes to be created) immaterial substances, while the five others create corporeal forms.

†† The same may be said of them as of the 'Dhyānibuddhas'; since the Bodhisattvas are not in *Dhyāna*, the word can only mean 'born of dhyāna.'

‡‡ There is a list in the Little Vehicle of seven human Buddhas who are also worshipped in Nepāl (Wilson ii., Bauddha tracts).

five Buddhas of contemplation. They are not, however, incarnations of them, but rather 'reflexes,' *pratibimba*, 'magical projections,' *nirmāṇakāya*.

2. It is difficult to date Hodgson's sources.* The same difficulty exists with regard to the poetical version of the Kāraṇḍavyūha, of which the *terminus a quo* will perhaps be supplied by the date of the Tibetan translation of the prose version of the same text. In this prose edition, the only one which the Tibetans have known or have cared about, there is, indeed, a passage wanting, namely the passage of the verse edition where Ādibuddha, Svayambhū, Ādinātha (first protector) appears at the beginning (ādisamudbhūta) in the form of light (jyotirūpa).

He gives himself to 'meditation on the creation of the universe,' and begets Avalokiteśvara as demiurge. It is not said that he creates the Buddhas, but rather that he is 'made up of the parts of the five Buddhas.' †

3. The name 'Ādibuddha' or 'Paramādibuddha' appears in more ancient documents. According to Csoma, who was the first and only one to determine this chronology, this name and the system to which it is attached are closely connected with the Śrīkālachakratantra, a tantra openly Śaivite in its inspiration, which was probably 'introduced (?) into India in the 10th cent. and into Tibet in the 11th century.' ‡

Now, however, it is a recognized fact that the Tantras are much older than used to be thought.§ It should at least be noticed that Mañjuśrī (*q.v.*) is called Ādibuddha in the Nāmasaṅgīti (vv. 55. 100), a book undoubtedly earlier than the 10th cent., if it is the case, as Tāranātha believes, that Chandragomin, a contemporary of Chandrakīrti (7th cent.) wrote a commentary upon it. ‖ It is not necessary to discuss the question whether the interpretation, given in the commentaries of the Nāmasaṅgīti and numerous tantric works,¶ was accepted at the time when, according to this tradition, the work itself was composed.

There were good reasons for ascribing to Mañjuśrī the character of an Ādibuddha, inasmuch as he is the personification of the knowledge whence Buddhas originate, and since he is more than a Bodhisattva, viz., a 'Jñānasattva,' in other words the *Dharmakāya* (see below) or the *Dharmadhātuvāgīśvara*. His attributes, in iconography, are the sword which destroys ignorance and the book of the Prajñāpāramitā, 'the supreme book.' King of sages (Vādirāj), Lord of the Holy Word (Vagīśvara), he is in his eternity (*trikāla*) a symbolic Ādibuddha, with a symbolism transparent enough, in the same way as the Prajñāpāramitā (later known as the Ādiprajñā) in very orthodox texts is called the mother of the Buddhas. Even if, as the texts inform us, he is 'made up of a part of the Tathāgatas,' or, conversely, the five Buddhas emanate from his person; or if the icons place the five Buddhas on his head, or in the halo of radiance with which he is crowned; if his four faces, together with the fact that he is the spouse of Sarasvatī, bring him singularly close to Brahmā,* these are conceptions which do not alter his original character any more than does his accidental identification with Anaṅga, the god of Love, or with Śiva, etc. Mañjuśrī is Ādibuddha, because he is the king of the Prajñā.†

4. Although in certain documents Mañjuśrī is a tantric Ādibuddha, his origin is on the side of purely philosophical speculation. The Tantras have an Ādibuddha of a different nature, nearer to Śiva-Brahmā than to Brahmā or Viṣṇu, viz. Vajrasattva-Vajradhara, whom later on we shall have occasion briefly to discuss.

II. *ANTECEDENTS OF THE ĀDIBUDDHA SYSTEM.*—By more or less well-defined steps we can follow the evolution of Buddhism from its origin (Little Vehicle) down to the conceptions which have just been discussed. There remain for examination the conceptions of the Buddha in nirvāṇa, and of the Bodhisattva, the confusion of the Buddha and the Bodhisattva, the doctrine of the three bodies and the Dhyānibuddhas.

1. *Buddha in quasi-nirvāṇa*.—(1) We shall see (AGNOSTICISM [in Buddhism]) that, according to the doctrine of the Vaibhājyavādins, and perhaps the Sthaviras, *nirvāṇa* can scarcely be anything else than annihilation. The canonical texts, however, are much less definite. It is said that 'the Buddha in *nirvāṇa* evades the grasp of the intelligence, just as it is impossible to measure the waters of the ocean, they are too many.' From this the conclusion may be, and has been, drawn that *nirvāṇa* is an undefinable state, but very different from nothingness. This is, moreover, the old meaning of the word *nirvāṇa*.

(2) It is not, however, necessary, as a matter of fact, to sift the question of *nirvāṇa*, and to solve it in an unorthodox and Brāhmanical way, in order to people the heavens with divine Buddhas. For a 'sutta' of the first order represents Śākyamuni as possessed of the power of prolonging his earthly existence to the end of the *kalpa* (see AGES OF THE WORLD [Buddhist]). There is no doubt that it was early believed that he continued to live 'invisible to gods and men,' and the new theology proved less timid than the old. According to the Sukhāvatī (§ 2), a Buddha lives for a hundred thousand *niyutas* (millions) of *koṭis* (ten millions) of kalpas, or more, without the beauty of his complexion being marred. Śākyamuni did not live eighty years! Only the Tathāgatas understand the vast duration of his life.‡

(3) The Mahāvastu relates that Śākyamuni, and as a rule any Buddha, or even a future Buddha

* Especially the Svayambhūpurāṇa (ed. *Bibl. Indica*). See on its date Haraprasād Śāstrī, *JBTS* II. 2, p. 33, and Lévi (later than 1460); and for the contents Rājendralāl, 249; Hodgson, 115; Burnouf, 539, 540; Lévi, *Népal*, I. 212; Foucher, *Cat. des peintures népalaises*, pp. 17 ff. Hodgson mentions also the Nāmasaṅgīti, Sādhanamālā, Bhadrakalpāvadāna, Divyāvadāna.

† See Burnouf, *Introd.* pp. 211–230.

‡ See Bendall, *Catalogue*, p. 69; Cowell and Eggeling, *Catalogue*, No. 49; Kandjur, *Rgyud*, i. 3: Paramādibuddhodhṛtaśrīkālachakra nāma tantrarājaḥ (Csoma-Feer, p. 292); the *Essays* by Csoma; Rémusat, *Mélanges*, p. 421; and, on a Hindu *Kālachakra*, Haraprasād, *Cat. Durbar Library*, 1905, p. lx.; last, but not least, Grünwedel, *Myth.*, pp. 44, 45, 60. Suchandra, who has the title of Kulika (*rigs-ldan*), the title of the Zhambhala kings, received it from Buddha at Dhānyakaṭaka (Orissa), and, returning to his own country, he composed the Kālachakra mūlatantra in 965 A.D. The Śambhala [Grünwedel has Zhambhala; the Tibetan is *bde-hbyuṅ*, corresponding to *bde-byed*, Śaṅkara; then *hbyuṅ* = *bhava* = *bhala* (Dr. P. Cordier); see Sarat Chandra, *Tib. Dict.* pp. 1231 and 670; MS Hodgson, *RAS*, 49, I., st. 26, 150, 156, etc.] should be located on the Jaxartes. It is from that country that the Tibetan calendar comes, and every one admits the influence of Upper Asia (Khotan, etc., or Mahāchīna, as the Chinese say) on the fate of Buddhism. According to Grünwedel, the book presents a distinctly Vaiṣṇavite appearance; the date is fixed by the mention of Islām and Muhammad (Madhumati), and of Mecca (Makha), where the religion of the Barbarians (*mlechha*) is prevalent. Tāranātha, p. 305.

The whole of the text preserved in the London and Cambridge MS (*Śrīdvādaśasāhasrikādibuddhoddhṛte śrīmati kālachakre*) is composed in a complicated metre, and professes to be only a recension of the Ādibuddha [tantra]. It ascribes to this book the honour of being the first to explain the *kuliśapada*, and therefore gives to it the title of *tantrottara*. The god Kālachakra receives the titles of *jinapati, jinendra, viśvabhartṛ, jinajanaka*, Father, King, Teacher of the Buddhas, Bearer of the Universe; but this Ādibuddha is at the same time the son of all the Buddhas, just as he remains young in spite of his old age, *vṛddho 'pi tvam kumāraḥ sakalajinasuto 'py ādibuddhas tvam ādau*.

§ Haraprasād Śāstrī, *Report*, 1895–1900; *Proc. Be. RAS*, 1900, August (Niśvāsasattvasaṁhitā, about 800 A.D.).

‖ Tāranātha, p. 152.

¶ Namely, in the Piṇḍikrama, published as the first chapter of the Pañchakrama (Ghent, 1896).

* *Devātideva: brahmātmakatvāt*, elsewhere *devendra: viṣṇusvabhāvatvāt*.

† See Foucher, *Iconographie bouddhique*, Part II., and Jñānasattvamañjuśrī-ādibuddhasādhana, *Rgyud* 61. Mañjuśrī is also the patron of arts, architecture, and image-makers; see Haraprasād Śāstrī, *Cat. Durbar Library*, lxvii.

‡ He is *nityakāya*. As regards the office and work of a Buddha before nirvāṇa, according to the Little Vehicle, see *Divya*, 150, 17; *Mahāvastu*, i. 51; compare and contrast the vows of Amitābha in the Sukhāvatīvyūha.

(Bodhisattva) during his last existence, has the appearance of hesitating, thinking, speaking, acting, suffering as we do. This, however, is wholly due to his condescension. In reality this marvellous being is superior to all such emotions, and remains a stranger to them. To maintain the contrary is heresy. The body of the future Buddhas is entirely spiritual. There is nothing 'mundane' in them. A Bodhisattva has really no father, no mother, no son, etc.

This 'hyperphysical' system (*lokottaravāda*) is more precisely set forth in the Vetulyaka school. According to their teaching, Śākyamuni did not appear in person in the world, but deputed an image of himself to represent him (cf. DOCETISM).

(4) The Mahāvastu says that many ages ago Śākyamuni took the vow of Bodhi in the presence of another ancient Śākyamuni. The same book speaks of eight thousand Buddhas of the name of Dīpaṅkara, . . . of three hundred millions of Śākyamunis.* If we identify this ancient Buddha with ours, make all the Dīpaṅkaras, all the Śākyamunis, all the Dhvajottamas, etc., into one single Dīpaṅkara, one single Śākyamuni, and adopt the docetic theory of the Vetulyakas, we obtain the system of the 'Lotus of the True Law.' Countless ages ago, nay rather in the beginning, Śākyamuni became Buddha; his appearances on earth, in which he seems to become Buddha, to enter into *nirvāṇa*, etc., are purely magical.†

Although it was quite late when the Mahāvastu received its final shape, the characteristics to which we have drawn attention seem to be ancient. For the Lotus the *terminus ad quem* is A.D. 265. As for the docetic theory, it is held to have been condemned at the Council of Pāṭaliputra (*circa* B.C. 246). Although the historical existence of the Council may be doubtful, the impression remains that the Buddhists had early reached the following conceptions:—

(*a*) Śākyamuni survives his earthly *parinirvāṇa*, and prolongs the 'trance' (*dhyāna*), from which he has never in reality issued since the moment that he became Buddha. There is no occasion, therefore, for reference, in addition, to the moment when he will enter really into *nirvāṇa*. 'The Blessed Buddhas, well equipped with knowledge and merit, fields of benevolence and compassion, shelters of the multitudes of beings, holding a perpetual concentration of mind, are neither in the *saṁsāra* (world of becoming) nor in *nirvāṇa*' (*saṁsāranirvāṇavimuktāḥ*). So it is said in the Dharmasaṅgītisūtra.‡

(*b*) In the orthodox theory (Vaibhājyavādin), Śākyamuni on becoming Buddha entered '*nirvāṇa* with residue,' the residue being the body without an active 'soul' or thinking organism, which nevertheless continues to live and speak. But no speaking is possible in *dhyāna*, therefore this body is only magical. Very probably the Buddhists soon came to believe that Śākyamuni during the whole of his earthly existence had only been the magical substitute of the real Śākyamuni, who had long since entered into eternal Buddhahood.

The steps are as follows:—The Bodhisattva comes from the heaven of the Tuṣitas to enter a human womb. The Buddha remains in the Tuṣita heaven [Is it there that he became Buddha? We do not know], and produces a double of himself. The Buddha, who has been Buddha from all time, or for such a long time that it comes to the same thing, reigns high up far beyond the Tuṣitas; if he acts and saves creatures, it is because he is not deprived of all compassion by becoming Buddha, and is, in fact, still a 'Bodhisattva'* (cf. Waddell, 'Sambhogakāya,' in *Buddhism of Tibet*, pp. 127, 347).

2. *The celestial Bodhisattvas.*—It will be seen that one of the principal doctrines of the Great Vehicle is that of the Bodhisattva, a compassionate being, who, out of pure love, refrains from entering into nirvāṇa in order to save created beings and to act the part of Providence (see BODHISATTVA and AVALOKITEŚVARA). In strict orthodoxy, the worship of a Buddha produces spiritual results only by a process which is entirely subjective and in which the Buddha counts for nothing; for the Buddha is either extinct or plunged in egoistic *dhyāna*. It is different with the Bodhisattvas, and Chandrakīrti says in so many words that, just as the new moon is celebrated and not the full moon, so must the Bodhisattvas be worshipped and not the Buddhas, even though the latter are of greater dignity. The Buddhas have more majesty, the Bodhisattvas more influence.†

The Buddhas derive their origin from the Bodhisattvas. For, in the first place, every Buddha has been a Bodhisattva before becoming a Buddha; and secondly, it is through the intervention of the celestial Bodhisattva (Mañjuśrī) that the future Buddha takes the vow to become a Buddha.‡

On the other hand, the Bodhisattvas are sons of the Buddhas (*jinaputra*), for, unlike the Pratyekabuddhas, they owe their knowledge of the Buddhist truth to the teaching of the Buddhas; they are, 'spiritually' speaking, begotten by the Buddhas.

In the doctrine of the Little Vehicle every future Buddha receives from a Buddha the announcement that he is to become a Buddha (*vyākaraṇa*). It is the mere statement of a fact. To the *vyākaraṇa*, however, might be, and has been, assigned an effective share in the attainment of the end in view. In the Laṅkāvatāra the Bodhisattva receives not only an announcement but a consecration (*abhiṣeka*). Conversely, it will be noticed in the Gāndhāra sculptures that the Bodhisattvas bear the phial which is to become the phial of consecration; and in the later iconography the same Amitābha, sometimes in the form of the meditating Buddha, sometimes in the form of Bodhisattva, is seen carrying the same phial.§

In theory, every Buddha begets innumerable Bodhisattvas to a spiritual life. But the Bodhisattvas, the usual companions of a Buddha, his associates in the spiritual administration of a *Buddhakṣetra*, a 'field of Buddha,' do not very often appear as his spiritual sons; they are, we might rather say, younger brothers, since they commence their long term of existence as Bodhisattvas about the same time that the future Buddha enters upon his career.

In certain texts which recall the two great Śrāvakas of the Little Vehicle, every Buddha has two chief Bodhisattvas (Karuṇāpuṇḍarīka). The Amitāyurdhyānasūtra connects Avalokiteśvara (*q.v.*) and Mahāsthānaprāpta with Amitābha; and Śākya at Buddh Gayā is represented between Avalokita and Maitreya. Sometimes a Buddha is seen surrounded by eight Bodhisattvas; and even when the system of the five 'Dhyāni-

* See Kern, *Manual*, 66, n. 2. The buddhology and mythology of the Mahāvastu are confused; see, for instance, iii. 508, where the five (human) Buddhas are confronted with the thousand Buddhas. Cf. Barth, *Journ. des Savants*, 1899.

† The same doctrine is found in the Suvarṇaprabhāsa.

‡ Śikṣās, p. 322. Cf. *na buddhaḥ parinirvāti na dharmaḥ parihīyate* (Suvarṇaprabhāsa). The identification of 'nirvāṇa' with some state of beatific meditation is clearly indicated by the *Lotus of the True Law*, ch. xi; cf. Kern, *Geschiedenis*, ii. 145. Elsewhere *dharmakāya* = *samādhikāya*.

* Celestial Buddhas are, in fact, no more real than their magical reflexes. From the very moment that a Bodhisattva becomes Buddha he is merged in 'nirvāṇa' or 'voidness'; but, owing to his merits, he still appears as a brilliant body among the Bodhisattvas who behold him. Thus it can be said with Waddell (*Buddhism of Tibet*, p. 357) that the Buddhas have two 'real' bodies, a *nirvāṇa*-body (= a non-body) and a glorious body. See art. MAHĀYĀNA.

† The Bodhisattvas tend to become real gods, superior to the Buddhas, bearing the same relation to the Buddhas as Śākyamuni bore to the Arhats.

‡ Contrast *Lalita*, 184. 19, where the Bodhisattva has to be 'excited' by the Buddhas of the ten regions.

§ Concerning the phial *kalaśa*, see Grünwedel, *Buddh. Art in India*, p. 191 ff.; Foucher, *Art bouddhique*, p. 34. The consecration of a Bodhisattva as crown-prince is the fifth and last duty of a Buddha (*Mahāvastu*, i. 51. 5).

buddhas' was fixed, the number was not very uniformly observed. At one time eight or nine Bodhisattvas of the first rank are shared very unequally among the Buddhas; at another, each Buddha has a single Bodhisattva, whose name is usually colourless and seems to be derived from the sculptures.

3. *Confusion of the Buddha and the Bodhisattva.*—From the preceding discussion it follows that the relations between Buddhas and Bodhisattvas are complex and do not lend themselves to precise definition; there is often a confusion between the two concepts, and traces of this confusion are early found. In the Mahāvastu the Bodhisattvas, from the very first stages of their spiritual development, receive the title of 'perfect Buddhas.' In the Bodhicharyāvatāra, the work of a very careful theologian, the *Jinas*, or the Buddhas who have attained Buddhahood and are in enjoyment of a *quasi-nirvāṇa*, endeavour to save the world; they are entreated to delay their *parinirvāṇa*. Avalokita, a Bodhisattva by nature, is at least once termed Bhagavat, and there are numerous texts in which the Buddhas are active. Perhaps, however, it is necessary to come down as far as the Kāraṇḍavyūha (p. 91, 8) to read in so many words that *nirvāṇa* is accompanied by thought.

We have seen that, spiritually regarded, the Buddhas are at the same time the fathers and the sons of the Bodhisattvas. This relationship, from the mystic and ontological point of view, may be, and has been, interpreted upon a twofold principle. The first, which is at one and the same time Buddhist and Brāhmanical (see p. 98[a]), is that of the identity of the Jina and the Jinaputra; the second, genuinely Hindu, is that of procession or emanation (see p. 100). These two principles are in other respects very closely connected.

Concerning this mysterious relationship between the Buddhas and the Bodhisattvas there is valuable information to be got, on the one hand, from the sculptures of Gandhāra, Magadha, etc.; and, on the other, from texts clearly related to iconography, whether they inspired the latter or were themselves inspired by it. We shall begin with the evidence of the texts.

In the Amitāyurdhyānasūtra, Avalokita, who is only a Bodhisattva, besides the hundreds of 'magical' Buddhas (see p. 98[a]) radiating from his body, bears on his head a colossal Buddha, also magical, that is to say, emanating from Avalokita.

Mañjuśrī, a Bodhisattva raised to the dignity of Ādibuddha, sometimes bears on his head small figures of the five Dhyānibuddhas, to signify that he proceeds from them and comprehends them. Conversely, the five Buddhas separate themselves from him (*sphuratpañchatathāgata*); and the carving that illustrates this expression actually represents them ranged above his head, following the profile of the statue; which is merely another way of setting them in order in the generating halo.*

On the other hand, the ancient sculpture places five Buddhas in the attitude of meditation in the frieze above five Bodhisattvas.† It is, we think, reasonable to recognize in these five Buddhas Śākyamuni, his three predecessors, and Maitreya, *i.e.* the 'historical' Buddhas of our age.‡ They are not saints who have attained *nirvāṇa*, for the Lotus distinguishes clearly between the Buddhas who have passed away and of whom only stūpas remain,§ and the Buddhas 'provisionally eternal,' whose contemplative existence is indefinitely prolonged, such as Amitābha and Śākyamuni. Some would recognize in them the so-called Dhyānibuddhas, and assign to one of them the name of Amitābha. This seems to be a hazardous inference, even when the idea of 'procession,' which is wrongly attached to the word Dhyānibuddha, is rejected, and it is in harmony with the doctrines of the Lotus to suppose that the Buddhas are here represented in the *quasi*-nirvāṇa which is their rational state. If, further, they assume the attitude of teaching, this is referable to their human double (see p. 98[a]); and if they act and save creatures, it is because a Buddha always preserves some of the characteristics of a Bodhisattva.

This activity, however, is not their proper function; and the Bodhisattvas, placed below them in the relief, are their servants for the present and their successors in the future, having entered later and independently of them on the road that leads to Buddhahood. Nevertheless, in these motionless saints, placed above the Bodhisattvas and provided with lotus and thunderbolt, we have the prototypes of the Jinas and Dhyānibodhisattvas of Hodgson.

Somewhat later, apparently, we find in sculpture a symbol which draws closer the bonds between the Buddha and the Bodhisattva. We refer to the practice (perhaps of Greek origin, for it is met with at Palmyra) of placing a miniature image of a Buddha in the tiara of the future Buddha. It was, we believe, first employed in the case of Avalokita, who bears on his head a small figure of Amitābha. We shall see that Avalokita is not even the spiritual son of Amita, but rather his right arm, who provides his paradise, an active Amitābha. The small image, which is perhaps not without some connexion with the colossal Buddha which emanates from the head of Avalokita in the Amitāyurdhyāna, is not that of a Buddha-father, but rather that of a Buddha-patron. And this interpretation, which we believe is founded on the literature, justifies that which we have propounded above regarding the Buddhas in the Gāndhāra frieze.

If we come down to the time attested by the *sādhanas*, or tantric incantations, and perhaps it will not be necessary to come down very far, the practice of thus placing a small figure in the tiara has become classical, and the position of the five Dhyānibuddhas is fully established.* They are seen on the heads of numerous divinities, especially upon those of the Tārās, where undoubtedly they figure as husbands rather than fathers. A sixth Buddha, Vajrasattva, also appears (see p. 99[b]). In the case of Mañjuśrī, as we have seen, the five Buddhas are all united in a single head-dress.

4. *Doctrine of the Three Bodies.*—The contradictory data which have just been set forth are fused into a theology, or rather a Buddhology, which, taking them all into account, justifies especially the antithesis of the Dhyānibuddha, the so-called human Buddha, and the Bodhisattva. But this theology goes beyond the mythological and polytheistic conceptions of the Buddhism of the Great Vehicle, and tends towards the unitarian systems which form the subject of this article.

The Buddhology of the Great Vehicle is summarized in the doctrine of the 'three bodies' (*trikāya*). This doctrine has been alluded to above, and we shall now state it in its least unorthodox form, which is undoubtedly the most ancient.

Buddha has three bodies: *dharmakāya, sambhogakāya, nirmāṇakāya.*†

* Foucher, *Iconographie*, ii. 34.

† See Burgess, 'Elura Cave Temples' in *ASWI*, vol. 5, pl. 20; Grünwedel, *Buddh. Kunst* 2, p. 170 (Eng. trans. p. 196).

‡ Cf. *Mahāvastu*, iii. 330. When the Bodhisattva is going to preach the Law, five thrones miraculously appear.

§ Kern, *Lotus*, p. 412.

* For the five Dhyānibuddhas in Japan, see *Si-do-in-dzou*, Musée Guimet, 1899; at Java, in 779, *Minutes of the Batavian Society*, April 1886, and Takakusu, *I-Tsing*, p. xlviii.

† The Tantras, however, assign to him four or five (see TANTRAS). This doctrine of the three bodies was stated for the first time by Schmidt, *Grundlehre des Buddhaismus*. See also Kern, *Inscriptie uit Battambang* (Fr. trans. *Muséon*, 1906, 1), and the present writer's essay in *JRAS*, 1906, p. 943 ff. *Trikāya* (=*trimūrti*) is a name of the Buddha (Trikṣ.). The Buddha, as identified with the Hindu Trimūrti (Brahmā-Viṣṇu-Iśvara), is called Tripuruṣa (Kern, *Vermenging*, 32). But, in the present writer's opinion, this conception of the Triad (Dharma, Buddha,

The *dharmakāya*, or 'body of the law,' is the real identical nature of every Buddha, and of every being. The ancients, without using the word, gave to the thing the name of *dharmāṇām dharmatā*, 'the manner of being of that which is,' that is to say, of being produced by a cause and of being transitory. The Mādhyamika, one of the two branches of the scholastic Great Vehicle, and evidently the older, made it clear that by this term must be understood the 'void,' *śūnyatā*. There is no difference between *nirvāṇa* and *saṁsāra*, the latter expressing the successive existence of phenomena which have no true reality. Every character, every individuality, is mere appearance. On entering *nirvāṇa* the individual takes possession of his *dharmakāya*, which is, as we have seen, the 'void.' But under the name of 'void,' which was identical with the 'element of things' (*dharmadhātu*), it was easy to understand a real substratum, free from any form which could be understood or expressed in words. The Mādhyamikas themselves are not always on their guard;* and the Yogāchāras, who form the other great school of the Great Vehicle, have no hesitation in taking 'void' to mean 'unreality of the phenomena,' 'reality of the absolute,' or the 'mere thing' (*vastumātra*).† Admitting the existence of thought alone, they saw in the *dharmakāya*, which is the 'womb of the Tathāgatas' (*tathāgatagarbha*) and the identical nature of all beings (*bhūtatathātā*, *dharmadhātu*), thought in its quiescent state (*ālayavijñāna*), whence issue, by a series of illusions, all individualities and all characters.

The *nirmāṇakāya*, or magical body, like the different illusions which every magician can produce, is the body which Sākyamuni displays to men from the moment when he became Buddha.‡

The 'real' body of the Buddhas (the body of the law not being a body at all) is the body of bliss (*sambhogakāya*), a supermundane body, marked with the thirty-two signs, etc., in which the Buddhas enjoy their full majesty, virtue, knowledge, and blessedness. It is the privilege of saints to perceive this body, which belongs to the world of form, in the same way as the human Kṛṣṇa (who is only a *nirmāṇakāya*) showed his 'true' form to Arjuna. It is a marvellous sight, a symphony of light and jewels, a symphony of knowledge and sound, for it ceaselessly proclaims the voice of the True Law (*rutarāśi*). It is the source of the joy of the Bodhisattvas. Its home is in the *Akaniṣṭha* (*Akaniṣṭhabhavana*, elsewhere *Sukhāvatī*, Vulture Peak, etc.). Yet the first person, from a chronological point of view, to whom a *sambhogakāya*, a 'body of bliss,' is ascribed, is not, as the present writer understands it, a Buddha, but a Bodhisattva, viz. Avalokita. And it is remarkable that the classical doctrine of the three bodies is silent upon the glorious form of the Bodhisattvas in general. These distinctions, however, on which our Western philology is wont to dwell, are, in reality, of no importance. All these conceptions merge into one another, and in exact theology the *sambhogakāya* is just as illusory, on its side, as the *nirmāṇakāya*. The latter is a transient illusion imposed upon men; the former is the cosmic illusion, which embraces the Bodhisattvas also, and is similar to the representation which the one Being makes to himself. It is the *ālayavijñāna*, 'quiescent intelligence,' the great and unique substratum, hidden under a glorious and eternal disguise, while ordinary creatures are the same *ālayavijñāna* separated into individual consciousnesses (*prativikalpavijñāna*).*

5. *Dhyānibuddhas.*—At first, however, the progress made in mythological and religious speculation is neither so great nor so rapid as in ontological. Sākyamuni was at first regarded as a man in whom every germ of rebirth had been by himself destroyed; who survived the destruction of the germ of rebirth as the 'living emancipated one,' and at death entered into *nirvāṇa*, nothingness or mystery. He was afterwards assigned a place among the 'never-reborn saints,'† termed in Pāli *Akaniṭṭhagāmins*, who attain *nirvāṇa* after having ascended from one heaven to another to the summit of the world of forms. He therefore possessed an acquired and perishable *sambhogakāya*. When it was understood that he had been Buddha almost from the beginning of time, and when the theory of the *kalpas* (Ages of the World) had been largely manipulated to suit this view, the *sambhogakāya* became his permanent and natural body. Mystic speculation, however, did not all at once arrive at unanimous conclusions. In principle there has never been but one *dharmakāya*, while the worlds are inhabited by millions of Buddhas, who have a right to this *dharmakāya*, and succeed more or less in appropriating it, and who in their *sambhogakāya* are so many celestial Jinas or Dhyānibuddhas. Each of them, as such, has control of a 'Buddha field' (*Buddhakṣetra*), of a world more or less blessed according as he has conceived his mission as Bodhisattva. Moreover, every Buddha in his own domain appears, when he pleases, in his magical body (*nirmāṇa*), or is replaced for this purpose by a worthy Bodhisattva.‡

The imagination which runs riot through the universe is subordinated to religious instinct. There must be gods, but there need not be too many. Among the innumerable Buddhas § there is one, Amitābha, the Buddha of the setting sun, the god of Infinite Light, who, thanks to his ancient vow, has won for himself the happy office of presiding over a universe in which there is no 'evil destiny.' The men of that country are equal to the gods of ours. There are none but Bodhisattvas, and only a few Arhats. That world is a

Saṅgha) has nothing to do with the Three Bodies. An icon is raised to the dignity of representing the dharmakāya by a special consecration, and particularly by the introduction of relics, of bands covered with *dhāraṇīs*, etc. (Grünwedel, *Myth.* 112).

* This *śūnyatā* is termed *vajra* in the mystic and tantric school.

† 'The real extremity' or 'end of the being,' *bhūtakoṭi*, the place where the being ceases, that is, the *śūnyatā*, *nirvāṇa*. But at the same time it is the crown of things and their first principle (primary cause). Compare what the Chinese have made of the *śūnyatākoṭi*, 'apex of nothingness,' a creator who resembles Ādibuddha (De Groot, *Sectarianism*, i. 176).

‡ It is clear that this body, since it has neither blood nor bones, cannot leave any remains; its *nirvāṇa* is only illusion, *na buddhaḥ parinirvāti* (Suvarṇaprabhāsa).

* For further details see *JRAS*, 1906, p. 943 ff. The one *brāhman* is at once Śiva, the various forms of Śiva, and the multitude of created beings. It is worthy of note that, according to Wassilieff, the Sautrāntikas (of the Little Vehicle) acknowledge the *sambhogakāya*.

† Köppen (ii. 26) is of opinion that there is some relation between the five so-called Dhyānibuddhas on the one hand and the four trances and the Anāgāmins (never-reborn saints) on the other. There is no evidence in support of this view. But the Anāgāmins seem to furnish a good illustration of what a Buddha may be after his 'apparent' *nirvāṇa* on this earth.

‡ The doctrinal theories, therefore, undergo several modifications. Amitābha, a visible form, is *sambhogakāya*. He is, however, described as *dharmakāya*, a qualification which belongs to him only in so far as he is *Vajradharma*, according to the passage cited by Foucher, *Iconographie*, ii. 24; and, regarded as *sambhoga*, he receives the name of Amitāyus. In the same way Akṣobhya is the name of the *dharmakāya*, whose beatific appearance is called *Vajrasattva*. Again, there are distinguished two Vairochanas and two Ratnasambhavas. A very unorthodox relationship is thus established between the three bodies and the three worlds of formlessness, of form, and of desire (*arūpa*, *rūpa*, *kāma*). But the *dharmakāya* is in principle quite a different thing from the *arūpa*.

§ Among the most curious enumerations, that of the thousand Buddhas of our age, published by Schmidt (*Mém. Ac. de St. Pet.*, 6th ser. ii.), in which Vairochana recurs four times (Nos. 20, 167, 351, 999), gives a fairly clear idea of the system of the reincarnations of a similar *quasi*-eternal Buddha. The thousand Buddhas are well known to the Chinese pilgrims (Beal, *Buddhist Records*, lxxviii. 99; and *JBTS* iii. 1). See further, *Mahāvastu*, iii. 330, where Vairochanaprabha is the most glorious Buddha.

'Happy Land,' a *Sukhāvatī*, or, as the Viṣṇupurāṇa says, a *Sukhā*. Although Maitreya has a paradise,* our true paradise is the land to which Amitābha calls his elect, and to which he conveys them with the help of his two 'Great Bodhisattvas.' Amitābha, at one time quite distinct from an eternal Śākyamuni (*Lotus of the True Law*), comes to be regarded as the *quasi*-eternal Buddha who was incarnated under the illusory appearance of the human Śākyamuni. He will be the *Jina* or *dhyānibuddha* of Śākyamuni. By the side of Amitābha there are four other Buddhas who at different times attracted the attention, now of religion, now of mythology, or again of mysticism. From among the myriads of Buddhas they are chosen to represent at one and the same time the *dharmakāya* and the *sambhogakāya*. As they are connected with the five human Buddhas, the five magical appearances of our age, it may easily be inferred that the number five originates in this ancient enumeration; and that just as the human Buddhas, as such, have no further ontological or religious importance, so their human names seemed ill fitted to designate their sublime 'substrata.'† In the same way as Śākyamuni, as eternal, bears the name of Amitāyus, and as uncreated light, of Amitābha, so also Kanakamuni will be called Akṣobhya, and Maitreya Amoghasiddhi.‡ But Kern has warned us repeatedly that it is dangerous to be too euhemeristic; and as the Dhyānibodhisattvas have taken the place of Bodhisattvas, much better attested in literature and more historical, so the Dhyānibuddhas, who are called the Brilliant (Vairochana), the Imperturbable (Akṣobhya), the Jewel-born (Ratnasambhava), the Sure-Success (Amoghasiddhi), are in the first instance 'names' (*nomina, numina*). Seeing that there are five Indras, five Rudras, five Kuśikas, Kern suggests that for the same reasons there are five Dhyānibuddhas. And we are quite willing to believe that it is in mysticism, in idolatry, in the solar cosmogony, etc., that we must look for the predominating factors in this divine πεντάς.§

Such is the polytheistic system of the Dhyānibuddhas. Even when Vajradhara is given only a secondary place, as the second body of Akṣobhya, the tantric element always constitutes an integral part of it. Every Buddha, at least in his 'blissful' form (*sambhoga*), has a wife, and begets a Bodhisattva; he is brought into relation with a *maṇḍala*, with a *dhāraṇī*, an element, etc.

III. Harmony was attained in various ways, either by raising to the presidency one of the five Buddhas, usually Vairochana,‖ the god of the Zenith,¶ or by interposing a sixth person, whether Mañjuśrī (as we saw above), or Vajradhara, or merely the Ādibuddha, not otherwise defined. The two last-mentioned conceptions demand a further brief consideration.

1. Vajradhara, 'Holder of the Thunderbolt,' is the *dharmakāya*; Vajrasattva, 'Thunderbolt-being,' is his beatific form; but the two names and the two things become confused (Wassilieff, 187). On the other hand, Vajrapāṇi, 'Thunderbolt in hand,' is the Bodhisattva.* In every instance, however, in the iconography, and usually in magic, the last-named takes the place of his doubles. He is a Bodhisattva of fairly ancient date; for it is certainly he that is represented on a gigantic scale, with four other Bodhisattvas, placed beneath five Buddhas on a Gāndhāra monument. The same sculpture regarded him essentially as merely an acolyte, and the personal attendant of Śākyamuni. He is also an entirely orthodox Bodhisattva, for Śāntideva invokes him with great energy. But he is not a Bodhisattva like the others, since he is by birth the bearer of the thunderbolt. In his person, moreover, the lexicons and Grünwedel recognize Indra.† He is a deity adopted by Buddhism, and not an original Buddhist saint. Vajradhara-Vajrasattva is the same individual raised to the dignity of a Buddha, and a supreme Buddha—the result, in fact, of the word *Vajra*.

'Vajra,' hard as adamant, clear as 'emptiness,' thunderbolt and weapon against the demons, and also a mystic synonym of the *liṅga*, has taken the place of Dharma and of Bodhi.‡ The Tāntrikas superimpose the Vajrakāya upon the Dharmakāya, and without hesitation replace the Bodhisattvas or the Śrībodhisattvas by Vajrabodhisattvas. The Vajra is a divine and supernatural thing; Vajradhara, or better still Vajrasattva, who is his incarnation, is a tantric Brahman.

The various Buddhas or Bodhisattvas are, in reality, only this Vajrasattva in different rôles.§ He is, moreover, self-sufficient. To Vairochana and his brethren there correspond an element, a *skandha*, a sense, an object of sense, a wife, a mythological and mystic family (*kula*), accessory divinities and formulæ, and above all a special part of the body, a 'vital breath,' knowledge (*jñāna*), and a particular sensation (*ānanda*) of the *maithuna*. Here, then, we are chiefly concerned with the *chakras*, or regions delineated on the body, with *prāṇāyāma*, regulation or suppression of the respiration, and with *lingayit* rites. Vajrasattva is, according to circumstances, a sixth element, a sixth *skandha*, a sixth joy (*ānanda*), a sixth Buddha, or at times a combination of the five elements, the five *skandhas*, or the five Buddhas. His wife is Vajradhātvīśvarī. The whole of this system may ultimately be reduced to a psychology which is essentially practical, with its physiological presumptions quite clearly defined, and aiming at the reinstatement of the faithful into his true nature, and his transformation into Vajrasattva. He has but to take possession, by means of the combined rites, of the 'body of bliss' (*ānandakāya*), or of the 'thunderbolt-body' (*vajrakāya*) in its most perfect form.‖

2. The Ādibuddha system consists, properly speaking, in superimposing on the five or six Buddhas (Vajrasattva included) a Being who, however invisible and inactive he may be in principle, is

* It is into the paradise of Maitreya that Hiuen-Tsiang would fain be reborn. Sometimes Śākyamuni appears to be the king of Sukhāvatī (Csoma-Feer, p. 333).

† Vipaśyin appears at least once in a list of the Dhyānibuddhas.

‡ We have Amitābha (*snaṅ-ba-mtha-yas*), Amitāyus (*tshe-dpag-med*), Amitābha (*hod-dpag-med*)—Grünwedel, *Myth.* 120, 211, n. 81, *Buddhist Art in India*, p. 195.

§ There are sometimes six or seven Dhyānibuddhas, a double or triple Akṣobhya (see Foucher, *Catalogue*, pp. 15, 29). On the other hand, in the Suvarṇaprabhāsa (p. 4) there are four Dhyānibuddhas, viz. Akṣobhya (an ancient Dharmachāṇaka), Ratnaketu, Amitābha, and Dundubhīśvara.

‖ The universal 'illuminating' Vairochana, or Virochana (*sarvāsām parsadām madhye virochyate dīpyata iti vairochana*). It is a name of the sun.

¶ In the Vairochanābhisambodhitantra (Wass. p. 187), Vairochana is a great deity who gives to Siddhārtha (?) the Vajrābhiṣeka, and who by meditation creates Vajrabodhisattvas of many kinds (Vajrapāṇi, etc.; Vajrapāśabodhisattva, etc.); but who worships Vajradhara 'of the hundred names,' learns the maṇḍalas from him, etc.

In the Nāmasaṅgīti, Vairochana with his circle (*chakra*) of 181 Buddhas and Bodhisattvas has no priority over the other Jinas.

In the Javanese book Kuñjarakarṇa, Vairochana is not only the *primus inter pares*, but he is supreme lord to whom other Jinas give heed. The doctrine he teaches is that of identity: 'I am You, You are I'; and if there are, in fact, so few monks who attain emancipation, the reason is that they refuse to recognize that Buddha, *i.e.* Vairochana, is identical with Śiva. On Vairochana as an *Asura*, see Vyut, 171, 5; as a *Nīlakāyika* god in Lalitavistara, see Monier-Williams' *Dict.* p. 1025. On the pre-eminence of Vairochana consult also Eitel, *Handbook*, p. 179, and *Si-do-in-dzou*; on the Japanese sects, Tendai et Siṅgon, 1272 A.D. (Musée Guimet, *Bibl. d'Études*, t. viii.).

* According to Waddell, 'the established church of Tibet regards Vajrasattva-Vajradhara as a reflex from Śākyamuni, as a god analogous to the Ādibuddha of the old (??) school Waddell himself, however, on the other hand, represents them as 'bodhisat-reflexes' from Akṣobhya (*Lāmaism*, p. 352).

† *Buddhist Art in India*, pp. 38, 90 f.

‡ See especially Senart, 'Vajrapāṇi dans les sculptures du Gandhāra,' in *Congrès d'Alger*.

§ Śākyamuni = Mahāvairochana = Vajradhara (Nāmasaṅgīti, v. 23).

‖ This is the more easy because the Guru, *Vajraguru* or *Vajrāchārya*, is Vajrasattva incarnate. He gives the Vajravrata, the Vajrasattvābhiṣeka, to whomsoever he pleases. In the ultimate analysis, therefore, the whole is comprised in the Gurvārādhana, in the worship of the teacher, the initiator, the master of the novices.

The Svayambhūpurāṇa gives some information about the Ādibuddhamaṇḍala. The commentaries of the Nāmasaṅgīti (25) describe in full the magical performances: *idānīṁ tasyādibuddhasya hṛdaye prajñāchakraṁ vibhāvayet. . . .* The *chakra* has four girdles (*mekhalā*) and is divided into six sections, the whole crowded with gods and formulæ.

nevertheless a god. His body, which is a 'body of law,' is called *samantabhadra*, 'universally propitious,'* a title borrowed from the Bodhisattva of that name. There are attributed to him the thirty-two marks, etc., of the Buddhas and of Great Men, which are, as we saw, the characteristics of the beatific body.† More fortunate than Brahmā, he is worshipped.‡ The ordinary Buddhas, etc., are not his 'reflections' in an inferior world; he is different from them, for they proceed from him at a fixed moment of his existence. In place, therefore, of the underlying and scarcely veiled identity of the tantric or purely ontological system of the five Buddhas, there is substituted emanation or creation by means of dhyāna.

It is evident that such a doctrine of the Ādibuddha is as much theistic as Buddhistic.

We must not, however, be led astray by words. If there is a shade of difference here, it is only a shade. True theism, as far as Buddhism knew it, is to be found not in the Ādibuddha creed of the *Aiśvarikas*, but in the worship of the celestial Bodhisattvas.

The doctrine of emanation, although it has its connecting links and its ultimate origin on the side of Hinduism, has, nevertheless, a *raison d'être* in Buddhism. Here we see the final step of the speculations which transformed Śākyamuni into a magician, and Avalokiteśvara, Vairochana, etc., into still greater magicians, Yogīśvaras, 'lords of the Yogis.' This character becomes evident when it is noticed that cosmic emanation is fashioned on the pattern of the creations by means of *dhyāna*.

What, then, is the ultimate difference between the system of emanation and the orthodox doctrine of the Great Vehicle? The Great Vehicle taught identity and the essential nothingness of things; but, while thus far very orthodox, it considered individual beings to be distinct from their very beginning. The *saṁsāra* has no beginning; it is the result of ignorance (*avidyā*), which is primeval. The *saṁsāra* is the same thing as nirvāṇa, but nirvāṇa will not be realized until the end.§

On the other hand, the Great Vehicle does not confuse magical creations (*nirmitakas*) with real 'beings.' The latter do not actually exist under the form which they adopt and by which they are known. But at least they are known, and they are truly existent illusions; while there is no real thought in magical creations.

As regards the first point, however, nothing was more logical than to suppose the 'womb of the Tathāgatas' originally virgin, to make the cosmos issue therefrom, and to represent it as returning again in *nirvāṇa*. The Brāhmans had paved the way, and this system fitted in admirably with the doctrine of cosmic revolutions in the course of the ages. And, as far as the second point is concerned, although ancient speculation, comparatively sober and self-confident as it was, refused to ascribe thought to the magical creations of magicians, it is doubtful whether we are justified in drawing the same conclusion when the magician is the *dharmakāya* personified under the form of a meditative Buddha. What he sees in his meditation is real and, as it were, autonomous, since nothing exists except this meditation and we ourselves are thought.‖ The absolute idealism of the Yogāchāras and the nihilistic monism of the Mādhyamikas entail all these consequences whenever they are brought into cosmogonic mythology.

* At least in the Tibetan 'ancient sects,' according to Grünwedel, *Myth.* p. 143; Waddell describes them as 'the wholly unreformed section or the old school.'

† On the other hand, Ādibuddha resembles Brahmā. The Tantras issue from his five mouths, as the four Vedas from the four mouths of Brahmā, etc.

‡ Under the name of Svayambhū.

§ In the language of the Brāhmans, it is the system of the *Advaita*, with a *vivarta* conceived as primitive.

‖ In the language of the Brāhmans, the system of the *dṛṣṭi-sṛṣṭi*.

LITERATURE.—Brian H. Hodgson, *Essays on the Languages, Literature and Religion of Nepal and Tibet*, London, 1874; Abel Rémusat, *J. des Savants*, May 1831, *Mélanges posthumes*, pp. 25, 152, etc; J. J. Schmidt, 'Ueber einigen Grundlehren des Buddhaismus,' *Mém. de l'Acad. de St. Petersburg*, 6th ser. i. 1831–32; A. Csoma de Körös, *As. Res.* xx. 488, 564, 'On the Origin of the Kālachakra System,' *JRASBe*, ii. 57, *Grammar*, p. 192; Csoma-Feer, p. 383; E. Burnouf, *Introduction*2 (1876) and *Lotus de la Bonne Loi*; C. F. Köppen, *Die Religion des Buddha*, 1857–59; H. Kern, *Geschiedenis* (Fr. trans. by G. Huet, Musée Guimet, *Bibl. d'Études*, t. x. and xi.), *Manual of Buddhism*, *GIAP*, Strassburg, 1896, *Saddharmapuṇḍarīka*, or 'The Lotus of the True Law,' *SBE*, xxi., Oxford, *Over den Aanhef eener Buddhistische Inscriptie uit Battambang*, Versl. der K. Ak. van Amsterdam, 4th R. iii. 1899, pp. 65–81, *Over de Vermenging van Çiwaïsme en Buddhisme op Java*, . . . *ib.* 3rd R. iv. 1888, pp. 8–43, *De Legende van Kuñjarakarṇa*, Verhand. of the same Academy, Nieuwe reeks, iii. 3, 1901. [These three last memoirs will shortly appear in French in the *Muséon*]; W. Wassilieff, *Der Buddhismus, seine Dogmen . . . aus dem Russischen übersetzt*, 1860; E. Schlagintweit, *Buddhism in Tibet*, London, 1868; L. A. Waddell, *The Buddhism of Tibet or Lāmaism*, London, 1895, *Lhasa and its Mysteries*, London, 1905, ch. xvii. ff.; A. Grünwedel, *Buddhistische Kunst in Indien*2, 1900 (Eng. trans. *Buddhist Art in India*, London, 1901), *Mythologie du Buddhisme au Tibet et en Mongolie* (French [very incorrect] and German editions), Leipzig, 1900 (an inexhaustible mine of all kinds of information); A. Foucher, 'L'art bouddhique' in *RHR*, 1895, *Catal. des peintures népalaises et tibétaines de la collection B. H. Hodgson* . . ., Mémoires de l'Acad. des Inscr. 1st ser. t. xi., I. 1897, *Études sur l'iconographie bouddhique*, i. and ii., École des hautes Études, 1900 and 1905; S. Lévi, *Le Népal*, Musée Guimet, t. xvii. xviii.; Monier-Williams, *Buddhism*, London, 1889, chh. ix. x.; W. W. Rockhill, *Life of the Buddha*, 1884, p. 200 ff. [See also artt. AVALOKITEŚVARA, BODHISATTVA, MAHĀYĀNA].

L. DE LA VALLÉE POUSSIN.

ADMIRATION.—1. An emotional reaction or feeling in regard to some agent who manifests unusual excellence or worth in the region of human activities. An individual is admired solely on account of his intrinsic worth, and this is determined by reference to an ideal of conduct which is approved in and for itself. Strength or force of will is implied in worth, but mere force of will, regardless of the end to which it is directed, does not excite admiration. The emotion thus indicates the existence of an ultimate ideal of conduct in whose realization we are interested. It concentrates attention on concrete examples, and in this way exercises an important influence on conduct. Wonder is usually a concomitant of admiration, but is not an integral part of the emotion as such. It is a purely intellectual state occasioned by anything striking or unusual. It may, for instance, be aroused by unusual unworthiness, and may therefore be associated with scorn as well as with admiration. See also RESPECT.

2. The term 'admiration' sometimes signifies æsthetic approval. The intimate relation which exists ultimately between the ideals of beauty and goodness partly accounts for this use of the word. See SCORN.

LITERATURE.—Bain, *Emotions and Will*3 (1875), ch. vii.; Martineau, *Types of Ethical Theory*2 (1886), 152–160; Ribot, *Psychology of the Emotions* (1897), Pt. II. ch. xi.; Martensen, *Chr. Ethics* (*Indiv.*), [Eng. tr. 1881] § 109.

DAVID IRONS.

ADMONITION.—Among the repressive measures resorted to by all kinds of societies for the protection of themselves and the discipline of their members, the lightest is the admonition of the offender. Admonition, when addressed to one who has committed an offence, is a punishment of a purely moral character. It does not deprive the offender of his property, like a fine; it does not deprive him of his liberty, like imprisonment; it inflicts no temporary or permanent indignity on his person, like corporal punishment. It is an appeal, a warning, a censure addressed solely to the highest elements in his character,—his reason and conscience. The value and limitations of admonition as an instrument of social order and discipline are admirably expressed in the religious philosophy of the Hebrews: 'A rebuke entereth deeper into one that hath understanding than an hundred stripes into a fool' (Pr 17[10]).

1. Admonition, as a means of maintaining social discipline, whether in the family or in larger social groups, has occupied a place among the laws and customs of peoples in almost all stages of civilization. It exists among the primitive races of the Indian peninsula; it is a recognized part of Muhammadan penal law, and it held a place in the penal code of ancient Rome (Post, *Ethnol. Jurisprudenz* (1894), ii. 28). When the Christians of Apostolic times began to form themselves into organized communities, admonition was one of the principal methods of upholding and enforcing ecclesiastical discipline. Admonition was a duty that devolved upon all Christian teachers and all Christian communities (Gal 2[14], 1 Th 2[2], 1 Ti 4[13], 2 Ti 4[2]; Hermas, *Vis.* ii. 43), and it was incumbent on every believer to admonish a brother overtaken in a fault (1 Th 5[14]). Admonition in the primitive Church was of two kinds: (*a*) private, pastoral admonition, and (*b*) public admonition before the assembled congregation. Public admonition consisted either in a solemn exhortation to the offender to amend (2 Co 2[5]), or, in extreme cases, in a warning to leave the Church (1 Clem. *ad Cor.* 54. 2; Sohm, *Kirchenrecht*, 33 f.). The object of admonition in the primitive Church was to perfect the Christian character (Col 1[28]), and it was to be administered not in anger, but in a spirit of anxious, paternal, affectionate solicitude (1 Co 4[14]).

2. When we consider the extent and importance of admonition in the primitive Church, as well as the existence of this principle in the ancient Roman penal code, it is natural to expect that admonition would find a place when the Church of later ages ultimately elaborated a complicated and comprehensive legal code of its own. Admonition formed a part of Canon Law; it was not regarded in this system of law as a punishment, but as a warning. This warning preceded the actual punishment, which consisted in the excommunication of the offender, and it was usual in ordinary cases to repeat the warning three days before resorting to the final act of excommunication (*Corpus juris canonici*, Editio Romana, 1582 [editions of Richter, 1839, and Friedberg, 1881]; Kahl, *Lehrsystem des Kirchenrechts und der Kirchenpolitik*, Freiburg, 1894, p. 142; *Actes du Congrès pénitentiaire international*, Rome, tome i. 182–183). Admonition holds a more or less definite place in the ecclesiastical constitution of most Protestant Churches.

3. Admonition as a means of dealing with offences against the secular law exists in several modern penal codes. The old Italian and French systems of criminal law admitted the principle of admonition, and at the present time it exists in a more or less restricted form in the penal codes of a considerable number of European communities. In some States admonition is applicable only when the offence has been committed by a juvenile, in others it is applicable in the case of adults as well. As used in penal law it is not the advice, warning, reprimand or exhortation which a judge is always at liberty to give when a prisoner is before him, whether he has been acquitted or convicted. It is to be regarded as a real punishment, solemnly pronounced by a judicial tribunal, and requiring a proper observance of all the rules of legal procedure. Admonition in this sense does not exist in English law [Prins, *Science pénale* (1899), p. 468; Alimena, *Revista penale*, xxvii. p. 557].

Admonition is a form of punishment which must always be of very limited application in cases which come before the criminal courts. Most cases which are of so trivial a character that they can be satisfactorily disposed of by a resort to admonition, are cases which are seldom brought before a judge at all. Owing to this fact, admonition is very little used in some of the countries where it exists as a penalty on the statute book. The prominence which the practice of admonition has acquired in recent years is to be attributed to a great and growing reaction against the abuse of short terms of imprisonment for petty and insignificant offences. Many of these offences are not, strictly speaking, criminal in character; they are for the most part offences against highway acts, police regulations, education acts, municipal regulations. The growth of large cities has increased offences of this kind enormously, inasmuch as crowded populations require a much more complicated network of regulations than thinly populated communities; and the growth of regulations is always accompanied by an increase in the number of petty offences. Petty offences of this kind are usually dealt with by the infliction of a fine; and when the offender is able to pay the fine, or when the fine falls upon himself, this penalty is perhaps the best and most effective method of dealing with them. But many cases occur in which the offender is unable to pay a fine, or, as in the case of juveniles, in which the fine falls upon the parents; in most of these cases the only alternative to a fine is imprisonment, and imprisonment, inflicting as it does a stigma which can never be removed, is felt to be too severe a penalty for the trivial nature of the offence. Hence the demand for some form of punishment which will avoid the odium of imprisonment for offenders unable to pay a fine. To some extent English law does deal with such cases. For example, where a charge is proved against an accused person, but the offence is so trivial that it is inexpedient to inflict punishment, the court may dismiss the information altogether, or it may convict the offender and discharge him conditionally on his giving security, with or without sureties, to be of good behaviour, or to appear for sentence when called upon (Summary Jurisdiction Act, 1879, sec. 16; Probation of First Offenders Act, 1887, sec. 1). These humane provisions of the English criminal law to a great extent supply the place of judicial admonition as used in some Continental States, but they do not succeed in abolishing short sentences of imprisonment, which are the bane of all existing penal arrangements, and which perhaps produce more evils than they cure. W. D. MORRISON.

ADOLESCENCE (*adolescere* = 'to grow up').—The period of growth that intervenes between mere childhood and complete adulthood or maturity. The term was formerly restricted to the latter part of this period (from 18 to 25), but later writers have followed a suggestion of Clouston (*Clinical Lectures on Mental Diseases*, Philadelphia, 1884, p. 375 [3rd ed., Lond. 1892]) that the term should be extended so as to cover the entire transition. Accordingly, adolescence extends from about the age of 12, when premonitory mental symptoms of puberty appear, to about 25 for males and 21 for females, when the reproductive powers are ripe. The phenomena of these years display a sufficiently definite progression to justify a subdivision of the period into early, middle, and later adolescence, the middle sub-period covering the two or three years from about the age of 15 during which the transition is most rapid and the mental life most inchoate. All these age-boundaries are necessarily only average and approximate.

1. The most obvious mark of adolescence is the attainment of reproductive power. But this is only a centre for a remarkable group of phenomena. The curve of growth, both for weight and for

height, takes a new direction; the proportions of bodily parts and organs change; hereditary tendencies crop out; new instincts appear; there are characteristic disorders, particularly of the mind and nervous system; new intellectual interests and powers spring up spontaneously; the moral sense is more or less transformed; emotion greatly increases in quantity and variety; and appreciations (literary, artistic, ethical, religious) multiply in number and depth.

These phenomena have the deepest significance for both the organic and the personal life. In respect to the personal life, which is here our chief concern, adolescence presents a peculiar state of flux or plasticity of all the faculties, followed by the assumption of a new type of organization. As a general rule the 'set' that character now takes remains through life. Even the vocational and other special interests that distinguish one's mature years commonly take their rise here. It is a time of peculiar responsiveness to religious impressions, and conversely it is the period when nearly all careers of criminality, viciousness, or incompetency are begun. [The practical importance of adolescence for moral and religious growth is so great that a special article will be devoted to this topic. (See GROWTH [MORAL AND RELIGIOUS, PERIODS OF]). Certain abnormal tendencies of adolescence will be treated in the article on MORBIDNESS. The remainder of the present article offers only such general description as may assist towards a correct perspective for the manifold problems of morals and religion that have their centre here].

2. For *physiology* the importance of adolescence lies in the ripening of a new organic function, that of sex. If we carry forward this physiological notion in the direction of biology, we perceive that adolescence marks a change in the relation of an individual to the species. The significant fact now becomes the attainment of racial, as distinguished from merely individual, functions. Extending our horizon, in the next place, from biology to sociology, we note that adolescence is the period in which individual life becomes socialized. Here begins the possibility of the family and of all the derivatives from family life that are summed up in the terms 'society' and 'the State.' But the genesis of complete social existence is likewise the genesis of complete individuality. In infancy and childhood, though individualistic impulses predominate, there is dependence upon others for nutrition, protection, and knowledge; the mind is receptive rather than critical; conscience is dominated by external authority; and, though spontaneous activities are numerous, in only a minor degree are they self-consciously guided or organized. With the adolescent all this changes. He becomes free from parental control, attains to complete responsibility under the laws of the State, under popular governments acquires the franchise; and all these external facts normally have, as their mental side, a decided access of intellectual and ethical independence, and of self-conscious purposes of relatively wide sweep.

3. Advancing, now, to the *ethical* aspect of these relations, we may say that adolescence tends toward the attainment of complete ethical personality, through release from a predominantly egoistic motivation of life. Self-realization now advances beyond a series of particular egoistic satisfactions (a characteristic of childhood), and requires the organization of the self into a larger whole as a member of it. This involves at once increased self-guidance, yet a deeper sense of obligation; a heightened individualism, yet an individualism that is transfigured into social self-realization. This movement outward from the merely particular self is of the highest importance for religion. For the movement may, and, wherever adolescence has been carefully studied, does go on to include the individual's relations not only to human society, but also to nature, and to God or the gods. It is characteristic of adolescence to become interested in the whole 'other-than-myself,' to feel its mystery, and to endeavour to construe it in terms of selfhood and sympathy.

Viewed from the standpoint of the Christian consciousness, adolescence is the normal period for attaining complete individual existence in and through the organization of the self into larger social wholes such as the family, society, the State, humanity, and the all-inclusive social relationship that Jesus called the Kingdom of God. But this is only the culmination of a view of adolescence that is present, more or less clearly, in all religions. The custom of signalizing the arrival of puberty by initiation into the tribe and its religion by means of symbolic ceremonies, bodily markings and mutilations, or by other civil and religious exercises, is world-wide, and it reaches through all strata of cultural development (see Hall, *Adolescence*, ch. xiii., and an art. by A. H. Daniels, 'The New Life,' in *Amer. Jour. Psy.* vol. vi. p. 61 ff.).

4. The close time-relation here existing between sexual development and the growth of the highest sentiments and impulses cannot be a mere coincidence. It is too constant, and the parallel between the biological and the psychological transformation is too close to permit a serious doubt that these two lines of growth need to be included under a single concept. Living organisms display two fundamental functions, nutrition and reproduction, the former of which attains its immediate end in the individual, the latter in the species. They are the physiological bases of Egoism and Altruism respectively. The physiological and the ethical here present a single law manifesting itself on two planes. In infancy and childhood we have a type of life that, in the main, presents on the physiological side a predominance of the nutritive function, and on the ethical side a predominance of self-regard, while in adolescence nutritive and reproductive functions are blended and unified, just as are also egoistic and social impulses. Of course, childhood is not exclusively egoistic, for family training and the pressure of a social environment guide conduct and even habits of feeling into social channels; but the inner, emotional, self-conscious realization of one's social nature waits for adolescence. Now, the mental states that characterize this change directly reflect the new physiological condition, though they pass beyond it, as though it were only a door of entrance. The new interest in the opposite sex tends to humanize the adolescent's whole world. All heroism becomes lovely, not merely the heroic devotion of a lover; Nature at large begins to reveal her beauty; in fact, all the ideal qualities that a lover aspires to possess in himself or to find in the object of his love,—all the sympathy, purity, truth, fidelity,—these are found or looked for in the whole sphere of being. Thus the ripening of sexual capacity and the coming of the larger ethical and spiritual capacities constitute a single process going on at two distinct levels.

The evidence of this connexion thus derived from normal growth is strengthened by abnormal and pathological phenomena. Persons who are made eunuchs in childhood commonly display a peculiar insensibility to social and religious motives. Further, nothing tends more positively towards the production of morbid moral and religious states during adolescence than defective physiological conditions or misuse of physiological power (see MORBIDNESS).

The tendency of all these data is towards the view that sexual capacity is in general the physiological basis of all the higher and finer qualities of personality, both ethical and religious. This does not reduce religion to terms of physiology, or subordinate it to something more nearly primary. Rather, it reveals in the biological and physiological realm a spiritual law that tends to transfigure the whole notion of life. We must interpret the whole biological development in the light of its highest stages, and physiological functions by their place in the highest self-consciousness.

The only serious objection to this view has been raised by Henry Drummond, who makes conjugal affection merely a secondary product of maternal affection (*The Ascent of Man*, London, 1894, chs. vii., ix.). However maternal affection originated, it can hardly be the sole origin of the higher sentiments. In the first place, the relation between a mother and a helpless infant lacks too much of mutual responsiveness or reciprocity to be the source of the humanizing of the world, to which reference has been made. Again, a large mass of evidence goes to show that this humanizing process does spring directly from the relationship of sex as its ideal expression. In addition to the evidence already adduced from adolescence, it will be appropriate to add an item from the general evolution of sex. Geddes and Thomson, tracing the evolution of the reproductive process, declare that, from its beginning in simple cell-division, 'the primitive hunger and love become the starting-points of divergent lines of egoistic and altruistic emotion and activity' (*The Evolution of Sex*, London, 1890, ch. xiii.). Consequently, as Mercier says, 'the sexual emotion includes as an integral, fundamental, and preponderating element in its constitution, the desire for self-sacrifice' (*Sanity and Insanity*, London, 1895, p. 220). In the adolescent period this universal law of life comes to self-consciousness, rises to the ethical plane, and goes on to complete itself in the all-inclusive ideas, aspirations, and self-consecrations of religion.

LITERATURE.—Although from of old the bloom-time of youth has been a favourite subject of literary art, scientific analysis of adolescent phenomena goes back little more than two decades. The stimulus for such analysis has come partly from pathology (see work of T. S. Clouston already cited; also his *Neuroses of Development*, Edinburgh, 1891, and his art. on 'Developmental Insanities and Psychoses' in Tuke's *Dictionary of Psychological Medicine*, London, 1892; likewise chs. i.–vii. of Hall's *Adolescence*), but more largely from educational needs and the general extension of psychology in physiological and biological directions. In the spheres of education and psychology, the study of adolescence has been greatly stimulated by G. Stanley Hall, President of Clark University, at Worcester, Mass., U.S.A. The *American Journal of Psychology* and the *Pedagogical Seminary*, both founded by him and published at Worcester, have devoted much space to articles on adolescence, largely from Dr. Hall and his immediate pupils. These publications, and others of a more popular sort, have represented and stimulated an extensive child-study movement in America. This movement, which has adolescence as one of its chief foci, is one cause of an extremely active ferment of educational reform. The very large literature of this subject is listed and indexed from year to year since 1898 by Louis N. Wilson in a *Bibliography of Child-Study*, also published at Worcester. In 1904 appeared G. Stanley Hall's *Adolescence: Its Psychology and its Relations to Physiology, Anthropology, Sociology, Sex, Crime, Religion, and Education*, in two large volumes (New York). The wide range of this work, the fulness of its materials, its abundant citations from sources, and the stimulating points of view of the author (though they often display the heat of an educational reformer), combine to make this by far the most notable product of the movement for the study of adolescence. In addition to these few very general references, consult the Bibliography appended to the articles on GROWTH and MORBIDNESS already referred to.

GEORGE A. COE.

ADOPTIANISM.—The name Adoptianism should, strictly speaking, be confined to a heresy which arose in Spain in the 8th century. But the wide circulation of Harnack's *History of Dogma* has familiarized us with the idea of tracing an Adoptianist Christology to an earlier period. We propose, therefore, to treat of Adoptianism in the broadest sense, bringing under this head all writings which speak of Christ as the adopted Son of God.

1. The keynote of the Christology of the 2nd cent. is struck in the opening words of the ancient homily known as *2 Clement*: 'Brethren, we ought so to think of Jesus Christ, as of God, as of the Judge of quick and dead.' *Ignatius* asserts the Divinity of the Lord no less emphatically than His true manhood; *e.g. ad Eph.* 18: 'For our God, Jesus the Christ, was conceived in the womb by Mary according to a dispensation, of the seed of David but also of the Holy Ghost.'

Harnack, however, contrasts with such teaching, to which he gives the name 'Pneumatic Christology,' the teaching of such a writer as *Hermas*, whom he claims as a teacher of Adoptianist Christology. Whereas Ignatius and Clement and others carry on the tradition of a pre-existent Christ on the lines of NT writings (Ep. Hebrews, Ephesians, Johannine writings), Harnack regards Hermas as a witness to a truer doctrine. According to the *Shepherd* of Hermas (see *Sim.* v. and ix. 1. 12), in Harnack's words (*Hist. of Dogma* [Eng. tr.] i. 191 n.):

> 'The Holy Spirit—it is not certain whether He is identified with the chief Archangel—is regarded as the pre-existent Son of God, who is older than creation, nay, was God's counsellor at creation. The Redeemer is the virtuous man chosen by God, with whom that Spirit of God was united. As He did not defile the Spirit, but kept Him constantly as His companion, and carried out the work to which the Deity had called Him, nay, did more than He was commanded, He was, in virtue of a Divine decree, adopted as a son and exalted to μεγάλη ἐξουσία καὶ κυριότης.'

We may agree with Lightfoot and others that Hermas sometimes confuses the Persons of the Son and of the Spirit, but this is as far as the evidence leads us. Is it surprising that an obscure shopkeeper without philosophical training should make slips in the work of analysis of Christian experience, which is the great task of Christian theology? In *Sim.* v. Hermas distinguishes accurately enough between the Lord of the vineyard; the Servant, under which figure Hermas speaks of the Son; and the Son, referring to the Holy Ghost. And when he writes (vi. 5) that God sent the Holy Ghost to dwell in the flesh of Christ, he does not mean that the Holy Ghost is the power of the Godhead in Christ, but that the pre-existent Christ was 'a spirit being.' Such teaching is found in Ignatius (Aristides, *Apol.*) and in later writers (Irenæus, *adv. Hær.* v. 1, 2; Tertullian, *Apol.* 21, *adv. Prax.* 8. 26).

As Dorner (*Doct. of Person of Christ* [Eng. tr.], I. i. 131) writes:

> 'So far is Hermas from Ebionism . . . that he rather seeks in part to retract the representation of the Son as a servant in the Similitude, and even to represent His earthly work as power and majesty; whilst what remains of His humiliation, such as His sufferings, he treats as the work of His free love, as the means of the taking away of our sins, and as the point of passage to a higher perfection.'

What Harnack reads into the Christology of Hermas is really the teaching of a much later writer, Paul of Samosata. No doubt it is true that the pre-existence of Christ was ignored or denied in some quarters. One class of Ebionites held a low conception of the Person of Christ, regarding Him as an ordinary man though superior to other men (Euseb. *HE* iii. 27). Some writers held that the Baptism was the beginning of His Divine Sonship.

2. This tendency to minimize the Divine glory of Christ reached a climax in the writings of *Paul of Samosata*, a rationalist Monarchian, who laid stress on the unity of God as a single Person, denying any distinction of the Wisdom or Word of God. 'A real incarnation of the Logos was thus impossible; He existed in Jesus not essentially or personally, but only as a quality. The personality of Jesus was entirely human; it was not that the Son of God came down from heaven, but that the Son of man ascended up on high' (Bethune-Baker, *Hist. Christian Doctrine* (1903), p. 101). Whether He was deified after His Baptism or His Resurrection was not clearly taught, but the union between God and Christ was, according to this view, one of disposition and will only.

3. The truth is that this tendency to minimize, which comes out again in the later Arians, Nestorians, and Adoptianists, was in continual conflict with its opposite extreme, which recurs in Sabellianism, Apollinarism, and Eutychianism. But between the two extremes the Church held on her 'tranquil way,' and the ultimate test of her belief in Christ's Divinity lies in the fact that she never ceased to offer prayer to Christ with the Father.

4. We find in the teaching of *Theodore of Mopsuestia* a connecting link with the later Adoptianism as well as the basis of Nestorian teaching, because it is probable that Latin translations of his works were read in Spain from the 6th century.

Theodore discusses the indwelling of God in Christ, in his work 'On the Incarnation.' What is in holy men an indwelling of approval only, was in Christ not merely of a higher degree, but brought Him into a close relation to God on a higher plane. From His Birth the co-operation of the Divine Word with the man Jesus raised Him to the level of perfect virtue. 'The Man Christ . . . is thus the visible image of the invisible Godhead; and on account of His union with the true Son of God, He possesses the privileges of a unique adoption, so that to Him also the title of Son of God belongs' (Swete, *Theod. of Mopsuestia on Minor Epp. of S. Paul*, i. lxxxi). Theodore seems to prefer the term 'conjunction' of natures rather than 'union,' and uses the metaphor of the union of husband and wife in marriage to express the union of two Natures in one Person. But in his desire to avoid Apollinarian error he opened the way for the theories of Nestorius, who taught that there was only 'a conjunction of the two Natures, an indwelling of the Godhead in the manhood united morally or by sympathy.' Such a union is mechanical, not vital. 'I separate the natures,' said Nestorius, 'but the reverence I pay them is just.' The strong point in his theory was the recognition of the Lord's true manhood. As Bright puts it, 'Nestorianism was really Trinitarian in one aspect, but in another it was inevitably, under whatever disguise, Humanitarian, or, in modern phrase, "Adoptianist"' (*Age of the Fathers* (1903), ii. 268).

5. We pass on to consider *the links which bound the later Spanish Adoptianism to earlier heresies.* There seems no doubt that Muhammadan rulers were inclined to patronize Nestorian Christians as more enlightened than their brethren. When the Arabs overthrew the Persian kingdom, they found Nestorian Christians strong. Muhammad himself is said to have cultivated the literary friendship of a Nestorian monk Sergius, and he gave privileges to Nestorians. They followed the Arabs everywhere, the Khalīfs appreciating their learning, and probably followed the Moors into Spain. Gams (*Kirchengesch. Spaniens*, ii. 2. 264) suggests that the mysterious 'Brothers of Cordova,' whom Elipandus, the first teacher of the heresy, quoted as writing much to him (he wrote to Felix in 799), were Nestorians. Alcuin traces the origin of the new error to Cordova (writing to Leidrat, he says: 'Maxime origo hujus perfidiæ de Corduba civitate processit'). And if they were not fully persuaded Nestorians, they may very well have been students of Theodore of Mopsuestia, whose works were read in the West. Gams also points out (*op. cit.*) that in his controversy with Migetius, Elipandus quoted Efren (=Ephraim the Syrian), suggesting that knowledge of his works seems to imply the presence of Nestorians in Spain.

6. *Elipandus*, Metropolitan of Toledo, was an old man when the trouble began (*c.* A.D. 780). It appears that he had successfully opposed the obscure heresy of Migetius, in which we can trace a lurking remnant of Priscillianism. Migetius taught that God was revealed in David (as Father), in Jesus (as Son), in St. Paul (as Holy Ghost), on the basis of an absurdly literal exegesis. (Thus he quotes David in Ps 44[2] (45[1]), 'Eructauit cor meum uerbum bonum'). From this extreme Elipandus turned to its opposite, and taught what with vehemence he declared to be the teaching of all the Fathers and of the Councils. Both he and his abler ally, Felix, bp. of Urgel, intended to teach the unity of Christ's Person while strictly distinguishing the Natures. They found the term 'adoption' in common use in their Spanish Liturgy,* and they argued that it was a fitting term to express the raising of the human nature to the dignity of Divinity. They taught that the Son is 'adoptive in His humanity, but not in His Divinity.'

It does not appear that the term 'adoption' in the Liturgy meant more than 'assumption.' Elipandus was rightly concerned to guard the reality of the human nature assumed, but overstated the case in his antithesis, teaching a double Sonship: as God, Christ is Son *genere et natura*; as man, He is Son *adoptione et gratia*. He roundly accused his opponents of teaching Eutychianism, that the manhood was derived from the being of the Father.

7. *Felix* followed on the same path. He transferred to the Person what was true of the nature. He taught that Christ as a servant needed grace, was not omniscient or omnipotent. As the Only-begotten Son, Christ says, 'I and the Father are one' (Jn 10[30]). As the 'First-born among many brethren' (Ro 8[29]) He is adopted with the adopted sons. Only thus can we be certain of our adoption.

Felix applied the phrase 'true and peculiar Son' (*uerus et proprius filius*) to the God-Logos alone, and did not shrink from the proposition 'the Son is believed one in two forms'; he distinguished between 'the one' and 'the other,' 'this one' and 'that,' nay, he called the Son of Man God by adoption (*nuncupatiuus deus*: meaning that He became God). He taught a dwelling of God in man, of the man who is united with Deity (Harnack, *op. cit.* v. 285). The Son of Man has two births, a natural birth of the Virgin, a spiritual birth by adoption and grace, begun in Baptism, completed in the Resurrection. Felix, indeed, taught that Christ was sinless, but that 'the old man,' *i.e.* our sinful nature, is regenerated in Him. Alcuin (ii. 18) found it difficult to believe that Felix was sincere when he seemed to regard Christ as needing regeneration.

8. When Elipandus published his theory in letters, the Abbot *Beatus* and the Bishop *Etherius* (Eterius, Heterius) entered the lists against him. He was amazed at their rashness. Toledo was not accustomed to take lessons from Asturias! He called his opponents names, of which 'servants of Antichrist' is a mild specimen. The controversy extended from Spain to France; and the Pope, Hadrian I., was drawn into it, not unwilling to deal with an independent Metropolitan. When Felix joined in the fray, the Synod of Regensburg was summoned, in A.D. 792. Felix defended himself in the presence of Charles the Great, but was vanquished in debate, and was sent in the company of Abbot Angilbert to the Pope. In Rome he signed a recantation; but when he returned to Urgel he repented of it, and fled into Saracen territory.

9. On his return from England, *Alcuin* wrote his first treatise against Felix. About the same time Elipandus and the Spanish bishops sent a treatise to the bishops of Gaul, Aquitania, and Asturias, and appealed to Charles to reinstate Felix. The Council of Frankfort met in the summer of A.D. 794, and was attended by representatives of the Pope as

* In the first passage quoted by Elipandus the text was doubtful (Alcuin, *adv. El.* ii. 7). In others the word did not mean more than *assumptio*. In *Missa in ascensione Domini*: 'Hodie saluator noster post adoptionem carnis sedem repetiit Deitatis. Hodie hominem suum intulit patri, quem obtulit passioni.'

well as by English theologians. It produced two dogmatic treatises—one by Frankish and German bishops; the other by the bishops of Upper Italy, led by Paulinus of Aquileia. They were sent by Charles to Elipandus, together with a treatise of Pope Hadrian. He begged him not to separate from the unity of the Church. In the spring of A.D. 798, Alcuin received a treatise from Felix, and asked Charles to invite replies from Paulinus of Aquileia, Richbod of Trèves, and Theodulf of Orleans, preparing also a reply of his own.

10. In the meantime Leidrat of Lyons, who with Nefridius of Narbonne and Abbot Benedict of Aniane had been conducting an active mission against the heresy in the district, met Felix and persuaded him to come to Court. In June A.D. 799 he met Alcuin at Aachen, and, after much discussion, was received back into the Church. He was put in charge of Leidrat, and remained at Lyons till his death. But Leidrat's successor, Agobard, after the death of Felix, found a posthumous treatise, in which some of the old errors were restated, and published a refutation, dealing particularly with the erroneous speculations of Felix on our Lord's ignorance (Agnoetism).

The heresy soon died out in the 9th cent. in the Frankish empire, though it is mentioned in the letters of Alvar of Cordova as surviving in his neighbourhood (*c.* A.D. 850). In the 11th and 12th cents. it was revived by some of the schoolmen, but did not become popular.

11. The chief result of the controversy was the fateful legacy of a theory of transubstantiation of the human personality in Christ, which the orthodox writers bequeathed to their successors, preparing the way for a theory of transubstantiation in the Eucharist. Alcuin (*c. Felic.* ii. 12) taught that '*in adsumptione carnis a deo, persona perit hominis, non natura.*' The idea was inherited from the Gallican Faustus of Riez, who had taught: '*Persona personam consumere potest*' (under the name Paschasius, *de Sp. sco.* ii. 4, quoted by Hooker in a famous passage, *Eccl. Pol.* v. 52. 3). Faustus had the legal conception of personality = ownership, most probably, in his mind, not a sort of semi-physical conception of consumption, as when the wick of a candle is consumed in the flame. There is danger in all such metaphors if they are pressed too far.

In every Christological controversy sacramental teaching has been involved. In Arian times, Hilary of Poitiers (*de Trin.* viii. 13) pleaded standard Eucharistic doctrine as a witness against error. Etherius and Beatus were right to show that the assumptions of their opponents brought about serious misunderstandings in Eucharistic teaching. But Harnack overstates their position when he argues that 'even in the instance of Beatus, the realistic conception of the Lord's Supper turns out to be a decisive motive against Adoptianism' (*op. cit.* v. 291).

12. In conclusion, it is pleasant to note that Alcuin (*Ep. ad Elip.*) wrote warmly in praise of the character of Felix, whose charm was also admitted after his death by Agobard (*op. cit.* 2).

LITERATURE.—Letters of Elipandus, *España Sagrada*, v. 524; *Etherii et Beati adv. Elip.* Lib. 2 [Migne, *Patr. Lat.* 96]; Alcuinus, *adv. Elip.*, *adv. Felic.* [Migne, 100, 101], Paulinus, Lib. 3 [Migne, 99], Agobardus [Migne, 104]; Gams, *Kirchengeschichte Spaniens*, ii. 2, 261 ff.; Baudissin, *Eulogius u. Alvar*; Möller, art. 'Adoptianismus' in *PRE*³.

A. E. BURN.

ADOPTION.

ADOPTION (among lower races).—1. Artificial kinship is a well-recognized and widely practised mode of strengthening societies founded, as savage and barbarous societies are, on real or pretended community of blood. By means of artificial kinship, strangers are adopted into a clan or kindred. Various methods are employed for this purpose, of which the most celebrated is the Blood Covenant (wh. see). In all societies based on blood-kinship, children are a common asset of great value, for the continuance of the society depends on them. Wealth of children is the supreme desire of families, and it matters comparatively little whether they are legitimate, or even whether they really have the family blood in their veins or not. Where natural means of obtaining children fail, therefore, artificial means are often freely resorted to. Moreover, the importance of children to the society leads to their being regarded with special tenderness and consideration; and even where there is no want of issue, children are adopted from motives of compassion. This is the case, to mention only two examples, among peoples as widely severed by race, environment, and culture as the Papuans and the North American Indians. Of the natives of Logea, an island off the coast of British New Guinea, we are told that on the occasion of a blood-feud after a successful raid, when it is customary to torture to death and eat the prisoners, the leader of the raid, being the owner of the prisoners, will sometimes save their lives and adopt them, according to sex and age, as father, mother, brother, sister, or child (Colonial Rep., No. 168, *Brit. New Guinea Annual Rep.* 1894–1895, p. 51). Elsewhere in New Guinea and the adjacent islands the purchase of children for adoption by women, either childless or with only small families or widows, or by families with children of one sex only, is a common practice (Kohler, in *ZVRW*, xiv. 365). So among the Osages and Kansas of North America 'children and women taken prisoners are preserved and adopted, especially into such families among their captors as have lost any of their members, either by sickness or war' (Hunter, *Memoirs of a Captivity*, 249). The Omahas practise adoption when a child, grandchild, nephew or niece has died, and some living person bears a real or fancied resemblance to the deceased (Dorsey, in 3rd Report of *BE*, 265).*

2. The effect of adoption is to transfer the child from the old kinship to the new. He ceases to be a member of the family to which he belongs by birth. He loses all rights, and is divested of all duties with regard to his real parents and kinsmen, and instead enters upon new duties and acquires new rights as the child of the family to which he is transferred, and of which he is now regarded in all respects as a native-born member. Very early in the development of the family as a social unit, in addition to the care of a parent during sickness and old age, the due performance of his funeral ceremonies and the cult of the ancestral *manes* were reckoned among the most important duties of a child. These are not always mentioned by ethnographical writers among the reasons for adoption; yet, where the religion of the people described lays stress upon them, they must always be taken into account. Thus the old Moravian writer Crantz, in describing the customs of the Eskimos

* Some of the North American tribes occasionally extended the practice of adoption so as to make it by analogy a transaction between entire groups of persons. Thus the Five Nations adopted the Tuscarora on their expulsion from North Carolina, about the year 1726, and admitted them, first as a boy, then through successive stages, as if they had been a single person, up to full equality. The Iroquois seem to have adopted the Delawares in a similar manner. In both cases the object was purely political, and the form of alliance (for such in effect it was) was probably dictated by circumstances (Hewitt in *Handbk. Amer. Ind.*, art. 'Adoption').

of Greenland, assigns as the only reason for adoption of children that the family has no children or only little ones, and that the husband in such a case adopts one or two orphan boys 'to assist him in providing food and to take care of his family in future times,' adding that 'the wife does the same with a girl or a widow' (Crantz, *History of Greenland*, i. 165); whereas we know from his own statements elsewhere in the book (pp. 205, 237), as well as from others, that an elaborate burial was given to a deceased Eskimo, that ghosts manifested themselves in various ways, asking for food by a singing in the ears; and that the dead were 'a kind of guardian spirits to their children and grandchildren' (Rink, *Tales and Traditions of the Eskimo*, 44, 63). Hence we may be led to infer that the reasons enumerated by Crantz were by no means the only reasons for adoption in Greenland. The inference is greatly strengthened by the express testimony of a careful observer about the Eskimos of Behring Strait, that 'a childless pair frequently adopt a child, either a girl or a boy, preferably the latter. This is done so that when they die there will be some one left whose duty it will be to make the customary feast and offerings to their shades at the festival of the dead. All of the Eskimos appear to have great dread of dying without being assured that their shades will be remembered during the festivals, fearing that, if neglected, they would thereby suffer destitution in the future life' (Nelson, in 18th Report of *BE*, 290).

3. Whatever may be the case among the Eskimos of Greenland, therefore, it is quite certain that those of Behring Strait practise adoption for reasons which include the perpetuation of the cult of the ancestral *manes*. At the other end of the habitable world the Bantus are distinguished by their devotion to the worship of ancestors. The race is so prolific that it rarely happens that a man dies without issue. When among the Baronga of Delagoa Bay the head of a kraal passes away without leaving a son, it is said that his village has departed, his name is broken. This is regarded as a supreme misfortune; and to avoid it the childless man has one means at his disposal, namely, the adoption of his sister's son. He gets a sister who is expecting to become a mother to come to his village, and there to give birth to her child. If a boy be born, he is made the heir, and is said to have restored his grandfather's village. For this purpose a chief may, it seems (though one below the rank of chief cannot), even adopt a stranger (Junod, *Les Baronga*, 121). The misfortune involved in the breaking of the name by the failure of children appears more clearly from a Zulu prayer to the family *manes*.

The worshipper says: 'Ye of such a place, which did such and such great actions, I ask of you that I may get cattle and children and wives, and have children by them, that your name may not perish, but it may still be said, "That is the village of so-and-so yonder." If I am alone, it may be I shall live long on the earth; if I have no children, at my death my name will come to an end; and you will be in trouble when you have to eat grasshoppers; for at the time of my death my village will come to an end, and you will have no place into which you can enter; you will die of cold on the mountains' (Callaway, *Religious Syst. of the Amazulu*, 224).

The Zulus are a people closely related, as well as geographically contiguous, to the Baronga. From what is here explicitly set forth concerning Zulu ideas, it may be legitimately concluded that the underlying motive for adopting a son in the manner practised by the Baronga, is that of providing for the worship of the dead by means of the sacrifices to be offered from time to time by the adopted son and his descendants.

4. It is, however, among races of higher civilization than the Eskimos or the Bantus that the connexion of adoption with the family cult is most clearly visible. Without anticipating what will be said below in special articles, it may be noted that the adoption ceremony often bears witness to this connexion. In Cambodia a solemn ceremony, though not absolutely essential to the validity of adoption, is often performed, and plays a great part in Cambodian custom. It is needless to relate the ceremony in detail. Suffice it to say that the following invocation is therein repeated:

'To-day, at a propitious hour, this man who, in consequence no doubt of a mistake on the part of nature, was born of other entrails, asks to be the son of so-and-so. Let so-and-so be his father, so-and-so his mother! It becomes us now to inform you of the matter, O deceased ancestors! Give us your benediction! Grant us favours and prosperity!' The formal adoption then takes place by the adoptive father or some other person on his behalf asperging the adopted son with water, counting nine, and crying: 'Come hither, run, O nineteen vital spirits!' Finally, the cotton threads with which the water has been sprinkled are bound to the wrists of the son thus admitted into the family (Aymonier, in *Excursions et Reconnaissances*, xiv. 189).

5. The ceremony of adoption has varied greatly. There is reason to believe that it originally consisted of a formal simulation of the natural act of birth, or of suckling. The former, as appears from the legend of the adoption of Herakles by Hera, recounted by Diodorus, was known in early times in Greece, and the same writer expressly tells us that it was still the practice of the barbarians. The Roman form seems to have been similar. It is still observed by the Turks in Bosnia; and a Slavonic folksong exhibits an empress as taking the son to be adopted into the palace and passing him through her silken vest that he might be called her heart's child (Krauss, *Sitte und Brauch der Süd-slaven*, 599 f.). The symbolism is, if crude, so natural that we need not be surprised at finding it very widespread. A story of the Tsimshians, a British Columbian tribe, represents a woman who purposed to adopt a child as sitting down and having the child placed between her legs, as if she had just given birth to it (Boas, *Indianische Sagen*, 275). Some of the Indian castes place the child in the lap of the person adopting it (Crooke, *Tribes and Castes of the N.W. Provinces and Oudh*, i. 59, 89). Saint Dominic was the adopted son of the Blessed Virgin. Accordingly, Roman Catholic painters have not hesitated to represent 'the whole countless host of Dominicans crowded under her dress' (Milman, *History of Lat. Christianity*[4], vi. 22 note). Although in England adoption has not been recognized within the historical period, a vulgar belief, which is said to have lingered into recent times, that a mother might legitimate her children born before marriage by taking them under her clothes during the marriage ceremony, seems to point to the existence at an earlier period of a rite of adoption simulating the act of birth.

6. Among the races of the North of Africa the ancient rite was by suckling. It is constantly alluded to in Berber and Kabyle stories. It is mentioned in stories told to-day in Egypt, and was probably the usual form among the ancient Egyptians (Basset, *Nouveaux Contes Berbères*, 128, 339; Wiedemann in *Am Urquell*, iii. 239). The development of the paternal at the expense of the maternal line of descent has in Africa and elsewhere transferred the rite to the man who adopts a son. Among the Gallas at Kambat, in the Eastern Horn of Africa, the son to be adopted sucks blood from the breast of his adoptive father (Paulitschke, *Ethnographie Nordost-Afrikas*, i. 193). In Abyssinia the son to be adopted takes the hand of the adoptive father and sucks one of his fingers, declaring himself to be his child by adoption. Sir George Robertson was thus constituted his adopted father by an old Kafir in the Hindu-Kush. On another occasion a man desirous of being his adopted son smeared butter on his left breast and sucked it (Robertson, *Káfirs of the*

Hindu-Kush, 203, 30). The Circassians practise adoption by the suckling rite. The woman offers her breast to the son to be adopted. So far is this carried, that if a murderer can by any means, even by force, succeed in sucking the breast of the mother of one whom he has slain, he becomes her son; and it ends a vendetta if the offender can simply manage to plant three kisses on the breast of the mother of the injured man (Darinsky, in *ZVRW*, xiv. 168; *L'Anthropologie*, vii. 229).

These crude ceremonies, of course, disappeared from the higher culture long before the custom of adoption itself passed away.

E. SIDNEY HARTLAND.

ADOPTION (Chinese).—Adoption is in China principally a religious institution, based upon ancestor-worship, which demands perpetuation of the family and the tribe.

The most sacred duty of a child, inculcated by the ancient classics, consists in absolute obedience and submission to the will of its parents, combined with the highest degree of affection and devotion. This duty, called *hiao*, naturally does not terminate with death. Father and mother, having entered the spiritual state, then become the patron divinities of their offspring. They reside in their tombs, and also at home on the altar, in wooden tablets inscribed with their names. The sons and their wives have to feed and clothe them by means of sacrifices prescribed with great precision by formal customary law, in order to protect them from hunger and cold, privation and misery, and themselves from punishment and misfortune. The *hiao* extends also to grandparents, and still more remote ancestors of the family, who likewise are tutelary divinities. Lest the sacrifices should cease, it is both a necessity and a duty for everybody to have sons, in order that they may continue the ancestor-worship. The saying of Mencius, 'Three things are unfilial, and the worst is to have no sons,' is a dogma of social and religious life to this day. Daughters are of no use in this respect; for, in accordance with the peremptory law of exogamy dominating China's social life probably from the earliest times, a daughter leaves her paternal tribe to enter that of her husband, and this secession means the adoption of her husband's ancestors.

A married man who has no son, either by his principal wife or by a concubine, is therefore bound to obtain one by adoption. According to ancient custom, confirmed by the laws of the State, he may adopt only a son of his brother, or a grandson of his father's brother, or a great-grandson of his paternal grand-uncle, and so on; in other words, an adopted successor must be a member of the same tribe, and thus a bearer of the adopter's tribe-name; and moreover, he must be a member of the generation following that of the adopter.

An adopted successor holds the position of a genuine son: he possesses the same rights, and has the same duties to perform.

Adoption is unusual, and at any rate not necessary, for those who have sons of their own; and it is unlawful for any man who has only one son to give him away for adoption.

The adoption of a son may, of course, be sealed by means of a written contract, but in most cases no such contract is made. It is an important event for the family, and, like all such events, is superintended by the elders of the family, whose tacit sanction is necessary. The intervention of the authorities is neither asked nor given, and so long as no glaring transgression of the laws of adoption is committed, and no complaints are lodged by the elders, they will not interfere. The consummation of the event is in the main religious, being solemnly announced to the soul-tablets in both homes by the respective fathers; and the son has, with prostrations and incense-offering, to take leave of those in his father's house, and in the same way to introduce himself to those in the house of his adoptive father. Should his natural father and his adoptive father have the same family-altar, there is, of course, only the one announcement before it.

J. J. M. DE GROOT.

ADOPTION (Greek).—**1. Origin and meaning of the institution.**—In the minds of the Greeks and Romans there were three things closely, and at first inseparably, connected,—the family organization, the family worship (that is, the worship of the dead ancestors of the family back to the common ancestor of the group of families constituting the clan or *γένος*, *gens*), and the family estate. It was the rule in both Greek and Roman law that the property could not be acquired without the obligations of the cultus, nor the cultus without the property or some share in it (Plato, *Laws*, v. 740, calls the heir *διάδοχος θεῶν*; Isæus, vi. 51: *πότερον δεῖ τὸν ἐκ ταύτης τῶν Φιλοκτήμονος εἶναι κληρόνομον καὶ ἐπὶ τὰ μνήματα ἰέναι χεόμενον καὶ ἐναγιοῦντα*; Cic. *de Leg*. ii. 19). It was imperative that the family should not die out, and the family cultus thus become extinct. To ordinary Greek sentiment, neglect in the grave was a calamity almost as much to be dreaded as the total omission of sepulchral rites (Eur. *Suppl*. 540: *δειλίαν γὰρ εἰσφέρει τοῖς ἀλκίμοισιν*, *sc*. to lie unburied). Hence the prayer of the pious for children, as a guarantee that the spirit should not be 'an unfed and famished citizen of the other world, for lack of friends or kinsmen on earth' (Luc. *de Luct*. 9). In the perpetuity of the family the corporation of the *gens* and the State itself were both directly interested (Is. vii. 30: *νόμῳ γὰρ τῷ ἄρχοντι τῶν οἴκων, ὅπως ἂν μὴ ἐξερήμωνται, προστάττει τὴν ἐπιμέλειαν*—according to the usual interpretation, which is, however, very doubtful). It was, however, a principle equally fundamental that the family and the cult could be continued only through males; a daughter could not continue the cult, because on marriage she passed into her husband's family. A legitimate son was therefore the prime object of marriage. It was from these principles that the regulations concerning inheritance and the institution of adoption sprang.

The institution of adoption was thus a necessary outcome of the desire to perpetuate the family and the family cultus. 'Adoption is the factitious creation of blood-relationship' (Maine, *Anc. Law*, new ed. 1906, p. 206), and is the earliest and most extensively employed of legal fictions (*ib*. p. 133). For Greece, adoption is apparently ascribed by Aristotle to Philolaos,* a Corinthian who migrated to Thebes and 'gave the Thebans laws respecting parentage, the laws of adoption (*νόμοι θετικοί*) as they are called . . . which were meant to preserve the number of allotments without change' (Ar. *Pol*. ii. 9, p. 1274*b*). In Athens adoption is older than Solon's legislation (B.C. 594), as is clear from the important law several times cited by the orators (*e.g*. Demos. xlvi. 14: *ὅσοι μὴ ἐπεποίηντο, ὥστε μήτε ἀπειπεῖν μήτε ἐπιδικάσασθαι, ὅτε Σόλων εἰσῄει τὴν ἀρχήν, κ.τ.λ.*). In Sparta it is older than Herodotus (about B.C. 480), who cites the regulation that adoptions must take place before the kings (vi. 57); in Crete it is older than the great inscription known as the Code of Gortyna,† which was inscribed about B.C. 450, but contains much earlier matter. Isæus (ii. 13) speaks of the right of adoption as being founded upon Solon's law of testament; but this is to invert the order of development. The institution is, in fact, much older than we have records to show, and was one of the most primitive factors in ancient life. Our knowledge of its regulations being derived mainly from the extant orations, especially those of Isæus and those ascribed to Demosthenes, in cases of disputed inheritance, is chiefly limited to Athenian law; but the Code of Gortyna shows considerable differences, and makes it probable that there were wide divergences in details in the various Greek States.

2. Adoption a form of will.—The primitive idea of the institution—that of an authorized fiction of direct descent, 'demanding of religion and law

* The date of Philolaos was about B.C. 725.

† Fabricius in *Mittheil. Ath.* 1885, p. 362 f. The regulations concerning adoption are given in full, with tr. and comments, in Roberts, *Introd. to Greek Epigraphy*, Part i. p. 326 f.

that which Nature had denied' (Cic. *pro Dom.* xiii. 14)—is frequently expressed by the orators (cf. Is. ii. 10: *ὅς τις ζῶντα τε γηροτροφήσοι καὶ τελευτήσαντα θάψοι αὐτὸν καὶ εἰς τὸν ἔπειτα χρόνον τὰ νομιζόμενα αὐτῷ ποιήσοι*. *Id.* ii. 46: *ἄπαιδα δὲ τὸν τελευτήσαντα καὶ ἀνώνυμον βούλεται καταστῆσαι, ἵνα μήτε τὰ ἱερὰ τὰ πατρῷα ὑπὲρ ἐκείνου μηδεὶς τιμᾷ μήτ' ἐναγίζῃ αὐτῷ καθ' ἕκαστον ἐνιαυτόν,* ἀλλ' ἀφαιρῆται τὰς τιμὰς τὰς ἐκείνου*). Nevertheless, this idea became overlaid with others as rationalism prevailed. The Athenian of the days of Isæus adopted a son, in very many cases at least, primarily in order to leave him property, or for other reasons. In other words, adoption, gradually losing to a large extent its early significance as a means of supplementing nature (Demos. xliv. 43: *ὅπως ἂν ὁ οἶκος μὴ ἐξερημωθῇ*), was used as a means of testamentary bequest, thereby overcoming a legal disability. For it must be remembered that 'Intestate Inheritance is a more ancient institution than Testamentary Succession' (Maine, *op. cit.* p. 207), and that normally (*i.e.* if he had a legitimate son) an Athenian could not make a will †—so the law is usually stated, but it may be doubted whether it was strictly enforced, at least in the 4th cent. B.C. (cf. Meier u. Schömann, *Der attische Process*[2], p. 591 f.; Wyse on Is. iii. 42 and vi. 28). If he died without legitimate male issue, and without a will, the relatives of the deceased, in an order fixed by law, were his heirs. The Athenian will, therefore, though only an 'inchoate testament' (Maine, *op. cit.* p. 208), together with adoption, which was the form in which testamentary disposition of property was as a rule made, interrupted the ordinary course of descent of family and property. In other words, an Athenian, availing himself of the right of adoption *inter vivos* or by testament, very often was actuated by the desire of *disinheriting* some one of his possible heirs-at-law (Demos. xliv. 63: *ὁρᾶτε γὰρ ὅτι ταῖς κολακείαις οἱ πλεῖστοι φυγαγωγούμενοι καὶ ταῖς πρὸς τοὺς οἰκείους διαφοραῖς πολλάκις φιλονεικοῦντες ποιητοὺς υἱεῖς ποιοῦνται*). This fact explains not only the frequency of disputes over wills and inheritances at Athens, but also the method of handling such followed by the pleaders, *e.g.* Isæus. The impression gathered from the speeches is that it was perhaps impossible for an Athenian to safeguard the heir of his choice against the assaults of disappointed relatives. And, herein a great contrast to the Roman courts, the tendency of Athenian juries was to 'vote for the relatives rather than for the will' (Arist. *Prob.* xxix. 3).

3. Methods of adoption.—In Athens there were three methods of adoption: (1) adoption *inter vivos*, i.e. during lifetime (cf. Is. ii. 14: *διδόντων οὖν τῶν νόμων αὐτῷ ποιεῖσθαι διὰ τὸ εἶναι ἄπαιδα, ἐμὲ ποιεῖται, οὐκ ἐν διαθήκαις γράψας, μέλλων ἀποθνήσκειν, ὥσπερ ἄλλοι τινές*); (2) adoption by will, taking effect only on death of the testator (see quotation above); (3) 'posthumous adoption,' by which if a man died without legitimate male issue, and without having adopted a son, the next-of-kin succeeding to the estate, or his issue, was adopted into the family of the deceased as his son. (The rules of this mode of adoption are not known, and our evidence is meagre. Instances are the following—Is. xi. 49, vii. 31; Demos. xliii. 11, this last an example of such adoption deferred for many years, and performed in the end simply as a manœuvre in view of a lawsuit. See Wyse, note on Is. x. 8). In Gortyna the procedure of adoption is of archaic simplicity, the act being public and oral, as its name there (*ἄνφανσις*, 'announcement') denotes—'Announcement of adoption shall be made in the Agora, when the citizens are assembled, from the stone from which speeches are made. And the adopter shall give to his *ἑταιρία* a victim and a pitcher of wine.' The Spartan mode (Herod. vi. 57) must have been similar.

4. Conditions regulating adoption.—The conditions under which adoption in Athens was possible were as follows. Since adoption was in reality a sort of willing, it could be performed only by him who was competent to make a will, that is, by a man only, not by a woman, nor by a minor * (*i.e.* one under the age of eighteen—Ar. *Ath. Pol.* 42). The adopter must be in full possession of his faculties, and not acting under undue influence (the vagueness of this last condition afforded a loophole for litigation, cf. Ar. *Ath. Pol.* 35). The proviso that the adopting citizen should have no legitimate son living, or, if he had, that he might then effect only a provisional adoption by will, followed directly from the underlying idea of the institution (Demos. xlvi. 24: *ὅ τι ἂν γνησίων ὄντων υἱέων ὁ πατὴρ διαθῆται, ἐὰν ἀποθάνωσιν οἱ υἱεῖς πρὶν ἐπὶ διετὲς ἡβᾶν, τὴν τοῦ πατρὸς διαθήκην κυρίαν εἶναι*. Cf. Plato, *Laws*, xi. 923 E). The adopted son must be a citizen of citizen parents, acting with his own consent, if of age, or that of his guardian (*κύριος*) if a minor. Neither party must stand under accountability to the State (*ὑπεύθυνος*) for conduct of office (Æschin. *in Ctes.* 21). Penal loss of civic rights (*ἀτιμία*) on either side would practically prevent adoption, especially as certain forms of such disfranchisement (*e.g.* the disabilities of a debtor to the Treasury) were transmitted to children and heirs until their removal (Demos. xliii. 58. Cf. the decree against Antiphon and his associates—*καὶ ἄτιμον εἶναι Ἀρχεπτόλεμον καὶ Ἀντιφῶντα, καὶ γένος τὸ ἐκ τούτοιν, καὶ νόθους καὶ γνησίους· καὶ ἐὰν ποιήσηταί τινα τῶν ἐξ Ἀρχεπτολέμου καὶ Ἀντιφῶντος, ἄτιμος ἔστω ὁ ποιησάμενος*). Hence men who had reason to fear condemnation involving such *ἀτιμία* were fain to secure previous adoption of their sons (Æschin. *in Ctes.* 21; Is. x. 17: *ἕτεροι μέν, ὅταν περὶ χρήματα δυστυχῶσι, τοὺς σφετέρους αὐτῶν παῖδας εἰς ἑτέρους οἴκους εἰσποιοῦσιν, ἵνα μὴ μετασχῶσι τῆς τοῦ πατρὸς ἀτιμίας*). The field of choice was legally unrestricted, at any rate after the time of Solon, though probably most men naturally looked for an adoptive son within the circle of their relatives.

5. The formalities of adoption.—As regards the ceremonies of adoption, the following procedure is spoken of by the orators, but it was perhaps neither universal nor legally enjoined (Is. vii. 15). The adoptive son was introduced to the members of his adoptive father's *phratry*—probably on the third and last day of the *Apaturia* (=October, roughly), as was the case with children of the body. The father offered the customary sacrifice (*μεῖον*), and took oath that his adoptive son was a genuine Athenian citizen; thereafter, with the consent of the assembled *phratries*,† the son's name was enrolled on the register of the *phratry* (*κοινόν* or *φρατορικὸν γραμματεῖον*; cf. Demos. xliv. 41). Subsequently (and if the adopted son was a minor, not until he came of age), and purely as a civic, not religious, act, the name was entered by the head of the father's *deme* on the *deme* roll (*ληξιαρχικὸν γραμματεῖον*) with the consent of the members of the *deme* (Demos. xliv. 39). These two enrolments, the one *quasi*-religious, the other purely political, gave the necessary opportunities for interference on the part of those who on public or private grounds had reason to oppose the adoption. The

* For these annual offerings to the dead, see Wyse, *The Speeches of Isæus*, note *in loc.*

† So in Gortyna testaments are unknown, even in the rudimentary form introduced at Athens by Solon. The code seems, in fact, concerned to combat the tendencies which produced the testament.

* These two conditions of sex and age are insisted upon in the Gortynian Code.

† At Gortyna there is no hint that the citizens are anything but witnesses, or that the *ἑταιρία* has any right of refusal of entry of the adopted son.

adopted son usually retained his old name, altering only the name of his father in writing his full signature, and if necessary that of his *deme* (see Keil in *Rhein. Mus.* xx. [1865] p. 539 f.).

6. Rights and duties of an adopted son.—The adopted son stepped at once from the family of his natural father into that of his adoptive father; he lost his relationship to his natural father, and all rights inherent therein (Is. ix. 33: οὐδεὶς γὰρ πώποτε ἐκποίητος γενόμενος ἐκληρονόμησε τοῦ οἴκου ὅθεν ἐξεποιήθη, ἐὰν μὴ ἐπανέλθῃ κατὰ τὸν νόμον); but he did not lose his relationship to his mother (if we may trust the statement of Is. vii. 25: μητρὸς δ' οὐδεὶς ἐστιν ἐκποίητος, ἀλλ' ὁμοίως ὑπάρχει τὴν αὐτὴν εἶναι μητέρα, κἂν ἐν τῷ πατρῴῳ μένῃ τις οἴκῳ κἂν ἐκποιηθῇ—which would seem to mean that an adopted son still retained his rights of next-of-kin so far as they belonged to him through his mother). He became the legal and necessary heir of his adoptive father, taking up and continuing the *sacra* of his new family, and possessing the right of burial in its sepulchre. Like a legitimate son of the body, he was entitled to enter without legal formalities into possession of his estate upon his adoptive father's death (Demos. xliv. 19: ἐνεβάτευσεν οὕτως εἰς τὴν οὐσίαν ὡς ὑπ' ἐκείνου ζῶντος ἔτι εἰσποιηθείς). Collaterals (ἀγχιστεῖς) and testamentary heirs, on the other hand, were forbidden to enter on occupation before their claim had been established in a court of law (ἐπιδικασία. Cf. Is. *frg.* iii. 6: οὐ δεῖ τὸν ἐπίδικον κρατεῖσθαι κλῆρον πρὸ δίκης. *Id.* vi. 3: λαχόντος δὲ τοῦ Χαιρεστράτου κατὰ τὸν νόμον τοῦ κλήρου, ἐξὸν ἀμφισβητῆσαι Ἀθηναίων τῷ βουλομένῳ, and cf. *ib.* iii. 60). Like a son of the body, an adopted son had no option of refusal of the inheritance, as had heirs-at-law (Demos. xxxv. 4. *Att. Proc.*[2] 573, *n.* 252).* Even if legitimate male children were born to his adoptive father subsequently to the adoption, the adopted son ranked with them for equal share of the property according to the law of inheritance (Is. vi. 63: καὶ διαρρήδην ἐν τῷ νόμῳ γέγραπται, ἐὰν ποιησαμένῳ παῖδες ἐπιγένωνται, τὸ μέρος ἑκάτερον ἔχειν τῆς οὐσίας καὶ κληρονομεῖν ὁμοίως ἀμφοτέρους. *Id.* vi. 25: τοῦ νόμου κελεύοντος ἅπαντας τοὺς γνησίους ἰσομοίρους εἶναι τῶν πατρῴων).†

The inheritance of a son adopted *inter vivos* could not be diminished, for after the act of adoption the father's limited power of testamentary disposition was, theoretically at least, *ipso facto* abrogated; only in the case of a testamentary adoption could any control over the disposition of the property be exercised, and that only in a general way (Is. v. 6: καὶ ἐπὶ μὲν τῷ τρίτῳ μέρει τοῦ κλήρου Δικαιογένης ὅδε τῷ Μενεξένου Δικαιογένει υἱὸς ἐγίγνετο ποιητός). If the adopted son left behind him a legitimate son of his body (γνήσιος υἱός) in the house of his adoptive father, thereby fulfilling the object of his adoption, he might return to his natural father's house, and there resume all the rights and duties of a son, relinquishing all such claims in respect of his adoptive father's estate (Harpocr. *s.v.* ὅτι: ὅτι οἱ ποιητοὶ παῖδες ἐπανελθεῖν εἰς τὸν πατρῷον οἶκον οὐκ ἦσαν κύριοι, εἰ μὴ παῖδας γνησίους καταλίποιεν ἐν τῷ οἴκῳ τοῦ ποιησαμένου). He could not, however, so leave behind him an adopted son; he had, in fact, no power himself of adoption, either in his lifetime or by will, so long as his own status was that of an adopted son; he transmitted the estate only to an heir of his body (Demos. xliv. 63: οὐ δίκαιον δήπου τὸν ποιητὸν υἱὸν ποιητοὺς ἑτέρους εἰσάγειν, ἀλλ' ἐγκαταλείπειν μὲν γιγνομένους, ὅταν δὲ τοῦτ' ἐπιλείπῃ, τοῖς γένεσιν ἀποδιδόναι τὰς κληρονομίας. *Ib.* 68: τοῖς δὲ ποιηθεῖσιν οὐκ ἐξὸν διαθέσθαι, ἀλλὰ ζῶντας ἐγκαταλιπόντας υἱὸν γνήσιον ἐπανιέναι, ἢ τελευτήσαντας ἀποδιδόναι τὴν κληρονομίαν τοῖς ἐξ ἀρχῆς οἰκείοις οὖσι τοῦ ποιησαμένου). Nor, on the other hand, could he restore the line of his natural father by putting back one of his own sons; he must return himself if he wished to keep alive his father's house (Is. x. 11). In this way the law protected the rights of the next-of-kin (ἀγχιστεῖς). If the adopted son died without male issue, or by consent of his adoptive father returned to his natural family, the οἶκος of his adoptive father fell at the death of the latter to the heirs *ab intestato* (ἀγχιστεῖς), as before the adoption—provided that no new adoption had been made either *inter vivos* or by testament (Demos. xliv. 68, and xliv. 47: ὁ δ' ἐγκαταλειφθεὶς ὑπὸ τούτου τελευταῖος ἁπάντων τῶν εἰσποιηθέντων τετελεύτηκεν ἄπαις, ὥστε γίγνεται ἔρημος ὁ οἶκος καὶ ἐπανελήλυθεν ἡ κληρονομία πάλιν εἰς τοὺς ἐξ ἀρχῆς ἐγγύτατα γένους ὄντας).* Apparently mutual consent was necessary for the repudiation of an adoption once made; it is doubtful how far an adoptive father could act alone herein, *e.g.* in case of unfilial conduct (in fact, a father's right of repudiation—ἀποκήρυξις—of a son, either adoptive or child of his body, may be a pure fiction; in any case, it is certain that he could not disinherit him by testament).† It seems that the Gortynian Code allowed one-sided repudiation of the bond; this is in accord with its whole treatment of the institution.

The law protected the rights not only of the next-of-kin, as above, but also of the female children of a father who adopted a son. The estate could not be willed away from a daughter, either by testament or by adoption; it must go 'with her' (Is. iii. 68: ὁ γὰρ νόμος διαρρήδην λέγει ἐξεῖναι διαθέσθαι ὅπως ἂν ἐθέλῃ τις τὰ αὑτοῦ, ἐὰν μὴ παῖδας γνησίους καταλίπῃ ἄρρενας· ἂν δὲ θηλείας καταλίπῃ, σὺν ταύταις. οὐκοῦν μετὰ θυγατέρων ἔστι δοῦναι καὶ διαθέσθαι τὰ αὑτοῦ· ἄνευ δὲ τῶν γνησίων θυγατέρων οὐχ οἷόν τε οὔτε ποιήσασθαι οὔτε δοῦναι οὐδενὶ οὐδὲν τῶν ἑαυτοῦ. Cf. Is. x. 13; Demos. xliii. 51). On the other hand, a daughter was incapable of performing the worship which was a condition of tenure of the estate. From the conflict of these two principles sprang the strange regulations concerning heiresses (ἐπίκληροι, lit. 'those on the estate'). He who took the estate (κλῆρος) took also the daughter who was 'on the estate' (ἐπίκληρος). A son, therefore, adopted during lifetime, generally espoused a daughter of his adoptive father, if there was one of marriageable age, even if it were not legally required of him to do so (Demos. xli. 3); a son adopted by will was legally bound to marry the testator's legitimate daughter, otherwise the will and the adoption became invalid, and a door was opened to the claim of the next-of-kin both to the daughter and the estate (Is. iii. 42, x. 13). We do not know what a father could lawfully do if, his daughters being already married, he wished to adopt a man who was not his son-in-law. The son, not the husband, of an heiress became heir to the estate of her father, but the husband enjoyed the usufruct until the son came of age (Demos. xlvi. 20: καὶ ἐὰν ἐξ ἐπικλήρου τις γένηται, καὶ ἅμα ἡβήσῃ ἐπὶ διετές, κρατεῖν τῶν χρημάτων, τὸν δὲ σῖτον μετρεῖν τῇ μητρί. Cf. Is. iii. 50). Posthumous adoption of the heir into the house of his maternal grandfather as his son was probably usual, but cannot be proved to have been a legal obligation.

* The Gortynian Code allows the adopted son to repudiate his inheritance.

† The Gortynian Code treats the adopted son less generously, giving him only the rights of a daughter when the adoptive father leaves legitimate children; that is to say, if there are other sons, he is to receive half a son's portion; if there are daughters only, he is to share equally with his adoptive sisters. The Code is concerned to depose the artificial son from a position of equality with natural heirs.

* So in the Gortynian law.

† Consult Mitteis, *Reichsrecht und Volksrecht*, p. 336; also Ramsay, *Histor. Com. on Galatians*, pp. 337 f. and 349 f. But the latter makes several sweeping assertions which are hardly capable of proof, or at best based upon the Roman-Syrian Law-Book of the 5th cent. A.D. Even the quotation from Lucian, *Abdic.* 12, can hardly prove anything for Athens of the 4th cent. B.C.

It is obvious that by adopting a daughter's son a man could guard against contentions for the hand of his daughter, and defeat the designs of rapacious relatives; nevertheless, instances of adoption of a grandson (son of a daughter) on the part of a grandfather are rare (Wyse on Is. viii. 36).

7. Decay of the institution of adoption.—Was it possible under Athenian law to adopt a daughter? A woman could not perpetuate in her own person the house and its cult, which was one of the main objects of adoption. Nevertheless, examples of the adoption of a daughter are found. Isæus furnishes two examples of the adoption of a niece by will (xi. 8 and 41); but in the first case the niece was perhaps also heiress *ab intestato*, apart from the adoption, and it is also doubtful whether the adoption was not *inter vivos*. A third example puzzles the lawyers (Is. vii. 9: *διέθετο τὴν οὐσίαν καὶ ἔδωκε τῇ ἐκείνου μὲν θυγατρί, ἐμῇ δὲ μητρί, αὐτοῦ δὲ ἀδελφῇ, διδοὺς αὐτὴν Λακρατείδῃ*). It is generally taken to mean that in his will Apollodoros adopted his half-sister, who was also his heiress *ab intestato*, thus acquiring the right of a father to dispose of his daughter in marriage (*Att. Proc.*[2] 505, *n.* 75). But Apollodoros had not become the adoptive father of the girl when he made his will and settled the marriage, since the adoption was only to take effect in the event of his death on foreign service (an event which did not occur).

The adoption of a daughter (*θυγατροποιΐα*), certainly not contemplated in earlier times, but never expressly forbidden, probably grew to be practised (though to what extent we know not) largely as a family manœuvre, as public sentiment became less strict, and the definitely religious aspect of the institution tended to fade from view. There are other traces of this change. Thus in the fragmentary speech of Isæus in defence of Euphiletos there is a reference to the adoption of non-Athenians irregularly for personal reasons (Is. xii. 2: *διὰ πενίαν ἀναγκαζομένους ξένους ἀνθρώπους εἰσποιεῖσθαι, ὅπως ὠφελῶνταί τι ἀπ' αὐτῶν δι' αὐτοὺς Ἀθηναίων γεγονότων*). Similarly, the necessity of providing a male descendant came to be felt less strongly. It is clear that many Athenians in the 4th cent. B.C. died unmarried and without troubling to adopt a son (Is. xi. 49; Demos. xliv. 18). The Code of Gortyna exhibits the same change. It is by no means certain that by it adoption was not permissible even when a man already had both sons and daughters. Its less stringent regulations concerning heiresses (*πατρωιῶκοι = ἐπίκληροι*); the fact that the next-of-kin might, as at Athens, shirk his spiritual duties to the deceased if he cared to waive his claim to the estate; the ease with which the bond created by adoption could be broken (by simple announcement from the stone in the Agora before the assembled citizens); and, above all, the fact that the adopted son might eventually decline his inheritance (which was his only on the express condition that he took over all the spiritual and temporal obligations of the deceased)—all testify to the gradual transformation and decay of the old institution.

W. J. WOODHOUSE.

ADOPTION (Hindu).—The adoption of a son (*putrasaṅgraha*) amongst the Aryan Hindus, as observed by Sir R. West, is essentially a religious act. The ceremonies in an adoption, as described in the Sanskrit lawbooks, resemble the formalities at a wedding; adoption consisting, like marriage, in the transfer of paternal dominion over a child, which passes to the adopter in the one case and to the husband in the other. One desirous of adopting a son has to procure two garments, two earrings and a finger-ring, a learned priest, sacred grass, and fuel of sacred wood. He has next to give notice to the king (or to the king's representative in the village), and convene the kindred, no doubt for the purpose of giving publicity to the transaction, and of having the son acknowledged as their relative by the kindred. The adopter has to say to the natural father, 'Give me thy son.' The father replies, 'I give him'; whereupon the adopter declares, 'I accept thee for the fulfilment of religion, I take thee for the continuation of lineage.' After that, the adopter adorns the boy with the two garments, the two earrings, and the finger-ring, and performs the *Vyāhṛti-Homa* or *Datta-Homa*, *i.e.* a burnt-sacrifice coupled with certain invocations, apparently from the idea that the conversion of one man's child into the son of another cannot be effected without the intervention of the gods. The learned priest obtains the two garments, the earrings, and the finger-ring as his sacrificial fee. Where the ceremony of tonsure [see TONSURE (Hindu)] has already been performed for the boy in his natural family, a special ceremony called *putreṣṭi*, or sacrifice for male issue, has to be performed in addition to the burnt-sacrifice, in order to undo the effects of the tonsure rite. The motive for adoption assigned in the Sanskrit commentaries is a purely religious one, viz. the conferring of spiritual benefits upon the adopter and his ancestors by means of the ceremony of ancestor-worship. The Code of Manu (ix. 138) has a fanciful derivation of the word *putra*, 'a son,' as denoting 'the deliverer from the infernal region called *put*.' In the same way, it is declared by Vasiṣṭha (xvii. 1) that 'if a father sees the face of a son born and living, he throws his debts on him and obtains immortality.' Another ancient text says, 'Heaven awaits not one who has no male issue.' These and other texts, laudatory of the celestial bliss derived from the male issue, are cited by eminent commentators in support of the obligation to adopt on failure of male posterity. The importance of this practice was enhanced by writers on adoption, who declared as obsolete in the present age (*Kaliyuga*) the other ancient devices for obtaining a substitute for a legitimate son of the body, such as appointing a widow to raise issue to her deceased husband, or a daughter to her sonless father, or legitimatizing the illegitimate son of one's wife, etc. These writers are unanimous in declaring that none but the legitimate son of the body (*aurasa*) and the adopted son (*dattaka*) are sons in the proper sense of the term and entitled to inherit. Adoption, no doubt, has continued, down to the present day, one of the most important institutions of the Indian Family Law, and its leading principles, as developed in the writings of Indian commentators, are fully recognized by the British courts, and form the basis of the modern case-law on the subject. On the other hand, it must not be supposed that the religious motive for adoption in India has ever in reality excluded or prevailed over the secular motive. The existence of adoption among the Jainas and other Hindu dissenters, who do not offer the oblations to the dead that form the foundation of the spiritual benefit conferred by sons, proves that the custom of adoption did not arise from the religious belief that a son is necessary for the salvation of man. In the Panjāb, adoption is common to the Jats, Sikhs, and even to the Muhammadans; but with them the object is simply to make an heir.

LITERATURE.—Stokes, *Hindu Law Books*, Madras, 1865; G. Bühler, 'The Sacred Laws of the Aryans,' part ii. in *SBE*, vol. xiv.; West and Bühler, *A Digest of the Hindu Law*[3], 2 vols., Bombay, 1887; Mayne, *Hindu Law and Usage*[6], Madras, 1900; G. Sarkar, *The Hindu Law of Adoption*, Tagore Law Lectures, Calcutta, 1891; Jolly, *Recht und Sitte*, Strassburg, 1896. See Hindu section of artt. SLAVERY, LAW AND LAW-BOOKS, INSTITUTIONS.

J. JOLLY.

ADOPTION (Japanese).—Adoption, now widely prevalent in Japan, is not a native institution. It was first introduced from China for a political purpose during the rule of the Hōjō Regents (1205–1333). Its importance is chiefly social and legal. The legal unit in Japan is the family and not the individual; hence, when there is no natural-born heir, adoption becomes necessary in order to provide a representative in whose person it shall be continued. But the religious point of view is by no means overlooked. The adopted son, on the death of his foster-father, takes charge of the family tombs and attends to the domestic religious observances, whether Shinto, Buddhist, or ancestral, just as if he were the real son. Their neglect, for want of an heir, would be considered a great calamity. There is no ceremony of adoption, but registration at the public office of the district is essential.

LITERATURE.—Gubbins, *Civil Code of Japan*, pt. ii.; Lloyd, 'A Japanese Problem-play' in the *Transactions of the Asiatic Society of Japan*, 1905. W. G. ASTON.

ADOPTION (Muhammadan).—In Arabia, in the days of Muhammad, a man could adopt another person as his son (Arab. *tabannâ*, تبنّى). The Prophet himself adopted Zaid ibn Ḥāritha. The latter was carried away in his youth as a slave and came into Muhammad's possession in Mecca. Some of his own tribesmen recognized Zaid and told his father Ḥāritha, who went to Mecca to offer a ransom for his son. Zaid, however, chose to remain with the Prophet, upon which the latter gave him his freedom and adopted him as his son, saying, 'He shall be my heir and I his.' Since that time he was called Zaid ibn Muhammad.

Many other instances of adoption are known in Arabic literature. But as a rule it does not appear that in Arabia adoption was practised exclusively for the purpose of saving the family from extinction. Often the idea apparently was merely to incorporate a certain person into a family, for one reason or another; as, *e.g.*, when a man, on marrying a woman who already had children from a former marriage, adopted her children as his own. Children of slave girls, begotten by the owner, were regarded as slaves, but it sometimes occurred that the father adopted them as his own children (as was the case with the famous poet 'Antara when he had given proof of ability). He who, having shed blood, fled from his tribe and found a protector in another tribe, was sometimes adopted by his protector as a son. Miqdād ibn al-Aswad, for example, who belonged to those who had accepted Islām in the very beginning of Muhammad's preaching, had fled originally from his tribe Bahrā, and later on was adopted in Mecca by al-Aswad, his protector. His real name was Miqdād ibn 'Amr. (Cf. Robertson Smith, *Kinship and Marriage in Early Arabia*[2], 1903, pp. 52–55, 135 ff.).

It is to be understood that at that time an adopted son was regarded as in all respects the equal of a real son. The following event, however, caused Muhammad to abolish the old rule, and to declare that adoption was only a fiction and did not entail any consequences as regards rights. Zainab, the wife of the above-named Zaid, Muhammad's adopted son, had aroused the Prophet's passion to such a degree, that he persuaded Zaid to repudiate her, upon which he married her himself. This caused great scandal. It was objected that by the law laid down in the Qur'ān (*Sura*, iv. 27) it was incest for a father to marry a woman who had been his son's wife. Then the verses of Qur'ān xxxiii. 1–5 and 37 were revealed, in which it was expressly announced to the faithful, that an adopted son (Arab. *da'î* دعىّ) was not a real son, so that to call an adopted son a real son was wrong, inasmuch as the process of adoption could never create any bonds of blood-relationship. Marriage with the repudiated wife of an adopted son was therefore not contrary to the will of Allah.

This passage in the Qur'ān has been the accidental cause of adoption not being regarded in the canonical orthodoxy of Islām as a valid institution with binding legal consequences.

TH. W. JUYNBOLL.

ADOPTION (Roman). — The remarks made above concerning the importance attached by the Greeks to the perpetuation of the family and the family worship must be understood to apply with equal force to Rome, at least in her earlier history. The general idea of adoption, and the general effects of the act, were the same in Rome as in Athens,* but some modification in details was introduced by the peculiarly Roman conception of paternal authority (*patria potestas*), and also by the Roman distinction between agnatic, or legal, and cognatic, or natural, relationships and rights. Their more sharply defined conception of legal status also led the Romans to a multitude of corollaries or regulations concerning adoption which find, so far as we know, no parallel in Greece, and opened up several questions which taxed the ingenuity of lawyers.

I. *TWO DISTINCT METHODS OF ADOPTION IN ROME.*—There were two entirely distinct methods of adoption among the Romans during the Republican period, according as the person adopted was, or was not, *sui iuris*, i.e. independent of his father's legal control (*patria potestas*). Although Cicero, for example, uses the word *adoptio* (*adoptatio*) to cover both methods, the proper term for the adoption of one who is *sui iuris* is that used by Gaius and A. Gellius—*adrogatio* (*arrogatio*), the term *adoptio* being properly restricted to the adoption of one who is under *patria potestas* (Gell. v. 19: 'quod per prætorem fit, adoptatio dicitur; quod per populum, adrogatio').

1. Adrogatio.—Adrogation, therefore, was the method by which the head of a family voluntarily submitted himself to the *potestas* of another. It involved a preliminary investigation on the part of the priestly college touching the purity of the reasons for the adoption, its suitability to the dignity of the families interested, and, above all, the security for the maintenance of the family and clan worship (*sacra domestica* and *gentilicia*) of the house which was about to lose its representative (Cic. *de Dom.* 34: 'quæ deinde causa cuique sit adoptionis, quæ ratio generum ac dignitatis, quæ sacrorum, quæri a pontificum collegio solet').

The adoption, by this method, of P. Clodius by M. Fonteius, a much younger man, is evidence of the way in which in the decay of the Republic the old safeguards of the institution could be misused, in the interests of political manœuvring; for the object of Clodius, a patrician, in securing adoption by Fonteius, a plebeian, was to become eligible for the Tribunate of the Commons.

If the priestly college approved the adoption, there followed the *detestatio sacrorum*, a public renunciation of the cultus of the family (and *gens*) of his birth on the part of him who was about to pass into a new family, and perhaps a new *gens* (Serv. on Verg. *Aen.* ii. 156: 'consuetudo apud antiquos fuit, ut qui in familiam vel gentem transiret, prius se abdicaret ab ea in qua fuerat et sic ab alia acciperetur'). Next, a bill (*rogatio*) authorizing the transition was introduced to the Assembly of the Curiæ (*Comitia Curiata*) by the Pontifex Maximus and voted upon in the usual manner.

Such was the procedure followed under the Republic, even when the Curiate assembly was a mere form, being represented

* Cf. Cic. *de Legibus*, ii. 19, 'ritus familiæ patrumque servanto.'

only by thirty lictors (Cic. *Leg. Agr.* ii. 31). For the words of Tacitus (*Hist.* i. 15: 'si te privatus lege curiata apud pontifices, ut moris est, adoptarem'—used by Galba) cannot be made to justify the view that the formalities of *adrogatio* at that date took place before the pontifices alone. This ancient method continued in use into Imperial times. Augustus so adopted Tiberius (Suet. *Aug.* 65: 'Tiberium adoptavit in foro lege curiata'; cf. Suet. *Tib.* 15; Tac. *Hist.* i. 15); the last example is that of Hadrian's adoption of Commodus (νόμῳ, says Dio Cass. lxix. 20).

An easier mode of *adrogatio* was gradually adopted. The first example of this was given by Galba, who adopted Piso by simple declaration (*nuncupatio pro contione*), before the army (Suet. *Galb.* 17: 'filiumque appellans perduxit in castra ac pro contione adoptavit'; Tac. *Hist.* i. 15 f.; and Dio Cass. lxviii. 3, Trajan's adoption by Nerva). This innovation, partly due to the Emperor's autocratic power, was assisted by the fact that the Emperor was also Pontifex Maximus (see Greenidge, *Roman Public Life*, p. 350). The method was extended to other cases, and the older formalities were largely abandoned in favour of a mode of adrogation effected by Imperial rescript (*per rescriptum principis*) and issued after preliminary investigation before a Prætor (or before the Governor in the Provinces, where adoption by Roman forms now first becomes possible). The older method indeed long survived, for Gaius mentions a rescript addressed by the Emperor Antoninus Pius to the pontifices, permitting the adrogation of a minor under certain regulations which need not here be specified. It was not until A.D. 286 that a Constitution of Diocletian entirely abolished the old method and substituted for it the Imperial rescript.

(*a*) *Some effects of adrogatio.*—The effect of adrogation was the loss of his own *patria potestas* on the part of the adopted, and immediate subjection to that of his adoptive father, whose legal son (*iustus filius*) he became. It conferred upon the adopter immediate universal succession to the property * and rights of the adopted. Seeing that, technically, *adrogatio* involved a certain loss of legal personality (*minima capitis deminutio*),† some rights vested in the adopted perished at once, *e.g.* any usufruct vested in him, or sworn obligation of service on the part of freedmen. In the same way, from the strictly legal point of view, all personal debts of the adopted were extinguished by his adoption (but here the prætorian equity gave his creditors the right to sell his property to the amount of their claims); if the debt was owing as a burden upon an estate to which the adopted had succeeded as heir, it was transferred with it to his adoptive father. Personal dignities of the adopted (*e.g.* magisterial powers) remained entirely unaffected in all their consequences. It is obvious that adrogation would annul any will previously made by the adopted. If the person adrogated had himself children under his *potestas*, these also fell into subjection to the adopter, and became legally his grandchildren. Hence Tiberius was compelled to adopt Germanicus before he himself was adopted by *adrogatio* by Augustus (Suet. *Tib.* 15: 'coactus prius ipse Germanicum fratris sui filium adoptare. Nec quicquam postea pro patre familias egit aut ius, quod amiserat, ex ulla parte retinuit. Nam neque donavit neque manumisit, ne hereditatem quidem aut legata percepit ulla aliter quam ut peculio referret accepta').

(*b*) *Adrogatio originally and always confined to patricians.*—It must be remarked that the above mode of adoption was essentially a religious mode, and applicable only to patricians, who alone were organized in true *gentes* (cf. Greenidge, *op. cit.* p. 9), as is evident from the fact that the assembled *Curiæ* and the priestly college were the chief actors in the ceremony. On the other hand, the restriction of this mode of adoption to those who were *sui iuris* cannot be regarded as a primitive characteristic, for the reason that the prime end of adoption, the continuation of the family cultus which was in danger of extinction through failure of natural heirs, could just as well be effected through the adoption of a *filius familias*, i.e. one who was still under *patria potestas*, provided that he had reached the age of puberty, for on the death of his adoptive father he would himself become the *pater familias*. And again, it is impossible to believe that the Rome of the regal period actually possessed no means of adoption save of those who were *sui iuris*—rather would it be probably of somewhat rare occurrence that one already *sui iuris* should put himself by *adrogatio* in the *potestas* of another. If, then, the ceremonies of *adrogatio* were originally also not applicable to sons still subject to their father's *potestas*, we shall be driven to confess that the mode of adoption of such, sanctioned by patrician law, is totally unknown to us; for the earliest method that we hear of as applicable to persons *alieni iuris*, is the purely civil and probably originally plebeian form by threefold sale hereafter described. Originally, then, *adrogatio* was probably applicable both to those who were *sui iuris* and to those who were under *patria potestas*. In historical times, however, it had come to be restricted to the former and relatively much less frequent case, while for the other the fictitious sale offered a more ready means of adoption.

2. Adoptio properly so called.—Adoption in its more proper sense, that is to say, the transference of a *filius familias* from the *potestas* of his natural father to that of an adoptive father, was accomplished by the aid of legal fictions in two distinct acts—(1) the dissolution of the link with the natural father, by means of fictitious sale, *mancipatio*; (2) the transference of the son to the *potestas* of the adoptive father by the procedure called *cessio in iure*.

According to the law of the Twelve Tables, a son thrice transferred by his father to another, under the solemn forms of the *mancipatio*, or sale *per æs et libram*, 'by the copper and the scales,' was freed from paternal control ('pater si filium ter venum duit, filius a patre liber esto'). The father, therefore, so sold his son to the person adopting, or to another; the son being forthwith emancipated by his purchaser, fell back under his father's *potestas*. The ceremony was immediately repeated with the same result. By a third sale the father finally destroyed his paternal rights over his son, who now remained in the lawful possession (*in mancipio*) of the purchaser. The usual custom was for the purchaser then to remancipate (*remancipare*) the son to his natural father, who thus for a moment held him in his turn *in mancipio* * (no longer as *filius familias*, subject to his *potestas*). Then followed the second act, completing the adoption. This took the form of a fictitious process of law (*legis actio*) before a magistrate—the Prætor at Rome, the Governor in the Provinces. The adoptive father instituted a *vindicatio filii in potestatem*, claiming him as his son. He who was holding him for the moment *in mancipio* (the natural father, therefore, if *remancipatio* had taken place) making no demur to the claim,

* Justinian allowed the adoptive father only the usufruct, unless the adopted son died not having been emancipated from his adoptive father's control.

† Gaius, i. 162: 'minima capitis deminutio est, cum et civitas et libertas retinetur, sed status hominis commutatur; quod accidit in his qui adoptantur.'

* If this were not done, the father would, of course, take no further part in the ceremony, his place being taken for the second act of the proceedings by the third person, to whom the *mancipatio* had been made. It was a deduction of the lawyers, from the words of the Twelve Tables, that a single sale sufficed to break the bond of *patria potestas* in the case of a daughter or grandson. See Mommsen, *Staatsrecht*, iii. 37[2].

the magistrate adjudged (*addixit*) the adopted to the claimant as his *filius*, subject to his *patria potestas*. Hence this form of adoption is spoken of as *adoptio apud prætorem*, as contrasted with *adrogatio*, which is *per* (or *apud*) *populum*. It is this form of adoption that is alluded to by Cicero (*de Fin.* 24: 'in eo filio . . . quem in adoptionem D. Silano emancipaverat'), and by which Augustus adopted Gaius and Lucius, his grandsons, in B.C. 17 (Suet. *Aug.* 64: 'Gaium et Lucium adoptavit, domi per assem et libram emptos a patre Agrippa').*

These complicated forms were gradually simplified, and finally Justinian made simple declaration on the part of the two principals before a magistrate sufficient, the son to be adopted also being present and consenting.

Some effects of adoptio.—Like *adrogatio*, true adoption involved a *capitis deminutio*, destroying the agnatic rights of the adopted in his natural family; but he still retained his rights as a cognate therein, and as such was entitled to succeed in the third degree to the estate of an intestate natural father. In his adoptive family he gained the rights both of an agnate and of a cognate; but if he were emancipated by his adoptive father, he reverted to the position and rights of an emancipated son of his natural father. Justinian altered this to the effect that (except in cases where the adopter was grandfather of the adopted) the adopted son remained in his natural family and under the control of his natural father, the adoption conferring on him simply the right of intestate succession to his adoptive father (*adoptio minus plena*).

The children, if any, of a son adopted before the prætor did not, as in *adrogatio*, pass with him into the *potestas* of his adoptive father. Emancipation of an adopted child broke all connexion between him and his adoptive family, save that marriage between the adopter and an adopted daughter or granddaughter, even after emancipation, remained illegal. Readoption by the same person was impossible.

II. *REGULATIONS CONCERNING ADOPTION.*—A person might be adopted, not into the place of a son, but into that of a grandson; the same applies to the adoption of a female. If he was adopted as grandson, the natural sons, if any, of the adopter became legally uncles of the adopted; but one of them might consent to stand as father to him, in which case that son's children became legally the brothers and sisters of the adopted. It was also open to the adopter to give his adopted son in adoption to a third person.

1. Age.—A debated question was as to the proper relative ages of the father and the adopted son. In the notorious case of the adoption of P. Clodius by M. Fonteius the adopted son was older than the adopter, and Cicero makes a point of this (Cic. *de Dom.* 35 f.: 'Factus es eius filius contra fas, cuius per ætatem pater esse potuisti'). The original idea was that adoption should imitate nature (cf. Cic. *ib.* 36: 'ut hæc simulata adoptio filii quam maxime veritatem illam suscipiendorum liberorum imitata esse videatur'), and this was the view of the later jurisconsults, who decided that the adopter should be older than the adopted by at least eighteen years (*plena pubertas*). In the case of *adrogatio* it was held that the *adrogator* should be sixty years of age, except in special cases of health or intimacy. Until the time of Antoninus Pius, a person under the age of puberty (*impubes* or *pupillus*) could not be adopted by *adrogatio*; but if under *patria potestas*, true *adoptio* was, of course, applicable to him.

* Gell. v. 19: 'Adoptantur autem cum a parente in cuius potestate sunt, tertia mancipatione in iure ceduntur, atque ab eo qui adoptat, apud eum apud quem legis actio est vindicantur.'

2. Adoption of females.—Women properly could not adopt, either by *adrogatio* or by *mancipatio*, as they could not possess *patria potestas*. But in A.D. 291 Diocletian allowed a woman to adopt her stepson (*privignus*) to replace deceased children. The adopted in this case acquired rights of inheritance. Females of any age could be adopted, originally not properly by *adrogatio*, though not for the reason assigned by Aulus Gellius ('cum feminis nulla comitiorum communio'), but because the marriage ceremony of *confarreatio* provided for them a mode of entrance into another family. Finally, however, *adrogatio* by Imperial rescript became applicable to women also.

The permission to adopt a female marked, it is clear, a decaying sense of the real significance of the institution. For if, as was, perhaps, most often the case, the adopted daughter was of marriageable age, she would, if subsequently given in marriage, by certain forms, at any rate, fall into the *potestas* of her husband, and become a member of his family and *gens* (see Greenidge, *op. cit.* p. 17). The same evidence of decay is seen in the abuse of the institution for political purposes by Clodius, which assuredly could not have happened had the feeling of the community been seriously concerned. Under the early Empire, adoption was practised to enable persons to escape the penalties of childlessness and to qualify under the provisions of the Lex Julia and Papia Poppæa, which prescribed that a candidate for office who had children, or who had more children, was to be preferred to one who had none or fewer (see Tac. *Ann.* ed. Furneaux, vol. i. p. 439 f.). In A.D. 62 it became necessary for the Senate to decree that pretended adoption for this purpose (manumission having at once followed the adoption) should be null and void (Tac. *Ann.* xv. 19: 'percrebuerat ea tempestate pravissimus mos, cum propinquis comitiis aut sorte provinciarum plerique orbi fictis adoptionibus adsciscerent filios, præturasque et provincias inter patres sortiti statim emitterent manu, quos adoptaverant').

The general impression given is that, at Rome, as compared with Greece, the institution of adoption more rapidly and completely lost its connexion with religious thought and practice.

3. Name.—Among the Romans, adoption introduced a peculiar modification of the name. The person adopted laid aside his original names and assumed those of his adoptive father, adding, however, an epithet to mark the *gens* out of which he had passed; that is to say, he retained his gentile name in an adjectival form. Thus C. Octavius, when adopted by the will of his maternal granduncle Cæsar, became 'C. Julius Cæsar Octavianus.' But the system was not uniformly observed, and in a few cases the epithet is derived from the name of the *Familia*, not from that of the *Gens*. The case of M. Junius Brutus is an example of another anomaly.

4. Imperial adoption.—The power of continuing the family by adoption gained a peculiar significance in connexion with the early Empire. For theoretically the *princeps* could not name his successor, though he might do much to guide the choice of the Senate and army. Neither designation nor heredity was recognized. Constitutionally, however, it was open to the *princeps* to appoint a consort in the Imperial power, who, on the death of the reigning Emperor, would have a practical, though not a legal, claim to be elected his successor. The natural course was to appoint a son to that position; but if the Emperor had no son, he could adopt whomsoever he chose as his virtual successor, the danger of such a course being minimized by the paternal control he possessed over his adopted son. The act of adoption by the *princeps* is figuratively called, therefore, by Tacitus, *comitia imperii* (*Hist.* i. 14); but the custom hardly attains its full significance until the adoption of Trajan. The accident of the childlessness of Augustus gave the institution its prominence in early Imperial history (cf. Suet. *Aug.* 64, 65; Tac. *Ann.* xii. 26; Suet. *Galb.* 17; Dio Cass. lxviii. 3).

5. Adoptio testamentaria.—There remains to be noticed a species of adoption spoken of by Pliny as *adoptio testamentaria*. The most conspicuous example is the will of Julius Cæsar adopting Octavius (Suet. *Cæs.* 83: 'in ima cera C. Octavium etiam in familiam nomenque adoptavit'). The adopted in such a case could not fall under the *patria potestas* of the adopter, who was dead; hence the adopted could not become heir or acquire agnatic rights, and had, in fact, no claim to the deceased's estate, except in so far as the will specifically granted such. The only legal effect, then, was to permit the adopted to bear the name and call himself son of the testator (*adsumere in nomen*). Octavius, it is true, availed himself of his testamentary adoption by Cæsar to secure a *privilegium* from the *Curiæ* adrogating him to the testator (Appian, *Bell. Civ.* iii. 94: ἀπὸ δὲ τῶν θυσιῶν, ἑαυτὸν εἰσεποιεῖτο τῷ πατρὶ αὖθις κατὰ νόμον Κουριάτιον. . . . Γαΐῳ δ' ἦν τά τε ἄλλα λαμπρὰ, καὶ ἐξελεύθεροι πολλοί τε καὶ πλούσιοι, καὶ διὰ τόδ' ἴσως μάλιστα ὁ Καῖσαρ, ἐπὶ τῇ προτέρᾳ θέσει, κατὰ διαθήκας οἱ γενομένῃ, καὶ τῆσδε ἐδεήθη. Cf. Dio Cass. xliv. 35, xlv. 5, xlvi. 47); but his is an exceptional case. By his will Augustus so adopted Livia (Tac. *Ann.* i. 8: 'Livia in familiam Juliam nomenque Augustae adsumebatur'), and at the same time constituted her and Tiberius his heirs. In later times this species of adoption took the form of devising an inheritance under condition of bearing the testator's name. This mode was, in fact, in use as early as Cicero's time and before it (cf. Cic. *Brutus*, 212: 'Crassum istius Liciniæ filium, Crassi testamento qui fuit adoptatus'). Atticus, the friend of Cicero, was adopted by the will of his uncle, and so became Q. Cæcilius Pomponianus Atticus, his uncle's name having been Q. Cæcilius; he also got 10,000,000 sesterces (Cic. *ad Att.* iii. 20). Dolabella was so adopted by a woman, but Cicero had his doubts as to the propriety of this—though, as he humorously remarks, he will be better able to decide when he knows the amount of the bequest (Cic. *ad Att.* vii. 8: 'Dolabellam vides Liviæ testamento cum duobus coheredibus esse in triente, sed iuberi mutare nomen. Est πολιτικὸν σκέμμα, rectumne sit nobili adulescenti mutare nomen mulieris testamento; sed id φιλοσοφώτερον διευκρινήσομεν, cum sciemus, quantum quasi sit in trientis triente'). Whether Dolabella accepted the bequest we do not know; at any rate he did not change his name. Later, Tiberius found no difficulty in accepting an inheritance without observing the condition (Suet. *Tib.* 6: 'Post reditum in urbem a M. Gallio senatore testamento adoptatus, hereditate adita mox nomine abstinuit, quod Gallius adversarum Augusto partium fuerat'). For other examples of this method of adoption, see Suet. *Galb.* 4; Dio Cass. xl. 51; Pliny, *Hist. Nat.* xxxv. ii. 2.

LITERATURE.—Meier-Lipsius, *Der Attische Process*, 539 ff.; *Speeches of Isæus*, ed. Wyse, Cambr. 1904, *pass.*; L. Beauchet, *Hist. du droit privé de la répub. Athén.*; E. Hruza, *Beiträge zur Gesch. des griech. und röm. Familienrechtes*; Caillemer, *Droit de succession légitime*; Ihering, *Geist des röm. Rechts*; Scheurls, *de modis liberos in adoptionem dandi*, Erlangen, 1850; artt. 'Adoptio' and 'Adrogatio,' in various Dictionaries of Classical Antiquities.

W. J. WOODHOUSE.

ADOPTION (Semitic).—

1. Adoption in Babylonia.—In the great Babylonian Law Code (Code of Ḫammurabi), adoption of various kinds is referred to and regulated.

(1) *Reasons for the custom.*—An obvious reason for the custom might seem to exist in its meeting the needs of childless persons, who desired to provide themselves with an heir, that the family patrimony might not be alienated. But in Babylonia, as in old Israel, a man whose wife was childless could take a concubine, or might, with his wife's acquiescence, enter into relations with a maid-servant for this purpose. And these alternatives sufficed in Israel to meet such cases so well that adoption was entirely unknown. Besides, adopted children in Babylonia were sometimes taken into a family where sons and daughters were living. Johns* suggests that 'the real cause most often was that the adopting parents had lost by marriage all their own children and were left with no child to look after them. They then adopted a child whose parents would be glad to see him provided for, to look after them until they died, leaving him the property they had left after portioning their own children.' But this was by no means the only operative cause. Sometimes children were adopted where an heir was desired, sometimes as a matter of convenience;† in some cases a child was apparently adopted as an apprentice; slaves could be taken for the purposes of adoption, and in the process gained their freedom; and not only sons, but daughters, could be thus secured.

(2) *Method.*—Adoption was effected and legally safeguarded by a deed in the usual form of a 'tablet of adoption' or 'sonship' (*duppu aplutišu, marutišu*). This was sealed by the adoptive parents, duly sworn to, and witnessed. The rights and obligations of the contracting parties were fully set forth, and so long as the tablet remained unbroken, and the seal intact, the position of the adopted child was secure. In cases of informal adoption, where no deed had been properly drawn up, the relationship was not legally binding, and the child could return to its own father's house. An exception was, however, made in the case of an artisan who took a child to bring up, and taught him a handicraft. Under these circumstances the child could not be reclaimed.

The term *aplûtu* is interesting. It is the abstract of *aplu*, 'son,' and therefore lit. = 'sonship.' It was, however, used to denote the filial relation generally (being applied to that of a daughter to a parent), and thus came to have the general meaning 'share' (that which belonged to a son or daughter by inheritance). *Aplûtu* might be granted by a father to a son during the lifetime of the former, the father handing over his property to the son, only stipulating for maintenance during his life.

(3) *Conditions and kinds of adoption.* — The conditions were fully set forth in the 'tablet of adoption' or defined by the Code. The obligation resting on the child might be to support the adoptive parent (details of the 'sustenance' to be supplied in such cases are given in many tablets); or one of service (as when a lady adopts a maid to serve her for life and inherit a certain house‡). The adoption of a child (*e.g.* a daughter) by a lady of fortune was evidently regarded as a good settlement for the child. Certain classes of people appear to have had no legal claim to their own children. These were the palace-favourite (or warder?) and the courtezan.§ If the children of such, after being adopted, attempted to repudiate their adoptive parents, the action was punished with the greatest severity (*C.H.* §§ 192, 193). In other cases, however, the possibility of repudiation of the relationship on one side or the other was contemplated. It appears that a clause implying repudiation (on the part of parents of a son, or *vice versâ*) was regularly inserted in the contract, though it could be enforced only by direct appeal to a law-court. Thus parents, according to the contracts, could repudiate adopted sons if they so

* *Babylonian and Assyrian Laws*, p. 154.

† The complicated issues that might arise may be well illustrated by a case cited by Mr. S. A. Cook (*Laws of Moses and Code of Hammurabi*, p. 131 f.): 'Bel-kâṣir, son of Nâdin, who had been adopted by his uncle, married a widow with one son: he has no children, and proposes to adopt the stepson. The uncle, however, objects, since under this arrangement his property would pass through Bel-kâṣir into the hand of strangers, and it is accordingly agreed that if the marriage continues to be without children, Bel-kâṣir must adopt his own brother as heir.'

‡ Cited by Johns, *op. cit.* p. 159.

§ *C.H.* (= *Code of Ḫammurabi*) § 187; cf. Cook, *op. cit.* p. 134, note.

wished, the son taking a son's share and departing. This looks like an attempt to contract outside the law. Failure on the part of the adopted child to carry out his obligations was good ground for disinheritance; but the penalty could be inflicted only with the consent of the judges, who felt bound, in the first place, to do all in their power to reconcile the parties. With this object in view, judgment was sometimes reserved.

The votary and the courtezan formed a class by themselves, and were the subject of special legislation. 'They were not supposed to have children of their own, but possessed the right to nominate their heir within limits. In return for exercising this right in favour of a certain person, they usually stipulated that such person shall maintain them as long as they live and otherwise care for them' (Johns, *op. cit.* p. 158*).

2. Adoption not practised by the Hebrews.—As has already been pointed out, no mention of the practice of adoption occurs in any of the Hebrew Law Codes. No term corresponding to υἱοθεσία exists in Hebrew,† nor does the Greek term (υἱοθεσία) occur in the LXX, while in the Greek Testament it occurs only in the Pauline Epistles. In fact, the practice of adoption would have endangered the principle of maintaining property in the possession of the original tribe, which was the object of such painful solicitude in the Mosaic Code (cf. Nu 27[8-11]). It is obvious that the reasons which operated in Babylonia were not active in Hebrew life. Babylonian civilization was much more complex and highly developed. Among the Israelites the risk of childlessness was met in the earlier period by polygamy, in the later by facility of divorce. [See, further, MARRIAGE].

In the Biblical history of the patriarchs the practice of polygamy is explicitly attested. Sarah, being barren, requests Abraham to contract a second (inferior) marriage with Hagar (Gn 16[2]); cf. also the case of Rachel and her maid Bilhah, and Leah and Zilpah (Gn 30[4. 9]).‡

Isolated cases of possible adoption, or something analogous, are, however, met with in the OT literature. Thus, (1) three cases of informal adoption can plausibly be said to occur in the OT—those of Moses, adopted (Vulg. *adoptavit*) by the Egyptian princess (Ex 2[10]); of Genubath, possibly (1 K 11[20]); and of Esther, who was adopted (Vulg. *adoptavit*) by her father's nephew Mordecai (Est 2[7. 15]). It is noticeable that in all three cases the *locale* is outside Palestine, and the influence of foreign ideas is apparent. Further, (2) something analogous to adoption seems to be implied in the case of Ephraim and Manasseh, sons of Joseph, to whom Jacob is represented as giving the status of his own sons (Gn 48[5] 'And now thy two sons . . . are mine; Ephraim and Manasseh, even as Reuben and Simeon, shall be mine'). As a full son of Jacob each receives a share in the division of the land under Joshua, Joseph thus (in the person of his two sons) receiving a double portion. This, however, is not really a case of adoption, but one where the rights of the firstborn were transferred (for sufficiently grave reasons) to a younger son (cf. Gn 49[4] for the sin of Reuben, vv.[22-26] for Joseph's elevation). To Joseph in effect are transferred the privileges of the eldest son; cf. further 1 Ch 5[1. 2]. (3) The levirate law has also some points of contact with adoption. The brother of a man dying without children entered into a union with the widow, in order to provide the dead man with an heir. The firstborn in this case received the name and the heritage of the deceased. Some of the Church Fathers (*e.g.* Augustine) have actually given the name of 'adoption' to this Mosaic ordinance. But the two things are obviously distinguished by fundamental differences. In real adoption the adopting parent exercises an

* Cf. S. A. Cook, *op. cit.* pp. 134, 147 f.

† In Delitzsch's *Heb. NT* it is rendered משפט הבנים (*e.g.* Ro 9[4]).

‡ See further on this point *EBi*, *s.v.* 'Family,' § 7 (vol. ii. col. 1502).

act of deliberate choice. Thus the levirate law is not a case of adoption in any real sense, but 'the legal substitution, made for sufficient reasons, of a fictitious for a natural father' (Many).

3. Legal adoption unknown among the Arabs.—Of adoption as a recognized institution among the Arabs no clear and certain traces exist. The practice of polygamy was sufficient to meet cases where the need of adoption might have been felt. See, further, art. ADOPTION (Muhammadan), above.

4. Theological application of the idea of adoption.—Adoption as an institution was evidently unfamiliar in Palestine during the NT period. None of the NT writers uses the technical Greek term υἱοθεσία except St. Paul. He doubtless employed the term because, having been born in Cilicia, he had received a partially Greek education, and was acquainted with the institutions and terminology of the Greeks, among whom adoption was commonly practised.

Among Gr. profane authors, from Pindar and Herodotus downwards, θετὸς υἱός or θετὸς παῖς, 'adopted son,' is regularly found.

Theologically the conception of adoption is applied by St. Paul to the special relation existing between God and His people, or between God and redeemed individuals. For the former sense, cf. Ro 9[4] ('Israelites . . . whose is the *adoption*, and the glory, and the covenants, and the giving of the law, and the service of God, and the promises'). Here the people of Israel as a whole is thought of. The redemption from Egyptian bondage was specially associated with the thought of Israel's becoming a nation and Jahweh's son. In this sense the people is sometimes called Jahweh's son (cf. Hos 11[1], Ex 4[22f.] 'Israel is my son, my firstborn,' etc.). The same thought is also prominently expressed in the Synagogue Liturgy (esp. in the Thanksgiving for redemption from Egypt which immediately follows the recitation of the *Shema'*: cf. Singer, *Heb.-Eng. Prayer-Book*, pp. 42–44, 98–99). In the four other passages in St. Paul's Epp. where the word υἱοθεσία occurs, it has an individual application, and an ethical sense, denoting 'the nature and condition of the true disciples of Christ, who by receiving the spirit of God into their souls become the sons of God' (Thayer), cf. Ro 8[15], Gal 4[5], Eph 1[5]; in Ro 8[23] the phrase 'to wait for the adoption' (ἀπεκδέχεσθαι υἱοθεσίαν) includes the future, when the full ethical effects of having become God's adopted sons will be made manifest in their completeness.*

Adoption in this sense implies the distinction that exists between the redeemed and Christ. 'We are sons by grace; He is so by nature.' 'Adoptionem propterea dicit,' says Augustine, 'ut distincte intelligamus unicum Dei filium.'† The thought of ethical adoption is finely expressed in Jn 1[12. 13].

In later ecclesiastical language υἱοθεσία became a synonym for baptism (cf. Suicer, *s.v.*). According to Suicer, Hesychius thus defines the term: ὅταν τις θετὸν υἱὸν λαμβάνῃ, καὶ τὸ ἅγιον βάπτισμα.

LITERATURE.—C. H. W. Johns, *Bab. and Assyr. Laws* (1904), ch. xv. ('Adoption'); Vigouroux, *Dict. de la Bible*, vol. i. (1895) art. 'Adoption' (by S. Many); S. A. Cook, *The Laws of Moses and the Code of Hammurabi* (1903), pp. 131 f., 134 f., 140; *EBi*, art. 'Family,' § 14 (cols. 1504–1505); the Gr. Lexx. *s.v.* υἱοθεσία (esp. Grimm-Thayer and Cremer); the Comm. (esp. Ramsay, *Historical Com. on Galatians*). Reference should also be made here to the great Syrian-Roman Law Code, edited by Bruns and Sachau (*Syr.-Röm. Rechtsbuch aus dem fünften Jahrhundert*, Leipzig, 1880). G. H. BOX.

ADORATION.—As this word is used, both in literature and in common practice, it seems to imply, on the one hand, admiration of qualities that are good and beautiful, and, on the other, a recognition of power in what possesses them. Further, it usually carries with it the idea that the object of adoration is immensely greater than the being who adores.

* In Galatians, adoption of the Greek type may be in the Apostle's mind; in Romans, of the Roman type.

† Lightfoot on Gal 4[5].

It is natural to speak of adoring God or a god, and of adoring Nature: somewhat less natural to speak of adoring another human being: hardly natural at all to speak of adoring a mere ideal, unless—and this is important—the ideal is conceived of as in some way possessing an intrinsic force of its own. Kant, for instance, might possibly have adored his Categorical Imperative, 'the Moral Law within,' which he compares in majesty to 'the starry heavens without,' for he seems to conceive it as something more than that which apprehends it.

The etymology,—*ad oro*, 'I pray to,'—is, in short, still felt in the word. Prayer, however, commonly implies the belief in some gain to him who prays, and this need not be felt in adoration. Indeed, it may be said that the pre-eminent characteristic of the adoring mood is the merging of self in the rapt contemplation of other goodness. The whole temper of the word is admirably illustrated in Browning's lines about the

'love that spends itself
In silent mad idolatry of some
Pre-eminent mortal, some great soul of souls,
That ne'er will know how well it is adored.'
Paracelsus, part iii. *ad fin.*

It is well to note expressly that admiration must reach a certain pitch before the term 'adoration' is felt to be appropriate. The bare recognition of power is, of course, never enough. Admiration of some kind must always be an element, even if it is only the admiration of such power, as in devil-worship. It is, indeed, this element of admiration that appears to give the principle of division between magic and religion. But in the lower forms of worship, as in the one just mentioned, the admiration being incomplete, the adoration is felt to be incomplete also. For its completion we seem to require, on the one hand, an embodiment of all that would satisfy our own ideal, and, on the other, the presence of a force that is more than ourselves.

The types of adoration, therefore, complete and incomplete, are as diverse as the diverse types of those religions that definitely worship a power beyond the worshipper. Strictly speaking, it would appear that religions such as Buddhism, which do not recognize such a power, should be excluded from this class, and that adoration, as we have defined it, has no place in them. But for the Semites and the Europeans at least, history plainly shows how vital an element it has been in their religious development. The whole growth of Hebrew monotheism out of the surrounding idolatry, until its final sharp separation, is one struggle to get away from weak and unworthy objects into the presence of what was truly to be adored.

Lack of power on the one hand, lack of righteousness on the other, are sure signs that the true God has not been found. Anything that suggests either deficiency must be cut away. The gods of the heathen are but the work of men's hands (Is 37[19]); and Israel must not turn His glory into 'the similitude of an ox that eateth grass' (Ps 106[20]). The god that makes a man's son pass through the fire is Molech, not Jahweh (Jer 7[31]). No such god may stand beside Him.

It is this belief in a completely satisfactory object of worship, and this passion to show it to other men, that have been among the great moving forces in Muhammadanism, as in every missionary enterprise since missions began. But the Hebrews, above all nations, have felt the rapture of this mood, and have given it the most complete expression in poetry.

The break-up of Greek religion was directly due to the fact that the old mythology provided images too imperfect to satisfy the heart's longing to adore. Plato and Euripides show the bitter dissatisfaction with their forefathers' imaginings, and the search, never fully satisfied, for something better (see, *e.g.*, Plato, *Euthyphro*; Euripides, *Bacchæ*, *Troades*).

The same dissatisfaction and the same search are manifest during the early days of the Roman Empire, only in a far more prosaic form, inasmuch as the age was far less imaginative. The eager acceptance of strange worships at Rome, and the attempt of Augustus to set up the worship of the Emperor above them all, are proofs of this, as pitiful as they are ludicrous.

Christianity, it might be thought, would have solved all these difficulties for those who accepted it. And it is noteworthy that perhaps the only expression of pure adoration in literature worthy to be set beside the Hebrew, is to be found in the vision of the Christian Paradise at the end of Dante's poem. It may be added that the liturgies of the Church have always been particularly successful in the place they have given to praise as distinguished from prayer. But not to speak of the profound and complicated controversies on the Trinitarian and Unitarian conceptions, it is clear that the fierce quarrels over the use of images and the honour due to the Saints exhibit the essential features of former struggles. The Iconoclasts and Reformers fear any devotion to what is not absolutely the highest, as tending to weaken the powers of real adoration. The Roman Catholics, on the other hand, deny that the reverence paid to the Saints is the same as, or in any way conflicts with, the worship of the one God.

Thus art. 'Saints,' by Mattès, in *Dict. Encyc. de la Théol. Cathol.* (Paris, 1870): 'The Saints are not honoured like God, and are not adored, but they are more honoured, more reverenced, than any men alive on earth. . . . Gradually the term δουλεία, *veneratio*, was fixed upon to denote the cult of the Saints, as distinct from λατρεία, *adoratio*, the word used to denote the worship offered to God, as distinct from the varying forms of expression that may indicate the respect, the deference, the homage paid to men on earth.'

A word should perhaps be said in conclusion about the attitude of those outside the Churches in the present day. For the vast majority of these there is no object of complete adoration, and this because of the divorce that is feared to exist between Power and Goodness. The cosmos, as known to Science, shows power, immense and overwhelming, but is the power good? The ideals of man—justice and mercy and love—are good, but have they a force in themselves? Only those can adore in the full sense who, like Wordsworth, definitely make the leap and unite Nature with God.

LITERATURE.—F. B. Jevons, *An Introduction to the History of Religion*, London, 1896; C. P. Tiele, *Elements of the Science of Rel.*, Edin. 1899, ii. 198 ff.; E. B. Tylor, *Primitive Culture*[3] (1891), esp. vol. ii.; W. Robertson Smith, *The Religion of the Semites*[2] (1894); G. Lowes Dickinson, *The Greek View of Life*, London, 1896; T. H. Green, *The Witness of God and Faith* (1889).

F. MELIAN STAWELL.

ADORATION (Biblical).—**1.** One of the simpler and lower forms of a sentiment approaching to adoration is that which is felt in presence of a fellow-man mightier and more majestic than oneself. Kings and conquerors, in the days when might was right, were always anxious to inspire their subjects with a profound dread of their person, and insisted on a cringing, self-debasing attitude in their presence. Ages of tyranny and submission made servile fear and abjectness almost universal in Oriental lands. Dread in the presence of conscious superiority produced homage indicative of lowly self-abasement. We see this in the case of Ruth before Boaz (Ru 2[10]); the Shunammite before Elisha (2 K 4[37]); Abigail (1 S 25[23]), Mephibosheth (2 S 9[6]), and Joab (2 S 14[22]) before David; and in the 'reverence' paid to Haman by all the king's servants save Mordecai (Est 3[2]).

2. These instances do not seem to furnish us with any sentiment higher and worthier than mere dread of power: and in presence of the indications of power *in nature* men have ever been wont to pay homage akin to that rendered to rulers and lords. The sun is certainly the most wonderful object in nature, and has called forth adoration in every age. Though this was discouraged and forbidden by the monotheistic leaders of Israel (Dt 4[19] 17[3]), it could not be entirely suppressed. Even in the times of the Exile, in the

Temple at Jerusalem, there were those who turned their faces to the east and worshipped the sun (Ezk 8^{16}); and in 'the Oath of Clearing' Job protests that when he beheld the sun and moon, his heart had *not* been secretly enticed, and he had not kissed his hand to them ($31^{26f.}$). The stars also, which move through the heavens in silent majesty, and evoke incessant wonder and awe, have for millenniums received devout adoration, and have been believed to rule the destinies of men. Even in Israel 'the host of heaven' received worship in the time of the kings (2 K 17^{16} 21^{3}). Similarly, when anything mysterious suddenly occurred, it was regarded with dread and reverence, especially when it was conceived of as the manifestation of a terrible Power behind all things. At the dedication of the Tabernacle, when fire came forth and consumed the burnt-offerings upon the altar, all the people fell on their faces (Lv 9^{24}). And in Elijah's time, when fire fell and consumed the prophet's burnt-offering and the wood and the stones, the people fell on their faces and cried, 'Jahweh, he is God' (1 K $18^{38f.}$). Similarly, Ezekiel fell on his face when he beheld the cherubim (1^{28}); and when he saw the glory of the Lord returning from the east to inhabit again the visionary Temple (43^{3}); and especially when 'the glory of the Lord filled the house of the Lord' (44^{4}).

3. The appearance of angels is stated on several occasions to have caused great dread and the outward manifestations of adoration: as when Abraham (Gn 18^{2}), and also Lot (19^{1}), bowed themselves with their faces to the earth. So when Manoah and his wife saw the angel 'ascend in the flame of the altar,' they fell on their faces to the ground (Jg 13^{20}). The same is narrated of Balaam after his eyes were opened and he saw the angel of the Lord standing in the way (Nu 22^{31}), and of the women at the tomb of our Lord when they saw the 'two men in dazzling apparel' (Lk 24^{4}). It was a sentiment more of abject terror, with less of reverence, that caused Saul to 'fall straightway his full length upon the earth' when he saw what he considered to be the ghost of Samuel (1 S 28^{20}).

4. Idolatry evoked in Israel the same outward signs of servile adoration as in other nations. The image was believed to be indwelt by the genius or divinity, and was usually treated with deep reverence; as when the vast multitudes on the plains of Dura prostrated themselves before the image which Nebuchadnezzar set up (Dn 3), and when Naaman spoke of bowing himself in the house of Rimmon (2 K 5^{18}). If not a deterioration from reverence, it must be a survival of a very early stage of idolatry, when we read of men *kissing* the image (Hos 13^{2}, 1 K 19^{18}; cf. the *stroking* (?) *the face* referred to in 1 S 13^{12}).

5. The loftier our conception of God becomes, the more profound is our sentiment of adoration. So long as men conceive of God as such an one as themselves, their adoration of Him is closely akin to that of a ruler or monarch; but as God recedes beyond our comprehension, the more sincere and profoundly reverent does our homage become. And when at length the term 'boundless,' or 'infinite,' employed either in a spatial, temporal, or ethical sense, is applied to God, then adoration reaches its ideal. There is an excellent drastic influence in the conception of Infinitude. 'Mystery,' as Dr. Martineau says, 'is the great redeeming power that purifies the intellect of its egotism and the heart of its pride' (*Essays* (1891), iii. 217). But the contemplation of the abstraction, 'the Infinite' or 'the Absolute,' can scarcely evoke adoration. It is when we realize that Infinitude is not a void, but is permeated with the energy of an Eternal Mind, that we prostrate our souls in holy adoration. When the OT saints could rise to the attitude of conceiving of God as 'the high and lofty One that *inhabiteth eternity*, whose name is Holy' (Is 57^{15}); and when in the prayer of Solomon we read 'heaven and the heaven of heavens cannot contain thee; how much less this house that I have builded' (1 K 8^{27}), we have as sublime instances of adoration as the OT furnishes.

6. Mystery is the mother of adoration. It is true that in a sense adoration is based on knowledge: 'we worship what we know': but it is an essential of sincere adoration that we should *not fully* know. Even on the lower human plane, what we revere is higher than we. If there is any one before whom we are inclined to bow the knee, and yield the veneration of hero-worship, it is the man of overpowering intellect, transcendent wisdom, or superlative goodness. Similarly, the very mysteries of the Divine foster adoration and evoke worship. The writer of Ps 8 was in a genuine state of adoration when he considered the heavens the work of God's fingers, the moon and the stars which He had ordained, and then exclaimed, 'What is man!' Self-abasement in the presence of majesty is an essential element in adoration, and the magnificence of God's work suggested to the Psalmist the incomparable magnificence of the Workman. This finds sublime expression in that most beautiful of the Nature-Psalms, Ps 29. The subject is a thunderstorm which gathers over Lebanon, and passes southward until it dies away in the wilderness of Paran. The storm-cloud is Jahweh's chariot, and as the advancing cloud tips one after another the mountain-tops of Palestine, the Psalmist sees therein Jahweh treading on His high-places, and causing the mountains to quake before Him. As the storm dies away, the setting sun gilds the gathering clouds with tints of preternatural splendour, and to the Psalmist it seems the very entrance to the temple and palace of God. The beauty of the scene entrances him. He sees a door opened in heaven. In imagination he is with the angels, who, like himself, have been enraptured with the marvellous spectacle, and he exclaims, 'In his temple everything saith, Glory.' It is to these celestial beings, who, like himself, are filled with adoration at the majesty of God, that the Psalmist addresses the words, 'Give unto Jahweh, O ye sons of the mighty, give unto Jahweh glory and strength.'

Equally sublime is the adoration of the Divine omniscience in Ps 139. The consideration of the intimacy of God's knowledge of him, wherever he is and whatever he does, produces in the mind of the Psalmist the self-abasement which prompts him to hide himself from God's presence (v.^{7}); the fascinating sense of mystery: 'Such knowledge is too wonderful for me' (v.^{6}); and also of adoring love: 'How precious also are thy thoughts unto me, O God' (v.^{17}).

The most worship-filled of the Psalms is a group of seven, containing 93 and 95–100. They have a common theme: the recent enthronization of the Divine King on Zion; and one might say that the keynote of the entire group is to be found in the words: 'O come, let us worship and bow down; let us kneel before the Lord our Maker' (95^{6}). This group contains the passage which most readily comes to our lips when we desire to express the *mystery* of God's dealings and yet wish to 'comfort ourselves against sorrow': 'Clouds and darkness are round about him: righteousness and judgment are the foundation of his throne' (97^{2}), and it gives to us the ideal of adoration: 'O worship the Lord in the beauty of holiness' (96^{9}). The attributes of God which evoke the adoration of the author, or authors, of these Psalms are these: (1) *The majesty of God*: 93^{1} 95^{3} $96^{3f.}$ 99^{1-3}; (2) *His providential care*: $95^{7ff.}$ 99^{6-8} 100^{3}; (3) *His creative power*: 95^{5} 96^{10} 100^{3b}; (4) *His righteousness and holiness*: 97^{6} $98^{2f.}$ $99^{3.5}$.

7. The effect of the contemplation of the Divine *holiness* is best seen in the vision of the youthful prophet Isaiah (ch. 6). The sight of the holiest beings in heaven, veiling their faces with their wings in view of the eternal Light of the excellent Glory, filled Isaiah with profound awe; and the sound of the antiphonal song of these holy ones, celebrating the infinitely superior holiness of God, filled him with such abasement that the only words he could utter were, 'Woe is me, for I am undone.' It was at his lips that the consciousness of his own impurity caught him. 'I am a man of unclean lips,' he cried; and it was there that the cauterizing stone from off the altar was applied—after which he felt able to join in the worship of the holy ones, and to become a messenger of the Lord of Hosts.

8. In the NT there is no very marked advance in the adoration rendered to God, because the attributes of God which usually evoke our adoration were almost as fully revealed in the OT as in the NT. We note, however, that the disparity between God and man is more completely realized, so that the prostration of adoration is considered to be fittingly rendered to God only, and is refused by others on that ground. When Cornelius was so much overawed by the mysterious circumstances in which Peter was sent for and came to Cæsarea, that he fell down at Peter's feet in lowliest reverence, Peter refused such obeisance as being excessive to a fellow-man. 'Peter raised him, saying, Stand up; I myself also am a man' (Ac 10^{26}); and in the Apocalypse of John, an angel rejects the same obeisance, on the ground that he is a fellow-servant with John and with all who obey God's words, significantly adding, 'Worship God' (Rev 22^{9}). And yet we find that the Lord Jesus never refused lowly homage, which implies the consciousness that adoration was fittingly paid to Him. The recorded instances of reverence paid to Christ are deeply interesting, especially the consideration of the motives which prompted it. There was probably a conflict of feelings in Peter's mind when he fell down at Jesus' knees, saying, 'Depart from me; for I am a sinful man, O Lord' (Lk 5^{8}), but it is clear that he was impressed by Christ's superior holiness. When Mary 'fell down at his feet, saying, Lord, if thou hadst been here, my brother had not died' (Jn 11^{32}), the sentiment was one of adoring love, which invests its beloved one with undefined power. The sense of need clinging vehemently to One who, they believe, has love and power enough to reach to the depth of their misery and need, was the sentiment most apparent in those who came to Jesus for His miraculous help, *e.g.* the leper (Mt 8^{2}), Jairus (9^{18}), the Syro-Phœnician woman (15^{25}), and the Gadarene demoniac (Mk 5^{6}), respecting all of whom we read that they 'came and worshipped him': while of the father of the demoniac boy we read that 'he came kneeling down to him' (Mt 17^{14}). Adoration of superhuman power was the feeling uppermost in the minds of the disciples, when, after Christ had come to the ship, walking on the sea, they 'worshipped him, saying, Of a truth thou art the Son of God' (14^{33}). Not only power but love also was present to the thoughts of the blind beggar who had been excommunicated from the synagogue when he paid adoration to the Lord Jesus (Jn 9^{38}). Jesus heard that they had cast him out, and sought the poor outcast; and when Jesus revealed Himself to him as the Son of God, he said, 'Lord, I believe,' and worshipped Him (*ib.*). And there was a deep adoring love in the minds of the disciples when they were met by the risen Lord, and they 'held him by the feet and worshipped him' (Mt 28^{9}).

9. Adoration of the Lord Jesus became more profound in the Christian community as their knowledge and faith increased. It was with devout adoration that the dying Stephen beheld Jesus standing at the right hand of God, and said, 'Lord Jesus, receive my spirit' (Ac $7^{55.59}$). There was incipient adoration in the words of St. Paul, who, when he saw the ascended Christ, 'fell to the earth, and trembling and astonished said, Lord, what wilt thou have me to do?' (9^{4-6}). There was a deeper adoration when in the Temple he prayed so long and so fervently that in ecstasy he saw his Lord again, and received from Him the definite commission to devote his life to the Gentiles (22^{17-21}). But how much richer was the knowledge, and more intense the love, and more profound the adoration, when he could say to the Ephesians: 'For this cause I bow my knees unto the Father of our Lord Jesus Christ, that ye, being rooted and grounded in love, may . . . know the love of Christ which passeth knowledge' (Eph $3^{14ff.}$).

The Revelation of St. John is filled with adoration to 'him who sitteth on the throne, and to the Lamb.' The vision of the exalted Lord as walking among the candlesticks caused the seer to fall at His feet as dead (Rev 1^{17}). In ch. 4 we read of the living creatures and the elders before the throne of God, who habitually adore and worship God. The four living creatures adore the holiness of God, and the elders habitually adore the creative power and wisdom of God, and cast their crowns before the throne in lowly reverence; but when the Lamb appears in the midst of the throne, bearing the marks of His suffering and death, they both break off from their accustomed song, and join in a '*new* song,' celebrating the greater wonders of redemption ($5^{9f.}$). This is followed by the song of adoration of the angels, who are equally impressed by the wonders of Christ's death, and join in the song, 'Worthy is the Lamb that was slain,' etc. ($5^{11f.}$). In ch. 7 we have two other songs of adoration: first, that of the redeemed, the 'multitude which no man could number' ($7^{9f.}$), and then that of the angels, who fall before the throne on their faces and worship God ($7^{11f.}$). In $11^{16f.}$ we again read of the lowly adoration of the 24 elders, and in 14^{3} we read of the song of the 144,000 'who had been redeemed from the earth.' All through this book partial knowledge, eagerness for more knowledge, and withal a profound mystery, combine to produce the loftiest type of adoration which the creatures of God, terrestrial or celestial, can experience and render.

10. It remains now that we should tabulate the various attitudes of adoration which are mentioned in the OT and NT. They are the same as are found in other Oriental countries. (1) *Prostration* (Heb. הִשְׁתַּחֲוָה, Gr. προσκυνεῖν), in which the one who was paying homage lay down abjectly with his face on the ground, as if to permit his lord to place his foot on his neck (Jos 10^{24}, Ps 110^{1}). This attitude is mentioned in 1 S 25^{24}, 2 K 4^{37}, Est 8^{3}, Mk 5^{22}, Lk 8^{41}. (2) *Standing*, as slaves stand in presence of their master. The Pharisee '*stood* and prayed' (Lk 18^{11}), and many of the Pharisees prayed standing in the corners of the streets (Mt 6^{5}). (3) *Sitting*, *i.e.* kneeling with the body resting on the heels or the sides of the feet. It was thus that 'David *sat* before the Lord' when he was filled with amazement at the message of Nathan, announcing the eternal establishment of his kingdom (2 S 7^{18} ‖ 1 Ch 17^{16}). (4) *Kneeling* (Heb. בָּרַךְ [2 Ch 6^{13}, Ps 95^{6}], כָּרַע [1 K 8^{54}, Jos 7^{6}, Ezr 9^{5}], Gr. γονυπετεῖν), with the body erect, or bent forward so that the head touched the ground. Solomon, at the dedication of the Temple, 'knelt on his knees, with his hands spread forth towards heaven.' The prediction of Messianic days is that 'every knee shall bow' to the Lord (Is 45[23], Ro 14[11], Ph 2[10]). The Lord Jesus in Gethsemane 'kneeled down' (Lk 22[41]), and also 'fell on the ground' (Mk 14[35]). St. Paul kneeled in the building used as a church at Miletus (Ac 20[36]), and also on the beach at Tyre (21[5]). (5) *Bowing the head*, so as to rest the chin on the chest (Heb. קָדַד, Gr. κλίνειν): used of Eliezer when he found that God had directed his way (Gn 24[26. 48]); of the elders of Israel when Moses told the story of the burning bush (Ex 4[31]), and when they received injunction as to the celebration of the Passover (12[27]); of Moses when Jahweh proclaimed His Name before him (34[8]); of Balaam (Nu 22[31]) and of Jehoshaphat (2 Ch 20[18]). (6) *Uplifting the hands*: used of Solomon at the dedication of the Temple (1 K 8[22. 54]; cf. also Is 1[15], La 3[41], 1 Ti 2[8]). Then, as we have said, there is one reference to 'kissing the hand' to the sun or moon as a sign of adoration (Job 31[27]).

LITERATURE.—Art. 'Adoration' in Hastings' *DB* and *Single-vol. DB*, *Jewish Encyc.*, Smith, and Kitto; art. 'Anbetung' in Herzog, and Schenkel; also Marti, *Isr. Rel.* § 10; Benzinger, *Heb. Arch.* (1894) § 68; Macfadyen, *Messages of the Psalmists* (1904), p. 33.

J. T. MARSHALL.

ADORATION (Jewish and Christian, post-Biblical).—**I. Jewish.**—(1) The *outward posture* of adoration did not differ from what had gone before (see above), only in post-Biblical literature its various forms were more strictly prescribed. This was a natural consequence of the predominance of the Pharisaic party, with its love of the details of ritualistic observance. It was ordered that on entering the Sanctuary the worshipper should make thirteen prostrations (השתחויות), a form of adoration which consisted in the spreading out of hands and feet while the face had to touch the ground. Another outward act of adoration was kneeling with the head bent forward so that the forehead touched the ground; a like posture, accompanied by kissing the ground, was an intensifying of the act. The most exaggerated form of adoration, however, was when, on the Day of Atonement, the high priest uttered the Holy Name of God (Jahweh); at the mention of this name every one present threw himself prostrate upon the ground, face downwards (Jerus. *Yoma* iii. 40 *d*).* The importance attached to the outward expression of adoration is also exemplified by the dispute that took place at the beginning of the Christian era between the Hillelites and the Shammaites as to the posture which ought to be assumed while reciting the *Shema'*. The Shammaites, who regarded standing as the most fitting attitude, won the day, and at the present time the Jews recite it standing. The same position is assumed during the saying of the *Shemōnē 'Esrē* (the 'Eighteen Benedictions'), which is one of the central parts of the Jewish liturgy;† indeed, its technical name is *'Amidah* ('Standing'), because, as it is one of the chief acts of adoration, the most appropriate attitude is that of standing while it is being recited (cf. for the position assumed during prayer, Mt 6[5], Lk 18[11]). Throughout the Middle Ages, down to the present day, the Talmudic prescriptions regarding attitudes of adoration have been observed. Thus, the throwing of oneself at full length upon the ground took place only on the Day of Atonement,‡ while at other times it consisted in bowing the head or standing, or, less frequently, kneeling.* A notable exception to this is, however, afforded by the Karaites; these professed in all things to reject Rabbinical traditions and to revert to Biblical usage only; they regarded eight external attitudes in adoration as indispensable, *viz.* 'bending the head, bending the upper part of the body until it touched the knees, kneeling, violent bowing of the head, complete prostration, raising the hands, standing, and raising the eyes to heaven.'† It will be noticed that kissing the ground or any object is not included among these, no doubt because in the OT this act of adoration was usually connected with non-Jahwistic worship (see preced. art. § 4).

(2) God alone is adored by the Jews, though the veneration paid to the *Torah* ('Law') both as an abstract thing of perfection,‡ and also in its material form ('the scroll of the Law'), reaches sometimes an extravagant pitch. One can see not infrequently in the Synagogue, worshippers stretching out their hands to touch the roll of the Law when carried in solemn procession to and from the 'Ark.' The hand that has touched the sacred roll is then kissed; moreover, during the ceremony of the *Hagbaa*, *i.e.* the 'elevation' of the scroll of the Law, the whole congregation stands up in its honour; this act is regarded as a special privilege or *miṣvah*.§ There are certain intermediate beings between God and men to whom great veneration, bordering on adoration, is paid; indeed, in some passages these intermediate beings are identified with God, and in so far can truly be said to be worshipped; but the later Jewish teaching on these beings is so contradictory —sometimes they are spoken of as personalities, at other times as abstract forces, at other times as Divine attributes—that it would be precarious to regard them definitely as objects of adoration. They are: *Metatron*, the *Memra* ('Word') of Jahweh, the *Shekhinah*, and the *Ruaḥ haḳḳodesh* ('Holy Spirit');‖ to these must be added the Messiah, in so far as He is represented as the incarnation of the Divine Wisdom, which existed before the world was created.¶

2. Christian.—(1) The *attitudes* of adoration among the early Christians were borrowed, as one would expect, from the Jews; an instance of how minutely the Jewish custom was followed is seen in Tertullian's description of Christian worship, given in *de Corona Militis* iii. He says that on Sunday and the whole week of the festival of Pentecost, prayer was not to be said kneeling. This is thoroughly in accordance with Jewish precedent, for 'the synagogal custom (*minhag*), as old as the first Christian century, omits the prostration on all festivals and semi-festivals.'**

(2) Adoration among Christians, almost from the commencement, has not been confined to the adoration of the Deity. It is true that in the Roman Catholic Church degrees of adoration are officially recognized (see above, p. 116[b]), but in actual practice this differentiation has not always been observed. Apart from worship offered to God, adoration is offered in the following instances:—

(*a*) *Adoration of the Eucharistic elements.*—The doctrine of Transubstantiation was held centuries before it was officially declared to be a dogma of

* *JE* i. 210; Weber, *Jüd. Theol.* . . .[2] pp. 41, 42. The whole of the first five sections of the tractate *Berakhoth* deal with prayer and its accompanying posture, mental preparation, etc.

† Singer, *Authorized Daily Prayer-Book*, pp. 44–54.

‡ This is, however, now done on New Year's Day as well.

* This refers to European Jews; those who live in the East follow, like the Muhammadans, the practice of prostration as in earlier ages.

† *JE* i. 211.

‡ A very small acquaintance with the Jewish religion will show that this is no exaggeration.

§ In the Synagogue this word is used in the technical sense of 'privilege,' not in the Biblical sense of 'command' (cf. *bar-Miṣvah*). See, further, Oesterley, *Church and Synagogue*, viii. (1906) p. 1 ff.

‖ *Ib.* vii. p. 153 ff. viii. pp. 70 ff. 112 ff.

¶ Cf. Hamburger, *RE* i. 739 ff.

** *JE* i. 211.

the Roman Catholic Church; from it followed of necessity the adoration of the 'Eucharistic Christ.'* Roman Catholics, of course, maintain that inasmuch as the elements of bread and wine in the Mass become the actual body and blood of Christ, they worship Christ, and Him alone, in the Mass. The adoration of the elements takes place at their elevation, *i.e.* after the consecration; † and the adoration is of the highest kind, viz. *cultus latriæ*. Communities, many in number, exist for the purpose of offering perpetual adoration to the consecrated elements; day and night, at least one person has to be present before these in prayer and silent adoration. In these communities ‡ each member has a particular hour assigned to him or her at which regular attendance is required for this purpose in the church or private chapel. The *raison d'être* of this perpetual adoration is that it should be in imitation of the holy angels and glorified saints who serve the Lamb 'day and night in his temple' (Rev 7^{11-15}).

(*b*) *Adoration of the Cross.*—As early as the time of Tertullian the Christians were accused of worshipping the Cross;§ and the evidence of Cassian (d. 435) points to a tendency which, as the witness of later writers shows, soon became a settled practice. He says: 'Quod quidam districtissimi monachorum, habentes quidem zelum Dei sed non secundum scientiam, simpliciter intelligentes, fecerunt sibi cruces ligneas, easque jugiter humeris circumferentes, non ædificationem, sed risum cunctis videntibus intulerunt.' ‖ St. Aldhelm (7th cent.) speaks of certain Christians as *Crucicolæ*, and, indeed, not without reason, if it be true that Alcuin, who lived at the same period, was in the habit of saying before the Cross: 'Tuam crucem adoramus, Domine, tuam gloriosam recolimus passionem; miserere nostri.' ¶ Moreover, stone crosses have been found at Mainz, belonging to the second half of the 8th cent., bearing the inscription: 'S̄c̄a Crux nos salva.' ** It was, therefore, not without reason that *latria* to the Cross was forbidden by the second Council of Nicæa (787).†† Two festivals in honour of the Cross were observed in very early days, and are kept up to the present day. The one is the 'Invention of the Cross,' which is observed on May 3 in memory of the alleged finding of the true cross by Queen Helena; the fact of the 'Invention' is testified to by Rufinus, Socrates, Sozomen, and Theodoret.‡‡ According to the story, Helena sent the nails, the inscription, and part of the Cross to Constantine; the rest was kept at Jerusalem in a silver case, which was carried in procession and worshipped by the faithful on certain days in the year. This custom had died out by the time of the patriarch Sophronius (d. 640); it was, however, continued in St. Sophia's at Constantinople till the 8th century. The other festival is that of the 'Exaltation of the Cross,'§§ kept on Sept. 14, in memory of the Emperor Constantine's vision of the Cross.‖‖ At the present day supposed pieces of the true Cross are possessed

* Cf. the words of St. Ambrose: 'It is the flesh of Christ . . . which we adore to-day in these mysteries,' quoted in Wetzer-Welte's *Dict. Encycl. de la Théol. Cath.* (1878) i. 78.

† Cf. the ancient Jewish custom, according to which the priest prostrates himself after he has offered a sacrifice.

‡ The most celebrated of these was that founded at Marseilles in the 18th cent. by the Dominican monk Antoine Le Quien.

§ *Apol.* 16. The word 'adore' with respect to the Cross occurs in Lactantius, as quoted by Benedict XIV. in *de Fest.* i. § 329, referred to in Addis-Arnold's *Catholic Dictionary*[6], *s.v.*

‖ Quoted by Bingham, *Antiq. of Christian Church*, ii. 362 (Oxford, 1855).

¶ Cf. Lingard, *Antiq. of Anglo-Saxon Church*, p. 174.

** Kraus, *Die Christl. Inschriften*, ii. 107.

†† Landon, *Manual of Councils*, Nic. 2.

‡‡ See Fleury, *Hist. Ecclés.* xi. 32 (Paris, 1722–1738).

§§ Called 'Holy Cross Day' in the Calendar of the English Prayer-Book.

‖‖ Eusebius, *de Vita Const.* i. 27–32.

by some churches; the piece of wood (sometimes very minute) is placed in a glass case, resembling a 'monstrance,' which is sealed up by the Pope or the Bishop; the glass case is kissed and adored by the faithful, and is also used for blessing the congregation. What must have materially contributed to the adoration of crosses and crucifixes was the custom of putting relics inside them, for veneration.

In spite of Conciliar prohibition, St. Thomas Aquinas taught that the Cross was to be adored with *latria*, *i.e.* supreme worship, and argued that one might regard a cross or an image in two ways: (1) in itself, as a piece of wood or the like, and so no reverence is given to a cross or to an image of Christ; (2) as representing something else, and in this way we may give to the Cross *relatively*—*i.e.* to the Cross as carrying on our mind to Christ—the same honour as we give to Christ *absolutely*, *i.e.* in Himself.*

(*c*) *Adoration of the Sacred Heart.*—This cult originated with the mystic, Margaret Mary Alacoque (d. 1690). In the year 1675 she announced that she had had a vision, and that our Lord had Himself appeared to her, and showed her 'His most holy heart upon a throne of flames, encircled with thorns, and over it a Cross'; that it had been revealed to her that Christ desired that His heart should be specially honoured, as satisfaction for the many offences that had been committed against Him in the Holy Sacrament; and that special adoration should be offered to it on the Friday after the octave of the festival of Corpus Christi.

The idea of the adoration of the heart of Christ had, however, already been expressed, for in the 16th cent. the Carthusian monk Lansperg had recommended pious Christians to assist their devotion by using a figure of the Sacred Heart.† The cult was at first vehemently attacked,—the term *cardiolatræ* was applied to those who practised it; but in spite of this it grew in popularity, and in 1765 a special office and Mass were accorded it,‡ with the condition that the 'Heart of Jesus' was to be regarded only as the symbol of His goodness and love, '. . . intelligens hujus missæ et officii celebratione non aliud agi, quam ampliari cultum jam institutum et symbolice renovari memoriam illius divini amoris, quo Unigenitus Dei Filius humanam suscepit naturam, et factus obediens usque ad mortem, præbere se dixit exemplum hominibus, quod esset mitis et humilis corde.'§ A little later, an explanation of the principle underlying the cult was put forth in the bull 'Auctorem fidei' (1794), in which it is said that the faithful worship with supreme adoration the physical heart of Christ, considered 'not as mere flesh, but as united to the Divinity'; they adore it as 'the heart of the Person of the Word, to which it is inseparably united.' Stress is laid on the distinction between 'objectum formale et materiale.' ‖ The cult became more and more popular under the influence and through the activity of the Jesuits; through their instrumentality the whole month of June was dedicated to the Sacred Heart. In 1856, at the desire of the French bishops, Pius IX. raised the festival of the 'Heart of Jesus' to a *Festum duplex majus*, and ordered it to be observed by the whole Church. In August 1864, Margaret Mary Alacoque was canonized, an act which still further popularized the cult.

* Quoted from his *Works* (III. xxv. a. 3 et 4) by Addis-Arnold, *op. cit.* art. 'Adoration of the Cross.'

† Addis-Arnold, *op. cit.* p. 426.

‡ By Pope Clement XIII.

§ N. Nilles, *De rationibus Festorum sacratissimi Cordis Jesu et Purissimi Cordis Mariæ, e fontibus juris canonici erutis*, libri iv. . . . Innsbruck, 1885, quoted by T. Kolde in *PRE*[3] vii. p. 778.

‖ Cf. Addis-Arnold, *op. cit.*, *s.v.*; Wetzer-Welte, *op. cit.* *s.v.*

In spite of the fact that officially a distinction is made between the material and the symbolic, and that the whole cult is declared to be only an expression of the dogma of the adoration of Christ's humanity united with His Divinity in the heart, it is certain that among very many devout, though uncultured, believers the adoration of Christ's heart is characterized by gross materialism; for the heart which is adored is spoken of as that which was pierced by the spear upon the Cross; and, in urging the excellence of this devotion, the late Bp. Martin of Paderborn (d. 1878) wrote thus: 'The real object of meditation concerning the most holy heart of Jesus, as the name itself implies, is the actual heart of Jesus,—the actual heart of Jesus, and not merely His love symbolized by this heart. . . . It is the real, bodily heart of Jesus which is placed before my eyes as an object of adoration (*Verehrung*) by means of the ordinary bodily representation of the same.' *

(*d*) *The adoration of the Heart of Mary Immaculate.*—It was inevitable that this should follow the adoration of the Sacred Heart. This devotion was first propagated by John Eudes, who founded a congregation of priests called, after him, Eudists; it was accorded official recognition in 1799. As with the Sacred Heart, so in this case it is explained that 'the physical heart is taken as a natural symbol of charity and of the inner life.' † The heart of St. Mary is adored with *Hyperdulia*, and what was said under the foregoing section as to materialistic conceptions applies here also.

(*e*) *The adoration of Saints and Images.*—According to the second Council of Nicæa (787), *δουλεία* (*veneratio*) is offered to the Saints, as distinct from *λατρεία* (*adoratio*); and in the Greek Orthodox Church it is said (*Conf. Orthod.* iii. 52): *ἐπικαλούμεθα αὐτοὺς* (*i.e. τοὺς ἁγίους*) *οὐχὶ ὡς θεούς τινας, ἀλλ' ὡς φίλους αὐτοῦ* (*i.e. θεοῦ*). In the same way, according to the Council of Trent, 'veneration' is offered to the Saints in their images and relics. It is insisted that Saints are not honoured like God, or adored, though they are more honoured and more venerated than any living man on earth. The Council of Nicæa, furthermore, ordered that respect and honour were to be accorded to the *images* of Saints, only in so far as they brought to mind their prototypes; in the same way the Greek Orthodox Church orders that worship is not to be offered them: *οὐ μὲν τὴν κατὰ πίστιν ἡμῶν ἀληθινὴν λατρείαν, ἣ πρέπει μόνῃ τῃ θείᾳ φύσει.*

But here again, whether it be to the Virgin Mary, or to St. Joseph (a more modern cult), or to any lesser Saint, however carefully official documents may differentiate between what is due to God alone and what is due to Saints or their images, it is no exaggeration to say that among the ignorant ‡ the Virgin Mary and the Saints take the place of God Almighty in the popular worship; and the images and relics of Saints are believed to possess miraculous powers in not a few cases, and receive adoration accordingly. In numbers of agricultural districts of European countries, the system of Saint-worship does not differ materially from that which obtained in pre-Reformation days, and that was in many cases an adaptation of heathen cults. § English documents of the Reformation period prove conclusively that among the things protested against were the rendering to the Virgin Mary and the Saints the honour that was due to God alone; the belief that these were able to give gifts which are in reality Divine; the belief that the ears of the Saints were more readily opened to the requests of men; and, finally, the practice of regarding Saints as tutelary deities. ‖

One other point must be briefly referred to: the word 'adoration' is used in reference to a newly elected Pope. Immediately after election the Pope is placed upon the altar; the Cardinals, who then come and render him homage, are said to go 'to the Adoration.' Again, when a Pope is elected spontaneously and unanimously, without the 'scrutiny' having been made beforehand, he is said to be elected 'by adoration.' ¶

W. O. E. OESTERLEY.

ADULTERATION.—Adulteration may be defined as the use of cheaper materials in the production of an article so as to transform it into an inferior article which is not by the purchaser or consumer readily distinguishable as inferior. There is not necessarily in the production the intention to deceive; and the substitute is not necessarily deleterious. Indeed, in some cases the technically inferior article may be more wholesome than the poorer qualities of the counterfeited article, as in the case of margarine and other substitutes for butter. The essential point is that the consumer does not get what he is paying for and intends to buy. We must, however, carefully distinguish between what by improved processes of production is really cheaper and what merely seems so; for it is the craze for cheapness that is largely responsible for the extent to which adulteration is practised. Owing to imperfect education and an often consequent misguided social ambition which lead people to ape the habits of those better off than themselves, without either the taste or the means to indulge in those habits, there is a very great demand for substitutes or imitations of articles of luxury, which gives the opportunity to the dishonest dealer, already disposed by self-interest and by pressure of competition and by the difficulty of detection, to adulterate.

The evil is not entirely modern. Even in the Middle Ages, under the guild system, regulations were required to secure that for a fair price an honest article was given. Night work, for instance, was forbidden, and a workman was required to show evidence of skill before he was permitted to practise his trade. Publicity was in the main the remedy against dishonest dealing, and owing to the simplicity of wants and to the simple character of the processes of manufacture, and to the close relation of producer and consumer, the remedy was tolerably effectual. In modern times these conditions are absent, and the practice is so prevalent, that, in defiance of the doctrine *caveat emptor*, legislation has been required to protect the consumer. The ignorance of the consumer, the impossibility of educating a taste that is continually being debased by the consumption of adulterated articles, and the frequent danger to life and health, have necessitated this departure from the doctrine of *laissez faire*, particularly with regard to articles of food. The consumer is still at the mercy of the vendor of shoddy clothes, etc., but in food and drugs at least he is protected, although it must be admitted that the penalties inflicted are often inadequate and the laws ineffective, owing to the absence of a standard quality (cf. the recent prosecutions for adulteration of brandy). Mr. Devus (*Political Economy*, p. 70) quotes a public analyst's report to the effect that of samples of milk 43 per cent., of mustard 16, of coffee 14, of spirits 11, of butter 11, and of disinfectants 75, were adulterated.

Legislation against adulteration takes various forms, of which the activity of the public analyst, through official inspectors who take samples, is perhaps the best known and most effective. It is unfortunate that the use of preservatives for milk and meat especially is not subject to precise regulation, for the repeated addition by successive dealers of preservatives to milk, for instance, converts what might be a laudable and economic practice into a deleterious adulteration. Fiscal legislation is often used for the purpose of excluding, or at least restricting, the use of poorer qualities and adulterated goods. Thus Canada increases the taxation on molasses as the quality deteriorates, for the avowed purpose of excluding 'black jack,' as it is called, which a paternal finance Minister declared 'no man should put into his mouth and think he is taking molasses.' In other ways, *e.g.* by prescribing that all goods and packages should be marked with the country of origin, the Government inter-

* Quoted in *PRE*[3] vii. 780.

† Addis-Arnold, *op. cit.* p. 427.

‡ The reference is to Roman and Greek Catholics.

§ For a popular presentation of the facts, see the earlier volumes of Freytag's *Die Ahnen*, a work which may be regarded as a classic.

‖ See the article on the subject in the *Church Times*, Aug. 31, 1906.

¶ Migne's *Troisième Encyc. théol.* ('Dict. des Savants et des Ignorants') xlvi. 87, Paris, 1859.

feres to prevent fraud and adulteration. This plan ('made in Germany,' etc.) has in the United Kingdom not been very successful, for the alleged poorer quality of goods imported has not been established, and the result has in some cases been an advertisement for the foreign producer.

It is necessary, in considering the demand for legislation to suppress adulteration, that we should be on our guard against class interests which may demand the prohibition or regulation of the sale of some cheaper but not less useful article than that which they produce. Thus in some agricultural countries the importation or manufacture of margarine is prohibited in the interests of the farmers, and the importation of live cattle from Canada into Great Britain is [1907] forbidden on the alleged ground that disease exists among Canadian herds. See Ashley's *Economic History* for mediæval regulations and ideas, and Marshall's address to the Co-operative Congress, 1889. J. DAVIDSON.

ADULTERY.

ADULTERY (Primitive and Savage Peoples).—**1. Woman in primitive society.**—A survey of the notions entertained by savage peoples regarding adultery tends to show that, in the earliest times, it could not have been regarded in any other light than as the interference of another with the woman over whom a man had, or conceived himself to have, certain rights. It was not considered as an act of impurity, for the idea of purity had not yet been evolved. Nor was it a breach of contract, for it is improbable that anything corresponding to marriage rites was yet in use. Nor was it a breach of social law, for men were not yet organized in social groups. Woman being conceived as belonging to man, any interference with her would immediately outrage man's instinctive sense of property, and would at once arouse his jealousy. He would, therefore, try to recover his property from the thief; and this could be done only by assaulting or killing him, in other words, by punishing him for his theft. Recognizing, too, that the woman, differing from other possessions of his, was a sentient being, and therefore to some extent a consenting party to the theft, he would also vent his anger upon her, even putting her to death in cases of extreme rage. Among animals precisely similar ideas with respect to the females may be found. Where an animal collects a number of females round him, as in the case of certain apes, he acts as a despot over them; young males born to him are, after a time, expelled, and the approach of a possible rival is at once resented (Darwin, *Descent of Man*, 591). Thus it must be admitted that, at the earliest stage of human history, adultery could have been nothing but a breach of proprietary rights, to be followed, when discovered, by a more or less savage act of private revenge upon both the culprits. Among most existing savages hardly any other idea of it exists, as we shall presently see. Woman before and after marriage is the property, first of her father or guardian, next of her husband. Among peoples who allow licence before marriage, none is permitted after it, when the husband assumes proprietary rights over the woman. And where such licence is not allowed, any unchastity is punished by inflicting a fine or death on the man who has depreciated the value of the woman in her guardian's or prospective husband's eyes. This idea of a husband's proprietary rights in the woman would be increased where she was the captive of his bow and spear, or where he had to undergo a period of servitude for her, or, much more usually, had to acquire her by purchase. Here it may be remarked that adultery is not confined to cases where a ceremony of marriage exists: wherever a man and a woman enter into a union more or less lasting, and the man treats her as his property, it may occur. But it need not be inferred that it is a common occurrence among all savage races. It is abhorrent to some peoples, *e.g.* the Andamanese, with whom conjugal fidelity is the rule (Man, *JAI* xii. 135), the people of Uea in the Loyalty Islands (Erskine, *Western Pacific*, 341), the Abipones (Dobrizhoffer, *Account of the Abipones*, ii. 153), and others.

Certain facts are often alleged against the idea that woman is not a free agent in primitive or savage society. Thus, a woman's consent is often required before marriage: yet even here the consent of her guardian is also necessary, and this right of choice on her part need not argue anything as to her future freedom of action, while it is counterbalanced by the overwhelming weight of evidence regarding the woman's position as a being owned first by her guardian, then by her husband. Again, in cases where, after marriage, the woman has considerable influence over her husband or in the tribe, this hardly affects the fact that her legal status is not that of the man, nor does it give her equal rights with him. This influence may frequently arise from the fact that women have their own sphere of action, that they have been the earliest civilizers, that they possess much of the tribal lore, and that they are feared as dangerous (magically) at certain crises of their lives. All this limits the husband's power in many ways; but so far as concerns interference with her sexually, his power is unlimited. Here, any attempt at independence on her part arouses at once that jealousy, that underlying fact of man's proprietary rights in the woman, which her innate superiority or her occasional influence does not abate. Even where the matriarchate exists, and where the man goes to live with the woman's people, this seldom takes away his power of life and death over her, especially where adultery is concerned (Haddon, *Head-Hunters*, 160, says that though in the Torres Straits islands a woman asks the man to marry her, and he goes to live with her parents, he can kill her if she causes trouble; cf. Powers, *Tribes of California*, 382). In effect all such exceptional cases are overruled by the fact that universally the woman's power of licence ceases at marriage, that universally unchastity on her part is regarded by the husband as a breach of his proprietary rights, that frequently the husband has the power to kill his wife for any such breach, that well-nigh universally he can lend his wife to another man, and that generally adultery on the husband's part cannot be punished in any way by the wife.

2. Adultery under different conditions of marriage.—It is now generally admitted that *promiscuity* was not the earliest form of human sexual relations. But even had it been so, the idea of adultery based upon jealousy and the sense of property would still have been conceivable. Men and women being collected into groups for the sake of defence or of facilitating the supply of food, the men would resent the approach of members of other similar groups, while any interference with the women of the group would be jealously guarded against by all the males of the group, to whom *ex hypothesi* all the females of the group belonged in common. Promiscuity, however, as a theory of marriage, is baseless, and has frequently been confused with what is known as *group marriage*, an entirely different thing. In this case, found in actual practice among certain Australian tribes, the men of one definite group are potential husbands of the women of another definite group; the husband of any one woman has only a preferential right in her, and the men of his group may have access to her on certain occasions. But here the husband's consent must first be given; and though it is practically never withheld, and a man is looked upon as churlish who does withhold it, this points to the existence of individual marriage underlying this mixed polyandrous and polygamous system, rather than to its being a systematized form of earlier promiscuity. The consent of the husband being necessary implies a certain proprietary right in the woman on his part; he sanctions her union with other men only on certain ceremonial occasions. If the woman dared to consort with a man not of the group, this would be resented by her actual and potential husbands; it would be incest rather than adultery (see § 5; Spencer-Gillen[a], 62, 63, 110, do.[b] 73, 140; Howitt, *JAI* xx. 53). Again, where *polyandry* exists, adultery is still possible, since the husbands of the woman are usually well defined, and their rights over her are arranged according to strict rule. Where, as in the Tibetan type of polyandry, a woman is the wife of several brothers, it is obvious that they will resent the approach of any other man to their wife, while contrariwise the woman is extremely jealous of her own conjugal rights (*Hist. Univ. des Voyages*, xxxi. 434). The story told by Strabo (xvi. 4. 25) of the custom of fraternal polyandry among the ancient Arabs, shows that adultery with another man was punishable, and similar cases might be cited (see § 4, Tibet). Among the Nairs, with whom polyandry assumes another form, the woman is not allowed to have any later sexual relations with the man who first consummates the marriage, while any relations with a man not of her caste is *ipso facto* adultery, and was formerly punished by death (Reclus, *Primitive Folk*, 162, 164).

A modified form of polyandry exists where the custom of providing a 'secondary husband' (the cicisbeate) exists. In this case, the secondary husband must contribute to the support of the household, and takes the place of the husband with the wife only in his absence. This is found among some Eskimo tribes (M'Lennan, *Studies in Ancient History*, 2nd ser. 376; Reclus, 66), where frequently the secondary husband is a younger brother. With them, therefore, the system is akin to that of the Todas, where the eldest of a group of brothers is the husband, but the younger brothers have rights over the wife also (*TES* vii. 240). It occurs among some Polynesian peoples (*ZVK*, 1900, 334) and others, as it did in ancient Sparta (Xenophon, *Rep. Lac.* i. 9). Sometimes, where adultery takes place, a man is forced to become a secondary husband, to do the work of the house and obey the husband, while he may now associate freely with the wife, as among the Konyagas (Reclus, 67).

3. Adultery under polygamy and monogamy.—But it is especially among peoples with whom polygamy or monogamy is the rule that we see the working of jealousy and the idea of property in the woman existing most emphatically. Jealousy of their wives exists among the lowest savages, and with them and among higher savage and barbaric tribes the utmost precautions are taken to prevent the approach of another man. Dire punishments are frequently meted out to the wife even on the slightest suspicion, or, as among the Negroes of Calabar, the wives are at intervals put through a trying ordeal to test their faithfulness (Miss Kingsley, *Travels in W. Africa*, 497). The universality of the feeling of jealousy among the lower races, the rigour of its action, and its extreme vigilance, go far to show, as Westermarck (*Human Marriage*, 117 ff.) points out, that there never was a time when man was devoid of it, and that it is a strong argument against the existence of a primitive promiscuity. When adultery has actually taken place and has been discovered, the husband, with few exceptions, can himself punish the offending woman and her paramour, without necessarily invoking the local tribunal. Indeed, that tribunal or the tribal custom expects him to do so, or fully approves his act, though in some instances he may be retaliated upon by the relatives of the woman or the man, where he has killed either or both. Punishment varies, but very frequently death is meted out in cases of detected adultery; in other places the woman is disfigured or mutilated by shaving off her hair, cutting off her nose, ears, etc., or she is chastised more or less seriously, or she is repudiated or divorced, or treated as a prostitute. In such cases the husband's jealousy or anger turns against his offending property, even though his act of revenge deprives him of his wife, or of her attractive qualities. Towards the offending man who has invaded his rights of property his attitude varies: he may kill him, emasculate, mutilate, wound, or flog him, or make him his slave, or force him to pay a fine, or to have his wife outraged in turn. Especially noticeable is the idea of theft in adultery, where, as in Africa, the man's hands are cut off, as if he were a thief (Waitz, *Anthropologie der Naturvölker*, ii. 472); in the fact that in the Torres Straits there is no word for adultery apart from theft (*puru*), and all irregular connexion was called 'stealing a woman' (*Camb. Exped. to Torres Straits*, 275); and that among the Arunta a man who commits adultery with a woman of the class from which he might choose a wife is called *atna mylkura*, 'vulva-thief,' because he has stolen property (Spencer-Gillen[a], 99). The same idea also emerges where, as among some Negro tribes, it is held to be adultery for a man to lay his hand on or brush accidentally against a chief's wife (Miss Kingsley, *Travels*, 497). The conception of the wife as property is also seen, not only in the common custom of slaying her at her husband's death, but, where she is allowed to survive him, in the belief entertained by savage and barbaric peoples that second marriage is wrong, or, if permitted, that any unchastity during a certain period after the husband's death is equivalent to adultery, or should be punished as such (Amer. Indians, Kukis, Patagonians, Ainus, etc.). Among some Amer. Indian tribes, the widow cannot even appear in public without being regarded as an adulteress (Adair, *Amer. Indians*, 186). For a certain time at least, sometimes for the rest of her life, the woman is still her husband's property; and as ghosts have power over the living, it may be presumed that the dead husband might still retaliate in case of any transgression.

4. Punishments for adultery.—The following examples will show the nature of the punishments for adultery meted out among different races by the outraged husband, or permitted to him by common consent or actual law:—

Among the Wotjobaluk of Victoria both the woman and her lover are killed; among the Yerkla-mining of S. Australia the woman was branded with a firestick for the first offence, speared in the leg for the second, and killed for the third; among some tribes the punishment consisted in handing her over to all comers (Howitt, *Nat. Tribes of S.E. Aust.* 245, 257, 207). A childless wife who misconducted herself could be repudiated in W. Victoria (Dawson, *Aust. Aborigines*, 33). In Tasmania the most cruel punishments were meted out to the woman (Bonwick, *Daily Life of the Tasmanians*, 72). In the Andaman Islands adultery is rare, but when it occurs it is punished by the husband, on whom, however, the friends of the injured party may retaliate (*JAI* xii. 135). In New Guinea adultery is capitally punished (Waitz-Gerland, *Anthrop. der Naturvölker*, vi. 661); elsewhere throughout the Indian archipelago it is a cause, and frequently the only cause, of repudiation (*Cambridge Exped. to Torres Straits*, 246; Westermarck, *Marriage*, 437, 523). With the Melanesian tribes the woman was brutally treated, and the paramour was killed by the husband or executed, though he was sometimes fined for what was regarded as a robbery, or had his wife violated by all the men of the village (De Rochas, *Nouv. Caléd.* 262; *BSAP*, ser. iii. vol. viii. 361). Death was the usual punishment in New Zealand (*Voyage of the Astrolabe*, 360); in other Polynesian islands the woman was variously punished. With the Hottentots the woman was killed or flogged (Alexander, *Exped. into Interior of Africa*, i. 98; *ZVK*, 1902, 344); and killing the guilty wife, and frequently her paramour also, is usual among both Bantu and Negro tribes (*Kafirs* [M'Lean, *Kafir Laws*, 111], *Wakamba* [Decle, *Three Years in Savage Africa*, 487], *Waganda* [Wilson and Felkin, *Uganda*, i. 201]). Lesser punishments were here also administered—chastisement, disfigurement, or repudiation of the woman, marrying her to a slave, and fining the guilty man (Post, *Afrik. Juris.* i. 401, ii. 30; Bowdich, *Miss. to Ashanti*, 170; Du Chaillu, *Afrique Equat.* 67, 435; Johnston, *Uganda Protec.* 590, 689, 746, 882; Waitz, ii. 110, 115). Death, mutilation and disfigurement, abandonment, and delivery of the woman to the men of the tribe, were common among the N. Amer. tribes, with whom also the aggressor was killed, mutilated, or fined (Bancroft, *Native Races*, i. 350, 412, 514; *Ann. Rep. BE*, iii. 364; Schoolcraft, ii. 132, v. 683 ff.). Tortures and death were meted out to both parties in Yucatan (Bancroft, ii. 674); in Mexico the woman had her nose and ears cut off, and was stoned to death (Herrera, *W. Indies*, iv. 338; Prescott, *Peru*, 21); in Guatemala the woman was repudiated and her paramour fined (Bancroft, ii. 673); in Nicaragua she could be divorced for nothing but adultery (Waitz, iv. 278). Among the Fuegians the husband could kill his wife, but was liable to be killed in turn by her family (Hyades and Deniker, *apud* Hobbouse, i. 46). Woman and paramour might be killed by the husband among many of the native tribes of India (Dalton, *Eth. of Bengal*, 45; M'Pherson, *Memor. of Service in India*, 83). Among the nomad Tatars the woman is frequently killed and the man forced to pay the husband a number of cattle; elsewhere in Tibet the woman is punished and the man pays a fine to the husband or group of husbands (*Hist. Univ. des Voyages*, xxxi. 437, xxxiii. 341). In Japan, woman and paramour are killed by the husband, the law supporting his act (Letourneau, 217). In China the law permits this punishment if it is meted out on the spot, otherwise the husband would be punished for the crime; but where adultery is proved he can repudiate or otherwise punish his wife (Alabaster, *Chinese Criminal Law*, 187, 251; Pauthier, *Chine Moderne*, 239).

Frequently, too, the gravity of the offence is proportionate to the rank of the husband with whose wife it is committed; in other words, the value of the woman belonging to him is greater. In New Caledonia, death was meted out to a man who merely looked at the wife of a chief. Among the Banyoro (Bantu), with whom the male delinquent was usually fined, in the case of adultery with a chief's or king's wife, he was put to death (Johnston, *op. cit.* 590); while in Uganda, where whipping was the usual punishment, the king's wife and her paramour were chopped to pieces (*ib.* 669); in Ashanti, intrigue with the king's slaves is punished by emasculation (Ellis, *Tshi-speaking Peoples*, 287). So in Peru, where death was the ordinary punishment, adultery with the Inca's wife resulted in the burning of the guilty man, the death of his parents, and the destruction of his property (Letourneau, *Evol. of Marriage*, 215). Similarly, adultery with the wife of a prince among the Tatars involved the punishment of the man's relatives as well as himself: generally speaking, this distinction holds good among most savage peoples, while a further distinction may be made between adultery with the principal wife and with a subordinate wife—the value of the former being, of course, greater.

The punishment of adultery among savage and barbaric peoples is thus largely in the hands of the aggrieved husband, and evidently originated out of the desire for personal revenge. But what was at first a mere arbitrary personal vengeance has now generally become an act which is supported by tribal custom. The husband slays the aggressor, but he knows that in so doing he will be backed by public opinion, and may even call in others to assist him. He is allowed or expected to administer punishment. Frequently, too, adultery is taken cognizance of as an offence by the laws of a tribe or people, whether administered by the old men, a council, a chief, or by the State. In such cases the husband might appeal to any of these to decide what the punishment should be or to administer it. Thus in Australia, among the Kamilaroi, the husband's complaint is carried before the headman, who gives sentence; and among the tribes of N. S. Wales a similar process is found (Howitt, *op. cit.* 207; Fraser, *Abor. of N. S. Wales*, 39). Other instances of adultery being punishable judicially rather than by private revenge among peoples who also punish it in the latter way, are found among the Kanakas of New Caledonia, where the aggressor is led before the chief and his council, and executed by their sentence (De Rochas, *Nouv. Caléd.* 262); among the Caribs, Samoans, Mishmis, in New Guinea, and in parts of Negro Africa (Steinmetz, *Rechtsverhältnisse*, 727 ff.; Turner, *Samoa*, 178; Chalmers, *Pioneering in N. G.* 179; Letourneau, 211). In such cases, however, the law may simply order the husband to execute the punishment, as in parts of ancient Mexico and in Central America (Bancroft, ii. 465; Biart, *Les Aztèques*, 168). And even where the offence is strictly a legal one, should the husband take the matter into his own hands, and, *e.g.*, slay both offenders at once, he would still be considered to be acting within his own rights, or would be subject only to a slight penalty, as in China, Japan, ancient Peru (where it was held that Manco Capac had decreed death to adulterers, Garcilasso, *Royal Comm.* i. 81). Or if the husband does not act according to the judicial sentence, he himself may suffer. Thus among the Tatars, if he does not punish his wife, the chief takes the cattle which her accomplice has paid the husband (Letourneau, 216); and in China, if he does not repudiate his wife he is whipped (Pauthier, *op. cit.* 239). But we also find that, where the offence is a legal one, there is a tendency to stay the husband's desire for the worst acts of vengeance. This has probably originated the frequent system of compensation by fine; it also accounts for cases, as among the Kafirs or the Bakwiri, where the husband must not kill the offending wife, and if he does so is punished as a murderer (M'Lean, *op. cit.* 117; Post, *Afrik. Jurisp.* i. 401); and, as among the Wakamba and other peoples, where the husband is allowed to slay the parties only when taken *flagrante delicto*.

The birth of twins is with many savage peoples regarded as uncanny, and one or both are put to death. The reason for this belief is not always certain, but in some cases it is thought, probably as a result of the further belief that a man can be the father of no more than one child, that a god has had intercourse with the woman. Such a belief is found among the Negroes (some of whom, however, regard the birth as lucky for this reason), South American tribes, and Melanesians (Ellis, *Yoruba-speaking Peoples*, 67; Codrington, *Melanesians*, 235). In such cases we have the idea that the wife has committed adultery with a divinity or spirit, as in the Greek myths of Alcmene and Leda. But it is sometimes held as a proof of adultery with another man (*S. American tribes* [Waitz, iii. 394, 480], *Teutons* [Westermarck, *Moral Ideas*, i. 408]). See Rendel Harris, *Cult of Heavenly Twins*.

5. Adultery within the prohibited degrees.—Among all races, marriage or sexual union is absolutely forbidden between certain persons, whether blood-relations or members of the same group, clan, totem, or tribe, as the case may be. Any offence against such a law is, to the savage mind, one of the worst forms of adultery; indeed, it should rather be called incest. It is not a trespass upon another's property, but a breach of tabu, and thus approaches our idea of impurity; while it is believed to bring ill-luck or disaster upon the family, clan, or tribe. As any breach of such a law is thus believed to affect the whole group, it is therefore punished by the group or by those to whom the administration of justice is delegated. There is no question of private revenge. Any such offence is regarded as so horrible, so disgraceful, and even so obnoxious to the gods (Turner, *Samoa*, 92), that it is usually unheard of, and no one thinks of committing it. But where it is committed, the punishment is usually death to both offenders, as in Australia, New Britain, New Hebrides, and among the Amer. Indians (Spencer-Gillen[a], 15, do.[b] 140; Westermarck, *Marriage*, 300; *JAI* xviii. 282; Macdonald, *Oceania*, 181; Frazer, *Totemism*, 59). In Yucatan the man was looked upon as an outcast (Bancroft, ii. 665); and a fine was levied among the Dyaks, Chukmas, and others (St. John, *Forests of the Far East*, ii. 198; Lewin, *Wild Races of S.E. India*, 186).

6. Adultery of the husband.—That, at the lower stages of civilization, adultery is regarded as an offence against the proprietary rights of the husband, is borne witness to by the fact that it is an offence only from the husband's point of view. With the rarest exceptions has the wife any redress when the husband himself offends, and it is only at higher levels of civilization that she has any general *right* to complain. Of course, where the husband commits adultery, he is always in danger of death or fine at the hands of the guardian or husband of his paramour, but this does not affect his wife's position in the matter. Where the wife has the power of complaining to a tribunal or of causing the husband to be punished (and probably wherever the woman has any influence at all, she will complain freely to her husband), the cases are probably to be classed with those where she can obtain redress for other offences, *e.g.* ill-usage. But the cases are so exceptional that no law can be framed from them, though they may foreshadow the dawning of the idea of the equal rights of wife and husband, and of the ethical belief that adultery is wrong.

Among the people of W. Victoria the wife can get an adulterous husband punished by complaining to the elders of the tribe, who send him away for a short period (Howard, *Matrim. Inst.* i. 229; Nieboer, *Slavery*, 18). In Africa, the husband in Great Bassam pays a fine to the wife for unfaithfulness (Post, *Afrik. Juris.* ii. 72), and among the Mariana he is severely punished (Waitz, ii. 106). With the Khonds of Orissa, where polyandry exists, and the woman can set a higher price upon herself, the husband cannot strike her for infidelity, whereas he is punished or is held to have dishonoured himself (Westermarck in *Sociol. Papers* (1904), 152). The Omaha wife could revenge herself on the husband and his paramour; and among the Sioux and Dakotas she could leave her husband for unfaithfulness (Dorsey, *BE*, 1885, 364; Howard, i. 239). Divorce for unfaithfulness on the husband's part might be obtained by the wife occasionally, as among some of the peoples of the Indian archipelago, the Shans, and others (Westermarck, *Marriage*, 527). But with these few exceptions savage mankind has scarcely recognized the fact that the adultery of the husband is a wrong done to his wife. Though it might be thought that the matriarchate would give the wife some power over her husband's infidelities, this is not supported by evidence, save in a few particular cases. These are where the royal succession was through a woman, who usually married a man of lower rank than herself, and remained his superior. His adultery was punishable, but she claimed greater licence. Thus among the Tænsas of North America, where the chief was looked on as a demi-god, his sister's son succeeded him. She, being thus also divine, treated her husband as a slave, killed him if he were unfaithful, but allowed herself great licence (M'Lennan, 420). Similarly in Loango a princess might be licentious, but would have her husband's head chopped off if he even looked at another woman (Pinkerton, xvi. 569). This did not apply to any other classes, and is on a level with the severity of the punishment meted out to a man committing adultery with the wife of a chief. It should be noted, however, that with a few peoples, the wife may have a ground for divorcing her husband if he takes a second wife or a concubine (Hobhouse, *Morals in Evolution*, i. 136); while, even where polygamy is practised, the feeling of jealousy on a wife's part, though it may not affect her husband directly or stay his desire of introducing another wife to his household, is frequently directed against the new-comer to her hurt, and in some cases the wife will commit suicide (Westermarck, *Marriage*, 497 ff.).

7. Permissible adultery.—Adultery among the lower races is considered wrong, *viz.* an offence against the rights of the husband, when it is committed apart from his will. There are occasions on which he commands or sanctions it, or when it is, so to say, legalized by social or religious custom. The custom of lending wives either to friends or strangers emphasizes once more the view that the wife is the husband's property. Here she acts at his will, as in the other case she infringes his rights. Here for the time the feeling of jealousy is in abeyance, even where it exists most strongly, and the husband decides that the wife may commit adultery. We thus see that adultery has not the precise meaning to the savage which it has to the civilized man.

The custom of lending wives is well-nigh universal among savages (Westermarck, *Marriage*, 74, 130), but various reasons exist for it, nor is it always to be explained as the outcome of hospitality. (*a*) In cases where a wife is lent to a friend, it may be done out of sheer friendliness or as an act of gratitude, but generally the lender will expect a similar favour to be shown to him. In other words, there will be reciprocity, as among the Columbian Indians, who barter wives as a sign of friendship (*Hist. Univ. des Voy.* xiii. 375), the Eskimos, Polynesians, and others (M'Lennan, *Studies*, 2nd Ser., 376; Letourneau, 212). The practice of lending wives is sometimes reduced to a system, as in those Australian tribes with whom group marriage prevails, and generally there are limits to the system of lending among most Australian peoples. Thus, where individual marriage prevails, the man can lend his wife only to men belonging to his own group, *i.e.* to those alone to whom his wife would have been marriageable (Spencer-Gillen[b], 141). This applies also to the tribes actually practising group marriage, the Urabunna and Dieri, since here the right of access to the woman to whom one man has a 'preferential right' is strictly limited to the men of his own group (*ib.* 73, 140). Some cases of polyandry, as where a brother permits relations with his wife to younger brothers, as well as the system of secondary husbands, might rather be classed as instances of lending.

(*b*) Sometimes it is done by way of sealing a covenant of friendship between two men, who then exchange their wives, as in Timor (*Deutsche Geog. Blätt.* x. 230); or after a quarrel between tribesmen, as in N. S. Wales (*JAI* xiv. 353). In all such cases the friends would belong to the same tribe or clan, and the act would have a more or less sacred significance.

(*c*) Where the custom of lending a wife to a stranger is concerned, it is usually assumed that hospitality alone is the cause (Westermarck, *Marriage*, 74); and though this may frequently be true, it is doubtful whether it covers all such cases, or if the husband would for this reason alone relinquish his rights over his wife. The reason is perhaps to be sought in the common idea that the stranger is, *ipso facto*, a dangerous person. Magical and other ceremonies are often used on his arrival to neutralize the danger (*GB*[2] i. 299 ff.), and respectful treatment throughout his stay is necessary for the same end. Thus the extremely common custom of lending a wife or other woman to a stranger may justly be assumed to be but one of many acts which are intended to ward off his evil powers. It tends to placate him, while, by bringing him into direct relation with the man who offers his wife, it makes him one with him. This view seems to be confirmed by the fact that among the Merekedeh, an Arab tribe, the stranger who would not accept the woman offered him was driven away by the women with hoots and contumely (*Hist. Univ. des Voy.* xxxii. 380). It was desirable to get rid of a guest who was not only dangerous, but evidently disposed to act dangerously. This custom of lending wives to strangers is found practically among all savage tribes (Letourneau, *op. cit. passim*).

(*d*) Occasionally the idea that the woman was ennobled by the embraces of a stranger may have prevailed, especially where he was a white man. This was believed by the Tasmanians (Wake, *Evol. of Morality*, i. 77), and probably underlies the fact that many peoples—Australians, Negroes, Sandwich Islanders, and some Eskimos—who are jealous of their own tribesmen, show no jealousy of white men, and freely allow them to have intercourse with their wives (Westermarck, *Marriage*, 131). On the whole, this idea corresponds to the custom of allowing the medicine man or priest to cohabit with the wife to ensure offspring, or to confer magical or religious virtues. This is found among the Eskimos, who believe that it is an honour for wife and husband that the *angekok* should have intercourse with the former (Egede, *Descr. of Greenland*, 140), among the Kalmuks (Moore, *Marr. Customs*, 182), in the Philippines, India, and Egypt (Reclus, *Prim. Folk*, 172–173). It is perhaps an extension of the custom of defloration by another than the husband, frequently a priest or chief, or of allowing several persons to have access to the newly-married virgin, in order to lessen the danger of sexual tabu for the husband (Crawley, *Mystic Rose*, 347 ff.; Spencer-Gillen[a], 93 ff.; Teulon, *Orig. de la Famille*, 69; Westermarck, 76 ff.)—a custom not to be confounded with the claim made by a chief or feudal lord over all marriageable women, the *jus primæ noctis*.

(*e*) Another cause which will override the feeling of jealousy is the love of gain—the husband trading with his wife to strangers or others. The Yumas of New Mexico and other Amer. Indians, the tribes of tropical S. America, the Eskimos, the Tahitians, and other Polynesian tribes, Negroes, Australians, and others (Bancroft, i. 218, 514; Powers, *Tribes of California*, 413; *ZVRW*, 1898, 297; Lisiansky, *Voyage Round World*, 82, 128; Bosman in Pinkerton, xvi. 525) freely offer their wives for money or its equivalent. But it is to be observed that this revolting practice, though not unknown as between savages themselves, has frequently been introduced or largely increased through contact with men of a higher civilization (Nansen, *Eskimo Life*, 166; Westermarck, 131).

(*f*) Adultery is further sanctioned by social and religious custom, especially at festivals or at other times, when a wife is lent or a general exchange of wives takes place. This apparent promiscuity has usually a distinct end in view, very frequently of a magical character—to ensure the smooth working of the ceremonies about to be observed, or by way of beginning a new life by, so to say, exchanging identity for the time being, or to procure fertility for the soil, or to avert trouble or sickness, or to insure the unified relationship of those practising this promiscuity. Such general exchange is found in Australia (Spencer-Gillen[a], 98, do.[b] 137, 141), in Fiji (*JAI* xiv. 28), among the Eskimos (*Ann. Rep. BE*, vi. 693), and among other peoples (Crawley, *op. cit.* 286). It has probably been of universal occurrence at such times, and in Europe relics of it are found in the folk-festivals, at which considerable licence still prevails.

(*g*) Religious prostitution usually occurred before marriage, and was associated with the worship of divinities of fertility; but in some cases a wife had to devote herself occasionally for this purpose and in order (as in a province of China) to secure magically the fertility of the land (Eusebius, *Vita Const.* iii. 58; Marco Polo, Yule's ed. i. 212).

See also for lending of wives, Starcke, *Primitive Family*, 122; Waitz, ii. 105, iii. 111; Post, *Afrik. Jurisp.* i. 471–472.

8. Adultery as an offence against purity and religion.—It has been seen that, to the savage, adultery is mainly a breach of the husband's proprietary rights. Whether any further ethical idea was imported into it, making it an act of impurity, is a question which it is difficult to answer. But it is not improbable that savages, who are quite aware that it is wrong, may attach some idea of impurity to its committal. If so, this conception may have arisen out of the idea of sexual tabu, the danger existing in intimate relations between man and woman—a danger existing even in marriage. This danger, implying a material contagion, would naturally be increased where a man had no right of access to a woman; it is most dangerous of all where adultery occurs within the forbidden degrees (§ 5). Out of this danger and material contagion the idea of sin and of impurity might easily arise; and we can hardly doubt that, in the evolution of moral ideas, it has so arisen (Crawley, *Mystic Rose*, 214). On this ground, therefore, it might be claimed that adultery is known by savages to be an act of impurity. They certainly believe that there are occasions when it is magically dangerous; that certain penalties will befall the transgressor, either automatically or, possibly, by the act of higher powers.

Ethical teaching among savages has hardly been made the subject of inquiry by actual observers, yet it is curious to note that among some of the lowest races—Australians and Andamans—adultery is held to be a grave moral offence, and, with the former, is taught to be so to the youths at initiation, while with both it is obnoxious to their high god, and will be punished by him (Man, *JAI* xiii. 450, 459; Howitt, *JAI* xii. 156–157, *Native Tribes*, 500). Elsewhere, as among the Indians of Guiana, the fear of spirits prevents them 'from offending against the rights of others,' and this would probably include adultery (*JAI* xi. 382). With the Fuegians, also, 'adultery and lewdness are condemned as evil' (Westermarck, 58). We cannot say, however, that it is with these peoples an offence against purity. Perhaps only at a higher stage is this conception really reached: thus it is said to have been a maxim in ancient Mexico that 'he who looks too curiously on a woman commits adultery with his eyes' (Sahagun, *Hist. gen. de las cosas de Nueva Espagna*, ii. 147), and both in Mexico and Peru a more ethical view of sin obtained. Among the rare cases where savages believe that in the future life retributive justice will follow their evil actions, it is also likely that adultery would be included in such actions. In those cases where the sins of the living are annually transferred to an animal or a human victim, or where this is done on behalf of a dead person as part of the funeral rites, adultery is frequently one of those sins, as among the Niger tribes, the Todas, and Badagas, and others (Crowther and Taylor, *Gospel on Banks of Niger*, 344; Reclus, 208). At the bush festival of the Creek Indians, men who had violated the marriage law were not allowed to take part in the fast, and the new fire was believed to atone for all crimes except murder (Frazer, *GB*² ii. 330). In such cases, however, sin is rather a material than a spiritual contagion, though the particular sin may involve the idea of incipient ethical impurity, and, as such, be obnoxious to higher powers. Again, the magical view of the danger of adultery at certain times is generally mixed up with the danger of lawful connexion at such times, but occasionally a distinction is made. During hunting, fishing, and especially in time of war, men are in a state of tabu, and must have no intercourse with women—a rule found among most savages, and one which must not be broken, lest ill-luck follow. The danger is here magical; but it is interesting to find it becoming more or less religious, as with the Aleuts, who fear that their own or their wives' unfaithfulness during whale-fishing would be punished by the whale, which is an object of reverence to them (Reclus, 52); and with some Amer. Indian tribes, *e.g.* the Dakotas, who think that the violation of captives would be resented by the spirits of the dead; and the Winnebagos, who observe continence because it was commanded by the 'Great Spirit' (Schoolcraft, *Ind. Tribes*, iv. 63; Drake, *Ind. Tribes*, i. 188). A saying of the Eskimos at Angmagsalik may also be cited, that 'the whale, the musk-ox, and the reindeer left the country because men had too much to do with other men's wives' (Nansen, *Eskimo Life*, 173). Occasionally, too, the vengeance of a mysterious god worshipped by males in their private mysteries is invoked, to deter women from adultery among certain Negro tribes, with whom a man representing the god enters the assembled crowd by night, seizes a suspected woman, and scourges her (Letourneau, 128).

It should be noted that the frequent appreciation of the chastity of unmarried women entertained by many savages, while connected with the idea that they are the property of their guardians or prospective husbands, may also be due to respect for sexual tabu. With some peoples, unchastity is considered absolutely disgraceful, and both parties are punished; while in Loango it is held to bring ruin on the country, and with some of the Sea Dyaks it is believed to be offensive to the higher powers (Pinkerton, xvi. 568; St. John, *Forests of Far East*, i. 52).

LITERATURE.—L. T. Hobhouse, *Morals in Evolution*, 1906; C. Letourneau, *L'Evolution du Mariage et de la Famille*, 1888 [Eng. tr. 1897]; A. H. Post, *Afrikan. Jurisprudenz*, 1887, *Grundriss der ethnol. Jurisprudenz*, 1894; M. Steinmetz, *Ethnol. Studien zur ersten Entwicklung der Strafe*; E. Westermarck, *History of Human Marriage*, 1891, *Origin and Development of the Moral Ideas*, 1906.

J. A. MACCULLOCH.

ADULTERY (Buddhist).—The last of the five Precepts binding on a Buddhist layman is not to act wrongly in respect of fleshly lusts (*Anguttara*, 3. 212). In a very ancient paraphrase of these Precepts in verse (*Sutta Nipāta*, 393–398), this one is expressed as follows: 'Let the wise man avoid unchastity as if it were a pit of live coals. Should he be unable to be celibate, let him not offend with regard to the wife of another.' This is evidence not so much of Buddhist ethics as of the general standard of ethics in the 6th cent. B.C., in Kosala and Magadha. In the Buddhist Canon Law we find a regulation to be followed by members of the Order, when on their rounds for alms, in order to prevent the possibility of suspicion or slander in this respect (*Pācittiya*, 43, translated in *Vinaya Texts*, 1. 41). An adulterer taken in the act might be wounded or slain on the spot. This explains the implication of the words used in *Samyutta*, 2. 188. But adultery was also an offence against the State, and an offender could be arrested by the police, and brought up for trial and judgment (Commentary on Dhammapada, 300). In such texts of the law administered in Buddhist countries as have so far been made accessible to us, the view taken of adultery is based on these ancient customs. So, for instance, of the Siṁhalese, Panabokke says (*Nīti Nighaṇḍuwa*, p. xxix) that adultery, unless committed in the king's palace, was seldom punished by the Kandian judges; (1) because the husband was loath, by complaint, to publish his disgrace; and (2) because he was allowed to take vengeance himself if the offender were caught under such circumstances that adultery was presumable. (See also Richardson, *The Dhammathat*, Burmese text and English translation, Rangoon, 1906). Nothing is said in the Buddhist law-books of any punishment to be inflicted, either by the husband or by the State, on the adulteress. Buddhist influence in this matter, except in so far as it mitigated severity against the woman, was therefore confined to the maintenance of pre-Buddhistic ideas and customs.

T. W. RHYS DAVIDS.

ADULTERY (Egyptian).—That adultery with a married woman was looked upon as a sin in Egypt is shown by the Negative Confession (part of ch. 125 of the Book of the Dead, a chapter that has not yet been found earlier than the 18th Dyn.). Here, in the 19th clause, we read, 'I have not defiled the wife of a husband' (*v.l.* 'the wife of another man'). That it was also against the law is implied by a text of the reign of Ramses V. (*c.* 1150 B.C.) containing a long list of crimes charged against a shipmaster at Elephantine, amongst them being that of adultery with two women, each of whom is described as 'mother of M. and wife of Ṇ.' (Pleyte, *Pap. de Turin*, pl. li ff.; Spiegelberg, *ZÄ*, 1891, 82). The didactic papyri warn against adultery as well as fornication. Ptahhotep says, 'If thou desirest to prolong friendship in a house which thou enterest as master, as colleague, or as friend, or wheresoever thou enterest, avoid approaching the women; no place prospereth where that is done. . . . A thousand men have been destroyed to enjoy a short moment like a dream: one attaineth death in knowing it' (*Prisse Pap.* ix. 7–12; Gunn, *Instruc-*

tion of Ptahhotep, p. 49). This text is not later than the Middle Kingdom. Another, of the period of the Deltaic dynasties, charges the youth to remember that 'the woman whose husband is afar off (or possibly 'the woman whose husband has freed himself from her,' *i.e.* 'divorced her'), behold she adorneth herself for thee daily. If there is no witness with her, she standeth and spreadeth her net. O crime worthy of death if one listens!' (*Pap. de Boulaq*, i. 16; Erman, *Life in Ancient Egypt*, 155). The story of Ubaaner turns on the infidelity of his wife with a peasant, who is eventually handed over to a magic crocodile to devour, the woman being taken to the north side of the palace (evidently a place of public assembly) and burned, and her ashes cast into the river (Erman, *Pap. Westcar*, p. 1 ff.; Petrie, *Tales*, i. p. 97; Maspero, *Contes Pop.*[3] p. 24). One of Herodotus' Egyptian tales is of king Pheron, who gathered his unfaithful wives into one town and destroyed all together by fire (Hdt. ii. 111). But it would not be safe to conclude that burning was ever the established penalty for adultery. In the New-Kingdom Story of the Two Brothers (Petrie, *Tales*, ii. p. 36; Maspero, p. 1), Bito, the younger brother, is solicited by the wife of the elder brother Anûp, like Joseph by the wife of Potiphar, and reproves her with the words, 'thou art as a mother unto me, and thy husband as a father.' Anûp, when convinced of her guilt—which was doubledyed, since in her fear she had accused Bito to him, and endeavoured to persuade him to kill Bito—slew her and cast her to the dogs. What the legal penalty for adultery was in real life, or by whom it was exacted, is not known. In two contracts of the time of the 26th Dyn., the earliest marriage contracts yet discovered in Egypt, the husband declares, 'If I leave the woman N., whether desiring to leave her from dislike (?) or desiring another woman than her, apart from the *great crime* that is found in woman, I will restore to her' the dowry, etc. The implication is that the husband had at least no obligation to the wife if he had divorced her for adultery. These contracts were written at Thebes in 589 and 549 B.C. respectively. Later marriage contracts, those of the reign of Darius and the numerous Egyptian contracts of Ptolemaic date, contain no definite reference to adultery (for all these see Griffith, *Catalogue of the John Rylands Papyri*, pp. 114 ff., 134 ff.); on the other hand, in the rarer Ptolemaic contracts written in Greek (Grenfell and Hunt, *Tebtunis Papyri*, i. 449) adultery and all forms of conjugal infidelity are forbidden to both husband and wife. The penalty for the husband is the forfeiture of the dowry, but that for the wife is not specified; perhaps one may gather that she was left absolutely at her husband's mercy. The contracts of Roman date, all of which are written in Greek, prescribe a blameless life on both sides, but in less detail.

A chapter of the very ancient Pyramid texts, as found in the pyramid of Unas (Onnos), after describing the divinity of the dead king and the continued activity of his bodily functions, ends strangely: 'Unas is a generator who carrieth off women from their husbands to any place that he wisheth, when his heart moveth him.' This idea is hardly to be reconciled with a highly developed moral sense in the nation, unless the divinity of kings invested them with special privileges that would be contrary to all good manners for their subjects.

F. LL. GRIFFITH.

ADULTERY (Greek).—In Athens, adultery (μοιχεία) on the part of the wife implied criminal intercourse with any man other than her husband. On the part of the husband it was, strictly speaking, criminal intercourse with the wife, sister, or mother of a fellow-citizen, or with his concubine, if she were a native Athenian (Dem. *Aristocr.* p. 637, § 53).

This strict interpretation was in the classical period widened so as to include offences committed against maidens and widows. On neither side is the offence regarded as a violation of the sanctity of a binding obligation, but as an offence against the family. Hence the special severity with which the wife was treated as compared with the husband. Any act of misconduct on her side might introduce alien blood into the family and pollute the worship of its ancestors. Marital infidelity involved no such dangers to a man's own family, and was condoned by law, except in so far as it infringed the rights of other families. There are traces, however, which show that the best opinion condemned it (Isocrates, *Nicocles*, § 42; Aristot. *Pol.* 1336*a*. 1; Plaut. *Merc.* 817 f., where the reference is to Greek and not Roman life).

1. Punishment of the man.—If the husband caught the offender *flagrante delicto* (ἄρθρ' ἐν ἄρθροις ἔχων, Lucian, *Eun.* 10), he might kill him at once (Dem. *Aristocr.* § 53). That this law was no mere antiquated survival can be seen from Lysias, *de cæde Eratosth.* § 23 ff., where an account will be found of the killing of the adulterer Eratosthenes by the injured husband Euphiletus, who, it should be noticed, is careful to secure the presence of witnesses to his act. The husband, however, might content himself with punishment short of death, *e.g.* παρατιλμός and ῥαφανίδωσις (Suid. *s.v.* ῥαφανίς and Λακιάδαι; Schol. Aristoph. *Nub.* 1083, *Plut.* 168, *Eccl.* 722); or he might agree to accept a sum of money in compensation for the wrong done to him. He was allowed to keep the offender prisoner until satisfactory guarantees were given that the sum promised would be paid ([Dem.] *in Neær.* § 65; Lys. *de cæde Eratosth.* § 25: ἱκέτευε μὴ ἀποκτεῖναι ἀλλ' ἀργύριον πράξασθαι). If the alleged adulterer denied the offence, he could bring an action for unjust detention (ἀδικῶς εἱρχθῆναι ὡς μοιχόν) before the Thesmothetæ. Should he fail to prove his case, the Court directed his sureties to hand him over to the offended husband, who might inflict whatever chastisement he chose within the precincts of the Court, provided that sword or dagger was not used (ἄνευ ἐγχειριδίου, *in Neær.* § 66). If the offender escaped, or had not been taken in the act, the husband or, in the case of maidens and widows, the guardian (κύριος) could bring an action for adultery (γραφὴ μοιχείας) before the Thesmothetæ. It is doubtful if any one unconnected with the family could bring such an action. It is not known exactly what penalty was inflicted, but in all probability it was disfranchisement (ἀτιμία), either total or partial.

2. Punishment of the woman.—If misconduct was proved, the husband was required to repudiate his wife, under the penalty of himself suffering ἀτιμία. She was excluded from public temples, and, if she refused compliance, could be expelled with impunity by any citizen. Such assailant might tear off her clothes and ornaments, but might not maim or kill her (*in Neær.* § 87; Æschin. *in Timarch.* § 183). Heliodorus (*Æthiop.* i. 11) is mistaken in stating that an adulteress was punished by death.

Little is known of the practice of other Greek communities in dealing with adultery. That it was everywhere regarded as a grave crime is clear from Xen. *Hiero*, iii. 3, where it is stated that many cities allowed the adulterer to be killed with impunity. Zaleucus, the Locrian legislator, ordained the punishment of blinding (Æl. *Var. Hist.* xiii. 24. 5); at Cyme and in Pisidia the adulteress was paraded on an ass (Plut. *Quæst. Gr.* 2; Stob. *Anth.* xliv. 41); and at various other cities, *e.g.*

Lepreon, Gortyn, and Tenedos, the offenders were either fined, pilloried, or disfranchised.

LITERATURE.—Meier and Schömann, *Der Attische Process*, ed. J.H. Lipsius, pp. 404–409; W. A. Becker, *Charikles*, ed. Göll. iii. p. 394 ff.; L. Beauchet, *Hist. du droit privé de la Répub. Athén.* i. p. 232 f. The chief passages from Greek authors are collected in I. B. Télfy, *Corpus Juris Attici*, No. 1169–1184.

F. W. HALL.

ADULTERY (Hindu).—The view which Hindus take of adultery is founded upon their conception of the nature of woman and marriage. The whole of Hindu literature is pervaded by the pessimistic idea of the inconstancy of the female character, by complaints of woman's unbridled indulgence of passion, and by demands for the maintenance of a strict oversight upon her. The practice of polygamy, which has existed from ancient times in India by the side of monogamy, and the consequently slight esteem in which the Hindu woman has been held up to the present day, must necessarily have led to the occurrence of adultery, and to a lenient judgment being passed upon the fault. On the other hand, it should be noted that we do find, even if not so frequently, an especially high value set upon the wife who proves true to her husband (*pativratā*), and that the law threatens adultery with severe punishment.

As early as the oldest historical period, the Indian people, on the testimony of the Rigveda, are by no means found, as is sometimes represented, in a condition of patriarchal simplicity and of austere moral habit. The word 'adultery' is unknown to the Veda. But numerous indications point to the fact that the highly developed culture did not fail to produce its ordinary consequences in corruption of character and moral laxity. Women who betray their husbands (*patiripaḥ*) are mentioned by way of comparison in Rigv. iv. 5. 5: 'Evil-doers . . . who walk in evil ways, like women who betray their husbands, shall be consumed by Agni.' In verse 4 of the didactic poem Rigv. x. 34, it is said that 'others lay hands on the wife of the man who abandons himself to the dice.' If from these passages we may infer on the one hand a censure upon the transgression of the marriage vow, on the other hand matrimonial infidelity is spoken of as something in itself intelligible and of daily occurrence. To this effect are the numerous stories which relate the intrigues of the gods with married women, *e.g.* of Indra with the wife of Vṛṣanaśva (Rigv. i. 51. 13, combined with Sāṭyāyana-Brāhmana by Sāyaṇa *in l.c.*; Ṣaḍviṁśa-Br. i. 1. 16; Maitrāyaṇīsaṁhitā ii. 5. 5), with Apālā Ātreyī (Rigv. viii. 91, and Sāṭy. Br. in *l.c.*), and with Ahalyā, the wife of Gautama (Ṣaḍv. Br. i. 1. 19–20); of the Aśvin with Sukanyā, the wife of Chyavana (Śatap. Br. iv. 1. 5), etc. The conduct of the gods is not here made a matter of reproach; and as little in other passages is adultery regarded from the ethical standpoint. It is because the Brāhman is in possession of the secret whereby he can by his curse inflict harm, that *therefore* men must refrain from illicit intercourse with the wife of a Brāhman (Śatap. Br. xiv. 9. 4, 11; Bṛhadār. vi. 4. 12; Pārask. Gṛh. Sūt. i. 11. 6). Adultery is mentioned in a similar connexion in the Atharvaveda, *viz.* in the magical spells and imprecations by which, for example, wives soothe the jealousy of their husbands, or keep their rivals at a distance, or by which the husband seeks to win back his unfaithful wife (Atharv. vi. 18; iii. 18; vi. 77).

The following passages throw a light that is altogether unfavourable on the ethical conditions of the Vedic period:—

In the *varuṇapraghāsa* the wife of the sacrificer is required by the priest to name her paramour.* 'Who cares whether the wife is unchaste (*paraḥpuṁsā*) or no?'* In Ts. v. 6. 8, 3 a special penance is appointed for the man who for the first time has performed the sacred *agnichayanam*; he is not again to have intercourse with a *rāmā* (the wife of a Śūdra). And he who has performed it for the second time must abstain henceforth from intercourse with the wife of another man.† Such conditions, comparable with hetairism, must have exercised an unfavourable influence on the purity of the race, and have rendered illusory the detailed pedigrees which were essential for ancestor-worship and other ritual purposes. That men were conscious of the actual unreliability of the lists of ancestors is shown by Nidānasūtra, iii. 8: 'Inconstant are the ways of women. Of whomsoever (as father) I shall call myself the son before both gods and men as witnesses, his son I shall be; and those whom I shall name as (my) sons, they will be my sons.' The attempt, however, was of course made in ancient times to provide against this ignorance by strict oversight of the woman; for the begetting of a son of the body (*vijāvan*) is regarded even in the Rigveda as necessary for the preservation of the race.‡ A proof of this is afforded by an ancient *gāthā* quoted in Āpastamba, ii. 13. 7, and Baudhāyana, ii. 3. 34, which is taken from a dialogue between Aupajandhani, a teacher of the white Yajurveda, and the mythical king Janaka: 'Now am I jealous for my wife, O Janaka, though (I was) not before; for in Yama's house the son is awarded to him who begat him. The begetter leads the son after his death into the dwelling-place of Yama. Therefore they protect their wives carefully, who dread the seed of strangers. Watch jealously this propagation of (your) race, let no strange seed fall on your field. When he passes into the other world, the son belongs to him who begat him; it is in vain that the husband (the nominal father) accomplishes this perpetuation of his race.'

A contrast between an earlier period of laxity and a later of austere morals can hardly be derived from the passages quoted. Even when in later times a strict marriage law was developed, and in the *Smṛtis* legal regulations were formulated with regard to adultery (*strīsaṅgrahaṇa*), polygamy and prostitution continued to exist, and the frequent mention of the son 'born secretly,'§ who may be heir to his mother's husband, though he is her illegitimate son by some other man, does not testify to a high regard for the marriage vow. A change of view was effected in course of time only so far as under the increasing influence of priestly theories adultery was seen to involve a danger to the caste system established by the Brāhmans, and an attempt was made to obviate this by the threat of severe punishments. It is essentially from the standpoint of caste distinctions that adultery is condemned in the *Smṛtis*. 'Whatever woman betrays‖ her husband, proud of her beauty and her descent, the king shall cause to be torn in pieces by dogs in an open place. The paramour shall be roasted on an iron bed; brushwood shall men throw (upon the fire); there shall the evil-doer be consumed.'¶ If these words implied merely the condemnation of adultery in general, they would be in contradiction to the comparatively lenient punishments prescribed later on.** The crime which demands an expiation so terrible is certainly the intercourse of a Brāhman woman with a man belonging to one of the three lower castes. This is proved by the similar regulations of other lawgivers,†† and the parallel passages of the Mahābhārata and Agnipurāṇa:

'Whatever woman abandons the nobler husband (*i.e.* a Brāhman, according to the commentator Nīlakaṇṭha) and seeks another inferior marriage couch (*svavarṇān nīchavarṇam*, 'inferior as regards caste,' Nīlakaṇṭha), the king shall cause to be torn in pieces by dogs in an open place.'‡‡ 'Whoever being lower (in caste) has sexual intercourse with a woman higher (in caste) deserves death. But the woman, who betrays her husband, shall he (the king) cause to be torn in pieces by dogs.'§§

* *Kena charasi*, 'with whom do you go?' Śat. ii. 5. 2, 20; cf. Kāty. v. 5. 6–10.

* Yājñavalkya in Śat. i. 3. 1, 21.

† *Na dvitīyaṁ chitvā 'nyasya striyam upeyāt.*

‡ Rigv. iii. 1. 23, vii. 4. 7.

§ *Gūḍhaja, gūḍhotpanna.*

‖ *Laṅghayet*, properly 'sets herself up above'; according to the commentators, *anyapuruṣagamanena* (Nārāyaṇa), *puruṣāntaropagamanena* (Kullūka), deceives him 'by intercourse with another man.'

¶ Manu, viii. 371 f.

** Manu, viii. 374 ff.

†† Āpastamba, ii. 10. 27, 8, 9; Gautama, xxiii. 14, 15; Yājñavalkya, ii. 286.

‡‡ *Śreyāṁsaṁ śayanaṁ hitvā yānyam pāpam nigachchhati, śvabhis tām ardayed rājā saṁsthāne bahuvistare*, Mahābh. xii. 165. 64.

§§ *Uttamāṁ sevamānaḥ strīṁ jaghanyo vadham arhati, bhartāraṁ laṅghayed yā tāṁ śvabhiḥ saṅghātayet striyam*, Agni-Pur. 227 42

By the side of these savage penalties the punishments assigned in the following verses of the Agni-P. in expiation of adultery seem altogether ludicrous: 'The woman misused by a man belonging to an equal caste shall be allowed to eat only sufficient to sustain life; the woman misused by a man of a higher caste shall have her head shaved. A Brāhman for intercourse with a Vaiśya woman, a Kṣatriya for intercourse with a woman of lower caste, a Kṣatriya or a Vaiśya for the first offence of intercourse with a Śūdra woman, shall be fined.'

The punishments in Manu are similarly graded according to the caste to which the offenders belong. For adultery with the wife of a man of one of the three higher castes, a Śūdra is to be punished with confiscation of property and the cutting off of his organ of generation; if she were guarded,—a condition to which great importance is attached,—the penalty may even be death. In this latter case a similar punishment overtakes the Vaiśya or Kṣatriya who is guilty with a Brāhman woman; otherwise they escape with heavy fines, imprisonment, shaving of the head, and watering of the head with urine. A Brāhman, on the contrary, who is guilty of a similar offence, is only condemned to fines, which are lower than in the case of a Kṣatriya.*

The wife guilty of adultery may justly be repudiated, and expulsion from caste also usually follows. Since, however, divorce is opposed to the principle of Hindu law, which regards it as a sin for husband and wife to be separated on the ground of mutual aversion,† and according to the testimony of al-Bīrūnī did not occur,‡ we must assume that, as a rule, the adultery was not allowed to come to light, and that the rule of Viṣṇu was observed, according to which the tribunals were to interfere only when the husband was unable without assistance to manage his wife.§ In the view of certain *Smṛtis* also, absolute repudiation of the wife was not always the consequence of adultery. Pāraskara ordains that repudiation is to be resorted to only where the adulterous connexion has not been without result, or the woman has separated herself permanently from her family.‖ Hārīta even declares himself expressly against the repudiation of the adulteress.¶ Other passages make mention of merely temporary and insignificant penances, such as the use of inferior food and clothing, sleeping on the ground, and performance of the servile tasks of scouring and sweeping.**

Statements which appear strange, but which are based upon the inferior position of the Hindu woman and the restraint to which she is subjected, regard as adultery conversations in an improper place or at an improper time, personal contact, playing and jesting, even the rendering of attentions and gifts of clothing, ornaments, flowers, etc.††

Undoubtedly more of theory than reality underlies these legal prescriptions. How little they corresponded to generally accepted ideas of morality is shown, for example, by the paragraph of the Kāmasūtra which treats of intercourse with married women. Among the reasons which deter a woman from adultery, regard for morals is mentioned only in the last place. Even the stern penalties which the law ordains for adultery between those belonging to different castes are to be ascribed, in the first instance, to the endeavour of the Brāhmans to give support to the social order which they had themselves evolved, and to assert the precedence to which they laid claim. Actual examples, nevertheless, of the infliction of savage punishments upon adulteresses are found in the popular literature. Instances are on record where the king is enjoined to have the nose and ears of the adulterous wife cut off.‡‡ In a narrative of the Pañchatantra §§ the aggrieved husband himself administers correction by cutting off his wife's nose and repudiating her. This kind of penalty seems to have been quite usual in the Middle Ages, even

* Manu, viii. 374–378. † Nārada, xii. 90. ‡ *India*, ii. 154.
§ Viṣṇu, v. 18. ‖ Pār. x. 15. ¶ Hār. iii. 13.
** Gautama, xxii. 35; Vasiṣṭha, xxi. 8, 35; Yājñavalkya, i. 70; Nārada, xii. 91.
†† Nārada, xii. 62–68.
‡‡ *e.g.* Kathāsaritsāgara, 61. §§ Pañch. iii. 16.

as it is to-day. It meets us again, at least as a threat, in the legendary literature of the Buddhists. 'And of this evil woman cut off the ears and nose from her living body.'* As here the threatened punishment is not carried out, so elsewhere throughout the Jātakas a very mild conception of adultery is presented. In the Pabbatūpatthara Jātaka † the king begs his wife, whom he loves, and the minister with whom she has had guilty intercourse, not to sin again, and forgives them. Another king, who has been betrayed by his wife with all the sixty-four messengers whom he has sent to her during the campaign, gives orders for the guilty parties to be beheaded. The future Buddha, however, obtains their pardon by pointing out to the king that the men were led astray by the queen, and that she has only followed her nature, since women are insatiable in the indulgence of their passions.‡ Elsewhere a minister who has transgressed in the royal harem, and is caught *flagrante delicto*, is banished from the realm.§

This lenient judgment of adultery as it is found in the Jātakas is, nevertheless, not to be traced to an intentional relaxation on the part of the Buddhists of the Brāhman law of marriage, but rather to the fact that the narratives, which arose in popular circles and were transmitted orally, reflect the Hindu view better than the Brāhman theory as formulated in the *Smṛtis*. Among the peoples, moreover, who adopted Buddhism, marriage law and custom, like prescriptive rights and usages in general, underwent no essential change. Abstinence from adultery was one of the rules the observance of which was enjoined by the Congregation on the youths of the laity.‖ 'The taking of life,' it is said in the Sīgālovādasutta, which minutely describes the duties of the laity, 'the appropriation of another's possessions, and falsehood are named (as offences); the wise do not commend intercourse with the wife of another man (*paradāragamanam*).'

According to the traditional accounts of the indigenous customary law of Ceylon, open punishment for adultery was usual only when the wives of the king were involved. In other cases the husband was at liberty, if he had caught the seducer in the act, to beat, wound, or even kill him. If the husband laid a complaint on the ground of adultery, the accused, in the absence of proof, was to be dismissed with reproof and warnings; but if convicted, to be condemned to light bodily punishment, with imprisonment and fine.¶

The legal principles, also, which are in force in Burma, and which are traceable to Hindu law but little modified by Buddhism, do not in general recognize the severe penalties threatened in the Brāhman law-books. Members of the lower castes guilty of adultery with a Brāhman woman are to be punished with 100 blows of a stick, but with 1000 blows in case of intercourse with a Kṣatriya. More stern punishments, however, such as burning alive, may be inflicted.** In other cases fines suffice for expiation, the amount varying with the caste of the parties concerned. Should the offender, however, be unable to pay, he is reduced to slavery. The seducer must further apologize, and give his promise not to repeat the offence. Should he break his promise, he is excluded, if a Kṣatriya, from intercourse with his relatives; if a Brāhman, he is excommunicated from his caste, and reduced to the condition of a Chaṇḍāla.†† According to another passage of the

* Cullapadumajāt. 193. † Pabb. 195.
‡ Akālarāvijāt. 119.
§ Ghatajāt. 355, and similarly Seyyajāt. 282.
‖ *Michchhāchārā virāmo*; cf. Dhammikasutta, Sutta Nipāta, 66 f.
¶ *Nīti-Nighaṇḍuva*, Introd. p. xxix f.
** Menu Kyay, vi. 30. †† *Ib.* vi. 8.

same law-book,* which exhibits in general a remarkable contrast to Hindu law, the Brāhman who is guilty of adultery with a woman of his own caste shall have his head shaved and be banished, or excommunicated from his caste.

The husband may separate himself from his adulterous wife, and may retain all her possessions.† The right to leave the unfaithful husband belongs also to the wife,‡ but she has no claim to the whole property.

In modern India adultery is regarded in the same light as in ancient times, since the regulations of the Brāhman law-books are still valid, and the social position of woman has undergone little change. It is true that even by the Hindu of to-day the chaste wife who remains loyal to her husband is looked upon as the incarnation of Lakṣmī, the goddess of wealth and good fortune; § but how little confidence the Hindus place in the faithfulness of their wives is shown by the close watch to which now, as formerly, they are subjected. The fear of punishment is regarded at the present time also as the best security for the observance of the marriage vow. 'No punishment is thought too brutal for unfaithfulness, and of this fact the women are well aware. I have myself seen instances, especially in the North-West Provinces, where a husband has cut off the nose of his wife, not even upon actual proof, but upon mere suspicion. Hands are sometimes cut off, and other horrible forms of mutilation are resorted to. . . . The woman, robbed of her fair looks, is ruthlessly cast out.' ‖ Even if this picture is overdrawn, yet other travellers confirm the fact that stern jurisdiction is sometimes exercised by the husband. In Nepāl the aggrieved husband has the right openly to cut down the seducer when found guilty; and here, as well as among certain Chittagong Hill Tribes, a wife whom infidelity has betrayed into guilt is deprived of nose and ears.

Divorce on the ground of adultery is allowed, according to the Madras Census Report for 1891. The Census Report, also, of the North-West Provinces and Oudh for 1901 mentions that the lower as well as the higher castes permit the divorce of the wife for unchastity. If, nevertheless, instances of divorce are rare, the cause is to be found less in a lofty morality than in the endeavour of the Hindus to withdraw their family life as much as possible from publicity.

LITERATURE.—J. Jolly, 'Recht u. Sitte,' in *GIAP* ii. 8, Strassburg, 1896, pp. 66, 121, 128; H. Zimmer, *Altindisches Leben*, 1870, pp. 306 ff., 331 f.; A. Weber, *Indische Studien*, x. 1868, p. 83 f.; Pischel and Geldner, *Vedische Studien*, i. 1889, p. xxv; E. Hopkins, 'Social and Military Position of the Ruling Caste in Ancient India,' in *JAOS*, vol. xiii. 1889, pp. 107, 367; *Nīti-Nighaṇḍuva*, or *Vocabulary of the Law in the Kandyan Kingdom*, tr. by Le Mesurier and Panabokke, 1880, p. xix f.; Jardine and Forschhammer, *Notes on Buddhist Law*, Rangoon, 1882; Rich. Schmidt, *Liebe u. Ehe im alten u. mod. Indien*, 1904, p. 433; J. A. Dubois, *Hindu Manners, Customs, and Ceremonies*[2], tr. by H. R. Beauchamp, 1889, p. 313; S. C. Bose, *Hindoos as they are*[2], 1883, p. 288; M. F. Billington, *Woman in India*, London, 1895, p. 123; K. Boeck, *Durch Indien ins verschlossene Land Nepal*, 1903, p. 286; E. Westermarck, *History of Human Marriage*, 1891, p. 122.

R. FICK.

ADULTERY (Jewish).—The substitution of monogamy for polygamy made no change in the Jewish law on adultery. From the time of the Babylonian Exile, monogamy became the prevalent custom in Jewish life. But the law continued to regard as adultery only the intercourse of a married woman with any man other than her husband. Thus a married man was not regarded as guilty of adultery unless he had intercourse with a *married* woman other than his wife. For in theory he might have several wives, and an unmarried woman with whom he had intercourse might become his wife. In fact, according to the Rabbinic law, such intercourse might be construed into a legal marriage. But concubinage was severely condemned (*Leviticus Rabba*, ch. xxv.). Yet the difference between the legal position of the male and the female adulterer (using the term in its now current sense) was considerably affected by the abolition of the Jewish power to pronounce or inflict capital punishment. This occurred, according to the Jewish sources (Jerus. *Sanh.* 18*a*, 24*b*; Bab. *Sanh.* 41*a*), forty years before the destruction of the Temple (*i.e.* in the year A.D. 30); but whatever be thought of this exact date, there is no doubt that the death penalty was neither pronounced nor inflicted for adultery in the time of Christ. Hence it is generally conceded that the case of the woman taken in adultery (Jn 8^{1-11}) does not imply that the woman would actually have been stoned. In the first place, the law of Moses does not prescribe stoning except where a betrothed virgin had intercourse with a man other than her affianced husband (Dt $22^{23.24}$). In other cases (Lv 20^{10}, Dt 22^{22}) the method of execution is not defined, and in all such cases, according to Jewish tradition, the criminal was executed not by stoning, but by strangulation (Mishna *Sanh.* xi. 1). Secondly, it will be observed that the woman had not yet been tried by the court. Finally, as indicated above, the death penalty had long ceased to be inflicted for adultery. The point of the incident in the Gospel of St. John was just the attempt to put Jesus into a dilemma, as the commentators point out. It may well be that the irregularities indicated above were an intentional aggravation of the record.

The punishment for adultery was modified into the divorce of the woman, who lost all her rights under the marriage settlement; the man was scourged. The husband of the adulteress was not permitted to cohabit with her; he was compelled to divorce her (Mishna, *Soṭa* vi. 1; Maimonides, *Hilch. Ishuth*, xxiv. 6). The adulteress was not allowed to marry her paramour (*Soṭa* v. 1). In case of the man's adultery, he was compelled to grant a divorce on his wife's application; the woman, of course, could not initiate divorce proceedings, but in the view of some of the mediæval authorities the Court would compel the husband to divorce her in case of his habitual licentiousness (*Eben ha-'Ezer*, § 154, 1 gloss). The 'ordeal of the bitter waters' (Nu 5^{11-31}) was abolished by Jochanan ben Zakkai during the Roman invasion (Mishna, *Soṭa* ix. 9), though Queen Helena of Adiabene—a proselyte to Judaism in the 1st cent. A.D.—sought to restore it (Mishna, *Yoma* iii. 10; Tosefta, *Yoma* ii. 3). Of the ordeal itself, R. Aḳiba (2nd cent. A.D.) remarks: 'Only when the (suspicious) husband is himself free from guilt will the waters be an effective test of his wife's guilt or innocence; but if he has himself been guilty of illicit intercourse, the waters will have no effect' (Sifrē, *Nasō*, 21; *Soṭa*, 47*b*). Mr. Amram (*Jewish Encyc.* vol. i. p. 217) comments on this passage as follows: 'In the light of this rabbinical dictum, the saying of Jesus in the case of the woman taken in adultery acquires a new meaning. To those asking for her punishment, he replied: "He that is without sin among you, let him first cast a stone at her" (Jn 8^{7}).' The abolition of the ordeal is attributed in the Mishna to the great prevalence of adultery; and it may be that in the disturbed conditions due to the Roman régime laxity of morals intruded itself.

But if so, it was but a temporary lapse. The records of Jewish life give evidence of remarkable purity in marital relations (cf. Abrahams, *Jewish Life in the Middle Ages*, 1896, 90 f.). The sanctity of marriage was upheld as the essential condition for social happiness and virtue. The moral abhorrence felt against the crime of adultery is shown in many

* Menu Kyay, vi. 31.
† *Ib.* xii. 43.
‡ Manoo Woonnana Dhammathat, 176.
§ Bose, p. 288.
‖ Billington, *Woman in India*, p. 123.

Rabbinical utterances. Not all a man's other virtues would save him from Gehenna if he committed adultery (*Soṭa*, 4*b*). Even lustful desire was condemned as a moral offence (*Eben ha-'Ezer*, § 21; cf. Mt 5[27. 28]). Perhaps the most remarkable testimony to the Jewish detestation of the crime is to be found in the Talmud (*Sanh.* 74*a*). In the year A.D. 135, at the crisis of the disastrous revolt against Hadrian, a meeting was held at Lydda. The assembly was attended by several famous Rabbis (including Aḳiba), and the question was discussed as to the extent of conformity with Roman demands which might justifiably be made rather than face the alternative of death. It was decided that every Jew must surrender his life rather than commit any of the three offences, idolatry, murder, or *gillui 'ărāyôth* (גִּלּוּי עֲרָיוֹת). This latter phrase includes both adultery and incest (Graetz, *Hist. of the Jews*, English tr., ii. ch. xvi.).

LITERATURE.—Z. Frankel, *Grundlinien des Mosaisch-Talmudischen Eherechts* (Breslau, 1860); D. W. Amram, *Jewish Law of Divorce* (1896); and the same author's art. 'Adultery' in *Jewish Encyc.* vol. i.

I. ABRAHAMS.

ADULTERY (Muslim).—In the year 4 of the Hijra, the Prophet was accompanied on one of his military expeditions by his wife, 'A'isha. One day, at the removal from the camp towards night, she remained behind and reached Muhammad's caravan only on the following morning, in the company of a man. This circumstance caused great scandal. Even the Prophet at first suspected his wife of adultery. Afterwards, however, it was revealed to him that she had been falsely accused, and he was again reconciled to her. The verses of the Qur'ān that have reference to this occurrence, namely, *Sūr.* xxiv. 1–5, contain, amongst other statements, the following words: 'As for the whore and the whoremonger, scourge each of them with a hundred stripes, and do not let pity for them take hold of you in Allah's religion. . . . But as for those who cast (imputations) on chaste women and do not bring four witnesses, scourge them with eighty stripes, and do not receive any testimony of theirs for ever' (cf. Th. Nöldeke, *Gesch. des Qorâns*, p. 156; A. Sprenger, *Das Leben und die Lehre des Mohammad*, iii. 63 ff.; D. S. Margoliouth, *Mohammed and the Rise of Islam*, p. 341; *The Koran*, Sale's Eng. tr., ed. 1825, ii. 180).

In Islām, therefore, according to these verses of the Qur'ān, incontinence should be punished with one hundred stripes. Originally, however, Muhammad had commanded that those who had been found guilty of this misdemeanour should be put to death by stoning—a punishment which he had probably derived from Judaism. In the Muslim tradition, various instances are mentioned in which this punishment is said to have been inflicted at Muhammad's command (cf. A. N. Matthews, *Mishkât-ul-Maṣâbîḥ*, ii. 182–186, Calcutta, 1810; I. Goldziher, 'Mohammedanisches Recht in Theorie und Wirklichkeit' (*Zeitschr. f. vergl. Rechtswissensch.* viii. 466 ff.). It may thus be understood that the Prophet had designedly mitigated the punishment attached to adultery out of affection for 'A'isha.

After Muhammad's death, a difference of opinion arose amongst the faithful with respect to this point. Many thought that the punishment of stoning to death was abrogated by the verses of Qur'ān xxiv. 1–5. But the second Khalīf, 'Umar, set his face very strongly against this view. According to him, adultery in Islām should be punished with stoning. 'Thus hath the Prophet ordained it,' said he, 'and thus have we acted on his command. Some people say that they find no injunction to this effect in Allah's book; but in the days of Muhammad we were accustomed in the recitation of the Qur'ān to recite also a verse in which the punishment of stoning was undoubtedly denounced against the violator of the marriage bond.' Indeed, according to Muslim tradition, such a verse is said to have formed originally a part of the thirty-third *Sūra* (cf. Nöldeke, *op. cit.* p. 185).

In the Muslim law-books, both punishments, stoning as well as scourging, are found threatened against the offence of fornication (Arab. *zinâ*). By this offence, the Muslim jurists understand not only adultery, but any sexual intercourse between two persons who do not stand to one another in the relation of husband and wife or master and slave. For those who are not yet married, if they render themselves guilty of this offence, scourging is thought sufficient; all others must in that case be put to death by stoning. An individual belonging to the latter group of persons is in Arabic called *muḥṣan*. The original signification of this word is 'well-guarded,' but in Arabic it came to be employed metaphorically to signify a married woman, and later a married person in general (cf. J. Wellhausen, 'Die Ehe bei den Arabern,' *Nachrichten der königl. Gesellsch. der Wissensch. in Göttingen*, 1893, No. 11, p. 447). According to the jurists, however, a person remains *muḥṣan*, even though his marriage may have been dissolved at a later period. If he thereafter renders himself guilty of *zinâ*, he must be stoned. In Islām, stoning is thus not a punishment exclusively of adultery, as was often incorrectly supposed (cf. Snouck Hurgronje, review of E. Sachau's *Mohammedanisches Recht* in *ZDMG* liii. 161 ff.).

On various matters of detail, as, for example, the question whether those who are to be stoned must also be scourged, etc., many go into different scholastic minutiæ. The evidence of *zinâ*, however, according to Qur'ān xxiv. 1–5, cannot be presented except by the testimony of four male witnesses, who are able to confirm the truth of the accusation by details. In fact, a condemnation for *zinâ* is thereby rendered impossible, unless the guilty person makes a confession, and thus becomes willingly subjected to the punishment.

When a man takes his wife in the act of adultery, he may put her to death at once, along with her paramour. If he suspects her of adultery, he is not required to bring forward any witnesses. The law permits him to take an oath that his wife has been unfaithful to him. When, however, the wife on her part swears under oath that she is innocent, she is not punished. Nevertheless, the marriage is then dissolved; and if the wife brings a child into the world, the legitimacy can be disowned by the husband. The swearing of this oath is in Arabic called *li'ân*. Cf. Qur'ān xxiv. 6–9: 'They who accuse their wives (of adultery) and shall have no witnesses (thereof) besides themselves, the testimony (which shall be required) of one of them (shall be) that he swear four times by God that he speaketh the truth and the fifth time (that he imprecate) the curse of God on him if he be a liar. And it shall avert the punishment (from the wife) if she swear four times by God that he is a liar and if the fifth time (she imprecate) the wrath of God on her if he speaketh the truth.'

Slaves are not stoned for *zinâ*, but only punished with fifty stripes.

LITERATURE.—E. Sachau, *Mohammedanisches Recht nach Schafiitischer Lehre*, pp. 14, 73 ff., 809, 815 ff., and other translations of Muslim Law Books; J. Krcsmárik, 'Beiträge zur Beleuchtung des islamitischen Strafrechts mit Rücksicht auf Theorie und Praxis in der Turkei,' *ZDMG* lviii. 101 ff.

TH. W. JUYNBOLL.

ADULTERY (Christian). — **I. Teaching of Jesus and the Apostles.** — It is sometimes said that the Law of Moses deals only with outward actions, while the Sermon on the Mount teaches us to think of the inward disposition, and the motives that prompt to action. The Decalogue, it is said, like other ancient codes of laws, forbids the sinful act by which the marriage bond is violated, but takes no account of the character or disposition. Jesus, on the other hand, shows us that the inward disposition which renders the sinful act impossible is the one thing of importance in the sight of God. A moment's consideration will convince us that, whatever element of truth there may be in this statement, it cannot be taken as a complete and satisfactory account of our Lord's comment on the Seventh Commandment (Mt 5^{27-30}), inasmuch as it is simply untrue to say that the Decalogue takes no account of inward disposition or motives. The command, 'Thou shalt not covet thy neighbour's wife,' goes behind the outward act, and condemns the sinful desire which leads to adultery. It is true, nevertheless, that in this passage in the Sermon on the Mount our Lord goes beyond the teaching of the Decalogue, and gives a new and deeper meaning to the command, 'Thou shalt not commit adultery'; that He does not merely recall to men's minds the teaching of the Tenth Commandment, which had been overlooked or forgotten in the Jewish schools, but that He lays down a great principle of the righteousness required in the Kingdom of heaven, from which obedience to the letter of the command will follow as a matter of course. The Tenth Commandment forbids the sinful desire, mainly because it tends to conduct which will injure one's neighbour; it is a safeguard against injury, and the thought of the injury done to one's neighbour is the prominent thought. In the passage in the Sermon on the Mount, on the other hand, our thoughts are centred on the moral injury to the man himself. 'If thy right eye causeth thee to stumble, pluck it out, and cast it from thee: for it is profitable for thee that one of thy members should perish, and not that thy whole body be cast into hell.' The indulgence in sinful thoughts and desires is not a minor offence tending to the injury of others, but is already the soul-destroying sin of adultery committed in the man's own heart.

It is now easy to understand why it is that, while throughout the NT sins of the flesh are unsparingly denounced, we have no detailed classification of such sins; and very little account is taken of the various distinctions—as between adultery, fornication, *stuprum*, etc. etc.—which are so often treated of at unedifying length in writings on these subjects. The word used most frequently in the NT for such sins is πορνεία, 'fornication.'* This serves to include all those 'lusts of the flesh which war against the soul' (1 P 2^{11}); and but little account is taken of the distinction between fornication and what we naturally regard as the graver offence of μοιχεία, or adultery proper, which involves the violation of the marriage bond. Some writers in modern times have found a difficulty in our Lord's words which forbid the dissolution of the marriage bond—παρεκτὸς λόγου πορνείας (Mt 5^{32}), μὴ ἐπὶ πορνείᾳ (19^9); and Döllinger (*Christenthum und Kirche*) made a not very successful attempt to show that the word πορνεία in these passages must refer to some offence committed before marriage, rendering the marriage itself null and void *ab initio*. It is a sufficient refutation of this view that such an interpretation was not thought of by the writers of the first four centuries, and that no difficulty was found in recognizing πορνεία as a general term, including in itself all sins of the flesh, and in this particular instance applying to adultery.

The passage in 1 Th 4^6, in which St. Paul deals directly with the sin of adultery, may be placed side by side with these passages from Mt., as affording an interesting illustration of the same principle. The Apostle does not ignore our duty towards our neighbour. Adultery is sinful because it is a kind of theft (τὸ μὴ ὑπερβαίνειν καὶ πλεονεκτεῖν ἐν τῷ πράγματι τὸν ἀδελφὸν αὐτοῦ). But he seems to dwell on this aspect of the matter only in passing, while his exhortation is occupied mainly with the need for purity and sanctification, and the danger of that fornication (τῆς πορνείας—note the use of the article) which was so common a feature in the life of the Græco-Roman world. St. Paul, no doubt, would have been quite ready to acknowledge that adultery, as inflicting a more grievous or irreparable wrong, was a graver offence than simple fornication, just as he recognized fully the gravity of the case of incest in Corinth (1 Co 5^1); but, in general, the object of the gospel was not primarily to develop a system of casuistry, but to call men to newness of life, and to produce a character which should make sin in all shapes and forms impossible. For the Christian, therefore, the Seventh Commandment is, before everything else, a law of chastity, and the sin of adultery includes every kind of unlawful sensual indulgence, whether in thought or deed. Marriage is, first of all, a spiritual union between those who are 'heirs together of the grace of life' (1 P 3^7); and all other objects must be considered as subordinate to the promotion of that social life which is absolutely necessary to man's well-being.

2. Ecclesiastical discipline. — The case of the incestuous Corinthian (1 Co 5) gives us our first example of the exercise of ecclesiastical discipline by a Christian community; and the Epistles to the Corinthians make it plain that, while the Christian Church from the very beginning was accustomed to exercise a stern discipline over the lives and conduct of its members, the idea that the offence of adultery necessarily involved final and irrevocable exclusion from the Church was unknown in the days of the Apostles.

Tertullian's statement, therefore, that from the beginning gross sins of the flesh were visited with final exclusion from the Church, must be regarded as an exaggeration, so far as the Apostolic age is concerned. Indeed, all the evidence goes to show that we have here rather the ideal picture of the glories of the primitive age, as conceived by the enthusiastic Montanist, than a sober statement of fact.*

Towards the close of the 2nd cent. there seems to be no doubt that the discipline in the Churches of Africa and Italy, with which Tertullian was most familiar, was exceedingly strict; but the evidence available appears to show that there was no uniform or clearly defined system of discipline established throughout the whole of Christendom.

Irenæus (*c. Hœr.* I. i. 13) tells us of certain women in the Church of Lyons who had been found guilty of adultery, and subjected to penance. As he speaks of only one of these as not being finally restored to communion, it may be inferred that the others had been received back; hence we may conclude that the system of discipline in the Gallic Church was somewhat less strict than that which prevailed in Italy or Africa. During the whole of the sub-Apostolic age, and down, at all events, to the close of the 2nd cent., the high standard of morality which we find in the Apostolic age was well maintained throughout the Christian communities. If any Christian fell away to vicious or immoral courses, he would in all probability forsake the Church and relapse to heathenism. Hence cases of grave offences calling for ecclesiastical censure would be of rare occurrence, and the conditions required for the establishment of a well-defined system of penitential discipline would not arise.

With the expansion of the Church and also, perhaps, as a consequence of the fading away of the early enthusiasm, it became necessary, if the Church was to maintain her position and carry on her work in the world, to relax somewhat the extreme severity of discipline, to make provision for the restoration of penitent sinners, and, at the same time, to make the Church's rules on such matters clear and distinct.

* St. Paul uses πορνεία and derivatives about eighteen times: μοιχεία does not occur, while μοιχός (and derivatives) occurs only five times in his Epistles, and two of these instances are quotations from the Decalogue, viz. Ro 2^{22} 13^9.

* *adv. Marc.* iv. 9. Tertullian here enumerates 'seven deadly sins which exclude from communion,' viz. *idololatria, blasphemia, homicidium, adulterium, stuprum, falsum testimonium, fraus.*

Pope Calixtus I. (c. 220) was probably neither the monster of iniquity depicted by his enemies, nor yet an enthusiastic exponent of evangelical principles, but simply a ruler of practical wisdom and foresight, who saw clearly what was required by the circumstances of the time. His famous edict: 'Ego et mœchiæ et fornicationis delicta iunctis pœnitentia dimitto,' however, provoked a stormy controversy, and was assailed with much vigour and bitterness by Tertullian in his treatise *de Pudicitia*. In this contest, and in the Novatian dispute which followed, the victory remained with those who maintained the laxer policy, and experience showed that the high but impracticable ideals of what seemed to be the more strictly religious party were unsuited to the new conditions and circumstances of the Church.

From the beginning of the 4th cent. down to the very close of the Middle Ages, a long series of Conciliar decrees and other authoritative enactments bears witness to the fact that throughout this period the Church was called upon to deal practically and effectively with a widely prevalent immorality, and to solve the problem of combining due severity against sinners with the mercy enjoined by the gospel.

The Canons of the Council of Illiberis (Elvira in Spain), which met A.D. 305, seem to have furnished a type and regulating principle for the ecclesiastical legislation of succeeding ages, and may well serve to indicate the conditions with which the Church had to deal and the principles adopted in dealing with them.

Canon 9 declares that a woman who has divorced her husband for adultery ought not to marry again during the husband's lifetime. Should she do so, she is to be excluded from communion until after the first husband's death, at all events unless she should be seized with a dangerous illness.

Canon 13 decrees perpetual exclusion from communion in the case of *consecrated* virgins who have fallen, and who show no true sense of the seriousness of their loss (*non intelligentes quid amiserint*). Such virgins, if repentant, may be restored to communion in the hour of death.

Canon 14. *Virgines sæculares*, guilty of fornication, to undergo a year's penance and to marry their seducers.

Canon 15 condemns marriage with Jews, pagans, or heretics as akin to adultery.

Canon 18 condemns adultery committed by a clergyman. Bishops, priests, or deacons found guilty of adultery are never, even to the end of their lives, to be restored to communion, both because of the enormity of the offence and because of the scandal to the Church ['et propter scandalum et propter nefandum crimen'].*

Canon 69 imposes five years' penance for a single act of adultery.

Canon 64 imposes ten years for adultery persisted in for any length of time, and enacts that there must be no restoration to communion so long as the sinner persists in the sinful life.

Canon 72. A *widow* who commits *adultery* (sic) must undergo a penance of five years, and, if practicable, must marry her seducer.

It is worth noting that in these decrees the words *mœchia* and *adulterium* are used in the broad NT sense to include sins of the flesh of every description.

3. Christianity and the civil law.—It may or may not have been a mistaken zeal for Christian religion and morality that induced Constantine and Constans to revive the old capital penalties for adultery which had been obsolete since the days of Augustus Cæsar.† In any case, it seems certain that the attempt to return to barbarous methods was a failure, since we find that in the time of Theodosius I. a milder, if scarcely less degrading, method of dealing with adulteresses was prevalent, at all events in the city of Rome. We learn from the Church historian Socrates (*HE* v. 18) that in the time of the Emperor Theodosius the Great these unhappy sinners were punished by confinement in the public brothels under circumstances of shameful and disgusting ignominy. The Emperor is praised for putting a stop to this barbarous practice on the occasion of his visit to the capital. Under Justinian the death penalty was finally abolished, and the Lex Julia restored with certain modifications. By this legislation the guilty wife, if not received back by her husband within two years, was condemned to be shut up for life in a convent.

* The refusal of absolution implies that the offence committed is one with respect to which the Church has no authority to promise the Divine pardon, but does not imply a claim to limit God's power to grant forgiveness, and must not be taken as a declaration that the guilty person will *certainly* be finally lost.

† The law of Constantine condemned the adulteress to death, but the penalty might be mitigated to banishment. The paramour was to be beheaded if a freeman, and if a slave, burned to death (Cod. Justin. I. ix. tit. 11). Constans decreed against both guilty parties the penalty inflicted on parricides, viz. to be burned alive, or else drowned in a sack (*ib.* I. vii. tit. 65).

Whatever we may think of the influence of Christianity upon the civil law of the older Empire, we can have no doubt that its influence upon the laws of the new nations that overran the Provinces of the Empire in the 5th and following centuries was wholly beneficent. The barbarous severities of the old national laws against adultery were mitigated. Divorce, pecuniary fines and—for guilty women—confinement in convents gradually took the place of the death sentence or the infliction of cruel mutilations.

The code of Theodoric decreed death for adultery. A married man who seduced a virgin was mulcted in a third part of his property as damages. The unmarried seducer was bound to marry his victim and endow her with a fifth of his estate. In the Burgundian code the adulterer was punished with death, and the adulteress, if not put to death, was treated as an infamous person. By the Visigothic code the adulteress and her paramour were given up to the injured husband to be punished with death or otherwise—according to his free pleasure. Flogging, mutilation, and other barbarous punishments were in force amongst the Danes and Saxons. In England the death penalty was not formally abolished until the reign of Canute. (See Milman, *Hist. of Latin Christianity*, Bk. III. ch. v.).

There was, indeed, one custom of the Northern nations which yielded very slowly, and only after many conflicts, to the influence of Christian teaching. In general the tone of morality—especially in all that relates to married life—amongst those nations was very high, much higher than in the Roman world which they conquered. Monogamy was the rule, and conjugal fidelity was strictly enforced. An exception, however, was made in the case of princes, who, as a mark of dignity, were allowed to maintain a plurality of wives or concubines. It is perhaps not wonderful that after their conversion these rude chiefs found it hard to accept the Christian view, and to regard this practice as sinful adultery, or that zealous Christian teachers should have often found the task of contending against this practice beset with much difficulty and danger.

4. Divorce.—The adultery of the wife has at all times been regarded as a sufficient ground for divorce; but differences of opinion have prevailed as to whether the same rule applies to the case of adultery committed by the husband. By the civil law of England, a wife cannot obtain a decree for divorce on the sole ground of the husband's adultery: there must be other circumstances, as, *e.g.*, cruelty or neglect. In Scotland, on the other hand, the adultery of either partner is itself a sufficient ground for divorce. The subject of divorce will be more fully treated in a separate article. For the present it may be sufficient to note that in the Roman Catholic Church, and by the canons of the English Church, divorced persons, whether innocent or guilty, are not allowed to marry again during the lifetime of the other partner. Remarriage is permitted in the Greek Church and in most Reformed Churches.

LITERATURE.—Von Dobschütz, *Christian Life in the Primitive Church* (Williams & Norgate, 1904); Lecky, *History of European Morals*; Harnack, *Gesch. der altchristl. Literatur* (Leipzig, 1893); Funk, *Altchristl. Bussdisciplin* (Paderborn, 1897); see also Letourneau, *L'évolution du mariage et de la famille*, Paris, 1888 [Eng. tr. in *Contemporary Science* series]; Westermarck, *Hist. of Human Marriage* (Macmillan, 1891); art. 'Adultère' in Cabrol's *Dict. d'Archéol. Chrét.* etc., and in Vacant's *Dict. de Théol. Catholique*.

W. M. FOLEY.

ADULTERY (Parsi).—The ancient Iranians attached much importance to marriage, and hence they looked upon adultery with horror. In the Gāthā Ushtavaiti (*Yasna*, liii. 7) there is a carefully worded warning against what Mills calls 'solicitations to vice,' * etc. The female Yazata Ashi (*Yasht*, xvii. 57–60) inveighs bitterly against this vice. She says that it 'is the worst deed that men and tyrants do,' † when they seduce maidens from the path of virtue. In some parts of the Avesta and in the Pahlavi books adultery is personified as 'Jahi.' The Yazata Haoma is entreated to withstand the evil influence of vicious women, whose lustful, wavering mind is like a cloud, which changes the direction of its motion according to the direction of the wind (*Yasna*, ix. 32). The Amesha Spenta *Asha Vahishtā* ('Best Righteousness') is similarly appealed to (*Yasht*, iii. 9). An adulterer or adulteress is, as it were, an opponent of Gao, the good spirit of the earth or the animal creation, the idea being that such a person comes in the way of the progress of the world (*Vendīdād*, xxi. 1). The progress of the world in the different spheres of activity, physical and mental, acts against these evil-doers (*ib.* xxi. 17). Eredaṭ-Fedri is the name of a good, pious maiden who is considered as a prototype of maidenly virtue, and whose guardian spirit is invoked to withstand the evil machinations of Jahi, the personification of adultery (*Yasht*, xiii. 142).

In the Pahlavi *Bundahish* (ch. iii.) this Jahi (Pahlavi *Jēh*) is said to be an accomplice of Ahriman himself. Her work is 'to cause that conflict in the world, the distress and injury from which will become those of Auhurmazd and the archangels.' ‡ In the Pahlavi *Daṭīstān-ī-Dēnīg* (71st question) § adultery is spoken of as one of the most heinous sins. The mother of Zohāk is said to be the first woman in the world who committed this offence. It is described as a sin which disturbs all lineage, which puts an end to all self-control and to the legitimate authority of a husband. It is more heinous than theft or spoliation (77th question). ‖ It is a crime which leads at times to murder, because the woman sometimes brings about abortion. ¶ There is another way in which adultery leads to murder. It is noted in the account of pregnancy ** that sexual intercourse during pregnancy is prohibited, because it is understood that it leads to injury to the life of the child in the womb. Now, a woman who yields to lust and gives herself up to an adulterous life is likely to commit adultery even in pregnancy. Such intercourse may cause the loss of the life of the child in the womb. ††

Adultery is a canker in society in another way. When a man commits adultery with a woman, according to the injunction of the *Vendīdād* he is bound to support the woman whom he has seduced and the children that may be born of the illicit intercourse. It is his duty to bring up his illegitimate children along with his legitimate children. But then the company of the illegitimate children is likely to spoil the good manners and morals of the legitimate children. And, on the other hand, if he does not bring up the illegitimate children properly, if he does not give them proper training, he is responsible for, and guilty of, all the wrongful acts and sins that the children may commit in their childhood or when they are grown up.

The sin of adultery was too heinous to be fully atoned for. But what little atonement could be made for it was directed to be done by the following good acts (*Daṭīstān-ī-Dēnīg*, lxxviii. 17–19):

(*a*) The guilty person, especially the adulterer, must help, *i.e.* by money or otherwise, in bringing about the marriage of four poor couples. (*b*) He must assist with money poor children who are not cared for by others, and bring them up decently and educate them. (*c*) If he sees others in society leading a vicious life, he must do his best to retrieve them. (*d*) He must perform certain religious rites, like those of the Dvāzhdah-Hōmāst.

In the *Vīrāf-Nāmak* the adulterer is represented as punished by being thrown into a steaming brazen caldron (ch. lx.), the adulteress as gashing her own bosom and breasts (ch. lxii.). * The adulteress who brings about abortion meets with worse punishment (ch. lxiv.). In all cases of adultery the *Vendīdād* (xv. 18) requires that the person seducing a woman, whether married or unmarried, shall maintain her and the children that may be born of her until they come of age. Any attempt at abortion was considered a great sin (*Vend.* xv. 11–14).

JIVANJI JAMSHEDJI MODI.

* *SBE* xxxi. 189.
† *Ib.* xxiii. 281.
‡ *Ib.* v. p. 15.
§ *Ib.* vol. xviii. ch. lxxii. § 5.
‖ *Ib.* ch. lxxviii. § 3.
¶ *Ib.* § 5.
** See BIRTH.
†† *SBE*, vol. xviii. ch. lxxviii. § 9

ADULTERY (Roman).—**1. Under the Republic.**—The word *adulterium* is a noun-derivative of *adulterare*, which is probably *ad alterum* (*se convertere*). The offence on the part of the wife is sexual intercourse with any man other than her lawful husband. On the part of the husband it has a narrow meaning, and is confined to misconduct with married women, misconduct with other than married women being designated by the general term *stuprum*. The unequal treatment of husband and wife is bluntly expressed by Cato in Aul. Gell. x. 23: 'In adulterio uxorem tuam si prehendisses, sine iudicio impune necares: illa te, si adulterares . . . digito non auderet contingere, neque ius est.' From this passage it is clear that the old right of self-help survived into the times of the Republic. There is no evidence, however, that the adulterer could be killed as well as the woman, if taken in the act. Originally the offence was dealt with not by the State (except in cases where it passed all bounds, and became, like open immorality, a matter for the police jurisdiction of the censors and ædiles), but by the *iudicium domesticum*, or family council, in which near relatives took part, with the head of the family as president in virtue of his *patria potestas*. This council could inflict what punishment it chose (Dionys. ii. 25; Suet. *Tib.* § 35. Cf. Plin. *HN* xiv. 13 ff.: 'matronam a suis inedia mori coactam,' where the charge brought is intemperance). If a wife was divorced on the ground of adultery, it was left to a civil court to decide what part of her dowry she should retain. Such a trial was termed a *iudicium de moribus*. The procedure followed is not accurately known, and cannot be recovered with any certainty from the evidence of the later lawyers, who are our only authorities.

2. Under the Empire: *The Lex Julia.*—By the end of the Republic, owing, among other causes, to the absence of effective legislation, immorality became so rife at Rome that the Government became alarmed at the prospect of a shrinkage in the population of Italy. In consequence of this, Augustus in 736/18 carried through the measure known (though the title is doubtful) as the *Lex Julia de adulteriis coercendis* (Hor. *Car.* iv. 5. 21–24; Suet. *Aug.* § 34). This, as its opening clause shows ('*ne quis posthac stuprum adulteriumve facito sciens dolo malo*'), was directed against immorality in general as well as against adultery. But now for the first time Roman law recognized adultery as an act done in contravention of the law of the State, and allowed others than the father or husband of the adulteress to prosecute. For this purpose a new court (*quæstio perpetua*) was established (Dio, liv. 30). The fragments of the law that survive will be found in Bruns, *Fontes Juris Antiqui*[6], p. 114. Adultery on the part of wife or concubine was declared punishable by the law, while marital misconduct was taken to include offences knowingly (*dolo malo*) committed against

* Hoshangji and Haug, *Vīrāf-Nāmak*, pp. 186, 187.

any *matrona honesta*, as well as against a married woman (*materfamilias*). It should be noticed that the *concubinatus*, or inferior marriage, though of great antiquity, was now for the first time recognized as a permanent legal relationship, doubtless in order to prevent such connexions from being penalized under the clauses against *stuprum*. The law fined the adulteress in one half of her dowry and one third of her property. The adulterer lost the half of his property. Both were interdicted fire and water, a punishment soon replaced by exile or deportation to an island. There is no ground for supposing that the death-penalty was sanctioned by the original terms of the *Lex Julia* (Paul. Sent. ii. 26. 14). Conviction entailed *infamia* (Dig. iii. 2. 2, 3), and the condemned became incapable of giving evidence (*intestabiles*, Dig. xxii. 5. 14, 18). The adulteress could not marry again (Dig. xxiii. 2. 26), but she was not debarred from entering the condition of *concubinatus* (Mart. vi. 22). The dissolution of the marriage was a necessary preliminary to any action taken against the wife or her paramour, and if her husband did not divorce his wife, he rendered himself liable to the charge of procuration (*lenocinium*). For sixty days after the dissolution of the marriage the right to prosecute was reserved to the husband or father of the woman (Dig. xlviii. 5. 2, § 8). If these took no action within this period of time, any one unconnected with the family (*extraneus*) could prosecute (Tac. *Ann.* ii. 85). Both offenders could not be prosecuted at once, and the trial of the one had to be completed before that of the other was begun. If the man was acquitted, the woman could not be charged. A period of limitation was prescribed within which an action must be brought,—six months in the case of the woman, five years in the case of the man. The ancient right of self-help was never entirely abolished, but the exercise of it was severely restricted. A father who surprised his daughter *in ipsa turpitudine* might kill her and her paramour, if he did so *in continenti*, which was held to mean 'almost by one and the same blow.' The husband's right to kill his wife when taken in the act was withdrawn. Here we seem to see an attempt to abolish the right of self-help by restricting it to the person least likely to act on the impulse of the moment. The only fragment which the husband retained of his former power was the right to kill the adulterer if a freedman of the family or a *persona vilis* (*e.g.* an actor), and if found in the house. The husband could detain the adulterer for twenty hours in order to secure evidence of the offence (*rei testandæ causa*).

The *Lex Julia* formed the basis of all subsequent legislation against adultery. It was not seriously modified till Constantine, under the influence of Christian ideas, introduced the penalty of death for the adulterer, and, by a curious reaction, once more confined the right of prosecution to the near relatives of the adulteress. The death penalty was maintained during the reigns of succeeding emperors. It was confirmed by Justinian (*Inst.* iv. 18. 4), who imposed on the adulteress the penalty of lifelong imprisonment in a nunnery, unless the offended husband cared to reclaim her within two years.

LITERATURE.—W. Rein, *Das Criminalrecht der Römer*, 1844, p. 835 ff.; Th. Mommsen, *Röm. Strafrecht*, 1899, p. 688 ff.; A. du Boys, *Hist. du droit criminel des peuples anciens*, 1845, pp. 400 ff., 677 ff.

F. W. HALL.

ADULTERY (Semitic).—The treatment of infidelity among the Semites can be illustrated by a great variety of evidence, extending from the codified legislation of Ḥammurabi, king of Babylonia (*c.* 2250), to the unwritten, though no less authoritative, tribal laws of the present day. So far as women are concerned—and, as elsewhere, the infidelity of the man was only tardily recognized as blameworthy—it must be understood that the offence implies a particular type of marriage, since it is obvious that where the woman has liberty of choice, does not leave her own kin, and may receive her suitors when or as long as she will, adultery is out of the question. Such a union is entirely one of a personal character, and gives the man no legitimate offspring.* But the prevailing type in the Semitic world is that wherein the woman follows the husband, who has paid a 'bride-price' (Arab. *mahr*, Heb. *mōhar*) to her kin, whereby he has compensated them for the loss of her services, and has acquired the right of possessing sons who shall belong to his tribe. By this act the man has practically acquired the exclusive property-rights, and deprives the woman of the right of disposing of her own person. Further, it must be recognized that this does not imply that paternity always meant what it does to us. The evidence goes to show that the man is at first only the father of all the children of the woman he has taken; and he might transfer or dispose of her temporarily in a way that is quite repugnant to all ideas of chastity. At this stage, therefore, a distinction could be, and was, drawn between authorized and unauthorized laxity, and in the circumstances the term 'adultery' could be applied only to those acts of infidelity which were done without the husband's consent or knowledge. It required a great advance before any breaking of the union between husband and wife could be regarded as a desecration.† See MARRIAGE.

In tracing the growing strictness of ideas of chastity in the Semitic world, it is to be observed that there was a gradual development of institutions of law and justice. Primarily, all offences against a man are matters for him and for his kin or tribe to settle; adultery may thus be privately avenged, and it is not until society has taken many steps forward in government that the matter is taken out of private hands and referred to a judicial inquiry. There is a great social gap, therefore, between the parental authority of Judah in Gn 38, and the recognition that immorality is an offence to be punished by judges, in Job 31¹¹.

It is undeniable that there was much in early Semitic life that cannot be judged in the light of modern ideas, and that primitive usages which were hardly thought to be dishonourable (Gn 19⁷ᶠ·, cf. Jg 19²³ᶠ·)—for which parallels could easily be found—bespeak a lack of refinement which leads to the inference that adultery, if recognized at all, could only have been the unauthorized infidelity referred to above. But a general advance in custom can be traced, and is peculiarly illustrated by three stories of the patriarchs: there is a distinct growth in morals in the account of Isaac's adventure at Gerar (Gn 26) as compared with the duplicate narrative of Abraham in Egypt (ch. 12), and these stories from the Jahwist or Judæan source are overshadowed by the Elohist or Ephraimite account of Abraham at Gerar (ch. 20), where the iniquity of adultery is forcibly realized.

Under the ordinary type of marriage, known as the *baal* or marriage of subjection, the Semitic woman, if unmarried, is entirely under the authority of her father; if betrothed or married, of her husband. It is necessary, therefore, to observe that, if adultery is primarily an infringement of the husband's rights, seduction is no less a matter for the father of the unbetrothed virgin. According to the old Hebrew law (Ex 22¹⁶ᶠ·), the man who was

* See Robertson Smith, *Kinship and Marriage in Early Arabia*², pp. 79–99.

† Robertson Smith's researches are supplemented by Wellhausen (*GGN*, 1893), who has observed that among the Arabs mistrust and jealousy spring less from love or ethical considerations than from ideas of property.

guilty of seduction was obliged to pay the *mōhar* or bride-price and marry his victim;* the later code (Dt 22[28f.]) fixes the amount at fifty shekels, and characteristically prevents the man from turning his newly-made wife adrift, by removing from him the right of divorce. How the law worked in ancient Israel can be gathered from the account in Gn 34, where, although little of the oldest narrative has been retained, it seems clear that compensation was required, and dispute or high-handed action would lead to furious intertribal conflicts.† The usual penalty for adultery was compensation, but frequently the offender was put to death. Modern custom permits the guilty pair, if caught, to be killed at once, or, at the sentence of the sheikhs, all the men take an equal share in the execution. The last point is important, since bloodshed according to primitive thought is a responsibility which all members of the community must share. The old form of exacting the death-penalty is parallel, as Robertson Smith has observed, to the ancient ritual of sacrifice. In both, every member of the kin should as far as possible participate in the act.‡ The particular form of death-penalty may vary between stoning, strangling, impaling, burning, and—at the present day—even shooting.

Mere suspicion of adultery is not enough, and terrible consequences may result from unsupported denunciation. Hebrew law required two witnesses, and (by an extension of the *talio*) the false accuser would bring upon himself the punishment his charge would have entailed upon another. It is noteworthy that the law in Dt 22[22] specifically provides that the guilty ones are 'found' in the act. The law in question belongs to a group which reflects that stage where moral ideas have become so advanced that the husband attaches importance to the chastity of his newly-married wife (the restrictions of Lv 21[7. 14] apply only to the priests). The procedure (Dt 22[13-21]) is detailed, and states that if the accusation of impurity brought against the bride is true, she is stoned to death by 'the men of the city'; if false, the man must pay a hundred shekels to the father, and is not permitted to divorce his wife.§ It is intelligible that, in the former event the girl is treated as an adulteress, since from the time that she was betrothed she is regarded *de facto* as a married woman. The same code in its treatment of betrothed women makes a noteworthy distinction in the *scene* of the offence. Should it be committed in the city, both are stoned; whereas, if it be in the open country, the woman goes free, since it is assumed that she cried for help and found no protector (vv.[23-27]).‖

The Babylonian code of Ḫammurabi implies a more advanced state of culture than the oldest Hebrew. The position of the married woman was secured by a contract which could specify the penalty for her infidelity and possibly vouched for her purity at the time of marriage.¶ The following laws require notice:—The man who is caught ravishing a betrothed virgin who is living in her father's house is put to death, whilst she herself goes free. If she was betrothed to his own son, a distinction is drawn dependent upon whether the marriage had or had not been consummated. In the latter event, the man must pay half a mina of silver and give her her personal property, and she is free to marry whom she will. In the former event, the man is strangled; the treatment of the girl is uncertain in the text.* Drowning was the ordinary legal penalty, although, according to a somewhat obscure law, the man might pardon his wife and the king the adulterer at their will. The Babylonian procedure in cases where absolute proof was not at hand is characteristic. In all ordinary cases the wife could take an oath and swear her innocence, and was allowed to return (or was sent?) to her (father's) house; but 'if the finger had been pointed at her on account of another,' and she is obviously the subject of scandal, she must undergo ordeal by water. Robertson Smith has cited the Arabian story of Hind bint 'Utba, whose husband sent her back to her father on suspicion of unchastity, and it appears that the case could not rest there, her treatment being clearly regarded as an insult; and from another incident it would seem that suspected wives could be conducted under ignominious circumstances to the Ka'ba and there swear seventy oaths.† The ordeal and oath reappear in the antique ordeal preserved in a late source, Nu 5[11-31], where the suspected wife is conducted to the priest, who brings her in humiliating attire before Jahweh. There the priest charges her by an oath which she accepts with the formula 'Amen,' and prepares a potion of holy water and the dust of the floor of the sanctuary,‡ in which have been washed the words of the oath. The procedure, which does not prescribe any punishment for unjust accusation, is treated at greater length in the Mishna (*Soṭa*; cf. also Jos. *Ant.* III. xi. 6), and is said to have been abolished towards the close of the 1st cent. A.D. (cf., further, OATH, ORDEAL).

The old Babylonian code handles acts of adultery in the case where the husband is a captive away from home. If he had left means of livelihood (lit. maintenance), and the wife enters the house of another, she is condemned to be drowned,—his family perhaps bring the charge,—whilst, failing these means, her desertion is not blameworthy; only, should the man regain his city she must leave the second husband (and children, if any) and return. Not unconnected with the subject is the further law that the woman who brought about her husband's death in order to marry another is to be killed. In Talmudic law, moreover, the adulteress who is divorced may not marry her accomplice. The charge against the widow in Gn 38, as the narrative shows, comes under the case of betrothed women, but the penalty (burning) is exceptional.§ When the woman was of low standing, *e.g.* a slave, the death-sentence was not demanded (Lv 19[20ff.]).

Naturally, the extreme sentence was not always carried out. Usage varied according to the tone of public opinion and private interests. A man might not care to parade his wife's disgrace (Mt 1[19]), and the woman in Jn 8 who was taken in adultery ultimately departs unpunished. Cosmopolitan life in Palestine in the last centuries of the pre-Christian era was scarcely conducive to purity, and the writer in Pr 6[32ff.] emphasizes not so much the immorality as the folly of the man who provokes the jealousy and wrath of the husband in a way which is likely to have unpleasant consequences for himself (cf. also Sir 23[18-26]). No doubt the teaching of the Hebrew prophets always outstripped contemporary morals.

* The payment, 'according to the bride-price of virgins,' which the man must make in the event of the father's refusal, is apparently an additional compensation.

† Cf. Doughty, *Arabia Deserta*, ii. 114 (see Bennett, *The Century Bible*, 'Genesis,' p. 318 f.).

‡ *Religion of the Semites*², pp. 285, 485 ff.

§ See, further, Driver, *ICC*, 'Deut.' p. 255.

‖ Cf. with this Boaz and Ruth (Ru 2[8. 9. 22]).

¶ See the contract, Pinches, *The Old Testament*² (1903), p. 173. It will be noticed that in Dt 22[15ff.] the accusation of impurity is regarded as a distinct reflexion upon the parents.

* For 'one shall cast *her* into the water' we should probably read '*him*' (Scheil, Winckler, Harper, etc.); see S. A. Cook, *Laws of Moses*, etc. (1903) 100 f. In that case 'strangled' should preferably be 'bound.'

† *Kinship*², p. 123; *Rel. Sem.*² p. 180.

‡ For Semitic parallels cf. the Syriac *ḥenānā* and *sheyāgtā*, and see *JQR*, 1902, p. 431; *JRAS*, 1903, p. 595.

§ For daughters of priests (Lv 21[9]), for all cases of immorality (Jub 20[4] 41[25f.]) and for incest (Code of Ḫammurabi).

The great advance upon primitive thought was the insistence upon the fact that adultery is as immoral in the husband as in the wife; previous to this the adulterer suffered only in so far as he had been the object of the injured husband's revenge. Accordingly the Decalogue and related teaching mark a great step in ethics in denouncing adultery, and in their warning against the covetousness from which lust springs (cf. the development of the truth in Mt 5[27ff.]).

The peculiar character of Nature-worship and the native cults of Baal and Ashtoreth were direct incentives to impurity, and whatever may have influenced growth of refinement in this scattered field, it is evident that the purer conception of Jahweh among the Hebrew prophets went hand in hand with the refinement of moral ideas in Israel. The relation between worshipper and God was typified by the marriage-relation, and Jahweh was His people's *baal* even as the husband was the *baal* of his wife. It was impossible not to perceive that intercourse with aliens tended inevitably to participation in foreign rites, and the symbolical use of such terms as 'jealousy,' 'fornication,' or 'adultery' becomes characteristic of the religious life of Israel, bound as it was to its God as surely as the wife was bound to her husband. Hosea's doctrine was thus in accordance with well-established belief, and lays stress upon the fact that, whatever may have been the customary attitude towards adultery in everyday life, Jahweh had neither destroyed nor utterly forsaken His adulterous people, but was willing to receive them again and pay the betrothal price of 'faithfulness.'

LITERATURE.—A. B. Davidson, art. 'Hosea' in Hastings' *DB*; *PEFSt*, 1897, p. 126 ff., 1901, p. 175 ff., 1905, p. 350; and the works referred to in the course of the above article. For the OT laws consult C. F. Kent, *Messages of Israel's Lawgivers* (1902), p. 92.

STANLEY A. COOK.

ADVAITA.—*Advaita*, derived from *a* privative and *dvaita*, 'duality' or 'dualism' (from Skr. *dvi*= 'two'), in its philosophic applications means *non-dualism*, and is used to designate the fundamental principle of the Vedānta (see art. VEDĀNTA), which asserts that the only reality is *brahman*; that the dualism set up between self and the world, between spirit and matter, is the result of illusion (*māyā*), or of ignorance (*avidyā*). The manifold world with its changing phenomena is unreal; the only reality is *brahman*, which is identified with *ātman* or self. The view which accepts as real both the Ego and the non-Ego in their distinction and opposition is *dvaita* or dualism; that which denies this dualism is *advaita*.

It is important to note the negative form of this philosophic term. It would have been easy to find a positive term if the intention had been to assert dogmatically the oneness of all reality as a positive conclusion. The *advaita* does not positively assert this oneness; it simply denies the dualism which presents itself in our ordinary thinking. This distinction is not only of importance in defining the precise meaning of the *advaita*, but it also throws light on the process of development by which Indian philosophy arrived at this result.

Just as the ideal philosophy of Greece was preceded by attempts to reach the basis of things along quite other lines, so the *advaita* solution of the Indian problem was the culmination of a long series of philosophic systems. These are generally described as the six *darśanas*, the six recognized systems.

The predominant interest in all of these was religious, not philosophic. The Nyāya taught its logic in order that man by finding out truth might attain to the bliss of emancipation through the favour of *īśvara* (God), whose existence can be demonstrated by inference. The Vaiśeṣika school sought to enlarge our means of knowledge by an elaborate classification of existence. The Sāṅkhya called in question these classifications, and reduced all existences to *one*, which it called *prakṛti*, dead matter, out of which all other substances were formed by the spontaneous action of its three qualities (see art. SĀṄKHYA). The explanation of life it sought in a *puruṣa* (soul), always in, but not of, *prakṛti*. Unwilling to admit the presence of a Creator, it thinks to secure the same result by the joint action of this *puruṣa* and *prakṛti*. *Puruṣa* cannot create; *prakṛti* cannot move; the one is lame, the other is blind. But the cripple and the blind work together for the benefit of the cripple. *Puruṣa* believes himself to be miserable as being bound in *prakṛti*; but when, by the destruction of *karma* (action), he is set free from the influence of *prakṛti* and attains to a correct understanding of the course of nature, he is set free from misery. The Yoga restored to this atheistic system the idea of a self-existent *īśvara*, through whose guidance alone *puruṣa* could find his way to salvation. This result, however, could be achieved only through a long process of physical discipline based on a knowledge of the occult processes of nature (see art. YOGA). The Pūrva Mīmāṁsā was a return to the authority of Vedic ritual and ceremony, while the Uttara Mīmāṁsā devoted itself to an exposition of the rationalism of the Upaniṣads, in which are found the germs of those conceptions which are peculiar to the *advaita* teaching (see art. VEDĀNTA).

This latest of the six schools, basing itself on revelation (*śṛti*), asserts that revelation not justified by reason and not corroborated by common sense experience will not lead to any real knowledge. It addresses itself to a criticism of the creation theory, and the evolution theory of the Vaiśeṣika and the Sāṅkhya systems above mentioned. It calls in question the very nature of our perceptions of *prakṛti*, and asserts that we are never conscious of anything beyond our own consciousness of phenomena, whether objective or subjective. Thought and being are, in fact, so inseparably united, that the attempt to separate the one from the other is like trying to mount on one's own shoulders. Thought can never transcend thought, and all we are cognizant of is *thought*. Real existence (*sat*) is the same as thought (*chit*). We are cognizant of phenomena under various forms, and we ascribe to them various names, but that of which they are the names and forms we do not know. The *substratum* of phenomena is *per se* incapable of definition, it is indescribable (*anirvachanīya*). Nor can it be maintained that these phenomena are evolved from thought, for to assert that thought changes itself into phenomena would be to contradict our experience of the essential nature of thought as one and the same in all states and under all conditions.

Abandoning, therefore, the theories of creation and evolution, the *advaita* has recourse to what it calls *vivarta*, the mere unaccountable assumption of the phenomenal in thought. Thought and Being having been shown to be inseparable, the supreme genus is a compound of both, which is named *brahman*. Thus the *advaita* proclaims itself a philosophy of non-dualism. It recognizes *phenomena* as *phenomena*; but it refuses to penetrate into the ultimate nature of their *substratum*, which it declares to be a profound mystery. Matter without mind and mind without matter are alike unthinkable. *Dvaita*, duality, is an entire misconception. The philosophical accuracy, therefore, of the term *advaita*, which was selected to designate this philosophical position, is apparent. It does not assert that all is *one*; it denies duality without asserting the convertibility of mind and matter. According to the *advaita* doctrine, the test of supreme or ultimate reality is unchangeableness. The eye does not change with the phenomena which it perceives; but it can be cognized as phenomenal by the mind, which can discern the changing conditions of the eye, the mind itself remaining unchanged throughout the process. But the mind, with its various phenomena of reason, volition, feeling, etc., is cognized as phenomenal by something which cannot be cognized by anything else, for it is unchanging and unique. This something is the ultimate self-cognizant and constant fact in all our perceptions. In and through it everything is. It is unconditioned, and therefore indescribable. It is neither *he* nor *she*; it is *it*.

Of it is all real being (*sat*), all thought (*chit*), all joy (*ānanda*). Hence the formula which defines *brahman—sach-chid-ānanda* = being, thought, joy.

It is to be noted that the *advaita* does not deny the existence of matter, it simply regards it as *per se* unknowable, and therefore indescribable. We can know it only in the forms in which it is phenomenally present in thought. All our knowledge contains two elements, one constant and eternal, which is the true, the real; the other changing and transitory, which is the untrue, the unreal.

The precise meaning of *māyā* becomes clearer when regarded from this point of view. *Māyā* is illusion, but not illusion without a basis. This basis is not thought which is changing, but the indescribable, the unknowable substratum of phenomena. That this unknowable must exist is a necessity of thought. Some metaphysicians speak of it as if it were an illusion out and out, sent forth from within the bosom of thought itself; but this is a view which is not necessitated by the teaching of the *advaita* as expounded above. *Māyā* cannot mean illusion out and out, but only so far as the phenomenal presentation is concerned. The *Advaitin* is concerned only in maintaining that thought and being are inseparable; it is quite in harmony with this position to maintain that a substratum of phenomena, regarding which nothing is or can be known, exists.

The name given to the complex whole, thought and being as reality, *brahman*, has been variously explained. (See art. BRAHMAN). The most satisfactory explanation is that which traces it to the rise of the term in the Rigveda to describe the elevating and inspiring power of prayer, resulting in an elevation of spirit which seems to lift the soul out of the consciousness of its individual separate existence. It is also designated *ātman* (self), not as implying individuality, for the consciousness of individuality must vanish in the contemplation of *brahman*, but because the sphere within which these higher processes of thought, which rise above the phenomenal self, have their being is that of the thinking subject. *Brahman* is the Supreme, the unconditioned Self, transcending all individuality. The relation of this *brahman* to the illusions that present themselves in our consciousness is illustrated by familiar examples—the mirage assumed to be water, the rope assumed to be a snake, etc. As in some of these instances want of proper light is the source of the illusion, so want of right knowledge is the cause of our mistaking phenomena for realities.

The *Advaitins* were fully conscious of the gravity of the problem which still remained unsolved, viz. the real origin of these illusions. In many of their attempts at explanation they contradict the fundamental principle of their system. We are told that *māyā* is only a creation of the mind; the mind is led away to these false notions. But this explanation, which seems to give definite objective existence to these false notions, is subversive of advaitism. The attempt is made to evade this difficulty by asserting that the mind has within itself from eternity ideas which it only reflects or dreams out. It thus only perceives itself. But eternal ideas seem also to constitute a separate reality. Others find the origin of *māyā* in the limitations imposed upon the unlimited. These limits, which give rise to the phenomena of perception, are the creation of the individual as an individual; in *brahman*, the unlimited, there is no individualization. To be emancipated from all sense of separate individuality is real knowledge, real bliss. This is the emancipation which finds expression in the formula *tat-tvam-asi*, 'thou art it.'

Others, again, have recourse to the theory of reflexion, viz. that the varying phenomena of perception emerge through the reflexion of *brahman* in nature. But what is it that reflects? Here again we have duality. The most generally accepted solution is that which despairs of the solution, which contents itself with saying that separate existence in every form is false, all is as it is, all is *brahman*. It illustrates its position by the story of Yājñavalkya, the ancient sage, who, when asked by one of his pupils in a question, thrice repeated, to describe the *advaita*, gave no answer; and, when pressed, replied that the *advaita* is best described by silence, for all describing means *dvaita* or dualism.*

Religion having furnished the chief stimulus to Indian philosophic thought, we naturally expect to find the root and germ of its leading conceptions in the Indian sacred writings. A line of thought leading up to the Vedāntic or *advaita* conception can be distinctly traced in the Brāhmaṇas based upon the Vedas, and in subsequent writings reckoned as inspired scripture.

Starting from a worship of personified nature-powers, the religious mind of the ancient Indians pressed on to seek that on which the gods and the worlds depended for their creation and their support. It found it in that elevation of soul experienced in prayer, which enabled it to transcend its individual existence, to which it gave the name *brahman*.

In the Taittirīya-Brāhmaṇa, 2, 8, 9, 6, the question of the Rigveda, 'Who is the supporter of the bearers of the world?' is answered. *Brahman* is declared to be 'that out of which earth and heaven have been formed, and that which upholds the bearers of the world.'

In the Kāṭhaka-Upaniṣad, v. 1–3, which represents a later stage in this process of thought, the *brahman* is described as the most inward and the noblest element in all the manifestations of nature, 'the sun in the firmament, God in the heavens,' as dwelling everywhere, as born everywhere, and he only is free from suffering and sure of salvation who reveres 'the unborn, the unchangeably spiritual' that dwells within him.

In the Chāndogya-Upaniṣad is set forth in the clearest terms this exaltation of the *ātman*, or self, in its identification with *brahman*. 'This Universe is *brahman*. Its material is spirit, life is its body, light its form . . . all-embracing, silent, undisturbed—this is my soul (*ātman*) in the inmost heart, smaller than a seed of grain—this is my soul in the inmost heart, greater than the earth, greater than the heavens, greater than all these worlds . . . this is *brahman*; to it shall I, when I go hence, be united.'† The self in this sense is 'the real,' 'the one without a second (*advitīya*).' It is that out of which the whole world has been formed, of which the world is a mere transformation. He who knows *the one* knows *all*.

The parallel movements of thought in the ancient and modern philosophies of the West have been frequently pointed out. The early Greek philosophy was inspired by the longing to discover a principle of unity in the manifoldness of the phenomenal world. The earlier attempts resulted in the assumption of some one common physical principle, out of which this variety was developed; the later attempts sought it in a spiritual cause. Xenophanes proclaimed the unity of the Divine, and his disciple Parmenides, denying to this Divine principle personality and change, reduced it to *Being*. To the unity thus reached by the path of pure abstraction he opposed the world of phenomena as *non-being* (τὸ μὴ ὄν). The correspondence between these successive stages in Greek thought and the course of Indian thought outlined above is interesting and suggestive. The other parallel is that presented by the Kantian philosophy. By a different path from that of mere abstraction, Kant pursued the same metaphysical quest. Having subjected to a minute critical analysis the faculties of human knowledge, he arrived at the result that 'the thing in itself' (*das Ding an sich*) is not accessible to human knowledge, as all knowledge of the external objective world is realized through the application of certain categories of thought, the categories of space, time, and causality, which inhere in the mind of the thinking subject. Reality in itself, therefore, so far as these faculties are our means of knowledge, is unknowable.

One cannot fail to recognize here also a remarkable similarity between Kant's critical position and the real *advaita* doctrine. But there is this important difference to be noted in regard to

* Śankara on *Brahmasūtra*, iii. 2. 17; Deussen, *Upanishads*, Eng. tr. (1906) p. 156 f.

† Chānd.-Up. iii. 14, cf. Śatap.-Br. x. 6. 3.

method. The *advaita* presents us with no critical analysis of the process of knowledge, for we can scarcely dignify with such a name the arbitrary and fanciful methods above indicated, by which the *Advaitin* sought to explain the fact of *māyā* in our perception of phenomena. So far as the *advaita* is to be regarded as a philosophy, it is a philosophy of a purely abstract and speculative nature. By one supreme effort of mind it advances to a position which other philosophies have sought to establish by a patient and laborious examination of the facts of experience. In its religious aspect it exhibits similar characteristics, and its religious aspect is more important than its speculative interest. It is a doctrine of salvation through the attainment of the true *knowledge*, and this knowledge is to be realized in the *advaita* conclusion. By a purely intellectual effort the emancipation of the soul from evil is to be achieved. In this solution of a deep moral problem we see the same impatience of facts, the same summary method of reaching the desired goal, as marks the speculative side of this philosophy. How far this philosophy has sounded the depths of the problem may be gathered from the illustration which it employs to describe it. One who wears a jewel round his neck is distressed when, forgetting that he has it, he searches here and there to find it. His peace is restored when he discovers that it has never been lost. So, we are told, the distressed soul finds salvation in the knowledge that there is no diversity, no evil, no separateness. Pleasure and pain are merely the results of this false sense of individuality and separateness. The mind of the individual may be conscious of evil and of suffering; but the great mind *brahman* knows nothing of these. Identification with *brahman* is the source of all bliss, the sense of separateness is the root of all evil.

LITERATURE.—See art. VEDĀNTA. The view of Advaitism given above will be found fully expounded in M. N. Dvivedi's *Monism or Advaitism?* Bombay, 1889.

D. MACKICHAN.

ADVOCATE.—The etymological meaning of 'advocate' (Lat. *advocatus*) is *one called to*, *i.e.* one called to another's aid. It may be used of one called in to assist another in any business, as, *e.g.*, when an official appointed to defend the rights and revenues of the church was called *advocatus ecclesiæ*. In legal phraseology an advocate is one called in to assist another's cause in a court of justice. The Lat. *advocatus* had a wider significance than 'advocate' connotes in modern English; in Cicero's time it denoted a backer, hence any legal assistant: not an advocate as in later authors (cf. *Phil.* i. § 16, *pro Cæc.* §§ 24, 43). Like παράκλητος in classical Greek, *advocatus* might refer to any 'friend of the accused person, called to speak to his character, or otherwise enlist the sympathy of the judges (or, as we should call them, the jury) in his favour.'

Field (*Notes on Translation of NT*, 1899, 102) supports the above statement by the following apposite quotation from Asconius, *ad Cic. in Q. Cæcil*: 'Qui defendit alterum in iudicio, aut *patronus* dicitur si orator est; aut *advocatus*, si aut ius suggerit, aut præsentiam suam commodat amico.' For a similar use of παράκλητος he refers to Dem. *de F. L. init.* p. 341. 10; Diog. Laert. *Vit. Bionis*, iv. 50. In Philo, *de Opif. M.* § 6 'the office intended is that of a *monitor* or *adviser* . . . but still preserving the leading idea of *amicus advocatus in consilium*.'

'Advocate,' as a judicial term, now generally signifies *pleader*. This is a natural development of meaning, for assistance in courts of law usually takes the form of speaking on behalf of one who is accused. As thus employed the word practically corresponds to the English 'barrister,' whose office it is to plead the cause of his client.

Five uses of advocate fall within the limits of this article, viz.:—

1. In the New Testament:
   (*a*) Jesus Christ 'an Advocate.'
   (*b*) The Holy Spirit 'another Advocate.'
2. In Church History:
   (*a*) *Advocatus ecclesiæ*.
   (*b*) *Advocatus diaboli*.
   (*c*) *Advocatus Dei*.

I. *'ADVOCATE' IN NT.*—(*a*) **Jesus Christ 'an Advocate.'**—There is general agreement that in 1 Jn 2[1] ('If any man sin, we have an Advocate with the Father, Jesus Christ the righteous'), 'Advocate' is a better rendering of παράκλητος than either 'Comforter' or 'Helper,' the alternatives suggested in RVm. Wyclif, following the Vulgate, has 'We han an aduocat anentis the fadir.' In considering the NT use of this word, Jewish as well as classical authors should be consulted. In Rabbinical literature *pᵉraglîṭā'*—the Aramaic transliteration of παράκλητος (cf. 'paraclete')—is not infrequently found. Buxtorf quotes 'An advocate is a good intercessor before a magistrate or king' (cf. *JE* vol. ix. p. 514 f.). Doubtless the word sometimes occurs in Jewish writers with a wider meaning, as in the Targum on Job 16[20] and 33[23], where it represents the Hebrew word for 'interpreter' (*mēlîṣ*); but its use to designate 'pleader' is well established. The antithesis between advocate and accuser is, for example, clearly marked in *Pirqe Aboth*, iv. 11: 'He who performs one good deed has gotten to himself one advocate [paraclete], and he who commits one transgression has gotten to himself one accuser.' Field (*op. cit.*) has good grounds for saying that Rabbinical writers use *paraclete* 'precisely in the same way as St. John in his Epistle, and as the Latin *patronus* which they also adopt.' This judgment accords with the conclusion already drawn from the history of the word. Though there is no evidence that the *patronus* was ever called *advocatus*, 'advocate' was, in its later usage, extended in meaning so as to include the function of the Roman *patron*, who was liable to be called to the side of his *client* 'to represent him before the tribunals when he became involved in litigation' (Muirhead, *Roman Law*, p. 9). Clement of Rome (1 *Ep. ad Cor.* i. 36) applies to our Lord the title προστάτης=*patronus*.

In 1 Jn 2[1] the thoughts suggested by the comparison of Christ to the Advocate must be interpreted in harmony with the context. When the believer is charged with having sinned, and Satan presses the charge in the presence of the 'Father . . . who judgeth' (1 P 1[17]), Christ pleads for the accused; because He is 'righteous' His advocacy is well-pleasing to the Father; and His plea that God would show forth His righteousness in the sinner's forgiveness is based upon the fact that He Himself is more than the sinner's Advocate, even the 'propitiation' for his sins (1 Jn 2[2], cf. Ro 3[25]). 'Faith in the forgiveness of sins cannot be religiously and ethically innocuous unless it is associated with faith in the propitiation' (Rothe, *ExpT*, i. [1890] p. 209).

(*b*) **The Holy Spirit 'another Advocate.'**—There has been much controversy in regard to the rendering of παράκλητος in Jn 14[16. 26] 15[26] 16[7]. In all four places Wyclif and the chief English versions translate it 'Comforter'; the Rhemish has 'Paraclete.' In RVm 'Advocate' is the first alternative. Beza, however, has *advocatus* both in the Epistle and in the Gospel; he rightly explains its application to the Holy Spirit 'by a reference to St. Paul's words (Ro 8[34]) about the Spirit as making intercession for us. The same explanation is given by Pearson on the eighth article of the Creed' (Hare, *The Mission of the Comforter*, 1846, note k. Hare's own preference is for 'Comforter,' not in its secondary sense as Consoler, but in its primary sense as Strengthener). Amongst modern scholars there is a growing consensus of opinion in favour of 'Advocate' as a title of the Holy Spirit as well as of Jesus Christ.

'Christ is our Advocate on high,
Thou art our Advocate within.'

The arguments in support of this view are succinctly stated by Field (*op. cit.* p. 103): '(1) "Another Advocate," *i.e.* besides Myself. (2) The word is only known from St. John's writings, here and in 1 Jn 2[1], where "advocate" is, by general consent, the right word in the right place. (3) Etymologically, advocate and παράκλητος are identical. (4) This is the only rendering which accounts for the passive form.'

The question is, 'Does the work of the Holy Spirit as described in the above four passages correspond to the functions of an advocate?' In three of them (Jn 14[16. 26] 15[26]) the Holy Spirit is the 'Advocate within' the hearts of Christ's disciples; as an Advocate he 'pleads the truth and makes reply to every argument of sin' (14[16]); His pleading is with power because He brings to remembrance the Saviour's words, unfolds their teaching (14[26]), and bears witness to His glory (15[26]). No strain is put upon the context of these passages by this interpretation; the disciples themselves will be 'judges against their own unbelieving hearts, and Christ will be triumphantly acquitted and declared to be the Son of God with power' (Hastings, *ExpT*, x. [1899] p. 170). The remaining passage (16[7]) describes the Holy Spirit's work in convicting the world. He is Christ's Advocate, and 'for the Apostles themselves the pleading of the Advocate was a sovereign vindication of their cause. In the great trial they were shown to have the right, whether their testimony was received or rejected' (Westcott, *Com. in loc.*).

Zahn (*Einleit.* vol. i. p. 45) finds a difficulty in accepting the rendering 'another Advocate' in Jn 14[16]. 'Another,' he argues, implies that Christ Himself had already been His disciples' Advocate, whereas He had rather been their Teacher or their Interpreter. But there is no need to give precisely the same meaning to 'Advocate' when it is applied to Christ's earthly intercourse with His disciples and to His heavenly intercession on their behalf. The difficulty seems to be sufficiently met by saying that on earth Christ was ever pleading God's cause with the men who had been given Him out of the world, whilst in heaven He is ever pleading their cause with God (cf. Cremer, *Bibl.-Theol. Lex. of NT Gr.* p. 337).

All admit that 'Advocate' does not adequately represent the varied work of the Holy Spirit. As a descriptive general title rather than as a precise tr. of the word in the passages discussed above, the felicitous suggestion of Dr. E. A. Abbott may be gladly accepted: 'Perhaps the best periphrasis of Paraclete for modern readers would be "The Friend in need"' (*Paradosis*, 1413*a*).

2. *'ADVOCATE' IN CHURCH HISTORY.*—(*a*) **Advocatus ecclesiæ.**—The 'Church's advocate' was a civilian officially charged with the duty of defending ecclesiastical rights and revenues. At the sixth Council of Carthage (A.D. 401) it was resolved (Canon 10) that 'the Emperors shall be prayed to appoint, in union with the bishops, protectors (*defensores*) for the Church.' At the eleventh Council of Carthage (A.D. 407) it was decreed (Canon 2c) that 'for the necessities of the Church five *executores* or *exactores* shall be demanded of the Emperor to collect the revenues of the Church' (Hefele, *Hist. of Church Councils*, vol. ii. pp. 425, 442). At different periods the duties of the *advocati ecclesiæ*—sometimes designated as *agentes, defensores*, or *exactores*—included not only the defence and maintenance of the secular and legal rights of the Church, but also the protection of the poor and of orphans, the exercise of jurisdiction, including police functions and the power to levy soldiers from among the vassals of ecclesiastics who claimed immunity from the service of the State.

At first the office of *advocatus ecclesiæ* was not hereditary, but Hinschius states (*PRE*[3] i. 199) that before the end of the 9th cent. founders of monasteries, etc., sometimes stipulated that it should be retained for themselves and for their heirs. In Charlemagne's time the right of nomination belonged to the king; but to some ecclesiastical corporations the power of free choice was given, with the proviso that the secular authority of the district—the duke or count—had the right to reject the nominee of the Church.

When the office of advocate was held by unscrupulous men, it became an instrument of oppression and extortion. Historians record many charges brought against these officials of plundering the property of the Church and misappropriating its revenues. Kurtz does not overstate the facts when he says: 'Many advocates assumed arbitrary powers, and dealt with the property of the Church and its proceeds just as they chose' (*Church History*, § 86). Hinschius (*op. cit.*) says that it was Pope Innocent III. who, in his negotiations with Otto IV. and Frederick II., first secured a promise that the State should protect the Church against the oppression of the *advocati ecclesiæ*.

(*b*) **Advocatus diaboli.**—In the Roman Catholic Church, when it is proposed to honour a departed saint by Beatification or Canonization,* it is the duty of the 'Devil's advocate' to plead against the proposal and to bring forward every possible objection to it. These objections may lie either against the saint's reputation for 'heroic' virtue, the orthodoxy of his writings, or the genuineness of the miracles with which he is credited. They may also have reference to technical errors of procedure, or to flaws in the evidence.

Von Moy, in an article which has the approval of the Roman Catholic authorities, says that papal canonizations are not certainly known to have taken place before the time of Pope John XV. (A.D. 993). At first bishops sanctioned beatifications without consulting the Pope, but in consequence of abuses Pope Alexander III. decreed (1170) that henceforth papal consent should in all cases be obtained. This decree, known as *Audivimus* (the word with which it begins), is the basis of the present regulations in regard to Beatification and Canonization. The edict of Pope Urban VIII. (1634) made it beyond dispute that it is the Pope's exclusive prerogative to beatify as well as to canonize, these acts being forbidden not only to bishops, archbishops, etc., but even to a papal legate, a council unless it has the Pope's consent, and the college of cardinals assembled when the papal throne is empty (Wetzer-Welte, *Kirchenlexikon*[2], vol. ii. p. 140 ff.).

In the process of Beatification a preliminary inquiry is instituted by the bishop of the diocese concerned. If the result is favourable to the *postulatores* who desire the Beatification, the proposal is forwarded to the *congregatio rituum* in Rome. At the various meetings of this congregation the *advocatus diaboli* or *promotor fidei* is required to bring forward all the objections that can be urged against the proposition of the *postulatores*. The decision is taken after both sides have been fully heard. Between the first and second meetings of the *congregatio rituum* ten years must elapse. The Beatification of a saint cannot take place less than fifty years after his death. Canonization may follow after an interval, if it can be shown that 'since beatification at least two miracles have been wrought by God in answer to the intercessions of the saint' (Von Moy, *op. cit.*). In the processes preliminary to Canonization the 'Devil's advocate' discharges the duties of his office in the manner already described.

The official regulations under which the *advocatus diaboli* acts provide for the strict application of the most stringent tests to the claims of the saint whom it is proposed to beatify or to canonize; moreover, the final decision, as in all *causæ majores*, rests with the Pope. It is claimed that 'in modern times the court of Rome has shown itself extremely averse to promiscuous canonization; and since the days of Benedict XIV., the promoter of the faith,

* Beatification differs from Canonization in that it permits but does not enjoin the honouring (*cultus*) of a saint, and that it applies to a particular diocese, province, or order, but not to the whole Roman Catholic world.

popularly known as the devil's advocate, has exercised extreme severity in sifting the claims of aspirants' (Foye, *Romish Rites*, p. 406 f.). This statement, however true of the procedure under some Popes, needs qualification. Alzog, an orthodox writer of 'correct' opinions, testifies that Pius IX. 'performed more beatifications and canonizations than any of his predecessors'; and Nippold, who quotes this testimony, adds that the Beatifications of this Pope show him to have been 'entirely in the hands of the Jesuits,' and that the biographies of the worthies beatified by him are 'full of unnatural asceticism and unnatural miracles.' The same historian states that the virgin Clara of Montefalco was canonized by Leo XIII. on the ground that 'not only was the body of the saint well preserved since her death in 1308, but that more especially her heart showed traces of the instruments of the passion.' At the public celebration of Dec. 8, 1881 there were exhibited in the gallery connected with the Vatican 'twelve pictures, of which six treated of the miracles performed by Clara' (*The Papacy in the Nineteenth Century*, Schwab's tr., pp. 128, 147, 198).

(*c*) **Advocatus Dei.**—In the Roman Catholic Church this title is given to the *procurator* whose duty it is to refute the objections raised by the *advocatus diaboli* against the Beatification or Canonization of a saint. Von Moy (*op. cit.*) states that 'God's advocate' is always a man of high rank, and that he is chosen from the province or from the order to which the saint belonged. Just before the solemn moment of canonization, the *advocatus Dei* approaches the papal throne, accompanied by an advocate of the consistory, who, from the lowest step of the throne, presents to the Pope, in the name of 'God's advocate,' an earnest request that it may please His Holiness to canonize the saint.

LITERATURE.—For 'Advocate' in NT see bibliography given in art. HOLY SPIRIT. Of special value is Westcott's Additional Note on Jn 14^{16} in his *Com.* on this Gospel. For *advocatus ecclesiæ* the best sources are mentioned by Hinschius (*PRE*[3] i. 198). Amongst them are Böhmer, *Observationes juris canonici*, Obs. vi.; Happ, *de Advocatia Ecclesiastica*; Brunner, *Deutsche Rechtsgeschichte*; Lamprecht, *Deutsche Wirthschaftsgeschichte*. For *advocatus diaboli* and *advocatus Dei* the chief authority is Prosper de Lambertini (Benedict XIV.), *de Servorum Dei Beatificatione et Beatorum Canonizatione*. This work is the only source mentioned by Von Moy in his art. 'Beatification und Canonization' in Wetzer-Welte's *Kirchenlexikon oder Encykl. der kathol. Theol. und ihrer Hülfswissenschaften*. See also Du Cange, *Glossarium*, *s.v.* 'Canonizare'; Milman, *Hist. of Lat. Christianity*, vol. ix. p. 71 f.; Alban Butler, *Lives of the Saints*; F. W. Faber, *Essay on Beatification, Canonization*, etc.

J. G. TASKER.

ÆGEAN RELIGION.—By this is meant the religion of the coasts and isles of the Ægean Sea in the Bronze and earlier Ages. 'Ægean' civilization was commonly known till recently as 'Mycenæan.' Now, however, that Mycenæ has been shown to have been probably neither the centre of it nor the scene of its earlier developments, the wider and non-committal name 'Ægean' has come into use, to include the 'Mycenæan' of Schliemann, the 'pre-Mycenæan' of his earlier critics, the 'Cycladic' of Blinkenberg and others, and the 'Minoan' of Evans. The first revelation of this forgotten civilization occupied the last quarter of the 19th cent., and begot, as was inevitable, more wonder and curiosity than science. Scholars were not able all at once to comprehend and co-ordinate the mass of novel raw material accumulating on their hands; and it took time to make the necessary comparisons between the Ægean civilization and other civilizations, contemporary and posterior. Among its institutions none remained so long obscure as the religious. Up to almost the end of the century no sacred building had been recognized among Ægean remains, and no undoubted idol of a divinity. Of the small number of unquestioned cult objects discovered, almost all were still ascribed by many scholars to foreign importation. The few ritual scenes represented on intaglios were, some of them, not observed to be religious at all, while others were ill understood for want of known parallels and of a sound general conception of Ægean cult. Perrot and Chipiez in their volume on the Art of Primitive Greece, issued in 1895, found hardly anything to say on religious representations; and Evans, when about to show in 1900 how much light could be thrown on the religion by certain classes of small objects, not till then adequately remarked, had to confess that 'among the more important monuments of the Mycenæan world' very little was to be found 'having a clear and obvious relation to religious belief.'* Since that date, however, the inquiry has been revolutionized by the exploration of Crete; and we now have a mass of monumental evidence upon Ægean religious belief, cult, and ritual from which knowledge of the broad principles and much ritual detail have been obtained. Upon this class of evidence any general account of the religion of a prehistoric civilization must of necessity be based; and only in the second instance should contemporary and posterior cults be introduced into the inquiry. For the present purpose no account will be taken of possible racial changes during the Ægean period, since the civilization evidently remained of one type throughout, and the popular religion shows development only, not essential change.

i. GENERAL NATURE OF ÆGEAN RELIGION.—We have ample evidence that Ægean religion and ritual had originally both a *natural aniconic* and an *artificial aniconic* character. In the first state, man, conscious of a dominant unseen Spirit, and impelled by his instinct to locate it in some visible object in permanent relation to his own daily life, finds its dwelling in imposing features of Nature, *e.g.* the sun, a mountain, a wood, a stream, and even a single tree or rock. In the second, he attempts to take the Spirit under his own control, and to bring it into particular and exclusive relation to himself by placing its dwelling in smaller and even portable objects: in stones of singular natural appearance, or fashioned by himself into pillars; in trees or bushes of his own planting, weapons, animal forms, and all kinds of object known to us as fetishes. The transition from these to idols is easy. Having become familiar with the Spirit, and conceiving it more and more in his own image, he passes to the *iconic* state, and in that will remain till the advanced point of mental development at which he ceases to demand a visible home for his god.

These states, however, are not to be regarded as always successive. With primitive man they are often contemporaneous, the usages and ritual proper to one coexisting with those proper to another, and making his religious life more full and various. The facts of an early state can therefore be learned from a later; and this is fortunate for the student of an extinct religion, since man seldom reaches the point of making monumental records of his cult before he has passed almost out of the primitive states. Nor can the peculiar character of his religion become certainly intelligible to us till he has expressed his conception in some theoanthropic presentation. In the case of the Ægean religion, our monumental evidence hardly begins until the full iconic state is well in sight. But from that point it is sufficiently full and intelligible to

* 'Mycen. Tree and Pillar Cult' in *JHS*, 1901, p. 99 (hereinafter referred to as *TPC*).

inform us not only how the deity was conceived and how worshipped from the beginning of theoanthropism, but how worshipped previously, before being endued with human attributes on the monuments, or perhaps with any very precise attributes whatever in the minds of worshippers. Moreover, more than most religions, the Ægean remained to the end full of aniconic cult-practices.

Ægean religion, then, was from the first a Nature cult, in which the heavenly bodies and imposing terrestrial features were objects of worship, while at the same time a Divine Spirit was understood to have its dwelling therein. From this state there survived in the Ægean religious art of a later stage such cult objects as the solar disc, the lunar crescent, the star symbol passing into various forms of cross,* the rocky mountain, and the grove; while from the other state, the artificial aniconic, persisted the single tree or group of trees, generally three in number, the pillar, single, triple, or many, sacred animals, weapons, conspicuously the *bipennis*, or double war-axe (chosen as a fetish very probably from its obvious likeness to the star dwelling), the large body shield, and other objects, notably a pair of horns, perhaps a trophy, symbolic of a sacrificial bull. All these accidents of the primitive religion will be dealt with more fully below in the section on the Cult; but in order to discern its essential idea, dependent as we are for all first-hand information on artistic monuments, we must pass at once to the iconic stage and inquire how Ægean man, so soon as he had clearly conceived the Divine Spirit, represented it in terms of his own nature.

ii. THE DEITY.—It has been said that, previous to the exploration of Crete, no idol or icon of a deity had been certainly recognized among Ægean remains. It must be borne in mind that in dealing with novel monuments of a prehistoric civilization, it is not legitimate to presume that a representation of the human figure is intended to be Divine until and unless it be found with clear concomitant indications of the supernatural—unless, for

FIG. 1.—GOLD RING FROM MYCENÆ.

example, it be represented as emitting light, or accompanied by wild beasts, such as lions or large serpents, fatal to ordinary humanity, or, again, of superhuman relative stature, or, lastly, receiving adoration. In the cult-scenes found first, *e.g.* those on the bezel of a gold ring found in the Acropolis treasure at Mycenæ (fig. 1), on impressed glass plaques, on a painted stela from the same site, and on other monuments, a manifest deity was not generally recognized, although there were undoubted religious votaries, even monstrous demonic forms,* and at least one figure accompanied by doves. Acute observers, however, familiar with the monuments of other Near Eastern religions, had already noted the prominence of female figures in these cult-scenes, and begun to guess that the Ægean peoples embodied their principal conception of the deity in feminine form. In particular, Evans had been observing a class of gem and ring subjects which showed a female between lions, goats, etc.† As the excavation of Knossos proceeded, this female form, represented under circumstances implying divinity, appeared with increasing frequency on a class of objects first found there, and of great value in this connexion, viz. well-preserved clay impressions of intaglio gems. On several such impressions the female figure is seen seated (fig. 1), while other figures stand in attitudes of adoration or pour libations before it; on one found in 1901 the figure is standing on a mountain peak, while lions mount guard on either hand and an adorer stands below; on another the figure in flounced dress lays her hands on the backs of two lions;‡ on another the figure, holding a spear, is accompanied by a lion regardant;§ on another the figure bears on her shoulder the sacred *bipennis*.‖ This female figure with the axe appears also on a schist mould found in East Crete. And, lastly, on one found by Halbherr at Haghia Triadha, in the south of Crete, a female of relatively gigantic stature stands between two smaller females before a shrine.¶ In the third year of the Cretan excavations the discovery of actual shrines began. In the first found, a miniature shrine of early date, there were no idols, but among other obviously sacred objects was a triad of terra-cotta 'bætylic' pillars with doves perched atop; and presently, in the same season, an actual chapel, very small, but sufficient for its purpose, which was no doubt domestic, was opened and found to contain, in company with sacred axes on pedestals and 'horns of consecration' (see below), three feminine idols in painted terra cotta and semi-anthropomorphic, of which the largest had a dove perched on her head. In the same year other and ruder idols of the same sex and type, but with snakes coiled about them, were brought to light at Gournia, an Ægean site in eastern Crete, dug by Miss H. A. Boyd, and also at Priniás in the Cretan Messará. This snake-goddess was not found at Knossos till 1903, and then she appeared as a faience idol, which is among Mr. Evans' greatest prizes. Three serpents coil about her and form her girdle, while a fourth rears its head above her tiara (fig. 2). That this figure, whether shown on intaglios or as an idol, is a goddess there is no manner of doubt; and that she is one and the same, whether accompanied by doves or serpents, has been conclusively proved by excavations in East Crete carried out in 1904. At Palaikastro the remains of a shrine were discovered wherein a goddess held a triple snake in her arms, while votaries danced round her, and doves perched on pillars hard by.**

This goddess, however, is not alone. In a much smaller number of intaglio impressions a youthful male figure has been observed, accompanied by

* The 'Swastika' (*crux gammata*), the cross *patée*, and the plain Greek cross.

* The latter, often observed on gems, were not credited with much significance owing to doubts, not only of the indigenous nature of the objects on which they appeared, but also of their being other than human votaries engaged in a theriomorphic ritual. Cf. A. B. Cook in *JHS* xiv. p. 81.

† *TPC* § 22, figs. 44, 45. Cf. Annual Brit. School at Athens (*BSA*), vi. p. 43 n.

‡ *BSA* vii. pp. 18, 19, 29, 101.

§ *Ib.* ix. fig. 37.

‖ *Ib.* viii. fig. 59.

¶ *Mon. Antichi*, xiii., *Resti*, etc. fig. 37. Cf. the gigantic seated female on a Zakro seal, *JHS* xxii. p. 77, fig. 2.

** *BSA* x. p. 223. This ritual dance seems also to be figured on an impression from Haghia Triadha (*Resti*, etc., *cit. supra*, fig. 33).

lions, and sometimes armed (fig. 3).* On a gold signet of Knossos such a figure with hair flying loose behind is seen in the upper field, and is supposed by Evans to be the deity descending on his shrine.† But no actual idol of a god has come to light, unless the male of short stature offering a dove to the goddess in the little chapel at Knossos‡ is to be interpreted as a Divine figure.

This list is not exhaustive. The goddess is probably to be recognized in many other intaglio scenes, *e.g.* those wherein a female holds up goats by the legs,§ as elsewhere she holds lions; and perhaps in certain other feminine idols. But it includes all undoubted representations of a deity so far found, and is more than enough to prove how the Ægean peoples, when they arrived at the iconic stage of religion, conceived divinity. They personified the Supreme Principle as a woman, to whom was subordinated a young male, less in honour and probably later in time. There is no evidence for more deities than these. The religion was what may be called a Dual Monotheism.

FIG. 2.—SNAKE-CROWNED GODDESS FROM KNOSSOS.

iii. CULT.—There is evidence for several classes of cult-objects, considered to be dwelling-places of the Divine Spirit, and surviving through the theoanthropic age as fetishes; for inanimate accessories of various kinds, of which the origin and later significance are often obscure; and for animate accessories of cult, perhaps also at first dwelling-places of the Spirit, but tending more and more to be regarded as symbolic. These all played a part in a customary ritual, of whose practices, strikingly uniform over the Ægean area, we have many illustrations.

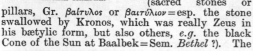

FIG. 3.—SEAL IMPRESSION FROM HAGHIA TRIADHA.

1. Dwelling-places of the Spirit (fetishes). — (*a*) *Bætyls* (sacred stones or pillars, Gr. βαίτυλος or βαιτύλιον = esp. the stone swallowed by Kronos, which was really Zeus in his bætylic form, but also others, *e.g.* the black Cone of the Sun at Baalbek = Sem. *Bethel* ?). The character and use of Ægean sacred stones have been very fully treated by Evans in *TPC*, and subsequent Cretan discoveries have added little but confirmation. There can be small doubt that, as cult-objects, they represented in a convenient fetish form the original Divine *mountain*, still seen in intaglio cult-scenes of a late period. They themselves became in time the origin both of altars and of iconic statues, passing through gradations of rude shaping. A remarkable example of this transition has come to light latterly at Knossos in the large building to the west of the palace, where lay several natural stone freaks, roughly resembling human forms, and evidently carefully preserved in a shrine. Whether pillars or wooden posts, descended from sacred trees, eventually acquired a symbolic significance as *phalli*, is less certain. An upright object impaling a triangle occurs in any case in gem-scenes, and is strongly suggestive of a *phallus* in connexion with a *vulva*. Further, there is reason to think that bætyls originated upright tombstones, which from being Divine or ghostly dwelling-places became merely commemorative in a late age.

Bætyls passed in Ægean cult through various modifications, retaining their significance as dwelling-places of the Spirit. At first unshaped single rocks or cairns, we find them developed in the majority of earlier Ægean cult-scenes into pillars, monolithic or built up. The Divine pillar stands alone, sometimes, as over the Mycenæ Gate, between sacred animals, a position wherein it precedes the iconic figures of a later period; often also in front of a shrine, while a votary adores before it; and it is very often associated with trees. Almost equally often it does not appear singly, but in groups of three, and less commonly of more.* Occasionally the dove is seen either descending towards it or perched upon it; more rarely rays issue from it. Thereafter the pillar, from standing free, becomes a support,—a 'pillar of the house,'—but is still bætylic, and its double function is sometimes shown by the free pillar bearing a fragment of superstructure. It is seen rising from behind 'horns of consecration' in fresco pictures of the façades of shrines, and in one case bearing sacred axe-heads affixed to its capital;† and it props up 'tables of offering,' with accessory supports round it.‡ It is possible that such sacred 'pillars of the house' have actually been found in certain chambers at Knossos and elsewhere, which seem too small to have needed a central prop for purely architectural reasons, and the probability is heightened by the fact that the blocks of which two such pillars in the Knossian palace are made, are marked with the sacred sign of the double axe.§ There is reason to think that the original Ægean sanctity of pillar supports has something to do with the later Greek fashion of using a redundancy of columns in sacred architecture.

(*b*) *Triliths* (dolmens).—These are much less frequently represented than *bætyls*, but sufficiently often to leave no doubt that the triad of stones forming a free standing portal had a sacred character in Ægean as in so many other lands.‖ They are seen framing a bætyl or standing before a sacred tree. On a remarkable gem impression from Zakro¶ in East Crete, such a trilith is well shown with lions couchant on either hand.

(*c*) *Trees* (Sem. *ashera*).—These, being perishable, are now to be looked for only in cult representations, and especially on intaglio impressions. There they are as frequent as bætyls, and they

* *TPC* fig. 43; *BSA* ix. fig. 38, vii. p. 101. Cf. Haghia Triadha seal (*Resti*, etc. fig. 40).
† *TPC* fig. 48.
‡ *BSA* viii. p. 100, fig. 56.
§ *e.g.* Zakro (*JHS* xxii. p. 77, fig. 3), Vaphio (Furtwängler, *Ant. Gem.* pl. ii. 25), Haghia Triadha (*Resti*, etc. fig. 42).

* *BSA* viii. 29, fig. 14. † *BSA* x. fig. 14 and pl. 2.
‡ *TPC* figs. 7, 9. These objects are supposed to be the origin of the sacred tripods of Greek cult.
§ *TPC* fig. 5. ‖ See *TPC* § 26.
¶ *JHS* xxii. 87, fig. 28.

occur singly or in triads (very common) or in groves. They are often seen growing out of the shrine itself, or in close proximity to an altar. The goddess sometimes sits under the shade (fig. 1); at other times she plucks the fruit. Many botanical varieties can be distinguished, the palm, the fig, the cypress, the pine, the plane, the vine; but the first three are most frequent. As has been said already, the tree occurs very often in the same scene with the pillar, a coincidence frequently observed in the case of megalithic monuments elsewhere.

(*d*) *Weapons.*—The great *body-shield*, curved inwards at the waist, which is so often used as a decorative motive in Ægean relief work, occurs in cult-representations as an independent object, lying before a shrine, or suspended in mid-air. Compare two gem-impressions from Zakro, which show shields lying, in the one case, before a group of five pillars (probably not towers, as stated in the text); in the other, before the façade of a shrine.* The most decisive monument is a small painted *stela* found at Mycenæ, whereon is depicted a great shield between two adoring votaries.† Miniature shields in clay and ivory, found at Knossos, were evidently cult-objects or amulets.

Figures of both the goddess and the god bear *spears*, but we have no evidence yet for the use of either that weapon or the *sword* as a cult-object.

With the *bipennis* or double-axe the case is very different. The evidence for its cult-use is overwhelming. It is seen in the field of a gem-impression with a votary adoring;‡ it forms the central object of a cult-scene painted on a clay coffin found at Palaikastro; and is being adored in both the chief scenes on the great Haghia Triadha sarcophagus,§ where it is seen in conjunction with sacred palm-trees and doves, and stands upright on a stepped pyramidal base, similar to the basis with socket for a staff, found in the palace at Knossos. In the small chapel on the latter site, it evidently stood between the sacred 'horns of consecration,'‖ a position in which it is often shown on intaglios (cf. fig. 4). Sometimes it appears in a reduplicated form, as in a steatite example from the small shrine at Knossos; on the gold signet from Mycenæ (fig. 1); and on the schist mould from East Crete, mentioned already: and, *à propos*, Evans recalls the fact that, since it appears in the hand of the goddess on a Knossian gem, and in company with her idols in the small shrine, it was at least as much her weapon as the god's. The dual axe is, he thinks, the fetish of a bi-sexual god. Miniature axes in bronze have often been found on Cretan sites, *e.g.* in the lower part of the holy cave on Mt. Dicte, and were evidently very common fetishes or cult-offerings. The sign of the axe is found more often than any other on Knossian blocks, whether as a symbol of consecration or as a mason's mark. It is not impossible that its name *labrys* is to be detected in that of the Cretan *labyrinth.*¶

2. Other inanimate accessories of cult.—Certain other objects are represented in cult-scenes, or have actually been found in connexion with shrines, about which it is less safe to say that they were dwelling-places of the Spirit. Even if originally so, and long in use as fetishes, they seem in the iconic stage to have become rather articles of ritualistic furniture.

* *JHS* xxii. figs. 29, 30.
† Perrot-Chipiez, *Hist. de l'Art*, 'La Grèce Prim.' fig. 440.
‡ From Zakro, *JHS*, *l.c.* fig. 5.
§ Paribeni, *Rendiconti R. Acc. Lincei*, xii. fasc. 70, p. 30.
‖ *BSA* viii. 100.
¶ So Kretschmer and Max Mayer quoted by Evans, *TPC* p. 109, n. 6.

(*a*) '*Horns of consecration.*'—These long misunderstood objects, of commonest occurrence in gem and fresco cult-scenes, and found modelled in stucco, clay, terra-cotta, and stone, were almost certainly fetishes at the first. They consist simply of a base with two erect horns, which, in the more elaborate examples represented, bend outwards at the tips, like the horns of oxen (fig. 4).* They are seen either on the top of a shrine or altar,† or beside sacred pillars or trees, which in some cases seem to rise out of them (cf. figs. 5, 6). Also they support in the same way the sacred *bipennis*, actual examples having been found in the small shrine at Knossos with sockets for axe-shafts. Upon a vase from Enkomi (Old Salamis) in Cyprus the picture shows not only one *bipennis* so rising from these horns, but two other axes fixed between the horns of actual *bucrania*, depicted in full (fig. 5).‡ This seems to confirm the inference, which in any case suggests itself, that the conventional sacred horns are a convenient reduction of an original *bucranium*, itself a reduction of the entire bull, known from abundant evidence to have been a sacred animal, and probably a Divine

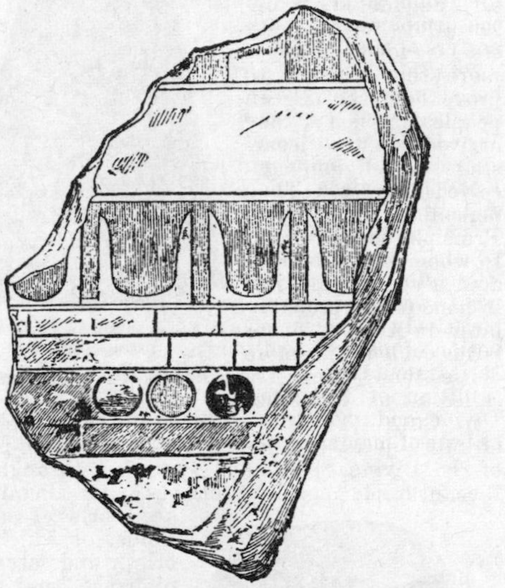

FIG. 4.—FRESCO FROM KNOSSOS.

dwelling. The horns-object serves to stamp any scene as religious, and its very frequent appearance is of great importance as a clue to the sacred character of other objects.

(*b*) *The knotted tie or zone.*—A representation of a knotted scarf or tassel seems also to have sacred significance. Found modelled in alabaster by Schliemann in the Mycenæan Acropolis graves, and supposed to be merely a fragment of wall decoration, it turned up again in the small shrine at Knossos as an independent object. It is possible that this 'tie' is a votive model of a zone, dedicated with a sexual significance, as in later Hellas. On a ring found at Mycenæ these knots are seen suspended from the capital of a lion-guarded pillar; and on a gem from the Argive Heræum they perhaps appear on either side of a bucranium.§

(*c*) *The cross.*—A cross in marble was found in a Knossian shrine; and the cross sign is common on gems and seal impressions.

* See, *e.g.*, the coloured plate appended to *TPC*, showing a fresco painting of a Knossian shrine.
† Paribeni, *l.c.* p. 5. Model altars with horns attached were found in the sacred Temenos near the royal villa of Haghia Triadha.
‡ *TPC* fig. 3.
§ Halbherr doubts this (*Resti*, etc. p. 42), preferring to interpret the objects as corslets.

3. Animate accessories of cult.—What are known in late stages of religion as animals sacred to such and such a divinity, in art appearing as mere attributes, and in real life devoted to the Divine pleasure, whether by being preserved as 'tabu' in the sacred precincts, or by being sacrificed that they may pass to the world invisible, have probably all a common origin as Divine dwelling-places or fetishes. In Ægean cult there were many such sacred animals:

(*a*) *Serpents*, seen twined about the person of the goddess (fig. 2), or held in the hands of her votaries. These were probably her original dwelling-place as an earth (chthonian) spirit.

(*b*) *Doves*, settled on her person or offered by votaries; also settled on, or seen approaching, bætyls, shrines (fig. 6), trees, and axes. They represent probably her original dwelling-place as a spirit of the sky.

(*c*) *Lions and lionesses*, which, in the iconic stage, are represented as the companions, guardians, or supporters of the deity.

(*d*) *Bulls, cows, and calves.*—The bull is most frequent. He is seen crowned with the sacred axe (fig. 5). In a magnificent relief, he guarded the main portal of the Knossian palace, and both there and at Tiryns appears again and again in fresco or on intaglios charging and tossing maidens and youths. Evans interprets these as circus scenes (the later ταυροκαθαψία); but it is possible that what was represented was not so much a comparatively harmless sport as a scene of the devotion of maidens and youths to the Divine beast. It is inevitable in this connexion to recall the tradition of the Knossian Minotaur, the semi-Divine and monstrous bull to which an annual tribute of maidens was devoted. Monstrous figures

FIG. 6.—GOLD SHRINE FROM MYCENÆ.

of minotaur type actually appear on Ægean intaglios,* proving that the legend is of prehistoric Ægean origin.

The cow and calf, very frequent on intaglios, seem to have typified the goddess's maternity.

(*e*) *Goats, nannies, and kids.*—The goat is very frequently held by the leg in the hand of the goddess, or accompanies her. A clay goat was found in the west shrine at Knossos. The nanny and kids seem to have the same significance as the cow and calf.

(*f*) *Deer and eagles* are frequent intaglio subjects; but beyond the fact that all Ægean engraved gems were probably in some degree amulets, we cannot adduce evidence of the sacred character of these animals.

(*g*) *Fishes* appear in fresco paintings at Knossos and Phylakopi in Melos, in two cases at least in possible connexion with shrines, recalling their

FIG. 5.—VASE PAINTING FROM SALAMIS, CYPRUS.

well-known connexion with the Semitic goddess.

(*h*) *Monstrous animals.*—Not only the *Minotaur*, but the *Griffin*, the *Sphinx* (two sphinxes draw a chariot on the Haghia Triadha sarcophagus), and various *composite monsters* appear in intaglios and on frescoes. Lion-headed demons are seen performing ritual acts, as, *e.g.*, pouring libations. Human figures with heads of *asses*, *lions*, *goats*, *birds*, and *bulls* occur, *e.g.* on a carved shell found at Phæstos.* A procession of ass-headed figures bearing a pole on their shoulders, in a Mycenæan fresco painting, has been interpreted as a scene of votaries wearing skins and engaged in *theriomorphic* rites; but this is an unsupported guess. An extraordinary variety of wildly monstrous combinations was found on intaglio impressions at Zakro; but it is possible that these were the product of heraldic fancy, and owed their variety to the necessity of differentiating signet types.

4. Temples and ritual.—There is no good Ægean evidence as yet for the existence of such large free-standing structures, having no relation to domestic buildings and devoted to Divine worship, as were the temples of the Hellenic period, although intaglio scenes show *small shrines*, either isodomic or of the dolmen type, standing apparently within enclosures or *temenoi*, and containing bætyls, sacred trees, and 'horns of consecration.' Such constructed shrines as have actually been found are *small plain chambers* enclosed in palace blocks, as at Knossos, and, possibly, at Palaikastro and Phylakopi in Melos. These, if they do not contain a sacred pillar, show only a ledge or platform at one end, upon which fetishes, idols, and other sacred objects stood. Such domestic 'shrines,' even if beautifully decorated with frescoes like the Melian chamber, can be regarded as little more than mere repositories for *sacra*. As for the representation of shrines, characterized by bætyls and horns, seen through openings in the façade, and in almost all cases tripartite, it is very doubtful if they are intended to show distinct temples,

* Knossos, *BSA* vii. figs. 7 b, c; Zakro, *ib.* fig. 45.

* *JHS* xxii. p. 92.

and not rather parts, or the whole, of a palace or other domestic structure. We have such representations in the Knossian frescoes, on intaglios, and in beaten metal (the gold miniature dove shrine of Mycenæ, fig. 6). It seems clear that certain parts of the Knossian Palace had a peculiarly sacred character;* and if it be admitted that the whole block of this 'Labyrinth' was the sacred house of the 'Labrys,' and that Minoan rulers were priest-kings (which is very probable), *the whole palace is perhaps to be regarded as a temple*, and we may assume that palaces and temples had not yet been differentiated. *Cave-sanctuaries* there certainly were, wherein Nature often provided bætyls ready made in the form of stalactites and stalagmites, as in the lower grotto of the Dictæan Cavern. Crete has supplied the most notable instances of caves so far; but parallels to the Idæan and Dictæan grottoes, and those near Sybrita and Kamares (southern face of Ida) and the mouth of the Knossos river, will probably be found ere long on the Greek mainland and in other islands. Such discoveries as the Temenos near Haghia Triadha and the deposits of votive objects found by Myres at Petsofa on the hills near Palaikastro, seem, however, to show that there were sacred places, distinct from domestic buildings, where cult was practised and votive objects were dedicated: but whether these were marked by constructed shrines or were mere enclosures (*temenoi*), or, again, open spots, possibly sanctified by a sacred tree or natural bætyl, we do not yet know. The evidence now available is rather in favour of the last alternative.

Free-standing *altars*, probably evolved from the bætyl, and retaining, perhaps, its self-contained sanctity and its significance, were, however, in ritual use. One, hewn out of rock, stands before the Idæan Cave; the foundations of three were found within the Knossian Palace on three sides of a quarter apparently indicated by its contents as peculiarly sacred; and they are often shown on intaglios and reliefs,† sometimes crowned with 'horns of consecration,' like the actual models found in the Temenos of Haghia Triadha (see above). Altars appear in pictures as rectangular structures of moderate height (fig. 7). The cupped 'table of offerings,' found, as has been already said, in some cases superimposed on a bætyl, is a convenient reduction of the altar.‡

We have no good evidence yet for a class of *priests* or *priestesses*; but it is quite possible that certain figures shown in such cult-scenes as those on the Haghia Triadha sarcophagus are intended to be sacerdotal.

As to *ritual*, various acts are represented. Votaries pour libations, raise hands in postures of adoration, call down the Divinity to his fetish dwelling by blowing through a triton shell, dance round the goddess (the 'Chorus of Ariadne'), brandish *sacra* (as does the faience votary of the snake-goddess of Knossos), play on stringed and wind instruments (Haghia Triadha sarcophagus), offer flowers and perhaps fruit (fig. 1), doves, etc., and slay animals in sacrifice (an ox on the Haghia Triadha sarcophagus, and perhaps goats, as in many intaglio scenes). There is no good evidence for *burnt* sacrifice; and the question of *human* victims cannot be determined at present. It depends on the interpretation of the *ταυροκαθαψία* scenes and of the Minotaur legend.

Dedication both of real articles of personal property and of *simulacra* was extensively practised. The Dictæan Cavern yielded hundreds of spear-heads, arrow-points, knives, sword-blades, razors, tweezers, hairpins, rings, and other bronze objects, taken off the persons of worshippers and offered to the Deity. It also yielded *simulacra* of weapons, *e.g.* especially the double-axe, a miniature chariot, miniature oxen, sheep, and goats, and figures of men and women. The latter figures belong to a large and widespread class of Ægean remains, found in silver, bronze, lead, terra-cotta, ivory, and faience, and of every grade of art. They are conventional representations of worshippers, dedicated to the Deity and placed in the Divine precinct to ensure Divine protection and a share in the Divine life for the dedicator. Even when placed in tombs, as at Kampos in Laconia, such statuettes were probably not *ushabti* (servants to answer the dead man's call in another world), but *simulacra* of surviving relatives who wished to be under the protection of the deceased and the Deity to whom he had gone. Less common objects of *ex voto* dedication are models of garments, *e.g.* skirts and girdles (found in the faience deposit at Knossos), and of human limbs, birds, and vermin (found in terra-cotta at Petsofa near Palaikastro). The Temenos of Haghia Triadha yielded a great variety of *simulacra* of all kinds.

FIG. 7.—PYXIS FROM KNOSSOS.

Perished *vegetable* substances have often been observed in little clay cups, in one locality (a 'pillar room' in a private Knossian house) lying *under* up-turned cups, disposed in orderly rows round the pillar. Certain long-stemmed vases with a spreading bowl, often richly painted, and always perforated to allow liquid to run away, which have been found on many Ægean sites (*e.g.* Knossos, Phylakopi), and were of frequent occurrence in the Dictæan Cave deposit, are supposed to have served for offerings of fruit. Corn was found in the cists containing the faience objects at Knossos. *Animal* remains lay thick in all strata of the Dictæan Cave, being chiefly the horns and bones of oxen, sheep, goats, and birds, which must be assumed to have been dedicated, cooked or raw; and stags' horns occurred with the sacred faience objects at Knossos.

It remains to be added that on the sarcophagus of Haghia Triadha, a scene is represented which has been interpreted as an act of worship to the mummified corpse of a dead man. The particular interpretation is not certain; but we have long had evidence of a practice of *ancestor worship* in the shape of the altar found above the Acropolis graves

* Evans in *BSA* ix. pp. 9, 35.

† *E.g.* on the steatite pyxis from Knossos, *TPC* fig. 2, fig. 7 above.

‡ See the specimens from the Dictæan Cave (*BSA* vi. pl. xi.) and Knossos (*BSA* ix. fig. 20).

at Mycenæ. Such a cult is quite compatible with that of the Divine Spirit, however personified, and indeed is almost always found as a subordinate practice in primitive religions. The dead, who are gone to the Great Mother or the Great Father, acquire a derivative sanctity, and are considered as able to exert powerful influence with the Deity for their surviving kin, and upon the lives of that kin. It would appear that the dead, who were not burned in the Ægean Age, and not certainly mummified, were supposed to continue to live as spirits in their tomb-houses on earth. Hence magnificent sepulchres were constructed, such as the great 'bee-hive' tombs of Mycenæ.

iv. SIGNIFICANCE OF ÆGEAN RELIGION.—The religious character and use of a great body of Ægean cult-objects having now been established, without reference to alien evidence, we may safely inquire whether a comparison of neighbouring and succeeding cults will explain the significance of the religion to which they pertained—a religion, be it remembered, which has no literary history of its own, and no literary records that can yet be deciphered. In this place the comparisons must be very briefly made. First, in regard to the Ægean *Divine Spirit* itself, personified in the iconic stage as a goddess and a young god, the student of comparative religion finds himself on very familiar ground. A goddess with a young subordinate god is known in early times on every coast of the Mediterranean which looked towards Crete. In Punic Africa she is Tanit with her son; in Egypt, Isis with Horus; in Phœnicia, Ashtaroth with Tammuz (Adonis); in Asia Minor, Cybele with Attis; in Greece (and especially in Greek Crete itself), Rhea with the young Zeus. Everywhere she is παρθένος, *i.e.* unwed, but made the mother first of her companion by immaculate conception, and then of the gods and all life by the embrace of her own son. In memory of these original facts, her cult (especially the more esoteric mysteries of it) is marked by various practices and observances symbolic of the negation of true marriage and obliteration of sex. A part of her male votaries are castrated; and her female votaries must ignore their married state when in her personal service, and often practise ceremonial promiscuity. As there is no ordinary human birth, so there is no ordinary human death. The Divine son Tammuz, Attis Melicertes, or Zeus himself in Crete (where his tomb was shown), dies, but comes again to life, as does Nature from summer to winter and winter to summer. The goddess is therefore the Spirit of Nature, constantly renewing herself in her own offspring. Of this universal Deity of all the Near East the Ægean goddess with her son was, beyond all question, a manifestation. If we are to give a name to her, it must be *Rhea*;* and if to her son and companion, it must be Zeus, remembering that, by Hellenic tradition, the coming into being of Zeus was laid peculiarly in Crete. In the primitive story he embraces his own mother.† Knossos, as Diodorus Siculus indicates,‡ was associated from dim antiquity with Rhea; and a curious piece of direct evidence connecting the Ægean goddess with the cult of Rhea has lately been adduced. A clay vessel of very peculiar form, the *kernos*, is stated by an ancient commentator § to have been for the use of worshippers of Rhea. The only vessels answering his description have come to light on Ægean sites, and one in particular was found at Palaikastro, in Crete, among the hoard of sacred objects accompanying a snake-goddess described above.

The spiritual community between Ægean and other Near Eastern religions being so close, it is not surprising that almost every recognizable cult-feature in the former can be paralleled in the latter. The indwelling of the Deity in stones, whether natural *bœtyls*, cairns, pillars, or triliths, and in trees, is a most familiar Semitic belief, and one which left numerous traces on Hellenic worship. A cult of weapons appears to have existed in early Asia Minor among the Hittites of Pteria and the Carians of Labranda, not to go so far afield as the Alani on the Eastern Euxine, who in a late age adored a standing blade.* The 'horns of consecration' are seen in Semitic sacred representations, and appear in Hebrew ritual as 'horns of the altar.' The 'sacred animals' are all widely related. The serpent as an embodiment of chthonian Divinity is not only Greek but Egyptian (snake-form of Nekhebst); the dove as the vehicle of the Divine spirit from on high has survived from Semitic literal belief into the symbolism of Christianity. The great *felidæ* were guardians and supporters of Anatolian Cybele. The bull, as a dwelling of Divinity in Egypt, has his counterpart in the Greek legends of Zeus: and the cow of Hathor is known to all. The infant Zeus is wrapped in the goat-skin, and the goat continued to a late time peculiarly sacred in the cult of western Asia Minor. The monsters of Ægean cult-scenes have so many affinities with the Egyptian (those on the Phæstian shell actually carry the Nilotic life-sign, the *ankh*) that they have all been referred to an Egyptian original, the maternity personification, Thueris, the hippo, reared on her hind-quarters. The parallelism in ritual observance is too extensive and obvious to need detailed mention.

It is not to be understood, however, that such parallelism implies the derivative character of Ægean religion, least of all derivation from any single civilization, such as the Semitic or the Egyptian. If there be parentage between Semitic and Ægean civilization, it is the former that is the offspring, given the comparative youth of its art and its system of writing;† while, as for Egyptian religion, though there is good reason to think that it came to exercise a considerable influence on Ægean iconic representation, and even a little on the ideas which that in turn produced, no one, comparing the complexity of early Egyptian cult with the simplicity of the early Ægean, could suppose the one derived bodily from the other. It is needless, indeed, to look for the derivation of the essential features of Ægean cult at any later epoch than that of the primeval expansion of mankind. Its fundamental religious ideas were those of a vast proportion of the common human stock, and they continue to be so to the present day. The Ægean race sought Divinity in the life principle of Nature, spontaneously originated and reproducing itself to eternity. It placed that Divinity in great features of Nature visibly related to human life. When it came to define its idea in terms of man, being yet in that social stage in which man in relation to reproduction held his naturally subordinate place, it represented the principle of life as an unwedded woman, its property of reproduction as a son unbegotten, and its relation to the humanity resultant from this woman and man as an unseen Spirit, descending on wings and indwelling in certain material objects, the choice of which was to some degree determined by their inherent suggestion either of great natural features or human organs of life. From these fundamental

* But she unites many attributes afterwards distributed between different impersonations of the mother-goddess, *e.g.* Demeter-Erinys; Eileithyia, known in East Crete as Dictynna-Britomartis; and Aphrodite-Ariadne.

† Cf. Clem. Alex. *Protrept.* ii. p. 76.

‡ v. 66.

§ Gloss on Nikander, *Alexipharmaka*, v. 217. See Dawkins in *BSA* x. p. 221.

* Amm. Marc. xxxi. 2, 21; cf. *TPC* p. 9.

† Some influence actually passed from Crete to Philistine Gaza, commemorated by a cult of Zeus Kretagenes.

ideas all the features of Ægean cult representation and ritual practice known to us can very well have proceeded naturally and independently.

D. G. HOGARTH.

AEGIS.—In Greek mythology, the aegis is an attribute of magic power, which seems to belong originally to Zeus, the supreme god, who is therefore called αἰγίοχος. It seems to have the power both of protecting its wearer and of inspiring terror in his enemies; and for this purpose, according to Homer, it is borrowed both by Athene and by Apollo. Its form is not easy to realize in the earlier descriptions, of which we find the fullest in *Il.* v. 738, where Athene puts it on.

'About her shoulders cast she the tasselled aegis terrible, whereon is panic as a crown all about, and strife is therein, and valour and horrible onslaught withal, and therein is the dreadful monster's Gorgon head, dreadful and grim, portent of aegis-bearing Zeus.'

Here it appears to be some sort of defensive mantle, like what is worn by Athene in later art; it is provided with 'a hundred tassels of pure gold' (*Il.* ii. 448), and is also described as ἀμφιδάσεια, fringed all round or hairy on both sides, as if it were a skin of some sort, but it was made by the smith-god Hephæstus (xv. 309); when it is shaken, it scatters terror on all around. It is used by Apollo (xxiv. 20) to wrap round the dead body of Hector, and so protect it from injury.

The views both of the Greeks themselves and of modern mythologists as to the form and meaning of the aegis have been greatly influenced by opinions as to the etymology of the word. The Greeks often associated it with αἰγέα or αἰγίς, 'a goat-skin'; and Herodotus (iv. 189) suggests that the aegis of Athene was derived from the tasselled goat-skins worn by the Libyan women near Lake Tritonis. It was interpreted by later Greek mythologists as either the skin of the goat Amalthea, which had suckled Zeus in his infancy, or that of a monster slain by Athene. Modern mythologists have usually preferred the connexion with ἀΐσσειν, 'to rush,' αἰγίς or καταιγίς, 'a squall'; but their interpretation of it as symbolical of the thundercloud, though found in many modern books, is not supported by any satisfactory evidence of early date; though Zeus thunders while he shakes the aegis (*Il.* xvii. 593), the two actions are not necessarily related as cause and effect; for a clear example of the aegis as causing a thunderstorm no earlier authority can be quoted than Silius Italicus (xii. 720); Virgil (*Æn.* viii. 352) connects it with clouds. Such instances are, of course, of no mythological value, but represent later theorizing.

In artistic representations the aegis regularly appears as the attribute of Athene; there is no certain example of its being associated with Zeus, and the restoration of the Apollo Belvedere as holding it is more than doubtful. In early representations of Athene it is a kind of scaly cloak, fringed with serpents, and with the Gorgon's head fixed in it; it extends over the left arm, and so can be held up as a shield. In other cases it takes the form of a short breast-plate with similar adjuncts, and this is the usual form in later art; sometimes it is abridged to a mere band across the breast of the goddess.

ERNEST A. GARDNER.

ÆONS (Gr. αἰῶνες='ages,' 'periods,' 'dispensations,' probably related to αἰεί='always,' 'for ever').—This term was employed by the opponents of Gnosticism, and by some of the Gnostics themselves, to designate the successive emanations from the Absolute Being. The problem of accounting for the existence of the actual world-order, when it is regarded as unreal and illusory, without ascribing it directly to the Absolute One, is common to all Oriental theosophical systems; and the philosophers of most of them attempted its solution by an evolutionary (devolutionary) series of æons or emanations. Close parallels to the Gnostic æons may be found in Japanese Shintoism, Mahāyānistic Buddhism, Zoroastrianism, the Platonic *Ideas*, Philo's *Powers*, the Stoic *Logoi*, etc. The Shinto system (as set forth in the *Kojiki*) seems to rest upon pure pantheism. To gain a starting-point for the devolutionary process, the infinite becomes differentiated into the male and female principles Izanagi and Izanami, personified and conceived of as grossly lustful. These procreative æons are thought to be derived from certain abstract deities that are merged in the infinite. These produce, first, three other deities (æons), representing the great powers of nature; and these still others, some working for the good and some for the evil of man. In the Buddhism of the Northern School the Ādibuddha (*q.v.*) produces the five 'Buddhas of Contemplation,' Vairochana, Akṣobhya, Ratnasambhava, Amitābha, and Amoghasiddhi; from whom, in their turn, emanate five 'Future Buddhas of Contemplation,' the sources of the five worlds which successively make up the universe. This number five may perhaps be compared with the five elements, earth, water, fire, air, and ether, of orthodox Brahmanism. Zoroastrianism has a similar, but twofold, system of æons in the Kingdom of Light and the Kingdom of Darkness, the head of the former being Ahuramazda and that of the latter being Ahriman. From each of these is evolved a graduated host of personified powers of nature, those proceeding from the former working for good, and those proceeding from the latter working evil, the two hosts being in perpetual conflict the one with the other. Philo, who regarded the Supreme Being as exalted above all possibility of contact with matter, which he characterized as 'lifeless, erroneous, divisible, unequal,' and hence as fundamentally evil, sought to bridge over the gulf between God and the world by the hypothesis of certain 'creative and regulative Powers.' These Powers are represented as God's thoughts, as the heavenly archetypes of earthly things, as that which gives life, reality, and durability to matter, as the breath of God's mouth. He sometimes seems to regard them as personalities. His Logos doctrine is particularly significant in relation to Gnostic æons. The Logos is designated 'Eternal Wisdom' (cf. the Gnostic æon *Sophia*), and 'the Sum of the Thoughts of God' (Gnostic æon *Ennoia*, or *Synesis*).

Plato (*Timæus*, 37 D) applies the name αἰών to the eternal Being which has Time as its counterpart in the world of sense. Aristotle in like manner describes the ultimate principle which sums up in itself all existence, as αἰών (ἀπὸ τοῦ ἀεὶ εἶναι, *de Mundo*, i. 9. 11). These and similar speculations of Greek metaphysic exercised a profound influence on later Gnostic theory; but it may now be regarded as almost certain that the Gnostic doctrine of the Æons was immediately derived from Mithraism. At the head of the Mithraic hierarchy, as in the earlier Zarvanite heresy of Zoroastrianism, from which this trait in it is derived, stood Infinite Time. This supreme god, inconceivable and ineffable, was worshipped under the name of *Aion*, and was represented in sculpture as a figure whose body was inscribed with the signs of the Zodiac and encircled by a serpent, which typified the course of the sun in the ecliptic.

The earlier Gnosticism, like the cult of Mithra, appears to have known of only a single Æon, which was conceived impersonally—sometimes as the Absolute itself, sometimes as the sphere of the Absolute. Thus in the account of the 'Gnostics' (specifically so called) which is given by Irenæus (*adv. Hær.* i. 30) we read of an ascent εἰς τὸν ἄφθαρτον αἰῶνα,—and similar language is employed by Epiphanius (*Hær.* xxxviii. 1) in his description of the Cainites. Traces of this original doctrine continue to reappear in the more highly developed Gnostic systems. Valentinus himself (Frag. 5) speaks of the 'living Æon' as of a unity, although he discovers a principle of distinction within this primordial unity. It belongs, indeed, to the essence of Gnostic speculation that the Æons remain ideally one, while they manifest themselves as a plurality.

In later Gnosticism the Æons are represented as a system or confederacy of Divine existences, which proceed in pairs of male and female (syzygies) from the supreme Father. Each pair originates another, and each descends in dignity as it stands more remote from the source of being. The doctrine of syzygies has its analogies in Mithraism as in the other Eastern religions mentioned above; but it was no doubt borrowed by the Gnostics from that Babylonian tradition to which they were indebted for so many details in their cosmology. In Gnosticism, however, the Babylonian idea of a physical generation is softened and rationalized. The successive pairs are not begotten, but are projected or emanated. They are the self-unfolding of the Divine nature; and in their totality they form its perfect manifestation. Hence they constitute the Pleroma,—the 'fulness' in which the Godhead exhausts its hidden potentialities. The Pleroma, composed of the several Æons, is the world of Light or higher reality; and is divided by a great gulf from the 'darkness' of phenomenal being.

The different Gnostic systems are widely at variance in their accounts of the number and arrangement of the Æons. Basilides (if we accept Irenæus and Hippolytus I. as our authorities for his teaching) would seem to acknowledge only six (Πατήρ, Νοῦς, Λόγος, Φρόνησις, Δύναμις, Σοφία). The *Pistis Sophia* assumes thirteen, and conceives of the Æons as the spheres inhabited by the Divine powers, rather than as the powers themselves. Valentinus enumerates thirty Æons, which are grouped in three divisions—the Ogdoad, the Decad, the Dodecad. Ideas of a geometrical nature are probably involved in this grouping; while the number 30 is apparently suggested by the thirty *yazatas* (angels) of Zoroastrianism. In the various systems which branch off from the main stem of Valentinianism, the Pleroma of 30 Æons is normative, but this number is subject to continual modifications.

A brief account of the system of Valentinus will suffice to illustrate the general character of the Gnostic Æonology. He starts with *Bythos* (depth) the Absolute One, and *Sige* (silence) as his female companion. These generate *Nous* (mind) and *Aletheia* (truth). These in turn project *Logos* (word) and *Zoe* (life), and these *Anthropos* (man) and *Ecclesia* (church). *Nous* and *Aletheia* afterwards produce ten æons (a perfect number) as an offering to the Father. *Logos* and *Zoe* follow in the production of æons, but produce twelve (not a perfect number), including Faith, Hope, Love, and the Lower Wisdom (*Achamoth*). This last, being unduly ambitious, and aspiring to produce æons without conjunction with a male æon, brought forth a 'formless and undigested substance' (the Demiurge), which evolved into the present order of things, with its mixture of good and evil, and with man in whom spirit is enslaved by matter. This disturbance of the Pleroma alarmed the other æons and deeply distressed Achamoth. In response to the tears of Achamoth and the supplications of the other æons, the Father permitted Nous and Aletheia to project Christ and the Holy Spirit for the restoration of form, the destruction of the Demiurge, and the comfort of Achamoth. These have for their task the separation of the life and light that have become imprisoned in humanity, from dead, evil matter, through a long series of magical rites (mysteries), and through the promotion of ascetical living.

In Gnosticism generally, as in the teaching of Valentinus, the creation of the lower world is explained by the hypothesis of a disturbance within the Pleroma. The error, or the undue ambition, of one of the Æons results in the origin of an inferior power, who in his turn originates others, until a whole world of darkness and illusion comes into being. Nevertheless, since the process has its beginning within the Pleroma itself, some portion of the higher essence becomes intermingled with the baser elements, from which it yearns to be delivered. The Redemption, according to the Gnostic thinkers, consists in the sifting out of this higher essence and its restoration to the Pleroma. In order that this may be accomplished, an Æon of supreme dignity descends into the phenomenal world and becomes identified, really or in seeming, with the man Jesus.

The Æonic theory, as we have seen, was in the first instance derived from the Zarvanite idea of Infinite Time as the ultimate fact in nature. Thus it was allied from the beginning with speculations of a purely physical character, and from these it never succeeded in entirely freeing itself. The greater Gnostics, and Valentinus more especially, sought to resolve the Æons into spiritual facts or processes. They were construed as modes of the Divine Being, activities in which the Absolute One unfolds and manifests His inward life. It proved impossible, however, to effect a complete transformation of a theory which was, in its essence, physical. Valentinus himself wavers in his conception of the Æons,—regarding them now as ideas, now as heavenly Persons, now as creative forces. His philosophical construction loses itself at every turn in primitive astrology and cosmical speculation. To this may be attributed the eventual failure of Gnosticism, alike as a philosophy and as a religion. While it professed to open a way out of the bondage of the natural world, it was itself grounded in ideas derived from nature-worship. See, further, GNOSTICISM.

LITERATURE.—Cumont, *The Mysteries of Mithra* (Eng. tr. 1903); Hilgenfeld, *Ketzergesch. des Urchristentums* (1884); Mead, *Fragments of a Faith Forgotten* (new ed. 1906); Schmidt, *Die Gnosis* (1903); Liechtenhan, *Die Offenbarung im Gnosticismus* (1901), pp. 105–141; E. Buckley, *Universal Religion* (Chicago, 1897).

ALBERT H. NEWMAN and ERNEST F. SCOTT.

ÆSCHYLUS.—Æschylus, son of Euphorion, an eupatrid of Eleusis, was born B.C. 525, commenced as a dramatist *c.* 499, gained his first victory in 484 and his last (with the *Oresteia*) in 458, and died at Gela in 456. He fought at the battles of Marathon, Artemisium, Salamis, and Platæa. From about 476, when he composed for Hiero of Syracuse *The Women of Ætna* at the foundation of that town, he was frequently in Sicily. There is no satisfactory explanation of the statement of Heraclides Ponticus that he was tried on a charge of revealing the Mysteries in a play, and acquitted on the ground of ignorance (cf. Aristotle, *Eth. Nic.* iii. 2); the further details are probably unauthentic. Partizanship in politics can hardly be imputed to him on the strength of the supposed reference to Aristides in the description of Amphiaraus (*Sept.* 592–594),* still less on the theory that Prometheus, *son of Themis*, stands for Themistocles. His eulogy of the Areopagus, however, in the *Eumenides* (esp. 681–706) testifies to conservative sentiments. In the same play (754–777), as well

* All references are to the text of Sidgwick (*Script. Class. Bibl. Oxon.*), whose numbering hardly differs from that of Dindorf, Wecklein, and most modern editors. Hermann, Paley, and a few others use their own special notation.

as in the *Supplices*, he approves of the democratic friendship between Athens and Argos. He expresses the strongest detestation of tyranny in all forms (*Pers.*, *Prom.*, *Ag.* 953–955, *Eum.* 185–190); but has no objection to constitutional monarchy (*Supp.* 398, 517, 600), or to moderate democracy (*Pers.* 242, *Supp.* 485–489). His general ideal is a balance of order and liberty (*Eum.* 526–528).

Æschylus may be called the Father of Tragedy (Philostr. *Vita Apoll.* p. 220), in the sense that he first perceived the possibilities of the drama as a branch of literature, rather than as ritual or ceremonial, for the expression of views as to life and character. His plays are *τεμάχη τῶν Ὁμήρου μεγάλων δείπνων*, because the personages are derived mainly from the Epic cycle; but he drew upon other 'sagas' as well, and upon contemporary history; and he dealt very freely with the plots. He was evidently acquainted with Hesiod and other cosmological writers. In a few cases he cites the gnomic moralists (*Prom.* 890); more often (*Sept.* 439, *Ag.* 1331, *Cho.* 60, *Eum.* 529) he expresses similar sentiments about wealth, fortune, pride, moderation, etc. He has much in common with his contemporary Pindar; and his general attitude towards the popular mythology was almost certainly influenced by the poems of Solon and Theognis. The common statements that he was indebted to Orphic or to Pythagorean doctrines cannot be seriously supported from the extant plays or fragments.

Of the 80 to 90 plays attributed to Æschylus, many of which can be grouped in trilogies or tetralogies, the majority are cited only by the lexicographers; little is known of their plots or the views contained in them, except in the case of the *Prometheus Solutus*. The *Danaids*, *Myrmidons*, and *Niobe* seem to have dealt with various aspects of the passion of love. Certain gnomic fragments (Nos. 70, 156, 159, 161, 177, 255, 266, 301, 353, 395, 401, 475, Sidgwick), which are striking aphorisms about the nature of the gods, good and evil, life and death, do not necessarily express the mind of the poet himself. His own moral and religious doctrines must be sought in (1) the general tendencies, (2) the choric odes, (3) the emphasized speeches of the favoured characters, in the seven extant plays. The selection of these, made apparently not later than the 5th cent. A.D., if not entirely accidental, may be due partly to celebrity and partly to special reasons. The *Oresteia* (*Agam.*, *Choëph.*, and *Eum.*) constitutes his masterpiece in all respects. The *Persae* and the *Septem contra Thebas* are cited by Aristophanes for their literary and patriotic qualities. The structure and style postulate an early date for the *Supplices*, though the theology is already remarkably mature; either of these features may have saved it. The *Prometheus Vinctus*, which might easily have aroused popular suspicions of impiety, appealed to the popular fancy for the marvellous in spectacle and narration. From these plays, after all allowances for the exigencies of dramatic form and popular taste, there emerges a body of gradually developed views attributable to Æschylus himself. His philosophy, in which the ethical cannot be sharply demarcated from the theological, may be discussed in the order of its development, as it deals with (1) the Divine nature, (2) the Divine agencies, (3) the moral nature and action of man, (4) the special questions of responsibility and heredity, the family curse, and the blood-feud, while (5) the nature of the problem dramatized in the *Prometheus* requires separate consideration.

I. In the earlier plays the Olympian gods are invoked jointly as a *πανήγυρις* (*Sept.* 220), or a *κοινοβωμία* (*Supp.* 222); they are *θεοὶ ἐγχώριοι, γενέθλιοι, πολισσοῦχοι, ἀστικοί, ἀγώνιοι*, with temples, altars, and images (*βρέτη*). The Theban maidens pray to Pallas, Poseidon, Ares, Cypris, Lyceius, Artemis, Hera, Apollo, and the local Pallas Onca (*Sept.* 126–180), as *παναρκεῖς, τέλειοι, λυτήριοι*, but also *Διογενεῖς*, under Zeus as the *πατὴρ παντελής* (116); Eteocles adds Earth and the *Ἀρὰ Ἐρινύς* of Œdipus (70). Popular language is used of augury, oracles, sacrifice, river-gods, and Hades (26, 379, 618, 269, 272, 854–860). But the same play finely describes Justice as the virgin daughter of Zeus (662); both the piety of Amphiaraus and the impiety of Polynices have moral elements; no *δαίμων* could involve Eteocles in *ἄτη* but for the *ὕβρις* of his determination to defend the gate attacked by his brother (677–708, 949–956). Similarly, in the *Supplices* the fugitives appeal to Artemis, Ares, Poseidon, Apollo, Hermes, and especially (*Supp.* 1034–1042) to Aphrodite, by whom Hypermnestra was perhaps defended (*Fr.* 44); also to Zeus as *ξένιος, σωτήρ, αἰδοῖος, ἱκέσιος, κλάριος, κτήσιος*, etc.; and to local deities, as the hero Apis (117, 263). With the *ὕπατοι θεοί* are coupled the *βαρύτιμοι χθόνιοι θῆκας κατέχοντες* (24–25); if Artemis is deaf, the suppliants will turn 'to the Zeus of the earth below, the host of all those whose work is done, if we fail to reach the Olympian gods' (154–161). But the coarser side of the myth of Io seems to be treated sarcastically (291–315); it is tentatively moralized by the insistence on Zeus as the eventual deliverer and founder of a royal race (574–593). The chthonian Zeus, who 'judges the sins of men by final judgments among the dead' (230), is deliberately identified with the Zeus who is *τέλειος, γαιάοχος*, and *παγκρατής* (816), who is also the son of Earth (892) and allied with Themis (360). The slightest association of injustice with the gods is impiety (921; cf. 395); and everywhere the lyrics extol the power and righteousness of Zeus, with the fervour of Hebrew prophecy. He is 'king of kings, most perfect in strength of the powers that make perfect' (524–526); 'hospitable in the highest, he directs destiny by venerable enactment' (673); 'he beholds violent deeds not gladly, but with eyes of justice' (812); 'the beam of his balance is over all' (822); 'what is fated, that will be; there is no transgressing the mighty, the limitless will of Zeus' (1047–1049). This is not merely poetical optimism:

> 'The desire of Zeus is not made to be easily grasped. Everywhere it glows, even in the gloom, with fortune that is sombre to mortal races. . . . For dark and dusky wend the ways of his mind, unobservable by human gaze. He hurleth men to utter destruction from their towering hopes, though he array no force against them; deity does nothing with labour. What his spirit has once designed, he works out withal, from above, from his holy seat' (87–103).

Such theology is in essentials that of the *Oresteia*, though the more ethical conceptions are tentative and far from correlated.

The theology of the *Persae* (?472 B.C.) is dramatically Oriental. Zeus and Phoebus and the Sun are invoked; Pallas has favoured Athens. The ritual of the dead (*οἱ φθιτοί*, *Pers.* 219, 523, 607–622) is supplemented by appeals to Earth, Hermes, and Hades-Aïdoneus, who *λαβεῖν ἀμείνους εἰσὶν ἢ μεθιέναι* (690), though Darius as a *δαίμων* or even *θεός* has a *δυναστεία* below. The repeated *ex parte* allegations of a Divine Nemesis or *φθόνος*, arbitrarily afflicting excessive wealth or happiness (163, 354, 373, 842), are akin to the fatalism of Herodotus's famous legends; and all the characters arraign a deity who deludes men to their ruin (*ἀπάτη θεοῦ*, 93, cf. *Fr.* 301; *νόσος φρενῶν*, 750; *ἔψευσας φρενῶν*, 472), or at least abets their folly (*ἀλλ' ὅταν σπεύδῃ τις αὐτός, χὠ θεὸς συνάπτεται*, 742). But both Darius and the Persian elders charge Xerxes with provocative *ὕβρις* in binding the sacred Hellespont (745, 72), and in destroying images and temples (807–815, 830), and blame him rather than the alleged δαίμων (924 *v.* 910, 933). It is insolence (ὕβρις) which 'flowers and is full in the ear with ruin (ἄτη), from which it reaps a harvest of lamentation' (821). Cyrus was right-minded and so was not afflicted (θεὸς γὰρ οὐκ ἤχθηρεν, ὡς εὔφρων ἔφυ, 722). Athens survives as the higher civilization.

So far the moralization of Homeric or popular theology has not been violent. In the *Oresteia* there is a marked advance in boldness of expression: 'le polythéisme subsiste, mais épuré, moralisé, presque purgé d'anthropomorphisme' (E. de Faye, p. 34). The allusions to Uranus and Kronos (*Ag.* 167–172, 640) possibly indicate development in the Universe; the chthonian cults of Earth, Night, the Dead and their agents (*Cho.* 399; *Eum.* 115, 321) are subordinated to the conception of deity as moral and rational. Sacrifices and ceremonies of purification are little in comparison with the observance of justice and self-restraint. Venerable legends of conflicting divinities are even re-written (*Eum.* 1–19). Of the Olympians, Apollo as the giver of oracles and ἐξηγητής of rites, and Athene as the inspirer of political wisdom, retain some genuine personality with impaired divinity; perhaps Hermes also and Artemis, for whose interference with the winds at Aulis Æschylus attempts to provide a decent motive (*Ag.* 134–155). Zeus is too great for the stage, even in the Prometheus plays. Theology is to be sought not in mythology, but in history (πάρεστι τοῦτό γ' ἐξιχνεῦσαι, *Ag.* 368), and in conscience (μνησιπήμων πόνος, *Ag.* 180; cf. 975–983). The supreme deity is not only all-powerful but all-just; thus Electra craves for Orestes the support of 'Strength and Justice with him who is the third (*i.e.* Ζεὺς σωτήρ), Zeus the greatest of all' (*Cho.* 244). To Zeus are applied not the old departmental names, but such epithets as πανόπτης, παγκρατής, πάντα κραίνων, παναίτιος, and δικηφόρος. There is surely more than an 'illusion du monothéisme' in the first theological passage of the *Agamemnon* (160–178):

'Zeus, whoe'er he be, if by this name 'tis his pleasure to be called, this name I address to him. Weighing all things well, I can conjecture nought but Zeus, if the burden of this vanity is in truth to be cast off from my mind. . . . But whoso heartily giveth titles of victory to Zeus shall hit the mark of wisdom full; even to Zeus, who hath guided mortals in the ways of wisdom, who hath established "learning by suffering" as an ordinance for ever.'

To those only who have learnt on these lines to know and do justice, 'Zeus the all-seeing and Fate (Μοῖρα) have condescended' (*Eum.* 1046).

Thus, in harmony with the conception of deity as normally personal, there emerges the conception, increasingly impersonal, of universal order. As physical law this is Μοῖρα, τὸ μόρσιμον, τὸ πεπρωμένον, ἡ πεπρωμένη, αἶσα, ἀνάγκη; as moral law it is θέμις, δίκη, νόμος θεῶν; but these terms admit of many degrees of personification, and not only overlap, but not uncommonly involve the *circulus in definiendo* to which idealistic systems are liable. The statement that Zeus is weaker than the Μοῖραι and Ἐρινύες (*Prom.* 515–518) is isolated and controversial; generally the established order is the expression not so much of the will of God as of His being. God is subject only to the law of His own nature as consistent and just. He *cannot* be on the side of evil (κρατεῖται δέ πως τὸ θεῖον τὸ μὴ ὑπουργεῖν κακοῖς, *Cho.* 957); He must be partial (ἑτερορρεπής) *morally* either way (νέμων εἰκότως ἄδικα μὲν κακοῖς, ὅσια δ' ἐννόμοις, *Supp.* 403). The working of this supreme authority is described in many combinations of terms, personally and impersonally. When in defiance of Right (Θέμις) men trample on the majesty of Zeus (Διὸς σέβας), then 'Justice sets up her anvil and Destiny forges the sword' (προχαλκεύει δ' Αἶσα φασγανουργός, *Cho.* 641–647). 'For each fresh deed of injury, justice is whetted by Fate (Μοῖρα) upon a fresh whetstone' (*Ag.* 1535, 1536). The μεγάλαι Μοῖραι are besought (*Cho.* 306–314) 'to grant success from Zeus to that cause to which Justice (τὸ δίκαιον) has gone over. For words of hate let words of hate be rendered; so Justice proclaims aloud as she exacts her due. For a bloody stroke let him repay a bloody stroke. That "the doers must suffer," there speaks a saying thrice ancient.' Even Clytæmnestra's 'thoughtfulness not overcome by sleep shall order justly everything that has been foreordained with Divine sanction' (δικαίως σὺν θεοῖς εἱμαρμένα, *Ag.* 912). Themis the Titaness and the παλαιγενεῖς Μοῖραι administer the νόμος θεῶν (*Eum.* 171) no less than Justice, the daughter of Zeus.

2. The determinations of this supreme authority are intimated to man not only in history and in conscience, but by direct agencies. Positively, Æschylus attaches importance to dreams; the visions of Atossa, Io, and Clytæmnestra reflect popular beliefs. 'For the mind in sleep is bright in its vision, though in daytime Fate is undiscernible by mortals' (*Eum.* 104). His attitude towards oracles is ambiguous. There seems to be some *arrière-pensée* in his treatment of the relations between Apollo and Orestes; Athens and not Delphi has the final word in the termination of the blood-guilt of the house of Atreus.* Negatively, the Erinyes are all-important. The meaning of the word fluctuates considerably in the extant plays, and evidently has a long history behind it. It is hardly likely that Æschylus himself first identified the Avengers of the underworld with the Benign or Venerable earth-goddesses of Athens and Sicyon (Εὐμενίδες or Σεμναί); but he certainly accentuated both factors of this conflation,† and, while first investing the Furies with the archaic horrors of Gorgons, etc. (Paus. i. 28, 6), was also conscious of a development from objective to subjective associations, from punishment as retributive to punishment as remedial. The Ἐρινύς is the activity of Divine justice in the presence of lawlessness. Zeus is a constant θεωρός (*Cho.* 246); even for birds robbed of their young, 'a god on high, some Apollo or Pan or Zeus, hears the shrill complaint of his denizens; and sooner or later sends on the transgressors a Fury of requital' (*Ag.* 55–59). Much less for Paris's breach of the laws of hospitality will Zeus shoot an arrow in vain, either short of the mark or too high in heaven (*Ag.* 365). 'One said that the gods do not deign to trouble about men by whom the honour of sacred things (χάρις ἀθίκτων) is trampled on; but he was not pious' (*Ag.* 372). Helen herself becomes for the house of Priam 'by the sending of Zeus, the lord of hospitality, a Fury of weeping to other brides' (*Ag.* 749). The Erinyes apply the laws of retributive and educational suffering. 'We deem ourselves,' sings their chorus (*Eum.* 312–320), 'to be direct in the course of justice. On the man who holds out pure hands, there comes no wrath from us; unscathed he traverses the way of life. But if one in guilt, like this man, hides his gory hands, we appear as honest witnesses for the dead, and visibly to the uttermost exact from him the price of blood.' Again, 'Great power have the awful Erinyes both with the gods immortal and with those below the earth; and in their dealings with men they fully and visibly bring things to pass, to some giving songs of joy, but to others a life blurred by tears' (950–955). As the play draws to a close, they serve to link Μοῖρα and Δίκη; and in their final metamorphosis there is as much conscious symbolism as the dramatic form permits.

3. If, then, innocence is rewarded and guilt punished, at any rate, in the long run (*Ag.* 750–771; *Eum.* 526–565), human morality must be based on

* See U. von Wilamowitz-Möllendorf's Introduction to the *Choëphoroi*, 1896.

† See Harrison and Verrall, *Mythology and Monuments of Ancient Athens*, pp. 558–564, and Haigh, pp. 120, 121.

universal law as applied to the life of the family and the city. By Æschylus, as by Dante, types of good and bad character are exhibited rather than analyzed. The dignity of individuality is drawn on a grand scale even in the case of Clytæmnestra, without casuistry or sophistry. There is the same note of distinction about the characters which are presented for admiration, the king of Argos, Eteocles as patriot, Orestes, Electra, and, above all, Prometheus. The whole range of Greek piety is displayed in the choruses of the Oceanids, Danaids, captive women, Persian and Argive elders. The fine series of contrasts in the *Septem* shows the poet's concurrence in the normal Greek ideas of αἰδώς, αἰσχύνη, σωφροσύνη, and εὐσέβεια; also in the connexion of morality with religion. He does not absolutely avoid the popular language which makes ἁμαρτία a disease of the intellect (νόσος φρενῶν, *Pers.* 751; σὺν φοίτῳ φρενῶν, *Sept.* 661; παραφορὰ φρενοδαλής, *Eum.* 330; ἀποσφαλεὶς φρενῶν, *Prom.* 473); but in his own view passion at least is bestial in character and originates where there is no law. The lustful 'have the tempers of random and unholy brutes' (*Supp.* 762); and 'the inordinate love which masters the female mind *both in brutes and in men* wins a perverse victory over the fellowship of wedlock,' and involves calamities (*Cho.* 598–601). Generally sin is ὕβρις, immorality *plus* impiety, as the wilful transgression (παραβασία) of the fixed limits of human action. It is ἄνομον and μάταιον, and its fruit is ἄτη, the criminal infatuation which is its own punishment. Ἄτη is δόλιος, μελανόζυξ, ὑστερόποινος; the moment of its supervention may be inevitable, but it is neither less nor more voluntary than happiness as the reward of virtue (*Eum.* 532–537). Moral pathology has never been more convincingly expounded than in the *locus classicus* on ὕβρις (*Ag.* 750–771):—

> 'An ancient saying has been fashioned in the generations of old, that a man's prosperity, when it has waxed great, brings forth and does not die without issue, but that out of good fortune springs up for the family an insatiate misery. But I hold my own mind apart from the rest on this. 'Tis the impious deed that gives birth to more after it, more, and like to their own breed; but the fate of righteous houses has ever a fair progeny. But old insolence is wont to beget an insolence with the vigour of youth in mortal ills, this day or that, when the time of birth has come due, yea and a fiend, against whom there is no battle, no war, unholy boldness; and these are the black banes (ἄτας) unto mansions, and like are they to their progenitors.'

Nor has the moral ever been drawn more relentlessly than by him:—

> 'Reverence the altar of Justice, nor trample it down at the sight of gain with godless foot; for retribution will ensue. The right issue abides in force. Wherefore let a man put in the place of honour, piety towards parents, and pay reverence to the claims of strangers to hospitality. He who is just of his own will without constraint, will not be unprosperous; utterly ruined he will never be. But I say that the transgressor who dares to offend, and is laden with goods all amassed without justice, shall perforce in time haul down his mainsail, when trouble seizes him and his yardarm is splintered. And he calls on those who hear him not and struggles in the midst of the swirl; but the god mocks at the hot-headed man, seeing him who boasted he should never be powerless now in helpless woes nor able to weather the point. And so, for ever wrecking his former prosperity on the reef of justice, he perishes unwept, unseen' (*Eum.* 539–565).

A religious moralist is sure to emphasize the inevitableness of ἄτη (*e.g. Ag.* 1566; *Cho.* 1076), but there are careful *caveats* against fatalism:—

> 'Instruct my son plausibly,' says Darius, 'warned from heaven as he has been to be wise in time, that he leave off from offending against God in overboastful boldness' (*Pers.* 831).

The murderers of the house of Atreus are even freer agents than the avengers. But if there has been no repentance and no purification, vengeance pursues the sinner even to the world below:—

> 'For this office has piercing Fate allotted to us to hold for ever, that all mortals to whom befall wanton deeds of blood, we should attend, until the guilty pass beneath the earth; but even in death he is not over free' (*Eum.* 334–340).

Æschylus's allusions to life after death are marked by a reserve unusual in poetical descriptions of Hades; as to continued consciousness he is perhaps consistent (*Cho.* 517); but he recognizes the possibilities of prolonged retribution and of remorseful memory, such as that indicated in Clytæmnestra's terrible sarcasm about Iphigenia's reception of her father (*Ag.* 1555–1559). Apart from the functions of an Alastor (*Supp.* 416) or an Erinys (*Eum.* 267), there may be a judgment in Hades by a presiding deity (*Supp.* 228–231). The ghost of Orestes will punish or reward his countrymen according as they deal with Athens (*Eum.* 767–777). The curses of the slain subsist by the survival of their personalities (ἴδετε πολυκρατεῖς ἀραὶ τεθυμένων, *Cho.* 406); the Erinyes themselves are called Ἀραί in the underworld (*Eum.* 417).*

4. But the more vividly sin is pictured as prolific and its effects as incalculable, the more difficulty there is in escaping from fatalistic theories, such as those implied in the popular ideas of the ancestral curse and the *jus talionis* developing into a blood feud. These subjects specially fascinated the mind of Æschylus. In the *Supplices* there is a simple warning of the danger of starting a curse: 'For your children and your house, in whichever way you determine, it remains to pay in full a corresponding penalty' (433–436); and in the sequel there was some purification from blood-guilt. In the *Septem* the children of Œdipus are involved in a curse not clearly defined as invoked or inherited by him (832–833), nor always alluded to in the same way (for the various phrases see *Sept.* 70, 654, 695, 709, 720–726, 887, 977–979). The curses (ἀραί, κατεύγματα) produce in the γένος a criminal propensity (ἄτη), sometimes personified as an evil spirit (δαίμων, ἐρινύς, ἀλάστωρ, even μοῖρα or κήρ) hounding it to destruction and infectious by its ὁμιλία κακή: 'the field of criminal folly produces a harvest of death' (*Sept.* 601). The chorus, indeed, makes Eteocles a responsible agent on account of his savage desire to shed unlawful blood (αἵματος οὐ θεμιστοῦ, 689–694), but to the question τίς ἂν καθαρμοὺς πόροι, the poet has not yet found his solution: οὐκ ἔστι γῆρας τοῦδε τοῦ μιάσματος (682), unless one is indicated in the self-sacrifice of Antigone. But ten years later the double problem of hereditary criminality and blood-guiltiness is treated in the *Oresteia* with a breadth of design which is not only poetic but 'prophetic.' There is little reason to suppose that early tragedy was necessarily written in trilogies, but the scheme is admirably suited to Æschylus's exposition of the origin, transmission, and extinction of a πρώταρχος ἄτη (*Ag.* 1192). The principal terms, ἀρά, ἐρινύς, ἄτη, are developing specific meanings; beside them are vaguer phrases (μῆνις, *Ag.* 155; μύσος, *Eum.* 378; ἄγος, *Cho.* 155; παρακοπή, *Ag.* 218; πῆμα, *Ag.* 346; ποινή, *Cho.* 947, etc.). The phenomena are best stated in *Cho.* 400–405: 'Law it is that drops of gore spilt upon the ground demand the shedding of other blood. For Havoc cries on the avenging Fury, who brings up from those slain before calamity (ἄτην) to attend upon calamity'; and then 'who will expel from the house the breed of the curse?' κεκόλληται γένος πρὸς ἄτᾳ (*Ag.* 1566). The story of the house of Pelops is not laboured; but a sufficient number of points—the adultery of Thyestes, Atreus's horrid revenge, the sacrifice of Iphigenia—lead up to the murder of Agamemnon. At each point the chain might have been broken, but each link is fresh riveted: 'Where will the force of this Ἄτη make an end? where will it cease and be lulled to rest?' (*Cho.* 1075). Has the curse acquired a personality as the τριπάχυντος δαίμων γέννης (*Ag.* 1476), demanding new blood before the old is dry, or as the παλαιὸς δριμὺς ἀλάστωρ (*Ag.* 1501), masquerading as the murderous adulteress, and yet all

* If the Areopagus is really the Hill not of Ares but of the Arae (Harrison and Verrall, p. 563), the Erinyes as well as the Eumenides have their ancient home in its chasms.

along the instrument of justice? (*Cho.* 641). Yet among the consequences may come a deed which, though terrible, is really innocent, an ἀνεπίμομφος ἄτη (*Cho.* 830); and the chorus of elders, even while declaring that the house is 'fast-bound,' grasps the truth that saves the morality of the situation. All retribution is and must be *deserved*; 'The robber is robbed, the murderer makes payment in full. There abides, while Zeus abides on his throne, the rule that the doer must suffer; this is the eternal law' (*Ag.* 1562–1564). The curse, then, is not an overwhelming fatality, but a hereditary predisposition which may be worked out in the race and even in the individual. The original transgressor was free to sin, and his descendant is free to adopt the prescribed means of purification. The actual development of this theme in connexion with the traditional obligation of the blood-feud is perhaps confused by a political motive; and the special pleading in the *Eumenides* about the nature of kinship is certainly frigid, as also the insistence on legal forms (ἀνάκρισις, μαρτυρία, σύνδικοι). The idea of blood for blood was so deeply rooted in popular sentiment and religious institutions, that Æschylus, no less than the legislators of his time, may have been puzzled to discriminate degrees of guilt, except by instinct. If the law is simply τοὺς κτανόντας ἀντικατθανεῖν (*Cho.* 144), Clytæmnestra may be allowed to swear that she sacrificed her husband to the Δίκη, Ἄτη, and Ἐρινύς of their daughter (*Ag.* 1433). If not, how can Orestes ever say that his mother's blood 'sleeps and is fading away from his hand, and the pollution is being washed out'? (*Eum.* 280). No libations are of any use (*Cho.* 521), especially if the blood is κοινόν (*Cho.* 1038); the spirit of the dead is not tamed by the funeral fires, φαίνει δ' ὕστερον ὀργάς (*Cho.* 326); and the feud would go on for ever, or till the family became extinct. In Æschylus's solution of the problem there are really two stages, of which the latter is the more important. Orestes can plead innocence because he acts under the 'interpretation' (ὁ μάντις ἐξηγεῖτό σοι ματροκτονεῖν, *Eum.* 595) and even threats (*Cho.* 283–298) of Apollo-Loxias, and is ready to perform the ritual purifications (*Cho.* 1059); and the Delphic oracle had since the 8th century really exercised an ethical and educational influence in Greece. On the other hand, Æschylus felt that neither the payment of blood-money nor the performance of ritual can quiet the conscience or carry civilization very far. It is perhaps too much to say that Apollo is 'kein guter Gott'; but the ultimate and really moral solution is to be found in the judicial decision of Athene on the divided vote of the Areopagus, which she herself represents as the victory of the *vox populi* regarded as the *vox Dei*; ἀλλ' ἐκράτησε Ζεὺς ἀγοραῖος (*Eum.* 978). The *Oresteia*, then, is certainly a 'tendency' poem to this extent, that it expresses a view in the moral and religious speculations of the age as to heredity and responsibility, though it is not merely didactic on any particular question of justice or equity.*

5. In the *Oresteia* the final reconciliation is provided by the gods; in the *Prometheus* they sustain the whole drama. Except in a few details attributable to a re-reading of his *Supplices*, the surviving play of the set (probably *two* tragedies with a satyric play) is totally opposed to Æschylus's theology in all its stages. Prometheus, son of Themis or Earth (212), secured Zeus's triumph over the older dynasty (221), but is now tortured for having saved the human race by the gift of fire, the chief instrument of civilization, of augury and medicine, and of other means of providing for the future, and of Hope as the mainspring of effort (249–256, 442–506). All who visit the victim, whether as Zeus's agents—Strength, Hephaestus, and Hermes—or as sympathizers—the Oceanids, Oceanus, and Io—have suffered more or less in person or in character from Zeus, who is a νέος τύραννος, governing gods and men arbitrarily (παρ' ἑαυτῷ, 189; ἰδίοις νόμοις, 404), unjustly (ἀθέτως, 150; πέρα δίκης, 30), and odiously (975). But Prometheus, by virtue of his parentage, knows a secret; if Zeus contracts a certain marriage,* his son will be greater than the sire (768, 907–927); in this respect Zeus is weaker than the Fates and Erinyes (515–520). The fragments of the *Solutus* indicate close parallelism in form and episodes to the *Vinctus*; in the solution Zeus and Prometheus meet one another half-way in a reconciliation, of which the agents are Heracles and Chiron the Centaur (cf. *Prom. Vinct.* 188–194, 1026–1029). Now this conception of a Zeus, inferior both in righteousness and in power, is out of all relation to the *Supplices* and the *Oresteia* alike, and no theory of the poet's meaning can be accepted which minimizes this fact. Apart from purely fanciful explanations of the plays as political or scientific allegory, two views have been very commonly held.

(*a*) A tragedian was at liberty to develop his dramatic situations freely, provided he kept to the main lines of some recognized myth. Æschylus found Hesiod's story of Prometheus suitable for the exhibition of character as affected by injustice, and susceptible of brilliant episodes about geography, anthropology, etc. This view, as developed by (*e.g.*) Patin and Paley, may be called the literary explanation. Wecklein's theory, that Zeus is in the right and Prometheus violent and shortsighted, but a tragic hero by virtue of a certain dignity of character, like Milton's Satan, comes under the same head. But no such theory really explains the boldness of the idea, the conflation of myths, or the intensity of the passion with which the hero is supported.

Accordingly, (*b*) most modern scholars, including E. de Faye, regard Æschylus as deliberately inculcating the position that even the supreme personal authority in the Universe is itself subject to the eternal laws (Μοῖραι) which constitute the ultimate necessity (Ἀνάγκη). Prometheus, the mythical representative of these forces, is, then, really in the right, and Zeus is in the wrong with him and with Io; but Zeus's submission is effected by the educational value of time (ἀλλ' ἐκδιδάσκει πάνθ' ὁ γηράσκων χρόνος, 981); and Prometheus, too, can yield without loss of dignity to an improved Zeus. This view gives an adequate meaning to the play as a whole, but it seems to lay undue stress on lines occurring in mere dialogue and not specially emphasized, and also to ignore the human personality of the protagonist. Moreover, it is difficult to imagine the author of the *Oresteia* and its epithets for Zeus acquiescing even temporarily in the idea of such development in the godhead.

Those, therefore (*c*), who hold the view first enunciated by a brother poet, Shelley, that Prometheus stands for Man, anxious to be moral and religious as well as rational, but convinced that he is the victim of forces incompletely understood, of the *de facto* supremacy of 'Nature,' prefer to trace in this drama the Greek parallel to the Book of Job. Æschylus was too great a poet to be a mere allegorist; but when his mind was occupied with *the problem of undeserved evil*, he found in the arch-allegorizer Hesiod that the origin of evil was the gift of fire and the creation of woman by Prometheus. He selected with a free hand from

* This view of the *Eumenides* seems less liable to objections than that which makes the Furies represent law, Apollo and Zeus equity, and Athene mercy, in a special question of moral casuistry. For that view see Haigh, p. 119.

* This is a marked instance of Æschylus's syncretism; the story of Peleus and Thetis has even less connexion than Io with the myth of Prometheus, which was apparently an ætiological explanation of certain fire ceremonies.

this and other myths the more dramatic parts of the symbolism. The mention of Heracles may have suggested the insertion of his ancestress Io, the passive as a foil to the actively-resisting victim. The anthropology and geography are not episodical if they bring out the dignity of human reason and the universality of human suffering. The heroic sympathy of the Oceanids illustrates the value of simple and instinctive morality. The philosophical answer seems to be indicated in the words *αὐθαδία*, repeated at every point of the play (see 64, 79, 436, 907, 964, 1012, 1034–1038), and *εὐβουλία*, the special quality of Themis, set in antithesis to it in the last lines of the dialogue. In the two recitative passages assigned to the hero in the Exodos, the boast *πάντως ἐμέ γ' οὐ θανατώσει* (1053) must have special significance as balancing the protest *ἐσορᾷς μ' ὡς ἔκδικα πάσχω*. But it is likely enough that the solution of the problem, like the conclusion of the Book of Job, was too formal a compromise to be altogether satisfactory; and that may be the reason why it has perished. The whole tendency of Æschylus's mind is so strongly optimistic in theology, that it would right itself naturally after a reactionary period of what is *pessimism* rather than *scepticism*, however dramatically intensified.

Æschylus's originality as a thinker consists, then, in his attempts to moralize the traditional beliefs, embodied in myths and institutions, by the light of certain religious presuppositions and certain moral convictions which have been illustrated above. In his main ideas there is little variation, except in their poetical expression; in the detailed application of them his language fluctuates too much to admit of exact and consistent analysis. His doctrines left hardly any mark, though his dramas continued to be popular for their antique simplicity and dignity; even Aristophanes's vindication of his literary merit against the criticism of the next generation takes lower ground than it might. Neither the piety of Sophocles nor the impiety of Euripides felt the force of his protest against a fatalistic theory of morals. In philosophy, intellect and state-law took the place of conscience and Divine law so completely, that Plato could employ the myth of Prometheus without reference to a treatment of the subject which the modern world has long considered one of the most sublime efforts of poetic genius.

LITERATURE.—Besides the introductions to editions of Æschylus, sections on him are to be found in all the general works on Greek literature or theology. The most useful summary in English is A. E. Haigh's *Tragic Drama of the Greeks*, ch. ii. (1896). Of the innumerable essays on Æschylus those by J. A. Symonds (*The Greek Poets*, 2nd series) and E. Myers (*Hellenica*) are best known. Of older books the most frequently referred to are K. O. Müller's *Dissertations on the Eumenides* (Eng. tr. revised, 1853), F. Welcker's *Griech. Götterlehre* (1857), and K. F. Nägelsbach's *Nachhomerische Theologie* (1857). The principal monographs are Klausen's *Theologumena Æschyli* (1829); G. Dronke's *Religiöse und sittliche Vorstellungen des Æschylos* (*und Sophocles*) (1861); E. Buchholz's *Sittliche Weltanschauung des* (*Pindaros und*) *Æschylos* (1869); and E. de Faye's *Étude sur les Idées religieuses et morales d'Eschyle* (1884).

HERBERT E. D. BLAKISTON.

ÆSTHETICISM (*αἴσθησις*, 'sense perception').—The theory of life which fails to distinguish moral from æsthetic values, or subordinates the moral to the æsthetic. Ordinarily the term is not used as a distinctive title for specific theories, but as denoting a tendency of theories otherwise named. Three usages of the term may be conveniently distinguished:

1. Æstheticism may denote *the identification of moral goodness with beauty*, such as is suggested in the common Greek phrase 'beautiful and good.' Morality and art may be looked upon as the realization of a common principle, that of order or harmony. The good man, like the musician to whom Aristotle is fond of comparing him, is the man who can introduce harmony into his subject, who can maintain that balance and symmetry of parts essential to the highest music, whether of conduct or of sound. The musician works with a different material from the good man, but their purpose and principle are the same, the good life is a work of art. And the impulse toward creation may also be the same. The artist works from love of the beautiful, from an instinctive passion for the beautiful itself. He recognizes no compulsion in his work, for he has no other desire than to create. So, too, the moral man creates from love of the good, from his instinctive desire to realize a complete and perfect life. Morality does not come to him in the form of a law constraining him to walk contrary to his nature. The good life is the life which realizes all the possibilities of man, the most completely human life. The good man is beauty realized in flesh and blood and action rather than in stone, but he is beautiful none the less.

That æstheticism in this sense characterized the Greek view of life is to a certain extent true, but not unreservedly so. It is true that the Greeks did not work out a clear distinction between the beautiful and the good. Aristotle (*Metaph.* xiii. 3) notes that the term 'good' is limited to certain actions, whereas beauty pertains also to that which is unmoved, but he gives no more exact *differentia*. Yet it is far from true that the Greeks altogether ignored the more severe, dualistic aspect of the moral life. To Plato, certainly, moral development is not a mere unfolding of the life of instinct, but the acquiring of a rational control over desires. The good is a reality recognized by reason, and independent of the individual's appreciation of it. As such an independent reality it stands over against the individual as the law of his action, demanding realization in his life. The moral life shows struggle and discord rather than the calm unity of a work of art. But this difference fails to find adequate expression in Greek theory, and as a consequence the fields of ethics and æsthetics remain confused. Were one to characterize this condition, it would perhaps be truer to say, not that their moral theory is æsthetic, but that their æsthetics is moralistic.

This confusion of the two fields is continued in the English Moral Sense School, which inherits the Platonic tradition, but in these later writers the Utilitarian principle is beginning to supplement the more æsthetic aspect. This is partially true of Shaftesbury, but more completely so of Hutcheson and Hume.

2. Æstheticism may also be used to denote the theory that *all ultimate values are æsthetic*, moral good being a means towards an ultimate æsthetic good. Under this conception the moral life is not itself beautiful, but it exists for the sake of æsthetic enjoyment. Morality, with its sense of obligation, is a result of mal-adjustment, in consequence of which we are compelled to do much which we do not value for its own sake, but as the necessary means towards an enjoyment which itself has no further use.

This conception finds literary expression in the writings of Mr. Walter Pater, in which the end of life is stated as richness of experience. This richness of experience is best realized in the life of æsthetic enjoyment.

3. Æstheticism also denotes *the divorce of art and morals*, usually implied in the popular use of the phrase 'art for art's sake.' Beauty is held to be independent of goodness, the technical aspect of a work of art being emphasized at the expense of its human significance. Art thus becomes a kind of higher morality, free from the objective laws which hold in the lower. The immoral may thus enter into the beautiful on the ground of its immediate value for perception.

LITERATURE.—Zeller, *Aristotle and the Earlier Peripatetics* (1897), ii. ch. xv.; Muirhead, *Chapters from Aristotle's Ethics* (1900), ch. v. § 5; Martineau, *Types of Ethical Theory*² (1886), i. bk. i. branch 1; Santayana, *Sense of Beauty* (1896), pt. 1; Pater, *The Renaissance* (1873), conclusion, also *Marius the Epicurean* (1885); Shaftesbury, *Characteristics* (1711); Bosanquet, *History of Æsthetic* (new ed. 1900), ch. iv.

NORMAN WILDE.

ÆSTHETICS.—Æsthetics is the philosophical study of beauty regarded in itself and in its application to art and nature. (1) *Meaning of the word.*—Considered solely from the etymological point of view (*αἴσθησις, αἰσθάνομαι*, to perceive by the senses), the word means the study of sense-perceptions. Kant remains faithful to this etymological acceptation when he applies the name of 'Transcendental Æsthetics' to the chapter of his *Critique* in which he discusses the sense-perceptions Time and Space. Baumgarten was the first to use the word 'Æsthetics' for the science of the beautiful; and the change that has taken place in the history of the term may be understood when it is recollected that, according to Baumgarten, the beautiful exists in the obscure regions of the lower consciousness, that it belongs to the rank of sensations, and is opposed to the 'clear thinking' of the intellect. To-day the term 'Æsthetics' has lost this connexion with *sensation*, and denotes in general the philosophy of the beautiful.

(2) *Place of Æsthetics in philosophy.*—The philosophy of the beautiful is bound up with and forms an integral part of a general system of philosophy. But Æsthetics is one thing in Plotinus or Thomas Aquinas, and quite another in Kant or Taine, because the philosophical systems of these scholars are so widely divergent. In the opinion of the present writer, Æsthetics is a mixed science, borrowing its principles from both metaphysics and psychology; so that (see art. BEAUTY) it includes two classes of questions, the one class bearing on the *subjective* feeling that beauty produces in the person affected by its charm, and the other relating to the *qualities of the things* to which we ascribe beauty.

(3) *History.*—Ancient writers devoted special attention to the objective side of beauty. Plato and Aristotle consider the beautiful as identical with order and proportion; Plotinus and the Neo-Platonic school make it an attribute of everything that exists *as such.* The Middle Ages changed the aspect of the doctrine of Æsthetics. While sharing largely in the *objective* theories of the beautiful, they supplemented them by a study of impression or *æsthetic pleasure.* Modern philosophy, on the contrary, takes its stand almost exclusively on the psychological side of beauty, and regards it as a purely *subjective* phenomenon. With Kant, for instance, beauty does not belong to the object itself, but only to our perception of it. Contemporary Æsthetics perpetuates and emphasizes these ultra-subjective tendencies.

LITERATURE.—See under BEAUTY.

MAURICE DE WULF.

ÆTHER.—Derived from a root signifying *to burn*, Æther is a term appropriated in Greek literature to the blue vault of the upper firmament, as contrasted with *aër*, which is applied to mist and vapour. In Homer æther is the abode of Zeus (*Il.* ii. 412, etc.). In Hesiod (*Theog.* 124) Æther and Day are the offspring of Night, and in at least one of the Orphic cosmologies, Æther, as representing light or fire, is contrasted with Chaos, and proceeds from Kronos (see Gomperz, *Greek Thinkers*, Eng. tr. 1901, i. 92 f.). Pherecydes, who occupies the borderland between the mythical and the scientific, traces the origin of all things to Zeus, Earth, and Kronos, and identifies the first of these with æther (Diels, *Vorsokratiker*, p. 508, No. 71, A 9).

The current conception of æther passed into the keeping of the philosophers, by whom it was variously defined and modified. In the Fragments of Parmenides æther is found as the region of the fixed stars (*Fr.* 10. 1, Diels), and as the fiery element of which their substance is composed (*Fr.* 11. 2, Diels); and although Aëtius indicates a distinction between æther as the outermost covering of the universe and the subjacent fiery heaven, we cannot attach much weight to his authority (ii. 7. 1; cf. ii. 15. 7, and see Krische, *Forschungen*, pp. 114, 115). Empedocles treats æther as a synonym of aër, except in one doubtful passage (*Fr.* 38. 4, Diels). On the other hand, Anaxagoras regarded aër and æther as the two primary differentiations of being —the cold and dark contrasted with the bright and warm (*Fr.* 1. 2, Diels). Indeed, we are informed that he employed æther as synonymous with fire (A 73, Diels). In the formation of the world, the dense, wet, cold, and dark sank into the centre, while the rare, hot, and dry went to join the enveloping æther (*Fr.* 15, Diels). From Anaxagoras it is convenient to pass to Euripides, who is said to have been largely influenced by his teaching (Diod. i. 7. 7.). There are various references to æther in Euripides, which may be the reflexion either of popular fancies or of current science, or of both. Thus the identification of Zeus with æther carries us back to Pherecydes, and anticipates the pantheism of the Stoa (*Fr.* 935; cf. Æsch. *Fr.* 65*a*). The conception of Æther as the husband of Earth, quickening all things into life by his fertilizing showers, is the common property of many poets and philosophers (Eur. *Frs.* 488, 836; and see Munro on Lucr. i. 250). Similar to this is the notion that the vital breath is derived from æther, and that the soul, retaining its consciousness after death, is absorbed in the source from which it sprang (*Hel.* 1014; *Suppl.* 531; cf. Lucr. v. 318). Though it has often been supposed that Euripides was here borrowing from Anaxagoras, it is noteworthy that the same thought is found in the inscription over those who fell at Potidæa (*CIA* i. 442), and may well be due, as has been recently suggested (*ClR* xv. 431), to a popular belief which arose in connexion with the practice of cremation. The soul of the dead man was thought to ascend with the smoke which rose from the burning corpse.

By the side of the four elements generally recognized in philosophy, from the time of Empedocles onwards,—fire, air, water, and earth,—æther ultimately came to be admitted as a fifth; but it is still open to question whether this view was derived by the Platonic school from the Pythagoreans (Zeller, *Pre-Socratics*, vol. i. p. 318, n.). Plato, in the *Timæus*, does not adopt this position (58 D); and though there is strong evidence that it formed part of his oral doctrine (Xenocrates, *ap.* Simplic. *Physic.* 268*a*), and it is accepted by the author of the *Epinomis* (981C), its definite establishment is generally connected with the name of Aristotle, from whose statement of the theory through the scholastic *quinta essentia* is derived our word *quintessence.* Eternal and immutable, providing the substance of the heavenly spheres and stars, ceaselessly rotating round the world, but transcending the strife of the terrestrial elements (*de Caelo*, 1. 2. 269*a* 30. 1. 3. 270*a* 13, *b* 1), æther was at once material and divine. The Stoics took a further step by identifying the substance of æther with God. It is described as fiery breath or creative fire, the rarest and most subtle of all bodies (Chrysipp. *ap.* Ar. Did. *Fr.* 31, Diels), which produces out of itself the phenomenal world, passing through the medium of the elements. The universe, subject to a law of ceaseless flux and reflux, moves either in creative progress or towards periodic conflagration. When everything is consumed by fire, the world-soul and the world are united in the single essence of æther (Chrysipp. *ap.* Plut. *Comm. Not.* 36). But when, by the equipoise of its constituent forces, the created world is in existence, the ruling power resides in the outermost periphery of æther (Diog. Laert. vii. 139; Ar. Did. *Fr.* 29, Diels). Then, as the world-soul, it permeates every part of the universe, and is the immanent cause of all individual existence (Diog. Laert. vii. 138). Thus may be justified the summary assertion of Chrysippus, that æther is everything, being at once father and son (Philodem. *de Piet.* c. 13, p. 80. 26 G).

A. C. PEARSON.

ÆTIOLOGY (αἰτιολογία).—The doctrine of causes. The latter part of the *Categories* of Aristotle (chs. 10–15), early suspected, but possibly compiled from Aristotelian fragments (Zeller's *Aristotle*, Eng. tr. vol. i. p. 66), contains the *Post-prædicamenta* which give the clue to the subsequent position and treatment of ætiology. In the treatises on *Metaphysics* which are based on the scholastic philosophy, 'General Metaphysics' is distinguished from 'Special Metaphysics,' notwithstanding the difference of standpoint, precisely as 'General Philosophy' is distinguished from 'Special Philosophy' by H. Spencer (*First Principles*, § 38). General metaphysics treats of—(1) Being and its properties; (2) the highest kinds of beings, *i.e.* the categories; (3) the relations of beings to each other. The third head embraces the same subject as the *Post-prædicamenta*, the whole division being foreshadowed by the *Ante-prædicamenta* (due to Abelard), *Prædicamenta* and *Post-prædicamenta* of the mediæval logic. Of the five relations treated of in the *Post-prædicamenta*—*oppositio*, *prioritas*, *simultas*, *motus*, and *habere*—two, *prioritas* and *simultas*, are especially concerned with causality. The first two divisions of general metaphysics, dealing with universals, the six transcendents, the nature of being, the supreme classes of finite beings, are sometimes regarded as constituting Ontology. The third division, which deals with the relations of finite beings to each other and to the Infinite, will thus contain as its most important part the doctrine of causes—Ætiology.

If we turn to modern philosophy, the position of ætiology is not different. In the contents of Burgersdyk's *Institutiones Metaphysicæ* (Mansel, *Metaph.* p. 288), the doctrine of causes occupies a similar position. It holds a like place in Wolf's *Ontologia*. K. Rosenkranz (*Wissenschaft d. log. Idee*) divides metaphysics into Ontology, Ætiology, Teleology (Erdmann's *Hist. of Philosophy*, tr. vol. iii. § 346. 11). E. von Hartmann (*Kategorienlehre*), under the categories of speculative thought, puts Causality (Ætiology), Finality (Teleology), Substantiality (Ontology).

We do not propose to enter into an examination of the various forms and shades of meaning which ætiology assumes in these several systems. Nor does it belong to this article to view the subject of causation from the point of view of the theory of knowledge and of the criticism of the causal concept. We shall confine ourselves to considering simply the leading forms of the theory of the nature and classification of causes in the successive periods of the history of philosophy. For this purpose the history of philosophy may be considered as divided into three periods—the ancient, the mediæval, and the modern. The leading characteristic of each of these periods is as follows: in ancient philosophy (Greek) the antithesis of subject and object, of mind and matter, as two substances over against each other, is absent. Thought and being, the one and the many, are equally objective. In the second period, owing to the development of Greek philosophy itself, and the spread of the Roman conceptions of authoritative law and duty, but above all, owing to the influence of Christianity, the spiritual and material are conceived as antithetically opposed existences, and the attempt is made under this altered point of view to retain the Greek solution of the problem. The substance of this solution is dogmatically affirmed in Scholasticism. What is not shown is that it is possible under the changed point of view. Modern philosophy consists in the constant effort to prove the possibility of the solution, to explain the manner in which spiritual and material being interpenetrate, affect, and condition each other. In modern philosophy, not the dogmatic result itself, but the way in which it is obtained, is the leading interest. The ætiological problem becomes an essentially different one in each of these periods.

In Greek philosophy the antithesis of subject and object is absent. Nature is instinct with motion, life, reason. The notion of personality is undeveloped, but at the same time the tendency to personification is omnipresent (see Jowett's *Plato*, vol. i. p. xiv). Thought is not a modification of a conscious mind, but consciousness is the accident, a ripple on the surface of nature (see Martineau's *Types of Ethical Theory*, vol. i. p. 23). From this point of view the antitheses with which Greek philosophy dealt—the one and the many, the real and the apparent, thought and being—are all reconcilable by one concept—that of mixture. 'There is only a mingling, and then a separation of the mingled' (Empedocles, v. 38). This mingling, or, as Plato termed it, 'participation' (μέθεξις), when conceived as the union of the one and the many, of form and matter, εἶδος and ὕλη, gives the well-known fourfold classification of causes of Aristotle—the formal, material, efficient, and final (ἡ οὐσία καὶ τό τι ἦν εἶναι· ἡ ὕλη καὶ τὸ ὑποκείμενον· ὅθεν ἡ ἀρχὴ τῆς κινήσεως· τὸ οὗ ἕνεκεν καὶ τὸ ἀγαθόν (*Metaph.* i. 3)). The principles intermingled are form and matter; the agency by which the composition is effected, and the end to be realized by the process, are the efficient and final causes. The latter causes, however, are never considered as distinct from the principles intermingled. The individual Greek thinkers illustrate this position. Aristotle has pointed out that the early ætiologists recognized only the material cause (*ib.*). The water of Thales, the air of Anaximenes, were material principles; but the active forces, the causal energies, are either the living matter itself, or its rarefaction and condensation. The same is true of the fire of Heraclitus (Zeller, *Pre-Socratic Philosophy*, Eng. tr. vol. i. pp. 222, 223, vol. ii. pp. 27, 28). In like manner, even when the efficient cause begins to receive distinct recognition, as in the love and hate of Empedocles, or the νοῦς of Anaxagoras, it still is not separate from the material cause. The νοῦς of Anaxagoras must not be conceived as a mere prime mover, a distinct agency detached from the universe to which it communicates motion. It passes into things. It is in all essences entirely homogeneous. It is not mixed with them in the coarse sense, but it permeates them (cf. Zeller, *Pre-Socratic Philosophy*, vol. ii. pp. 343 ff.). When Socrates, in the *Phædo*, complains that Anaxagoras did not make full use of his principle (Aristotle makes the same complaint), this is not an *ignoratio elenchi*, as Lewes (*Hist. of Philosophy*, vol. i. p. 84) represents it. Socrates does not desiderate a physico-teleological theory of the universe in the modern sense. It is only to be expected that νοῦς, in moving the universe, should impart something of its own sublime rational nature to things, should more or less pass over into them. The Platonic idea does no less. Socrates and Plato thus bring to light the formal cause.

As is well known, the causal activity of the ideas is the crux of the Platonic philosophy. In one of its forms, at any rate, the formal cause is naturally regarded as the moving principle. The efficient cause is identified with the form, the Idea. The demiurge in Plato is most probably to be viewed, not as the exclusive activity of the highest idea, the idea of the Good, the One (as by Martineau, *Types of Ethical Theory*, vol. i. pp. 45 ff.), but as the personification of the principle of activity or efficiency flowing from the Good, and pervading the whole world of ideas. We thus see that efficiency, action, may be identified with either the matter or the form.

When Aristotle brought down form from the far-off τόπος νοητός, or intelligible world of Plato, and incorporated it in matter, the problem still remained, to which side action, efficiency, was to be attributed, and Aristotle is generally interpreted as assigning it exclusively to form. In favour of this view is his celebrated definition of the Absolute as νόησις νοήσεως, the thought of thought; but the interpretation is probably one-sided. There is much in Aristotle to lead us to regard the Absolute as dwelling in a sort of supersensuous sensuous world, as related to the real world—which in all its various grades is a σύνολον, a compositum of matter and form—not merely through the element of form, but also through that of matter. In *Metaph.* viii. (ix.) 8, end, the argument against the ideal theory contends that the ideas, as such, are mere potentialities (δυνάμεις). This view would help to solve the ancient controversy as to the pantheism or monotheism of Aristotle, the immanence or transcendence of the νοῦς.

In the Neo-Platonic philosophy the ideal world of Plato and the Divine νοῦς of Aristotle are hypostasized into a series of personal beings. This philosophy represents the innate tendency of Greek philosophy itself to pass over into that antithesis which dominates Christian philosophy—the antithesis of subject and object, spirit and nature. St. Augustine views the Platonic ideas no longer as independent substances, but as ideas in the mind of God. The hierarchy of ideas and emanations yields to the heavenly hierarchy. With this change of view the combination or composition of form and matter, of idea and reality, becomes a most difficult problem. The community of idea and reality, the intercourse of mind and matter, can no longer be conceived as a mere mingling or composition of the two, if the idea as universal dwells in a separate substance—mind. The great controversy of the Middle Ages, of Realism and Nominalism regarding universals, is the struggle with this problem. Yet in regard to ætiology, the real interest does not lie in this problem, but in a greater one connected with it. Granting that reality is the union of matter and form, which factor in this union is the active one? Thomas Aquinas answers, 'form': 'Forma est agendi principium' (Stöckl, *Gesch. der Philos. des Mittelalters*, vol. ii. p. 451). It is diverse views of the relation of the causal power in the universe to those principles of matter and form, the union of which to the Scholastic as much as to Aristotle constitutes the nature of things, that underlie the great rival systems of Thomas Aquinas and Duns Scotus, and from which their other differences proceed. In Scotus the union proceeds from the side of the matter, not the form. The latter is the efficient, the causal factor (de Gérando, *Systèmes de Philosophie*, vol. iv. p. 577; Rousselot, *Études sur la Philosophie dans le Moyen Age*, iii. p. 56). Duns Scotus's philosophy here encounters the same difficulties as have been urged against H. Spencer. In both Aquinas and Scotus, however, the source of the efficiency is transcendent, whether it be the Divine intellect or will which determines it.

Modern philosophy, from Descartes and Spinoza to Hegel and Hartmann, Spencer and Lewes, is engaged on the problem of explaining how the intercommunication of mind and matter, spirit and nature, takes place. It has been remarked by Bayle and Rousselot that Spinoza's philosophy is contained in that of Scotus. This is true in a sense. But the ultimate causal principle is in Scotus transcendent, in Spinoza immanent. This difference is characteristic of modern philosophy. The solution is no longer taken from the transcendent sphere. If the Absolute is called in, it is, as in Spinoza, Leibniz, Schelling, Hegel, an immanent, not transcendent Absolute.

Of the problem thus handed down it cannot be said that the solution has yet been reached. In the Monadology of Leibniz and the Absolute Idea of Hegel it is form, the ideal side, that contains the principle of all causal agency throughout the universe. These principles differ from the Platonic idea in this, that they are subjects, have the objective world over against them, even if that world have no being apart and be a nullity or contradiction at the core. In Schopenhauer and Hartmann only the Will, the material side, actualizes the representation or idea. The 'willing to will' of Hartmann answers to the *materia primo-prima* of Duns Scotus. It is the same in our English philosophy. Out of the unknowable Absolute of Spencer, and the known Absolute of Lewes, the material, organic, and mental worlds proceed. Yet the relation of these higher forms to the primordial matter and motion is unsolved. Psychophysical parallelism is but the statement of the enigma. The question remains, Which is the efficient—form, matter, or both? In what ways do they co-operate, and how? The ætiological and teleological problems are still unsolved.

LITERATURE. — Aristotle, *Organon* and *Metaphysics*; H. Ritter et L. Preller, *Hist. philos. Gr. et Rom.*; Fairbanks, *First Philosophers of Greece*; Ferrier, *Lectures on Gr. Philosophy*; Zeller, *Philos. der Griechen*; Stöckl, *Gesch. der Philos. des Mittelalters*; Fichte, *Wissenschaftslehre*; Schelling, *Syst. des transcend. Idealismus*; Hegel, *Logik* (*Werke*, iii., iv., v.); Karl Rosenkranz, *Syst. der Wissenschaft, Wissenschaft der logischen Idee*; von Hartmann, *Philos. des Unbewussten, Religion des Geistes, Kategorienlehre.*

GEORGE J. STOKES.

AFFECTION.—That aspect of psychic life which comes to consciousness as concrete states of Feeling (which see); the abstract *quale* of feeling consciousness. In the newer divisions of the fundamental or rudimentary aspects of conscious process it has been found necessary to distinguish the concrete given states of mind, characterized as Knowledge, Feeling or Emotion, and Will, from those abstract and largely hypothetical *quales* which, although never found alone, nevertheless serve to define the concrete states. For example, a state of feeling is always or usually one both of knowledge of an object and of active tendency or will. Since never realized in its purity, it becomes necessary, therefore, to define such a state by what it would be if so realized. The characteristic aspect of consciousness whereby it is not knowledge or will, but feeling, is what is called 'affection.' It is the differentia of a state of feeling or emotion. Similarly, a state of knowledge is never feelingless nor will-less; its differentia as knowledge is its reference to an object; it is called 'cognition.' With active process, or in a large sense Will, the same sort of distinction leads us to the determination of its *differentia* as a certain active quality called 'conation.' Affection, cognition, and conation are therefore the three fundamental aspects of conscious process, considered as irreducible phases of what in a case of concrete happening is, usually at least, all three. Cf. Baldwin's *Dictionary of Philosophy and Psychology*, artt. 'Affection,' 'Cognition,' 'Conation,' and 'Classification of the Mental Functions' (by Stout). J. MARK BALDWIN.

AFFIRMATION.—I. In *legal parlance* an affirmation is distinguished from an oath in that no penalty is invoked upon himself for false witness by the person affirming. It seems to have arisen in the scruples of those who felt the danger of invoking the name of the Deity in case a mistake of memory or statement led to unforeseen consequences. Courts, seeing that testimony from persons of this character might be quite as reliable as any supported by an oath, finally accepted affirmation in lieu of more strongly attested allegations. The tendency to substitute affirmation for an oath will be proportioned to the decline of the belief that oaths have any more sacredness than a simple asseveration, and to the decline of the belief that the invocation of the Deity affects the efficacy of an oath. Where an appeal to the Deity and His punitive disposition or habits is supposed to influence human veracity, the oath will prevail; but it is not necessary where veracity is respected for itself. No doubt the efficacy of the oath in one period of human history was much influenced by a belief in future punishment, but that has ceased to exercise the influence it once possessed, and the community must rely upon one of two motives to assure veracity. The first is natural human penalties, and the second is respect for the truth. In either of these there will be no necessity for the oath where any scruple exists about invoking the Deity.

2. Affirmation, in *logical and philosophical diction*, is distinguished from negation or denial. It thus means the statement of a fact. It may represent nothing more than a belief that a given thing is a fact, but, so long as it takes the form of a positive statement, it is called an affirmation. To assert, to posit, to asseverate, to declare are the equivalents of affirmation, and, of course, mean at least the formal assurance that the thing affirmed is a fact. In formal logic, affirmation is a name for a certain type of judgment which is distinguished by the grammatical form or mode of statement, and not by the meaning or content of the sentence, or by the particular state of mind out of which the statement issues. Psychologically speaking, however, affirmation denotes a degree of tenacity in conviction which looks towards assurance, and it expresses that state of mind. Negation or denial expresses the same kind of mental state, while doubt is the opposite of both affirmation and negation. Hence psychologically there is no difference between affirmation and negation, in so far as assurance is concerned, but only a difference in reference to the relation between the ideas involved in the mental process of comparison and judgment. That is, the difference between affirmation and negation concerns the content of the judgment, and not its mental state of conviction. Affirmation implies a certain kind of connexion between subject and predicate, and negation excludes it.

JAMES H. HYSLOP.

AFGHANISTAN.—Afghanistan (lit. 'land of the Afghans') is a country of south-central Asia, whose location and political importance have led to its playing a part in the religious history of the Orient from the time of Zoroaster to the appearance of Muhammad. The present boundaries of this mountainous land are political rather than geographical, as they are largely defined by the fact that Afghanistan is a buffer-country between the English empire of India on the south and south-east and the Russian provinces of Bokhara and Turkistan on the north, while Persia and Baluchistan limit its western and southern frontiers.

In the first chapter of the Avesta (Vd. i. 7) the ancient northern capital Balkh (Bākhdhi) is referred to as a beautiful city with banners floating from its high walls, and there is a persistent tradition that the city was a strong religious centre, the abode of Lohrasp, the father of Vishtasp, patron of Zoroaster, and that Zoroaster himself was slain there when the Turanians stormed Balkh during the Holy War which Iran had started against Turan. The modern capital Kābul (Kāvul in the Pahlavi treatise *Shatroihā-i Airān*, 34) appears in the Avesta (Vd. i. 9) as Vaēkereta, and the region of the Helmand, the chief river of Afghanistan, the Etymandros of the Greeks, is called Haētumant (Phl. Hētūmand) in the same Zoroastrian law-book (Vd. i. 13). The modern lowland district of Seistan in south-western Afghanistan was the home of the Zoroastrian dynasty of the Kaianians and the place of the holy lake Kansaoya (mod. Hāmun) of the Avesta, from whose waters the Saviour (Av. Saoshyant) was to arise at the Millennium. Zoroastrianism appears also to have prevailed in the land during the Parthian and Sasanian eras, from B.C. 250 to A.D. 650, although some Greek religious influences may have followed in the wake of Alexander's invasion. Buddhism made some progress in Afghanistan, being traceable chiefly to Indians who emigrated from the Indus to the Helmand region after the Scythian invasion, and who carried with them, among their sacred treasures, the water-pot of the blessed Buddha himself. This relic was preserved in a shrine near the ancient site of Kandahar, and is described by Bellew, who saw it, as 'a huge bowl carved out of a solid block of dark green serpentine' (see *Races of Afghanistan*, p. 22).

The conquest of the country by the Arabs in the 7th cent. destroyed all previous religious foundations, and cleared the ground anew for the building up of Islām. Muhammadanism became the national faith of the Afghans, and has remained, mainly in its Sunnite form, their creed and chief bond of union, although they acknowledge the political headship of an Amir over their loosely connected tribes.

The Afghan nation consists of a number of tribes considerably divergent in their character, with a population variously estimated at between 3,000,000 and 6,000,000. Most important are the Afghans and Paṭhāns, who constitute the chief element of the population, together with the clans known as Ghilzais in the east, Yusufzais and Afridis on the Indian border, the Duranis to the west, and the Tajiks, Hazarahs, Usbegs, and Aimaks, mostly showing traces of Mongolian blood, to the north and north-west. The great majority of the Afghans belong ethnologically to the Iranian stock; and although there is an intermixture of blood, especially on the borders, there is no good reason for accepting the view that they were of Semitic origin, while they may preserve some such tradition from a later date and show certain slight Semitic traces.

The language of the country is generally called Afghan, but often Pukhtun or Pushtun, the former (Pukhtun) being North Afghan, the latter (Pushtun) South Afghan. The literature of the people is but scanty, and no monuments have been traced farther back than the 16th century. Most interesting among the remains are the Afghan folksongs, a collection of which has been made by the French scholar Darmesteter, and among these ballads are a number that deal with religion.

LITERATURE.—A comprehensive bibliography of works relating to Afghanistan, its language, history, and religion, will be found in the German work by Geiger and Kuhn, *Grundriss der Iranischen Philologie*, i. pt. 2, 201–230 (Geiger), ii. 612–15 (Jackson). Of general interest are: Elphinstone, *Account of the Kingdom of Caubul*, London, 1815; Spiegel, *Eranische Alterthumskunde*, i. 307–25, Leipzig, 1871; Bellew, *The Races of Afghanistan*, 1880; Roskoschny, *Afghanistan*, 2 vols. Leipzig, 1885–6; Darmesteter, *Chants populaires des Afghans*, Paris, 1888–90; Forbes, *The Afghan Wars*, London, 1892; Roberts, *Forty-Nine Years in India*, London, 1897; Yate, *Northern Afghanistan*, London, 1888, *Khurasan and Sistan*, London, 1900; Sultan Mahomed Khan, *The Life of Abdur Rahman, Amir of Afghanistan*, 2 vols., London, 1900; Hamilton, *Afghanistan*, London, 1906.

A. V. WILLIAMS JACKSON.

The name 'Afghan,' first appearing in literature in al-Bīrūnī's *India* (tr. Sachau, i. 208), is of uncertain signification; and the Afghans themselves prefer the designation Pushtūn or Pukhtūn, older form Pashtūn, Pakhtūn (whence their Indian name

Paṭhān)—a term which Lassen (*Ind. Altertumskunde*[2], Leipzig, 1867, i. 513) connected with the Πάκτυες of Herodotus (iii. 93, 102, iv. 44, vii. 68); while Darmesteter (*Chants populaires des Afghans*, Paris, 1888, i., Introd. 182) has suggested that the Afghans may also be implied by the Παρσυῆται of Ptolemy (vi. 18. 3, 20. 3). At all events, the native appellation Pushtūn signifies 'mountaineers,' and may be implied by the passage in Arrian's *Anabasis*, iii. 8. 4: Βαρσαέντης δὲ 'Αραχώτων σατράπης 'Αραχώτους τε ἦγε καὶ τοὺς ὀρείους 'Ινδοὺς καλουμένους. Several other names are given by Dorn (ii. 62–64), the most interesting being Sulaimānī (doubtless from their residence in the Koh-i-Sulaiman), Banī Aṣif (Aṣif being the cousin of Afghāna), Banī Isrāīl, and, of course, Rohillas ('mountaineers').

Though pre-Islāmitic Afghanistan has no real history, it is rich in legends of its origin. The best known of these traditions, to which allusion has already been made in the preceding article, is preserved in a Persian history of the Afghans by Ni'amat Allah, an author of the 16th cent. (tr. Dorn, *History of the Afghans*, 2 vols., London, 1829–36). According to his account, the eponymous hero of the Afghans was Afghāna ibn Irmia ibn Ṭālūt (Saul). Afghāna himself was the commander-in-chief of Solomon's army, and through his executive ability he was enabled to complete the Temple at Jerusalem. When, however, the Israelites were scattered abroad by Nebuchadrezzar, Afghāna and his children (numbering forty) were also dispersed; and some settled around Ghor and others near Mecca, where they remained for fifteen hundred years, obeying the Torah in all things. With the advent of Muhammad, the contemporary head of the Afghans or 'Israelites,' Khalid ibn Valid, embraced Islām, and after a long and victorious career, which included exploits in Persia, sent letters to the Afghans at Ghor concerning the coming of Muhammad, whereupon several of their chiefs, headed by Kais, went to Medina and there accepted the new faith, spreading it in Afghanistan on their return. The historic worthlessness of this legend is beyond question; and equally absurd is the tradition recounted by Firishta, tracing the Afghans to descendants of Pharaoh's nobles, who, after his fall, emigrated to India and settled in the Sulaiman Mountains. Many joined Abraha in his attack on Mecca, but were converted, and later returned to the neighbourhood of their early home.

Turn from legends to facts. Afghanistan was traversed by Alexander the Great in his march to India, and it is alluded to by Strabo (p. 699) as Γανδαρίς. This latter term is of particular interest, in that it represents the Sanskrit *Gandhāra*, which 'lay on both sides of the Kabul river, immediately above its junction with the Indus' (McCrindle, *Ancient India as described in Classical Literature*, Westminster, 1901, p. 31, n. 4). After Alexander, this region came under the sway of his successors, and thus formed part of the dominions of the Græco-Bactrian and Indo-Scythian dynasties. With the latter line of kings a new religious influence was introduced into Afghanistan, particularly by Kanishka (1st cent. A.D.)—the faith of the Buddha. By this time nearly all trace of Zoroastrianism had probably disappeared, though even in the middle of the 19th cent. local tradition at Herat told of the destruction of a fire temple there by Muhammadans in the reign of the Ṭāhirid Abdallah (d. 844) (Ferrier, *Caravan Journeyings and Wanderings*, London, 1857, p. 181); while Zoroastrians seem to have flourished in the Pamirs as late as the 13th cent., ruins of three forts ascribed to them still existing in Wakhan (Gordon, *Roof of the World*, Edinburgh, 1876, p. 141), where the natives even now treat fire with reverence, being reluctant to blow out a light (Wood, *Journey to the Sources of the River Oxus*, new ed., London, 1872, p. 333). Buddhism, however, has left not only many small figures at Hidda and Kabul (Vigne, *Personal Narrative of a Visit to Ghuzni, Kabul, and Afghanistan*, London, 1840, p. 207), but also some sixty topes, dating mostly from the 4th and 5th cent. A.D., and found chiefly at Darunta, Chahar Bagh, Hidda, Kabul, Koh Daman, and Kohwat; as well as ruins of elaborate monasteries at Jamalgiri, Takht-i-Bahi, and Sahri Bhalol, which show distinct influence of Greek art. Sculptures of the Buddha have also been found at Bamian (Wilson, in Vigne, *op. cit.* pp. 187–192); and the Chinese travellers Fa Hsien (tr. Legge, Oxford, 1886, pp. 33–40) and Hiuen Tsiang (tr. Beal, London, 1884, i. 98–103) both describe Kanishka's magnificent dagoba at Peshawar.

Modern Afghanistan, as noted in the preceding article, is wholly Muhammadan. Besides official Sunnite orthodoxy, however, there exists a mixture of Semitic and Indian folk-belief. To this category belongs the vast number of saint-shrines (*ziārat*), which consist either of the domed tomb of some saint or of a heap of stones, enclosed by a wall and usually surrounded by trees or bushes (Bellew, *Journal of a Political Mission to Afghanistan*, London, 1862, pp. 70–71, 107–109, 386)—a religious phenomenon common amongst both the modern Semites and Hindus (Curtiss, *Primitive Semitic Religion To-day*, New York, 1902, *passim*; Crooke, *Popular Religion and Folk-Lore of Northern India*, Westminster, 1896, i. 183–185, 189–229). Again, levirate marriage is practised, and it is a grievous affront not to ask the brother's consent if the widow be again married, though, if she have children, it is considered more honourable for her to remain unwedded (Elphinstone, *Account of the Kingdom of Caubul*, London, 1815, i. 236). Amongst some tribes, moreover, it is customary for the suitor to serve the father of his would-be bride for many years, as Jacob served Laban for Rachel's sake (*ib.* p. 240; Bellew, *Journal*, p. 27). The blood-feud, as amongst the Semites, is a sacred duty (Elphinstone, *op. cit.* i. 220–221; Conolly, *Journey to the North of India*[2], London, 1838, ii. 163–165); and blasphemers, as amongst the Hebrews, are stoned to death (Bellew, *Journal*, p. 68). In time of pestilence a buffalo or cow is led through or around the village or camp. The sins of the community are then ceremonially transferred to the victim's head, after which it is either slaughtered and its flesh divided between the priests and the poor, or it is driven into the wilderness (Bellew, *loc. cit.*). This practice, familiar from the Hebrew scapegoat, is also found extensively in Northern India (Crooke, *op. cit.* i. 142, 166–167, 169–170).

Dreams, the evil eye, exorcism, ordeals, and omens are, of course, attentively regarded by the Afghans; so that a high wind for three days is a sign that a murder has been committed, since, when Cain slew Abel, there was a similar commotion of the elements (Conolly, *op. cit.* ii. 137–146). The popular demons of Afghan folk-belief are *jinns*, *peris*, *āls*, and *parṛaīs*. The *jinns* and *peris* are common to all popular Muhammadan mythology, but the *āls* and *parṛaīs* (the latter word a semasiologic variation of *parī*, 'peri') are plainly Indian in origin. The *āl*, described as a woman about twenty years of age, with long teeth and nails, eyes curving down the side of the nose, feet turned heel foremost, and feeding on corpses (Vigne, *op. cit.* pp. 211–212), is manifestly the *churel* of Northern India (Crooke, *op. cit.* i. 269–271; *Calcutta Review*, No. cliii. p. 180 ff.), who, though she may assume a beautiful form, is in reality 'very ugly and black, breastless, protruding in stomach and navel, and feet turned back' (Steel and Temple, *Wide-Awake Stories*, Bombay, 1884, p. 318). In Armenian folk-lore the *āl* is also found, though differing materially from the Indo-Afghan concept (cf. Abeghian, *Armen. Volksglaube*, Leipzig, 1899, pp. 118–120). The *parṛaī*, a huge monster, with flabby breasts thrown back over her shoulders, stretching out her hairy arms to any length, and devouring those who answer her plaintive cry for help (Darmesteter, *op. cit.* i. 254–255), is clearly the Indian *rakshasī* (Crooke, *op. cit.* i. 246–253), who plays an important part in Hindu folk-tales. Though the Afghans are essentially an Iranian people (Deniker, *Races of Man*, London, 1901, p. 420), they thus exhibit a total loss of Iranian concepts, for which they have substituted an amalgam of Semitic and Indian beliefs.

LITERATURE.—In addition to the works cited in the previous article, mention may be made of Lassen, *Ind. Altertumskunde*[2], i. 503–515, ii. 289–360 (Leipzig, 1867–74); Masson, 'Topes and Sepulchral Monuments of Afghanistan' in Wilson, *Ariana Antiqua*, pp. 55–118 (London, 1841); Fergusson, *Hist. of Indian and Eastern Architecture*, pp. 72–79, 169–184 (London, 1876); Bellew, *Journal of a Political Mission to Afghanistan*, pp. 46–77 (London, 1862); Conolly, *Journey to the North of India*[2], ii. 136–150 (London, 1838); Ni'amat Allah, *Hist. of the Afghans* (tr. Dorn, 2 vols., London, 1829–36); Modi, 'The Afghanistan of the Amir and the Ancient Mazdayaçnāns' in *East and West*, 1907; Raverty, *Poetry of the Afghans* (1862), and *Notes on Afghanistan* (1881); Malleson, *Hist. of Afghanistan* (1879); Sultan Mahomed Khan, *The Constitution and Laws of Afghanistan* (London, 1900); Ibbetson, *Punjab Census Report* (Calcutta, 1882) [for the Afghans in British India or on its border].

LOUIS H. GRAY.

AFRICA.—[The purpose of this article is to give a *general* account of the ethnology, religions, and ethics of Africa. A detailed description of the various religions will be found in the following articles: BANTUS AND S. AFRICA, BERBERS AND N. AFRICA, HAMITES AND E. AFRICA, NEGROES AND W. AFRICA].

A line drawn from the mouth of the Senegal river, through Timbuktu, eastwards to Khartum, then southwards to the equator, and along the equator again eastwards to the Indian Ocean, will roughly divide Africa into two main ethnical sections of nearly equal areas—*Caucasic* in the north and *Ethiopic* or *Negro* in the south (for the sense in which these and other general ethnical terms are here taken see art. ETHNOLOGY [Conspectus]). Of the northern section, which comprises the Mediterranean seaboard from Morocco to Egypt, the Saharan and Libyan deserts from the Atlantic to the Red Sea, Abyssinia and the Galla, Masai and Somali lands, there are two great divisions—the *Hamitic Caucasians*, who are here indigenous, and the *Semitic Caucasians*, who are later immigrants from Asia, but have long been almost everywhere in the closest contact with the Hamitic aborigines. Most probably the two races originally constituted a single Hamito-Semitic group, whose primeval home was North Africa, whence some moved in remote times across the Red Sea to South-West Asia, and here became specialized as Semites; while others—Iberians, Ligurians, Pelasgians—ranged northwards into Europe by the land-connexions still persisting in the Old and New Stone Ages at various points across the Mediterranean. In those days the Saharan wastes were not a marine bed since upraised, as is popularly supposed, but, on the contrary, a plateau which was higher than at present, enjoyed a genial climate, was traversed by great rivers (now reduced to dry wadys), and clothed with a rich subtropical vegetation; in a word, a region in every way suited for the evolution of the highest (Caucasic) division of the human family. In North Africa this evolution has from prehistoric times been represented by the ancestry of the present Hamitic populations, who are still found in possession of all the inhabitable parts, either exclusively or in association with their Semitic kindred who have returned at different times to the common cradle-land.

The Hamites, who are called *Libyans* (Africans) by Herodotus, and recognized by him as the one autochthonous people in the north (iv. 197), have throughout all recorded time formed not merely the substratum but the great majority of the inhabitants between the Atlantic and the Red Sea, and from the Mediterranean to the Sudan. They are the *Tamahu* of the Egyptian temple-inscriptions (B.C. 1500–1300), and the *Maxyes* of Herodotus (iv. 191, 193), this term and its later forms as given by Ptolemy, *Masices, Mazices*, being identical with *Amzigh* (plur. *Imazighen*), 'free' or 'noble,' which is still the collective name of all the Mauritanian Hamites. There are three well-defined divisions, which, with their chief sub-groups, may here be tabulated:

I. EASTERN HAMITES:
- *Ancient Egyptians and Copts*; Nile valley from the Delta to Nubia.
- *Bejas* (Ababdeh, Bishāri, Hadendāwa, Homrān, Beni-Amer); from Upper Egypt to Abyssinia, between the Nile and the Red Sea.
- *Afars* (Dankali, pl. Danākil); the steppe between Abyssinia and the Red Sea.
- *Agaos, Khamants, Falashas* (?), *Funji*; Abyssinia, Senaar.
- *Gallas* (Ilm'orma), *Somali*; Galla and Somali lands.
- *Turkanas, Masai, Wa-huma*; Lake Rudolf, Mau plateau, Uganda.

II. WESTERN HAMITES:
- *Imazighen* (Atlas or Mauritanian Berbers), *Kabyles, Riffs, Shluhs, Shawias, Zenagas, Mzabs, Khumirs, Haratins, Wajila*; Morocco, Algeria, Tunis, Tripoli, Siwa oasis.
- *Tuaregs* (Saharan Berbers); *Askar* (Azjar) group, *Ahaggar* (Hoggar) group, *Kel-Owi* group, *Kel-Geres* group, *Awelimmiden* group, *Trarsas* and *Braknas*; Western Sahara.

III. CENTRAL HAMITES:
- *Tibus* (Tedas, Dazas, Baeles, Zoghawas); Tibesti uplands, Ennedi, Wanyanga, Borku, Kanem.

During the historic period the Semites have been represented in North Africa by the Phœnicians from Syria, the Jews from Palestine, the Himyaritic Arabs from Yemen, and the Muslim Arabs from Central and North Arabia. The *Phœnicians*, founders of Carthage, Leptis, Utica, and numerous other settlements on the north coast, have long been extinct. The *Jews*, who began to arrive some time after the Babylonian captivity, are still found in small communities along the seaboard, from Egypt to Morocco. In Tripolitana some have become troglodytes, dwelling in the limestone caves of the Ghurian uplands, south of Tripoli. These subterranean habitations appear 'to have originated principally with the Jews, who from time immemorial had become intimately connected with the Berbers, many of the Berber tribes having adopted the Jewish creed' (Barth, *Travels*, i. p. 48). The Jews also penetrated at an unknown date into the heart of Abyssinia, where they are supposed to be still represented by the Judaizing *Falashas* of the Simen district, who claim to be of the 'House of Israel,' and are often called the 'Jews of Abyssinia.' But these Falashas—that is, 'Emigrants'—can no longer be called Jews, since they are now completely assimilated in speech and appearance to the surrounding Agao Hamites. They have no knowledge of Hebrew, and even their Bible is the Ge'ez (Himyaritic) version common to all the Abyssinian Christians.

This term *Ge'ez*, properly *Aga'zi*, has reference to Aksum, capital of the Aksumite empire, founded probably about the beginning of the Christian era by the *Himyaritic Semites*, who had already crossed over from South Arabia, and have since then been politically dominant in Abyssinia. Aksum soon became a great centre of Himyaritic culture, which was further developed under Hellenic influences about 450, when Christianity was introduced by the apostle Frumentius from Alexandria. Then the Bible was translated into Ge'ez (*v. supra*), which was at that time the current, as it is still the liturgical, language of the country; and this tongue has preserved some early Christian documents, the Greek or Syriac originals of which have been lost.

Having received its teachings from Alexandria, the Abyssinian Church is a branch of the Coptic, and consequently professes the Monophysite doctrine of Eutyches accepted by the Alexandrian patriarchs in the 6th cent. The *Abuna*, or spiritual head of the Abyssinian Christians, is always consecrated by the patriarch of Alexandria, and for the last 700 years has even been of Coptic nationality. But his possibly dangerous political influence is neutralized by the *Etsh'ege*, a kind of national high priest at the head of the regular clergy, and of the *debtura*, or men of letters. These literati, although laymen, enjoy special ecclesiastical privileges, and thus serve to check the action both of the *Abuna* and of the religious orders, which are very numerous, and own a large part of the land. Like the mosques in Muhammadan lands, the churches and monasteries are the schools of the country, and over these the *debtura* have complete control. But education is in a rudimentary state, and the only art still cultivated is painting, which was introduced in Byzantine times, and is employed exclusively for the decoration of the churches. A traditional canon of the art requires all orthodox Christians, saints, and good people to be represented in full face; all others in profile. Among the latter are included all their enemies, the Jews, the devils, and especially the Falashas, who are popularly believed to be magicians, capable, like the European wer-wolves, of assuming the guise of dangerous animals, such as lions, panthers, or hyænas. These and many other old pagan notions are still rife beneath the thin lacquer of Abyssinian Christianity.

After the 6th cent. the Aksumite empire disappeared from history, and was successively followed by those of *Tigrē* in the north, *Amhara* in the centre, and *Shoa* in the south. Menilek, present king of Shoa, rules the whole land in absolute sovereignty, and all his Himyaritic subjects are being slowly merged in a single Abyssinian nationality, differing little in their physical and mental characters, and speaking two distinct modern forms of the old Ge'ez language—Tigriña in the north and Amharic in the south, the parting line being the Takkazē river. But all these historical Himyarites of the plateau are to be distinguished from the *Zabalat Himyarites*, who probably preceded them in this region, and have been settled from time immemorial in the district between the Blue Nile and its Dender affluent east of Senaar. These Zabalats never came under Hellenic or later Muslim influences like their Funji neighbours, and hence are neither Christians nor Muhammadans, but appear still to practise the same Semitic rites as their Minæan and Sabæan forefathers. They are called 'fire-worshippers,' but do not worship the fire itself, which they regard only as a great purifier and as an emblem of a Supreme Being, who reveals himself in this element as well as in the heavenly bodies. Hence they turn in prayer to the stars or towards the rising and the setting sun, and kindle great fires over the graves of the dead. But there is also a supreme demon, whose wrath has to be averted by offerings and sacrifices. The two principles of good and evil would thus appear to be recognized, as in so many other religions which can have had no direct contact with the old Zoroastrian system. The Zabalats differ from the Muslim Arabs in many other respects, being strict monogamists, keeping no slaves, and recognizing no hereditary sheikhs.

Even before the great Muslim irruptions of the 7th and later centuries, the northern *Arabs*, mostly, no doubt, Bedawîn from the Nejd plateau, had ranged into North Africa, and mention is made of the *Ruadites*, who had already penetrated westwards to Mauritania before the rise of Islām. But the great movements which have made the Arab race, language, and religion dominant throughout North Africa, began with the conquest of Egypt in the 7th century. Later came the peaceful but ethnically more important immigration of North Arabian tribes, instigated by Ahmed ibn-Ali, who died in 1045. Then took place that tremendous dislocation of the indigenous populations during which a large section of the Berbers withdrew from the plains to the Mauritanian uplands, while others retired to the Saharan oases. Here they were followed later by the Arabs themselves; so that at present the pure Arab and mixed Arabo-Berber tribes form the great majority of the inhabitants of Tripoli, Mauritania, and the Sahara; while the Arab language and the Muslim religion prevail almost exclusively amongst the native populations in all the large towns along the Mediterranean seaboard, from Marakesh and Fez to Cairo and Alexandria. The old Hamitic languages, however, still persist amongst the Muhammadans of the Sahara (Tuaregs, Tibus), the tribes of the Siwa and Aujila oases (Cyrenaica), and many of the Berber groups in the Atlas uplands.

Islām, long the exclusive religion of Arabs, Berbers, and Tibus, presents few special features, except where it assumes a political aspect, as among the *Senūsīya* brotherhood, or else becomes affected by the primitive beliefs and superstitions of the aborigines, as in Tibesti and Senaar. There are numerous small groups which enjoy great repute either as *shurfa* (pl. of *sharīf*, 'noble,' 'high-born,' a title assumed by those claiming descent from the Prophet), or *marabouts* (saints, recluses, charlatans, claiming supernatural powers like shamans or medicine-men), or *khwān*, the literati, who now constitute the *Senūsīya* confraternity, a politico-religious body which has acquired immense influence throughout the Muhammadan world. It is so named from the Algerian sheikh Senūsi, who set up as a zealous preacher or reformer, first in Mecca, then at Bengazi in 1843, and in 1855 removed to the Faredgha oasis, where he died 'in the odour of sanctity.' Since then the brotherhood has continued to flourish under his successors, the Mahdi ('guided'), who are destined to restore the power of Islām to its former splendour. Numerous *zawiyas* (convents), each a little centre of religious fervour, industry, and even culture, have sprung up in Tripoli and the Saharan oases, and the Faredgha 'mother-house'—convent, mosque, school, hospital, and stronghold combined—has thus become the headquarters of a powerful organization, which numbers millions of devoted adherents, and makes its influence felt from Mauritania to Mesopotamia. The society continues to expand throughout North Africa; and although it looked askance at the late Nubian Mahdi and his Khalīfian successor at Omdurman, that was only through jealousy, and because its time had not yet come.

Of the strange interminglings of Muhammadanism with primitive religions, some instances are given in art. ABORIGINES. The same tendencies may be observed amongst the Saharan *Tibus*, who represent the ancient Garamantes, and were nearly all pagans till they became at least nominal Musalmāns in the 18th century. Some still practise heathen rites openly, and amongst the Baeles of the

Ennedi district Allah has not yet been dethroned by Yīdo, the native name of the Supreme Being. In the same district a kind of *mana* or supernatural virtue is ascribed to the *kūntok*, a species of mottled stone of somewhat rare occurrence in the country. During the prayers addressed to Yīdo this stone is sprinkled with flour and with the blood of a sacrificed sheep, and it then secures for its fortunate owner the success of all his projects and confusion to all his enemies (Nachtigal, *Sahăra u. Sudan*, ii. p. 176). Polygamy is not controlled by the Qur'ānic law, the number of wives being merely a question of ways and means, while the son is obliged to marry all his father's wives except his own mother. Matriarchal custom persists, as is shown by the fact that the wife continues to reside in her parents' home till the birth of the first child, and permanently if there is no issue; in which case the husband receives back the camels paid to his father-in-law for his bride.

Although passing for good Muhammadans, the *Tedas* (Northern Tibus) do not abstain from *lakbi* (palm wine), and now and then sacrifice a goat for rain or other favours. All wear amulets attached to various parts of the body, and think that ailments may be cured by drinking the water used for washing out Qur'ānic texts written on the inside of a cup. Similar texts contained in little leather bags make their spears and other weapons more deadly, and also protect horses and camels from the evil eye. Their half-Arabized Fezzanese cousins put great faith in the marabouts, who are more numerous and influential in Fezzan than elsewhere. They are much employed as sorcerers in thwarting the machinations of the great demon Iblis or Shaitān and the innumerable other wicked jinns, common enemies of mankind, against whom Allah appears to be powerless. In the Timbuktu district the marabouts are, or were formerly, replaced by the *santons*, a sort of African shamans, who employed music to work themselves into a state of ecstasy, in which they pretended to hold communion with the souls of departed Muslim saints. From these they received instructions as to the proper animals—a white or red cock, a hen, a gazelle, a goat, or an ostrich—to be sacrificed for the recovery of the sick. In such cases incense was burned, and the cooked meat was served to the patient and those present, the blood, the bones, and feathers being buried as a sacrificial offering to the dead saint.

Amongst the Muslim *Tuaregs* the belief is universal that below the surface the Sahara is everywhere peopled by a class of supernatural beings called *Ahl at-Trab*, who delight in playing mischievous pranks on wayfarers in the desert. They seize and pull down the camels' feet, causing them to sink in the soft sands; they gnaw off the roots of the desert plants, thus killing the scanty vegetation; on the approach of the thirsty traveller, they drink up the water of springs and wells; they even come to the surface and assume bodily forms to deceive and torment the living. All unexplained natural phenomena, such as the pillars of sand raised by the whirlwind, are referred to invisible agencies, and the mysterious droning heard on a still night in many parts of the wilderness is the voice of the jinns conversing among themselves (Harding King, *A Search for the Masked Tawareks*, pp. 39, 42).

Although little influenced by the teachings of Islām, the moral character of the Tuaregs and Mauritanian Berbers is greatly superior to that of their Arab neighbours. Apart from the blood-feuds, vendettas, and predatory expeditions permitted by tribal usage, 'the vices so common amongst the Moors are unknown in the homes of the Berbers. They seem to possess none of that uncontrollable passion that is so large a feature in the Arab character, and its place is taken by affection and sincerity. No doubt, to a great extent the moral character of the Berbers is due to the fact that their women are allowed entire liberty, do not veil their faces, and mix on almost all occasions with the men' (W. B. Harris, *Tafilet*, p. 160). The Arab, still a nomad herdsman, who holds that the ploughshare and shame enter hand in hand into the family, remains a fanatic ever to be feared, because he blindly obeys the will of Allah proclaimed by his prophets, marabouts, and mahdis. He is ruled by a despotic and theocratic sheikh, in accordance with the precepts of the Qur'ān; whereas the agricultural Berber, with his *jam'a* (public assembly) and unwritten code, feels himself a freeman, is a born sceptic, cares little for theological dogmas, and is far less of a fatalist than his Semitic neighbour. Although many of the Mauritanian tribes have adopted the Arabic language, the process of assimilation appears to be arrested, and the Berber is now everywhere gaining on the Arab. 'He is the race of the future, as of the past' (Dr. Malbot).

In a remarkable ethnological generalization, Herodotus tells us (iv. 197) that the Africa known to him was occupied by four distinct peoples,—two indigenous, the Libyans (our Hamites) and the Ethiopians (our Negroes); and two intruders, the Phœnicians and the Hellenes. Since then other intruders (ἐπήλυδες), such as the Romans, Vandals, Bulgarians, and Cherkesses, have come and gone, while other later arrivals—Arabs, Jews, Turks, Italians, Iberians, French, Britons, Dutch, Belgians, Germans—have settled round the seaboard, and, by occupying their respective 'Hinterlands,' have made nearly the whole continent a political dependency of Europe. But these movements have scarcely affected the ethnical relations, and the statement of Herodotus regarding two indigenous races (αὐτόχθονες)—Libyans in the north and Ethiopians in the south—still holds good. Thus the Libyan (Hamitic) domain, as above described, is everywhere conterminous with the Ethiopic (Negro), which comprises the section of the mainland south of the parting line indicated at the beginning of this article, together with the adjacent island of Madagascar. Amid the great mass of black humanity there are extensive and long-standing interminglings,—Arabo-Berbers and Fulahs in the north, Malayans in Madagascar,—and also some aberrant elements, such as the Negritoes in the forest zone of the Congo, the Bushman-Hottentots in the southern steppe lands, and the utterly degraded Vaalpens of the Limpopo basin. But, taken as a whole, these Negro and Negroid populations present sufficient uniformity in their physical, and still more in their mental, characters to be grouped together as one main division of mankind. More, perhaps, on linguistic than on ethnical grounds, they are usually divided into two great sections: *Sudanese Negroes*, of diverse speech, north of the equator; and *Bantu Negroes*, of one speech, thence southwards.

Sudan—that is, the region which stretches south of the Sahara between the Atlantic Ocean and Abyssinia—is commonly regarded as the original home of the Negro stock; hence its Arabic name, *Bilād as-Sūdān*, 'Land of the Blacks,' the Nigritia or Negroland of our early writers. Although it has been largely encroached upon by Hamites and Semites from the north and east, here are still found many of the most typical Negro populations, such as the Serers, Felups, Timni, and Krumen of the West Coast; the Tshi, Ewe, and Yorubas of the Gold and Slave Coasts; the Bauchi, Mosgus, Michi, and Yedinas of Central Sudan; the Igarras, Ibos, and Benins of Southern Nigeria; the Mabas, Nubas, Denkas, Golos, Shilluks, Bari, Bongos, and Nuers of East Sudan and the White Nile; and the Zandehs (Niam-niam), Mangbattus, Monfus, A-Barambos, and A-Babuas of the Welle basin. These are all uncivilized pagans, who speak a great number of radically distinct Negro languages, and exhibit Negro physical traits, often to an exaggerated degree. These traits, which prevail with marked uniformity over wide areas, were already specialized in remote times, as we see from the portraits depicted on the early Egyptian monuments, and as we find them graphically summed up in the description of a negress attributed to Vergil (*Moretum*, 32–35):

> 'Afra genus, tota patriam testante figura,
> Torta comam labroque tumens et fusca colore,
> Pectore lata, iacens mammis, compressior alvo,
> Cruribus exilis, spatiosa prodiga planta.'

Standing out in marked contrast to all these primitive peoples are the relatively civilized Hamito-Negro or Semito-Negro nations, such as the Mandingos, Songhais, and Fulahs in the west; the Hausas, Kanuri, Baghirmi, and Mabas of Wadai in the centre; and the Furs and Nubians in the east, who are all Muhammadans, and of diversely modified Negroid type, but still speak independent languages of Negro stock. From these striking contrasts between the pure Negro and the mixed Negroid peoples the inference has been drawn that the Negro left to himself remains a Negro in every sense of the term, and without miscegenation is incapable of making any advance beyond a low social and intellectual level. For this arrest of progress seen everywhere in Africa and the New World (West Indies, Southern United States), a physiological explanation has been sought in the early closing of the cranial sutures, preventing any further expansion of the brain after puberty. 'A cet arrêt intellectuel doit correspondre la soudure de la boîte cervicale; le développement du crâne s'arrête et empêche le cerveau de se dilater davantage' (Binger, *du Niger au Golfe de Guinée*, ii. p. 246). Hence it is that the Negroes often display in early life a degree of intelligence even superior to that of European children. 'They acquire knowledge with facility till they arrive at the age of puberty, when the physical nature masters the intellect, and frequently completely deadens it. This peculiarity has been attributed by some physiologists to the early closing of the sutures of the cranium, and it is worthy of note that throughout West Africa it is by no means rare to find skulls without any apparent transverse or longitudinal sutures' (Ellis, *The Ewe-Speaking Peoples*, p. 9).

The chief subdivisions of both the Sudanese and the Bantu sections will be found in art. ETHNOLOGY (Conspectus). Between the two sections the most conspicuous difference is the linguistic confusion which prevails in Sudan and the linguistic unity which is the dominant feature in Bantuland. Except in the south-western Bushman-Hottentot territory, in Madagascar, where a Malayo-Polynesian tongue is exclusively spoken, and perhaps amongst the Negritoes of the forest zone, all the current idioms are closely related members of a common stock language. And as the tribes themselves are not so closely related, but, on the contrary, often present considerable physical differences, it follows that Bantu is far more intelligible as a linguistic than as an ethnical expression. In fact, a Bantu is, strictly speaking, nothing more than a full-blood or more often a half-blood Negro of Bantu speech. In general, all are mestizos, showing every shade of transition between the Negro and the Caucasic (Hamitic and Semitic) elements. The Negro has apparently everywhere formed the substratum, which has, so to say, been leavened in diverse proportions by very old and later Caucasic infiltrations from the north. These interminglings have resulted in endless modifications of the physical characters, but have left the original Bantu form of speech untouched, as is always the case where two or more races are merged in one. The ethnical groups form new combinations by miscegenation, while the languages, being incapable of miscegenation, all perish except one. Hence it is that in the Bantu domain we have many physical blends with only one unblended form of speech. 'There are many mixed races; indeed, all races are mixed; but there are no mixed languages, but only mixed vocabularies' (A. H. Keane, *Ethnology*, 1896, p. 199; also M. L. Lapicque: 'Les langues se tuent; les peuples se mêlent,' MS note). For details see art. BANTUS AND S. AFRICA.

From the religious and ethical standpoints there is not much to choose between the pagan Sudanese and the Bantu peoples. Everywhere amongst both sections are met the same crude animistic notions, gross superstitions, cruel practices associated with ancestor-worship, ordeals, omens, witchcraft, fetishism, human sacrifices, and other observances which are specially characteristic of all primitive African cults. Everywhere also is noticed the clear line of demarcation which is drawn by all the natives between their religious practices and their rules of conduct. Here is plainly seen how religion and morals belonged originally to two different orders of thought, and how the one is made subservient to the other, as when the invisible powers are asked to aid and co-operate in deeds of violence, murder, vendetta, rape, theft, plunder, and other acts regarded as immoralities in higher social systems. Thus on the Gold Coast 'religion is not in any way allied with moral ideas, whose source is indeed essentially distinct, although the two become associated when man attains a higher degree of civilization. Murder, theft, and all offences against the person or against property are matters in which the gods have no immediate concern, and in which they take no interest, except in the case when, bribed by a valuable offering, they take up the quarrel in the interests of some faithful worshipper. The most atrocious crimes, committed as between man and man, the gods can view with equanimity. These are man's concerns, and must be rectified or punished by man' (Ellis, *The Tshi-speaking Peoples*, p. 11). In fact, all these gods are themselves originally malignant superhuman beings, born of fear, and authors of all evil, as is even indicated by some of their names, such as that of the Ashanti god *Bohsum*, said to mean 'Producer of Calamities.' Hence sickness, death, and all other miseries are attributed to them, either directly, or indirectly through witchcraft, since 'it is from them that wizards and witches obtain assistance and mysterious knowledge' (*ib.* p. 13). From such venal deities no correct views of right and wrong could ever have been acquired, and it must be obvious that 'moral ideas flow from an essentially different source than religion,' that both 'cannot have sprung from a common root' (Th. Waitz, *Introd. to Anthropology*, Eng. ed. i. 279).

Ancestor-worship appears to be the most outstanding feature of all African primitive religious systems. That the spirits of the dead are the gods of the living is a formula that applies equally to the Sudanese natives of Upper Guinea, and to the Bantu populations of Uganda, the eastern coastlands, and Damaraland. Amongst the Gold and Slave Coast peoples there are many local and general personifications of the powers of nature; but these were held in slight esteem compared with the ancestral gods to whom hecatombs of human victims were immolated at the periodical 'Customs' during the flourishing days of the kingdoms of Ashanti, Dahomi, and Benin. It was the same in Uganda, where the former kings of the national dynasty were revered as demi-gods. Their souls were supposed to dwell in and inspire the witch-doctors; shrines were raised over their graves, the maintenance of which was a religious duty, and here were offered the human sacrifices, as many as two thousand by the late King Mtesa. The demon Ndaula, whose abode is on the Gambaragara heights, whence he plagues the people with smallpox and other evils, is also a departed spirit, identified with one of the early members of the Uganda dynasty. The trees planted round the ancestral graves were sedulously tended by wise women, whose oracles, like those of the Pythian priestess, were taken as decisive in certain political crises. The course of events was thus still controlled by the deceased rulers of the land, while the very trees overshadowing their tombs gradually acquired that sacred character which led eventually to general tree-worship.

Along the eastern seaboard the dominant spirit was Munkulunkulu, who ruled, under endless variants, from the Tānā river round the Cape to the Cunene. He is often spoken of as the 'Supreme Being'; but such a concept was not grasped by the African aborigines, and the fundamental idea is revealed in the root *inkulu*='old,' 'great' (cf. Lat. *alt-us*, cognate with Teutonic *alt*, 'old'); so that the word really connotes a deification of the great departed, and is thus a direct outcome of the universal ancestor-worship. This is also fully in accordance with the view of Bleek, who holds that the term originally meant 'great ancestor.' Thus, as in Celebes, where *empung* (='grandfather') is the generic name of the gods, *Unkulunkulu* becomes the Divine progenitor of the Zulu-Xosa Bantus; while of *Mulungu*, the form current in Nyasaland, the Rev. Duff Macdonald writes: 'In all our translations of Scripture where we found the word "God" we used *Mulungu*; but this word is chiefly used by the natives as a general name for spirit. The spirit of a deceased man is called Mulungu, and all the prayers and offerings of the living are presented to such spirits of the dead. It is here that we find the great centre of the native religion. The spirits of the dead are the gods of the living' (*Africana*, i. p. 59). And again: 'Their god is not the body in the grave, but the spirit [Mulungu], and they seek the spirit at the place where their departed kinsman last lived among them. It is the great tree at the verandah (*kwipenu*) of the dead man's house that is their *temple*; and if no tree grow here they erect a little shrine, and there perform their simple rites' (*ib.* p. 60). Here we have the very incipient stage itself of ancestor-worship again closely interwoven with the tree element. Then comes a further development, in which the departed spirit reveals himself first in dreams, and later through the *juakuweweta*, the priestess or prophetess, as in Uganda and Hellas. 'The god comes to her with his commands at night. She delivers the message in a kind of ecstasy. She speaks (as her name implies) with the utterance of a person raving with excitement. During the night of the communication her ravings are heard sounding all over the village in a high key' (*ib.* p. 61). We seem to be reading an extract from Pausanias on the Delphic Oracle. And the broad statement is made that 'the spirit of every deceased man and woman, with the solitary exception of wizards and witches [who become hyænas], becomes an object of religious homage. The gods of the natives, then, are nearly as numerous as their dead' (p. 68).

In some parts of Nyasaland, as in Uganda and elsewhere, ancestor-worship eventually became associated with human sacrifice. 'If the deceased owned several slaves, an enormous hole is dug for a grave. The slaves that were caught immediately on his death are now brought forward. They may be either cast into the pit alive [being made fast to slave-sticks], or the undertakers may cut all their throats. The body of their master or their mistress is then laid down to rest above theirs, and the grave is covered in' (*ib.* p. 107). We know from Commander Cameron and most other early travellers that similar and even worse atrocities were of constant occurrence all over the Bantu lands, before their suppression by the European Powers in 1884. It is thus again seen that in these respects the Bantus stand on the same low social level as the Sudanese negroes.

On the West Coast nature-worship was, as a rule, perhaps more prevalent than on the east side. Here Munkulunkulu was generally replaced by *Nzambi*, who also has many variants, and is similarly described by some observers as a 'Supreme Being.' But this is denied by the Rev. W. H. Bentley, our best authority on the subject, who rejects the far-fetched explanations of Kolbe and others, adding that 'the knowledge of God is most vague, scarcely more than nominal. There is no worship paid to God' [in Kongoland] (*Dict. and Gram. of the Kongo Language*, p. 96). Farther south, Mulungu reappears, under the form *Mukuru*, amongst the Bantu Hereros of Damaraland, and it is noteworthy that here also ancestor-worship prevails almost exclusively. 'The best missionaries who have worked among the Hereros could find nothing going beyond the simplest ancestor-worship. Their chief deity, Mukuru, that is, the "Ancient," is a spirit whose dwelling is placed in the Far North. His grave is regarded as a sacred spot in many places. Every tribe has its own Mukuru [exactly as in Nyasaland], to whom all superstitious usages and customs are referred. Above all, he sends rain and sunshine. Mukuru's "grave" certainly points to the weight assigned to ancestor-worship among these people, and many other facts confirm this' (Ratzel, *Hist. of Mankind*, ii. 358). Here also the worship is connected with trees, since 'the Hereros in their sacrifices use sacred sticks from trees or bushes consecrated to the ancestors. Many keep these sticks, which are perhaps the last relics of ancestor-worship, in bundles, hung with amulets, upon the branches of the bush makera, which stands at the place of sacrifice, and represents the altar' (*ib.* p. 361). Farther on, the highly-developed tree-cult of the Hereros is shown to be 'a direct offshoot of ancestor-worship, for it ultimately leads to the tale that a sacred tree gave their origin to the Ova-herero, the Bushmen, oxen, and zebras' (*ib.* p. 481). One particular species is specially reverenced, and, when seen from afar, is hailed with the words, 'Holy art thou, our ancestor.' The evolution is thus obvious. A given tree is first respected for the sake of the man who was attached to it when alive, or else buried beneath its shade in death. Then the tribe during its wanderings meets the same tree elsewhere, and by association of ideas transfers to it the reverence or worship formerly paid to the now perhaps forgotten ancestor. But a tree is always something visible and tangible. Hence, under changed conditions, tree-cult may well outlive the ancestor-worship in which it originated. Here it may be noted that the selection of the bush *makera* for special homage was probably due to a popular etymology confusing this term with *Mukuru*, the Herero form of *Mulungu*, the 'Ancient.'

Other more or less characteristic features of the African religious systems and superstitions—fetishism, human sacrifices, omens, ordeals, talismans, cannibalism, wer-animals, witchcraft—are dealt with in separate articles.

LITERATURE.—H. Barth, *Travels in Africa*, 5 vols., 1857; D. Livingstone, *Missionary Travels*, etc. 1857, *Last Journals*, 1874; H. M. Stanley, *Through the Dark Continent*, 1878; F. L. James, *The Wild Tribes of Sudan*, 1883; J. Macdonald, *Light in Africa*, 1890; F. Manetta, *La Razza Negra*, Turin, 1864; F. Ratzel, *Hist. of Mankind*, vol. ii. 1897; A. H. Keane, art. 'Negro' in *Encyc. Brit.*9, *Ethnology*, 1896, *Man*

Past and Present, 1900; Spencer St. John, *Hayti: or, The Black Republic*, 1884; Duff Macdonald, *Africana*, 1882; A. B. Ellis, *The Tshi-speaking Peoples of the Gold Coast*, 1887, *The Ewe-speaking Peoples of the Slave Coast*, 1890, *The Yoruba-speaking Peoples of the Slave Coast*, 1894; W. Junker, *Travels in Africa*, 3 vols. [Keane's Eng. ed. 1890–1892]; J. F. van Oordt, *The Origin of the Bantu*, Cape Town, 1907.

A. H. KEANE.

ĀGAMA.—In the oldest Buddhist writings this is the standing word for 'tradition' (*Vinaya*, ii. 249; *Aṅguttara*, ii. 147). This usage is maintained in the *Milinda* (215, 414) and in the *Mahāvastu* (ii. 21). But from the 5th cent. A.D. onwards the word means usually a division of the Sutta Piṭaka—the same portion as was, in the older phraseology (*Vinaya*, ii. 287), called a *nikāya*. The reason for this change was that the latter word (*nikāya*) had come to be used also in the sense of a division of disciples, a school or sect, and had therefore become ambiguous. In Buddhist Sanskrit books this later use of *āgama* seems to have supplanted entirely the use of *nikāya*; but our edited texts are not sufficient in extent to enable us, as yet, to state this with certainty.

T. W. RHYS DAVIDS.

AGAOS.—**1.** The Agaos or **Agows**, a name applied to various groups of Hamites who do not possess any collective name, form part of the primitive Hamitic population of Abyssinia. Formerly they occupied a large extent of the plateau, but were gradually driven, in prehistoric times, towards the south and west by incoming peoples—the Himyaritic Semites speaking the Ge'ez tongue. The latter are now divided into the Tigrē and Amhara branches, but the Amhara, who crossed the Takkazē, are much mixed with the Hamitic element, while their Ge'ez speech has been greatly modified by the primitive language, if indeed it is not that primitive speech itself modified by the Semitic language of the conquerors. At present the Agaos, whose name means 'the free,' are composed of several groups scattered throughout the region between the Takkazē and the Abai, mainly in subjection to the rule of the Negus Negust, but retaining their own customs and speech. They are found chiefly in the province of Lasta, on the upper Takkazē (where they were completely reduced only in the 17th cent. by the Emperor of Abyssinia), and in the districts to the south-west of Lake Tānā or Tzana (where they give their name to one province, Agaomidir or Agao-land, which is almost entirely peopled by them). They are characterized by broad faces and high cheek-bones, yellow complexion, and strong, coarse, straight hair, and are of the Caucasic type, like their Semitic conquerors, from whom they do not differ much in appearance. The name Agaos is probably to be found in the *Athagaō* of the inscription at Adulis, dating from the beginning of the 2nd cent. A.D., discovered and preserved by Cosmas. This may be the district of Addago on the Takkazē, with a population of Agao blood. Cosmas (A.D. 523) refers to the Ἀγαῦ, and says they acknowledged the authority of the kings of Aksum. About 400 years later, the Agaos of Semen, under their queen, Judith, were strong enough to expel the Menilek dynasty from the throne of Aksum (*JA*, 1863). The Agao speech is said by Beke to be the language of the people of Abyssinia, as Amharic is that of the court, the army, and commerce. It is spoken from the Sanhait district in the N.E. to Gojam and Shoa in the south, under different names and in a variety of dialects, and in some provinces is almost exclusively in use. By the people themselves in Lasta it is known as *Khamtinja*; this group also call themselves *Hamra*, now found in the name Amhara borne by the district between the Takkazē and the Abai, and suggesting that the present Himyaritic Amhara people may have borrowed their name from that of some of the Hamitic aborigines. D'Abbadie calls the Lasta Hamites *Khamta*—a word connected with *Khamtinja* (*Athenæum*, 1845, 359); while Beke (*JRGS* xiv. 56) calls their language *Hhamera*. *Khamta*, still borne by the Khamants of Lake Tānā, and *Hhamera* were probably names of earlier dominant Agao tribes.

2. The principal divisions of the peoples who may be classed as Agaos are the Agaos of Lasta (Bruce's 'Tcheratz Agaos'), including the Khamants; those of Agaomidir and the surrounding districts enclosed in the sweep of the Abai as it issues from Lake Tānā; and the Falashas. Both the first groups are divided into seven tribes, probably from some sacredness in this number. The second group call themselves Aghaghā, according to Beke (*JRGS* xiv. 10). The **Falashas,** whose language closely resembles the Agao, are found scattered through the province of Semen and neighbouring districts, as well as in Agaomidir. They claim to be descended from Jews who came from Judæa with the Queen of Sheba, and follow the rites of Judaism. Hence they are frequently called the Jews of Abyssinia. But they are certainly not Jews by descent, nor are their features Semitic, since in physiognomy they closely resemble the Agaos. Possibly their Jewish faith is the survival of some earlier diffusion of Judaism through Abyssinia before the introduction of Christianity, as there is no record of their conversion. They are divided into three sects, each with its high priest; they hold themselves aloof from the other peoples of the land, do not practise polygamy, and never marry out of their own tribe. Entering a Christian house is strictly forbidden; when this has been done, ritual purification is necessary. Their places of worship or *masjīds* are distinguished by a red earthenware pot placed on a pinnacle. They are divided into three compartments, each of different sanctity, as in the Jewish tabernacle, and admission to each is strictly regulated by the Levitical law. Behind is a small enclosure with a stone on which sacrificial victims are slaughtered. Though they have incorporated with their customs several ceremonies drawn from Christian sources, they carefully observe the Law, especially in the ritual of purification and of feasts and keeping the Sabbath. Some of their sacrifices, however, differ from those of the Jewish law. They observe great ritual scrupulosity. The dying and the unclean are taken to a hut set apart for this purpose. They fast twice a week, as well as for forty days before Easter. Their ideas about the Messiah are vague, but they believe that Jerusalem will again be rebuilt. The priests must observe several tabus from which the people are free; some of them are great ascetics, passing years in dismal swamps, and sometimes in a frenzy throwing themselves into the waters. As a people the Falashas are inoffensive. They are devoted to agriculture, are metal-workers, and furnish skilful artisans in various towns of the province (see D'Abbadie in *Nouvelles Annales des Voyages*, iii. 84 ff.; Stern, *Wanderings among the Falashas*, 1862; Beke, *JRGS* xiv. 8).

3. The other branches of the Agaos were pagans, or possibly pagans with a veneer of Judaism, as the name of their queen, Judith, would suggest, until the advent of the Portuguese missionaries in the 16th and 17th centuries. By them they were in part converted to Christianity of a nominal type, and the process was probably completed by their final subjugation to the Abyssinian emperors. Like the rest of the Abyssinians, they are of the Monophysite sect, and assert their orthodoxy as strongly as any; but it is probable that, beneath their nominal adhesion to the faith, there are many survivals of their earlier paganism with its cult of sun and moon, trees, rivers, and animals, of which the cow was the chief. No complete account of that primitive paganism is now available, but it was evidently nature-worship of no high order, and in its observances the fertility of the land was aimed at. Hence the worship of rivers, and especially of the Takkazē and Abai, was prominent. Survivals of these rites are described by Lobo and Bruce. The springs from which the Nile rises were the scene of an annual gathering of the tribes for this cult. A small mound formed the altar upon which the sacrifices were placed. To this place once a year, on the appearance of the star Sirius, the *shum* or priest called the heads of the Agao clans. A black heifer which had never borne a calf was slain, its head cut off and plunged into one of the springs, and then wrapped up in the hide, which was sprinkled with the sacred water. The carcase was laid on the mound, washed with water, and divided into as many pieces as there were heads of clans. Each head received a piece, and the flesh was eaten raw, with draughts of the Nile water. Lobo says that each then sacrificed one or more cows. The bones were collected into a heap, and the priest, having anointed himself with the fat, sat down on the heap, which was then set on fire. As the flames increased, he harangued them, the fire doing him no injury. When all was consumed, each person present made him an offering. The head of the animal was carried to a cave, where other ceremonies were performed, apparently for the purpose of ensuring rain and good seasons. The spirit of the river was called by the highest Divine names—Eye of the World, the Everlasting God, etc., and the priest told Bruce that it had appeared to him in bodily shape like a venerable man (Lobo, *Voyage to Abyssinia*, Eng. tr. 1735, 99; Bruce, *Travels*, iii. 730). This cult is obviously based upon the importance of the river to the whole region through which it passes, and is not unlike the rites performed by the ancient Egyptians at the rising of the Nile and the appearance of Sirius, the star of Isis (Frazer, *Adonis, Attis, Osiris*, 228). Similar rites were practised by other tribes (*La grande Encyc.* i. 177), and human sacrifices to river-divinities are also spoken of; these also occurred in Egypt (Johnston, *Travels in S. Abyssinia*, 119). A modified form of these rites still prevailed in Beke's time (1804), and sick persons are still brought to the sources of the Abai, and left there for seven days in hope of their recovery (Beke, *JRGS* xiv. 13). Serpent-worship was prevalent in Abyssinia in earlier times, and a great serpent called Arwē figures in the early history of the people. Some remains of this cult are found among the Agaos. The preservation of serpents was prayed for; they were believed to give oracles, and in some cases they were kept in the houses of the people and fed. If the animal did not eat, ill-luck was at hand (Bruce, iii. 732–4). Miraculous stories of serpents are found in the legendary lives of Abyssinian saints (Parkyns, *Life in Abyssinia*, 298). Other relics of earlier animal-worship may be seen in the claim of the Agaos of Lasta to understand the language of birds, by the interpretation of which they regulate their affairs (Plowden, *Travels in Abyssinia*, 124). The Falashas, on account of their skill in metal working, and some of the Agaos, are regarded as sorcerers and *bandas* or wer-wolves. They are believed to take possession of their victims, who exhibit curious symptoms of hysteria, and try to get into the forest, where their persecutor, in hyæna shape, devours them (see LYCANTHROPY).

4. The Khamants, scattered through Amhara and Shoa, claim descent from Moses, but are regarded as pagans by both the Falashas and the Abyssinians. They are said to believe in God and in a future state, but are called worshippers of forests from the rites performed by them under trees. Other 'secret acts of devotion' at certain rocks are also spoken of. A scheme of King Theodore's for their compulsory conversion was overruled by his advisers (Stern, 43; *La grande Encyc.* i. 177; Reclus, *Univ. Geog.* x. 147). It is uncertain whether the Waïto, dwelling on the eastern shore of Lake Tānā, belong to the Agao race. They speak the Agao language, but are an extremely primitive people, supporting themselves by hunting and fishing, and eating animals regarded by the other tribes as unclean. By them, therefore, they are called 'idolaters,' a vague term, but they call themselves Christians (Keane, *Africa*, 494; St. Martin, *Géog. Univ.* i. 36).

LITERATURE.—F. Jer. Lobo, *Voyage to Abyssinia*, 1735; James Bruce, *Travels to discover the Source of the Nile*, 1790; C. T. Beke, various papers in *JRGS*, vols. x. xii. xiv.; Antoine d'Abbadie, papers contributed to various Journals; H. A. Stern, *Wanderings among the Falashas in Abyssinia*, 1862; V. de Saint-Martin, *Nouveau Dict. de Géog. Universelle*, 1879, *s.v.* 'Agaos'; A. H. Keane, *Africa*, vol. i. 1895, *Ethnology*[2], 1901.

J. A. MACCULLOCH.

AGAPE.—

i. Summary of theories.
ii. Evidence for Christian common meals and for their connexion with the Eucharist:
1. New Testament.
2. Ecclesiastical writings to the end of the 3rd cent.; *Didache*; Ignatius; Pliny; Justin Martyr; Celsus; Minucius Felix; Lucian; *Epistle to Diognetus*; *Acts of Paul and Thecla*; *Acts of Perpetua and Felicitas*; Irenæus; Clement of Alexandria; Tertullian; *Canons of Hippolytus*; *Acts of James and Marianus*; Origen; Cyprian; *Acts of Pionius*; the older *Didascalia*.
3. Writings of 4th cent. and later: 'Church Orders'; Councils of Laodicea, Carthage No. 3, Gangra; pseudo-Pionius; Chrysostom; pseudo-Jerome; Theodoret; Augustine; Socrates; Sozomen; Trullan Council.
4. Funeral and commemorative Agapæ.
5. Archæological and epigraphic evidence.
iii. Review of the evidence.
(*a*) General deductions.
(*b*) Relative order of Agape and Eucharist when united.
(*c*) The name 'Agape.'
(*d*) Materials for the Agape.
iv. Origin of the Agape.
Literature.

i. SUMMARY OF THEORIES. — The Christian Agape or Love-Feast is one of those subjects which are apparently easy, but which are shown by careful study to be exceedingly difficult. At one time there was little doubt about its origin and history; but in the last few years it has attracted much attention, not only in Great Britain and in Germany, but also more especially in France; and views which were formerly held almost as a matter of course have been emphatically called in question, with the result that there is at present nothing like unanimity among scholars as to the origin and history of this curious custom of Christian antiquity. It may be well, by way of preface, to state briefly, and as far as possible in general terms, the views that have been put forward, classing together those which differ only in minor details. (*a*) The view which was almost universal, and which is still by far the most common, is that from the first the Christians celebrated the Eucharist and also a common meal to which some liturgical importance was attached, and which was called, from at least the latter part of the 1st cent., the 'Agape'; that the Eucharist and the Agape were at first united, but that, by reason either of abuses or of external persecution, they were disjoined at some time in the latter half of the 1st or the first quarter of the 2nd cent., though the time of the separation was not the same in all countries. (*b*) An entirely different view has lately (1902) been published by Mgr. Batiffol, who thinks that the Agape itself did not exist till the 3rd cent., beginning as a private charity supper, and becoming a more public organization in the 4th cent.; that though in the earliest ages the Christians sometimes had meals in common, these did not, except as an abuse, have any connexion with the Eucharist, and that the name 'Agape' in writings of the first two centuries was another designation of the Eucharist itself. (*c*) A view which has found much favour in Germany is that the Agape was the original institution, and that the Eucharist itself grew out of it, or that there was no real distinction between them (Spitta, Jülicher). (*d*) Ladeuze and Ermoni consider that both the Agape and the Eucharist are Apostolic, but that they were in reality perfectly distinct rites, though sometimes joined as in 1 Co 11. (*e*) Dean Armitage Robinson and a writer in the *Church Quarterly Review* (July 1902) hold a somewhat undefined but perhaps intermediate position, being dissatisfied with the first of the views enumerated above. Dr. Robinson (*Encyc. Bibl. s.v.* 'Eucharist') suggests that every meal was probably hallowed by Eucharistic acts, especially the daily meal for the poor (Ac 6^1), but that these should be distinguished from formal Eucharists like that in Ac 20^7. The Christians had stated charity suppers, he thinks, parallel to those of Greek guilds; these cannot always be distinguished from Eucharists. The Eucharist was gradually separated from a common meal; the original institution developed in two ways, liturgically into the Eucharist, and socially into the Supper; and the more these two sides developed, the more decided became the separation. Such are the various theories that have been maintained; we shall return to them when we have cited the evidence.

ii. EVIDENCE FOR CHRISTIAN COMMON MEALS AND FOR THEIR CONNEXION WITH OR SEPARATION FROM THE EUCHARIST.—It is proposed to gather together here all the evidence; for it seems unreasonable to put out of view, as is suggested by the *Church Quarterly* Reviewer, all evidence of suppers where the word 'Agape' is not found. We shall discuss later the name 'Agape' itself; here it may be remarked that the most important matter to be considered is the thing implied. The name need not necessarily have been universal; or, if it was universal, there is no special reason why it should have been mentioned in all the authorities, many of whom allude only incidentally to the custom now under discussion.

1. The New Testament.—(*a*) We may first take Acts, as indicating the earliest Christian customs, though the book itself was written later than 1 Corinthians, which we will next consider. In neither of these books is the *name* 'Agape' mentioned, but in Acts probably, and in 1 Corinthians certainly, there are allusions to a common meal having some connexion with the Eucharist. In Ac 2^{42} we read that the Christians continued steadfastly in the Apostles' teaching and fellowship (κοινωνία) — or perhaps 'in fellowship' — in the breaking of bread and the prayers (τῇ κλάσει τοῦ ἄρτου καὶ ταῖς προσευχαῖς), and in v.^{46}, that they 'day by day continuing . . . in the temple, and breaking bread at home (κλῶντές τε κατ' οἶκον ἄρτον), did take their food (τροφῆς) with gladness and singleness of heart, praising God,' etc. The expression 'to break bread' is found also in Ac $20^{7.11}$, where St. Paul, at Troas, after preaching till midnight on the 'first day of the week,' and after the Eutychus incident, broke bread and ate (κλάσας τὸν ἄρτον καὶ γευσάμενος), and 'talked with them . . . till break of day'—apparently an Eucharist with or without a meal, though Alford (*Gr. Test. in loc.*) and Bp. J. Wordsworth (*Ministry of Grace*, p. 316) think that γευσάμενος certainly means a meal (cf. Ac 10^{10}),—and in Ac 27^{35}, where an ordinary meal is almost certainly spoken of. The phrase was used by the Jews (Jer 16^7, La 4^4), and we find it, or the corresponding substantive, in NT in connexion with the Feedings (Mt 14^{19} 15^{36} and ‖ Mk.), the meal at Emmaus (Lk 24^{35}), and the Eucharist (Mt 26^{26} and ‖ Mk. Lk. and 1 Co 10^{16} 11^{24}, in the last of which verses, however, κλώμενον agreeing with σῶμα must doubtless be omitted, with ABCℵ). In view of these facts, we must conclude that 'to break bread' (κλάσαι ἄρτον or τὸν ἄ.) was used in the Apostolic age sometimes of an ordinary meal and sometimes as a technical name of the Eucharist, or perhaps of the Eucharist and a meal combined. In Ac 2^{42} the article ('*the* breaking of bread') shows that an ordinary meal is not meant, and we have to take the reference to be to the Eucharist, with or without a religious meal eaten in common, and the word 'food' (τροφή) in v.^{46} will probably lead us to think that the Eucharist *with* a meal is meant. The Peshiṭta reading in v.^{42} ('the breaking of the Eucharist') goes the other way, but seems to be a mere gloss due to later ideas. The phrase κατ' οἶκον in v.^{46} (*i.e.* 'at home' or 'in a private house') has probably no bearing on the matter, as being merely opposed to 'the Temple'; it is not likely that there is any reference to a supposed custom of going from house to house to partake of a common meal.

(*b*) In 1 Co 11^{17-34} we have an undoubted reference to a meal taken in common (δεῖπνον, probably, though not necessarily, an *evening* meal) and combined with the Eucharist, when the Corinthians were in meeting assembled (ἐν ἐκκλησίᾳ, v.^{18}); abuses of greed and drunkenness are censured, and St. Paul promises to 'set the rest in order' whensoever he comes. From this passage most writers have concluded that the earliest custom was for the Christians to combine the Eucharist with a meal taken in common. Lightfoot (*Apost. Fath.*^{2} pt. 2, ii. 313) and Duchesne (*Origines*, p. 48, in Eng. ed. p. 49 n.) further deduce that the meal came first and the Eucharist 'at a late stage in the entertainment'; this (apparently) being suggested by the emphasis laid by St. Paul on our Lord's having taken the Eucharistic cup 'after supper' (μετὰ τὸ δειπνῆσαι, v.^{25}). Batiffol (*Études*, 1st ser. p. 281) thinks that the union of meal and Eucharist was an innovation of the Corinthians, and that it is the union itself that St. Paul censures. If so, we cannot argue any common custom from this passage. Against this view, Ermoni (*L'Agapé*, p. 9 ff.) truly remarks that St. Paul does not attack the thing itself, but only the abuse of greed and drunkenness, seeing that each one ate what he had brought, not partaking with others. St. Paul would not, Ermoni says, have bidden them wait for one another if the meal itself, in union with the Eucharist, were the thing condemned. All knew that the Eucharist began when the community were assembled. And, further, the Fathers who comment on the passage all see in it the Agape and Eucharist combined, — Chrysostom, Theodoret, Augustine, Jerome,—though Chrysostom, imbued as he is with the discipline of his own time (of fasting communion), puts the Eucharist first; Augustine says that it was St. Paul that gave the rule of fasting communion in consequence of the abuse at Corinth (*Ep.* cxviii. [liv., Bened.] *ad Januarium*, § 8).

(*c*) In Jude, and probably in 2 Peter, we have the first trace of the *name* 'Agape.' In Jude ^{12} we read of 'hidden rocks in your love-feasts when they feast with you, shepherds that without fear feed themselves' (οἱ ἐν ταῖς ἀγάπαις ὑμῶν σπιλάδες, συνευωχούμενοι, κ.τ.λ.). The reading ἀγάπαις (BKLℵ, etc.) is no doubt correct, and is supported by the

Vulgate (*epulis*) and the Syriac (ܒܫܪܘܬ̈ܗܘܢ), but AC have ἀπάταις, influenced by the *v.l.* in 2 P 2^{13}. Here, then, we have a common feast called Agape, but nothing is said of the Eucharist. There is no necessary connexion of the feast with the Eucharist in Jude, nor yet any necessary separation. Batiffol endeavours to get over this witness to the Agape by translating ἀγάπαι by 'love,' saying that Jude elsewhere has ἀγάπη in this sense (v.^{21}; cf. ἀγαπητοί, vv.$^{3.\ 17}$), and that he uses plurals for singulars elsewhere,—in v.^{8} δόξας (Vulg. *majestatem*, Syr. also has singular), and in v.^{13} αἰσχύνας (Vulg. *confusiones*, but Syr. has singular). There is, however, no reason for taking these plurals as singular in meaning; in the former case 'dignities' makes the only good sense, and in the latter the plural, as meaning 'each his own shame,' is very suitable. Thus Batiffol's translation in v.^{12} can hardly be accepted. But in any case the common feast itself (if not the name 'Agape') is borne witness to by Jude. In the parallel passage 2 P 2^{13} we have at least one variation: 'Spots (σπῖλοι) and blemishes, revelling in their love-feasts (ἀγάπαις) while they feast with you' (συνευωχούμενοι ὑμῖν). Here we note the variation of σπιλάδες and σπῖλοι; and the reading ἀγάπαις, which is supported by B and by the A corrector, the Vulgate, Pocock's Syriac (the Peshitta does not contain Jude or 2 Peter), Sahidic, and Ethiopic, is disputed by A*C, which have ἀπάταις both here and in Jude. Deissmann (*Bibl. Stud.* p. 365) and Batiffol (*op. cit.* p. 283) assume the latter to be the true reading without even mentioning the former; and Batiffol builds an argument on ἀπάταις—that the writer of 2 Peter did not see any reference to the Agape in the Jude passage that was before him. On the other hand, Lightfoot (*op. cit.* ii. 313) and Bigg (*Internat. Crit. Com. in loc.*) treat ἀπάταις as an obvious error; and this is probably true, ΑΓΑΠΑΙΣ passing very easily into ΑΠΑΤΑΙΣ.

2. Ecclesiastical writings up to A.D. 300.—(*a*) We may pass over Clement of Rome (though his mention in § 44 of the presbyters 'offering the gifts of the episcopate' is thought by Lightfoot to include contributions to the Agape) and come to the *Didache*, which, in common with almost all writers, we may date very early in the 2nd century. In this work (§ 9) we find, after instructions on baptism, fasting, and prayer, directions for the 'Eucharist' (περὶ δὲ τῆς εὐχαριστίας οὕτω εὐχαριστήσατε), with thanksgivings first over the cup and then over the 'broken bread' (κλάσμα); to the latter is attached a prayer that the Church may be gathered together. In these formulas we have no reference to our Lord's words at the Last Supper, or to the sacrament of His body and blood; nor is there anything in common between them and the Eucharistic passages of Ignatius and Justin Martyr. After them follows a prohibition against any of the unbaptized eating and drinking of the 'Eucharist,' and we then read (§ 10): 'After ye are *satisfied* (μετὰ τὸ ἐμπλησθῆναι), thus give ye thanks,' and the thanksgiving is for God's holy name, for the 'knowledge, faith, and immortality made known,' for God's power, and because the Creator had given food and drink for enjoyment (εἰς ἀπόλαυσιν), and had bestowed spiritual food and drink and eternal life. A prayer is added for the protection and gathering in of the Church, ending with 'Hosanna.' Then comes a 'fencing of the tables' and 'Maranatha.' But prophets may 'give thanks' as much as they desire (εὐχαριστεῖν ὅσα θέλουσιν). Of all this there are many interpretations. Batiffol (*op. cit.* p. 284) thinks that the Eucharist alone is here referred to; he takes the words 'after ye are satisfied' metaphorically, as a souvenir of Jn 6^{12} (though that tells against his view). He considers that as only the cup and the bread are mentioned, we cannot have here an Agape; while in the thanksgiving after 'being satisfied' spiritual nourishment is spoken of, which would be inapplicable to an Agape. Dom Leclercq also (*Dict. d'Archéol. Chrét.*, *s.v.* 'Agape,' col. 792) thinks that the *Didache* does not mention the Agape, but that it does not contradict the supposition of its existence; he does not, however, consider that the first formulas are the words used to *consecrate* the bread and wine. Mr. Box likewise (*JThSt*, iii. 363 ff.) holds that the *Didache* formulas are for the Eucharist, but he believes that the Agape followed the Eucharist and must be inserted before the words 'after ye are satisfied.' Prof. Ermoni, on the other hand, holds (*op. cit.* p. 17 ff.) that, as the *Didache* in § 14 speaks of the Sunday Eucharist ('gather yourselves together and break bread and give thanks,—*or* celebrate the Eucharist, εὐχαριστήσατε,—first confessing your transgressions, that your sacrifice may be pure'), the earlier sections must speak only of the Agape; and he concludes that the two ordinances were then separate, all the baptized being allowed to attend the Agape, but only the pure and holy (§ 15) the Eucharist. He takes εὐχαριστία in §§ 9, 10 as meaning no more than 'thanksgiving.' None of these theories appears to be so probable as that of Bp. Lightfoot (*op. cit.* ii. 313) and Dr. Keating (*The Agape*, p. 53), that the *Didache* writer means that the Agape was joined on to and preceded the Eucharist. The reference in §§ 9, 10 would then be to the two combined; the mention of the Sunday *synaxis* in § 14 does not really militate against this. The Agape probably, in the *Didache* as in 1 Co 11, came first, with the formulas given there as graces before and after meat (so Bp. J. Wordsworth, *Holy Communion*, p. 46); and after the people were satisfied came the fencing of the tables (§ 10 *s.f.*), which, as Zahn (*Forsch. zur Gesch. des NT Kanons*, 3rd pt. p. 293 f.) suggests, would be the connecting link between Agape and Eucharist. The prayers for the Eucharist, on this view, are not given; but prophets might use any words which they thought suitable. It is not improbable that the earliest Eucharistic worship was, in the main, extemporaneous. This theory makes εὐχαριστία in the *Didache* include the Agape. As the common meal was holy and so closely joined to the Eucharist, there was not in the thought of the writer such a sharp distinction between the two that one name might not be applied to both (cf. Ignatius below), or that the meal itself should not be conceived of as giving a spiritual blessing, as in the thanksgiving 'after being satisfied.' It is remarkable that the writer of the *Apostolic Constitutions* (vii. 25 f.), owing to the changed conditions of his day, in adapting the *Didache* turns this thanksgiving into a thanksgiving 'after partaking' (μετάληψιν) of the Eucharist.—There is another passage in the *Didache* (§ 11) which should be noticed. A prophet who 'orders a table (ὁρίζων τράπεζαν) in the Spirit' must not eat of it. The Eucharist therefore cannot be referred to. The phrase may be applied to an Agape, but Batiffol is probably right in thinking that merely gifts to the poor are meant, and that there is nothing liturgical about this passage.

(*b*) Ignatius (*c.* 110 A.D.) speaks (*Ephes.* 20) of 'breaking one bread, which is the medicine of immortality and the antidote that we should not die but live for ever in Jesus Christ'; and in *Rom.* 7 says: 'I desire the bread of God, which is the flesh of Christ . . . and for a draught I desire His blood, which is love (ἀγάπη) incorruptible' (see below, iii. *c*). In *Smyrn.* 8 he says: 'Let that be a valid Eucharist which is under the bishop . . . it is not lawful apart from the bishop either to baptize or to hold a love-feast (οὔτε ἀγάπην ποιεῖν).' In the first two passages Ignatius clearly speaks of the Eucharist, and it is remarkable that he uses ἀγάπη in connexion with it; while the most obvious interpretation of the last passage is that ἀγάπη includes both the love-feast and the Eucharist, which would therefore be held together in Ignatius' time. This is Lightfoot's conclusion (*op. cit.* i. 400 f., ii. 312 f.). But Batiffol takes ἀγάπη here of the Eucharist, 'par une abstraction,' and thinks that the metaphorical use of the word in *Rom.* 7 bears out his view. He denies that 'Agape' was at this early time used of a feast. He also says that the 4th cent. interpolator of Ignatius took the words in question to mean the Eucharist [the interpolator being probably the writer of the *Apostolic Constitutions*, see Brightman, *Lit. E. and W.* p. xxxiv ff., though Lightfoot gives an argument to the contrary, *op. cit.* i. 265 n.]. The interpolator has, 'not to baptize, nor to make an oblation (προσφέρειν), nor to offer (προσκομίζειν) sacrifice, nor to celebrate a feast (δοχήν).' Here the Eucharist and the love-feast are spoken of as quite separate. This was obviously the case in the 4th cent., and the interpolator is only introducing the customs of his own day; but this has no bearing on the sense of the true Ignatius [δοχή = ἀγάπη frequently in the 4th cent., see, *e.g.*, Lightfoot, ii. 312, and below (*r*)]. Robinson (*Encyc. Bibl. s.v.* 'Eucharist') does not think that Eucharist and Agape are in Ignatius convertible terms; if, he says, the Agape required the presence or sanction of the bishop, *a fortiori* so would the Eucharist. This does not really explain why Ignatius should join baptism and the Agape without mentioning the Eucharist, as would be the case if his ἀγάπη does not include the Eucharist. Lightfoot's opinion, then, seems to be by far the most probable. The phrase 'to baptize and hold the Agape' would be nearly equivalent to Tertullian's 'to dip and offer.' A woman may not, that Father says, 'tinguere nec offerre,' *i.e.* baptize or celebrate the Eucharist (*de Virg. Vel.* 9; cf. *de Exh. Cast.* 7: 'et offers et tinguis et sacerdos es tibi solus').

(*c*) Pliny's letter (*Ep.* xcvi.) to Trajan (A.D. 112) may next be considered, so far as it bears on the Agape. He says that certain Christian renegades had stated to him that the Christians were wont on a fixed day (*stato die*) to assemble before dawn and to repeat antiphonally a hymn to Christ as to a god, and to bind themselves by an oath (*sacramento*) not to commit any wrong . . . ; which done, they had been accustomed to separate and to come together again to take food, but that ordinary and innocent (*promiscuum tamen et innoxium*); and even this they had ceased to do after [Pliny's] edict, in which he had forbidden guilds (*hetærias*) according to [Trajan's] command. Thus there was a morning religious service and a meal later in the day (which, however, was innocent, and gave no countenance to the charge of indiscriminate immorality made against the Christians), and the second meeting was given up. Various views of the meaning of this passage have been held. With Lightfoot (*op. cit.* i. 13 ff., 50 ff.,—a long and careful account,—ii. 313) and Probst (*Lehre und Gebet*, p. 350 f.), we may consider the morning service to have been the Eucharist, and that there is some confusion between the double meaning of the word *sacramentum* ('oath' and 'sacrament'), or that the two sacraments of baptism and the Eucharist are confused; while the later meeting was for the Agape, which, in consequence of Trajan's action, was given up in Bithynia. The separation between Agape and Eucharist would either have taken place some time before Pliny,—perhaps, as Probst thinks (following Augustine), in St. Paul's time,—or else have been recent, and due to Trajan's well-known hostility to clubs. It is inconceivable that the Christians should have given up the Eucharist, and this consideration is against Batiffol's idea (*op. cit.* p. 288), that the first meeting was only for praise and prayer, and the second only for the Eucharist,—that being the meaning, he says, of 'ordinary and innocent food,'—the Agape not yet existing. He thinks that the Eucharist no less than the Agape would be contrary to Trajan's edict; and that, had the Eucharist been celebrated at the morning meeting, the apostates would have said so, for they had no reason for hiding anything. Dr. Armitage Robinson thinks (*op. cit.* § 17) that we cannot deduce from Pliny's letter that the Eucharist and the Agape had once been united, and that they were at that time, or had been at some previous time, separated; he considers that the renegades had given up the common meal, but that the Christians, as far as we know, had given up nothing. The renegades, however, had given up Christianity altogether, and they spoke of what had been given up before the persecution broke out,—they can hardly refer to any but the whole body of Christians in Bithynia. Dom Leclercq (*op. cit.* col. 795) thinks that the early meeting was the one which was given up; but the Latin will hardly bear this construction. None of these criticisms seems to the present writer to have shaken Lightfoot's position,

(*d*) Justin Martyr (*Apol.* 65–67) openly describes the Eucharist; for, as Batiffol shows (*Etudes*, 1st ser. p. 18), the *disciplina arcani* hardly existed in his day; but he does not mention the Agape. Leclercq (*op. cit.* col. 796) thinks that his silence does not exclude it, for he had only to defend what was attacked. But surely the Agape was a ground of attack? Keating (*op. cit.* p. 59) thinks that it had been given up generally, because of Trajan's edict; and with this opinion we may agree. The unessential nature and partial existence of the Agape are the conclusions to which the early evidence points.

(*e*) The date of Celsus is disputed. Keim, Funk, Aubé, Renan, and Mozley place it *c.* 177 A.D. For a careful discussion see Lightfoot, *Ap. Fath.* pt. 2, i. 530 f.; he gives reasons for thinking that the date should be put before A.D. 161. Origen (*c. Cels.* i. 1) says that Celsus' first accusation against the Christians was 'that they were accustomed to hold secret meetings among themselves, forbidden by the laws (ὡς συνθήκας κρύβδην πρὸς ἀλλήλους ποιουμένων, κ.τ.λ.). . . . And he would calumniate the so-called Agape of the Christians among themselves (καὶ βούλεται διαβαλεῖν τὴν καλουμένην ἀγάπην Χριστιάνων πρὸς ἀλλήλους) as taking its rise from the common danger,' etc. Batiffol (Letter in the *Guardian*, Jan. 7, 1903) argues that ἀγάπη must mean 'love' here, since πρὸς ἀλλήλους follows. No doubt the phrase 'Agape among themselves' is not an elegant one, but Batiffol's interpretation makes καλουμένην meaningless; 'so-called love' has no sense. The expression is parallel to the phrase above (συνθήκας κρύβδην πρ. ἀλλ.). May there not be a *double entendre* in the second phrase, the word ἀγάπη being used in its technical sense, with an ironical reference to the primary one? Celsus would mean 'the so-called Agape of the Christians, the feast of mutual love.' He could not intend to condemn Christian love as 'arising from the common danger and having a power that transcends oaths.' Origen clearly understands him to refer to the Agape, and this seems to be the only possible meaning of his words.

(*f*) Minucius Felix (for the date see Lightfoot, *op. cit.* i. 534, who puts it at *c.* 160 A.D.; and Salmon in Smith-Wace, *Dict. Chr. Biog.*, who puts it at 234; Keim gives 177) combats accusations of the heathen with regard to Christian assemblies. He says (*Octavius*, xxxi. 5): 'The feasts (*convivia*) which we hold (*colimus*) are chaste and temperate; we neither indulge ourselves in luxurious repasts (*epulis*) nor protract our feast (*convivium*) with strong drink, but we blend cheerfulness with gravity.' This can only refer to a meal, not to the Eucharist, to which the accusations of drunkenness and greed could not refer, though Batiffol thinks that Minucius is here alluding to it alone.

(*g*) Lucian in his satire *de Morte Peregrini*, § 12 (written probably not long after A.D. 165, Lightfoot, *op. cit.* i. 141, 345), says that when Peregrinus was in prison, 'old women—widows they are called—and orphan children might be seen waiting about the doors of the prison. . . . Then various meals were brought in and sacred formularies (λόγοι ἱεροί) of theirs were repeated.' Whether Lucian was primarily satirizing the Christians or the Cynics, we have probably here, as elsewhere, allusions to Christian history and customs, and in this case to the Agape (see below, *i*).

(*h*) The *Epistle to Diognetus* (date uncertain; probably *c.* 170 A.D., though some argue for a later date) says of the Christians that 'they partake of the same table, not of the same bed' (τράπεζαν κοινὴν παρατίθενται, ἀλλ' οὐ κοίτην), evidently alluding to the accusation of Œdipodean incests made against the Christians. As Leclercq (*op. cit.* col. 796) observes, this accusation seems to refer to the Agape, while that of Thyestean banquets refers to the Eucharist, the feeding on the body and blood of Christ being misunderstood; and the τράπεζα κοινή would apply less to an Eucharist than to a repast where the guests lay at meat, there being a paronomasia between κοινή and κοίτη.

(*i*) In some texts of the *Acts of Paul and Thecla* (§ 25), in connexion with a meal of bread with vegetables, salt, and water, we read: 'There was within the tomb a great Agape' (or 'much love,' ἀγάπη πολλή, Lat. *gaudium magnum*). But in the uncertainty as to the date of the writing, which has probably a very early substratum, though in its present form it is a late work, we can lay no stress on this quotation, especially for the name 'Agape' (see Ramsay. *Ch. in Rom. Emp.* ch. xvi.; also Conybeare, *Mon. of Early Christianity*, p. 75, who strangely takes this meal for a primitive Eucharist).—In the *Acts of Perpetua and Felicitas* (§ 17, Ruinart, *Act. Mart. Sinc.*^{2} p. 100), which must be dated probably at the very end of the 2nd cent., we have a reference to the custom of publicly entertaining at a free meal those condemned to wild beasts (cf. Tertullian, *Apol.* 42 [*Patr. Lat.* i. 556]). Perpetua and her companions turned the entertainment into an Agape ('non cœnam liberam sed agapen cœnarent').

(*j*) Irenæus does not mention the Agape. Dom Leclercq (*op. cit.* col. 796) thinks that this does not exclude its existence in Gaul; this Father's treatise being an exposition of Christian doctrine, no mention of the Agape is to be expected. And Dr. Keating comes to the same conclusion, believing that no connexion between Agape and Eucharist had survived in Gaul. But Batiffol takes Irenæus' silence as disproving the existence of the Agape anywhere.

(*k*) Clement of Alexandria undoubtedly refers to meals taken in common, and to their being called 'Agapæ.' He denounces the drunkenness and greed which disgraced some such repasts (*Pæd.* ii. 1): 'They . . . dare to apply the name Agape to pitiful suppers redolent of savour and sauces, dishonouring the good and saving work of the Word, the consecrated Agape, with pots and pourings of sauce. . . . Gatherings for the sake of mirth . . . we name rightly suppers . . . but such entertainments (ἑστιάσεις) the Lord has not called Agapæ.' So in *Strom.* iii. 2 he denounces the licentiousness of the feasts of some heretics (perhaps the cause of the heathen slanders), and says that he will not call them 'Agapæ.' According to the *Church Quarterly* Reviewer (July 1902, p. 500), Clement protests against the use of the word 'Agape' at all for common meals, and not only against its application to these feasts of drunkenness and revelling; but this hardly appears from Clement's own words. A more probable interpretation is that meals taken in common were ordinarily called 'Agapæ' in his time, and that he would not allow the name where abuses were rife. In any case, he is a witness for the ordinary use of the name, whether he approved of it or not. For Clement and the Agape see Bigg's *Christian Platonists of Alexandria*, p. 102 f. He inclines to the idea that the Eucharist and the Agape were celebrated together in Clement's time at Alexandria, in the evening. In connexion with the passages from Jude and 2 Peter, Dr. Bigg points out (*Internat. Crit. Com. in loc.*) that Clement uses εὐωχία of the Agape (*Pæd.* ii. 1), which he also calls ἡ ἐν λόγῳ τρυφή (*ib.* 12, aliter 1), using τρ. in a good sense as opposed to ἡδονή, the pleasure of eating and drinking; though it is also just possible, as Dr. Keating suggests (*The Agape*, p. 86), that Clement is referring by this latter phrase to the Eucharist as preceding the Agape ('public banquets *after* the rich fare which is in the Word,' μετὰ τὴν ἐν λόγῳ τρυφήν). But see below, iii. (*b*).

(*l*) Tertullian refers more than once to the Agape, or as he also, translating, calls it, 'dilectio.' He gives a full account of it in *Apol.* 39 (*Patr. Lat.* i. 531 ff.), and says: 'Among the Greeks our supper is called *dilectio*.' In § 9 he had dealt with Thyestean banquets; in § 39 he returns to the heathen accusations, dealing with the charge of incest, and the words used (*e.g.* 'triclinium,' 'discumbere,' 'cœnula') show that a meal in common is referred to, though Batiffol understands him to be speaking symbolically of the Eucharist throughout. In the treatise *ad Martyres* (§ 2, *Patr. Lat.* i. 696), Tertullian speaks of the consolations of Christians in prison 'through the care of the Church, the brethren's Agape' (cf. *Acts of Perpetua*, above); but here the meaning probably is 'love' merely, though the Greek word is used. In his Montanist days he brings against the Catholics the very accusations which he had refuted in his *Apologeticus*. In *de Jejuniis*, 17 (*Patr. Lat.* ii. 1029, *c.* 217 A.D.?), he accuses them of licentiousness in the Agape: 'Apud te agape in cacabis fervet: fides in culinis calet, spes in ferculis iacet. *Sed maior his est agape*, qui per hanc adolescentes tui cum sororibus dormiunt,' etc. This cannot possibly refer to the Eucharist.—Tertullian's style is so difficult that it is not surprising if scholars do not agree in interpreting his words; but it is hard to escape the conclusion, especially from the *Apologeticus* passage, that the Agape, as we generally understand the term, was in common use in his time. We read here of preliminary prayers, sitting at meat, handwashing, the lighting of the lamps, psalms and hymns, prayer and dismissal; a collection was taken for the poor. This description shows that the Agape was held in the evening. On the other hand, the Eucharist in Tertullian's time was in the morning (*de Cor. Mil.* 3 [*Patr. Lat.* ii. 99], *etiam antelucanis coetibus*, where *etiam* perhaps means that the usual custom was to celebrate the Eucharist *after* dawn, save in time of persecution; cf. *de Fuga in Persec.* 14 [*Patr. Lat.* ii. 141], where the same is implied; see J. Wordsworth, *Min. of Grace*, p. 317). For a full discussion of Tertullian and the Agape, see Keating, p. 62 ff., Batiffol, p. 291 ff., Leclercq, col. 802 ff.; Ermoni, p. 28 ff.

(*m*) There is not much that need detain us after

this till the end of the 3rd cent., but the *Canons of Hippolytus* are important as introducing a whole series of 4th cent. 'Church Orders,' which are, as some think, derived from these *Canons*, or more probably are their collateral descendants. For the date, etc., see Achelis, *Die Canones Hippolyti* (*TU* vi. 4), p. 212 ff., and Funk, *Didasc. et Const. Ap.*, 1906. The latter thinks that the *Canons* are of the 6th cent. or later, and derived from *Apost. Const.* bk. viii.; but most writers take them to be a somewhat interpolated work either of the Roman or of the Alexandrian Church early in the 3rd cent. (so Achelis, Duchesne, J. Wordsworth, Brightman, Morin). We know the work only in an Arabic translation. In these *Canons* (§§ 164–177, ed. Achelis), the Agape, 'if there is one,' is to be on Sunday at lamplighting, the bishop being present and praying, and psalms being sung; the people are to be dismissed before dark. The feast is described as 'prepared for the poor.' The catechumens receive the 'bread of exorcism' but are forbidden to eat at the 'meal of the Lord.' Christians are to eat and drink to satiety, not to drunkenness or scandal. The exhortations of the bishop at the meal (he speaks sitting) are referred to. It is not, however, correct to say that the *Canons* use the *name* 'Agape' ('in agapis κυριακαῖς,' Achelis, Haneberg); for, as Riedel (*Die Kirchenrechtsquellen des Patr. Alex.*, 1900, p. 221 ff.) points out, the Arabic *wălîmah* does not mean anything more than a meal or feast; it is not equivalent to the technical 'Agape.'

(*n*) In the *Acts of James and Marianus* († 259 A.D.), James, speaking of the heavenly banquet and a martyr Agapius, says: 'Ad Agapium cæterorumque martyrum beatorum pergo convivium. . . . Quo cum . . . quasi ad agapen spiritu dilectionis et caritatis raperemur,' etc. (Ruinart², p. 228). Here the heavenly feast is the antitype of the earthly Agape.

(*o*) Origen, except in the quotation from Celsus given above, hardly refers to the Agape, but deals at length with the Eucharist. Probably the Agape was, at least for the time, less common in his day. We find, however, in a work ascribed to Origen, references to the funeral agapæ, for which see below, § 4.

(*p*) Cyprian (*Ep.* lxii. [lxiii.] 16, *c.* 253 A.D.) explains why the Eucharist (*dominicum*) is celebrated in the morning and not after supper. While it was right, he says, for Christ to 'offer [the mingled cup] about the evening of the day, that the very hour of sacrifice might symbolize the setting and the evening of the world,' yet 'we celebrate the resurrection of the Lord in the morning.' Elsewhere (*ad Donatum*, 16) Cyprian describes the supper in common, the 'temperate meal' (*convivium sobrium*) resounding with psalms. Thus the Agape and the Eucharist were quite distinct in his day. For other allusions to the Agape in Cyprian, see Keating, *op. cit.* p. 102 f.

(*q*) In the *Acts of Pionius*, § 3 († 250 A.D.; see Ruinart², p. 140), we read of what appears to be a Saturday Agape with solemn prayer ('facta ergo oratione solemni cum die sabbato sanctum panem et aquam degustavissent'). The 'bread and water' could not be the Eucharist.

(*r*) The older form of the *Didascalia* (as given by Dr. Hauler in the *Verona Fragments*, xxvi. p. 38), which perhaps belongs to the 3rd cent. or the beginning of the 4th, speaks of the Agape by name. It is a feast given to old women (*aniculis*); a portion is to be given to the bishop (*sacerdoti*), even if he be not present at the Agapæ and distributions (*in agapis et erogationibus*), and so also to the other clergy. Similarly the Syriac *Didascalia*, edited by Mrs. Gibson (Eng. tr. p. 48), which has 'widows' for 'old women'; and also the parallel passage of the *Apostolic Constitutions* (ii. 28, *c.* 375 A.D.), which has 'agape or entertainment' (ἀγάπην ἤτοι δοχήν, cf. the Ignatian interpolation above, **2** (*b*)), and expands the *Didascalia* without adding to the sense.

3. Evidence of the 4th cent. and later.—It is not disputed that in the 4th cent. there was a custom of having meals in common and of calling them 'Agapæ'; and also that the Eucharist was absolutely distinct from them.

(*a*) The 'Church Orders' make this plain. [For a description of them and for their dates, see Cooper-Maclean, *The Testament of our Lord*, pp. 7 ff., 25 ff.; Funk believes that the dates of most of them are later than those there given]. The *Egyptian Church Order* (*c.* 310 A.D.), found in the *Sahidic Ecclesiastical Canons* or *Egyptian Heptateuch*, the *Ethiopic Church Order* (*c.* 335 A.D.), found in the *Ethiopic Statutes* (lately published by Mr. Horner), and the Latin *Verona Fragments* (*c.* 340 A.D.), edited by Dr. Hauler, and the *Testament of our Lord* (*c.* 350 A.D.; some think that it was edited in its present form *c.* 400 A.D., though this seems less likely), all speak of the common meal, which the *Egyptian Church Order* and the *Verona Fragments* call 'the Lord's Supper.' They all forbid the catechumens to partake of it, though they allow them to receive the 'bread of exorcism' [Ethiopic: 'of blessing'] and a cup (the bread and cup are omitted in the *Testament*). The bishop presides and exhorts; all eat abundantly, but soberly and in silence; drunkenness is strongly forbidden, and scandal is not to be brought on the host. We must also notice that the Egyptian and Ethiopic books say that the people are each to receive a portion of bread, and 'this is a blessing, and not an Eucharist like the body of the Lord' (the *Testament* has a similar phrase). This partaking of *eulogiæ* ('blessings'), or loaves given by the people at the offertory in the Eucharist, but not consecrated, afterwards became and still is very common in the East, and it is just possible that it may be a relic of the Agape. Perhaps the 'bread of exorcism' is something of this sort. In these Church Orders the Agape is a feast provided by the rich for the whole community; but it is not represented as being merely a 'charity supper' or a form of alms to the poor.

(*b*) The Agape is mentioned in three 4th cent. Councils. That of Laodicea in Phrygia (*c.* 370?) forbade the 'so-called Agape' to be held in the Lord's houses (κυριακοῖς) or in churches (*can.* 28), probably because of the prevalent abuses. The Third Council of Carthage (A.D. 397) made the same rule (*can.* 30, aliter 29; following one which orders that the 'sacrament of the altar shall always be celebrated fasting' except on Maundy Thursday). The Council of Gangra in Paphlagonia (date uncertain) endeavoured to restore the Agape to its former dignity, and forbade any to despise those who in the faith solemnized it (*can.* 11). This shows that the abuses of the Agape were leading to its discontinuance in Asia Minor.

(*c*) Pseudo-Pionius' *Life of Polycarp* can be used as evidence only for the 4th cent. (see Lightfoot, *Ap. Fath.* pt. 2, iii. 429 f.). The writer relates how Polycarp visited a certain bishop named Daphnus, who made an offering in his presence to a number of brethren, and set a little cask full of wine in the midst of them, which miraculously remained full though they drank from it. Here an Agape seems to be meant.

(*d*) The comment of Chrysostom on 1 Co 11 (*Hom.* 27) does not appear to give us any sure indication about the ordinary Agape in his own day. He uses the past tense, and from his language here, if taken alone, we might have supposed that the Agape had ceased in his time. In

Hom. 22 he describes how, after instruction, prayer, and 'communion of the mysteries,' the rich had been accustomed to bring materials for a feast from their houses to the church, and to entertain the poor there. Pseudo-Jerome and Theodoret in their comments on 1 Co 11 follow Chrysostom. Their evidence is good for what was the tradition of former custom, though not necessarily for that of Apostolic times (see above, § 1). In the same *Hom.* 27 and in *Hom.* 31 Chrysostom refers to the funeral-Agape of his own day (see below, § 4).

(*e*) Augustine speaks of the Agape in his own time as a charity supper (*c. Faust.* xx. 20). Faustus the Manichæan had represented the Christians as converting the heathen sacrifices into their Agapæ. Augustine denies this, and says that the Agape is a feeding of the poor ('agapes enim nostræ pauperes pascunt') with fruits or flesh meat. But whether the Agape was in his day celebrated regularly, or only as a funeral feast (see below § 4), we cannot say.

(*f*) The Agape in Egypt in the 5th cent., united with the Eucharist, is apparently attested by Socrates and Sozomen. The former says (*HE* v. 22): 'The Egyptians near Alexandria and the inhabitants of the Thebaid hold their religious assembly on the sabbath, but do not participate in the mysteries in the manner usual among Christians in general; for, having eaten and satisfied themselves with food of all kinds, making their offering (*προσφέροντες*, *i.e.* celebrating the Eucharist, as often) in the evening they partake of the mysteries.' Sozomen (*HE* vii. 19) says: 'There are several cities and villages in Egypt where, contrary to the usage established elsewhere, the people meet together on sabbath evenings, and, although they have dined previously, partake of the mysteries.' [For the Saturday Agape cf. the *Acts of Pionius*, above, 2 (*q*)]. Dom Leclercq (*op. cit.* col. 822) thinks that in Socrates and Sozomen there is no trace of an Agape, only of an Eucharist. But the words 'eating and satisfying themselves' certainly point to one, and the whole object of this exceptional custom would appear to be to keep up the example of the Last Supper.

(*g*) We notice, lastly, that as late as the Trullan Council (A.D. 692) the 'African practice of receiving the Eucharist on Maundy Thursday after a meal' is disapproved (*can.* 29), and Agapæ within the churches are forbidden (*can.* 74).

4. Funeral and Commemorative Agapæ.—These should probably be treated separately from the ordinary Agapæ, as being quite distinct in origin, and as having arisen later (Duchesne, *Origines*, p. 49 n., Eng. tr.). It will be a question whether some of the references already given should not have been placed under this head. The commemorative Agape was a Christianized form of the heathen *parentalia* or festival in honour of dead relatives (cf. Augustine, *Ep.* xxix. 9 *ad Alypium*); and the custom probably was, first to celebrate the Eucharist with prayer for the departed, and later in the day to hold an Agape. In the references to this custom in Tertullian and Cyprian, the Eucharist alone is explicitly mentioned; but probably an Agape is intended as well, as the Hippolytean *Canons* show. The custom seems to have spread as the veneration for the martyrs grew.

In the *Martyrdom of Polycarp* (§ 18) the Smyrnæans look forward to 'celebrating the birthday of his martyrdom, for the commemoration of those that have already fought in the contest,' etc. But we are not told *how* the commemoration was to be celebrated. The Leucian *Acts of John* (Gnostic; *c.* 170 A.D.? or perhaps earlier) speak of going 'to the tomb to break bread' (ed. Zahn, p. 231). This may be an Agape or the Eucharist. Tertullian (*de Cor. Mil.* 3 [*Patr. Lat.* ii. 99]), immediately before describing baptism and the Eucharist, says: 'We make oblations for the departed annually for their birthdays'; and in *de Monogam.* 10 (*Patr. Lat.* ii. 992) the widow 'prays for his [her husband's] soul . . . and offers (*i.e.* the Eucharist) on the anniversary of his falling asleep.' So in *de Exhort. Cast.* 11 [*Patr. Lat.* ii. 975], addressed to a widower about his departed wife, we read: 'For whose spirit thou prayest, and for whom thou offerest annual oblations.' The *Canons of Hippolytus* (above, 2 (*m*)) have this direction (§§ 169, 170): 'If there is a memorial of the dead, before they sit (at meat) let them partake of the mysteries, though not on the first day of the week ('neque tamen die prima'). After the oblation, let the bread of exorcism be distributed to them before they sit down.' This comes after the directions for the Sunday Agape, and before general rules for meals taken in common. We may notice here that the parallel passage in the *Apostolic Constitutions* (*c.* 375 A.D.), which follows an office for the departed, refers to the commemorative feasts *only*, not to the Sunday Agape (viii. 44; Lagarde, p. 276), and rebukes faults of drunkenness. In Cyprian (*Ep.* xxxiii. [xxxix.] 3, *ad clerum* [*Patr. Lat.* iv. 323]) we read of sacrifices being offered ('sacrificia offerimus') for martyrs and their anniversaries kept, and the last words probably refer to an Agape (so elsewhere in the Epistles). For many years after Cyprian's death they danced and sang round his grave, till this was stopped by Aurelius, bishop of Carthage (Augustine, *Serm.* cccxi. 5 [*Patr. Lat.* iv. 328 f.]); a feast is probably implied. The *Commentary on Job*, ascribed to Origen (Bk. iii. p. 238, ed. Lommatsch), speaks of these commemorations of the departed as being an opportunity for feeding the poor. In the 4th cent. we have an obscure canon of Elvira in Spain (*c.* 305 A.D.), forbidding lights in cemeteries 'per diem,' as disturbing the souls of the dead (*can.* 34). This may refer to a funeral Agape; the lamp-lighting rather points to this. Later, Gregory of Nazianzus (*Orat.* vi. 4 ff.) and Chrysostom (*Hom.* 47, *On Julian the Martyr*) bewail the drunkenness that was rife at these entertainments (cf. also Chrys. *Hom.* 27 *in* 1 *Cor.* 11, *Hom.* 31 *in Mt.* 9). Augustine tells us of the pious custom of his mother Monica at Milan, of bringing food 'ad memorias sanctorum,' as was usual in Africa; but that Ambrose had forbidden it (*Confess.* vi. 2), no doubt because of the 'revelries and lavish repasts in cemeteries,' which Augustine himself deplores (*Ep.* xxii. 6, *ad Aurelium*). He forbade these commemorative feasts himself in A.D. 392, and says that they were not universal in Italy, and that where they were customary they were abolished by the bishops (*ib.* 4, 5). Theodoret, however, in the 5th cent., tells us of yearly feasts in honour of martyrs; and the sermons ascribed to Eusebius of Alexandria (5th or 6th cent.? see Smith-Wace, *Dict. Chr. Biog.* iii. 305 f.) describe banquets given to the poor on Saints' days, 'the hosts considering that they are entertaining the martyrs themselves.' These sermons speak of the disorders and drunken revels going on till daybreak; 'while aside the priest prays for them and consecrates the body of Christ, they separate' (Migne, *Patr. Gr.* lxxxvi. 357 f., 364 f., quoted by Leclercq). At the funeral itself feasts were common. Paulinus (*Ep.* xiii. 11, A.D. 397) tells us of a funeral banquet at Rome called an Agape, given for the poor in the basilica of St. Peter, by Pammachius.

In Syriac writers Agapæ are called *nyāḥāthā*, lit. 'rests' or 'refreshments'; so in Jude and 2 Peter. This word, however, has no special reference to the dead, nor can it be argued from it that the Syriac translator of Jude and 2 Peter took the meaning of ἀγάπαι to be 'commemorations of the dead.' On the other hand (see Payne-Smith, *Thesaurus Syriacus, s.v.*), the word is often in Syriac writings coupled with *dūkhrānê*, the ordinary word for 'Saints' days,' and then the reference is without doubt to commemorative Agapæ.

5. Archæological and epigraphic evidence.—This seems to the present writer not to carry us far. It is too vague, and the dates are too uncertain to lead us to any sure conclusion about the Agape. Reference may, however, be made to Dom Leclercq's art. in the *Dictionnaire d'Archéologie Chrétienne*, where this side of the subject is treated very fully with excellent illustrations. It will suffice here to mention one or two examples of evidence adduced by the author. There is a fresco in the Capella Greca of the Cemetery of St. Priscilla near Rome, discovered in 1893. The multiplication of the loaves and fishes is represented as a banquet, with seven persons lying at meat. Dom Leclercq thinks that this shows that at the time of the fresco the Agape and the Eucharist were united. But this is very precarious. Of inscriptions alluding to the heavenly Agape may be mentioned πῖε ἐν Θεῷ (Leclercq, *op. cit.* col. 832) and 'Anima dulcis pie zeses in Deo: dulcis anima pie zeses vivas,' where probably 'pie'=πῖε, 'zeses'=ζήσῃς, and perhaps 'vivas'='bibas' (*ib.* col. 833).

iii. Review of the evidence.—(*a*) **General deductions.**—Looking back at the quotations and references detailed above, we may obtain some idea of the history of the Agape. To the present writer it appears, after a careful consideration of what has been written in the last few years, that Bp. Lightfoot's view of the matter has not, in the main, been shaken. The evidence seems to point to the Apostles, probably because of the precedent of the Last Supper, having combined the Eucharist with a common meal, which before long was called the Agape. Yet the Agape was not universal. It was dropped, in some places earlier than in others, and then resumed under somewhat different forms. At first, as the evidence seems to show, the Agape was a meal for the whole community. To call it always a 'charity supper,' as it undoubtedly became in some or in most places later on, is a little misleading. It was a supper for all, rich and poor alike, though no doubt provided almost entirely by the rich, a sign of Christian unity and marked by liturgical forms. Later, the thought of the rich providing for the poor and of the Agape being a charity became prominent; and this was perhaps largely due to the rise of funeral or commemorative feasts, in which the relatives of the deceased gave in his honour, or rich people generally gave in honour of a martyr, a banquet to the poor. These commemorative feasts and the ordinary Agapæ seem to have been confused, at least in many places, during the 4th century. It is important to bear in mind that the custom of the Agape, being a non-essential, varied in different countries. Perhaps it was never quite universal; certainly it was of only partial adoption for the greater part of the first four centuries.

To summarize the evidence, we may say that in Acts and 1 Corinthians the Eucharist and the Agape seem to have been combined; in Jude and 2 Peter perhaps dissociated. In the *Didache* and Ignatius they were probably combined, and perhaps also in Bithynia quite up to the time of Pliny, when they were separated and the Agape dropped. In Justin the Agape does not seem to have been actually existent, perhaps on account of Trajan's Edict. In Celsus, Minucius Felix, and the *Epistle to Diognetus* it is found existing. In Gaul, at the end of the 2nd cent. it had probably been dropped, as it is not mentioned by Irenæus. Lucian's satire and the *Acts of Perpetua* probably testify to the custom of a 'prison Agape.' Clement of Alexandria, Tertullian, Cyprian, the *Canons of Hippolytus*, and some *Acts of Martyrs* in the 3rd cent., attest the Agape as existing and separate from the Eucharist; the old *Didascalia* describes it as a feast to old women. In the 4th cent. 'Church Orders' the Agape is a common meal, not *only* a charity supper; it is entirely separate from the Eucharist. From the canons of the Councils of Laodicea, Gangra, and Carthage (No. 3), we gather that it was held in churches; perhaps the evidence shows a tendency for it to disappear at this time. Augustine treats it as a charity supper, 'a feeding of the poor.' In the 5th cent. there is the remarkable testimony of Socrates and Sozomen to the exceptional case of Agape and Eucharist combined in Egypt; but there is nothing to show that this custom had always existed there. It may, on the one hand, be a relic of old custom; or, on the other, it may be a revival, a piece of out-of-date antiquarianism. In the 7th cent. the Trullan Council shows that the Agape still existed.—Funeral or commemorative Agapæ are probably referred to by Tertullian, the *Acts of John*, and Cyprian, certainly in the *Canons of Hippolytus*, in the *Commentary on Job* (by Origen?), by Gregory of Nazianzus, Augustine, Chrysostom, and others.

(*b*) **Relative order of Agape and Eucharist when united.**—Did the Agape or the Eucharist come first? On the one hand, we have the precedent of the Last Supper, where the Eucharist followed the meal, and the suggestion in 1 Co 11 that the Corinthian Agape came first (see above, ii. 1). In the *Didache*, if the view taken above (ii. 2) be right, the Agape precedes, and the 'fencing of the tables' is followed by the Eucharist. In the exceptional case in the Thebaid in the 5th cent., the Agape (if there was one) clearly came first. On the other hand, in Ac 20^{11} we have the order, 'breaking bread' and 'eating.' If the former means the Eucharist and the latter the Agape, the order is reversed. It is quite possible, however, that 'breaking bread' and 'eating' are here one and the same thing, and refer to the Eucharist and the meal combined; in which case we can make no deduction from the words. As has been seen, Chrysostom, in his homily on 1 Corinthians, makes the Eucharist precede, *i.e.* not in his own day merely, but in the primitive ages. We need perhaps lay no great stress on the late evidence of the Thebaid on the one hand, or of Chrysostom on the other. The Fathers of the 4th or 5th cent. probably had no more knowledge of Christian antiquities in this department than we have. Chrysostom was no doubt influenced in his view of the Apostolic age by the customs of his own day, and the Christians of the Thebaid may have been merely trying to follow what appeared to them to have been the custom at the Last Supper. Confining ourselves, then, to the early evidence of NT and the *Didache*, it certainly seems more probable than not that the Agape came first, and that the Eucharist immediately followed. This is Bp. Lightfoot's view. Dr. Lock (in Hastings' *DB*, *s.v.* 'Love-feasts') inclines the other way; and so, more decidedly, does Mr. Box (*op. cit.*).

(*c*) **The name 'Agape.'**—It is important to consider why this word was applied to a meal. The Greek ἀγάπη is apparently first found in the LXX. Before NT it is exclusively found in Jewish documents. It is not, however, *only* biblical. Deissmann (*Bibl. Stud.* p. 199, Eng. tr.) quotes a passage in Philo (*Quod Deus immut.* § 14), who probably took the word from the LXX; the meaning is 'love to God.' ἀγάπη is also found in a scholium on Thucydides, but we do not know if the glossator was a Christian or not (see Deissmann, *op. cit.* p. 200). In OT and NT, except in the two passages Jude 12, 2 P 2[13], the word always means 'love.'

How, then, did it acquire its technical sense? Dr. Keating (paper in the *Guardian*, Dec. 24, 1902) suggests that it was because of the new commandment given at the Last Supper (Jn 13[34] ἵνα ἀγαπᾶτε ἀλλήλους); and this may very probably be the case. At any rate, the feast would be called 'love,' because it was the bond which united Christians together; and when (as in Ignatius) the name was applied to the Eucharist and the meal jointly, it would be especially suitable, because Christians are thus united to their Saviour. That this was the main idea of the name is confirmed by the phrase 'kiss of love,' φίλημα ἀγάπης (1 P 5[14]; cf. φίλ. ἅγιον, Ro 16[16], 1 Co 16[20], 2 Co 13[12], 1 Th 5[26]), which was no doubt in early times as in later ages, and as it is still in the East, one of the most significant features of Christian assemblies; by it the worshippers reminded themselves of their brotherhood. As the idea of a charity supper became prominent, after the separation of Eucharist and Agape, the name came to imply 'benevolence' rather than 'brotherly love.' Sometimes in Latin, and perhaps in Greek, *agape* came to mean no more than 'alms.' Thus Jerome speaks of widows being fond of display at Rome—'cum ad agapen vocaverint, præco conducitur' (*Ep.* xxii. 32, A.D. 384), and in the *Apostolic Constitutions* ἀγάπη is used of a charitable gift to a widow, apart from a supper. But this is not certain. The degeneration of the word is exactly parallel to that of our English 'charity.'

It is noteworthy that the name 'Agape' is very seldom given to commemorative feasts. In the passage of Paulinus given above (ii. § 4), however, the feast is so called.

As will be seen from the evidence produced above, the name 'Agape' is applied to a meal taken in common, if the deductions made in this article are correct, in the following: Jude, 2 Peter (probably), Ignatius, Celsus (probably), *Acts of Paul and Thecla* (perhaps), *Acts of Perpetua and Felicitas*, Clement of Alexandria, Tertullian, Origen (quoting Celsus), *Acts of James and Marianus*, the older *Didascalia*, and in the 4th cent. writers *passim*.

As in the case of other technical terms, it is probable that a double reference was not uncommon. Just as 'Agape' was used of a meal with an implied reference to Christian love, so it and its corresponding verb were sometimes used of Christian love with an implied reference to the love-feast. Thus in the Celsus passage (above, ii. 2 (*e*)) the reference is probably double. So in Ignatius, *Rom.* 7 (above, ii. 2 (*b*)), an Eucharistic passage ('I desire His blood, which is love incorruptible'), the primary reference is to love, but there is probably a secondary one to the Agape. And similarly in *Smyrn.* 7, the passage which immediately precedes that already quoted (ii. 2 (*b*)), though the words συνέφερεν δὲ αὐτοῖς ἀγαπᾶν must probably be rendered: 'It were expedient for them to have love,' and not, as Zahn and others suggest, 'to celebrate the Agape' (as if ἀγαπᾶν were equivalent to ἀγάπην ποιεῖν), yet the passage would seem to have an indirect allusion to the combined Eucharist and love-feast (see Lightfoot's note, *op. cit.* ii. 307).

(*d*) **Materials for the Agape.**—As to these we have very little evidence. In the *Didache* only a cup [of wine] and bread are explicitly mentioned. In the *Acts of Paul and Thecla*, § 25, 'five loaves of bread, with vegetables and salt besides, and water' are spoken of (Conybeare, *Monuments of Early Christianity*, p. 75); in the *Acts of Pionius*, only bread and water. Later on, Augustine mentions meat, poultry, cheese, milk, honey (*c. Faust.* xx. 20). Dean Plumptre (Smith-Cheetham, *Dict. Chr. Ant. s.v.* 'Agapae') suggests, from archæological evidence, that fish was commonly used. He adds that 'bread and wine were of course indispensable'; but this, as far as the wine is concerned, is not obvious, except when the Eucharist was combined with the Agape.

iv. ORIGIN OF THE AGAPE.—Many suggestions have been made on this subject. Most writers have seen in the custom an endeavour to follow the precedent of the Last Supper, when the Eucharist was combined with a meal. It is also thought that the early Christians were copying the Jews, who had social meals, or the Greeks and Romans, who had clubs, of which banquets were a prominent feature. The origin of the Agape has also been looked for in the funeral feasts which were common among both Jews and Gentiles. Or it has been thought to have arisen simply from the early communism of the Apostolic Church (Ac 4[32]).

These suggestions are not all mutually exclusive, and probably all of them have a solid foundation. It would be difficult to deny all association with the Last Supper. In that action of our Lord the Christians would find ample justification for joining their Agape to the Eucharist, or for making the Eucharist a part of the Agape. But then it is necessary to ask, What was the exact significance of the Supper celebrated by Jesus? This question is made difficult by the apparent discrepancy between the Gospel accounts, St. John suggesting that the Supper was celebrated some twenty-four hours before the Paschal lambs were killed, while the Synoptists would lead us to think that the Supper was the Passover itself. This difficulty cannot be fully considered here (see the discussion in Dr. Sanday's article 'Jesus Christ' in Hastings' *DB* ii. 633 ff.—the article has been republished in book form, 1904—and the literature enumerated there, *ib.* p. 638), but whatever view be taken of the Last Supper, that observance cannot fully account for the rise of the Agape. For, first, suppose that our Lord ate the real Paschal Supper on Maundy Thursday; if the Apostles had instituted the Agape in imitation of the Last Supper, it seems almost certain that the love-feast would have been held only once a year, at Easter. [We cannot use this as an argument for the Johannine account of the disputed chronology, for the connexion between the Agape and the Last Supper is assumed. But it is probable for other reasons (see Sanday, *loc. cit.*) that the Last Supper did not synchronize with the regular Paschal meal]. Next, suppose that the Last Supper was an anticipated Passover; then, if the Agape depends entirely on it, the difficulty just mentioned as to its being frequent instead of annual would not be taken away. Thirdly, let us take Mr. Box's suggestion (*JThSt*, iii. 360 ff.), that the Last Supper had its origin in the Jewish *Qiddūsh* or weekly sanctification of the Sabbath, an ancient Rabbinical observance, and still a feature of the home life of the Jews. The family sit at table after the synagogue service at the beginning of the Sabbath (*i.e.* our Friday evening), and on the table are placed two loaves and wine. The father blesses the cup, and all the family drink of it; handwashing follows, and the bread is blessed and distributed. Then follows the Sabbath meal. This ceremony is not confined to the Sabbath, but also precedes other festivals, such as the Passover. This is certainly an attractive suggestion, and one which, if the Agape depended solely on the Last Supper, would account for its frequent, instead of annual, occurrence in the Christian Church. But there are several objections to it. Dr. Lambert (*JThSt*, iv. 184 ff.) has brought forward some of them. Two considerations seem fatal to it. It assumes that the Eucharist followed by the Agape (for Mr. Box believes the Eucharist to have come first) represented the Jewish *Qiddûsh* followed by a festive meal. But at the Last Supper the Eucharist certainly *followed* the meal (1 Co 11[25]); and the balance of the argument appears to be against the order required by this theory for the Christian Agape (see above, iii. (*b*)). And, further, the Paschal character of the Last Supper seems too prominent for us to be convinced that it was not *in some sense* a Paschal meal. If so, our difficulty as to the origin of the Agape remains, and we must look elsewhere for it, without indeed denying the influence of the Last Supper on the custom under discussion.

The environment of the Apostolic Church must certainly be considered in judging of the origin of the Agape. To the Jews common meals were quite familiar. The Essenes made a practice of them, living a sort of community life (Philo, *Quod omnis probus liber*; Jos. *BJ* ii. 8; Hippolytus, *Ref. Hær.* ix. 18 ff.). For other Jewish illustrations see Keating, *op. cit.* p. 20 ff. We may also cite the allusion to the heavenly banquet in 2 Es 2[38], 'Behold the number of those that be sealed in the feast of the Lord.' The guilds and associations in the heathen world at the beginning of our era were also very common; of these, banquets were usually a prominent feature (Lightfoot, *op. cit.* i. 18 ff.; Keating, p. 1 ff.). Funeral feasts were common in the heathen world (Tacitus, *Ann.* vi. 5, *Hist.* ii. 95; cf. Tertullian, *de Res. Carn.* 1 [*Patr. Lat.* ii. 841]); they were part of the obsequies, and were offerings to the dead. They were common in Egypt, Asia Minor, and indeed throughout the countries touched by Christianity. The Jews were familiar with them (2 S 3[35] was a delayed funeral banquet; cf. Jer 16[7], Ezk 24[17], Hos 9[4], To 4[17], Bar 6[32]). For a full account of them see Dom Leclercq's article, which, however, appears to make them too exclusively the origin of the Christian Agape. He seems to look on the Last Supper as a funeral banquet, celebrated before our Lord's death, and on the Agape as having that aspect throughout. The evidence does not show this. We do not read of Christian funeral or commemorative feasts till the time of Tertullian, at least; and there is nothing to connect them with the Eucharist or with the Last Supper. They would seem rather to have arisen after the almost total separation of Agape and Eucharist.

The most probable account of the origin of the Agape would seem to be that the Christians of the Apostolic age, desirous of showing their unity and brotherly love, imitated the Jewish and heathen custom of having common meals; they could not join the heathen guilds because of the idolatry that would be involved in doing so, and therefore they had what corresponded to these guilds among themselves, namely, the Agapæ. The connexion with the Eucharist—which in itself was quite a distinct act—would be a further step. They remembered that our Lord had associated the first Eucharist with a meal, and this was their justification in joining the Agape with it, so that the name 'Eucharist' could be said to include the Agape, as in the *Didache*, or the name 'Agape' the Eucharist, as in Ignatius. Indeed, in this way they would seem to be carrying out our Lord's injunction most fully. That the meal partaken of by our Lord was a Paschal meal—probably one specially instituted by Him in anticipation, but that is immaterial—would not affect the matter. There was nothing Paschal about the Agape, but the point of similarity between it and the Last Supper would be the connexion with the Eucharist. These two points, then, seem to stand out—(1) the frequent Agape was at first due to the early communism of the Church at Jerusalem, and carried on by the Gentile Churches in imitation of those without; (2) its connexion with the Eucharist was based on the fact that our Lord instituted that sacrament after a common meal. That the origin and history of the Agape are plain cannot for a moment be maintained; but that the explanation here given fits the known facts, appears to be at least probable.

LITERATURE.—Lightfoot, *Apostolic Fathers*[2], pt. 2 ('Ignatius and Polycarp'), 1889, i. 52 n., 400 f., ii. 312 f., iii. 457; Keating, *The Agape and the Eucharist*, 1901, and art. and letter in the *Guardian*, Dec. 24, 1902, Jan. 7, 1903; Batiffol, *Études d'Histoire et de Théologie positive*, 1st ser., Paris, 1902 (reply to Dr. Keating), letter in the *Guardian*, Jan. 7, 1903, and art. 'Agape' in *Dictionnaire de Théologie Catholique* (an earlier exposition, the views of which have since been much modified by the writer); the *Church Quarterly Review* for July 1902, notice of Dr. Keating's book; Lock, art. 'Love-feasts' in Hastings' *DB* vol. iii. 1900; Armitage-Robinson, art. 'Eucharist' in *Encyc. Bibl.* vol. ii. 1900; Zahn, art. 'Agapen' in *PRE*[3], 1896, and *Brot und Wein*, Leipzig, 1892 (reply to Dr. Ad. Harnack); Ramsay, *Church in the Roman Empire*[6], pp. 219, 358; Cooper and Maclean, *The Testament of our Lord*, 1902, p. 228 f. (for the Church Orders); J. Wordsworth, *Holy Communion*, 1891, pp. 44–46, 57–60, and *Ministry of Grace*, 1901, ch. vi.; Bingham, *Christian Antiquities*, xv. 7; Suicer, *Thesaurus*, *s.v.* 'Agape'; Plumptre, art. 'Agapae' in Smith and Cheetham's *Dictionary of Christian Antiquities*; Leclercq, art. 'Agape' in Cabrol's *Dictionnaire d'Archéologie Chrétienne et de Liturgie* (esp. for epigraphy and pictorial representations); Ermoni, *L'Agape dans l'Eglise primitive*, Paris, 1904 (a reply to Batiffol); Funk, 'L'Agape' in *Revue d'histoire ecclésiastique*, Jan. 15, 1903 (Louvain); Adolf Harnack, 'Brod und Wasser,' *TU*, vii. 2 (Leipzig, 1892); Kraus, artt. 'Agapen' and 'Mahle' in *RE der Christl. Altertümer*; Ladeuze, 'L'Eucharistie et les repas communs des fidèles dans le Didaché' (*Revue de l'Orient Chrétien*, 1902, No. 3); Spitta, *Zur Geschichte und Litteratur des Urchristentums*, i. (Göttingen, 1893); Jülicher, 'Zur Geschichte des Abendmahls' (*Theolog. Abhandl.*), 1892; Percy Gardner, *Origin of the Lord's Supper*, 1893; Thayer, 'Recent discussions respecting the Lord's Supper,' 1899 (*JBL* xviii. 110–131); Box, 'The Jewish antecedents of the Eucharist' (*JThSt*, iii. 357); Lambert, 'The Passover and the Lord's Supper' (*JThSt*, iv. 184); Th. Harnack, *Der Christliche Gemeinde Gottesdienst*, p. 213 f.; Wright, *NT Problems*, p. 134 ff.

A. J. MACLEAN.

AGAPĒMONE ('Abode of Love'). — Henry James Prince, the founder of Agapēmonism, was born January 13, 1811. After being articled to a medical man in Wells, Somerset, he resolved to take Holy Orders in the Church of England. In his 26th year he entered St. David's College, Lampeter (March, 1836). The connexion with the Welsh college led to the new sect being called the 'Lampeter Brethren.'

This, however, was misleading, for the Lampeter Brethren, eleven alumni of that institution, were a devout and earnest band of Episcopalian ministers who met for mutual edification, but who afterwards felt 'compelled to come to the calm, deliberate, and final, though most distressing, conclusion that Prince is awfully in error.'

During his college course Prince was an exemplary student. His brother-in-law and fellow-student, Rev. A. A. Rees, wrote that, till 1843, he never saw or heard of an individual more thoroughly devoted to God.

Prince was ordained in 1840 to the curacy of the agricultural parish of Charlynch, near Bridgwater, Somerset. The rector's name was Starky.* The careers of these two men now became identified. Starky, like Prince, was a man of extraordinary gifts of speech, but the rector soon acknowledged his curate as the very voice of God. His zeal on behalf of Agapēmonism led to its adherents in Weymouth and other parts of the south country being called 'Starkyites.' A wonderful revival of religion began in Charlynch and the district in October 1841. Prince published a record of it in 1842. It is a diary of most earnest work on behalf of souls. In six months the whole parish had professed conversion. Yet we find that, as early as May 4, 1841, the Bishop of Bath and Wells had revoked Prince's licence to preach, on the ground of his labouring in neighbouring parishes, admitting

* His Christian name appears to have been lost. In the B.M. Cat. the name stands 'Starky (——),' and on the title-page of his book in the Museum it is given as Br. Starky.

to the Lord's Table before Confirmation, and refusing the Sacrament to persons of evil lives. The diary is an instructive and edifying book, but it reveals the subtle and almost hypnotic power of Prince over his rector and the parishioners. While so absorbed in seeking the salvation of his people that he can think of nothing else, the emotion he expresses strikes the reader as unpleasant and unnatural. *The Charlynch Revival* was published because Prince thought it 'calculated, under the Divine blessing, to stir up the hearts of the Lord's people, and especially of His ministers, to expect great things from God.' With a few emendations it might be reissued as a model of pastoral labours. Before its publication in August 1842, Prince had already sent out two small works, *Letters to his Christian Brethren in St. David's College, Lampeter*, and *Strength in Jesus*, both of which ran to more than one edition.

The date of the beginning of his delusions seems to have been early in 1843. In May of that year he wrote to Mr. Rees a long letter in which he expounded the steps by which the Holy Ghost came to be settled and fixed in the personality of H. J. Prince. In the same year he desired his Lampeter brethren to believe (1) that he was the Holy Ghost personified; (2) that the Holy Ghost suffered and died in him; (3) that this suffering and death obtained for them what he called 'my spirit,' or, as he also phrased it, 'a modification of the Holy Ghost.' About the same time he also published *Testimony Hymns*, religious parodies on certain popular ballads, to back up his own pretensions,—wretched doggerel, like almost all his hymns,—in which he seemed to be losing all consciousness of other things and persons than himself. This was the beginning of his own self-proclaimed apotheosis.

Prince had been inhibited by the Bishop of Bath and Wells, and presently the same lot befell him at the hands of the Bishop of Salisbury. When he attempted to officiate as curate at Stoke-by-Clare, in Suffolk, he suffered once more at the hands of the Bishop of Ely. He appealed to the Archbishop, but could get no redress. Then, to use his own words, 'prevented from preaching *within* the pale of the Established Church, Bro. Prince, after some months' waiting on God for guidance in faith and prayer, proceeded to preach *without* it.' He became most energetic in denouncing priestcraft, but apparently without having observed that there were fellow-Christians who felt as strongly as himself upon this subject. Starky and Prince began to preach in barns at Charlynch. What was practically a Free Church was formed at Spaxton, a mile away. Crowds came to hear them. The twain asserted that they were the Two Witnesses of Rev 11, and Prince published several brochures in regard to the 'Two Anointed Ones.' He declared that community of goods was still binding on believers. Thereupon they sold their lands, and brought the money, 'laying it at Bro. Prince's feet.' About this period also he asserted that he was the prophet Elijah, that this had been made known to him by direct revelation, and that 'people were not to consider what they heard from him as an ordinary sermon, nor to think of him as an ordinary preacher; on the contrary, he was come from the courts of heaven, from the bosom of eternity.'

A crop of opposing pamphlets immediately sprang from the press, written for the most part by men who had been his personal friends. It is clear from some of his actions at this time, and particularly from the ballads which he penned and made his congregation sing, that his phenomenal self-love had passed beyond eccentricity into unsoundness of mind.

Prince and Starky now set up the Agapēmone, which they opened in 1849 at the entrance to the village of Spaxton. Money was poured into the treasury by their credulous followers. Freehold land was bought, and a beautiful and spacious residence erected upon it (for a description of it see Hepworth Dixon, *op. cit. infra*). The whole of the Princeite propagandism centred in the Agapēmone. It was the residence of Prince until his death on January 5, 1899, when he had almost completed his 88th year.

Throughout the movement it was very noticeable that Prince acquired influence over wealthy persons. They renounced the world, deposited their money at the Bank of England in the name of Brother Prince, and took up their abode at the Agapēmone. A wave of fanaticism seemed to sweep across the district about Bridgwater. Many intelligent persons believed him when Prince announced himself as the Final Revelation of the will of God to mankind. Christ had come again in the person of His messenger, first to judgment, and then to convince the world of righteousness. In him the Holy Ghost was to destroy the works of the flesh, and to cast out the devil. Whether he took the title of 'Lord,' or only accepted it, without deprecating its application to himself, seems uncertain. Some who retired from the Agapēmone blame his followers as much as they do Prince. Said one of them, 'They were simply mad about him, and were ready to fall down and worship him as if he were God.' Letters passed through the post addressed to 'Our Holy Lord God at Spaxton.' There is no evidence that Prince objected to this profane and wicked adulation. He stood at his throne in the auditorium, defying all the powers of evil,—sin, death, hell, the devil,—speaking as if he were master of all, until the doubters among the assembly quailed and trembled lest sudden judgment should fall upon him and upon them. He announced that neither he nor any that attached themselves to him could die, or suffer grief or sickness, because the Lord had come in his person to redeem the flesh. He began to set up royal state. Having purchased the Queen-Dowager's equipage and four cream-coloured horses, he was accustomed to drive rapidly about Bridgwater and the neighbourhood, accompanied by bloodhounds, whose presence lent the element of fear to the spectacle. In 1851, when he brought a party of believers to see the Great Exhibition, he drove about the parks and streets in an open carriage, preceded and attended by outriders, all of them bareheaded because they were in the presence of 'The Lord. After the catastrophe which we have now to relate, he fixed upon the title of 'The Beloved' as his own, because we are 'accepted in the Beloved.' His books and tracts were signed with a 'B,' as the initial letter of his pontifical title. Presentation copies bore the words 'From Beloved,' and the inscription, 'I have chosen you out of the world.'

It was inevitable that a movement begun in pride and profanity should develop into ungodliness. The habit of ostentation, luxury, boisterous hilarity, drinking to excess, gaiety, amusements, and the pursuit of wealth had become the order of the day. Disturbances arose out of lawsuits brought by some who seceded from the Agapēmone, horror-stricken at what they had witnessed and suffered there. One of these cases, *Nottidge* v. *Prince* (British Museum, Vol. Law Reports, 29 L.J.Ch. 857) brought about a complete exposure of the methods by which Prince and his henchmen 'crept into houses, leading captive silly women,' and 'turning the grace of our Lord Jesus Christ into licentiousness.' The suit was heard before Vice-Chancellor Stuart in the Court of Chancery, and occupied in hearing June 4–8, and July 25, 1860, when judgment was given. The bill was filed to recover from Prince £5,728, the property of Louisa Jane Nottidge, and the like amounts on behalf of two of her sisters. The report of the trial is the most trustworthy and complete history of the shameful condition of the Agapēmone from 1848 to 1860, when Prince was at the summit of his power and arrogance.

Whether Prince proclaimed or allowed 'free-love' at the Agapēmone cannot be proved. But the cross-examination in Court revealed the fact that, up to 1856, at any rate, grave disorders occurred, and the Vice-Chancellor referred in the strongest terms to the disgraceful revelations.

We have said that there is much in Prince's writings that is commendable and edifying. In the *Journal* of three years' spiritual experience he bows low before God under the sense of sin, or enjoys ecstatic communion with his Saviour. *The*

Man Christ Jesus is an enthusiastic review of the life of the Lord, though verbose, dreamy, obscure, and exclamatory,—exhausting all the Orientalism of Holy Scripture that can be used in a luscious and erotic sense to express devotion to Christ. *Leaves from the Tree of Life*, and *The Shutters taken down from the Windows of Heaven* contain much that needs to be said in regard to spiritual, as opposed to sacerdotal, religion. But the books, like the man himself, are stealthy and deceptive. While devout Christians can approve large portions of his writings, the latter are completely marred by the sudden introduction of his own theories, and by the application to himself personally of the words used by our Lord about His own nature and work. Next to the *Journal* the most important book is *The Counsel of God in Judgment, or Br. Prince's Testimony to the Closing of the Gospel Dispensation*, published when he was 77 years old. It declares the doom of Christendom, the fulfilment of all grace in Prince, his rejection by the Church, and the consequent withdrawal of the Holy Ghost from the Church and the world to Prince and the Agapēmone. But he will have to be judged by *The Little Book Open.* The note to the copy in the British Museum, 4th October 1856, is that an order went forth from the Agapēmone that all copies should be destroyed,—so strong was the public sentiment about it. It consists of a collection of the 'Voices.' In one of them Prince profanely manipulates Holy Scripture to cover and justify his own adulteries. All this loathsome uncleanness stands dressed in fervid and glowing language which vainly endeavours to conceal its crime.

After the trial in the Chancery Court, comparative silence fell upon the Agapēmone. Prince lived a very retired life. The funds of the brotherhood also seemed to be failing them, until in the late eighties a windfall came in the person of a wealthy London merchant, who presented to Prince all his property, and served the brotherhood in the humble capacity of butler. For the last ten years of his life Prince was very feeble. He outlived all his principal followers. He was buried on the 11th of January 1899, in the grounds behind the Agapēmone.

In 1890 and for a few years later there was a remarkable recrudescence of this fanaticism. Several prominent members of the Salvation Army cast in their lot with Prince. A mission to Norway was reported to be very successful. But, above all, Clapton, in the N.E. of London, became the scene of this renewed activity. The 'Children of the Resurrection,' as they named themselves, built, in 1892, 'The Ark of the Covenant,' an elaborate structure, seating about 400 persons, at a cost of £16,000. The preacher, at its opening in 1896, was the Rev. J. H. Smyth-Pigott, the official successor of Prince. Smyth-Pigott, who is of good family, was formerly a curate of St. Jude's, Mildmay Park. He has also served in the Salvation Army. In his opening sermon he declared he expected Christ to come that very day to judgment, but did not explain why, in that case, this expensive church was being dedicated. In September 1902, Smyth-Pigott proclaimed himself to be Jesus Christ; with the result that most riotous scenes took place for several weeks.

Since the tumultuous scenes which accompanied the making of this announcement, Smyth-Pigott has lived in retirement at his house in Upper Clapton, or at the Agapēmone at Spaxton, worshipped as Divine by the little company who accept his pretensions. 'The Ark of the Covenant' remained closed to the public during 1903 and 1904, private services being held at rare intervals. It needs only to be added that the present tenants of the Agapēmone are a quiet, blameless, and elderly company, numbering about 35 persons, whose praise is sung throughout the whole neighbourhood for their unquestioned piety and fervent charity [1907].

LITERATURE.—Prince's own *Journal: or, An Account of the Destruction of the Works of the Devil in the Human Soul, by the Lord Jesus Christ, through the Gospel*, published in 1859, but relating to the period between 1835 and 1839, also *The Charlynch Revival: or, An Account of the Remarkable Work of Grace at Charlynch*, 1842; J. G. Dick, *A Word of Warning: The Heresy of Mr. Prince*, London, 1845; Rees, *The Rise and Progress of the Heresy of Rev. H. J. Prince*, Weymouth, 1845; O. Piers, *The Door not Shut: or, Three Reasons for not believing Mr. Prince to be a True Prophet*, 1846; Hepworth Dixon, *Spiritual Wives*, chapter on Visit to the Agapēmone, 1868; Prince, *A Hook in the Nose of Leviathan*, 1877, also, *A Sword in the Heart of Leviathan*, 1877, and *The Man Christ Jesus*, London, 1886; *The Counsel of God in Judgment: or, Br. Prince's Testimony to the Closing of the Gospel Dispensation, and the Revelation of Jesus Christ as the Son of Man*, 1887; also a variety of pamphlets of a painful nature, printed for private circulation only.

EDWIN J. DUKES.

AGAPĒTÆ.—A name applied to female Christian ascetics who lived together with men, although both parties had taken the vow of continency, and were animated with the earnest desire to keep it. They were also known by the nickname of *Virgines Subintroductæ* or *Syneisaktoi*, which arose at a comparatively late date, after the custom had fallen into disfavour, and has tended not a little to confuse the judgment regarding this form of sexual asceticism. In reality, this spiritual marriage was one of the most remarkable phenomena which asceticism called forth on Christian soil — a fruit of overwhelming enthusiasm for the ascetic ideal. Our sources justify us in saying that the custom was widespread during the whole of Christian antiquity. In Antioch the bishop Paul of Samosata had several young maidens in his immediate neighbourhood (Eusebius, *HE* vii. 30. 12 ff.). At the time of Cyprian, virgins who were dedicated to God lived in the most intimate relationship with confessors, priests, and laymen (*Epist.* 4. 13. 14); and the rigorous Tertullian advises well-to-do Christians to take into their houses one or more widows 'as spiritual spouses,' who were 'beautiful by their faith, endowed with their poverty, sealed by their age.' . . . 'It is well pleasing to God to have several such wives' (*de Exhort. Castit.* 12; *de Monog.* 16). We hear the same regarding heretics: several heads of the Valentinian sect lived together with 'sisters' (Irenæus, *Hær.* i. 6. 3), the Montanist martyr Alexander was united in spiritual marriage with a prophetess (Euseb. *HE* v. 18. 6 ff.), and the Marcionite Apelles had in the same way two spiritual wives, one of whom was the prophetess Philumene (Tertullian, *de Præscr.* 30).

As spiritual marriage arose from ascetic motives, it had its proper place in monasticism, and has there preserved its original form. From the first initiators or forerunners of the monastic life onwards — among the Encratites of Tatian, the Origenists and Hieracites—to the anchorites whom Jerome and Gregory knew, we hear again and again that many monks lived together with women, and we need not wonder if we meet with traces of Syneisaktism proper on monastic soil till late in the Middle Ages. In the desert, where the ascetic was alone with his companion, the relation often took the form of the woman becoming his servant, and assisting him in the many varied ways in which the man of antiquity allowed himself to be waited on by his servants. We must not, however, on this account allow ourselves to be misled as to the main point, viz. that the reason why the monk and the nun had retired into the desert is to be sought in their ascetic ideal, which they had in common, and which they aimed at realizing in separation from the world. In the struggle for life and in the conflict against their own flesh they sought power in a union of souls, which was supposed to bring them nearer to God.

The old Irish Church had made this kind of asceticism a foundation-pillar of its organization. According to the primitive Christian custom, no difference was then made between man and woman (cf. Gal 3[28]), and both were allowed to take part in Church functions. In the monastic houses, moreover, the priestly monks lived together with the priestly nuns, according to an old anonymous reporter, up to the year 543: '*Mulierum administrationem et consortia non respuebant, quia super petram Christi fundati ventum tentationis non timebant*' (Haddan-Stubbs, *Councils and Ecclesiastical Documents*, ii. 2, p. 292). At the time, too, when the Irish, with their mission, undertook a forward movement towards Brittany, the Gallican bishops found it especially blameworthy in the incomers that they were accompanied by women, who, like the men, assumed to themselves sacramental functions (cf. the letter of the three bishops in the *Revue de Bretagne et de Vendée*, 1885, i. p. 5 ff.); they did not know that the Irish-Breton Church had preserved customs and principles of the most ancient Christian Church.

After the well-to-do circles in the large cities had become Christian, there was developed a new form of spiritual marriage. It happened frequently that rich widows and young women, in accordance with the tendency of the time, refused marriage, and in order to provide a master for their large houses, caused clergymen or monks to bind themselves to them in spiritual marriage. This is a variety of Syneisaktism, but an unfortunate one. The rôles seem to be reversed. The woman had the upper hand, because she remained the mistress of her large possessions, and in addition she enjoyed the repute of virginity. On the other hand, the position of the priest was difficult, and often precarious. However seriously asceticism and the union of souls might be taken, still the fact could not be lost sight of that the priest was a subordinate, and his position may have varied between house steward, domestic chaplain, and spiritual lover. This is the rôle which the *abbé* in France had in the 17th and 18th centuries. At the time of Chrysostom this evil custom was widespread in Constantinople (Migne, xlvii. col. 495 ff.); likewise at the same time in Gaul, as Jerome (*Ep.* 117) discloses. It is therefore to be regarded as a peculiar product of Christianity.

The spiritual marriage of the clergy is most frequently mentioned, and therefore best known; so much so that it has been widely believed that only the clergy of the ancient Church lived with Syneisaktoi. And it cannot be denied that the custom, just as in the case of Monasticism, found its especial home here. It stands parallel with celibacy, which, in like manner, in Christianity was not created for the clergy, but none the less became a ruling custom among them, and at a later date was elevated to a law, because people judged marriage to be inferior, and imposed the highest and most ideal demands on the clergy. Now, as the clergy who withdrew from marriage became more numerous, their choice of a companion for spiritual wedlock, in order professedly to live a life of asceticism, was of much more frequent occurrence. And as time went on, the ideal nature of the relationship seems to have disappeared in face of practical motives. Out of the ascetic and the bride of the soul there arose imperceptibly the housekeeper, who was suspected to be also the mistress. No doubt the common judgment on this form of asceticism had changed in course of time. Men's minds had become more alert and sane, and the priest who lived together with a woman was looked on with other eyes than at an earlier date. It seems, however, as if Syneisaktism itself had degenerated. The housekeepers of the clergy were called *mulieres extraneæ*, and placed on the same footing as servant maids. Spanish synods, about the year 600, even ordered that the *extraneæ* should be sold as slaves, and the proceeds given to the poor (*can.* 5 Toledo, 589; *can.* 3 Hispalis, 590; *can.* 42, 43 Toledo, 633). In the Decretals of Gregory IX., iii. 2, *de cohabitatione clericorum et mulierum*, the concubinage of the clergy is forbidden. In the East the same development can be proved. Even in the later synods the Syneisaktoi are alluded to; but it is evident that it was really a question of female servants of the clergy; and to the Greek canonists of the 12th cent. the name Syneisaktos means no more than the housekeeper of a clergyman. Syneisaktism must, therefore, have undergone a transition. Even in the later centuries clergy lived together with women without being married to them, just as in earlier times; but people regarded this living together differently. In the early times man and woman had taken the vow of virginity, and had struggled in a union of souls to attain the common ideal; in later times the practical requirements of life came to the front. The clergyman needed a woman to look after his household, who was faithful and devoted to him. The natural way of marriage was barred to him by the ordinance of celibacy; but if he took a young woman into his house without marrying her, he was exposed to evil report. Without doubt, even in later times the ideal motives of the community of life may in many cases have been alive, as formerly. On the whole, the development which has been sketched is thoroughly natural. An ascetic enthusiasm which proposes to itself such high aims must, in the course of time, evaporate and make room for the sober realities of the day. Such an heroic ideal may perhaps be suitable as a way to heaven for a few specially favoured natures; but it becomes questionable, and even pernicious, as soon as it is made a rule to be followed by a large class of men.

The different forms of Syneisaktism arose under the influence of social conditions. In the loneliness of the desert, the nun became the maidservant of the hermit; in the cities and villages, the soul-friend of the well-to-do priest degenerated into his housekeeper, just as, on the other hand, rich widows assigned to their spiritual friends the rôle of steward; and if in Ireland monks and nuns lived together in large companies, that was caused by the peculiar conditions of the Irish missionary church, which was a monastic church. The difference of the forms, however, allows us to see plainly the original form. The original motive was in all cases a religious one—more precisely, an ascetic one; brotherly love was supposed to take the place of the love of marriage. Syneisaktism was the natural product of two opposing tendencies in ancient Christianity. On the one hand, brotherly love, in all its forms of expression, was most highly prized, so that it was declared to be the proper palladium of religion (cf. 1 Co 13), and the exclusiveness of the small and intimate congregations favoured the rise of a narrow social life and close friendly relationship between Christians who were widely separated in age and social position. We can see, from the example of the Irish religious houses, how great an influence the idea of community must have had. On the other hand, there was a strong aversion, based on religious feelings, to sexual intercourse. Marriage was regarded as a not very honourable concession to the sensual nature of mankind, and people revered the ascetics without inquiring what sacrifices they paid for their ideals. Owing to the conflict of social ideals, which bound men most closely with each other and yet threatened to estrange man and woman, there arose the unnatural combination of asceticism and brotherly love, which meets us in Syneisaktism. A form of intimate social life of the sexes was created, which was not marriage either in reality or in intention, and was blind to its own dangers, because those who adopted it trusted everything, even the quite impossible, to the power of the Spirit animating the Christian.

Thus it is only natural that it was just the spiritually elevated Christians, the leaders of the communities — the prophets, confessors, bishops, and clergy—who lived in spiritual marriage. In the same way the *uxores spirituales* of the earlier times were always such women as enjoyed a special position of honour in the community as 'brides of Christ,'—the virgins, widows, or even prophetesses. What they undertook was not hidden in a corner, but was generally admired as a glorious example of Christian love and continency. But in course of time the judgment of the ancient Church regarding the Syneisaktoi changed.

Hermas seems to regard spiritual marriage, in all its forms, as a precious characteristic of the life of the Christian community (*Simil.* x. 3). Irenæus does not disapprove of it (*Hær.* i. 6. 3 *fin.*). Tertullian regards it as the most desirable form of cohabitation of man and woman (see above). Paul of Samosata values it highly, and practises it himself. His opponents at the Synod of Antioch (Eusebius, *HE* vii. 30. 12 ff.), and, shortly before that, Cyprian (*Ep.* 4. 13. 14), are the first to express themselves against it. The Synods of the 4th cent.—Elvira *can.* 27, Ancyra *can.* 19, and Nicæa *can.* 3—forbid the clergy to have women in their houses, and after that date prohibitions of Syneisaktism are never absent from the Church ordinances. In cases of disobedience the clergy are punished or even deposed. In the case of laymen or monks, strict admonitions are, as a rule, regarded as sufficient.

The different attitudes taken up by the Church on the question are explained by the development which she had undergone. In the first three centuries she had spread very widely, and the communities had in places become very numerous. There were many elements in her that did not take the moral precepts of Christianity seriously. The strict prohibitions regarding sins of the flesh were, owing to the necessity of the case, weakened and modified in the 3rd century. The Roman bishop Callistus likened the Church to Noah's ark, in which there were clean and unclean beasts (Hippolyt. *Philos.* ix. 12). Then such a custom as spiritual marriage had to be abolished,—a custom which, if feasible at all, was so only in small intimate communities, where each one knew the other and all were under supervision and discipline. It proved, however, excessively difficult to root out Syneisaktism, as we may learn from the ever repeated prohibitions, which become more and more strict as time goes on. How very deep the opposition to it went can be gathered from the fact that the later bishop of Antioch, Leontius, castrated himself in order to be permitted to retain his house companion. Yet people were in many places convinced of the innocence and the justice of such a relationship, and even produced proofs from writers who justified the Syneisaktoi by quoting Biblical examples from the Old and New Testaments (Achelis, *Virg. Subintrod.* p. 42 f.).

That spiritual marriage was in course of time regarded in a different light, is proved further by the changes of designation.

Tertullian calls the female ascetic, who lives with a man, his *uxor spiritualis*—which is the appropriate name in the sense of early days. Then there occurs the term *conhospita.* The spiritual marriage seems to have been called ἀδελφότης. On the other hand, the inhabitants of Antioch invented for the female friends of Paul of Samosata the nickname συνείσακτοι, and this name afterwards stuck to female ascetics who lived together with like-minded male friends. The term was carried over into the Latin Church in the translation *subintroductæ* (Roman Synod *a.* 743 in Mansi, xii. 381). More frequently still the general designation, *mulieres extraneæ*, is used.

In regard to the question of the age of spiritual marriage, the *Shepherd* of Hermas comes especially under consideration. Hermas knows the custom of Christian men and women being united to each other by a bond of special affinity, even when they are separated from each other by all kinds of relationships in life (*Vis.* i. 1. 1); he presupposes that virgins find shelter in the houses of Christian brothers (*Sim.* x. 3); and, finally, knows the intimate forms of intercourse which were usual between the spiritually betrothed (*Sim.* ix. 11. 3, 7). He reports, of course, not facts but visions, but he would not have been able to introduce the situations he describes in such a matter-of-fact way, if he had not regarded them as characteristics of Christian brotherly love, of which he was proud.

The passage 1 Co 7 has also to be considered, since it has been brought by Ed. Grafe into connexion with the question of the Syneisaktoi. According to the interpretation suggested by Grafe, 1 Co 7[36] refers to the awakening love between a Christian householder and a young girl residing in his house, who are bound by a common vow; the Apostle recommends that an end be put to the precarious situation by marriage. But, on the other hand, in v.[37] he praises the Christian who, in the like situation, understands how to control himself; while v.[38] unites both decisions. The matter, then, does not concern father and daughter, as has generally been held by exegetes, but is a case of spiritual marriage—the same situation as we found above in the case of the bishop and clergy of Antioch, as we must presuppose in Hermas, and as we saw in the letters of Cyprian. What was so inevitable took place at Corinth (although it was avoided in other places), viz. that the peculiar relation between the guardian and his spiritual bride became too intimate to be endurable for any length of time. According to Grafe, St. Paul advised both to marry, while the present writer finds it more in accordance with the wording of the text (cf. the repeated γαμίζων) and also with the supposed situation, to think that he advised the young woman to leave the house and be married to some other Christian. If the words of St. Paul have a concrete case of Syneisaktism in view, such as prevailed at the episcopal court of Antioch, that is almost the only conceivable solution. In ancient times young girls were married without much ceremony, and for a female ascetic, who had had a disappointing experience, a marriage was certainly the best way. It must, however, be granted that this interpretation of the passage in Corinthians is not beyond question, especially as the text is not quite certain.

Lastly, the *de Vita Contemplativa* must be mentioned. This may be regarded as a genuine work of Philo. The Therapeutæ in Egypt, who are there described, and who tabued marriage and sexual enjoyment, lived in union with female companions, just as the Christian monks did at a later date. It is the same combination of sexual asceticism and brotherly communion as in Syneisaktism, only that the personal intimacy between the individual pairs is wanting; the brotherly love is just the specifically Christian factor in the spiritual marriage. This makes it possible to place the beginnings of Syneisaktism in the Apostolic Age. The ascetic cohabitation of man and woman had already had its prototype in Hellenistic Judaism. It can, however, on more general grounds, hardly be doubted that spiritual marriage with its extravagances belongs to the earliest Christian times, when 'the Spirit' ruled the community, and the 'first love' still burned. At that time the communities were small and intimate, and had had no disappointing experiences with regard to themselves; asceticism made its way into the Church; and so all the conditions for the rise of Syneisaktism were present. This must be so if Syneisaktism is conceived of, as it has been by us above, as an attempt to substitute for marriage Christian brotherly love. If we seek to derive it, in the way formerly adopted, from the celibacy of the clergy or from Monasticism, then we are driven to a much later date for its origin. But in face of the testimony of the most ancient Christian authors, that can hardly be maintained.

LITERATURE.—The question was first raised by **Henry Dodwell**, *Dissertationes Cyprianicæ*, iii. (Oxford, 1682). Thereupon a small literature on the subject grew up. The titles of the contributions are given by **J. E. Volbeding**, *Index dissertationum* (Lipsiæ, 1849), p. 167. So far as is known to the present writer, all the authors held Syneisaktism to be an error of the corrupt Church of the 3rd century. The above mentioned discussion of 1 Co 7[36-38] by **Ed. Grafe**, 'Geistliche Verlöbnisse bei Paulus,' followed a notice of **Weizsäcker**, and appeared in *Theol. Arbeiten aus dem rheinischen wissenschaftl. Prediger-Verein*, N.S., iii. (Freiburg, 1899). This interpretation has found considerable approval. The conception of Syneisaktism given above is proved in detail by **H. Achelis**, *Virgines Subintroductæ; Ein Beitrag zu 1 Cor.* 7 (Leipzig, 1902).

H. ACHELIS.

AGARIĀ, AGAR, AGARĪ.—An Indian tribe which, at the Census of 1901, numbered 270,370, of whom the vast majority are found in Bombay, the Central Provinces, and Bengal, with a few in other parts of N. India. The ethnography of this tribe is very obscure, and, as collected under one heading in the Census returns, it includes at least three different communities, who may, however, agree in being of common Dravidian or Muṇḍā origin. In Chota Nāgpur and the adjoining district of Mirzapur the Agariā practise the old rude Dravidian method of smelting iron. In the Tributary Mahāls of Bengal and in the Sambalpur district of the Central Provinces they are a fair, good-looking race, who claim to have once been Rājputs in the neighbourhood of Agra, whence they say they derive their name. The legend runs that they refused to bow the head before the Muhammadan emperor of Delhi, and were compelled to leave their original settlements and migrate southwards. These the Census returns describe under the name of *Agharīā*, in order to distinguish them from the *Agariā*, who are pure Dravidians. In the Mandla district of the same province they are described as a subdivision of the Goṇḍs (wh. see), and among the laziest and most drunken of that race. In Bombay another branch practise in some places the business of salt-making, and derive their name from the pit (Hind. Mahr. *agar*, Skr. *ākara*, 'a mine') in which the brine is evaporated.

It is only the tribe in Chota Nāgpur and the immediate neighbourhood that preserves its original beliefs. Generally they have a well-marked totemistic division into sub-castes; a vague form of ancestor-worship, which is confined to propitiating the dead of the preceding generation; and a respect for the Sāl tree (*Shorea robusta*), which is used at their marriages. In Mirzapur they neglect the ordinary Hindu gods, and have a special worship of Lohāsur Devī, the Mother-goddess who presides over the smelting furnace. To her the *baigā*, or village officiant, sacrifices a goat which has never borne a kid, and burns a few scraps of cake, the meat and the remainder of the bread being consumed by the worshippers. In Palamāu, according to Forbes, their worship is of a still lower type. 'They appear,' he writes, 'to have no deities, and to have no knowledge of the Supreme Being, though some of them appear to have heard of the universal Devī; but I do not think they worshipped her in any way. On certain days of the year they offer up sacrifices to propitiate the spirits of the departed members of the family.' This ceremony is called Mūā,' *i.e.* 'the Dead.' They generally also worship the Dih or local gods of the village in which they happen to settle. In Bengal their women have the reputation of being notorious witches. Dalton was told that 'in Gangpur there are old women, professors of witchcraft, who stealthily instruct the young girls. The latter are all eager to be taught, and are not considered proficient till a fine forest tree, selected to be experimented upon, is destroyed by the potency of their "mantras" or charms, so that the wife a man takes to his bosom has probably done her tree, and is confident in the belief that she can, if she pleases, dispose of her husband in the same manner if he makes himself obnoxious.'

A closely allied tribe of the E. Muṇḍās in Lohārdaga—the Āsurs, who speak the same language as the Agariā—worship Andhariyā Devatā, the Earth-god. The sacrificer places a fowl with its head on the anvil, and, holding it in position with the forge pincers, strikes its head with a hammer, praying that the goddess will protect the worshipper from injury by the sparks which fly from red-hot iron. These people also worship Boṛ Pahāṛī Bongā, the great Hill-god, with the sacrifice of a brown goat, and Pandrā Devatā, the Sun, with a mottled fowl.

The Agariā of the Central Provinces and the allied tribe in Bombay are practically Hindus, worshipping in particular Hanumanta, the monkey-god, and all the village gods and goddesses. But they still preserve traces of the original pre-Aryan beliefs in representing these deities by stones and white ant hills, and by performing their worship through their own headman, and not by a Brāhman officiant.

LITERATURE.—For Bengal and the United Provinces: **Dalton**, *Ethnology of Bengal* (1872), 196, 322 ff.; **Forbes**, *Settlement Report on Palamāu*, quoted in *North Indian Notes and Queries*, iv. 43; **Crooke**, *Tribes and Castes* (1896) i. 1 ff. For Central Provinces: *Census Report*, 1901, i. 196, 322 f.; *Gazetteer*, i. 273 f. 457. For Bombay: *Gazetteer*, xv. pt. i. 360. For the Asurs: *JASB* lvii. pt. i. 8; *Census Report*, 1901, i. 283.

W. CROOKE.

AGASTYA (or Agasti).—The reputed author of some Vedic hymns (*Rigveda*, i. 165–191). In the Rigveda he is sometimes mentioned, and some particulars are alluded to, notably his miraculous origin and his relation to Lopāmudrā, his wife (see E. Sieg, *Sagenstoffe des Rigveda*, i. 105–129). In Hindu mythology* he is regarded as the patron saint of Southern India, where places sacred to him abound; still, his hermitage was shown on the Yamunā near Prayāga.† He originated from the seed of Mitra and Varuṇa, which they had dropped into a water-jar on seeing the heavenly nymph Urvaśī.‡ From his double parentage he is called Maitrāvaruṇi, and from his being born from a jar he got the names Kumbhasambhava, Kalaśayoni, and similar ones denoting 'jar-born.' A Vedic name of Agastya is Mānya.

Agastya, growing old as an ascetic, was admonished by his ancestors to beget a son in order to save himself and them from perdition. He therefore produced, by magic power, a beautiful maiden, Lopāmudrā, from the best part of all creatures, and gave her to the king of Vidarbha to be his daughter. Nobody daring, on account of her supernatural beauty, to pretend to her hand, Agastya at last demanded her in marriage. The king, fearing his wrath, acceded to his wish, and Lopāmudrā became the wife of the ascetic. When, however, after a course of penances in Gangādvāra, Agastya desired to embrace his wife, she refused to do his will unless she was decked out in such splendid robes and costly ornaments as she had been accustomed to in her father's house. In order to satisfy her demand, Agastya applied to different kings for treasures; but he ascertained that their budgets were just balanced, so that they might not bestow wealth on him. On their advice and in their company he went to the king of Maṇimatī, the Dānava Ilvala, who was famous for his riches.

* See Holtzmann's paper on Agastya in the *Mahābhārata* in *ZDMG* xxxiv. p. 589 ff.
† *Mahābhārata*, iii. 87.
‡ *Bṛhaddevatā*, v. 30; *Rāmāyaṇa*, vii. 57.

Now Ilvala, an enemy of the Brāhmans, had a brother, Vātāpi, whom, on the arrival of a Brāhman, he used to kill and then to prepare as a meal. When the unsuspecting guest had finished his dinner, Ilvala, by his magical power, called Vātāpi to life again, and in this way killed his victim. The Dānava tried this trick on Agastya, but his incantation failed to revive Vātāpi, whom Agastya had already completely digested. So Ilvala was fain to give Agastya such treasures as satisfied the desires of Lopāmudrā. According to the *Rāmāyaṇa* (iii. 11. 66), however, Agastya, on this occasion, reduced the Dānava to ashes by fire issuing from his eye. The Riṣi had by Lopāmudrā a son called Dṛdhasyu or Idhmavāha.*

Another famous deed of Agastya was his having caused the fall of Nahuṣa.

When, after vanquishing Vṛtra, Indra, polluted with the sin of *brahmahatyā*, or killing of a Brāhman, fled and hid himself, the gods made Nahuṣa ruler of the skies. But Nahuṣa soon became overbearing and desired to make Śachī, Indra's wife, his own. She, however, would not consent unless he came to her on a car drawn by the seven Riṣis. Nahuṣa therefore yoked them to his car, and made them draw it. During his ride, he, for some cause, differently stated in different places, kicked Agastya on the head, whereupon the Riṣi turned him, by his curse, into a serpent, until Yudhiṣṭhira should release him from the curse.†

Most frequently Agastya is mentioned in Sanskrit works as having stayed the abnormal growth of the Vindhya range, and as having drunk up the ocean.

The Vindhya was jealous of Mount Meru, round which sun and moon and stars were always revolving. In order to force the heavenly bodies to go round him too, Vindhya began to grow, and rose to such a height that the gods became alarmed. They therefore asked Agastya to prevent the mountain from obstructing the path of the sun. Accordingly the Ṛṣi went with his family to the Vindhya, and, pretending to have something to do in the South, he asked the mountain to cease growing till he should return; and when the Vindhya had agreed, he passed on and took up his abode in the South for ever.‡ His hermitage was near the Godāvarī and Pampā, where Rāma and Sītā were his guests.§ The Rāmāyaṇa, however, takes apparently no heed of Agastya's resolve never to leave the South, for in Bk. vii. it is related that he visited Rāma in Ayodhyā, and there told him the early history of Rāvaṇa and Hanuman.

The drinking up of the ocean is thus related in the *Mahābhārata* (iii. 103 ff.):

The Kālakeyas or Kāleyas, a class of Asuras, had fought under Vṛtra against the gods. After the death of their leader they hid themselves in the ocean where the gods could not reach them, and determined to extirpate the Brāhmans and holy men; for thus, they thought, they would bring about the end of the world. The gods, alarmed by their raids, were advised by Viṣṇu to implore Agastya for help. The Riṣi, accordingly, drank up the water of the ocean and thus laid bare the Kālakeyas, who were then slain by the gods. The ocean continued a void till Bhagīratha led the Gangā to it and thus filled it again with water.

A curious trait of our saint is that he was a famous hunter and archer. For this reason, probably, Manu (v. 22) adduces Agastya as an authority for killing deer and birds for sacrificial purposes and for servants' food.

After his death Agastya was placed among the stars‖ as Canopus, the most brilliant star in the southern heavens except Sirius. The heliacal rising of this star, while the sun is in the asterism Hastā, marks the setting in of autumn after the close of the rains.¶

Agastya seems, in popular belief, to represent that force of nature which makes an end of the monsoon,—in mythological language, drinks up the waters of the ocean,—and which brings back the sun, temporarily hidden by the clouds of the rainy season, or, turned mythologically, stays the growth of Vindhya obstructing the path of the sun. As a rain-godling, 'who is supposed to have power to stop the rain,' he is still invoked in Muzaffarnagar.*

In Southern India, Agastya 'is venerated as the earliest teacher of science and literature'; he is the reputed author of many Tamil works; 'he is believed to be still alive, though invisible to ordinary eyes, and to reside somewhere on the fine conical mountain in Travancore commonly called Agastya's hill, from which the Porunei, or Tāmraparṇī, the sacred river of Tinnevelli, takes its rise.'† See also VEDIC RELIGION (4 B b).

H. JACOBI.

* *Mahābhārata*, iii. 96–99.
† *Mahābhārata*, v. 17 ff., xii. 342 ff.; and, with some variations, xiii. 99 ff.
‡ *Mahābhārata*, iii. 103.
§ *Rāmāyaṇa*, iii. 11 f.; *Kādambarī*, ed. Peterson, p. 21 ff.
‖ *Taittirīya Āraṇyaka*, i. 11. 2.
¶ *Varāha Mihira*, *Bṛhat Saṁhitā*, xii. 7 ff.

AGE.—In most animals there is a normal specific size to which the great majority of the adult members of the species closely approximate. In a large collection representing a species there may be a few giants and a few dwarfs, but most of the members show a close approximation to the same limit of growth, and there are good reasons for believing that the normal specific size is *adaptive*, *i.e.* that it has been slowly established in the course of selection as the fittest size for the given organization and the given conditions of life. In some cases, *e.g.* many fishes, there is no such definite limit of growth; thus haddocks are often found as large as cods.

Similarly, in many animals that have been carefully studied, we find that there is a normal potential duration of life,—an age which is rarely exceeded, though it may be seldom attained. This normal 'lease of life' is in most cases known only in a general way, though in many cases we are able to say that the living creature in question never lives *longer* than a few months, or a year, or a few years. Statistics from forms kept in captivity are obviously vitiated by the artificial conditions, and the life of animals in their natural conditions is so often ended by a 'violent death'—coming sooner or later according to the varying intensity of the struggle for existence—that it is difficult to say what the normal potential duration of life really is. But a critical survey of a large body of facts led Weismann in his essay on 'The Duration of Life' (1889) to the conclusion that this, like size, is an adaptive character, gradually defined by selection in relation to the external conditions of life.

Attempts have often been made to correlate the duration of life with certain structural and functional characteristics of the type discussed, *e.g.* with size, with the duration of the growing period, with rapidity or sluggishness of life, but none of these correlations can be generalized, and there is much to be said for Weismann's more cautious thesis, that the length of life is determined in relation to the needs of the species. Given a certain rate of reproduction and a certain average mortality, the duration of life that survives is that which is fittest to the conditions. (See ADAPTATION.) In the same essay Weismann pointed out that unicellular organisms, which have no 'body' to keep up, which can continually make good their waste by repair, and which have very simple inexpensive modes of reproduction, are practically 'immortal,' *i.e.* they are not subject to *natural* death as higher organisms are. Epigrammatically expressed, natural death is the price paid for a 'body.'

In the case of man, we must clearly distinguish between the *average specific longevity*, about 34 years in Europe—but happily raisable with decreasing infantile mortality, improved sanitation, decreasing warfare, increasing temperance and carefulness,—and the *potential specific longevity*, which for the present race is normally between

* Crooke, *The Popular Religion and Folklore of Northern India*, i. 76.
† Caldwell, *Compar. Gram. of Dravidian Languages*[2], 119 f.

seventy and one hundred years. There is no warrant for fixing any precise limit, either for the past or the future. All that we can scientifically say is that there are few well-established instances of a greater human longevity than 104 years. Sir George Cornewall Lewis did good service (1862) in destructively criticising numerous alleged cases of centenarianism, the occurrence of which he at first regarded as quite unproved, but even he finally admitted that men do sometimes reach a hundred years, and that some have reached one hundred and three or four. The famous cases of Thomas Parr, Henry Jenkins, and the Countess of Desmond, said to be 152, 169, and 140 respectively, were ruled out of court by Mr. Thoms, who edited *Notes and Queries* at the time when Sir G. C. Lewis's wholesome scepticism created much stir. As man is a slowly varying organism, as regards physical characters at least, it is extremely unlikely that his longevity was ever much greater than it is now. Monsters in age and monsters in size are alike incredible.

Prof. E. Metchnikoff is one of the few modern biologists who would deal generously with Biblical and other old records of great human longevity. He apparently thinks there has been some misunderstanding in regard to Methuselah's 969 years and Noah's 950, but he accepts the great ages of 175, 180, and 147 years ascribed to Abraham, Isaac, and Jacob. Similarly, he accepts the 185 years with which St. Mungo of Glasgow has been credited. And as he is generous in regard to the past, he is hopeful in regard to the future, believing that a more careful and temperate life, as well as an enlightened recognition of the disharmonies of our bodily frame, may bring about a time when man will no longer, as Buffon says, 'die of disappointment,' but attain everywhere 'a hundred years.' 'Humanity,' Metchnikoff says, 'would make a great stride towards longevity could it put an end to syphilis, which is the cause of one-fifth of the cases of arterial sclerosis. The suppression of alcoholism, the second great factor in the production of senile degeneration of the arteries, will produce a still more marked extension of the term of life. Scientific study of old age and of the means of modifying its pathological character will make life longer and happier.' He also quotes the theoretically simple conclusion of Pflüger's essay on 'The Art of prolonging Human Life':—'Avoid the things that are harmful, and be moderate in all things.'

A fact of much interest is the statistical evidence that such a subtle character as 'longevity,' that is to say, a tendency to a certain lease of life, be it long or short, is heritable like other inborn characters, though it rests, of course, to some extent with the individual or his environment to determine whether the inherited tendency is realized or not. Just as stature is a heritable quality, so is potential longevity, but the degree of expression is in part determined by 'nurture'—taking the word in the widest sense.

There is, as we have hinted, reason to believe that natural death is not to be regarded simply as an intrinsic necessity—the fate of all life; we can carry the analysis further, and say that it is incident on the complexity of the bodily machinery, which makes complete recuperation well-nigh impossible, and almost forces the organism to accumulate arrears, to go into debt to itself; that it is incident on the limits which are set to the multiplication and renewal of cells within the body, thus nerve-cells in higher animals cannot be added to after an early stage in development; and it is incident on the occurrence of organically expensive modes of reproduction, for reproduction is often the beginning of death. At the same time, it seems difficult to rest satisfied with these and other physiological reasons, and we fall back on the selectionist view that the duration of life has been, in part at least, punctuated from without and in reference to large issues; it has been gradually regulated in adaptation to the welfare of the species.

It seems to us suggestive to recognize four categories of phenomena in connexion with age. The first is that of the immortal unicellular animals which never grow old, which seem exempt from natural death. The second is that of many wild animals, which reach the length of their life's tether without any hint of ageing, and pass off the scene—or are shoved off—victims of violent death. In many fishes and reptiles, for instance, which are old in years, there is not in their organs or tissues the least hint of age-degeneration. The third is that of the majority of civilized human beings, some domesticated, and some wild animals, in which the decline of life is marked by normal *senescence.* The fourth is that of many human beings, not a few domesticated animals, *e.g.* horse, dog, cat, and some semi-domesticated animals, notably bees, in which the close of life is marked by distinctively pathological *senility.* It seems certain that wild animals rarely exhibit more than a slight senescence, while man often exhibits a bathos of senility. What is the explanation of this?

The majority of wild animals seem to die a violent death, before there is time for senescence, much less senility. The character of old age depends upon the nature of the physiological bad debts, some of which are more unnatural than others, much more unnatural in tamed than in wild animals, much more unnatural in man than in animals. Furthermore, civilized man, sheltered from the extreme physical forms of the struggle for existence, can live for a long time with a very defective hereditary constitution, which may end in a period of very undesirable senility. Man is also very deficient in the resting instinct, and seldom takes much thought about resting habits. In many cases, too, there has come about in human societies a system of protective agencies which allow the weak to survive through a period of prolonged senility. We cannot, perhaps, do otherwise in regard to those we love; but it is plain that our better ambition would be to heighten the standard of vitality rather than merely to prolong existence, so that if we have an old age it may be without senility. Those whom the gods love die young.

LITERATURE.—Ebstein, *Die Kunst das menschliche Leben zu verlängern*, Wiesbaden, 1891; Flourens, *De la Longévité humaine*², Paris, 1855; G. M. Humphry, *Old Age, and Changes incidental to it*, Cambridge, 1885; E. Ray Lankester, 'Centenarianism,' in *The Advancement of Science*, London, 1890, also *Comparative Longevity in Man and Animals*, London, 1870; Lejoncourt, *Galerie des centenaires anciens et modernes*, Paris, 1842; E. Metchnikoff, 'Études Biologiques sur la Vieillesse,' in *Annales Inst. Pasteur*, i. (1901) p. 865, ii. (1902) p. 912, also *The Nature of Man* [tr. 1903], esp. ch. x., 'The Scientific Study of Old Age'; Karl Pearson, *The Chances of Death*, vol. i., London, 1897; Pflüger, *Ueber die Kunst der Verlängerung des menschlichen Lebens*, Bonn, 1890; W. J. Thoms, *Human Longevity*, 1873; J. Arthur Thomson, 'On Growing Old,' in *London Quart. Rev.*, April 1903; H. de Varigny, art 'Croissance' in Richet's *Dict. de Physiologie*, iv., 1900; August Weismann, 'The Duration of Life,' in *Essays upon Heredity*, Oxford, 1889.

J. ARTHUR THOMSON.

AGED.—See ABANDONMENT AND EXPOSURE, OLD AGE.

AGES OF THE WORLD.

AGES OF THE WORLD (Primitive and American).—**1.** The conception of a series of cosmic eras, mutually related, yet separated from each other by cataclysms destroying the entire known world and forming the basis for an essentially new creation, is peculiar to a high degree of religious development. The idea of creation is common to practically all religious systems (see art. COSMOGONY), and at a later, though still relatively primitive, period is evolved the notion of a cosmic cataclysm which is to annihilate the world. Still later, it would seem, comes the doctrine that after this cosmic annihilation there is to be a new world, a belief which is found, for instance, in systems so divergent as the Iranian and the Norse. Closely connected with the belief in the regeneration of the world is the well-nigh universal doctrine that the entire earth has already been destroyed by a flood (see DELUGE). The theory of Ages of the World has been carried still further by the phase which holds that the present cosmic era has been preceded by others, and the Greek, Hindu, and Buddhist systems have even evolved a series of cycles each of which contains four Ages, and which have been and are to be repeated in infinite succession.

2. The most familiar example of the belief in Ages of the World is, of course, the philosophized Greek view presented by Hesiod (*Works and Days*, 109–201), according to whom there have been four Ages—golden, silver, brass, and iron—each worse than the one preceding. Equally pessimistic is the Hindu system of Ages, where the four *yugas*, or Ages of a 'day of Brahma' (12,000 years), are successively shorter in duration and increasingly degenerate. Among primitive peoples such a series of Ages of the World seems to be unknown, yet it is noteworthy that among the South American Indians it is generally held that the world has already been destroyed twice, once by fire and again by flood, as among the eastern Tupis and the Arawaks of Guiana. In like manner, the ancient Peruvians fancied not only that two cosmic cataclysms had occurred, but that the world was again to be destroyed, so that they stood in terror of every lunar and solar eclipse.

3. Outside the great culture nations of Asia, Northern Africa, and Europe, however, only the Aztecs of ancient Mexico, perhaps under the influence of the still more highly developed Mayas of Yucatan, evolved a doctrine of Ages of the World. This marvellous people held that the present era, which bore no special name, was preceded by four Ages or 'Suns': the Sun of Earth, the Sun of Fire, the Sun of Air, and the Sun of Water. Each of these cycles had been terminated by a fearful and universal cataclysm, and the Aztecs looked forward with dread to the end of the present era. At the close of each cycle of fifty-two years they were filled with special fear; every fire was extinguished, and all the priests, followed by the people, marched in solemn procession to a mountain two leagues from the capital. There they watched with bated breath for the rising of the Pleiades, and when this constellation was seen, the priests rekindled fires by the friction of two pieces of wood, one of which was placed on the breast of a human sacrifice, while the multitude rejoiced in the assurance that the world would surely survive for another cycle of fifty-two years. It is noteworthy that Aztec sources vary widely with regard to both the length and the sequence of the cosmic eras, the latter being given not only as stated above, but also as Water, Air, Fire, Earth; Earth, Air, Fire, Water; Water, Earth, Air, Fire; and Water, Air, Earth, Fire. In like manner, the order of the cataclysms which terminated the several eras varies according to the different sources, but it is certain at least that the Sun of Earth was terminated by famine, the Sun of Fire by conflagration, the Sun of Air by a hurricane, and the Sun of Water by a flood.

4. The basis of this Aztec belief in Ages of the World is not altogether certain. It has been suggested that it was due, at least in part, to the tremendous natural phenomena of a tropical country, and also to the political and social revolutions which took place in ancient Mexico. The former explanation is doubtless the one to be preferred, implying a reminiscence of some remote catastrophe, mythopoetically magnified by successive generations, especially as this hypothesis also explains the characteristic South American belief in a twofold destruction of the world by fire and flood.

LITERATURE.—Waitz, *Anthropologie der Naturvölker*, iv. 161–163 (Leipzig, 1864); Brinton, *Myths of the New World*², pp. 229–233 (New York, 1876); Réville, *Native Religions of Mexico and Peru*, pp. 113–118 (London, 1884); Ehrenreich, *Mythen und Legenden der südamer. Urvölker*, pp. 30–31 (Berlin, 1905).

LOUIS H. GRAY.

AGES OF THE WORLD (Babylonian).—Even before the discovery of the cuneiform inscriptions, it was known that the Babylonians had reflected on the course of the world's history, and that they regulated the Ages of the World according to the movements of the planets. Seneca * reports a statement of Berosus, who under the rule of the Seleucids was priest in the Marduk temple of Babylon, and whose lost historical work *Chaldaica* was intended to prove the commencement of a new world period under the Seleucids or under Alexander.

'Berosus says that everything takes place according to the course of the planets, and he maintains this so confidently that he determines the times for the conflagration of the world and for the flood. He asserts that the world will burn when all the planets which now move in different courses come together in the Crab,† so that they all stand in a straight line in the same sign, and that the future flood will take place when the same conjunction occurs in Capricorn. For the former is the constellation of the summer solstice, the latter of the winter solstice; they are the decisive signs of the zodiac, because the turning-points of the year lie in them.'

These accounts of Berosus have here, as well as in the narratives of the Creation and the Flood, been proved thoroughly reliable. The teaching which underlies them regarding the course of the world corresponds to the accounts which we can read from the cuneiform inscriptions.

* *Fragm. hist. Græc.* ii. 50.

† The sign of the Crab in the zodiac is the turning-point of the summer sun, if the vernal equinox lies in the Ram; the corresponding turning-point of the winter sun is Capricorn. Our calendar has retained the designations, although the vernal equinox has long ago moved into the Fish.

The Babylonian doctrine, which we find popularized in myths, dramatic and festive customs, and games, inquires into the origin of things and the development of the world from its beginnings in chaos to its renewal in future æons. The doctrine has spread over the whole world. We find it again in Egypt, in the religion of the Avesta, and in India; traces of it are discovered in China, as well as in Mexico and among the savage nations of South America. To refer these phenomena back to 'elementary ideas' (Bastian, *Völkeridee*), such as may arise independently among different peoples, will not hold good in view of the circumstance that we have to do with ideas connected with definite facts which rest on continued astronomical observations. Babylonia was, moreover, according to a constant tradition, the home of astronomy ('Chaldean wisdom'), and there the science of the stars formed the basis of all intellectual culture.

In the Babylonian conception of the universe, which regards everything earthly as a copy of a heavenly prototype, the zodiac is considered the most important part of the whole universe. The zodiac (*šupuk šamê*) is the broad 'Way' on the heavens, *c.* 20 degrees, upon which the sun, the moon, Venus and the four other moving stars (planets) known to antiquity, trace out their course; while the other stars, the fixed stars, seem to stand still on the ball of the revolving heavens. The moving stars were regarded as interpreters of the Divine will. The heaven of fixed stars was related to them like a commentary written on the margin of a book of revelation.

The rulers of the zodiac are the sun, the moon, and Venus. In a mythological text (*WAI.* iv. pl. 5) we are told that Bel placed them to rule the *šupuk šamê*. The four remaining planets, Marduk-Jupiter, Nebo-Mercury, Ninib-Mars, and Nergal-Saturn, correspond to the quarter appearances of the three, and have their special place of revelation at the four quarter points of the cycle, or, speaking in terms of space, at the four corners of the world. Every one of the astral divinities represents the whole Divine power. Polytheism rests on myth, which popularizes the teaching, and on worship, which again is a product of the mythology. The temple-teaching at every place of worship serves to prove that the divinity reveals itself at a particular place in a definite form and shape, such as result from the relation of that place to the corresponding sacred region of the heavens (*τόπος*, *templum*). The local god is *summus deus* for the region; the other gods are like wonder-working saints.

Seeing, however, that the Divine power reveals itself in the zodiac, the theory involves a triadic conception of the godhead. The triad—sun, moon, and Venus—in their relation to each other, as well as each of these three bodies individually, comprehends the whole being of the godhead. In the case of every mythological phenomenon, the question must be raised whether the divinity in the particular place or in the expression of its worship stands for the sun, the moon, or the Venus- (Ištar-) character. In each case, however, the deity represents at the same time the whole cycle, which repeats its phenomena in every microcosm of the natural world. The same is true of Marduk, Nebo, Ninib, and Nergal. In the teaching of Babylon, which is best known to us, the chief points in the sun's track belong to them in a special sense as well as the quarter appearances of the sun's course. They can thus be designated sun-gods, but they can equally well be represented as forms of the moon or of Venus as they appear in their course. In like manner, they are representatives of the course of the cycle of nature (Tammuz in the upper and under world), which runs parallel with the astral phenomena in the changes of the year. Marduk and Nebo as the embodiments of the spring and harvest phenomena, or Ninib and Nergal as the embodiments of the phenomena of summer and winter, could occupy the place of Tammuz in both halves of his cycle.

The Babylonian sages reached the profound conception that time and space are identical.* Both are revelations of the Divine power, and have therefore the same principles of division.

The course of the world cycle is consummated in the struggle of the two powers of the world system, light and darkness, the upper and the under world, the summer of the world and the winter of the world. In the myths the sun and the moon are the combatants. The moon is, according to the Babylonian teaching, the star of the upper world (the reverse holds in Egypt). She dies and rises again from the dead (*inbu ša ina rammaniša ibbanû*, 'fruit, which produces itself out of itself'); she symbolizes the power of life from the dead. The sun, which, in opposition to the moon, stands at the low point, and in which the stars disappear, is the power of the under world. 'Ištar desires to become the queen of heaven.' In the myth she is the heavenly virgin (in the zodiac she is represented by the figure of the Virgin with the ear of corn or with the child) who gives birth to the sun-child or the moon-child, which then overcomes the dragon of darkness and thereby brings in the new era,—but then at the highest point of the course dies and sinks down into the under world; or she is the Venus, who descends into the under world and brings up the fallen ones. The four planets of the four points of the world, which indicate in the gyration the turning-points of the sun (Ninib and Nergal) and the equinoctial points (Marduk and Nebo), are made use of in the mythology in the following manner: Marduk is the bringer in of the new time (the spring sun), Nebo (Hermes with the balance of the dead) is the guide to the dark half of the lower world, Ninib (Mars) brings the doom of the change of the summer sun (death of Tammuz by the boar, the sacred animal of Ninib), Nergal is lord of the dark half of the under world. Thus Marduk and Nebo exchange places under the precedence of Babylon, whose local god is Marduk. The rôle of bringing in the new time belongs in reality to Nebo. His name indicates that he is the 'prophet' of the new time (Nebo-Mercury is the morning-star; in the word lies the root of the official name *nebî*, 'prophet,' *i.e.* one who announces the new age).†

The change of the arc of day and the arc of night, the summer and winter courses of the stars, and the related change of life and death in nature, result in the doctrine of the *change of the Ages*. The change of the seasons corresponds to the succession of day and night. According to the principle that the microcosm everywhere reflects the macrocosm, the year is a copy of the greater period of time, in which the evolution of the world is consummated, and the seasons correspond to Ages of the World.

The acceptance of Ages of the World must go back to the observation of the stages of the sun's course. Before we speak of these Sun Ages of the World, we shall give a survey of traces of Ages of the World in which the connexion with these stages is not at first apparent.

The cuneiform texts mention 'kings before the Flood' in opposition to 'kings after the Flood.' They are thought of as in past time:—

* The Assyr.-Bab. *'âlam*, 'world,' is the Heb. *ôlām*, 'primeval time,' 'eternity.'

† Jupiter, as a planet, has in itself no claim to special emphasis. In our order of the days of the week it occupies the fifth place (Thursday, *Jeudi*, *Jovis dies*). The fact that the classical peoples raise him to the rank of *summus deus* is an indication of the wide diffusion of the Babylonian conception of the world.

1. *Lam abûbi*, **'the time before the Flood.'** In the time before the Flood there lived the heroes, who (according to the Gilgameš Epic, which on the 11th table tells the story of the Flood) dwell in the under world, or, like the Babylonian Noah, are removed into the heavenly world. At that time there lived, too, the (seven) sages. Ašurbanipal speaks of inscriptions of the time before the Flood. A magical text mentions a saying of an old sage before the Flood. *WAI.* v. 44, 20*a*, speaks of 'kings after the Flood.' Berosus indicates along with the sages the early kings, who together lived 120 years.

1. Aloros (=Bab. *Arûru*?).
2. Alaporos (Adaporos)=*adapa*, *i.e.* Marduk, the son of Ea in the heroic age, who, as the bringer in of the new age (cf. Ἀδὰμ μέλλων), Marduk as fighting with the dragon, will introduce the new age of the world.*
3. Amêlon=*amêlu*, 'man.' As Adapa corresponds to the Biblical patriarch Seth, Amêlon in like manner corresponds to Enosh (*i.e.* man).
4. Ammenon = *ummânu* ('workmaster') = Cain (Cainan), 'smith' (cf. Aram. *qainâya*—'smith').
5. Megalaros=?.
6. Daonos=?.
7. Evedorachos=*Enmeduranki*, 'favourite of the great gods,' who taught his son the secret of heaven and earth; *i.e.* Enoch, who walked with God, and after a life of 365 years (the number of the sun) was taken away. The Jewish feast of the turning of the winter sun (*Ḥanukkah*, 'feast,' later applied to the dedication of the Temple) was connected with Enoch. Jubilees (4[21]) says of him: 'Enoch was among the angels of God six jubilees; and they showed him all that the *rule of the sun* is in heaven and on the earth, and he wrote it all down.'
8. Amempsinos=*amel-Sin*, 'man of the god Sin'=Methuselah. There is a Babylonian text which communicates 'the secrets' of Amel-Sin.
9. Otiartes (Opartes?)=*Ubara-Tutu*, father of the Babylonian Noah (Utnapištim, Ḥasisatra, in Berosus *Xisuthros*).

Berosus relates that Kronos before the Flood had ordered Xisuthros to engrave with letter-signs all things according to their beginning, middle, and end (engraving on tablets with cuneiform letters is meant), and to deposit them in Sippar. After the Flood his children and relatives had gone to Babylon, taken the writings from Sippar, and circulated them among the people.

2. The historic period, which again unfolds itself in Ages. The division of the Ages into periods before and after the Flood is also connected with the course of the stars. The Golden Age of early times corresponds to the time in which the vernal equinox in the zodiac goes through the dominion of Anu (four figures). The Flood brought the course of the world through the dominion of Ea (four figures, water-region); the historical period corresponds with Bel's realm of the zodiac. For the track of the zodiac is portioned out to Anu, Bel, and Ea, the triad of Divine power in the whole universe of space, corresponding on the zodiac to Sin, Šamaš, and Ištar. The restoration of the world after the Flood corresponds to the fashioning of the world after the original chaos, which also appears as the power of the waters (in the myth the water-dragon had been subdued); the world after the Flood corresponds to the primeval world after the Creation.†

The application of Ages of the World to the periods of the evolution of the æon of mankind is connected in a special way with the teaching about the calendar, which is based on observation of the *precession of the equinoxes.*

By the precession of the equinoxes is meant the gradual displacement of the same point of day in the ecliptic, the middle line of the zodiac, which the sun's track marks out. The inclination of the axis of the earth to the plane of the sun is variable. In accordance with this, the point of intersection of the apparent plane of the sun and of the equator recedes for the spectator For the observation of the ancients this resulted in the following phenomenon: The position of the sun in the same spring days recedes from year to year farther towards the east. In 72 years the displacement amounts to a day, in every 2200 years therefore, about a figure in the zodiac. The vernal equinox traverses once in 12×2200 years the water-region (Flood) and the fire-region. On this fact rests the teaching of Berosus given above (p. 183[b]).

In the region of further Asia, the earliest historical time of which we can find traces in the original sources had placed the cult of the god of the moon in the forefront. Sargon says, in his State inscription of the king of Meluḫḫa, that his fathers had, from distant times, since the æon of the moon-god (*Adî Nannar*), sent no more messengers to his predecessors. In the scheme of the partition of the world between the moon and the sun (moon=star of the upper world, sun =the star of the under world; see above, p. 184[b]), Nebo would, in the pre-Babylonian order, correspond to the moon, Marduk to the sun. Nebo, too, in accordance with his character, is the 'prophet'; and, according to the nature of the doctrine regarding him, also the victor over the power of darkness, the bearer of the tablets of fate. Under the influence of the supremacy of Babylon he has exchanged his rôle with Marduk; and this, by the way, agrees with the principle of the Babylonian doctrine, according to which opposites pass over into one another (east and west, south and north, summer and winter, day and night, exchange their rôles). We could thus speak of an *Age of the moon* or an *Age of Nebo*, to which in the epoch of the supremacy of Babylon an *Age of the sun* or an *Age of Marduk* would correspond. But if there was a theory which reckoned in this way, still the latter is at least subsequently regarded as the Age of the moon; *i.e.* the Nebo Age, which preceded the rule of Marduk of Babylon, has been transposed in the teaching of the calendar, which was reckoned according to the precession.

(*a*) *Age of the Twins.*—In the Age before the rise of Babylon (about B.C. 5000–2800) the sun stood in the zodiacal sign called the Twins. If we were to make additional use of this circumstance in the theory of the Ages of the World, as we are inclined to do, the two phases of the waxing and waning moon would in harmony with it correspond to these twins. The moon also is called repeatedly *ellamonê*, *i.e.* 'twins'; and the hieroglyphics of the zodiac, which even to-day indicate the Twins in the calendar, consist of the picture of the waxing and waning moon, just as the Romans represented Janus, who bears the character of the moon, as the two half-moons with human faces.

This Age of the Twins was for Babylon the age of the settlement of the Semitic Babylonians.

The Twins (*Dioscuri*) thus supply the ruling motive for all the myths which indicate the beginning of a new epoch (Cyrus, Cambyses, Romulus, Remus, etc.). And if any one in the time of the Assyrian predominance wished to dispose of the claims of Babylon, he went back to the archaic form of calculation. Either Nebo was deliberately raised to a more prominent place than Marduk, or (*e.g.*, under Sargon) Sivan, the month of the moon-god, was regarded as the first month of the year. In the same way the Roman calendar was made archaic by beginning the year with Janus (January), although the last month was called December (*i.e.* the tenth month).

* Marduk and Adapa are both *abkallu*, *i.e.* 'sages' in the Divine sense. Sennacherib, who, by the destruction of Babylon and the raising of Nineveh into prominence by violent means, sought to inaugurate a new era, allows himself to be glorified as Adapa. He says (*K.* 270, 1*a*): 'Assur spoke in a dream to the grandfather of the king, my lord "*abkallu*": "the king, the king of kings (Ašurbanipal), is the grandson of the *abkallu* and Adapa."' See p. 186[b] for the inauguration of a new Age with Ašurbanipal.

† The Biblical story of the Flood still shows traces of the notion found in the Babylonian narrative of the flooding of the whole world. The mountain where the ark landed is originally the mountain of the world. The report of the Priests' Code (Gn 8[4f.] 13) gives the precise height of the mountain. On its top stands the tree of life (olive tree) from which the dove brings the leaf. The ark of the Indian Flood also lands on the mountain of the world.

One would expect an Age of the sun to follow an Age of the moon (the sun and the moon are also twins). As a matter of fact, the reckoning of the calendar, which was changed about B.C. 2800, on the basis of the precession into the next figure of the zodiac, was so adjusted that in the zodiac the figure of the Bull followed the Twins.

(*b*) *Age of the Bull.*—This reform of the calendar was assisted by the actual state of affairs. The time of its introduction corresponds with the period in which Babylon became the metropolis of the world. Marduk, the god of the city of Babylon, the 'farmer of Babylon' (Nebuchadrezzar calls himself *Ikkaru ša Babili*, as representative of the god on earth), is symbolized by the bull, which corresponds to the figure of the Bull in the heavens.* In this way the Age of the sun came at the same time to its rights, for Marduk as the representative of the Divine power is in an especial sense the sun-god. Ḫammurabi took advantage of the reform of the calendar to glorify his rule as a new epoch of the world. He says that he has succeeded in 'exalting Marduk.' The priests of Babylon celebrate Marduk as the fighter with the dragon and as the demiurge, and found the claim of Babylon to world empire on the rôle of Marduk as creator of the world. The honour which belonged to Nebo as the lord of the destinies is transferred to Marduk. He determines on New Year's day the fate of the world. Nebo, who in the older teaching carried the tablets of fate, is now recorder of the destinies.

The calendar which corresponded to the Age of the Bull must have reckoned the beginning of the year a month earlier, so that the year began with Iyyar and closed with Nisan; for the world-epoch embracing a sign of the zodiac corresponds to the course of the sun through a sign of the zodiac, *i.e.* one month. That it was so reckoned can, of course, be proved only indirectly. The king of Assyria allowed himself to be invested in office in the month Iyyar. The investiture is a ceremony which took place also in Babylon, and therefore according to Babylonian law. The king seized the hands of Bel-Marduk, and by this act his rule obtained its ratification and consecration. This inauguration was still observed in Iyyar after Nisan must have long been regarded as the first month. Under Sargon and Nebuchadrezzar the inauguration took place in Nisan. The new calendar had thus in the meantime secured recognition for its claims.

The mythological motives of the Age of the Bull had to be taken from the myths of Marduk. Seeing that Marduk is regarded as the child of the sun (the ideogram signifies 'son of the sun'), the motive of the mysterious birth is connected with his appearance as well as the motive of the persecution by the dragon (exposure and rescue). The myths of Marduk which are as yet known have not supplied evidence for his birth from the virgin queen of heaven (see above, p. 184[b]). But the myths tell of the marriage of Marduk. The child of the sun in the course of the cycle becomes the lover and the husband of the queen of heaven (Ištar). Every historical celebrity who, in the Bull age, was distinguished as a ruler of the world, a founder of dynasties, etc., was furnished with the Marduk motive, if some antiquated method corresponding to the age of the Twins did not prefer the motive of the Dioscuri (see above, p. 185[b]). In this way we can explain the mythical setting of the history of Sargon I., who founded Babylon, and in all probability was the first to introduce the Marduk method of reckoning.

* In the Babylonian ideogram of the planets, Jupiter signifies 'bull of the sun,' and is explained as the 'furrow of the heavens' which the bull of the sun ploughs.

'Sargon the mighty king of Agada am I. My mother was a vestal,* my father of the lower class. . . . My vestal mother conceived me, in secret did she bear me. She laid me in an ark of bulrushes, closed my doors with pitch, laid me in the river. . . . The river bore me downwards to Akki, the water-carrier. Akki, the water-carrier, received me in the friendliness of his heart, brought me up as his child, made me his gardener. During my activity Ištar fell in love with me. . . . For years I enjoyed sovereign power.'

It is related of the hero of the Babylonian Gilgameš Epic how Ištar seeks to win his love. Ælian, however (*Hist. Anim.* xii. 21), says his mother had been a king's daughter, who conceived the hero by means of an insignificant man.

Gudea, the South Babylonian priestly prince, says to the goddess, who stands by his side, 'I have no mother, thou art my mother; I have no father, thou art my father; in a secret place hast thou borne me.'

Ninib appears in an epic poem as the hero, who will allow his royal power to extend to the bounds of heaven and earth. He is a child of Ištar, he is called 'My father know I not.'

Ašurnaṣirpal allows the following story to be told of himself:

'I was born in the midst of mountains, which no man knoweth; thou hast, O Ištar, with the glance of thine eyes chosen me, hast longed for my supremacy, hast brought me forth from the mountains, and called me as ruler of men.'

Ašurbanipal wishes to be regarded as a child of Ištar, who had once nourished him. The writers of his tablets represent his Age as the Golden Age of the world (cf. p. 187[b]).

(*c*) *Age of the Ram.*—The recognition of the fact that the calendar must now be arranged according to the Ram as the vernal equinox, and the fixing of it so, give to the otherwise unimportant king Nabonassar (Nabû-nasir, 797–734) a special significance. The framers of the calendar in his time have dated a new age from Nabonassar. Syncellus relates (*Chronographia*, 207) that Nabonassar, according to the testimony of Alexander Polyhistor and Berosus, destroyed all historical documents relating to his predecessors, in order that dates might be reckoned only according to his time (*συναγάγων τὰς πράξεις τῶν πρὸ αὐτοῦ βασιλέων ἠφάνισεν, ὅπως ἀπ' αὐτοῦ ἡ καθαρίθμησις γένηται τῶν Χαλδαίων βασιλέων*).

The breaking of the tablets is not to be taken literally. It is the same as the *burning of the books* in reforms of other ages, in Persia under Alexander, in China, B.C. 213, under Chin-shi-hoang. In the case of the burning of the libraries of Alexandria, too, this motive must be taken into consideration. It signifies the beginning of a new era of Islām in Egypt under Omar.

This is the reason why the Babylonian chronology contained in the extant inscriptions begins with Nabonassar. The Ptolemaic canon, too, which, as is well known, did not follow historical ends, but represented a calendar with astronomical limits,† had begun with Nabonassar. The misunderstanding of Syncellus can also be explained in this way; the *Chronographia* (267) says the Babylonians had from the time of Nabonassar written down the periods of the courses of the stars (*ἀπὸ Ναβονασάρου τοὺς χρόνους τῆς τῶν ἀστέρων κινήσεως Χαλδαῖοι ἠκρίβωσαν*).

In Babylon itself the reform of the Age of the Ram never obtained full recognition, because the Age of Nabonassar coincided with the fall of Babylon. The old Babylonian reckoning kept its hold here. Still Berosus, under the rule of the Seleucids, reckons, as we saw (p. 183[b]), with the Age of the Ram. The new reckoning seems to have found its chief support in Egypt. Just as the Bull Age received recognition by emphasizing Marduk of Babylon, in the same way the Age of the Ram served the purpose of glorifying Jupiter Amon, who is represented with the head of a

* *Enîtu*, the 'sister of god,' in the Code of Ḫammurabi, the priestly representative of the sister-wife of Marduk, Ištar.

† It was carried further for several centuries after Christ. Claudius Ptolemæus is by no means the author; he had collected the traditions and preserved them in their true form.

ram, although he is in his nature identical with Marduk. Alexander the Great, who allowed himself to be celebrated by contemporary writers as lord of worlds, and to be painted by Apelles as Jupiter, consulted the oracle in the oasis of Jupiter Amon. Manetho says that under Bocchoris 'a ram (ἀρνίον) spoke.'

The doctrine of the Ages of the World, as may already have been inferred from the preceding explanation, is connected with the **expectation of a deliverer**. As deliverer there appears the Divine power, which reveals itself in the spring equinox. It is Marduk-Adapa, it is the 'ram,' which, according to the Age, overcomes the power of darkness. In 4 Ezra (11^{44-46}) the seer reflects on the ways of the Highest:

'Then the Highest looked at his times; lo, they were at an end, and his æons (*sæcula*) were full. . . . Now the earth will be refreshed and return . . . and trust in the judgment and mercy of her creator.'

In these words lies the fundamental religious idea of the doctrine of the Ages of the World. 'The æons were full.' 'The time is fulfilled.'*

The connexion of the doctrine of the Ages of the World with the expectation of a deliverer produces the following characteristic opinions, which meet us at once as axioms:

1. *The Age of perfection lies at the beginning.* Just as pure knowledge, revealed by the godhead, lies at the beginning, so that it is the task of science to discover the original truth by observation of the book of revelation written down in the stars, and to obtain freedom from the errors which have crept in through human guilt, so also the Age of pure happiness lies at the beginning.

This fundamental idea has produced a special theory regarding the doctrine of the Ages of the World which is based on the connexion of the planets with the *metals*. Silver is the metal of the moon, gold the metal of the sun,† copper the metal of Ištar. According to the reckoning which begins with the Age of the moon, the silver must have been the first Age, on which a less valuable then followed. We know from classical antiquity the succession: Golden, Silver, Copper (Iron) Ages (Hesiod, *Works and Days*, 90 ff., and Ovid, *Metam.* i. 89 ff.). The succession of the Ages of the World lies also at the basis of the Book of Daniel. The commencement with the Golden Age points to Egypt, where the sun predominates (see above, p. 184b). It may, however, point to the Babylonian conception, which gives the first place to Marduk as a sun-phenomenon, just as the planetal series of our days of the week places Sunday before Monday. The Golden Age is also called the Age of Saturn. Owing to the change of the heptagram into a pentagram, Saturn is represented by the sun, as Mars is by the moon; and an astronomical text of the Babylonians, which has been handed down to us from the time of the Arsacids, expressly says that Saturn and the sun are identical.‡ As far as the rest are concerned, the order of succession corresponds to the astral theory. The third, the Copper Age, corresponds to Ištar-Venus, the third figure among the rulers of the zodiac.

The succession gold, silver, copper, brings the second characteristic at the same time into view. It is as follows:

2. *The times are becoming worse.*—This is much more strongly expressed when the theory departs from the scheme provided by the planets with regard to the fourth Age, and allows an *Iron* Age, corresponding to the distress of the present time, to follow after the Golden, the Silver, and the Copper Ages. The end of these evil times, which precedes the destruction of the world, is a time of cursing, a time of tribulation, and the reversal of the natural order. The Babylonian omens often speak of this time of cursing, which stands in opposition to the time the deliverer brings (see above): 'When such and such things happen in heaven, then will the clear become dull, the pure dirty, the lands will fall into confusion, prayers will not be heard, the signs of the prophets will become unfavourable.' In a form of curse which speaks of princes who do not obey the commands of the gods, we have the following:

'Under his rule the one will devour the other, the people will sell their children for gold, the husband will desert his wife, the wife her husband, the mother will bolt the door against her daughter.'

In the Atarhases myth, the text of which originates in the 3rd mill. (the time of Ammizaduga), the distresses which precede the Flood are related. In the Ira myth the coming of the deliverer after the time of cursing is expected:

'The seacoast shall not spare the seacoast, Mesopotamia shall not spare Mesopotamia, nor Assyria Assyria, the Elamite the Elamites, the Carsite the Carsites, the Sutæan the Sutæans, the Cutæan the Cutæans, the Lulubæan the Lulubæans, one land another land, one man other men, one brother another, but they shall strike each other dead. But after that shall come the Akkada, who shall lay them all low and overwhelm them severally.'*

Signs in the sun and in the moon proclaim the end. In a hymn we have the following:

'Oh, father Bel . . . oh, lord of the land, the ewe rejects her lamb, the she-goat her kid. How much longer in thy faithful city shall the mother reject her son, the wife her husband? Heaven and earth are laid low, there is no light with us. The sun does not rise with his radiance over the land, the moon does not rise with her light over the land. Sun and moon do not rise with their radiance over the land.'

The time of the curse corresponds to the rule of the powers of the lower world. It is like the time of the descent of Ištar to Hades. When Venus is in the lower world, all life is dead. As it is in the small year, so is it in the world year.

But then comes the great revolution:

3. *The happy time of the beginning comes back.* The Babylonian texts seldom speak of this time of blessing. It is only from the description of the happy rule of kings, who are praised by the writers of the tablets as the bringers in of a new Age, that we can extract the motives of the time of blessing. Especially is this the case with Ašurbanipal.

'Since the time the gods in their friendliness did set me on the throne of my fathers, Ramman has sent forth his rain, Ea opened the springs; the grain was five ells high in the ear, the ears were five-sixths ells long, the harvest was plentiful, the corn was abundant, the seed shot up, the trees bore rich fruits, the cattle multiplied exceedingly. During my reign there was great abundance, under my rule rich blessing streamed down.'

LITERATURE.—A. Jeremias, *Das AT im Lichte des alten Orients*², Leipzig, 1906 (ch. i. 'Die altorientalische Lehre und das altorientalische Weltbild'), *Babylonisches im NT*, do. 1905; Schrader, *KAT* (3rd ed. revised by Zimmern and Winckler, Berlin, 1903), 332 ff., 380 ff.; H. Winckler, *Altorientalische Forschungen*, iii. 179 ff., 274 ff., *Die Weltanschauung des alten Orients*, *Altorientalische Geschichtsauffassung*, *Ex oriente lux*, i. 1, ii. 2 (Leipzig, ed. Pfeiffer), 'Himmelsbild und Weltenbild bei den Babyloniern' in *Der alte Orient*, iii. 213, Leipzig.

ALFRED JEREMIAS.

AGES OF THE WORLD (Buddhist).—The views of the Buddhists on periods of cosmical destruction and renovation were matters of vivid interest to the first Orientalists, as will be seen from the bibliography on p. 190. This interest has rather languished since the publication of the *Religion des Buddha* of Köppen, the last who has dealt thoroughly with this topic.

* *Ūmē imlû*, 'the days are full,' are the words in an oracle which Ašurbanipal receives in Susa, according to which he is said to have been prophesied 1635 years before as the saviour of Nana, the queen of heaven.

† Therefore the relation of the value of silver and gold in antiquity is 1 : 13⅓, *i.e.* the relation of the course of the moon to that of the sun (27 : 360). The remains of colours, which Rawlinson found on the planet steps of the Nebo temple in Borsippa, were for the moon silver (white), for the sun golden, for Venus light-yellow.

‡ Cf. for this, the present writer's *Das AT im Lichte des alten Orients*, p. 13.

* Note how the whole world is embraced in the range of vision.

The fanciful theories of the *Kalpas* or *Ages of the World* do not appear to be essential to Buddhism, whether looked upon as a religion or as a philosophy. Nor are they of mythological moment, being rather matter of 'secular knowledge,' or, as a Buddhist would say, *lokāyatika*. Nevertheless, as they can be proved to be very old; as they are made use of when the myriads of Buddhas of the Great Vehicle are honoured, and have been duly recorded by the Buddhists of every country, Sinhalese as well as Mongolian; as, moreover, some bits of philosophical or religious reflexion are interwoven with them, we may be allowed to consider the subject in all its aspects.

There is no beginning of transmigration (or *saṁsāra*); there will be no end to it: on these two points all Buddhist schools agree. But, without mentioning that speculations on the beginning or the end of the cosmos are forbidden by the Buddha in some texts (see AGNOSTICISM [Buddhist]), it must be observed that there is an end to transmigration for the Arhats, who rightly say at the time of dying, 'This existence is for me the last one.' Moreover, in the Buddhism of the Great Vehicle, Avalokita, for instance (see AVALOKITA), resolved to postpone his entering into Nirvāṇa till every creature should, by his own really divine exertion, have been carried into the peace of salvation. The problem, where the texts are silent, or rather, contradictory, will probably have to be solved as it has been by the Sāṅkhya: the number of the souls being infinite, there will never come a time when all will have attained Nirvāṇa. Hence there need be no despondency, for *we* can be among the elect, if only we care for it.

Theories on the revolutions of the world are said, in the *Brahmajālasutta*, to be extraneous to Buddhism, and even alien to its spirit. But they soon became naturalized; and, while originally very like the Brāhmanical theories, they were worked after a new plan.

There is mention in the fourth edict of Aśoka of the next destruction of the Universe. 'The pious king hopes that his sons and grandsons, and so on, will maintain good practices till the age of cosmical destruction (*saṁvaṭṭakappa*).' This text does not, however, prove that the belief in the very speedy disappearance of Buddhism was still unknown.

The canonical Pāli texts do not furnish us with the complete theory now to be stated. These afford only hints or allusions, from which it is difficult to draw any conclusion as to the conditions of the elaboration of the doctrine. These hints, however, will be carefully pointed out. So far as the Buddhism of the South is concerned, we derive our knowledge from the Commentaries, of which the materials are much older than Buddhaghoṣa, their official compiler; and for the Buddhism of the North from Mongolian, Tibetan, and Chinese sources, confirmed by the *Abhidharma* literature.

The general lines are as follows:

A 'Period' (*kappa*), or 'Great Period' (*mahākappa°, kalpa*) of cosmical evolution, is to be divided into four 'Incalculables' (*asaṅkheyya*) or 'Incalculable Periods' (*asaṅkheyyakappa, asaṅkhyeyakalpa*). These last are always mentioned in the following order: (1) Period of destruction (*saṁvaṭṭakappa, saṁvartakalpa*); (2) of duration of the destruction (*saṁvaṭṭatthāyin, saṁvartasthāyin*, when the world remains destroyed); (3) of renovation, or rather revolution (*vivaṭṭa°, vivarta°*); (4) of duration of the world renovated (*Aṅguttara*, ii. 142, iv. 100; *Majjh.* i. 35).

How long is an 'Incalculable' period? The answer given by Buddha himself is a very good one: It is difficult, *i.e.* impossible, to exhaust an 'Incalculable' by numbering hundreds of thousands of years. In *Saṁyutta*, ii. 181–2, there is a simile which has found its way into the Chinese and Sinhalese records: 'Suppose a mountain of iron to be touched every hundred years by a muslin veil; the mountain will be destroyed before the Incalculable is at an end—and the *saṁsāra* has no common measure with the Incalculables, nay, with hundreds of thousands of Incalculables': the *saṁsāra* being 'infinite,' as we should say, and the 'Incalculables' indefinite.

The same problem occurs in the *Mahāvastu* (i. 77). It is said that the future Buddha must, before becoming a Buddha, pass through 'stages' or 'terraces' of immeasurable duration (*aparimita, aprameya*). 'If it be so,' asks Kātyāyana, 'how will the future Buddha ever attain the higher stage?' Answer: 'It is the same with the Ages of the World: each of them is immeasurable, and nevertheless there are many Ages.'

Notwithstanding these very clear statements, Buddhists and moderns have tried to calculate the 'Incalculable.' 'Asaṅkhyeya,' like many other words of the same meaning (and there are plenty of words in Sanskrit to express 'incalculable'), has been used to indicate an exact number. But the lists of 'high numbers,' the so-called *paṅkti*, are constructed on different principles: the progression being sometimes by multiples (10, 100, 1000; or 10, 10,000, 1,000,000 . . .), sometimes by squares, and the *asaṅkhyeya* does not always hold the same place in the lists. A. Rémusat said that an 'Incalculable'=1 followed by 17 ciphers (100,000,000,000,000,000) years. But these figures give a *parārdha*, not an *asaṅkhyeya*. From the *Dhammapadīpikā*, Burnouf and Hardy admit 1 followed by 97 ciphers; and there is, according to the first named, a very ingenious combination of the first 'nombres premiers' in the formation of this number. Joinville (Sinhalese unnamed sources) has 1 followed by 63 ciphers. From Burmese sources, Pallegoix has 1 followed by 168 ciphers, and Burnouf, 1+140 ciphers. According to the Northern *Abhidharma* list, *asaṅkhyeya* being the 53rd of a geometric progression (1, 10, 100 . . .), we have 1 followed by 52 ciphers. Lastly, the *Buddhāvataṁsaka* list gives a much larger number of ciphers. Given a progression, 10, 10^2, 10^4, 10^8, . . . *asaṅkhyeya* is the 104th term: to write the number thus described we should require 352 septillions of kilometres of ciphers, allowing that one cipher occupies a length of 0.001 m. That suggests in some degree the vastness of an 'Incalculable.'

Theoretically, each 'Incalculable' is divided into twenty *Antarakalpas* (*°kappa*) or 'Intermediate Periods.' But the advantage of this division is not very clear, except in the third Incalculable.

When the Great Period begins, of which the Destruction Age is the first part, the average duration of human life is 80,000 years. Gradually there is moral deterioration, with a corresponding decrease in the age of man (see *infra*, p. 189^b). The destruction is near at hand. A hundred thousand years before it is to begin, a *Deva* or Angel (a 'Buddhist Noah,' as he has been called) gives to the world of conscious creatures a warning about the forthcoming calamity.* In course of time all the creatures, with the exception just to be noted, attain reincarnation in higher worlds, *i.e.* in spheres which will not be overtaken by the destruction. The time for a higher reward may be said to have come for the great majority of creatures, after numerous migrations amongst ordinary good and bad births. They alone 'in whom the root of merit is destroyed' by adhesion to wrong views, and for whom 'the word of deliverance has utterly perished,' cannot by any means ascend into the higher realms; and as the hell in which they are tormented is going to be annihilated, they will take rebirth in the hell of some universe whose destruction is not imminent. Elsewhere it is said that there are self-made hells for them. In the old sources it would seem that only Devadatta, the cousin and rival of Śākyamuni, will endure 'for an age,' or 'for ages' (*kappaṭṭha*) in a state of pain.

This gradual disappearing of the animate world (*sattaloka*) fulfils the first Intermediate Period of the Age of Destruction. Now begins the Destruction of the 'receptacle-world' (*bhājanaloka*) itself, by fire (*tejaḥsaṁvartanī*), by water (*ap°*), or by wind (*vāyu°*).† There is a complete set of 64 Great Periods, in regular succession; seven destructions by fire, then one by water, then seven by fire, then one by water, and so on, the last, *i.e.* the 64th, being by wind. We are told that the destruction by fire does not reach so high in the various spheres of the cosmos as does the destruction by water; and the

* All the gods called Lokabyūhas hold this office of Noah, according to the *Visuddhimagga* (Warren, p. 322).

† *Visuddhimagga*, xiii.; āposaṁvaṭṭa, tejo°, vāyu° (*JPTS*, 1891, p. 118). For the Brāhmanical speculations, see 'Matsyapurāṇa,' *ap.* Aufrecht, *Cat. Oxoniensis*, p. 346; Böhtl.-Roth, *s.vv.* 'Saṁvarta, Saṁvartaka.'

destruction by wind is greater than the destruction by water (*saṁvaṭṭasīmā*, limit of destruction).*

But there are discrepancies between the European authorities, and probably also between the sources. Köppen has a very ingenious theory, stating that there are great, mean, and little destructions by fire, and so on. He goes so far as to ascertain the order in which they will succeed, though he confessedly fails to find any authority to support his views. Does the destruction by fire annihilate only the worlds up to the abode of the Mahābrahmans, including the sphere of the first meditation? Or does it annihilate the two abodes immediately superior belonging to the second Dhyāna (*Parittaśubhas* and *Apramāṇābhas*)? Does the Water-Destruction, which in any case destroys the three second Dhyāna abodes, destroy also the two first third Dhyāna abodes?† Hardy, misunderstood by Köppen, gives a third opinion: the water destroys the first third Dhyāna abode. Lastly, there seems to be a general agreement as regards the Wind which overthrows the worlds up to the second fourth Dhyāna abode. The matter would be a little too fanciful to detain our attention if we did not find in the *Brahmajāla*, the first Sutta of the *Dighanikāya*, the origin of the contest. Buddha, explaining the origination of the universe, states that, during the period of destruction, beings have mostly been reborn in the World of Radiance (*i.e.* in the third second Dhyāna abode)—hence the opinion that the fire (the fire must be meant, as it is the more frequent) reaches up to the second second Dhyāna abode; but Buddha adds that, at the origin of time, the Palace of Brahmā with Mahābrahmā appears, this being fallen from the World of Radiance. There is no mention here of the two first second Dhyāna abodes, which would have been necessary steps of decadence; hence the opinion that the destruction does not go higher than Brahma Palace—*i.e.* the apex of the second meditation.

We may conclude that the theory of the celestial abodes was not perfectly elaborated when the *Brahmajāla* was compiled.

Details ‡ are given of the destruction by Fire, wrought by seven suns, well known in the Brāhmanical literature. All water is dried up, beginning with the small rivers; and the appearance of the seventh sun gives rise to the general conflagration. As regards Water, the *Śikṣāsamuchchaya* is the only text to give us the names of the four Dragon-Kings who pour drops always increasing in size, each for five Intermediate Periods: Iṣādhāra, Gajaprameha, Acchinnadhāra, Sthūlabinduka.§ It treats the matter from a philosophical point of view: 'Whence comes the water?' it is asked. 'From nowhere.' 'And where does it go when the deluge is at an end?' 'To nowhere.' The destruction is also said to reach the Brahma-heaven, but it is not said to go higher. The destruction by winds is parallel. The Pāli commentator gives the name of one of them, *prachchanda*.

Nothing is known of the Second Period. The world remains chaotic, or, if we prefer it, a pure nothing: 'The upper regions of space become one with those below, and wholly dark.' There are no ashes left by the fire; no dust by the wind. One would assume that the water (which, being very acid, disintegrates the Iron or Crystal Mountains) does not annihilate itself. On the contrary, 'the water does not settle so long as anything remains, but everything becomes impregnated with water and then suddenly settles and disappears.'

When the time of renovation is come again, *i.e.* when the former merit of the beings born in higher abodes is exhausted, and they have to be reborn in inferior regions, first (in the case of destruction by fire) appears the abode of Brahmā (Brahmavimāna), with its threefold division of inhabitants, coming from the Ābhāsvara abode; then in order the three Deva abodes of the Parinirmitavaśavartins, the Nirmāṇaratis and the Yāmyavimāna (gods, Yāmas, the Tuṣitas, etc., are not named); then the Circle of the Wind (*vāyumaṇḍala*) on which is established the Circle of Water, etc., with Mount Meru and its heavenly inhabitants, with the sun and the moon, etc.: all this is called the *bhājanaloka* or the 'receptacle-world.' And that is the end of the first Intermediate Period of the 'Incalculable of Renovation.'

During the nineteen following periods the inferior parts of the *bhājanaloka* are successively peopled by men, and so on. First the men are said to be *aparimitāyu*, *i.e.* 'of immeasurable life.' Such they remain to the end of the Period of Renovation, according to the *Abhidharmakośa*. The sources known to Hardy and Köppen agree in stating a decrease to 80,000 or 84,000 years. When the infernal beings have appeared, the Incalculable Period of Renovation (*vivartamānāvasthā*) is finished.

The following Period of Duration (*vivṛttāvasthā prārabdhā*) is divided into twenty well-characterized Intermediate Periods. During the first, the whole of which is of decrease, the average duration of human life falls from 'immeasurable length' (or from 80,000 years) to ten years. The eighteen following are divided into two parts: the first of increase (*utkarṣakalpa*, *ūrdhvamukha*), during which life increases from ten years to 80,000 years; the second of decrease (*apakarṣakalpa*, *adhomukha*) inversely to the first. The twentieth and last is only of increase. We do not know if the first and the last are shorter than the remaining ones, but that seems probable.

Here the Brāhmanic theory of the Four *yugas* finds a place: the increasing will be divided into the Iron, Bronze, Silver, and Golden Ages; and the decreasing will be parallel (Kali, Dvāpara, Tretā, Kṛta). We are now (A.D. 1907) in the Iron Age of the first Intermediate Period of the Period of Stability (this Intermediate is only decreasing). From a hundred years, the highest attained in the Iron Age, life is declining to ten.

When the decreasing Kali Age begins, the five calamities (*kaṣāya*) begin to prevail; but when life is reduced to ten years (*daśavarṣāyuḥ kalpaḥ*) the destiny of men is worse. At the end of every Intermediate Period (except the last, or the 20th, which is only of increase) the greater number of living beings pass away by hunger, epidemics, and sword. Some say that these three plagues work together, some that they appear in succession, as in the *Abhidharmakośa* and the *Mahāvyutpatti*; and this same diversity of opinion manifests itself in the Mongolian and Chinese sources. Spence Hardy establishes a connexion between prevailing vices, plagues, and forthcoming destruction: Love, Epidemic, Fire; Hate, Sword, Water; Delusion, Hunger, and Wind. It would follow, as Destruction is coming only after many Intermediate Periods, that during the whole of the 'Incalculable,' every Intermediate has epidemics, etc., according to the final modes of passing away.* The majority of the creatures being dead, the remaining ones are 'converted,' and the age of man increases again. A new intermediate Age has begun.

If we except the speculations on the 'creation' by the united merit of all sentient existence, and on the 'repopulation' of the worlds, which are perfectly free from pantheistic views, and, being built on the doctrine of *karma*, are perfectly Buddhistic, there is not much Buddhism in the cosmogony we have studied. We must add some details which are part of the Buddhist's own mythology.

Periods (*i.e.* great Periods) are said to be 'void' (*śūnyakalpa*) if no Buddha appears in them. They are 'non-void' or 'Buddha-periods' in the opposite

* To understand the following, the reader is referred to the Cosmology. We give below the necessary ideas:

Above the world of desire (*i.e.* the four continents, Mount Meru with its divine inhabitants) begins the world of form, consisting of three (or two) heavens of the first meditation, three of the second, three of the third, eight of the fourth. Above are the four heavens of non-form. The worlds are organized in such a way that the second meditation realms are established above a thousand first meditation realms (Little Chiliocosm); that the third meditation realms cover a thousand second meditation realms (Middle Chiliocosm); that the fourth meditation realms cover a thousand third meditation realms (Great Chiliocosm). For one universe, in the proper sense of the word, there are 1,000,000,000 first meditation abodes (Brahma-heavens), 1,000,000,000 Mount Merus. One universe is the 'field of a Buddha.' The authorities are not very consistent. For instance, we learn that the destructions by fire, etc., destroy the same number of worlds (1,000,000,000). 'In lateral expansion the world-cycle always perishes to the extent of a Buddha's domain' (*Visuddhim.* xiii., in Warren, p. 321).

† The latter opinion is better supported by the texts at our command (*JPTS* 1891, p. 118).

‡ For particulars see Spence Hardy, ***Manual***; Köppen and Warren, *locc. citt.*

§ In the 'Matsyapurāṇa,' *Cat. Oxon.* 347*b*, 33, there are seven clouds 'to give the destruction-water'; the first is named 'destruction' (*saṁvarta*).

* See Köppen, 282, n. 1. He adds that, according to 'some,' these plagues appear only in the Intermediate Period immediately preceding the Destruction.

case. Sometimes a great Period elapses between two appearances of a Buddha; sometimes an incalculable number of great Periods; sometimes, on the contrary, there are in the same period many Buddhas. We have 'substantial'-periods (*sāra°*), with one Buddha; 'curd'-periods (*maṇḍa°*), with two; 'excellent' (*vara°*), with three; 'substantial-curd'-periods (*sāramaṇḍa°*), with four; 'auspicious' (*bhadra°*) or 'greatly auspicious,' with five. Such is the present Period. There have been twenty-nine 'void' Periods before it. So far the old tradition. The redactors, moreover, of the *Mahāvastu* (iii. 330), the Chinese Buddhist pilgrims, etc., are already aware that in the Bhadrakalpa a thousand Buddhas are wanted.

At the beginning of the Universe, when the primordial water (see above, 189ᵇ) is about to give way for the appearance of the solid world, a lotus appears at the place where the sacred tree of Buddha has been and will be.* There is no flower if the period is to be void; there are as many flowers as forthcoming Buddhas.† Compare the Brāhmanical flower.

Another point of interest is the description of the first men, or, as it has been called, the Buddhist Genesis.‡ Originally, falling as they did from the Ābhāsvara-abode, human beings retained the attributes of their former existence. Born by 'apparitional-birth,' self-radiant, with joy as their only food, and with spiritual bodies, such beings are evidently meant by the 'men of immeasurable life' referred to above (see p. 189ᵇ). There is neither sun nor moon. As time goes on, earth appears on the surface of the primeval ocean. It is a savoury earth, and, as it were, a foam. Men eat it, and their radiance is lost for ever. Sun and stars furnish some light. Then follows the eating of some honey-moss, of creepers, of a marvellous rice. It is a long decadence. When this last has become a regular food, organs of sex appear; and with the institution of marriage, of private property, and of caste, begins the organization of human society. Interesting for general folklore (especially the details on marriage), the story is certainly very old, and was adapted before the classification of the celestial abodes. That in falling from the Ābhāsvara-abode the beings do not go through the heavens of Brahmā and the Devas, and that these are utterly ignored, are significant facts. But it is more astonishing that the 'self-appearing' men do possess the attributes of the Ābhāsvaras. We might assume that there was originally no connexion between these first men and any sort of degenerated gods. The first men were regarded as *ābhāsvaras*, *i.e.* 'resplendent,' and the Ābhāsvara gods themselves may be derived from this old conception.

LITERATURE.—1. Deshauterayes, 'Recherches sur la Religion de Fo' in *JAS* viii. 281; A. Rémusat, 'Essais sur la Cosmographie et la Cosmogonie des Buddhistes,' 1831, in *Mélanges Posthumes*, pp. 65–131, 'Fo-Koue-Ki'; I. J. Schmidt, 'Über die Tausend Buddhas' in *Mem. Acad. St. Petersburg*, 6, ii. p. 41; G. Turnour, 'An Examination of the Pāli Buddhistical Annals,' *JASB* vii., No. 3, 686–701; Burnouf, *Lotus de la bonne Loi*, pp. 314, 324–329; R. Spence Hardy, *Manual of Budhism*², 1880, pp. 1, 5–8, 28–35, 94–97, *Legends* (1881), pp. 80, 153; C. F. Köppen, *Die Rel. des Buddha* (1857–9), i. 266–289; Childers, *Pāli Dict.* p. 185; Eitel, *Hand-book* (1888), 68.

2. Indian Sources.—*Visuddhimagga*, xiii., trans. by Warren, *Buddhism in Translations* (1900), p. 321 ff.; the Sarvāstivādin treatise entitled *Lokaprajñapti*, known in the Tibetan version (*hjigrten-gdags-pa*, Tandjur, Mdo. lxii. 1–107), regarded by the Vaibhāṣikas as forming part of the Scriptures, but in reality constituting a *Śāstra*; the *Lokaprajñapti-abhidharma-śāstra* (Nanjio 1297), said to be closely related to it (see Takakusu 'On the Abhidharma Lit.' in *JPTS*, 1905, pp. 77 n., 143); neither the Tibetan nor the Chinese treatise seems to have been directly studied. It is the tradition of these books of *Abhidharma*, doubtless, that is found in the *Abhidharmakośavyākhyā*, fol. 262 of the MS. of the French Asiatic Society, which has been consulted for the present article.

L. DE LA VALLÉE POUSSIN.

* On the intervention of the *vajrāsana* see Beal, *Buddhist Records*, ii. 116.

† In the late records a thousand lotuses appear at the beginning of the Bhadrakalpa.

‡ By Prof. Rhys Davids, *Dial. of the Buddha*, p. 105, and by A. J. Edmunds, 'A Buddhist Genesis,' *Monist*, xiv. 207–214. The text is the *Aggaññasutta* (Dīgha xxvii.); it is translated from the Chinese by S. Beal, *Four Lectures*, pp. 151–155, and it is found in the *Mahāvastu* (Sacred Book of the Mahāsāṅghikas), i. 338–348. See E. Hardy, *Buddha*, p. 81.

AGES OF THE WORLD (Christian*).—The poets and the philosophers of pagan antiquity have, as a rule, represented the evolution of man as a gradual but inexorable decay, putting the happy era at the beginning, and asserting that the world would end in complete destruction. The Christian idea is exactly the opposite; and this is quite natural, for Jesus Christ caused a great hope to shine on humanity, groaning in the darkness of paganism. The prophets of Israel had already flung out some rays of this hope, in foretelling the coming of the Messiah, who would establish on earth an era of true religion, of peace and happiness. In short, while pagans placed the Golden Age in the past, Christians put it in the future; they have described the history of the world as an ascent, if not continuous, at least intermittently progressive, and finally triumphant, towards good and happiness. The writer of the Apocalypse (ch. 20) describes in an imaginative style the last phases of this historical drama.

St. Augustine is the first Father of the Church who explicitly mentions **Seven Ages** in the history of man, and all the theologians who followed him were more or less inspired by his idea. His plan is derived from the 'Days of the Creation' in Genesis. The passage is *de Civitate Dei*, xxii. 30 *ad fin.*

Paulus Orosius, a Spanish priest (d. 418), the friend and admirer of St. Augustine, to whom he dedicated his *Historiæ*, besides trying to prove incidentally the Bishop of Hippo's theory of the government of God in history, divided his work into seven books, which, however, correspond to different epochs. He had clearly come under the influence of Roman history. The founding of Rome, the taking of the city by the Gauls, the death of Alexander, the taking of Carthage, the Servile War, the reign of Cæsar Augustus, with which he makes coincident the birth of Jesus Christ,—these are the memorable events which form the boundaries of his periods.†

The **Venerable Bede** (d. 735), who in his *Chronicles* owes much to Paulus Orosius, also adopts seven Ages, and surmises that the last one, ending with the year 1000, will mark the end of the world.

Adson, abbot of Montier-en-Der, in his treatise,

* [As the Jews were accustomed to distinguish the age before, from the age after, the advent of the Messiah, so the majority of NT writers distinguish ὁ αἰὼν οὗτος from αἰὼν ὁ μέλλων. In both cases an ethical is always superimposed upon the temporal meaning. The former age is the period which shall elapse before the appointed Parousia of Christ, 'the period of instability, weakness, impiety, wickedness, calamity, misery' (Thayer); the latter is the age after Christ has come again in power to establish the Kingdom of God definitively, with all its blessings. It is inaugurated by the resurrection of the dead, and it answers, in scope and nature, to the completed work of Christ. The present world, as being material and transient, is under subjection to angels, who mediate the Law; the world to come (ἡ οἰκουμένη ἡ μέλλουσα, He 2⁵), on the other hand, is viewed as already existent, in a sphere transcending this earth, out of which it will come down as a new and divine order of things. The term 'world' (οἰκουμένη) expresses the constitution of that state of things which as 'age' (αἰών) is viewed more in relation to its development in time. The tone of the NT in speaking of the present age is almost invariably one of censure. The gulf between the two ages, however, is not conceived as being quite absolute. 'The powers of the age to come' (He 6⁵) project themselves in manifold ways into the present age, diffusing harmony and order throughout what is otherwise a chaos, and preparing ultimately to supersede the laws of the present dispensation. H. R. MACKINTOSH.]

† See the Anglo-Saxon version of the *Historiæ* of Orosius by Alfred the Great, ed. Bosworth, London, 1859.

de Antichristo, dedicated to queen Gerberge (954), sketches the preliminaries of the final judgment, which will follow the apostasy predicted by St. Paul, and the struggle against Antichrist; and he puts off the end of the world until this epoch.

Bernard, a hermit of Thuringia (d. 960), announces, on the contrary, that the end of the world is near. He and a great number of preachers in the 10th cent., through their allegorical interpretation of the Apocalypse, spread the belief in the immediate coming of Antichrist and the end of the world. Nevertheless their position was combated as an error by Abbo, abbot of Fleury-sur-Loire, the most learned monk of his time.

Scotus Erigena (d. *circa* 890) groups the first six Ages into three epochs, each marked by a different priesthood. The first epoch, comprising the first five Ages of St. Augustine, was contemporary with the patriarchs and priests of the OT. The second, beginning with Jesus Christ, was marked by the priesthood of the NT. Erigena foretells a third in the everlasting life, when all the faithful will serve as priests, and will see God face to face.

Joachim of Floris (d. 1202), the famous visionary hermit of Calabria, in his book, *de Concordia*, adopts Erigena's division into three Ages or religious conditions, and places each under the control of one person of the Trinity; but, differing from his predecessors, he holds that these periods overlap each other. The Age of the Father extends, according to him as well as to Scotus Erigena, from Adam to Christ. The Age of the Son starts from Elisha, and reaches as far as 1260. The last Age, that of the Holy Spirit, takes its origin from St. Benedict and the establishing of the monks in the West, and will last until the end of the world.

'The first era,' says Joachim, 'was that of knowledge, the second that of wisdom, the third will be that of complete intelligence. The first was servile obedience, the second was filial servitude, the third will be liberty. The first was the trial, the second action, the third will be contemplation. The first was fear, the second faith, the third will be love. The first was the age of slaves, the second that of sons, the third will be that of friends. The first was the Age of old men, the second that of young people, the third will be that of children. The first passed under the light of the stars, the second was the dawn, the third will be broad daylight. The first was winter, the second the beginning of spring, the third will be summer. The first bore nettles, the second thorns, the third will yield wheat. The first gave water, the second wine, the third will give oil. The first is connected with Septuagesima, the second with Quadragesima, the third will be Easter. The first Age refers, then, to the Father, who is the originator of all things; the second to the Son, who condescended to put on our clay; the third will be the Age of the Holy Spirit, of whom the Apostle has said, *Where the spirit of the Lord is, there is liberty*' (*de Concordia*, lib. v. c. 84).

Dante does not number the Ages of the World, but, borrowing the form of his prophecy from the figures of the Apocalypse, foretells the vengeance of God against the Dragon, which has broken the wheel of the Chariot of the Church, and announces that the one sent by God, whose number is 510 (=DVX), will kill the foul thief and the giant who sins with her (*Divina Commedia*, Purg. xxxiii. 43 ff.).

Bossuet, in his *Discours sur l'histoire universelle* (1681), returns to the seven Ages of the *City of God*, but considerably modifies the divisions of St. Augustine. According to him, the first Age, from Adam to Noah, comprises the creation and the beginnings of man. The second, from Noah to Abraham, was marked by the Flood and the first punishment of man, and opens the era of the bloody conquests. The third Age, from Abraham to Moses, was contemporaneous with the beginning of the OT. The fourth stretches from Moses to the building of the Temple at Jerusalem by Solomon. The fifth goes to the end of the captivity of Babylon; the sixth runs from Cyrus to Jesus; the seventh, and last, reaches from the Nativity up to our time. It is evident that Bossuet looked only at the past; he did not borrow the Bishop of Hippo's beautiful prophecy of a seventh Age,—the Age of rest and of face to face contemplation of God, when Christ has triumphed over His enemies, and God is all in all.

The Neapolitan **Vico** (d. 1744), in his *Scienza Nuova*, distinguishes three Ages in the history of the different nations. The Divine Age, or, so to speak, the infancy of man, where all is divinity and authority, belongs to the priests; the Heroic Age, where the conquerors rule by brute force; and the Human Age, the period of civilization, after which men will return to their primitive state. Mankind, according to him, will turn round perpetually in this circle—a theory similar to that of the Stoics.

It was the privilege of a Frenchman, more famous as an economist than as a theologian, to return to the Christian idea of a progressive development. **Turgot**, a prior in the Sorbonne, at the age of twenty-three (1750), in his *Discours sur le progrès successif de l'esprit humain*, established the contrast between the pagan notion of a Golden Age at the beginning of the world, and the idea of the perfecting of mankind. In the same way as sons and heirs profit by the knowledge and advantages acquired by their fathers and grandfathers, so, according to Turgot, there is a heritage of truth, of intellectual, moral, and economic progress, which, in each new generation, enriches the patrimony of humanity. Hence comes progress.

In the 18th and 19th cents. the idea of the development of the Ages of the World, *i.e.* of mankind, by analogy with the ages of human life, was renewed by some Christian philosophers. **J. G. Herder**, in *Ideen zur Philos. d. Gesch. der Menschheit* (1784), admits that there are in the evolution of races and nations, as in the life of plants, periods of growth and blossoming, of fruit-bearing, and, lastly, of withering. Mankind tends, by the reciprocal influence of the nations, to the realization of that blessed Age announced by Christ under the name of the 'Kingdom of Heaven.'

The founder of positivism, **Auguste Comte** (d. 1857), thinks that religion is contemporary with the infancy of humanity.

'Following the very nature of the human mind,' he says, 'each branch of knowledge must pass through different stages: the theological stage, which is the age of fiction; the metaphysical stage, which is that of abstraction; and the scientific stage, which is the positive age' (*Cours de philosophie positive*, iii., Appendix, p. 77).

Henrik Ibsen maintains that man evolves in turn through three phases:

'the kingdom founded on the tree of knowledge; the kingdom founded on the tree of the Cross; and, lastly, the kingdom founded on these two trees at once, for the sources of its life are in the paradise of Adam and at Golgotha' (*Emperor and Galilœan*, 1st Part, Act iii.).

Drummond, in his *Ascent of Man* (1894), distinguishes three ages in the evolution of the world: the first, in which the Vegetable Kingdom was led to produce the flowering plants; the second, the evolution of the Animal Kingdom, where the possibilities of organization were exhausted in the Mammalia; lastly, the third, which comprises the ascent of man and of society, and is bound up with the struggle for the life of others. 'This is the Further Evolution, the page of history that lies before us, the closing act of the drama of Man' (p. 443).

This is a short sketch of the Christian theories of the Ages of the World. In opposition to the pagan conception of a fateful decay of man, ending in annihilation, the Christian conception, derived from the Messianic idea of the Hebrews, shows the ascent, the progress of man, though not without falls, towards more truth, more justice, and more happiness. The socialists of the present day have unwittingly adopted the Christian idea of the 'Millennium.'

Pascal summed up the Christian conception of the Ages of the World very well when he said: 'The whole race of men, during the course of so many centuries, ought to be considered as being the same man always living and continually learning' (*Fragment d'un traité du Vide*, Paris, 1897, p. 436).

LITERATURE.—Rev 20; Augustine, *de Civitate Dei*, xxii. 30 *ad fin.*; Paul Orosius, *Historiarum mundi, libri vii. adversus paganos, sive Ormesta*; Bede, *Chronicus, sive de sex œtatibus mundi*; Scotus Erigena, *Homilia in prologum Johannis evangelii*; Joachim de Floris, *Liber de Concordia*, v. 84; Vico, *Principj di una Scienza Nuova d'intorno alla comune natura della nazioni* (1725); Turgot, *Discours sur le progrès de l'humanité* (1750); J. G. Herder, *Ideen zur Philosophie der Gesch. der Menschheit* (1784); Auguste Comte, *Cours de philosophie positive* (1830–42), iv., App. 77; H. Ibsen, *Emperor and Galilœan* (1873); Jules Roy, *L'an mille*, Paris (1885); Drummond, *The Ascent of Man* (1894).

GASTON BONET-MAURY.

AGES OF THE WORLD (Egyptian).—In their literature the Egyptians have not left any formal description of the world and its ways as they imagined it to have been in past ages. Manetho (*c.* B.C. 300), enumerating the rulers of Egypt, records in the period before Menes two dynasties of gods, followed by four others the character of which is not defined, and finally a dynasty of νέκυες, demigods. The fragments of the Turin Papyrus of kings prove that such a view was already established in the 14th cent. B.C., although the details cannot yet be recovered. Hephæstus, the creator-god, heads the list in Manetho, and he is immediately succeeded by the sun-god. These two correspond in Egyptian to Ptaḥ and Rêʿ, the latter being the organizer of the world. An inscription of the Tenth Dynasty says of the temple of Siut that it was 'built by the fingers of Ptaḥ and founded by Thoth for Ophois,' the local god; and a Ptolemaic text ascribes to the sun-god, during his reign on earth, the building of most of the Egyptian cities and their shrines. Stories of the time of the rule of the gods on earth are seen in the mythology (*e.g.* the myth of Osiris, and the legend of Hathor's massacre, and the Heavenly Cow) and in the popular tales (vaguely in the story of the Two Brothers). 'Since the time of the god' and 'since the time of Rêʿ' are old formulas for expressing immemorial antiquity; so also is 'since the time of the worshippers of Horus.' These last correspond to Manetho's νέκυες, and have been shown by Sethe to be historical personages, representing the kings of Upper and Lower Egypt before Menes united the two lands. Their records, when they had not perished altogether, were written in so primitive a style as to be undecipherable to the Egyptians of the third millennium B.C., and these 'worshippers of Horus' entered early into the realm of the legendary. The Turin Papyrus appears to give 23,200 + x years to the god-kings, and 2100 + x years to a dynasty of 19 'worshippers of Horus.' The wise Ptaḥḥotep, in his rather cryptic proverbs dating from the Old Kingdom, seems to refer to 'the counsels of them of old, of them who listened to gods'; and the 'worshippers of Horus' are the type of virtue rewarded in the same collection of proverbs: 'An obedient son is like a worshipper of Horus, he hath happiness in consequence of his obedience; he groweth old, and attaineth to the honour of great age.' Thus there was some idea of a more perfect condition having prevailed in primeval times. None the less, the myths show rebellion, deceit, and wickedness of all kinds appearing amongst both gods (*e.g.* Seth) and men in the age of Divine rule.

LITERATURE.—Meyer, *Ægyp. Chronol.* p. 115; Sethe, *Beitr. z. älteste Gesch. Æg.* i. p. 3; Maspero, *Dawn of Civilization*[4] (1901) p. 160.

F. LL. GRIFFITH.

AGES OF THE WORLD (Greek and Roman).*—The Greeks, and after them the Romans, were especially interested in this subject, and it is largely to their speculations that we owe those familiar references to the Ages which we find in the literary tradition of our Western civilization. In the Græco-Roman world this theme was actively discussed for nearly a millennium. During that long period the theory of the Ages was worked over again and again by the various schools of philosophy, by manifold attempts to harmonize conflicting authorities or to incorporate new ideas, by the lore of the people, by the fictions of the poets, even by the embellishments of mere rhetoric. The result is that a complete and detailed examination of the question is not to be expected in the space at our command.

Every theory upon this subject belongs to one of two types. The first assumes that man has risen from his former estate; the second, that he has fallen. Both of these occupy an important position in the history of ancient thought, but, so far as the present inquiry is concerned, the theory of descent, that belief in the progressive degeneration of mankind which is cherished by the folk of many races, was at all times the dominating type. The well-known lines of Horace (*Odes*, III. vi. 46–48),

> 'Ætas parentum, peior avis, tulit
> Nos nequiores, mox daturos
> Progeniem vitiosiorem,'

are the expression of a view which recurs again and again in the Græco-Roman world, from the Homeric poems (*Il.* i. 272, v. 304; *Od.* ii. 276, etc.) to the last words of Classical Literature.

A strictly chronological development of our subject is impracticable. The blanks in our surviving tradition are so large, especially in the departments most important to us, that no definite date for the inception of any one article of doctrine may be assumed with safety. Indeed, practically every idea by which the later tradition is distinguished will be found upon examination to possess a high antiquity. We may assert, however, that three periods of formative influence are especially prominent. The first is represented by Hesiod, the second by the Stoics and their predecessors, the third by the revival of Mysticism in the 2nd cent. B.C.

I. Hesiod.—The position of Hesiod was always paramount. The influence of Hesiod upon our theme is very much the same as was the influence of Homer upon the form and content of Greek Literature. The account of the Ages which we find in his *Works and Days* (109–201) is our earliest classical authority upon the subject. It is, also, to a remarkable extent, the centre and ultimate source of the later development. There were several other accounts of the early history of man, and some of them were evidently folk-legends of a high antiquity. None of them, however, is of any great importance to us. A few have contributed a detail here and there to the development of the Hesiodic norm, but most of them languish in comparative obscurity. Such being the case, it will be advisable to make Hesiod our basis, and to begin with a summary of his famous account.

First of all, the Olympian gods made the 'Golden Race of men.' These men lived when Kronos was king in heaven. They fared like the gods themselves, always making merry, and untroubled by toil or care, for the teeming earth bore of its own accord an abundance of all good things, and there was no old age. Even death itself, when at last it came, stole upon these men like a pleasant slumber. When this race passed away, Zeus made them the good spirits that live above the earth and are the invisible guardians and helpers of mortal man.

Then the Olympians made a second race, the men of the Silver Age. These were far inferior to the Golden Race, for they remained little children a hundred years, and when they finally reached maturity they straightway perished by their own folly, for they slew each other and refused to worship the immortals as men ought to do. Therefore Zeus was wroth, and put them

* There is no extended treatment of this subject as a whole. Among the three or four briefer accounts, the only one of any real value is by **O. Gruppe**, in his *Gr. Mythol. und Religionsgesch.*, Munich, 1902, pp. 447–450 (Müller's *Hdb. der Klass. Altertumswissensch.* vol. v.).

away. But even these men were honoured, for they were made the good spirits that live below the earth.

Then Zeus made another and a third race, the men of the Brazen Age. They were sprung from the ash-trees, and were strong and terrible, eating no corn, lovers of war and violence, and knowing nought of pity. Their weapons and their houses were of bronze, and they wrought in bronze. There was no iron. These men, too, fell by the work of their own hands and fared to Hades, nameless and unhonoured. Mighty they were, but dark death laid hold of them, and they left the bright light of the sun.

Then Zeus made a fourth race, better and more just. These were the Heroes of the elder days, such as fought at Troy and at Thebes. We call them the Demigods. And when they perished, Zeus gave them a life and an abiding-place at the ends of the earth. There they dwell in careless ease in the Isles of the Blest, hard by the deep-eddying stream of Ocean, and thrice a year the earth bears them fair fruit.

Would that I had not been allotted to the fifth period, but might have died earlier, or else have been born later! For this is the Age of Iron. There shall be no surcease from labour and sorrow by day or by night, and the gods will lay bitter burdens upon us. But, even yet, not all will be bad. This race shall Zeus destroy, when men are born with hoary hair, when fathers strive with sons and sons with fathers, guest with host and friend with friend; when brothers cease to be dear, when goodness, justice, and piety are no longer regarded. . . .

Then Aidos and Nemesis, whose fair bodies are clothed in pure white raiment, shall depart to heaven, and men shall find no succour in their grievous calamity.

The inconsistencies in this account were perceived by the ancients themselves, and in modern times an extensive literature has gathered about the subject.* For our present purpose, however, it is enough to say that these inconsistencies are due to the fact that Hesiod's version is a composite structure, the main support of which is an ancient division of the history of mankind into four Ages. No reference to this version is found in the Homeric poems, but, even at that early period, some form of it was probably current among the Greeks.

The designation of these four Ages by the four metals—gold, silver, bronze, iron, in the order named—is, in itself, an indication that the theory of descent is the fundamental idea of the legend. True, the causes and symptoms of descent, the coefficients of degradation, so to speak, are by no means clear at first sight. This, however, is, in itself, a striking proof of the high antiquity of the theory. Our long familiarity with the later phases of the legend naturally suggests the ethical *motif* as the standard of measurement here. But in the primitive stages of a myth like this, neither morality nor moral responsibility is of much account. The Golden Age is a replica of heaven, a mortal reflexion of the glory of the immortals. The men of those days were superior to us simply because they were made so. They were nearer the gods than we. Their position was a matter of powers and privileges, not of character. The long descent from those happier days has been measured by the gradual loss of those powers and privileges. The causes of it are in the will of the gods themselves. The idea of moral responsibility as a factor in the problem belongs to a period of more mature reflexion, and we see the first beginnings of it in Hesiod's own account. Peace and plenty in the first Age are followed by brutish anarchy and violence in the second. The third sees organized violence and deliberate cruelty; the fourth, crime of every sort and description. The steps, however, are none too clear, and the old description of the Ages was not yet in harmony with the new standard.

During the subsequent history of our discussion, more and more emphasis was given to the ethical *motif*. The basis of it continued to be the assumption of a descent from innocence and happiness to guilt and misery, the adumbration of which has already been observed in Hesiod. More specific details of the process frequently reflect the philosophical tenets of the writer, and may, also, be freely manipulated in the interests of rhetoric or for other purposes.

The principal difficulty with Hesiod's account arises from the fact that there was no place in the old four-fold scheme for the Heroic Age. As a matter of fact, the Heroic Age belongs to another and a different account of the development of mankind. Neither of these accounts, however, could be neglected, and in Hesiod we see the first known attempt to combine and harmonize the two. The deduction upon which it was based seems tolerably clear. According to the old four-fold system, the Brazen Age immediately preceded our own. On the other hand, it was also generally accepted that the Heroic Age immediately preceded our own. Consequently, the Heroic Age of the one scheme ought to coincide with the Brazen Age of the other. This, however, is impossible, as any one may see by comparing the two. Hesiod, therefore, inserted the Heroic Age between the Brazen and the Iron Ages of the old scheme, and re-numbered accordingly. The result was a system of five Ages, the inconsistency of which was usually clear enough to the ancient critics themselves.* For example, the famous accounts given by Aratus and Ovid indicate a full realization of the fact that the only way of harmonizing the two systems was either to revise Hesiod's conception of the Four Ages in such a way that the Heroes could find a place in the last of them, or, better still, to shift all four Ages to the past. In that event, our own race, of which the Heroes are, in any case, the earlier and better exemplars, may be assigned to the period between the close of the Iron Age and the present day.

As we have already seen, the presence of the Heroic Age in Hesiod's account upsets the principle of progressive degeneration, a fundamental idea of the old four-fold scheme. It also runs counter to the belief that each one of the Ages is represented by its own separate and distinct race of men. It was not until the rise of the Cyclic Theory that this idea was in any way disturbed, and, even then, the process was one of revision rather than destruction. Much less was the doctrine of successive races affected by the later intrusion of the Flood Legend. At first thought, we might esteem ourselves the descendants of Deucalion and Pyrrha, who were themselves survivors from the previous Age. But the story itself reminds us that we are really *terrigenæ*, a new race sprung from the earth.

We now come to one of the most notable and, doubtless, one of the most ancient features of our legend. This is the significant association of it with the great dynastic change of Olympus. The Golden Age was under the sway of Kronos. Since then, his son Zeus has ruled the world in his stead. On this basis, the Four Ages are sometimes reduced to two, the Age of Kronos and the Age of Zeus, the old régime and the new, the happy past and the unhappy present. This may well be an older and a simpler version. But it occurs only in the later writers,† and, so far as they are concerned, is probably for brevity, or to score a rhetorical point.

Real variations from this feature of the old account are especially characteristic of the philosophers, and may best be taken up in connexion

* Preller, *Gr. Mythol.* p. 87; E. Rohde, *Psyche*³, i. 91–110; Bergk, *Gesch. der Gr. Lit.* i. 947 ff.; Alfred Nutt, *Voyage of Bran*, i. 269 ff.; Grote, *Hist. of Greece*, ch. ii. Among the older authorities the most important are: K. F. Hermann, *Verhandl. d. Philologenversammlung*, etc., *zu Gotha*, iii. 62 ff.; Bamberger, *Rhein. Mus.*, new ser., i. 524–534; Schömann, *Opuscula*, ii. 305–319; Buttmann, *Mythologus*, ii. 1–27.

* Rohde, *l.c.*, contends that the principle followed by Hesiod in his classification and discussion of the Five Races was not their condition in this world, but their status in the world to come. This view has not met with approval, and in any case it has no direct bearing upon the points which are of real importance to us.

† *e.g.* Vergil, *Georg.* i. 121 f.; Tibullus, i. 3. 35; Dio Cassius, lxxi. 36; Maximus Tyr. xxxvi. 2; Ausonius, xvi. 2. 27 (p. 175, ed. Schenkl).

with the Cyclic Theory. But the Hesiodic version of this *motif*, above all, the primitive association of Kronos with the Golden Age, persisted until a late date, not only in the genuine folk-tradition to which it really belongs, but also, to a large extent, in the literature. In fact, the Golden Age is often designated simply as 'the Age of Kronos,' 'the Days when Saturn was King,' etc.*

THE GOLDEN AGE.—No part of our subject has been so thoroughly investigated by modern scholarship as the Golden Age.† It is, perhaps, the most important element in Hesiod's own account, and, for obvious reasons, the theme was extremely popular in the literary tradition of later times.‡ And, with the exception of certain details to be taken up in another connexion, these descriptions all bear a strong family resemblance to each other. Not less striking is their resemblance to what we hear about Elysium, the Garden of the Gods, the Hyperboreans, and similar conceptions.§ Indeed, as Dieterich has shown in his interesting monograph, *Nekyia*, the traditional *motifs* common to all these themes passed over to the early Christian writers, and were applied by them to their descriptions of heaven.

The main reason for such a similarity is, of course, not far to seek. In all cases, the theme is ideal happiness, and whether we locate it in the past or somewhere in the present, in this world or in the next, the details which make up the vision of unfulfilled desire are, for the average man, very much the same. Nor should we fail to remind ourselves that in the speculations of the folk there is no impassable barrier between our life and the life of those beyond the grave. Nothing was more certain than that the Golden Age and the race who had lived in those happier days had both passed beyond our ken; but that they still existed somewhere, and that, even now, a mere mortal man might be able to find them again, was not felt to be utterly beyond the bounds of possibility. Odysseus had returned alive from Hades, and it is a well-known historical fact that the gallant Sertorius ‖ was, at one time, actually on the eve of setting sail for the Fortunate Isles in the Western Ocean, just as, many centuries later, Ponce de Leon took the same direction in his search for the Fountain of Youth. The same association of ideas is clearly seen in Hesiod's account. In fact, this is one of the most ancient and primitive aspects of the legend. Hesiod's Golden Age, when Kronos ruled a race of men who have since departed, is in all essential particulars a mere replica of Hesiod's Isles of the Blest, where dwell those sons of the gods who have passed alive beyond the grave. Moreover, the foundation of both is material which had long been traditional, even at the time when the Homeric poems were composed.* Indeed, even as Hesiod tells the story, it still reflects with remarkable fidelity the old folk-tale of a Lost Paradise before the simple beauty of the legend had been marred by the intrusion of moral lessons and specific philosophical doctrines. Men lived long, never grew old, and died a painless, *i.e.* a natural death. Meanwhile, they passed their days like the gods, in innocence, peace, and fabulous plenty, making merry continually, and knowing nothing of labour, disease, or sorrow.

Such are the principal *motifs* of the old legend of the Golden Age, and they usually form the basis of all versions. The variations or additional details which we find in later accounts are, for the most part, due either to philosophical speculation, the incorporation of allied myths, or manipulation for literary purposes.

By far the most important of these is the first. In fact, the growing prominence of the ethical element, the most notable feature in the later development of the Golden Age, is very largely due to the philosophers. The earliest of them were the Orphics of the 6th cent. B.C. The body of doctrine developed by these nameless mystics was probably long the possession of a few, and, when we consider the strange figures of speech in which its real meaning was often concealed, we can hardly wonder that it was long misunderstood or derided by the many. The kernel of it, however, the great idea for which they were slowly preparing, was destined to grow in strength, and, in the far future, to bear abundant fruit. This was the belief that not alone the sons of the gods, but, by a lifetime of merit, the sons of men, might find their reward, even in the dark house of Hades. Naturally, therefore, not only among the Orphics and their disciples, but also among their opponents, the ideal of the Lost Paradise became more and more prominent. Discussion or description of the Golden Age, more especially of its analogue beyond the grave,—the Golden Age, so to speak, of the future—continued to grow in importance and interest. We hear many echoes of it in Plato. But, especially, to the writers of the Old Comedy the Orphics and their doctrines were a never-failing subject for parody and satiric comment.

One of the plainest signs of Orphic influence upon this discussion was the marked improvement in the present position of Kronos. According to the popular belief, old 'King' Kronos had been in the Golden Age a sort of divine *Roi d'Yvetot*, afterwards consigned to nethermost Tartarus, and, ever since then, a synonym of extreme old age and harmless senility.† This view, however, was deliberately opposed by the Orphics. Their teaching was that Kronos had long since been freed from his shameful captivity. Moreover, he is not old and weak. On the contrary, he is for ever young and vigorous, and now rules in Elysium, the land of those who have gone hence. There, in a world of eternal youth and joy, he is surrounded not only by the heroes of old, but also by the spirits of just men made perfect—after the Orphic pattern—and, indeed, as some say, by a remnant of men from those golden days when he was king in heaven.‡

Piety and justice as *motifs* in the ideal of happiness had been ascribed, long before Hesiod's time, to peoples living beyond the limits of the known world. Such were Homer's *Abioi* (*Il.* xiii. 6), 'the most righteous of men,' and, to give one more

* *e.g.* Plato, *Polit.* 269 A, 271 C, 276 A, *Hipp.* 269 B; Philodemus, *de Pietate*, p. 51; Vergil, *Ecl.* iv. 6; Tibullus, i. 3. 35; Propert. ii. (iii.), 32. 52; Ovid, *Amor.* iii. 8. 35, *Heroid.* iv. 132, etc.

† See esp. Eichhoff, *Jahrbüch. f. Philol.* cxx. 581 ff.; E. Graf, 'ad Aureæ Ætatis Fabulam Symbola,' *Leipz. Stud. z. Class. Philol.* viii. (1885) 1–85; A. Dieterich, *Nekyia*, Leipzig, 1893; E. Rohde, *Psyche*, Leipzig, 1903, i. p. 106 ff.; A. Nutt, *Voyage of Bran*, London, 1895.

‡ The earliest known reference after Hesiod is a line quoted by Philodemus from the old epic, *Alcmæon* (see Kinkel, *Epic. Græc. Fragm.*, Leipzig, 1877, p. 313). Theognis, 1135 ff., is the source of Ovid, *F.* i. 6. 29. The author of the *Ætna*, writing in the 1st cent. A.D., says that descriptions of the Golden Age may be expected from every poet, and are so common that—

'Non cessit cuiquam melius sua tempora nosse.'

The present writer has noted nearly a hundred references to it during the course of this investigation.

§ The result is that in cases where only a fragment of description has survived, it is sometimes impossible to decide which conception the author had in mind. Compare, *e.g.*, Solon, frag. 38, ed. Bergk; Cratinus, frag. 160, ed. Kock; Crates, frag. 228, ed. Kock; Lucilius, 978 ff., ed. Marx. See also Dieterich's *Nekyia*, and Waser in Pauly-Wissowa, v. pp. 2470–2475.

‖ Sallust, *Hist.* frag. 192, 193, ed. Maurenbrecher; Horace, *Epod.* xvi. 42, and schol.; Plutarch, *Sertorius*, 8.

* *e.g.* Homer, *Il.* xiii. 5, *Od.* iv. 85, vii. 201 and 88, iv. 563, vi. 41, ix. 108. See Graf, *l.c.* p. 4 ff.

† See M. Mayer in Roscher, ii. 1456 ff.

‡ Pindar, *Olymp.* ii. 124, *Pyth.* iv. 291; Æschyl. frag. 190, ed. Nauck; Teleclides, frag. 1, ed. Kock; Varro, *de Re Rust.* iii. 1, 5; Horace, *Epod.* xvi. 63; *Orphica*, frag. 245, ed. Abel.

example, the Hyperboreans,* so long famous in the literature and legend of the Græco-Roman world. This idea was now emphasized in the analogous legend of the Golden Age—the ideal world of the past—and on the basis of it not only the Orphics but other schools of philosophy exploited their specific views regarding the nature of righteousness and the indispensable conditions of happiness. In other words, as the Golden Age ceased to be an article of faith, it became, more and more, the field in which these thinkers aired their theories of what the world ought to be. From this sort of thing it was only a step to that long line of Utopian romances which were quite as characteristic of late antiquity as they are of the present day.†

Among the various bits of specific theory imported into the Golden Age by the philosophers, one of the oldest and most important was the doctrine of vegetarianism.‡ This doctrine doubtless goes back to the elder Orphics, but the most prominent representatives of it in antiquity were the Pythagoreans. The earliest reference to it now surviving is a fragment of Empedocles (127 D), and the most complete discussion of it in connexion with the Golden Age is Ovid, *Met.* xv. 96 f.§ In this famous passage Ovid introduces Pythagoras himself as the expounder of his own doctrine. The essence of it is that, in the Golden Age, men lived upon the fruits of the earth, and that the degeneration of later Ages is marked by the departure from this rule.

That the Golden Age was distinctively the era of perfect love and peace is easily inferred from Hesiod's account, but the later development is marked by a much stronger emphasis upon this feature. This was partly due to the influence of the Cyclic Theory, in which, as we shall see later, it was the necessary result of the Platonic conception of harmony. The first to lay stress upon it—and probably in this connexion—was Plato's predecessor Empedocles.‖ This, no doubt, is the reason why he made Aphrodite instead of Kronos ruler of the Golden Age.

Among those not interested in any cyclic theory—poets, for the most part—the favourite method of bringing out the peace and harmony of the Golden Age was to emphasize the contrast with later times by dilating upon war, violence, and bloodshed as both causes and symptoms of degeneration in the succeeding ages of mankind. This diatribe on war first comes to the front during the Alexandrian age. It is characteristic of Roman poetry, especially of the Elegy, and, in the end, became a mere rhetorical commonplace.¶

Another important line of development in later times was inspired by the varying use and interpretation of one of the most persistent and characteristic peculiarities of the genuine folk-legend. We refer to the belief that in the Golden Age all the imaginable blessings of life come of their own accord. In this way we have an ideal combination of fabulous plenty with luxurious idleness.

* See esp. **O. Crusius** in Roscher, i. p. 2895 ff., and the references.

† **Henkel**, *Philologus*, ix. 402, gives a long list, beginning with the *Republic* of Protagoras. See **E. Rohde**, *Der Gr. Roman*[2], Leipzig, 1900, p. 210 ff. with references.

‡ See Graf, *l.c.* p. 20 ff., for an extended discussion, and cf. Porphyr. *de Abstinentia*, ii. 21 ff.; Plato, *Leg.* vi. 782 E. Seneca, *Epist.* cviii. (Sotion); Clemens Alex. *Strom.* vii. 32, etc. For similar ideas in the East, Gruppe (*Gr. Mythol.* p. 448, note 2) refers to Gn 1[29] 2[16]; cf. Windischmann, *Zoroastr. Stud.* p. 212. Connected with this discussion is the old tradition that men talked with the animals in the Golden Age. The references to it are, Crates, 14, ed. Kock; Plato, *Polit.* 272 B; Xen. *Mem.* ii. 7, 13; Babrius, *procem.*

§ See esp. **Schmekel**, *de Ovid. Pythag. Adumbratione*, Diss., Greifswald, 1885.

‖ So, too, Aratus, 108, and freq. in the Roman poets, *e.g.* Vergil, *Ecl.* iv. 18, *Georg.* i. 125 and ii. 539; Tibullus, i. 10. 7; Ovid, *Met.* i. 97; Seneca, *Her. Œt.* 1056; Juvenal, xv. 168; Claudian, *de Raptu Proserp.* ii. 25, *procem.*, *Laud. Seren.* 70; Sidon. Apoll. *Pan.* 105, etc.

¶ *E.g.* Aratus, 131; Vergil, *Ecl.* iv. 32, *Georg.* ii. 540, and Servius; Tibullus, i. 3. 36 and 47; Juvenal, xv. 168; Ovid, *Met.* i. 99, etc.

When treated seriously, either for literary or for didactic purposes, this *motif* led directly and inevitably to the conclusion that the ideal condition of human society was communism.* Several commonplaces which the Roman poets inherited from the Alexandrian age might be included here.† We know, too, for example, that this theme was developed at some length by the historian Ephoros in his account of the idealized nations of the North.‡

When treated by the satirists and by other people of a less serious turn of mind, the same *motif* led quite as directly to one of the most important and interesting developments in the literary history of this legend. This is the treatment of the Golden Age or its analogues in this world and the next as a comic theme. It makes its first appearance in the writers of the Old Comedy, and was primarily intended by them to satirize the peculiar tenets of the Orphics. But the story of Topsy-Turvy Land (*das Märchen des Schlaraffenlandes*, as the Germans call it) was certainly not invented by the Comic Dramatists. It is rather a folk-variation of the old story of the Golden Age, and references to it turn up now and then from the old Comedy of Greece to the present day.§ The comedy in these descriptions is usually produced by pushing the automatous element, occasionally too, the theory of communism, to its perfectly logical, and yet, at the same time, its utterly absurd conclusion. The result is a Lost Paradise of the *bon-vivant*, the votary of ease, and the irresponsible bachelor The nearest congener of this type is the conception of the Golden Age especially affected by the idyllic-erotic poets of the Alexandrian age and by their Roman imitators. The same automatous and communistic features are prominent, and the examples by which they are illustrated are sometimes so nearly the same that the difference between the two departments is hardly more than a matter of mood.¶ At first sight this is surprising. It ceases to be so, however, as soon as we remind ourselves that the pathetic exaggeration so characteristic of the idyllic-erotic sphere is largely due to the fact that the author himself is rarely more than half convinced of the truth, or even of the possibility, of his own statements. It is an easy step from this state of mind to that ironical extravagance of humorous unbelief—and this, too, has its pathetic side—to which we are indebted for the old tale of Topsy-Turvy Land.

On the philosophical side, the growing distrust of everything in Hesiod's account that savoured of the supernatural served to bring out still another aspect of the Golden Age more and more clearly. Before taking up this point, however, we should remind ourselves that the counter-theory of ascent was, meanwhile, being supported by a party of such activity and intelligence that it could not be ignored.** The theory of ascent was also backed by folk-legends of great antiquity, and for centuries all classes seem to have been interested in discussing the various inventions by which the rise of mankind from utter savagery to our present stage of civilization has been marked.

It is evident that until the account of Hesiod was revised the two parties were utterly irreconcilable. If one did not believe Hesiod, the most

* See Graf, *l.c.* p. 60, and compare such passages, *e.g.*, as Plato, *Critias*, 110 C, but esp. the *Republic*, 415, 417, 424, 451–465, with the notes and references in the edition of Adam, Cambridge, 1902. Plato went further in this respect than any of his predecessors. He looked upon communism as one of the indispensable conditions of an ideal State, and the reflexion of this view may be seen in what he has to say of the Golden Age.

† Vergil, *Georg.* i. 126, *Æn.* ix. 569, and Servius; Tibullus, i. 3. 43, ii. 3. 73; Ovid, *Met.* i. 132; Juvenal, vi. 18; Seneca, *Phædra*, 539, *Epist.* xc. 41; Justinus, xliii. 1. 3, etc.

‡ Frag. 76 in Müller's *Fragm. Histor. Græc.* vol. i. p. 256.

§ **Friedländer**, *Sittengesch. Roms*[5], i. 537, Leipzig, 1888; **O. Crusius**, 'Märchenreminiscenzen im antiken Sprichwort' in *Verhandlungen der 40ten Philologenversammlung*, 1890, pp. 31–47; **Rohde**, *Psyche*, i. 315. 2, *Griech. Roman*[2], p. 206, n. 4; **J. Pöschel**, *Das Märchen vom Schlaraffenland*. The version best known to us, through numerous imitations, is the one given by the old Trouvère in his lay of the 'Land of Cocagne' (text in Barbazan, *Fabliaux et Contes*, 1784 [new ed. by Méon, 1880, ii. p. 175], tr. by G. L. Way, *Fabliaux or Tales*, etc., London, 1800, ii. p. 81; abstract by Legrand d'Aussy, *Fabliaux ou Contes*, etc., Paris, 1829, i. p. 302).

‖ Teleclides, 1 ed. Kock; Pherecrates, 108 K; Cratinus, 165 K; Crates, 14 K; Eupolis, 277 K; Athen. vi. 267 E; Lucilius, 978, ed. Marx; Petronius, 45; Lucian, *Sat.* 7, *Vera Hist.* i. 7, etc.

¶ Vergil, *Georg.* i. 132, *Ecl.* iv. 21; Horace, *Epod.* xvi. 49; Tibullus, i. 3. 45; Ovid, *Met.* i. 111; Dioscorides, *Anth. Pal.* vii. 31, etc.

** **Rohde**, *Griech. Roman*[2], p. 216, n. 2; **Eichhoff**, *l.c.* p. 587; Graf, *l.c.* p. 57; Æschylus, *Prom.* 440–455; Moschion, frag. 7, ed. Nauck; Critias, frag. 1, ed. Nauck; Athen. frag. 1, ed. Kock; Democritus, p. 237, ed. Mullach; Aristotle, *Met.* i. 2, and Zeller, *Phil. der Griechen*[4], i. p. 826. 3; Lucretius, v. 925; Diodorus, i. 8 and ii. 38; Horace, *Sat.* I. iii. 99; Lucian, *Amores*, 33. 34; Aristides, i. p. 32, ed. Dind.; Ovid, *Ars. Amat.* ii. 473; Tibullus, II. i. 39; Cic. *pro. Sext.* 42; Lobeck, *Aglaopham.* p. 246 (*Orphica*).

logical course was to agree with the Epicureans, who denied the account of Hesiod *in toto*, and replaced it by their own view, which is the nearest approach in antiquity to our modern theory of evolution. This denial, which lies implicit in the famous passage of Lucretius (v. 925 f.), is stated positively, for example, by Diodorus, who (i. 8 f.) describes the theory of Epicurus upon this point, and (v. 66 f.) implies that the Golden Age was a mere invention of the Cretans. But this summary disposition of the difficulty is of no value to us. We are more interested in the process of reconciliation. The most important force in this process, so far as it was accomplished at all, was a gradual realization among thoughtful men of the fact that the ideal of life traditionally associated with the Golden Age, though it seemed attractive, was, in reality, unfit to pose as the highest development in any theory of descent.

2. Cynics, Stoics, etc.—At this point, certain Stoic modifications of Cynic doctrine are of especial value to us. The great representative passage to be considered in this connexion is Aratus, *Phænomena*, 97–140.* The version of the Ages by this famous Alexandrian poet of the 3rd cent. B.C. was one of the best known in the ancient world, and undoubted traces of its influence are to be found in most of the later accounts. Briefly described, it is a revision of Hesiod under Stoic influence. The object of the author was not only to reconcile the discrepancies of the old version, but also to remove whatever was irrelevant to a theme which he proposed to treat not as an independent account, as Hesiod had done, but as a rhetorical episode suggested by his mention of the constellation Virgo, *i.e.* Astræa, whom Aratus, following an old tradition, identifies with the Nemesis of Hesiod, and calls *Dike*.

Dike was comparatively unimportant in Hesiod. Owing to the exigencies of rhetoric, she now becomes the central figure. Moreover, after the true Stoic fashion, she is made to assume the functions of both Zeus and Kronos in the traditional version. The five ages of Hesiod are reduced to three—an Age of Gold, of Silver, and of Bronze.

The men of the Golden Age are described as peaceful tillers of the soil, with no knowledge of civil strife or of the vexations of the law. Moreover, they were far removed from the perils of the sea. In those days there were no ships to bring the luxuries of life from abroad. The goddess mingled freely with these simple souls, and taught them how men should live with reference to each other.

The Silver Age was more sophisticated. Nevertheless, the goddess still remained upon earth, although she now retired to the mountains, and was seen but rarely.

The Brazen Age saw the first swords, and the first slaughter of the oxen for food. Then *Dike*, utterly hating that race of men, finally departed to heaven and took her place among the stars.

It will be seen that one of the most notable signs of revision here is the disappearance of the old folk-element of marvel. In its place we have a conception in which the Stoics are mainly responsible for the emphasis laid upon the ethical *motif*, especially upon the relation of man to his fellows, to the world about him, and to the State.

The underlying principle in such a theory of the Ages is the conclusion that the ascent of man in the arts of civilization is accompanied, at all events beyond a certain point, by a corresponding descent in moral and even in physical fibre. Why is this the case? The reply was that to be healthy in mind and body, and therefore, happy, we must live in harmony with nature. But civilization beyond a certain point is not in harmony with nature. Accordingly, beyond a certain stage of civilization, we can be neither healthy, virtuous, nor happy. Now, as journeying into the future should bring us finally to a state of ideal misery, so journeying into the past should take us back finally to a state of ideal happiness. That state of ideal happiness was, of course, the Golden Age. The Golden Age of the past was, therefore, the ideal simple life of the past.

Such in substance was the general drift of the Cynic argument as modified by the Stoics, and, as a matter of fact, the Golden Age of Aratus is really an idealization of the agricultural and pastoral stage of human society *—a theme which always comes to the front in any period of over-cultivation, as soon as men begin to stagger under the burden of their own inventions. So conceived, the theory of the Ages was not only quite consistent with the evolution of civilization from the crudest beginnings, but agreed with the Epicureans in presupposing such a process. But, as regarded the various inventions and discoveries by which that process has been marked, it loved to dwell upon those very devices, and to lay great stress on the view that they had been the most conspicuous cause of the downfall of man himself. The favourite examples are those chosen by Aratus. They are the first sword and the first ship.

The first sword † is a characteristic introduction to the topic of war which we have already mentioned. The first ship is also a favourite way of connecting the discussion of the Ages with the diatribe on navigation so frequently found in the later writers, especially among the Romans. In fact, it is a commonplace of modern criticism that the Romans were afraid of the sea. As, however, the opinion is a generalization, founded, for the most part, upon these very passages, we need not take it too seriously. The sailor's impious challenge of the treacherous and relentless deep was a subject inspired not so much by national character as by literary tradition. It is fully developed in the *Works and Days* of the old Bœotian poet, a conventional theme of the Greek epigram at all periods, a regular *motif* in the poetry of the Augustan age, and by the 1st cent. of our era a mere rhetorical commonplace.‡

In order to understand better the attitude of the Epicureans towards the theory of the Ages, as presented, for example, by Aratus, we must return for a moment to the underlying principle upon which, according to Stoic reasoning, that theory was founded. We mean the conclusion stated above, that advance in the arts of civilization is at the expense of the character, health, and happiness of the individual. Now, when we consider the Stoic argument by which this conclusion was made to yield the theory that the Golden Age of

* Another representative passage is Seneca, *Epist.* xc. 5 ff., in which he quotes from Posidonius the description of an ideal past of the Stoics, in which the philosophers take the place of Kronos.

* Horace, *Epod.* ii.; Propert. iii. 13. 25; Seneca, *Medea*, 333; Plutarch, *de Nobil.* 20, etc. etc. This interpretation of the Golden Age was especially welcome to the Romans, not only because of their temperamental Stoicism, but because it agreed more nearly with their own tradition of early times and with the character and attributes of Saturn before he was identified with the Greek Kronos.

† *e.g.* Vergil, *Georg.* ii. 540; Ovid, *Met.* i. 99; Juvenal, xv. 168; Tibullus, i. 3. 47. The rhetorical question of Tibullus (i. 10. 1) states a maxim of the philosophers which is often repeated. See, *e.g.*, Seneca, *N.Q.* v. 18. 15: 'Nihil invenimus tam manifestæ utilitatis quod non in contrarium transeat culpa. So Ovid, *Met.* xv. 106, speaking in the person of Pythagoras. Opponents of the theory of descent, especially the Epicureans, contended that the sword merely marked one period in the long chronicle of homicide. It was the successor of the club and the large rough stone (Lucretius, v. 966). Cf. also Hor. *Sat.* i. 3. 100; Valer. Flacc. v. 145, and esp. Plato, *Rep.* 358 E (war the natural condition of mankind), and the commentary of Adam.

‡ Among the most important of the numberless references are, Stobæus, 57 (who gives a number of quotations); Hesiod, *W. and D.* 236; Sophocles, *Antig.* 332; Seneca, *Medea*, 301 and 607; Tibullus, i. 3. 37 and ii. 3. 39; Propert. i. 17. 13 and iii. 7. 29; Ovid, *Amor.* ii. 11. 1; Statius, *Thebaid*, vi. 19 and *Achilleid*, i. 62; Claudian, *de Raptu Pros.* i., *proœm.* The final conclusion, after generations of discussion, was that the one great cause of the downfall of man had been his greed and his selfishness. It was clear to the poets and philosophers themselves, especially to the Romans, that all their commonplaces on the fall of man were really just so many illustrations of this one *motif*. It drove him to war, it suggested the first ship, it urged him on to explore the earth for treasures better hid, it devised the vexations of the law and brought about the injustice of wealth and poverty; through crime and self-indulgence it has made him acquainted with sorrow, disease, and all the ills that flesh is heir to. The result is that he has not only shortened his life by his own devices, but, what with anxiety, dyspepsia, and a bad conscience, with marriage a failure and children a burden, the little life he has left is no pleasure to him.

the past was the ideal simple life of the past, we perceive that it is founded on two assumptions. The first is that this conclusion, that advance in the arts is at the expense of the individual, is a truth of universal application, and not to be modified. The second is that the twin process to which it refers has operated continuously, and will go on doing so. The Stoics could make these assumptions without hesitation, since both of them followed, inevitably, from that cyclic theory of the Ages to which this school of philosophers gave its enthusiastic support. Not so the Epicureans. The Epicureans agreed that the growth of civilization had been accompanied by certain signs of degeneration in man himself, but they denied that the principle was capable of universal application. They insisted that every stage of civilization, in its own particular fashion, has been unfavourable to the individual. In other ways it has been favourable. There is no such thing, therefore, as progressive degeneration in the strict sense of the word. Such a theory would imply a period of ideal happiness at one extreme, followed by a period of ideal misery at the other extreme. Both are superhuman, and therefore impossible. In other words, there never was a Golden Age, even if we adopt the Stoic revision of the old legend.

Another method of reconciling the difficulties in Hesiod's account is illustrated by Vergil, *Georg.* i. 121 ff. The primary purpose of this version was to enhance the dignity of labour. The history of mankind is divided into two periods—the Age of Saturn, and the Age of Jove. The Golden Age, when good old Saturn was King, agrees entirely with Hesiod. The second period, however, is not an age of degeneration, but an age of reform. Jupiter, the divine father of our race and of all our higher aspirations, purposely did away with the *far niente* of the old régime, not out of a petty resentment against Prometheus—as the old folk-legend (*e.g.* Hesiod, *W. and D.* 42 f.) would have us believe—but rather,

> 'curis acuens mortalia corda,
> Nec torpere gravi passus sua regna veterno,'

because he was well aware that, unless men have difficulties to meet and overcome, they can never grow strong in any sense. In this characteristically noble conception, it is interesting to see to what an extent Vergil succeeded in meeting the demands of contemporary thought without sacrificing the traditional account of the Golden Age so dear to the poets.

The famous account of the Ages which Ovid gives in the first book of his *Metamorphoses*, 89–162, and the version best known to the modern world, is one of the earliest surviving attempts to incorporate the Flood Legend. Otherwise, it is chiefly remarkable as an illustration of the poet's characteristic skill in combining and harmonizing the views of preceding thinkers. The Four Ages (Gold, Silver, Bronze, and Iron) are all in the past. The Age to which we belong is a fifth. The Flood is the great catastrophe by which the wicked and godless race of the Iron Age was destroyed. The history of our own race, therefore, begins with the earth-born children of Deucalion and Pyrrha. In this way, the Flood Legend, the theory of descent, the theory of ascent, the traditional account of the Golden Age, the Heroes, and, with only a slight modification, even Hesiod's quintuple division of the Ages, were all made to dwell together in peace and unity.

CYCLIC THEORY.—Let us now turn our attention to the Cyclic Theory, the most important element, in the long run perhaps the one really vital and vitalizing element, in the history of our subject. The Cyclic Theory of the Ages was founded on the belief that, after the analogy of day and night, of the waxing and waning of the moon, and of the eternal round of the seasons, the entire Universe itself is subject to an ever-recurring cycle of change. This ancient Babylonian doctrine* of the world-year, the *magnus annus*, as it was called by the Romans, makes its earliest known appearance on Greek soil with Heraclitus,† was thoroughly discussed by the later philosophers, and finally became known to the world at large. Indeed, it may be called the prototype of some of our most recent views suggested by the nebular hypothesis.‡

The association of this idea with the old folk-legend of the Ages was inevitable, and appears at a very early period in the history of Greek speculative thought. In fact, it has often been stated, though without sufficient warrant, that belief in a cyclic theory of the Ages is the explanation of Hesiod's wish that he had died earlier or could have been born later.§ The fragments, however, of Empedocles show, in spite of their scantiness, that at that time the process had already begun.‖ But the most important discussion, so far as we are concerned, the one, too, which had the strongest influence upon later times, is developed or touched upon in various dialogues of Plato,¶ more especially in the *Polit.*, *Timæus*, and *Republic*.

According to Plato's definition,—and this much, at least, appears to have remained unchanged in later times—a *magnus annus* means the period which elapses before the eight circles, each revolving about the earth in an orbit of its own, arrive simultaneously at the point from which they started at the beginning of our cycle.** Further details of the Platonic theory—and these underwent considerable revision in later times—apparently rest on the assumption that each complete revolution of the Universe is followed by a counter revolution in the opposite direction. A motion forward, as it were, is followed by a motion backward. The history of mankind is directly affected by this motion, and especially by the alternation of it.

The motion forward is the Age of Kronos and the direction of harmony. During all this period the great Helmsman of the Universe is at his post, and we have the Golden Age of the poets. As the motion is the reverse of that which prevails in our time, it is naïvely assumed that the conditions of life are to a large extent the opposite of those with which we are familiar. The men of that age are born old, with hoary hair,†† and instead of growing older continue to grow younger, until they finally disappear. Moreover, they are born from the earth, and the earth feeds them. There is no toil, no pain, no war, there are no women ‡‡ and no children of women. Yet with all their advantages these men do not attain unto wisdom.

When the forward motion is completed, the Helmsman retires from his post, and the Universe, left to itself, yields to the force of gravity, as it were, and begins its backward revolution, which is in the direction of discord. The point at which the motion is reversed is always signalized by fire, flood, or some other cosmic upheaval, involving a terrific destruction of organic life. The few men who survive cease growing young and begin to grow old, those just born from the earth with hoary hair die, and return to the earth from which they came. Men are no longer born from the earth, as before, but even as

* Gomperz, *Griech. Denker*, Leipzig, 1896, i. p. 115, with note and references on p. 438; Lenormant-Babelon, *Hist. de l'Orient*, v. 175; *supra*, p. 183 ff.

† Gomperz, *l.c.* pp. 54 and 428; Diels, *Herakleitos von Ephesos*, Berlin, 1901, frag. 66 (26, Bywater).

‡ Gomperz, *l.c.* p. 117.

§ Hesiod, *W. and D.* 174–5. See the editions of Rzach, Leipzig, 1902, p. 158, and of Goettling-Flach, Leipzig, 1878, p. 201, with notes and references; Graf, *l.c.* p. 11; Schoell-Studemund, *Anecdota Graeco-Latina*, ii.

‖ Diels, *Poetarum Philosophorum Fragmenta*, Berlin, 1901, pp. 88 and 112 ff.

¶ Plato, *Polit.* 269 C, *Tim.* 39 D ff., *Rep.* 545 C ff.; Cic. *Timæus*, 34 ff. For a good discussion of this theory and of the Platonic Number with which it is closely associated, and also for a selected bibliography of the enormous literature which has gathered about it, see Adam's ed. of the *Republic*, ii. p. 264 ff.

** *Tim.* 39 D; Cic. *Timæus*, 33; Macrob., *Som. Scipionis*, ii. 2, 19; Stobæus, *Eclog.* i. 264 (vol. i. p. 107, Hense). See esp. Usener, *Rhein. Mus.* xxviii. 395; Ritter and Preller, *Hist. Philos. Græc.*, Gotha, 1888, p. 404; Reitzenstein, *Poimandres*, Leipzig, 1904, p. 50, n. 2.

†† The likeness to Hesiod, *W. and D.* 180 ff., has been pointed out and discussed by Adam in the *ClR* v. 445.

‡‡ *Polit.* 271 F; *Leg.* iv. 713 C ff. It has been observed by Eichhoff (*l.c.* p. 589) and others that the story of Pandora as told by Hesiod (*Theog.* 570, and *W. and D.* 70) implies that there was no woman in the Golden Age, and that it was through her that this happy period came to an end. See also, Grimm, *Deutsche Mythologie*, p. 540.

the Universe is now left to itself, so are all and several of its parts; and each race is propagated in the manner familiar to us who belong to that period. The continuance of the motion backward increases and accelerates the process of disorganization, until, by the time the Universe again reaches the point of departure, it is ready to fly off at a tangent and disappear for ever in the infinite space of discord. At this point, however, the Helmsman again resumes his post, reverses the direction of the Universe, and with the change again to harmony the Golden Age necessarily returns as before. The few who survive from the preceding period suffer change in sympathy with the whole. Again the old begin to grow young, and continue to do so until they finally disappear. Again the new generations are born with hoary hair, and not from each other, but from the earth. In fact, it is those who died in the preceding period of discord and were buried in the earth that now rise again from the dead, and in their turn are born old, grow young, and finally vanish.

It will be seen at once that, according to this remarkably suggestive theory, which, of course, owes much to earlier thinkers,* the sum of human experience is measured by two world-years. During the first the Universe moves forward, during the second, backward, to the place of beginning. Each *magnus annus* is therefore one of the two Ages into which the history of mankind is divided; and this alternation of Ages will continue so long as the Universe endures. As with the whole, so with each and all of its parts. The Ages of man, the life of man himself, are closely connected with this eternal oscillation of the Universe. All move in a cycle. The Golden Age of the long ago will surely come again some day. Moreover, every one of us shall rise again to another life in that Golden Age. Thus, regret for the past was balanced by hope for the future. In the later history of our theme, this association of ideas was of the utmost importance, and served to identify the theory of the Ages more and more closely with its ancient analogue, the doctrine of a future life beyond the grave.

The Stoic theory† of cycles occupies an important place in their systems. Here, their acknowledged dependence upon Heraclitus is clearly seen in the prominence they give to his doctrine of ἐκπύρωσις, the elemental fire into which the world is periodically resolved, and from which it is periodically born anew.

After the old world has been completely consumed, the four primal elements,—fire, air, water, earth,—which are indestructible, gradually assume their previous relations to each other, and in this way a new world comes into being exactly like the old. As soon as the proper point is reached in the process of reconstruction, every sort of living thing is born from the earth, and from that time proceeds to increase after its kind.‡ Man, too, is here, 'knowing nothing of wrong and born under better auspices.' But this Golden Age of innocence is never for long. 'Villainy steals on apace. Virtue is hard to find out: it needs a leader and a guide. The vices are learned without a master.'§ So the process of degeneration goes on until the time comes for the next ἐκπύρωσις. Then the world is destroyed and built anew, as before.

An ἐκπύρωσις occurs each time that the eight circles are in conjunction at the place of beginning.‖ For the Stoics, therefore, every *magnus annus* is the measure of one complete life, as it were, of the Universe. It follows that the totality of human experience must, also, lie between those impassable barriers of flame by which every great year is divided from its fellows. The soul outlives the body, but even the soul of the ideal Stoic¶ cannot survive the ἐκπύρωσις. Nothing emerges from this trial by fire except the primal elements from which all things are made.**

In one sense, however, we all have a personal interest in every period of the world's existence, for the reason that, according to the Stoic doctrine of εἱμαρμένη,* the history of every *magnus annus* is, necessarily, the exact counterpart of the history of every other *magnus annus*. The chain of existence and of consciousness is parted by the ἐκπύρωσις; but all begins anew, just as it did in the previous epoch; and every thing down to the slightest detail is exactly repeated.† To quote a favourite illustration of the Stoics themselves, every *magnus annus* will see Socrates. In every *magnus annus* he will marry Xanthippe, drink the hemlock, and die.‡

In the later stages of the Cyclic Theory we have also to reckon with the manipulations of the Orphic philosophers.§ It is extremely difficult to extract a definite answer to any question connected with the history of this movement. The *floruit* of the elder Orphics was not far from the 6th cent. B.C. With the great revival of Mysticism, four or five hundred years later, the old doctrine of the Orphics again came to the front, and was more or less revised or extended in conformity with similar ideas in other systems of thought—more especially Plato, the Stoics, and the Orient. Both periods were characterized by great literary activity. Unfortunately, however, our present knowledge of it is, for the most part, confined to chance quotations in the Neo-Platonists and the still later scholiasts, and their references are generally so vague and indefinite that, in the absence of other testimony, it is often impossible to distinguish the earlier product from the later. We may be fairly certain, however, that the two following theories, both of which are ascribed to the Orphics, are not a product of the earlier school.

The first is mentioned by Servius on Vergil, *Ecl.* iv. 10. In this note, Nigidius Figulus (*de Diis*, lib. iv.) is quoted for the statement: 'According to Orpheus, the ruler of the First Age is Saturn; of the Second, Jupiter; of the Third, Neptune; of the Fourth, Pluto.' An apparent reference to the same theory is found in two hexameters quoted from some Orphic poem by Lactantius, *Instit.* i. 13. 11 (Abel, *Orphica*, frag. 243).

As we shall see shortly, the four gods in this system are merely personifications of the four elements. The number points either to the Stoics or to the common source of both. Moreover, the formal association of the four elements with the Four Ages of man is an item of speculation which, so far as the Greeks are concerned, cannot be carried back beyond the Alexandrian period. Finally, this is certainly a cyclic theory, and it cannot be shown that the elder Orphics ever carried their doctrine of the re-birth of the soul any further. The extension of it to a periodical re-birth of the Universe itself, and the establishment of a close connexion between the two, belong to a subsequent development in the history of the Orphic movement.

The second theory is much more Orphic in character. The substance of it is given by Proclus in a note on Plato's *Republic*, 38. 5, ed. Schöll.

'The theologian Orpheus,' he says, 'taught that there were three Ages of man. The first or Golden Age was ruled by Phanes. Most mighty Kronos was ruler of the second or Silver Age. The third is the Titanic. The ruler of it is Zeus, and it is called Titanic because the men of that age were created by him from the remains of the Titans. The idea of Orpheus is that these three periods comprise every stage in the history of the human race.'

The Orphic elements in this account receive their best illustration from an Orphic theogony, the fragments of which are arranged and discussed by Gruppe in Roscher, iii. 1139 ff. The naïve crudity of the imagery in this poem strongly reminds one of the teleological speculations of the savage or semi-barbarous races.‖ The underlying thought, however, seems to be clear enough. It is a belief that the creation of the Cosmos was brought about by a series of emanations from the universal essence (Phanes), and that from time to time the Cosmos returns to its primeval form. The souls of men themselves are so many sparks which trickle down, as it were, from the divine fire above. But we are much more remote from the first Phanes, the primal All-Soul, than the first men were. Since then the backward path has steadily grown longer and more indirect. At all events, this seems to be what Proclus means when he says (*Orph.* frag. 244, ed. Abel) that, according to Orpheus, the men of the Golden Age lived κατὰ νοῦν μόνον, the men of the Silver Age κατὰ τὸν καθαρὸν λόγον; whereas all that we can appeal to is that small portion of Dionysus-Phanes which the

* See the two preceding notes, and Adam, *Repub.* ii. p. 296, n. 6, p. 297, n. 1-4, and references.

† Ritter and Preller, *l.c.* pp. 28 ff. and 398-405; Zeller, *Grundriss der Gesch. der Gr. Phil.*, Leipzig, 1905, p. 214; Zeno, frag. 107-109, and Chrysippus, frag. 596-632, in van Arnim's *Stoicorum Veterum Fragmenta*, Leipzig, 1905.

‡ Cleanthes, frag. 497, ed. van Arnim.

§ Seneca, *N.Q.* iii. 30. 8.

‖ Nemes. *de Nat. Hom.* 38 (quoted by Ritter and Preller, *l.c.* p. 404).

¶ Diog. Laert. (vii. 156) says that 'the Stoics claim that the soul is the spirit which is a part of ourselves. It is, therefore, corporeal, and though it survives our death, it is not immortal. . . . Cleanthes, therefore, thinks that all souls, Chrysippus, that only souls of the "wise," last until the ἐκπύρωσις.' Cf. also vii. 151; *Doxographi Græci*, 393, ed. Diels, etc.

** But see Ritter and Preller, *l.c.* p. 401 B.

* Diog. Laert. vii. 147 ff., and Ritter and Preller, *l.c.* p. 412.

† Eudemus, ed. Spengel, Berlin, 1866, pp. 73-74; Chrysippus, frag. 623-627, ed. van Arnim; Gomperz, *l.c.* pp. 113 and 116 ff.

‡ Nemes. *de Nat. Hom.* 38.

§ See esp. O. Gruppe in Roscher, iii. 1117-1154, who discusses the subject at length, and refers to all the important literature connected with it. A new edition of the Orphic remains is much needed. The latest edition, and the only one now generally available, is Abel, *Orphica*, Leipzig, 1885. This, however, is not entirely satisfactory, and does not supersede the monumental work of Lobeck (*Aglaophamos*).

‖ See Gomperz, *l.c.* pp. 193 and 109 ff.

Titans had eaten before they were slain by Zeus, and which, therefore, still lingered in the remains from which we of the third race were afterwards created.

The coefficient of descent in this version of the Ages is the ever-increasing distance from that to which the gods themselves owe their being. On the whole, we may characterize the account which Proclus summarizes as a theory of double emanation, the chief object of which was to lead up to the birth of Dionysus, the Orphic redeemer. In other words, we have the somewhat vague idea of a cyclic theory of the Universe attached to a much more highly developed doctrine of the re-birth of the soul and of the means whereby it may some day return to the god who gave it.

The doctrine of an ἐκπύρωσις, irrespective of its philosophical meaning, makes a strong appeal to the imagination. It was at all times, therefore, one of the most prominent features of the Cyclic Theory. By the 2nd cent. B.C., owing to the widespread activity of its most enthusiastic exponents, the Stoic popular preachers, no item of philosophical speculation could have been more familiar to the average man. Finally, together with much else that had been identified with the Stoics, it passed over to the Christian thinkers; and, long after the period with which we are here concerned, we find the Church Fathers undertaking to derive the doctrine of the ἐκπύρωσις from the Book of Genesis.*

But, long before the Stoics, the ἐκπύρωσις had begun to be associated with other great cosmic disasters of a different nature. The origin and progress of this development are better understood as soon as we observe the process of reasoning by which they were inspired and directed. In the first place, the cycle of the Universe had been called a year. This led to the natural but quite illogical assumption that, for that very reason, it must necessarily possess all the attributes of its prototype and namesake, the solar year. Second, the present condition of the world depends upon the maintenance of the elements in a certain state of equilibrium. Any disturbance of it is at once reflected in the world about us. If the disturbance is sufficiently severe, the result is cosmic disaster. The character of the disaster is determined by whichever one of the elements has gained the upper hand. Finally, great significance was attached to the fact that there were four Elements, four Seasons, four Ages of man.

The conquests of Alexander drew the East and the West closer to each other than they had ever been before, and this *rapprochement* was not disturbed by the Imperial policy of Rome. The phase of our subject now under consideration is especially marked by the more or less direct influence of Oriental speculations. Conversely, therefore, this aspect of the Cyclic Theory did not become especially prominent until the Alexandrian age. The first step was to associate the Flood Legend with the Cyclic Theory, and to set it over against the ἐκπύρωσις as a second recurrent catastrophe of the *magnus annus*. This doctrine of the regular alternation between a destruction by fire and a destruction by water was already an old story in the time of Plato (*e.g. Tim.* 22, C). There are no signs of this doctrine in the fragments of Zeno, Cleanthes, and the earlier Stoics. We know, however, that it was familiar to their contemporaries. Moreover, as early at least as Cicero's time, the doctrine had been adopted by the Stoics themselves, and henceforward we hear much of it.† Compare, for example, the vivid description of the great cyclic *diluvium* which Seneca gives us in his *Nat. Quæst.* iii. 27 ff.

The idea that these two contrasted disasters occur at certain definite points in the *magnus annus* is also of Oriental origin, and, doubtless, of a high antiquity. On the Greek side, the first to mention it is Aristotle. The quotation, which we owe to Censorinus, xviii. 11, was probably from Aristotle's lost *Protrept.*, the model of Cicero's famous dialogue, the *Hortensius*, which is also lost.* No doubt it was largely through the *Hortensius* that the Romans became familiar with Aristotle's observation that the two disasters of the *magnus annus*, or, as he termed it, the *maximus annus*, occur at the solstices: the *conflagratio* at the summer solstice, the *diluvium* at the winter solstice.† In other words, the solar year has solstices; it also has summer and winter—the one, hot and dry, the other, cold and wet. Therefore the great year has the same peculiarities. This being granted, the *conflagratio* is put in the great summer, simply because the great summer is hot and dry, and the *diluvium* in the great winter, because the great winter is cold and wet.

We should not expect this sort of logic from Aristotle, and, as a matter of fact, the idea was not his own. Indeed, as the *Protrept.* was a discussion in the form of a dialogue, we do not know that he approved of the view at all. That his information went back to some Eastern source is indicated by a fragment from the voluminous history of his much younger contemporary, the Chaldæan priest Berosus. The passage is quoted by Seneca, *Naturales Quæstiones*, iii. 29. 1 ff. 'Berosus,' he says, 'qui Belum interpretatus est,' insists that he can set the time for the *conflagratio* and the *diluvium*. The earth will burn up, he claims, when all the stars, which now move in different orbits, are in conjunction in the constellation of Cancer. The Flood will take place when the same stars reach conjunction in the constellation of Capricorn. 'Illic solstitium, hic bruma conficitur.' Conjunction in Cancer produces the *conflagratio*, conjunction in Capricorn the *diluvium*. This touch of astrology makes the statement very impressive, and these Chaldæans were nothing if not impressive. But, as Gomperz has already observed,‡ the actual foundation of the statement is nothing but the fact that the summer and winter solstices of the ordinary solar year are presided over by Cancer and Capricorn respectively. When this flimsy assumption of profundity is removed, the theory of Berosus is probably identical with the one mentioned by Aristotle.

Now that fire and water had acquired a definite and important position in the cyclic scheme, it followed inevitably that the two remaining elements, air and earth, ought to be put on the same plane. The line of development followed was largely suggested by the fact that there were four Elements, four Seasons, four Ages of man. The four seasons of the ordinary year are spring, summer, autumn, and winter—a series which has always been associated with man's own descent from youth to hoary eld, from strength and happiness to weakness and sorrow. So the four seasons of the great year are the four Ages of man, another series with which the idea of descent had always been associated. As the springtime of the little year of our life is the golden youth of man, so the springtime of that greater year was the golden youth of all mankind.§ Finally, the traditional order of the four elements—fire, air, water, earth—is also one of descent from the lighter to the heavier, from pure spirit to the earth, earthy.

If, now, we associate the four elements in their regular order with the corresponding Ages of man in their regular order, the dominating element during the Golden Age will be fire, during the Silver Age, air, during the Brazen Age, water, and during the Iron Age, earth. The conclusion of this is that the descent of man himself is due to his ever-increasing distance, so to speak, from the Divine fire. We are thus brought back to the Orphics again, and, as a matter of fact, the Stoic-Orphic theory reported by Nigidius Figulus, in which, as we have already seen, the *magnus annus* was equipped with four seasons, each ruled by the appropriate element, is a complete illustration of the tendencies we have just been discussing.

A theory ascribed to the Magi by Dio Chrysostom and partially reported by him (xxxvi. 43 ff.), should also be mentioned here. The Magi tell us, he says, that the Lord of the world rides in a chariot drawn by four horses which are sacred to Zeus, Hera, Poseidon, and Hestia respectively. In other words, the four horses are the four elements, fire, air, water, and earth. As a rule they are tractable. Now and then, however, the first steed becomes restive and sets fire to the other three. This is the origin of the story of Phaethon told by the Greeks. Again it is the steed of Poseidon that becomes

* See Windischmann, *Zoroastr. Stud.* p. 259.

† Cic. *Rep.* vi. 23, cf. Macrob. *Som. Scip.* ii. 10. 10 ff.; Lucret. v. 338; Luc. vii. 812, as interpreted by the *Commenta Lucani*, ed. Usener, p. 252 (frag. 608, vol. ii. p. 186, ed. van Arnim); Seneca, *Dial.* vi. 26. 6, etc.

* Usener, *Rhein. Mus.* xxviii. 391 ff.

† For an echo of this statement see the *Meteorologica*, i. 14.

‡ *Griechische Denker*, i. 115.

§ Vergil, *Georg.* ii. 336 ff.; Ovid, *Met.* i. 107; *Pervigilium Veneris*, 2 ff. etc.

restive, and the drops of his sweat are sprinkled upon the other three. This, again, is the source from which the Greeks derived their story of Deucalion's flood.

If one were to insist upon completing the analogy between the four Elements, the four Ages of man, and the four Seasons of the great year, the Ages presided over by air and by earth, as was already the case with the Ages of fire and water, should each be marked by a cosmic disaster appropriate to its nature. We know that this was actually done, but as these attempts lie outside the sphere with which this article is concerned, they do not require discussion here.*

3. **Revival of Mysticism in 2nd cent. B.C.**—The last important stage in the long history of our subject is the era of the prophets. The rapid growth of Mysticism which began early in the Alexandrian age reached its culmination in the 2nd cent. B.C. One of the most striking features of the movement, and a significant comment upon the mental and spiritual condition of the entire Græco-Roman world, was the rapid production of apocryphal works. It is probably fair to assume that the production of this literature was much encouraged, if not actually suggested, by the then widespread belief that the life of mankind moves in cycles. At all events, one of the most characteristic features of all these visions and prophecies was the emphasis given to some cyclic theory of the Ages. It would be quite unnecessary here, even if they were still available to us, to examine these works in detail. Their chief importance to us would be derived not from their contents, but from the point of view which, by virtue of their very nature, they all possess in common. These visions and prophecies, like all other works of the same class, appealed more to faith and the emotions than they did to reason and the understanding. The author tells his readers that this last Age has nearly run its course, and that the great change is near at hand. He does not state it as an opinion or a theory, capable of being discussed as such. He states it as oracular utterance, as inspired prophecy, the truth of which is already foreshadowed in current events and cannot be questioned. In this way the Cyclic Theory of the Ages was transformed from a rhetorical and philosophical theme into a Divine assurance of the joy soon to come. As a class, these compositions contributed almost nothing to the development of the Cyclic Theory itself. A word or two, however, should be given to the Sibyl.

The *Oracles of the Sibyl* have been ascribed to about the middle of the 2nd cent. B.C. They were well known to the Romans for the next 200 years; but at the time when the collection now bearing that name† was composed, the earlier had apparently ceased to exist. Meanwhile, however, they had won a sort of secondary immortality through the influence they had exerted upon the fourth *Eclogue* of Vergil,‡ the most famous literary work ever inspired by any aspect of our theme. From this poem and the ancient comment upon it, it appears that the Sibyl adopted the Stoic-Orphic identification of the Four Ages of man with the four seasons of the *magnus annus*. In addition to this, she—or her authority—was inspired by the analogy of the ancient solar year to divide the great year into ten great months, each of which was the length of a *sæculum* and presided over by a god. Ever since the time of Sulla there had been rumours afloat that the Sibyl's last *sæculum* was drawing to a close, and that the Golden Age was at hand. One cannot read the fourth *Eclogue* without feeling that Vergil was himself impressed by a prophecy so much in harmony with the aspirations of his own lofty soul. Nevertheless, we must not forget that the poem is really a poem of congratulation upon the birth of a son, into which, as Marx has clearly demonstrated,* Vergil introduced the topic of the Ages in accordance with the specific suggestion of the rhetoricians for poems of this type, and developed it in strict conformity with the rules laid down by them. The most famous line in the poem,

'Iam nova progenies cælo demittitur alto,'

is a clear reflexion of the cyclic theories which we have just been discussing. That, in itself, it should also foreshadow quite as clearly the great central article of the Christian faith, is an excellent illustration of the fact that there has never been any break between ancient and modern culture. The foundation of the most enlightened Christian thought, quite as much as the foundation of Vergil's thought, was that gradual blending of the Orient with the speculations of the Greek philosophers, more especially Plato and the Stoics, which moulded the doctrine of the Ages in its final form, and which, ever since then, has played such an important part in the mental and spiritual consciousness of the civilized world. It is, therefore, no matter for surprise that for more than 1500 years this last great document in the long history of the Cyclic Theory of the Ages was firmly believed to be a prophecy of the coming of Christ.†

KIRBY FLOWER SMITH.

* O. Gruppe, *Gr. Mythol.* p. 450, n. 1, also his *Gr. Kulte und Mythen in ihren Beziehungen zu den orient. Religionen*, Leipzig, 1887, p. 670, n. 8, and 695, n. 22, with references.

† The two modern editions of the *Oracula Sibyllina* are by Rzach, Vienna, 1891, and by Geffcken, Berlin, 1902. See also Christ, *Gesch. der Gr. Lit.*, Munich, 1905, p. 822, and references.

‡ O. Gruppe, *Gr. Kulte*, etc., p. 687ff., and references: A. Cartault, *Étude sur les Bucol. de Virg.*, Paris, 1897, p. 210ff.; W. W. Fowler, *Harvard Studies*, xiv. 19ff. etc.

* F. Marx, *Neue Jahrbüch. f. das klass. Altertum*, i. (1898), pp. 105–128.

† Comparetti, *Virgilio nel medio evo*, 1896, i. 129–138, and ii. 90–99; Mayor, etc., *Virgil's Messianic Eclogue*, 1907.

AGES OF THE WORLD (Indian).—The Hindu doctrine of the Ages of the World (*yugas*) is combined with that of two other great periods, the *manvantaras* and *kalpas*, into a fanciful system of universal chronology, which passes for orthodox. Its basis is the yugas; they are, therefore, treated here in connexion with the other elements of the chronological system. Orthodox Hindus recognize four Ages of the World (*yugas*), roughly corresponding to the Gold, Silver, Brass, and Iron Ages of the ancients. They are called *kṛta, tretā, dvāpara*, and *kali* after the sides of a die; *kṛta*, the lucky one, being the side marked with four dots; *tretā* that with three; *dvāpara* with two; *kali*, the losing one, with one dot. These names occur in the period of the Brāhmaṇas as names of throws at dice, and in one verse of the Aitareya Brāhmaṇa (7, 14) they are already referred, by the commentator, to the yugas. In the epics and the Purāṇas the belief with regard to the four yugas has become a fully established doctrine. The general idea, the same in all Brāhmanical sources, is that the character, or, if the expression may be used, the proportion of virtue, and the length of each yuga conform to the number on the side of a die, after which it is named. In the *kṛtayuga*, virtue (*dharma*) was fully present in men, with all four feet, as it is expressed, but it diminished by one quarter or foot in every succeeding age, till in the *kaliyuga* only one foot of dharma remains. The same proportion holds good with regard to the duration of the several Ages. The kṛtayuga lasts 4000 years, to which a dawn and a twilight of 400 years each are added; the same items in tretā are 3000 and 300, in dvāpara 2000 and 200, in kali 1000 and 100 years. Thus the period of the four yugas together, technically called a *mahāyuga* or *chaturyuga*, though commonly a *yuga*, lasts 12,000 years (Manu, i. 69 ff. =

Mahābhārata, iii. 12,826 ff.). The years in this statement are interpreted as Divine years, consisting each of 360 human years, giving thus a total of 4,320,000 years in each *mahāyuga*, and this interpretation, once adopted in the Purāṇas, became a dogma. The usual descriptions of the kṛta- (or satya-) yuga reveal to us a happy state of mankind, when life lasted 4000 years, when there were no quarrels nor wars, when the rules of caste and the precepts of the Vedas were strictly obeyed, when, in short, virtue reigned paramount. In the kali- (or tiṣya-) yuga just the reverse prevails. There is a confusion of castes and *āśramas*. The Veda and good conduct gradually fall into neglect; all kinds of vices creep in; diseases afflict mankind; the term of life grows shorter and shorter, and is quite uncertain; barbarians occupy the land, and people kill one another in continual strife, till at the end of the yuga some mighty king extinguishes the infidels. From these extremes the character of the intermediate yugas may be imagined.* The dawns and twilights of the several Ages are periods of transition from one Age to the next, when the character of the one is not yet entirely lost, and that of the other not yet fully established.

It seems natural to presume that originally the mahāyuga comprised the whole existence of the world; indications, indeed, of such a belief are not wanting, as will be noticed later. Still, the common doctrine is that one mahāyuga followed on another, one thousand of them forming a single *kalpa*. The kalpa, then, is the length of time from a creation to a destruction of the world. The belief in periodical creations and destructions of the world is very old; and its existence in the Vedic period may be inferred from Atharvaveda, x. 8. 39, 40. It is combined as follows with that in the four Ages. In the first kṛtayuga, after the creation of the earth, Brahman created a thousand pairs of twins from his mouth, breast, thighs, and feet respectively. They lived without houses; all desires which they conceived were directly fulfilled; and the earth produced of itself delicious food for them, since animals and plants were not yet in existence. Each pair of twins brought forth at the end of their life a pair exactly like them. As everybody did his duty and nothing else, there was no distinction between good and bad acts. But this state of things changed at the end of the Age; the first rain fell and trees grew up. These produced honey and whatever the primitive people desired. In the first tretāyuga, mankind consisted no longer of pairs of twins, but of men and women. Being now for the first time subject to cold and heat, they began to build houses, and they quarrelled about the miraculous trees. The trees, however, disappeared, and herbs became the food of men. Now trade was introduced, and personal property, unknown before, caused the social distinctions. Then Brahman established the four castes and the four *āśramas*, and fixed the duties peculiar to each of them. Afterwards he created spiritual sons, who were the ancestors of gods, demons, serpents, inhabitants of hell, etc.† At the end of the last kaliyuga of a kalpa, the heat of the sun becomes fierce and dries up the whole earth; and by it the three worlds are set on fire and consumed. At last enormous clouds appear and rain for hundreds of years, and deluge the whole world till the waters inundate heaven.‡ As the latter signs are frequently alluded to, in the form of similes in the Epics, etc., as occurring at the end of a yuga (instead of at the end of a kalpa), it is most probable that originally the yuga ended with the destruction, and consequently began with the creation of the world. A similar belief seems to have been expressed by the term 'kalpa,' but perhaps with this difference, that the concept of a yuga was intimately connected with the idea of the four stages through which mankind must pass, analogous to the four ages of man, viz. childhood, youth, adult life, and old age, while this idea was not necessarily implied in the concept of the kalpa. The combination of both these popular beliefs, with regard to the kalpa and the yuga, in the form described above, was probably due to the systematizing efforts of the Paurāṇikas.

* Cf. J. Muir, *Original Sanscrit Texts*3, vol. i. p. 143 ff.
† Vāyu Purāṇa, i. 8.
‡ Viṣṇu Purāṇa, vi. 3 *al.*

There is still a third kind of long period, the *manvantara*, fourteen of which go to the kalpa. Each manvantara contains 71 mahāyugas, and 14 manvantaras are therefore equivalent to 994 (14×71) mahāyugas. The remainder of 6 mahāyugas required to make up the kalpa (=1000 mahāyugas, *sup.* p. 200) is so distributed that the first manvantara is preceded by a dawn of the length of one kṛtayuga (=0·4 mahāyuga), and each manvantara is followed by a twilight of equal length (15 × 0·4 = 6 mahāyugas). The twilight of the manvantara is, according to Sūrya Siddhānta, i. 18, a deluge (*jalaplava*). This artificial system of the manvantaras was probably introduced in order to account for the different patronymics of Manu, such as Vaivasvata, Svāyambhuva, Sāṁvarana, which occur already in different Vedic works. These early caused a belief in the existence of several distinct Manus.* The Paurāṇikas systematized these notions as described. Since Manu was thought to have introduced the social and moral order of things, and to have played a part in the creation of gods and men, 'the seven Ṛṣis, certain (secondary) divinities, Indra, Manu, and the kings, his sons, are created and perish' in each manvantara;† and the details of these recurring events in each manvantara are given, *e.g.*, in the same Purāṇa.‡ Artificial as these manvantaras appear to be, still they are given as one of the five characteristic topics of the Purāṇa in a verse found in several Purāṇas.§ And the whole system of yugas, etc., is regarded as orthodox to such a degree that all the astronomical works, the Siddhāntas, have adopted them, except the Romaka Siddhānta, which for that reason is stigmatized as not orthodox.‖

The astronomical aspect of the yuga is that, in its commencement, sun, moon, and planets stood in conjunction in the initial point of the ecliptic, and returned to the same point at the end of the age. The popular belief on which this notion is based is older than Hindu astronomy.¶ The current yuga is the 457th of the present varāha-kalpa, or kalpa of the Boar, the 28th of the present manvantara (that of Manu Vaivasvata), which itself is the 7th of this kalpa. We are now in the kaliyuga, which began Feb. 17, B.C. 3102, the epoch of the still used era of the kaliyuga. At the end of the last tretāyuga lived Rāma, the son of Daśaratha, and at the end of the last dvāparayuga took place the great war of the Pāṇḍavas and Kauravas, described in the Mahābhārata.

A kalpa is called a day of Brahman, and his night is of equal length. At the close of the night he creates the world anew. Of such days and nights a year of Brahman is composed; and a hundred such years constitute his whole life. This longest period is called a *para*, half of which, a

* Cf. *SBE* xxv. p. lxiv f.
† Wilson, *Viṣṇu Purāṇa*, i. p. 50.
‡ Wilson, *l.c.* iii. p. 1 ff.
§ Wilson, *l.c.*, Pref. p. vii, note 1.
‖ Thibaut, *Pañchasiddhāntikā*, Introd. p. xxviii.
¶ See *Actes du X. Congrès International des Orientalistes*, p. 104. For details of the astronomical use of the yugas, the reader is referred to the translation of the Sūrya Siddhānta, *JAOS* vi. p. 15 ff.

parārdha, had elapsed at the beginning of the present kalpa.*

The notions of the Buddhists about the Ages of the World (*yugas*) and about the larger periods (*kalpas*) are similar to those of the orthodox Hindus, but still more fanciful. The names of the four yugas are the same, but their arrangement is different. They begin with kaliyuga and go up to kṛtayuga,† and then, in reversed order, go down to kaliyuga.‡ Thus, instead of a mahāyuga of four Ages, the Buddhists assume a period of eight Ages, which is called an *antarakalpa*. An *antarakalpa* is 'the interval that elapses while the age of man increases from ten years to an *asaṅkheyya* (*asaṅkhyeya* = $10{,}000{,}000^{20}$), and then decreases again to ten years; this period is of immense length.'§ According to some authorities, it has a length of 1,680,000 years.‖ Together with the age, the moral state of mankind increases and decreases. Twenty antarakalpas form one *asaṅkhyeya kalpa* (Pali *asaṅkheyya kappa*), and four asaṅkhyeya kalpas constitute one *mahākalpa*. The first asaṅkhyeya kalpa is called *saṁvarta* (P. *saṁvaṭṭa*), during which a world or sphere (*chakravāla*, P. *cakkavāla*) is completely destroyed by fire, water, or wind. In the second (*saṁvartasthāyin*, P. *saṁvaṭṭaṭṭhāyin*) the state of void continues. In the third (*vivarta*, P. *vivaṭṭa*) the world is being built up again; and in the fourth (*vivartasthāyin*, P. *vivaṭṭaṭṭhāyin*) the world continues to exist.

It is during this last period that the world becomes first inhabited, by *ābhāsvara* gods of the Brahmaloka being born on earth. These self-luminous beings lost their lustre when they first began to feed on a delicious juice produced by the earth. They then created the sun, the moon, and the stars. While these beings gradually degenerated, the earth ceased to yield this first kind of food, and produced a kind of cream-like fungus. This was followed by a climbing plant, and this again by an extraordinary kind of rice. When this rice was used as food, sexual intercourse began. The rice deteriorated, and at last ceased to grow of itself. At the same time other vices were introduced, and personal property, till at last the present order of mankind was established.¶ Then comes the period of the twenty antarakalpas, described above. A hundred thousand years before the end of the mahākalpa, a god appears and warns mankind of the coming event, exhorting them to amend. And after that time the destruction of the earth—nay, of a billion of worlds or *chakravālas*—sets in by fire, water, or wind.** The mahākalpas are either empty (*śūnya*) kalpas—those in which there is no Buddha—or Buddha kalpas. The latter are of five kinds, *sāra-*, *maṇḍa-*, *vara-*, *sāramaṇḍa-*, and *bhadrakalpas*, according as one, two, three, four, or five Buddhas appear. The present kalpa is a bhadrakalpa; for four Buddhas have already appeared—Krakucchanda (Kakusandha), Kanakamuni (Koṇāgamana), Kāśyapa (Kassapa), and Gotama; and the fifth, Maitreya (Metteyya), has yet to come (see above, pp. 187-190).

The notions of the *Jainas* about the Ages of the World are not quite unlike, yet curiously different from, those described above. The Jainas liken time to a wheel with twelve spokes; the descending half of the wheel is called the *avasarpiṇī* period, the ascending half *utsarpiṇī*. Each half is divided into six Ages (*āra* = 'spoke'). The *āras* are, in avasarpiṇī, the following:—(1) suṣamasuṣamā, the duration of which is 400,000,000,000,000 oceans of years (*sāgaropamā*); (2) suṣamā, 300 billions of oceans of years; (3) suṣamaduṣamā, 200 billions of oceans of years; (4) duṣamasuṣamā, 100 billions of oceans of years, less 42,000 common years; (5) duṣamā, 21,000 years; (6) duṣamaduṣamā, likewise 21,000 years. The same Ages recur in the utsarpiṇī period, but in reversed order. In the first Age men lived three *palyas* or *palyopamās*, a long period not to be expressed in a definite number of years (one billion of palyas go to one ocean of years), and men grew to a height of three *gavyūtis*, a *gavyūti* being about two miles. Men were born in pairs, and each pair gave birth to a pair of twins, who married. There were ten kinds of miraculous trees (*kalpavṛkṣa*), which furnished men with all they wanted. The earth was as sweet as sugar, and the water as delicious as wine. This state of things continued through the first three Ages, but gradually age after age the length of life declined, and was only two *palyas* at the beginning of the second, and one *palya* at the beginning of the third Age, while correspondingly the height of the body diminished to two and one *gavyūti*. Furthermore, the power of the trees and the quality of earth and water deteriorated at the same rate. In the third Age the trees more slowly satisfied the wants of men, who therefore claimed them severally as personal property. Vimalavāhana was appointed to keep order among men, and he became the first patriarch (*kulakara*). The seventh patriarch, Nābhi, was the father of Ṛṣabha, who was anointed the first king, and who introduced the principal institutions of mankind. Ṛṣabha became the first *tīrthakara*, or prophet of the Jainas. His nirvāṇa occurred 3 years 8½ months before the end of the third Age. In the fourth Age the order of things was similar to the present one, except, of course, that everything gradually deteriorated with the lapse of time. The life of man lasted a krore of *pūrvas* (a *pūrva* = $8{,}400{,}000^2$ years) at the beginning, and diminished to a hundred years at the end of the Age; and, similarly, the height of men decreased from 2000 cubits to 7 cubits. 23 *tīrthakaras* were born in the fourth Age, the last of whom, Mahāvīra, died 3 years 8½ months before the beginning of the fifth Age, which began in B.C. 522. In the fifth and sixth Ages length of life will diminish down to 16 years, and the height of men to 1 cubit. There will be no *tīrthakaras* in the last two Ages of the avasarpiṇī period. In the succeeding utsarpiṇī period the same Ages will recur, but in reversed order. In this way an infinite number of avasarpiṇīs and utsarpiṇīs follow each other.*

The idea on which the notion of these periods seems to be based is apparently the year. The avasarpiṇī and utsarpiṇī correspond to the two *ayanas*, the southern and northern course of the sun; and the six *āras* of each period to the six months of the *ayana*.† On the other hand, the first three *āras*, with their pairs of twins, with the miraculous trees for their subsistence, much resemble the first kṛtayuga of the Purāṇas, while the remaining three *āras* may be compared to the tretā, dvāpara, and kali yugas. A peculiar feature of the Jaina system, however, is the great disparity in length between the last two Ages and the first four, while the relative length of the four yugas is reproduced in the *āras*, if we consider the fourth, fifth, and sixth *āras* as one.

On the whole, there is an unmistakable family likeness between the notions of the orthodox Hindus, the Buddhists, and the Jainas, as described above, though they have developed on different lines.

LITERATURE.—Besides the works referred to throughout this article, consult the Literature given at the end of the article AGES OF THE WORLD (Buddhist).

H. JACOBI.

* Wilson, *Viṣṇu Purāṇa*, i. p. 53.
† *Utsarpani yugas*; see Hardy, *Manual of Budhism*, p. 7.
‡ *Arpani*, apparently for *avasarpiṇī*, *ib.*
§ Childers, *Pali Dictionary*, *s.v.* 'Kappa.'
‖ Burnouf, *Lotus de la bonne Loi*, p. 324 f.
¶ Hardy, *l.c.* p. 64 ff.
** Hardy, *l.c.* p. 28 ff.

* Hemacandra, *Ādīśvara-charitra*, 2. 113 ff.
† Cf. *SBE* xlv. p. 16, note 1.

AGES OF THE WORLD (Jewish).—**1.** The Heb. word *yôm* (יום), 'day,' is frequently applied in both Biblical and post-Biblical literature in a sense closely allied to that of an Age of the World. *Levit. Rab.* 19 and *Sanh.* 19, referring to Ps 90[4], say God's 'day' is a thousand years. Philo in *de Opificio Mundi*, i. 3, etc., treats 'the Days of Creation' as covering an epoch. He denies that the story of Genesis is to be taken literally as meaning an actual creation in six ordinary days. Creation was not in time: the six days described the arrangement or order of creation, much in the same sense as scientists talk of the geological orders. Midrash *Ber. Rab.* xii. deals with the time occupied in creation. 'The day of the Lord' (Mal 4[5]) 'that day' (היום ההוא, Zec 14[9]), 'the great day' (Mal 4[5]), 'the day of judgment,' 'the day of vengeance' (Jer 46[10]), 'the day of rebuke' (Hos 5[9]), are all expressions for the Last Judgment, sometimes covering the future world (עולם הבא) which will succeed it. יומנא, 'our day,' is used as a synonym for עולם הוה, 'this world' (Targum for 'days' in Ps 34[12]). 'The days of the kings' (Dn 2[44]) means the everlasting kingdom of the future world. 'The days of the Messiah' (*Sanh.* 99*a*) is used in the Talmud and Midrash for the Messianic Age; 'the days of the life of the world to come,' for the future world which follows. 'The day which is all Sabbath,' 'the day which is altogether good,' 'the day which is altogether long,' 'the day whereon the righteous sit with crowns upon their head and enjoy the splendour of the Divine presence,' are expressions in the Jewish Liturgy (in the grace after meat for Sabbaths and Festivals, especially Passover) which also connote the future world.

2. Before this world existed there had been successive creations (*Gen. Rab.* 1, *Ab. R.N.* xxxvii.). 'Seven things were created before the world was created, and these are they: the Law, Repentance, the Garden of Eden, Gehenna, the Throne of Glory, the Temple, and the Messiah's name' (*Pes.* 54*a*). There were 974 generations before Adam, which with the 26 generations between Adam and Moses make up a thousand (*Shab.* 88*b*, *Ḥag.* 13*b*, 14*a*). The Mishna discourages such cosmogonic speculations. 'Two together should not study the Creation nor even one the Chariot' (*Ḥag.* cap. ii.). The Gemārā *ad loc.* (*ib.* 11[6]) forbids inquiry into what was before the world was, basing this on the limitations of Dt 4[32].

3. In the Bible narrative there are traces of a Golden Age in the account of the Garden of Eden, where Adam dwelt till the Fall. As to the length of his sojourn the Rabbis differ. The Bible narrative presents some striking parallels to the Assyrian story, just as the post-Biblical does to Zarathushtrian speculations. But, as Goldziher points out in his *Mythology among the Hebrews*, even if its cosmogony had been derived from Iranian sources, it is an essential part of *their* system, whereas the Pentateuch makes no further use of it. It is notable that the later Jewish view is that *Gan Eden* (Paradise) will be the reward for good conduct after death. This is no devolution from a Golden to an Iron Age (for traces of which in Dn 2, see below), and no evolution in an opposite sense, but rather a sort of endless cycle; 'the thing that hath been, it is that which shall be' (Ec 1[9]).

4. The Pentateuch is almost exclusively concerned with the history of Israel, and the first age of persecution (afterwards known as a גָּלוּת, *gālûth*, or 'captivity') is that of Egypt. According to Gn 15[13], Abraham's seed is to be afflicted 400 years. In Jg 11[26] a period of 300 years is given as the interval between the Exodus and Jephthah, during which the children of Israel were left in undisturbed possession of the other side of the Jordan. In 1 K 6[1] the period between the Exodus and the building of the Temple is fixed at 480 years.

5. The Prophets, before the Assyrian captivity, are concerned only with the immediate future. They deal with practical politics, and warn the people to repent in view of disasters that are imminent. The Day of the Lord, which in the post-captivity literature of the Bible becomes the Day of Judgment, occurs already in Amos (5[16-20]), the earliest of the later prophets, as well as in Isaiah (cf. W. R. Smith, *Proph.* 131 f.).

6. In the post-exilic literature of the Bible we first meet with a distinct promise of an ultimate, not immediate, Messianic Age, in which all wrongs will be righted. The return under Zerubbabel had proved a disappointment. The autonomy of the Jews had not been satisfactorily re-established. The Jews did not occupy their proper position in the world. The people were dissatisfied with their leaders, and thus the notion of an ideal Messiah rather than a political one seems to have become evolved. Zechariah (ch. 14), when he proclaims: 'One day which shall be known to the Lord, not day, nor night . . . there shall be no more the Canaanite in the house of the Lord of Hosts,' represents a Messianic Age distant but sure. Malachi is much more practical. He preaches against the sins of his day, but even he does not threaten with immediate disaster. His 'day that I [the Lord] do make' (Mal 4[3])—the great and dreadful day of the Lord (4[5])—is the Day of Judgment, and here first is Elijah the prophet promised as a precursor of that day. Daniel is written in a different spirit. Despite its mysticism, it is a political pamphlet. It is almost certainly late, and intended to encourage those who were suffering under the Syrian oppression. Ben Sira is perhaps earlier. He, too, prays for redemption (ch. 36), and, like some of the Psalms and post-exilic prophets, looks forward to the Kingdom of God. The Apocalyptic literature, of which Enoch is certainly, and the Book of Jub. is perhaps, pre-Christian, is overweighted by the gloomy events of the time. The Messianic Age is increasingly needed, and national impatience insists on fixing its date.

7. The destruction of Jerusalem gave a mighty impetus to apocalyptic literature. The era of Messiahs and Prophets produced such men as Theudas in B.C. 44, under Fadus; 'the Egyptian' was another such under Felix; under Hadrian appeared Bar Cochba 'the Son of the Star,' who persuaded even an 'Aḳiba to join him in insensate revolt against Rome; and so on through a long succession of pseudo-Messiahs down to Sabbatai Zebi (whose advent in the mystic year 1666 caused such excitement both in and out of Jewry), and even to Mari Shooker Kohail, an impostor who so lately as 1870 excited wild hopes among some Arabian Jews of Aden. The Diaspora seemed to lay stress on individual rather than national hopes of reward and punishment after death. But Messianic hopes are traceable even in Philo, who looks to a future re-assembly of the Diaspora in Palestine, and echoes of this view are to be met with in the 4th *Eclogue* of Vergil. The Kingdom of God and His people (see Ps 145[11], Wis 10[10]) is of the future (cf. Is 52[7], Mic 4[4], Zec 14[9]). Contrast the national view of Is 24[23], 'The Lord of Hosts shall reign in Mount Zion, and in Jerusalem,' with the universalistic concept of *Orac. Sib.* iii. 767, 'His everlasting Kingdom shall be over all creatures,' and the Jewish Liturgy for the New Year and Atonement, 'all works shall fear thee . . . joy to thy land . . . shining light to the Son of Jesse thine anointed . . . when thou makest the dominion of Arrogance to pass away from the earth' (Singer's *Prayer Book*, 239). But such universalistic ideas are comparatively rare. God's

Kingdom is also that of His people (Dn 2^{44} 7^{27}). And this idea prevails throughout the Jewish apocalyptic writings, *e.g.* Assump. Mos., Enoch (Eth. and Slav.), 4 Ezra: God's enemies, whole peoples, will be previously destroyed. It is perhaps based on Ezekiel's Vision of Gog and Magog (38 and 39) as the first prophecy of this stage. After this world-war comes the Judgment (Jl 3^{12}). Meantime the people of Israel will be hidden away in safety (Is 26^{20}, Zec 14^{5}, Apoc. Bar 29^{2}, and Mk 13^{14-20}). The precursors of the Messiah are Elijah (Mal 4^{5}, Sir 48^{10-12}, *Orac. Sib.* ii., *Edujoth*, viii. 7), Moses (Dt 18^{15}), Enoch (Gn 5^{24}, Eth. Enoch). The Messianic Kingdom is predominatingly particularistic. The Diaspora will be reunited, Jerusalem rebuilt, the heathen converted.

8. In the Apocalyptic literature, and first in Daniel, we get the universalist idea of 'this world' and 'the next' as parallel to the tribal idea of the Present Age and the Messianic Age. The Æon of עולם הזה (*ὁ νῦν αἰών*, 1 Ti 6^{17}) is 5000 years in Assump. Mos.; 10,000 in Eth. En 16^{1} 18^{16} 21^{6}, Jub 1^{29}; 7000 in *Sanh.* 97*a*, where R. Katina says the world will last 6000 years and in the seventh will be destroyed; of the 6000, 2000 years are 'Tohu' (chaos), 2000 Torah, and 2000 Messianic. This theory is based on the 6 days of Creation. 'As the sabbatical year is remitted once in 7 years, so is the world remitted 1 chiliasm in 7' (cf. Bacher, *Agada der Tannaiten*, i. 139 ff. [2nd ed. 133 ff.]).

Daniel's theory of year-weeks (ch. 9) is based on the 70 of Jer 25^{12} 29^{10}. (The Babylonian year was divided into 72 weeks of 5 days each). Daniel's 4 metals (ch. 2) and his 4 great beasts (7^{3}) seem based on the classical conception of this world's division into the Gold, Silver, Bronze, and Iron Ages. Eth. Enoch also divides the period of the 70 shepherds into 4 ages ('*cursus alter*' is divided into 4 *horæ*, meaning perhaps 4 Roman Emperors).

9. The division into 7 millenniums for the duration of 'this world' is made in Eth. Enoch, Test. Abr., R. Katina (*Sanh.* 97*a*). The preceding tribulations of the Messiah are to last 7 years, says R. Simeon ben Jochai (*Der. Eretz zut.* 10). In $3\frac{1}{2}$ periods (Dn 12^{7}) 'all these things shall be finished.' 4 Ezra divides the world into 12 portions. All these figures, 4, 7, $\frac{7}{2}$, 70 (72), and 12 have an astronomical basis, and correspond to the seasons, the days of the week, the weeks of the Babylonian year, and the signs of the Zodiac.

10. The mathematical determination of the end of 'this world' and the beginning of the next was eventually discarded by the Rabbis after all such calculations had proved false. 'Rab says, All the terms (קצין) have ceased, and the matter resteth only upon repentance and good works' (*Sanh.* 97*b*, cf. Am 5^{18}). Before God renews His world (מחדש עולמו), the Messianic Age will come. It is interpolated between this world and the next. The time of Messianic tribulations (חבלי משיח) is the precursor of the change of Æon. Men will be weaker (4 Ezr 5^{54-55}). They will suffer terrible diseases (*Orac. Sib.* iii. 538), children will be born with white hair (Jub 23^{25}), women will be barren (*Orac. Sib.* ii. 164). Fields will not fructify (4 Ezr 6^{22}), poverty and famine will prevail (Eth. En 99^{5}, Apoc. Bar 27), universal war will rage (4 Ezr 9^{3}), the wise shall be silent and fools shall speak (Apoc. Bar 70^{5}). Then will come the Judgment (יום הדין), when God will weigh sins and virtues, but even here the Messiah, Prince of Peace, emerges (Apoc. Bar 29 and 73); and after all this travail the time of the Messiah shall be revealed, though He is here no longer the national hero but the renewer of Paradise, the restorer of the Golden Age. Next will follow the Resurrection of the Dead (Is 26^{19}). God will destroy death (Dn 12^{2} 'Many of them that sleep in the dust of the earth shall awake'). En 51^{1-3}, 4 Ezr 7^{32}, and Apoc. Bar 50^{2} point to a universal resurrection. Others limit this to the righteous (*Test. of Judah*, xxv., cf. Jos. *Ant.* xviii. § 14 [ed. Niese]). The Rabbis throughout their literature rebuke the scepticism of the Sadducees who deny this dogma (*Sanh.* xi. 1: 'He hath no portion in the world to come who denies that the Resurrection of the Dead is in the Torah'). The righteous obtain eternal life (חיי עולם, *Baba Bathra* 11*a*). After the Resurrection comes the Renewal of the World. Is 65^{17} foretells the creation of 'new heavens and a new earth'; Jub 1^{29} speaks of the New Creation; *Mekhilta* 51*b* on Ex 16^{25} describes this עולם חדש, 'the new world.'

11. The discordance of ideas between the earthly Paradise of the Messianic Kingdom and the transcendental New Jerusalem induced a belief in an interregnum (cf. Eth. En 91). The Ages of the World are 10 weeks; the 8th, that of the sword and rebuilding of Jerusalem, is the Messianic period. The 9th and 10th are those of the Last Judgment, at the end of which comes the New Creation. In the Apocalypse of John (ch. 20) this Messianic interregnum is to last 1000 years, whence the Christian doctrine of the Chiliasm (cf. *Orac. Sib.* iii., 4 Ezra, and Apoc. of Baruch). In 4 Ezr 7^{28} the Messianic period lasts 400 years, after which Christ returns to heaven, and the general Resurrection follows.

In the Talmud the Messianic period is to last a 'fixed time' (*Zebaḥim* 118*b*, *Arakhin* 13*b*, *Pes.* 68*a*). Periods mentioned are 40, 70, 365, 400, 1000, and 2000 years. Only Ben Zoma in *Ber.* 1. 5 contrasts this world with the Days of the Messiah. But in the 2nd cent. a clear distinction is drawn between the Days of the Messiah and the Future World (cf. *Shab.* 151*b*, *Pes.* 68*b*, *Sanh.* 91*b*, *Ber.* 34*b*). The Samaritan Messiah, Ta'eb, dies 'after a long reign.' 'All the prophets,' say R. Chijja bar Abba and R. Jochanan, 'prophesied only as to the days of the Messiah, but, as for the Future World, no eye but thine, O Lord, hath seen it' (*Ber.* 34*b*).

Maimonides in his *Yemen Epistle* gives the following order: Resurrection, Future World, Death, and a second Resurrection. In his *Moreh* 11, 29, and 30 he endeavours to prove that the world is eternal, and in his *Mishne Torah* on 'Repentance' (8) he declares that the future world is already existent. Nachmanides (in his *Torath Adam*, 'Reward and Punishment,' שער הגמול) and the Raabad dispute this, and declare that Gn 8^{22} 'while the earth remaineth' suggests its destruction. The world is to return to *tohu bohu* (chaos), and the Almighty will renew it. So too Azaria de Rossi (*Meor Enayim*, xliv. 54). When Ecclesiastes says (1^{4}) 'the world abideth for ever,' he only means the world Jubilee. Baḥya ben Asher in his Com. on Lv 25^{2}, 'then shall the land keep a Sabbath unto the Lord,' takes this to support the view of the Qabbālā as referring to the destruction of the world (וחד חריב). The rest eternal is the future world after the Resurrection. In Lv 25^{8}, 'seven times seven years,' the second seven 'hints' (רמז) at the Great Jubilee, which is the end of the world. The Qabbālā, though the idea predominates therein of the world-wheel (*gilgal*), implying the endless recurrence of all things, is directed less to time than to space. The notion of space is older than that of time. Even beasts distinguish things by their space. The discrimination of things by time does not follow till relatively late. But even the mysticism of the Qabbālā has a bearing on the Jewish view of the future life. It is, without doubt, Christologically tinged, and, though highly venerated by the Eastern Jews, is practically neglected nowadays by those of the West.

In the *Zohar* on Gn 26^{1} it is said that Adam should have lived 1000 years, but gave up 70 for David (alluding to Ps 21^{4}).

12. Bible chronology has always presented difficulties. The discrepancies between the chronology of the Massoretic and Samaritan texts and the Septuagint are dealt with by Dr. Jacob of Göttingen. He explains one chief variation as due to a desire to date Noah exactly 1000 years after Adam. *Pirqe Aboth* (v. 2, ed. Taylor) draws attention to the fact that there were ten generations from Adam to Noah, and ten from Noah to Abraham. The chronology of Genesis would seem to have been based on years according to the solar system, but the Jews reverted to the lunar system after the Exodus, as seen from Ex $12^{1f.}$

13. The conservative Jewish view is still expressed in the following passages in its Liturgy. The 12th Creed expresses belief 'in the coming of the Messiah, and, though he tarry, I will wait daily for his coming'; the 13th, 'that there will be a resurrection of the dead at the time when it shall please the Creator' (Singer's *Prayer Book*, p. 90); in the *Qaddish* (*ib.* p. 37), 'May he establish his Kingdom in your days . . . speedily!' (cf. *Orac. Sib.* iii. 767). In the Sabbath Morning's Service (*ib.* p. 129) the following antitheses bring out Jewish belief in the four cosmic stages or Ages of the World: 'There is none to be compared unto thee, O Lord our God, in this world, neither is there any beside thee, O our King, for the life of the world to come; there is none but thee, O our Redeemer, for the days of the Messiah; neither is there any like unto thee, O our Saviour, for the resurrection of the dead.'

LITERATURE.—Bacher, *Agada der Tannaiten*, vol. i. 1884; Bousset, *Rel. d. Judentums* 2, 1906, pt. iv. pp. 233–346 (cf. the list of authorities cited by him); Schürer, *GJV* 3, ii. 496–556; R. H. Charles, *A Crit. Hist. of the Doct. of a Future Life in Israel*, London, 1899; Loewy, 'Messiaszeit and Zukünftige Welt' in *MGWJ*, 1897, 392–409; *Sanh.* c. 11; Maimonides, אגרת תימן, *Yemen Epistle*; Nachmanides, *Torath Adam*, 'Sha'ar Ha Gemul'; Maimonides, *Guide to the Perplexed*, ii. 29, 30, also his *Mishne Torah, Hilchot Teshuböh*, viii.; Azaria di Rossi, *Meor Enayim*, xliv. 54; Lipschütz, *Mishna*, תפארת ישראל; An Excursus on the Future Life (based on *Nezikin*).

E. N. ADLER.

AGES OF THE WORLD (Muhammadan).—See COSMOGONY (Muhammadan).

AGES OF THE WORLD (Teutonic).—See COSMOGONY (Teutonic).

AGES OF THE WORLD (Zoroastrian).—**1.** By far the most detailed account of Iranian cosmology is afforded by the Pahlavi *Bûndahishn*, a work which, though dating in its present form from the post-Muhammadan period, undoubtedly contains material of far greater antiquity. According to it, Aûharmazd (Ormazd) 'produced spiritually the creatures which were necessary for those means [his complete victory over evil], and they remained three thousand years in a spiritual state, so that they were unthinking [or invulnerable] and unmoving, with intangible bodies' (i. 8). . . . 'And Aûharmazd spoke to the evil spirit thus: "Appoint a period, so that the intermingling of the conflict may be for nine thousand years." For he knew that by appointing this period the evil spirit would be undone. Thus the evil spirit, unobservant and through ignorance, was content with that agreement; just like two men quarrelling together, who propose a time thus: "Let us appoint such-and-such a day for a fight." Aûharmazd also knew this, through omniscience, that within these nine thousand years, for three thousand years everything proceeds by the will of Aûharmazd, three thousand years there is an intermingling of the wills of Aûharmazd and Aharman, and the last three thousand years the evil spirit is disabled, and the adversary is kept away from the creatures' (i. 18–20, West's tr.). Then Ahura Mazda (Pahlavi *Aûharmazd*) recited the *Ahunavar*, and exhibited to the evil spirit his own triumph in the end; the evil spirit, perceiving his own impotence and the annihilation of the demons, became confounded and remained three thousand years in confusion, that is, the second trimillennium of time. During the confusion of the evil spirit, Ahura Mazda created Good Thought (Pahlavi *Vohûman*), as well as the five other archangels. Ahriman (wh. see) produced in opposition to them six corresponding evil powers. Of the creatures of the world Ahura Mazda produced first, the sky (and the light of the world); second, water; third, earth; fourth, plants; fifth, animals; and sixth, mankind (*ib.* i. 21–28). The spirits of men, their *fravashis* and their consciousness, had already been created in the beginning. Now Ormazd deliberated with them, asking them if they would assume a bodily form in order to contend with the fiend Ahriman, and in the end become wholly immortal and perfect for ever, whereupon they consented (ii. 10–11). According to the third chapter, the confounding of the evil spirit and his demons was due to 'the righteous man,' a phrase which doubtless designates Gaya-maretan (Pahlavi *Gâyômarț*), the primeval man, who existed undisturbed, during the same second trimillennium, with the primeval ox.

The evil spirit now rushed into creation, and the seventh millennium, or the third trimillennium, began. The elements, the primeval ox, and the primeval man were successively attacked by the Evil One. But the appointed time for Gaya-maretan had not yet arrived. He lived and ruled for thirty years more, although the destroyer had come (iii. 22 f.). Attacked by Ahriman, the ox fell to the right; from his body and his limbs the plants were produced, and the animals from his seed (iv. 1, x. 1–3, xiv. 1–3).* Gaya-maretan fell on the left side in passing away, and from one portion of his seed received by the earth the first human couple, Mâshya and Mâshyôî, grew up for forty years as a plant, and were then changed into the shape of a man and a woman (iv. 1, xv. 1–5). The history of mankind, which then began, occupies the second half of the 12,000 years.

The 34th chapter of the original *Bûndahishn* sums up the first two trimillenniums of the creation as follows: 'Time was for twelve thousand years; and it says in revelation, that three thousand years was the duration of the spiritual state, where the creatures were unthinking, unmoving, and intangible; and three thousand years was the duration of Gâyômarț, with the ox, in the world.' Those three millenniums are immediately connected with three of the constellations of the zodiac: Cancer, Leo, and Virgo.

The first millennium of the human race is distributed as follows in the same chapter:—

Gâyômarț, 30 years.
Mâshya and *Mâshyôî* growing up during 40 years (*Bûnd.* 15. 2).
" " living without desire for intercourse, 50 years.
" " living as husband and wife, 93 years, until
Hôshyang (Av. *Haoshyangha*), great-grandson of Mâshya, came, 40 years (and six months, according to Windischmann).
Takhmôrup (Av. *Takhma-urupa*; Shâh-nâmah *Tahmûras*), great grandson of Hôshyang, 30 years.
Yim (Av. *Yima*; Shâh-nâmah *Jamshîd*), brother of Takhmôrup, 616 years and six months, until the divine power or glory of the Iranian rulers left him, in the shape of a bird, because he took pleasure in words of falsehood and error (*Yasht*, xix. 34), and made himself something more than a man.
Then he lived in concealment for 100 years.
Total, 999 years and six months (or 1000 years).

The next millennium, the second of human history, and the eighth of the creation, was under the sway of Dahâk, whose lineage on his mother's side is traced, by *Bûnd.* xxxi. 6, nine degrees from the evil spirit himself. Dahâk is the Azhi Dahâka, the dragon with three heads, of the Avesta, who tried to seize the kingly power-substance, the *khwarenah*, as it left Yima, who had become too proud owing to his happy paradise-reign; but Atar, the fire, saved it (*Yasht*, xix. 47 ff.).

According to another tradition in the same *Yasht* (xix. 35), the *khwarenah*, in leaving Yima, went in three parts: one to Mithra; the second to Thraêtaona, who killed the dragon Azhi Dahâka; and the third to Keresâspa, the great hero, who is to be the successful adversary of the dragon at the end of the time. Those three guardians of the 'kingly glory' are regarded as succeeding each other, so that Mithra preserves it during the reign of the fiend, until Thraêtaona comes—as, in the other version, just mentioned, Atar is said to save the kingly glory, which takes refuge in the waters of the sea Vouru-Kasha.

After the millennium of Dahâk, who is assigned

* The twenty-seventh chapter of the *Bûndahishn* presupposes the existence of plants before the attack of the fiend: 'it says in revelation, that, before the coming of the destroyer, vegetation had no thorn and bark about it.'

by *Bûnd.* xxxiv. 5 to Scorpio, the sovereignty devolved on Frêṭûn, the Thraêtaona of the Avesta, the Frîdûn of the Shâh-nâmah, who killed the terrible usurper and introduced the third millennium of mankind and of the third trimillennium of creation. This millennium is assigned by the *Bûndahishn* to Sagittarius, and contains the names of the heroic legends of ancient Irân. The *Bûndahishn* makes the following calculation (xxxiv. 6–7):—

Frêṭûn, contemporary of the 12 years of Airîc, 500 years.
Mânûshcîhar (Av. *Manushcithra*), contemporary of the Turanian adversary Frâsîyâb, the Franhrasyan of the Avesta, who made Mânûshcîhar and the Iranians captive in the mountain-range Padashkhvâr, south of the Caspian, 120 years.
Zôb, Aûzôbô (Av. *Uzava;* Shâh-nâmah *Zav*), grandson of Mânûshcîhar, expelled Frâsîyâb from Iran, and reigned 5 years; adopted
Kaî-Kabâṭ (Av. *Kavi Kavâta*), founder of the most renowned royal race of Iran, the Kavis, who retained the *khwarenah*, the spiritual substance of the kingship of Irân, during several generations, 15 years.
Kaî-Kâûs (Av. *Kavi Usadhan*), grandson of Kaî-Kabâṭ, 150 years.
His grandson Kaî-Khûsrâv (Av. *Kavi Husravah*), who was received into heaven without death, 60 years.
Kaî-Lôrâsp (Av. *Kavi Aurvaṭ-aspa*), 120 years; and his son
Kaî-Vishtâsp (Av. *Kavi Vishtâspa*), the protector of Zarathushtra, until the coming of the religion, 30 years.
Total, 1000 years.

So far the last chapter of the *Bûndahishn.* It accordingly gives only a short chronology of the millennium of the Zarathushtrian faith,—ruled by Capricorn,—in which period the present generation is thought to live. After the coming of religion it reckons (xxiv. 7–9):—

For the Achæmenians . . .	258 years.
,, Alexander	14 ,,
,, the Ashkânians (Arsacides) . .	284 ,,
,, the Sasanians	460 ,,
Total	1016 ,,

Then the sovereignty is said to have fallen to the Arabs (cf. the somewhat older list of the Iranian kings in the Mandæan *Ginzā*; Louis H. Gray, 'The Kings of Early Irân according to the *Sidrā Rabbā*,' in *ZA*, xix. 272 ff.).

In this chronological table the successors of Alexander and the Parthian kingdom until Ardashir, the founder of the Sasanian dynasty, occupy only 284 years, instead of at least 547. On the other hand, the Sasanians have too many, 460 years instead of 425 or 427. This double mistake is perhaps unintentional. Although the total of the historical chronology is thus shortened by the writer of *Bûndahishn*, xxxiv., the millennium should be finished and the expected Saviour should have come, as we have seen, sixteen years before the Arabs. This millennium, which must contain the whole history since the revelation to Zarathushtra, has been a puzzle to the Zarathushtrians. The *Bahman Yasht* (Pahlavi), which has, in its present form, a complicated literary history behind it, shows the difficulty caused by the old traditional statement of the sacred writings that a son of the prophet should be born in a supernatural way and appear a thousand years after the beginning of the new dispensation. The popular belief awaited rather a valiant warrior, Bahram Varjâvand, the Iranian Messiah. Indeed, we read in the Pahlavi *Bahman Yasht*, iii. 44 ('Pahlavi Texts,' tr. by E. W. West, *SBE* v. p. 231): 'Regarding Hûshêṭar it is declared that he will be born in 1600.' This must mean 1600 years after Zarathushtra. That is 600 years too late—but it brings us only to the beginning of the 13th cent. A.D., according to the traditional Zarathushtrian chronology. (See the introduction of E. W. West to his tr. of *Bahman Yasht*; and Bousset, 'Beiträge zur Gesch. der Eschatologie' in *Ztschr. f. Kirchengesch.*, xx. 122 ff.; N. Söderblom, *La Vie future*, 271 ff.; and art. ESCHATOLOGY [Parsi]).

It is evident, as E. W. West has pointed out in his most important introduction to vol. v. of his tr. of Pahlavi Texts (*SBE* xlvii.), that this system of chronology must have been made before the year that should finish the millennium of the actual history of mankind after Zarathushtra. The first revelation to the prophet being dated by the Pahlavi tradition 300 years before Alexander, or about 630 B.C., that means about 370 A.D.

Amongst other statements and calculations to be found in Pahlavi writings about the first thousand years of the last or fourth trimillennium, besides the short notice at the end of the *Bûndahishn*, two have an interest for our present purpose.

(1) The period of mankind being fixed at 6000 years, Zarathushtra, who was born thirty years before the end of the former 3000 years, and whose first intercourse with the celestial beings begins the second trimillennium, makes his appearance in the middle of human history. According to the *Sad Dar*, lxxxi. 4–5, it is declared in revelation that the Creator spoke to Zarathushtra thus (*SBE* xxiv. 345):

'I have created thee at the present time, in the middle period; for it is three thousand years from the days of Gâyômard till now, and from now till the resurrection are the three thousand years that remain. . . . For whatever is in the middle is more precious and better and more valuable, . . . as the heart is in the middle of the whole body, . . . and as the land of Irân is more valuable than other lands, for the reason that it is in the middle.'

(2) The *Dînkarṭ*, ix. 8, a compilation of the 9th cent., renders the contents of the seventh *fargarṭ* of the now lost *Sûṭkar Nask* of the Sasanian Avesta thus (*SBE* xxxvii. 181):

'The seventh *fargarṭ* is about the exhibition to Zaratûsht of the nature of the four periods in the millennium of Zaratûsht. First, the golden, that in which Aûharmazd displayed the religion to Zaratûsht. Second, the silver, that in which Vishtâsp received the religion from Zaratûsht. Third, the steel, the period within which the organizer of righteousness, Âtûrpâṭ, son of Mâraspend, was born [or Adarbâd, the great champion of orthodoxy in the 4th cent., who offered to undergo the ordeal of pouring molten brass on his chest in order to prove the truth of the Mazdayasnian faith]. Fourth, the period mingled with iron is this, in which there is much propagation of the authority of the apostate and other villains, as regards the destruction of the reign of religion, the decay of every kind of goodness and virtue, and the disappearance of honour and wisdom from the countries of Irân.'

It is not possible to say how much of this account belonged to the text of the *Sûṭkar Nask* and what is taken from its 'Zend' (its translation and Pahlavi paraphrase, used by the compiler). The events described need not come down later than the time after the death of the great Shâhpûhr II. in 379. His grandson Yazdgard I. (399–420) was called by the priests the 'sinner' because of his tolerance in quarrels about religion. At all events, it is scarcely likely that the whole scheme of the four [Metal] Ages, known in India, Greece, Rome, etc., should have been wholly introduced by the Pahlavi paraphrase. In the Pahlavi *Bahman Yasht*, i. 6, it is expressly said that the appearance of the accursed Mazdîk [the heretic who flourished during the reign of Kôbâd (488–531), and who was put to death by his son Khûsrô Nôshirsân] during 'this time' (the Iron Age), is mentioned in the lost Zend commentary on three *Yashts* of the Avesta, although the two of these three *Yashts* still extant (the Avesta *Bahman Yasht* being lost) do not contain anything about the matter.

In the same context of the Pahlavi *Bahman Yasht* the historical standpoint is a later one than in the *Dinkarṭ's* rendering of *Sûṭkar Nask*, and three of the four Ages are applied to other epochs. That of Gold means the conversation of Ahura Mazda and his prophet, and King Vishtâspa's acceptance of the religion. That of Silver is the reign of the Kayanian *Arṭakhshîr*, generally identified with Artaxerxes Longimanus (465–424)—perhaps including the reigns of Xerxes II., Darius II., and Artaxerxes Mnemon (404–358). That of Steel is the reign of the glorified Khûsrô, son of Kôbâd (531–579), the greatest of the Sasanians, during whose reign the Pahlavi literature flourished (F. Justi in *Grundriss der iran. Philologie*, ii. 539). In ii. 21–22 there is allusion to the great merit of the Steel Age king: 'when he keeps away from this religion the accursed Mazdik. . . . And that which was mixed with iron is the reign of the demons with dishevelled hair of the race of Wrath, when it is the end of the ten-hundredth winter of thy millennium, O Zaratûsht, the Spîtâmân!' The speaker is Ormazd.

In another passage of our Pahlavi commentary or paraphrase of the *Bahman Yasht* (ii. 15–22) the Metal Ages are increased to seven. Zarathushtra had seen in a dream a tree with seven branches; one golden, one of silver, one bronze, one of copper, one of tin, one of steel, and one mixed up with iron. The Lord explains the dream thus: The seven branches are the seven periods to come. The Golden one means the reign of King Vishtâsp; that of Silver is the reign of Arṭashîr the Kayân (= Artaxerxes Longimanus); the Bronze Age represents the first two Sasanian monarchs, Arṭashîr (226–241) and his son Shâhpûhr I. (241–227), and the restorer of true religion, Âtarôpât Mâraspand ('with the prepared brass'), under Shâhpûhr II. (309–379). The Copper Age is evidently out of its order, as it puts us back from the Sasanian dynasty to the Parthians, to 'the reign of the Ashkânian king' [we do not know which] who removes from the world the heterodoxy which existed; while the wicked *Akandgar-i Kilisyâkîh* [probably = 'Alexander the Christian,' an anachronism that need not surprise us on the part of a Pahlavi writer, who identifies the two great enemies of the Mazdayasnian faith coming from the West (Alexander the Great and the Christian Roman empire)] is utterly destroyed by this religion, and passes unseen and unknown from the world. The Tin Age brings us to the powerful Sasanian monarch, Bahrâm v. (420–438), 'when he makes the spirit of pleasure and joy manifest, and Aharman with the wizards [*i.e.* the heretics] rushes back to darkness and gloom.' The Steel Age represents the persecutor of Mazdik, King Khûsrô, and the one mixed with Iron is characterized as in the first chapter.

As we have seen, the four original Ages are the same, but between the Silver one (= Artaxerxes I. and II.) and the Steel one (=Khûsrô Anoshirvan) three supplementary periods are intercalated. The Copper Age is out of place, and should probably be put before the Bronze Age. The number four is thus changed into seven.

At the end of Zarathushtra's millennium Ukhshyatereta (Pahlavi *Hûshêṭar*), 'the one who makes piety grow,' shall be born, in a marvellous way, from the prophet's seed. When thirty years old, he enters on his ministry to restore the religion (*Bûndahishn*, xxxii. 8; *Bahman Yasht*, iii. 44; *Dînkarṭ*, vii. 8, 51–60). The second millennium of the post-Zarathushtrian trimillennium begins. In the 5th cent. of that millennium (*Dînkarṭ*, vii. 9, 3 [*SBE* xlvii. 108]) the wizard Mahrkûsh, mentioned in an extant fragment (*Westergaard*, viii. 2) of the Avesta as Mahrkûsha, will appear for seven years, and produce a terrible winter, that will, 'within three winters and in the fourth,' destroy the greater part of mankind and of animals.

Those winters are mentioned in the second *fargarṭ* of the *Vendîdâd* without the name of Mahrkûsha, the demon or the wizard of frost and snow. Yima, the paradise-king, is told by Ormazd to prepare an enclosure, a *vara*, and to live in it himself with a chosen host of men, animals, plants, and fires, in order to be preserved during the winters that will invade the earth.

When in Hûshêtar's millennium the enclosure made by Yima is opened, mankind and animals will issue from it and arrange the world again, and there will be a time of fulness and prosperity (*Dînkarṭ*, vii. 9, 3 f.; *Maînôg-î Khraṭ*, xxvii. 27–31). New beings thus come back miraculously for the restoration of the world (*Dâṭistân-î Dînîk*, xxxvii. 95 [*SBE* xviii. 109–110]).

A thousand years after Hûshêṭar, a second son of Zarathushtra will be born, Ukhshyatnemah, 'he who makes the prayer grow' (Pahlavi *Hushêṭarmâh*). When thirty years old, he will confer with the archangels. That is the beginning of the last millennium of the world (*Bûndahishn*, xxxii. 8; *Dînkarṭ*, vii. 9, 18–23). After its end the third miraculous son of the prophet shall be born in the same way by a third virgin, pregnant from the water of the lake Kansava, which holds the seed of Zarathushtra (*Bûndahishn*, xxxii. 8; *Dînkarṭ*, vii. 10, 15–18).

The usual translation of his name *Astvat-ereta*, 'he who raises the [dead] bodies,' seems very unlikely. The second part of the name, *ereta*, which means in the name of the first son of the prophet 'righteousness,' being the Iranian equivalent of the Skr. *ṛta* (which appears otherwise in the Avesta as *asha*), would then be a verbal form in the third name. More probable is Bartholomæ's rendering (*Altiran. Wörterbuch*, col. 215), 'he who is the personified righteousness' or 'piety.' But the analogy with the former two names: *Ukhshyat-ereta* and *Ukhshyat-nemah*, makes one think that the first half also of this third name is a verbal form, an act. particip. of *stav-*, 'to praise,' with a preceding *ā*. If, indeed, the initial *a* were long, the name might be translated, 'he who praises righteousness.'

More frequently the third expected restorer of religion is called *Saoshyant* 'the saviour,' 'the helper,' originally and generally in the Avesta an appellative applied to the zealous Mazdayasnians and promoters of religion.

Now the last conflict breaks out; resurrection and purification open the way to eternal blissful existence. The time preceding the coming of the three restorers of faith will be marked by misery and impiety (*Spend Nask*, according to *Dînkarṭ*, viii. 14, 11 ff.). We recall the four Ages that mark a successive deterioration in Zarathushtra's millennium. The Pahlavi apocalyptics paint the time before Hûshêtar's coming in dreadful colours borrowed from history. At the end of the last thousand years Azhi Dahâka will break his fetters. But, on the other hand, the end of those three Ages is described as an advance towards the glorious consummation (*Dînkarṭ*, ix. 41, 4–8). We have seen how the opening of the gate of Yima's enclosure will produce a new prosperity before Hushêṭar-mâh's appearance. After the 5th cent. of Hûshêtar's millennium two-thirds of the population of Irân are righteous and one-third wicked (*Dînkarṭ*, vii. 9, 13). In the last millennium 'no one passes away, other than those whom they smite with a scaffold weapon, and those who pass away from old age. When fifty-three years of that millennium of his still remain, the sweetness and oiliness of milk and vegetables are so perfect, that, on account of the freedom of mankind from desire for meat, they shall leave off the eating of meat, and their food becomes milk and vegetables. When three years remain, they shall leave off even the drinking of milk, and their (food and drink become water and vegetables' (*Dînkarṭ*, vii. 10, 7 ff.). The milk of one cow shall be sufficient for a thousand men. As hunger and thirst diminish, men shall be satisfied with one meal every third day. Old age shall not be weak any more and life shall become longer. Humility and peace shall be multiplied in the world.

The Greeks were acquainted with the optimistic Mazdayasnian doctrine of the spiritualizing of mankind towards the end. Men, at the end of the world, will need no food, and they will cast no shadow (Theopompus-Plutarch). The eighteenth *fargarṭ* of the *Varshtmânsar Nask* of the Sasanian Avesta told, according to *Dînkarṭ*, ix. 41, 4, 'about the triumph of the sacred beings over the demons at the end' of the three last periods of the world.

These 12,000 years form the long period of creation, divided into four great Ages. It is bounded by eternity on both sides, by 'time without end.' The 'Great,' or 'Iranian,' *Bûndahishn*, which appears to be a later development of the more commonly known *Bûndahishn*, says about Time (Darmesteter, *Le Zend Avesta*, ii. 310–311): 'It was without limits up to the creation, and it was created limited to the end, that is, to the reducing of the evil spirit to impotence. After this, Time resumes its infiniteness for ever and ever.' This later theological speculation about the personified Time (*Zrvan*) is found in the Avesta itself, which distinguishes between 'Time without limits' (*Zrvan akarana*), and the 'Time long, self-determined' (*Zrvan dareghô-khvadhâta*) (*Nyâish*, i. 8). In *Vendîdâd*, xix. 9, Zarathushtra answers the Evil One: 'The beneficent spirit created in the time without limits.' 'Time without limits' was made later on, in order to weaken the dualism to an eternal Divine Being, from whom the two opposite spirits emanate.

The distribution of *Time* into the endless Time before and after the 'long, self-determined Time' has its exact *local* equivalent in the strictly organized Mazdayasnian theology. The region of light where Ormazd dwells is called 'endless light.' The region where the Evil Spirit resides is called the 'endless dark.' 'Between them was empty space, that is, what they call "air," in which is now their meeting' (*Bûnd.* i. 2–4) [cf. Plutarch's words, *de Is. et Os.* 46, about Mithra as μεσίτης between the two 'gods']. The air or atmosphere, *Vayu* (Pahlavi *Vâi*) is deified as well as *Zrvan* (Time), and is designated exactly as Time: *dareghô-khvadhâta* (*Nyâish*, l. 1), 'long, self-determined.' The Great *Bûndahishn* (Darmesteter, *loc. cit.*) distinguishes between the good Vâi and the bad Vâi—space as well as time being divided according to the dualistic principle. Already the Avesta knew such a distinction, *Yasht*, xv. invoking 'that part of thee, O Vayu, which belongs to the Good Spirit.'

2. Date of the Zoroastrian system of Ages of the World.—(*a*) As we have already seen, most of the names and legends and ideas that belong to the Pahlavi accounts of the Ages of the World are to be found in the Avesta. As to the system itself divided into four periods, the principal contents of the lost *Dâmdâṭ Nask*, the book 'about the production of the beneficial creatures,' of the Sasanian Avesta, from which the *Bûndahishn*, 'the original creation,' is derived, are very shortly reproduced in the following terms in the *Dînkarṭ*, viii. 5 (*SBE* xxxvii. 13–14).

'Amid the *Dâmdâṭ* are particulars about the maintenance of action and the production of the beneficial creatures. First, as to the spiritual existence, and how much and how is the maintenance in the spiritual existence; and the production of the worldly existence therefrom, qualified and constructed for descending into the combat with the destroyer, and accomplishing the associated necessity for the end and circumvention of destructiveness' (West's tr.).

An extant Avesta fragment, quoted in the Pahlavi *Vendîdâd*, ii. 20, runs: 'How long time lasted the holy spiritual creation' (*cvantem zrvânem mainyava stish ashaoni dâta as*). It shows that the complete Avesta knew the system of four times three thousand years.

Except for the events at the end of Zarathushtra's millennium, the Sasanian Avesta must have known all the principal features of the world-chronology now described, with its environment of 'the endless time.'

(*b*) Plutarch brings us further back, to about 300 B.C., but speaks only of two or three of the four periods (*de Is. et Os.* 47), expressly quoting Theopompus, Philip of Macedon's historian:

Θεόπομπος δὲ φησὶ κατὰ τοὺς μάγους ἀνὰ μέρος τρισχίλια ἔτη τὸν μὲν κρατεῖν τὸν δὲ κρατεῖσθαι τῶν θεῶν, ἄλλα δὲ τρισχίλια μάχεσθαι καὶ πολεμεῖν καὶ ἀναλύειν τὰ τοῦ ἑτέρου τὸν ἕτερον· τέλος δ' ἀπολείπεσθαι τὸν Ἅιδην, καὶ τοὺς μὲν ἀνθρώπους εὐδαίμονας ἔσεσθαι, μήτε τροφῆς δεομένους μήτε σκιὰν ποιοῦντας. τὸν δὲ ταῦτα μηχανησάμενον θεὸν ἠρεμεῖν καὶ ἀναπαύεσθαι χρόνον, καλῶς μὲν οὐ πολὺν τῷ θεῷ, ὥσπερ δ' ἀνθρώπῳ κοιμωμένῳ μέτριον. Bernardakis, in his edition of the *Moralia*, reads after χρόνον: ἄλλως μὲν οὐ πολὺν ὡς θεῷ, etc.

The first part of this quotation* agrees with the Mazdayasnian record of the last nine thousand years (*Bûnd.* i. 20).

Lagrange ('La Religion des Perses' in *RB*, 1904, p. 35) understands ἀνὰ μέρος as indicating *two* periods: one with Ahura Mazda as ruler, another with Angra Mainyu as ruler; then follows their fight in a third and last period, ended by the defeat of evil. It is possible to translate ἀνὰ μέρος in that way. But, as the phrase runs, it is more natural to apply the two 'turns' to the two different trimillenniums mentioned. ἀνὰ μέρος belongs to both the following statements. The μάχεσθαι καὶ πολεμεῖν comes, as the second 'turn' of the two gods' relation, after τὸν μὲν κρατεῖν τὸν δὲ κρατεῖσθαι. The tr. of Lagrange has another drawback. It would be quite an isolated statement in opposition to all other records about Mazdayasnian chronology.

Some slight misunderstanding may easily have been perpetrated either by Theopompus or by Plutarch in quoting him. But it seems impossible not to recognize (1) the impotence of Ahriman, (2) the conflict, and (3) the victory of Ormazd—making up the well-known Mazdayasnian scheme.

The second part of the quotation from Theopompus offers some difficulty. The last words after χρόνον have been more or less ingeniously changed by various conjectures. The phrase should mean: 'The god who has brought about these things [the defeat of Hades (identified with Ἀρειμάνιος also by Diog. Laërt. *Proœm.* 6) and the blessed state of mankind] keeps still and reposes himself during a period not very great for the god, as [it would be] moderate for a sleeping man.' But the end of the phrase is not tolerable Greek, and must be corrupted in some way. The meaning compels us to think of a rest of Ahura Mazda after the consummation of the destiny of the world. Such an idea is not necessarily inconsistent with the opposition of later Mazdayasnian theology (*Shikand-gûmânik vijâr*, xiii. 102–105 [*SBE* xxiv. 217]) to the Jewish doctrine of a rest of God after the *Creation*. But we know nothing of a Divine repose after the *frashôkereti*, the fulfilment at the end. Theopompus is supposed to have thought of another being, Keresâspa, who is to awake from his long sleep in order to kill the unfettered Azhi Dahâka; or of Saoshyant, 'sleeping' as the prophet's holy seed in the lake Kansava waiting for his virgin mother; or of Yima, expecting in his *vara* the end of the desolation caused by the great winter—but not reposing! The context excludes, as far as the present writer can see, the introduction of a *third* god, after the two enemies spoken of. But it might be that the Greek author has applied to Ahura Mazda some misunderstood statement regarding another figure in the final drama.

(*c*) The elder Pliny writes (*HN* xxx. 2. 1): 'Eudoxus, qui inter sapientiæ sectas clarissimam

* 1. 'One of those gods reigned and the other was under his dominion during three thousand years. 2. During another three thousand years they battle and fight and destroy each other's works. 3. At the end Hades (Angra Mainyu, who was indeed originally probably a god of the infernal regions and of the dead) succumbs, and men shall be happy, needing no food and throwing no shadow.'

utilissimamque eam intelligi voluit, Zoroastrem hunc sex millibus annorum ante Platonis mortem fuisse prodidit. Sic et Aristoteles.' Thus Greek authors of the 4th cent. B.C. placed Zarathushtra 6000 years before B.C. 347. Hermodorus, in the same century, and Hermippus, a century later, put him 5000 years before the Trojan war. Xanthus of Lydia, perhaps a century earlier, seems to have stated that the prophet lived 6000 years before Xerxes. These fanciful dates are the more astonishing the older they are,—that is, the nearer they approach to Zarathushtra's lifetime, which the Mazdayasnian tradition places in the 7th cent. B.C., and which can scarcely have been many centuries earlier at least.*

A. V. Williams Jackson ingeniously suggests that the placing of Zarathushtra 6000–7000 years before Christ is due to the Greeks having misunderstood the statements of the Persians, according to which the spiritual prototype of Zarathuṣtra was created several thousands of years before the prophet himself. ('On the Date of Zoroaster,' in *Zoroaster, the Prophet of Ancient Iran*, p. 152 ff.). This view has been supported by West, 'Pahlavi Texts,' v. [*SBE* xlvii. p. xl ff.].

Dînkarṭ, vii. 2, 15 f., in rendering the contents of *Spend Nask*, tells: 'Again, too, revelation says that, when the separation of the third millennium occurred, at the end of the 3000 years of spiritual existence without a destroyer (after the creatures were in spiritual existence, and before the arrival of the fiend), then the archangels framed Zaratûsht together, and they seated the guardian spirit [the *fravashi*, already in existence for 3000 years] within, having a mouth, having a tongue, and the proclaimer of the celestial mansions' (cf. *Dinkarṭ*, viii. 14, 1). Thus the spiritual body of Zarathushtra is framed together two trimillenniums before his birth, at the end of the ninth millennium, *i.e.* B.C. 6630, according to Mazdayasnian tradition. If this striking explanation of the fanciful Greek dates for Zarathushtra be right, even this special feature of the Mazdayasnian chronology—the pre-formation of Zarathushtra's body 6000 years before his birth—must have been heard of by Greek writers as early as the 5th cent. B.C., which does not seem very probable. At all events, nothing is to be found in these Greek records about 'the holy spiritual creation,' the first of the four trimillenniums.

3. Composite character of the Mazdayasnian system of Ages of the World.—This is evident. The means are lacking for the reconstruction of its formation. But certain points may be noted.

(*a*) The whole Yima legend must drop out. Originally it was an independent scheme of Ages of the World, like the old Norse Fimbulvetr, 'great winter,' which ends this Age and brings about a new mankind, whose ancestors, Līf and Līfthraser, are hidden during the desolating winter in Mimir's grove. Mahrkûsha's winter and the new humanity arising from Yima's *vara* have evidently no *raison d'être* whatever in the complete historical system of the Avestan theology. It has been rather awkwardly put aside in Ukhshyatereta's millennium, because it must not be omitted. The Yima legend in *Vendîdâd*, ii., does not know the 12,000 years' system, and excludes it, at least in its complete form, although the old mythic Yima has been duly transformed into a forerunner of Zarathushtra.

The blessed paradise-reign of Yima was a very popular legend in old Irân. Several Avesta texts mention it (*Yasna*, ix. 4 f.; *Yasht*, ix. 9 ff., xiii. 130, xv. 15 f., xvii. 29 ff., xix. 32 ff.), besides *Vendîdâd*, ii. Under his rule death and sickness and all adversities were unknown. The older tradition gives him a thousand years. In the *Vendîdâd* he enlarges the earth by one-third of its space, 'the cattle and mankind and dogs and birds and red burning fires' being after 300 years too crowded. After another 300 years he has to repeat the enlargement. When he has done this three times, that is, after 900 years, the tale passes on to the preparation of the *vara* for the coming winters. The analogy—300 years after each enlargement—should give us 1200 years. But the author might have imagined a hundred years after the third enlargement for the making of the enclosure, thus keeping the old tradition of a happy age of a thousand years in the old time. The later learned chronological system in *Bûndahishn*, xxxiv. 4, and *Maînôg-î Khraṭ*, xxvii. 24, 25, gives 616 years and 6 months.

The Yima legend gives three Ages of the World: the paradise-Age; the present time, which will close with a catastrophe; the frost-demons' win-

* Pliny also mentions another Zarathushtra, who is said to have lived shortly before B.C. 500.

ters, and the restoring of the living world from Yima's *vara*—after the well-known scheme :

'Past and to come seems best ; things present worst'
(*2 Henry IV.* I. iii. 108).

It is impossible to say whether this system of three Ages ever existed as a theory by itself. But there are several traces of the greater importance of Yima Khshaêta, 'the radiant,' Jamshîd in pre-Zarathushtrian legend (cf. Blochet, *Le messianisme dans l'hétérodoxie musulmane*, p. 126 f.). He seems to have been once considered as the first man and the first ruler. For further discussion see Söderblom, *La Vie Future*, 175–187.

(*b*) The heroic lore of Irân knew a list of heroes and old rulers, which is preserved in the extant parts of the Avesta, especially in the fifth *Yasht*, consecrated to the goddess Ardvî Sûra Anâhita, in the dramatic history of the *khwarenah* (the spiritual substance-power of the Iranian kingship), as given in *Yasht*, xiv., and in the ecclesiastical lists of saints of the *Yasht*, xiii. These legends have been, *tant bien que mal*, amalgamated with and adopted into the Zarathushtrian system.

(*c*) The division of the present millennium into the common Metal Ages is a combination of two systems, of which the Mazdayasnian tradition evidently adopted or borrowed the second one at a later period.

(*d*) The real existence of mankind from Mâshya-Mâshyôî until the coming of the Saoshyant comprises only 6000 years,—as in Talmudic and Christian literature (Böklen, *Die Verwandschaft der jüd.-christl. mit der pars. Eschatologie*, 82–84), where the duration of the world is fixed on the analogy of the six days of creation, a thousand years being with God as one day. Theopompus-Plutarch also seems to reckon 6000 years, but in a different way : 3000 for Ahura Mazda's supremacy (=Gâyômarṭ's trimillennium), and 3000 for the conflict (=until Zarathushtra), the two periods being ended by the final victory and eternal bliss (and the rest of God, which looks like a Jewish-Christian Sabbath of the world ; cf. Ep. Barn. 15).

The last trimillennium, from Zarathushtra to the Saoshyant, of the final Zarathushtrian chronology seems to have been understood by Theopompus as the time of fulfilment, rather than as a new period. It is possible that the doctrine had this aspect earlier. That would better suit the spirit of the *Gâthâs*, where the final renovation of the world seems, in some texts at least, to be soon expected. In any case, Theopompus' record agrees, as to the main contents, with the last 9000 years of the *Bûndahishn*. Those 9000 years *alone* are mentioned in the *Arṭâ Vîrâf Nâmah*, xviii. and liv. : the damned souls complain that they are not delivered from hell although 9000 years have gone —one day or three days in hell seeming to them as long as the whole duration of the world. The author of the *Arṭâ Vîrâf Nâmah* must have known the first trimillennium, as the period of 'the holy spiritual creation' is mentioned in the Avestan fragment Pahl. *Vend.* ii. 20. But it is not unlikely that *Arṭâ Vîrâf's* 9000 years, which are to be compared with Theopompus' statement, represent an older chronology containing three parts : (1) a good ruler, (2) the present intermingled state, and (3) the great restoration, corresponding to our reconstruction of the Yima legend. The first of the four great epochs will then have been added in order to get the number four, or the twelve thousand years.

We are not sufficiently acquainted with the old Babylonian divisions of the existence of the world. But probably the 12,000 years of the *Bûndahishn*—as well as the same age of the world predicted by Mani (Kessler, *Mani*, i. 343 ; the number 12 is fundamental in Mani's doctrine, see Kessler, art. 'Mani' in *PRE*[3]), and by the Etrurians [according to Suidas], like the 12 parts of the existence of the world in 2 Es 14[10ff.] and Apoc. Bar 53, are derived from a Babylonian cycle. This probability comes very near demonstration when we remark that both the Etrurian belief, as reported by Suidas, and the *Bûndahishn* combine the twelve millenniums with the zodiacal signs. The Mazdayasnian theologians owed their astronomical science to the Babylonians and to the Egyptians (J. Marquart, *Philologus*, Sup. x. 1. 192 ff.).

(*e*) The *Gâthâs* represent an epoch in which this doctrine of periods did not belong to the Zarathushtrian faith. If periods were already known in Irân, this must have been outside the Zarathushtrian reform. The long waiting is incompatible with the preaching of the *Gâthâs*. Time, as in both Jewish and Christian prophecy and apocalyptics, is rather sharply divided into two Ages : the present era of struggle and difficulty, and the happy reign of theocracy and justice after the longed-for separation by fire.

4. Meaning of the periods.—The beliefs outlined in the foregoing pages represent the original and characteristic feature of the Mazdayasnian system of Ages of the World, and must be derived from the Zoroastrian idea, expressed in the *Gâthâs*, of Ahura Mazda as the ruler of the future destiny of mankind. The division into Ages does not imply merely a distinction between the present and the old time—as *e.g.* in the *alcheringa* (wh. see) of the Australians. Nor does it signify a deterioration, as, for example, in the Ages of Hesiod and Ovid. Something resembling a pessimistic view of the course of time might be gathered from three phases of the Mazdayasnian religion : (1) the monster of the old myth will be unfettered ; (2) the sharp opposition implied in the Zarathushtrian reform, and the earnest appeal to choose the way of Asha, sometimes give a dark colouring to the Gâthic view ; (3) several thousand years later, when the glorious line of history was already pointed out by Avestan and Pahlavi theology, the tragic events under the last Sasanians and after the Arabian conquest taught a sombre lesson of the end of Zarathushtra's millennium before the advent of the expected helper, who never came. The four Ages of Gold, Silver, Steel, and Iron were adopted, at first probably by an orthodox compiler, during the early controversies with Manichæism and other heresies ; then history filled out the Iron-mingled Age in different ways. The Great *Bûndahishn* kept open its chapter 'On the calamities which have invaded Irân in different ages' (Blochet, *l.c.* 45). But the Metal Ages are only episodes in *one* millennium, and give no idea of the destiny of the world. In both cases the general optimistic character of the Zarathushtrian faith prevails : the victory of Ormazd is the surest thing in the world, known and predicted since the beginning. The worldly corporeal existence and human affairs are no enemies of piety, but pure elements and duties, the diligent fulfilment of which formally constitutes each Mazdayasnian a fellow-worker with Ormazd, a helper, saviour (*saoshyant*), and *frashôcaretar*, 'a renewer' of humanity and of the world. These functions he discharges in company with the great heroes, from Kaî-Khûsrâv—without whose destruction of the idolatrous temples behind the lake of Caêcasta the renovation of the world could never have been carried out (*Maînôg-î Khraṭ*, ii. 95)—to the last *saoshyant*. The world is a realm of conflict, where impurity constantly threatens and demons are ever on the watch. But it is a noteworthy fact that the period of confusion and strife is not *the present Age*. That period ended with the appearance of Zarathushtra. We already live in the Age of the victory of Ormazd.

The Persian periods do not imply an eternal repetition, as in the developments of Aryan speculation and religion in India and Greece, and sometimes in modern thought (*e.g.* Nietzsche, and, in a less pedantic way, Sv. Arrhenius)—the same causes combining to produce in eternal cycles the same effect—

'When this world shall be *former*, underground,
Thrown topsy-turvy, twisted, crisp'd, and curl'd,
Baked, fried, or burnt, turn'd inside-out, or drown'd,
Like all the worlds before, which have been hurl'd
First out of, and then back again to chaos,
The superstratum which will overlay us.'
—(*Don Juan*, canto ix. stanza xxxvii.).

Nothing can be more characteristic than the placing of the Metal Ages and this Iron Age only in one, the present, Mazdayasnian millennium, while the millenniums form together a progress towards an end, whereas in the Indian conception the four *yugas* and the present evil *kali* Age form the constant feature of periods which emerge and pass away in endless similarity. The system of periods in Irân did not unite, as in India, with the popular belief in the transmigration of souls — a belief worked out into a fundamental philosophical doctrine in Indian systems of periods.

The Mazdayasnian scheme expresses, in a somewhat scholastic way, the idea implied in the word *history*: that is to say, 'something happens in what happens' (E. G. Geijer), so that the intricate mass of events has a meaning and a goal beyond the actual combinations and situation. The real kernel of history is a 'forward,' not a 'see-saw,' and not a 'backward,' although it may seem so to human eyes. This profound conception has arisen only twice in the history of human thought—in the only two ancient prophetic religions, one Aryan, one Semitic—in Zarathushtrianism and in Mosaism. Neither seems to have borrowed it from the other. Christianity inherited it from Mosaism, and it has become prevalent in the Western civilization in the form of belief in a Divine purport in history, in progressive evolution, or in a redeeming crisis, and constitutes one of the most significant features and influential factors in the civilization of Europe and America, as distinguished from the great civilizations of India and of the Far East. It is so deeply rooted in the Western mind, that even so sincere and acute an admirer of and believer in the Indian conception as Schopenhauer unconsciously yields to it (cf. his *Sämmtliche Werke*, v. 224). To have originated faith in the significance and purpose of history may fittingly be called Zarathushtra's greatest gift to mankind.

LITERATURE.—E. W. West, Introductions and Translations of Pahlavi Texts i. and v. (*SBE* v. and xlvii.); *Grundriss d. iran. Phil.* ii. 100 f.; J. Darmesteter, *Le Zend Avesta*, 1892-93; Fr. Windischmann, *Zoroastrische Studien*, 1863; C. P. Tiele, *Geschiedenis van den Godsdienst in de Oudheid*, ii. 1902; A. V. W. Jackson, *Zoroaster, the Prophet of Ancient Iran*, 1899, *Grundriss d. iran. Phil.* ii. 668 ff.; J. H. Moulton, 'Zoroastrianism' in Hastings' *Dict. of the Bible*; W. Bousset, 'Beiträge zur Gesch. der Eschatologie' in *Ztschr. f. Kircheng.* xx. 122 ff.; E. Stave, *Einfluss des Parsismus auf das Judentum*, 1898; E. Böklen, *Die Verwandschaft der jüd.-christl. mit der pars. Eschatologie*, 1902; N. Söderblom, 'La Vie Future d'après le Mazdéisme,' *A. M. G. Bibl. d'Études*, ix. 1901; E. Blochet, *Le messianisme dans l'hétérodoxie musulmane*, 1903; J. Marquart, 'Untersuchungen zur Geschichte von Eran' (*Philologus*), 1905; Louis H. Gray, 'The Kings of Early Iran' in *ZA* xix. 272 ff.; Ch. Bartholomae, *Altiran. Wörterb.* 1006 ff., *Zum Air Wb.* 197 f., 1906; E. Lehmann, *Zarathushtra*, 1899-1902.

NATHAN SÖDERBLOM.

AGHORĪ, AGHORAPANTHĪ, AUGAR, AUGHAR. — These are names applied to a sect of ascetics in India who have for a long time attracted attention on account of their habit of cannibalism and other abominable practices.

1. *Meaning of name.*—Their name indicates connexion with the cult of Śiva, being derived from Skr. *a-ghora*, 'not terrific,' one of the euphemistic titles of the god. *Aghorapanthī* means 'one who follows the path' (Skr. *pantha*) or cult of Śiva in this form. The worship of Śiva as Aghoriśvara, 'the non-terrific Lord,' is practised at a fine temple at Ikkeri, in Mysore, and in many other places.

2. *Distribution.*—The present distribution of the sect is a question of some difficulty. According to the Census of 1901, they number within the Empire 5580, of whom the vast majority (5185) are found in Bihār or W. Bengal, the remainder in Ajmīr-Mhairwāra and Berār, with 2 convicts in the Andaman Islands. This differs widely from the Census figures of 1891, when 630 Aghorī and 4317 Augars were recorded in the United Provinces, 3877 Aghorī in Bengal, and 436 Augars in the Panjāb. The explanation of this discrepancy lies partly in the fact that, like all ascetics of the kind, they are constantly wandering from one part of the country to another to attend bathing fairs and visit places of pilgrimage. Secondly, the unpopularity of the sect doubtless induces them at the time of the Census to record themselves under other and more reputable titles. The chief centres of the sect, where a monastery (*maṭha*) of some kind was assigned to them, used in former times to be Mount Ābū, Girnār, Bodh Gayā, Benares, and Hinglāj — the last the most western point to which Indian polytheism extends. But they have now disappeared from Mount Ābū, and they seem to have no recognized establishments at any of the other holy places, which, however, they still occasionally visit.*

3. *History of the sect.* — The first account of ascetics following the rule of the modern Aghorī is found in the *Travels* of the Buddhist pilgrim, Hiuen Tsiang. He speaks of 'naked ascetics, and others who cover themselves with ashes, and some who make chaplets of bones, which they wear as crowns on their heads' (Beal, *Si-yu-ki, Buddhist Records of the W. World*, i. 55; Watters, *Yuan Chwang's Travels in India*, i. 123). In another passage he speaks of the Kāpāladhārin, or 'wearers of skulls,' some of whom have no clothes, 'but go naked (*nirgranthas*); some wear leaf or bark garments' (Beal, *op. cit.* i. 76; Watters, *op. cit.* i. 149). When we come to later times, we have more particular accounts of these Kāpālika or Kāpāladhārin (Skr. *kāpāla*, 'a skull,' *dhārin*, 'carrying'). Ānandagiri, in his *Śaṅkara-vijaya*, thus describes the Kāpālika: 'His body is smeared with ashes from a funeral pile, around his neck hangs a string of human skulls, his forehead is streaked with a black line, his hair is woven into the matted braid, his loins are clothed with a tiger's skin, a hollow skull is in his left hand (for a cup), and in his right hand he carries a bell, which he rings incessantly, exclaiming aloud, "Ho Śambhu, Bhairava, ho lord of Kālī!" titles of Śiva' (H. H. Wilson, *Essays*, i. 264 n.). Again, the poet Bhavabhūti, who wrote in the first half of the 8th cent. A.D., in his drama *Mālatī and Mādhava*, Act v., gives a vivid account of the rescue by Mādhava of his mistress from the clutches of the Aghora Ghanṭa, who is about to sacrifice her at the altar of the goddess Chāmuṇḍā, who represents Devī in one of her most terrible forms. Within the temple the human-sacrificing priest circles in his Tantric dance round his victims, while he invokes the goddess, round whose neck is a garland of human skulls (Wilson, *Theatre of the Hindus*, ii. 55; Frazer, *Lit. Hist. of India*, 289 ff.). A vivid description of this Kāpālika-vrata, or worship of the terrific forms of Śiva and his consort Durgā, is given in the *Prabodha Chandrodaya*, or 'Moon of Intellect' (Eng. tr. J. Taylor, 38 ff.). In the *Dabistān* (Eng. tr. Shea-Troyer, ii. 129), the author of which died about 1670, we have an account of the 'sect of the Yogīs, who know no prohibited food. . . . They also kill and eat men. . . . There are some of this sect who, having mixed their excretions and filtered them through a piece of cloth, drink them, and say that such an act renders a man capable of great affairs, and they pretend to know strange things. They call the performance of this act *Atilia* and also *Akhori*. They have all originated from Gorakhnāth. The author of this work saw a man, who, singing the customary song, sat upon a corpse, which he kept unburied until it came into a state of dissolution, and then ate the flesh of it; this act they hold extremely meritorious.' Gorakhnāth is the great mediæval Hindu saint, of whom many

* Havell, in 1905, found an Augar at Benares seated in a stone cell raised high above the burning-*ghāṭ*. The sect still maintains here its evil reputation, but this black-robed ascetic, who is shown in the photograph studying a sacred book, proved to be quite inoffensive. He bestowed his blessing upon the prying tourist, but contemptuously refused to accept a present (*Benares, The Sacred City*, 119 f.).

marvellous tales are told, and from whom some of the *yogī* Orders trace their origin.*

4. *The sect in modern times.*—There are numerous accounts of the disgusting practices of these ascetics in modern times. M. Thevenot, whose *Travels* were republished in London in 1687, alludes to what was apparently a community of Aghorī cannibals, who during his time were established at a place which he calls 'Debca,' in the Broach district of the Bombay Presidency; but his statements must be received with caution. Ward (*View of the Hindoos* [1815], ii. 373) mentions, among other ascetics, the 'Ughoru-punthee.'

'These mendicants, born in the western parts of Hindoos'thanu, wander about naked or nearly so, carrying in the left hand a human skull containing urine and ordure, and a pan of burning coals in the right. If these marks of self-denial do not extort the alms they expect, they profess to eat the ordure out of the skull, in the presence of the persons from whom they are begging.'

Tod (*Travels in W. India* [1839], p. 83 ff.) gives a vivid description of a colony of Aghorī at Mount Ābū (wh. see). One of the most famous of them, named Fatehpurī, was finally, by his own instructions, immured in the cave which he had occupied for many years. A native gentleman informed Tod that a short time previously, when he was conveying the dead body of his brother to the burning-ground, an Aghorī begged to be allowed to remove the corpse, saying that it would make excellent chutney (*chatnī*), the relish used with curry. He further refers (p. 383) to the terror felt regarding such wretches, who resided near the shrine of Kālikā Mātā, the Mother-goddess, another form of Devī, where a stranger visiting the place was met by a personage, who after a while explained that she was the dread Mother-goddess herself. But this was really the disguise of an Aghorī cannibal, who captured his victims in this way. Buchanan (Martin, *E. India*, ii. 492 f.) tells of an Aghorī who appeared at Gorakhpur in the United Provinces early in the 19th century. He thrust himself into the house of the local Rājāh, whom he bespattered with filth. The Rājāh complained to Mr. Ahmuty, the judge of the district, who ordered the expulsion of the Aghorī from the place. But soon after, when Mr. Ahmuty himself fell sick and the Rājāh's heir died, every one of the Hindu population attributed these misfortunes to the curse of the offended saint.

The same feeling of horror caused by the practices of these wretches is graphically pictured in a curious book, *The Revelations of an Orderly*, published at Benares in 1849. The author (reprint 1866, p. 66) speaks of the *ghāṭs*, or bathing-steps, on the river Ganges at Benares being frequented by—

'Aghorpunth faqueers (Anglicé, ogres), practical philosophers, who affect to disbelieve that there is any difference between things, and to avow that any difference depends upon the imagination. A cuff or a kick is as immaterial to them as a blessing. They go about *in puris naturalibus* with a fresh human skull in their hands (off which they have previously eaten the putrid flesh, and from which afterwards with their fingers they scoop out the brain and eyes), into which is poured whatsoever is given them to drink. They pretend to be indifferent whether it be ardent spirits, or milk, or foul water. Their food is the first thing that offers, whether it be a putrid corpse, cooked food, or ordure. With matted hair, blood-red eyes, and body covered with filth and vermin, the Aghorī is an object of terror and disgust to everybody. He looks rather like a wolf, ready to destroy and devour his prey, than a human being. I once saw a wretch of this fraternity eating the head of a putrid corpse, and as I passed by he howled and pointed to me; and then scooped out the eyes and ate them before me. I had my matchlock in my hand, and was within an ace of putting a ball into his head; for I deemed him a wolf, and, in fact, he was a brute.'

The author, really a European in the disguise of a Hindu, ends by appealing to the Government to suppress such abominable exhibitions. Since the time when this book was written, the custom of ascetics wandering about nude has been repressed by police regulations, and, as will be seen later on, the habit of cannibalism, as practised by the Aghorī, has been prohibited by special legislation within British territories. But as late as 1887 we have an account of a gang who appeared at a fair held at the sacred city of Ujjain in the native State of Gwālior in Central India. 'On demanding some goats from the authorities, they were refused. On this, they proceeded to the burning-*ghāṭ*, and, taking a corpse from the pile, began to devour it. The horrified spectators summoned the police, but the naked fanatics only desisted on being promised the goats which had been before refused them' (*Panjāb Notes and Queries*, iv. 142).

5. *Life history of an Aghorī.*—A full account of the life history of a modern Aghorī, based on inquiries by an Indian Medical Officer, Drake Brockman, was contributed by H. Balfour (*JAI* [1897] xxvi. 340 ff.). This man was by caste a *lohār*, or blacksmith, from the Native State of Patiāla, in the Panjāb. He started life as a beggar, and was adopted as a disciple by an Aghorī. He wandered to the Śaiva shrine of Badarinārāyan in the lower Himālaya, and thence to Nepāl. He then made a pilgrimage to Jagannāth in Orissa, and came finally to Mathura and Bharatpur, at which last place he was found and examined. 'I now receive,' he stated, 'food from every caste and tribe, and have no caste prejudices. I can eat from every one's hand. I do not myself eat human flesh, but some of my sect have the power to eat human flesh and then make it alive again; some have success with charms, and they eat the flesh of the human body; but I have not this power, as I was not successful with the charms. This much I do, I eat and drink out of a human skull. I also eat the flesh of every dead animal, with the exception of the horse, which we are forbidden to devour; all my brotherhood eat the flesh of all dead animals but the horse.'

It has been a subject of much debate why the flesh of the horse is specially prohibited. Some have believed that the reason is that the Hindī name of the horse (*ghorā*) may be connected by its members with the title of the sect. But this seems hardly probable. On the other hand, the horse has long been a sacred animal in India, and its sanctity possibly dates from a period earlier than that of the cow. In the Aśvamedha or horse-sacrificial rite, it was regarded as an emblem of Virāj, the primeval and universally manifested Being, and even at the present day there is considerable evidence of the sanctity of the animal (Colebrooke, *Essays*, ed. 1858, 36; Crooke, *Pop. Religion*, ii. 204 ff.). As a coincidence it may be noted that Pliny (*HN* xxviii. 9) specially points out that when a horse was sacrificed at public ceremonials the *flamen* was forbidden to touch it.

6. *Relations of the Aghorī to other Hindu sects.*—The Aghorī are naturally so reticent about their sectarial organization that their relation to other Hindu sects is as yet imperfectly known. The sect in modern times, or at least that branch of it which has its headquarters at Benares, assigns its origin to one Kinna Rām, who was initiated by one Kālu Rām, an ascetic from Girnār, towards the close of the 18th cent. (Crooke, *Tribes and Castes*, i. 26). Hence they are sometimes known under the title of Kinnarāmī. In religious belief the Aghorī is closely allied to the Paramahaṁsa, who

'is solely occupied with the investigation of Brahma, or spirit, and who is equally indifferent to pleasure or pain, insensible to heat or cold, and incapable of satiety or want. Agreeably to this definition, individuals are sometimes met with who pretend to have attained such a degree of perfection; in proof of it they go naked in all weathers, never speak, and never indicate any natural want; what is brought to them as alms or food, by any person, is received by the attendants, whom their supposed sanctity or a confederation of interest attaches to them, and by these attendants they are fed and served on all occasions, as if they were as helpless as infants' (Wilson, *Essays*, i. 232).

Another sect of the same class, which displays an equal disregard of the decencies of life, is the Sarbhangi (Crooke, *op. cit.* iv. 292). But the dis-

* For the Kāpālika, also, see Monier-Williams, *Hinduism and Brāhmanism*, p. 59; Barth, *Religions of India*, Eng. tr., p. 59; Wilson, *Essays*, i. 21, 264; Buchanan, in Martin, *Eastern India*, ii. 484.

regard of the ordinary needs of life shown by these two sects is very different from the abominable practices of the Aghorī. Their relations, again, to the Aughar *yogīs* of the Panjāb have not been clearly ascertained. It would seem that to the general licence of the latter, the former add the occasional eating of human flesh and filth.

7. *Cannibalism and eating of filth.*—The questions of importance in connexion with the Aghorī are: first, the eating of human flesh and filth; secondly, the use of the human skulls from which they eat and drink. The practice of human sacrifice and cannibalism in India has always been chiefly associated with the Tantric rites of the Śākta worshippers of Devī, the Mother-goddess, in one or other of her various forms, as Kālī, Durgā, Chāmuṇḍā, and others. This cult is supposed to have had its origin in E. Bengal or Assam about the 5th cent. A.D. The Kālika Purāna distinctly recommends the immolation of human beings, for which at the present time pigeons, goats, and, more rarely, buffaloes are substituted. It may be suspected that Hinduism, in this form, assimilated some of the rites of the non-Aryan races; but from the place of its origin it is more probable that these practices were adopted from the E. tribes rather than from the Bhīls, to whom they have been attributed by Hopkins (*Rel. of India*, 490, 533), and others (Gait, *Census Rep. Bengal*, 1901, i. 181 f.). Human sacrifice in this ritual form still prevails in dark corners of the land, as in Assam, and the more remote forest tracts of the Central hill ranges (Gait, *Census Rep. Assam*, 1891, i. 80; Crooke, *Pop. Rel.* ii. 169 ff.). With this side of Hinduism the Aghorī sect is closely connected. There are, again, as in the case of the Śrāddha, or annual Hindu feast of the dead, fairly obvious survivals of the primitive custom of the sacramental eating of the dead, as well as that of devouring the bodies of old or eminent persons for the sake of keeping in the family their valour or other virtues (Hartland, *Legend of Perseus*, ii. 278 ff.). But none of these motives accounts for the cannibalism of the Aghorī.

It is perhaps possible to account for these practices in another way. We find among some savage races instances of wizards or medicine-men eating substances which are in themselves disgusting and revolting, or poisonous or medicinal in nature, with a view to enhancing the spiritual exaltation of the eater.

Thus, according to Haddon (*Report Cambridge Exped.* v. 321), at Mabuiag in Torres Straits, the Maidelaig, or sorcerer, 'made a practice of eating anything that was disgusting and revolting in character, or poisonous or medicinal in nature, not only during the course of instruction, but subsequently whenever about to perform a special act of sorcery. For instance, they were said frequently to eat flesh of corpses, or to mix the juices of corpses with their food. One effect of this diet was to make them "wild" so that they did not care for any one, and all affection temporarily ceased for relatives, wife, and children; and on being angered by any of them they would not hesitate to commit murder.' In parts of Melanesia, according to Codrington, *Mana*, or spiritual exaltation, is gained by eating human flesh; and in this way people obtain the power of becoming vampires, the ghost of the corpse which was eaten entering into friendly relations with the eater (*JAI* x. 305; *Melanesians*, 222). In Central Africa, according to Macdonald, witches and wizards feed on human flesh, and any one tasting a morsel of such food becomes himself a wizard (*JAI* xxii. 107). Among nearly all the Bantu negro races there is a lingering suspicion that the sorcerer, or person desiring to become a sorcerer, is a corpse-eater, a ghoul who digs up the bodies of dead persons to eat them, either from a morbid taste, or in the belief that this action will invest him with magical powers. In Uganda, as well as in many parts of Bantu Africa, there is believed to exist a secret society of such ghouls, who assemble at midnight for the purpose of disinterring and eating corpses. People cursed with this morbid taste are in Uganda called *basezi* (Johnston, *Uganda*, ii. 578, 692 f.). The same story is repeatedly told of witches in India, who frequent cemeteries, and by eating human flesh gain the power of flying in the air and performing other wonders (Tawney, *Katha-sarit-sagara*, i. 158, ii. 450, 594). Stories of the same kind are still told in India (*Panjāb Notes and Queries*, ii. 75; Temple-Steel, *Wideawake Stories*, 418). Even at the present day the Oḍī magicians in Malabar are said to eat filth as a means of acquiring power (Fawcett, *Bulletin of the Madras Museum*, iii. 311).

Belief of this kind may have been the real origin of the practice, and the explanation which the modern Aghorī gives, that according to the Śaiva rule all things are equal and all immaterial, may be a recent development.

8. *Use of human skulls as cups and vessels.*—The same motive possibly accounts for the use of the human *calvaria* for purposes of eating and drinking. In many places the skull used in this way is believed to possess special magical qualities. Thus, among the Wadoe of E. Africa, at the appointment of a chief, a stranger is killed, and the skull of the victim is used as a drinking-cup at the inauguration rite (*Man*, ii. 61). The new priest of the king of the Baganda drinks out of the skull of his predecessor, whose ghost thus enters into him (*JAI* xxxii. 45). In the same way the Zulus make the skull of a noted enemy into a bowl for holding the 'charming-medicine' with which the war-doctor sprinkles the soldiers before a campaign (*ib.* xix. 285). Similarly, in the Indian Himālaya, the skulls of some women killed in a snowstorm were made into drums for summoning devils (Waddell, *Among the Himalayas*, 401). In these and in many other instances of the practice collected by Balfour (*JAI* xxvi. 347 ff.), it is clear that the skull has been carefully selected as that of some eminent or notorious person, or of one whose death has occurred under tragical circumstances. The custom of the Aghorī, if it originated in this way, appears, therefore, in a debased form, for they do not seem to exercise any special care in selecting the skulls which they use. Several bowls of this kind, procured in India, Ashanti, Australia, China, Tibet, and the lower Himālayas, have been figured and described by Balfour (*JAI* xxvi. 357). Waddell gives a picture of one used in Tibetan devil-worship, as well as a drawing of a modern Tibetan hermit, an exact representation of the Aghorī, drinking out of such a bowl (*Lhasa and its Mysteries*, 220, 239, 243, 370).* In fact, Tibet, with its remarkable colony of immured hermits described by Waddell (*op. cit.* 237 ff.), appears to exhibit more closely than even modern India the course of austerity practised by the early Hindu ascetics. The fat, comfortable appearance of the modern *yogī* or *sannyāsī* proves that austerity is not a part of his way of life.

This habit of using skulls as drinking-cups shows itself even in Europe. It was a custom of the old Germans, and Livy (xxiii. 24) tells the same tale of the Celts. Paulus Diaconus (*Hist. Langob.* ii. 28 in Gummere, *Germ. Orig.* 120) tells how Alboin met his death when he insisted on his queen drinking out of a cup made of the skull of her father. It is still a common belief that epilepsy may be cured by drinking out of a cup made from the skull of a suicide (*Folk-lore*, vii. 276, xiv. 370; Mitchell, *The Past in the Present*, 154; Rogers, *Social Life in Scotland*, iii. 225). The powder made from human skulls, and even the moss growing on them, are valued as a styptic in cases of hæmorrhage (Black, *Folk Medicine*, 96).

9. *Punishment of Aghorī.*—There are numerous cases of members of the sect convicted in modern times by Indian courts of law, on charges of outraging and eating human corpses. In 1862 the Sessions Judge of Ghāzipur in the United Provinces convicted and sentenced an Aghorī to one year's rigorous imprisonment, under sections 270–297 of the Indian Penal Code, on a charge of dragging a corpse along a road. A similar case, in which cannibalism was proved, occurred at Rohtak in the Panjāb in 1882, and in Dehrā Dūn of the United Provinces in 1884. In 1884 two Europeans detected an Aghorī eating human flesh on an island in the Ganges. Several skulls, one of which had been recently severed from the trunk, were found

* In Nepāl, Buchanan Hamilton saw people of the Got or gardener caste, in the worship of Bhawānī in the Tantric form, drinking spirits out of human skulls, until they danced in a state of drunken excitement, which was supposed to proceed from inspiration (*Account of the Kingdom of Nepal*, 35).

impaled on bamboo posts round his hermitage (*PASB* iii. 209 f., 300 ff.).

10. *Initiation rites of the Aghorī.*—Ascetic Orders usually guard as secret the methods of initiation and the formula which is whispered in the ear of the neophyte. Hence the accounts of the initiation rites of the Aghorī are, from their general unpopularity, to be received with some degree of caution. According to one, and that perhaps the most authoritative account, the *guru*, or head of the Order, blows a conch-shell accompanied by rude music performed by a hired band. He then micturates into a human skull and pours the contents over the head of the candidate, whose hair is then shaved by a barber. The neophyte next drinks some spirits and eats food which has been collected as alms from the lowest castes, and assumes the ochre-coloured, scanty waist-cloth, and the stick of the ascetic. During the rite the *guru* whispers mystic formulæ (*mantra*) into the ear of his disciple. In some cases it is reported that eating human flesh is part of the rite, and two necklaces, one made of the tusks of the wild boar and the other of the vertebræ of the cobra, are placed round the neck of the disciple (*PASB* iii. 241 f.). According to another account, five glasses filled with spirits in which meat has been mixed with flowers are placed upon the altar. A piece of cloth is tied over the eyes of the neophyte; he is then led before two *gurus*, who light a lamp; the cup of initiation is served to all present; his eyes are opened, and he is told to look for the 'divine light,' while the spell (*mantra*) is whispered into his ear (*North Indian Notes and Queries*, ii. 31). According to a third account, the initiation takes place in Benares at the tomb of Kinna Rām, the founder of the Order, on which cups of hemp liquor (*bhang*) and spirits are placed. Those who wish to retain their caste drink only the hemp; those who solicit complete initiation drink both the hemp and spirits. A sacrifice of fruits is then made on the holy fire, which has continued lighted since the days of Kinna Rām, and an animal, usually a goat, is sacrificed. It is believed that the victim often comes to life, and that the cups on the tombstone miraculously raise themselves to the lips of the candidates for admission into the Order. The rite ends with the shaving of the head of the neophyte, the hair being previously moistened with urine, and a feast is given to the assembled brethren. Full admission to the Order is said to be granted only after a probation lasting twelve years.

11. *Dress and appearance.*—The Aghorī, of whom photographs were collected by Leith for the Anthropological Society of Bombay, is represented as covered with ashes taken from a funeral pyre. He seems to wear frontal marks denoting the unity of the deities Brahmā, Viṣṇu, and Śiva. He wears the rosary of Rudrāksha beads made of the seeds of the tree *Elæocarpus ganitrus*, a necklace made of the bones of a snake, and the tusks of a wild boar, and carries a skull in his hand. Some members of the Order are said to wear necklaces made of human teeth (*PASB* iii. 348 ff.).

LITERATURE.—The chief authorities have been quoted in the course of this article. The most complete accounts of the sect are those of H. Balfour, 'The Life History of an Aghori Fakir,' *JAI* xxvi. [1897] 340 ff.; H. W. Barrow, 'Aghoris and Aghorapanthis,' from the MS collections of E. T. Leith, *PASB* iii. [1893] 197 ff.; Crooke, *Tribes and Castes of the N.W. Provinces* [1896], i. 26 ff.

W. CROOKE.

AGITATION.—**1.** The methods of the agitator are usually considered to be a modern phenomenon, and although this is not an entirely accurate view of the case, it is at least so far true that the conditions of social life have recently become such as to bring his labours into startling prominence. It is possible to trace the rudiments of this device far back into the past, since the ringer of the tocsin bell, the lighter of the beacon-fire, and the bearer of the flaming torch may fairly be regarded as forerunners of a Mazzini or a Shaftesbury. But there is a pregnant distinction. The message of the tocsin bell in mediæval Florence was an agitating one, but it was single, definite, and predetermined, announcing a bare fact, but conveying no new idea. A developed agitation, on the contrary, depends almost entirely on popularizing a new thought; it applies fresh moral judgments to facts which may have been familiar enough. The present writer has elsewhere described this instrument of collective action as 'an attempt to act mediately on social abuses by acting directly on a social conscience' (*History of Eng. Philanthropy*, p. 172). Even in this, its developed form, agitation can be discovered in so-called ancient as well as in modern history. Whether judged by its results or by the splendid vigour of its onset, no greater agitation has been witnessed than the reconstruction of Western society by the enthusiastic promulgation of the Christian faith. Nor is any more instructive description of the effect of the agitator's art to be found than 'These that have turned the world upside down are come hither also' (Ac 17[6]).

Nevertheless, agitation is characteristically modern. There is not much opportunity for its successful use, unless a 'public opinion' exists to which its appeal can be directed. Public opinion itself has existed in some shape for many centuries, but it continually gains in power and effectiveness. In the more definite form of what Professor Dicey calls 'law-making public opinion' it is not yet evolved except in the more progressive nations. The formation of public opinion in its modern sense has been referred to the era of the first printing-presses, and its mature growth to that of the periodical press (Tarde, *L'Opinion et la Foule*, pp. 7–9). This is also the period of democracy, and it is precisely in democratic societies that agitation is found to be a potent and familiar weapon. We have to appraise its ethical value. If we are to do this with any precision, we shall be compelled to limit the range of the discussion, and to treat not all agitations, but only one leading group. The present article, then, is immediately germane to agitation as an instrument of the humanitarian spirit, and may require some modification in details before being applied to purely political movements, as for the franchise, or class struggles, as of Trade Unionism.

2. The most obstinate labour of public life is to make institutions (*e.g.* laws or customs) match with the ethical ideal. The agitator's function is to facilitate the task. Accordingly, any good agitation should possess the following characteristics. (1) It is *the antithesis of quietism*, for it is necessarily based on the conviction that objects of social concern are the proper concern of the individual also; it denies the distinction between public and private interests, and asserts the duty of each to share in the life of all. It is directed to the removal of abuses; but, so far from being caused directly by the *existence* of a wrong, it springs from the *perception* of the evil. Successful agitation is, therefore, an index of moral sensitiveness. Men treated animals with cruelty long before the Kindness to Animals campaign began (Society for the Prevention of Cruelty to Animals, A.D. 1824). (2) Agitation is a leading method of *popularizing higher moral standards*. In the instance just referred to, the matter of judgment was simple enough. Frequently, however, the full significance of the end to be pursued is discovered only in the course of the agitation itself. This was notably the case with Prison Reform and

Factory Legislation, so that what was at first a goal to be reached becomes repeatedly the starting-point for fresh effort. (3) Agitation *appeals to the unselfish impulses and strengthens the social imagination.* Most of us live largely in a world of personal aims purified and enriched only by consideration for the aims of a few neighbours. Into this mind marked by narrow (not necessarily poor) sympathies strikes the impetus of a larger claim. It may be a Dreyfus affair, the appeal for justice to one;* or Emancipation, the appeal of the enslaved Negro race; or the ideal of Italian unity. In every instance individuals are driven into the larger realm of public sympathy. (4) *Agitation is a means of social peace.* This is in the nature of paradox, because the first result is always controversy and strife. But even in the turmoil something is gained when social imagination is stirred. Through the effort to remove particular wrong there emerges forefeeling of and admiration for the ideal human society in which remediable wrongs will be remedied. Opposition to the bad is one form of loyalty to the good, and those who enter on the conflict prepare the type of mind fit for the better life of social peace.

3. So far we have rather ignored the foibles, prejudices, and inconsistencies of actual men. No agitation proceeds with much sweet reason, and there is something in strong zeal which accentuates our native quarrelsomeness. In other words, agitation is not a perfect instrument in the hands of imperfect men. Agitators even for worthiest ends are not immune from bitter envying and strife in their hearts. Of course, there are drawbacks, but the only question which need now detain us is whether they are of such a kind as to discredit the use of a powerful instrument of ethical gain. Two serious criticisms are adduced, neither of which can be entirely rebutted. (1) Agitation is rooted in exaggeration, and appeals to an unhealthy sensationalism. Thus the higher powers of the intelligence are swamped under orgiastic emotion. This is the danger of all enthusiasm. It would be more than serious enough if Le Bon's indictment of the 'crowd' could be accepted. Agitation does appeal to half-instructed emotions with incalculable results. Yet such an appeal may very well lead to right conduct, and even to truer thought. For in respect of the disinterested response of the 'public' it must be noted that (*a*) it is set to ponder larger issues; (*b*) its thinking (or feeling) becomes more incisive; (*c*) the thought may not be very clear, but were its sympathies not warmly engaged, it would hardly think at all on great affairs of ethical concern. (2) Popular movements, it is objected, are liable to be vitiated by the ignorance of those to whom appeal is made. Agitation which is effective as a stimulant is inapt for instruction; it is certainly no method for producing philosophers. This fact is serious chiefly as it affects the results of agitation. Something is accomplished, but the whole thought is rarely worked out before the fervour begins to fade. Agitation can achieve more in the field of criticism than in that of construction, or, to finish with a truism, agitation cannot be the only instrument of reform. But it has its function. A final judgment as to its precise worth will depend on the value attached to 'correct thinking' and 'the good will' respectively. The difficulty of improving and perfecting this instrument is a part of the general problem of how to maximize correct thinking and good will in the same persons at the same time and for a single ideal end.

* It is instructive to contrast this world-wide agitation with Voltaire's similar effort on behalf of Calas when popular interest was less largely evoked. The difference marks the enhanced modern facility for agitation.

LITERATURE.—A. V. Dicey, *Law and Public Opinion in England*, 1905; B. K. Gray, *History of Eng. Philanthropy*, 1905 (esp. ch. viii. 'The Philanthropist as Agitator'); G. Le Bon, *Psychologie des Foules*, 1899; G. Tarde, *L'Opinion et la Foule*, 1899 (esp. § i. 'Le Public et la Foule'); I. Taylor, *Nat. Hist. of Enthusiasm*, 1842.

B. KIRKMAN GRAY.

AGNOIOLOGY.—A term coined by Professor J. F. Ferrier in his *Institutes of Metaphysics* (1854), to denote the Theory of Ignorance in contrast to Epistemology (*q.v.*), also a term apparently coined by him (p. 48) to denote the Theory of Knowing. The conception of Agnoiology, as well as the name, was originated by Ferrier (pp. 50–51, 406, 435). Agnoiology is intended to meet the plea by which Ontology is often baffled, that Absolute Being—that which truly is—may be something of which we are ignorant (pp. 50, 406–408). This plea is met by showing that ignorance is an intellectual defect, and must, therefore, admit of a possible remedy. Consequently we cannot be ignorant of anything which cannot possibly be known. We cannot, for example, be ignorant of two straight lines enclosing a space. To be ignorant of them would imply that our ignorance might possibly be removed, and that they might thus be known. But they cannot be known, for they are contradictions, absurdities; and therefore also they cannot be things of which we are ignorant. For the same reason, matter by itself, that is, an object which is not related to any conscious intelligence, contradicts the very nature of knowledge. It is something which we cannot possibly know, and therefore cannot be ignorant of. Accordingly the conclusion of Agnoiology is that the only object of which we can be said to be ignorant is, like the real object of all knowledge, not what is commonly spoken of as an object in contradistinction from a subject, but that object in relation to an intelligent subject by whom it is known. Thus matter *and* mind, some object *plus* some subject, is the complete object of all ignorance as well as of all knowledge (p. 432). From this the ontological inference is that, as Absolute existence must be either that which we know or that of which we are ignorant, it can never be an object by itself or a subject by itself, but must always be a synthesis of the two (pp. 511–521).

The Agnoiology of Ferrier is thus by anticipation a critique of the system which soon afterwards came to be known as Agnosticism (*q.v.*). Ferrier's work appeared six years before Spencer's exposition of Agnosticism in his *First Principles*, and double that period before Huxley gave the system its unclassical name. Yet neither of these writers has attempted to grapple with Ferrier's critique, and in the vast literature of Agnosticism the critique has failed to receive the recognition which it certainly deserves. There is, therefore, no work to be consulted for Agnoiology besides the *Institutes of Metaphysics*. The above references are to the pages of the 3rd edition (1875).

J. CLARK MURRAY.

AGNOSTICISM.—**1. Meaning.**—The origin of the term is described by Huxley as follows:—

'When I reached intellectual maturity, and began to ask myself whether I was an atheist, a theist, or a pantheist; a materialist or an idealist; a Christian or a freethinker, I found that the more I learned and reflected, the less ready was the answer; until at last I came to the conclusion that I had neither art nor part with any of these denominations, except the last. The one thing in which most of these good people were agreed was the one thing in which I differed from them. They were quite sure they had attained a certain "gnosis"—had more or less successfully solved the problem of existence; while I was quite sure I had not, and had a pretty strong conviction that the problem was insoluble. And, with Hume and Kant on my side, I could not think myself presumptuous in holding fast by that opinion. This was my situation when I had the good fortune to find a place among the members of that remarkable confraternity of antagonists, long since deceased, but of green and pious memory, the Metaphysical Society. Every variety of philosophical and theological opinion was represented there, and expressed itself with entire openness; most of my colleagues were *-ists* of one sort or another; and, however kind and friendly they might be, I, the man without a rag of a label to cover himself with, could not fail to have some of the uneasy feeling which must have beset the historical fox when, after leaving the trap in which his tail remained, he presented himself to his normally elongated companions. So I took thought, and invented what I conceived to be the appropriate title of "agnostic." It came into my head as suggestively antithetic to the "gnostic" of Church history, who professed to know so much about the very things of which I was ignorant; and I took the earliest opportunity of parading it at our Society, to show that I, too, had a tail, like the other foxes. To my great satisfaction, the term took; and when the *Spectator* had stood godfather to it, any suspicion in the minds of respectable people that a knowledge of its parentage might have awakened was, of course, completely lulled' (*Collected Essays*, vol. v. pp. 239, 240).

Mr. R. H. Hutton has given a slightly different account; he states that the word was 'suggested by Professor Huxley at a party held previous to the formation of the now defunct Metaphysical Society, at Mr. James Knowles' house on Clapham Common, one evening in 1869, in my hearing. He took it from St. Paul's mention of the altar to "the Unknown God"' (Murray's *New English Dictionary*).

These accounts demand a few brief comments. The inscription on the altar was 'the unknown,' not 'the unknowable God' (ἀγνώστῳ, not ἀγνωστικῷ θεῷ), and the term 'agnostic' is said to be linguistically incorrect. The Gnostics of Church History were so called in contempt because they opposed their extravagant speculations to the historical testimony of the Church; and in opposing Agnosticism to the knowledge of God claimed by Christian theism, Huxley suggests that it is an equally baseless fabric. There was no necessity for the introduction of the new term, as the familiar term 'scepticism' is almost synonymous with it, although Agnosticism restricts its doubt to a narrower sphere; not the possibility of all knowledge is denied, but only the possibility of any knowledge of ultimate reality. This restriction the term does not, however, indicate; nor has Huxley proved his right to impose on the term this arbitrary restriction. The flippancy also of the account must produce a painful impression.

It is as a refuge from the dread of Materialism that Huxley offers us this doubt of Agnosticism.

'For what, after all,' he asks, 'do we know of this terrible "matter," except as a name for the unknown and hypothetical cause of states of our own consciousness? And what do we know of that "spirit" over whose threatened extinction by matter a great lamentation is arising . . . except that it also is a name for an unknown and hypothetical cause, or condition, of states of consciousness? And what is the dire necessity and "iron" law under which men groan? Truly, most gratuitously invented bugbears. . . . Fact I know, and Law I know; but what is this necessity save an empty shadow of my own mind's throwing—something illegitimately thrust into the perfectly legitimate conception of law?'

Refusing to attempt any solution of the problem of ultimate reality, he very confidently declares the terms in which the immediate reality is to be interpreted.

'It is in itself of little moment whether we express the phenomena of matter in terms of spirit, or the phenomena of spirit in terms of matter—each statement has a certain relative truth. But with a view to the progress of science, the materialistic terminology is in every way to be preferred. For it connects thought with the other phenomena of the universe . . . whereas the alternative, or spiritualistic, terminology is utterly barren, and leads to nothing but obscurity and confusion of ideas. Thus there can be little doubt that the further science advances, the more extensively and consistently will all the phenomena of Nature be represented by materialistic formulæ and symbols' (*Collected Essays*, i. p. 159 ff.).

In the supposed interests of science he is prepared to sacrifice the real interests of morality and religion, although in determining the mode of explaining the world these supreme interests of the life of man have surely a prior right to be taken into consideration. Not only so, but he assumes that from the standpoint of 'spirit,' science will not get its due, whereas an idealist philosophy has no interest in traversing the conclusions of science in its own sphere—the explanation of phenomena. It is only when science attempts to be a philosophy of ultimate reality as well, that it comes into necessary conflict with a spiritualistic interpretation of the Universe. If all the phenomena of the Universe are known only as they exist for thought, it is not necessary to connect thought with these phenomena by reducing it to them, for there must ever be the essential connexion between it and them of the subject which knows and the objects which are known. Thought is not an alien in the Universe to be made at home only by a proof of its kinship with the material phenomena it knows. Nay, rather it alone holds the secret of relationship among all these phenomena; for Huxley is entirely without warrant in his assumption that a complete and adequate and consistent account of the Universe, even as phenomenal, can be given in the materialistic terminology. Life and Mind alike cannot be resolved into matter and force. This line of criticism belongs to the article on MATERIALISM; but it was necessary to indicate it so far in order to show on what unproved assumptions Huxley's agnosticism rests. The materialistic explanation, even he recognizes, cannot be accepted as a solution of the problem of ultimate reality. It is because he refuses to treat as seriously as it deserves, on account of its own sufficiency as well as for the interests it protects (morality, religion, etc.), the spiritualistic explanation, which does offer the solution, that he is compelled to assume, and even to make a boast of, his attitude of nescience.

2. Hume.—To understand *Agnosticism* as the modern phase of scepticism, it is not necessary to go further back than Hume, to whom Huxley confidently appeals: 'The fundamental doctrines of materialism, like those of spiritualism and most other "isms," lie outside the limits of philosophical inquiry; and David Hume's great service to humanity is his irrefragable demonstration of what these limits are.' Whether the demonstration is as irrefragable as Huxley thinks, we may inquire. Hume reduces all the contents of consciousness to 'perceptions,' and divides perceptions into 'impressions' and 'ideas.' The former include 'all our sensations, passions, and emotions' which are given us with a peculiar 'force and liveliness' by which we distinguish them from the latter, which are but their faint copies. In thinking, we connect impressions and ideas with one another, by such conceptions as causality and substance and subject. These cannot be derived from our sensations, the ultimate and exclusive source of knowledge. How does Hume account for these conceptions? He derives all such conceptions from custom. 'Because we are accustomed to see that one thing follows another in time, we conceive the idea that it *must* follow, and *from* it; of a relation of succession we make a relation of causality' (Schwegler's *Hist. of Philos.* p. 183). That any such connexion necessarily exists we have no right to affirm. 'All events,' Hume says, 'seem entirely loose and separate. One event follows another, but we can never observe any tie between them. They seem conjoined, but never connected' (*Works*, A. & C. Black, 1854, iv. p. 84). 'Necessity,' he says elsewhere, 'is something that exists in the mind, not in objects' (i. p. 212). Without attempting to offer an ultimate reason for this custom, he recognizes it as a *universal principle of human nature*. Substance is explained in a similar way. 'The idea of a substance as well as that of a mode, is nothing but a collection of simple ideas, that are united by the imagination, and have a particular name assigned to them, by which we are able to recall, either to ourselves or others, that collection' (i. 31, 32). A consequence of this definition of substance is the denial of the reality of the external world. 'The opinion of external existence, if rested on natural instinct, is contrary to reason, and, if referred to reason, is contrary to natural instinct, and carries no natural evidence with it to convince an impartial inquirer' (iv. 177). The subject fares no better. 'What we call a mind,' he says, 'is nothing but a heap or collection of different perceptions, united together by certain relations, and supposed, though falsely, to be endowed with perfect simplicity and identity' (i. 260). Such radical scepticism could not offer any solid basis for a rational theism. While Hume expressed his satisfaction that 'our most holy religion is founded on Faith, not on Reason,' and personally professed belief in the existence of God; yet in his *Natural History of Religion* he sought to trace back the origin of belief in God to ignorance and superstitious fears; and in his *Dialogues concerning Natural Religion* there can be little doubt he endeavoured to throw discredit on the theistic evidences. This apparently inconsistent position may be explained by the fact that his own scepticism, in spite of his philosophical principles and the conclusions which he so frankly and boldly drew from them, was not absolute, but mitigated; for he recognized, in practical life at least, 'the strong power of natural instinct' as lending sanction to common beliefs, for which no rational proof could be given.

3. Kant.—Although Kant set himself the task of answering Hume, yet his answer was so incomplete that Huxley claims Kant as well as Hume on his side. Opposed to Hume's scepticism in regard to the forms of sense and the categories of the understanding, Kant himself becomes sceptical as regards the ideas of reason.

'He conclusively showed that knowledge could not be reduced to sensations, and that intelligence implied in all its operations necessary conditions as well as contingent impressions, and so far he substantially disposed of the scepticism of Hume by proving its dependence on an inadequate and erroneous psychology. But when he proceeded to argue that the constitutive principles involved in knowledge have to do only with phenomena or states of conscious experience, but are wholly incapable of placing us face to face with things; that they have a merely subjective and relative value, but give us no information as to external reality; that, while useful in coordinating and unifying our perceptions, they in no degree justify our affirming that there is anything corresponding to these perceptions,—then he virtually undid his own work, and became not the conqueror, but the lineal successor of Hume' (Flint, *Agnosticism*, p. 141).

Into the details of Kant's criticism of Hume's scepticism it is unnecessary to enter (see KANT). Suffice it to say that Kant has shown once for all that the connective principles, by which the contents of consciousness are combined in an intelligible, rational unity, belong of necessity to the mind itself. Sensation does not give them; custom cannot bring them into being; the very possibility of consciousness depends on them; they are not casual results of, but necessary conditions for, any experience. Nevertheless he distinguishes the 'thing-in-itself' from the thing as it is for our knowledge; and thus the necessary constitution of the mind makes a knowledge of the reality as it is impossible. This sceptical element appears more prominently in Kant's treatment of the ideas of the reason. 'The mind from the very nature of its intellectual constitution necessarily assumes the unity of the soul, the existence of the universe (the totality of phenomena), and the reality of a First Cause' (*ib.* p. 163), and nevertheless the ideas are only *regulative*, and not *constitutive*. By them we can give the rational unity to our experience which is the aim of all thinking; but we are not at liberty to regard these ideas as clues to reality, or as proofs of the existence of world, self, or God. Kant's criticism of the rational theology of the age (the cosmological, teleological, and ontological arguments) will be duly taken account of in the treatment of Theism. Here it need not further concern us. It is true that in his *Critique of the Practical Reason* he restores the ideas of God, freedom and immortality, as postulates of the moral consciousness; yet his conception of reason as theoretical is in its final issue sceptical. German idealism laid hold on the antisceptical aspect of the Kantian philosophy; but in more recent Neo-Kantian movements the sceptical aspects have again come to the front. Against Kant's position it may be urged that the reason which, by its very constitution, is debarred from knowing reality as it is, and which in its final unifying exercise is necessarily illusive, is so grotesque a conception, that so great a thinker can be excused its creation only on the ground that, as a pioneer in new ways of thinking, he could not himself realize whither he was allowing himself by his tortuous reasoning to be led. The division of the mind into sense, understanding, reason, is an unreal abstraction; the separation of the pure from the practical reason is opposed to more recent developments of psychology, which recognize the control of the *cognitive* by the *conative* aspect of personality. If mind be a unity, the illusiveness of the ideas of the pure reason would attach to the postulates of the practical reason; and the categories of understanding and forms of sense must fall under the same condemnation. What the Hegelian Logic does is to develop the most concrete conceptions out of the simplest, and to identify this mental process with the evolution of the Universe—some interpreters would say even of God Himself. If here 'vaulting ambition doth o'erleap itself,' yet, with greater modesty, it may be claimed that experience itself warrants the assumption that in the process of thinking the mind does penetrate more deeply into the reality of things; for the system of nature which science builds is not contradicted, but confirmed, by the course of nature itself. That the world is one and the self is one is an assumption that is ever finding verification in experience. Not only is the self one as the subject of consciousness, but it is one as a character which is being formed, as a personality which is being developed. If this be so, then the practical as well as the theoretical need of a final unification of the world and life in the conception of God, fully justifies the assumption of God's existence. What makes reality as we know it most intelligible cannot, without an absolute scepticism, such as the positive elements of Kant's analysis forbid, be denied reality. Kant should have been more, or not at all, sceptical.

4. Comte.—The positivism of Comte is necessarily agnostic; but as it is discussed in another article (see POSITIVISM), all that need be said about it in this connexion may be put in a few sentences. Both the theological and the metaphysical explanations of the world are condemned as superseded stages in the development of human thought. The positive stage does not connect phenomena by the principles of causality and substance; it only observes sequences and resemblance. The custom, which Hume recognizes as universal, of thus connecting phenomena is in positive thought to be expressly avoided. Nevertheless, Comte assumes the uniformity and constancy of the laws of phenomena, as taught by experience, although what warrant can be given for such an assumption, if no objective connexion of phenomena may be asserted, it would be impossible to discover. With glaring inconsistency he resolves mental into material phenomena, thus applying the category of causality which he himself had relegated to the metaphysical stage. Kant's vindication of the necessity for thought of these connective principles is a convincing answer to Comte's positivism.

5. Hamilton.—Hamilton, although in his general philosophical position a follower of Reid, had read Kant without thoroughly understanding him, and developed the sceptical elements in his system. While the Divine nature cannot be known, the Divine existence may be believed, as our moral nature and the Scriptures testify. We can believe *that* God is, without knowing *what* He is. He goes so far as to affirm that 'to think that God is as we can think Him to be is blasphemy. The last and highest consecration of all true religion must be an altar ἀγνώστῳ θεῷ, To the unknown and unknowable God.' That there is no warrant for such an application of the inscription on the altar at Athens, has already been shown. If the endeavour to think what God is is blasphemy, then not only all theology but even all religion must be convicted of it. The recognition in all humility and sincerity that God cannot be perfectly known by the imperfect mind of man is characteristic of all genuine piety; but that does not involve the admission, which is something altogether different, that God cannot be known at all. Hamilton must turn elsewhere than to religion, and theology as its interpreter, for a justification of his sweeping statement. From his own philosophy he draws the following arguments: (1) As all knowledge is relative in two senses, all objects being related to one another, and also related to the subject knowing, God as the absolute, out of all relations, cannot be known. But to think God as absolute is not to think of Him as out of all relations, but as Himself constituting all His relations; and His relation as object to the thinking mind as subject is not necessarily one in which He, as He really is, is concealed and not revealed; for, as Creator, it is more likely He would make mind capable of knowing Him. As has already been insisted on in criticising Kant, the thing-in-itself, reality as it is, has not a foreign distorting and obscuring element added to it when it is known; but even from the data of sense the thinking mind can construct the object as it is. The *phenomenal* as perceived is completed in the *noumenal* as conceived, and in the latter reality is known as it is, which is not the case in the former. (2) As the only possible object of knowledge and positive thought is the conditioned and the limited, the Infinite as *the unconditionally unlimited*, and the Absolute as *the unconditionally limited* cannot be known or positively thought. But is there any justification for so defining the Infinite and Absolute, and still more for identifying such verbal abstractions with the conception of God? God has a definite nature, distinct attributes, characteristic operations, and to think God is not to think an abstraction at all. His infinitude and absoluteness mean self-limitation and self-conditioning. Since for our knowledge and our thought all existence, save God, is conditioned and limited by other existence, the mind cannot find rest until it conceives such self-limitation and self-determination. It may be said that the mind not only can but must think the Infinite and Absolute, that is, God. (3) As has already been indicated, the Infinite and Absolute are both so defined as to be a mere 'negation of thought'; but as the necessity and legitimacy of so defining these terms have been challenged, his conclusion that God as Infinite and Absolute cannot be known or thought falls to the ground. Both are positive conceptions, and both are necessary to complete our positive thinking about the world as conditioned and limited. As correlative conceptions, finite and infinite, relative and absolute, may claim to be equally known and mutually illuminative. (4) He concedes that although by reason we may not know God, yet we believe that God is an authority, which yields us 'the original data of reason.' This faith rests on 'a mental impotency.' To state his amazing argument in his own words: 'The conditioned is the mean between two extremes—two inconditionates exclusive of each other, neither of which can be conceived as possible, but of which, on the principle of contradiction, and excluded middle, one must be admitted as necessary. We are thus warned from recognizing the domain of our knowledge as necessarily coextensive with the horizon of our faith. And by a *wonderful revelation* we are thus, in the very consciousness of our inability to conceive aught above the relative and the finite, *inspired with a belief in* the existence of something unconditioned beyond the sphere of all comprehensible reality' (*Discussions*, p. 15). It has already been shown that the Infinite and Absolute are not *inconditionates*; but if they were, how can positive thought be the mean of notions that are 'a mere negation of thought'? How to these can there be applied any of the laws of thought? If we cannot define these notions, how can we affirm that they contradict or exclude one another? Or, in fact, how can we base any sort of argument on the unknowable and unthinkable? One cannot but feel that most of this argument is merely verbal jugglery.

6. **Mansel.**—Nevertheless, Hamilton found a follower in Mansel, who adopted his philosophy so far as he could use it for an avowedly apologetic Christian purpose. He believed that he could best cut the ground from under the feet of any objectors to the Christian revelation, by showing that in these matters human reason was quite incapable of offering an opinion. He set himself to answer in the negative this question: 'Whether the human mind be capable of acquiring such a knowledge as can warrant it in deciding either *for* or *against* the claims of any professed revelation, as containing a true or a false representation of the Divine Nature and Attributes?' (1) The first argument Mansel advances is that reason is not entitled to criticise the contents of revealed religion unless it can prove itself capable of conceiving the nature of God, that is, of constructing a philosophy of the Infinite and the Absolute. This is an extravagant demand. The moral insight and spiritual discernment which qualify a man to judge of a doctrine, whether it be of God or not, are very much more general and simple than the speculative capacity, not to say audacity, which can and dares undertake to find out God unto perfection. (2) Having made this demand, he seeks in his second argument to prove that neither psychologically—from a study of the mental faculties of man—nor metaphysically—from the knowledge man can get of the nature of God—can it be met. This second argument loses its validity with the disproof of the first. Both by looking within and by turning without can man get such glimpses of God as make real religion possible; and he need not, therefore, concern himself about the question whether he can or can not construct a philosophy of the Infinite and Absolute. (3) Having demanded a philosophy of the Infinite and Absolute, and demonstrated its impossibility, Mansel next concentrates attention on the conceptions of the Infinite and Absolute, and seeks to show how contradictory they are. How can human thought distinguish in the Absolute, as one and simple, a plurality of attributes? If the Infinite is free of all possible limitations, how can it coexist with the finite? The conception of God as First Cause, as involving the limitation of its effect, is irreconcilable with the conception of the Infinite. But all this playing with words fails to mislead, if we look steadily at realities and keep our eyes off abstractions. If we define, as we may and should, the Infinite and Absolute as the fulness of being, life, mind, power, which is distinguished from relative and finite existence in that it is self-conditioned and self-limited, not determined either positively

or negatively by that which is not itself, this whole scholastic structure falls to the ground. (4) Turning from these conceptions, Mansel then seeks by an analysis of the universal conditions of human consciousness to prove that the Infinite and Absolute cannot be its object. 'Consciousness is the relation of an object to a subject and to other objects, but the idea of the Absolute precludes all such relation. Further, our consciousness is subject to the laws of space and time, and cannot therefore think the thought of a Being not likewise subject to them' (Pfleiderer's *Development of Theology*², 1893, p. 327). But to be known by a mind which He has endowed with the capacity of knowing Him is no limitation of God's Infinitude. As the Absolute, God is not without relations, but only as related to Him do all things exist, consist, persist. Man's consciousness of time and space implies the correlative conceptions of eternity and immensity. This argument, further, is inconsistent with the claim that man may and should believe *that* God is, even although he cannot know *what* God is, as belief is a state of consciousness, even as knowledge is. (5) Mansel denied, to state briefly some of his conclusions, the moral likeness between God and man, and therefore the possibility of man's judging by reason or conscience what claimed to be the revealed mind and will of God; he admitted the possibility of moral as of physical miracle, that is, the suspension of the laws of right as of force; he rested the claim of the Scriptures to be accepted entirely on external evidences; he thus sought to protect the orthodoxy of his time from attack by a moral and religious scepticism, which, if taken seriously, would be fatal alike to goodness and godliness.

7. Herbert Spencer.—Herbert Spencer attaches himself in some of his arguments to Hamilton and Mansel; but his interest is altogether different from theirs. He is not seeking to protect revealed religion against attack from philosophy, but to vindicate the materialistic method of modern science as the only valid method of interpreting the Universe. His motive is not, however, irreligious, as his desire is to reconcile religion and science, and he is confident that he has called a truce to their age-long conflict. As the most influential of the exponents of Agnosticism, he claims a fuller treatment and closer criticism than any of the writers already mentioned. Following step by step his discussion of the Unknowable in his *First Principles*, we must consider the following questions:—(1) Does he correctly indicate the relation of science and religion, so as to be warranted in his assumption of the conception which alone can reconcile them? (2) Does the inconceivability of the ultimate religious and scientific ideas lie in their very nature, or only in his statement of them? (3) Is his use of the doctrine of the relativity of knowledge valid, and does it strengthen his conclusion that God is unknowable? (4) Does this reconciliation of science and religion do justice to religion?

(1) In the first chapter Spencer argues that science and religion are co-ordinate, the sphere of the former being what is known, and of the latter that which, though in consciousness, yet transcends knowledge; that each must 'recognize the claims of the other as standing for truths that cannot be ignored'; and that a reconciliation can be effected only by the discovery that what is the ultimate fact, and the first principle of each, is common to both. It is in the most abstract truth of religion and the most abstract truth of science that, he holds, the two coalesce. His claim that science occupies the whole realm of the knowable, so that for religion is left only the region of the unknowable, must at once be challenged. For the self-conscious personality the categories of science—force, matter, law—are not adequate; and within the realm of the knowable even categories—life, mind, will—must be employed to which physical science does not do justice. Religion contributes a conception, God, to the interpretation of the knowable, which cannot be got rid of by this arbitrary division of the provinces of science and religion. Not a truth common to science and religion is what we have to look for, still less the most abstract truth; but, on the contrary, the abstract categories of science must be supplemented and corrected by the much more concrete categories of philosophy, morality, and religion. It is the same reality which science explains and religion interprets; but the explanation of science is completed in the interpretation of religion. Matter, force, law are less intelligible conceptions than mind, will, personality, God; for the self-conscious spirit of man finds itself in the latter as it cannot in the former. To confine knowledge to objects of sense and such connexions between them as the understanding, with its categories of quantity, quality, relation (substance and causality), may constitute, and to exclude from knowledge the larger and loftier conceptions of a teleology of nature, of a personality in man, and, above all, of the all-embracing, all-sustaining, all-directing, and all-illuminating reality, God, is altogether an arbitrary proceeding. It has already been criticised in dealing with Kant's scepticism regarding the ideas of the pure reason. To deny all value to the knowledge religion claims is necessarily to challenge the validity of the knowledge allowed to science.

(2) Spencer's proof in the second chapter, that science must end in nescience, and religion must be content with awe of the Unknowable, is as follows:

(*a*) Conceptions are symbolic, when their whole content cannot at once be represented to the mind. These are legitimate, if we can assure ourselves 'by some cumulative or indirect process of thought, or by the fulfilment of predictions based on them,' that there are actualities corresponding to them. Otherwise they are to be condemned as vicious and illusive, and cannot be distinguished from pure fictions. Here, it is evident, he tries to limit conception to representation (*Vorstellung*), and to exclude the idea or notion (*Begriff*). But regarding this restriction, which, it must be emphatically stated, the world's greatest thinkers have not denied because it never occurred to them that it could be made, there are some questions which may reasonably be asked. Is man's thought to be limited to what he can image to himself? Having started from sense-objects, is that alone knowledge for him which can be referred to sense-objects? Or, beginning with these, has he not the right, nay, does it not rest on him as a necessity of his mind, to bring into clearness of consciousness all that is implied in this rudimentary knowledge, whether the ideas so attained have corresponding images or not? Does not his own inner life furnish him with spiritual conceptions, which, although they have no corresponding sensible actualities, are not only bound up with his most real and permanent personal interests, but even make more intelligible to him the world of sense around him, and help him to discover its meaning, worth, and aim? As Kant has surely conclusively shown, the mind has its own connective principles, which, underived from and inexplicable by experience, are yet necessary to experience. If knowledge were as Spencer restricts it, the conditions of its possibility would be excluded from it.

(*b*) Having prejudged the question by this definition of the conceivable, Spencer proceeds to deal with the ultimate religious conceptions concerning the origin and the nature of the Universe, and maintains that 'a critical examination will prove not only that no current hypothesis is tenable, but also that no tenable hypothesis can be framed' (p. 30). The Atheistic hypothesis of a self-existent Universe is inconceivable, as it explains one mystery by another; so is the Pantheistic, for 'really to conceive self-existence is to conceive potential existence passing into actual existence by some inherent necessity, which we cannot do.' As regards the Theistic hypothesis, the analogy with human art is properly set aside, as this does not produce its own materials. 'The production of matter out of nothing is the mystery.' Granted an 'external agency,' that must be accounted for; and we must assume 'self-existence,' and that is 'rigorously inconceivable.'

This statement calls for several comments. *First*, it is altogether illegitimate to identify the ultimate religious conceptions with theories of the origin of the Universe; for these theories hold an altogether secondary place in religion, and religion possesses an inward witness of kinship and fellowship with God which is quite independent of them. *Secondly*, what Spencer calls the theistic solution is rather the deistic, for which God is an 'external agency,' and the solution of Christian theism combines the thesis of pantheism (immanence) and the antithesis of deism (transcendence) in the synthesis of a conception of God as unity-in-difference—a conception which certainly does not conform to Spencer's arbitrary rule of conceivability, but which for many thinkers of clear vision is altogether luminous. *Thirdly*, theism is not required to conceive the production of matter out of nothing, as it is not committed to the assertion of an ultimate, absolute dualism of matter and mind, but can conceive the possibility of matter as in God as Spirit. *Lastly*, that 'self-existence is rigorously inconceivable' is an unwarranted assertion, as dependent existence inevitably leads thought to conceive an existence on which there is dependence, but which is not itself dependent. It is because the existence that explains itself can alone satisfy our thought that we are led, by the application of the category of causality, to seek for existence that does not so explain itself an explanation beyond itself.

(*c*) After having thus endeavoured to show that all theories of the origin of the Universe are untenable, Spencer fixes his attention on the nature of the Universe. We must assume a First Cause, which is Infinite and Absolute; and, nevertheless, these concepts, all equally necessary, are yet mutually contradictory. Here he borrows freely from Mansel, and indulges in the same verbal jugglery, the futility of which has already been shown. The conclusion, which is supported by such arguments, is put forward as having the support of the religious consciousness itself. 'Not only is the omnipresence of something which passes comprehension that most abstract belief which is common to all religions, which becomes the more distinct in proportion as they develop, and which remains after their discordant elements have been mutually cancelled, but it is that belief which the most unsparing criticism of each leaves unquestionable, or rather makes it ever clearer' (p. 45). Although it may be admitted that the conception of God has changed, as it necessarily must, since man's thought is dependent on experience, yet it must be maintained that the progress has been mainly positive and not negative. Growing knowledge of self and of the world does necessarily correct the conception of God, bringing it into closer harmony with experience; but this conception of God is not less but more rational, moral, spiritual; it answers the question of the mind, the longings of the heart, and the needs of the life more and not less adequately. The religious consciousness will assuredly not sustain the contention that 'this deepest, widest, and most certain of facts that the Power which the Universe manifests to us is utterly inscrutable.'

(*d*) It is not necessary for the present purpose to follow Spencer in his proof, in the third chapter, that the ultimate scientific ideas are also inconceivable; a closer examination would show that all the difficulties are due to an inadequate method of thought, which tries in vain to reduce the concrete complexity of existence to an abstract simplicity of conception. To give but one instance, he tries to prove that the self which knows cannot itself be known, for the relativity of knowledge involves as ultimate the distinction of subject and object. But that subject and object may be discriminated, it is necessary that both be embraced in the unity of consciousness; in self-consciousness that unity is still unity-in-difference, as the self is object to itself as subject; and it is mere word-play to affirm that the self cannot both be intelligible and intelligent. In fact, self-consciousness is the ideal knowledge, the perfect accord of thinking and being. Assuming for the sake of argument that the ultimate ideas of science are inconceivable, why does Spencer not draw the same conclusion for science and religion? Science with inconceivable ultimate ideas possesses the realm of the knowable; religion with inconceivable ultimate ideas must content itself with the unknowable. How can a system of knowledge be based on inconceivable ideas in one case, and nescience be the necessary result in the other? The proximate ideas of religion—the phenomena of the religious life—have as much claim to be treated as data of knowledge as the perceptions of the outer world with which science occupies itself. This scepticism regarding ultimate ideas undermines science as much as religion.

(3) The argument in the fourth chapter, based on the relativity of knowledge, is borrowed from Hamilton and Mansel. 'The inference,' says Spencer, 'which we find forced upon us when we analyse the product of thought as exhibited objectively in scientific generalization, is equally forced upon us by an analysis of the process of thought as exhibited subjectively in consciousness' (p. 74).

(*a*) The analysis of the product of thought leads to this conclusion. 'Of necessity, therefore, our explanation must eventually bring us down to the inexplicable. The deepest truth which we can get at must be unaccountable. Comprehension must become something other than comprehension before the ultimate fact can be comprehended.' This ultimate fact, he assumes, will be 'some highly general fact respecting the constitution of matter of which chemical, electrical, and thermal facts are merely different manifestations.' The method of explanation here taken for granted is entirely false. To discover what is common to all phenomena, and to ignore their differences from one another, is not to explain them. The logical universal does not at all account for the particulars it embraces. The abstraction man does not help us to comprehend Cæsar, Paul, Luther, Napoleon. It is the most concrete unity—that which combines the most numerous and varied differences in a system within itself—that is the ultimate fact which not only explains all, but is itself explicable. Not in the divorce of existence and intelligence can thought be brought to a halt; but only in such a conception as makes reality most fully rational can its goal be found. Spencer, in looking away from concrete differences to an abstract unity, is looking in the wrong direction for the ultimate fact. Explanation, to be adequate, must be synthetic and not analytic; it must end not in a generalization, but in a system.

(*b*) In the analysis of consciousness, the relativity of knowledge is said to imply two kinds of relation—the relation of object to subject, and the relation of objects to one another. Because a thing is known only in such relations, Spencer argues that it cannot be known in itself, whatever that may mean. This assumption, that the knowledge of reality adds to reality an element so foreign that consequently as known it is other than it is as unknown, is an absurdity which has already been sufficiently exposed. Spencer adopts Hamilton's objection, that God as the Absolute must be known either as subject or as object, or as the indifference of both. But what forbids our thinking of God—the object of our knowledge—in so far as God Himself has distinguished our consciousness from His own—as the subject which thinks all things as existent by His will? We as subjects knowing God are, for God, objects which do not limit His infinitude, or determine His absoluteness, because He knows us as existent in distinction from Himself by His own self-determination and self-limitation. Our intelligence which seeks God as its object, and which, on the assumption that the Universe is a manifestation and not a concealment of God, believes that it knows God, must be by God's act delusive, if God does not manifest Himself as He is. It would require much more cogent arguments than these verbal juggleries of Spencer to convince us that God made intelligences in such wise that He Himself could never become intelligible to them. Enough has already been said also about the second sense in which the relativity of knowledge is used. To conceive God is not to think a Being out of all relations, but a Being whose reality is revealed in His relations, constituted by Himself.

(*c*) While agreeing with Hamilton in this argument from the relativity of knowledge, Spencer differs from him in asserting that the unrelated, though inconceivable, is yet a constituent element of thought. 'Our notion of the Limited,' he says, 'is composed, firstly, of a consciousness of some kind of being, and, secondly, of the consciousness of the limits under which it is known. In the antithetical notion of the Unlimited, the consciousness of limits is abolished, but not the consciousness of some kind of being. It is quite true that in the absence of conceived limits this conciousness ceases to be a concept properly so called, but it is none the less true that it remains as a mode of consciousness' (p. 90). He then tells us that this something is constituted by 'combining successive concepts deprived of their limits and conditions' (p. 95). Here a logical abstraction is supposed to be a reality, and even the reality that explains all; but, as has already been shown, God, to explain the Universe, must be conceived as the concrete unity which embraces all differences, and relates them to one another.

(4) Spencer hopes, in the fifth chapter, that 'in the assertion of a Reality utterly inscrutable in nature,' science and religion will be reconciled. Science is to admit the existence, religion the inscrutable nature of this reality. He thinks that this will not be a vain appeal, as his understanding of the history of religion is that it is developing in this direction. How mistaken he is needs no proof. The religious consciousness does recognize that the abysmal depths of the Divine cannot be fathomed by the human mind; but it does not admit that the truth about God it claims to possess is an illusion. Religious knowledge is valid and valuable, though imperfect and incomplete. Spencer requires religion to give up the conception of God as personal. 'It is just possible,' he says, 'that there is a mode of being as much transcending Intelligence and Will as these transcend mechanical motion.' Nevertheless, he insists on interpreting the Universe which is the manifestation of the ultimate reality as mechanical motion. Rejecting the highest conceivable category as too low for the reality, he insists on applying to its manifestations the lowest conceivable category. He represents the inscrutable mystery as *causal energy*, while declining to describe it as Intelligent Will. His system is materialistic rather than idealistic. He gets rid of the personality of religion to substitute not a higher but a lower conception in interpreting the Universe. In surrendering the personality of God, religion surrenders everything; in admitting the existence of this reality, science is in no way restrained in its explanation of the world in terms of matter and motion. In this reconciliation religion loses, science gains, everything.

In the criticism of the authors passed in review the objections to Agnosticism have been stated. But a brief summary may be allowed at the close. The materialistic explanation for which it seeks to find room is inadequate to account for life, mind, morality, religion. The idealistic explanation which it seeks to shut out not only does justice to the highest interests of life, but makes more intelligible the whole process of the Universe as an evolution of spirit. The theory of knowledge on which it rests is sceptical in its result, and this scepticism must extend to science as well as to philosophy and theology. The trust in the reason of man, on which the proof of God's existence rests, is as necessary to give validity to the conclusions of science. The arguments from the relativity of knowledge, the conditionateness of thought, the negative character of the conceptions of the Infinite and Absolute, have the futility of scholastic abstractions and verbal subtleties, and show no direct contact with any intelligible reality. The religious consciousness is altogether misrepresented when it is claimed as confirming the conclusion of the inscrutable nature of the alternate reality. More recent philosophical developments encourage the expectation that Agnosticism will soon be a superseded mode of thought.

LITERATURE.—The works of the authors discussed should be consulted; also Leslie Stephen's *An Agnostic's Apology* (1893). In all books of Christian Apologetics some attention is given to the subject. Specially to be commended are Flint's *Agnosticism* (1903), and Ward's *Naturalism and Agnosticism*[2] (1903).

ALFRED E. GARVIE.

AGNOSTICISM (Buddhist). — One of the most important and, in some ways, most obscure questions in Buddhism is whether the Buddha was an agnostic, in the sense that he refused to express an opinion upon a future life (transmigration) and on the state of the Buddha after death, and preached only the attainment of '*nirvāṇa* upon earth.' We propose, in the first instance, to describe the authorities bearing upon this question, then to discuss them, and finally to draw conclusions.

I. **Authorities.**—1. When Buddha is asked by King Ajātaśatru what are the actual fruits of a 'religious life' (or life of a monk, *śrāmaṇya*),* he gives an answer in which there is nothing metaphysical. He regards the question, as his interlocutor desires, from the point of view of the present life. In the first place, the monastic state confers a great dignity on the person who assumes it. The slave who has become a monk is honoured by his former master; in the same way the free man is relieved from private cares. There is, however, something better: good conduct, mastery over oneself, food and clothing in sufficiency but without excess, produce a rich contentment.† And there is something better still: the practice of successive 'trances' (*dhyāna*), the knowledge which accompanies them, and the annihilation of all passion, the attainment, in a word, of the state of an *arhat* or of *nirvāṇa* upon earth—these are the sublime fruits of the monastic life.

* See the *Sāmaññaphalasutta*, Dīgha, i. pp. 47–86, translated by various scholars, and recently by Rhys Davids, *Dialogues of the Buddha*, pp. 56–95, with an Introduction.

† There are many charming descriptions of the happiness of life in the forest among the trees, which are more kindly and complaisant than men (see *Śikṣāsamuchchaya*, ch. ix.).

2. This sketch of the monastic life will perhaps be more correctly understood if compared with the sentiments expressed by the Buddha when he is questioned on metaphysical subjects. The examples are numerous, and at times widely divergent. We shall confine ourselves to a discussion of the most remarkable. Perhaps the most characteristic is that related in the *Mahāvagga*.* The Buddha is addressed as follows: 'You are said to teach the doctrine of annihilation [that is to say, that there is no life after death, and no future retribution for the deeds done upon earth]. Is that true?' 'I teach,' replied the master, 'the annihilation of desire. . . .' There is thus a kind of play upon words; and this passage, in which the problem of the future life is curtly dismissed, confirms the impression left by the dialogue as summarized above.

3. In the 'Net of Brahmā'† the Buddha enunciates a series of propositions, of which some at least are of historical and doctrinal worth. They are presented as strange and alien to Buddhism; and, while some are more specifically condemned, the series as a whole is rejected. The following is the order:—

(1) (*a*) The universe and the soul are eternal (*śāśvatavāda*) in the sense that they have had no beginning,—a belief founded upon the fact that some saints have memory of their previous existences.

(*b*) The universe and the soul are, at one and the same time, eternal and non-eternal, either because Brahmā, the creator of the universe, has neither beginning nor end, while other beings are perishable, or because the soul is eternal and the body perishable.

(2) The universe is (*a*) limited in space, (*b*) unlimited, (*c*) unlimited at the sides and limited towards the top and the bottom, (*d*) neither limited nor unlimited [the contradiction is not explained].

(3) It is possible to refuse to choose between four propositions (affirmation, denial, simultaneous affirmation of the affirmative and negative, simultaneous denial of the affirmative and the negative) with reference to (*a*) the existence of another world, (*b*) the reality of 'apparitional beings,'‡ (*c*) the fruit of actions, (*d*) the renewed life of the man who is set free from desire, *i.e.* of the *arhat*. This refusal is said to be a sign of stupidity and sophistry. Teachers of such doctrine are 'slippery as eels.'

(4) The soul has no cause, that is, it appears in the present world without having passed through a previous existence. In the same way the present evolution of the universe has had no antecedents.§

(5) The soul has, after death, (*a*) conscious existence, conceived under sixteen different aspects; (*b*) unconscious existence, under eight different aspects; (*c*) existence neither conscious nor unconscious, under eight different aspects; or (*d*) it is annihilated at death (seven distinct theories, corresponding to seven classes of souls).

(6) Some maintain that *nirvāṇa* is attained in this life (*diṭṭhadhammanibbāna*), conceived as the possession either of the pleasures of the senses,* or of the first, etc., up to the fourth ecstasy (*dhyāna*).†

These opinions regarding the past and the future are theories (*dṛṣṭi*=θεωρία).‡ The Buddha knows the consequences which they entail upon those who adopt them; they form the net in which the ignorant are caught, beginning with Brahmā, who believes himself to be eternal! The Buddha knows far better things, viz., the origin and the end of sensations, and the means of escaping them. He ends by saying that he has destroyed every germ of re-birth in himself; so long as his body lives, it is seen by gods and men; after his death neither gods nor men will see him.

4. Of all the questions raised in the 'Net of Brahmā' only ten appear in the *Majjhima Nikāya*, i. 426.§ These are especially important, for with slight modifications they constitute the list of fourteen questions to which no reply is allowed.‖

(1) Eternity of the universe: Is it eternal? Is it non-eternal?

(2) Infinity of the universe: Is it infinite? Is it finite?

(3) The vital principle (*jīva*) and the body: Are they identical? Are they non-identical?

(4) Continued life of the Tathāgata, *i.e.* the *arhat*, the saint, 'he whose thought is emancipated': Does he survive death? Does he not survive? Must we assert of such an one at the same time survival and non-survival of death? Must we deny both?

Māluṅkya is sufficiently curious to insist on obtaining an answer to these questions, which he regards as fundamental. The Buddha refuses to reply. He has withheld information on the questions of the eternity or otherwise of the universe,

* vi. 31; trans. in Vinaya Texts, *SBE* xvii. p. 108 ff.

† *Brahmajālasutta*, Dīghanikāya, i. pp. 1–46, trans. by Rhys Davids, *Dialogues*: 'The Perfect Net.' A Sanskrit redaction of this sūtra is known by a quotation in the *Abhidharmakośa*, see Minayeff, *Mélanges Asiatiques de St. Pétersbourg*, vi. 577 ff. The sūtra seems to get its name from the fact that it explains how Brahmā, believing himself to be the creator, is caught in the net of error. On the same principle a series of errors is explained. Possibly the Sanskrit sūtra did not contain the first part of the Pāli edition, as it is quoted as *śīlaskandhikā* (*JRAS*, 1906, pp. 444–446), and occurs in several suttas of the Dīgha.

‡ Those that appear without being begotten according to ordinary laws. Either they issue from lotuses, as was the case with the heroes of numerous legends, or the reference is to the first beings, or the inhabitants of such and such a paradise, etc. . . . or perhaps the Bodhisattva in his last birth, as he takes up his abode of his own free will in the womb of Māyādevī. In the later dogmatism, to deny the other world, apparitional beings, actions (good or bad), or the arhat, is *mithyādṛṣṭi* (heresy), which destroys the roots of merit.

§ The Brāhmans very often object to Buddhism that it admits the production of being out of not-being (*asataḥ saj jāyate*). But this objection is not supported by any Buddhist authorities.

* As a matter of fact, the pseudo-Buddhism of the Tantras identifies supreme bliss or *nirvāṇa* with sexual enjoyment.

† Strictly speaking, the possession of the fourth trance is not '*nirvāṇa* upon earth,' because this possession is a momentary one. But we may assume that this definition of '*nirvāṇa* upon earth' is very like the orthodox conception.

‡ That is to say, erroneous views and speculations; not that there may not be, in a certain sense, a past and a future, a conscious future life, a '*nirvāṇa* upon earth,' but this past and this future are not the past and future of an *ego* given as permanent. This comment follows the *Madhyamakavṛtti*, ch. xxvii., and the dogmatic teaching of the Pāli Suttas.

§ *Chūla-māluṅkya-ovāda*, translated by Warren, *Buddhism in Translations*, p. 117, and by Oldenberg, *Buddha*, p. 274 f. See also 'Mahālisutta,' in *Dialogues*, p. 187.

‖ The fourteen 'unelucidated topics' (*avyākṛtavastu*) of the Sanskrit Buddhist literature are the same as these, with the addition of four concerning the eternity and the infinity of the universe (viz., Is it at one and the same time eternal and non-eternal? or is it neither eternal nor non-eternal?), and the difference that the questions concerning the Tathāgata precede those on the vital principle (see below, p. 224, note ‡).

Oldenberg has proved that, in many cases, 'world' must be interpreted as the 'ego' (*Buddha*, p. 271, Fr. trans.[2] p. 263). In any case *loka* means *sattvaloka*, world of the living, and not *bhājanaloka*, world-receptacle of living beings. On the other hand, we have seen that 'eternal' is equivalent to 'without beginning.' It is noteworthy that the Sanskrit authorities define 'infinite' as 'having no end in time,' contrary to the interpretation of the Sutta quoted above. The questions, then, regarding infinity will be understood as follows: Will all beings attain *nirvāṇa*? Will no being attain *nirvāṇa*? Will some beings attain *nirvāṇa*, while others will not? Is it false to say that some beings attain *nirvāṇa* and that others do not?

As regards the relations of the *jīva* and *śarīra*, it is difficult to determine the original meaning of the words and the bearing of the question. Certainly nothing is more alien to Buddhist doctrine than to identify the 'vital organ' or 'vital principle' (*jīvitendriya*) with the body. By *jīva* Buddhism understands the personal and so-called permanent principle denoted by the technical word *pudgala*. *Śarīra* denotes the *rūpaskandha*, 'the element of form,' and, by extension, the other *skandhas* (bodily elements under different aspects: sensation, etc.). From the very remarkable fact that the Buddha, on the subject of the *jīva-śarīra*, condemned both the denial and the affirmation of their identity, but was silent upon the doctrines of 'identity and non-identity' and 'neither identity nor non-identity,' the etc., because knowledge on this point does not help in any way towards the annihilation of the passions.

5. In the 'Dialogue of Vaccha'* we observe a slightly different attitude on the part of Buddha. When questioned as to the ten points above specified, he condemns the ten 'theories'; they produce suffering, and do not help towards the annihilation of the passions. He himself has no 'theories' (*diṭṭhi*); his teaching (*diṭṭha*, his knowledge) embraces the *skandhas* only (Pāli *khandhas*), the constituent elements of beings, their beginning and their end. In fact, as has been pointed out, all the 'theories' connected with the past or future, and the identity or survival after death of the Ego, presuppose the existence of the Ego. But this Ego does not exist in itself; there is only an aggregation, a complex of *skandhas*.

Vaccha insists, and returning to the four questions concerning the existence after death of the Tathāgata, who is here denoted by a descriptive term, *vimuttachitta*, 'he whose thought is set free,' he receives a formal answer: 'It is wrong to say that the Tathāgata exists after death, wrong to say that he does not exist, wrong to assert survival and the contrary, wrong to deny both.' Vaccha fails to comprehend this, and the Buddha explains: 'Can it be said of an extinguished flame that it has gone to the right or to the left . . . ? Similarly in the Tathāgata there exists no matter, no *skandha* which one could name when speaking of the Tathāgata; and being alien to every conception of matter and *skandhas*, the Tathāgata is deep, immeasurable,† unfathomable, like the great ocean. It is wrong to say that he exists after death, wrong to say that he does not exist . . .'

That is to say, if we understand correctly, it is impossible either to assert or deny, or to say anything about what does not exist, inasmuch as it is not an object of knowledge. But the *skandhas* are the only objects of knowledge, and the *skandhas*, which constituted the man 'whose thought is set free,' have no existence after death, the emancipation of the thought consisting in this, that the thought does not reconstitute the *skandhas* in a new grouping.

6. This comparison of the Tathāgata with the great ocean is repeated in a passage in which it seems to be interpreted in a mystical sense.‡ 'Why has the Buddha not revealed whether he exists or not . . . after death?' To this question, asked by King Pasenadi, a learned nun replies: 'Hast thou a mathematician who could measure the water of the ocean? . . . The ocean is deep, immeasurable, unfathomable. In the same way there exists no matter in the Tathāgata . . .' (as above, § 5).

On examining the comparison more closely, however, we see that it does not hold. The water of the ocean evades measurement because it is too vast, while the Tathāgata after death cannot be calculated, measured, or fathomed because there no longer remains in him anything capable of being calculated or measured, or, more exactly, anything capable of being known and described.

But why is it heresy to maintain the annihilation of the Tathāgata? Because there is no opportunity of distinguishing between the Tathāgata living and the Tathāgata after death.* And just as it is wrong to assert that the Tathāgata, during his lifetime, is either distinct from or identical with the *skandhas* either united or singly,—the Tathāgata, even during life, cannot be 'really apprehended,' there is nothing real in him, Buddha is only a name,—so what is true of the Tathāgata is true of the Ego, of any Ego whatever; the Ego does not exist in itself.† This way of looking at the problem is precisely that adopted by the *Nāgārjuna* and the *Mādhyamika* schools. The Tathāgata has no further existence, because there is no Tathāgata. It is the same *in reality* with all the other so-called Egos. The Buddha has nothing to say about them, because it is impossible to speak about what does not exist.‡

II. **Discussion.**—We have thus given an account of the chief authorities on which the study of the problem of agnosticism ought to be based. These documents, the agnostic statements of the Buddha bearing upon various problems, and assuming slightly different forms, admit apparently of three different, and even contradictory, interpretations: (1) They furnish us with the ultimate underlying belief in the mind of the Buddha assumed to be an agnostic, and with the official doctrine of the Order, which is 'positivist' in the modern sense of the word. (2) They conceal, for reasons of a practical kind, an implied affirmation touching the future life of ordinary men quite as much as the existence after death of the 'emancipated.' (3) They constitute a formal denial both of the existence of the 'emancipated' and of the Ego.

It is obvious that in itself the strange system, which consists in distinguishing four hypotheses,—affirmative, negative, affirmative and negative, neither affirmative nor negative,—and whose earliest application appears in the passages quoted, is capable of this threefold interpretation. It is a method either (1) of evading an answer, the policy of the 'slippery eel,' as Buddha says, or (2) of asserting the existence of the mystery, but forbidding its discussion, or (3) of denying both the existence and the conceivability of the object in question by closing up 'all joinings and loopholes by which the true facts of the case might escape being caught in the logical net.' §

Let us examine the three interpretations.

1. *Agnosticism.*—The first constitutes one of the most remarkable amongst the numerous systems that Western analysis has recently disentangled from those precepts of the Buddha which are more or less faithfully preserved in the Pāli writings. It is remarkable quite as much for its own sake as for the contrast which it presents to the pre-

Sammitīyas, not without reason, drew the conclusion that the *pudgala* exists, without any one being able to state what relation it bears to the *skandhas*. This is the theory of *avāchyatva* ('inexpressibility'), which is controverted by the *Abhidharmakośa* and the *Mādhyamikas* (see next col. note †). Buddha (*Saṁ. N.* iv. 400) refuses to say whether there is, or is not, a self (see IDENTITY).

* *Majjhimanikāya*, i. p. 483; translated by Warren, p. 123. The reason of the silence is explained in *Saṁyuttanikāya*, iv. 400; on the Ego, cf. Oldenberg, pp. 272, 273.

† *Appameyyo*, 'immeasurable,' also means 'not within the range of knowledge.' The context, however, does not seem to allow this acceptation of the term here. Plays upon words are very frequent in Hindu metaphysics, and the simile of the ocean is the justification in the present instance.

‡ *Saṁyuttanikāya*, iii. 109; Warren, p. 138; also Oldenberg, p. 280. Although the conception of the present article, even more than its conclusions, departs from the views expressed by this eminent Indian scholar, it is the writer's duty to acknowledge to the full the obligation under which he lies to him.

* Dialogue between Yamaka and Sāriputta, *Saṁyuttanikāya*, iii. p. 112; Oldenberg, *Buddha*, p. 281 f., Fr. tr. p. 279; Warren, p. 138; cf. *Saṁyuttanikāya*, iv. 380. *Anupalabbhamāna*, according to Oldenberg (*Buddha*, Fr. tr. p. 272, note), means 'not to be conceived,' and Warren renders 'you fail to make out and establish the existence of the saint in the present life' (p. 141). In Buddhist logic, *anupalabdhi* is 'the non-perception of what ought to be perceived'; there is no jar because, all the conditions necessary to the perception of a jar being fulfilled (light, proximity, acuteness of sight, etc.), I do not perceive a jar.

† According to another school, that of the *Sammitīyas*, the Ego stands in no definite relation to the *skandhas*, but none the less exists, though 'unnameable' (*avāchya*).

‡ We have seen that all Buddhists do not deny the reality of the self, and that the Buddhists who believe in a self call it *pudgala*—the commonest word in the sacred literature for 'somebody,' 'an individual'—in order to avoid the suspicion of heresy which the use of the Brāhmanical word *ātman* would necessarily involve.

§ Oldenberg, *Buddha*, p. 278. It is thus that the 'four-branched syllogism' is dexterously employed by the *Mādhyamikas*, the best example of which has reference to the origin of things. An object is not produced by itself, nor by anything else, nor by itself together with something else, nor without causes; therefore no object is ever produced. The two last hypotheses, affirmative and negative, neither affirmative nor negative, are usually rejected as absurd, being self-contradictory.

vailing spirit of Hindu religions. Amid the luxuriant mythological, dogmatic, mystic, penitential, and ritualistic growth which the period of the Brāhmaṇas and the Upaniṣads, and of Jainism exhibited, the Buddha had established his Order with stern simplicity and as a strictly moral régime.* As a matter of fact, mysticism, with the four famous ecstasies (*dhyāna*), which were regarded by the early Buddhists as older than Buddhism,† is one of the chief features of this régime. Buddhists, however, do not claim that *dhyāna* by itself affords any valuable superior knowledge, any supernatural virtue or insight into the Divine. Without disparaging the 'divine eye,' the memory of former births, the passing through walls, etc., which are the natural results of ecstasy, their chief aim is to produce by mental rather than physical means a state of mind full of restfulness and moral insight, to the reality of which experience should testify, and which, in the classical country of the *yogīs*, a 'positivist' doctrine, whose only concern is moral happiness, need not be ashamed to own.

The point of view ascribed to the Buddha is exactly that of Ajātaśatru: 'Of what use in the present world is the monastic life, and in general the practice of virtue, the excellent practice?' To this question by itself the reply will be that the importance of the monastic life is essentially in 'this visible world.' It is indeed possible, Buddha seems to say, that virtue may be beneficial in another existence, but experience has clearly proved that, practised as I teach it, and following a middle course between excess and the sorrowful life of penance which Nigaṇṭha (founder of the order of the Jainas) preaches, being possessed of all that is necessary,—for the attainment of the condition of an *arhat* is difficult and requires bodily vigour,‡—then virtue produces perfect happiness upon earth. What more do you wish? If you are not satisfied, go elsewhere; sham physicians are legion.

Such, in broad outline and apart from the theory of ecstasy, is the essence of the Buddhism which our neo-Buddhists preach. These conclusions can be reached only by 'doctoring' tradition, and by ignoring in particular all that our authorities say concerning the reward of actions in future births; and *that* is certainly genuine Buddhism.

It should be noted further (and this gives special colour to his so-called agnosticism) that Buddha never says, 'I do not know.' He sometimes says, 'You are to know nothing about it.' That is entirely different.§ The tradition consistently claims that the Buddha was omniscient (*sarvajña*) not only in the narrow sense of the term, possessing the knowledge of what was necessary for salvation, knowledge of the means which lead to the emancipation of thought—a knowledge which he shared with the Pratyekabuddhas, etc.—but also universal omniscience (*sarvākārajñatva*), the knowledge of all that was and is and is to come.‖

* From the very beginning Buddhism claims to be a 'middle way.' This middle way, according to many authorities, consists in avoiding the two goals (or extremes) of doctrine—affirmation and denial of a self, existence after death, etc. But the word, in its earlier use, seems to refer to disciplinary or penitential moderation. The Buddhist monk does not indulge in sensual pleasures, but he keeps himself free from the morbid exaggerations of asceticism. See Rhys Davids, *Dialogues*, p. 207.

† Rhys Davids, *Dialogues*, p. 51, n. 1.

‡ See *Dialogues*, p. 209.

§ This remark, the interest of which is evident, was pointed out to the present writer by A. Barth.

‖ The only passage within the writer's knowledge in which a contrary opinion is suggested is the discussion in the *Tantravārttika*, a work by the Brāhman Kumārila, on the omniscience of the Buddha. Kumārila maintains that all knowledge is derived from the Veda, and not from the teaching of Buddha. And he represents the Buddhist, his antagonist, responding to him in words to this effect: 'Granted that the Buddha does not know the number of the insects, etc., what does that matter? He knows, and he alone was able to impart to us, saving truth' (see *JRAS*, 1902, pp. 363 ff.).

It will be noticed that, in the older narrative, Buddha, having attained to *bodhi*, thinks of three persons in succession who are worthy to be the first to receive his teaching. The gods have to inform him of the death of these three persons, of which he is ignorant. Moreover, Buddha hesitates to preach the law, and has to be encouraged by Brahmā. These discrepancies were afterwards explained to have been mere affectation on the part of Buddha, who was anxious to comply with 'worldly ways' (*lokānuvartana*).

2. *The agnostic statements may conceal positive affirmations.*—(1) The texts themselves invite us to study the reasons, opportune or otherwise, which justified the Buddha in refusing to answer certain questions of a cosmological or metaphysical nature.

On one occasion the Buddha declares that the world is inconsistent with him, but that he is not inconsistent with the world; that he assents to all to which the world assents, so far as it is based on sound reasons. And, in fact, he sometimes affirms that, since discord and quarrelling are the worst evils, and the absence of discord is the essential characteristic of a monk, one ought to refrain from expressing any opinion.* Moreover, moral therapeutics, directed towards the emancipation of thought, demands the regular purification of the mind, progressive suppression of all the ideas to which the mind can cling, extending even to unconsciousness of the end in view, since this can be attained only in the suppression of thought. 'To long for nirvāṇa is sheer folly and an invincible obstacle to its attainment.' Thus, on the one hand, the Buddhist should try to win the favour of all, and to choose the more advantageous course or that which involves less evil. 'Just as it is necessary to speak to each in his own language, and to preach to barbarians in the language of the barbarians,' so it is necessary to avoid hurting or offending any one, and to guide each on that path of progress which he is capable of following, to the neglect even of the real truth, that is to say, even by inexact statements. And, on the other hand, the belief, the 'view' (*dṛṣṭi*), which is in itself perfectly justified, that we have passed through innumerable existences before arriving at the present one, must be abandoned, because it is inimical to salvation, inasmuch as it suggests the idea of the permanence of the individual. It is, moreover, in reality false, the test of the truth of any proposition being its accord with the end in view.

(2) Two points, moreover, of capital importance rest upon the most definite testimony. It is certain, on the ground of tradition, that Buddha adopted a very distinct attitude towards the question of action (*karma* [which see]), and consequently the question of existence after death. To quote the texts would be impossible, and perhaps it is of greater interest to recall the historical example of the friendly relations existing between the Order and the sects (Aggikas, Jaṭilas) who accepted the doctrine of the fruit of works.†

The early Buddhists believed in retribution for actions, in the influence which earlier existences exercised upon the present, and in a future life conditioned by the accumulated and imputable effects of previous actions.

There is no less evidence that they believed in the possibility of escaping from the circle or whirlpool of existence to the rest of *nirvāṇa*. 'In the language of that time,' as a very competent judge affirms, 'the word *nirvāṇa* always denoted supreme happiness, apart from any idea of annihilation.'

* Burnouf, *Introduction*, p. 458; Kern, *Geschiedenis*, i. p. 276.

† *Mahāvagga*, i. 38. 11 (Vinaya Texts, *SBE* xiii. p. 190): 'If fire-worshippers and Jaṭilas come to you, O monks, they are to receive the ordination (directly), and no noviciate period is to be imposed upon them. And for what reason? These, O monks, hold the doctrine that actions receive their reward, and that our deeds have their results (according to their moral merit).' From this it may be inferred that the chief dogmatic tenet of the primitive Church was the doctrine of *karma*.

It seems, indeed, quite probable that, in the dogmatics of Buddhism, the conception of *nirvāṇa* had been identified, or almost so, with that of annihilation, certain reservations being always made; but that, however far, from the very first, the Buddhists diverted the word *nirvāṇa* from its ordinary acceptation, the ancient definition held its ground—supreme happiness, subject to no re-birth or renewed death.

In spite of the texts which attach a peculiar importance to the conception of '*nirvāṇa* upon earth,' or, as the Brāhmans say, 'of emancipation during this life' (*jīvanmukti*), it would be an unjustifiable limitation of Buddhism and departure from the normal conditions of Indian religions to restrict the word altogether, or, for the most part, to the attainment of that perfect calm denoted by the name of *arhat*-ship, or '*nirvāṇa* upon earth.' *

One text declares: 'The disciple who has put off lust and desire, rich in wisdom, has here on earth attained deliverance from death, repose, nirvāṇa, immortality.' It is undoubtedly right to say that *nirvāṇa* is not merely the hereafter which awaits the emancipated saint, but the perfection which he enjoys in this life. But if the Buddhist aspires to this release from the passions, in which *arhat*-ship consists, it is, above all, because, like the *jīvanmukti*, this is the pledge of true and final *nirvāṇa*. If the monk 'whose thought is emancipated' is said to have attained deliverance from death, it is really by anticipation, for it does not imply that he will not die: 'All life ends in death'; this really signifies that after death he will enter the abode where death is no more.†

It cannot be denied that Buddhism has a very definite theory concerning a hereafter, the nature of which cannot be explained. Whatever the everlasting abode may be, it is the aim and the essence of religion. It may be conceived as a prolongation of the state of the *arhat*. All other good is said to be purely negative, the removal or the alleviation of suffering, but *nirvāṇa* is good absolute. Would this be so, however, if it were nothing more than *arhat*-ship doomed to extinction at death, which, moreover, according to the ancient texts, does not prevent former wicked deeds from receiving their due punishment?

(3) If, then, Buddha at times refuses to answer, it is not in the manner of the evasive sophist who is slippery as an eel. Nor is it that he himself is ignorant or wishes his disciples to remain in ignorance. But the essential point is that his disciples should learn to distinguish profitable knowledge and thoughts. What is the use of indulging in those idle dreams concerning the universe, past or future existence, or *nirvāṇa*? In the same way the author of the *Imitation*, who assuredly subscribed to the Nicene creed, cuts short his meditations on the Trinity: 'What is the use of being trained in the mysteries of the Trinity if you sin against the Trinity?' What can the Buddha tell concerning the manner of life of the emancipated saint, when emancipation can be attained only by ridding the mind of all thought and all desire? He refuses to satisfy useless curiosity, for *nirvāṇa* is a state essentially indefinable.‡

3. *The agnostic statements are formal denials.*—In the two preceding pages tradition has been treated selectively; the theory of the *skandhas* has been laid aside. This theory is found in connexion with almost all the ancient and modern texts. It is consistent with the denial of an Ego. It admits the existence of a phenomenal Ego, which prolongs its existence as long as thought is not 'emancipated.' After emancipation the phenomenal Ego dissolves, the *skandhas* are no longer associated to form the illusory Ego; there no longer exists anything.

The Tathāgata, therefore, does not exist after death; so that the assertions relating to the Tathāgata after death must be understood in the sense of a radical denial, as has been done by the writers of the various dialogues in the *Majjhima* and the *Saṁyutta* above mentioned.

Moreover, if there is no Ego in the emancipated Tathāgata, there is none in Tathāgata living,—there is no Ego in any being. All speculation concerning the future and the past of the Ego is, therefore, absurd, and what is said about the eternity of the world, etc., must be understood as a formal denial. This is the system of the *Mādhyamikas* openly professed in the *Suttantas*.

It seems clear, then, that if we admit the primitive character of the theory of the *skandhas*, and assume the absolute consistency of the early Buddhist speculations, we must ascribe a purely negative value to the Buddha's statements. Thus is obtained a doctrine entirely coherent, identifying *nirvāṇa* with annihilation. All the statements on the one side or the other will find their explanation in practical considerations. On the other hand, the agnostic hypothesis, as far as it concerns the future existence of ordinary men, will be set aside, for the theory of the *skandhas* implies the teaching with regard to actions and transmigration. The question is whether, by such an exegesis, we are not building a new Buddhism on old principles, as the *Mādhyamikas* have confessedly done.

III. Conclusion. — Of the three systems expounded above, the third is the system of a large number of *Suttantas*, that is to say, the orthodox doctrine of the Pāli canon, and of the *Mādhyamikas*. The second is very probably that of popular Buddhism and of the 'pudgalavādins';* while the first has nothing to support it save the texts above cited and the sympathy of several European scholars. The present writer does not conceal his preference for the second. In order to establish it, or rather to reconcile it with traditional assumptions, a comparative estimate is needed. To this let us finally proceed.

It is generally believed that the earliest Bud-

* The present writer will not conceal his opinion that the expression 'nirvāṇa upon earth' (*diṭṭhadhammanibbāna*) possibly conveys a meaning very different from that skilfully pointed out by Carpenter, Rhys Davids, and Oldenberg. It signifies, in contradistinction to the *nirvāṇa* to be attained during a future life, etc. (*upapadyanirvāṇa*, *antarāparinirvāṇa*, etc.), the *nirvāṇa* to be attained at the end of the present existence. With regard to the state of an *arhat*, it should be observed (1) that there is not actual cessation of suffering (*dukkhavūpasama* = nibbāna, *Sumaṅgalavilāsinī* vii. 121), and (2) that it is called 'nirvāṇa with a residue,' in contrast to the real nirvāṇa.

† Cf. Oldenberg, *Buddha*, p. 264 f., whose judgment, according to the present writer, ought to be slightly modified. From the earliest texts we are led to think that the Tathāgata and the saints in general were able to prolong their life for an 'age of the world' [see AGES OF THE WORLD (Buddhist)]. This is very like immortality. On the Vedic beliefs concerning the immortality of the soul and the gradual formation of the doctrine of renewed death (*punarmṛtyu*, *i.e.* transmigration), see A. M. Boyer's very instructive art. in *JA*, 1901, ii. p. 451 ff. He states that ordinary immortality means 'long life after death,' and that everlasting immortality is reserved for the saints (p. 474).

‡ At least so far as human powers of understanding are concerned. The intelligent Buddhist sometimes examines the topics of religion, and sometimes adheres to them without pondering over them: 'These matters are understood only by the Tathāgata.' 'Only the Tathāgata knows, we do not know' (*Bodhisattvabhūmi*).

On the remaining 'non-elucidated topics' it may be said:—

(1) As regards the existence of the Ego and of the universe from eternity, all the texts and the best attested dogmas entirely dismiss the idea that the Ego and the universe are uncaused.

(2) As far as the 'infinity of the universe' is concerned, the text quoted (p. 221) understands by infinity (*ananta*) 'limitless extension in space.' It is very probable that this is the original meaning of the word, and that the word *śaśvata*, 'eternal,' refers to the future as well as the past. In fact, Buddhist cosmology is acquainted with an infinite number of universes. By the term *ananta* the Mādhyamikas mean 'endless duration in time' (cf. *Saṁ. N.* i. 62; Oldenberg, p. 263). *Anta* is 'end' as contrasted with *ādi*, 'beginning.' The orthodox reply is that the world will continue until the last being has attained emancipation. This moment will probably never come. But in each individual 'the end of the world' (*lokasya anta*) may be achieved by the emancipation.

(3) As to the relation between the *jīva* and the *śarīra*, it will be noticed that in the list of the fourteen non-elucidated questions, only the two hypotheses of identity and non-identity are examined. The scholastic doctrine explains *jīva* as equivalent to *sattva*, *pudgala*, *ātman*, permanent principle; and denies its existence, in the course of a discussion of its relations, not with the body (*śarīra*), but with the *skandhas*. It acknowledges also *jīvitendriya*, vital faculty, which is not destroyed with the body in the sense that existence is prolonged by the 'vital faculty' of the succeeding life (except where the re-birth has taken place in certain heavens).

* See above, p. 221b, n. ||, and 222b, n. ‡.

dhism did not lay any claim to originality of doctrine; it shared with the whole of India the belief in the imputation and the retributive effects of action (*karma*), the concatenation of causes, and the possibility of attaining *nirvāṇa*. Nor is there anything to prove that by *nirvāṇa* the Buddhists understood something different from what all others understood by it—a state certainly very difficult to define, but quite distinct from nothingness. Moreover, the Buddha was distinguished, as the texts studied lead us to believe, by a certain contempt for speculation; whence we may conclude that the theory of the *skandhas*, if it existed in germ, had not attained its final form. In the Order there were monks who were opposed, as no doubt the Buddha himself had been, to cosmological or metaphysical speculations; there were also philosophers and 'Abhidharmists,' and it is to these Abhidharmists that we owe the Pāli writings as well as the writings of the Sarvāstivādins.

The question of *nirvāṇa* having been raised, the earliest documents (from Buddha himself ?) had given the reply that nothing could be asserted on the subject, either existence or non-existence, etc.—an answer perhaps childish from the Aristotelian point of view, but sufficiently frank to declare at one and the same time that it is a mystery and that inquiry into it is unnecessary. Such a rejoinder is, in any case, parallel to that suggested with regard to the eternity of the universe; and the former no more seeks to deny the existence of the Tathāgata after death than the latter the actual existence of the universe, or even its eternity. Buddha's only wish, as is said in so many words, was to forbid idle or harmful speculations. It was the philosophers who developed the doctrine of the *skandhas*, the direct result of which is the denial of the Ego (*Suttantas*), and the indirect result the denial of all phenomena in themselves, and the 'universal void' (*Mādhyamikas*). It is no wonder that the philosophers put an entirely new meaning into the old answer:—Nothing can be said of the Buddha after his death, because there is no longer any Buddha, because there never has been a Buddha even during his lifetime; the two things go together, as the *Suttanta* expressly states. It is scarcely conceivable that this was the original Buddhist doctrine. But if it had been, it is most probable that a less ambiguous formula would have been found for its expression.

The Buddhist who accepts the revealed texts as they stand cannot have any doubt as to his choice. He must adhere to the third interpretation, the only one which is orthodox and in harmony with accepted teaching. The choice of the historian of religions is more difficult, for it is modified by the manner in which he conceives the orthodox view to have grown up. The present writer confesses to a reluctance to exercise a definite option, but if a choice be required,—which is by no means the case,—he believes that the second interpretation is to be preferred. L. DE LA VALLÉE POUSSIN.

AGRA, the famous Mughal capital, is situated on the right bank of the R. Jumnā, in the United Provinces of Agra and Oudh. Agra does not appear to have been a sacred place to the Hindus, and its religious interest depends on a splendid series of mosques and tombs. On the left bank of the river stood an ancient Hindu town, of which little now remains but traces of the foundations. The Muhammadans first occupied the place in the time of Sikandar Lodi (A.D. 1505). Bābar, the founder of the Mughal Empire, died here in 1530, but neither he nor his son Humāyūn left any monument of their reigns. Akbar founded the modern city in 1558, and the splendid buildings which now adorn it are the work of himself, his son Jahāngīr, and his grandson Shāhjahān. Akbar built the Agra Fort about 1566, and four years later commenced the erection of his new capital at Fathpur-Sīkrī, 23 miles from Agra, which was occupied for only seventeen years and then abandoned. The site was selected because a famous Musalmān ascetic of the place, Sheikh Salīm Chistī, resided there, and Akbar believed that it was through his intercession that he obtained an heir in Prince Salīm, afterwards known as the Emperor Jahāngīr. At Agra no important religious buildings survive which were the work of Akbar; but to him we owe the splendid Jāmi' Masjid, or 'Cathedral Mosque,' at Fathpur-Sīkrī, and its magnificent gate, the Buland Darwāza, or 'High Portal,' with a touching inscription, which were completed respectively in 1571 and 1602.

Akbar died at Agra in 1605, and was buried at Sikandra, 5 miles from the capital, in a splendid mausoleum, which he himself had commenced. It differs in plan from every other Mughal monument, the design, according to Fergusson, being borrowed from a Hindu, or more probably from a Buddhist, model. Akbar's revolt from orthodox Islām is marked by the fact that the head of his tomb is turned towards the rising sun, not towards Mecca. The original design was modified by Jahāngīr, and the building in its present shape gives the impression of incompleteness. It was finished in 1613. The beautiful tomb of Itmād-ad-daula, Mirza Ghiās Beg, on the left bank of the Jumnā opposite Agra, was the work of his daughter, the famous Nūr Mahal, the favourite queen of the Emperor Jahāngīr. But it is to the Emperor Shāhjahān, the son of Jahāngīr, that we owe the famous buildings which are now the glory of Agra. The **Tāj Mahal** was erected by him as the mausoleum of his beloved wife, Arjumand Banū Begam, better known as Mumtāz-i-Mahal, 'Eminent of the Palace,' who was married to him in 1612, and died in childbirth at Burhānpur in the Deccan in 1630. It was commenced soon after her death, but was not finished till 1648. This splendid structure is too well known to need further description here. Another beautiful religious building erected by Shāhjahān is the famous Motī Masjid, or 'Pearl Mosque,' which was intended to be the Court Chapel of the Palace. To his eldest daughter, Jahānārā Begam, who tended her unhappy father in the troubles of his later years, is due the Jāmi' Masjid, or 'Cathedral Mosque' of Agra, built opposite the Delhi Gate of the Fort. This was completed in 1644. On the accession of Aurangzeb, who deposed his father Shāhjahān in 1658, the architectural history of Agra closed.

LITERATURE.—Fergusson, *Hist. of Indian and E. Architecture*, 569 ff.; Havell, *Handbook to Agra and the Taj*; Führer, *Monumental Antiquities and Inscriptions of the N.W.P. and Oudh*, 53 ff.; Heber, *Journal*, ed. 1861, ii. 9 ff.; Sleeman, *Rambles and Recollections*, ed. V. A. Smith, i. 377 ff.

W. CROOKE.

AGRAULIDS.—Euripides, in *Ion* 23 and 496, speaks of the three 'daughters of Agraulos,' who, according to Apollodorus (iii. § 180), are called Aglauros,* Herse, and Pandrosos. A rich banquet, the *Deipnophoria*, was offered to them together (Bekker, *Anecdota*, i. 239). They danced, Euripides tells us (*l.c.*), on the northern descent of the Athenian Acropolis, on the green meadow before the temple of Athene, beside the Apollo grotto and the seat of Pan, who piped to them. This is the picture which the votive-reliefs represent, some of which have been found on the spot in question (*Athen. Mitth.* iii. 200). In fact, there lay there beside each other the caves of Apollo and Pan under the Erechtheum, and the temple of Athene;

* Aglauros or Agraulos—both forms have been used throughout the article. It will be observed also that in the spelling of proper names the Greek forms have been employed, except in familiar words like Erechtheum, Cecrops.

and there, too, lay the sanctuary of Agraulos Pausanias, i. 18. 2; Herodotus, viii. 53; Jahn-Michaelis, *Arx Athenarum*, Table vii. and xvi. 3). In it the Attic youth swore allegiance to the standard, calling, above all, on Agraulos (Pollux, vii. 106).

Aglauros is thus an ancient and very sacred goddess of Athens. Her name and her connexion with Pandrosos and Herse, the dewy sisters, show that she was a goddess of agriculture. Later she is, in the same way as Pandrosos, so united with Athene that both appear as secondary names of Athene, or that Agraulos is designated the first priestess of Athene. At quite an early date their connexion was very close; the dismal feast of atonement and cleansing sacred to Athene, the *Plynteria* in Thargelion (May), stood also in relation to Agraulos (Hesych.; Bekker, *Anecdota*, i. 270); the *Arrhephoria* or *Hersephoria* was associated with Athene and Herse (Istros in scholium to Aristophanes, *Lysistrate*, 642); and the Pandroseion, with the sacred olive tree of Athene, was closely connected with the Erechtheum (Pausanias, i. 27. 2). Athene herself had once been a goddess of agriculture. Aglauros, however, is also united with Demeter, and is regarded as a secondary name for her (*CIA* iii. 372). This proves that Aglauros was originally an independent goddess, who, however, disappeared more and more in consciousness, and for this reason was united with a greater related goddess. This was the case with many other deities who were originally independent. Their memory was, in the end, preserved only in secondary names of related divinities. The important signification of Aglauros is seen, too, in the fact that at Salamis in Cyprus, where she, along with Athene and Diomedes had a common sanctuary, human sacrifice was down to a late date offered to her (Porphyry, *de Abstinentia*, ii. 54). In Athens there were secret rites in her worship (Athenagoras, *Leg. pro Christ.* 1), which the family of the Praxiergidoi seems to have practised (Töpffer, *Attische Genealogie*, p. 133).

In accordance with the serious nature of the feast of Agraulos, the *Plynteria*, her secret rites, and her human sacrifices, is the legend which has developed out of her worship. This we find in a threefold form. (1) Agraulos, along with Herse and Pandrosos, receives from Athene the boy Erichthonios in a chest, with the command not to open it. Aglauros and Herse open it notwithstanding, and in maddened frenzy cast themselves down from the Acropolis (Pausanias, i. 18. 2; Apollodorus, iii. 189). This is obviously meant, too, to explain the situation of their sanctuaries below the Acropolis, while that of Pandrosos was on the top. (2) Aglauros casts herself from the Acropolis in order that she may, in accordance with an oracle, secure the victory for her country against Eumolpos; for this reason a sanctuary to her was founded there (Philochoros, *Frg.* 14). (3) Aglauros is changed by Hermes into a stone, because, being incited by Athene to jealousy, she had refused him access to her sister (Ovid, *Metam.* ii. 708 ff.).

From all this we have as the result that the Agraulids resemble the Horæ and the Graces. They nurse the child Erichthonios, the seed-corn, entrusted to them by Athene, just as Demeter does Triptolemos. In the month Thargelion (May), when the dew ceases and the harvest begins, Aglauros dies.

Aglauros appears in the tradition twice: (1) as the mother of the Agraulids, daughter of Actæus; (2) as their oldest sister, and daughter of Cecrops. Connected with Aglauros are Alkippe, her daughter by Ares, who was seduced by Halirrhothios the son of Poseidon, and Keryx, her son by Hermes, the head of the Eleusinian family of the Kerykes, who is, however, also called the son of Pandrosos or Herse (Töpffer, *Attische Genealogie*, 81 ff.).

LITERATURE.—Preller-Robert, *Griech. Mythologie*, i. 199 ff.; Robert in *Commentationes Mommsen.* 143 ff.

E. BETHE.

AGRICULTURE.—I. Until recently the theory was held that the human race passed from the life of the hunter to that of the nomad shepherd, and from that again to the life of the tiller of the ground. As a sweeping generalization it is no longer possible to hold this theory; that it is not altogether untrue is shown by what is happening to the Bashkir Tatars at the present day. In their case agriculture has been forced upon them by the danger of starvation. Russian civilization has encroached upon them from the north and west, and the Ural Cossacks from the east, so that the area of their pasture lands, and, as a consequence, the amount of live stock they are able to maintain, have much diminished. Before resorting to agriculture themselves, they employed Russians to farm for them, and farmed part of their land on the *métayage* system. But when the virgin soil is exhausted, the master, who loves the easy life of the shepherd and disdains the hard toil of agriculture, is no longer able to pay for hired labour, and perforce must himself put his hand to the plough (Wallace, *Russia*, new ed. i. p. 265 ff.). The same observation was made regarding the Tatars of the Crimea in 1794 (Pallas, *Travels*, Eng. ed. 1802–3, ii. p. 383). In those parts of the world, however, which are best known to us, there is evidence of a settled agricultural population from the earliest period. Not only in Neolithic times, but from the earlier Stone Age, there is evidence, supplied largely by the excavations of Ed. Piette in various cave-shelters in France, that agricultural plants, and animals at least partially domesticated, were well known (see DOMESTICATION). In Egypt and in Babylon there is evidence of agriculture going back, at a moderate calculation, to the early part of the third millennium B.C., and possibly to a much earlier period. Mesopotamia is the only area for which there is good evidence that some kinds of common cereals grow wild [de Candolle, *Origin of Cultivated Plants*, 1884, p. 358 (common wheat); p. 364 (spelt)]. It is in countries with a rich alluvial soil, like Egypt and Mesopotamia, that we should *a priori* expect agriculture to begin. In Egypt a primitive agriculture along the banks of the Nile would be possible merely by casting seed upon the mud left behind by the river when it subsides after flood. Agriculture in the earliest times was probably thus practised before the invention of the plough, the seed being left to sink into the soft mud, or, as represented on Egyptian monuments, being trodden in by cattle.

It is, however, to be remembered that when we consider primitive agriculture, we must discard all generally accepted notions as to its practice. Agriculture at the present day, as practised in most countries of Europe, may be defined as (1) the regular cultivation by the plough and other well-known implements, and with the addition of manure, of (2) definite areas of (3) arable land, held as (4) freehold or (5) on a legally defined tenancy, (6) such cultivation being for the most part in the hands of males. But if we may deduce primitive methods from the practice of such tribes in modern times as combine some agriculture with hunting, and appear to be only in the first stages of agricultural development, primitive cultivation preceded all implements except those of stone and wood. Thus the Navajos and many tribes of New Mexico, who grow [Indian] 'corn, beans, pumpkins, melons, and other vegetables, and also some wheat,' and make some attempts at irrigation, dibble the ground: 'with a short sharp-pointed stick small holes are dug in the ground, into which they drop the seeds, and no further care is given to the crop except to keep it partially free from weeds' (Bancroft, *Native Races of Pacific States*, i. p. 489; cf. H. Ling Roth, *Sarawak*, i. p. 402). In Northern Honduras at an earlier period, the natives, according to Herrera, cleared the ground with stone axes, and turned the sod by main strength with a forked pole or with sharp wooden spades (Bancroft, i. p. 719). Dibbling alone is found sufficient in the Amazon area, the ground never being turned up or manured (Wallace, *Travels on the Amazon*, p. 335). In Melanesia, where horticulture rather than agriculture is the form of cultivation, and has reached a high degree of excellence, adzes of stone or shell were used before the introduction of metals. In the New Hebrides and in most of the Solomon Islands the natives use stone; 'the Santa Cruz people, Torres islanders, and Banks' islanders used shell, for adzes the giant clam shell' (Codrington, *The Melanesians*, p. 313). Stone adzes, which may have been used by the early inhabitants of France, were found by Piette (*L'Anthropologie*, vii. p. 1 ff.), and stone sickles have been discovered in many places. Early Egyptian stone adzes are figured by De Morgan (*Recherches sur les origines de l'Egypte*, ii. p. 96).

Nor are definite areas of arable land held by individuals. The savage is regularly communistic in his ideas; the land tilled belongs in the first instance to the tribe, though, when a man reclaims virgin forest, what he reclaims is his own heritable property (*Sarawak*, i. p. 419 ff.). Areas that are reclaimed from the primeval forest by the joint efforts of the community are naturally regarded as joint property. How this is done is well described by Wallace (*Travels on the Amazon*, p. 217): 'Imagine the trees of a virgin forest cut down so as to fall across each other in every conceivable direction. After lying a few months they are burnt; the fire, however, only consumes the leaves and fine twigs and branches; all the rest remains entire, but blackened and charred. The mandioca is then planted without any further preparation.' If the ground continues to be cultivated and roughly weeded, the trees soon rot, so that they can be removed; grass then springs up, which, if kept grazed, remains open (Wallace, p. 334). In other countries, however, it is not so; in Sarawak new land of this nature has to be planted every year, as the tough grass which succeeds a crop of paddy is too difficult for the Dayak to break up till the land has once more become jungle (*Sarawak*, i. p. 397 ff.). The landholding systems of the peoples of antiquity and the Teutonic three-field system are descended from a similar system of communistic landholdings (Maine, *Village Communities*, Lect. iii.).

But even wandering tribes may engage to some extent in agriculture. Waitz (*Anthropologie der Naturvölker*, vol. i. p. 406) observes that in North America such tribes would plant a crop, wait to gather it, and go on again. And, even where they are more settled, tribes must from time to time change their habitations, because, as they do not manure their lands, these gradually become exhausted.

From all this it is clear that five of our conditions of modern cultivation (p. 226b) do not hold for primitive times, as illustrated by the last survivors of uncivilized races. Nor is the sixth point more true. Primitive agriculture is not altogether, nor to any large extent, in the hands of males. As von den Steinen remarks of the Bakairi of Central Brazil, it is woman that has invented agriculture. Its beginnings, no doubt, arose where hunting and fishing were difficult or unproductive. Just as we have seen that it is with the greatest reluctance that a pastoral people becomes agricultural, so is it with the change from hunting to agriculture. Amongst the most primitive of the native tribes of America it is noticeable that where game is scanty, or the men are ineffective hunters, agriculture is most developed. Dibbling with a pointed stick and hoeing with a stone axe were possible for the women and children in the neighbourhood of their huts, while the men wandered farther afield as hunters or on the war-path. Hence agriculture reaches an advanced stage before the women hand over the greater part of the operations to the men. The Dayak men of Sarawak help in sowing the seed and in reaping the harvest; the hard intermediate toil of weeding is left to the women and children (*Sarawak*, i. p. 405). Amongst the South Sea islanders local custom settles the respective shares of the men and women in the garden work (Codrington, p. 303). If a man has another occupation, he regularly leaves a large part of the agricultural work to the women, as may still be seen in the Peloponnese and elsewhere in Eastern Europe and in the West Highlands of Scotland. In more advanced parts of the British Isles it is only the rapid development of agricultural machinery in the last forty years that has gradually banished women from field-work. But the agricultural duties of primitive woman also brought her important rights. Her labour gave her a right to the soil, which, as the importance of agriculture became more marked, brought her many other privileges in its train, and these privileges had the greatest influence upon the history of family relations (Grosse, *Die Formen der Familie und die Formen der Wirthschaft*, p. 159 ff.). Superstition also recommended leaving agriculture in the hands of women. 'When the women plant maize,' said an Indian to the Jesuit Gumilla, 'the stalk produces two or three ears. Why? Because women know how to produce children. They only know how to plant corn to ensure its germinating. Then let them plant it; they know more than we know' (J. E. Harrison, *Prolegomena to the Study of Greek Religion*, p. 272, quoting from Payne, *History of the New World*, ii. p. 7). This side of agriculture has been worked out in much greater detail by E. Hahn in *Demeter und Baubo* and elsewhere. (For Africa, see the references in Jevons, *Introduction to the History of Religion*, p. 240).

2. **The earliest cultivated plants** are not easy to define. The carvings on reindeer horns figured by Piette in his *L'Art pendant l'âge du Renne* (plates 17 and 14), and from him by Hoops (*Waldbäume und Kulturpflanzen*, pp. 278–9), come from Meso-Palæolithic strata, and undoubtedly represent ears of corn. From a late Palæolithic stratum representations of an ear of winter barley (*escourgeon*), as still grown in France, have been discovered (Piette, in Hoops, *op. cit.* p. 280). In the rock-shelter of Mas-d'Azil, on the left bank of the Arise, Piette found in a transitional stratum between Palæolithic and Neolithic a small heap of short oval grains of wheat, the precise character of which could not be determined, as, on being exposed, they turned to dust (Hoops, p. 281). From another transitional stratum at Campigny, in the north of France, the print of a grain of barley has been found on a potsherd. From this period stones for grinding corn have also been discovered. From the Neolithic pile-dwellings at Wangen, on the Lake of Constance, 'two varieties of wheat and the two-rowed barley were distinctly recognized both in whole ears and in the separate grain, the latter in quantities that could be measured in bushels' (Munro, *Lake Dwellings of Europe*, p. 497). Before the end of the Stone Age three species of wheat (*Triticum vulgare, dicoccum, monococcum*), probably three species of barley (*Hordeum hexastichum*,—this was the most widely spread,—*distichum, tetrastichum*), and two species of millet (*Panicum miliaceum* and *italicum*), were grown in Europe—naturally in greater variety in the south than in the north of Central Europe. Not only was flax cultivated, but weaving was practised [the fabrics are figured in Forrer and Messikommer's *Praehistorische Varia* (Zürich, 1889), [plates iv. and x.]. Vegetables—lentils, peas, beans, parsnips, and carrots—and poppies were cultivated, as well as vines and fruit trees (Heer, *Pflanzen der Pfahlbauten*; and, more recent and more general, Hoops as above, and Buschan, *Vorgeschichtliche Botanik*). The precise characters of the grain figured on early Egyptian monuments cannot, it is said, be identified. But both in Egypt and in Chaldæa it early became the practice to express the value of land in terms of wheat (Maspero, *L'Orient classique*, i. p. 761, n. 2). As already pointed out, botanists regard Mesopotamia and the countries bordering upon it as probably the original home of wheat and barley. As the earliest cultiva-

tion of them in Europe appears in the warmer intervals between successive ages of ice, in the earlier of which ice probably extended as far as the Alps, in the latter to the latitude of London and Berlin, they clearly must have been introduced from the Mediterranean basin. It is hardly to be expected that evidence of grain cultivation will be found in the British Isles or other parts of Northern Europe in strata corresponding to those in which Piette has found them in the south of France, for, as Nehring has shown (*Über Tundren und Steppen der Jetzt- und Vorzeit*, 1890), a period when these countries consisted of *tundras* and steppes like those of modern Siberia must be postulated as existing for some considerable time after the end of the Ice Age. In such an area, where ice still exists below the surface, agriculture would be impossible. Importation, moreover, from Asia through Russia would have been equally impossible at this period, the Caspian then extending much farther to the north and west, while the northern Ægean did not exist (see Ratzel's map in *SSGW*, 1900). From the earliest literature of the Indo-Germanic peoples—the Vedas—it is clear that, though the early Hindus of this stock had large flocks and herds, they also practised agriculture. But the meaning of the word *yava-s* which they apply to grain, and which is etymologically identical with the Greek ζειά, 'spelt,' is hard to define. Its modern representative in Persia, Baluchistan, and India seems always to mean barley. A word for *corn*, however, is very likely to vary its meaning according to latitude. Thus, in English, *corn* means to an Englishman wheat, to a Scotsman oats, to an American of the United States maize. The same word amongst other peoples of the same stock is variously applied, meaning to a North German rye, and in Scandinavia barley. The Greeks knew and cultivated wheat, barley, and two kinds of millet. In the classical period the Romans cultivated the same cereals, though the poets write of *far*, 'spelt,' as being the grain which formed the food of the early Romans. The Roman word for wheat, *triticum*, is in origin an adjective, and must have originally meant the threshed or milled grain, from *tero*, 'rub, pound.' Oats and rye are not suitable for warm countries, and were not cultivated by the Greeks and Romans. Oats (βρόμος) and rye (βρίζα) were both known to the Greeks from Thrace. From the former, Dionysos, who came into Greece from Thrace, got the epithet of βρόμιος, as being in his northern home a god of beer, not, as in Greece, of wine (J. E. Harrison, *Prolegomena*, p. 416). Schrader (in Hehn's *Kulturpflanzen und Haustiere*[7], p. 553) quotes Dieuches, a doctor of the 4th cent. B.C., for oat meal, which was regarded as superior to barley meal. In both Greece and Rome, probably, barley played a great part in early times. It is to be noticed that *far* is etymologically identical with the English *bere* and *bar*-ley. The most plausible explanation of the name of the Greek goddess Persephone or Pherrephatta (the name occurs in a great variety of forms in the different Greek dialects) was 'the barley-killer,' the first element in the name being from the same root as *far* and *bere*. This harmonizes well with the functions of Persephone, who is queen of the under world during the four months which elapse between the planting of the autumn-sown grain and spring.

3. Implements.—The operations of the farmer vary according to the season of the year, and the character of the implements varies according to the nature of the operations. For Europe the earliest description is given by Homer. On the shield of Achilles four rural scenes are depicted, three of which represent the seasons when the farmer's life is busiest (*Iliad*, xviii. 541 ff.). On the first is shown a rich fallow in which many ploughmen are driving their teams this way and that: *many* because, according to Professor Ridgeway's explanation of the scene (*JHS* vi. p. 336), the land that is being ploughed is the common land of the community, and the ploughing must be begun by all the holders at the same time—an ancient practice which is still commemorated in England by Plough Monday, the first Monday after Twelfth Night. The field is broad, and is for triple ploughing (εὐρεῖαν τρίπολον, 542). When the ploughers reach the headland (τέλσον ἀρούρης), a man comes forward and offers them a drink. 'They then turn their team along the furrow, eager to reach the headland of the deep fallow.' This eagerness is sometimes explained, rather naïvely, as arising from the prospect of a drink at the other end. More probably the emphasis rests upon the epithet *deep*. A fallow speedily becomes covered with grass and weeds, which, with the very ineffective plough that is still used in Greece, makes ploughing a hard task, even for a strong man. In modern times, even with the best plough, the breaking up of old pasture (which with improved implements would be a task of a similar nature) is a very difficult matter. The threefold ploughing was required partly, no doubt, because the ancient plough was so ineffective. In Egypt, where the ploughing was done in a much more yielding soil, a man is represented (not in the earliest art) as preceding the plough with a mattock, for the plough has no coulter. That Homer looked upon ploughing fallow as very hard work is clear from other passages, in which we are told that 'he who has been holding the plough (πηκτὸν ἄροτρον) in a fallow all day is glad when the sun goes down and he can hie him home to supper, though his knees totter beneath him as he goes' (*Od.* xiii. 31–34). The oxen in the yoke also feel the strain (*Il.* xiii. 705). Hence, with the development of the plough and of a system of tillage, agriculture of necessity passed more into the hands of men. Moreover, when a pastoral people turns to agriculture, it objects to women having to do with the cattle. 'Among the Bechuanas the men never allow the women to touch their cattle. The ploughs cannot be used except by the help of cattle, and therefore the men have now to do the heavy work' (E. Holub, *JAI* x. p. 11). In countries where cultivation is carried on in gardens rather than in fields, the hoe or mattock remains the regular implement of cultivation. Such countries are the South Sea Islands and a great part of China. So also in the world of the gods, Demeter handed over agriculture, so far as ploughing was concerned, to Triptolemus, who, as the Homeric hymn to Demeter tells us, till then was but a prince (θεμιστοπόλος βασιλεύς, 473) of Eleusis. Henceforth his name, whatever its original meaning, is identified with τρίπολος, the word for the triple ploughing. It is, however, probably only Athenian pride that makes ploughing take its rise in the little plain of Eleusis. In such little plains in the Hebrides, the *caschrom*, the little crooked spade, is hardly yet extinct. The plough, in all probability, took its origin in larger areas with deeper soil. Such an area was Bœotia, from which comes the earliest European poem on agriculture, Hesiod's *Works and Days*. A still better example of an area suited for the plough is Thessaly, the bed of an earlier inland sea, drained when the Peneus cut its way through the vale of Tempe. Eleusis had traditions of a connexion with the far north of Greece and Thrace, and it is significant that the word *Triptolemus* by its *pt* instead of *p* preserves a feature which, in historical names, is specially characteristic of Northern Greece.

It is unnecessary to suppose that the *plough* was invented only in one place. Its simplest form is a forked stick with one of the limbs cut off short. The stump with its sharp point forms the sole and the cutting edge of the plough, the long branch forms the handle. In this form, pushed along by the handle, the plough is able only to make a shallow groove. The next stage in its development is either to find a tree with two branches so arranged that one may form the handle * and the other penetrate the ground, while the trunk forms the pole, or to attach to the simpler forked stick another branch at right angles. This forms the pole, and by means of it some powerful pulling force may be applied. This force may either be boys, as in an Egyptian representation of ploughing, or some of the lower animals,—cows, bullocks, buffaloes, or mules. In Egyptian art the ass is never represented in the plough; but Varro (i. 20. 4) says the ass was used in Campania. The Greeks preferred the mule to the ox as speedier, according to Homer (*Il.* x. 352–353). In Sarawak a wooden plough is drawn by a buffalo. Its action is like that of a pointed stick dragged through the land to a depth of four inches (*Sarawak*, i. p. 422). The Greeks had not discarded the plough made of a forked stick (αὐτόγυον) in Hesiod's time, though both he and Homer know a more elaborate form, the mortised plough (πηκτὸν ἄροτρον). Hesiod (*W. and D.* 432–434) advises the farmer to have one of each kind in case of accidents. The more primitive form is to be of holm-oak, which is fitted into a shoe (ἔλυμα), to the front end of which the share, when it had been discovered, was attached. In Hesiod's time the pole was connected to the rest of the plough by wooden pegs; in the Egyptian plough it is simply bound fast by a rope (for full details of the Egyptian plough, see an article by H. Schäfer in the *Annual of the British School at Athens*, x. p. 127 ff.). The wood for the plough is to be cut in the autumn, because it is then less likely to suffer from dry-rot. A piece of the proper shape may not be easy to find. The pole is to be of bay or elm, the shoe of oak. Hesiod is a cautious farmer, and wishes everything to be steady. His yoke of oxen are to be nine years old, his ploughman forty. Such oxen will not be restive, such a ploughman will attend to his work and not gaze after his comrades (444).

To a similar or even less advanced stage of civilization belong the primitive ploughs which are represented in rock drawings on the borders of France and Italy and in Sweden. In these the plough consists of (1) a bent branch to which (2) the pole is attached. Near the end of the pole a cross-bar is attached which crosses the foreheads of the oxen, and, as in ancient Greece and Egypt, and largely in the East still, is fixed to the horns (see the figures in Sophus Müller's *Urgeschichte Europas*, p. 147). There are no reins; as is shown in one of the scenes represented, a second man leads the oxen. By the time of the Roman writers the form of the plough had developed considerably. Cato and Varro give no details, but the elder Pliny was acquainted with the coulter and with several varieties of ploughshare. In his time a recent improvement had been made in Rhætia by adding two wheels. A plough of this kind is figured by Dr. E. B. Tylor (*JAI* x. p. 79). As he says, the modern English plough 'improves upon this rather in details of construction and material than in essential principle.' But the descendant of this is the 'grubber,' or the drill plough; the ordinary plough arises from the first type by the addition of a mould-board.

Needless to say, this and all other operations of husbandry were regulated by the stars. Certain days were fortunate for certain operations, and others not, as is expounded in the latter part of Hesiod's *Works and Days*, and is observed in all countries.

The earliest form of harrowing is, no doubt, represented by the man with a mattock, who follows the Egyptian ploughman and breaks the clods. 'Let the slave who follows a little behind,' says Hesiod of the same practice in his country, 'give the birds some trouble by covering the seed.' Pliny says the Egyptians once trod in the seed with swine (xviii. 47). In Egyptian art only sheep are so represented (Erman, *Life in Ancient Egypt*, p. 429), though Herodotus (ii. 14) says that below Memphis swine were regularly so used. On the Isthmus of Panama it is possible to dispense with harrowing, because the brushwood is left lying on the ground, and the seeds are scattered amongst it (Bancroft, i. p. 759). In St. Kilda, Martin observed that the harrow, which was entirely of wood, had teeth only at the front end, because wood was so scarce. The place of others was taken by 'long tangles of sea-ware tied to the harrow by the small ends; the roots hanging loose behind scatter the clods broken by the wooden teeth' (*A Voyage to St. Kilda* (1753), p. 18). Pliny (xviii. 20) recognizes both a hurdle and a mattock (*rastrum*) for this purpose.

The scene upon the shield of Achilles to represent summer is the cutting of the corn on a prince's private estate (τέμενος βασιλήιον, 550). Some were cutting with *sickles* (δρεπάνας), others were engaged in binding into sheaves the handfuls which boys brought them from the reapers. Similar scenes are represented in Egyptian art, where the sickle was serrated. Such serrated sickles go back to the Stone Age (Flinders Petrie, *Illahun, Kahun, and Gurob*, Pl. vii. Fig. 27). The early Greek sickle must also have been serrated, as χαράσσω is the verb used of sharpening it in Hesiod (see *Works and Days*, 387, with Paley's note). Some Egyptian figures are represented as pulling the grain up by the roots. This may have been to avoid wasting the straw, which, according to Pliny (xviii. 47), was only about a cubit long, owing to the dry sandy subsoil. In St. Kilda, according to Martin, the corn was pulled up by the roots in order to have it as long as possible for thatch. As a rule, in ancient times, most of the straw was left on the ground, and this when set on fire or ploughed in helped to manure the ground. Pliny observed (xviii. 72) that the stubble was left long except where straw was required for thatch or for fodder.

Between seedtime and harvest in most countries *hoeing* has to be done. Where the crops have to be hoed, this work is often left to women. In Greek agriculture, at least of the 5th and later centuries B.C., this work was done by men, and to leave it undone was regarded as very bad farming (Xenophon, *Oeconomicus*, xvii. 12; Theocritus, x. 14).

For all the operations of husbandry a *cart* or waggon is of importance. The employment of the cart is slower in developing than that of the plough, partly because extended use of it demands good roads. The prudent Hesiod advises the farmer to have his cart ready in good time against the spring, 'for it is easy to say, "Let me have a pair of oxen and a cart," and it is easy to answer, "No, my oxen have field work to do." The man wise in his own conceit says he will make a cart for himself, poor fool, and does not even know that there are a hundred pieces of wood in a cart, which he must take care to have in store by him beforehand' (*op. cit.* 453–457). Yet in some parts of the British Islands which are now famous for agriculture there were few or no carts as late as the middle of the 18th century. In Aberdeenshire, crops were even then carried from the field and manure from the farmyard in *currachs*, a sort of wicker panniers hung on either side of a *crook saddle*, while corn was taken to the mill or the seaport in sacks upon horseback (Pratt, *Buchan*[2], p. 19). Pennant observed in Caithness that the beasts of burden were the women. 'They turn their patient backs to the dunghills, and receive in their *keizes*, or baskets, as much as their lords and masters think fit to fling in with their pitchforks, and then trudge to the fields in droves of sixty or seventy' (*Tour in Scotland in 1769*, 3rd ed. p. 168). The first mechanical method of transporting heavy weights was, no doubt, upon a sled, a rough frame of wood with stout cross-bars, or a hurdle. A good specimen of the Egyptian sled for carrying corn-sacks is figured in H. Schäfer's article in the *Annual of the British School at Athens*, x. p. 139). Varro tells us that manure was taken to the fields upon hurdles for the purpose (*crates stercorariae*, i. 22, 3). This was an old Roman practice, as the list of necessaries for a farm which he is quoting is taken from Cato (*de Agricultura*, x.). Cato, however, also provides three asses with panniers for this purpose (*asinos ornatos clitellarios qui stercus vectent tris*), so that the *crates*, as they are mentioned next to the *irpex*, a kind of rake, may have been used for harrowing in the manure after it was spread upon the fields.

A cart without wheels was formerly widely used in the mountainous parts of Britain, and is still used in Ireland, the shafts being continued to form the frame, with their ends resting on the ground. The body of the cart was formed by two semicircular bows of wood, the ends of which were fastened to the shaft poles. These bows were kept in position by a bar running between their apices. The shaft poles were kept in position by cross-bars, and the bows also had cross-pieces; so that the shape of the body was that of a tilt-cart (these are illustrated in Dr. Haddon's *Study of Man*, 165 ff.).

A great advance in the development of the cart is marked by the introduction of wheels. The early history of the wheel is not clear. As, in the early heavy waggon, the axle and wheels turn together, it is obvious that wheels and axle in one block might have developed out of rollers. This view is adopted by Dr. Tylor (*JAI* x. p. 79), and doubtfully by Dr. Haddon (*Study of Man*, p. 173). Such a primitive arrangement is still to be found in Portugal. On the other hand, Professor Ridgeway contends (*Origin and Influence of the Thoroughbred Horse*, p. 488) that the war chariot with spoked wheels is earlier than the ox cart, which

* In Sir C. Fellows' sketch (*Journal written during an Excursion in Asia Minor*, p. 71), the stump is the part on which the share is fitted. The same kind of plough is still used in some of the Greek islands.

was modelled upon it. The body of the cart was a creel of wicker work, which could be removed at will. Of farm carts the Romans had two kinds—two-wheeled (*plaustrum*) and four-wheeled (*plaustrum maius*). Since they are termed *stridentia plaustra* (Virgil, *Georgics*, iii. 536), it is evident that they moved with much creaking, like the 'groaning' or 'singing' carts of Spain and Portugal (Haddon, *Study of Man*, p. 186 ff.). The noise is caused by 'the friction of the axle against the wedges in the floor of the waggon which keep it in its place' (Haddon, p. 189). The cattle were harnessed to the pole by a yoke which was fastened by a pin near the end of the pole, and lashed tightly with a thong or cord. Some kind of strap was fastened across under the neck of the animals. The modern forms are figured by Sir C. Fellows (*Journal*, p. 71), the ancient Egyptian by Schäfer in the article already mentioned.

4. Since in the countries round the Eastern Mediterranean the corn harvest comes on in May and June, the industry of autumn is the ingathering of tree fruit and the making of wine and olive oil, just as the making of cider is a characteristic autumn occupation of England, and on the Saxon font at Burnham Deepdale, in Norfolk (which has twelve scenes representing the months), is taken as the typical occupation for October. Hence the vintage is taken for the autumn scene upon the shield of Achilles. The young men and maidens carry the fruit in wicker baskets, a lad plays on the lyre and sings to them, and they join in singing and dancing (*Il.* xviii. 561 ff.). The vine grows wild round the Mediterranean, and in Asia as far as the Himalayas. Grape seeds have been found in pile-dwellings of the later Stone Age in Italy, and of at least the Bronze Age in Switzerland, and vine leaves have been discovered in the tufa round Montpellier and Meyrargue in Provence (de Candolle, *Cultivated Plants*, p. 192). The use of wine was probably introduced to the Greeks from Asia Minor or Thrace. Hesiod contemplates that his farmer may make a voyage after harvest, but adjures him not to wait for the new wine, in case of bad weather (*op. cit.* 663 ff.). Such a voyage from Bœotia would probably be to Lesbos, or the adjacent mainland, which was famous for its wine. According to all tradition, the use of wine and the culture of the grape were later in Italy, still more so in the countries north of the Alps (Schrader, *Reallexikon*, *s.v.* 'Wein').

The last of the crops which had more than a local importance was that of the *olive*. According to de Candolle (*Origin of Cultivated Plants*, p. 283), 'its prehistoric area probably extended from Syria towards Greece.' At Athens, till the development of the mines at Laurium, the trade in olive oil was the only important export industry, the soil being thin and ill adapted for agriculture. The olive, indeed, was supposed to be the special gift of the patron goddess Athene, and the sacred olive trees were protected from harm by heavy penalties. No doubt in early times such heavy penalties alone protected all produce, whether of domesticated plants or animals, against the instinct of primitive savagery to seize it for immediate use without regard to future loss (see TABU and TOTEMISM). The olive, as the Latin form of the word shows, spread from Greece to Italy, and from Italy again to the north of Europe. It is clear from Cato and Varro that in their time the vine and olive crops were regarded as of much greater importance than the growing of cereals. This was the result of the second Punic war. Hannibal devastated rural Italy; the agricultural population had to flee to the towns for protection, and stay there for half a generation while the war lasted, and the farmers themselves were drafted into the army. When the war was over, the rustics had no capital wherewith to restore their farms; the State was unable to help them, and the wealthy quietly annexed the derelict farms of the poor. With the development of an Empire outside Italy, corn came in payment of taxes from the subject States. With curious lack of economic insight, Gaius Gracchus, who was anxious to restore the rural population, caused this imported corn to be sold at less than its market value, with the result of making it impossible to grow corn for sale in Italy.

It is impossible to enter here into the more advanced departments of agriculture, the use of *irrigation*, which developed early in Egypt and Mesopotamia, and which is also recognized by Homer; and the cultivation of fruit trees by pruning and grafting. Wallace observed (*Travels*, p. 335) that the natives on the Amazon never pruned or did anything else to their fruit trees. On the other hand, the labourers imported from Melanesia into Queensland were much surprised to find black men who had no garden. In the Melanesian islands, in Sarawak, and elsewhere, irrigation has long been practised (Codrington, *The Melanesians*, p. 303; *Sarawak*, i. p. 406).

After the corn harvest was finished, the corn had to be *threshed*. This was done by oxen treading it out on the hard threshing-floor [for the making of which Varro and Virgil (*Georgics*, i. 178–180) give careful directions], or by dragging over it a sledge or heavy toothed plank, as was the Roman practice, and as is still done in Asia Minor (Fellows, *Travels*, p. 51). (Prehistoric methods were probably much simpler, the corn possibly being stripped from the ear by hand). The corn was stored for winter use in carefully plastered underground chambers, so as to escape, as far as possible, the ravages of vermin. As we have seen, corn was stored even in the Stone Age.

The last task in the preparation of corn for food prior to cooking it was the *making of it into meal or flour*. Piette found rubbing stones in a late stratum of the Palæolithic Age (Hoops, p. 280), though these were not necessarily used for corn. Bancroft's description (i. 653) of the methods of the aborigines of Yucatan probably represents approximately very ancient practice. The grain is first soaked, and then bruised on the rubbing stone and wetted occasionally till it becomes soft paste. From the rubbing stone develop the pestle and mortar of later times, which are often mentioned in the life of ancient Athens. But the handmill, with its heavy under stone and its lighter upper stone, which turns upon the other, goes back to the Stone Age (Hoops, p. 301 f.; Schrader, *Reallexikon*, *s.v.* 'Mahlen'). As they are often found in the graves of women, it is evident that this also was one of the duties of early woman, as indeed is clear from the literature of all countries from the earliest times.

LITERATURE.—For Mesopotamia and Egypt the representations in art: **Perrot-Chipiez** for both; the illustrations in **Wilkinson** (the text is out of date) and **Lepsius**, *Denkmäler aus Aegypten*; and the books mentioned in the text. For Greece: **Hesiod**, and incidentally **Homer**; **Theophrastus**, *Hist. of Plants*, etc, and *de Causis Plantarum*; with many allusions in **Aristotle**, **Xenophon**, and elsewhere (the *Geoponica* belongs to the late Roman Empire, but contains information from earlier sources). For Rome: **Cato** (its present is not the original form of the work); **Varro**, who professes to have read Phœnician, Greek, and Latin works on the subject, and was himself competent; **Virgil**, who, as a farmer's son, and himself a farmer, writes in the *Georgics* with knowledge and interest, though not, of course, in technical fashion [the *Moretum* attributed to him gives an excellent account of a day in the life of a simple rustic]; **Columella**, elaborate but inexact; **Palladius**, the greater part of whose work is arranged as a farmer's year, and had much influence in the Middle Ages. Detailed accounts of Greek and Roman agriculture will be found in **Baumeister's** *Denkmäler des klass. Altertums*, *s.v.* 'Ackerbau;' Smith's *Gr.-Rom. Ant.*, and Pauly, *s.v.* 'Ackerbau' [this, though old, still contains much that is useful]. The agriculture of the Semitic nations is treated in the various Bible Dictionaries; Indian agriculture in the Vedic Age by Zimmer, *Altindisches Leben.* General accounts, specially for the Indo-Germanic peoples, are given, with full references to literature, in Schrader's *Sprachvergleichung und Urgeschichte* [a new edition is in course of publication] and *Reallexikon der indogermanischen Altertumskunde.* Cf. also Behlen, *Der Pflug und das Pflügen bei den Römern und in Mittel Europa in vorgeschichtlicher Zeit* (Dillenburg, 1904); Meringer, *Indo-germanische Forschungen,* xvi. 183 ff., xvii. 100 ff. (with many illustrations). The cultivated plants are treated by de Candolle (*Origin of Cultivated Plants,* 1884), by Hehn (*Kulturpflanzen und Hausthiere*[7] (ed. by Schrader, 1902), and by Hoops (*Waldbäume und Kulturpflanzen im germanischen Altertum,* 1905). These works give full references to other literature. The origins of agriculture are treated also by Hahn, *Die Haustiere,* 1896, *Demeter und Baubo,* 1896, and *Das Alter der wirthschaftlichen Kultur der Menschheit,* 1905; by Sophus Müller, *Urgeschichte Europas,* 1905; and by Hirt, *Die Indogermanen,* i., 1905. Mucke's book (*Urgeschichte des Ackerbaues und der Viehzucht: Eine neue Theorie,* 1898) must be used with caution.

P. GILES.

AHERIA (Skr. *akheṭika,* 'a hunter').—A Dravidian tribe of hunters, fowlers, and thieves, found in North India to the number of 35,447, of whom the majority inhabit the United Provinces and the Panjāb. Their religion is of the animistic type, and they worship a host of minor gods or godlings, and spirits not included in the orthodox Hindu pantheon. Some, who are more influenced by Hinduism, follow Devī, the Mother-goddess; but in the United Provinces their tribal god is Mekhāsura (Skr. *mesha-āsura,* 'the ram spirit'), of which they can give no account, but which probably represents a primitive form of theriolatry. Gūga or Zāhir Pīr, the famous saint round whom has been collected a curious cycle of legend, is worshipped by the agency of a Musalmān officiant (Crooke, *Popular Religion,* i. 211 f.). Another Muhammadan saint worshipped by them is the Miyāṅ or Mīrāṅ Sāḥib of Amroha in the Morādābād district, of whom also strange legends are told (Shea-Troyer, *Dabistān,* iii. 235; Crooke, *op. cit.* i. 217). In a lower stage of animism is Jakhiya, who is apparently a deified sweeper, a member of which caste attends his shrine. To him a pig is sacrificed, and the sweeper officiant rubs a little of the blood upon the foreheads of children to repel evil spirits. Barai and Chāmar, two of the common village godlings, are also worshipped. To the latter the offering is a cake of wheat, but in serious cases a ram is offered, the flesh of which is then and there consumed in the presence of the god. It is a curious fact that the Aherias have appropriated as their patron saint Vālmīki, the mythical compiler of the epic of the Rāmāyaṇa. The sacrifices to the tribal godlings are generally performed by a member of the family which makes the offering, not by a regular priest. In some cases where the victim is not actually slain, it is released after blood has been drawn from its ear. The Aherias stand in great fear of the ghosts of the dead; and when they cremate a corpse, they fling pebbles in the direction of the pyre as they return home, in order to prevent the spirit from accompanying them.

LITERATURE.—Crooke, *Tribes and Castes of the North-Western Provinces and Oudh,* 1896, i. 45 ff., *Popular Religion and Folklore of Northern India,* new ed. 1896, ii. 57.

W. CROOKE.

AHIṀSĀ.—*Ahiṁsā* is the Indian doctrine of non-injury, that is, to all living things (men and animals). It first finds expression in a mystical passage in the Chāndogya Upanishad (3. 17), where five ethical qualities, one being *ahiṁsā,* are said to be equivalent to a part of the sacrifice of which the whole life of man is made an epitome. This is not exactly the same as the Hebrew prophet's 'I will have mercy and not sacrifice,' but it comes near to it. The date of this document may be the 7th cent. B.C. This was also the probable time of the rise of the Jains, who made the non-injury doctrine a leading tenet of their school. (See, for instance, Āchārānga Sutta 1. 4. 2, translated by Jacobi, *Jaina Sūtras,* 1. 39). It is the first of the five vows of the Jain ascetics (*ib.* p. xxiii.); and they carried it to great extremes, not driving away vermin from their clothes or bodies, and carrying a filter and a broom to save minute insects in the water they drank or on the ground where they sat (*ib.* p. xxvii).

The doctrine has been common ground in all Indian sects from that time to the present. But each school of thought looks at it in a different way, and carries it out in practice in different degrees. The early Buddhists adopted it fully, but drew the line at what we should now call ordinary, reasonable humanity. It occurs twice in the eightfold path,—no doubt the very essence of Buddhism,—first under right aspiration, and again under right conduct (Majjhima iii. 251 = Saṁyutta v. 9). It is the first in the Ten Precepts for the Order (*sikkhāpadāni*), and therefore of the five rules of conduct for laymen (*pañcha sīlāni*), which correspond to the first five of the Precepts (Vinaya i. 83, Aṅguttara iii. 203). It is the subject of the first paragraph of the old tract on conduct, the Sīlas, which is certainly one of the very oldest of extant Buddhist documents, and is incorporated bodily into so many of the Suttantas (Rhys Davids, *Dialogues of the Buddha,* i. 3, 4). Asoka made it the subject of the first and second of the Rock Edicts in which he recommended his religion to his people, and refers again to it in the fourth. But he had long been a Buddhist before, in the first Edict, he proclaimed himself a vegetarian. The rule of the Buddhist Order was to accept any food offered to them on their round for alms; when Devadatta demanded a more stringent rule, the Buddha expressly refused to make any change (*Vinaya Texts,* ii. 117, iii. 253); and a much-quoted hymn, the Āmagandha Sutta (translated by Fausböll, *SBE* x. 40), put into the mouth of Kassapa the Buddha, lays down that it is not the eating of flesh that defiles a man, but the doing of evil deeds. The Buddhist application of the principle differs, therefore, from the Jain.

It would be a long, and not very useful, task to trace the different degrees in which the theory has been subsequently held. It is sufficient to note that the less stringent view has prevailed. At the end of the long Buddhist domination the practice of animal sacrifices had ceased, and though with the revival of Brāhman influence an attempt was made to restore them, it failed. The use of meat as food had been given up, and has never revived. But the Indians have not become strict vegetarians. Dried fish is still widely eaten; and though there is a deep-rooted aversion to taking animal life of any other kind, the treatment of living animals, draught oxen and camels for instance, is not always thoughtful. Nowhere else, however, has the doctrine of *ahiṁsā* had so great and long-continued an influence on national character.

T. W. RHYS DAVIDS.

AḤIQĀR, THE STORY OF.—In several versions of the *Thousand and One Nights,* the story of the sage Aḥiqār (Ḥaikār, Ḥikār, etc.; cf. on the original form of the name, Lidzb. in *ThLZ,* 1899, col. 608) is to be found. The tale is derived from a compilation which was circulated especially among the Christians of Syria (cf. Lidzb. in *ZDMG* i. 1896, p. 152). The contents of the story are as follows:—Aḥiqār is minister of Sennacherib, king of Assyria. He is already sixty years old, and has sixty wives in sixty palaces, but no son. He has recourse to the gods (in the Armenian version, to Belshim, Shimil and Shamin; cf. on this Lidzb. in *Ephem.* i. p. 259) and prays for children, but receives the reply that they have been denied to him, and is advised to adopt his nephew Nadan, and to bring him up instead of a son. Aḥiqār does so, devoting the greatest care to the physical and intellectual culture of his nephew, but the young man turns out a failure. He squanders the property of Aḥiqār and commits all kinds of crimes. When he is on this account called in question by Aḥiqār, Nadan seeks to devise means to remove his uncle. He contrives an intrigue to represent him as a traitor to the king. The king is deceived, and condemns Aḥiqār to death. However, Aḥiqār and his wife Ashfeghni succeed in influencing the executioner to spare his life, and to execute in his stead a slave who had been condemned to death. Aḥiqār is kept concealed by his wife, and is generally supposed to be dead. The news, too, reaches the ears of Sennacherib's rival, Pharaoh of Egypt, and encourages him to impose on Sennacherib the task of building him a palace between heaven and earth. If Sennacherib should be able to carry out this demand, he would pay to him the income of his empire for three years; but if not, Sennacherib must do the same to him. Of all the advisers of the king, no one is able to comply with the demand of Pharaoh—least of all, Nadan. The king is in the greatest extremity, and bitterly repents the removal of Aḥiqār. Then the executioner discloses the fact that he, at the time of the command of the king, did not carry out Aḥiqār's execution, and that he is still alive. On hearing this, the king is highly delighted, releases Aḥiqār, and sends him to Egypt. He easily solves all problems proposed by Pharaoh, and the latter has to pay the tribute and still other sums to Sennacherib. After his return home, Aḥiqār is again installed in his old position, and his nephew is unconditionally handed over to him. Aḥiqār reproaches him for his actions, and the effect on Nadan is so strong that he 'swelled up like a skin' and burst asunder.

The importance of this narrative, from the side of the history of religion, consists in the fact that, in all likelihood, it belongs to the lost literature of the Aramæans of the pre-Christian era (cf. Lidzb. in *ThLZ* and *Ephem. l.c.*). That the story had arisen in ancient times can be concluded from the consideration that the contents of the tale, with the names of both the principal heroes, are alluded to in the Book of Tobit (14^{10}). The connexion of this passage in the Book of Tobit with the story of Aḥiqār was first recognized by G. Hoffmann (*Auszüge aus syrischen Akten persischer Märtyrer*, p. 182), but he adopted the view that the story took its rise first in the Middle Ages under the influence of the passage in Tobit. However, the various versions of the story discovered since then make this supposition untenable, and the priority of the story of Aḥiqār is now generally recognized. The heathen character of the tale, too, cannot be mistaken, and this is especially prominent in the Armenian version. Among the gods mentioned in the text, the 'God of heaven' takes the first place. He is B'elšamin, whose worship was widely diffused among the Semitic peoples in the last centuries B.C. and the first A.D. Especially instructive is the passage in which Aḥiqār emphasizes the ascendency of B'elšamin as the 'God of heaven' over Bel, sun and moon (cf. *Ephem.* i. p. 259).

LITERATURE.—In addition to the works mentioned in the text, cf. Benfey, *Kleinere Schriften*, iii. p. 186 ff.; Salhani, *Contes arabes* (1890), p. 1 ff. (Arabic version); Jagič, *Byzant. Zeitschr.* i. (1892) p. 107 ff. (Slavonic version); Kuhn, in the same, p. 127 ff.; Meissner, *ZDMG* xlviii. (1894) p. 171 ff.; Lidzbarski, in the same, p. 671 ff.; Lidzbarski, *Die neuaramäischen Handschriften der Kgl. Bibliothek zu Berlin* (1896), i. ii. p. 1 ff. (Arabic and new Aramaic version); Dillon, *The Contemp. Rev.* lxxiii. (1898) p. 362 ff.; F. C. Conybeare, J. Rendel Harris, and Agnes Smith Lewis, *The Story of Aḥikar*, London, 1898 (Syriac, Arabic, Armenian, and Slavonic versions); Cosquin, *RB* viii. (1899) p. 50 ff., 510 ff.; Th. Reinach, *REJ* xxxviii. (1899) p. 1 ff.; Halévy, *RS* viii. (1900) p. 23 ff.; Gaster, *JRAS*, N. S. xxxii. (1900) p. 301 ff. (Roumanian version); J. Dashian, *Kurze bibliographische Untersuchungen u. Texte*, ii. (1901) p. 1 ff.; *JE* i. (1901) p. 287 ff.; P. Vetter, *Theol. Quartalschrift*, lxxxvi. (1904) pp. 321 ff., 512 ff., lxxxvii. (1905) pp. 321 ff., 497 ff.; Bousset, *ZNTW* vi. (1905) p. 180 ff.; de Moor, *Muséon*, N. S. ii. (1901) p. 445 ff.

M. LIDZBARSKI.

AHĪR.—An important tribe of agriculturists and breeders of cattle, which at the Census of 1901 numbered 9,806,475, of whom the vast majority are found in Bengal (where it is by far the largest caste), the United and Central Provinces, and in smaller numbers throughout N. India. Their name connects them with the Abhīras, a people occupying the Indus valley; and Lassen's view, that the Śūdras, or servile caste of the Hindu polity, with the Abhīras and Nishādas, were a black, long-haired Indian race, occupying what is now the valley of Sind, is perhaps correct. Another suggestion, which would connect them with a Scythian tribe, the Abars, who are believed to have entered India in the 1st or 2nd cent. B.C., is less probable. In N. India their traditions connect them with Mathura, the holy land of Krishṇa; and the Jādūbansī, one of their subdivisions, claim descent from the Yādava tribe to which Krishṇa is said to have belonged; while another, the Nandbansī of the United Provinces, the Nanda Ghosh of Bengal, claims as its ancestor Nanda, the foster-father of the divine child.

1. *Bengal.*—In Bengal the caste is known as Goālā (Skr. *gopāla*, 'a cowherd'), and in accordance with the legend of their descent they are generally worshippers of Krishṇa, and therefore members of the Vaishnava sect. But their cult is of a much lower type than the pietistic form of Vaishnavism associated in Bengal with the teaching of Chaitanya. Thus, they have a special feast, known as the Govardhan-pūjā, which takes its name from the holy Mathura hill associated with the cult of Krishṇa, at which they pray to a heap of boiled rice which is supposed to represent the hill, and make an offering of food, red-lead, turmeric, and flowers to every cow which they possess. In other parts the worship is paid to a mass of cowdung made to represent a human form, presumably that of Krishṇa. A still more primitive rite is that described by Buchanan (in Martin, *E. India*, i. 194), when at the *Divālī*, or Feast of Lamps, they tie together the feet of a pig, and drive their cattle over the wretched animal until it is killed, after which they boil and eat the flesh in the fields, though on other occasions they are not permitted to taste pork. Here the pig was probably originally a sacred animal, and is sacramentally slain to promote the fertility of the fields (Frazer, *Golden Bough*², ii. 366 ff.).

It is a curious proof of the sympathy which even Hindus of high caste and social position exhibit towards the coarser side of Hinduism, that when, in 1895, the English officer in charge of the Santāl country prohibited this brutal rite, a protest was immediately made in the Legislative Council of Bengal by one of its members. It is satisfactory to find that the Lieutenant-Governor supported the action of his subordinate (*North Indian Notes and Queries*, v. 38).

In W. Bengal they have special reverence for the hero Lorik, round whom a cycle of curious legend centres, and for Kāśī Bābā or Kāśīnāth, the ghost of a murdered Brāhman, which is greatly feared. If he be not propitiated, he brings disease upon the cattle; and Risley describes how, when the plague appears, 'the village cattle are massed together, and cotton seed sprinkled over them. The fattest and sleekest animal being singled out, it is severely beaten with rods. The herd, scared by the noise, scamper off to the nearest shelter, followed by the scape-bull; and by this means it is thought the murrain is stayed.'

2. *United Provinces.*—In the United Provinces, those members of the caste who are initiated into any of the orthodox sects are either Vaishnavas or Śaivas, the former preferring the cult of Krishṇa, the latter that of Śiva or of his consort Devī in some one of her many forms, in preference the goddess known as the Vindhyabāsinī Devī, who has her temple at Vindhyāchal in the Mirzapur district, and is supposed to be the guardian goddess of the Vindhyan Hills. In Sahāranpur they have two deities who preside over marriage—Brahm Devatā and Baṛ Devatā, the former representing the great Hindu god Brahmā, who has an image of gold in human form; the latter the banyan tree (Hind. *baṛ*, Skr. *vaṭa*). On the night of the wedding the image of Brahm Devatā is brought by the goldsmith and placed upon the marriage-platform. When the binding portion of the rite has been performed, the bride and bridegroom offer to the image sandalwood, rice, flowers, incense, sweetmeats, and cakes, and light lamps before it. The women of the household then bury the image in the kitchen, and raise an earthen platform over it. The members of the family worship this daily by pouring water over it, and on feast days offerings of milk and rich cakes are made to it. This is done until a second marriage takes place in the family, when it is dug up and removed, and its place is taken by a new image. This is a very curious survival of Brahmā worship among a people where we were unlikely to suspect its existence. Except in a few temples specially dedicated to this, the head of the Hindu triad, his cult has now largely fallen into disuse. The worship of the banyan tree is closely connected with the custom of tree-marriage (Crooke, *Popular Religion and Folk-lore of N. India*, ii. 115). Among the Ahīr the bridegroom marks the trunk of the tree with vermilion at the same time as he marks the parting of the bride's hair with the same substance—a rite which is an obvious survival of the blood-covenant, marking the reception of the bride into a new kith and kin different from her own.

They also worship the Pāñchoṅpīr (see PACHPIRIYAS) and various minor local gods, the most popular of whom is Kāśīnāth, a deified ghost, at whose festival pots of milk are set to boil for the refreshment of the godling; and one man, becoming possessed by the deity, pours the contents over his shoulder, and is said never to be scalded. Their special cattle-god in the eastern parts of these Provinces is Bīrnāth (Skr. *vīra-nātha*, 'hero-lord'), who is represented by a collection of five wooden images rudely carved into human form.

3. *Central Provinces.*—A similar quintette of gods of disease is worshipped in the Central Provinces. Here their principal deities are Dūlhā Deo, said to be a deified bridegroom who died on his wedding-day (see DRAVIDIANS), and Budhā Deo, the chief god of the Gonds. As in Bengal, their chief festival is the Divālī, when they go about bedecked with strings of cowry shells, singing and dancing. They also pay much respect to a deified man, Haridās Bābā. He is said to have been a *yogī* ascetic, and to have possessed the power of separating his soul from his body at pleasure. One day he went in spirit to Benares, and left his body in the house of one of his disciples, an Ahīr. As he did not return, and the people ascertained that a dead body was lying in this house, they insisted that it should be burned. After this was done, Haridās returned, and when he found that his body had been burned, he entered into another man, and through him informed the people what a terrible mistake had been made. In atonement for their error, they worship him to this day. We have here an excellent example of the world-wide belief in the separable soul. The beliefs of the Ahīr in this Province are of a very primitive type, and Russell points to obvious survivals of totemism in the titles of some of the sub-castes.

4. *Deccan.*—In the Deccan the Ahīr are known as Gāvlī, which is the equivalent of *Goālā*, explained above. Here they are worshippers of the ordinary Hindu gods,—in particular of Śiva—and their priests are *jaṅgams*, or officiants of the Lingāyat (wh. see) sect. Those known as Marāṭha Gopāls worship the Mother-goddess, the Devī of Tuljapur in the Nizām's dominions, Kānhoba, Khandoba of Jejuri in the Poona district, and Mahāsoba, with offerings of sandal paste, flowers, and food. Each family dedicates a she-buffalo to Kānhoba, or Krishna, rears her with care, and does not load her or sell her milk and butter, but presents these to a Brāhman. Further south in Kāṇara, the Gollar, a kindred tribe, worship Krishṇa, Śiva under the form of the terrible Kāla Bhairava, and his consort Pārvatī. The rites in honour of these deities are performed after the Lingāyat rule.

5. *Gaddī, Ghosī.*—In N. India, when Ahīr are converted to Islām, they are known as *Ghosī* ('a shouter,' Skr. *ghush*, 'to shout after cattle') or *Gaddī*, and follow the Muhammadan rule, with some admixture of Dravidian animism. In Bombay they use many Hindu rites at marriage and birth, worship an image of the goddess Devī at the Dasahrā festival, and of Lakshmī, the goddess of good luck, at the Divālī, when they also adore the Tulasī or holy basil plant, as at the Holī they worship the castor-oil plant.

Quite distinct from these are the Gaddī of the Panjāb Hills, of whose beliefs Rose has given a full account. They are nominally Hindus by religion, worshipping Śiva by preference, and, in addition to him, Nāgas or serpent gods, Siddhas or deified ascetics, Bīrs or heroes, and Devīs or Mother-goddesses. The Nāgas, probably as representing the earth in serpent form, receive an offering of beestings, male kids and lambs, first-fruits of all crops, incense, and small cakes. The Siddhas, as befits their wandering life, are presented with a sack, stick, crutch, sandals, and thick bread cakes; the Bīrs receive a he-goat, a thick woollen cloak, waistband, cap, and fine bread. They and the Siddhas are thus conceived as living a life in another world, much the same as that which they enjoyed on earth. The Devīs, as female deities, receive vermilion and trinkets beloved by women, ardent spirits, and a goat. Women have their special worship of Kailū, who is a Bīr and the *numen* of abortion. Kailung is one of the chief Nāgas or serpent gods. Like Śiva, he is adored under the form of a sickle, which the god always carries when grazing his flocks. Besides these objects of worship, there are the *autārs* (Skr. *avatāra*, 'an incarnation of one of the greater gods'), a term here applied to the ghost of a person who has died childless, and who therefore is malignant and causes sickness. To propitiate this spirit, the sick person puts on clothes which are specially made for him, and wears an image of the spirit round his neck. Thus clad, he worships the *autār*, an image of which is always kept near a stream. The clothes and image are worn as a memorial of the dead man, to keep him in mind and conciliate him. Besides these, they worship a host of malignant spirits—*bātal*, the sprites of rivers and streams; *yoginīs*, or rock spirits; *rakshanīs* and *banasats*, who are here regarded as akin to the *yoginīs*, but are probably in their origin female demons (Skr. *rākshasī*); and spirits of the wood (Skr. *vanaspati*, 'king of the wood'). This would be quite in accordance with the belief of forest tribes, who naturally worship the spirits of trees, rocks, or rivers by which they are surrounded. Chungū is another demon who inhabits trees. He sucks the milk of cattle, and is propitiated with an offering of a coco-nut—a frequent form of commutation of the original human victim, the coco-nut representing the skull—, a plough handle, almonds, and grapes—the usual farmer's gifts. His effigy is made in flour, and to this incense is offered. Gungā, the demon who causes cattle disease, is propitiated by setting aside a griddle cake of bread until the final offerings can be made. Then a piece of iron, something like a hockey stick, is made, and the deity embodied in this is taken into the cattle shed, where he is worshipped by the sacred fire on a Thursday. A he-goat is killed, and a few drops of the blood sprinkled on the iron. At the same time cakes are offered, and some are eaten by *one* member of the household, but not by more than one, or the scourge will not abate; the rest are buried in the earth. Every fourth year the deity is worshipped in the same fashion. Kailū is a demon worshipped by women after childbirth, by putting up a stone under a tree, which is sanctified by magic formulæ (*mantra*) and then worshipped. A white goat, which may have a black head, is offered up to the demon by making an incision in the right ear and letting the blood fall on a white cloth—a good example of the commutation of the blood sacrifice. The woman eats some coarse sugar and dons the cloth, which she must wear until it is worn out, thus maintaining a sacramental communion between the demon and herself. If any other woman should happen to wear the cloth, it would cause her divers bodily ills. These facts regarding Gaddī religion are specially interesting, as being one of the best extant accounts of Indian animism as shown in the Panjāb Hills.

LITERATURE.—For Bengal: Dalton, *Descriptive Ethnology*, 314 f.; Risley, *Tribes and Castes*, i. 289; Buchanan Hamilton, in Martin, *Eastern India*, i. 194 f., ii. 133. For the cult of Lorik and Kāśī Bābā: Gait, *Bengal Census*, 1901, i. 197; Crooke, *Popular Religion and Folk-lore*, ii. 160; Risley, *op. cit.* i. 132; *North Indian Notes and Queries*, v. 77. For the United Provinces: Crooke, *Tribes and Castes*, i. 63, ii. 370, 419. For Rājputāna: *Census Report*, 1901, i. 139. For the Central Provinces; *Census Report*, 1901, i. 80, 189; *PASB* lviii. pt. i. 297. For the Deccan and Concan: *Bombay Gazetteer*, xv. pt. i. 297, xvii. 151, 184; *PASB* i. 42. For the Panjāb: Rose, *Census Report*, 1901, i. 119 ff.

W. CROOKE.

AḤMADĀBĀD, AḤMEDĀBĀD.—Chief city of the district of that name in the province of Gujarāt; founded in A.D. 1413 by Aḥmad Shāh, from whom it takes its name, and during the 16th and 17th cents. one of the most splendid cities of W. India. The religious buildings illustrate the conflict of the Muhammadan style with that of the Jains to which it succeeded.

'The truth of the matter,' writes Fergusson, 'is, the Mahomedans had forced themselves upon the most civilized and most essentially building race at that time in India, and the Chalukyas conquered their conquerors, and forced them to adopt forms and ornaments which were superior to any the invaders knew or could have introduced. The result is a style which combines all the elegance and finish of Jaina and Chalukyan art, with a certain largeness of conception which the Hindu never quite attained, but which is characteristic of the people who at that time were subjecting all India to their sway.'

Among these buildings the Jāmi' Masjid, or Cathedral Mosque, though not remarkable for size, is one of the most beautiful mosques in the East. This and other buildings of the same class, following 'the most elegant and instructive of Indo-Saracenic styles,' were built during the century and a half of independent rule (A.D. 1413–1573). Their tombs are equally remarkable, that of the King Mahmūd Begaḍā being one of the most splendid sepulchres in India.

LITERATURE.—Fergusson, *Hist. of Indian and Eastern Architecture*, 526 ff.; *Bombay Gazetteer*, iv. 262 ff., ix. pt. i. 131.

W. CROOKE.

ĀHOMS.—The Āhoms are Shāns belonging to the great Tai family of the human race. This family extends from the Gulf of Siam northwards into Yūn-nan and thence westward to Assam. It comprises several divisions, viz. the Siamese, Laos, Shāns, Tai Mau or Tai Khē (Chinese Shāns), Khāmtī and Āhom.* According to Dr. Grierson, the Tai race, in its different branches, is beyond all question the most widely spread of any in the Indo-Chinese Peninsula, and even in parts beyond the Peninsula, and it is certainly the most numerous. Its members are to be found from Assam to far into the Chinese province of Kwang-si, and from Bangkok to the interior of Yūn-nan.* The Āhoms used to call themselves not 'Āhom,' but, like the Northern Shāns, 'Tai.' Regarding the etymology of the word 'Āhom' there has been some discussion, and various views have been expressed. Dr. Grierson seems to incline to the opinion that the word is a corruption of *Ashām*. *Shān* is the Burmese corruption of *Shām*, which is the true spelling and pronunciation of the name of the well-known tribe. We have not, however, been able to ascertain what is the force of the initial A. The Muhammadan historians called the Āhoms 'Āsām.' They say, when mentioning them, that 'Āsām did this and that.' If this suggestion is correct, 'Āhom' must be a, comparatively speaking, modern corruption.† It is very probable that this tribe gave the modern name to our Province of Assam, the old name for the country being Saumarpīṭh.‡

* Introduction to Dr. Cushing's *Shān Grammar* (Rangoon, 1871).

History.—Gait, in his extremely valuable work, *A History of Assam*, gives a detailed historical account of the tribe. All that need be stated here is that the Āhoms invaded Assam, under the leadership of Chukāphā, from the Shān States in the 13th century. The Āhom *buranjis*, or chronicles, give the exact date, which has been computed by us from their reckoning to be A.D. 1228. The conquest of Yūn-nan by Khūblai Khān took place in the year A.D. 1253,§ but it is possible that the Chinese inroads into Yūn-nan began some years previous to the final conquest of the country, and the general disturbance of the people which took place in consequence caused some of the Shāns to migrate to other countries, as was the case with the Āhom branch. Probably, however, the Āhoms required but little encouragement to shift their quarters, for the Shāns are restless by nature, and are constantly moving from place to place, even in times of peace. The Āhoms, passing over the Pātkai‖ range, which divides Assam from Upper Burma, subdued in turn the different Bārā tribes, *i.e.* the Morāns, Borāhīs, and Chutiyās, which they found in possession of the Brahmapūtra valley. Although it would seem that the Āhoms, when they first appeared in the Province, were not large in numbers, they must have increased considerably afterwards, for they gradually extended their dominions until in the time of Rudra Singha (1696–1714) they were in possession of practically the whole valley of Assam, and were, moreover, able more than once to repel the Muhammadans who had invaded the country on several occasions, and to defeat the great Kacharī king Nara Nārāyaṇ, as well as the Raja of Jaintia. The Āhoms probably received a certain number of recruits from their Shān relatives beyond the Pātkai; but they seem to have admitted the Bārā people of the country largely into their tribe, and by this means also they probably increased their numbers. At the Census of 1901 those who returned themselves as Āhoms amounted to 178,049, the greater portion of this number being resident in the two upper Assam districts of Sibsagar and Lakhimpur.

The Āhom legend that two brothers, Khūnlūng and Khūnlai, from whom they claim descent, came down from heaven and established themselves at a place called Mūng-Ri-Mūng-Rang, seems to be identical with the Shān legend mentioned by Dr. Cushing,¶ except that the *habitat* of the Shāns is said to have been the Shweli valley. Mūng-Ri-Mūng-Rang is thought by Sir George Scott to have some connexion with Mōng-Hi-Mōng-Ham, a place in the Hsephsawng Panna on the bank of the river Mekong in the Chinese Shān States. Wherever may have been the exact abode of the Āhoms before they entered Assam, it is very probable that they formed one of the tribes included in the Shān kingdom of Mūng Mau, which at that time was very large and powerful.** This kingdom was probably identical with what was known to the Manipuris as the kingdom of Pong.††

Physical Characteristics.—The description of the physical characteristics of the Shāns given by Dr. Cushing ‡‡ is equally applicable to the Āhoms, except that it should be stated that the Āhoms of the Assam valley, owing to intermarriage with the Bārā tribes, which are of Tibeto-Burman origin, exhibit probably fewer Shān characteristics than the people of the Shān States. The statement of the Muhammadan historian, quoted on p. 139 of Gait's *History of Assam*, that the Āhom women are 'very black,' is scarcely accurate, for the Āhom women are among the fairest in Assam, and show a pleasing contrast to the

* General Introduction to 'Tai Group' in *Linguistic Survey of India* (Calcutta, 1904), vol. ii. p. 59.

† In Assamese, *s* and *sh* become a guttural *h*.

‡ See p. 61 of General Introduction to 'Tai Group' in *Linguistic Survey of India*, vol. ii.; also pp. 240, 241 of *A History of Assam* (E. A. Gait).

§ Dr. Cushing's note in the *Burma Census Report* of 1891, p. 201.

‖ Said to take its name from the Āhom words *pāt*, 'to cut,' and *kai*, 'fowl,' it being the Āhom custom to seek auguries by examining the legs of fowls.

¶ *Burma Census Report*, 1891, p. 202.

** See note by Dr. Cushing in the *Burma Census Report* of 1891.

†† For derivation of '*Pong*' see *Burma Census Report*, 1891, p. 203.

‡‡ Cushing in *Burma Census Report*, 1891.

ordinary Kachārī * woman of the plains, whose skin is frequently dusky in hue, and whose features are hard and ill favoured. Though more muscular, and certainly more capable of bearing fatigue than the Assamese Hindu of Aryan or semi-Aryan extraction, the Āhom, by long residence in the steamy plains of Assam, and by inordinate use of opium, has physically deteriorated, and has become as incorrigibly lazy as the ordinary Assamese *rāyat*. Āhoms are heavy drinkers, consuming large quantities of rice beer, called by them *lau*,† which they brew in their own villages. The *Bihus*, or harvest and sowing festivals, are celebrated by more than usually heavy potations.‡ The *deodhais*, or Āhom priests, distil a spirit from rice in out of the way localities, often in defiance of the Excise laws. The evils of the gambling habit, which affect other races of Indo-Chinese origin,§ do not, so far, appear to have spread among them. In educational matters the Āhoms are more backward than even the ordinary Assamese Hindus, which is saying a good deal. In consequence, both the Āhoms and the Assamese Hindus stand in great danger of being elbowed out of all Government as well as industrial employment by the people of Eastern Bengal. The condition of the old Āhom aristocracy becomes worse and worse each year, owing chiefly to the failure of its members to realize the new conditions of life. Families in Sibsagar which a generation or two back held positions of power and comparative wealth at the Āhom Raja's court are now practically destitute.

Dress.—The dress of the Āhom tribesman at the present time possesses nothing to distinguish it from that worn by the Assamese cultivator. It was the Āhoms, however, who probably introduced into Assam the large broad-brimmed hat or *jhāpi*, which is an adaptation of the Shān head covering. The dress of an Āhom nobleman used to consist of a turban of silk or a cap called *jema*, a short coat, *mirjai*, made of Assamese *mūghā* or *pāt* silk, reaching to the waist, a long coat, also of silk, worn over the *mirjai* reaching down to the ankles, and a *churiā* or silken waist cloth. Āhom females dress in a similar manner to ordinary Assamese women, wearing either silk (varying in texture) or cotton, according to the circumstances of the wearer. All this silk is spun and woven in the Assamese homesteads. Women as well as men nowadays wear the *jhāpi*, a specially large and gaily decorated hat being reserved for the bride on her wedding-day. Formerly the *jhāpi* was an emblem of authority, and none but the great were allowed to wear it in the presence of the Raja. Jewellery is much the same as that ordinarily met with in the valley, although the different articles are sometimes called by different names. The girls of the Deodhai, or priestly clan, tattoo star-shaped devices on their hands and arms, the dye used being prepared in the Āhom or Norā villages. Tattooing takes place when a girl has reached about ten years of age. The Norās, another Shān tribe of Assam, who possess a few settlements in the valley, observe a similar custom.

Houses and Villages.—Āhom villages do not differ from those of the ordinary cultivator of the valley, but the houses of the priests (Deodhais), who are in all matters more conservative than the rest of the tribe, are built on piles about 5 to 6 ft. from the ground, the dwelling of the ordinary cultivator being either set up on an earthen plinth or flush with the ground. The Deodhai houses are divided into three compartments, *maren* or cook-room, *chāngku* or sleeping-room, and *chāmku* or dining-room. The spaces immediately below these three chambers are used for the loom, cowshed, and pig-sty respectively.

Food and drink.—Pigs and fowls abound in the Deodhai villages. Āhoms who have not been Hinduized, sometimes even those who have become the disciples of Vaiṣnavite gosains, eat pork and fowls, and drink rice beer and rice spirit, much to the scandal of their sanctimonious Assamese Hindu neighbours, who regard them with horror. The Āhoms cultivate rice in the same fashion, using the same primitive plough, as the other peasants of the valley, but, owing to their extremely lethargic habits, fail to reap anything like full benefits from the magnificently rich soil. A large quantity of grain is used up by them in the manufacture of *lau* (rice beer), and they spend probably quite as much money in buying opium as in paying the Government land revenue.

Exogamous groups.—The Āhoms are divided into a number of exogamous groups called *phoids* or *khels*, the principal ones being seven in number, hence the term *sātghariā* ('belonging to seven houses') which is nowadays applied to them. The composition of these seven principal divisions has varied from time to time, but they are said to have originally consisted of the following: the Royal Family, the Buragohain, Bargohain, Chiring, Deodhai, Mohan, and Bailong *phoids*.‖ The whole of the superior exogamous groups are divided, further, into two main divisions, called Gohains and Gogois, but there are some decidedly inferior *phoids*, such as the Chaodangs, who were the public executioners in the old days, as well as Likchans, Gharfaleas and others, with whom Āhoms of the upper classes will not intermarry. For a description of the Āhom system of government, State and social organization, and particularly the *pāik* system, the reader is referred to ch. ix. of Gait's *History of Assam*.

Marriage.—Āhoms who have become Hindus observe a modified Hindu marriage ceremony, but the real Ahom rite is the *saklang*. The ritual is contained in a holy book called the *saklang pūthi* (unfortunately no longer available). As the actual ceremony is conducted with some secrecy, and as it is said to be forbidden to divulge its details to anyone but an Āhom, the writer had considerable difficulty in finding out what actually occurs on the occasion; but two reliable authorities, Srijuts Kanakeswar Borpatra Gohain and Radha Kanta Sandikai, E.A.C., were good enough to give him the following description. The bridegroom sits in the courtyard; the bride is brought in, and she walks seven times round the bridegroom. She then sits down by his side. After this both rise and proceed to a room screened off from the guests. Here one end of a cloth is tied round the neck of the bride, the other being fastened to the bridegroom's waist. They walk to a corner, where nine vessels full of water have been placed on plantain leaves, the Chiring Phukan (or master of the ceremonies) reads from the *saklang pūthi*, and three cups containing milk, honey and ghee, and rice frumenty, are produced, which the bride and bridegroom have to smell. Some uncooked rice is then brought in a basket, into which, after the bride and bridegroom have exchanged knives, rings are plunged by bride and bridegroom respectively, unknown to one another, it being the intention that each should discover the other's ring and wear it on the finger. The exchange of the knives and the rings is the binding part of the ceremony. Bride and bridegroom are then taken outside and do *sewa* (homage) to the bride's parents and to the people assembled, and the marriage is complete.

Āhoms used to be polygamous, but one wife is said to be more correct now. Āhom girls are not married till they reach a nubile age—sometimes much later. The marriage expenses seem to be quite out of proportion to the means of the people; for instance, a Deodhai marriage in Sibsagar was reported to the writer to have cost more than Rs. 200 (bridegroom's expenses).

Death.—Āhoms generally bury their dead; formerly they invariably did so, but now those who have accepted the Hindu religion resort to cremation. The following is a brief description of the old Āhom rites. The corpses of the poor are buried in the ground without coffins. Those of the rich are reverently laid in boxes; a water-pot, cup, *dā* (stick), *jhāpi* (or large hat), and a *pirā* (or wooden stool) are put inside the box with the corpse. These articles are intended for the use of the deceased's spirit in the next world. The coffin is then lowered into the grave, which is filled in, a large earthen tumulus (*moidām*) being thrown up over it. The Āhom kings were buried at Choraideo in the Sibsagar district, their funeral obsequies being of a much more elaborate nature. A *buranji*, (Āhom chronicle) describes how at the funeral of Raja Gadādhar Singha, who died in A.D. 1696,* a number of living persons, who had been the deceased's attendants, were interred with the corpse, together with many articles of food and raiment, and ornaments. It is stated that sometimes horses and even elephants were interred alive with a dead king.

Religion.—As the Āhoms are now almost entirely Hinduized, and there are very few of the old

* Kachāris call themselves Bārā.
† Assamese *lao pāni*.
‡ The *Bihus* are Bārā festivals which the Āhoms have adopted.
§ *E.g.* the Khassis.
‖ This statement is made on the authority of Srijut Golab Chandra Barua, late Āhom translator to the Government.

* Gait, *History of Assam*, p. 163.

Deodhais (the only persons who possess any knowledge of the ancient ritual) who remember the ancient religious customs, it is well-nigh impossible to give an accurate and connected account of the Āhom religion.

The writer has been unable to trace Buddhistic influences. Possibly Buddhism had not penetrated so far as the Upper Mekong before the Āhoms left Müng-Ri-Müng-Rang, their ancient site; or Buddhism had become so inextricably mixed with the worship of the gods of earth and sky as to become indiscernible. Apart from the god Chumseng or Chung Deo, whose worship was conducted by the Āhom king, assisted by the Chiring Phukan, as will afterwards be described, the Āhoms possessed various gods, amongst whom the following seem to have been the more important: Along or Phu-Ra-Ta-Ra (God the creator), Lengdon (god of heaven, the Hindu Indra), Kaokham (god of water, the old Vedic deity Varuṇa), Lengbin and Lengdin (god and goddess of the earth), and Phai (god of fire, Hindu Agni). Chumseng, who was daily worshipped at the king's house, was not regarded as a god himself; for, according to Āhom tradition, Chumseng was given to the Āhom progenitors, Khūnlūng and Khūnlai, by Lengdon, god of heaven. Chumseng was worshipped more as a fetish—something supernatural, possessing the power to do good to the king and his people. Chumseng was perhaps an ammonite, something of the nature of the Hindu *sālgrām*, or even a precious stone (which the etymology of the name, i.e. *chum* = 'precious' and *seng* = 'stone,' would certainly suggest). The stone or image, whatever it was, could not have been large, as at the coronation ceremony it was hung round the king's neck. The worship was conducted with secrecy, none but the king being allowed to view Chumseng. The king could see him only twice a year. The mysticism attached to the Chumseng worship accounts for the doubt as to what Chumseng actually is. Old people say that Chumseng lies concealed somewhere in Assam at the present day.

The Āhoms performed ceremonies called *saifa* and *umpha* for the good of the crops and the State, the latter being on a grander scale than the former, and conducted by the king himself. A ceremony called *sarkai*, the object of which was the scaring away of evil spirits from the country, was also performed, the peculiarity of this observance being that a man who had lost several wives by death was offered up as a sacrifice. The **rikkhwan**, or expiation ceremony (lit. *rik* = 'call,' and *khwan* = 'life'), was 'generally performed at the installation of a new king, in times of danger, or after a victory. The procedure was as follows. The king sat in full dress on a platform, and the priests and astrologers poured holy water over his head, whence it ran down his body through a hole in the platform on to the chief *bailong* or astrologer, who was standing below. The king then changed his clothes, giving those which he had been wearing and all his ornaments to the chief *bailong*.'* Gait says that the same ceremony, on a smaller scale, was also frequently performed by the common people, and still is, on certain occasions, *e.g.* when a child is drowned. Much the same ceremony seems to have been celebrated in Manipur State.

Priesthood.—The priests, as has already been stated, were called *deodhais*. Probably this name was applied to them after the conversion of the king and his court to Hinduism, for in the Āhom language the priests were called *sāngmun*. The Deodhais claim descent from Laokhri, who is said to have been the companion of the two princes Khūnlūng and Khūnlai when they descended from heaven to earth, and to have acted in the dual capacity of priest and councillor. Although in the old days of Āhom rule the Deodhais composed the king's Privy Council, they were afterwards restricted to priestly duties and to divining events, the latter being thought by the Āhoms a matter of very great importance. Tradition runs that the heavenly princes brought from above the *kai-chan-müng*, or heavenly fowls; hence the sanctity which is attached to these birds. Some Deodhais near Luckwa (in Sibsagar district) once performed the divination ceremony for the writer's benefit. It was as follows. An altar of plantain trees and bamboos was set up (*mebenga*); plantain leaves and fruit, rice, sugar-cane, and liquor (*lau*) were brought, and a lamp. Three fowls and three fowls' eggs were placed upon the altar. The officiating priest sprinkled holy water on the spectators with a sprig of *blāk singpha* (the King flower). Prayers were then offered up to Jasingpha (the god of learning), and the fowls' necks were wrung. The flesh was scraped off the fowls' legs until the latter were quite clean, and then search was made for any small holes that existed in the bones. When the holes were found, small splinters of bamboo were inserted in them; and the bones were held up, with the bamboo splinters sticking in them, and closely compared with diagrams in a holy book which the priest had ready at hand. This book contained diagrams of all sorts of combinations of positions of splinters stuck in fowls' legs, and each meant something, the meaning appearing in verses written in the Āhom character, which were duly droned out by the Deodhai. The Āhom kings placed great faith in such omens, and the position of diviner was one of no small profit. Even now many Āhoms consult such soothsayers.

Coronation.—The Royal Coronation ceremony was celebrated with great pomp at Choraideo hill in the Sibsagar district, the *Swargadeo** and his principal queen riding on elephants. On such occasions the sacred Chumseng was brought out from the Royal *arcana* and hung round the neck of the king, who was girt about with the sword *hengdang* (the Āhom 'excalibur'), three feathers of the sacred birds (*kai-chan-müng*) being placed in his turban. After planting two banyan trees on Choraideo hill, the king returned and took his seat on a bamboo stage (*holong ghar*), under which had been placed a specimen of every living creature, including man. The king was bathed with holy water, which fell upon the collection below. Then the king, taking the sacred sword, killed a man, a criminal being selected for the purpose.† A great feast was afterwards given to the people, all of whom assembled to do homage to the new king.

As Gait says, 'The Āhoms were endowed with the historical faculty in a very high degree; and their priests and leading families possessed *buranjis* or histories, which were periodically brought up to date. They were written on oblong strips of bark, and were very carefully preserved and handed down from father to son.' ‡

A detailed description of the Āhom system of chronology will be found on p. 361 of Gait's *History of Assam*. It is interesting to find that it is of like character to that employed by the Chinese, Japanese, and other Mongols. This fact is another link in the chain of evidence in favour of China having been the cradle of the Shān race.§

It is beyond the province of this article to give a sketch of the Āhom language, nor, indeed, is this necessary, since the treasures of the 'Linguistic Survey' of India have been made available to the student. Not only in vol. ii. of this series, but also in a separate monograph,‖ Dr. Grierson has fully described the language. According to Dr. Grierson, Āhom is one of the oldest forms, if not the oldest, of the Shān languages. It is more akin to Siamese than any of the more modern Shān vernaculars.

* Gait, *History of Assam*, p. 86.

* Lit. 'god of heaven,' a title given to the kings by their subjects. It is a literal translation of the Āhom *chaopha*—cf. the Shān title of *tsawbwaw*.

† Raja Rudra Singha substituted a buffalo. This was the custom also afterwards.

‡ Gait, *History of Assam*, p. 4.

§ Dr. Cushing very clearly states this theory in his note on the Shāns (*Burma Census Report*, 1891, pp. 201–204).

‖ *Notes on Āhom* (1902).

What is extraordinary, considering the power which the Âhoms wielded, and that they were for centuries the ruling race in Assam, is the completeness with which their language has disappeared. In the present Assamese language, we have it on the authority of Dr. Grierson, there are barely fifty words in common use which can be traced to an Âhom origin. From the time when the Âhom kings accepted Hinduism and imported Hindu priests from Nadiya in Bengal and elsewhere, the Âhom language commenced to disappear, slowly at first, but in the end very rapidly, until at the present day there are probably not more than a few dozen men all told who possess even a smattering of the ancient tongue. It is perhaps due to the irony of fate that Assamese, the language which displaced Âhom, seems also fated to share the same destiny; for, since the addition to Assam of Eastern Bengal with its teeming millions of Bengali-speaking inhabitants, it seems impossible that a weak vernacular like Assamese will be able to withstand a powerful Bengali onslaught, unless special measures are taken to protect it from being crushed out.

LITERATURE.—E. A. Gait, *A History of Assam* (1906); G. A. Grierson, *Linguistic Survey of India* (1904), ii. 59–140, also 'Notes on Âhom' in *ZDMG* (1902) lvi. 1–59, and 'An Âhom Cosmogony' in *JRAS*, April 1904; J. M. Foster, 'Note on Ghargaon' in *JASB*, vol. xli. (1872); E. A. Gait, 'Abstract of the Contents of one of the Âhom Pūthis,' *ib.* vol. lxiii. (1894) pt. i. pp. 108–111, and 'Notes on some Âhom Coins,' *ib.* vol. lxiv. (1895) pt. i. pp. 286–289; *Assam Census Reports* of 1881, 1891, and 1901; *Burma Census Report* of 1891; Nathan Brown, 'Comparison of Indo-Chinese Languages' in *JASB* vi. (1837) 1023 ff. (contains an account of the Âhom alphabet, and a comparison of the language with others of the group. It also contains an Âhom account of the Cosmogony, of which a translation, together with a verbal analysis by Major F. Jenkins, is given in *JASB* xli. 980); B. H. Hodgson, 'Aborigines of the North-East Frontier,' in *JASB* xix. (1850) 309 ff., reprinted in *Essays relating to Indian Subjects* (1880), ii. 11 ff. (contains an Ahom vocabulary); E. T. Dalton, *Descriptive Ethnology of Bengal* (1872, with Vocabulary on p. 69 ff.); P. R. Gurdon, 'On the Khāmtīs' in *JRAS* xxvii. (1895) 157 ff., 163 (contains a brief list of words compared with Shān, Khāmtī, Lao, and Siamese) For a fuller bibliography, see *T'oung Pao*, No. 2, May 1906.

P. R. GURDON.

AHRIMAN.—The later Persian designation by which the devil, or principle of evil, is known in the religion of Zoroaster. The ancient form of the name is *Angra Mainyu* in Gâthic Avesta *Aṅra Mainyu* in Younger Avesta, *Ahraman* in Pahlavi, and *Ahriman* in Modern Persian, whence the current designation 'Ahriman.' The Greeks, as early as Aristotle, were familiar with the Persian appellation as Ἀρειμάνιος, which the Latins adopted as *Arimanius*. The original meaning of the term appears to be 'Enemy-Spirit,' 'Spiritual Foe' (*aṅra*, 'inimical,' *mainyu*, 'spirit'), although the exact etymology of the title *aṅra* is not yet clear.

In the Gâthâs, *Angra Mainyu* generally stands in opposition to *Spenta Mainyu*, the 'Holy Spirit' of *Ahura Mazda*. But in the Younger Avesta this distinction between the Holy Spirit and God is not preserved, both being identified, so that the opposition thenceforth stands between *Aṅra Mainyu* and *Ahura Mazda*. *Angra Mainyu* is not mentioned in the Old Persian inscriptions, but the evil principle is there designated by *Drauga*, 'Falsehood' (*Bh.* i. 34, iv. 34, 37; *Dar. Pers.* d. 17, 20).

Although Aṅra Mainyu is coeval with Ahura Mazda (*Dâṭistân-î-Dênîg*, xxxvii. 21, 26), he is not regarded as being co-eternal with him, for it is he who will cease to be (*Bûndahišn*, i. 3). The nature of Ahriman, as portrayed in the Zoroastrian scriptures from the earliest to the later times, is that of the very essence of evil, an entity (more or less personified) that chooses by preference to do wrong and oppose the spirit of goodness, because of being ignorant, deceitful, malicious, and perverse (*e.g.* *Yasna*, xxx. 3–6, xlv. 1–2, xlvi. 7, xxxi. 12). He arose from the abyss of endless darkness (*Bûndahišn*, i. 9), his abode being in the northern regions (*Vendîdâd*, xix. 1). He did not know for some time of the existence of Ormazd (*Bûndahišn*, i. 9; *Zâṭ-Sparam*, i. 2); nor, being ignorant and blind (*Bûndahišn*, i. 19), did he foresee his future doom (*Dīnkarṭ*, tr. Sanjana, p. 258). Accordingly, being absolutely unaware of what is to befall him at the end of time, he is unable to adopt any means to guard himself (*ib.* p. 462). He is absolute evil without any goodness (*Zâṭ-Sparam*, i. 17; *Dâṭistân-î-Dênîg*, xxxvii. 28; *Sad Dar*, lxii. 3), but he is not a fallen angel, like his counterpart in Christianity. His standing epithet is 'the demon of demons' (*Vendîdâd*, xix. 1); and he is the destroyer of the world (*Arṭâ-Vîrâf Nâmak*, ch. c.) and full of malice (*Bûndahišn*, i. 10). As a pernicious power, Ahriman is represented, especially in the Younger Avesta and the Pahlavi books, as thwarting the beneficent influence of Ormazd by means of antagonistic creations (*e.g. Vendîdâd*, i. 1 f.; *Yasht*, xiii. 77; *Yasna*, ix. 8; *Bûndahišn*, i. 1–28), and as in constant struggle with the spirit of light (*e.g. Yasht*, x. 97, xiii. 13, xviii. 2, xix. 46, 96; *Yasna*, x. 15). He strives to persuade men to be hostile to Ormazd and win them over to his own side (*Bûndahišn*, i. 14; *Zâṭ-Sparam*, i. 8), and his greatest victory consists in inciting a human soul to rebel against Ormazd. His complete satisfaction is found in securing a human soul on his side (*Dînâ-î-Maînôg-î-Khraṭ*, xlvi. 4, 5). So mighty is he, moreover, that even the Yazatas, or 'Angels,' did not succeed in overpowering him, and it was only Zarathushtra who confounded him (*Yasht*, xvii. 19, 20; *Vendîdâd*, xix.; *Dīnkarṭ*, vii. 4, 36–41). From Ahriman proceeds all disorder, and he is the source of all disease and of death (*Yasna*, xxx. 5; *Vendîdâd*, xx. 3, xxii. 2, ii. 29; *Yasht*, iii. 13–14). He attacks the creations of Ormazd, and introduces imperfections, disease, and death. He killed *Gâyômarṭ*, the primeval man, and *Gôshûrvan*, the primordial ox (*Bûndahišn*, iii. 17; *Zâṭ-Sparam*, iv. 3; *Dâṭistân-î-Dênîg*, xxxvii. 82); he introduced all physical and moral imperfections into creation; he created hosts of demons to accomplish his work of destruction in the kingdom of goodness (*Bûndahišn*, i. 10, 24, 27); he formed Azhi Dahâka for the destruction of the world of righteousness (*Yasht*, ix. 14, xvii. 34). Ahriman is the head of a ribald crew of demons, fiends, and arch-fiends, who are mentioned hundreds of times as *daēvas* (Mod. Pers. *dīv*, 'demon') and *drujas* in the Avesta and later literature, and conceived of as abiding in hell, in 'endless darkness,' 'the worst life, the abode of Deceit and of the Worst Thought' (*Yasna*, xxxi. 20, xxxii. 13; *Vendîdâd*, iii. 35). The final defeat of Ahriman and his evil progeny is to be brought about by man. At the resurrection, Ahriman, being impotent and helpless, will bow down before the good spirits (*Yasht*, xix. 96), and his doom, according to the later books, is to be utter annihilation (*Dâṭistân-î-Dênîg*, xxxvii. 20, 59, 71, 114, 120), for the Zoroastrian religion postulates the ultimate triumph of good over evil and the final eradication of sin from the world (*Dâṭistân-î-Dênîg*, xxxvii. 120–122). At that time Ahriman will be driven from mankind (*Dīnkarṭ*, tr. Sanjana, p. 445), and, rushing to darkness and gloom in his impotence (*Bûndahišn*, xxx. 30), will be forced to seek refuge in the earth (Westergaard Fragments, iv. 3), where he will be imprisoned (*Dīnkarṭ*, tr. Sanjana, p. 151) or destroyed (*Cama Memorial Volume*, 128–129).

Attempts have been made to trace resemblances between Ahriman and Ahi, the sky-serpent of ancient India, as also with the Māra of Buddhism, but these are too few and too remote to deserve much consideration. The nearest resemblance is that between Ahriman and Satan.

Owing to the emphasis which the Avesta and later books lay upon recognizing the principle of evil as an active agent in the life of the world, Zoroastrianism is frequently spoken of as Dualism. The Parsis, or modern followers of the faith, however, vigorously reject the application of the term to their religion, and their most advanced teachers deny attributing any personality to Ahriman except as a principle or force. Further discussion of this problem, and the attitude in ancient as well as modern times with regard to the subject, is reserved for the article on DUALISM. See also ORMAZD, ZOROASTRIANISM.

LITERATURE.—For detailed bibliographical references on the subject, consult Jackson, 'Die iranische Religion' in Geiger and Kuhn's *Grundriss der iran. Philol.* ii. 646–668, including also Spiegel, *Eranische Alterthumskunde*, ii. 119–126, Leipzig, 1873; Darmesteter, *Ormazd et Ahriman*, Paris, 1887; Casartelli, *The Mazdayasnian Religion under the Sassanids* [tr. from French into English by Firoz Jamaspji], pp. 50–68, Bombay, 1889; Tiele, *Gesch. der Religion im Altertum*, ii. 153–163, Gotha, 1898, and *Geschiedenis van den Godsdienst in de Oudheid*, ii. 264–271, Amsterdam, 1901; Stave, *Über den Einfluss des Parsismus*, p. 235 ff., Haarlem, 1898; Rustomji Peshotanji Sanjana, *Zarathushtra and Zarathushtrianism in the Avesta*, Bombay and Leipzig, 1906; *JE* i. 294–297.

A. V. WILLIAMS JACKSON.

AHUNA-VAIRYA.—A formulated name* taken from the first words of a prayer or solemn declaration, collected from scattered parts of the *Gāthās*, and always held in the highest veneration by the followers of Zarathuštra. It is of much factitious and also of much real importance, for it has received unusual attention both from experts in Zend philology and from non-experts interested in the history of theological doctrines,—this last owing to the erroneous supposition that it represents the original of the Philonian-Johannine Logos. Its chief occurrence, as our texts now stand, appears at the close of *Yasna* xxvii., just preceding the beginning of the *Gāthā Ahunavaiti*. It consists of three lines which may once have numbered twenty-one words, and may still be so reckoned by counting the particles. These twenty-one words were supposed, or were later made, to correspond to the twenty-one *nasks*, or books of the Avesta, most of which, as complete documents, have now perished.

1. Dialect and other characteristics.—The *Ahunavēr* is composed in the so-called *Gāthic* dialect, or, more correctly, in the original Avestan language, of which all outside of the *Gāthās* should be considered a dialect; but the differences are not very great, particularly now that we have begun to discover† that the *Avesta* forms themselves partake somewhat of that multiphonous character which leaves the Pahlavi language at times so inscrutable. The *Ahunavēr* preserves the metre of the *Gāthā Ahunavaiti*, which, though properly the original of both the substance and metre of this brief piece, yet curiously enough derives its name from its own offspring. For the *Gāthā* from which these lines were collected bears their name, and is called *Ahunavaiti*, i.e. 'having the Ahuna with it,' probably referring to the accidental position of this formula in the fixed course of the *Yasna* recital.

Though preserving unmistakable traces of having been somewhat artificially constructed, both as to metre and contents, the little group of words is well worthy of its parentage in the *Gāthā*. A careful translation of it would be as follows, all discussion being here omitted:—

'As the Ahū is to be chosen,
So (let) the Ratu (be) from every legal fitness,
A Creator of mental goodness,
And of life's actions done for Mazda;
And the kingdom (be) to Ahura,
Whom (the Ahū, or the Ratu) He has appointed as nourisher to the poor.'

The immediate sources of the expressions may be said to be such as *Yasna* xxix. 6, xxxi. 8, 16, 21, xxxiv. 5, xliv. 4, liii. 9—all being Gāthic passages.

2. Interpretation.—*The moral idea in the Ahunavēr as a testimony to its presence elsewhere.*—In view of their priority in age and of other circumstances, the *Gāthās* have been supposed to be the original sources of the moral idea as well as of the now accepted eschatology. They have been confidently held to be the most prominent early literature in which those conceptions are manifested. And apart, perhaps, from our Semitic Scriptures, they most certainly possess this claim, especially when it is remembered that the Hebrew exilic Scriptures have been widely and reasonably thought to have been influenced by those Persian ideas which are most incisively expressed in the *Gāthās* and the rest of the genuine Avesta. They (the *Gāthās*) therefore constitute a principal focus of light for the history of religious experience. But we must by no means take all their high claims at once for granted without the most searching investigation at every step. They do indeed prove to be what at the first glance they seem to be; and they stand almost isolated in this respect, as being in their day among the most serious records of religious conviction and sentiment. But they imperatively demand all possible corroboration as to their value in regard to the vital consideration in question. Now the *Ahunavēr* is one of their most important supports. Hence the high scientific value of its interpretation. The facts relating to the *Ahunavēr*, as also to the *Gāthās*, certainly prove that the moral idea prevailed extensively in Iran as well as in India. This is extremely interesting simply as a matter of psychological experience; but it implies beyond all question a widely felt and practical religious influence of the moral idea upon the sentiments and lives of the populations amidst which this lore prevailed. Here we have a point of momentous consequence, which possibly explains also why Cyrus was so ready to further the religious as well as the political prosperity of the Jews, with all that this entailed in the return of the people and in the restoration of their sacred Temple with their established faith.

It is apparent from the translation given above that all ideas save the moral one are actually and instinctively excluded from the lines. Neither Aša, nor Vohuman, nor Khšathra is here used even in its high secondary sense as the name of one of the archangels themselves, each a personification of the supreme ideas of Truth, Benevolence, and Lawful Order,—while the closing words refer to the first altruistic act of the moral instinct—the care of the afflicted; and, almost strange to say, there is not a trace of any allusion to ceremonies. If we are correct in placing the *Ahunavēr* next after the *Gāthās* in order of time, say about one hundred years later, then their exclusively moral point of view tends to prove the vital energy of the moral idea in the *Gāthic* hymns themselves—a matter of extreme scientific interest in view of the facts.

3. Later sanctity.—The *Ahunavēr*, having acquired a singular sanctity for the reasons given, was freely used by the religious fancy of a somewhat later age. Like the 'sword of the Spirit,' it becomes a weapon in the hand of saints and angels. *Zarathuštra* himself, in his later traditional rôle, and in his Temptation, repels *Angra Mainyu* with it, while *Sraoša* wields it as his *snaithiš*, *i.e.* as his 'halbert.' It would, however, be precarious simply to assert that the above-noted characteristic of the formula was the effective and immediate cause of the somewhat excessive importance afterwards attributed to it. Its sacrosanct character, if one might so express it, was probably owing to its brevity plus its allusions to the *Gāthās*, or even to some purely accidental intellectual circumstance, and it was doubtless often used perfunctorily like the *Pater Noster*, if not indeed almost as a potent instrument of magic.

4. Relation of the Ahunavēr to the History of Religion.—The allusions to this formula which occur in the commentary upon it in *Yasna* xix.

* *Ahunavēr*, *Honover*, are Pahlavi and Parsi abbreviations, *ahuna* representing *ahū*, and *-vēr* representing *vairyō* (some would write *-vair*, *ahunavair*).

† See *ZDMG* lii. (1898) 436 ff.

have been widely exploited in critical and semi-critical studies upon the subject of the *Philonian-Johannine Logos*; and it certainly constitutes a secondary factor to be reckoned with in our decision as to the history of exegesis at the places indicated. Such expressions as the *Ahunavēr* being 'the word uttered before the heaven, the earth,' etc., do indeed recall the terms in the Prologue of St. John: 'In the beginning was the Word.' It has been supposed that these expressions in *Yasna* xix. gave the idea to this 'Word' of St. John. Oppert, we believe, first suggested the connexion. But *possible* as such an initiative might be, the present writer does not regard it as at all *probable*, in view of the Greek *Logos* with which Philo was so familiar. Besides, there is no saying what the date of *Yasna* xix. may be; it may even have been Sasanian. Commentary of course appeared almost as soon as a text was issued; and our Pahlavi commentary texts, however late they received their present forms, as 'edited with all the manuscripts collated,' cannot fail to have preserved hints from the very earliest ages. Naturally, these were sometimes much covered up by over-growths; and this *Yasna* xix. must certainly have had predecessors. Philo may also have acquired some information as to Avestan doctrine from the semi-Persian books of the Bible, from the Apocrypha, and from the exilic Talmud, so far as they were then current, and from the many related documents of which we have never known even the existence; for echoes of such religious doctrines must have reached both Jerusalem and Greek Egypt; but to suppose that *Yasna* xix. influenced this Philonian-Johannine Logos of the Prologue seems to us utterly out of the question, in view of the history of Philo's development. See artt. LOGOS and PHILO JUDÆUS.

LITERATURE.—The texts of the Avesta at *Yasna* xxvii.; the Pahlavi text of *Yasna* xxvii. (see Spiegel's text, tr., and Com.); Anquetil du Perron, *Zend-Avesta*, i. pt. 2, p. 81; Oppert, 'L'Honover, le verbe créateur de Zoroastre' in *Annales de la philos. chrét.*, Jan. 1862; Kossowicz, *Decem Zendavestæ excerpta*, 1868; Justi, *Handbuch der Zendsprache*, p. 258; Haug, *Essays on the Parsis* 3, p. 141, n. 2; Haug and West, *Glossary . . . of Arda Viraf*, pp. 256–257; *Avesta, Livre Sacré du Zoroastrianisme*, tr. by C. de Harlez, p. 301; Roth, *ZDMG*, xxxviii. 437; Bartholomae, *Altiran. Wörterb.* cols. 282, 707, 778, and refs.; Darmesteter, *SBE* v.[2] 129, xxiii. 23, Zend-Avesta, i. 162 ff.; L. H. Mills, *SBE* xxxi. 281 (somewhat modified above in the article, more point being seen in *ašātčit hačā*); West's translation of the Pahlavi text of the Ahunavēr (Ahunavair) in *SBE*, xxvii. 5–6, note; Zartoshti, *Meher*, 1273 A.H. No. 3, p. 253; K. F. Geldner, *SBAW* xxxviii. (1904); H. G. Smith in *ARW* vi. 233–243.

L. H. MILLS.

AHURA MAZDA.—See ORMAZD.

AINUS.

[J. BATCHELOR].

1. The Ainu habitat.—The few Ainus now living—and at the present time there are less than 20,000 of them left—may be looked upon as the very last remnant of a great pre-historic race, which was, without doubt, once spread over an area extending from Siberia in the north down to the southernmost limits of old Japan. An indisputable proof of this lies in the fact that very many geographical names in Siberia and throughout the whole of the Japanese empire, Formosa excluded, are discovered to be of Ainu origin.* Moreover, Japanese mythology, as contained in their book entitled *Kojiki*, or 'Records of Ancient Matters,'† and Japanese history as found in their *Nihongi*, or 'Chronicles of Japan,'‡ both of which works date back to the 8th cent. A.D., bear unmistakable evidence to the fact of the Ainus being an aboriginal race of Japan.

2. The Ainu religion pre-historic.—There is no great difficulty in determining the descent, nature, and relationship of such religions as have arisen during historical times; such as, for example, Judaism, Muhammadanism, Christianity, Brāhmanism, Buddhism, Taoism, and others of less importance. But a vast majority of ancient religions, of which there are still to be found some living examples left among scattered tribes and races, had their origin in pre-historic times, concerning which neither specific documents nor trustworthy traditions are to be had. The Ainu religion is one of these. Indeed, like indigenous Japanese Shintoism, it is a religion without any known historical beginning, and has no recognized founder.

3. The native religion still unchanged.—That the Ainu religion is the same to-day in all essentials as it was in pre-historic times, may be inferred from the inherent genius of the language, as well as gathered by way of auxiliary from the customs of the people and their present-day practices of rites and ceremonies. It is on record that in the year 1620 the Jesuit Father Hieronymus de Angelis paid a visit to the Island of Saghalien (the whole of which was then reckoned part of the Japanese empire), from Nagasaki; and from his description of the Ainus, written two years later, it is found that their manners and customs were the same then as those of their descendants now. Also, in June 1643, Captain Vries of the ship *Castricum* saw them, and his report bears the same testimony as that of the Jesuit Father. The *Matsumæ Manuscripts*, the *Ezo Isan Monogatari*, and other Japanese works also speak to the same effect. Ancient and modern lists of words, whether written in English or German, Japanese or Russian, and dating back hundreds of years (Batchelor, *Dict.* 5), show that the language of this race has not materially changed since they were collected.

The name of the famous mountain *Fuji* itself is not Japanese, as many have supposed it to be, but is of Ainu origin, like so many other places in its locality. It is a name which carries us back to pre-historic times, and plunges us at once right down into the very heart of Ainu religion. As written by the Japanese, who do so, it should be remembered, by means of Chinese hieroglyphics used phonetically and without the least regard to meaning, *Fuji* is generally made to mean 'Mountain of wealth,' 'Peerless,' or 'Not-two.' In Ainu, however, *Fuji* means 'fire,' and is the name especially applied to this element when being worshipped. *Fuji* is, in truth, the name of the goddess of fire. Hence it may well be concluded that in pre-historic times this beautiful, peerless *Fuji no yama* was regarded by the Ainus as one of their nature-deities, and, as such, worshipped. Volcanoes are also frequently worshipped by this race at the present day. Furthermore, *Fuji* is a dormant volcano. To-day fire is worshipped upon the hearth in every Ainu hut (where the occupants are not Christian), and, when worshipped, always has the appellation *Fuji*, or *Huchi*, or *Unji*, according to dialect, applied to it. The common word for 'fire' in its ordinary uses is *Abe*.

4. The Ainu religion originally monotheistic.—*The term for 'God' defined.*—Although the Ainu religion, as now developed, is found to be extremely polytheistic, yet the very word in use for 'God,' being of the singular number, seems to indicate that in its beginning it was monotheistic in nature. This word is *Kamui*. This is a compound of three distinct roots, the chief of which is *ka*, whose meaning is 'over,' 'above,' 'top,' and so forth. It is like *super* and ὑπέρ. It occurs in *kando*, 'heaven,' 'sky'; and is found in many words where the sense of *super* is to be conveyed. The fundamental meaning of *mu* is 'spreading,' 'creeping'; and *kamu*, which is the oldest Japanese word for 'God,'* means, in Ainu, 'covering,'

* See Batchelor, *An Ainu-Eng.-Jap. Dict. and Gram.*, Tokio, 1905, pt. ii. pp. 15–77.

† See tr. by Chamberlain, *TASJ*, Supplement, 1882.

‡ *TASJ*, Supplement, 1896, by W. G. Aston.

* Aston in his *Shinto*, London, 1905, p. 7, gives practically the same derivation for the Japanese word *kami*, stating that it is probably connected with *kaburu*, 'to cover,' and has the general meaning of 'above,' 'superior.'

'creeping over.' *I* is a particle which has the power of changing some parts of speech into nouns, as well as being a personal pronoun meaning 'he, 'she,' or 'it.' Thus by derivation *Kamui* means 'that which' or 'he who covers' or 'overshadows.' And so our thoughts are made to revert to the *οὐρανός* of the Aryans and to the *Tien*, 'heaven,' of the Chinese.

The term *Kamui* is of wide application, and may be used as a noun or adjective at will. But, however employed, it never loses its root meaning of chief in station, quality, or power. Thus, used as an adjective, it has the following shades of meaning. *Kamui nupuri*, 'a great or high mountain'; *Kamui rera*, 'a strong' or 'mighty wind,' or 'a beautiful wind'; *Kamui nonno*, 'a pretty flower'; *Kamui chikoikip*, 'a large animal,' and so forth. When used as a suffix, *Kamui* is always a noun, *e.g.* *Nupuri Kamui*, 'the gods of the mountains'; *Chikuni Kamui*, 'the gods of trees.' Also *Ya-un-Kamui*, 'gods upon the land'; *Rep-un-Kamui*, 'gods in the sea.' It is not the mountain or tree or flower or land or sea that is called 'God' and worshipped, but the spirit or spirits supposed to dwell in these objects. Otherwise the construction of the term would have to be changed; as, for example, *Nupuri Kamui* should be changed into *Nupuri-ne-kamui*, and *Chikuni Kamui* into *Chikuni-ne-kamui*.

5. The Supreme God distinguished.—After monotheism had given place to polytheism, it became necessary for the Ainus to distinguish between the deities. Making gods many rendered it imperative to have some term by which to designate the Supreme God. Hence, when speaking of the 'God of Gods,' the Ainus gave Him the name of *Pase-Kamui*, 'Creator and Possessor of heaven.' All the rest are termed *Yaiyan Kamui* or 'common deities,' also 'near' and 'distant deities.' *Pase* is an adjective, and points to rank and authority, its first meaning being 'weighty,' 'true,' and 'superior in rank.' And so *Pase Kamui* may well be translated by the word 'chief' or 'true God'; or, as the Hebrews would have said, 'God over all.'* Thus far, then, we have reached a real basis for two articles of Ainu belief, viz. (*a*) 'I believe in one supreme God, the Creator of all worlds and places, who is the Possessor of heaven, whom we call *Pase Kamui*, "The true God," and whom we speak of as *Kotan kara Kamui, Moshiri kara Kamui, Kando koro Kamui*'; (*b*) 'I believe also in the existence of a multitude of inferior deities (*Kamui*), all subject to this one Creator, who are His servants, who receive their life and power from Him, and who act and govern the world under Him.'

6. Special names given to the Creator.—In asking for proof of the existence of a Creator, the Ainus point to the flash of lightning and call it the shining forth of God's glory, and to the thunder and say it is the sound of His voice. The Milky Way is called His river. Two specially favourite names one sometimes hears applied to Him are *Tuntu* and *Shinda*. The first of these, *Tuntu*, may be translated by 'brace,' 'support,' 'pillar,' 'sustainer,' 'upholder.' God is addressed by it often in prayer when the thought uppermost in the mind of the worshipper is that of God as the upholder and sustainer of all things. The second word, *Shinda*, means 'cradle.' The Creator is so named because He is looked upon as the God in whose hands we rest. He is also called upon as 'our nourisher' (Batchelor, *The Ainu and their Folklore*, London, 1901, p. 582 ff.).

7. Evil spirits called Kamui.—Bearing the meaning it does, it is not surprising to find that the term *Kamui* is applied to evil spirits as well as good. Satan and all his angels are called *Nitne Kamui*. *Nitne* means 'stiff,' 'oppressive,' 'heavy' as dough. Evil spirits are thus naturally looked upon as the oppressors and enemies of mankind. Indeed, as the Ainus quaintly put it, 'they are very difficult to get along with.' They are extremely numerous and quite ubiquitous. And they even are expressly

* See Batchelor, *Dict.* pt. ii. p. 20, *s.v.* 'Kamui.'

said to inhabit the very same objects, in many instances, as the better deities themselves. Hence the good and evil genii of trees are brought to notice. Tree-blight and all accidents from trees, for example, are caused by the evil genii; while the buds, leaves, flowers, and useful fruits grow, it is supposed, through the favour of the good ones.

8. Special meanings of the term Kamui.—A careful analysis of the word *Kamui*, taken in connexion with the various objects to which it is applied, makes the following facts clear: (*a*) When applied to spirits supposed to be good, it expresses the quality of being useful, beneficent, divine. (*b*) When referred to supposed evil spirits, it indicates that which is bad and most to be dreaded. (*c*) When applied to reptiles, devils, and evil diseases, it signifies the most hateful, abominable, repulsive, and harmful. (*d*) When applied especially as a prefix to animals, fishes, or birds, it represents the greatest or most fierce, or the most useful for food or clothing, as the case may be. (*e*) When applied to persons, it is a mere title of respect expressive of honour, dignity, and rank. But it should be noted that, because an object has the term *Kamui* applied to it, this in no way implies that it is looked upon as divine or as necessarily worshipped. Demons are called by this term, but many of them are not even revered, though, out of fear, they may be propitiated with offerings. Men are often called *Kamui*, but they never have divine worship paid them.

9. God and Creation.—It has been seen (§ 5) that the supreme God is sometimes spoken of as Creator. But, to save confusion of thought, the method of creation should be explained. According to Ainu ideas, matter of all kinds is considered to have existed from all eternity, and other things to have been evolved out of it. *Ex nihilo nihil fit* is the motto of this people, so that one is prepared to find certain ideas connected with the metamorphistic cult lurking in their theories anent the origin of things. But with the Ainus metamorphism is by no means a natural change, for upon examination it is found to partake in some instances of the nature of special creative acts performed for the specific purpose of stocking the earth, while in others it is made to take place as a predetermined punishment by a stronger power for some evil done.

Thus, for example, deer and fishes of some kinds are said to have been made to develop out of hairs, bones, and scales of similar creatures cast out of heaven after a celestial feast (427, 298).* Some snakes, so theory asserts, came out of a pole, and others out of a log of wood (364); one woman, we learn, was changed into a frog as a punishment for some misdemeanour (26), another into a flower (260), and a child into a goat-sucker (183); the hazel-hen came from a piece of deer skin (447), and a Japanese who had lost his way in the mountains was metamorphosed into a green pigeon (444); some bears, demons, foxes, and cats were developed, so we are informed, from sparks of fire and ashes (467, 501), while hares were evolved from hairs cast out of heaven (514); in some instances, eels, we learn, came out of twisted grass (525), and in others from a piece of wood (365); squirrels, the Ainu would have us believe, were made to come out of a pair of old cast-away sandals (500); gnats, mosquitoes, and gadflies are said to have been evolved from the ashes of a goblin (74), and so on.

God and the production of dry land.—The legend concerning the first appearance of dry land is peculiar, and, inasmuch as a bird is supposed to have assisted in bringing it forth by hovering over the original substance, it is worth quoting. In the beginning the world was a great slushy quagmire. The waters were hopelessly mixed up with the earth, and nothing was to be seen but a mighty ocean of bare sloppy swamp. All the land was mixed up with, and aimlessly floating about in, the endless seas. All around was death and stillness. Nothing existed in this chaotic mass, for it was altogether incapable of sustaining animal life; nor were there any living fowls flying in the airy expanse above. All was cold, solitary, and desolate. However, the clouds had their demons, and the Creator lived in the highest heavens, with a host of subordinate deities. At last, the true God determined to make the earth habitable. He therefore made a water-wagtail, and sent him down from heaven to produce the earth. When this bird saw the dreadful condition the world was in, he was almost at his wits' end to know how to perform his allotted task. He fluttered over the water with his wings, trampled upon the muddy matter with his feet, and beat

* The numbers refer to pages of *The Ainu and their Folklore*, hereafter cited as *AF*.

it down with his tail. After a very long time of hovering, trampling, and tail-wagging, dry places began to appear, and the waters gradually became the ocean. And so the worlds were in time raised out of the waters, and caused to float upon them. Therefore the Ainus call the earth by the name *Moshiri*, i.e. 'floating land,' and hold the wagtail in great esteem.

10. Animism the root of Ainu polytheistic notions.—It was stated in § 4 that there are grounds for concluding the Ainu religion to have been monotheistic in nature at the commencement, and to have gradually developed later into polytheism. The moving cause of this evolution of dogma becomes very apparent when it is taken into consideration that the one great principle underlying Ainu theological notions in all their parts may be summed up in the one word, *Animism*—not animism as formerly employed in biology simply to denote the theory, of which Stahl is the chief exponent, that the soul (*anima*) is the vital principle, and the cause both of the normal phenomena of life and also of the abnormal phenomena of disease. It is this and very much more. Animism is here used in the wide sense given it by E. B. Tylor (*Prim. Cult.* chs. xi.–xvii.), as including the whole doctrine of souls and other spirit-entities, whether they be conceived of as being good, bad, or indifferent in nature and action.

According to universal Ainu ideas, not only are men and women, beasts, fishes, and fowls, trees and all plants, supposed to be animated with soul-life, but all other objects as well. Indeed, animism, as found to be developed among this people, is as uniform and comprehensive as the great τὸ πᾶν of the pantheistic creed, for it holds all nature in its embrace; yet so multiform is it, that it allows a distinct individual race and class of spirits to every order of phenomena. Accordingly, almost every conceivable object, whether visible or invisible, animate or inanimate, organic or inorganic, is endowed with a distinct personal, intelligent, and never-ending life. It is this conscious entity which works in and through it, that governs it and keeps it in its normal condition. Hence the bubbling spring and rippling rivulet, the rushing torrent, the flying clouds, whistling winds, pouring rain, roaring storm, and restless ocean,—all such things, together with animal and vegetable life, have their governing spirits within them, which must be treated with due respect by all men. This philosophy also asserts as one of its dogmas that even such objects as rocks and stones, lumps of clay, and grains of sand and dust, all have their separate class-life; and manufactured articles also, such as clothing and weapons, farming and fishing implements, eating and drinking utensils, and even entire huts, are supposed to have separate governing spirits of their own, which will live in the other world. This is not pantheism proper, for there is no trace of such a thing being thought of as one life naturally and of course swallowing up another; spiritual immortality is with them a personal immortality, and *Nirvāṇa* is quite unknown in their midst.

It is part of the animistic creed to look upon spirit-entities as having various degrees of intellect and higher and lower qualities of moral nature. And the more intelligent or the more beneficial to mankind any supposed spirit is thought to be, the higher is his station as a deity; while the less beneficent such an entity is conceived to be to the world in general, and, among men, to the Ainus in particular, and the more practical harm he does or is thought to be capable of doing, the greater demon is he considered to be. Thus, as beneficent objects said to contain personal, intelligent entities, springs of cool drinking water and sulphur baths are held in especial esteem; while, inasmuch as storms and diseases do damage and work death and destruction, they are looked upon as containing demons, some of a higher and some of a lower degree of moral nature and power.

11. All things supposed to be of dual parts.—According to Ainu statements, the people imagine all things to have two parts: the one inner, invisible, and ethereal in nature, and the other (corresponding to it) an outer, visible, and substantial, though not necessarily material, form—a form by which it reveals itself, through which it acts, and by which it makes itself felt. These two naturally go together, though they may be separated for a while at times (as in dreams, for example, when the soul is supposed to leave the body for a time), owing to special causes or for particular purposes. But the normal condition is for them to act together, the inner essence through the outer form. Further, the inner spirit may, if necessary to carry out some extraordinary purpose, even assume the outer form of an object not belonging to its class, and make itself seen and heard through it. In this we discover the basis for the thought of demoniacal or other possession.

12. Ainu ideas about anthropomorphism.—Nuttall, in his Standard Dictionary, defines anthropomorphism as being the ascription (*a*) of a human form to deity, (*b*) of human qualities and affections to deities, and (*c*) of human faculties to the lower animals. This definition is quite Occidental. An Ainu would not think of putting it in that way. He would certainly change the order by making it clear that man is the recipient and God the giver. He does not say, for example, that the deities are anthropomorphic, but that man is theomorphic in so far as his higher nature is concerned, and demon-like in everything that is evil about him. To all spirit-powers superior to man, whether in good or evil, are ascribed the most beautiful and the most hideous attributes of mankind. But it must not be supposed that because the people think of an object as being endowed with a personal, conscious life which can think and will and act for good or ill as it pleases, it is therefore in every instance anthropomorphic in structure. The inward and outer forms differ, and both will, it is thought, differ for ever. The outward form will always remain the same, whatever may be thought of the spirit form. It will be the same with all animals and trees, or with a blade of grass or a stone. As they are here, so will they be for ever in the next world. There is to be no change in form, and no extinction. The only *natural* change that can take place will be in the qualities of good and evil, for then evil will become more evil and goodness better.

13. The word for 'spirit' defined.—In discussing Ainu religion, it is always necessary to keep in mind the meaning of the word in use for 'spirit' or 'soul.' The term is peculiarly interesting, and deserves careful consideration. Its root has nothing whatever to do with such expressions as רוּחַ, σκιά, *umbra*, 'shade,' 'breath,' and so forth. It suggests quite a different set of ideas. It is *ramat* or *ramachi*, to which the Japanese term *tamashii* or *tama* is in all probability allied. But the root of *ramat* is *ram*, which is a noun meaning 'mind,' 'understanding,' 'intellect,' and then 'spirit,' 'soul,' 'essence,' the 'meaning of a word.' The final *at*, which at times is heard as *chi*, signifies existence, the root being *a*, 'to be.' Hence it is that gods and devils, elves, fairies, gnomes, goblins, and all spirits, of whatever race or order they be, are looked at from the side of intelligence rather than that of life alone (cf. § 10).

14. The sun a nature-god.—The Ainu religion, then, being thus animistic (see § 10) and anthropomorphic (see § 12) in principle, and each spirit agency being necessarily conceived of as endowed with *mind* or understanding (§ 13), the process of religious development becomes natural and easy, and nature-gods may be created both *ad libitum* and *ad infinitum*. The sun above us, for example, is seen to move; there is nothing haphazard about him; he rises and sets with the utmost regularity, and shines with surpassing splendour and with the evident good purpose of dispensing his welcome light and genial heat to the world. There is, therefore, it is thought, a living light-giving spirit (*ramat*) within the body or *num*,* i.e. 'ball,' of the sun, by whose influence he shines and by whose power he moves. He is one, indeed, who reminds us much of the Egyptian *Ra*,† for he too was supposed to be directed by a divine agency and personal will. In his own sphere among the lesser lights of heaven this stupendous and mysterious orb is chief and king, and the region of the east, whence he rises, is held sacred.

Inferior to the Creator (see § 5) yet superior to the sun in power is another spirit, malignant in nature. It is he who is supposed to be the cause of solar eclipses, and he is thought to be the very incarnation of diseases and other bodily evils. When the sun is eclipsed, this orb is supposed to be dying. That is to say, his intelligent life—*i.e.* his *ramat*—is departing from the outer visible substance and leaving the *num* black, cold, and dead. Yet he is never allowed quite to die, for a good superior spirit, who is either the Creator himself or His deputy, always, out of a kindly regard for mankind, graciously brings him back to his normal condition.‡

15. The moon.—The moon, who is said to be the wife of the sun, is not worshipped. There is a legend about her which runs as follows:

'The sun and moon are husband and wife. They are divine beings whose province it is to rule the heavens and the earth. The male is appointed to do his work in the daytime only, and the female at night. Sometimes, however, they may be seen travelling across the heavens in company. The divine sun is the larger of the two, has the brightest and best clothing to wear, and shines the most clearly. The moon is round like a cake of millet, and is clothed in dark and white garments which are worn one over the other. Now, the moon is sometimes invisible. When this is the case, it is because she has gone to visit her husband.'

16. Dualism.—In mentioning the supposed cause of solar eclipses (see § 14) we were brought face to face with the fact that dualistic ideas are rampant in the Ainu religion. Indeed, they are as much in evidence there as they are in the Avesta, where the struggle between Ormazd and Ahriman is so clearly depicted; or as they are in the Rig Veda, where Indra and Vṛtra form so constant a burden. The basis of dualistic ideas may be found (in so far as the Ainus are concerned) in their conception of spirit as defined in § 13, and of anthropomorphism as explained in § 12, taken in connexion with the antitheses of nature. The Ainus see so many contrary things ever present both within and outside of themselves, fighting, as they suppose, so much and so often against one another. Thus, light gives place to darkness, and bad weather to fine; rejoicing may be with us to-day, but to-morrow men must weep; this morning a child is born, and in the evening it dies; disease follows health, and good is succeeded by evil. Why, the Ainu asks, is this so? The explanation is simple. He who is the origin of light and life, of health and all good, is Himself the good true God (*Pase Kamui*, see § 5); while the source of disease, death, and all harm and evil in every degree and kind is naturally thought to be the *Nitne Kamui*, and all his agents the demons (see § 7).

* The Samoyedes believe in a supreme God of heaven called by this very name. The Tibetan name for God is *Nam*. Is it possible that these are all connected?

† Hardwick, *Christ and other Masters*, London, 1863, p. 443.

‡ For an account of an eclipse of the sun and the Ainu method of curing it, see *TASJ*, vol. xvi. part i. 1887.

No clearer illustration of the doctrine of dualism can be found than that exhibited by Ainu notions of the *Kamui* or superior spirits of the sea. The chief of these are two in number, named *Mo-acha* and *Shi-acha*. They are exactly the opposite of each other in character, and together with all the spirits of the ocean are called *Rep-un-Kamui*, i.e. 'deities in the sea.' *Shi-acha*, i.e. 'wild,' 'rough,' 'strong Uncle,' is always restless, and is continually pursuing his brother *Mo-acha*, i.e. 'Uncle of peace,' or 'calm.' *Mo-acha* is good, and is beloved and worshipped; while *Shi-acha* is dreaded and disliked as being evil. Though he is not thankfully worshipped, he is often propitiated by means of adulatory speeches and offerings. *Shi-acha* is said to be the cause of all harm done by and upon the sea, while his brother rules the calm. Another good illustration of this subject is afforded by the account the Ainus give of the devil's attempt to swallow the sun. (See *AF* 69).

17. Fire-worship.—It has already been pointed out in § 14 that the greatest visible nature deity of the heights is the sun. Of like nature is the chief deity of the terrestrial globe, fire. The personal essence of fire, that is to say, its supposed spirit, when upon the hearth, is said to be of the feminine gender, and, besides being called *Fuji*, *Unji*, or *Huchi* as the case may be (see § 3), is also named *Iresu-Kamui*, *i.e.* 'the divine being who rears us,' and *Iresu-Huchi*, i.e. 'the ancestress who rears us'—*Fuji* or *Huchi* meaning 'grandmother' or 'ancestress,' and *Iresu* 'to sustain' or 'to bring up.' She is the chief in her sphere and class, and is sometimes spoken of as a disease-destroying and body-purifying spirit. As she is of so great importance, and holds so high a position, it is not surprising to find that fire is in comparison most often worshipped. Indeed, so high is she supposed to be, that she is sometimes spoken of as the 'Governor of the world.' With respect to her, there are several tabued things which go to show how she is reverenced. Thus, for example, a burning log must not be struck with anything; the ashes must not be knocked out of a pipe into it; nothing must be taken out of it with a knife; a pair of scissors must not be placed near it; nail parings, saliva, and refuse of any kind must not be suffered to fall into it. That this goddess is looked upon as superintending matters connected with the house in which she dwells and is burning, may be gathered from such a prayer as the following: 'O thou divine goddess of fire, have mercy upon us and take care of this house.' And that she is thought to attend to the wants of the family is proved by the following address and prayer made to her at the time of a marriage: 'We have now settled to marry our son and daughter; therefore, O thou goddess of fire, hear thou and be witness thereto. Keep this couple from sickness, and watch over them till they grow old.' And that she is feared is proved by the fact that she is supposed to be the chief witness for or against a person in the day of judgment (see § 40). When that takes place, it is said that she will present the great Judge of all with a perfect picture of every word spoken and action done by each individual being, and from her there can be no appeal.

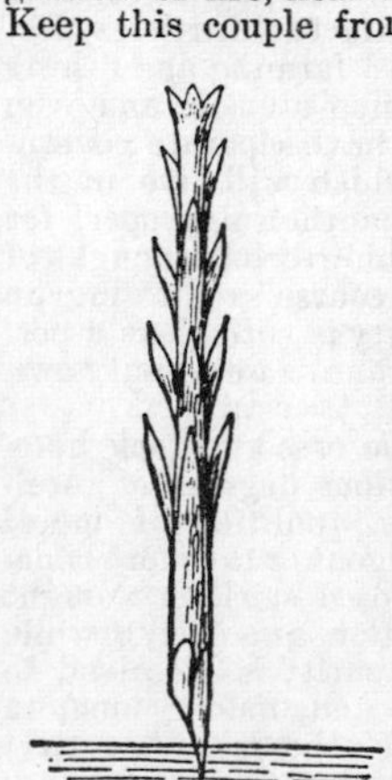

INUMBA-SHUTU-INAO OR REFINING-CLUB FETISH.

But not only are prayers said to the goddess of fire, offerings also are sent to her by means of fetishes, and libations are poured out for her acceptance. Whenever beer is brewed, which is mostly done at the end of the millet harvest, and immediately before the seed-sowing time, the Ainus always make a kind of *inao* or fetish out of wood, which they call *inumba-*

shutu-inao, i.e. 'refining-club fetish.' This instrument is used as a messenger to the spirit of fire, and is sent to her with some lees at the time of refining. It will be seen in the illustration here given that a hollow place is left at the top of the fetish. This is called the 'seat' or 'nest,' and is made so as to hold the lees presented. When these have been put on the 'seat,' drops of beer are offered to the various deities, and the fire is worshipped as follows: 'O divine grandmother, we drink beer to thee; we offer thee *inao*. Bless this household, and drive evil away. O keep us from all harm.' After this, prayer is offered to the spirit of the fetish itself thus: 'O refining-club fetish, take the lees now placed upon thee to the goddess of fire, and thank her on our behalf for all the blessings she has bestowed upon us. Tell her of our estate and welfare, and solicit her continual help and favour.' After having been thus offered and addressed, the fetishes are sometimes reverently burnt upon the hearth while prayer is being said, and so, in a way, the manes are sent to the spirit world. Sometimes, however, they are not burnt, but set up by the doorway as offerings to the deities of doors. The husband of the goddess of fire, that is to say, 'the household *inao*' mentioned in § 24, is also associated with his consort in the prayers said on such occasions.

18. Various nature-deities.—Before treating of the subject now incidentally mentioned, viz. fetishism, it will be well to mention some other nature-deities. After the goddess of fire, the chief of these seems to be one called *Toi-kuru-puni-kuru*, or 'He who rises from the surface of the earth.' He is said to have a wife who is called *Toi-kuru-puni-mat*, or 'She who rises from the surface of the earth.' These, it may be said, represent that class of deities whose province it is to attend to the well-being of vegetation. They are said to be of a good nature and disposition, and are consequently worshipped. This couple seem to represent the male and female principles of nature. The natural law by which rain descends and clears away is represented by one called *Pe-konchi-koro-guru*, or 'He who wears the water-cap.' The Ainus say that this deity appears as a great rain-cloud. He is considered good, and ought therefore to be worshipped. There is a legend concerning him which runs as follows: 'Once upon a time the Ainus were at war. The enemy had pressed them very hard, and had set fire to their houses. Upon this, the people called upon all the deities they could think of for deliverance. Soon a large cloud arose from the mountains, and, floating directly to the burning village, rained heavily upon it and extinguished the flames. They then learned for the first time that this cloud was a god. He has been worshipped ever since this event, and the name "He who wears the water-cap" was then given him.' Another class is represented by one called *Ikoro-koro-guru*, or 'He who possesses great treasure.' Another name given him is *Nupuri-koro-Kamui*, or 'The divine possessor of the mountains.' He has yet a third name by which he is known, and that is *San-ru-e-poro-Kamui*, or 'The divinity with the large footprints.' This deity is the representative of such animals as are worshipped. When he makes himself visible, he is said to come always in the bodily form of a bear, and it is supposed to be his special business to attend to the wants and general welfare of the forests and mountains.

19. The spirits of the air.—Like the gods of the earth, the deities of the air are found to be very numerous. And they too may in some cases be regarded as personifications of the laws of nature. After the god of the sun mentioned in § 14 comes one called *Shi-nish-e-ran-guru*, or 'The person who comes down to the highest clouds.' He has a consort whose name is *Shi-nish-e-ran-mat*, or 'She who comes down to the highest clouds.' These are both worshipped, and they are supposed to move the clouds which they inhabit. Then follow *Nochiu-e-ran-guru* and his consort *Nochiu-e-ran-mat*, i.e. 'He' or 'She who comes down to the constellations.' It is their joint duty to attend to the shining and well-being of the stars. These also are worshipped. The last class to be mentioned is supposed to attend to the lower clouds and fogs, and is represented by a pair called *Urara-e-ran-guru* and *Urara-e-ran-mat*, i.e. 'He' or 'She who descends in fogs.' They are said to be worshipped by some.

20. The demons of land and air.—In all things the Ainus are firm believers in an almost co-ordinated array of hostile deities who manifest their malignant nature by creating disease, death, and every kind of evil. Speaking of these matters, an Ainu once said to the present writer: 'As the demons of the air are so near this earth, it is possible for them to pay us frequent visits, and even to dwell among us. This accounts for so much that is evil in the world.' Referring to the dryads of the forests, he said: 'There are a great number of them. The genii who work evil to men are part of these; and though dwelling in the forests and mountains, they have their real home in the air around us. They are the servants of the prince of devils.' Whirlwinds also, however small they may be, are looked upon as embodiments of evil spirits.

One of the chief demons of the earth is called *Nitat-unarabe*, or 'Aunt of swamps *or* marshes.' And she, as her name implies, is supposed to have her home in fens, moors, and other damp places. Very many of the evilly disposed demons, ghosts, and ghouls are thought to be her offspring, and those which owe their origin to her go by the name of *Toi-hekunra*. The following legend gives a fair idea as to what the people consider them to be like:

All ghosts are closely related to the demon of swamps. They are very large and have extraordinarily big heads, while their hair is always rough. When seen, it is nearly always found to be standing upright. However, as they appear only after dark, and are but dimly seen, one cannot tell exactly what they are like. When they reveal themselves, it is only in order to bewitch people, and to do them harm. They are dreadful creatures, and, as they are true demons, are much to be feared. They came by their origin in this way. After God had finished making the world, He threw His mattocks away among the mountains, and left them there to rot. But as they decayed, they changed themselves into demons and ghosts. They should be carefully avoided, for if a person catches but a glimpse of one, possession immediately follows, even though the demons themselves should not see the persons who have observed them. These ghosts walk only at night; it is, therefore, best for all people not to go out of doors after dark. Such, indeed, is the command of the ancients. Now, if a person should have the misfortune to meet one of these creatures, he should hasten to say the following words: 'O you demon, I have been desiring to see and speak with you for a very long time, and now at last we have fortunately met. What I wanted to tell you is this. At the other end of the world there is a certain demon called *Moshiri-shinnai-sam* who has been most grievously backbiting you. He says: "There is a demon inhabiting the marshes who is unbearably proud. She had better be careful, for if ever I come across her path, I will give her such a sound whipping that she will never forget it." Now, therefore, hasten away, for if he catches you, you will be flogged, and it will go hard with you, for he is a mighty one.' If one addresses the demon in this way, she will believe it and set out at once, filled with wrath, to take vengeance. These words are spoken to deceive the demon, and so frustrate her evil designs; and, unless they are said in her hearing, the person to whom she appears will immediately fall down and die. So say the ancients. This legend, when stripped of all verbiage, and considered in connexion with the general run of Ainu thought, shows the demon of the swamps to be merely malaria and ague personified.

After the evil principle which is supposed to reside in marshes, the chief of the demons appears to be one called *Kina-shut-un-guru*, or 'The person dwelling among the grass roots.' The demons which follow are very difficult to define, and are very numerous. *Toi-pok-un-chiri*, i.e. 'The underground bird,' is especially called upon for help by hunters in times of danger; but whom he represents, no one appears to know. Akin to this one is *Toikunrari-kuru*, with whom is associated his wife *Toikunrari-mat*. These names mean 'He (or She) close upon the surface of the earth.' These two are looked upon as the friends of hunters, and are called upon in times of danger. *Hopokike-ush*, who stands next in order, is said to be the demon who causes stones to rattle down the cliffs and mountain sides. These are but classes of demons, for such creatures are very numerous indeed. They inhabit all kinds of places, such as the tops and bottoms of mountains, the flat surfaces of rocks, all kinds of flora, stony places, and localities where dust or sand prevails. The winds also have their demons, good and bad, and so have rain, mist, snow, hail, sleet, frost, ice, etc. (see *AF*, ch. 51).

21. Gods and demons of the sea and rivers.—All the larger kinds of fishes and sea animals have divine honours paid them, as, for example, whales, sea-leopards, sea-lions, sword-fish, salmon, trout, sea-tortoises, and so forth. These are all worshipped. So far as one can learn, the principal deities of the sea are as follows:—*Rep-un-riri-kata inao uk Kamui*, 'The god upon the waves of the sea who receives fetishes.' Whenever he allows himself to be seen, it is said to be in the form of a whale. He is looked upon as the head of all sea-deities, and has many servants, of whom the tortoise and the albatross are his favourites. Prayers are said to this god quite frequently, and the two servants just mentioned are said to act as go-betweens. Messages are conveyed through them and offerings of fetishes and beer are sent by them to him. The heads of these creatures are often to be seen kept as charms, and worshipped by the fishermen. The deity who is supposed to be next in order is called *Kai-pe-chupka-un-kuru*, i.e. 'The person who resides in the eastern surf.' As the name implies, he is said to have his home somewhere near the shore towards the east. We are informed that in bodily form he is like a large fish of some kind; but what kind of fish is not now known. He is supposed to be very good, and is therefore often worshipped, and given presents of fetishes and beer. The spirits next in order are the *Shi-acha* and *Mo-acha* mentioned in § 16.

There is an Ainu controversy about this couple, for by some the two names are said to represent one object only, and that object the whale! *Mo*, meaning 'peace' or 'calm,' is made to apply to the lee side of him, and *shi*, which means 'great' or 'rough,' is said to be his weather side. Or, some say again that he is called *mo* because he is gentle, and *shi* because he is very large. A legend regarding him is as follows. 'Once upon a time two Ainus were out at sea fishing, when they were suddenly overtaken by a severe storm. As their boat was in great danger of being swamped, they gave themselves to earnest prayer. Every known god of the sea was called upon for help, but all to no purpose. At length a very large whale, a whale as big as a mountain, was seen to rise out of the water, and gradually came to the side of the boat. It remained there till the storm was over, sheltering the boat from the wind and waves. This was no other than *Mo-acha* or *Shi-acha*. He was not known before that time, but has ever since been honoured with the prayers of the Ainu fishermen.' Other names given him are *Mo-acha-ahunge-guru*, 'The bringer in of the uncle of peace,' and *Shi-acha-ahunge-guru*, 'The bringer in of the uncle of roughness' or 'storm.'

The next deity of the sea is a goddess who is known by the name of *Chiwash-ekot-mat*. This name means 'The female possessor of the places where the fresh and salt waters mingle.' It is said to be her duty to watch at the mouths of rivers and allow the fish, particularly the spring and autumn salmon, to go in and out.

The specially evil demons of the sea are numerous. The name of the chief is *Ko-notu-ran-guru*, or 'He who descends upon the calm sea.' He, it is said, causes storms. Any abnormal fish, whether it be abnormal in form or colour, is supposed to be unlucky, and to belong to this demon. When caught, such fish are immediately tossed back into the sea. They are called *Ikonnup*, or 'things of misfortune.' This demon is married, and his wife's name is the same as his own, excepting that it has a feminine suffix. All mermaids are supposed to be her offspring, and are called *Ruru-koshinpuk* and *Atui-koshinpuk*.

These names mean 'Salt-water' and 'Sea-mermaids.' A young fisherman gave the present writer the following fact illustrating this matter. He said that he and his father while fishing once caught a kind of tortoise which the Ainus call *kinapo*. On examination it was found to have one foot very much whiter than the others, and this the father considered ought not to have been. On making the discovery, the old man declared it to be 'a misfortune-giving thing.' He therefore cut the foot off, and, letting the tortoise drop into the sea, said, '*Nani Ko-notu-ran-guru akore na, pirika no eyam yan*; 'O Ko-notu-ran-guru, I give this directly to you, take good care of it.' Next follows the demon called *Kai-pok-un-guru*. He is married, and together with his consort is said to 'reside under the surf' upon the seashore. *Ota-patche-guru* and his wife come next, and they are supposed to be the spirits who 'make the sand fly.'

The river demons are also very numerous, and their names indicate their work. They are: *Konupki-ot-guru*, or 'dwellers in muddy places.' They are said to reside specially near the river banks. *Chiuka-pinne Kamui rametok* ('the brave and divine male current') comes next. Then there are *Chiu-range guru* and his wife ('they who send the current'), and *Kochiu-tunash guru* with his wife, *i.e.* 'persons of the swift current,' and others too numerous to mention. The river deities are called *Wakka-ush-Kamui* ('water gods'). All rivulets and tributaries are said to be their offspring. They are named *Kamui poteke*, i.e. 'the little hands of the deities,' and *Kamui matnepo*, *i.e.* 'daughters of God.' Then there is *Petru-ush-mat* ('the female of the waterways'), together with *Pet-etok-mat* ('the female source of rivers'). Mermaids are called *Pe-boso-ko-shinpuk*, i.e. 'mermaids who pass through the water.' They are also called *Mimtuchi* and *tumnunchi*, i.e. 'fat' and 'fleshy devils.'

22. The demons of diseases.—Although, as was shown in § 20, many demons are supposed to have their origin and homes in marshes, yet the Ainus believe that demons of disease come in great measure from the sea, as the following lore shows:

'Various diseases from time to time attack the body. Such, for example, are ague, fever, heavy colds, stomach-ache, and consumption. Now, when these complaints arise, the men should meet together and go to the villages up and down the rivers, and take from each hut a small quantity of millet, fish, tobacco, skunk-cabbage, and cow-parsnip. These should all be brought to an appointed place, where the men should also come together and pray. After prayer they should carry them to the seashore, and, having made fetishes, reverently place them by their side. When this has been done, they should pray, saying, "O ye demons of sea harbours, have mercy upon us. O ye demons of disease, ye are fearful beings: we have, therefore, with one accord met together and decided to enrich you with fetishes and various kinds of food. Do ye wait upon those of your kind who have afflicted us, and on our behalf entreat them to take their departure. We present these articles of food for you to eat, and the fetishes are paid as fines. O all ye demons who watch over the harbours, cause the demons of disease to be taken away from our village."'

23. Fetishism.—The specific doctrines of Ainu religion as relating to the nature of their supposed superior spirits being such as that now stated (see especially §§ 10–13, 16, 17), the way to fetishism is short, direct, and logical. But fetishism is a term which has its difficulties, and must, to save confusion of thought, be defined before going further. The name is a Portuguese term derived from *feitiços*, and has long been in use in Portugal to designate the relics of saints, amulets, and charms in general use by the Roman Catholics. It was applied by Portuguese merchants to objects of many varieties to which the natives of the West Coast of Africa paid religious honour.* In

* See Jevons, *Introduction to the History of Religion*, London, 1896, p. 169.

Rouquetti's Portuguese Dictionary *feitiços* is explained by the French equivalent *sortilège*, *maléfice*, *enchantement*, *charme*. The term *Fétichisme*, as the name of the corresponding religion, was first employed by President de Brosses in his *Du culte des Dieux Fétiches* (1760). Among the Ainus a fetish is looked upon as a medium employed by a person by which one spirit (*ramat*, see § 13) is caused to act upon another for good or ill. It may be, and often is, by way of courtesy called a *Kamui* ('deity'), but it is only a deity of a lower order, and simply used as a go-between. Thus, for example, should a man desire to worship a good river deity or to propitiate an evil one, or should he wish to harm another person or have him blessed, he would make some fetishes out of sticks of wood or other substance and send them with messages to the gods or demons. This is the use of fetishes among the Ainus. They may, therefore, well be called media, for they are just as much media as persons who take verbal messages from one to another. The term by which the principal fetishes are known in Ainu quite agrees with this definition. It is *inao*, i.e. 'message-bearer.' Its roots are *ina* ('message,' 'request'), and *o* ('bear,' 'contain'). It appears to lie at the root of the word for prayer, which is *inonno* in Ainu and *inori* in Japanese. It is curious to remark that in ancient Japanese *inori* meant 'to curse.' As the word carries this meaning, we are not at all surprised,—nay, we should rather expect to find Ainu fetishes used for both good and evil purposes, and sent to gods and demons alike.

24. Fetishism in Ancestor-worship.—One of the most important and relatively highest fetishes the Ainus possess—and every family must have this one—is called *Chisei koro inao* ('the fetish who possesses the house'), also called *Chisei epungine ekashi* ('ancestral caretaker of the house'). It is the province of the spirit of this fetish to assist the goddess of the fire (see § 17) in looking after the general well-being of the family. His special abiding-place is in the sacred north-east corner of the hut, at the back of the family heirlooms. He is not only worshipped where he stands, but is also sometimes brought out from his abiding-place and stuck in a corner of the hearth, where prayers are actually addressed to him as the husband of the fire, which in its turn is called the 'ancestress,' i.e. *fuji* or *huchi*. The way this fetish is made is as follows: A piece of hard wood, such as lilac, say an inch or two in diameter, is taken. This is to form the stem, and is usually about two feet in length. One part is shaved with a sharp knife from top to bottom to represent the front. Near the top a gash is cut across in imitation of a mouth, and a little below this the so-called heart is carefully bound in. This heart, when first given to it, consists of a warm black cinder freshly taken from the hearth and firmly tied with a string made of twisted willow shavings to the stem, which is called the *netoba*, i.e. 'body.' After the heart has been bound in, a number of willow shavings are hung all round so that the stem with its mouth and heart is quite hidden from view. After it has been respectfully made, it is reverently stuck in the ground by the fireside, and the following dedicatory prayer is devoutly said to it: 'O fetish, you are henceforth to reside in this house with the goddess of fire; you are her husband, and your place will be in the treasure corner. Please help her to watch over us, and do you bless us.'

All this reminds us forcibly of the *Lares* and *Penates* of the ancient Romans, the one great difference being that the 'fire' and 'household' gods of the Ainus are more clearly defined by their names. At the present day the Ainus do not seem to look upon this as ancestor-worship; they do not, indeed, know what it is. But the names given them go to show that in its origin it was such.

A curious thing about the fetish is the fact that it is thought to be connected in some psychological way with the present living head of the family in which it has been dedicated. The following piece of lore explains this:

'The chief fetish should be made, in so far as its stem is concerned, of lilac, because this is found to be a hard kind of wood and does not quickly decay, even if stuck in the damp ground out of doors. It is not considered wise to use any other wood than lilac for this purpose, for in olden times a certain man made one of *cercidiphyllum*, the end of which rotted after a short time, so that it fell over. Not many months after, the owner himself became weak and died. This was owing to the influence of the fetish having been withdrawn. For this reason it is now known that the stem should be made of lilac only, that being the most durable wood of all. However, should a person happen to be in a place where he cannot obtain lilac, he may use either willow or *cercidiphyllum*, but these must not be kept long for fear they should rot away. When they become a little old, they should either be cast right away into the forest or reverently burnt upon the hearth before they have a chance of decaying. Others should then be made in their place.'

THE STEM.

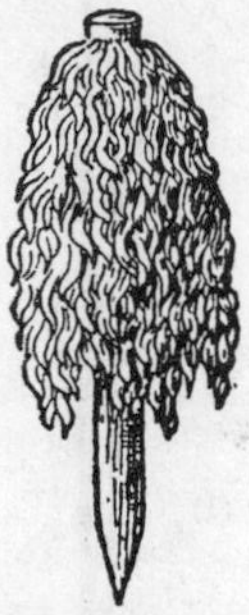

THE HOUSEHOLD FETISH.

25. Ancestor-worship in general.—Prayers to the dead form a fairly strong feature in Ainu religion. The necessity for them is taught the people thus:

'If a person cultivates a spirit of selfishness, and offers nothing by way of food and drink to his deceased ancestors, the elders of the people should warn him, saying, "Foolish and wicked person, thou art a fool, and thou dost not understand; thou shalt die a hard death." If this be said, all the people, young and old alike, will be careful to worship the dead.' Another short counsel runs thus: 'Should a person leave his home and go away and die in a strange land, some of his relatives must surely go to his grave and there worship and offer libations. The dead observe all deeds, good and bad. Those who do what is right are blessed, and those who do what is evil are cursed by them.'

Women are not allowed to take part in religious exercises in so far as the deities are concerned, but they are commanded to make offerings to their deceased husbands and ancestors. The words they are usually taught to say on such occasions are as follows: 'O ye honourable ancestors, I am sent to present this beer and food to you.' On being asked why this ceremony should take place, an Ainu gave this piece of lore:

'The divine *Aioina* said, "If the people do good while upon the earth and not evil, though they die young they go to heaven. When there, they have good hunting." It is good for people on this earth to offer those who have gone before to Paradise food, beer, and lees. Not to do so shows lack of filial respect. Those who have departed still live and take an interest in those left behind. They should, therefore, be reverenced; unless respect is paid to them, they will come to this earth again and bring misfortune. When, therefore, ye have food, remember your ancestors. This will please them, and they will send you good health and prosperity! So spake *Aioina*.'

The ceremony of ancestor-worship is called *shinnurappa*, i.e. 'libation-dropping,' and takes place outside the huts by the east-end window and a little towards the west. Fetishes and beer are offered, and a prayer such as this said: 'O ye ancestors now dwelling in the underworld, we offer you beer and lees; receive them and rejoice.

Your grandchildren have met together specially to offer these things. Rejoice. Watch over us, and keep us from sickness. Give us a long life so that we may continue to offer such gifts.'

26. Private or tutelary fetish.—The fetish mentioned in § 24 was shown to belong to the family as a whole, but there is another very important one which is quite personal. It is always made of willow. Why it is regarded as of so high importance the following legend will show: 'When God made man, He formed his body of earth, his hair of chickweed, and his spine of a stick of willow.' And so, the backbone being regarded as the principal part of the human body, it is looked upon as the seat of life. It is said that no warrior of old could be killed unless his spine was injured.

When a child has been born, some very near blood relative of the male sex gets a nice clean stick of willow and shapes it into a fetish. When it is made, he proceeds to worship it, after which he reverently carries it to the bedside, and there

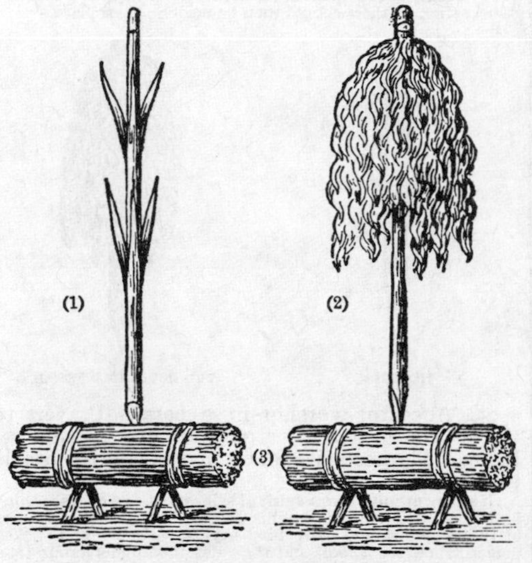

TUTELARY FETISH.

sets it up as the tutelary deity of the child. The accompanying illustrations show what it is like. That marked (1) is the willow stick itself, and is called the *shutu*, i.e. 'club'; that marked (2) is the club with the willow shavings attached, which are called *inao-kike*, i.e. 'fetish shavings'; the bundle of reeds marked (3) is called *Kamui-set*, 'the divine seat' or 'throne.' The end is stuck into this so as to keep it dry, and thus prevent it from rotting. That this fetish may be rightly called the angel of the child's growth the following folklore makes clear:

'As the backbone of man is made of willow wood, the men should hasten to make *inao* of this tree as soon as a child has been born. After it has been properly whittled, it should be addressed thus: "As thou, O fetish, art divine, we worship before thee. When God formed man in the beginning, He made his spine out of a piece of willow wood. We therefore call upon thee, O willow fetish, to watch over this child while he is growing up. Guard him and give him strength, together with long life." After this prayer has been said, the fetish should be reverently stuck in its "seat" and placed by the child's side. When the child has grown up, he should frequently procure beer and worship this, his guardian angel.' As might be expected, this fetish is particularly worshipped in time of sickness by the individual for whom it was made. The following is a prayer taught some children for their use on such an occasion: 'O thou willow god, as thou art my spine and backbone, do thou hasten to heal me and make me strong. O thou dear deity, I am ill, and my body is weak; pray help me soon.' If this prayer is said devoutly, it is supposed that the sufferer will soon recover from his malady.

So, too, when older people fall sick, willow fetishes are made by the old men and worshipped, after which some of them are sent to the Creator and other superior deities with messages. And, when all is done, they are taken outside to the sacred place at the eastern end of the hut. Here they are carefully stuck in the ground, and libations of beer offered them. It is, therefore, not surprising to find that the Ainus formerly used to reverence the willow almost as much as the Papuans did the *waringen* tree; who, we are told, had such an affection for it that the wilder tribes of Ceram used to lodge, and almost live, among its branches (Earl, *Papuans*, 116, 160).

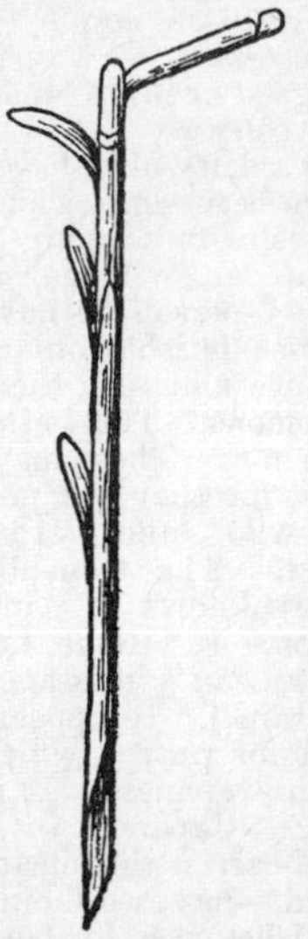

NITNE-INAO, OR 'EVIL FETISH.'

27. Demon-worship.—The worship of demons is one of fear among this people, and is as a rule performed by way of propitiation. This becomes very clear when a certain kind of fetish called *nitne-inao* or *nitne-hash-inao*, i.e. 'evil fetish' or 'evil bush fetish,' is made and used. The purpose of it may be gathered from the prayer which follows. This kind of fetish is used especially in times of sickness, for on such occasions an afflicted person is supposed to be possessed by a demon of disease. It is called an evil fetish, not because it is itself regarded as being of an evil nature, but rather because the occasion on which it is used is a bad one. It is sent to the wicked demon of disease; this is why it is called evil. When it is made, a kind of stew called *nitne-haru*, i.e. 'evil stew,' is prepared and offered with it. This consists of bones of fish, some vegetables, and the remnants of any kind of food, mixed together and well boiled. When all has been prepared, the fetish is stuck in the ground upon the hearth, and the stew, which has by no means an inviting smell, is placed before it. Then a so-called prayer is said as follows:

'O evil fetish, take this evil food, together with the disease of this sick person, and also the demon who has possessed him, and go with them to hell. When you arrive there, please make it so that the demon will not return to this earth again.

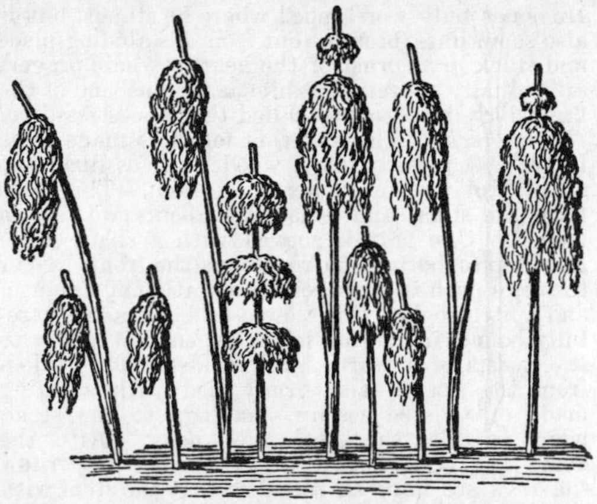

NUSA, OR CLUSTER OF INAO.

I have supplied you with food; take it to the demon and propitiate him; please feed him with it.'

After this the patient is beaten with *takusa*, a bunch of grass; and if the fetish is successful in his errand, it is supposed that a cure will follow. After the worship has been performed, the fetish is taken outside the hut and stuck up at the *nusa* place, where the stew is set before it. Here the following prayer is said to the demon of the rubbish-heap: 'O thou angry demon, O thou demon of the rubbish-heap, accept this fetish and food; make haste and heal this sick person.' The man who officiates at this ceremony then returns to the hut, where he again exorcizes the demon by brushing the patient down with the *takusa* mentioned above.

Fetishes of the following shape are also sometimes used for this purpose. The present writer has several times seen them set up in the huts of sick people, and very earnestly worshipped. After having been prayed to, the spirit of the fetish is supposed to wander about in the earth and visit the various demons of evil on behalf of the sick man, and, after having found them, is said to consult with them as to what is best to be done for the patient.

SHUTU-INAO, *i.e.* 'CLUB FETISH.'

28. Special fetishes for epidemic disease.—In the event of any village being attacked by an epidemic disease, but more especially if the disease be of a severe and dangerous nature, as, for example, smallpox, the Ainus of the villages immediately surrounding the infected one get sticks of elder or cladrastis, about four feet in length, and make them into fetishes or charms. These instruments are called *chikappo-chiko-mesup*, i.e. 'little carved birds,' by some, and *rui-shutu-inao*, i.e. 'thick club fetish,' by others. They are also named *kotan-kikkara-inao*, i.e. 'fetishes for village defence.' As soon as set up they are devoutly worshipped, when the people call upon them to drive the dread disease away. They are supposed to represent the eagle-owl, which is thought to have power over this particular evil. The slit in the top of the fetish given in the illustration is said to represent the mouth, and the shavings left on the sides are intended for feathers. Food is sometimes placed in the mouth as an offering to the demons to whom the fetish is sent. That which the writer has seen consisted in one case of putrified fish mixed with brimstone, and in another of *cynanchum Caudutum.* It is said that the

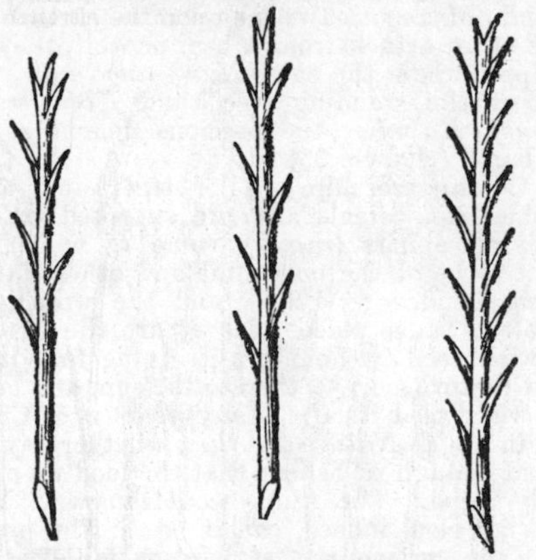

CHIKAPPO-CHIKO-MESUP, OR 'LITTLE CARVED BIRDS.'

demons, being unable to withstand the smell of these things, will flee from them.

29. Fetishes for the sea-gods.—The fishermen have one kind of fetish which is a special favourite with them. It is called *hash-inao*, i.e. 'bush fetish.' This kind is made by cutting a short stick, and either splitting it at one end and inserting a shaving in the opening so made, or else by cutting a few gashes in it in an upward direction, as shown in the illustration. The gashes cut across the top are said to represent the mouth. Though willow is the favourite wood used, yet they may be made of dogwood, lilac, cercidiphyllum, ash, magnolia, or oak—indeed, of almost any wood which happens to be nearest to hand. When being set up, a good representative prayer said to them runs thus: 'O ye gods who govern the waters, O ye water deities, we are now about to go fishing. Please accept

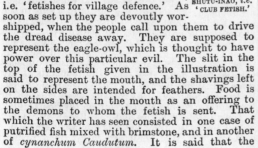

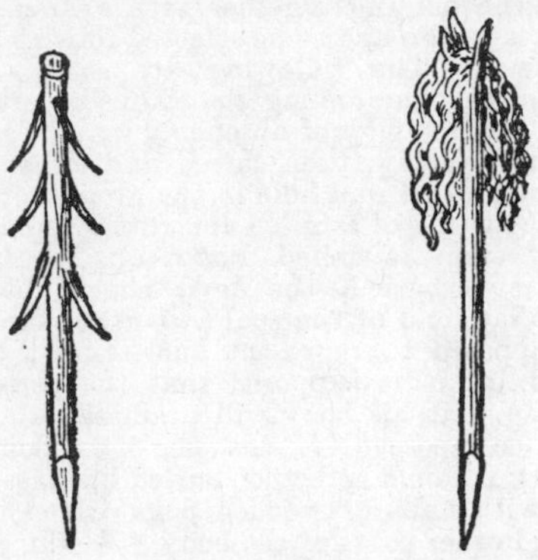

HASH-INAO

these fetishes and watch over us. Grant that we may catch many fish to-day.'

30. Religious charms.—In so far as their purpose is concerned, the dividing line between the fetishes mentioned in the preceding sections and the various kinds of charms in use among this people is not very clearly defined, so that it is often most difficult to distinguish between them; that is to say, he would be a bold person who should venture to put his finger first on one and say, 'This is a fetish,' and then on another and say, 'This is a charm'; for either may be both, and both either, according to the time and purpose for which they are made. The charms are very numerous, and are used for many purposes. Among other objects, rocks *in situ* and also stones of various shapes and sizes may be found employed both for purposes of personal protection against evil, and as a means for working harm to others (*AF* 398); the skins, bones, feathers, and beaks of birds are sometimes kept as love-charms (75, 76); snake skin is thought to be a special talisman, energetic, if properly treated, in working good in the storehouses and garden seeds (209); birds' eggs and nests are special cereal charms, while the heads of some kinds of birds are kept and used for driving away disease (219); the heart of the 'dipper' is a charm supposed to bestow eloquence and quick sight (336); bears' eyes swallowed whole are said to produce long and clear sight in hunters. The skulls of bears, foxes, bats, falcons, owls, kites, and the fore-feet of hares are also all worshipped at times and used as charms (*AF*, ch. 34). The horns of deer, and the stones sometimes found in the bladders of animals, are also thought much of as charms supposed to bring good luck to the happy finder and possessor (401).

31. Magic.—Following close upon the subject of fetishes and charms, and very nearly related to these objects in principle and nature, comes magic, sometimes called sympathetic magic. This has been defined by Zimmern as 'the attempt on man's part to influence, persuade, or compel spiritual beings to comply with certain requests or demands' (see Aston's *Shinto*, London, 1905, p. 327). Bearing in mind the meaning of the word for 'spirit' (*ramat*; § 13), and that all things are supposed to have spirit in them, and remembering the definition of *Kamui* (God) and the various objects to which this term is applied (§ 4), and not forgetting the fact that the Ainus do not so much worship the visible objects to which their prayers are addressed, as pray to the spirits, good and evil, supposed to animate them, we find this definition very apt in so far as this people is concerned.

The Ainu terms for magic are *ichashkara*, i.e. 'a shutting up,' or 'enclosing in a fence,' and *ishirishina*, i.e. 'binding up tightly,' and it usually implies the binding together with a curse of two objects, a person and some selected fetish supposed to be evil. The following are some common methods in vogue among the Ainus of practising this art. The effigy of an enemy may be made of mugwort or straw, then cursed and either buried head downwards in a hole in the ground or placed under the trunk of a fallen and rotting tree. This kind of effigy is called *inoka*, i.e. 'the image.' When it is buried, the devil should be called upon to lay hold of the soul (*ramat*) of the person it is supposed to represent and take it to hell. By this act it is supposed that the person will sicken so that his body will gradually die as the image decomposes (*AF*, chs. 30, 31). Sometimes the effigy is found to be not buried but fastened to a tree with nails or wooden pegs driven into its head and other parts of the body. Again, another plan is to make an *inao* fetish of the guelder-rose and ask it to depart at once with the soul to the region inhabited by the demons. Sometimes a little boat is made of rotten wood, and the effigy of an enemy is placed in it together with an idol supposed to be a demon. When made, the demon is worshipped and asked to row the soul of the cursed one to hell. Sometimes, again, the head-dress of a person is taken, wrapped up in a bag in the shape of a corpse prepared for burial, and placed in a hole in the ground to rot. It is supposed that as this decomposes, the enemy to whom it belonged will sicken and die. The demons of some kinds of trees are also at times asked to curse one's enemies by seizing their souls and turning them into devils.

But magic, as one would naturally expect, may also be used for good purposes. Thus, for example, upon returning one very cold night from a journey with the Ainu head of a family, we found some convolvulus roots set up in a warm place before the fire upon the hearth. Upon making inquiries as to the meaning of this, we were informed that it was intended as a charm to prevent our feet from being frozen during the journey. Of the frequent use of trees in magic, a full account may be found in *AF*, ch. 30; cf. also § 33 below.

32. Bewitching, divination, and exorcism.—That bewitching people, exorcizing demons, and finding out things by divination are integral parts of Ainu religious superstitions cannot be doubted. A case of bewitching, by cutting holes in the garments of another person with a pair of scissors, which came under the writer's own observation, will be found in *AF*, p. 341 ff. Similarly a case of divination, by means of a fox's skull, is recorded (*ib.* pp. 350, 379 ff.). A case of exorcism by means of a tree, together with cutting clothes and beating with mugwort, will be found described on p. 315 of *AF*; while an account of a curious method of exorcizing the demon in madmen, by cutting their bodies with a sharp stone, shell, knife, or razor, and then thoroughly dipping them in a river, will be found set forth on p. 312. Cats are supposed to bewitch people in some instances (294, 507); dogs in some (507); and birds, such as the cuckoo, woodpecker, night-hawk, goat-sucker, and owl, in others (409); while such animals as hares (515), squirrels (500), otters (512), and various kinds of fish (522) are also supposed to possess this power. Indeed, there is no reason to suppose that there is any living creature in the earth which cannot bewitch, should it desire to do so.

33. Tree-worship.—The Ainus suppose not only that every tree has its own personal spirit (*ramat*), but that the roots also, the stem, bark, wood, heart, forks, knots, buds, leaves, twigs, crown, and every other part as well, are themselves each peopled with innumerable spirits, some of a good, and others of an evil, disposition. That the willow is regarded as a deity, and as such worshipped, has already been shown in § 26. Other kinds of trees also, such as the actinidia and grape vines, which are supposed to have had their origin in Paradise (156–158), dogwood, oak, spruce, spindle-wood, prunus, hornbeam, black alder, lilac, magnolia, yew, ash, azalia, cercidiphyllum, chestnut and mulberry, and others, are all worshipped on occasion (380). Some of these, as has already been shown in §§ 31, 32, are also used in cursing people and for the purpose of witchcraft, being at such times entreated to bring misfortune to one's enemies. For this purpose the guelder-rose, alder, poplar, elm, birch, hydrangea, and walnut are particularly employed (331, 332, 281). There are, however, other purposes, and those good religious ones, to which the Ainus put trees. The general name one usually hears applied to this cult is *Kim-o-chipaskuma*, i.e. 'the doctrine of the mountains,' and this particular part of it is named *Chikuni-akoshiratki orushpe*, i.e. 'news about preservation by trees.' Regarding this the Ainus say: 'When those Ainus who are acquainted with the cult of the mountains are about to start on a hunting expedition, they first, after having worshipped at the *nusa** cluster, go and select a large tree and worship its spirit, saying: "O thou great possessor of the soil, we are about to go and kill animals, pray help us; O see that we meet with no accidents, and prosper us." After this has been done, they set out fully expecting to come across much game.' This is tree-worship in its baldest form (cf. also § 26), and we see by it that the hunters regard the tree genii, for the time being, as their tutelary deities and guardians. In times of sickness, also, trees are worshipped. On such occasions the tree genii are called upon under various names, as, for instance, *Topochi*, 'the wise one,' and *Shirampa*, 'the one upon the earth.' Or, in case of an attack from a bear or wolf, they are worshipped under the name *Niashrange guru*, 'the person of the standing tree,' and *Kisara-range shinupuru Kamui*, 'the precious demon of the rough bark' (*AF*, ch. 33).

34. Cereal worship.—Like trees and other vegetable life, cereals also are supposed to contain living spirits (*ramat*), some of which are thought to be of the masculine and others of the feminine gender (*AF* 204), and the worship of them often takes place. Never are the gardens sown with seed without prayer being first made to the Creator (see § 5), then to the sun, and lastly to the very seed itself. Many years ago, Cicero asked, in his *de Natura Deorum*, whether any one was mad enough to believe that the food we eat is actually a god. The Ainus would answer, 'Yes,' and 'What else, indeed, can it be?' The prayer used at the ceremony of eating new millet at the harvest thanksgiving is very interesting, and shows clearly that it is the spirit of the food partaken of that is worshipped, and not God, the Giver of all good gifts. The prayer runs thus:

'O thou cereal deity, we worship thee. Thou hast grown very well this year, and thy flavour will be sweet. Thou art good. The goddess of fire will be glad, and we also shall rejoice greatly. O thou God! O thou divine cereal! do thou nourish the people.' The person who officiates then continues, 'I now partake of thee. I worship thee and give thee thanks.' After having thus prayed, the persons present take a cake and eat it among them, and from this time the new millet is common food. Commenting on this, Aston says (*Shinto*, p. 160): 'Gratitude in the first place to, and then for, our daily bread, is an important factor in the early growth of religion. Without it

* See illustration under § 27.

we should have had no Roman Ceres, no Mexican Maize-god Centliotl, and no Ukemochi' (cf. also p. 277, Nihi-name).

But eating the god is by no means limited to cereals among the Ainus, for the bear sacrifice partakes of quite the same nature, to which subject we shall now proceed.

35. The bear festival.—Although animals of many kinds, and birds also (see *AF*, chs. 36–39), even down to a tiny sparrow, are at times first worshipped and then killed in sacrifice, it is (when considering this phase of the subject) to the bear festival that we must look for the highest expression of Ainu religion. The general name given for 'sacrifice' is *iyomande*, which means 'to send away,' so we must expect that when a living object is sacrificed, the spirit is supposed to be 'sent' somewhere, and for some purpose. And here it may be well to ask, To whom is the bear sent, and why? To this question it must be replied in the first place that, so far as can be ascertained, there is now (whatever there may have been in olden times) no idea of substitution underlying the practice; nor, secondly, is it piacular, for the people know nothing of the 'shedding of blood for the remission of sins.' All thoughts, therefore, connected with the old Jewish notion of sacrifice must be left out of the question when considering Ainu ideas concerning it. The very essence of Ainu religion consists in communion with the greater powers, and the people imagine that the most complete communion they can possibly hold with some of their gods—animals and birds, to wit*—is by a visible and carnal partaking of their very flesh and substance in sacrifice. At the time of offering, the living victim is said to be sent to his ancestors in another place. Still, at the same time, the bear festival is a kind of mutual feast—a feast of friendship and kinship—in which Bruin himself also participates. Indeed, the bear is offered to himself and his worshippers in common, and they are supposed to have a good happy time of communion together. But as this is a very difficult and, in some ways, a very important subject, it has been thought best to give a simple description of the festival as now practised, and let it speak for itself.

That the Ainus rear bear cubs in cages and often pay them divine honours is a well-known fact. The present writer once visited a village where as many as ten cubs were caged. After they have come to the age of two, or rarely three, years, and it has been decided that a sacrifice is to take place, the owner sends out an invitation to the people, which runs thus: 'I, so and so, am about to sacrifice the dear little divine thing from among the mountains. My friends and masters, come ye to the feast; we will then unite in the great pleasure of *iyomande*, "sending the god away." Come.' This is certain to be heartily responded to. When the guests have all arrived, the men make many fetishes (*inao*), stick them in the hearth, and perform worship. When this has been properly done, most of the *inao* are reverently taken up and carried by the men to the *nusa* place outside the hut and there stuck up. Next, two long, thickish poles are carefully laid at their base. The men now come reverently out of the hut, ornamented with their crowns, and solemnly approach the cage containing the bear. The women and children follow singing, dancing, and clapping their hands, for all are in anticipation of having a jolly time. Having reached their appointed place, all sit in a circle, the old men in front and the women and children behind. After all this has been arranged, an Ainu is chosen, who, having approached the bear, sits down before it and tells it that they are about to send it forth to its ancestors. He prays pardon for what they are about to do, hopes it will not be angry, tells it what an honour is about to be conferred upon it, and comforts it with the consolation that a large number of *inao* and plenty of wine, cakes, and other good cheer will be sent along with it. He also informs it that if it be a good and proper bear, it will appear again later to be treated in like manner. The last address we heard of ran thus: 'O thou divine one, thou wast sent into the world for us to hunt. O thou precious little divinity, we worship thee; pray hear our prayer. We have nourished thee and brought thee up with a deal of pains and trouble, all because we love thee so. Now, as thou hast grown big, we are about to send thee to thy father and mother. When thou comest to them, please speak well of us and tell them how kind we have been; please come to us again, and we will once more sacrifice thee.' After such a prayer the bear is taken out of its cage with ropes and made to walk about in the circle formed by the people. Here it is shot at for some time with blunt arrows called *hepere-ai*, i.e. 'cub-arrows,' and so teased till it becomes quite furious. After this the poor animal is securely tied to a stake for

HEPERE-AI.

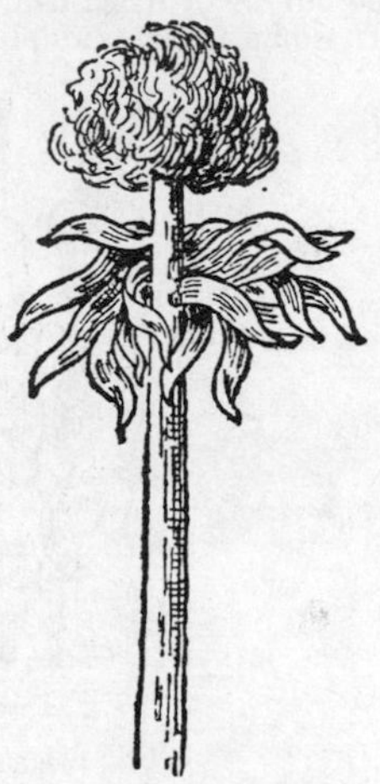

TUSH-OP-NI.

the last scene before its death. This stake, which is ornamented at the top with tufts of arundinaria, is called *tush-op-ni*, *i.e.* 'tree with rope affixed.' After it has been further worried, a young Ainu previously selected suddenly rushes forward and seizes the brute by the ears and fur of the face, while at the same time a second man rushes behind and lays hold of its hind quarters. Next a third man runs forward with a stick, about two feet in length and two inches in diameter, which he thrusts between the jaws of the cub. Next two other men come and catch hold of the two hind legs while others seize the forefeet. When all this has been done, the two long poles which were laid by the *nusa*, and which are called *ok-numba-ni*, i.e. 'poles for the strangling,' are brought forward. One of these is placed under the brute's throat, and the other upon the nape of its neck. A good shot with the bow now comes forward and shoots an arrow into the beast's heart, and so ends its misery. In some instances, however, the bear is shot before its head is placed between the poles. But this seems to be the case only when the animal is dangerous. Care has to be taken so to strike the bear that no blood is allowed to fall upon the earth. Should any be spilled, it must be quickly wiped up with some of the sacred willow shavings.

* The same principle holds good with regard to cereals; see § 34.

Why the shedding of blood should be thus tabued no one seems to know.* In some instances, however, the men (particularly those who are hunters) catch the blood in their cups and drink it while reeking warm. This is said to be done with the object of thereby obtaining the courage and other virtues possessed by the victim. On one or two occasions some of the blood taken at a feast has been sent, sprinkled on paper, to sick Ainus staying in our house! It has been smelled and licked with great eagerness, the recipient expecting to receive great bodily and spiritual good from it. Indeed, even the writer himself has, to his great astonishment, had some reserved and sent him.

As soon as dead, the victim is skinned and its head cut off, the skin, however, being left attached to the head. This is taken to the east window and placed upon a mat called *inao-so*, and ornamented with shavings, ear-rings, beads, and other things. On one occasion the present writer even saw a Japanese mirror placed before it, and some old sword hilts and guards! After all this has been performed, a piece of the animal's flesh is cut off and placed under its own snout. This is called *Not-pok-omap*, i.e. 'that under the jaw.' Then a piece of dried fish called *Sat-chep-shike*, i.e. 'the bundle of dried fish,' and a moustache lifter, with some millet dumplings, some strong drink,

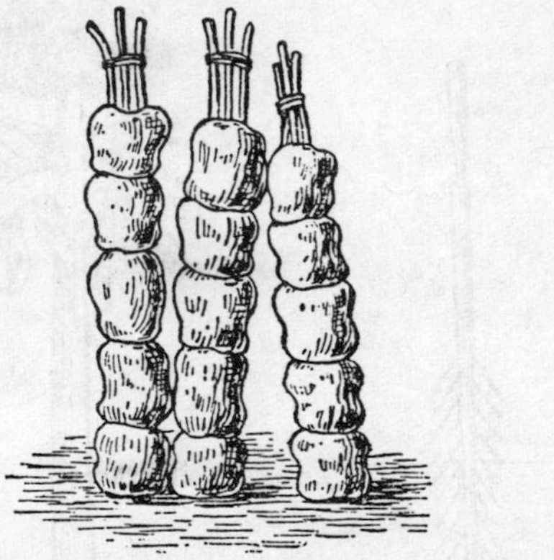

IMOKA-SHIKE.

either rice or millet beer, and a cup of its own flesh boiled, are placed before it. The cup of boiled meat is called *Marapto-itangi*, i.e. 'the cup of the feast.' This having been finished, a man worships, saying: 'O Cub, we give you these fetishes, cakes, and dried fish; take them to your parents, and say: "I have been nourished for a long time by an Ainu father and mother, and have been kept from all trouble and harm. As I am now grown big, I am come to thee. I have brought these *inao*, cakes, and dried fish. Please rejoice." If you say this to them, they will be very glad.' This prayer is only representative; others are said, but all are after the same model. Next, millet dumplings are threaded on sticks and placed by the head. These are said to be for the feast in the new world, for it would never do for the cubs to appear before their ancestors without a small present to provide viands for another meal. They are called *Imoka-shike*, i.e. 'remnants of the feast.' This having been finished and the dancing over, the people return to the hut, where new fetishes (*inao*) are made and placed reverently upon the bear's head. In the meantime some of the cub's flesh has been boiled. A cup of this is now taken and set before the beast's snout, and he is then said to be partaking of the *marapto-itangi*, 'the cup of the feast,' and *ipuni-itangi*, 'the cup of offering.' After a little time has elapsed, the man who presides at the feast says: 'The little divinity has now finished eating; come, ye friends, let us worship.' He then takes the cup, salutes it, and divides the contents—to every guest a very small portion—for it seems to be absolutely essential that each person should take a little. Other parts of the beast are stewed and eaten, while the entrails are cut up fine, sprinkled with salt, and eaten raw. This, like the drinking of the blood, is said to be for the purpose of obtaining the prowess and other virtues of the bear. For the same reason also some of the men besmear themselves and their clothes with blood. This latter custom is called *yai-isho-ushi*, i.e. 'besmearing oneself with good sport.'

The head of the brute is at length detached from the skin and taken to the *nusa* heap, where it is set up upon a pole called *Ke-omande-ni*, i.e. 'the pole for sending away.' All the skulls of animals set up along with that of the bear, and there are many of them, are called *Akoshiratki Kamui*, i.e. 'Divine preservers,' and are at times worshipped. The feast lasts several days as a rule; indeed, it is not quite over till the whole of the cub has been devoured and all the strong drink swallowed.

KE-OMANDE-NI.

36. **Totemism.** — The word 'totem' is said to be derived from the Ojibwa (Chippewa) word *totam* (see *EBr*, art. 'Totemism'). 'As distinguished from a fetish, the totem is never an isolated individual, but always a class of objects, generally a species of animals or plants, more rarely a class of inanimate natural objects, very rarely a class of artificial objects.' Judging from the very few survivals of totemism still in existence among this people, and from their language, one is led to the conclusion that this cult never attained the proportions among them that it did among Africans, or South Australians, or the North American Indians. The Ainus, for example, are very seldom heard to speak of themselves or others as belonging to a bear, a wolf, a turtle, a snipe, a hawk, or an eagle clan, and never of any vegetable clan. Still, there are some grounds for believing that their faith was, in the distant past, somewhat tinged with the totemistic superstition. But it was a totemism which differed from that of the Indians and many others, inasmuch as the Ainus in some instances think it a praiseworthy act to kill and eat their totem if it be an animal (see § 35), and cook and eat it if it be a cereal (see § 34; and cf. *AF* p. 206). According to the general ideas of totemism as practised elsewhere, this ought not so to be. For among the Indians it was thought that, the connexion between the man and his totem being mutually beneficent, the totem protecting the man and the man respecting the totem, it should not be killed if it was an animal, or cut if it was a plant. But the Ainus consider it a very great mutual benefit to kill and eat their totem where possible. Indeed, by feeding upon it they imagine they can get the closest communion with it,—their totem and their god,—sometimes, for example, the bear.

The clearest instance of a genuine belief in totemistic descent the present writer has ever come across among the Ainus was that of a young man who held that his forbears were, one or

* The same tabu is found in other religious systems, and seems based on the belief that the ground is rendered tabu by the sacred blood falling upon it (Jevons, *Introduction to the History of Religion*, pp. 73–74; Frazer, *GB* i. 178 ff.).

both, descended from an eagle. (The account of this will be found on p. 10 of *AF*). Just as the bear may very possibly have represented the national totem of the Ainus, so the present illustration may be an example showing the eagle to have been the totem of a family. An example of the individual totem is found in the willow tree, with which it is shown the Ainus consider themselves to be very closely connected (*AF* 83 ff.). The vines, grape and actinidia, used for ear-rings (156), also seem to have been looked upon as totems; while the images of foxes, wolves, birds, and fish sometimes found carved on the moustache lifters used by the men when drinking, and upon the crowns worn by them at their feasts (158–159), may point to clan totemism.

37. Ophiolatry.—Although snake-worship is still practised to some extent among the Ainus, there is not sufficient evidence to go upon to justify us in saying that this cult ever attained such elaborate proportions of worship as that among the Danhglwe in the serpents' house at Dahomey,* or among the Indians, or even among the ancient Japanese.† Nevertheless, that which is now seen is probably the last remnant of what was once a somewhat complete system.

According to Ainu ideas, the first snake that ever was, belonged not to this earth but came down from heaven, though others of the ophidian tribe had their origin otherwise. In this we are reminded of St. John in Rev 12⁷⁻⁹; and also of Zoroastrian mythology, in which Ahriman descended earthwards in the form of a serpent.‡ But among the Ainus the original serpent is supposed to have been a good being, and in this respect differs from that of both St. John and the Persians (*AF*, ch. 32).

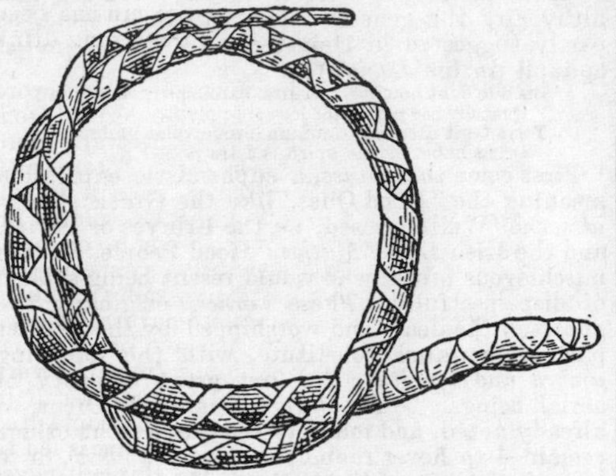

IMOKA KAMUI, OR IMAGE OF SNAKE USED FOR WORSHIP.

Serpents are worshipped most frequently at the time of childbirth, but especially when there is any difficulty in the matter. On such occasions the image of a snake, which is called *Imoka Kamui*, i.e. 'the divine image,' is made out of sedge (*Carex rhynchaphysa*), worshipped, and then suddenly placed upon the shoulders of the patient. The reason given for this is said to be that, according to Ainu belief, all such difficulties are brought about by the king of the evil offspring of serpents himself; and they say that rather than propitiate the evil one, they should go directly to the chief serpent and ask him to keep his wicked subordinates in check and remove the evil they have done.

In cases of ague also snake-worship has taken place, as well as in instances of snake-bite. These reptiles are also sometimes worshipped as a means for cursing people, being asked to bite one's enemies. The prayer said to them on such an occasion takes some such form as the following:

'O snake, I have a word to say to you: pray listen. I have an enemy So-and-so by name. Remember the name. If you ever see him coming along this road, please bite him, possess him, poison him, and kill him. I will then make *inao* out of walnut wood, and also offer you many libations. Pay attention to what I say.'

* Bouley, *Religions of the Africans*, p. 46.
† Griffis, *The Religions of Japan*, New York, 1895, pp. 30, 33, 278.
‡ Hardwick, *Christ and other Masters*, p. 553.

Snake-possession is called *okokko-parat*, i.e. 'snake punishment,' and the women especially are very much afraid of it. There is no particularly specified manner in which it shows itself, for almost any disease may, so they think, be owing to possession by one or more of these reptiles.

Ophiomancy also appears to have left traces behind. The writer of this article once knew of a woman who professed to foretell future events by means of the image of a snake she kept stowed away in a box near by. She called it her guardian angel, and used to pray to it frequently. By its inspiration she professed to be able to tell the reasons for any sickness people were afflicted with, and to discover the proper remedies for them. But, so far as real ophiomancy is concerned, we have never yet heard of any Ainu, man or woman, who professed to predict future events by means of a genuine serpent, dead or alive, whether by its manner of eating or by its coils.

38. Tabu.—Besides the various small matters forbidden in relation to one's attitude towards fire (see § 17), the Ainus have other tabus of a religious and semi-religious nature which should be mentioned. Thus the blood of a bear must not be spilt at a bear-feast (see § 35); a woman must not pronounce the name of her husband lest she thereby cause him harm in some way (*AF*, 252); the cry of certain birds, as, for instance, the cuckoo, woodpecker, night-hawk, goat-sucker, and owl, should not be imitated for fear of being bewitched by them (409, 427); at childbirth also *couvade* is practised, during part of which time the father of the child is forbidden to eat and drink except very sparingly; nor must he worship the gods, hunt, fish, or work till after the purification of the wife, which takes place on the seventh day after parturition (235–241).

39. The future life.—There is no idea more firmly fixed in the Ainu mind than the notion that the spirit is appointed to live for ever in another world —a world which, for the good, is the counterpart of this, only much better, and free from pain, and, for the evil, is dark, wet, cold, and dreary. The very word in use for the spirit (*ramat*) demands that such a place as heaven should exist, for a living being can neither, it is thought, lose his life nor get rid of his own proper personality for ever (see § 13). But the spirit is there supposed to be clothed with a spiritualized body resembling the present, and to exist under like conditions to those of the present life. In the other world the spirit will require a house to live in, tools to work with, as well as boats and hunting and fishing implements. That the Ainus really think this is proved not merely from their words, but also from some of their customs practised at the time of death. The most common word for 'to die' is *ra-i oman*, i.e. 'a going to the lower place.' This does not necessarily mean that the spirit is in every case supposed to descend into the bowels of the earth (*pokna moshiri*, 'the lower world') when it leaves the body, though sometimes it may do so;* and, to hear the people talk, one might be tempted to believe that the Ainus think heaven itself to be in Hades. But, according to their expressed cosmological ideas, they really suppose there are six (*AF* 60) heavens above and six hells (ᾅδαι) below us, and that the best place is in heaven above and the worst in Gehenna below. *Ra-i oman*, 'a going to the lower place,' is not the only term for death. There are others, such as 'to pierce the skies'; 'to make a clearance'; 'to have space for thought'; 'to sleep the other sleep,' and so on (548).

When a person is about to be buried, whether it be a man, woman, or child, the spirit is still spoken to as if it were present in the corpse, and is supposed to partake of the burial feast together with

* Stories of supposed journeys to Hades may be seen recorded both in *AF* (570, 572) and in 'The Language, Mythology, and Geographical Nomenclature of Japan viewed in the light of Ainu studies,' *Memoirs of the Literature College, Imperial University of Japan*, No. 1.

the mourners. Many of the possessions belonging to the deceased, such as bows and arrows, clothing, means for obtaining fire, pipes, tobacco boxes, knives, cups, ornaments, and so forth, are killed (!) by being cut or broken, and so sent to the nether world for future use (*AF* 554–566). Huts too, which, as has already been pointed out, are supposed to be living creatures (117–132), are sent off to the other world by being burned; they are to be for the use of those who occupied them in this life.

40. The future judgment.—After death the Ainus assuredly look for judgment. All must appear, they say, before the tribunal where God the Creator is said to be the judge of all men, and the goddess of fire the chief witness for or against them (see § 17). Those who are accounted worthy go to the happy land, called *Kamui-kotan* or *Kamui-moshiri*, i.e. 'the land' or 'country of the gods'; while the wicked must be sent to *Tei-nei-pokna-moshiri*, i.e. 'the wet underground place,' where they will be for ever unhappy and perhaps frozen up in a block of ice. Whether the punishment will be in reality fire, ice, or swamp, the Ainus are not certain and do not pretend to know; but that their Gehenna is not the same as the hell of the Buddhist is very clear, for there are no purgatorial fires thought of among them.

LITERATURE.—No books have been specially devoted to Ainu religion, though notices of the subject occur in almost all works which touch upon the Ainus. In the year 1893, A. H. Savage Landor published his *Alone with the hairy Ainu*. This book is sometimes quoted as authoritative on the matter, and, were all his remarks true to fact, it would be of the utmost importance. In ch. xxviii. Landor says that the Ainus recognize no 'supreme God and no intelligent creator.' . . . 'The Ainu worship nothing.' . . . 'The Ainu have no religion.' . . . 'They are decidedly not moral, for nothing is immoral with them,' and much more to the same effect. On p. 282, again, he says: 'The Ainu language is as poor in words as the Ainu brain is deficient in thoughts. Thus it is no easy matter to explain to an Ainu what is meant by "religion," by "divinities," and by "worship."' But the Ainu language is by no means so deficient in words as Landor imagined. Dobrotvorsky gives as many as 10,930 words and phrases in his *Ainsko-Russkiü Slovar* (Kazan, 1875), while nearly 14,000 words alone are to be found in Batchelor's *Ainu-Eng.-Jap. Dictionary*[2] (Tokio, 1905). Landor's idea of the Ainus as a non-religious people will not bear looking into.

A much less pretentious, but far more reliable, work on the subject is that written by B. Douglas Howard, in 1893, and entitled *Life with the Trans-Siberian Savages*. This is a pleasantly written little book of 209 pages, and treats mostly of the Saghalien Ainus. The account therein contained shows the religion of these people to be the same as that of the Yezo Ainus; and subsequent personal contact with them has shown Mr. Howard to be correct in his description and generally reliable in his deductions. Indeed, so much alike did he find the two tribes in the matter of religion and religious practices, that he was, by reading the present writer's work, *The Ainu of Japan*, able to give the 'probable meaning' of what he saw and heard on that island (Howard, p. 17).

Miss Bird also, in her very pleasantly written *Unbeaten Tracks* (1885, abridged, Letter 37, pp. 273, 277), speaks of Ainu religion. She says, 'There can be nothing more vague and destitute of cohesion than Ainu religious notions.' . . . 'They have no definite ideas concerning a future state, and the subject is evidently not a pleasing one to them.' . . . 'Such notions as they have are few and confused.' All this is not quite correct; and it would be unreasonable to suppose that Miss Bird could—even had she claimed to do so—in the short three weeks she was actually with the Ainus, have explored every dark nook and corner in the mind of the people. She laboured under the great disadvantage also of being obliged to obtain all her information at second hand through a Japanese interpreter; and if there is any one thing the Ainus are naturally reticent and secretive about before strangers, it is their religion.

J. BATCHELOR.

AIR and GODS OF THE AIR.—Here it is proposed to deal only with those invisible beings who are supposed to hover between heaven and earth,—that is, whose proper abode is the circumambient atmosphere. They are called *Air-gods* rather than *Sky-gods*, the better to distinguish them from the true celestial deities who dwell aloft in the ethereal regions, either in or above the blue vault of heaven, and have no direct contact with the earth and its enveloping waters. But the air is the least stable of the elements, ever fluctuating to and fro, with upward and downward contacts, and restlessly filling all the intermediate spaces, so that the world itself was by our imaginative forefathers called the *middangeard*—the middle region floating in the boundless ether. Hence there are necessarily continuous overlappings and interminglings everywhere, and it often becomes difficult or impossible to draw a clear line between the aërial and celestial deities on the one hand and the aërial, the earthly, and even the underground gods on the other. How true this is may be seen in the protean forms attributed by the ancients to the Olympian Jove himself. Although Zeus was primarily a sky-god, he also filled many other functions, as shown by such epithets as Χθόνιος, Ὄμβριος, Θαλάσσιος (Earth-, Rain-, Sea-god), while Homer speaks even of the Ζεὺς καταχθόνιος, the 'Underground Zeus' (*Il.* ix. 457). So also his consort, the earth-goddess Dione, whose 'variations show how readily sky-goddess, sea-goddess, and earth-goddess might pass from one province into another' (A. B. Cook, *ClR*, April 1903, where the subject is dealt with fully).

Of the aërial beings proper, such as those spirits dismissed by Prospero 'into air, into thin air,' or those others who 'on the beached margent of the sea . . . dance their ringlets to the whistling wind,' or those again who 'hover through the fog and filthy air,' the genesis appears to be twofold, as partly suggested in Hemsterhuis's oft misquoted epitaph (in his *Lucian*):

> 'Bis duo sunt homines; manes, caro, spiritus, umbra;
> Quatuor has partes tot loca suscipiunt.
> Terra tegit carnem, tumulum circumvolat umbra,
> Orcus habet manes, spiritus astra petit.'

First come the *manes*, a euphemistic expression meaning the 'Good Ones,' like the Greek *eumenides*, the 'Well-disposed,' *i.e.* the Erinyes or Furies, and the Irish *Duine Matha*, 'Good People,' *i.e.* the mischievous fairies who would resent being spoken of disrespectfully. These *manes*, originally the ghosts of the dead, and worshipped by the greater part of mankind, constitute, with the following *umbra* and *spiritus*, the first great category of aërial beings. Many were consigned to Orcus, as already noted, and many to the grave; but others remained to hover round the tombs (*umbra*), or to be wafted aloft as the 'other-self' (*spiritus*), and fill the aërial spaces with good and evil genii. (For these distinctions between the personal soul and the other associated entities, see art. ETHNOLOGY, § 9).

Here it should be noted that the *umbra*—the human shadow—was originally regarded as a distinct being, and the belief still survives, even amongst cultured peoples, as in the English saying, 'No man can escape from his shadow.' So also Lucian: 'They [the shadows], when we die, become accusers and witnesses against us, and convictors of crimes perpetrated during life, and they have the reputation of being exceedingly trustworthy, since they are always associated with and never separated from our bodies' (*Menippus, or the Oracle of the Dead* in H. Williams' *Lucian*, p. 273).

Naturally these arbiters of human destinies eventually received divine honours, although it was found impossible to assign any fixed abodes either to them or to the other spirits of the air belonging to the first category, that is, those representing departed souls and their concomitants. They are, however, very numerous, and the Talmudists, who have taken the trouble of counting them, find that the bad ones (only about 7,406,000) are vastly outnumbered by the good, who are roughly estimated at 1 quadrillion, 64 trillions, and 340 billions.

If not so numerous, the aërial gods belonging to the second category, *i.e.* those derived directly from the air itself, may be regarded as by far the more important of the two classes. These may, by contra-distinction, be called the Wind-gods in a pre-eminent sense, and among them must be included the winds themselves. Thus the very first of the six groups mentioned by Epicharmos are the winds: Ὁ *μὲν Ἐπίχαρμος τοὺς θεοὺς εἶναι λέγει ἀνέμους, ὕδωρ, γῆν, ἥλιον, πῦρ, ἀστέρας* (Stobæus, *Floril.* xci. 29), and the deification of the four quarters whence blew the chief winds formed the very basis of the religious systems of many primitive peoples.

This was specially the case in the New World, wheret he Virginian Algonquians had only five gods, and of these four were the 'Four Winds which keep the four corners of the earth' (see art. AMERICA). Constant reference is made to these four deities of the cardinal points, the fundamental idea being that they are the props of the universe, controllers of the seasons and the weather, and senders of rain and sunshine, on whom, in fact, all good and evil things depended. Hence in *Hiawatha* (xiv):

> 'Gitche Manito the Mighty,
> He, the Master of Life, was painted
> As an egg, with points projecting
> To the four winds of the heavens';

and to him is opposed

> 'Mitche Manito the Mighty,
> He the dreadful Spirit of Evil,' etc.

Ratzel, a leading authority on these questions, remarks comprehensively that 'in the place held by the winds among the precursors of creation, based upon the association between breath (or soul) and wind, the pervading sanctity of the number four in the quarters of the heaven, and generally the elements of astronomy and meteorology are alike conspicuous. The Winnebagoes [a Siouan people] say that the Great Spirit created four men and one woman, and that the former created the four winds, the latter the earth. Everywhere they are among the beneficent creative spirits, and often they precede in time even sun, moon, and stars. As to the sun, so also to the four quarters of the world, tobacco is offered from the sacred pipe. The winds, as messengers of the sun, who bring rain, growth, and refreshment, have their share of veneration next after the moon. We further meet with four servants of the Mexican Air- and Sun-god (Quetzalcoatl), four supporters of the earth, who survived the deluge, four corners of the world—whence the Sioux get their pipe of council, four brothers who produced the floor [read vault, sky]—as in the Arawak legend, and so forth. Hence was developed the universal notion of the sanctity of four and its multiples, and hence the cross on American monuments' (*Hist. of Mankind*, ii. p. 146). In their creation legend the Hare Amerinds, members of the Athapascan family, tell us how the Father dwells overhead, and the Mother underfoot, while the Sun moves up and down in mid-air between them, and thus becomes an aërial god. One day, during his wanderings in the heavens, he noticed the earth, a mere islet lost in boundless space, and thereupon cried out: 'O my father on high, kindle thy heavenly fire for my brothers on that little island who have long been unhappy. Look on them, father, and take pity on men.' Then the sun became the day-star, and gladdened the sight of mortals. Amongst other Amerinds the encompassing air is peopled, not by pure spirits, but by disembodied souls, which flit about, for example, above the Chiloe Islands, while in French Guiana the Rucuyenne Caribs send the good to the haven of bliss and envelop the wicked in the clouds as in a kind of purgatory.

In the myths and traditions of the Hopi (Moqui) Pueblos, leading parts are played by the great cloud-god Cotokinuñwû, who dwells in the firmament, and by the four quarters, which have their animal embodiments—Puma, Bear, Wildcat, and Wolf—for N., W., S., and E., with the corresponding colours, yellow, green or blue, red, and white for the several cloud-gods. Thus, in the myth of the Maiden and the Coyote, the Yellow Cloud Chief, the Blue Cloud Chief, the Red Cloud Chief, and the White Cloud Chief try, each in his turn, to win the heroine of the story, but all without success (H. R. Voth, *The Traditions of the Hopi*, p. 157).

But it was in Mexico and Central America, where astronomic lore had made such marked progress, that these notions acquired their greatest expansion and almost formed the very framework of the more advanced religious systems. Everywhere the *teocalli* (temples always erected on pyramids) faced the four cardinal points which supported the heavens; in the Aztec cosmology one of the four cataclysms was caused by the air; and Orozco y Berra identifies Quetzalcoatl himself with *el dios de los vientos* ('the god of the winds'), since he was often represented as moving through the air laden with a wind-bag which was always inflated with destructive gales, and he was born of the cloud-snake Mixcoatl, or at least of his consort Coatlicue—she of the 'snake-robe.'

To Quetzalcoatl corresponds the Kukulcan of the Mayas, a universal deity of many functions, enthroned on the clouds of heaven and on the cross-shaped tree of the four points of the compass, also figured in the pictorial codices as dwelling in the air, above rain, storm, and the death-bringing clouds from which the lightning falls. He is associated, too, with the four colours—yellow, red, white, and black—which, as in the Hopi myth (see above), though in a different way, correspond to the cardinal points—yellow, air; red, fire; white, water; black, earth. 'Kukulcan,' writes Dr. P. Schellhas, 'is represented with all the *four cardinal points*; he appears as ruler of all the points of the compass; north, south, east, and west, as well as air, fire, water, and earth are subject to him' (*Deities of the Maya MSS*, p. 17). Here we see the interminglings of divers functions and provinces above referred to. It may be added that Kukulcan shares his many-sidedness with three other Maya gods, one unnamed who is connected with the symbolic colours of the cardinal points, a second the war-god, of frequent occurrence in the codices, and a third identified by Förstemann with a storm-deity, whose features are intended to symbolize the blast of the tempest. Thus each of the four winds would appear to have been originally deified, or presided over by divinities whose functions and ethereal realms afterwards became confused.

Lastly, the Cakchiquels, one of the most cultured Maya-Quiché nations of Guatemala, paid special homage to the four wind-gods, to whom even human sacrifices were offered. 'Sanchēz y Leon states that the most usual sacrifice was a child. The heart was taken out, and the blood was sprinkled toward the four cardinal points, as an act of adoration to the Four Winds, copal being burned at the same time as an incense' (*Historia de Guatemala*, quoted by Brinton in the *Annals of the Cakchiquels*, p. 45).

In Madagascar the Four Winds are, or were, fully recognized, and, as amongst the northern Amerinds, worshipped in their order next after the supreme deity. Little is now heard of them, and they are scarcely mentioned in the missionary records; but in Robert Drury's time (early in the 18th cent.) they were invoked in all solemn oaths, thus: 'I swear by the great God above, by the Four Gods of the Four Quarters of the World, by the Spirits of my Forefathers, that,' etc. (*Journal*, p. 103 of Oliver's ed.). And Drury tells us that at their meals the people 'take a bit of meat and throw it over their heads, saying, "There's a bit for the Spirit." Then they cut four more little bits, and throw to the lords of the four quarters of the earth' (*ib.* p. 280).

It is, however, to be noted that this belief may have been introduced by the later (Hova) immigrants from Malaysia, where the worship of the wind-gods had long been established under Hindu influences. In the island of Bali, east of Java, where alone Brāhmanism and Buddhism still persist, the four have expanded, as later in Greece (Aristotle, *Meteorologia*), to eight, that is, the eight gods or demi-gods of the Rāmāyaṇa — Indra, Yama, Sūrya (for Nirriti), Chandra (for Ishāni), Anila, Kubera, Varuṇa, and Agni. Of these, however, only three — Indra, Yama, and Varuṇa —are still worshipped, and these as forms of Śiva, and since in Bali the worship of Śiva has in a way absorbed that of all the other gods of the Hindu pantheon, the eight cardinal points themselves are now also attributed to corresponding forms of Śiva. Of the three specially mentioned, Indra has been raised to the heights of Olympus, just as Jupiter has become a chthonic and katachthonic god (see above). Nevertheless, it would be incorrect to regard Indra as the supreme object of adoration in the Vedic system, and he still remains a true rain and air god with his cortège of maruts and storm devas, since his heaven (Indraloka or Svarga) lies beneath that of Viṣṇu, and Viṣṇu's beneath that of Śiva, where at last the soul attains repose and release from transmigration. In fact, Svarga still has earth contacts athwart the empyrean; its inhabitants are liable to become mortal again, and Indra himself is only the prince of these devas, who need the *amṛta* (ambrosia) to keep them alive, yet may still be attacked and vanquished by demons, or by ascetics who acquire supernatural power by self-mortification.

In North Celebes the four wind-gods are held in honour, and play a great part in the local cosmogonies.

Lumimuüt, mother of mankind, met the rock-born priestess Kareima, who ordered her to turn her face to the south. 'While she did this the priestess prayed, "O Cause of the East Wind, fertilize this woman." Lumimuüt, however, perceived nothing. Then, on the command of the priestess, she turned to the east, to the north, and finally to the west, and each time the priestess prayed that the deity of the wind would fertilize her. Her prayer was answered, and Lumimuüt by the god of the west wind begat a son named Toar. When Toar grew up, Kareima took two sticks, one of the plant called *tuis* and one of the plant called *assa*, and cutting them of the same length gave one (tuis) to Lumimuüt and one (assa) to Toar, saying, "See, here are two sticks of the same length. Go you, Lumimuüt, to the right, and you, Toar, to the left, and whenever you meet any one measure sticks. Then if they are of the same length you are mother and son, but if one is longer than the other come to me immediately at the centre of the earth."' Both went on their way, but after a time Lumimuüt and Toar met without knowing one another, and on measuring sticks they found that Lumimuüt's was longer than Toar's, for the tuis stick had sprouted out and grown. Thereupon they returned to Kareima, and when she had measured the sticks she said, 'You are not mother and son, therefore you must become man and wife. Be fruitful and populate the earth.' So Lumimuüt and Toar begat many children, twice nine, three times seven, and once three. The three are the Pasijowan, of whom one was the priest at Warendukan *in the air*; from the other two the people of Minahassa [North Celebes] trace their descent. This legend of the origin of the earth and its people is full of interest to the student of cosmologies. The story of the conception of Lumimuüt by the god of the West Wind exhibits traces of the very common myth of the marriage of Heaven and Earth. Lumimuüt is the earth goddess, the fruitful mother of all things; the West Wind is the one which brings the rain and fertilizes the earth (S. J. Hickson, *A Naturalist in North Celebes*, p. 241).

In Celebes, besides the four wind-gods, there are numerous aërial beings, which are somewhat vaguely described as 'free wandering spiritual forms of various ranks, powers, and capabilities for good or evil.' These are distinguished from the spirits by which certain trees, rocks, waterfalls, and other objects are supposed to be animated, and, as 'the religion of the Minahassers was a differentiated form of Animism' (*ib.* p. 247), it may be conjectured that the wandering forms are believed to be disembodied souls of the dead rather than spirits derived directly from the air. This view is strengthened by the further statement that the spiritual world is inhabited by the souls of deceased chiefs, who live for ever 'in the form of wandering ghosts haunting the scenes of their former triumphs and experiences. They believed in a series of ancestral ghosts of the rank of first-class gods, and in a crowd of lesser deities, protecting spirits and demons' (*ib.* p. 248). And as all alike were called *Empung*, the generic name for the gods, but literally meaning a 'grandfather' (cf. the African *Munkulunkulu*, which has the same meaning), it is obvious that ancestor-worship prevailed over pure psycholatry in Celebes, and that the ancestral spirits dwelt to a great extent in the ethereal regions. In fact, four heavenly villages were expressly set apart as their residence, and these villages—Kasosoran, Kalawakan, Kasendukan, and Karondoran—were so contiguous to the earth that formerly the empungs would often return and mingle with mortals, rich blessings ever following in their footsteps. In these celestial villages rice was grown, and it was from this source that the cereal now thriving in Minahassa was orginally procured.

Now, the return of the departed spirits is dreaded, and at funerals the relatives blacken each others' faces with charcoal. This custom is called *mahawuwuringan*, and the object is to prevent any recognition by the ghosts who may be hovering about the graves or returning to their former abodes. Obviously for the same reason black peoples, such as the Australians and Andamanese, often try to disguise themselves by daubing their faces with white bands or patches, and white is the mourning colour in China. On this subject Hickson aptly remarks that 'whatever they may be intended to express in civilized communities, there can be little doubt that the customary suits of solemn black originated, not in grief or respect for the departed friend, but in the fear of his returning spirit. At the funeral the priest drives it away with a sword, and the maiden who sits upon the bier [in Minahassa] frightens it by the sound of bells. Then everything is done to confuse the spirit if it attempts to return to its accustomed haunts. The ghost is always supposed to come back to the house by the same route by which the corpse was taken away. We can see the reason, then, why the corpse is let down through a hole in the floor and carried three times round the house before being conveyed to the grave. The spirit is so much more perplexed in finding its way back home by this circuitous route. Then, again, the nearest relatives do not attend the funeral, in order that the ghost, if it is hovering around, may not suspect that it is its own funeral that is taking place. Care must be taken, too, that if the spirit should return to the house, it should not recognize the inmates. The friends and relatives, therefore, disguise themselves by painting their faces black [the Minahassers are Indonesians of a light brown or cinnamon colour], by wearing black hats, leaving their hair loose and unkempt, and in other ways. It must not be supposed that black is the universal mourning colour. Among white and fair-skinned people it naturally is, because it affords them the most effectual disguise. Among the black-skinned Andamanese white is the mourning colour. They paint themselves with stripes of white paint. The Spaniards at the time of the conquest of the Philippines found that many of the inhabitants used white as a mourning colour. Many of the races of Luzon and the Sulu islands use white to the present day for this purpose' (*op. cit.* p. 299).

Another curious survival—the almost universal custom of whistling for the wind—finds its explanation in the belief of the Minahassers that the souls of the living as well as of the dead may at times take refuge in the surrounding atmosphere. This is especially the case with sick people, whose ailments are supposed to be caused by their spirits leaving the body and fluttering about somewhere in the neighbourhood. Then the *walian* (priest or shaman) is sent for to diagnose the patient, while all his friends go out to the fields and villages to look for his soul. 'They make a fire in a likely spot, and entice the spirit back by cooking rice and chicken, or by whistling and calling as they would for a dog, whilst the priest goes through the list of gods and gives the ceremony a religious character. This goes on for some time; a rich patient who can afford many chickens has usually to wait a longer time for his spirit to return than a poor one. At last the walian sees it! It shows itself clearly here or there by a movement in the grass or by some other sign. The walian advances with the greatest caution, and catches it in a sarong [the broad Malay cloth worn as a wrap], just as a schoolboy catches a butterfly in his hat. They now turn homewards; a child leads the way, carrying a woka leaf (*Livistonia*) to prevent the priest and spirit from getting wet; the priest follows, carrying the spirit in the sarong, and then another priest armed with *sago-sago* and *mumu* [swords and sticks], which he swings backwards and forwards to keep away the spiteful *sakits* [demons of the air] who wish to recapture the patient's spirit. When they have reached the chamber, the priest opens the sarong over the head of the patient, and says with great satisfaction and assurance, "Now is your soul returned." This being done, the patient should get well again, but if he does not, it is a sign that his time has come, and his spirit can no longer be retained' (*ib.* p. 295). Thus we see that whistling for the wind, still practised by all seafaring peoples, from the English captain to the Malay skipper, originally meant whistling for the truant souls lurking in the wind. Innumerable other survivals, could they be traced to their source, would also be found to be deeply rooted in the superstitious beliefs of primitive man.

Nowhere can this be seen better than in China, where the aërial spaces still swarm with countless good and evil spirits, the belief in which has influenced the development of the very arts, especially of architecture. The fundamental notion is that the good spirits move through the air in curved, the bad in straight, lines. Hence the former are welcomed, the latter baffled by the curved form given to the roofs of the houses, pagodas, gateways, and all other conspicuous structures. For the same reason, no straight highways can be laid down, and partly on this ground great objections were for years raised against the development of railway enterprise. The danger of desecrating the ancestral graves was also urged; but both difficulties were overcome when it was pointed out that the burial-places could be avoided by cleverly designed curves, and that these curves would at the same time serve to thwart the wicked and encourage the beneficent genii.

So also in Korea the air is infested by many malevolent beings, such as the smallpox devil, the typhus devil, and the cholera devil. As after death some of these might again enter the corpse and revive it to kill the living, they are scared off by the vigorous beating of gongs, drums, pots and cans, which is kept up incessantly for three days and nights after the funeral. These demons always travel on the north wind, and the good spirits on the south wind. Hence the graves are usually situated on the sunny slopes of a hill, whither all good influences are wafted on the balmy southern breeze. The family vaults of the better classes are also sheltered from the evil spirits by horseshoe-shaped mounds turned northwards, that is, towards the quarter whence come the demons riding on the icy arctic blasts. Here again we seem to divine why the horseshoe is still a lucky object even among the cultured peoples of the West, where it is nailed to the stable door to protect the farmyard from evil influences. Originally there were no horseshoes; hence it was not the shoe itself, but its peculiar shape, that was regarded as propitious, because earthworks so constructed may have been thought favourable to the good and adverse to the evil genii.

That the demons of epidemics wander about in mid-air is a belief not confined to Korea, but pervading the religious thought of the whole Eastern world. To the Chins of Upper Burma cholera and smallpox are real devils who 'hover through the fog and filthy air,' and when some of the tribe visited Rangoon in 1895 they carried their *dahs* (knives) unsheathed to scare off the pestilent *nat*, and passed the day hiding under bushes to escape its notice. Some even wanted to pacify it by the sacrifice of a slave boy, but were talked over to substitute a few pariah dogs (Carey and Tuck, *The Chin Hills*, i. *passim*). So also in India, the belief in the same cholera and smallpox demons, who 'are supposed to be always wandering about in mid-air' (*Census Report* for 1901), is almost universal amongst the Kolarian and Dravidian aborigines. For details the reader must be referred to art. ASIA.

In Greece the four chief winds were known to Homer, who in the *Iliad* groups them in pairs (Εὖρός τε Νότος τε, ii. 145; Βορρῆς καὶ Ζέφυρος, ix. 5), and in the *Od.* (v. 295–296) mentions them consecutively:—

Σὺν δ' Εὖρός τε Νότος τ' ἔπεσον Ζέφυρός τε δυσαὴς
Καὶ Βορέης αἰθρηγενέτης, μέγα κῦμα κυλίνδων.

Here all are personified poetically, but not yet deified, unless the 'ether-born' Boreas is already to be taken as an air-god. Even their king Æolus is still only the 'friend of the gods,' as in *Od.* x. 2:—

Αἴολος Ἱπποτάδης, φίλος ἀθανάτοισι θεοῖσιν

whereas in the *Æneid* he is enthroned amongst the Immortals ('celsa sedet Æolus arce, sceptra tenens,' i. 56–57), although still subordinate to Neptune ('Non illi imperium pelagi, sævumque tridentem, sed mihi, sorte datum,' i. 138–139). But in the interval between Homer and Virgil the rich Hellenic mythology was developed, and then, of course, divine or semi-divine origins and genealogies were discovered for all the winds personified by Homer. Thus Herodotus tells us (vii. 189) that by his marriage with Oreithyia, daughter of their (legendary) king Erechtheus, the Athenians claimed kinship with Boreas, and that they invoked and offered sacrifices both to him and to his consort (ἔθυόν τε καὶ ἐπεκαλέοντο τόν τε Βορῆν καὶ τὴν Ὠρειθυίην). Another highly honoured wind-god was balmy *Zephyrus*, bearer of fruits and flowers, who, with *Notus* and others, was born of the Titan Astræus and the goddess Eos (Aurora). To Zephyrus the Athenians raised a temple, where his effigy was that of a gentle winged youth wreathed in flowers. Later, under the discriminating analysis of Aristotle, the four became eight and even twelve (*Meteorol.* 2–9). Of the last four little is afterwards heard; but the eight appear to have retained their rank as air-gods at Athens, where was raised to them the still existing octagonal Horologium of Antonius Cyrrhestes, popularly known as the 'Temple of the Winds.' On each of the eight walls a bas-relief symbolizes the wind which it faces, and 'an additional element of interest is supplied by the dress and accompaniments of these figures, by which the character attributed by the Greeks to the winds which they represent is described. Boreas, for instance, is depicted as a bearded man of stern aspect, richly clad and wearing strong buskins, and he blows a conch shell as a sign of his tempestuous character. Cæcias, another cold and inclement wind, carries a shield, the lower part of which is full of hailstones. Notus, the most rainy wind, holds an inverted urn, the whole contents of which he is pouring out upon the earth. Zephyrus, on the other hand, who is the harbinger of spring, appears as a graceful youth, almost unclothed, with the fold of his robe filled with flowers' (H. F. Tozer, *Hist. of Anc. Geography*, p. 195).

Italy also had its complete category of wind-gods, quite independently of the Greek, as shown by their old Italic names, such as *Corus*, *Aquilo*, *Auster*, and *Favonius*. To Zephyrus corresponded Favonius, of whom Horace sings (*Od.* I. iv. 1) that 'Solvitur acris hiemps grata vice veris et Favoni,' and whom Plautus contrasts with 'rainy Auster': 'Hic Favonius serenu'st, istic auster imbricus: hic facit tranquillitatem, iste omnis fluctus conciet' (*Mercator*, V. ii. 35, 36). From this we see that Auster answers to the Greek Notus, while Virgil makes it equally clear that Aquilo represents Boreas, as in *Geor.* iii. 196—

'Qualis Hyperboreis Aquilo cum densus ab oris
Incubuit, Scythiaeque hiemes atque arida differt
Nubila.'

It may here be stated that in Italy, as in Greece, Olympian Jove himself had at an early date extended his sway to the earth, or rather to the nether world. Of Umbrian, a sister language of Latin, some lengthy liturgical texts survive on the seven *Tabulæ Iguvinæ* found in 1444 at Gubbio, where they are still preserved in the town-hall. On Tab. II., which may date from B.C. 500, the epithet *hunte* is twice applied to Jove (*Hunte Iuvie ampentu*, l. 21; and *Hunte Iuvie vestikatu*, l. 35), and this epithet, being clearly connected with *hondra*=infra, means 'Infernus,' so that Hunte Iuvie answers exactly to the Homeric Ζεὺς καταχθόνιος. With this compare the stem *huntro-*, which in Oscan, another sister tongue, means *inferus*, leaving no doubt as to the force of Hunte (*The Curse of Vibia*, l. 11 in R. S. Conway's *Italic Dialects*, i. p. 127).

A few miscellaneous references may now be given to complete the subject, and show how thickly primitive peoples packed the encompassing atmosphere with gods, demons, and spirits of all kinds. These are nowhere more numerous and varied than in Arabia and surrounding lands, where the most dreaded are the ghouls (properly غول=*ghul*), who, however, are denizens not so much of the air as of woods and deserts. They assume divers shapes and colours, and show a certain kinship with both the wer-wolf and the vampire, being supposed to devour men, animals, and dead bodies. These ghouls range through Persia and Muslim India into the Malay lands, where there is a special 'storm fiend who rides the whirlwind,' and also 'a vile fiend called *penangalan* who takes possession of the forms of women, turns them into witches, and compels them to quit the greater part of their bodies, and fly away at night to gratify a vampire craving for human blood. This is very like one of the ghoul stories in the *Arabian Nights' Entertainments*' (Miss Bird, *The Golden Chersonese*, p. 354).

The other supernatural beings of the Arabs, and now generally of all Muslim peoples—Iblis 'Prince of Darkness,' the afrīts, sheitāns, and the whole host of jinns—existed in pre-Muhammadan times, as is evident from Job 1^6, where הַשָּׂטָן is rendered ὁ διάβολος in LXX and *Satan* in the Vulgate. So universal was the belief in their existence, that they had to be admitted with modifications into the Muhammadan system, which recognizes three created intelligences under Allah—the angels formed of light, the jinns of subtle fire, and man of the dust of the earth. The jinns are commonly supposed to be mischievous goblins hostile to man. Some, no doubt, are wicked elves or demons, whose chief is the fallen angel Iblis. These reside in the lowest firmament, that is, the surrounding air, and haunt the caves, the wells, the woods, the hill-tops, and the wilderness. They have the power of putting on any form they please, but not grosser than the essence fire and smoke, and of thus making themselves visible to mortals. They may even take possession of living people, from whom they have then to be exorcised by charms and incantations. But others bear a good character, and frequent the habitations of man in a friendly way; they are addressed by him in kindly language; and they, too, in virtue of their subtle essence, pervade the solid mass of the earth and the whole space of the firmament. They are also believed to inhabit rivers, wells, ruined houses, ovens, and other places, and in letting down a bucket to a well, or in lighting a fire, the magic formula is pronounced, 'Permission, ye blessed' (Featherman, *Social Hist. of the Races of Mankind*, iv. p. 388). Jaffeer Shurreef, who speaks from personal knowledge, goes so far as to say that the belief of the Indian Muhammadans is that it is not a jinn, but a sheitān, who does evil deeds (*Moosulmans of India*, pp. 324–325). This, however, does not apply to Arabia, where the bad certainly predominate over the good genii, and where the above-quoted 'soft words' may be merely euphemistic. In any case, both classes belong to our second category, inasmuch as they are not of human origin but are directly created by Allah.

In general, witches and magicians, who have the power of assuming strange forms, everywhere infest the air as well as the land and water. In Aurora, Pentecost, and other Melanesian Islands, they fly about disguised as owls, eagles, or even blow-flies, and then they are most dangerous. 'In Lepers' Island the wizards who practise it [the magic art] are believed to have the power of changing their shape. The friends of any one suffering from sickness are always afraid lest the wizard who has caused the disease should come in some form, as of a blow-fly, and strike the patient; they sit with him, therefore, and use counter-charms to guard him, and drive carefully away all flies, lest his enemy should come in that form' (R. H. Codrington, *The Melanesians*, p. 207). This observer mentions the case of Molitavile, a noted magician who turned himself into an eagle, or rather whose soul went out of him, and in this shape flew a long way after a ship which had carried off some natives of Lepers' Island, and in that way was able to tell their relatives what had become of them. He reported that all had fared well except one who had died. 'Long afterwards, when some of those who were then on board returned, they said that he had brought back the truth, one of them by that time had died' (*ib.* p. 208).

In Guiana, not only the sun and moon, but also the wind and storms are deified, or, it would be more correct to say, are 'humanized' by indwelling spirits of an essentially anthropomorphic type. 'On one occasion, during an eclipse of the sun, the Arawak men among whom I happened to be rushed from their houses with loud shouts and yells. They explained that a fight was going on between the sun and moon, and that they shouted to frighten and so part the combatants. In many other countries exactly this proceeding of making a noise to separate the sun-spirit and the moon-spirit, or the sun-god and the moon-god, has been noticed; and it is generally supposed that in such cases a high degree of authority is attributed to these spirits. But I see nothing in this or in anything else which shows that savages distinguish, by attributing greater authority to them, such beings as sun and moon, and very many other natural phenomena, as wind and storms, from men and other animals, plants and other inanimate objects, or from any other being whatsoever. All beings—and under this heading are included all personified natural phenomena—are, in fact, of the same kind, each with a body and a spirit. It is the old story—they differ from each other only in that some are more powerful than others in the mere matter of brute force, and none have any sort of authority over others' (E. im Thurn, *Among the Indians of Guiana*, p. 364). By the Brazilian Botocudos the air is well stocked with spirits, mostly of a malevolent disposition—thunder-gods, storm-gods, and the moon itself, the 'night-fire' (*toru-guenket*), which they look upon as a sort of evil principle. All baneful manifestations are attributed to the moon, which causes the thunderstorm, and is supposed at times itself to fall on the earth, crushing the hill-tops, flooding the plains, and destroying multitudes of people. During storms and eclipses arrows are shot upwards, not, as by the Caribs and Arawaks, to frighten the sun, the 'day-fire' (*toru-shompek*), which for the Botocudos is the beneficent principle of good, but to scare away the demons of the air, just as the Indo-Chinese wild tribes shoot skyward at the devouring dragon trying to swallow both sun and moon in the mid-day darkness (A. H. Keane, 'The Botocudos,' in *JAI*, Nov. 1883).

Among the Eskimos the air, usually reserved for departed souls, is replaced by the surrounding ice-fields as the chief abode of the hosts of wicked trolls and goblins. The Greenlander especially has a superstitious terror of the inland ice-cap. 'It is the home of his evil spirits, his ghosts, his apparitions and shades (*tarajuatsiak*), his trolls (*timersek* and *erkilik*), his ice-men who are supposed to be twice as tall as ordinary people, and a whole host of other supernatural beings' (Brögger and Rolfsen's *Fridtiof Nansen*, p. 130). In pagan times there were numerous *bugalak*, or good genii, whom the Western Greenlanders, since their conversion to Christianity, have degraded to evil spirits now inhabiting the lower regions of the atmosphere and the nether world, while Torngarsuk, the Great Spirit, has become the Christian Satan. Elsewhere the souls of the departed sometimes lead a restless existence in their aërial abodes, and during their hunting expeditions the Alaskan Eskimos often see phantoms gliding over the heights; these are the ghosts of the departed returning to scare or injure their living relatives. The people of the Barrow Point district are much troubled by such apparitions, as also by Kiolya, the demon of the aurora borealis, and by Tunya, the Eskimo Zeus, who, like his classical prototype, reigns in the earth, the water, and the heavens. This is one of those numerous instances of overlapping where it becomes impossible to distinguish clearly between chthonic, celestial, and air gods.

LITERATURE.—There appears to be no work specially devoted to the subject of this article. Hence the references must be to a few of the more important treatises in which incidental mention is made of the gods of the air. Such are—A. B. Cook, 'Zeus, Jupiter, and the Oak,' in *ClR*, April 1903; Lucian, ed. Hemsterhuis and H. Williams; Stobæus, *Florilegium*; F. Ratzel, *Hist. of Mankind*, Eng. ed. 4 vols. 1897; H. R. Voth, *The Traditions of the Hopi*, 1905; P. Schellhas, *Deities of the Maya Manuscripts*, 1905; D. G. Brinton, *Annals of the Cakchiquels*, 1885; R. Drury, *Madagascar Journal*, etc., ed. P. Oliver, 1890; S. J. Hickson, *A Naturalist in North Celebes*, 1889; T. Belt, *A Naturalist in Nicaragua*, 1874; Brögger and Rolfsen, *Fridtiof Nansen*, 1896; R. Friedrich, 'Bali' in *Papers relating to Indo-China*, 1887; *Anales del Museo Nacional de Mexico*, 1900–1907; Carey and Tuck, *The Chin Hills*, etc. 1896; H. F. Tozer, *A Hist. of Anc. Geography*, 1897; R. S. Conway, *The Italic Dialects*, 2 vols. 1897; A. Featherman, *Social Hist. of the Races of Mankind*, 4 vols. 1885–1891; R. H. Codrington, *The Melanesians*, 1885; E. im Thurn, *Among the Indians of Guiana*, 1883; A. H. Keane, *The Botocudos*, and *Man, Past and Present*, 1900; H. Rink, *The Eskimo Tribes*, 1887.

A. H. KEANE.

AIYANAR.—Among the most widely known and popular of the deities of the village, the *grāma-devatā*, of Southern India is Aiyanar, the tutelary god of the fields, who protects the crops from harm and drives off from them by night the evil spirits of blight and ruin. His name and worship seem to be little, if at all, known north of the Deccan. In the south, however, almost every village has its shrine dedicated to Aiyanar, where offerings are presented and prayers made for the safety of the crops from drought and disease. Grouped around the shrine, and near the village, are usually to be found rude models in terra-cotta of horses, often life-size, or more rarely of elephants, on which Aiyanar with his troop of attendants is supposed to ride when in mad career he chases away the demons. The Indian villager avoids approaching the shrine of Aiyanar after dark, lest he should be mistaken for a demon and slain.

The god is represented roughly carved in human form, either seated with crown and sceptre, or on horseback, and is sometimes accompanied by his two wives, Pūranī and Pudkalā, who join him in the rout of the evil spirits. He is also propitiated in times of distress or pestilence, when animal sacrifices are offered on rude stone altars in front of the shrine and libations are poured out. The priests who officiate belong invariably to the lowest castes. The clay models of the horses are presented by the villagers in acknowledgment of aid rendered, as thank-offerings for recovery from sickness, or in fulfilment of a vow. Except, however, at harvest-time, there do not seem to be any regular festivals held in his honour, or any definite periods of worship prescribed. Sir Monier Williams' account of his visit to Aiyanar's shrine at Parmagudi, on the road from Madura to Rāmnād, may serve in general as a description which would apply to the majority of the places sacred to the god in Southern India.

The shrine 'was situated close to a grove of small trees not far from the village. Under a rough stone canopy was a rudely-carved stone male idol. . . . About twenty-five toy-like terra-cotta horses, some as large as life, were ranged on each side. . . . I saw no signs of any recent offerings, nor was a single worshipper of the god to be seen anywhere. I noticed, indeed, that all the shrines of A. had a deserted appearance, the fact being that he is never worshipped, in our sense of the word. He is only propitiated in emergencies. Every year after harvest-time a festival is kept in his honour, when numerous animals are sacrificed, and images of the god are decorated with ornaments, and drawn about through the village streets on the rude clay horses' (*Brāhmanism and Hinduism*[4], p. 219 f.).

The name *Aiyanar* is said to be a combination or corruption of the two names *Hari-Hara*, or Viṣṇu-Śiva; and the god is popularly regarded as the son of Śiva by Viṣṇu, when the latter had assumed a female form. It is more probable, however, that he represents a primitive Dravidian deity, recognized and more or less adopted by the incoming Āryans, and provided with an orthodox parentage. A figure of Gaṇeśa, one of the other two sons of Śiva, sometimes stands near his shrine. But, unlike his brother, Aiyanar does not seem ever to be invoked in the strict sense of the term, or to have prayers addressed to him for blessing or positive good.

LITERATURE.—Papers on Religious Reform, I. *Popular Hinduism*, Madras, 1887, p. 8 f.; Monier Williams, *Brāhmanism and Hinduism*[4], London, 1891, pp. 209, 218–220, 245; W. Crooke, *Popular Religion and Folk-lore of Northern India*, new edition, 1896, vol. i. pp. 97, 262, quoting from Oppert, 'Original Inhabitants,' p. 505.

A. S. GEDEN.

AJANTA.—Ajanta is the Anglo-Indian form of the native name Ājuṇṭhā, a village and ravine celebrated for its cave temples, situated in N. lat. 20° 32′ 30″, E. long. 75° 48′, near the frontier of the British province of Berār, but within the dominions of the Nizām of Hyderābād. It lies at the head of one of the passes (*ghāṭ*) that lead down from the Indhyādrī hills, dividing the table-land of the Deccan from the British district of Khāndesh in the valley of the Tāptī. The only early reference to the caves is that of the Buddhist pilgrim Hiuen-Tsiang, or as Watters, the latest translator and editor of his journal, transliterates his name, Yüan Chwâng. He writes, speaking of the kingdom of Mo-ha-la-cha (Mahāraṭṭha): 'In the east of this country was a mountain range, ridges one above another in succession, tiers of peaks and sheer summits. Here was a monastery, the base of which was in a dark defile, and its lofty halls were quarried in the cliff and rested on the peak, its tiers of halls and storied terraces had the cliff on their back, and faced the ravine. This monastery had been built by the A-chē-lo (Āchāra [or perhaps rather Achala]) of Western India.' The pilgrim then relates the circumstances in Āchāra's life which led to the building of the monastery. 'Within the establishment,' he adds, 'was a large temple above 100 feet high, in which was a stone image of the Buddha above 70 feet high; the image was surmounted by a tier of seven canopies unattached and unsupported, each canopy separated from the one above it by the space of 3 feet. The walls of this temple had depicted upon them the incidents of the Buddha's career as Bodhisattva, including the circumstances of his attaining Bodhi, and the omens attending his final passing away; all, great and small, were here delineated. Outside the gate of the monastery, on either side north and south, was a stone elephant, and the pilgrim was informed that the bellowing of these elephants caused earthquakes' (Watters, ii. 239 f.).

Burgess and other authorities believe that this account, dated A.D. 642, refers to the Ajanta caves. Watters admits that this view is probable, but he doubts whether the Achala of the inscription recorded by Burgess is the A-chē-lo of the pilgrim's narrative. This inscription merely states that 'the ascetic Sthavira Achala, who glorified the faith and was grateful, caused to be built a mountain-dwelling for the Teacher, though his wishes were fulfilled.'

The place was visited for the first time by Europeans in 1819, and the earliest account of its monuments, by Alexander, appeared ten years later (*Trans. R. A. S.* 1829). The first scientific survey was made by Fergusson, and appeared in the same journal in 1843. His account of the wall-paintings aroused much interest, and led to an appeal to the Indian Government that careful copies of them should be made. This was done by Major R. Gill; but his drawings, except the five last executed, were unfortunately destroyed in a fire at the Crystal Palace, where they were being exhibited, in 1866. All that remains of his work now seems to be small copies, in Mrs. Spiers' *Ancient India*, of two of his pictures and of eight detached fragments from others. In 1872 the work of copying the frescoes was started afresh by Griffith, and his work, in two splendid volumes, was published by the Secretary of State for India in 1896–97.

The caves are excavated in the face of an almost perpendicular rocky scarp, about 250 feet high, sweeping round in a semicircle, and forming the north side of a wild glen traversed by a small stream, the Vāghur. Above the caves the valley terminates abruptly at a waterfall with seven leaps, the total height being about 200 feet. The site is lonely and picturesque, and, at the same time, close to a main line of ancient traffic, thus combining the three leading characteristics which guided the excavators of the rock caves of Western India in selecting places for their establishments.

The series consists of 24 monasteries (*vihāra*) and 5 temples or meeting-halls (*chaitya*). According to Burgess, who has made a careful survey and compiled an exhaustive report on the caves (*Arch. Survey Reports, W. India*, iv. 43 ff.), the earliest group consists of two Chaitya caves (numbered IX., X., according to Fergusson's plan of the site) and two Vihāras (XI., XII.), all of which were excavated certainly before the commencement of the Christian era. Of the later caves, Burgess forms two groups. Nine (VI., VII., VIII., XV. to XX.) range in date from the 5th to the end of the 6th cent. A.D. The second group (I. to V., XXI. to XXVII.) were all excavated, or at least finished, within the limits of the 7th century. This second, and by far the largest, series belongs to the Mahāyāna school of Buddhism, and can be distinctly marked off from those of the earlier group. Cave No. I. is specially to be noted. Burgess describes it as the most handsomely ornamented Vihāra at Ajanta, or, indeed, in all India, and at the same time it is one of the most modern, having been constructed probably in the beginning of the 7th cent., and not completely finished before A.D. 650.

The most interesting and valuable of the remains at Ajanta are the series of frescoes in the caves. These generally represent passages from the legendary history of Buddha, and from the Jātakas, or stories of the Buddha's former births, the visit of Asita to the infant Buddha, his temptation by Māra and his forces, legends of the Nāgas, or serpent race, hunting scenes, battle pieces, the carrying of the relics to Ceylon, and other incidents in the Buddhist legend. Many of the frescoes represent incidents taken from the Jātakas, of which some twelve have been identified by S. F. Oldenburg (*Journ. American Oriental Society*, xvii. 183 f.; *JRAS*, 1896, p. 324). Of these, perhaps the most important are the Ummadantī Jātaka of king Sibi or Sivi (Cowell's Cambridge trans. v. 107 ff.) and the Chaddanta Jātaka, or tale of the six-tusked elephant (*ib.* v. 20 ff.). A recent discovery in one of these caves has brought to light a picture which depicts the Nidānas, or Causes, in concrete form. This picture, supplemented by Tibetan versions and Lamaistic explanations, is certainly a diagram of human life in the form of the wheel (Waddell, *JRAS*, 1894, p. 367; *Buddhism of Tibet*, 105 ff.). In the mountain scenery of the frescoes are depicted figures of birds and monkeys, and sometimes of Bhīls and other forest tribes, and the fabled inhabitants of the hills—Guhyakas, Kirātas, and Kinnaras, the last of whom are musicians to the mountain gods, with human busts and legs and tails of birds. The whole series of frescoes is of the greatest historical value as illustrating the religious and social life of India between the 3rd and 8th cents. of the Christian era.

All critics have fully recognized the artistic value of these frescoes. 'The condition of mind,' writes Griffith (in Burgess, *Notes*, 4 f.), 'which originated and executed these paintings at Ajanta must have been very similar to that which produced the early Italian paintings of the 14th cent., as we find much that is common to both. Little attention paid to the science of art—a general crowding of figures into a subject; regard being had more to the truthful rendering of a story than to a beautiful rendering of it; not that they discarded beauty, but they did not make it the primary motive for representation. There is a want of aërial perspective, the parts are delicately shaded, not forced by light and shade, giving the whole a look of flatness, a quality to be desired in mural decoration. Whoever were the authors of these paintings, they must have constantly mixed with the world. Scenes of everyday life, such as preparing food, carrying water, buying and selling, processions, hunting scenes, elephant fights, men and women engaged in singing, dancing, and playing on musical instruments. Many are most gracefully, and all most graphically depicted upon these walls; and they could only have been done by men who were constant spectators of such scenes; by men of keen observation and retentive memories.' Of the famous painting of the 'Dying Princess,' in cave XVI., the same authority writes: 'For pathos and sentiment and the unmistakable way of telling its story, this picture, I consider, cannot be surpassed in the history of art. The Florentine could have put better drawing, and the Venetian better colour, but neither could have thrown greater expression into it' (*ib.* 58 f.).

In many of the paintings there is ample evidence of Sasanian or Persian influence. One wall scene (Griffith's drawing No. 5) appears to represent the reception of a Persian embassy at the Court of an Indian king, and, according to Burgess (*ib.* 27), can hardly be earlier than the 7th cent. of our era.

LITERATURE.—The literature dealing with the Ajanta caves and their wall-paintings is very extensive. References to the older accounts of travellers and the comments of critics upon their narratives have been collected by Campbell, *Bombay Gazetteer*, xii. 480, where a good account of the site will be found. The later and better authorities are: J. Burgess, *Notes on the Bauddha Rock-Temples of Ajanta*, Bombay, 1879, in *Archæological Survey of Western India*, No. ix.; J. Fergusson and J. Burgess, *The Cave Temples of India*, London, 1880, pp. 280–347; J. Burgess and Bhagwanlal Indraji, *Inscriptions from the Cave-Temples of Western India*, Bombay, 1881; J. Burgess, *Report on the Cave-Temples and their Inscriptions*, London, 1883; L. A. Waddell, 'Note on the Ajanta Paintings' in *Indian Antiquary*, xxii. 8 ff. The wall-paintings are reproduced by J. Griffith, *The Paintings in the Buddhist Cave-Temples of Ajanta, Khandesh*, 2 vols., London, 1896–97.

W. CROOKE.

ĀJĪVIKAS.*

[A. F. R. HOERNLE].

1. Introduction.—The sacred books, both of the Buddhists (*e.g.* *A.N.* iii. 276; *Dial.* pp. 71, 220) and the Jains, inform us of the existence, contemporary with the foundation of Buddhism and Jainism, about the end of the 6th cent. B.C., of a community of religious mendicants, whom they call Ājīvikas. From certain Jain Scriptures we further learn that the founder of this community was a man called Gosāla Maṅkhali-putta (Pāli *Makkhali-putta*, Skr. *Maskari-putra*). In the seventh Aṅga (*U.D.* ii. 133), a man, Saddāla-putta, is said to have been received by Gosāla into the Ājīvika community, and the *Bhagavatī Sūtra*, the fifth Aṅga, gives us an account of the life of Gosāla, as the acknowledged head of that community. Though the Buddhist Scriptures (*e.g.* *M.N.* i. 198, 250, 515; *S.N.* i. 68, iv. 398; *D.N.* i. 52; *Jāt.* v. 246) also frequently mention Gosāla Makkhali-putta as one of the leaders of the six religious mendicant communities whom Buddha singles out for special animadversion, they never explicitly connect him with the Ājīvikas, or state that he was their leader. But that on this point the Buddhist tradition did not really differ from the Jain, is shown by the fact that both attribute to him the holding of the religio-philosophical doctrine of the negation of free will and moral responsibility.

On the exact signification of the name 'Ājīvika' we have no information. The Skr. word *ājīva* means the mode of life, or profession, of any particular class of people, whether they live as 'householders' in the world or, as religious mendicants, have renounced the world. Thus 'right-livelihood' (*saṁyag-ājīva*) was in the Buddhist system (*Dial.* 221; *B.S.* 147; O.B. 146) one of the eight 'paths' incumbent on the mendicant. The word *ājīvika*, being a derivative of *ājīva*, means one who observes the mode of living appropriate to his class. We shall see in the sequel that there is some ground for believing that Gosāla held peculiar views as to the *ājīva* of a mendicant who was truly liberated from the fetters of *karma*. It was probably for this reason that he and his adherents came to be known as *Ājīvikas*, or the men who held the peculiar doctrine of *ājīva*. All the indications that we have tend to show that, as usual in such cases, the name was not taken by themselves, but given to them by their opponents, and that in their mouth it was meant to be opprobrious. As we shall see, Gosāla, by his conduct, laid himself open to the charge of insincerity, in that he practised religious mendicancy, not as a means of salvation (*mokṣa*), but as a means of gaining a livelihood, as a mere profession (*ājīva*). The name 'Ājīvika,' it appears, was originally meant to stigmatize Gosāla and his followers as 'professionals'; though, no doubt, in later times, when it became the distinctive name of a mendicant Order, it no longer carried that offensive meaning.

2. Personal History of Gosāla.—The fifth Aṅga of the Jains, commonly known as the *Bhagavatī Sūtra*, gives us a fairly connected and detailed account of the life of Gosāla (*Bh.S.* xv. 1, tr. in *U.D.* App. 1). According to this account, Gosāla's father was a *maṅkha*, a kind of professional beggar, whose name was Maṅkhali. Hence he was known as the *Maṅkhali-putta* or the son of Maṅkhali. His other name, Gosāla, he received from the circumstance of having been born in a cowshed (*gośālā*), in which his parents, failing to obtain any other refuge during a certain rainy season, had taken shelter. When he grew up, he adopted his father's profession of a *maṅkha*. In the course of his journeyings he repeatedly fell in with Mahāvīra, who, just about that time, had commenced the wandering life of a *Niggantha** ascetic. Seeing the great respect in which Mahāvīra was held by the people, Gosāla determined to attach himself to him. Though at first repulsed, he succeeded at last by his importunity in being accepted as a disciple by Mahāvīra. But the two men were so different in character and temper, that after six years, owing to the insincerity and trickery of Gosāla, the companionship was dissolved. Gosāla now set up as the rival leader of a separate community of religious mendicants, called *Ājīvikas*, and with his followers established his headquarters on the premises of a potter woman in the town of Sāvatthī (Śrāvastī). After the lapse of sixteen years, Mahāvīra, who never in the meantime appears to have met his former companion, happened to visit Sāvatthī, and, hearing of the influence which Gosāla was wielding there, he took occasion to expose the false character of the professing ascetic. On learning this, Gosāla, threatening vengeance, at once proceeded with his followers to where Mahāvīra with his Nigganthas was lodging. Here he began the dispute by putting forward an ingenious argument to prove that Mahāvīra was mistaken in his identity, and that, in reality, he was a totally different person from the Gosāla whom Mahāvīra had once known as his companion. On Mahāvīra contemptuously brushing aside this sophistry, the infuriated Gosāla grossly abused his adversary; and the two rival factions came to blows. In the fight two of Mahāvīra's disciples were disabled, but in the end Gosāla, being discomfited by Mahāvīra in a personal encounter, was compelled to retire in disgrace. The taunts of his rivals, and the consequent distrust of the townspeople, now made Gosāla's position in Sāvatthī untenable. This preyed on his mind so much that it became utterly unhinged, and, throwing aside all ascetic restraint, he gave himself up to drinking, singing, dancing, soliciting the potter woman, and besprinkling himself with the cool muddy water of the potter's shop. Six months of this riotous living brought on his end; and with it came a momentary return of

* The following special abbreviations are used in this article:

A.N.	=	Aṅguttara Nikāya.
A.S.	=	Āchārāṅga Sutta.
B. and R.	=	Böhtlingk and Rieu's edition of the Abhidhāna Chintāmaṇi.
B.S.	=	Buddhist Suttas, in *SBE*, vol. xi.
Bh.Rep.	=	Bhandarkar's Report on the Search for Sanskrit MSS, 1883–84.
Bh.S.	=	Bhagavatī Sūtra, Calcutta edition.
C.B.	=	Bp. Copleston's Buddhism.
D.N.	=	Dīgha Nikāya.
Dial.	=	Dialogues of the Buddha, translated by T. W. Rhys Davids.
Ep.Ind.	=	Epigraphia Indica.
J.S.	=	Jaina Sūtras, Parts i. and ii., in *SBE*, vols. xxii. and xlv.
Jāt.	=	Jātakas.
K.Mah.	=	Kielhorn's edition of the Mahābhashya.
K.S.	=	Kalpa Sūtra, ed. Hermann Jacobi.
M.N.	=	Majjhima Nikāya.
N.R.	=	Neumann's Reden Gotama Buddhas.
N.S.	=	Nirayāvalīya Sutta, ed. Dr. S. Warren.
O.B.	=	Oldenberg's Buddha.
Oman	=	The Mystics, Ascetics, and Saints of India, by J. C. Oman.
R.L.B.	=	Rockhill's Life of Buddha[4].
S.A.	=	Smith's Aśoka, in Rulers of India Series.
S.I.Inscr.	=	South Indian Inscriptions, in Archæological Survey of India.
S.I.P.	=	Senart's Inscriptions de Piyadassi.
S.K.	=	Sūtra-kṛtāṅga, in Jaina Sūtras, Part ii.
S.N.	=	Saṁyutta Nikāya.
S.V.	=	Sumaṅgala Vilāsinī.
T.Mv.	=	Turner's ed. of the Mahāvaṁśa.
Tr.C.O.	=	Transactions of the Sixth International Congress of Orientalists.
U.D.	=	Uvāsaga Dasāo, ed. by R. Hoernle, in the Bibliotheca Indica.
V.O.J.	=	Vienna Oriental Journal.
V.P.Tr.	=	Vinaya Piṭaka, tr. in *SBE*, vols. xiii., xvii., and xx.
W.I.St.	=	Weber's Indische Studien.
W.M.H.	=	Wilkin's Modern Hinduism.

* Also spelled *Nigaṇṭha*; see *J.S.* ii. p. xiv, footnote 8.

reason and the sense of remorse. His last act was to acknowledge to his disciples the truth of Mahāvīra's statement respecting himself, and to instruct them to bury him with every mark of dishonour and publicly to proclaim his shame. The disciples, it is added, refrained from carrying out the dying instructions of their master.

Such is the substance of the story of Gosāla's life in the Bhagavatī Sūtra. The Buddhist references to his life are much briefer. Buddhaghoṣa (*c.* 410 A.D.), in his commentary on the Dīgha Nikāya (*S.V.* pp. 143, 144, tr. in *U.D.* App. II.), tells us that Maṅkhali was the name of Gosāla, and that the latter name was given to him because he was born in a cowshed. Having broken an oil vessel through carelessness, and fearing chastisement from his angry master, who had caught him, he broke away, leaving his garments in his master's hands. He fled naked to a village, where the people offered him clothes; but he refused them, hoping to make a better living as a naked *arhat*, or holy man.

The two accounts—so far as we are able to judge—are quite independent of each other. One is Buddhist, the other is Jain; and the Buddhists and Jains, being antagonistic sects, would not adopt each other's views. Moreover, Buddhaghoṣa wrote in Ceylon, while the Jain Scriptures, as we now have them, were composed probably in Western India. All the more valuable are the two accounts, both in respect of the points in which they agree and in which they differ. They agree in two points: first, that Gosāla was born of low parentage in a cowshed, and subsequently took up the profession of a naked religious mendicant; and, secondly, that this profession of his was not sincere, but adopted merely for the sake of getting an idle living. The ground for the belief in Gosāla's insincerity, as will be shown in the sequel, was, according to both the Buddhists and the Jains, that Gosāla not only taught but also practised antinomian doctrines.

The point on which the two accounts differ is the meaning of the name 'Maṅkhali' or 'Maṅkhali-putta.' According to the Jains, Maṅkhali is the name of Gosāla's father, and a derivative from *maṅkha*. According to the Buddhists, it is the name of Gosāla himself. The derivation from *maṅkha* is indefensible. The Prākrit word *maṅkhali* is the equivalent of the Skr. word *maskarin*; but there exists no word *maska*, the equivalent of *maṅkha*. The latter word, in fact, has not been found anywhere but in the passage of the Bhagavatī Sūtra which adduces it as the source of the name Maṅkhali, and it is presumably an invention *ad hoc*. Moreover, the meaning of the hypothetical word *maṅkha* was not certainly known to the old commentators. Thus, while Abhaya Deva (*c.* 1050 A.D.), in his commentary on the Bhagavatī Sūtra, explains it to mean 'a kind of beggar that tries to extract alms from the people by showing them pictures of (malignant) deities which he carries about with him,' Hemachandra (*c.* 1140 A.D.), in his commentary on the Abhidhāna Chintāmaṇi (B. and R. verse 795), says that it is a synonym of the well-known word *magadha*, 'a bard.' The truth, no doubt, is that *maṅkhali-putta* is a formation like *Nāya-putta*, 'a man of the Nāya-clan' (the epithet of Mahāvīra), or *Nigganṭha-putta*, 'a mendicant of the Nigganṭha Order.' It describes Gosāla as having originally belonged to the Maṅkhali, or Maskarin, class of religious mendicants. The very early existence of this kind of mendicant in India is proved by the fact that the celebrated grammarian Pāṇini (*c.* 350 B.C.), in his *Grammar* (vi. 1, 154), explains the formation of the name. According to him, a Maskarin was so called because he carried in his hand a bamboo staff (*maskara*). On account of this practice of carrying a staff, he was known also as *Eka-daṇḍin*, or a 'one-staff-man.' Patañjali, in his comments on Pāṇini's statement (K.Mah. iii. 96), further explains that this kind of wandering mendicant (*parivrājaka*) was called Maskarin not so much because he carried a staff, as because he professed to have renounced all activities. The reference in these two statements is to the fact that there were two grades of these Maskarins or *Eka-daṇḍins*. In the lower grade, the ascetic carried an actual staff, in addition to a begging bowl and a strip of loin-cloth (*kaṭi-bandhana*). In the higher grade of *Paramahaṁsa*, he abandoned even these three possessions, claiming absolute renunciation as his only staff of reliance (W.I.St. ii. 174–75).

In ancient India, at one time, the tendency appears to have been very prevalent to adopt the life of a homeless wandering ascetic. Often this life was adopted from sincere religious motives; but probably as often it was due to a mere love of vagrancy and dislike of honest work. It was not limited to any particular class of people; but it was probably more prevalent among the lower classes. Among the upper classes (the so-called 'twice-born') the Brahmanic law-givers attempted to regulate it by enacting that the early years should be devoted to education and the middle years to rearing a family and pursuing a profession, while only the declining years might be given up to the ascetic life. It may be doubted whether this wholesome regulation ever was much observed in Indian society; the tendency to devote the whole life to religious mendicancy was too strong among the people. The Maskarin, as a rule, led a solitary life, and the adoption of this manner of life was open to very grave abuses. Hence some men of commanding personality conceived the task of regulating the tendency to the ascetic life, not by checking it, or restricting it to a certain period of life, but by organizing the mendicants into communities governed by strict rules of conduct. Such men were the founders of Buddhism and Jainism. Gosāla, from all accounts, was hardly a man of that stamp. He seems, by natural disposition, to have belonged to the baser sort of Maskarins, who made religious mendicancy a pretext for an idle and self-indulgent life. The existence of this baser sort of mendicants in ancient India is vouched for by a curious piece of folklore. It occurs in the Tittira Jātaka (No. 438 in *Jāt.* iii. 542). The verses occurring in the Buddhist Jātakas embody the most ancient folklore—of a much older date than Buddhism itself. In the 12th and 13th verses of that *Jātaka* a mendicant of the baser sort is described, among other things, as carrying a bamboo staff (*vet-āchāra*), which shows that he must have belonged to the class of mendicants who were known as Eka-daṇḍins, or Maskarins. But what gives particular significance to this notice is that the much later commentary identifies that mendicant as an Ājīvika. It is clear that in the mouth of the Buddhists, 'Ājīvika' was a term of reproach applicable to a Maskarin or Eka-daṇḍin of the baser sort. This seems to explain why it was that both Buddhists and Jains call Gosāla a Maṅkhali, and say that he was a leader of Ājīvikas; and very possibly he was not only himself a Maṅkhali, but also, as the Jains say, the illegitimate son of a Maṅkhali.

It is difficult to determine the motive which induced Gosāla to attach himself to Mahāvīra. It may be that the contact with that religious enthusiast temporarily woke up the better instincts in Gosāla's nature; or it may be that, as the Jain account suggests, he hoped to learn from Mahāvīra more potent 'tricks of his trade.' In the former alternative, his association with Mahāvīra had no permanent effect on him. There seems to be no reason seriously to question the truth of the Jain statement that Gosāla took up his headquarters on the premises of a potter woman. That act of open defiance of one of the strictest rules of religious mendicancy, confirmed as it is by Buddha's well-known abhorrence of Gosāla, throws an informing light on the real character of the man. There is, no doubt, something tragic in the closing scene of Gosāla's life: the open exposure of his shame by Mahāvīra in the face of his own disciples and fellow-townspeople, the consequent mental derangement, and the final momentary remorse. But the feeling of pity will be measured by the view taken of Gosāla's real character.

The Bhagavatī Sūtra (fol. 1250*a*, 1269*a*) states that Mahāvīra survived Gosāla sixteen years. It also states that Gosāla's death was coincident with the great war which King Kuṇiya (Ajātaśatru) of Magadha waged with King Cheḍaga of Vaiśālī for the possession of an extraordinary elephant (*U.D.*, App. I. p. 7). From these two statements the year of Gosāla's death may be approximately determined. The traditional date of Mahāvīra's death is B.C. 527. This would place Gosāla's death in B.C. 543. But that date is rather too early. The elephant above mentioned was given by King Seṇiya (Bimbisāra) of Magadha to his younger son Vehalla in disregard of the superior claim of his elder son Kuṇiya. It may be assumed as certain that Kuṇiya only awaited his entrance into the exercise of regal power before commencing the war for the possession of the elephant. Now Seṇiya made over the throne to his son Kuṇiya some years before the latter murdered him by a slow course of starvation. This murder happened in the year B.C. 490, or eight years before the death of Buddha, which itself took place, as is now practically certain, in B.C. 482. Mahāvīra died some time, it is not known how long, before Buddha. But Gosāla died sixteen years before Mahāvīra, in the year of the war, and that war must have taken place in the year of Kuṇiya's accession to regal power, and that accession cannot well be placed at a very long interval before the murder of Seṇiya. All these conditions are best satisfied by assuming that Mahāvīra died in B.C. 484, two years earlier than Buddha, and that consequently the death of Gosāla and the war took place in B.C. 500, sixteen years before the death of Mahāvīra, and ten years before the murder of Seṇiya. Accordingly that year, B.C. 500, may be taken as the approximate date of the death of Gosāla.

3. Doctrines and practices of Gosāla.—Neither Gosāla nor any of his Ājīvika followers has left us any record of their doctrines and practices. Accordingly we are reduced to the necessity of forming our opinion on those two points from the occasional references to them in the records of their rivals, the Buddhists and Jains. Their statements must, of course, be accepted with some caution; but their general trustworthiness is guaranteed by their agreement in all essential points. This agreement possesses all the more value, as the statements, coming from two mutually hostile sects, constitute two independent sources of information.

In the Buddhist Majjhima Nikāya (i. 514 ff., N.R. ii. 284) there occurs a very instructive statement. Buddha is represented as dividing the ascetic systems which differed from his own into eight classes. Four of these he condemns as 'living in incontinency' (*abrahma-charya-vāsa*); of the four others he says only that they are 'unsatisfying' (*anassāsika*). Among the latter he classes the system of Mahāvīra, while among the former he places the system of Gosāla. The distinction is clear. Buddha objected to Gosāla on ethical grounds—for holding principles theoretically and practically immoral. His system, indeed, he conceived to be the most mischievous (*A.N.* i. 286; O.B. 82, 199; *Dial.* 71), and its author he stigmatized as 'the bad man' (*mogha-purisa*), who, like a fisherman, caught men merely to destroy them.

The fundamental thesis of the system of Gosāla is stated, in the Buddhist and Jain Scriptures alike, in slightly varying but substantially identical phraseology. The Jain Uvāsaga Dasāo (i. 97, 115, ii. 111, 132) gives it as follows: 'There is no such thing as exertion or labour, or power, or energy, or human strength; all things are unalterably fixed' (cf. *S.N.* iii. 210; *A.N.* i. 286). In the Buddhist Dīgha Nikāya (p. 53; *Dial.* 71) the pith of Gosāla's system is more fully stated as follows:

'There is no cause, either proximate or remote, for the depravity of beings; they become depraved without reason or cause. There is no cause, either proximate or remote, for the purity of beings; they become pure without reason or cause. Nothing depends either on one's own efforts or on the efforts of others; in short, nothing depends on any human effort, for there is no such thing as power or energy, or human exertion or human strength. Everything that thinks (*i.e.* the higher animals), everything that has senses (*i.e.* the lower animals), everything that is procreated (*i.e.* all animals), everything that lives (*i.e.* all plants), is destitute of force, power, or energy. Their varying conditions, at any time, are due to fate, to their environment, and their own nature; and it is in accordance with their position in one or other of the six classes (see below, p. 262[a]) that men experience ease or pain.'

How this system, in its theoretical aspect, was worked out in detail, we do not know. The Buddhist and Jain Scriptures give us no further information. It is evident, however, that, in principle, it was a thorough-going kind of determinism, denying the free will of man and his moral responsibility for any so-called good and evil. It is equally obvious that, if carried out in practice, the principle would be most mischievous. Both the Buddhists and the Jains agree that Gosāla did carry his principle into practice. Buddha, as before stated, charged him with incontinency. Mahāvīra is equally emphatic. He accuses him of teaching that 'an ascetic commits no sin if he has intercourse with women' (*J.S.* ii. 411). He charges his followers with being 'the slaves of women' (*ib.* ii. 270), and says that 'they do not lead a life of chastity' (*ib.* ii. 245). To this charge Gosāla laid himself open by his own action in choosing for his headquarters the premises of a woman.

From the fact that the Jain Scriptures maintain that originally Gosāla was a disciple (*śiṣya*) of Mahāvīra, it would appear that, beyond his determinism with its practical application, there was, in the main, no difference between his doctrines and those of Mahāvīra. This conclusion is also suggested by the statement of the Jain Bhagavatī Sūtra (*U.D.*, App. I. p. 4), that Gosāla's system was 'taken from the eight Mahānimittas, a portion of the Puvvas.' These Puvvas (*Pūrvas*), or 'Originals,' were believed to be the original sacred texts taught by Mahāvīra himself to his disciples (*IA* xvii. 280, xx. 170, 171). The general identity of Gosāla's system with that of Mahāvīra is further confirmed by a curious scheme of classification of 'all beings' (*sarva-sattva*), which in the Buddhist Dīgha Nikāya (p. 54; *Dial.* 72) is attributed to Gosāla. The extreme conciseness with which the scheme is stated makes it very difficult to understand it, and to compare it effectively with the system of Mahāvīra as set forth at large in the Jain Scriptures. But two important particulars can be definitely identified which are specially claimed by the Jains as doctrines of Mahāvīra.

In this connexion it is worth noting that the very same scheme, with the exception of Gosāla's concluding moral, is, in the Buddhist Majjhima Nikāya (*M.N.* i. 517, N.R. ii. 289) and Saṁyutta Nikāya (*S.N.* iii. 211, 212), attributed to the religious mendicant Pakudha Kachchāyana, and in the Tibetan Dulva (R.L.B. p. 103) to the religious mendicant Ajita Kesa-kambala. These two men, together with Gosāla Maṅkhali-putta, belonged to that group of six mendicant leaders whom Buddha often prominently names as his rivals. The other three were Mahāvīra Nātaputta, the leader of the Nigganthas, Pūraṇa Kassapa, and Sañjaya Belatthiputta. It would appear, therefore, that that classificatory scheme was in reality common to all the six mendicant leaders, but that each gave to it an application peculiar to himself. In the case of Gosāla the application took the determinist line; and this, indeed, is explicitly suggested by the determinist moral appended to the scheme in the Dīgha Nikāya. With regard to one item of the scheme,—that which refers to the 'conscious soul' (*saññi*, Skr. *sañjñi*)—its general agreement, with differences in detail, is directly affirmed by the Buddhist Scriptures. In the Majjhima Nikāya (iv. 398), as explained in the Dīgha Nikāya (p. 31; *Dial.* 44, 45), it is stated that all the six mendicant leaders alike taught, in opposition to Buddha, that the conscious soul continues to exist after death, though they differed among themselves as to the exact mode of existence. Gosāla is said (by Buddhaghoṣa) to have held that the soul 'had form' (*rūpī*), while Mahāvīra held that it was 'formless' (*arūpī*), but what these terms exactly imported we do not know.

The scheme of classification itself is as follows (*D.N.* 54; *Dial.* 72; cf. *U.D.*, App. II. pp. 17–29): 'There are 1,400,000 principal sorts of birth, and again 6000 (or 60,000 according to the Dulva, R.L.B. p. 103) others, and again 600. There are 500 sorts of *karma*, and again 5 (according to the 5 senses), and again 3 (according to act, word, and thought); and there is a whole *karma* and a half *karma* (the whole being a *karma* of act or word, the half a *karma* of thought). There are 62 modes of conduct, 62 periods, 6 classes (*abhijāti*) among men, 8 stages of a man's life, 4900 sorts of livelihood (*ājīva*), 4900 sorts of wandering mendicants, 4900 regions inhabited by Nāgas, 2000 faculties, 3000 purgatories, 36 dust depositories, 7 productions from conscious souls (*saññi*), 7 from unconscious beings, and 7 from parts between two joints (*e.g.* of sugar-cane), 7 sorts of devas, 7 of men, 7 of *paiśāchas* (goblins), 7 of lakes, 7 large and 700 minor precipices, 7 important and 700 unimportant dreams. There are 8,400,000 great periods during which both fools and wise alike, wandering in transmigration, shall at last make an end of pain.' To this scheme Gosāla is represented as appending his own determinist warning: 'Though the wise should hope that by some particular virtue or performance of duty or penance or righteousness he may make mature the (inherited) *karma*, that is not yet mature, or though the fool should hope by the same means to get rid of *karma* that has matured, neither of them can do it. The ease and pain, measured out as it were with a measure, cannot be altered in the course of transmigration; there can be neither increase nor decrease thereof, neither excess nor deficiency. Just as a ball of string, when it is cast forth, will spread out just as far as and no farther than it can unwind, so both fools and wise alike, wandering in transmigration exactly for the allotted term, shall then, and only then, make an end of pain.'

The two items in the foregoing scheme which can definitely be identified in the Jain system are —(1) the division of all living beings into those possessing one, two, three, four, or five senses, which is fully set out in the Jain *Uttarādhyayana Sūtra* (*J.S.* ii. 213, 219; also *ib.* i. 3, footnote 2); and (2) the division of mankind into six classes (*abhijāti*). The latter division, as held by Gosāla, is explained by Buddhaghoṣa in his commentary on the Buddhist *Dīgha Nikāya* (*S.V.* 162, tr. in *U.D.*, App. II. p. 21). According to his account, Gosāla distinguished the six classes by six colours—black, blue, red, yellow, white, and supremely white. The black class were the hunters, butchers, murderers, thieves, in short, all evil-doers. The blue were the mendicants known as Bhikṣu, that is, the Buddhist monks. The red were the mendicants known as Nigganṭha, who wore (at least) a strip of loin-cloth. The yellow were the lay adherents of the mendicants known as Achelaka, that is, those mendicants who wore no clothing whatsoever. The white were the mendicants, male as well as female, who were known as the Ājīvikas. The supremely white were the leaders of the latter: Nanda Vachchha, Kissa Saṅkichcha, and Gosāla Maṅkhali-putta.

In Mahāvīra's system, the six classes, which he termed *leśyā*, were also distinguished by a series of six colours differing but slightly—black, blue, grey, red, yellow, and white (*J.S.* ii. 196). In the interpretation of these colours, the two systems, on the first view, seem to differ considerably; but the underlying principle is, on closer inspection, seen to be the same. According to Mahāvīra, the black are those who injure living beings, *i.e.* those who contravene the first of the five vows of the Law (*ahiṁsā*). The blue are those who indulge their greed or their passions, *i.e.* those who contravene the fourth and fifth of the vows (*akiñchana* and *brahma-charya*). The grey are those who are deceitful and thieving, *i.e.* those who contravene the second and third of the vows (*satya* and *asteya*). The red are those who strive to control themselves so as to keep the law, *i.e.* the lay adherents. The yellow are those who are firm in controlling themselves, *i.e.* the 'professed' mendicants. The white are those who have attained absolute self-control, *i.e.* the so-called *Jina-kalpika*, like Mahāvīra himself (*J.S.* ii. 199, 200). Gosāla's interpretation is practically the same, with the exception that he illustrates his meaning by quoting types. Thus for him the Buddhists, or Bhikṣus, are the type of the blue class: for among their rivals the Buddhists had the reputation of being 'the preachers of ease' (*sāta-vādin*) who favoured 'the way of comfort' (*puṣṭi-mārga*, *J.S.* ii. 269, footnote 3; and *V.O.J.* iii. 332, footnote 2). The Nigganthas were the type of the red class; for they were superior to the Buddhists in renouncing comfort, but inferior to the Ājīvikas in adhering to a loin-cloth. The lay adherents of himself, the Achelaka, or 'totally naked' leader, were the type of the yellow (or Mahāvīra's red) class. The 'professed' adherents of himself, the so-called Ajīvikas, who apparently also walked totally naked, were the type of the white (or Mahāvīra's yellow) class. He himself, and other leaders, who walked totally naked, were the type of the supremely white class. In this connexion it is interesting to note that Buddhaghoṣa's interpretation of Gosāla's classification is based on the Aṅguttara Nikāya (iii. 383), where, however, it is attributed to the mendicant leader Pūraṇa Kassapa. If this is not a mere textual error, it confirms the observation already made that the classificatory scheme was common to all the six prominent rivals of Buddha (cf. *Mahābhārata*, xii. 280, v. 33 ff.).

It has already been stated (above, p. 261[b]) that, in the main, there was no doctrinal difference between Gosāla and Mahāvīra. There was, however, one point on which, according to the Jain tradition, there was a marked difference between them. They both accepted the so-called *Puvvas*, or Original Sayings. These were, later on, embodied in the *Dṛṣṭivāda*, or the twelfth Aṅga of the Jains. The first portion of this Aṅga is said to have explained 'the preparations necessary to grasp the meaning of Mahāvīra's system correctly' (*IA* xx. 173). With respect to this preparatory discipline (*parikamma*) we are told that some counted six, while others counted seven groups. The former count was that of the orthodox Jains, while the latter belonged to certain schismatics, called Ājīvikas or Terāsiyas, that is, as Abhayadeva (*c.* 1050 A.D.) explains, to the sect (*pāsaṇḍa*) founded by Gosāla. These men had their name *terāsiya* (Skr. *trairāśika*) from their practice of treating everything under three aspects (*tray-ātmaka*)—assertion, negation, and indifference. Thus they would say, *e.g.* that a thing may be true, or untrue, or partake of both while being neither (*sat*, *asat*, *sad-asat*). This tenet, technically known as the *syādvāda*, or the 'it may be' principle, is distinctive of the Jains generally. It follows that the Terāsiyas must have made use of it in some special way, and that this special way constituted their seventh group of preparatory discipline (*parikamma*). It may further be surmised that this seventh group was concerned with the *ājīva*, or 'profession' of men; and that for this reason the Terāsiyas had received their alternative name of Ājīvikas, or 'Professionals.' The substance of their teaching on this head is explained by Śīlāṅka (*c.* 876 A.D.) to have been that, besides the two states of man (admitted by Mahāvīra), in which he was 'bound' by *karma*, and in which he was 'liberated' from *karma*, there was a third state in which he was neither truly bound nor truly liberated (*J.S.* ii. 245, footnote 2). The men of the 'bound' state were those who lived in the world. To the intermediate state belonged those who had renounced the world (like Mahāvīra); but these men, owing to their spiritual arrogance, were not truly liberated; they had yet to pass through an innumerable series of transmigrations before they could reach that state of true liberation from *karma* which Gosāla claimed himself to have attained. In the Bhagavatī Sūtra (fols. 1237–1252; R.L.B. p. 253; *U.D.*, App. II. p. 18; see also *Dial.* 72) the latter is represented as himself explaining his theory of transmigration.

'According to my doctrine,' he says, 'all those who have become, or are now becoming, or will hereafter become, perfected, have to finish 8,400,000 great periods (*mahākalpa*), during which they have to be born, in regular alternation, seven times as a deva in a firmament (*sañjūha*) and seven times as a 'conscious being' (*saṇṇigabbha*, man) on earth, finishing up with seven reanimations in seven different bodies; and having, in the course of these re-births, rid themselves of the effects of the five sorts of *karma*, and of the three sorts of *karma*, and of the fraction of a *karma* (see above, p. 261[b]) in the proportion, respectively, of 100,000 and 60,000 and 600 (of the 8,400,000 great periods) they attain final perfection.'

To give an idea of the immeasurable length of time involved in this process, Gosāla adds:

'The bed of the river Ganges measures 500 *yojanas* in length, half a *yojana* in breadth, and 50 *dhanu* in depth (a *yojana* = 4½ miles, a *dhanu* = 6 feet). Taking a series of seven Ganges rivers of which each succeeding has seven times the dimensions of the preceding, the last of the series is equal to 117,649 Ganges rivers. If now every hundred years one grain of sand be removed, the time required to exhaust the whole of the sand of those seven Ganges rivers would be one *saras* period; and 300,000 of such *saras* periods make one *mahākalpa*, or great period' (*U.D.*, App. II. p. 27, footnote 21).

In the course of its last conscious existence on earth, the soul has to pass through seven changes of body by re-animation; that is to say, the soul successively passes into, and thus re-animates, the dead body of seven different persons. In his own case, Gosāla explains, he left near the town of Rājagiha the body of Udāī Kuṇḍiyāyaṇīya (when the latter died), and passed into the (dead) body of Enejjaga, re-animating it for the space of 22 years. When the latter died, he passed into and re-animated the body of Mallarāma for 21 years. Similarly, he re-animated in succession the four dead bodies of Maṇḍiya, Roha, Bhāraddāī, and Ajjuṇaga Goyamaputta for the space of 20, 19, 18, and 17 years respectively. 'Finally,' Gosāla continues, 'with the seventh change I left in Sāvatthī, on the premises of the potter woman, the body of Ajjuṇaga, and entered that of Gosāla Maṅkhali-putta for the space of 16 years. So I have fulfilled the seven changes in the course of 133 years, according to my doctrine.'

This insistence by Gosāla on the theory of re-animation being his own doctrine is of particular importance. It is one of those theories which Jain tradition states to have been quite peculiar to Gosāla, and to have originated in connexion with certain incidents in his life. It is clearly a somewhat incongruous supplement made by Gosāla to his general theory of transmigration. It must have been added for a particular purpose. What that purpose was is practically admitted by Gosāla himself. It was to refute Mahāvīra's aspersions on his character. In the Bhagavatī Sūtra (fol. 1237; *U.D.*, App. I. p. 5) we are informed that, in his last encounter with Mahāvīra in Sāvatthī, Gosāla said to him:

'You have called me your pupil, but that pupil of yours, Gosāla Maṅkhali-putta, is long since dead and re-born in the world of Devas, while I, who am really Udāī Kuṇḍiyāyaṇiya, have only in the seventh of the changes of body entered into the re-animated body of Gosāla, which body I am still retaining.'

This repudiation of identity certainly seems to suggest that the dissolution of the early companionship of the two men had taken place not so much by reason of a mere theoretical difference in doctrine, as on the ground of some course of conduct which was regarded by Mahāvīra, as well as by the people generally, as discreditable and unworthy of an ascetic.

Though the theory of re-animation was employed by Gosāla for the purpose of repudiating his identity, the incident which suggested it to him occurred, according to the Bhagavatī Sūtra (fol. 1214 ff.; *U.D.*, App. I. p. 3), at an earlier time, when Gosāla was still associated with Mahāvīra.

Once, while wandering together from Siddhatthagāma to Kummagāma, the two men passed a large sesame shrub in full bloom. Seeing it, Gosāla asked Mahāvīra whether or not the shrub would perish, and where its seeds would reappear. Mahāvīra replied that the shrub would perish, but that seeds would form in seed-vessels of the same shrub. Gosāla would not believe it; so, thinking to prove him a liar, he quietly returned to the shrub, tore it up by the roots, and threw it away. As chance would have it, just then a shower of rain fell. In consequence of it, the shrub was able again to take root; and so the seeds after all formed in its seed-vessels. In the meantime the two men had passed on to Kummagāma. On their return some time afterwards they passed the identical sesame shrub; and seeing it, Gosāla reminded Mahāvīra of his prophecy, adding that it was clear that the shrub had not died, and that the seeds had not formed. Mahāvīra replied that his prophecy had come true; for the shrub had perished, seeing that Gosāla himself had pulled it out by the roots and thrown it away, but that owing to a timely fall of rain the shrub had come to life again, and the seeds had formed in the seed-vessels. He added that similarly all plants were capable of re-animation. Still Gosāla would not believe it, and went up to the plant to examine its seed-vessel; but finding, on opening it, that Mahāvīra had been correct, he drew the further conclusion that not only plants but in fact all living beings (*jīva*, 'souls') were capable of re-animation. To this generalization of the theory of re-animation, however, Mahāvīra would not assent.

In this connexion another doctrine may be mentioned which is stated in the Bhagavatī Sūtra (fols. 1254, 1255; *U.D.*, App. I. p. 7) to have been quite peculiar to the Ājīvika followers of Gosāla. It was known as 'the Eight Finalities' (*aṭṭha charamāiṁ*), that is, the doctrine of the last drink, the last song, the last dance, the last solicitation, the last tornado, the last sprinkling elephant, the last fight with big stones as missiles, and the last Tirthāṅkara, viz. Maṅkhali-putta himself. The incidents which gave rise to this doctrine are those which attended the closing days of Gosāla's life. The first four were his last personal acts as related already in the story of his life (above, p. 259 f.). The next three are said to have been remarkable events which happened just about the time of Gosāla's death. The tornado refers to one of those fierce cyclonic storms, accompanied with torrential rain, which still occasionally visit Bengal, but which are almost unknown in other parts of Northern India. The 'sprinkling elephant' is said to have been a huge creature which had been trained to amuse the ladies of the royal harem when they bathed in the river Ganges, and the claim to the possession of which, as has already been related, occasioned a war between the kings of Magadha and Vaiśālī. In this war those stone missiles are said to have been employed (*N.S.* § 17 ff.) which evidently must have been thrown by some kind of powerful catapult. The *raison d'être* of this curious doctrine, no doubt, is that the dubious death of their master was felt by his disciples to require investment with some kind of rehabilitating glamour.

The incidents attending Gosāla's death gave rise to another peculiar doctrine, reported in the Bhagavatī Sūtra (fol. 1255 ff.; *U.D.*, App. I. pp. 8, 9). In the heat of his feverish excitement, Gosāla is said to have held a mango in his hand, and to have wetted himself with the muddy water which is always present on a potter's premises. This action is said to have suggested the doctrine of 'the Four Potables and the Four Impotables' (*chattāri pāṇagāiṁ, chattāri apāṇagāiṁ*), that is, the four things that may be used as drinks, and the four things that may be touched, but may not be drunk. The former refer to what is excreted by the cow, what is soiled by the hand (*e.g.* water in a potter's vessel), what is heated by the sun, and what drips from a rock. The latter refer to such things as water-jars, mangos, beans, etc.

With regard to the practices of the Ājīvikas, we have an instructive statement in the Buddhist Majjhima Nikāya. In the 36th chapter (*M.N.* i. 238; N.R. i. 376), Sachchaka, a member of the Nigganṭha community, is represented as explaining to Buddha the practices observed among the adherents of Gosāla Maṅkhali-putta and his friends Nanda Vachchha and Kissa Saṅkichcha. These three men, as we have seen (above, p. 262[a], also below, p. 267[a]), were the leaders of the Ājīvikas. Respecting them and their adherents, Sachchaka says:

'They discard all clothing (*achelaka*); they dispense with all decent habits (*muttāchāra*); they lick their food out of their hands (*hatthāpalekhaṇa*, p. 265[a]); they listen to no call to come or wait for food; they permit no food to be brought to them, or to be specially prepared for them, or to be received by them on invitation; they accept no food from the mouth of the pot or pan in which it is cooked, nor food placed within the threshold or among the firewood or among the pestles, nor food from a couple eating together, or from a woman with child, or a woman giving suck, or a woman in intercourse with a man; nor food which is reduced (in times of drought), or when a dog is standing by, or where flies are swarming round; they will not eat fish or flesh, nor drink liquor made from rice or the flowers of *Woodfordia floribunda*, nor sour gruel made of unhusked barley; some of them beg only at one house and accept but one handful of food, others beg at two houses and accept two handfuls, others beg at seven houses and accept seven handfuls; some subsist on one gift of food, others on two, others on seven; some take food only once a day, others only once every two days, others only once every seven days, others only once every half-month; in this manner they observe various routines of fasting.'

In the Digha Nikāya (p. 166; *Dial.* 227) this account of the Ājīvika practices is placed in the mouth of a naked ascetic (*achelaka*) Kassapa. This may refer to the mendicant leader Pūraṇa Kassapa (above, p. 261[b]), one of the six rivals of Buddha; and it may indicate that the practices in question were more or less common to all those six rival communities of religious mendicants, thus confirming what has already been said with regard to their common doctrines. In any case, with respect to Mahāvīra and his Nigganthas, the identity of several of their observances with those of the Ājīvikas has been pointed out by Professor Jacobi in his Introduction to the Jaina *Uttarādhyayana* (*J.S.* ii. p. xxxi).

Another point is worth noticing in connexion with Sachchaka's statement of the Ājīvika practices. When he had finished it, Buddha inquired whether the Ājīvikas were really able to sustain life on such conditions, and Sachchaka contemptuously replied that, of course, at other times they indulged in copious and excellent food and drink, and thus regained bodily vigour and grew fat. This remark is significant of the repute in which the sincerity of Gosāla and his Ājīvikas was held by their contemporaries. It only serves to confirm the suspicion of Gosāla's insincerity on the far more serious point of sexual conduct, which, there is good reason to believe, caused the rupture between him and Mahāvīra.

From the way the Terāsiyas, or Ājīvikas, with their peculiar doctrine respecting the seventh group of preparatory discipline (above, p. 262[b]), are spoken of, it is clear that they were not regarded as outside the pale of the Niggantha community. Their doctrine might not be acceptable to the majority, it might even be schismatic, but it was not condemned as heretical. It might cause friction between its propounder, Gosāla, and his associate, Mahāvīra, who rejected it; but it would not have caused that total separation and intense hostility which we see taking the place of the early association of the two men. For this change clearly there must have existed a special cause not essentially connected with the Terāsiya or Ājīvika doctrine. What this cause was we are nowhere explicitly told. The Buddhists are silent on the point. Buddha, we know, disliked Gosāla, but he had never been in personal touch with him, and the quarrel of Gosāla with Mahāvīra did not greatly interest him or the Buddhists. It was different with Mahāvīra. In the earlier years of their ascetic life he and Gosāla had been associates. The subsequent difference and total separation could not but be a matter of importance to the Jains. Yet even in their Scriptures—so far as we know them at present—no explicit statement of the cause or reason of the separation is recorded. We are left to draw conclusions from some indirect indications; nor are these at all obscure in their suggestiveness. The reported choice of Gosāla's headquarters on the premises of a woman, and his attempt to repudiate his identity, clearly point to, not a doctrinal, but a practical ground of separation, to some discreditable feature in the conduct of Gosāla. What this feature was is plainly enough indicated in the Sūtra-kṛtāṅga (*J.S.* ii. 245). Answering the contention of Gosāla (above, p. 262), that men who, like Mahāvīra, had renounced the world belonged to the intermediate state, and were still liable to be involved in *karma*, just as clarified water again becomes defiled, while he, Gosāla himself, had reached the state of perfect liberation, Mahāvīra points to the conduct of Gosāla and his followers: 'These men do not lead a life of chastity.' That fact, he means to say, should be enough to satisfy 'a wise man' as to the truth, or otherwise, of Gosāla's contention. In this connexion it may be noted that, in the Bhagavatī Sūtra (fols. 1275–1291; *U.D.*, App. I. pp. 11–14), Mahāvīra is represented as ironically applying to Gosāla his own doctrine of transmigrations, and showing how Gosāla, instead of being in the state of true liberation, had after his death to pass through an interminable transmigratory series, the several steps of which he specifies, before he really attained perfection.

There is, however, a passage in the Sūtra-kṛtāṅga which is even more explicit in its suggestiveness. It records (*J.S.* ii. 409–413) a disputation which Ārdraka, a follower of Mahāvīra, held with Gosāla respecting the points on which the latter differed from Mahāvīra. These are, first, a charge of inconsistency against Mahāvīra, that he at first wandered about as a single monk, but afterwards surrounded himself with many monks; secondly, a charge of misplaced severity, that he insisted on four restrictions which Gosāla rejected; thirdly, a charge of spiritual arrogance as well as spiritual cowardice. The four restrictions refer to:

(1) Drinking of cold water.
(2) Eating of (unboiled) seeds.
(3) Accepting things specially prepared.
(4) Having intercourse with women.

Mahāvīra forbade these actions as sinful, but Gosāla maintained that an ascetic committed no sin in doing them. The same four restrictions are mentioned in another place of the same Sūtra-kṛtāṅga (*J.S.* ii. 267), though with a notable difference. Here they run as follows:

(1) Drinking cold water.
(2) Eating (unboiled) seeds.
(3) Accepting things specially prepared.
(4) Serving a sick brother with food brought to him in the vessel of a householder.

The ethical item of sexual intercourse is here replaced by the ceremonial item of eating from the vessel of a lay adherent. The significance of this difference will be explained in the sequel (p. 267[a]). At this point it is important to notice only that none of the matters in dispute is concerned with doctrine; they are all concerned with conduct.

Considering that it was the conduct of religious ascetics that was in question, the most striking point in dispute is that respecting sexual intercourse. To understand the position, we must remember that Pārśva, the precursor of Mahāvīra, had enjoined only four vows (*vrata*) on his followers (*J.S.* ii. 121). These were—(1) not to injure life (*ahiṁsā*), (2) to speak the truth (*sūnṛtā* or *satya*), (3) not to steal (*asteya*), (4) not to own property (*aparigraha* or *akiñchana*). That is, Pārśva enjoined the vows of kindness, truth, honesty, and poverty. To these Mahāvīra added the fifth vow of chastity (*brahma-charya*, *ib.* ii. 91, 109, 139, 204). His reason for making this addition is explained in the Uttarādhyayana Sūtra (*ib.* ii. 122, 123). Before Mahāvīra it had been understood that chastity was implicitly enjoined by the other vows; but in reality they left a loop-hole. The wife being accounted a species of property, marriage was forbidden by the vow of poverty, and adultery by the vow of honesty; but the case of fornication was left open. On this specious ground, laxity of morals crept in among the intellectually or morally weaker members of the Niggantha community founded by Pārśva. Mahāvīra's fifth vow of chastity was designed to reform that evil. On this point he encountered the opposition of his associate, Gosāla. The latter sympathized with the lax party; and he appears to have justified his own and their laxity of morals by the double argument that the truly 'liberated' ascetic could commit no sin, and that, as there was no free will, there was no moral responsibility. Indeed, there is good ground for believing that it was this very laxity of conduct on the part of Gosāla that gave the occasion to Mahāvīra to introduce the fifth vow, and thus to force the withdrawal of Gosāla. It will be noticed that the two statements of the four restrictions, above quoted, have the first three restrictions in common, while they vary with respect to the fourth. This points to something peculiar in those three restrictions. Now, in one place of the Sūtra-kṛtāṅga (*J.S.* ii. 313) these particular three restrictions (regarding cold water, seed, and non-acceptance of specially prepared food) alone are mentioned, and in the Āchārāṅga Sūtra (*J.S.* i. 63) we find Mahāvīra described as 'the wise man who enjoined three restrictions' (*yāmā tiṇṇi**). On the other hand, in the Buddhist Dīgha Nikāya (p. 57; *Dial.* 74), Mahāvīra is made to describe himself as 'the man of four restrictions' (*chatur-yāma*). The explanation of this discrepancy which suggests itself is that Mahāvīra originally enjoined only three restrictions on his followers, and that he added the fourth at a later time when he quarrelled with Gosāla. This fourth restriction respecting intercourse with women is, in fact, identical with Mahāvīra's fifth vow of chastity, which, as has already been remarked, is an addition made by him to the four vows of Pārśva. If the surmise is correct that it was Gosāla who provided the occasion for the institution of the fourth restriction (*yāma*), that is to say, the fifth vow (*vrata*) of Mahāvīra's system, it goes a long way to prove that it was Gosāla's laxity

* In *J.S.* i. 63 the phrase is wrongly translated by 'three vows,' following herein the commentators; but *vrata*, 'vow,' is something different from *yāma*, 'restriction.'

of morals that was the real cause of Mahāvīra's separation from him. Speaking on the ascetic's duty to avoid intercourse with women, Mahāvīra is represented in the Sūtra-kṛtāṅga (*J.S.* ii. 273) as saying concerning Gosāla: 'In the assembly of the monks he pronounces holy words, yet secretly he commits sin; but the wise know him to be a deceiver and great rogue.' It was Gosāla's hypocrisy in the matter of sexual conduct that caused the breach between him and Mahāvīra.

This, then, was the main cause; but, no doubt, there were other subsidiary causes which exacerbated the friction between the two men. They had reference to the three restrictions regarding the use of cold water and unboiled seeds, and the acceptance of specially prepared food. In order to realize the significance of these seemingly trivial matters, we must remember that among all Indian ascetics abstention from action (*karma*) was held to be the paramount rule of conduct, because *karma* bound the soul in the cycle of transmigrations. But to this rule there was one exception: seeing that without the body one cannot go through the whole of the discipline which secures salvation (*mokṣa, nirvāṇa*), such actions as are necessary for the preservation of the body (*dharm-ādhāra-śarīra-rakṣaṇāya* in the commentary to *S.K.* ii. 6, § 7, in *J.S.* ii. 411), *e.g.* the begging and eating of food, are innocuous and do not operate as a fetter (*karma-bandha*; see Bh. Rep. pp. 94, 99). Every vow (*vrata*) or restriction (*yāma*) taken on himself by the ascetic was considered tacitly subject to that rule and its exception. The differences among the ascetics arose when it came to the practical application of this tacit reference. Thus, while all agreed that storing food was forbidden, but that begging one's daily allowance of food was permitted, some ascetics qualified that permission by certain restrictions (*yāma*). Mahāvīra forbade the use of cold water and of seeds in their natural state, lest injury should be done to any 'life' (*jīva*) in either; both should be used only after boiling, or other safeguarding process. He also forbade the acceptance of any food specially prepared for the mendicant, lest the privilege of begging should degenerate into indulgence. Gosāla, on the other hand, rejected these three restrictions.

Again, while all ascetics were agreed that besides the body the ascetic should own no other possessions, Mahāvīra permitted the possession of a bowl for the reception of the begged food. Gosāla denied the justice of this permission, because the ascetic could and should make use of his hand for that purpose (cf. *J.S.* i. 57, footnote 2, and ii. 267, footnote 2). The food should be received into the bowl made by the palms of the joined hands, and out of this natural bowl it should be licked up. Hence ascetics of this stricter observance were known as the 'hand-lickers' (*hatthāpalekhana*, *D.N.* 166; *Dial.* 227). If food, however, was required for a sick monk, it was to be carried to him in the vessel of the householder. Mahāvīra objected to this practice as open to the risk of injury to any 'life' that might be in the householder's vessel (*J.S.* ii. 303).

In this connexion the treatment of the question of clothing may be mentioned. Some ascetics (like Pārśva) permitted the use of wrappers; others permitted only the irreducible minimum of a pudic cover (*kaṭi-bandhana*); while, again, others went about absolutely naked. To the second class appear to have belonged the Nigganthas, or the immediate followers of Mahāvīra (*J.S.* i. 73), who, accordingly, are called by Gosāla the 'one-strip men' (*eka-sāṭaka*), and placed in his red class (above, p. 262[a]). Though conceding to his Nigganthas the use of a loin-cloth, for himself Mahāvīra discarded the use of all clothing. On this point there was no difference between him and Gosāla; both were mendicants of the *achelaka*, or 'clothless,' class. Indeed, it is just possible that on this point Mahāvīra may have been influenced by Gosāla. For we are told in the Jain Scriptures that at first, when Mahāvīra adopted the ascetic life, he attached himself to the clothed community of Pārśva; it was only in the second year of that life, about the time when he fell in with Gosāla, that he adopted the strictest observance of absolute nakedness. The coincidence suggests that Mahāvīra adopted that observance from Gosāla, and that it was this circumstance that formed the bond of their early companionship, until the discovery of Gosāla's hypocrisy caused the subsequent and final separation. It appears probable, however, that within the Niggantha community the general rule was to wear the loin-cloth, and the practice of total nakedness was limited to that section of it which formed the party of Gosāla, and had adopted his doctrine on *ājīva* as formulated in the seventh group of the preparatory discipline (above, p. 262[b]), and which hence was known as the Ājīvikas.

On this point there is an instructive story related in the Buddhist *Vinaya Piṭaka* (i. 291; *V.P.Tr.* ii. 216 ff.). Once, when Buddha was staying in Sāvatthī, he and his Bhikṣus were invited by a wealthy woman, Visākhā, to a meal in her house. When the meal was ready, she sent her maidservant to call her guests. While the maid went on her errand, a heavy shower of rain fell, and on her arrival at Buddha's lodging she found the Bhikṣus standing disrobed and enjoying the rain. Thinking that there was a mistake, she returned to inform her mistress that at the place to which she had been directed there were no Bhikṣus, but Ājīvikas. The misunderstanding, of course, was cleared up; but the incident, which happened at Sāvatthī, shows that the Ājīvikas were naked monks, and that they were the followers of Gosāla, who, as we have seen, had established his headquarters at Sāvatthī, after he had separated from Mahāvīra. The same point is illustrated by Gosāla's sixfold classification of men (above, p. 262[a]), in which the white class is represented by his own party, the naked Ājīvikas, while the red class is typified by the party of Mahāvīra, the one-strip 'Nigganthas.' Total nakedness, however, must have been the mark of the whole Ājīvika party among the Nigganthas; not only of that portion which seceded with Gosāla, but also of the other portion which continued in the connexion. For, as will appear in the sequel, it was the latter that formed the nucleus, from which, at a later date, the Digambara Order took its rise (below, p. 266[b]).

It remains briefly to consider the two other charges preferred by Gosāla against Mahāvīra (above, p. 264[b]). The reference in the first of these is not quite clear. Mahāvīra is accused of having first 'wandered about as a single monk,' but having afterwards 'surrounded himself with many monks' (*J.S.* ii. 409, 410). On the other hand, Gosāla claims to 'live alone and single' (*ib.* p. 411). As a fact, however, Gosāla also was 'surrounded by many monks,' who were known as the Ājīvikas. It is clear, therefore, that the mere fact that a leader wandered about or lived with a company of personal disciples did not count as an offence. The gravamen of Mahāvīra's procedure, in the eyes of Gosāla, appears to have been that, like Buddha, he instituted an Order (*saṅgha*) of monks. The followers of Mahāvīra were scattered in various places in larger or smaller groups, but they were all organized in one community, under one Law, and one leader (Mahāvīra). Gosāla's followers formed but a small group that always accompanied its leader. There were, indeed, other groups of ascetics of a similarly dubious character who also bore the name of Ājīvikas, or 'Professionals,' but they lived apart under separate leaders, the names of two of whom, Kissa Saṅkichcha and Nanda Vachchha, are recorded in the Buddhist Scriptures (*M.N.* i. 238, 524; *A.N.* iii. 384). But the Ājīvikas of this dubious kind, who must be distinguished from the later Ājīvika Order of monks (below, p. 268), formed no organized community like the Nigganthas (or Jains) and Buddhists. It is obvious that the antinomian tenets and practices of Gosāla, and other men of his way of thinking, would form a natural bar to the formation of a widespread public organization. It may have been the consciousness of his disability in this respect that prompted Gosāla's accusation against his more successful rival.

The second of the two charges against Mahāvīra accused him at once of spiritual arrogance and spiritual cowardice. The reference in this charge is to Gosāla's theory of the three spiritual states of men (see above, p. 262[b]). According to him, Mahāvīra was in the intermediate state; his soul, though free from *karma* in a sense, was not truly liberated, for it was full of spiritual arrogance in thinking that his system alone was correct and condemning those who differed from him (*J.S.* ii. 411, §§ 11–14, and Śīlāṅka's comment on Sūtra-kṛtāṅga, i. 1, 3, § 12; *J.S.* ii. 245). It was also full of spiritual cowardice in being eager to win converts among the common people, but afraid to meet learned men who might refute him (*J.S.* ii. p. 412, §§ 15–18, and p. 413, §§ 19–25). The advocate of Mahāvīra replies that, first, his master only teaches, as others do, what he believes to be true and right, and while condemning false doctrines, he does not condemn those who entertain them. Secondly, he never refuses to meet honest and worthy opponents, and is void of hypocrisy himself, while trying to win people for his doctrines.

4. History of the Ājīvikas.—The earliest mention of the Ājīvikas occurs in a brief record incised on the walls of two rock-hewn caves on Barabar Hill near Gayā (*IA* xx. 361 ff.; S.A. 144). According to its own statement, it was made in the 13th year of the reign of the Emperor Aśoka, that is to say, in B.C. 251. It runs as follows: 'King Piyadassi, in the 13th year of his reign, bestowed this cave on the Ājīvikas.'

The next mention occurs in the seventh of the celebrated Pillar Edicts of the same Emperor Aśoka, incised in the 28th year of his reign, or in B.C. 236 (S.I.P. ii. 82, 97; *Ep. Ind.* ii. 270, 272, 274; S.A. 155). It runs as follows: 'I have arranged that my Censors of the Law of Piety shall be occupied with the affairs of the Buddhist Order (*saṅgha*) as well as with the Brāhman (ascetics), the Ājīvikas, the Nigganthas, and, in fact, with all the various mendicant communities (*pāsaṇḍa*).'

A further early mention occurs in a brief record, incised on the walls of three rock-hewn caves on Nagarjuni Hill in the first year of the reign of Aśoka's successor Daśaratha, that is, in B.C. 227 (*IA* xx. 361 ff.; S.A. 145). It runs as follows: 'This cave was bestowed by his Majesty Daśaratha, immediately after his accession, on the venerable Ājīvikas, to be a dwelling-place for them as long as the sun and moon endure.'

After this we meet with no mention of the Ājīvikas till we come to the 6th cent. A.D. In that century, about A.D. 550, Varāha Mihira, in his astrological works Bṛhaj-jātaka (xv. 1) and Laghu-jātaka (ix. 12), names them as one of seven classes of religious mendicants. These are—(1) the Śākyas or Raktapaṭas (men of the red robe), *i.e.* the Buddhist monks; (2) the Ājīvikas, or, as the commentator Bhaṭṭotpala (*c.* 950 A.D.) explains, the Ekadaṇḍins, or 'men of one staff'; (3) the Nirgranthas, or Jaina monks; (4) the Tāpasas (ascetics) or Vanyāśanas (eaters of wild fruits), *i.e.* Brāhmans of the third *āśrama*, living as hermits in the forest; (5) Bhikṣus (mendicants), *i.e.* Brāhmans of the fourth *āśrama*, living as homeless wanderers, and following, according to the commentator, the Mīmāṁsā system; (6) the Vṛddha-śrāvakas; and (7) the Charakas, who appear also to have been two kinds of wandering religious mendicants. That these seven classes of devotees, and therefore the Ājīvikas among them, were actually existing in Varāha Mihira's time, is evident from the fact that he teaches that a person is destined to enter into one of them according to the indications of his horoscope.

In the 9th cent. we have the testimony of the great Jain commentator Śīlāṅka (*c.* 876 A.D.) to the continued existence of the Ājīvikas. And here we first meet with the interesting fact of the identity of the Ājīvikas with the Digambara Jains. Commenting on the objection made by some to Mahāvīra's four 'restrictions' in the Sūtra-kṛtāṅga (*J.S.* ii. 267), Śīlāṅka states that the reference is to the Ājīvikas or Digambaras. Seeing that, in his comment on another passage of the same work (*ib.* ii. 245), he identifies the followers of Gosāla, that is, the Ājīvikas, with the Terāsiyas (Sanskr. Trairāśikas), it follows that in Śīlāṅka's view the followers of Gosāla, the Ājīvikas, the Terāsiyas, and the Digambaras were the same class of religious mendicants.

In the 10th cent. we have a further testimony to the identity of the Ājīvikas and the Digambaras. In his vocabulary, called the Abhidhāna Ratnamālā (ii. 189, 190), Halāyudha (*c.* 950 A.D.) enumerates a large number of names of the two Jain divisions, the Śvetāmbaras (or white-clothed ones) and the Digambaras (or sky-clad, *i.e.* naked ones), or, as he calls them, the Śvetavāsas and Digvāsas. The latter, he says, are also known as the Ājīva, which is only a shorter form of Ājīvika.

Lastly, in the 13th cent. we have, in certain temple records, a mention of the Ājīvikas as a sect then actually existing in South India. These records are inscriptions on the walls of the Perumāl Temple at Poygai near Virinchipuram (*S.I.Inscr.* i. 88, 89, 92, 108). They refer to grants of land to the temple together with 'the tax on Ājīvikas,' made by the Chola king Rājarāja in the years A.D. 1238, 1239, 1243, 1259. By the editor of the inscriptions these Ājīvikas are, on the authority of modern Tamil dictionaries, identified with the Jains. This, of course, means the Digambara sect of the Jains; for it is this sect whose principal seat, in those times, was in Southern India, and colonies of them are still to be found there (*IA* xxxii. 459; *JGOS* xxxviii. 17). The statements on the subject in the Tamil dictionaries appear to be based on the Tamil literature, and possibly on modern usage. The older Tamil literature (*teste* Dr. Pope) certainly uses the term Ājīvika in speaking of the Jains, *i.e.* the Digambaras. There can be no doubt, therefore, that since the 6th cent. A.D., when Varāha Mihira used the term, the name has signified the Digambara sect of the Jains.

As to Varāha Mihira's use of the term, it is to be noted that his commentator Bhaṭṭotpala, whose date is about A.D. 950, identifies the Ājīvikas with the Ekadaṇḍins. This identification is based on a Prākrit verse which he quotes from a Jain writer called Kālakāchārya. That writer, who lived about A.D. 450, that is, about a century earlier than Varāha Mihira, names the same seven classes of ascetics with the one exception that he writes Ekadaṇḍins for Ājīvikas (*Tr.C.O.* iii. 2, p. 553). Bhaṭṭotpala on his own part adds that the Ekadaṇḍins or Ājīvikas are devotees of Nārāyaṇa, that is, of Viṣṇu. On the other hand, Śīlāṅka, speaking of the Ekadaṇḍins in another connexion, declares them to be devotees of Śiva (*J.S.* ii. 245, 417). It is clear from this apparent discrepancy that what these two commentators had in their mind was the class of ascetics who are still known as the Daṇḍins, or 'Men of the Staff.' These ascetics are usually classed as belonging to the Śaivite division of Hindus; but they are rather eclectics, in that they invoke not only Śiva but also Viṣṇu as Nārāyaṇa. They carry a staff (*daṇḍa*) with a piece of reddish cloth attached to its top, wear only a narrow strip of cloth or go entirely naked, and are enjoined to live solitary. They hold Vedāntist doctrines; and any man, caste or no caste, may join them (*BG* ix. pt. i. 542). They must not be confounded with the Daśanāmī Daṇḍins, who are a comparatively modern class of ascetics, having been founded by the reformer Śaṅkarāchārya and his disciples in the 9th cent. A.D., and who live in convents (*maṭha*), and pay some regard to caste in the matter of admission (*JBAS* lix. 55, note).

From the fact that Gosāla is called Maṅkhaliputta, or Maṅkhali (Maskarin), *i.e.* the man of the bamboo-staff, it is clear that originally he belonged to the class of Ekadaṇḍin (or Daṇḍin) ascetics; and, though he afterwards joined Mahāvīra and adopted his system, he held some distinguishing tenets of his own, and also retained his old distinguishing mark, the bamboo-staff. On account of these distinctions his party within the Nigganṯha community was known as the Terāsiya or Ājīvika (above, p. 262), and apparently also as the Ekadaṇḍin, or the One-staff men. Still later, by reason of his evil life, when it was discovered, Gosāla was expelled by Mahāvīra from the community; and with him, it would appear, were ejected also a few others of the Ājīvika party who were his intimate friends and shared his evil practices. The Buddhist Scriptures name two of these friends, Kissa Saṅkichcha and Nanda Vachchha (above, p. 263[b]). These three men, after separating from Mahāvīra, appear to have lived a comparatively solitary life at Sāvatthī at the head of small groups of like-minded followers. But there is no reason to believe that, with the expulsion of the black sheep, the Ājīvika or Terāsiya party as such ceased to exist within the Nigganṭha Order. In fact, whatever evidence there is points the other way. Thus, in this connexion, the difference already noted (above, p. 264[b]) between the two versions of the 'four restrictions' possesses a peculiar significance. The reference to sexual delinquency occurs in that version which is concerned more especially with Gosāla and his faction; while the other version, which substitutes the reference to the use of the householder's vessel, is, according to the commentator Sīlāṅka, concerned with the Ājīvikas or Digambaras. The discrimination, in the two versions, tends to show that there was a portion of the Ājīvika party within the Nigganṭha Order which was not implicated in the antinomies of Gosāla's faction. As a matter of fact, the Digambaras differ, to the present day, from the Śvetāmbaras on the points implied in the four restrictions. Thus the restrictions respecting the use of cold water and natural seeds were intended to enforce extreme regard for any kind of 'life' (*jīva*); but the Digambaras are said to be 'only moderately careful of animal life,' while the Śvetāmbaras are extremely so (*IA* xxxii. 460). With respect to the fourth restriction, while both sects insist on the vow of chastity, they differ in regard to the possession of the alms bowl. While the bowl belongs to the regular outfit of the Śvetāmbara monks, the Digambaras are not permitted to carry it, but must receive their food in the palms of their hands (Oman, p. 151). As to the point of nakedness, the difference between the two divisions is sufficiently indicated by their names.

Further evidence in the same direction is afforded by the subsequent revival of the Terāsiya trouble within the Nigganṭha community, and by the retention to this day of the distinguishing mark of the staff among the Digambaras. On admission, we are told, 'the novice is supplied with the articles allowed to an ascetic by the Jain Scriptures, a black rod or *daṇḍ* about five feet long,' etc., and 'the Sādhu (or professed monk) always carries his staff (*daṇḍ*)' (*BG* ix. pt. i. p. 107).

The case, then, stands thus: Ekadaṇḍin is a general term for a class of ascetics which includes two subdivisions, the orthodox Śaivite Daṇḍins and the heterodox Jain Ājīvikas or Digambaras. The Jain writer Kālakāchārya, of course, meant to indicate the latter by the word Ekadaṇḍin; and Varāha Mihira, therefore, to preclude misunderstanding, substituted the more definite term Ājīvika. The orthodox commentator, Bhaṭṭotpala, misunderstanding the position, confused the heterodox Ājīvika with the orthodox Daṇḍin.

According to the tradition of the Digambaras, an acute antagonism between their own party and the party of the Śvetāmbaras arose during the life of Bhadrabāhu, who appears to have been the last head of the united Nigganṭha, or Jain community (*JGOS* xxxviii. 14, xl. 92; *IA* xxi. 59). Soon after his death, about B.C. 314 (*i.e.* 170 years after Mahāvīra's demise in B.C. 484, above, p. 261[b]), the differences between the two parties grew into a final and definite rupture, which the Śvetāmbara tradition in the Kalpa Sūtra (*J.S.* i. 290) ascribes to a man called Chhaluka Rohagupta. This man is said to have been a disciple of Mahāgiri, who was at the head of the Śvetāmbaras from 269 to 239 B.C., and it was he who is said to have founded the Terāsiya schism. The Terāsiyas, as we have seen (above, p. 262), are the same as the Ājīvikas, and the latter are identical with the Digambaras. It follows, therefore, that the Ājīvika or Digambara Order was already in existence in B.C. 251, when Aśoka dedicated the Barabar Hill cave to the Ājīvikas. As to Aśoka's successor Daśaratha (or Samprati, as the Jains call him), we are expressly told that he was converted to Jainism. It is true that the Śvetāmbaras claim him as a convert of their own leader Suhastin (*K.S.* 10; *J.S.* i. 290), a contemporary (B.C. 269–223) and co-leader with the above-mentioned Mahāgiri (*JGOS*, xxxvii. 501). But from the fact that Daśaratha dedicated, in B.C. 227, the Nagarjuni Hill caves to the Ājīvikas, perhaps his conversion is to be placed to the credit rather of the Digambaras; although, of course, he may, like his predecessor Aśoka, have distributed his favours impartially to the principal mendicant Orders of his time. Of Aśoka we know from his seventh Pillar Edict that he was a patron equally of the Buddhists, Nigganthas, Ājīvikas, and Brāhmaṇas. It is evident now, from what has been said, that the terms Nigganṭha and Ājīvika denote the two Jain Orders which are known to us as the Śvetāmbaras and Digambaras. It has been asserted (by Professors Kern and Bühler, *Ep. Ind.* ii. 274, *IA* xx. 362) that the term Brāhmaṇa in the Edict qualifies the Ājīvikas, describing them as being a 'Brāhmanical' Order. Irrespective of the difficulty whether at that early time there existed any orthodox Brāhmanical Order similar to the Buddhist and Jain (Nigganṭha), the Edict speaks of 'Brāhmaṇas.' That word does not mean 'a person connected in some way with Brāhmanism,' but it denotes 'a person of the Brāhman caste,' and in the context of the Edict it means 'a Brāhman ascetic,' that is, a person of the Brāhman caste who had adopted the rule of the fourth Brāhmanic *āśrama* or way of living. Such a person took on himself to live a homeless wandering life as a religious mendicant. The appeal to the statement of Bhaṭṭotpala, as has been already shown (above, p. 266), is unavailing. A Vaiṣṇava or Saiva ascetic may belong (or rather, may have belonged before joining) to any caste (W.M.H. pp. 59 ff., 83 ff.). These men may be said to be 'Brāhmanical' ascetics because they profess to be devotees of Brāhmanical deities, but no Indian would call them 'Brāhmaṇas.' The word 'brāhmanical' expresses a Western idea, quite foreign to the word *brāhmaṇa*.

The history of the Ājīvikas may be briefly summed up as follows: Gosāla commenced his ascetic life as a Maṅkhali, or Maskarin, that is, as an individual of the ancient well-known class of religious mendicants which was distinguished by the carrying of a bamboo staff. After a time he made the acquaintance of Mahāvīra, who belonged to another class of religious mendicants known as the Nigganthas, or Unfettered Ones (*i.e.* unfettered from the bonds of *karma*), the followers of Pārśvanātha. The two men, holding kindred views on the stringency of ascetic requirements (*e.g.* on the point of nakedness [*achelaka*]), associated, and elaborated a common system, to which, however, Gosāla added some particulars of his own. Each of them had his own party among their common following; and Gosāla's party was known as the Ājīvikas, or 'Professionals,' on account of its leader's peculiar views on the *ājīva*, or 'profession,' of a religious mendicant. In course of time Gosāla developed antinomian proclivities; and this produced ill-feeling between the two associates and ultimately led to a total rupture. Gosāla departed, together with those of the Ājīvika party who actively sympathized with him. There is no reason to suppose that the seceders formed a large group, or that as a group they survived the death of their leader Gosāla. The others of the Ājīvika party who had not shared Gosāla's antinomian tenets and practices remained within the Nigganṭha community; but they retained their peculiar views on the points of total nakedness, non-possession of a bowl, imperfect regard for life, distinctive mark of a staff, and probably other matters. On account of these differences, there no doubt existed some amount of friction between the Ājīvika party and the rest of the Nigganṭha community. It manifested itself especially in the time of Bhadrabāhu, whose sympathies appear to have been rather with the Ājīvikas. But the friction came to a head only in the earlier part of the 3rd cent. B.C., when that party, which was known also as the Terāsiya (Trairāśika), definitely and finally separated to form the distinct Order which is now known as the Digambaras. It thus appears that the Jain division into Digambaras and Śvetāmbaras may be traced back to the very beginning of Jainism, it being indirectly due to the antagonism of the two associated leaders, Mahāvīra and Gosāla, who are the representatives of the two hostile sections.

It remains only to notice a few detached references to Ājīvika mendicants occurring in the Buddhist Scriptures and elsewhere. The Vinaya Piṭaka (i. 8; *SBE* xiii. 90) and Majjhima Nikāya (i. 170; N.R. i. 271, ii. 454) relate how Buddha, immediately after his enlightenment, met an Ājīvika of the name of Upaka, who, however, received Buddha's account of his spiritual experiences rather contemptuously. The Majjhima Nikāya (i. 31; N.R. i. 45) further relates the story of an Ājīvika Paṇḍuputta who had been originally a carriage-builder, and who was converted by Buddha to his own belief. In the Vinaya Piṭaka (ii. 284; *SBE* xx. 370) we are told also of an anonymous Ājīvika mendicant who gave the Buddhist monk Kassapa the first information of his master's death. These three men probably were members of the Ājīvika party in the Nigganṭha community. In another place the Vinaya Piṭaka (ii. 130; *V.P.Tr.* xx. 132) relates how on one occasion certain Ājīvikas, meeting with some Buddhist monks who walked under the protection of sunshades, jeered at the un-ascetic conduct of their rivals. In the Mahāvaṁsa (T.Mv. 67) there is a curious notice of a group of Ājīvikas which existed in Ceylon in the time of King Paṇḍukabhaya about B.C. 426, and on whose behalf that king is said to have built a house (*gaha*). This notice, however, considering the very early date to which it refers, must be accepted with much reserve. Another very curious notice of the Ājīvikas occurs in a little book on *Hindu Logic as preserved in China and Japan*, by Sadajiro Sugiura (ed. by Mr. Edgar A. Singer, jr., in the Philosophical Series [No. 4] of the Publications of the University of Pennsylvania).

In the Introduction, p. 16, the author says: 'Two more schools are frequently included by Chinese and Japanese authors among the great ones (*i.e.* the well-known six Indian). They are called Nikendabtra and Ashibika, and are quite similar to each other. They both hold that the penalty of a sinful life must sooner or later be paid; and since it is impossible to escape from it, it is better that it should be paid as soon as possible, so that the life to come may be free for enjoyment. Thus their practices were ascetic: fasting, silence, immovability, and the burying of themselves to the neck (*Nyakuron-so*, i. 22), were their expressions of penance. They were probably offshoots of the Jainist or some other Hindu sect.'

The 'Nikendabtra and Ashibika' of this statement are obviously the Nigganthas and Ājīvikas, that is, the Śvetāmbara and Digambara Jains.

LITERATURE.—There exists no connected account of the Ājīvikas; but, in addition to the works mentioned in the text, short detached remarks on the sect occur in the following works:—Bühler, *Epigraphia Indica* (Calcutta, 1894), ii. 272, 274, 323, and *IA* xx. 361 ff.; Burnouf, *Lotus de la bonne loi* (Paris, 1852); Grimblot, 'Sept Suttas Pālis' in *IA* (Bombay, 1879), viii. 312; Jacobi, 'Jaina Sūtras,' *SBE*, vols. xxii. and xlv. (Oxford, 1884–95), pt. i. pp. 16, 18, pt. ii. pp. 19, 22–26, 29–32, and *IA* ix. 161 ff.; H. Kern, *Hist. de Bouddhisme*, i. (Paris, 1901–3), 15, 121, 151, ii. 6, 41, 337, and *Manual of Indian Buddhism* (Strassburg, 1896), pp. 72 and n. 2, 74, 82, 112, 116; Leumann, *V.O.J.* iii. (Vienna, 1889), 328 ff., *Actes du Sixième Congrès Or.* 1883, pt. iii. p. 554 ff., and *Aupapātika Sūtra* (Leipzig, 1883), pt. i. p. 80, par. 120; Oldenberg, *Buddha* (4th ed., 1903), pp. 82, 93, 199; O. Schrader, *Stand der Ind. Philosophie* (Strassburg, 1902), pp. 12, 34 ff.; Rhys Davids, *Buddhist India* (London, 1903), pp. 143, 146, 290, and *Dialogues of the Buddha* (London, 1899), pp. 71, 219, 220, 227, 232; Rockhill, *Life of the Buddha* (London, 1884), pp. 101, 249 ff.; Senart, *Inscriptions de Piyadassi* (Paris, 1886), ii. p. 209 ff.; V. A. Smith, *Asoka* (Oxford, 1901), pp. 106, 144 f.; Weber, *Catalogue of the Royal Library, Berlin, Index*, p. 1280 (1892).

A. F. R. HOERNLE.

AJMĒR, AJMĪR (the *meru*, or sacred mountain, of Ajayarājā, who is said to have founded the city in the 2nd cent. A.D.).—The capital of the British district of Ajmēr-Mhairwārā, in the province of Rājputāna. It is noted for two important religious buildings, a mosque, and the shrine of a noted faqīr, or Musalmān saint. The former, which bears the name of Arhāī Din kā Jhoñpṛā, 'the shed of two and a half days,' is a converted Jaina temple; and the most probable explanation of the name is that the Sultān Quṭb-ad-dīn or Altamsh, when he visited the place, ordered that within that period the original Jaina temple should be converted into a mosque for his devotions. It is now the finest existing specimen of the early style of Musalmān mosque in India. Inscriptions fix the date of its erection between A.D. 1211 and 1236, in the reign of Altamsh. It is thus of the same age as the celebrated mosque near the Kuth Minār in Old Delhi, and Cunningham supposes that both were probably planned by the same architect and erected by the same body of workmen.

The faqīr's shrine, or *dargāh*, marks the resting place of the famous Musalmān saint, Khwājah Mu'īn ad-dīn Ḥasan Chishtī (A.D. 1142–1236), who was born in Sijistān or Sīstān, eastern Persia, whence he journeyed to India in 1193, and retired to the seclusion of a hermitage at Ajmēr. In the mass of hagiologic literature which has grown up round this personage, many wonders and miracles wrought by him are recorded. The Emperor Akbar made a pilgrimage to his tomb, and to the present time the merchants of the Dargāh Bāzār, which adjoins the tomb of the saint, daily lay their keys on the steps of the shrine before they open their shops. The custody of the shrine is in the hands of the eldest lineal descendant of the holy man, and all the descendants of the Khwājah still enjoy such consideration throughout India that the Nizām of Hyderābād will not sit in their presence, and even the Hindu Mahārājās of Jaipur, Gwālior, and Jodhpur place them on the same seat with themselves. The annual festival of the Saint is held in the month Rajab, when enormous cauldrons of rice, butter, and other condiments are filled at the expense of rich pilgrims to the shrine, and while the food is still in a state of boiling heat it is scrambled for by the mob of fanatical devotees who attend the fair, and who highly value even a small particle of the sacred food. It is counted among the miracles of the Saint that no lives have been lost on such occasions, though burns are frequent.

LITERATURE.—La Touche, in *Rajputana Gazetteer* (1879), ii. 61 ff.; Fergusson, *Hist. of Ind. and Eastern Architecture* (1899), 263, 510 ff.; *Indian Antiquary* (1897), xxvi. 164. For the history of the saint, *Ain-i-Akbari*, tr. Jarrett (1894), iii. 361.

W. CROOKE.

AKĀLĪS.—The sect of the *Akālīs* differs essentially from all the other Sikh orders in being a militant organization, corresponding to the Nāgas or Gosains among the Hindus. Their foundation is ascribed to Guru Govind * himself, and they steadfastly opposed Banda's attempted innovations. The term *akālī*, or 'immortal,' is said † to be derived from *akālī-puruṣa*, 'worshippers of the eternal,' but probably it is a self-assumed title, bearing its obvious meaning. The Akālīs wear blue chequered dresses,‡ with bangles or bracelets of steel round their wrists, and quoits of steel in their lofty conical blue turbans, together with miniature daggers, knives, and an iron chain.§

* The tenth and last Guru of the Sikhs, 1675–1708.

† Murray's *Hist. of the Panjāb*, i. p. 130; Cunningham's *Hist. of the Sikhs*, p. 117. But *akāl* means 'deathless,' *i.e.* 'God,' and *Akālī* is simply 'God's worshipper.'

‡ Malcolm points out that Kṛṣṇa's elder brother, Bala Rām, wore blue clothes, whence he is called Nīlāmbar, or 'clad in dark blue,' and Śitivas, or 'the blue clad' (*Asiatic Researches*, xi. p. 221).

§ A few Akālīs wear the *jaṭā* or top-knot, but not all. Those who do not, only use '*ḍur* and *loṭā*' water; and also smoke,

In their military capacity the Akālīs were called Nihangs, or reckless,* and played a considerable part in Sikh history, forming the Shahīds, or first of the four *dehṛas*. At the siege of Multān in 1818 a few Akālī fanatics † carried the fausse-braye by surprise, and precipitated the fall of that fortress. The career of Phūlā Singh illustrates both their defects and their qualities. This Akālī first came into notice as the leader of the attack on Metcalfe's escort at Amritsar in 1809. He was then employed by Ranjīt Singh, who stood in considerable awe of him, as a leader in the Indus valley, where he was guilty of atrocious cruelty towards the Muhammadan population, and in Kashmīr.‡ Finally, Phūlā Singh and his Akālīs contributed to, or rather virtually won for Ranjīt Singh, the great Sikh victory over the Yūsufzais at Terī in 1823. In this battle Phūlā Singh met with a heroic death, and his tomb at Naushahra is now an object of pilgrimage to Hindus and Muhammadans alike.

Under Phūlā Singh's earlier leadership, and perhaps before his rise, the Akālīs had become a terror to friends and foes alike, and they were dreaded by the Sikh chiefs, from whom they often levied contributions by force.§ Ranjīt Singh, after 1823, did much to reduce their power, and the order lost its importance.

The Akālī headquarters were the Akāl Būnga ‖ at Amritsar, where they assumed the direction of religious ceremonies ¶ and the duty of convoking the Gurūmatā; indeed, they laid claim to exercise a general leadership of the Khālsa. Since Ranjīt Singh's time Anandpur has been their real headquarters, but their influence has to a large extent passed away, and some of them have degenerated into mere buffoons.

As an order the Akālīs are celibate. They have, says Trumpp, no regular chief or disciple, yet one hears of their *gurus*, whose leavings are eaten by their disciples (*sewak* or *chela*). They do not eat meat or drink spirits, as other Sikhs do, but consume inordinate quantities of *bhang*.

LITERATURE.—The general histories of the Sikhs, see art. SIKHS; J. C. Oman, *Mystics, Ascetics, and Saints of India*, London, 1903, pp. 153, 198–201; A. Barth, *Religions of India*², London, 1889, p. 248 f.; Monier Williams, *Brāhmanism and Hinduism*⁴, London, 1891, p. 175; W. Crooke, *Things Indian*, London, 1906, p. 431; Panjāb Census Reports, Sir Denzil Ibbetson (1881) and E. D. Maclagan (1891).

H. A. ROSE.

AKBAR.—1. *Life.*—The emperor Akbar, whose full name was Abū-l-fatḥ (or Abū-l-Moẓaffar) Jalāl-ad-dīn Akbar Ghāzī, was born at Umarkoṭ ('the fort of Umar') in Sind on 15 Oct., O.S., 1542. His birthday was on a Sunday, a circumstance to which importance was afterwards attached, as it seemed to connect him with the sun and with the Messiah, whose birth was traditionally said to have taken place on that day. He was the son of Humāyūn, the second king of India of the Moghul dynasty, and grandson of Bābar, the conqueror of India. His mother, Ḥamīda Bānū, was of Persian origin, and was descended from the famous saint Aḥmad of Jām, and she was also related to Sulṭān Ḥusain Baiqara, the celebrated king of Herāt. But though of noble lineage, her father was neither rich nor distinguished, and was in the service of Mīrzā Hindāl, a younger brother of Humāyūn, as a religious teacher.

After his father's defeats by the Afghans and flight from his brother 'Askarī, the infant Akbar was left behind in camp, and was taken possession of by his uncle 'Askarī and conveyed to Kandahār. He was then about fifteen months old, and did not see his parents again till he was four or five years of age. This was when Humāyūn succeeded, with the aid of the king of Persia, in defeating his brothers and in establishing himself in Afghanistan. When Akbar was twelve or thirteen years of age, he accompanied his father on his expedition to India, and was present at the decisive battle of Machīwārah, Jan. 1555, when Humāyūn, or rather his general Bairām Khān, defeated the Afghan Sikandar Sūr. This was followed by Humāyūn's entry into Delhi and his resumption of power; but his good fortune was not of long continuance. In Jan. 1556 he was killed by falling down the steps leading from the roof of his library, and Akbar, who was then in the Panjāb with his guardian Bairām Khān, was crowned at Kalānūr on 14 Feb. 1556. On 5 Nov. following, Akbar and his guardian Bairām Khān won a victory at Pānīpat—the Indian Armageddon—over Hemū, the Hindu general of the Afghan king; and though the boy Akbar refused, like Gideon's sons, to slay Hemū with his own hands, he earned the title of *ghāzī*, or 'holy warrior,' and retained it to his death, in spite of all his changes of creed. For some years after this Bairām was regent; but in 1560 a palace-intrigue enabled Akbar to rid himself of his guardian and to assume direct power. For a time, however, he deferred greatly to his nurse Māham Anaga, a Turkish lady of great ability. But the misconduct and punishment of her son Adham Khān put an end to her power and her life in 1561, and after this Akbar became really his own master. From that time forward his career was one of almost uninterrupted success. He gradually became master of Upper India, including Kashmīr and Afghanistan, as well as of Bengal, Bihār and Orissa, Gujarāt and Sind, and part of the Deccan. He died, after a reign of fifty years, on his birthday or the day following, in 1605, at Agra, and was buried at Sikandra.

2. *Religious opinions.*—This side of Akbar's character has received what is perhaps a disproportionate amount of attention. No doubt the question of his beliefs is a most interesting one, but the almost exclusive attention which has been paid to it has tended to obscure the emperor's real greatness. After all, Akbar was a king immersed in affairs, and religion was only the occupation of his leisure hours. He was a great conqueror and administrator, and was more in his place at the head of his troops, or when engaged in revenue-reforms, than when seated in his Hall of Worship. It is certain, too, that he never seriously entertained the idea of becoming a Christian, and that the devoted Italian and Portuguese missionaries were sadly deceived in their hopes about him.

which the *jaṭā*-wearers may not do. Others, again, wear a yellow turban beneath the blue one, so as to show a yellow band across the forehead. The story goes that a Khatrī of Delhi (Nand Lāl, author of the Zindagā-nīma) desired to see the Guru in yellow, and Govind Singh gratified his wish. Many Sikhs wear the yellow turban at the Basant Panchmī. A couplet erroneously ascribed to Bhai Gurdās says:

Siāh, sufed, surkh, zardāe,
Jo pahne, soi Gurbhāī.

'They who wear dark blue (the Akālīs), white (the Nirmalas), red (the Udāsīs), or yellow, are all brothers in the Guru.'

* Ibbetson, § 522. Cunningham (p. 379) says *nihang* = 'naked' or 'pure,' and it has that meaning literally (cf. Platts, *s.v.*); but in Sikh parlance the word undoubtedly means 'free from care,' 'careless,' and so 'reckless.' In Hinduism it bears its original meaning.

† They were headed by one Jassa Singh, called Mālā ('rosary') Singh, from his piety. 'He denied himself the use of *bhang*, the only intoxicating drug in use among the Akālīs.' See Carmichael Smyth's *Reigning Family of Lahore*, p. 188.

‡ Prinsep, on the *Sikh Power in the Panjāb*, p. 111, and *Phoola Singh, the Akālī*, in Carmichael Smyth, *op. cit.* 185–192.

§ Contemporary writers had a low opinion of their character. *E.g.* Osborne describes their insolence and violence (*Court and Camp of Ranjīt Singh*, pp. 143–146, 181).

‖ One of the *takhts*, or thrones, of the Sikhs.

¶ M'Gregor (*Hist. of the Sikhs*, i. 238) says that on visiting the *temple* (*sic*) of the Akālīs at Amritsar, the stranger presents a few rupees, and in return receives some sugar, while a small mirror is held before his face so as to reflect his image. This practice, if it ever existed, is now obsolete.

Father Goldie very sensibly remarks: 'How far Akbar was sincere in his search for truth, how far he had towards it a feeling akin to the agnosticism of our day, or whether he was merely bent, from the very first, on making for his subjects an eclectic religion, which would fuse into one the various creeds under his sceptre, and over which he determined to place himself as the supreme prophet and infallible teacher, it is hard to say. Certain it is that Blessed Rudolf, to whom such universal toleration was a new experience, very naturally made the same mistake about Akbar that many a zealous foreign priest makes about English non-Catholics when first he meets with them, and is captivated by their courteous respect for his views, and their kind interest in his work. The sovereign was quite willing to pay homage to the Holy Scriptures, and pleased to see the 'ulamā beaten on their own ground. But from this to submission in heart and deed to the authority of the Church was a long step, and one of which he very probably never dreamt.'

Akbar's religious opinions have been discussed by Hindus, Muhammadans, Parsis, Christians, and freethinkers, and we have details about them in the Akbar-Nāmah, Badayūnī, the Dabistān, and in the writings of Du Jarric, Bartoli, Vans Kennedy, Wilson, Elphinstone, Rehatsek, Blochmann, Count Noer, General Maclagan, and others. We have also Tennyson's poem *Akbar's Dream.* Undoubtedly Akbar has received more credit than he deserves for the depth and fervour of his religious feelings. He had an active mind and delighted in discussions. As he himself said, 'Discourses on philosophy have such a charm for me that they distract me from all else, and I forcibly restrain myself from listening to them, lest the necessaries of the hour should be neglected.' But he was the reverse of a fanatic or an enthusiast. He was, before all things, a man of the world.* His real belief was that forms of religion were of little consequence. He saw that men were good or bad from causes quite remote from their religious tenets, and that there were good men in all religions. He had no overpowering conviction that there was salvation or destruction in any creed; and not being a one-sided enthusiast himself, he could not establish a new religion or make any ardent proselytes. He was a sincere inquirer after truth, but he was not a profound thinker, and his book-knowledge was exceedingly small. Altogether, he was very badly equipped for religious or philosophical discussions; for, as Badāyūnī says, though he had an acute † mind and was a seeker after truth, he was exceedingly ignorant. He had not, like Julian the Apostate, studied in the schools, and was not competent, therefore, to arbitrate between contending sects. At the same time he was wiser and less superstitious than Julian, and did not, like him, try to turn the clock back and to revive a dead paganism. Julian was a fanatical polytheist, and disliked freethinkers as much as he disliked Christians; but Akbar was made of calmer stuff.

Though Badāyūnī in one place (Lowe, 312) ascribes Akbar's heresies to his having been associated from boyhood with Hindus and to his early marriages with Rajput princesses, there seems to be no doubt that Akbar, like many other freethinkers, began by being pious after an orthodox fashion. But perhaps Badāyūnī, by his jingling expression *Hinūd ranūd*, does not mean so much that the Hindus with whom Akbar associated were men of bad character, as that they were devotees and ascetics, for *ranūd* is the plural of *rand*, a word which has a double meaning, and signifies both a libertine and a devotee. In this sense the charge is true, for Akbar was from his youth up fond of the society of *yogīs* and *sannyāsīs*. Writing of the sixth year, when Akbar was still under twenty, Abū-l-Faẓl tells us that one night Akbar went out from his palace in Agra incognito, in order to mix with the crowd of good and bad people who were assembled together to make a pilgrimage to Bahraich in Oudh to the shrine of Sālār Mas'ūd. He was nearly recognized by one of the vagabonds, but escaped by improvising a squint. In the same year he went off one night from Agra on a hunting expedition, and at Mandakhor, a place between Agra and Fatḥpūr, he fell in with some singers who were chanting in Hindu ballads the praises of Mu'īn ad-dīn, the great saint of Ajmīr. He had often listened to tales of this saint, and now the songs inspired him with a desire to visit his tomb. He felt what Abū-l-Faẓl calls *jāzibat tawajjuh*, or 'attraction towards visiting'; and in that same year he accomplished the journey to Ajmīr, in spite of the remonstrances of his courtiers. For many years afterwards he paid an annual visit to the same shrine. Though in both these instances the gathering was ostensibly Muhammadan, yet then, as now, many Hindus took part in it, and doubtless Akbar met many Hindus on such occasions.

In 983 Hijra (A.D. 1575), Akbar built his '*Ibādatḫāna* or Hall of Worship. Badāyūnī tells us that the cause of this was that Akbar had been filled with gratitude to God for his successes.

'Victory had followed upon victory, and the extent of his empire had increased daily. Not a single enemy remained. He associated much with *faqīrs*, and spent much time in discussions about the Word of God and the word of the Prophet. He engaged in questions about *Ṣūfiism* and theology, and spent many nights in repeating the name of God (*Ẕikr*) and in uttering the words *Yā Hū* and *Yā Hādi*, "O He" and "O Guide," in which exercises he had become skilful.'

At this time too Akbar would often seat himself in solitude on a stone bench near his palace in Fatḥpūr, and spend the hours of the early dawn in prayer and contemplation.* It seems that Akbar, who was always of an imitative turn of mind, was induced to make these exercises by what he heard about Sulaimān Kararānī,† the able ruler of Bengal, Bihār and Orissa, who used to spend the later hours of the night in prayer and in the company of 150 *sheikhs* and *'ulamā*. He was also influenced by the news that his aged relative, Sulaimān Mīrzā of Badakhshān, was coming to visit him. Sulaimān was an old warrior who had fought seventy-two battles with the Uzbegs, but he became a *ṣūfī* in his later years, and used to discuss points of ritual with Badāyūnī.

In the following year, 984 (or 1576), Akbar's devotion carried him so far that he wished to make a pilgrimage to Mecca, and was restrained only by the remonstrances of his officers. As it was, he made a show of going, polled his hair, bared his head and feet, donned the pilgrim's dress, and walked some distance with the caravan. He also appointed a *mīr ḥajj*, or superintendent of pilgrims, supplied him with funds, built or purchased pilgrim-ships, and otherwise assisted his subjects to go to Mecca. In 1575 he had also shown his interest in pilgrimages by enabling his aunt Gulbadan Begam, and one of his chief wives, Selīma Begam, and other ladies to proceed to Mecca *via* Surat.

In the 23rd year of his reign, May, 1578, Akbar

* On one occasion he remarked, 'Divine worship in monarchs consists in their justice and good administration'; and added that mortifications of the body and spirit were for the elect (Jarrett, iii. 399).

† '*Jauharī nafīs u ṭālib-i-ḥaqq būd ammā amī maḥẓ*,' lit. 'He was a rare jeweller (*i.e.* a connoisseur), and a seeker after truth, but totally ignorant.' Akbar was ambitious of the character of a prophet or an apostle, and seems to have flattered himself that his own ignorance was an advantage for playing such a part. One of his sayings (Jarrett, iii. 385) is: 'The prophets were all illiterate. Believers should therefore retain one of their sons in that condition.'

* The Jesuits, who had studied Akbar carefully, reported of him that 'Il était mélancolique de sa nature et sujet au mal caduc, tellement que pour se tenir joyeux il s'entretenait en divers exercices, plaisirs et récréatifs, comme à voir combattre des éléphants, etc.' (Du Jarric). Compare also Akbar's saying, 'On the completion of my twentieth year, I experienced an internal bitterness, and from the lack of spiritual provision for my last journey, my soul was seized with exceeding sorrow' (Jarrett, iii. 38b). [The reading seems doubtful, and perhaps the 20th year means the 20th year of the reign]. Cf. also Jarrett, iii. 388: 'One night my heart was weary of the burden of life.'

† Sulaimān Kararānī died in 980, some three years before the '*Ibādatḫāna* was begun. So Badāyūnī must either be confusing things new and old, or he must be referring to some posthumous accounts of Sulaimān's behaviour.

had a remarkable experience which is described as a case of *jazba*, or attraction. He had gone out to the banks of the Jhelum—the Hydaspes of Alexander—to enjoy hunting, and had appointed officers to organize an immense *qamargāh*, or battue. It was to extend over some fifty miles of country from Girjāk—supposed to be the Bucephala of Alexander—to old Bhera. They were ten days engaged in driving the game, and had nearly completed the work, when something came over Akbar, and he suddenly broke up the hunt and set free all the animals, even, says Abū-l-Faẓl, to the finches. Niẓām ad-dīn, who by mistake puts the event into the 24th year, calls it a case of a strong attraction (*jazba qawī*), and says that Akbar bestowed alms on *faqīrs* and others, and ordered a garden to be laid out and a house built on the spot where he had sat under a tree and experienced the call. Shortly afterwards he made a rapid ride to Ajmīr, in order to pay his annual visit to the shrine and to be present at the anniversary of the saint's death. In this year also he revived the discussions in the '*Ibādathāna*, and we are told that the Ṣūfī, the philosopher, the rhetorician, the lawyer, the Sunnite, the Shī'ite, the Brāhman, the Yātī, the Buddhist, the atheist, the Christian, the Jew, the Sabæan, the Zoroastrian, and others enjoyed the pleasure of seeing Akbar place himself in the pulpit and preside over the debates. The date given for the commencement of these discussions is 20 Mihr A.H. 986 or 3 Oct. 1578. Abū-l-Faẓl puts Father Rudolf Acquaviva's appearance in the Hall of Worship into this year, and tells an apocryphal story about the Father's challenging the Muhammadan doctors to the ordeal of fire; but unless Abū-l-Faẓl is giving a consecutive account of the discussions and so has departed from a chronological order, there is a mistake in his narrative, for Acquaviva did not arrive at Fathpūr till February, 1580. According to Abū-l-Faẓl, Akbar spoke at one of the meetings as follows:

'Formerly, from assenting to the opinions of specious, wicked men, we thought that outward conformity and the letter of Muhammadanism profited even in the absence of inward conviction. Hence we by fear and force compelled many believers in the Brāhman (*i.e.* Hindu) religion to adopt the faith of our ancestors. Now that the light of truth has shone upon our soul, the brilliant illumination has possessed us that in this distressful spot of contrarieties (the world), where the darkness of understanding and the blackness of presumption are gathered together, fold upon fold, a single step cannot be taken without the torch of proof, and that creed only is profitable which is adopted with the approval of the intellect. To repeat the words of a creed, to remove a patch of skin (*i.e.* to become circumcised), and to place the extremity of one's bones (*i.e.* the adoring head) on the ground out of dread of the Sultan is not the seeking after God.

'Obedience is not the placing your forehead in the dust;
Put Truth forward,* for sincerity does not dwell in the forehead.

'The first step in this perilous desert is with a high courage and a lofty resolve to do battle with the protean and presumptuous carnal soul, and by rigorous self-knowledge to bring Anger and Lust into subjection to Sultan Reason, and to erase from the soul the images of evil habits. Mayhap the Sun of Proof shall emerge from behind the veil of Error and convert one into a worshipper of the Truth. Afterwards, he may by inward influences draw to himself some inquirer after the Path. Such loadstones are quarried in the mines of asceticism. Or he may, by virtue of a talisman and might of incantations, bring him into his circle. Should the latter, by an error of judgment, fall into the pit of heresy, assuredly he shall not be stained with the dust of blame. We blame ourselves for what we did in accordance with old rules and before the real truth about Faith had been made known to us.'

These words may be compared with two sentences in Akbar's Memorabilia at the end of the '*Ain*. 'Formerly,' he states, 'I persecuted men into conformity with my faith and deemed it Islām. As I grew in knowledge, I was overwhelmed with shame. Not being a Muslim myself, it was unmeet to force others to become such. What constancy is to be expected from proselytes on compulsion?' . . . 'The first step in this long road is not to give the rein to desire and anger, but to take a measured rule and align one's actions thereon.'†

Akbar went on to introduce the subject of the tenets of opposed religions, and described their

* There is a play here on the words *pesh* and *peshānī*.
† Jarrett, iii. 384.

various excellences. He gave no weight, says Abū-l-Faẓl, to the foolish talk of the vulgar, but seized upon whatever was good in any religion. He often said, 'He is truly a man who makes Justice his leader in the path of inquiry, and who culls from every sect whatever Reason approves of. Perchance in this way that lock whose key has been lost may be opened.' In this connexion he praised the truth-choosing of the natives of India, and eloquently described their comradeship in the day of disaster, and how they played away, in the shade of Fidelity, Goods, Life, Reputation, and Religion—those four things which are prized above all others in the world's market. He also dwelt on the wonderful way in which the women of India reduce themselves to ashes whenever the day of calamity arrives. To the learned Christians he said:

'Since you reckon the reverencing of woman part of your religion, and allow not more than one wife to a man, it would not be wonderful if such fidelity and self-sacrifice were found among your women. The extraordinary thing is that it occurs among those of the Hindu religion. There are many concubines, and many of them are neglected and unappreciated, and spend their days unfructuously in the privy chamber of chastity, yet in spite of such bitterness of life they are flambeaux of love and friendship.'

In the 24th year of his reign, in the month of Bahman, Jan. 1580, he sent a force under Quṭb ad-dīn to capture the ports held by the Portuguese, on the ground that they hindered the pilgrims on their journey. Probably this refers to the exactions which the Portuguese made under the guise of the issue of safe-conducts, and also to their issuing tickets bearing representations of the Virgin and Child. Zealous Musalmāns objected to these as being marks of idolatry. A remarkable thing is that at about the very time that Akbar was organizing this expedition against the Portuguese, Rudolf Acquaviva, the Italian priest, and his companions were, at Akbar's request, journeying from Goa to his court, and were indulging in fond hopes of his conversion! His invitation had been received in Sept. 1579, and they left in November of that year and arrived at Fathpūr in Feb. 1580. They came therefore too late to make any impression on Akbar, or at least too late to persuade him to be a Christian. The great year of Akbar's change was 1579, when he mounted the pulpit one Friday at Fathpūr Sīkrī and recited a stanza of Faiẓī's, and when he obtained a document from the '*ulamā* certifying that he was more than a *mujtahid* and that the people were bound by his religious decrees. Apparently the pulpit-incident took place in June 1579, and the signing of the document was in September of the same year. According to Abū-l-Faẓl, the idea of becoming supreme pontiff occurred to Akbar at an even earlier period. In describing the events of the 23rd year (986 or 1578), he says that about this time the idea of the primacy (*peshwāī*) of the spiritual world took possession of him. He seems to ascribe this to the influence of music. Further on in the same chapter he mentions the wonderful effect produced upon Akbar by the singing of one Bakhshū, or Bachū, who was perhaps the famous minstrel of Bahādur Shāh of Gujrāt.

The document seems to have been signed by the 'ulamā on 2 September 1579. Copies of it are given by Niẓām ad-dīn and Badāyūnī, but Abū-l-Faẓl contents himself with giving a short abstract of it, and, curiously enough, he says nothing about his father Mubārak's share in it, though, according to Badāyūnī, he was the prime mover in the matter, and the person who drafted the paper. It certainly was an extraordinary document, and one which did little credit to Mubārak as an honest man. It declared that Akbar (who could neither read nor write) was a most learned theologian ('*alam ba Allah*), and that, if *mujtahids* differed in opinion about any religious point, he could decide between them, and that his decision was final; also that if he issued any new order, the nation was bound to obey it, provided that it was not opposed to the Qur'ān, and should be for the public benefit. If any one opposed such an order, he would be ruined spiritually and physically, and be subject to final damnation.

Badāyūnī tells us that the 'ulamā, with the

exception of Mubārak, signed this document unwillingly, but that Mubārak added to his signature the statement that he was heart and soul in agreement with the paper, and that he had for years been awaiting its execution. Badāyūnī adds that after Akbar had procured this document, the road of *ijtihād* (decree-giving) became open, the supremacy of the *imām's* intellect was established, and no place remained for opposition. There was an end to the resolving of questions and to prohibitions. The intellect of the *imām* became the Law, and Islām was called bigotry.

Abū-l-Faẓl's account of the execution of the document and of its effects is naturally very different from Badāyūnī's. According to him, all the doctors were eager for its execution, and the reluctance was on the part of Akbar, who was unwilling, as he expresses it, to come out from behind the veil. He yielded to their entreaties only because he came to perceive that, in leaving his position as commander of the spiritual world, and accepting the rank of *mujtahid*, he was in reality placing a veil over himself. The result of the document was, he says, that the wanderers in the desert of doubt attained certitude, and that distracted souls obtained repose. Almost immediately afterwards, however, he admits that Akbar's conduct gave rise to many misconceptions, and that he was accused of claiming the Godhead, of disliking the Muhammadan religion, and of being a Hindu. He says that one special reason for such ideas was the appearance of Christian philosophers in the meetings, and the discomfiture by them of the pretenders of learning.

It was probably in order to counteract these ideas that Akbar, shortly after this, paid a visit to the shrine at Ajmīr * (he did not go there at the usual time, that is, at the saint's anniversary), and that he paid extraordinary reverence to a stone which was brought from Mecca and was said to bear an impression of the Prophet's foot. Abū-l-Faẓl tells us that the impression was not genuine and that Akbar knew this, yet that he completely silenced calumnies by his politic conduct on this occasion.

Akbar's innovations in religion, added to his interference with the fief-holders, led to the rebellion of Bihār and Bengal. Maulānā Muhammad Yezdī, the chancellor of Jaunpūr, issued a decree to the effect that it was a duty to rebel against Akbar. Akbar retaliated by having him and another leading rebel—Mu'izz al-mulk of Mashhad —arrested, and contrived that they should be drowned in the Jumna. This rebellion made Akbar proceed more carefully with his new religion, and the Christian missionaries found him less disposed to listen to them. After the rebellion was suppressed, however, he advanced further in the path of heresy, and formally instituted the Divine Faith and practised sun-worship. At the same time he was intolerant to some heretics. A sect calling themselves *Ilāhīs* sprang up, but Akbar had the members seized and sent off to Sind and Afghanistan, where they were bartered for horses!

Akbar had a theory that the Muhammadan religion could last for only a thousand years from its origin. This was apparently a part of the Mahdavī movement which, as Blochmann's preface to the translation of the *'Ain* shows, began in A.H. 900, that is, at the beginning of the 10th cent. (Muham.). In accordance with his belief in the approaching termination of the Muhammadan religion, Akbar proceeded in the year A.H. 990 still further with his innovations. Among other things,

he ordered a history to be written which he called the *Tārīkh Alfī*, or 'Chronicle of a thousand years.' At this time only ten years were wanting to complete the chiliad according to the ordinary reckoning from the Flight to Medina, but Akbar disliked this era, on the ostensible ground that the word 'Flight' was of ill omen, and that it implied the success of the enemies of the Faith. He therefore directed that the history should begin ten years later, from Muhammad's death. It appears, however, from a passage in the *Dabistān*, that he was also inclined to date the thousand years from the commencement of Muhammad's apostleship, *i.e.* when he was forty years old. If this were the date, then the thousand years would begin in A.D. 610; and so in 1582 the thousand Muhammadan years were more than complete, for each of them is eleven days shorter than the solar year. Next, he prohibited the killing of cows, and interdicted, or at least greatly restricted the use of, beef. In the same year, also, he wrote to Goa, asking for missionaries and for copies of the Pentateuch, the Psalms, and the Gospels in Arabic and Persian. This letter has been translated by Rehatsek in the *Indian Antiquary*, but it first appeared in an English dress in James Fraser's *History of Nadir Shāh*, London, 1742.

Elphinstone remarks that Akbar's religion seems to have been pure Deism, in addition to which some ceremonies were permitted in consideration of human infirmity. This, however, is too favourable a view of the matter. Akbar mixed up a good deal of Hindu and Parsi superstition with his Deism, and, like Muhammad, he was unable to dispense with what Gibbon terms a necessary fiction. If his creed was that there was only one God, he added to it that Akbar was God's Vicar. He even went further than Muhammad, for he claimed to have the power of working miracles. In the beginning of his religious career, indeed, he had the good sense to refuse to pray for rain, on the ground that God knew, without being asked, what men had need of. But flattery gradually corrupted him, and he claimed to have the power of healing diseases, of causing rain to fall or to cease, and allowed it to be said of him that he had spoken in his cradle. This last was intended as a proof that he was like Jesus Christ (*Masīḥwār*, 'like the Messiah'), regarding whom a similar tradition existed. It would seem that Akbar was ambitious of establishing the fact of such a resemblance. He was born on a Sunday, which was the traditional birthday of Jesus Christ, and he styled his mother, or at least approved of her being styled, *Miriam-makānī*, i.e. 'of the household of Mary.' It must also be said that Akbar carried the principle of being all things to all men very far. His biographer, Abū-l-Faẓl, *more suo*, makes this a virtue, saying in *Akbar-Nāmah*, iii. 260, that Akbar kept such a guard over himself that every one, whether a secularist or a spiritualist, thought that he was his own peculiar leader. But most people will regard it as a proof that he was not strongly attached to any form of religion. The letter to the Jesuits at Goa is immediately preceded in the collection of Abū-l-Faẓl's letters, by one to the *sharīfs* at Mecca, in which he expresses great reverence for Muhammad, etc., and indignantly repudiates the charge that some one had addressed an unorthodox writing to him. The juxtaposition of these two letters does not prove that they were written about the same time, but this is evident from other circumstances. The letter to the Jesuits was written in Rabi'-al-awwal, A.H. 990,* Apr. 1582;

---

* On his way back from Ajmīr, Akbar seems to have been ostentatiously pious, fitting up a large tent furnished with prayer-niches, and praying in the congregation five times a day. Cf. extracts from the *Zubdatu-i-Tawarīkh* (Elliot, vi. 189).

* The date of the letter to the Jesuit Fathers is, however, not quite certain. One MS. (B. M. Add. 16, 844) gives the date as 999, and if it be true that Jerome Xavier was sent in consequence of this letter, this date is likely to be correct.

that to the *sharīfs* is not dated, but it evidently was written about the same time, for it refers to the year 989 as having passed away.

Some years afterwards, viz. in A.H. 994 (1586), we find him writing a letter repelling the charge of impiety brought against him by 'Abdullāh Khān, the ruler of Transoxiana. 'Abdullāh had been so dissatisfied by the reports about Akbar's heresies that he had dropped correspondence with him. In reply Akbar wrote two long letters to him, denying the charge and asserting his orthodoxy. Blochmann (p. 468) represents Akbar as contenting himself with sending an Arabic quatrain which 'Abdullāh could construe into a denial of his apostasy ; but the letter goes farther than this, and is a serious denial, backed by supposed proofs, of the charge that he was no good Muslim. In it he appeals to his temporal successes as proofs of his being sound in the Faith, for otherwise God would not have favoured his arms ; he refers to his having introduced Islām into places where it was previously unknown, and speaks of churches and temples of infidels and heretics having been turned by his instrumentality into mosques and holy shrines for the orthodox. He also speaks of his great desire to destroy the Feringhis, *i.e.* the Portuguese, who oppressed the pilgrims to Mecca. The truth probably is that, though Akbar had become disgusted with the *'ulamā* on account of their greed and their quarrels among themselves, and also because they held that he had more wives than the Law allowed, and though he was determined to be the head of the Church and the supreme arbiter in religious matters, he never entirely divested himself of his early religious beliefs. He was a *dipsychus*, like his secretary and panegyrist Abū-l-Faẓl, who, while professing a new religion, and presiding over a fire-temple, was yet secretly engaged in the pious work of multiplying copies of the Qur'ān, and was sending copies of his father's commentary thereon to foreign princes. Akbar, too, was before all things a politician and a man of the world, and was in no mood to endanger his sovereignty for the cause of religious truth. He was willing that his followers should exhibit what he called the four degrees of devotion, *i.e.* to sacrifice Life and Property, Religion and Reputation for him, but he showed no eagerness to make such sacrifices himself. He was not an enthusiast about the Divine Religion, and hence, though he was a mighty monarch, he was far less successful than his humble contemporary Bayāzīd in making proselytes, and founded no enduring school.

In the *Dabistān-al-Maẓāhib*, a singular work written in the time of his grandson Dārā Shikoh by a Sūfī who apparently professed Muhammadanism, but was at heart a Parsi or a follower of the *Dīn Ilāhī* of Akbar, we have what purports to be a specimen of the disputes which were carried on in the *'Ibādatḫāna*, but they are probably imaginary. For real accounts of them we must go to Badāyūnī and Abū-l-Faẓl. The chapters in the *'Ain* (Blochmann's tr.) which bear on the point are the *'Ain* 18 of the 1st book, on 'Illuminations,' and *'Ain* 77 of the same book on 'His Majesty as the Spiritual Guide of the People.' To the latter there is a short supplement entitled 'Ordinances of the Divine Faith.' There are also two valuable chapters on the subject in the third volume of the historical part of the *Akbar-nāmah*. The gist of them is Monotheism, but then this was combined with a worship of light and fire, especially as represented by the sun, which is not to be distinguished from the religion of the Parsis. Indeed, it was Parsis from Nausārī in Gujrāt and from Persia who taught Akbar. Upon this point the interesting article on 'The Parsis at the Court of Akbar' by Jivānjī Jamshedjī Modī, Bomb. Branch of the *RAS* (1902 f.) may be consulted. Reference, too, may be made to the chapter in the *Dabistān* on the worship of the constellations and planets. As Blochmann remarks in a note (p. 210), the author gives prominence to the idea that the successes of Chingiz Khān and his descendants were due to their worship of the stars, and that conversion to Islām brought about their decline.

Akbar never published any catechism of his religion, and, though Abū-l-Faẓl meditated writing a separate book on the subject, he never did so. We therefore have to draw our knowledge of his

tenets from scattered passages in Badāyūnī and from the short section in the *'Ain* entitled 'Ordinances of the Divine Faith' (Blochmann, 166). Akbar called his religion *Dīn Ilāhī*, or 'the Divine Faith,' and also the *Tauḥīd-i-Ilāhī*, or 'Divine Monotheism,' in allusion to his leading doctrine of the Oneness of the Deity. With this, however, he coupled the statement that Akbar was God's *Khalīf*, or Vicar. Badāyūnī writes : 'His Majesty had now (A.H. 987, or A.D. 1579) determined to use publicly the formula "There is no God but God, and Akbar is God's representative." But as this led to commotions, he thought better of it, and restricted the use of the formula to a few people in the Harem.' Akbar also adopted the doctrine of transmigration, and observed : ' There is no religion in which the doctrine of transmigration has not taken firm root.' Perhaps, in making this remark, he was thinking not only of the Hindu and Buddhist religions, but also of the Nuṣairis, who, as we learn from the work of Réné Dussaud (p. 120), have always strongly held the doctrine. At p. 271 of the *Akbar-nāmah*, vol. iii., Abū-l-Faẓl refers to the presence at Fatḥpūr of adherents of Nuṣair, and says that the language used by them led some people to suppose that Akbar was claiming to be God. Certainly the expressions used by Abū-l-Faẓl and his brother might well give rise to Mullā Sherī's sarcasm—

'The King this year has laid claim to be a Prophet ;
  After the lapse of a year, please God, he will become God.'

Akbar paid homage to the sun, and it is difficult to say that he did not worship it. Abū-l-Faẓl says in the *'Ain* (Blochmann, p. 48): 'His Majesty maintains that it is a religious duty and Divine praise to worship fire and light ; surly, ignorant men consider it forgetfulness of the Almighty, and fire-worship. But the deep-sighted know better.' He also believed that Royalty was a light emanating from God, and a ray from the sun. ' Modern language calls this light *farr-īzidī*, "the Divine light," and the tongue of antiquity called it *Kiyān Khwarah*, "the sublime halo"' (Blochmann, iii.). Evidently Persia and the old Persian religion had a strong influence over him. Parsīs came to him from Nausārī in Gujrāt, and he also sent to Persia and fetched a learned Zoroastrian named Ardashīr. He adopted the Persian Naurūz (New Year) festival and some twelve others, and enjoined their observance on his provincial officers (see his *firmān* of A.H. 992 [1584], *Akbar-nāmah*, iii. 10, and his instructions to the viceroys and to the police [Jarrett, iii. 41, etc.]). In the *firmān* he also gives his reasons for establishing a new era, which he called the Divine era, and in his instructions to the kotwal (Jarrett, iii. 43) he becomes so bigoted in his asceticism as to direct that whoever should eat or drink with a butcher should lose his hand. If the association did not go so far as this, the penalty was the loss of a finger. This, as Elphinstone well remarks, was a law worthy of Manu, and no doubt it was prompted by the zeal of his Hindu advisers who wished to put down the killing of cows. Widows were not to be compelled to perform *satī*, but were not to be prevented from voluntary immolation. Circumcision was to be deferred till the age of twelve, the object being not to make children Musalmāns until they could judge for themselves.

Some of the flatterers suggested that he should introduce the New Faith by force, but his natural mildness and tolerance prevented him from following their advice. As Badāyūnī says, 'His Majesty was convinced that confidence in him as a leader was a matter of time and good counsel, and did not require the sword.'

The mode of initiation into the new religion is described in the *'Ain* (Blochmann, 165). Akbar, we are told, did not readily admit disciples, but if one showed earnestness of purpose he was accepted, and the ceremony took place on a Sunday when the sun was in the meridian. In the *Akbar-nāmah*, iii. 354, one instance of such initiation is recorded. Fatḥ Dost, the son of the Bārbegī or Master of Requests, importuned Abū-l-Fazl and Akbar to be admitted, and at length Akbar consented and recited over him the formula 'The pure *shast* and the pure glance err not.' But the initiation was not a success, for two days afterwards Fatḥ Dost was caught and killed under such disgraceful circumstances that his father declined to prosecute (Iqbālnāma).

Father Rudolf Acquaviva left when he found Akbar bent on establishing a new faith. He and other missionaries saw they made no impression on Akbar, who refused to accept Christianity unless the mysteries of the Trinity and of the Sonship of Jesus Christ were made intelligible to him. He also withdrew from their society when he found that his alleged heresies were provoking a rebellion in Bengal. He returned to playing with the subject when the danger was over, and Father Jerome Xavier was with him to the end, and wrote for him a Life of Christ and a Life of St. Peter, and also some controversial tracts. But Akbar never was so well-disposed to Christianity as his son Jahāngīr, and died as he had lived—a sceptic.

LITERATURE.—*Akbarnāma*, Bib. Ind. ed. iii. pp. 252, 268; *'Ain-Akbari*, Blochmann and Jarrett's tr.; Badayūnī, Lowe's tr.; *Dabistān-al-mazāhib*, Shea and Troyer's tr.; Abū-l-Fazl's *Letters*, book i.; *Khāfi Khān*, Bib. Ind. ed. i. 197; Elliot, *Hist. of India*, vi. 59 and 189; Pierre Du Jarric of Toulouse, *L'Histoire des choses plus mémorables*, etc., Bordeaux, 1608–1614; *Missione al Gran Mogol dal Daniello Bartoli*, Piacenza, 1819; Jerome Xavier, *Hist. Christi, etc., Latine reddita a Ludovico de Dieu*, Leyden, 1639; S. Lee, *Controversial Tracts on Christianity and Muhammadanism*, Cambridge, 1824; Father Goldie, *First Christian Mission to the Great Mogul*, Dublin, 1897; artt. by General Vans Kennedy in *Transact. Bomb. Lit. Soc.*, and by H. H. Wilson in *Calcutta Quarterly Oriental Magazine*; art. 'The Parsis at the Court of Akbar,' by Jīvānjī Jamshedjī Modī in Bomb. Branch of *RAS* for 1902, and App. 1903, p. 537, also published separately, Bombay, 1903; General Maclagan, 'Jesuit Missions to the Emperor Akbar and Observations thereon,' in *JASB* for 1896 and 1904; Graf von Noer, *The Emperor Akbar*, tr. by Mrs. Beveridge, Calcutta, 1890; Shamsu-l-ulama Maulvī Muhammad Husain, *Darbār-Akbari* (*Urdu*), Lahore, 1898.

H. BEVERIDGE.

AḲIBA BEN JOSEPH (50–135 A.D.).—A great Rabbi who largely modified Jewish thought after the destruction of Jerusalem, and was not without influence on the early Christians. Graetz describes Aḳiba as beyond doubt the most gifted and influential of the Tannaim. Much legendary material clusters round his early history. He was a great traveller. He went to Rome in the autumn of 95 as one of an embassy to dissuade Domitian from a cruel edict, only stopped by the emperor's death. His companions were Gamaliel, Eliezer ben Asaria, and Joshua (*Erubin*, 84; and *Sukka*, 23). When on board ship, he erected a tabernacle, which was blown down in a gale, and his companions laughed at him for being over-righteous. At Rome he was in favour at the court of the Emperor Nerva, where Flavius Clemens (consul and Domitian's nephew) and Domitilla and Akylas (or Aquila), afterwards Aḳiba's pupil, became proselytes. But when Trajan succeeded, bad times arose for the Jews, and he returned to Palestine. Thence he went to Babylon, and preached and taught in Nehardea (see *Jebamoth, ad fin.*). Afterwards he lived at Gazakha (*'Ab. Zara*, 34*a*).

Before the outbreak of Bar Cochba's rebellion, Aḳiba made a final journey throughout Parthia and Asia Minor, and spread the Messianic propaganda, preaching against Hadrian and his legions. We read of him as in Phrygia, Galatia, Galicia, and Cappadocia (*Rosh Hashanah*, 26*a*; *Jebamoth*, 121*a*; *Baba ḳamma*, 113*a*; *Sifre*, Nu 5[8]). The earthquake which had just destroyed Cæsarea inspired Aḳiba and the Jewish rebels with confidence; for as its rise had coincided with Jerusalem's fall, so should its fall result in the restoration of the Jewish capital.

The disastrous failure of Bar Cochba's rebellion resulted in Aḳiba's imprisonment and execution by the Romans.

E. A. Abbott, in *From Letter to Spirit*, quotes the Talmudic description of his martyrdom. The Talmud Babli (*Berakh.* 61*b*) tells how, when Aḳiba 'was being led out to execution, it was the time for reciting the Shema' ("Hear, O Israel, the Lord our God is ONE GOD"), and they were combing his flesh with combs of iron; but he persisted in reciting it. His disciples remonstrated with him, saying that he had endured enough. Aḳiba replied, "All my days I have been troubled about this verse: Thou shalt love the Lord with all thy soul (or life), even if He should take away thy spirit (or breath). When, said I, will it be in my power to fulfil this? Now that I have the occasion, shall I not fulfil it?" As he was lengthening out the word ONE, till he expired at ONE, the Bath Ḳol went forth, saying, "Happy art thou, Aḳiba, that thy spirit went forth at ONE."'

It is interesting to compare this with the account in the Jerus. Talmud (*Berakh.* ix. 7): 'R. Aḳiba was on the point of undergoing the extremity of the law in the presence of the impious Turnus Rufus, when the moment arrived for reciting the Shema'. He began it, and it filled him with joy. "Old man, old man!" cried the pro-consul, "art thou a sorcerer (so that thy tortures cause thee no suffering), or dost thou defy me by showing joy in the midst of thy pains?" "Calm thyself," replied Aḳiba; "I am neither sorcerer nor mocker; but all my life long I have read this verse of the Pentateuch, and sorrowfully said to myself, When shall I fulfil the three ways of worshipping God set forth in this profession of faith: Thou shalt love the Lord thy God with all thy heart, with all thy soul, and with all thy powers? I have proved that I love him with all my heart and with all my means, but I had not yet undergone the test of love with all my soul, as I undergo it at this moment, and that is the moment in which I thus recite the Shema'. I delight in this occasion of proving my faith; and I have shown my joy." With these final words he gave up his soul (to God).'

The story of the 'ten martyrs,' including Aḳiba, still forms the theme of a touching *Seliḥa*, and of an elegy in the Jewish ritual for the Day of Atonement and the Fast of the Ninth of Ab.

But legend does not leave Aḳiba with his death. As with so many saints, there is something miraculous about his burial. A Midrash, quoted by Jellinek (vi. 27. 8), tells how, after Aḳiba's execution, Elijah, accompanied by Aḳiba's faithful disciple Joshua, entered the prison where the body lay, removed it thence, and, escorted by many angels, brought it to Cæsarea. They entered a cavern containing a bed, table, chair, and lamp, and laid the body on the bed. No sooner had they left the cave than it closed of its own accord, and no man has ever seen it since. A hundred years after Aḳiba's death, about 250, we get the first mention of a Messiah ben Joseph, in contradistinction to the Messiah ben David. R. Dosa tells of this in *Sukka*, 52*a*. The Messiah ben Joseph must die first, and then will be the advent of the real Messiah. This idea is perhaps due to the legendary talk which encircled either Jesus or Aḳiba, and genuine Jewish folk-lore is at the bottom of it.

Aḳiba was much opposed to the new Christian heresy, and it is not surprising that Jerome puts him at the head and front of the offending Rabbis.

'Duas domus Nazarei—duas familias interpretantur Saummai et Hillel ex quibus orti sunt scribæ et Pharisæi, quorum suscepit scholam Achibas (quem magistrum Aquilæ proselytæ autumant) et post eum Meir cui successit Johanan filius Zachai et post eum Eliezer, et post ordinem Delphon (=Tarphon) et rursum Joseph Galileus, et usque ad captivitatem Jerusalem Josue.'

Perhaps his most famous pupil was Aquila, whose literally literal translation of the Hebrew text of Scripture was held in high esteem by all Jews, though Jerome sneers at it. Every enclitic את is translated by σὺν. And the Talmud of Jerusalem (*Ḳidd.* i. 59[a]) says: 'Aquilas the proselyte made his Targum (תרגם) in Aḳiba's presence.' This was because of his practice of Aḳiba's theory, and accounts for the popularity of his translation amongst the Jews, who in Talmud and Haggādah quote Aquila no less than fourteen times (see de Rossi, *Meor Enaiim*, vi. 45). But that popularity did not preserve his Targum, for the Jews soon forgot their Greek; and it was not till 1903 that Burkitt was able to rescue and identify an important fragment out of the Cairo Genizah. Of Aḳiba's other pupils, we must mention the Jewish Æsop, Meir, who was the link between his Mishna and ours, and Simeon ben Jochai the mystic, to whom the foundation of the Ḳabbala is attributed.

With mysticism, however, as with gnosticism, Aḳiba had no sympathy. He is the only one of the four Rabbis who is said to have entered the פרדס, the mystic garden, and come out again without hurt. One died, one became insane, and one an apostate —probably to Christianity. The last was the famous Aḥer, Elisha ben Abuyah. There was much coquetting with Christianity in those times. Even the famous Eliezer ben Hyrcanus, Aḳiba's teacher, was taunted with being a Christian because he listened with pleasure to a parable recited to him in the name of Jesus. But Aḳiba's was an exact science which left no room for eschatological speculations. He sought for mathematical proofs of his principles of the Jewish religion, and found them in the apparently superfluous terms, words, letters, and ornaments of Scripture upon which tradition and usage were to found new legislation. This method he derived from his teacher, Nahum of Gimzo, but Philo had applied it a century earlier to the relations of ethics and philosophy. Akiba applied it to Halākhah, and Aḳiba's view ultimately prevailed in the Talmud. It is in reference to this doctrine that Mt 5^{18} and Lk 16^{17} record that 'till heaven and earth pass, one jot or one tittle shall in no wise pass from the law' (ἰῶτα ἓν ἢ μία κεραία and τοῦ νόμου μίαν κεραίαν πεσεῖν). Sharpe translates κεραία by 'one tip of a letter.'

Aḳiba's chief antagonist was **R. Ishmael.** The two are throughout Rabbinical literature regarded as opponents, like Hillel and Shammai, and other pairs such as those described in *Aboth*, cap. 1. The fundamental distinction between them was in their treatment of pleonasms in Scripture: Ishmael regarded these as the mere rhetoric of ordinary language, Aḳiba held them to be essential portions of the Law. He never took the particle את as a sign of inflexion, but 'expounded (דורש) all the אתין in the Torah,' and his pupil Nehemiah of Emmaus seceded from his school in consequence of the risk which such an interpretation involved in such a passage as 'Thou shalt fear (את) the Lord thy God,' which, according to R. Aḳiba's view, implied fearing somebody or something *with* the Lord. Aḳiba said this meant the Torah, but, objected his pupil, it might just as well mean another god. Another of such rules was that dealing with the word 'saying' (לאמור): 'Wherever the word לאמר is used it must be expounded' (*Sifre*, Nu 5^6). Finally, he interpreted the letters ה and ו wherever they seemed pleonastic in the text. 'R. Aḳiba expounded the ווין' (*Jebamoth*, 586). A further difference between the men was that whereas R. Aḳiba did, R. Ishmael did not allow himself to treat conclusions out of Scripture as the premises for further conclusions (Jerus. *Ḳidd.* i. 2, and *Nazir*, 57*a*).

It was in opposition to this perhaps extravagant mode of interpretation that the more sober R. Ishmael altered all rules of interpretation to his famous 13 *Middoth*, so that he represented logic and his great opponent allegory. These thirteen principles are really based upon the seven rules laid down by Hillel.

The *Middoth* were originally drawn up as abstract rules by Hillel, and were variously interpreted and modified by his successors, but Aḳiba and Ishmael and their scholars specially contributed to their definition, Aḳiba on the grammatical and exegetical side, and Ishmael on the logical. In their final form these *Middoth* are seven of the thirteen exegetical principles by which the Law is expounded, and which constitute the *Baraitha de R. Ishmael* to be found in the Jewish Daily Prayer-Book.

(1) The inference from minor to major.

(2) The inference from similarity of phrases.

(3) and (4) A general law derived by induction from a common feature in (*a*) the same passage, (*b*) different passages.

(5) If an enumeration of particulars succeeds a general proposition, such general proposition is limited to articles *ejusdem generis*, but if it precedes, the general proposition may be extended.

(6) Interpreting a passage according to one of similar content in another place.

(7) Deducing a passage from its context.

In (5) and (7) Aḳiba and Ishmael disagree. Where two Scripture passages conflict, a third passage would be adduced to confirm one of the two conflicting dicta and reject the other, but Ishmael would thereby modify both such dicta. This opposition of the two schools gradually decreased and finally vanished, so that the later Tannaim do not discriminate between Aḳiba's axioms and Ishmael's.

The effect of Aḳiba's system was epoch-making. He really gave his contemporaries a new point of view. The Temple had been destroyed, the country vanquished, and the Jews of the time were like sheep without a shepherd, having lost all hope and all belief. Scripture seemed insufficient to provide for one's daily needs or satisfy anybody's ideals. The Oral Law was doubted. It had enemies without and within. The forces of barbarism and Rome had conquered, and Christianity was a redoubtable foe from within, which, with its Messianic mysticism, must have offered comfort to the hopeless exiles. Then came R. Aḳiba, and showed that there was authority for all the Oral Law. He gave the solid rock of Scripture as the foundation for all the structure of observances, rules, and usages prevalent in his time, and at the same time enabled his pupils and followers to build up afresh. No wonder he surprised and dazzled his contemporaries, and even his teachers, so that R. Joshua, once his teacher, could ask (*Sota*, 27*b*), 'Who will remove the earth from the eyes of R. Jochanan ben Zaccai, so that he may see how vain was his fear that Halākhah would have to be abandoned because it wanted Scripture support. Behold R. Aḳiba hath found Scripture support.' Everybody agreed that, but for R. Aḳiba, the whole Law must have been forgotten or, at any rate, neglected. Aḳiba's literalism not only justified tradition, it enabled the Oral Law to be rounded off and ordered and completed, and thus he is the true Father of the Talmud. His mnemonic method was twofold: first, to divide the laws according to their subject-matter, property, marriage, divorce, Sabbath, and so on, each such division constituting a treatise (*Masekhta*); and, secondly, to arrange the material for each treatise according to numbers, so as to make them easier to remember. Thus there are *four* kinds of damage to property, there are *five* classes of people who may not enjoy the Priests' *terūmah*, *fifteen* women are excluded from the levirate, *thirty-six* crimes are punishable with excision. This arrangement of the Halākhah was called *Mishna*, afterwards known as R. Aḳiba's Mishna, to distinguish it from the Mishna now extant, and this was translated by the Christian theologians, such as Epiphanius, as Aḳiba's *Deuterosis*. There had been other Mishnas earlier in date, but Aḳiba's superseded all. Thus it is frequently stated in the Talmud that 'This (meaning the dogma there set forth as the Law) is R. Akiba's Mishna, but the first Mishna said . . .' (cf. *Sanhedrin*, 27*a*, and *Rosh Hashanah*, 17).

Mnemonic grouping, into numbers, was applied by Aḳiba to his ethical sayings also. These, collected by Bacher in his *Agada der Tannaïten*, throw considerable light upon the social conditions of the Palestine of Aḳiba's time. Some of them are culled from Sirach, an interesting fact, when it is remembered that Aḳiba was one of the Rabbis who settled the canon of Scripture, and objected to the use of extraneous books, including Ben Sira. In something like the spirit of Omar he said that Scripture was enough. If books contravene Scripture, destroy them; if they support Scripture, they are not needed. Some of Aḳiba's logia are given in the 3rd chapter of *Aboth*, but his ethics is scattered throughout Talmud and Midrash. Specimens of these are the following:—

'Three people are happy, and their consciences may be tranquil, namely, (1) he whose prayer is glib in his mouth, for prayer must come free from the heart, not from the mouth; (2) he in whom men have satisfaction, God has satisfaction, and he in whom men have not satisfaction, God has not satisfaction; (3) he who is satisfied with that he possesses, that is a good sign for him; but he who is dissatisfied, that is a bad sign.

As for sin, at first it is like a thread of a spider's web, but in the end it is as strong as a ship's rope. He who in anger tears his clothes and breaks his crockery, he will serve idols in the end, for this is how the evil inclination works. It says to-day "tear thy clothes," and to-morrow "serve idols."'

Aḳiba is very hard upon passionate anger. 'He who in anger throws his bread on the ground and scatters his money, he will not leave the world before he has had to beg his neighbours for bread and for money.' Aḳiba mocked at the weaklings who could not withstand the inclination to sin, but there is an Aramaic legend to the effect that he himself had once nearly succumbed to temptation (*Ḳidd.* 81*a*), when Satan presented himself to him in the guise of a lovely woman.

Like Hillel's, Aḳiba's great principle was that of Lv 19[18], 'Love thy neighbour as thyself,' and this principle he applied with characteristic ingenuity to marriage. An unequal match he condemns as offending against this principle. 'He that marries a wife who is not fitting to him commits five sins. He transgresses the three commandments, not to bear a grudge, or hate his brother in his heart, as well as the two as to loving one's neighbour. If he hates his wife, he defeats the object of marriage.' It is better to save one's own life rather than that of a stranger, because it is said, 'Fear thy God that thy brother may live with thee.' 'The greatest sin is usury, the greatest virtue visiting the sick.' At Gazaka Aḳiba noticed three things that pleased him much. 'The Medians carve at table, they kiss the hand only, their meetings are in the open field.' (These preferences reflect his fears as a conspirator against Rome).

'There are five persons whose sin can never be forgiven: (1) he who is always repenting and repeating his sin; (2) he who sins much; (3) he who sins in pious times; (4) he who sins in order to repent; (5) he who desecrates God's name by his sin.'

Aḳiba was no laughing philosopher. He lived in serious times, and therefore it is that he says laughter and levity lead to immorality, and, further, that tradition is a fence for the Law, vows for piety, silence for wisdom.

To his son Joshua he gave the following seven rules of life (*Pesaḥim*, 112*a*): (1) 'Do not live in the heights of the city; (2) do not live in a city whose ruler is a learned man; (3) do not enter a house suddenly—either a stranger's or thine own; (4) do not walk barefooted; (5) eat an early breakfast, in summer because of the heat, in winter because of the cold; (6) better do without a Sabbath meal than take charity from thy neighbours; (7) keep friendly with the man whose hour smiles upon him.'

Five rules he gave to his pupil Simeon ben Jochai when he was in the Roman prison: (1) 'If thou wouldst hang thyself, hang on a large tree; (2) teach thy son out of a correct book; (3) do not cook in a pot in which thy neighbour has cooked; (4) seek to keep thy capital and have an income besides; (5) it is both mirth and pleasure to have a wife and children.' In *Aboth de R. Nathan* other six rules are laid down: (1) 'Go not into the society of mockers, lest thou learn from their actions; (2) eat not at the table of a priest who is an idiot, lest he give thee that which is not holy; (3) be not free with thy promises, lest thou break thine oath; (4) accustom not thyself to be a guest with others, lest thou have to eat at the kitchen of the poor; (5) commit not thyself to doubtful things, lest thou art found wanting in that of which there is no doubt; (6) go not to foreign countries, lest thou be tempted to serve strange gods.'

With regard to diet he advised (*Sanh.* 17. v), 'Live only in a city where there is fruit, for fruit is good for the eyes. He that eats foods that disagree with him transgresses three commandments. He disgraces himself, he disgraces the food, and he makes a *Berākhah* (blessing) in vain.'

'Shameful is he who allows his daughter to remain at home unmarried.'

'Take heed of him who gives advice without being asked for it.'

LITERATURE.—*Talmud* and *Midrash* and Wünsche, *Bibliotheca Rabbinica*; Schürer, *HJP*[3], vol. ii.; Graetz, *Hist. Jews*, vol. iv.; Bacher, *Agada der Tannaïten*; I. H. Weiss, דור דור ודורשין, *zur Geschichte der Jüdischen Tradition* (Vienna, 1871–1887); Gastfreund, *Toldoth R. Akiba* (Lemberg, 1871); Strack, *Einleitung zum Talmud*.

E. N. ADLER.

ALAKHNĀMĪS, ALAKHGĪRS, or ALAKHIYĀS (Skr. *alakṣya*, 'unseeable,' and *nāman*, 'name'; hence Hindūstānī *Alakh-nāmī*, 'one who calls upon the name of the Unseeable.' In *Alakhgīr*, *gīr*=Skr. *giri*, an honorific title employed by one of the orders of the *Dasnāmī* Śaiva sect. *Alakhiyā* is simply a Hindūstānī derivative of *Alakh*, meaning 'a follower of the Unseeable').—A name applied in Northern India to various sects of Śaiva mendicants. The name *Alakhiyā* is applied to all, but *Alakhnāmī* is generally reserved for those who claim to be a subdivision of the Purī division of the Dasnāmī sect, while *Alakhgīr* is reserved for those belonging to the Giri division. They are all popularly known as *Alakh-kō jagānēwālē*, or 'Wakers of the Unseeable,' in allusion to their habit of crying out His name. Adherents of other Śaiva forms of belief also call themselves Alakhiyā, but the true Alakhiyās consider themselves as belonging to a sect apart, and do not follow customs (such as slitting the ears among Gōrakhpanthīs [*q.v.*]) which are retained by Alakhiyās of other professions.

All these Alakhiyās have tenets much in common, based on the central idea that the Supreme Deity is incomprehensible, or, as they say, 'unseeable.' In this respect Powlett's account (see Literature at end) of the Alakhgīrs of Bīkānēr in Rājputānā may be taken as applying to all. This particular sect was founded by a Chamār (or low-caste leather worker) named Lāl, to whom his followers gave the title of Lāl-gīr. He denounced idolatry, and taught his followers to call only upon 'the Unseeable.' Their sole worship consisted in repeatedly ejaculating the name *Alakh*. Charity was to be practised; the taking of life and the use of meat as food were forbidden; asceticism was encouraged. His doctrine was that there is no future state. All perishes with the body, which is finally dissolved into the elements. The sole rewards which he held out to his disciples were confined to this life, and consisted in the attainment of purity, untroubled contemplation, and serenity. There being no future life, heaven and hell (or, in other words, happiness and misery) were within the man himself.

Alakhiyās wear a peculiar garb, consisting of a long blanket coat and a round, or high conical, cap. Although mendicants, they never beg directly. They come to a man's door and raise their characteristic cry of '*Alakh kahō; Alakh-kō lakhō*,' 'Tell of the Unseeable; see the Unseeable.' If alms are then offered, they accept them; otherwise they go away at once. They are looked upon as a quiet, harmless class of beggars.

Lāl-gīr's date is unknown, nor is there any record of the origin of the special theory which is the basis of the religion. That the Supreme Deity is indiscrete, void of all qualities, and incomprehensible, is a commonplace of nearly all phases of Hindu belief, but this has been materially qualified during the past thousand years by the spread of the Bhakti-mārga [*q.v.*], which superadds to it the idea of devotion to a personal God, who is the Supreme Deity become incarnate in cognizable form out of pity for man's weakness and sin. The greatest exponent of the Bhakti-mārga, Tulsī Dās (1532–1623 A.D.), was never weary of dwelling on the incomprehensible nature of the Supreme Deity, and arguing from the fact that He was *mana-krama-bachana-agōchara* (*i.e.* beyond the reach of thought, act, and speech) to the conclusion that the only way of salvation open to finite beings was the exclusive worship of a personal incarnation of that Deity under the form of Rāma. The tenets of the Alakhiyās, based as they are upon the rejection of the idea of a personal God, may well have been put forward as a protest against the view of the Bhakti-mārga, and as a counter attempt to popularize the idealistic theology of the *advaita* Vedānta philosophy, the aim of which is knowledge of the unknowable, rather than the adoration of the comprehensible. In this connexion the termination *gīr* in 'Lāl-gīr,' 'Alakh-gīr,' is important, as, amongst Śaivas, it is employed only by those who claim spiritual descent from Śaṅkarāchārya [*q.v.*], the great founder of the *advaita* Vedānta. Lāl-gīr was also probably influenced by the doctrine of the Jains (with which his teaching has much in common), who are a numerous and influential body in Rājputānā. Still more striking is the agreement of his teaching with some of the doctrines of Buddhism, but we have no reason to suppose that he can have been alive when that religion flourished in India. The earliest mention of the Alakhiyās that the present writer has seen is in a short poem attributed to Tulsī Dās. That reformer is said to have entered into a controversy with one of them, and his argument, as contained in the poem, was that the only way to 'see the Unseen' was to see him through the personality of Rāma.

A modern sect, akin to the Alakhiyās, was founded about the year 1850, in Orissa, by one Mukund Dās, who was, according to his followers, an incarnation of Alēkh (*sic*) himself. He, however, claimed only to be in special communication with this Alēkh, whom he described as a formless, spiritual being, omnipresent and omniscient. In other respects his teaching was identical with that of the Alakhiyās of Northern India. He died in 1875, and the sect then dwindled, but is still in existence in some force in the district of Sambalpur, immediately to the west of Orissa.

LITERATURE.—Regarding Lāl-gīr, see p. 195 of the *Gazetteer of Bikānēr*, by Major P. W. Powlett (1879); also W. Crooke, *The Tribes and Castes of the North-Western Provinces and Oudh* (1896), i. p. 78 (mostly based on Powlett); cf. also H. H. Wilson, *Essays on the Religion of the Hindus* (ed. 1861), i. pp. 235, 236, 238; and the present writer's 'Notes on Tulsī Dās' in *Indian Antiquary*, xxii. (1893) p. 271. As for the followers of the Alēkh sect, see *Proceedings of the Bengal Asiatic Society* for 1882, p. 2 ff.

GEORGE A. GRIERSON.

ALAKNANDĀ (Skr. *alaknandā*, 'a young girl').—A sacred river in the district of British Gaṛhwāl, one of the tributaries of the Ganges. It has several sacred junctions (*saṅgama*) along its banks, at which religious bathing fairs are held—Nandprayāg, where it is joined by the Nandākinī; Karnaprayāg, by the Pindar; Rudraprayāg, by the Mandākinī; Devaprayāg, by the Bhāgīrathī, after which it is styled the Ganges (which see). Though the Alaknandā in volume and position is superior to the Bhāgīrathī, the latter is popularly regarded as the source of the sacred river.

LITERATURE.—Raper in 11th vol. of *Asiatic Researches*; Oakley, *Holy Himalaya* (1905), 141 f.

W. CROOKE.

ALBIGENSES.—A sect which derived its name from the cathedral city of Albi (Lat. *Albiga*), situated on the south bank of a confluent of the Garonne in France called the Tarn, which gives its name to the modern department. The 'civitas' of the bishopric was conterminous with those of Carcassonne and Toulouse, all the three dioceses being in the province of Narbonne, and owing a common allegiance to the metropolitan of that city (Longnon, *Géog. de la Gaule*, pp. 520–521; Devic and Vaissètte [ed. 1872], vi. 6). The associations of Albi were consequently chiefly with the country to the south; but when, in the 11th cent., it was placed under the rule of a vicomte, his jurisdiction extended north as far as the course of the Aveyron. Its earlier history, however, like that of Toulouse, is connected mainly with that of Septimania, the extensive region between the Rhone and the Pyrenees.

As early as the 5th cent. St. Amarand had been the patron saint of Albi, and with his worship was associated that of Eugenius, the bones of both being interred at Vieux, some 18 miles west of the city. Diogenianus, its third bishop, is the first with respect to whom we have any information; he is referred to by Gregory of Tours (*Hist. Franc.* ii. 12) as one of the ablest guardians of the faith in the first half of the 5th century. Septimania, from the 5th to the 8th cent., was ruled by the Visigoth, who had his capital at Toulouse, and the territory is consequently, at this period, often referred to as Gothia. The Goths professed the Arian faith, and supported it, although not coercively, among the populations whom they had reduced to subjection, but whom they aimed at assimilating rather than effacing. They were themselves industrious cultivators of the soil, and understood the working of metals; the Roman cities remained intact beneath their sway, and the Roman law was administered concurrently with their own. The chief impediment to peaceful relations between the two races was the pertinacity with which the Catholic bishops of the conquered opposed the religious creed of the conquerors. Arianism, however, continued to spread, and, during the reign of Theodoric II. (453–466), became the national faith of the Suevi in northern Spain and of the populations of Cantabria and the Spanish March. If, indeed, the same conciliatory spirit towards the Roman clergy as was shown by Theodoric the Ostrogoth in Italy, had been shown by the Catholic bishop towards the upholders of the Arian creed in Septimania, it is probable that the Albigensian crusade would have been averted. In the 5th cent., under King Euric, the Visigoths had extended their rule over the greater part of the Spanish peninsula, while in Gaul it reached the Loire; but the persistently aggressive policy of the Catholic towards the Arian clergy roused the latter to a retaliatory course of action, which still further embittered the relations between the respective adherents of the two chief religions of Western Christendom. In the following century, on the other hand, the envoy of the Ostrogoths in Italy to Belisarius, could defy their enemies to prove that their monarch had ever resorted to unprovoked aggression on those professing the Catholic faith (Procopius, *de Bell. Goth.* ii. 6), while the rule of Theodoric the Great was characterized by such exceptional tolerance towards his Jewish subjects as to make them his firm supporters against the common enemy (Vaissètte, *Hist. de Languedoc*, i. 656–660; Dahn, *Urgesch. d. german. u. roman. Völker*, i. 362–368, 240–250; Milman, *Lat. Christianity*[4], bk. iii. ch. 3).

It is to be noted, again, that political aims weighed considerably with Clovis, the Frankish monarch, when, after his defeat of the Alemanni in 496, he embraced the Catholic form of the Christian belief. Ten years later, when he marched against the Visigoths, it was as 'Arian heretics' that he proposed to sweep them out of the land (Gregory of Tours, ii. 27), and the immediate result, consequently, was to rouse the Burgundian and other Teutonic monarchies, which professed Arianism, to a common resistance. From the struggle which ensued, Theodoric emerged lord of Provence as well as of Italy, while Gothia became yet more closely allied to the Visigothic power in Spain. In both these great monarchies, aversion from, and a spirit of resistance to, the Frankish invader became a tradition alike with the Teutonic conqueror and the native element—an element which in turn was largely modified by ethnic admixture.

The Albigeois, probably recovered by the Goths in the early part of the 6th cent., was again wrested from them a few years later, and the capture by the Franks of Alais, Uzès, Lodève, (*Luteva*), and Carcassonne followed shortly after. The last-named city was thus constituted a Catholic see,—Sergius, the first bishop, afterwards appearing as a supporter of the Roman creed at the third Council of Toledo in 589, over which Reccared, the Visigothic monarch, presided. Reccared had recently been converted to Catholicism; and, stimulated by his example, and aided by the great preponderance of the ecclesiastical over the lay element, the Roman party secured on that memorable occasion an easy victory, eight bishops of Septimania, those of Maguelonne, Lodève, Agde, Beziers, Narbonne, Carcassonne, and Elne, headed by the metropolitan of Nîmes, making their submission and subscribing the condemnation of their former Arian tenets. Reccared's example was reluctantly followed, however, by many of his subjects, and in Septimania frequent risings ensued [Mansi, *Concilia* (ed. 1644), xiii. 128–130; Dahn, *op. cit.* i. 393–394].

Early in the 8th cent. the kingdom of the Visigoths was overthrown by the Saracen, and the new conqueror maintained his ground in Gothia for fifty years. In certain features, Muhammadanism and Arianism are alike, especially in their common denial of the Divinity of Christ, and also in the aversion with which both regarded the innovations which were then taking place in the Roman Church, in the direction of saint-worship and the concomitant veneration of images and relics. The new conquest was attended also by another racial admixture which would imperceptibly incline the population of Septimania to listen favourably to the discourse of those Paulician teachers from whom many of them were, before long, to imbibe the doctrines of Manichæism. Fauriel has pointed out how, during this period, the industries, architecture, language, and learning of Septimania were modified by the influence of the dominant race (*Hist. de la Poésie Provençale*, iii. 312–316). Of this approximation between the two races, an historical incident and a traditional reproach afford alike a noteworthy illustration. In the following century, a leader of the Paulicians is to be found advancing to battle side by side with a Saracen emir, to join in the defeating of the forces of the Catholic Greek beneath the walls of Samosata (Cedrenus, ii. 153; Zonaras, ii. lib. xiv.). In the 12th cent., the Catholic persecutor could assume it as a recognized fact that, in consequence of the Gothic and Saracen occupations, the inhabitants of Septimania, and more especially those of the Toulousain, had inherited a taint of heresy from which many of them were still unpurged (Peter de Cernay, Migne, *PL* ccxiii. 541; Milman, *op. cit.* v. 439; Luchaire, *Innocent III., la Croisade des Albigeois*, 159).

The obscurity which attaches to the history of the different Italian States in the 10th cent. and the earlier part of the 11th renders it impossible to trace with precision the dates and circumstances of those successive migrations of Paulicians (or 'Publicani,' as they are frequently termed), who, quitting their homes in Bulgaria (or Thrace), appeared at this era in Italy and from thence passed on to Western and Central Europe. The connexion between these emigrants from the Eastern Empire (or its dependencies) and the Albigenses of a later period, was first pointed out by Ussher, and more fully afterwards by Limborch (*Hist. Inquisitionis*, Amsterdam, 1592; tr. by Chandler, 1731), who also explained the features of divergence or agreement between the Albigenses and the Waldenses. But a more critical account of both sects and of the literature relating to them appeared in 1832 from the pen of S. R. Maitland, who, following up the line of inquiry indicated by Gibbon (in his 54th chap.), argued from evidence derived from *place*, *time*, and *name*, that 'the persons called Albigenses, in the south of France, were Paulician emigrants' (*Facts and Documents*, p. 92). 'In all essentials,' says Lea, 'the doctrine of the Paulicians was identical with that of the Albigenses' (*Hist. of the Inquisition in the Middle Ages*, i. 91). A recent critic, however—Professor Karl Müller of Giessen—is of opinion that the tenets of the **Cathari** (as we must now term them) are to be regarded as the outcome of a fusion of Paulician doctrines with those of the Euchites, a process which he considers had been brought to completion in Thrace (or Bulgaria), and subsequent to which the same emigrants, proceeding westward, carried with them doctrines which had a Gnostic-dualistic tendency (*ThLZ* (1890) p. 355).

As early as 1012, when the Emperor Henry II. was at Mainz, 'refutata est insania quorundam hæreticorum,' whom Hauck (*Kirchengesch.* iii. 431) assumes to have been Manichæans (Pertz, *Monumenta Germ. Hist.*, iii. p. 81); but the earliest authentic instance appears to belong to 1017, when certain canons of Orleans and other ecclesiastics of that city, thirteen in number, were brought before a specially convened Synod, and on being convicted of Manichæan tenets, which they refused to abjure, were burnt outside the city gates. Various features gave to this case a peculiar interest,—the fame of Orleans as a seat of learning, the facts that King Robert himself caused the inquiry to be instituted, that the heresy had been imported from Italy and Perigueux, and not least that it was by artifice, on the part of a Norman knight, that the necessary evidence was ultimately obtained from the admissions made by the victims themselves. The heresies to which they confessed—as involved in the denial of the Virgin-birth of Christ, of the efficacy of baptism, and of prayers to the saints, of the Real Presence in the Eucharist, and of the lawfulness and duty of marriage (in opposition to the Petrobrusians) —were unquestionably those of the Albigenses (D'Achéry [1723], i. 604–605; Döllinger, *Beiträge*, i. 62–65; Bouquet, *Recueil*, x. 36–38).

There is, however, strong presumptive evidence of the existence of such doctrines in northern France before the 11th century. In 991, the eminent Gerbert, on being consecrated to the archbishopric of Rheims, made solemn declaration of his belief in the articles of the Catholic faith, at the same time expressly specifying certain other tenets which he accepted with no less sincerity,— the resurrection of Christ and also that of all mankind, the Divinely inspired origin of both the OT and the NT, the existence of an evil spirit (which was evil *non per conditionem sed per arbitrium*), the lawfulness of marriage and of second marriage, and of the eating of meat, the remission of original sin by the rite of baptism (*Gerberti Epistolæ*, ed. Havet, 161–162; *ib.* ed. Olleris, 245–250; Schmidt (C.), *Hist. et Doct. des Cathares ou Albigeois*, i. 33). As all these were tenets specially repudiated by the Cathari, it is difficult not to concur in the view of Schmidt, Havet, and others, that Gerbert's declaration was designed as a protest against the growing activity of the sect in the province which he had been called upon to administer. As uttered by the metropolitan of the French kingdom, Gerbert's pronouncement acquired special importance, and it is probable that any manifestations of such heresy within the royal domain were repressed with exceptional rigour. But all around the comparatively circumscribed limits of the realm of France in those days, we have evidence that the doctrines of the Cathari were spreading rapidly. At Arras, in Flanders (whose counts rendered to the French Crown a homage that was purely external), there appeared in 1025 an Italian named Gundulf, whose preaching attracted so large a following that Reginald, the bishop of the city, ordered his arrest. He succeeded, however, in effecting his escape, and the bishop decreed it politic to deal mercifully with the perverts. He condescended to argument, but was baffled by the discovery that they admitted no written authority in doctrine save the NT, while they altogether rejected the OT. His inquiries failed to elicit any expression of opinions which could be pronounced

Manichæan, a fact which Schmidt (i. 36) explains by supposing that the humble *textores* of Arras were not yet fully initiated. Yielding to Reginald's gentle persuasions, they abjured their errors and implored forgiveness, whereupon they were again admitted to the fold. Among the tenets to which they confessed was the denial of the worship of the Cross and of its use as a sign—an early instance of opposition to this feature in the Roman ritual (Mansi, *Concilia* (1759), xix. 423; Schmidt, *op. cit.* i. 35; Döllinger, *Beiträge*, i. 66–67). In 1043, we find Roger, bishop of Chalons-sur-Marne, consulting Wazon, bishop of Liège (an ecclesiastic in high repute both for his learning and piety), with respect to certain *secret meetings* frequently held by the Cathari in his diocese, especially at the fortress of Montwimer, near Chalons. Wazon advised that, in the first instance, Roger should limit his interference to simply instructing the faithful throughout his diocese to abstain from communion and intercourse with such as were known to attend the gatherings. As, however, no satisfactory result followed, the Council of Rheims, in 1049, determined to issue a sentence of excommunication against not only those who were known to be members of the sect, but also against all who should encourage or protect them (Mansi, *op. cit.* xix. 742). This stringent measure appears to have had the designed effect; and, for some sixty years after, all traces of Catharists in northern France entirely disappear.

The above instances may here suffice to exemplify the treatment of heresy under the earlier Capets—a treatment far more rigorous than that to be noted, in the 11th cent., elsewhere. Both Hugh and his son Robert II. were strenuous supporters of the Church, while the archbishops of Rheims and Sens were immediate feudal lords of not a few of the civil magnates in the French kingdom. In Burgundy, Normandy, and Aquitaine, on the other hand,—provinces which in the 11th and 12th cents. were held by their rulers in what was virtual independence of the French Crown,—although there is evidence of a continuous growth of Catharist doctrines, the evidence that would have necessarily resulted from active measures for their repression appears to be comparatively rare. A decree of the Council convened at Toulouse by Calixtus II. in 1119, and reenacted at the Lateran Council of 1139, throws considerable light on the general situation. The 'secular powers' are thereby enjoined to take active measures against those whom the Church has visited with its anathema; should they, on the contrary, endeavour to protect them, they are to be regarded as accomplices (Mansi, *op. cit.* xxi. 226, 532). The researches of Luchaire supply an excellent commentary on those edicts. The attitude of the seigneur in his fief, as well as that of the citizen in his walled town, was at this time becoming less and less friendly towards the Church; the former often found his territorial claims in conflict with those of the bishop, or with those of some adjacent monastery exempted from local control by virtue of papal charter, while the latter's chief pride was in the newly acquired freedom and privileges of his *ville franche*; both were thus inclined to sympathize with the persecuted sectary rather than with the imperious persecutor. In 1147, Bernard of Clairvaux, accompanied by the cardinal legate of Ostia, made a progress through Septimania, in the hope that, by means of his powerful oratory, he might succeed in winning back the population to the paths of orthodoxy. He found the churches deserted, for the most part, by their congregations, and in many cases by their clergy. The laity, on the other hand, whether seigneurs or artizans, were firm supporters of heresy, if not actually professed schismatics, while the powerful count of Toulouse and the almost equally powerful vicomte of Beziers could only be regarded as sympathizers with the movement [*Opera* (ed. 1719), i. 238]. According, indeed, to William of Neuburg, writing in 1160, the Cathari, 'commonly called Publicani,' existed in 'countless numbers' not only in France, but also in Spain, Italy, and Germany (*Hist. Rerum Anglic.*, ed. Hamilton, i. 120). And at nearly the same time, Hildegarda, the 'inspired' abbess of St. Rupert's Mount, near Bingen, addressed to the clergy of Mainz and Cologne her fervid appeals; enjoining them, 'if they would not that destruction should come upon them,' to eject from their territories these 'nefarious men, worse than Jews, and like unto the Sadducees,' whom she further describes as 'contemptuous of the Divine command to increase and multiply,' 'meagre with much fasting and yet addicted to incestuous lusts,' and 'despisers not only of God's commands as made known through Moses and the Prophets, but also of those of Christ' (Migne, *PL* xcvii., *Epp.* 47 and 48, pp. 247–253; Trithemius, *de Viris Illus. Ord. S. Benedicti*, ii. 119). At the Council of Tours in 1163, like tenets are described as emanating from Toulouse and extending over southern France, and bishops are enjoined to use all possible means to prevent their flocks from being brought under the influence of the preachers of such heresy (Mansi, *op. cit.* xxi. 1177). At the Lateran Council of 1179, Alexander III. enacted a sentence of excommunication against both preacher and pervert, and commanded the secular power to proceed against these heretics,—'quos alii Catharos, alii Patrinos, alii Publicanos, alii aliis nominibus vocant'—while all are forbidden, under peril of incurring an anathema, to give them shelter, either in their houses or on their lands (Mansi, *Concilia* [1644], xxvii. 460–461). If we may trust the Church History published at Leyden in 1599 with the sanction of the Vigniers, large numbers of heretics, *bearing the same appellations*, were burned in Flanders and various parts of France about the year 1183 (Vignier, *Hist. de l'Église*, p. 391). Two years later, we find the cardinal bishop of Albano placing himself at the head of an armed force with a view to their forcible suppression. But the first organized measures of this kind date from the decree of the Council of Verona in 1184, where, although the Cathari are indicated only in general terms, the doctrines prescribed are those by which they were especially distinguished, and the bishop of each diocese is instructed to *search out heretics*, and, on due further inquiry, to hand them over to be dealt with by the secular authorities (Lavisse and Rambaud, ii. 272).

It was not, however, until the pontificate of Innocent III. (1198–1216) that the decree of the Council of Verona appears to have been put into execution. A member of an illustrious Roman house, he applied himself with singular ability and penetration to the task of building up a spiritual despotism. Even Otto IV. was constrained to promise his co-operation in a religious Crusade before he could receive his imperial crown in Rome (Oct. 1209), and by that time the dangers which confronted the Church had assumed a yet more menacing aspect, for the Catharists now represented a movement which threatened the Roman pontificate itself with overthrow. From their various centres in southern Europe, following the courses of the great rivers,—the Danube, the Rhone, the Rhine, and the Saone,—they appeared, in yet greater numbers than before, in Picardy and Flanders. Industry, and especially the weaver's craft, attracted them to the more important industrial centres,—the desire of convincing their foes by argument, to the famous schools of Paris, Chartres, Chalons, Orleans, Rheims, and Soissons (Hauréau, *Innocent III.*, p. 12). In Spain, it was rumoured, they were seeking to form an alliance with the Saracen against Christianity, and, like Hildegarda, the pontiff in Rome and the troubadour in Languedoc alike denounced their heresy as the worse of the two (Joachim *in Apocalyp.*, f. 134 ; Fauriel, *Hist. de la poésie provençale*, i. 77).

It is now that the territory of the Albigeois, having become their chief centre in Languedoc, appears first to have given its name to the sect ; but in distant centres or districts they were still generally known as Cathari, and often, specifically, by some local name, wherever they congregated in large numbers—in Flanders and Picardy, for example, as *Piphili*, a corruption of Pauliciani ; farther south, as *Bulgari* or *Bougres*. But their most widely spread designation, after that of Cathari, was **Patarini**, the name which they had brought with them from Italy, where again, at certain centres, they sometimes bore a local appellation, such as *Concorricci*, from Concorrazzo near Monza, *Albanenses*, from Alba in Piedmont, and *Bagnolenses*, from Bagnolo near Brescia. Even Agen, though but a few miles distant from the Albigeois, gave them a distinctive appellation,—*Agennenses* [see in Döllinger's *Beiträge* (ii. 53–84), the text of a MS compiled in 1235, and entitled *Supra Stella*].

It does not, however, appear that these widely scattered communities were at variance among themselves, as was notably the case, in the 17th cent., with those Puritan representatives of the Cathari who settled, as exiles, in Holland and in Germany. They are rather to be regarded as successive waves of a great exodus from Hungary, Croatia, Bosnia, Bulgaria, and Dalmatia, breaking now on the north-western shores of the Adriatic (where Venice became their chief centre), and now on the coast of Apulia, but finding, both among the rising communes of Lombardy and the unruly barons of the south, a sympathy which deepened into admiration and bore fruit in numerous converts to their doctrines. The state of the Catholic Church, indeed, whether in the lands which these exiles had quitted or in those in which they settled, was not such as to inspire them with much reverence for its institutions. In Bosnia there was but one Catholic bishop, and the clergy were poor and ignorant. In Hungary, a public official might be a Jew, a Muhammadan, or a pagan ; and the monasteries there, which professed the Benedictine rule, were fain to seek their novices in Germany and Italy, and existed in almost complete isolation from the surrounding populations. Those of the Greek Church, on the other hand, while regarded with dislike by the Latin clergy, often sheltered within their walls not a few for whom the refined subtleties of the Manichæistic dualism possessed almost a fascination ; while over those rude natives to whom the Perfects of the Cathari were able to preach in the vernacular, their simpler faith and ascetic life exercised a scarcely less potent influence. Among those of them who became converts to Bogomilism (see BOGOMILS) the aversion from the doctrines and example of the Old Rome was so strong that large numbers became converts to Muhammadanism. The Paulicians, however, who formed an important body in the New Rome, migrated to Italy and to France. With regard to what might there be observed of the life of the higher ecclesiastics and the state of discipline in the Church at large, it may here be sufficient to cite the declarations of a contemporary Pope and the candid admissions of a living Catholic prelate. It was in May, 1204, that Innocent III. addressed to his legate in Narbonne a letter calling attention to the demoralized condition of the clergy in that province, a state which he attributes largely to the misrule of the metropolitan, Berenger II. He describes the superior clergy as 'dumb dogs who had forgot how to bark, simoniacs who sold justice, absolving the rich and condemning the poor, themselves regardless of the laws of the Church, accumulators of benefices in their own hands, conferring dignities on unworthy priests or illiterate lads.' '*And hence*,' he adds, '*the insolence of the heretics* and the prevailing contempt both of seigneurs and the people for God and for His Church.' 'Nothing,' he goes on to say, 'was more common than for monks even, and regular canons, to cast aside their attire, take to gambling and hunting, consort with concubines, and turn jugglers or doctors' (*Epist.* bk. vii. No. 75, Migne, *PL* cciv. 355–357). 'We are bound, in good faith, to admit,' writes Mgr. Douais, 'that the clergy of the 12th cent. were not simply wanting in the power to withstand the revolutionary designs of the new Manichæans, *but themselves afforded them at once a pretext and an excuse*' (*Les Albigeois*[2] [1880], p. 287). In the year in which Innocent himself was elected Pope, the citizens of Lodève, in the territory of Beziers, had plundered the palace of their bishop, and compelled him, by threats on his life, to grant them fresh privileges (Luchaire, *Innocent, III.*, p. 27). It is, indeed, undeniable that at this time most of the chief seigneurs in Languedoc regarded Catholicism with indifference, if not hostility, and were friendly at heart to the Catharists ; while, if their arch-accuser, Peter of Cernay, may be credited, the counts of Foix, Beziers, Toulouse, and Béarn took special delight in encouraging the desecration of churches and in offering insults to the officiating clergy (*Historia Albigensium*, Migne, *PL* ccxiii. cols. 565, 566, 579, 600–602). That such outrages were instigated by the Catharists themselves, or that they were the result of their teaching, is, however, at least doubtful, although there certainly are instances of similar action on their part under extreme provocation. But, generally speaking, by the admission of the same writer, they were known among their supporters as the *boni homines*, the 'bons hommes,' whose simple blameless life offered, in most respects, the strongest contrast alike to the self-seeking and self-indulgent habits of the clergy, and to the dissolute and reckless careers of the majority of the seigneurs (*ib.* col. 553).

Prior to the reign of Louis VII. (1130–1180), the counts of Toulouse had been among the most independent of all the vassals of the French Crown ; but in 1154 the marriage of Raymond V. with Constance, the sister of Louis, ushered in a material change in these relations. Shortly after, and for the first time within a century, a French monarch visited Languedoc in person ; in 1158 his aid was invoked to repel the forces of Henry II. of England from the Toulousain. From that day, it became the policy of Louis and of his successor, Philip Augustus, to cultivate direct and friendly relations with the clergy of these southern provinces; and a series of charters granted to the bishops of Maguelonne, Narbonne, Nîmes, Uzès, and Agde, and to the churches and abbeys of Toulouse, raised them to comparative independence of the local seigneurs with respect to their temporalities,—the King and the Pope thenceforth representing their suzerains (Luchaire, *Instit. des premiers Capétiens*, ii. 281).

It was at the time when this important political change was becoming operative, about the year 1167, that the chief leader of the Paulicians in Constantinople, whose name was Nicetas (or Niquinta), arrived in the Toulousain to preside over a Synod of the teachers of the Catharists which had been convened in St. Felix de Caraman near Toulouse. His account of the prospects of the sister Churches in the East was well calculated at once to reassure those whom he addressed, and to rouse the apprehensions of those of the local Catholic clergy to whose ears it might come. His own church of Melangia, in close proximity to Constantinople, stood firm; as also did each of four others, among which he had made a visitation before crossing the Mediterranean: (1) that known as the Drugurian, (2) that in Roumania, (3) the Bulgarian (with Philippopolis as its centre), (4) the Dalmatian,—at the head of each being its duly appointed bishop, duly fortified for the spiritual life by the reception of the *Consolamentum*. Before he left the Tousousain, Nicetas had either confirmed or instituted five new bishops for Septimania and the adjacent counties, among whom was Sicard Cellerier, bishop of Albi (Vignier, *Histoire de l'Église*, 1601; Döllinger, *Beiträge*, i. 116, 121, 123 and n.).

According to Döllinger (*ib.* p. 200), the above-named Synod reasserted the Manichæistic doctrines of the sect in their most aggressive form; and in 1201, another 'Perfectus,' one Julian of Palermo, a teacher of the same school, appeared at Albi. He had long been known by his labours among the warlike race which sheltered in the gloomy gorges of Albania, and his fervid oratory now so wrought upon the Albigenses, that almost the entire population accepted his teaching, while his emissaries were received with open arms in most of the chief towns of Septimania. It is to be noted, accordingly, that at the very time when Innocent resolved upon the Crusade in Languedoc, the doctrines of the Cathari had assumed a form which can only be described as subversive, not merely of the teaching of the Western Church, but of Christianity itself.

The Church of the Cathari most resembled, perhaps, that of Rome, with respect to its organization. It appears to have had its Pope, although this is somewhat doubtful (see Schmidt, *Histoire*, ii. 145); but it is certain that, in the New Rome, Niquinta had been styled 'Papa,' and Julian of Palermo, known as *Maior Hæreticorum*, appears to have been regarded as his successor. The functions of the Catholic bishop were vested in the Perfectus, the person in each separate community or congregation of *credentes* who, by virtue of a lengthened course of ascetic discipline which included periods of complete isolation from society, had won for himself the recognized right to bear a designation which implied his superiority to human frailties and passions. Under his teaching his flock learned to repudiate the Divinely instituted ordinance of marriage and to ignore the rights of individual proprietorship, the ties of social existence and of civic organization being alike thus cast aside. Self-detachment from the world, while engaging in secular duties and pursuits, appears, indeed, to have been their dominant conception of the religious life, all contact with the material involving a certain defilement, while life itself was a kind of purgatory, of which the Catharists rejected the Roman doctrine, maintaining that the soul, after death, entered forthwith into a state either of perfect happiness or of eternal suffering (see Eckbertus, Migne, *PL* clxxii. col. 15). Their abstention (of Manichæistic origin) from all animal food included even milk and eggs, all matter being regarded as the creation of the Spirit of Evil, but especially that which was the outcome of sexual propagation. Labour was justifiable so far as it served to sustain life; carried beyond that point, it was useless for those who were debarred from the possession of anything that could be called personalty (Schmidt, ii. 84, 85). Such was the creed imposed by the Perfectus on the believers (*credentes*); but besides the believers there were the 'hearers' (*auditores*), who listened to the words of the teacher but failed adequately to put in practice what he taught. With regard to their theology, the evidence is perplexing, not to say contradictory. Their Christology, while evidently influenced by Arianism, differed from it in some important respects. Christ, they held, was not God, but a creation of the Divine Nature, and one with it only in respect of will and intention,—an Archangel among the angels and appearing upon earth in this celestial form (see DOCETISM), but neither Incarnate nor Ascended, the very miracles which He wrought being explained away as purely metaphorical, and designed simply to symbolize the power of the spiritual over the earthly nature. At the time of the commencement of the Crusade, indeed, the dualistic and anti-materialistic theory had obtained such influence in Languedoc, owing, possibly, to the teaching of Nicetas and Julian, that, according to some teachers, the Christ of the Evangelists was really an emanation of the Spirit of Evil, permitted to appear on earth as the Tempter, seeking to lead mankind astray and to undo that work of man's salvation which was being accomplished by the true Christ in heaven (Peter of Cernay, *op. cit.* col. 546; Schmidt, ii. 37). The views inculcated with respect to the Third Person in the Trinity, so far as discernible, are not altogether intelligible, and the dualist can hardly but have found his main theory accompanied with exceptional difficulties in connexion with this question.

If the above tenets were calculated to scandalize and alarm the devout Catholic, the theory of the *Consolamentum* must have added yet further to his dismay, supplanting as it did the ordinances of the Church in relation to baptism, to the Eucharist, and to absolution. This singular and elaborate ceremony, described at length by Schmidt (ii. 119–129), commencing with the renunciation of the Church of Rome and followed by a declaration of acceptance of the Catharist faith, and a solemn promise to observe all the conditions imposed with regard to chastity, diet, and companionship, terminated in the formal admission of the believer into the number of the Perfecti. He then, after a rigid fast extending over three days, retired for forty days more into complete solitude. In cases where the *Consolamentum* had been granted to one who was seriously ill, the individual, we are told, would not infrequently refuse all food, and either voluntarily or at the behest of the Perfecti submit himself to the *endura*, so as to die of starvation, and thereby expedite his immediate passage into eternal felicity (*Liber Sentent. Inquisitionis Tolosanæ*, p. 134; Schmidt, ii. 102, 129). With the *Consolamentum* were associated two other doctrines which may be said to have completed the alienation of the Catharist from all that savoured of Roman Catholicism,—the above-mentioned repudiation of the doctrine of Purgatory, and the theory that the efficacy of the ceremony would be lost, if the officiating Perfectus were not himself pure from sin. The admiration, indeed, with which the teaching of the Perfecti was listened to, alike by the seigneurs of Septimania and the citizens of Milan and Toulouse, is largely to be attributed to the fact that the Perfecti actually exemplified in their lives the austere virtues which they inculcated, thereby presenting a marked contrast to the life and aims of the great majority of the Roman clergy. The attitude, again, of the Catharist towards those who were not of his persuasion cannot be described as intolerant; he preached and he prayed, but he did not persecute; and here, again, he contrasted favourably with the Catholic, and won the sympathy of the seigneur. It is, indeed, implied by William of Puylaurens (*Chronica*, *passim*), that under the protection of the knights of Languedoc a man could profess almost any religion that he pleased. To Innocent III., however, such laxity of belief and diversity of tenets appeared only to call imperatively for intervention; and his experiences, since his accession, in his own dominions might well seem to show that such intervention, if judiciously carried out, might be relied upon to accomplish the desired results. In Italy itself the increasing numbers of the Patarini and the defiant attitude of many of their leaders had already roused him to active measures. At Verona, on the petition of the archbishop, he had promulgated a sentence of excommunication, but it had been treated with contempt (Baluze, ed. Mansi, i. 191). It was yet more ominous when, within the limits of the Patrimony itself, a succession of cities had given evidence of like infection. At Orvieto, in 1200, his intervention having been solicited by the Catholic party, he had sent Parentio, a high-spirited young Roman noble, to assume the office of *podestà*; but the unsparing severity with which his representative had exerted his authority had given rise to a conspiracy, and Parentio had been dragged from his house and put to death outside the city walls (*Acta SS.* vol. lxviii. Mai). At Viterbo (one of his favourite residences), in 1205, several Catharists had been elected consuls, and their Perfectus, one John Tiniosi, had been returned for the office of papal chamberlain. Remonstrances having proved ineffectual, Innocent himself, in 1207, had repaired to the city; the leaders fled on his approach; he commanded that their houses should forthwith be demolished and their property confiscated; while the podestà and the consuls were compelled to swear that, in future, they themselves would mete out like punishment to all heretics (*Epist.* x. Nos. 105, 130, 139; Migne, *PL* ccxv. cols. 1200, 1220, 1231). Like punishment was inflicted on Orvieto, and with the close of the year 1207 the submission of the cities was complete, and penitent Viterbo had been raised to the rank of a cathedral city; while Innocent was now able to direct his attention to where it seemed most required, namely, to Languedoc. His intervention in that province was materially aided by a political change which had taken place since his accession (Schmidt, i. 148–149).

In 1137, the kingdom of Aragon had been acquired by the count of Barcelona, Raymond-Berenger IV., and the crown had become hereditary in his house. In 1204, his descendant, Pedro II., following the example of the French monarch, had proclaimed himself the vassal of the Roman pontiff; and, in consequence, various fiefs which had before done homage to the counts of Toulouse (among them those of Carcassonne, Albi, and Nîmes) became detached from their former fealty to that of the kings of Aragon, the first two cities, it is to be noted, being in the same episcopal province, with Narbonne as their common metropolis (B. Hauréau, *Bernard Délicieux*, p. 12).

It was now, therefore,—when the Fourth Crusade had resulted in the reduction of the Eastern Empire to the condition of a French dependency, when the disastrous ten years' war between France and Germany had been ended, and Otto IV., under solemn promise to restore the lands which he had wrested from the Holy See, was looking forward to his coronation in Rome,—that the time seemed to have arrived for effective measures in the Toulousain.

Throughout his letters, Innocent lays emphasis on the fact that his great aim is the conversion of the heretic, not his destruction; and in Nov., 1206, three legates had been sent by him from Rome to Narbonne instructed to make yet another attempt to bring the Cathari to reason by force of argument. They were at the same time directed to lay aside all pomp and ostentation, and to aim at winning the sympathy of observers by a humble demeanour, to go meanly clad, imitating the poverty of their great exemplar, and by the force of their own example and convincing speech (*documentum sermonis*) to recall the heretic from his errors (*Epist.* ix. No. 185). It is noted by Luchaire that four months before this letter was written, Diègo de Acevedo, the bishop of Osma in Spain, accompanied by Dominic de Guzlan, the founder of the Dominican Order, had had audience of Innocent in Rome, and on their return journey had, by accident, fallen in with the above three legates (one of whom was Peter of Castelnau) at Castelnau, when the bishop of Osma had given them much the same advice as that which soon after reached them as a mandate from Rome. As Dominic was one of the bishop's chapter, and was present when this advice was given, we may fairly accept the assertion of Vignier that the self-denial, self-devotion, and fervid oratory which distinguished the Dominican friars were, to a great extent, evoked by the urgent necessity of combating the success which had attended the exhibition of the same characteristics on the part of the teachers of the Catharists (*Histoire de l'Église*, p. 405; Luchaire, *Innocent III.*, 90–91). Dividing themselves into little bands, the Dominicans now appeared at different centres,—Servian, Beziers, Verfeil, Montréal, and Pamiers,—inviting the leaders of the Catharists to amicable disputation on the chief points of disagreement. At each of these centres the disputation extended over from seven to fourteen days, and was listened to with intense interest by crowded audiences; but as the only accounts which have come down to us are those preserved in Catholic sources, they can hardly be supposed to be impartial. But if it be true that at Montréal, Oton, the Catharist protagonist, affirmed and maintained as his *quæstio* the identity of the Church of Rome with the Babylon of the Apocalypse, and even ventured to style the former 'the Synagogue of the Devil' (Vignier, pp. 407, 410), the Catharist can hardly be credited with any real desire to conciliate his opponent [Devic and Vaissètte (1879), vi. 249]. At the expiration of two years thus spent, Dominic is recorded to have expressed himself deeply chagrined at the small result of their collective labours (Pierre de Cernay, *op. cit.* cc. 1–5; Schmidt, i. 211–217; Luchaire, *Innocent III.*, 92–99).

But however sanguine Innocent may originally have been of their success, he had already determined on the employment of other means, and, early in 1207, Peter of Castelnau had received instructions to urge upon certain seigneurs of Septimania (of whom Raymond of Toulouse himself was one) that they should lay aside the feuds which, unhappily, were rife among themselves, and combine in a Crusade against the heretics. That it was designed, by this proposal, to isolate Raymond admits of little doubt, and he was himself fully aware of the net that was now closing round him. The other barons, allured by the prospect of rich plunder, to be reaped at small risk, readily assented; but the count of Toulouse, apart from his open sympathy with the Cathari, who composed a large proportion of his own subjects, recoiled from the prospect of seeing his own domains overrun by the enemies of his house, and very naturally refused. Thereupon Peter pronounced him excommunicate, and placed his territory under an interdict, at the same time justifying this extreme course by alleging the count's laxity and extortion in the administration of his seigneury,—laxity, as shown in his partiality to Jews and heretics; extortion, as attested by his encroachments on the temporalities of the Church (Vaissètte, iii. 146; Devic and Vaissètte [1879], vi. 249-250). Innocent followed up the action of his legate by confirming the sentence of excommunication, and, addressing to Raymond a letter in which he upbraided him with seeking 'to preserve peace with his neighbours while he allied himself with the foes of Catholic truth' (*Epist.* x. No. 99; cf. Devic and Vaissètte, *op. cit.* vi. 255-257).

In the first instance, Raymond is said to have feigned submission, but he failed to give practical effect to the promises which he is alleged to have made; and Innocent now, for the fourth time, proceeded to invoke the aid of King Philip, entreating him to come in person and place himself at the head of the Crusade. The latter, although himself involved in hostilities with John Lackland, at length feigned compliance, but in doing so he stipulated that Innocent, in turn, should undertake to bring about a two years' truce between France and England, and should also decree the levying of a subsidy from the clergy and nobles of the French kingdom to defray the expenses of the Crusade. This, however, was altogether beyond Innocent's power; and it was while he was probably hesitating as to the course he should next pursue that his perplexities were suddenly terminated by the assassination of Peter of Castelnau, when on his way to St. Gilles, by one of Count Raymond's officers. The incident itself is enveloped in obscurity, and not less so the extent of the count's complicity in the deed. But, according to the statement made by Innocent to King Philip, Raymond, feigning penitence, had invited Peter to St. Gilles, there to receive his submission, and had then contrived the murder. But this statement is invalidated, to a certain extent, by the pontiff's admission, when referring to the subject some four years later, that positive proof was wanting (*Epist.* xi. No. 26, xii. No. 106). His immediate action, however, assumed the count's complicity, and in a circular letter (10 March, 1208) to the churches of Languedoc, Raymond was again excommunicated, his person and his territory were declared to be no longer under the protection of the law, and his subjects and allies alike absolved from their vows of fidelity or compact (*Epist.* xi. No. 26). Should he, however, give proof of his penitence, he might even yet be received again into the bosom of the Church, but only on condition that he expelled the heretic from his dominions (*ib.* Migne, *PL* ccxv. col. 1557).

A Crusade was then proclaimed, Arnold Amalric being appointed chief leader, with Simon de Montfort as his lieutenant, while all who refused to listen to the summons were forbidden the enjoyments of social life and interdicted from Christian burial at their death. To the Dominicans was confided the duty of preaching the great expedition throughout the realm, and for the fifth time an appeal was made to Philip (Devic and Vaissètte, vi. 263-267). The king, however, still stipulated that the two conditions which he had before specified should be carried out, while he at the same time intimated (in a letter subsequently erased from the royal registers) that, as he was advised by his councillors (Raymond's guilt as a heretic being still unproven), the pontiff had exceeded his powers in declaring his lands subject to confiscation. Such, indeed, was the attitude which he continued to maintain until his death, influenced partly by his disinclination to appear personally as the abettor of religious bigotry, but still more by the desire to employ the military resources at his command for other purposes, and not least by the apprehension lest, under the rule of a too powerful vassal, Languedoc might recover its former virtual independence (Luchaire, *u.s.* 126-127).

The first phase of the Crusade, accordingly, was that of a religious war, directed mainly by the papal legate and headed by French nobles, among whom, next to de Montfort, the duke of Burgundy, and the counts of Nevers, Auxerre, St. Pol, and Geneva, were the most conspicuous,—the Dominican, like Peter the Hermit more than a century before, lending his aid as an orator to rouse the enthusiasm of the multitude, while his efforts were seconded by the Troubadour, who, in his *Chanson de la Croisade*, vaunted that more than 20,000 fully armed knights and 200,000 foot had rallied to the standard of the Cross (*ib.* p. 129). Raymond himself, completely dismayed, now again made his submission, and (18 June, 1209), after a humiliating ceremony, was reconciled to the Church by the papal legate in the cathedral at St. Gilles; he was compelled to swear on the Gospels and in the presence of holy relics that he would treat all heretics as personal foes, expel the Jews, proclaim a Truce of God, and himself take part in the Crusade (for the oaths taken by Raymond and Milo, the legate, on this occasion, see Devic and Vaissètte, vi. 277-279; Migne, *PL* ccvi. cols. 90-91). A like submission made by the vicomte of Beziers was not accepted, although he was a nephew of Raymond and brother-in-law of Peter, the king of Aragon. In July, Beziers itself was taken by storm, when a general massacre of the inhabitants took place. Raymond Roger, the vicomte, fled to Carcassonne, and shortly after died a prisoner in the fortress, not without suspicion of foul means having been employed. It was at the capture of Beziers that Arnold, the papal legate, on being appealed to by the soldiery to guide them in the work of butchery (for fear that loyal Catholics might otherwise perish unrecognized) is narrated to have made reply, 'Slay them all, the Lord will recognize his own.' The story, however, is at least doubtful (Hurter, *Gesch. Pabst Innocenz des Dritten*[2], ii. 343; Devic and Vaissètte, vi. 288-289, 313; Migne, *PL* ccxvi. cols. 138-141). Narbonne saved itself from a like fate only by an anticipatory execution of a number of the Cathari. Montpellier, owing to its long and approved loyalty to the Church, altogether escaped; but Innocent could vaunt that 500 towns and castles had been wrested from the enemies of the Faith, while the greater part of Septimania was reduced to the appearance of a desert. So great, indeed, was the scarcity of supplies, that the French leaders, having completed their forty days' term of service, and seeing no prospect of further plunder, were fain to return home. Simon de Montfort, fourth earl of Leicester, alone remained. In the Île de France he held only a petty seigneury, and having been appointed successor to Raymond Roger in the viscounty of Beziers and Carcassonne, he found himself virtually an autocrat in the government of the desolated province. Although he was by education and conviction an ardent Catholic, his religious enthusiasm was probably fanned by a sense of personal wrong. In 1107 he had been mulcted by John of England of all the estates which he inherited through his mother in that country. Raymond of Toulouse, on the other hand, had married Joan, John's sister, and daughter of Eleanor of Aquitaine. If we add to these considerations the fact that King John of England was at this very time excommunicate, owing to his maltreatment and defiance in England of that same episcopal order whose power de Montfort was pledged to restore in Languedoc, we cannot but see that hatred of heresy can hardly have been the sole motive which urged on the stern Norman knight in his merciless career. Before the year 1210 had passed, John himself received intimation that his own barons were plotting to place the crown which he wore on the head of Simon de Montfort].

The circumstances under which Simon was now called upon to administer his territory were, however, sufficiently discouraging. Funds began entirely to fail him, and this at the very time when the few knights who had remained with him were demanding double pay, to indemnify them for the absence of the plunder which the country no longer afforded. In his difficulties he appealed to Innocent. The pontiff, already overburdened by the demands consequent upon the Fourth Crusade (see CRUSADES), was unable to respond with pecuniary aid, but wrote to the Emperor Otto, the Kings of Aragon and Castille, and 'numerous powerful knights and ladies,' to invoke their assistance (Migne, *PL* ccvi. cols. 141–157). At the same time, we find him gratefully acknowledging the service which Simon had rendered in restoring to the papal exchequer the hearth tax of three pennies *per annum* which the lawless barons of Languedoc had, in many cases, been diverting to their own uses.

In the meantime, Raymond, sorely pressed by the demands imposed on him by the papal envoys, was reduced almost to desperation by being for a third time excommunicated, the sentence having been pronounced by a Council at Avignon, 6 Sept., 1209. He resolved on a personal appeal to Innocent, before whom (Jan., 1210), having been admitted to an audience in the Lateran, he laid a statement of his grievances. Accounts differ with regard to what actually took place on this occasion; but it is probable that the pontiff deemed it prudent to disown, to some extent, the relentless proceedings of his legates, one of whom, Milo, had just died, and he now enjoined that Raymond, who had complied with all the conditions originally imposed, should be reinstated in possession of his castles, and that his lands should be relieved from further requisitions (Migne, *PL*, *ib.* cols. 171–173). His instructions, however, either arrived too late, or were wilfully disregarded by his legates, to whom Toulouse was now called upon to surrender its count. But the dwellers in the city and in the faubourg alike, holding themselves bound by their oath of allegiance to their seigneurs, refused compliance; and it was with difficulty that the archbishop of the city, a staunch supporter of Simon, succeeded in inducing a certain number of the citizens to support the latter, under whose leadership there now ensued, throughout the Toulousain and Septimania (June, 1210 to Sept., 1212), a long series of plunderings and massacres, accompanied by almost unprecedented atrocities, wherever the defenceless victims refused to abjure their errors. At the strong fortress of Minerve, near Narbonne, 140 Perfecti were hurled or threw themselves on to the burning pyre (Devic and Vaissètte, vi. 329–331). At Lavaur, taken after a stubborn defence, the well is still shown into which the widowed 'Lady of the City,' the bounteous Giralda, and her daughter, were flung, and stones rolled down upon their bodies. The governor and eighty knights were either suspended on the gallows or put to the sword. Termes, Castres, and other towns were the scenes of similar horrors, Toulouse and Montauban being, eventually, the only two which remained in the possession of Raymond [Guillelmi de Podio Laurentii *Hist. Albig.*, cc. 17, 18 [in Duchesne (A.), *Hist. Franc. Script.*, v.]; Devic and Vaissètte, vi. 342, 356–358, 384; Peter of Cernay, Migne, *PL* ccxiii. cc. 37, 52, 53; *La Chanson de la Croisade*, stanzas lxvii.–lxxiv. (ed. Paul Meyer, ii. 83–91); *Voyage en France* (35ème série), 269].

The war itself must now be regarded as assuming another phase, and Innocent himself became aware that a reaction was setting in throughout Languedoc, as, to quote the expression of Paul Meyer, 'it became clear that the Crusade was designed to accomplish nothing less than the substitution of some enterprising adventurers from France for the ancient seigniorial families of the South' (*La Chanson*, etc., Introd. p. xxiv; Fauriel, *Hist. de la Croisade*, Introd. pp. xlviii–l).

The doctrines of the Catharist were again openly espoused, as a powerful incentive to renewed resistance. The Count de Foix, Raymond Roger, reverted to his former defiant attitude. The Catholic leaders, on the other hand, perceiving how closely political supremacy was involved in the suppression of heresy, began to assert their position with increased emphasis. Arnold Amalric, the abbot of Citeaux, usurped to himself the title of duke of Narbonne (Luchaire, *Innocent III.*, p. 188), and imposed oaths of fidelity and homage on the former subjects of Raymond of Toulouse. Simon, however, with his habitual astuteness, professed, in the first instance, to ignore his own position, and, writing to Philip (Aug., 1211), said that he had instructed his envoys to assume possession of all the territory wrested from Raymond, and to hold the same until the rightful owner should be declared (*ib.* 178). By the middle of the following year, however, his representatives in Rome preferred the demand for his recognition as lord of Languedoc; in a charter of 14 Sept., 1212, granted by the abbot of Moissac, that dignitary expressly declared that 'God has justly assigned to Simon de Montfort the territory of his adversary' (*ib.* 189). In the following December, Simon himself convened an assembly at Pamiers, to which the seigneurs, the clergy, and the citizens of the province were alike summoned,—the great political revolution which was in process being thinly disguised by their being themselves invited to become members of the Commission which was then appointed, and by whose action the 'customs' of Paris, the 'use' of Northern France, and the supremacy of the Church (acting through its ecclesiastical courts), were substituted for the feudal liberties and the civic freedom which had before existed. As Luchaire points out, however, Simon de Montfort posed as the saviour of the land, whose mission it was to establish order, centralization, and peace; and for a time there were those who firmly believed that they should obtain these blessings at his hands.

The king of Aragon was still Simon's suzerain, and, with the support of Innocent, was able to assert his rights. He regarded with no small alarm his great vassal's monopoly of influence and the impending political changes. As soon, accordingly, as the Crusade was pronounced by Innocent to be at an end (Jan., 1213), Peter's first endeavour was to submit to a Council convened at Lavaur (16 Jan.) a memorandum, drawn up with the design of showing that Raymond himself had never been proved a heretic, and that neither he nor his cousin, the count of Comminges, nor the count of Foix, nor Gaston de Béarn, had ever accepted the Albigensian doctrines. It was the design of the Council, however, to complete the count's ruin rather than to afford him the opportunity of regaining the confidence of Innocent, and counter-representations were made at the Lateran, couched in terms of such urgency, that the pontiff, notwithstanding his distrust of Simon and the Norman party, was prevailed upon to change his attitude completely. 'The supporters of heresy,' he now wrote to King Peter, 'are more dangerous than the heretics themselves,' at the same time plainly intimating that further obduracy would be visited with another Crusade (*Epist.* xvi. No. 48; Migne, *PL* ccxvi. col. 851). Soon after, hostilities were resumed; and Peter, along with his allies, now appeared at the head of a great army outside the walls of the strong fortress of Muret, where Simon, with a small body of knights, awaited their attack. The disastrous defeat which the confederates there sustained, involving, as it did, the death of the king and the dispersion of his forces (12 Sept., 1213), sealed the fate of Raymond's party. He himself is next heard of at the court of John Lackland, at Périgueux, proffering a now worthless homage. Simon's son, Amaury, now married Beatrice, the heiress of Dauphiny; Toulouse surrendered to Montfort, and the whole of southern France became incorporated with the French kingdom. Towards the close of the year, the Troubadour, William of Tudela, gives place (line 2768) to his successor in the *Chanson*, which henceforth becomes of primary value as a contemporary historical source, being at once highly original and always to be trusted (P. Meyer, Introd. vol. i. xci–xciii).

In 1214, Innocent rescinded the prohibition to preach the Crusade, and in the course of the year a hundred thousand 'pilgrims' poured into Languedoc. Their first military achievement was the capture of Maurillac, on which occasion we find a reference to the Waldenses, seven of whom were burnt 'with great joy' as incorrigible in the attestation of their errors (Devic and Vaissètte, vi. 445). Concurrently with this movement, the victory achieved by the royal forces over Otto IV. at Bouvines (27 July, 1214) broke the power of the barons throughout the realm, and was hailed by the clergy as an auspicious triumph for the cause of unity in the Church. At the Council of Montpellier (8 Jan., 1215), Simon was unanimously elected 'prince and sovereign' of Languedoc; and in the following April, Prince Louis, accompanied by the new lord of the province and by Peter of Beneventum, the new papal legate, set out on a progress through the scenes of the war. The towns, still secretly hostile to de Montfort, threw open their gates to the representatives of the Crown and the Holy See. Innocent, however, although he formally acknowledged the new governor of the conquered territory, would never recognize him as its rightful lord, and subsequently, when called upon to arbitrate in the fierce contention between Simon and the abbot Arnold for the dukedom of Narbonne, gave his decision in favour of the monastic dignitary.

At the memorable Lateran Council of Nov., 1215, Raymond was once more, and finally, confronted with his accusers; and here, again, we find the pontiff strongly urging that the exiled count should be reinstated in the Toulousain. His advice was supported by a small minority of bishops, whose counsel Peter of Cernay does not scruple to stigmatize as that of an 'Ahithophel' (*Hist. Albig.* c. 83; Migne, *PL* ccxiii. col. 700), and it was rejected by a vast majority. The brief allusion of the monkish chronicler to the fact of this divergence of opinion is illustrated at length by the contemporary Troubadour, in a manner which brings home to us the fact that this famous Council, to quote the language of Fauriel, was really 'nothing less than a great political congress, at which the passions, ideas, ambitions, and secular aims of the time are to be discerned, for the moment, in actual open conflict' (*Hist. de la Poésie Provençale*, iii. 159). In the sequel, Innocent himself was under the necessity of issuing a decree whereby Raymond was adjudged to have forfeited his right to govern, and condemned to pass the remainder of his life as a penitent, only a small annuity being granted him, which, together with his wife's dowry, was deemed sufficient for his maintenance. The Council assigned to de Montfort all the territory which he had wrested from the heretics, along with Toulouse and Montauban, but it was ordered that the unconquered lands 'in Provincia' (beyond the Rhone) should, for a time, be held in commission, and that in the event of the count's only son (a youth of fifteen, against whom no imputation of heresy had been preferred) giving proof, by his 'fidelity and upright conversation,' of genuine merit, provision should ultimately be made for him therefrom (*Hist. Albig.*, col. 701; Guill. de Pod. Laur., c. 34; Vaissètte, iii. 280; Devic and Vaissètte, vi. 475, 477).

To all outward seeming, Raymond was now permanently excluded from a public career. The decisions of the Lateran Council had, however, been received throughout both the Toulousain and Provence with a general dissatisfaction which emboldened both father and son to sail, in the spring of 1216, for Marseilles, where they were received with enthusiasm, and a rising in their favour took place, which forthwith extended up the Rhone and into Aragon, while large subsidies arrived from England. A conflict ensued, of which the Provençal poet supplies us with an animated description, but the incidents of which are of military rather than religious interest; though it is deserving of notice that the weapons of ecclesiastical approval and censure were wielded by both parties, in entire contempt for the attitude of the Roman pontiff. At Beaucaire (*Bellumquadrum*) the insurgents, after capturing that important fortress, were stimulated to the work of reconstructing the defences by the promise of indulgences held out by Raymond's chaplain, and both knights and ladies applied themselves assiduously to the toil; while, in the following year, when Simon de Montfort appeared outside the walls of revolted Toulouse, he stood scarcely in happier relations to the Church than Raymond himself, having been excommunicated by his own ecclesiastical superior, Arnold, duke of Narbonne, on some pretext arising out of their bitter contention for the dukedom (Fauriel, *Hist. de la Croisade*, 3995–4014; Lea, *Hist. of the Inquisit.* i. 184). As Innocent had died in the preceding year (July, 1216), and his successor, Honorius III., sustained his policy in Languedoc with increased vigour, it is evident that the broader questions at issue were almost lost sight of in those of purely local importance.

On commencing operations, for the third time, against Toulouse, Simon prayed that if he failed to recapture the city he might perish in the attempt, while, if successful, he vowed that he would reduce it to ashes (Fauriel, *ib.* 7835–7855). The citizens, on the other hand, conscious that mercy was not to be looked for at his hands, repelled his attacks with a desperate energy, which, after a siege of nine months, was rewarded by his being killed (25 June, 1218) by a huge stone hurled from the wall by a mangonel, his brother Guy having only a minute before fallen by his side,—*Ez escridan la joya, car es Dieus mercenars* ('shouts of joy arise, for God is merciful'), exclaims the Troubadour (*ib.* 8434–8456, 8475; Meyer, i. 342, also ii. 421; Sandys, *Hist. of Classical Scholarship*[2], i. 549). At the news of the tyrant's death, the Catharists and their supporters now flew to arms throughout Languedoc; and Honorius, alarmed at the prospect, addressed to Philip an urgent remonstrance, which resulted in the appearance of Prince Louis at the head of an army, whose achievements in the field are remembered only by the massacre at Marmande, when 5000 men, women, and children were put to death by order of the bishop of Saintes, on the sole ground of their assumed heretical beliefs, and the city itself was burnt (Guill. de Pod. Laur. p. 685; Fauriel, *ib.* 9306–9320). An endeavour to inflict like exemplary punishment on Toulouse was baffled, and, after laying siege to the city for forty days, on 1 Aug., 1219 Louis struck his camp and returned to France. The Albigeois took fresh heart, and many of the towns which had been wrested from them by the sword of Simon were now recovered. Eventually, after a war extending over two more years, Amaury de Montfort was fain to bribe the French monarch to renewed interference, by offering to surrender to him the entire territory which had been adjudged to his late father. It was at this juncture that Raymond VI. died (Aug., 1222); his interment in consecrated ground was forbidden; and for nearly a century and a half the remains, denied the rites of burial, were exposed to sight within the precincts of the Hospital of the Knights of St. John, outside Toulouse (C. Molinier, *L'Ensevelissement de Raimond VI.*).

During Simon's rule, large numbers of the Catharists had fled to Bulgaria and Croatia,—to return, at his death, inspired with renewed zeal by the exhortations of their Pope, or metropolitan, in those regions,—while they were encouraged and sustained in the renewal of the conflict in the Narbonnaise by the teachings of his delegate, one Bartholomew of Carcassonne (Devic and Vaissètte, vi. 567–568). The disputations with the Catholics were again held; and in the years 1225–1226 the famous Franciscan, Antony of Padua, had appeared in the Toulousain and the Narbonnaise to urge on the persecutor the resumption of hostilities (*ib.* vi. 591–595). In the national archives of Paris are still to be seen the letters, written in 1227 by the metropolitan of Sens and the bishop of Chartres, offering contributions towards a new Crusade against the Albigenses (Lea, *Hist. of the Inquisition*, i. 201). Eventually, after a long and gallant struggle, Raymond VII. submitted; and was compelled, by the Treaty of Meaux (1229), to accept a series of onerous and humiliating conditions — the demolition of the greater part of the walls of Toulouse, the cession to the French Crown of territory amounting to two-thirds of his father's dominions (of which, however, a part had been included in the surrender, above mentioned, by Amaury), the cession to the Roman See of the marquisate of Provence (the portion of Provence on the left bank of the Rhone), while in Toulouse itself he was required to institute a school of studies, which subsequently developed into the university, but was now conceived on lines designed to ensure the predominance of strictly Catholic teaching (Martin, *Hist. de France*[4], iv. 149–150).

In assenting to the foregoing conditions, Raymond can have been actuated by no other sentiment than a conviction of the political unwisdom of prolonging a racial conflict against forces which were overwhelming; but in promising his active and unsparing co-operation in the extirpation of heresy, and subsequently befriending the two great Mendicant Orders (he is said even to have urged on the papal legate in the work of organizing the Inquisition within his own diminished territory), it is probable that he was giving expression to a contrite sense of the paternal folly which had brought such ruin on his house, and that the manner in which Innocent had compassionated his helpless boyhood may have instilled into the young count a genuine admiration of his protector, and sympathy with his designs. That sagacious pontiff had seen very clearly, some years before his death, that, however effective fire and sword might prove in the temporary effacement of heresy, something more was needed to prevent the recrudescence of an ancient faith sincerely, however wrongly, held. Notwithstanding his habitual tendency to temporize, he had accordingly drawn up a series of instructions which represent an important innovation upon preceding methods (Douais, *L'Inquisition*, 1906, p. 6). The mode of procedure in a judge's court, at that time, was still that of the old Roman tribunal; the magistrate always awaited the appearance of an accuser before he intervened to punish the malefactor. But, however adequate such a method might be found in dealing with offences against the person or against property, Innocent perceived that it failed altogether to reach a particular class of citizens, distinguished generally by their blameless life and inoffensive conduct, but lying under grave suspicion owing to their abstention from the prescribed forms of public worship, and their secret gatherings. If such conduct were really a shelter for rumoured malpractices, it was certain that stronger motives were required to induce the *accusator* to come forward, and hence the institution of the *inquisitio*, a system of inquiry, authorized in legal form and terminology, for bringing home to the offender a definite charge. As early as 1183, Lucius III. had enjoined upon the bishop of each diocese the necessity of seeking out and passing sentence on heretics (Mansi [1644], xxviii. 6), although Luchaire appears to be in error in supposing that his instructions were actually formulated as a decretal (Douais, *op. cit.* pp. 18–20); the *inquisitio*, moreover, postulated the *inquisitor*, and it was not until the wide-spread activity and devotion of the Dominican Order had become manifest that Innocent could discern the instrumentality for which he had been looking. Between the years 1204 and 1213 he issued four decretals [subsequently re-enacted by Gregory IX. (1227–1241)], in which the system of *secret inquiry* was formally recognized (*ib. op. cit.* 6, 7), and direction given that investigations should be instituted throughout the province of Arles, and in the dioceses of Agde, Lodève, Verceil, Tarragona, and Geneva (Potthast, *Regesta*, 2516, 2672, 2876, 4628). It is, however, maintained by Douais that even these instructions were general in their scope, specifying, as they do, no particular offence or persons. But when the dioceses to which they were sent (as specified by himself, pp. 6–8), together with the time of their promulgation, are considered, it is difficult not to infer that they must have been directly aimed at the Albigensian heresy. By the machinery thus brought into operation, the Inquisition (which may be considered to date from the year 1229) obtained the evidence on which its first proceedings were grounded, and was enabled to arrogate to itself a function beyond the power of the already existing ecclesiastical courts; while the Inquisitor, if we accept the view of Douais, represented an authority which the supreme pontiff alone had the power to delegate (*L'Inquisition*, pp. 9–13).

From the year 1229, accordingly, the history of the Albigenses becomes mainly associated with the proceedings of the Inquisition, and will be found treated under that heading; while for an admirable illustration of this later period, the experiences of *Bernard Délicieux*, as described by B. Hauréau (1877), should also be consulted. With the advance of the fourteenth century, the Catharist almost disappears in Western Europe, although occasionally showing a bold front against the Dominicans in Toulouse. In the East, in their ancient home in Bosnia, on the other hand, they more than held their ground, even compelling the Franciscans to retire from the kingdom (see BOGOMILS); and so recently as 1875 a paragraph in *Le Temps* stated that members of the sect were still to be found in that country. They were also to be met with, long after the Inquisition had done its work, secluded in the valleys of the Pyrenees; but for the last four centuries they have often been confused with the Waldenses, and their independent existence becomes, in consequence, more difficult to trace. In Germany the Catharist becomes lost in the 'Ketzer' [Schmidt, *Hist.* i. 141, ii. 232–233; Lombard (Alex.), *Pauliciens*, etc. (1899), 269–275]. In Albi itself, their final disappearance may, perhaps, be inferred from the fact that in 1404 the bishop of Amboise is to be found giving orders that the bones of St. Amarand should be brought from Vieux (*supra*, p. 277a) and deposited in the cathedral church of St. Cecilia, as in a city no longer tainted with heresy (Gregory of Tours, ed. Ruinart, col. 787–788 n.).

LITERATURE. — I. *CONTEMPORARY.* — (i.) **Anna Comnena**, *Alexias*, lib. iv. ch. 4, xiv. cc. 8 and 9, xv. ch. 8. (ii.) **Peter of Vaux-Cernay** (Petrus Sarnensis), *De factis et triumphis Simonis comitis de Monteforti* (to Simon's death in 1218), Migne, *PL* ccxiii., Paris, 1855. Peter was the nephew of Guy, the abbot of the monastery of Vaux-Cernay, with whom he went to Provence in 1206; he was the partial admirer of Simon, and is his apologist throughout. (iii.) **William de Puylaurens** (Guillelmus de Podio Laurentii), *Historia Albigensium* (to the year 1272). William was chaplain to Count Raymond VII., and wrote long after the Crusade. Although not always strictly impartial, he is entitled to the highest credit as an accurate and honest writer. (iv.) *La Chanson de la Croisade contre les Albigeois*, first made known and edited by C. Fauriel (Paris, 1837). This edition is altogether superseded by that of Paul Meyer (2 vols., Paris, 1875–1879); the editor in his Preface (i–cxix) has established the following conclusions: (1) The *Chanson* is the production of two writers, differing considerably in their diction, style, and ideas, the former being one William of Tudela (in Navarre), an ardent partisan of the Crusaders; the latter, who commences line 2768 and carries on the narrative to the siege of Toulouse (June, 1219), was a native of that city, and shows himself throughout a devoted adherent of the party of the seigneurs who opposed the Crusade. Notwithstanding some important omissions, he supplies us with a narrative of the highest value in relation to the subject and of great historical merit. (2) In the course of the 15th cent. the whole poem was reproduced in a prose version (which, like the original, is in a mixture of Provençal and Romanic). This version is generally cited as by *L'Anonyme*, and is printed by Devic and Vaissètte among the *Preuves* (vol. viii. 1–203). It has small literary merit, and, since its claim to be regarded as an original production has been thus refuted, can no longer be regarded as of any historical value. (v.) The Letters, or Registers, of Innocent III. (Migne, *PL* ccxiv.–ccxvii.) are of primary importance. (vi.) The treatise by **Eckbert**, abbot of Schaunang, in the diocese of Trèves, entitled, *Sermones XIII. adversus pestiferos fœdissimosque Catharorum damnatos errores et hæreses* (Migne, *PL* cxcv. 11), and the Letter of **Everwein** of Steinfeld to Bernard of Clairvaux, *De hæreticis sui temporis* (Migne, *PL* clxxxii. 676), both written *circ.* 1150, are recognized sources for the doctrinal belief of the Catharists of that period. That of **Alanus de Insulis**, bishop of Auxerre, *De Fide Catholica contra hæreticos sui temporis* (*ib.* ccx. 305) deals specially with the Albigensian heresy. It appeared towards the close of the century, and was shortly followed by the *Libellus contra Catharos* (*ib.* cciv. 772–792) of **Bonacursus**, a heretic who had returned to the Church, and who gives, along with the doctrines of the Catharists, the recognized arguments for their refutation. It was owing to a conviction that the arguments advanced by **Monéta** in his *adversus Catharos et Waldenses Libri V.* (Rome, 1743) were also largely applicable to Lutheran tenets, that the Dominican Ricchini first published this treatise, together with two noteworthy dissertations on the Catharists and Waldenses. The *Summa de Catharis et Leonistis* of **Reinerius Sacchoni** (*cir.* 1300) is printed in Martène et Durand, *Thesaurus Novus*, vol. v.; and another text, largely interpolated and with a different title, is given by the Jesuit Gretser (*Opera*, XII. ii.).

II. *MANUSCRIPTS.*—Chiefly the collection Doat, now in the Bibliothèque Nationale in Paris, forming 258 vols. in folio; these relate solely to the proceedings of the Inquisition. For critical account of same, see Molinier (Chas.), *L'Inquisition, etc. Étude sur les sources de son Histoire*, Paris, 1881.

III. *MODERN LITERATURE.*—**Catel (G. de)**, *Histoire des Comtes de Toulouse*, Toulouse, 1623; **Benoist (Jean)**, a Dominican, published at Paris in 1691 his *Histoire des Albigeois et des Vaudois*, 2 vols. [a eulogium of persecution, containing, however, important documents]; **Limborch (Phil.)**, *Historia Inquisitionis*, Amsterdam, 1692; **D'Achéry**, *Spicilegium veterum aliquot Scriptorum*, ed. de la Barre, 3 vols., Paris, 1723; **Jas (P.)**, *de Waldensium secta ab Albigensibus bene distinguenda*, Leyden, 1834; **Maitland (S. R.)**, *Facts and Documents illustrative of the History, Doctrine, and Rites of the ancient Albigenses and Waldenses*, London, 1838; **Compayré**, *Études historiques et documents inédits sur l'Albigeois*, etc., 1841; **Hurter (Fried.)**, *Gesch. Pabst Innocenz des Dritten*, 4 vols., Hamburg, 1842; **Schmidt (C.)**, *Histoire et doctrine de la Secte des Cathares ou Albigeois*, 2 vols., Paris, 1849; **Teulet and de Laborde**, *Layettes du Trésor des Chartes*, 3 vols., Paris, 1863–1875; **Devic and Vaissètte**, *Histoire générale de Languedoc*, 1872–1890, 10 vols., Toulouse, 1873 [this edition refers to the corresponding passages in the edition of 1733–1755, and embodies in the *Preuves* a large amount of new material]; the *Annuaire* for 1879 of *Bull. de la Soc. de l'Hist. de France* (pp. 233–285) contains *Le Débat d'Izarn et de Sicart de Figueiras* with Introd., notes, and tr. by Paul Meyer. The 'disputation' (in Provençal) is between an Inquisitor (Izarn) and a heretic bishop (Sicart), and turns successively on nine of the chief Catharist tenets held heretical by the Church; **Hauréau (B.)**, *Bernard Délicieux et L'Inquisition Albigeoise*, Paris, 1877; **Lombard (Alex.)**, *Pauliciens, Bulgares et Bons-Hommes en Orient et en Occident*, Geneva, 1879; **Molinier (Charles)**, *L'Inquisition dans le Midi de la France au xiiie et au xive siècle*, Paris, 1881; **Douais (Mgr.)**, *Les Albigeois, leurs Origines* 2, etc., Paris, 1880, *L'Albigéisme et les Frères Prêcheurs à Narbonne au xiiie siècle*, Paris, 1894, *L'Inquisition: ses Origines, sa Procédure*, Paris, 1906; **Lea (H. C.)**, *History of the Inquisition in the Middle Ages*, 3 vols., London, 1880; **Luchaire (Achille)**, *Innocent III., Rome et Italie*, Paris, 1905; *Innocent III., la Croisade des Albigeois*, Paris, 1905; **Cartellieri (Alex.)**, *Philipp II. August.* vols. i. and ii., Leipzig, 1906; **Guiraud (J.)**, *Cartulaire de Notre-Dame de Prouille*, 2 vols. Paris, 1907 [the first volume contains an *Étude sur l'Albigéisme Languedocien aux xiie & xiiie Siècles* by M. Guiraud, grounded chiefly on the MSS Doat, with criticisms on the original sources, and also notes on the following questions:—The distinctive features of the Albigenses and the Waldenses; the latter, the writer points out, sometimes upheld the teaching of the Church in opposition to the former (pp. xxix–xxx); the universal belief of the Catharists that there was no salvation within the pale of the Jewish Church, not excepting even the Patriarchs (xlix–lvii); their estimate of the Catholic Church as absolutely corrupt and incapable of originating either what was morally good or socially salutary (xlix, lx); the *endura*, as a faintly disguised mode of suicide,—although the writer admits that such a charge finds no support in the indictments of the Inquisition (lxiii); he holds, however, that the Catharists, by their rejection of the sacraments of the Church and their denial of the lawfulness of marriage, of oaths, and of capital punishment, undermined the foundations of social life as conceived in the Middle Ages (lxxx–lxxxiv). In the sixth ch. he defines more precisely the limits and activity of the Catharist Churches both in France and in Germany; in the ninth he represents the whole movement as originating in the ancient faiths of the East, through the media of Gnostic and Manichæistic teaching]; *Acta Aragonensia: Quellen zur Kirchen- u. Kulturgeschichte aus der diplomatischen Korrespondenz Jaymes II.* (1291–1327), ed. **H. Finke** (Berlin, 1907).

J. BASS MULLINGER.

ALCHEMY (Greek and Roman).—At present our knowledge of ancient alchemy is based upon a collection of chemical recipes in a Leyden Papyrus (X, ed. Leemans, *Papyri Musei Lugduno-Bataviensis*, ii., 1885), and a number of manuscripts in several libraries, containing a Byzantine and Mediæval collection of chemical treatises. Chief among these are a Marcianus in Venice, dating from the 10th or 11th cent., and a Parisinus in the Bibliothèque Nationale, written in 1473. The material contained in these manuscripts was edited by Berthelot and Ruelle in the *Collection des Alchimistes Grecs*, Paris, 1888. Unfortunately, this latter edition is without any critical value, not only as regards the constitution of the text, but as regards the writings of the most important among the authors contained in the collection. For, instead of retaining the order, or at least the treatises as they are given in the MS, the editors have attempted an arrangement by ages; and to attain this aim they have cut up the collection, so that it is with the greatest difficulty that one can obtain an idea of the treatises as they were given in the original collection. The difficulty is increased by the fact that even our best manuscript, the Marcianus, is in reality a second edition, with omissions and additions, of an earlier collection, perhaps of the 9th cent., while the younger codices contain much material of very doubtful character. A final judgment must therefore be postponed until some scholar has re-edited the *Corpus Chemicorum* in a manner to conform to modern demands. (On this question compare W. Meyer, *Verzeichnis der Handschriften im preussischen Staate*, i. 1, 5, 1893).

The notices of the ancients themselves in regard to the history of alchemy are scarce. The alleged mentions of the 'science' in the poet Manilius (under Tiberius), iv. 243 ff., and in Pliny's *HN* xxxiii. 79, referring to an attempt of Caligula to make gold, are more than doubtful. The first authentic testimony points to the time of Diocletian. According to Suidas (Διοκλητιανός and Χημεία), the emperor ordered all Egyptian books on the making of gold and silver to be burnt. We are thus taken back to the beginning of the 3rd cent. of our era, a period which teemed with secret, magical, and astrological writings. To the same time points a notice of the Byzantine historian Georgios Synkellos (8–9 cent.), that Julius Africanus mentioned the science of chemistry (676, 10, ed. Bonn). During the 4th cent. the possibility of alchemy was denied by Themistius (*Or.* iv. 214, ed. Petau), and Æneas of Gaza (5th cent.) is undoubtedly well acquainted with its existence. None of these authors, however, uses the modern name. This was formerly believed to be secured by a passage in the astrologer and Christian writer Firmicus Maternus (5th cent.), but the passage is a late interpolation (cf. the edition by Kroll-Skutsch, Leipzig, 1898).

The notice in Suidas points to Egypt as the original home of alchemy. To the same country the legendary history of the pseudo-science also points. The ancient alchemists knew a great many stories about the mystic origin of their art. It was said to have been taught by the fallen angels, by Isis, by Miriam the sister of Moses (the last trace of that legend has been preserved in the 'bain-marie' of modern chemistry), and so forth. But even their best tradition ascribed the invention of the 'holy mystery' to the philosopher Democritus of Greece. This tradition takes us at once to Alexandria, where a luxuriant growth of forgeries under the name of the atomistic philosopher had sprung up, largely ascribed to a certain Bolos of Mendes, living about the beginning of our era. (The literature in Berthelot, *Hist. de l'alchimie grecque*, Paris, 1885; cf. Pauly-Wissowa, i. *s.v.* 'Alchemie'). To Egypt the very name also points (Hoffmann, *Hdwtb. der Chemie*, ii. 516 ff., and Wissowa, *l.c.*).

The extant works on alchemy fall into two classes, roughly represented by the Leyden Papyrus and by the Collection. The former class is purely technical, not yet infected by mystical ideas, and designed for practical purposes. The second class starts likewise from practical work, but from the outset is indissolubly interwoven with mystical thoughts. As time went on without bringing the alchemists any nearer to the solution of the eagerly sought mystery, speculations and fantastic hallucinations overlay the practical nucleus in ever increasing masses, until towards the end of the Middle Ages the writings of the adepts had become one vast farrago of allegories, each one in its turn calling forth a still more allegorical commentary, until the 18th cent. brought about a revolution and a return to practical work, and began the modern science of chemistry.

We shall now rapidly pass in review the extant works. The Leyden Papyrus belongs to a group of papyri found together in Egypt in the early part of the 19th cent. and purchased by the Leyden Museum. Among these, three stand out prominent as a related group. They are known by the letters X (our papyrus), V, and W. The last two have of late come into greater prominence by the excellent treatment to which they have been subjected by Albrecht Dieterich ('Papyrus Magica V' in *Jahrb. f. Philologie*, Suppl. xvi.; *Abraxas, Studien zur Religionsgesch. des späteren Altertums*, 1891). They are our most valuable source for studying the syncretistic religion of later antiquity as reflected in the mind of the vulgar. With these our X must be grouped, as it was found with them. The great mass of its recipes, it is true, contain nothing but prescriptions for the apprentices of some cheating gold- and silver-smith. But these prescriptions are interspersed with others referring to superstition. Small wonder, for the art of the metal-worker from the earliest times was considered to be specially connected with magic; witness the legends of the miraculous creations of Hephæstus, of his Telchines and Daktyloi (see on these Roscher's *Lex. der gr. u. röm. Mythologie, s.v.*), and the northern legends of the smith Wieland. Traces of this belief have lasted into our own times. Even to-day the village blacksmith is usually 'the wise man,' if not actually the wizard, of his village.

Alchemy in the proper sense of the word cannot be said to be found in X. But a large number of its recipes have for their end to produce an alloy of baser metals which cannot be distinguished from the genuine article, so much so that even a member of the guild shall not be able to detect the fraud. But two of its prescriptions use a 'never-ending material' and a special kind of *asemon*. This *asemon*, originally the Egyptian name (*asem*) of an alloy of gold and silver, perhaps the so-called *elektron*, is here conceived as a material which can give the *qualities* of the precious metals to the base ones. It acts, so to speak, as a leaven, changing the base foundation into gold as leaven changes flour into bread; in other words, we are face to face with a real *chemical* action.

At this point the second group of chemical literature sets in. Its most important, nay fundamental, treatise indeed, that of 'Democritus,' bears in its recipes the closest resemblance to the prescriptions of the papyrus (cf. Berthelot's analysis, both in the *Histoire* and in the Introduction to the *Collection*). In close analogy to the papyrus, this treatise also included originally not only the science of commutation of metals, but likewise that of imitating precious stones, and of dyeing cloth. The mystic element, however, is already in full force. Not only is the technical part proper introduced by a fabulous tale, giving the miraculous history of the alleged recovery of the treatise from a secret vault, but it repeats again and again, in the fashion of a refrain, the mystic saying: 'Nature rejoices in nature, nature conquers nature, nature rules over nature'—a saying to which we shall return later on. Other pieces, too, in the *Collection*, according to Berthelot's expert analysis, are more or less closely related to the papyrus, but as some of them do not occur in the oldest MS, we shall leave them undiscussed. One step forward, it is true, has been taken by the author of the pseudo-Democritean work; he is no longer conscious of the fraudulent character of his practices, but honestly believes in the possibility of transmutation.

We have called the above work fundamental. And so, indeed, it must be called, in view of the fact that after its existence nothing new was written, and that all successors either had no higher ambition than to comment upon it, or started from it as their basis. Here belong the works of Synesius (not the Cyrenæan bishop of this name, although a contemporary of his), of Olympiodorus (of doubtful age, but perhaps living under Justinian), and of Zosimus (the most important of them all, though the most elusive). The question of the latter's personality, as well as of his time, is so perplexing because for his writings more than for anything else the editorial method of the French Collection has been confusing. In the several hundred quarto pages filled by pieces ascribed to him, many parallel and even contradictory pieces from old as well as from new codices are jumbled together. This much is sure, however, and borne out by the Index of the Marcianus, that of all the commentators he was the most important. Certain indications in his writings allow us to conjecture that he lived after the philosopher Porphyrius, and before Olympiodorus. He also seems to allude to Mani, the founder of Manichæism. We shall therefore not err very much one way or the other, if we assign him to the early years of the 4th cent. of our era. Suidas (*s.v.*) tells us that he came from Panopolis in Egypt, and lived in Alexandria.

The later Greek alchemists can find only a passing mention in this article. Such are Stephanos, contemporary of the emperor Heraclianus, and the alchemistic poets, four in number, who in Byzantine trimeters revamp the scanty ideas of Stephanos. Numerous smaller treatises, preserved in MSS, cannot even be mentioned here. The question of their value is indissolubly bound up with that of the value of our tradition.

We shall now be able to trace in a very few words the development of alchemy. Starting from the purely practical basis of fraudulent craftsmanship, in Egypt, famed from olden times for her knowledge of metalwork and crude chemical knowledge (cf. the Egyptian porcelains and glasses), it found its further development in that home of all mystic humbug, Alexandria. Here it fell under the influence of that mixture of religions, of mysticism, and of philosophy which we call either Syncretism or Gnosis, and pursuing that kind of knowledge found its 'Bible' in the forged treatise ascribed to Democritus. Also in the manner of that kind of literature, counter-claim met claim; hence the various traditions as to the real inventors of alchemy. Conforming partly in ideas and in expressions to Christianity, it escaped the fate of other superstitions,—the condemnation of the Church,—was carried to Constantinople, and there vegetated in peace in the dust of libraries. On the other hand, through Syrian translations it found its way to the Muslims, was by them carried to the West, and so reached Europe, where it was received with credulous avidity, and flourished until superseded by truly scientific methods, thus finally flowing into the broad stream of true and modern chemistry.

It remains now to speak of the relations between alchemy and philosophy and religion. The researches of Usener (*Religionsgeschichtl. Untersuchungen*, Bonn, 1889–1897), of Dieterich (*l.c.*), and of Schmekel (*Untersuchungen zur Geschichte der Mittlern Stoa*) have shown how enormous was the influence of the Stoic school on the development of popular beliefs in the last cent. B.C. and the 1st cent. A.D. In regard to alchemy, however, the proof had been furnished as early as 1856 by Prantl (*Deutsche Vierteljahrsschrift*, 1856) in an article which still contains the best exposition of the philosophical elements in ancient alchemy. The Stoics, in their endeavour to prove that the whole cosmos was permeated by the Divine, and that all phenomena of life were only emanations of it, could not afford to reject any claim to the supernatural raised by these pseudo-sciences, and so they became the ardent defenders of magic, alchemy, and astrology (for the latter see Bouché-Leclercq, *Hist. de l'Astrologie grecque*). *Vice versa* these sciences gratefully adopted the apparent aid to be got from the Stoic arsenal of proofs. When the Democritean theory constantly harps on the refrain: 'Nature overcomes nature, nature rejoices in nature, nature rules over nature,' the alchemists simply followed Stoic precedent. Nay, this very tenet is considerably older than the extant works on gold-making. It is ascribed to the mythical Egyptian king Nechepsos, the patron saint of astrology, whose forged works found their entrance into the world of letters about the beginning of our era. The maxim, too, upon which the Leyden Papyrus bases its prescriptions, that a little leaven leavens a whole loaf, belongs here. When later, in the 2nd and 3rd cents. of our era, that jumble of all philosophies, from the Ionians to Neo-Platonism, which we call Hermetic philosophy, gained ascendency, it too was eagerly adopted by the alchemists. Hermes now becomes the great protagonist and inventor of the science. Nor were the alchemists averse to borrowing from other pseudo-sciences. They were deeply indebted to Astrology, again under the influence of Stoic ideas. Not only do some treatises take account of favourable planetary aspects, but the theory that the planets exercise a profound sympathetic influence over the component parts of the universe found its expression in the small but significant fact that the metals are written in the manuscripts by a sort of planetary notation: for gold they wrote the sign of the sun, for silver that of the moon, and for quicksilver that of Hermes, whence the English name 'mercury.' No less strong is the influence of that syncretism which we are accustomed to call Gnosis. The greatest of all commentators, Zosimus, explains the title of his last chapter, *Omega*, by telling us that it belongs to the sphere of Kronos, but only *κατὰ ἔνσωμον φράσιν*, while the *ἀσώματος φράσις* is known only to the great and hidden Nikotheos. Not only the name itself is Gnostic, but still more so the distinctions between a corporeal and an incorporeal expression; for this distinction between Jesus in the body and without a visible body forms the very foundation of Gnostic speculations.

This leads us into the sphere of religion. Now we must not expect to find in the alchemists any new information about the religious speculations of their time. These men, locked up as they were in their narrow laboratories, were simply receptive, and only reflected what was saturating the air around them. In this sense only may we go to the alchemists as a source of religious information. And here we find what we should expect. All religions have been jumbled into a great chaotic mass. Everything is 'One and All.' But nevertheless, individual deities, like Hermes, Kronos, Aphrodite, play their part. Nor were the alchemists averse to calling in the help of Judaism, and of Christianity as it appeared to them. Zosimus embodied in his commentary a piece containing highly interesting speculations about Adam. But, on the whole, we may repeat what Usener says about the speculations of the Gnosis: like a sultry breath of air carrying to us wondrous scents from an unapproachable garden, such is the impression of the Gnostic (and alchemistic) teachings.

LITERATURE.—Kopp, *Beiträge zur Gesch. der Chemie*, 1869; Leemans, *Papyri Græci Musei Lugduno-Batavensis*, ii. 1885; Dieterich, 'Papyrus Magica V,' *Jahrb. f. Philologie*, Suppl. xvi., and *Abraxas*, 1891; Berthelot, *Origines de l'Alchimie*, 1885, *Journal des Savants*, 1884, 1893; Berthelot and Ruelle, *Les Alchimistes Grecs*, 1888 (partly reprinted, with independent pagination, in Berthelot, *La Chimie au moyen âge*); Hoffmann in Ladenburg, *Hdwtb. der Chemie*, ii. under 'Chemie'; Tannery, *Revue des Études Grecques*, iii.; Jahn, *Revue de Philologie*, xv.; Bouché-Leclercq, *Hist. de l'Astrologie Grecque*; Schaefer, *Die Alchemie*, 1887; Pauly-Wissowa, i. *s.v.* 'Alchemie.'

E. RIESS.

ALCHEMY (Muhammadan). — **I. Authors.** — The most ancient Arabic author who wrote about alchemy was a royal personage — Ḫālid, son of Yazīd, son of Mu'āwīya—who died A.H. 85 (A.D. 704). There are three letters on alchemy ascribed to him; his master is said to have been a Syrian monk, Morienus or Marianus, and to have dedicated a treatise on alchemy to him: *Liber de compositione Alchemiæ, quem edidit Morienus Romanus Calid regi Ægyptorum*, tr. in 1182 by Robert Castrensis (cf. Leclerc, i. 64). Compositions ascribed to Ḫālid and translated into Latin are published in the *Theatrum Chemicum* and in the *Bibliotheca Chemica*; the Arabic text of these is not extant.

The historian Ibn Ḫaldūn, in his *Prolegomena* (iii. 207 in de Slane's Fr. translation), questioned the authenticity of the alchemical works of Ḫālid the Umayyad, on the ground that this prince was a Bedawī Arab who lived before the time of the scientific activity of the Arabs, and that therefore he could not have been acquainted with such a complicated science as alchemy. However, the tradition is very exact, both in the *Book of Songs* (*Kitāb al-Aghānī*, xvi. 88–98), and in Mas'ūdī (*Les Prairies d'or*, ed. and tr. into Fr. by Barbier de Meynard, viii. 176). This historian says that alchemists acknowledge Ḫālid, son of Yazīd the Umayyad, as one of their elder brothers.

The second name to be mentioned is that of Geber. This famous person, who became illustrious and legendary in the Christian Middle Ages, is known under the Arab name of Abū Mūsā Jābir, son of Ḥaiyān; his tribal name is 'the Azdite'; from the place of his birth he is named 'of Ṭūs' or 'of Ṭarṭūs'; he is sometimes called al-Ḥarrānī, which agrees with the tradition connecting him with the Sabæans of Ḥarrān. The surname 'al-Umawī, the Umayyad,' which is sometimes given him, represents a tradition according to which he had Ḫālid, son of Yazīd, as master; but other accounts describe him as a pupil of Ja'far aṣ-Ṣādiq, who is also credited with a profound knowledge of occult sciences, and to whom bibliographers ascribe works on science and divination (cf. Hajjī Ḫalfa, v. 277, 280; Ibn Ḫallihān, No. 130). Lastly, there is occasionally coupled with the name of Geber the epithet 'Ṣūfī'; this is explained by the fact that Geber, having been converted from Sabæism to Islām, is said to have exhibited great zeal for the Musalmān faith; the title must have been added, however, at a later period.

We should clearly pay no heed to a view mentioned in the *Fihrist* (p. 354 ff.), according to which

Geber is a mythical personage. This famous alchemist did certainly exist; but very little is known about his life. A reliable tradition represents him as usually residing at Kūfa; he is sometimes connected with the Barmecides (*Fihrist* and Hajjī Ḥalfa, iii. p. 588). He flourished about the year A.H. 160 (A.D. 776). A whole series of works is attributed to him; their titles are generally symbolical, and their number exceeds two hundred. There are twenty-two Arabic works placed under his name in our libraries. Berthelot and Houdas have published five of these treatises under the titles of: *Book of Royalty; Small Book of Balances; Book of Mercy*, a work revised by a pupil; extracts from the *Book of Concentration*; and *Book of Oriental Mercury*. The Latin treatises ascribed to Geber do not correspond to the Arabic works; besides, they exhibit a more advanced stage of chemical science. Some of these are: *Geberi regis Arabum summa perfectionis ministerii*, Gedani (Dantzig), 1682; *Geberi philosophi de alchemia libri iii.*, Nuremberg, 1545 (cf. Steinschneider, *ZDMG* xiii. 649). The Latin treatise, entitled *Book of the Seventy* of Jo (John), is the only one which seems to have preserved some fragments of Geber or his pupils, judging from the resemblance between the titles of its chapters and those of a work of the same name which the *Fihrist* mentions and ascribes to Geber (Latin MS 7156, Paris; cf. Berthelot, *La Chimie au moyen âge*, i. 323).

There were several alchemists in the 3rd cent. A.H.; the two most famous are the ascetic Dhū-n-Nūn al-Miṣrī of Ikhmīm (d. 245=A.D. 859) and Ibn al-Waḥshīya, the imaginative author of the *Nabatæan Agriculture*, who wrote during the second half of that century. We possess three works of Dhū-n-Nūn on alchemy—in poetry, dialogue, and miscellany (cf. R. A. Nicholson in *JRAS*, 1906, p. 311 ff.). We have various works of Ibn al-Waḥshīya, especially a *Treasury of Wisdom* or *Secrets* (*Kanz al-ḥikma* or *Kanz al-asrār*), which is a system of alchemy. We may add to these names that of Muḥammad, son of Umail (rather than Amyal) at-Tamīmī, who composed, among other things, an essay on ancient Egyptian paintings; and that of Uthmān, son of Suwaid al-Ikhmīmi, who disputed with Ibn al-Waḥshīya.

In the 4th cent. (10th A.D.) appears the medical philosopher 'Razes,' Abū Bakr Muḥammad, son of Zakarīya ar-Rāzī. He was an enthusiastic student of alchemy, and almost a martyr to this science. As he had dedicated his famous book on medicine, *al-Manṣūri*, to the Sāmānid prince Abū Ṣāliḥ Manṣūr, son of Isḥāḳ, he afterwards also presented him with his plea, 'The Establishment of Alchemy' (*Kitāb ithbāt al-kīmīya*). The prince asked him to verify some of his experiments, and, finding him unable to do so, he struck him across the face with a whip, and blinded him. He died in A.H. 311 or 320. We may mention his *Kitāb al-asrār*, 'Book of Secrets,' on alchemy; a *Preparatio Salis Aromatici*, placed under his name, is published in the *Theatrum Chemicum*, iii. No. 64.

To the same century belongs another important writer, Maslama al-Majrīṭī, *i.e.* of Madrid. This learned encyclopædist (d. 395 or 398=A.D. 1004 or 1007), after travelling in the East, brought thence to his native country a collection of the famous works of the 'Brethren of Purity,' of which he probably made a new recension. Being skilled in alchemy, he wrote specially on this subject a *Kanz al-faḍā'il*, 'Treasury of Accomplishments,' dated 348.

We may mention in passing another prince, who was reputed to be an alchemist, the celebrated Fāṭimid Ḥalīfa al-Manṣūr al-Ḥākim (d. 411=A.D. 1020), the founder of the religion of the Druzes. The only famous names that we find after him are those of Ghazzālī the great philosopher, Ṭughrā'ī, and Jildakī. Ghazzālī (451–505=A.D. 1111) believed in alchemy, and wrote some articles on the subject; one of them is extant at Berlin, *Maqāla al-fauz*, 'Lecture on Preservation.' Ṭughrā'ī (al-Ḥasān, son of 'Alī), who died about 515, wazīr of the Seleucid Sultan Mas'ūd at Mosul, became famous as an alchemist, wrote on alchemy, *Jāmi' al-asrār*, 'Compendium of Secrets,' an article on the philosopher's stone, and a commentary on Geber's *Book of Mercy*. Jildakī ('Ali, son of Aidamur, son of 'Alī), who died in 743=A.D. 1342), is the author of several works on alchemy and the search for 'the elixir' (cf. on this author S. de Sacy, *Notices et extraits*, iv. 108; Leclerc, ii. 280).

Alchemical studies continued in Islām during the time of the literary decline and down to the present day. In the 10th cent. A.H. (16th A.D.) authors like Muṣliḥ ad-Dīn Bostān Efendi of Aidin, or 'Alī Beg of Iznīq, are found writing 'Alchemies,' and in the 11th cent. the physician Maulā Ṣāliḥ, son of Naṣrallāh al-Ḥalabī, adapted Paracelsus. It is said that there are still alchemists in Morocco and at Mecca.

2. Doctrine.—The doctrine of alchemy appears among the Arabs under very philosophical aspects; it implies certain ideas on the nature of physical matter which are derived from general philosophy. This connexion with philosophy is so very close, that we come upon treatises beginning with real philosophical introductions; *e.g.* the 'Treatise on Concentration' goes so far as to speak expressly of the doctrine of the 'categories,' which it ascribes to Pythagoras, saying that there are ten things which form the universe: essence and its nine accidents.

It is not difficult to see with what philosophical school the alchemists are, as a rule, connected. It is with the great school of Neo-Platonic origin, which developed in the Musalmān world when the Greek sciences were being studied there, and attained its height about the 10th cent. of the Christian era (4th A.H.). The alchemists are connected more especially with the branches of this school which professed the so-called 'illuminative' doctrines. In these sects a disposition to syncretism prevailed: according to them, truth was possessed in the different nations by wise men who expressed it in different ways, and who are at one time mythical personages, at another well-known philosophers of very different opinions. The same inclination towards syncretism is shown in the alchemical writings. The alchemistic authors do not know whether they owe their art to Egypt rather than Persia, or to India rather than China. The ancestors whom they claim are at one time quite mythical, *e.g.* Hermes and Agathodæmon; at another historical or semi-historical, *e.g.* Qārūn, the Korah of the Bible, brother-in-law of Moses, whose treasures are mentioned in the Qur'ān (xxviii. 76, 79, xxix. 38, xl. 25); or, again, queen Cleopatra, the emperor Heraclius, or Bilqīs, the queen of Sheba. To these soothsayers and kings the alchemists add the philosophers and scholars of classical antiquity, especially Pythagoras, Plato, Aristotle, Democritus, Dioscorides, and Galen. This grouping would not give any very clear information, if we did not know from the history of philosophy that the list is framed according to the usage of the Alexandrians and the Sabæans, and that therefore it was in these two groups of scholars that the Muslims found their masters. As regards the Sabæans, we have already remarked that Geber probably belonged to their sect; they carried the practice of syncretism to a great length; they collected and fixed a large number of legends of various origins. The addition of the Talmudic legends of Qārūn and of Bilqīs, of the Persian names of Jāmāsp and of

Maghis the sage, to the Egyptian legends of Hermes and Agathodæmon, must have been their work. More especially Alexandrian are the legends, of frequent occurrence in the alchemical writings, which refer to the Pyramids and the great ruins of Egypt, and represent these monuments as ancient laboratories, or at least as having been used as deposits for the secrets of the sciences. The tradition which makes Cleopatra a scientist is undoubtedly Alexandrian, as is also the one which represents another woman, Mary the Copt, as lecturing on alchemy in the presence of various learned men (cf. Kopp, *Beiträge*, i. p. 402; Steinschneider, *Mathem.* § 140; Berthelot, *La Chimie au moyen âge*, iii. *passim*). One of the Arabic treatises published by Berthelot and Houdas bears the name of an Egyptian sage Ostanes.

Another tendency which appears from time to time in the alchemical writings certainly arises from Neo-Platonism, viz. the tendency to mysticism. It makes itself evident in two ways: (1) by founding the art of alchemy on a revelation which was received by the ancient prophets, *e.g.* by Hermes or by Qārūn; or (2) by making moral conditions intervene in the production of the great work: God co-operates in the undertaking, and the alchemist must prepare himself for this Divine co-operation by purity of heart. Even in the cases in which this condition is not formally laid down, the alchemistic writings bear a strongly religious stamp.

It is a very wide-spread custom among writers on occult subjects to connect the metals with the planets. Gold is held to correspond with the sun, silver with the moon; the other metals, mercury, iron, tin, lead, correspond respectively to Mercury, Mars, Jupiter, and Saturn. This connexion was made long ago, but the Muslims ascribe it more especially to the Sabæans; and this provides a new proof of the important part which that sect took in the transmission of ancient ideas, Greek as well as Jewish and Chaldæan.

The part played by Syrian scholars in this work of preserving and handing down scientific knowledge was greater even than that of the Sabæans; and it is better known. It was through Syrian works that the Muslims became acquainted with the chief Greek alchemists, especially Zosimus (cf. Berthelot, *La Chimie au moyen âge*, ii.).

Now, what exactly is the doctrine, or rather the postulate, on which alchemy is based? This postulate, in its essential elements, is very simple. It holds that metals differ from each other in degree, but not in nature, and that any one of the baser metals, like lead or copper, may be transmuted into a more perfect metal like silver or gold. This postulate is connected with or implies a curious idea frequently expressed by alchemists, that of the 'life' of the mineral. The metal or the mineral is really regarded as a living being, which is engendered and develops in the womb of the earth, where it is subjected to various conditions, such as help or hinder its perfection. This theory is expressed, *e.g.*, in the treatise of the 'Brethren of Purity' devoted to mineralogy. Dieterici, the editor of that treatise, remarks that it is conceived on Aristotelian, one might say rather, Neo-Platonic principles, and that it is inserted in a series of treatises based on those of Aristotle, although we do not know any work on minerals by that philosopher.

In that treatise the doctrine is presented thus. From the elements which lie like potentialities in the womb of the earth, there are first of all formed, as energies, mercury and sulphur; from those two there are afterwards formed, as entelechies, metals which are good or bad, noble or base, according to circumstances. It is only in consequence of certain injuries undergone that the material does not become silver or gold instead of lead or tin. Alchemy endeavours to repair these injuries (Dieterici, *Die Abhandlungen der Ikhwān es-Safā*, Leipzig, 1886, Vorwort, p. 13, and text, p. 137). The same idea is expressed in the *Cosmography* of Qazwīnī (ed. Wüstenfeld, i. p. 207), and in this work also it is ascribed to Aristotle; the metals in their mines undergo certain injuries which cause their imperfections: *e.g.* lead is a kind of silver which has three defects—an unpleasant odour, softness, and a disagreeable sound. In this book also, means of getting rid of these defects are suggested.

In the works of Geber published by Berthelot, and especially in the *Book of Mercy*, whose authenticity appears most certain, this notion of the life of metals is consistently expounded; a regular anthropomorphic theory is applied to mineralogy; not only the idea of 'generation' applies to metal, but also the ideas of 'marriage, pregnancy, and education'; all these conditions, it is said, are necessarily the same as in the case of a human being. This doctrine is expressed with equal force in the treatise by al-Ḥabīb, published in the same collection and apparently quite ancient. According to these various alchemists, the formation and the life of metals require time, like our own; to bring the metal in the womb of the earth to its perfect state, which is the state of gold, nature takes a very long time, more than a thousand years, according to the most wide-spread alchemistic tradition; the work of alchemy is to imitate nature, and at the same time to discover more rapid means than hers for the development of the metal.

The anthropomorphic theory of alchemists has one more aspect; it applies to chemical bodies the ideas of life and death, of body and soul, of matter and mind. In this sense the idea of occult forces is very interesting; these subtle, intangible, invisible forces are compared to 'spiritual forces'; the force of the magnet, which attracts iron through other materials, and that of poison, which permeates the organism, are called 'spiritual forces' (Berthelot, *Geber: 'Traité de la miséricorde,'* p. 175). In bodies there are some substances earthly and gross, and others pure and light; the former are called 'dead,' the latter 'living'; these notions of death and life are also employed in a relative way: *e.g.* sulphur and arsenic are living when they are mixed with substances inferior to them, such as talc; but they appear earthly and dead when they are united with live mercury (*ib.* p. 178). In every body, and *a fortiori* in every combination, it may be supposed that there is a material part and a spiritual part, a soul and a body. The soul is infused into the body; its nature is superior to that of the body, refines it, and gives it a kind of immateriality. A common task for chemists consists in giving a soul to each body, by first purifying souls and bodies, and then infusing into each body the soul which suits it. Geber, still following the idea that there were certain injuries caused by nature, even speaks of 'restoring' to the body the soul which 'has gone out of it'; this is another aspect of a chemical operation; thus, mercury is the soul which suits gold and the other metals. The spirit also is capable of a sort of education; not only must it be fit to unite forcibly with its body, and for that reason be pure, but it must also be firm, it must resist fire, and to this end must, as far as possible, partake of the nature of fire.

In practice, the aim of the alchemist's efforts is to find the substance, a living substance, 'elixir' or spirit, which, when combined with the body of the imperfect metal, previously prepared and purified, will change it into perfect metal. Alchemists use various means, and look in various places to find this substance; they do not regard it as exclusively mineral; they even make use of organic bodies in its preparation; they discuss whether it is 'excrement, blood, hair, or egg'; as a rule, they describe it as a stone; it is 'the Philosopher's stone, the very precious stone.' This stone is afterwards ground down, and during the grinding it is sprinkled with water mixed with drugs and simples. The liquid obtained in this way is the 'elixir.'

3. Discussions of the doctrine. — During the course of Arabic literary history, various persons assumed an attitude of opposition to the alchemical doctrine. This opposition led to discussions. It must, however, be stated that the objections raised were not directed against the study of bodies and their properties, but only against the assumption peculiar to alchemists, concerning the possibility of the transmutation of metals. In the 3rd cent. A.H. the philosopher al-Kindī declared himself against the alchemists. He wrote a treatise on 'the error of those who think that gold and silver can be obtained otherwise than in their mines,' and another on 'the deceits of alchemists.' A pupil of al-Kindī, Dubais, took up the cause of the alchemists, however, and wrote two treatises on their science, cited in the *Fihrist*. Razes composed a 'refutation' of the objections of al-Kindī. Fārābī believed in alchemy, but Avicenna (Ibn Sīnā), was opposed to it (see AVICENNA). Ṭughrā'ī afterwards defended alchemy against Avicenna.

Avicenna's chief objection consisted in saying that the seven metals differ in their specific qualities, each of them forming a definite species with real characteristics; Fārābī believed, on the contrary, like the alchemists, that all metals were of the same species, and he considered their qualities merely as accidents. Ṭughrā'ī, bringing in the Divine power, observes, in addition, that it is not a question of producing a specific difference in the metal treated, but of making it fit to receive this difference from its Creator. Avicenna also objects, like al-Kindī, that it is incredible that there can be a shorter way of bringing metals to their perfect state than that which is followed by nature.

The other objections brought forward against alchemy are: that no one has ever been pointed out with certainty as having achieved the great work; that it is especially poor people who study alchemy; that alchemists circulate counterfeit gold, and in that way wrong the public, and are liable to punishment by law. This latter accusation refers to the cases in which alchemists succeeded in giving to metal what they called a dye, *i.e.* in covering it with a layer which had the appearance and some of the properties of gold. The alchemists replied, weakly enough, it is true, to these objections, by saying that this 'dye' was fast, and would last several centuries.

The cosmographer Dimishqī (ed. Fraehn, p. 97) and the historian Ibn Ḥaldūn (*Prolegomena*, de Slane's Fr. tr. iii. 207 ff.), opponents of alchemy, speak in an interesting way about alchemists, and relate the objections which were raised against them.

4. Special contribution of Muslims to alchemy. —It is very difficult to determine exactly the share due to Muslims in the progress of chemical discoveries. It was, apparently, very slender. The most ancient Arabic works are adaptations of, or commentaries on, Greek works; that of Crates is typical. The discoveries which Western tradition has ascribed to Geber, those of *aqua regalis*, of sulphuric acid, nitric acid, and nitrate of silver, are not found in the Arabic works placed under this alchemist's name, but only in some Latin pamphlets at the end of the 13th cent.; it seems, therefore, that the admiration affected by the Western peoples for Muslim alchemists is due not so much to their real worth, as to the general custom of looking to the East for masters, especially of the occult sciences.

It is probable, however, that Muslims made progress in chemistry as applied to medicine, in dyeing, and in the art of enamelling. Al-Kindī, besides others, wrote about colouring matters, glass-making, the processes of removing stains from cloth, and other similar subjects. These particular industries have not yet been studied minutely enough.

Every one knows that our languages are indebted to Arabic chemistry for certain words, which are in some cases Arabic words, in others Greek words preceded by the Arabic article; *e.g. alchemy, alembic, aludel, alcohol, elixir*. The word *alchemy* has been derived from χυμεία, 'mixture.' Wiedemann has shown that this word originally denoted the very substance which has the property of accomplishing transmutation, the elixir, and not the sum of the ways which help to find it (Wiedemann, *Beiträge*, ii. p. 351; J. Gildemeister, *ZDMG*, 1876). The *koḥl*, which has given its name to alcohol, was originally a very fine powder; it is the black powder which Oriental ladies use for blackening round their eyes. The use of the word was generalized and extended to various powders and to liquids. *Elixir* is said to be derived from Greek ξήριον, 'dry powder' (J. Gildemeister, *l.c.*); it is possible, however, from the point of view of the grammatical form, that it is an Arabic word and belongs to the root *kasara*, 'to grind,' *al-iksīr* being 'the thing ground,' 'the powder.'

LITERATURE. — Berthelot, *La Chimie au moyen âge*, 1885, pt. i., *Essai sur la transmission de la science antique au moyen âge*, Paris, 1893, pt. iii. with the collaboration of O. Houdas, *L'Alchimie arabe*, 1893; Eilhard Wiedemann, *Beiträge zur Gesch. der Naturwissenschaften*, i.–iv., Erlangen, 1904–1905. On the Arabic authors see Brockelmann, *Gesch. der arab. Litteratur*, 2 vols., Weimar and Berlin, 1897–1902. Latin works on alchemy given as translations from Arabic are found in the following collections: *Theatrum Chemicum*, 6 vols., Strassburg, 1659–61; *Bibliotheca Chemica*, Geneva, 1702; *Artis auriferæ quam chemiam vocant duo vol.*, Bâle, 1572; *Artis chemicæ principes*, Bâle, 1572. A famous work, entitled *Turba philosophorum*, is found in two different versions in the collection *Artis auriferæ*; an 'Alchemy' ascribed to Avicenna, *Liber Abuali Abincinæ de anima in arte Alchimiæ*, is found in the *Artis chemicæ principes*. On several of these works and on mineralogy, cf. F. de Mély, *Les Lapidaires de l'antiquité et du moyen âge*, pt. iii. No. 1, Introduction, Paris, 1902.

BON. CARRA DE VAUX.

ALCHEMY (European).—The study of alchemy in Europe is traceable to the schools of Spain. J. Ferguson, in his notes to the 'Catalogue of the Alchemical, Chemical, and Pharmaceutical books of James Young of Kelly and Durris,' notes which form the latest storehouse of information on the history of alchemy in Europe, says, under the head of Michael Scott: 'It was in Spain, to which it had been brought by the Arabs, that the art first found place in Europe' (*Bibliotheca Chemica*, Glasgow, 1906).

The Khalifate of Cordova reached its highest splendour under the rule of Abderrahman III. (A.D. 912–961) and Al-Ḥakam II. (961–976). The libraries of the rulers, the nobles, and persons of importance, numbering in some cases 400,000 volumes, attracted students from all parts of Europe (Rafael Altamira of Crevea, *Historia de España*, i. 275).

1. Among the first to profit by this revival of learning was **Gerbert**, afterwards Pope Sylvester II. (999–1003). While still a student in the Abbey of Arvillac in Auvergne, he attracted the attention of Borel, Count of Barcelona. He returned with him to Spain, and is said to have visited Cordova during the reign of Al-Ḥakam II. It was in the schools of Spain that he studied the sciences of arithmetic, geometry, astrology, and chemistry, which at a later date brought him into disrepute as a wizard. During the Papacy of John XIII. (965–973) he visited Rome in the company of Count Borel and Hatto, Bishop of Vich. He then made the acquaintance of the Emperor Otho I., and was recommended by him to the notice of Adalbero, Archbishop of Rheims. By Otho II. (973–983) he was appointed Abbot of Bobbio. Driven from Bobbio by the neighbouring nobles, he returned to Rheims, where he taught the 'whole range of human science.' On the degradation of Arnulf, he was made Archbishop of Rheims in 991. Forced to resign the see in 996, he took refuge at the Court of Otho III. (983–1002), and by his influence in 998 he became Archbishop of Ravenna. In the following year he succeeded to the Papacy. Thus by the close of the 10th cent. the learning of Spain was introduced into France and Italy and the Imperial Court (Milman, *Lat. Chr.* iii. pp. 331–345).

2. The influence of Gerbert did not end with his death. His pupil, **Fulbert of Chartres** (1007–1028), carried on his work. Adelmannus, Bishop of Brescia, in a letter to Berengarius, speaks of their joint studies 'in Academia Carnotensi, sub nostro illo venerabili Socrate, nempe Fulberto' (Bar. *Ann. Eccl.* 1004, 6). The Schools of Berengarius in Tours and Angers to some extent carried on the same work. Behind the theological controversy of the early Scholasticism of the 11th cent., the tradition of the wide learning of Gerbert may be traced as one cause of the recognition of the philosophical studies of Spain in the 12th cent. (Neander, *Gesch. der Chr. Rel. u. Kirche*, iv. 283).

3. The fall of the Khalīfate of Cordova in 1031 did not check the progress of learning in Spain. The kings of Seville, Cordova, Malaga, Granada, Almeria, Denia, Zaragoza, Toledo, and Badajos vied with one another in the patronage they gave to philosophy and science. The studies of the former period were continued, and special attention was given to the natural sciences—medicine, chemistry, botany, and astronomy. Ibn al-Baiṭar of Malaga made a large collection of minerals and plants, and under the Muwaḥḥid Khalīf Ya'qūb al-Manṣūr (1196) the Giralda of Seville became the chief observatory in Europe. In philosophy, Averroës of Cordova (1126–1198) won a European reputation as the commentator of Aristotle and Plato.

4. The conquest of Toledo by Alfonso VI. of Castile in 1085 was another step in the propagation of the Arabic learning in Europe. A school of translators was founded at Toledo which reached the highest point of its fame in the reign of Alfonso VII. (1130–1150). Among those who were attracted to Spain were Hermann of Dalmatia and Hermann of Germany, Gerard of Cremona, the Englishmen Daniel of Morlay, Robert the Archdeacon, and Michael Scott (Raf. Altamira Crevea, *op. cit.* i. 484–514). It was in 1182 that Robert Castrensis translated the *Liber de compositione Alchemiæ*, associated with the names of Ḫālid and Morienus. To the same period belongs the teaching of Alain de Lille, known as 'Doctor universalis,' who had been a monk at Clairvaux, and was afterwards Bishop of Auxerre.

5. Michael Scott was among the first to bring alchemy into prominence in Europe under the patronage of Frederick II. (1194–1250). He dedicated his *de Secretis* to Frederick in 1209. He studied Arabic in Sicily, and spent ten years in Spain. At Toledo he translated Aristotle's treatise on Natural History from the Arabic, with the help of a Jew. In 1217 he translated an Arabic work on the sphere. This is a link with the studies of Gerbert, who in a letter to Remigius, a monk of Trèves, excuses himself for not sending a sphere, owing to his time being occupied with civil business.

'Sphæram tibi nullam misimus, nec ad præsens ullam habemus, nec est res parvi laboris tam occupatis in civilibus causis. Si ergo te cura tantarum detinet rerum, volumen Achilleidos Statii diligenter compositum nobis dirige, ut Sphæram, quam gratis propter difficultatem sui non poteritis habere, tuo munere valeas extorquere' (Gerberti *Ep.* 134, *ap.* Duchesne, *Hist. Franc. Script.* ii. 820).

From Toledo he went to Cordova; in 1220 he returned to Sicily, and in 1230 he was at Oxford. He died in 1235. Ferguson says of him:

'At Toledo he learnt magic for which the city was famous—natural magic or experimental physics or jugglery, as well as black magic, involving the invocation of the infernal powers. There, too, he experimented in Alchemy' (*Bibl. Chem.*, art. 'Michael Scott').

His *Liber de Alchimia* is the result of these studies.

6. Albert the Great has the merit of having brought the study of alchemy as a branch of philosophy into touch with the Scholasticism of the Middle Ages. The Great Chronicle of Belgium in 1480 speaks of him as 'magnus in magia, major in philosophia, maximus in theologia.' Born at Lauingen in Swabia, he studied at Paris and Padua, and in the early part of the 13th cent. taught in the Schools at Cologne. In 1228 he was called to Paris, but after three years returned to Cologne. He was the most distinguished amongst the Dominicans of Germany. In 1260 he was summoned to Rome by Pope Alexander IV., and was made Bishop of Ratisbon. He resigned the see after three years, and retired again to his studies and his lectures at Cologne, where he died in 1280. He was the master of Thomas Aquinas (Milman, *Lat. Chr.* ix. 122). His *Libellus de Alchimia* (Alb. Magn. *opp. omn.*, Paris, vol. xxxvii.) is a practical treatise on the transmutation of metals, the structure of furnaces, and the various methods to be used in the study of alchemy. The Preface is valuable as indicating the wide-spread interest which was then shown by all classes in the study:

'Inveni multos prædivites litteratos, Abbates, Præpositos, Canonicos, Physicos, et illiteratos, qui pro eadem arte magnas fecerunt expensas atque labores, et tandem deficiebant quoniam artem investigare non valebant.'

He persevered where others had failed:

'Ego vero non desperavi, quin facerem labores et expensas infinitas' (*Lib. de Alch.*, Præf.).

He considers it a true art:

'Probat artem Alchimiæ esse veram' (*l.c.* c. 3).

He believes all metals can be transmuted into gold and silver, represented in astrological terms as Sun and Moon:

'Et ut breviter dicam, omnia metalla transubstantiantur in Solem et Lunam' (*ib.* c. 10).

He speaks of the Elixir:

'De his quatuor spiritibus fit tinctura quæ dicitur Elixir arabice, fermentum latine' (*ib.* c. 10).

Fermentation and chemical reaction seem to be used as equivalent terms.

7. Thomas Aquinas was the pupil of Albert the Great at Cologne and at Paris. He, like his master, was a member of the Dominican Order. He graduated at Paris, and taught not only at Cologne under Albert, but at Paris, at Rome, and at other cities in Italy. He refused the Archbishopric of Naples, and died at the Abbey of Fossa Nuova near Piperno on his way to the Council of Lyons in 1274. Ferguson, in his *Bibl. Chem.*, discusses the authenticity of the *Thesaurus Alchemiæ secretissimus ad fratrem Reinaldum* which is attributed to him, and leaves it an open question. The *Summa* contains one or two passages which directly or indirectly refer to alchemy, although his similes are drawn from animal and plant life rather than from the mineral world. The principle of the transmutation of metals may be inferred from one of the earliest definitions of the *Summa*:

'Respondeo dicendum quod solus Deus est omnino immutabilis, omnis autem creatura aliquo modo est mutabilis. Sciendum est enim, quod mutabile potest aliquid dici dupliciter. Uno modo per potentiam, quæ in ipso est. Alio modo per potentiam, quæ in altero est' (*Summa*, pt. i. qu. ix. art. ii.).

God alone is immutable; all else is mutable, in different ways. In one place Aquinas refers to the relation that exists between the minerals and the stars:

'Ad primum ergo dicendum, quod effectus aliquis invenitur assimilari causæ agenti dupliciter. Uno modo secundum eandem speciem, ut homo generatur ab homine, et ignis ab igne. Alio modo secundum virtualem continentiam: prout scilicet forma effectus virtualiter continetur in causa. Et sic animalia ex putrefactione generata, et plantæ et corpora mineralia [assimilantur soli et stellis, quorum virtute generantur' (*Summa*, pt. i. qu. cv. art. i.).]

In discussing the question of the sale of adulterated goods, he says that to sell gold and silver made by the alchemist, if it have not the nature of true gold and silver, is a fraudulent transaction. If, however, this gold of the alchemist is true gold, the transaction is lawful. He recognizes the possibility of fraud, but at the same time witnesses to his belief in the production of gold by the art of the alchemist. The passage is sometimes only partially quoted. It is of importance in its bearing on the alchemical knowledge of Thomas Aquinas:

'Ad primum ergo dicendum quod aurum et argentum non solum cara sunt propter utilitatem vasorum, quæ ex eis fabricantur, aut aliorum hujusmodi; sed etiam propter dignitatem et puritatem substantiæ ipsorum. Et ideo si aurum vel argentum ab alchimicis factum, veram speciem non habeat auri et argenti, est fraudulenta et injusta venditio; præsertim cum sint aliquæ utilitates auri et argenti veri, secundum naturalem operationem ipsorum, quæ non conveniunt auro per alchimiam sophisticato. Sicut quod habet proprietatem lætificandi, et contra quasdam infirmitates medicinaliter juvat. Frequentius etiam potest poni in operatione, et diutius in sua puritate permanet aurum verum quam aurum sophisticatum.'

This contrast between real gold and counterfeit gold implies some knowledge and experience of the art of alchemy:

'Si autem per alchimiam fieret aurum verum, non esset illicitum ipsum pro vero vendere, quia nihil prohibet artem uti aliquibus naturalibus causis ad producendum naturales et veros effectus: sicut August. dicit in 3. *de Trinit.* de his quæ arte dæmonum fiunt.'

The art of alchemy is not unlawful if it confine itself to the investigation of natural causes and natural effects, though some think it demoniacal (pt. ii. 2, qu. lxxvii. art. ii.).

8. **Roger Bacon**, born about 1214, spent his youth at Oxford before joining the Franciscan Order. He began his studies in alchemy and the kindred sciences before 1250, and by 1267 had spent more than 2000 libræ 'on secret books and various experiments and languages and instruments and tables.' He left Oxford for Paris some time before 1245, and returned to Oxford soon after 1250. About 1257 he was exiled, and placed under strict supervision at Paris for ten years. On June 22, 1266, Clement IV. wrote to him, bidding him send him his works secretly and without delay, notwithstanding any restrictions of the Order. Within fifteen or eighteen months he sent to the Pope the *Opus Majus*, the *Opus Minus*, and the *Opus Tertium*. By the Pope's influence he returned to Oxford and began to labour at a great Summa Scientiæ, the *Compendium Philosophiæ*. In 1278 he was condemned 'propter quasdam novitates,' and remained in prison for fourteen years. His last known work was written in 1292.

The *Opus Majus* is silent on the subject of alchemy. The *Opus Minus*, of which only fragments exist in the Bodleian (Brewer, *Opera Inedita*, 311–390), deals with practical alchemy in pt. ii., and speculative alchemy, or *de rerum generationibus*, in pt. v. There is no reference to it in the *Opus Tertium*, but in the *Compendium Philosophiæ* it is the subject of bk. iii. of vol. iii. Speculative alchemy, according to the definition of Roger Bacon, is the science of the generation of things from elements; practical alchemy teaches 'how to make noble metals and colours,' and 'the art of prolonging life.' Some other works of his on alchemy are regarded as genuine.

The different titles of the *Breve Breviarium* give some idea of the scope and aim of his work; it is entitled, *De naturis metallorum in ratione alkimica et artificiali transformatione*, or *Cœlestis alchymia*, or *De naturis metallorum et ipsorum transmutatione*. The date is uncertain. On the subject of old age is the *Libellus Rogerii Baconi . . . de retardandis senectutis accidentibus et de sensibus conservandis*. It is assigned to the year 1276. The *Antidotarius* is a second part of this work. The *De consideratione quintæ essentiæ*, the *Speculum alchemiæ*, the *Speculum secretorum*, the *Secretum secretorum naturæ de laude lapidis Philosophorum*, the *Semita recta alchemiæ*, and the *Thesaurus spirituum*, are wrongly attributed to Bacon (Little, 'The Grey Friars in Oxford,' *Oxf. Hist. Soc. Publ.* vol. xx. pp. 191–211).

9. The most prominent names among the alchemists of the last part of the 13th cent. are **Raymondus Lullius** and **Arnold of Villanova**. The former of these, the Raymond Lully of the later English alchemists, was born of noble parentage in Catalonia, and held, in his early years, a high position in the Court of Aragon. Disappointed in a romantic attachment, he renounced the world, and gave himself up to a life of study and mission work in Africa. His work witnesses to a remarkable combination of spiritual devotion and scientific research, with a passionate enthusiasm for the conversion of the Moors. He devoted himself at first to the study of Arabic. He undertook his first mission to Africa in 1271, but met with little success. He was at Paris in 1281, where he became acquainted with Arnold Villanova. In 1287 he visited Rome, and in 1291 Montpellier. During these years he wrote his great works, the *Ars Generalis sive Magna* and the *Libri xii. Principiorum Philosophiæ contra Averroistas*. In 1292 he went to Africa a second time, and was imprisoned at Tunis. In 1293 he was in Naples; and after journeying to Cyprus and Armenia he was again in Paris in 1308, where he is supposed to have met Duns Scotus. In 1309 he made another missionary journey to Africa, and succeeded in converting seventy disciples of Averroës at Bona, the ancient Hippo, the see of St. Augustine. Once again, as an old man of eighty, he made a last journey to Africa, in 1315, to be stoned and maltreated at Bugia. He lived only to see the shores of the island of Majorca, where he was buried in a chapel on one of his own estates. In his last will, the *Codicillus seu Vade Mecum quo fontes alchemicæ artis ac philosophiæ reconditioris traduntur*, he says that he converted 22 tons of quicksilver, lead, and tin into gold. The tradition that he was brought from Rome by Cremer, Abbot of Westminster, and that he coined the rose-nobles for Edward III., does not seem to rest on historical fact (Ferguson, *Bibl. Chem.*).

Arnold of Villanova, his contemporary, was probably also a Spaniard. He was born in 1245, and died in 1310. He studied amongst the Arabs of Spain; and it is stated, on the authority of John André, that he succeeded in the genuine conversion of iron bars into pure gold at Rome (*Bibl. Chem.* p. 95). At least these alchemists of the 13th cent. in their researches seem to have discovered the secret of a long and useful and strenuous life. Albert the Great died at the age of 87, Roger Bacon at about 78, Raymond Lully at 80, and Arnold Villanova at 65, at a period when the average life was not so long as it is now.

10. The most distinguished pupil of Lully and Villanova was **Pope John XXII.** (1316–1334), who also lived to the age of 90. He worked at alchemy in the Papal palace at Avignon, and is said to have left behind him 25,000,000 florins. At the same time he wrote a letter in which he censured the black magic which was practised 'in nostra curia' by certain clergy,—Joannes de Lemovicis, Jacobus dictus Brabantinus,' and a barber-surgeon, described as 'Joannes de Amanto, medicus,' or, in another place, 'barberius' (Raynald, *Ann. Eccl.* 1317, 53).

11. The practice of the art of alchemy was continued throughout Europe in the 14th cent. on the lines laid down by the masters of the 13th cent. **John Cremer**, Abbot of Westminster, after studying the art for thirty years, worked at Westminster in the reign of Edward III. (1327–1377). **John**

Rupecissa, or Jean de Roquetaillade, was a Franciscan of Aurillac in Aquitaine. He was imprisoned by Innocent VI. in 1356–1357. He quotes Geber, Lullius, and Villanova. In his *Liber lucis* is the picture of a furnace, in which was practised 'the incubation of the philosophic egg whence issued the marvellous quintessence.' **Petrus Bonus** of Ferrara was the author of the *Preciosa Margarita novella de Thesauro ac pretiosissimo Philosophorum Lapide*. It was written in 1330, and published at Venice in 1546. The term 'fermentum,' used by Albert the Great as the Latin of elixir, is applied by Petrus Bonus to the philosopher's stone. It is also used as the means of perfecting it:

'Apud philosophos fermentum dupliciter videtur dici: uno modo ipse lapis philosophorum et suis elementis compositus et completus in comparatione ad metalla; alio modo illud quod est perficiens lapidem et ipsum complens.'

The chemical reactions due to it are compared with the working of yeast:

'De primo modo dicimus quod sicut fermentum pastæ vincit pastam et ad se convertit semper, sic et lapis convertit ad se metalla reliqua. Et sicut una pars fermenti pastæ habet convertere partes pastæ et non converti, sic et hic lapis habet convertere plurimas partes metallorum ad se, et non converti' (Petrus Bonus, *ap.* P. Schützenberger, *On Fermentation*, p. 11). Schützenberger adds: 'This property of transmitting a force to a large mass without being itself weakened by the process was precisely that which ought to characterize the philosopher's stone, which was so much sought after.' Since these words were written, the discovery of radium has given to chemistry an element which also appears to have the property 'convertere plurimas partes metallorum ad se, et non converti.'

Nicolas Flamel belonged to the latter part of the 14th century. He was born in Pontoise about 1330, and died in 1418 at the age of 88. His discovery of the elixir of life in 1382 seems to have met with its reward.

12. Among the prominent names of the 15th cent. are **Basil Valentine** and **Isaac of Holland.** The former is considered the author of the *Triumphal Car of Antimony*, but there is considerable doubt as to the facts of his life and the authorship of the works attributed to him. The chief fact is a record in an Erfurt Chronicle under the year 1413: 'Eadem ætate Basilius Valentinus in Divi Petri monasterio vixit.' There is a similar doubt as to the identity of Isaac of Holland. The life of **Bernard, Count of Treviso,** covers the whole century. Born in 1406, he died in 1490 at the age of 84, another instance of the secret of long life won by the alchemists probably by means of study, method, and application to work. He distinguishes between the results of the labour of the true alchemist and the counterfeit products of sophistical alchemists. Here there is some echo of the phrase of Thomas Aquinas: 'aurum sophisticatum.'

England produced three prominent alchemists in this century. **George Ripley** was born about 1415, and was a Canon Regular of St. Augustine at Bridlington. He visited Rome in 1477, and returned in 1478 after having discovered the secret of transmutation. He is the author of *The Compound of Alchemy, or the Ancient Hidden Art of Alchemie: Containing the right and perfectest Means to make the Philosopher's Stone, Aurum potabile, with other excellent Compounds.* His Twelve Gates of Alchemy give some insight into the methods of the art in England in the 15th century. They are: Calcination, Solution, Separation, Conjunction, Putrefaction, Congelation, Cibation, Sublimation, Fermentation, Exaltation, Multiplication, Projection. He died in 1490 at the age of 75. **Thomas Dalton** lived in the middle of the century, and received a powder from a Canon of Lichfield under a promise not to use it until after his death. **Thomas Norton** of Bristol wrote his *Crede Mihi*, or *Ordinal of Alchemy*, in 1477. He says:

'I made also the Elixir of life,
Which me bereft a merchant's wife;
The Quintessens I made also,
With other secrets many moe,
Which sinful people took me fro
To my great pain and much more woe.'

13. The 16th cent. saw a further development of alchemy into the more exact sciences of chemistry and medicine. **Paracelsus**, in his student wanderings an alchemist, became by practice a physician, by experience a chemist. He was at once adept and wizard, sceptic and critic. He wrecked his work by his bombast, his life by his self-indulgence. At the same time, to use Browning's words, 'the title of Paracelsus to be considered the father of modern chemistry is indisputable.' Gerardus Vossius says of him: 'Nobilem hanc medicinæ partem, diu sepultam avorum ætate, quasi ab orco revocavit Th. Parcelsus' (*de Philosophia et Phil. sectis*, ix. 9). It appears also from his treatise *de Phlebotomia* that he had discovered the circulation of the blood. Lavater says that 'though an astrological enthusiast,' he was 'a man of prodigious genius' (*de Natura Rerum*, Holcroft's tr., vol. iii. p. 179). There is a reference to his use of laudanum on the evidence of his secretary, Oporinus:

'Alii illud quod in capulo habuit, ab ipso Azoth appellatum, medicinam fuisse præstantissimam aut lapidem Philosophicum putant' (Melch. Adam). Browning adds: 'This famous sword was no laughing matter in those days, and it is now a material feature in the popular idea of Paracelsus. . . . This Azoth was simply "laudanum suum." But in his time he was commonly believed to possess the double tincture—the power of curing diseases and transmuting metals. Oporinus often witnessed, as he declares, both these effects, as did also Franciscus, the servant of Paracelsus, who describes, in a letter to Neander, a successful projection at which he was present, and the results of which, good golden ingots, were confided to his keeping.'

Paracelsus, otherwise Philippus Aureolus Theophrastus Bombastus ab Hohenheim, was born at Einsiedeln in 1493. He studied medicine under his father at Villach, and alchemy under Tritheim, Bishop of Spanheim, at Würzburg. The character of his studies at Würzburg is best seen in the letter dedicatory, written in 1510, by Agrippa to Tritheim:

'Quam nuper tecum, R. P. in cœnobio tuo apud Herbipolim (Würzburg) aliquandiu conversatus, multa de chymicis, multa de magicis, multa de cabalisticis, caeterisque quæ adhuc in occulto delitescunt, arcanis scientiis atque artibus una contulissemus,' etc.

It was partly in rebellion against these traditional methods, partly to gain as wide an experience as possible, that Paracelsus spent his early life in travel:

'Patris auxilio primum, deinde propria industria doctissimos viros in Germania, Italia, Gallia, Hispania, aliisque Europæ regionibus, nactus est præceptores' (Melch. Adam, in *Vit. Germ. Medic.*). The passage illustrates the wide interest in alchemy throughout Europe at the close of the 15th century.

Under the patronage of Sigismond Fugger, Paracelsus learnt much in the mines of Bohemia, and himself speaks of his researches into folk-lore:

'Ecce amatorem adolescentem difficillimi itineris haud piget, ut venustam saltem puellam vel fœminam aspiciat' (*Defensiones Septem adv. æmulos suos*, 1573: 'de peregrinationibus et exilio').

In 1526 he was called to a chair of physic and surgery at Basel. Here his over-bold denunciation of Avicenna and Galen made him many enemies. In 1528 his fall was brought about in the case of a canon of Basel named Liechtenfels. This man was cured by Paracelsus, but refused to pay the recognized fee. His refusal was supported by the magistrates, and Paracelsus fled to Colmar. He was at Nuremberg in 1529, at St. Gall in 1531, at Pfeffers in 1535, and at Augsburg in 1536. He then visited Moravia, Arabia, and Hungary. In 1538, when at Villach, he dedicated his 'Chronicle' to the States of Carinthia, in gratitude for the many kindnesses with which they had honoured his father. He died at Salzburg in 1541, at the early age of 48. He seems to have been generous in the practice of medicine. His epitaph says of him: 'Bona sua in pauperes distribuenda collocandaque erogavit.' A sceptic and fierce critic in alchemy, he appears to have been no less so in theology. Quenstedt says of him: 'Nec tantum novæ medicinæ, verum etiam novæ theologiæ autor est' (*de Patr. Doct.*). Delrio places him among those who were: 'partim atheos, partim hæreticos' (*Disquis. Magicar.* i. 3). At the same time, Browning is justified in the last words he places in the mouth of Paracelsus:

'If I stoop
Into a dark tremendous sea of cloud,
It is but for a time; I press God's lamp
Close to my breast; its splendour, soon or late,
Will pierce the gloom: I shall emerge one day.
You understand me? I have said enough?'

An inventory taken at his death shows that the only books he left were the Bible, the New Testament, the Commentaries of St. Jerome on the Gospels, a printed volume on medicine, and seven manuscripts. His works were published by F. Bitiskius in 3 vols. fol. in 1658; the Hermetic and Alchemical writings by A. E. Waite in 2 vols. in 1894. Jules Andrieu says of him: 'He is the pioneer of modern chemists, and the prophet of a revolution in general science' (*Encyc. Brit.* art. 'Alchemy'). Browning sums up his study of Paracelsus in the words:

'Meanwhile, I have done well, though not all well.
As yet men cannot do without contempt;
'Tis for their good, and therefore fit awhile
That they reject the weak, and scorn the false,
Rather than praise the strong and true, in me:
But after, they will know me.'
(*Paracelsus*, 1835, and notes).

The new influence in the 16th cent. is shown by the violent death of **Beuther,** who was alchemist to the Elector Augustus of Saxony from 1575 to 1582, and in the title of **Libavius'** great work published in 1595—*Alchymia recognita, emendita, et aucta.* It has been called the 'first text-book of chemistry.' It contains a chapter on the philosopher's stone. In England, **Thomas Charnock** published his *Breviary of Philosophy* in 1557, his *Exigue of Alchemy* in 1572, and his *Memorandum* in 1574. He was instructed in the use of gold-making powder by Bird, who received it from Ripley. It was only those who were well-to-do who could carry on these experiments. The furnace alone cost Charnock £3 a week. The *Alchemical Testament* of **John Gybbys** of Exeter in the time of Elizabeth has been published by James O. Halliwell (London, 1854).

There does not seem to have been much interest taken in alchemy at Oxford in the early part of the century. The Day Book of John Donne in 1520 contains but few references to alchemical works. There is one copy of the *Commentum Arnoldi de Villanova* (fol. 3, a. 1); there are three copies of a *Chiromantia de manu* (fols. 1. a. 1, 8. b. 2, 13. a. 1), and two copies of Albertus, *de mineralibus* (13. a. 1, 13. b. 2). There is also a copy of *Theoretica planetarum* (15. b. 1) (Fletcher, *Collectanea Oxf. Hist. Soc.* vol. v. p. 71 ff.). In the catalogue of books belonging to William Grocyn, drawn up by his executor, Linacre, in the same year, there is the same absence of such books (Mont. Burrows, *Collect. Oxf. Hist. Soc.* vol. xvi. p. 317 ff.). Oxford had at this time other interests, especially the new learning associated with the names of Grocyn, Linacre, Foxe, and others. The training of Linacre, the founder of the English College of Physicians, the friend of Politian and Chalcondylas, and the great Venetian publisher, Aldus Manutius, is in marked contrast to the restless wanderings of Paracelsus.

14. It was long before the new sciences cut themselves altogether adrift from the ideas of the alchemists. In the early part of the 17th cent. the brotherhood of the Hermetic philosophers known as the Rosicrucians (wh. see) brought the occult mysteries of the earlier alchemists again into notice. The brotherhood claimed descent from **Christian Rosencreutz** in 1459; but no evidence for this exists beyond their own publications. The controversy centred round a work entitled, *Chymische Hochzeit Christiani Rosencreutz anno 1459,* written by **Johann Valentin Andreä** in 1616, and published at Strassburg. Among the most prominent of the Rosicrucian brotherhood was **Michael Maier,** physician to the Emperor Rudolph II. (1576–1612). He published *Examen fucorum Pseudo-chymicorum* in 1617, *Atalanta fugiens* in 1618, *Symbola aureæ mensæ* in 1617, and the *Tripus aureus* containing three treatises—the *Basilii Valentini Practica ex Germanica,* the *Crede Mihi seu Ordinale* of Thomas Norton, and the *Testamentum* of Cremer, Abbot of Westminster. **Robert Fludd** introduced the brotherhood to the notice of English physicians. Born in Kent in 1574, he matriculated at St. John's, Oxford, on November 10, 1592, and took his M.A. degree in 1598. One of the three questions discussed by him for Inception in Medicine in 1605 was: 'Chymicum extractum minus molestiæ et periculi affert quam quod integrum et naturale' ('Reg. Univ. Oxon.,' *Oxf. Hist. Soc.* vol. ii. pt. i. 193, ii. 191, iii. 194). In the same year is discussed in Comitiis: 'Incantatio non valet ad curam morbi.' Fludd went abroad and studied the works of Paracelsus and the mysteries of the Rosicrucians. On his return he practised as a physician in London, and died in 1637.

The Hon. **Robert Boyle,** one of the first promoters of modern chemistry, and a leading member of the Royal Society on its incorporation in 1662, believed in the transmutation of metals. In 1659 he brought to Oxford 'the noted chemist and Rosicrucian, Peter Sthael of Strasburgh.' Anthony Wood began a 'course of chemistry' under him April 23, 1663, paying 30s. in advance, and the balance of 30s. at the conclusion of the class, May 30, 1663. 'A. W. got some knowledge and experience; but his mind was still busy after antiquities and music.' Among the members of this famous chemistry class at Oxford was 'John Lock, a man of turbulent spirit, clamorous, and never contented,' and 'Mr. Christopher Wren, afterwards a knight, and an eminent virtuoso.' In 1664, Mr. Sthael was called away to London, and became operator to the Royal Society; and continuing there till 1670, he returned to Oxford in November. (Clark, 'Wood's Life and Times,' *Oxf. Hist. Soc.* vol. xix. pp. 290, 472). The *Sceptical Chemist,* by Robert Boyle (Oxford, 1680), contains the first statement of the molecular or atomic idea in chemical philosophy (H. C. Bolton, *Catalogue of Works on Alchemy and Chemistry,* exhibited at the Grolier Club, New York, 1891). He was made 'Dr. of Phisicke' in 1665, and died in 1691.

The Rosicrucian ideas and alchemistical methods survived to some extent at Oxford. **Elias Ashmole** was the contemporary of Robert Boyle at Oxford, but as a member of Brazenose, and not as 'a sojourner.' In 1650 he edited a work of Dr. John Dee, who died *c.* 1608, of whom Wood says: 'I have heard some say that he was a mere mountebank in his profession' ('Wood's Life and Times,' *Oxf. Hist. Soc.* vol. xix. p. 308). In 1654, Ashmole wrote *The Way to Bliss in three books.* 'The author says that motion is the father of heat, and doth beget and purchase it of nothing, theoretically anticipating modern doctrines' (Bolton, *Catalogue*). Bk. iii. ch. ii. treats of the Philosopher's Stone. In 1677 he offered his curios and MSS to the University, on the condition that it would build a Museum and Chemical Laboratory. The foundation-stone was laid September 14, 1679, and the building was finished March 20, 1682–1683.

The inscription describes this first public laboratory in Oxford: 'Musæum Ashmoleanum: Schola Naturalis Historiæ: Officina Chemica.' The three largest rooms were public: 'The uppermost . . . *Musæum Ashmoleanum.* The middle room is the *School of Natural Historie*, where the professor of chymistry, who is at present Dr. Robert Plot, reads three times a week. The lower room, a cellar . . . is the Laboratory, perchance one of the most beautiful and useful in the world' ('Wood's Life and Times,' *ib.* vol. xxvi. p. 55).

It was thus under the direction of Ashmole, perhaps the last of the Oxford alchemists, that the study of chemistry was placed on a sound and public footing. Ashmole died in June 1692, a year after Robert Boyle.

In the sister University, at the same period, **Newton**, who became Fellow of Trinity in 1667, directed his studies for some little time to alchemistical methods, and investigated the Philosopher's Stone. But at Cambridge, as at Oxford, the newer scientific methods set aside the dreams and theories of the older alchemists, and opened the way to modern chemistry.

15. In the 18th cent. alchemy was finally discredited in the person of **Dr. Price of Guildford**, the last of the alchemists, a distinguished amateur chemist, and Fellow of the Royal Society. In May 1782 he professed to transmute mercury into silver and gold in the presence of a select company. Some of the gold thus obtained was presented to George III., and Price was made M.D. of Oxford. The Royal Society then pressed him to repeat the experiments in their presence. He hesitated, refused, and only on the pressure of the President, Sir Joseph Banks, at last reluctantly consented. He withdrew to Guildford, prepared an ample amount of laurel water, and then began to manufacture his projection powder. On the 3rd of August he invited the Royal Society to Guildford. Only three Fellows responded to the invitation. He received them, and then committed suicide in their presence.

In Germany, alchemy was laughed out in the person of **Semler.** He received the 'Salt of Life' from Baron Hirschen, and, treating it as the Philosopher's Stone, was surprised to find gold deposited in the crucible. Klaproth analyzed the 'Salt of Life,' and found it to consist of Glauber's salt and sulphate of magnesia. In the 'Salt' sent by Semler, however, Klaproth discovered gold, though not in combination. Klaproth again consented to analyze Semler's solution before the Court, when, instead of gold he found a kind of brass called tombac. On further investigation, it was discovered that Semler's old servant, eager to humour his master, had slipped pieces of gold leaf into Semler's chemical mixtures. The servant entrusted the secret to his wife, that in his absence she might purchase the gold leaf as before. She, however, bought brass instead of gold, and spent the balance on drink. In this way alchemy was laughed out of Germany (Chambers, *Book of Days*, i. 602).

The theories of the alchemists did not die out at once. They were still held by the adepts at the close of the 18th century. The Antiquary says that Dousterswivel 'exhibits himself as a perfect charlatan—talks of the *magisterium*—of sympathies and antipathies—of the cabala—of the divining-rod—and all the trumpery with which the Rosicrucians cheated a darker age, and which, to our eternal disgrace, has in some degree revived in our own' (Scott, *Antiquary*, ch. xiii.). The *Lives of the Adepts in Alchemystical Philosophy* was published in London in 1814, and contained reports and extracts of many works on alchemy. Bulwer Lytton's *Zanoni* was written in 1842 as a study in the mysteries of the Rosicrucians.—George Eliot in 1871 wrote: 'Doubtless a vigorous error vigorously pursued has kept the embryos of truth a-breathing: the quest of gold being at the same time a questioning of substances, the body of Chemistry is prepared for its soul, and Lavoisier is born' (*Middlemarch*, vol. iii. ch. xlviii.).

16. But it was the establishment of the Atomic Theory by Dalton in the beginning of the 19th cent. as a working hypothesis in practical chemistry that set on one side the theories of the alchemists:

The observation of the Law of Equivalents and the Law of Multiples 'led to the idea that the elementary bodies are made up of indivisible particles called *atoms*, each having a constant weight peculiar to itself; and that chemical combination takes place by the juxtaposition of these atoms, 1 to 1, 1 to 2, 1 to 3, 2 to 3, etc., a group of atoms thus united being called a *molecule*. This is the atomic hypothesis of Dalton' (H. Watt, *Inorganic Chemistry*, 1883, p. 267).

Immutability has been the recognized law of the elements:

'Our molecules, on the other hand, are unalterable by way of the processes which go on in the present state of things, and every individual of each species is of exactly the same magnitude. . . . In speculating on the cause of this equality, we are debarred from imagining any cause of equalization, on account of the immutability of each individual molecule. It is difficult, on the other hand, to conceive of selection and elimination of intermediate varieties, for where can these eliminated molecules have gone to, if, as we have reason to believe, the hydrogen, etc., of the fixed stars is composed of molecules identical in all respects with our own?' (Clark-Maxwell, *Theory of Heat*, 1885, p. 331).

Thus, under the most advanced theory of Chemistry and Physics in the 19th cent., the transmutation of elements was inconceivable. Yet there were masters of chemical philosophy who entered a caution against the exclusion of possibilities.

Tilden writes: 'The molecular theory has been adopted in a somewhat rigid form, not by reason of any special conviction of my own regarding its permanence as a scientific truth, but because I am satisfied by long experience that, whatever form it may ultimately assume, it is even now a most important and almost indispensable aid to teaching chemistry' (*Introd. to Chemical Philosophy*, London, 1876, p. vii). In treating of the Periodic Law and Mendelejeff's Table, he says: 'This table requires a few remarks. In the first place, there are some elements, as, for instance, copper, silver, and gold, for which a place cannot readily be found. Silver is undoubtedly allied, though not very closely, with sodium, whilst it is also connected with copper on the one hand and with mercury on the other. Gold again is unquestionably triad, whilst the platinum metals to which it is most nearly related exhibit even atomicity' (*ib.* p. 243). There still remained something behind which was not altogether clear, and this, too, in the important metals, silver and gold.

17. The discoveries of the Becquerel rays and the isolation of the element radium by M. and Mme. Curie in the opening years of the 20th cent. have opened up far-reaching possibilities, and have induced many leading chemists to conceive the idea of the transmutation of the elements. At the Leicester Meeting of the British Association on Aug. 1, 1907, Lord Kelvin challenged these inferences. He maintained that it was almost absolutely certain that there are many different kinds of atom, each eternally invariable in its own specific quality, and that different substances, such as gold, silver, lead, iron, etc., consist each of them of atoms of one invariable quality, and that any one of them is incapable of being transmuted into any other. He thus combated the recent assertion regarding the transmutation of metals, and continued to regard an atom as the ultimate indivisible unit of matter, and the electron, or electrion, as an electrical atom.

The discussion on 3rd Aug. 1907 was an event in the history of chemical science. Professor Rutherford, in opening the debate, held that the discovery of the electron had not as yet disproved the atomic theory. All attempts to find an electron with a positive charge of electricity had failed. 'Though we can liberate the electrons of matter very freely, there is no evidence that the liberation of the electron tends to the disintegration of an atom.' Sir William Ramsay, as a chemist, disagreed with Lord Kelvin and Professor Rutherford. The latter had said that there was no evidence that the loss of electrons altered the atom. Perhaps not. *But there was evidence that the gain of electrons did so.* He declared that, by placing radium hermetically closed in a glass vessel, the electrons, emanating from the radium through the glass, and falling on a nickel bar placed in juxtaposition, had the effect, after a certain time, of covering the bar with a film of radioactive matter, which could be separated by chemical treatment. His conclusion was that some kind of transmutation took place, converting the nickel into some other substance, this being characterized by its radio-activity. Lord Kelvin, in his reply, said that the discovery of the properties of radium had been most suggestive, and had opened our eyes to other discoveries, never suspected or dreamed of. Sir William Ramsay then announced a further discovery. He had proved that when radium was isolated in a bottle, after a lapse of time it gave off an emanation, and the new gas helium. When again that emanation was isolated, it produced helium and something else, which is conjectured on possible grounds to be lead. Again, when that emanation was dissolved in copper solution it produced the new element called argon, but now, when the radium emanation was dissolved in water, and the gases were extracted from the water, the resulting production was not helium, but its kindred element neon. These marvellous properties of radium thus described by Sir William Ramsay seem almost to realize the ancient dreams of the alchemists. Has it after all been reserved for the chemists of the 20th cent. to find in radium the Philosopher's Stone, and to prove it to have the power of transmuting yet unknown elements into gold?

LITERATURE.—M. Berthelot, *Les Origines de l'Alchimie*, Paris, 1885; J. Ferguson, *Bibliotheca Chemica: a Catalogue of the Alchemical, Chemical, and Pharmaceutical books in the Collection of the late James Young of Kelly and Durris, Esq.*, 2 vols., Glasgow, 1906; H. C. Bolton, *Catalogue of works on Alchemy and Chemistry exhibited at the Grolier Club*, New York, 1891; Anon., *Lives of the Adepts in Alchemystical Philosophy*, London, 1814; A. E. Waite, *The Hermetic and Alchemical Writings of Philippus Aureolus Theophrastus Bombast, of Hohenheim, called Paracelsus the Great*, 2 vols., London, 1894.

THOMAS BARNS.

ALCHERINGA.—The name applied by the Arunta, Kaitish, and Unmatjera tribes of Central Australia to the mythical past in which their ancestors were formed, and their ceremonies and regulations instituted. According to Spencer-Gillen (*Nor. Tr.* p. 745), the word *alcheri* means 'dream' (but cf. *FL* xvi. 430), and *Alcheringa* is equivalent to 'Dream Times.' Analogous beliefs are found in other tribes to the north of the Arunta; the Warramunga term corresponding to *Alcheringa* is *Wingara*.

1. In the Alcheringa existed at the outset, according to the Arunta myth, the ancestors whose spirits they regard as incarnated in the men of the present day; they were at most semi-human, but possessed more than human powers, and are credited with the formation of natural features such as the Macdonnell Ranges; in the Alcheringa period these amorphous *inapertwa*, who were transformed into human beings and later underwent initiation ceremonies, travelled over the country in totem companies, each carrying a *churinga* (see AUSTRALIANS), and at the spots where they camped are the present *oknanikilla*, or local totem centres. The Arunta distinguish four Alcheringa periods: (*a*) creation of man from the *inapertwa*; (*b*) institution of circumcision with the stone knife; (*c*) of the *ariltha* or mica operation; (*d*) of regulations regarding marriage. Originally the country was covered with salt water, which was withdrawn towards the north; two *ungambikula* (='self-existing') in the western sky saw to the east some *inapertwa*; with their knives they released the half-formed arms and legs, slit the eyelids and so on; after circumcising the men they became lizards. Some of the uncircumcised men were eaten by *oruncha* (evil spirits), who were killed by men of the lizard totem. In the next two stages an *oknirabata* (sage) introduced circumcision with the stone knife, and taught the little hawk totem group to perform the operation; they also formed the four intermarrying classes, but without associating them with marriage regulations. More *inapertwa* were transformed; men of the wild cat totem instituted the mica ceremony, and the order of the initiation ceremonies was arranged. Finally, the Emu people introduced the present marriage restrictions. According to the Unmatjera and Kaitish, the *inmintera* (the Arunta *inapertwa*) were formed into human beings by an old crow; he returned to get his stone knife with which to circumcise them, and in his absence two lizard men from the south circumcised and subincised the men, and performed the corresponding operation on the women. Another Kaitish tradition makes the transformers two boys to whom Atnatu (a god) sent down stone knives. Some of the ancestors were men (*ertwa*) when they were first formed. In the Kaitish tribe the travels of the groups of totemic ancestors are almost wanting, or possibly forgotten; the various spots are said to have been peopled by one or two ancestors, who sometimes carried *churinga*.

2. The Urabunna, the neighbours of the Arunta on the other side, also have their mythic period, named Ularaka; the ancestors of the totemic groups were semi-human and lived on the earth or beneath it; they had superhuman powers. The ancestors of each totemic group at the present day were few in number, and there is no myth of the *churinga* being carried. The Urabunna belief thus differs widely from that of the Arunta and Kaitish, and comes near that of the Warramunga (see below). The semi-human ancestors wandered about the country putting *mai-aurli* (spirit individuals) into rocks and pools, and these subsequently became men and women, who formed the first totem groups. These *mai-aurli* are continually undergoing re-incarnation; as a rule, with the Arunta they inhabit different localities according to their totem; but in the Urabunna and other tribes those of two or more totems may inhabit the same place. Each re-incarnated individual is held to change his phratry, totem, and sex on re-incarnation; after death he goes back to the spot where he was left in the Ularaka, and this regardless of the totem to which he may for the time being belong. In the Wonkgongaru tribe, north-west of Lake Eyre, the Urabunna beliefs prevail, with the exception that they accept the Arunta belief as to the *inapertwa*.

3. The Unmatjera hold that every totemic ancestor had his class as well as his totem; the totem changes in their belief, as in that of the Arunta, in successive incarnations, the class seldom or never.

4. The Warramunga, Walpari, Tjingilli, and other tribes hold that every one is the incarnation of a Wingara ancestor; but these latter are regarded as having been fully formed men, and all the members of a totemic group at the present day are looked on as the descendants of one ancestor who wandered over the country leaving spirit children in trees and rocks; they believe that if a woman strikes one of these trees with an axe, the spirit child will enter her body. The ancestor began his travels under ground, and then came up to the surface; *churinga* are known in this tribe, but not associated with individuals. These beliefs are shared by the Umbaia and Gnanji, but the latter hold that women have no *moidna*, or spirit part; consequently spirit female children, though they exist, do not take human form. The Binbinga also hold that one totemic ancestor formed members of a group, and left Ulanji spirits which emanated from his own body.

5. In the Arunta tribe at the present day a man marries a woman of his own or any other totem; in the other tribes totemic exogamy is enforced. Tradition says that in the Alcheringa times men invariably married women of their own totem; the classes, too, were originally non-exogamous, and the present regulations came down from the north. It seems clear that the progress of social changes from north to south corresponds with the facts; but there is much division of opinion as to the value of the remainder of the myths. They are treated as mere ætiological myths by Andrew Lang and others, as genuine historical traditions by Spencer and others. It seems clear that some part of them cannot be historically true; for the totem groups are represented as living exclusively upon their totems; and some of these, such as grubs and plants, are not in season for more than a portion of the year.

LITERATURE.—Spencer-Gillen, *Native Tribes*, 1899, pp. 119-127, 387-422, *Northern Tribes*, 1904, pp. 145-175, etc. *FL* xvi. 428-433, gives the views of the Southern Arunta. For remarks on the Alcheringa legends see Lang, *Social Origins*, 1903, and *Secret of the Totem*; Durkheim's art. in *ASoc* iii. (1901) 20, etc.; see also Van Gennep, *Mythes et Légendes d'Australie*, 1906, p. xliv f.

N. W. THOMAS.

ALCOHOL.—The use of alcohol in some form or other has been familiar to man from a very early period in his race-existence; in all ages of which we have any record, in all climates, amongst tribes of the most varied degrees of culture, it has been and still is an agent with marked effects on the individual and the race. The name is Arabic in origin (*al-koḥl*, 'collyrium,' the fine powder used to stain the eyelids).

Alcohol, as we know it in ordinary use, is properly named 'ethyl alcohol,' and is one of a series—distinguished in their properties from one another by their boiling point, their specific gravity, and their poisonous effect—consisting of carbon, hydrogen, and oxygen. Their names and chemical formulæ are:—Methyl alcohol (CH_3OH), ethyl alcohol (C_2H_5OH), propyl alcohol (C_3H_7OH), butyl alcohol (C_4H_9OH), and amyl alcohol ($C_5H_{11}OH$). Methyl alcohol is obtained from distillation of wood, and, being nauseous in taste, it is added to ethyl alcohol, so that the latter may be sold for industrial purposes without tax as methylated spirits. Fusel oil contains amyl and ethyl alcohol as well as other by-products of fermentation, and is usually present along with other analogous substances in distilled alcoholic liquors; but as their amount is small and their action subsidiary, they will not be further referred to.

Alcohol is formed from sugar by the action of the yeast-fungus, a unicellular organism which excites fermentation in saccharine solutions. A molecule of sugar is thus split up into alcohol and carbonic acid (along with some collateral products). There is a natural limit to the strength of the alcoholic liquor which is thus formed (apart from the amount of sugar present); when alcohol reaches a strength of 16 p.c. by volume, it stops further fermentation. Most 'natural' wines, such as claret, contain only from 8 to 12 p.c. alcohol, as it is but rarely that the grape-juice is sugary enough to allow of the formation of alcohol to the highest possible extent. Stronger wines, such as port and sherry, are 'fortified' by the addition of alcohol. It should be noted that mankind has in all ages made naturally fermented drinks from any available material. By more complicated processes, beer or ale is produced either from barley-malt or some substitute, the strength in alcohol varying from 3 p.c. or less up to 8 or 9 p.c. The strongest drinks, such as brandy, whisky, rum, gin, and liqueurs, are manufactured with the aid of distillation.

1. Physiological effects of alcohol.—Alcohol is a poison for protoplasm, that is, for the soft plastic material which is the essential constituent of every one of the minute cells that make up living organisms, whether animal or vegetable. Its poisonous effect in very dilute solution is easily shown on lowly organisms (Ridge, *Med. Temp. Review*, 1898, vol. i. p. 148; Woodhead, 'Pathology of Alcoholism' in Kelynack's *Drink Problem*, pp. 52–56), and the more finely organized cells are most susceptible (Overton, *Studien über die Narkose*, Jena, 1901). Let us briefly trace the effects of alcohol when taken into the human body in moderate quantity.

(1) With the feeling of warmth in the stomach, there is an increased secretion of gastric juice such as is produced by any irritant. Of the two constituents of the gastric juice, it is not so much the pepsin as the hydrochloric acid that is thus secreted, and recent research indicates that the digestive quality of the secretion depends very largely on the nature of the stimulus. Hence it is probable that alcohol is of but slight value as a digestive aid. By quickening the movements of the stomach and intestines, it helps the expulsion of gases. If taken in concentrated form or in too great quantity, it decidedly retards digestion, and frequent repetition of such doses is apt to bring on gastric catarrh.

(2) Alcohol passes in about 15 minutes into the blood and lymph vessels, and is thus rapidly diffused through the various tissues; it forms a compound with the colouring matter of the blood which takes up and gives off oxygen less readily (Woodhead, *l.c.* p. 57). Hence the normal changes in the tissue cells are interfered with, and this is one of the causes of the accumulation of fat in certain alcoholics. The waste products are apt to be retained too long by the cells.

(3) The nerve-cells of the brain, the most highly organized and delicate of the tissues, very early show the effect of alcohol. Many of the best observers of their own mental processes, such as Helmholtz and Huxley, have expressed themselves strongly as to the harmful effect of minute doses of alcohol on brain work. It would seem that the 'stimulating' effect is really due to paralysis of the very highest nerve-centres, so that cheerfulness, wit, and recklessness have freer play. Large numbers of psychometric experiments under conditions of the greatest accuracy prove that alcohol in small dietetic doses exercises a distinctly paralyzing effect on the working of the brain. Some mental processes are quickened for a short time, and then a retarding effect shows itself, which is prolonged and much more than cancels the apparent beneficial result. With the early facility there is apt to be loss of accuracy (Horsley, 'Effects of Alcohol on the Human Brain,' *Brit. Journ. of Inebriety*, Oct. 1905; Rüdin, *Psychol. Arbeiten*, ed. E. Kraepelin, 1901–1902; Neild, 'Psychometric Tests on the Action of Alcohol,' *Brit. Journ. of Inebr.*, Oct. 1903). The greater the demands made on psychic activity, the more marked is the interference caused by alcohol. An invariable result is that the person experimented on has the delusion that he is doing better with alcohol than without it. The depressing results of a slight intoxication may last from 24 to 36 hours (Fürer, *Transactions of the Internat. Anti-alcohol Congress*, Basel, 1906). The effect of the regular consumption of alcohol—say 1 to 2 litres of lager beer *per diem*—is distinctly prejudicial to all kinds of intellectual effort (Kürz and Kraepelin, *Psychol. Arbeiten*, 1900); and in general the more difficult mental operations are more impaired than the easier. As for the idea that habituation produces a certain immunity to alcohol, this is probably due to a blunting of the nerves. Such a result is apt to be associated with a dangerous tendency to augment the dose in order to experience the agreeable effect, just as with morphine (Kraepelin, *Münch. Med. Woch.*, 17th April, 1906). Experiments on the *sensory* functions (sight, hearing, simple touch, etc.) show, from the first, diminution in accuracy and rapidity. The *motor* functions of the body are generally influenced favourably by alcohol at first (Frey, *Alcohol und Muskelermüdung*, Leipzig, 1903; Schnyder, Pflüger's *Archiv*, 1903; Destrée, *Journ. Méd. de Bruxelles*, 1897); the amount of work is increased, and is more easily performed; but after a brief period extending at most to 20 or 30 minutes, there comes a prolonged reaction, so that the total effect is distinctly disadvantageous. The popular belief that alcohol strengthens and increases working capacity is accountable for a vast amount of drinking among the working classes.

(4) The effect of alcohol on the circulation (Monro and Findlay, 'Critical Review of work on Alcohol and the Cardio-Vascular System,' *Med. Temp. Rev.* 1903–1904; Abel, 'Pharmacological Action of Ethyl Alcohol,' *Med. Temp. Rev.* 1904–1905) is to cause first a dilatation of the small vessels, especially of the skin, shown by flushing of the face and a feeling of warmth. A slight acceleration of the pulse is frequently, but not always, produced by small doses, but the average for the whole day may be lowered. If the pulse tension is low to begin with, alcohol will not raise it. On the whole, experiments show that alcohol does not

strengthen the heart, but rather the reverse. There may be a short stimulating effect through reflex action just after its administration. Large doses are strongly depressive.

(5) The tissues, we have seen, have their oxidation interfered with by alcohol. There is, further, increased loss of heat from the body, with lowering of temperature through the dilatation (paralysis) of the blood-vessels. Hence comes quickened and deeper respiration, so that alcohol is indirectly a respiratory stimulant (Binz, *Therapie d. Gegenwart*, 1899).

(6) The *nutritive* value of alcohol is still the subject of keen discussion (Rosemann, Pflüger's *Archiv*, 1901, vol. 86, also vols. 94, 99, and 100). All admit that large quantities of alcohol are poisonous, and it would seem that the most minute doses that have any demonstrable effect act prejudicially on the nervous tissues. Still it is conceivable that in other ways alcohol may be serviceable to the body. In small doses, from 90 to 98 p.c. is oxidized; heat is thereby produced, and alcohol, it is said, can thus take the place of other materials, such as fat or carbohydrate (Atwater and Benedikt, *Experiments on Metabolism of Matter and Energy*, Washington, 1898). The same may be said about glycerine, or fusel oil (amylic alcohol), whose total effect is distinctly poisonous. Alcohol can neither build up nor repair the tissues, and any favourable action that it has in producing energy is probably much more than counterbalanced by its poisonous effect, either directly or by means of intermediate products, while the tissues are dealing with it (Schäfer, *Textbook of Physiology*, vol. i. p. 882). This conclusion of physiological science is in harmony with the experiences in actual life of army leaders, travellers, climbers, employers of labour, etc. The good effects of alcohol are similar to those obtained from other more or less dangerous stimulants and narcotics.

2. Acute alcoholism (Intoxication).—When enough alcohol is taken to produce intoxication, judgment, self-control, perception, and the other higher faculties are affected first. With greater facility in thought and speech, there is a certain disregard of the environment; a quiet person may become lively and witty, unwonted confidences are given, and there may be assertiveness and quarrelsomeness. Singing, shouting, and other noisy demonstrations indicate the free play of the emotions; then comes motor impairment, shown by indistinct speech and staggering gait; drowsiness, muscular paralysis, and even coma may supervene; the temperature may become dangerously low, and in the worst cases respiration and circulation may be paralyzed. Short of this, after 6 to 12 hours the man awakens from his drunken sleep with furred tongue, loss of appetite, thirst, flushed face and eyes, headache, and mental confusion. These phenomena vary according to the amount, strength, and purity of the liquor, the time occupied in consuming it, and the stability or resisting power of the person imbibing. Persons with a special cerebral susceptibility may develop wild maniacal excitement with a comparatively small dose. Such persons may suffer from an insane or alcoholic heredity, epilepsy, injuries to the head, or antecedent insanity. An automatic dream-state, in which complicated, it may be criminal, actions are performed quite unconsciously, is sometimes induced by acute alcoholism (Sullivan, *Alcoholism*, pp. 41–43).

3. Chronic alcoholism.—Excess has been defined as anything over that amount of alcohol which the body can completely dispose of in 24 hours, but a complete definition must include cases where any permanent mischief is produced during a lifetime. Since 1864, when Anstie declared 1½ oz. of absolute alcohol to be the physiological limit, the tendency amongst scientific writers has been steadily towards reduction of this. Abel (*l.c.* Sept. 1905, p. 275) concludes that the 'moderate' or average permissible quantity of alcohol is represented by one, or at most two, glasses of wine (10 p.c.) in the 24 hours; that is about half an ounce of absolute alcohol at the outside. Others (*e.g.* Max Grüber, quoted by Woodhead, *Brit. Journ. of Inebriety*, Jan. 1904, p. 166) hold that as even such a small quantity may impair function, it would be rash to assert that this would be harmless to the vast majority of mankind if taken habitually and indefinitely. The ordinary signs of chronic alcoholism are due to the habitual taking of much larger quantities. Such are loss of appetite, especially for breakfast, foul tongue, bad breath, with often a peculiar easily recognizable odour, morning vomiting, expectoration of yellow tough mucus, dyspeptic and intestinal disorders. Very fine tremors, most marked in the morning, are present in tongue, fingers, and lower limbs. Sleeplessness is frequent; speech shows a loss of crispness; memory, especially for names, is defective; there is a difficulty in coming to a decision or in concentrating the attention, and a disinclination for bodily or mental exertion. The victim of alcohol shows a want of initiative, and may give promises with the intention, but without the power, of keeping them. Self-respect becomes impaired, and by selfishness, neglect of wife, children, and other dependants, loosening of self-control and want of truthfulness, the moral deterioration is signalized.

Dipsomania, or periodical inebriety, is more frequently shown in women than in men. After an interval of abstinence, complete or relative, comes an overmastering impulse to drink. The time of recurrence may be quite irregular, in other cases it may be every week, fortnight, month, or at even longer intervals, and the duration of the attack is also variable. We are all subject to periodicity, even in regard to our brain force, and in dipsomaniacs there is usually a more than average instability of nerve. They show a close analogy to the condition found in epileptics.

Delirium tremens is a form of acute alcoholism supervening almost invariably on a chronic condition. There may have been a period of specially heavy drinking without taking food, or the onset may have been precipitated by some shock to the nervous system (mental, physical, or acute disease such as pneumonia). A frequent early symptom is distaste for drink, whilst hallucinations, with restlessness, nervousness, and insomnia, become more and more marked. The hands are constantly at work, picking at the bedclothes, going through the actions of some occupation, etc. Tremors become coarser, and are present all over the body. The mind is incessantly active, talking incoherently, seeing horrifying visions, hearing whispers, plottings, insults. Terror and suspicion are constant; the bodily functions are all deranged, the temperature is raised, and complicating diseases are apt to supervene. After an acute stage of 3 or 4 days the patient usually falls into a refreshing sleep, and awakes a different man. But the risk of a fatal result increases with each succeeding attack. *Delirium tremens* is comparatively rare in women, and is much more common amongst drinkers of spirits than amongst those who take wine or beer. Closely allied to *delirium tremens* is a form of continuous alcoholic delirium (*delirium ebriosum, mania a potu*), which often sends patients to asylums. *Alcoholic dementia* is not uncommon as the final state of chronic drinkers of alcohol; the symptoms point to an exaggeration of the ordinary mental state, developed by alcohol, as described above. Loss of memory, irritability, lowering of mental tone, and loss of self-control may become so marked as to require asylum treatment.

Besides those definite forms of alcoholic insanity, alcohol may be the *exciting* cause in various forms of mental disorder. It is probably the most powerful *predisposing* factor, after syphilis, in causing general paralysis of the insane. Kraepelin (*Münch. Med. Woch.*, April 1906) argues that 80 p.c. of cases of general paralysis would not occur if alcohol were banished from the world. The exact percentage of asylum inmates due to alcohol is somewhat difficult to ascertain, owing to varying ways of compiling statistics, and difficulties in getting at the facts of the patients' history. From 15 to 20 p.c. of the insane are so through drink, and in recent years this percentage has tended to increase, especially in large cities (Clouston, *Mental Diseases* [6], p. 483). The proportion of women to men thus afflicted is in Italy 1 to 11, in Germany 1 to 16, in Austria 1 to 5, in New York City 1 to 2, in Paris and Edinburgh about the same. Taking Great Britain all over, the proportion of women to men is about 1 to 2½, significant evidence of the amount of drinking amongst women in this country (Hoppe, *Tatsachen*, etc. p. 274 ff.; Rowntree and Sherwell, *Temp. Problem*, Appendix, p. 465). Allowance must be made for the likelihood that many who succumb to alcohol would in its absence break down mentally in some other way, in virtue of their unstable nervous system, and it has been noted that the habitual inebriates of the London police courts rarely become certifiably insane (Carswell, *Scottish Med. and Surg. Journ.* 1903, ii. p. 385). Genuine epilepsy may be produced by alcohol; if present already, it is inevitably made worse by drink. Not seldom one sees cases of epileptiform convulsions coming on after a long course of inebriety; they are induced by a specially severe bout. Not the brain only, but the other divisions of the nervous system, are very apt to be damaged by chronic alcoholism. Most characteristic is *multiple neuritis*, an inflammation of the nerves beginning in the feet and hands, and advancing upwards if the cause persists, till a fatal result occurs. There are changes in sensation, such as numbness, 'needles and pins,' pains, great muscular tenderness, diminished sensibility to touch; there is loss of power going on to complete paralysis, and there is mental deterioration. The disease may be brought on by alcohol in any form; it is often associated with the steady secret drinking of women. It is much aggravated by small quantities of arsenic, as was shown in an epidemic which occurred recently in Liverpool, Manchester, and other towns in the north of England. The cause here was the excessive drinking of beer manufactured from invert-sugar, in which arsenic was present as an impurity. Several other neuralgic and spinal-cord affections are caused or aggravated by chronic alcoholism.

4. Tissue changes caused by alcohol.—Most of the disorders that we have been describing are associated with pathological changes, easily recognized through the microscope. The various parts of the body are able to recover from the poisonous effect of even a large dose of alcohol. And, so far, the functional disturbance in the cell eludes the best methods of examination that we possess. If, however, the poisonous dose is repeated indefinitely, there comes a time when organic changes occur, and these are usually irremediable. Thus degeneration, indicated by changed microscopic appearance, may be found in the cells of the brain, cord or spinal nerves, in the heart muscle, the walls of the blood-vessels, the liver-cells, etc.; and at the same time there may be an increase of fibrous tissue, 'the lowest structure in the body' (Woodhead in Kelynack's *Drink Problem*).

5. The effect of alcohol on morbidity.—Besides the purely alcoholic forms of disease, such as cirrhosis of the liver and alcoholic neuritis, a large proportion of the illness found in hospital and in private practice is indirectly due to alcohol (Jacquet, *Presse Méd.*, 1899, p. 338). Not only are the tissues directly damaged, but the resisting power of the body to disease is greatly lowered by excessive drinking.

Acute pneumonia, for instance, is more apt to occur, and more likely to be fatal, in alcoholic persons. If the body is weakened in its resisting power, by starvation, by chill, or by a poison such as alcohol, microbes get a lodging in the system. Pneumonia in drinkers is about 3 times as fatal as amongst the temperate. So also with cholera, plague, yellow fever, malaria, and other microbe diseases. As for tuberculosis, the great mass of present-day medical opinion is opposed to the view that alcohol diminishes the likelihood of its onset. If the nervous system is lowered in tone, alcohol greatly helps the development of the disease. This is proved by the death-rate from phthisis in alcoholic insanity (R. Jones). Amongst traders in drink, tubercle is from 1½ to 3 times more frequent in every organ of the body liable to it than amongst persons following other occupations (Dickinson, *Transactions of Path. Soc.* vol. xl. 1889). When one further takes account of the unhealthy conditions in which chronic alcoholics live, one cannot doubt that drink is largely responsible for the wide-spread prevalence of tuberculosis. Venereal diseases are very frequently acquired in the intoxicated state, when the lower passions become supreme. In the army they are much less frequent among abstaining soldiers than among non-abstainers. In their treatment, abstinence from alcohol is usually enjoined. Syphilis is much more destructive among chronic drinkers. From the *surgeon's* point of view, the worst cases for operation are those of chronic drinkers. They take anæsthetics badly, their tissues do not heal well, and they are liable to septic complications. Clinical experience is confirmed by numerous experiments on animals; rabbits, guinea-pigs, fowls, etc., have been shown, if treated for a time with alcohol in even moderate doses, to be much more susceptible to the germs of tetanus, splenic fever, tuberculosis, diphtheria, etc., than non-alcoholized animals (Abbot, Déléarde, Laitinen—work summarized by Woodhead in *loc. cit.*).

Certain Friendly Societies in the United Kingdom consist entirely of total abstainers, and the amount of sickness amongst them is, to a marked degree, less than in Societies where abstinence is not compulsory, although in both classes the men are medically selected, and show, by the very fact that they join those Societies, that they are prudent and careful. The average duration of sickness per member among abstainers (Rechabites, Sons of Temperance, etc.) is only from a half to a third of that in other Societies. Alcoholics, when once put on the books of Trade Societies, whether through disease or injury, are notoriously slow in recovering.

6. Alcoholism and mortality.—The mortality returns of the United Kingdom give a very imperfect idea of the number of deaths due to alcohol (Vacher, *Practitioner*, Nov. 1902). Seeing that certificates of death are not treated as confidential documents belonging to the State, deaths are often attributed to diseases of the liver, kidneys, lungs, or nervous system, instead of to their primary cause—alcoholism. The Swiss returns of mortality, on the other hand, are reliable, and they show a death-rate from alcoholism, amongst men, of 10 p.c. or more. In Swiss communities of over 5000 inhabitants, there dies between the ages of 20 and 40 every seventh or eighth man directly or indirectly from alcohol, and between 40 and 60 every sixth, and above 60 every seventeenth man (Hoppe, p. 230). It is estimated that in this country alcohol accounts for 100,000 to 120,000 deaths per annum (Kerr, *Inebriety*, p. 381).

Certain British Insurance Societies have separate columns for abstainers and non-abstainers. In both sections the members are drawn from precisely the same class in all essential and important particulars, and the non-abstainers assured are good average lives. But the abstaining section in all cases shows a very much greater longevity. Thus in the United Kingdom Temperance and General Provident Institution the mortality in the general section has been, on an average, 36 p.c. higher than in the temperance section (Whittaker, 'Alcoholic Beverages and Longevity,' *Contemp. Rev.*, March 1904). Of course the 'general section' represents an average which includes at one end of the scale men who are extremely moderate, and at the other those who are free drinkers. In the absence of any accepted standard of moderation, the class of 'moderate drinkers' must suffer statistically.

7. Alcoholism and crime.—There is universal testimony as to the close relationship between excessive drinking and breaches of the moral law and the laws of the State. This is a direct consequence of the paralysis of the higher faculties, intellectual and moral, and the resulting free play given to the lower inclinations. Alcohol is not only a direct cause of crime, but it acts powerfully along with other conditions, such as hereditary nervous weakness or instability of the brain. Again, crime may be due to loss of work, poverty, and starvation, so often the results of indulgence in alcohol.

A distinction has rightly been drawn between the lighter and the graver violations of the law which are due to drink. It is fortunately true that the great majority are of the former class. To them, however,—in order to give some idea of the degrading effect of excessive drinking,—we must add the vast number of cases where similar offences are committed with impunity, escaping the notice of the police through the sheltering influence of friends. Moreover, these offences are so common that there is a disposition on the part of the police, magistrates, the public generally, and the relatives to regard them with the utmost leniency. The large proportion of habitual inebriates charged time after time shows that many, perhaps most, of the petty offences are really due to chronic alcoholism plus a heavier bout than usual. In 9 cases out of 10, the drunkard of our police courts figures also as the wife-beater, the beggar, the prostitute, or the thief. As for the graver offences, the bulk of crimes of acquisitiveness are not connected with alcoholism. On the other hand, alcoholism is probably the cause of some 60 p.c.

of homicidal offences, and of a smaller, though still considerable, proportion of crimes of lust. Nearly always in homicidal crimes, and very frequently in sexual crimes, the alcoholic condition which generates the criminal impulse is chronic intoxication and not casual drunkenness. (Sullivan, *Alcoholism*, 1906, ch. ix.).

8. Alcoholism and the future of the race.—Alcohol is specially dangerous to children, as their delicate tissues are highly susceptible to the poison. Most disastrous results follow its administration in the early years of life—a practice which is far from uncommon amongst the ignorant. Besides the direct effects, such as stunting of growth, blunting of intellectual and moral faculties, and organic changes, we must attribute to alcohol the multifarious evil influences of the social environment in drinking families. Hence the incidence of sickness and mortality in the families of parents who are one or both given to drink is extremely heavy.

The Report on Physical Deterioration (1904) remarks on the increase of drinking amongst women of the working-classes, with consequences extremely prejudicial to the care of the offspring, not to speak of the possibility of children being born permanently disabled. If the mother drinks heavily during lactation, the quality of her milk is much impaired, and there may be present in it a certain amount of alcohol. Still more serious for the child is drinking on the part of the mother during pregnancy. Not only is the fœtus badly nourished, but alcohol is found to pass freely into its blood from the mother's. Hence we find in such conditions a great predisposition to abortion and premature labour; and if the infant is born viable, it is apt to be the subject of disease or deformity. There is passed on in many cases not only a nervous excitability, but a tendency to give way to drink sooner or later. While it may be true that 80 to 85 p.c. of all children are born apparently healthy, whatever the antecedent condition of the mother, it is highly probable that the first 10 or 15 years of life, even under the best conditions, would reveal diseased tendencies that were present in a latent condition from the first. Notwithstanding the ancient and wide-spread belief that the condition of intoxication in one or both parents at the time of conception has a malign influence on the germ-plasm, this cannot be said to be scientifically proved. The prevailing scientific view is that no acquired characters can be transmitted from parents to child; but when poisons are circulating in the blood, such as the syphilitic or alcoholic, it is practically certain that they have a modifying effect on the germ-cells (Saleeby, *Heredity*, p. 73). On the other hand, the tendency to degeneration through alcohol would be at once arrested by the removal of the cause, and civilized races would rapidly improve in physique. Races that have been accustomed only to their own fermented drinks, such as the North American Indians and the West Africans (Külz, *Archiv für Rassen- und Gesellsch. Biologie*, ii. 1905), have shown a tendency to die out when habitually taking imported distilled liquor. Previously there was no race alcoholism under conditions which had lasted for hundreds of years, their relatively weak drink being obtainable only at special seasons of the year, and on special occasions. The undoubted increase in insanity in this and other countries is largely due, according to the best authorities, to alcoholism. Mott's investigations (*Alcohol and Insanity*, London, 1906) show clearly that those who become insane in this way have their balance upset by an amount of alcohol much less than can be taken with comparative impunity by persons of more stable nervous system. In such cases alcohol reveals some latent defect, just as in other cases the imbecile, the epileptic, or the degenerate, through marked susceptibility to alcohol, join the criminal classes. *Suicide* (Sullivan, *Alcoholism*; Prinzing, *Trunksucht und Selbstmord*, Leipzig, 1895) has become more frequent in recent years in almost all civilized States, its rate being specially heavy amongst persons who are exposed to alcoholism. Great Britain has a larger proportion of women suicides than other lands, this being connected with the greater amount of female drunkenness. 80 p.c. of all cases of attempted suicide in England are alcoholic, while only 30 p.c. of cases of completed suicide are so classified. Alcoholic suicide may result from one of the diseased mental states, such as *delirium tremens*, melancholia, the automatic dream-state, or some other condition associated with hallucinations; or it may come from the poverty, misery, and indifference to life that alcohol is apt to produce. The association of alcohol with *accidents* of all sorts is brought home to us by the daily newspapers and otherwise, but no statistics can show the vast number of cases where lowering of the mental functions by alcohol without admitted excess, is responsible for some catastrophe. Many railway companies in America have an absolute rule against drinking on the part of their officials, and more or less strict measures of this nature are taken by British companies. Comparatively slight impairment of attention, presence of mind, and efficiency in the railway servant may endanger hundreds besides himself. The more strict the rule against drinking on any particular railway, the more free is it from accident. Again, accidents are much more common on Saturdays and holidays; any hospital can prove this, and also that the reason for this is drink. Accident insurance societies often give abstainers a discount of 10 p.c.

9. Alcoholism and poverty.—Drink, according to Charles Booth (*Pauperism and the Endowment of Old Age*), is the most prolific cause of pauperism, and it is the least necessary. From one-third to one-half of those who receive poor relief owe their position directly to drunkenness as the principal cause. (The total cost of poor relief in England and Wales annually is about £12,000,000). To this should be added a large percentage in which drink is the indirect cause of pauperism, through disease or injury; and besides this, just above the pauper class is the enormous amount of comparative poverty from misspent earnings, loss of working time, and general impairment of efficiency. It is calculated that at least half the taxes accruing from drink are expended by the State in preventing, punishing, and repairing evils which are the direct consequence of the consumption of that drink. Of the £170,000,000 or so annually spent in this country on liquors, about £100,000,000 come from the pockets of the working-classes. Many working men spend 6s. or 7s. a week on drink, and some very much more. The average drink expenditure per head in 1905 was £3, 15s. 11½d., and per family of 5 persons £18, 19s. 9½d.; but it must be remembered that millions of adults drink no alcoholic liquor, and that over 15,000,000 of the population are children. Hence amongst those who take drink to excess the expenditure is enormous, and means such a deduction from an income which is little better than a living wage, that not enough is left for food, clothing, good housing, etc. Here we are face to face with the tremendous waste of earnings, which, spent productively, would raise the general standard of living, check physical deterioration, provide better houses, clothing, food, furniture, and stimulate the desire for healthier and higher recreations. Greater demands on the genuine productive industries of the country would have to be satisfied, and the tremendous addition to the national efficiency would help to solve the grave social and industrial problems with which we are confronted.

10. Treatment.—In dealing with *acute alcoholism*, the skill of the physician and attendants is often severely taxed. Apart from purely medical measures, the main reliance is to be placed in complete withdrawal of alcohol, administration of liquid nourishment in abundance, and the procuring of mental and bodily rest. In *chronic alcoholism* the patient may be helped by full explanations of the action of alcohol on the body, by appeals to his better nature, by any measure that will strengthen the will power, whether religious or social (such as joining a temperance society), or by being removed for a sufficiently long time (one to three years) from temptation. In the way of prevention much is to be hoped for from the wider diffusion of scientific knowledge, along with the spread of education (see 'The Teaching of Temperance,' by E. Claude Taylor in Kelynack's *Drink Problem* [a good bibliography of teaching manuals is given]). Improvements in housing and domestic cookery, higher rates of pay, and the consequent bettering of bodily, mental, and moral health, all favour temperance. Total abstinence should be enjoined on certain classes: those who are hereditarily predisposed, through inebriety in parents or in grandparents, or through want of nerve stability; those whose occupations are closely associated with a heavy drink mortality; those who have given way to drink; persons who have suffered from diseases of the brain or nerves, or injuries to the head; and all children and juveniles. See also artt. DRUNKENNESS, INEBRIATE ASYLUMS.

LITERATURE.—In addition to references already given, the following may be consulted: Abderhalden, *Bibliog. d. Alkoholismus*, 1904; Amer. Assoc. for the study and cure of Inebriety, *Disease of Inebriety*, 1893; A. Baer, *Der Alkoholismus*, 1878; John Burns, *Labour and Drink*, 1904; T. S. Clouston, *The Hygiene of Mind*, 1906; N. S. Davis, 'American Experiments on Alcohol,' *Med. Temp. Review*, 1900; M. Helenius, *Die Alkoholfrage*, 1903; Hugo Hoppe, *Die Tatsachen über den Alkohol*, 1904 (a comprehensive work; literature very fully

given); V. Horsley and M. D. Sturge, *Alcohol and the Human Body*, 1907; R. Hutchison, *Food and Dietetics*, 1900; T. N. Kelynack, *The Alcohol Problem in its Biological Aspect*, 1906 [he also edits *The Drink Problem*, 1907, containing special articles by 14 physicians]; Norman Kerr, *Inebriety*, 1888; Lancereaux, 'Intoxication par les boissons alcooliques' in *Nouveau Traité de Médecine*, 1907; W. Bevan Lewis, *Textbook of Mental Diseases*, 1899; Ploetz, 'Zur Bedeutung des Alkohols für Leben und Entwickelung der Rasse,' *Archiv für Rassen- u. Gesellsch. Biologie*, i. 229 (1903); *The Practitioner*, November 1902 (special alcohol number); G. Archdall Reid, *Principles of Heredity*, 1906, *Alcoholism, a Study in Heredity*, 1901; W. Ford Robertson, 'Pathology of Chronic Alcoholism' (*British Journ. of Inebriety*), 1904; H. D. Rolleston, 'Alcoholism' (Allbutt's *System of Medicine*), 1897; Rowntree and Sherwell, *Temperance Problem and Social Reform*, 1899; C. W. Saleeby, *Heredity* (Jack's Scientific Series), 1906; Samuelson, *History of Drink*, 1878; Shadwell, *Drink, Temperance, and Legislation*, 1902; Sullivan, *Alcoholism: A Chapter in Social Pathology*, 1906; Triboulet, Mathieu and Mignot, *Traité de l'alcoolisme*, 1905; G. Sims Woodhead, *Recent Researches on the Action of Alcohol in Health and Sickness* (Lees and Raper Memorial Lecture), 1904; J. Mackie Whyte, 'Some Recent Researches on Alcohol, their bearing on Treatment,' *Med. Temp. Rev.*, May 1901; *Final Report of Royal Commission on Licensing Laws* (Peel Commission), 1899; *Report from the Departmental Committee on Habitual Offenders*, etc., 1895; *Report of the Interdepartmental Committee on Physical Deterioration*, 1904; *Report of the Proceedings of the Nat. Conf. on Infantile Mortality held at Westminster, June 13 and 14, 1906; The Brit. Journ. of Inebriety* (pub. quarterly for the Society for the Study of Inebriety); *The Med. Temp. Rev.* (pub. monthly for the Brit. Med. Temp. Assoc.); *The Amer. Quart. Journ. of Inebriety*.
J. Mackie Whyte.

ALEUTS.—**1.** The religion, mythology, and folk-lore of the natives of the Aleutian Islands—the 'stepping-stones' from Alaska to Kamtchatka—and of the north shore of the long narrow peninsula of Alaska as far as the river Ugashik, are especially important, since their long isolation in a peculiar environment has caused them 'to develop in particular directions more than any other known branch of the Innuit (Eskimo) stem,' this variation being 'especially evident in their language, religious exercises, and certain details of handiwork, such as embroidery and grass-fibre weaving' (Dall). The language is rich in verbal forms and has many peculiarities of vocabulary, but is, nevertheless, undoubtedly Eskimoan in type, not 'transitional between Samoyed and Eskimo' (Henry). The harpoon attains in the southern portions of the Aleutian area 'a *finesse* in structure and appearance nowhere else seen'; the arrow also is 'delicately complex,' neat and beautiful; and the 'exquisite weaving' displayed in the Aleutian beach-grass work 'will compare with that of any basketmakers in the world' (Mason). The *kayak*, the characteristic skin-boat of the Eskimo men, reaches the minimum in size and height among the Aleuts. The lamp, which with the Eskimos generally is the analogue of the fireplace, or the hearth, with many other peoples, is crudest and rudest among the Aleuts,—'the most primitive lamps on earth are those of the ancient Aleuts; many of them are merely unmodified rock fragments' (Hough). Yet the modern Aleuts use small lamps in their fishing boats at sea for warming chilled hands and bodies. They seem to have used the lamp mostly outside the house, preferring, when possible, a fire in the open air, though they are said to have done much less cooking than the other Eskimo tribes. When first discovered by the whites, both men and women among the Aleuts wore labrets, or lip-ornaments, a custom borrowed, perhaps, from the adjacent American Indians, and primarily confined to the female sex. Dall reports the practice of wearing labrets as having 'died out within two generations' (*ante* 1878). Besides labrets, the Aleuts possessed masks, which figured in their dances and religious ceremonies, and were also placed on the faces of the dead. In physical type the Aleuts differ somewhat from the Eskimos proper, being rather brachycephalic and of darker complexion; in facial expression also some difference has been noted. Their constant use of the *kayak* and the cramped position they are forced to assume for long hours have affected their gait and the condition of their limbs. In the management of these boats the Aleuts have been very skilful. Veniaminov, the Russian priest who was among them in the early part of the 19th cent., styled them 'sea Cossacks, riders of marine mares'; they were bow-legged, too, like the famous horsemen of the Czar. The Aleuts have been in their present environment, into which they came from the interior of Alaska (the probable scene of the primitive dispersion of the Eskimo race, or, at least, of a considerable part of it), for a very long time. Dall's investigations of the ancient village-sites, shell-heaps, mummy-caves, etc., of the Aleutian Islands demonstrate the continuity of occupation of the region by this people, and their apparent progress through three periods of culture (littoral, fishing, hunting). The earliest forms of some of their art-objects (*e.g.* labrets) are preserved in the burial-caves and shell-heaps, and their variations may be traced down to the times of the modern Aleuts and the advent of white influences, in consequence of which their ancient culture has tended more and more to disappear.

Like the Eskimos of continental Alaska, the Aleuts seem to have been influenced in several ways by the peoples of north-eastern Asia. To such contact Dr. Franz Boas attributes the use of property-marks on arrows, harpoons, etc., something as yet unrecorded of the Eskimo tribes outside of Alaska (*Amer. Anthrop.* vol. i., N.S., 1899, p. 613). By inspection of the harpoons in a dead, stranded whale, it is possible to discover the community to which the killer belongs, who, when notified, takes possession of the animal, dividing it with the finders. These property-marks 'occur almost exclusively on weapons used in hunting, which, after being despatched, remain in the bodies of large game,' and 'in each village the natives of a certain group—a boat's crew, family, house community, or any other social unit—use a certain decoration for their implements, which, in connexion with certain lines, forms their property-mark.' From the Russians, through the Siberian natives, and not from the Indians, the Aleuts and Alaskan Eskimos acquired the knowledge and use of tobacco, according to Murdoch (*Amer. Anthrop.* vol. i., 1888, p. 328). The modern Aleuts 'use nothing but civilized methods of smoking,' and are great smokers. The absence of ceremonial connected with the use of tobacco among the Aleuts, is another evidence of the non-American mode of its introducton. On the other hand, the Aleuts have adopted something from the American Indian tribes, as, *e.g.*, in all probability, the habit, just mentioned, of wearing lip-ornaments, some art-*motifs*, etc. The institution of slavery prevailed among them as it did among certain Indian tribes of the North Pacific coast.

2. The *puberty-ceremonies* and *marriage-customs* of the Aleuts are of special interest. When a girl reaches the age of puberty, she is isolated from the rest of the community in a small *barrabarra*, or hut, and no one except her slave, if she possesses one, is permitted to visit her. This confinement lasts seven days, and the breaking of the tabu by a man is the theme of one of the most wide-spread tales, which has many variants.

The couple concerned are often brother and sister, and sometimes the woman is forcibly ravished, while at other times she yields consent readily enough. After the discovery of the offence the two young people flee, pursued by their parents and others (who resent the infraction of the tabu as an unpardonable crime), and ultimately hurl themselves from a cliff into the sea, becoming the first two sea-otters, or (in some versions) hair-seals. In one version of the tale, reported by Golder, the girl, who is ravished in the dark, after the fire has gone out, cuts the sinews of her assaulter's legs as he escapes through the roof. The man, who dies from a fall on the rocks, turns out to be her own brother. She finds him dead on the floor of her parents' house, with all his friends mourning. Instead of taking part in the mourning herself, she sings a joyous song, the burden of which is, 'Get up, my brother, get up!' and, approaching her brother's corpse, uncovers herself. Gradually movement returns to him; first, his toes wriggle, then, as she dances and sings again, the life-colour re-enters his cheeks; and, when she has gone through her conjuration a third time, he suddenly jumps up and seeks to embrace her. She flees, pursued by him, and both followed by the people, until, reaching a cliff overhanging the sea, the brother and sister are compelled to leap from it into the water, and, when they are caught sight of again, they have become two sea-otters, the first of those creatures known in the world. In another tale, the first sea-otters are represented to be a woman and her paramour (the nephew of her husband), with whom she has sworn to die. The sun and moon legend of the Greenland Eskimos seems to belong, partly at least, to this cycle. It is curious to find among the Aleutians that improper sexual relations are connected with the violation of the tabu of girls at the age of puberty. The version of the legend with this theme is perhaps the oldest, as it is the most detailed form. The early Aleuts, Veniaminov informs us, looked upon incest with horror (later accounts disagree on this point), esteeming it the worst of crimes. Such intercourse was believed to result always in monstrous offspring (children disfigured with the tusks and beard of sea-animals, etc.). They had no prejudice against the intermarriage of cousins.

The Aleuts had no marriage ceremony, apparently, though children were sometimes betrothed to each other. The recognition of the marriage came with the birth of a child. The primitive custom seems to have been for a man to take to wife a young woman from the next village (or one not his own), but not to set up housekeeping with her until she had borne him a child. Until that event happened, the woman remained at the house of her father, where she was visited from time to time by her husband. Among the early Aleuts, girls, or married females, giving birth to illegitimate children, were put to death, and their bodies hidden away, so much was such conduct despised. Infanticide was regarded as something likely to cause great misfortune to the whole community. Wives were exchanged sometimes for food, clothes, etc., and were often lent as a mark of hospitality. They could also be divorced or sent home, when unsatisfactory to the husband. In some cases, the children were taken by the mother. The re-marriage either of widowers or widows was not permitted until some time had elapsed since the death of their consorts. Both polyandry and polygamy seem to have occurred among the Aleuts. With those of Unalaska, in cases of polyandry the husbands agreed amicably to the terms upon which they were to share the woman, or, the first married was the chief husband, the second, and inferior, being 'a hunter or wandering trader.' Since polygamous families depended for their maintenance upon the wealth of a single husband, it appears to have been permissible for him to return his wives to their parents, if his fortune decreased to such an extent as to make it impossible for him to support them all properly. Wives could be obtained by purchase and by rendering services to the father; but, in the case of purchase, certain other relatives besides the father had to be compensated. Marriage by capture was reported by Coxe, at the close of the 18th cent., among the natives of Unimak, the largest island of the Archipelago. With certain of the Aleuts (*e.g.* those of Atkha) the man took the widow of his dead brother, such action being compulsory rather than facultative. Among these natives great jealousy is said to have existed. From various parts of the Aleutian area the existence was reported of men who adopted the ways and habits of women, dressing like them, etc., and never marrying.

3. The *burial customs* of the Aleuts also deserve special mention, by reason of the great care often bestowed on the disposal of the dead. Memorial feasts, lasting sometimes for several days, were held, and, according to the details in the stories, slaves were often sacrificed. The bodies of the dead were sometimes hung up in the hut, or suspended in the open air from a pole to which the cradle or mat was attached. When the bodies were laid away in some rock-shelter, protective masks were often put over their faces to guard them from the too inquisitive glances of the spirits. The bodies of certain rich individuals and people of importance in the tribe were washed in running water after the entrails had been removed, then dried, wrapped in furs, grass-matting, etc., and hung up in some cave, or other place dry and sheltered from the rain. Some of these mummies are very old, being found with all the marks of great age. Sometimes the dead Aleuts were placed in these caves and rock-shelters in lifelike postures, dressed and armed, as if active in some favourite occupation—hunting, fishing, sewing, or the like; and with them were placed figures representing the animals of the chase, wooden imitations of their weapons, etc. According to Elliott, the mummified bodies of celebrated whale-hunters used to be removed from their resting-places in the caves and dipped in the running water of streams, those about to venture forth on the hunt drinking of the water that flowed over the remains, to obtain the good-luck and the skill of the dead. It is also said that sometimes the body of a celebrated whale-hunter, who had died, was cut into small pieces, each living hunter taking one, which, when carefully dried, was kept for the purpose of rubbing the head of the whale-spear. The Aleuts seem to have had other superstitious proceedings of a similar nature connected with the transference of the qualities of the great dead to the living. Famous hunters and mighty chiefs were especially honoured in this way.

4. The early Aleuts had very many *songs*, the old stories being nearly always accompanied by or containing some. According to Veniaminov and Golder, there were historical songs, songs of ancestors and heroes, songs used only on religious occasions (strictly religious songs accompanying the spirit-ceremonies, etc.), and songs dealing with the ordinary affairs of life. Very often songs were extemporized. Golder is of opinion that the democratic shamanistic *régime* which 'allowed any Aleut to think he could compose a song,' is 'a condition of degeneracy as compared with the earlier time when the making of the songs was more or less in the hands of shamans of distinction'; but this is hardly the case. As both men and women could be shamans, they were likewise both song-makers. There were numerous conjuring-songs for hunting, fishing, 'raising the dead,' calling and dispersing the spirits, etc. Songs were accompanied by the drum, the only musical instrument of the Aleuts. Stories were usually accompanied by one or more songs, but the Aleuts of to-day have forgotten the songs, though they continue to narrate some of the stories.

5. The early Aleuts were very fond of *dances* and *dance-festivals*, some of which were carried out by the whole village, with other villages as guests, or participants to some extent. After the evening meal the men are said sometimes to have danced naked until exhausted. Dances of naked men, and of naked women, from which the other sex was rigidly excluded on pain of death, and masked dances of various kinds were in vogue. Successive dances of children, naked women, and women in curious attire, which were followed by shamanistic incantations, feasting, etc., are also reported as having occurred among the Aleutians. The dances in which the sexes took part together are reputed to have been more decorous. Their most

remarkable performance of this sort, however, was the great moonlight dance held in December, which had considerable religious significance. In connexion with these dances, wooden figures or images were set up, one for the women and one for the men. The sexes danced apart from each other, masked and naked, on the snow under the moonlight. The huge masks employed on these occasions were so made that the wearer could look only at the ground, since to see or look at the images, upon which the spirits were believed to descend during the ceremonies, was death to the individuals so doing. After the dance was over, the images and masks, which seem generally to have been made for the particular occasion, were broken in pieces and thrown into the sea. Although mention is made of wooden figures carried from island to island, and associated with certain ceremonies, permanent 'idols' and 'temples' hardly existed. There were, it appears, certain 'sacred' high places, or rocks, where, with mysterious ceremonies, old men, or men only (women and youths not being allowed to approach these spots), made offerings. Events like the casting up of a whale on the beach were the cause of dancing and other festivities. In some of the dances the participants put on all their ornaments and finery, while in others they danced naked, except for the large wooden masks, which came down to their shoulders, and often represented various sea-animals. The masks used in the ordinary dances were different from those used in religious ceremonies, the former being evidently copied from the Aleut type of face, while the others, when human faces are represented, seem to differ much from it. The dancing-masks are often grotesque. Some of the carved masks used in certain ceremonies were deposited in caves. Masked ceremonies were also connected with the spring-time festivals.

6. Besides their religious dances and like ceremonies, the Aleuts had others of a *dramatic* and *educational* nature. Myths and legends were acted out in pantomime and dance by the members of one village, who would invite the inhabitants of another to witness the 'play.' On such occasions special songs would be composed and sung. In these 'plays' men and animals alike were imitated and represented. Similar events on a smaller scale took place in individual huts, the larger ones in the 'village-house.' Veniaminov and Golder give an account of a performance called *kugan agalik*, or 'the appearance of the devils,' the object of which was to frighten the women into obedience and 'keep them under' properly. The essentials of the performance were as follows:—When it was thought necessary to impress the women and girls, certain of the men left the village on a pretended hunt. At night, after they had been gone a few days, the men at home made believe some calamity was about to overtake the community, and, by pretending great fear, made the women remain in the huts. While they were thus frightened, strange noises were heard, and the 'devils' arrived, against whom the men made the show of a valiant defence. After the 'devils' had been driven away, it was found that one of the villagers was missing, and a woman, previously agreed upon, was carried out as a ransom for him. By and by both were brought back, the man apparently dead. He was gradually revived by being beaten with inflated bladders, addressed with invocations, etc., and was given by his relatives to the woman who had saved him. The lost hunters then came in and expressed surprise at what had occurred. This 'play' is clearly analogous to the 'Mumbo Jumbo' ceremonies of the Negroes of West Africa and to the initiation rites of the Australian aborigines.

7. The early Aleuts had very many *stories* and *legends* and much *folk-lore*. According to Veniaminov and Golder, their tales and legends were chiefly of three kinds: purely narrative, satiric or moralizing, and mythological. Comparatively few of the stories of the Aleuts have been preserved,—of those recorded nearly all are due to Veniaminov (1820–1840), and Golder at the close of the last century.

One of the Aleutian ancestor stories tells of the adventures, so disastrous to the people, of Chief Agitaligak of Adus and his son Kayulinach. Another is concerned with the doings of the son of 'the woman fond of intestines.' One of the origin-legends ascribes the beginnings of the Aleuts to a being who fell down from the sky in the form of a dog. Another version of this myth of canine ancestry, found also elsewhere in the Eskimo territory, makes the Aleuts descend from a female dog belonging to Unalaska and a great dog which swam over to her from the island of Kadiak. Still another account traces them back to the dog-mother, called Mahakh, and an old man named Iraghdadakh, who came from the north to visit her. Another legend makes the ancestors of the Aleuts two curious creatures, male and female, half-man and half-fox,—the name of the male being Acagnikakh. Some legends also attribute to the 'Old Man' the power to create human beings by throwing stones on the earth; birds, beasts, and fishes being made by throwing stones over the land, into the water, etc.

Golder calls attention to the fact that the Aleutian stories are very realistic, there being 'not a single story that could not have happened in real life.' Supernatural incidents occur, to be sure, but they come in only at the end of the tale. It is, as Golder remarks, 'as if the gods were called in to help out the story-teller, when he gets into a tight place.'

8. As may be seen from their religious ceremonies and other practices, as well as from the evidence in their tales and legends, the Aleutians had much *spirit-lore*. The shamans were able to obtain the assistance of spirits by their incantations, and the spirits (*kugan*) of power descended into the 'idols' during the great religious dances. The Aleuts believed that their dead relatives acted as guardian spirits, helping them out in all dangerous situations and trying conditions. They also relied much upon these spirits in their schemes of revenge, etc. Belief in amulets of various kinds was common,—the warrior, *e.g.*, wore a belt of sea-weed with magic knots. Mention is also made of the *tkhimkee*, a marvellous pebble, which all animals were unable to resist when it was thrown into the sea. The Aleuts of to-day have little of the rich mythology and folk-lore of their ancestors, the conversion to the Greek Church, which took place in the time of Veniaminov, and the course pursued by the Russian priesthood having resulted in the passing away of institutions and beliefs, ceremonies, customs, and habits of the olden time. To this process the Aleuts appear to have taken somewhat readily, a fact which further hastened the disappearance of what was purely national and racial.

LITERATURE.—H. H. Bancroft, *Native Races of the Pacific States*, i. [1883] 87–95, iii. 104–105, 144–145, 508, 577–580; W. H. Dall, 'Tribes of the Extreme North-West,' *N. Amer. Ethnol.* i. [1877] 1–106, *Alaska and its Resources*, Boston, 1870, see pp. 388–390, 'Remains of late Prehistoric Man . . . of the Aleutian Islands,' *Smithson. Contrib. to Knowl.*, No. 318, 1878, 28–32, 'On Masks, Labrets,' etc., *Third Ann. Rep. BE*, 1881–1882, 67–202, esp. 137–143; H. W. Elliott, *An Arctic Province*, London, 1886; J. G. Georgi, *Beschreibung aller Nationen des russ. Reiches*, St. Petersburg, 1776; F. A. Golder, 'Aleutian Tales,' *JAFL* xviii. [1905] 215–222, see also vol. xx.; V. Henry, *Esquisse d'une gram. raisonnée de la langue Aléoute*, Paris, 1879; I. Petroff, 'Report on the Population, Industries, and Resources of Alaska,' *Rep. U.S. Census*, 1880, iii. 1–189; A. Pfizmaier, 'Die Sprache der Aleuten und Fuchsinseln,' *SBAW Phil.-hist. Kl.* 1884, pp. 801–880; J. C. Pilling, *Bibliog. of the Eskimo Language*, Washington, 1887; A. L. Pinart, 'Les Aléoutes, leurs origines et leurs légendes,' *Actes de la Soc. d'Ethnog.*, Paris, 1872–1873, pp. 87–92, *La Caverne d'Aknanh, Isle d'Ounga*, Paris, 1875; E. Reclus, *Primitive Folk*, London, 1890, ch. ii. 48–122, on 'The Western Innoits, especially the Aleutians'; I. Veniaminov, *Notes on the Islands of the Unalaskan District* (in Russian), 2 vols., St. Petersburg, 1840, with a 3rd vol. *Notes on the Atkhan Aleuts* (also in Russian); *Bulletin 30, BE*, Washington, 1907, pp. 36–37.

ALEXANDER F. CHAMBERLAIN.

ALEXANDER OF ABONOTEICHOS in Paphlagonia owes his fame to a treatise of Lucian, who was his contemporary. The piece is full of the minutest details of Alexander's life. But Lucian makes no concealment of the contempt and hatred which he felt for one whom he regarded as a venal and impudent impostor, trading on the selfish superstition of an ignorant and credulous people. In his war against the credulity of his age, Lucian has evidently exerted all his art to blacken the character of one who seemed to him to represent its worst excesses of superstition. Yet, apart from the charges against Alexander's morals, Lucian's life of Alexander is probably more trustworthy than his life of Peregrinus.

Alexander was a Greek of Abonoteichos, with splendid gifts of mind and body, and a charm of manner which, Lucian admits, left on casual acquaintances the impression of a high and simple character. He began his career with a wizard physician connected with the circle of Apollonius of Tyana. On his death, Alexander formed a partnership with a Byzantine adventurer, and during their travels in Macedonia, the pair, seeing the passion of the time for any means of forecasting the future, determined to exploit its hopes and fears by founding an oracle which should rival the fame and wealth of the old seats of prophecy. They brought a tame serpent from Macedonia, and in the precincts of Apollo at Chalcedon they buried two tablets, predicting that Asklepios would come to Pontus with his father, and make his home at Abonoteichos. Alexander knew his countrymen. The promise of the epiphany soon spread, and the people of Abonoteichos at once began to build a temple for the coming god. Soon Alexander appeared among them, with white tunic and purple cloak, and a scimitar in his hand, reciting an oracle which proclaimed him 'the seed of Perseus, dear to Apollo.' Fits of prophetic frenzy still further raised the general excitement. One morning at dawn, almost naked and scimitar in hand, he bounded into the market-place in all the orgiastic excitement of a votary of the Great Mother, leapt upon the altar, and, with a strange jumble of Hebrew or Chaldæan phrases, announced the coming of the god. He then rushed to a ditch which ran round the foundations of the new temple, fished up a goose's egg in which a young snake had been skilfully enclosed, broke the shell, and displayed to the awestruck crowd the nascent deity.

Multitudes thronged to Abonoteichos, and Alexander, sitting on a divan, held a levée, in which he displayed, coiled about his shoulders, the trained serpent from Macedonia, to which a very simple art had attached a human head. Crowds poured through the darkened room, jostling one another to see the new god so miraculously mature, so human and so divine. The great miracle drew crowds from Bithynia, Thrace, and Galatia, and even from remote barbarian regions. Artists flocked to the spot to express the likeness of the new deity in colours, or bronze or silver, 'Glycon the third of the seed of Zeus, a light to men.'

Alexander had studied the system of the older oracles, and he determined to found a new one, while he carefully displayed a reverence for the ancient seats of Claros or Didyma. For a small fee of 2 obols he received on stated days sealed packets, which he ceremoniously returned apparently unopened, with the needed answer. A hot needle and a delicate hand concealed the imposture, although Lucian by means of an obstinate seal once exposed the fraud. The oracle, like so many of the time, was mainly one of healing, and, skilfully managed, with an army of officials and interested envoys and missionaries to spread the fame of its efficacy throughout the Empire, it gathered in a revenue of nearly £7000 a year. Its fame spread to Rome, and great nobles like Severianus the governor of Cappadocia, and Rutilianus, one of the most experienced statesmen of the age, were drawn into the net. Alexander had many questions of a dangerous political curiosity put to him, which would not bear disclosure. Rutilianus, at the mature age of sixty, even condescended to marry Alexander's daughter, his boasted offspring by an amour with Selene, who had been captivated as by another Endymion.

In the great plague of A.D. 167, a magical verse, dictated by the new oracle, was inscribed over the doors of houses throughout the Roman world. Even the circle of the philosophic Emperor yielded to the imposture. When the Marcomannic war was at its height, an oracle from Abonoteichos was received at headquarters, ordering two lions to be thrown into the Danube. The ceremony was followed by a disaster to the Roman arms, which was glibly explained by classical precedent.

Alexander, with all his daring and ingenuity, was scrupulously conservative in adhesion to ancient forms. He crowned his achievements by establishing mysteries on the approved model, from which Christians and Epicurean freethinkers were excluded under a solemn ban. The ceremonies lasted for three days. Scenes from old and new mythologies were presented with striking effect—the labour of Leto, the birth of Apollo and Asklepios, the epiphany of Glycon, and the celestial origin of Alexander himself. Lucian believed that the new religion was tainted with the foulest immorality. Alexander had many enemies, and there is no doubt that he was surrounded by large numbers who, like Lucian, scorned and derided the superstition of the time. They openly assailed the new oracle, and strove to convict it of deceit. For his own scornful incredulity, Lucian once nearly paid with his life. And Alexander, by the mouth of the god, ordered that the blasphemies of the atheists should be punished by stoning. He finally triumphed over all opposition, and rose even to divine honours. His statue was an object of worship at Parium in the time of Athenagoras. Inscriptions of Dacia and Mœsia attest the wide extent of his influence. In the third century, the religion of Glycon still flourished at Ionopolis, the new name which Alexander had given Abonoteichos, and which still survives under altered form. Coins of Nicomedia and Ionopolis bear the device of the serpent with a human head.

LITERATURE.—Lucian, *Alexander*; Athenagoras, *Legatio pro Christianis*, ch. 26; *CIL* iii. 1021 f.; 'Ephem. Epigr.' in *CIL*, suppl. ii. 331; Renan, *L'Église chrétienne* (1878), 428 f., and *M. Aurèle* (1880), 50; Gregorovius, *Hadrian* (1884), ii. ch. 15.

S. DILL.

ALEXANDER THE GREAT (his place in the history of religion and ethics).—**I. Synopsis of his reign.**—Alexander III., afterwards surnamed the Great, was born at Pella, B.C. 356. He was the son of Philip II., king of Macedonia, and Olympias, a Molossian princess. In 336 he succeeded to the throne, and two years afterwards set out on his Eastern expedition. S.W. Asia was subdued by his victories at the Granicus (B.C. 334) and at Issus (B.C. 333). His attention was then turned to Egypt, and in the course of the expedition an opportunity occurred for a visit to Jerusalem, which may perhaps be regarded as historical. Alexandria was founded in B.C. 331. Campaigns against the northern provinces of Bactria and Sogdiana followed, and gradually all the districts over which the kings of Persia exercised sovereignty were subdued. Alexander then forced the Khyber Pass, or, more probably, another pass 80 miles to the north-east, crossed the Indus, and occupied the Panjāb; but his further designs were thwarted by the discontent of his army, and in 323 at Babylon his brief and meteoric career was brought to a close.

2. Preparations for Alexander's work.—Alexander's greatest work was the spread of Greek influence, less from set purpose than as a result of his methods of recruiting his armies and organizing his conquests, and in ways that made this influence permanent and controlling. The conception of such spread may be found before his day as a part of the political theories of men who were feeling the defects of the various kinds of autonomy prevalent within Greece, or were eager for a fuller and richer life than was possible there. Isocrates in his letter to Philip of Macedon transcends the limits of city patriotism, and contemplates the spread of Greek culture, possibly also of the Greek race, by means of conquest. The school of Socrates was familiar with wide views, and impatient of parochial strife and politics. Xenophon was one of his disciples, who never ceased to be a Greek, but yet considered travel and military service abroad, with eventual settlement in some district where he might at once rule in comfort and disseminate his own views, as the natural career for a man of ambition or leisure. The employment of Greek soldiers as mercenaries by Eastern sovereigns was an ancient practice in the days of Cyrus; and, whilst among these soldiers poor Greeks formed the more numerous section, there were included also adventurers from the leading cities, who were men of parts as well as enterprise. Whatever their treatment was at first, they had ceased before the days of Alexander to be regarded merely as means of defending a weak satrap or adding to the dominions of a strong one. To Cyrus and his associates and successors they were friends to be courted; and a Persian policy of encouraging Greek settlements coincided with the increasing Greek demand for expansion. Emergence from the narrow area and narrower interests of the little native cities was becoming a necessity. Agesilaus might have effected it but for the dissensions and rivalries that showed the impossibility of Greek overlordship on any large scale. And in political theory on the part of thinkers, both as a practical means of escape from the *impasse* to which the affairs of Greece had been brought, and as the continuation of a process that had been going on for several generations, a preparation for Alexander's schemes of conquest was laid long before he was born.

3. Policy of Alexander, and its general results.—The rapidity of Alexander's conquests was too great to allow of the establishment of a fully organized administration in the districts which he traversed and subdued. At first he appears to have appointed merely a military governor and a fiscal agent, who were supported by a small band of veterans capable of acting as minor officials in the maintenance of order, in the collection of the taxes, and in the training of recruits. As opportunity served, this temporary arrangement was supplemented and made effective by the foundation of a number of settlements or cities, each of which was designed to serve as a centre of defence or influence. Seventy such cities, ranging from Kandahar to Alexandria, were founded by Alexander himself, and claim in various dialects to perpetuate his name. The inhabitants were partly Macedonian and partly Greek,—veterans, discontented troops, camp followers,—with natives swept in from the neighbouring villages or transported from remote and unmanageable lands. Some of these cities were intended to be outposts or garrison towns, others were placed as convenient marts upon the great trade routes; but all were invested with the privileges of partial autonomy. In military affairs the Macedonian element predominated, whilst the Greeks were put in charge of the local administration, and made themselves felt supremely in matters of thought and culture. A similar policy was followed by Alexander's successors, with the difference that the distinction between Macedonian and Greek gradually disappeared. One result was that Greek became the language of politics, trade, and intellectual intercourse from Macedonia to Persia and from Bactria to Egypt. Before his birth Greece had supplied Macedonia herself with the standard of excellence in taste and civilization; and at his death the joint Græco-Macedonian influence was the rising factor in the whole evolution of private life, and strengthened the bond of union supplied in the Eastern world by a common language.

4. The philosophical schools, and their relative influence. — Amongst the changes of position in philosophic thought and its estimation during this period, two are of special importance in the history of the process of Hellenization. (*a*) On the one hand, the philosopher, though neither ceasing to indulge in abstract speculation, nor allowing himself to be drawn into the thick of political strife, becomes the adviser of all parties, and the person to whom appeal is addressed in emergency. Aristotle was one of the teachers of Alexander, but does not appear to have been consulted by the king in any difficulty; and the *Politics*, with its catalogue of one hundred and fifty political constitutions, was conceivably an object of amusement to the practical man. Yet two philosophers were selected to rouse the king out of the gloom and remorse into which he was plunged by the murder of Clitus. Xenocrates took no active part in the faction strife of Athens; yet the Athenians more than once chose him as their emissary to Philip, just as afterwards they used him in a similar capacity during the Lamian war. In later times the practice continued. The leading philosophers thus became a class or group of men outside the political arena and above it; they were consulted in practical emergency as well as in speculative perplexity, and their influence in spreading the culture they represented was both detached from dangerous entanglements and quickened by association with general human interests. (*b*) The period of Alexander witnessed a considerable change in the relative amount of attention given to the principal philosophic groups. Metaphysic for a time yielded the ground to ethic. Plato and Aristotle proved less attractive than men who were inferior to both in range and keenness of intellect, but who touched actual life at more points that the ordinary busy man could appreciate. The retirement of the princely thinkers was but temporary, and before many centuries passed they re-emerged in new guises or relationships, of which the number is not yet exhausted. They were both theorists and transcendentalists; and what the Greek world wanted at a time when it was busily engaged in spreading and rooting itself everywhere was not so much speculation as experience, a law of duty rather than a guide to exact thought. As soon as the conditions of life became favourable, for Plato and for Aristotle alike a splendid revival was fated; but the philosophy of Hellenism in its first progress eastwards, as in its later subjugation of Rome and Italy, was of another type.

5. Pyrrhonism, Stoicism, Epicureanism.—Pyrrho is said to have taken part in Alexander's expedition to India (Diog. Laert. ix. 63), but it is not until afterwards that traces of his teaching can be found to any extent in Greek thought. The rise of the New Academy, with its blending of the two schools of Plato and Pyrrho, is in reality the date when the Greek mind began to take refuge in conclusions that were other than positive; for the appeal of scepticism is of necessity met in a practical age with a tardy response, and the discomfort caused by the disturbance of earlier beliefs is an unwelcome diversion when the mind is bent on activities. Pyrrho's importance in this period is twofold. He scattered seed, of which the fruit was late in appearing; but, when it did appear, the crop was plentiful; and the sceptical or captious inquirer, interested in every form of thought but captivated by none, became a not infrequent product of the Hellenistic genius. And he illustrates the reflex influence upon Greek culture of the beliefs of some of the districts which Alexander traversed or visited. That Pyrrho learnt his theories in Persia or India rests upon the statement of an early writer, whose name alone is known, and is probably incorrect (Diog. Laert. ix. 61). With more confidence it may be asserted that his natural equanimity was raised by his Eastern experiences into the worship of imperturbability. The Greek joyousness was transformed into a careless immobility, upon which in part may well be based alike the fatalism of various later creeds and the independence of external circumstance which the Stoic coveted and the Cynic mingled with bitterness.

During Alexander's reign the only schools of philosophy that could be regarded as of appreciable present value were the Stoic and the Epicurean, of which the former, especially, gradually became identified with the extension of Greek culture. Epicurus was a dozen years younger than Alexander, but, according to his own account, he entered seriously upon his philosophical studies at the age of fourteen. He claimed to be independent of his predecessors, but was certainly influenced by the teaching of Democritus, and he articulated in a system conceptions and tendencies that were floating in the air and creating the intellectual climate of the Greek world in Alexander's days. Zeno, too, was probably a little younger than the great king; but his teaching also links itself on to that of Socrates and the Cynics, and, as developed by his immediate successors, it soon became the standard of Greek ethical thought in its spread among the nations. Both schools indulged but little in abstract speculation, but endeavoured to teach men how to secure the happiness which was, in their view, a better and more natural end than knowledge. Epicureanism denied the existence of anything like Providence, declined to anticipate a judicial readjustment of experiences after death, and bade the sage carefully balance all possible present pleasures, and choose the path of prudence. Stoicism, on the other hand, had an elementary theology as well as an ethic. Other knowledge was held to be attainable than that given by the senses. The so-called gods were manifestations of a Supreme God, who ruled over human lives and ordained for each man the part he should play in the world. Happiness was to be reached indirectly by the discharge of duty, without much consideration of conditions or consequences. Wisdom and peace lay in keeping touch with the Divine ruler and plan of life; in which case a man became, whatever his outward circumstance, royal and free. Such a philosophy, unlike the Epicurean, involved the fusion of all distinctions of creed or race or custom, and was exactly appropriate to a period when civilizations also were fusing, and a rule of life was in request that could survive national decay and still serve for guidance in any change of fortune. Stoicism may be regarded as the leading philosophy in the Greek culture that became cosmopolitan. It succeeded in establishing itself at length on the banks of the Tiber, and penetrated even through the thick shell of Hebraism, affecting the thought and the phrases of St. Paul himself.

6. Alexander and the Jews.—Though Alexander possibly visited Jerusalem, according to the tradition preserved in the Talmud as well as by Josephus (*Ant.* IX. viii. 3–6), and though he enrolled Jews in his armies, granted them special privileges, used them as an intelligence department, and settled many favourably in his new towns and colonies, there are no indications of any direct or immediate influence upon their creed or practice. Indirectly, he opened or reopened the channels of communication by which the East and the West were brought into contact both with one another and with Egypt and Cœle-Syria. Along those roads, in subsequent ages, came teachers from India and Persia as well as from Greece; but the Hebrew did not readily assimilate any foreign belief or custom. The cause is to be found in the strictness of his monotheism as well as in the exceptional solidarity of the race. The Greek language was tolerated and even adopted in the course of time, but Greek culture was regarded with abhorrence in the inner circles where Jewish traditions were most sacredly preserved; and the complete coalescence of Hellenism with Hebraism proper has not yet taken place.

LITERATURE.—Freeman, *Hist. Essays*, 2nd ser. (4th ed. 1892). Essay 5 discusses the sources of Alexander's history. For the Rabbinical traditions see Derenbourg, *Hist. de la Pal.* (1867) i. 41 ff.; Hamburger, *RE* ii. (1883) 44 ff.; and *JE* i. 341–343. For relations with India see *JRAS* (1903) 685 ff. and (1894) 677 ff. Droysen, *Gesch. Alex. des Grossen* (1837) and *Gesch. des Hellenismus* (1877) are of special value. Wilamowitz, *Antigonus von Karystos* (1894), is brilliant for some of the philosophical tendencies. Add Mahaffy, *Gr. Life and Thought* (1896), *Progress of Hellenism in Alexander's Empire* (1905), and *Story of Alexander's Empire* (1900) (elementary, but well supplied with maps); Bevan, *Jerus. under High Priests* (1904); and Susemihl, *Lit. der Alexandrinerzeit* (1892).

R. W. MOSS.

ALEXANDRIAN THEOLOGY.

[W. R. INGE].

Scope of the Article.—Some of the best-known histories of 'Alexandrianism,' or 'the School of Alexandria,' have been really histories of Neo-Platonism. This is a mistake. Neo-Platonism, which will be dealt with in this Encyclopædia under its own name, is the latest stage in the development of Greek thought. Its connexion with Alexandria is less than is commonly supposed. In this article the local limit will be observed.

Secondly, this article will deal with theology, not with philosophy. Although Neo-Platonism was essentially a religious philosophy, and Alexandrian theology a philosophical religion, it is possible to maintain the distinction. And we may speak of an Alexandrian theology, though not of an Alexandrian philosophy.

Thirdly, the Hellenic schools of religious thought which flourished at Alexandria are omitted, as belonging rather to the precursors of Neo-Platonism than to our present subject. The justification for omitting them lies in their subordination of positive religion to philosophy, which was almost an axiom among the Pagans; *e.g.* Galen expresses surprise that some Christians, who cannot follow philosophical arguments, 'have progressed as far in self-control and the ardent pursuit of virtue as genuine philosophers.' Moreover, in spite of the resemblance in metaphysical and especially in ethical principles between these Hellenic schools and the Judæo-Christian Alexandrians, their attitude towards Greek tradition and culture is decisive. There is a great cleavage in this respect even between Clement and Plotinus. In reformed Pagan circles it seems to have been a matter of good taste not to mention Christianity, and Judaism was regarded with equal contempt. It is very doubtful whether the Jewish-Alexandrian theology had any direct influence upon Neo-Platonism. In fact, national and, still more, religious prejudices counteracted the cosmopolitan tendency of thought which began under the successors of Alexander. In spite of the common parentage of many ideas, and the parallelism of development under similar conditions, the separation is sharp between the three forms which religious philosophy assumed in the 2nd and 3rd centuries: (1) Jewish and Christian Platonism, both of which stand on the basis of Jewish monotheism; (2) the Hellenic religious philosophy, of which the best representative is Plotinus; (3) the barbaric Platonism of the Gnostics. In all these systems or schools there appear the following characteristics, though often qualified by other tendencies: (*a*) an abstract notion of God as the transcendent, absolute Unity, (*b*) a tendency to call in intermediary powers (the Logos, spirits, etc.) to bridge over the chasm between God and the world, (*c*) a tendency to connect matter with the evil principle, (*d*) self-discipline as a means to clearer vision of Divine truths. But the emphasis which was laid on these several doctrines differed widely in the three classes above named.

This article deals only with the first—Jewish and Christian Platonism, as developed at Alexandria. And the three representative names, round which our discussion must range, are Philo, Clement, and Origen.

1. Precursors of Philo.—It was inevitable that the Judaism of the Diaspora should diverge further and further from the Palestinian tradition. In Egypt especially, where the Jews comprised nearly half the population of the capital, and were numerous throughout the country, a vigorous independent life was sure to appear in all departments of mental activity. The Egyptian Jews could not maintain an attitude of aloofness from the secular culture of the world around them. To say that they were Hellenized is only to say that they were not self-excluded from the civilization of the period, for Hellenism was a factor in all the religion, philosophy, and ethics of the lands where Greek culture penetrated. But when we speak of the Hellenizing of Judaism, we mean more than the pervasive influence of the secular civilization. There was a definite attempt made by the Jews to interpret their own religion in a form acceptable to the Greeks, from which cannot be separated an attempt to interpret Hellenism to themselves by stretching it upon a framework of Jewish orthodoxy. This latter design was rendered necessary by the rapid decay of faith in the statutory Judaism among the educated, a decay which was exhibited both by the increasing inwardness and spirituality of the really religious, and by the increasing externality and hypocrisy of the cult among the official class. In the Diaspora, a liberal Judaism sprang up which was merely a cultured Unitarianism with strong ethical convictions. The old dream of a theocracy was forgotten, and Messianism aroused no interest. The Greek doctrine of immortality was given a moral turn by conceiving of the future life as primarily the scene of rewards and punishments; and the national hatred of Rome (after the Roman conquest of the East) was gratified by the belief in a day of universal destruction, ushering in the great assize. The statutory basis of this religion was furnished by the Old Testament, which was asserted to contain the sum total of all Divine and human wisdom. The 'books of Moses,' in particular, were treated with unlimited reverence.

The *Septuagint* is perhaps our earliest specimen of Jewish-Alexandrian literature, for the traces of Greek influence in Sirach are very disputable. Dähne has shown that the translators frequently modify the naïve anthropomorphism of the Old Testament, substituting, *e.g.*, the 'power' for the 'hand' of God, and His 'glory' for His 'robe' in Is 6^1. In Gn 1^2 they seize the opportunity to introduce the Platonic distinction of matter and form, and in Ps 51^{12} the Stoical ἡγεμονικόν intrudes itself. The third book of the so-called *Sibylline Oracles*, which probably dates from the middle of the 2nd cent. B.C., is a remarkable proof of growing respect for Greek thought and religion, since the main object of the composition is to support Jewish monotheism and Jewish national hopes, under the form of heathen prophecy. But the characteristic features of Alexandrianism, enumerated above, are not prominent in the *Sibylline Oracles*. Neither allegorism, nor ecstasy, nor asceticism, can be found in them. In the so-called *Wisdom of Solomon*, though the form is that of Hebrew poetry, the matter is far more Hellenic. The half-personified 'Wisdom' is almost identical with Philo's Logos, and the 'Spirit' is also half-personified, being, indeed, only 'Wisdom' itself under a slightly different aspect. The 'Word,' on the other hand, is used, as in the Old Testament books, for the expression of the will of God; there is no approximation to the Philonic use of 'Logos,' even in 18^{14-16}, where there is a poetical personification. On Messianic hopes the author is silent, like the other Wisdom-writers; the book was not written for Palestinian Jews, and was not accepted by them as Scripture. The influence of Greek (Platonic and Stoic) philosophy appears chiefly in the conception of a harmonious and beautifully ordered world directed by an immanent principle (Wisdom). The most striking deviation from orthodoxy is to be found in the doctrine of pre-existence, which is clearly stated in $8^{19.20}$ 'I was a child of comely parts, and had obtained a good soul; or rather, being good, I entered into an undefiled body.' This can only mean that the soul has displayed goodness in a previous state of existence. The body is thus no essential part of the personality, a view which leads easily to the notion that it is, if not the source of moral evil, yet the 'muddy vesture of decay' which presses down the soul. The eschatology is vague. There will be no bodily resurrection; but the souls of the righteous will be rewarded, at the 'inspection,' with everlasting felicity, while those of the wicked will be excluded from their true life, and cast into eternal darkness.

2. Philo.—Passing by the Letter of the pseudo-Aristeas, a manifest forgery, and the fragments of Aristobulus (a Jewish Peripatetic who lived in the middle of the 2nd cent. B.C.), which have also been suspected, we come to Philo. Philo (born about 20 B.C.) was a member of a well-known Alexandrian family, being brother of Alexander the Alabarch, the head of the Jewish community in the Egyptian capital. Philo himself lived a life of retirement and contemplation, until an outbreak of anti-Jewish fanaticism, fomented by the Roman governor Flaccus, led to his being sent to Rome with a deputation from the Jewish community (A.D. 39–40). He was then elderly, and had already written most of his books.

Philo believed himself to be, and was accepted by his contemporaries as being, an orthodox Jew. He is an apologist, who wishes to defend Judaism against atheism, polytheism, and scepticism. More particularly, since Judaism for the Alexandrian Jew was a book-religion, he was concerned to prove that the highest forms of revelation and of human wisdom were contained within the compass of the Old Testament. Disrespect to the sacred text is in his opinion a crime of the deepest dye: he knows of an impious man who, after laughing at some story in Genesis, soon after hanged himself for no particular reason—a manifest judgment (*de Mut. Nom.* 8). His theory of inspiration is that God speaks through the prophet, who is merely a passive instrument. This inspiration takes place when the instrument is in a kind of trance, such as Philo himself has experienced. His mind suddenly becomes full of images, and ideas pour forth from it, while he is insensible to all externals (*de Migrat.*

Abrah. 7). The description resembles Böhme's account of his manner of writing. At the head of all the prophets is Moses, who alone had seen God face to face. In his writings the sum of human wisdom is contained.

This conception of revelation, as given once for all in its entirety, led Philo into great difficulties. If he had been content to argue that the more spiritual faith of his day was contained implicitly, in germ, in the Pentateuch, he might have made out a good case. But the doctrine of development, even in the limited application afterwards made by St. Paul, was unknown to him. He can admit no inferiority in Genesis as compared with Isaiah. And since the OT, understood in its natural sense, contained many things which could not but shock the conscience as well as the intelligence of a cultivated Alexandrian acquainted with Greek philosophy, the expedient of *allegorism* was necessary (see ALLEGORY). This method was no invention of Philo, or of his contemporaries. Greek moralists had long treated Homer in this way, quoting lines from him as we quote verses from the Bible, to enforce moral truths. The system was elaborated by the Sophists, and still more by the school of Anaxagoras; but it is rejected by Plato, who will not admit unedifying myths into his State, 'either with or without allegories.' It may be said that to a certain extent this kind of exposition is justified. In the higher kinds of literature, the perception of some sort of allegory or double meaning is almost necessary. The mere literal or grammatical sense cannot satisfy the student of any poetry or imaginative prose. But when Homer is made by the Stoic to prove such philosophic theses as that virtue can be taught, or that the sage is 'apathetic'; by the Pythagorean to teach that silence is golden, and by the Epicurean that pleasure is the guide of life; and when Moses is made by Philo to indicate the eternal motion of the heavens under the figure of the cherubim's flaming sword, we have a right to protest. So arbitrary and unscientific an exegesis is a fatal obstacle to understanding the religious books of mankind—a task in which we cannot succeed unless we realize that the thoughts of the past are relative to the past, and must be interpreted by it. Philo himself calls it the method of the Greek mysteries. In these rites everything was represented as being at once a thing and the covering of a thing, an outward sign and an inward truth.

Allegorism, then, is simply the sacramental method applied to history and literature. It was becoming the common property of all the higher religions, and was the easiest refuge for educated men who wished to belong to an established religious body, without forcing themselves to accept immoral or absurd beliefs. The general view was that all revelation is a Divine cryptogram, which serves the double purpose of concealing the truth from those who are unworthy to receive it, and of magnifying it, for the choicer spirits, by an indirect and mysterious mode of presentation (*ἡ κρύψις ἡ μυστικὴ σεμνοποιεῖ τὸ θεῖον*).

The following summary of Philo's principles of exegesis may give some idea of the method in practice. (1) When nouns are repeated, a hidden meaning is indicated. In Lv 18⁶ 'man,' 'man,' shows 'that what is meant is not the man possessed of body and soul, but he only who is possessed of virtue.' Similarly, pleonasms are significant. In Gn 15⁵ *ἐξήγαγεν ἔξω* means that Abraham was delivered from the trammels of the flesh. There can be no tautology in Scripture, and no change of a word without meaning. If Moses says 'shepherd' in one place, and 'keeper of sheep' in another, he means to distinguish between a good and a bad kind. (2) Plays on words are frequent, *e.g.* ὄνος is meant to indicate πόνος, and πρόβατον to indicate προβαίνειν. (3) Double meanings of words often give the clue to the higher meaning, *e.g.* since 'rib' is sometimes used for 'strength,' the words about Adam's rib mean that the αἰσθητικὴ δύναμις comes forth out of the νοῦς. (4) Numbers are always important: *one* is the number of God, *two* of the creature, *three* of the body, *four* of potential completeness, *five* of the sensuous life, and so on. (5) Animals are symbolic: the camel of memory, the ass of the irrational nature, the snake of lust. Inanimate objects are treated in the same way. (6) The proper names in the Pentateuch are allegorized according to their fancied etymological affinities. Philo speaks of allegorism as the 'moral,' as opposed to the 'natural' interpretation.

It is plain that the principle of allegorism offered great temptations to evading the letter of the Mosaic law. This misuse of the method is condemned by Philo, who protests against those who thus 'spiritualized' the ceremonies enjoined in the Pentateuch (*de Migrat. Abrah.* 16). He also distrusts the symbolic study of nature, as raising more problems than it solves. We shall learn more by studying our own minds, and the sacred literature.

In considering Philo's theology, we must expect to find the Greek and Hebrew elements imperfectly fused. It would surpass the genius of any man to harmonize the logical, analytic thought of the Greek with the vague, indefinite intuitions of Hebrew prophecy. But the way had been prepared for him by approximations from both sides. The Jews of Alexandria had universalized Jahweh till He had lost the characteristics of the tribal God of the Hebrews; and, on the other hand, Greek thought was now more favourably disposed to the transcendence of God than when Stoicism reigned supreme. Philo has no difficulty in explaining the anthropomorphisms of the Pentateuch as mere accommodations. God is, in truth, not a Being who can feel anger, jealousy, or repentance. He is without body, invisible, the most universal of beings, above goodness, above knowledge, above even the absolute Good and Beautiful. We apprehend His existence partly by analogy: as we have an invisible mind, which is sovereign over the body, so must the Universe be guided by an invisible mind, which is God (*de Mundi Opif.* 23). Also, the world shows traces of design; but the principle of causality cannot reside in matter, which has nothing noble in itself, but only the potentiality of becoming all things (*de Mundi Opif.* 5).

A higher mode of apprehending God is by spiritual intuition, which under certain conditions culminates in knowledge of Him. But, since like only can know like, we are precluded by the limitations of our finitude from forming an adequate conception of the mind of the Universe. We cannot get out of ourselves, and underived existence is incomprehensible to us. 'We must first become God, which is impossible, in order to be able to comprehend God' (*Fragm.* ii. 654). We approach most nearly to the truth when we strip off from our idea of God all that is characteristic of finite existence. This process still leaves Him with the attributes of goodness, freedom, and activity. Creative activity (τὸ ποιεῖν) is as characteristic of God as receptivity (τὸ πάσχειν) is of the creature, and God 'never ceases working.' The *via negativa* logically leads to a God who is without qualities (ἄποιος *); but Philo here takes refuge in agnosticism. 'God has revealed his nature to none, and we cannot say that the First Cause is material or immaterial, with or without qualities' (*Leg. All.* iii. 73). The bare fact of His existence (ψιλὴν ἄνευ χαρακτῆρος ὕπαρξιν, *Quod Deus immut.* 11) the mind can apprehend, but no more. He was revealed to Moses as the Nameless Existing. Nevertheless, we can without contradiction ascribe to God the attributes of omnipotence, omniscience, and the like, which can be applied only to the Supreme Being; and such attributes as goodness, which in their full meaning can be applied only to Him. 'Those things which among men are called truth and justice, are symbols only; but those which are

* But properly ἄποιος means not 'having no attributes,' but 'incapable of being classified': God does not belong to any class or order of being, but is above all classification, being unique.

so with God are prototypes or ideas.' God is 'the most generic' as excluding nothing; but He transcends even the highest genus, τὸ λογικόν. He is 'older than the monad'; by which Philo means that the unity of God is not merely the negation of plurality, but that His nature is the archetype of the mathematician's unity.

One of the most difficult parts of Philo's system is the doctrine of the Divine 'Powers.' These Powers could be fully apprehended only by pure Intelligence; to us they are revealed in their action. They are not, however, exhausted in the created world, for they are infinite, like God Himself. Their function is to give to matter those forms in virtue of which we are able to say that things exist. In themselves, the Powers are the eternal forms of God's thought; their activity is stamped on the whole order of nature, which in the regularity of its changes reflects the persistence of the creative ideas. These Powers, or ideas, are not of equal rank. The highest of them is the Logos, which stands nearest to the Godhead, even as the reasonable soul of man is that part of him which reaches most nearly to the Divine.

It has been usual with critics of Philo to condemn with great severity this conception of 'Powers.' It is said that he uses them as an expedient to mediate between two irreconcilables, God and the world, and that the contradiction reappears, in no way softened, in the qualities assigned to the mediating agencies. The Powers are sometimes identified with God, and sometimes separated from Him. They are (it is said) a transparent device to bring God again into contact with the finite, from which He has been jealously excluded by another line of argument. It is perhaps worth considering whether any theistic system which regards God as something more than a finite spirit among other spirits, has succeeded in explaining how an almighty, omnipresent, and eternal Being can really act in space and time. Philo is possibly not more successful than others who have attempted to do so; but a fair estimate of his teaching will acquit him of the puerile expedient of creating substitutes to act in God's place. 'God, being outside creation, has none the less filled the universe with *Himself*,' he says in one place (*de Post. Cain.* 5); and this is not an isolated acknowledgment of the Divine immanence in the world. He 'extends' His Powers over creation just as man is said to 'extend' the energies of his soul to God. It is true that we read that 'the Blessed One must not come into contact with indeterminate matter; and this is why He used the immaterial Powers, whose real name is ideas, that every genus might be taken possession of by its proper form.' But surely this is merely to assert the transcendence of God, without denying His immanence. The notion of the Powers as subordinate *persons* is quite foreign to Philo's mind, and cannot even be discussed without wandering far from his standpoint. Drummond quotes a very apposite parallel from Athanasius: 'The Logos is, as it were, *in* all creation, outside of the whole in his essence, but in all things by his powers . . . containing the whole of things and not contained, being wholly and in all respects *within* his own Father, and him only.' Both in Philo and Athanasius the phrases denoting spatial externality and its opposite are well understood to be metaphors. In the same way, when the Powers are symbolized as the agents and ministers of God, the poetical form ought not to have been misunderstood as a literal statement of fact. Philo is extremely fond of personification: *e.g.* for him 'all the virtues are virgins,' just as, *par revanche*, the wives of the patriarchs are 'not women but virtues.' Nothing can prove more strongly that Philo did not ascribe personality to the Powers, than the fact that he everywhere distinguishes them from the angels (in spite of Zeller and others). The angels are incorporeal souls, created, finite, and localized: they are 'powers,' no doubt, doing God's will, but they are entirely different from 'the Powers' or Divine Ideas. These latter are the active manifestations of the energy of God, which give to creation all the reality, as well as all the order and beauty, which it possesses.

In the hierarchy of Powers, the Logos of God is, as already remarked, second to God Himself (*Leg. Alleg.* ii. 21). The name Logos comes from Stoicism, but for the content of the word Philo is more indebted to Plato. The Stoical notion of Logos as active and quickening force is less prominent than the Platonic expressions 'idea of ideas' and 'archetypal idea.' The Logos of Philo, in fact, coincides with the Platonic Νοῦς, and the intelligible world is the mode which he assumes in creating: 'in the Logos are inscribed and engraved the constitutions of all other things.' As the principle of orderly differentiation in the natural world, he is called the 'Cutter' (τομεύς). The inferior ideas, gathered up in the Logos, constitute the multiplicity in unity of God's creation. A difficult question is raised by the distinction between the inward (ἐνδιάθετος) and the uttered (προφορικός) Logos in man, which corresponds to a distinction in the universal Logos. 'The Logos is double both in the universe and in the nature of man' (*Vit. Mos.* iii. 13). The 'seal' of the Logos upon matter—the expressed thought of God—is not called the 'uttered Word'; but the distinction in the universal Logos seems to be between the thought of God in itself and the same thought made objective.

Another problem is the relation of the Logos to the half-personified 'Wisdom' of the early Jewish-Alexandrian literature. Philo disliked the gender of 'Wisdom'; and though he explains that 'its nature is masculine, not feminine,' he found the word less dignified as well as less plastic than Logos. 'Wisdom' is chiefly used by Philo of the Logos as informing the human soul, hardly ever of God's creative power. The word 'Spirit' is sparingly used of the Logos or Wisdom inhabiting the soul of man. The question as to the personality of the Logos is better undiscussed. Neither Philo nor any Greek cared to define personality, a concept which has no name in the Greek language. He sometimes speaks of 'Logoi' in the plural, with no more hesitation than when we speak indifferently of 'the law' or 'the laws' of nature. For this very reason he employs poetical or mythical personification quite freely. The Logos is the constitutive principle of human individuality; he is not himself an individual. The Logos-doctrine of Philo is therefore nearer to what, in Christianity, became Monarchianism than to the Arianism with which it has been compared, or to Athanasian orthodoxy. See, further, the article LOGOS.

As the Logos of God is the archetype of human reason, the mind of man is nearer to God than any other created thing. The human soul is the only worthy temple of God; those in whom God dwells may justly be called His sons. Knowledge of God, gained by imitation of Him and likeness to Him, is the highest good for man. Evil consists in separation from God, and ignorance of Him; the cause or fountainhead of moral evil is selfishness (φιλαυτία), especially when combined with arrogance and conceit (μεγαλαυχία). 'To speak, like Esau, of "*my* birthright" and "*my* blessing," is proof of boundless ignorance, and of a mean, servile disposition; for it belongs to God alone to say "Mine"' (*Leg. Alleg.* iii. 70). Philo does not identify evil with ignorance; for he clearly teaches that sins committed in ignorance are pardonable; but he is careful to distinguish between the ignorance which we cannot help and that which is due to pride or selfishness. The corruptible body always tends to press down the soul; not that it is evil in itself, for matter has no moral significance, good or bad, apart from our use of it; but, as a matter of experience, the bodily needs and appetites are a clog upon spirituality. The 'powers' of sense, though Divine gifts, are irrational, urging us to their own gratification without thought of consequences; but to make this gratification our object is wrong and ruinous. The passions (πάθη) for the most part operate in opposition to reason, and are therefore bad; but the good man is not destitute of such μισοπόνηρα πάθη as pity and love.

The great helper of mankind in the ascent to God is the Logos; and here Philo tries to unite his Jewish reverence for the written 'Word' of God with his Platonic idealism. His description of the virtuous life is on the whole very modern in sentiment. Self-discipline is not an end in itself. Such exercises as fasting, abstinence from the bath, and sleeping on the ground are useless and unprofitable labours, which injure the soul as well as the body (*Quod. det. pot.* 7). It is true that we have a war to wage, 'the most difficult and troublesome of all wars,' against our bodily appetites, and that in practice we must often regard our bodies as by nature evil; but Philo advises neither ascetical austerities nor withdrawal from the world. 'The serpent, pleasure, bites us in the wilderness'; it is safer to live in the world, to accept responsibilities and dignities, and show how such a career can be followed without contamination and to the good of others. 'Those who assume a squalid and melancholy appearance, and say that they despise glory and pleasure, are hypocrites.' Unworldliness is to be gained only by knowledge of the world. At the same time, such luxury as was prevalent among the wealthier classes in Egypt is wrong. The good things of the world should be used sparingly, that the soul may not be entangled in the corruptible elements. Truthfulness in speech is strongly insisted on, and taking oaths is deprecated as needless for an honourable man, whose word ought to be sufficient. The only acceptable worship is that of the soul, and truth the only sacrifice (*Quod. det. pot.* 7); ceremonial observances and rich offerings do not make a man pious. Piety and justice seem to share the throne as the chief of the virtues. The soul is in its essence immortal, and will be rewarded or punished in a future state for its life here; but Philo discourages this line of thought; virtue and vice are their own reward and punishment; heaven and hell are within us. To enjoy an innocent and quiet mind, free from unruly passions; to feel the presence of the Holy Spirit of Wisdom within us; to share at last in the peace which passes all understanding, and to see God as He is—this is the goal which Philo sets before himself and his readers. 'The climax of blessedness is to stand steadfastly and steadily in God alone.' A resurrection of the body has no place whatever in his creed.

Philo has been very variously estimated as a thinker. Dähne treats him with contempt; Zeller thinks that his whole system is vitiated by a fundamental contradiction—the attempt to achieve union with a Being whose very notion makes such union impossible. Such a scheme, he suggests, could be the creation only of a consciousness at discord with itself and the world. Vacherot emphasizes the inconsistency of borrowing now from Plato and now from the Stoics, the result being an 'incoherent syncretism' dragged into the service of Judaism. Siegfried is impressed by his complete abandonment of the old Jewish religion, which nevertheless he affects to defend in words. 'No Jewish writer contributed so much to the dissolution of Judaism. The history of his people becomes in his hands mainly a didactic symbolic poem, by which he inculcates the doctrine that man attains to the vision of God by mortifying the flesh. The God of Philo was an imaginary Being, who, in order to gain power over the world, had need of a Logos, to whom the palladium of Israel, the unity of God, was sacrificed.' E. Caird, criticizing Philo's whole system from the Hegelian standpoint, shows that he had no conception of a historical process of evolution, and objects that his world is regarded as related to God, but not God to the world. (For a consideration of this criticism, which affects Plotinus more than Philo, see the article on NEO-PLATONISM). A more favourable estimate than any of these is given by Drummond, whose exhaustive treatise takes rank, with Siegfried's book, as the most valuable exposition of Philo's theology. No sane critic could place Philo in the same rank as a great original thinker like Plotinus; but the unfavourable estimates of him have proceeded mostly from critics who extend their condemnation to the school of Plato generally, in the interests of some rival system. The 'inconsistencies' which have been so freely attributed to Philo are mainly the difficulties which all who believe in a God at once transcendent and immanent must be prepared to face, though some of them are mere misunderstandings due to an unsympathetic and sometimes superficial study of his writings. His belief in the possibility of immediate communion with 'the first God' in visions is the result of personal experience. He describes, modestly and clearly, 'what has happened to himself a thousand times' (*de Migrat. Abrah.* 7). In the face of this passage it is difficult to maintain that in Philo God 'is not related to the world,' or, with Dähne, that he 'robs the human race of their God.'

The extent of the influence exercised by Philo's writings in the first century, and early part of the second, is very difficult to determine. As regards pagan philosophy, he remained both then and afterwards outside the pale. Neo-Platonism, so far as we can judge, is not directly indebted to him. The question whether St. Paul and the author of the Fourth Gospel had read Philo has not been decided. As regards the latter, a strong case may be made out on either side. That the author of the Gospel was steeped in the philosophy of the Jewish Alexandrian school is certain; but his standpoint differs from that of Philo in several particulars, and many of the most characteristic Philonic words are absent from the Gospel, so that direct dependence cannot be proved. The same may be said of the Epistle to the Hebrews. The Epistle of Barnabas, as Siegfried shows, follows the Philonic rules for allegorical interpretation. Justin Martyr's Logos-doctrine is nearer to Philo's than that of the Fourth Gospel; and there are parallels which suggest a direct knowledge of Philo's writings. It is probable also that he was read by some of the Gnostics of the 2nd century. Clement was well acquainted with Philo, and seems to borrow from him not only many fanciful applications of the allegorical method, but several characteristic theological and philosophical terms; though these latter may be part of the common stock of ideas at Alexandria. The same may be said of Origen, between whom and Philo many correspondences are discovered by Siegfried. Eusebius frequently quotes Philo; and, to come to the Latin Fathers, Ambrose conveys whole sentences from him into his writings, so that a Jewish commentator has (much too strongly) called Ambrose 'Philo Christianus.' Jerome is also much influenced by Philo's interpretations of the Old Testament.

LITERATURE.—Text of Philo: Richter (1851–53). The best critical expositions of his system are in Dähne, *Geschichtl. Darstellung der Jüdisch-alexandrinischen Religionsphilosophie* (1834); Zeller, *Die Philosophie der Griechen*, iii. 2 (1881); Siegfried, *Philo von Alexandria* (1875); J. Drummond, *Philo Judæus*, 2 vols. (1888). Of these the most trustworthy are Siegfried and Drummond. Dähne's book is marred not only by want of sympathy with his subject, but by some strange errors, *e.g.* that Philo anticipated the Johannine identification of the Logos with the Messiah. There is an excellent article on Philo in the *Jewish Encyclopedia* (x. 6–18).

3. Alexandrian Christianity.—Until the age of Clement, the Christian Church at Alexandria lay in obscurity. Our information is so scanty that we cannot even say whether the ideas of Philo and his school were a factor in Alexandrian Christianity during the greater part of the 2nd century. The Church in the Egyptian capital retained a democratic constitution until Clement's lifetime, perhaps even consecrating its patriarchs by the hands of its college of presbyters. It had at this period no fixed liturgy, and no definite distinction between the Eucharist and the Agape. In contrast with this primitive organization, there grew into importance, in the later half of the century, the remarkable Catechetical School, the earliest διδασκαλεῖον in close relation to the Church. (The schools of the Apologists — Justin, Tatian, etc. — were private ventures). The oldest Gnostic schools for the study of religious philosophy were in Egypt, and the Christian Catechetical School may have been modelled partly upon these and partly upon the Jewish high schools (cf. Euseb. *HE* v. 10, ἐξ ἀρχαίου ἔθους διδασκαλείου τῶν ἱερῶν λόγων παρ' αὐτοῖς συνεστῶτος). The school emerges from darkness under Pantænus; but we know very little about its management either under him or under Clement. There were no class-rooms or collegiate buildings. The head of the school gave informal instruction in his own house, sometimes by lectures, sometimes by conversation classes (Orig. *c. Cels.* vi. 10). The usual course was three years (*Const. Ecc. Egyp.* iii. 42). No fees were charged. The lecturer was supported by free gifts from rich students. The education was on much the same lines as that advocated by Philo. The aim was the acquisition of γνῶσις—the higher theology and religion. The preparation consisted partly of moral discipline and partly of the study of philosophy, to which must be added the art of expounding, in accordance with the principles of allegorism, the books which contain the special revelation. The Christian teachers placed Greek philosophy and the Old Testament Scriptures side by side as propædeutic to the higher knowledge; and among philosophers, though the Platonists and Stoics were most studied, none were excluded except the 'godless Epicureans.' The commentaries of Origen show that Biblical study held a very important place in the course. The list of Heads of the School is given as follows:—Pantænus, Clement, Origen, Heraclas, Dionysius, Pierius, Theognostus, Serapion, Petrus, Macarius (?), . . . Didymus, Rhodon. (Arius, according to Theodoret [*HE* i. 1], was catechist; but it is very unlikely that he was ever Head of the School). The Catechetical School lost its importance during the Arian controversy, and was further weakened by the attacks upon Origen's orthodoxy. It was destroyed in the unhappy struggle between Theophilus of Alexandria and the barbarous orthodoxy of the Egyptian monks.

(*a*) **Pantænus,** the first Head of the School, is said by Eusebius to have been a Stoic, by Philip of Side to have been 'an Athenian, a Peripatetic.' In any case, he was learned in Greek philosophy, and, according to a doubtful tradition, visited India as a missionary before his appointment at Alexandria. The notices of his teaching indicate that he led the way in the allegorical interpretation of Scripture. His work seems to have been more catechetical than literary, and the most interesting fragment of his teaching has been preserved in the form of question and answer. 'Pantænus, being asked in what manner Christians suppose God to know reality, replied, He neither knows sensible things by sense, nor intelligible things by intellect. For it is not possible that He who is above the things that are should apprehend the things that are according to the things that are. We say that He knows things that are as acts of His own will' (ὡς ἴδια θελήματα, Maximus Conf., *Schol. in Greg. Naz.*). Clement was almost certainly a hearer of Pantænus (not *vice versa*, as Philip of Side says); and it is highly probable that Pantænus is the 'Sicilian bee' whom Clement discovered 'hiding himself' in Egypt, and in whom he 'found rest.'

(*b*) **Clement of Alexandria.** — Titus Flavius Clemens was born about A.D. 150, not at Alexandria; perhaps at Athens (Epiphanius). After many years of leisurely travelling in Italy, Greece, and the East, he came to Alexandria, where, about 200, he succeeded Pantænus as Head of the Catechetical School. In 202 or 203 he was compelled by the persecution under Severus to quit Alexandria, probably for Palestine and Syria. He was still living in 211, but dead in 216. We do not know at what period of his life he embraced Christianity, or what were the stages of his conversion.

The works of Clement are—

(1) The Λόγος Προτρεπτικὸς πρὸς Ἕλληνας, an exhortation to the Greeks (not 'Gentiles,' as Jerome mistranslates it) to abandon paganism. This treatise was probably written about 190. (2) The Παιδαγωγός, written after the last-named, a practical instruction dealing chiefly with the conduct of social and personal life. The 'Tutor' is Christ Himself, the great Instructor of all mankind. (3) The Στρωματεῖς (title in full κατὰ τὴν ἀληθῆ φιλοσοφίαν γνωστικῶν ὑπομνημάτων στρωματεῖς, *Strom.* i. 29), *Miscellanies*, a much longer treatise, in seven, or eight (Photius, Jerome) books. (The fragment of a logical treatise called Book viii. does not seem to belong to the Στρωματεῖς,* and the end of Book vii. promises another treatise rather than another Book: ἀπ' ἄλλης ἀρχῆς ποιησόμεθα τὸν λόγον). The *Miscellanies*, which are issued 'in studied disorder,' that the mysteries of knowledge may not be made too plain to readers who are unfit for them, expound the principles of a reasonable and philosophic faith. The treatise was probably designed to lead up to another, which Clement intended to be called Διδάσκαλος. (This intention is implied in *Pæd.* ii. 76, iii. 97, and other places). This would have completed the series begun in the Προτρεπτικός and continued in the Παιδαγωγός, initiating the reader into the higher γνῶσις. But Clement probably found that he could not publish such a work without violating his principle of reserve in communicating religious truths. Some have identified the Στρωματεῖς with the promised Διδάσκαλος; but de Faye and Mayor have shown that several promises are unfulfilled in the Στρωματεῖς, and that the work has no appearance of finality. It was probably a sort of *hors d'œuvre*, forming no part of the original scheme. (4) Ὑποτυπώσεις or *Outlines*, in eight books. These were notes and comments on the Old and New Testaments, including, says Eusebius, contested books such as Jude, Barnabas, Apocalypse of Peter, but not the whole of the Old Testament. Photius passes some severe strictures on this work, in which Clement, he says, teaches that 'matter is timeless,' that the Son is a creature, that there were many worlds before Adam, that there are two Λόγοι, of whom only the lower, a Power or Effluence of the Divine, was incarnate; together with metempsychosis and docetism. (5) Τίς ὁ σωζόμενος πλούσιος, still extant; an interesting sermon, ending with the well-known story of St. John and the robber. (6) Several other treatises are mentioned by Eusebius and Jerome, and (as subjects on which he intended to write) by Clement himself.

The view adopted above as to the character of the *Miscellanies* and the non-fulfilment of the design for a *Didascalus* is of great importance for the understanding of Clement's theology. In *Strom.* iv. 1 he announces his intention, after dealing with other subjects, of introducing his readers to the 'true gnostic science of nature,' initiating them first into the lesser and then into the greater mysteries. But from such initiation he carefully refrains in the *Miscellanies*, for, as he says, 'to put everything into a book is as bad as to put a sword into a child's hand.' We have, then, to conclude that Clement has suppressed what he considered the highest part of his teaching. It is safest, he says, to learn and teach such things orally. What was this esoteric teaching? It is safe to guess that it was mainly connected with Biblical exegesis. Clement believed in an authoritative tradition of interpretation, handed down from Christ Himself through Peter, and James, and John, and Paul. It probably allegorized narratives which the *simpliciores* treasured as bare facts. Besides this, the 'Gnostic' doubtless allowed himself to develop a mystical philosophy of religion, which could not be fully imparted or even made intelligible to the public.

The conception of the earthly life of Christ as a grand symbolic drama or Divine mystery-play for the enlightenment of humanity, was quite in accordance with Alexandrian philosophy. And though no objection was taken to the supernatural element, as such, in either the OT or the NT, the esoteric teaching undoubtedly was that certain details in the former which were morally objectionable had only a symbolical truth. With regard to the philosophy of religion in its wider aspects,

* The critical problems raised by this fragment, the *Eclogæ*, and the *Excerpta ex Theodoto*, have been discussed with different results by Zahn, Ruben, von Arnim, and de Faye.

it is seldom necessary to read between the lines in Clement. He was not a profound thinker, but a well-read and able man, who accepted in an intelligent manner the syncretistic philosophy popular in learned circles at Alexandria. He has been called cloudy and rhetorical, and has been accused of taking his quotations from anthologies of elegant extracts. But the obscurity is rather of arrangement than of thought, and the rhetoric is not often obtrusive. In Clement an ardent and impetuous imagination is joined to a serene soul and a clear intelligence. In fact it is worth observing, in view of the often repeated statement that rhetoric, 'the evil genius of Greece,' infected Greek Christianity, that Minucius and Tertullian are much more 'rhetorical' than Justin or Clement.

Clement, as a Christian philosopher, is aware that he has to encounter prejudice and mistrust. Gnosticism, at this time, was much more dreaded in the Church than fifty years earlier, when it was really a formidable intellectual force. At the end of the 2nd cent. the Christians were better educated, and the growth of rationalism and speculation in the Church alarmed many. Tertullian argues that, since 'hæreses a philosophia subornantur' (*de Præscript.* 7), philosophy should be banished from the Church; and Clement is well aware that the majority agree with him. 'Philosophy,' he protests, 'is not a goblin who wants to run away with us, as the vulgar think' (*Strom.* vi. 10). It is not the privilege of the few; 'with us, philosophers are those who love Wisdom, the Author and Teacher of all things' (*Strom.* vi. 7). But he feels that the obscurantists, with their cry of *μόνη καὶ ψιλὴ πίστις* (*Strom.* i. 43), are formidable: he must even vindicate his right to publish a book at all! Must literature be left only to pagans and atheists?, he asks. Must teaching be only by word of mouth? His doctrine is not his own, but handed down from the Apostles; and, lastly, people are not obliged to read him. Such a defence throws much light on the Christian distrust of culture even at Alexandria.

To turn to Clement's theology. God is a Being (*οὐσία*), but above space and time, 'beyond even the One and the Monad,' and strictly nameless, though we are obliged to give Him names. In a doubtful fragment (on which see Bigg, *Bampton Lectures* [1886], p. 64) he has been thought to deny to God consciousness of the external world; but probably Clement only means that God knows reality *not* as external to Himself. He certainly does not teach that the Father has no consciousness except through the Son. God takes pleasure in our salvation, and in that only (*Strom.* vii. 3; *Protrept.* 94, 95, 116): His nature is profoundly *moral*: He is good because He *wills* to do good, not like fire, which radiates heat automatically (*Strom.* vii. 42, and esp. *Strom.* vi. 104, *ἐπεὶ καὶ ὁ θεὸς οὐχ ᾗ φύσει ἀγαθὸς ἐστι, ταύτῃ μένει μακάριος καὶ ἄφθαρτος . . . ποιῶν δὲ ἰδίως ἀγαθά, θεὸς ὄντως καὶ πατὴρ ἀγαθὸς ὤν.*). Such passages must be considered as well as those in which he tries to outdo Plato in emphasizing the transcendence of God.

Nevertheless he insists that no man cometh to the Father except through Christ, the Logos. He rejects the Stoic pretension to 'resemble God' (cf. however, *Strom.* vi. 113, quoted below), and quotes very pertinently the words of Christ Himself, 'It is enough for the disciple to be as his master.' His Logos-doctrine, which is the basis of his Christology, is less metaphysical and more religious than that of Philo. Although the direct dependence of Clement on Philo, as regards his conception of the Logos no less than in his principles of allegorism, has been conclusively established by Siegfried, it is plain that, while Philo is mainly preoccupied with the desire to explain the formation and government of the universe, Clement is much more interested in religious psychology. In the 150 years which elapsed between the two writers, the centre of gravity in 'philosophy' had changed from metaphysics and cosmology to religion and ethics (*ὅσα εἴρηται . . . δικαιοσύνην μετὰ εὐσεβοῦς ἐπιστήμης ἐκδιδάσκοντα, τοῦτο . . . φιλοσοφίαν λέγω*, he says). The immanent Logos of the Stoics was now more thought of than the Platonic 'Idea of Ideas.' Clement's attempt to combine the two conceptions may be the excuse for Photius' charge that he taught 'two Logoi.' Or perhaps Clement was perplexed by problems about the Father's consciousness while the Son was incarnate. But the 'two Logoi' do not appear in his extant treatises. The Logos in Clement is the instrument in creation (He is often called 'creator'); He introduces harmony into the universe, of which He is the 'pilot.' He created man in His own image. He is spoken of as 'the Will of God,' 'a power, or energy, of God,' and in particular as 'Saviour,' a term to which, we think, there is no parallel in Philo. He was a 'lover of mankind' from the beginning (*Protr.* 6); it was He who revealed Himself in the OT theophanies. Since the Incarnation, He has been the 'Saviour,' 'Tutor,' and 'Teacher' of Christians, of those, that is, who have been 'initiated' by the laver of illumination (*Pæd.* i. 26) into the true mysteries. In his soteriology, baptism is decidedly more prominent than redemption by the blood of Christ. Very characteristic is the presentment of salvation as an *educational* process, by the side of the other conception—equally characteristic of the period—of salvation as the acquisition of immortality.

Of the Third Person of the Trinity, Clement says but little. The Alexandrians, in point of fact, hardly needed a Third Person; for the functions of the World-Soul, the Third Person of the Platonic Trinity and the God of the Stoics, were discharged by the Logos in addition to those of the Platonic Νοῦς; and, were it not so, there was no close resemblance between the Holy Ghost of Christianity and the Neo-Platonic Psyche. Clement makes the orthodox statements about the Person of the Holy Ghost, and, for the rest, puts the subject aside as a *θαῦμα μυστικόν*.

Clement's psychology is Platonic. There are three parts of the soul—the irrational soul, the rational soul, and the *σπέρμα πνευματικόν*. The third is evidently identical with the *κέντρον ψυχῆς* of Plotinus, and the *synteresis* of mediæval mysticism. But Clement ascribes so much Divine inspiration to the rational soul that the tripartite classification seems hardly necessary. Origen discards it. Clement guards himself against the common tendency to associate evil with matter. The body is not naturally evil, he says, nor is the soul naturally good. Rather the soul is that which wills, the body that which acts. On preexistence there is no definite statement. It was regarded as an open question in the Church, and probably Clement, like Origen, was inclined to believe it, though without accepting the Platonic doctrine of metempsychosis. He admits no hereditary guilt. God punishes only voluntary sins; the sins forgiven in Baptism are actual transgressions; infant Baptism is not mentioned (Bigg, p. 81).

The most distinctive feature of Clement's ethics is his doctrine of the Two Lives. This classification was common to most of the religious and philosophical teaching of the time, and was exaggerated into an absolute difference by the Gnostics. Clement is as much opposed to Gnosticism as he is anxious to utilize and harmonize Platonic and Stoic doctrine. Faith and knowledge, the principles of the lower and higher life respectively, are necessary to each other, and closely related. Faith is defined as 'a voluntary anticipation (πρόληψις) of things unseen,' 'an uniting assent to an unseen object,' 'the foundation of rational choice.' 'Voluntarily to follow what is useful is the first condition of understanding it.' Unless knowledge is based on faith, it remains merely intellectual assent, and is neither stable nor effective. The motive powers of faith are hope and filial awe. 'God is just, because He is merciful.' Faith, however, must go hand in hand with inquiry (ζήτησις): it is the nature of living faith to develop into knowledge (γνῶσις). The perfect Christian, therefore, is the 'Gnostic,' a word which Clement will not abandon to the sectarians who at last monopolized it. The portrait of the Gnostic is given in *Strom.* vii. It is of supreme importance for the understanding of Clement as a teacher, because it anticipates the final part of his scheme, which was never executed. He does not expound his Gnosticism, but he does show us its fruits. The Gnostic is the man whose character has been formed by the complete religious philosophy for which the earlier books of the *Stromateis* are a preparation only.

The aim of the Gnostic is to 'become like to God.' Clement is not afraid, speaking as a Greek, to say that he μελετᾷ εἶναι θεός (*Strom.* vi. 113). The Divine attribute of which he is thinking in such expressions is the higher knowledge, that which has for its object the 'intelligible world.' In one place (*Strom.* ii. 47) he says in more Christian language that the highest contemplation is knowledge of God, which is inseparable from likeness to Him. In Stoical form he says (*Strom.* iv. 39) that Gnosis is the purification of the ruling faculty of the soul; and everywhere the necessity of moral even more than intellectual training is insisted on. In the seventh book the 'canons' of the Gnostic character are said to be 'gentleness, kindness, and noble devoutness,' and the 'achievements of the Gnostic faculty' are 'to know what is right, to do what is right, and to help others to do it.' 'He is the true athlete, who in the great stadium, this beautiful world, is crowned for the great victory over all his passions.' 'He is persuaded that for souls that have chosen virtue, progress is always towards something better, till they are brought to the Great High Priest, in the vestibule of the Father.' Especial prominence is given to the two words ἀπάθεια and ἀγάπη, the former of which is the perfected work of temperance, when the passions are no longer even felt: οὕτως ζῆσαι ὡς ἄσαρκος (*Strom.* vii. 79; and still stronger *Strom.* vi. 75): and the latter is the climax of the whole Christian life, the end which, like the beginning, faith, is not matter of teaching (τὰ ἄκρα οὐ διδάσκεται). The statement that Clement exalts the intellect above the affections is untrue. The words κυριωτάτη πάσης ἐπιστήμης ἀγάπη (*Strom.* vii. 68) are typical. The 'intellectual love of God' affords perfect satisfaction to all our faculties, and unifies the entire personality. 'Conduct follows knowledge as surely as the shadow the body.' The will is not neglected. Faith in the first instance is an affair of the will, and is the necessary foundation of knowledge, the superstructure (*Strom.* ii. 11, v. 2, vii. 55): 'but both are Christ, the foundation and the superstructure too.' Faith exists in a higher and a lower form—πίστις ἐπιστημονική and π. δοξαστική (*Strom.* ii. 48).

As a thinker, Clement is most important as the author of a syncretistic philosophy of religion, fusing Platonism and Stoicism in a Christian mould. In Stoicism he found a natural religion, rationalism, moralism, and a predominant interest in psychology and apologetics, in Platonism a cosmology, doctrines of revelation, redemption and salvation, and contemplation as the highest state. 'In Clement,' says Hort, 'Christian theology in some important respects reaches its highest point. . . . There was no one whose vision of what the faith of Jesus Christ was intended to do for mankind was so full or so true' (*Ante-Nicene Fathers*, p. 93).

LITERATURE.—The best edition of the text of Clement is in Stählin, *Gr. christl. Schriftsteller der drei ersten Jahrhunderte* (1905). Important for the study of Clement are Zahn, *Forschungen zur Geschichte des Neutestamentlichen Kanons*, etc., vol. iii. (1884); Bigg, *Christian Platonists of Alexandria* (1886); P. M. Barnard, *Quis Dives Salvetur* (1897); de Faye, *Clément d'Alexandrie* (1898); Capitaine, *Die Moral des Clemens von Alexandria* (1903); Hort and J. B. Mayor, *Clem. of Alex. Miscellanies*, Book vii. Cf. also an article by the present writer in *Church Quarterly Rev.* for July 1904.

(*c*) **Origen** (Origenes Adamantius—the latter a real name) is said by Epiphanius to have been 'an Egyptian by race,' which probably does not mean a Copt. Porphyry calls him 'a Greek,' and his father, the martyr Leonides, has a Greek name. He was born about 185, was carefully brought up as a Christian, became a pupil of Pantænus and Clement, and already in his 18th year occupied informally the position of Head of the Catechetical School, the older teachers having been scattered by the persecution under Severus. For many years he was occupied in laborious study and teaching, mainly on the Bible; but he attended the lectures of Ammonius Saccas, and was himself consulted by many non-Christians. In 215 he was driven from Egypt by mob-violence, and taught for some time at Cæsarea, even preaching in the churches, though still a layman, till Demetrius recalled him to Alexandria. On his return he devoted himself mainly to writing Biblical commentaries, leaving to his coadjutor Heraclas most of the catechetical teaching. Meanwhile his relations with Demetrius became strained, and he availed himself of invitations to visit Palestine, Greece, and Asia Minor (about 227). In Palestine he received orders from the bishops there, without the consent of Demetrius. That prelate resented his action as contumacious, and Origen left Alexandria for the last time in 231. The Egyptian Synod condemned him, and even declared his priesthood invalid; but the sentence was disregarded in Palestine, where Origen laboured (at Cæsarea) for the last twenty years of his life. He was tortured and imprisoned in the Decian persecution (250), and, broken in health, died at Tyre in 253.

A complete list of Origen's works would occupy too much space here. The following are the probable dates of the most important treatises:

220–228. Commencement of *Hexapla*. Com. on Canticles.
228–231. Commentaries on St. John, Genesis, etc.; *Miscellanies; de Principiis.*
232–238. Commentaries continued; *Exhortation to Martyrdom.*
238–240. Commentaries on Ezekiel.
240. *Letter to Julius Africanus*; Commentaries on Canticles (10 books).
241–248. Homilies on OT; New Testament Commentaries; *Hexapla* finished.
249. The eight books *contra Celsum.*

Of these the most valuable for an understanding of Origen's theology and philosophy are the *de Principiis*, the *Commentary on St. John*, and the *contra Celsum*; to which may be added the beautiful treatise *On Prayer* (date uncertain; before 231), and the collection of extracts from his writings called *Philocalia*, made by Gregory of Nazianzus and Basil.

Principles of exegesis.—Allegorism in Origen is an instrument of apologetics, and at the same time a device to gain freedom of thought. He insists that no word or letter of Scripture can lack a profound meaning, and that every historical text has a body, soul, and spirit, *i.e.* a literal, moral, and spiritual sense. History is compared to a ladder, of which the literal facts are the lowest rungs (*in Joh.* i. 20).

This metaphor would bind us to do justice to the literal meaning first. But Origen, like Philo, at times expresses almost contempt for the literal narrative. 'What man of sense,' he asks, 'will suppose that the first and second and third day, and the evening and morning, existed without a sun and moon and stars? Or that God walked in a garden in the evening, and that Adam hid himself under a tree? Or that the devil took Jesus into a high mountain, whence He could see the kingdoms of the Persians and Scythians and Indians?' (*de Princ.* i. 16). All such passages are valuable only for their higher meanings. 'There are some passages,' he says, 'which are not literally true, but absurd and impossible' (*de Princ.* iv. 18). So 'some of the laws of Moses are absurd and others impossible.' Moses orders the sacrifice of an animal (the τραγέλαφος) which does not exist in nature. 'I should blush to admit that God has given such commands, which are inferior to many human enactments.' 'Scripture contains an unhistorical element, inwoven with the history,' in order that the worthlessness of the latter may drive us to seek the spiritual meaning.

We may wonder that Origen did not make more use of the theory of a progressive and gradual revelation, which he asserts in several places. But his main object was to save the OT (which was attacked and ridiculed by the Gnostics) for the Church, while at the same time repudiating the obligation to obey the Law, which was still pressed on the Christians by the Jews. The allegoric method served both ends. It must also be remembered that the 'homily,' as established by custom at Alexandria, necessitated a very plastic treatment of the text. The preacher or lecturer was expected to go straight through some book of the OT, extracting something edifying from each chapter. What could he say about Joshua but that the Canaanite kings were 'non tam reges quam vitiorum nomina'? The tone of these interpretations is often half-ironical, though the moral lesson is pressed home with all seriousness. His treatment of NT difficulties shows even greater boldness, and is quite startling. The discrepancies between the four Evangelists are, he thinks, fatal to their credit unless we look for their truth in the 'spiritual sense.' There is (so Jerome makes him say) an Eternal Gospel, of which the actual Gospel is only the shadow. We must separate the αἰσθητὸν εὐαγγέλιον from the νοητὸν καὶ πνευματικόν. Thus he interprets the Fourth Gospel as a symbolic treatise, much as Loisy and others do now. But in his eyes all this exegesis was not the work of human ingenuity, but the gift of the Holy Spirit. Much of it was traditional: Clement seems always to copy, not to invent, his allegorisms. Origen, without making any boastful claim, believes himself to be illuminated.

Doctrine of God.—As 'Spirit' and 'Light,' 'God is a simple intellectual nature, in whom is no greater nor less, higher nor lower, the Monad, Unit, Mind, and Fountain of all Mind' (*de Princ.* 1). As against the Christian Stoics, he asserts that God is incorporeal, and he is more careful than Clement to avoid Stoical phrases savouring of materialistic pantheism. God is spaceless and timeless, 'everywhere and nowhere,' 'natura simplex et tota mens.' Being unchangeable, He cannot feel anger, hatred, or repentance. Punishment is not His work, but the necessary consequence of sin. And yet He is long-suffering, merciful, and pitiful: He has 'the passion of love' (*in Ezech. Hom.* vi. 6, Bigg, p. 158). God is not infinite, but self-limiting (*in Matt.* xiii. 569): His almightiness is limited by His goodness and wisdom (*c. Cels.* iii. 493). Origen has not solved the problem of reconciling these moral attributes with the Platonic transcendence; for a fine but vague passage on the subject see *in Num. Hom.* xxiii. 2. He has less confidence than Clement in the *via negativa* as a path to reality; the most intimate knowledge of God is gained not by abstraction, but by direct revelation; grace is implanted in the soul μετά τινος ἐνθουσιασμοῦ. On this side he is more of a mystic than Clement. Moreover, by emphasizing the attribute of Goodness (ἀγαθότης) rather than that of self-existent Being, he gives the idea of God a richer and more ethical content.

But the doctrine of God in Origen involves at every point the problem of the Trinity. The Son or Logos is the centre of his theology. He is co-eternal and co-equal with the Father. 'There never can have been a time when He was not. For when was the Divine Light destitute of its effulgence? . . . Let him who dares to say there was a time when the Son was not, consider that this is the same as to say there was a time when Wisdom, the Word, and life were not' (*de Princ.* iv. 28). But we must distinguish between those attributes (ἐπίνοιαι) which belong to the Son essentially, and those which are assumed for the purpose of redemption. To the former class belong Wisdom, Word, Life, Truth; to the latter, Firstborn from the dead, Propitiation, Light, Shepherd. The former class are νοητά, the latter αἰσθητά. 'Happy are they who need the Son of God no longer as Physician, Shepherd, Redemption, but as Wisdom, Word, Justice, and the other perfect attributes' (*in Joh.* i. 22). He is willing to identify the Logos with the Platonic κόσμος νοητός (*in Joh.* xix. 5; *c. Cels.* vi. 63), only protesting against subjective idealism (*de Princ.* ii. 3, *mundum in sola phantasia et cogitationum lubrico consistentem*). The Son is therefore essentially eternal and unchanging, not merely the λόγος προφορικός of God; He '*was* (not 'became') with God,' as St. John says. He is absolute Truth, Righteousness, and Wisdom; but the text, 'none is good save one, that is God,' forbids us to call Him the absolute Good, though 'in regard to us He is the absolute Good.' Prayer may be addressed to the Son or to the Spirit, but the highest prayer is that which is addressed to the Father in Christ's name.

The charge of subordinationism in Origen's Christology cannot be maintained. It is unlikely that he used the word ὁμοούσιος, in the Nicene sense, of the Son, because for a Platonist it is hardly correct to speak of the οὐσία of God, who is ὑπερούσιος; but words like οὐ κατὰ μετουσίαν ἀλλὰ κατ' οὐσίαν ἐστὶ θεός (*Sel. in Psalm.* 135) should have been enough to establish his orthodoxy on this side. The doctrine of ἐπίνοιαι (see above), varying with the grade of spirituality attained by the believer, explains some apparent inconsistencies of expression, and his reverence for Scripture (*e.g.* 'My Father is greater than I') explains others. The subordination which he teaches is one of person and office, not of essence. 'The Son is less than the Father, as reaching only to rational beings; while the Father, holding all things together, reaches to everything. The Holy Spirit is less [than the Son], as extending to the saints only' (*de Princ.* i. 3). In the Incarnation the Son united Himself with a soul which had remained absolutely pure in its pre-existent state (*de Princ.* ii. 6). Like other souls, it was eternally united to the Word. It was free, like other souls, but so perfectly and inseparably did it cleave to the Word from the beginning, that the union of the two is like a molten mass of metal always radiating a white heat. By this union it was saved from all possibility of sin. His body was also pure and perfect. It was real flesh and blood, but of transparent beauty to those whose spiritual sight was purged. He rose from the dead, not in this flesh, but with that 'spiritual body' of which St. Paul speaks. 'Origen's view of the God-Man—a term which he first employed—differs from the ordinary view, generally speaking, only in so far as it is conditioned by his opinions of the pre-existence of the Soul and of the nature of the resurrection body' (Bigg, p. 189).

Origen speaks with much hesitation about the nature and office of the Holy Spirit. As a Person of the Trinity, He is co-eternal and co-equal with the Father and Son. 'The Spirit of the Father and the Spirit of the Son is one and the same' (*in Rom.* vi. 13). He understood St. Paul well enough to observe that no distinction is made by him between the action of the Spirit and of the Son (*de Princ.* i. 3). But in one remarkable passage (*in Joh.* ii. 6) he raises the question whether the Spirit came into being through the Word (διὰ τοῦ λόγου ἐγένετο), or whether He has no separate essence (ἑτέραν οὐσίαν) from the Father and the Son. These speculations are so inconsistent with the strong Trinitarian doctrine elsewhere maintained, that they cause surprise. They show how fluid dogma still was when Origen wrote. But the influence of his teaching (in spite of the charges brought against him) certainly operated *against* subordinationism. With some hesitation he pointed to the true view that the sources of Essence, of Revelation, and of Inspiration must be completely equal—must be God in the same degree. The opposite view removes the supreme God from life and experience, and makes Him finally unknowable. Other significant *dicta* about the Trinity are that 'the Father begets, the Son comprehends, the Holy Ghost penetrates all'; and that 'things derive their essence from the Father, reason from the Son, and holiness from the Holy Ghost' (*in Rom.* vii. 13; *de Princ.* i. 3).

Cosmology and Psychology.—The world began in unity, and will end in unity. In this sense the end will be 'like the beginning,' but not identical with it, inasmuch as the beginning is the desire for a perfection which is only implicitly contained in the scheme, as designed by perfect Wisdom. God created the world 'out of nothing': matter, the lowest of the creatures, was created by Him immediately after the 'fall of the souls,' to prevent the world from being dissolved' (*de Princ.* ii. 1). God is neither the whole nor a part of the whole: the former conception contradicts His simplicity, the latter His sovereignty. His Spirit is no all-pervading subtle element, like the Stoic πνεῦμα. The world is distinct from God; it is His creation. It is eternal in the sense that it had no beginning in time; the entire scheme that we know is only a brief phase in an innumerable series of worlds. The original creation, Origen teaches, was of innocent spirits, who shared 'accidentally' or precariously the perfection which God possesses 'essentially.' Their fall from perfection was voluntary. Some (the angels and the stars, to which Origen attributes souls) remained in their first estate; others (sinful men and evil spirits) fell in various degrees, and can be restored only through the discipline of suffering. This world is constructed as the appropriate scene of their training, affording scope for the treatment proper to every degree of guilt. The fall of the souls was thus antenatal, but Origen teaches no metempsychosis. The story of the Fall in Genesis he is disposed to treat as mere allegory (*c. Cels.* iv. 40). The most succinct statement of his doctrine is in *de Princ.* ii. 8, ending νοῦς πως οὖν γέγονε ψυχή, καὶ ψυχὴ κατορθωθεῖσα γίνεται νοῦς, words which throw light on his psychology. 'Soul' is 'mind' in a fallen state; it is an adventitious principle, intermediate between 'flesh' and 'mind' or 'spirit.' In reality his psychology is dichotomic, though out of respect to St. Paul he preserves in words the distinction between 'soul' and 'spirit' (see esp. *in Joh.* xxxii. 2; *in Levit. Hom.* ii. 2).

The discussion as to whether Origen teaches the immateriality of the soul has been conducted on wrong lines. The soul for Origen is certainly immaterial, but it implies a body. 'The spirit,' he says, 'is with the soul as a master and director, associated with it to remind it of the good, and to accuse and punish it for its faults. If the soul is disobedient and obstinate in revolt, it will be divided from the spirit after it leaves the body' (*in Rom.* ii. 9). The soul which is exalted by following the spirit, and not only following but being transformed into spirit, must put off its nature as soul, and become spiritual (*de Orat.* 10). Here the 'spirit' resembles the impersonal νοῦς of Neo-Platonism; but the question whether it belongs or does not belong to our *ego* can be answered neither for Origen nor for any other mystical thinker. It is an essential part of his teaching that the existence of God and other fundamental truths of religion are 'sown in the soul' as matters of immediate apprehension (αἴσθησις). 'So long as we keep them, the Logos never leaves us' (*in Joh.* xix. 3). This θεία αἴσθησις is made to cover such sensuous experiences (of sight, hearing, smell) as the later Catholicism accepts under the name of mystical phenomena (*c. Cels.* i. 48); but such communications, though from a Divine source, are only externalized by our minds; 'God never speaks to us from outside' (*in Psalm.* xxvii. 1). From these 'seeds' spring the flowers and fruits of Divine knowledge, Christ revealing Himself under various aspects as the soul is able to receive Him. Corresponding to this psychological dispensation is the historical economy which, after the partial theophanies of OT, culminated in the Incarnation. The two are parallel aspects of the same Divine plan; it is meaningless to ask whether the historical Incarnation is the 'cause' of the soul's restoration. At the same time it must be admitted that Origen has a less firm grasp of the ideas of progress and development than Clement. He gives too much importance to the 'fall of Adam,' and in consequence his philosophy of history is both gloomier and less scientific than Clement's. His view of secular culture is also much less sympathetic.

Eschatology.—Clement had represented men in the future life as placed in different grades according to their moral deserts. The wicked will be subjected to disciplinary punishments till they are forced to own their guilt. Origen developed further the notion that all punishment must be disciplinary, since 'God can hate nothing,' and it is no part of His nature to render evil for evil. Moreover, immortal spirits (νοεραὶ φύσεις) cannot be consigned to perdition.

Here it is plain that Origen encountered great difficulties in reconciling his philosophy with the traditional Church teaching on the resurrection, last judgment, heaven, and hell. It is clear, he says, that the Gospels must not be understood literally. 'The stars' could not 'fall from heaven' upon the earth, for they are much larger than the earth. Our material bodies, which are dispersed among other organisms, cannot be reconstituted in the resurrection. Can we suppose that the damned will literally 'gnash their teeth'? No, he says; it is the 'spark,' or vital principle, which survives, and will make a new abode for itself, the resurrection body. Even when the soul becomes pure spirit, it will need a kind of body, for God alone is incorporeal spirit. Purgation must continue after death; 'even Paul or Peter must come into that fire.' But will any remain in torment for ever? Origen hopes and thinks not, but will not dogmatize; he remembers the guest who was cast into outer darkness, with no promise of pardon. There are passages in Origen which imply at least a *pœna damni* never to be made good; but he would himself have disclaimed any certitude on the subject. Only he insists that promises like 'love never faileth,' 'God shall be all in all,' must somehow be fulfilled. Even the devil *might* find salvation, as a spirit made in the image of God, though, as devil, he would be destroyed (*in Rom.* v. 3). The final consummation is complete likeness to God: 'God shall be all in all'; *i.e.* He will be all in each individual (*de Princ.* v. 6). Then there will be no more diversity, when all shall have reached the highest degree of perfection.

Esoteric Christianity.—Origen believes that the Logos enlightens all men according to their capacities. Current Christianity is the best that the average man can assimilate. It includes mythical stories, which exist both in OT and NT; it offers rewards and punishments as inducements to virtue, and communicates truths in veiled forms and images. But it is not a matter of indifference what symbols are presented to the 'common man'; it is the religion of Christ alone which must be accepted by all, though under different aspects. The Gnostic learns that the objects of religious knowledge have only a supramundane history: the 'eternal' or 'spiritual' Gospel 'places clearly before men's minds all things concerning the Son of God, both the mysteries shown by His words, and the things of which His acts were the riddles' (*in Joh.* i. 9).

Such passages have been harshly interpreted as implying that the Gnostic has no further need of the historic Christ; but this is true only in the same sense in which it might be said of St. Paul—in other words, the statement is quite misleading. The innate knowledge of God, which he asserts, is the work of the Logos-Christ, who first fully disclosed Himself in the historic Incarnation. On the actual effect of the death of Christ, as a transaction, Origen suggests various views, already current, in a tentative manner: among others, the idea of a ransom paid to the devil, which was popular at this time. He certainly did not regard the historic work of Christ as a mere appearance or exhibition, though, for the Gnostic, Christ *in* us is far more important than Christ *for* us.

Influence of Origen.—The double achievement of Origen (carrying on what Clement began) was to destroy Gnosticism, and to give philosophy a recognized place in the creeds of the Church. The second was the price which the conservatives had to pay for the first. Henceforth the Church possessed a theology and a philosophy of religion which were far more attractive to the educated mind than the barbaric Platonism of the Gnostics. It was, of course, neither possible nor desirable to teach the philosophy to the masses, for whose benefit the Catholic system, with its apparatus of cultus, miracle, and sensuous symbolism, was developed side by side with the progress of scientific theology. In their relation to tradition, the Alexandrians mark a stage in a conflict which ended in a compromise. The great Gnostics of the 2nd cent. had been unable to maintain their footing in the Church. Clement succeeded in doing so, though not without suspicion; Origen, after much hesitation, was condemned. The Cappadocians endeavoured to reconcile faith and knowledge by mutual concessions, a process which was completed, after a fashion, by Cyril of Alexandria and by the theologians of the 6th century (Harnack, *Hist. of Dogma*, iii. 5).

The first conflict in which Origen's theology was deeply involved was against Sabellianism. Dionysius, bishop of Alexandria, in attacking the Monarchians fell under the charge of Tritheism, the Roman see pronouncing against him, and laying down a *via media* between the Alexandrian and the Sabellian doctrines. This condemnation had no effect at Alexandria, where the school of Origen flourished almost unchallenged till the end of the 3rd century. Modifications, however, were introduced, involving a doctrine of subordination in the Trinity of the Neo-Platonic type, and upholding continence (ἐγκράτεια) as the great original contribution of Christianity to ethics. Gregory Thaumaturgus (who is said to have called the Son a κτίσμα) taught the Trinitarian doctrine of Origen in a form nearer to Monarchianism than to Tritheism.

The first serious attack on Origen was that of Methodius, who, however, in spite of his bitterness, seems only to advocate a compromise between his teaching and the rule of faith. In the controversies that followed in the 4th cent., which need not be described in detail, we mark a gradual hardening and crystallizing of theological thought under the chilling breath of authority. Origen's teaching was disintegrated, selections being made from it without regard to consistency, and he himself was at last condemned as a heretic. After Athanasius the Logos-doctrine began to decay in importance, as the notion of an economic and relative Trinity gave place to that of an absolute Trinity. The identification of the Logos-Christ with the spirit of the cosmic process fell more and more out of sight. This change may also be described as part of a transition from Platonism to Aristotelianism in the Church. The school of Antioch led a revolt against the Alexandrian exegesis of Holy Scripture, and founded a more critical method, in which the literal sense was always at least considered, and the Messianic allusions in OT very much curtailed. Origen's idea of pre-existence had still many supporters in the 4th cent., but was more and more discredited, till it was finally condemned at Constantinople in 533. The rival theories—that the soul is begotten with the body, and that God creates souls and plants them in the embryos—were left to contend with each other. The doctrine of the Fall of Man, based on Genesis, resumed its importance when the theory of an extramundane Fall was excluded. The question whether Christ would have become incarnate if Adam had not sinned is never, we think, discussed at length except by those who answer it in the negative; but the idea of an Incarnation as an essential part of the Divine plan is certainly in accordance with Alexandrianism, and has been revived by modern thinkers (*e.g.* Westcott), who are in general sympathy with Clement and Origen. It was part of the teaching of Pelagius, and may have been discredited on that account.

One of the most important of Origen's contributions to theology was his teaching on the death of Christ, which combined rather than reconciled the notions of expiatory sacrifice—of a propitiatory death of God vanquishing the death decreed by Him—and of the revelation of a redemption really effected in the eternal world. Both ideas were familiar to the Greek mysteries. The idea of *substitution* could not be emphasized by an Alexandrian; the Logos-doctrine makes it meaningless, but after Cyril it became prominent.

In the long Arian controversy the name of Origen played a curious part. The Adoptianist theory of a Jesus who gradually becomes God was totally at variance with Origen's doctrine; but Arius found in the Neo-Platonic cosmology a support for his theory of a *mediating* Logos, between the inaccessible Father and the world. But in denying to the Logos any *essential* unity with the Father he abandoned decisively the Alexandrian Christology. 'With Arius, Christ belongs in every sense to the world of created things' (Harnack); with Athanasius He belongs in every sense to God, the cosmical aspect being virtually shelved. Athanasius was not a scientific theologian, and the restatement of Alexandrian theology, necessitated by his labours, fell to the Cappadocians, of whom Gregory of Nyssa is most in sympathy with Origen. This writer avoids some of the most obnoxious speculations of his master, but on the whole reproduces his teaching, which in this way has found and maintained a footing in the Catholic Church, for Gregory of Nyssa has never been condemned.

But the growing power of 'tradition' had already begun to kill religious philosophy; and the progressive degradation of Christianity into a religion of cultus affected Christian Platonism in precisely the same way in which Neo-Platonism suffered between Plotinus and Jamblichus. Dionysius the Areopagite is the representative of this application of Alexandrian allegorism to ritual and dogma. The first vogue of this extraordinary writer coincided with a reaction in favour of Origen. Among later developments of Christian Platonism, which owed some of their inspiration to the Alexandrian theology, it is necessary to mention only the philosophical mysticism of Eckhart and his successors, the 'Cambridge Platonism' of the 17th cent., and in our own day the theology of F. D. Maurice, Westcott, etc. Among philosophers, Leibniz has many points of resemblance to Origen.

LITERATURE.—Redepenning, *Origenes* (1841–1846); Denis, *De la Philosophie d'Origène* (1884); Westcott, art. 'Origenes' in *Dict. Christ. Biogr.*; Harnack, *Dogmengeschichte*; Bigg, *Christian Platonists of Alexandria* (1886); text: Lommatzsch (1831–1847).

Permanent value of the Alexandrian Theology.—Was the attempt of the Alexandrians to Christianize the current philosophy of their age legitimate? The question has been very diversely answered. Writers like Deissmann, Wernle, and Hatch, and the Ritschlian school generally, regard the 'Hellenizing' of Christian doctrine as an alien graft upon the enthusiastic revivalism of primitive Christianity, and deplore, with Harnack, the 'secularizing' and 'depotentiation' of the religion which they ascribe to the influence of Alexandria. On the other side, it has been pointed out that, unless we ignore St. Paul's Epistles, the Epistle to the Hebrews, and the Fourth Gospel, there is much of 'Hellenism' in the NT; and also that philosophy in the first two centuries had ceased to be 'secular' and had become religious. The later Stoics and Platonists were 'not far from the kingdom of God,' and were by no means inclined to undervalue strictness of conduct. Moreover, the fusion of Greek and Jewish thought was so inevitable that to deplore it is to take a pessimistic view of human development. Finally, revivalism is in its nature a brief phase; an intellectual system must follow it, or the whole effects of the movement must disappear. The Alexandrians satisfied the legitimate need of their age by providing 'a scientific doctrine of religion which, while not contradicting the faith, does not merely support or explain it in a few places, but raises it to another and higher intellectual sphere, namely, out of the province of authority and obedience into that of clear knowledge and inward intellectual assent emanating from love to God' (Harnack, *History of Dogma*, Eng. trans., vol. ii., pp. 324 f.). This recognition, from a writer whose view of religion is strongly anti-intellectualist, is remarkable, and it does no more than justice to the great constructive effort of Clement and Origen, by which the best of Platonism and Stoicism was incorporated in Christianity. The permanent value of their syncretistic schemes will always be differently judged while men continue to be 'born either Platonists or Aristotelians'; those who would oust metaphysics from theology can have but scanty sympathy with the Alexandrians. But if speculation on Divine truths is permissible or even necessary, no Christian theologians deserve a higher place than Clement and Origen, who made a serious and not unsuccessful attempt to combine in their creed the immanence and transcendence of God, universal law and human freedom, the universal and the particular in revelation, a lofty standard of practical ethics and world-forgetting contemplation. Hort's opinion of Clement's contribution to Christian theology has been quoted. Westcott says of Origen, 'We have not yet made good the positions which he marked out as belonging to the domain of Christian philosophy' (*Rel. Thought in the West*, 252).

W. R. INGE.

ALGONQUINS.

ALGONQUINS (Eastern).—**I. Divisions.**—The existing representatives of the Algonquin or Algic race may be separated linguistically into three divisions: the Blackfeet of the extreme western part of North America, whose idiom differs most from that of all the other Algonquin tribes; the Cree-Ojibwas of the middle west, whose language embraces a number of closely allied linguistic variations; and the so-called *Wabanaki* races of the north-eastern American coast, with whom the present article is especially concerned.

The term *Wabanaki* or *Oñbanaki* means both 'land of the dawn *or* east' and 'man *or* person from the east.' The name is at present applied to five distinct clans; viz., the Passamaquoddies, Penobscots, Canadian Abenakis or St. Francis Indians, Micmacs, and Delawares, all of whom are plainly descended from one common family which probably first established organized tribal relations along the Canadian and New England north-eastern coast. There is no reason to consider that the term 'Easterners = *Wabanakis*' has any meaning going farther back than this into the origin of these peoples, who, in all probability, came eastward at a comparatively early date from some unknown western *habitat*. Unless modern Americanists are to be driven to accept the impracticable theory that the eastern tribes crossed from Europe by way of some long since vanished land-bridge, the theory of a western origin for all the Indian coast-races is literally forced upon us. It will be seen, therefore, that the name '*Wabanakis* = Easterner' must have for us a geographical rather than a racial-historical signification.

(1) The Passamaquoddy Indians of Pleasant Point, Maine, now numbering about 500 in all, are identical with the Milicetes or Etchemins of New Brunswick and Nova Scotia, Canada. The name *Passamaquoddy* is a purely local term, meaning 'spearers of pollock-fish' (*peskátum*). The correct form is *Pestumokádyik*, which has been corrupted by the whites into *Passamaquoddy*. These Indians are by far the most interesting remnant of the Wabanakis, as they still retain an unusually extensive oral literature, including love poems, legends, and historical tales of considerable value. It should be stated that the nucleus of the material relating to the primitive religious conceptions of the *Wabanakis* has been collected by the present writer from the Passamaquoddies primarily, and secondarily from the Micmacs.

(2) The Penobscot Indians of Maine now number not more than 350, most of whom live at the Indian village of Oldtown on Penobscot River near Bangor, Maine. These people still speak a characteristic Algonquin language, which is more closely allied to the idiom of the Abenakis of St. Francis, near Pierreville, Quebec, Canada, than it is to that of the geographically nearer neighbours of the Penobscots, the Passamaquoddies. In short, there can be no doubt that both the Penobscot and the Abenaki dialects are sister idioms which have sprung from a common original at a very recent date (cf. the present writer in *Kulóskap the Master*, p. 30).

(3) It is well known that the Abenakis of Canada are the direct descendants, of course with some admixture of French and other blood, of the majority of the savages who escaped from the great battle of the Kennebec in Maine, when the English commander Bradford overthrew their tribe on 3rd December, 1679. Many of the survivors at once fled to French Canada, where they established their *habitat* at their present village of St. Francis, near Pierreville, Quebec. Others again may have wandered into Canada at a slightly later date. There can be no doubt that the Indians now called Penobscots, from their residence near the river of that name, are the descendants of those of the early Abenakis who eventually submitted themselves to their English conquerors. The Canadian Abenaki is the only one of the Wabanaki clans which calls itself generically by the comprehensive name *Wabanaki* (*Kulóskap*, p. 31).

(4) The Micmacs are the easternmost and by far the most numerous to-day of the Wabanaki remnants. They are to be found in various places in the Canadian provinces of Quebec, New Brunswick, Nova Scotia, Prince Edward's Island, and Newfoundland. Their grade of intelligence is much lower than that of the other members of the same family, but they still possess a vast store of folklore, legends, and poems, which is perishing for want of interested collectors. Their language differs so greatly from the dialects of the Passamaquoddies, Penobscots, and Abenakis, that the members of these clans always use French or English when communicating with their Micmac neighbours, while an intelligent Passamaquoddy can without difficulty be understood by a Penobscot or Abenaki, if the dialect is pronounced slowly.

(5) The story of the enforced westward wanderings of the ill-fated Delawares or *Lenâpe* has been told in detail by a distinguished authority, the late Dr. D. G. Brinton, in his comprehensive work, *The Lenâpe and their Legends*, pp. 122–126. At the present day, this famous tribe, around which a certain glamour of romance has been cast by the well known American author, Fenimore Cooper, in his *Leatherstocking Tales*, is scattered literally to the four winds of heaven. The three Delaware clans, the *Minsi*, the *Unami* and the *Unalachtigo*, who were once the dominant native race in Delaware, Pennsylvania, New Jersey, and parts of New York State, are now represented by a few bands living in Indian Territory, in Western Canada, and in Ontario, Canada. The Delawares of Indian Territory, numbering about 500 persons, have quite lost their tribal identity, as they have been incorporated by the Cherokee nation, by whose chief and council they are governed. In Ontario there are only about 300 in all: 100 situated at Hagersville on the Reserve of the Six Nations (Iroquois), 100 at Munceytown, and the same number at Moraviantown, which is the seat of a Moravian mission.

2. Religious conceptions. — All the Wabanaki clans at present existing, save only the Delawares, are, with very few individual exceptions, of the Roman Catholic faith, a fact which is most fortunate for students of comparative religion, as the Catholic priests have made little if any effort to stifle the ancient ideas regarding witchcraft and spirits, which formed the chief elements of the earlier shamanistic faith. For this reason, nearly all our material, upon which this and other studies of Algonquin religious ideas are based, comes from the Catholic tribes, and not from the Delawares, who are all Protestants, belonging for the most part to the Church of England or to the Moravians.

The religious system of the primitive eastern Algonquins was, as already indicated, purely shamanistic, viz. a faith which, although admitting in a vague way the existence of a Supreme Being, laid its chief stress on the government of the world by an indefinite number of secondary spirits or deities, both benevolent and malevolent towards man. These beings, in whose hands lay the real power, had therefore to be propitiated by all sorts of magic rites and spells, which gave rise to a caste of conjurors and wizards, who were themselves endowed with preternatural powers. In the lore of the Wabanakis, the general principle of good may be said to be represented by the rather clown-like being known to the Passamaquoddies as *Kulóskap* and to the Penobscots as *Klûskâbe*, who, as Mr. Leland has aptly put it, personifies the principle of good nature rather than of goodness. *Kulóskap's* twin brother, *Malsum* the wolf, was the evil genius of the Indians, and may perhaps be called the *Ahriman* of the Wabanakis, although this is almost too dignified a term. It is highly interesting to notice that these twins were born from an unknown divine mother, the good *Kulóskap* in the natural manner, and the evil wolf through the woman's side, a method which he maliciously chose in order to kill his mother. In spite of his name, which means 'the liar,' the tendency of *Kulóskap* was essentially benevolent (*op. cit.* p. 34). He was called 'the deceiver,' not because he deceived or injured man, but because he was clever enough to lead his enemies astray—the highest possible virtue to the early American mind.

Kulóskap was at once the creator and the friend of man, and, strangely enough, he made the Indian (or man—the terms are synonymous) out of the ash tree. The present writer, in collaboration with the late Charles Godfrey Leland, has published a work entitled *Kulóskap the Master* (New York, 1902), which gives in translation a number of songs and narrative poems relating to this being's career and exploits. In this collection, which gives the history of *Kulóskap* almost in epic form, it will be noticed that the hero or demi-god is born from a divine mother, and that he is the creator of man and all the animals, a special poem being devoted to the origin of the rattlesnakes, who were primitively bad Indians. *Kulóskap* then named the animals, and discovered that man was the lord of them all. Traces of Christian influence are so evident even in the titles of these poems as to need little elaboration. It will be noticed, however, that although the general outline has undoubtedly been affected by the teachings of the missionaries, the details remain distinctly native. *Kulóskap* then became the kindly teacher of man, who came into the world an absolutely ignorant being. When man was first created, there was no light at all, and the god's first act was to bring about the 'daybreak and the dawn.' Here again we see Biblical influence. *Kulóskap* at once proceeded to instruct man in hunting, fishing, and trapping, and in the arts of building huts and canoes. He showed man the hidden virtues of 'plants, roots, and blossoms.' He taught him the use of weapons, and even the names of the stars, and the origin of the planets. He recounted to his apt pupils 'all the wonderful stories and the very old traditions,' thus becoming the Indian father of history. He was prodigal in magic gifts to his special favourites, and became, in short, a veritable demiurge, whose special care was the welfare of mankind.

The epic, if so loosely connected a series may be so called, concludes with a number of tales relating to the magic power of the god, who, although almost omnipotent, was on one occasion conquered by an unusual enemy—the baby! When the god was boasting of his powers to a certain woman, she replied: 'One there still remains whom no man has ever yet overcome in any strife,' indicating her baby who sat 'upon the floor in baby peace profound, sucking a piece of maple sugar sweet; greatly content and troubling nobody.' The Master then proceeded to attempt to cajole the baby to come to him, using at first all his blandishments. When these failed, for the baby remained immovable, he had recourse to sorcery, 'and used the awful spells, and sang the songs which raise the dead, and fright the devils wild, and send the witches howling to their graves.' But the baby 'peacefully as ever kept his place' (*op. cit.* p. 107). This story, which seems to be a genuine native production, is a good illustration of the Indian sense of humour, which, contrary to accepted opinion, is very highly developed.

In the end, owing to the evil ways of man, *Kulóskap* 'sailed away over the water, the shining waves of Minas; and they looked in silence at him, until they could see him no more. Yet when they had ceased to behold him they still heard his voice in song, the wonderful voice of the Master! But the sounds grew fainter and fainter and softer in the distance, till at last they died away. Then over them all was silence, till a wonder came to pass: for all the beasts, which before had used but one common language, now talked in different tongues!' Here again we seem to have a perverted echo from the missionaries. After *Kulóskap* had left the land, the bird which had loved him most, the Great Snowy Owl, 'went far into the North, into the deep dark forest, where to this day his children sing to the night "Kûkûskûûs," which meaneth in our language "sorrow, sorrow, sorrow." And the loons who had been his huntsmen go back and forth o'er the waters, seeking in vain for their master, the lord whom they cannot meet; ever wailing, wailing sadly, because they find him not' (*op. cit.* p. 216). Micmac tradition in various forms still associates Kulóskap (or Glooscap, as he is there called) with Cape Blomidon, a bold headland projecting into the Bay of Minas, Nova Scotia.

It will be evident even from the above very brief sketch, that *Kulóskap*, as he at present exists in the memories of his former children, is a mixture of traditions. The element of the Christian God has entered very markedly into this lore, curiously compounded with what are undoubtedly native elements. For example, it is quite clear that all the stories of the exploits of the demi-god are based on the conception that he was a supernatural Indian and the father of all the conjurors, a class which still exists among the Catholic Wabanakis. This same culture-hero appears in the legends of the entire Algonquin family, although often under another name. It is highly probable, therefore, that the idea of a great Divine man was brought by these eastern Indians from their primitive western home.

The Wabanakis saw a spirit in every tree and waterfall, and a malignant or benevolent influence in many animals; and, in order to propitiate these beings, the class of sorcerers became, of course, a positive necessity. These people, who are called by the Passamaquoddies *m'deolinwuk*, 'drum-beaters,' from their methods of exorcism, had very peculiar powers. We see from the tales that the conjuror could transform himself into an animal at will; that he could cast a spell on an enemy, even though the latter might also be a *m'deolin*; that he could violate the laws of nature so far as to walk in hard ground, sinking up to the ankles or knees at every step; and, finally, that the wizards could communicate with each other telepathically. One need hardly comment on the first two or the fourth of these wonders, as they are common among all shamanistic conjurors; but the third phenomenon, the power to sink into hard ground while walking, seems to be characteristically American. Rink states that this is not an unusual feat among the conjurors of the Greenland Eskimos, who frequently sink into rocky or frozen ground 'as if in snow.' The trick is probably done by some peculiar method of stooping, or else is merely suggested by means of hypnotic influence. Leland compares here, however, the Old Norse statements regarding their wizards, who occasionally sank into the ground, and who had power to pass through earth with the same ease as through air and water (*Algonquin Legends*, p. 342). It seems hardly permissible to draw a parallel between the ancient Norsemen and the northern Indians on this account, as the case Leland cites is that of a conjuror who disappeared into the ground head downwards when stabbed at by a foe. The present writer has been told by old Passamaquoddies that they had personally seen conjurors 'soften the ground' without any apparent means of performing the wonder. On this account, the theory of suggestive hypnosis seems the most acceptable one.

Religious cannibalism appears also to have existed among the Wabanakis. In one tale, the wizards eat their murdered comrade, evidently with the idea of absorbing into themselves some or all of his power. As is well known, the Fijis and the New Zealand Maoris often ate their enemies with the same object in view; viz., to become as brave as the fallen foe had been. All authorities tend to show, however, that cannibalism was extremely rare among the American races, and was resorted to only in isolated cases such as the one here noted. In one Delaware tale, the wizard, who is also an evil spirit, desires to devour a very old worn-out man. This seems to be a relic from primitive times, when it was probably not unusual to devour the aged, perhaps for a double purpose: both to get rid of them, as was the case until recently among the islanders of Tierra del Fuego, and also possibly to absorb sacramentally into the living members of the family the essence of the dead parent, whose soul is thus prevented from becoming entirely extinct.

Especial attention should be called at this point to the remarkable ideas prevalent among the Wabanakis regarding the cohabitation of women with serpents (*Kulóskap*, p. 225). Such a conception may seem strange, coming as it does from a land where there are no ophidians large enough to warrant such a superstition. Although running the risk of seeming fanciful, the present writer deems it not impossible that we have in these hideous tales some relic of far distant pre-historic days when huge serpents were not unknown. It should be added, moreover, that in every case of such sexual relations between serpents and human beings among the Wabanakis, the serpent was always a wizard in disguise,—a fact which shows that, in the later superstition at least, the unusual character of such monstrous serpents was fully appreciated.*

It will appear evident from this sketch of the religious ideas of the Eastern Algonquins, that the legends of these people are well worthy of preservation, from the point of view both of primitive poetry and of science. Mr. Leland, in his preface to *Kulóskap the Master* (p. 14), remarks on the very common reproach of Europeans, that Americans have a land without ancient legends or song. He adds: 'We bewailed our wretched poverty when we had in our lap a casket full of treasure which we would not take the pains to open.' The fact is that almost every hill and dale of New England has or had its romantic native legend, its often beautiful poem or curious myth. Many of these fancies have disappeared for ever through the deliberate ignorance of the average white settler, who even to-day, when the Indian has almost vanished from the land, is inclined to preserve the old feeling that 'the only good Indian is a dead Indian.' Rand's *Legends of the Micmacs* (New York, 1894), Leland's *Algonquin Legends of New England* (Boston, 1885), *Kulóskap the Master*, and the present article must perhaps suffice, then, to present to the English-speaking public a few interesting and characteristic specimens of the religious traditions of the rapidly disappearing race of the Wabanakis,—a race which, fifty years hence, will, in all probability, have hardly a single living representative who shall know its language or lore.

J. DYNELEY PRINCE.

*It may be noted that similar marital relations between serpents and mankind, though generally with a different *motif*, are found not only among other stocks of North and South America, but also in Europe, Asia, Africa, and Polynesia (cf. MacCulloch, *The Childhood of Fiction*, London, 1905, pp. 253–259, 264–267).

ALGONQUINS (Prairie Tribes, viz. the **Kickapoos, Pottawatomies, Sacs, and Foxes**).—These tribes, together with their Algonquin allies, the Chippewas, and their Siouan friends, the Osages and Iowas, have their strongest bond of union in their return, between the years 1880 and 1884, to their ancient beliefs. Many of them had been, in name at least, Roman Catholics, a few were Presbyterians and Methodists, though all, except the Pottawatomies, revered the clan totems as saints, and all continued to wear their medicine-bags, and to guide their actions by their dreams. Those who remained heathen in name as well as in practice had seemed to have forgotten the old gods, and merely showed a superstitious faith in the power of their 'medicine,' as their fetishes were called, the incantations of their *shamans* or wizards, the 'warnings' of their dreams, and a vague impression that somewhere, above the firmament or in the bowels of the earth, dwelt a company of immortal, gigantic animals—the totems, or ancestors—from whom the various clans of the tribes were descended.

As early as the middle of the 17th cent., the Jesuits endured every sort of hardship and danger to convert these peoples, who, at that time, were living at the head of the Green Bay of Lake Michigan (Parkman, *La Salle and the Discovery of the Great West*, p. 34), and they had some reason to believe that they had succeeded. In 1673, Father Marquette wrote that, when he and M. Joliet went among the tribes of the Green Bay Indians, he was rejoiced to find in one of their villages a great cross set up, adorned with white skins, red girdles, and bows and arrows, as votive offerings (Marquette, *A Discovery of some New Countries and Nations in the Northern America*, printed as an appendix to Hennepin's *America*, p. 323)—a proof to him of the success of the mission of Allouez and Dablon, established in 1669–70. Hennepin, the Franciscan friar, had, however, not much confidence in these conversions. He avers that these 'salvages' would 'suffer themselves baptized six times a Day for a Glass of *Aqua Vitæ* or a Pipe of Tobacco' (*America*, pt. ii. p. 56), and adds this statement as to what they really did believe: 'Some of 'em acknowledge the Sun for their God. . . . Others will have a Spirit that commands, say they, in the Air. Some among 'em look upon the Skie as a kind of Divinity, others as an Otkon or Manitou, either good or evil. . . . Dreams with them supply all other defects, and serve instead of Prophecy, Inspiration, Laws, Commands, and Rules, either for undertakings in War, Peace, Trade, or Hunting. Nay, they are a kind of Oracles in their Eyes. You would say, to see 'em at their Devotion, that they were of the Sect of the Pretended Inspir'd. The Belief they have in their Dreams imposes upon them a kind of Necessity of believing likewise, that they are forewarned by an Universal Mind of what they ought to do or avoid. Nay, this Infatuation prevails upon 'em so far that if they were persuaded in their Dreams to kill a Man, or commit any other Enormous Crime, they would immediately do it with the greatest alacrity, and make Atonement for it by the means which we shall hereafter relate. Parents' Dreams generally serve for the Observation of their Children, and Captains' for those of their Villages. There are some among 'em as pretend to interpret Dreams. . . . When they meet with any great Fall of Water, which is either difficult to pass or dangerous to avoid, they throw into it a Bever's skin, Tobacco, Porcelane, or the like, by way of Sacrifice, to appease and engage the Deity that there presides. . . . There is no nation among 'em which has not a sort of Juglers or Conjurers, which some look upon to be wizards. . . . They are, in a Word, extremely bewitch'd of these Juglers, though they so plainly and frequently appear to deceive 'em. These Impostors cause themselves to be reverenced as Prophets which fore-tell futurity. They will needs be looked upon to have an unlimited Power. They boast of being able to make it Wet or Dry; to cause a Calm or a Storm; to render Land Fruitful or Barren; and, in a Word, to make Hunters Fortunate or Unfortunate. They also pretend to Physic and to apply Medicines, but which are such that they have little or no Virtue at all in 'em. . . . It is impossible to imagine the horrible Howlings and strange Contortions that these Juglers make of their Bodies, when they are disposing themselves to Conjure, or raise their Enchantments. . . . They will do nothing without either Presents or Hire. But however 'tis certain that if these Impostors have not skill enough to procure themselves Credit, or to find something to say in case of a Failure in their Art by their Patients' Death, 'tis ten to one but that they are killed on the spot without any further formality.

'These poor blind Wretches are, moreover, engaged in several other Superstitions, which the Devil makes use of to Ensnare 'em. They believe there are many living Creatures which have Rational Souls. They have a very unaccountable veneration for certain Bones of Elks, Bevers, and other Beasts, and therefor never give them to their dogs, but lay 'em up in Repositories with a great deal of Care: These they never throw into Rivers but with great Reluctancy. They say that the Souls of these Animals observe how they deal by their Bodies, and consequently advertise both the Living and the Dead of that kind thereof, so that if they treat 'em ill, they must not expect that those sorts of Beasts will ever suffer themselves to be taken by them either in this or the other world' (*America*, pt. ii. pp. 56–60). In addition, there are scattered through the two parts of the book descriptions of the various feasts and dances for the living and the dead, which might have been written to-day, so little change has time wrought, and on p. 112 the author says of the 'medicine' or fetish: 'These people admit of some Sort of Genius in all things: they all believe there is a Master of Life, as they call him, but hereof they make various Applications: some of them have a lean Raven, which they carry along with them, and which they say is the Master of their Life; others have a Bone or Sea-Shell, or some such thing.' He also details at some length the story of the woman who fell down from Heaven and bore two sons, one of whom, after a time, retired to Heaven. This, of course, is a fragment of the legend of Hiawatha, Manibosho, or Nanabush (all names of the same supernatural personage).

The revival of the old religion, either modified by contact with Christianity or else having always had observances which had escaped the notice of the missionaries, was brought about by the Chippewas. According to their story, a band of their people was surprised by the Sioux and exterminated. From the setting of the sun till its rising all lay dead, but when its beams fell on the Woman—her name is too sacred to be spoken—she revived, and heard a voice saying to her, 'Get up and take the drum.' When this command had been four times repeated, she rose up and found a drum and twelve drumsticks beside her. She took a stick and began to beat on the drum, and immediately the other sticks began to beat as if hands held them. At once her strength was restored, and her scalp-lock, which had been torn away, was renewed,—a most important miracle, as the soul is supposed to be in the small bulb which lies at the roots of the scalp-lock, and one is a slave in the spirit land to the holder of the scalp. Then the voice spoke again, 'Go to the other band of the Chippewas and to all who will be my friends'; so she set out, travelling night and day, feeling no need of food or rest, and listening to the instructions of the Voice. Thus she travelled for eighty days, at the end of which time she reached her people, called them together by the roll of her drum, and told them that Geechee Manitou wished them to take leave of the gods of the white people, politely, and turn again to him. He desired a dance house built for him, and a dance, to be called the Remembrance or Religion dance (*Ow-wah-see-chee*), to be performed in it by strong young men, without physical blemish, who had practised, prayed, and denied themselves all pleasures for eighty days. This dance was to continue four, seven, or twenty-one days, to the accompaniment of the drum and songs of praise to the manitou (pronounced 'manito-ah' by the Indians), while all the people feasted and made offerings of the smoke of tobacco and the steam of cooked food, beginning with the offering of a white dog. In addition, all the old customs were to be revived, and an effort was to be made to induce all other Indians to conform to them again. When the people had purified themselves by fasting and by being sweated in the sweat-lodge (a small close hut having a great stone in it which is heated and then drenched with cold water to produce a vapour in which the devotee stands naked to have the devils that produce disease or wickedness sweated out of him while he recites his prayers); and after they had built a dance house, and had honoured Geechee Manitou by prayers and praises, she taught them the Religion dance, put them in mind of some forgotten beliefs, and then disappeared, no one knew whither; nor did she ever return. At once the Chippewas had a great revival of old practices, to which they invited their relatives the Pottawatomies, who in turn proselytized the Kickapoos and their friends and neighbours, the Osages, Sacs, and Foxes. A little later the Sacs won over the Iowas and Otoes, but in spite of strenuous efforts they have never been able to add any other Siouan tribes to this coalition.

Besides Geechee Manitou, these tribes believe in three great gods. He is the first, the creator, and he lives in a golden boat, which we call the sun. Meechee Manitou is the god who lives in the cold, wet, slippery cavern in which the souls of the wicked wander and shiver for ever. He is not now very active in mischief, but he is the father of an innumerable number of devils that produce war, pestilence, famine, aches, pains, quarrels, and all other ills of body and soul. Some of these are the offspring of witches with whom he has consorted; others sprang from his breath, his sweat, his saliva, even his words and the scent of his footsteps. The Brothers, 'twin sons of the woman who fell down from heaven,' spend their time, one in ruling over the happy hunting-ground, or place of the happy dead; the other in sitting in the road the ghosts go over, at the point where it divides, his business being to show the good their way to the happy hunting-ground, and the bad their way to the cavern of Meechee Manitou. These Brothers lived a long time on earth, destroyed many devils and wizards (some tribes were in the world before these two gods, and had become very wicked), received additional physical and spiritual power from the totems, founded the Fox tribe, and then took their way—one to the spirit land, the other to the road that leads to it. The occasion of their leaving the world was this: on account of the good works of the Brothers, the devils and wizards endeavoured to destroy them, and succeeded in killing the younger, Cold Hand; but when the elder, Hot Hand, mourned so terribly as to flood the earth with his tears, and draw it, which had hitherto been flat, into hills and valleys by his sobs, the devils and wizards, terrified by the commotion, worked four days and nights with their enchantments to 'make the dead alive.' When he was made alive, he went to his brother, but Hot Hand was not pleased. He said he was ashamed, because he had been heard to mourn so terribly, and he went into his wigwam and shut Cold Hand out. Presently he thrust forth a kettle, fire-sticks, tobacco, and a whistle to call ghosts. Cold Hand took these things and went away. He sat down on the edge of the world to dream. When he came out of his dream, he 'made a place for good souls. Before that they had no place; they blew about in the wind. Since that time, death has been better than life' (M. A. Owen, *Folk-Lore of the Musquakie Indians*, p. 15).

The totems are patron saints. Each clan or subdivision of the tribe is named from the giant animal from which it is supposed to be descended. Judging from the old legends told by tribe historians, all the tribes at one time had many clans, each with its clan Secret Society which did homage to its totem, as its *shaman* or medicine-man directed; but so many clans were exterminated by their wars with white and red men that in some tribes the totemic system is only a memory, and in others there are many more sticks to the sacred drum than there are drummers to hold them—each clan having but one drummer playing at a time.

The hereditary chief is the high priest of the faith, nominally, but he does nothing without first consulting the *shamans*, who are presidents of the totem societies, prophets, physicians, and exorcists all in one, besides filling some other offices (referred to by Hennepin). When it is understood that the earth and air are supposed to be peopled with an infinite number of malignant devils and sprites, as well as vampire ghosts, which are always on the alert to do mischief except when rendered torpid by extreme cold, and as only the *shamans* know the secret of casting them out or spell-binding them, it will be readily comprehended that, so long as the ancient beliefs prevail, the *shamans* will be the real autocrats of the tribes. Generally a son succeeds his father, as in the case of the chieftainship, but sometimes the son is not clever enough to be a *shaman*; in that case, any boy in the clan may be selected to be trained, thus keeping the succession in the family, as everyone in the clan is related. Sometimes, when an especially clever boy is found in another clan, the *shaman* takes possession of him, and, in rare cases, a boy has been brought from another tribe. In the latter case he is adopted by a member of the *shaman's* tribe who has lately lost a son of about the same age.

The white witches of the tribe are the 'women-with-spots-on-their-faces.' These spots are round daubs of vermilion, and each one stands for a Religion dance given for the woman-with-spots-on-her-face, at puberty, by her father. These dances and the severe usage to which she is subjected from a very early age, make her a healer and a bringer of good fortune. She insures safe delivery to women in childbirth, not by being present, but by chanting and praying at a distance and refusing to hear all entreaties to be present; she names the newborn infants after something that belongs to the father's clan (this is the real name, not much used, not the nickname given from some exploit or peculiarity); she heals the sick, and interprets the confused dreams of the women; any one with whom she is friendly is lucky, any one with whom she is unfriendly may look for misfortunes.

The ceremonials of the faith may almost be described by a word—'dancing.' There are fasts, prayers, and hymns before dancing, and feasts, prayers, and hymns during dancing; these are parts of the same thing. There are dances for planting and dances for harvest, dances to bring rain and to cause it to cease, for peace, for war, for puberty, to restore health, and to honour the dead, totem dances, and dances for every great event in the life of the tribe and individual except birth, marriage, and the too frequent divorces.

Kickapoos.—The Kickapoos consider themselves foreigners. 'This is the only tribe among all our Indians who claim for themselves a foreign origin,' says Thomas L. M'Kenney, formerly of the Indian Department, Washington, U.S.A., speaking of the Shawnee tribe, of which the Kickapoo is a division. 'Most of the aborigines of the continent believe their forefathers ascended from holes in the earth; and many of them assign a local habitation to these traditionary places of the nativity of their race; resembling, in this respect, some of the traditions of antiquity, and derived, perhaps, from that remote period when barbarous tribes were troglodytes, subsisting upon the spontaneous productions of the earth. The Shawanese believe their ancestors inhabited a foreign land, which, for some unknown cause, they determined to abandon. They collected their people together, and marched to the seashore. Here various persons were selected to lead them, but they declined the duty, until it was undertaken by one of the Turtle tribe. He placed himself at the head of the procession, and walked into the sea. The waters immediately divided, and they passed along the bottom of the ocean until they reached this "*island*"' (M'Kenney, *North American Indians*, vol. ii. pp. 263–264). This writer goes on to state, what the traditions of the Kickapoos confirm, that the Shawnees were, in their days of power, divided into twelve tribes, and these again into 'families,' such as the Eagle, the Turtle, etc., each named from its totem or ancestral animal; but two of the tribes were annihilated, six were merged, and four kept their names and tribal government. These four were the Kickapoos, Pickaways, Chilicothes, and Makostrakes.

It is not known exactly when these people were driven, by the Iroquois, southward to the Savannah river, nor is it known when they left that region and separated the tribes. In 1673, Father Marquette found the Kickapoos on a river which flowed into the Bay of Puans (the Green Bay of Lake Michigan, or, as it was then called, the Lake of the Illinois), and he refers to Father Allouez as having a mission among them. He adds that, in comparison with their neighbours, the Miamis, they are boors (Marquette, *A Discovery of some New Countries and Nations in the Northern America*, in Hennepin's *America*, pt. ii. p. 323). On Hennepin's map, published in 1698, they are north of Lake Winnebago, but, in his account of the retreat of Tonti when he was endeavouring to lead his little company back to M. La Salle after the destruction of Fort Crèvecœur (A.D. 1680), he speaks of their home as being on the west side of the Bay of Puans (*America*, pt. i. ch. 75, headed 'The Savages Kikapoux murther Father Gabriel de la Ribourde, a Recollect Missionary'), though bands of their young men were wandering in the south-east in the hope of surprising small companies of their enemies, the Iroquois. Hermann Moll's map, published before 1716, shows them on the west side of the bay. In 1763, when they were engaged in the conspiracy of Pontiac to form a federation of all the Indian tribes with the intention of preventing the encroachments of the whites or destroying them, they were living on the Miami and Scioto rivers (Parkman, *Conspiracy of Pontiac*, vol. ii. p. 198 and map). Colonel Bouquet reported, when he had forced the Indians to sue for peace (1764), that the 'Kickapoux' had three hundred warriors and a total population of fifteen hundred. He placed them on the 'Ouabache' (Wabash) river (*19th Annual Report of the Bureau of American Ethnology*, p. 1108). On May 22, 1804, Captain William Clark, of the Lewis and Clark Expedition, wrote as follows: 'This tribe resides on the heads of the Kaskaskia and Illinois rivers, on the other (east) side of the Mississippi, but occasionally hunt in Missouri' (Elliott Coues, *The History of the Lewis and Clark Expedition*, vol. i. p. 7); but this could have been but one band of them, for, in 1808, the Pottawatomies and Kickapoos gave to Tecumseh and his brother, the Prophet, a tract of land in Indiana, lying along the Tippecanoe river. These two most distinguished Kickapoos, Tecumseh, or Flying Panther, and the Prophet Tens-kwau-taw-waw, endeavoured to form a confederacy like the one Pontiac projected, and, in 1811, became engaged in a war with the whites, which terminated disastrously for the Indians at the battle of Tippecanoe, much to the surprise of the red men, who had believed that the incantations of the Prophet had rendered them bullet-proof. In the war of 1812, Tecumseh and his people joined forces with the British (Eggleston and Seelye, *Tecumseh*, chs. xxii.–xxxiii.). Catlin visited the Prophet and his people in Illinois in 1831, but his map, printed in 1840, shows them on the west side of the Missouri river. During the Civil War, one band, with a band of Pottawatomies, went to Mexico, but have since returned. *Smithsonian Report*, pt. ii. p. 185, states: 'Kickapoos at Pottawatomie and Great Nemaha Reservation, in Brown County, Kansas, August 20, 1885, 235. Kickapoo, Mexican (mixed band with Pottawatomie), Indian Territory, 346.' The numbers are at this time much smaller, so that the report of the Commissioner for Indian Affairs for 1901 gives the number of Kickapoos in Kansas as 199, and of Mexican Kickapoos in Indian Territory as 221. It is a dying people.

The Kickapoos are sickly, melancholy, and severely religious. In addition to a dance house, they have a 'house of silence'—a wooden structure which was built, as a chief was commanded in a dream, in silence and fasting. It is used for prayer and praise, but not for dances. Another revelation of late years causes them to flog their children for misdemeanours—something unknown in other tribes, where children are whipped only at puberty as a trial of endurance. A flogger is chosen once a year by lot, and his duty is to make the rounds of the wigwams every Saturday with a mask over his face. In consequence, no one is at home on Saturday but the culprits; the rest of the family sit among the bushes on the river bank and weep. The culprits do not weep during this (supposedly) religious exercise. These people have but one council-fire and three totems. This refers to the Brown County Kickapoos, not to the Mexican, who prefer to be considered Pottawatomies. They pay more reverence to the Rain Serpent than other Indians, and this may partly account for their sickliness, as their reservation is so infested with venomous reptiles as to render cattle-raising almost an impossibility, in consequence of which their staple flesh diet is pork. (It is well known that the bite of a serpent has no effect on a hog). As an antidote for themselves and their ponies, they make use of a tea and wash of infused leaves, roots, and blossoms of the arrow-leaved violet (*Viola sagittata*). Violet was once a maid, sister to Rattlesnake, and as good as he was wicked; whomsoever he poisoned, she healed. In rage at this he killed her. Geechee Manitou, compassionating her and those she could befriend, changed her into this healing plant. It grows wild in great abundance all over the reservation. Another cause of their inferior physique may be their marrying in the clan—something contrary to the religious scruples of most other Indians. Their tribal name means 'smooth,' and undoubtedly refers to some stream by which they have lived, and not to their tempers.

Pottawatomies.—These people have no legend of ever having lived anywhere but in the North-West. The French missionaries and fur traders found them, during their first explorations, in what is now the State of Michigan. 'Early in 1600 the Pottawatomies were occupying the lower peninsula of Michigan, in scattered bands, whence they were driven westward by the Iroquois, and settled about Green Bay. The French acquired much influence over them, whom they joined in their wars with the Iroquois' (*Smithsonian Report, 1885*, p. 135). The *Jesuit Relation*, 1658, refers to them as being the nearest tribe to the settlement of St. Michael, near the head of Green Bay. A band of them accompanied Marquette when, in 1674, he set out to found a new mission, the Immaculate Conception, at the principal town of the Illinois; and it was the Ottawas, the elder branch of this family of Indians, that, in 1676, carried the bones of Marquette to St. Ignace in a grand procession of thirty canoes, and took part in the funeral services (Parkman, *La Salle and the Discovery of the Great West*, pp. 68–71). It is evident, therefore, that they were considered Christians; but when they joined in Pontiac's conspiracy, nearly a hundred years later, reliable witnesses declared that they ate the bodies of their most valiant enemies. Again, in the war of 1812, they were guilty of the same practices. One of the best attested instances is that of Captain Wells, who was killed after the capture of Chicago in 1812. 'This man, who had been a long time among the Indians, having been taken prisoner by them at the age of thirteen, had acquired a great reputation for courage, and his name is still mentioned as that of the bravest white man with whom they ever met. He had almost become one of their number. . . . At the commencement of hostilities . . . he sided with his own countrymen . . . Wells was killed. . . . His body was divided, and his heart was shared as being the most certain spell for courage, and part of it was sent to the various tribes in alliance with the Pottawatomies, while they themselves feasted upon the rest. . . . Mr. Barron has seen the Pottawatomies with the hands and limbs of both white men and Cherokees, which they were about to devour. . . . Among some tribes cannibalism is universal, but it appears that among the Pottawatomies it is generally restricted to a society or fraternity, whose privilege and duty it is, on all occasions, to eat of the enemies' flesh; at least one individual must be eaten. The flesh is sometimes dried and taken to the village. Not only are the members of this fraternity endued with great virtues, but it is said they can impart them, by means of spells, to any individual they wish to favour' (W. H. Keating, *Keating's Narrative*, compiled from the notes of Major Long and Messrs. Say, Keating, and Calhoun, vol. i. pp. 102, 103).

Since Keating's narrative was written (1825), missionaries have again laboured among these people, and with considerable success. Among those who still cling to tribal life there are Methodists, Presbyterians, and Roman Catholics, as well as worshippers of the Manitous; but it is impossible to tell what proportion of the tribe has responded to the efforts of Christian teachers, as some appear to participate in the exercises of both religions. Another reason for the apparent predominance of the heathen element is that the Christian contingent leaves the tribe and is lost among the whites. This is the reason, also, why the tribe appears so small,—never numbering quite fifteen hundred,—although the Pottawatomies are large, handsome, healthy, prolific people, and not in any sense victims of encroaching civilization. One band is at the Sac and Fox Agency, Indian Territory; and another at the Pottawatomie and Great Nemaha Reservation, Kansas; while possibly three hundred are in Michigan, Wisconsin, and Iowa. When the tribe disappears, it will be from disintegration, owing to the fact that these extraordinarily keen traders do not care to hold their goods in common. Their boast is that they have followed and bartered with the whites from the time they met the first French fur-traders, and always to their own advantage, except when they sold the site of the city of Chicago. Briefly put, trading brings segregation, segregation civilization, civilization Christianity, an unusual conversion, but one likely to be permanent. The name *Potta-wat-um-ees* signifies 'those-who-make-or-keep-a-fire,' and refers to their having started a council-fire for themselves when they and the Ojibwas, or Chippewas, separated from the Ottawas. They seem to have no totems, though the old people recite folk-tales which indicate that there was a time when they possessed them, and a few have claimed that they are descended from a dog. This is not to be taken seriously, as they partake of the dog feast, and no Indian eats the animal named from his totem.

Sacs and Foxes.—These people are classed as one tribe in Government reports, very much to their dissatisfaction. They have never been under the same chieftainship, but have kept up their separate council-fires, and have a different number of totems (the Sacs have one that the Foxes consider unworthy of any descendants but women, the Tree or Dryad totem). Their traditions of migration from the Atlantic seaboard to the region of the Great Lakes are about the same, and so are their accounts of reverses at the hands of the Iroquois on the east and the Sioux on the west; but the Foxes have a legend of a mysterious white buffalo leading them to join forces with the Sacs, which the latter ridicule. The Jesuits found them living as distinct tribes in the neighbourhood of Lake Michigan. Both tribes fought the Hurons and Illinois. In 1712 the Foxes, or, as they were generally called, the Outagamies or Musquakies, with their allies, attacked the French at Detroit, but were defeated with great slaughter, by the aid of the Sacs, Hurons, Ottawas, Mascoutins, Illinois, and other tribes (Parkman, *A Half-Century of Conflict*, pp. 279–286). In 1732 another determined effort was made by the French and their Indian allies to destroy these terrible fighters; and it was so nearly successful that, about 1736, eighty warriors and their families joined themselves to the Sacs, these being all that were left of this 'scourge of the West,' as they had long been called. Jonathan Carver, in 1766, found the two tribes in neighbouring villages on the 'Ouisconsin' (Wisconsin) river. He describes the Saukie town as the best Indian town he ever saw, having ninety houses, each large enough for several families, well built of hewn plank, and having sheds before the doors. The streets were wide, he adds, and the land round about so well cultivated that traders made this an outfitting station. The principal business of the warriors was to engage in forays among the Illinois and Pawnees for the purpose of procuring slaves. This appeared to him to be the reason the tribe did not increase in numbers more rapidly, for their adversaries quickly retaliated. The Outagamie or Fox town was almost deserted (Carver, *Travels*, pp. 46–49). Both tribes were too busy fighting the Sioux and Chippewas to take part in the war of the Revolution, but the Foxes and part of the Sacs were on the side of the British in the war of 1812. The same division took place in the Black Hawk War (1831–32), when the band of Sacs under Keokuk refused to fight the U.S. There are at the present time between four and five hundred Sacs in Indian Territory, whose last recognized chief Ke-wah-ko-uk (Keokuk) died in Aug. 1903, and about two hundred on the Pottawatomie and Great Nemaha Reservation, in Kansas, under Margrave, a Pennsylvania German, to whom they gave the place of the hereditary chief, deposed for drunkenness. The Foxes are at Tama, Iowa: a small, rich tribe, numbering scarcely more than three hundred, if we exclude visiting Pottawatomies. As to this division, the agent wrote, August 1885: 'Our Indians, the Sac and Fox of the Mississippi, disclaim any connexion whatever with the Sac tribe, and claim most earnestly that they are Foxes only.' Later, the Sacs expelled the few Foxes in their midst. The Sacs are more agreeable than pious, the Foxes more pious than agreeable. The Sacs are great lovers of fun, the Foxes great sticklers for dignity. The Sacs are stalwart, and with a leaning towards civilization; the Foxes sickly, and with a profound regard for the wisdom of their ancestors. The Sacs have eight totems from which they are descended; the Foxes have seven totems from which they are not descended, since they trace their lineage to a boy and girl, one of whom came from the shoulder of one of the Brothers, the other from the side of his twin. *Saukie* is said to mean 'yellow clay,' while *o-saukie* means 'mouth of the river,' and *Outagamie* connotes 'red clay.' *Musquakie*, the name by which the Foxes call themselves, means 'fox.'

LITERATURE.—**Jonathan Carver**, *Travels through the Interior Parts of North America in the Years 1766, 1767, and 1768*, London, 1778; **Elliott Coues**, *The History of the Lewis and Clark Expedition*, New York, 1893; **Edward Eggleston and Lillie Eggleston Seelye**, *Tecumseh and the Shawnee Prophet*, New York, 1878; **Louis Hennepin**, *A New Discovery of a Vast Country in America*, London, 1698; **W. H. Keating**, *Keating's Narrative*, London, 1825; **Father Jaques Marquette**, *A Discovery of some New Countries and Nations in the Northern America*, printed as an Appendix to Hennepin's *America*, London, 1698; **Thos. L. M'Kenney**, *North American Indians*, Philadelphia, 1874; *Jesuit Relations* (Thwaite's translation), Cleveland, 1896–1901; **M. A. Owen**, *Folk-Lore of the Musquakie Indians*, London, 1904; **Francis Parkman**, *A Half-Century of Conflict, Conspiracy of Pontiac*, and *La Salle and the Discovery of the Great West*, Boston, 1894; *19th Report of the American BE*, Washington, U.S.A.; *Smithsonian Report*, 1885; *Bulletin 30 BE*, pp. 38–43.

MARY A. OWEN.

ALLĀH is the proper name of God among Muslims, corresponding in usage to Jehovah (Jahweh) among the Hebrews. Thus it is not to be regarded as a common noun meaning 'God' (or 'god'), and the Muslim must use another word or form if he wishes to indicate any other than his own peculiar deity. Similarly, no plural can be formed from it, and though the liberal Muslim may admit that Christians or Jews call upon Allāh, he could never speak of the Allāh of the Christians or the Allāh of the Jews. Among Christians, too, a similar usage holds. In the current Arabic Bible versions, 'God' (אלהים) is uniformly rendered *Allāh*, but when 'the Lord God' (יְהוָֹה אלהים) occurs, it is rendered *ar-rabbu-l-ilāhu*, 'the Lord, the *Ilāh*,' where 'the *Ilāh*' is an uncontracted form, retaining its force of a common noun with the article, from which *Allāh* has been shortened through usage. The Muslim, too, who usually derives and explains *Ilāh* as meaning 'worshipped,' uses it and its plural *Āliha* in the broadest way, of any god, explaining that such is possible because worshippers believe that their god has a claim to worship, and 'names follow beliefs, not what the thing is in itself' (*Lisān*, xvii. 358). But more ordinarily, in referring to the gods of the heathen, a Muslim speaks simply of their images or idols, *aṣnām, authān*.

The origin of this goes back to pre-Muslim times, as Prof. Nöldeke has shown below (art. ARABS [RELIGION OF THE ANCIENT]). Muhammad found the Meccans believing in a supreme God whom they called Allāh, thus already contracted. With Allāh, however, they associated other minor deities, some evidently tribal, others called daughters of Allāh. Muhammad's reform was to assert the solitary existence of Allāh. The first article of the Muslim creed, therefore,—*Lā ilāha illā-llāhu*,—means only, as addressed by him to the Meccans, 'There exists no God except the one whom you already call Allāh.'

Naturally, this precise historical origin is not clear to the Muslim exegetes and theologians. But that Allāh is a proper name, applicable only to their peculiar God, they are certain, and they mostly recognize that its force as a proper name has arisen through contraction in form and limitation in usage.

Aṭ-Ṭabarī (d. A.H. 310 = A.D. 923), the greatest commentator on the Qur'ān of the old traditional school, seems to have very little on the word. He gives only one derivation, namely, that it means 'the worshipped, the served,' and contents himself with proving the existence of such a root in Arabic and the possibility of the contraction of *al-ilāh* to *Allāh* (*Tafsīr*, i. 40). Apparently neither the etymological nor the metaphysical question had become important for his time. It is very different in the next greatest Qur'ān commentary which we have, that by ar-Rāzī, the great systematic theologian, who died in A.H. 608 (= A.D. 1209). He deals with it twice, in one passage considering whether God can have a known proper name (*Mafātīḥ al-ghaib*, i. 61), and in another, the meaning, derivation, etc., of Allāh (i. 83 ff.). The first position, he says, the earlier philosophers denied. The object of a name was to distinguish the thing named from other things; but if the thing named could not be known, as in the case of the peculiar essence of God, there was no use for the name. Certainly, if God gave knowledge of Himself to some particularly chosen beings, He might have a name for them. As this name, then, would be the greatest of all names, he who knew it could control all things and beings, material and spiritual. It would be, in fact, the Most Great Name of God, the ineffable name of the Jews, by which miracles could be wrought, and of which Muhammad had evidently heard. That such a name exists ar-Rāzī believes; traditions from Muhammad assert its existence among the names given in the Qur'ān, but are vague and contradictory as to which it is; and as it cannot be a name involving a quality, but must be the name of God's essence, it can be nothing else than Allāh, God's proper name. His consideration, then, of Allāh he divides into five sections (i. 83 ff.). 1. The preferable view is that Allāh is a proper name of God, and has no derivation; this he defends with arguments based on the undoubted usage of the Qur'ān and the impossibility of making a common noun apply to an individual only. 2. The various derivations alleged by those who hold that it comes from a common noun. Eight of these are given, with theological and metaphysical refutations of an *a priori* kind; the facts of the language have little consideration. 3. The linguistic possibility of derivation. Some held that it was from Hebrew or Syriac; but it was known by the Arabs in the time of Muhammad as a plain Arabic word, and as such most accept it. Of the others, those who say it is a name need no derivation, and those who derive it are of two schools, on which a reference to Lane, *Lexicon*, pp. 82*b* ff., will suffice. 4. Broadly, Allāh is used of the true God only, as also, in the first instance, *al-ilāh*; but the latter can by extension be applied to any god, as Allāh Himself applies it in the Qur'ān. [This, of course, is a complete reversal of the historical fact.] 5. Certain peculiarities of this Divine Name which distinguish it from all other names of God; *e.g.* as letter by letter is cut from it, the remainder continues significant for God, and the formal confession of the Muslim faith can take place only through this name, and not through any of the descriptive epithets, such as 'the Merciful One,' 'the Holy One,' etc.

With the Qur'ān commentary of Baidāwī (d. A.H. 685 = A.D. 1286) we reach, again, saner air. Modelled on that of az-Zamakhsharī (d. A.H. 538 = A.D. 1143)—a combination of rationalism and precise grammatical and lexicographical interpretation—it has no room for *a priori* theories or dreams of a wonder-working Name. Allāh is a contraction of *al-ilāh*, and has come to be used as a proper name, though a common noun in origin. A number of possible derivations are given with examples of such transformation. It is shown that God's essence in itself, taken without reference to some other thing, real or imagined, is unintelligible to mankind, and so cannot be indicated by a separate word, even though especially revealed to His saints, as ar-Rāzī suggests; nor does derivation from a root involve *shirk* in the theological sense, one thing having part in another; it means only that the two expressions have part in a common idea and formation. The Syriac derivation is mentioned without criticism.

Other commentaries give modifications only of the two attitudes of ar-Rāzī and al-Baiḍāwī. Thus Abū-s-Su'ūd (d. A.H. 982 = A.D. 1574) paraphrases and elucidates al-Baiḍāwī. The following statement from him (margin of *Mafātīḥ al-ghaib*, i. 19) shows how far this interpretation could attain: 'Know that what is meant by the negation in the first article of the creed, *Lā ilāha illā-llāhu*, is that He is the rightfully worshipped One, and the sense of that article of the creed is, "No rightfully worshipped individual exists except that rightfully worshipped One."' Similarly, Niẓām ad-Dīn al-Naisabūrī (d. *circ.* A.H. 710 = A.D. 1310) abbreviates from ar-Rāzī, but is disposed to regard the difference as verbal (*lafẓī*) only, a hard saying (margin of aṭ-Ṭabarī's *Tafsīr*, i. 53 ff. and 63 ff.). All these are generally accepted and respected commentaries. See art. GOD (Muslim).

LITERATURE.—There is little in Western languages on this subject. Cf. Fleischer, *Kleinere Schriften*, i. 154, 170; Sprenger, *Leben und Lehre des Mohammad*, i. 286 ff., ii. 33; Palmer's *Qur'ān*, i., xii. ff., lxvi.; Hughes, *Dictionary of Islām*, *s.vv.* 'God,' 'Da'wah'; Grimme, *Mohammed*, ii. 36.

D. B. MACDONALD.

ALLĀHĀBĀD.—An important Indian city, capital of the United Provinces of Agra and Oudh. The original Hindu name of the place is Prayāga, '*the* place of sacrifice,' a name which is applied to three other sacred bathing-places on the Alaknandā (wh. see), one of the upper waters of the Ganges. Allāhābād is specially holy, as it is supposed to be the triple junction (*triveṇī*) of three sacred rivers—Ganges (Gangā), Jumnā (Yamunā), and Saraswatī, the last being supposed to have an underground connexion with the others. The name *Allāhābād*, 'abode of Allāh,' was conferred upon the place by the Emperor Akbar, who in A.D. 1572 built his fort commanding the junction of the two rivers, and named it *Illāhābās*, which was changed to Allāhābād by his grandson Shāhjahān. But the place had been regarded as sacred from the very earliest times. It first appears in history as the site where Aśoka erected one of his edict-pillars about B.C. 240. Fa Hsien, the Buddhist pilgrim, about A.D. 414 found it included in the kingdom of Kośala; and the name Prayāga appears in the *Travels* of his successor, Hiuen-Tsiang in the 7th century. He found Buddhism prevailing here side by side with Brāhmanism, and he notes that in the midst of the city was a famous temple of the latter faith, in front of which was a large tree with wide-spreading branches, which was said to be the dwelling of an anthropophagous demon. This tree was surrounded with human bones, the remains of pilgrims who, according to immemorial custom, were in the habit of sacrificing their lives by jumping from its boughs into the holy stream. This tree is now almost certainly represented by one of its successors—the Akshaya Vaṭa, or 'undying Banyan-tree,' which is still one of the chief objects of Hindu worship. It stands in an underground temple, probably part of the edifice described by Hiuen-Tsiang, or built on the same site. This building is now within the Fort, and owing to the accumulation of rubbish the whole of the lower part has disappeared underground. Early in the 14th cent. the historian Rashīd-ud-dīn mentions the sacred tree 'of Prāg' at the confluence of the Ganges and Jumnā. About the time of Akbar, 'Abd al-Qādir speaks of 'the tree from which people cast themselves into the river.' From these accounts it is clear that in the interval between the time of Hiuen-Tsiang and Akbar the rivers had cut away the land near their junction so that the sacred tree, once in the centre of the city, had been brought close to the water. This accounts for the fact that, except the famous Pillar of Aśoka, no relics of the Buddhist and Brahmanical monuments described by the traveller of the 7th cent. now survive.

The chief bathing fair at Allāhābād is what is called the *Māgh Melā*, Māgh (Jan.-Feb.) being the month in which it is held. The chief bathing day is that of the new moon (*amāvasyā*), and the fair is held in the sandy bed at the river junction, which is left dry at the close of each rainy season. Every twelfth year here and at Hardwār, when the sun is in the sign of Kumbha or Aquarius, bathing is specially efficacious, and enormous crowds of pilgrims assemble from all parts of India. To these are added large numbers of ascetics, and beggars who display their infirmities to the charitable parties of bathers. Specially remarkable are fanatics like the *ūrdhvabāhu*, who extend one arm or both arms above the head until the muscles become withered through disuse, and the *ākāśamukhin*, who keep their necks bent back looking at the sky. To these are added numbers of traders and sellers of all kinds of goods who supply the wants of the pilgrims. The maintenance of sanitation and the prevention of outbreaks of epidemic disease are in the hands of a special European staff. This is the chief danger resulting from gatherings of this kind, the attendance at which has greatly increased since the railways offered facilities to the pilgrims. The people are so orderly and law-abiding that little work falls upon the police force. The bathing at these fairs is controlled by a body of local Brāhmans, who take their name, *prayāgwāl*, from the place, and have a bad reputation for insolence, rapacity, and licentiousness.

LITERATURE.—Cunningham, *Archæological Reports*, i. 296 ff., abstracted and supplemented by Führer, *Monumental Antiquities and Inscriptions of the North-western Provinces and Oudh*, 127 ff.; *Imperial Gazetteer of India*, *s.v.*

W. CROOKE.

ALLEGORY, ALLEGORICAL INTERPRETATION.—The word 'allegory' is derived from the terminology of Greek rhetoric, and means primarily a series of metaphors ('Iam cum fluxerunt continuæ plures tralationes, alia plane fit oratio. Itaque genus hoc Græci appellant ἀλληγορίαν': Cicero, *Orator*, xxvii. 94; cf. *de Oratore*, iii. 166). Seeing that the later classical poets studied in the schools of rhetoric, it is not surprising that Horace, in the ode in which he compares the State to a ship (*Od.* i. 14), had an allegory in view, as is recognized by the rhetorician Quintilian (viii. 6, 44). Thus we see that the conception of allegory as formulated in rhetoric, and, owing to the close connexion between ancient rhetoric and hermeneutics, as used also in explaining a work of literature, has a rather narrow range. The term is by no means applied in that wide sense which it has to-day when we speak, for instance, of allegorical figures in art. On the contrary, we must keep in view that allegory is a form of representation which a reader believes himself to find in a piece of writing which is more or less in need of interpretation. As such an interpretation, however, is in reality justified only where the author of the writing, as, for instance, Horace, or Goethe in the second part of *Faust*, had a secret meaning in mind, the rule comes to be that in allegorical interpretation an entirely foreign subjective meaning is read into the passage which has to be explained. In this way allegory is almost always a relative, not an absolute, conception, which has nothing to do with the actual truth of the matter, and for the most part springs from the natural desire to conserve some idea which, owing to its age, has come to be regarded as sacred.

These remarks are necessary for the proper understanding of allegory among the nations of antiquity. It is a misuse of the word to find in Homer and the poets of the subsequent period unconscious allegorical ideas, as is done, *e.g.*, by Decharme (*La critique des traditions religieuses chez les Grecs des origines au temps de Plutarque*, p. 279 ff.). The use in Homer (*Il.* ii. 426), in Archilochus (*Fragm.* 12), or in Sophocles (*Antig.* 1007) of Ἥφαιστος for fire is neither allegory nor a conscious substitution of the gift of the god for his name (Plutarch,

Quom. adol. poet. aud. deb. p. 23*ab*), but a direct identification of the god with his earliest form of earthly manifestation. Hephæstus is here, to adopt Usener's terminology, the 'divinity of the moment' (*Götternamen*, p. 279 ff.). A similar explanation must be given of the Cyclops—Brontes, Steropes, Arges (Hesiod, *Theog.* 140), and of Scamander, which in Homer is both god and stream, as well as of Uranos, Gaia, Demeter, Chaos, etc. There are figures, which in the later evolution unite themselves to the elementary divinities, whose names and natures are identical, *e.g.*, Eris (*Il.* iv. 440, v. 518, 740, xi. 3 f., xviii. 535, xx. 48; Hesiod, *Op.* 16, 24, 28, 804, *Theog.* 225, etc.), Phobos, Deimos, Kydoimos (*Il.* iv. 440, xiii. 299, xv. 119, v. 593, xviii. 535), Zelos, Nike (Hesiod, *Theog.* 384), and others. Only the most superficial consideration, however, can call such a usage allegorical. It is simply owing to the difficulty we have in analyzing such a pantheon of abstract conceptions and such a theology, and for want of a better term, that we call them personifications. It is quite impossible in such cases to speak of an allegory, seeing that in Homer and Hesiod we are dealing with a world of ideas still comparatively naïve. Allegory is much more the child of a reflective epoch.

The assertion that piety is the mother of allegorical explanation is entirely correct (cf., *e.g.*, Gomperz, *Griechische Denker*, i. 305). The 6th cent. before Christ rejected the gods of Homer and Hesiod. Xenophanes (*Fragm.* 11, 12, Diels), Pythagoras (Diog. Laert. viii. 19, 21), and Heraclitus (*Fragm.* 42 D) attack with all their energy the religious views of their predecessors and contemporaries. But the piety of the faithful was not brought by means of these attacks to give up its ideals then any more than it is to-day; it had recourse to the method, so often practised since, of reading a new meaning into the sacred tradition, and thus protecting it from the satire of its critics. Quite a number of men meet us in this connexion, who sought, often by very childlike or indeed childish means, to succour the ancient tradition, but who themselves regarded their undertaking with religious earnestness. The oldest of these was Theagenes of Rhegium, who flourished at the time of Cambyses (Tatian, *adv. Græcos*, 31). He wrote an 'Apology' for the Homeric poetry (Schol. Hom. *Il.* xx. 67), and probably (cf. Schrader, *Porphyrii quæstionum Homericarum ad Iliadem pertinentium reliquiæ*, Leipzig, 1880, p. 384) sought to save the battle of the gods in the twentieth book of the Iliad by a physical and ethical interpretation. Others are said to have made similar attempts. The philosopher Anaxagoras interpreted Homer's poetry in a purely ethical way (Favorinus in Diog. Laert. ii. 3. 11), and his pupil Metrodorus of Lampsacus followed a similar method in his physical explanation of the Homeric figures. For him Demeter was the liver, Dionysus the spleen, Apollo the gall; Hector signified the moon, Achilles the sun, Agamemnon the earth, Helena the air (cf. the passages in Diels, *Die Fragmente der Vorsokratiker*, p. 339). Diogenes of Apollonia went on similar lines (Philodem. *de Piet. c.* 6*b*) when he found in Homer not myths but truth, and identified Zeus with the air. Democritus of Abdera too, an enthusiastic admirer of Homer (*Fragm.* 18, 21, Diels), inclined to an allegorical interpretation of the gods (*Fragm.* 30 D). When we consider, further, how much interest religious questions excited in Athens in the middle of the 5th cent., how, for instance, Aristophanes ridiculed the new doctrines of philosophy (*Nub.* 828, 380 ff.), and when we remember that the rationalistic historians from Hecatæus and Herodotus onwards had stripped the old miraculous legends as far as possible of their supernatural character, it is easy to understand that a related, if not an entirely identical, movement had to make itself felt in poetry as well. Euripides, the pupil of Anaxagoras (cf. *Fragm.* 487, 839, 877, Nauck), is by no means an allegorist, although he, too, resolves Zeus into ether (*Troades*, 884; *Fragm.* 941). The true allegorist, as we have seen, has a fixed system. The poet Euripides, moved as he is by doubts, appears now as a believer, and again as a sceptic. In his later years he wrote the *Bacchæ*, in which he gives a purely rationalistic explanation of the birth of Dionysus (vv. 286 ff.). This is also a way of saving the old tradition, but it is not, properly speaking, allegorical. In the place of a silly fable we find a new and no less silly myth. Such a proceeding, however, is not allegorizing (cf. also Decharme, *l.c.* 295).

Up to this point we have constantly spoken of 'allegory,' as if this expression were found in the philosophers themselves. This is, however, by no means the case. We find a number of writers giving allegorical interpretations, who never use the word itself. The older expression, which was used till 'allegory' occurs in the 1st cent. B.C. (cf. Cicero, *Orator*, 94; Plutarch, *Quom. adol. poet. aud. deb.* p. 19 f.), was ὑπόνοια. Thus Xenophon uses the word in the well-known passage of his *Symposium* (iii. 6), where he adduces Stesimbrotus of Thasos and Anaximander (cf. also Plato, *Ion*, 530 D, who mentions Glaucon by the side of Metrodorus and Stesimbrotus) as teachers of Antisthenes in this method of explaining Homer. As a matter of fact, the Cynical school had with conscious purpose reduced the allegorical interpretation of Homer to a system. The writings of Antisthenes were largely occupied with the poetry of Homer and the figures it contained (Diog. Laert. vi. 1, 17 f.); and we learn from the fifty-third oration of Dio Chrysostom (p. 276 R), that he distinguished in Homer between δόξα and ἀλήθεια, and that he allegorized the poet (cf. Schrader, *l.c.* 387 f.; Dio Chrysost. viii. 283 R; Xenoph. *Memor.* i. 3. 7; Dümmler, *Antisthenica*, 22 ff.) In spite of their utter denial of the existence of a plurality of gods, and their emphatic rejection of the figures of mythology, the Cynics were quite unable to free themselves from the spell of the Homeric poetry. Plato is the opponent of Homer and Antisthenes; he often treats with playful sarcasm the attempts of the 'great Homer experts' to interpret the names and actions of the gods allegorically (*Cratyl.* p. 407 A; *Phædr.* 229 C; *Repub.* 378 D, where again the word ὑπόνοια appears).

Thus the beginning of a system of allegorizing had been made. The Stoics undertook its completion, and their views passed on later to the Jews and the Christians, and thence more or less directly to our own time. The passage from Dio referred to above mentions the Stoic Zeno as the follower of Antisthenes in his method of explaining Homer, and the fragments we possess from the hand of the founder of the Stoical school bear witness to his allegorical point of view (Arnim, *Stoicorum veterum fragmenta*, i. pp. 43, 167 ff.). Chrysippus, the head of the Stoical school, has, of course, taken great delight in working out the method.

Zeus is for him the Logos, who orders all things; he derives his name from his life-giving activity (ζῆν). Male and female divinities do not exist: Ares is war, Hephæstus fire, Kronos the stream, Rhea the earth, Zeus ether, Hermes reason. Almost all the names of the gods suggest such an interpretation, as Rhea comes from ῥεῖν, Themis from θέσις, Kronos from χρόνος or κρᾶν (κιρνᾶν), Apollo from the circumstance that he was οὐχὶ τῶν πολλῶν καὶ φαύλων οὐσιῶν τοῦ πυρός (cf. Arnim, *l.c.* ii.; *Fragm.* 1076, 1079, 1084, 1087, 1090, 1095).

It serves no purpose to refer to the many (often self-contradictory) interpretations of the Stoics (cf. Chrysippus), but we may mention in passing that in the person of Crates of Mallus this method of interpretation extended itself to the exposition of Homer as a whole (Wachsmuth, *de Cratete Mallota*, p. 62). Two unsatisfactory though not uninteresting writings which are still extant, the *Allegoriæ Homericæ* of Heraclitus and the *Theologiæ Græcæ compendium* of Cornutus, prove to us the wide diffusion of these views, and show of what excesses the allegorical method of interpretation is capable. Of the two, Heraclitus is the less annoying; he at least has some feeling; he hates Plato and Epicurus (cap. 4), in fact all those who are not enthusiastic admirers of his beloved Homer. Accordingly, he endeavours to meet the old objections raised against the weakness and sins of the Homeric gods.

Thus the chaining of Hera (*Il.* iii. 277) is explained as the union of the elements (23); the hurling of Hephæstus through the air (i. 592) signifies the earthly fire, which is weaker than the heavenly flame (thus Hephæstus is χωλός) (26); the wounding of Aphrodite and of Ares (v. 336 ff., 858 ff.) is to be understood as the defeat of the barbarian army (ἀφροσύνη = Ἀφροδίτη), which sends forth unearthly noises (30, 31); the union of Aphrodite and Ares (*Od.* viii. 266 ff.) is the combination of love and strife in harmony. These interpretations are so general that even Apollodorus, the great Athenian student of Greek religion, grants them his recognition (Cornutus, p. 49, 4; Münzel, *Quæstiones mythographæ*, p. 17). Other testimonies to the allegorical usage are given, for instance, by Strabo (p. 18), and by the author of the pseudo-Plutarchic writing, *de Vita et poesi Homeri*; but it would serve no purpose to follow this out in detail.

In spite, however, of the strength of this movement, it had by this time reached a very definite limit. Plato, as we saw above, derided the attempts of Antisthenes to defend Homer allegorically. His followers, the members of the so-called Middle Academy, along with the Epicureans, made use of sceptical arguments, and renewed the conflict against the Stoics, the successors of the Cynical school. The chief representative of this line of thought is Carneades, who practically advocated the views of his teacher, Arcesilaus; his attack is contained in the third book of Cicero's *de Natura Deorum*, and in Sextus Empiricus, *adv. Mathem.* ix. He regarded the interpretation of the myths as entirely meaningless, and reproached the Stoics for regarding as wise the inventors of such disreputable stories (Cicero, *l.c.* iii. 24, 62). The Epicureans expressed themselves to the same effect; they found all those allegorical gods of the Stoa nothing but absurdities, and they applied the term 'godless' to the mode of procedure of the sect, for the effect of these very interpretations was to make the gods appear as perishable (Philodem. *de Piet.* cap. 18). These opinions were then, to a large extent, taken over by the Christians, although they, in like manner, early fell under the spell of allegory.

The attack was keenly maintained, but a great movement has never yet been checked by harsh contradiction. The 1st cent. before and after Christ is the great era of the Stoa, which at a later date even occupied the Imperial throne in the person of Marcus Aurelius. But, what is more important, these views made their way into Judaism. The Wisdom of Solomon is under the influence of the Stoa, and the allegorical interpretation of the Jewish law is found in the letter of Aristeas (§ 143 ff.), just as symbolical explanations occur among the Essenes (Philo, *Qu. omn. prob. lib.* ii. p. 458, Mangey). Philo, however, is the chief representative of this direction of thought. Attempts have been made to trace back his allegorical exposition of the Scriptures to the Haggada. And this much, at any rate, is certain, that there were interpreters before Philo who made use of the same method of explanation, for he frequently refers to such expositions of the Old Testament.

Those 'Physicists' had explained Abraham as the νοῦς, and Sarah as virtue (Philo, *de Abrah.* ii. 15, Mangey); again, the king of Egypt was the νοῦς as ruler of the body (*de Jos.* ii. p. 63, Mangey); they interpreted the rite of the Passover as referring either to the purification of soul or to the creation of the world (*de Septen.* ii. 291); and in this way a number of Scripture passages obtained a moral interpretation (*e.g.* Gn 21[23], Dt 25[11]; cf. *de Plant. Noë*, i. 337; *de Spec. Leg.* ii. 329); there were even definite rules for this exegesis (*de Somn.* i. 631, 611, 660).

But Philo not merely followed in the footsteps of his predecessors; his aim rather was to reduce the allegorical explanation to a kind of system. There is no writer who shows more clearly than he the origin of the allegorical method. Philo tells us often of the different attacks which the opponents of the Scriptures, *i.e.* the Greeks, made on the Biblical narratives. He reprimands the detestable people who express amazement at God's changing His opinion, and writes against them the pamphlet, *Quod Deus sit immutabilis*; he is well aware that the same persons mock at the tower of Babel (*de Conf. Ling.* i. 405), smile at the serpent in Paradise (*de Mund. Op.* i. 38), explain the swearing or wrathful God of Israel as a monster (*Leg. all.* i. 128; *Quod Deus s. imm.* i. 282), and make merry over Joseph's dreams (*de Jos.* ii. 59). This Greek criticism, which lasted from the days of Philo till the fall of paganism, compelled the Jews, and after them the Christians, to give an allegorical meaning, a ὑπόνοια, to the sacred Scriptures, just as, at an earlier date, it had compelled the faithful among the pagans. But, besides that, by Philo the Scriptures are best regarded as an allegory (*de Jos.* ii. 46; here, again, the term ὑπόνοια is used); the allegorical exposition is the soul of the sacred text, the literal meaning only its body (*de Migr. Abr.* i. 450), a comparison which Origen later adopts (see below). The literal meaning of a passage would, according to Philo, lead to absurdity and impiety,—here, too, Origen is his pupil,—and literal obedience to the precepts of the Law would be preposterous (*e.g. Leg. all.* i. 44; *de Conf. Ling.* i. 425; *de Somn.* 634; *de Spec. Leg.* ii. 329; *de Agric.* i. 324, etc.). We cannot here go on to speak of the reasons which, according to Philo, caused the Deity to give such incomplete representations of Himself, nor is it possible to introduce a large number of individual allegories. The history of allegorical exegesis is tedious enough owing to the want of diversity in the method. Accordingly it may suffice to give a few instances, which any one can easily amplify for himself, from Siegfried's book, *Philo von Alexandria als Ausleger des AT.* pp. 160–272.

Philo recognizes in Paradise the ἡγεμονικόν of the soul, in the tree of life the fear of God, in the tree of knowledge the φρόνησις (*de Mund. Op.* i. 37; *Leg. all.* i. 56); the four rivers of Paradise are the four cardinal virtues (*de Post. Caini*, i. 250; *Leg. all.* i. 56); Abel is pure piety without intellectual culture, Cain the egoist, Seth the virtue which is imbued with wisdom (*Qu. det. pot. ins.* i. 197; *de Sacrif. Ab.* i. 163; *de Post. Caini*, i. 249), Enoch hope (*Qu. det. pot. ins.* i. 217; *de Præm. et Pœn.* ii. 410), etc.; Hagar signifies the ἐγκύκλιος παιδεία, Sarah virtue and wisdom (*de Cherub.* i. 139 f.); Joseph is the type of the statesman (*de Jos.* ii. 41); his coat of many colours indicates that his political policy is intricate and difficult to unravel (*Qu. det. pot. ins.* i. 192); in the Law (Dt 21[15-17]) the one beloved wife is pleasure, the other who is hated is virtue (*de Sacrif. Ab. et Caini*, i. 167); and so on.

Seeing that the allegories crowd in on Philo in such a way, it is natural for him to interpret the same passage in different allegorical ways (*de Prof.* i. 572); moreover, the same facile hand occasionally changes the text, just when it suits his allegory to do so (*Qu. det. pot. ins.* i. 200).

The Jewish method of interpretation was carried over into *Christian* exegesis, although the influence of Philo did not make itself particularly felt till the 2nd and 3rd centuries. Thus St. Paul, as well as the writer of the Epistle to the Hebrews, makes ready use of allegorical exegesis (cf. Gal 4[24] 3[16], 1 Co 9[9]); and the Epistle of Barnabas, with its search for a spiritual meaning behind the letter, is a product of the Jewish tradition. This need of allegorizing is seen still more plainly in the Apologists.

This is particularly true of Justin Martyr, who interprets a number of Old Testament prophecies in a most daring fashion: thus Gn 49[11], 'he hath washed his garments in wine, and his vesture in the blood of grapes,' means that he will purify the faithful in whom the Logos dwells, with his blood, which, like the juice of the grape, comes from God (*Apol.* i. 32); when it is said, 'the government shall be upon his shoulder' (Is 9[6]), the meaning is that Christ would be hung on the cross. The Gnostics go still further. They allegorize in their Oriental manner not only the Old Testament, but also the New, discovering in the simplest words and incidents ever anew their 'Demiurge,' their 'Bythos,' their 'Achamoth,' and their 'eternal Wisdom' (Irenæus, i. 1. 17, 15; Hatch, *Influence of Gr. Ideas and Usages upon the Christian Church*, p. 75).

The enormous syncretism of the 2nd cent. drew allegory into its circle. When we see Greeks and Christians contending with one another, we become quite bewildered with the confusion of terms. The Apologists unite with the Sceptics in their opposition to allegory (Aristides, xiii. 7, Seeberg; Tatian, *adv. Græc.* 21; pseudo-Clem. Rom. *Hom.* vi. 17, etc.); but they themselves calmly use allegorical interpretation. Celsus is perfectly justified in his attack on this method, which he designates as a retreat of shame at the immoral stories of the Bible (Origen, *c. Cels.* i. 17, iv. 48 ff.). But, again, Celsus is an allegorist himself (*l.c.* vi. 42), and so both parties, Greeks as well as Christians, tread the same erroneous path.

Allegory had, in fact, become to the men of this time a religious requirement. Although Irenæus and Tertullian scornfully reject the Gnostic interpretations, yet the method took firmer hold, and, along Philo's lines, developed just as luxuriantly as in the Græco-Judæan empire. The language of Clement of Alexandria, revelling as it does in symbolic pictures, at once betrays the allegorist; but it is not worth our while to go into his individual allegorical interpretations here (*Strom.* i. 3. 23, vi. 11. 94; *Pæd.* ii. 8. 62), as they do not essentially differ from those of other Theosophists. Then, Hippolytus is an allegorist, in the full sense of the term, in his commentary on Daniel (cf. i. ch. 13 ff.), and especially in the Canticles, where the interpretation follows that of the Jewish Rabbi Aḳiba. Origen gave the allegorical method a kind of scientific basis. He also commented on the Canticles, and here we see the influence of Philo more definitely than in his predecessors (cf. p. 8). For it is with the influence of Philo that we have here to deal, not that of Cornutus, as Porphyry, the opponent of Origen, asserts (Eusebius, *HE* vi. 19. 8). According to Origen, then, as to the Hellenistic Jews, there is a threefold conception of Scripture,—the simple man is edified by means of the 'flesh' of the Bible, the advanced by means of its 'soul,' the perfected by the pneumatic νόμος, which has a shadow of good things to come (*de Princ.* iv. 11). Thus the understanding of Scripture stands in the most intimate relationship to human nature. There are, however, in Scripture all kinds of σκάνδαλα, προσκόμματα, and historical impossibilities. Origen, well instructed in the heathen polemics, agrees that there could have been no days before the creation of the stars, and that God could not, like a gardener, plant trees or take walks. It was also impossible to talk of God's face, from which Cain hid himself. Then the Gospels, as well as the OT law, contain precepts which are not to be literally followed (*e.g.* Lk 10[4], Mt 5[39. 29]; cf. 1 Co 7[18]). And there is no lack of stories which are absurd when taken literally, as, *e.g.*, that Satan brought Jesus to the top of a high mountain (Mt 4[8ff.]). Now it would be quite false to reject the whole on account of such peculiarities; on the contrary, where the literal meaning is unworthy of the wisdom of revelation, it is the proper thing to look for the ὑπόνοια. The πνευματικόν, but not the σωματικόν, goes through the whole of the Scriptures; in some passages the latter is impossible. Thus the allegorical wisdom received its academical consecration, and it made little difference that Porphyry, the passionate opponent of Christianity, declared himself against the method (Eusebius, *HE* vi. 19. 4), seeing he himself, as is well known, did no better (cf. the case of Celsus, above). A more threatening opposition arose from another quarter, from the camp of the Christians themselves. We know quite a succession of ecclesiastical writers who declared themselves against Origen's allegorical system. These are the representatives of the school of Antioch (Julius Africanus): Lucian, Eustathius of Antioch (*de Engastrimytho*, ed. Jahn, *Texte und Untersuchungen*, ii. 4; cf. especially ch. xxi. f.), Diodorus of Tarsus (τίς διαφορὰ θεωρίας καὶ ἀλληγορίας), Isidorus of Pelusium, and, above all, Theodore of Mopsuestia, who wrote, among other works, five whole volumes against the allegorists (cf. for him, Kihn, *Theodor von Mopsuhestia und Junilius Africanus als Exegeten*). These men, of course, did not think of bluntly rejecting the pneumatical exegesis as unjustified; they only sought, by calling in question the sole supremacy of the allegorical interpretation, to restore the historical basis which had been destroyed by the allegorists. This they did by attempting to disclose the *typical* meaning after having ascertained the verbal signification. But they could not in this way really reach consistency. The allegorical method was, after all, more logical than the exegesis of the school of Antioch, which, in recognizing typology and in distinguishing a double meaning in Scripture, again came nearer to the allegorical interpretation, and, particularly by accepting Messianic passages in the OT, made its own position untenable. Theodore himself is the best example of this. It is quite refreshing to learn his opinions regarding the Book of Job and the Canticles (Migne, *Patrologia Græca*, lxvi. 697 ff.): the former resembles a Greek drama, the latter a love poem, in which Solomon celebrates his marriage with an Egyptian woman. The Psalms, too, were explained historically by Theodore. But then, again, comes the reaction. Although Theodore does not deny that, *e.g.*, Zec 9[8-10] refers to Zerubbabel, and although he expresses himself strongly against those who interpret one part of the prophet's words as applying to him, and another part as referring to Christ, still he finds a kind of mediation in the thought that a considerable part of the prophetic message is to be understood 'hyperbolically,' *i.e.* its full truth was first found in Jesus Christ (cf. *Comment. in Zach.* ix. p. 554 f. 11). Similarly, too, he interprets Ps 54 as referring to Onias, but, at the same time, as being a σκιαγραφία (cf. above, Origen, and Theodore himself [p. 555]) of the sufferings of our Lord. Another excellent example (Jl 2[28-32]) is given more fully by Kihn, *loc. cit.* 137. Theodore's exegesis continued to flourish in the school of Nisibis, and obtained, by means of Julius Africanus, an entrance into the West (Kihn, *loc. cit.* p. 215 ff.).

The allegorical method was not emphatically enough combated by this new method, which in the place of the one ὑπόνοια only set another, notwithstanding the vigour with which the champions of the doctrine of Antioch in thoroughly Greek style carried on the conflict. It was now no longer possible to overthrow the system; it had already become far too necessary an element in Greek thought. Gregory of Nyssa seems to have quite made up his mind not to reduce the Scriptures to an allegory (*Hexæmeron*, i. p. 6. 42, 43); but then, again, he takes a delight in all allegorical representations, and gives some himself, particularly in his explanation of the Canticles. Gregory of Nazianzus, who, like all the Apologists, opposes the heathen allegories, wishes to adopt in the interpretation of Scripture a *via media* between the *παχύτεροι τὴν διάνοιαν* and the allegorists (*Orat.* xlv. 12), but he also declares: *ἔνδυμα τῆς ἀσεβείας ἐστὶν ἡ φιλία τοῦ γράμματος* (*Orat.* xxxi. 3).

Allegorical interpretation flourished also in the West. Its rules had been taught at an early date in the rhetorical schools (Jerome, *Com.* on *Ep. ad Gal.* ii. 4. 24). Alongside of Hilary and Ambrose, the great name to be mentioned here is that of Jerome, who lays down the maxim (*Comment. in Mal* 1[10ff.], vi. 952, Migne): 'Regula scripturarum est: ubi manifestissima prophetia de futuris texitur, per incerta allegoriæ non extenuare quæ scripta sunt,' but who at the same time explains Leah as Judaism, Rachel as Christianity (*Ep.* cxxiii. 13, i. p. 910, Migne), and declares (*ad Am.* lib. i. 2. 1 ff., vi. 238, Migne): 'Qui legit introiisse Judam ad Thamar meretricem et ex ea duos filios procreasse, si *turpitudinem* sequatur *litteræ* et non ascendet ad decorem *intellegentiæ spiritalis*, comburat ossa regis Idumææ.' Augustine here, as in all other departments, occupies a prominent place. He follows in his writing, *de Doctrina Christiana*, the seven hermeneutic rules of the Donatist Tychonius (iii. 30), and gives a lively and delightful representation of the duties of the expositor. In spite, however, of the breadth of his view, he too appeals to the old text, 2 Co 3[6], that the letter killeth (iii. 5); and thus we kill our souls when, in following the letter, we subject our *intellegentia* to the flesh (cf. Origen, above). But Augustine in many Biblical passages recognizes not so much an allegorical meaning as *figurata locutio* (xi. 15): 'Servabitur ergo in locutionibus figuratis regula huiusmodi, ut tamdiu versetur diligenti consideratione quod legitur, donec ad regnum caritatis interpretatio perducatur.' It requires, however, no more than these seven rules of Tychonius to show us that Biblical exegesis was threatened with a schematism which, in a short time, prevailed. Cassiodorus, who in like manner makes use of Tychonius, postulates in his book *Institutiones divinarum et sæcularium literarum* six *modi intellegentiæ*; and Eucherius proceeds according to the same example in his *Formulæ spiritalis intellegentiæ*, which now furnish us with a copious table of individual allegories. Thus a special meaning is afforded when Scripture speaks of the features of God—the eyes of God are His insight, His mouth is His speech, and so on.

But, in addition to that, every individual thing has its definite meaning: the ice is = *durities peccatorum*; the winds = *animæ sanctorum*; the shadow = *protectio divina*; the stones = either Christ or *sancti*; roses are = *martyres a rubore sanguinis*; the fishes = *sancti*; the raven = *nigredo peccatoris vel dæmonis*; the lion = *dominus*; the bear = *diabolus aut duces sævi*, but the wolf and the wild boar are also representations of the devil; the tiger is = *feminea interdum interrogantia*; the camel = *divites rebus sæculi onusti vel moribus distorti.*

After winning these triumphs, the Middle Ages fell asleep, and it is impossible for us here to trace the vagaries of allegorical interpretation further. The interpretation, which finds expression in the following well-known couplet, becomes quite a fixed rule:—

'Littera gesta docet, quid credas *allegoria*,
Moralis quid agas, quo tendas analogia.'

Bernard of Clairvaux is an enthusiastic allegorist of the Canticles. Thomas Aquinas (*Summa Theol.* i. art. 10) distinguishes the *sensus historicus vel litteralis* from the *sensus spiritualis, qui super litteralem fundatur et eum supponit*, and this distinction prevailed for centuries. It was not till the Reformation that this way of interpreting was called in question. Luther, who confesses that as monk he had allegorized everything, seeks, along with the other Reformers, only for the *sensus litteralis* (Heinrici, in Hauck, *PRE*[3], vii. art. 'Hermeneutik'). Of course he still interprets Canticles allegorically, but does not express himself so enthusiastically regarding it as either the theologians of the Middle Ages or many later exegetes. The Canticles, in fact, have been to a large extent the test for the later Biblical interpretation. Generally speaking, the allegorical method has in modern times fallen into disuse. Men like Cocceius belong to the exceptions, and Biblical criticism on a historical and grammatical basis has, particularly since the end of the 18th cent., almost annihilated allegorical exegesis. Still the interpretation of the Canticles, which held its place in the Canon, has again and again raised up friends of the old method. Although H. Grotius, as early as the 17th cent., treated the poem to a large extent historically and grammatically, and Herder, at the end of the 18th cent., offered a purely historical and literary explanation, still there have been even in our times men like O. von Gerlach and Hengstenberg, who have more or less preferred the old interpretation of the Canticles as referring to Christ and the Church. This is the exegesis which still prevails in the Roman Catholic Church.

A few words remain yet to be said with regard to the Jewish allegorists. The 2nd cent. of our era produced quite a succession of these exegetes. We have already noted above (p. 330[a]) that the allegorical interpretation of the Canticles is due originally to R. Aḳiba. Among the Jews, no less than among the Christians, keen controversies have raged, and the 13th cent. in particular is remarkable for the passions which this dispute called forth. Among the Jewish interpreters of the Bible at the present day the allegorical method is the method of interpretation which finds most general favour. JOH. GEFFCKEN.

ALL FOOLS' DAY.—This has been authoritatively defined as a humorous name for the First of April, the day which has been popularly appropriated to the custom of playing the fool by means of practical jokes at the expense of a person's credulity. The term is of comparatively modern use; the practice is wide-spread, but of obscure origin.

The phrase is used by Swift in 1712: 'A due donation for All Fools' Day' (Hone's *Every Day Book*, i. 205). It occurs in 1760 in *Poor Robin's Almanack*: 'The First of April some do say Is set apart for All Fools' Day' (Brand, *Pop. Antt.*). Charles Lamb uses the expression: 'All Fools' Day. The compliments of the season to my worthy masters.'

The custom is wide-spread. Hearne, in his diary, under April 2, 1712, writes: 'Yesterday being the first of April (a day remarkable in England for making of April Fools),' etc. (Hearne's *Collection*, vol. iii. Oxf. Hist. Soc. 1888). Congreve in 1687 refers to the fools'-errands practised on the First of April: 'That's one of Love's April-fools, is always upon some errand that's to no purpose.' There is also in the *Oxf. Eng. Dictionary* a reference as early as 1609, from Dekker's *Gull's Hornebook* (ed. Grosart, ii. 209): 'To the intent I may aptly furnish this feast of Fooles.' There is no distinct reference to the practice in Shakespeare, unless, in the light of the Congreve quotation above, the following from *As You Like It* may be taken as an allusion to it:

'*Ros.* Now tell me how long you would have her after you have possessed her.
Orl. For ever and a day.
Ros. Say "a day" without the "ever." No, no, Orlando; men are April when they woo, December when they wed.'—IV. i. 143.

Brockhaus (*Konv. Lexikon*) says that the practice is unknown to German antiquity, and appears to have been introduced from France.

The origin of the practice is obscure. It is clear from Dekker that it was widely prevalent at the close of the 16th century. It seems difficult, therefore, to accept the theory that it was due to the transference of New Year's Day from the First of April to the First of January. In France this is said to have been due to an order of Charles IX. in 1564, and it is suggested that for the *étrennes*, or New Year's gifts which were transferred to the First of January—

'on ne fit plus que des félicitations de plaisanterie aux personnes qui s'accommodaient avec regret au nouveau régime. On fit mieux encore; on s'amuse à les mystifier par des cadeaux simulés ou par des faux messages, et finalement, comme au mois d'avril le soleil quitte le signe zodiacal des Poissons, nos aïeux donnèrent à ces simulacres le nom de poissons d'avril' (*Nouv. Dict. Larousse Illust.*).

But is not this itself a *plaisanterie*? New Year's gifts were, at least in England, given at the beginning of January before 1564. It is on record that they were presented to Henry VI. between Christmas Day and 4th Feb. 1428 (Rymer's *Fœdera*, x. 387). And 'Sol in piscibus' stood of old in the calendars much as the phrase 'Sun enters the sign Pisces' stands in the calendar for 1907 against 19th Feb. The *poissons d'avril* were caught under the Ram. They cannot even come under the category of the Irish Bull.

Other suggestions have been made as to the origin of this practice of making an April-fool, or 'hunting the gowk,' as it is termed in Scotland. Some have seen in it a parody of the changeableness of April weather. Others regard it as a reminiscence of the solemn fooling in the Miracle Plays. Another sees in it a relic of the Roman *Cerealia*, held at the beginning of April.

'The tale is that Proserpine was sporting in the Elysian meadows, and had just filled her lap with daffodils, when Pluto carried her off to the lower world. Her mother Ceres heard the echo of her screams, and went in search of the voice; but her search was a fool's errand,—it was hunting the gowk or looking for the echo of a scream' (Brewer, *Dict. of Phrase and Fable*).

May not this be numbered among the fables, the *Cerealia* being kept from April 12 to 19?

Fooling similar to that which characterizes the First of April takes place at the Holī Festival in India; and Maurice (*Ind. Ant.* vi. 71) says:

'The First of April in England and the Holī Festival in India had their origin in the ancient practice of celebrating the Vernal Equinox.'

The similarity of the fooling in India and the Celtic lands of Western Europe, taken together with affinities in religion and folklore, illustrated by the cross-legged figure of the Celtic deity Cernunnos in the Bordeaux Museum, points to a common origin in very early times, and supports Maurice's conclusion. The same conclusion is expressed in other words in Brockhaus' *Konvers. Lex.*:

'dass er der Rest eines alten heidnischen vielleicht altkeltischen Festes ist, welches mit dem Beginn des Frühlinges im Zusammenhange stand.'

In whose honour this old Celtic Festival was held, and what religious mystery or rite underlay the fooling, has yet to be traced. It is only possible to suggest the lines along which the solution may be found.

Two points have to be noted. The rite—if such fooling may be dignified by the name of rite—must be performed at the passing of March, *i.e.* on the First of April. It must also be finished before noon. These points are confirmed by two rhymes. In North Staffordshire, if the joke is played in the afternoon, those who are trying to practise the joke are met with the retort:

'March is gone, and April come;
You're a fool, and I'm none.'

In South Staffordshire the rhyme runs:

'April-fool's dead and gone,
You're ten fools to make me one.'

These rhymes, preserved in a district still strongly versed in old Celtic folklore, point not only to the antiquity of the custom, but to its being associated with some ancient pagan rite, celebrated between the evening of the last day of March and the morning of the First of April.

Is there any means of tracing the origin and affinity of the rite? The First of April was kept in ancient Rome as the Feast of Venus and Fortuna Virilis. Ovid says that Fortuna Virilis was worshipped by women that she might preserve their charms, and thus enable them to please their husbands (*Fasti*, iv. 145–149). How the men occupied themselves during the time the women were worshipping at the shrine of Fortuna Virilis, or whether they suspected they were being fooled by the women, cannot be known. As Fortuna Virilis was also the goddess of boys and youths, it is not impossible that the old game of 'blind-man's buff,' or 'hoodman-blind,' as it is in Shakespeare, may be a relic of the rite practised by the men on the occasion of this Festival. Or the fooling may be specially associated with this Spring Festival of Venus. It is on record that Q. Fabius Gurges, the Consul, at the close of the Samnite War, founded the worship of Venus Obsequens and Postvorta (Smith, *Class. Dict.* art. 'Venus'). Fuller details may be found in Livy (*Hist.* xi.).

It is to some Celtic form of this worship of Venus on the First of April that the origin of All Fools' Day must be traced. Rhys in his Hibbert Lectures shows an affinity between Venus and the maiden-mother Arianrhod, the daughter of Don.

'These remarks on the parallelism between the Celtic Sun-god and Balder would be incomplete without a word respecting the latter's mother, Frigg. She is proved, by the Anglo-Saxon word Frigedæg, now Friday, and by the old Norse habit of calling the planet Venus Frigg's Star, to have been treated to a certain extent as a counterpart of the Latin Venus. Her dwelling in a mansion called Fensal, the Hall of the Fen or Swamp, recalls Lleu's mother, Arianrhod, and her sea-girt castle' (Rhys, *Hibb. Lect.* p. 543).

And perhaps it is not merely accident that some of the most exquisite fooling in the *Mabinogion* is in 'Math, the son of Mathonwy.' Arianrhod was the mistress of the Culture Hero, Gwydion, son of Don. By her he had two sons, Llew or Lleu, the Sun-hero of Celtic mythology, and Dylan. The boy Llew was reared at Dinas Dinlle, on the Carnarvon coast near the southern end of the Menai Straits. A little distance to the south-west is a sunken reef known as Caer Arionrhod, the sea-girt Castle of Arianrhod in the *Mabinogion*. This was the scene of the magic fooling by which Gwydion won a name for his son Llew, and forced Arianrhod to invest him in the armour in which he was to shine. Llew's twin-brother was christened by order of Math, and immediately made for the sea. 'He swam as well as the best fish in its waters, and for this reason was called Dylan, the son of the wave' (Guest's *Mabinogion*, ed. Nutt, pp. 66–71). His name is commemorated in the headland Maenddulan on the same coast.

Llew and Dylan are held by Rhys to represent the principles of light and darkness, and it would be natural that any rite connected with the victory of the Sun-god Llew over Arianrhod and his twin-brother Dylan should be associated with the First of April. This suggestion also affords an explanation of the French phrase. Those who were fooled on the First of April, and suffered the discomfiture of Dylan, would suitably be named after his fish-like propensities, 'poissons d'avril.'

All Fools' Day may therefore be the relic of a Spring Festival of Llew. In the shining armour of the Sun, which he had won by his magic from Arianrhod, he triumphed at this season of the year over the cold gloom of the winter sunlight personified in his brother Dylan. These early myths took shape in religious rites, and were preserved in folklore and in popular rhymes and customs. Rhys, writing of the feast held on the First of August in honour of Lug, another name of the Sun-hero Llew, says:

'Look at the position of these places [Lyons, Laon, Leyden, all variants of the older Lugdunum] on the map, and take into account those of Dinlleu in Arvon and Dinlle in the Wrekin district of Shropshire, also the places where the Lugnassad were celebrated in Ireland, and you will readily admit that the name Lugus, Lug, or Lleu was that of a divinity whose cult was practised by all probably of the Celts both on the Continent and in these islands' (*Hib. Lect.* p. 420).

Such a cult would almost of necessity involve a Spring Festival in which Llew would be associated with Arianrhod and his brother Dylan. And it may be noted that it is within sight of the Wrekin that the North Staffordshire rhyme runs:

'March is gone, and April come;
You're a fool, and I'm none.'

The lines point to the triumph of Llew and the discomfiture or fooling of Dylan.

LITERATURE.—Murray, *New Eng. Dict. s.v.*; Larousse, *Nouv. Dict. Illust.*; Brockhaus, *Konv. Lexikon*; Brewer, *Dict. of Phrase and Fable*; Chambers, *Book of Days*; Rhys, 'Celtic Heathendom,' *Hib. Lect.*, 1886; Guest, *Mabinogion*[2] (1904).

THOMAS BARNS.

ALMSGIVING.—See CHARITY.

ALTAR.

IN the most general sense of the term, an altar may be defined as a surface, usually elevated, but occasionally level with the ground, or even depressed beneath it, prepared or adapted to receive a sacrifice. It is thus, by implication, intimately connected with sacrifice (*q.v.*), and has seemingly been developed as a ritual adjunct to the oblation. Sacrifices are, however, not uncommonly made to natural objects by casting the offering into them. Thus, amongst the Nicaraguans, the human sacrifices to the volcano Masaya or Popogatepec were cast into the crater of the mountain, and amongst the Hurons tobacco was thrust into the crevice of a rock in which a spirit was believed to dwell (Tylor, *Pr. Cult.*[3] ii. 207–208); while, in similar fashion, pins and other trifles are dropped into holy wells in Cornwall and Armenia; and in Swabia, the Tyrol, and the Upper Palatinate, meal is flung into the face of the gale to placate the storm-demon (*ib.* pp. 214, 269; cf. also pp. 210–211; and Abeghian, *Armen. Volksglaube*, Leipzig, 1899, p. 58). The common Greek practice of making offerings to water deities, even to Poseidon himself, by permitting the blood of the sacrifice to flow immediately from the victim into the water, is too well known to require more than an allusion, and it is again exemplified both in Guinea and North America; while, in like manner, offerings are made to the earth by burying the sacrifice, as amongst the Khonds of Orissa (a mode of sacrifice which also occurs elsewhere in offerings to the dead), and to the fire by casting the offering into it, as amongst the Yakuts and the Carinthians (Tylor, *op. cit.* ii. 377–378, 407–408). Sacrifice to the dead may be made simply by casting the offering away at random, as in Melanesia (Codrington, *Melanesians*, Oxford, 1891, p. 128).

Sacrifices may also be offered either by placing the offering simply on the ground, as amongst the Indians of Brazil and the African negroes (cf. Jevons, *Introd. to Hist. of Rel.*, London, 1896, pp. 134–135); or by hanging the oblation on trees or poles, as amongst the ancient Swedes and the modern Semites, Armenians, Hindus, and some of the African tribes (cf. Tylor, *op. cit.* ii. 228; Curtiss, *Prim. Semit. Rel. To-day*, New York, 1902, pp. 91–92; Abeghian, *op. cit.* p. 59; Crooke, *Pop. Rel. and Folklore of N. India*, London, 1896, ii. 99–100, 102; Ellis, *Ewe-Speaking Peoples*, London, 1890, p. 42).

In considering the primitive purpose of the altar, it may not be amiss to discuss the etymology of the words denoting it in Semitic and Indo-Germanic. In the former group of languages 'altar' is represented by the Hebrew *mizbēaḥ* (Arab. *madhbaḥ*), a derivative of זבח (Assyr. *zibû*, Arab. *dhabaḥa*, etc.), 'to slaughter,' thus clearly indicating that the Semitic altar was for the slaughtered victim or its blood, not for the burnt-offering (the burnt-offering being of later development amongst the Semites; cf. W. R. Smith, pp. 350 ff.); and this is curiously confirmed by the fact that amongst the modern Semites there are no burnt-offerings, but only the slaughter of victims without burning (Curtiss, *op. cit.* p. 229).

But if we turn to the Indo-Germanic words for 'altar,' a striking diversity of terms awaits us. First and foremost is the Latin *altāre*, borrowed in many languages (*e.g.* Old High German *altāri*, Old Pruss. *altars*, Old Church Slav. *olŭtarĭ*, Lith. *altõrius*, Russ. *altarĭ*), and defined by Festus as follows: 'altaria sunt in quibus igne adoletur.' The word is commonly derived from *altus*, 'high'; but this must be rejected, since not only is the meaning unsatisfactory, but linguistic evidence is against it, *-āris* (*-ālis*) being used in Latin only to form an adjectival or nominal derivative from a noun (cf. *limināris* for an inferred *liminālis*, 'relating to the threshold,' from *limen*). It should plainly be connected with *ad-oleo*, 'to burn a sacrifice,' unaccented Lat. *a* in post-tonic syllables (the primitive form of *adoleo* being *ádaleo*) becoming *o* before *l* and labials, and probably stands, by dissimilation, for an inferred *altālis*, 'fiery' (cf. for this etymology and other Indo-Germanic cognates, Walde, *Lat. etymol. Wörterbuch*, Heidelberg, 1906, p. 9; the *t*, however, makes the derivation of *altāre* from the root *alē* very difficult, unless one may assume in it the presence of a 'root-determinative' *t* [cf. Persson, *Wurzelerweiterung und Wurzelvariation*, Upsala, 1891, pp. 28–35], though this method of etymologizing is rejected by many scholars). The second Lat. term for 'altar' is *ara*, Oscan *aasa*, Umbrian *asa*, which is most probably connected with *areo*, 'burn' (Walde, *op. cit.* p. 40).

The Greek terms for 'altar' are βωμός, θυμέλη, and θυσιαστήριον. The first of these, which stands in *Ablaut*-relation with Doric βᾶμα (Attic βῆμα), 'step,' itself occasionally means 'step' (*e.g. Odyss.* vii. 100); while the last two are both connected with θύω, 'to sacrifice,' especially by burning (cf. Latin *suf-fio*, 'fumigate,' etc.). Finally, in Germanic we have the Icelandic *stalli*, Anglo-

Saxon *weofod* or *wihbed*, and Gothic *hunslastaþs*, the first being etymologically akin to the Eng. *stall*, 'place,' the second denoting 'idol-table,' and the third 'place of sacrifice, housel-stead.' Finally, it may be noted that a modern Russian term for 'altar,' *žertveniikŭ*, also means 'place of sacrifice,' being a derivative of *žertva*, 'sacrifice'; but it must be borne in mind that this root is ultimately connected with Skr. *gar*, 'to praise,' so that the Slav. group, including Old Church Slav. *žrěti*, 'to sacrifice,' *žrŭtva*, 'sacrifice,' and *žirĭcŭ*, 'priest,' seems to have regarded the sacrifice primarily as praise (cf. Miklosich, *Etymol. Wörterbuch der slav. Sprachen*, Vienna, 1886, p. 410)—a concept which is, perhaps, borrowed from Christianity.

It is thus evident that amongst the Semites the altar was primarily the place where the victim was slaughtered, and amongst the Indo-Germanic peoples the place where it was burnt.

It is clear from what has already been said that the altar, essentially an adjunct of the sacrifice, has been evolved later than the oblation, for many peoples have sacrificed, or made their offerings, and still do so, without altars; and there are considerable areas, particularly in Africa and South America, where the altar is entirely unknown, while the late development of the altar amongst the Indo-Germanic peoples is a commonplace (cf. Schrader, *RE der indogerm. Altertumskunde*, Strassburg, 1901, pp. 855, 861), and receives a striking exemplification in the relatively late evolution of the Indian *vedi* (see ALTAR [Hindu]). The latter represents, indeed, a curious type of altar, in that it is primarily a fire altar in a trench strewn with grass, evolving later into the common form of a raised altar for burnt-offerings. Its development thus shows all three forms of the altar — depressed below the ground, practically level with the ground, and elevated above the ground (cf. Ludwig, *Der Rigveda*, iii., Prague, 1878, p. 364 f.; Hillebrandt, *Ritual-Litteratur*, Strassburg, 1897, p. 14).

Allusion has already been made to the widespread custom of hanging offerings on sacred trees, and oblations are likewise placed on sacred stones. The best example of the latter phenomenon is perhaps found in the case of the Heb. *maṣṣēbāh*, 'upright stone, pillar' (from נצב, 'to take one's stand'; cf. Arab. *naṣaba*, 'to set up,' *nuṣb*, 'object set up, idol': for other cognates and for literature, cf. *Oxf. Heb. Lex.* pp. 662–663), which was regarded as a Divine abode and anointed with oil (*e.g.* Gn 28[18]). In like manner the Arab. *anṣāb* (plural of *nuṣb*, 'idol,' which is derived from *naṣaba* = נצב, and is thus linguistically connected with *maṣṣēbāh*) were anointed with blood (W. R. Smith, pp. 184, 321).

It is held by many that the sacred stone or tree and the altar 'originally were identical in use and purpose' (cf. Jevons, *op. cit.* pp. 134–135); but this view seems at least open to question, despite the support given to it by the history of the Semitic altar. Though the distinction may be deemed academic and subtle, the present writer feels that, while the deity is believed to be in the sacred stone or the sacred tree, he is never held to dwell in the altar. The altar is, in other words, from its very inception, the table on which the offering to the god is slaughtered, burnt, or deposited. The oil and blood on the sacred stone please and feed the deity, the rags on the sacred tree adorn him; but the offerings on the altar are taken by him, not placed upon him. In no sense, then, can the sacred tree or stone be considered identical with the altar, unless one is ready to regard the Ægæan Sea as an altar because offerings were cast into it in honour of Poseidon, or the crater of Mauna Loa as an altar since human sacrifices to Pele were hurled into its depths; for there seems to be no differentiation of kind between the besmearing of the sacred stone and the casting of an oblation into the ocean or into a crater.

The evolution of the altar will be considered more fully in the following sections devoted to it amongst individual peoples, but a brief allusion may be made to two forms of altar not always recognized as such. In the opening sentence it has been stated that the altar may sometimes be 'level with the ground, or even depressed beneath it.' In the former case we have a very primitive type indeed—but a step removed from the mere placing of offerings on the ground by interposing a layer of sand which serves as an altar. The typical example of this form is the Hopi altar, which is discussed in ALTAR (American), though an analogue may be traced in the Semitic use of the threshold as an altar (see Trumbull, *The Threshold Covenant*, London, 1896, *passim*), or in the mat-altars of the ancient Egyptians; as well as in the herbs on which the flesh of slaughtered victims was laid by the Persians (Herodotus, i. 132; Strabo, p. 732 f.).

The altar depressed below the ground is more than the mere trench which often surrounds the altar to receive the blood which flows from the sacrifice slaughtered upon it (cf. 1 K 18[32]; Wellhausen, *Reste des arab. Heidentums*[2], Berlin, 1897, p. 105), even as the altar itself frequently has hollows artificially made or modified in its upper surface to receive or carry off the blood (cf. Curtiss, *op. cit.* pp. 235–236). This form of depressed altar was particularly appropriate in sacrificing to the *manes*, and is admirably exemplified in the sacrifice made by Odysseus in order to enter Hades (*Odyss.* xi. 24–47; cf. Lucian, *Charon*, 22; Pausanias, x. 4–10); or again in the ancient Persian form of sacrifice to water (Strabo, *loc. cit.*), where, as in the Indian *vedi* (see above), we find the trench combined with the *quasi*-mat (for further instances of the Indo-Germanic trench-altar see art. ARYAN RELIGION). With all this may be compared the distinction in Chinese ritual between the victims sacrificed to earth and those offered to Heaven, the former being buried and the latter burnt.

The trench-altar is interestingly combined with the more usual form in the round altar with a hollow centre, through which the blood might flow immediately into the earth, found at Mycenæ, and corresponding with the hollow, round ἐσχάρα, 'hearth,' level with the ground, ἐφ' ἧς τοῖς ἥρωσιν ἀποθύομεν (Pollux, *Onomasticon*, i. 8; see Schuchhardt, *Schliemann's Excavations*, tr. Sellers, London, 1891, pp. 156–157); while the connecting bond between the two forms seems to be given by an altar discovered by Schliemann at Tiryns, consisting of a quadrangular block of masonry laid on the ground, with a round hole in the centre, lined with masonry to a depth of three feet, beneath being a rough earthen pit (Schuchhardt, *op. cit.* p. 107).

The probable general development of the altar may, in the light of what has been said, be sketched briefly as follows. Offerings were originally set upon the ground before the divinity, or placed upon the object in which he was believed to dwell, but as yet there was no altar. With the further evolution of the concept of sacrifice as a meal, either exclusively for the divinity or to be shared by him with his worshippers (for full details see art. SACRIFICE), and with the development of the idol-concept (see art. IMAGES AND IDOLS), natural objects, chiefly poles and stones, of appropriate shape were placed before the idol in which the deity was held to reside, and there received the offerings; or a thin substance was placed upon the ground to remove the offering from direct contact with the ground—thus giving the most primitive forms of the altar, which might also be made of a pile of stones, or even of earth. As the shrine or temple (*q.v.*) was evolved, the altar was placed at first outside it, because of the small dimensions of the primitive shrine; but later it resumed its original place in front of the object in which the divinity was believed to dwell, or which symbolized the deity to whom sacrifice was made. With the development of art, the altar, which had long ceased to be left in its natural shape, despite the conservative character of religious ritual (cf. Ex 20[25]), became varied in form, and was ornamented in accord with the best abilities of those who constructed it. The theory of the altar, however, is unchanged, whether victims be slaughtered on it, or whether it be used for burnt-offerings, or to receive and bear animal, vegetable, or other oblations (as in the Roman *lectisternium*, the Jewish table of shewbread, or many Polynesian altars), these distinctions belonging properly to the subject of sacrifice (*q.v.*). The human body has been used in at least two cults as an altar. In the Aztec Ochpaniztli, or broom feast, the woman who was to be sacrificed by decapitation was held by a priest on his back, he thus constituting an altar (*Bulletin 28 BE*, p. 174); while in Satanism (*q.v.*) the body of a nude woman forms the altar on which the Mass is parodied.

LITERATURE.—Jevons, *Introd. to Hist. of Rel.* (London, 1896) pp. 130–143; and see at end of following articles.

LOUIS H. GRAY.

ALTAR (African).—Nowhere, except in South America, is there so general a lack of the altar as in Africa—a phenomenon which closely corresponds to, and is in part indicative of, the primitive religious conditions of that continent, and also finds a partial explanation in the simplicity characterizing fetishism (*q.v.*), the prevailing type of religion there; though temples, or 'fetish huts,' are by no means unknown, even amongst tribes which have no altars, such as the Bantu Basogas (cf. Waitz, *Anthropol. der Naturvölker*, ii., Leipzig, 1860, pp. 184–185; Johnston, *Uganda Protectorate*, London, 1902, pp. 717–718). Thus, amongst the Hottentots, and even the Hovas of Madagascar, we find no traces of the altar (Waitz, *op. cit.* pp. 342, 440); while amongst the tribes of the West Coast, whose religion has been perhaps the most carefully studied, this feature of the cult plays relatively a very minor rôle. Attention should here be directed, however, to the sacrifices which are made by the Ewe-speaking peoples to Legba, the phallic deity, to whom 'on extraordinary occasions a human sacrifice is offered, the victim is disembowelled, the entrails placed in a dish or calabash before the image, and the body suspended on a tree or post in front of the shrine, where it is suffered to remain till it rots and falls to pieces' (Ellis, *Ewe-Speaking Peoples*, London, 1890, p. 42). Here both the dish and the tree (or post) represent a primitive form of altar, and in like manner we may regard the post on which a girl was impaled at Lagos to secure fertility for the ensuing year (Waitz, *op. cit.* p. 197) as a crude altar.

On the other hand, in the 'customs' of Dahomey (cf. Ellis, *op. cit.* pp. 120–138), the sacrificial victims were merely slaughtered on the ground; nor can the usage of burying living human beings when houses or villages were set up in Grand Bassam, Yarriba, and Dahomey (cf. the same custom in Polynesia), or the practice of staking out a victim in the path of a threatened invasion, where he was left to starve to death to deter the foe, be cited as referring in any way to the altar. Nevertheless, in Dahomey a rude form of altar is found in the small piles of earth placed at the foot of trees, the turning of roads, the entrance to houses or villages, and in open spaces, on which are set manioc, maize, palm-oil, and the like, as offerings to the spirits (Schneider, *Rel. der afrikan. Naturvölker*, Münster, 1891, p. 115).

Amongst the Tshi-speaking peoples of the Guinea Coast the country stool (*egwah*) of the god, 'which is the local symbol of authority,' is washed with the blood of human victims sacrificed in honour of the deity, whose own image receives a similar ablution, this being expressly recorded of the divinities Bobowissi, Ihtúri, Bons'ahnu, Behnya, and Prah (Ellis, *Tshi-Speaking Peoples*, London, 1887, pp. 23, 51–53, 65). But neither the stool nor the image can properly be termed an altar, any more than the elevations on which the idols are set in Dahomey temples, where 'the images of the gods are placed inside, usually on a raised rectangular platform of clay; and before them are the earthen pots and vessels, smeared with the blood, eggs, and palm-oil of countless offerings' (Ellis, *Ewe-Speaking Peoples*, p. 81).

Against this rather negative material may be set at least one African altar of a degree of development approximating to that found, for instance, in Polynesia. This is the one in the 'ju-ju house' at Bonny, thus described by de Cardi (in Mary Kingsley's *West African Studies*, London, 1899, p. 515):

'The altar looked very much like an ordinary kitchen plate rack with the edges of the plate shelves picked out with goat skulls. There were three rows of these, and on the three plate shelves a row of grinning human skulls; under the bottom shelf, and between it and the top of what would be in a kitchen the dresser, were eight uprights garnished with rows of goats' skulls, the two middle uprights being supplied with a double row; below the top of the dresser, which was garnished with a board painted blue and white, was arranged a kind of drapery of filaments of palm fronds, drawn asunder from the centre, exposing a round hole with a raised rim of clay surrounding it, ostensibly to receive the blood of the victims and libations of palm wine. To one side, and near the altar, was a kind of roughly made table fixed on four straight legs; upon this was displayed a number of human bones and several skulls; leaning against this table was a frame looking very like a chicken walk on to the table; this also was garnished with horizontal rows of human skulls—here and there were to be seen human skulls lying about; outside the ju-ju house, upon a kind of trellis work, were a number of shrivelled portions of human flesh.'

LOUIS H. GRAY.

ALTAR (American).—I. Among *the Indians of N. America* the altar played an important part, although, curiously enough, the Jesuit missionaries in New France make no mention of this adjunct of religious cult. This silence may be explained, at least in part, not only by the fact that these heroic and devoted souls were not trained observers, but also by the circumstance that the Algonquian and Iroquoian stocks among whom they laboured were essentially nomadic, and thus had neither temples nor altars sufficiently striking to attract the missionaries' attention. We know, however, that the Indians of Virginia had 'altars, which they call Pawcorances, placed in their fields, where they sacrifice blood and fat of savage beasts, and offer tobacco when they return from war or the chase' (de Laet, *L'Hist. du Nouveau Monde*, Leyden, 1640, iii. ch. 18). The Natchez, moreover, had a large temple, in the centre of which was an altar with a perpetual fire; while the Cadoan Assinai temples contained a wooden altar, on which stood leathern coffers, filled with leather dishes and musical instruments (Waitz, *Anthropol. der Naturvölker*, iii. 204, 220–221). The perpetual fire, it may be noted, was also maintained in Louisiana and amongst the Muskhogees (*ib.* pp. 203, 208).

Altar-mounds, found in connexion with many of the structures of the 'mound-builders,' contain altars of clay or, more rarely, of stone. They vary greatly in size and shape, but are seldom over twenty inches high, and are near the ground in the centre of the mound; while in their top is a basin-shaped hollow, usually filled with ashes (Bancroft, *Nat. Races of the Pacif. States*, iv. 774; cf. Thomas, *RBEW* v. pp. 57–58 [West Virginia]; Holmes, *ib.* xx. pp. 36–37). Here, again, numerous variations from the general type are known. Thus, on the top of a mound near Sterling, Ill., was found 'an oval altar 6 ft. long and 4½ wide. It was composed of flat pieces of limestone which had been burned red, some portions having been almost converted into lime. On and about this altar I found abundance of charcoal. At the sides of the altar were fragments of human bones, some of which had been charred' (Holbrooke, quoted by Yarrow, *Introd. to Study of Mortuary Customs among the N. Amer. Indians*, Washington, 1880, p. 23).

In his *Mœurs des sauvages amériquains* (Paris, 1724, ii. 327) the Jesuit Lafitau advances the theory that the calumet, or 'pipe of peace,' was an altar. This statement, perhaps surprising at first, is not so absurd as it may appear, for the calumet certainly contains, in some instances, a burnt-offering in honour of a deity. Among the Southern Talapouches and Alabamons the head priest went forward each morning before sunrise with the calumet, and blew the first puff of smoke towards the east. The Natchez custom was very similar, except that the head priest thrice prostrated himself to the east, and honoured not only that quarter, but also the three others with whiffs of smoke. Like customs are found amongst many N. American Indian tribes, such as the Kisteneaux, Sioux, Shoshones, Omahas, Poncas, Blackfeet, Pottawatomies, and Hopis (M'Guire, 'American Aboriginal Pipes and Smoking Customs' in *Report of the United States National Museum*, 1897, pp. 351–646, especially pp. 563–571).

By far the most elaborate modern N. American Indian altars, however, are those of the Hopis and kindred Pueblo tribes, whose snake, antelope, and flute altars have been carefully described by Fewkes (*RBEW* xv. p. 270; *ib.* xvi. pp. 278–279, 287–288, 290–292; xix. pp. 966–969, 980–983, 989–996, 1001–1002). These altars are of special interest in that, unlike any others known, they embody primarily the principle of sympathetic magic, especially as 'at present the ritual is performed for the purpose of bringing abundant rain and successful crops' (Fewkes, *ib.* xix. p. 963, cf. pp. 1009–1111). The Hopi altar, which, of course, presents unessential variations in different places and ceremonies, is composed of sand, the square interior white, with bordering strips of yellow, green, red, and white, symbolizing the four cardinal points. At the top of the central square are four symbolic figures of each of the four rain-clouds, from which depend four serpents, typifying lightning, while on the top outer white sand border are lines of black sand, representing rain. At the bottom of the altar are four water-gourds (the number again typifying the four quarters of the sky), separated by ears of maize, and at the top is a vase with maize-stalks. Rattles and bull-roarers, symbolizing thunder, are scattered around the edges of the altar, and a pouch of tobacco (the smoke typifying the rain-cloud), a water-gourd, and a 'medicine-bowl,' into which an aspergill is dipped to symbolize the falling rain, are also prominent features. The lines of meal drawn across the sand seem to represent the fertilization proceeding from the rain-clouds to the external world; while *tipones*, or totemistic emblems of the clans celebrating the ritual, form the most sacred objects of the altar. Figures of aquatic animals are also found frequently, together with other objects whose precise significance is not yet fully known.

Many of these Hopi-Zuñi altars, it should be noted, have a more or less elaborate reredos, that of the Cakwaleñya ('Blue Flute' society) at the Tusayan pueblo of Mishongnovi, for example, being described by Fewkes (*RBEW* xix. pp. 991–992) as consisting 'of uprights and transverse slats of wood, the former decorated with ten rain-cloud pictures, five on each side, one above the other. These symbols had square outlines, each angle decorated with a figure of a feather, and depending from each rain-cloud figure, parallel lines, representing falling rain, were painted. The transverse slat bore a row of nine rain-cloud figures of semicircular form. Four zigzag sticks, representing lightning, hung from the transverse slat between the vertical or lateral slats of the reredos. Two supplementary uprights were fastened to the main reredos, one on either side. These were decorated at their bases with symbolic pictures representing maize, surmounted by rain-cloud figures. The ridge of sand between the uprights of the altar supported many smaller rods and slats, the one in the middle being decorated with a picture of an ear of corn.' Despite the elaborate character of these reredoses, however, they are obviously subordinate to the sand-altars placed before them, and of which they are palpable imitations; even though, as in some of the Zuñi altars described by Mrs. Stevenson, the reredos is *quasi*-permanent, while the sand-altar must be remade for each ceremony.

Amongst the Zuñi, as already intimated, we likewise find elaborate altars showing the same general type as their Hopi congeners. In all of them the principle of sympathetic magic seems to be present, as is clear from Mrs. Stevenson's detailed description of them (*RBEW* xxiii. pp. 245–246, 428, 432–434, 454, 491, 529, 543, 550, 551).

2. Turn to *Mexico* and *Central America*. The altar in the great temple at the City of Mexico in honour of Huitzilopochtli, the god of war and the chief Aztec deity, was a green block, probably of jasper, 5 ft. long by 3 broad and high, curved convexly on the top, so that the human sacrifice slaughtered upon it might be in the best position for the excision of the heart (Bancroft, *Nat. Races of the Pacif. States*, ii. 582–583). The Aztec altar, moreover, had an adjunct, not found elsewhere, in the sacrificial yoke, a heavy stone of green jasper, curved in a ∩-shape, and placed over the neck of the human sacrifice at the time of his immolation, to assist the priests who held his arms and legs, to keep him in a proper position for the chief celebrant.

Our general knowledge of the details of the Aztec altar must, however, be drawn from the sacrificial stones of neighbouring peoples, which may be inferred to have been analogous. The Maya altars, as found in the ruins of Copan, Honduras, and of Quirigua, Guatemala, are 6 or 7 ft. square and about 4 ft. high, taking a variety of forms and being covered with sculpture somewhat less elaborate than the statues of the divinities themselves (Bancroft, *op. cit.* ii. 689, iv. 94). As in many Semitic altars, their tops were intersected with grooves to receive the blood of the sacrifices offered upon them (*ib.* iv. 94–99, 111–114, 541). Besides formal altars, the ancient Mexicans, Mayas, and Guatemalans also had braziers and small altars in which copal, which here corresponded to the Oriental incense, was burnt in honour of the gods, one of these smaller structures, found at Palenque in the Mexican State of Chiapas, being 16 in. high and 4 ft. in circumference (*ib.* i. 697, ii. 584, 690, iii. 336, iv. 345–346). Like the 'mound-builders' of N. America, the Mayas erected altars on the graves of the dead (*ib.* ii. 799), and in Nicaragua flat stones have been discovered which apparently served as altars (*ib.* iv. 32, 61–62).

Both in Mexico and in Central America generally, the altar, like the temple itself, was placed on the summit of the *teocalli*, or 'god-house,' a pyramid of considerable elevation; so that it has been not inaptly said that 'a Mexican temple was essentially a gigantic altar, of pyramidal form, built in several stages, contracting as they approached the summit' (Réville, *Native Religions of Mexico and Peru*, London, 1884, pp. 47–48). In places, however, as at Quemada, in the Mexican State of Zacatecas, a small structure, 5 ft. high and with a base 7 ft. square, was set in front of a pyramid, apparently as an altar (Bancroft, *op. cit.* iv. 587–588).

3. In *South America* the altar seems to be unknown, thus giving yet another proof of the cultic inferiority of the South American Indians to those of North and Central America. Even the archæological remains of Peru present no example of the altar, so seeming to confirm the words of Garcilasso de la Vega (*Royal Commentaries of the Yncas*, iii. 20, tr. Markham, London, 1869, i. 271) that 'these Indians did not know anything of building an altar.' Nevertheless, there are not infrequent allusions to sacrifice, in the works of the early Spanish *conquistadores*, both of fruits and animals, so that it would seem, in view of the high civilization of the empire of the Incas, as though the Peruvians may very probably have known of the altar, despite the lack of archæological evidence.

LITERATURE.—Hough in *Handbook of American Indians* (*Bulletin 30 BE*), i. 46–47 (Washington, 1907); Waitz, *Anthropologie der Naturvölker*, iii. (Leipzig, 1862); Bancroft, *Native Races of the Pacific States*, iv. (San Francisco, 1883).

LOUIS H. GRAY.

ALTAR (Celtic). — The data concerning the Celtic altar are extremely scanty, since all native records of the pre-Christian period are lacking, while the altars still preserved date from the Roman period, and are modelled upon Roman originals. The chief sources, then, for a knowledge of the altar, as of other portions of Celtic cult, are a few early classical authors. Cæsar, in his brief account of Druidism (*de Bello Gallico*, vi. 13–18), makes no mention of any altar, and is followed in this silence, which may not be without significance, by Strabo (iv. 4. 4–5). On the other hand, Tacitus (*Annales*, xiv. 30) distinctly states that the Druids of Mona 'held it right to besmear the altars with captive blood'; and this practice is extended to the whole of Gaul by Pomponius Mela (iii. 18). By far the most famous passage, however, in this connexion, is found in Lucan's *Pharsalia* (i. 443–445):

> 'Et quibus immitis placatur sanguine diro
> Teutates, horrensque feris altaribus Hesus,
> Et Taranis Scythicæ non mitior ara Dianæ.'

(On the identification of these divinities, see Rhys, *Lectures on the Origin and Growth of Religion as illustrated by Celtic Heathendom*, pp. 44–47, 61–73). The same poem contains a brief description of a Druid temple (iii. 399–452) at Marseilles, which was destroyed by Cæsar. It seems to have consisted simply of a gloomy wood, the oak being mentioned as one of the trees, which contained 'altars built with offerings to the dead' (*structæ sacris feralibus aræ*) and rude, artless images of the gods, roughly hewn from logs. Although Cæsar expressly states that the Gauls differed widely from the Germans in cult (*de Bello Gallico*, vi. 21), Lucan's description of the temple of Marseilles recalls involuntarily the statement of Tacitus (*Germania*, 9), that the ancient Teutons made neither images nor temples for the gods, but worshipped them in groves.

A large number of Celtic altars of the Roman period have been preserved, but are practically valueless, as being modelled entirely on classical prototypes. It was supposed by older archæologists that the dolmens or cromlechs, formed by laying a flat stone across two or three others which had been placed erect, were Druidical altars, a hypothesis now abandoned, since these structures are rather sepulchral chambers which were frequently covered to a greater or less extent with earth. It is probable, moreover, that the dolmens date from the neolithic period, and it is impossible, therefore, to state that they are specifically Celtic. The only conclusion which can be reached, in the light of the data now available, concerning Celtic altars is that the Druids probably had simple structures placed in their sacred groves and used for sacrifice, though the altar was not indispensable, since the wooden and osier cages filled with men and other victims and burned as a holocaust (Cæsar, *de Bello Gallico*, vi. 16; Strabo, iv. 4. 5) could scarcely have been offered on any but a special structure or on the ground.

LITERATURE.—De Belloguet, *Ethnogénie gauloise*, iii. (Paris, 1868); D'Arbois de Jubainville, *Introduction à l'étude de la littérature celtique* (Paris, 1883); O'Curry, *Manners and Customs of the Ancient Irish*, ii. (London, 1873); Dottin, *Manuel pour servir à l'étude de l'antiquité celtique* (Paris, 1906).

LOUIS H. GRAY.

ALTAR (Chinese).—The Chinese sacred books inform us that burnt-offerings were made to Shang-ti, the Supreme Ruler, upon mountain-tops from time immemorial; and the fact that, even to the present day, the worship of Heaven or Shang-ti is conducted upon a circular mound would seem to be a reminiscence of this ancient practice. As early as the days of the Emperor Shun (B.C. 2300), a distinction appears to have been made between the 'round' altar upon which the sacrifices—arranged in a circle, and hence called the '*round sacrifice*'—were offered to God, *i.e.* Shang-ti, and the '*spread-out sacrifice*,' and others, which were associated with the worship of subordinate deities or spirits, and which, as the names imply, were arranged in other ways. The distinction between the shape of the altar of heaven and that of earth is observable even now in China, and may serve to illustrate the early methods as represented in the classical books.

The celebrated 'Altar of Heaven,' in the Chinese quarter of Peking, stands in a beautiful park some 3 miles in circuit, and is a magnificent structure of white marble, 27 feet high, composed of 3 circular terraces, the lowest of which is 210 feet in diameter, the middle 150, and the upper 90 feet.* It is approached by 4 flights of steps, corresponding to the 4 points of the compass. Each terrace is protected by a marble balustrade. The top is paved with marble slabs arranged in concentric circles, the innermost slab being round in shape,—corresponding to the shape of Heaven,—around which is arranged a circle of slabs, 9 in number, and, outside of this, other circles in multiples of 9 until the square of 9 is reached in the outermost ring. Five marble stands support the altar furniture, consisting of censers, candlesticks, and vases. Close to the altar there is a furnace of green tiles, 9 feet high by 7 feet wide, approached by steps on three sides, intended for the reception of the sacrificial offerings which are here burned on the great occasions when the Emperor represents the whole nation in his high-priestly capacity. In the chapels adjoining, where the tablets of Shang-ti and the Imperial ancestors are preserved, this circular arrangement is also maintained.

The 'Altar of Earth,' as described in the *Law of Sacrifices*, was a square mound in which the victims were buried, while those offered to Heaven were burnt. The passage reads as follows: 'With a blazing pile of wood on the grand altar they sacrificed to Heaven; by burying in the grand mound they sacrificed to the Earth.' The Great 'Altar of Earth,' in the Chinese quarter of the city of Peking, consists of 2 terraces of marble, each 6 feet high. The lower terrace is 100 feet square, and the upper one 60 feet. The altar is situated in a park on the north side of that which contains the 'Altar of Heaven' above described. The coping of the wall which encloses the park is of yellow tiling, corresponding to the colour of earth.

The 'Altar of Prayer for Grain,' popularly known as the 'Temple of Heaven,' is separated by a low wall from the 'Altar of Heaven.' It also is circular in shape, but is protected by a triple roof of blue tiling, 100 feet in height.

The local altars on which sacrifices to Earth are periodically offered consist of low mounds of earth, about 5 feet square, and perhaps a foot high. They

* An engraving of the altar, from a photograph, is given in *Bible in the World*, March 1907, p. 79.

are not ornamented or distinguished in any way, except at the time of sacrifice, when they are specially prepared for the occasion.

In Chinese temples, whether Confucian or Buddhist, the altar usually consists of a stone table, rectangular in shape, the proportions varying with the size of the building. The altar furniture includes a censer, two candlesticks, and sometimes a pair of vases of bronze, porcelain, or stone. When Ancestor Worship is conducted in private houses, the offerings are laid out upon ordinary dining tables placed close together.

Permanent altars are erected in front of tombs for the half-yearly sacrifice to the spirits of the dead. They consist of a single stone slab supported by two others, thus forming a table. A smaller altar of similar construction is found at grave sides, intended for the sacrifices to the local spirits or demons.

In the majority of Chinese dwellings there are to be seen miniature altars, where incense is burned, and small offerings of food presented, either to the spirits of deceased relatives, or such popular divinities as the 'God of Wealth.'

LITERATURE.—*Chinese Classics*, trans. by J. Legge, vol. iii., 'Shu King, or Book of Historical Documents,' Oxford; also 'Texts of Confucianism,' *SBE*, vols. iii. xvi. xxvii. xxviii.; S. W. Williams, *Middle Kingdom*, revised ed., 2 vols., London, 1883; E. H. Parker, *China and Religion*, London, 1905, and the literature there cited; H. A. Giles, *Religions of Ancient China*, London, 1905, pp. 28 f., 45; G. Owen, 'Confucian Classics' in *Bible in the World*, March 1907, p. 79 ff.; Mrs. Archibald Little, *Intimate China*, London n. d., p. 341 ff. [description of worship at the Temple of Heaven]; P. D. Chantepie de la Saussaye, *Lehrbuch der Religionsgeschichte* 3, Tübingen, 1905, vol. i. pp. 60 ff., 83 ff.

W. GILBERT WALSHE.

ALTAR (Christian). — **I. Nomenclature.** — (*a*) *GREEK.*—St. Paul, in a passage dealing with the Eucharist, uses the phrase τράπεζα Κυρίου (1 Co 10[21])—a term frequently employed by the Greek Fathers after the 3rd cent., and constantly by Eastern liturgical documents, as a designation of the Christian altar. The word θυσιαστήριον—the ordinary equivalent of LXX for מִזְבֵּחַ—occurs in his writings (1 Co 9[13] 10[18]), but only with reference to the altar of the old dispensation. The writer, however, of the Epistle to the Hebrews may refer to the Eucharist when he says, 'We have an altar (θυσιαστήριον), whereof they have no right to eat which serve the tabernacle' (He 13[10]); but most commentators explain this passage otherwise (cf. Rev 8[3-5]). There is no other reference to the Christian altar in the NT.

[See Probst, *Liturgie der drei ersten christlichen Jahrhunderte*, pp. 20, 21, 37, 38; F. E. Warren, *Liturgy and Ritual of the Ante-Nicene Church*, pp. 78–82; Westcott, *Heb.* 455–463].

In the sub-Apostolic age it is difficult to find any direct reference to the altar. The *Didache* is silent on the point, but in the letters of Ignatius the word θυσιαστήριον occurs in passages dealing with the Eucharist; and this writer in at least one passage (*ad Philad.* 4) appears definitely to apply this word to the Eucharistic altar.

[See *ad Philad.* 4, *ad Magnes.* 7; cf. also *ad Ephes.* 5, *ad Trall.* 7 (in these latter passages θυσιαστήριον is applied figuratively to the Christian community; see Lightfoot, *Philippians*, p. 263)].

Later in the same century, Irenæus (*c. Hær.* iv. 18. 6) writes that the sacrifice of bread and wine should be frequently offered on the altar. Eusebius designates the altar of the basilica at Tyre, dedicated in the year A.D. 314, as ἁγίων ἅγιον θυσιαστήριον (*HE* x. 444), and speaks in the same place of the altars (θυσιαστήρια) erected throughout the world after the Peace of the Church. The word τράπεζα also is defined by pseudo-Athanasius as θυσιαστήριον (*Disput. cont. Arian.* xvii.).

τράπεζα, not θυσιαστήριον, is the term usually employed in the liturgies; it is also common in many of the Greek Fathers. Sometimes the word stands alone—ἡ τράπεζα, 'the table' *par excellence* (*e.g.* Chrys. *Hom. iii. in Epist. ad Ephes.*). Sometimes, as in 1 Co 10[21], it is τράπεζα Κυρίου (*e.g.* Orig. *c. Cels.* viii. 24). But very often adjectives are added, such as ἱερά, ἁγία, μυστική, and the like.

βωμός, as contrasted with θυσιαστήριον, is used in the OT for heathen altars: *e.g.* 1 Mac 1[59] ἐπὶ τὸν βωμὸν ὃς ἦν ἐπὶ τοῦ θυσιαστηρίου (note the use of the word in Ac 17[23]—the only place in which it occurs in the NT). This usage is generally followed by Christian writers. Exceptions, however, are met with, *e.g.*, in Synesius (*Katastasis*, 19 [Migne, *PG* lxvi. coll. 1572, 1573]), who speaks of βωμὸς ὁ ἀναίμακτος. Clement of Alexandria and Origen also use the word βωμός, but in a figurative sense, when they say that the soul of the faithful is the true Christian altar.

[Clem. Alex. *Strom.* vii. 31–32; Orig. *c. Cels.* viii. 17; for τράπεζα see Dionys. Alex. *Ep.*, *ap.* Eusebius, *HE* vii. 9].

In the passage just quoted from Origen he expressly admits the charge of Celsus that Christians had no material altars. This admission, coupled with the fact that so few references to the altar are to be found in early Christian literature, might suggest that the altar was not in early times an adjunct of Christian worship. Nor is Origen alone in his admission; other writers say practically the same thing. But the prevalence of the *Disciplina Arcani* during this period sufficiently accounts for the reticence of ecclesiastical writers on this as on all other subjects connected with Christian worship and the administration of the sacraments. Further, it must be remembered that the same writers, who appear to deny the existence of altars, deny also the existence of temples, stating that God can be worshipped in any place, and that His best temple is in the heart of man. It would appear, then, that the same arguments could be used to disprove the existence of churches in the period now under discussion, and we have positive evidence in disproof of any such statement (see Duchesne, *Christian Worship* [Eng. tr.], ch. xii.). The object of these writers, no doubt, was to differentiate between the pagan sacrifices and the 'unbloody sacrifice' of the Church. In the pagan sense, it is true, Christians had neither temples nor altars.

With the passage cited from Orig. may be compared Minucius Felix, *Octavius*, c. x.; Arnobius, *adv. Gent.* vii. 3).

The word *madhbᵉha* is employed by the Syrians, both Jacobites and Nestorians, *manershōoushi* by the Copts, and *khoran* by the Armenians, to designate the altar (see Brightman, *Lit.* i. 569).

(*b*) *LATIN.*—The term usually employed by the Latin Fathers and Western liturgical documents to designate the altar is *altare*. This word is used already by Tertullian, who describes the Lord's Table as *altare* (*de Exhort. Castit.* ch. 10). Cyprian also frequently uses this term, and applies to it an exclusively Christian significance, contrasting '*aras* Diaboli' with '*altare* Dei' (*Ep.* 64 [65]); nevertheless, in one passage of his writings we find the phrase 'Diaboli altaria' (*Ep.* 59 [65]). *Altare* is also commonly used by Ambrose (e.g. *de Virgin.* ch. 18) and Augustine (e.g. *Sermo* 159, par. 1). The appellation *Mensa Domini* or *Mensa Dominica* is also employed by Augustine (*e.g. Sermo* 90, par. 5) and other Latin Fathers.

Ara, the Vulg. rendering of βωμός, is not applied to the Christian altar by any early ecclesiastical writer except Tertullian, who uses the phrase 'ara Dei' (*de Orat.* 14 [19]). The word *ara* is, however, used occasionally in inscriptions: *e.g.* in one generally supposed to be of Christian origin and of early date—ARAM DEO SANCTO ÆTERNO (*CIL*, vol. viii. n. 9704). Minucius Felix, in a well-known passage, writes: 'Delubra et aras non habemus' (*Oct.* ch. 32). Prudentius uses *ara* as the designation of the base of the altar: 'Altaris aram funditus pessumdare' (περὶ Στεφάνων, x. 49); and in this usage he is followed by other writers. The plural *altaria* is sometimes used with the significance of a singular. The singular *altarium* is used sometimes by late writers for *altare*. *Altarium* is also used as a designation of the free space around the altar.

The word *mensa* came to be applied to the slab itself on which the Elements were placed.

Altaria occurs, *e.g.*, in Cæsarius of Arles, *Hom.* vii.: the elements to be consecrated '*sacris altaribus imponuntur*.' Possibly the plural is used in this way by Ambrose [*Ep.* 20, *ad Marcellinam*] in a passage which has been quoted to prove that his church contained more than one altar (see below, § 4). For *altarium*, cf. Council of Auxerre (A.D. 578), *can.* 10: Mass is not to be said more than once a day, '*super uno altario*.' For the use of *altarium* to designate the space around the altar, cf. Greg. Tur. (*Hist.* ii. 14), who speaks of a church having *fenestras in altario triginta duas*; cf. also Mone, *Messen*, p. 6.

2. Material and form of the altar.—Altars were constructed of wood, stone, or metal.

(1) *Altars of wood.*—It is generally agreed that the earliest altars were made of wood. This would appear from the following considerations. The earliest churches were, no doubt, ordinary dwelling-houses adapted to the special requirements of Christian worship (see Duchesne, *op. cit.* ch. xii. p. 399 ff.), and it would seem probable that in the beginning the Eucharist was celebrated at the tables usually to be found in such houses. It is also known that at the beginning of this era such tables were usually made of wood, either square or round in shape. This view is supported by certain very early frescoes which have survived, and which have for their subject the consecration of the Eucharist. One of these, known as the *Fractio Panis*, is attributed to the first half of the 2nd cent.; and another, discovered in the cemetery of Calixtus, belongs to the latter half of the same century.

[Reproductions of both these frescoes will be found in vol. i. of *DACL*. The *Fractio Panis* is reproduced as Fig. 172, the fresco from the cemetery of Calixtus as Fig. 1123].

From both these frescoes it would appear that in very early times the Eucharist was consecrated at a small three-legged table, similar in form to those in use at the period for purposes of repast. No doubt, at a comparatively early date, special tables were reserved for the Eucharist, and their form was differentiated from that of those ordinarily in use; but for this period of transition we have no definite evidence. That these tables were made of wood is further attested by certain relics preserved at Rome in the churches of St. John Lateran and St. Pudenziana. These are alleged to be the table used at the Last Supper, and altars used by St. Peter. For our purpose the only point which deserves attention is that these relics are of wood, thus evidencing the traditional belief that the earliest altars were of that material. A number of passages of an incidental character in the writings of both Greek and Latin Fathers give the ultimate confirmation of this view. Optatus, Augustine, and Athanasius all mention altars of wood.

[See Optat. *de Schism. Donatist.* vi. 1, where he says that the Donatists used the altars of the Catholics as firewood; also Aug. *Ep.* 185, par. 27, who states that the orthodox bishop Maximianus was beaten with the wood of the altar. Athanasius, *ad Monach.*, expressly states of the altar destroyed at Alexandria by the Count Heraclius, that it was of wood (ξυλίνη γὰρ ἦν); these words, however, may imply that he was familiar with altars made of other materials].

It will, then, seem fair to conclude that in the earliest period altars were of wood, round or square in shape, and resembling the ordinary tables used for domestic purposes, from which they were gradually differentiated.

It was not till after a considerable period that wooden altars were altogether superseded by those of stone or metal. Although condemned by the local Council of Epaona (A.D. 517), they continued in some places to be used for several centuries later. In England it is related that the ancient wooden altars were demolished by the order of St. Wulstan, bishop of Worcester (A.D. 1062–1095), and there is evidence of their occasional retention in France and Spain at a later period.

In the East the material of the altar does not seem to have been regarded as of great importance; it is, however, stated that the use of altars of wood was forbidden by the Nestorian Patriarch, John bar-Algari, at the end of the 9th century.

[See Council of Epaona, *can.* 26—the earliest decree on the subject; also Capitulary of Charlemagne (A.D. 769), c. 14 [Migne, *PL* xcvii. 124]. For England, William of Malmesbury, *de Gestis Pontif. Angl.*, who relates the demolition by St. Wulstan of '*altaria lignea jam inde a priscis diebus in Anglia*.' For France, see the anonymous author of the *Miracula S. Dionysii* quoted below, p. 341b, and the case of the altar of the monastery of St. Cornelius quoted by Dom Martène, *de Antiquis Ecclesiæ Ritibus*, i. p. 111. For Spain, Hardouin, *Concilia*, vi.*a* col. 1026. For the East, Assemani, *Biblioth. Orient.* iii. p. 238].

(2) *Altars of stone.*—It is certain that from a very early date stone altars were in use, and it is scarcely to be doubted that there is a very close connexion between them and the tombs of martyrs. It would seem that probably, during the same period at which the Eucharist was celebrated at the wooden tables described above, in the houses which served in early times for the purposes of Christian worship, it was also celebrated on the stone slabs (*mensæ*) which covered the relics of martyrs and formed part of their tombs (*arcosolia*). That the celebration of the Eucharist in cemeteries was a custom of great antiquity is indisputable; it is expressly ordered in the *Apostolic Constitutions*, where (iv. 17) the faithful are commanded to assemble in the cemeteries for the reading of Scripture and recitation of Psalms (*i.e.* for the observance of the nocturnal vigil) for the martyrs, saints, and all the faithful departed, and also to offer the Eucharistic sacrifice in churches and cemeteries. It is possible that the same custom is referred to as early as A.D. 155 in the *Letter of the Smyrneans* relating the martyrdom of St. Polycarp. After mentioning that they have placed the relics of the martyr in a suitable place, they pray that they may be permitted to gather themselves together in that place, and to celebrate the anniversary of his martyrdom (*Martyr. Polycarp.* c. 18). In the *Liber Pontificalis* it is stated of Pope Felix I. (A.D. 269–275): 'Hic constituit supra memorias (*al.* sepulcra) martyrum missas celebrari.' It seems, however, probable that this means only that he regulated an already existing practice. (See *Lib. Pontif.*, ed. Duchesne, i. p. 156). The cemeteries themselves afford abundant evidence of the existence of altars, but it is impossible here to enter into any discussion of the many disputed points arising from the investigation of these monuments. It is certain that not all the tombs (*arcosolia*) now existing were used for the celebration of the Eucharist, but it is agreed on all hands that many were used for this purpose; and instances occur of the slab covering the tomb being provided with rings, which would enable it to be drawn out for the purpose of the Eucharist. The intimate connexion between altars and the relics of martyrs is evidenced by such passages as the words of the author of the treatise *de Aleatoribus*, who writes: 'Martyribus præsentibus supra mensam Dominicam' (*CIL* i. pt. 3, p. 103); or of Augustine, who thus writes of the altar erected on the site of the martyrdom of Cyprian: 'Mensa Deo constructa est: et tamen mensa dicitur Cypriani . . . quia ipsa immolatione sua paravit hanc mensam, non in qua pascat sive pascatur, sed in qua sacrificium Deo, cui et ipse oblatus est, offeratur' (Aug. *Sermo* cccx. p. 2, in *Nat. Cyp.* 2). In this connexion may also be quoted the famous lines of Prudentius on the altar and tomb of the martyr Hippolytus:

'Talibus Hippolyti corpus mandatur opertis,
Propter ubi adposita est ara dicata Deo.

Illa sacramenti donatrix mensa eademque
Custos fida sui martyris adposita
Servat ad æterni spem iudicis ossa sepulcro,
Pascit item sanctis Tibricolas dapibus.'
(Prudent. περὶ Στεφάνων, xi. 169–174).

During the era of persecution, while the churches were for the most part in private houses, it was necessary for the faithful to betake themselves to the cemeteries and catacombs for the purpose of celebrating the Eucharist at the time of interment, or on the anniversaries of the martyrdoms. But after the Peace of the Church the custom arose of building churches immediately over the sites of the martyrdom of famous saints, or of translating their relics to churches prepared for their reception; as also, at a somewhat later period, of burying ecclesiastical personages beneath or in proximity to the altar in already existing churches. It was not considered necessary to possess the entire body of a saint or martyr; fragments of it would suffice, or even a piece of linen soaked in his blood. These relics were placed within the altar, so that its tomb-like character was for the most part preserved. In later times it was considered unlawful to consecrate an altar without relics; and if these could not be obtained, a leaf of the Gospels, or even a consecrated Host, was placed within it. (See Duchesne, *op. cit.* p. 403, and *canon* 2 of Council of Celichyth [Chelsea] quoted there).

Two forms of stone altar appear to have existed in early times—the one square, resembling a table; the other oblong, and resembling a tomb. It appears, however, that from the 4th cent. onwards many forms were in use. We meet with several instances of the table form supported by one or more columns, and sometimes with a combination of tomb and table form. An instance of this latter is the altar of St. Alexander, consisting of a table-like structure, the *mensa* of porphyry supported on columns of marble, having a substructure, in the form of a tomb, containing the relics of the saint. Generally speaking, however, the altar was probably of the form of a cube, and in the East it has retained this form. The present oblong form, common in the West, dates from the period when it was customary to place relics of saints in a sarcophagus situated at right angles to the altar and immediately behind it, having its end looking westward and supported by the altar itself. (See § 3, and Ed. Bishop, *On the History of the Christian Altar*, p. 14 ff.).

[A very full description of large numbers of these altars will be found in the *DACL*. Much information will be found in the art. 'Autel,' but more detailed accounts are given under the names of the localities where the particular altars are preserved. See, *e.g.*, 'Auriol (Autel d'),' i. col. 3151 ff., with its representation of the famous one-legged stone altar preserved there. See also the bibliography at the end of the present article].

(3) *Altars of metal.*—The earliest notice of an altar of metal is probably to be found in Sozomen (*HE* ix. 1), who mentions the altar of gold presented to the Church of St. Sophia at Constantinople, by Pulcheria, daughter of Arcadius, in the early part of the 5th century. In the next century we have a very full account of the magnificent altar presented by Justinian to the new basilica of St. Sophia, constructed by him between the years 532 and 563. We are indebted for this description to Paul the Silentiary, who tells us that the Holy Table was of gold, adorned with precious stones, resting upon pillars of gold, and that it was surmounted by a dome or *ciborium*, supported by pillars of silver gilt, and terminating in a great cross of gold (Paul Silent., *Descript. St. Sophiæ*, ed. Bona, vv. 682 ff.). In the West also, at about the same date, we have mention of altars of precious metal; but it is not clear whether they were constructed of metal or of wood which was covered with metal. These notices occur in the *Liber Pontificalis*, and date probably from the latter half of the 5th century. Especially worthy of mention in this connexion is the altar of St. Ambrose at Milan, probably erected before the year A.D. 835. It is 7 ft. 3 in. in length, 4 ft. 1 in. in height, and the *mensa* is 4 ft. 4 in. wide. The front is of gold, the back and sides of silver, and it is decorated with panels containing subjects in relief and with enamel work. It is probably the most elaborate specimen of its kind which has survived.

[For a reproduction see *DACL*, fig. 1130; and for the extensive literature connected with this altar see the same work, vol. i. col. 3171, n. 8].

3. Site and accessories of the altar.—The earliest Christian churches were of the form of a basilica, and the altar was usually placed on the chord of the apse. Around the apse were arranged the seats for the clergy, the bishop's throne being placed in the centre, behind the altar. Sometimes, however, it was placed more forward, nearer the centre of the church; but this was not common. Usually it was raised on steps, and separated from the body of the church by a low screen or railing, not of sufficient height to hide it from the view of the congregation. In later times, beneath the steps of the altar, was constructed a small vault (*confessio*) to contain the relics of a saint. It became customary from an early date for the altar to be covered by a canopy, usually dome-shaped and supported on pillars, called the *ciborium* (κιβώριον). The *ciborium* was made of metal or stone, and richly ornamented. It served a double purpose. Firstly, being provided with curtains hung between the pillars, it served to veil the altar at certain points in the service. Secondly, it did honour to the altar, providing it with a canopy or *umbraculum*, as in that period was customary with the seats of great personages. The date of the introduction of the *ciborium* is uncertain; it must, however, have been considerably earlier than the 6th century. A distinction must be made between the custom of the East and the West. In the West it had been, and for the most part is, customary to allow the altar to stand well in view of the people. In the East, at least from the 4th cent. onwards, the reverse has been the case. The *ciborium* with its veils is found in the West probably from about the 6th cent. onwards, and possibly owing to Byzantine influence. Among other reasons which tended to cause its disuse was the change in the shape of the altar, and the custom of placing a shrine containing relics upon it. The *ciborium* was well suited to the original cube-like altars, which, as we have seen, were in use in early times, but quite unsuited to the oblong altars evolved in the Middle Ages in the West. The *ikonostasis*, or heavy screen, hiding the *bema* from the rest of the church, and in general use in the East at the present day, represents to some extent the veil of the *ciborium*.

In early times nothing was placed upon the altar except the cloths and sacred vessels necessary for the Eucharist, and the book of the Gospels. Not even relics or the reserved Sacrament might be placed upon it. This custom appears to have prevailed in the West for some centuries, but in the 9th cent. a homily or pastoral charge, attributed to Leo IV. (A.D. 855), permits a shrine containing relics, the book of the Gospels, and a pyx or tabernacle containing the Lord's body, for purposes of the viaticum. From this period onwards, in the West, the ornaments which had formerly decorated the *ciborium* were transferred to the altar. At first these appear to have been placed on the altar only during the celebration of the liturgy, but gradually it became customary to place them there permanently. Thus the cross, which had surmounted the dome of the *ciborium* and had depended from it, was placed on the altar itself. In the same way with lights, first a single candlestick was placed on one side of the altar opposite to the cross, later two candlesticks are found, one on either side of it. All this had been accomplished by the 13th century. Meantime, the *ciborium* having practically disappeared in the West, and the altar becoming more and more loaded with tabernacle reliquaries, candles, etc., and having generally been placed as far back as possible against the east wall, the reredos begins to make its appearance,—as also the small canopy now generally in use,—which may be regarded as directly descended from the *ciborium* and all that we now have to represent it.

[The earliest description of the interior of a Christian church is a passage in the *Didascalia Apostolorum*, incorporated in the *Apostolic Constitutions*, bk. ii. c. 57. For the ancient custom with regard to relics, cf. St. Ambrose (*Ep.* xxii. 13): 'Ille [Christus] super altare . . . isti [martyres] sub altari.' The homily attributed to Leo IV. is probably a document of Gallic origin, and is the ground-work of the address of the presiding bishop in the *Ordo ad Synodum* of the present Roman pontifical. It will be found in Migne, *PL* cxv. 677. For this section see especially Edmund Bishop, *On the History of the Christian Altar*].

4. Number of altars.—The primitive custom appears to have been that each church should have only one altar. This custom has prevailed in the East to the present day, although altars are found in παρεκκλησίαι, or side-chapels—these being regarded as separate buildings. In the West the multiplication of altars has been common from a comparatively early date.

[Cf. Ignat. *ad Philad.* 4, cited above: σπουδάσατε οὖν μιᾷ εὐχαριστίᾳ . . . ἓν θυσιαστήριον ὡς εἷς ἐπίσκοπος . . . Eusebius mentions only one altar in his description of the great basilica at Tyre (*HE* x. 4). The passage from Augustine, sometimes quoted in this connexion, proves nothing. He speaks of the existence of two churches in one town (*civitas*) as a visible sign of the Donatist schism (*in Epist. Joh. ad Parthos*, Tract. iii. 5), but his words obviously refer to schismatic worship in general. Contrast St. Basil (*Hom.* xix.), who speaks of more than one altar in a single town. For Eastern custom, cf. Renaudot, *Lit. Orient. Collect.* i. pp. 164, 311, 477, 499; also G. M. Neale, *Introd. to the Hist. of the Holy Eastern Church*, p. 183].

It has been suggested that the multiplication of altars in a single church originated in the cemetery chapels, in some of which several *arcosolia*, or altar tombs, are to be found. But it is dangerous to draw any inference from this fact, because it is generally agreed that many of these *arcosolia* were never used for the purpose of celebrating the Eucharist. More probably the reason is to be sought, on the one hand, in the growth of the Christian population subsequent to the Peace of the Church, and an attempt to meet their increasing needs; and, on the other hand, in the increasing desire of the clergy to celebrate, rather than only to communicate, as often as possible. It is, however, difficult to find passages which imply the existence of more than one altar in a single church earlier than the 6th century. It is not till the time of St. Gregory the Great that we have definite evidence; but it is clear that by that time the custom was well established, because at the request of a correspondent, Palladius, bishop of Saintonge, the pope sent relics for the consecration of four of the thirteen altars which Palladius had set up in his church (Greg. Magn. *Epist.* vi. 49). From this time onward the evidence for the multiplication of altars in a single church is abundant.

[The passage from St. Ambrose, cited above, p. 339a, is inconclusive: 'militis irruentis in altaria, osculis significare pacis insigne' (*Ep.* 20); cf. also St. Paulinus of Nola, *Ep.* xxxi. par. 6. For later evidence see Greg. Tur. *de Gloria Martyrum*, i. 33; Bede (*HE* v. 20), who states that Acca, bishop of Hexham (deposed A.D. 732), having collected a number of relics of apostles and martyrs, exposed them for veneration, 'altaria, distinctis porticibus in hoc ipsum intra muros ejusdem ecclesiæ.' In the 9th cent. the plan of the church of St. Gall, in Switzerland, provided for the erection of seventeen altars. See also Council of Auxerre, *can.* 10, quoted above; Walafrid Strabo, *de Reb. Eccl.* c. xxi.; *Capitularia Regum Francorum*, ed. Baluze, i. 422].

5. Portable altars and 'antimensium.'—The oldest example of a portable altar which has survived is that which was found with the bones of St. Cuthbert, and is now preserved in the Cathedral Library at Durham. It measures 6 in. × 5¾ in., and is made of wood covered with very thin silver. On the wood are found two crosses and part of an inscription, IN HONOR . . . S . . . PETRV. The earliest writer who certainly refers to portable altars is Bede, who relates (*HE* iii. 10) that, in the year 692, two English missionaries to the Saxons on the Continent carried with them an altar stone ('tabulam altaris vice dedicatam'). The following description is given of the portable altar of St. Willebrord: 'Hoc altare Willebrordus in honore Domini Salvatoris consecravit, supra quod in itinere Missarum oblationes Deo offerre consuevit, in quo et continetur de ligno crucis Christi, et de sudore capitis ejus' (Brower, *Annal. Treviren.*, an. 718, p. 364). From this and other passages it would appear that portable altars contained also relics. Portable altars are designated *altaria portabilia, gestatoria, viatica.* Sometimes *ara* is used for a portable altar.

[It has been suggested that portable altars were in use in the time of St. Cyprian, but the passage quoted from his writings (*Ep.* iv. 2), in which he makes provision for celebration in the prison, is inconclusive. A portable altar is preserved at Rome in the church of St. Maria, in Campitelli, said to have belonged to St. Gregory of Nazianzus; but it is not regarded as authentic. We also find other portable altars mentioned at a fairly early date, as that of St. Wulfran (*circ.* 740), the apostle of Frisia (Surius, *Vitæ Sanctorum*, ii. 294) and of St. Boniface. Mention is also made of a wooden board, covered with a linen cloth, used by the monks of St. Denys, who accompanied Charlemagne in his campaign against the Saxons (*Mirac. St. Dionys.* i. 20; *Acta SS. OSB.*, ed. Paris, 1672, vol. iv. p. 350)].

In the East, in place of a portable altar, the *antimensium* (Gr. ἀντιμίνσιον, a word of somewhat doubtful origin) is used. It consists of a piece of cloth consecrated, with various ceremonies, at the time of the consecration of a church. It is to be used apparently in oratories which do not possess a properly consecrated altar, and in other places where it is doubtful if the altar has received consecration.

[See Bona, *de Reb. Lit.* I. xx. 2 (end); Neale, *op. cit.* p. 186 f.; Goar, *Euchologia*, p. 648. See also Suicer, *Thesaurus*, *s.v.*, and the authorities there cited; also Renaudot, *op. cit.* i. 182].

6. Consecration of altars.—It would appear that prior to the 6th cent. the dedication of a church was accomplished simply by the solemn celebration of the Eucharist in it. No special form of consecration existed. But in the case of churches destined to contain relics,—and in the latter part of this period nearly all churches possessed them,—these had to be solemnly enclosed in the altar before the celebration of the first mass in the church. Indeed it is possible that the later forms of dedication originated to a great extent in the ceremonial accompanying this *depositio* of the relics (*pignora*) of saints, and, as these rites illustrate the history of the altar, they may be briefly mentioned here. A study of the earliest liturgical documents, dealing with the consecration of churches with their altars, reveals the fact that in the West two types of service existed side by side—the Roman and the Gallican; the latter, as might be expected, closely resembling the Byzantine formulæ of dedication. Briefly it may be said, with regard to the ceremonies of the consecration of the altar, that the Roman rite is of a funerary character, while the Gallican and Eastern rites resemble the ceremonies of Christian initiation. In the latter the altar is first consecrated by lustration with holy water and anointing with chrism, these corresponding to the rites of baptism and confirmation. These ceremonies having been performed by the bishop in the presence of the people, he leaves the church and proceeds to the spot where the relics are awaiting him. Having brought them to the church, he takes them to the altar. But before the *depositio* a veil is let down, so that the concluding ceremony of enclosing the relics within the altar is not witnessed by the people—who meanwhile chant the Psalm, *Cantate Domino canticum novum* with the Antiphon *Exultabunt Sancti in gloria*. In the Roman rite, which is of a funerary character, the bishop first enters the church and washes the altar once with water, then, returning to the door of the church, receives the *pignora*, and, accompanied by the people, proceeds to the altar, where he performs the ceremonies of the *depositio* in a far more elaborate fashion, these constituting the main feature of the consecration.

[See Duchesne, *op. cit.* p. 399 ff. (cf. the letter from Pope Vigilius to Profuturus of Braga cited on p. 97). The earliest *Ordines* of consecration are: (1) that published by F. Bianchini, *Anastas. Bibliothec.* iii. p. xlviii; and (2) the *Ordo of S. Amand*, published by Duchesne, *op. cit.* p. 478; cf. also the Gelasian *Sacramenta Muratori*, i. p. 635; see also *Monumenta Liturg.* Ambr. vol. i.; and for the Eastern rites, Goar, *Euchalog.* p. 832].

LITERATURE.—D. Bartolini, *Sopra l'antichissimo altare de legno rinchiuso nell' altare papale della sagrosanta arcibasilica lataranese*, Rome, 1852; E. Bishop, 'On the History of the Christian Altar' in *Downside Review*, n. 71, July 1905 (privately reprinted); J. Blackburne, *A brief Historical Enquiry into the Introduction of Stone Altars into the Christian Church*, Cambridge, 1844; Cardinal Bona, *de Reb. Liturg. Ant.* 1677; J. Corblet, *Hist. dogmat. liturg. et archéol. du Sacrament de l'Eucharistie*, Paris, 1886, ii. pp. 59–220; J. B. de Rossi, *Roma Sotterranea*, Paris, 1877, iii. pp. 488–495; L. Duchesne, *Christian Worship: its Origin and Evolution* [Eng. tr.], London, 1903; J. A. Fabricius, *de Aris veterum Christianorum*, Helmstadt, 1697; A. Heales, *The Archæology of the Christian Altar*, London, 1881; Fr. Laib and F. G. Schwarz, *Studien über Gesch. des Christl. Altars*, Stuttgart, 1858; J. Mede, 'On the name Altar, anciently given to the Holy Table,' *Works*, London, 1864, ii. 486–500; F. Probst, *Liturgie der drei ersten Christl. Jahrhunderte*, Tübingen, 1870; W. E. Scudamore, *Notitia Eucharistica*, 1876; J. B. Thiers, *Dissertation sur les principaux autels, la clôture du chœur et les jubés des églises*, Paris, 1655; F. E. Warren, *The Liturgy and Ritual of the Ante-Nicene Church*, London, 1897.

H. LEONARD PASS.

ALTAR (Egyptian). — According to the sculptures, offerings were laid on mats or stands. A common form of the latter was a pillar-shaped upright of wood or stone, on which a bowl, censer, or tray could rest, and sometimes the bowl or tray was made in one piece with the upright. In tombs and temples the typical scene of offering shows a tray-stand  covered with sliced loaves of bread , or with meat, vegetables, and other food, placed before the deceased man or the god; such stands are often accompanied by a variety of food on mats. At el-Amarna the stands of provisions to which the sun-god Aton stretches his radiating hands are often surmounted by flaming bowls, perhaps censers, perhaps lamps. The food, drink, incense, and water were provided for the god or the deceased, as they would have been for the banquets of a living man; most flesh and vegetables seem to have been eaten raw, but in the standard lists of offerings roast meat was included. Amongst the varieties of the symbol *khêwi*, 'altar,' in the New Kingdom, is , the picture of a stand with a flaming vessel upon it; and in the scenes of that age the offerer sometimes presents such a stand in his hand, with a plucked goose in the midst of the flames. Possibly this represents a kind of burnt sacrifice rather than a summary kind of cooking. The root of the name *khêwi* is spelt by the figure of a bivalve shell , which suggests that a shell may sometimes have replaced the bowl as the receptacle for the offering. Another kind of stand for offerings—a wooden frame to hold jars of liquid —was named *uthu*, this name being equally applied to those used at banquets.

In early tombs a flat slab for offerings, commonly called a 'table of offerings,' was placed before the niche containing a statue of the deceased, or in some other place corresponding. The table was oblong, with a projection like a spout in front. It was generally sculptured with 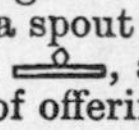, a loaf upon a mat, and often with a number of offerings in detail. The special name for this type was probably *hotep*. Such tables are also found in the ruins of temples, where they may have been placed for the service of the dedicator's statue rather than for that of the god. The type persisted down to the Roman period; it is rare during the New Kingdom, but was revived after its fall.

Temple altars on a large scale are very rare in Egypt. Down to the present time only four examples have been discovered, and none have survived in the Ptolemaic temples. The earliest is of the Fifth Dynasty, in the temple of the Sun at Abusir (Borchardt, *Das Re-Heiligthum des Königs Ne-Woser-Re*, i. pp. 14, 43). It is formed of five great blocks of alabaster; in the middle is a slightly raised circular slab, with four  around it, oriented precisely to the cardinal points. Its extreme measures are some 15 ft. each way. Most of the surroundings are now destroyed to the level of the ground. The altar stood in a court before the great obelisk-shaped monument, and was raised only a few inches above the level of the floor; beside it was an area specially prepared for the slaughter and cutting up of victims. At Karnak, in an upper chamber close to the Festal Hall of Tethmosis III., is a great oblong rectangular altar or altar-base of white felspar, bearing the name of Rameses III. (Dyn. XX.), having each side shaped as a *hotep*. Tethmosis himself is recorded to have dedicated a similar one.

A different type of temple altar is a raised rectangular platform, reached by a flight of steps. There is a well-preserved example in the temple of Hatshepsut at Deir el-Bahari (Naville, *Deir el-Bahari*, i. Pl. 8; see also plan of temple in *Archæological Report*, 1894–95, or in Baedeker's *Egypt*). It measures about 16 by 13 ft., and stands in the centre of a small court about 5 ft. above the floor. The usual Egyptian cavetto cornice runs round it, and the top is flat except for some slight coping or cresting near the edge. Built of white limestone, it is dedicated to the sun-god, and is called a *khêwi* in the inscription, like the stands of offering. Another raised altar is at Karnak, dedicated by Tethmosis III.; and a third is stated to be in the largest temple of Gebel Barkal, dating from the early Ethiopian Kingdom in the 8th or 7th cent. B.C. (Borchardt, *l.c.*). These are all that are known to exist. The sculptures in the tombs of el-Amarna show the chief altars of Aton to have been of this form (Lepsius, *Denkmäler* iii. 96, 102; Davies, *El Amarna*, i. Pl. 12, 25, 27–28, ii. Pl. 18, iii. Pl. 8, 10). It seems as if the sun-gods in particular (Re, Aton, Amen-Re) were honoured by great altars.

F. LL. GRIFFITH.

ALTAR (Greek).—The altar, in Greek religion, is a raised place, usually an artificial structure, which is used for the purpose of making offerings to a god or gods. It is thus to be distinguished, on the one hand, from a sacrificial *trench* or *pit*, such as was often used for offerings to the dead, to heroes, or to the infernal deities; and, on the other, from a *table* for offerings such as was often placed in a temple or before a god at a ceremonial banquet.

But there is no very strict line of demarcation in either case. The distinction sometimes made between βωμός as an altar for the Olympian gods and ἐσχάρα for offerings to heroes, though laid down by Pollux (i. 8) and others, is not strictly observed by classical authors. And, on the other hand, a portable altar, such as was often used for incense or minor offerings, is not easy to distinguish from a sacred table.

A more essential distinction, at first sight, might seem to depend on the *nature of the offerings* for which an altar was used,—whether, for example, it was only for bloodless libations, for incense, and for gifts of fruit and flowers, or for the slaughter of victims, of which portions were burnt upon it. The ritual and offerings admissible in each case were prescribed by the nature of the deity worshipped and by the sacred regulations of the local cult, and the shape and construction of the altar must have depended upon these. But, apart from purely practical considerations, there does not seem to be any essential distinction observed in the form of the altar according to the various purposes for which it was intended.

Some confusion of thought is found in the case of sacred stones or other objects that were anointed with offerings of blood, oil, or other liquids, bound with sacred woollen fillets, and otherwise treated in much the same way as altars. This fact has led some writers to assert that an altar was sometimes regarded not merely as the symbol of the god, but as having him immanent in it. These sacred stones, which are a survival from primitive religious beliefs, are not, however, properly to be regarded as altars, though they may have been sometimes so thought of when religious thought had advanced to less crude conceptions of the deities.

Apart from these, an altar seems to derive its sanctity merely from its association with a god, or its dedication to him. There was nothing in Greek religion to prevent a sacrifice being made to a god on any occasion or in any place ; and, in such cases, the convenience of the sacrifice would suggest the use of any outstanding rock or natural mound, or, in the absence of such help, the piling together of stones or sods to make an improvised altar (αὐτοσχεδία ἐσχάρα, Paus. v. 13. 5); and a similar primitive form, often heaped together out of the ashes of victims, was retained by many of the most famous altars, such as those of Zeus at Olympia and of Hera at Samos. This, however, implies the repetition of sacrifices at the same place ; the selection of such places was due to various causes. These may best be classified, according to Hermann's well-known division, as natural, social, and historical; but before we examine instances of these three classes, it is necessary to consider the relation of the altar to other objects connected with worship, especially the precinct, the image, and the temple.

The normal equipment of a sacred place in Greece consisted of a *temple*, an *altar*, and a *precinct*. In later times the temple was the most conspicuous and the most important, and usually contained the image of the god ; but even then the altar was the essential thing for ritual purposes. If possible, it was placed in front of the temple, and in its main axis ; but so that the person sacrificing faced east, with his back to the temple. Examples of this are numerous ; *e.g.* the altars in front of the temples of Aphæa at Ægina, of Apollo at Delphi, and of Aphrodite at Naucratis. Often, however, it was difficult or inconvenient to place the altar in this position, and it was placed elsewhere in the neighbourhood, as in the case of the altar of Zeus at Olympia, and of Athene on the Acropolis at Athens. In addition to the main altar, there might be others in the precinct, whether dedicated to the same god as the main altar or to other deities. An extreme case is offered by Olympia, where as many as 69 other altars are recorded as existing in the sacred *Altis* of Zeus. There was usually, in all probability, a small altar for incense and small offerings within the temple ; traces of such altars have rarely been found (an example is in the temple of Sarapis on Delos [*BCH* vi. 299]) ; but they may often have been small portable ones.

It must always be borne in mind in this connexion that a temple in Greece was not usually intended for the performance of services or ritual acts, much less for congregational use ; it served chiefly to house the image of the god and his most precious offerings. Assemblies and services, including sacrifices of all kinds, took place for the most part outside, around the altar which was their real centre ; provision was sometimes made close to the altar for the accommodation of worshippers or spectators. Thus at Oropus there are curved steps above the altar in the Amphiaræum, and at Olympia there was accommodation for spectators near the great altar of Zeus. Round the altar of Artemis Orthia at Sparta, where the ceremonial flogging of the Spartan youths took place, a regular amphitheatre was erected in Roman times. An earlier and more important example of the association of an altar with the provision of accommodation for spectators is the θυμέλη placed in the orchestra of the theatre. Here the altar was the original centre round which were placed first provisional seats, and afterwards the great buildings which we find as theatres on numerous Greek sites. At Priene, where alone the *thymele* is still extant, it is placed on the side of the orchestra farthest from the stage.

Altars were, however, not always associated with temples. An altar might be set up on any sacred spot, with or without a precinct of some sort around it ; and altars were also connected with the life of men, especially in domestic and civil surroundings. It was usual to have an altar of Zeus Ἑρκεῖος, the protector of the enclosure, in the courtyard of every house ; traces of such an altar are found even in the palace at Tiryns. Here it was usual for the head of the house to offer sacrifice, especially on festival days. In addition to this there was the *hestia* or hearth, usually circular, and sacred to the goddess of the same name. Such a hearth is usually found in the hall of palaces of the Mycenæan age : its position in the house of historical times is doubtful. We should expect to find it in the *pastas* or open recess opposite the entrance, according to Galen's description of the primitive house ; but some suppose it to have been placed in the ἀνδρών or dining-room. The hearth was the centre of domestic life, and it was accordingly sought by a suppliant who claimed the right of hospitality ; at a wedding, fire from it was carried to the *hestia* in the new home by the bride's mother, thus ensuring the continuity of the domestic worship. The hearth of the royal palace was the centre of the worship and hospitality of the State in monarchical times. It was natural that, with the growth of democratic feeling, this should be transferred to the hearth of the State as the focus of civic life ; such a hearth, itself usually circular, was often enclosed in a circular building called a *tholos* ; and the Prytaneum, where public hospitality was dispensed, was associated with it. The original character of the public hearth as an altar of Hestia was not, however, lost sight of ; the Prytanes at Athens regularly offered sacrifice there. On the sacred hearth in the Prytaneum at Olympia the fire was always kept burning day and night. It was also customary to set up altars in a market-place (*agora*), a gateway, or other places of concourse ; and the sacrifices which preceded any assembly for political or other purposes implied the provision of an altar for offering them. Such altars frequently stood by themselves, without being attached to any particular temple or precinct.

This summary of the relation of altars to other appliances or conditions of religious or social life suffices, to a great extent, as a comment on the classification of the reasons that led to the choice of various places for altars. We may assign to natural causes the erection of altars on mountain-tops or in groves, beneath sacred trees, in caves, beside springs, or in other situations distinguished by their natural surroundings; to the same category may be assigned altars dedicated to Zeus Καταιβάτης where lightning had struck, and others in commemoration of extraordinary phenomena; *e.g.* the altar to Phosphorus—perhaps an epithet of Artemis—dedicated by Thrasybulus in honour of the miraculous light that led his adventurous band from Phyle to Munychia. Examples of altars which owe their origin to social causes have already been given, especially those of the house and of the agora. In addition to the usual gods of the market-place (ἀγοραῖοι θεοί) we sometimes find altars of more abstract ethical significance, such as the altars of ἔλεος (pity) and of αἰδώς (sense of honour) at Athens. Many of the altars attached to temples or in precincts would belong to this class. Altars that owe their origin to historical causes are not so common; a good example is the altar dedicated by the Greeks to Zeus Eleutherius at Platæa after their victory over the Persians. This class might be indefinitely enlarged if we include in it all altars that were set up for a special sacrifice and left as a memorial of it. Such were especially common in later times; a familiar example is offered by the 'taurobolic' altars of Roman date.

The *form* and *size* of altars vary very greatly, from a small portable block or table to a structure a stadium in length, and from a mere mound of earth to an elaborate combination of architecture and sculpture like the great altar at Pergamus. The form of a round or oval mound, with the addition probably, in larger examples, of a retaining wall of some sort to hold it together, was to be found in many of the oldest and most sacred altars. That of Zeus at Olympia, which was constructed of the ashes of victims, including those brought from the sacrifices on the sacred hearth at the Prytaneum, had a circumference, on its lower platform, of 125 ft., and of 32 on its upper portion, and a total height of 22 feet. The altar of Apollo at Delos, which was counted one of the seven wonders of the world, was said to be constructed of the horns of victims (κεράτινος βωμός). The other form of altar which may be regarded as primitive is an upstanding mass of rock, either in its rough state or cut to a rectangular form. The great altar of Athene on the Acropolis at Athens was a tract of natural rock, quite uneven on the top, but cut to a more or less square shape at the sides; it was about 80 or 90 feet square. Another rock-cut altar, of a more regular shape, with a platform and steps, is that in the middle of the Pnyx from which the orators addressed the people. Altars were, however, more frequently made of stone or marble, cut from a single block if they were small, or built up like any other structure if they were large. Small altars might be either round or rectangular; there does not seem to be any ritual distinction between the two, except that the hearth (ἑστία) was usually circular; and so, perhaps, were the low altars suitable to heroes, and called by later authorities ἐσχάραι; but rectangular altars to heroes were not unusual, *e.g.* that in the Heroum at Olympia.

When the altar was of any size and importance, the rectangular form prevailed; and the altar was usually mounted on a basis which projected on one side, and so provided a platform (πρόθυσις) on which the sacrificer stood. This was usually so placed that he faced towards the east; thus, in the normal positions of altar and temple, he would turn his back on the image of the deity in the temple,—a fact which alone would suffice to prove that the altar was the most primitive and most essential object in religious rites. This platform was of considerable extent in great altars, and was the place where the victims were slaughtered, the portions that were selected to be burnt being consumed on the altar itself. Altars intended for the sacrifice of many victims at once, or for hecatombs, were necessarily of very large size. The dimensions of the great altar built by Hieron II. of Syracuse (which is about 215 yards in length and about 25 yards in width), of the altars of Zeus at Olympia and of Athene at Athens, have already been mentioned; another example, of medium size, is an altar near the theatre at Megalopolis, which measures about 36 ft. by 6 ft. 6 inches.

Where stone was not readily available, an altar might be constructed of other materials; thus at Naucratis the altar, with its steps and *prothysis*, in the precinct of Aphrodite, is built, like the temple, of unbaked brick and faced with stucco. Altars of any considerable size usually consisted of a mere outer shell of masonry, the inside being filled with rubble or with the ashes from sacrifice; they thus offered a convenient surface on which to kindle the sacrificial fire. In the case of small stone altars which were used for burnt-offerings, some special arrangement was necessary to place on the top. As a rule, extant small altars are flat on the top. Sometimes they are hollowed into basins, as if to hold libations or drink-offerings; occasionally we find a drain to let the liquid run away, as in the altar found at Paphos (*JHS* ix. 239). Sometimes an altar had the form of a table supported upon stone legs. A good early example of this type was found in the early Dionysion west of the Acropolis at Athens. The Bœotians used to build an altar of wood on the summit of Mount Cithæron, and to let it be consumed together with the sacrifice.

It was usual to give some architectural form to an altar, if only in the step or steps on which it was raised and the moulding that ornamented it at top and bottom. Where something more elaborate was attempted, it often took the form of Ionic volutes at each end of the top moulding; these were often joined at the sides by rolls such as we see on the capitals of Ionic columns. Large built altars are sometimes ornamented by a Doric frieze of triglyphs and metopes, occupying the whole height of the structure; an example of this occurs in the large altar already mentioned at Megalopolis. Often in later times the decoration of an altar, in architecture and sculpture, became more elaborate. The altar of Athene at Priene was decorated with an attached Ionic colonnade, and with figures in relief between the columns. The altar of Artemis of Ephesus is said to have been full of the work of Praxiteles. The great altar of Asklepios at Cos was an elaborate structure; but the chief example of this kind was the great altar of Zeus at Pergamus. This consisted of a great basis, about 100 ft. square, ornamented with the well-known frieze of the gigantomachy. A broad flight of steps on the west side led up to the top of this basis, which was surrounded by a colonnade; in this space was the altar proper, consisting of heaped up ashes. An even larger altar than this is said to have existed at Parium on the Propontis. A remarkable architectural development of the circular altar is to be seen in the *Tholos* or *Thymele* (its official name) at Epidaurus; it has the form of a circular temple, with colonnades inside and outside.

Inscriptions are not usually found on altars in Greece. An early example is the altar with ἥρῶος or ἡρώων painted on its stucco face in the Heroum at Olympia. The chief altar attached to a temple or precinct would not require any such means of identification, though, where it was a special dedication, this might be recorded, *e.g.* the great altar of Apollo at Delphi states that it was dedicated by the Chians, and a smaller inscription on its corner adds that the Chians received the privilege of προμαντεία for their gift. In the case of altars to other gods than the one to whom the precinct belonged, inscriptions would be useful, but were by no means universal. They would be required also on altars in public places; *e.g.* the inscribed altar in the Dipylon gateway at Athens, dedicated to Zeus Herkeios, Hermes, and Acamas. Where the object of an altar was commemorative rather than for practical use, the inscription would of course be essential. But ritual ordinances as to sacrifices were usually inscribed, not on the altar itself, but on a stela or slab set up beside it, or on some other convenient place in its immediate vicinity.

For the ritual of sacrifice, and the manner in which altars were used in connexion with it, see SACRIFICE. But it should be added here that an altar was usually dedicated to the service of a particular god, and was not used for offerings to any other. A good example of this is seen in the sixty-nine altars of Olympia, each of which had its proper destination, and was visited in its proper turn in the monthly order of sacrifices. This rule did not, however, preclude a common dedication to several gods of one altar (σύμβωμοι, ὁμοβώμιοι θεοί). There existed altars of all the gods, or of the twelve gods; an interesting example, probably to ensure the worship of some powers that might otherwise be overlooked, is offered by the altar of 'the unknown gods' at Olympia. The example of this title quoted by St. Paul at Athens (Ac 17[23]) was, however, in the singular. Frequently two gods were worshipped at the same altar; a classical instance is provided by the six twin altars mentioned by Pindar in *Ol.* v. 12 (see Schol. *ad loc.*). In Athens, Poseidon and Erechtheus shared a common altar in the Erechtheum, and in the Amphiaræum at Oropus the altar has been enlarged so as to accommodate several deities (Πρακτικὰ Ἀρχ. Ἑτ. 1804, p. 91).

In addition to their use for the ritual of sacrifice, altars were also sought by *suppliants*, who often sat upon the steps, and especially by *those seeking sanctuary*. The altar in a house, whether the *hestia* or that of Zeus Herkeios, often served this purpose; and in a temple a suppliant would naturally place himself under the protection of the god either by clasping his image or by seating himself on the altar or beside it. It does not, however, appear that in Greek religion there was any peculiar power in this connexion that belonged to the altar more than to any other part of a temple or precinct. The right of sanctuary usually had clearly defined limits within which it was inviolable. It is worthy of note that when Cylon's followers had to go outside these limits, it was to the early image, not to the altar, that they attached the rope to which they trusted for protection.

LITERATURE.—See end of art. ALTAR (Roman).

ERNEST A. GARDNER.

ALTAR (Hindu).—Altars, or raised platforms, play an important part in the Hindu ceremonial. The Sanskrit for a Hindu altar is *vedi*, which is defined as 'an altar or raised place made of Kuśa grass, or strewed with it, and prepared for an oblation, for placing the vessels used at a sacrifice, a place or ground prepared for sacrifice' (Monier Williams, *s.v.*). The original *vedi* was a trench of varied shape, in which the sacrificial fires were kept, dug in the sacrificial ground. In early times in India, when the gods were worshipped by each man at his own fireplace, it was a duty incumbent on every householder to keep the sacred fire in the altar, from the very day on which the ceremony of the Agnyādhāna, or the setting up of sacrificial fires, had been performed. On that important occasion the sacrificer chose his four priests, and erected sheds or fire-houses for the Gārhapatya and the Āhavanīya fires respectively. A circle was marked for the Gārhapatya fire, and a square for the Āhavanīya fire; a semicircular area for the Dakṣiṇāgni or southern fire, if that also was required. The *adhvaryu* or officiating priest then procured a temporary fire, either producing it by friction, or obtaining it from the village, and, after the usual fivefold lustration of the Gārhapatya fireplace, he laid down the fire thereon, and in the evening handed two pieces of wood, called *araṇi*, to the sacrificer and his wife, for the purpose of producing by attrition the Āhavanīya fire the next morning.

There were different *vedis* for different kinds of offering, as, *e.g.*, the large Soma altar (*mahāvedi*) and the *pāśukī vedi*, used for animal sacrifice, which resembled the *uttarā vedi*, or 'northern altar'; the latter was an altar raised with earth excavated in forming what is called a *chātvāla*, or hole. The Śatapatha Brāhmaṇa compares the shape of an altar to that of a woman: 'The altar should be broad on the western side, contracted in the middle, and broad again on the eastern side; for thus shaped they praise a woman.' The shape of sacrificial altars was considered a matter of so much importance that there were special manuals in Sanskrit, called Śulbasūtras, which form part of the ancient Śrautasūtras, and give the measurements necessary for the construction of the altars. The different shapes in which brick altars might be constructed are mentioned as early as in the Taittirīya Saṁhitā. Thus there is a falcon-shaped altar built of square bricks, or an altar of the shape of a falcon with curved wings and outspread tail; a heron-shaped altar with two feet; one of the shape of the forepart of the poles of a chariot, an equilateral triangle; another of the form of two such triangles joined at their bases; several wheel-shaped or circular altars, tortoise-shaped, etc. The area of the earliest species of altars was to be 7½ square *puruṣas*, the term *puruṣa* denoting the height of a man with uplifted arms. The area remained the same when a different shape of altar was required. This and other changes could not be effected without a considerable knowledge of geometry. As stated by Thibaut, 'squares had to be found which would be equal to two or more given squares, or equal to the difference of two given squares; oblongs had to be turned into squares and squares into oblongs . . .; the last task, and not the least, was that of finding a circle the area of which might equal as closely as possible that of a given square.' The result of these operations was the compilation of a series of geometrical rules which are contained in the above-mentioned Śulbasūtras.

A lively controversy has been going on as to whether these geometrical rules are of Indian growth, or due to Greek influence, the numerous coincidences between the Sanskrit texts and the writings of Heron favouring the latter view, whereas the apparent antiquity of the Śulbasūtras, and their close connexion with the ancient sacrificial rites of the Brāhmans, would seem to render their native origin the more probable alternative.

Though offerings in the ancient Vedic fashion have become very rare in India, various kinds of altars continue in common use for religious purposes. Thus the present writer saw a square *vedi* made of earth or clay, on which an open fire for oblations of butter had been kindled, at the consecration of a public tank near Calcutta. Hindu altars are also erected at some of the Saṁskāras or family celebrations of the Brāhmans. Thus among the Deshasth Brāhmans in Dharwar, it is customary, a few days before the ceremony of thread-girding, to raise a porch in front of the house, on the western side of which an altar is set up facing east. On the day of the ceremony the boy is bathed and is seated on a low wooden stool which is placed upon the altar, and his father and mother sit on either side. The chief priest kindles on the altar a sacred fire, into which he throws offerings. On the occasion of a marriage in the same caste, an altar about six feet square and one foot high is raised. The bride and bridegroom are led to the marriage altar, and two men hold a cloth between them. At the lucky moment the cloth is drawn aside, and each for the first time time sees the other's face. Afterwards the priest kindles a sacred fire on the altar, and clarified butter and parched grain are thrown in. The married couple walk thrice round the fire. Seven heaps of rice are made on the altar, and a betelnut is placed on each of the heaps. The bridegroom lifting the bride's right foot places it on each of the seven heaps successively. Among the Deshasth Brāhmans of Bijāpur, boys on their initiation are led to an altar called *bahule*, where the priest girds them with the sacred thread, to which a small piece of deerskin is tied.

LITERATURE.—Eggeling's transl. of the Śatapatha Brāhmaṇa in *SBE*, vols. xii. xxvi. (1882, 1886, with plan of sacrificial ground with *vedi*); R. C. Dutt, *History of Civilization in Ancient India*, 3 vols., Calcutta, 1889–1890; J. Thibaut, 'On the Śulvasūtras' in *JRASBe*, vol. xliv., 'Astronomie, Astrologie, und Mathematik' in *GIAP*, Strassburg, 1899; A. Hillebrandt, 'Rituallitteratur,' *ib.*, Strassburg, 1897; A. Bürk, 'Das Āpastamba-Śulba-Sūtra' in *ZDMG*, vols. lv. lvi., 1901, 1902; *BG*, vol. xxii. Dharwar, and vol. xxiii. Bijāpur; Monier Williams, *Brāhmanism and Hinduism*⁴, London, 1891, p. 308.

J. JOLLY.

ALTAR (Japanese).—In Japan little distinction is made between the table and the altar. No special sanctity attaches to the latter. In Buddhist temples there is a stand on which incense is burnt, called *kōdan* or *kōdzukuye* ('incense-table'). Shinto offerings are placed on small tables of unpainted wood. The old ritual prescribed that in the case of Greater Shrines the offerings should be placed on tables (or altars); in the case of Lesser Shrines, on mats spread on the earth.

Each house may have its Buddhist domestic altar, or rather shrine (*butsudan*)—a miniature cupboard or shelf where an image of a Buddha is deposited, or a Shinto altar (*kamidana*) where Shinto tokens, pictures, or other objects of devotion are kept.

W. G. ASTON.

ALTAR (Persian).—**1.** In none of the ancient Persian records, whether literary or inscriptional, do we find a generic term for 'altar.'* Nevertheless, to infer from the absence of such a term in the extant records that no kind of altar was employed in the Zoroastrian ritual during the period represented by the Inscriptions and the Avesta, would be to press the argument from negative evidence too far. Moreover, if the limited vocabulary of the Inscriptions contains no *word* for 'altar,' yet the royal sculptor has left an unequivocal witness of the existence of altars in the Mazdaism of the early Achæmenians, in the representation of the altar itself in bas-relief over the entrance of the tomb of Darius Hystaspis on the rocks at Naksh i Rustam.†

The statements of Greek and Roman authors as to the absence of altars, and of temples and images, in early Persian worship, would seem, on the first view, more difficult of a satisfactory explanation.‡ Herodotus, claiming to speak from personal observation and research, states (i. 131 ff.) that the Persians 'think it unlawful to build temples or altars, imputing folly to those who do so.' Therefore, 'when about to sacrifice, they neither erect altars nor kindle fire.' Strabo (born *c.* 60 B.C.), writing some four hundred and fifty years later, reiterates (XV. iii. 13) the testimony of Herodotus, though, in regard to the phenomena of his own time, he afterwards modifies its application (see *loc. cit.* §§ 14–15).

It is generally agreed, however, by this time, that the kind of altar with which Herodotus, as a Greek, was familiar—a raised platform in masonry, with steps to ascend, erected in front of the temple and under the shadow of the sculptured statue of the deity to whom the temple was dedicated, and upon which animal sacrifices were immolated—was quite unknown amongst the Persians for a long period after Herodotus wrote his *History*. This is not intended to imply that animal sacrifices as well were foreign to the Persian worship of the 5th cent. B.C. For, in the same passage, Herodotus describes the customs observed in such sacrifices: 'If any intends to sacrifice to a god, he leads the animal to a consecrated place.' 'Then dividing the victim into parts, he boils the flesh, and lays it upon the most tender herbs, especially trefoil.' The herbs must certainly be regarded as serving the purpose of an altar, upon which the flesh is presented for the acceptance of the deity; for while it lies there, the *Magus*, we are told, performs the religious service (cf., in some respects, the use of the altar of peace-offering amongst the Hebrews).

The same custom was observed in the cult of certain Persian divinities even in Strabo's time. 'They sacrifice to water by going to a lake, river, or fountain; having dug a trench, they slaughter the victim over it . . .; then they lay the flesh in order upon myrtle or laurel branches' (*loc. cit.* § 14). Here we meet with an Iranian substitute for the Greek βωμός, or raised altar for immolating the victim, namely, the *trench*, which, indeed, is highly suggestive of the antiquity of the method of sacrificing to some of these natural divinities. We have before us what is, probably, a relic of an ancient method of sacrificing which goes back to the Indo-Iranian period, the trench being the Zoroastrian counterpart of the *vedi* of the Vedic ritual.*

There is another fact in connexion with ancient Persian substitutes for altars mentioned by Herodotus, which is interesting, and not, it would appear, without its significance. 'The consecrated places' in the open air whither the victims for some of their sacrifices were led for slaughter, were on the tops of the highest mountains.† Remembering this and the fact that the chief god of the Persians was a sky-god, do we not here perceive their true reason, or, at least, an additional reason on their part for reproaching with folly, as they did, those who erected artificial platforms for sacrificing? In these mountains the pious Zoroastrians saw the altars which their God had provided, which dwarfed and rendered superfluous all other altars, and upon which He seemed ever to dwell as they gazed upon them from their distant homes.

On the other hand, the bas-relief sculpture over the royal tomb at Naksh i Rustam does not represent a sacrificial altar, or indicate any substitute whatsoever for the Greek βωμός, such as the trench was. Its purpose and significance are entirely different. If we wish to find amongst another people anything like a parallel to it, we must turn, not to the Greeks, but to the ancient Hebrews. Like the Ark of the Covenant amongst the Israelites, it was not an instrument for presenting anything to the deity, but the resting-place of the most perfect

* The *dāitya gātu* of the Avesta (*Vendīdād*, viii. 81, 85; xiii. 17) forms no real exception; for, etymologically, it means no more than 'legal or consecrated place,' and is synonymous rather with *temple* than with *altar*. See, however, Jackson, *Grundr. iran. Phil.*, ii. 701; *Persia, Past and Present*, p. 303, by the same author.

† See Dieulafoy, *L'Acropole de Suse*, p. 392.

‡ See art. TEMPLES.

* See 'Das Āpastamba-Śulba-Sūtra: Übersetzung von Bürk; Die altindischen Altäre und das geometrische Wissen welches ihre Konstruktion voraussetzt,' *ZDMG*, vol. lv. p. 543 ff., vol. lvi. p. 327 ff.

† Compare the use of 'high places' (*bāmōth*) amongst the Hebrews (1 K 3[4], 2 K 17[11]. See also Gn 22[14]).

symbol and truest visible manifestation of the presence of that divinity, namely, the sacred fire. The figure on the rock is, therefore, a Fire-altar, attesting the use of such altars amongst the Persians long before the death of Darius.

Of the fact that the Persian reverence for fire goes back to a very early period, there can be no doubt.* The prominence of the *Agni*-cult amongst the Indians as well as the Iranians shows conclusively that it was part of that common heritage which the Indo-Iranian period bequeathed to them. And the reform of Zoroaster had, no doubt, as one of its results, the intensification and extension of the reverence for that element.†

When we remember that the divine flame had to be preserved with the most scrupulous care from all possibility of contamination,‡ as well as maintained ever unextinguished, it is natural to conclude not only that from early times there must have been a protection from climatic and atmospheric dangers, in the form of roofed and walled edifices (see TEMPLES), but that it would be equally necessary to circumscribe it in some vessel, and raise it sufficiently high from the floor, so as to guard it from being polluted by dust or insects. And in the representation on the rock these conditions are fulfilled.

In formation, judging from the bas-relief altar,§ the Achæmenian Fire-altar seems to have consisted of (*a*) a massive plinth or pedestal, with (*b*) what appears like a stone slab, of some inches in depth, resting upon it, and which may very naturally be regarded as the prototype of what is now so well known as the *Ādōsht* ; ‖ (*c*) crowning all, the sacred urn, now called the *Ātash-dān*, the 'fire-container,' wherein the divine and eternal fire burned.

Even in those early days, probably, just as in the time of Strabo ¶ and Pausanias ** (*c.* 180 A.D.), and in modern Fire-temples, this sacred vessel was full to its utmost capacity with the ashes of preceding days, and upon these the sacred flame was kept burning day and night with incense and sandalwood.

Moreover, from the days of Cyrus onwards the divine fire burned, not only in the sacred vase concealed in the seclusion of the *Ātash-gāh*, but it, or at least an inferior form of it,†† invariably formed part of the religious processions and royal progresses of the Persian kings. Xenophon, in describing these processions (*Cyrop.* VIII. iii. 11–13), tells us that 'after the third chariot men followed carrying fire on a large altar' (ἐπ' ἐσχάρας μεγάλης).

In what respect, if at all, the ἐσχάρα differed in form from the altar of the *Ātash-gāh*, we are unable to say. The word ἐσχάρα, which Xenophon employs, is variously translated in passages where it occurs as 'hearth,' 'unraised altar,' 'brasier.' One would scarcely think that this portable altar would include the massive support which seems to have characterized the temple altar * (but see on Sasanian altars, below, § 2).

Sebēos (wrote *c.* 650–675 A.D.) states that the portable altar was less elaborate than that in use in the *Ātash-gāh.** Quintus Curtius (*c.* 64 A.D.), however, asserts that these royal altars were made of silver.† The latter statement may refer only to the *Ātash-dān*. Tabari, the Arabic historian (*b.* 839 A.D.), relates how Yazdijird III., the last of the Sasanian kings, carefully deported with him the sacred fire, in its fit receptacle, from place to place in his hurried flight before the conquering Arabs.

From the representations on the coins of the period,‡ we learn that the sacred fire was not extinguished upon the altar during the Parthian domination (B.C. 250–A.D. 226). Unfortunately, these coins do not assist us very materially in ascertaining the conformation of the altar at this time. Although the Fire-altar is a common type on the reverse of the pieces of the period, they contain only the *Ātash-dān*, having as support the lower part of the Fire-temple or *Ātash-gāh* ; that is, it is only a convention. Still they serve sufficiently to show that in its main element, the *Ātash-dān*, the Fire-altar of the Achæmenians had persisted and survived the shock given to Zoroastrian ritual by the conquest of Alexander and the rule of the Arsacids.

It is possible, though this is by no means certain, that it was during this period § that the sacred places on the high mountains, under the influence of foreign cults, gave room to temples, in the classical sense (ἱερόν), and consequently there arose the accompanying altar (βωμός) for animal sacrifices (cf. Strabo, *loc. cit.* § 15, also XI. viii. 4 ; Pausanias, *loc. cit.*).

Other high authorities ‖ are strongly inclined to assign what are, admittedly, the extant remains of one of these temples, the famous temple at Kangavar, to the time of Artaxerxes II. (Mnemon) (404–358 B.C.), when, as we learn from several sources, there was a serious decadence from orthodox Zoroastrianism, and a recrudescence of ancient cults (cf. J. H. Moulton, *Thinker*, 1892, vol. ii. pp. 498–499). The last word on this matter is yet to be written.

On any theory, we are certain that in the first century before our era two classes of altars, at least, were used in Zoroastrian ritual, namely, the Fire-altar of the *Ātash-gāh*, and the sacrificial altar attached to the temples erected to specific Persian divinities.

Was there not yet another altar in use at this period? Certain statements in the terse account which Strabo gives (*loc. cit.*) of the religious practices of the Persians would seem to justify the inference.

We know that the temples of those Persian

* See von Ferdinand Justi, 'Die älteste iranische Religion und ihr Stifter Zarathustra' in *Preussische Jahrbücher*, vol. lxxxviii. pp. 84, 85, 86. Also, Shahrastani, ed. Haarbrücker, Halle, 1850, i. pp. 281, 298 ; and Gottheil, 'References to Zoroaster in Syriac and Arabic Literature' in *Classical Studies in Honour of Henry Drisler*, pp. 44–47.

† See Jackson, *Zoroaster, the Prophet of Ancient Iran*, pp. 98–100.

‡ See Dieulafoy, *L'Acropole de Suse*, p. 392, n. 1.

§ There is no reason to think that the two large real Fire-altars hewn out of the rock at Naksh i Rustam were typical of those in use in the regular worship at any period in the history of the Zoroastrian religion. (See Jackson, *Persia, Past and Present*, p. 303, and illustration, p. 305).

‖ 'Âdôsht, Pehlevi âtîshto (Dâdistân 48. 15), probablement formé de *âtar-sta*, "où se tient le feu"' (Darmesteter, *Le Zend Avesta*, vol. i. p. lxi, note 3).

¶ 'In the middle of these (the fire-temples) is an altar, on which is a great quantity of ashes' (Strabo, *loc. cit.* § 15).

** 'In the temples of the Persians there is a room where ashes of a colour other than that of ordinary ashes are found. . . . He puts dry wood upon the altar . . . the wood is to be ignited on the ashes without fire' (Pausanias, v. 27. 5).

†† Dieulafoy, *L'Acropole de Suse*, p. 399 ; Tiele, *Geschiedenis van den Godsdienst in den Oudheid*, Deel ii. 2de Stuk, pp. 363–4, Amsterdam, 1901.

* 'Outre les somptueux pyrées construits dans les villes, il existait encore des pyrées ambulants pour lesquels on disposait une tente spéciale, et le roi n'entrait jamais en campagne autrement qu'accompagné de mages et de pyrées' (*Journal Asiatique*, 1866, p. 113 [Sebēos, p. 50]). For a somewhat different version of this passage, see Dr. Heinrich Hübschmann, *Zur Geschichte Armeniens und der ersten Kriege der Araber* (*aus dem Armenischen des Sebēos*), Leipzig, 1873, p. 7, n. 1.

† 'Ordo autem agminis erat talis. Ignis, quem ipsi sacrum et æternum vocabant, argenteis altaribus præferebatur. Magi proximi patrium carmen canebant' (iii. 3, 9 f.).

‡ These coins were not part of the national issues, but belonged, probably, to the semi-independent kings of Persia—Persia in the narrower sense. See *Numismata Orientalia*, 'Parthian Coinage,' by Percy Gardner, p. 20 ; *Num. Chron.* vol. vii. pp. 237, 242, 244 ; and especially Justi, *Grundr. iran. Phil.* ii. pp. 486–87 ; *Corolla Numismatica*, Oxford, 1906, *Étude sur la Numismatique de la Perside*, pp. 63–97, Pl. iii. by Allotte de la Füye ; Dorn, *Collection des monnaies sassanides de feu le lieutenant-général J. de Bartholomæi*, St. Petersburg, 1873, *passim*.

§ See Dieulafoy, *L'Art Antique de la Perse*, pt. v. 7–8, 10–11, 207.

‖ See Jackson, *Persia, Past and Present*, pp. 236–242.

divinities were separate and distinct from the Fire-temples or *Ātash-gāhs* (Strabo, *loc. cit.* § 15). But Strabo adds that to whatever divinity the Persians sacrificed, they first addressed a prayer to fire, all their devotions then, as now, being performed in the presence of the sacred element. Further, in describing the sacrifice to water as mentioned above, he adds that they took great care lest any of the blood should spurt into the fire. The fire, in this case, cannot have been that of the *Ātash-gāh*, but a fire on some kind of altar or brasier present at the place of sacrifice (§ 14). This fire would naturally be of an inferior grade to that used in the *Ātash-gāh*, and consequently it is quite conceivable that it may have served both for boiling the flesh * and for representing the fire of the *Ātash-gāh* as the symbol of the nature and presence of the deity. (See below, § 3).

If the inference is correct, we have here the parent, so to speak, of the Fire-altar employed at the present day in the *Izashnah-Gāh*, or place where the religious rites are performed.

2. On Sasanian coins of all periods, the Fire-altar is a constant type, modified, as it is, from time to time. On some of the earlier pieces we observe that there are, attached to the sides of the altar, metal feet † in the form of lions' paws, which seem to rest upon what were probably intended for handles wherewith to carry the altar. It is, however, conceivable that these were a feature of only the movable altar already described, but were not characteristic of the altar of the *Ātash-gāh*. However, in the later coins of the period this feature disappears, and we have merely the central support in the form of a short column with a base, and crowned, as in the older coins, by the *Ādōsht*, which, in turn, supports the *Ātash-dān*.‡

Whether it was the great reform of Zoroastrianism inaugurated and developed by the Sasanian kings that abolished the practice of animal sacrifice, or whether it had fallen into disuse before the rise of that dynasty (cf. Dieulafoy, *L'Acropole de Suse*, p. 402, Note 2), there can be no doubt that from Sasanian times onwards no places for real sacrifices are to be counted among Zoroastrian altars.

The *dāitya-gātu* was no doubt more extensive than a mere shrine for the *Ātash-dān* of the Bahram Fire, but its remaining part was the shelter of another, only inferior, Fire-altar, already conjectured to exist in earlier times, namely, the small Fire-altar of the *Izashnah-Gāh* (as witness of this, see the elaborate ritual of Avesta, *Vend.* v. 39, etc.). These are the two classes of altars in use among the Zoroastrians of Persia and the Parsis of India at the present day.

3. Modern Fire-altars, while always retaining the two most essential out of the three parts of which Sasanian and, probably, as we have seen, earlier altars consisted, namely, the *Ādōsht* and the *Ātash-dān*, vary somewhat in the form of the latter from those found on the coins and sculptures.

The *Ātash-dāns* seen by Anquetil du Perron at Surat (see *Zend Avesta*, ii. pl. x.; Darmesteter, *Le Zend Avesta*, i. pl. iii.), consisted of large round vases of metal, much like our garden flower-vases, with a foot like a goblet and widening upwards, the larger one measuring three and a half feet in height, and three in diameter at the brim. Each stood upon its *Ādōsht*, about six inches in height. The size and degree of elaboration which characterize the *Ātash-dān* depend in the first place upon the wealth of the community worshipping at its shrine, and especially upon the quality of the fire it contains: whether it is the Bahram Fire, the purest and most sacred of all earthly fires, or the *Ātash i Ādarān*, the fire of the second grade, or only that used in the *Izashnah-khānah*.

The larger of the two fire-altars which Anquetil saw was that of an *Ātash i Ādarān*, placed, of course, in the *Ātash-gāh*; the smaller one was that in use in the *Izashnah-Gāh*. The latter contains the lowest grade of the hierarchy of sacred fires; it is the representative, though not the equal, of the fires of the *Ātash-gāh* (Darmesteter, *Le Zend Avesta*, i. p. lxiii). In front of this altar the priestly rites and religious ceremonies are performed (see SACRIFICE and OFFERINGS). In large temples, such as that at Kolaba, described by Darmesteter (*op. cit.*), there are as many as six of these small altars, where as many pairs of priests are able, simultaneously, to perform their ministrations. This is the class of altar found in the numerous *dādgāhs*, or small chapels, which have no *Ātash-gāh* attached.

Unlike the sacred fire on the altars of the *Ātash-gāhs*, the fire of these altars may be allowed to go out, and be kindled again whenever the faithful Zoroastrians assemble to perform their devotions and ceremonies. A small altar of this class is found also in all pious and orthodox Zoroastrian homes (see Dieulafoy, *L'Acropole de Suse*, Pl. xvi.).

LITERATURE.—The principal works have already been referred to in the body of the article. Dieulafoy's *L'Acropole de Suse*, p. 350 ff. (Paris, 1890–92), is the only work which treats, with anything like fulness, of *ancient* as well as *modern altars*. Scattered references in Greek and Roman authors have been collected and translated by (1) Wilson, *Parsi Religion*, p. 182 ff., Bombay, 1843; (2) Haug, *Essays on the Sacred Language . . . and Religion of the Parsis*, p. 7 ff., London, 1884. These two works contain other relevant matter. On *modern altars*, see Anquetil du Perron, *Zend Avesta, Ouvrage de Zoroastre*, vol. ii. pp. 531, 568–71, Pl. x., Paris, 1771; C. de Harlez, *Avesta, Livre Sacré des Sectateurs de Zoroastre*, vol. ii. p. 10 ff.; Darmesteter, *Le Zend Avesta*, vol. i. p. lix-lxiii, Pl. ii.–iv., vi., Paris, 1892.

E. EDWARDS.

ALTAR (Polynesian). — The Polynesian altar, or *fata*, was essentially a table for the gods, and was constructed of wood, thus forming a striking contrast to the stone altars found in practically all other parts of the world. In Tahiti, the altar was situated either before or in the *marœ*, or temple (Moerenhout, *Voyages aux îles du Grand Océan*, Paris, 1837, i. 470–471); while in Hawaii, where the pyramidal *marœ* was replaced by the *heiau*, the figure of the god was put in the inner apartment to the left of the door, with the altar immediately in front of it (Ellis, *Polynesian Researches*, 2nd ed. London, 1832–1836, iv. 89). The usual type of the Polynesian altar is admirably described by the missionary William Ellis, as follows (i. 344–345; cf. Cook, *Troisième Voyage*, Paris, 1785, ii. 152–153, 350, iii. 388): 'Domestic altars, or those erected near the corpse of a departed friend, were small wicker structures; those in the public temples were large, and usually eight or ten feet high. The surface of the altar was supported by a number of wooden posts or pillars, often curiously carved and polished. The altars were covered with sacred boughs, and ornamented with a border or fringe of rich yellow plantain leaves. Beside these, there were smaller altars connected with the temples; some resembling a small round table, supported by a single post fixed in the ground. Occasionally, the carcase of the hog presented in sacrifice was placed on the large altar, while the heart and some other internal parts were laid on this smaller altar, which was called a *fata aiai*. Offerings and sacrifices of every kind, whether dressed or not, were placed upon the altar, and remained there till decomposed.' A Tahitian altar is described and pictured by Wilson (*Missionary Voyage to the Southern*

* See Rawlinson, *Five Great Monarchies of the Ancient Eastern World*, vol. iii. p. 359, London, 1871.

† See *Num. Chron.*, New Series, vol. xii. 'Sasanian Coins,' Pl. i.

‡ See *Num. Chron.* vol. xii. pl. ii.–v, and, in general, Dorn, *op. cit.*

Pacific Ocean, London, 1799, p. 211) as being forty feet long and seven wide, and resting on sixteen wooden pillars eight feet in height. It was covered with thick matting which hung down the side in fringes, and on it was a rotting pile of hogs, turtles, fish, plantains, coconuts, and other offerings. Since the Polynesians had no burnt-offerings, and since the sacrifices to the gods were, of course, *tabu*, this unsavoury procedure was unavoidable. In Tahiti, the victim was usually dead when placed on the *fata*, and there were also stone altars on which the heads of human victims were placed. The type of altars here described did not differ materially from the class represented by the Hawaiian *rere*, on which human victims were laid face downward, covered with sacrifices of sacred pig, and left to decay (Ellis, iv. 162).

The same distinction which prevails among the Melanesians (wh. see), is found in the Polynesian altars, which include not only the *fata* here described, but also the *fata tupapau*, or altar for the dead, which was six or seven feet in height, and received a corpse immediately after death. This *fata tupapau* was covered by a cloth which protected the dead body from the elements (Moerenhout, i. 470–471, 547); to the corpse food was offered daily for six weeks or two months. This covering is also extended in the Marquesas, where altars to the *tikis* and spirits of the dead are frequent along the roads and by the houses (Waitz-Gerland, *Anthropologie der Naturvölker*, vi. 387, Leipzig, 1872; cf. Cook, ii. 301), to the small *maræ* (Seraut in *L'Anthropologie*, xvi. 475–484). At the *maui fata*, or altar raising, the altar was decorated with mero branches and coconut leaves, while the offerings were pigs, plantains, and the like, but not human sacrifices (Ellis, i. 349).

LITERATURE.—Waitz-Gerland, *Anthropologie der Naturvölker*, vi. 378, 384, 387–388 (Leipzig, 1872).

LOUIS H. GRAY.

ALTAR (Roman).—Much of what has been said about altars in Greek religion applies to Roman religion also, especially in the case of customs or rituals borrowed from Greece. Indeed, most treatises or articles do not make any distinction between the two. Here only those cases will be mentioned as to which we have independent evidence for Roman practice, or in which Roman practice differed from Greek.

1. As to *names*, Varro (as quoted by Servius, *Æn.* ii. 535) asserts: 'Diis superis altaria, terrestribus aras, inferis focos dicari.' But this distinction, like that between βωμός and ἐσχάρα in Greek, is by no means universally observed by Latin writers, though there seems to be a general impression, in accordance with the etymology, that *altaria* are usually higher structures than *aræ*. Lofty altars were thought suitable to Jupiter and the gods of heaven, low ones to Vesta and Earth. Natural or improvised altars, especially those built of turf, are familiar in Latin literature (*e.g.* Horace, *Od.* III. viii. 3–4: 'Positusque carbo in cæspite vivo'). Such altars were set up all over the country, especially in connexion with sacred groves or trees; but they tended, as Greek influence spread, to be superseded by altars of stone or marble. Some of the earliest and most sacred altars in Rome seem not to have been attached to any particular temple; among these were the *ara maxima*, sacred to Hercules, and the mysterious subterranean altar of Consus, which was uncovered only once or twice in the year during festivals.

2. When altars are associated with temples, their *position* varies. Vitruvius (IV. viii.) states that altars ought to face east, and should be placed on a lower level than the images of the gods in the temple, in order that the worshippers may look up to them. The orientation of temples being much more varied in Italy than in Greece, that of the altar varies also. Roman temples are usually raised upon a high substructure approached by steps; and the altars at Pompeii are usually placed either in the open area in front of the steps or on a platform part of the way up. The sacrificer appears, from the position of the altars, to have stood, in some cases, with his side to the temple, in some cases with his back to it. Here, as in Greece, the usage seems to show that sacrifices offered to a god on his altar were not directly offered to the image which symbolized his presence,—that, in short, we have not cases of genuine 'idolatry.' But, in the scenes of sacrifice frequently represented on Roman reliefs, it is common for either a recognizable temple or a small statue of a god to be indicated behind the altar, probably as an artistic device to show to whom the sacrifice is offered.

3. There were also altars in Roman *houses*. It appears that, in primitive houses in Italy, the hearth served both for sacrifices to the domestic gods and for cooking purposes; this must have been in the atrium or central living-room. In farmhouses, where the kitchen with its hearth was still the principal room, we find a survival of this arrangement in the shrine for the household gods affixed to the wall close by the hearth; an example occurs in the villa at Bosco Reale. In Pompeiian houses the hearth has been transferred, for practical purposes, from the atrium to the kitchen; and that its religious functions accompanied it is shown by the fact that here also a shrine or painted figures of the domestic gods are often found in the kitchen near the hearth. More frequently, however, the household worship was more conveniently carried on at a small shrine provided for the purpose, either in a special room or in various positions in the atrium, peristyle, or garden. Such shrines usually consisted of a niche, with either statuettes or painted images of the domestic gods, the *lares* and *penates*, the genius of the house, and serpents; and in front was placed a small altar of a usual type. In one case a small fixed altar was found in a dining-room; probably portable altars were generally employed for the offerings which usually accompanied all meals, when they were no longer held in the common living-room or kitchen.

4. Of the *common hearth of a city* we have the most familiar example in that of Vesta at Rome, where the undying fire was tended by the Vestal Virgins. This was, doubtless, circular, as was the temple that contained it. Small altars were commonly placed in the streets, usually with a niche, or at least a painting on the wall behind, to indicate the gods to whom the altar was dedicated—sometimes the *lares compitales* or street gods, sometimes other deities.

5. As regards the *form* of altars in early Italian religion, we have not much information. The Ara Volcani, discovered in the recent excavations of the Forum, was an oblong mass of natural rock, with its sides scarped away; it was restored with stone and covered with stucco after some damage in quite early times, possibly at the Gallic invasion. Among the primitive objects of cult found underneath the famous black stone was a rectangular block, which was probably an altar. Roman altars were probably influenced in form considerably by Etruscan custom, which seems, from vase paintings and other evidence, to have favoured some curious and fantastic shapes. But we have little evidence of this in Roman monuments. From Imperial times the evidence is abundant; the forms are in their origin dependent upon those of Greece, though they soon enter on an independent development of their own. The magnificent architectural structures of Hellenistic times found a counterpart in the Ara Pacis Augustæ, which was surrounded by

reliefs with allegorized and ceremonial scenes, and is perhaps the most characteristic example of the sculpture of the Augustan age. Smaller altars, both round and square, are provided with artistic decoration in the naturalistic garlands carved in the marble, where the Greeks would have hung real ones, and in the reliefs, frequently representing sacrifices, but including many other appropriate subjects. In these it is possible to trace a development which, however, concerns the history of sculpture rather than that of religion. Simpler architectural decorations follow the Greek models; raised rolls at each end, faced by Ionic volutes, and bands of triglyph ornamentation, are very common. We also find sometimes on reliefs an ornamental canopy built on the top of an altar. In Roman custom, altars were far more frequently than in Greece erected merely in commemoration of a sacrifice, whether actually made upon them or not; in such cases the inscription was the essential thing, the altar form being little more than a convention. On the other hand, altars for actual use were frequently supplied with arrangements convenient in practice, such as basins to receive libations, and ducts to carry away the liquids.

6. Smaller *portable* altars, either for incense or for minor offerings, were frequently used; some have been found at Pompeii and elsewhere, but they are not easy to distinguish from tripods or other tables. It is doubtful whether the *gartibulum* or marble table, frequently found behind the impluvium in the atrium of Pompeiian houses, should be considered as an altar in origin. If, as has been suggested, it originally stood beside the hearth, it may have served this purpose, though it may have been merely a dresser. A peculiar interest attaches to this table in the matter of religious evolution, if we accept its sacred significance; for it plays an important part in the theory of the development of the plan of the primitive Christian church from the atrium of the dwelling-house.

'Between the tablinum and the open part of the atrium stood an ornamental stone table, the only reminder of the sacred hearth. It is a very striking fact that this is precisely the position of the holy table in the basilica; when we take into account the similarity of many of these tables with the most ancient [Christian] altars, we can hardly fail to admit a close relation between them' (Lowry, *Christian Art and Archæology*, London, 1901, p. 100).

7. The association of altars with *tombs* in Roman custom is somewhat confusing. Tombs frequently take a form resembling an altar (*cippus*); and it is natural to associate this with offerings to the dead, even if the altars be merely commemorative and not intended for actual use; the word *ara* is even applied to tombstones in inscriptions. On the other hand, Vergil describes a funeral pyre as 'ara sepulcri' (*Æn.* vi. 177). This altar, on which offerings to the dead were consumed together with his body, may be symbolically represented by the altar-tomb.

LITERATURE.—The fullest and most recent account of altars, Greek and Roman, is that by Reisch in Pauly-Wissowa, *s.v.* 'Altar,' where references to earlier authorities are given. An article with illustration is in Daremberg-Saglio, *Dict. des Antiquités, s.v.* 'Ara.' For Pompeian altars see Mau, *Pompeii*, 1899; for the decoration of Roman altars, Mrs. Strong, *Roman Sculpture*, 1907. See also the Handbooks of Antiquities, such as Hermann, *Lehrbuch*, ii. 'Gottesdienstliche Alterthümer'; Iwan Müller, *Handb. der klass. Altertumswissenschaft*, v. 3 'Griech. Sakralaltertümer' (Stengel, pp. 10–15), v. 4 'Religion und Cultus der Römer (Wissowa), and Indexes of these works. See also A. de Molin, *De Ara apud Græcos* (Berlin, 1884).

E. A. GARDNER.

ALTAR (Semitic).—**1. Primitive conditions.**—The primitive Semites regarded trees, crags or rocks, and springs as deities, and in the earliest times brought their gifts into direct contact with the god by hanging them on the tree, rubbing them on the rock, or throwing them into the spring or well. Evidences of the survival of these customs in Arabia, the primitive Semitic home, are known, and some of them survive even beyond its borders. Both in Arabia and in Palestine trees are found hung with the relics of such offerings.* Gifts were thrown into the Zemzem at Mecca,† and into other springs.‡ That they were also brought into contact with rocks, appears from the ritual of the *maṣṣēbāh* described below. The simplest altar was a natural rock, the top of which contained a channel by which the blood was conveyed to a sacred cave below, as was the case with the sacred rock in the Mosque of Omar at Jerusalem. Such rocks are still used by the Arabs as places of sacrifice (see Curtiss, *Bibl. World*, xxi. 255, 256). Sometimes the blood was conveyed by a rivulet to a sacred well. Such a rivulet was the *Ghabghab* at Mecca, which flowed into the Zemzem.§ No doubt in the earliest times the deity was supposed to dwell in or be identical with a crag, one part of which was taken as an altar because of its natural formation. Out of these primitive conditions there were two lines of development, one of which produced the altars of later times, and the other the *maṣṣēbāh*.

2. Stone altars.—The earliest altar of artificial construction was apparently a rough heap of stones, which represented a mountain-top or a crag in which the god had been thought to dwell. Such altars were made of unhewn stones, and were sometimes surrounded by artificial trenches (1 K 18^{32}). Traces of such altars are found among the Israelites and the Aramæans (cf. 2 K $16^{10ff.}$, Ezk 43^{13}, and 1 Mac $4^{45ff.}$). They were probably at first rude cairns, which suggested a mountain peak. The remains of such cairns may still be seen at Suf and on Mount Nebo, as well as in many other parts of the East (see Conder, *Heth and Moab*, 181 ff.; and Barton, *A Year's Wandering*, 143).

3. Altars of earth.—In lieu of such an altar as this, it was possible in early times to make an altar of earth. Such an altar is permitted in the 'Book of the Covenant,' Ex 20^{24-26} (E), though we have no description of one in the OT. Possibly Macalister is right in thinking that he discovered an altar of this type at Gezer, for in connexion with the high place there he found a bank of earth about 11 ft. in length, which was baked so hard that it was exceedingly difficult for the workmen to cut through it.‖ Underneath this bank were a number of human skulls. As human sacrifice formed a part of early Semitic worship, it is possible that this bank once served as such an altar. Though by no means certain, this is a suggestive possibility. Light on the altar of earth may possibly be obtained from the Samaritans. The writer in 1903 saw their preparations on Mt. Gerizim for the Passover, and when he asked if they had an altar, they said 'yes,' and showed him a hole dug in the ground—perhaps 18 in. in diameter and 10 in. deep. From this a conduit of oblong shape led off. Over the hole the sheep were killed, and the blood flowed into the conduit to be soaked up by the earth. Analogy with the rock-cut altar at Petra described below shows, however, that this is not a complete altar, but only the slaughter-place. The complete earthen altar was a mound of earth, plus one of these earthen slaughter-places.

4. Maṣṣēbāhs.—Another development from the primitive crag was the Arabic *nuṣb* or Hebrew *maṣṣēbāh*. This was a stone pillar of conical shape, frequently resembling in a rough way a phallus, in which the god was supposed to dwell. The fat and oil of sacrifices were smeared on this

* See Doughty, *Arabia Deserta*, i. 449 ff.; and Barton, *A Year's Wandering in Bible Lands*, 162.

† See Barton, *Semitic Origins*, 235.

‡ Cf. W. R. Smith, *Rel. of Sem.*², 177.

§ See Wellhausen, *Reste arab. Heidentums*², 103 ff.

‖ *Bible Side-Lights from the Mound of Gezer*, 56.

stone, so that it served at once as an emblem of deity and as an altar. It was a *bethel* (Gn $28^{17ff.}$). Sometimes such a pillar stood alone, sometimes one or two honorific stones were placed by it,* sometimes the number of stones was made seven,† and at Gezer the whole number of these standing pillars was ten.‡ High places adorned with such stones have in recent years been discovered at Tell es-Safi,* at Petra,§ at Megiddo,§ and at Gezer.‖ When the number of stones is more than one, it is usually easy to identify the *bethel*, as it is worn smooth from the contact of offerings. These pillars were common to both the Hamitic and the Semitic world,¶ and developed in course of time into the Egyptian obelisk.

5. Meat cooked in a pot hung on three sticks.—At this early time probably the larger part of each sacrifice was cooked and eaten by the worshipper, as in 1 S $1^{4.5ff.}$ 2^{13-16}. Probably in the earliest period the flesh was boiled in a pot, as described in Samuel, and as represented on some early Bab. seals and in an early hieroglyphic Bab. inscription.** The Bab. pictures represent the pot as resting in the crotch of crossed sticks, as in course of time the fashion of roasting the meat instead of boiling it came in. The transition in Israel is noted in 1 S 2^{14-16}. It is quite probable that this transition marked a stage of culture which was attained at different periods in different parts of the Semitic world, and that one of its consequences was the institution of burnt-offerings—or offerings consumed by fire, of which the deity was supposed to inhale the smoke. This transition led to the creation of fire-altars. These were ultimately of several kinds, and the evolution of them proceeded along two lines.

6. Ariels.—One way of making a fire-altar was to add a fire-hearth to a *maṣṣēbāh*. This was actually done at Aksum in Abyssinia, where such structures have been found.†† Perhaps the 'ariels' of Moab, mentioned in 2 S 23^{20} and on the Moabite Stone (lines 12 and 17), were structures of this nature. They were structures which could be dragged away, and were connected with the shrines of Jahweh, as well as with those of other deities. This is evident from line 17 of the Moabite Stone, and from Is $29^{1.2.7}$, where the name is figuratively applied to Jerusalem.

W. R. Smith supposed that the pillars of Jachin and Boaz, which stood before the temple of Solomon at Jerusalem, were used as fire-altars also.‡‡ Herodotus (ii. 44) tells us of two similar pillars at Tyre, one of emerald and the other of gold, which shone brightly at night. This latter fact was possibly due to some sort of fire, fed either by burning fat or some similar substance, connected with them. Possibly all these pillars were developed, like the altar-*maṣṣēbāhs* of Aksum, out of the primitive pillar.

7. Rock-cut altars.—Another development from the primitive mountain crag was the rock-cut altar. This represents a later stage of culture than the altar of unhewn stones. That was an artificial imitation of a mountain crag, but it was built of stones on which man had lifted up no tool. Human labour had placed the stones one upon another, but was confined to that alone. Rock-cut altars, on the other hand, are projections of native rock which human hands have fashioned into a form better suited to the purposes of sacrifice. One such was unearthed by Sellin at Taanach.* This consists of a stone about half the height of a man, roughly rounded at the top, but square at the base. At the corners rude steps have been cut in the stone, and the top is slightly hollow. It appears to have been used for libations only, and never for fire offerings.

Another example of a rock-cut altar is found in the rock-cut high-place which was discovered at Petra in the year 1900.† This altar is 9 ft. 1 in. long, 6 ft. 2 in. wide, and 3 ft. high. It is approached on the east side by a flight of steps, on the top of which the officiating priest could stand. On the top of the altar is a depression 3 ft. 8 in. long, 1 ft. 2 in. wide, and 3½ in. deep. This was apparently the fire-pan of the altar. On three corners of this altar there are depressions cut, which have suggested to some the possibility that, when complete, it was adorned at the corners with horns of bronze. This is, of course, only conjectural.

Just to the south of this altar, and separated from it only by a passage-way, is a platform which seems to have been used for the preparation of sacrifices. It is 11 ft. 9 in. long from north to south, 16 ft. 6 in. wide, and 2 ft. 9 in. high. It is ascended by four steps at the north-east corner. In the top of this platform there are cut two concentric circular pans, the larger of which is 3 ft. 8 in. in diameter and 3 in. deep, and the smaller 1 ft. 5 in. in diameter and 2 in. deep. From the lower pan a rock-cut conduit, 3 ft. 2 in. long, 2 in. wide, and 3 in. deep, leads away. This platform was, no doubt, used for the slaughter of the victims, and these basins were designed to catch the blood, and the conduit to conduct it away.‡

When we remember the importance attached to the blood by the early Semites, and their feeling that it should be offered to the deity (cf. 1 S $14^{33.34}$ and Dt $12^{16.23-25.27}$), it becomes clear that this platform was as important a part of the altar as the other. Some scholars have called it, because of the circular basins cut in it, the 'round altar.'§ Analogy makes it clear that the trench of the Samaritans, referred to above, is in reality a part of an altar. Probably every altar of earth in ancient times was accompanied by a slaughtering-place similar to the one seen on Mount Gerizim.

8. Altars of incense.—A still later form of the altar—later from the standpoint of cultural development—was a small portable altar carved out of a stone. Such altars were developed in many parts of the Semitic world, and are described more fully below in connexion with the altars of the different nations. They were used for the burning of fat or of sweet-smelling incense, and probably came into use at a time when, in ordinary sacrifices, such parts of the offering only were given directly to the deity, the other and more edible parts becoming the property of the priests.

9. Bronze altars.—At the farthest remove culturally from the primitive Semitic altar stands the bronze altar. Not made of an unmanufactured product like stone, it is an altar of a civilized, and not of a primitive, people. Such altars are found among the Babylonians, Assyrians, Phœnicians, and Hebrews. Our knowledge of their forms is set forth below in describing the altars of these nations.

10. Arabian altars.—The only large altar that can in any sense be called Arabian which has, so far as the writer knows, been studied by Europeans,

* Cf. Bliss and Macalister, *Excavations in Palestine*, 32.
† See Herod. iii. 8, who says the Arabs had seven.
‡ Macalister, *op. cit.* 57.
§ See Robinson, *Biblical World*, xvii. 6 ff.; Curtiss, *PEFSt*, 1900, 350 ff.; Libbey and Hoskins, *Jordan Valley and Petra*, ii. 175–187. For Megiddo, cf. *Nachrichten der Zeit. Deut. Paläs. Ver.*, 1903, 47.
‖ Macalister, *Bible Side-Lights from the Mound of Gezer*, 56.
¶ See the Fifth Dynasty temple restored in Erman's *Ägypt. Rel.* 45.
** See Scheil, *Délégation en Perse*, ii. 130, and compare Barton in *JAOS* xxii. 122 n. 31, and 128 n. 9. A similar scene is figured on a seal in the writer's possession.
†† See Theodore Bent, *Sacred City of the Ethiopians*, 180 ff.
‡‡ *Rel. of Sem.*², 488 ff.

* See Sellin, *Tell Ta'anek*, p. 36.
† Cf. *PEFSt*, 1900, p. 350 ff.; *Bibl. World*, vol. xvii. p. 6 ff.; Brünnow and Domaszewski, *Provincia Arabia*, i. 241, 242; and Nielsen, *Altarab. Mondreligion*, 172–177.
‡ See the references in note †.
§ So Wilson and Robinson; see Brünnow and Domaszewski, *op. cit.* p. 243.

is the great altar at Petra, described above (§ 7). That rock-cut altar may, however, be an Edomite or Nabatæan work, and indicative of their civilizations rather than of the civilization of the Arabs. Indeed, the use of tools upon it makes it probable that it was constructed by people who had lost the primitive simplicity and poverty of thought which attached to all things Arabian in early times.

The purely Arabian altars were, as they still are, spurs of natural crags, or stones containing hollows to receive the blood (see Curtiss, *Bibl. World*, xxi. 255, 256).

From South Arabia a very interesting altar of incense has come, which is now in the Berlin Museum.* It is a little over 2 ft. high. It tapers slightly as it rises, until within about 7½ in. from the top. At this point a slight shoulder projects, above which the stone broadens again. On one side, in an ornamental framework carved in stone, rises a pyramid, the blunt apex of which is surmounted by the thin crescent of the moon. The horns of the crescent are turned upward, and a star or representation of the sun-disc occupies its centre.

Petrie discovered three such altars of incense in the temple at Serabit el-Khadem in Sinai.† It is true that this was ostensibly an Egyptian temple, but there can be little doubt that Semitic customs and practices found their way into it. Of the altars found here, the highest was 22 inches. It had on the top a cup hollow, 3½ in. wide and 1 in. deep. One of these altars presented on the top a burnt surface, about ¼ in. deep, and its sides were blackened. All of them were cut so as roughly to resemble an hour-glass in shape, though one of them continued to taper well up to the top.

11. Aramæan altars.—In 2 K 16[10ff.] we are told of an altar in Damascus which the Judæan king Ahaz saw, and which so pleased him that he had one made like it and placed in the Temple at Jerusalem. Probably the altar described by Ezekiel (43[13-17]) is a description of it. If so, it was built of stones, and consisted ‡ of a base 27 ft. square and 18 in. high, along the top of which ran a moulding 9 in. wide. On this arose a square of 24 ft., which was 3 ft. high; on this a square of 21 ft., which was 6 ft. in height; and above this arose the hearth of the altar, 16 ft. square and 6 ft. high. It was approached by steps on the east side. The whole structure was about 17 ft. high, and at its corners were projections of some kind called 'horns.' It is only by inference that we carry these dimensions back to the altar at Damascus. Of course, between Ahaz and Ezekiel there may have been modifications, but when the influence of religious conservatism is taken into account, our inference seems to be justified.

As noted above (§ 10), the altar at Petra was perhaps a Nabatæan structure. If so, it should be counted an Aramæan altar.

A few smaller Nabatæan altars, of the kind called altars of incense above, have been discovered. One such was found at Kanatha, and bears a Nabatæan inscription. On one side of it a bullock is carved in a rather primitive type of art.§ Another Nabatæan altar of similar type from Palmyra has two hands carved on its side below an inscription.‖ A fragment of a basaltic altar found at Kanatha, carved with the head of a bullock,* betrays such excellent artistic workmanship that it can hardly be Nabatæan, but is probably Greek. Another Nabatæan altar, found by the Princeton expedition, is pictured by Littmann.† It consists of a straight stone, the shoulders of which are rounded as the top is approached. This is set in a larger base. The upper edge of the base is carved into a moulding. Another Palmyrene altar ‡ has straight sides, and at its top an ornamental moulding projects, making the top larger than the body of the altar. Altars of similar structure, probably of Nabatæan workmanship, may now be seen in Muhammadan cemeteries at Palmyra.§ All these Nabatæan incense-altars known to the present writer have a perpendicular pillar-like form. None of them is shaped like an hour-glass, as are the Arabian altars. Sometimes the base is larger than the stem of the altar, and sometimes a moulding makes the top larger, but the lines of the intervening part are perpendicular.

12. Babylonian altars.—Our knowledge of early Bab. altars comes in part from the pictures on old Bab. seals. These altars may not be purely Semitic, as the Semites there were mixed with the Sumerians,‖ but the Semites were in the country before the dawn of history and early mingled with the Sumerians, so that it is often difficult to disentangle the strands of their civilization.¶ The earliest altars pictured may be Sumerian in origin, but they were employed by Semites at so early a time that we shall treat them as Semitic.**

At the very dawn of Babylonian history the only altars pictured belong to the class called above 'altars of incense.' They are of two forms, each of which appears on seals as archaic as those picturing the other. One of these was apparently a block of stone, shaped thus . The seals which portray it represent the notch as a kind of hearth in which the fire was built. Probably the high portion was hollowed out. One seal represents this style of altar as constructed of large bricks.††

Equally ancient, so far as appears, was the altar of the hour-glass shape.‡‡ These were not all exactly alike. Sometimes the middle of an altar was small, sometimes it was large; sometimes the top was larger than the bottom, and sometimes the reverse was the case; sometimes the narrowest portion was almost at the top, sometimes it was nearer the bottom; but the hour-glass form describes them all.

A third altar, figured on a seal of the de Clercq collection,§§ is perhaps older than either. It consists of flat stones, or possibly large flat bricks, placed above one another in a simple pile.

Still other forms appear on later seals. One such altar ‖‖ is of stone, and is triangular in form, broad at the base, sloping toward the top, and surmounted by a fire-pan. Just below the fire-pan runs an ornamental ledge. That the Babylonians had bronze altars is made probable by another seal, showing a low structure supported by three legs, on which a sacrificial fire burns.¶¶

That the Babylonians had larger altars corresponding in function to the rock-cut altar at Petra is not only probable *a priori*, but is confirmed by the explorations of Dr. Haynes at Nippur. This

* See Mordtmann, *Himjar. Inschriften und Alterthümer*, Pl. iii.; and Nielsen, *Altarab. Mondreligion*, 135.
† See Petrie, *Researches in Sinai*, 133–135.
‡ Cf. Toy, 'Ezekiel,' p. 101 in Haupt's *SBOT*.
§ See Sachau, *SBAW* (1896) 1056 and Pl. x.; Clermont-Ganneau, *Recueil d'archéologie orientale*, iii. 75 and Pl. I., also *ib.* ii. 108 ff.; Littmann, *Semitic Inscriptions*, p. 84.
‖ Cf. Clermont-Ganneau, *op. cit.* i. 117 and Pl. I.

* See Merrill, *East of the Jordan*, 42.
† *Op. cit.* p. 66. ‡ Littmann, *ib.* p. 30.
§ *Ib.* p. 82.
‖ Cf. Meyer, *Sumerien und Semiten in Babylonien*.
¶ See Barton, *Semitic Origins*, ch. v.
** The best description of these is by William Hayes Ward in Appendix G of S. I. Curtiss' *Primitive Semitic Religion Today*.
†† See Ward, *op. cit.* 267–269. For the brick altar, fig. 3, p. 268.
‡‡ Cf. Ward, *ib.* pp. 270–275. §§ No. 141.
‖‖ *Collection de Clercq*, No. 308. ¶¶ *Ib.* No. 392.

excavator found a structure built of sun-dried bricks, 13 ft. long and 8 ft. wide. A ridge of bitumen 7 in. high ran around the top. The structure was covered with a layer of white ashes several inches deep, and was separated from the surrounding space by a low wall or curb. Near it was a bin containing several bushels of ashes. Dr. Haynes rightly regarded this as an altar. He found it 3 ft. below the pavement of Naram-Sin, so that it belongs to the pre-Sargonic period.*

Herodotus (i. 183) bears witness to the fact that two kinds of altars stood in the temple at Babylon. He says the smaller altar was of gold, but is silent as to the material of which the larger altar was constructed. These correspond to the 'altar of burnt-offering' and the 'altar of incense.'

13. **Assyrian altars.**—The altars of the Assyrians consisted, no doubt, of the two varieties employed by the Babylonians. Those which explorations have brought to light belong to the smaller type, or the class of 'altars of incense.' These are sometimes of stone and sometimes of bronze.

The stone altars are of three forms. The oldest is from the time of Adad-nirari III. (B.C. 812–783), and is in the British Museum. It consists of an oblong stone 55 cm. long and of the same height, so carved that the top presents the appearance of a sofa without a back. The lower part is ornamented by a few horizontal symmetrical lines.† The second type is made of a block of stone so carved that its base is triangular, and is ornamented by two horizontal ledges. At the corners between these ledges a lion's foot is carved. This base is surmounted by a circular top.‡ The third altar is shaped much like the Nabatæan altars, but with a castellated top.‡ Both these last are from the palace of Sargon (B.C. 722–705), and are in the Louvre.

The Assyrian bronze altar is pictured for us on the bronze gates of Balawat,§ on a sculpture of Ashurbanipal,‖ and on other sculptures.¶ These altars, in spite of variations in detail, were built on the same pattern. Each was a table-like structure, sometimes half the height of a man, sometimes a little higher. The legs at each corner were moulded, somewhat like the legs of a modern piano. The legs were joined to one another by horizontal bars. Sometimes there was one, sometimes two, and sometimes three of these, and their distance from the ground was determined by the fancy of the maker. From the middle of the side of the altar (or from the centre of it, the perspective is so imperfect that it might be either) a leg descended to the lowest of these cross-bars. The top of the table was slightly hollow and formed the fire-pan. One of the representations shows the sacrifice burning on it. Such an altar could be taken with the army on a campaign, as is shown by the bronze gates of Balawat.

14. **Canaanite altars.**—In ancient Canaan the altars of burnt-offering were sometimes of native rock, as at Taanach (see § 7), sometimes structures of unhewn stone (§ 2), and sometimes heaps of earth (§ 3). These have already been sufficiently described (§§ 2, 3, 7). A Canaanite altar of incense was, however, found at Taanach, which is unique. It was made of earth moulded into a rounded trunk, broad at the base and tapering considerably toward the top. It was ornamented by many heads—both human and animal—in relief.**

* See Clay, *Light on the OT from Babel*, 110.
† Cf. Perrot and Chipiez, *Hist. de l'art dans l'antiquité*, ii. 260.
‡ Perrot and Chipiez, *ib.* p. 268.
§ See Birch and Pinches, *Bronze Ornaments from the Palace Gates of Balawat*, Pl. B 1 and 2; cf. also Ball, *Light from the East*, 164; Perrot and Chipiez, *op. cit.* 429 ff.
‖ Cf. Ball, *op. cit.* 200.
¶ *e.g.* cf. Layard, *Nineveh and its Remains*, ii. 354.
** See Sellin, *Tell Ta'anek*, 75.

15. **Phœnician altars.**—The Phœnician altars which have survived are all 'altars of incense.' They present a variety of forms. Sometimes they are square with a large base and top, the central portion, though smaller, being of the same size all the way up.* Sometimes they are of the same general shape except that they are round, and the base and top join the central portion in an abrupt shoulder instead of being tapered down to it. Such is an altar found at Malta.† Another altar found at the same place has its central portion carved into panelled faces in which a vine is cut for ornamentation.‡ Still others are variations of the hour-glass form.§

Bronze altars are mentioned in Phœnician inscriptions as having been erected at Gebal, Kition, Larnax Lapethos, at the Piræus, and in Sardinia,‖ but we have no knowledge of their form. Perhaps they were made on the pattern of Assyrian bronze altars. We know that in many ways the Phœnicians copied Assyrian art.

16. **Hebrew altars.**—According to Ex 20^{24-26}, early Israelitish altars were constructed either of earth or stone. These have been described in §§ 2, 3. Solomon, when he erected his temple, introduced a brazen altar after Phœnician fashion. The description of this has been omitted by redactors from 1 K 6, because it was not made of orthodox material (so Wellhausen and Stade). Its presence is vouched for by the story of 2 K $16^{11ff.}$ and by the late and confused insertion (so Kittel), 1 K 8^{64}. The Chronicler (2 Ch 4^{1}) makes it a gigantic structure 30 ft. square and 15 ft. high, and modern scholars have often followed his statements.¶ As the altar had perished long before the Chronicler's time, and as it was smaller than the large stone altar which Ahaz built near it (2 K $16^{14.15}$), and which was but 27 ft. square at the base, we may conclude that the Chronicler's measurements are unhistorical. It is much more likely that Solomon's brazen altar was of the Assyrian pattern. If it was, we can better understand why king Ahaz was so eager to supplant it with a stone altar which would be better adapted to the offering of large sacrifices. This bronze altar had disappeared by the time of the Exile. The stone altar of Ahaz is described above (§ 11). Such an altar, built of unhewn stones, continued to exist down to the destruction of the Temple by Titus (cf. 1 Mac 4^{45-47} and Jos. *BJ* v. v. 6).

According to 1 K 6^{22} 7^{48}, a golden altar, apparently of incense, stood before the Holy of Holies in Solomon's temple, but we have no description of its form.

The altars described in the Priestly document as made for the Tabernacle were the altar of burnt-offerings (Ex 27), made of acacia wood and overlaid with bronze, and the altar of incense (Ex 30) made of acacia wood and overlaid with gold. Modern scholars regard both of these as fancies of priestly writers, as it is clear that neither of them would stand a sacrificial fire. The altar of incense of this passage was possibly patterned on that of the Temple. If so, it gives us its dimensions. It was 18 in. square and 3 ft. high.

17. **Horns of the altar.**—Various explanations have been offered for the 'horns of the altar.' Stade ** suggested that they arose in an attempt to carve the altar into the form of an ox, while W. R. Smith †† believed that they were substituted for the horns of real victims, which at an earlier time had been hung upon the altar. Josephus (*BJ* v. v. 6) says of the altar of Herod's temple that 'it

* See Renan, *Mission de Phénicie*, 163.
† Cf. Perrot and Chipiez, *op. cit.* iii. 304 (fig. 220).
‡ *Ib.* fig. 228.
§ *Ib.* 252 (fig. 191); Renan, *op. cit.* 229.
‖ See *CIS* i. Nos. 1, 10, 95, 118, 143.
¶ So Benzinger, *Heb. Arch.* 588.
** *Gesch.* i. 465.
†† *Rel of Sem.*^{2} 436.

had corners like horns,'* suggesting that the term was figuratively applied to some ornamentation which surmounted the corners. As no horns appear upon any Semitic altar yet discovered, but the altar frequently appears surmounted with ornaments, it is probable that, as in Jer 17[1], the word 'horns' is figurative.

The Hebrew 'table of shewbread,' a counterpart to which is figured in Assyrian reliefs, might in one sense be called an altar, but, strictly speaking, it is an altar only in a secondary sense.

LITERATURE.—Nearly all the literature has been mentioned above. In addition, mention may be made of art. 'Altar' by Addis in *EBi*, that by Kennedy in Hastings' *DB*, and that by Barton in the *JE*; also Nowack, *Heb. Arch.* (1894) ii. 17 ff.; Benzinger, *Heb. Arch.* (1894) 378 ff.; Curtiss, 'Places of Sacrifice among the Primitive Semites' in *Biblical World*, vol. xxi. 248 ff.; Greene, 'Hebrew Rock Altars,' *ib.* vol. ix. 329 ff.; and W. H. Ward, 'Altars and Sacrifices in the Primitive Art of Babylonia' in Curtiss' *Primitive Semitic Religion To-day* (1902), Appendix G.

GEORGE A. BARTON.

ALTAR (Slavonic).—There is a considerable number of texts relating to the temples of the Baltic Slavs, but they do not furnish any details about altars. The words denoting 'altar' among the Slavonic nations are borrowed, through the Old High German *altāri*, from the Latin *altare*. The Old Church Slavic *žrŭtva*, 'sacrifice' (cf. *žirĭcŭ*, 'sacrificer, priest'), compared with its Russian derivative *žertveniikŭ*, which is employed in the sense of 'altar' in the Biblical texts, seems to indicate that the altar was the place in the temple where the victims were sacrificed. Perhaps it is simply the translation of the Greek θυσιαστήριον. The entire group of words associated with *žrŭtva* primarily means only 'praise' (Vondrák, *Altkirchenslavische Grammatik*, Berlin, 1900, p. 129). Mention may likewise be made of Old Church Slavic *trěbište* (connected with *trěba*, 'negotium'), 'altar, θυσιαστήριον, σέβασμα'; and *krada*, 'rogus, fornax.'

LITERATURE.—Miklosich, *DWAW* xxiv. 18.

L. LEGER.

ALTAR (Teutonic).—There seems to be no doubt that in heathen times the Teutonic peoples made use of altars; but our information with regard to these is very meagre, since the majority of the references give no details.

The bulk of the evidence is obtained from the Icelandic sagas. In these *stalli* appears to be the regular term for an altar within a temple: we are told that the *stalli* was set up in the centre of the sanctuary [the *afhús*—see TEMPLES (Teutonic)]; and it is described by the Christian writer of the Eyrbyggia Saga as 'like unto an altar.' The materials of its construction are nowhere stated, and there is practically no indication as to whether it was built of earth, stone, or wood. There are references in the sagas to a custom among the Icelandic settlers of carrying with them from Norway 'the earth under the altar'; and in the Kialnesinga Saga the *stalli* is described as made with much skill, and covered above with iron. If the material was wood, the iron would be necessary, since the writer goes on to say that upon the *stalli* burnt the sacred fire that was never allowed to go out. There is some evidence that the figures of the gods stood upon the *stalli*; it is certain that it carried the oath-ring and the great copper bowl (the *hlaut-bolli*) into which was collected all the blood of the victims slain at the sacrifice. Within the bowl were the *hlaut* twigs, by means of which the walls of the temple, within and without, were sprinkled with the blood, and the altar reddened all over.

We hear further of altars within sanctuaries in England and elsewhere: in Anglo-Saxon the regular Christian term for 'altar' was *wihbed* (earlier form, *weofod*), which had probably come down from heathen times. In Gothic the word for 'altar' is *hunslastaþs*, lit. 'place of sacrifice.'

There is mention also in the sagas of a sacrificial stone, called Thor's stone, which stood in the midst of the place of assembly, and on which the men who were sacrificed to Thor had their backs broken. With this we may compare the altars mentioned by Tacitus (*Ann.* i. 61) in the forest of Teutoburgium, where the officers of the army of Varus were sacrificed by the Cherusci in A.D. 9. We hear elsewhere of sacred stones, especially in the Dane Law in England.

Many writers have supposed that the *hörg* of the sagas was some kind of stone altar, mainly on the strength of the passage in Hyndluliódh, where Ottar is said to have built for Frey a *hörg* of stone, which he made glassy with the blood of cattle. But other passages clearly indicate that the *hörg* was of the nature of a room; while the Old German glosses give the corresponding form *haruc* as a translation of *lucus* and *nemus* as well as of *ara*. It is perhaps safer, therefore, to regard the *hörg* simply as a sanctuary. It was apparently often in the charge of women, and seems to have been used especially in connexion with the cult of the dead, while the sacrifices at it took place, sometimes at least, by night.

C. J. GASKELL.

ALTER.—The social 'other,' fellow, or *socius* of the personal 'ego.' In current social Psychology and Ethics the 'alter' is the fellow of the social environment or situation in which the personal self finds itself. It is a contrast-meaning with 'ego.' The term 'altruism' shows historically an earlier use of the same word, meaning conduct or disposition favouring or advancing the interests of another rather than those considered advantageous for oneself. The development of less individualistic views in Sociology, Psychology, and Ethics has rendered important, indeed indispensable, the notion of personality as in some sense more comprehensive than individualism was able to allow. Various views of collectivism, social solidarity, general will and self, rest upon a concept of the 'ego' which essentially involves and identifies itself with its social fellow. The present writer has developed (reference below) such a view in detail, using the term 'socius' for the bipolar self which comprehends both 'ego' and 'alter.' On such a view, the 'ego' as a conscious content is identical in its matter—and also, in consequence, in its attitudes, sympathetic, emotional, ethical, etc.—with the 'alter.' The self-thought is one, a normal growth in the interplay of the influences of the social *milieu*; and the individual is not a social 'unit,' to be brought into social relationships, but an 'outcome' of the social forces working to differentiate and organize common self-material. The altruistic or 'other-seeking' impulses are on this view normal and natural, because in fact identical with the 'ego-seeking'; both are differentiations of the common group of less specialized movements in the process that constitutes personal consciousness in general. Recent work in Social Psychology has shown the place of imitative and other processes whereby the 'ego-alter' or 'socius' meaning is developed.

LITERATURE.—Rousseau, *Contrat social*; Bosanquet, *Philosophical Theory of the State* (1899); Baldwin, *Social and Ethical Interpretations* (1897), and *Dictionary of Philosophy and Psychology, in locis.*

J. MARK BALDWIN.

ALTRUISM.—The use of the term 'Altruism' is due to Comte, who adopted it to describe those dispositions, tendencies, and actions which have the good of others as their object. He contrasted it with 'Egoism' (wh. see), which has self-interest

* κερατοειδεῖς προανέχων γωνίας.

as its direct object. Comte maintained that 'the chief problem of our existence is to subordinate as far as possible egoism to altruism.' Herbert Spencer adopted the term, and gives considerable space in his *Data of Ethics* to the discussion of the contrasted elements of Egoism and Altruism, and to their reconciliation. Briefly, the contrast set forth in the terms 'Egoism' and 'Altruism' was indicated by former writers on Psychology and Ethics by the distinction between self-regarding and other-regarding, that is, benevolent or disinterested tendencies.

The two terms have been widely used by more recent writers. We may distinguish between the use of the terms in Psychology and in Ethics. In Psychology 'Altruism' means the disposition which has as its object the good of another. Some are disposed to limit the meaning of the word to those dispositions which are consciously directed towards an object, and to deny the application of the term to mere spontaneous and unreflective action. In other words, they limit Altruism to conscious beings, and to them when they have attained to powers of reflexion, and have learned to constitute objects for themselves. They exclude from the sphere of Altruism also the gregarious and instinctive grouping together of animals for attack and defence. In Ethics, 'Altruism' is used to denote those dispositions and actions which have the welfare of others or another for their motive and object. It lays stress here, of course, on the ethical aspect of the disposition.

While many would limit the use of the terms 'Egoism' and 'Altruism' to dispositions and actions which arise only within a self-conscious being, and arise as the outcome of a process of reflexion, there are others who strive to trace the origin of egoistic and altruistic tendencies backwards to those instincts of love and hunger, the rudiments of which seem to be present in all forms of life. The conception of Evolution and the acceptance of it as a working hypothesis, at least, by all manner of workers, tend to lay great stress on this line of investigation. Evolutionists tend to regard the behaviour of each species of animals as illustrative of an ethical code relative to that species; and some of them, like Professors Geddes and Thomson, look on the processes of life as a 'materialized ethical process.' Professor Henry Drummond laid stress on the two great struggles; namely, the struggle for the life of self, and the struggle for the life of others.

Writers on this topic from the point of view of Evolution may be divided into two classes. There are those who, with Professor Huxley, describe the process of Evolution as a gladiatorial show, and nature as 'red in tooth and claw with ravin.' They affirm that the very existence of ethical life depends on the possibility of man's ability to combat the cosmic process. In popular literature, in scientific articles, in learned treatises, it has been affirmed that the animal world consists of a struggle between half-starved animals striving for food. 'Woe to the vanquished!' was put forward as the universal cry. Competition was described as strongest between animals of the same kind, and it was through this competition and the premium set on success that species was supposed to advance. On the other hand, there were those who questioned the reality of the struggle, and who questioned whether the struggle for existence is the only law of life and the only rule of progress. While the followers of Darwin laid stress on the struggle for existence, developed it, and painted it in ever darker colours, they apparently forgot that he had written in other terms in the *Descent of Man*. In this work he had set the problem before him of tracing the evolution of man from simpler forms of life, and an evolution of all the features of human life, physical, psychological, ethical. Thus he was led to lay stress on the social character of many animals, on their co-operation, on the evolution of sympathy and mutual helpfulness, until in certain parts that kind of struggle which was prominent in the *Origin of Species* tended almost to disappear. The unit in the struggle changes before our eyes; it is no longer the individual who struggles, gains an advantage, it is 'those communities which included the greatest number of the most sympathetic members that would flourish best, and rear the greatest number of offspring' (*Descent of Man*^{2}, 163). Even from Darwin's point of view here is a new factor introduced into the struggle for existence. Sympathy, mutual help, or union between members of the same species for attack or defence, has been recognized as a decisive factor in the evolution of life. The community has taken the place of the individual, and mutual help is as much a fact of life as mutual competition.

While many evolutionists had apparently forgotten that Darwin had set forth the great influence of the social factor in the evolution of higher forms of life, others took up the hint, and traced the various forms and kinds of social mutual helpfulness in the lower forms of life, and their influence on the development of altruistic affections. Nature did not appear to them to be a mere gladiatorial show; it was a sphere of co-operation, in which each was for all, and all for each. They delighted to trace co-operation throughout the sphere of life, they pointed out to men such forms of co-operation as *symbiosis*, as the co-operation of bacteria with wheat, with various forms of trees, alliances between trees and insects, and generally they were able to show that, competition notwithstanding, the world was a system that worked together. Then they pointed to the evolution of socialistic tendencies in gregarious animals. They showed us a herd of cattle banded together for defence, with the cows and calves in the centre, and the bulls to the front. They showed us a pack of dogs under the rule of a leader, organized for hunting, with the social order dominating the individual, and obeyed by the individual, with sanctions for obedience and penalties for disobedience. Then they traced for us the evolution of those psychological qualities the ethical character of which we distinctly recognize when they appear in self-conscious beings. Trust, obedience, recognition of the order of the pack, or of the herd, consciousness of fault and expulsion from the herd if the order is disregarded, are all depicted by those who trace for us the social evolution of life.

Stress has been laid by some on the relation of parents and children, on the care for offspring as the source of social affection; and attention has been called to the fact that a prolonged infancy calls forth a great development of parental care. As individuation increases, fertility lessens, and with the increase of individuation there goes the increase of the period of helplessness in infancy; and thus they are able to indicate an increase of social affection. Still this source of Altruism does not carry us very far, for the relation of parent and offspring is only temporary, and does not form the basis of a lasting relationship.

It is in the aggregation of animals together for mutual benefit that most evolutionists look for the source of Altruism. It is not possible to enter here into the controversy between those who hold that acquired qualities can be transmitted through heredity, and those who maintain that such transmission has never been proved. It is an important question in itself and in its consequences. But for our purpose it is not needful to take a side on the question. For the present purpose, the denial of the possibility of a transmission of acquired qualities has directed attention to, and stimulated inquiry into, the possibility of social transmission of acquired attainments from generation to generation. Is there a tradition among animals? Is there social transmission of the mental and intellectual gains of a species? Or is the only way of transmission that of organic change inherited from parents by their offspring? We quote the following from Professor J. Mark Baldwin:

'Wallace and Hudson have pointed out the wide operation of imitation in carrying on the habits of certain species; Weismann shows the importance of tradition as against Spencer's claim that mental gains are inherited; Lloyd Morgan has observed in great detail the action of social transmission in actually keeping young fowls alive and so allowing the perpetuation of the species; and Wesley Mills has shown the imperfection of instinct in many cases, with the accompanying dependence of the creatures upon social, imitative, and intelligent action.' He adds: 'It gives a transition from animal to human organization, and from biological to social evolution, which does not involve a break in the chain of influences already present in all the evolution of life' (*Development and Evolution*, 1902, p. 148).

Nurture, imitation, social transmission seem to count for something in the evolution of life, and specially of social life among animals. While it is true that a chicken almost before it has shaken itself free from the shell will peck at a fly and catch it, yet there is evidence to show that in other forms of life the young have to learn from parental example; and it even appears that direct instruction of a kind is given. There is sufficient evidence, at all events, to affirm that the higher animals, whose young need parental care for some time ere they can provide for themselves, have to learn how to make their living. Parent birds teach their young to fly, and teach them to recognize the approach of danger. On this there is no need to dwell, save to remark that in such races of life, where parents and offspring are for a time associated, where parents care for offspring and offspring depend on parents, there is room and there is need for the exercise of what may be called social affections. Nor need we object to the fact that we find in lower forms of life the germ and the promise of what comes to flower and fruit in self-conscious beings. We have learnt that life is one, and that the laws of life are similar in all the ranges of life. It seems to proceed on one plan, and we need not be surprised that rudimentary forms of the higher may be found in the lower layers of life. But the full meaning of the social relations between living beings does not appear till we come to self-conscious beings who can look before and after, and reflect on their own experience.

While, therefore, we receive with gratitude the testimony of the students of life to the existence of the germs of social life in the lower spheres of living beings, it must be insisted on here that the advent of self-conscious beings into the world has made a great difference. The advent of rationality has given a new meaning to all the phenomena of life as these are manifested in beings lower than man. Appetites, passions, desires, affections are no longer what they were in lower forms of life. Appetite is a different thing in an animal which eats only for the sake of hunger, and drinks only to assuage thirst, from what it is in civilized man, who brings the wealth of his artistic nature and the powers of his memory and imagination to enhance the beauty of his festival. Even into appetite the wealth of his whole nature may enter. If this is the case with appetite, it is still more true of the emotions, such as fear, desire, and so on. Take *surprise*, and we find that while we call by the same name the similar phenomena of an animal and a man, yet surprise is relative to the experience of the individual. We are not surprised at railways, telegraphs, telephones, motor cars; these have become the commonplaces of civilization. Thus Comparative Psychology has in all its comparisons to remember what a difference self-consciousness has made in the character of the feelings, and to make allowance accordingly.

Thus in the discussion of Egoism and Altruism, while help of a kind can be obtained from a study of the lower life, that help does not carry us very far. In the lower forms of life the individual is sacrificed to the species: in a beehive the hive seems to be all-in-all, and the individual bees, whatever their function is, are steadily sacrificed to the good of the whole. Numerous other illustrations are at hand. But in a human society such a solution must be found that neither shall the individual be sacrificed to the whole nor the whole to the individual. The individual has a claim on the whole for the opportunity of living a full, rich, and gracious life; and society has a claim on the individual for devoted and whole-hearted service.

Looking at the history of our subject, and at the actual history of man, we find many curious things. Early societies steadily sacrificed the individual to the tribe, and the individual scarcely seemed to have any but a tribal consciousness. The discovery of the individual seems to be a late discovery. The individual must not in any way depart from the custom of the tribe; he must believe their beliefs, follow their customs, wear their totem, and in no way think or act spontaneously. Individual worth and freedom were neither recognized as desirable, nor tolerated, because inimical to the welfare of the tribe. Late in history, and mainly through religious influences, the worth and value of the individual won recognition, human life was recognized as sacred, and freedom found a place amid human worths and interests. In truth, we find in history the pendulum swinging from one extreme to another; now the individual is in bondage to society, and then the individual tends to make society impossible. Here there are long stretches of history where the authority of society dominates the individual, and then a reaction, when men regard the individual as the sole reality and society as a tyranny and trouble. If any one casts his eye back to the beginning of modern philosophy and reads Hobbes and Descartes, and follows out the principle of individualism to the French Revolution, its culminating period in modern history, he will find that the individual in all his naked simplicity, in all the grandeur of his so-called rights, is the object of all study, the beginning of all speculative thought. He is real, his rights are his own, and he is prepared to defend them against all comers. He is in a state of war, he is a free and independent creature, and if he is to live in society he will do so only when he has made terms with his neighbour. So he makes a social contract, he surrenders so much, and he obtains a guarantee for the others. He is supposed to be naturally selfish, egoistic, and to regard others only as instruments for his own good.

Looking at man from this point of view, those who hold it are laid under the heavy burden of attempting to derive Altruism from Egoism, and it need hardly be said that they have failed in the task. Altruism can no more be derived from Egoism than Egoism can be derived from Altruism. The truth seems to be that each of them goes down to the very foundations of life, and life can scarcely be conceived in the absence of either. If it be true that life comes only from life, then life must be sacrificed in order to produce fresh life. That is Altruism, whether it is conscious Altruism or not. It is vain to ask for the genesis of Altruism, it is as deep as life; it is vain to ask for the beginning of Egoism, for it is proverbial that self-preservation is the first law of life. In fact we are here, as we are so often, the victims of our own abstractions. We cannot really separate the individual from society, or society from the individual.

It may be well, at this stage, to point out that what we may distinctively call the Ego feelings have also a social reference. In one sense all feelings which refer to the interests of the individual are Ego feelings. Personal pains and pleasures, desires and aversions, exist only for him who feels them. It would on the whole be an improvement in our use of words if we limited the title 'Ego feelings' to those feelings which belong to a self-conscious subject, and which depend not upon consciousness, but on self-consciousness. 'Ego feelings' thus would mean, not passive pain or pleasure, but feelings actively related to our self-esteem, to our self-assertion, or to any manifestation of the activity of the self by which the impression of its own worth is enhanced. In these feelings the Ego is at once the subject which feels them and the object of which they are qualities.

Limiting Ego feelings to those which thus refer to the self, we observe that it is precisely this reference to self that determines the value of an experience in our mental life. Pleasures and pains depend largely on being connected with self as their subject. Any worthy achievement, any feat performed, is estimated not by the passive sensations accompanying it, or by the physical endurance, but by the exaltation of self-feeling which is aroused. The man who does a daring deed, or performs a notable task, has a sense of power and efficiency, and delights in the deed as his own. Men delight in deeds and rejoice in things accomplished, not so much for their inherent worth, as for the fact that the deeds are their own. Our experiences are of value, and we account them of abiding worth, not because they gratify our sensibility, but because we have put so much of ourselves, of our personality, into them. Thus we can never form pleasures into a sum and measure their value quantitatively as Hedonism tries to do. All values in experience are constituted by their reference to self in self-consciousness.

Self-knowledge, self-reverence, self-control, the activity of self in constituting its objects, are thus determining elements in pleasure and pain. The passive pleasures are almost without value; one chooses the nobler part, though the choice may bring pain with it. A slave may have little of the anxiety, the care, the hardship of the free man, but then a slave can never have the exaltation of self-feeling and self-respect which comes from knowledge and freedom and manhood. It is, then, the reference to self that gives to rational pleasure its distinctive note. But it is next to be observed that even the reference to self has its social aspect. It always refers, even in its most egoistic mood, to a social standard. In fact, the social reference enhances the significance of pain and pleasure in an immeasurable degree. Man sees himself as with the eyes of others. 'As Nature teaches the spectators to assume the circumstances of the person principally concerned, so she teaches this last in some measure to assume those of spectators' (Adam Smith, *Moral Sentiments*, p. 29). The self looks at itself from a spectator's point of view, and estimates itself accordingly. Thus it may have an added misery: social slights, feeling of poverty, looked at from a spectator's point of view and reflected by the self on itself, enhance the feeling of misery till it may become unbearable. On the other hand, a sense of social appreciation, a looking at one's self through the eyes of others, may enhance pleasure till it becomes ecstasy. Pride, vanity, ambition, and other Ego feelings of the same kind need the reference to self for their justification, and yet without the social reference the reference to self would lose its value.

Without the reference to self, values would cease to have a meaning, and pleasure would be merely of the passive sort. As, however, pleasure and pain, the meaning of life and the worth of life, can exist for each person only in his own consciousness, and without the conscious possession of these in his own life a man can never enter into sympathy with others, so a full, broad, intense Ego life is the condition of a full, deep, and wide social life. The chief problem of our life is thus not, as Comte said, 'to subordinate egoism to altruism,' but to develop Egoism to its proper proportions, in the belief that the higher and fuller a personality is, the more he has to contribute to the happiness of mankind. Selfishness does not consist in a man valuing himself according to his intrinsic and social worth, but in ignoring or denying the rights, claims, and worth of others: 'Thou shalt love thy neighbour as thyself.'

Egoistic feelings would lose their value without the social reference. So also the social feelings would lose their value were there not the reference to the self to give them value. There is no necessity for any lengthened reference to the abstract man who has figured so picturesquely in philosophical treatises from Hobbes downwards. Nor is he quite dead yet. This abstract man is a being endowed only with egoistic impulses. Self-preservation is for him the only law of life: his natural life is a state of war. How is such a being to be constrained to live in society? He may be made social in various ways: by a force from above or from without urging him, by means he does not know, to become social even when his reason compels him to think that selfishness is his highest interest. But usually the way to make a selfish being social is to endow him with a desire for approbation, to make him seek society to win approval, or to make him see that others are needful to him if he is to carry out his purposes; and a wise selfishness takes the form of benevolence. The attempt is very subtle and very penetrating, but it is a failure. Men never became social in that way. They are social from the beginning. All that can be said is that man is naturally selfish and naturally social, and the field for the exercise of the Ego feelings and of the social feelings is to be found in society alone.

Look at the individual from any point of view we please, everywhere we meet the social reference. Begotten by social union, born within society, he grows up within society, and is equipped by society for the battle of life. The achievements of society form his inheritance. Social customs are learned by him before he is aware of the process; social beliefs become his beliefs, thought becomes possible because it is embodied in the action, in the language, in the converse of the people with whom the individual lives. In this social sphere the individual lives, here he learns, makes himself heir to the treasures of learning, science, and knowledge, without which individual life would be only rudimentary. A human being in isolation would not be a human being at all.

Jeremy Bentham in the beginning of his *Principles of Morals and Legislation* says, 'A community is a fictitious body, composed of individual persons who are considered as constituting, as it were, its members.' It is a characteristic definition. Nor does that phase of thought appear in Jeremy Bentham alone. It is characteristic of the century in which it appeared. No body of any kind is constituted by the members alone. Any unity has to be looked at from two points of view, and is never the sum of its parts. Regard must be had to the wholeness of the whole as well as to the parts. But society or a people is not a fictitious body, of which individuals are the fictitious parts or members; a people is a unity, an organic whole, and the individuals are so in relation to the whole.

'Just as the organs are produced by the whole and exist in it alone, so the individuals are produced by the people, and live and move in it alone; they function as its organs, they speak its language, they think its thoughts, they are interested in its welfare, they desire its life; they propagate and rear offspring and so perpetuate the race. And this objective relation of the individual to the whole manifests itself subjectively in his volitional and emotional life. Everywhere the circles of the ego and the non-ego intersect. The fact is universally accepted; only in moral philosophy we still find persons who do not see it, but insist on regarding the antithesis between altruism and egoism as an absolute one. I should like to show how little the facts agree with this view; in our actual life and practice there is no such isolation of individuals; the motives and effects of action are constantly intersecting the boundaries of egoism and altruism' (Paulsen, *A System of Ethics* [Eng. tr.], pp. 381–3.

Professor Paulsen proceeds to show that every duty towards individual life can be construed as a duty towards others as well. Care of one's own health might appear to be purely selfish, yet on reflexion it appears that the possession of good health may add to the happiness of a community.

'The ill-humour which results from an improper mode of life, or a neglect of self, is not confined to the guilty person; he is cross and irritable, and his moodiness and moroseness are a source of annoyance to the whole household. In case of serious illness the family becomes uneasy and anxious, and perhaps suffers materially from a diminished income and an increase of expenditure. When the patient is an official, his colleagues are made to suffer; they have to do his work; if he has absolutely ruined his health, he becomes a pensioner, and so increases the public burdens' (*ib.* pp. 383–4).

It is not possible really to separate self-interest from the interest of society. The worths, values, and interests of the individual are inseparably bound up with those of society. It is society that gives life, warmth, and colour to the Ego feelings, and the life, warmth, and colour of the Ego feelings, their intensity and| their sweetness, are needed for the vitalization of society. The analogy of the organism holds good with regard to the social organism. But the idea of a social organism as a systematic whole, indeed the idea of a world as a systematic whole, can exist only for a being who is conscious of the unity of his individual life as connected with an organism which is a unity. But to pursue this further would open up issues wider than fall to be discussed here. The observation has been made to show that from the metaphysical point of view, as well as from the psychological and the ethical, the individual cannot be severed from the whole, and that the antithesis between Egoism and Altruism is both misleading and ultimately unthinkable.

It is not our purpose to name, far less to discuss, the various forms of Hedonism. It may be observed, however, that from Butler's time an enlightened self-regard is recognized to be a legitimate form of moral sentiment; while a regard for the welfare of others enters also into all forms of virtue. A rational regard for the welfare of others expresses itself in every one of what by way of eminence are called the cardinal virtues;—in courage, temperance, and constancy; in wisdom, justice, and truth; in kindness and benevolence. But, again, these virtues are concrete facts which have their being in some individual person. They are not something in the air, or something that has merely an abstract existence. And then, just as they belong to some individual, so they flourish only as he finds himself rooted in society. The higher features of human character, which make these virtues possible in the individual, have emerged in human history through the social effort of man. The higher faculties of man, and the virtues evolved with them and through them, grew in him as a social being,—a being who must live with his kind, who works with his mates, who can come to himself and to his fruition only in fellowship with his fellow-men.

The antithesis may be put, finally, in another way. The individual seeks his own good, his own happiness, his own satisfaction. But what does he mean by these terms? A desire for good is not a desire for mere pleasant feeling. It is a desire for self-satisfaction, for a better, truer, more real self; for a self which shall approach nearer to that ideal of a self which has dawned upon his intelligence. A wider thought and a truer thought, a deeper and a purer feeling; a power of activity which shall bring his ideal to reality—these express some aspect of the good a man desires. But it is only through the social bond and by means of social effort that the making of such a self is possible. It is not too much to say that it is only through social effort and through social life that man becomes a living soul.

It is in virtue of the social solidarity of mankind that the individual man enters into the inheritance of all the past. It is through this social bond and effort that he has subdued the earth and made it his servant. It is in his social life that man has come to the conclusion that he is the crown and sum of things, that the cosmos has toiled and worked upwards towards him, and in him has become conscious of itself and its meaning. In association man feels that he can make physical powers fetch and carry for him, make the winds his messengers, and harness the lightning to his carriage. It is not necessary to enumerate the social achievements of man. But there is not one of them which has not originated in the thought of a solitary mind, and then become the common possession of many minds. Yet the thought would never have come to the solitary thinker unless he had previously been prepared to think through his social environment, and by the great tradition of the ages. It is on this fact that we lay stress as the reconciliation of Egoism and Altruism, for it is the refutation of the idea which persists in so many quarters that man is inherently selfish, and has regard only to his self-interest, that he is naturally egoistic, and altruistic only in a secondary and fictitious fashion. Even Reason has been so spoken of, and the Synthetic Reason has been described as a selfish, analytic, destructive faculty, a weapon cunningly devised to enable its possessor to survive in the struggle for existence.

LITERATURE.—Butler, *Sermons*; Adam Smith, *Moral Sentiments*; Darwin, *Descent of Man*[2], 1871; H. Spencer, *Data of Ethics*[1], 1879; Stephen, *Science of Ethics*, 1882; Ladd, *Philosophy of Conduct*, 1902; Mackenzie, *Introduction to Social Philosophy*[2], 1890; Bowne, *Introduction to Psychological Theory*, 1886; Paulsen, *System of Ethics*, 1899. See also the works of J. S. Mill, Sidgwick, and Bain; and specially Albee, *History of English Utilitarianism*, 1902, and Villa, *Contemporary Psychology*, 1903.

JAMES IVERACH.

AMANA SOCIETY.—The Amana Society, or Community of True Inspiration, is an organized community of about 1800 German people who live in seven villages on the banks of the Iowa River in Iowa County, Iowa. This unique society owns 26,000 acres of land, which, together with personal property, is held in common. Indeed, the Amana Society is thoroughly communistic both in spirit and in organization. And yet it is in no sense a product of communistic philosophy. Primarily and fundamentally the Community of True Inspiration is a Church, organized for religious purposes, to work out the salvation of souls through the love of God (Constitution of the Society, Art. I.). The communism of Amana, therefore, is neither a political tenet, nor an economic theory, nor yet a social panacea, but simply a means of serving God 'in the inward and outward bond of union according to His laws and His requirements' (*ib.* Art. I.).

1. **History.**—As a Church, or distinct religious sect, the Community of True Inspiration traces its origin back to the year 1714 and to the writings of Eberhard Ludwig Gruber and Johann Friedrich Rock, who are regarded as the founders or 'Fathers' of the 'New Spiritual Economy' of True Inspiration. Both Gruber and Rock were members of the Lutheran Church who had become interested in the teachings of the early Mystics and Pietists. Having studied the philosophy of Spener, they endeavoured to improve upon and formulate especially the doctrines of that little band of Pietists whose followers during the last quarter of the 17th cent. were called 'Inspirationists,' and who are said to have 'prophesied like the prophets of old' (cf. Perkins and Wick, *Hist. of the Amana Soc.*).

The unique fundamental doctrine of the founders of the 'New Spiritual Economy' was *present-day inspiration.* To be sure, Gruber and Rock believed profoundly in the inspiration of the Bible; but they argued:

'Does not the same God live to-day? And is it not reasonable to believe that He will inspire His followers now as then? There is no reason to believe that God has in any way changed His methods of communication; and as He revealed hidden things through visions, dreams, and by revelations in olden times, He will lead His people to-day by the words of His Inspiration if they but listen to His voice' (Gruber, *Characteristics of the Divine Origin of True Inspiration*).

Divine inspiration did not come, however, to all members of the Community, but only through those who were especially endowed by the Lord with the 'miraculous gift of inspiration.' These especially endowed individuals, called *Werkzeuge* ('Instruments'), were simply passive agencies through whom the Lord testified and spoke to His children (Gruber, *Divine Nature of Inspiration*).

The nature of the 'new word and testimony,' as revealed through the *Werkzeuge*, and its relation to the earlier revelations of the Heb. prophets are clearly set forth by Gruber in these words: 'Its truths are in common with the written word of the prophets and the apostles. . . . It aspires for no preference; on the contrary, it gives the preference to the word of the witnesses first chosen [prophets and apostles] just after the likeness of two sons or brothers, in which case the oldest son as the first-born has the preference before the younger son who was born after him, though they are both equal and children begotten of one and the same father.' Again he says: 'Both the old and the new revelation, of which we here speak, are of divine origin and the testimonies of one and the same Spirit of God and of Jesus Christ, just as the sons mentioned above are equally children of one and the same father though there exists through the natural birth a slight difference between them' (Gruber, *Characteristics of the Divine Origin of True Inspiration*).

Not all, however, who aspired to prophecy and felt called upon to testify were to be accorded the privilege. For there were false as well as true spirits. Gruber, who wrote much concerning true and false inspiration, records in his *Autobiography* his own sensations in detecting the presence of a false spirit:

'This strange thing happened. If perchance a false spirit was among them [the congregation] and wished to assail me in disguise, or if an insincere member wished to distinguish himself at our meeting in prayer or in some other manner, then I was befallen by an extraordinary shaking of the head and shivering of the mouth; and it has been proven a hundred times that such was not without significance, but indeed a true warning, whatever he who is unskilled and inexperienced in these matters may deem of it according to his academic precepts and literal conclusions of reasons' ('Articles and Narrations of the Work of the Lord' given in *Inspirations-Historie*, vol. ii. p. 33).

That the appearance of false spirits was not uncommon is evidenced by the many instances, given in the *Year Books*, or *Testimonies of the Spirit of the Lord*, where aspiring *Werkzeuge* are condemned, and by the fact that Gruber's son was 'especially employed [by the Lord] to detect false spirits wherever they made themselves conspicuous, and to admonish them with earnestness to true repentance and change of heart' (*IH* * ii. 41).

* *IH* will be used in this art. for *Inspirations-Historie*.

Gruber and Rock, who had 'the spirit and gfit of revelation and inspiration . . . went about preaching and testifying as they were directed by the Lord.' They travelled extensively through Germany, Switzerland, Holland, and other European countries, establishing small congregations of followers. Those desiring to share in the 'New Spiritual Economy' and enjoy the blessings of 'True Inspiration' were asked such questions as—

(1) 'Whether he (or she) intends to behave as a true member of the Community of Jesus Christ towards the members, and also in respect to the public Prayer Meetings and the arrangement of the same? (2) Whether he (or she) be ready to suffer all inward and external pain, and to risk cheerfully through the mercy of God everything, even body and soul? (3) Whether he (or she) had obtained Divine conviction with regard to the work and word of inspiration, and whether he for his purification and sanctification would submit to the same? (4) Whether he (or she) was in a state of reconciliation, or in some disagreement with some brother or sister; also if he had anything to say against any one, or if any one had anything to say against him' (*IH* i. 50).

Although the number of congregations established during the time of Rock and Gruber was not large, considerable religious fervour was aroused by their teachings. Moreover, their attacks upon 'the utter hollowness and formality' of the established Church, and their bold denunciation of the 'godless and immoral lives' of many of the clergy of that day, aroused the authorities of the orthodox Church to active opposition. They also encountered the opposition of the political authorities, because they refused to perform military service or to take the required oath of allegiance. They refused to 'serve the State as soldiers, because a Christian cannot murder his enemy, much less his friend.' On the other hand, they refused to take the legal oath as a result of their literal adherence to the commands given in Mt $5^{34.37}$: 'But I say unto you, Swear not at all'; and 'Let your communication be, Yea, yea; Nay, nay: for whatsoever is more than these cometh of evil.'

Concerning the arrest of himself and his companions, because they would not upon one occasion take the prescribed oath, the younger Gruber, writing in 1717, says: 'Before the city gate the executioner untied us in the presence of the sheriff. The latter held in his hand a parchment with the oath written upon it and bade us to raise three fingers and to repeat it. We replied that we should not swear. He urged us forcibly with many threats. The brother (H. S. Gleim) repeated again that we should not swear; we should give a promise with hand-shake and our word should be as good as an oath, yet he would leave to me the freedom to do as I pleased. I affirmed then likewise I should not swear, since our Saviour had forbidden it' (*IH* ii. 124).

Furthermore, both the Church and the Government were irritated by the refusal of the Inspirationists to send their children to the schools which were conducted by the Lutheran clergy. Opposition soon grew into persecution and prosecution. And so the believers in 'True Inspiration' were fined, pilloried, flogged, imprisoned, and stripped of their possessions. In Zürich, Switzerland, 'their literature was by order of the city council burned in public by the executioner' (*IH* i. 65). Naturally, as their persecution became more severe, the congregations of Inspirationists sought refuge in Hesse—one of the most liberal and tolerant of the German states of the 18th century.

The *Tagebuch* for the year 1728 records that on Dec. 11, 'after a blessed period of two times seven years spent in the service of this Brotherhood and Community into which the Lord through His holy Inspiration had led him, the time came to pass when it pleased the Lord to recall His faithful worker and servant E. L. Gruber from this life and to transplant him into a blissful eternity.' Twenty-one years later, on March 2, occurred the death of J. F. Rock, which is recorded in this characteristic fashion: 'The time of his pilgrimage on earth was 10 times 7, or 70 years, 3 months and 3 days. In the year 1707, when he was 4 times 7 years old, he emigrated with Brother E. L. Gruber from his native country. In the year 1714, when he counted 5 times 7 years, there came to him the gift of the Spirit and of Prophecy, and he made until 1742, in 4 times 7 years, over 100 lesser and great journeys in this service. In the year 1728, when he was 7 times 7 years old, he lost his faithful brother, E. L. Gruber. And in 1742, when he counted 9 times 7, or 63 years, he ceased to travel into distant countries and spent the remaining 7 years (of his life) largely at home' (*Testimonies of the Spirit of the Lord*, 1749).

With the death of Rock in 1749 the congregations of the 'New Spiritual Economy' began to decline. Left without a *Werkzeug*, the members relied chiefly upon the writings and testimonies of Rock and Gruber for guidance and spiritual consolation.

'At the beginning of the 19th cent. but few of the once large congregations remained; even these few had fallen back into the ways of the common world, more or less, preferring the easy-going way to the trials and tribulations suffered by their fathers' (Noe, *Brief Hist. of the Amana Soc. or Community of True Inspiration*, Amana, Iowa, 1900, p. 6).

The decline continued until 1817, when it is recorded that 'a new and greater period dawned for the Community' (*IH* i. 429), and that 'Michael Kraussert was the first *Werkzeug* which the Lord employed for the now commencing revival.'

The 'Revival,' 'Awakening,' or 'Reawakening' of 1817 began with the testimonies of Kraussert, whose first inspired utterance was given to the congregation at Ronneburg on September 11, 1817, as a summons in these words: 'Oh Ronneburg, Ronneburg, where are thy former champions, the old defenders of faith? They no longer are at this present day, and effeminates dwell in the citadel. Well, then! Do ye not desire to become strong? The eternal power is offered to you' (*Testimonies of the Spirit of the Lord*, 1817).

Michael Kraussert was a journeyman tailor of Strassburg, who had been converted to the faith of the Inspirationists through the writings and testimonies of Rock. With great zeal and much religious fervour he seems to have played an important part in the 'Reawakening.' And yet it is recorded that he lacked courage in the face of persecution; that 'at the arrest and subsequent examination at Bergzabern he showed fear of men and resulting weakness'; that in the presence of hostile elders he 'became timid and undecided, and ran, so to speak, before he was chased'; and that 'through such fear of men and reluctance for suffering he lost his inner firmness in the mercy of the Lord, went gradually astray from the Divine guidance, and soon fell back into the world' (*IH* iii. 34, 429).

After the 'fall' of Kraussert (whose connexion with the Inspirationists was therewith severed), the spiritual affairs of the Community were directed by the *Werkzeuge* Christian Metz and Barbara Heinemann, who came to be regarded as the founders and leaders of what is sometimes called in the records the 'New Community.'

When Michael Kraussert, Christian Metz, and Barbara Heinemann appeared as *Werkzeuge* at the time of the 'Reawakening,' a century had elapsed since Gruber and Rock preached the doctrines of the 'New Spiritual Economy.' But the persecution of independents in religious thought had not ceased; and so these new prophets were repeatedly arrested, and their followers 'were attacked and insulted on the streets and elsewhere' (*IH* iii. 70).

As a century before, so now the growing congregations of Inspirationists sought refuge in Hesse, where on October 31, 1831, it is recorded, 'the Lord sent a message to the Grand Duke of Hesse-Darmstadt as a promise of grace and blessing because he had given protection to the Community in his country' (*IH* iii. 96). It was at this time that the far-sighted Christian Metz conceived the idea of leasing some large estate in common which should serve as a refuge for the faithful, where each could be given 'an opportunity to earn his living according to his calling or inclination.'

And so, in the year 1826, 'it came about through the mediation of the Landrath of Büdingen that a part of the castle at Marienborn was given in rent by the noble family of Meerholz, which was very convenient for the Community, since it lay near Ronneburg,' the home of the principal elders (*IH* iii. 68).

In all, four estates were rented, and to the administration of these four estates, located within a radius of a few miles and placed under one common management, are traced the beginnings of the communistic life of the Inspirationists. Communism, however, formed no part of their religious doctrines. It was simply a natural development out of the conditions under which they were forced to live in their efforts to maintain the integrity of their religion. Under a common roof they hoped to live simply and peacefully the true Christian life. And so rich and poor, educated and uneducated, professional man, merchant, manufacturer, artizan, farmer, and labourer met together as a religious brotherhood to worship and plan the labours of the day.

But independence and prosperity were not yet fully won. The day of complete religious and economic freedom for which they hoped had not come. Cherished liberties relative to military service, legal oaths, and separate schools were still denied. Rents became exorbitant, while excessive heat and drought destroyed the harvests.

It was in the midst of their depression that 'the Lord revealed through His instrument, Christian Metz, that He would lead them out of this land of adversity to one where they and their children could live in peace and liberty' (Noe, *Brief History*, p. 15). Indeed, this 'hidden prophecy,' uttered by Christian Metz on May 20, 1826, was now recalled: 'I proceed in mysterious ways, saith thy God, and my foot is seldom seen openly. I found my dwelling in the depths, and my path leadeth through great waters. I prepare for me a place in the wilderness, and establish for me a dwelling where there was none' (*Testimonies of the Spirit of the Lord*, 1826).* This was interpreted as pointing the way to America. And so there was much discussion concerning emigration to the wildernesses of the New World. Finally, there came through the *Werkzeug*, Christian Metz, these words from the Lord: 'Your goal and your way shall lead towards the west, to the land which still is open to you and your faith. I am with you, and shall lead you over the sea. Hold Me and call upon Me through your prayers when storms or temptations arise. . . . Four may then prepare themselves' (*TSL*, July 26, 1842). Thereupon Christian Metz and three others were named through inspiration to visit America; and they were given 'full power to act for all the members, and to purchase land where they deemed best' (Noe, *Brief History*, p. 15).

After a voyage of many hardships and privations, the committee of Inspirationists reached New York City on October 26, 1842. After three months of careful deliberation they purchased a tract of five thousand acres of the Seneca Indian Reservation lands in Erie County, New York. Within four months of the purchase the first village of the Community was laid out and peopled. They called it Ebenezer.

Other villages were soon founded, and under the name of 'Ebenezer Society' the Community was

* Hereafter referred to as *TSL*.

formally organized with a written constitution. It is recorded that during 'the planting and building of the new home' the Lord 'gave precepts, directions, and explanations concerning the external and internal affairs of that time' through His 'holy word and testimony' (*IH* iii. 329).

With the transplanting of the Community of True Inspiration to America there came a serious consideration of communism as a plan for organizing and conducting the economic life of the Society. To live simply as a Christian congregation, or church, was, of course, the fundamental aim of the Community. But they had found the practice of communism conducive to that end. Besides, 'the Lord had gradually announced more and more clearly that it was His intention and pleasure, nay His most holy will, that everything should be and remain in common' (*IH* iii. 367).

It was in the midst of the discussion over communism that 'a very important revelation occurred again at Mittel Ebenezer on October 23, 1850, in which the Lord expressed His grief and displeasure over the discontent of many members with regard to common possession' (*TSL*, 1850). And on March 19, 1852, the 'Lord testified most emphatically and earnestly to put to shame those who would not believe and trust in the Lord and the Brethren. He announced that it was not His holy will, and never should be, that communism should be abolished; and He pronounced His curse upon all those who would attempt it, but gave a most gracious promise to those who would faithfully preserve it.' This testimony, which was given through Christian Metz, reads in part as follows: 'As truly as I live, saith the Lord, it is at no time my will to dissolve the ties of the Community in such manner, or to suffer its dissolution, neither through artful devices or skill and diplomacy, nor cunning or power of men. Nay, the faith which hath love and the bond of peace for its essence and foundation shall continue to exist. And there shall come eternal disgrace, shame, and disfavour upon those who cause it; their children shall suffer want and be without blessing in time and eternity. Their material possessions shall melt away, and the divine treasure they have disavowed; therefore the Lord is against them' (*TSL*, 1852, No. 12). And thereupon the erring Brethren 'did repent concerning it,' and signed the amendment to the Constitution providing for the adoption of absolute communism. This amendment, moreover, was incorporated in the new constitution adopted in the State of Iowa, and communism has ever since been one of the fundamental principles of the Community.

Thus it is evident that the object of the Community of True Inspiration is the worship of God in freedom according to their peculiar faith. Communism was adopted as one of the means to that end, but not in accordance with any understanding on the part of the Inspirationists of the social theories of Jesus. It has solved the problem of furnishing remunerative labour to the members, and has given them leisure 'to think upon the things that are of the Lord.'

Although more than eight hundred members had come from Germany to Ebenezer, many had remained in the old home. Those who came were largely of the peasant class. But they were men and women of character who were possessed of the enthusiasm born of moral earnestness. In their new home they enjoyed spiritual freedom, and were rewarded with a large measure of material prosperity.

As time went on, however, certain undesirable features of the location of their villages became more and more evident. In the first place, they suffered no little molestation from the Seneca Indians, who were tardy in leaving the Reservation. Then the rapid growth of the city of Buffalo (only five miles distant) caused such an advance in the price of real estate that the purchase of additional land to accommodate the growing Community was out of the question. And, finally, it became evident that the young people of the Community were too near the worldly influence of Buffalo to persevere in the injunction of Gruber, who said: 'Have no intercourse with worldly minded men, that ye be not tempted and be led astray.'

And so a committee was directed to go to the new State of Iowa, and there inspect the Government lands which were for sale. Out of one of the garden spots of Iowa they selected and purchased eighteen thousand acres of contiguous land.

A better selection for the new home could scarcely have been made. Through it meandered the beautiful Iowa River, bordered with the black soil of its fertile valley. On one side of the river the bluffs and uplands were covered with timber for fuel and building. Quarries there were of sandstone and limestone, while the clay of the hills was unexcelled for the making of brick. On the other side of the river stretched the rolling prairie land. To this splendid new domain, all ready for the plough and axe, the Inspirationists brought enthusiasm, industry, moral earnestness, and religious zeal.

The first village on the Iowa purchase was laid out during the summer of 1855. 'The time had now come,' writes Gottlieb Scheuner in his *IH*, 'that the new settlement in Iowa was to receive a name.' When the Community emigrated from Germany and settled near Buffalo in the State of New York, the Lord called that place Ebenezer, that is, 'Hitherto hath the Lord helped us.' Now He again led them out from there to a new place, which, as the work proceeded, was to be called 'Bleibtreu.' This had been laid into the heart of the *Werkzeug*, Christian Metz, who later poured it forth in a song beginning thus:

'Bleibtreu soll der Name sein
Dort in Iowa der Gemein.'

Since, however, it was difficult to express this word or name in English, it was proposed instead to use the Biblical name 'Amana,' which signifies *glaub' treu* ('believe faithfully') (cf. Song of Sol. 4^8). To this, it is recorded, the Lord gave His approval in a song on September 23, 1855. Henceforth the new home of the Community was known as Amana (*TSL*, 1855).

The removal from the old home to the new, from Ebenezer to Amana, covered a period of ten years. In addition to the first village, which had been given the name Amana, five additional villages were laid out by the year 1862—West Amana, South Amana, High Amana, East Amana, and Middle Amana. It was at this time that the Society, in order to secure railroad facilities, purchased the small village of Homestead. Twelve hundred members had come from Ebenezer; and by the time the sale of the Ebenezer lands had been completed, the Society's territory in Iowa consisted of twenty-six thousand acres.

In the year 1859 the Community was incorporated in accordance with the Laws of the State of Iowa under the name of 'The Amana Society.' The Constitution, which was also revised, came into force on the first day of January, 1860. This instrument is not a 'Declaration of Mental Independence,' nor a scheme for a 'One World-wide Socialistic Fraternal Brotherhood,' but a very simple, business-like document of ten articles.

On July 27, 1867, six years after the establishment of the last of the seven Iowa villages, and two years after the completion of the Ebenezer sale and the removal of the last detail of the Community to the new home in the West, Christian Metz, the *so hoch begabte und begnadigte* brother, 'through whom the weightiest and greatest things were wrought and accomplished,' was, after 'fifty years of effort and labour, recalled from the field of his endeavour' at the age of 72 years, 6 months, and 24 days (*IH* iii. 878).

Half a century—the most eventful years of the Community's inspiring history—bridges the interval between the 'bestowal of God's mercy' on Michael Kraussert at the time of the 'Reawakening' and the 'blessed departure and release' of Christian Metz in 1867. During that period the Community was never without a *Werkzeug*. 'Great undertakings and changes occurred,' and material progress unparalleled in communistic history was theirs.

After the death of Christian Metz 'the work of grace' was carried on by Barbara Heinemann, now Landmann (who lost her gift at the time of her marriage in 1823, but regained it in 1849 and retained it to the time of her death in 1883 at the age of ninety), and by the elders in whom the 'Lord manifested Himself so strongly and powerfully during the last illness of Brother Christian Metz.' Since the death of Barbara Landmann no *Werkzeug* has been called in the Community; but, as in the period following the death of Rock, 'well founded Brethren endowed with divine mercy, who are still living witnesses of the great blessing of Inspiration, carry on the work of the Lord in the Community.' How long the coming generations will 'fill the widening gap' with no *Werkzeug* for their spiritual guidance, and with the breaking of the link in the 'passing into eternity of these faithful witnesses and Elders,' which binds them to the past with its inspiring history, 'is ordained only in the hidden counsel of God.'

2. **Religion.**—Although communism may appear to the casual observer to be the most characteristic feature of the Amana Society, a careful study of the history and spirit of the Inspirationists reveals the fact that the real Amana is Amana the Church — Amana the Community of True Inspiration. Religion has always been the dominating factor in the life of the Community.

The basal doctrine of the Amana Church is *present-day inspiration and revelation.* That is, to use the words of the *Werkzeug* Eberhard Ludwig Gruber, 'God is ever present in the world, and He will lead His people to-day as in olden times by the words of His Inspiration if they but listen to His voice.' Indeed, it is the belief of these people that, ever since the beginning of the 'New Spiritual Economy,' the spiritual and temporal affairs of the Community have been immediately under Divine direction according to the 'decisive word of the Lord' as revealed through His specially endowed instruments the *Werkzeuge.* And so it appears throughout their history that in all 'important undertakings and changes, nay in the whole external and internal leadership of the Community, the *Werkzeug* had to bear the bulk of the burden and care, since the Lord ordained and directed everything through him directly.' Thus Divine inspiration and revelation came through the *Werkzeuge* (*IH* iii. 878).

Perhaps the best exposition of the nature of Inspiration, as understood by the Inspirationists, is found in Eberhard Ludwig Gruber's *Divine Nature of Inspiration*, where, in reply to the charge that he was an 'instrument of the Devil,' he sets forth his own 'convictions' as follows:

'Because I have not light-headedly and without test and experience come to the approval of these things.

'Because the testimonies of the inspired persons, although being at first adverse to me, have not in the least troubled me, nor aroused and stirred my emotions, as certainly would have happened to some extent if they had originated from a wicked and dark spirit.

'Because I have not been hindered thereby in the usual quiet introspective prayer granted to me by the mercy of God.

'Because during such a deep and earnest self-examination all scruples and objections to this matter were, without effort on my part, so completely removed and dispersed that not one remained which irritated me or which I could not comprehend.

'Because such prayer, which was absolutely without prejudice in the matter, has again won for me the precious gift of tears, which had become almost unknown to me.

'Because the Spirit of Inspiration penetrated into and laid bare those things which occurred in the most hidden corners of my heart, so that no creature could know them, and because it (the Spirit of Inspiration) also approved and commended those ways of mercy and sanctification in which the Lord had hitherto led me in affairs external and internal.

'Because the promises pronounced in regard to myself have not dazzled me or made me vain.

'Because at the same time the extinguished love was again renewed in the hearts of many.

'Because the assemblies of prayer recommended by the Spirit, and up to that time vainly striven for, were at once established to our joy and bliss, and without opposition of the then well-disposed individuals.

'Because I was led into the severest struggle for purification, instead of expecting at once the fulfilment of the great promises given me.

'Because this struggle searched my innermost self and has deeply impressed upon me the most vivid lessons of complete denial and negation of myself.

'Because in this matter also all external hindrances were removed, and I indeed was made willing and confident to throw them behind me, and to take upon me all the disgrace and suffering of this service, often confirming my faith under tests and with proofs not mentioned here, but known to God and also to others.

'Because the inner word was laid open and led forth from the depths of my heart, whither no divine creature, much less a satanic spirit, could reach, deeper and more abundantly than I ever possessed it before.

'Because those inner emotions known to me from my youth, but now become stronger and more numerous, have ever either held me back from some evil deed, or encouraged and urged me to some good act.

'Because they (inner emotions) often must with certainty reveal to me the presence of hidden false spirits rising against me or others.

'Because in all this I do not found my conclusions on the inspiration alone, as may be the case with others, but upon the undeniable work of God in my soul, which has gone on there for long years out of sheer mercy, and which under this new economy and revival is becoming ever more powerful.

'Because my son, together with many others, has been brought into a state of deepest repentance and wholesome anxiety of mind through the powerful Testimony of the Spirit in the inspired persons.

'Because the Word of the Lord was unsealed to him (the son) by the very first emotions (of the inspired one).

'Because the Spirit of Inspiration promptly appeared, as when it had been foretold that a certain married woman (*die Melchiorin*) would testify on the day mentioned in Bergheim.

'Because my son came to testify (make utterance) with great fear and trembling, nay even through the severest struggle, and surely not through his wish and vain desire.

'Because he was enabled and compelled in his first testimony, as a foreshadowing of the future, to denounce with great certainty an impure spirit, to the sincere humiliation of the latter.

'Because he (the son) was led in these ways of Inspiration, contrary to inclination and habit of his youth, to deep introspection and seclusion, and was also endowed with many extraordinary gifts of mercy.

'Because he made, far beyond his natural abilities, such pure, clear, and penetrating statements (utterances) that many well learned in divine and natural things were led to wonder.'

According to the belief of the Community of True Inspiration, the word and will of the Lord are communicated to the faithful through the specially endowed *Werkzeuge*, whose inspired utterances are in fact the *Bezeugungen*, that is, the Testimonies of the Lord. These are either written or oral. The gift of oral prophecy or testimony (*Aussprache*), being regarded as the highest form of inspiration, was not enjoyed by all the *Werkzeuge.* Indeed, the 'miraculous gift of *Aussprache*' was sometimes preceded by the humbler gift of *Einsprache*, when the *Werkzeug*, unable to give voice to his inspiration, committed his testimonies to writing. Thus the 'specially endowed' *Werkzeug*, Christian Metz, seems to have entered upon the 'service of the Lord' with simply the gift of *Einsprache*, which was later followed by the gift of *Aussprache*, and still later by the combined gifts of *Einsprache* and *Aussprache.* Sometimes the *Werkzeuge* were deprived of the gracious gifts of *Einsprache* and *Aussprache*, which were restored only after a period of deepest humility.

The inspired testimonies of the *Werkzeuge*, as recorded in the *Year Books*, or *Testimonies of the Spirit of the Lord*, vary in length from a few sentences to many pages. Some were uttered in rhyme; and there are instances where a testimony is given through two *Werkzeuge* speaking alternately. Under the date of Jan. 12, 1819, such a testimony was given by Michael Kraussert and Barbara Heinemann (*TSL*, 1819). From the records it appears that testimonies were addressed sometimes to the whole congregation of the Community, and sometimes to individual members.

As to content, the Testimonies touch a great variety of subjects, from the routine affairs of daily existence to impassioned admonitions to live the holy life. Many contain promises of the love and mercy of the Lord. Others take the form of appeals of the 'God of Salvation' for more spiritual life. Some are warnings against *Lichtsinn*, pride, self-righteousness, and self-will; and especially are the *selbstständig* and *eigenmächtig* warned against the wrath of God. There are vigorous denunciations of the wicked, and there are threats of 'the hellish torture' and the 'gloomy abyss' for those who do not repent. But many more there are that teach and preach humility, obedience to the will of the Lord, self-negation, and repentance. Throughout, the testimonies suggest a wide familiarity with the language of the Bible, especially of the Old Testament.

The testimony of Christian Metz, given as a warning and admonition to Kraussert, is typical of the utterances of the *Werkzeuge.* It runs thus:

'Thus speaketh the eternal God: I will give a word of testimony to my servant Kraussert, who knoweth not now how to begin, so bewildered he is. But listen, then. What hath prompted thee to act and deal thus according to thine own inclinations? Thou hast run before thou wast sent away, saith the almighty God of Love. Alas, how troubled is my spirit, that thou hast failed thus, and dost not want to be found again! Oh come back again and resign thyself in and to the faithful tie of brotherhood which I have established, and which I have again strengthened through thee. Thou runnest about thus, and art like a hireling who hath seen the wolf and hath abandoned to him his flock and deserted. Is this the true faithfulness of the shepherd? Do faithful servants act thus, when the wolf cometh that they run away and step not into the gap to ward off harm? . . . Canst thou, then, say that I have deserted thee a single time, when thou wast persecuted for holy causes alone? Have I not ever helped thee again and satisfied thee? . . . Hear, then, what the God of Eternal Love furthermore testifieth in regard to thee: Thou art, then, not as faithful in thine office and service as thou wast, and thou dost not sufficiently submit thyself in and to my will; thou hast become too self-willed, and thou dost not want to heed the others, whom, too, I have summoned, and through whom I instruct thee. Alas, I do not wish to make known and have recorded all that I have to record against thee, saith the mighty God. But, nevertheless, thou shalt never succeed in this manner if thou returnest not soon and quickly again in and to the training of my love, and dost not more carefully tend my flock than at present. Oh, I still love thee and see thee in thine erring state; return, then, and care more diligently for the souls whom I have called.

'Indeed I shall help and always have helped thee! Why, then, dost thou lose courage now and desert ere thou wast sent away? Hath it ever been heard of, that my witnesses whom I have called from time to time have not also thus believed that they knew no fear? And though the whole world should rise and appear in the field against them, and they themselves should be so weak that they could hardly stand on their feet, I will still be their God and their mighty protector, if they trust me in all things. Thus thou mayest see that I take no pleasure at all in thy present course of action.

'Alas, my soul is troubled that the wild beasts have broken in in such number. Wilt thou then, too, turn a hireling and scatter the sheep which I so miraculously have led together? saith the mighty God. Alas, return then again and lead them on as a faithful servant and shepherd; with the staff of the true love of the shepherd seize firmly upon faith; then I will assist thee again and give back the inward peace, love, and simplicity. Submit cheerfully to this punishment, for it is my will that it may become known thus that no mortal may boast of his importance' (*TSL*, 1819).

The giving or uttering of oral testimonies by the *Werkzeug* seems to have been accompanied by a more or less violent shaking of the body (*Bewegung*), which is described by one of the scribes in these words:

'With regard to the *Bewegungen*, the *Werkzeuge* were not alike; although they were all moved by one Spirit, there was considerable difference in regard to their gifts and commotions or convulsions. When they had to announce punishments and judgments of God, they all did it with great force, majestic gestures, strong motions, and with a true voice of thunder, especially if this occurred on the public streets or in churches. But when they had to speak of the love of God and the glory of the children of God, then their motions were gentle and the gestures pleasing; but all, and in all attitudes assumed by them, spoke with closed eyes. Often they had, some time previous to the *Bewegung*, a feeling of its approach. Again they were seized suddenly, often at their meals, by day and by night. At times they were aroused from their slumber, and had to testify frequently on the public highways, in fields and forests. In short, they were instruments in the hands of the Lord, and had no control over themselves.

'Violent as the commotions of the body often were, still they did no harm to the body; on the contrary, they served often as remedies if the *Werkzeuge* were ill, as on the occasion of the *Werkzeug* who on a journey lay seriously ill at Halle, Saxony, and was very weak in body, when he suddenly, to the terror of those present, was seized with violent convulsions and had to testify. In the utterance he received orders to start on the journey, at which all were surprised. After the testimony the *Werkzeug* arose and was well at the very moment, and on the following day they departed' (*IH*, ii. 295).

The belief in the genuineness and Divine nature of the *Bewegungen* is set forth in an account of an interesting interview which took place between the younger Gruber and his *Schreiber* and two Jewish Rabbis in a synagogue at Prague. The account, which is recorded under the date of Jan. 30, 1716, is a comparison of the manner of prophesying by the *Werkzeuge* of the Inspirationists and the old Hebrew prophets. It reads in part:

'Hereupon came two old grey-headed Rabbis and questioned us. This is the reason why I have recorded the happenings. They asked, in the first place, where we had our home. Answer: Near Frankfort. Question: Of what religion? Answer: We call ourselves Christians. They said they believed that, and that they knew full well that not all are Christians who call themselves Christians, just as, among themselves, not all were Jews who called themselves Jews; and that they asked only for the sake of the outer distinction. Thereupon I replied that one of us had been reared in the Reformed Church, the other among the Lutherans. They asked: Which of you is, then, the Prophet of the Lord? I pointed to Gruber. Now they questioned further: How does the word of the Lord come to this Prophet? Does it come through an external voice into the ears, or from within? Reply: Not from without, but from within, and, to be explicit, in the following manner: The *Werkzeug*, or the Prophet, feels at first in his innermost being a gentle and pleasant glow, which gradually becomes more intense and also fills the external body; thereupon results an inflation of the nose and a trembling of the whole body; at last, violent motions of the whole body, often attended by kicking with hands and feet and shaking of the head; and in the centre of this internal fire the word of the Lord is born; and the Prophet is enabled, through the *Bewegungen*, to pronounce the word of the Lord without fear or awe, such as it was born in him, at times syllable by syllable, at times word by word, now slowly, now rapidly, so that the *Werkzeug* has no choice of his own, but is used solely as a passive instrument in the hand of the Lord.

'Now you will be able to inform us,—we said to them—since you are better acquainted with the Hebrew language than we, whether the old Prophets among the people of Israel also announced the word of the Lord through such strange gestures of the body and through *Bewegungen*? They replied, in kindness and humility: The word of the Lord had not been made known to them otherwise than from within; and if you should have said that the word of the Lord came to the Prophets of the present day from without, we should have rejected it. Nor do the commotions of the body surprise us at all, since this has been a positive characteristic of the old Prophets; for he who spoke without these commotions of the body was not considered a true Prophet; wherefore we, in imitation of the Prophets of old, unceasingly move when we sing our psalms' (*IH*, ii.).

Ever since the time of the founders (Rock and Gruber) of the 'New Spiritual Economy' the testimonies of the *Werkzeuge* have been 'correctly written down from day to day and in weal or woe' by specially appointed scribes. Indeed, the *Werkzeug* was usually accompanied by a scribe, whose duty it was faithfully to record all inspired utterances. Moreover, the testimonies of the *Werkzeuge* have been printed by the Community in yearly volumes, entitled: 'Year Book of the Community of True Inspiration, or Testimonies of the Spirit of the Lord wherewith the Lord has Blessed and Endowed His Community Anew, Revealed and Uttered through,' etc., with the name of the *Werkzeug*, the year, and the number of the collection (*Sammlung*). In these volumes, which have been distributed only among the members of the Community, each testimony is numbered and briefly introduced as:

'No. 54 (20th Collection).—*Nieder Ebenezer*, October 12, 1845. Sunday afternoon, in the meeting of the Sisters, Brother Christian Metz fell into inspiration while an old testimony was being read, and he had to utter the following testimony from the Lord to the members of this meeting.' Or—

'No. 39 (53rd Collection).—*Heimstätte*, February 27, 1878. When on the afternoon of this day all the elders from the other settlements had met with the elders of this place and Sister Barbara Landmann, in order to begin the examination (*Unterredung*) still to be held in this Community, Sister Barbara Landmann fell at the very start into inspiration, and there occurred a decision through the word concerning Brother —— because of his attachment to the teachings of Swedenborg. Then followed an admonition to the other elders to work in harmony, and to promote the work of the Lord in the same spiritual love of souls.'

The Community of True Inspiration is without a creed, but professes the 'literal word of God' as found in the Bible and in the Testimonies of the *Werkzeuge*. As to its ethical and religious standards of conduct, these are, perhaps, best set forth in the 'One and Twenty Rules for the Examination of our Daily Lives,' by Eberhard Ludwig Gruber, published in 1715, and in the 'Twenty-four Rules for True Godliness,' revealed through Johann Adam Gruber in 1716, 'according to which the new communities were established and received into the gracious covenant of the Lord.' The 'Rules for the Examination of our Daily Lives' are as follows:

'I. To obey God without reasoning, and, through God, our superiors.

'II. To study quiet, or serenity, within and without.

'III. Within, to rule and master your thoughts.

'IV. Without, to avoid all unnecessary words, and still to study silence and quiet.

'V. To abandon self, with all its desires, knowledge, and power.

'VI. Do not criticize others, either for good or evil, either to judge or to imitate them; therefore contain yourself, remain at home, in the house and in your heart.

'VII. Do not disturb your serenity or peace of mind—hence neither desire nor grieve.

'VIII. Live in love and pity toward your neighbour, and indulge neither anger nor impatience in your spirit.

'IX. Be honest and sincere, and avoid all deceit and even secretiveness.

'X. Count every word, thought, and deed as done in the immediate presence of God, in sleeping or waking, eating, drinking, etc., and give Him at once an account of it, to see if all is done in His fear and love.

'XI. Be in all things sober, without levity or laughter, and without vain and idle words, deeds, or thoughts, much less heedless or idle.

'XII. Never think or speak of God without the deepest reverence, fear, and love, and therefore deal reverently with all spiritual things.

'XIII. Bear all inward and outward sufferings in silence, complaining only to God; and accept all from Him in deepest reverence and obedience.

'XIV. Notice carefully all that God permits to happen to you in your inward and outward life, in order that you may not fail to comprehend His will and to be led by it.

'XV. Have nothing to do with unholy, and particularly with needless, business affairs.

'XVI. Have no intercourse with worldly-minded men; never seek their society; speak little with them, and never without need; and then not without fear and trembling.

'XVII. Therefore, what you have to do with such men, do in haste; do not waste time in public places and worldly society, lest you be tempted and led away.

'XVIII. Fly from the society of women-kind as much as possible, as a very highly dangerous magnet and magical fire.

'XIX. Avoid obeisance and the fear of men; these are dangerous ways.

'XX. Dinners, weddings, feasts, avoid entirely; at the best there is sin.

'XXI. Constantly practise abstinence and temperance, so that you may be as wakeful after eating as before.'

The 'Twenty-four Rules for True Godliness' appear as a part of a lengthy testimony in which the Lord commands a renewal of the Covenant 'before my holy face and in the presence of my holy angels and of the members of your community,' which ceremony is still observed in the community by shaking hands with the presiding elder in open meeting. The concluding paragraph of the admonitory introduction and the 'Twenty-four Rules for True Godliness' are as follows:—

'Hear then what I say unto you. I, the Lord your God, am holy! and therefore ye, too, shall be and become a holy community, if I am to abide in your midst as ye desire. And therefore you shall henceforth resolve:

'I. To tear all crude and all subtle idols out of your hearts, that they may no longer befool you and mislead further to idolatry against your God, so that His name be not defamed and He go not suddenly forth, and avenge and save the glory of His name.

'II. I desire that ye shall have nought in common with the fruitless works of darkness; neither with the grave sins, and sinners, nor with the subtle within and without you. For what relationship and likeness hath My holy temple with the temples of pride, unchastity, ambition, and seeking for power, and of the useless, superfluous, condemning prattling, which stealeth time away from me? How could the light unite with the darkness? How can ye as children of the light unite with the ungodly, the liars and their works, the scoffers and blasphemers, who are nothing but darkness?

'III. Ye shall henceforth in your external life conduct yourselves so that those standing without find no longer cause for ill reports and for defaming My name. Rather suffer wrong if ye are abused. But above all flee from associations which hinder you from growing in godliness. All mockers and scoffers, and those who recommend you unto vanity, ye shall shun, and have no dealings with them.

'IV. Ye shall also perform your earthly task the longer and more according to the dictates of your conscience, and gladly desist from that which My Spirit showeth you to be sinful —not heeding your own loss, for I am the Lord, Who can and will care and provide for the needs of your body—that through this ye may not give cause for censure to the scoffer. The time which I still grant you here is very short; therefore, see to it well that My hand may bring forth and create a real harvest within you.

'V. Let, I warn you, be far from you all falseness, lying, and hypocrisy. For I say unto you that I will give the spirit of discernment and shall lay open such vices unto you through Him and the Spirit of Prophecy. For to what end shall clay and metal be together? Would it not make for me a useless vessel, which I could not use and should have to cast away with the refuse? Behold, my children, I have chosen you before many, many, many, and have promised to be unto you a fiery entrenchment against the defiance of your inner and outer enemies. Verily! Verily! I shall keep My promises, if ye only endeavour to fulfil what ye have promised and are promising.

'VI. Ye shall, therefore, none of you, strive for particular gifts, and envy the one or the other to whom I give, perchance, the gift of prayer or maybe of wisdom. For such the enemy of My glory seeketh ever to instil into you, especially into the passionate and fickle souls, to impart to you thereby a poison destructive to the soul. Ye shall, all, all, all of you be filled with My pure and holy Spirit when the time shall come to pass, if ye shall let yourselves be prepared in humility and patience according to my will. Then ye, too, shall speak with tongues different from the tongues ye now speak with. Then I shall be able to communicate with you most intimately.

'VII. Put aside henceforth all backbiting, and all malice of the heart toward each other, which ye have harboured hitherto! None of you are free from it. Behold I shall command the Spirit of My love, that He, as often as ye assemble for prayer in true simplicity of heart and in humility, be in your very midst with His influence and may flow through the channels of His love into the hearts he findeth empty.

'VIII. Ye must make yourselves willing for all outer and inner suffering. For Satan will not cease to show unto you his rancour through his servants and through his invisible power. It is also pleasing to Me and absolutely necessary for you that ye be tried through continuous sorrow, suffering, and the cross, and be made firm and precious in My crucible. And he who doth not dare—but none must be indolent himself in this—to exert all his physical and spiritual powers through My strength, let him depart, that he may not be later a blemishing spot upon My glory.

'IX. Do not in future lend your ears to suspicion and prejudice and, because of your lack of self-knowledge, find offence in each other, where there is none. But each one among you shall become a mirror for the other. Ye shall, moreover, also endeavour to stand every day and hour before the Lord as a unity, as a city or a light on a high mountain, which near and far shineth bright and pure.

'X. At the same time practise more and more outer and inner quiet. Seek ever, though it will be for the natural man which is inexperienced in this a hard death, to hide yourselves in humility in the inner and undermost chamber of your nothingness, that in this soil I may bring to a befitting growth My seed, which I have concealed therein.

'XI. Behold, My people! I make with you this day a covenant which I bid you to keep faithfully and sacredly. I will daily wander amongst you and visit your place of rest, that I may see how ye are disposed toward Me.

'XII. Guard yourselves! I, the Lord, warn you against indifference towards this covenant of grace and against negligence, indolence, and laziness, which thus far have been for the most part your rulers and have controlled your heart. I shall not depart from your side nor from your midst, but shall Myself, on the contrary, reveal Myself ever more powerful, holier, and more glorious through the light of My face in and among you, as long as ye will bring forth to meet Me the honest and sincere powers of your will. This shall be the tie with which ye can bind and hold Me. Behold I accept you this day as slaves of My will, as free-born of My kingdom, as possessors of My heart. Therefore let yourselves gladly and willingly be bound with the ties of My love, and the power of love shall never be wanting unto you.

'XIII. And ye who are the heads and fathers of households, hear what I say unto you: The Lord hath now chosen you as members of His community, with whom He desireth to associate and dwell day by day. See therefore to this, that ye prove truly heads and lights of your households, which, however, always stand under their faithful Head, your King. See that ye may bring your help-mates to true conduct and fear of God through your own way of living, which ye shall strive to make ever more faultless, more earnest, and manly.

'XIV. Your children, ye who have any, ye shall endeavour with all your power to sacrifice to Me and lead to Me. I shall give you in abundance, if ye only keep close to Me inwardly, wisdom, courage, understanding, bravery, and earnestness mingled with love, that ye yourselves may be able to live before them in the fear of God, and that your training may be blessed, that is, in those who wish to submit to My hand in and through Me. But those who scorn you and do not heed My voice, in and through you and otherwise, shall have their blood come upon their own heads. But ye shall never abandon hope, but wrestle for them with earnest prayer, struggle, and toil, which are the pangs of spiritual birth. But if ye neglect them through indifference, negligence, half-heartedness, and laziness, then every such soul shall verily be demanded of such a father.

'XV. Do now your part as I command you from without and frequently inwardly through My Spirit; do not desist, just as I never cease to work on you, My disobedient children; then ye shall abide in My grace and save your souls. And such women and children shall bear the fruits of their sins as do not wish to bow themselves under you and Me. I will henceforth no longer tolerate those grave offences among you and in your houses about which the world and the children of wrath and disbelief have so much to say; but I have commanded the Spirit of My living breath that He pass through all your houses and breathe upon every soul which doth not wantonly close itself to Him. The dew of blessing shall flow from the blessed head of your High Priest and Prince of Peace upon every male or head among you, and through them it shall flow upon and into your help-mates, and through both man and wife into the offspring and children, so that all your seed shall be acceptable, pure, and holy before the Lord, since He Himself hath nourished and will nourish the same among you.

'XVI. And none of your grown-up children shall be permitted to attend your meetings who have not previously received from their parents a good testimony according to the truth, not appearance, and without self-deception, as also from the elders and leaders, especially from the one who with his fellow-workers hath to watch over the training of the children, which is to be carried on with earnestness and love, but without severity and harshness. This training is to be watched over with all earnestness, and should the parents be negligent and the case require it, then shall the latter be temporarily excluded [from the prayer meetings] for their humiliation.

'XVII. Prove yourselves as the people whom I have established for an eternal monument to Me, and whom I shall impress upon My heart as an eternal seal, so that the Spirit of My Love may dwell upon you and within you, and work according to His desire.

'XVIII. And this is the word which the Lord speaketh of these strangers who so often visit you and cause so much disturbance. None whom ye find to be a scoffer, hypocrite, mocker, sinner, derider, and unrepenting sinner, shall ye admit to your community and prayer meetings. Once for all they are to be excluded, that My refreshing dew and the shadow of My love be never prevented from manifesting themselves among you. But if some should come to you with honest intentions, who are not knowingly scoffers, hypocrites, and deriders, though it be one of those whom ye call of the world, if he to your knowledge doth not come with deceitful intentions, then ye may well admit him. I shall give you, My faithful servants and witnesses, especially the spirit of discrimination, and give you an exact feeling whether they are sincere and come with honest intentions or otherwise.

'XIX. If they then desire to visit you more frequently, ye shall first acquaint them with your rules, and ask them whether they will submit to these rules and to the test of the elders. And then ye shall read to them My laws and commands, which I give unto you; and if ye see that they are earnestly concerned about their souls, then ye shall gladly receive the weak, and become weak with them for a while, that is, ye shall, with them and for them, repent and make their repentance your own. But if a scoffer or mocker declare that he repenteth, him ye should admit only after considerable time and close scrutiny and examination of his conduct, if ye find the latter to be righteous. For Satan will not cease to try to launch at you his fatal arrows through such people. Be therefore on your guard, and watch lest the wolf come among you and scatter, or even devour, the sheep.

'XX. And those who pledge themselves with hand and mouth after the aforesaid manner to you shall make public profession before the community, and also make an open confession of their resolve, and I shall indeed show you if this latter cometh from their hearts; the conduct of those ye shall watch closely, whether they live according to their profession and promise or not, lest the dragon defile your garments.

'XXI. (To the elders.) Thus my elder and his fellow-workers shall frequently visit the members of the community and see how things are in their homes and how it standeth concerning their hearts. I shall give to you My servant (the *Werkzeug*) and to your brothers keen eyes, if ye only pray for it. And if ye find that one is in uncalled sadness, or liveth in negligence, impudence, licentiousness, or the like, then ye shall admonish him in love. If he repent, ye shall rejoice. But if after repeated admonition he doth not mend his ways, then ye shall put him to shame openly before the community; and if even this doth not help, then ye shall exclude him for a while. Yet I shall ever seek My sheep, those who are already excluded and those who in future, because of their own guilt, must be excluded, and I shall ever try to lead them in their nothingness into My pasture.

'XXII. And to all of you I still give this warning: let none of you reject brotherly admonition and punishment, lest secret pride grow like a poisonous thorn in such a member and torment and poison his whole heart.

'XXIII. Ye shall not form a habit of anything of the external exercises (forms of worship) and the duties commended to you; or I shall be compelled to forbid them again. On the contrary, your meetings shall make you ever more fervent, more earnest, more zealous, in the true simple love towards each other, fervent and united in Me, the true Prince of Peace.

'XXIV. This the members and brethren of the community shall sincerely and honestly pledge with hand and mouth to My elders, openly in the assembly, after they have carefully considered it, and it shall be kept sacred ever after' (*TSL*, 1819–1823).

From the records it appears that the members of the Community of True Inspiration are graded spiritually into three orders (*Abtheilungen*) according to the degree of their piety. Ordinarily, the spiritual rank of the individual is determined by age, since piety increases with years of 'sincere repentance and striving for salvation and deep humility of spirit.' Nevertheless, it remains for the Great Council of the Brethren at the yearly spiritual examination to judge of the spiritual condition of the members irrespective of age, and to 'take out of the middle order, here and there, some into the first, and out of the third into the second, not according to favour and prejudice, but according to their grace and conduct' (*The Supper of Love and Remembrance of the Suffering and Death of our Lord and Saviour Jesus Christ for 1855*). Moreover, reduction in spiritual rank follows the loss of piety, or as a punishment for evil doing. During the days of the *Werkzeuge* this spiritual classification of the members into *Abtheilungen* was made with 'great accuracy' through Inspiration.

There are three important religious ceremonies which are observed by the Community of True Inspiration with great solemnity. These are the renewing of the covenant (*Bundesschliessung*), the spiritual examination (*Untersuchung* or *Unterredung*), and the Lord's Supper or Love-feast (*Liebesmahl*).

Formerly the ceremony of renewing the covenant (*Bundesschliessung*) was appointed and arranged by the *Werkzeuge*; but it is recorded in *IH* iii. 872 that in 1863, 'when the annual common Thanksgiving Day [ordinarily the last Thursday of November] of the land came round, the Lord gave direction through His word that henceforth this day should annually be observed solemnly in the Communities as a day of Covenant, which has been and is still observed.' Every member of the Community, and every boy and girl fifteen years of age or more, take part in this ceremony. Following the usual religious exercises of hymn, silent prayer, reading from the Bible, and an exhortation by the head elder, the elders pass in turn to the head elder, who gives them a solemn shake of the hand, signifying a renewed allegiance to the faith and a pledge to 'cleave unto the ways of the Lord, that they may dwell in the land which the Lord sware unto their fathers.' Then the brethren one by one and according to age and spiritual rank, come forward and similarly pledge themselves by shaking the hand of the head elder and his associates. Finally, the sisters come forward, and in the same manner renew their allegiance to the work of the Lord.

The spiritual examination (*Untersuchung*), which is held annually, seems to be based upon the words of the Bible (Ja 5^{16}), which read: 'Confess your faults one to another, and pray one for another, that ye may be healed.' It serves as a preparation for the Love-feast (*Liebesmahl*) which follows. This ceremony of confession, with its sanctification and purification, seems to be participated in by every man, woman, and child in the Community. It is now conducted by the first brethren, although formerly it was the office of the *Werkzeuge* to ask the appropriate questions and to judge of the spiritual condition of each individual. Nor did the *Werkzeuge* hesitate to condemn the shortcomings of the members as revealed in this examination. And frequent were the exhortations to holier living, such as: 'Oh that ye were not given to the external, and that your eyes were directed inward! Pray the Lord, the God of your salvation, and live more sincerely for the true spirit of humility' (*TSL*, 1845).

Through the *Untersuchung* the people of the Community were prepared for the most elaborate and solemn of all the ceremonies of the Inspirationists, namely, the Lord's Supper or Love-Feast (*Liebesmahl*), which is now celebrated but once in two years. A special feature of the Love-feast as carried out by the Community of True Inspiration is the ceremony of foot-washing, which is observed at this time by the higher spiritual orders. Gottlieb Scheuner, the scribe, records, in reference to a particular Love-feast, the following:—

'The entire membership, excluding the young people under 15, was divided into three classes according to the conviction and insight of the brethren and the *Werkzeug* (Barbara Landmann) concerning the spiritual state of the respective people. Likewise the servants for the foot-washing, for the breaking of the bread, and for the distribution of bread and wine, also those who were to wait at the supper, as well as the singers and scribes, had to be chosen and arranged. . . . The number of those who were to serve had to be determined in proportion to the great membership. Thus there were appointed for the foot-washing at the first Love-feast 13 brothers and 12 sisters. . . . For the second Love-feast likewise 13 brothers and 14 sisters from the first class. . . . For the breaking of the bread and the passing of the wine two times 12 brethren were selected. . . . For the leading and the support of the singing 8 brethren and 4 sisters were chosen. Besides those, many of the best singers among the brethren and sisters of their respective class were selected and joined to the leaders, so that the whole choir consisted of 20, sometimes 22, persons, who in the afternoon during the meal had their place at a separate table in the middle of the hall. To write down the testimonies of the Lord, those then being teachers at the different communities were appointed' (*IH* iv. 57).

The regular or ordinary religious exercises of the Community of True Inspiration are extremely simple, for the Inspirationists believe that 'forms and ceremonies are of no value, and will never take a man to heaven.' In the several villages prayer meetings are held every evening in rooms set aside for the purpose. On Wednesday, Saturday, and Sunday mornings the people meet by orders (*Abtheilungen*), while on Sunday afternoon there is held from time to time a general meeting. Thus, exclusive of special exercises, there are eleven religious services held each week in the Community.

With the exception of the prayer-meetings, all the religious gatherings are held in the churches, of which there is one in each village. The church is very much like the ordinary dwelling-house, except that it is longer. The interior is severely plain. White-washed walls, bare floors, and unpainted benches bespeak the simple unpretentious faith of the Community. In the general meetings the elders sit in front facing the congregation, which is divided—the men on one side and the women on the other.

The services are all solemn, dignified, and impressive, and never accompanied by excitement. There is no regular pastor or priest. In the exercises, which are conducted by the elders, there is really nothing peculiar. The silent prayer is followed by a hymn sung by the congregation. Then the presiding elder reads from the Bible or from the testimonies. Again there is prayer, which is sometimes given extemporaneously and sometimes read, or else is given in the form of supplicatory verses by the members of the congregation. The presiding elder announces a chapter in the Bible, which is read verse by verse by the members of the congregation. There is, of course, no sermon—simply a brief address of exhortation from an elder. After the singing of a hymn and the pronouncing of a benediction by the presiding elder, the people leave the church, the women going first and the men following. Nothing could be more earnest, more devout, more reverent, more sincerely genuine than the church services of the Community of True Inspiration.

As texts for religious instruction, the Community has published two Catechisms, one for the instruction of the youth, the other for the use of the members of the Community. The former was re-edited in the year 1872, and the latter in 1871. The title-pages are almost identical, and read: 'Catechetical Instruction of the Teachings of Salvation presented according to the Statements of the Holy Scriptures, and founded upon the Evangelic-Apostolic Interpretation of the Spirit of God for the Blessed Use of the Youth (or Members) of the Communities of True Inspiration.'

The one supreme object of 'the pilgrimage on earth' in the Inspirationist's system of theology is the salvation of the soul. The Community is but a school of preparation for the next world. The awful fate, after death, of the soul that has not been thoroughly purified and sanctified during its earthly sojourn is perhaps best described in an old *Bezeugung*, which reads: 'Such souls will wander in pathless desolation; they will seek and not find; they will have to endure much torment and grief, and be wretchedly plagued, tortured, and tormented by misleading stars' (*TSL*, 9th Collection, 2nd ed. p. 104).

'Behold how good and how pleasant it is for brethren to dwell together in unity,' said Gruber to his congregation of followers two centuries ago. And nowhere, perhaps, is this simple Amana doctrine of 'brothers all as God's children' more impressively expressed than in the Amana cemetery, where there are no family lots or monuments, but where the departed members of the Community are buried side by side in the order of their death, regardless of natural ties. Each grave is marked by a low stone or a white painted head-board, with only the name and date of death on the side facing the grave. There lies the great-hearted Christian Metz by the side of the humblest brother.

3. Religious and moral instruction.—The stability of the Community of True Inspiration and the perpetuity of the faith of the 'New Spiritual Economy' for nearly two centuries are due in a measure to the instruction and training of the youth; for the Inspirationists have always insisted on training their children in their own way according to the faith of the fathers (*Urgrosseltern*).

To-day there is in each village of the Community a school organized under the laws of the State and sharing in the public school fund. But since the whole of Amana Township is owned by the Society, the Society levies its own school tax, builds its own school houses, chooses its own school directors, and employs its own teachers. Thus the education of the youth of Amana is under the immediate guidance and direction of the Community.

To preserve the earnestness and religious zeal of the fathers (*Urgrosseltern*) is the real mission of the Community school. Here learning is of less account than piety. 'What our youth need more than text-book knowledge,' says the *Kinderlehrer*, 'is to learn to live holy lives, to learn God's commandments out of the Bible, to learn submission to His will, and to love Him.' Indeed, 'to love the ways of humility and simplicity,' and never to reject or despise the good and sincere admonitions of the brethren, constitute the foundation of the ethical and religious training of the Amana child, who, between the ages of five and fourteen, is compelled to attend school six days in the week and fifty-two weeks in the year. In addition to the branches that are usually taught in grammar schools outside of the Community, there is daily instruction at the Amana schools in the Bible and the catechism. Nor is this religious instruction slighted or performed in a perfunctory manner. Said one of the Community schoolmasters: 'It is my profound belief that no other children on the whole earth are more richly instructed in religion than ours.'

The spirit as well as the scope and character of the instruction and training of the youth of Amana is beautifully expressed in the 'Sixty-six Rules for the Conduct of Children' which are given in the catechism. To live up to these rules is indeed the first step towards salvation.

In order to ascertain and promote the spiritual condition of the youth in the schools, there are held each year two 'solemn religious meetings,' which are conducted by the first brethren. One of these meetings, the *Kinderlehre*, consists of a thorough review of the principles and doctrines of the Community and of the supreme importance of keeping the faith. The other, called the *Kinder Unterredung*, is indeed the children's part of the yearly spiritual examination (*Untersuchung*).

Graduation from the schools of the Community, which may take place either in the autumn or in the spring, is attended with solemn religious exercises. The children who are about to leave the schools are carefully examined as to their knowledge of both spiritual and temporal things. It is at this meeting that each child reads his 'graduation essay,' which is a simple child-like review of his school life, of his faults, of his aspirations, and of his intentions as a member of the Community.

Graduation from the schools is, in a sense, a preparation for the *Bundesschliessung* which follows, and in which the children are first permitted to take part at the age of fifteen. It is not, however, until the boys and girls come to the legal age of twenty-one and eighteen respectively that they are admitted as full members of the Society.

4. Membership.—Besides those born in the Community, who become members by signing the Constitution when they have arrived at the legal age, any outsider may join after a probation of two years, during which he agrees to labour faithfully, abide by the regulations of the Community, and demand no wages. If, at the close of this period, the candidate gives 'proof of being fully in accord with the religious doctrines of the Society,' he is admitted to full membership, after conveying to the Society all his property, taking part in the *Bundesschliessung*, and signing the Constitution. Members who 'may recede from the Society either by their own choice or by expulsion, shall be entitled to receive back the moneys paid into the common fund and to interest thereon at a rate not exceeding 5 per cent. per annum from the time of the adjustment of their accounts until the repayment of their credits' (Constitution, Art. VIII.). Few, however, withdraw from the Society; and most of those who do leave return in the course of time. The records show that formerly many outsiders (from Germany) were admitted; but in recent years the increase is almost wholly from within.

'Every member of the Society is,' according to Art. VI. of the Constitution, 'besides the free board, dwelling, support, and care secured to him in his old age, sickness and infirmity, further entitled out of the common fund to an annual sum of maintenance for him or herself, children, and relatives in the Society; and these annual allowances shall be fixed by the Trustees for each member single or in families according to justice and equity, and shall be from time to time revised and fixed anew.'

5. Government. — The entire conduct of the affairs of the Amana Society rests with a board of trustees consisting of thirteen members, who are elected annually by popular vote out of the whole number of elders in the Community. The members of the board of trustees are the spiritual as well as the temporal leaders of the Community of True Inspiration, and as such are called 'The Great Council of the Brethren.' Out of their own number the trustees elect annually a president, a vice-president, and a secretary.

With a view to keeping the members informed concerning the business affairs of the Society, the board of trustees exhibits annually in the month of June to the voting members of the Community a full statement of 'the personal and real estate of the Society.' The board itself meets on the first Tuesday of each month. Besides its general supervision of the affairs of the Community, the board of trustees acts as a sort of court of appeal to which complaints and disagreements are referred. With their decision the case is finally and emphatically closed.

Each village is governed by a group of from seven to nineteen elders, who were formerly appointed by Inspiration, but who are now (there being no *Werkzeug*) appointed by the board of trustees. Each village has at least one resident trustee, who recommends to the Great Council, of which he is a member, a list of elders from the most spiritual of the members of his village. From these lists the Great Council appoints the elders for each village according to spiritual rank. The governing board of each village is known as the 'Little Council,' and is composed of the resident trustee and a number of the leading elders, who call into conference the foremen of the different branches of industry and such other members of the Community as may, on occasion, be of assistance in arranging the village work.

It is this Little Council of the village that appoints the foremen for the different industries and departments of labour, and assigns to any individual his apportioned task. To them each person desiring more money, more house room, an extra holiday, or lighter work, must appeal; for these allotments are, as occasion requires, 'revised and fixed anew.'

The highest authority in matters spiritual in the village is the head elder; in matters temporal, the resident trustee. And although the trustee is a member of the Great Council itself, which is the spiritual head of the Community, in the village church the head elder ranks above the trustee.

Each village keeps its own books and manages its own affairs; but all accounts are finally sent to the headquarters at Amana, where they are inspected, and the balance of profit or loss discovered. The system of government is thus a sort of federation, wherein each village maintains its local independence, but is under the general supervision of a central governing authority, the board of trustees.

6. The Amana Villages.—The seven villages of the Community of True Inspiration lie from a mile and a half to four miles apart; but all are within a radius of six miles from 'Old Amana.' They are connected with one another, as well as with most of the important towns and cities of the State, by telephone. Each village is a cluster of from forty to one hundred houses arranged in the manner of the German *Dorf*, with one long straggling street and several irregular off-shoots. At one end are the village barns and sheds, at the other the factories and workshops; and on either side lie the orchards, the vineyards, and the gardens.

Each village has its own church and school, its bakery, its dairy, and its general store, as well as its own sawmill for the working up of hard wood. The lumber used is obtained largely from the Society's timber land. At the railway stations there are grain houses and lumber yards. The station agents at the several Amana railway stations and the four postmasters are all members of the Society. The establishment of hotels, in no way a part of the original village plan, has been made necessary by the hundreds of strangers who visit the villages every year.

7. The Amana Homes.—The homes of the Amana people are in two-story houses built of wood, brick, or a peculiar brown sandstone which is found in the vicinity. The houses are all quite unpretentious; and it has been the aim of the Society to construct them as nearly alike as possible, each one being as desirable as the other. The frame-houses are never painted, since it is believed to be more economical to rebuild than to preserve with paint. Then, too, painted houses are a trifle worldly in appearance. The style of architecture is the same throughout the entire Community—plain, square (or rectangular) structures with gable roofs. There are no porches, verandas, or bay windows; but everywhere the houses are (in the summer time) half hidden with grape vines and native ivy. The uniformity is so marked that it is only with the aid of an inconspicuous weather-beaten sign that the stranger is able to distinguish the 'hotel' or 'store' from the school, church, or private dwelling. Grass lawns are not maintained about the buildings, but in season they are surrounded with a riotous profusion of flower beds.

In the private dwelling-house there is no kitchen, no dining room, no parlour—just a series of 'sitting rooms' and bed rooms, which are furnished by the Society in the plainest and simplest manner. Each house is occupied by one, two, or sometimes three families. But each family is assigned certain rooms which constitute the family home; and in this home each member has his or her own room or rooms. There is no crowding in the Amanas; for the same spirit which led the Society to adopt the village system has led it to provide plenty of house room for its members.

8. Domestic Life.—At the time of its inception the 'New Spiritual Economy' does not seem to have had rigid precepts relative to marriage. But with increasing religious fervour among the Inspirationists celibacy came to be regarded with much favour; while marriages were in certain special cases prevented by the *Werkzeuge*. It does not appear, however, that marriage (although discouraged) was ever absolutely prohibited. To-day there seems to be no opposition; and the young people marry freely, notwithstanding the admonition that 'a single life is ever a pleasure to the Lord, and that He has bestowed upon it a special promise and great mercy' (*TSL*, 1850, No. 74). The newly married pair are, indeed, still reduced to the lowest spiritual order. A young man does not marry until he has reached the age of twenty-four years, and then only after permission has been given by the Great Council of the brethren one year in advance. Marriage in the Community of True Inspiration is a religious ceremony which is performed in the church by the presiding elder.

Divorce is not recognized in the Community of True Inspiration. The married couple are expected to abide by the step they have taken throughout life. But if, for good and sufficient reason, such a life union is impossible, 'then one of them, mostly the man, is told to separate himself from the Community and go into the world.' Second marriage is not regarded with favour.

The number of children in the Amana family is never large—ranging usually from one to four. Indeed, with the birth of each child the parents suffer a reduction in spiritual rank. There are, however, very few childless families in the Community.

The newly married couple begin their home life in rooms which are provided and furnished by the Society. Housekeeping with them, however, is a very simple matter, since there are neither meals nor cooking in the home. At more or less regular intervals in each village there is a 'kitchen house,' at which the meals for the families in the immediate neighbourhood are prepared and served. At each of these common eating places provision is made for from sixteen to forty persons. The preparation of the food and the serving of the meals are done by the women.

In their dress the members of the Society are and always have been very 'plain.' There is nothing distinctive about the clothes of the men. Their 'best clothes' are made by the Community tailor, but ordinarily they wear ready-made garments—except a few of the elder brethren, who still wear trousers with the old-fashioned broad fall front, and a coat without lapels. With the women utility and comfort (instead of adornment) are chiefly regarded. Plain calicoes of gray or blue or brown are worn for the most part. The bodice is short and very plain; while the skirt is long and full. An apron of moderate length, a shoulder-shawl, and a small black cap complete the summer costume. The only headdress is a sun-bonnet with a long cape. The winter dress differs from this only in being made of flannel; while a hood takes the place of the sun-bonnet. Every woman makes her own clothes; and every mother makes the clothing for her children.

9. Industrial Life.—Agriculture, which is one of the chief industries of the Community, is carried on, with the German proneness for system, according to the most modern and scientific methods. The general plan of the field work is determined by the board of trustees; but a field 'boss' or superintendent is responsible to the Society for the proper execution of their orders. He sees that the farm machinery is kept in good condition, he appeals to the elders for more men to work in the fields when necessary, and he obtains from the 'boss' of the barns and stables the horses that are needed. From fifteen to eighteen ox teams are still used for the heavy hauling.

The Amana Society is perhaps best known in the business world through its woollen mills, which have been in active operation for forty-two years. Over half a million pounds of raw wool are consumed in these mills annually. It has always been the aim of the Society to manufacture 'honest goods,' and they have found a ready market from the Atlantic to the Pacific coast. The hours of labour in the woollen mills during the greater part of the year are the usual Amana hours of 7 to 11 in the morning and 12.30 to 6 in the afternoon. But during the summer months, when the orders for the fall trade are being executed, the mills run from half-past four in the morning to eleven at night (the factories being lighted throughout by electricity).

In spite of the long hours and the busy machinery, there is a very unusual factory air about the Amana mills. The rooms are light and airy. There is a cushioned chair or stool for every worker 'between times.' An occasional spray of blossoms on a loom frame reflects the spirit of the workers. Here and there in different parts of the factory are well-equipped cupboards and lunch tables, where the different groups of workers eat their luncheon in the middle of each half-day. In the villages where the factories are located the boys of thirteen or fourteen years of age who are about to leave school are employed in the mills for a few hours each afternoon 'to learn.' If the work is congenial, they are carefully trained and are given every opportunity to 'work up'; but if this employment is not agreeable, they are at liberty to choose some other line of work.

In Old Amana there is a calico printing establishment, where four thousand five hundred yards of calico are dyed and printed daily. The patterns for the calico are designed and made by a member of the Society. This 'colony calico,' as it is called, is sold throughout the United States and Canada, and is quite as favourably known as the woollen goods.

The industrial efficiency of the operative in the Amana mills and factories is noticeably great even to the casual observer. Each worker labours with the air of a man in physical comfort and peace of mind, and with the energy of a man who is working for himself and expects to enjoy all the fruits of his labour.

Besides these mills and factories, the Society owns and operates seven saw mills, two machine shops, one soap factory, and one printing office and bookbindery. The job work for the stores and mills, the text books used in the schools, the hymn books used in the churches, and other religious books commonly read in the community, are all printed at the Amana printing office. The Society publishes no newspaper or magazine, official or otherwise, although it subscribes for several trade journals.

In three of the villages there are licensed pharmacies. The quantity of drugs prepared for the outside market is not large, as no effort has ever been made to build up a drug trade. As a rule, only special orders are executed. Some physicians of the State prefer to get their supplies here rather than to send farther east for them. The Society were the first people west of Chicago to manufacture pepsin, and their manufacture is still considered one of the best in the market.

In addition to the aforenamed industries, each village has its shoemaker, tailor, harness-maker, carpenter, blacksmith, tool-smith, waggon-maker, etc. These tradesmen, as a rule, do not devote their entire time to their occupations, but only make and repair what is needed in their line by the people of the village. During the busy season they stand ready to be called to the factory or the field as circumstances demand. The physicians, pharmacists, and mechanics are trained at the expense of the Society.

LITERATURE.—*Constitution and Bye-Laws of the Community of True Inspiration; Life and Essays* of Eberhard Ludwig Gruber; *Autobiography* of Johann Friedrich Rock; *Year Books* of the Community of True Inspiration [published by the Society each year during the lifetime of the *Werkzeuge* and containing the *Bezeugungen* in the order of their utterance, with brief introductions relating the circumstances under which the *Bezeugungen* were given]; *Brief Relation of the Circumstances of the Awaking and the first Divine guidance of Barbara Heinemann; Historical Description of the Community of True Inspiration* . . . recorded by Brother Christian Metz. *Extracts from the Day Book* of Brother Christian Metz; *Inspirations-Historie*—compiled from various accounts, some of them printed, some written by Gottlieb Scheuner, 4 parts or vols. :—[Vol. i.] Historical account of the founding of the Prayer-Meetings and Communities; [vol. ii.] Various articles and narrations of the work of the Lord in His ways of Inspiration; [vol. iii.] Historical Account of the New Revival, Gathering, and Founding of the Community of True Inspiration; [vol. iv.] Description of the works of the mercy of the Lord in the Communities of True Inspiration; *Catechetical Instruction of the Teachings of Salvation*, part i. for the youth of the Community, part ii. for the members; *Psalms after the manner of David for the Children of Zion: . . . particularly for the Congregation of the Lord; The Supper of Love and Remembrance of the Suffering and Death of our Lord and Saviour Jesus Christ* [published during the lifetime of the *Werkzeuge* after each Love-Feast, and containing a full account of the meetings and the *Bezeugungen* uttered during the solemn ceremonies]; numerous pamphlets and essays found only in the records and libraries of the Society. These works are all in German, and printed chiefly at Ebenezer, N.Y., and Amana, Iowa. Reference may also be made to Nordhoff, *Communistic Societies of the United States*, pp. 25-59 (New York, 1875); Hinds, *American Communities*, pp. 263-286 (Chicago, 1902); Knortz, *Die wahre Inspirationsgemeinde in Iowa* (Leipzig, 1896); and Perkins and Wick, *History of the Amana Society* (Iowa City, Ia., 1891).

BERTHA M. H. SHAMBAUGH.

AMARĀVATĪ.—A small town (lat. 16° 34′ 45″ N., long. 80° 24′ 21″ E.) on the south bank of the Kistna (Krishṇā) River in the Kistna District, Madras Presidency, the ancient Dharaṇikoṭa, or Dhānyakaṭaka. It is famous as the site which has supplied a multitude of fine sculptures, chiefly bas-reliefs, of the highest importance for the history of both Indian art and Buddhist iconography. The sculptures, executed almost without exception in white marble, formed the decorations of a *stūpa*, which was totally destroyed at the end of the 18th and the beginning of the 19th cents. by a local landholder, who used the materials for building purposes. The surviving slabs are only a small fraction of the works which were in existence about a century ago. Most of the specimens rescued from the lime-kiln are in either the British Museum or the Madras Museum. The body of the *stūpa* was cased with marble slabs and surrounded by two railings or screens, of which the outer and earlier stood 13 or 14 feet in height above the pavement, the inner and later one being only six feet high. The casing slabs, and every stone of both railings, including the plinth and coping, were covered with finely executed bas-reliefs. The basal diameter of the *stūpa* was 138 feet, the circumference of the inner rail was 521 feet, and that of the outer rail 803 feet. It is estimated that the separate figures on the outer rail must have numbered 12,000 or 14,000. The multitude of figures on the inner rail, carved on a minute scale suggesting ivory work, was still greater. The outer rail was constructed of upright slabs connected by three cross-bars between each pair of uprights, which stood on a plinth and supported a coping about two feet nine inches in height. On the outer face each upright was adorned with a full disc in the centre and a half-disc at top and bottom, with minor sculptures filling the interspaces. Similar but ever-varying discs decorated the cross-bars, and the coping was ornamented with a long wavy flower-roll carried by men, numerous figures being inserted in the open spaces. The plinth exhibited a frieze of animals and boys, generally in comic or ludicrous attitudes. The decorations on the inner side were even more elaborate, the coping presenting a continued series of bas-reliefs, and the central discs of both bars and pillars being filled with beautiful sculptures, treating every topic of Buddhist legend. The Amarāvatī railings are by far the most splendid examples of their class, and the sculptures, even in their present fragmentary state, are invaluable as documents in the history of both art and religion. Fortunately, their date can be determined with a near approach to precision. Dedicatory inscriptions recorded during the reigns of the Āndhra kings Pulumāyi (A.D. 138–170) and Yajña Srī (A.D. 184–213) fix the time of the erection of the outer rail as the middle or latter part of the 2nd cent. A.D. This inference agrees well with the statement of Tāranāth, the Tibetan historian of Buddhism (Schiefner, *Tāranāthas Gesch. d. Buddhismus in Ind., St. Petersburg*, 1869, pp. 71, 142), that the Buddhist patriarch Nāgārjuna surrounded the great *chaitya* of Dhanaśrīdvīpa or Srī Dhānyakaṭaka with a wall or screen (*Mauer*). The ecclesiastical rule of this patriarch, who is said to have been contemporary with Kanishka, is placed by Dr. Eitel between A.D. 137 and 194; and the most probable scheme of Indian chronology assigns Kanishka to the period A.D. 120–150. We may therefore assume with confidence that the great outer rail was erected and decorated between the years A.D. 140 and 200. Of course, the work must have occupied many years. The inner rail is somewhat later in date, and may not have been finished before A.D. 300. A few fragments of ancient sculpture prove that the *stūpa* in its original form dated from very early times, about B.C. 200.

The Indian art of relief sculpture drew its inspiration from two sources, Alexandria and Asia Minor. The ancient school (B.C. 250–A.D. 50), of which the Bharhut (*q.v.*), Sānchi, and Bodh Gayā works are the leading examples, evolved a thoroughly Indianized adaptation of Alexandrian *motifs*, so completely disguised in Indian trappings that the foreign origin of the art has not been generally recognized. The composition is characterized by excessive crowding and compression, and the execution by extreme naïveté and realism, the purpose of the sculpture being directed to edification rather than to making an æsthetic impression. The works of this school were produced from the time of Aśoka (B.C. 250) down to about the Christian era, or a little later. The so-called Græco-Buddhist art of Gandhāra, or the Peshāwar region, on the contrary, was influenced, not directly by Alexandria, but chiefly by the schools of Pergamum and other cities of Asia Minor, which practised a cosmopolitan style of art, sometimes designated as Græco-Roman. The balanced composition of the Gandhāra reliefs closely resembles that of many Roman works, Pagan or Christian, and is as much superior to that of the ancient Indian school as is the execution of individual figures. The Gandhāra draperies follow classical models, and are often treated with much skill. The special value of the Amarāvatī sculptures to the historian of art is that they form a connecting link between the two schools above named. Their basis is the old Indian art of Alexandrian origin, but that is freely modified in respect of the composition, execution, and drapery by the influence of the contemporary Gandhāra school, the best work of which may be assigned to the period A.D. 100-300. From the religious, as from the artistic, point of view the sculptures of Amarāvatī occupy a position intermediate between those of Sānchi and Gandhāra. The artists of the ancient school never attempted to delineate the figure of the Buddha, and were content to indicate his felt but unseen presence by the empty chair, the print of his footsteps, or other significant symbols. Gandhāra art, on the other hand, is characterized by inordinate repetition of the image of the Master, sitting, standing, or engaged in various incidents as related in the books of legends. The Amarāvatī sculptures frequently made use of the symbolical notation of their predecessors at Sānchi and Bharhut, but also freely adopted the foreign innovation, and often introduced isolated images of the Buddha, either standing or sitting, clad in Greek drapery. Such images seem to be more common on the later inner rail than on the earlier outer one. Scenes representing the Buddha in action are rare at Amarāvatī.

LITERATURE.—The sculptures are fully illustrated and described by Fergusson, *Tree and Serpent Worship*[2] (1873), and Burgess, *The Buddhist Stūpas of Amarāvatī and Jaggayyapeta* (being vol. vi. of the New Imp. Ser. of Archæol. Rep., London, 1887). Full references to special reports are given by Sewell, *Lists of the Antiquarian Remains in the Presidency of Madras* (1882), i. 63. See also Fergusson, *History of Indian and Eastern Architecture* (1899); Grünwedel, *Buddhist Art*, tr. Burgess and Gibson (1899); and Foucher, *L'Art Bouddhique du Gandhâra*, i. (1905). The evidence proving the Alexandrian origin of the ancient Indian art has not yet been fully published.

VINCENT A. SMITH.

AMARKANṬAK (Skr. *amara-kanṭaka*, 'peak of the immortals').—A hill in the Bilāspur district of the Central Provinces, India, lat. 22° 40′ 15″ N., long. 81° 48′ 15″ E. It is on the watershed of Central India, three great rivers having their sources from it,—the Narbada, flowing westward to the Indian Ocean; the Johilla, shortly joining the Son, one of the tributaries of the Ganges; while the Arpa mingles with the Mahānadi, which drains the plain of Chhattīsgaṛh, and, like the Ganges, flows eastward into the Bay of Bengal. As the source of the Narbada, which local legend declares will by and by surpass the sanctity of the Ganges, Amarkanṭak is an important place of pilgrimage.

'If the peninsula,' writes Sir R. Temple, 'may be imagined as a shield, and if any spot be the boss of such a shield, then Amarkanṭak is that spot. South of the Himālayas there is no place of equal celebrity so isolated on every side from habitation and civilization. To the east and to the north, hundreds of miles of sparsely populated hills and forests intervene between it and the Gangetic countries. On the west there extend hilly, roadless uplands of what are now called the Sātpura regions. To the south, indeed, there is the partly cultivated plateau of Chhattīsgaṛh, but that, after all, is only an oasis in the midst of the great wilderness. It is among these mighty solitudes that the Narbada first sees the light' (*Cent. Prov. Gaz.* 346 f.).

Formerly difficult of access, it has now been rendered approachable by the railway between the Bilāspur and Katni Junctions, and cultivation has rapidly advanced in Chhattīsgaṛh. The place where the Narbada rises is enclosed by a wall of masonry, and, as the name of the site implies, it is surrounded by temples dedicated to the cult of Śiva.

LITERATURE.—Forsyth, *Highlands of Central India*[2] (1889), 403; *Central Provinces Gazetteer* (1870), 347.

W. CROOKE.

AMARNĀTH or **AMBARNĀTH** (Skr. *amaranātha*, 'the immortal Lord,' a title of Śiva).—A place situated in the Thāna district of the Bombay Presidency, famous as the site of an ancient Hindu temple. The temple is without history, written or traditional. An inscription translated by Bhau Daji (*JRASBo* ix. 220) gives its date as A.D. 860; but it seems probable that the existing building is a restoration, or has been rebuilt from the materials of that erected in A.D. 860. It faces west, with doors to north and south in a hall in front of the shrine (*maṇḍap, antarāla*), supported by four pillars, elegant in conception and general beauty of details. At the west entrance is a defaced bull (*nandi*), showing that the shrine was dedicated to Śiva. The roof of the hall is supported by columns, of which the sculpture is so rich and varied that no description can give a correct idea of its beauty. The temple is remarkable for a three-headed figure, known as a *trimūrti*, of a male with a female on his knee, probably representing Śiva and his spouse Pārvatī. The sculpture, as a whole, shows a degree of skill that is not surpassed by any temple in the Bombay Presidency. It has been fully described, with a series of plates, by J. Burgess (*IA* iii. 316 ff.).

W. CROOKE.

AMAZONS.—**1.** The Amazons were a mythical race of women, dwelling in the northern part of Asia Minor, or still farther north, who had proved their prowess in conflict with the greater heroes of Greece. Something about the conception of feminine warriors made it very attractive to the Greek story-teller. Women who had asserted their independence of conventional bonds, and who kept their power by maiming or blinding their male children; women who wore a man's short *chitōn*, and who had cut away the right breast that they might the more freely handle arms; withal beautiful women to inspire with love those Greek heroes who fought against them—such were the Amazons. According to Pherekydes (*frag.* 25), their nature was explained by the fact that they were descended from Ares and the naiad nymph Harmonia; Hellanikos (*frag.* 146) makes them a race of women living apart from men and perpetuating their kind by visits to neighbouring people. Thus they were both 'man-haters' (Æsch. *Prom.* 724) and 'man-like' (Hom. *Il.* iii. 189).

In the epics they use the same arms as do other warriors. Pindar (*Ol.* xiii. 125) and Æschylus (*Suppl.* 288) speak of them as skilled with the bow, and in art they ordinarily wear a quiver. Their proper weapon in later myth was the axe—either the axe with blade and point, such as Xenophon found in use in the mountains of Armenia (*Anab.* iv. 4. 16), or the double-headed axe, πέλεκυς (Plut. *Quæst. Græc.* 45, 301 F.). The Latin poets (*e.g.* Virg. *Æn.* xi. 611) refer to them as fighting from war-chariots, but Greek poetry and art represent them as going into battle on horseback (Eur. *Hipp.* 307, 582, etc.).

The story of their mutilated breasts is probably due to a false etymology (α- privative and μαζός 'breast'). What the name did originally mean is not quite clear; with some probability Göttling (*Comment. de Amaz.* 1848) has suggested that it referred to their unfeminine character in that they have nothing to do with men (α- and μάσσειν). The names of individual Amazons are in the main genuine Greek names, added as the myth found favour among the Greeks.

2. The *Iliad* mentions two wars in which the Amazons were involved—a war with the Lycians, which led the king of the Lycians, Isobates, to send Bellerophon against them (vi. 186), and a war with the Phrygians, in which Priam fought on the side of the Phrygians (iii. 189). Strabo (xii. 552) notes the inconsistency of this story with the account of Penthesileia and her companions. According to the later epic, the *Aithiopis* of Arktinos, she came to Troy after the death of Hector to aid the forces of Priam. Achilles inflicted a mortal wound on Penthesileia, only to be touched with love at her beauty as she lay dying in his arms.

The story of Herakles and Hippolyte is a later myth about an earlier generation. It was one of the twelve labours of Herakles to fetch the girdle of Hippolyte, queen of the Amazons, for Admete, Eurystheus' daughter. According to Apollodorus (*Bibl.* ii. 5. 9. 7), the queen fell in love with Herakles, and gave him the girdle; but as he went to board his ship the other Amazons, invited by Hera, attacked him. Suspecting treachery on the part of Hippolyte, Herakles shot her with an arrow and sailed away. In the more common form of the story, sometimes connected with the Argonautic expedition, Herakles made war on the Amazons, overcame them in battle, and triumphantly carried off the girdle (Diod. Sic. iv. 16; Apoll. Rhod. ii. 967).

A somewhat similar story is told of Theseus and Antiope, namely, that Theseus made an expedition against the Amazons, and either by love or by force won Antiope to be his bride. The importance of this expedition was that it furnished the occasion for the expedition of the Amazons against Athens. As the story is told by Plutarch (*Thes.* 27), its form is determined by several Amazon shrines at Athens, by the position of the Areopagus in front of the Acropolis, and by a place called *Horkomosion*, where a treaty of peace was made. In this war Antiope met her death, and was buried by the Itonian gate of Athens. The story was significant in that it furnished Attic orators and artists with another instance of the superiority of civilization to barbarism, as in the battle of gods and giants and in the war between Athens and Persia.

3. *Locality.*—On the north coast of Asia Minor and well towards the east, the town of Themiskyra by the river Thermodon was the generally accepted seat of the Amazons. Rarely were they located farther to the north or north-east. It should be noted, further, that either one Amazon or a band of Amazons finds a place in the local legends of very many cities on the north coast and the west coast of Asia Minor. 'Herakles turned over to the Amazons the region between Pitane and Mykale' (Herakleid. Pont. *frag.* 34); and such cities as Smyrna and Ephesus are most important local centres of Amazon legend. In Greece proper, on the other hand, there are graves of Amazons and places which they visited, but they are present only as visitors from outside.

4. *Explanation.*—Any effort to understand the Amazons must start from three facts. (1) The Amazons were warriors, armed with weapons such as the Greeks associated with eastern Asia Minor and regions still farther to the east and north. They were closely associated with the 'Thracian' god Ares; he was their reputed father, they sacrificed horses to him, and their camp at Athens was on the hill of Ares. (2) They were also connected with Artemis, especially the Ephesian Artemis. It is said that this cult was established by the Amazons, and that here they performed war dances and choral dances in honour of the goddess (Paus. vii. 2. 7; Kallim. *Hymn to Artemis*, 237 f.; cf. *Il.* ii. 814). (3) The legends of the Amazons are in the main connected with the coast towns on the north and west of Asia Minor.

K. O. Müller suggested (*Dorier*, i. 390 f.) that the conception arose from the large number of *hierodouloi* connected with the worship of Artemis at Ephesus and elsewhere in Asia Minor. It is more probable that the presence of women with these peculiar weapons in the armies of northern and eastern races started the legends, that incursions of these races into Asia Minor determined the locality with which they were associated, and that war dances performed by women in the worship of Ares, Artemis, etc., aided the growth of the legends. To bring the Amazons into conflict with Bellerophon, Achilles, Herakles, and Theseus was the natural means of emphasizing the prowess of feminine warriors.

LITERATURE.—Bergmann, *Les Amazones dans l'histoire et dans la fable*, Colmar; W. Stricker, *Die Amazonen in Sage und Geschichte*, Berlin, 1868; Klügmann, *Die Amazonen in der alten Litteratur und Kunst*, Stuttgart, 1875.

ARTHUR FAIRBANKS.

AMBĒR.—An ancient, now ruinous, city in the native State of Jaipur in Rājputāna. Formerly it was held by the non-Aryan Mīnās, from whom the Kachhwāhā sept of Rājputs conquered it in 1037 A.D. It then became their capital, and so continued to be until 1728, when Jai Singh II. founded the present city of Jaipur, and Ambēr became deserted. It was in olden days much frequented by pilgrims from all parts of India, but its glory has departed. At a temple of Kālī within the ruined city a goat is daily sacrificed, a substitute, as is believed, for the human victim offered in former times to the goddess.

LITERATURE.—For the history: Tod, *Annals of Rajasthan*, Calcutta reprint, 1884, ii. 381 ff. For a description of the remains: Major Baylay, in *Rājputāna Gazetteer*, ii. 154 f.; Rousselet, *India and its Native Princes*, 1890, ch. xx.; Fergusson, *Hist. of Indian and Eastern Architecture*, 1899, p. 480.

W. CROOKE.

AMBITION.—'Ambition,' derived from Lat. *ambitio*, the 'going round' of a candidate for office canvassing for votes, signifies primarily a desire for a position of power or dignity; thence a desire for eminence of any kind, and so, by an easy but well-defined and recognized extension (in the absence of any other word to cover the idea), the will to attain, obtain, or perform anything regarded by the user of the word as high or difficult. The same term thus becomes applicable to Jaques' 'ambition for a motley coat,' and the desire of Milton to write something which the aftertimes would not willingly let die. It is obvious that almost any desire may in certain circumstances become our 'ambition' in this third sense, which may, therefore, be dismissed at once—especially as in default of a qualifying term one of the first two is always intended. The present article will accordingly be confined to these. The motive in question holds a unique position for two reasons: its moral position is more uncertain in general estimation than that of any other, and it is reported by tradition to have been the first sin. These points will be taken in order.

1. Bacon, in his essay, 'Of Ambition,' says of it that it 'is like choler, which is an humour that maketh men active, earnest, full of alacritie, and stirring, if it be not stopped; but if it be stopped and cannot have his way, it becommeth adust, and thereby maligne and venomous.' Spinoza (who defines it, however, as 'an excessive love of glory') says: 'Ambition is a Desire by which all the Affections are nourished and strengthened; and on that account this particular Affection can hardly be overcome. For so long as a man is influenced by any Desire at all, he is inevitably influenced by this' (*Ethics*, pt. iii. Appendix). The opinions of these high authorities imply no particular censure. A reference to any Dictionary of Quotations, however, will reveal it indeed as

'divine' and 'accursed,' 'blind' and 'eagle-eyed,' 'base' and 'sublime'; but for one epithet of honour ten will be found of blame. At the same time, this proportion does not appear accurately to represent the average man's feeling towards it, which may be described as two parts of fear and distrust to one of secret admiration. Now, amid this clash of opinion, it is clear that ambition is in itself non-moral; for power is never, in the last analysis, desired for itself, but always from an ulterior motive, namely, for the *opportunities* it affords, whether for enhanced activity, for the exercise of peculiar faculties possessed, for the furtherance of a desired end, or the gratification of vanity. Logically, therefore, it should be judged by the motive behind; and, in fact, the soundest defence of it may be based upon this consideration. But such a plea avails little against the prosecutor, whose main, if often unrealized, ground of attack (apart from religion) rests upon the means by which the ambitious are tempted to gain their ends.

The reasons for the conflicting views entertained on the subject may be summed up thus, the attitude of religion being reserved for separate treatment. From the point of view of society, it is natural and right that public opinion should be directed to check rather than to encourage ambition, as the danger of an excess of it is greater than that of a deficient supply. Morally, such a desire can in no case be generally considered virtuous, in view of the obvious personal advantages which power, from whatever motive sought, confers upon the possessor. To many philosophers, again, it is especially anathema as a chief enemy of that peace of mind and independence of externals which is the Nirvāṇa of their creed. These reasons apply to the desire for power in any degree of development; but what is after all perhaps the chief cause of the invidious sense attaching to the word 'ambition' lies in a subtle implication which modifies the meaning, without equally restricting the use, of the term itself. In the words of Aristotle (*Ethics*, ii. 7), 'There is such a thing as a due and proper desire for distinction; the desire may also be excessive or defective: the man who is excessive in this desire is called "ambitious," the man who is deficient, "unambitious"; *for the middle state there is no name.*' This desire is, in fact, present in some degree in almost all members of the white races, and hence the definite term 'ambitious' is applied only to those in whom it is prominent, and therefore over-developed. It stands, in short, self-condemned as excessive, in which condition it is pregnant with danger alike to the State, the neighbour, and the morality of its subject, and lies justly under the censure of political, ethical, and philosophic thought. At the same time it is viewed by many, even when in excess, with a certain reluctant admiration as the infirmity of a *noble* mind. For, whatever its own demerits, it is generally found in company with the qualities most admired in Western civilization—ability and energy. It implies also a certain length and largeness of view, in themselves admirable, and in many cases can only with difficulty be distinguished from its twin-virtue—aspiration. Finally, it is a motive with which, though perhaps faulty, the world, in the present condition of religion and morals, could ill afford to dispense; for positions of power are after all generally given to those who not only desire, but also in some degree at least deserve them, and the noble actions, prompted either wholly or in part by ambition, fill not a few of the most distinguished pages in history. 'Licet ipsa vitium sit, tamen frequenter causa virtutum est' (Quintilian).

The verdict of religion upon worldly self-aggrandizement could hardly be doubtful, and in all countries it is unanimous in condemnation. For Greek religious thought it was the direct forerunner of ὕβρις, which is visited upon the children to the third and fourth generation; in Buddhism it is a wile of *mâya*, entangling the soul in the world of becoming and desire; for Confucius it is an enemy of peace; to the Muhammadan it is a choosing of this present life and its braveries, for which there is nothing in the next world but the fire.

In the Bible the word itself does not occur, and in the OT hardly even the idea. The Jewish historians confined themselves practically to the acts of kings, lesser men being introduced only when they came into contact or conflict with the king. But a violent change in the kingship of a people essentially and always theocratic, in the view of the writers, was ascribed as a rule to the direct intervention of God using a man as His instrument; and any private motives of such an instrument were disregarded. Thus it is not unlikely that such men as Jeroboam or Jehu were ambitious, but they are set in action by the word of a prophet. The Prophets again scourge the sins of the people, of which ambition was not one. The absence of any reference to it in the 'Wisdom-literature' of the nation (Proverbs, etc.) is more remarkable. Even Ecclesiastes, in considering the vanity of human wishes, travels round the idea rather than refers to it directly, in a way which suggests that power as a direct object of desire was unfamiliar to the author. The view of the NT, so far as expressed, is uncompromising. In the Christian community there is no room for ambition. The 'Kingdom of Heaven,' or Church of Christ, is for the poor in spirit (Mt 5^3); 'Whosoever would become great among you shall be your minister' (20^{26}); 'Set not your mind on high things, but condescend to things that are lowly' (Ro 12^{16}). Quotations need not be multiplied: the humility and renunciation of the things of the flesh, which are the badge of the followers of Christ, leave little room for the self-assertion inseparable from ambition. What (if any) modifications of this rigorous doctrine may be involved in or justified by the transition of Christ's Church from a limited and purely religious community to the creed of nations, it is not within the province of this article to discuss.

2. It is a current belief that ambition was the first sin which disturbed the harmony of heaven. 'Cromwell, I charge thee, fling away ambition: by that sin fell the angels' (*Henry VIII.* III. ii. 440). The origin of this tradition, which has no authority in the Bible, is obscure; but it may perhaps be traced to the old identification of the 'king of Tyre' in Ezk 28 with Satan. ('Thine heart is lifted up, and thou hast said, I am a god, I sit in the seat of God' [v.^{2}]. 'Therefore . . . strangers . . . shall bring thee down to the pit' [vv.$^{7, 8}$]. 'Thou hast been in Eden, the garden of God . . . thou wast the anointed cherub that covereth' [vv.$^{13, 14}$], etc.). According to the more elaborate version of Milton, however (*Paradise Lost*, v. 660 ff.), pride claims precedence. For it was jealousy of Christ, whose begetting threatened the archangel's pre-eminence in heaven, that stirred Satan's ambitious aim against the throne and monarchy of God. Dante appears to adopt the same tradition ('di cui è la invidia tanto pianta,' *Par.* ix. 129; 'principio del cader fu il maladetto superbir di colui,' etc., *ib.* xxix. 55). (For an elaborate discussion of the point see the *Dict. Encyclopéd. de la Théol. Cathol.*, *s.v.* 'Diable'). It is worth noting in this connexion that the first step in the process of declension of Plato's ideal State is marked by the appearance of a ruffling and ambitious spirit (φιλονεικίαι καὶ φιλοτιμίαι, *Repub.* viii. 4).

LITERATURE.—Besides the works mentioned, reference may be made to Fowler and Wilson, *Principles of Morals* (1894), 43 ff., 169; A. H. Strong, *Christ in Creation and Ethical Monism* (1899), 480; Dobschütz, *Chr. Life in the Prim. Church* (Eng. tr. 1904), 215, 221; J. B. Lightfoot, *Camb. Sermons* (1890), 317; A. L. Moore, *From Advent to Advent* (1892), 239; J. T. Jacob, *Christ the Indweller* (1902), 135.

C. D. ROBERTSON.

AMBROSE OF MILAN.—I. Life.—Ambrose was born, probably, at Trèves, the seat of government of his father, the Prætorian prefect of the Gauls. The family was noble; his father was one of the four highest officers in the empire; his elder brother Satyrus became the governor of a province, name unknown (*de excessu Satyri*, i. 49, 58). The family was also Christian in sympathy; Ambrose's great-aunt Sotheris had suffered as a martyr in the persecution of Diocletian (*de Virgin.* iii. 7; *Exhort. Virg.* xii. 82). The year of Ambrose's birth is a little uncertain. Either 333 or 340 A.D. will suit the data given in his letters (*Ep.* lix. 3, 4; see *PL* xiv. 68, for a full discussion). But probably 340 best meets all the circumstances. On the death of his father, his mother removed with her family to Rome (352), and there Ambrose received the usual liberal education. Of Latin authors Vergil was his favourite; he was also well read in Greek literature. In the doctrines of Christianity he was instructed by Simplicianus, whom he loved as a father (*Ep.* xxxvii.; not to be confused with the Simplicianus who succeeded him). Adopting the law as a profession, he rose very rapidly. When he was but little over 30 (372), Valentinian I., on the advice of the Christian Probus, the prefect of Italy, appointed him 'consular' of Liguria and Æmilia, an office which he discharged with great ability and integrity. In 374 both Dionysius the Catholic and Auxentius the Arian bishop *de facto* died. Both parties strove hard to secure the election of the successor, for at that time Milan was perhaps the first city in Europe in population and importance. Ambrose, in whose province it lay, went to preside at the election, and to suppress the customary tumults. But while the consular was addressing the people in the church on the duty of maintaining order, a voice was heard proclaiming, 'Ambrose is bishop.' The cry, according to Paulinus, first started by a child, was taken up by Arians and Catholics. In spite of the protests of Ambrose—on which Paulinus enlarges *con amore*, with disregard both to truth and to the good name of his hero, judged, that is, by modern ideas—the sanction of Valentinian was given to this irregular election, which won the approval also of the bishops of East and West (Basil, *Ep.* lv.; for Ambrose's statements about the election see *de Offic.* i. 1, 4, *Ep.* lxiii. 65, *de Pœnit.* ii. 8, 72. Ambrose says that Valentinian promised him 'quietem futuram,' *Ep.* xxi. 7). Ambrose was as yet only a catechumen; he had shrunk from baptism under the common feeling of the day which led so many to postpone the same until near death—the dread lest he should lose the baptismal grace. Within eight days of his baptism he was consecrated bishop (Dec. 7, 374, Migne, xiv. 71). His first step was to give his property to the poor and the Church. The administration of his household was handed over to Satyrus († 379), who left his province that he might serve his younger brother (*de excessu Satyri*, i. 20 f.)

Ambrose's life as a bishop was one of incessant work. His moments of leisure were filled with self-culture in theology, which, however, for the most part he learned by teaching (*de Offic.* i. 1, 4). Throughout his diocese Arianism almost ceased to exist, largely through his constant preaching and the care he bestowed on the preparation of catechumens. The Arians, thus bitterly disappointed in the bishop they had elected, found an opportunity for attacking him in his sale of Church plate to provide funds for the release of Roman prisoners captured in Illyricum and Thrace by the Goths, after their great victory at Adrianople (Aug. 9, 378). Ambrose's reply was characteristic: Which did they consider to be the more valuable, church plate or living souls? (*de Offic.* ii. c. 28).

Of his life at this time Augustine has given us a delightful picture (*Conf.* vi. 3, *Ep.* xlvii. 1):

'He was surrounded by an army of needy persons who kept me from him. He was the servant of their infirmities, and, when they spared him a few minutes for himself, he gave his body the food necessary, and nourished his soul with reading. . . . Often when I entered his retreat I found him reading softly to himself. I would sit down, and, after waiting and watching him for a long time in silence (for who would have dared to disturb attention so profound?), I would withdraw, fearing to importune him if I troubled him in the short time he rescued to himself out of the tumult of his multifarious business.'

In his opposition to the Arians, Ambrose did not limit his efforts to his own diocese. At Sirmium in 380, in spite of the threats of Aviana Justina, the Arian widow of Valentinian I. (†Nov. 17, 375), Ambrose succeeded in carrying the election of the Catholic Anemius to the see. In 381 the young emperor Gratian—who from 378–381 lived chiefly at Milan, and followed in most things the advice of Ambrose, whom he called his *parens*, and who composed for his instruction (see *de Fide*, i. prol. iii. 1) his treatise against Arianism, entitled *de Fide* (378)—summoned a Western council, which met in September at Aquileia. Through the influence of Ambrose, who presided, the council deposed two more Arian bishops, Palladius and Secundinus [see the *Gesta Conc. Aq.* inserted in Ambrose, *Op.* after *Ep.* viii. (Migne, xvi. 916), or, more fully, Mansi, iii. 599 ff., and cf. *Epp.* i. ix.–xii.]. If in the following year he attended the abortive council at Rome, he seems to have taken no part in its deliberations. (For this somewhat uncertain council, see Mansi, iii. *s.v.*).

The murder of Gratian, who had estranged the soldiers by foolish and unpatriotic conduct, at Lyons (Aug. 25, 383) by the agents of the British usurper Maximus, led Justina, acting for her young son Valentinian II., to persuade Ambrose to journey to Trèves as her ambassador (*de Obitu Valent.* 28). As the result of his visit (winter, 383), or rather of the delays caused thereby, and the knowledge that behind Ambrose would be, if necessary, the forces of Theodosius, Italy seems to have been secured for Valentinian II., Spain, however, falling to the usurper (*Ep.* xxiv. 6, 7).

On his return to Milan, Ambrose came into collision with Q. Aurelius Symmachus, the prefect of Rome, Pontifex Maximus, Princeps Senatus, the leader in the Senate of the conservative and pagan majority (on this question of the majority, Ambrose, *Ep.* xvii. 10, 11, is untrustworthy). In 384, Symmachus had sought from Valentinian II. the restoration to the Senate of the ancient golden statue and altar of Victory, whose removal had been ordered by Gratian (382). This *Relatio Symmachi* (*Op. Sym.*, ed. Seeck, x. 3, in M.G.H.; see also Migne, *PL* xvi. 966), or defence of paganism, followed the usual line of argument of the times. Symmachus traced the greatness of Rome to the help of the gods; her decline and recent disasters, including a famine in the previous year, to the new creeds. He eloquently appealed to the charm of old traditions and customs. Ambrose's answer (*Ep.* xvii. a hasty appeal to Valentinian; *Ep.* xviii. more matured; cf. *Ep.* lvii. 2, 3) is not altogether happy in its claim that Rome owed her greatness not to her religion, but to her own intrinsic energy—a weak concession to secularism. For the rest, he dwells on paganism as the world's childhood, Christianity as the evolutionary and progressive factor and result. The request of Symmachus was refused, as also were three other similar requests [382 to Gratian, 388 or 391 to Theodosius, 392 to Valentinian II. (Amb. *Ep.* lvii. 5)], chiefly through the zeal of Ambrose and the zealous orthodoxy of Theodosius. To Theodosius we owe the final triumph of Christianity by the series of his edicts which prohibited pagan rites, culminating, so far as sacrifices were concerned, in the deadly *nullus omnino* of Nov. 8, 392 (*Cod. Theod.* xvi. t. x. §§ 12, 13). The difficulties which the usurpation of Eugenius (see *infra*) threw in the way of the carrying out of this edict in the West explain Ambrose's antagonism to this shadow of an emperor.

But the great conflict of Ambrose was with the Arian court. Under the influence of a Scythian Arian, Mercurinus, better known by his name of Auxentius, adopted from the Arian bishop whom Ambrose had succeeded, the empress Justina demanded from Ambrose (Easter, 385) the surrender, first of the Portian basilica, now the Church of St. Victor, then of the new basilica (see *infra*), for the use of the Arians. Ambrose refused this, as well as all later requests (*Epp.* xx. xxi.). On Jan. 23, 386, Justina retorted by a decree drawn up by Auxentius, giving the Arians full freedom to hold religious assemblies in all churches. The edict was a failure. So Justina sent orders that Ambrose should either allow the dispute between Auxentius and himself to be settled by (secular) arbiters, or should leave Milan. Ambrose declined to do either. To employ the people who guarded the Portian basilica, in which he was in a way imprisoned, Ambrose introduced among them at this time the Eastern custom of antiphonal song [*Sermo de basilicis tradendis* (Migne, xvi. 1007), esp. c. 34; August. *Conf.* ix. 7].

Ambrose's victory over Justina was completed by the miracles (especially the alleged healing of a blind butcher named Severus) attending his discovery of some gigantic bones, which he believed to be those of two brother martyrs, Protasius and Gervasius, and of whose location he had a 'presage' or vision. The discovery of these relics was welcomed with enthusiasm by a church somewhat barren of local martyrs. In spite of Arian sneers, they were solemnly deposited under the altar of the new basilica then awaiting dedication, which Justina had claimed, and which Ambrose now called by their name [*Ep.* xxii.; August. *Civ. Dei*, xxii. 8, *Conf.* ix. 7; Paulin. *Vita*, cc. 14, 15; for Ambrose's view of the miracles, *Ep.* xxii. 17–20].

Realizing its hopelessness, Justina abandoned the struggle, the more readily that she needed the bishop's help. In 387 she requested Ambrose again to act as her ambassador with Maximus (*de Obitu Valent.* 28). It was probably on this second visit to Trèves that Ambrose refused to communicate with the followers of the Spanish bishops Ithacius and Idatius, because they had persuaded Maximus to sentence and torture to death Priscillian and certain of his followers as heretics (see PRISCILLIANISM), and also because they held communion with Maximus, the slayer of Gratian. We see the same resoluteness in his refusal to give Maximus at the first interview the customary kiss of peace, and in his demand for the body of Gratian. We need not wonder that his embassy was unsuccessful, and that Ambrose was 'himself thrust out' of Trèves (*Ep.* xxiv.; and for Ithacius, etc., cf. *Ep.* xxvi. 3).

Maximus crossed the Alps (Aug. 387), and for a short time occupied Milan itself. During this usurpation Ambrose withdrew from the city, while the death at that time (Bury's *Gibbon*, iii. 177 n.) of the exiled Justina rid the bishop of all further trouble from the Arians. As regards Ithacius, it may be added that Ambrose presided in the spring of 390 over a council of bishops from Gaul and Northern Italy at Milan which approved of his excommunication.

After the defeat and execution of Maximus at Aquileia (Aug. 27, 388), the great Catholic emperor Theodosius took up his abode at Milan. Emperor and bishop were soon in conflict. The first struggle is of some moment in the history of the growth of intolerance. The Christians of Callinicum in Mesopotamia had burnt down a conventicle of the Valentinians and a Jewish synagogue. Theodosius ordered the bishop of Callinicum to rebuild the same at his own expense. Ambrose protested in a long letter written at Aquileia (*Ep.* xl.); he seemed to glory in the act; for the Church to rebuild the synagogue would be a triumph for the enemies of Christ. On his appealing to Theodosius in a verbose and rambling sermon at Milan (in *Ep.* xli.), the emperor yielded. 'Had he not done so,' Ambrose wrote to his sister, 'I would not have consecrated the elements' (*Ep.* xli. 28). In such incidents as these we see the beginnings of the claims which culminated in Hildebrand and Innocent III. Of almost equal importance is it to notice the intolerance which treats the Valentinian village chapel as if it were no better than a heathen temple (*Ep.* xl. 16), and considers the death of Maximus to be the Divine retribution for his ordering in 387 the rebuilding of a synagogue in Rome (*Ep.* xl. 23).

Whatever may be thought of his arrogance and intolerance in this matter of Callinicum, in his next conflict with Theodosius Ambrose was grandly in the right. The story is too familiar to need much detail. Angered by the murder of Botherich, the barbarian governor of Illyria, by the people of Thessalonica, Theodosius gave orders, retracted all too late, that the whole populace should be put to death. The gates of the circus were closed; for three hours the massacre went on of those within (April 30, 390). According to Theodoret, 7000 perished. On learning the news, Ambrose wrote to Theodosius a noble and tender letter exhorting him to repentance (*Ep.* li.). What answer Theodosius returned we know not; but on his presenting himself at Milan at the door of the church (*S. Ambrogio*), Ambrose met him in the porch, rebuked him for his sin, and bade him depart until he had given proofs of his penitence. For eight months, if we may trust Theodoret, Theodosius absented himself from all worship (Theodoret, v. 18). He felt his exclusion bitterly. 'The Church of God,' he said to Rufinus his minister, 'is open to slaves and beggars. To me it is closed, and with it the gates of heaven.' The intercession of Rufinus was in vain; so Theodosius laid aside his pride, and, prostrate on the floor of the church, confessed his sin, a forerunner in a worthier struggle of Henry IV. at Canossa and Henry II. at Canterbury. On receiving absolution, Theodosius mounted the chancel steps to present his offering. Ambrose refused to allow him to remain. 'The purple,' he said, 'makes emperors, not priests.' Ambrose claimed the chancel for the clergy alone. In all this we see not merely the final triumph of the Christian religion over the Empire, but the beginnings of the subjection of the laity to the priesthood. [On this Thessalonican matter and Ambrose's action, see Ambrose, *Ep.* li.; Theodoret, v. 17, 18 (needs care); Sozomen, vii. 25; Rufin. ii. 18; August. *Civ. Dei*, v. 26; Paulin. *Vit. Amb.* 24; and for the penance of Theodosius, Amb. *de obitu Theodos.* 34].

The relations of Theodosius and Ambrose were

henceforth undisturbed. During the usurpation of Eugenius (392–394), whom Arbogast the Frank, after strangling Valentinian II. at Vienna (May 15, 392), had elevated from the professor's chair to the purple, Ambrose retired to Bologna and Florence and stood loyally by Theodosius, in spite of all the friendly overtures of Eugenius. In Eugenius he rightly detected the danger of the recrudescence of paganism, as part of his political programme (*Ep.* lvii.; Paulin. *Vita*, 26, 31). No one, therefore, rejoiced more than Ambrose in Theodosius' victory over the puppet emperor at Heidenschafft (or Wipbach ?), Sept. 6, 394 (*Epp.* lxi. and lvii.; *Enarr. in* Psalm xxxvi. 22; Paulin. *Vita*, 26–34; August. *Civ. Dei*, v. 26), though he was careful to intercede with Theodosius not to punish the people in general. A few months later Theodosius died at Milan (Jan. 17, 395), in his last hours sending for Ambrose and commending his sons Arcadius and Honorius to his care (Amb. *de Obitu Theod.* 35). It was Ambrose also who in the presence of Honorius pronounced over the dead Theodosius the funeral oration. The death of Ambrose two years later (Good Friday, April 4, 397) was more than the passing of a great bishop: 'It is a death-blow for Italy,' exclaimed the valiant but ill-fated Stilicho (Paulin. *Vita*, 45). Ambrose was buried under the altar of the great church which he had built and consecrated to Protasius and Gervasius (see *supra*), but which now bears his own name (S. Ambrogio).

2. Influence.—The reputation of Ambrose must always rest upon his courage and skill as a practical administrator of the Church in most troublous times. In spite of sacerdotal claims which later were to bear much fruit, few would grudge him the tribute of their admiration. He combined the loftiest qualities of the Roman senator with the goodness and self-denial of the true Christian. Though his methods may not always commend themselves to our modern notions, in his results Ambrose was usually in the right. He saved Italy from Arianism, and restored her to the faith. Even the growth of sacerdotal claims was not without its services. In the approaching barbarian deluge it was no small gain to civilization that there was a power before which tyranny should quail. This is one side of his famous saying at the Council of Aquileia, 'Sacerdotes de laicis judicare debent, non laici de sacerdotibus' (*Gesta Conc. Aquil.* 51; see *supra*, p. 373[b]). The other side is its development into the deeds and theories of Hildebrand.

By his introduction of antiphonal singing (on the details of which see Groves' *Dict. Music*, new ed. *s.v.* 'Antiphony, Ambrosian, Gregorian'), Ambrose enriched the Western Church for ever. His own hymns, though repeatedly imitated in later days (see the full list of hymns falsely attributed to Ambrose, Migne, *PL* xvii. 1171–1222), are few in number, according to the Benedictine editors not more than twelve in all (printed in Migne, xvi. 1410), but of great interest and value. Their construction is uniform: 8 strophes in Iambic acatalectic dimeter (◡—◡—◡—◡—). The ascription to him of the *Te Deum* as composed at the baptism of St. Augustine is a legend of late growth. His morning hymns, *Æterne rerum conditor*, *Splendor paternæ gloriæ* ('O Jesu, Lord of heavenly grace'), his evening hymn, *Deus creator omnium*, his Christmas hymn, *Veni redemptor gentium*, and his hymn, *O lux beata Trinitas*, are permanent possessions of the Church universal (Trench, *Sacred Lat. Poetry*, 80–86; Julian, *Dict. Hymn.* 56 and *s.v.*).

The reputation of Ambrose as a writer and thinker must not be rated high, in spite of his being regarded as one of the four Latin Fathers of the Church. Gibbon is correct: 'Ambrose could act better than he could write. His compositions are . . . without the spirit of Tertullian, the copious elegance of Lactantius, the lively wit of Jerome, or the grave energy of Augustine' (iii. 175 n.). As a thinker he is completely overshadowed by his great convert St. Augustine, whose baptism in S. Ambrogio, at his hands, is one of the great spiritual events of the world (April 25, 387). But his influence was strongly exerted in certain directions, some of which we may deplore, all of which had later developments. His extravagant regard for relics (Gervasius, *supra*), and his enthusiasm for virginity (see especially the three books *de Virginibus* addressed to his sister Marcellina) and asceticism were signs of the times and indications of the future. His theory of the Sacraments (*de Sacramentis libri sex*) tended to the emphasis of materialistic conceptions; for instance, he praises his brother Satyrus for tying a portion of the Eucharist round his neck when shipwrecked (*de excessu Satyri*, i. 43, 46). He deduces the necessity of daily communion from the clause of the Lord's Prayer (ἐπιούσιος; *supersubstantialis*, Vulg. *quotidianus* [*de Sacr.* vi. 21], a view much developed in mediæval theology; cf. ABELARD, *supra*, p. 16[b]). His sermons are remarkable for their manliness and sober practicalness, enforced at times by felicitous eloquence. His letters are more valuable as materials for the historian than because of any charm or personal revelation. His exegetic writings, as we might expect from his lack of special study, contain little that is original, and are excessively allegorical after the fashion introduced by Origen (cf. August. *Conf.* vi. 4). But his knowledge of Greek enabled Ambrose to enrich Latin theology with many quotations from the Eastern Fathers, *e.g.* Basil and Gregory of Nyssa. Jerome, in fact, by reason of his dependence on these sources, especially Basil, compares him to a crow decked out in alien feathers (Rufinus, *Invect.* ii.). We see this dependence in his *de Bono Mortis* (the Blessing of Death), written about 387, in which his exceedingly mild view of the future punishment of the wicked is plainly indebted to *Fourth Esdras*. 'It is more serious,' he writes, 'to live in sin than to die in sin' (*op. cit.* 28). Nevertheless he 'does not deny that there are punishments after death' (*ib.* 33).

As a moral teacher Ambrose is seen at his best. His *de Officiis Ministrorum*, founded on the *de Officiis* of Cicero, is an attempt to establish a Christian ethic on the basis of the old philosophic classification of four cardinal virtues (*virtutes principales*)—*prudentia* or *sapientia*, *justitia*, *fortitudo*, and *temperantia* (*l.c.* i. 24). Of these he identifies *prudentia* with a man's relation to God ('pietas in Deum'; *de Offic.* i. 27). The classification is essentially faulty, as it leaves no place for humility, a grace unrecognized by pagan writers, and which Ambrose has difficulty in bringing in (*de Offic.* ii. 27). Virtue, he claims, is not the *summum bonum* of the Stoics, but rather the means to it. Ambrose further follows the Stoics in distinguishing between perfect and imperfect duties ['officium medium aut perfectum'; *consilia evangelica* and *præcepta* (*de Offic.* i. 11, 36 ff.; iii. 2)], a doctrine later developed into the mediæval 'works of supererogation.' His exegesis of the Sermon on the Mount is literal. The taking of interest is unconditionally rejected; the Christian should not even defend himself against robbers (*l.c.* iii. 4), though, remembering his Old Testament, he does not go so far as absolutely to condemn the soldier (*l.c.* i. 40). As was usual in the early Church, he disapproves of capital punishment, though he shows that he was somewhat embarrassed by the position in the matter of Christian judges (*Ep.* xxv.). We see his leanings to monasticism in his declaration that private property is *usurpatio* (*de Offic.* i. c. 28); charity is thus the partial adjustment of a wrong, and, as such, able to cancel sin (*de Elia et jejuniis*, c. 20, from Tobit 12[9]; *Sermo de eleemosynis*, 30, 31). We see the new note of humanity in his declaration that strangers must not be expelled from a city in time of famine (*de Offic.* iii. 7).

LITERATURE.—*A.* For the life of Ambrose we are dependent on the materials to be found in his own works (first arranged by Baronius) and on the *Vita* of Paulinus, his secretary. This work, dedicated to Augustine, is most unsatisfactory, and full of the absurdest prodigies [with which cf. the contemporary Sulpic. Severus, *Vita Martini* (ed. Halm, *CSEL*), cc. 1, § 9; 7, 8, 16; *Dial.* i. 24, 25, ii. 4, iii. 5, § 5]. It will be found in Migne, *PL* xiv. 27-46, or ed. Bened. App. An anonymous life in Greek (Migne, *PL* xiv. 46-66) is valueless. Other sources of knowledge from Augustine, etc., are indicated in the text.

B. The chief editions of the works of Ambrose, including a great many that are spurious, are (1) the editions of Erasmus, esp. the Basel ed. of Froben in 1527; (2) the Roman ed. in 6 vols. 1580-1587; (3) the Benedictine ed. of du Frische and le Nourry, Paris, 1686-1690; (4) Migne, *PL* xiv.-xvii. [the last vol. mostly spurious; Migne has excellent notes]; (5) the new ed. in progress (text only) in the Vienna *CSEL* (the Epp. unfortunately as yet [1907] not printed); (6) the ed. of Ballerini (Milan, 1875).

C. Of modern works, mention may be made of Th. Förster, *Amb. B. v. Mailand* (1884); Ihm, *Studia Ambrosiana* (1889); Pruner, *Die Theol. d. Amb.* (1862); Deutsch, *Des Amb. Lehre von d. Sünde und Sündentilgung* (1867); P. Ewald, *Der Einfluss der stoisch-ciceron. Moral auf die Ethik bei Amb.* (1881). For the historic setting, Gibbon, ed. Bury; and Hodgkin, *Italy and her Invaders* (1880, vol. i.), are indispensable.

H. B. WORKMAN.

AMERICA (Ethnology, Religion, and Ethics *).—Although many of the ethnical questions presented by the *Amerinds* or *Amerindians*, as some now propose to call the American aborigines, wrongly named 'Indians' by the Spanish discoverers, still await solution, the more fundamental problems affecting their origin and cultural development may be regarded as finally settled. Little is now heard of the 'Asiatic school,' which derived the Amerinds and all their works from the Eastern Hemisphere in comparatively recent times, that is, when the inhabitants of the Old World—Egyptians, Babylonians, Malays, Hindus, Chinese, Japanese—were already highly specialized. Such an assumption necessarily gave way when a more critical study of the American physical and mental characters, religious and social systems, failed to discover any close contact with those of the Old World, but pointed rather to independent local growths, owing nothing to foreign influences except the common germs of all human activities. Direct contact or importation might, for instance, be shown by the survival of some language clearly traceable to an Eastern source; or some old buildings obviously constructed on Egyptian, Chinese, or other foreign models; or any inscriptions on such buildings as might be interpreted by the aid of some Asiatic or European script; or some sailing craft like the Greek trireme, the Chinese junk, or Malay prau, or even the Polynesian outrigger; or some such economic plants and products as wheat, barley, rice, silk, iron; or domestic animals such as the ox, goat, sheep, pig; or poultry; things which, not being indigenous, might supply an argument at least for later intercourse. But nothing of all this has ever been found; and the list might be prolonged indefinitely without discovering any cultural links between the two hemispheres beyond such as may be traced to the Stone Ages, or to the common psychic unity of mankind. Mention is made of the oil-lamp, which, however, is confined to the Eskimo fringe, and was no doubt borrowed from the early Norse settlers in Greenland. There are also the Mexican pyramids, which have been likened to those of Memphis by archæologists who overlook the fundamentally different details, and forget that the Egyptians had ceased to build pyramids some 3000 years before the Mexican teocalli were raised by the Toltecs. Lastly, recourse is had to the Aztec and Maya calendric systems, although they prove, not Oriental borrowings, as Humboldt wrongly thought, but normal local developments on lines totally different from those of the Eastern astronomers.

Mainly on these grounds, the late J. W. Powell finally rejected the Asiatic theory, holding that there is no evidence that any of the native arts were introduced from the East; that stone implements are found in the Pleistocene deposits everywhere throughout America; that the industrial arts of America were born in America; that the forms of government, languages, mythological and religious notions were not derived from the Old, but developed in the New World (*Forum*, Feb. 1898). Mr. F. S. Dellenbaugh goes even further. He sets back the peopling of the continent to the Pre-Glacial epoch, while the climate was mild; and concludes that the Amerind race was 'early cut off on this hemisphere from intercourse with the remainder of the world, and held in isolation by a change in land distribution and by the continued glaciation of the northern portion of the continent'; and thus 'welded into an ethnic unity, which was unimpressed by outside influences till modern times' (*The North Americans of Yesterday*, 1901, p. 458). Hence the general homogeneity of type, customs, social and religious institutions, 'which separates the Amerindian races from the rest of the world, and argues an immense period of isolation from all other peoples' (*ib.* p. 358).

Recent exploration, especially in South America, supports the view that this 'general homogeneity' is not primordial, but the result of a somewhat imperfect fusion of two original elements—long-headed Europeans and round-headed Asiatics—which reached the New World in pre- and inter-glacial times by now vanished or broken land connexions. The Europeans, who most probably came first by the Faroe-Iceland-Greenland route available in the Pleistocene (Quaternary) Age, occupied the eastern side of the continent, and ranged in remote times from the Eskimo domain to the extreme south, where they are still represented by the Botocudos, Fuegians, and some other long-headed isolated groups. Thus the veteran palæo-ethnologist, G. de Mortillet, suggests that the Palæolithic men, moving with the reindeer from Gaul northwards, passed by the then existing land bridge into America, where they became the ancestors of the Eskimos. This view is anticipated by Topinard on anatomical grounds, and now confirmed for South America by A. Nehring and F. P. Outes. Nehring produces a long-headed skull from a Brazilian shell-mound at Santos, which presents characters like those both of the European Neanderthal and of the still older Javanese *Pithecanthropus erectus* (*Verhandl. Berlin. Anthrop. Ges.* 1896, p. 710). And in Patagonia, Outes describes eight undoubted Palæolithic stations and two Pleistocene types,—a long-headed arriving from the North-east and a short-headed from the North-west (*La Edad de la Piedra en Patagonia*, Buenos Ayres, 1905, section ii.).

The two streams of migration—Asiatic short-heads (North-west) and European long-heads (North-east)—are thus seen to commingle in the extreme south as early as the Old Stone Age; that is, prior to any marked somatic and cultural specializations

* This art. is offered as a general introduction to the Religion and Ethics of the American tribes. The tribes of North America will be grouped under the titles NORTH PACIFIC COAST; CALIFORNIA; MIDDLE AND SOUTHERN PLAINS; PUEBLOS; ALGONQUINS; DENES; ATLANTIC SEACOAST; ESKIMOS AND THE N.W. COAST; and some important tribes will be more fully described under their own names. An art. on the Mexican tribes will be found under MEXICO. The present art. is followed by a separate sketch of the religion of the South American tribes; on which see, further, ANDEANS, etc.

in the Eastern Hemisphere. The Asiatics, following the still bridged Bering route, appear to have arrived a little later, but in larger bodies, which explains the predominance of round heads along the Pacific seaboard from Alaska to Chili. But interminglings were inevitable, and the result is that the Amerinds as a whole are a composite race, in which the Mongolic (Asiatic) characters are perhaps more marked than the Caucasic (European). Thus the complexion is reddish-brown, coppery, olive or yellowish, never white; while the hair is uniformly black, lank, often very long and round in section, like that of all Mongols. The high cheek-bones, too, point to Mongol descent, as does also the low stature—5 feet and under to 5 feet 6 inches—in the west (Thlinkets, Eskimos, Haidas, Pueblos, Aztecs, Peruvians, Aymaras, Araucanians). On the other hand, the large convex or aquiline nose; the straight though rather small eyes, never oblique; the tall stature (5 feet 8 inches to 6 feet and upwards), especially of the Prairie Redskins, the Brazilian Bororos, and the Patagonians, as well as a curious Caucasic expression often noticed even amongst the Amazonian aborigines, bespeak a European origin, more particularly for the eastern and central groups. The constituent elements of the Amerinds would therefore appear to be proto-Europeans of the Old Stone Age—that is, a somewhat generalized primitive Caucasic type—and proto-Asiatics of the early New Stone Age,—that is, a somewhat generalized primitive Mongolic type,—both elements still preserving many features of the common Pleistocene precursors (see art. ETHNOLOGY, § 4).

Coming now to the *mental qualities*, as illustrated by language, the industrial arts, social and religious institutions, and ethical standards, we shall find that in all these respects the Amerinds show far greater divergences from their Eurasian progenitors than is the case with their somatic characters. The reason is obvious. The physical traits brought with them from the East are, so to say, indelible and, apart from slight modifications due to miscegenation, climate, and heredity, necessarily persist as witnesses to their ethnical origins. But the mental phenomena and cultural processes were all in a rudimentary state when the Amerinds were cut off from the Eurasians in the Ice Age, and since then the very rudiments have almost been obliterated during their normal evolution in the New World. Dellenbaugh deals fully with such industries as basketry, pottery, carving, weaving, and, without any reference to Eastern prototypes, is able to follow their regular development in America from the rudest beginnings to the finished Pueblo and Californian waterproof wickerwork, and the highly artistic earthenware and basalt carvings of the Chiriqui district, near Panama. And that these are all purely local products, uninspired by any extraneous influences, is evident from the fact that, as we shall see, they are exclusively 'dominated by the customs and religious ideas of the Amerind race, which were practically the same everywhere in different stages of development. As in picture-writing we trace the growth of letters, so by the aid of Amerind sculpture and carving we have a line of art progress from infancy to the present time' (*op. cit.* p. 192 f.).

Perhaps even a stronger proof of independent growth in a long-secluded region is presented by the Amerind languages, not one of which has yet been traced to a foreign source. From all other forms of speech they differ not merely in their general phonetic, lexical, and structural features: they differ in their very morphology, which is neither agglutinating, inflecting, nor isolating, like those of the Old World, but holophrastic or polysynthetic, with a tendency to fuse all the elements of the sentence in a single word, often of prodigious length. Here culture makes no difference, and the same holophrastic character is everywhere presented by the rudest as well as by the most highly cultivated tongues current between Alaska and Fuegia, by Aztec, Mayan, and Quichuan (Peruvian) no less than by Eskimo, Algonquin, Cherokee, Amazonian, Ipurina, and Tehuelche of Patagonia. Yet of this remarkable linguistic phenomenon not a single instance is to be found anywhere in the Eastern Hemisphere. There is incorporation with the verb, as in Basque and the Mongolo-Turkic family, always limited, however, to pronominal and purely formative elements. But in Amerind speech there is no such limitation; and not merely the pronouns, which are restricted in number, but the nouns, with their attributes, which are practically numberless, all enter necessarily into the verbal paradigm. Thus the Tarascan of Mexico cannot say *hoponi*, 'to wash,' but only *hopocuni*, 'to wash the hands,' *hopodini*, 'to wash the ears,' and so on, always in one synthetic form, which is conjugated throughout, so that the conjugation of a Dakotan, Cree, Aztec, or any other Amerind verb is endless. Specimens only can be given, and they fill many pages of the native grammars without even approximately exhausting a theme for which six or eight pages suffice, for instance, in English or Danish. The process also involves much clipping and phonetic change, as in the colloquial English *hap'oth*='halfpenny worth,' *I'd*='I would,' etc., forms which give just a faint idea of the Amerind permutations.

It is obvious that such a linguistic evolution from a common rudimentary condition of speech, as in the Pleistocene Age, implies complete isolation from foreign contacts, by which the cumbrous process would have been disturbed and broken up, and also a very long period of time, to expand and consolidate the system throughout Amerindia. But time is perhaps still more imperiously demanded by the vast number of stock languages which form another remarkable feature of the American linguistic field. Some are known to have died out since the Discovery; but many others, variously estimated at from one to two hundred, or perhaps more than are found in the whole of the Eastern Hemisphere, are still current, all differing radically in their phonology, vocabulary, and general structure—in fact, having little in common beyond the extraordinary holophrastic mould in which they are cast. But even this statement conveys a far from adequate idea of the astonishing diversity of speech prevailing in this truly linguistic Babel. Powell, who has determined nearly sixty stocks for North America alone, shows that the practically distinct idioms are far more numerous than might be inferred even from such a large number of mother-tongues. Thus in the Algonquian family there are quite forty members differing one from the other as much as, and sometimes even more than, for instance, English from German: in Siouan, over twenty; in Athapascan, from thirty to forty; and in Shoshonean, a still greater number (*op. cit.* and *Indian Linguistic Families of America North of Mexico*, Washington, 1891). For the stocks Powell adopts the convenient ending *-an* attached to a typical or leading member, such as *Algonquin*, which for the whole group becomes *Algonquian*; and the principle has been extended by Dr. N. León to the Mexican and Central American families, and by A. H. Keane to those of South America. León's list, based on the latest information, comprises seventeen stocks, including the great and widespread Nahuatlan (Aztecan) and Maya-Quichéan families, and ranging from Lower California and the Rio Grande del Norte southwards to Panama (*Familias Linguisticas de Mexico*, etc., Museo Nacional, 1902). The imperfectly explored South American section has already yielded over fifty stocks, of which the more important are the Quichua-Aymaran, the Tupi-Guaranian, the Cariban, Arawakan, Gesan, and Araucan. But some of these are lumped together in large groups, such as the Ticunan, Moxosan, and Purusan, each of which will, on more careful analysis, probably be found to comprise several stocks (Keane, *Central and South America*, 1901, vol. i. ch. ii.).

So uniform are the physical characters, that systematists have failed to establish an intelligible classification of the Amerind races on strictly anthropological data. Hence all current classifications are mainly linguistic, and make no claim to scientific accuracy. Thus Sir E. im Thurn declares that for Guiana, where 'it is not very easy to describe the distinguishing physical characters,' and where 'there are no very great differences other than those of language,' this factor 'must be adopted as the base of classification' (*Among the Indians of Guiana*, 1883, p. 161). At the same time, the linguistic grouping is convenient, and often even informing, as we see in the northern fringe, where, owing to the astonishing tenacity with which the Eskimos cling to their highly polysynthetic language, their pre-historic migrations may still be easily followed from Greenland and Labrador round the shores of the frozen ocean to Alaska, and even across the Bering waters to the opposite Asiatic mainland. So with the Algonquians, whose cradle is shown to lie about the Hudson Bay lands, where Cree, the most archaic of all Algonquian tongues, still survives.

Perhaps even more striking is the case of the Siouans (Dakotans), hitherto supposed to have been originally located in the prairie region west of the Mississippi, but now proved to have migrated thither from the Atlantic slope of the Alleghany uplands, where the Catawbas, Tutelos, Woccons, and other Virginian tribes still spoke highly archaic forms of Siouan speech within the memory of man. So also the Niquirans, Pipils, and others of Guatemala and Nicaragua, who are known to be of Nahuatlan stock, not from their somatic characteristics, but solely from the corrupt Aztec language which they have always spoken.

As the tribe is thus identified only or mainly by its speech, it becomes important to determine the distribution of the Amerind tongues in their several areas. It is noteworthy that the great majority of Powell's families, about forty altogether, are crowded in great confusion along the narrow strip of seaboard between the coast ranges and the Pacific from Alaska to California: ten are dotted round the Gulf of Mexico from Florida to the Rio Grande, and two disposed round the Gulf of California, while nearly all the rest of the land—some six million square miles—is held by the six widely-diffused Eskimoan, Athapascan, Algonquian, Iroquoian, Siouan, and Shoshonean families. Similarly in Mexico, Central and South America, about a dozen stocks—Opata-Piman, Nahuatlan, Maya-Quichéan, Chorotegan in the north; Cariban, Arawakan, Tupi-Guaranian, Tapuyan (Gesan), Tacanan, Aymara-Quichuan, Araucan in the south—are spread over many millions of square miles, while scores of others are restricted to extremely narrow areas. Various theories have been advanced to explain this strangely irregular distribution, and, at least in the North American prairie lands, the Venezuelan savannahs, and the Argentine pampas, a potent determining cause must have been the scouring action of fierce, predatory steppe nomads, so that here, as in Central Asia, most of the heterogeneous groups huddled together in contracted areas may perhaps be regarded as 'the sweepings of the plains.' The chief stocks, with their more important sub-groups, will be found in art. ETHNOLOGY, *Conspectus*.

None of the Amerind languages has ever been reduced to written form except by the missionaries, and in one instance by a Cherokee native (Sequoyah or George Guest), working under European influences and on Old-World prototypes. Even the cultured Peruvians had nothing but the *quipo*, knotted strings of varying thickness, colour, and length, used for recording dates, statistics, and events. The more artistic, but less serviceable, Algonquian *wampum* sometimes answered the same purpose, as in the historical treaty between Penn and the Delaware Indians. But various rude pictographic systems, inscribed or painted on rocks, skins, earthenware, or calabashes, were almost universal, ranging from the extreme north (Eskimos) to Argentina and Central Brazil. The Matto Grosso aborigines, recently visited by the Bohemian explorer, V. Fric, have developed quite an ingenious method of 'taking notes,' using dried calabashes for the purpose. Everybody goes about with one of these, which may be called his diary, all important incidents being inscribed on it pictorially. The art is perhaps the most perfect of the kind anywhere devised, since the scratchings are quite legible, and handed round to be read as we might hand round printed or written matter. True perspective and proportion are observed, as by the Bushmen in their cave paintings; and the evil spirits which swarm everywhere are also thwarted by being sketched in fanciful forms on the calabashes (*Science*, July 1906).

Far more advanced than any of these primitive methods are the Aztec, the Zapotec, and especially the Maya pictorial codices, painted in diverse colours on real native (maguey) paper, and mainly of a calendric or astrological character. Several have been reproduced in facsimile with long commentaries by Förstemann and Seler, but still remain undeciphered, although they express numerals quite clearly. They had also reached the *rebus* state, but apparently fell short of a true phonetic system, despite the claim of Bishop Landa's 'alphabet' to be regarded as such. There are also long mural inscriptions on many of the temples and other structures at Palenque, Uxmal, Chichen-Itza, and elsewhere in Chiapas, Yucatan, and Honduras. But these also have so far baffled the attempts of Mr. Cyrus Thomas and others to interpret them, although the calculiform ('pebble-like') characters present the appearance of a real script. It is admitted that many have phonetic value, but only as rebuses, and the transition from the rebus to true syllabic and alphabetic systems had apparently not been made by any of the Amerinds. But even so, these codices and wall writings, believed to embody calendric systems on a level with the reformed Julian, represent their highest intellectual achievements, while the palaces and temples in the above-mentioned districts rank as their greatest architectural triumphs, rivalled only by those of the Chimus, Quichuas, and Aymaras in Peru and on the shores of Lake Titicaca.

Elsewhere there is nothing comparable to these monumental remains of Central and South America, and the less cultured Amerinds of North America have little to show of æsthetic interest beyond their beautiful ceramic and wickerwork products, the earth-mounds thickly strewn over the Ohio valley and some other parts of the Mississippi basin, and the *casas grandes* of the Pueblo Indians in New Mexico and Arizona. On the origin of the *casas grandes*—huge stone structures large enough to accommodate the whole community—no question arises. They are undoubtedly the work of their present occupants, the Hopi (Moki), Tañoan,

Keresan, and Zuñian tribes, driven to the southern uplands by the Apaches, Navajos, and other predatory nomads of the plains. Their communal houses or strongholds grew out of the local conditions, and the complete adaptation of Pueblo architecture to the physical environment is quite obvious. The circular chambers called *estufas* or *kivas* occurring in some districts are still the council houses and temples, the 'medicine lodges,' in which the religious and social affairs of the community are transacted, and their very form recalls the time when the tribe dwelt in round huts or tents on the plains. Some are very old, some quite recent; yet the structures do not differ from one another, and in all cases 'the result is so rude that no sound inference of sequence can be drawn from the study of individual examples; but in the study of large aggregations of rooms we find some clues. The unit of Pueblo construction is the single room, even in the large many-storied villages. This unit is quite as rude in modern as in ancient work, and both are very close to the result which would be produced by any Indian tribes who came into the country and were left free to work out their own ideas. Starting with this unit, the whole system of Pueblo architecture is a natural product of the country and of the conditions of life known to have affected the people by whom it was practised' (Cosmos Mindeleff in Sixteenth An. Report of *BE*, Washington, 1897, p. 192).

This applies with equal force to the *cliff-dwellings* of the neighbouring Colorado cañons, in which the same peaceful Pueblo peoples have taken refuge against the same marauding Prairie Indians. 'Along the cliff lines slabs of rock suitable for building abound; and the primitive ancients, dependent as they were on environment, naturally produced the cliff-dwellings. The tendency towards this type was strengthened by inter-tribal relations; the cliff-dwellers were probably descended from agricultural or semi-agricultural villagers who sought protection against enemies, and the control of land and water through aggregation in communities' (*ib.* p. 94).

In the same way many of the Ohio mounds, which often present the aspect of fortresses, may have been raised by the more settled Cherokee (Iroquoian) tribes as earthworks against the lawless nomads of the surrounding plains. In any case the long controversy regarding their origin may now be taken as closed, and the view that they were constructed, not by any unknown pre-historic race, but by the present Amerinds, is generally accepted as beyond reasonable doubt. Mr. W. K. Moorehead, one of the best observers, recognizes two distinct mound-building races, the earlier long-heads of the Muskingum valley, and the later round-heads whose chief centre lay about the sources of the Ohio river. From the sepulchral and other mounds of the long-heads have been recovered pottery, slate and hematite objects, copper bracelets and other ornaments, all generally inferior to those of the round-heads. Fort Ancient, the largest of the earthworks in Ohio, is nearly a mile long with over 10 miles of artificial knolls, and Chillicothe on the Scioto river is the centre of several extensive groups, such as the Hopewell and Hopeton works, and the Mound City, that have yielded potteries of artistic design, finely wrought flints, and some copper, but no bronze or iron implements—another proof that nearly the whole of America was still in the Stone Age at the time of the Discovery. Moorehead concludes that none of the mound-builders attained more than a high state of savagery; that they were skilled in several arts, but excelled in none; that they were not even semi-civilized, much less possessed of the 'lost civilization with which they have been credited' (*Primitive Man in Ohio*, 1892, *passim*). Hence the general inference of Cyrus Thomas that there is nothing in the mounds that the Amerinds could not have done, that many have been erected or continued in post-Columbian times, consequently by the present aborigines, and that there is therefore no reason for ascribing them to any other race of which we have no knowledge (Twelfth An. Report of *BE*, Washington, 1894). Taking a broader view of the whole horizon, Dr. Hamy ventures to suggest that the mound-builders, the Pueblo Indians, and the cliff-dwellers 'all belong to one and the same race,' whose prototype may be a fossil Californian skull from the Calaveras auriferous gravels assumed to be of Pleistocene age (*L'Anthropologie*, 1896, p. 140).

For most of these Northern Amerinds a higher moral standard may perhaps be claimed than for the more civilized Central and South American peoples. Our general impression of the native American, writes Mr. Dellenbaugh, who knows them well, is that he is a kind of human demon or wild animal, never to be trusted, unable to keep a compact, and always thirsting for blood. But it is not so. If treated fairly he may nearly always be trusted. The Iroquois League maintained the 'covenant chain' with the British unbroken for over a century; the Delawares never broke faith with Penn; and for two hundred years the Hudson Bay Company have traded all over the northern part of the continent, without a serious rupture with any of the Chipewyan, Cree, and other rude Athapascan and Algonquian tribes.

'We are blind to our own shortcomings, and exaggerate those of the Amerind. In estimating their traits we do not regard them enough from their own standpoint, and without so regarding them we cannot understand them. His daily life in the earlier days was by no means bloodthirsty, and the scalping-knife was no more the emblem of pre-Columbian society than the bayonet is of ours. In most localities he achieved for all, what all are with us still dreaming to obtain—"liberty and a living," and his methods of government possessed admirable qualities' (*op. cit.* p. 353 f.).

The aborigines, however, were not free from the taint of cannibalism, which, if it assumed a somewhat ceremonious aspect in the north, was widely practised by many of the Brazilian, Andean, Colombian, and Amazonian tribes in the south, without any such religious motive. Thus the nearly extinct Catios, between the Atrato and Cauca rivers, were reported, like the Congo negroes, to 'fatten their captives for the table.' Their Darien neighbours stole the women of hostile tribes, cohabited with them, and brought up the children till their fourteenth year, when they were eaten with much rejoicing, the mothers ultimately sharing the same fate (Cieza de León). The Cocomas along the Rio Marañon ate their own dead, grinding the bones to drink in their fermented liquor, and explaining that 'it was better to be inside a friend than to be swallowed up by the cold earth' (Markham, *JAI*, 1895, 235 f.). The very word *cannibal* is a variant of *caribal*, derived from the man-eating Caribs; and so universal was the custom in New Granada, that 'the living were the grave of the dead; for the husband has been seen to eat his wife, the brother his brother or sister, the son his father; captives also are eaten roasted' (Steinmetz, *Endokannibalismus*, p. 19). But the lowest depths of the horrible in this respect were touched by what J. Nieuwehof relates of the wide-spread East Brazilian Tapuya savages, although something nearly as bad is told by Dobrizhoffer of some of the primitive Guarani tribes in Paraguay (*ib.* pp. 17–18). The Seri people of Sonora, most debased of all the Northern Amerinds, are certainly cannibals (McGee). But elsewhere in the north, anthropophagy has either long since died out, or else survives here and there apparently only as a ceremonial rite. 'Cannibalism of this kind prevailed in many tribes; *always, ostensibly*, a religious ceremony, not a means of satisfying hunger. The victims were often richly feasted and generously treated for some time before being executed' (Dellenbaugh, p. 368). Yet Payne declares that the Aztec custom of consuming captives at religious feasts was in reality a means of procuring animal food resulting from the limited meat supply, and that perpetual war was waged mainly to obtain prisoners for this purpose (*History of the New World*, etc., ii. pp. 495, 499, 501).

The more favourable picture presented by the northern aborigines is specially applicable to the Iroquois, in many respects the finest of all the Amerinds, — unsurpassed, says Brinton, by any other on the continent, 'and I may even say by any other people in the world. In legislation, in eloquence, in fortitude, and in military sagacity they had no equals. They represented the highest development the Indian ever reached in the hunter state. Crimes and offences were so infrequent under their social system that the Iroquois can scarcely be said to have a criminal code. Theft was barely known, and on all occasions, and at whatever price, the Iroquois spoke the truth without fear and without hesitation' (*The American Race*, p. 82). Even in the literary sphere they rank high, as attested by Sequoyah's most ingenious syllabic script (see above), and by the stirring poetic effusions of Miss Pauline Johnson (Tekahionwake), who can thus sing of the departed Amerind's 'Happy Hunting Grounds':

'Into the rose-gold westland its yellow prairies roll,
World of the bison's freedom, home of the Indian's soul.
Roll out, O seas, in sunlight bathed,
Your plains wind-tossed, and grass-enswathed. . . .
Who would his lovely faith condole?
Who envies not the Red-skin's soul
Sailing into the cloudland, sailing into the sun,
Into the crimson portals ajar when life is done.'
(*The White Wampum*, 1906).

This vision of a cloudland, the glorified abode of departed souls, is a purely anthropomorphic notion common to all the primitive Amerind peoples. It has nothing to do with the supernatural, or with rewards and penalties after death, or even with the immortality of the higher creeds, but is to be conceived as a purely natural continuation of the present life, freed from its cares and troubles. Skyland is only a distant part of this world, which is better than the tribal territory, and in which the departed continue to live in a state of absolutely material comfort and happiness, exempt from all present anxieties, and, so to say, without a thought for the morrow.

'The key to the whole matter may be provided by remembering that these [Guiana] Indians look on the spirit-world as exactly parallel to, or more properly as a part of, the material world known to them. Spirits, like material beings, differ from each other only, if the phrase be allowed, in their varying degrees of brute force and brute cunning, and none are distinguished by the possession of anything like divine attributes. Indians therefore regard disembodied spirits not otherwise than the beings still in the body whom they see around them' (Sir E. im Thurn, *Among the Indians of Guiana*, 1883, p. 358).

Such is the first stage of the purely animistic religions common to the more primitive Amerind peoples in North and South America. The essential point is that men remain men in the after world, where they continue to follow their ordinary pursuits under more pleasant conditions. Thus the Eskimo has his kayak, his harpoons, and great schools of cetaceans; the prairie redskin his tomahawk, his bow and arrows, and countless herds of bisons, and so on. Thus is explained the secondary part played by ancestor-worship, and also the great variety of burial rites amongst the Amerinds. If a man remains a man, he cannot be deified or worshipped; and if he is still interested in human pursuits, he needs attendance and attendants. The Guiana native is buried in his house, which is then deserted, so that he may visit his former dwelling without interference from his survivors. He will also need his hammock and other necessaries, which are accordingly buried with him. In the north-west he was accompanied by a slave, who, if not dead in three days, was strangled by another slave. In Mexico, the custom of burying live slaves with the dead was general. Elsewhere they were wrapped in fine furs, or in less costly grasses and matting, to keep them warm. Then there were burials in pits, mounds, cists, caves; also cremation, embalming, and sepulture in trees or on scaffolds, or in the water, or in canoes that were then turned adrift. In Tennessee, old graves are found which were made by lining a rectangular space with slabs of stone, exactly as during the reindeer period in France. And in Ancon, on the coast of Peru, whole families were mummified, clothed in their ordinary garb, and then put together in a common tightly corded pack with suitable outward adornments, and all kinds of domestic objects inside (Reiss and Strübel, *The Necropolis of Ancon in Peru*, A. H. Keane's Eng. ed. 3 vols., 1880–1887).

In the evolution of the Amerind Hades, the next step is the recognition of two separate departments, —one for the good, usually left in cloudland; the other for the wicked, more often consigned to the nether world, but both at times relegated to the same shadowy region of difficult access beyond the grave. Thus the Saponi (eastern Siouans) hold that after death both good and bad people are conducted by a strong guard into a great road, along which they journey together for some time, till the road forks into two paths — one extremely level, the other stony and mountainous. Here they are parted by a flash of lightning, the good taking to the right, while the bad are hurried away to the left. The right-hand road leads to a delightful warm land of perennial spring, where the people are bright as stars and the women never scold. Here are deer, turkeys, elks, and bisons innumerable, always fat and gentle, while the trees yield delicious fruits all the year round. The rugged left-hand path leads to a dark and wintry land covered with perpetual snow, where the trees yield nothing but icicles. Here the wicked are tormented a certain number of years, according to their several degrees of guilt, and then sent back to the world to give them a chance of meriting a place next time in the region of bliss (J. Mooney, *The Siouan Tribes*, etc. p. 48).

This discrimination between the two abodes thus obviously coincides with the growth of a higher ethical standard, such as is seen even amongst the pitiless Aztecs with their frightful religious orgies. If the Spanish historian, Sahagun, can be trusted, their moral sense was sufficiently awakened to distinguish between sin and crime, and they even recognized a kind of original sin, which was washed away by cleansing waters. Xochiquetzal, the 'Mexican Eve,' the 'first sinner,' was depicted weeping for her lost happiness, when driven from Paradise for plucking a flower; and the Earth-goddess Tlaçolteotl was represented as an embodiment of sin, which was 'from the beginning of time.' Hence the newborn babe is subjected to a ceremonial washing, with the words, 'My son, come unto thy mother, the Goddess of Water, Chalchiuhtlicue, thy father, the Lord Chalchiuhtlatonac; enter the water, the blue, the yellow; may it cleanse thee from the evil which thou hast from the beginning of the world' (E. Seler, *Aubin Tonalamatl*, A. H. Keane's Eng. ed., 1901).

A further development of the after-life, still in association with a corresponding growth of the moral sense, is seen in the beautiful vision of the Araucanian people, who consign the departed spirits, not to an invisible heaven or hell, but to the visible constellations of the starry firmament. Their forefathers are the bright orbs which move along the Milky Way, and from these ethereal heights are still able to look down and keep watch over their earthly children. Under their ever vigilant gaze, these Southern Amerinds had a far higher motive than the hope of reward or the fear of punishment, to avoid wrong-doing and to practise all the virtues, that is, all the tribal usages sanctioned by tradition. Thus, without any legal codes, pains, or penalties, the social interests were safeguarded, while even personal conduct was controlled; for who would dare to wrong his neighbour beneath the glittering eyes of his ancestors? Scarcely any more complete fusion of the ethical and religious systems has elsewhere been realized (*RAnth*, 1884).

It will be seen at once that these Araucanian ancestors, though wafted aloft, still remained human, with human cares and interests, and hence could not be worshipped as gods. The Delawares also would say to a dying man, to comfort him, 'You are about to visit your ancestors,' or, as we might say, to join the majority, without attaching any sense of an apotheosis to the expression. So it is nearly everywhere amongst the Amerinds, and Herbert Spencer's broad generalization that all religions have their origin in ancestor-worship ('ghost propitiation') does not apply at all to the New World. His further statement (*Eccles. Institutions*, p. 687), that 'nature-worship is but an aberrant form of ghost-worship,' has here to be reversed, since the prevailing Amerindian religions were various forms of what American writers designate as *zoötheism*, that is, the deification, not of men, but of animals. Dellenbaugh says emphatically: 'Savage races worship animal gods and natural objects personified as animals . . . as in the case of the thunder and lightning generally attributed by the Amerinds to the mysterious "thunder-bird"' (*op. cit.* p. 393). In their creation myths the aborigines themselves are sprung from animals: three, say the Mohegans, a bear, a deer, and a wolf; one, say the Delawares, the 'Great Hare,' called the 'Grandfather of the Indians.' Their personal and totemic gods were everywhere conceived to be in the form of animals, and to these various acts of homage were made, thus leading up to the universal zoötheism common to most Amerinds.

But there is no absolute uniformity, and amongst some of the more advanced nations there occur instances of what may be called hero-worship, resulting, as elsewhere, in some form of apotheosis or ancestor-worship. Thus the Aztecs have their *Quetzalcoatl*, answering to the Mayan *Kukulcan*, both meaning the 'bright-feathered snake,' and both appearing under two forms, as a deity and as an historical person. Hence they may very well have been real men who arose as teachers and civilizers amongst their people, and became deified as their good deeds became traditions and memories. To them corresponded the Quiché *Gukumatz* (same meaning), one of the four chief gods who created the world; *Votan*, the eponymous hero of the Tzendals; the Algonquian *Michabo*; the Iroquoian *Ioskeha*, and many others. But the Amerind pantheon was essentially limited. In the three extant Maya codices—the Dresden, Paris, and Madrid—Dr. P. Schellhas could find only 'about fifteen figures of gods in human form and about half as many in animal form,' and these figures 'embody the essential part of the religious conceptions of the Maya peoples in a tolerably complete form' (*Deities of the Maya Manuscripts*, 1905, p. 7). Most of the gods here figured—the Death-god, Itzamná (the Maya culture hero), the Moon-, Night-, Sun-, War-, Snake-, Water-, and Storm-gods—find their counterpart in the Aztec Olympus, which may have a few others of its own. But the more primitive Amerind religions cannot boast of more than five or six; and in 1616, before contact with Europeans, the chief of the Potomac Algonquians told Captain Argoll that they had only 'five gods in all; our chief god appears often unto us in the form of a mighty great hare [see above]; the other four have no visible shape, but are indeed the four winds, which keep the four corners of the earth' (W. Strachey, *Historie of Travaile into Virginia*, p. 98). Frequent mention occurs of these four deities of the Four Cardinal Points, or of the Four Winds, or of four invisible powers, bringers of rain and sunshine, rulers of the seasons and the weather, with a fifth represented as greater than all, 'who is above,' and is identified by Brinton with the god of Light, of whom 'both Sun and Fire were only material emblems' (*The Lenâpé and their Legends*, 1885, p. 65). This is the *Manitou* of the early writers, who is described by the missionaries as the Creator, the Supreme Being, the true God of the really monotheistic aborigines. But this Manitou with many variants is the Devil of the New Jersey natives (*Amer. Hist. Record*, i. 1872), and in the Delaware *Walam Olum*, edited by Brinton (Philadelphia, 1885), there are all kinds of Manitous—a Great Manitou who speaks 'a manitou to manitous,' who was 'a manitou to men and their grandfather,' and 'an evil Manitou,' who makes 'evil beings only, monsters, flies, gnats,' and so on. The claim of this Manitou, the 'grandfather' of the Delawares, to rank as the *Ens Supremum* must therefore be dismissed with the like claims of the Dakotan 'Wakanda' and other Amerindian candidates for the highest honours. On the general question of a Supreme Being it is pointed out by Gatschet that the deities of the early Algonquian natives are better known than the so-called 'gods' of most of the present North American aborigines. This is due to the observations made by Capt. John Smith, Strachey, Roger Williams, and a few other pioneers prior to Christian influences. The first preachers translated 'God' and 'Jahweh' by the Algonquian terms *manit*, *mundtu*, 'he is god'; also *manittw* (whence our *manitou*), which simply means 'ghost' or 'spirit,' so that the plural form *manittowok* served to express the *gods* of the Bible. Here *m* is an impersonal prefix which is dropped in polysynthetic composition (see p. 377[b]), leaving the root *anit*, *ant*, *and*, i.e. any spirit, not *the Spirit* in a pre-eminent sense. It was equally applicable to one and all of the *genii loci*, and to restrict it to *one* was reading into it a meaning puzzling to the natives, though required for the right understanding of the Christian and Biblical concepts. One of these genii was *Kaut-antow-wit*, the great south-west spirit, to whose blissful abode all departed souls migrated, and whence came their corn and beans. The same root appears in *Kehteanit*, the 'Great Spirit, which by the epithet *kehte* (='great') acquired sufficient pre-eminence to be used by the missionaries for 'God' and 'Jahweh.' But *great* is relative, not absolute, and does not necessarily involve the idea of an *Ens Supremum*. *Kehteanit* again is the *Kiehtan* of Eliot's Massachusetts Bible, and also the *Tantum* (contraction of *Keitanitom*, 'our great god') of the Penobscots, who associated him with *Hobbamoco*, the Evil One, thus suggesting the two principles of good and evil as more fully developed in the *Walam Olum*, and among the Araucanians and others. E. Winslow (*Good News from New Eng.*, 1624) thinks *Kiehtan* was the chief god of the Algonquins, maker of all the other gods, and himself made by none. But if there were other gods, by whomsoever made, then *Kiehtan* was merely the head of a pantheon, the Zeus or Diespiter of the New World. Hence he naturally dwells above, in the heavens towards the setting sun, whither all go after death. But he had a rival, *Squantam*, 'whom they acknowledge,' says Josselyn, 'but worship him they do not.' In any case he was more to be feared than loved, for *squantam* comes from the verb *musquantam* (='he is wrathful'), which explains the Narraganset remark at any casual mishap, *musquantam mánit*, 'God was angry and did it' (*JAFL* vol. xii.).

Respecting the Dakotan *Wakanda*, also supposed to rank as the Supreme Being, W. J. McGee clearly shows that he is not a personality at all, much less a deity, but a vague entity, an essence, a virtue, a subtle force like the Polynesian *mana*, which inheres in certain objects and renders them efficacious for good or evil. 'Even a man, especially a shaman, may be wakanda. So, too, the fetishes, and the ceremonial objects and decorations, — various animals, the horse among the prairie tribes, many natural objects and places of striking character, — though it is easy to understand how the superficial inquirer, dominated by definite spiritual concepts, perhaps deceived by crafty native informants, came to adopt and perpetuate the erroneous interpretation' (Fifteenth An. Report of *BE*, Washington, 1897, p. 182).

Nobody pretends that the sublime notion of a Creator had been grasped by the Pueblos with their undisguised animal-cult, ceremonial snake dances, and gross symbolism; or by the Cheyennes, Poncas, and allied groups, whose elaborate animal and sun dances have been so fully described by G. A. Dorsey (*Field Columbian Museum Publications*, Chicago, 1905). Hence nothing more is heard of a Supreme Deity till we are confronted by the Mexican Tonacatecutli who was represented as the one true god of the Aztecs, the maker of the world, the supreme Lord, to whom no offerings were made because he needed none. But in so describing him it is suggested that the early interpreters were biassed by Biblical conceptions. A more plausible view, advanced by Seler, is that Tonacatecutli was a later invention of the Nahuan rationalists, 'the outcome of philosophic speculation, of the need of a principle of causality, such, for instance, as the God of our modern theosophistic systems' (Seler, *Aubin Tonalamatl*, 39). The Mayas also, however advanced in other respects, were but indifferent theologians with whom the local tutelary deities still survived under Christian names. Appeal is likewise made to the 'Feather-Snake' god of the Huaxtecs, creator of man, but also father of the Tlapallan people, and founder of the Tollan empire, whereby his universal godhead is destroyed (see art. TOLTECS); and to Piyexoo, chief deity of the Zapotecs, the Creator, the uncreated *Pitao-Cozaana*, who, however, was only the first amongst many patrons of all the virtues and of all the vices, to whom horrible sacrifices were made (de Nadaillac, *Prehistoric America*, p. 363). The *Bochica* of the Chibchas was almost certainly an eponymous hero (see art. CHIBCHAS), and this Colombian nation were really Sun-worshippers, like the neighbouring Quichuas (Peruvians), amongst whom it would be idle to look for an *Ens Supremum*. We are indeed told that one of the Incas had his doubts about the divinity of the sun, while a mysterious being, a *Deus ignotus* or supreme god, is spoken of who was worshipped under the name of *Pachacamac* or *Viracocha*, the sun, moon, and stars being merely the symbols under which he revealed himself to his creatures. But for the mystification involved in this conception the reader must be referred to art. VIRACOCHA.

Thus a rapid survey of the whole field has failed to discover an *Ens Supremum* amongst the Amerinds, whose primitive beliefs were essentially animistic, the worship of animals greatly predominating over that of ancestral spirits, which plays a very subordinate part in the American systems. Conspicuous features are totemism and shamanism in the north, true polytheism in the higher religions of Mexico and Central America, solar worship in those of South America, and various forms of lycanthropy everywhere. These subjects have here been barely touched upon, as they will be found fully treated in special articles.

LITERATURE.—E. J. Payne, *Hist. of the New World called America*, 2 vols. 1892, 1898; A. D'Orbigny, *L'Homme Américain*, 2 vols. 1839; H. H. Bancroft, *The Native Races of the Pacific States of N. America*, 5 vols. 1875–76; H. R. Schoolcraft, *Hist., etc., of the Indian Tribes of the United States*, 3 vols. 1851–53; D. G. Brinton, *The American Race*, 1891; J. W. Powell, *Indian Linguistic Families North of Mexico*, 1891; N. León, *Familias Linguisticas de Mexico*, 1902; M. de Nadaillac, *Prehistoric America*, 1885; F. S. Dellenbaugh, *The North Americans of Yesterday*, 1901; A. H. Keane, *Man Past and Present*, 1900; W. Bollaert, *Researches in New Granada, Ecuador*, etc. 1860; J. J. von Tschudi, *Reisen durch Südamerika*, 5 vols. 1866–69; P. Ehrenreich, *Die Urbewohner Brasiliens*, 1897; K. von den Steinen, *Durch Central-Brasilien*, 1886; The Annual Reports of the Smithsonian Institution, Washington, and the Publications of the Peabody Museum, Cambridge, Massachusetts.

A. H. KEANE.

AMERICA, SOUTH.—The religious ideas of the savage peoples of South America are, in comparison with those of the North Americans, strikingly undeveloped. They have not advanced beyond the crudest forms of belief in ghosts, such as are produced by the vague fear of the souls of the dead, or of the demons, which express themselves in certain natural occurrences. Their religious beliefs are thus not essentially superior to those of the Australians or the Papuans. The want of a belief in gods, in the proper sense of the term, speaks less for the low stage of religious culture than the almost total absence of forms of worship that are no more than mere magic practices, as, *e.g.*, prayers, sacrifices, idols, and sanctuaries. The few undoubted traces of a real cult belong to tribes in whose case we are inclined to suspect that influence has been brought to bear on them from the side of the civilized and half-civilized peoples of the region of the Andes and of Central America.

We find such traces among the Arhuacos (Köggaba) of Colombia, the Tainos of the Antilles, the Tacanas of Eastern Bolivia, the Araucans and several nations of the Chacos and the Pampas, which are in connexion with them, especially the Guaycuru group, who have also adopted numerous elements of Peruvian culture.

Of course the mythology of the South Americans can tell us of creators and world figures, but still these are without the character of gods. They are legendary figures without religious significance, without influence on man and his fate, and thus also devoid of religious worship or veneration. The Peruvian religion was the first to raise the heroes of the legends, so far as they were personifications of the sun or moon, to the position of divinities. Among the Chibchas of Colombia are to be found the first approaches to this.

The earliest reports regarding the religious ideas of the savage tribes of the time of the Conquest and the first missionaries are, in general, obscure and contradictory. While some deny all religious feeling to the Indians, others tell of reverence for God, or at least of devil-worship, and others again of the dualistic opposition of a good and an evil spirit.

On the other hand, reverence for one all-ruling highest being was expressly ascribed to many tribes.

In particular the following are named: Tupan among the eastern Tupis, Sume among the southern Tupis or the Guaranis, Pillan among the Araucans, Gualichu among the Puelches, Queevet among the Abipones, Soychu among the Patagonians, and others. As a matter of fact, we have in all these cases by no means to do with more elevated ideas of God. These beings are, on the contrary, mere natural demons or deified ancestors or heroes of the tribe.

Without doubt, the demonic figures which took part in the masked dances of the Indians have often been regarded by the missionaries as gods or devils. The festive huts, the houses of the community or of the bachelors, in which the masks were preserved, were supposed to be 'temples.' And yet, all the contemporary observers even at that date emphasize the absence of specific actions of worship (prayer and sacrifice), except in the above-mentioned cases of probable foreign influence from regions of higher culture. Still, the masked dances might be regarded as the first traces of a primitive culture. As the analogies among other savage peoples teach us, the ceremonies are in the main directed towards exerting a magical influence on animals or animal spirits (in the sense of an allurement, defence, or multiplication), or towards driving out destructive demons that manifest themselves in natural phenomena.

Often too, of course, they are primitive dramatic representations of achievements of the tribe and of the legends of the heroes, as, *e.g.*, those connected with the Yurupari or Izi mysteries of the tribe of the Uaupés, and probably those of the Passē and Tikuna, and those of the Chiquitos of Bolivia, which were described at an early date. The sacred dances of the Tainos in Cuba and Hispaniola (Haiti), the so-called Areitos, were of this nature.

These masquerades seem to be especially important at the initiation ceremony of the young men, at funeral celebrations, and at the laying out of new settlements. The use of masks seems to have been confined to the basin of the Amazon. In Guiana and Venezuela, the Orinoco region, the east coast, and farther south than 15° south latitude their existence has not been proved.

We know more particularly only those of the Marañon (Tikuna), those of Uaupé and Yapura (Tariana and Betoya tribes), those of the upper Xingu (Bakairi, Mehinaku, Auetö, and Trumai) and of Araguay, those of the Karaya (which present a striking resemblance to the so-called dukduk masks of New Britain).

Idols of wood and stone belonging to a more ancient period are frequently mentioned in the Antilles, in Darien, Venezuela, and on the Amazon; still, we are ignorant of their appearance or signification. Only with regard to the Tainos do we know that they represented their ancestral gods (*Zemes*) in grotesque figures of wood and cotton, of which a few have been preserved. On the lower Amazon various peculiarly formed sculptures of men and animals have been found, whose style points to the Columbian sphere of culture (according to Barboza Rodriguez and R. Andree). The so-called idols of the Takana of Eastern Bolivia have not yet been more closely investigated. The wooden 'Santos' of the Caduves (Guaycuru) are in all probability representations of ancestors, but perhaps influenced by Christianity.

In the older literature actual divinities of individual peoples are mentioned; in particular Tupan, the 'god of the eastern Tupi,' whose name was adopted in the popular language as the general designation of God, and, through the influence of religious instruction carried over to many tribes of the interior. Thus he frequently obtained the signification of 'the God of the white man.' In reality *Tupan* is simply 'the flash,' *i.e.* a thunder-demon of the Tupis, who, however, pay him all sorts of worship. In the magic rattle (*maraka*) his worshippers believed that they heard his voice, and so it came about that Hans Staden pronounces this rattle to be nothing else than the god of the tribe. In his nature he has absolutely nothing to do with the one God in the Christian sense of the term.

In other cases the supposed divine beings are of a purely mythical nature, the ancestors of the tribe, or culture-heroes, who are active as demiurges, like Tamoi or Sume of the Tupi-Guaranis, whom even the missionaries identified with St. Thomas, who in some mysterious fashion was reported to have been the first to bring religion and civilization to America.

Other similar figures are Quetzalcoatl and Kukulcan in Central America, Bochica in Colombia, and Viracocha in Peru. The same is also true of Aguarachi of the Abipones, the Rueevet or Huecubu of the Puelches and Araucans, and the fox-god of the Chiriguanos (according to Campana).

We can thus gather exceedingly little positive information from the older references. The more recent material for observation is also still scanty and incomplete. The following may be regarded as certain, so far as it goes. The belief in souls (animism) forms for these peoples the basis of all their supernatural ideas. The spirits of the dead are thought of as demons which are for the most part hostile, or at least terrifying—seldom indifferent,—or good spirits stand over against these evil demons.

Of such a nature are the Opoyen and Mapoyen of the Caribbean Islands, the Anhangas of the Tupis, the Kamyry of the Ipurinas. Only among the Tainos do we find a completely systematized spirit worship of the *Zemes*, which are represented by idols.

The belief in the incarnation of the souls of the dead in animals is widely diffused. Jaguars, snakes, and in particular birds like *araras*, hawks, eagles, are such soul-animals. Besides these there are everywhere spiritual beings of an indefinite nature; cobolds, which appear in animal or in grotesque human forms, but as a rule invisible to the eye, manifest themselves in certain natural sounds, such as in the echo, in the rustling of the wood, or in nightly sounds of an indefinite kind, or have their seat in remarkable rock formations. The best known are the forest demons of the Tupis —Kaapora, Kurupira, and Yurupari—which were adopted in the popular superstition of the colonists. Similar beings dwell in the water as gigantic snakes or crab-like monsters.

Where a special 'land of the fathers' in heaven, or more seldom in the lower world, is accepted, the souls of the dead return to it. Among the Chaco tribes the stars are the souls of warriors, which combat one another in the thunder-storm. As falling stars, they change their places. Certain constellations—in particular Orion, the Cross, Pleiades, the Milky Way—are regarded as representations of beings or objects of mythical significance belonging to the primeval time. They illustrate in this way incidents in the activity of the culture-heroes in the cosmogonical legend.

These peoples have not advanced to a deification of cosmic bodies and natural powers. Even the sun and the moon have remained, in spite of their personification in the myth, without significance for the religious ideas. Atmospheric phenomena, too, have been little observed, a fact which probably is connected with the great regularity of the rainfall and thunderstorms throughout the whole continent. In a few cases proof can be given that demons or spirits of nature were supposed to manifest themselves in these phenomena.

Among the eastern Tupis, Tupan reveals himself in the lightning flash; among the Machakalis, Akjanam shakes the rain out of his beard. The Caribbean islanders know demons who control the sea, the wind, and the rain. The rainbow, too, is widely regarded as an evil spirit that brings sickness (*yolok*, 'devil,' of the Caribbean peoples of Guiana). Among other peoples he is a mythical animal, snake (*Ipurina*) or electric eel (*Karaya*).

Tendencies towards the development of actual divinities and divine cults are to be found among the Tainos, who, besides the spirits of their ancestors, revered the sun and the moon; and probably also among the old tribes of Darien and of the north coast (according to Peter Martyr, Oviedo, Gomara, and others). In later times, among the Takanas of Eastern Bolivia, gods of water, of fire, of sicknesses, etc. are mentioned, and their images were worshipped in temples by means of sacrifices and dances (according to Col. Labre and P. Armentia). But these details have not yet obtained scientific confirmation. Again, with regard to the sacrifice of horses which the Patagonians or tribes of the Pampas are said to offer, we have no exact information. In individual cases the mighty phenomena of volcanic action have led to divine worship of active volcanoes.

Thus the Jivaro of Ecuador are supposed to look upon the volcano Cayambé as the seat of a mighty spirit, to whom they offer prayer. Among the Araucans, Pillan is the god of thunder and of volcanoes. Subordinate to him are the Cherruves, the inciters of the summer lightning, who in like manner are thought of as dwelling in volcanoes.

The cause of this imperfect development of the belief in gods is probably to be sought in the entirely primitive condition of agriculture in the whole of South America, with the exception of the slopes of the Andes. Agricultural rites of a magical nature, from which, as a rule, divine cults are developed, do not easily arise among tribes who, though practising primitive agriculture, may yet be said to follow an almost purely hunting or fishing life, and owing to the perfectly regular change of kinds of weather and the certainty of copious showers, do not require heavenly helpers. Only under the more niggardly natural conditions of the high lands of the Andes in Peru and Bolivia did the farmer recognize his dependence on higher powers, at the head of which he placed the sun-, or light-god.

The *mythology* of the South Americans, now unfortunately only partially known to us, seems to have been more plentiful than might have been expected from their crude religious ideas. The most that we know comes from more recent times; still, even from the 16th cent. we possess a comparatively complete cosmogony and cycle of heroic legend of the eastern Tupis, related by Thevet, *Cosmographie*, Paris, 1574 (in extracts in Dénis' *Fête brésilienne*, Paris, 1851). Further, we have fragments of a creation-legend of the Tainos, according to Peter Martyr. The subsequent missionary period has supplied us only with scattered and unreliable material.

It was not till recent times that more valuable sources were again furnished by the investigations of travellers, such as D'Orbigny (for the Yurakaré of Bolivia), Brett and E. im Thurn (for the tribes of Guiana), Cardus (for the Guarayos of Bolivia), von den Steinen and Ehrenreich (for the Bakairis, Paressis, and Karayas of Central Brazil), Lenz (for the Araikans), Borba (for the Kaingang of the Ges linguistic stock of South Brazil), and others. Of great importance is the so-called Iurupari myth of the Uaupé tribe, communicated by Stradelli (*Bol. soc. geogr. Ital.*, Rome, 1890), the only complete legend handed down regarding the worship of a secret society. A critical collection of all the materials discovered up to the present time was given by Ehrenreich in his *Mythen und Legenden der südamer. Urvölker*, Berlin, 1905. The myths deal in the main with cosmogony, the work of creation of the culture hero or heroes, conceived of as brothers, who bring to mankind the useful plants, fire, and other possessions, and appoint the course of sun and moon. The sun or highest heavenly being, thought of as a magician, is placed at times, as the procreator of the heroes, at the beginning of the genealogy, *e.g.* Monan of the Tupis, Kamushini of the Bakairis. A destruction of the world by flood or by world-conflagration occurs more than once (see Andree, *Flutsagen*). The story of the birth of the hero brothers with the motive of the immaculate conception, the death of their mother, their combats with monsters and with one another, their ascension into heaven or descent into the lower world, offers many parallels with myths of the old world. Still, these can be explained from the similarity of the view of nature lying at the basis of all these myths, which is always connected with the sun and moon and their relation to each other. The heroes themselves are often immediately recognizable as personifications of these stars, as, *e.g.*, the pair of brothers Keri and Kame among the Bakairis.

On the other hand, there are undoubtedly many North American and even East Asiatic legendary elements which have wandered to South America, probably following the Pacific Coast. In like manner there are common elements in the stories of the heroes of Peru and Eastern Brazil which can be explained only by immediate influence of the one people on the other.

LITERATURE.—J. G. Müller, *Gesch. der amerikan. Urreligionen*, Basel, 1867; E. im Thurn, *Among the Indians of Guiana*, London, 1883; Barboza Rodriguez, *Paranduba amazonense*, Rio, 1890; K. von den Steinen, *Unter den Naturvölkern Zentralbrasiliens*, Berlin, 1893; P. Ehrenreich, *Mythen und Legenden der südamericanischen Urvölker*, Berlin, 1905. This work contains abundant bibliographical material. For older literature, see Waitz, *Anthropologie der Naturvölker*, iii. Leipzig, 1862; cf. also the various anthropological manuals, *e.g.* Keane, *Man Past and Present*, Cambridge, 1900, p. 416 ff.

P. EHRENREICH.

AMESHA SPENTAS.—A designation for a specific class of beings in the Zoroastrian religion, corresponding to the idea of archangels in Judaism and Christianity. The name literally means 'Immortal Beneficent Ones,' from Av. *ameša* (read *amereta-*), 'undying' and *spenta*, 'bountiful, beneficent' (from root *su-*, 'to increase, benefit'), and the form appears in Pahlavi as *Amhraspand*, read in later Persian as *Amshaspand*. As a class-designation the title *Amesha Spenta* does not occur in the metrical Gāthās, although the Amesha Spentas themselves are constantly referred to singly, or in company, throughout these older hymns; but the actual title does occur in the prose Gāthā of the Yasna Haptanghāitī (*Yasna*, xxxix. 3; cf. xlii. 6), and is met with often in the Younger Avesta and in the subsequent Zoroastrian literature.

The Amesha Spentas are conceived of as attendant ministers waiting as servitors upon their supreme lord and sovereign, Ahura Mazda, or Ormazd (cf. Phl. *Yōsht-ī Fryānō*, ii. 55–59; *Bahman Yasht*, iii. 31), with whom they make up a sevenfold group, to which number the divine being Sraosha is also often added (cf. *Yasht*, ii. 1–3, xix. 16=xiii. 83, x. 139, iii. 1; *Yasna*, lvii. 12; *Bundahishn*, xxx. 29). In later usage the term *Amshaspand* is more loosely employed, and some of the angels are called by this designation. Besides Sraosha, who is admitted to the group, and who works in unison with them (*Bundahishn*, xxx. 29), Ātar, the Fire of Ahura Mazda, is spoken of as an Amshaspand (*Yasna*, i. 2). Gōšūrvan, the soul of the primeval ox, though usually spoken of as an angel, is called an Amshaspand in *Shāyast lā-Shāyast*, xxii. 14. A later 'Kusti' formula even speaks of *sī u se*, 'thirty-three,' Amshaspands. Their nature is that of virtues and abstract qualities personified, and their names are *Vohu Manah* 'Good Thought,' *Asha Vahishta* 'Perfect Righteousness,' *Khshathra Vairya* 'Wished-for Kingdom,' *Spenta Armaitī* 'Holy Harmony,' *Haurvatāt* and *Ameretāt* 'Saving Health and Immortality.' The Greek writer Plutarch, in the 1st cent. A.D., alluded to them as 'six gods' (*ἓξ θεούς*, *de Is. et Os.* 47), and rendered their names respectively as *εὔνοια, ἀλήθεια, εὐνομία, σοφία, πλοῦτος, ὁ τῶν ἐπὶ τοῖς καλοῖς ἡδέων δημιοῦργος* (see Tiele, 'Plutarchus over de Amšaspands,' in *Feestbundel Prof. Boot*, pp. 117–119, Leyden, 1901). He once mentions Ameretāt by name as *'Αμάρδατος* (miswritten as *'Ανάδατος*), and a century earlier Strabo (xi. 8. 4, xv. 3. 15) unquestionably refers to Vohu Manah under the name *'Ωμανής* (see Windischmann, 'Die persische Anahita, oder Anaïtis,' in *Abhandlungen d. bayr. Akad.*, phil.-philol. Classe, viii. part 1, p. 36, Munich, 1856), all which goes to prove that the conception was well known at that period. This latter fact, among numerous others, is of weight in disproving the theory advanced by Darmesteter, that the conception of the Amesha Spentas in Zoroastrianism was late, and owed its origin to the influence of Philo Judæus.

The various attributes which the Zoroastrian scriptures apply to the Amesha Spentas are in harmony with the spiritual qualities represented by these allegorical personifications. This will be manifest at a glance, if reference be made to the Avesta (*e.g. Yasna*, xxxix. 3; *Visparad*, ix. 4, xi. 12; *Yasna*, iv. 4, xxiv. 9, lviii. 5; *Yasht*, xiii. 82–84). The Gāthic adjectives *vohu* 'good,' *vahišta* 'best,' *vairya* 'wished-for,' *spenta* 'holy,' which are the most common titles of the first four Amesha Spentas in the earlier period of the religion, become in later times standing epithets, practically indispensable to the qualities to which they are added by way of nearer definition. The last two personifications, Haurvatāt and Ameretāt, have no standing attributes, but are commonly mentioned together as a pair.

The Amesha Spentas were Ahura Mazda's own creation (*Yasht*, i. 25; *Dīnkarț*, tr. Sanjana, p. 103), and their function is to aid him in the guidance of the world (*Yasht*, xix. 16, i. 25, ii. 1–15; *Vendīdād*, xix. 9; *Bundahishn*, i. 23–28). They are invisible and immortal (*Dīnkarț*, tr. Sanjana, pp. 47–48), good rulers, givers of good, ever living and ever bestowing (*Yasna*, xxiv. 9). They have their Fravashis, which are invoked (*Yasht*, xiii. 82). They receive special worship in the ritual, and are said to descend to the oblations upon paths of light (*Yasht*, xiii. 84, xix. 17). They dwell in paradise, where at least one of them, Vohu Manah, sits on a throne of gold (*Vendīdād*, xix. 32); but they are not infinite and unproportioned like their Lord, Ormazd (*Dīnkarț*, tr. Sanjana, p. 114). They are spoken of as the givers and rulers, moulders and overseers, protectors and preservers of the creation of Ormazd (*Yasht*, xix. 18). For that reason the guardianship of some special element in the universe is assigned to each. To Vohu Manah is entrusted the care of useful animals; to Asha Vahishta, the fire; to Khshathra Vairya, the supervision of metals; to Spenta Armaitī, the guardianship of the earth, whose spirit she is; and to Haurvatāt and Ameretāt, the care of water and vegetation (*Shāyast lā-Shāyast*, xv. 5; *Great Bundahishn*, tr. Darmesteter, in *Le Zend-Avesta*, ii. 305–322). The precise nature of the relation, in each case, between tutelary genius and element, has been variously explained, according to the stress laid upon the physical or the spiritual side of the concept; but it is certain that the association and the double nature are old, because the twofold character may be seen foreshadowed in the Gāthās, and becomes pronounced, in the later texts especially, on its physical side. Each Amesha Spenta has a special month assigned to his honour (*Bundahishn*, xxv. 20). Each has a special day as holy day (*Sīrōzā*, i. 1–7). Each has a special flower, *e.g.*, white jasmine sacred to Vohu Manah, the 'basil-royal' to Khshathra Vairya, musk to Spenta Armaitī (*Bundahishn*, xxvii. 24). It is impossible here to enter into a detailed discussion of the functions of each of the Amesha Spentas, the first three of which celestial group are males (or rather, neuter according to the grammatical gender, not sex), and the last three females; but it is sufficient to indicate the fact that these exalted personifications play an important rôle as archangels throughout the entire history of the Zoroastrian religion, and are opposed (more particularly in the later development of the faith) by six antagonists, or corresponding archfiends, *Aka Manah, Indra, Sauru, Nāoṅhaithya, Tauru*, and *Zairi* (*Vendīdād*, x. 9–10, xix. 43; *Yasht*, xix. 96). The Amshaspands will, nevertheless, vanquish these opponents at the time of the resurrection (*Yasht*, xix. 96; *Bundahishn*, xxx. 29).

To draw parallels between the conception of the Amesha Spentas as a spiritual band higher than the angels (Av. *Yazatas*), yet lower than the Supreme Being, Ahura Mazda, and the Biblical doctrine of archangels, is natural and has been done by some scholars, while others have emphasized the likenesses to the idea of the Ādityas in ancient India. Opinions vary as to whether the resemblances are due to borrowing, or to some common source, or, again, to natural developments. It is premature, as yet, to attempt to give a decision on this question, which is but a part of the whole problem of the influence of Zoroastrianism on other religions or its kinship with them.

LITERATURE.—Fuller references will be found in Jackson, *Die iranische Religion*, in Geiger and Kuhn's *Grundriss der iran. Philologie*, ii. 633–640; Spiegel, *Eranische Alterthumskunde*, ii. 28–41, Leipzig, 1873; Darmesteter, *Haurvatāț et Ameretāț*, Paris, 1875, *Ormazd et Ahriman*, pp. 38–43, 246–249, Paris, 1879, *Le Zend-Avesta, traduction nouvelle*, Paris, 1892–93; C. de Harlez, *Des Origines du Zoroastrianisme*, pp. 49–93, Paris, 1878–79, *Avesta traduit*, Introd. pp. 90–94, Paris, 1881; Casartelli, *Mazdayasnian Religion under the Sasanids* [tr. from French into English by Firoz Jamaspji], pp. 42–49, 74–75, Bombay, 1889; Justi, 'Die älteste iranische Religion' in *Preuss. Jahrb.* 88. 72–77; Tiele, *Gesch. der Religion im Altertum bis auf die Zeit Alexanders des Grossen*, ii. 139–155; Lehmann, *Zarathustra*, ii. 44–62; Gray, 'The Double Nature of the Iranian Archangels' in *ARW* vii. 345–372.

A. V. WILLIAMS JACKSON.

'AM HA-AREṢ (עַם הָאָרֶץ).—A term used in Rabbinic Hebrew to designate, either collectively or individually, those who were ignorant of the Law, and careless as to its observance. It is almost invariably a term of reproach. Its literal meaning, 'people of the land,' may suggest that its origin is similar to that of the words 'pagan' or 'heathen.' In the OT it occurs several times, but never with the significance which it afterwards acquired (cf. 2 K 24[14], Ezr 9[1], Neh 10[31]).

Our chief authority for the use of the term is the Mishna, where it frequently occurs (see list of passages given below), and in these passages the *'Am ha-areṣ* is, as a rule, contrasted with the *Ḥābhēr* (companion) who had bound himself to a very strict observance of the Law. In all matters regarding questions of tithe or of 'clean and unclean' the *'Am ha-areṣ* is not to be trusted. Thus we find it stated in the Mishna: 'He who takes it upon himself to be a *Ḥābhēr* sells neither fresh nor dry fruits to the *'Am ha-areṣ*, buys from them no fresh, does not enter into their house as a guest, or receive them as guests within his walls' (*Demai*, ii. 3). The majority of the passages in the Mishna deal with similar topics in connexion with the *'Am ha-areṣ*, viz. the fact that he must not be trusted in matters concerning the agrarian laws and ritual purity. One passage, however, is a notable exception to this, and is of peculiar interest as showing the feelings of the earlier Rabbis on this point. It is the well-known saying of Hillel: 'No boor (בור) is a sin-fearer, nor is the *'Am ha-areṣ* pious' (*Aboth*, ii. 6). In order, however, to obtain a definition of the *'Am ha-areṣ*, we must turn to the Bab. Talmud, where the following passage occurs (*Berākhōth*, 47*b*):

'"Who is an *'Am ha-areṣ*? One that does not eat his ordinary food in a state of ritual purity." These are the words of R. Meir; but the Ḥekhāmîm say, "He that does not tithe his fruits properly." "Who is an *'Am ha-areṣ*? One that does not read the Shema' morning and evening." These are the words of R. Eliezer. R. Joshua says, "One that does not put on the phylacteries." Ben Azzai says, "One that has not the fringes on his garment." R. Nathan says, "One that has not a Mezuza on his door." R. Nathan ben Joseph says, "One that has children, and does not educate them in the study of the Law." Others say, "Even if he have read and learnt, yet if he have not associated with wise men he is an *'Am ha-areṣ*."' (Cf. also Bab. *Soța*, 23*b*, *Gițțin*, 61*a*, where this passage occurs with some variations).

From this passage it would appear that the *'Am ha-areṣ* was regarded by the Rabbis as a person who was accustomed to neglect the various enactments of the Law, and the general attitude of the Pharisees towards him was one of contempt and hostility. As we have seen, the *Ḥābhêr* is warned against having intercourse with him, and it naturally followed that intermarriage between the two classes was regarded with the greatest disfavour. 'One that gives his daughter in marriage to an *'Am ha-areṣ*,' R. Meir used to say, 'is as if he had bound her and set her before a lion' (Bab. *Pesaḥ*, 49*b*). In another place it is stated that the *'Am ha-areṣ* is disqualified for acting in certain capacities, which are enumerated under six heads, viz. (1) he must not be appointed to receive evidence; (2) his own evidence is not to be accepted; (3) a secret must not be confided to him; (4) he must not be appointed as the guardian to orphans; (5) he must not be appointed as overseer of the charity box; (6) it is not right to accompany him on a journey (Bab. *Pesaḥ*, 49*b*, and Rashi's comment, *ad loc.*). The attitude of hostility was apparently mutual, as would appear, among other passages, from the saying of R. 'Aqiba which occurs just before the passage cited above. He is reported to have said, 'When I was an *'Am ha-areṣ* I used to say, "Would that I had a *talmîd ḥākhām* ('disciple of the wise,' 'scholar'), and I would bite him like an ass."' Or again, a little later, 'The hatred with which the *'Am ha-areṣ* hates the *talmîdê ḥᵉkhāmîm* is greater than the hatred with which the heathen hates Israel' (Bab. *loc. cit.*). These passages offer a sufficient explanation of the words in Jn 7[49] 'This people who knoweth not the law are accursed,' in which we may probably see a reference to the attitude of the Pharisees towards the *'Am ha-areṣ*. Some difference of opinion exists as to the identity of the *Ḥābhêr*, with whom the *'Am ha-areṣ* is so frequently contrasted in the Mishna. Schürer and others identify the *Ḥābhêr* with the Pharisees, making the two terms practically synonymous. Others are rather inclined to regard the *Ḥābhêr* as a member of some kind of religious guild bound to a strict observance of the Law. But one thing is perfectly clear, viz. that the *Ḥābhêr* was not necessarily himself a *talmîd ḥākhām*, though he might incidentally be one. This would appear from the following passage: 'He who would take upon himself the decrees of the association (*ḥabheruth*) must do so in the presence of three *ḥăbhêrîm*; even if he is a *talmîd ḥākhām*, he must do it in the presence of three *ḥăbhêrîm*' (Bab. *Bekhor.* 30*b*).

Two passages may be cited which appear to indicate a less hostile attitude towards the *'Am ha-areṣ*. The first one is from *Aboth de R. Nathan* (ed. Schechter, p. 64*b*), the other is from the Midrash *Shir ha-Shirim Rabba*. In the first of these we are told that it is not right for a man to say, 'Love the wise man, but hate the disciples, love the disciples, but hate the *'Am ha-areṣ*'; but love them all, and hate the heretics and apostates and informers.

An attempt has been made to mitigate the severity of the statements concerning the *'Am ha-areṣ* which have been quoted above, by suggesting that in reality they refer to informers and political enemies (see Montefiore [*Hibbert Lectures*] and Rosenthal, cited below), but sufficient evidence for this is not forthcoming; and the quotation given above from *Aboth de R. Nathan* seems to point in the contrary direction. This also appears to be the view of the writer in the *JE*, who states as his opinion that 'there can be no doubt it was this contemptuous and hostile attitude of the Pharisaic schools towards the masses that was the chief cause of the triumphant power of the Christian Church.' A new and independent investigation of many points connected with the *'Am ha-areṣ* is to be found in the recently published work of A. Büchler, cited below.

LITERATURE.—Mishna, *Demai*, i. 2, 3, ii. 2, 3, iii. 4, vi. 9, 12, *Shebiith*, v. 9, *Ma'aser sheni*, iii. 3, iv. 6, *Ḥagiga*, ii. 7, *Giṭṭin*, v. 9, *Eduyoth*, i. 14, *Aboth*, ii. 5, iii. 10, *Horayoth*, iii. 8, *Qinnim*, iii. 6, *Tohāroth*, iv. 5, vii. 1, 2, 4, 5, viii. 1, 2, 3, 5, *Makhshirin*, vi. 3, *Ṭebul Yom*, iv. 5; Jerus. *Hor.* iii. 48*a*; Bab. *Bᵉrākh.* 47*b*, *Shab.* 32*a*, *Soṭa*, 22*a*, *Giṭṭin*, 61*a*, *Baba mez.* 85*a*, *Baba bath.* 8*a*, *Leviticus Rabba*, 37, *Aboth de R. Nathan*, ed. Schechter, 16, 64; *Shir ha-Shirim Rabba*; Schürer, *GJV*[3] ii. p. 520 ff.; Hamburger, *RE* 54–59; Geiger, *Urschrift* (1857), 151; Rosenthal, *Zeit u. Schule R. Akibas* (1885), 25–29; Montefiore, *Hibb. Lect.* 1892, pp. 497–502; *JE*, *s.v.*; Friedländer, *Entstehungsgesch. d. Christenthums* (1894), ch. ii.; Ad. Büchler, *Das galiläisch 'Am ha-areṣ* (1906).

H. LEONARD PASS.

AMIABILITY.—The adjective 'amiable' is obviously the Lat. *amabilis* modified in transmission through the French. It is thus etymologically equivalent to *lovable*, denoting that which is adapted to excite the sentiment of love in any of its varied forms. It has therefore been occasionally applied even to things, as, *e.g.*, in Ps. 84[1], 'How amiable are thy tabernacles!' But now it is used almost exclusively to describe persons and personal characteristics. In this use it has fortunately never degenerated by application to characteristics that are loved by corrupt minds. Thus, in its psychological aspect, amiability comprehends both the natural dispositions and the acquired habits which, being themselves of the nature of love, are calculated to evoke the same sentiment in others. In ethical and religious value amiability may therefore claim the rank that is accorded to love; and the evolution of moral intelligence has always tended towards that ideal in which love is recognized as the supreme principle and inspiration of all morality.

J. CLARK MURRAY.

AMITĀYUS or APARIMITĀYUS (Tibetan *Tse-dpag-med*), 'The Boundless or Everlasting Life,' is one of the mystical or superhuman Buddhas invented in the theistic development of Buddhism in India. His worship was wide-spread in India in the Middle Ages, although hitherto unnoticed, for the writer found his image frequent in the ruins of mediæval Buddhist temples in mid-India. In Tibet, where the cult of a class of divinities with similar attributes, namely, the Sages of Longevity, had long been prevalent, his worship has become very popular as a supposed means of prolonging the earthly life of votaries. His image is to be seen in nearly every temple in Tibet; it is also worn in amulets, and carved on rocks by the wayside. He is specifically invoked in the prayer-flags which flutter from every point of the compass, and he is specially worshipped in that sacramental rite, the so-called 'Eucharist of Lāmaism,' where consecrated bread is solemnly partaken of by the congregation.

He is considered to be an active reflex or emanation of the divinely meditative Buddha, Amitābha (see ADIBUDDHA), who sits impassively in the Western Paradise (*Sukhāvatī*).

He is represented in the same posture as his prototype Amitābha, not, however, as an ascetic Buddha, but crowned and adorned with thirteen ornaments, and holding in his hands the vase of life-giving ambrosia, which is one of the eight luck-compelling symbols (*mangala*) of ancient India, and the vessel for holy water on Tibetan altars.

LITERATURE.—E. Schlagintweit, *Buddhism in Tibet*, Lond. 1868, p. 129; L. A. Waddell, *Buddhism of Tibet*, Lond. 1895, pp. 348, 352, 444, also *Lhasa and its Mysteries*, Lond. 1905, pp. 86, 214, 393.

L. A. WADDELL.

'AMM, 'AMMI.—The word *'amm* (עַם, عَمّ, ܥܡܐ, etc.) is common to all the Semitic languages, and must have been found in the original tongue from which they are sprung. A comparison of its meanings in the dialects, together with a study of the social organization and religious beliefs of the several races, leads to the conclusion that the word denoted originally a male relative in the preceding generation. The Semites passed once through a stage of fraternal polyandry, and in such a society the distinction between father and paternal uncle is impossible. The mother's polyandrous husband, who might be either father or uncle, was known by the child as *'amm*. Cf. Gn 19^{38} where *Ben-'ammi* is equivalent to 'son of my father,' and the phrase נאסף אל עמיו which alternates with נאסף אל אבתיו. The name 'uncle' was naturally applied to male deities, as 'father' was in later times. Long after polyandry had passed away *'amm* continued to be used as a title of deity; and as it lost its primitive associations, it tended more and more, like Baal, Adon, Melek, and other epithets, to become a proper name. The Ḳatabân people in South Arabia designate themselves in their inscriptions as 'Children of 'Amm' (ולד עם), just as their neighbours the Sabæans designate themselves as *Walad Ilmaḳah*, showing that among them *'Amm* had become a Divine name (cf. Hommel, *ZDMG*, 1895, p. 525; Glaser, *Mitteilungen der vorderasiatischen Gesellschaft*, 1899, ii. p. 21). According to II. Rawl. 54, 65, V. 46, 11, Emu (= Nergal) was a god of the land of Suḫi on the west side of the Euphrates (cf. Sayce, *RP*, 2nd ser. iii. p. xi; KAT^3 481). According to King (*Ḫammurabi*, iii. p. lxv), Ḫammu = 'Ammi is written with the determinative for 'god' in the name of the king Ḫammurabi. The proper name Dur-'Ammi, 'Fortress of 'Amm,' also indicates that 'Amm is regarded as a deity (*ib.* p. 252). A trace of this meaning also lingers in Heb. in the formula לחי עם, 'by the life of the Uncle,' which is parallel to לחי ראי and חי יהוה.

How far this process went can be determined only by a study of the proper names compounded with *'amm* in all the Semitic dialects. Here the problem is complicated by the fact that *'amm* has developed a number of secondary meanings, and so it is not easy to determine what is its significance in any given compound. When fraternal polyandry gave place to monogamy and polygamy, and the father became a recognizable relative, *abu*, which hitherto had meant 'husband' (cf. Jer 3^4, and old Bab. usage), came to mean 'father,' and *'amm* received the more specific meaning of 'paternal uncle.' This is a common meaning in Arab. (cf. *bint 'amm* for 'wife,' lit. daughter of 'paternal uncle'), also in Min. and Sabæan. From this *'amm* came to mean any relative in the ascending line on the father's side, just as 'father' was used to denote a remoter ancestor; then it was used for 'relative' in general. It is used in this sense in one of the Tell el-Amarna letters (Winckler, 45^{32}). Jensen also cites an instance in Babylonian (*LCBl*, 1902, col. 695 f.). In Gn 17^{14}, Lv $7^{20f.\ 25.\ 27}$ 23^{29}, Nu 9^{13} 15^{30}, Ex 31^{14}, Lv 19^{16} 21^{1-4} *'amm* cannot mean 'people,' but only 'kinsman.' *Lo-'ammi*, the name of Hosea's child, must mean primarily 'Not my kin,' inasmuch as it was given with reference to the mother's adultery. The Carthaginian proper name עמא (*CIS* 384) and Nabatæan עמיו, Οὔμεια (Euting, *Sin. Inschr.* 90^{27} 358^5 355), may mean 'kinsman' or 'uncle,' but cannot mean 'people' (cf. Aram.-Talm. אבא as a personal name). The final stage in the development of meaning was reached when *'amm* came to denote 'race' or 'people'—a common usage both in Hebrew and Arabic.

The question now arises, Which of these meanings is found in the numerous proper names compounded with *'amm*? These names are widely scattered through the Semitic races, and must have been one of the earliest types of name formation; it is natural, therefore, to conjecture that in them *'amm* has its primitive meaning of 'father-uncle,' and is used in some cases at least as a title of the Deity. Whether this is the fact can be determined only by an inductive study of the names in question.

1. The first class of 'Ammi-names consists of those in which 'Ammi is *followed by a noun*, as in *'Ammi-hud*. In most of these the translation 'people' for 'Ammi gives a very unlikely name for an individual, *e.g.* *'Ammi-el*, 'people of God,' or 'people is God'; *'Amme-ba'ali*, 'people of Baal,' or 'people is Baal'; and so with the other names given below. It is generally admitted, accordingly, that in all names of this class *'Ammi* has the sense of 'kinsman' or 'uncle.' This view is confirmed by the fact that compounds with *Abi*, 'father,' and *Aḥi*, 'brother,' run parallel to names with *'Ammi*, *e.g.* *Abi-el*, *'Ammi-el*; *Abi-hud*, *Aḥi-hud*, *'Ammi-hud*. The next question is, whether the epithet 'uncle' or 'kinsman' is understood of a human being or of a divinity. The answer to this question depends upon the grammatical relation in which *'Ammi* stands to the following noun. There is high authority for the view that it is a construct with the old genitive ending which frequently survives in the construct state, *i.e.* *'Ammi-hud* means 'kinsman of glory,' which, like *Abi-hud*, 'father of glory,' means 'glorious one.' This theory is open to many serious objections: (1) This construction is a pure Arabism, and there is no evidence that it existed in the other dialects. (2) It is very unlikely that any man should have been named *Abi-El* in the sense of 'father of God,' *Abi-Yah* in the sense of 'father of Yah,' *Abi-Ba'al* in the sense of 'father of Baal,' or *Abi-Melek* in the sense of 'father of Melek'; and it is just as unlikely that *'Ammi-El*, *'Ammi-Ba'al*, *'Ammi-Sin*, *'Ammi-Shaddai* mean respectively 'uncle (older kinsman) of God, Baal, Sin, Shaddai.' (3) These names are paralleled by names in which the same elements occur in reverse order, *e.g.* *Eli-'am* (2 S 11^3 = 1 Ch 3^5 *'Ammiel*), *Ba'al-'am*, *Aa-'am* (*Yah-'am*?), *Nabu-imme*, *Shulmanu-imme*, *Shamash-imme*. There is no reason to suppose that *Eli-'am* differs in meaning from *'Ammi-El* or *Ba'al-'am* from *'Ammi-Ba'al*. If the elements in these names are regarded as standing in the construct relation, they will mean respectively 'God of uncle,' 'Lord of uncle.' These have no relation to their inverted counterparts, and are most unlikely personal names. If, on the other hand, the nouns are regarded as standing in the relation of subject and predicate, the compounds are synonymous whatever be the order of the elements: *'Ammi-El* means 'uncle is God,' and *Eli-'am* means 'God is uncle.' (4) Conclusive evidence that *'Ammi*, *Abi*, *Aḥi*, *Dod* ('uncle'), *Ḫal* ('maternal uncle'), *Ḫam* ('father-in-law') are not constructs before the following nouns, is found in the fact that they are used in forming the names of *women*. *Abi-gal*, *Abi-noam*, *Ḫamu-ṭal* cannot mean 'father of joy,' 'father of pleasantness,' 'father-in-law of dew,' but must mean 'father is joy,' 'father is pleasantness,' 'father-in-law is dew' (cf. *Abi-ṭal*).

If *'Ammi* is not in the construct before the following noun but is the subject of a sentence, a further problem arises as to the meaning of the vowel *î* which appears not only in Hebrew but also in Canaanite names in the Tell el-Amarna letters and in Babylonian. Many regard it as the suffix of the first pers.; but against this view are the facts that no other pronominal suffixes are used in forming proper names, that the analogy of other names leads us to expect a general affirmation in regard to the Deity rather than the expression of a personal relation to Him, and that the *î* is omitted in parallel forms, *e.g. Eli-'am* = *'Ammi-El*, *'Ammi-Ba'al*=*Ba'al-'am*, *Ab-shalom*=*Abi-shalom*, *Ab-ram*=*Abi-ram*. Probably, therefore, *î* should be regarded as a modification of the original *û*, the nom. ending. The ending *û* still appears in *Ammu-ladin*, *Ammu-nira*, *Ammu-rabi*, and other names in Bab. and Assyr. records (cf. Heb. *Ḥamû-ṭal*). If this be so, *'Ammi-el* must be translated, not 'my uncle is God,' but 'uncle is God.'

From this conclusion it follows that *'Ammi* in all these names is not a designation of a human relative, but of the Deity. In such names as 'uncle is God,' 'uncle is glory,' 'uncle is Lord,' 'uncle' can only be a title of a divinity. This conclusion is confirmed by the facts that *Abi*, *Aḥi*, and other names of relationship, except *Ben* 'son' and *Bint*, *Bath* 'daughter,' invariably refer to a god; *'Amm* forms compounds also that are parallel to compounds with Yah, cf. *'Ammi-El* and *Jo-El*, *'Ammi-hud* and *Hud-Yah*. The substitution of *Eli-'am* in 2 S 11^{3} for *'Ammi-El* of 1 Ch 3^{5} also shows consciousness that 'Ammi at the beginning of a compound is a Divine name. The change is analogous to the various substitutions for Baal in the Book of Samuel. Cf. also *Abi-ḥail* in the Heb. text of Est 2^{15} 9^{29} instead of *'Ammi-nadab* of the Gr. text.

The following names belong to this class:—*'Ammi-El*, 'uncle is God' (Nu 13^{12}, 2 S $9^{4.5}$ 17^{27}, 1 Ch 3^{5} 26^{5})=*Imi-ilu* (Obelisk of Manishtusu, Scheil, *Textes Élam.-Sém.* p. 6 ff.); *Amme-Ba'ali*, 'uncle is Lord,' an Aramæan of the middle Euphrates region (Ashurnaṣirpal, ii. 12, 118 f.); *'Ammi-hud*, 'uncle is glory' (2 S 13^{37} *Q'rê*, a king of Geshur, Nu 1^{10} 2^{18} $7^{48.53}$ 10^{22} $34^{20.28}$, 1 Ch 9^{4}); *'Ammi-hur*, 'uncle is white'? (2 S 13^{37} *Kethib*); *'Ammi-ia* (עמי־יה?), the name of a land in the Tell el-Amarna letters (Winckler, 119^{11} 120^{15} etc., cf. *Abi-Yah* and *Aa-am*); *Ami-li'ti*, 'uncle is might' (Rm. 77, rev. 10; Harper, *Letters*, No. 414); *'Ammu-nira*, 'uncle is light,' king of Beirut in the Amarna letters (Winckler, 96^{29} 128–130=*Ḫamu-niri*, $71^{15.66.69}$ $91^{53.133}$); *'Am-'ād* (meaning?), a town of Asher (Jos 19^{26}); *Ama-Sin*, 'uncle is Sin' (Ob. of Manishtusu, A, v. 3)=*Imi-Sin* (*ib.* Scheil, *Textes Élam.-Sém.* p. 6 ff.); *'Ammi-Shaddai*, 'uncle is Shaddai' (Nu 1^{12} 2^{25} $7^{66.71}$ 10^{25}); *'Am-shai*, 'uncle is a gift' (1 Ch 6^{10-20} 11^{20}: read עמשי, cf. אבישי).

2. A second class of 'Ammi-compounds consists of names in which 'Ammi is *followed by a word that may be either a verb in the perf. 3 sing. or a verbal noun*, e.g. *'Ammi-nadab*. In names of this class, as of the preceding, *'Ammi* cannot be translated 'people.' Such combinations as 'people has bestowed,' or 'people of bestowing,' 'people is generous,' 'people is friendly,' have no sense as names of individuals. *'Ammi* must here be translated 'uncle,' or 'kinsman,' and is clearly a title of the Divinity that has given the child. Nearly all the names with *'Ammi* of this class are paralleled by compounds with *Abi* and *Aḥi*, where also the name of relationship is a title of the deity; cf. *'Ammi-nadab*, *Abi-nadab*, *Aḥi-nadab*; *'Am-ram*, *Abi-ram*, *Aḥi-ram*. The parallelism between *'Ammi-zabad* and *Jeho-zabad*; *'Am-ram* and *Jeho-ram*; *'Ammi-nadab*, *Jeho-nadab*, *Chemosh-nadab*; also shows that *'Ammi* is treated as a Divine name. Mention has already been made of the fact that *Ḫammu*, the Bab. equivalent of *'Ammi*, is written with the determinative of 'god' in the name Ḫammurabi.

Those who take *'Ammi* as a construct in the preceding class of names take it also as a construct in this class, and translate *'Ammi-nadab* as 'uncle of generosity'; but all the objections urged against this view in the last class hold good here. *Jeho-nadab*, *Chemosh-nadab*, *Jehoram* can only be translated 'Jahweh is generous,' 'Chemosh is generous,' 'Jahweh is high'; and on this analogy the only natural translations for *'Ammi-nadab* and *'Am-ram* are 'uncle is generous,' 'uncle is high.'

Names of this formation are as follows:—*'Ammi-amara*, a Sabæan (Hommel, *AHT* 84); *'Am-mue'-en-shi* (עמיאנש), sheikh of Upper Tenu in the Egyptian tale of Sinuhe (*c.* B.C. 1970), apparently the same as the Sabæan name *'Ammi-anisa* (*CIS* 13; Halévy, 155 [=156, 158], 176, 243) and *'Ammi-anas*, a god of the Khaulan (Wellhausen, *Reste*^{2}, 23); *'Ammi-ditana* (*satana*?), one of the kings of the I Dyn. of Babylon; *Ammi-zabad*, 'uncle has presented' (1 Ch 27^{6}); *'Ammi-za'da*, 'uncle has terrified'; *Ammi-dhara'a*, 'uncle has sown'; *'Ammi-yada'a*, 'uncle knows'; *'Ammi-yapiya*, 'uncle is perfect' (all S. Arab names, Hommel, *AHT* 84); *'Ammi-yathi'a*, 'uncle has helped,' a Sabæan (Hommel, *AHT* 84) = *Am-yate'u*, an Assyrian (*WAI* iii. 46, No. 6=Johns, *Deeds*, No. 229, rev. 5)=*Amme-'ta'*, an Arab (*WAI* iv. 47, No. 1^{15}; Delitzsch, *Paradies*, p. 303; cf. *Abi-yate'* in Ashurbanipal, *Rassam*, vii. 97); *'Ammi-kariba*, 'uncle has blessed,' a Sabæan (*CIS* iv. 73); *'Ammu-ladin*, 'uncle is near,' a king of Kedar (Ashurbanipal, *Rassam*, viii. 15); *Ammi-nadab*, 'uncle has been generous' (Ex 6^{23}, Nu 1^{7} 2^{3} $7^{12.17}$ 10^{14}, Ru 4^{19}, 1 Ch 2^{10} 6^{22}, Est 2^{15} 9^{29} [acc. to LXX]), also a king of Ammon mentioned by Ashurbanipal (*KB* ii. p. 240); *'Ammi-amuqa*, 'uncle is wise,' a Sabæan (cf. Heb. עמוק); *'Ammi-ṣaduqa*, 'uncle is righteous,' a Sabæan (Hal. 535),= *'Ammi-saduga*, a king of the I Dyn. of Babylon; *'Ammu-rabi*, or *Ḫammu-rabi*, 'uncle is great,' a king of the I Dyn. of Babylon; *'Am-ram*, 'uncle is high' (Nu 3^{17-19} 26^{59}, Ex 16^{18-20}, 1 Ch $6^{2.3.18}$, Ezr 10^{34}), also an Assyrian (Johns, *Deeds*, 59, rev. 2); *'Ammi-sami'a*, 'uncle has heard,' a Sabæan (Hommel, *AHT* 84); *'Ammi-shapaka*, 'uncle has bestowed,' a Sabæan (*CIS* 37).

3. A third class of 'Ammi-formations contains names in which 'Ammi is *preceded by a noun*; e.g. *Eli-'am*. Here also the translation 'people' for *'Ammi* gives no good sense, and the noun which precedes is not construct, but absolute. *Eli-'am* does not mean 'God of the people,' nor 'God is a people,' both of which would be impossible names for an individual, but it means 'God is uncle.' Once more the parallelism between *Eli-'am* and *Eli-Yah*, *Baal-'am* and *Baal-Yah*, shows that *'am* is a Divine name.

The following names belong to this formation:—*Eli'am* (2 S 11^{3} 23^{34}), also in a Phœn. inscription (*CIS* 147), and in the Bab. name *Ilu-Imme* (Johns, *Deeds*, 162^{5}); *Ani-'am* (1 Ch 7^{19}; meaning?, perhaps = *Anu-'am*, 'Anu is uncle'); *Beli-am*, 'Beli is uncle' (Ob. of Manishtusu, C, xv. 3; Scheil, *Textes Élam.-Sém.*), =prob. בלעם, Balaam; *Ben-'ammi*, 'son of uncle,' the progenitor of the Ammonites (Gn 19^{38}; cf. art. AMMONITES); *Bir-amma*, 'Bir is uncle,' an Assyrian (Johns, *Deeds*, 476, rev. 5; 855, rev. 8); *Zimri-ḫammu*, 'mountain-sheep is uncle,' a totemic Assyr. name (*Cun. Texts Brit. Mus.* iv. 1*a*, line 8); *Aa-amme* (perhaps =*Yah-am*, 'Jahweh is uncle,' an Assyr. name (Johns, *Deeds*, 296^{3}); *Yithre-'am*, 'abundance is uncle' (2 S 3^{5}, 1 Ch 3^{3}) = *Atar-ḫamu*? (Johns, *Deeds*, 198, obv. 3; Bezold, *Catalogue*, v. 1982); *Nabu-ḫamme*, 'Nebo is uncle,' a Bab. name interchanging with *Nabu-amme* and *Nabu-imme* (Strassmaier, *Nabuchodonosor*, p. 18 f.); *Shulmanu-imme*, 'Shulman is uncle,' an Assyr. name (Johns, *Deeds*, 284^{3}); *Shamash-imme*, 'Shamash is uncle' (Johns, *Deeds*, 248^{1}); *Se-imme*, 'gift is uncle' (cf. עמשי), an Assyr. name (Johns, *Deeds*, Nos. 126, 282 f.).

4. A fourth formation, in which *a verb in the perf. 3 sing. precedes* 'Ammi, is represented, so far as the present writer knows, only by רחבעם, Rehoboam (1 K 11^{43} etc.), and (=Φιλόπατρις) as a cognomen of the Nabatæan king Ḥâriṭat (Euting, *Nab. Inschr.* 25, etc.). This is perhaps a late formation, and in it *'am* may have the late sense of 'people'; but the meaning '(Divine) uncle' is also possible, and is favoured by the parallel Rehab-Yahu. The name will then mean 'uncle is large.'

5. A fifth formation is found when 'Ammi *is preceded by a verb in the imperf. 3 sing.* Here belong the Heb. personal names, יקמעם, ירבעם, ישבעם, and five town names. These are commonly believed to be a late formation peculiar to the Heb., and *'am* in them is supposed to mean 'people'; but *Yashdi-ḫammu*, ''Ammi is lofty,' occurs in an Assyr. text (*Cun. Texts Brit. Mus.* iv. 2, line 21); and יקמעם is parallel to יקמיה, and ישבעם to ישביה; so that, even in this class, the primitive meaning of 'uncle' may still survive.

From the foregoing investigation it appears that *'Amm* is one of the earliest and widest spread of the Semitic designations of deity. It appears in the Obelisk of Manishtusu, which Scheil dates B.C. 4500, and in the earliest period of all the other Semitic languages. It was originally a title like El, Baal, Adon, Melek, and most other Divine names; but in a number of places where its primitive meaning was forgotten it developed into a true personal name. Among the Hebrews it was treated, like Baal, Adon, and Melek, as a title of Jahweh. It is found most frequently in the early period, and no new names of this sort were coined during the period covered by the OT. See AMMONITES.

LITERATURE.—Derenbourg, *REJ* ii. 123; De Jong, *Over de met ab, ach, enz. zamengestelde Hebreeuwsche Eigennamen*, 1880; G. B. Gray, *Studies in Hebrew Proper Names*, 1896, pp. 41–60, 75–86; Grünwald, *Eigennamen des AT*, 1895, p. 46 f.; Hommel, *Altisr. Überlieferung*, 1897, p. 83 ff., *Aufsätze und Abhandlungen*, 1892, p. 154, *ZDMG* xlix (1895); Jensen, *ZA* x. 342 f., *GGA*, 1900, p. 979, *LCBl*, 1902, col. 695 f.; Kerber, *Die religionsgesch. Bedeutung der heb. Eigennamen*, 1897, p. 5 ff.; Krenkel, 'Das Verwandtschaftswort עם,' *ZATW*, 1888, p. 280 ff.; Lenormant, *Lettres Assyriologiques*, 1872, 1 ser. ii. 84; Mordtmann, *ZDMG*, 1872, p. 427; Nestle, *Die isr. Eigennamen*, 1876; Neubauer in *Studia Biblica*, 1885, i. 225; Prätorius, *ZDMG*, 1872, p. 427, *Neue Beiträge zur Erklärung der him. Inschriften*, 1873, p. 25; Sayce, *RP*, 2 ser. iii. p. xi; W. R. Smith, *Kinship*², 1903, p. 71 f.; Wellhausen, *GGN*, 1893, p. 480 f.; *KAT*³, 1902, p. 480 ff.

LEWIS BAYLES PATON.

AMMONITES.—During the period covered by the Old Testament literature the Ammonites occupied the eastern portion of the region now known as the Belḳā. Dt 2^{37} describes their territory as 'the whole side of the torrent of Jabbōq, and the cities of the hill-country,' *i.e.* the region about the upper course of the modern Wādy Zerḳā (cf. Dt 3^{16}, Jos 12^{2}). Jos 13^{25} speaks of the towns of Ja'zēr and 'Ărō'ēr as marking the frontier between Ammon and Israel. Ja'zēr is also named in Nu 21^{24} according to the Gr. text (BAFL). It is described by Eusebius and Jerome as lying 10 R.m. west of Philadelphia (Rabbah) and 15 R.m. from Heshbon. Its precise location and also that of 'Ărō'ēr have not yet been determined. The capital city of the country was Rabbāh, or Rabbath benê-'Ammôn, at the head-waters of the Jabbōq (cf. Dt 3^{11}, Jos 13^{25}, 2 S 11^{1} 12^{26-29} 17^{27}, 1 Ch 20^{1}, Jer $49^{2f.}$, Ezk $21^{25(20)}$ 25^{5}, Am 1^{14}). It was rebuilt by Ptolemy Philadelphus (B.C. 285–247), and received from him its Greek name of Philadelphia. Its modern Arabic name of 'Ammān is a survival of the ancient name of the land. The other towns Minnîth and Ābēl-cheramîm are mentioned in Jg 11^{33}.

In regard to this people there are no native sources of information. Even inscriptions are wholly lacking. Our knowledge of their religion, accordingly, must be derived from the scanty notices of the OT and from the allusions in certain Assyrian inscriptions.

According to Gn 19^{33-38}, the ancestors of Moab and Ammon were sons of Lot by his two daughters. They were thus nearly related to Israel (cf. Dt $2^{9.19}$). In the case of the Moabites this opinion is sustained by proper names and by the Mesha Inscription, which is written in a dialect almost identical with Hebrew. In the case of the Ammonites it is sustained by the proper names Nāhāsh (1 S 11^{1}), Hānûn (2 S 10^{1}), Shōbî (17^{27}), Zelek (23^{37}), Na'āmāh (1 K 14^{21}), Ba'sa and Ruḥub (Shalmaneser, *Monolith*, ii. 95), Sanipu (Tiglath Pileser, *Clay Tablet Ins.*, rev. 10), Puduilu (Sennacherib, *Prism*, ii. 52; Esarhaddon, *Broken Prism*, v. 18), Amminadbi (Ashurbanipal, 'Fragment,' in *Keilinschrift. Bibl.* ii. p. 240), Ba'ălîs (Jer 40^{14}), Tōbîāh (Neh 2^{19}); also by the divine name Milcōm, and the city names Rabbāh, 'Ărō'ēr, Minnîth, Ābēl-cherāmîm, all of which are easily interpreted from the Hebrew.

The Ammonites were a part of the same wave of Semitic migration to which Israel belonged, and their settlement east of the Jordan did not long precede Israel's occupation of Canaan. According to Dt $2^{20f.}$, they dispossessed a people known as the Zamzummîm, a branch of the Rephaim, which it has been proposed to identify with the Zuzim in Ham of Gn 14^{5} (cf. Dt 3^{11}). According to Jg 11^{13-22}, Jos 13^{25}, they occupied originally the whole of the region east of the Jordan, but were driven out of the western half of this by the Amorites (cf. Nu 21^{25-31}). The Amorite kingdom of Sihon the Israelites conquered, but the land of the Ammonites they did not disturb (Nu 21^{24}, Dt $2^{19.37}$ 3^{16}, Jg 11^{15}). Dt $23^{4(3)f.}$ represents the Ammonites as participating with the Moabites in hiring Balaam to curse Israel, and, according to Nu 22^{5}, Balaam came from the land of the children of Ammon (read *'Ammôn* with Sam., Syr., Vulg., instead of *'ammô*, 'his people'). According to Jg 3^{13}, the Ammonites assisted Eglon, king of Moab, in his conquest, and, according to 10^{7}–11^{33}, they disputed the possession of Gilead with the Israelites. A similar attack upon Gilead by Nahash, king of Ammon, was warded off by Saul, and was the occasion of his elevation to the throne, according to the older source of the Book of Samuel (1 S 11^{1-11}). Nahash 'showed kindness' unto David, *i.e.* kept peace with him and paid his tribute, but his son Hanun, trusting to the help of the Aramæans of the adjacent regions of Beth-Rehob, Zobah, and Maacah, revolted, and had to be conquered by David (2 S 10^{1}–11^{1} 12^{26-31}, 1 Ch 19^{1}–20^{3}). The spoil of this campaign David dedicated to Jahweh (2 S 8^{12} = 1 Ch 18^{11}), and the Ammonites remained tributary during the rest of his reign and during the reign of his successor. Zelek the Ammonite appears in the list of David's bodyguard (2 S 23^{37}). Solomon cultivated friendly relations by marrying a wife from this nation (1 K 11^{1}), and this account is confirmed by the fact that the mother of Rehoboam was an Ammonitess ($14^{21.31}$). According to one recension of the LXX, she was the daughter of Hanun, son of Nahash. For her benefit the cult of Milcōm, the god of Ammon, was established on a hill near Jerusalem (1 K $11^{5.7.33}$, 2 K 23^{13}). After the death of Solomon, the Ammonites appear to have regained their independence, and to have remained free until they fell beneath the yoke of the Assyrians along with the other small nations of Western Asia. The victories of Jehoshaphat, Uzziah, and Jotham over them rest only upon the authority of the Chronicler (2 Ch 20. 26^{8} 27^{5}). In B.C. 854, Ba'sa (Baasha), son of Ruḥub (Reḥōb), with 1000 men, came to the help of the king of Damascus against Shalmaneser II., along with Ahab of Israel and ten other kings of Syria (Shalmaneser, *Monolith*, ii. 95). In the reign of Jeroboam II. (*c.* 760 B.C.), Amos denounces the Ammonites because of the atrocities that they have committed in Gilead (Am 1^{13}). In B.C. 734, Tiglath Pileser III. records that he received the tribute of Sanipu of Bit-'Ammān (Bēth-'Ammôn), along with that of Ahaz of Judah (*Clay Tablet Ins.*, rev. 10). From Zeph $2^{9f.}$, Jer $9^{25(26)}$ 49^{1-6}, it appears that after the deportation of the Israelites east of the Jordan by Tiglath Pileser III. in 734 (2 K 15^{29}), the Ammonites moved in and occupied their land. Sennacherib (*Prism*, ii. 52) records that he received the tribute of Puduilu (Padahel) of Bit-'Ammān at the time of his invasion of Syria in 701. This same Puduilu is mentioned by Esarhaddon (*Broken Prism*, v. 18) as one of the twenty-two kings of the 'land of the Hittites' who furnished building materials for one of his palaces. In his place in a similar list of twenty-two kings Ashurbanipal names Amminadbi (Amminadab) (*Keilinschriftliche Bibliothek*, ii. p. 240, l. 11). At the time of Nebuchadrezzar's first invasion of Syria the Ammonites assisted him (2 K 24^{2}). Subsequently they joined a league against him (Jer 27^{3}, Ezk $21^{20.28}$), but before they were attacked they managed to make peace, and participated in his assault upon Jerusalem (Ezk $25^{1-7.10}$). In spite of this, many of the Jews took refuge among them at the time of the siege, and Ishmael was incited by Baalis, king of Ammon, to murder Gedaliah, the governor whom Nebuchadrezzar had appointed at the time of the fall of the city (Jer $40^{11.14}$ 41^{10}). The name Kephar hā-'Ammônai in Jos 18^{24} (P), as one of the villages of Benjamin, suggests that during the Exile the Ammonites, like the Edomites, made settlements west of the Jordan. If so, this will explain the denunciation of the exilic prophecy, Is 11^{14}. As early as the time of Ashurbanipal, two main divisions of the Arabians, Kedar and Nebaioth, were menacing the old lands of Edom, Moab, and Ammon, and were prevented from overrunning them only by the activity of the Assyrian monarch. Ezk 25 anticipates that these 'children of the East' will bring these three nations to an end (cf. Ob 1^{7}); and, as a matter of fact, after the Exile we find, instead of Moab and Edom, Geshem the Arabian as the chief enemy of the Jews (Neh 2^{19} 4^{7} $6^{1.6}$). Ammonites are still mentioned, but they seem to lead no independent national existence. Tobiah, the Ammonite who opposed Nehemiah ($2^{10.19}$ $4^{3.7}$ 6^{17} 13^{4}), bore a name compounded with Jahweh, he and his son both had Jewish wives, he was connected by marriage with the high priest, and he appears regularly in company with Sanballat the Horonite and the Samaritans. Apparently he had nothing to do with the old land of Ammon, but was a resident of Kephar hā-'Ammônai (Jos 18^{24}). No king of Ammon is named after the Exile, and it seems probable that this people perished as a nation, along with Moab and Edom, at the time of the Nabatæan Arabian migration. Survivors of these nations found refuge in Judah, and gave rise to the problem of mixed marriages, which caused Nehemiah and Ezra so much trouble (Ezr 9^{1}, Neh $13^{1.23}$). Where Ammonites are mentioned in the later history, we have merely an application of an old geographical term to a new race. The Ammonites under Timotheus (1 Mac 5^{6-8}), and the Ammonites of Ps 83^{7} and Dn 11^{41}, are Nabatæans or Greeks living in the old land of Ammon.

We must now endeavour to construct from these meagre sources a picture of the religion of the ancient Ammonites. From 1 K $11^{5.33}$, 2 K 23^{13}, it appears that **Milcōm** was their chief national god, just as Chemosh was the god of Moab, Kozai of Edom, and Jahweh of Israel. In 2 S 12^{30} = 1 Ch 20^{2} the LXX reads *Milcōm* instead of *malcām*, 'their king.' This is the reading of the Talmud (*'Ăbōdā zārā*, 44*a*), of the old Jewish commentators, and of most modern authorities. In that case the passage reads, 'And he took the crown of Milcōm from off his head, its weight was a talent of gold, and on it there was a precious stone. It David placed upon his own head.' From this it appears that Milcōm was represented by an idol of human size which was adorned with the insignia of royalty like other ancient images. In Jer $49^{1.3}$, LXX, Vulg., Syr. also read *Milcōm* instead of MT *malcām*, and this reading is undoubtedly correct, so that the passage should be translated, 'Hath

Israel no sons? hath he no heir? why then doth Milcōm inherit Gad, and his people dwell in the cities thereof? . . . Milcōm shall go into captivity, his priests and his princes together.' This shows that Milcōm bore a relation to Ammon similar to that which Jahweh bore to Israel, and that he had a priesthood that was the counterpart of the Jahweh priesthood. In 2 S 12^{31}, Am 1^{15} 5^{26}, Zeph 1^{5}, some of the versions and certain commentators also read *Milcōm* instead of *malcēn* and *malcām*, but these emendations are less probable. Apart from these passages in the OT no mention of Milcōm is known.

The name Milcōm is with Baudissin (*Jahve et Moloch*, 30) and Lagarde (*Übersicht über die . . . Bildung der Nomina*, p. 190) to be regarded as *milk* 'king' (Phœn. *milk*, Heb. *mélek*) with the old nominative ending and mimmation. It means, therefore, simply 'the king.' Others regard it as compounded of *mélek* and *'am*, and as meaning 'king of the people' (so Kuenen, *Theol. Tijdschrift*, ii. 1868, 555–598), or 'Am is king' (so Eerdmans, *Melekdienst*, 112); but these explanations are unsatisfactory, because they do not account for the disappearance of the ע. In etymology and meaning accordingly, Milcōm is identical with **Molech**, the god wroshipped by the Israelites, according to Lv 18^{21} 20^{2-5}, 2 K 23^{10}, Jer 32^{35}. The vowels of this word are generally believed to be those of *bōsheth* 'shame,' and to have been added by the Massoretes to express their abhorrence of the cult. The original pronunciation was Mélek. The name is always accompanied by the article (except in 1 K 11^{7}, where the text is corrupt), and means 'the king.' In Is 30^{33} 57^{9} it is probable that 'the king' refers to this god, and there are other passages in the OT where it is possible that the expression has the same meaning.

On the basis of the similarity of form and meaning of Milcōm and Molech it has been conjectured that the two gods are identical, and that Molech-worship was borrowed by Israel from the Ammonites. If so, we can learn something in regard to Milcōm from a study of Molech. In support of this theory it is claimed that the only passages in the OT which mention Molech-worship (2 K 23^{10}, Jer 32^{35}, Lv 18^{21} 20^{2-5}, Is 30^{33} 57^{9}) were written after the time of Manasseh, and have his abuses in mind. This seems to show that Molech-worship was an innovation introduced from Ammon. There are several difficulties in the way of this view. Even if we grant that Molech was a borrowed divinity, it is not clear why he should have been borrowed from the Ammonites. They had no such political importance in the time of Manasseh that their god should have been sought as a refuge against the Assyrians. If Molech was borrowed from them, why did he not retain his original name of Milcōm? Mélek as a divine name is found in all branches of the Semitic race. In Babylonia and Assyria it appears as Malik (Jastrow, *Rel. of Bab. and Assyr.* 176 f.); among the people of Sepharvaim as Adram-Mélek and Anam-Mélek (2 K 17^{31}); in Palmyra as Malak-Bel (Baudissin, *Studien*, ii. 193); in Phœnicia, as Melḳart (=מלך־קרית); in Edom, in the proper name Malik-rammu (Sennacherib, *Prism*, ii. 54). If Molech-worship is really a borrowed cult in Israel, it may have been derived from any one of these sources quite as well as from the Ammonites.

It is not certain, however, that Molech-worship was an innovation introduced by Manasseh. Mélek is a title frequently applied to Jahweh Himself (*e.g.* Ps $5^{3(2)}$ 10^{16} $20^{10(9)}$ 24^{7} 29^{10} $44^{5(4)}$ $47^{3(2)}$ $48^{3(2)}$ $68^{25(24)}$ 74^{12} $84^{4(3)}$ 95^{3} 98^{6}, Is 6^{5} 33^{22}, Jer 8^{19} 10^{10} 46^{18}, Mic 4^{9}, Zeph 1^{5}, Zec 14^{17}, Mal 1^{14}, and proper names such as Malkishua, 1 S 14^{49}). A characteristic feature of the Mélek cult was child-sacrifice, and this is known to have been an element of the early Jahweh religion. The Book of the Covenant in Ex $22^{28(29)}$ enacts, 'The firstborn of thy sons shalt thou give unto me,' and contains no provision for redemption, such as we find in 13^{13} and 34^{20}. The story of Abraham's sacrifice of Isaac in Gn 22 (E) shows that child-sacrifice was practised in the early religion of Jahweh, but that the conviction was growing in prophetic circles that Jahweh did not demand these offerings. In spite of prophetic opposition, however, they continued to be brought (cf. 1 K 16^{34}, and Winckler, *Gesch. Isr.* i. 163, n. 3; 2 K 16^{3}, 2 Ch 28^{3}). Jeremiah repeatedly insists that Jahweh does not require these sacrifices (Jer 7^{31} 19^{5} 32^{35}), and this indicates that in the popular conception they were part of His requirements. The Holiness Code (Lv 18^{21}) also suggests that Molech sacrifices were popularly regarded as Jahweh sacrifices. Ezekiel goes so far as to quote the law of Ex 13^{12}, 'Thou shalt sacrifice unto Jahweh everything that openeth the womb,' and to say that Jahweh gave this commandment in wrath to destroy the nation because it would not keep the good statutes that he had previously given it (Ezk $20^{24-26.\,31}$). These facts make it clear that Molech-worship was no new thing in Israel, and that by the nation in general it was regarded as one form of Jahweh-worship. The absence of early prophetic polemic against child-sacrifice is, accordingly, to be explained by the fact that the prophets included it in their repudiation of all sacrifice. Jeremiah and Ezekiel, who hold the Deuteronomic standpoint in regard to sacrifice, are obliged to specify that Jahweh does not require child-sacrifice, although He requires animal-sacrifice. If Molech-worship is ancient in Israel, then it cannot have been borrowed from the Ammonites in the time of Manasseh.

Another theory which identifies Milcōm with Molech supposes that this cult was introduced into Israel by Solomon. This opinion makes its appearance as early as the Gr. versions, and has been the source of much textual corruption. It seems to be supported by 1 K $11^{7.\,33}$, which speaks of 'Milcōm, the abomination of the Ammonites,' as worshipped by Solomon after his marriage with an Ammonite wife (cf. 2 K 23^{13}, 1 K $14^{21.\,31}$); and by 1 K 11^{7}, which calls this god Molech. Granting the historicity of Solomon's worship of Milcōm, which is disputed by a number of critics, it appears from 1 K 11^{7}, 2 K 23^{13}, that the high place of Milcōm was on the right hand of the Mount of Destruction east of Jerusalem, *i.e.* somewhere on the ridge of the Mount of Olives; but the high place of Molech, according to all the OT references, was in the Valley of Hinnom (cf. 2 K 23^{10}, Jer 2^{23} 7^{31} 19^{6} 32^{35}, 2 Ch 28^{3} 33^{6}). From this it is clear that Milcōm and Molech were not identified by the ancient Israelites (cf. Baethgen, *Beiträge*, 15). The substitution of Molech for Milcōm in 1 K 11^{7} is evidently a textual error; the MT points without the article, and Lucian's recension of the LXX reads Milcōm.

A third theory is that there was a primitive Semitic god, Mélek, of which Milcōm and Molech are local variants. Against this view is the fact that Milcōm and Molech are not personal names, but titles, like Baal, 'owner'; Adon, 'master'; Marna, 'our lord.' There was no primitive Semitic god Baal, whose cult came down in the various branches of the Semitic race, but there was a multitude of Baalim who presided over various holy places and who were distinguished from one another as the Baal of this place or the Baal of that place. These Baalim were different in functions and might have different personal names. In like manner there were as many Melākîm as there were nations, and there is no reason why the Mélek of Ammon, or the Mélek of Israel, or the Mélek of Tyre, or the Mélek of Palmyra should be identified with one another, any more than why their human rulers should be identified because they all bore the name of 'king.'

Although there was no primitive god Mélek, it is probable, however, that all the various Mᵉlākîm of the Semitic races bore a family resemblance to one another, just as the Baalim bore a family resemblance, so that it is possible to draw inferences from the character of one Mélek to that of another. The Baalim were gods of nature. They manifested themselves in springs and streams and trees. They gave the fruits of the earth, and they were worshipped with offerings of firstfruits. The Mᵉlākîm, on the other hand, were tribal gods conceived after the analogy of human rulers. They gave the fruit of the womb; and, accordingly, they were worshipped with firstborn children and firstborn animals. Wherever we know anything of the cult of the Mᵉlākîm, child-sacrifice is its most conspicuous feature. When this rite was practised in Israel it was always in the name of the Mélek, even though this might be understood as a title of Jahweh. From Dt 12^{31} $18^{9.10}$, Lv $18^{21.24}$, Ezk 16^{20}, Ps 106^{38}, it appears that this sort of sacrifice was also offered by the Canaanites, and this testimony is confirmed by the excavations at Gezer, Megiddo, and Taanach, where the remains of sacrificed infants have been found in large numbers. Child-sacrifice was a conspicuous element in the cult of the Tyrian and Carthaginian Melḳart, and 2 K 17^{31} states that the people of Sepharvaim sacrificed their children to Adram-Mélek, and Anam-Mélek. These facts seem to show that sacrifice of infants was intimately connected with the conception of deity as Mélek, or ruler of the tribe; and we are probably warranted in thinking that wherever a god was called by this name this sort of sacrifice was celebrated in his honour. In the case of Milcōm, accordingly, infant-sacrifice is probable, although this is never mentioned in the OT; and this opinion is confirmed by the fact that the closely related Moabites sacrificed children in honour of their god Chemosh (2 K 3^{27}).

In regard to the manner in which children were sacrificed we have only the analogy of Molech-worship in Israel to guide us. The technical name for the rite was 'making over children to the King by fire' (Lv 18^{21} 20^{2-4}, Dt 18^{10}, 2 K 16^{3} 17^{17} 21^{6}, 2 Ch 33^{6}, Ezk 20^{31}). The same expression is used of 'making over' the firstborn to Jahweh in Ex 13^{12}. From Gn 22^{10}, Ezk 16^{20}, Is 57^{5}, *et al.*, it appears that children were slain like other sacrifices, and from Dt 12^{31} 18^{10}, 2 K 17^{31}, Jer 3^{24} 7^{31} 19^{4-6} 32^{35}, that their bodies were afterwards burnt in a place known as *Tᵉphāth* (*Tōpheth*, with the vowels of *bōsheth*, 'shame'). Analogous rites are found among the Phœnicians and Carthaginians, and we may perhaps assume that they existed also among the Ammonites.

Besides Milcōm there is no clear evidence that the Ammonites worshipped any other god. Jg 10^{6} speaks of 'the gods of the children of Ammon,' but this is a late editorial passage. From Jg 11^{24} it has been inferred that Chemosh was a god of the Ammonites as well as of the Moabites, or else that Chemosh and Milcōm were identified; but it is now generally recognized that the section Jg 11^{12-28} has nothing to do with Jephthah's dispute with the Ammonites. It is a fragment of a narrative of a dispute between Israel and the Moabites which has been combined with the Jephthah story by the compiler of the Book of Judges (cf. Moore, *Judges*, 283).

More can be said in favour of the view that the Ammonites worshipped a god called 'Am or 'Ammi. The name 'Ammôn (Assyr. Ammân) is apparently a diminutive or pet-name from 'Am, as Shimshôn (Samson) is from Shemesh. Ammon alone is never used as a tribal name, except in the late passages, Ps 83^{7} and 1 S 11^{11}, where the Gr. reads τοὺς υἱοὺς Ἀμμών. The regular expression is 'children of Ammon.' Even the ancestor of the race is not called Ammon, but Ben-'Ammî (Gn 19^{38}). 'Am means primarily 'father-uncle' in a polyandrous society, then 'paternal uncle,' then 'kinsman,' then 'people.' The narrator in Gn 19^{38} has chosen the meaning 'father-uncle,' and has derived from this the story of the incestuous origin of the Ammonites. Their ancestor, he thinks, was called Ben-'Ammî, 'son of my father-uncle,' because his father was also his mother's father. It is more likely, however, that 'Ammî was used here originally with reference to a god who was called the 'father-uncle,' or 'kinsman' of the tribe.

This use of 'Ammî as a divine name is wide-spread in the Semitic dialects. In Heb. we find it as the first element of the proper names 'Ammiel, 'Ammihud, 'Ammihur, 'Amminadab, 'Ammishadai, 'Ammizabad, 'Ammiad; and as the final element in the names Ani'am, Eli'am, Ithre'am, Jashobe'am, Jekame'am, Jeroboam, Rehoboam, Jible'am, Jokde'am, Jokme'am, Jokne'am, Jorke'am. In Babylonia it appears in names of kings of the first dynasty, 'Ammisatana, 'Ammisaduga, Ḫammurabi (or 'Ammurabi), and in South Arabia in 'Amḳarib and other proper names. One of the kings of Ammon mentioned by Ashurbanipal bore the name Amminadbi (Amminadab), 'my father-uncle is generous,' where 'Ammî is clearly the name of a deity. Bala'am is also a name compounded with 'Am, and one tradition in Nu 22^{5} (read '*Ammôn* instead of '*ammô*, 'his people'), makes Balaam come from the land of the children of Ammon (cf. Dt $23^{4\,(3)\,f.}$. Rehoboam also bears a name compounded with 'Am, and he was the son of an Ammonite mother (1 K $14^{21.31}$).

On the basis of some of these facts, Derenbourg, in *REJ* (1880) i. 123, proposed the theory that 'Am, or 'Ammi, was the name of the national god of the Ammonites. This theory is correct, if we regard 'Am as merely a title applied to Milcōm by the Ammonites, as it was applied to Jahweh by the Israelites; but it is not correct if we regard 'Am as a separate deity. There is no evidence that there was a primitive Semitic god 'Am, any more than that there was a primitive Semitic god Baal or Mélek. 'Paternal uncle' is a title like 'father,' 'brother,' 'king,' 'lord,' that might be applied to the most diverse gods (see 'AMM, 'AMMI).

The word Ilu, or El, which appears in the name of the Ammonite king Pudu-ilu (cf. Padah-El, 'God has redeemed,' Nu 34^{28}), is also generic, and may refer to Milcōm, as it does to Jahweh in the parallel Heb. form (cf. Pedaiah, 2 K 23^{36}). Baalis (בעליס), the name borne by the king of Ammon at the time of the fall of Jerusalem, is of doubtful etymology. Grätz regards it as abbreviated out of Ben-'ālîṣ (בן־עליץ), 'son of exultation.' Baethgen (*Beiträge*, 16) regards it as equivalent to Baal-Isis, 'husband of Isis,' or 'Isis is Baal,' and compares Abd-is, 'servant of Isis' (*CIS* 308). Both interpretations are exceedingly doubtful, and all that can be gathered from this name is that Baal was in use as a generic name for deity among the Ammonites as among the other Semites. Tobiah the Ammonite and his son Jehohanan (Neh 2^{10} $6^{17f.}$) have names compounded with Jahweh, and this has been made a basis for the conjecture that Jahweh was one of the gods of the Ammonites, as of the people of Hamath (cf. Joram, 2 S 8^{10}, and Yau-bi'di in the inscriptions of Sargon), and of the people of Ya'udi in Northern Syria (cf. Azri-yau in the inscriptions of Tiglath Pileser III.). The conclusion is, however, not valid, because, as previously pointed out, the Ammonites settled in the land of Israel during the Exile and adopted the cult of the god of the land. The other Ammonite names that have come down to us are not theophorous, and, therefore, yield no information in regard to the religion of this race. Stephen of Byzantium (cited by Baethgen, *Beiträge*, 16) states that the original name of the capital of Ammon was Ammana, then it was called Astarte, and finally Philadelphia. If this be true, it indicates the worship of the primitive Semitic goddess Ashtart. From the mention of the gigantic sarcophagus of Og that was preserved at Rabbah (Dt 3^{11}), we may, perhaps, infer that ancestor-worship was practised among the Ammonites as among other branches of the Semitic race.

From the foregoing survey it appears that there is no convincing evidence of the worship of any other god than Milcōm among the Ammonites. It would be rash, however, to infer from this lack of evidence, which is due to the scantiness of our sources, that Milcōm occupied the same unique place in Ammon as Jahweh did in Israel; and to use this, as Renan did, as proof of a tendency to monotheism in that branch of the Semitic race to which Israel belonged. In all probability the Ammonites were polytheists, like their neighbours and near relatives the Moabites and Edomites, and it is merely an accident that we know the name of only the head god of their pantheon.

In regard to the rites of their religion we know practically nothing, except what we may infer from the analogy of the religions of kindred races. Jer 9^{26} shows that they practised the rite of circumcision, in common with the Egyptians, Israelites, Edomites, and Moabites. In other respects probably their customs did not differ widely from those of ancient Israel. From Gn 19^{36-38} Delitzsch (*Com. on Gen.*) infers that the Ammonites and Moabites were characterized by an extreme lewdness that aroused the moral repugnance of Israel; and he appeals to Nu 25 for proof of this in the case of the Moabites; but Gn 19^{36-38} is so evidently derived from a fanciful popular etymology of the names Moab and Ben-'Ammî that no historical conclusions can be based upon it.

LITERATURE.—Ewald, *Hist. of Isr.* (London, 1876), ii. pp. 295, 336, 393 ff., iii. (1878), p. 24; Stade, *GVI* (1881), i. pp. 113–126; Wellhausen, *Isr. u. jüd. Gesch.* (1895), p. 7 ff.; Winckler, *Gesch. Isr.* (1895), i. pp. 213–216; Kautzsch, art. 'Ammon' in Riehm's *HWB* (1884); Macpherson, art. 'Ammon' in Hastings' *DB* (1899); Buhl, art. 'Ammon' in *PRE*³; Moore, art. 'Milcom' in *EBi*; and the literature under MOLECH, AMMI in this work.

LEWIS BAYLES PATON.

AMNESTY.—The word is used somewhat loosely by modern writers with reference to several episodes in Greek history. Strictly and properly, it is the word used by writers of the post-classical age to describe the resolution adopted by the Athenians after the expulsion of the so-called Thirty Tyrants, when, in the summer of B.C. 403, a reconciliation was effected, through the mediation of the Spartan king Pausanias, between the oligarchical party of the city and the democrats of the Piræus, upon the following basis:

'All persons who, having remained in the City during the oligarchical régime, were anxious to leave it, were to be free to settle at Eleusis, retaining their full civil rights, and possessing full and independent rights of self-government, with free enjoyment of their personal property. . . . There should be a universal amnesty concerning past events towards all persons (τῶν δὲ παρεληλυθότων μηδενὶ πρὸς μηδένα μνησικακεῖν ἐξεῖναι), except the Thirty, the Ten (who were their successors), the Eleven (who had carried out their decrees of execution), and the magistrates (ten in number) of the Piræus; and these should also be included if they should submit to give an account of their official acts (ἐὰν διδῶσιν εὐθύνας) in the usual way' (Arist. *Ath. Pol.* 39 [Kenyon's tr.]; cf. Xen. *Hell.* ii. 4. 38, and reference in Aristoph. *Plut.* 1146: μὴ μνησικακήσῃς, εἰ σὺ Φυλὴν κατέλαβες. 'Αλλὰ ξύνοικον πρὸς θεῶν δέξασθέ με).

That the children of the Thirty were included under the amnesty is testified by Demosthenes *Or.* xl. 32: νυνὶ δ' ὑμεῖς μὲν οὕτως ἐστὲ κοινοὶ καὶ φιλάνθρωποι, ὥστ' οὐδὲ τοὺς τῶν τριάκοντα υἱεῖς φυγαδεῦσαι ἐκ τῆς πόλεως ἠξιώσατε—which was in striking contrast with the practice usual in Greek political strife.* This agreement of harmony was ratified by the oath of the whole people, and for some years at least it seems to have been incorporated with the oath of office taken by members of the Council and the Heliasts—the senators swearing not to admit any information (ἔνδειξις) or to allow any arrest (ἀπαγωγή) founded on any fact prior to the archonship of Eukleides, excepting only in the case of the persons expressly excluded from the amnesty (πλὴν τῶν φυγόντων); the dikasts swearing neither to remember past wrongs, nor to yield to any solicitation to do so, but to give their verdict in accordance with the revised code dating from the restoration of the democracy (Andoc. *de Myst.* 90: οὐ μνησικακήσω, οὐδὲ ἄλλῳ πείσομαι, ψηφιοῦμαι δὲ κατὰ τοὺς κειμένους νόμους. See Grote, *Hist. of Greece* [vol. xii. ed. 1884], viii. 100 n.).*

* *e.g.* at Corcyra (Thuc. iii. 70 f.); at Argos (Grote, *Hist. of Greece*, ix. 418); see Thonissen, *Le droit pénal*, p. 153, and cf. Dio Cass. xliv. 26. 5.

The amnesty, as above described, seems to have been renewed two years later with the secessionists at Eleusis (Arist. *l.c.*; Xen. *Hell.* ii. 4. 43: καὶ ὀμόσαντες ὅρκους ἦ μὴν μὴ μνησικακήσειν ἔτι καὶ νῦν ὁμοῦ τε πολιτεύονται καὶ τοῖς ὅρκοις ἐμμένει ὁ δῆμος). The energetic but high-handed action of Archinos was a powerful factor in maintaining the amnesty. When one of the returned exiles began to violate the agreement, Archinos haled him before the Council, and persuaded the Councillors to put the man to death without trial (Arist. *l.c.*: ἄκριτον ἀποκτεῖναι), telling them that they had now an opportunity of showing whether they wished to preserve the democracy and abide by their oath. Archinos also carried a measure giving every one accused in violation of the amnesty the right to raise a special plea in bar of action (παραγραφή. See Isocr. *Or.* xviii. 2: ἄν τις δικάζηται παρὰ τοὺς ὅρκους, ἐξεῖναι τῷ φεύγοντι παραγράψασθαι . . . ἵν' οἱ τολμῶντες μνησικακεῖν μὴ μόνον ἐπιορκοῦντες ἐξελέγχοιντο κ.τ.λ.).†

It must be noticed that the terms used of the above events by the classical writers are αἱ διαλύσεις or αἱ διαλλαγαί, αἱ διαθῆκαι, οἱ ὅρκοι—the 'reconciliation,' the 'covenant,' the 'oath'; while for the specific content of the oath the phrase μὴ μνησικακεῖν, 'not to remember past wrongs,' is ordinarily used (corresponding to the phrase τὰς περὶ τῶν προτέρων αἰτίας ἐξήλειψαν used in Arist. *Ath. Pol.* xl. 3). Compare the account given by the Latin compilers, *e.g.* Corn. Nep. *Thras.* iii. 2: 'legem tulit, ne quis ante actarum rerum accusaretur neve multaretur, eamque illi oblivionis appellarunt'; Justin, v. 10. 10: 'atque ita per multa membra civitas dissipata in unum tandem corpus redigitur, et ne qua dissensio ex ante actis nasceretur, omnes iure iurando obstringuntur, discordiarum oblivionem fore.' The Greek word ἀμνηστία, translating the Latin *oblivio*, is first used in Val. Max. iv. 1. 4: 'hæc oblivio, quam Athenienses ἀμνηστίαν vocant'; and by Plutarch (*Cic.* 42): Κικέρων . . . ἔπεισε τὴν σύγκλητον Ἀθηναίους μιμησαμένην ἀμνηστίαν τῶν ἐπὶ Καίσαρι ψηφίσασθαι (cf. Plut. *Præc. Pol.* 17: τὸ ψήφισμα τὸ τῆς ἀμνηστίας ἐπὶ τοῖς τριάκοντα: and Hist. Aug. *Aurel.* 39: 'amnestia etiam sub eo delictorum publicorum decreta est de exemplo Atheniensium'). It was probably the classical phrase μὴ μνησικακεῖν that was in Cicero's mind in the opening of his First Philippic (*Phil.* i. 1: 'in quo templo, quantum in me fuit, ieci fundamenta pacis, Atheniensiumque renovavi vetus exemplum: græcum etiam verbum usurpavi, quo tum in sedandis discordiis usa erat civitas illa, atque omnem memoriam discordiarum oblivione sempiterna delendam censui'—where, however, the Berne MS reads 'amnestiam' before 'usurpavi').

A similar example of an Act of oblivion, though no details are known, is furnished by the restored democracy of Samos in B.C. 411 (Thuc. viii. 73: καὶ τριάκοντα μέν τινας ἀπέκτειναν τῶν τριακοσίων, τρεῖς δὲ τοὺς αἰτιωτάτους φυγῇ ἐζημίωσαν· τοῖς δ' ἄλλοις οὐ μνησικακοῦντες δημοκρατούμενοι τὸ λοιπὸν ξυνεπολίτευον). An abortive attempt to re-establish harmony on the basis of amnesty was made at Megara in B.C. 424 (Thuc. iv. 74).

It is clear that the above Acts of oblivion differ from those examples to which the word 'amnesty' is also applied by modern writers—that is to say, those resolutions, of which several instances are

* Cf. Dio Cass. xliv. 26. 2: στασιάσαντές ποτε . . . καὶ τυραννηθέντες, οὐ πρότερον ἀπηλλάγησαν τῶν κακῶν πρὶν συνθέσθαι καὶ διομολογήσασθαι τῶν τε συμβεβηκότων σφίσι . . . ἐπιλήσεσθαι, καὶ μηδὲν τὸ παράπαν ὑπὲρ αὐτῶν μήτε ἐγκαλέσειν ποτὲ μήτε μνησικακήσειν τινί.

† Whether this belongs to the year B.C. 403 or to B.C. 401 is doubtful—probably to the latter year; so the present writer would arrange the events, rejecting Breitenbach's attempt (ed. of Xen. *Hell.* ed. 2, note on *Hell.* ii. 4. 43) to prove that the oath as given by Andocides (above quoted) belongs to the second and final act of reconciliation, and that hence arises its difference from the oath as given by Xen. *Hell.* ii. 4. 38.

known from Greek history, taken in times of great danger, with the object of stilling disputes and uniting all forces in defence, by which political exiles were recalled and civic rights conferred upon those who had been partially or wholly disfranchised as a penal measure. The Athenians adopted this measure shortly before the battle of Salamis (Andoc. *de Myst.* 107 : ἔγνωσαν τούς τε φεύγοντας καταδέξασθαι καὶ τοὺς ἀτίμους ἐπιτίμους ποιῆσαι. Cf. Arist. *Ath. Pol.* 22 : κατεδέξαντο πάντας τοὺς ὠστρακισμένους . . . διὰ τὴν Ξέρξου στρατείαν). Again, a similar resolution was passed at the time of the siege of Athens by Lysander, on the motion of Patrokleides (Andoc. *op. cit.* 73 : ἐπεὶ γὰρ αἱ νῆες διεφθάρησαν καὶ ἡ πολιορκία ἐγένετο, ἐβουλεύσασθε περὶ ὁμονοίας, καὶ ἔδοξεν ὑμῖν τοὺς ἀτίμους ἐπιτίμους ποιῆσαι : see § 77 for the full text of the decree). A third example is furnished by the proposal of Hypereides after the defeat at Chæroneia, that exiles should be recalled and public debtors and other ἄτιμοι be restored to their civic status on condition of military service (Lycurg. *Leocr.* 41 ; Hyper. *frg.* 29 ; Demos. *Or.* xxvi. 12 : ὅτε γὰρ Ὑπερείδης ἔγραψε, τῶν περὶ Χαιρώνειαν ἀτυχημάτων τοῖς Ἕλλησι γενομένων . . . εἶναι τοὺς ἀτίμους ἐπιτίμους, ἵν' ὁμονοοῦντες ἅπαντες ὑπὲρ τῆς ἐλευθερίας προθύμως ἀγωνίζωνται). To these examples may be added the measure of Solon (Plut. *Sol.* 19), which restored civil rights to all who before his archonship (B.C. 594) had been visited with disfranchisement, with the exception of certain categories of persons which need not here be specified. Such acts of grace were known with reference to individuals, *e.g.*, the recall of Alcibiades (Xen. *Hell.* i. 4. 11, his return in B.C. 408 ; the vote of recall actually passed in B.C. 411, Thuc. viii. 97) and of Demosthenes in B.C. 323 (Plut. *Dem.* 27), as well as of the historian Thucydides—to take only conspicuous examples in Athenian history.

Such acts of grace or pardon on the part of the sovereign people in reference to individuals or comparatively small groups or classes are clearly different in their nature from Acts of oblivion, where, in Greek history at any rate, the sovereign body itself has been sundered in twain upon a conflict of principle concerning the forms of government. Both, again, are to be clearly distinguished (and the confusion is not uncommon in the books of reference) from what the Greeks called ἄδεια, which corresponds to our Bill of Indemnity. Such ἄδεια or guarantee against penal consequences was always necessary to enable anyone to exercise any privilege that did not properly belong to his status, *i.e.* to enable slaves, resident aliens or disfranchised citizens to perform those higher functions which were part and parcel of the notion of civic status. It was also necessary before a proposal for the State to forego any of its rights against individuals, as, for example, a proposal for the removal of *atimia* or disfranchisement (Dem. *Or.* xxiv. 47 : ἄλλος οὗτος νόμος, οὐκ ἐῶν περὶ τῶν ἀτίμων οὐδὲ τῶν ὀφειλόντων λέγειν οὐδὲ χρηματίζειν περὶ ἀφέσεως τῶν ὀφλημάτων οὐδὲ τάξεως, ἂν μὴ τῆς ἀδείας δοθείσης, καὶ ταύτης μὴ ἐλάττων ἢ ἑξακισχιλίων ψηφισαμένων. Cf. *CIA* i. 180–183, and i. 32). A vote of ἄδεια also guaranteed informers against punishment for crimes in which they might have been participators; but their evidence must be truthful. In general, ἄδεια was a preliminary surrender of specific rights of the State in favour of an individual for a particular purpose (see Goldstaub, *De ἀδείας notione et usu in iure publico Attico*, Breslau, 1888).

We must distinguish, then, the following three categories : (1) ἄδεια, indemnity for acts which involve or may involve penal consequences ; in general, prospective ; only when retrospective does it coincide in practical effect with amnesty. (2) Pardon, in cases in which the penal consequences are already in operation. In this sense the word 'amnesty' is incorrectly used, as above explained. The Greeks apparently possessed no single term to cover this sense. (3) μὴ μνησικακεῖν (= Lat. *oblivio* and late Gr. ἀμνηστία ; Eng. 'amnesty' in its correct use), an Act of oblivion, or refusal to make investigation of matters of fact with a view to punishment.

LITERATURE.—Grasser, 'Amnestie des Jahres 403,' Munich, 1868, *Jahrb. f. Philologie*, xcix. 193 fol. ; Lübbert, *De Amnestia anno CCCCIII a. Chr. ab Atheniensibus decreta*, Kiel, 1881 ; J. M. Stahl in *Rheinisches Museum*, 1890, p. 275 fol.

W. J. WOODHOUSE.

AMPHIARAUS.—A seer and, along with Adrastus, the chief hero of the legend of the Seven against Thebes. He had early become the subject of heroic legend, and his character was portrayed in legend in Argos as well as round about Thebes. These local legends had been, too, at an early date united to the Theban cycle of legends by the two Homeric epics, 'The expedition of Amphiaraus' and the 'Thebaid.' But his cult is older than the legend.

Amphiaraus was worshipped in the Peloponnesus (Sparta, Pausanias, iii. 12. 5 ; Argos, Pausan. ii. 23. 2 ; Phlius, Pausan. ii. 13. 7 ; and the colony of Byzantium, *FHG* iv. 149. 16), and especially in Oropus near Thebes, where his sanctuary has been excavated (Pauly-Wissowa, i. 1893 ff.). He was worshipped as a god of the lower world, often at his own grave, where he gave oracles. That is the original form of the belief regarding him. This is the reason, too, why he is a seer in the heroic legend, and why he does not die but descends alive into the depths of the earth.

As seer, Amphiaraus was genealogically connected with the famous seer Melampus (Homer, *Od.* xv. 225 ff.), and later with Apollo (Hygin. *Fab.* 70, 128). Argos was regarded as his home. An all but forgotten legend represents him as an Argive king and enemy of Adrastus, whose brother Pronax he kills. Adrastus flees to Sicyon to his grandfather Polybus, but returns victorious and makes peace with Amphiaraus. The latter marries Eriphyle, the sister of Adrastus ; and both parties are bound to accept her decision. When Polynices was seeking allies for the war against Thebes, Adrastus his father-in-law bribed Eriphyle, who compelled Amphiaraus, against his will, to march with them (Pindar, *Nem.* ix. with Scholium 30 and 35 ; Herodotus, v. 67 ; Hygin. *Fab.* 73). A later version of the legend, which probably originated from the epic Thebaid, related that Amphiaraos concealed himself in his house in order not to be compelled to take the field against Thebes, where he knew he must die, but was betrayed by his wife Eriphyle, who had been bribed by Polynices with the necklace of Harmony. Thus did Eriphyle become guilty of the death of Amphiaraus, who at his departure instructed his youthful son Amphilochus to wreak vengeance on Eriphyle for his death (Homer, *Od.* xv. 243 ff. with Scholium 246 ; Sophocles, *Elec.* 836 with Scholium ; Apollodorus, *Bibliotheca*, iii. § 60 ff. ; Hygin. *Fab.* 73). This leave-taking was represented on the Cypselus chest in Olympia (Pausan. v. 17. 4), and the picture on the Corinthian bowl (κρατήρ) corresponds with it (*Monumenti d. Instituto*, x. 4. 5).

In Nemea also, which lies on the road between Argos and Thebes, there were legends of Amphiaraus, traces of which have been preserved in the legends of the founding of the Nemean Games, especially in the 3rd *Hypothesis* in Pindar's Nemean Odes ; Aelian, *Var. Hist.* iv. 5 ; Pausanias, iii. 18. 12, ii. 15. 2 ; Apollodorus, *Bibliotheca*, iii. 6. 4.

In the war against Thebes, Amphiaraus slays the powerful Theban hero Melanippus (Herodotus, v. 67 ; Pausanias, ix. 18. 1). But he cannot withstand Periclymenus, and flees from him; however, as the latter is about to stab him in the back, Zeus divides the earth with a lightning flash, and sinks Amphiaraus with his chariot alive into the depths. This tradition is a unity, and thus probably derived from the epic Thebaid (Pindar, *Nem.* ix. 24; Euripides, *Supp.* 925; Apollodorus, *Bibliotheca*, iii. § 77).

There are mirrored in these legends struggles of the time of the settlement of the Greek peoples in Argos as well as round about Thebes. The people who worshipped Amphiaraus had brought his cult with them from Argos over Phlius and Nemea towards the north, where its last remnants were preserved between Attica and Bœotia. These historical recollections in connexion with the cult, which remained ever living, have provided the material of the legend and determined its character.

LITERATURE.—Welcker, *Epischer Cyclus*, ii. 320 ff.; Bethe, *Thebanische Heldenlieder*, 42 ff., 76 ff.; Pauly-Wissowa, i. 1866 ff.

E. BETHE.

AMPHICTYONY.—An amphictyony was a union of different cities or peoples, centred in a temple for the common performance of certain religious duties. The name is derived from ἀμφικτίονες (with a variant form in later times, ἀμφικτύονες), which, with its equivalent περικτίονες, is used by early writers (Homeric Hymn, Pindar, Thucydides) in the sense of 'dwellers round.' The word ἀμφικτυονία is not expressly defined by any Greek writer; it is not frequent in the classical authors, although the substantive ἀμφικτύονες and the adjective ἀμφικτυονικός are often used. The ideas attached to these words were coloured by the history and constitution of the Delphian amphictyony, and we need not assume that all amphictyonic unions were similar in organization or function. Many local unions in early times which were formed on a religious basis, and would fall within the definition given above, are not expressly described as amphictyonies. This may be accidental, for some amphictyonic unions are mentioned only once in ancient literature, and there were primitive religious leagues, which did not survive in later times, that seem to have possessed the characteristics generally regarded as amphictyonic, and we know of no essential difference which should exclude them from the present survey.

The simplest form of union which can be traced in the earliest times is the union of people of kindred race within a continuous area round a common temple.

Such a federation is perhaps implied in the beginning of *Odyss.* iii., where the men of Pylos in their companies feast and offer sacrifice to Poseidon. So Strabo records (viii. 343) that the Tryphilians met at Samicum in the grove of the Samian Poseidon, had the sacred truce proclaimed, and united in sacrifice. So also the twelve Ionian cities of the Peloponnesus, before the Ionian migration, combined in a religious league centred in the temple of Poseidon at Helice (Strabo, viii. 384), and on this league was modelled the federation of the Ionian colonies in Asia. Strabo (ix. 412) refers to the 'amphictyonic' league of Onchestus, whose meeting-place was the grove of Poseidon in the territory of Haliartus, founded perhaps before the immigration of the Boeotians. The Boeotians, after their conquest, celebrated at the temple of Itonian Athene, in the plain of Coronea, the festival of the Pamboeotia (Strabo, ix. 411); and we may assume that their league had an amphictyonic character. It may have been the original basis of the political federation of later times.

Strabo (viii. 374) also records an 'amphictyony' of Calauria, an island off the coast of Troezen. This met, probably at a very early period, at the temple of Poseidon (which was always an asylum), and included the following cities: Hermione, Epidaurus, Aegina, Athens, Prasiae, Nauplia, and the Minyan Orchomenus. At a later time Argos and Sparta took the plaee of Nauplia and Prasiae. This league combined states which were not neighbours. Whether it had any objects other than religious we do not know; but it is possible, as is generally assumed, that it was a union of sea-states, designed to secure intercourse by sea.

The amphictyony of Pylae, which afterwards became so important from its connexion with Delphi, was originally a combination of different races (not cities), united in the worship of Demeter. Its history will be studied in detail below.

There are possible references to an amphictyony of Dorian states centred in Argos (Paus. iv. 5. 2; Plut. *Parall.* 3), presumably meeting at the temple of Apollo Pythaeus. The allusion in Pindar (*Nem.* vi. 44) to the festival of the 'amphictyons' in the grove of Poseidon is held by some to imply a Corinthian amphictyony, but the word may be used in a general sense. It has been suggested that we should assume a Euboean amphictyony meeting in the temple of Amarynthian Artemis, as there is evidence of the Euboean cities combining in a festival there (Strabo, x. 448; Livy, xxxv. 38).

Of these religious leagues centred on the mainland of Greece, those meeting at Samicum, Helice, Coronea, and Amarynthus are not expressly described as amphictyonies. Of the federations of the Greek colonies, in the Aegean or in Asia, we have warrant for calling only that of Delos an amphictyony. This league from a very early date united the Ionians of the islands in the worship of Apollo, and its history will be considered below. There are other leagues which have amphictyonic characteristics. The twelve Ionian colonies of Asia Minor (of which a list is given in Herod. i. 142) met at the Panionium, a precinct on the promontory of Mycale dedicated to the Heliconian Poseidon, and celebrated a festival called Panionia (Herod. i. 148; cf. Strabo, viii. 384; Diod. xv. 49). The league, which was probably founded on the model of the original league of the Ionian cities in the Peloponnesus, had also political objects, and the meetings at the Panionium were used for the discussion of questions of common policy and to promote joint action (Herod. i. 170, vi. 7). Ephesus was also a place of common festival for the Ionians (Thuc. iii. 104; cf. Dionys. Hal. iv. 25, who says the precinct of Artemis was the place of meeting, and Diod. xv. 49, who says the πανήγυρις was transferred from the Panionium to Ephesus). The grove of Poseidon at Tenos seems to have been the site of a πανήγυρις (Strabo, x. 487).

The three Dorian cities of Rhodes (Lindus, Ialysus, and Camirus), Cos, and Cnidus, with Halicarnassus (which was afterwards excluded from the union), celebrated a festival on the Triopian promontory at the temple of Apollo (Herod. i. 144). Dionysius (*l.c.*) says that these Dorians and the Ionians meeting at Ephesus took the great amphictyony as their model, and attributes to their leagues, besides religious functions, powers of jurisdiction and control of policy for which we have no evidence elsewhere.

The religious leagues in Greece and the colonies which come within the definition of an amphictyony, as given above, have been mentioned. It is possible that there were other similar federations in early times of which all trace is lost.

Before discussing the Delian and the Delphian amphictyonies, each of which had a special character, it will be best to consider the general functions of such religious leagues.

It is clear that the amphictyony was a primitive form of union, the origin of which in all probability preceded the coming of the Achaean invaders. The gods whose temples supplied the meeting-places are for the most part the gods of the earliest inhabitants. Poseidon appears at Samicum, Helice, Onchestus, Calauria, and the Isthmus (if we interpret Pindar's allusion as showing the existence of an amphictyony), and at Mycale and Tenos. At Pylae, Demeter was the presiding goddess. The primary purpose was the common worship, at set times, of the god; and the offering of a common sacrifice and the celebration of a common festival were essential elements. (Terms like τὰ Παμβοιώτια, τὰ Πανιώνια, τὰ Ἐφέσια, τὰ Δήλια might denote the festival generally, or the sacrifice; cf. Strabo, viii. 384, θύουσι ἐκεῖ τὰ Πανιώνια).

At the meeting (πανήγυρις) a sacred truce (ἐκεχειρία) was proclaimed. The cities or peoples participating sent sacred envoys (θεωροί, in some instances denoted by special titles, Πυθαϊσταί, Δηλιασταί), but many of the ordinary citizens flocked to the gatherings. Usually there were athletic and musical contests, and it is possible that the great games of Greece had their origin in amphictyonic meetings (see Gilbert, *Griech. Staatsaltertümer*, ii. p. 406).

The gathering often served other purposes: fairs were held, and some of them became important markets. Peaceful intercourse between the states was encouraged, and combination for political purposes was facilitated by these meetings, which were sometimes used for definite political ends. Thus the Ionians discussed their common interests, and resolved on united action at the Panionium; the Boeotian confederation may have been the outcome of the religious league at Coronea, and events caused the Delian and the Delphian amphictyonies to assume political importance. In spite, however, of the exaggerated statements of some ancient writers (Dionys. Hal. iv. 25), there is not sufficient evidence to justify us in assuming that the original purpose of the amphictyonic gatherings was other than religious. But the indirect results were of great moment both in religion and politics. The Greek tendency to disunion was in some measure corrected. Co-operation in the worship of a tribal god gave expression to the idea of kinship; intercourse at the sacrifices, festivals, and marts tended to break down the barriers between different states, and on occasion prepared the way for permanent peace and political union. The names Pamboeotia and Panionia, given to two of these gatherings, emphasize the idea of unity. When the amphictyony included cities which were not neighbours, or which did not recognize the bond of kinship, its function was even more important. The association of different peoples in the worship of a common god broke through the exclusiveness of local cults, and tended to found that religious unity which was regarded as one of the bases of Hellenic nationality (Herod. viii. 144). The Delphian amphictyony certainly contributed to the idea of Hellenism, and, in concert with the oracle, had great influence in establishing common religious observances among the Greeks. Its political importance was in some sense accidental; its religious functions it shared with the other amphictyonies, whose importance in the history of religion rests on their work in uniting different states in the common worship of the same gods.

The Delian amphictyony.—Delos, the sacred island, hallowed as the birthplace of Apollo, was from early times a religious centre for the Ionians of the Aegean. The legends spoke of a transfer of the island from Poseidon to Apollo (Strabo, viii. 373), and of Theseus instituting a festival (Paus. viii. 48. 3; cf. Plut. *Thes.* 21). It is thought that the connexion of Theseus with the festival was an invention in the time of the Athenian domination; but, at least from the time of Solon, Athens sent sacred envoys, Δηλιασταί, chosen from certain Eupatrid families (Athen. vi. 234). There is evidence for the existence of the πανήγυρις at a comparatively early date, in the Homeric Hymn to the Delian Apollo (i. 146–164; cf. Thuc. iii. 104, ἦν δέ ποτε καὶ τὸ πάλαι μεγάλη ξύνοδος ἐς τὴν Δῆλον τῶν Ἰώνων τε καὶ περικτιόνων νησιωτῶν, and Strabo, x. 485). To Delos came the 'Ionians in their trailing robes,' with their wives and their children. There they offered sacrifice, performed sacred dances and hymns, and engaged in contests. Doubtless a sacred truce was proclaimed, and a fair was held upon the seashore, where the visitors to the festival exchanged their goods. The union of the states celebrating the festival probably bore the name of an amphictyony. Although it is not expressly described as such, the existence in later times of officials called Ἀμφικτύονες is best explained on the theory that the title is a survival from earlier days (see below, and cf. Thuc. *l.c.* περικτίονες). As Mycale and Ephesus rose in importance as meeting-places for the Ionians of Asia Minor and of the islands near the coast, the festival at Delos waned. The islanders (presumably of the Cyclades) and the Athenians continued to send their bands of singers and their sacrifices, but in the troublous times of the 6th and 5th centuries the great festivals were abandoned (Thuc. *l.c.*).

Delos was too small in extent and population to possess any political strength. Hence it was liable to come under the patronage or the sway of dominant powers. Pisistratus had purified the island, and Polycrates had shown it favour (Thuc. *l.c.*). The Athenians, on the institution of their confederacy in 477, chose Delos as the meeting-place. Political reasons may have moved them, but it is probable that their choice was partly determined by the desire to represent their league as an amphictyony, centred in what had been a holy place of the Ionian race, of which Athens claimed to be the natural head. At Delos the meetings of the allies were held, and the federal funds were stored. With the growth of Athenian domination and the transfer of the treasury to Athens (in 454), Delos lost its importance in the confederacy, until, in 426–5, the Athenians purified the island, and established a great festival, to be held every four years. Whether the amphictyony had hitherto in form survived or not, we do not know, but the Athenians seem to have wished to represent it as still existing. Thus, although the temple and its funds were controlled by Athenian magistrates (the earliest direct evidence refers to the year 434–3, *CIA* i. 283), these bore the title Ἀμφικτύονες or Ἀμφικτύονες Ἀθηναίων (*BCH* viii. p. 283). The probable explanation of this name is that the title had at some time been borne by the representatives of other states, and that although (with one or two exceptions in the 4th cent.) only the Athenians appointed such magistrates, the fiction of amphictyonic government was kept up. (Our knowledge is based on inscriptions; the only allusion to such officials in literature is in Athenaeus, iv. 173, ὁ τῶν Ἀμφικτυόνων νόμος).

The amphictyony of Delos thus ceased to be a religious union of independent states, and became an instrument of Athenian supremacy, so that its history is bound up with the varying fortunes of Athens.

The festival (Δήλια) was celebrated in the spring of the third year of each Olympiad. (A lesser festival took place every year). It was regulated and presided over by the Athenians (Aristotle, *Ath. Pol.* 54. 7, refers to it as if it were an Athenian festival); the Athenians sent a θεωρία in the sacred ship, and at every celebration an offering of a gold crown was made to Apollo (ἀριστεῖον τοῦ θεοῦ, *CIA* ii. 814); and from the number of crowns recorded in the inventories, the number of celebrations can be estimated. The festival was modelled on the great Pan-Hellenic festivals, and was doubtless open to all the states of the Aegean, possibly to all the Greeks. To the old athletic and musical contests the Athenians added horse races. (For the order of proceedings see Plut. *Nic.* 3). Banquets concluded the festival, at which the Delians served the tables, and hence bore the title of Ἐλεοδύται (Athen. iv. 173).

The first celebration was in 425, and was probably the occasion of the magnificent θεωρία of Nicias (Plut. *Nic.* 3; others attribute this to 417). The Delians seem to have resented the rule of the Athenians, and in 422 the Athenians expelled them from the island (Thuc. v. 1), intending, no doubt, to make it a mere appanage of Athens. But in 420, at the bidding of the Delphian oracle, they were restored.

The festival was celebrated every four years during the Peloponnesian war. An inscription of 410–409 (*BCH* viii. p. 283) shows Delian νεωκόροι sharing in the administration with the four Ἀθηναίων Ἀμφικτύονες (for whose title this is the earliest definite evidence). After the fall of Athens, Delos regained its independence (the fragment of an inscription, *IGA* 91, probably refers to this); the great πεντετηρίς was abandoned, but the annual festival was celebrated by the Delians, and to this the Athenians still sent their θεωρία (Xen. *Mem.* iv. 8. 2).

Soon after the battle of Cnidus, when the Athenians were striving to re-establish a federation of sea-states, they seem to have regained the control of the Delian temple (*CIA* iv. 2. 813*b*), and the festival was renewed probably in 388 (in the 4th cent. its date was changed to the second year of the Olympiad). The Athenian control was interrupted for a time (the banishment of Delians recorded in *CIA* ii. 814 may be connected with this epoch), and probably the festival was omitted in 380; but with the foundation of their second confederacy the Athenians were again masters of the Aegean. The inscription containing the accounts from 377 to 374 (known as the Sandwich marble, *CIA* ii. 814) throws much light on temple property and administration. From 377 to 375 the sacred property was administered by four Ἀμφικτύονες Ἀθηναίων: in 374 five Athenian commissioners were appointed and five Ἀνδρίων Ἀμφικτύονες. This recognition of the allies is consistent with the principles of the confederacy, but in only one other inscription do the Andrian commissioners appear (*BCH* viii. 367), and the Athenians, aided by Delian subordinate officials (Βουλὴ Δηλίων καὶ ἱεροποιοί mentioned in an inventory of 364–3, *BCH* x. 461), continued to administer the temple and the sacred property. The festival was regularly celebrated with the usual offering of a golden crown. The resentment of the Delians was manifested in the banishment (probably about 350) of an Athenian partisan (*CIA* ii. 115*b*); and, in 345–4 or 344–3, the Delians appealed to the arbitration of the Delphian amphictyony to regain control of the temple (see below, p. 398). The decision was favourable to the Athenians; even after the collapse of her power, Athens retained her control of Delos until at least 315. Before 308 Delos was independent, and the nominal amphictyony had come to an end. (For date, see von Schöffer in Pauly-Wissowa, iv. 2482).

The Delphian amphictyony.—The chief amphictyony is usually referred to by modern writers as 'the Delphian' or 'the Pythian,' because in historical times Delphi was its most important place of meeting. It met also at Anthela, near Thermopylae. The ancients regard it as *the* amphictyony; allusions to it are usually connected with the substantive Ἀμφικτύονες or the adjective Ἀμφικτυονικός (with σύνοδος, σύστημα, συνέδριον), and the collective substantive Ἀμφικτυονία is comparatively rare (Dem. vi. 19, xi. 4). The substantive Ἀμφικτύονες is used either of the amphictyonic peoples generally, or of their representatives at the amphictyonic meetings, or of the actual council of Hieromnemones.

Its early history is legendary (Strabo, ix. 420, τὰ πάλαι μὲν οὖν ἀγνοεῖται), and the legends are diversely interpreted. The foundation was ascribed to an eponymous hero, Amphictyon, usually described as the son of Deucalion and brother of Hellen (by Dionysius, iv. 25, as the son of Hellen), some 300 years before the Trojan war. He, being king at Thermopylae, united the neighbouring peoples in the festival of Pylaea. Other accounts explained the name Ἀμφικτύονες as meaning 'the neighbouring peoples,' and connected the institution with Delphi (for the authorities see Bürgel, *Die pyläisch-delphische Amphiktyonie*, p. 4 ff.). The rival claims of Thermopylae and Delphi, as the place of origin, were reconciled in the legend that Acrisius, summoned from Argos to help the Delphians, instituted a συνέδριον at Delphi on the model of that at Pylae, and organized the constitution of the amphictyony (Schol. to Eur. *Orest.* 1093; cf. Strabo, ix. 420). Little further is recorded until the first Sacred War (B.C. 595), when the amphictyonic peoples are said to have attacked Crisa for injury done to Delphi and transgression of the amphictyonic ordinances (Æschines, iii. 107–8; Strabo, ix. 419). After the destruction of Crisa, the Pythian games were instituted.

The truth underlying the legends may be somewhat as follows. At a remote period, probably before the great migrations within Greece, the peoples then settled near Thermopylae combined in the worship of Demeter, the festival possibly being connected with the harvest. That Pylae was the original meeting-place is probable on the following grounds. The cult of Demeter Amphictyonis was always maintained at Pylae; the meetings of the amphictyony, whether at Pylae or Delphi, bore the name Πυλαία, and Πυλαγόροι was the title of the official envoys; the peoples in after times belonging to the amphictyony were largely those grouped round Thermopylae. It is a matter of speculation which of these peoples originally belonged to the amphictyony. There were, no doubt, fresh accessions consequent on the migrations, and, by the end of the 7th cent., probably most of the peoples in eastern Greece between Thessaly and Laconia had been admitted. The Thessalians were presidents. At some period before the first Sacred War, Delphi had been taken under the protection of the amphictyony, and became a second place of meeting. (Legend placed this at a very early date, and the tradition of the Greeks undoubtedly set it before the Sacred War. Bürgel argues that the war was not conducted by the amphictyony, which, he thinks, was opened to new states after the war). The war with Crisa marks an epoch; henceforth the history of the league rests on surer information; it is more closely identified with Delphi, whose shrine and property came under the protection of the amphictyonic council, which also had the superintendence of the Pythian games.

(*a*) *Members.*—The amphictyony was a league of twelve peoples (ἔθνη, called γένη by Paus. x. 8. 2; Strabo, ix. 420, wrongly speaks of πόλεις). Whatever changes in the composition of the amphictyony took place, the number of the peoples was constant. The earliest list that has come down to us is that of Aeschines (ii. 116), who professes to give twelve names, though only eleven appear in the text. These are the Thessalians, Boeotians, Dorians, Ionians, Perrhaebians, Magnetians, Locrians, Oetaeans, Phthians, Malians, and Phocians. It is generally believed that the Dolopes should be added to complete the list, and that Aeschines describes as Oetaeans the people who more usually appear as Aenianes (Herod. vii. 132, in a list of nine peoples who submitted to Xerxes, cites only amphictyonic peoples). From 346 to 345 the Macedonian king took the place of the Phocians, and the Delphians were admitted, room being made for them by uniting the Perrhaebians and the Dolopes as one people. (An inscription gives us a list of the peoples in 344–3. See E. Bourguet, *L'Administration financière du sanctuaire pythique au IVe siècle avant Jésus-Christ*, p. 145 ff., and *BCH* xxi. p. 322). The subsequent changes after the Aetolians were admitted need not be followed here.

While there was at all periods a conservative adherence to the principle that races and not states should be members of the amphictyony, a measure ascribed to Acrisius, and certainly adopted at an early date, regulated the participation of separate states in the amphictyonic council. Each of the twelve peoples admitted to membership had two votes (Aesch. ii. 116), and in some cases these votes were divided between different branches of the same race (*e.g.* the Locrians and the Malians), or between states belonging to the same race; thus we find the Ionian votes shared by Athens and one of the Euboean states; the Dorian votes divided between the Dorians of the metropolis and the Dorians of the Peloponnesus, or at another time between the Lacedaemonians and some other state of the Peloponnesus (*BCH* xx. p. 197 ff.); and the Boeotian votes between the different cities of Boeotia (Thebes being usually represented). The exclusion of a particular state from the amphictyony might be effected without diminishing the representation of the race to which it belonged, as its vote could be transferred to another state. We have no information as to how the apportionment of votes to the individual states or sections of the people was effected. While the decision of amphictyonic business was thus entrusted to the representatives of the states qualified for the time to vote, other states not so represented, or even states which had no right to a vote, might take part in the amphictyonic meetings, and send sacred embassies.

(*b*) *Meetings and representatives.*—The meetings were held twice a year, in spring and autumn (*πυλαία εἰαρινὴ καὶ μετοπωρινή*, Strabo, ix. 420), and on each occasion at both Anthela and Delphi. Extraordinary meetings might be called (Aesch. iii. 124). Any members of the amphictyonic peoples might attend; sacred embassies (*θεωρίαι*) were probably sent by the amphictyonic peoples, and there were also Πυλαγόροι (in some writers Πυλαγόραι) and Ἱερομνήμονες, who represented the interests of the states or peoples qualified to vote. From the 3rd century Ἀγορατροί seem to have taken the place of the Πυλαγόροι.

There is some uncertainty as to the respective duties of the Πυλαγόροι and the Ἱερομνήμονες at different dates. In the early years of the 5th cent. the Πυλαγόροι are represented as the executive and deliberative power (Herod. vii. 213; Plut. *Them.* 20. Strabo ix. 420 does not mention any other officials). Towards the end of the century we can trace Ἱερομνήμονες (Aristoph. *Nub.* 623). Inscriptions and literary evidence (the account of the meeting of the amphictyony in Aeschines, iii. 115 ff., is our chief authority) show that in the 4th cent. the Hieromnemones (who were twenty-four in number, two for each amphictyonic people) formed the council of the amphictyony. Pylagori were still appointed, but had not voting power, and were perhaps not limited in number. Thus, Athens sent three to Delphi in 339. The method of appointing these officials may have been left to the discretion of the different states. At Athens we find the Hieromnemones appointed by lot (Aristophanes, *l.c.*) and the Pylagori elected. Prominent statesmen were sometimes appointed (*e.g.* Demosthenes and Aeschines), perhaps to watch over the political interests of their state at the amphictyony. From the narrative of the meeting in 339 (Aeschines, *l.c.*) it would appear that the Hieromnemones formed the council (*συνέδριον*) of the amphictyony, and that the individual Hieromnemon might seek advice and support from the Pylagori of his state. Thus Aeschines, who was one of the Athenian Pylagori, was admitted to the council of the Hieromnemones when the other Pylagori had withdrawn, and after defending the cause of Athens, retired before the vote took place. In the council of Hieromnemones, all power, deliberative, judicial, and executive, was vested, and it was apparently sometimes described as *τὸ κοινὸν τῶν Ἀμφικτιόνων* (*CIA* ii. 551, l. 41; cf. Aesch. ii. 139). The president is referred to as *ὁ τὰς γνώμας ἐπιψηφίζων* (Aesch. iii. 124). The decisions of the council were called *δόγματα* or *τὰ δεδογμένα*. It was open to the council to call an *ἐκκλησία* of all who were attending the meeting (*οἱ συνθύοντες καὶ χρώμενοι τῷ θεῷ*, Aesch. *l.c.*), presumably to announce the course of action proposed, or to ratify the decision of the council.

For the special boards of *ναοποιοί* and *ταμίαι* see below.

(*c*) *Competence of the amphictyony.* — It is difficult precisely to define the competence of the amphictyony. There is no general statement in ancient writers that can be relied upon (Dionys. Hal. iv. 25, vaguely exaggerates), and its powers, so far as they cannot be inferred from the original aims, must in the main be deduced from the historical instances of its activity. It should be noted that the influence and the importance of the amphictyony varied greatly at different periods. As most of its members were politically insignificant, states such as Athens and Sparta at the height of their power had little respect for its authority. On the other hand, when a strong state commanded a majority of votes and so became predominant in the council, it could use the amphictyony for its own ends, and find pretexts to justify an extension of amphictyonic action. It is possible here to give only broad results without detail.

We may assume that, probably from the first, the amphictyony had two main objects: the union of different peoples for common religious purposes, and the common observance of certain rules affecting the relations between those peoples. Two causes combined to increase the importance of these objects. As the amphictyony came to include representatives from most of the peoples of Greece, it tended to assume an Hellenic character, and when Delphi was taken under its protection and became its most important meeting-place, the universal recognition of the oracle and of the cult of Apollo increased the prestige and importance of the amphictyony. It is not always easy to distinguish the relative spheres of Delphi and of the amphictyony, but it must be remembered that the oracle, though under the protection of the amphictyony, was independent, and many institutions or observances which owed their origin to Delphi should not be credited to the amphictyony.

The members of the amphictyony united in common religious observances at both Anthela and Delphi. At Anthela they worshipped Demeter (with the title Ἀμφικτυονίς or Πυλαία) and the hero Amphictyon. We know that there were meetings in spring and autumn protected by the proclamation of a holy truce (*ἐκεχειρία*); sacrifice was offered, and probably a festival was celebrated with its usual accompaniment of contests and market. An important inscription (*CIA* ii. 545) gives us much information as to the relations of the amphictyony with Delphi. The inscription dates from B.C. 380, and the assertion of the amphictyonic rules and duties may mark a recent restoration of the power of the amphictyony, perhaps under the protection of Sparta, then at the height of her power (Bürgel, *op. cit.* p. 252; Bourguet, *op. cit.* pp. 158–9). At Delphi Leto, Artemis, and Athena Pronaia (or Pronoia) were associated with Apollo as Amphictyonic deities (Aesch. iii. 108, 111), to whom sacrifice was offered at the spring and autumn meetings.

In the procession preceding the sacrifice, among other beasts an ox of great price was led (this is the βοῦς τοῦ ἥρωος of *CIA* ii. 545, l. 32; cf. Xen. *Hell.* vi. 4. 29, βοῦς ἡγεμών. Some think this beast was a special offering at the great Pythia). The amphictyony superintended the meetings and festivals, including the great Pythia, which took place every four years, and the annual Pythia. To these festivals the amphictyonic states sent envoys (perhaps the πυθαϊσταί of Strabo, ix. 404; cf. *CIA* ii. 545. 45, where Böckh restored πυθαϊστάς). The amphictyony was responsible for the care of the sacred rites, of the property consecrated to the gods, the temples and other buildings, and the sacred land. In the inscription referred to provision is made for a circuit of the sacred land (πέροδος, cf. Dem. xviii. 150, περιελθεῖν), and penalties are imposed on any one taking it into cultivation (cf. Aesch. iii. 109, 119). The Hieromnemones are to keep the buildings at Delphi in repair. The roads and bridges (presumably on the routes leading to Delphi) are to be kept up by the amphictyons (usually interpreted as the different peoples belonging to the amphictyony).

More important duties fell to the amphictyony when the great temple had to be rebuilt. In the 6th cent., after it had been destroyed by fire, the rebuilding was entrusted to the Alcmaeonidae, as contractors (Herod. ii. 180, v. 62). In 373 the temple was again burnt down, and under the amphictyonic law of 380 the Hieromnemones undertook its reconstruction. We have much detailed information on the procedure from inscriptions recently found at Delphi. (The results are summarized in E. Bourguet, *L'Administration financière du sanctuaire pythique au IVe siècle avant Jésus-Christ*). The restoration of the temple undertaken in 369 was not completed for thirty years. The work was interrupted by the Sacred War, but the heavy fine imposed upon the Phocians supplied funds, which enabled the work to be carried through. In connexion with this work two new colleges of amphictyonic magistrates were instituted. From 369 we can trace the activity of the ναοποιοί. The members of the College belonged to amphictyonic peoples, but the total number, as well as the numbers from the different states, varied widely. Some of the states represented in the amphictyonic council appointed none, while Delphi had a ναοποιός before it secured a vote in the council. The ναοποιοί met twice a year at the ordinary meetings of the amphictyony; they collected funds for the expense of rebuilding, and made contracts in accordance with the specifications (συγγραφαί) drawn up for the different parts of the work. (For details of the contracts, methods of payment, etc., see Bourguet, *op. cit.* p. 95 ff.). After the completion of the temple, the ναοποιοί were charged with the maintenance of the fabric, and their activity can be traced for a century and a half.

In 339, at the autumn session, a college of twenty-four ταμίαι was instituted (see Bourguet, p. 110 ff.). It is thought that the institution may have been proposed in the interest of Philip, who was anxious to increase his influence in the amphictyony. The result was to make the work of the ναοποιοί subordinate, and to concentrate the control of expenditure in the hands of the new college. The composition of the college was identical with that of the council of the Hieromnemones; the same states were represented, and the lists of both were drawn up in the same order. The ταμίαι, from the sums assigned to them, met not only the expenses of rebuilding the temple (the money for which was paid over to the ναοποιοί), but the other expenses of the amphictyony, both at Delphi and Pylae (see Bourguet, p. 126 ff.). This board was, however, only a temporary institution, and when the last instalment of the Phocian fine had been paid and the temple at Delphi was finished, their work probably ceased. Before 310, and possibly as early as 326, they were no longer acting.

Inscriptions thus enable us to realize in detail the activity of the amphictyony in the case of the sacred property. The protection of the property of the god is one of the objects guaranteed by the amphictyonic oath recited by Aeschines (ii. 115). The other clauses of the oath remind us of another obligation of the amphictyony, the observance of certain common principles, the violation of which was a sin visited by amphictyonic vengeance. Aeschines mentions the oath not to raze any amphictyonic city to the ground, or to cut off running water in war or peace. The purpose of those prohibitions, which may go back to the origin of the amphictyony, is not to prevent war altogether, but to modify its harshness and to encourage peaceful intercourse. We do not know whether there were other general obligations of a similar character recognized by the amphictyony. Dionysius (iv. 25) refers to κοινοὶ νόμοι called amphictyonic, and other writers refer to the laws or deliberations of the amphictyony (Strabo, ix. 420; Schol. to Eur. *Orest.* 1093). If we could accept the vague statements of these late writers, we might assume a much wider competence of the amphictyony in regulating the relations of the Greek states to one another, and it is possible that there were κοινὰ νόμιμα or νόμοι τῶν Ἑλλήνων other than those mentioned by Aeschines, which were sanctioned by the amphictyony (see Bürgel, *op. cit.* p. 198, for certain regulations, possibly but not demonstrably amphictyonic). There are instances of charges being brought before the amphictyony which may have been based on the supposed violation of general rules, though we lack definite testimony. Among the historical incidents quoted in this connexion are the condemnation of the Dolopes of Scyros for piracy (Plut. *Cim.* 8); the price put upon the head of Ephialtes after the second Persian War (Herod. vii. 213); the condemnation of the Spartans, who were fined and excluded from the amphictyony for the seizure of the Cadmea (Diod. xvi. 23); and the charge threatened against Athens by the Amphissians in 339 (Aesch. iii. 116).

Charges brought before the amphictyony were tried by the council, which might fine the offenders or exclude them from the league, or in more serious cases proclaim a holy war against the offending state. As we do not know the scope of the amphictyonic laws, we cannot say whether the charges were always based on a supposed transgression of them. Probably some pretext was assumed to bring them within the jurisdiction, but the competence of the amphictyony might be extended by the admission of charges which did not properly come before its court. Thus an Athenian decree of 363 (*CIA* ii. 54) asserts that Astycrates has been condemned παρὰ τοὺς νόμους τῶν Ἀμφικτιόνων, and in 335 Alexander apparently demanded that the orators of Athens should be tried before the amphictyony (Dem. xviii. 322). Apart from this, disputes might be referred by consent to the arbitration of the amphictyony, and we probably have an instance of this in the submission by the Athenians and Delians of their controversy respecting the Delian temple in 345–4 or 344–3 (Dem. xviii. 134, xix. 65).

The amphictyony might pass votes referring to individuals, as in the honours accorded to the heroes of Thermopylae (Herod. vii. 228) and to Scyllias (Paus. x. 19. 1), and in the grants of ἀτέλεια and ἀσυλία to the guilds of Dionysiac artists (*CIA* ii. 551—at some date after 279).

We may conclude that the competence of the amphictyony was not rigidly restricted, at least in practice. It was open to a power possessing a dominant influence to extend its functions, and Alexander induced the council to confer upon him the command of the war against Persia (Diod. xvii. 4).

(*d*) *Importance of the amphictyony.* — The amphictyony in its constitution, its objects, and its possibilities involved important principles. It united many different peoples of Greece on the basis of a common Hellenism; and this union was realized by a system of representation by which equal votes were accorded to the several members. It fulfilled the purpose common to amphictyonies generally, of maintaining certain religious institutions and rites, while it enforced the recognition of rules regulating the relations of its members. In this respect it tended to establish in the Greek world a system of *quasi*-international law, with a court to enforce it, comparable in our own days to the purpose of the Concert of Europe. In its constitution it might seem to prepare the way for a federal system, if not for a Pan-Hellenic national union. This may explain why, on different occasions, the amphictyony might act as the representative of Greek feeling or policy, and why it was sometimes described as if it included the whole nation (cf. Soph. *Trach.* 638, Ἑλλάνων ἀγοραὶ Πυλάτιδες; Herod. vii. 214, οἱ τῶν Ἑλλήνων Πυλαγόροι; Aesch. iii. 161, 254, συνέδριον τῶν Ἑλλήνων).

But the disruptive forces which dominated the Greek political system counteracted these tendencies. The influence of the amphictyony (apart from the oracle) in the sphere of religion scarcely extended beyond its own meetings. The rules of humanity which it laid down were not enforced, and amphictyonic cities were razed to the ground without vengeance or protest. The amphictyony had little effect in correcting the separate autonomy of the great states. Composed as it was in great part of peoples of small political or military significance, it could not impose its will on powerful states, which overshadowed it or made it a mere instrument of policy. Thus in the greater part of the 5th cent., while Sparta and Athens divided the allegiance and controlled the fortunes of the other Greeks, the amphictyony receded into the background. In the 4th cent., from 380 at least, the amphictyony assumed a greater importance, mainly because it came under the influence and served the purposes of the most powerful states—at first Sparta, then Thebes, and later the Macedonian king. The amphictyony became the scene of intrigues, and the Sacred Wars, waged nominally in the cause of the amphictyony, were critical for Greek history. It is precisely at this period that Demosthenes describes the league as ἡ ἐν Δελφοῖς σκιά (v. 25). The subservience to the policy of the dominant state became still more marked when the Aetolians controlled the amphictyony.

LITERATURE. — For amphictyonies in general, the proper sections in G. Busolt, *Griech. Staalsaltertümer*[2] (1892); G. Gilbert, *Griech. Staatsaltertümer*, ii. (1885); G. F. Schömann, *Griech. Altertümer*, ii. (4th ed. by J. H. Lipsius, 1902), should be consulted. See also F. Cauer, 'Amphiktyonien' in Pauly-Wissowa, i. (1905 ff.). For the Delian amphictyony see von Schöffer in Pauly-Wissowa, iv. 2459 ff.; for the Delphian amphictyony, H. Bürgel, *Die pyläisch-delphische Amphiktyonie*, Munich, 1877. The French excavations at Delos and Delphi have brought many fresh inscriptions to light. These have been published in the successive volumes of the *BCH*. The financial history of the Delphian amphictyony is summarized in E. Bourguet, *L'Administration financière du sanctuaire pythique au IVe siècle avant Jésus-Christ* (Paris, 1905).

LEONARD WHIBLEY.

AMRITSAR.—Amritsar, in the Panjāb, is one of the religious centres of India and the chief city of the Sikhs. It lies in what is known as the Mānjha country, about 32 miles east of Lahore, and contained at the census of 1901 a population of 162,429, of whom 40 per cent. were Hindus, 48 per cent. Muhammadans, and 11 per cent. Sikhs. It is the chief commercial town of the Panjāb proper; but its commercial importance is based less on any advantages of position than on the fact that the city is built round the celebrated 'Tank of Nectar' or 'Tank of the Immortals,' *i.e.* the gods (Sanskrit, *Amṛtasaras*), in the centre of which is situated the Golden Temple, the central shrine of the Sikh religion. There are stories of the spot having been visited by the first Sikh Guru, Nānak (A.D. 1469–1538), and by the third Guru, Amardās (A.D. 1552–1574); but the actual purchase of the site and excavation of the tank are believed to have been undertaken by the fourth Guru, Rāmdās, in A.D. 1577, and the masonry work was begun by the fifth Guru, Arjan, in A.D. 1588. The remaining five Gurus seem to have paid little or no attention to the place, but after the death of the last Guru in A.D. 1708, and during the turbulent period which preceded the breaking up of the Mughal empire, the shrine began to obtain considerable popularity and to be recognized as the national centre of the Sikh confederacies. The Muhammadan Government took every precaution to prevent access to the shrine; but so great was the attachment of the Sikhs to it that the Sikh horsemen would frequently risk their lives by galloping through the Mughal lines for a sight of the sacred tank. In A.D. 1762, the Afghan leader, Ahmad Shāh, blew up the sacred shrine with gunpowder, and polluted the sanctuary with the blood of kine; but four years later, in A.D. 1766, the shrine was reconstructed on its present basis. The Sikh leaders then began to build round it a number of separate fortified quarters which formed the nucleus of the present city of Amritsar, and the city has since continued to flourish under Mahārājāh Ranjit Singh (A.D. 1801 – 1839) and the British Government (since 1849).

There are five sacred tanks in the city, but the most celebrated is the 'Tank of Amritsar' proper, in which the Golden Temple lies. The form of the tank is nearly square, the sides at the top being 510 feet in length, and it is fed by water from the Bārī Doāb Canal. The Temple occupies a small island in the centre of the tank, 65½ feet square, which is connected with the west side by a fine causeway 227 feet long and 18 feet broad. The central shrine is known as the *Har-mandar* or 'Temple of God,' and consists of a single room, covering a square of 40½ feet, with four doors, one opening to each side. The lower part of the outer walls is adorned with marble inlay, resembling that of the Tāj Mahal at Agra, and the upper walls and roof are covered with plates of copper heavily gilt, from which the place has obtained among Europeans the name of the 'Golden Temple.' Among the Sikhs themselves the shrine and its precincts are known as the *Darbār Sāhib* or 'Sacred Audience'; and this title owes its origin to the fact that the *Granth*, or Sacred Book, is looked upon as a living Person, who daily in this shrine receives his subjects in solemn audience. The book is brought every morning with considerable pomp from the *Akālbūnga* (see p. 400ᵃ) across the causeway to the shrine, and returns at night with similar ceremony. It is installed in the shrine below a canopy, and a *granthī* sits behind it all day waving a *chauri*, or yak's tail, over it, as a servant does over the head of an Indian Prince. On the south sit a selection from the *pūjārīs*, or hereditary incumbents of the Temple, and on the north sit the musicians (*rāgīs* and *rabābīs* — the latter, strange to say, being Muhammadans), who from time to time sing hymns from the Granth to the accompaniment of divers native instruments. In front of the book is the cloth upon which the faithful deposit their offerings. Although the outer precincts have since 1898 been lit by electric light, the shrine itself is lit with clarified butter or candles only. The wearing of shoes within the precincts, and, of course, smoking of any kind, are strictly prohibited; and as the Granth is always installed upon the ground, it is considered irreverent for any one within the precincts to sit upon a chair or stool.

Round all four sides of the tank runs a paved walk 30 feet broad, known as the *Prakarama* (properly *Parikrama*), which is frequented by the worshippers who come to bathe, by pandits or ascetics of various kinds, and by vendors of religious and other trinkets. At the south-east corner of this walk, where the water issues from the tank, is the bathing-place assigned to the Mazhabis, or low-caste converts, whom the bulk of the Sikhs still decline to admit to their religion on equal terms. Round the outside of the walk rise a number of picturesque buildings, known as *būngas* or hospices, which were for the most part built by the Sikh chiefs in the latter part of the 18th cent. for the accommodation of themselves and their followers when visiting Amritsar; and among these the *būnga* of the Rāmgarhia Sirdārs is prominent by its two large towers, which dominate the city and neighbourhood of Amritsar.

Attached to the main shrine are three subsidiary institutions, which are of considerable importance in the eyes of the Sikhs. The first of these is the *Akālbūnga*, or 'Hospice of the Immortal,' which adjoins the shrine on the west side of the causeway, and is the traditional centre of the fanatical sect known as the Nihangs or Akālīs. The *Granth Sāhib* is kept here at night, and the building also contains a fine collection of the weapons of Guru Har Govind and other Sikh Gurus and chiefs. The courtyard in front of the *Akālbūnga* is a favourite place for the administration of the *pahal*, or religious baptism of the Sikh creed; the ceremony may, however, be performed anywhere in the presence of the Granth, and the number of persons baptized at the *Akālbūnga* does not exceed 1200 annually. The second of the well-known subsidiary institutions is the *Bābā Atal*, a shrine surmounted by a tower, which lies a few hundred yards to the south-east of the Har-mandar. This shrine was commenced in A.D. 1729 in memory of Bābā Atal, the young son of Guru Har Govind (A.D. 1606–1645), and is surrounded by the cenotaphs of many of the old Sikh nobility. The third institution subsidiary to the Golden Temple is the shrine of *Taran Tāran*, which lies 13 miles south of Amritsar, and which was founded by the fifth Guru, Arjan (A.D. 1581–1606). The Taran Tāran shrine, which also is built on an island in a large tank, is the scene of a considerable monthly fair, and the Amritsar temple, too, is the centre of two exceedingly large fairs, the Baisākhī and Diwālī, which are held in the spring and autumn respectively, and are attended by immense numbers of persons, both for religious and for commercial purposes, from the whole of northern India.

The actual building of the Golden Temple and its precincts is maintained from the proceeds of a *jāgir*, or assignment of land revenue from certain neighbouring villages. The *granthīs* who read the sacred volume are three in number, and are supported by offerings made directly to them by worshippers at the shrine. The *pūjārīs*, or incumbents, are a very large body of men to whom the general offerings at the shrine are distributed, after deducting a fixed sum for the temple establishment,—that is to say, the musicians, office-bearers, menials, and so forth. The whole institution and its subsidiaries are supervised by a manager, who is generally a Sikh gentleman of position appointed by the Government. The funds of the temple, as well as a certain number of precious ornaments, are kept in a somewhat primitive manner in a treasury over the main gate.

The whole importance of Amritsar from a religious point of view lies in the Golden Temple, and there is little of religious importance in the town outside the precincts of the *Darbār Sāhib*. Mention may, however, be made of two recent institutions, namely the Sāragarhī memorial and the Khālsa College. The former is a memorial in the form of a Sikh shrine, which was erected in A.D. 1902 in the centre of the city by the British Government in memory of the gallant manner in which a small body of the 36th Sikh Regiment held the fort of Sāragarhī on the North-West Frontier against an Afghan enemy in the Tīrāh campaign of 1897. The latter is a denominational college which was started some twelve years ago for the encouragement of learning among the Sikhs. It lies some two miles out of the city, and is largely supported by the Sikh States of the Panjāb as well as by private donors.

LITERATURE.—Murray's *Handbook for India and Ceylon*, 4th ed., 1901, p. 196; Hunter's *Imperial Gazetteer for India*, s.v. Amritsar; Sirdār Sundar Singh Rāmgarhia, *Guide to the Golden Temple*.

E. D. MACLAGAN.

AMULETS.—See CHARMS.

AMUSEMENTS.—A. 1. In the category of 'amusements' it is usual to include all sorts of pleasant occupations, both mental and physical, by which the attention is disengaged from the serious pursuits of life. Strictly speaking, however, an amusement is a light form of enjoyment in which little exertion either of the body or of the mind is required. In this respect amusements differ from **recreation**, which is a word of a higher order, inasmuch as recreation implies some considerable expenditure of energy, either mental or physical or both, although in the nature of the case the exertion is agreeable and refreshing. Both amusement and recreation are designed to serve the same end, the recuperation of one's jaded mental and physical powers; but amusement secures that by turning the mind into channels where the time passes pleasantly without the need of special exertion, whereas recreation effects its purpose by an agreeable change of occupation, by calling into activity other faculties and muscles than those engaged in work. Amusement, in short, is a form of enjoyment in its nature akin to relaxation; recreation is pleasurable exercise in which the energies, set free from work, are allowed to play in other directions (see RECREATION).

2. The slight demands which amusements make on the mental and physical activities, and their character as a means of lightly beguiling the time and drawing off the attention from the more important concerns of life, no doubt explain why in a serious age the word was used in a depreciatory sense. At the close of the 17th cent. we find *amusement* defined as 'any idle employment to spin away time' (Phillips, quoted in *Oxf. Dict.*). It may readily be allowed that anything which has no further aim than to kill time and to render men oblivious of the higher ends of life deserves to be condemned; and the use of the word **pastime** as synonymous with amusement has been regarded as an unconscious and melancholy confession that amusements have no other object and serve no other end than to fill up the emptiness of a life which is devoid of nobler interests, and to make men forget themselves. This pessimistic view of

amusements finds unquestionably some justification in the actual state of things. It cannot be doubted that amusements are often greedily sought after by those who find in the true business of life, in noble aims and strivings, nothing to excite their interest and to afford them joy; and they are indulged in with the object of appeasing the natural craving for happiness which finds no satisfaction in higher pursuits. Where this is the case, the passion for amusement is a pathetic witness to the misery of a life which has missed its true joy. But when a depreciatory estimate of amusements is based on the view that life itself, in the duties and relationships to which men are called, is so rich in delights that any other form of enjoyment is unnecessary, the ground is less secure. It is a severe and exacting philosophy which affirms that, to all who are conscious of the satisfactions which attend the pursuit of high moral aims, life is an absorbing interest which takes the place of all amusements. 'Where men are rightly occupied, their amusement grows out of their work' (Ruskin, *Sesame and Lilies*, 100). This, it must be confessed, is somewhat too highly pitched for ordinary human nature. It is this view of amusements which has commonly been associated with Puritanism, not altogether with justice. To begin with, at least, it was no aversion to pleasant things, arising out of an austere philosophy of life, that called forth the Puritan protest against the amusements of the time. Amusements were condemned, not because they were considered too trifling for men who had the serious business of life on hand, but because they were either sinful in themselves or closely associated with sinful accessories. This was the case, for instance, in the matter of dramatic representations. 'In the days of Elizabeth, the Puritan Stubbes held that some plays were "very honest and commendable exercises," and "may be used in time and place convenient as conducible to example of life and reformation of manners"; but the gross corruption of the seventeenth century stage drove Prynne and the majority of the Puritan party to extremer views' (Traill, *Social England*, iv. 165). It was the unfortunate association of evil with so many forms of amusement that disposed the Puritans in their later days to look askance at mirth and enjoyments perfectly innocent; their abhorrence of tainted pleasures led them to regard with suspicion every form of gaiety in which 'the enjoying nature' of their neighbours found expression, and fostered the growth of an austere and sombre spirit, which regarded life as too serious a business to permit of indulgence in light and pleasant diversions.

3. The Puritanic 'gospel of earnestness' is too narrow and one-sided to do justice to human nature. Healthy-minded men refuse to be satisfied with any view of life which ignores the natural instinct for play, and regards participation in amusements as a weakness which will be outgrown when men have tasted the more solid joys which duty brings. It is, no doubt, true that, wherever duty engages the conscience for its faithful and honourable discharge, it becomes, if one cannot say the chief amusement, at least the chief interest in life. But that does not mean more than the recognition of the subsidiary place which amusements should occupy. It does not justify an ascetic attitude towards amusements. Human nature has an instinct for joys of a light and entertaining kind, and the proper method of dealing with that instinct is not disparagement and repression, but a wise control and a large-hearted recognition of the part its gratification may play in the culture of life. The Christian view of life has room for laughter and mirth, for pleasures which stand in no immediate relation to life's duties, but minister to our natural capacity for enjoyment. And the supreme justification of this generous attitude to amusements lies in this, that where they are wisely indulged in, they serve a high end, and cannot be banished without loss. They give a zest to life; they pleasantly engage the mind and give it relief from the strain of duty, and enable it to recover its elasticity and tone. However interesting work may be, however congenial the more serious pursuits in which men engage may prove, the necessity arises, if the freshness of interest is to be maintained, of laying the work aside and seeking other interests. Human nature requires something more than rest for its refreshment; it requires that we should seek diversion for the sheer joy of it—some diversion which shall pleasurably occupy the mind and relax the energies, and afford an opportunity for escaping from the deadening influences of routine. The appetite for enjoyment must be wisely gratified, if the vitality necessary for good work is not to be impaired. *Cito rumpes arcum si tensum habueris.*

4. The main ethical justification of amusements lies, accordingly, in their fitness to renew and refresh our powers for the duties of life. But they serve other ends which are ethically important. They have a *social* value—many of them at least. The fact that we are thrown into pleasant association with others constitutes one of the charms of amusement; and, apart from the refreshing influences of such intercourse, there is a further gain in the growth and consolidation of friendship, and in the forging of links which bind us more closely together. There may be indeed, and there are, experiences shared with others which have a far greater uniting power than fellowship in the social pleasures of life, but the latter has its honourable place, and the value of it is deserving of recognition. Moreover, amusements, like everything else which draws us into association with others, serve as an opportunity for the culture of social virtues—unselfishness, equanimity, courtesy, and the like; while, if we extend our definition of amusements to include the great national games, they afford a discipline for the growth of such qualities as patience, self-restraint, magnanimity, alertness, readiness to seize an opportunity. Then, further, the pursuit of amusements is a bulwark against the temptations of the leisure hour. Nothing exposes the heart to the inroads of evil like the want of some healthy interest; and an honest love of innocent pleasure, if it served no other end, would be valuable as a moral safeguard.

5. All this must be freely acknowledged. Amusements have an undeniable ethical worth when they are wisely engaged in. But they cease to be ethically valuable, and indulgence in them becomes a dissipation, when they are sought after without due regard to the serious interests of life. When they are allowed to engross the mind and to become the main business in which pleasure is found, when their pursuit prejudices the performance of duty and the cultivation of higher interests, when they encroach on time which should be devoted to more serious matters, or make one indisposed to engage in one's proper work, they become harmful and morally reprehensible. There is no amusement, however innocent in itself, that cannot be changed into a means of self-indulgence through the excessive or untimely pursuit of it. Its pursuit is untimely when there is work waiting to be done. The pleasures of amusement are stolen pleasures, if they are enjoyed at the cost of neglect of duty. 'Sport and merriment are at times allowable; but we must enjoy them, as we enjoy sleep and other kinds of repose, when we have performed our weighty and important affairs' (Cicero, *de Off.* i. 29, 103). But the abuse of amusements lies not

only in their untimeliness, but also in their excess. They are frequently allowed to bulk so largely in life that serious occupations become distasteful. If, after participation in amusements, we are unable to pass with ease to more important concerns, and, instead of feeling refreshed for duty, have an aversion to it, we may fairly conclude that we have transgressed the limits of legitimate enjoyment, and have fallen into self-indulgence. That these limits are frequently overpassed is not a matter for doubt. There is no question that at the present day the desire for amusement has in many instances become a passion which is seriously prejudicing the culture of the higher life. In the opinion of competent judges, there is a waning of intellectual interests, a decay of any genuine love for those pursuits which enlarge and enrich the mind, a growing unconcern for the graver matters of religion and social service, and in some degree at least this is to be attributed to the immoderate indulgence in lighter pleasures. The fault of our age is not in seeking amusement, but in not knowing where to draw the line. *Nec lusisse pudet, sed non incidere ludum* (Horace, *Epist.* I. xiv. 36).

6. The nemesis of excessive addiction to amusements is not only the destruction of the taste for serious pursuits, but the decay of any genuine pleasure in life. The rationale of amusements is their power to send us back to work re-vitalized and capable of finding joy in it. But when they usurp the throne of our desires, and so dominate our thoughts and interest that work is felt to be a wearisome and uninviting interlude, they kill joy in that region of life where joy is all-important, where alone joy can be solid and lasting. A predominant craving for amusement defeats its own end; it renders joyless the whole stretch of life which of necessity must be given to work, and it speedily exhausts the enjoyment that amusement itself can give. Excessive pleasure-seeking brings satiety. Amusements, when they become the chief object of pursuit, lose their power of amusing. There is a world of truth in the well-known saying, uttered in reference to the excitements of a London season: 'Life would be tolerably agreeable, if it were not for its amusements.' Excess of pleasure nauseates and takes the joy out of life.

7. In the choice of amusements, and in the determination of the extent of their indulgence, there are other than personal considerations to be taken into account. From the individual's point of view, it is important that he should learn to avoid every form of pleasure which is physically harmful or morally debasing, and to allow himself only that measure of enjoyment which is consistent with the proper discharge of his work, and with a due concern for higher personal interests, such as self-culture and religious worship. But the question of amusements must be considered also in the light of the obligations which we have towards others. To some extent, of course, a consideration of that kind is always involved. Our conduct is never, strictly speaking, merely self-regarding; faithfulness in work, for instance, with which our amusements should never be allowed to interfere, is not simply a personal matter — it affects all others whom our work is calculated to benefit. But as members of a family, or of a church, or of society in general, we have duties to others—duties of love, helpfulness, consideration, service; and these must be kept in mind in determining the extent and nature of our amusements. Indulgence in pleasures the most innocent is illegitimate when it leads to the neglect of our social obligations. A man has no right to seek amusement to the detriment of those offices of love and fellowship which he owes to those of his own family circle. Similarly, one may spend so much time or money on the gratification of one's desire for enjoyment as to render impossible the honourable discharge of one's duties to society. Those most closely identified with religious and philanthropic work are unanimous in the opinion that one of the chief difficulties in finding money for its adequate maintenance arises from the increasing expenditure on amusements. Further, there may be occasions when our obligations to others raise the question whether we should not deny ourselves the gratification of an amusement which to us is perfectly innocent, but which is a cause of offence to those with whom we are closely associated. The duty which we owe to 'weaker brethren' cannot be entirely ignored, although there must be limits set to it. One may feel constrained in certain circumstances to renounce a form of enjoyment which harms another or offends his conscience; but, in the interests of moral education, it should be recognized that one has also a duty of vindicating the freedom of conscience, and of showing that amusements which to some are obnoxious, and even injurious, may be indulged in with perfect loyalty to high ethical standards. But, in still another way, our obligations towards others are bound up with the question of amusements. In these days the provision of amusement is very largely in the hands of professional classes, and it has been maintained that the moral danger to which men and women belonging to these classes are exposed is so great, that the amusements provided by them should not be countenanced by those who have the welfare of their fellows at heart. This is perhaps the chief reason why many refuse to enter a theatre. It should be frankly acknowledged that if, as is frequently alleged, the theatrical career puts the souls of men and women in needless jeopardy, and exposes them to temptations such as no one should be called upon to face; if the conditions and atmosphere of an actor's calling are so lowering to the moral tone as to make a loose manner of life practically inevitable, the enjoyment furnished by dramatic representations is a form of amusement which a good man will refuse to countenance. Now, that there are moral risks of a peculiar kind attending the theatrical profession, it would be idle to deny; but the fact of risk does not necessarily condemn it, any more than the inevitable risks attending all kinds of worldly business condemn them. Nevertheless it is a consideration which cannot be left out of account in determining our attitude to the theatre; each individual is bound not only to think of the effects of a dramatic entertainment on himself, but also to consider, on the grounds of the fullest knowledge at his command, whether those who provide the entertainment are prejudicially affected in character.

8. In the last resort, the question of amusement is for each individual to decide. It is impossible to lay down hard-and-fast rules which will have universal validity. The science of ethics is one of the most individual of all the sciences. The determination of duty is a matter for the earnest and enlightened conscience of each person for himself. It is not to be denied that the method, which has been largely favoured in some quarters, of drawing up lists of allowable and proscribed amusements has a certain practical utility; the deliberate judgment of good men in reference to pleasures, whose worth for the ethical ends of life is a matter of debate, is not rashly to be set aside; nevertheless, in all such matters the individual conscience must be the final judge. The free life of the spirit must not be bound; only it should be remembered that, for a wise settlement of the question of amusements, the individual must have a clear apprehension of the moral obligations resting upon him, and be guided by a spirit of devotion to a lofty ideal of life. 'He that is spiritual judgeth all things.' Let a man realize the true ethical ends of life, let him recognize that life is a gift to be honourably used for self-culture and service, and the question of amusements may be left to settle itself. He who walks according to 'the law of the spirit of life in Christ Jesus' will never find himself in serious difficulty. He will not ask himself in what amusements he may indulge, or to what extent he may indulge in them, without doing wrong; he will be so intent on seeking the true ends of life that only those amusements will be desired which are in harmony with these ends, and only that measure of indulgence will be allowed which helps towards their attainment. In the most natural way, amusements will take their fitting place as a means of refreshment. They will be the lighter breathings of an earnest spirit, which finds in them a new zest for duty and a preparation for more exacting pursuits. The ethical ideal which gives unity to life will govern them and lend them value; so that pleasures, which in those indifferent to high aims are simply the frivolous exercise of a low-toned spirit, are the sparkle on the surface of a deep and earnest nature, the instinctive playfulness of a heart that finds in relaxation a help for serious work.

B. 1. So far we have been concerned with the general principles which should control the choice and pursuit of amusements; we turn now to consider their character and place in our modern life. It was inevitable that the vast changes which have taken place in business and industrial life within the last two or three generations should affect in a large degree the habits of men in their hours of leisure. The decay of intellectual interests has been incidentally referred to as one of the regrettable results of the increasing desire for lighter forms of amusement, but it must be confessed that it is hard to see how that was altogether to be avoided. The growing strain which the conditions of modern life have imposed on those engaged in business, the exacting demands made on brain and physical endurance by the sharpness of competition as well as by the necessity for providing the comforts and æsthetic refinements of a higher standard of living, have made such inroads on the energies of men that their pleasures have inevitably taken the form of amusements which agreeably relax the tension of the mind. In former days, when the strain was less severe, it was possible in moments of leisure to devote oneself to interests which required some intellectual effort; but under the conditions of present-day life the tension in the case of very many is so great that, if the balance is to be redressed and the powers re-energized for the proper discharge of work, amusements must often be of a nature to quicken sensation and act as an agreeable opiate to serious thought. This may be regretted in the interests of wide and harmonious self-culture, but it is part of the price which must be paid for the overdriven activity of modern life. The same consideration is a fair answer to the criticism which decries the craving for spectacular amusement in the name of robuster methods of recreation. It is blindness to the facts of modern life that leads to the wholesale condemnation of pleasurable excitement which is not accompanied by the healthy glow of exercise. That some measure of recreation in its nobler sense is both desirable and necessary for health of body and mind may be freely allowed; but it cannot be questioned that for the vast proportion of the toilers in our cities what is needed is not so much a further expenditure of energy, as some form of diversion which will quicken the pulse of life by its appeal to the imagination through the senses; and the hard-driven poor ought to be able to secure this in ways that are free from moral danger. Nothing, indeed, is of greater importance for the true welfare of those who are exposed to the strain of city life than the establishment of centres where healthy amusement, freed from all contaminating associations, can be had at a small cost. The Churches are moving in this direction already, and the time should not be far distant when municipalities will realize that it is their highest interest to devote some attention to the amusements of the people.

2. It is not merely the strain which our modern civilization imposes that makes the question of amusements of such vital importance; it is much more the unnatural conditions which have been created by the highly specialized character of modern industry. For large sections of the population there is under present conditions nothing in the nature of their work itself to excite any deep and genuine interest. In earlier days, handicraftsmen found in the varied operations of their calling, and in the freedom in which their skill found scope, a zest which in our mechanical age is almost entirely lacking. It is by no means surprising that men have sought an escape from the colourless routine of uninspiring work along the path of least resistance, and have endeavoured to satisfy their craving for a wider and more joyous life by indulgence in vicious pleasures or in forms of excitement which sap instead of renewing the energies. In these circumstances the great problem is to make activity pleasurable again, to find some way by which interest may be re-awakened in the performance of work which in itself is largely devoid of interest. Unquestionably the noblest way of attaining this end is to endeavour to implant in men's minds a new sense of the deeper meanings of work, a feeling for its ethical significance to the individual himself, and for its significance as the contribution which he is able to make to society in return for the privileges which society confers upon him. But the same end may be served in another way. It has been remarked that 'the most powerful moralizing influences are not always those which are directly moral' (MacCunn, *Making of Character*, 58). Accordingly, interest in work, with the formation of good habits which that implies, may be secured by the provision of healthy amusement which will stir the imagination and satisfy the instinctive desire for a larger life. While the love of life is at present largely exploited by private individuals, with results that are frequently far from beneficial, the aim of the community ought to be to supply forms of entertainment which shall prove a stronger attraction than questionable and vicious pleasures, and shall so enlarge the horizon of men's better desires that they will feel a new inducement to enter into work with all the energies at their command. As an indirect means of attaining moral ends, amusements have a worth which is deserving of greater attention than they have received. Professor Patten (*The New Basis of Civilization*) closes a suggestive discussion of this question with these words: 'Amusement is stronger than vice, and can stifle the lust of it. It is a base of economic efficiency upon which depends the progress of multitudes. When men and women have withstood the allurements of vice and learned work habits, then the steps beyond are fairly well paved. The Church and home can moralize and induce character, the school can clarify purpose, and the settlement can socialize the material ready in the industrial world' (p. 143). See also GAMES.

LITERATURE.—Martensen, *Chr. Ethics* (*Gen.*), 1885, p. 415 ff., *ib.* (*Soc.*), 1882, ii. 77 ff., 254 ff.; Schleiermacher, *Die chr. Sitte*; Rothe, *Chr. Ethik*; Richard Baxter, *Christian Directory*;

Lecky, *Map of Life*, 1899; Patten, *The New Basis of Civilization*, 1907; Dale, *Week-Day Sermons*, 1867; Bushnell, *Serm. on Living Subjects*, 1872; Munger, *On the Threshold*, 1881; Horton, '*This Do*,' 1892; Lambert, *The Omnipotent Cross*, 1899; Brierley, *Ourselves and the Universe*, 1906; Dickie, *Life's Ideals*, 1907; Cameron Lees, *Life and Conduct*, 1892.

A. F. FINDLAY.

AMYRALDISM was the name given, more generally, to the theology of Moyse Amyraut (Moses Amyraldus, the Amiro of Baillie's *Letters*), and, more particularly, to his way of defining the doctrine of Predestination. In the latter sense it was called, not quite appropriately, *Hypothetical Universalism*. It was one of three attempts (the others being Arminianism and the Covenant Theology) made during the 17th cent. to break through the iron ring of Predestination within which the Reformed Scholastic of that century had enclosed the theology of the Reformed Church. To understand the theory it is necessary to know something of the workings of that Scholastic, and something too of the life and aims of Amyraut.

The second leads naturally to the first. Moyse Amyraut was born at Bourgeil in Touraine in 1596. His family belonged to the Reformed religion. The boy was destined to a lawyer's career. He had begun his studies, and had attained to the grade of licentiate, when the reading of Calvin's *Institutio* turned all his thoughts to theology. He entered the Theological College of Saumur, where the teaching of the celebrated Scoto-French theologian, John Cameron, made a profound impression on him—second only to that already produced by the study of the *Institutio*. After a short ministry at Aignan, in Paris, he became minister at Saumur (1626). He had rapidly acquired a high position in the Reformed Church of France, and was deputed by the National Synod, which met at Charenton in 1631, to carry their respectful congratulations to King Louis XIII. At Court he attracted the attention of Cardinal Richelieu, and retained his friendship. In 1633 he was appointed Professor of Theology in Saumur, having as colleagues, appointed at the same time, Josué de la Place and Louis Cappel. All three had been students under Cameron, and all had a fervid admiration for the theology of Calvin as that was exhibited in the *Institutio*. All three believed that the so-called Calvinism of the day differed widely from the teaching of the master, and they were not slow to let this be known in their lectures. The College soon acquired a great reputation. Students came to it from the Reformed Churches beyond France, especially from Switzerland. Then doubts began to arise about the orthodoxy of its teaching, both in France and in Switzerland. The individual churches of the latter country began to withdraw their students, and that 'after-birth' of Reformed creed-making, the *Formula Consensus Helvetica*, was framed for the purpose of denouncing the doctrine of the three professors of Saumur.

The critics of Amyraut were right if orthodoxy was to be tested by the Reformed Scholastic of the day. It was his aim to bring back the Calvinism of the *Institutio*, which differed widely from the Scholastic, and in nothing more than in the doctrine of Predestination. With Calvin, predestination is not set forth at the beginning of his theological system; it is never used as the fundamental thought under which everything else is to be classed. It is simply an explanation of the sovereignty of grace, which overrides man's sin and man's weakness. Still, in spite of the smaller place and special position which the word and idea of predestination held in the *Institutio*, there was a master-thought running through Calvin's theological thinking which might easily be displaced by the conception of predestination. The devout imagination has never made grander or loftier flight than in the thought of the *purpose of God* moving slowly down the ages, making for redemption and the establishment of the Kingdom of God. This is the master-thought in the *Institutio*. It was full of life and movement, and had for issue a living thing, the Kingdom of God. If this conception of the Kingdom of God be kept in view, it is impossible to crystallize or stereotype the living thought of purpose. The Kingdom comes into being in such a variety of ways, none of them able to be expressed in exact definition. Its conception can never be summed up in a few dry propositions. It is something which from its very nature stretches forward to and melts in the infinite. But if a keen and narrow intellect, coming to Calvin's theology, fastens on its nerve thought of *purpose*, and manipulates it according to the presuppositions and formulæ of the second-rate metaphysics within which his mind works, it is possible to transform the thought of purpose into a theory of predestination which will master the whole system of theological thinking.

This is what the Reformed Scholastics of the 17th cent. did with the experimental theology of the 16th century. They made it a second-rate metaphysic dominated by what they called the Divine decree. Moreover, they effected the transformation in the very same way that the mediæval Schoolmen had treated the experimental theology of Augustine. They began with a definition of God borrowed from the Aristotelian philosophy, and put this abstraction in the place which ought to be occupied by the Father, who has revealed Himself in Jesus Christ. The *Principium Essendi* was their starting-point. The abstraction which did service for God in the Aristotelian philosophy needed another abstraction to bring it into relation to the universe of men and things. The Aristotelian thought which mediated between the principle of existence and the variety of life and motion in the universe was the category of Substance. Substance, the first and unique category, collected everything into a unity of being, and so brought the *All* into relation with the *One*. A second abstraction was also needed by the Reformed Scholastic. This was found in the Divine decree. It was the highest category, embracing all existence, including everything knowable, everything which proceeds from the One Principle of Being. The essential existence of God (Trinity) is alone outside this decree; everything else lives, moves, and has its being within the circle of the Divine decree. It is the channel through which God delivers Himself in action outside His essential nature. It includes, it *is*, all existence, still immanent within the Godhead. Within it are all things arranged in *eternal* providence, and all men, and the election of some and the reprobation of others. When existence emerges, it comes forth on the lines laid down within the Deity in the Divine decree, which includes all creation, all actual providence, all Divine work of redemption.

It was this Scholastic that Amyraut and his colleagues protested against—this enclosing everything thinkable within the ring-fence of a Divine decree, which was simply the Aristotelian category of Substance under another name. They wished to get back to the experimental theology of the Reformation age as that was exhibited in its greatest master. They felt that the first thing to be done was to break through this ring-fence, within which the metaphysic of the time made all theological thought move. The attempt made before them, which went by the name of Arminianism, did not appeal to them. It had nothing to do with the experimental theology of Calvin, and was simply the revolt of a shallower metaphysic against a deeper. They accepted the decisions of the Synod of Dordrecht. But they wished to bring theology back to life, to connect it with the needs of men and women.

The special doctrine of Amyraut is known as *Hypothetical Universalism*, or the *Double Reference Theory of the Atonement*. It was suggested by, if not based on, Cameron's doctrine of Conversion. That doctrine, as Amyraut understood it, was: Conversion may be described as a special case of the ordinary action of the intelligence on the will. According to the psychology of the day, it was held that the will acts only in so far as it is influenced by the intellect—action follows enlightenment, and that only. Conversion is a special case of this action of intellect upon will—special, because in this case the Holy Spirit enlightens the intellect, and the intellect, charged with this spiritual enlightenment, acts upon the will. Conversion is thus an instance of the ordinary action of the intelligence on the will, and yet is, at the same time, an altogether extraordinary work of supernatural grace. The grace of God, which is supernatural when it acts upon the will in conversion, follows the ordinary psychological laws. This relation between the intellect and the will in conversion suggested to Amyraut a similar parallel between Providence and Election, and between Creation and Redemption. Providence may be looked on as belonging to the course of nature; but Election is a special instance of Providence and at the same time the peculiar and gracious work of God. Creation belongs to the ordinary course of nature, and Redemption is a special instance of Creation, and is nevertheless a unique and gracious work of God. Just as the relation of the intellect to the will may be called the universal of conversion, so Election may be looked at as set in the environment of Providence, and Redemption in the environment of Creation.

Amyraut, whose devotion to Calvin was unbounded, insisted that these thoughts of his were the legitimate and historical development of ideas presented in the *Institutio*. He keeps to Calvin's great thought of the purpose of God unfolding itself down through the ages. This purpose of grace, when viewed out of all relation to time, is universally Creation, specially it is Redemption; viewed historically, it is Providence and Election; viewed individually, it is Intellect acting on Will and Conversion. He has thus three pairs of ideas —the one universal and natural, the other special and of grace; and that which is of grace is always set in the environment of the natural.

This mode of thought, however, embodied a practical ecclesiastical purpose. In those days Germany was being devastated by the Thirty Years' War—a struggle hideously prolonged, all men saw, in consequence of the mutual jealousies between Calvinists and Lutherans. Since the Synod of Dordrecht, the Lutherans had grown more embittered against the Calvinists. They believed that its doctrinal conclusions had been directed against them indirectly. Amyraut hoped to make it plain to the Lutherans that Calvinist theology could be stated in a form which might be more acceptable to them. He saw that the Lutherans took special objection to the Calvinist doctrine of a limited reference in the Atonement, and he hoped to overcome that difficulty.

Two modes of dealing with the Lutherans were possible to Reformed theologians. (1) They might have insisted that Lutheran theology was quite distinct from Arminianism, and that the condemnation of the Arminians at Dordrecht was not meant to, and did not, involve a condemnation of the Lutherans; that the particular point raised in the Arminian controversy had never been before the Lutheran Churches, and had never been settled by it; and that in any attempt to bring the Lutheran and the Reformed Churches closer to each other, this particular doctrine of a limited reference in the Atonement might be left an open question. This was the view of the great French Reformed theologians Claude and Jurieu. (2) They might, while adhering strictly to the Reformed doctrine as laid down at the Synod of Dordrecht, have endeavoured to shape that doctrine so as to make it approach the Lutheran type in statement at least. Amyraldus selected the latter method. He tried to show that there might be the general reference in the Atonement to all men, which the Lutherans insisted on retaining, while the Reformed thought of a limited reference was also correct. He worked out his scheme of conciliation by the use he made of the three pairs of ideas already mentioned. The purpose in Creation, he said, was Redemption; the purpose in Providence was Election; the purpose in the gift of intellectual endowment was Conversion. Applying this to the matter in hand, he declared that, if the whole design of God in Providence is to make all things work together for the good of them that are called, Providence itself is but a wider election—an election which may be described as universal.

His argument condensed was somewhat as follows: The essential nature of God is goodness; and by goodness Amyraut means love *plus* morality—love limited by the conditions which the universal moral law must impose upon it. This Divine goodness shines forth on man in Creation and in Providence, which is simply Creation become continuous. But sin has through man entered into creation, and has destroyed the true end and aim of man's life. In presence of sin God's goodness shines on, but it must, from its very nature as love *plus* morality, take a somewhat different form. It becomes righteousness, which is goodness in the presence of sin; and this righteousness demands the Atonement, Christ's work of satisfaction, through which men are saved from the consequences of their sin. The goodness of God remains unchanged; it is seen in the desire to *save*; but the presence of sin has made it appear under a special form. When this thought is applied to assort the theological ideas of the 17th cent. Calvinism, it is seen that the purpose of God in salvation is really *infra-lapsarian*, because it arises from goodness in the presence of sin, and therefore face to ace with the thought of the Fall. But it may also be regarded as *supra-lapsarian*, because it is simply a continuation of the original goodness of God. In this purpose of God there is no theoretical limitation save what is implied in the means which the goodness of God in presence of sin is morally compelled to take, *i.e.* the work of Christ. The purpose of God to save is simply the carrying out of the original and universal goodness of God. The work of Redemption is thus the carrying out of the original work of creation. The purpose to redeem is set in the environment of the original purpose to create. When looked at from the point of view of Creation, the *supra-lapsarian*, there is a universal reference in the work of Christ. But when we look at this purpose of God in presence of sin, and when we know that some men do die impenitent and therefore are not saved—when we take the *infra-lapsarian* purpose to save—we see that the theoretically universal reference is limited practically by the fact that some are not saved. The universal reference is theoretical or *hypothetical*; the limited reference to the elect is practical and *real*. Christ's work has real reference only to the some who are saved. This placing a hypothetical universal reference round the limited reference in the work of Christ is *the* distinctive feature in the theology of Amyraldus.

Amyraut, however, applied this general thought in a threefold way:—(1) He broke through the strict idea of salvation limited to the elect—to whom all reference of the work of Christ was limited in 17th cent. Reformed theology—by making the goodness of God, which has regard to *all* men universally, still active in His righteousness (which is His goodness in the presence of sin). He declared that this thought lay implicitly in the well-known phrase of the divines at Dordrecht: '*Christum mortuum esse sufficienter pro omnibus, sed efficaciter pro electis*'; and to make plain what he believed to be its meaning, he changed it to: '*Christum mortuum esse sufficienter sed non actualiter pro omnibus.*' This gave him a hypothetical universalism and a real limitation to those actually saved. (2) He broke down the barrier which 17th cent. divines had reared against the possibility of the salvation of the heathen, by their statement that those to whom the external call is not addressed cannot be held to be recipients of the benefits of the saving work of Christ. He taught, following Zwingli, that God in providence did bestow upon pious heathen what in their case did amount to an external call. This gave a real and not a hypothetical, universal, external call, and with it the offer of salvation to those who had not heard the Gospel message. (3) He widened the precisely fixed sphere of conversion by insisting that every illumination of the intellect was an analogue and prophecy of the spiritual enlightenment which produces conversion.

But while all these three conceptions were discussed in his many treatises on Predestination, the controversy which followed the publication of his views was really confined to the first line of thought. The question was asked, What changes this hypothetical universal reference into a real particular reference? Is it the action of God or of man? If the change arises from man's power to resist what God has purposed to do for all, then Amyraut was an Arminian, as the Dutch and the Swiss theologians asserted. Did the mystery of the change lie hidden in God? Then his theology did not differ substantially from that of the divines of Dordrecht, save perhaps in sentiment. The latter was the view taken by the French Reformed Church. Amyraut was summoned before the

National Synod of 1637 along with his friend Paul Testard, pastor at Blois. The accused were energetically defended, and allowed full liberty to explain their position. They were acquitted of all heresy. The accusation was renewed at the National Synods of 1644 and 1645, with the same result. The Swiss theologians were not satisfied. Their *Formula Consensus Ecclesiarum Helveticarum Reformatarum* (1676) witnessed their protest.

The doctrine of Amyraut has maintained a firm hold on many evangelical Calvinists since his day. It was professed by Baxter, Vines, and Calamy in the days of the Westminster Assembly. It was not, as we can learn from the minutes, meant to be excluded by the definitions in the Westminster Confession. It was taught by Professors Balmer and Brown within the Secession Church in Scotland. It is part of much modern evangelical theology.

LITERATURE.—*Traité de la Prédestination et de ses principes* (Saumur, 1634); *Echantillon de la doctrine de Calvin sur la Prédestination* (Saumur, 1637, consists of six sermons); *De la Justification* (Saumur, 1638); *De Providentia Dei in malo* (Saumur, 1638); *Defensio doctrinæ J. Calvini de absoluto reprobationis decreto* (Saumur, 1641); *Dissertationes theologicæ quatuor* (Saumur, 1645, in the Theses Salmurenses); *Exercitatio de gratia universali* (Saumur, 1646); *Declaratio fidei contra errores Arminianorum* (Saumur, 1646, also in French); *Disputatio de libero hominis arbitrio* (Saumur, 1647); Quick, *Synodicon* (London, 1692), pp. 352, 455, etc. Later books: J. J. Hottinger, *Succincta et solida ac genuina Formulæ Consensus . . . historia* (Zürich, 1723); Walch, *Religionsstreitigkeiten ausserhalb der luther. Kirche* (Jena, 1733), i. p. 454 ff.; Schweitzer, *Die Prot. Centraldogmen in ihrer Entwicklung der Reform. Kirche* (Zürich, 1856); Ebrard, *Reform. Kirchenzeitung* (1853); Edmund Saigey, *Amyraut, sa vie et ses écrits* (Paris, 1849); also Bayle's *Dict.*, art. 'Amyraut.' THOMAS M. LINDSAY.

ANABAPTISM.—I. *HISTORY.*—The Anabaptists, or Katabaptists (*Wiedertäufer* or *Täufer*) rose in close connexion with the early Reformers at Zürich, Wittenberg, and possibly elsewhere. They spread swiftly over those parts of Europe affected by the Reformation, making a profound impression in the early years of that movement. All the leading Reformers (Luther, Zwingli, Bucer, Oecolampadius, Calvin, Knox, and many others) combated their views in one or more publications and disputations; their doctrines are condemned explicitly or by implication in all the leading creeds of the 16th and 17th cents. (Augsburg, Part I. Artt. ix. xvi.; Trent. Sess. v. 4, 'On Bapt.,' Can. xiii.; French, xxxv.; 2nd Helv. Conf., Artt. xx. xxx.; Belgic Conf., Art. xxxiv.; Scotch Conf., Art. xxiii.; Formula of Concord, Art. xii.; Thirty-nine Artt. xxvii. xxxvii. xxxix.; Westminster Conf. xxviii.); and Calvin's *Institutes* were originally written largely to prove to Francis I. that the Reformers were not all Anabaptists; they were put under the ban by the Diet of the Empire in 1529; and most other civil governments, including that of England, took action against them.

They were the radical party of the Reformation period, regarding Luther and Zwingli as half-reformers who had pulled down the old house without rebuilding in its place. Despairing of reforming the old Church, they sought to build anew on the foundation of Scripture literally interpreted, without the help of the State or any other existing institution; this religious ideal involved fundamental social and political changes (Beck, *Geschichtsbücher d. Wiedertäufer*, p. 12). They differed considerably among themselves in spirit, aim, and many more or less important points of doctrine, but strove together towards a great and far-reaching reform. They sought to reform the work of the Reformers.

The striking similarity between many of their doctrines and those of some earlier sects has led to an effort to show some historical connexion. Ritschl (*Gesch. d. Pietismus*) has sought to trace their doctrines to the spiritual Franciscans; Ludwig Keller and others have sought to show some connexion with the Waldenses, who a little earlier were widely scattered over central Europe. The similarity in doctrines, spirit, and organization is so marked as almost to compel belief in some sort of historical succession; and yet the effort to trace this connexion has not so far been successful. Moreover, several considerations militate against such a conclusion. (1) The Anabaptists themselves were not conscious of such connexion, regarding themselves as the spiritual children of a renewed study of the Bible. (2) All their leaders, so far as their lives are known, came out of the Catholic Church. (3) They had little or no communion with older sects after their rise. These considerations render it probable that they, like the sects of the Middle Ages, are the offspring of a renewed Bible study, and that the similarity is the result of independent Bible study under similar circumstances and controlling ideas.

The history of the party can perhaps be best followed by dividing them into German, Swiss-Moravian, and Dutch Anabaptists. These divisions overlap more or less, but they are largely distinct types.

I. The German Anabaptists.—It is commonly held that the German Anabaptists rose with Thomas Münzer and Nicholas Storch at Zwickau in eastern Saxony. Münzer, a well-educated man, deeply imbued with the mysticism of the later Middle Ages, a friend and follower of Luther, became pastor at Zwickau in 1520. Here he came under the influence of Nicholas Storch, a weaver, who had become deeply tinged with Bohemian views: chiliasm; the rejection of oaths, magistracy, warfare, and infant baptism; and the insistence on community of goods. Under this influence he at once began drastic reforms. With his approval Storch set up a new church on the Bohemian model, claiming new revelations and the special guidance of the Spirit. Their socialistic teachings and revolutionary proceedings soon forced them to leave. Storch, in company with a former Wittenberg student named Stübner, proceeded to Wittenberg in the hope of winning the support of the University for their views. Luther was then in hiding at the Wartburg; Carlstadt and Cellarius, two of the professors of the University, were speedily won over by the new prophets, and even Melanchthon was deeply moved. Various reforms were put into effect immediately. Luther, hearing of these radical proceedings, and believing they would bring the whole reform movement to ruin, hastened to Wittenberg in spite of the protest of his friends, and in eight powerful sermons succeeded in suppressing the movement at that place. Storch and eventually the two professors whom he had won to his views were driven away, Melanchthon was saved, and the radical reforms revoked. Henceforth Luther was one of the most powerful and uncompromising opponents of the Anabaptists. Storch now wandered from place to place, and finally disappeared about 1525.

In the meantime Münzer had visited Prague for several months, had then laboured as pastor and agitator at several places in Thuringia, and had made a visit to southern Germany and the border of Switzerland in the interest of his views. He was becoming more socialistic, more chiliastic, more bitter towards the ruling and upper classes. At last in 1525 the peasant uprising broke out. It had his enthusiastic support, and shortly after its overthrow at Frankenhausen he was arrested and executed. With this catastrophe the Anabaptist cause in Germany suffered a permanent defeat. Henceforth Anabaptism was associated in the minds of Germans with the wild socialism and chiliasm of Münzer and the horrors of the Peasant War. And yet neither Münzer nor Storch is known to have been re-baptized or to have practised believers' baptism. Both opposed infant baptism, but Münzer specially provides for it in a German service which he drew up for the church of Alstedt in 1523. It is impossible to determine the extent to which these men preached the necessity of believers' baptism, and thereby became the founders of the Anabaptism of Hesse and other regions of western Germany. They were chiefly interested in socialistic-chiliastic ideas, and probably did not press the demand for re-baptism. If this be true, the Anabaptists of the Rhine region had another origin, to be traced later.

2. The Swiss-Moravian Anabaptists.—Bullinger says that the Swiss Anabaptists sucked their Anabaptism from Münzer (*Refor. Gesch.* i. p. 224 f.). But this is improbable. Münzer, as we have seen, did visit the border of Switzerland in 1524, and was in conference with some men who later adopted Anabaptism; but in a letter still preserved (Cornelius, *Gesch. d. Münst. Aufruhrs,* ii. Beil. 1), written September 5, 1524, they show marked independence, even chiding Münzer for some of his views. Moreover, the whole tone and spirit of the Swiss was different from that of Münzer. Chiliasm and violence had no place in their scheme, and socialistic tendencies were much less prominent. Besides, there was in southern Germany and Switzerland at this time wide-spread doubt of the Scripturalness of infant baptism, Bucer, Oecolampadius, and even Zwingli being in doubt ('Vom Tauf, vom Widertauf,' etc., *Opp.* ii. p. 245, *ib.* i. p. 239 f.; Egli, *Actensammlung,* 655, 692).

These Anabaptists rose from the circle of Zwingli's intimate friends and associates at Zürich. Zwingli had become pastor there on 1st Jan. 1519, and by his powerful evangelical preaching had by 1523 brought many of the population to a readiness to abolish Catholic worship and doctrines. But he was anxious to avoid division and strife, and delayed action, hoping to convince the whole mass of the people and then proceed to reform with the authority of the cantonal government. Under these circumstances there sprang up a radical party who favoured proceeding at once with reform 'without tarrying for any.' Moreover, their convictions on some points were in advance of Zwingli's. They urged him to remove or destroy the images, abolish the Mass, begin the celebration of the Supper in both kinds, and finally, to set up a church composed of saints (believers) only. His delay in adopting their earlier demands and his flat refusal to entertain the last led to a final break with the party in 1523 or 1524 (Bullinger, *Der Wiedertäufer Ursprung,* Bl. 9).

The more prominent members of the party at this time were Simon Stumpf pastor at Höngg, Froschauer the famous printer, Heine Aberli, Andreas Castelberg a cripple, Conrad Grebel a young man of aristocratic family, Felix Manz, Wilhelm Reublin pastor at Wytikon, Ludwig Hätzer an excellent Hebraist and later translator of the Prophets, and Georg Blaurock a converted monk who was the most powerful popular preacher among them. Grebel and Manz were the real leaders of the party at Zürich. Grebel was trained at Vienna and Paris, and possessed a fine Greek culture; Manz was an excellent Hebrew scholar, habitually using his Hebrew Bible in preaching. These men held private meetings for Bible study, and here their views were gradually developed and perfected (Egli, *op. cit.* No. 623). Early in 1524 they reached the conclusion that infant baptism was without warrant in Scripture, was an invention of the Pope, yea of Satan himself; it was therefore invalid, was no baptism, and hence the duty of beginning anew the baptism of believers was felt to rest upon them. This they proceeded to do in Dec. 1524 or Jan. 1525, when in a private house Grebel baptized Blaurock, who in turn took a dipper (*aimer*) and baptized several others in the name of the Trinity (Egli, 636, 646). This was followed by the celebration of the Supper in the same simple way.

The civil authorities now resorted to repressive measures. After a public disputation with the Anabaptists (17th Jan. 1525), it was decreed that all infants should be baptized within eight days, that all private religious meetings be abandoned, and that all foreign Anabaptists be banished. Soon afterwards several were arrested, warned, threatened, and released. Continuing their activity, they were again arrested, thrown into prison, and a second ineffective disputation was held on 20th March. On 5th April most of them escaped from prison, and leaving for a brief period the Canton of Zürich comparatively quiet, they spread their views far and wide in other cantons. Renewed activity in Zürich was met by increasing severity on the part of the authorities. In Jan. 1526 the fine to be imposed for re-baptizing was raised to five pounds, and in March eighteen persons were thrown into prison and ordered to be fed on bread and water till they 'die and rot.' Further, baptizing or aiding and abetting the same was to be punished by drowning. Soon afterwards the prisoners were released, on what terms is unknown. Manz and Blaurock were again arrested in the territory of Zürich early in 1527. Soon afterwards Manz was drowned, while Blaurock was beaten through the streets and sent into banishment with the death penalty hanging over him in case of return.

In August 1527, Zürich proposed the adoption of uniform measures for the suppression of the Anabaptists by the cantons affected, viz. Basel, Berne, Schaffhausen, Chur, Appenzell, and St. Gall. These cantons had probably all received these views from Zürich (but see Müller, *Gesch. d. Ber. Täufer,* p. 52 f.) in the early stages of the movement.

The Anabaptists appeared in Basel in the summer of 1525, and for nearly a year enjoyed comparative peace. In June 1526 they were banished five miles from the city, and a month later attendance on their secret meetings was forbidden. Notwithstanding fines, imprisonment, and public floggings, they multiplied rapidly in the country districts throughout the year 1527. They first appeared in the territory of Berne in 1525, but gave little trouble before 1527, when persecution in Basel and elsewhere drove them into this canton in great numbers. In St. Gall they are found early, and achieved a signal success. The founder and leader was Wolfgang Uolimann, who was converted and baptized (immersed naked) in the Rhine at Schaffhausen in Feb. 1525. Grebel himself preached in St. Gall for two weeks in March with great power and success. By Easter the Anabaptists numbered five hundred souls, and their influence was so great that the authorities felt compelled to deal gently with them. The foreign Anabaptists were banished, and the native ones were persuaded to cease baptizing until the matter could be decided by the Council. Zwingli was alarmed by the rapidity of their growth, and persuaded Vadian, who was the leading statesman of the canton and a brother-in-law of Grebel, to oppose them, dedicating his book *Vom Tauf,* etc., to Vadian at the end of May. Notwithstanding the earnest entreaties of Grebel (Cornelius, *Gesch. Münster. Aufruhrs,* ii. 250), Vadian turned against them. After a disputation early in June, the Council ordered the Anabaptists to cease baptizing altogether, and to cease teaching outside one of the churches which was opened to them. Severe measures were enforced against them, and by 1527 the strength of the movement was broken.

In similar ways Anabaptism had been planted in Chur, Appenzell, and Schaffhausen. In Schaffhausen it seemed for a time that Dr. Sebastian Hofmeister, the leading preacher of the canton, would be won for the Anabaptists (Egli, 674).

The efforts of Zürich to secure the adoption of uniform regulations against the Anabaptists in August 1527 were unsuccessful; but all the cantons agreed to proceed more strenuously towards their extermination. It now became very difficult for the leaders to find hiding-places in Switzerland, and the emigration to the Austrian lands and Moravia which had begun several months earlier was greatly accelerated. Still many lingered and worked in Switzerland, and still the measures for their suppression increased in severity. In the canton of Zürich six were executed between 1527 and 1532, and one in the Catholic canton of Zug (Nitsche, *Gesch. d. Wiedertaufer* (1885), p. 97). Twenty years later, Bullinger still complains bitterly of their great numbers, and the time of their complete disappearance from the canton is unknown.

After the Reformation was legally introduced into Basel in 1529, the government proceeded against the Anabaptists more vigorously. On 12th Jan. 1530, Hans Ludi was beheaded, and a year later two others were drowned (Burckhardt, p. 41). Others, both men and women, were exposed in the pillory, ducked, beaten, and banished, and it is probable that others were executed (Burckhardt, p. 43). This broke their power, but they lingered on amid perpetual persecution through the 16th and 17th centuries.

Berne proceeded against the Anabaptists more vigorously after 1527. In 1528, during the great disputation which led this canton to accept the Reformation, eight Anabaptists were arrested and thrown into prison. When Zwingli and others failed to convince them of their errors, they were banished under penalty of death if they returned. During the years 1528–1529 frequent cases were brought before the authorities;

disputations with Pfister Meyer in 1531 and at Zofingen in 1532 failed to retard their growth. Berne then proceeded to blood, and between the years 1528 and 1571 no fewer than forty were executed (Müller, p. 78 f.). But even this severity was not sufficient to root them out of this canton. During the succeeding centuries they were sent to the galleys, deported, banished, persecuted; but they have maintained their existence to the present time.

In St. Gall, persecution drove the Anabaptists, especially the women, to the most absurd and childish and even immoral practices (Kessler, *Sabbata*). One case in particular wrought disaster to the Anabaptist name and cause. On 7th Feb. 1526, a half-witted man named Schugger struck off his brother's head 'by the will of God.' Later Anabaptists denied all connexion with this incident, but they could not escape the consequences of the deed. Anabaptists lingered in this canton till the 17th century.

By 1532 all the leaders, such as Grebel, Manz, Blaurock, Denck, Hätzer, and Hübmaier, were dead, hundreds had been forced to recant, many had died in prison, and perhaps thousands had been driven from the country. The movement in Switzerland lay in ruins, destroyed by the civil power. The causes of this bitter persecution are not far to seek. The Anabaptists in this region, with few exceptions, were quiet, pious, law-abiding people, with some oddities due to their strictness (Kessler, *Sabbata*, i. 272). Even Bullinger admits that they had the appearance of unusual piety. But they made what seemed at that time impossible demands: a Church composed of believers only, rigid discipline for moral offences, complete freedom for the Church and the individual conscience. Failing to obtain their demands, they divided and weakened the Reformers, causing endless strife and difficulty. Their refusal to bear arms, to serve as civil officers or take the oath, made them dangerous to the State, while their attitude towards property, usury, and certain forms of taxes threatened the whole social order. Hence suppression and extermination were felt to be the only paths to safety.

The intimate relations of the south German cities with Switzerland made them peculiarly susceptible to all spiritual and religious movements in that country. Accordingly we find large Anabaptist circles in Strassburg, Worms, Nuremberg, and Augsburg quite early. In these circles such leaders as Ludwig Hätzer, Hans Denck, and Hans Hut were won for the Anabaptist cause. One of the most important conquests was in the small border town of Waldshut in Austrian territory. Here Dr. Balthasar Hübmaier, a gifted scholar and eloquent preacher, some time rector of the University of Ingolstadt and Cathedral preacher at Regensburg, was the leading pastor. He was early converted to Reformed views, and in 1524 succeeded in introducing them into the city. But he was unable to stop here. Gradually he found himself compelled to accept Anabaptist views; about Easter 1525 he and some sixty members of his church were re-baptized. This was followed soon afterwards by the baptism of several hundred others, and the Anabaptists seemed to be in a fair way to win the town. But for some months the Austrian authorities, who were strict Catholics, had been threatening to punish the town for its evangelical doings. Hitherto the support of Zürich had emboldened Waldshut to persevere. The Anabaptist defection caused the withdrawal of this support, and in December the storm broke over the devoted city. Hübmaier fled to Zürich, was arrested as an Anabaptist, imprisoned, and forced to recant as the price of liberty. Released on 11th April, 1526, he fled through Constance to Augsburg, and thence in June to Nikolsburg in Moravia, where his persecuted brethren were already gathering.

Driven from Switzerland, the Anabaptists fled eastward into the Austrian lands from 1526 onwards. Their doctrines found ready acceptance, and soon large bodies had been gathered at Rottenberg, Kitzbüchl, Brixen, Bozen, Linz, Steyer, and elsewhere. Here they came under Catholic governments which hunted them down, if possible, even more strenuously than the Swiss. King Ferdinand himself was very active in the work of extermination, and in a few years hundreds had suffered martyrdom. Protected by the character of the country and the sympathy of the common people, the Anabaptists continued to maintain an existence for more than a century, until the Catholic reaction swept all forms of evangelical life in these regions out of existence.

Persecution in the Austrian lands drove the Anabaptists onward into Moravia, Bohemia, and Poland. The religious history and the social and political condition of these lands made them an asylum for various sects, and here for a brief period the Anabaptists found rest and safety. At Nikolsburg, under the protection of the lords of Lichtenstein, they found 'a goodly land,' a new Jerusalem, from 1526 onwards. Thither they streamed in great numbers from Switzerland, the Austrian lands, Germany, and elsewhere; natives were converted to their views, and soon they numbered thousands. Among the first to arrive was Hübmaier. Learned, eloquent, free from fanaticism, without rancour in debate, a careful exegete, possessed of an excellent literary style, he was the chief ornament of the sect. Within little more than a year he published no fewer than fifteen tracts, in which he set forth with force and clearness the great principles that characterized his people. Had he lived, their history might have been different. But the Austrian authorities soon learned of the presence in their dominions of this fugitive from Waldshut, and demanded his apprehension as a traitor. After some delay, the lords of Lichtenstein delivered him up in July, 1527. He was imprisoned at Vienna, where he was burned at the stake on 10th March, 1528. Thus perished the most important of all the Anabaptist leaders.

The community in Nikolsburg could ill afford to lose a man of such wisdom and sanity. Already in 1526 Hans Hut, one of Münzer's followers who had escaped from Germany, appeared among the brethren as a powerful and impressive herald of Christ's speedy return, a determined opponent of magistracy and war. Others soon began to agitate in favour of community of goods. Hübmaier had opposed all these views, but Hut's enthusiasm had won many of the brethren before his expulsion by the Lichtensteins. They soon felt compelled to banish his followers, who were now perhaps a majority of the brethren. The moderates remained at Nikolsburg under the leadership of Spitalmaier as chief pastor, but they were never again the most influential party. The radicals settled at Austerlitz, and soon became a thriving community, with branches at Brünn and elsewhere. Chiefly through the missionary labours of Jacob Huter, a noble and zealous leader, their persecuted brethren in the Austrian lands were induced to immigrate in large numbers. They built great communal houses, became experts in agriculture and stock-raising, and in the manufacture of many important articles of commerce. Their value was recognized by their lords, who protected them as far as possible; but after the Münster horror in 1535 a terrible persecution broke over them. Their houses were broken up, and they were driven forth into other lands. As persecution subsided, they returned and took up their work again. After another period of persecution, which lasted with more or less severity from 1547 to 1554, they enjoyed great prosperity till 1592, when they probably numbered some 70,000 souls. They had suffered from frequent internal strifes, and were now caught in the great Catholic reaction led by the Jesuits, and gradually declined. Greatly reduced by the Thirty Years' War, they were completely ruined by later invasions of Turks and others, as well as by persecution. Some of them fled to Hungary and Transylvania, where they disappear in the 18th century. Others fled to southern Russia, whence a remnant removed in 1874 to South Dakota, in the United States, where they still preserve their communal life.

The Anabaptists of two other regions, both with some relations to the Swiss-Moravian movement, must be mentioned in this connexion. About 1526, in connexion with the work of Schwenckfeldt, the Anabaptists appeared in Silesia. Soon they had flourishing congregations in several important cities, but persecution from 1528 onwards gradually exterminated them.

By the middle of the 16th cent. there was a strong Anabaptist body in N.E. Italy, chiefly anti-Trinitarian in Christology. The Inquisition then got on their track, and in a few years the movement was stifled. Many of them fled to Poland, where they built up a flourishing connexion. In 1605 they issued the Racovian Catechism, which provides for immersion as the mode of baptism. Though they were Socinians, they believed in the authority of Scripture and the lordship of Christ. They suffered the fortunes of the other evangelicals in this region during the Counter-Reformation.

3. The Anabaptists of the Rhine regions.—As far as their history can be traced, the Anabaptists of the lower Rhine-lands owe their origin and peculiarities chiefly to Melchior Hoffmann. This wonderful man was born in Hall, Swabia, and was a furrier by trade. He early accepted Luther's views, and by 1523 was a zealous evangelical preacher in North Germany. He was without education, but early acquired a remarkable knowledge of the text of Scripture, along with an intense interest in the prophetic and apocalyptic portions. He developed a burning enthusiasm as well as a powerful eloquence in propagating the Lutheran views. His zeal and power usually aroused intense opposition, and frequently occasioned riot and sometimes bloodshed. He moved rapidly from place to place, and always made a profound impression. In 1523 he was in Wolmar, in Livonia; banished from there, in 1524 he was in Dorpat; in 1526 he was in Sweden, at Stockholm; in 1527, at Lübeck; then at Kiel, where he made a profound impression on King Frederick I. of Denmark. Banished from there, he entered East Friesland, with Carlstadt, where he threw himself into the controversy between the followers of Luther and Zwingli over the Supper, supporting the latter party, and by his power and eloquence carrying the day for his views. In June 1529 he reached Strassburg. By this time he had devoloped most of the peculiarities of his system, including the allegorical method of interpreting Scripture, a glowing chiliasm which fixed the beginning of the reign of Christ on earth in the year 1533, the assertion that the human nature of Christ was not derived from Mary, and, therefore, not ordinary flesh, a denial of the oath, etc. During this visit he is supposed to have come in contact with Anabaptists, who were then numerous in Strassburg, and to have been baptized into their fellowship. Returning to East Friesland in May, 1530, he began a truly wonderful Anabaptist propaganda, which extended, with brief interruptions, to 1533, and covered much of the Low Countries. Most of the Lutheran and Zwinglian work was swept away, and it is probable that the majority of Evangelicals in the Netherlands from 1533 to 1566 were of the Hofmannite type. In 1531 he suspended baptisms for two years, intimating that the Lord would then come to assume the reins of government at Strassburg, and bring the era of righteousness and peace for all the oppressed. The effect was magical, the religious and social excitement intense. In order to be present when the Lord came, he quietly returned to Strassburg early in 1533. He was soon apprehended and thrown into prison, where he died ten years later. But the seed which Münzer and others had sown was destined to bear some horrible fruit.

The episcopal city of Münster, in Westphalia, had been ruled by a succession of exceedingly dissolute and oppressive bishops, who, however, succeeded in holding reform at bay for several years. But in 1529 Bernard Rothmann, a gifted young preacher near Münster, began to preach evangelical doctrines. He was suspended, but returned to his work in 1531, and soon made an alliance with Knipperdollinck and the social democracy of the city. The bishop was driven away in 1532, and the next year reform was introduced. Persecuted Evangelicals from surrounding regions found their way into Münster, and there was great rejoicing and naturally great excitement over this new triumph of the truth. Heinrich Roll, a fugitive from Cleve, became an advocate of believers' baptism in 1532, and the next year Rothmann reached the same conclusion, and began a crusade against infant baptism. He was followed by a number of the leading men of the city. The City Council undertook to force the preachers to administer infant baptism, but popular sentiment was so strong as to prevent the execution of their will. This was the tense and excited condition of the city towards the end of 1533; Anabaptists, Lutherans, Catholics, and social democrats were all struggling for supremacy, when a horde of still more excited Anabaptists poured into the city from the Netherlands, believing it to be the hour for setting up Christ's kingdom at Münster as the New Jerusalem.

Jan Matthys, a baker of Haarlem, a disciple of Hofmann, inspired with a fanatical hatred of the upper classes, now proclaimed himself the promised prophet Enoch, and ordered the resumption of baptism as a final preparation for the coming King. In a short time thousands were baptized. In January 1534 two of his missionaries entered Münster, where they baptized Rothmann and other leaders, and announced the setting up of the earthly kingdom, in which there should be no magistracy, no law, no marriage, and no private property. Soon John of Leyden, a gifted young man of twenty-five years, appeared and took over the leadership of the new theocracy. Catholics and Lutherans fled, and the city fell completely into the hands of these fanatical Anabaptists. Matthys now declared Münster to be the New Jerusalem, and invited all the oppressed Anabaptists thither. Thousands of deluded and persecuted people sought to reach this place of safety and happiness, only to be destroyed on the way or ruined at last in the city. The city was soon besieged by the forces of the bishop, assisted by neighbouring princes, while within its walls murder, polygamy, and crime ran riot. After more than a year of ever increasing shame, the terrible orgy ended in massacre and cruel torture in 1535.

The effect of this Münster kingdom was most disastrous to the Anabaptists. Everywhere persecuting measures were sharpened, and the name became a byword and a hissing throughout Europe. This episode was regarded as the legitimate outcome of Anabaptist principles.

Menno Simons gathered up the fragments of

the quiet Anabaptists and re-organized them in 1536, at the same time disclaiming all connexion with the Münster fanatics. From him they have been called Mennonites (wh. see), and in Holland and America they still constitute a respectable folk.

Before and after the Münster episode some Anabaptists found their way to the eastern sections of England, where they were severely persecuted. It is possible, indeed probable, that there is some connexion between them and the Independents, English Baptists, and Quakers, all of whom show some of the peculiarities of the Anabaptists.

II. *SYSTEM.*—Anabaptism affords a case of arrested development with scarcely a parallel in Christian history. Arising spontaneously at different points, the movement seized Central Europe with a powerful grip, and bade fair to divide the population with other forms of Protestantism. But the machinery of ecclesiastical and civil government was soon set in motion to suppress it, and in ten years there remained only a persecuted, fanatical remnant of the once powerful movement. Without any great leader to crystallize its doctrines, and suffering persecution from the beginning, the party never attained unity and harmony. It is, therefore, often necessary to set forth the prevailing tendency, and at the same time to point out important variations from the general trend.

The immediate, direct accountability of each individual soul to God in all religious things was the fundamental principle of the Anabaptists. No institution, sacred or secular, no ordinance, no parent or priest, could mediate between the soul and God. Communication between the two was open; they must approach each other through Jesus Christ. This principle determined the character of their religious views; and its corollary, the absolute brotherhood of believers, determined their conception of all human relations, their attitude towards society and the State. Both these principles they regarded as revealed and illuminated by the Scriptures, which, when properly interpreted, were authoritative for all the relations and duties of life. For their proper interpretation, only piety and spiritual enlightenment were necessary; learning might be useful or harmful, according to the spirit of the interpreter. In order to set forth their tenets in more detail, it is best to group them under the three heads of Religious, Political, and Social.

1. Religious views.—(1) In general, the Anabaptists accepted the common Catholic and Protestant doctrine of God as set forth in the Apostles' and the Nicene Creeds. A few, like Denck and Hätzer, doubted, or denied, the essential Deity of Christ; and, on the other hand, Melchior Hofmann and his followers denied the humanity of Christ, maintaining that His was a sort of heavenly flesh, descended through Mary, but without essential relations to humanity.

(2) They opposed the Augustinian theology of the Reformers, insisting vehemently on the freedom of the will and complete moral responsibility. The theology of Luther, Zwingli, and Calvin appeared to them to be contrary to the Scriptures, dishonouring to God, and dangerous to morality. In these views they anticipated Arminius by almost a century.

(3) The Anabaptists maintained the right of the individual to interpret Scripture for himself; and some of them, at least, asserted the superior authority and sanctity of the NT over the OT as the fuller, clearer revelation of God, thus approximating to the modern view of a progressive revelation. Pfister Meier says: 'I obey that in the Old Testament which I find confirmed in the New.' The chief qualification for correct interpretation of the Scripture was the illumination of the Holy Spirit—a doctrine which was strongly emphasized. It was charged that they claimed to have revelations and visions which they regarded as more important than Scripture; but this charge was probably an exaggeration of their real belief in the fact and importance of spiritual illumination.

(4) The true Church was composed of believers only—'saints.' Despairing of bringing the State Church to this standard, they proceeded to set up a new Church on this model, thereby introducing schism into the Protestant ranks. The purity of the Church was to be secured by the baptism of believers only, and preserved by the exercise of strict discipline. (*a*) Infant baptism was regarded as without warrant in Scripture, contrary to the principle of voluntary action in religion, an invention of the devil, and the chief source of the corruption in the Church and of its subjection to the State. In its stead they practised believers' baptism, administering the rite to those who had been baptized in infancy, thus winning the name 'Anabaptists'—re-baptizers—from their opponents; but the name and its implication they earnestly repudiated, declaring that so-called baptism in infancy was no baptism, and claiming for themselves the name of 'brethren' or 'disciples.' Infant baptism, the repudiation of which was the most obvious characteristic of the sect, became the chief battle-ground of the parties. The *mode* of baptism was never a matter of discussion. Most of them practised affusion, the form then prevalent on the Continent; but some of the Swiss and Polish Anabaptists insisted on immersion as the only admissible form, thus anticipating the modern Baptist position. (*b*) The means of preserving the Church pure was the constant application of rigid discipline for moral offences. Unconverted and immoral members were severed from the body relentlessly, the party doubtless going to extremes in this respect. Discipline was exercised by the democratic action of the congregation rather than by the officers of the Church or by the civil power. On all these points they came into sharp collision with the State Church. They strove to reproduce in themselves the life of Christ, and in their Church the life of primitive Christianity, laying great emphasis on the imitation of Christ. While admitting that they had the appearance of unusual purity of life, their opponents declared them to be hypocrites and guilty of grave moral lapses. A few cases, due to fanaticism, especially among the followers of John of Leyden and others of what may be termed the 'fanatical' Anabaptist school, seem to be proven; but, beyond dispute, they in general lived quiet and harmless lives, in striking contrast to the society about them.

(5) The ordinances of Baptism and the Lord's Supper had no sacramental significance. Baptism was rather a declaration of faith and forgiveness than a sacrament of cleansing or regeneration. They were charged with laying an over-emphasis on baptism; but, as a matter of fact, its place in their scheme was not so important as in that of Luther. They insisted on believers' baptism, because they regarded it as Scriptural and necessary to the purity of the Church; Luther insisted on infant baptism, because he regarded it as necessary to the regeneration of the individual. They believed that infants dying in infancy are saved without the necessity of baptism. They agreed with Zwingli in regarding the Supper as a memorial ordinance, rejecting Catholic, Lutheran, and Calvinistic views.

(6) Not much is known of the officers and organization of the Anabaptists. Ordination seems to have been in abeyance in the earlier stages of the

movement, which was a great outburst of missionary activity among laymen. When charged with preaching in improper places and without proper authority, they claimed the authority of a Divine call which needed no ecclesiastical ordination or State authorization. Later abuses in their own ranks forced them to adopt ordination. Preachers were chosen by lot and ordained by the congregation as a recognition of the Divine call, which they still regarded as the necessary part of their qualification for preaching. They rejected with decision the principle of State support in every form, and claimed that preachers ought to be supported by the free-will offerings of the congregation when located, and by Christian hospitality when travelling. They reproached the ministers of the State Church with inactivity and want of care for the people, among whom they should go as shepherds among the sheep.

(7) On eschatology there were great differences of opinion. The majority, perhaps, held sane and Biblical views; but expectation of the early return of Christ bred the wildest fanaticism in others. From the belief of Hofmann that Christ was soon to set up His Kingdom on earth and destroy the wicked, it was but a step to an effort to set up the Kingdom by destroying the wicked, and we have the 'fanatical' Anabaptists and John of Leyden's horrible 'kingdom' at Münster as the outcome. Thomas Münzer also had believed in the use of the sword, and his powerful personality had given the whole movement in Germany a fanatical and dangerous chiliastic bent, which brought ruin on his cause.

(8) Anabaptist worship was necessarily very simple. Persecution and the lack of church buildings made it necessary to worship in small companies, in such a fashion as to attract as little attention as possible. In the earlier years worship probably consisted almost wholly of prayer and instruction; later, singing occupied a large place. Their own compositions were set to popular music and sung far and wide. These songs, often written in prison, reveal profound religious feeling and unwavering faith and hope (cf. Wolkan, *Lieder der Wiedertäufer; Aus Bundt*).

2. Political views.—(1) The Anabaptists regarded the State as a necessary evil, ordained of God indeed, and therefore to be obeyed where its obligations were not in conflict with conscience. The charge that they were opposed to magistracy altogether is without foundation in fact. They denied the supremacy of the State in the realm of conscience, and resisted its assumption of authority here, even to death; as to other things they inculcated obedience. The conscience was absolutely free under God. The State had no religious duties; it was needed only to protect the good and punish the wicked. This doctrine involved complete disestablishment; universal toleration; freedom of worship, organization, and teaching. These views came to full, clear, and vigorous expression in Hübmaier especially. Repudiated and execrated then, this contention has been adopted in modern times with more or less completeness by all civilized lands.

(2) Many of the Anabaptists maintained that no Christian could hold civil office, because such elevation was in conflict with the principle of Christian brotherhood and equality; besides, it often required the infliction of capital punishment, and to kill was under no circumstances permissible to a Christian. This tenet, regarded by their opponents as destructive of all government, was not so understood by themselves. They did not believe capital punishment was necessary to the suppression of crime, nor did they regard all who bore the Christian name as Christians. Their opponents said: 'If no Christian can act as magistrate, we must go to the heathen or Turks for governors.' 'No,' replied the Anabaptists, 'there are but few Christians even in Christian lands, and hosts of men are left for rulers.' The different meanings attached by the two parties to the word 'Christian' were the source of the misunderstanding. Their anticipation of the modern movement for the abolition of capital punishment is noteworthy. Hübmaier and others, however, maintained the right of a Christian to hold civil office.

(3) They opposed the oath under any and all circumstances, on purely Biblical grounds (Mt 5^{34}). This, again, was regarded by Zwingli and others as destructive of civil government, which was thought to rest upon the inviolability of the oath. No such importance and sacredness were attached to it by the Anabaptists, who taught that one's assertion should be as sacredly kept as the oath. Under the threat of execution they sometimes took the oath; but it was not regarded as binding, because taken under duress.

(4) The Anabaptists were relentless opponents of war as the great destroyer of human life, which they held to be inviolable. Under pressure they paid war taxes, assisted in building fortifications, and rendered other services of this kind; but they suffered imprisonment and death rather than bear arms. The Münster kingdom was a hideous caricature of the whole movement, and cannot be cited in opposition to this statement. Indeed, the Anabaptists' insistence upon peace was the main cause of the constant war made upon them. The military basis of society in the 16th cent. made such advocates of peace appear exceedingly dangerous to national existence; but this cause of bitter denunciation and persecution may yet become their crown of glory as the world swings into the era of universal peace.

3. Social and economic views.—(1) In imitation of the primitive Christian Church, the Anabaptists were strongly inclined to a voluntary and benevolent communism in the acquisition and administration of property (Ac $2^{44f.}$). This opinion, which appears in the earliest stages of the movement, was fully developed in Moravia, where many of them lived and worked in great communal settlements (Loserth, *Communismus*, etc.). Among the German and Dutch Anabaptists appeared a tendency towards enforced communism, as seen in Thomas Münzer and in the Münster kingdom. But a large part, perhaps a majority, of the Anabaptists, did not favour actual communism in any form; they strenuously maintained, however, that all property belonged primarily to the Lord, and must be freely used in ministering to the needy. They conceived themselves in the position of stewards, under solemn obligation to administer the Lord's money for the highest good of mankind.

(2) They opposed the lending of money at interest, refused to accept interest themselves, and paid it unwillingly to others. Money, they held, should be lent for the benefit of the borrower rather than the lender. Proper fraternal relations forbade the exploitation of the needs of a brother; besides, the practice was regarded as contrary to the explicit teaching of Scripture (Dt $23^{19f.}$, Ps 15^{5}).

(3) They refused to pay ecclesiastical taxes, believing that religion should be supported by the voluntary gifts of religious people.

Glancing backwards over their views, we see that the Anabaptists were several centuries in advance of their age. They were the modern men of their time. Some of their tenets, then universally anathematized and persecuted, have been adopted by all civilized lands, *e.g.* universal religious toleration; others have been widely incorporated in the newer lands (America and Australia), and are making headway in the older societies, *e.g.* complete separation of Church and State; yet others are still objects of endeavour, only seen as far-off boons, as, for example, abolition of war; some, as communism, are not likely ever to be adopted widely. It is remarkable that these simple people should have drawn from a fresh study of the Bible so many great ideas that still float before the race as high and distant ideals.

LITERATURE.—Anabaptist writings and disputations, now very rare and widely scattered in the libraries of Europe, of which but few have been reprinted or translated; the pertinent writings of their opponents in 16th cent.; various court records, published and unpublished, and a few chronicles. The earlier writers on the Anabaptists, such as Fischer, Gast, Meschovius, Ottius, Sender, and others, are more or less partisan and unreliable. The large recent literature, of which only a few of the more important works can be mentioned, is more just. The first-hand treatments are in German for the most part, though there are several excellent works in English and a few in French.—**H. Barge**, *Andreas Bodenstein von Karlstadt*, Leipzig, 1905; **J. von Beck**, *Geschichtsbücher d. Wiedertäufer in Oesterreich-Ungarn von 1526 bis 1785*, Vienna, 1883; **K. W. Bouterwek**, *Zur Lit. u. Gesch. d. Wiedertäufer, besonders in den Rheinlanden*, Bonn, 1864; **P. Burckhardt**, *Die Basler Täufer*, Basel, 1898; **H. S. Burrage**, *Hist. of the Anabaptists in Switzerland*, Philadelphia, 1881; **C. A. Cornelius**, *Berichte d. Augenzeugen über das Münsterische Wiedertäuferreich*, 1853, *Gesch. d. Münsterischen Aufruhrs*, Leipzig, 1855; **H. Detmer**, *Bernhard Rothmann*, Münster, 1904; **E. Egli**, *Actensammlung z. Gesch. d. Züricher Reformation*, Zurich, 1879, also *Die St. Galler Täufer*, Zurich, 1887, and *Die Züricher Wiedertäufer zur Reformationszeit*, Zurich, 1878; **M. Geisberg**, *Die Münsterischen Wiedertäufer*, Strassburg, 1907; **C. Gerbert**, *Gesch. d. Strassburger Sectenbewegung z. Zeit d. Reformation, 1524–34*, Strassburg, 1889; **K. Hase**, *Das Reich d. Wiedertäufer*, Leipzig, 1860; **R. Heath**, *Anabaptism from its Rise at Zwickau to its Fall at Münster, 1521 to 1536*, London, 1895; **L. Keller**, *Ein Apostel d. Wiedertäufer* (Denck), Leipzig, 1882, and *Gesch. d. Wiedertäufer u. ihres Reichs zu Münster*, Münster, 1880; **J. Loserth**, *Der Anabaptismus in Tirol*, Vienna, 1892, also *Communismus d. Mährischen Wiedertäufer in 16 u. 17 Jahrhundert*, Vienna, 1894, *Die Stadt Waldshut u. d. vorderösterreichische Regierung in d. Jahren, 1523–6*, Vienna, 1891, *Doctor Balthasar Hübmaier u. d. Anfänge d. Wiedertaufe in Mähren*, Brünn, 1893, *Georg Blaurock u. d. Anfänge d. Anabaptismus in Graubündten u. Tirol*, Berlin, 1899; **O. Merx**, *Thomas Münzer u. H. Pfeiffer*, Göttingen, 1889; **E. Müller**, *Gesch. d. Bernischen Täufer*, Frauenfeld, 1895; **A. H. Newman**, *Hist. of Anti-Pedobaptism from the Rise of Pedobaptism to A.D. 1609*, Philadelphia, 1897; **A. Nicoladoni**, *Joh. Bünderlin v. Linz*, etc., Berlin, 1893; **E. C. Pike**, *The Story of the Anabaptists*, London; **K. Rembert**, *Die Wiedertäufer in Herzogthum Jülich*, Münster, 1893; **T. W. Röhrich**, *Zur Gesch. d. Strassburgischen Wiedertäufer in d. Jahren 1527–43*; **J. K. Seidemann**, *Thomas Münzer*, Dresden, 1842; **Vedder**, *Balthasar Hübmaier, the Leader of the Anabaptists*, New York, 1905; **R. Wolkan**, *Die Lieder d. Wiedertäufer*, Berlin, 1903; **F. O. zur Linden**, *Melchior Hofmann*, etc., Haarlem, 1885. Besides the above, many valuable articles will be found in Cyclopædias and Journals of History and Theology, as well as brief treatments in all the Church Histories (fullest in **Lindsay**, *History of the Reformation*, ii. [1907] 430–469).

W. J. M'GLOTHLIN.

ANÆSTHESIA.—Dioscorides in treating of mandragora gives a description of its virtues as an anæsthetic, and prescriptions for its use. Of one preparation he says that it is given to produce anæsthesia (βούλονται ἀναισθησίαν ποιῆσαι) in patients to be cut or cauterized; and of another, that the patient can be put to sleep for three or four hours so as to be cut or cauterized, feeling nothing (αἰσθησόμενον οὐδένος). Before his day and since, various drugs have been used to produce insensibility to suffering. The most efficacious of them, besides mandragora, were opium, Indian hemp, hemlock, henbane, belladona. They were usually given internally in the form of infusions, tinctures, and extracts. More rarely they were smoked when incandescent, or inhaled in the form of hot vapours. When chemistry took the place of alchemy and produced more definitely volatile substances, it was found that among them were some possessed of sedative properties; and in 1795, Dr. Pearson advocated the use of sulphuric ether to relieve the cough in cases of asthma. When the various gases came to be differentiated and their properties investigated, Sir Humphry Davy found that nitrous oxide—'laughing-gas,' as it was called—had the power of alleviating pain; and in 1800 he said, 'As nitrous oxide in its extensive operation appears capable of destroying physical pain, it may probably be used in surgical operations in which no great effusion of blood takes place.' His suggestion was not taken up. Laughing-gas continued, however, to be administered from time to time in chemical class-rooms and at public entertainments. In 1844, Dr. Horace Wells, a dentist in Hartford, Connecticut, observed that individuals might be injured when under the influence of the gas without being conscious of any pain. He conceived the idea of testing its effects during the extraction of teeth, and got his assistant, Dr. Rigg, to extract one of his own molars after he had produced insensibility in himself by the inhalation of nitrous oxide. After having proved its efficacy in a series of cases, he went to Boston to give a demonstration of its value in the Massachusetts General Hospital. In the test case, by some mischance, the anæsthesia produced was imperfect, and he was dismissed with something of contempt. His health broke down, and he went to Europe to recruit.

On 16th October 1846, Dr. William Thomas Green Morton, who had been assistant to Wells, put to sleep with sulphuric ether, in the same Boston Hospital, a patient on whom Professor J. C. Warren operated for removal of a small tumour in the neck, and on the day following he put to sleep another patient operated on painlessly by Dr. Hayward. Morton had consulted Wells, after his return to Hartford, as to the preparation of nitrous oxide, and had been advised to get from Professor Jackson, Professor of Chemistry in Harvard University, the necessary directions. Professor Jackson suggested that instead of nitrous oxide he should make trial of sulphuric ether, and Dr. Morton had experimented on himself and some of his dental patients before he offered to demonstrate its effects in the public theatre. He called his preparation *lethēon*, and took out a patent for its use. He associated Dr. Jackson with himself in obtaining the patent, and admitted that Dr. Smilie, who had previously anæsthetized a patient by causing inhalation of sulphuric ether with opium dissolved in it, might continue the use of his preparation without infringement of the patent. It was Morton's demonstration on the 16th of October 1846 that truly marked the beginning of the era of anæsthesia, and gave the impulse to its adoption in all branches of the profession throughout the world. But for a time there was unseemly strife as to priority of the discovery, Jackson and Wells both disputing the claim of Morton to be the discoverer of the new mode of producing insensibility to pain. So that, although a monument in honour of the great event was set up in Boston, years passed ere it was finally decided to inscribe on it the solitary name of Dr. Morton, and Wendell Holmes is credited with having made the suggestion that E(I)THER might do.

Meanwhile news had come to Europe of the great discovery that the inhalation of ether vapour could be employed with safety so as surely to control the pain of surgical operations, and surgeons in Great Britain and the Continent began to make trial of it in all directions. On the 17th of January 1847, James Young Simpson, Professor of Midwifery in the University of Edinburgh, etherized a woman in labour. The benefit of etherization in surgery was established. But would it be safe to apply it in midwifery cases? Would the pain of labour be removed without interference with the labour effects? Could the patient be kept for the necessary time under the influence of the narcotic? What might be the after effects? What of the child? The test case was one in which Simpson had predetermined, because of pelvic deformity, to extract the child by turning, and the result showed that labour could go on in its course although the sensations of pain usually attendant on it were for the time being altogether abrogated. When the virtue of the anæsthetic had been proved in other cases of both natural and instrumental labour, he claimed for women the right to be relieved of this sorest of all human suffering—their labour-pains. There had been misgivings in some minds as to the propriety of the administration of ether to surgical patients, and when it was proposed further to abolish the pains of labour, there arose a perfect storm of opposition to the practice. Simpson had to bear the stress of it because of his application of it in midwifery, and because some months later, searching for a substance that might be free from some of the drawbacks of ether, he discovered, on the 4th of November 1847, the anæsthetic virtue of chloroform, and introduced it as a substitute for the earlier anæsthetic. Oliver Wendell Holmes had suggested that the term 'anæsthesia' should be applied to the process; but Simpson's papers, like those of most of the other writers up till the end of 1847, spoke of 'Etherization in Surgery,' 'The Inhalation of Sulphuric Ether in Midwifery,' and such-like. It was only after the new narcotic began to be used that it became necessary to fall back on the Greek expression which would be applicable to the effect of any agent; and when at a later period Simpson traced the history of narcosis and narcotics, and found Theocritus speaking of Antigone having a painless labour because Lucina poured *νοδυνία* over her, he regretted that he had not adopted the terms 'nodynia' and 'nodynic' rather than 'anæsthesia' and 'anæsthetic.'

The occasional deaths resulting from the use of both ether and chloroform led to fresh experiments with nitrous oxide, which has been found especially safe and satisfactory in operations of short duration, as in tooth-pulling, so that it is now the anæsthetic most frequently employed in dentistry. Other volatile liquids have also been found to be possessed of anæsthetic properties, such as amylene, ethidene, bichloride of mythylene, etc. But none of them is free from danger, and none of them is so serviceable as chloroform in the ease and rapidity with which patients can be anæsthetized with relatively small quantities of the drug, and in the comfort which attends the subsequent awakening. There is still much discussion as to the relative values of ether and chloroform. For, whilst the former requires special apparatus in its administration and is apt to have troublesome *sequelæ*, the proportion of fatal cases is distinctly less than is met with in the use of chloroform. So that members of the profession who specialize as anæsthetists prefer its use in hospital practice and for patients undergoing the major operations of surgery, whilst chloroform remains the favourite anæsthetic in hot climates, in the lying-in room, and in the hands of military surgeons and busy general practitioners in their ordinary round of daily work. The writer has in the course of more than half a century seen some thousands of patients under the influence of anæsthetics—commonly of chloroform, and he has not seen a fatal case; but he knows that any day the record may be closed.

Some have sought to avoid the danger associated with all means of producing general anæsthesia by the superinduction of local anæsthesia. The skin has been rendered insensible by applications of ice, of ether spray, as suggested by Sir Benjamin Ward Richardson, or of ethyl chloride so as to freeze the surface. Alone, or conjoined with freezing processes, electricity, cocaine, eucaine, and other analgesics have been applied to the surface or injected hypodermically so as to produce a more lasting degree of local anæsthesia. Ovariotomy has been performed on a patient who lay still and made no complaint of suffering during the operation, when the seat of incision in the abdominal wall had been rendered insensible by freezing with ethyl chloride and hypodermic injections of cocaine. Such measures are, as a rule, however, only applicable for minor operations. A wider and more lasting form of localized anæsthesia was introduced by Dr. Corning of New York, in 1885, who found that injections of cocaine into the arachnoid space in the lumbar region of the spinal chord produced anæsthesia in the lower half of the body, of sufficient intensity and duration to allow of the carrying out without pain of amputations of the lower limbs and other grave operations in the lower half of the abdomen. Cocaine and its derivates and also stovaine with adrenalin have been used in this way with results in midwifery and in various surgical procedures that give hope of a great future for this method of superinduction of localized anæsthesia.

It should be added that from time to time insensibility to pain has been produced by means that were not medicinal, but purely mental. In the 18th cent., Mesmer produced, by what he supposed was an animal magnetism, a series of phenomena which were more carefully investigated in the middle of last century by Mr. J. Braid. Under the designation 'hypnotism,' Braid described a state of the system into which individuals could be brought by having their attention fixed on a given object for a length of time until there ensued an exhaustion of some elements in the nervous system and the subject became amenable to the control of the operator. The person thus hypnotized can be made insensible to suffering at the suggestion of the hypnotizer. Dr. Esdaile and other surgeons in the Indian medical service reported a series of cases where operations, both major and minor, were performed on patients in a condition of unconsciousness thus produced. But hypnotism has been found applicable mainly to cases where there is disturbance in the nervous system; and its use for the relief of the pain of surgical operations is restricted by the circumstances (1) that not every patient can be hypnotized, and (2) that the patient may have to be experimented on repeatedly before the hypnotizer gains sufficient control to command the necessary degree of anæsthesia. The practice has not sufficiently commended itself to the medical profession, even so far as to encourage more than a few members of it to try for themselves whether they were capable of exercising a hypnotic influence.

LITERATURE.—Henry J. Bigelow, *Ether and Chloroform*, Boston, 1848; James Braid, *On Hypnotism or Nervous Sleep*, 1843; H. Braun, 'Ueber Infiltrationsanæsthesie und regioniäre Anæsthesie,' Volkmann's *Sammlung*, 228; J. Leonard Corning, *Headaches and Neuralgia*, 1890; Doloris and Malartic, 'Analgésie obstétricale par injections de cocaine dans l'arachnoide lombaire,' *Comptes rendus de la Société d'Obstétrique*, 1900; James Esdaile, *Mesmerism as an Anæsthetic in India*, 1852; George Foy, *Anæsthetics, Ancient and Modern*, 1889; James Miller, *Surgical Experience of Chloroform*, 1848; W. T. G. Morton, *Historical Memoranda relative to the Discovery of Etherization*, 1871; Johann Müller, *Anæsthetika*, 1898; Report of Select Committee of U.S. Senate on the 'Discovery of the means by which the human body is rendered insensible to pain,' Feb. 1853, 32nd Congress; Semi-Centennial of Anæsthesia, Massachusetts General Hospital, Boston, 1897; T. Hookham Silvester, 'The Administration of Anæsthetics in Former Times,' *London Medical Gazette*, 1848; A. R. Simpson, 'The Jubilee of Anæsthetic Midwifery,' *Glasgow Medical Journ.*, March 1897; J. Y. Simpson, *Works*, vol. ii. 'Anæsthesia'; T. R. Smilie, *On the History of the Original Application of Anæsthetic Agents*, 1848; Edward Warren, *Some Account of the Lethēon; or, Who is the Discoverer?* 1847; J. Collins Warren, 'The Influence of Anæsthesia on the Surgery of the Nineteenth Century,' *Transactions of the American Surgical Association*, 1897.

A. R. SIMPSON.

ANĀGATA VAṀSA ('Record of the Future').—A Pāli poem of 142 stanzas on the future Buddha, Metteyya. It is stated in the *Gandha Vaṁsa* (*JPTS*, 1886, p. 61) that it was written by Kassapa; and in the *Sāsana Vaṁsa Dīpa* (v.[1204]) we are told that he was a poet who lived in the Chola country. We may probably conclude that he did not reside at Kāñchipura, the Chola capital, as in that case the name Kāñchipura, which would have suited the metre equally well, would probably have been put in the place of Chola-raṭṭha. The further statement (*Gandha Vaṁsa, l.c.*), that he also wrote the *Buddha Vaṁsa*, seems to be a mistake. And we know nothing either of his date or of the other books attributed to him. The poem has been edited for the Pāli Text Society by the late Professor Minayeff (*JPTS*, 1886, pp. 33–53), with extracts from the commentary, which is by Upatissa (see *Gandha Vaṁsa*, p. 72). Of the latter writer also nothing is at present known, unless he be identical with the author of the *Mahā Bodhi Vaṁsa* who wrote in Ceylon about A.D. 970.*

Our ignorance about the date of the *Anāgata Vaṁsa* is regrettable, as the question of the origin and growth of the belief held by the later Buddhists in this future Buddha, Metteyya, is important. As is well known, there are statements in the *Nikāyas* (*e.g. Dīgha*, II. 83, 144, 255) that future Buddhas would arise, but, with one exception, neither the *Nikāyas* nor any book in the *Piṭakas* mention Metteyya. His name occurs, it is true, in the concluding stanza of the *Buddha Vaṁsa*, but this is an addition by a later hand, and does not belong to the work itself. Neither is Metteyya mentioned in the *Netti Pakaraṇa*. The exception referred to is a passage in the 26th Dialogue of the *Dīgha* which records a prophecy, put into the Buddha's mouth, that Metteyya would have thousands of followers where the Buddha himself had only hundreds. This passage is quoted in the *Milinda* (p. 159); but the *Milinda* does not refer anywhere else to Metteyya. In the *Mahāvastu* (one of the earliest extant works in Buddhist Sanskrit) the legend is in full vogue. Metteyya is mentioned eleven times, two or three of the passages giving details about him. One of these agrees with the *Anāgata Vaṁsa* in its statement of the size of his city, Ketumatī (*Mahāv.* iii. 240 = *Anāg. Vaṁ.* 8); but discrepancies exist between the others (*Mahāv.* iii. 246 and iii. 330 differ from *Anāg. Vaṁ.* 78 and 107). It is in this poem that we find the fullest and most complete account of the tradition, which evidently varied in different times and places.

This is really conclusive as to the comparatively late date of the poem. In earlier times it was enough to say that future Buddhas would arise; then a few details, one after another, were invented about the immediately succeeding Buddha. When in the south of India the advancing wave of ritualism and mythology threatened to overwhelm the ancient simplicity of the faith, a despairing hope looked for the time of the next Buddha, and decked out his story with lavish completeness.

Three points of importance are quite clear from the statements in this work. (1) There is little or nothing original in the tradition of which it is the main evidence. It is simply built up in strict imitation of the early forms of the Buddha legend, only names and numbers differing. But it is the old form, both of legend and of doctrine.

(2) There is sufficient justification for the comparison between Metteyya and the Western idea of a Messiah. The ideas are, of course, not at all the same; but there are several points of analogy. The time of Metteyya is described as a Golden Age in which kings, ministers, and people will vie one with another in maintaining the reign of righteousness and the victory of the truth. It should be added, however, that the teachings of the future Buddha also, like that of every other Buddha, will suffer corruption, and pass away in time.

(3) We can remove a misconception as to the meaning of the name. *Metteyya Buddha* does not mean 'the Buddha of Love.' *Metteyya* is simply his *gotra* name, that is, the name of the *gens* to which his ancestors belonged—something like our family name. It is probably, like *Gotama*, a patronymic, and means 'descendant of Mettayu.' Another Metteyya, in the *Sutta Nipāta*, asks the Buddha questions, and is doubtless a historical person. We can admit only that whoever first used this as the family name of the future Buddha may very likely have associated, and probably did associate, it in his mind with the other word *mettā*, which means 'love.' It would only be one of those plays upon words which are so constantly met with in early Indian literature. The personal name of the future Buddha is given in the poem, and elsewhere also, as *Ajita*, 'unconquered.'

The poem in one MS has the fuller title *Anāgata-Buddhassa Vaṇṇanā*, 'Record of the future Buddha' (*JPTS*, 1886, p. 37). There is another work, quite different from the one here described, though the title is the same. It gives an account, apparently, in prose and verse, of ten future Buddhas, of whom Metteyya is one (*ib.* p. 39). This work is still unedited.

LITERATURE.—H. C. Warren, *Buddhism in Translations*, Cambridge, Mass., 1896, pp. 481–486, has translated a summary of one recension of this work.

T. W. RHYS DAVIDS.

ANĀHITA (Gr. Ἀναεῖτις).—Anāhita is one of the chief deities in Mazdaism, and we get fairly accurate information about her character from a complete *Yašt* (v) and numerous other passages in the Avesta. Ardvī Surā Anāhita, that is, undoubtedly, 'the high, powerful, immaculate one,' is a goddess of fertilizing waters, and more particularly of a supernatural spring, located in the region of the stars, from which all the rivers of the world flow (Darmesteter). The fertility which the divine water caused in the earth was extended to the animal kingdom, and, according to the Avesta, Anāhita 'purifies the seed of males and the womb and the milk of females' (*Vendīdād*, vii. 16; *Yašt*, v. 5), and is invoked by marriageable girls, and by women at the time of childbirth (*Yašt*, v.). At the same time she is thought of as a goddess of war, who rides in a chariot drawn by four white horses (*Yašt*, v. 11, 13), which are wind, rain, cloud, and hail (*Yašt*, v. 120), and she bestows victory on the combatants, and gives them sturdy teams and brave companions. The Avestan hymn, after enumerating all the heroes of the past who sacrificed to Anāhita, including Zoroaster, whom she instructed in her worship, concludes with a very exact description of her appearance and her dress (*Yašt*, v. 126 ff.). 'She is a beautiful maiden, powerful and tall, her girdle fastened high, wrapped in a gold-embroidered cloak, wearing earrings, a necklace, and a crown of gold, and adorned with thirty otter skins.' These minute details are undoubtedly inspired by a sculptural type, and this passage of the Avesta has rightly been connected with the famous text of Berossus (Clem. Alex. *Protrept.* 5), which says that Artaxerxes Mnemon (B.C. 404–361) was the first to teach the Persians to worship anthropomorphic statues in the temples of Babylon, Susa (cf. Pliny, *Hist. Nat.* vi. 27, 135), and Ecbatana (cf. Plutarch, *Vit. Artax.* 27; Polybius, x. 27. 12), in Persia, Bactriana, Damascus, and Sardis. These statues were probably reproductions of a Babylonian original, and perhaps, as has been suggested, Anāhita might even be identical with the Semitic goddess Anat. This would account for the passage in Herodotus (i. 131), according to which 'the Persians learned from the Assyrians to sacrifice to the "heavenly" Aphrodite, whom they

* Geiger, *Mahavaṁsa und Dipavaṁsa*, Leipzig, 1905, p. 88.

call Mithra.' The ancient historian had probably written 'Mithra' by mistake for 'Anāhita.' As a matter of fact, the two divinities are united, and form, so to speak, a pair in the cuneiform inscriptions of the Achæmenians, in which they figure precisely from the reign of Artaxerxes Mnemon (Weissbach-Bang, *Die altpersischen Keilinschriften*, 1893, 44, 46).

The information of Berossus on the diffusion of the Anāhita cult throughout the Persian empire is confirmed by a mass of evidence. Outside of Iran, the goddess is found in Armenia (Gelzer, *Sit. Gesellsch. Wiss. Leipzig*, 1896, 111 ff.; see also art. ARMENIA [Zoroastrian]). She had temples at Artaxata, at Yashtishat in Tauranitis, and especially at Erēz in Akilisene, the whole region of which was consecrated to her (*Anaetica regio*, Pliny, v. 83). The Erēz sanctuary, which contained a golden statue of Anāhita, was famous for its wealth, and the daughters of the noble families of Armenia used to go there and prostitute themselves to strangers before their marriage (Strabo, xi. 532 C). This sacred custom, which is probably of Semitic origin, seems to be a modification of the ancient exogamy (cf. Cumont, *Religions orientales*, Paris, 1907, 287). Old traditions continued to hold ground at Erēz under the Romans; the sacred buffaloes of Anāhita wandered at liberty in Akilisene, and the victims for sacrifice had to be captured by hunting (*RA*, 1905, i. 25 ff.).

The Persian goddess was worshipped also in Pontus and in Cappadocia (Strabo, xi. 512 C, xii. 559 C, xv. 733 C), perhaps also at Castabala in Cilicia (Strabo, xii. 537 C). In these districts she became identified with the great autochthonous divinity Mā, and her temples were attended by a number of sacred slaves (ἱερόδουλοι) of both sexes. At Zela in Pontus, a festival, the Sacæa, which was probably of Babylonian origin, was held annually.

It is especially in Lydia that Anāhita has left numerous traces of her presence. She was probably, as Berossus states (cf. above), brought into Sardis by Artaxerxes II., and there became amalgamated with Kybebe (Cybele), the Great Mother honoured throughout the country. The well-known figures of a winged goddess holding a lion in either hand, to which the designation 'Persian Artemis' has been given, really represent this syncretic divinity worshipped as 'mistress of the beasts' (πότνια θηρῶν) (Radet, *CAIBL*, 1906, p. 285). Descriptions of her noisy rites exist as early as in the works of the tragic poet Diogenes of Athens (Nauck, *Trag. Græc. Fragm.* 776). Her principal temples were at Hierocæsarea (Paus. v. 27. 5, vii. 6. 6; Tac. *Ann.* iii. 62: 'delubrum rege Cyro dicatum'; cf. *Bull. Corr. hellén.* xi. 95), and at Hypæpa (Paus. *l.c.*; cf. *RA*, 1885, ii. 114; Dittenberger, *Orientis Græci Inscriptiones Selectæ*, 1903–05, 470); but her name also appears in a large number of inscriptions in this vicinity (Reinach, *Chroniques d'Orient*, 157 ff., 215 ff.; Buresch, *Aus Lydien*, 1898, 28, 66 ff., 128; Roscher, *Lexikon der Mythologie, s.v.* 'Persike'; Wright, *Harvard Studies*, 1895, vi. 55 ff.). The conception formed of the goddess and the ceremonies by means of which she was worshipped seem to have remained faithful to the ancient Iranian traditions; she was always regarded as the goddess of sacred waters (Ἀναεῖτιν τὴν ἀπὸ τοῦ ἱεροῦ ὕδατος, Buresch, *l.c.* p. 118), and her liturgy was repeated in a 'barbarian' language (Pausanias, v. 27. 5).

The Greeks identified Anāhita, on the one hand, on account of her warlike character, with Athene, and, on the other, as a goddess of fertility, with Aphrodite (Berossus, *l.c.*; Agathias, ii. 24; Photius, *Bibl.* 94). Already, in Iran, as noted above, under the influence of the Chaldæan star-worship, Anāhita had become the planet Venus. But the name usually applied to her in the West was 'Persian Artemis' or 'Persian Diana' (Ἄρτεμις Περσική or Περσία, 'Diana Persica') (Pausanias, vii. 6. 6; *Bull. Corr. hellén.* xi. 65; Diodorus, v. 77; Plutarch, *Lucull.* 24; Tacitus, *Ann.* iii. 62). As the bull was sacred to her, she was confounded especially with 'Artemis Tauropolos' in Lydia, as well as in Armenia and Cappadocia. It was probably from this composite cult of the Asiatic Tauropolos that the 'taurobolium' penetrated into the Roman world (Pauly-Wissowa, *s.v.* 'Anaïtis'; *RA*, 1905, i. 28 ff.). In the Latin countries, the Persian goddess, assimilated with the *Magna Mater* of Phrygia, certainly remained in close connexion with Mithra, whose mysteries spread to the West after the 1st cent. of our era (Cumont, *Textes et monuments figurés relatifs aux mystères de Mithra*, i. 333 ff. and *passim*).

LITERATURE.—Windischmann, 'Die persische Anāhita,' *Sitzungsb. Akad. München*, 1856; Spiegel, *Eranische Altertumskunde*, 1873, ii. 54 ff.; Darmesteter, *Zend-Avesta*, 1893, ii. 363 and *passim*; Roscher, *Lexikon der Mythol. s.vv.* 'Anaïtis' (Ed. Meyer) and 'Persike' (Höfer). FR. CUMONT.

ANALOGY.—The determination of the limits within which validity belongs to the argument from analogy is a problem of long standing. Though the discussion of the question properly falls within the sphere of logic rather than of theology, yet the latter science is intimately concerned with its decision. So long as arguments from analogy occur with such frequency and have so important a part to play alike in the defence and in the exposition of revelation, the theologian will not be easy unless his confidence in this logical process be firmly established. Moreover, even the warmest advocate of the argument from analogy will admit that as an instrument of thought it is specially liable to abuse, and that its employment involves at least risks of error which require to be explicitly recognized in order to be avoided. In this article the subject of treatment will be the use of analogy in theology; but in the interest of clearness of statement it will be necessary to begin with some brief reference to general principles.

I. Analogy: its definition in logic.—At the outset we are confronted with a considerable lack of agreement among logicians as to the correct definition of analogy. Some authorities, content to fall in with popular usage, identify the argument from analogy with the argument from resemblances. Such, for example, is the position adopted by J. S. Mill, who explains it to be the inference that when one object resembles another in a certain number of known points it will probably resemble it in some further unknown points also. Such a logical procedure is akin to induction, but is distinguishable therefrom by the circumstance that no causal or necessary connexion has yet been established between the known points of resemblance and the further points whose resemblance is only inferred. The conclusion is, therefore, not demonstrable but probable, and the amount of probability will vary in accordance with the number and the importance of the resemblances which have been observed, and will be correspondingly diminished by any ascertained points of dissimilarity between the two objects. In estimating the extent of the probability, account must be taken of the proportion borne by the number of ascertained resemblances to the supposed number of unknown properties (cf. Mill, *System of Logic*, III. xx.).

This conception of analogy is, however, repudiated by other logicians as altogether too lax and unscientific. Influenced by the meaning of the word in the original Greek, and by its primary use as a term of mathematics, they insist that analogy is a resemblance not between things, but only between relations.

'Two things,' writes Dr. Whately, 'may be connected together by analogy, though they have in themselves no resemblance; for analogy is the resemblance of ratios or relations; thus, as a sweet taste gratifies the palate, so does a sweet sound gratify the ear, hence the word sweet is applied to both, though no flavour can resemble a sound in itself' (*Elements of Logic*[2], p. 168).

The last words of the sentence are noteworthy. They indicate that upon this view of analogy no legitimate inference can be drawn from the nature of the one pair of related terms to the nature of the other pair. The relation between palate and taste may be strictly similar to the relation between ear and sound, but we cannot therefore draw inferences as to the nature of the one from what we know of the other. This is an important contention with far-reaching consequences, and its influence upon theological argument will appear presently.

This definition of analogy has the merit of scientific exactness, and of being in strict accordance with the type exhibited by mathematics, but it is at the same time open to serious criticism. The restrictions which it imposes upon the function of analogy are such as would almost entirely invalidate the use of the argument in practical life. Men in their daily concerns do not confine their analogical arguments to the consideration of mere relations, but freely draw inferences as to the nature of things. Although this is a merely practical objection, it is not without support in the theory of analogy. It has been pointed out that *some* identity of nature is always postulated in every analogy. In mathematical analogy, for example, it is at least necessary that both pairs of terms should be magnitudes. And, again, in the analogy between sound and taste, though in a sense there is no resemblance between them, yet they are both sensations. The heterogeneity is not absolute. Exception, therefore, may fairly be taken to the extreme statement of Whately, that no inference is permissible from the nature of the one to the nature of the other. And the theologian will press the point; for in his hands the argument from analogy is usually of the more flexible and practical form, which cannot be confined within the narrow limits set by the type of mathematical analogy. It is concerned with realities rather than with abstract relations.

2. Analogy in religious vocabulary.—The entire vocabulary of religion is based upon the perception of analogies between the material and the spiritual worlds. Words which now bear an immaterial and spiritual significance were originally used to denote visible and tangible objects. If in many languages the word for breath or wind has come to be used for the soul, it is because at an early stage of their development men became conscious of an analogy between the lightness and invisibility of air and the supposed properties of the human spirit. To a later and more critical age the analogy may appear thin and crude; but it must be remembered that the initiation of a religious vocabulary dates from the childhood of the race. In the gradual evolution of religion, crudities have been refined away, until the original meaning of many words now used exclusively with a spiritual significance has been forgotten. But throughout the whole course of the development the necessity for finding analogical words as a vehicle for the expression of spiritual truth has never been outgrown. The innermost secret of religion is still put into speech by means of the analogy of human fatherhood. Thus witness is borne in all ages to the instinctive readiness with which men assume a parallelism between the things which are seen and the things which are not seen. To what extent that parallelism really exists and how far it affords us grounds of inference to the real nature of the spiritual world, is the problem which every philosophy of religion sets out to solve.

3. Analogy as a means to the knowledge of the spiritual world.—Not only the vocabulary but the content of natural religion are derived from the source of analogical reasoning. For natural religion begins with the assumption of a resemblance between God and the world, sufficient to justify the inference that the wonder and majesty of Creation will in some sort reflect the wonder and majesty of the Creator (cf. Wis 13[5] 'For by the greatness and beauty of the creatures proportionably [ἀναλόγως] the maker of them is seen'). Though this is the only Biblical passage in which the word 'analogy' appears in this connexion, yet the thought of the world as the visible expression of the attributes of the invisible God is of constant recurrence in Scripture. It is familiar to the Psalmist (Ps 19). It is stated explicitly by St. Paul: 'For the invisible things of him from the creation of the world are clearly seen, being understood by the things that are made, even his eternal power and Godhead' (Ro 1[20]). This assumption of a significant analogy between God and the world is not argumentatively justified in the Bible. Like the other principles of natural religion, it is taken as accepted truth. And the belief culminates in the doctrine of man's creation in the image of God. It is impossible to overestimate the formative influence of this conception of human nature as the true analogue of the Divine. As it was one of the controlling factors in the development of Jewish religion, so has it exercised an even more dominant influence upon Christian thought, supplying, as it does, the philosophic basis for the doctrine of the Incarnation. Throughout the whole history of Christian doctrine the question of the reality of the likeness of man to God, *i.e.* of the truth of the analogy between Divine and human nature, has been one of the pivots of controversy. Men have arranged themselves in opposite camps according as they have been more or less ready to accept this belief.

4. Analogy in Patristic writings.—The great theologians of the early centuries, following the precedent of Scripture, made free use of analogy for the double purpose of defence and exposition. It was to them a convenient means of exposing the hollowness of many commonly urged objections, and a ready method of illustrating the difficulties of abstract theology by means of familiar and concrete examples. Illustrations of so frequent a practice are scarcely necessary. But perhaps a single example from East and West may not be out of place.

The following quotation from Gregory of Nyssa indicates how clearly he recognized the character of the logical process which he was employing: Ὥσπερ δὲ τὸν Λόγον ἐκ τῶν καθ' ἡμᾶς ἀναλογικῶς (*v.l.* ἀναγωκικῶς) ἐπὶ τῆς ὑπερκειμένης ἔγνωμεν φύσεως, κατὰ τὸν αὐτὸν τρόπον καὶ τῇ περὶ τοῦ πνεύματος ἐννοίᾳ προσαχθησόμεθα, σκιάς τινας καὶ μιμήματα τῆς ἀφράστου δυνάμεως ἐν τῇ καθ' ἡμᾶς θεωροῦντες φύσει (*Serm. Cat.* ii.). In the short treatise, *De fide rerum quæ non videntur*, ascribed to St. Augustine, the objection to the requirement of religious faith is met by insistence on the analogy of the actual necessity of faith in ordinary human intercourse. And in his work, *De Trinitate*, the mysteries of the Triune Being of God are repeatedly illustrated by the analogous mysteries of human psychology.

5. Analogy in Scholastic theology.—But however legitimately and successfully this method of argument was employed by the Fathers, it was not by them subjected to reflective criticism. A real advance was therefore made when the Schoolmen entered upon a rigorous examination of the limits of the analogical method with particular reference to its use in theology. Among the reasons which led them to undertake the task was their desire to find a philosophic justification for the anthropomorphic language of Scripture. Such language obviously could not be taken literally, nor yet be summarily dismissed as merely metaphorical, and therefore implying no real likeness between God and His creatures. The Schoolmen's answer to the problem is to be found in their theory of analogy, which concerns itself not only with the explanation of the analogical use of language, but also with the far deeper and more important question of the reality and the extent of the analogy between the finite and the infinite, and the legitimacy of inference from one to the other.

With regard to language, it was pointed out that a distinction must be made between the univocal, the equivocal, and the analogical use of words. A word is univocally employed when in two or more propositions it conveys precisely the same meaning; equivocally when used in two entirely different senses. But where two things are connected by some relation, the same word may be applied to them both in a related, though not precisely identical, sense. This last is the analogical use. Thus—the instance is as old as Aristotle—the word 'healthy' is analogically applied to the body which is sound, and to the food which is the cause of soundness. Similarly, the term 'being' is analogically applied to God who exists absolutely, and to man whose existence is contingent and dependent.

Upon the basis of this distinction was established the justification of the use of human terms about the Deity. When, for example, we speak of the wisdom of man and the wisdom of God, the word 'wisdom' is not used univocally. For if so, we should be denying any difference in kind between human and Divine wisdom, and our statement would be obviously opposed to the Christian teaching about God. Nor yet is the use of the word equivocal. For then we should be asserting the essential unlikeness of human and Divine wisdom, and it would be impossible to argue from the nature of the one to the nature of the other. Such a position would be untenable, because if a similar objection were supposed to hold good in all parallel cases, every inference from the creature to the Creator would be vitiated by the fallacy of equivocation. A way of escape from these opposite difficulties is provided by the recognition of the analogical use of the word. It is implied that there is a relation or proportion existing between the wisdom of man and the wisdom of God. What is partial and incomplete in man is perfect in God. (Cf. Thom. Aq., *Summa*, I. xiii. 6).

This distinction between the univocal and the analogical use of words was a sufficient reply to the reproach of anthropomorphism, but it left untouched the deeper question of the extent of the analogy or resemblance between God and His creatures. Accordingly, in the effort to reach greater clearness of thought with reference to this fundamental problem of religion, the Schoolmen proceeded to introduce further distinctions into their conception of analogy. These may be sufficiently illustrated from the scheme of Suarez (*Disput. Metaphys.* xxviii. sec. iii.). He distinguished two kinds of analogy, viz. that of proportion and that of attribution. To the former of these not much interest attaches. It amounts to little more than a mere resemblance, seized upon by the mind as justification for the use of a metaphor. Though such an analogy of proportion may appeal to the imagination, and therefore be of use in the way of illustration, it does not go far enough to warrant any inference in argument. The analogy of attribution, on the other hand, is established by the existence of a resemblance in the nature of things, and is valid for purposes of inference. When this resemblance consists in the possession by two subjects of the same quality in different degrees, the analogy is styled intrinsic. This is the highest grade of analogy, *analogia attributionis intrinseca*, and of this kind is the analogy between God and His creatures as regards, for example, the property of existence. Existence is predicated of Him and them. Their existence, however, is not of the same degree as His. Yet is it so far the same as to allow of some inferences being drawn, from what we know of finite existence, as to the nature of infinite existence. These distinctions may possibly appear needlessly subtle and technical, but the consideration of them will at least serve the purpose of calling the attention of the student to the possibility of some confusions of thought that have been actually responsible for the failure of much analogical argument.

6. Analogy in post-Reformation theology.—When the questions of theology ceased to be confined to the schools, and became the subject of popular debate, it was natural that the problem of analogy should be handled in accordance with the new methods, and in a manner intelligible to a larger public. A general advance in intellectual enlightenment brought the question once more to the front. At a time when man's knowledge of the world was being rapidly extended in many directions, he was inevitably brought once more face to face with the issue, whether Nature was in any true sense the analogue of God. Hence at the beginning of the 18th cent. we find that the theory of analogy was occupying the attention of some of the foremost theological writers.

Among the books on the subject which specially deserve mention may be noticed a *Discourse on Predestination*, by Dr. King, Archbishop of Dublin (1709). By this writer a somewhat extreme form of religious agnosticism was advocated. Desiring to allay the bitterness of theological controversy, he laid stress on the principle that all our notions about the Deity are inevitably limited by our human and finite capacity. 'If we know anything about Him at all, it must be by analogy and comparison, by resembling Him to something we do know and are acquainted with' (Whately's reprint of King in Appendix to Bampton Lectures, 3rd ed. p. 480). Our notions of God are really as far from the truth as a map is different from actual land and sea. A chart, while it provides instruction sufficient for the purpose of the traveller, does not actually resemble the country conventionally represented. Similarly, Scripture teaching about God may give us information about Him adequate for the purposes of this present life, without revealing Him to us as He is. This depreciation of man's capacity for acquiring a true knowledge of God was intended in the interest of theological peace. It became, however, the occasion of controversy. Bp. Browne, of Cork, contributed several books to the discussion of the question. In an early work he maintained that—

'Our ideas of God and divine things . . . are a sort of composition we make up from our ideas of worldly objects, which at the utmost amount to no more than a type or figure by which something in another world is signified, of which we have no more notion than a blind man hath of light' (quoted in Introduction to *Procedure*, etc.).

Adhering to these principles in his *Procedure, Extent, and Limits of the Human Understanding* (1728), he accepted without demur King's somewhat extreme conclusions:

'That we have no direct or proper notions or conceptions of God in His attributes, or of any other things of another world; that they are all described and spoken of in the language of revelation, by way of analogy and accommodation to our capacities; that we want faculties to discern them' (*op. cit.* p. 11).

At the same time he criticized King for failing to distinguish between metaphor and analogy, and for thus suggesting the inference that our statements about God are merely metaphorical, and as unreal as the ascription to Him of human passions or human limbs. To the exposition of this distinction he devotes a chapter (bk. i. ch. ix.), explaining that metaphor expresses only an imaginary resemblance or correspondence, whereas in analogy the correspondence or resemblance is real. The same theme is worked out at greater length in his later book, *Things Divine and Supernatural conceived by Analogy with Things Natural and Human* (1733). Our knowledge of the spiritual order is strictly relative to our capacities.

'God does not raise up our minds to any direct or immediate view of the things of another world, . . . but brings them down to the level of our understanding' (p. 32). 'What just and sufficient knowledge of God we have in this life is obtained by analogy or similitude with those perfections we find in ourselves' (p. 39).

The question naturally attracted the attention of Berkeley, who handled it with characteristic acuteness and precision in *Alciphron*, Dial. iv. ch. xxi. Familiar with the Scholastic definitions of analogy, he does not shrink from the conclusion that all our knowledge of God is strictly analogical. It is not, however, on that account to be reckoned as worthless. Human passions, indeed, are attributed to God by metaphorical analogy only, and involve no statement as to His nature. On the other hand,

'Knowledge, for example, in the proper formal meaning of the word, may be attributed to God proportionably, that is, preserving a proportion to the infinite nature of God. We may say, therefore, that as God is infinitely above man, so is the knowledge of God infinitely above the knowledge of man, and this is . . . *analogia proprie facta*. And after this same analogy we must understand all those attributes to belong to the Deity which in themselves simply and as such denote perfection' (ed. 1732, i. p. 257).

Berkeley, while recognizing the incompleteness of our spiritual knowledge, lays the emphasis on its trustworthiness rather than on its inadequacy.

'This doctrine of analogical perfection in God, or our knowing God by analogy, seems very much misunderstood and misapplied by those who would infer from thence that we cannot frame any direct or proper notion, though never so inadequate, of knowledge or wisdom as they are in the Deity, or understand any more of them than one born blind can of light or colour.'

Such was Berkeley's repudiation of the attempt to make religious truth unassailable by assuming it to be unintelligible.

It is remarkable that Butler, whose work is still the classical example of the application of the argument from analogy to theology, should have deliberately abstained from any prefatory justification or explanation of the theory of the instrument which he wielded with so much effect. Such, however, is the case. Declaring at the outset that he will not take it upon him to say how far the extent, compass, and force of analogical reasoning can be reduced to general heads and rules, he curtly brushes aside objections to this kind of argument with the remark that it is undeniably adopted by all in practical life. 'It is enough to the present purpose to observe that this kind of general way of arguing is evidently natural, just, and conclusive.' Others, as we have seen, were discussing these very points at the time when Butler was engaged in the composition of the *Analogy*. Perhaps he distrusted such speculations as essentially unpractical. Whatever the reason may have been, they are absent from his own work. He applies, he does not analyze, the argument from analogy. What gives his work its pre-eminent position in apologetic literature is not his selection of this particular kind of argument, but the steady patience, the scrupulous exactitude, and the transparent honesty with which he applied it to the controversies of his day. He offers a striking contrast alike to those writers who denounced analogical reasoning as worthless and those others who belauded it as the key to all difficulties. The claim that he makes on its behalf is modest in its scope. Positively it can never (so he tells us) afford more than a probable proof; negatively it can expose the latent insincerity of much unbelief, by showing that circumstances often considered to be conclusive objections to religion are strictly parallel with analogous circumstances in nature, the acknowledged handiwork of God. Analogy in Butler's hands provided no vindication of the character of God (*Works*, ed. W. E. Gladstone, i. 359), but it was fitted to open the eyes of men to their obligations, leaving them without intellectual excuse if they failed to consider with appropriate seriousness the arguments urged on behalf of religious belief.

The full effectiveness of Butler's argument will not be appreciated unless it be remembered that he says he is arguing upon the principles of others, not his own (*ib.* p. 367). Convinced that the proper proof of religion was to be found in the principles of liberty and general fitness, he nevertheless avoided reference to these principles, and limited himself to the consideration of religion as a matter of fact and practice. Upon this lower ground he met his adversaries, the Deist and the indifferentist. Against them he turned the weapon of analogy with complete logical success. Deistic objections against Christianity crumble away under his analysis. It is, of course, true that since his day the incidence of the critical attack upon religion has shifted its position. Hence many of his arguments need re-statement in accommodation to modern requirements. But, whatever alterations in detail may be thought necessary, time has not altered the general verdict in favour of the soundness and cogency of his argument.

7. Analogy since Kant.—Discussion of the nature and extent of man's analogical knowledge of God will always hold a principal place in apologetics, and for that reason will be sensitive to any change in the general philosophic attitude towards the ultimate questions of metaphysics. Hence it was that the whole statement and treatment of the problem were profoundly affected by the influence of the critical philosophy of Kant. That influence, however, was slow to exhibit itself in English theology, and until the 19th cent. was well advanced the discussion continued along the traditional lines. A controversy between Copleston and Grinfield in 1821 brought out once more the possibilities of disagreement over the place to be assigned to analogy. The two writers, representing respectively the lower and the higher estimate of the value of analogy, reproduce with curious exactness the points which had been made a century before by Archbp. King and Bp. Browne. Explicit acknowledgment was made of the debt due to these earlier writers; and Whately, Copleston's friend and disciple, reprinted with notes and high commendation King's famous *Discourse on Predestination*, in which the limitations of human reason had been so rigorously insisted upon. A different attitude towards the fundamental question at issue revealed itself in Mansel's Lectures on the *Limits of Religious Thought* (1858). The title of the book recalls that of Bp. Browne's *The Procedure, Extent, and Limits of the Human Understanding*. And the resemblance is more than superficial. In both writers there is the same tendency to dwell on the inadequacy of the human intelligence to probe the mysteries of the Divine Nature. But Mansel, under the influence of Kantian principles as to man's ignorance of things in themselves, attacks the problem from a different side, and goes far beyond the point reached by his predecessor. Whereas Bp. Browne had urged the relativity and consequent incompleteness of man's analogical knowledge of God, Mansel went so far as to say that, of God's real nature, we, under our finite conditions, are, and must remain, totally ignorant. It is an ignorance so complete as to exclude the possibility of either affirmation or denial.

'We cannot say that our conception of the Divine Nature exactly resembles that Nature in its absolute existence; for we know not what that absolute existence is. But, for the same reason, we are equally unable to say that it does not resemble; for, if we know not the Absolute and Infinite at all, we cannot say how far it is or is not capable of likeness or unlikeness to the Relative and Finite' (3rd ed. p. 146).

This is not the place in which to take notice of those further considerations with regard to the distinction between regulative and speculative truth, by which Mansel sought to establish religious faith upon this basis of philosophic scepticism. It is enough to give attention to the line which he adopted with respect to analogy. Repudiating on metaphysical grounds the analogy between the Finite and the Infinite, and consequently rejecting the customary philosophic proofs of religion, he found a negative defence for belief in the analogous difficulties of religion and philosophy. In so doing he claimed to be following in the footsteps of Bp. Butler, and to be adding another chapter to his argument on the analogy between religion and the course of nature. His principle he declares to be, that there is no rational difficulty in Christian theology which has not its counterpart in philosophy; and, further, that the stumbling-blocks which the rationalist professes to find in the doctrines of revealed religion arise, not from defects peculiar to revelation, but from the laws and limits of human thought (*ib.* p. 170). His work certainly resembles that of Butler in being an eminent example of the way in which the argument from analogy can be used for defensive purposes. He showed conclusively enough that many of the objections urged against revelation are applicable with equal force against the commonly accepted principles of thought and action. If the creed of theism contains its antinomies, so also does the creed of philosophy. In both cases explanation is equally impossible.

But the emphasis which Mansel placed upon our ignorance of the Divine Nature as it is, and his insistence on the absence of any necessary analogy between the goodness of man and of God, were the occasion of vigorous protests at the time, and eventually proved partly responsible for results very different from those which he desired. The assertion of man's ignorance, made by him and by other religious thinkers in the interest of revelation, was one of the exciting causes of the agnosticism, explicitly opposed to religion, which gained currency in the latter half of the 19th century.

8. Renewed confidence in Analogy.—In recent years there has been a distinct revival of confidence in the reality and the significance of the analogy between the Creator and His creation, and in the possibility of passing from the knowledge of one to the knowledge of the other. Among the causes which have contributed to this result must be counted the advance of the idealistic philosophy, and the increased attention given to the study of human personality. Instead of attempting to evade the reproach of anthropomorphism by conceding to the agnostic the inscrutability of the Divine Nature, the modern apologist is not afraid to avow the anthropomorphic character of theology, while he insists that in this respect theology is in the same position as every other department of human thought. 'Personality is thus the gateway through which all knowledge must inevitably pass. . . . It follows that philosophy and science are, in the strict sense of the word, precisely as anthropomorphic as theology, since they are alike limited by the conditions of human personality, and controlled by the forms of thought which human personality provides' (Illingworth, *Personality Human and Divine*, p. 25). In the book from which these words are quoted, human personality is deliberately taken as the analogical symbol of the Divine Nature, on the ground that God possesses, in transcendent perfection, the attributes which are imperfectly possessed by man. Thus what might appear to be the damaging effect of the admission of an anthropomorphic element in theology is neutralized by the correspondent assertion of a theomorphic doctrine of human nature. The supposition of an absolute and insuperable heterogeneity between the Finite and the Infinite, which has always been the basis of philosophic scepticism, whether in alliance with or in opposition to orthodoxy, is denied. The reality and the inexhaustible significance of the analogy between God and man are explicitly re-asserted.

LITERATURE.—Cajetan, *De nominum analogia; Opuscula*, Tom. iii. Tract v., Lyons, 1562; Suarez, *Disp. Metaphys.* xxviii. sec. iii., *De analogia entis ad Deum et creaturam*, Cologne, 1614; W. King, *Discourse on Predestination*, 1709 [reprint by Whately, 1859]; P. Browne, *Procedure, Extent, and Limits of the Human Understanding*, 1728, also *Things Divine and Supernatural conceived by Analogy with Things Natural and Human*, 1733; J. Butler, *Analogy of Religion to the Constitution and Course of Nature*, 1736; E. Copleston, *Enquiry into the Doctrines of Necessity and Predestination*, 1821; E. W. Grinfield, *Vindiciæ Analogicæ*, 1822; H. L. Mansel, *Limits of Religious Thought*[3], 1859; J. Buchanan, *Analogy considered as a Guide to Truth*[2], 1865; J. R. Illingworth, *Personality Human and Divine*, 1894; J. S. Mill, *Logic*, bk. iii. ch. xx., 1843, also *Hamilton's Philos. examined*, 1872, p. 111 ff.; Vacant, *Dict. de Théol. Cathol.*, art. 'Analogie,' 1900; Sigwart, *Logic* [Eng. tr.], 'Analogy' in Index.

G. C. JOYCE.

ĀNANDA.—One of the principal early disciples of the Buddha. He was the Buddha's first cousin, and is described as being devoted to him with especial fervour in a simple, childlike way, and serving as his personal attendant (*upaṭṭhāka*). A panegyric on him is put into the mouth of the Buddha just before his (the Buddha's) death (*Mahā Parinibbāna Suttanta*, in *Dīgha*, ii. 144–146). But it is for his popularity among the people and in the Order, and for his pleasant way of speaking on the religion, not for intellectual gifts or power of insight. So, in the same book (*l.c.* 157), the stanza put into Anuruddha's mouth at the death of the Buddha is thoughtful; while that put into Ānanda's mouth is a simple outcry of human sorrow. Though all the other disciples had attained to *arhat*-ship long before this, Ānanda remained still a 'learner' (*sekha*); and at the council said to have been held after the Buddha's death, Ānanda is described as the only one of the first hundred members selected to take part in it who was not an *arhat* (*Vinaya*, ii. 285). He became one before the council met (*ib.* 286), and took a prominent part in it; but that did not prevent the council from admonishing him for certain faults of inadvertence he had previously committed. Other passages of a similar tendency might be quoted (*e.g. Majjhima*, No. 32); but these are perhaps sufficient to show that the picture drawn of him is of a man lovable and earnest, but withal somewhat dense.

T. W. RHYS DAVIDS.

ANARCHY, ANARCHISM.—Anarchy means, as writers like Kropotkin understand it, the perfectly unfettered self-government of the individual, and, as a result, the absence of any kind of external rule. It is the widest possible application of the doctrine of *laissez faire*. Government, it declares, is something that human nature should not be asked to submit to. If men were but left to themselves, they would form themselves into co-operative producing groups, which would live in perfect harmony with one another. Each individuality would have unlimited powers of expansion, and the rigid moulds would vanish into which at present human nature is forced with infinite hurt to itself.

Anarchy as a theory must therefore be separated from Anarchism as a historical movement. The popular idea of Anarchy is that it is concerned only with bomb-throwing and Terrorism. But Anarchy as a theory of existence has been proclaimed by some of the gentlest and most cultured spirits in Europe; and although, in the case of a writer such as Bakunin, the thinker and the active revolutionary are merged, it will be convenient to consider first the theory and then the history of the movement.

i. THEORY. — On its economic side Anarchy is a branch of Socialism or Collectivism. It regards the day of private ownership and of capitalism as drawing to a close. It believes that the wage *nexus* between employer and employee is evil, and must sooner or later cease. Its view of the remuneration of labour varies between payment by labour time and the taking by each of what he wants from the common stock of production. When the workers are living in free associations, each will see that his own interest is the interest of the association, and the present tragic struggle for the increased share will cease.

The political basis of Anarchy is, negatively, that the possession of mere electoral and voting power is quite illusory as a means of social redemption for the many. Liberalism has been a failure. Even universal suffrage could lead but to the deeper enslavement of the worker. Representative government has had its full trial, and has failed; its defects are inherent in itself, and never can be cured. It is impossible for a Parliament to attend to all the numberless affairs of the community. More and more Parliament shows this inability in the congestion of business, and in the increasing extent to which local affairs are delegated to local authorities. It is this process of decentralization that is so full of hope to the philosophic Anarchist. He takes it to foreshadow the day when every little group will settle its own affairs, when there will be no rulers and no subjects, when each individual will have free play within his group, and each group free play in its relation to all other groups.

Anarchy has been extremely anxious to place itself on a scientific basis. In its modern form it has claimed Herbert Spencer as intellectual sponsor. It declares itself to be acting along the lines of evolution in that it is conforming to those two great tendencies which Spencer discerns in present-day conditions—the tendency to integrate labour for the production of all wealth in common, so that no individual shall be able to say what portion of the total result is due to his toil; and the tendency towards the fullest freedom of the individual for the prosecution of all aims beneficial both for himself and for society at large. Throughout organic nature the capacities for life in common are growing in proportion as the integration of organisms into compound aggregates becomes more and more complete. The struggle for existence, Kropotkin asserts, is not merely the struggle for the existence of the individual, but also the progressive adaptation of all individuals of the species to the best conditions for the survival of the species. The conditions must, therefore, be modified, so that man will be able to live the normal free life, instead of being forced by positive law to hold a place in a system of things which gives him neither freedom nor opportunity.

ii. HISTORY. — The view that authority is in itself a thing undesirable, and that man reaches the full measure of his stature only when he is allowed to develop his individuality absolutely unchecked, is by no means new. It appeared in several of the Mystic and Anabaptist sects of the later Middle Ages and post-Reformation period. In the 13th cent. there was a sect of the Beghards, calling themselves Brethren and Sisters of the Free Spirit, who professed pantheistic views. It claimed the utmost liberty on the ground that, as God inhabited each, the will of each was the will of God. In their preaching the Brethren advocated community of goods and community of women; they insisted on a personal equality, and rejected all forms of authority. In the period immediately preceding the French Revolution the idea was widely spread that the normal condition of life was that represented by 'Paul and Virginia,' a condition under which men were self-sufficing and independent, owning no other authority than that of their own wills. In 1795, William Godwin wrote his *Inquiry concerning Political Justice*, advocating community of goods, the self-government of mankind according to the laws of justice, the abolition of all forms of government, and the abolition of marriage.

The real founder of Anarchy as a living modern movement was Pierre Joseph **Proudhon**, a Frenchman of humble parentage, born in 1809. The attention Proudhon attracted was due, not only to his great ability, but to the fact that he lived in the stormy middle years of the 19th cent., when all constituted forms of government were on their trial, and to his acceptance of the dominant Hegelianism as the vehicle of his thought. His first work, *What is Property?* was published in 1840, and the answer he gave to his own question was that property was theft. The conclusion reached had evidently much in common with Marx's view that capital was crystallized labour, wealth of which the workman had been defrauded in the process of production. Labour, Proudhon held, is the source of value, and the value of labour should be measured by its duration. So far he followed the ordinary Socialist views of his time. It was when he asked himself the question how the poor man was to be raised from his poverty that he diverged from many of his contemporaries, and began that rift in the Communistic ranks that now has become the gulf between the policies of State Socialism and Anarchy. Proudhon, with Marx and Louis Blanc, wished to secure for labour the whole product of labour. Blanc hoped to attain this end by organizing labour under the authority of the State; Proudhon thought that the same result could be reached by the free initiative of the people unassisted in any way by the State. Governments, he declared, were the scourge of God, introduced in order to keep the world in discipline and order. It was not their function to produce movements, but to keep them back. Progress would be made not by revolution, but by evolution. As the people became more enlightened, they would gradually learn to dispense with government. The constitution would have to be revised continuously and unceasingly; so gradually, by the formation of independent and interacting groups, Anarchy would be introduced.

It was in the ranks of the 'International Association of Working Men' that the conflict between State Socialism which wished to make government co-terminous with human activity, and Anarchy which wished to eliminate government altogether, came to be fought out. Before this struggle commenced, the 'International' had had a long and somewhat confused history. In 1836 a number of Germans, exiled in Paris, formed a communistic society which they called the League of the Just. Becoming involved in trouble with the French Government, they removed to London in 1839. Amid the mixture of races in London, the Society, as a matter of course, came to be of an international character. The influence of Marx began to tell upon it. It accepted his view that economic conditions determined the social structure, and that every vital change in society must be brought about by a change not so much in political conditions as in economic. This change could be wrought only along the lines of social development. In 1847 the Society began to call itself the Communist League, its aim being 'the founding of a new society without classes and without private property.' The manifesto that the League put forth did not a little to give vigour to the various revolutionary movements of 1848; but, in the reaction following upon that time of enthusiasm, the League died. During the London International Exhibition of 1862 views were exchanged between French workmen visiting the Exhibition and their English fellows; popular sympathy with the Polish insurrection of 1863 helped the movement; and so, in 1864, the 'International Association of Working Men' was formed, with **Karl Marx** as its ruling spirit. His influence led the Association to the acceptance of State Socialism. State ownership of the land, as well as of the means of transport and communication, was early agreed upon as an object for which the Association should strive, although a proposal to abolish the right of inheritance did not find a majority.

But the disintegration of the International was at hand. In 1869, Bakunin and a number of the Russian Anarchists had joined it, and at once they began to attack the centralizing views of Marx. Then the Franco-German war broke out, and national feeling could not be eliminated even from an International Association. The Commune in Paris raised hopes that were almost immediately dashed in very dreadful fashion. In 1871 it became evident that there were two definitely marked groups in the Association, and the line of cleavage, as Kropotkin has pointed out, was not only an economic, but a racial one. The Germans, who now had received Parliamentary government, wished to work along electoral lines. 'The conquest of power within the existing status' became the watchword of the party which took the name of the 'Social Democrats.' The Latin and Slav elements in the Association gathered themselves together, under the leadership of Bakunin, in advocating the abolition of all paternal government, and the free action of the people through separate groups. In 1872 the Anarchists were expelled from the Association, and henceforth uttered their views through the 'Jura Federation.' This expulsion of the Anarchists was almost the last action of the International. It moved the seat of its General Council to New York, held one other Congress in Geneva in 1873, and then died. The Jura Federation and the Anarchists had a stormier history, owing to the influence of their leader.

Michael Bakunin (1814–1876) was an aristocrat and an officer. Horrified by the repressive duties he had to perform in Poland, he left the army and became a revolutionary. From 1849 to 1855 he was almost constantly in prison. In 1855 he was exiled to Siberia, but escaped in 1861 to America, and thence made his way to London. It was at this time that Russia seemed to be on the verge of a crucial constitutional change. The Czar in 1857 had promised the emancipation of the serfs, but after he had announced his intention the reactionary party induced him to impose upon the serfs an enormous redemption price for the land, and to postpone the emancipation till 1863. But in 1863 there broke out the insurrection in Poland. It was repressed with the utmost cruelty; tens of thousands of Poles were exiled to Siberia. Up to this time Russian social reformers had wrought mainly by going among the artizans and peasantry, indoctrinating them with their liberal and revolutionary views. This propaganda was now rendered almost impossible. After the attempt on the Czar's life by Karakozoff in 1866, the reformers had to hide their heads. Thousands fled the country, and settled in Switzerland and elsewhere.

It was among those exiles that Bakunin developed his Anarchist views. His object was the destruction of the existing order of things in faith, morals, economics, and politics. He refused to consider the question of reconstruction; 'all talk about the future is criminal, for it hinders pure destruction, and stems the course of revolution.'

The programme of the International Social Democratic Alliance which he founded gives the most succinct statement of his views. 'The Alliance professes atheism; it aims at the abolition of religious services, the replacement of belief by knowledge, and Divine by human justice; the abolition of marriage as a political, religious, judicial, and civic arrangement. Before all, it aims at the definite and complete abolition of all classes, and the political, economic, and social equality of the individual of either sex; and to attain this end it demands, before all, the abolition of inheritance, in order that, for the future, usufruct may depend on what each produces, so that . . . the land, the instruments of production, as well as all other capital, shall only be used by the workers, *i.e.* by the agricultural and industrial communities.' All children were from birth to be brought up on a uniform system, with the same means of instruction, so that there might disappear 'all those artificial inequalities which are the historic products of a social organization which is as false as it is unjust.' It rejected 'all political action which does not aim directly and immediately at the triumph of the cause of labour over capital.' It repudiated 'so-called patriotism and the rivalry of nations,' and desired the universal association of all local associations by means of freedom.

Bakunin's ideas were developed by his disciple **Netschajeff**, the son of a Court official in St. Petersburg, and born there in 1846. Netschajeff was much more a Terrorist than an Anarchist. Anarchy is, at all events, a reasoned system of things. It believes that life will be not only possible, but desirable, under the conditions it seeks to establish. But Netschajeff had regard purely to a destructive movement. His views were expounded in the Revolutionary Catechism, which was at first supposed to be the work of Bakunin, but is now, with more likelihood, held to have been by Netschajeff himself. According to this Catechism, the revolutionary must let nothing stand between him and the work of destruction. 'If he continues to live in this world, it is only in order to annihilate it all the more surely. A revolutionary despises everything doctrinaire, and renounces the science and knowledge of this world in order to leave it to future generations; he knows but one science—that of destruction. For that, and that only, he studies mechanics, physics, chemistry, and even medicine. . . . The object remains always the same—the greatest and most effective way possible of destroying the existing order.' The Catechism makes no ambiguity as to its methods. Differential treatment is to be meted out to the different classes of society; the rich are to be spared, but their wealth is to be used for the purposes of revolution; the former owners of wealth are to become the slaves of the proletariat. But rulers are not to be dealt with thus considerately. 'In the first place, we must put out of the world those who stand most in the way of the revolutionary organization and its work.' There is to be no attempt to set things right upon their present basis. Every effort is to be made 'to heighten and increase the evils and sorrows which will at length wear out the patience of the people, and encourage an insurrection *en masse.*' Active Terrorism is part of Netschajeff's programme. 'All is not action that is so called; for example, the modest and too cautious organization of secret societies, without external announcement to outsiders, is in our eyes merely ridiculous and intolerable child's play. By external announcements we mean a series of actions that positively destroy something—a person, a cause, a condition that hinders the emancipation of the people. Without sparing our lives, we must break into the life of the people with a series of rash, even senseless actions, and inspire them with a belief in their powers, awake them, unite them, and lead them on to the triumph of their cause.' This is the attitude that the plain man understands by Anarchism. It is claimed, of course, by the Anarchist thinkers that to allow this extravagant utterance of the Revolutionary Catechism to stand as representative of the whole movement is to do it an injustice, and to confound extreme applications of a general principle with the principle itself. 'To confuse Nihilism with Terrorism is,' says Kropotkin, 'as wrong as to confuse a philosophical movement, like Stoicism or Positivism, with a political movement, such as, for example, Republicanism.' But, in answer, it may be said that all Anarchists are not thinkers, and it is teaching of the Bakunist character that has had, as it was intended to have, the most startling results. The assassination of Alexander II., of the Empress of Austria, of King Humbert, of President M'Kinley, the bomb outrages in Chicago in 1887, in the French Chamber of Deputies in 1893, in a theatre in Barcelona in 1894, the attack on King Edward VII. at Brussels in 1900, the attempt, on their wedding day, upon the young King and Queen of Spain, are the things which 'break into the life of the people with a series of rash, even senseless actions,' and make the whole movement hateful to those who feel that any organized form of society, however it may violate the rights of individuals, is preferable to a state of things in which the most irresponsible make the greatest noise and have the greatest power to do mischief. It must be allowed, too, that this irresponsible Terrorism is the dominant form of Anarchism at the present time. In 1882 the Anarchists, in conference at Geneva, cut themselves adrift from all political parties. They declared the enmity of the Anarchists to the law. 'We declare ourselves allies of every man, group, or society which denies the law by a revolutionary act. We reject all legal methods. We spurn the suffrage called universal. . . . Every social product is the result of collective work, to which all are equally entitled. We are, therefore, Communists; we recognize that without the destruction of family, communal, provincial, and national boundaries the work will always have to be done over again.'

It is, at first sight, not a little difficult to find any relation between this extravagant propaganda which has had such appalling results and **Prince Kropotkin**, the man of high birth, of splendid ability, of gentle and noble and self-sacrificing life. Kropotkin has told his own story in the *Memoirs of a Revolutionist*, and whoever would seek to understand Anarchism should read this book, along with the account of the trial of the Anarchists at Lyons in 1883 (*Le Procès des Anarchistes*). Such a reading will explain how it is that the more recent developments of Anarchism go so far beyond the conceptions of Proudhon. If Russians who have suffered, as Bakunin and Stepniak and Kropotkin and tens of thousands of others have done, can find no solution of the social situation other than the utter destruction, by any means, of the present condition of affairs in Russia, it is not to be wondered at. The Russian Anarchists imagine that they reach their conclusions as a necessary inference from certain scientific propositions. In reality it is the Russian bureaucracy that has conditioned their thinking. Kropotkin was born at Moscow in 1842, a member of one of the most ancient and distinguished families in the Empire. He was brought up as a page at Court; but already, on his father's estates and in his father's house, he had seen enough of the life of the serf to make him an ardent advocate of the liberal views that were in the air before the actual date of emancipation. Instead of following out the career that was open to him, as a courtier and an officer of the Household Brigade, he chose service in Siberia, and spent four years there, being occupied most of the time in geographical and geological work. In Siberia he recognized the absolute impossibility of doing anything really useful for the masses of the Russian people by means of the existing administrative machinery, and became convinced that the only future for mankind lay in an entirely free Communism. On returning to St. Petersburg, full of ardour for his country's freedom, he found that the liberal movement of the earlier years of Alexander II. had died. Turguenieff's 'Smoke' is its epitaph. Kropotkin accordingly set to work to renew the Anarchist zeal, and strove, through companions whose earnestness and utter disregard of self almost disarm criticism, to spread among the working classes of the capital revolutionary opinions. His activity was discovered. For three years he was imprisoned in the fortress of SS. Peter and Paul, but finally escaped. For the next few years he moved between Switzerland, France, and England, and, becoming involved in the Anarchist rising in Lyons in 1883, was sentenced to five years penal servitude. Since his liberation at the end of three years he has lived mostly in England.

Kropotkin's main idea is that, as the present system of government and competition and private property cannot be mended without being ended, society must fly asunder into its primary elements and begin to re-aggregate itself. The right of private property he denies, on the ground that if we go back to the uncivilized condition of things we find no such right. Land has been made what it is by draining and cultivation in past generations. Production to-day is the result of innumerable inventions that have now become merged in the general producing machinery. We can produce now only as a consequence of what past generations have done. 'Who is, then, the individual who has the right to step forward and, laying his hands on the smallest part of this immense whole, to say, I have produced this; it belongs to me?' This argument, by which he thinks he has proved the illegitimacy of private property, occurs again and again in his writings. An ironmaster, he declares, deals with and uses the discoveries of those who have gone before, and the discoveries of to-day that he can buy up. 'British industry is the work of the British nation, —nay, of Europe and India taken together,—not of separate individuals.' But where government has once been destroyed and individuals have been left free to re-aggregate themselves, each man will take his place in the group he prefers; and those groups, retaining their own freedom, will at the same time act with mutual helpfulness and consideration, without any constraint from a government. The working agreements that have been arrived at by railways suggest themselves to him as the kind of thing that will be reached under Anarchism. The result is to be a great increase in production. At present 'the owners of capital are certainly endeavouring to limit the production in order to sell at higher prices.' Kropotkin seems to think that the economics of the diamond industry apply, in this regard, to agriculture and cotton-spinning, quite oblivious of the fact of the general economy of large production. If it be asked how labour is to be organized, or to be rewarded, Kropotkin is sufficiently vague. Under the system of free groups each man would naturally turn to the work he could do; but what assurance would there be that he would stand to any agreement he had made? The Anarchist answer is that there will be no necessity to hold him to his agreement. As the agreement has been freely entered into, there will be no need of any authority to enforce it. The labourer will be remunerated by helping himself to that portion of the joint product which he requires. The problem of the idler is easily settled :—there are not likely to be idlers in such a society. Work is natural to man, and the feeling of brotherhood and mutual responsibility will result in greatly improved labour. 'We consider that an equitable organization of society can arise only when every wage system is abandoned and when everyone contributing for the common well-being, according to the full extent of his capacities, shall enjoy also from the common stock of society to the fullest possible extent of his needs.'

To the questions that present themselves to the objector, Kropotkin has the most indefinite of answers. It may be asked, for instance, how, under any such free associations, any large public works are to be undertaken. We have heard not infrequently of such undertakings resulting in losses to the contractor, and, finally, being carried through not by that mutual agreement which is apart from law, but by the insistence of the law that a contract entered into shall be fulfilled. When a group finds difficulty in building, let us say, another Forth Bridge, who is to insist that the work shall be finished so that gross waste shall not ensue? And will not that ideal unity between group and group be very soon broken when matters of this kind come to be discussed and settled?

Then, again, with regard to the remuneration of labour, it may be granted that the wages system is not an ideal method of assessing the value of each man's contribution. But what would be the result on production, distribution, and industrial peace when each man was taking from the general heap exactly what he wished? The alternative on the Anarchist view is that he should be paid according to the labour time spent on his work. But what would become of art, music, literature, under such a system? The labourer is not, as a rule, prepared to acknowledge that anything is work which is not manual work. Far from granting that the value of an hour's work of Lord Kelvin or Mr. Edison was the equal of his own, he would deny to it the very name of work. Under this system the family would disappear as a matter of course. The notion of a permanent alliance between man and woman, enforceable by law, would be impossible. The relationship between husband and wife would be absolutely free; and this, unless human nature were to be altogether changed, would mean that the woman was to be placed at the mercy of the man and have assurance neither of home nor of sustenance. Children would require to be in charge of the group, not of the parents, and equality would necessitate that they should all be brought up in common.

Kropotkin assures the critic that the dreaded evils are imaginary. The solidarity of the human race will prevent them. The condition of things that is to be established not by law but by the sheer dignity of man, after bloodshed and revolution have done their work, is the idyllic one of perfect peace, and the solidarity of the human race. The Romanoff and the serf will vie with each other in praying the other first to take his portion of the heap.

On its theoretical and economic side Anarchism is a dream. It postulates an unreal world in which all men will live at peace, and work without thought of self. Nor is there any ground for the hope that under a system where men would be working for their group and not for their own advantage, production would be increased. One method of apportionment of wages—payment according to labour time — might have some chance of success under State Socialism, but none under a system where each man was absolutely free. The loafer and the malingerer would have found their paradise. But, anxious as Kropotkin is to dispense with government, his own scheme would involve government with an iron hand. Paternal feeling, one of the primary instincts of mankind, would have to be dead if men did not try to do their best for their own children. The rights of parentage would not be surrendered by those who were most worthy of being parents unless under the strongest compulsion. Only the sensual and the reckless would be satisfied. The great postulate of the whole system is that national feeling shall become extinct. A society organized in productive and socialist groups would clearly be unable to defend itself against a foe armed and organized as the great powers of to-day are. It would be necessary, therefore, not only that the groups within any one race should live at unity among themselves, but that they should be devoid of jealousy for the groups in any other race.

The history of Anarchism as a movement is the history of innumerable 'associations' flying to pieces, of innumerable congresses effecting nothing. Among the Teutonic peoples the movement has made no headway, for order and system is the genius of these peoples. Among the Latin and Slav races it has had a hearing. That a Russian who has suffered under the bureaucracy should be an Anarchist is no surprise. He may naturally feel that the dissolution of society into its elements is the postulate of any reconstruction. But that Anarchism shall ever establish itself as an organization of society under which men and women shall be able to live is impossible. What is even remotely practical in it, the taking of the means of production out of private hands, has already been adopted as the fundamental element of their policy by the State Socialists. The broad difference between those two great branches of Communism is that, while in the one it is realized that government will require to have much more extensive functions than it has at present, so that it may regulate those relationships which now are settled by private contract, in the other it is expected that the solidarity of the human race will be such that the will of the individual shall become the will of the group apart from all interference by government. That the former view better fits the facts as we know them, hardly admits of dispute.

LITERATURE.—Proudhon, *Qu'est-ce que la Propriété?* (1840), *De la Justice dans le Révolution et dans l'Église* (1858); Bakunin, *La Revolution Sociale ou la Dictature Militaire* (1871), *God and the State* (1894); Kropotkin, *La Conquête du Pain* (1891), *Fields, Factories, and Workshops* (1904), 'Scientific Bases of Anarchy' in the *Nineteenth Cent.*, Feb. 1887, 'The Coming Anarchy,' *ib.* Aug. 1887, *Memoirs of a Revolutionist*[2] (1906); Stepniak, *Underground Russia* (1883), *Career of a Nihilist* (1889); Kennan, *Siberia* (1891); C. Zenker, *Anarchism* (1898); Kirkup, *History of Socialism*[2] (1907); G. Plechanoff, *Anarchism and Socialism* (1906); *Le Procès des Anarchistes* (1883); P. Latouche, *Anarchy! An Authentic Exposition of the Methods of Anarchists and the Aims of Anarchism*, London, 1908.

R. BRUCE TAYLOR.

ANAXAGORAS, son of Hegesibulus, was born about B.C. 500 at Clazomenæ on the southern shore of the Gulf of Smyrna. He brought philosophy and natural science from Ionia to Greece, and marks an era in the history of Greek thought, being the first known advocate of a distinct psychical principle, called the *Nous* (Mind). He taught also an original theory of the constitution of matter.

Anaxagoras belonged to a family of wealth and position, but neglected his inheritance to follow science. Tradition asserts that he was a pupil of Anaximenes. This is chronologically impossible, as Anaximenes died before B.C. 520. He probably belonged to the school of Anaximenes, for scholarship in Ionia was not unorganized; the relation among groups of congenial thinkers foreshadowed the development in Greece of chartered schools of philosophy (θίασοι) (Diels, *Ueber die ältesten Philosophenschulen der Griechen*, Leipz. 1887; Wilamowitz-Möllendorf, *Antigonos von Karystos*, p. 263 ff.). Theophrastus states that Anaxagoras was 'an associate of the philosophy of Anaximenes' (Arist. *Phys. Op.* fr. 4; Diels, *Doxographi Græci*, p. 478). Anaxagoras migrated to Athens about B.C. 460, the first philosopher to take up his abode there. The intimate friend and teacher of Pericles (Plato, *Phædrus*, 270), he taught in Athens thirty years, numbering among his pupils Euripides, Thucydides, Archelaus, and Metrodorus of Lampsacus. His influence was far-reaching in introducing rationalism into Greece.

His chief work, entitled περὶ Φύσεως ('on Nature'), complete in several volumes, was published, probably in Athens, after B.C. 467, the year of the great fall of meteorites which he mentions. It was written in prose, and was the first Greek book, with the exception of geometrical writings, to be illustrated with diagrams. Considerable fragments survive, most of which are found in Simplicius' commentary on Aristotle's *Physics*.

At the beginning of the Peloponnesian war, when Pericles' popularity began to wane, Anaxagoras was arraigned for impiety, accused of denying the godhead of the sun and moon, and of saying that the sun was burning stone, and the moon earth (Plato, *Apol.* 26 D). Pericles saved him, but he was exiled to Lampsacus, on the southern shore of the Hellespont, about B.C. 430. There he had many disciples, and died in B.C. 428. A stone was erected to his memory bearing on one side the word Νοῦς and on the other 'Αλήθεια (Arist. *Rhet.* Bk. II. cap. 23).

That matter is neither generated nor destroyed had been the doctrine of the Ionian physicists for a full century. Heraclitus brought the idea of becoming into prominence, but Anaxagoras believed absolute change impossible. 'The Hellenes,' he said, 'are wrong in using the expressions "coming into being" and "perishing"; for nothing comes into being or perishes, but there is mixture and separation of things that are.' To Anaxagoras the eternity of matter involved the eternity of all its qualities, therefore the problem that confronted him was the origin of force. The three great systems of Empedocles, the Atomists, and Anaxagoras, all accepted the unchanging character of particles of matter and the separation of matter and force; Anaxagoras' book shows acquaintance with both of the other systems. Anaxagoras posited the *Nous* to satisfy his strongly developed sense of causation, to account for order in the universe, and to solve a definite mechanical problem.

In the beginning was chaos, which contained original particles of all existing objects, for 'How could hair come from not-hair, and flesh from not-flesh?' (Diels, cf. *Hermes*, xiii. 4). Anaxagoras calls the particles 'seeds' or 'things' (σπέρματα or χρήματα, Fr. 4 [Schorn]); but they were called *homœomeriæ* by a later half-Aristotelian phraseology. All things were together and occupied all space. There was no empty space. The action of the *Nous* upon some point of chaos produced rotation of inconceivable rapidity, which, ever widening in extent, caused the union of homogeneous particles. The impulse of the *Nous* was initial. Revolution followed and separation by force and speed, 'and speed makes force' (Fr. 11 [Schorn]). The earth was formed in the centre of this movement. The sun, moon, and stars were separated by the violence of the motion, and the celestial globe increased in circumference as ever-increasing masses of matter were included in the rotation. Homogeneous seeds combine to form objects as we know them, but there is never absolute freedom from disparate seeds. Objects become so by the kind of matter prevailing in them. Earth, water, air, and fire are complex substances containing particles belonging to all objects. The sun is a mass of ignited stone as large as, or larger than, the Peloponnesus. The earth is flat or a flat cylinder, resting on the air. Anaxagoras discovered with tolerable accuracy the cause of the phases of the moon and of eclipses, and he explained at length various meteorological and elemental phenomena. His observation in early manhood of a huge meteoric stone which fell at Ægospotami may have helped him to form his cosmological theories (Pliny, *HN* ii. 58; Diog. Laert. I. iii. 10).

Anaxagoras believed in the qualitative trustworthiness of sense-perception, but the senses, being weak, cannot discern the truth (Sext. Emp. *Math.* vii. 90). Sensation is produced by opposites, and is connected with pain (Theoph. *de Sens.* 27, 29; Diels, *Dox.* p. 507). That which is hot is also somewhat cold. Our senses show us the proportions that prevail. 'Snow must be dark, because the water from which it comes is dark' (Sext. Emp. *Hyp.* i. 33). The superiority of man lies in his possession of a hand. Death is a simple necessity of nature.

The *Nous* is the rarest and purest of all things, in its essence homogeneous, a kind of reasoning force, or thought-stuff. Personality is attributed to it in one fragment only, which speaks of its knowledge of the past, present, and things to come (Fr. 6 [Schorn]). The *Nous* was a possible first cause of motion from a dualistic standpoint, a *deus ex machina* according to Aristotle, and merited the disappointment which Plato in the *Phædo* attributes to Socrates regarding it. Yet it forms an important link in the shifting of interest from nature to man; and, although metaphysically an incomplete conception, the *Nous* of Anaxagoras was pronounced immaterial by Plato, Aristotle, and Theophrastus.

Anaxagoras' teaching regarding the laws of nature and unity in the cosmic process formed a marked contrast to the mythical ideas of his age. His great contribution to knowledge was in the scientific method employed and in referring order in the universe to a rational principle. Anaxagoras left no distinctly ethical or religious teachings. He considered contemplation of nature the highest task of man.

LITERATURE.—Schaubach, *Anaxagoras Clazomenae Fragmenta*, Leipzig, 1827; Schorn, *Anaxagoras Clazomenae et Diogenis Apolloniatae Fragmenta*, Bonn, 1829; Mullach, *Fragmenta Philosophorum Græcorum*, Paris, 1867; Diels, *Doxographi Græci*, Berlin, 1879; Heinze, 'Ueber den Νοῦς des Anax.' in *Ber. d. sächs. Gesell. d. Wiss.*, Feb. 1890; Burnet, *Early Gr. Philosophy*, London, 1892; Zeller, *Phil. der Griech.*, Leipz. 1893; Gomperz, *Griech. Denker*, Leipz. 1897; Ritter and Preller, *Hist. Phil. Græc.*, Gotha, 1898; Diels, *Frag. der Vorsokrat.*, Berlin, 1903; Caird, *Evolution of Theology in Greek Philosophers*, Glasgow, 1904; Adam, *The Religious Teachers of Greece*, Edinburgh, 1908. The literature is given more fully in Baldwin, *Dictionary of Philosophy and Psychology*, vol. iii. Pt. 1 (New York and London, 1905), p. 68.

MARY MILLS PATRICK.

ANCESTOR-WORSHIP AND CULT OF THE DEAD.

ANCESTOR-WORSHIP AND CULT OF THE DEAD.—The worship of the Manes, or ancestors, is, says Tylor (ii. 113), 'one of the great branches of the religion of mankind. Its principles are not difficult to understand, for they plainly keep up the social relations of the living world. The dead ancestor, now passed into a deity, simply goes on protecting his own family and receiving suit and service from them as of old; the dead chief still watches over his own tribe, still holds his authority by helping friends and harming enemies, still rewards the right and sharply punishes the wrong.' In this view of the case the departed ancestor is regarded as invariably kindly and well disposed towards his surviving relatives; and it may be said that this is the usual feeling of savage and barbaric man towards his kinsfolk who have passed into the other world. But there are, as will be seen, exceptions to this general rule; and the question of the attitude of the living towards the dead has formed the subject of controversy between two schools of anthropologists.

1. *The dead regarded as friendly.*—What may be called the totemistic school—that which regards totemism as the main source from which religion has been evolved—dwells specially upon the kindly relations between the deity and his worshippers. Thus, according to W. R. Smith (213–357), primitive sacrifice is an act of communion, the totem animal or beast sacred to the god being slain in order to renew or re-establish the bond of connexion between the clan and its supernatural ally. Hence he rejects the supposition that 'religion is born of fear.' 'However true,' he writes (p. 54), 'it is that savage man feels himself to be environed by innumerable dangers which he does not understand, and so personifies as invisible or mysterious enemies of more than human power, it is not true that the attempt to appease these powers is the foundation of religion. From the earliest times, religion, as distinct from magic or sorcery, addresses itself to kindred and friendly beings, who may indeed be angry with their people for a time, but are always placable except to the enemies of their worshippers or to renegade members of the community. It is not with a vague fear of unknown powers, but with a loving reverence for known gods who are knit to their worshippers by strong bonds of kinship, that religion in the only true sense of the word begins.'

This theory has been extended by Jevons (*Introd. Hist. Rel.* 54 ff.) to the cult of the dead. He contends that primitive man was 'ordinarily and naturally engaged in maintaining such [friendly] relations with the spirits of his deceased clansmen; that he was necessarily led to such relations by the operation of those natural affections which, owing to the prolonged, helpless infancy of the human being, were indispensable to the survival of the human race; and that the relations of the living clansman with the dead offered the type and pattern, in part, though only in part, of the relations to be established with other, more powerful, spirits.' In support of this position, he contends that the maintenance of the parental instincts and family affection was essential to the survival of primitive man in the struggle for existence; and he quotes instances of the grief felt by the survivors when a death occurs in the family; the provision of food and other necessaries for the use of the dead; the retention of the corpse in the dwelling-house for a considerable period after death, or its ultimate burial beside the hearth; the preservation of relics of the departed; the appeals of the mourners to the ghost, imploring it to return home; the adoption of cremation, which frees the soul from the body and thus enables it to revisit its friends; the custom of catching the departing soul; the periodical feasts which the dead are invited to attend; and so on (*op. cit.* 46 f.).

2. *The dead unfriendly to the living.*—On the other hand, the same writer (p. 53) admits that love was not 'the only feeling ever felt for the deceased. On the contrary, it is admitted that fear of the dead was and is equally wide-spread, and is equally "natural."' These two apparently opposite modes of thought in relation to the dead he explains by the supposition that primitive man draws a clear line of distinction between the ghost of the kinsman and that of the stranger; the one is kindly and protective, the other malignant, dangerous, and hence an object of fear. 'In fine,' he remarks (*op. cit.* 54), 'as we might reasonably expect, the man who was loved during his lifetime did not immediately cease to be loved even by savages, when he died, nor was he who was feared in life less feared when dead.' The many instances of the savage cult of the dead, when it is prompted by fear, he regards as due to 'mal-observation of the facts of savage life.'

But these cases are so numerous that it is impossible to account for them in this way. Thus it is universally admitted that the spirits of strangers and enemies are inimical, and the same feeling is extended to those who have perished by an untimely death, or in some unusual or tragical way. On this principle Frazer (*GB*² i. 331) explains the inconvenient restrictions imposed on the victors in their hour of triumph after a successful battle, in obedience to which the warrior is isolated for a period from his family, confined to a special hut, and compelled to undergo bodily and spiritual purification. For the same reason, on the return of the successful head-hunter in Timor, sacrifices are offered to propitiate the soul of the victim whose head has been taken, and it is generally believed that some misfortune would overtake the victor were such offerings omitted. For the same reason, the same feeling is very generally extended to the ghosts of kindred in the case of children, youths, or maidens snatched away in the prime of their strength and beauty. These are naturally supposed to cherish feelings of jealousy or hatred towards the survivors, who are in the enjoyment of blessings from which they are excluded. The same is the case with the ghosts of women dying in childbirth, who are almost universally regarded as specially dangerous. Equally malignant are the spirits of the murdered man, of one slain by a wild beast, or dying from snake-bite. This feeling is naturally extended to the ghosts of wizards or sorcerers, who were renowned during life on account of the mysterious powers which they were supposed to possess. Thus the Patagonians lived in terror of the souls of their sorcerers, who were believed to become evil demons after death; and the Turanian tribes of N. Asia dread their shamans even more when dead than when alive (Falkner, *Descript. of Patagonia,* 116; Castrén, *Finsk mytologi,* 124; Bastian, *Mensch in der Geschichte,* ii. 406; Karsten, *Origin of Worship,* 110).

Such cases may be easily explained; but the fear of the dead is not confined to spirits of the classes already enumerated. 'Death and life,' writes Tylor (ii. 25), 'dwell but ill together, and from savagery onward there is recorded many a device by which the survivors have sought to rid themselves of household ghosts.' He instances the habit of abandoning the dwelling-house to the ghost, which appears in some cases to be independent of horror, or of abnegation of all things belonging to the dead; and the removal of the corpse by a special door, so that it may not be able to find its way back. In some cases, again, the return of the ghost is barred by physical means. In parts of Russia and East Prussia, after the corpse is removed, an axe or a lock is laid on the threshold, or a knife is hung over the door; and in Germany all the doors and windows are shut, to prevent the return of the ghost. With the same object the Araucanians strew ashes behind the coffin as it is being borne to the grave, so that the ghost may miss the road; and Frazer suggests that the very general practice of closing the eyes of the dead was based upon the same principle, the corpse being blindfolded that it might not see the road by which it was borne to its last home (*JAI* xv. 68 ff.). In India the Aheriyas, after cremating the corpse, fling pebbles in the direction of the pyre to scare the ghost; and in the Himalayas one of the mourners, on returning from the funeral, places a thorny bush on the road wherever it is crossed by another path, and the nearest relative puts a stone on it, and, pressing it down with his feet, prays the spirit of the dead man not to trouble him (Crooke, *Pop. Religion,* ii. 57).

Appeals are often made to the spirit, imploring it not to return and vex its friends. Among the Limbus of Bengal, the officiant at the funeral delivers a brief address to the departed spirit on the general doom of mankind and the inevitable succession of life and death, concluding with an exhortation that he is to go where his fathers have already gone, and not come back to trouble the living in dreams (Risley, *Tribes and Castes of Bengal,* ii. 19). Similar appeals are made by the Chinese, Dakotas, and the Karieng (Frazer, *JAI* xv. 65). The Yoruba sorcerer wishes a safe journey to the ghost: 'May the road be open to you; may nothing evil meet you on the way; may you find the road good when you go in peace.' The house of death is abandoned or burned, the deceased is called upon by name, and adjured to depart and not haunt the dwellings of the living (Ellis, *Yoruba-speaking Peoples,* 156, 160). Even in India, a land where the worship of ancestors widely prevails, the Santāl believes that the ghostly crowd of spirits who flit disconsolately among the fields they once tilled, who stand on the banks of the mountain streams in which they fished, and glide in and out of the dwellings where they were born, grew up, and died, require to be pacified in many ways. He dreads, says Hunter, his Lares as much as his Penates (*Annals of Rural Bengal,* 1897, p. 183).

3. *Prevalence of Ancestor-worship.*—In the sectional articles which follow, the character and prevalence of ancestor-worship in various parts of the world will be considered. In Australia it seems to be in little more than an embryonic stage; and the same may be said of New Zealand and Tasmania. Throughout Polynesia and Melanesia the cult is well established. In the Malay Peninsula it appears in the primitive animistic form, influenced by Islām. In the Semitic sphere the evidence for its existence is inconclusive. In Africa it prevails widely among the Bantu tribes, and in W. Africa became the State cult of the kingdoms of Ashanti and Dahomey. The elaborate death cult of the Egyptians was probably largely influenced from the south and west of the continent. In various forms it appears throughout the American region. It is, however, in India and in China, whence it seems to have been carried to Japan, that it appears in the highest vigour.

4. *Worship defined.*—At the outset it is necessary to define with some approach to accuracy what we mean when we speak of the 'worship' of ancestors. There are few races in the world which do not practise what has been called a death cult in some form, that is to say, we notice everywhere in the methods of disposal of the dead, in the funeral rites, and in the solemnities performed either immediately after the removal of the corpse, or subsequently at periodical intervals, one of two predominant ideas. Some people seem to desire to put the dead man out of sight, and thus relieve the survivors from any danger which may result from the hostility of the spirit; in other cases we find the relatives animated by a desire to maintain affectionate or friendly relations with the departed dead, to placate or gratify them, to supply them with food and other necessaries needed to maintain them in the new state of life on which they have entered. The latter is probably the most primitive, and is certainly the most general attitude adopted by the survivors. But even if we admit that the survivors do thus endeavour to secure amicable relations with the spirits of their departed friends, and that on occasion they may, in return, solicit their aid and sympathy, we are as yet far from reaching what may be rightly called 'worship' of the dead. 'Religion,' in its narrowest sense, has been defined by Frazer (*GB*[2] i. 63) as 'a propitiation or conciliation of powers superior to man which are believed to direct and control the course of nature and of human life.' For our present purpose it is on the words in this definition 'superior to man' that the question depends. Savage or barbaric man usually regards his departed relatives as needing his ministration and aid, rather than thinks that he is dependent upon them for protection and support. He pictures the soul when it leaves the body as a diminutive, feeble entity, which must be carefully protected from injury, and for which a suitable refuge must be provided where it can await the period when it is finally admitted into death-land. Even there, as we see in Homer's Nekuia, the common dead are conceived to pass a weak and passionless existence, a feeble imitation of that which they enjoyed on earth. It is only certain heroic souls who acquire a higher degree of strength and vitality, and even they can be roused to meet and converse with their friends on earth only when they lap the blood of the victim from the sacrificial trench. When this conception of the

helpless life of the departed prevails, it is obvious that the loving sympathy and ministrations of the living to the departed do not rise to the dignity of 'worship.'

The distinction, then, between the worship and the placation, or tendance, of the dead is one of great importance, which many of our travellers and observers have failed to appreciate. There are cases in which the dead are worshipped; but those of placation and ministration to the needs of the departed in the other world are much more numerous. In the accounts which follow of the prevalence of this form of worship in various parts of the world, the evidence upon which they are based must be accepted with this preliminary reservation. This distinction, again, if kept steadily in view, will enable us to account in some degree for the remarkable differences of opinion which prevail regarding this form of belief. Hence we must receive with some degree of caution the accounts of travellers who report that certain tribes are exclusively devoted to the worship of their ancestors, or that this form of belief does not exist among them. Two things are liable to cause misconception. In the first place, the veil which the savage hangs round his most cherished beliefs and ritual is so closely woven that casual visitors to a savage or semi-savage tribe, or even persons who have resided amongst them for some time, and have acquired some considerable knowledge of their language and character, find great difficulty in penetrating the mysteries of their religion. In the second place, the death cultus, which ordinarily takes place at the grave, is of necessity a formal and public act, and is likely to be observed and investigated by the casual inquirer, who may remain in complete ignorance of what is really the vital part of the tribal beliefs.

5. *Ancestor-worship the basis of human religion.*—The theory which suggests that the cult of ancestors is the basis of all human religion is usually associated with the name of H. Spencer. This writer begins his summary of the conclusions at which he has arrived, by dealing with what may be called the hero cult. 'Anything,' he writes, 'which transcends the ordinary, a savage thinks of as supernatural or divine; the remarkable man among the rest. This remarkable man may be simply the remotest ancestor remembered as the founder of the tribe; he may be a chief famed for strength or bravery; he may be a medicine-man of great repute; he may be an inventor of something new. And then, instead of being a member of the tribe, he may be a superior being bringing arts or knowledge; or he may be one of a superior race predominating by conquest. Being at first one or other of these, regarded with awe during his life, he is regarded with increased awe after his death; and the propitiation of his ghost, becoming greater than the propitiation of ghosts less feared, develops into an established worship' (*Principles of Sociology*, i. 411).

This view of the hero cult may be accepted with some reservation. In the first place, there are grounds for believing that fear is not the only, or even the primary, reason for the deification of the hero. The cult of the distinguished dead was often founded, not so much upon awe as upon the desire of the survivors to maintain friendly relations with the spirits of the departed (Jevons, *Introd.* 106). Secondly, in those parts of the world where the hero cult is developed to its highest form, the devotion paid to the hero is of a degree inferior to that of the regular gods, who are often nature spirits, and not necessarily ghosts of the dead. This distinction is clearly marked in Greece, where the cult of Heracles or Asklepios is of a lower grade than that of deities like Athene or Zeus. The ritual of hero-worship is also clearly different from that used in the worship of the gods. The same is the case in India, where heroes like Rāma or Krishṇa, who have been elevated to the rank of gods, are found sheltering themselves as *avatāras*, or incarnations, of a great nature deity like Vishṇu.

But Spencer goes much further than to recognize a cult of the deified hero. Following the passage already quoted, he goes on to say: 'Using the phrase ancestor-worship in its broadest sense as comprehending all worship of the dead, be they of the same blood or not, we conclude that ancestor-worship is the root of every religion.' Even the most downright upholders of the Spencerian hypothesis are unable to accept it when thus extended. Thus Grant Allen (*Evolution of the Idea of God*, 36) observes: 'I do not wish to insist that every particular and individual god, national or naturalistic, must necessarily represent a particular ghost, the dead spirit of a single definite once-living person. It is enough to show, as Mr. Spencer has done, that the idea of the god, and the worship paid to the god, are directly derived from the idea of the ghost, and the offerings made to the ghost, without holding, as Mr. Spencer seems to hold, that every god is, and must be, in ultimate analysis the ghost of a particular human being.' And in another passage (*ib.* 42) he writes: 'Religion has one element within it still older, more fundamental than any mere belief in a god or gods—nay, even than the custom or practice of supplicating and appeasing ghosts or gods by gifts and observance. That element is the conception of the Life of the Dead. On the primitive belief in such life all religion ultimately bases itself. The belief is, in fact, the earliest thing to appear in religion, for there are savage tribes who have nothing worth calling gods, but have still a religion or cult of their dead relatives.' Elsewhere, in discussing the cult of Attis, he seems to suggest that the tree-spirit and the corn-spirit originate in the ghost of the deified ancestor (*Attis*, 33 and *passim*).

Needless to say, these views have not met with general acceptance. Thus Hartland (*Legend of Perseus*, i. 203) regards this Euhemerism of Spencer as 'a child (one among many) of his passion for explaining everything quite clearly, for stopping up all gaps and stubbing up all difficulties in his synthesis, rather than an all-sufficient account of the beginnings of religion.' Lang (*Myth, Ritual and Religion*, ed. 1899, i. 308 f.) attacks what he calls 'the current or popular anthropological theory of the evolution of gods,' on various grounds. He finds in this hypothesis a 'pure Euhemerism. Gods are but ghosts of dead men, raised to a higher and finally to the highest power.' Analogous to this, but not identical, is the theory of Tylor (ii. 334), which suggests that 'man first attains to the idea of spirit by reflexion on various physical, psychological, and psychical experiences, such as sleep, dreams, trances, shadows, hallucinations, breath and death, and he gradually extends the conception of soul or ghost till all nature is peopled with spirits. Of these spirits one is finally promoted to supremacy, where the conception of a supreme being occurs.' To this combined animistic and ghostly theory Lang replies (*ib.* i. 310) that all gods are not necessarily of animistic origin. 'Among certain of the lowest savages, although they believe in ghosts, the animistic conception, the spiritual idea, is not attached to the relatively supreme being of their faith. He is merely a powerful *being*, unborn, and not subject to death. The purely metaphysical question, "Was he a ghost?" does not seem always to have been asked. Consequently there is no logical reason why man's idea of a Maker should not be prior to man's idea that there are such things as souls, ghosts and spirits. Therefore the animistic theory is not necessary as material for the "god-idea." We cannot, of course, prove that the "god-idea" was historically prior to the "ghost-idea," for we know no savages who have a god and yet are ignorant of ghosts. But we can show that the idea of God may exist, in germ, without explicitly involving the idea of spirit. Thus gods *may* be prior in evolution to ghosts, and therefore the animistic theory of the origin of gods in ghosts need not necessarily be accepted.' Secondly, he urges that, in all known savage theological philosophy, the God, the Maker and Master, is regarded as a being who existed before death came into the world. Everywhere death is looked on as a comparatively late intruder, who entered this world not only after God was active, but after it had been populated by men and beasts. 'Thus the relatively supreme being, or beings, of religion are looked on as prior to Death, therefore, not as ghosts.' Thirdly, the Vui of Melanesia and the Atua of the Tongans are '*beings*, anthropomorphic, or (in myth and fable) very often bestial, "theriomorphic." It is manifest that a divine being envisaged thus need not have been evolved out of the theory of spirits or ghosts, and may even have been prior to the rise of the belief in ghosts.' Fourthly, as among the Andamanese, Fuegians, and Australians, 'these powerful, or omnipotent divine beings are looked on as guardians of morality, punishers of sin, rewarders of righteousness, both in this world and in a future life, in places where ghosts, though believed in, *are not worshipped, nor in receipt of sacrifice*, and where, great-grandfathers being forgotten, ancestral ghosts can scarcely swell into gods.' Such gods, not receiving sacrifice, 'lack the note of descent from hungry food-craving ghosts.' If to this it be replied that the Australians are degenerate and must once have had chiefs or kings whose surviving ghosts have become their gods, he answers that there is no evidence of Australian degeneration. They have, on the contrary, advanced 'when they supersede their beast or other totem by an eponymous human hero.' Lastly, the theory being thus found inadequate to explain the facts of the lowest 'savage' religions, it is equally inapplicable to the 'barbarian' stage of culture. Here we often find a highest deity who is seldom worshipped with sacrifice, who has become otiose, a mere name, finally a jest and a mockery; while 'ancestral ghosts, and gods framed on the same lines as ghosts, receive sacrifice of food and of human victims.' Besides this, the higher barbarian gods are localized, which is not the case with the high gods of low savages. This 'break or flaw in the strata of religion' he explains by 'the evolution through ghosts of "animistic" gods who retained the hunger and selfishness of these ancestral spirits whom the lowest savages are not known to worship.' Such gods, needing constant sacrifices, are easily bribed to overlook the moral delinquencies of their worshippers, or to forgive their sins. Thus animism 'is on its way to supplant or overlay a rude early form of theism,' and thus the current theory, which makes the highest god the latest in evolution from a ghost, breaks down. The tribal or national deity, as latest in evolution, ought to be the most powerful, whereas among barbarians he is 'usually the most disregarded.' This line of argument may be accepted without admitting the implication that monotheism is a primitive form of belief, and it is to this extent valid against the Spencerian hypothesis.

As for the gods of nature, it is difficult to understand how the belief in them could have arisen through an ancestor-cult. It is possibly true, as Ellis (*op. cit.* 282) observes, that they are sometimes blended with ghost-gods; 'the reverence paid to certain rivers, rocks, cliffs, etc., must have often dated from some fatal accident that occurred in connexion with them. It was this which first attracted attention, and primitive man would not be likely to discriminate between the ghost of the victim, which would haunt the spot where the latter lost his life, and the indwelling spirit of the natural feature.' But such cases could never have been common, and the reverence paid to any abnormal feature of natural scenery would generally be quite independent of any association with a ghost. Still more is this the case with gods of sky, sun, moon, wind, or rainbow. The animism which leads to the worship of phenomena like these cannot depend upon, and may be earlier than, the belief in the survival of the soul after death.

6. *Ancestors oracular.*—Ancestral spirits are believed to be able to give oracles to their descendants, who consult them in times of danger or trouble. At certain places deep chasms or openings in the earth were observed, through which the shades could rise from their subterranean home, and give responses to the living. The Greeks called such places oracles of the dead (*νεκυομαντεῖον, ψυχομαντεῖον, ψυχοπομπαῖον*). The most ancient oracle of this kind was that of Thesprotia, where Periander succeeded in conjuring up and questioning the ghost of his murdered wife, Melissa (Herod. v. 92; Paus. ix. 30. 3). There was another at Phigalia in Arcadia (Paus. iii. 17. 8, 9), and Italy possessed one at Lake Avernus (Diod. iv. 22; Strabo, v. 244). The regular mode of consulting such oracles was to offer up a sacrifice and then to sleep in the sacred place. The soul of the dead man then appeared to the sleeper in a dream, and gave his answer (Frazer, *Paus.* iii. 243). The same belief is found in many forms in other parts of the world. In Melanesia, 'after a burial they would take a bag and put Tahitian chestnut and scraped banana into it. Then a new bamboo some ten feet long was fixed to the bag, and tied with one end in the mouth of it, and the bag was laid upon the grave, the men engaged in the affair holding the bamboo in their hands. The names of the recently dead were then called, and the men holding the bamboo felt the bag become heavy with the entrance of the ghost, which then went up from the bag into the hollow of the bamboo. The bamboo and its contents being carried into the village, the names of the dead were called over to find out whose ghost it was. When wrong names were called, the free end of the bamboo moved from side to side, and the other was held tight. At the right name the end moved briskly round and round. Then questions were put to the enclosed ghost, Who stole such a thing? Who was guilty in such a case? The bamboo pointed of itself at the culprit if present, or made signs as before when names were called. This bamboo, they say, would run about with a man if he had it only lying on the palms of his hands; but it is remarked by my native informants, though it moved in men's hands it never moved when no one touched it' (Codrington, *Melanesians*, 211 f.). Among the Akikuyas of E. Africa, the medicine-man holds converse only with those recently dead, whose lives he had been unable to save. He goes out and visits the corpse when it has been thrown out into the jungle. He pours 'medicine' upon its hands, and calls on it to rise. When it rises, the wizard says: 'Revile your father, mother, and brothers.' It does so, and after the wizard has thrown more 'medicine' upon it, the conversation ceases. Persons so reviled get sick and die (*JAI* xxxiv. 262). In S. Africa the wizard in the same way gets into communication with the spirit world, and delivers oracles in the form of riddles and dark parables (*ib.* xx. 120). The Dayaks sometimes, like the Greeks, seek communion with the ancestral spirits by sleeping at their graves in the hope of getting some benefit from them (Roth, *Natives of Sarawak*,

i. 211). In Australia some specially gifted seers are able to see the disembodied spirit sitting on the spot where its body lies buried, and no longer able to retire into its accustomed habitation (*JAI* xvi. 54). In Lapland, according to Scheffer (Borlase, *Dolmens of Ireland*, ii. 477), the Lapps buried their dead in caves, sacrificed a reindeer in honour of the dead, and fasted for three days after the burial. When offering the sacrifice, they inquired the will of the Sitte or ancestral ghosts. They said: 'O ye Sitte, what will ye have?' Then they used to beat a drum on which a ring was laid, and if the ring fell on any creature pictured on its surface, they understood that this was what the spirit desired. They then took the animal thus selected, ran through its ear and tied round its horn a black woollen thread, and sacrificed it. Sometimes the wizard pretends to go in person to death-land to consult the ancestral spirits. Among the Dayaks he possesses a charm which ensures the aid of a kindly spirit when he goes to Sabayan, the under world, in search of the soul of a sick man (*JAI* xxxiii. 81). The Melanesians tell a similar story of a woman who went to Panoi to consult the dead, and the Australian wizard is able to bring back news from the dead, or he ascends the sky, visits Daramulun, and obtains magical power from him (*ib.* x. 283, xiii. 195). In W. Africa the Yoruba priest takes a young child, bathes his face in the 'water of purification,' and digs a hole in the earth within the sacred grove at midnight. When the child looks into the hole, he is able to see Dead-land, and can tell the priest what he sees. When his face is washed a second time, he forgets all that has happened (Ellis, *op. cit.* 141). Such powers, often gained under the influence of fasting, are claimed by shamans all over the world (Tylor, ii. 410 f.).

7. *Disease, etc., caused by ancestral spirits.*—When the attention of a tribe is fixed on the cultus of ancestors, it becomes a natural inference that disease or other misfortune is due to neglect of their worship. In Celebes, all sickness is ascribed to the ancestral spirits who have carried off the soul of the patient (Frazer, *GB*[2] i. 265). This reminds us of the Greek conception of the Keres and Harpies (Harrison, *Proleg.* 176 ff.). In the same way, wrathful ancestors are supposed to cause tempests; the thunder is their voice. In Peru, when parents who have lost a child hear thunder within three months of the death, they go and dance on the grave, howling in response to each clap, apparently believing that they hear the sighs and groans of their lost child in the rumble of the thunder (Frazer, *Lect. on Kingship*, 206 f.). In some cases the wrath of the spirit is attributed to causes which we can only regard as frivolous. In Natal we hear of a diviner announcing to his people that the spirits had caused disease because they did not approve of some persons living in the kraal of a relative, and wished them to have a house of their own (*JAI* i. 181). Sometimes, again, the spirit is provoked on account of a sin committed by his people. Among the Banyoros of Uganda, the death of a man by lightning is attributed to the anger of the Bachwezi, or ancestral spirits, on account of some sin committed by the dead man, or wrong-doing on the part of members of the clan. To appease them, a sacrifice is demanded (Johnston, *Uganda*, ii. 539 f.). In Florida, according to Codrington, 'it is a *tindalo*, that is, a ghost of power, that causes illness; it is a matter of conjecture which of the known *tindalos* it may be. Sometimes a person has reason to think, or fancies, that he has offended his dead father, uncle, or brother. In that case no special intercession is required; the patient himself or one of the family will sacrifice, and beg the *tindalo* to take the sickness away; it is a family affair.' But if the *tindalo* be that of a stranger, a doctor is called in to identify and propitiate it (Codrington, *Melanesians*, 194 f.). But generally the cause of offence to the spirit is that the relatives have neglected its wants. When a North American Indian fell into the fire, he believed that the spirits of his ancestors pushed him in because their worship was neglected (Schoolcraft, i. 39). Often, again, it is caused by jealousy of the spirits towards the living, or it arises because the ghosts are lonely in Dead-land and desire companionship. For this reason spirits which have recently departed this life are apt to carry off with them to the world of the dead the souls of their surviving relatives (Frazer, *GB*[2] ii. 345 f.). Miss Kingsley was assured that the danger of the ancestral ghost's injuring the members of the family, particularly children, 'comes not from malevolence, but from loneliness and the desire to have their company. . . . This desire for companionship is, of course, immensely greater in the spirit that is not definitely settled in the society of spiritdom, and it is therefore more dangerous to its own belongings, in fact, to all living society, while it is hanging about the other side of the grave, but this side Hades' (*W. African Studies*, 133). Ellis, from whom Miss Kingsley probably borrowed the fact, says that ancestors cause sickness because the ghost wants the services of his relatives in Dead-land, and so hastens their departure from this world (*Ewe-speaking Peoples*, 109). It is a common belief that the spirits of people who have died a violent death may return to earth if they can find a substitute, and hence they are offended with any one who prevents another soul from taking his place by rescuing a person from drowning (Black, *Folk Medicine*, 28 f.). In Ireland, according to Lady Wilde, 'it is believed that the spirit of the dead last buried has to watch in the churchyard until another corpse is laid there, or to perform menial offices in the spirit world, such as carrying wood and water, till the next spirit comes from earth. They are also sent on messages to earth, chiefly to announce the coming death of some relative, and at this they are glad, for their own time of peace and rest will come at last' (*Ancient Legends, etc., of Ireland*, 1887, 82 f.). So in China 'it is commonly believed that if the spirit of a murdered man can secure the violent death of some one else, he returns to earth as if nothing had happened, the spirit of his victim passing into the world below and suffering all the misery of a disembodied spirit in his stead' (Giles, *Strange Stories from a Chinese Studio*, 1880, ii. 365). Fortunately, however, the patient is not always left to the mercy of the spirits of his enraged relatives. In San Cristoval, it was believed that the friendly and unfriendly ghosts fight with spears over the sick man. The patient would suffer, die, or keep his health according to the issue of this unseen spectral battle (Codrington, *op. cit.* 196).

8. *Ancestors appearing in children.*—The belief that the child is nothing more or less than an ancestor re-born on earth is found almost throughout the world. The idea, of course, depends upon the resemblance of members of the same family in successive generations. It is the basis of the extraordinary theory held by the Arunta tribe in Central Australia regarding conception, and among the northern tribes of the same continent every new child is believed to be the incarnation or re-incarnation of spirit children left by remote ancestors (Spencer-Gillen[a], 51 f., 337; *FL* xv. 467). Among the Thlinkets of N. America, the spirit was 'believed to have the option of returning to this life, and generally entered the body of a female relative to form the soul of a coming infant. If the child resembled a deceased friend or relation, this embodiment was at once recognized, and the name of the dead person was given to it' (Bancroft, *Native Races*, iii. 517). In the same region the Nootkas accounted for the existence of a distant tribe speaking the same language as themselves by declaring them to be the re-incarnated spirits of their dead (*ib.* iii. 514). In W. Africa the Yorubas inquire of their family god which of the deceased ancestors has returned, in order to name the child after him, and its birth is greeted with the words 'Thou art come,' as if addressing some one who has returned; and their neighbours, the Ewe, believe that the only part of its body which a child receives from its mother is the lower jaw, the rest being derived from the ancestral spirit (Ellis, *op. cit.* 120, 131). The same procedure in naming children appears among the Khonds of India, where the priest drops grains of rice into a cup of water, naming with each grain a deceased ancestor. From the movement of the seed in the water and from observation of the child's person he decides which ancestor has re-appeared in it, and the name is usually given accordingly. Hence we can explain why in the islands of Watabela, Aaru, and the Sula Archipelago barren women and their husbands visit certain sacred graves to pray for offspring—the spirits of the sainted dead being thus re-incarnated (Ploss, *Das Weib*, 1887, i. 436 ff.). The same belief appears in W. Europe in the habit of young girls in the Pyrenees going to a dolmen to pray for a lover, and young brides for a child; in the erotic superstitions connected with rude stone monuments in Spain, Brittany, and Ireland; and in the cycle of Irish legend connected with the bed of Dermot and Grania (Borlase, *Dolmens of Ireland*, 580, 689, 845 f.). This leads immediately to the theory of metempsychosis, which is generally accepted among primitive races. In India it is doubtful whether this belief appears in the Vedas, but it is admitted in the later Purānic literature, and at the present day in the Panjāb it is quite logically accepted to explain the fact that, as the soul is transmitted from generation to generation, so with the life are transferred all attributes and powers of the progenitor. Hence we have numerous instances here of the transmission of the hereditary powers of curing disease or causing evil which are believed to be found in certain clans and families. 'This principle of inherited supernatural powers or sanctity is much more deeply rooted than that of caste. It is natural and fitting that a man should follow his father's trade, but he may change his occupation. . . . When once sanctity has been acquired by a family, it is next to impossible to shake it off. Social status is much less permanent. The original conception of the metempsychosis appears then to have been that the life or soul, with all its attributes, was transmitted by natural descent. This idea was developed into the doctrine that the soul transmigrated from one body to another independently of such descent, but this doctrine did not regard transmigration as something fitful and uncertain; on the contrary, religion held that it was subject to one set of rules, and magic that it could be regulated, but in neither sense was transmigration a matter of chance' (Rose, *Census Report, Panjāb*, 1901, i. 161 ff.). But, as Hartland remarks (*op. cit.* i. 220), 'the subtlety of savage metaphysics is marvellous. An acute observer points out that among the Tshi-speaking peoples of the Gold Coast and the Ewe-speaking tribes of the Slave Coast, a distinction is drawn between the ghostly self that continues the man's existence after death in the spirit-world, and his *kra* or *ñoli*, which is capable of being born again in a new human body. In the eastern Ewe districts and in Dahomey the soul is, by either an inconsistency or a subtlety, believed to remain in the land of the dead and to animate some new child of the family at one and the same time; but it never animates an embryo in a strange family.'

9. *Ancestor-worship and Totemism.*—The question of the relation of ancestor-worship to totemism has recently been discussed by Tylor, Hartland, and Frazer. Tylor (*JAI* xxviii. 146 f.) quotes from Wilken (*Het Animisme bij de Volken van den Indischen Archipel*, 1884–85, pt. i. p. 74 f.) cases of crocodiles being regarded as kindly and protective beings, to kill which is considered murder, as they may be man's near relatives. Offerings are made to them, and people look forward to the great blessedness of becoming crocodiles when they die. In the same way Sumatrans worship tigers, and call them ancestors. Some of the non-Aryan tribes of the central Indian hills believe that the ancestor is sometimes re-born in a calf, which in consequence of this connexion is well fed and treated with particular respect (Crooke, *Popular Religion*, i. 179). On this Tylor thus comments: 'Wilken sees in this transmigration of souls the link which connects totemism with ancestor-worship, and on considering his suggestion, we may see how much weight is to be given to the remarks made independently by Dr. Codrington as to Melanesia (*op. cit.* 32 f.). He found that the people in Ulawa would not eat or plant bananas, because an influential man had prohibited the eating of the banana after his death because he would be in it; the elder natives would say, we cannot eat so-and-so, and after a few years they would have said, we cannot eat our ancestor. . . . As to such details we may, I think, accept the cautious remark of Dr. Codrington, that in the Solomon Islands there are indeed no totems, but what throws light on them elsewhere. The difficulty in understanding the relation of a clan of men to a species of animals or plants is met by the transmigration of souls, which bridges over the gap between the two, so that the men and the animals become united by kinship and mutual alliance; an ancestor having lineal descendants among men and sharks, or men and owls, is thus the founder of a totem-family, which mere increase may convert into a totem-clan, already provided with its animal name. By thus finding in the world-wide doctrine of soul-transference an actual cause producing the two collateral lines of man and beast which constitute the necessary framework of totemism, we seem to reach at last something analogous to its real cause.'

Following on this discussion, Hartland considers the whole question in connexion with the tribes of S. Africa. He notices that the only branches of the Bantu race among which no certain traces of totemism and but few of mother-right are found are the Amazulus and their kindred tribes, the most advanced of the whole Bantu race. The Bechuanas, on the contrary, exhibit substantial remnants of totemism, and with them traces of mother-right. Thus in the lowest social stage of these races totemism is still flourishing, and patriarchal and pastoral institutions are struggling with it. Totemism is here, in fact, developing into ancestor-worship (Frazer, *Man*, i. 136), and the question is—How has ancestor-worship developed and supplanted totemism? This question Hartland answers by suggesting that it is entirely dependent upon the growth of the patriarchal system. 'The more absolute becomes the power of the head of a nation, and under him of the subordinate chiefs and the heads of families, the more the original totemism superstitions tend to disappear until they are altogether lost and forgotten.'

The same process seems to be going on in other parts of the world. Thus, in Yam, one of the islands in Torres Straits, the animal kindred come to be replaced by a definite effigy, the soul of which is kept in an external receptacle, and the effigy is further associated with a hero (Haddon, *Cambridge Exped.* v. 377f.; *Head-hunters*, 138). Haddon regards this materialization of a totem as unique; 'so important a development of totemism is practically to place it beyond the realm of pure totemism.' We find something of the same kind in a totem-post from British Columbia, where, as Tylor remarks, 'the figures go beyond mere representations of the totem animals, and depict a mythic incident in which the human ancestor is believed to have come into relation with the animal which was thence adopted as the totem of the clan' (*JAI* xxviii. 136). The development of totemism into ancestor-worship is also illustrated by the case of the Bhuiya tribe in Bengal. They show great reverence for the memory of Rikhmun or Rikhiāsan, whom they regard, some as a patron deity, others as a mythical ancestor, whose name distinguishes one of the divisions of the tribe. Risley believes it possible that in the earliest stage of belief Rikhmun was the bear-totem of a sept of the tribe, that later on he was transformed into an ancestral hero, and finally promoted to the rank of a tribal god (*Tribes and Castes of Bengal*, i. 112).

With our present limited knowledge of the origin and development of totemism, which may at any time be revolutionized by fresh information from the Australian or other primitive tribes, it would be premature here to do more than quote these examples of ancestor-worship developing out of totemism, with the more or less plausible explanations which have been suggested to account for it.

10. *Ancestor-worship and Idolatry.*—We have more satisfactory evidence of the development of ancestor-worship into idolatry, a term not in itself satisfactory, but preferable to that of 'fetishism,' which possesses no scientific value. The practice of erecting carved representations of deceased ancestors is one of the many sources from which the idol was probably evolved. Its analogue is to be found in the primitive stone pillar, in which the god was manifested when blood was sprinkled upon it (Jevons, *Introd.* 133). This custom of erecting memorial images is very common in Melanesia and the adjoining region. At Santa Cruz, 'when a man of distinction dies, his ghost becomes a *duka*. A stock of wood is set up in his house to represent him. This remains, and is from time to time renewed, until the man is forgotten, or the stock neglected by the transference of attention to some newer or more successful *duka*.' Offerings are made to it in times of danger at sea, at the planting of a garden, on recovery from sickness, when fruit is laid before it (Codrington, *op. cit.* 139). In the Solomon Islands, if a person of great consequence dies, 'a figure may be made of him after his death, for the ornamentation of a canoe-house, or of a stage put up at great feasts. These images are hardly idols, though food may sometimes be put before them, though to remove them would be thought to bring down punishment from the dead man upon those who should so insult him' (*ib. JAI* x. 302). In Ambrym, however, the large figures screened with bamboos, which would naturally be taken for idols, are set up in memory of persons of importance at a great feast perhaps a hundred days after death. 'That they do not represent ancestors is fairly certain; the very oldest can be but a few years old' (*JAI* x. 294). They generally represent figures of men, who would be loosely called ancestors by the powerful people of the village, and these would be treated with respect, food being placed before them. 'But these had no sacred character, further than that they were memorials of great men, whose ghosts, visiting their accustomed abodes, would be pleased at marks of memory and affection, and irritated by disrespect. There was no notion of the ghost of the dead man taking up his abode in the image, nor was the image supposed to have any supernatural efficacy in itself.'

In the New Hebrides, a model of the dead chief is made of bamboo; the head is smeared over with clay, shaped and painted so as to be often a fair likeness of the deceased, and placed on the bamboo model, the whole image being set up in the god's house or temple, with the weapons and personal effects of the dead man. Boyd, who describes these images (*JAI* xi. 76, 81), is doubtful whether they are objects of affectionate regard or of worship, and Somerville (*ib.* xxiii. 21, 392) does not ascribe any religious character to them. But it is obvious that an image set up as a memorial and propitiated with offerings of food may very easily develop into an idol. Haddon (*Head-hunters*, 91) describes similar models in wax on skulls of deceased relatives. They seem to be kept mainly for sentimental reasons, as the people are of an affectionate disposition, and like to have memorials of departed friends; but they are employed mainly as *zogos*, or potent instruments of divination by which a thief, stolen goods, or a person who by means of sorcery had made any one sick, should be detected. The model was taken in procession, and was believed to be able to guide him who bore it to the house of the offender. There is much difference of opinion regarding similar images from Easter Island, some denying that they are worshipped; others alleging that they represent chiefs and persons of note, and that they are given a place at feasts and ceremonies; others, again, suggesting that they are used for purposes of divination. In the case of a rude cultus like this it is possible that all three suggestions may represent the varying conditions of the devotion paid to them (*Man*, iv. 73 f.). In New Guinea the explorers found two roughly carved wooden men, with bushy hair on their heads. When asked to sell them, the natives said: 'No. They belong to our ancestors, and we cannot part with them' (Chalmers-Gill, *Work and Adventure*, 229).

In India the use of such images seems to be largely based on the principle of providing a refuge for the ghost during the period which elapses between death and the completion of the funeral rites. Among the lowest castes in North India a reed is very generally fixed for this purpose near a tank, and water libations are poured upon it during the days of mourning. Woodthorpe (*JAI* xi. 65) describes the curious images erected by the Nāgas of the N.E. frontier over their graves. These are sometimes executed with much skill, the wrists and elbow-joints indicated, emerald beetle wings representing the eyes and a row of white seeds the teeth. 'They were clad in all the garments of the deceased, with their shields fixed on the left side, two imitation bamboo spears standing on the right.' The Khariyas, according to Dalton (*Descriptive Ethnology*, 160), make images of the same kind. In South India the Nāyars make an image of the dead man out of palmyra leaf, and to this rice and other things are offered (Fawcett, *Bull. Madras Museum*, iii. 248). Among the Kāfirs of the Hindu-kush the veneration paid to images of this kind seems to amount to actual worship. Sacrifices are made before them, and their descendants, when suffering from sickness, sprinkle blood upon their pedestals. A straw figure of a warrior is venerated at his funeral, and effigies of the honoured dead are erected over their graves (Robertson, *Kafirs of Hindu-kush*, 414, 635, 648).

The Ostiaks of Siberia make similar figures. Among them the effigy is 'worshipped with divine adoration for such a period of time as may be determined by the Shaman or priest, not exceeding, however, three years, when the image is buried. Offerings of food are set before it at every meal; and if it represents a deceased husband, the widow embraces it from time to time, and lavishes upon it tokens of affectionate and passionate attachment. The image of a deceased Shaman is preserved from generation to generation; and 'by pretended oracular utterances and other artful impositions the priests manage to procure pious offerings as abundant as those laid on the altars of the acknowledged gods' (Featherman, *Ugro-Turanians*, 559, 575).

In America the same practice is well established. Of the Cemis or images raised by the aborigines of Hispaniola, Ferdinand Columbus states: 'They give the image a name, and I believe it is their father's or grandfather's, or both, for they have more than one, and some above ten, all in memory of their forefathers' (*JAI* xvi. 260). The grave-posts, roughly hewn into an image of the dead, appear among many tribes of the American Indians (Dorman, *Prim. Superstition*, 177 ff.). The Similkameen Indians of British Columbia place carved figures representing the dead on their graves. These are dressed in the clothes of the dead man, and when decayed are renewed (*JAI* xxi. 313). The Sioux set up a grave-post, recording the totem of the deceased warrior, with a record of his warlike expeditions and of the number of scalps taken by him, of which Schoolcraft gives illustrations (i. 356).

In Africa the Lindu, a forest tribe, have a distinct form of ancestor-worship, and are accustomed to remember the dead by placing roughly-carved dolls, supposed to represent the deceased person, in the abandoned hut in which he is buried (Johnston, *Uganda*, ii. 555). Miss Kingsley (*Travels*, 473) records a case where, on the death of a twin, an image of the child was carried about by the survivor as a habitation for the soul, so that it might not have to wander about, and being lonely call its companion to follow it.

When we come to races in a higher grade of culture, we find survivals of the same practice. The Roman noble exhibited in the wings which opened from his central hall the *imagines* or likenesses of his revered forefathers, which are believed to have been originally portrait-masks to cover the faces of the dead. These at funerals were fitted on to the faces of the actors who represented the dead man's ancestors, and when kept in the house were probably attached to busts (Smith, *Dict. Ant.*[3] ii. 992 ff.). The actors with these masks were seated on chairs of dignity at the funeral rites (Granger, *Worship of the Romans*, 65).

11. *Ancestor-worship in relation to the family.*—Ancestor-worship is primarily a family cult, based on the desire of the survivors to maintain friendly relations with the departed. But the family is a comparatively modern institution, and behind the modern family, organized on the principle of the maintenance of the *patria potestas* and succession in the male line, there is a long past, when possibly promiscuity and certainly polyandry or group-marriage, with the natural accompaniment of succession in the female line, must have prevailed. This is not the place to discuss the priority of father-right and mother-right. In Australia, at any rate, group-marriage is found to prevail where mother-right exists, and it is difficult to imagine how it could have arisen under conditions of father-right. Hence ancestor-worship cannot be regarded as a highly primitive belief. Jevons (*op. cit.* 194) is on less sure ground when he argues that it could not have arisen before the time when agriculture was started as the main industry of the human race. 'Originally,' he urges, 'the dead were supposed to suffer from hunger and thirst as the living do, and to require food—for which they were dependent on the living. Eventually the funeral feasts were interpreted on the analogy of those at which the gods feasted with their worshippers—and the dead were now no longer dependent on the living, but on a level with the gods. . . . It could not therefore have been until agricultural times that the funeral feast came to be interpreted on the analogy of the sacrificial feast.' It would, however, be unsafe to infer that the cult of ancestors is confined to tribes organized on the patriarchal system. Thus in South India the custom of tracing descent through the female seems to have widely prevailed, and the Nāyars, who still maintain this rule, are ancestor-worshippers. This they have not borrowed from the Hindus, but it has been derived by them from the primitive animism (Fawcett, *Bulletins Madras Museum*, iii. 157, 247, 253, 273). The same is the case with many of the lower castes in Northern India, among whom survivals of matriarchy can easily be traced, and with certain Melanesian races, who combine an ancestral cult with descent in the female line; as, for instance, the Pelew Islanders, the Ipalaoos of the Caroline Archipelago, the Chamorres of the Ladrones, and the Biaras of New Britain (Kubary, *Pelauer*, 39; Featherman, *Oc. Mel.* 356, 358, 396, 401, *Pap. Mel.* 52 ff.).

12. *Social Results of Ancestor-worship.*—It remains to consider briefly the effect of ancestor-worship on the social condition of the races which practise it. In the case of Japan, a writer in the *Times* (20th Nov. 1905) remarks: 'It is not difficult even for Europeans to understand how strong is the foundation, both for national and dynastic loyalty, which such a faith affords. It ensures that the whole Japanese people, from the highest to the lowest, shall ever bear in mind the existence and the strength of the innumerable ties which knit the present to the past. It is at once a safeguard against violent revolution and a guarantee of gradual progress. It is a conception which we cannot perhaps easily grasp in its fulness, but we can readily acknowledge its nobility and its simplicity, and we can feel how great and precious a factor it may be in moulding the hearts and minds of a nation.' To the same belief the sanctity of the household and, as a consequence, the inviolability of marriage, have been much indebted. The strong desire of every man to leave a son competent to perform the rites on which the happiness of his ancestors and of himself depended was one of the main foundations of that family life which is the basis of modern society, and, except in countries like India, where it conflicted with the prejudices of the priestly class, tended to raise the status of woman. On the other hand, in the ruder stages of society, the belief that the unappeased and angry soul of the father or kinsman hovered round the family hearth, and could be consoled by no propitiation save by the blood of the murderer slain by a member of the household, tended to foster the desire for revenge, to strengthen the feeling of hostility towards rival tribes, and to confirm the popular belief that 'stranger' and 'enemy' were synonymous terms.

LITERATURE.—The authorities have been freely quoted in the preceding pages. On the general subject see Spencer, *Principles of Sociology* (1877), pt. i. chs. xx. xxv.; Avebury, *Origin of Civilisation* (1870), 364 ff.; Tylor, *Primitive Culture*[3] (1891), ch. xiv.; de la Saussaye, *Manual of the Science of Religion*, 112 ff.; Jevons, *Introduction to the History of Religion* (1896), ch. xv.; Fustel de Coulanges, *La cité antique*; Howard, *History of Matrimonial Institutions* (1904); J. G. Frazer, *GB*[2] (1900), ii. 460, iii. 83; W. R. Smith, *Rel. of Sem.*[2] (1894), 213; Landtmann, *The Origin of Priesthood*, ch. ii.; Karsten, *The Origin of Worship, a Study in Primitive Religion* [the two last being academical dissertations addressed to the Alexander University of Finland]; Carpenter, 'The Gods Embodiments of the Race Memory' in *Hibbert Journal*, ii. 259 ff.

W. CROOKE.

ANCESTOR-WORSHIP AND CULT OF THE DEAD (American).—**1. Communion with spirits of the dead.**—Perhaps the most marked feature of the religion of the American Indians is the vivid belief in life after death, possessed by nearly all of the many tribes from Alaska to Patagonia.* There can be little doubt that this belief was based upon the equally general belief in communication between mankind and the spirits of the dead.

Whatever may be the true explanation of that modicum of genuine phenomena, which some attribute to the action of spirits, and others to the sub-conscious self, the phenomena were recognized by the Indians long prior to the advent of modern spiritualism, and, at least in many cases, prior to the earliest historical contact with Europeans. The tribes regarded these phenomena as caused by the spirits of the dead. As a rule they were friendly spirits, those of tribal ancestors, relatives, or friends who returned to earth to warn, protect, instruct, or amuse the living. They were treated with reverence and respect, seldom with fear. They could be seen by those who trained their senses above the normal plane, in accordance with methods handed down from the ancestors, or sometimes, under unusual circumstances, by ordinary mortals.

The power of seeing them was believed to be acquired in various ways—by continued solitary meditation, by the use of certain narcotic herbs, by crystal-gazing. Those who acquired this power became mediums, and were respected as the 'Medicine Men' (a term possibly derived from the mysteries of the Meda Societies), magicians, or priests. By the aid of the spirits they were enabled to foretell the future, and to describe events occurring at a distance. Evidently, therefore, the spirits were believed to possess superhuman knowledge and power, and intercourse with them was sought to obtain this, not for purposes of worship. Amongst many tribes those who acquired this power are distinguished by various names, according to the scope of their attainments, but the principal distinction is between those who are controlled by the unseen forces and those who control them. Only the masters were enabled to compel the spirits to do their bidding. No instances are given of the abuse of these powers. Like the spirits themselves, those who were supposed to hold intercourse with them seem to have been regarded only in a favourable light. As to the effect of these practices upon the medium personally, nothing is heard. Besides these methods of obtaining intercourse with spirits, some men were believed to be born gifted with this power, to some others it could be quickly or instantly imparted by masters. In dreams and visions and under unusual circumstances, spirits were believed to appear, without mediumistic interposition, to ordinary mortals.† There is hardly a tribe to-day which does not possess at least one member who believes that he is able to describe distant events at the time of their occurrence, or to perform some other apparently supernatural feat. In the myths of several southern tribes, mortals journey to the land of the dead, and return therefrom to relate their experiences.‡

2. The soul and the double.—

'The Iroquois and Algonkins believe that man has two souls—one of a vegetative character, which gives bodily life, and remains with the corpse after death until it is called to enter another body; another of more ethereal texture, which can depart from the body in sleep or trance and wander over the world, and at death goes directly to the land of spirits.'*

The Sioux recognize three souls—one goes to a hot place after death, one to a cold, while a third watches the body. The Dakotas claim four souls.† In most American Indian languages the word for 'soul' is allied to those for 'air,' 'wind,' 'breath,' the breath being thought to represent the animating principle derived from the Cosmic Spirit, or Soul, as amongst Hindus and Romans, though only the system of the Vedas analyzed this relationship.‡

The individual soul was regarded as part of this Cosmic Soul which formed the principal deity of the American Indians. The personified deities in Peru, and probably elsewhere as well, were recognized as special manifestations,§ although the adequate understanding of this concept was doubtless confined to the few, as in all places and times. The unconscious attempt of the missionaries to read monotheism into the concept of the Great Spirit, amongst the northern tribes, naturally prevented appreciation of its true nature, and led to vagueness in their statements.

A wide-spread belief assigned to each individual an attendant guardian spirit, or spiritual companion, independent of, but attached to, the physical self. It warned the self through intuitions of impending dangers, and the like. Such was the *tornak* of the Eskimos; the *oiaron* of the Iroquois, chosen after a period of solitary meditation in the woods, and symbolized by some object seen in a dream or vision; the *ochechag* of the Ojibwas; the *amei-malguen* of the Araucanians; the *huauque* or 'double' of the Peruvians, literally 'brother of a brother,' but also applied to twins and, significantly, to a friend. The Peruvians, moreover, gave this name to the false heads placed upon the mummies to which they expected that the departed spirits would return at some future time. It is probable that the word *huaca*, applied to all sacred objects, referred to the spiritual counterpart, from which, according to the Peruvians, all material objects were derived. Whether accidentally or otherwise, this word is repeated in the sacred Mexican city of *Teotihuacan*, and in the deities *Wakan* and *Wakonda* of North American tribes, as Brinton has shown.‖ It is possible that *Thunapa pachaca*, 'He who knows himself and all things,' one of the names applied to the Peruvian Cosmic Spirit, may apply to one who has mastered the relation of this double to the physical self. The Guiana tribes also assert that every human being consists of two parts—body, and soul or spirit.¶

3. Methods of communication.—The Micmacs, like the Natchez, Peruvians, and other tribes, kept the bodies of their dead in their homes or temples, believing that this would enable the spirits to warn them of the approach of enemies, and to advise with their priests about the affairs of the tribe. It was once usual for the young men of many tribes, at the approach of puberty, to go alone into the woods to meditate in solitude and without food, until they had visions of visiting spirits, and the like. In Peru a class of hermits dwelt alone upon the mountains, and were consulted as to many things, past, present, and future. The Eskimos also had their hermits, *kavigtok*,** and, according to the Micmacs, there are now several such hermits of their tribe dwelling on the mountains in the almost unexplored wilderness around Cape North, Cape Breton Island.

* Brinton mentions the Pend d'Oreilles of Idaho as the only exception, but others are now known.

† For details of such beliefs amongst Eskimos and Micmacs, see Rink, p. 58; Hagar in *Jour. of Am. Folk-Lore*, vol. ix. p. 170 ff.; Bancroft, iii. 147.

‡ Lafitau, i. 402.

* Brinton, p. 253.

† *Ib.* 49, 52, 55.

‡ See Oviedo, lib. xlii. cap. 2, 3.

§ See Molina, p. 29.

‖ Bancroft, iii. 199, 514; José de Acosta, lib. v. cap. vi.; Rink, 39; Lafitau, i. 336, 370; Molina, *Hist. of Chili*, p. 257; Hagar, *Peruvian Astronomy*, 'Gemini' chapter.

¶ Im Thurn, p. 346.

** Rink, 45.

4. Folk-lore of communication.—There is a general belief amongst the Indians that if you go into the woods on a calm day and listen, you will hear the light footsteps of the spirits, and sometimes the sound of an axe. Many of the spirits inhabit trees, from which they appear before the solitary traveller. The Brazilian tribes believe that they announce coming death. The Northern Lights represent to the Eskimos and other tribes the dance of the dead, and are thought to occur only when many have died. The origin legend of the Incas relates that Huanacauri having been walled up in a cave by his three brothers, his spirit accompanied them thence to Cuzco, flying through the air. In some parts of Peru the natives scattered flour or maize or quinua about the dwelling to see by the footsteps whether the spirits had been moving about.* The modern Mayas mark a path from the tomb to the hut with chalk, so that the returning spirit may find its pathway thither. The Peruvians seem to have believed that all their laws were revealed to their rulers by spirits who descended from the celestial world.†

5. Seances.—The Pottawatomies had recognized rules for communicating with the dead.‡ The spirits came with a 'sound like that of a distant strong wind sweeping through leafless trees, and intermingling with strange voices.' A Zuñi rain-priest said that a woman member of his fraternity having died in the sword-swallowing rite, 'her spirit troubled us so much with rapping that we placed live coals in the centre of the room and added piñon gum; the room was soon filled with smoke, which effectually rid us of the spirit.' Amongst practically every tribe with which the Spaniards came in contact, their writers describe certain men as talking with the devil, who appeared to them in divers shapes, and imparted supernatural information. Probably they referred to the demonstrations called by us 'seances.' In Cumana, they say, the *piaches*, or priests, informed them as to the exact day when relief ships would arrive from Spain, and as to the number of men, and the amount of supplies they would bring. The priest who made this prophecy

'went into a cave on a very dark night, took with him some bold youth, who stood while he sat. The priest called, cried out, repeated verses, shook rattles, sounded horns dismally, spoke some words of entreaty, and if the devil did not answer, sounded again, sang threats, and grew angry. When the devil came, which was known by the noise, the priest pounded hastily and loud, fell down, and showed that he was taken by the fiend by the faces and gestures that he made.§

According to Acosta, the Peruvians had conjurers who

'tell what hath passed in the fartherest parts before any news can come. As it has chanced since the Spaniards arrived there that in the distance of two or three hundred leagues, they have known the mutinies, battles, rebellions, and deaths, both of tyrants and those of the king's party, and of private men, the which have been known the same day they chanced or the day after, a thing impossible in the course of nature. To work this divination they shut themselves into a house and become drunk, until they lose their senses, A day after they answered to that which was demanded. They likewise show what has become of things stolen and lost.' ‖

In the provinces of Quito the devil in frightful shape appeared to the priests, who were much respected by all the other Indians.

'Among these one gave replies, and heard what the devil had to say, who, in order to preserve his credit, appeared in a threatening form. Then he let them know future events, and no battle or other event has taken place amongst ourselves that the Indians throughout the kingdom have not prophesied beforehand. There can be no doubt but that by an illusion of the devil the figures of persons who were dead, perhaps fathers or relations, appeared to those Indians in the fields in the dresses they wore when living.' ¶

Perhaps the most detailed account of a seance in America, recorded, it should be remembered, long before the advent of modern spiritualism, is given by Salcamayhua, an Aymara, of pure blood and noble lineage, who writes as follows:

'It happened one day that the Inca Ccapac Yupanqui wished to witness how the huacas conversed with their friends, so he entered the place selected, which was in a village of the Andes, called Capacuyo. When the young Inca entered among these idolaters, he asked why they closed the doors and windows, so as to leave them in the dark, and they all replied that in this way they could make the huaca come who was the enemy to God Almighty, and that there must be silence. When they had made an end of calling the Devil, he entered with a rush of wind that put them all into a cold sweat of horror. Then the young Inca ordered the doors and windows to be opened that he might know the shape of the thing for which they had waited with such veneration. But as soon as it was light, the Devil hid its face, and knew not how to answer. The dauntless Inca Ccapac Yupanqui said, "Tell me what you are called," and with much shame it replied what its name was. It fled out of the house raising shouts like thunder.'*

Seances are also described amongst the Caribs and other tribes.

A special and much venerated class of Peruvian priests, called *mallquit umu*, devoted themselves to communicating to the people information obtained from the spirits which had formerly inhabited the mummies placed in their keeping. They were also called *huaca rimachi*, 'those who make the sacred objects speak,' and *ayatapuc*, 'those who make the dead speak,' as they obliged the devil 'to enter into the corpses which they consult, or into the bodies of those whom they put to sleep by their sorceries.'† The famous temple of Rimac Mallqui, near Lima, seems to have been devoted to communion with the dead.

The suggestion of hypnotism is repeated in the snake-charming of the Zuñis, whose priests claim to be able to insert their own minds into the brains of the reptiles and to learn their ways.

6. Inducing visions.—To induce visions the Peruvians made use of the plant called *villca.*‡ Hernandez says that the Mexicans used an herb called *ololiuhqui*, or 'serpent-plant,' when they wished to consult with the spirits. By means of it they were enabled to behold a thousand visions, and the forms of hovering demons.§ The Micmacs similarly used their *mededesköoi* or serpent-plant. Amongst the Mayas the *h'menes* or priests were enabled by gazing into the *zaztun*, a crystal of quartz, or other translucent material, to behold reflected therein the past, present, and future, to locate lost articles, to see what was happening to absent ones, to learn by whose witchery sickness and disaster had been caused. Scarcely a village in Yucatan was without one of these stones.‖ The Cherokee magicians by means of their *oolunsade*, or crystals, obtained power to go to the spirit world and back. In them they beheld events anywhere at any time they wished. They also used them to call to their aid the invisible little people, who would accomplish almost anything for them, either good or evil. They would drive out the hostile spirits who caused illness or inflicted death; they would fly on errands over land and sea. One Cherokee, with every indication of good faith, informed the present writer that he possessed a crystal and could use it in all the ways stated. It must be fed by rubbing blood upon it, and if angry would cause injury to its owner. The Zuñi priests used crystals for like purposes. In Peru, though the use of crystals is not affirmed, a legend asserts that the Inca Yupanqui, while gazing into the clear depths of a spring, beheld a messenger from the celestial world, who told him many wonderful things.

7. Belief in life after death.—Whether the general belief in life after death amongst the American Indians was founded on their real or

* Arriaga, p. 39.
† S. Hagar, *Peruv. Astron* 'Scorpio' chapter.
‡ *Forum*, July 1898, p. 624. § Herrera, vol. iii. pp. 310, 311.
‖ Acosta, vol. ii. pp. 367, 368.
¶ Cieza de Leon, pt. i. p. 180.

* Salcamayhua, p. 85.
† Calancha, tome i. p. 411; Squier, p. 84, quoting Pinelo; Cieza de Leon, pt. i. ch. 91.
‡ See Lorente, p. 284. § *Popol Vuh*, p. 184 note.
‖ Brinton, *Essays of an Americanist*, p. 165.

supposed communion with the spirits of the dead, or *vice versa*, the intensity of this belief amongst the Cahrocs and in Peru is evidenced by the Druid-like custom of whispering in the ears of the dying messages to departed friends.* Algonquin women who desired to become mothers flocked to the couch of those about to die, in the hope that the vital principle, as it passed from the body, would enter them and fertilize their sterile wombs. The Aymara word *mallqui* meaning 'mummy' is also translated 'tree,' 'lord,' 'immortal,' 'a bush for transplanting,' 'a young bird about to leave its nest for life elsewhere.' The conventional expression amongst the Indians at the approach of death is 'My father calls me to rest with him.' Many tribes held the doctrine of re-incarnation. The Chinook says that when a man dies, his spirit passes to his son; the Thlinket, that the soul has the option of returning to life. In that case it generally enters the body of a female relative to form the soul of a coming infant. Some tribes of Southern California supposed that the dead returned to certain verdant isles in the sea while awaiting the birth of infants, whose souls they were to form. The Apaches taught the metempsychosis of souls into animals. The Nootkas, Pueblos, and Mayas also believed in re-incarnation.† The Dakota medicine-men profess to tell things which occurred in bodies previously inhabited for at least half a dozen generations. Many tribes preserved the bones of their dead, believing in the resurrection of the body.‡

8. Magic.—Feats of magic in which, however, the participation of spirits is not asserted, are reported amongst many tribes, the Mayas being especially proficient therein. See fully under art. MAGIC.

9. Mortuary customs.—The various tribes made use of very diverse methods of burial, including inhumation in natural or artificial cavities, in or on the ground, desiccation by tight wrapping, the remains being afterwards placed in or on the earth, deposition in urns, surface burial in hollow trees or caverns, cremation, aerial sepulture in lodges or elevated platforms, and aquatic burial beneath the water or in canoes which were afterwards turned adrift.§ Mummies, common in Peru, have also been found in many parts of North America, but it is still doubtful whether any artificial process of embalming was resorted to for preserving these bodies. A form of water burial, analogous to the Norse, was once practised by the Micmacs at the funeral of chiefs. It seems not to have been used by any other tribe on the Atlantic coast.

Food, clothing, tools, and cherished objects were generally buried with the body, and food and drink were afterwards left upon the grave, but this was the service of love seeking to provide for the material wants of the soul in the earth above. It was not worship. In Peru, as in India, even the wives and servants of the deceased, together with some of his domestic animals, were once buried with the deceased, but at the time of the conquest it had already become the general custom to substitute images of the required objects.

The Ojibwas believe that, when they partake of visible food at the grave, the spirit at the same time partakes of the spiritual element of that food.‖ The Mexicans had a similar belief.¶ So, often, as in Egypt, the pottery deposited on the grave was broken that its 'spirit' might escape to serve the deceased.** The Algonquins beat the walls near the corpse with a stick to frighten away the lingering ghost. But this was done only by the enemies of the deceased.*

10. Nature of life after death.—The land of souls amongst the American Indians was usually located in the sky, the sky-world being regarded as the world of origins, of which the earth is but an echo or counterpart. Life in the sky-world therefore was thought to differ little from life on earth. The soul continued to pursue the same objects that it had sought here. The Happy Hunting Ground was a literal ideal of the northern hunter tribes, but the concept rises amongst the Mayas to a place of eternal repose under the cool umbrageous shade of the sacred tree, *yaxche*.† Certain legends seem to localize the land of souls in or near the sun, and in the Pleiades,‡ but the sun merely represents the dwelling of the ruler of the sky-land.

Journey of souls.—The way thither is long and difficult. For four days and nights the soul toils onwards over a dark and dreary way, lighted only by the fires which are maintained on its grave during that period. First it journeys to the extremities of the earth, to the point where the Milky Way, the path or river of souls, touches the earth. At the entrance to the Galaxy, it passes a dog, or between two mountains which guard the way. Then, guided by the spirit of a dog or by a star, it leaves the earth and advances on this narrow path until it comes to a point where the path forks. Here the spirits of those who have been brave and courageous, and have led praiseworthy lives, reach the broad arm and quickly attain to the celestial goal, while those less commendable pass out upon the narrow arm and struggle on with bitter effort. Such is the real symbolic basis of the journey of souls. Though this symbolism is usually veiled, it is sometimes quite clearly stated, as by the Skidi Pawnees.§ Everywhere the soul must cross water, usually a torrential river, sometimes a series of streams, the ocean or a lake. Sometimes it does this on a narrow hair bridge, as in Peru and Colombia and amongst the Eskimos, sometimes on a slippery log, as amongst the Cherokees, Iroquois, and other northern tribes, on an enormous snake amongst Algonquins and Dakotas, on sea-lions on the Peruvian coast, on dogs in Mexico, in a stone canoe amongst the Ojibwas. The Mexicans, with marked inconsistency in view of their sanguinary rites, translated to heaven at once and without effort the souls of warriors and of women who died in childbirth. The Pawnees conceded to them a comparatively easy journey.

The Zuñis believe that

> 'the ghost hovers about the village four nights after death, and starts on its journey to Kothluwalawa (Abiding-place of the Council of the Gods) on the fifth morning. During the spirit's stay in the village, the door and hatchway of the house must be left ajar that it may pass in and out at will; should the door be closed the ghost would scratch upon it, and not be satisfied until it was opened. These shadow beings can be observed by seers and by others under certain conditions.'‖

Parents or sisters of a deceased person sleep at the side of the surviving spouse during the four nights that the spirit is supposed to remain in Zuñi. A grain of black corn or a bit of charcoal is put under the head of the women to ensure against dreaming of the lost one, whose ghost would appear should the sleeper awake.

11. Worship of ancestors and of the dead.—Strictly speaking, instances of true worship of ancestors or of the dead in America are rare. The dead are seldom confused or identified with the various deities, whose attributes, with

* Hill, vol. i. p. 260; Bancroft, iii. 200.
† Bancroft, iii. 53, 514, 517, 525, 527.
‡ S. R. Riggs in *AAOJ*, vol. v. p. 149.
§ Yarrow, pp. 92, 199.
‖ *Ib.* p. 191.
¶ Tylor, vol. ii. p. 35.
** Sayce in *Dawn of Civilization*, p. 195 note 1.

* Brinton, 255; Bancroft, iii. 199.
† Landa, pp. 200, 201.
‡ See Brinton, 261, 262; Bancroft, ii. 511; S. Hagar, *Peruv. Astron.* 'Taurus' chapter.
§ Dorsey, *op. cit.*
‖ *Bur. Am. Eth.*, 1904, 307.

few exceptions, clearly reveal their origin in the personification of natural phenomena. The American Indians as a race are typically nature-worshippers. The sun and moon, and other celestial bodies, the seasons, the six directions, the four supposed elements, all figure prominently and generally in their pantheon, but the cult of the dead, wide-spread though it be, is confined almost entirely to communication with the spirits of the departed. Fear is seldom an element of this cult. Its main motive seems to be merely the renewal of friendly relations with the spirits, who are regarded as leading in another world an individual life very similar to their earthly life, to which they are eventually destined to return. Superhuman knowledge of events distant in time or space is indeed attributed to the spirits, no greater perhaps than that conceded to certain living men, but these men themselves were thought to receive their knowledge from the spirits. It is a long step from such attributes to deification. Honours were paid to the dead individually, similar in degree to those due them when on earth; information was asked of them, seldom anything else. But there is slight evidence that the dead were regarded as superior beings.

The chief when living remained a chief when dead, as much below the deities then as before, except for greater knowledge. In Spanish writings of a period when apostles were asserted to have fought visibly against the heathen in Peru, spirits are said to have helped the Inca Yupanqui to overcome his enemies. If this be a Peruvian tradition, it is a rare example of a native legend which attributes to the spirits active intervention in the affairs of this world. Amongst the civilized tribes who offer elaborate petitions to their nature deities, very few are directed to the spirits. The legend of Manco Ccapac and Mama Oello of Peru, and the deities of the Popol Vuh, who, descending from the sky, after an active life on earth re-ascend to the sky and become stars, clearly reveal nature personification. Amongst a number of legends relating to caciques similarly translated and deified, none which present details can be otherwise classified.

The Paraguayans and the Powhatans of Virginia are said to have worshipped the skeletons of their forefathers,* but may merely have retained them to consult with the spirits which were believed in some sense to remain attached to the bodies. So the people of Comagre worshipped the bejewelled mummies of their ancestors.†

The Eskimo upper world is ruled by the souls of the dead, including those inhabiting the celestial bodies. These were once men, and occasionally returned to earth.‡ In Nayarit, the skeleton of a king received Divine honours, as did Pezelao, god of the dead in Oaxaca.§ But the worship of the deity who governs the dead is quite distinct from the worship of the spirits themselves. The Caribs held regular meetings to propitiate the spirits.‖ The Californian tribes believed that some of the dead became stars,¶ the Iroquois that the stars had all been mortals, or favoured animals, and birds. But the sun and moon existed before them.** In Peru, the malquis, or mummies, were petitioned to grant food, health, and life.†† According to Acosta, each ruling Inca after death was regarded as a god, and had his individual sacrifices, statues, etc.‡‡ Each month the coast people sacrificed children and anointed the tombs with their blood.§§

* Brinton, 274.
† Bancroft, iii. 500.
‡ Rink, p. 48.
§ Bancroft, iii. 457.
‖ *Ib.* 498.
¶ *Ib.* 523.
** Mrs. Erminie A. Smith.
†† Arriaga, p. 30.
‡‡ José de Acosta, lib. vi. cap. xii.
§§ F. de Xeres, *Reports*, p. 32.

The Chibchas and Guatemalan tribes buried a corpse in the foundation of each building that it might be protected by the spirit.* The Mexicans called their dead *teotl*, meaning 'divinity.'† Some asserted that their gods had been at first mere men, who had been deified either because of their rank, or some notable thing which they had done.‡ They set up in their temples statues of their victorious generals.§

12. Festival of the dead.—In many parts of America there was an annual or semi-annual festival in honour of the dead who, at this time, as in China, Japan, and many other countries, were believed to return to earth over the Milky Way to participate invisibly in the ceremonies. In Peru the Ayamarca, or Carrying of the Corpse, festival was celebrated annually for three days at the time of our Halloween, All Saints', and All Souls'. The supposed coincidence in time is but one of many similar analogies in the Peruvian ritual that are associated with ceremonials which have reached us from pre-historic times. During this festival the bodies of the deceased rulers of the Incas, with those of their principal wives or *ccoyas*, were clothed in new garments, and were brought forth from the temple in which they were deposited. Each mummy, followed by its special attendants, was then borne in ceremonial procession through the streets of the sacred city of Cuzco, after which food and drink were offered to it with all the honours due in life, in the belief that at this time the spirit did indeed return to the body, and reside therein during the time of the festival. The procession echoed on earth the passage of the sun through the zodiacal sign of the Mummy (Scorpio). At the same time fruits and flowers were placed upon all graves to refresh the returning spirits. The festival is also associated with the imparting of celestial wisdom.‖

The basis of this ritual, however, seems to have been rejoicing over the temporary renewal of intercourse with departed friends and relatives, and its object to welcome and please them with respect and courtesies. The element of worship of the dead as superior beings or the offering of prayers to them for aid is not prominent. The Mexicans held festivals in honour of the dead in August and November, when the souls hovered over and smelt of the food set out for them, sucking out its nutritive quality. The Mayas, Miztecs, Pueblos, and Eskimos performed similar rites in November, the Iroquois in spring and autumn.¶ The Hurons believed that the souls of the dead remained near to the bodies until the feast of the dead was celebrated. They then became free, and at once departed for the land of spirits.** The Chibchas and Peruvians repeated the curious Egyptian custom of introducing a mummy in the midst of a revel to suggest to the feasters the omnipresence of death.††

13. Demons.—The religion of the American Indians is not dualistic; good and evil alike are attributed to the Great Spirit. But the conflict, so far as it is recognized, depends rather upon physical and mental than upon moral qualities. No instance can be found in aboriginal America of a contest between a supreme good and a supreme

* Scherzer quoting Ximenez in note, p. 188; Padre Simon, p. 255.
† Motolinia, p. 31.
‡ Mendieta, p. 84; Camargo, iii. p. 154; see also Herrera, iii. p. 221.
§ Camargo, in *Nouv. Ann. des Voyages*, 4me ser., iii. p. 136.
‖ S. Hagar, *Peruv. Astron.* 'Scorpio' chapter.
¶ Bancroft, ii. 331, 335; Frazer in *Fortnightly Review*, Sept. 1906, p. 476 ff.; Morgan, i. 275; Tylor, *Primitive Culture*, ii. p. 45.
** Yarrow, 191; Stevenson; Lafitau, ii. 43; Charlevoix, 277.
†† Salcamayhua, 85; Uricoechea, 19.

evil power for dominion over souls or even for the control of the world. Mischievous, angry, and hostile spirits are recognized, and two heroes, respectively propitious and adverse to mankind, are sometimes contrasted in traditions, probably of native origin, though modified by Christianity. But there was no Satan in America, and the hostile spirits play a subordinate part. The attempts of the early missionaries to create a Satan in the various native languages are amusing. Generally the word used means simply 'spirit,' but in the list is included the beneficent Araucanian god dwelling in the Pleiades, numerous deities called evil only because associated with the dead, and the Peruvian *Supay*, which is only the name of the under world, shared by Haitians, Quichés, Pueblos, and, apparently, by the South Pacific Islanders and the Dayaks of Borneo.* This under world, as well as the sky-world, was undoubtedly viewed as the home of the spirits; and those who dwell in the former seem to be regarded as inferior and to some extent hostile, but there is no such contrast as between heaven and hell. There was no conception of a place of punishment. Such ideas are of missionary origin.

LITERATURE.—José de Acosta, *Nat. and Mor. Hist. of the Indies*, ed. Markham, Hakluyt Soc. pub., London, 1880; *Amer. Anthropologist*, Washington; *Amer. Antiquarian and Orient. Journ.*, Chicago; *Amer. Folk-Lore Society Memoirs*, Boston; Arriaga, *Extirp. de la Idolat. del Peru*, Lima, 1621; H. H. Bancroft, *Native Races of the Pacific States*, New York, 1875-76; D. G. Brinton, *Essays of an Americanist*, Philad. 1890, *Myths of the New World*[2], New York, 1876; *Bureau of American Ethnology*, Annual Reports, Washington; Antonio de la Calancha, *Coronica Moralizada del Orden de San Agustin en el Peru*, vol. i., Barcelona, 1639; Charlevoix, *Voyage to North America*, London, 1761; Clavigero, *Hist. of Mexico* (Eng. tr.), London, 1787; F. H. Cushing in *Song of the Ancient People*, 1893; G. A. Dorsey, 'Traditions of the Skidi Pawnee,' *Am. Folk-Lore Soc. Memoirs*, Boston, 1904; J. G. Frazer, *Golden Bough*[2], London, 1900; Stansbury Hagar, 'Cherokee Field Notes,' 'Micmac Field Notes,' 'Micmac Magic and Medicine' in *Journ. Am. Folk-Lore*, vol. ix. p. 170 f., *Peruvian Astronomy* (in course of publication); Hernandez in *Popol Vuh*; Antonio de Herrera [Stevens tr.], *General Hist. of the vast Continent and Islands of America*, London, 1725-26; S. S. Hill, *Travels in Peru*, London, 1860; Im Thurn, *Among the Indians of Guiana*, London, 1883; *Journal of American Folk-Lore*, Am. Fk-l. Soc., Boston; Kingsborough (Lord), *Antiquities of Mexico*, London, 1831-48; Lafitau, *Mœurs des Sauvages Amér.*, Paris, 1724; Diego de Landa, *Relacion des Choses de Yucatan*, ed. Brasseur de Bourbourg, Paris, 1869; Cieza de Leon, *Travels*, Hakluyt Soc., London, 1864; Sebastian Lorente, *Hist. Ant. del Peru*, Lima, 1860; Sir John Lubbock, *Prehistoric Times*[4], London, 1878; Maspero and Sayce, *Dawn of Civilization*, London, 1894; Geron de Mendieta, *Hist. Eccles. Ind.*, ed. Icazbalceta, Mexico, 1870; Molina, 'Hist. of Chili' in Kerr's *Voyages*, vol. v., London, 1809; *Narratives of the Rites and Laws of the Incas*, ed. Sir Clements R. Markham, Hakluyt Soc. pub., London, 1873; Morgan, *League of the Iroquois*, New York, 1901; Motolinia, *Hist. de los Indios de Nueva España*, ed. Icazbalceta, Mexico, 1858; *Nouvelles Annales des Voyages*, 4me Série, Paris (Camargo in); Manuel Orozco y Berra, *Geog. de las Lenguas y Carta Etnografica de Mexico*, Mexico, 1864; Oviedo y Valdes, *Hist. General y Natural de las Indias*, Madrid, 1851-55; Chief Simon Pokagon, in *Forum Mag.*, July, 1898; *Popol Vuh*, ed. Brasseur, Paris, 1861; *Relacion de la Nouvelle France*, 1636; H. Rink, *Tales and Traditions of the Eskimo*, ed. R. Brown, London and Edinburgh, 1875; Salcamayhua in *Rites and Laws of the Incas*; Padre Simon, *Not. Hist. de las Conquistas de Tierra Firme* in Kingsborough's *Antiquities of Mexico*, vol. viii.; Mrs. Erminie A. Smith in *Bureau of Am. Ethnol.*, 2nd Report; E. D. Proctor, *Song of the Ancient People*, Boston, 1893; Herbert Spencer, *Descriptive Sociology*, London, 1873-81; E. G. Squier, *Peru*, New York, 1877; Stevenson, *Travels in Peru*; Mrs. Matilda Stevenson, 'The Zuñi' in *Bureau of Am. Ethnol.*, 23rd Rep., Washington, 1905; Tylor, *Primitive Culture*[3], London, 1891; Uricoechea, *Memoria sobre las Antiguedades Neo-Granadinas*, Berlin, 1854; Ximenez, *Las Hist. del Origen de los Indios de Guatemala*, Vienna, 1857; H. C. Yarrow, 'Mortuary Customs of the North American Indians' in *Bureau of Am. Ethnol.*, 1st Rep., Washington, 1880.

STANSBURY HAGAR.

ANCESTOR-WORSHIP AND CULT OF THE DEAD (Babylonian).

—It is at the outset necessary to inquire how far the Babylonian beliefs and customs relating to the cult of the dead, and pointing to a form or forms of ancestor-worship, were in their origin Semitic. The answer depends on the attitude one takes towards the Sumero-Akkadian problem. The majority of Assyriologists, believing as they do in the existence of a distinctly pre-Semitic Sumero-Akkadian culture and language, naturally hold that the cult connected with the spirits of the departed, which was allowed to flourish by the side of the Babylonian State religion (or rather religions) was in its essence very largely, if not entirely, a popular survival of an ancient non-Semitic form of animism, and Sayce goes so far as to say that the ideas connected with this cult were 'never really assimilated by the Semitic settlers' (*Religions of Ancient Egypt and Babylonia*, 1902, p. 276). An entirely opposite opinion must, of course, be held by the smaller number of Assyriologists, who categorically deny the pre-Semitic civilization here referred to; and even a cautious writer like Jastrow maintains that there is no necessity 'to differentiate or to attempt to differentiate between Semitic and so-called non-Semitic elements' in Babylonian and Assyrian religion (*Religion of Babylonia and Assyria*, 1898, p. 24).

The non-Semitic origin of the cult appears at first sight to be confirmed by the many words of an entirely different linguistic stock that meet us in the texts relating to it, as, *e.g.*, *Ekur* and *Kigallu* (names of the under world), and apparently also *utukku* and *ekimmu* (kinds of ghosts). But Semitic terms are by no means absent, as *e.g.* *Allatu* (name of the goddess of the under world), *Shu'ālu** (one of the names of the under world), and, as it seems, also *Arālu*† (or *Arallu*), which is the most common designation of Hades.

It is, furthermore, safe to assume by analogy that, even on the theory of an early pre-Semitic civilization of Babylonia, the Semites may, on entering the country, have brought with them popular ideas regarding the dead which were not dissimilar from those they found among the natives, and that the adoption of Sumero-Akkadian terms (which, let it be remembered, are frequent in the Semitic state religions themselves) would in the process of adaptation follow as a matter of course. It must also be borne in mind that, historically speaking, we have so far to do almost entirely with Semites. We are therefore in the present state of our knowledge fully justified in—provisionally at any rate—treating the cult and the ideas connected with it as in the full sense of the word Semitic.

Besides the question of origin, many other uncertainties still obscure the problem; for there are so far not enough data for the formulation of a complete system of these ideas and customs. In the interpretation also of a number of facts one has often to rely on inference rather than actual proof. It may be assumed that fuller knowledge will be the result of further excavation and the complete decipherment of extant materials; but for the present it must suffice to systematize the information that has already been gained.

The extant data may be conveniently treated under the following three heads:—(1) deification, (2) sacrifices and offerings to the dead, (3) necromancy. Some cognate matters, which may help to elucidate the problem, can easily be mentioned in connexion with one or other of these three parts.

1. Deification.—The only instance so far known

* S. Hagar, *op. cit.* 'Scorpio' chapter.

* On *Shu'ālu* (Heb. *Shᵉ'ōl*) see § 3 below.

† Jeremias (*Bab.-Assyr. Vorstellungen vom Leben nach dem Tode*, p. 123) considers it to be the same as *Ariel* in Is 29[1ff.], both words apparently signifying (1) the mountain of the gods, the Heb. Zion; (2) a place of desolation and woe. The term *Arālu* would thus seem to point to a mountainous country (therefore not Babylonia) as the origin of the ideas connected with the under world. The same result is obtained from the use of the term *Ekur*, which among its various meanings includes that of the mountain of the gods.

in Babylonian mythology of mortals passing to immortality and deification without having previously died and gone down to the under world, is that of Sit-napishtin, the Babylonian Noah,* and his wife (or, according to Berossus, as reported by Alexander Polyhistor, also his daughter and his pilot †). When the deluge was over, Bel, whose wrath had been appeased by a speech of Ea, bestowed divine life on the pair, and assigned to them a dwelling afar off 'at the mouth of the streams.' The case of the hero Gilgamesh and that of Etana, before whose names the determinative for 'god' is always placed, are different; for both of them had first to pass through death, the common fate. Gilgamesh, as the epic bearing the name shows, endeavoured in vain to secure exemption from the fate of mortals by his visit to his ancestor ‡ Sit-napishtin; and with regard to Etana, it is only reasonable to assume that he was dashed to pieces when he fell from the heights of heaven with the eagle that bore him. In the case of Adapa, who, having broken the wings of Shūtu, the south-west wind, was summoned to heaven to answer the charge, deification and a place in the company of the gods of heaven would have been his share, if he had not refused to partake of the 'meat of life' and 'the water of life' which Anu had offered him. The ground for deification in the cases mentioned was no doubt the heroic character of the persons concerned; but the element of ancestor-worship was probably not absent, and it is in any case clear that such instances of deification cannot be dissociated from the cult connected with the departed.

Passing from legend (which may, however, be assumed to rest on some actual ancient events) to historic times, we find the names of Dungi and Gudea (probably before the middle of the 3rd millennium B.C.) 'written on tablets that belong to the centuries immediately following their reign, with the determinative that is placed before the names of gods. Festivals were celebrated in honour of these kings, sacrifices were offered to them, and their images were placed in temples. Again, Gimilsin (about 2500 B.C.), of the second dynasty of Ur, appears [like an Egyptian Pharaoh] to have been deified during his lifetime, and there was a temple at Lagash which was named after him' (Jastrow, *op. cit.* p. 561). In paying honour to deified kings and other great personages, the sons and other descendants would both naturally and in accordance with an established rule (see § 2) take the lead, and the people generally would share in the celebrations, so that we have here instances firstly of ancestor-worship in the strict sense of the word, and secondly in its wider, if looser, signification as homage paid to the departed kings and fathers of the people.

Some acts pointing to deification or semi-deification in later times will be mentioned in connexion with sacrifices and offerings to the dead, and it will there also be seen what form the cult of the dead took among the people in general; but it is necessary to inquire whether we are able to form a clear notion of what deification meant among the ancient Babylonians. Did the deified rulers and chiefs stay among the gloomy deities of the under world presided over by Nergal and his consort Allatu, or did they ascend to join the company of the supernal gods? A writer like Jastrow, who strongly emphasizes the impossibility of a disembodied human spirit escaping out of the Babylonian Hades, must adopt the former alternative, notwithstanding the various difficulties connected with this interpretation (as, *e.g.*, the instances of an *utukku* actually finding its way back to earth). The brightest view so far taken of the Babylonian doctrine bearing on this problem is that of A. Jeremias (*op. cit.* pp. 100–105, and elsewhere). With Sayce and others this writer takes the epithet 'raiser from the dead,'* given to Marduk and other deities, in its natural sense (as against the forced interpretation of Jastrow, who takes it in the sense of preventing death from overtaking the living), and attributes to the ancient Babylonians hopes of a much brighter existence than was to be had in the under world; and if this be so, there is nothing to prevent us from thinking that by their deification Gudea and others entered the luminous company of the gods of heaven instead of dwelling for ever in Hades, and that in consequence their descendants had bright and happy visions of the ancestors to whom they addressed worship. Confirmatory of this view is the fact that the 'water of life,' to which reference has already been made in the story of Adapa, is to be found even in Hades. If Ishtar could by the command of Ea be restored to the upper world by being sprinkled with this 'water of life' ('Descent of Ishtar,' reverse, l. 38 ff.), why not also departed mortals who were destined for deification? The truth, however, seems to be that we have here to deal with different streams of belief, some tending one way and some another. But in accepting this opinion it is not necessary at the same time to agree with Sayce, who assigns the gloomier doctrine of Hades to the Sumerians, and the supernal deification to the Semites, for it may well be that there were different streams of tradition among the Semites themselves. Development within the Semitic field is, of course, also an important factor to consider.

2. Sacrifices and offerings to the dead.—Mention has already been made of sacrifices offered to deified kings in early Babylonian history, and of festivals celebrated in their honour. The famous Stele of Vultures, which records the victories of Eannatuna, or Eannadu, an ancient king † of the city of Shirpurla, shows on one of the extant fragments the corpses of departed warriors laid in rows, whilst their surviving comrades are represented with baskets on their heads, which are generally understood to have contained funeral offerings ‡ for the dead. The fallen enemies, on the other hand, are refused burial, their remains being the food of struggling vultures (on the terrible meaning of this treatment, see below). An ancient bronze tablet, which represents a funeral scene, apparently watched over from the top by Nergal, and showing below the goddess Allatu in her bark, exhibits the dead person lying on a bier, attended by priests in fish-like garments, with a stand for burning incense not far from the head of the bier.§ 'On

* In reality Sit-napishtin (pronounced by some Par-napishtin, Pir-napishtin, or Ut-napishtim, and named Xisuthros [=Atra-khāsis, or Khāsisatra] by Berossus) appears to be a combination of the Biblical Noah and Enoch, the latter having also escaped death (Gn 5[24]).

† Or, perhaps, the ship's architect; see Euseb. *Chron.*, ed. Schoene, i. p. 22.

‡ In the Gilgamesh Epic, ix., beginning of col. iii., the hero says:—'Sit-napishtin, my father . . . who entered the assembly of the gods,' etc.

* Cf. 1 S 2[6] ('He bringeth down to Sheol and bringeth up').

† Probably before B.C. 4000 (see L. W. King, *Bab. Religion*, p. 48).

‡ The interpretation of the scene is, however, uncertain. The baskets may have contained more earth for the mound raised over the corpses. Jastrow (*op. cit.* p. 599) states that the Stele shows animal sacrifices being offered to the dead, and Maspero (*Dawn of Civilization*, p. 607) says that 'the sovereign deigns to kill with his own hand one of the principal chiefs of the enemy' in honour of the dead. Fragments of the Stele were first made known by de Sarzec, *Découvertes en Chaldée*, plates 3 and 4. For other literature, see Maspero, *loc. cit.*

§ See Jastrow, *op. cit.* p. 579; Maspero, *op. cit.* p. 690 ff.; L. W. King, *op. cit.* p. 37 ff. The exact interpretation of this tablet is also a matter of dispute, but there is no doubt about the burning of incense. The fish-like garments of the attendants or priests have apparently reference to the god Ea in his character as lord of the deep. This and the other bronze plates of the same class are by some supposed to have served as votive tablets in the graves of the dead.

the monuments of later Babylonian and Assyrian kings we do not find any representation of burial ceremonies' (L. W. King, *op. cit.* p. 48), but from a broken inscription of one of the later Assyrian kings, whose name has not been preserved, 'we learn that the king placed vessels of gold and silver in the grave as dedicatory offerings' to his departed father (*ib.* p. 49). Ashurbanipal (king of Assyria, B.C. 668–626), in a still more devout fashion, appears at the tombs of his ancestors with rent garments, pouring out a libation in memory of the dead, and addressing a prayer to them (see, *e.g.*, Jastrow, *op. cit.* p. 605).

It is necessary, however, to distinguish carefully between sacrifices in the proper sense of the word and offerings of various kinds made to the dead by way of providing for their proper maintenance in the under world. The former point to a form of deification and actual worship (though probably in most cases of a secondary kind), whilst the latter, which, roughly speaking, belong to the decidedly popular element of the cult, are generally understood to have had the object of keeping the ghosts of the departed in a sufficiently comfortable condition in the under world, so as not to risk their returning to molest their living relatives and acquaintances. One is inclined to include affection for the departed among the underlying motives, and some of the details to be mentioned presently would seem to support this view; but it is true that the motive of fear was exceedingly strong. The departed human spirit was best known by the dreaded name *ekimmu*. The difference between it and *utukku* cannot be accurately stated. It seems, however, that *utukku* was a general name for demon, for we hear of the *utukku* 'of the field,' 'of the sea,' etc., whilst *ekimmu* was (or became) the proper name for a departed human spirit. Sayce (*op. cit.* p. 284) would limit the meaning of *ekimmu* to the 'spirit of an unburied corpse over whose unsanctified remains the funeral rites had never been performed'; but R. C. Thompson (*The Devils and Evil Spirits of Babylonia*, i. p. xxvii. ff.) has shown that the name was also applied to ghosts who, though properly buried, had no one to provide them with the necessary sustenance in the under world, so that they were forced to return to the earth in order to seek for themselves some sort of maintenance among their former associates. When opportunity offered, the ghost would even enter the body of a living man, tormenting him until it should be exorcized by a priest. In order to guard against these dangers to the living, it was necessary, first of all, to perform the funeral rites, by means of which the human spirit was enabled to reach its destination in the realms of Arālu; and it was, secondly, required of the relatives, and more particularly of the eldest son and direct descendants of the deceased, to make provision for their proper maintenance in a region where, apart from the sustenance provided for them by their friends on earth, 'dust is their nourishment, their food clay,' and where 'over gate and bolt dust is scattered' (opening part of the 'Descent of Ishtar'). Offerings of this kind would, however, naturally assume a propitiatory character of a more or less definite kind, and a sufficiently close affinity with sacrifices proper would be the result.

The provision thus made for the departed differed, of course, in accordance with their condition during their life on earth, and was, besides, dependent on the means possessed by their living relatives. The occupant of the smaller chambers of burial 'was content to have with him his linen, his ornaments, some bronze arrowheads, and metal or clay vessels,' whilst others were provided with 'furniture, which, though not as complete as that found in Egyptian sepulchres, must have ministered to all the needs of the spirit' (Maspero, *op. cit.* p. 686). Special requirements were also thought of. Thus, 'beside the body of a woman or young girl was arranged an abundance of spare ornaments, flowers, scent-bottles, combs, cosmetic pencils, and cakes of the black paste with which they were accustomed to paint the eyebrows and the edges of the eyelids' (Maspero, *ib.*). 'Toys, too, are found in the graves, and we may assume that these were placed in the tombs of children' (Jastrow, *op. cit.* p. 598). Food and drink were, of course, the main requirements, and these all-important offerings were made to the dead not only at the time of burial, but also afterwards by surviving relatives; and the entrances to tombs that have been found (Peters, *Nippur*, ii. 173, and elsewhere) may be explained as an arrangement made for renewing these and other offerings. The son performed the office of pouring out water in memory of his father. The water-jar is indeed 'never absent in the old Babylonian tombs, and by the side of the jar the bowl of clay or bronze is found, which probably served the same purpose as a drinking utensil for the dead' (Jastrow, *op. cit.* p. 599). Remains of food of various kinds are, however, more frequent in the early graves than in those of later times. Among the other objects placed at the disposal of the dead are the staves which the owners carried about in their lifetime, and the seal-cylinders which persons of position were in the habit of using. How far the customary wailing for the dead, not only immediately after their departure, but also subsequently, included terms of homage and adoration, cannot be stated with any certainty; but it appears that the Festival of Tammuz was selected as a kind of 'All Souls' Day,' and some degree of adoration of the dead may have been combined with the ceremonies connected with the homage paid to the annually reviving god.

The grim side of this cycle of ideas is seen in the treatment of the corpses of enemies. By dragging the dead bodies out of their graves, mutilating their remains, and other indignities, their shades were deprived of their comfort and their rest, and their living relatives became at the same time exposed to the terrible molestation of the prowling and suffering ghosts. This explains the violence done to the remains of fallen enemies, as represented on the Stele of Vultures already referred to. In later times, Ashurbanipal expressly states that by destroying the graves of Elamite kings and dragging their bodies to Assyria he had made sure that no food should be tendered to them, and no sacrifices offered in their honour (see *e.g.* Jastrow, *op. cit.* p. 602; L. W. King, *op. cit.* p. 44). Similar revenge upon his enemies was taken by Sennacherib.

3. Necromancy.—Necromancy, which is an essential part of the cult of the dead, and which must also have been connected with the presentation of offerings to the shades consulted, undoubtedly held a prominent place among the magic arts of the Babylonians. 'A series of mythological texts shows that scenes such as that between Saul and the witch of Endor were familiar to Babylonian fancy also. Among the lists of the various orders of priests we find the offices of "exorcist of the spirits of the dead," the priest "who raises the Spirit of the dead," and the *Sha'ilu*, the "inquirer of the dead"' * (A. Jeremias, *Bab. Conception of Heaven and Hell*, p. 28). The argument, however, that

* Jeremias himself, however, states that the literature so far known to us has no example of the 'inquiry of the dead.' The case of Eabani was different, for Gilgamesh conversed with him like one person with another (see further on). It is to be noted here that in Ezk 21[26] [Eng. [21]] Nebuchadnezzar is represented as inquiring of the Terāphim, which some writers regard as images of ancestors. (See § 2 of the 'Hebrew' article).

has been urged by Jastrow (*op. cit.* p. 559) and others, that the name *Shu'ālu* (Heb. *She'ōl*) itself proves that inquiry of the dead was inseparable from the very notion of the under world thus designated, is by no means convincing; for the root *sha'al* (שׁאל) may be connected with *sha'al* (שׁעל), thus giving to *Shu'ālu* the meaning of 'hollowed out place' rather than that of 'place of inquiry' * (see *Oxf. Heb. Lex. s.v.*).

The classical, and so far solitary, clear instance of raising a dead person and conversing with him (analogous to the famous Biblical instance of Saul and Samuel) is that of the hero Gilgamesh and the shade of his friend Eabani, as related in the closing tablet of the Gilgamesh Epic. The help of Nergal himself had to be obtained in order to secure the desired effect. The god of Hades 'opened the hole of the earth, and let the *utukku* of Eabani come forth out of the earth like a wind' (Gilgamesh Epic, xii. col. 3, ll. 27–8). The conversation of the two friends turns on the condition of the departed in the regions of Hades.

As connected with this part of the subject omens may be mentioned. Mr. R. C. Thompson, in the work already referred to, writes as follows:—

'The belief in the *ekimmu* spirit had obtained such a hold over the Assyrians that they even went to the length of deducing omens from the appearance of such a ghost in a house. As a rule, it was held to be an evil omen, whether it was merely a silent apparition or whether it gibbered or uttered some words or awaited some response. . . . The threat that is held over the heads of all spectres of this class is that no rite shall be paid to them until they have departed' (vol. i. p. xxxv).

To sum up: the evidence, so far as it goes, shows clearly that even in historic times the cult of the dead and elements of ancestor-worship formed, more or less distinctly, part of Babylonian religious observances. As regards deification of deceased ancestors, sacrifices in the proper sense of the word, and festivals held in honour of the dead, the clear evidence, as was to be expected, relates to the ruling families only. It may, by analogy with the religious development of other races, be assumed that ancestor-worship and the cult of the dead were more prevalent in pre-historic times than later on. But whether this cult was in very ancient times the only or even the chief religious worship of the Babylonians—whether Sumerians or Semites, or a combination of both—is quite a different question. It surely is not improbable that it was but one among a variety of cults, and that the various *numina loci*, the heavenly bodies, the storm, the lightning, and other powers of nature played at least as great a part in the earliest Babylonian religion as the worship of the departed. There is at any rate nothing in the Babylonian cult to confirm the theory of Herbert Spencer, that ancestor-worship was the sole original worship of humanity, and that animism in its wider sense was developed out of it.

LITERATURE.—The principal literature used has been frequently quoted. The part relating to the subject in the German edition of Jastrow's *Religion of Babylonia and Assyria* had not come to hand when the article was written. The bibliography at the end of that edition will no doubt be the fullest. In the quotations from the 'Descent of Ishtar' and the 'Epic of Gilgamesh,' Jensen's edition (Schrader's *KB* vi.) has been followed.

G. MARGOLIOUTH.

ANCESTOR-WORSHIP AND CULT OF THE DEAD (Celtic).

—The meagre data preserved concerning the Celtic religions contain little evidence to show that the worship of ancestors prevailed in Gaul or the British Isles. The general existence of this cult throughout the Indo-Germanic peoples (see Schrader, *Reallexikon der indogermanischen Alterthumskunde*, Strassburg, 1901, pp. 21–33), however, renders it practically certain that the Celts, like the kindred stocks, worshipped their ancestors. The Druids are known to have taught not only immortality but also metempsychosis (Cæsar, *de Bello Gallico*, vi. 14; Lucan, *Pharsalia*, i. 454–458). Yet the only passages which in any way sanction the hypothesis of ancestor-worship are Cæsar, *de Bello Gallico*, vi. 19, and Pomponius Mela, *Chorographia*, iii. 19. The former author states that, 'in keeping with the cult of the Gauls, funerals are magnificent and sumptuous, and they cast upon the pyre all that they suppose pleasing to the living; even animals and, a short time ago, slaves and dependants who were evidently especially dear to the deceased were burned with them after the funeral rites had been duly performed.' Pomponius adds that, in consequence of the Gallic belief in immortality, 'they burn and bury with the dead things proper for the living,' and says that the human victims who were burned were either messengers (like the slaves killed to carry tidings to a deceased king in Dahomey) or faithful retainers who desired to continue life in the future world with their patrons. It is questionable, however, whether all this can be construed as ancestor-worship in the strict sense of the term.

LOUIS H. GRAY.

ANCESTOR-WORSHIP AND CULT OF THE DEAD (Egyptian).

—*A.* **Ancestor-worship.**—Of a developed ancestor-worship, like that of the Far East, there is in Egyptian religion little trace. Their knowledge of their long history disposed the Egyptians to revere the memory of their ancestors (*ṭepu-āui*), and we often hear 'the time of the ancestors' referred to with respect: such-and-such a temple was rebuilt 'as it had been in the time of the ancestors'; so wonderful a thing had never happened 'since the time of the ancestors,' and so forth. The kings naturally regarded their predecessors in the royal line with respect, and are depicted making offerings to their names, as at Abydos, where Seti I. and his son, the Prince Rameses (afterwards Rameses II.), offer incense before the two long rows of cartouches, each of which contains the name of a king whom Seti considered worthy of special honour. Incense is being offered much as it might be offered before Japanese *ihai*. But Egyptian ancestor-worship went little farther than this. The ordinary person did not specially venerate the names of his ancestors. He often commemorated them, but never as gods, except in so far that every dead man was a god in that he 'became Osiris.' But as a proof of his loyalty to the reigning dynasty, he venerated the ancient royal names which his king delighted to honour: at Saḳḳâra we find a private person, Tunur, offering to a series of kings' names, which is almost identical with that reverenced by Seti I. at Abydos. Such lists were purely commemorative. Seti I. did not regard his ancestors as gods because they were his ancestors, but because, as kings of Egypt, they had been gods; every king during his life was the 'good god' as the successor and representative on earth of the sky-god Horus, the oldest ruler of Egypt. Tunur regarded the ancient kings as gods for the same reason. He would never have represented himself offering to the *ihai* of his own ancestors as gods, because they never had been gods, nor did he regard them as gods except in so far as each was an Osiris.

Osiris-worship was not ancestor-worship. It is not probable that the Egyptians regarded even Osiris, the great god of the dead, with whom every dead man was identified, as a sort of original ancestor of the race, in spite of the belief that he had once reigned over Egypt as king. This Euhemeristic view is probably late, and was certainly of local origin, probably at Busiris in the Delta (see below). The older Egyptians had feared the

* Jeremias, *Leben nach dem Tode*, p. 62 renders 'place of decision' (*Entscheidungsort*), but the synonym *Mala-akki* which he quotes may itself be a mere guess of Babylonian etymologists.

magical power of the dead man, and had regarded him as a deity; every dead man was Osiris. So they worshipped him as Osiris and in the form of the god of the dead; not under his own name or in his own shape. Thus no real cult of ancestors as gods under their own names and in their own shapes ever grew up in Egypt. To venerate one's ancestors as Osirises was a very different thing from venerating them as ancestors. Filial piety demanded the mention of mother and father, perhaps of grand-parents, on one's gravestone; the son could put up a *stele* in memory of his parents 'as making their names to live upon earth.' But so also could a brother make the name of his brother or sister to live. No worship is implied.

Religious duty demanded the proper observance of certain ceremonies at the tomb by the hand of the 'servant of the ghost' (*ḥen-ka*), but these were not intended as worship of the ghost; they were meant to ensure his happy transit through all the terrors of the under world and the final reunion of the parts of his body and soul in the celestial boat of the sun-god. The religious texts inscribed upon the walls of the tombs had a similar signification. They are all magical spells designed to keep the spirit of the dead man from harm and wandering; and to enable him, by means of formulæ asserting his divine dignity, to win his way past all opposition to his position as a god and the equal of the gods. But no prayers are addressed to him as a god; and if they were, they would only be addressed to him as the god Osiris, not as an ancestor-god protecting his family and tribe. Of this conception we find no trace in Egyptian religion, except the position assigned to Horus, who, like his father Osiris, had reigned in Egypt, and was the predecessor, if not the progenitor, of its kings. But here again, as in the case of Osiris, the kings venerated their ancestor Horus, not because he was their ancestor and the founder of the monarchy, but because he was himself one of the great gods, and was also implicitly divine because he had been a king.

Thus it would appear that the deification of every dead man, or rather his identification with one particular deity, allowed no room for ancestor-worship, in the true sense, in Egyptian religion. No doubt possible traces of it may be discerned here and there in local beliefs, but in the main scheme of the national religion it had no place.

B. **Cult of the dead.**—As has been shown above, the deification of every dead man as himself the god Osiris resulted in the absence of any regular form of ancestor-worship in Egypt. The dead man was venerated as Osiris, not as an ancestor. Originally, however, this 'Osirian' doctrine was not common to the whole of Egypt. It seems to have originated at Dedu or Busiris, 'Osiris' town,' the modern Abusîr near Samanûd, in the Delta. Here Osiris, far back in the primitive period, must have been simply the protector-god of the local necropolis, as the god Ptah-Seker, or Sokari, was the protector of the necropolis of Memphis, and Anubis, the jackal (confused at a very early period with Upuaut, 'Opener of the Ways,' the wolf war-god of Siût), was the protector of that of Abydos. Anubis of Abydos was also identified with a shadowy deity, Khentamentiu, 'the Chief of the Westerners,' the latter being the dead, who were usually buried on the west bank of the Nile. Whether there was any idea among the primitive Egyptians that the Libyans of the western oases, who sometimes came within their ken, were the spirits of their dead in the West, and that the ruler of the dead was their chief, we cannot tell, but it seems probable that it was so. Khentamentiu, however, is never pictured, so we cannot tell what he was supposed to be like; he had already become identified with the jackal Anubis before the dawn of history.

While, however, the protector of the necropolis of Abydos was regarded as a jackal, because the jackal had his abode among the tombs and prowled around them at night, so that the childlike mind of the primitive Egyptian, in fear of him as the ravager of the graveyards, easily came to venerate him, and to desire to placate him by worship as its protector, the Memphite and Busirite gods of the dead were conceived of as dead men; in the northern view the dead were ruled by the dead. The Busirite and Memphite deities, Osiris and Ptah, were closely related. Both were represented as human mummies, the first carrying the whip and flail, emblems of sovereignty, and the second the symbols of power, stability, and life. If the legend of the foundation of Memphis at the beginning of the First Dynasty has a historical basis, it may be that the resemblance of the form of Ptah to that of Osiris is due simply to the fact that the worship of Busiris had penetrated so far southward at that time that, when the necropolis of Memphis was constituted, its protective deity was given a shape differing but little from that of Osiris. However this may be, the Osiride Ptah seems very soon to have come to be regarded as the god of the living city of Memphis rather than that of its necropolis, though his mummy form shows that he was originally a god of the dead almost identical with the Busirite Osiris. Then he was conceived as exercising his function of protector of the necropolis in the form of a dead and mummied hawk, placed upon a coffin. Hence, perhaps, his name of Ptah-Sekri, 'the coffined Ptah.' The hawk was an ancient symbol of divinity, and a dead hawk naturally symbolized a dead god. Later on, the peculiar Kabiric form of Ptah, which may really be older at Memphis than either the mummied man or the mummied hawk, and may, indeed, be the original form of the city-god before the Osiride form prevailed, was revered as 'Ptah-Socharis-Osiris.' This triple name combined Ptah, 'the coffined one,' and the Busirite Osiris proper, in one deity of the Memphite necropolis (now known as that of Saḳḳâra, the village whose name is that of the ancient god). At Memphis this Socharis-form of Osiris was never replaced by the regular Busirite form, which prevailed elsewhere in Egypt. Doubtless this was because, at Memphis, Osiris was entirely identified with Ptah-Seker, while at Abydos he was introduced from the north and merely displaced Anubis, the latter preserving his name and individuality, and only ceding his title of *Khentamentiu* to his superseder.

Thus at Abydos and everywhere else in Egypt, except at Memphis, Osiris was figured in his original Busirite form, as wearing the royal crown in his capacity of king of the dead, just as the living Pharaoh was king of the living. Indeed, as has been noted above, an Euhemeristic view regarded him as a very ancient dead king, who now ruled the shades as he had once ruled the living, and his wife and sister, Isis and Nephthys, as having been his actual wife and sister in life, who bewailed him as he lay on his bier after his death at the hands of his wicked brother Set, the half-foreign deity of the wild desert. Gradually the worship of Osiris spread southwards over all Egypt, and at Siût and Abydos the guardian wolf and jackal diminished into his sons and servants, preserving their individuality, but ceding to him their local sovereignty. At Abydos the title of *Khentamentiu* did not finally pass from Anubis to Osiris till about the time of the Twelfth Dynasty. Thenceforward Abydos became the great centre of Osiris-worship, and

Busiris degenerated into comparative unimportance. The only real rival of Abydos as the headquarters of Osiris was the northern city of Mendes, in the Delta, only a few miles east of Busiris, where the god had at an early period become identified with the local animal-deity, a goat, who was called 'Soul of the Lord of Dedu,' *Bi-neb-ded*, afterwards pronounced Bindidi, Mindid, whence Mendes and the modern Mendîd or Amdîd. It is uncertain whether the goat of Mendes was originally a god of the dead or not; probably he was not. The 'Lord of Dedu,' whose 'soul' he was called, is, of course, Osiris, lord of Busiris. This title of *Neb-Dedet* was recognized throughout Egypt as one of the chief titles of Osiris, and on the stelæ at Abydos it is always accorded to him side by side with the old appellation of the Abydene Anubis, *Khentamentiu*.

With the worship of Osiris went the peculiar doctrines associated with his cult: the belief in resurrection, in the springing of life out of death, which made him a deity of renewed life as well as of death, and so identified him with the green corn-bearing Nile land as opposed to the waste deserts of his brother Set; and, most important of all, the peculiar doctrine of the identification of every dead man with the god, which became at a very early period the cardinal tenet of Egyptian belief with regard to the dead. This Busirite dogma was held even under the Old Kingdom by every Egyptian, and we may find his *credo* in this regard in the well-known '*suten-di-ḥetep*' formula of prayer for the welfare of the dead man, which appears on every sarcophagus, and on every stele or gravestone, and in which the god, whether Anubis 'on the Serpent-Mountain, Lord of Sepa,' or Osiris, 'Lord of Dedet, Khentamentiu, Lord of Abydos,' is besought to give a 'king's offering' (*ḥetep-suten*) of 'thousands of flesh, fowl, and everything good and pure on which *the god there* liveth, to the *ka* of the venerated N, the justified.' The venerated and justified dead man is the *god there*, the deified Osiris N in the tomb, though he may not definitely be called 'the Osiris N.'

Even when other deities were invoked to give the offering, as Amen-Rā or Hathor in the Theban necropolis over which they ruled, or Geb the god of the earth and the Circle of the Nine Gods, the dead man is still Osiris; he is not identified with Amen-Rā, Hathor, or Geb, although the fact that he is Osiris is not always mentioned. On the *ushabtis* (see DEATH AND THE DISPOSAL OF THE DEAD [Egyptian]) he is always called Osiris, and in later times we find the formula definitely phrased thus, 'May Osiris . . . give a king's offering . . . to the Osiris N.' Osiris is asked to give an offering such as a king would give to himself, for every dead man was himself. The dead man was venerated, therefore, not as the dead N, a god because he was a dead ancestor, but as being one with Osiris. In this sense he was worshipped, and only in this sense may the Egyptians be said to have possessed a cult of the dead. Their cult of the dead was the cult of Osiris, and it was to Osiris that the *ḥen-ka*, or 'servant of the ghost' (usually a near relative of the deceased), made the offerings at the tomb, 'seeking to do honour to those there' [a polite periphrasis for the dead]. These offerings consist, in the words of the very interesting inscription on the stele put up by King Aahmes to the memory of his grandmother, Queen Teta-shera, 'in the pouring of water, the offering upon the altar, and the painting of the stele at the beginning of each season, at the Festival of the New Moon, at the feast of the month, the feast of the goingforth of the Sem-priest, the Ceremonies of the Night, the Feasts of the Fifth Day of the Month, and of the Sixth, the *Hak*-festival, the *Uag*-festival, the feast of Thoth, the beginning of every season of heaven and of earth.'

Originally, of course, these honours (see DEATH AND THE DISPOSAL OF THE DEAD [Egyptian]) were paid primarily to the *ka*, or 'double,' of the deceased, which was supposed to reside in the tomb, and, had it not been for the universal adoption of the Osirian doctrine, they would undoubtedly have developed into a regular form of ancestor-worship, the *ka* of each person 'there' being worshipped as a god. We may perhaps even say that before the general adoption of the Osirian doctrine, the southern Egyptians did worship the *kas* of the dead, or even the *sahus* (see DEATH, etc.). We do not know how ancient the beliefs in the other spiritual parts of the dead man, the *ba*, or soul proper, and the *khu*, or intelligence, are. In any case, these other spiritual portions of the man never were specially venerated. They required no sustenance, therefore no offerings were made to them, such as were made to the *ka*. These offerings were made by the members of the family of the deceased persons, whose names were commemorated on stelæ, together with those of their living descendants 'who make their name to live upon earth' (*se'ankh renusen tep ta*). Several generations of the dead are often thus 'made to live' on the stelæ (see DEATH, ETC. [Egyptian]). The Egyptian 'cult of the dead' amounted to no more than this.

The worship of the supreme god of the dead, Osiris himself, as apart from the offerings made to the individual Osirises, the dead, was carried on in the usual manner. He had two great temples, at Abydos and Busiris, which disputed the possession of his most holy relic, supposed to be his actual body; and at Abydos he was supposed to be buried in a tomb which, by a misunderstanding of a hieroglyph, was identified with the tomb of the early monarch Tjer, the sign of his name being misread as *Khent*, 'chief,' and so identified with 'Khentamentiu.' He was worshipped also as the ram at Mendes, and as the bull Apis and in the Kabiric form at Memphis. The temple at Abydos was originally not his. In its lowest strata we find that his predecessor Anubis is the sole deity mentioned. Later on, as we have seen, Anubis and his 'brother' Upuaut, the wolf of Siût (the 'Makedôn' of Diodorus), accompany him as his 'sons' and attendants. The wolf was originally not a god of the dead or of Abydos at all, but was a war-god, of whom the wolf was a good symbol, as the 'opener of the ways' to the pack. But the kinship of the wolf to the jackal soon caused Upuaut to be regarded also as a fellow-protector of the tombs with Anubis at Abydos, and in later times he is exclusively a god of the dead, the double of Anubis. Isis and Nephthys, with the child Horus, naturally accompanied Osiris from the Delta, where they also had their origin. But they did not come much forward till a comparatively late period, when the triad Osiris, Isis, and Harpocrates took the place of the Theban triad Amen, Mut, and Khensu, which had become somewhat discredited everywhere except at Thebes after the end of the Theban domination. During that period Osiris had degenerated from the position of king of the dead to that of merely their judge; his kingly functions were usurped by Amen-Rā, the Theban 'king of the gods,' who during the night was supposed to sail in his solar bark through the under world, giving light to the spirits and accompanied by them in his course. But in the Saïte period Osiris not only returned to his position as king of the dead, but became king of the living also, for he took the place of Amen-Rā as supreme deity of Egypt, and the whole set of myths connected with his name and those of Isis and Horus became the most important part of Egyptian religious belief. It was natural that this should be so then, when the centre of political gravity had shifted to the Delta, the original home of the Osirian religion. Later the Memphite sacred bull Apis, originally the animal of Ptah, but, on account of the confusion of the city-god with Socharis, also regarded as an incarnation of Osiris, came very much to the front, and the Ptolemaic Egyptians evolved a Græco-Egyptian deity, Sarapis (from *Asar-Ḥapi*, Osiris-Apis), out of the old Osiris, whose name now disappears. Finally, in the Roman period, Sarapis becomes identified with the old Nubian god of the dance and of music, Bes, and this godling, the most disreputable of the whole Egyptian pantheon, is venerated on the walls of ancient Abydos as the successor of Osiris, of Anubis, and of the primeval Khentamentiu.

LITERATURE.—Maspero, *Études de mythologie et d'archéologie égyptiennes*, ii. pp. 10, 359 and *passim*; Eduard Meyer, 'Die Entwickelung der Kulte von Abydos und die sogenannten Schakalsgötter' in *Ægyptische Zeitschrift*, xli. (1904), 97-107 [with regard to the origin and relations of the Osirian doctrine, and the history of Anubis and Upuaut]; Budge, *Hist. Eg.* i. p. 19 [on the identification of the 'Tomb of Osiris' at Abydos]; Petrie, *Abydos ii.* [on the temple of Osiris there]; Currelly and Gardiner in *Abydos iii.* [on the stele of Tetashera]; Hall in *PSBA*, Jan. 1908 [on the *Suten-di-ḥetep* formula, etc.]. Generally, on the cult of the dead, the works of Budge, Erman, and Wiedemann on Egyptian religion.

H. R. HALL.

ANCESTOR-WORSHIP AND CULT OF THE DEAD (Fijian).—The Fijian divinities fall naturally into two divisions—the *Kalou-vu* ('Root gods') and the *Kalou-yalo* ('Spirit gods,' *i.e.* deified mortals). There is much truth in Waterhouse's suggestion that the Kalou-vu were of Polynesian origin, carried into Fiji by immigrants from the east and imposed upon the conquered Melanesian tribes in addition to their own pantheon of deified ancestors; and that Ndengei, who was undoubtedly a Melanesian ancestor, was adopted by the immigrants, as the Etruscan gods were by the Romans. The Fijian's belief in his own tribal divinity did not entail denial of the gods of other tribes. To the Hebrew prophets the cult of Baal-peor was not so much a false as an impious creed. In giving their allegiance to the chiefs who conquered them, it was natural that the Fijians should admit the supremacy of their conquerors' gods, who, by giving the victory to their adherents, had proved themselves to be the more powerful. Wainua, the great war-god of Rewa, is said to have drifted from Tonga; and his priest, when inspired, gave his answers in the Tongan language. The Rewans had given the chief place in their pantheon to the god of mere visitors.

First among the Kalou-vu was Ndengei, primarily a god of Rakiraki on the north coast of Viti Levu, but known throughout Fiji except in the eastern islands of the Lau group. This god, evolving from the ancestor and tutelary deity of a joint family into a symbol of Creation and Eternity in serpent form, is a counterpart of Jupiter, the god of a Latin tribe, inflated with Etruscan and Greek myth until he overshadowed the ancient world as Jupiter Optimus Maximus. Ndengei and the personages associated with him are proved by the earliest myths of their home on the Ra coast to have been mortals deified as the first immigrants and founders of the race. If the Polynesian gods were originally deified ancestors, their deification took place at a period so remote that their descendants cannot be identified.

Ancestor-worship is the key to the Melanesian system of government. The Fijian's conception of human authority was based upon his religion. Patriarchy, if not the oldest, is certainly the most natural shape into which the religious instinct of primitive man would crystallize. First there was the family—and the Pacific islands were probably peopled by single families—ruled absolutely by the father, with his store of traditions brought from the land from which he came. His sons, knowing no laws but those which he had taught them, planting their crops, building their huts and their canoes under his direction, bringing their disputes to him for judgment, came to trust him for guidance in every detail of their lives. Suddenly he left them. They could not believe that he, whose anger they had feared but yesterday, had vanished like the flame of yesterday's fire. His spirit had left his body; yet somewhere it must still be watching them. In life he had threatened them with punishment for disobedience, and, even now, when they did the things of which he disapproved, punishment was sure to follow—the crops failed; a hurricane unroofed the hut; floods swept away the canoe. If an enemy prevailed against them, it was because they had neglected him; when the yams ripened to abundant harvest, he was rewarding their piety. In this natural creed was the germ of government. Each son of the dead father founded his own family, but still owed allegiance to the earthly representative—the eldest son—in whom dwelt a portion of the father's godhead. Generations came and went; the tribe increased from tens to hundreds, but still the eldest son of the eldest, who carried in his veins the purest blood of the ancestor, was venerated almost like a god. The ancestor was now regarded as a Kalou-vu, and had his temple and his priests, who became a hereditary caste, with the strong motive of self-interest for keeping his memory green. Priest and chief tacitly agreed to give one another mutual support, the one by threatening divine punishment for disobedience, the other by insisting upon regular offerings to the temple.

That the cult of a common ancestor persisted for many generations is shown by the custom of *tauvu*, which means literally 'sprung from the same root,' *i.e.* of a common origin. It is applied to two or more tribes who may live in different islands, speak different dialects, and have nothing in common but their god. They do not necessarily intermarry; they may have held no intercourse for generations; each may have forgotten the names of its chiefs of five generations back, the site of its ancient home, and the traditions of its migrations; and yet it never forgets the tribe with which it is *tauvu*. Members of that tribe may run riot in its village, slaughter its pigs, and ravage its plantations, while it sits smiling by, for the spoilers are its brothers, worshippers of a common ancestor, and are therefore entitled in the fullest sense to the 'freedom of the city.' Sometimes the bond can be traced back to its origin, the marriage of the daughter of a high chief with the head of a distant clan. Her rank was so transcendent that she brought into her husband's family a measure of the godhead of her ancestors, and her descendants have thenceforth reverenced her forefathers in preference to those of her husband. Generally the bond is so remote that the common ancestor is known by the name of an animal or of a natural object, and the fact that his worshippers may not eat the animal suggests a trace of totemism of a bygone age. In such cases a young band from an overcrowded island may have crossed the water to seek wider planting lands.

Among the Viti Levu tribes of Melanesian origin there was a peculiar ancestral cult known as the *mbaki*, primarily devoted to a thanksgiving for the first-fruits and to initiation. The rites were held in rectangular stone enclosures, called *nanga* ('bed,' *i.e.* of the ancestors). These were built close to the graves of dead chiefs, who were invoked to shower blessings on the tribe in ceremonies which degenerated into orgies of a sexual character. The rites were said to have been introduced by two old men who were found wandering on the sea-shore—strangers cast up by the sea, for they could not speak a word of Fijian. The initiated were sworn to secrecy, and the peculiarity of the rites was that initiated members of tribes with whom the owners of the *nanga* happened to be at war might attend the rites unharmed, and invoke the aid of spirits from whom they were not themselves descended.

The Fijians had a well-peopled mythology of the after life. The spirits of the dead had neither temples nor priests, for, as they left the living unmolested, the living were not called upon to make propitiatory sacrifices to them. They were kept alive by the professional story-tellers, who revived them after funerals, when men's thoughts were directed to the mystery of death. In a land where every stranger is an enemy, the idea of the naked shade, turned out friendless into eternity to find his own way to Bulotu, conjured up images of the perils that beset the lone wayfarer on earth, and the shade was made to run the gauntlet of fiends that were the incarnations of such perils. Though the story of the soul's last journey agreed in outline, the details were filled in by each tribe to suit its geographical position. There was generally water to cross, and a ghostly ferryman who treated his passengers with scant courtesy. There was Ghost-scatterer who stoned the shade, and Reed-spear who impaled him. Goddesses of frightful aspect peered at him and gnashed their teeth; Ravuravu, the god of murder, fell upon him; the Dismisser sifted out the real dead from the trance-smitten; fisher-fiends entangled cowards in their net; at every turn of the Long Road there was some malevolent being to put the shade to the ordeal; so that none but brave warriors who had died a violent death—the only sure passport to Bulotu—passed through unscathed. The shades of all Viti Levu and the contiguous islands and of a large part of Vanua Levu took the nearest road, either to the dwelling of Ndengei or to Naithombothombo, the 'jumping-off-place,' in Bua, and thence passed over the western ocean to Bulotu, the birthplace of the race. No belief was more natural for a primitive people than that the land of which their fathers had told them, where the air was warmer, the yams larger, and the soil more fruitful, was the goal of their spirits after death.

When a chief died, his body was washed and shrouded in bark-cloth. A whale's tooth was laid on his breast to throw at the ghostly pandanus tree. If he hit the mark, he sat down to wait for his wife, who he now knew would be strangled to his manes; but if he missed, he went forward weeping, for it proved that she had been unfaithful to him in life. His tomb became his shrine. A roof was built over it to protect him from the sun and the rain. Kava roots and cooked food were laid upon it, that his spirit might feed upon their spiritual essence. And with each presentation, prayers for his protection were repeated. Indolent or ignoble chiefs were soon forgotten, and in times of prosperity the grass began to grow rank even over the bones of a doughty and masterful chief, but at the first breath of adversity his tomb was carefully weeded, and the offerings became regular. Some member of the priestly family would then become possessed by his spirit, and would squeak oracles in a high falsetto. The process of evolution from the tomb to the temple would now be very short. The peculiarity of ancestor-worship in Fiji is that men worshipped not their own, but their chief's ancestors, to whom they themselves might have but a slender blood relationship.

BASIL THOMSON.

ANCESTOR-WORSHIP AND CULT OF THE DEAD (Hebrew).—The latest portions of the Hebrew Canon are, roughly speaking, contemporary with the earlier Jewish apocryphal writings; but it will for the present purpose be convenient to include the evidence of all the canonical writings of the OT under the heading 'Hebrew,' and to reserve the data found in the OT apocrypha, the Talmud, and other later works for the 'Jewish' section of the subject here dealt with. Probable dates of later Scriptures quoted in the section will, however, usually be given.

The question of ancestor-worship among the ancient Hebrews has been much discussed in recent times, the most systematic treatise on the affirmative side so far being Friedrich Schwally's *Das Leben nach dem Tode* (Giessen, 1892), which in the main follows the views previously laid down by Stade and Oort (see the literature at the end). A decisively negative answer is given in *Der Ahnenkultus und die Urreligion Israels* by Carl Grüneisen (Halle, 1900), who, whilst utilizing the arguments advanced in J. Frey's *Tod, Seelenglaube und Seelenkult in alten Israel* (Leipzig, 1889), attempts to establish his thesis on a more scientific basis than had been done before. This divergency of views rests, of course, not so much on questions of fact as on diverse modes of interpreting the many references to the departed found in the OT. The Hebrew Scriptures have, thanks partly to the relation they bear to all phases of life, and partly, no doubt, also to the judgment emphatically pronounced by Jahwism on other cults, preserved for us a far larger number of details connected with mourning and cognate matters than have so far come to light in the inscriptions of Babylonia and Assyria. It is highly probable, however, that a common stock of ideas underlies both these branches of early Semitic beliefs and customs; for it is becoming more and more clear that pre-Mosaic Hebraism was thoroughly rooted—not by borrowing, but by original affinities—in the widely spread traditions of the general Semitic family.

This branch of the subject will be treated under the following heads: (1) Translation to heaven; (2) Teraphim; (3) Sacrifices and offerings to the dead; (4) Sanctity of graves; (5) Mourning customs; (6) Levirate law; (7) Laws of uncleanness; (8) Necromancy.

1. Translation to heaven.—Deification, if the term were here allowed at all,* could not possibly mean the same in the religion of Jahweh as in the polytheistic Babylonian religion; and yet it seems impossible to resist the conclusion that the translation of Enoch recorded in Gn 5^{24} originally belonged to the same class of beliefs as the transference of the Babylonian Sit-napishtin to the society of the gods. It has already been remarked (see § 1 of 'Babylonian,' art. above) that Sit-napishtin is in reality a combination of the Biblical Noah and Enoch; or, more probably, Noah and Enoch represent a splitting up of the one original personality of Sit-napishtin. However this may be, Enoch, like Sit-napishtin, was spared death and the descent into Sheol, which are the common fate of mortals; and the legitimate meaning of the phrase 'Elohim took him' is that he was transferred to a condition of close association with the Deity. Under the Jahwistic system of religion this would mean that he joined

* The use of the term might seem justified by the designation *elohim* applied to the ghost of Samuel in 1 S 28^{13}, but it is there used only by the witch of Endor. Whether *elohim* = 'the dead' in Is 8^{19} is very doubtful. The idea of deification or semi-deification is, however, implied in a passage like Ps 82^{6}, though *elohim* is there used of the living.

the company of angelic beings (cherubim, seraphim, etc.) which in prophetic imagery * (see Is 6; Ezk 1 and 10) surrounded the throne of Jahweh.

Another clear instance of the translation of a mortal to the company of heavenly beings, without having died and gone down to Sheol, is Elijah,† who passed from earth to heaven in a whirlwind (2 K 2^{11}); and a veiled example of transference to heaven immediately after death (*i.e.* without having previously gone down to Sheol) is, according to Rabbinic tradition (see *Deut. Rabba*, xi. 6), contained in Dt 34^{6}, where the burial of Moses is apparently stated (see Driver, *in loco*) to have been undertaken by Jahweh Himself. Viewed in the light afforded by the translation of Enoch and Elijah, it seems likely that the Midrashic statements of the high favour accorded to Moses ‡ are based on a tradition of great antiquity.

Different from the above-named instances, because pointing to an anti-Jahwistic stratum of belief in deification or semi-deification, is Is 63^{16}, where the supremacy of Jahweh is emphasized by the admission made by the prophet on his own behalf or on that of the nation, that 'Abraham knoweth us not, and Israel doth not acknowledge us.' The clear inference is that Abraham and Israel (or Jacob) were, as the departed ancestors of the race, regarded, by at any rate a portion of the nation, as tutelary deities who interested themselves in the condition of the people, and on whom one could call for succour in times of distress (see, *e.g.*, Cheyne, *The Prophecies of Isaiah*, *in loco*, and *Last Words*; Ed. Meyer,§ *Die Israeliten und ihre Nachbarstämme*, 1906, p. 285). The ideas connected with the term 'Abraham's bosom' used in the parable of Dives and Lazarus (Lk $16^{22.23}$) may not unfairly be regarded as a development from the deification of Abraham implied in the Isaianic passage quoted (see R. Winterbotham, 'The Cultus of Father Abraham,' in *Expositor*, 1896, ii. pp. 177–186).

2. Teraphim.—It has been suggested (see, *e.g.*, Schwally, *op. cit.* p. 35 ff.; Charles, *Eschatology*, p. 21 ff.) that the Teraphim, of which pretty frequent mention is made in the OT, were originally images of ancestors. But there is, so far, nothing to prove the correctness of this proposition. The word itself is of uncertain origin. Schwally's suggestion that *Teraphim* comes from the same root as *Rephaim* ('shades') fails to recommend itself on philological or other grounds. Sayce ‖ connects it with a Babylonian word *tarpu* ('ghost'). Perhaps equally admissible would be a connexion with the Ethiopic *terāf* (pl. *terāfāt*), which among other meanings has that of *excellentia*, *præstantia*. The plural *Teraphim* in the sense of *excellentiæ* would then be analogous to that of *Elohim* in its original plural signification, but it would at the same time afford no clue ¶ as to what kind of exalted beings it represented. From 1 S $19^{13.16}$ (where Michal employs Teraphim to personate David on a sick-bed) we learn that the word was in the plural form used to denote a single image (thus lending itself, like *Elohim*, to a *pluralis majestatis*). The same passage shows that it bore a human form, but this fact by no means demonstrates its identity with an ancestral figure.* In Jg 17^{5} $18^{17ff.}$, at any rate, the Teraphim cannot denote a mere family deity, but the national God (Jahweh) Himself; for the image there spoken of belonged first to an Ephraimite and then to Danites, with a Levite as ministering priest in both cases (see the emphatic reference to a general cult in 18^{19}). Nor does the testimony borne by 1 S 19 to the fact of the Teraphim having formed part of the usual equipment of a well-to-do family ['observe *the* Teraphim,' Charles, *op. cit.* p. 22] necessarily imply a connexion with ancestor-worship; for it is quite as likely that the national God Himself was thus represented in houses of private families.† Still less decisive is the consultation of Teraphim as oracles (with the sanction of the prevalent religion, as, *e.g.*, Hos 3^{4}; or without it, as, *e.g.*, 2 K 23^{24}); for Jahweh Himself or any other deity could thus be consulted.

The *Elohim* before whom a Hebrew servant who wished to remain perpetually in his master's service was brought, in connexion with the ceremony of having his ear pierced with an awl at his master's door ‡ (Ex 21^{6}), have also been regarded by a number of scholars as images of ancestors and identified with the Teraphim. The momentary fixing of the servant's ear to his employer's door looks, indeed, like 'admission to the family cult with all its obligations and privileges,'§ and it is from this consideration that the idea of ancestral gods (or an ancestral god), being here represented by *Elohim*, derives its strength. But certain the conclusion is not; for the tutelary deity of the family need not necessarily be an ancestor, and may, in fact (as has already been remarked), be the national God Himself. Nor is it certain that images of any kind are here meant; for the term *Elohim* may bear the meaning of 'judges' (cf. Ex $22^{7.8.27}$ (Eng. vv.$^{8.9.28}$), and see LXX, Dillmann and the Rabbinical Commentaries, *in loco*), and the piercing of the ear may have been a symbol of obedience (for illustrations, see Dillmann, *in loco*). If, however, the *Elohim* in Ex 21^{6} were images of ancestors, either the Mosaic legislator must have felt no antagonism between Jahwism and this form of the ancestral cult, or the images must at the time in question have come to be regarded as representatives of Jahweh Himself. On the former supposition the omission of the *Elohim* in the parallel Deuteronomic passage (Dt 15^{12-18}) would point to a later effort made to eliminate the ancestral idea from the ceremony. On the latter supposition the Deuteronomist would have aimed at discarding images generally (even of Jahweh Himself).‖

There remain two references in the OT to Teraphim in connexion with non-Israelites, namely, the stealing of Laban's Teraphim by Rachel recorded in Gn 31, and the consultation of Teraphim by Nebuchadnezzar mentioned in Ezk 21^{26} (Eng. v.^{21}). From the fact of the apparent common worship of the Teraphim by Hebrews, Aramæans, and Babylonians, the conclusion has been drawn that ancestor-worship must be meant (see Schwally, *op. cit.* pp. 36, 37); for it would, so it has been argued, be difficult to find another cult that possessed the international character implied. Another such basis could, however, be easily imagined (any of the great powers of nature would indeed satisfy this requirement), and it is furthermore possible that the Teraphim (especially if the general meaning, *excellentiæ*, be adopted; see above) represented different kinds of deities among different nations. In the case of Ezk 21^{26} there is also the possibility that the prophet merely expressed Nebuchadnezzar's manner of consulting oracles in terms of Hebrew speech, and that

* These prophetic ideas were probably grounded on much earlier modes of religious contemplation. Isaiah and Ezekiel need only have given a special Jahwistic finish to certain more or less known forms of Divine imagery. In the case of Ezekiel, the influence of his Babylonian surroundings is clearly discernible.

† Charles (*Eschatology*, p. 56) regards the translation of Enoch and Elijah as a step preparatory to the higher doctrine of the soul developed by Jahwism; but an analogous higher belief probably existed also among the Babylonians (see A. Jeremias referred to in § 1 of Babylonian art.). The tradition regarding Enoch is, moreover, in all probability far too early to fall in with Charles's theory. The truth seems to be that diverse theories and beliefs existed side by side among both the Babylonians and the ancient Hebrews.

‡ In the Midrash referred to, as also elsewhere, the spirit of Moses is said to have been separated from the body, not by the intervention of the angel of death, but by a kiss of Jahweh. Immediately after death he was placed under the throne of glory amidst cherubim, seraphim, and other angelic beings.

§ This inference from Is 63^{16} is, of course, independent of Ed. Meyer's general theory regarding the original divinity of some of the patriarchs.

‖ See *Oxf. Heb. Lex.*, *s.v.*

¶ It would be too venturesome to base a theory on the root-meaning of the Ethiopic verb *tarafa*: *reliquum esse vel fieri*, so as to make it refer to the continued existence of the departed.

* The argument that an ancestral image must here be excluded by the very fact of David's firm adherence to Jahweh (Charles, *loc. cit.*) is not sufficiently convincing, for a certain degree of veneration paid to departed forefathers may be quite compatible with monotheism or (as in David's case) with henotheism.

† For illustrations, see Grüneisen, *op. cit.* p. 181.

‡ This interpretation goes with the theory that the Elohim were household gods; if (see farther on) judges are meant, the door or doorpost would be that of the sanctuary or court where they sat.

§ So Charles, *loc. cit.*; it would, however, be more correct to omit the word *all* from the sentence. The perpetual servant still continued in the status of a dependent, and fell short of the privileges of a son of the house (except, perhaps, under special circumstances, when there was no son; see Gn 15^{3}).

‖ If judges were meant by *Elohim*, their omission by the Deuteronomist might have been due to the use of the word in that sense having become obsolete, although it might be urged that *shôphᵉṭim* would in that case have been employed instead.

Teraphim in the usual OT meaning of the word were not actually used by him.

It would seem, therefore, that so far we have no clear indication as to what deity or deities the Teraphim represented. All that can be said is that they may originally have been images of ancestors, and the fact of their having been (in many cases at least) household gods would be in consonance with the idea, though it cannot be adduced as a proof of its correctness.

3. Sacrifices and offerings to the dead.—As a clear reference * to the offering of food to the dead Dt 26^{14} may be claimed; the tithe-giver there makes the following declaration: 'I have not eaten thereof in my mourning, neither have I put away thereof being unclean, *nor given thereof to the dead*.'† Oort, Stade, Schwally, and others see in this declaration a prohibition (and therefore an evidence of the custom) of sacrificial offerings to the dead, understanding the text to mean that the tithe sacred to Jahweh was not to be perverted to idolatrous practices connected with the worship of the dead; but the general bearing of the entire declaration suggests only the provision of sustenance. The evidence for sacrifices offered to the dead must therefore rest on other grounds (see farther on). The fact, however, that every single tithe-giver had to make the statement in question proves that the practice of feeding the dead, or a strong disposition towards it, was wide-spread among the people, and perhaps also in the higher grades of society.

This is one of the indications showing that the ancient Hebrews shared with their Babylonian kinsmen the belief in the continuance of the human personality after death, and in its need of sustenance in Sheol, the Hebrew equivalent of the Babylonian *Shu'ālu* or *Arālu*. But whilst in Babylonia and Assyria the early customs connected with the belief were allowed to flourish by the side of the State religions, Jahwism strove with all its might to suppress them. In a measure it succeeded; but popular ideas are not easily rooted out, and the practice continued for a considerable period of time in different parts of the country. The various and partly conflicting references to the dead met with in the OT are largely to be explained by this conflict of Jahwism with the ancient cult and the frequent recrudescence of heathen ideas in all their original force. That, however, Jahwism made substantial progress in the course of time, is shown by the fact that Jahweh, who was originally only a territorial God, gradually acquired authority even over Sheol, as is evidenced by His power of bringing up the dead from the under world mentioned in 1 S 2^{6} (hardly later than *c.* 700 B.C. [Driver]), and by the belief in His presence there recorded in Ps 139^{8} (close of Persian age [Cheyne]). There is here another point of contact with the (probably likewise later) Babylonian belief which regarded Marduk and other deities as 'raisers from the dead' (see § 1 of 'Babylonian' art.); but the chief interest of the fact lies in the slow but sure preparation for the higher Hebrew doctrine of monotheism and the later Jewish belief in the resurrection as taught in Dn 12 (probably Maccabæan) (see Charles, *op. cit.* p. 132 *passim*).

Of direct evidence for the presentation of sacrificial offerings to the dead there is not much. The reference to a family sacrifice in 1 S 20^{29} is not conclusive; for although there is much to be said in favour of the idea that the blood-relationship with an ancestral god lay at the base of such a family offering,* it is conceivable that a deity other than ancestral was in the case mentioned the object of common worship (see what has been said in § 2 on the family deity). The treasures found in the sepulchre of King David (Jos. *Ant.* XIII. viii. 4, XVI. vii. 1; *BJ* I. ii. 5), and doubtless also in those of other kings, may originally have had the character of a sacrificial offering (Schwally, *op. cit.* p. 24); but it is also possible that they were merely intended to serve as an ample provision for the dead monarch's needs. The divers kinds of spices with which the grave of King Asa was filled (2 Ch 16^{14}) might have been nothing but an extension of the use of spices in the preparation of the body for burial; but the 'very great burning' which was made for the same king would seem to point at least to the offering of incense † to the departed. The prevalence of the practice in the case of kings is attested by Jer 34^{5}; and its spread among the people is in all probability proved by the term *mesārephō* (מְסָרְפוֹ, 'he that makes a burning for him,' rather than 'he who burns him'; see *Oxf. Heb. Lex.*, *s.v.* שׂרף) in Am 6^{10}. Ezk 43^{7-9} offers very strong evidence of the idolatrous worship of departed kings (see § 7), and the offering of sacrificial gifts must have formed part of such worship.‡ The evidence from oracles (see § 8) points in the same direction, for an offering of some kind would naturally precede the consultation of the dead. On the probable offering of hair made to the dead, see § 5; and there is, besides, the tendency to connect a propitiatory purpose with the ordinary presentation of sustenance to the departed; and if the analogy from the Babylonian custom be taken into account, it becomes pretty certain that among the ancient (pre-Mosaic and anti-Jahwistic) Hebrews also sacrifices to the dead were, to say the least of it, not uncommon.

4. Sanctity of graves.—The question concerning the veneration of graves is closely connected with that of sacrifices to the dead; for if the latter question be answered in the affirmative, the graves of ancestors would have to be regarded as the places where the sacrificial offerings were made. Viewed in this light, there is much in favour of the opinion that the *maṣṣēbah* set up by Jacob on the grave of Rachel (Gn 35^{20}) was intended to mark it as a spot devoted to her worship.§ The name *Allon-bacuth* ('oak of weeping') given to the tree under which Rebekah's nurse, Deborah, was buried (Gn 35^{8}), proves nothing; and Cornill's conjecture (*ZATW* xi. pp. 15–21) that the erection of a *maṣṣēbah* and the libation of oil poured on it recorded in Gn 35^{14} referred in the original form of the text to Deborah's grave, cannot, of course, be treated as an ascertained fact. Nor can the circumstance mentioned by Schwally (*op. cit.* p. 58), that graves, like the sanctuaries of Jahweh Himself, were put on heights, be cited in favour of intended sacrificial worship there; for the same writer records the well-known fact that tombs in Palestine were, apparently for other reasons, generally rock-hewn.

The stress laid on family graves (as more especially the cave of Machpelah, Gn $23^{3ff.}$ etc.), with

* Schwally's attempt (*op. cit.* p. 22) to construe Jer 16^{7} into an evidence to the offering of sustenance, and even of sacrificial gifts to the dead, is not convincing (see Grüneisen, *op. cit.* p. 130); but so far as sustenance is concerned, the evidence of Dt 26^{14} is quite sufficient.

† Driver (*in loco*) does not decide between the claims of this rendering and that of '*for* the dead,' which might then be taken to refer to funeral repasts offered to the mourners by their friends. But the phrase would hardly be natural in that sense. Among the Rabbinic commentators, Abraham ibn Ezra suggested an idolatrous intention, introducing this explanation by 'and some say.'

* See W. R. Smith, *Rel. of Sem.*2, Lect. ii., *passim*.

† Unless it was merely intended to render the passage to Hades pleasant.

‡ The eating of sacrifices to the dead mentioned in Ps 106^{28} is brought in as a foreign custom (connected by parallelism with Baal-peor), but at the same time it shows a tendency among the Hebrews to adopt it.

§ Cf. the *maṣṣēbah* set up by Jacob at Bethel for the worship of Jahweh (Gn 28^{18}). The worship paid to Rachel would no doubt be of a secondary kind.

which the phrase 'being gathered to one's fathers' has been connected, may legitimately be regarded as a desire 'to introduce the departed into the society of his ancestors' (Charles, *op. cit.* p. 12); but the passages relating to these sepulchres contain (in the form at any rate in which the texts have been handed down to us) no reference to sacrifices or offerings of any kind.

There is, however, apart from family graves, the strong testimony of Is 65[4] ('who remain among the graves, and lodge in the monuments'), which, as an evidence of necromancy practised at graves (see § 8), demands not only the supposition that offerings were there made in order to obtain a hearing from the dead, but also that from the general idolatrous point of view such graves (declared doubly unclean by Jahwism; see § 7) were regarded as sacred. At least as strong is the evidence from Ezk 43[7-9]. On both passages, see § 7.

5. Mourning customs.—Several of the mourning customs of ancient Israel are very obscure, and a careful scrutiny is required before anything like a decision can be arrived at on any single point. It will therefore be best to consider these customs separately.

(*a*) *The mourner put on sackcloth.*—The sackcloth, with which the application of ashes or earth is sometimes mentioned, was in very early times in all probability a loin-cloth only, the tearing and entire putting off of the usual garments having preceded the 'girding on' of it (see esp. Is 32[11]). Mic 1[8] ('I will go stripped and naked'), especially if taken in conjunction with the phrase, 'in nakedness and shame' of v.[11], points to a still earlier custom, when the mourner went quite naked; but the general practice of putting on sackcloth as a substitute for all other garments must have set in pretty early, and considerable modifications * both in the form of the sackcloth and in the direction of putting on other apparel may have been gradually, though not universally, made in later Biblical times.

The putting on of sackcloth has been claimed as a mark of submission to a superior (cf. 1 K 20[31. 32]), and the fact of Isaiah having apparently worn it as his usual garment † (Is 20[2]) has been taken to show that it was also considered a holy garment (see Schwally, *op. cit.* p. 12). The practice would on either explanation point to one form or another of ancestor-worship. Jer 48[37], where the putting on of sackcloth is mentioned together with cuttings in the hands, etc., places it in the category of usages which have been claimed to possess a ritual value (see farther on). But it is, on the other hand, psychologically very probable that the meaning lying at the base of the practice is that of self-humiliation,‡—a sentiment which would equally accompany the attitude of submission to a superior, and the marks of grief at losing a beloved relative or companion, and which might also suit the prophet attending on Jahweh. The primitive entire nakedness of the mourner, to which reference has been made, reminds one of the fact that on the Stele of Vultures (see § 2 of the 'Babylonian' art.) the dead are shown to have been buried naked.§ The mourner might therefore have desired not to appear at greater advantage than the mourned dead. Later on, sackcloth would be assumed by the mourner in deference to the altered public sense of decency, and the modifications referred to would gradually follow. If this view be correct, the close association of the sackcloth with ritual usages (Jer 48[37]) may belong to later times. On the suggestion that the practice of wearing sackcloth was adopted with the object of deceiving the dead as to the identity of the mourner, see farther on.

(*b*) *The mourner put off his sandals.*—The putting off of one's sandals in connexion with mourning is not so frequently mentioned as the girding on of sackcloth, but it was no doubt meant to accompany it regularly (see, *e.g.*, Ezk 24[17], 2 S 15[30]). Passages like Ex 3[5], Jos 5[15] show that no sandals were to be worn at sacred places. Hence the supposition that it was essentially a ritual practice. But here again the original meaning was probably self-humiliation, which would suit both the grief of mourners and the attendance at sacred places.

(*c*) *The mourner cut off his hair, or beard, or both.*—The cutting off of the hair in connexion with mourning is mentioned, *e.g.*, in Mic 1[16] ('make thee bald and poll thee for the children of thy delight'); the removal of the beard as a sign of mourning for the destruction of Jerusalem is recorded in Jer 41[5]; the two together are found in Is 15[2]. The characteristic feature in cutting off hair on these occasions consisted in making a baldness 'between the eyes' (Dt 14[1]), which must mean over the middle part of the forehead (see Driver, *in loco*), although in different parts of the country hair from other parts of the head was probably also cut away. The beard was apparently cut off entirely.*

Tylor, Oort, W. R. Smith, and others favour the idea that the hair so cut off was designed as an offering to the dead—a theory which is strongly supported by numerous analogies from the customs of the Arabs † and other races. The offering of hair in the ritual of Jahweh is clearly attested in the case of the Nazirite (Nu 6[18]), and the practice would seem less strange in the ritual of the dead, who, according to old ideas, stood in need of all the things that appertained to the living.

Another plausible explanation would be that the cutting off of the hair from head and chin was a kind of adjunct to the removal of one's clothes. Everything, it may have been held, was to be discarded that served as an ornament or protection to the body, not only the clothes, but also the hair. The idea of self-humiliation, which might have been involved in the act, is supported by the fact that the cutting off of the beard (see 2 S 10[4], and the parallel passage 1 Ch 19[4]) was regarded as an indignity. This idea would, however, not be incompatible with the simultaneous sacrifice of the hair. The dead might be benefited, and the living at the same time humiliated.

A third explanation that has been offered of this and, in fact, of all the mourning customs connected with apparel and bodily mutilation, is that these rites had the object of deceiving the dead as to the identity of the living, so as to escape any evil which recognition might bring with it.‡ This idea seems, however, un-Semitic, and it certainly does not fit in with other notions regarding the dead in early Hebrew times. Beings who could be called *yiddeʻōnīm* (יִדְּעֹנִים 'knowing ones' §), and to whom one resorted for oracles, could hardly be deceived by a change of garments or other disguise on the part of the living. They certainly could not be deceived by taking off one's sandals, which is also pressed into the service. The examples, moreover, from the customs of other races (including the Romans), quoted by the supporters of this theory, are for the most part capable of another explanation. The opposite

* This supposition is borne out by the somewhat conflicting data regarding the wearing of sackcloth. The verb *ḥagar* which is used with *saḳ* appears to show that a loin-cloth was originally meant (cf. *ḥăgōrah* in Gn 3[7]), and the word *mothnaïm* ('loins') is expressly employed where *ḥagar* is not used. In as late a work as the Ascension of Isaiah (1st cent. A.D.) the prophets spoken of in 2[10] are said to be naked, notwithstanding the sackcloth that was on them. On the other hand, the verbs *lavash* and *kasah* are also used with *saḳ*, and *ḥagar* is also employed with *ēphod*, etc.; and a passage like 'to spread sackcloth and ashes under him' (Is 58[5]), clearly points to a different kind of cloth from that put round the loins. For a fuller discussion on this point, see on the one side Schwally (*op. cit.* p. 11 ff.), and on the other Grüneisen (*op. cit.* p. 79 ff.). Whether in any case the *saḳ* ever had the form of a corn-sack with a slit at the top (see Kamphausen in Riehm's *HWB*, art. 'Sack'), is a different question.

† Cheyne (*Prophecies of Isaiah, in loco*) regards it as an 'outer garment,' and explains the word 'naked' in, *e.g.*, 1 S 19[24] to mean 'without the outer garment.' But one can hardly accept this as a natural explanation of the term.

‡ See J. Frey, *Tod, Seelenglaube*, etc. p. 42.

§ It is, of course, possible that the circumstance was there due to the exigencies of war.

* This is required by the verbs *galaḥ* and *gadaʻ* used in the passages quoted. In 2 S 10[4] the verb *karath* is used, and *half* the beard is expressly mentioned (in 1 Ch 19[4] [parallel passage] the verb *galaḥ* is, however, used, and apparently the entire beard meant).

† See esp. W. R. Smith, pp. 323–326.

‡ For a full exposition of this view (adopted also by Kautzsch in Hastings' *DB*, Ext. Vol. 614[b]), see Grüneisen, *op. cit.* p. 95 ff. J. G. Frazer (*JAI* xv. p. 73 ff.), on whose remarks regarding Bohemian and other customs Grüneisen and others primarily based the theory, expresses himself, however, doubtful as to the meaning of the cutting off of the hair spoken of here (*ib.* p. 73).

§ The Biblical statements affirming the impotence and shadowy character of the dead are mainly due to the weakening influence exercised by Jahwism on the ancient cult; so in Job (probably time of Bab. captivity [Driver]) 14[21. 22], the dead are affirmed to know of nothing but their own pains, and in Ec 9[10] (*c.* 200 B.C. [Nöldeke and others]) Sheol is stated to be devoid of work, device, knowledge, and wisdom. Allowance must, of course, also be made for different streams of thought in very early times.

treatment of the hair by men and women in times of mourning (each adopting the unusual course, men, *e.g.*, covering their heads at funeral ceremonies, and women letting their hair fly loose about them) may surely be explained as a species of self-neglect expressive in each case of self-humiliation induced by grief; and a similar explanation would be applicable to several other customs.

The Jahwistic prohibition in Dt 14^1 of making a baldness between the eyes for the dead furnishes a strong presumption in favour of regarding the act as a ritual observance connected with the worship of the dead; and the ground of the prohibition ('ye are children of Jahweh,' and a 'holy people' to Him) strengthens the theory that it was directed against an opposing religious cult. The place described as lying between the eyes may have for this very reason been chosen for the *ṭōṭāphōth* * (Dt 11^{18} etc.), by which every Israelite was to be marked as a devotee of Jahweh, unless it was independently chosen as the most conspicuous part of the head. The absence of a prohibition regarding the removal of hair from other parts of the head and from the beard in connexion with mourning is probably owing to the fact that, according to Lv 19^{27}, it was prohibited under all circumstances.†

(*d*) *The mourner made cuttings in his flesh.*—Cuttings in the flesh, accompanied by removal of the beard and tearing of garments, appear as a general custom in Jer 41^5, notwithstanding its distinct prohibition in Dt 14^1, thus showing that the Deuteronomic legislation could make its way only very gradually. Instead of the verb *hithgōdēd* used in the two passages mentioned, and the form *g^e dūdōth* found in Jer 48^{37}, there is in Lv 19^{28} the command not to make a *séreṭ* (also tr. 'cutting') for a dead person, or to print any marks (writing of *ḳa'aḳa'*) on the flesh, the latter being evidently a kind of tatu. If the theory of making oneself unrecognizable by these disfigurements be discarded, there remains only the idea of thereby 'making an enduring covenant with the dead' (W. R. Smith, *Rel. of Sem.*[2] p. 322 f.).‡

That cuttings in the flesh were parts of religious ritual is, moreover, proved by the action of the priests of Baal recorded in 1 K 18^{28}. The fact that these incisions, as also the making of a baldness between the eyes, were prohibited by Jahwism, whilst the wearing of sackcloth, etc. was never interfered with, would seem to show that these groups of acts belonged to different categories, thus forming another reason for rejecting the theory that they had all the purpose of making the living unrecognizable to the dead.

(*e*) *The mourner covered his head or beard.*—The covering of the head (*e.g.* 2 S 15^{30}, Est 6^{12}) and the beard (Mic 3^7, Ezk 24^{17}) as a mark of mourning on account of death or other calamity might be explained, with Schwally and others, as a substitute for cutting off hair from head and beard. But the covering of the face in 2 S 19^5 [Eng. v.^{4}] (the clearest instance of actual mourning) reminds one of the same act performed in the presence of Jahweh (Ex 3^6, 1 K 19^{13}). As the covering of the face was there prompted by the fear of beholding the Deity (cf. Ex $33^{18ff.}$), it seems likely that the mourner was also afraid of seeing the ghost of the departed (which is, of course, different from deceiving the ghost by a disguise). It is possible, however, that the covering of the face was merely an extension of covering the hair, and the idea that the latter act was a substitute for removing the hair might therefore be maintained. As the hair of the head and beard was regarded as a personal ornament, the covering of it might, in any case, be expressive of self-neglect or self-humiliation occasioned by grief.

No evidence of ancestor-worship can be derived from the extant accounts of the two remaining* customs, namely, (*f*) the *lamentation over the dead*, with its accompaniment of weeping and striking different parts of the body with the hand; and (*g*) the *partaking of food and drink by the mourners*† in connexion with funeral ceremonies. The lamentations were natural or professional (see Jer 9^{16} [Eng. v.^{17}] expressions of grief, and need—so far as the texts in their present form go—neither have been ritually addressed in worship to the dead (Schwally, *op. cit.* p. 20 f.) nor intended to scare away the ghosts of the departed by much howling (Grüneisen, *op. cit.* p. 100). The lamentations of David over Saul and Jonathan and over Abner (2 S $1^{17ff.}$ $3^{33.34}$) certainly show no trace of either intention. With regard to funeral repasts, Schwally's attempt to construe Jer 16^7 into a decidedly ritual act has already been referred to (§ 3). The text, as it stands, speaks only of food and drink offered to the mourners by way of comfort. On the uncleanness connected with the 'bread of mourning' in Hos 9^4, see § 7.

6. Levirate law.‡—A close relationship has been claimed between ancestor-worship and the law of levirate, which, in the form given to it in Dt 25^{5-10}, enacts that when brothers 'dwell together,' and one of them dies without leaving male issue, the surviving brother (no doubt the eldest, if more than one) was to marry the widow, and that the first-born son of this union was to be considered the son of the departed brother, so 'that his name be not put out of Israel.' The supposition is that the original object of the institution was to provide the dead man with a son to carry on his cult (so, *e.g.*, Stade, Schwally, Charles)—an object which must be assumed to have been entirely forgotten in the time of the Deuteronomic legislator. In the case of Ruth (where the law is found to extend over the whole clan), the object is 'to raise up the name of the dead upon his inheritance' (Ru 4^5). Absalom (2 S 18^{18}) puts up for himself a pillar in his lifetime, because he had no son to keep his name in remembrance. In Gn 38 (where, under an older form of the law, all the children would have apparently belonged to the departed) the ground stated is merely that of raising up a posterity to the departed.§ But if the institution—as it is quite reasonable to suppose—had from the first, besides the desire of leaving a memorial of one's name, a close connexion with the law of inheritance, it is impossible to eliminate the idea of the cult of the departed altogether, as the son or sons thus provided for the dead man, as inheritors of his property, would, under pre-Mosaic religious notions, be expected to charge themselves with the sustenance (and probably also sacrificial offerings) due to the departed. This broader basis of the levirate law would seem to be required by the extant data and the considerations arising from them, and it also

* Usually translated 'frontlets'; see *Oxf. Heb. Lex.*, *s.v.* טטף. The modern *tephillim* (known as phylacteries) consist of a part for the left arm, and another to be placed over the middle part of the forehead.

† For the probable ground of this general prohibition, see Dillmann, *in loco*.

‡ Driver explains that 'the Israelites, being Jehovah's children, are not to disfigure their persons in passionate or extravagant grief' (on Dt $14^{1.2}$). But it is doubtful whether grief would have generally gone the length of these mutilations, and the ground assigned for the prohibition (see the text above) appears to indicate an opposing religious cult.

* An attempt has been made to connect the festival of Purim with the Persian *Farvardīgān*, which was a kind of All Souls' Day; but if so, the story of Esther must have been purposely altered beyond ordinary recognition. See, on the one side, Schwally, *op. cit.* p. 42 ff.; on the other, Grüneisen, *op. cit.* p. 188 ff. The other literature will be found in these works.

† The supposition that sympathizing friends and neighbours provided the mourners with this nourishment is strengthened by the fact of the same custom obtaining among the Jews at the present day.

‡ For the custom, under partly different rules, among other races, see esp. Westermarck, *Hist. of Human Marriage*, p. 510 f.

§ On J. F. M'Lennan's theory that the law originally rested on a polyandrous system of marriage, see Driver, *Deut.* p. 284.

does justice to the fairly complex state of society which already obtained in those early days. So far as the element of the cult of the dead is concerned, it is important to mention that the *Ḳaddish* (see § 3 in the 'Jewish' article), which, like acts of Jewish public worship in general, is to the present day confined to males, also seems to bear traces of a survival (in a much modified form) of the religious services rendered to the departed by his surviving sons.

7. Laws of uncleanness.—The laws of uncleanness relating to dead human bodies (see esp. Nu 19[14-16]) can be satisfactorily explained by the almost universal fear of contamination * arising from the contact or close vicinity of decaying bodies that obtained in ancient times. The ancient Egyptians,† it is true, busied themselves much with corpses, but then they took every possible care to prevent decay setting in. In the Mosaic law the abhorrence of dissolution also affected not only animals that were forbidden as food, but also clean ones if not slain in proper ritual fashion (Lv 11). Leprosy, which was similarly loathed, is also ritually unclean (Lv 13), though here the fear of contagion must have been an important factor.

It is likely that this fear of contamination was in early times merged into the general notion of savage races, that everything connected with birth, disease, and death involved the action of superhuman agencies of a dangerous kind (see W. R. Smith, *Rel. Sem.*[2] 444 f.), analysis and differentiation of causes being a product of gradual mental development; but it would be rash to identify these agencies with ancestral spirits. On the contrary, the fact that dead human bodies are regarded as unclean among a number of races with a strongly developed system of ancestor-worship (see Grüneisen, *op. cit.* p. 114) proves that the two are independent of each other. Worship may be given to the departed spirits of ancestors, and contamination may at the same time attach to their dead bodies. The regulation of Nu 19[15], that an open vessel with no covering round it, which has stood in the tent of a dead person, is unclean, whilst covered vessels remain clean, can be suitably explained by the idea that the covering protects the vessel from contracting contamination, and need not point to the fear that the ghost might take up its abode in the open vessel.

The pollution connected with the bread of mourners (לֶחֶם אוֹנִים) referred to in Hos 9[4] is also explicable without a reference to a Jahwistic opposition to ancestor-worship. For the meal offered to mourners by way of comfort may be all that is meant; and if so, the uncleanness would only be that of ordinary contamination contracted by contact with dissolution.

An additional tabu, arising from opposition to the religion of Jahweh, would come in only in cases where a sufficiently recognizable element of ancestor-worship or some other heathen form of the cult of the dead showed itself; and as such practices were demonstrably not uncommon among the ancient Hebrews (see esp. § 3), the additional tabu would be of a correspondingly wide application. But the dead body itself would probably in such cases be affected only in so far as the spirit may have been supposed to linger about it, for, as has already been remarked, the cult of the dead was not necessarily connected with the notions entertained of the body.

In the case of priests (Lv 21[1ff.]) greater restrictions against contact with dead bodies are imposed, because the contamination would make them for a time unfit for Jahweh's service. The ground of the main ordinance there given cannot be opposition to ancestor-worship, for the persons whose obsequies priests may attend (father, mother, etc.) are just those to whom the heathen cult of the dead would chiefly apply (see Grüneisen, *op. cit.* p. 112). The order, however, not to remove the hair from head and beard, or make cuttings in the flesh, appears (unless v.[5] be regarded as unconnected with the rule regarding obsequies) to have the meaning that, although priests may take part in the funeral rites of very near relatives, they must abstain from anything connected with heathen mourning ceremonies, more particularly as in their case this additional tabu, like that of uncleanness *per se*, would naturally be of greater stringency than in the case of laymen.

The strongest instance of the combined tabu of ordinary contamination and heathen worship appears in Ezk 43[7-9], where tombs of kings erected quite close to the sanctuary of Jahweh are clearly stated to have been places of a rival worship (note their *zᵉnūth*, a usual term of unfaithfulness to Jahweh, borrowed from the relationship of marriage), whereby the 'holy name' of God is defiled. A similar double tabu is presented by Is 65[4], where graves, which are unclean in themselves (Nu 19[16]), are used for purposes of necromancy.

8. Necromancy.—Though the Teraphim cannot be demonstrated to have been originally images of ancestors (see § 2), there is ample independent evidence of the practice of necromancy among the ancient Hebrews. The spirits of the departed were called *yiddᵉʿōnīm* ('knowing ones') by those addicted to the practice, and the *'ōbōth* (usually rendered 'familiar spirits') also represent a form of necromancy, the calling up of the spirit of Samuel on behalf of Saul (analogous to the calling up of Eabani by Gilgamesh) having been effected by a woman possessed of an *'ōb* (*baʿălath-'ōb*, 1 S 28[7]).* In Isaiah 8[19] the people are distinctly charged with inquiring of the dead on behalf of the living; and Is 65[4] may safely be regarded as a strong evidence of necromancy practised at graves.†

The practice was decidedly anti-Jahwistic, and is everywhere forbidden (whereas the inquiry of Teraphim is not always prohibited, see § 2). As has already been remarked, necromancy, which is in itself an important part of the cult of the dead, is, at the same time, an indirect evidence to the offering of propitiatory gifts to the spirits consulted.

Summary.—In summing up all the extant evidence, the same result is, in the main, obtained as in the Babylonian section. The OT embodies indubitable traces not only of the popular cult of the dead, but also of a certain degree of actual worship paid to ancestors and departed kings and heroes. But the importance of these practices has been much exaggerated. There is no ground for thinking that ancestor-worship was the only or even the chief religion of pre-Mosaic Israel. On the contrary, various parts of the OT show clearly that Jahwism had to maintain at least as keen a struggle against the worship of the heavenly bodies and of various other powers of nature as against the cult of the dead. It is also true that in a certain modified form the exaltation of departed heroes, more especially of the spiritual type, was from the first quite compatible with the religion of Jahweh; and the final monotheistic development of Mosaism left still more room for the glorification of great human personalities in one form or another.

LITERATURE.—Works of F. Schwally, C. Grüneisen, R. H. Charles, and others have been more or less frequently quoted. A very full bibliography will be found in Grüneisen's book. Add A. Lods, *La Croyance à la vie future et le culte des morts dans l'antiq.Isr.* (1906). Of earlier works in favour of ancestor-worship, notice esp. Oort, 'De doodenvereering bij de Israëliten,' *ThT* xv. p. 350 ff.; Stade, *GVI* i. pp. 387-427. W. R. Smith, *Rel. Sem.*[2], and other publications contain much that bears on the problem. J. Frey (*Tod, Seelenglaube*, etc.) tries to prove that though there was a belief in the soul, no cult of the dead (in the sense of paying homage to them) existed among the ancient Hebrews. Kautzsch (Hastings' *DB*, Ext. Vol. pp. 614-615) agrees in the main with Grüneisen [animism, but no ancestor-worship]. Among com-

* See Dillmann (*Die Bücher Ex. u. Lev.* p. 479), who also brings in the idea that Jahweh was a God of life, not of death. On the far-spread fear of contamination connected with death, see, *e.g.*, A. P. Bender in *JQR* viii. 109, 110. The removal of a corpse to the 'tower of silence,' lest it should pollute the sacred earth, is one of the most necessary duties of Parsiism.

† In the New World the Peruvians offered a fairly close parallel to the Egyptians in this respect (see Prescott, *Conquest of Peru*, book I. beg. of ch. iii.).

* The fact of Saul bowing to the ground at the appearance of the spirit of Samuel (1 S 28[14]) might be regarded as an evidence of worship paid to the dead, though perhaps it was still the prophet who was thus honoured.

† Cf. Cheyne, *The Prophecies of Isaiah, in loco.* At graves the spirits of the departed would be more naturally consulted than demons.

mentators (some of the leading modern commentaries have, as occasion required, been referred to), Solomon Yiṣḥâḳî, Abraham ibn Ezra, and David Ḳimḥi will on a number of points still be found helpful.
G. MARGOLIOUTH.

ANCESTOR-WORSHIP AND CULT OF THE DEAD (Indian).—**1.** In India the worship of ancestors lies at the root of all the funeral rites. As now explained by official Brāhmanism, the object of these is to provide the departed spirit with a kind of 'intermediate body interposed, as it were parenthetically, between the terrestrial gross body which has just been destroyed by fire, and the new terrestrial body which it is compelled ultimately to assume' (Monier-Williams, *Brāhmanism and Hinduism*[4], 277). This writer goes on to say that this intervenient body, composed of gross elements, though less gross than those of earth, 'becomes necessary, because the individualized spirit of man, after cremation of the terrestrial body, has nothing left to withhold it from re-absorption into the universal soul except its incombustible subtle body, which, as composed of the subtle elements, is not only proof against the fire of the funeral pile, but is incapable of any sensations in the temporary heaven or temporary hell, through one or other of which every separate human spirit is forced to pass before returning to earth and becoming re-invested with a terrestrial gross body.' Unless it be provided with this new body, the soul must, like the ghosts of the unburied Homeric dead (Homer, *Od.* xi. 54; *Il.* xxiii. 72), wander about as an impure *preta*, or ghost, on the earth or in the air, among demons and other evil spirits, into the state of which it will eventually pass unless it be protected by the performance of the Śrāddha provided by its relatives on earth. Further than this, the new body thus created for the spirit must be nourished and supported, and the spirit must be aided in its progress from lower to higher worlds and back to earth by the performance of the periodical Śrāddha rites. This duty of the relatives is among orthodox Hindus supposed to be finally discharged only when the rite is performed at some specially sacred place. Gayā in Bihār is the most appropriate place for these rites, while the Hindus of the west, for the obsequies of a mother, prefer Sidhpur in the Baroda State. Hence also arises the necessity of begetting a male heir, which is urgently felt by all Hindus, as is also the case in China. Using a folk-etymology, Manu (*Institutes*, ix. 138) derives the Skr. name of a son, *putra*, as if it were *puttra*, 'he that delivers his father from the hell called Put.'

2. *Feeding the dead.*—This orthodox conception of the Śrāddha—that it is intended to provide an 'intermediate' body for the departed soul—is a later development. The Śrāddha was really evolved from the custom of feeding the dead, a rite common among all savage and semi-savage races. 'Like the habit of dressing the dead in his best clothes, it probably originated in the selfish but not unkindly desire to induce the perturbed spirit to rest in the grave and not come plaguing the living for food and raiment' (Frazer, *JAI* xv. 74 f.). The custom is well established among many of the Indian tribes. Thus, among the Nāgas of Assam, the corpse is watched with great care, and when decomposition sets in, quantities of spirits are thrown over it. Whatever the deceased was in the habit of eating and drinking in his lifetime (such as rice, vegetables, and spirits) is placed once a month on the ground before the dead body. At the end of the period of mourning, a great feast, consisting of liquor, rice, and flesh of cows and buffaloes, is prepared, and the members of the clan in war dress partake of it. Among the Luhupa sept of the same tribe the cattle sacrificed are eaten, with the exception of one leg, which is buried under the head of the dead man to serve as food for him in the grave. Among the Angāmi sept, on the first day after a death, meat is distributed among the relatives and friends of the deceased. The next day they assemble at the house of the dead man, eat part of the meat, and each member of the sept of the deceased throws a piece of liver out of the house to the distance of some eight paces. On the third day portions of the cooked rice are tied up in leaves, and buried outside the house on the fourth day. On the fifth day the platter and cup of the dead man are hung up in the house and left there till thirty days have passed, when they are given to a friend of their former owner. The funeral rites end with the sacrifice of a cock, the flesh of which is eaten by all the members of the family (*JAI* xxvi. 196 f.).

Among a more civilized race, the Nāyars of Malabar, the Śeshakriyā, or rite of making offerings to the spirit of the dead, commences on the day after the cremation ceremony, and continues for seven days. All male members of the Taravād, or sept of the deceased, bathe, and the eldest mourner taking with him a strip of cloth which he has torn from the dead man's shroud (probably in order to maintain communion with the dead), and a piece of iron (to scare evil spirits), brings some half-boiled rice, curds, and other articles of food, and places them in the north-east corner of the courtyard, which is believed to be the abode of the spirit. A lamp, which is also probably intended to drive off demons, is lighted beside the food. A piece of palmyra leaf, about a foot long and a finger broad, is taken, and one end of it is knotted. The knotted end is placed in the ground, and the other left standing up. This represents the deceased, and to it the food is offered. 'The place where the piece of leaf is to be fixed has been cleaned carefully, and the leaf is placed in the centre of the prepared surface. The offerings made to it go direct to the spirit of the deceased, and the peace of the Taravād is secured' (Fawcett, *Bulletin Madras Museum*, iii. No. iii. 247 f.).

The custom of providing food for the dead is common among the lower castes in Northern India. In Bengal the funeral rites of the Gonds last for three days, after which the mourners purify themselves by bathing and shaving, and make offerings of bread and milk to the spirit of the departed. Among the Kāmis, the blacksmith caste of Nepāl, 'on the eleventh day a feast is prepared for the relatives of the deceased; but before they can partake of it a small portion of every dish must be put on a leaf-plate and taken out into the jungle for the spirit of the dead man, and carefully watched until a fly or other insect settles on it. The watcher then covers up the plate with a slab of stone, eats his own food, which he brings with him to the place, and returns to tell the relatives that the dead man's spirit has received the offering set for him. The feast can then begin.' The Bhakat Orāons preserve the bones of the dead, to be interred in the tribal cemetery. 'At this festival pigs and great quantities of rice are offered for the benefit of departed ancestors, who are also held in continual remembrance by fragments of rice or dāl [pulse] cast on the ground at every meal, and by a pinch of tobacco sprinkled whenever a man prepares his pipe' (Risley, *Tribes and Castes*, i. 293, 395, 92).

The Māl Pahāriās, who identify the Lares, or ancestors, with Gūmo Gosāin or Gūmo Deota, the gods of the wooden pillar which supports the main rafters of the house, perform the same rite in another way. 'Around this centre are grouped a number of balls of hardened clay, representing the ancestors of the family, to whom the first-fruits of the earth are offered, and the blood of goats or fowls poured forth at the foot of the pillar that the souls may not hunger in the world of the dead' (Risley, ii. 71). The custom of offering first-fruits to the ancestral spirits is very common, and has been fully illustrated by Frazer (*GB*² ii. 460, 462 ff.). The Mechs, again, adopt another method to secure that the offering may reach the etherealized souls of the dead. When the corpse is buried, 'a small fire is kindled upon the grave, in which food and drink are burned for the benefit of the deceased' (Risley, ii. 89 f.). The Māls provide for the needs of the departed in another way, by lighting on the night of the worship of the goddess Kālī, in the month of October–November, dried jute stems in honour of their deceased ancestors, 'and some even say that this is done to show their spirits the road to heaven' (*ib.* ii. 50).

In other parts of Northern India rites of the same kind are performed. The degraded Ghasiyas of Mirzapur, at the annual mind-rite for the dead, lay out five leaf-platters containing the usual food of the family, with the prayer: 'O ancestors, take this and be kind to our children and cattle' (Crooke, *Tribes and Castes*, ii. 417). The Kols, whenever there is a tribal feast, offer a fowl to the spirits of the dead, and pour a little liquor on the ground, with the prayer: 'Do not injure us or our children' (*ib.* iii. 311). The Rājis, who are perhaps the most degraded people in this part of India, content themselves with shaving the heads, beards, and moustaches of the sons and younger brothers of the dead man, and throwing the hair on the grave as an offering to the spirit (*ib.* iv. 213). The ritual of the Nats, a tribe of wandering acrobats, is more remarkable. The mourners cook food on a river-bank, and spread a cloth on which the ghost is supposed to sit. The nearest relative, taking an earthen cup and a knife in his hand, plunges into the water. The cup he places on his head with the knife upon the mouth of it, and then dives until the cup becomes filled with water. This he deposits under the cloth on which the spirit is supposed to sit, and lays a cup of water at each corner of the cloth. Within the enclosure thus made food is laid for the refreshment of the spirit, who is invited to partake of the meal. When the spirit is supposed to have done eating, they say: 'Go and join those who have departed before you' (*ib.* iv. 63 f.). Even more elaborate than this is the rite performed by the Musahars, a tribe which has hardly risen above the condition of wanderers in the jungle. After the corpse is flung into a river (which is their usual mode of disposing of the dead), a tree near the spot is selected as a refuge for the spirit, and food and water are laid at its foot for nine days in succession. At the time of presenting these offerings, the chief mourner invokes the dead: 'Come, O dead one, from the palace of Indra! Come and eat the food of this world! Take it and return to thy palace.' These offerings are allowed to lie for some time on the place where they were deposited, and are then removed by the mourner, who cooks and eats the food, throwing a morsel on the fire for the use of the dead, and repeating the invocation already made at the tree. The offerings are changed daily during the period of mourning, and the rite ends with a clan feast of the dead (*ib.* iv. 31 f.).

In the United Provinces, among the various branches of the outcast Dom tribe, the idea of feeding or propitiating the spirits of the dead is combined with that of barring or preventing the return of the ghost, which is believed to afflict the survivors. Thus, among the Basors, some sacrifice a hog in the name of the dead man, with the object of providing the spirit with food; while others kill the animal, cut off its legs, and bury the trunk in the courtyard of the house of death, as a sort of sympathetic charm to prevent the spirit from rising out of its grave and afflicting the family (Crooke, *op. cit.* i. 226). Very similar is the custom of the Dhāngars, among whom, on the tenth day after death, the mourner sacrifices a pig in the name of the deceased, and, cutting off its feet and snout, buries them under a stone in the courtyard, with the invocation to the spirit: 'I have buried you here, never to come out; you must rest here in spite of the spells of an exorcist, or of any one else who may try to wake you' (*ib.* ii. 269).

3. *Vicarious feeding of the dead.*—From this crude belief in the possibility of feeding the spirits of the dead, the transition to the theory that this can be done vicariously is easy. Among some of the Indian castes survivals of the primitive matriarchy are found in the custom of providing for the feeding of the spirits by the bestowal of food on relatives in the female line. The Bhoksas of the sub-Himalayan Tarāī, every year in the month set apart for mourning, feed the descendants of their daughters in order to propitiate the ghosts of the dead; and, for the same reason, the Juāngs of Bengal and other menial tribes of Northern India employ the maternal uncle of the person making the offering as priest (Crooke, *op. cit.* ii. 58; Risley, *op. cit.* i. 353). The next stage appears when the Paṭāri, or tribal priest of the non-Aryan peoples of the Vindhyan and Kaimūr ranges in the centre of the peninsula, is invited, as a right attaching to his office, to share in the funeral feast. When we reach the higher castes of Hindus in the Plains, we find the custom of feeding Brāhmans prevalent. The belief is that food consumed by them passes on to the spirits. In fact, all through Northern India, large numbers of Brāhmans, generally drawn from the younger members of the families which provide *purohits*, or family priests, or from those branches of the caste which have settled down to an agricultural life and have no body of religious clients, exist only to be fed. These people flock in numbers to attend the death rites of wealthy people. At places like Gayā, whither the pious journey to perform the final death rites of their friends, a special class of Brāhmans has the monopoly of attending to be fed on such occasions.

4. *Annual rites for the dead.*—The establishment of an annual celebration, like the All Souls' Day of Christendom, when the dead are specially remembered and offerings of food are provided for them, appears among the most primitive tribes. Thus the Luhupa Nāgas of Assam, once every year in the month of December, hold a solemn festival in each village in honour of those members of the community who have died during the preceding year. The village priests conduct the rites, which culminate on the night of the new moon. On this occasion, they believe, the spirits of the dead appear at a distance from the village in the faint moonlight, wending their way slowly over the hills, and driving before them the victims slain for them or the cattle which they have stolen during their lives. Finally, the procession disappears over the distant hills, amidst the wailing of those who have lost relatives during the year (*JAI* xxvi. 194). The period consecrated by orthodox Hindu usage to the propitiation of the spirits of the dead is known as the *Kanāgat*, so called because it takes place in the sign of Kanyā, or Virgo, or *pitra-paksha*, 'ancestors' fortnight,' occurring in the moonless half of the month Kuār (August–September). This fortnight is specially devoted to the death cult, and the pious offer sacred balls (*pinḍa*) in memory of their ancestors. During this time the pious fast; others abstain only from meat, or eat fish instead of it.

5. *Ancestor-worship among the non-Aryan tribes.*—The cult of the dead, so far as it extends to the provision of food for the spirits of the dead, is thus

not confined to the higher castes, but is widespread among the non-Aryan part of the population. Sometimes, as in the case of the wild Kurubārus of Mysore, this worship is one of fear, and is devoted to the propitiation of the Vīrika, or spirits of ancestors who have died unmarried, and are thus supposed to be malignant (Buchanan, *Journey*, i. 397). The Yerukalas, one of the forest tribes of the Nīlgirī Hills, sacrifice, in conjunction with other gods, to the Pitris, or Manes of their ancestors (Oppert, *Orig. Inhabit.* 204). In the Bombay Presidency many of the ruder Hindu tribes, such as the Dhor Kāthkaris and Vaitis of Thāna, the Kunbis of the Konkan, Atte Kunbis, and Halvakki Vakkals of Kānara, worship their ancestors, usually in the form of an unhusked coconut (*Gazetteer*, xiii. 165, 182, xv. 217, 249, 203). The Bhīls of Khāndesh combine the cult of their ancestors with that of the Mātās, or Divine Mothers, and the same is the case with the Central Indian branch of the tribe (*ib.* xii. 93; Malcolm, *Trans. Roy. As. Soc.* i. 72). Gonds in the Central Provinces worship the family dead on the third day after a death, and on every Saturday and feast day (Hislop, *Aboriginal Tribes*, 25; *Gazetteer*, 278). In Chota Nagpur the Kisāns and Bhuiyars adore their ancestors, 'but they have no notion that the latter are now spirits, or that there are spirits and ghosts, or a future state, or anything'; the Bhuiyas revere their ancestors under the name of Bīr or Vīra, 'hero,' a title which, as we have seen, is often applied to malignant spirits; the Kharrias put the ashes of their dead into an earthen pot and fling it into a river; afterwards they set up in the vicinity slabs of stone as a resting-place for them, and to these they make daily oblations; the only worship performed by the Korwas is to their dead relatives, but this statement of Dalton is more than doubtful (Dalton, *Descript. Ethnol.* 132 f., 139, 160, 229). Among the Khonds the cult is very highly developed. 'The beatified souls of men enjoy immediate communion with all the gods; they are in rank little inferior to minor gods, live with them, and much after their fashion. Every tribe invokes the souls of deceased ancestors in endless array at every ceremonial, after invoking the minor gods; and they especially remember those of men renowned for great or good actions, as for reclaiming waste lands, for extraordinary bravery, for wisdom in council, or for remarkable integrity of life. They believe that beatified souls, although wholly without power, may act as intercessors with some of the gods, as with Dinga Pennu, on the one point of inducing him to restore lost relations speedily to their homes' (Macpherson, *Memorials of Service*, 95).

Among that remarkable people the Kāfirs of the Hindu-kush, though the fact is denied by them, there are distinct traces of ancestor-worship. They have the custom of making straw effigies of the honoured dead, which are paraded at their funerals, and one year after his death an effigy is erected to the memory of every Kāfir of adult age. These images are of various kinds, carved out of wood with axes and knives on conventional models. 'The more ponderous kinds,' says Robertson, 'are roughly fashioned in the forest, and are then brought into the village to be finished. Some of the best images have a manikin seated on the left arm holding a pipe; others have similar little images perched on the chair-handle. Several of the large images have all manner of quaint designs and carving over their bodies. Some even look as if the carving were intended to imitate tatuing, such as the Burmese are so fond of. The people have a good deal of superstition about these effigies. Bad weather which occurred while a slave was carving some images for me to take to India, was ascribed to the fact that images were being taken from the country. . . . The images are often decorated with wisps of cloth bound round the head, and, where the juniper-cedar is easily obtainable, by sprigs of that tree fastened to the brows. The faces of the effigies are carved precisely like the idols, and similarly white round stones are used for the eyes, and vertical cuts for the mouth, or rather the teeth. The effigies are provided with matchlocks, or bows and arrows, axes and daggers, carefully but grotesquely carved, and commonly have a cart-wheel-shaped ornament in the middle of the back. The effigies of males are given turbans, while those of females have a peculiar head-dress, which is possibly a rough imitation of a horned cap. Before these images of the eminent dead sacrifices are made, and their pedestals are sprinkled with blood by their descendants when they are suffering from sickness. Long stones are also erected to serve as a kind of cenotaph, and a goat is always killed when the pillar is erected. The Kāfirs also celebrate a festival, known as Marnma, in honour of the illustrious dead; and the last two days of the Duban feast are devoted to dancing, feasting, and singing ballads in honour of the departed heroes of the tribe' (Robertson, *Kafirs of the Hindu-kush*, 636 ff., 414 f.).

6. *The Śrāddha.*—The mind-rite of orthodox Hindus, known as the Śrāddha (Sanskrit *śrat*, 'faith,' 'trust,' 'belief'), is a more highly developed form of the primitive funeral feast and of the custom of feeding the dead. Even so late as the time of Manu (*Institutes*, iii. 267–271) the idea of providing food for the dead was recognized. 'The ancestors of men,' he writes, 'are satisfied a whole month with sesamum, rice, barley, black lentils or vetches, water, roots, and fruit, given with prescribed ceremonies: two months with fish, three months with venison, four with mutton, five with the flesh of such birds as the twice-born may eat, six months with the flesh of kids, seven with that of spotted deer, eight with that of the deer or antelope called Eṇa, nine with that of the Ruru deer; ten months are they satisfied with the flesh of wild boars and wild buffaloes, eleven with that of hares and of tortoises, a whole year with the milk of cows and food made of that milk; from the flesh of the long-eared white goat their satisfaction endures twelve years. The pot-herb *Ocimum sanctum*, the prawn, the flesh of a rhinoceros or of the iron-coloured kid, honey, and all such forest grains as are eaten by hermits, are formed for their satisfaction without end.' He further directs (iii. 205 ff.) that an offering to the gods should be made at the beginning and end of a Śrāddha. 'It must not begin and end with an offering to ancestors; for he who begins and ends with an oblation to the Pitris quickly perishes with his progeny.' The Brāhman is directed to smear with cow-dung a purified and sequestered piece of ground, with a declivity towards the south. 'The divine manes are always pleased with an oblation in empty glades, naturally clear, on the banks of rivers, and in solitary spots.' The officiant is then to seat the assembled Brāhmans, and he is to honour them, 'having first honoured the gods with fragrant garlands and sweet odours.' The feeding of Brāhmans at the mind-rite was thus customary. As another lawgiver directs, 'Whatever mouthfuls at a Havyakavya (or Śrāddha) are eaten by the Brāhmans are eaten by the ancestors' (Wilson, *Indian Caste*, i. 366). To drop the oblation into the hands of a Brāhman is, Manu lays down, equivalent to putting it into fire. 'If his father be alive, let him offer the Śrāddha to his ancestors in three higher degrees; or let him cause his own father to eat as a Brāhman at the obsequies. Should his father be dead, and his grandfather be

living, let him, in performing the obsequies of his father, celebrate also his paternal grandfather. Having poured water with holy Kuśa grass and sesamum into the hands of the Brāhmans, let him give them the upper part of the cakes, saying, "Śrāddha to the Manes." That fool who, having eaten of the Śrāddha, gives the residue of it to a man of the servile class, falls headlong down to the hell named Kālasūtra. The superfluous Piṇḍas, or holy balls, may be given to a Brāhman, to a cow, to a kid, or consigned to fire' (iii. 220 f., 223, 249, 261).

The form of the modern Śrāddha rite is most intricate, and includes a number of minute observances, the ritual of which is elaborately prescribed. In the form of the rite known as Ekoddishṭa, which is performed for the benefit of a single deceased individual, for ten days after the cremation lamps are kept lighted for the benefit of the Manes, to light the ghost during its progress to join the Pitris or sainted dead, either in a temple, or under a sacred fig-tree, or on the spot where the obsequial rites are to be performed. These, technically called *Kriya-karma*, should take place near running water; and the spot is hence known as the *ghāṭ*, the usual term applied to the steps used for bathing at a river or tank. One condition is that it must not lie to the west of the house of death. This place, when selected, is carefully smeared with clay and cow-dung, a fireplace is erected, and beside it an altar of white clay, also smeared with the dung of the cow. The officiant, with his top-knot tied up, first bathes, and then standing with his face to the south, the land of spirits, offers a lamp, sesamum, barley, water, and sprigs of the sacred Kuśa grass (*Poa cynosuroides*), with a dedication to the Manes. The object of this rite is to allay the extreme heat and thirst which the spirit must undergo during cremation. This ends the ceremonies of the first day, and during the next ten days, either once or twice daily, the rite of feeding the spirit is performed. For Brāhmans rice, the original sacred grain, and for Kshatriyas, and the illegitimate sons of Brāhmans, barley-flour, are prescribed. These grains are boiled in a jar of copper, the old sacred metal, mixed with honey, milk, and sesamum, and then made into a small ball (*piṇḍa*), which is offered to the spirit with the invocation that it may obtain liberation, and reach the abodes of the blessed after crossing the hell called Rāurava (Manu, *Institutes*, iv. 88). By this rite the creation of a new body for the disembodied soul begins. On the first day one ball is offered, on the second two, and so on until during the observances of the ten days fifty-five balls have been offered.

The motive of the offerings appears in the numerous invocations which are made at various times in the service. One runs thus: 'Thou hast been burnt in the fire of the pyre and hast become severed from thy brethren; bathe in this water and drink this milk, thou that dwellest in the ether without stay or support, troubled by storms and malignant spirits; bathe and drink here, and having done so be happy.' Another hymn is as follows: 'Let the lower, the upper, the middle fathers, the offerers of soma, arise! May those fathers who have attained the higher life protect us in the invocations! Let this reverence be paid to-day to the fathers who departed first, to those who departed last, who are situated in the terrestrial sphere, or who are now among the powerful races, the gods. Do us no injury, O Father, on account of any offence which we, after the manner of men, may commit against you. Fathers! bestow this wealth upon your sons, now grant them sustenance. Do thou, O resplendent God, along with the fathers who, whether they have undergone cremation or not, are gladdened by our oblation, bless us' (Muir, *Original Sanskrit Texts*, v. 297).

By these ten days' rites the spirit has been enabled to escape from the same number of different hells, and gradually a new body with all its members has been created. The order in which the members of this new body are formed is sometimes thus defined. On the first day the dead man gains his head; on the second his ears, eyes, and nose; on the third his hands, breast, and neck; on the fourth his middle parts; on the fifth his legs and feet; on the sixth his vital organs; on the seventh his bones, marrow, veins, and arteries; on the eighth his nails, hair, and teeth; on the ninth all remaining limbs and organs and his manly strength. The rites of the tenth day are usually specially devoted to the task of removing the sensations of hunger and thirst which the new body then begins to experience. The house and the vessels which it contains are purified so as to remove the last taint of the death pollution; the fireplace at the scene of the obsequies is broken, and a handful of water is offered to the ether to assuage the thirst of the spirit. After bathing at a spot higher up the stream than that where the obsequies were performed, the officiant and other relatives go homewards, first being sprinkled with the five products of the sacred cow (*pañcha-gāvya*), and taking care to lay a ball of uncooked meal on the road behind them, so as to attract the attention of the ghost and dissuade it from returning in their company.

On the eleventh day the chief rites consist in the gift of a cow (*kapila-dāna*) to the chief Brāhman, and the loosing of a scape-bullock (*vṛṣotsarga*) in the name of the deceased. This seems to be partly a survival of the ancient rite of animal sacrifice, and partly a means of removing the tabu of death (Frazer, *GB*² iii. 13 ff.). It is released with the dedications: 'To father, mother, and relatives on the father's and mother's side, to the family priest (*purohita*), wife's relatives, those who have died without rites, and who have not had the due obsequial ceremonies performed, may salvation come by the loosing of the bullock!' At the present day the animal is usually branded with the divine emblems of the discus and trident, and henceforth is allowed to wander free in the village lands. Food is again cooked, and offered to the Manes, with the invocation: 'You have finished your course, and have reached the abodes of bliss. Be present, though invisible, at this rite.' The general effect of the ceremony is that the spirit ceases to be a disembodied ghost, and becomes enrolled among the sainted dead. On the twelfth day food is again offered, and water poured at the root of a sacred fig-tree for the refreshment of the spirit.

The rite done for the benefit of one individual person (*Ekoddishṭa Śrāddha*) is quite distinct from the annual propitiation of the Manes of the family. On the last day of this feast all ancestors are named and propitiated, but sacred food balls (*piṇḍa*) are offered only for the three male ancestors on the father's side—the father, grandfather, and great-grandfather. The idea prevails that the ancestor, once united with the sainted dead, needs no further special propitiation. The non-Aryan tribes believe that, like themselves, the spirits of the dead are mortal. What becomes of them after a couple of generations no one cares to say. But when that period has elapsed, they are supposed to be finally disposed of, and, being no longer objects of fear to the survivors, their worship is neglected, and attention is paid only to the more recent dead, whose powers of mischief are recognized. The Gonds propitiate only for one year the souls of their departed friends, and this is done even if they have been persons of no note in their lifetime.

But with worthies of the tribe the case is different, and if one of them has founded a village or been its headman or priest, he is regarded as a god for many years, and a small shrine of earth is erected to his memory, at which sacrifices are annually offered (Hislop, *op. cit.* 16 f.).

No Śrāddha is performed for girls who die unmarried, and for boys only if they have undergone initiation and investiture with the sacred thread. Special rites are performed in the case of those whose ghosts are universally regarded as malignant. Such cases are those of a woman dying in childbirth or in a state of impurity. Her corpse is generally anointed with the five products of the cow, sprinkled with water, a little fire is placed on the chest, and it is then either cremated or flung into running water. In such cases it is a common rule that no rites are performed until the ninth day after death, when, if the family can afford the cost, the ceremonies of the last few days, as already described, are performed. To these are added a special rite of expiation, which is intended to free the household from pollution. Similar rites of a special kind are performed when a man is drowned, dies on an unlucky day, or in the case of one originally a Hindu who becomes an outcast, a Christian, or a Musalmān. In this rite, which is known as Nārāyaṇa-bali, 'oblation to the god Nārāyaṇa,' the Śrāddha of expiation is usually performed over an image of the deceased, made of barley or some other grain (*Bombay Gazetteer*, xx. 522 f.; Risley, *op. cit.* i. 266, ii. 191; Crooke, *op. cit.* i. 90, 210, ii. 465).

The Śrāddha is performed throughout India with more or less variety of practice by all orthodox Hindus. Among the castes of a lower grade the primitive custom of feeding the dead has been to some degree extended after the example of their Hindu neighbours. The main point of difference is the abbreviation of the rite, which does not extend over a period so long protracted as in the case of the orthodox, and the ceremonial is very often limited to the last few days of the mourning season.

7. *Hindu worship of the Pitris.*—The question remains—how far the Hindus can be said to 'worship' the Pitris. In the earliest Vedic period the worship paid to the Manes was distinct from that of natural phenomena. 'It is not denied that the Hindus made gods of departed men. They did this long after the Vedic period. But there is no proof that all the Vedic gods, as claims Spencer, were the worshipped souls of the dead. No *argumentum a fero* can show in a Vedic dawn-hymn anything other than a hymn to personified Dawn, or make it probable that this dawn was ever a mortal's name' (Hopkins, *Religions of India*, p. 10). The general theory seems to have been that ancestors are of a class different from that of the gods, and that though they are divine and possessed of many godlike powers, so that the Vedic poet thus invokes them, 'O Fathers, may the sky-people grant us life; may we follow the course of the living,' yet they are distinct from the gods, and never confounded with them (*ib.* 143, 145). Hence, in the Vedic ritual of the Śrāddha, when the officiant invites the gods and ancestors to the feast, he does so with two separate invocations (Colebrooke, *Essays*, 114). Speaking of the Vedic conception of Yama, the god of death, Barth thus writes: 'It is there, at the remotest extremities of the heavens, the abode of light and the eternal waters, that he reigns henceforward in peace and in union with Varuṇa. There, by the sound of his flute, under the branches of the mythic tree, he assembles around him the dead who have lived nobly. They reach him in a crowd, conveyed by Agni, guided by Pūshan, and grimly scanned as they pass by the two monstrous dogs who are the guardians of the road. Clothed in a glorious body, and made to drink of the celestial soma, which renders them immortal, they enjoy henceforward by his side an endless felicity, seated at the same tables with the gods, gods themselves, and adored here below under the name of Pitris, or fathers' (*Religions of India*, Eng. tr. 22 ff.). When we come to the Atharva Veda, we first encounter the specific doctrine of the elevation of the Pitris. The due performance of rites raises them, we are told, to a higher state; in fact, if offerings are not given, the spirits do not go to heaven. This view was still further extended in a later period. It is when we reach the Epic period that we find a progressive identification of the gods and the Pitris. 'The divinities and the Manes are satisfied with the oblation in fire. The hosts of gods are waters; so, too, are the Manes. . . . They are both of one being' (*Mahābhārata* i. 7. 7 ff.). The poet speaks also of the Manes worshipping the Creator, Prajāpati Brahmā, in his Paradise. It is in the Purāṇic period, when the Indian religious imagination ran riot, and produced that vague and complex system which is the basis of modern Hinduism, that we find them mixed up with Vedic gods and a host of other objects of devotion, like the bird Garuḍa and the world-snake Śesha. But throughout this progressive development the Pitris seem invariably to lack that criterion of worship which we have already fixed. They are never regarded as independent divine beings; on the contrary, stress is always laid upon the fact that they depend upon their friends on earth for continuous aid and maintenance, and that their advancement to a higher stage is impossible without the due performance of rites done by their pious descendants.

LITERATURE.—The authorities have been freely quoted in the course of this article. The best authority on the funeral rites of Hindus is still Colebrooke's essay in *Asiatic Researches* (1801), vii. 232 ff.; reprinted in *Essays on the Religion and Philosophy of the Hindus*, ed. 1858, 93 ff. A good account of the modern rites will be found in Atkinson, *Gazetteer of the Himalayan Districts* (1882–84), ii. 853 f., 917 ff.; Grierson, *Bihār Peasant Life* (1885), 391 ff. Full details are given in the caste articles in the *Bombay Gazetteer*, edited by Sir J. Campbell.

W. CROOKE.

ANCESTOR-WORSHIP AND CULT OF THE DEAD (Iranian).—The Zarathushtrian religion, as known from the Avesta, comprises an elaborate system of religious thoughts and moral habits founded on the idea of two universal powers, one heavenly and pure, the world of Ahura Mazda (Ormazd), and its contrast, the bad and impure world of the devils, the head of whom is Angra Mainyu (Ahriman). In this religion, according to its theoretical scheme, the ancestors, or the souls of the dead, play no part; but practically, in the popular customs and beliefs, the cult of the dead still survives. Parsism not only permits this popular worship, but even finds room for it in the official ritual, so that in the Yashts of the later Avesta we read a voluminous litany to angels or ghosts, in whom, no doubt, are to be recognized the souls of the dead, especially those of the ancestors. But it must be observed that these primitive ghosts are difficult to recognize in the shape that is given them in this Avestan composition, being often placed in the epical evolution as heroes or kings of old, as patrons or protectors of persons, families, or provinces, or as heavenly angels or genii, fashioned after the national and religious ideas of the Iranians.

These ghosts are in the Avesta called Fravashis (Pahlavi *Farvardīn*), and are invoked in the 13th, or *Fravardīn*-Yasht. The word Fravashi means in the Avestan language 'confession,' the Fravashi being a personification of the belief of the pious, his genius or his *alter ego*, who protects him and takes care of him during his lifetime, and who will, in time, receive him in the other world. Under this theological fabric is no doubt concealed a more primitive idea of a being which in some way belongs to human nature as part of his soul or as the principle of his life, nourishing him and giving him growth. These original functions of the Fravashis may be traced in the Avesta itself, when it tells that Ormazd, through these angels, makes all plants and herbs spring out of the earth, gives offspring to the herds, shapes the child in the mother's womb, gives it all its limbs, lets it be born, and grants the mothers many children. Originally these beings may have conferred these boons themselves without the direction of any supreme god, thus fulfilling the functions that ordinarily belong to the province of the ancestors.

This character of ancestral patronage becomes yet more conspicuous when we read Yasht xiii. 64 ff. Here we see how the Fravashis, when drought menaces the land, hurry to the heavenly lake Vourukasha, and how they quarrel in order to procure water, 'each for his own family, his own village, his own tribe, his own country.'

That the Persians themselves looked upon the Fravashis as souls, we learn from Yasna xxvi. 7: 'We invoke the souls of the dead (*iristhānām urvano*), the Fravashis of the righteous, the Fravashis of all our kinsmen that have died in this house, the Fravashis of men and women, of both sexes we invoke' (similarly Yasna lxxi. 23). The little we know of the exterior of the Fravashis fits in with this definition. 'They come flying like a well-winged bird,' we read in Yasht xiii. 70. The souls, then, were imagined in the shape of birds; as the Egyptian *ba* and as the souls in the Assyrian hell are described; as the souls, according to Greek beliefs, left the bodies on the point of death under the guise of birds—the same idea as still confronts us in European folklore (cf. von Negelein, 'Seele als Vogel' in *Globus*, lxxix. 357–361, 381–384; Goldziher, *ib.* lxxxiii. 301–304).

The *cult* of the Fravashis has had its fixed place and its special time in Zoroastrianism; the time was the period Hamaspathmaêdaya, March 10th–20th, *i.e.* the five last days of the year plus the five intercalary days, which days the Indo-European peoples always were wont to consecrate to the souls of the dead. Further, the Fravashis are always invoked in the evening, viz. in the Aiwisrūthrima Aibigaya (cf. Yasna i. 6; Gāh. iv. 1–2), being the first part of the night from 6 to 12,—the usual time reserved for the cult of the dead by kindred nations. We derive our information about the customs of this cult from Yasht xiii. 49–52: 'We invoke the good, the mighty, the holy Fravashis of the righteous, who descend to the villages at the time of the Hamaspathmaêdaya and return thither every night for ten nights to ask for help. Will anybody praise us? Will anybody pay homage to us? Who will accept us amongst his own? Who will bless us? Who will receive us with a handful of meat and a garment, and with sacred reverence?' Everybody who fulfils his duty to these Fravashis—we are told in the same Yasht—shall have his house filled with good things during the coming year (Yasht xiii. 51 f.).

This custom survived far into the Middle Ages; the Arabian chronologist al-Bîrûnî testifies that the Persians during these days placed the meat in the rooms of the deceased, or on the roofs of the houses, believing that the dead conversed with the family; then they burnt juniper as incense in their honour (*i.e.* in reality to keep them away) (al-Bîrûnî, *Chronology*, transl. Sachau, London, 1879, p. 210 ff.).*

The Fravashis are not only invoked during the Hamaspathmaêdaya-period, but also commemorated on the 19th of every month; in the Persian calendar (see art. CALENDAR [Persian]) they have, further, their place as the protectors of the first month of the year (*Fravardîn*; cf. the Armenian loan-name of the twelfth month, *Hrotiç*; Hübschmann, *Armenische Grammatik*, 1895, i. 184 f.). Corresponding to this official position of the Fravashis, the Persian imagination elevated them into higher and higher spheres; and we often meet with them as the genii of the stars (*e.g.* Yasht xiii. 5–7; Maînôg-î Khraṭ xlix. 22 f.). Altogether they seem in later times to have taken up a place in the Persian cosmology similar to the δαίμονες in Greece.

Besides their place in the ritual, the Fravashis play a prominent part in the private cult of the Persians, especially in the funeral ceremony called *âfrîngân* ('homage'). It was a common meal to which the survivors invited both rich and poor; the priests attended the feast and performed several symbolical ceremonies. On that occasion cakes of meat and flour were offered to the spirit of the recently deceased. The origin of this feast seems to be a meal to the nourishment of the deceased. The same oblation is repeated at the festival in memory of the deceased, or the *Srōsh Darūn*, where cakes are offered to the angel of Death, *Srōsh*.

In *Armenia* the Persian ideas on the Fravashis and their cult have continued into modern times. They are commemorated on the Saturdays before the five great festivals of the year, and, upon the whole, every Saturday. They are imagined to dwell in the neighbourhood of the tombs and in the houses of their kinsmen, and the survivors burn incense and light candles in honour of them. At the tombs the Armenians celebrate a special commemoration of the dead, on which occasion they burn quantities of incense. The Manes dwell three days on earth; then they fly away to heaven, leaving behind their blessings to their descendants. Especially between fathers and sons there is a vivid communication at that time. The Armenians as well as the Persians imagine that souls are connected with the stars.

LITERATURE.—J. Darmesteter, *Le Zend-Avesta*, Paris, 1892–1893, ii. 152 ff., 500 ff.; N. Söderblom, 'Les Fravashis,' *RHR*, 1899; Manuk Abeghian, *Der armenische Volksglaube*, Leipzig, 1899, 23 ff.

ED. LEHMANN.

ANCESTOR-WORSHIP AND CULT OF THE DEAD (Japanese).

—In order to understand what the worship of ancestors and of the dead actually amounts to in Japan, we must distinguish clearly the true national religion, that is to say, the native primitive Shinto, as it existed during the first centuries of the Christian era, from the Shinto subsequently modified under the influence of Chinese ideas. This transformed Shinto indeed is of very little interest here, as it is only a shadow cast over Japan from the continent. Our task is to distinguish and emphasize the ideas that are really Japanese, original, and prior to this foreign influence; and to accomplish it we must examine only the most ancient documents, such as the *Kojiki* (*Records of Ancient Matters*, A.D. 712), the *Nihongi* (*Chronicles of Japan*, A.D. 720), the *Norito* (rituals which were not published until the beginning of the 10th cent., but were undoubtedly composed at a much earlier date), etc., being careful to eliminate, even in these documents, any traces of Chinese ideas which they may contain.

* Cf. also the metrical *Sad-dar*, dating probably from the end of the 15th cent., xiii., xxii., xli., tr. Hyde, *Hist. relig. veterum Persarum*, Oxford, 1700, pp. 444, 447 f., 456. There is likewise a record of the celebration of the feast in 538 (Hoffmann, *Auszüge aus syrischen Akten persischer Märtyrer*, Leipzig, 1880, p. 78 ff.); while in 565 Chosroës spent ten days at Nisibis to celebrate the Fravardagân: τὴν ἑορτὴν τὴν Φουρδίγαν προσαγορευομένην, ὅ ἐστιν ἑλληνιστὶ νεκυία (Menander, ed. Niebuhr, Bonn, 1829, p. 374).

It is on account of the neglect of these necessary precautions that Japanese writers, especially the great native philologians of the 18th and the beginning of the 19th cent., have represented their national religion as being mainly an ancestor-cult, while in reality it is mainly a cult of nature. For instance, the famous theologian Hirata (1776–1843), while claiming to restore the primitive Shinto, calls into existence a fanciful religion, into which he introduces, in an artificial way, ancestor-worship as practised by the Chinese: the worshippers must pray to the whole succession of their family ancestors in order that these Manes may protect their descendants and see to their happiness (*Tamadasuki*, vol. x.). From Japan this erroneous conception spread into Europe, where the writers have, one after another, repeated the statement that Shinto was chiefly an ancestor-cult. Even the most conscientious scholars have not escaped the influence of this prevailing idea. Sir Ernest Satow maintained in Murray's *Handbook for Japan*[2] (Introd. pp. 62, 69) that 'in its very earliest beginnings Shinto appears to have been ancestor-worship.' This eminent Japanese scholar has now, however, given up that theory. But more recently, Prof. B. H. Chamberlain wrote (*Things Japanese*[3], 1898, p. 358): 'Shinto is the name given to the mythology and vague ancestor- and nature-worship which preceded the introduction of Buddhism into Japan.' Dr. W. E. Griffis (*Religions of Japan*, 1895, p. 88) emphasizes the idea, saying that 'from the Emperor to the humblest believer, the God-way is founded on ancestor-worship, and has had grafted upon its ritual system nature-worship.' Capt. Brinkley sums up the whole in the very concise statement: 'Ancestor-worship was the basis of Shinto.'

This theory is, in the present writer's opinion, the reverse of the historical evolution as it actually took place. It is evident that at a certain period ancestor-worship was seen to be the dominant cult of Shinto, and when people in our time visit the temples which are dedicated for ever to illustrious ancestors or to certain nature-gods confounded with Imperial ancestors, they are tempted to see in them a confirmation of the general theory of Herbert Spencer. But if we get rid of these modern impressions, and also lay aside the conventional opinions of native commentators, and if we confine our attention simply to the ancient writings, we find that the oldest and most interesting parts of the *Kojiki* and the *Nihongi*, those relating to the 'age of the gods,' are essentially devoted to nature myths; that, moreover, the most important *Norito* celebrate the glory of the gods of nature, and that it is not animism but naturism that in Japan, as in so many other countries, constitutes the real basis of the primitive religion. Does this, however, mean that, as Dr. W. G. Aston maintains at the present time, 'Shinto, the old native religion of Japan, had no cult of true ancestors' (*Man*, 1906, No. 23, cf. his *Shinto*, 1905, p. 44 and *passim*; K. Florenz, *Nihongi, Zeitalter der Götter*, Tokio, 1901, p. 253, and art. SHINTO)? The present writer thinks rather that the truth lies between these two extremes, and that, if ancestor-worship did not appear until after nature-worship, and if it was then developed chiefly under the influence of Chinese ideas, it nevertheless existed in germ in the original Shinto as in the majority of primitive religions.

We shall not discuss the question as to whether cannibalism existed in pre-historic Japan, and if so, whether it was followed by a ceremonial anthropophagy, which is then explained by the desire to offer to certain ancestral gods the food they would most appreciate (see N. Gordon Munro, 'Primitive Culture in Japan,' in *Trans. of the Asiat. Soc. of Japan*, Dec. 1906, vol. xxxiv. pt. 2, pp. 73 ff. and 133 ff.). As a matter of fact, from the time that primitive man invests all the gods, if not with his own form, at least with his feelings, this moral anthropomorphism must lead him to offer to the gods, whoever they may be, the things which appear most precious to himself, and the gods for whom these sacrifices are intended may be gods of nature quite as well as ancestral spirits. We shall therefore dismiss this questionable interpretation of customs which are themselves doubtful, and confine ourselves wholly to the written documents.

These documents show us, in the first place, that the primitive Japanese had a vague belief in the immortality of the soul, without having, however, any precise or absolute idea on the subject. The *Nihongi*, when relating the story of the hero Tamichi, who appeared one day as a serpent with glaring eyes to punish the violators of his tomb, ascribes to the men of that time the thought: 'Although dead, Tamichi at last had his revenge. How can it be said that the dead have no knowledge?' This passage alone is sufficient to prove that there were supporters of another opinion, who doubted the sentient immortality of the dead. In general, however, they believed that the dead survived this life. The common people descended through the opening of the grave to a dark lower region, *Yomi*, *i.e.* 'the Land of Darkness,' where there were neither rewards nor punishments, but where all, good and bad alike, continued to lead a vague existence, regretting the life and light of the upper region. This is the dark kingdom, which swarms with the fierce deities of disease and death, the 'hideous and polluted land' where Izanagi, horror-stricken, found his wife Izanami in a state of putrefaction. Other persons, such as Izanagi himself, do not share this general destiny: it is on a terrestrial island amidst the living that this god chooses his resting-place. Lastly, many divine heroes and illustrious persons were translated to the 'Plain of High Heaven' (*Takama no hara*). Just as the first parents had sent the most beautiful of their children, the Sun and the Moon, to that upper region to illumine it with their brilliance, so men raised the objects of their admiration up to the stars. Like the deified Roman Emperors, they were 'sideribus recepti.' The dead whose brilliant career terminated in this final assumption were not, however, the most virtuous; they were the most illustrious, and their apotheosis was only the natural continuation of their former power. Thus, the particular abode of the dead depended chiefly upon their earthly dignity. Their future life, with which no moral consideration had to do, rested upon an idea that was purely aristocratic. The ladder of the ranks of men had a top which was lost in the clouds and leaned against the floor of the gods. In a word, the spirits of men found a place very readily in the society of the gods of nature. The heroic glory of the one corresponded to the physical brilliance of the other. They took up their abode in the same places, and in virtue of the same inherent sovereignty.

This being so, it follows that the cult of the dead was of a somewhat vague character, and that ancestors were worshipped mainly in proportion to the social position they had held during life. One old mythical account, in which there is a description of the burial of the god Ame-waka-hiko ('heaven-young-prince') by a flock of birds, which perform the various duties of the funeral ceremony, shows us clearly that the Japanese must have practised very complicated rites on such occasions. The existence of funeral sacrifices also shows that they rendered to their ancestors a worship intended to ensure their welfare, providing them with the objects, animals, and companions which they would require in the other life. The most important writing on this subject is one which relates how human sacrifices were suppressed—an event which the *Chronicles of Japan* place at a time corresponding to that of the birth of Christ, but which probably should be brought down to a more recent date, of the actual occurrence of which, however, there can be no doubt. One passage explains, first of all, why they thought of this suppression:

'28th year [of the reign of Suinin = 2 B.C.], 10th month, 5th day. Yamato-hiko no Mikoto, the Mikado's younger brother by the mother's side, died.

'11th month, 2nd day. Yamato-hiko was buried at Tsuki-zaka in Musa. Thereupon his personal attendants were assembled, and were all buried alive upright in the precinct of the tomb. For several days they died not, but wept and wailed day and night. At last they died and rotted. Dogs and crows gathered and ate them.

'The Emperor, hearing the sound of their weeping and wailing, was grieved at heart, and commanded his high officers, saying: "It is a very painful thing to force those whom one has loved in life to follow him in death. Though it be an ancient custom, why follow it if it is bad? From this time forward, take counsel so as to put a stop to the following of the dead."'

Another passage then tells how the reform was accomplished:

'32nd year [= 3 A.D.], 7th month, 6th day. The Empress Hibasu-hime no Mikoto died. Some time before the burial, the Emperor commanded his Ministers, saying: "We have already recognized that the following of the dead is not good. What should now be done in performing this burial?" Thereupon Nomi no Sukune came forward and said: "It is not good to bury living men upright at the tumulus of a prince. How can such a practice be handed down to posterity? I beg leave to propose an expedient which I will submit to your Majesty." So he sent messengers to summon up from the Land of Idzumo a hundred men of the clay-workers' Be [hereditary corporation]. He himself directed the men of the clay-workers' Be to take clay and form therewith shapes of men, horses, and various objects, which he presented to the Emperor, saying: "Henceforward let it be the law for future ages to substitute things of clay for living men, and to set them up at tumuli." Then the Emperor was greatly rejoiced, and commended Nomi no Sukune, saying: "Thy expedient hath greatly pleased Our heart." So the things of clay were first set up at the tomb of Hibasu-hime no Mikoto. And a name was given to these clay objects. They were called *haniwa*, or clay rings.

'Then a decree was issued, saying: "Henceforth these clay figures must be set up at tumuli: let not men be harmed." The Emperor bountifully rewarded Nomi no Sukune for this service, and also bestowed on him a kneading-place, and appointed him to the official charge of the clay-workers' Be. His original title was therefore changed, and he was called Hashi no Omi. This is how it came to pass that the Hashi no Muraji superintend the burials of the Emperors' (*Nihongi*, tr. by Aston, 1896, vol. i. p. 178 f.).

With regard to the other funeral offerings, we are sufficiently enlightened by the pottery, weapons, and ornaments brought to light by excavations in the ancient Japanese tombs. Aston interprets these customs as being 'partly a symbolical language addressed to the deceased, and partly . . . an appeal for sympathy by the mourners and a response by their friends.' The present writer thinks rather that we should see in them the proof of a belief in the continued sentient existence of the dead, and in the necessity for satisfying the needs which they still experience in the other world, *i.e.*, in a word, the existence of a real cult of the dead. Even to-day the majority of the Japanese scarcely think of a future life, and the conception of the immortality of the soul seems almost foreign to them; and yet towards their ancestors they perform no less rigorously the minute rites of the ancestor-worship borrowed by them from China. It is probable that the primitive Japanese also, who, as the ancient writings testify, were even at the hour of death not in the least concerned about a future life, felt none the less the desire to do all that they thought might still be useful for their dead relatives. It is true that the ancient documents do not make any direct reference to this point; but the fact must not be lost sight of that these are annals in which scarcely any but famous persons are described, and in which we could hardly expect to find information regarding the obscure life of the common people. They mention the human sacrifices offered at the tomb of an Imperial prince more readily than the humble offering of rice and water which poor families might make. But, on the other hand, with regard to heroes and illustrious personages, we find very clear cases of deification and of worship rendered to the far-off ancestors, gods of nature or human beings, who were regarded as the household gods (*ujigami*) of the great families of the 8th century. (For further details on this last point see the present writer's book, *Le Shinntoïsme*, Paris, 1907, p. 276 f.).

This cult of ancestors, which we can assert with certainty in some illustrious cases, and logically infer also among the poor people who were unknown to the court historiographers, was speedily developed and systematized under the influence of continental ideas. Then Chinese ancestor-worship came to be established with all the ceremonies which it involves and all the consequences it entails, beginning with the very important practice of adoption, which was intended to ensure the continuance of family sacrifices. But this evolution, which is quite distinct from real Japanese religious ideas, is beyond our subject. See CHINA.

MICHEL REVON.

ANCESTOR-WORSHIP AND CULT OF THE DEAD (Jewish).—As was to be expected, the final victory of monotheism made the conscious practice of forbidden or doubtful rites in connexion with the dead impossible to those who strictly followed the sober development of pure Mosaism in early post-Biblical times and the various periods of Rabbinism that followed. Ancient occultism retained, however, a hold on the minds of not a few in each generation; and the confluence of Eastern and Western mystical ideas which in mediæval times produced the theosophical systems of the Kabbalah, gave a further impetus to various essentially un-Mosaic notions about the dead, and even succeeded in partially invading the liturgical form of synagogue-worship.

The literary evidence, which is on some important points supported by practices prevalent at the present day, has here to be collected from (1) the Apocryphal and Pseudepigraphical writings attached to the OT; (2) the Talmudic and Midrashic literature; (3) the Liturgy; (4) the Kabbalah. Only the salient features need, however, be mentioned in each part.

I. Apocryphal and Pseudepigraphical literature.*—Taking the different parts of the subject, in so far as sufficiently important data exist, in the order followed in the 'Hebrew' article above, it must first be mentioned that the garden or Paradise assigned to Enoch and the other elect is, according to the *Book of Enoch* (32^2 65^2 106^8), imagined to be at the end of the earth towards the east. In it is the tree of wisdom ($32^{3.6}$), whose fruit the holy ones eat and attain high knowledge. In 47^2 'the holy ones who dwell in the heavens' are, however, spoken of. The well of righteousness mentioned in 48^1 is perhaps a reminiscence of the 'water of life' which is to be found in the Babylonian heaven and other mythical localities. Whether the pseudepigraphical work known as the *Assumption of Moses* originally contained in the lost portions at the end an account of the translation of Moses to heaven still remains doubtful, though a negative answer would seem to accord best with the facts of the case (see the introduction to that book in Kautzsch's edition). Josephus, however, clearly implies a belief in it (*Ant.* IV. viii. 48), and 11^8 in the *Ass. Mos.*

* The books contained in the *Variorum Apocrypha* (ed. C. J. Ball) are here quoted in the usual English form. For the other books, *Die Apokryphen und Pseudepigraphen des AT* (ed. Kautzsch, 1900) has been followed. The dates of the books range from about B.C. 200 (Sirach) to the earlier Christian period.

itself (ending, 'the whole world is thy grave') would seem to be in consonance with the idea. Concerning Baruch, the friend and disciple of Jeremiah, we are informed that he was to be preserved alive 'to the end of the times' (*Apoc. Bar.* 13^3 76^2), — a favour which appears to stand in some relation to the translation of the earlier saints.

In the ridicule of Babylonian idol-worship contained in the *Epistle of Jeremiah* is found the statement that they set gifts before the idols 'as unto dead men' (v.^{27}); but the practice of offering gifts to the dead thus implied may be understood to have been as purely Babylonian as the idol-worship itself. A direct warning against the heathen worship of the dead is contained in *Jubilees* 22^{17} ('Their sacrifices they slay to the dead, and pray to the demons, and eat upon the graves'); and it is natural to suppose that the warning would not have been needed, if there had been no tendency to adopt these practices among the Jews. The supposed reference to offerings made to the dead in Sir 30^{18} has been disproved by the Cairo Hebrew text (if here correct); for instead of 'messes of meat set upon *a grave*,' the Hebrew has 'heave-offerings placed before *an idol*' (*gillûl*).* The treatment of the dead spoken of in Sir 7^{33} and To 4^{17} may possibly refer to offerings made to the departed, but it is not unlikely that funeral rites only are meant in the former passage and funeral feasts in the latter (see the notes to the *Variorum Apocrypha*). It would seem indeed that the progress of monotheism had by that time made habitual offerings to the dead impossible, and that the transformation of the practice into what has not inaptly been called 'the new sacrificial cult of the dead' ('Das neue Totenopfer' [Schwally, *Das Leben nach dem Tode*, p. 188]) had already set in. In 2 Mac. $12^{42.\ 43}$, Judas Maccabæus is reported to have ordered the Jews under his command to offer up prayers and to send a large sum of money as a gift to Jerusalem, in order to effect an atonement for the Jewish soldiers killed in battle, under whose coats objects consecrated to idols—no doubt intended to serve as a magical protection—had been found. It has been suggested that the prayers and offerings of money were in reality intended by Judas and his companions to clear the survivors rather than the dead from the pollution of idolatry; but as the author or compiler of 2 Mac. interpreted the act as having been performed on behalf of the dead (see vv.$^{43b.\ 44.\ 45}$), the practice of trying to benefit the dead rather than paying homage to them must have been in vogue when the narrative assumed its present form (some time in the 1st cent. B.C.).

The references to *mourning customs* found here and there in the Old Test. Apocrypha and Pseudepigraphical writings in the main support the view that the objectionable practices mentioned in the 'Hebrew' article lay outside the range of topics contemplated by the authors. Even the picture of priests having 'their clothes rent, and their heads and beards shaven,' and roaring and crying before their gods 'as men do at the feast when one is dead' (*Ep. Jer.* vv.$^{31.\ 32}$), is taken from Babylonian idol-worship, and does not necessarily point to exactly similar practices among the Jews. With regard to the number of days given up to mourning, it is remarkable that, whilst Jth 16^{24} and Sir 22^{12} show that the practice of keeping seven days was usually continued, the *Life of Adam and Eve* speaks of six days' mourning, the seventh being (like a Sabbath) reserved for rest and joy. Ben-Sira (apparently inconsistent with himself) furthermore recommends (38^{17}) a day or two, 'lest thou be evil spoken of.'* If, therefore, Schwally's suggestion (*op. cit.* p. 41), that the seven days' mourning corresponds to the number of days assigned to great religious festivals, were adopted, it would at the same time follow that in the times to which the apocryphal books belong this idea had lost its hold upon the popular mind.

* In the OT, however, the plural only of this word is used. The Greek ἐπὶ (or ἐν) τάφῳ appears to rest on a misreading (*gōlēl* for *gillûl*); so also the Syriac.

Necromancy in its ordinary form also lies outside the range of topics dealt with by the writers of this literature. But the appearance of the high priest Onias and the prophet Jeremiah to Judas Maccabæus in a dream on the eve of his battle against Nicanor (2 Mac $15^{12ff.}$) represents a form of oneiromancy that is pretty closely related to necromancy (cf. the appearance of Alexander to his thrice married widow Glaphyra, recorded in Jos. *Ant.* XVII. xiii. 4; *BJ* II. vii. 4). Ben-Sira, representing, as he did, Hebraism pure and simple, declares, however, that 'divinations, and soothsayings, and dreams are vain' (Sir 34^5). The call addressed to the 'spirits and souls of the righteous' (Song of the three Children ^{64}) to join in the universal hymn of praise to the Creator has a poetic ring about it, but the whole Song might be brought into relation with animistic conceptions.

2. Talmudic and Midrashic literature.—It may at first sight seem strange that the number of persons who gained the distinction of being translated to heaven without having died and gone down to Sheol, is considerably increased in some of the later additions belonging to Talmudic, Midrashic, and allied literature. This advance is, however, in reality quite in keeping with the greater facility for the glorification of distinguished human personalities under the final monotheistic development of Mosaism referred to at the end of the 'Hebrew' article. In the minor Talmudical tractate *Derekh Ereṣ Zuṭṭa* (7th or 8th cent.), ch. i., seven (or, according to others, eight) others, besides Enoch and Elijah (including the Messiah; Eliezer, the servant of Abraham; Hiram, king of Tyre, etc.),† are accorded this honour. In *Yalḳuṭ Ezekiel*, § 367 (about 11th cent.), thirteen such translations are enumerated, the name of Methuselah being among those added to the preceding list. The *Alphabetum Siracidis* (ed. Steinschneider, Berlin, 1858) occupies a middle position between the two lists named, the number of translations being eleven (one of the number, however, being the posterity of the phœnix). Specially developed in Talmudic and Midrashic literature is what may fairly be called the cult of Elijah, who, according to Mal 4^5, was to be the herald of a new order of things, and whose expected appearance as the forerunner of the Messiah is referred to in the NT (*e.g.* Mt $17^{10ff.}$). Quite in keeping with this expectation is, for instance, the conversation of Elijah with R. Yōsē related in *Berākhōth*, 3*a*, where the grief caused to the Deity by Israel's captivity is so forcibly and characteristically described. On the Midrashic statements regarding the high favour accorded to Moses at his death, see § 1 in the 'Hebrew' article.

A very important concession to popular habits of thought is made in the minor Talmudical tractate *Semāḥōth* (prob. 7th or 8th cent.), ch. viii., where the custom of placing the dead person's pen (or reed) and ink as well as his key and writing-tablet by his side in the grave is countenanced, although the belief in the ability of the departed to use these things might be considered to be perpetuated thereby. The concession is indeed ex-

* The suggestion that mourning for distant relatives only is here meant does not seem to suit the context (see note in Kautzsch's edition).

† For the full enumeration of this and the following lists see A. P. Bender, 'Death, Burial, and Mourning,' etc., in *JQR* vi. (1894) 341 f.

pressly granted, notwithstanding its known approximation to 'Amorite' customs. In the *Shulḥān 'Arūkh* of Joseph Caro (*ob.* Safed, 1575), which is the accepted guide of strictly orthodox Judaism at the present day, the same practice is tolerated (see *Hilkhoth 'Abheluth*, § 350). Merely academic is, of course, the permission to make burnings for kings, but not for persons of inferior rank (*ib.* § 348; *Semāḥōth*, ch. viii.; cf. the 'Hebrew' article, § 3). One of the explanations suggested to account for the pouring away of all the water found in a house in which a death has taken place, is that an offering to the dead, or, at any rate, a provision of drink for them, was thereby intended (see A. P. Bender, *JQR* vii. [1895] p. 106 ff.). It is, however, more likely that the water was poured away because it was believed to have contracted contamination * (see § 7 in the 'Hebrew' article). A Karaite writer of the 10th cent. (Abu's-Sari b. Maṣliaḥ) declares that a number of Rabbinite Jews of his day were in the habit of burning candles and offering incense on the graves of the righteous.† A transformation of this custom similar to that noticed in 2 Mac. (see § 1) is found, *e.g.*, in *Midrash Tanḥūmah* on *Ha'ăzīnū* (the last weekly pericope but one in Deuteronomy), where the religious commemoration of the dead on the Sabbath is recommended in order to prevent their returning to Gehenna (cf. the remarks on *Ḳaddīsh* and *Hazkārath Neshāmōth* in the next §).

Not much that can be regarded as significant is here to be noted in connexion with *mourning customs*. The repast provided in modern times for mourners by their neighbours after a funeral is clearly understood to have the object of thus offering sympathy and consolation to the bereaved, who are, besides, naturally unable to make satisfactory provision for their own wants at such a time. The rending of the garments on the part of mourners is now generally but a slight ceremonial act, consisting in tearing the (left) lapel of the coat one is wearing. In Talmudical and subsequent times there was a custom of baring the shoulder and arm (see Bab. *Baba Qāma*, 17*a*, and cf. *Semāḥōth* ix.). A. Büchler (*ZATW*, 1901, pp. 81–92) regards this act as a sign of subjection of the living to the dead (see § 5 (*a*) in the 'Hebrew' article). If so, there would here be a survival of the cult of the dead in the old sense of the word.‡

Jastrow (*ZATW*, 1902, pp. 117–120) tries to controvert Büchler's opinion by showing that practices of this kind are a return to ancient habits of life, entire nakedness having, in fact, originally obtained in connexion with mourning (see § 5 (*a*) in the 'Hebrew' article), because a state of nudity was the primitive condition of man. In reality, however, the two explanations do not clash with each other, for the sense of self-humiliation and subjection to the departed spirit would be quite compatible with a reversion to an older and less dignified mode of existence.

All trace of ancestor-worship (supposing that there ever was any in it) has disappeared from the rather precarious working of the levirate law in modern times. Nor is there now any trace of a ritual tabu in the Rabbinical ideas bearing on the uncleanness of dead bodies, fear of contamination through contact with a decaying human organism being the explanation adopted. A certain kind of necromancy, on the other hand, reappears in, *e.g.*, Bab. *Berākhōth*, 18*b* (parallel passage in *'Abōth de-Rabbi Nathan*, ch. iii.), where a certain pietist, having on some occasions taken up his lodging at the cemetery, is reported to have overheard the conversation of two spirits regarding the success or failure of crops sown at different times of the year.

3. The Liturgy.—The high veneration, almost amounting to a cult, paid to Moses and Elijah, also finds expression in some parts of the Jewish ritual. A cup of wine is at the present time in many places reserved for Elijah in the Passover-night Service,* which, though celebrated in commemoration of the release from Egypt, also emphasizes the hope of future redemption by the Messiah, whose forerunner was to be Elijah. The same prophet is also assumed to preside at the ceremony of circumcision, the chair in which the actual operator sits being designated the 'chair of Elijah'† in the German and other forms of the ritual. In the *Pirḳē de-Rabbi Eliezer* (latter half of the 8th cent.), end of ch. xxix., this idea is brought into connexion with Elijah's well-known zeal for Jahweh, the child being by the rite of circumcision initiated into Israel's covenant with Jahweh. Moses, his work and his death, are the subject of a number of hymns in the *Maḥzōr* (extended Service Book) for the Feast of Weeks (in connexion with the giving of the Law on Sinai) and the Passover. The liturgical elaboration of the life and work of Moses is specially prominent in the ritual of the Karaites (sect founded about the middle of the 8th century).

The most important portions of the synagogue services to be noted here are, however, the *Ḳaddīsh* and *Hazkārath Neshāmōth*.

(*a*) The *Ḳaddish*, which is of the nature of a doxology and embodies the Messianic hope, but contains no mention of the dead, was primarily instituted for recitation after completing the study of a section of the Talmud and at the end of a Talmudic discourse or lecture. But as the merit of the study of the Torah (by which the Talmud as the authoritative exposition of the Torah was mainly understood) was considered exceedingly potent, the idea must have arisen early that the living might thereby benefit even the departed; and it probably thus came about that the doxology concluding such study was assigned to mourners. In *Massekheth Sōpherīm* (prob. 6th or 7th cent.), xix. 12, its use in this connexion appears firmly established, though its recitation is assigned to the cantor. Later on its recital was ordered to follow every burial (see Moses b. Naḥmān [*ob.* 1268 or 1269], *Tōrath ha-Adam*, ed. Venice, 1595, fol. 50*a*); and the mourners' *Ḳaddish* in the full modern sense of the word is mentioned in the French ritual known as *Maḥzōr Viṭry* (A.D. 1208). The *Ḳaddish* thus gradually became, though never exclusively so, an indirect prayer for the departed. Its original connexion with the study of the Torah was in this use of it (as indeed in several other of its uses) lost sight of, and the idea of benefiting the dead by the special act of worship on the part of the surviving son or sons became very prominent.‡

The practice thus connects itself in idea with the new or inverted cult of the dead which was

* Mr. Israel Abrahams, on the authority of Nissim Gerondi (*ob.* shortly after 1374), favours the view that the pouring away of water was a method of making known the occurrence of a death (*Jewish Life in the Middle Ages*, p. 334); but if so, what need was there of pouring away *all* the water in the house? The likelihood is that the practice, though primarily pointing to quite a different principle, naturally got to serve in a secondary way to indicate death by a kind of association of ideas.

† See Perles, *MGWJ*, 1861, p. 389.

‡ The report found in *Semāḥōth* ix., of R. 'Aḳiba striking his breast at the death of R. Eliezer until the blood gushed out, has apparently no ritual significance, the act having been merely an expression of great personal grief.

* This custom, of which no trace has so far been found in mediæval MSS and early printed liturgical books, is probably due to the influences of later Kabbalism, though—as stated in the text—it is capable of being reasonably based on an old tradition.

† It is possible that the 'chair of Moses' in the now demolished Jewish synagogue at Kai-feng-fu in China (see *JQR*, Oct. 1900, p. 29) was intended to serve the same purpose.

‡ Compare the development of the custom as stated in L. N. Dembitz, *Jewish Services in Synagogue and Home*, pp. 109–110; see also the art. 'Kaddish' in Hamburger's *RE* ii. A statement on the different forms of the *Ḳaddish* will also be found in these works.

already in vogue in Maccabæan times, or, at any rate, at the time to which the composition of 2 Mac. belongs (see § 1). Instead of seeking to obtain benefits through the agency of the dead, the living engage in actions calculated to improve the condition of the departed; and as the surviving son or sons are the most approved agents of this form of the cult, it is only natural for those who see in the law of levirate (see § 6 in the 'Hebrew' article) an original connexion with the ancient sacrificial cult of the dead, to bring this use of the *Ḳaddish* into relation with that law, and to refer the religious function obligatory on the descendants to the same motive in both sets of regulations. The objection that might be raised is that, if the *Ḳaddish* were really connected with the idea underlying the law of levirate and the ancient sacrificial ritual of the dead, one would have expected to find it in use in much earlier times than can be attested by the existing literary evidence, continuity in essence being one of the marks of gradual development. But it is, on the other hand, not against analogy to suppose that if —as is very likely to have been the case—the idea itself was never eradicated from the popular mind, it should, under certain favourable influences,* have been later on fully revived under the form of the *Ḳaddish Yāthōm* (orphan's *Ḳaddish*). Such a use of the doxology would be merely one more instance of the embodiment of old forms of thought in fresh and later shapes.

(*b*) The same may also be said of the most solemn office connected with the departed, *i.e.* the *Hazkārath Neshāmōth* ('remembrance of souls'), which forms part of the Ashkenāzi ritual for the eighth day of the Passover, the second day of Pentecost, the eighth day of the Feast of Tabernacles, and the Day of Atonement. In this office direct petitions for the well-being of departed parents and other relatives are offered,† thus more explicitly attesting the revival (though in a much modified form), since mediæval times, of an earlier idea that the living are capable of rendering substantial service to the departed. In the Spanish ritual the same idea, in the form of direct petitions, is embodied in the *Hashkabah* ('laying to rest') which forms part of the Burial Service, and is also —under certain special regulations—recited during the synagogue services.‡

Mention should also here be made of the 'Jahrzeit,' or annual commemoration of departed parents, at which the *Ḳaddish* forms the most important feature, a candle being also kept burning for twenty-four hours.§ But the Jewish Liturgy also embodies petitions in which the merit of the departed is, *vice versa*, pleaded on behalf of the living, thus coming nearer to the old idea of seeking support from the spirits of the dead rather than offering help to them. In the famous prayer *Abīnū Malkēnū* ('Our Father, our King'), the merit of the martyrs is claimed as a ground for obtaining favour from the Almighty. The frequently occurring idea of *Zekūth 'Abōth*‖ ('merit of the fathers') may indeed not unreasonably be attached to the invocation, in the ancient 'prayer of eighteen' (1st to 2nd cent. A.D. at the latest), of the God of Abraham, the God of Isaac, and the God of Jacob. In conclusion, the practice of asking pardon of the dead in a ceremony at the grave (see *Shulḥān 'Arūkh*, i. § 606) may be mentioned. The mystical or spiritual union of the living with the dead and the possibility of interaction between the two states of being are clearly expressed in this interesting ritual.

4. The Kabbalah.—The cult of Elijah is very prominent in Kabbalistic literature. The founders (12th cent.) of the developed form of mysticism which is more particularly designated by the term 'Kabbalah' claimed to have received their instruction from the prophet in person. In the *Zōhar* (a work compiled in the latter part of the 13th cent., but attributed to the Tanna Rabbi Simeon b. Yoḥai (2nd cent.), which is the great text-book of the Kabbalah, Elijah also often appears as instructor under the title *Sabha* (*i.e.* 'the ancient one'). Moses, under the title *Ra'ya Mehēmna* (*i.e.* 'faithful shepherd'), appears, in a section bearing the same title, in conference with Elijah and R. Simeon b. Yoḥai; Abraham, Isaac, Jacob, and other worthies being also present at the deliberations, which are honoured by the appearance of the Deity Himself. Meṭaṭrōn, who very frequently figures in the Kabbalah, but whose exact nature and origin have not yet been satisfactorily explained, is in many places identified with Enoch.* R. Simeon b. Yoḥai himself, designated *Būṣina Ḳaddisha* ('sacred light'), is almost deified, and great veneration is also paid to leaders of later Kabbalistic schools, more particularly Isaac Luria (*ob.* 1572) and Baal-shem (*ob.* 1761).

Connected with the honours paid to departed worthies is the doctrine of metempsychosis, which, though in origin and essence entirely foreign to Mosaism,† and indeed to Semitic thought in general, succeeded about the 8th cent. in passing from Greek (and Indian) thought into the tenets of certain Jewish sectaries, through the medium of Muhammadan mysticism. Sa'adyah Gaon (*ob.* 942), who appears to be the first to make mention of it in orthodox Jewish literature, protests strongly against it.‡ But it nevertheless gained a firm footing in the Kabbalah, and attained an extraordinary development in the comparatively modern Kabbalistic system of Isaac Luria, the works on *gilgūlīm* ('transmigrations') composed by himself and his followers, containing long lists of identifications of ancient personages with men and women of later date.§ An addition to the doctrine of metempsychosis made by the Kabbalists is the principle of *'ibbūr* ('impregnation'). If two souls (who may, of course, be spirits of the dead) do not separately feel equal to their several tasks, God unites them in one body, so that they may support and complete each other. This doctrine may have been suggested by the theory of incubation (see farther on), which is itself clearly connected with the belief in demoniacal possession, taking the term 'demon' in this instance to denote a spirit, without reference to its origin or moral qualities.

Pilgrimages to graves‖ are much encouraged by the later Kabbalists. The tomb of Simeon b.

* It may thus well be that, as some have thought, the *Ḳaddish* is in a way the Jewish counterpart of certain practices in the Roman Church; but the idea underlying it would at the same time go back to ancient truly Semitic habits of thought.

† For further details see, *e.g.*, L. N. Dembitz, *op. cit.* pp. 219–220.

‡ See Dr. Gaster's edition of the Spanish Services, vol. i. p. 200 ff.; L. N. Dembitz, *Jewish Encyclopedia*, vol. vi. p. 283 f.

§ The article 'Jahrzeit' in the *JE* (vol. vii.) will be found instructive, for both the modern and the ancient manner of observing it.

‖ The Samaritans often use the formula בעמל משה ('by the merit of Moses').

* See especially the passage in *Massekheth 'Aṣīlūth* (ed. Jellinek, *Ginzē*, etc. p. 3), where Metatron is stated to have been originally human (flesh and blood). For various attempts to explain the name and office of Metatron see *Literaturblatt des Orients*, 1847, coll. 282–283; Oesterley and Box, *Religion and Worship of the Synagogue* (1907), pp. 107–178.

† See A. Schmiedl, *Studien über jüdische Religionsphilosophie* (Vienna, 1869), pp. 159–166. The phrase μεταβαίνειν εἰς ἕτερον σῶμα, used by Josephus in connexion with the belief of the Pharisees (*BJ* II. viii. 14), must refer to the resurrection (comp. the parallel passage in *Ant.* XVIII. i. 3).

‡ *Emūnōth we-Dē'ōth*, ch. vi.

§ Compare the belief implied (though not countenanced in its literary sense) in Mt 11[14], Lk 1[17].

‖ On pilgrimages generally the art. 'Pilgrimage' in the *JE* (vol. x.) should be consulted.

Yoḥai at Meron near Safed is thus devoutly resorted to on the 33rd of 'Omar (*i.e.* the 33rd day from the 2nd day of Passover), when a great popular festival, at which illuminations are an important feature, is held in honour of the saint. Pilgrimages to the grave of Isaac Luria at Safed are made each new moon, and the persistence in many places of the popular custom of praying at stated times (as, *e.g.*, on the 9th of Ab) at the graves of departed relatives is probably also partly due to the influence of Kabbalistic ideas.

The efforts of 16th cent. and later Kabbalists to obtain inspiration from the souls of the departed by clinging with outstretched bodies to their graves, and thus in a manner to become incubated with the spirits of the dead, remind one of the practice of necromancy at graves condemned in Is 65[4] (see § 8 in the 'Hebrew' art.); but as the Kabbalists evidently arrived at this method by a new and largely borrowed line of thought, and as, furthermore, their object was not necromancy, but what they regarded as spiritual illumination, the custom cannot be regarded as a revival of the ancient practice. A species of oneiromancy is the same Kabbalists' belief that information of high import can be obtained through dream-visions of the departed.

Summary.—The general result obtained from a study of the Jewish part of the subject is, owing to the diverse forms of development undergone by the thoughts and practices of the people in different periods and widely scattered countries, far from homogeneous. The Talmudic and Midrashic literature thus exhibits a larger amount of reminiscence of, or reversion to, ancient thought than the Apocryphal and Pseudepigraphical writings, though these latter stood nearer in point of time to earlier Hebraism; and the Liturgy, influenced partly by the Kabbalah, and partly—as is not unlikely—by Christian practices, shows some interesting instances of the revival of old ideas in a much modified form. The Kabbalah itself, as has been shown, has added the doctrine of metempsychosis to the original Jewish and Hebrew stock of ideas, and it has in connexion with it furthermore introduced the theory of dual psychic personality in one body, thereby affecting the spirits of the departed in a manner previously unheard of in Judaism.

LITERATURE.—Besides the passages of the original sources (Apocrypha, etc.) referred to in the article, the following books, essays, or articles may be consulted with advantage. For Apocryphal and Pseudepigraphical literature, ch. iii. in F. Schwally's *Leben nach dem Tode*, 1892. From the Rabbinic point of view, J. Perles, 'Die Leichenfeierlichkeiten im nachbiblischen Judenthum' in *MGWJ* x. [1861] pp. 345 ff., 376 ff.; A. P. Bender, 'Beliefs, Rites, and Customs of the Jews, connected with Death, Burial, and Mourning' in *JQR* vi. [1894–5] 317 ff., 664, vii. 101 ff., 259 ff. [also discusses modern points of view]; A. Büchler, 'Das Entblössen der Schulter und des Armes als Zeichen der Trauer' in *ZATW*, 1901, pp. 81–92. For points in the Liturgy, the articles 'Seelenfeier,' 'Kaddish,' etc., in Hamburger's *RE*; L. N. Dembitz, *Jewish Services in Synagogue and Home* [the same author wrote the art. 'Kaddish,' etc., in the *JE*]. For metempsychosis, etc., L. Ginzberg's instructive art. 'Cabala' in *JE* iii. [requires, however, to be supplemented from other sources]; also I. Broydé's 'Transmigration of Souls' in *JE* xii. 231–234. Some other works dealing with the subject will be found in the literature given at the beginning of C. Grüneisen's *Der Ahnenkultus und die Urreligion Israels*, 1900. G. MARGOLIOUTH.

ANCESTOR-WORSHIP AND CULT OF THE DEAD (Polynesian and Tasmanian).—In Polynesia, ancestor-worship was far less important than in Melanesia or Micronesia. Throughout this group, moreover, it was only the nobles who retained an existence after death, the souls of the common people perishing immediately after dissolution (Waitz-Gerland, *Anthropologie der Naturvölker*, Leipzig, 1872, vi. 302; Dillon, *Narrative of a Voyage in the South Sea*, London, 1829, ii. 10–11). The ghosts of the dead might appear to the living and might work them either weal or woe, but they were in the main maleficent, and were accordingly, for the most part, objects of dread (Waitz-Gerland, pp. 315–316, 330, 332). Between the general worship of ghosts and the cult of ancestors a distinction should be drawn, evanescent though the line of demarcation often becomes. Ellis (*Polynesian Researches*, 2nd ed., London, 1832–1836, i. 334–336) expressly postulates the existence of *oramatuas*, or 'ancestors,' who ranked next to the *atuas*, or gods, and were often the spirits of deceased fathers, mothers, brothers, sisters, children, and other relatives, as well as of departed warriors who had been conspicuous for bravery. Although the *oramatuas* frequently helped in time of need, and opposed the malevolence of other ghosts or of hostile magic, they were, as a rule, cruel and irritable. It was thus necessary to place the corpse of the dead at a considerable height above the ground, this being apparently the origin of the *fata tupapau*, or altar for the dead (Moerenhout, *Voyages aux îles du Grand Océan*, Paris, 1837, i. 470–471). Food was brought daily to the dead for six weeks or two months, and if the deceased had been a man of eminence, a special priest, termed *haivatupapau*, visited the body for several weeks and offered it food. It was believed that the *oramatua* could smell the spiritual part of this offering, and, in case it returned, it would therefore be gratified and content, so that it would not desire to resume earthly life (Ellis, i. 404–405; Moerenhout, i. 547; Wilson, *Missionary Voyage to the Southern Pacific Ocean*, London, 1799, p. 345). At the burial of a chief a hole was often dug in which the hostility of the deceased against his family for their supposed malevolence, which had resulted in his death, was buried, thus obviating the possibility of his maleficent return to his surviving kinsmen (Moerenhout, i. 552). Connected in a sense with the cult of ancestors was the mourning for the dead, together with the self-mutilations practised by the survivors (Waitz-Gerland, vi. 401–404); and here, too, belong the human sacrifices of wives, slaves, and favourites at graves in New Zealand, Hawaii (Waitz-Gerland, vi. 404–405), and the Fiji Islands (Russel, *Polynesia*, Edinburgh, 1843, p. 72). The motive for both these latter features was either the gratification of the *oramatua* at the sight of the grief which his death had caused, or a provision for his needs in the future life.

The religion of the Tasmanians was at a much lower stage of development than that of the Polynesians; yet it is clear that they, too, believed in a life beyond the grave, and thought that the souls of the dead might return to bless or curse them. They accordingly carried a bone of the deceased as a charm; yet the 'shades' (*warawali*) of dead relatives and friends were regarded, on the whole, as more kindly than the gods. Of an actual cult of ancestors, however, little seems to be known (Ling Roth, *Aborigines of Tasmania*, 2nd ed., Halifax, 1899, pp. 54–55). LOUIS H. GRAY.

ANCESTOR-WORSHIP AND CULT OF THE DEAD (Roman).—The great extent of ancestor-worship among the Romans, and its equally great limitations, make it not only one of the most interesting problems in the field of Roman religion, but also a subject the understanding of which brings with it a grasp of the fundamental principles which governed the formation and the development of the religion of the Romans. As it is in the main a private worship (*sacra privata*) rather than a public one (*sacra publica*; for the distinction, cf. Wissowa, p. 334; Marquardt, p. 120 ff.), our sources for the Kingdom and the Republic are limited, and it is only in the

Empire, with its vast number of sepulchral inscriptions (*CIL* vi., *CIG* xiv., over 40,000 for Rome alone) that we have any extensive contemporary sources. For the earlier period, however, we have a sufficient number of literary sources to enable us to form a definite idea of the cult, inasmuch as the stereotyped character of all religious ceremonial justifies us in combining testimonies from various historical periods; and, though the underlying ideas did undoubtedly change somewhat from generation to generation, there was a certain conservative force at work too. It will be most convenient, therefore, to treat of the underlying ideas and the expressions of them in cult acts, first during the general period of the Republic, and then, secondly, to sketch the development of these ideas from the close of the Republic onwards during the course of the Empire.

I. From the Earliest Period to the Close of the Republic.

1. The first and most fundamental question which requires an answer is this, Are any of the Roman gods to be traced back to ancestor-worship as their origin? From Euhemerus (cf. Rohde, *Gr. Roman*, 220 ff.) down to Herbert Spencer (*Principles of Sociology*) it has been a favourite contention that many great deities were in origin nothing but deified ancestors. An examination of Roman religion in its earliest state shows that this was not the case in Rome. The religion of the earliest period reveals distinct traces of animism (cf. Tylor, *Primitive Culture*, i. 377 ff., ii. 1–377)—that belief common to all primitive peoples, which posits for all things, animate and inanimate, living and dead, a 'double,' or psychic parallel, which has an effect on the thing itself and must therefore be propitiated. These doubles are potentialities rather than individualities. They are interesting not so much for what they are as for what they do. Now, Roman religion is peculiarly interesting in this respect, because in it we see a development of animism one step further. Certain of these powers have advanced sufficiently towards individuality to acquire a name, but they are none of them as yet individuals thought of in the fashion of man (on the importance of names cf. Frazer, *Golden Bough*², i. 403 ff.); hence there was not, could not be, a native Roman mythology. They were advancing towards it when Greek influence placed her myths at Rome's disposal, so that she never developed any of her own. On the other hand, a great number of the gods of the earliest period were still mere potentialities, thought of in groups rather than as individuals, *e.g.* the *Di Penates*, powers who guarded the storeroom, the *Di Agrestes*, powers who looked after the crops. It was into one of these groups that the dead went, into the *Di Manes*, the 'good gods' (*manus*='good'; cf. Roscher, ii. 2316). It will be readily seen, therefore, that, far from its being the case that the dead were ever made great individual gods, they received such divinity as they had by the same processes of thought which made all gods, great and small.

If further proof is needed, it may be found in the total absence of hero-worship in Roman religion, as it was before Greek influence came; and in the significant fact that, when under Greek influence two great characters of Græco-Roman mythology, Æneas and Romulus, were elevated to the rank of gods, theologians found nothing better to do than to identify them with two already existing old Roman deities, Numicius and Quirinus respectively (for Æneas=Numicius, cf. Rossbach in Pauly-Wissowa, i. 1015; Aust in Roscher, iii. 475. For Romulus=Quirinus, cf. Wissowa, p. 141). Every attempt to make even the *Di Manes* the source of other deities has been a failure. It has been tried repeatedly, but in vain, in the case of the *Lar Familiaris* or protecting spirit of the house (cf. Fustel de Coulanges, *La Cité antique*, p. 20; Nissen, *Templum*, p. 148; Rohde, *Psyche*³, i. p. 254).

2. Having rid our discussion of any connexion between the deified dead and other individual deities of Rome, we must now try to make clear to ourselves what the concept of the **Di Manes** was, and how the Romans felt towards them. It has often been asserted that the Romans had from the beginning a persistent and continuous belief in the immortality of the soul. This statement is absolutely misleading. We have seen that the habit of thought of the early Romans posited a double for everything; the dead must therefore have a double as well as the living. This double, even though it was the double of the dead, was thought of as possessing a certain sort of life—it could at certain times return to earth and exercise an influence for ill upon the living. This potentiality, however, was simply one of a vast number of similar potentialities; there was nothing individual about it, except its relation to its own family represented by the living members. Subsequent centuries, saturated with Greek philosophy and filled with an idea of individuality which was totally lacking in the earlier days of Rome, identified this poor shadowy potentiality with the human soul, and read into the whole matter a belief in immortality.

In the presence of the mystery of death, a mystery which even the light of Christianity has not wished fully to remove, men's minds do not work logically, and there is no part of religious beliefs where contradictions are more abundant than in the beliefs concerning the dead. Roman religion, in spite of its generally logical character, is no exception to the rule. It will never be possible for us, even with all the sepulchral inscriptions in the world, to establish one formula which will cover all cases—for the simple reason that no such formula ever existed. We are, however, able to make a general statement which will represent fairly well the normal concept, apart from the very numerous and very contradictory deviations.

When a man died, he went over into the *Di Manes*,—the good gods,—entering their ranks and losing all individuality and all specific earthly relations, except that when the *Manes* returned to earth, they visited the living members of the family to which they had belonged on earth; and thus the family idea, so fundamental in the social structure of Rome, triumphed over the grave, and possessed an immortality which the individual failed to obtain. The inclusiveness of the term *Di Manes* is seen in the fact that the gods who ruled over the dead, as well as their subjects, the dead themselves as gods, were all included in the phrase, though it is equally significant of the mass-idea that the actual gods of the dead, though demonstrably present, never rose to great individual prominence until the Greek Pluto-Persephone came into Rome as *Dis-Proserpina*.

3. Upon this theory of the *Manes* the cult followed inevitably. If the dead were able to influence the affairs of the living, they must be propitiated, and inasmuch as their interference was primarily with the affairs of the family to which they had originally belonged, and still did belong, it was incumbent upon the living members of that family to see that they were propitiated. Thus the cult of the dead was in its origin an ancestor-worship, and may well have been originally a family matter exclusively. Further, it was incumbent upon each living member of the family not only to perform these sacrifices, but also to

provide those who would succeed to the sacrifices after his death, in other words, to propagate the family. As for the State itself, it was also a family; and thus in that macrocosm of family life which the early State religion shows,—with its Vesta and its Penates,—there might come also sacrifices for the dead, not only for the dead already provided for by their own families, but also for that ever-increasing number of 'ancestors' whose descendants, in spite of all precautions, had ceased, that homeless throng of spirits whose immediate claims on the world of the living had been removed, and who therefore all the more readily would turn their ill-will against the State at large, unless she gave them satisfaction. Thus it was that both the *sacra privata* and the *sacra publica* were in part a worship of the dead.

There are sufficient suggestions and recollections in the body of Roman law to warrant the assumption of this theory, which, as one readily recognizes, is a close parallel to the Hindu law; but there is also this distinction, that, whereas Hindu law is based directly upon a sacral foundation, Roman law, when we first meet it, is already in the dual stage of *jus divinum* and *jus humanum*, with their intricate interlocking, so that we have merely the shadow picture of what once was. But even the shadow picture is tolerably complete, and the *jus Manium* formed one of the regular topics of Roman law, especially in relation to heirs and inheritances. The cardinal principle was the continuity of family worship (*perpetua sacra sunto*). Thus Cicero (*de Legibus*, ii. 22) quotes an old law: 'Let private sacrifices continue forever,' 'Keep sacred the laws concerning the divine dead.' The heir was under obligations to continue the sacrifices, and this was a prior lien on any money which the inheritance might bring him. Similarly, cases of adoption were often motived by the desire of the adopter to obtain an heir to care for the sacrifices; and, though the process was a civil one, it was necessary, inasmuch as it involved the giving up of one set of sacrifices and the taking of another on the part of the adopted person, to discuss it in the oldest and most primitive of all the assemblies—the Comitia Curiata—and to obtain the consent of the Pontifex Maximus to the giving up of the one set of *sacra* (the so-called *detestatio sacrorum*, cf. Hunter, p. 766), a consent which was never given if the transfer left the one set of *sacra* destitute of an earthly representative (for a similar precaution in Hindu law, cf. Hunter, p. 205, note 2). We may also compare the old law ascribed to Romulus (Plut. *Rom.* 22), whereby whoever sells his wife is given over to the *Manes*, probably because this was a blow to the stability of the family, and hence to the continuity of sacrifices to the dead. The actuating motive underlying all the *jura Manium*, all the enactments concerning the dead, was neither a chivalrous pity nor primarily a regard for the comfort of the dead, but first and foremost a self-protective action on the part of the living. So fearful were men lest they might in some way have offended the gods of the other world, and lest the powers under the earth might hinder the gathering of the crops which had come out of the earth, that every year before the beginning of harvest a sow (*porca præcidanea*) was sacrificed to Tellus (and probably also to Ceres) 'by him who had not given the dead his due' (Paul. p. 223); later, by all men to Ceres and Tellus together, for fear they might have offended, so that eventually it began to be thought of merely as a sacrifice to Ceres for a good harvest (Wissowa, p. 160).

4. In its earlier stages the cult of the dead belonged to the religion of fear rather than the religion of love. The spirits of the dead were capable of doing injury; they must first be brought to rest in the lower world. There they were incapable of doing harm, and they could rise from there only on certain occasions, and on those occasions religion provided for their pacification. All the cult acts pertaining to the dead may be grouped, therefore, under these two ideas, the bringing of the spirits to rest, which must be done immediately after death, and the placating of the spirits on the regular annual occasions when they returned to earth again. Around this crude religion of fear the religion of love wound itself, breathing a new and better spirit into these old forms, and possibly instituting one or two festivals of its own. But we must deal first with the self-protective apotropaic side.

The ceremonies connected with death and burial do not as a whole concern us here, but merely those festivals which were strictly religious in character. These features seem, all of them, to go back to two ideas which are so intertwined that for us they are practically inseparable—possibly they always were. One is the offerings given to the dead as a newly formed member of the *Manes*, including a proper burial, as giving him a home, and the offerings of food, etc.; and the other is the ceremonies of purification which were necessary for the living, after their close contact with this lower world at the edge of the open grave (cf. the idea of the *Manes* coming for the dead, which occurs occasionally in inscriptions, *e.g.* *CIL* ii. 2255 [Corduba]: 'the Manes have taken Abullia'). There is a considerable degree of uncertainty attaching to the exact order and names for the various ceremonies connected with and following the funeral; writers of the Empire, who are practically our only authorities, seem to be confusing Greek and Roman ideas, and older with newer Roman customs, and possibly the details will never be fully straightened out. But in general the matter was as follows. The supreme duty towards the dead was burial. Doubtless an ethical motive of piety, a desire to give the dead a home for his own sake, often re-inforced this duty; but the fundamental motive was one of self-protection, on the principle that the ghost of the dead would continue to haunt the living until a place was provided for it (Tertullian, *de Anim.* 56: 'It was believed that the unburied did not descend to the world below before they had received their due,' *i.e.* burial). Curiously enough, in certain cases it seems to have been felt that the dead had forfeited the right of burial, *e.g.* in the case of suicides, of those lawfully put to death, and of those struck by lightning. Here it was an equally great duty to abstain from burial, and there seems to have been no fear of evil consequences from their shades. But in all other cases burial was an ethical imperative (Quintilian, *Decl.* v. 6: 'Because even upon unknown dead we heap earth, and no one ever is in too great a hurry to honour an unburied body by putting earth, be it ever so little, on it'). The question of burial *versus* cremation in the various epochs of Roman history does not concern us here, for in either case the grave was sacred; but burial seems always to have held at least a symbolic supremacy—owing to the *os resectum*, or the custom of burying at least a portion of the body, *e.g.* a finger, when the rest was cremated. The burial was the most important self-protective act; in comparison with it the other acts were of relatively minor importance; and most of these acts seem to have had more to do with the purification of the surviving members of the family than with the dead himself. One sacrifice of purification took place before the body was carried out for burial: the sacrifice to Ceres of a sow (*porca præsentanea*, not to be confused with the *porca præcidanea* above), 'for the sake of purifying the family' (Festus, p. 250; cf. Mar. Victor. p. 25). In all probability Tellus, Mother Earth, and not Ceres, was the original recipient of the sacrifice, which was transferred to Ceres under the influence of the Greek Demeter cult (cf. Wissowa, p. 161); and hence the sacrifice was probably originally a purification of the living by means of an additional propitiation for the dead. On the day of the funeral and at the grave itself a sacrificial banquet seems to have been offered to the dead (*silicernium*, cf. Marquardt, *Privatleben*, p. 378). It consisted probably of very much the same things as were offered at the regular annual celebration of the *Parentalia* (see below). The nine days immediately following the funeral were days of mourning and purification, the *sacrum novemdiale*, the same term that was decreed by the State for its extraordinary periods of devotion occasioned by some great calamity (on the number nine as a sacred number cf. Diels, *Sibyll. Blätter*, p. 41). On some of these days the *Feriæ Denicales* occurred, a celebration about which we know little, except that the attendance of the members of the family was considered so necessary that the military authorities recognized it as a valid excuse for the absence of a recruit from the enlistment inspection, 'provided it had not been set on that day for the purpose of serving as an excuse' (Gell. xvi. 4. 3 ff.). The period of mourning ceased on the ninth day with a final banquet, with offerings to the dead, the *cena novemdialis*; and if funeral games were celebrated at all, as they often were, they occurred on this day (*ludi novemdiales*). The spirit of the dead was now safely housed in the lower world, whence he could not return, except on stated occasions; and the Roman could go about his daily business, mindful only of these stated occasions when they arrived.

5. As regards the lower world itself, the Romans seem originally to have interested themselves very little in it. Every bit of description is given us by writers under Greek influence, and the details are identical with those of the lower world of the Greeks. Now, it is not likely that a strong Roman tradition could thus have been totally destroyed; we should certainly find traces of it somewhere. Hence it is probable that the Roman lower world was not furnished with the fittings of imagination until Greek mythology provided the models. There is nothing strange about this, when we realize that the half-animistic character of the Roman pantheon precluded the growth of mythology for both the greater and the lesser gods. From the time of the Punic wars onwards the Romans pictured to themselves the lower world in just the same form as the Greeks had done (cf. Rohde, *Psyche*³, vol. i.); and before that time, if they thought of it at all, and inevitably they must have done so to some slight extent, it was merely as a place of shadows and darkness. Their practical concern was the question of the eventual return of the spirits to trouble them; and hence their attention was concentrated not on the lower world in pleasant poetic fancies, but on the door between it and the upper world, the passage through which these divine dead came up. This entrance was the *mundus*, about which the Romans possessed original beliefs strong enough to remain even under the pressure of Greek thought. The *mundus* was the opening of the lower world; it was in the form of a trench into which sacrifices to the gods of the lower world, and to the dead as gods, could be thrown. In the centre of every town, at its foundation, such a trench was dug and sacrifices performed. The oldest *mundus* of Rome was that of the Palatine city (for its location cf. Richter, *Die älteste Wohnstätte des röm. Volkes*, Berlin, 1891, p. 7 ff.; Hülsen, *Röm. Mitt.* v. 76 ff., xi. 202 ff.). It was opened three days in the year: August 24, October 5, and November 8; probably the stone, and possibly some earth was removed (cf. Festus, p. 142; Macrobius, *Sat.* i. 16, 17 ff.). 'When,' as Varro says (cf. Macr. i. 1), 'the *mundus* is open, the door of the sad gods of the lower world is open, therefore it is not proper on those days for a battle to be fought, troops to be levied, the army to march forth, a ship to set sail, or a man to marry.' There were other sacred trenches of the same sort in Rome: one in the Forum, the Lacus Curtius, connected with the story of M. Curtius (recently discovered; cf. Hülsen, *Rom. Forum*, p. 139; and, in general, Gilbert, *Top.* i. 334 ff.), another the so-called 'grave of Tarpeia,' which was evidently opened on Feb. 13, when one of the Vestals made sacrifice there (cf. Mommsen, *CIL* i.² p. 309; Schwegler, *Röm. Gesch.* i. 486; and, in general, on Tarpeia as a forgotten goddess of the lower world, Wissowa, *Rel. der Röm.* 187, 188), and still another at the 'grave of Larenta' in the Velabrum, to which on Dec. 23 the Pontifices and the Flamen Quirinalis brought offerings (Varro, *Ling. Lat.* vi. 23 ff.; *Fast. Præn.* to Dec. 23; cf. Wissowa, p. 188 and note 1).

6. Apart from these special occasions for each particular *mundus*, there were two general occasions in the year when all the spirits of the dead were supposed to return to earth again, the nine days from Feb. 13–21, and the three days, May 9, 11, 13. The first was called the *Parentalia*, the second the *Lemuria*. These two occasions were so entirely different, and the *Parentalia* is on such an infinitely higher plane ethically than the *Lemuria*, that it is difficult to think of them as having the same origin; yet, when we compare All-souls' Day with Hallowe'en, we see the same divergence. The *Parentalia* kept pace with Rome's increase in culture, whereas all that was crudest in old folklore clung to the *Lemuria*.

Since the *Lemuria* represents a more primitive stage, it had better be discussed first. The most picturesque account is that given by Ovid (*Fasti*, v. 419 ff.), but we must be on our guard in using it, remembering that Greek ideas and a poetical imagination are present in everything that Ovid writes. The ceremony takes place at midnight. The father of the household, barefooted, passes through the house, throws black beans behind his back, and says nine times, 'These I give, and with these I redeem myself and my family.' Then he shakes cymbals and says again nine times, '*Manes exite paterni*,' 'Go forth, ye divine shades of my fathers.' The comparison of this ceremony with the 'driving out of the ghosts,' so common among primitive peoples of to-day, suggests itself immediately (cf. Frazer, *Golden Bough*², iii. 83 ff. Here, as everywhere else in this interesting and valuable book, the reader must exercise great care in examining the sources given, as they differ widely in scientific value; cf. also Rohde, *Psyche*³, i. p. 239).

The *Parentalia* presents quite a different picture. As its name implies, it is the festival of the *parentes*, or the making of offerings to one's ancestors. It began at noon of Feb. 13 and continued for nine days. The first eight days belonged only to the sphere of private worship, but the ninth day (Feb. 21) was also a public celebration, the *Feralia* (Varro, *op. cit.* 13; Paul. p. 85; cf. Marquardt, iii. 310 ff.). During all these nine days marriages were forbidden, the temples were shut, and the magistrates laid aside their official dress. Every family decorated the graves of its ancestors and made offerings there. Most appropriately, on the day after the close of the celebration, Feb. 22, a family festival, the *Caristia*, or *Cara Cognatio*, was held, when family quarrels were adjusted, and the peace which the individual member of the family had just made with the dead was now extended to the living members among themselves (cf. Ovid, *Fasti*, ii. 617; Val. Max. ii. 1, 8; *Calend. Philocal.*; cf. *CIL* i.² p. 258).

The attempt has been made to distinguish between the *Lemuria* and the *Parentalia* by considering the former as the festival of the unburied, and therefore hostile, dead, and the latter as the festival of the buried, and therefore friendly, dead (cf. Warde Fowler, *Roman Festivals*, p. 108). The idea of fear is certainly more prominent in the former than in the latter; but the *Lemures* are just the same ancestors as the *Di Parentes*, and the very fact that their interference, either for good or for ill, is confined to stated seasons, proves that they were buried, *i.e.* admitted into the lower world and resident there ordinarily.

Of the other yearly festivals of the dead we know but little: we hear of a festival of the *Carnaria* on the first of June, the 'Bean Calends' (*Calendæ Fabariæ*, Varro in Non. p. 341; Macr. *Sat.* i. 12, 31; Ovid, *Fasti*, vi. 101 ff.), so called from the offering of beans to the dead; but roses were also offered (*CIL* iii. 3893).

7. In one respect the spirit-worship of the Romans was in distinct contrast to that of the Greeks and of most other ancient peoples. The dead had the power of returning to earth again on stated occasions, but they could not be called up and consulted. 'Necromancy' was an altogether imported idea, and wherever we meet with references to it, foreign influence is present. The absence of this custom is no accident. The idea of prophecy was hardly present in any form in native Roman religion; their science of augury and of the *haruspices* was simply a means of ascertaining the approval or non-approval of the gods in regard to a certain action, merely of obtaining an answer to a categorical question. But if the dead might not be called up arbitrarily to give information, it was possible for certain individuals to be given over to them for punishment, as in the *consecratio*, or for certain individuals voluntarily to give themselves over to them, as in the *devotio*. *Consecratio* is the transfer of a person or thing out of the realm of the *jus humanum* into that of the *jus divinum*. Where a person is involved, it is, of course, a punishment. Persons or things might thus be given over to any deity or group of deities, and the *Di Manes* formed no exception; *e.g.* a man who sold his wife was *dis manibus sacer* (Plut. *Rom.* 22); also a child who struck his parent (Fest. p. 230); and the violator of a grave (*CIL* x. 4255). The characteristics of the *devotio*, on the other hand, are these. It is in the nature of a vow, made to the *Di Manes*, or Tellus and the *Di Manes*, whereby a man's life is given to the *Di Manes* in advance in order that other men's lives may be destroyed. We have semi-legendary accounts of three generals who offered their own lives that the enemy of the State might be destroyed: the first the case of Decius, the father, in the battle of Vesuvius, B.C. 340 (cf. esp. Livy, viii. 6. 8–16; 9. 1–11, and, in general, Münzer in Pauly-Wissowa, iv. 2280); the second that of Decius, the son, in the battle of Sentinum, B.C. 295; and the third that of Decius, the grandson, in the battle of Asculum, B.C. 279 (cf. Münzer, *ib.* iv. 2285; on the *devotio* proper cf. Panly-Wissowa, *ib.*, *s.v.*). The *devotio*, as a curse directed against private individuals, does not belong to this period, as it arose entirely under Greek influence, and does not seem to have been prevalent until the Empire.

II. From the Close of the Republic until the Establishment of Christianity.

1. In the earliest periods of Roman religion the *Di Manes* were quite as truly gods as any of the other gods of Rome, and quite as unlike the later god-concept as any other of the gods. They were all alike thought of animistically as mere potentialities; but the other gods were destined to develop and to obtain an individuality, whereas the *Di Manes* remained an unindividualized mass of spirits, into which the dead man went at death, losing, so far as the cult was concerned, all his individuality except merely his family relationship. To be sure, under Greek influence certain gods of the dead were adopted by the Romans, namely Dis and Proserpina, formed on the analogy of the gods of the upper world; but this had the effect of only emphasizing the more the undeveloped dense mass of the *Di Manes*. On the other hand, during these centuries of the Republic, another idea had been slowly developing—the idea of the **Genius** (or if a woman, the Juno), or divine double of the individual, accompanying him during all his lifetime. In the question as to what became of the *Genius* at the death of the individual, and in the answering of that question by ascribing to him a life after death, the idea of personal immortality had its rise in Rome. The statements of later writers are obscured, partly by purely philosophical ideas foreign to the real beliefs of the many, and partly by a desire to identify and generally systematize all forms of Roman belief; but we can dimly recognize the following development. Originally the *Genius* and the *Di Manes* had no connexion whatsoever, except the mere matter of sequence; so long as a man lived he had a *Genius*, an individuality, at first thought of as merely physical, later as psychological; but when he died, his individuality ceased, he was gathered to the majority (not the divine doubles of the individuals in it), the *Di Manes*. Now, in the course of time one of the effects of Greece on Rome was the development of individuality and of the idea of individuality. All these ideas centred in the *Genius*, and hence it was natural to think of the *Genius* as existing after death. It must, however, in that case stand in some relation to the *Manes*, it must be identical with at least a part of them, that part contributed by the individual at his death. It is not surprising then, that, beginning with the Augustan age (cf. Hübner, in Müller's *Handbuch*, i. p. 529, § 47), the idea of the individual makes itself felt in connexion with the *Manes*, and we have the form (which soon becomes the ordinary form), 'To the *Manes* of, or belonging to, such a man,' emphasized occasionally by the addition of the *Genius* (cf. *CIL* v. 246, etc.). Sometimes the *Manes* are left out entirely, and we have merely the *Genius* or the Juno of such a person (for the *Genius*, cf. *CIL* v. 246, ix. 5794; for the Juno, v. 160, x. 1009, 1023, 6597). This reinforcement by the *Genius* was the salvation of the *Manes*; it gave new life to the concept, and the *Di Manes* began to develop out of a mere mass of spirits into a host of individual protecting deities. The cult went on in its old forms, but a new spirit, a new idea, had been brought into it. It is along this line that the *Di Manes* had their effect on the two great religious developments of the Empire—the emperor-worship of the first two centuries, and Christianity in its later centuries.

2. *The worship of the dead and emperor-worship.*—The elevation of the Roman emperors into gods was caused by two entirely distinct sets of tendencies; the one coming from the Orient, a tendency which, in so far as it was not checked (as it always was by all the better emperors), made the emperors into gods during their lifetime as well as after death; the other a thoroughly Roman concept, the idea that during life not the man but only his *Genius* was divine, but that after death, when the *Genius* still lived as the individualized *Manes*, the offerings might be made to the individual as a god. The difference, therefore, between an emperor, who allowed himself to be worshipped merely within the limits authorized by Roman ideas, and an ordinary Roman citizen was this: during lifetime the *Genius* of each was an object of worship, but the emperor's *Genius* was always, in all cases, one of the regular gods of the State cult, whereas the *Genius* of the individual belonged purely to the private cult, usually confined to a man's household. After death, both the emperor and the private citizen were worshipped as gods, with a similar distinction, namely, that in the case of certain emperors the Senate, after examining their acts, decreed that they should be included among the regular gods of the State. The only real distinction, therefore, was the inclusion of the emperor's *Genius* among the gods of the State in every case, during life, and the inclusion of the emperor himself, *i.e.* his *Manes*, among the State gods in certain cases after death. There can be little doubt that emperor-worship had the effect of strengthening the worship of the dead in general.

3. *The worship of the dead and Christianity.*—Among the many difficult problems which the teachers of the Christian religion had to solve in

the Roman world, perhaps none was more difficult than that presented by the developed concept of the worship of the dead as protecting and helping deities. Polytheism, so far as the greater gods were concerned, had among the educated classes gone over into monotheism without the aid of Christianity, merely by the doctrine of a philosophical syncretism; but it was with inborn, almost instinctive beliefs, bred in the bone, such as the divinity of the dead, that the Church's real battle had to be fought. Her method was one of compromise; it was the authorization, nay the encouragement, of the worship of certain individuals, men and women who as martyrs had by one act set the seal upon their faith, or whose life had been holy to such a degree as to merit certain miraculous manifestations. The worship of these martyrs and saints was intended primarily to keep them as ensamples in the minds of the living. But this was not enough for a people who had worshipped the dead not so much because they had been good during their lives, as because these gods of the dead were useful to them, protecting and helping them in their hours of danger and need. The saints, too, must accomplish something for them. This also was granted by the Church, but merely in the sense that the saints acted as intermediaries, whose intercession with God would increase the probability of obtaining one's petition. Theology stopped there, but humanity went further. By that facile transfer of the means into the end, of the intermediary into the final, which is so characteristic of simple minds, aided too as they were in this case by a habit of thought which had made the dead into gods like other gods, these saintly intercessors soon became gods on their own account, and the legend of each became a cult-legend, indicating the circumstances in which each was especially powerful. Thus there arose, literally from the dead, a host of minor gods, a myriad of potentialities, like the old gods of the so-called *Indigitamenta*. Human frailty had, at least in the lower classes, triumphed over theology, and the real religious world of the Roman's latest descendants bore a startling resemblance to that of his peasant ancestors in the days of Romulus. See also art. ROMAN RELIGION.

LITERATURE.—Aust, *Religion der Römer*, 1899, pp. 179 ff., 225–232; De Marchi, *Il Culto Privato*, 1896, i. 180–208; W. Fowler, *Roman Festivals*, 1899, *passim*; Hunter, *Roman Law*, 745 f.; Marquardt, *Staatsverwaltung*, 310; Preller, *Röm. Mythologie*, 1858, ii. 61–119; Rohde, *Psyche*³, i. 216–258; Steuding, art. 'Manes' in Roscher; Tylor, *Primitive Culture*³, 1891, *passim*; Wissowa, *Religion der Römer*, 1902, 187–193, and his artt. 'Lemuria' and 'Larvæ' in Roscher.

JESSE BENEDICT CARTER.

ANCESTOR-WORSHIP AND CULT OF THE DEAD (Slavonic).

—We have only very few references to the cult of the dead among the pagan Slavs. The German chronicler Thietmar, who had not much sympathy with the Slavs, says (in the first Book of his Chronicles, § 14), 'They believe that everything ends with death' ('Omnia cum morte temporali putant finiri'). The Russian chronicler known by the name of Nestor, in the chapter in which he relates the conversion of the Russian prince Vladimir, puts into his mouth the words, 'The Greek priests say that there is another world,' which would seem to imply that the pagan Russians did not believe in that other world. On the other hand, the Bohemian chronicler, Cosmas of Prague, declares that the Christian prince Bretislav II., by an edict in 1092, suppressed 'sepulturas quæ fiebant in silvis et campis, atque scenas (or cœnas) quas ex gentili ritu faciebant in biviis et in triviis quasi ob animarum pausationem, item et iocos profanos quos super mortuos inanes cientes manes . . . exercebant.' This most probably refers to rites and festivals in honour of the dead. The phrase 'ob animarum pausationem' seems to have been influenced by the Christian idea of purgatory.

The idea of death is expressed in the Slav languages by the root *mer*, *mor*, which is common throughout the Indo-Germanic languages. The place to which people go after death is called by the name of *nav*, which is connected with a root meaning 'die' (Lettic *nāve*, 'dead'; Gothic *naus*, 'corpse'; Greek νέκυς, etc.). The Polish chronicler Dlugosz, speaking of the pagan Slavs, says that they called Pluto 'Nya,' and that they asked of him 'post mortem in meliores inferni sedes deduci.' Dlugosz, as well as Cosmas of Prague, admits that the Slavs believed in the immortality of the soul.

The ancient Russians held banquets, called *tryzna* or 'festivals,' in honour of the dead. The ancient Slavs had no places used expressly as burying-grounds. They practised both burial and cremation.

We have no definite texts on ancestor-worship, but folk-lore gives valuable hints regarding it. The Russian peasants believe in the existence of a *dĕdushka domovoi* ('grandfather of the house'), which evidently represents the soul of an ancestor. In White Russia, one of the most primitive parts of the Slav world, ancestor-worship is prevalent at the present day. In the 16th cent. the Polish poet Klonowicz, in a Latin poem entitled 'Roxolania,' described the offerings which were brought to the graves:

> '. . . Mos est morientum poscere Manes.
> Portari tepidos ad monumenta cibos.
> Creduntur volucres vesci nidoribus umbræ
> Ridiculaque fide carne putantur ali.'

The peasants of White Russia give the name of *dziady* ('ancestors') to the souls of dead relatives, even in the case of children who died in infancy. Feasts of an absolutely pagan kind are held in their honour. They are invited to eat, and a spoonful or a part of each dish is taken and put into a special vessel. This vessel is placed on the ledge of the window. The meal ends with an address to the ancestors, who are then advised to go back to the sky (see art. ARYAN RELIGION). It is these rites that the Polish poet Mickiewicz has described so well in his poem on the *Dziady* ('The Ancestors'). On the other hand, in Bohemia, vessels which must have contained food have been found in pagan (probably Slav) graves. These had evidently been placed there for the use of the dead in the life beyond the tomb. The kindred Letto-Lithuanians also had special deities of the dead—Kapu mâte and Wella mâte amongst the Letts, and Vielona amongst the Lithuanians. Sacrifices were offered not only to Vielona as goddess of the dead, but also to Žemyna, the Lithuanian earth-goddess (cf. Usener, *Götternamen*, Bonn, 1896, pp. 104–105, 107–108). It is furthermore noteworthy that the Lithuanians offered sacrifices to the dead on the anniversary of their decease, when, after a formal prayer to them, water and food were cast beneath the table of the feast in their honour, and lights were placed on it even at midday (Brückner, *Archiv für slavische Philologie*, ix. 33). See also art. ARYAN RELIGION.

LITERATURE.—Kotliarevsky, *The Funeral Rites of the Pagan Slavs* (in Russian), 2nd ed., St. Petersburg, 1891; L. Leger, *La Mythologie slave*, Paris, 1901.

L. LEGER.

ANCESTOR-WORSHIP AND CULT OF THE DEAD (Teutonic).

—There is abundant evidence for Manes-worship among all Teutonic peoples. As a rule, however, the authorities give no indication that participation in the rites was confined to descendants and relatives of the deceased, though it is not unlikely that the worship referred to in such passages as *Indic. Superstitionum*, Tit. 1 ('De sacrilegio ad sepulchra mortuorum'), was generally of this variety. In Scandinavian lands also we hear of worship paid to kings and other distinguished men, apparently at or near their tombs, but here again the cult appears to have been shared by the dead man's subjects or dependants.

Perhaps the nearest approach to strict ancestor-worship is to be found in the records of the colonists of Iceland, who believed that all members of their families would pass after death into certain hills. They regarded these places with special reverence, and constructed sacrificial shrines there. Again, the element of ancestor-worship may be said to enter into the cult of certain gods, from whom most royal families, in England as well as in the North, claimed descent. Yet in the case of deities whose cult was wide-spread, such as that of Woden-Othin (by far the most frequent case), it would be unsafe to assume that this was the original element. On the other hand, deities whose worship was more or less local, like Thórgerðr Hölgabrúðr, may very well have been regarded originally as ancestral spirits. In this connexion account is to be taken also of the *hamingiur*, or guardian-spirits of families, who are represented as similar to valkyries or warrior maidens.

Lastly, mention must be made of the *erfi*—a word which in other Teutonic languages means inherited property, but in Scandinavian a wake or feast in honour of a dead person, especially the head of the house. Such feasts were often held on an immense scale, and many hundreds of persons invited. Large quantities of ale were then drunk in memory of the deceased—whence the banquet was also called *erfi-öl*, a name which survived until recently in the northern English word *arval*. Towards the close of the feast the heir was for the first time allowed to occupy the vacant high seat. At religious festivals also it was customary to drink to departed relatives as well as to the gods.

The **Cult of the Dead** among the Teutons will be fully described under art. ARYAN RELIGION.

LITERATURE.—Golther, *Handbuch der germanischen Mythologie*, Leipzig, 1895, p. 90 ff.; Mogk, in Paul, *Grundriss der germ. Philologie*[2], Strassburg, 1900, iii. 249 ff.; Meyer, *Germanische Mythologie*, Berlin, 1891, p. 69 ff.; Chantepie de la Saussaye, *Religion of the Teutons*, Boston, 1902, p. 289 ff.

H. M. CHADWICK.

ANCESTOR-WORSHIP AND CULT OF THE DEAD (Ugro-Finnic).—Ancestor-worship and cult of the dead is, so far as we can judge, the oldest form of religion among the Ugro-Finnic peoples. It is almost the only form common to them all. Their places of sacrifice frequently stand in close proximity to their places of burial; their images are chiefly representations of the dead; their offerings are to be explained by the needs (food, clothes, etc.) of the dead; and their whole system of magic seems in the main to aim at a union with the spirits of the dead. See artt. FINNS, LAPPS, MORDVINIANS, OSTIAKS.

KAARLE KROHN.

ANDAMANS.—I. *The Country and the People.*—The Andamans form the Northern portion of a string of islands, seven hundred miles long (the Nicobars forming the Southern portion), stretching across the Eastern side of the Bay of Bengal, between Cape Negrais in Burma and Achin Head in Sumatra. Certain physiological facts, in combination with phenomena exhibited by the fauna and flora of the respective terminal countries, have long been held to point to the former existence of a continuous range of mountains, thought to be sub-aerial, between these two points. Assuming this opinion to be correct, the Andamans are, in their present condition, the summits of a submarine range, connected with the Arakan Yoma range of Burma, which has, at some time or other, become almost wholly submerged by a volcanic subsidence. This range need not have been more than the physically possible one of two hundred fathoms, to connect a long narrow peninsula jutting out from the Burma coast with the present Andaman group of islands.

These considerations are of importance for the present purpose, as, according to Portman (see Literature below), the tradition of the South Andaman, or Bojigngiji, group of tribes is that Maia Tomola, the ancestral chief of the nation from which they all sprang, dispersed them after a cataclysm, which caused a subsidence of parts of a great island, divided it up into the present Andaman Islands, and drowned large numbers of the old inhabitants, together with many large and fierce beasts that have since disappeared. He also notes, as tending to show the junction of the Andaman Islands with the mainland, that, besides the South Andaman tradition, the people of the Little Andaman have names for animals that do not now exist and which they cannot describe.

Lying as they do in the track of a great commerce, which has gone on for at least two thousand years, both from China and Japan westwards and from the Levant and India eastwards, the existence of the Andamans has been reported probably from the days of Ptolemy (McCrindle, *Ancient India as described by Ptolemy*, 1885, p. 236) under a variety of names, representing some form of *Andaman*, meaning a 'monkey' people, and indicating the savage aboriginal antagonists of the more civilized early population of India. As early as the 9th cent. the inhabitants of the islands were quite untruly described by Arab travellers as cannibals (Reinaud, *Relation des voyages*, 1845, i. 8)—a mistake that seems to have arisen from three observations of the old mariners. The Andamanese attacked and murdered without provocation every stranger they could seize on his landing, as one of the tribes does still; they burnt his body (as they did in fact that of every enemy); and they had weird all-night dances round fires. Combine these three observations with the unprovoked murder of one of themselves and the fear aroused in ignorant mariners' minds by such occurrences in a far land, century after century, and a persistent charge of cannibalism is almost certain to be the result. This is a consideration of cardinal importance, as this false charge led to the Andamans being left severely alone until 1857 (except for a brief period between 1789 and 1796), when the British Government was forced to take steps to put a stop to murders of shipwrecked crews by occupying the islands. The result is that there exists in the Andamans an aboriginal people uncontaminated by outside influences, whose religious ideas are of native growth and exhibit the phenomena of a truly untutored philosophy.

The Andamanese are naked pigmy savages, as low in civilization as almost any known upon earth, though close observation of them discloses the immense distance in mental development between them and the highest of the brute beasts, one most notable fact being that they eat nothing raw, cooking all their food, however slightly, and making pots for the purpose, and this from time immemorial. Their various tribes belong to one race, speaking varieties of one fundamental isolated language. They are the relics of a bygone Negrito population now represented by themselves, the Semangs of the Malay Peninsula, and the Aetas of the Philippines (these last two being much mixed with the surrounding peoples), who in very ancient times occupied the south-eastern portion of the Asiatic Continent and its outlying islands before the irruptions of the oldest of peoples whose existence, or traces of it, can now be found there. In this view the Andamanese are of extreme interest, as preserving in their persons and customs, owing to an indefinite number of centuries of complete isolation, the last pure remnant of the oldest kind of man in existence.

2. *Character of the People.*—In childhood the Andamanese are possessed of a bright intelligence, which, however, soon reaches its climax; and the adult may be compared in this respect with the civilized child of ten or twelve. He has never had any sort of agriculture, nor, until the English taught him the use of dogs, did he ever domesticate any kind of animal or bird, nor did he teach himself to turn turtle or to use hook and line in fishing. He cannot count, and all his ideas are hazy, inaccurate, and ill-defined. He has never developed, unaided, any idea of drawing or making a tally or record for any purpose, but he readily understands a sketch or plan when shown him. He soon becomes mentally tired, and is apt to break down physically under mental training.

He retains throughout life the main characteristics of the child: of very short but strong memory; suspicious of, but hospitable to, strangers; ungrateful, imitative, and watchful of his companions and neighbours; vain and, under the spur of vanity, industrious and persevering; teachable up to a quickly reached limit; fond of undefined games and practical jokes; too happy and careless to be affected in temperament by his superstitions; too careless, indeed, to store water even for a voyage; plucky but not courageous; reckless only from ignorance or inappreciation of danger; selfish, but not without generosity, chivalry, or a sense of honour; petulant, hasty of temper, entirely irresponsible and childish in action in his wrath, and equally quick to forget; affectionate, lively in his movements, and exceedingly taking in his moments of good temper. At these times the Andamanese are gentle and pleasant to each other, considerate to the aged, the weakly or the helpless, and to captives; kind to their wives and proud of their children, whom they often over-pet; but when angered, cruel, jealous, treacherous, and vindictive, and always unstable. They are bright and merry companions, talkative, inquisitive, and restless, busy in their own pursuits, keen sportsmen, and naturally independent, absorbed in the chase for sheer love of it and other physical occupations, and not lustful, indecent, or obscenely abusive.

As the years advance they are apt to become intractable, masterful, and quarrelsome—a people to like but not to trust. Exceedingly conservative and bound up in ancestral custom, and not amenable to civilization, all the teaching of years bestowed on some of them has introduced no abstract ideas among the tribesmen, and changed no habit in practical matters affecting comfort, health, and mode of life. Irresponsibility is a characteristic, though instances of a keen sense of responsibility are not wanting. The intelligence of the women is good, though not, as a rule, equal to that of the men. In old age, however, they frequently exhibit a considerable mental capacity which is respected.

There is no idea of government, but to each tribe and to every sept of it belongs a recognized chief, who commands a limited respect and such obedience as the self-interest of the other individual men of the tribe or sept dictates. There is no social status that is not personally acquired on account of some admitted superiority, mental or physical. Property is communal, as is all the land; and the ideas as to individual possessions, even as to children, are but rudimentary, and are accompanied by an incipient tabu of the property belonging to a chief. Custom is the only law, and the only explanation of social actions or of the form and adornment of manufactured articles. In the religious ideas of such a people as this, religion is seen in its most primitive form.

3. *Religion.*—The religion is simple animism, and consists of fear of the evil spirits of the wood, the sea, disease, and ancestors, and of avoidance of acts traditionally displeasing to them, and this in spite of an abundance of mythological tales told in a confused, disjointed manner. There is neither ceremonial worship nor propitiation. There is an anthropomorphic deity, Puluga, the cause of all things, whom it is not, however, necessary to propitiate, though sins, *i.e.* acts displeasing to him, are avoided for fear of damage to the products of the jungle. Puluga now dwells in the sky, but used to live on the top of Saddle Peak, their highest mountain. The Andamanese have an idea that the 'soul' after death will go under the earth by an aerial bridge, but there is no heaven or hell, nor any idea of a bodily resurrection in a religious sense. There is much active faith in dreams, which sometimes control subsequent conduct, and in the utterances of 'wise men,' dreamers of prophetic dreams, gifted with second sight and power to communicate with spirits and to bring about good and bad fortune. These practise an embryonic magic and witchcraft to such personal profit, by means of good things tabued to themselves, as these people appreciate. There are no oaths, covenants, or ordeals, nor are there any forms of appeal to supernatural powers.

Puluga, who is fundamentally identifiable with some definiteness with the storm (*wuluga*), despite his confusion with ancestral chiefs, has so many attributes of the Deity that it is fair to translate the term by 'God.' He has, however, a wife and a family of one son and many daughters. He transmits his orders through his son to his daughters the Morowin, who are his messengers. He has no authority over the evil spirits, and contents himself with pointing out to them offenders against himself. The two great evil, *i.e.* harmful, spirits are Erem-chauga of the forest and Juruwin of the sea. Like Puluga, both have wives and families. The minor evil spirits are Nila, and a numerous class, the Chol, who are practically spirits of disease. The sun is the wife of the moon, and the stars are their children, dwelling near Puluga; but there is no trace of sun-worship, though the Andamanese twang their bows and 'chaff' the moon during an eclipse; and a solar eclipse frightens them, keeping them silent.

The Andamanese idea of a soul arises out of his reflexion in water, and not out of his shadow which follows him about. His reflexion is his spirit, which goes after death to another jungle world (*chaitan*) under the earth, which is flat and supported on an immense palm tree. There the spirit repeats the life here, visits the earth occasionally, and has a distinct tendency to transmigration into other beings and creatures. Every child conceived has had a prior existence, and the theory of metempsychosis appears in many other superstitions, notably in naming a second child after a previous dead one (because the spirit of the former babe has been transferred to the present one), and in the recognition of all natives of India and the Far East as *chauga*, or persons endowed with the spirits of their ancestors.

4. *Superstitions.*—The superstitions and mythology of the Andamanese are the direct outcome of their beliefs in relation to spirits. Thus fire frightens Erem-chauga, *lit.* 'Forest-ghost,' so it is *always* carried (the practical reason is that the Andamanese are the only people known who have never been able to 'make' fire). To avoid offending the sun and the moon, they keep silence at their rise. Puluga shows himself in the storm, and so they appease him by throwing explosive leaves on the fire, and deter him by burning beeswax, because he does not like the smell. Earthquakes are the sport of the ancestors. There are lucky

and unlucky actions, but not many, and a few omens and charms. Animals and birds are credited with human capacities. For instance, murdered persons have been found with heavy stones placed on them, and with stones placed along the pathway. Every Andamanese knows that this is a warning to the birds not to tell the English that the men have been murdered, but that the murderers have passed along the path in front. Primitive simplicity here comes to the surface, as the presence of the stones tells an Englishman who understands the signs exactly what has happened.

5. *Mythology.*—The great bulk of the Andamanese mythology turns on Puluga and his doings with Tomo, the first ancestor; to him and his wife Puluga brought fire and taught all the arts, and for them he created everything. This line of belief is still alive, and everything natural that is new is attributed to Puluga. Thus, when the Andamanese were introduced to the volcano on Barren Island, seeing the smoke from the top, they at once named it *Molatarchona*, 'Smoke Island,' and said the fire was Puluga's. The next most important element in their mythology is the story of the cataclysm which engulfed the islands, and was, of course, caused by Puluga. It separated the population and destroyed the fire, which was afterwards stolen by Luratut, the kingfisher, and restored to the people. The population previous to the cataclysm became the *chauga*, or 'ghostly ancestors.' Other stories relate in a fanciful way the origin of customs (*e.g.* tatuing and dancing), the arts, articles of food, harmful spirits, and so on. An important ethnological item in these stories is the constant presence of the ideas of metempsychosis, and of metamorphosis into animals, fish, birds, stones, and other objects in nature. Indeed, the fauna chiefly known to the Andamanese are ancestors changed supernaturally into animals.

6. *Customs.*—There are rudimentary initiatory ceremonies for both males and females connected with arrival at puberty and marriageability, and pointing to a limited tabu, but they are not accompanied by the communication of any secrets or by any religious ceremony. The women also practise a limited tabu as to food during menstruation and pregnancy. The idea of tabu does undoubtedly exist as to food, and every man has through life his own tabued article. This is, however, usually something observed to disagree with him in childhood or to be unpalatable. Tatuing is partly ceremonial, and the perpetual evening dancing also becomes ceremonial on occasion. Neither has any religious significance, and the songs accompanying the dances rarely relate to beliefs and superstitions. Among the games, mock burials and 'ghost' hunts are favourites. Religion does not enter into the naming customs, except possibly into the 'flower' names for girls, which are bestowed after some one of sixteen selected trees which happen to be in flower at the time they reach puberty.

The Andamanese are monogamous, and by preference, but not necessarily, exogamous as regards sept, and endogamous as regards tribe, or more strictly, group. Marriages are not religious, but are attended with distinct ceremonies. Betrothal accounted as marriage is recognized, and the marriage relations are somewhat complicated, and quite as strictly observed as among civilized communities. Deaths occasion loud lamentations from all connected with the deceased. Burial in the ground and exposure in trees, as an honour, are practised. A death causes an encampment to be ceremonially marked, and to be deserted for about three months, and burial spots are also marked and avoided. Mourning is observed by smearing the head with grey clay and refraining from dancing for the above period. After some months the bones of the deceased are washed, broken up, and made into ornaments. To these great importance is attached as mementoes of the deceased, and they are believed to stop pain and cure diseases by simple application to the diseased part. The skull is tied round the neck and worn down the back, usually, but not always, by the widow, widower, or nearest relative. Mourning closes with a ceremonial dance and the removal of the clay. The ceremonies connected with the disposal of the dead are conventional, reverential, and by no means without elaboration in detail.

LITERATURE.—E. H. Man, *Aboriginal Inhabitants of the Andaman Islands*, London, 1883; M. V. Portman, *History of our Relations with the Andamanese*, Calcutta (Government), 1898; R. C. Temple, *Census of India*, 1901, vol. iii. ('The Andaman and Nicobar Islands'), Calcutta (Government), 1903.

R. C. TEMPLE.

ANDEANS.—1. The pre-Inca people.—For the study of the Andean religions it is necessary to take account of a civilization which flourished long before the rise of the Incas; because the later power inherited some of the names, and with them the religious belief, of the more ancient people. Near the south shore of Lake Titicaca, now over 12,000 feet above the sea-level, there are very extensive ruins of a most remarkable character. They are of such great extent that there must have been a very large population in the vicinity; the stones are of such size, and any possible quarry so distant, that the people must have been possessed of very remarkable mechanical skill; and they are cut and carved with such accuracy and precision that the workers must have been skilful masons. The mouldings and symmetrical ornamentation show most accurate measurements, and no want of artistic taste. There were numerous statues, and much detailed carving. The monoliths are so enormous, one of them 36 feet by 7, another 26 feet by 16 by 6, that they are excelled in size only by the obelisks and statues of Egypt.* The ancient people who built them may well receive the name of the monolithic people, forming a monolithic empire.† Universal tradition points to the south as the direction whence they came. The building of Tiahuanacu, as the ruins are now called, necessitated a great population, mechanical skill—the result of long ages of civilization—and abundant supplies of food.‡ It appears certain that the region could not have been at its present elevation. At 12,500 feet no corn will ripen, and the country can sustain only a very sparse population. The monolithic builders cannot have worked at that elevation, or anything like it. The early Spanish writers give unanimous evidence that the ruins of Tiahuanacu were built long before the time of the Incas.§

2. Pre-Inca religion.—The only clue to the religion of the monolithic people is to be found in a famous doorway cut out of one enormous stone. 'The masonry is excellent throughout, and all the lines are as straight, the angles as square, and the surfaces as level as could be produced by any good workman of the present day.'‖ The length of the

* *The Megalithic Age of Peru*, by Sir Clements Markham, American Congress, Stuttgart, 1904.

† The best recent accounts are by Richard Inwards, *The Temple of the Andes* (1889), and by Le Comte de Crequi Montfort, *Mission Scientifique Française, Travaux et Fouilles de Tiahuanaco*, 1903.

‡ See *Archæologia*, vol. lviii. (2nd series, p. 73), on the transport of monoliths for Stonehenge and in Egypt. All needful appliances existed in the Stone Age, but a large population or command of men was essential. The date of Stonehenge is now placed at 1800 B.C., or 3700 years ago.

§ Cieza de Leon, cap. cv. pp. 374-379; Garcilasso de la Vega, i. pp. 71, 75, 210, 212, ii. 307; Acosta, pp. 71, 416. These references are to the present writer's translations (Hakluyt Society). See also *Relaciones Geograficas de Indias*, ii. p. 56.

‖ Inwards. *The Temple of the Andes*, p. 21.

monolith is over 13 ft., and the opening of the doorway 4 ft. 6 in. by 2 ft. 9 in. Above the doorway there is much carving. There is a central figure with many symbols and accessories. There are rays round the head; in each hand there is a sort of sceptre ending with heads of birds, the marks on the dress are the same as those round a golden representation of the sun of the Incarial times, denoting the Inca months *Camay* and *Ccapac Raymi*. It is the work of a highly skilled mason, but not of a sculptor. On each side of the central figure there are three rows of kneeling figures, eight in each row. They all hold sceptres, and are crowned. Those on one side have the heads of men, and on the other those of birds. Underneath there is a beautifully designed ornament running along the length of the stone, consisting of rectangular patterns, ending with birds' heads, and three human heads similarly ornamented. This central figure may, the present writer thinks, be assumed to represent the deity worshipped by all the chiefs of the people and all the animal creation. But there must have been an interval of many centuries between the fall of the monolithic empire, caused by the region becoming uninhabitable for a large population, and the rise of that of the Incas. When the old empire fell to pieces, the Andean region must have been occupied by many tribes, and the old language naturally broken up into dialects. One, spoken in the basin of Lake Titicaca, received the name of *Aymara* from the Jesuit missionaries of Juli; another spoken in the region of the Incas was called Quichua by the first Spaniard who wrote its grammar; another dialect was spoken further north. Eventually, some five centuries before the arrival of the Spaniards, the Incas began to form another great empire, and their language prevailed over the others.

3. The Incas.—There had been a long interval of disintegration. Nevertheless, all memory of the monolithic empire had not been lost. There were myths telling how the great God first made Himself known at Lake Titicaca, how the sun first appeared there, and how the first man was created there.* But the main tradition was the revelation of the almighty God, named Viracocha, who is carved with his adoring worshippers on the monolithic doorway. His worship was maintained by chiefs and learned men, after the old empire had disappeared, and was inherited by the Incas. Some other names were handed down as attributes of the almighty God. The chief of these were *Con, Illa, Ticsi, Pachayachachi, Pachacamac*. The meaning of *Con* is unknown. *Illa* means light. *Ticsi* is said to be a founder. The anonymous Jesuit explains the word as *Principium rerum sine principio*. The derivation of *Viracocha* is lost to us. Two authorities† say that the first part of the word is a corruption of *pirua*, a depositary or abode. The primary meaning of *cocha* is a lake, but here it is said to mean an abyss, profundity, space—'Dweller in space.' *Pachayachachi* and *Pachacamac* are attributes of the deity. *Pacha* means time or place, also the universe, *yachachi* a teacher, *camac* to rule or govern—'The teacher and ruler of the universe.' The name Viracocha sufficed to convey to the minds of the Incas the idea of a Supreme Creator, yet they added other terms to it, intended to express some of the attributes of the deity.‡

4. Viracocha.—The Incas, with their *Amautas* (wise men) and *Quipucamayocs* (registrars), certainly worshipped the Supreme Being under the name of Viracocha, having received the tradition from remote ages, and they looked upon all other deities as his servants, ordained to do his will. An Inca Indian, named Pachacuti Yamqui Salcamayhua, who wrote early in the 17th cent., mentions another being as having been made known in the early times, whose fame was handed down by tradition. This was Tonapa, also called Tarapaca and Pachaccan. He is also mentioned by Sarmiento as a servant of Viracocha. The details about him are puerile. It is possible that Tonapa represents a solar myth. The name occurs with that of the creator in some of the Inca hymns.

The Incas certainly worshipped Viracocha, the supreme creator of all things, but they approached him as an unknown god, who to them was shrouded in mystery. They cried to him to be taught where he was, that they might know and understand him; and they recognized that the sun, the moon, and the seasons were ordained and ordered by him. They sought to know the will of the Deity, and prayed for comfort and support.

5. Some **hymns of the Incas** have been preserved by Salcamayhua, but in a very corrupt form, and it is difficult to make out their exact meaning in English;* but they are so important for a correct estimate of the Peruvian religion that it seems desirable to give English versions of two of the hymns.

I.

'O Viracocha! Lord of the Universe,
Now art thou male,
Now art thou female,
Lord of heat! Lord of generation!†
Can divination be employed
To learn where thou art?
If away, where art thou?
Whether thou art above,
Whether thou art below,
Whether thou art around
Thy royal throne and sceptre,
O hear me!
From the heaven above,
From the sea below,
Where'er thou art,
O Creator of the world,
O Maker of man,
Lord of all lords,
To thee alone,
With eyes that fail,
With longing to know thee,
I come to thee
To know thee,
To understand thee.
Thou seest me,
Thou knowest me.
The Sun, the Moon,
The day, the night,
Spring and winter,
They all travel,
Not ordained in vain,
From appointed places
To their destinations;
They duly arrive
Whithersoever may be ordained.
Thou holdest them
Under thy sceptre,
Thou holdest them.
O hear me!
Let me be thy chosen;
Do not suffer
That I should tire,
That I should die.'

* The Titicaca myths are related by Garcilasso de la Vega, Cieza de Leon, Molina, Betanzos, Salcamayhua, and the anonymous Jesuit, and in the official history of Sarmiento. They are not mentioned by Balboa, Montesinos, Acosta, or Santillana.

† Montesinos and the anonymous Jesuit.

‡ The best essay on the word *Viracocha* is by Don Leonardo Villar (Lima, 1887).

* They were originally printed in the corrupt Quichua, exactly as in the manuscript, in the present writer's translation of Salcamayhua (Hakluyt Society, 1873). Ximenez de la Espada brought out a Spanish edition in 1879, printing the hymns in Quichua in the same way. Don Samuel A. Lafone Quevedo then took the Quichua in hand, and, with the able assistance of Padre Mossi, the author of one of the latest Quichua dictionaries, numerous emendations were made, and still more corrections in the separations of words. The text was thus made sufficiently intelligible to bear translation into Spanish (*Ensayo Mitologico. Los Himnos sagrados de los Reyes del Cuzcos*, from S. A. Lafone Quevedo, Talleres del Museo de La Plata, 1892).

† Are these lines, conceivably, intended to convey an idea analogous to the Hindu *Linga* and *Yoni*?

II.

'Come, then,
Grand as the heavens,
Lord over the earth,
Creator of all things,
Creator of man!
Ever I adore thee;
Fainting, with my eyes
Hid under the lashes,
Thee am I seeking,
To look upon thee,
Like as on a river,*
Like as on the springs,
Gasping with thirst.
Comfort me, O Lord!
Acclaim thy will,
Help me, O Lord!
I raise my voice
With all praise,
Thinking on thy will
And doing it.
We will rejoice,
We will be glad,
So be it for evermore.'

6. Huacas.—Subordinate to Viracocha, to whom a temple was dedicated in the great square of Cuzco, the worship of the Sun, Moon, Lightning, and of certain deities, called *Huacas*, was ordained. When the empire of the Incas rose to greatness, there was a complicated ritual, with special ceremonies, festivals, and sacrifices for each month. Our information is mainly derived from the first Spaniards who came to Peru and wrote narratives. They were soldiers, lawyers, in two instances natives, but chiefly priests who were full of pre-conceived ideas.† It is not always easy to separate their pre-conceptions and the results of their leading questions from the actual facts they were told. It is still more difficult to reach the exact nature of the beliefs of a people, when we have reports only of their ceremonies and of their outward worship.

The people were divided into *ayllus* or tribes, which had a close analogy to the Roman *gens*. Every *ayllu* had a common *huaca* or sacred object of worship, which was called *paccarina*. The chief *paccarina* of the Inca *ayllu* was the Sun. The Incas were children of the Sun. But there was another very sacred *huaca*, which is often mentioned in Inca history, and to which a legend was attached.‡

The origin of the Incas is connected with this *huaca*. Four brothers and four sisters are said to have issued from 'windows' at a place called *Paccari-tampu* (some leagues south of Cuzco), two words meaning 'the tavern of the dawn.' Their leader was Manco Capac, the first sovereign Inca. They had many followers, and they advanced northwards to occupy the valley of Cuzco. During the march one of the brothers was turned to stone at a place called Huanacauri. This is the legend. Next to the celestial bodies, this *huaca* of Huanacauri became the most sacred object of worship. It was three miles from Cuzco. Very elaborate sacrifices were offered to it, and it was at Huanacauri that the great festival was celebrated, when the Inca youths went through their ordeals previous to receiving knighthood. But the exact position of the Huanacauri *huaca* in the Inca religion is not clear. It was certainly a very important one in the traditions of the Inca *ayllu*.

7. Ancestor-worship. — The other *ayllus* had various beasts or birds, natural objects or mummies, as their *paccarinas*. It was the worship of ancestors by the side of the worship of celestial bodies. The *mallquis*, or bodies of the dead, were preserved, and treated with the greatest respect. In the mountains round Cuzco and in the Yucay valley they were kept in caves faced with masonry. In the basin of Lake Titicaca they were preserved in towers called *chulpas*. Those at Sillustani are circular, and carefully built with ashlar masonry. In Quito the dead were interred in mounds called *tola*.

The bodies of the Incas were preserved with extreme care, and it is stated, in the official report of Sarmiento, that the special *huaca* or idol of each Inca was kept with the mummy (Sarmiento, *Hist.*). There were servants for the mummies of the sovereigns, and estates for their maintenance. The names of seven of the so-called idols have been preserved; and they do not support the idea that they were idols in our sense of the word, but rather insignia or commemorative ornaments, perhaps in the nature of *penates*, used by each sovereign in his lifetime. It was a custom, not only as regards the Inca *mallquis* but among all classes of the people, to place with the dead, offerings of food and other things required by them when living. This custom has never been eradicated, and even now it is practised secretly in many parts of Peru. The belief which originated this custom, and which has caused its continuance even to the present day, must have been very deeply seated. It is exceedingly difficult to acquire a complete understanding of the ideas of another race of people which give rise to special customs. But the present writer was well acquainted with an old priest, Dr. Pablo P. Justiniani, a lineal descendant of the Incas,* whose intense sympathy for his people enabled him to comprehend their ideas, if any one ever did so. He told the present writer that they felt a certainty that their dead continued to exist apart from their bodies, and that they had needs, but spiritual, not corporeal needs. They were certain of this because many of them had seen their dead. Don Pablo attributed this conviction to appearances in dreams and visions. Of a future state of rewards and punishments they do not appear to have had any idea in the time of the Incas, only the conviction that their ancestors continued to exist after death. In this state they were souls without bodies, but still with needs and requirements, not corporeal, but spiritual. Thence arose the strange belief that all things had souls as well as their material parts, and that the spirits of the dead needed the souls or spiritual parts of food, chicha, coca, llamas, even clothing. By placing the corporeal parts of these things with the dead, it was believed that their souls or spiritual essences were conveyed, through prayer and certain ceremonies, to the souls of the dead. This belief was so deeply impressed on the Inca people that it survived all subsequent persecution. The practice existed

* The same idea as in the 42nd Psalm.

† The most important work on the religion of Peru was written about 1575 by a priest named Cristoval de Molina, who lived at Cuzco, and was a master of the Quichua language. The present writer's translation, from the original manuscript, was printed for the Hakluyt Society in 1872.

In August, 1906, Dr. Pietschmann, the librarian of the Göttingen University, published the official history of the Incas, by Sarmiento. It was written in 1572 from information received from over 80 members of the Inca family, to whom the history was read, and whose suggestions and corrections were adopted. The manuscript had been in the Göttingen library since 1780. This work will be found to be the most authentic and valuable history of the Incas in existence.

‡ According to Arriaga, the word *paccarina* means 'worshipped.' It comes from *paccari*, 'the dawn,' whence *paccarisca*, 'birth' or 'origin'; and *paccarina* would be the 'original ancestor.'

* Inca Huayna Capac.
|
Manco Inca.
|
Maria Tupac Usca = Pedro Ortiz de Orue.
|
Catalina Ortiz = Luis Justiniani.
|
Luis Justiniani.
|
Nicolo Justiniani.
|
Justo Pastor Justiniani.
|
Dr. Don Pablo Policarpo Justiniani.

secretly fifty years ago to some extent, as Don Pablo informed us. The present writer is told by Baron Erland Nordenskiöld, who returned from Peru in the year 1906, that the practice still exists. This appears to have been the position of the Inca worship of their ancestors, possibly accompanied by some idea of intercession. Like the sovereign Incas, each *ayllu* had a *paccarina* or so-called idol, represented by a hill or other natural object, occasionally by an image. This was apart from the household *conopa*, to be noticed presently.

8. Priesthood.—The complicated ceremonial worship of the Incas necessitated a great body of priests and ministers. The *Villac umu* (lit. 'the head giving counsel') was the chief of the Inca hierarchy. Next in rank were the *Villcas*. Then there were the sacrificing priests, or *Harpaycuna*, special priests and virgins of the Sun, the priests and servants of the *huacas*, the soothsayers and wizards, the *Huacap Rimachi*, or receiver of oracles, and a host of recorders and servants. For the support of this hierarchy large revenues were assigned.

9. Festivals.—The Peruvian ceremonial system was very closely connected with the course of the year, the sowing and planting seasons, the irrigation, the harvest, and consequently with the course of the sun. The year was a solar year, divided into twelve months and some intercalary days, and it was necessary to ascertain the times of the equinoxes and solstices. Pillars were erected to determine the time of the solstices, and the time of the equinoxes was observed by a stone column in the centre of a circular level platform called Inti-huatana. There was one in the square before the Temple of the Sun at Cuzco, another at Pisac, and others in different parts of Peru. Each month had its special festival.

The first month, 22 June to 22 July, was called *Intip Raymi*. Many llamas were sacrificed to the Sun, amid ceremonies of great magnificence. The next month was called *Chahuarquiz*, the season of ploughing the land. It was also called *Tarpuy-quilla* or the sowing month. Prayers were made for a good harvest. The people chanted a song called *Yahuayra*, and sacrifices were offered. Next came the month *Yapaquis*, the season of sowing the land, when the *Situa* festival was solemnized. The rains commenced, and it was a time of sickness. Four hundred warriors stood in the great square, a hundred facing each of the cardinal points. The priests shouted, 'Go forth, all evils,' and the four parties started in four directions, shouting, 'Go forth, all evils.' They ran until they came to rivers, where they bathed and washed their arms. The Inca and the people also bathed, and there were ceremonies for driving away sickness at the doors of all the houses.

Ccoya-raymi was the Moon festival, the expiatory feast being at night. It was a time for weaving fine cloth. *Uma-raymi* was the month in which one of the great *huaca* festivals was celebrated for the initiation of aspirants. It took place at Huanacauri. The youths, after going through certain exercises and penances, were admitted to knighthood. The month of *Ayamarca* was in November and December. Next followed *Ccapac-raymi*, one of the three principal festivals of the year. There was another ceremony of admitting youths to manhood at Huanacauri, which was conducted with great magnificence. *Camay* was the month of martial exercises, and also the *hatun-poccoy*, or great ripening. The next month was *Pacha-poccoy*, or the small ripening, when the festival of the *mosoc nina* was celebrated, and the new fire for the altar before the Sun was kindled. The *Ayrihua* came next, being the beginning of harvest. The offerings of maize were brought to the temples of the Creator and of the Sun, youths and maidens, in procession, singing a harvest song called *yaravi*. The harvesting month was *Aymuray* in May and June.

10. Human sacrifice.—The religious ceremonies included burnt-offerings in great profusion. The present writer formerly held that the weight of evidence was, on the whole, that there were no human sacrifices. He felt this to be remarkable, for the idea of propitiatory sacrifice is to offer the best and most loved, as in the cases of Isaac and Jephthah's daughter. He held that the Peruvian sacrifices were more in the nature of thanksgiving than of propitiatory offerings. But the authoritative evidence of Molina and Sarmiento has led him to modify this view. On extraordinary occasions, two children, a male and a female, were first strangled and then included in the burnt-offerings. Such occasions were the celebration of great victories, or the commencement of wars, and the *Huaca* festival at Huanacauri.

11. Sun-worship. — Nearly all the ceremonies were connected with agriculture and with the course of the sun, so that it was natural that the sun should be the chief object of adoration with the people. But some shrewd remarks on the subject are recorded of one or two of the Incas (by Garcilasso de la Vega, *Comm. Real.*). Seeing that the Sun had to accomplish its circle every year, they concluded that it must have a master. It was the same thought as that of Omar Khayyam:

> 'And that inverted Bowl they call the Sky,
> Whereunder crawling coop'd, we live and die,
> Lift not your hands to *It* for help—for It
> As impotently moves as you or I.'

So they turned to Viracocha, the Creator obeyed by the sun and all living things, as the chief object of their adoration.

12. Government. — The religious beliefs of the people away from Cuzco were connected with their mode of life and their environment. It seems desirable to give a short account of the rural life of the people, and of the administrative organization of Inca rule. It was, in fact, pure socialism —a system which can exist only under a despotism. Several very able Spanish lawyers, notably Polo de Ondegardo and Santillana, were employed, soon after the conquest, to investigate and report upon the Incarial system of government. Reliance may be placed upon the correctness of the details they collected. It appears that the whole of the peoples were divided into ten classes, according to their ages and ability to work.

1. *Mosoc aparic* (baby), 'newly begun,' just born.
2. *Saya huarma* (child), 'standing boy,' age 2 to 6.
3. *Macta puric* (child that can walk), age 6 to 8.
4. *Ttanta requisic* (bread receiver), about 8.
5. *Pucllac huarma* (playing boy), 8 to 15.
6. *Cuca pellec* (coca picker), very light work, 15 to 20.
7. *Yma huayna* (as a youth), light work, 20 to 28.
8. *Puric* (able-bodied), tribute service, 28 to 50.
9. *Chaupi ruccu* (elderly), light work, 50 to 60.
10. *Puñuc ruccu* (dotage), no work, over 60.

The *Puric* was the unit of administration, the other classes being dependent on him. A *Pachaca* was 100 *Purics* under a *Pachaca-camayoc* or Centurion. 1000 *Purics* were under a *Huaranca-camayoc*, or officer over a thousand, and the *Hunu-camayoc* governed the whole *ayllu* or *gens* of 10,000 *Purics*. There were four Viceroys over the four provinces, who were called *Tucuyricoc* ('He who sees all'). There were also a reporter on vital statistics and an officer to investigate and report upon charges and accidents, one to each *ayllu*. The land belonged to the people in their *ayllus*. The produce was divided between the *Inca* (government), the *Huaca* (church), and the *Huaccha* (people). The flocks were divided between *Inca* (government) and *Huaccha* (the people). When the people worked for the Government, they were fed by the Inca, and not from their own share of the produce.

Thus the land belonged to the whole *ayllu*, and each able-bodied member, or *Puric*, had a right to his share of the harvest, provided that he had been present at the sowing. No one who had been absent at the sowing could receive a share of the harvest. The population was very great, and increased rapidly; but the evils of minute sub-division were avoided by the system of *Mitimaes*, or colonists.*

13. Various cults.—The worship of Viracocha, the Supreme Being, was restricted mainly to the Incas and learned men. The worship of the Sun was more extended, and was the religion of all who took part in the festivals of the Incas; but the religion of the mass of the people was different. Each *ayllu* had its *paccarina*, with its festival and worship. But each *Puric*, or head of a family, believed that all things in nature had an ideal or soul which ruled and guided them, and to which they might pray for help. Thus there was a soul or ideal of the maize and other harvests, of the llamas, and of all things that influenced their daily life. They made statues or other representations of these objects, and prayed and sacrificed to them for healthy flocks and abundant harvests. The statues were made of pottery or stone, sometimes of the precious metals, and were called *huaca* or *conopa*. In Huarochiri, and, no doubt, in other provinces, the people had mythological stories of great interest in the study of their folk-lore; and the discovery of the remaining reports on the extirpation of idolatry will throw further light on the religion of the Peruvian people.†

14. Oracles.—The valleys on the coast, from Nasca to the Rimac, were occupied by people of the same race and language as the Incas, and at Nasca there are marvellous irrigation works. Here the ocean and its inhabitants received the worship that was given to other powers of nature in the Sierra; and there were two or more famous oracles to which people resorted from great distances. One was at Rimac, whence the name of Lima, the modern capital of Peru. Another famous temple was on the coast, at a place called Pachacamac. Raised on an eminence, with an extensive city at its feet, the oracle itself appears to have been a fish *conopa*, which was supposed to give answers to the questions of pilgrims.

There was no temple to the Supreme Being at Pachacamac. The word is that of an attribute of the Almighty Creator. But in this case it was merely the name of the place. Many other places received names from deities or festivals. There was another *Pachacamac* near Tumipampa. *Vilca* (sacred), *Huaca* (church), and *Raymi* (festival) form parts of the names of several places in Peru. The great temple at Pachacamac on the coast was dedicated to two *conopas* of the coast people, a fish-deity and a fox-deity, which became famous oracles. Pilgrims came from great distances, and an extensive town rose up at the foot of the temple. It was falling to ruin when the Spaniards arrived.

15. An unknown civilized people conquered by the Incas.—There was another civilized people along the northern part of the coast of Peru, quite distinct from the Andean tribes, but finally conquered by the Incas. We have evidence of their civilization from the contents of the tombs examined by Reiss and Stübel at Ancon. We have further evidence in the great palace of the 'Gran Chimu' near Truxillo, and Balboa has preserved a tradition of their arrival by sea and landing at Lambayeque, which also throws a little light on their superstitions.‡ There is a grammar of their language, which is totally unlike any Andean dialect.* But there is no account of the religion of this strange civilized nation of the Peruvian coast, now practically extinct.

Quito was conquered by the last great and undisputed sovereign of the Inca dynasty; but though there is a work on the former Scyris rulers of Quito, the accounts in it are comparatively modern and of doubtful authority. We have no narratives giving details respecting the religious belief of the Quito people previous to the conquest by the Inca Huayna Ccapac. It is stated that they worshipped the Sun.†

16. The Chibchas.—Farther north there was a civilized people, the Chibchas, of whose religion there is some account. Their land is where the Andes divide into three cordilleras, with the three great rivers of Magdalena, Cauca, and Atrato flowing northwards between them into the Caribbean Sea. The Chibchas dwelt on the tablelands of Bogota and Tunja, with their river Funza flowing to the Magdalena, their eastern drainage being carried by the Meta to the Orinoco. This territory is about 150 miles in length, by 40 to 50 broad. It was ruled by two principal chiefs, the Zipa of Bogota and the Zaque of Tunja. The Zipa was striving for a paramount position before the arrival of the Spaniards, and had subjugated the chief of Guatavita. It is of this chief that the story is told that he held a great annual festival on the banks of the Lake of Guatavita, when he covered himself with grease, and then rolled in gold dust. Gilded and resplendent, he then entered a canoe, and was taken to the centre of the lake. Before all his people, he plunged into the water, and his bath was followed by feasting and dancing. This was the origin of the story of El Dorado.

The *religious beliefs* of the Chibchas are thus stated by the earliest writers. Light was originally enclosed in a receptacle called *chiminigagua*, and this receptacle appears to have been, in the conception of these people, the Supreme Creator. The Chibchas are said to have worshipped this almighty deity, but none the less they also worshipped the sun, the moon, the rainbow (called *cuchairra*), hills, lakes, rivers, trees, and many idols.‡ Human sacrifices appear to have been offered only to the Sun, as a deity to be feared and propitiated. The Chibchas had a tradition of a beneficent being named Bochica having appeared amongst them, and having taught them all they knew. He also was worshipped. He is said to have opened a channel for the river Funza, and to have formed the famous falls of Tequendama. The people had several curious myths, and they appear to have conducted their ceremonial worship with some magnificence. There was a procession in which the Zipa joined at the time of sowing, and another at harvest time. There is certainly a superficial resemblance between the religions of the Incas and that of the Chibchas.

There are two early authorities for Chibcha civilization. Padre Fray Pedro Simon wrote his *Noticias Historiales* in 1623, and the work was published at Cuenca in 1627. Dr. Don Lucas Fernandez Piedrahita, the Bishop of Santa Marta, wrote his *Historia General de las conquistas del nuevo reyno de Granada* in 1676. Simon is the best authority, being nearest to the time; but Piedrahita wrote well, and gives a brief but clear account of the Chibchas. He was descended from the Incas of Peru. There is a grammar of the Chibcha language by Fray Barnardo de Lugo, 1624. It is not now spoken. The best modern works on the subject are Humboldt in his *Vues des Cordillères*, Acosta in his *Compendio Historico* (Paris, 1848), and E. Uriacochea in his *Memoria sobre las antiguedades neo-granadinas* (Berlin, 1850).

The Chibcha language prevailed among all the

* Polo de Ondegardo, 162; Santillana.

† *Extirpacion de la idolatria del Peru*, por el Padre Pedro Pablo Joseph de Arriaga (Lima, 1621). Arriaga says he destroyed 600 *huacas* and 3418 *conopas* in one province. *Narratives of the False Gods and Superstitions of the Indians of the Province of Huarochiri*, by Dr. Francisco de Avila, 1608 (see the present writer's tr. for the Hakluyt Society).

‡ *Miscellanea Austral*, por Miguel Cavello Balboa, written between 1576 and 1586. Translated into French, and published in the series of Ternaux-Compans, 1840.

* *Arte de la lengua Yunga de los valles del Obispado de Truxillo*, por Don Fernando de la Carrera (Lima, 1644).

† *Historia del Reino de Quito*, por Juan de Velasco; also in the Ternaux-Compans series, 1840.

‡ *Ccuychi* is the Quichua for a rainbow. There may have been intercourse between the Incas and Chibchas, but there is no evidence beyond the identity of a few words.

tribes of the highlands, and they had all made advances in civilization, although those of Bogota and Tunja were far in advance of the rest. The general movement of the Chibcha tribes had been from south to north, and this race appears to have advanced its settlements beyond Panama, as far as Chiriqui. There is no evidence that any people of Aztec or Maya affinities ever entered South America or had relations with South American peoples.

17. **Originality of the Andean religion.**—The Andean races moved from the south northwards. Their civilization was of spontaneous growth, without any foreign aid, and uninfluenced by communication with other races. Elaborate attempts have been made to establish identity between Quichua words and words of similar meaning in Aryan languages, but a careful study of the subject cannot fail to produce the conviction that they are fanciful, and based on an insufficient knowledge of the Quichua language. The South American race naturally reached its highest development in the Andean region, where agriculture and the textile and other arts were necessary for the support and well-being of the people, and where a temperate climate conduced to the development of various civilizing influences and to a reasoning contemplation of the powers of nature, guided by religious instincts. It was in this way, and not by any foreign influences, that the Andean religions were developed by the races inhabiting the cordilleras of the Andes. In their highest form the Andean religions recognized the existence of a Supreme Creator of the universe, and sought to know his will by prayer and praise. The celestial bodies, the thunder and the rainbow, were revered as bringing good to man, but only as inferior deities obeying the mandates of the Creator. In the worship of the *paccarinas* and of ancestors there is a clear indication of a belief in a future existence; and the power attributed to the souls of animals and crops, and of inanimate objects, among the mass of the people, is peculiar to the Andean races in the form in which it prevailed amongst them. In whatever comparative position the Andean religion may be placed among the religions of the world, it must stand by itself as the unaided conception of the Andean people, uninfluenced by any communication with other races.

LITERATURE.—The works which give detailed accounts of the Andean religions do not include all the earlier works on the civilization and history of the native races. The first account is contained in the second part of the *Chronicle* of **Cieza de Leon**, tr. by Sir Clements R. Markham for the Hakluyt Society. The Spanish text was afterwards printed and edited by Ximenes de la Espada at Madrid. **Juan José de Betanzos** wrote his *Summary Narration* in 1551. He knew the Quichua language, and married an Inca princess. His work has been printed and edited at Madrid in 1880, but has not been translated. The two *Relaciones* of the learned lawyer **Polo de Ondegardo** are still in manuscript. But one of his reports has been translated and edited for the Hakluyt Society by Sir Clements R. Markham, 1872. **Fernando de Santillana** was a Judge of the Lima Audience in 1550. His valuable *Relacion* remained in manuscript until it was edited and printed by Ximenes de la Espada in 1879. The most detailed and best work on the religion of the Incas was written in about 1575 by a priest at Cuzco named **Cristoval de Molina**. The manuscript has been translated and edited for the Hakluyt Society by Sir Clements R. Markham in 1872. **Miguel Cavello Balboa** is the authority for the civilized people of the coast of Peru. He wrote his *Miscellanea Austral* at Quito between 1576 and 1586. It has been translated into French, and forms a volume of the Ternaux-Compans series (1840). **José de Acosta's** *Historia de las Indias* appeared in 1588. It was translated in 1604, and the Eng. tr. was edited by Sir Clements R. Markham for the Hakluyt Society (2 vols.), 1872. The works of **Fernando Montesinos**, entitled *Anales* and *Memorias Nuevas del Peru*, have a peculiar interest from the long list of sovereigns he gives, to be found nowhere else. He came to Peru in 1629. His work remained in manuscript until it was translated by Ternaux-Compans in 1840. The Spanish text was edited by Ximenes de la Espada in 1882. The *Relacion de los Costumbres Antiquas de los Naturales del Peru*, by an anonymous Jesuit, is a most valuable work. It remained in manuscript until it was edited by Ximenes de la Espada in 1879. The works on the extirpation of idolatry, by **Francisco de Avila**, written in 1608 (MS.), and **Pablo José de Arriaga** (Lima, 1621), are very important. Avila's report has been translated by Sir Clements R. Markham from the manuscript, for the Hakluyt Society, 1872. There is also information in the history of the order of St. Augustine in Peru (1638–1653), by **Antonio de la Calancha**. The *Commentarios Reales* by the **Inca Garcilasso de la Vega** are well known (1st ed. Lisbon, 1609, last ed. Madrid, 1723). Their value is much increased by the extracts from the lost work of the Jesuit Blas Valera. The work of Garcilasso de la Vega has been translated and edited for the Hakluyt Society by Sir Clements R. Markham, 1869. **Bernabé Cobo's** *Historia del Nuevo Mundo* (4 vols., Seville, 1890) was written in 1653. **Pachacuti Yamqui Salcamayhua**, an Indian of the Collao, wrote (*c.* 1620) a work entitled *Relacion de Antiguedades deste Reyno de Peru*. The manuscript was translated and edited by Sir Clements R. Markham (1872). The Spanish text was afterwards edited by Ximenes de la Espada (1879). By far the most valuable history of the Incas was written by **Pedro de Sarmiento**. The manuscript has been in the library of the University of Göttingen since 1780. The text was first printed by the librarian, Dr. Pietschmann, in August, 1906, with a learned introduction and notes. The work has been translated by Sir Clements R. Markham. The best essay on the word *Viracocha* is by **Don Leonardo Villar** (Lima, 1887). There are two authorities on the religion of the Chibchas of Bogota. **Fray Pedro Simon** wrote his *Noticias Historiales* in 1627. The *Historia General de las conquistas del nuevo regno de Granada*, by **Bishop Lucas Fernandez Piedrahita**, appeared in 1676. The work on the antiquities of New Granada by **Uriacochea** (Berlin, 1850) may also be consulted.

CLEMENTS R. MARKHAM.

ANGEL.—See SPIRITS.

ANGEL DANCERS.—A religious sect of Methodist origin, founded in Hackensack, New Jersey, about 1890, by Huntsman T. Mnason, with the aid of John M'Clintock ('John the Baptist'), Daniel Haines ('Silas the Pure'), Mary Stewart ('Thecla'), Jane Howell ('Phoebe'), Elias Berry, and Herman Storms, with his wife and their children, Mary and Richard (the latter a graduate of Rutgers College). At the age of fifty, Mnason, after a somewhat dissolute life, became converted at a Methodist revival meeting in New York City in 1888. On the night of his conversion he believed that he had a vision of Heaven and Hell, seeing both the Lord and the Devil. He chose the Lord and Heaven, and claimed direct Divine guidance in all his acts. After many privations, he wandered to Park Ridge, N.J. Here he claimed to have received the power of healing by the laying on of hands. His strange appearance, in which he sought to imitate the traditional portraits of Christ, and his wonderfully magnetic will power, aided by a musical voice, evident sincerity, and easy flow of speech, made a strong impression upon men and women alike. He next appeared in Hackensack, N.J., where he commenced the preaching of his new doctrine, which he and his followers still maintain.

Mnason and his followers have everything in common, and believe they shall be judged by their works, and not by their faith. They are careful to harm no living thing, and they adhere to a strict vegetarian diet. They do not believe in any form of marriage, whether civil or religious, and hold the most extreme ideas of free love. Their dress has no decoration of any kind. At the house of a farmer in Hackensack, named Herman Storms, Mnason gathered some followers, and gave the place the name of the 'Lord's Farm.' The house is open at any hour of the day or night, and any one is welcome, and may share food and clothing. This was carried to such an extreme that vagrants were entertained 'in the Lord's name,' thus constituting a menace to the neighbourhood.

Locally the sect is known as 'the Lord's Farm,' never as 'Angel Dancers.' When at the height of their influence, they used to hold outdoor meetings in neighbouring towns. It was during these meetings that the dancing occurred from which the name of 'Angel Dancers' was derived. The dance is a species of religious frenzy, brought on by the belief that the Devil is in their midst. It finds a ready parallel in many forms of religious ecstasy. It commonly begins after grace has been said before a meal, and a sign that the Devil is being vanquished lies in the ability to jump over the table! When directly questioned as to his denominational standing, Mnason claims to be an 'Old Style Methodist,' being opposed to all forms, and declares his religion to be based on the Book of Acts.

In May 1893, Mnason and some of his followers were arrested and put in jail for malicious mischief and maintaining a disorderly house. They refused, however, to defend themselves, and when speaking of each other styled themselves martyrs. At their trial in October of the same year, Mnason was sentenced to one year's hard labour. After his release the Storms took him back, and the 'Angel Dancers' continued their practices, their demeanour during their imprisonment having won them sympathy. Most of their time is spent in raising farm produce, which Mnason personally takes to market. They are noted for their industry and for their scrupulously honest dealings. Mnason never allows an angry word to be spoken to man or beast; and during both winter and summer he does a great deal of charitable work, going miles to carry aid, 'in the Lord's name,' to all who ask for it. At present only about twelve followers are left at the farm, where they quietly attend to their own affairs. F. D. VAN ARSDALE.

ANGER (Psychological and Ethical).—i. *PSYCHOLOGICAL.*—There are two ways, according to Aristotle (*de Anima*, i. 1), in which anger may be characterized. By the dialectician or speculative philosopher (διαλεκτικός), it may be defined as 'the desire of retaliation, or such like'; by the natural philosopher (φυσικός), as 'the boiling of blood about the heart, or of heat.' Neither of these two ways, taken by itself, does he regard as adequate; for the one has respect only to the 'form,' while the other takes account solely of the 'matter,' and the complete view requires that both form and matter be attended to. In other words, Aristotle is here exemplifying in a concrete instance the great psychological truth that the emotions are 'materialized notions' (λόγοι ἔνυλοι), that they have both an inward or psychical side and an outward or corporeal expression; and that each of these requires to be reckoned with, if the phenomenon is to be satisfactorily explained. We may even go a step farther, and maintain, with Darwin (*The Expression of the Emotions in Man and Animals*, p. 239), that 'most of our emotions are so closely connected with their expression, that they hardly exist if the body remains passive.' Certainly, the control of anger consists very much in conscious abstraction from the modes in which it physically embodies itself.

(1) *On the physical side*, anger, in the individual, manifests itself in marked disturbance of the bodily organism: *e.g.* the movements of hands and jaws become pronounced, respiration is quickened, the nostrils are dilated, the action of the heart is accelerated, the face changes colour, the eyes flash, the eyebrows are knit, the voice waxes loud, harsh, and discordant; and, in that species of anger which we know as **rage**, there is wild 'striking out,' vehement and uncontrolled, so that anger may not inaptly be designated (as by Horace, *Epist.* I. ii. 62) 'a brief madness' (*ira furor brevis est*).

These changes in the body are obvious to the spectator. But there are others that are invisible, which take place in the internal organs, giving rise to organic sensations which play a distinct part in the process, inasmuch as they react on the emotion, modifying, accentuating, or intensifying it, as the case may be. Hence, the organism has been likened by psychologists (*e.g.*, Bain, James, Stout) to a 'sounding-board,' on which the nervous excitement correlated with the emotion 'plays,' and which is in turn affected and modified by the organic 'resonance.' This organic factor is highly important; but we must not make too much of it, as has been done by Professor James, who, in his theory of emotion, reduces emotion to a kind of sensation begotten of organic disturbance.

'Our natural way of thinking about these coarser emotions [grief, fear, rage, love],' he says (*The Principles of Psychology*, ii. 449), 'is that the mental perception of some fact excites the mental affection called the emotion, and that this latter state of mind gives rise to the bodily expression. My theory, on the contrary, is that *the bodily changes follow directly the perception of the exciting fact, and that our feeling of the same changes as they occur* IS *the emotion.* Common sense says, we lose our fortune, are sorry, and weep; we meet a bear, are frightened, and run; we are insulted by a rival, are angry, and strike. The hypothesis here to be defended says that this order of sequence is incorrect, that the one mental state is not immediately induced by the other, that the bodily manifestations must first be interposed between, and that the more rational statement is that we feel sorry because we cry, angry because we strike, afraid because we tremble, and not that we cry, strike, or tremble, because we are sorry, angry, or fearful, as the case may be.'

'Angry because we strike!' That, surely, is to put the cart before the horse; for why do we strike at all? Is it not because the emotion of anger is already aroused, through perception of the kind of act that affects us, though there is no doubt that the organic sensations react upon the emotion and fan it—the 'resonance' has a real effect? If we are angry because we are insulted, it is because we first *feel* the insult; without this feeling, we should, in all likelihood, remain indifferent, and it is the function of delay and deliberation to calm the feeling and to produce indifference.

(2) Taken *on the psychical side*, anger is mental disturbance, displeasure, or discomposure, of a painful kind, arising from opposition, hurt, or harm received, operating like a reflex act, viz., by immediate active response, or reaction without deliberation, on recognition of the unacceptable or offending fact that arouses it. It has thus a necessary relation to the conative, as well as to the emotive, side of our being. What induces anger is something that has to be got rid of; and, in the angry state, our activity is strongly put forth, so that the riddance may be readily secured. Moreover, if the real cause of the offence cannot be reached at the moment, the ebullition vents itself on something else (thing or person) within reach—stool, chair, book: the pent-up energy must find discharge somehow—an 'explosion' is inevitable. 'Young children, when in a violent rage, roll on the ground on their backs or bellies, screaming, kicking, scratching, or biting everything within reach' (Darwin, *op. cit.*, p. 241). Thus anger may be said to be instinctive. It does not wait for reason (though it may be brought under the control of reason), and is, in itself, regardless of results. It is aroused in us by what opposes us, or thwarts us, by what we object to, by what offends and pains us (all such we *resent*); and it aims at repressing or suppressing the opposition, and at preventing its future operation. It is not, however, in itself *malignant* or *malevolent*, and, consequently, is not really a synonym for retaliation, as Aristotle's 'dialectician' would make it to be. Hence, such a definition as Locke's (*An Essay concerning Human Understanding*, ii. 20) must be rejected: 'Anger is uneasiness or discomposure of the mind, upon the receipt of an injury, with a present purpose of revenge.' The 'present purpose' is not of revenge, but simply of rebutting the offence or getting rid of it, and does not primarily intend to repay or injure the doer at all, although revenge may easily follow in the wake of it. Thus it is that we may very well be angry with a man without bearing him ill-will; and thus it is that anger is only of brief duration (thereby differing

from **wrath**, which is a settled disposition), although the choleric man is liable to repeated fits of it.

Like other 'passions,' anger lacks in moderation —transgresses limits, defies proportion. This indicates its danger as a motive power. When it acts like the wind, it exercises a useful function; when it becomes the whirlwind, it may do serious damage. On this account, its effects on the irate individual himself may be unsatisfactory; when the passion has ceased, depression frequently ensues, exhaustion thus taking its revenge.

Anger is a primary emotion of the human mind, and needs to be experienced in order to be known. It has a distinct quality of its own, different from that of every other emotion; and no one could, by mere description, make it intelligible to a man who had never himself been angry. Not only is it not derived from other emotions, it does not even presuppose experience of other emotions to give it being. Yet it enters itself into other emotions, — sometimes as their basis, sometimes as a subsidiary factor, — and so may be allied with 'affects' that are distinctly malevolent. It is an *egoistic* emotion, which may quite easily be transformed into one of *selfishness*; hence its ethical significance, to be considered presently.

The varieties of anger are irascibility and peevishness. **Irascibility** is the susceptibility to anger of a nervously excitable subject; and **peevishness** is undue sensibility to trifles, annoyance at them far beyond what their real value or significance warrants.

ii. *ETHICAL.*—Anger, as has just been said, is not in itself malevolent: it is simply a protection or defence against harm or hurt, and may be directed against things as well as against persons. It is a species of resentment, and operates instinctively, and, therefore, without due regard to consequences; hence the need of direction and restraint, and hence the ethical bearings of the emotion. As instinctive **resentment**, it is neither to be praised nor to be blamed, but is to be accepted as a part of the human constitution necessary to the welfare of the individual, and therefore ultimately to the good of the community. But inasmuch as the causes of anger are frequently human beings, and inasmuch as anger is apt to expend itself in excessive measure, and, in cases where the causes of it cannot be immediately reached, on objects that had no share in arousing it, it has to be brought under the control of reason. This is necessary, if anger is to be (as it ought to be) a help to justice. But, in thus rationalizing it, we are giving it a distinctively moral character, and are taking it in a wider signification than is accorded it by the psychologist. We are now estimating it in relation to its consequences, and assigning it a place in an ethical scheme of values. This means (to use Butler's famous analysis) that we are distinguishing between resentment that is sudden or instinctive and resentment that is deliberate, and appraising each in connexion with its social bearings.

Sudden or instinctive resentment, on the ethical side, is directed against injury, as discriminated from mere hurt or harm: it presupposes a conscious agent, intentionally doing an offending act for the purpose of injuring us. It consequently assumes the form of moral indignation, which is the spontaneous reaction of the conscience against what is wrong or evil, when the wrong or evil is designedly effected. It is the resentment of a healthy mind sensitive to injustice, and responding unreflectingly or immediately on the perception of the offence. Without this kind of anger, it is hardly conceivable how the moral nature could be effective at all.

When, on the other hand, we turn to deliberate resentment, we find that we are giving anger a different complexion, and are bringing it into relation with other phenomena of human nature that may or may not be conducive to men's highest interests. In so far as deliberate resentment means simply restraining the act that would naturally follow from the instinctive perception of the injury inflicted, till we have assured ourselves (in cases where some doubt may be possible) whether our resentment is just or not, and whether the consequences of our action may not be out of all proportion to the offence, it can only be right and commendable. But when, as is so frequently the case, deliberate resentment allies itself with our malevolent inclinations (with the savage or the fiend within us), then it becomes morally reprehensible, often in the highest degree. It is the nature of anger voluntarily nursed to magnify the offence that caused it: vanity and offended dignity come in to intensify and transform the emotion,—a grudge rankling in the bosom naturally exaggerates. Further, there can be little question that anger readily associates itself with that desire to injure others or to inflict pain on them that seems to be native to human beings, and so is easily changed into hatred, or retaliation, or revenge, or, keener still, vindictiveness. It is now exclusively aimed at persons, and is in its nature diametrically opposed to the sympathetic and humane sentiments, the tender emotions, that bind men together; it is the very antithesis of love, and, instead of attracting and cementing, alienates and repels. It is not only that the angry person, full of hate, is estranged from his fellow or resents his action; he also desires to inflict injury on him, to cause him pain, and gloats over and delights in his suffering. If he longs simply to pay him back or to requite him for the offence committed, his emotion is **retaliation**, proceeding on the principle of equivalents, the *lex talionis*—'an eye for an eye, and a tooth for a tooth,'—oblivious altogether of the promptings of generosity and mercy. When he harbours ill-will and cherishes his wrath, refusing to be pacified, meditating unmeasured requital and waiting for the favourable opportunity, it is **revenge**. Revenge is in its very nature inequitable and relentless, bloodthirsty and cruel, satisfied with nothing less than 'the head of John the Baptist in a charger.' When revenge pursues its object spitefully with unremitting persistence, and finds zest in every petty infliction of evil on him, it is **vindictiveness**. The spitefulness gives it a very despicable character.

Various questions concerning anger suggest themselves:

(1) A point that the earlier British psychologists (Butler, Thomas Reid, Dugald Stewart, Thomas Brown, etc.) delighted to investigate regarding anger and the malevolent affections, was their *use* or *final cause*. Accepting human nature as a given hierarchy of principles and faculties, and intending their philosophy to have practical value, they asked what end these seemingly destructive and objectionable forces served in the economy of man's being. They had little difficulty in showing that, given man and given his present circumstances, these forces minister both to the protection or self-preservation of the individual and to the good of the community. Sudden anger clearly conduces to the defence of the irate person against hurt or harm; and when the cause of the harm is another living person, it serves as a warning to him to desist: it is the Scottish Thistle fully displayed, with the significant motto, '*Nemo me impune lacessit*.' Even more strikingly is this purpose served by retaliation and revenge, when the vengeful person has to deal with others of like vengeful disposition as his own. His anger, being fierce, is both punitive and deterrent.

(2) In more recent times, another question has come prominently forward, viz.: *Whether the malevolence of human nature* (which nobody denies as a fact) *is really native to it?* The negative was ably upheld in *Mind*, a few years ago, by Mr. F. H. Bradley, who tried to reduce malevolence to excitement, or love of power, or self-assertion, or suchlike. This was strenuously opposed by Professor Bain, who insisted that, making all allowance for self-assertion and the love of power and similar strong emotions, there is a certain residuum that is unaccounted for, and this residuum is simply innate malevolence.

'Let us take, then, the examples where we are witnesses to suffering inflicted by others, and where we ourselves are noways concerned, or, at all events, very remotely. Why do multitudes delight in being spectators of punishments, including the gallows? In former days, when executions were public, when whippings, the pillory, and the stocks were open to everybody's gaze, what was the source of the fascination attending the spectacles? They were remotely connected with the security of the people generally, but they were most frequented by those that thought least of public security. . . . We can go a step farther. There are abundance of examples of delight in mischief of the most absolutely gratuitous kind, beginning in tender years, and continuing more or less until maturity. The love of teasing, of practical joking, of giving trouble and annoyance, without any cause whatever, is too manifest to be denied. . . . The demand for excitement of itself proves nothing. What we are to look at are the forms that it takes by preference, inasmuch as these are probably something more than mere excitement: they involve real and unambiguous pleasure. If the votaries of excitement are in the habit of seeking it by molesting, annoying, chaffing other people, the inference is that the excitement is a mere cover for a definite pleasure, the pleasure of malevolence. To sit on a road fence, and pass insulting and jeering remarks upon the innocent passers-by, is not to be slurred over as mere love of excitement: it arises from the deeper fountains of malignity. We may easily procure excitement in forms that hurt nobody; we may even find excitement, and pleasure too, in bestowing benefits; when we habitually seek it in the shape of inflicting pain, we must be credited with delighting in the pain. . . . The question ever recurs—Why is hatred such a source of consolatory feeling, if there be not a fountain of pleasure in connexion with the sufferings of others?' (Bain, *Dissertations on Leading Philosophical Topics*, pp. 84-104).

The strength of the argument seems to lie on the side of the affirmative; and, however unacceptable it may be, the fact must be recognized that man has an original tendency to inflict suffering on others, and derives real satisfaction and delight from contemplating the suffering that he inflicts.

(3) Our repugnance to this position may perhaps be mitigated, if we accept the explanation of the origin or source of the malevolent affections offered by the theory of Evolution. In his masterly work on *The Expression of the Emotions*, and elsewhere, Darwin has amassed materials to show that these affections originated, æons ago, in the predatory habits of the race, taken in connexion with those of the lower animals. They are the result of the necessity for combat and mutual warfare in the early struggle for existence. It was in these far back times that anger, retaliation, and revenge, with all the ways of giving outward expression to them, so significant of their animal origin, arose; and they are a heritage to us from the past. By this hypothesis, the wolf in man receives an explanation of a scientific kind, which, whether fully adequate or not, throws light on many points connected with malevolence that otherwise remain dark and puzzling. The philosophies of some countries (Oriental in particular) have tried to explain the phenomenon by the supposition of metempsychosis or transmigration of souls, especially the passage of the soul of a brute into the body of a man. The lower impulses and passions seem thereby to be accounted for, and man's baser nature to be so far justified. That is but the imaginative and non-scientific way of solving the problem; over against which has to be placed the scientific and reasoned mode of solution offered by Evolution.

LITERATURE.—Aristotle, *de Anima*, i. 1, and *Eth. Nic.* iv. 5; Seneca, *de Ira*; Butler, *Sermons*, viii. and ix.; Hume, *A Treatise of Human Nature*, Bk. ii. and Bk. iii. pt. 3; Thomas Reid, *Works* (Hamilton's ed.), pp. 568-570; Adam Smith, *The Theory of Moral Sentiments*, pt. ii. sec. 1; Dugald Stewart, *The Philosophy of the Active and Moral Powers of Man*, Bk. i. ch. iii. sec. 6; Thomas Brown, *Lectures on the Philosophy of the Human Mind*, Lect. lxiii.; Alexander Bain, *The Emotions and the Will*⁴, chs. ii. and ix., and *Dissertations on Leading Philosophical Topics* (1903), pp. 84-104; Herbert Spencer, *The Principles of Psychology*, vol. i. pt. iv. ch. 8, and vol. ii. pt. viii. ch. 4; Darwin, *The Expression of the Emotions in Man and Animals*, ch. x.; John Grote, *A Treatise on the Moral Ideals*, ch. xi., Appendix; W. James, *The Principles of Psychology*, vol. ii. ch. xxv.; G. F. Stout, *A Manual of Psychology* (1899), pp. 307-311, and *The Groundwork of Psychology* (1903), pp. 188-197; David Irons, *A Study in the Psychology of Ethics* (1903), pp. 78-83.

WILLIAM L. DAVIDSON.

ANGER (WRATH) OF GOD.—I. *THE DIVINE ANGER AS PRESENTED IN THE OT.*—God is revealed in the OT as a living Being, who has a merciful purpose toward the universe which He has made. During all the ages of human history, He is seeking to carry out this purpose to its consummation. In doing so, He is confronted by the ignorance and slowness of men, by their self-will and their hostility. These awaken in Him such feelings as would be stirred in the heart of a wise and good man, in view of the hindrances and oppositions with which he met in the course of some great and beneficent enterprise. The OT speaks freely of the grief, and jealousy, and anger of God. There are doubtless very grave difficulties in attributing these emotions, and, indeed, emotions of any kind, to One whose thoughts are not as the thoughts of men. But the writers of the OT, while guarding against an obvious abuse of this anthropomorphic method of conceiving the Divine nature (1 S 15[29]), do not stop to discuss such problems. They are chiefly concerned to make vivid and real the thought of God, as a living Person in whose image human beings have been made. Human qualities, accordingly, are attributed to God, because human nature is homogeneous with the Divine nature. In man these attributes and affections are marked by finitude and imperfection. In God they exist in absolute perfection. This makes a great difference between what is found in man and what is attributed to God, as the OT writers are well aware. But there is an identity deeper than the difference; and therefore even the latest and most spiritual of the prophets and psalmists make fearless use of anthropomorphic language. Had they failed to do so, they would have endangered, in the minds of their readers, the personality and the moral nature of God. Anger, accordingly, is found in the Divine character, as it is always found in any strong human character.

1. The nature of the Divine anger.—The OT describes it in terms which are laden with terror. What created thing can stand before the flame of that great anger (Dt 32[22]; cf. He 12[29], Ps 78[21] 88[16] 90[7. 9. 11])? The Divine anger, described in these and many other passages, is not to be confounded with the causeless and capricious fury which men have been wont to attribute to the objects of their ignorant and slavish fear. It is always to be understood by reference to the central truth of Jahweh's self-revelation. He is the covenant God of His people. He seeks their salvation. If He is angry, it is when the conditions under which alone He can work out that salvation are infringed, and His purpose of mercy is imperilled. The relation in which He stands to Israel necessarily implies that His holiness, *i.e.* His Godhead, be not violated in any of its manifestations. A God who is not holy and inviolable cannot be a Saviour. To invade His sanctity is to defeat His purpose. The anger of God is aroused, therefore, by any act which stands between Him and the end which He has in view.

Incidents are recorded which seem to bring the anger of Jahweh down to the level of the inexplicable rage of an unethical heathen god (*e.g.* 1 S 6^{19}, 2 S 6^{6-8}). Regulations are made which seem to connect the Divine anger with matters that are wholly outward, and, therefore, not fit occasions of wrath in a perfectly moral being (*e.g.* Lv 10^{6}, Nu 1^{53} 18^{5}; cf. Ex 12^{13} 30^{12}). All such cases, however, are to be understood by reference to the Divine purpose. It is endangered when the pride and self-will of man invade the sphere of the Divine holiness. What is at stake is not a ceremonial regulation as such, but the holiness, *i.e.* the very Divinity, of God Himself. By such acts as those referred to, therefore, the anger of God is kindled, and upon the perpetrators of them it descends in crushing might.

2. Its objects.—The objects of the Divine anger, accordingly, are men who oppose themselves to the Divine will. Such are all who are hostile to Israel, the people of God's choice, the realm wherein He rules:—the nations who rage, and the peoples who imagine a vain thing (Ps 2^{1}), the enemies that reproach, and the foolish people who blaspheme His name (Ps 74^{18}). Not these alone, however, nor these chiefly, provoke Him to anger. When Israel breaks the laws of righteousness, upon which the commonwealth of God is founded, or does dishonour to Him who redeemed His people, His heart is hot within Him; and He punishes, not with cold, unemotional, judicial exactitude, but with an intensity of indignation which, to an awakened conscience, is the most awful element in the penalty (Ps 5^{5}, Hab 1^{13}, Lv 26^{14-45}, Dt 12^{31}, Is 61^{8}). The long education of Israel, culminating in the teaching of the prophets, has burned into the conscience of men that sin is a reality for God, and that towards it He is moved with a just and terrible anger (Ps 11^{5}). The depth of God's feeling with regard to sin can be fathomed only by estimating aright the relation in which He stands to His people. He is their Saviour, and the tenderest and most sacred relation in which two human beings can stand to one another is not too close to figure forth His relation to them. He is their husband and Lord; they are His spouse. Sin on their part is conjugal infidelity, the most awful outrage that can be committed against love. In such figures the prophets depict the grief and jealousy of God, and seek to measure the fierceness of His wrath (Ezk 23, Am 3^{2}, Dt 4^{24} 5^{9}, Zeph 1^{18}, Ps 78^{58}).

3. Its manifestation.—The Divine anger, therefore, is an affection awakened in the Divine nature by the presence of evil. It is manifested in judgments following upon wicked deeds. Its instruments are to be found in the forces of nature, which are under the control of God, and in men, whose selfish pride or ambition may be made subservient to the will of God, so that it may, unconsciously, be the rod of Jahweh's anger (Is $10^{5f.}$). The prophets, however, clearly discern that God's operations, alike in mercy and in judgment, cannot be carried to completion in the state of the world as they know it. Not in any of these common days, which succeed one another with uncompleted significance, can the work of God be finished, but only in a Day, which completes the series, and at once reveals and fulfils the whole design of God. This Day of the Lord will be both the crown of salvation and the ultimate stroke of judgment. The unimaginable terrors of that Day haunt the visions of the prophets, confounding the self-righteousness of those who had expected it to bring them the gratification of their national and personal pride (Am 5^{18-20}, Zeph 1^{7-12}, Mal $3^{2.3}$). Thus the wrath of God gains a predominantly eschatological sense, not, however, to the exclusion of the view that it is a present quality of the Divine nature, and is continuously manifest in His attitude toward sin.

4. The turning away of the Divine anger.—Being under the control of the ultimate Divine purpose, which is love, the wrath of God may be restrained, or even entirely turned away, and give place to the unhindered outpourings of loving-kindness. It is, indeed, plain that, if God gave free vent to His anger, the objects of it would immediately be destroyed (Ps 130^{3}). Such an action on His part, however, would defeat His own ends. During the historic period, throughout which God is pursuing His aim, His wrath cannot be fully executed (Ps $78^{38.39}$). One consideration is paramount—the honour of His Name, *i.e.* the success of His design of mercy to Israel. God cannot submit to be taunted with failure (Ezk 20^{22}, Is 48^{9-11}). He is angry, and He punishes. But he waits to see if, by punishments restrained and controlled by mercy, sinners may learn, and turn to Him, and live. Beyond this period of discipline there lies an awful possibility of exhausted forbearance, and final and measureless doom. What, then, will avert this doom, and turn anger into acceptance and delight? The OT has no clear or full answer to give. The sacrifices, obviously, could not atone for sin, in its real spiritual significance; and their symbolism cannot have conveyed exact dogmatic teaching. The prophets, however, had grasped one great and fruitful thought: if a representative of the people be found who, standing in living relation to the nation, yet separating himself from the national trespass, shall deeply apprehend the sinfulness of the nation's sin, and the terror of the Divine judgment upon it, and shall make profound acknowledgment before God, in the name of the people, of their guilt and ill-desert, the Divine anger will be appeased, and God will return to His people in mercy (Gn 18^{23-33}, Ex 32^{9-14}, Nu 25^{10-13}). It is true that no perfectly competent representative can be found among the people themselves. Even a Moses or a Samuel would be insufficient for so great a work (Jer 15^{1}). Yet the principle of atonement through sin-bearing remained deep in the prophetic consciousness (Ezk 22^{30}, Jer 5^{1}, Is 65^{8}), and, in the great vision of Is 53, one is depicted capable of undertaking even this vocation of unspeakable suffering, and, through his faithful discharge of it, procuring deliverance for the transgressors.

II. *THE DIVINE ANGER AS PRESENTED IN THE NT.*—The OT and the NT are at one in their intense conviction that God is 'a Person, with ethical attributes,' a living Being, having moral powers and qualities, which are reflected and reproduced in man. They agree also in their presentation of the character of God. That full ethicizing of the idea of God which is seen in the prophets of the OT is assumed as fundamental truth by the teachers of the NT. Love and mercy, holiness and righteousness, are qualities which believing men, alike before and after the coming of Christ, discern in the character of God, and adore with reverence and joy.

So also the NT, like the OT, has no hesitation in attributing emotions to God. Peace, and pleasure, and gladness are all to be found in Him, and, through their effects in the hearts of believers, are part of the Christian's heritage of blessedness. The reality of these Divine emotions is so wrought into Christian experience, as expressed in the NT, that to question it or explain it away would deprive the experience itself of its life and joy.

1. It may be urged, however, that while it is true that the NT, like the OT, attributes emotions to God, it differs in not attributing to Him the emotion of anger. Is this true? Does anger disappear in NT teaching as an element in the character of God? It is well known that Ritschl and some theologians of his school maintain that the only NT use of the Divine anger is eschatological. Is this correct? (*a*) It is true that the NT usage is prevailingly eschatological. NT believers, like the prophets of the OT, had the Day of Wrath full in view. The Baptist made it the burden of his warning and appeal (Mt 3^{7}). However difficult the exegetical questions may be in connexion with certain portions of the tradition, it is certain that eschatology occupied a large place in the teaching of Jesus, and

that He used OT figures in describing the terrors of the Judgment. In the Apocalypse of St. John that final outpouring of the wrath of God weighs upon the soul with an awful sense of doom (*e.g.* 6[16ff.] 14[10]). The preaching of the Apostles is full of the terror of the Lord. To them and to their hearers the impending wrath was a terrible reality; and one element, not the greatest, yet very precious and wonderful, in the gospel, is that the Messiah saves from this unspeakable Judgment (1 Th 1[10], Ro 5[9]). (*b*) It is not true, however, that the usage is exclusively eschatological. It is to be observed, moreover, that while feelings of terror are readily awakened by references to the ultimate Judgment and its dread accompaniments, a deeper awe is aroused by the contemplation of a Judgment that is present and continuous, and an anger that is awake and abiding even now. This more solemn view of the wrath of God is not awanting in the NT. The teaching of Jesus is very far fron. depicting a God who is undisturbed at the sight of human pride and self-will. Sin is a reality for God, and there is one sin, which itself is the ultimate product of sin, which hath never forgiveness. Some of the parables are heavy with the weight of the Divine indignation (*e.g.* Mt 25[14-30]). More significant still than the words of Jesus were His own feelings and their outcome in act. He who said, 'He that hath seen me hath seen the Father' (Jn 14[9]), was not stoically cold or sublimely unmoved in presence of evil. Once and again He was filled with a great anger (Mk 3[5] 8[33] 11[15-17], Mt 23[1ff.]). In allowing Himself this emotion and its utterance, Jesus certainly did not regard Himself as out of harmony with the feeling and attitude of God toward the evils that so moved Him. This teaching is echoed throughout the NT. Sin always attracts to itself the wrath of God (Ro 1[18] 4[15] 9[22], Eph 2[3] 5[6]). Sin, in its inmost significance, is equivalent to rejection of the Divine mercy incarnate in the Son of God. 'He,' therefore, 'that obeyeth not the Son shall not see life, but the wrath of God abideth on him' (Jn 3[36]). When we remember what 'life' means, in the vocabulary of the Old and New Testaments, viz. the favour and fellowship of God, we are compelled to put into this saying the profoundest sense of a weight of holy indignation now resting upon the soul which is not standing in the obedience of Christ. It is possible to deny the doctrine thus conveyed, and to rid our hearts of the fear it conveys; but it is not possible to deny that NT writers held this doctrine, and owned this overwhelming terror.

2. The wrath of God, then, rests on the soul that rejects Christ; but upon the soul that is 'in Christ' no such awful load remains. The NT writers are at one in attributing this great deliverance to the saving work of Christ, and specifically to His death, which they regard as a sacrifice for sin. When Christ was raised from the dead, 'the cloud of Divine wrath—the ὀργή so long suspended and threatening to break (Ro 3[25. 26])—had passed away. This is the thought which lies at the bottom of Ro 6[7-10]' (Sanday on Ro 4[23ff.] in *ICC*). The penitent believer, looking to the cross of Christ, is certified, by the witness of the Spirit within him, that the anger of God, which once rested upon him, is now turned away from him. *Is it then the intention of the Biblical writers to convey the idea that Christ bore the wrath of God, that He endured the outpouring of the Divine anger?* Is it fitting for the redeemed to say:

> 'The Father lifted up His rod:
> O Christ, it fell on Thee'?

It is a remarkable fact that the NT never does, in words, connect the death of Christ with the Divine anger, even in passages where the line of argument might have seemed to culminate in such a thought. It seems as though the writers deliberately refrained from any language which might suggest that the Son became the subject of the Father's anger, or that His death was due to an ebullition of the Divine wrath, which, flashing forth in lightning stroke, smote the holy breast of Jesus. At the same time it is to be noted that experiences which are themselves expressions of the wrath of God are attributed to Christ, and our salvation is traced to them. In Gal 3[13] Christ is described as having become 'a curse for us,' and in 2 Co 5[21] as having been made 'sin' on our behalf. Whatever these mysterious expressions, 'become a curse,' 'made sin,' may mean, they cannot mean less than an actual experience, by the sinless One, of what sin involves; and that, without doubt, is the wrath of God. Yet the actual phrase is not used. It must be remembered, also, that Jesus, in dying, experienced an agony, whose source and bitterness we can never fully know; which, as it broke from Him in the cry of desertion, cannot have meant less than an unspeakable sense of the Divine judgment upon human sin (cf. Principal Garvie in *Studies in the Inner Life of Jesus*, London, 1908, p. 417 ff. Yet it does not appear, even in that cry of infinite pain, that He felt that God was angry with Him. Descriptions are given, implying that Jesus in death bore sin, through a profound realization of what it means, and of what the Divine attitude and feeling toward it, and the Divine judgment upon it, really are. In these very descriptions, however, phrases which might lead to inferences regarding the anger of God being endured by the Son of His love are carefully avoided. Christian faith is directed to One who was the Son of God, in whom the Father was well pleased, who hung upon the cross in fulfilment of the mission to which the Father summoned Him, and who must therefore have been, in that hour, the object of the Father's deep satisfaction and most tender love, who yet surrendered the comforts of the Father's fellowship, identified Himself with sinful men, and passed, Himself sinless, through the apprehension of God's sentence upon sin, acknowledging its justice, and approving, as in the holy life, so in the sacrificial death, the righteousness of God. The believer, when he commits himself to the crucified and risen Lord, receives from Him salvation, and enters upon the joy of those from whom the Divine anger is turned away, and who live in the Divine favour and fellowship. At the same time, being spiritually one with his Lord, he enters into the experiences in which Christ won his deliverance, realizes and acknowledges God's judgment upon sin, dies to sin as a power over him, and begins to live the new life of victory over sin; and in these experiences, which strangely reproduce both the passion and the glory of the Redeemer, the salvation, which he receives as a gift, is wrought out in a growing assimilation to Christ. He combines, in his own experience, what he has seen combined upon the Cross, the wrath of God against sin and the Divine mercy toward sinners. The terror of the Lord and the love of Christ are the two powers which operate within his soul, to make him flee from sin, and live unto Him who for his sake died and rose again. It may be possible to have a religious experience in which a sense of the wrath of God has no place; but it ought to be acknowledged that it would not be an experience which has the cross of Christ for its starting-point and the NT for its rule and guide.

III. *DOCTRINAL CONCLUSIONS.*—The Biblical usage warrants certain inferences, which require to have their place in any theology whose guiding principles are found in the Scriptures.

1. **The reality of the Divine anger.**—The passion of anger is implanted in man, and has for its end the prevention and remedy of injury and the miseries arising out of it. 'It is to be considered,' in the words of Bishop Butler in his famous Sermon on *Resentment* (§ 11), 'as a weapon, put into our hands by nature, against injury, injustice, and cruelty'; and 'it may be innocently employed and made use of.' We ascribe human qualities to God, not because we think of Him as a magnified man, but because we necessarily regard men as reflecting, under conditions of finitude and limitation, the qualities of the Divine nature. Human anger shares in the imperfection and sinfulness of man. The 'weapon put into our hands' we often use unwisely, forgetting, as we wield it, the claims of both righteousness and love. Divine anger is far removed from any such defect. It is an affection of One who is at once loving and righteous. It is completely under the control of

attributes which are themselves combined, without any opposition, in the harmony of the Divine character. But it is in God essentially what it is in man. In Him, also, it is a 'weapon' against injury; and its keen edge is turned against those who, in pride and self-will, seek to injure God. The classical theological statement of this position is to be found in Lactantius' *de Ira Dei.* The gods of Epicurus inhabit 'the lucid interspace of world and world,' where no 'sound of human sorrow mounts, to mar their sacred everlasting calm.' The God of Stoicism is another name for the Universal Reason embodied in the universe, and is lifted far above the throb of feeling. Against any such views of the apathy of the Divine nature, Lactantius sets the Christian conviction of the character of God as love, and announces the principle 'qui non odit, nec diligit.' 'If God is not angry with the impious and the unrighteous, it is clear that He does not love the pious and the righteous. Therefore the error of those is more consistent who take away at once both anger and kindness.' This line of argument has been often followed, *e.g.*, by Trench (*Synonyms*, p. 129): 'There is a wrath of God, who would not be good unless He hated evil, the two being inseparable, so that He must do both or neither.'

Objections to the reality of the Divine anger have arisen mainly from an intrusion of philosophical theory into the sphere of Christian thought; and for this, in the history of theology, Augustine is chiefly responsible. He is still very largely under the control of Neo-Platonism, and shares the dread, always entertained by mystical piety, of lowering the Divine nature, by connecting it with finite things, or of breaking in upon the ineffable bliss of God, by the impertinence of predicates taken from human experience. Thus in the *City of God* (bk. xv. ch. 25) he speaks of 'the anger of God, which does not inflame His mind, nor disturb His unchangeable tranquillity,' and identifies it with the sentence which God pronounces upon sin. 'The anger of God is not a disturbing emotion of His mind, but a judgment by which punishment is inflicted upon sin.' The language which in Scripture attributes anger to God, he regards as anthropopathic, and explains it as 'a condescension to man's finitude, insinuating itself into the minds of all classes of men, alarming the proud, arousing the careless, exercising the inquisitive, and satisfying the intelligent.' We may even trace something of the same hesitation in Dr. John Caird's estimate of the value and the defects of anthropomorphic language: '. . . when we are told of His wrath as being aroused or abated . . . the religious mind passes beyond the anthropomorphic figure to seize, in an indefinite but not unreal way, the hidden spiritual meaning. The representation conveys a general impression which is of the nature of knowledge, though, literally construed, it expresses what is untrue' (*Introd. to the Philosophy of Religion*, p. 174 f.). It is true that the religious mind refuses to take literally figurative descriptions, which seem to ascribe to God 'the ignorance and changefulness, even the desires and passions, of our finite sensuous nature.' But it is certain, also, that the religious mind, instructed by Scripture and by experience, will not permit a speculative construction to imperil the conception of the Divine personality. The difficulty of conceiving how God can be both the 'Absolute' and a living Person is, of course, very great. Probably we ought to direct our thoughts to a fresh study of the conception of the Absolute, particularly with the aim of freeing it from the immobility and sterility which an exclusive use of the category of Substance has imported into it. In any case, we must seek to do justice in our thinking to an absolute will of love, which determines the whole counsel and action of God; and, also, to His attitude toward that which conflicts with this will—an attitude which can be construed only as condemnation and wrath.

2. Sin and the Divine anger.—(1) The indignation of God against sin is real; and the passing away of wrath and the unhindered manifestation of love are real also. Theology, accordingly, in its effort to give reflective expression to the facts of Christian experience, cannot neglect the idea of the wrath of God, and the problems connected with it.

Ritschl, indeed, refuses to allow any theological value to the idea of the wrath of God. He speaks of it in his great work on *Justification and Reconciliation* as 'ein ebenso heimatloses wie gestaltloses Theologumenon' (vol. ii. p. 154). In vol. iii. p. 323 [Eng. tr.] he says: 'From the point of view of theology, no validity can be assigned to the idea of the wrath of God and His curse upon sinners as yet unreconciled; still less, from this theological standpoint, is any special mediation between the wrath and the love of God conceivable or necessary in order to explain the reconciliation of sinners with Him.' This view depends (*a*) on an interpretation of the Biblical usage, viz. that 'wrath' has a uniformly eschatological meaning, which is surely unsound; (*b*) on a conception of God as being absolutely and exclusively love, justice being excluded from the Divine essence, which imperils the ultimate distinctions of Good and Evil. 'When the Divine reason, clothed with omnipotence, has created morally free beings, the right of punitive justice cannot be refused to it without exposing the moral world to the danger of falling a prey to chaos' (Dorner, *System of Christian Doctrine*, vol. iv. p. 65). Guilt is more than a guilty feeling; and 'the impression of a change from Divine wrath to Divine mercy' (Ritschl, vol. iii. p. 323) is more than subjective. It is the reflexion, within the subject of redeeming grace, of an actual difference of attitude and feeling on the part of the personal Source and Author of redemption. Such an experience is real, and must not be so explained by theology, in its effort to maintain 'the view-point of eternity,' as to be explained away.

(2) The wrath of God against sin stands in the closest relation to all His ethical attributes, particularly to His holiness and His love. *His holy character* is outraged by the presence of moral evil. If it were not so, He would not be a God to worship, as the impersonation and the guardian of righteousness. A trained conscience bows before this righteous wrath of God against evil, recognizing it as an element in ideal excellence. That nature alone whose insight is blurred and whose judgment is perverted, fails to be angry at the sight of moral evil. 'A sinner,' says Dr. A. B. Davidson, 'is an ill judge of sin' (*Com. on Hebrews*, p. 108, on 4^{15}). God, knowing sin to its root, hates it with a perfect hatred. *His love* is not less affronted than His holiness. The welfare of men, which is the aim of His love, is ruined by moral evil. The highest good of men depends on the conquest of sin in them, and their conformity to the holy character of God. His love for men, therefore, intensifies the heat of His indignation against that in them which opposes the realization of His loving purpose for them.

Some theologians have pressed this close connexion between love and anger to the point of identifying them.

So Martensen: 'This wrath is holy love itself,' feeling itself 'restrained, hindered, and stayed through unrighteousness'; Oosterzee: 'Not without reason has this wrath been termed "the extreme burning point of the flame of love"'; and many modern writers, *e.g.*, Scott Lidgett: 'The manifestation of the Fatherhood of God is shut out, and because shut out, is turned to wrath; for the wrath of God is simply the love of the Fatherhood denied its purpose by rebellion'; and Stevens: 'The wrath of God is the reaction of His holy love against sin. It is not the opposite of love; it is a part or aspect of love.'

It may be doubted, however, whether this identification serves the purpose of clear thinking. Love, while incompatible with revenge, is certainly not inconsistent with resentment (cf. Butler, Sermon ix. § 10). It is possible to love those who have injured us, while feeling a deep and just indignation at the moral turpitude of their conduct. But our anger is certainly not a part or aspect of our love. Even a parent's anger at the evil conduct of a beloved child is not to be identified with his love for his child; though it is closely related to his love, being intensified by his desire to secure for his son the very highest moral results, and being, at the same time, controlled and directed by love in its manifestations. Anger is connected primarily with the attitude which a righteous man necessarily takes toward evil. He condemns it, and does so with a passion which is pure in proportion to the soundness of his moral character. To make it simply the impulse of disappointed love is to lower its moral quality, and make it selfish and unethical. A righteous man feels resentment toward evil, and is impelled to make that resentment clearly known and profoundly felt by the wrong-doer. He is constrained to do this not by revenge, but by his sense of the duty he owes to the principle of right itself, and to him who has invaded it. And this duty is not less binding, if the wrong-doer be a beloved child. The father's love and anger are real and distinct.

Their relations to each other constitute a problem the solution of which will tax his utmost wisdom.

It is after this analogy that the Biblical usage presents the Divine anger; and by it theological thought must be guided. God is full of love to the sinner, while at the same time He burns with just and awful resentment against his sin. His love and His wrath are alike real, and each has its distinctive place in the character of God. Their relations constitute a problem whose solution cannot be adequately set forth in terms of thought; while yet Christian faith grasps the solution in the cross of Christ.

Even Martensen, who identifies love and wrath, dwells upon 'the tension or apparent variance' which sin has produced between the Divine love and the Divine righteousness, and defines the idea of the Atonement as 'the solution of a certain antithesis in the very life of God as revealed to man, or of the apparent opposition between God's love and God's righteousness' (*Christian Dogmatics*, p. 303).

3. The turning away of wrath.—Scripture never suggests that there is any antagonism between the Divine love and the Divine anger, and nowhere countenances the idea that God was so angry with sinners that He felt it necessary to pour out His fury on someone before He could begin to love anyone. Theologians, who have kept close to Scripture, even while maintaining on scriptural grounds an 'objective' theory of the Atonement, have not failed to protest against this outrageous perversion of the truth. Calvin, whose expressions may often be criticised for their gloom and terror, is absolutely explicit upon this point: 'Our being reconciled by the death of Christ must not be understood as if the Son reconciled us, in order that the Father, then hating, might begin to love us, but that we were reconciled to Him, already loving, though at enmity with us because of sin' (*Institutes*, bk. ii. ch. xvi. § 4). The Divine love, accordingly, is the original impulse and the continual inspiration of the whole redemptive activity of God. Yet the Divine love cannot expunge and obliterate the Divine anger by a mere overflow of sentiment. The Divine anger can be turned away only when those against whom it is directed enter, with profound insight and entire assent, into its grounds and reasons, and submit themselves, with unmurmuring surrender, to the experiences in which the awful displeasure of the Holy One is manifested and realized. To say this, however, is to make the problem insoluble, and to seal upon sinners the unspeakable terrors of the Divine judgment. Suppose, however, that, in the centre of the human race, there should appear One so related to men that He was able to take upon Himself a service which no sinner can render for his brother, and no sinner can discharge in his own interests. Suppose that He should enter, without one shade of disparity or inadequacy, into the mind of God regarding sin, and submit Himself freely to the whole experience in which that mind is expressed, feeling, as He did so, an extremity of spiritual anguish for which no sinful soul has any complete measurement. Would not His suffering be a sacrifice for sin which the Divine love could accept without any infringement of its holiness, while the cloud of the Divine wrath would roll away for ever? Suppose, further, that such an One were the gift of God's love to the race, as indeed He would need to be, seeing that the race could not produce Him, and were in Himself the very Word of God, the express image of His Person, as He would need to be if He were to reveal God's mind toward sinners. Would He not be the living personal meeting-point of the Divine love and the Divine anger? But this is the message of the NT. In the sufferings of Christ, the love of God reaches its consummation, and by them the wrath of God is stilled for evermore. To the question whether the Son endured the wrath of God, we must, following the usage of Scripture and the obvious truth of the situation, give a negative answer. 'We do not,' says Calvin, commenting on the cry of desertion wrung from the anguish of Christ's inmost soul, 'insinuate that God was ever hostile to Him or angry with Him. How could He be angry with the beloved Son, with whom His soul was well pleased? Or how could He have appeased the Father by His intercession for others if He were hostile to Himself? But this we say, that He bore the weight of the Divine anger, that, smitten and afflicted, He experienced all the signs of an angry and avenging God' (*Institutes*, bk. ii. ch. xvi. § 11). The last phrase in this sentence is ill chosen. But the deep truth remains, that the Redeemer knew, in that hour of lonely and unknown agony, the whole meaning of sin, and apprehended it as the object of God's just condemnation and infinite resentment. Thus He bore our sin, and thus He turned away from us the wrath which was our due. The discussion of theories of Atonement is not here in place; but it is certain that no theory will be adequate which fails to give due weight to the fact which is presented in the narrative of the Passion, and in the teaching of the NT—that Christ in dying had laid upon His soul the very judgments of God (cf. Dorner, *System of Christian Doctrine*, iv. 114, 116).

The faith which apprehends Christ as Saviour means the transition from a condition which involves the hostility of God, while yet His love is devising means for the restoration of the sinner, to a state in which the Divine love may satisfy itself in accepting the penitent and crowning him with goodness. But it is to be noted that this spiritual act has for its object Christ in His experience of sin-bearing, and implies spiritual oneness with Christ in it. The penitent, as he first comes to Christ, will know but little of what was involved in that experience. But the most rudimentary faith implies that the sinner identifies himself with Christ, as Christ had identified Himself with him; that the Divine judgment upon sin which Christ bore and so vindicated for ever, the sinner accepts and ratifies, and thus, under the constraint of the love of Christ, dies to sin in its principle and power. Thus, though the sinner does not bear the anger of God in its outpouring upon sin, yet, taught by the suffering of Christ, he knows what that righteous indignation is from which he has been delivered, and enters with purged conscience upon the new life of fellowship and obedience.

4. The day of wrath.—The NT is occupied mainly with the proclamation of the gospel, and with opening to believers the wealth of opportunity and blessedness which is theirs in Christ. It has, accordingly, comparatively little material for a doctrine of the Last Things on its negative side. Yet the conclusion to which we are led admits of no doubt. If there remain, after the full period of probation is ended, those who persist in their opposition to God and their rejection of the Divine mercy, whose characters have attained a final fixity, the NT leaves no doubt as to what their condition must be. They have sinned an eternal sin (Mk 3^{29}). They must endure the utmost visitation of the wrath of God (1 Th 5^{9}, Ro $2^{5.8}$ 5^{9}). We are not called on to decide the question whether there shall be many such lost souls, or even whether any such shall be found at the time of the consummation. We are warned against attempted descriptions of what is, in its nature, unimaginable, the loss and the misery of such a state. But any serious consideration of human nature, and of the relations of God and man, leads to the conclusion that such fixity of opposition to God must be included in the possibilities of the development of human character, and that, if this possibility is ever realized, it must involve none other than this overwhelming judgment.

LITERATURE.—Monographs: Lactantius, *de Ira Dei*; Ritschl, *de Ira Dei* (1859); Weber, *Vom Zorne Gottes* (1862). Discussions in the Biblical Theologies, specially Davidson, Oehler, Schultz, Stevens; and in the Systematic Theologies, *e.g.* Martensen, Dorner, Kaftan, W. Adams Brown. Discussions in works on Atonement and Redemption: Ritschl, *Justification and Reconciliation* (Eng. tr. 1900); Dale, *The Atonement*[7] (1878); Simon, *The Redemption of Man*[2] (1906); M'Leod Campbell, *The Nature of the Atonement*[4] (1873); Moberly, *Atonement and Personality* (1901); Stevens, *The Christian Doctrine of Salvation* (1905); articles in *PRE*, and in Hastings' *DB* and *DCG*.

T. B. KILPATRICK.

ANGLO-ISRAELISM.—The theory that the inhabitants of England are the descendants of the 'lost' (?) Ten Tribes of Israel is held somewhat widely, and is said to have two million adherents in Great Britain and the United States. The Anglo-Israelites are, at any rate, sufficiently numerous to support one publisher, who devotes his business entirely to publications dealing with the subject. There are also several periodicals published in furtherance of the views of the Anglo-Israelites.

The earliest suggestions of an Israelitish ancestry of the English are to be found in John Sadler's *Rights of the Kingdom* (1649). These take the form of a series of parallels between English law and customs and those of the Hebrews and Jews. The name 'Britain' itself is traced to a Phœnician source, *Berat Anak* ('The Field of Tin and Lead'). Many of the legends attached to the Coronation Stone have also a Jewish tinge, and are traced back to a landing of fugitive Israelites, under the lead of Jeremiah and Baruch, in Ireland.

The modern movement owes its foundation to Richard Brothers (1757–1824), a half-pay officer of eccentric habits in the English navy. According to his account he was a Divinely appointed prophet. He described himself as a 'nephew of the Almighty,' and claimed descent from David. Among his prophecies were those of the imminent restoration of Israel to the Holy Land, and the elevation of himself as prince of the Hebrews and ruler of the world. Brothers was confined as a lunatic, but succeeded in obtaining many admirers, among them Nathaniel Brassey Halket, M.P. for Lymington. The non-fulfilment of his prophecies sorely tried the faith of the believers, but through good and ill repute he retained the loyalty of John Finlayson, previously a Scotch lawyer with an extensive and lucrative practice. According to the *Dictionary of National Biography*, Brothers printed in all fifteen volumes, chiefly in support of his theory of the Israelitish descent of most of the inhabitants of England. The more important of the volumes are *Revealed Knowledge of the Prophecies and Times* (1794), and *A Correct Account of the Invasion and Conquest of this Island by the Saxons* (1822). Prominent among the literature that followed upon Brothers' announcements were Finlayson's writings. In 1840 the theory was adopted by John Wilson, who lectured and wrote widely on the subject. His *Our Israelitish Origin* is the first coherent exposition of the theory. Other advocates in the nineteenth century were W. Carpenter (*Israelites Found*), F. R. A. Glover (*England the Remnant of Judah*), and C. Piazzi Smyth, the Astronomer-Royal for Scotland, who deduced from certain measurements of the Great Pyramid that the English were descended from the Lost Tribes. In 1871, Edward Hine published his *Identification of the British Nation with Lost Israel*, of which a quarter of a million copies are said to have been sold. In the United States the leaders of the movement have been W. H. Poole and G. W. Greenwood. The theory has also been adopted to a slight extent on the Continent, where, for instance, the hostility of the English to Napoleon and Russia, and the sympathy aroused by the Dreyfus case are attributed to this cause.

The advocates of the theory identify Israel with the *Khumri* of the Assyrians, the *Cimmerioi* of the Greeks, the *Cimbri* of the Romans, and the *Cymri*. All these forms, it is said, are variations of the same name, and traces of it are to be found in 'Crimea,' 'Cumberland,' 'Cambria,' and 'Gumri' (a Russian fortress on the banks of the Araxes, the place of the Israelitish exile). The Ten Tribes of the Assyrian Captivity on leaving the land of their sojourn are supposed to have wandered towards the west, while those of the Babylonian Captivity passed eastwards towards Afghanistan and India. It is claimed that evidence of the journey towards the north-west is to be found in the tombs, alleged to be of Israelitish origin, that stretch from the Caucasus westwards round the Euxine. The further passage westwards can be traced, we are told, in the river nomenclature of Russia: the *Don*, *Danez*, *D(a)nieper*, *D(a)niester*, and *Danube*. The theory goes on to state that these migrants were driven by Alexander over the Danube and settled in Dacia. There they were attacked by the Romans, whom they ultimately repulsed. Many of them, however, were driven farther north, and founded republics, on the Israelitish pattern, in the north and west of Europe. The Goths, who were also of Israelitish descent (Goth = Getæ = Gad) were driven by the Huns into the dominions of Rome, in which and beyond which they spread. In consequence of these events, almost the whole of Europe, as well as her colonies in other continents, is held to be peopled by descendants of Israel. Among the local identifications are the tribes of Simeon and Levi among the Ionians, Asher in the Etruscans, Dan in the Danes, Judah in the Jutes, and Manasseh in the Celts. The Lacedæmonians are also stated to have been descendants of Judah.

The Khumri are divided into the Scuthæ or Scythians — whence *Scots* — and the Sacæ — afterwards *Saxons* (sons of Isaac). The former, it is said, composed the migration of B.C. 670, when the tribes of Reuben and Gad, and half that of Manasseh, started on their wanderings. The latter consisted of the remainder of the victims of the captivity of nineteen years later. One branch of the tribe of Dan, however, escaped on ships, and ultimately settled in Spain and Ireland, where they were known as the *Tuatha-dé-Danann*. They arrived in Ireland under the lead of the scribe Baruch and possibly also of Jeremiah. Accompanying them, we are told, was an Israelitish princess who subsequently married a local chieftain, the couple being crowned on the Bethel stone, rescued from the ruins of the Temple. This stone, the *Lia-Fail*, it is claimed, accompanied the Scots to Scotland, was invariably made use of at coronations, was removed by Edward I. from Scone to Westminster, and is identical with that now used at English coronations. There is in reality considerable doubt whether the Coronation Stone is identical with the *Lia-Fail*.

In support of the theory many alleged identifications in respect of customs, traditions, beliefs, etc., have been adduced. These, without exception, depend upon very inadequate support. Similarities as authentic have been discovered between the various languages of the British Isles and Hebrew. The theorists choose safer ground when they point to England's influence and success, and suggest as a cause God's covenant with Abraham, fulfilled in the persons of his descendants, the English. It is also argued that the English must be the representatives of Israel, as otherwise the many Divine promises made to that race would be unfulfilled.

The theory relies to a very considerable extent on a very literal interpretation of certain passages in the Old Testament (Authorized Version). It is pointed out that Israel was to change his name (Hos 1[9]), increase beyond number, dwell in islands (Is 24[15]) to the north (Jer 3[12]) and the west, and be a great nation (Mic 5[8]). Israel would also extend beyond his new limits and found colonies (Is 49[19. 20] 54[3], Dt 28[1] and 32[7-9]). One of the tribes, Manasseh, was to become an independent nation (Gn 48[19]). From this tribe, we are told, the United States was derived. Reference is found to the lion and the unicorn in Nu 24[8. 9], and to the American eagle in Ezk 17[3]. The promise that Israel shall possess the gates of her enemies (Gn 22[17] 24[60]) is fulfilled in the case of Britain by the possession of Gibraltar, Aden, Singapore, etc.

LITERATURE.—The literature on the subject is enormous. The many works of Brothers and Hine are hardly readable. The most coherent account is to be found in John Wilson's *Our Israelitish Origin*[3] (1845). Other works explaining the theory, in addition to those already mentioned, are H. W. J. Senior's *British Israelites* and *The Ten Tribes* (1885); T. R. Howlett's *Anglo-Israel and the Jewish Problem* (1892); J. M. Williams' *The Sakai, Our Ancestors* (1882); H. H. Pain's *Englishmen Israelites* (1896); Oxonian's *Israel's Wanderings* (1881); H. A. Smith's *The Ten Tribes* (1887); C. A. L. Totten's *Our Race* (1896)[f]; and H. W. Poole's *Anglo-Israel* (1889). Other books that should be consulted are: C. Piazzi Smyth's *Our Inheritance in the Great Pyramid* (1864); R. Gorell's *English derived from Hebrew*, and *Identity of the Religions called Druidical and Hebrew* (London, 1829); F. C. Danvers' *Israel Redivivus* (1905). Cf. also Jacobs in *JE* i. 600 f. A very large number of books and pamphlets on the subject is published by Banks, Racquet Court, Fleet Street, London, E.C.

ALBERT M. HYAMSON.

ANGRA MAINYU.—See AHRIMAN.

AṄGUTTARA NIKĀYA.—The fourth of the five *Nikāyas*, or collections, which constitute the *Sutta Piṭaka*, the Basket of the tradition as to doctrine, the second of the three *Piṭakas* in the canon of the early Buddhists. The standing calculation in Buddhist books on the subject is that it consists of 9557 *suttas* or short passages.* Modern computations would be different. This large number is arrived at by counting as three separate *suttas* such a statement as: 'Earnestness, industry, and intellectual effort are necessary to progress in good things,' and so on. Thus in the first chapter, section 14, occurs the sentence: 'The following is the chief, brethren, of the brethren my disciples, in seniority, to wit, *Aññā Kondañña*.' The sentence is then repeated eighty times, giving the pre-eminence, in different ways, of eighty of the early followers of the Buddha, who were either brethren or sisters in the Order, or laymen or laywomen. In each case the necessary alterations in the main sentence are made. We should call it one *sutta*, giving a list of eighty persons preeminent, in one way or another, among the early disciples. According to the native method of repeating by rote, and therefore also of computation, it is eighty *suttas*. Making allowance for this, there are between two and three thousand *suttas*.† The work has been published in full by the Pāli Text Society, vols. i. and ii. edited by Morris, and vols. iii., iv., and v. by E. Hardy (London, 1885–1900).

The *suttas* vary in length from one line to three or four pages, the majority of them being very short; and in them all those points of Buddhist doctrine capable of being expressed in classes are set out in order. This practically includes most of the psychology and ethics of Buddhism, and the details of its system of self-training. For it is a distinguishing mark of the Dialogues themselves, which form the first two of the *Nikāyas*, to arrange the results arrived at in carefully systematized groups. We are familiar enough in the West with similar groups, summed up in such phrases as the Seven Deadly Sins, the Ten Commandments, the Thirty-nine Articles, the Twelve Apostles, the Four Cardinal Virtues, the Seven Sacraments, and a host of others. These numbered lists are, it is true, going out of fashion. The aid which they afford to memory is no longer required in an age in which books of reference abound. It was precisely as a help to memory that they were found so useful in the early Buddhist days, when the books were all learnt by heart and had never yet been written. And in the *Aṅguttara* we find set out in order first all the units, then all the pairs, then all the trios, and so on up to the eleven qualities necessary to reach Nirvāṇa, the eleven mental habits the culture of which leads to the best life, or the eleven conditions precedent to a knowledge of human passion.

The form, therefore, is conditioned by the necessities of the time. The matter also is influenced, to a large degree, by the same necessities. In a work that had to be learnt by heart it was not possible to have any reasoned argument, such as we should expect in a modern ethical treatise. The lists are curtly given, and sometimes curtly explained. But the explanations were mostly reserved for the oral comment of the teacher, and were handed down also by tradition. That traditional explanation has been preserved for us in the *Manoratha Pūraṇī* ('wish-fulfiller'), written down, in Pāli, by Buddhaghoṣa in the 5th cent. A.D. This has not yet been published.

The original book—for we must call it a book, though it is not a book in the modern sense of the word—was composed in North India by the early Buddhists shortly after the Buddha's death. How soon after we do not know. And the question of its age can be adequately discussed only in connexion with that of the age of the rest of the canonical works, which will be dealt with together in the art. LITERATURE (Buddhist).

LITERATURE.—An analysis of the contents of each *sutta*, in English, has been given by Edmund Hardy in vol. v. of his edition, pp. 371–416. A few *suttas* have been translated into English by H. C. Warren, *Buddhism in Translations*, Cambridge, Mass. 1896; and into German by K. E. Neumann, *Buddhistische Anthologie*, Leyden, 1882.

T. W. RHYS DAVIDS.

ANIMALS.

[NORTHCOTE W. THOMAS.]

Introduction.—It is a well-established fact that the complexity of the mental processes of animals is apt to be exaggerated even by professional psychologists, and this, though civilization, or perhaps rather education, has brought with it a sense of the great gulf that exists between man and the lower animals, not excluding those to which exceptional intelligence is, rightly or wrongly, attributed, such as the elephant and the anthropoid ape. In the lower stages of culture, whether they be found in races which are, as a whole, below the European level, or in the uncultured portion of civilized communities, the distinction between men and animals is not adequately, if at all, recognized, and more than one cause has contributed to this state of things. Just as we overestimate the complexity of the mental processes of animals, the savage, though for a different reason, attributes to the animal a vastly more complex set of thoughts and feelings, and a much greater range of knowledge and power, than it actually possesses. We are accustomed to show respect to the lifeless corpse of a human

* See *Aṅguttara*, v. 361; *Sumaṅgala Vilāsinī*, ed. Rhys Davids and Carpenter, London, 1886, p. 23; and *Gandha Vaṁsa*, p. 56.

† Professor Edmund Hardy (*Aṅguttara*, Part 5, vi.) makes the number 'about 2344.'

being; the savage, in his treatment of the game which has fallen a victim to the prowess of the hunter, shows evidence of a similar state of mind; he attributes to the soul of the slain beast an anxiety as to, and a knowledge of, the good or bad treatment of its mortal remains. When the animal is still alive, he regards it as open to argument; he will reproach the crocodile with having slain those who have done it no harm, and point out that the crocodiles, having been the aggressors, have only themselves to thank when man takes the offensive and exacts vengeance for his lost relatives and friends. He attributes to animals the power of speech, a power which in the case of the monkey is said to be put to no use, owing to the animal's fear that he might be made to work if he once began to talk. Both in fables and folk-tales, animals are represented as carrying on conversations and as being moved by the same motives as the human beings who narrate the stories (MacCulloch, *Childhood of Fiction*, pp. 38–41, 247–278); so much so, in fact, that in Africa the arguments in a judicial process not uncommonly turn on the question of what the crocodile said to the hen—in which form the negro embodies his precedents and leading cases. Even in Europe it is not hard to find traces of this primitive attitude of mind; there is a well-known custom of telling the bees when the master of the house dies; and few beliefs are more firmly rooted in the minds of country people than that neglect of this precaution will offend the insects, and deprive the new master or mistress of their labours. So, too, a knowledge of the moral character of those about them is attributed to the bees, with a corresponding influence on their activity. There is therefore no line of demarcation between man and beast, so that the North American Micmacs say: 'In the beginning of things, men were as animals and animals as men' (Leland, *Algonquin Legends*, p. 31). To the uncultured the difference is in the form, not in the nature, of things. The Indians of Guiana do not see any sharp line of distinction between man and other animals, between one kind of animal and another, or even between animals—man included—and inanimate objects. On the contrary, to the Indian all objects, animate and inanimate, seem exactly of the same nature, except that they differ in the accident of bodily form. Every object in the whole world is a being consisting of body and spirit, and differs from every other object in no respect save that of bodily form, and in the greater or less degree of brute cunning and brute power, consequent on the difference of bodily form and bodily habits (Im Thurn, *Among the Indians of Guiana*, p. 350).

But this doctrine of the essential similarity of all things, in spite of differences of form, does not embody the whole of the savage's creed. Perhaps still more essential is his belief in the impermanence of form. We find this exemplified even in Europe; few tales are more common than those of the transformation of an old witch into a cat or a hare. But magical powers are by no means essential to this change of form. To take only one example. There is a wide-spread belief that certain migratory birds, and especially the stork, assume human form in other lands; and no sense of incongruity is felt when the story is told of a traveller in foreign lands, being one day approached by an unknown man who displays great familiarity with his family affairs, inquires after the health of his children, and takes a general interest in what is going on in the distant Fatherland. The traveller's astonishment is allayed only when he learns that the stranger obtained his knowledge on the spot. His request for an explanation is met by the simple reply that the stranger is the stork who nests on the good man's roof. All the world over we find the same belief in the power of men, animals, plants, and even inanimate objects, to assume another form at will (cf. MacCulloch, pp. 149–187). It is therefore no wonder if the savage attitude towards nature is widely different from our own.

These transformations can take place during life. Of a slightly different nature, but almost equally important for the comprehension of the beliefs and customs of the uncultured, is the idea that death simply means the assumption of another form quite as material as the former. One of the great sources of the respect paid to animals is the belief that certain species are the embodiments of the souls of the dead, or even the very souls of the dead (for the view varies), and that these souls must receive respect, not only because they are ancestors or relatives, but also because their anger would mean the anger of the species of animals which their souls inhabit. Thus a kind of alliance springs up between certain human kins and certain species of animals, in which some writers have sought the germ of totemism. Less important, because more temporary, is the alliance sought at the initiation ceremony; here an individual provides himself with a tutelary genius, sometimes conceived as a spirit, sometimes as a living animal, on whose aid he relies in the battle of life.

Again, to the superior knowledge of animals, to their magical powers, or sometimes, and as a later development, to their position as messengers of a deity, are to be attributed the wide-spread augural beliefs and practices. To sum up, the savage has a very real sense of his kinship with animals; they are not merely his brothers, but his elder brothers; to them he looks for help and guidance. Not only so, but on them he depends for a great part of his subsistence—a fact which is far more vividly brought home to him than to the meat-eating human being of civilized societies, and in like manner he is far more liable than more cultured peoples to meet his death beneath the claws of a lion or a bear, or to succumb to the venom of the serpent. It is therefore small wonder that his attitude towards the animal creation is one of reverence rather than superiority.

1. *AGRICULTURE.*—The researches of Mannhardt have shown that the European peasant of to-day conceives that the life of the corn exists in the shape of an animal or human being apart from the corn itself. The animal **corn-spirit** is believed to take various forms,—pig, horse, dog, cat, goat, cow, etc.,—and is often conceived to lie in the last ears to be cut, the reaping of which is termed in some parts 'cutting the neck.' The corn-spirit is found not only in the harvest field, but also in the barn and the threshing-floor; the corn-spirit is killed in beating out the last grains from the ears. As a rite of sacralization of the eater, or of desacralization of the corn, the animal incarnation of the corn-spirit is eaten in a ritual meal at the harvest supper, at seedtime, or at other periods; the bones or parts of the flesh of this ritual food are used in magic to promote the fertility of the new crop. Sometimes the actual animal is not itself eaten; in its place we find the cake in animal form; but we cannot assume that this cake has taken the place of a former sacrifice of the animal, for it is made of the corn; the eating of the corn in the form of the animal is as effective a sacrament as the eating of the animal itself.

In Greece and other parts of the ancient world we find traces of the conception of the corn-spirit as an animal. Demeter was closely related to the pig, and was actually represented at Phigalia in the form of a horse, while her priests were called horses. In the case of Attis and other *prima facie* corn-deities a similar connexion with animals can be traced. Among the American Indians the corn-spirit is occasionally conceived in animal form (bison, deer, goat; see below). In other parts of the world an anthropomorphic or simply animistic conception is the rule.

Various theories have been advanced to account for the animal form of the corn-spirit. Frazer (*Golden Bough*², ii. 289) suggests that the animals which are driven into the last corn in the process of reaping may have suggested the idea. Marillier (*RHR* xxxvii. 381) holds, with more probability, that the animal form of the soul and of spirits generally was so familiar a conception that it was sufficient to suggest that the life of the corn must be in the form of an animal. Preuss explains some cases of the connexion of animals with corn or other vegetables, as their tutelary deities, on the ground that they were originally held to influence the supply of heat (*Am. Anth.*, N.S. iv. 40; *19th Ann. Rep. Bur. Ethn.* p. 308, etc.), from which, like other magical animals (*Globus*, lxxxvi. 116; *Arch. Anth.*, N.S. i. 142 f.), they become tutelary deities. Possibly, too, the belief in soul-animals (see p. 493ᵇ) may have had some influence; it is not uncommon to make offerings to ancestors in connexion with agriculture; these ancestors are sometimes conceived in the form of animals; it is therefore no long step to the concept of a corn-spirit in animal form. In Indo-China the ancestor is actually believed to guard the fields in the form of a toad at seedtime (*Miss. Cath.* 1894, p. 143). In Yucatan, spirits in the form of lynxes were believed to protect the cornfields (Brinton, *Essays*, p. 172). In central Java the wer-tiger is held to guard the plantations against wild pigs (*Tijdschr.* xli. 570).

Vegetation spirits generally are conceived in Europe to be in animal form; but in other parts of the world this idea is seldom found.

2. *ART (DECORATIVE).*—It is an almost universal custom to decorate weapons, pottery, clothing, etc., with designs, often so highly conventionalized as to be recognizable only on comparison with less stylicized forms. One of the main sources of decorative design is the animal world, and the object was, it may be assumed, magical in the first instance. In its later forms there is a combination of purposes, but this is usually where the animal has come to be associated with a god. In this case the use of the animal as an art *motif* is a form of worship; at the same time, if the animal is the emblem, for example, of rain, its use is equivalent to a prayer for rain. There are, however, innumerable instances of the use of animals in art, both in connexion with totemism and otherwise, for magical or non-theistic purposes. The totem posts of the Haidas have all sorts of decorative animal carvings, sometimes of genealogical significance; in New Guinea the totem is delineated on drums and pipes. The lizard (see below) is largely used in Africa and the Pacific, and the frigate bird in Melanesia. In Central Australia the sand is covered with delineations of animals; animals are figured at Australian and South African initiation ceremonies; and many Australian decorative designs are totemic, or at least animal *motifs*. Probably the skin markings (see 'Tatu' below) of the Australian and other peoples are largely conventionalized forms of similar motives. Where a religious significance has once attached to a design, the art *motif* may continue to be largely used merely for magical purposes and finally for luck. In Europe we are familiar with the use of animals in heraldry. See articles on ART.

3. *COLOUR.*—The colour of animals is highly important, both in magic (wh. see) and otherwise. In Europe the king of the snakes is said to be white. White horses (see below) were especially sacred. In Indo-China the cult of the white elephant is well known. In Japan white animals have a high importance (*Globus*, lxii. 272), and good fortune for the reigning house is inferred from their appearance. The daughter of a man who feeds 1000 white hares in his house will marry a prince. In Patagonia white cassowaries are sacrosanct; the Patagonians believe that the species would die out if they were to kill such white specimens; white horses and cows enjoy an equal respect (*ib.* lxi. 63). The white animal is often preferred as a victim. The Woguls offer a white horse in autumn; the officiants dance round it and stab it with their knives till it falls dead (*ib.* liv. 332). So, too, the Tcheremiss offer white animals (Erman, *Archiv*, i. 415). Among the Shans of Annam a white buffalo is sacrificed annually (*Miss. Cath.* 1896, 59), and the Battas also select white victims (Marsden, *Sumatra*, p. 385). In August or September the Situa festival was held in Peru; the priests received for sacrifice one of the holy white llamas, which were never shorn (*Ausland*, lxiv. 951). See also 'Bear,' etc., below.

For special purposes distinctive colours must be used. Thus the rain-cloud is black; in a sacrifice for rain, therefore, the victim must be in imitation of it. The Wambugwes of East Africa offer a black sheep and a black calf when they want rain; the Garos of Assam offer a black goat on the top of a very high mountain in time of drought; in Sumatra a black cat is thrown into a river and allowed to escape after swimming about for a time; the ancient Hindus set a black horse with its face to the west and rubbed it with a cloth till it neighed (*Golden Bough*², i. 101–2); and in the same way white animals must be sacrificed for sunshine (*ib.* p. 103). For an agricultural sacrifice at Rome red-haired puppies were chosen, in imitation of the colour of ripe corn (*ib.* ii. 311). In the same way in Egypt red-haired oxen were the chosen victims (*ib.* p. 142). The Iroquois sacrifice of the white dog (see below) may perhaps be set down as another example; for although white is not everywhere the emblem of purity, it is natural to connect with this idea the selection of a white dog for a piacular sacrifice.

4. *CREATOR.*—It is by no means self-evident to the savage mind that the functions of the Creator of the universe or of some part of it are necessarily united with those of its sustainer, or of a moral ruler of mankind, or even of a god. Hence, though we find cases in which the Creator is an object of worship, or at any rate respect (see 'Crow' below), we also find a share in creation assigned to animals which are not even specially sacred.

The Gros Ventre account of the origin of the world is that the world was once all water, inhabited only by a swan, which in some unaccountable way produced a crow, a wolf, and a water-hen. One day the crow proposed to the wolf to send down the water-hen to look for earth, for they would be so much happier if they had a little ground under their feet. The earth was brought, and while the wolf sang and performed on a rattle, the crow sprinkled the earth about on the waters and formed the globe as we have it to-day. Subsequently man was created, and the crow turned herself into an Indian (Coues, *Henry and Thompson, MS Jls.* p. 351). According to the Guaycurus of South America, they were called into existence after all the other nations by a decree of the caracara bird, but they show it no special respect (*Patriota*, 1814, p. 26). In some cases chance seems to have caused an animal to figure as Creator; in S. Australia the islands were said to have resulted from a blow of a great serpent's tail, but Noorele created other things (Eyre, *Expeditions*, ii. 356).

5. *CULT.*—Anthropological data are supplied in many cases by the chance remarks of a traveller, who, if he understands the true nature of the phenomena he is describing, does not always appreciate their importance, and consequently leaves us in the dark on points which are indispensable to the correct understanding of his information. This is especially the case when the information relates to the worship or supposed worship of animals; not only are the sources of such a cult extremely various, but it may be possible for actions which spring from purely utilitarian motives to wear the appearances which elsewhere characterize the ritual of an animal cult. We find, for example, that in ancient Egypt it was the practice to feed the sacred crocodiles, which were associated with the god Souchos (Sebek); in modern days we have a similar practice recorded in West Africa; but in the absence of information from those who give them food we can hardly inter-

pret the custom without fear of error. Prudence is a faculty commonly denied to the peoples in lower stages of culture; but it may well have happened that accident, if not reflexion, suggested to some one that a hungry crocodile is a far more dangerous neighbour than one which is in no need of food. We cannot, therefore, explain the modern custom, without more ado, as crocodile-worship; the possibility of the utilitarian explanation must also be kept in mind. Quite apart from this, there is a difficulty in the interpretation of the data which arises from the indefinite nature of many of the observances. Savage ritual is well-established, but the savage creed is often vague and fluctuating. At any rate, in the hands of European questioners, it is not uncommon for one native to assert one thing while another will maintain exactly the reverse; or one and the same man will put forward contradictory propositions either after an interval of time or even during a single interview. Where the ritual is unmistakably religious or magical, we can dispense with the commentary of the officiating priest or magician; but where there is room for doubt we can ill afford to do without this guidance, even though we know that the explanation given is not necessarily the original one.

The terms 'worship' and 'cult' are used, especially in dealing with animal superstitions, with extreme vagueness; and, moreover, the interpretation of the facts to which they are applied is in itself uncertain. At one end of the scale we find the real divine animal, commonly conceived as a 'god-body,' *i.e.* the temporary incarnation of a superior being, with a circle of worshippers. At the other end, separated from the real cult by imperceptible transitions, we find such practices as respect for the bones of slain animals, or the use of a respectful name for the living animal. The question is one with the general problem of the definition of religion; it cannot profitably be discussed in connexion with a single species of cult, and it is the less necessary to do so here, as we are concerned only with general principles and broad outlines.

Animal cults may be classified on two principles: (*a*) according to their outward form; (*b*) according to their genesis. The first kind of classification is important chiefly for the comprehension of the principles which underlie the evolution of animal worship into anthropomorphic cults; the second is primarily concerned with an earlier stage—that of the actual beginnings, it may be, of the religious sentiment or its manifestation.

(*a*) *Formal Classification.*—Animal cults may be broadly divided into two classes: (i.) the whole species without exception is sacred; (ii.) one or a fixed number of a species is sacred. In a certain number of cases the second class may be indistinguishable from the first; this is the case in the Bornean cult of the hawk; there were only thirty-three real omen birds among the Ibans of Borneo in olden days, but they were indistinguishable from their fellows.

Although it is by no means axiomatic that the cult of the species has in every case preceded the cult of the individual animal, it seems probable that we may regard this as the normal course of evolution. The transition may be effected in more than one way. (1) As in the case of the hawk (see below) among the Bornean peoples, *a simple progress from theriomorphic to anthropomorphic ideas* may suffice to explain the change. There is no reason to doubt that such a process may take place both without foreign influence and without any internal impulse due to the rise of sun-, moon-, or other cults of single deities, which would naturally tend to produce a species of syncretism in previously existing multiple cults. Among more than one Australian tribe, for example, the eagle-hawk seems to have been transformed into an anthropomorphic deity; but there is no reason to suspect either foreign influence or assimilation to other native cults, for the latter are admittedly non-existent. So, too, in Central Australia the Wollunqua totem animal is a mythical serpent; the totemic ceremonies are performed to keep him in a good humour, and not, as is the case with the other totems of the same tribe, to promote their increase; but when we reach acts intended to propitiate a single animal, mythical or otherwise, we are on the verge of worship, if indeed the boundary between totemism and animal cults proper has not long been overpassed. At the same time, not only may the rise of individual cults, such as those of the heavenly bodies, exert a deep influence on the multiple cults, but a specialization of function may, where multiple cults alone are present, aid to bring about the same result. The chief purpose for which the Bornean peoples require omens is to get directions for the conduct of their head-hunting expeditions; in other words, the conditions themselves made for the specialization of a war-god, either multiple or unified. Intertribal war tends to increase, if it does not call into existence, the power of the chief; from the human leadership on the war-path to the predominance of one individual among the omen birds is not a long step; and we actually find evidence that it was taken by the Ibans, while the Kayans have gone far in the same direction. Evidence of similar tendencies can readily be produced from many other areas; the Amerinds had, in the very early days of the Jesuit missions, already attained the conception of an 'Elder Brother' of each species, marvellously great and powerful (*Rel. des Jés.* 1634, p. 13). In California the Acagchemens worshipped the *panes* bird; each village sacrificed a different bird, and the sacrifice was annual; but the view which the worshippers took was that only one bird was sacrificed, each year the same, and the same in each village. In Samoa the process had not gone quite so far; the gods of the villages were incarnate in animals; each god was incarnate in all the animals of the species; consequently although respect was shown to the individual dead animal, the life of the god was in no way affected by its decease; he continued to survive in the remainder of the species (Turner, *Polynesia*, p. 242). Other examples will be found in Tylor (*Prim. Cult.*[3] ii. 243 ff.).

(2) The process of unification, as in the case of the Acagchemens, where mystical ideas have also played their part, may be hastened by *a custom of sacrificing the sacred animal annually.* The doctrines of reincarnation and identity of the sacrificial animal would undoubtedly be highly important for the history of this case of evolution, if it were not probable that they were later developments, if not actually due to the influence of European ideas. For an example of a stage in cult where the importance of sacrifice pure and simple is manifest we may turn to the Woguls. Once in each year they go in crowds into the woods and kill one of each species of animals, preferring the horse and the tiger as best; they flay off their skins, hang up the carcases on a tree, and in their way pray to them, falling prostrate on the earth; after which they eat the flesh together (Ides, *Three Years' Travels*, p. 7). In this example we are not, it is true, told what is done with the skins. But another traveller tells us (Strauss, *Reise*, pp. 93, 119) that the Crim Tatars and others hang the skin of the sacrificial animal on a pole and worship it. We find that the Egyptians clothed the image of Ammon in the

fleece of the ram which was sacrificed to him once a year. Intermediate stages are given by the Californian custom of preserving the *panes* skin and using it as the *tobet*, or cloak, of Chinigchinnich; and by the Floridian sacrifice of the goat (see below), whose skin was preserved for a year, until its place was taken by that of the next victim.

(3) In the folk-lore of modern Europe the corn-spirit is conceived to bear sometimes human, sometimes animal form; but in neither case has anything like unification made its way into the minds of the peasants who are the repositories of these primitive ideas. In Greece and Rome, on the other hand, we find the corn-spirit, as recorded in literature, no longer an undifferentiated, multiple divinity, who resides equally in every field and on every farm. A process of synthesis has unified the anonymous rustic animal and human gods, though in Greece we can still trace their features in survivals. How far this unification corresponded to anything in the nature of anthropomorphization and unification in the minds of the peasants whose gods they originally were, we do not know; but it may be suspected that the process did not go far. It may, of course, be true that the corn-spirit in modern Europe is but a degenerate descendant of Wodan, Ceridwen, Demeter, or whatever the name of the corn-deity was; but this explanation leaves us without a hint of how the former god came to be conceived as an animal. However this may be, it seems clear that the passage from multiplicity to unity may have come about by a process which implies a certain amount of philosophizing. Just as in Egypt there was a tendency to identify all the gods with Ra, so in Greece, in a minor degree, went on the process of identifying the local corn-gods with more central and systematized cults. The natural tendency was for the cult of a deity to spread beyond its original area and to swallow up less important or nameless objects of worship, and this went on in the case of animal no less than of other cults. At the same time, we must not overestimate the importance of the movement, which may have penetrated but slightly the lower strata of the population. It may be noted in passing that it is possible to have two distinct kinds of syncretism: (α) where one deity swallows up his fellows, all being of the same species, which probably occurred in the case of Demeter, complicated, however, by the fact that the horse as well as the pig was associated with her, thus leading to a double movement of synthesis—the unification of many local homogeneous corn-spirits, plus the unification of the different species of animals, the heterogeneous corn-spirits — from which we get Demeter as she is presented to us by classical authors; and (β) where there is no underlying unity of function. If the cult of Apollo Smintheus developed from an older cult of the mouse, we can indeed explain why the mouse-god should also be the sun-god, by saying that the mice devastate the fields under cover of darkness, and that the sun-god is the natural protector of the farmer against the plague of mice. But though we can explain syncretic movements on semi-rational lines in this case, it by no means follows that we have given the real explanation; and it would be far from easy to hit upon similarly obvious explanations of other syncretic processes.

(4) Side by side with the immolation of the victim, and sometimes supplementing the annual sacrifice as a cause of the sanctity of a special animal, may be placed *the custom of selecting an animal for special honour*. We find two types of this practice. The first, among pastoral peoples, consists in consecrating an animal which is thenceforth inviolate. Perhaps we may see in a custom of this sort the source of the Egyptian cult of the bull, which later came to be regarded as a 'god-body,' and was recognized by special marks. In the second type, the animal, so far from remaining inviolate, is sacrificed at the end of the year or after a certain period of time; but, unlike the cases referred to in a previous section, its sanctity terminates with its death, and its place is taken by another living animal. This form of worship may perhaps be due in the first instance to the commonly felt wish to apologize and do honour to the animal about to be slain, in order that its comrades, honoured in its person, may show no disinclination to fall victims to the hunter's dart.

(*b*) *Genetic Classification.* — In dealing with animal cults from *the genetic point of view*, it must not be forgotten that, while changes in ritual are at most but gradual, the explanations which are given of the acts are liable to change in a much greater degree. Foreign influences apart, development in creeds is often a slow process; but it may be taken as axiomatic, at any rate for the lower stages of culture, that belief changes far more rapidly than ritual. If, therefore, we find that at the present day a species of animals is held in reverence, it by no means follows that the explanation is the one which would have been given in pre-European days; yet even this more primitive interpretation may not throw any light on the real origin of the cult. The ætiological myth is particularly characteristic of savages, and the ætiological myth is not history but guesswork. To take a concrete example, the Barotse explain the fact that they have the baboon as their totem by a myth which involves the supposition, if it is to be regarded as real history, that they developed totemism after their passage from savagery to barbarism, marked by their acquisition of cultivated plants (*Folklore*, xv. 110). Not only is this highly improbable in itself, but the myth throws no light on the genesis of totemism in other parts of the world or among other South African kins, if indeed it be totemism with which we are confronted among the southern Bantus. Again, the southern Bantus as a whole explain their respect for the totem (?) animal, or *siboko*, by the story that the souls of their ancestors go to reside after death in the species which they respect. It does not follow that this is an original trait of their creed. True totemism seems to exist among other Bantu tribes, uncontaminated by any eschatological theories. It is by no means impossible that with the southern Bantus true totemism existed in the first instance; with the development of ancestor-worship, possibly a result of the change from female to male descent, there would be a tendency to bring other cults into relation with the predominant form of worship. The belief, but rarely found in other parts of the world, of transmigration into the totem animal may have taken the place of the belief in transmigration pure and simple, which is found in Australia without any connexion with totemism (*Man*, 1905, No. 28).

Again, the cults of pastoral tribes are commonly explained on the ground that they do honour to the species on which they depend for their subsistence. That may be so at the present day; but there is no proof that the cult of the animal in question does not date back to the days before it was domesticated or when it was only in process of domestication, which obviously must have been for reasons unconnected with its future usefulness. If, as is not impossible, the cult of the animal led to its domestication, the modern explanation is obviously late, and we can only guess at the causes which made the animal an object of worship in the first place.

Animal cults may be conveniently classified under ten specific heads, with another class for nondescript forms of unknown origin or meaning: (1) pastoral cults; (2) hunting cults; (3) cults of dangerous or noxious animals; (4) cults of animals conceived as human souls or their embodiment; (5) totemistic cults; (6) cults of secret societies, individual cults of tutelary animals; (7) tree and vegetation cults; (8) cults of ominous animals; (9) cults, probably derivative, of animals associated with certain deities; (10) cults of animals used in magic. Broadly speaking, it may be said that in the cases of (1), (2), and perhaps (7), the motive is mainly the material benefits which the animal confers on its worshippers; (3) and to some extent (5) and (10) are connected with fear of the consequences of refusing respect; (6) and (8) are connected with the assistance derived from the animal; and (9) with the fear of the wrath of a god; while (4) seems to be compounded of fear of the wrath of ancestors and desire for their help.

(1) The characteristics of the *pastoral* type are that a domestic animal, (*a*) is spared as a species, or (*b*) receives special honour in the person of an individual animal. (*a*) As an example of the first sub-type may be taken the Hindu respect for cattle, and, as a modified form, the attitude of the South African Bantus towards their herds. The latter are losing their respect for cattle; but whereas in pre-European days the sacrifice of cattle was permitted to the Hindu, at the present day he is absolutely forbidden to kill an animal of the species, though the prohibition is certainly of late development. (*b*) As an example of the second sub-type may be taken the Toda cult of the buffalo (see below), the Madi cult of the sheep (see below), and perhaps the West Asiatic cult of the camel (unless we should regard the rite described by Nilus in *PL* lxxi. as astral in its nature), since they fairly represent the class of pastoral cults in which honour is done to the species by sacrificing one of its members with special ceremony. In another class of pastoral cult the honour is done to the species by selecting one animal as its representative and letting it go free. As an example of this type may be taken the Kalmuk custom of setting free a ram lamb. But it may be noted that even here it is the practice to sacrifice the sacred animal eventually. This is only, however, when it is growing old, and Frazer explains it, like many other customs of a similar kind, as due to a wish that the god or divine animal may not grow old and thus lose, with the decay of his powers, the strength needed for the fulfilment of his functions.

(2) In *hunting* cults, on the other hand, the species which receives honour is habitually killed, and, in order to atone for the loss of individual members, (*a*) the species is considered to be represented by a single individual, which is itself finally killed, but not until it has, like the bear (see below) among the Ainus, received divine honours, and (*b*) each individual of the species at its death by the hand of the hunter is propitiated and receives offerings, or whatever treatment is conceived to be proper to make its feelings predominantly those of satisfaction, in order that its surviving fellows may show no unwillingness to present themselves in their turn. As examples of this sub-type may be taken the buffalo, and the bear (see below) among some peoples (cf. *Golden Bough*[2], ii. 404 ff.), and, in fact, most animals on which hunting or fishing tribes largely depend. In some cases the propitiation does not go farther than forbidding misuse of the bones of the dead animals, such as giving them to dogs, breaking them, etc., which may be a purely practical measure based on savage ideas of reproduction, rather than cult properly so called.

(3) The cult of *dangerous* animals is generally characterized by tabus before, during, and after the hunt, and by ceremonies intended to propitiate the slain animal. They are mainly practised in Africa and South Asia; as examples may be taken the cult of the leopard, lion, and tiger (see below). The dangers to be avoided are twofold: in the first place, the soul of the slain beast may take vengeance on the hunter, who therefore submits to the same tabus as are imposed on him during a season of mourning, with the idea of either deceiving or keeping at a distance the malevolent ghost; in the second place, as in the previous sections, the remainder of the species has to be kept in good humour or prevented from learning of the death of their comrade. To this end, in Sumatra, a magician is employed when a crocodile is to be hunted, and elaborate explanations are frequently given that the animal is to be or has been killed because it attacked a human being and thus broke the truce normally subsisting between man and the species. In Japan, a man who kills a snake should crush its head, or more will come; this seems to be intended as a means of preventing it from calling its fellows to avenge its death. Again, after hunting the leopard, it is the custom for the hunter to imitate the voice or the habits of the leopard; if this is not intended to deceive the spirit of the slain animal, it may be intended as a propitiatory act to appease the remainder of the species. Vermin are propitiated in various ways, and many of the practices are applied to mice (see below). In the Baltic island of Oesel an offering is made to a weevil, and they think less damage will then be done to the corn. In the island of Nias in the Dutch East Indies the ant is very destructive; at harvest time it is propitiated by being called Sibaia—the name of a good spirit which is supposed to protect the crop from harm. With the position of this spirit may be compared that of Apollo Smintheus (see 'Mouse' below), Dionysus Bassareus (see 'Fox' below), Baalzebub, and other deities whose names are associated with vermin. It is open to question how far we are justified in assuming that any cult of vermin is implied which has subsequently developed into the cult of a god or been united with it by a process of syncretism. In Central India the Waralis worship a stone which they call the lord of tigers (see below; see also 'Horse'), but there is no reason to suppose that they believe the stone to have been a tiger or to contain the spirit of a tiger; nor is any cult of the living tiger recorded among them. It does not necessarily follow that Apollo Smintheus must have been a mouse, or that a mouse cult must have been amalgamated with an independent cult unconnected with mice.

(4) We come to an entirely different set of ideas, in the respect shown to animals because they are regarded as the *abode of the souls of the dead*, or sometimes as *the actual souls of the dead, and even of the living* (*Rev. de l'H. des Rel.* xxxvii. 385; *Golden Bough*[2], iii. 409 f., 430 ff.; van Gennep, *Tabou, pass.*; *Folklore*, xi. 235; von den Steinen, *Unter den Naturvölkern*, pp. 512, 353, etc.) Some of the Celebes tribes perform a periodical ceremony in honour of the crocodiles, on the ground that their departed relatives take that form; they take provisions and musical instruments in a boat and row up and down, playing on the instruments, till a crocodile appears; they offer food to it and hope thereby to recommend themselves to their kindred (Hawkesworth, iii. 759). More especially among the Bantu tribes of South Africa and the Malagasy is the belief found that the dead pass into certain animals, which among the Bechuanas differ for each clan. What is sometimes regarded as totemism, is at the present day a system of ancestor-worship (*Man*, 1901, No. 111). With the South African facts should be compared the Madagascar beliefs (v. Gennep, *Tabou, pass.*). In the Solomon

Islands it appears to be the custom for a dying man to inform his family into what species of animal he proposes to migrate (*JAI* xxviii. 147). The abode thus taken up in an animal is commonly regarded as permanent, the soul of the dead man passing into another of the same species, if his particular animal is killed (*Man*, 1904, No. 118), but occasionally the soul is believed to pass on after a time to its final abode (*Folklore*, xii. 342). The belief is occasionally found in Africa that a chief has put his soul for safe keeping into an animal, which is therefore respected (*Golden Bough*², iii. 407; *JAI* xx. 13; see below, 'Goat,' 'Cattle').

If we are entitled to assume that the *siboko*ism of the South African Bantus is totemism, or has replaced an earlier stage of pure totemism, the soul-animal occupies a specially important place in the history of savage religion. In any case, the worship or respect for the soul-animal has probably been the starting-point of other cults; thus the Zulu and Masai respect for the serpent may represent the beginnings of serpent-worship. The association of the dog with the Lar at Rome probably points to a time when the dog was regarded as a form of the soul; at the same time it should not be forgotten that the Lar was also a household god, and that the dog might with special appropriateness be associated with it; the dog was likewise associated with Hecate, also apparently a family goddess.

(5) One of the most widely distributed animal cults is that known as *totemism*; it is, however, rather negative, consisting in abstinence from injuring the totem animal, than positive, showing itself in acts of worship. There are, however, exceptions; the Wollunqua totem is a single mythical animal; the Warramunga ceremonies with regard to it are at the present day devoted entirely to placating it, an attitude which can hardly be distinguished from the propitiation of a god. Among certain Central Australian tribes the totem animal is required to be eaten on certain occasions, although this is to be regarded as an aberrant form of totemism (Lang, *JAI* xxxv. 315–336). In America, too, we hear of sacrifices to the totem (Loskiel, *History*, i. 40; Maclean, *Twenty-five Years*, p. 186), unless, indeed, totem is here used in the sense of individual totem, offerings to which are frequent (Frazer, *Totemism*, p. 54). Under this head may be noticed the cult of certain animals in Australia, which are associated with all the males or all the females of a given tribe. They are frequently termed 'sex totems,' but 'animal brothers' would be a more intelligible term. Their real meaning may be said to be unknown. How far totemism tends to evolve into other forms of cult is a disputed question, but it seems probable that the totem of the chief, where the office is hereditary, will come to be respected by the whole tribe (*Miss. Cath.* 1888, 262; cf. *Tour du Monde*, 1895, p. 100). The segregation of totem kins leads to certain districts holding certain animals sacred, and may open the way to higher cults.

(6) In the case of the totem kin, the association of a human being with a species of animals is hereditary, and no choice in the matter is permitted to him. Of a more voluntary nature are *secret societies*. Even here inheritance has much to do with the acquisition of membership in a society, especially in N.W. America. At the same time, initiation seems to play a considerable rôle in the case of the secret society; in the absence of initiation ceremonies a man remains outside the society, but this can hardly be the case with a totem kin, for women, too, belong to it, though their initiation ceremonies, if performed at all, do not seem, any more than those of the males, and probably much less, to bear any relation to the totem. The fundamental idea of many secret societies is the acquisition of a tutelary animal. In the same way the individual gains an animal genius by his initiation fast. Closely connected with these 'naguals,' as they may conveniently be termed, are the familiars of witches and the wer-wolves, or other animal forms of wer-men.

(7) More especially in Greek and Roman mythology we find a number of woodland deities, which are very clearly *spirits of the woods in animal or partly animal form*. Bearing in mind the possibility of syncretism, it may be recognized that even if Dionysus and other deities commonly associated with vegetation cults are sometimes conceived in animal form, this is no proof that they were so conceived *qua* vegetation spirits; but this objection applies in a much less degree to Pan, the Satyrs, and Silenuses, while in the case of the Fauns there is a general agreement that they are spirits of the woods (Mannhardt, *Ant. Wald- u. Feldkulte*, p. 113). We have a parallel to them in modern European folklore; Lêshi, the wood-spirit, is believed in Russia to appear partly in human shape, but with the horns, ears, and legs of a goat (Mannhardt, *Baumkultus*, p. 138).

The frequent conception of the corn-spirit as an animal, and particularly as a pig, makes it highly probable that Frazer is correct in arguing that Proserpine, Attis, and Adonis were originally conceived as pigs, or, at any rate, that their cult developed from that of a corn-spirit in pig form. In European folklore there is little that can be termed worship or cult in the attitude towards the animal under whose form the corn-spirit is believed to appear; few or no ceremonies are performed, save those whose object is to placate the spirit injured by the reaping of the crop and to ensure the proper growth of the new crops when they are sown in the spring. More definite acts of worship are recorded of the Pawnees on the Upper Missouri (see 'Bison' below), and of some of the tribes in Florida.

(8) *Omens* are drawn from the cries and actions of birds, mammals, etc., all the world over; but developments like the cult of the hawk (see below) in Sarawak are probably rare. If we may assume that the present-day conditions in the tribes referred to represent three stages in the evolution of a god, there is no doubt that from an omen-giving bird has been evolved a specialized anthropomorphic deity, especially associated with warlike operations.

(9) The question of *the association of certain animals with certain deities* is a very difficult one. On the one hand, it is certainly impossible to prove that all such animals were sacred before they became connected with the god; and equally impossible to show that the god has actually been crystallized out of one or more sacred animals. On the other hand, we cannot point to any clear case of respect for an animal paid to it wholly and solely because it is associated with a certain deity. If the jackal was respected in Egypt because it was associated with Anubis, it may be argued, on the one hand, that this association was due to the fact that the jackal was formerly regarded as a soul-animal; on the other hand, we may with apparently equal justice argue that the jackal was frequently seen about the tombs, and that this led to its being associated with the god of tombs. The question seems to be in most cases insoluble.

(10) It can hardly be said that there is any cult proper of animals used in *magic*. Among the southern Bantus, however, the crocodile (see below) is sacrosanct. The explanation of this is not far to seek: the crocodile is used for evil by magicians; to kill a crocodile, therefore, would be to incur the suspicion of being a magician and possibly the penalty of death. It is therefore easy to see how the association of an animal with evil magic can lead to its being respected (for the view that magical animals become gods, see Preuss's articles in *Globus*, vol. lxxxvii. *passim*).

(11) In a comparatively large number of cases we are unable to trace the origin of a cult of

animals. First and foremost the facts of serpent-worship—the most widely spread of animal cults—are far from having been explained. The serpent is, in many cases, associated with a cult of ancestors; this is readily comprehensible where the species is a harmless one; the very fact of its harmlessness would mark it out as different from its fellows; so, too, where the snake inhabits the house or its immediate neighbourhood, we have an adequate cause for its association with the worship of the dead; among the Zulus, for example, not every snake is an *idhlozi*, but only those which are found in the neighbourhood of the kraal. Some part of serpent-worship may be put down to their association with water; one of the commonest forms of water-monster is the serpent. The water-snake is specially honoured among the Xosa-Kafirs, in order that cases of drowning may not be frequent (Merensky, *Erinnerungen*, p. 38). But these facts are far from sufficient to explain the wide distribution of serpent-worship. On the other hand, its cult is much more than the cult of a dangerous animal, as is readily seen by comparing serpent-worship with the cult of the wolf or the crocodile, and it seems doubtful if the mysterious nature of the serpent, which is sometimes invoked as an explanation, is sufficiently important to account for the preference given to the reptile. Probably a multiple origin may be assigned to it.

The relations of animals and gods in Australian religion are by no means clear. Baiame seems in some eastern tribes to occupy the same position which the bell-bird holds in the mythology of the central tribes; his opponent, Mudgegong, is conceived under the form of an eagle-hawk, thus reproducing the familiar mythical conflict which in other parts of Australia is narrated of the eagle-hawk and the crow. Farther south the eagle-hawk, under the name of Mullion, again figures as an evil spirit. The name of the god of some Victorian tribes is Pundjel, and the same name is applied to the eagle-hawk; possibly, however, both receive it simply as a title of respect. However that may be, it seems clear that a certain amount of anthropomorphization has gone on in Australia. What is not clear is the position of the animals from which the anthropomorphic gods or evil spirits seem to have been evolved. Both eagle-hawk and crow are phratry names; but, while the crow (see below) is respected, possibly as a soul-animal, there are few traces of a similar respect for the eagle-hawk. Yet we cannot find that the crow has been anthropomorphized into a deity, and the deities and demons are connected with animals in areas where the phratry names, at least at the present day, have nothing to do with these animals. On the other hand, the eagle-hawk is a common form of the wizard (Spencer and Gillen, *Native Tribes of Central Australia*, p. 533).

Howitt has maintained that Koin and other spirits which the European observers have regarded as demons are really gods. If this be so, if the god of the Australian is no more than a magnified medicine-man, we have a sufficient explanation of the position of the eagle-hawk. Even if Howitt's theory is not generally applicable, the fact that the medicine-man of one tribe may be erected into a god by them, and into a demon by their neighbours who suffer from his machinations, gives a not improbable explanation of the facts. It does not, of course, follow that any one medicine-man has been deified; just as the Ibans have deified a generalized hawk (see below), the Australians may have apotheosized a generalized eagle-hawk-medicine-man.

In view of the position of the eagle-hawk as head of one of the phratries, it is of some importance that on the north-west coast of America we find among the Thlinkets two deities, Yehl and Khanukh, whose names mean 'raven' and 'wolf'; at the same time they are divided into two phratries, which are also named after the raven and the wolf. It is true that Tylor has denied (*JAI* xxviii. 144) that Khanukh ever appears in wolf form; Yehl, on the other hand, assumes the bird form in many of his adventures. This does not, however, seem fatal to the view that the presiding animals of the phratries have somehow been developed into deities or demi-gods, for Yehl is little more than a culture hero; at the same time this theory leaves unexplained the spread of the two cults into the opposite phratry. For neither in America nor in Australia is there any trace of uni-phratriac deities, as there should be on the supposition that the presiding animal has become a god. It should not be forgotten that in some of the central tribes of Australia there are traces of species deities (*R.G.S.Aust., S. Aust. Br.* ii. 80). It is true that animal form is not expressly attributed to them; on the other hand, emu feet are attributed to the chief god of the southern Aruntas (MS note). It may therefore be that the deification of the eagle-hawk is due neither to its importance in magic nor to its position as a phratry animal, though these facts may have had influence in bringing about its preferred position.

Even were it established that phratry animals have been promoted to godship, it by no means follows that this is equivalent to the erection of a totem into a god. That phratry animals have ever been totems is a pure hypothesis, and no consistent account has yet been given of the process by which they became more than totems.

Another animal god of unexplained origin, whose importance marks him out for notice, is the Great Hare of the Algonquins (Strachey, *Historie of Travaile*, p. 98; Lang, *Myth*², ii. 79; Brinton, *Myths*³, p. 193), who, in his human form of Michabou or Manibosho, was the culture-hero of this important family of Amerinds. Brinton, emphasizing the connexion of the Great Hare with the East, has, on etymological grounds, explained it as the dawn. Meteorological explanations have ceased to be convincing; moreover, according to one form of the myth, the rabbit (which is Brinton's translation of the latter half of *Michabou = Manibosho*) was not in the east but in the north (Brinton, p. 196). To speak of the cult of the Great Hare as animal-worship is, according to Brinton, to make it senseless, meaningless brute-worship; but this is to view it from the point of view of Europe in A.D. 1900 rather than in the light of other primitive cults. It may safely be said that no attempt to explain away animal-cults on these lines can be successful in more than very small measure. Brinton's preference for a dawn myth cannot therefore carry the day against the natural meaning of the Algonquin legends. Moreover, no adequate account has ever been given of the process by which men came, on the score of a simple etymological misunderstanding, to turn a god in human shape into an animal.

Less important is the Bushman god Ikaggen or Cagn (see 'Mantis' below), who, according to the latest account, was believed to manifest himself in the form of the mantis (*ikaggen*), or the caterpillar (*ngo*). From this duplex form we may perhaps assume that he had made some progress in the direction of anthropomorphization. The problem of how one god comes to manifest himself in several animals is a complicated one, when it is a phenomenon of the religion of savage or barbarous peoples, among whom the syncretic processes, the working of which in Greece or Egypt is fairly obvious, cannot be assumed to have played a large part, if indeed they played any at all. We see the same phenomenon in Samoa, where one village-god was believed to be incarnate in two or three kinds of animals. In the latter case it is perhaps to local causes, such as the aggregation of villages under one chief, or the coming together of more than one clan in a single village, that we must look for the explanation. But such an explanation can hardly be applied to the god of the Bushmen, who are on the very lowest nomadic plane of culture. The question is complicated by problems of Bushman origin and history; for if they were once a more settled folk, who suffered dispersal and disorganization when the Bantu stream overflowed South Africa, it may well be due to their disintegration that the hypothesis of syncretism, as an explanation of the cult of Cagn, seems inappropriate. Perhaps material for the solution of the problem may be found in the still unpublished mass of material relating to the Bushmen collected by Dr. Bleek and Miss Lloyd.

Prominent among animal gods is the Hindu monkey-deity, Hanuman, who figures largely in the Rāmāyana. It has been argued that his cult is not primitive, but has been borrowed from some wild tribe; and this conclusion is based on the fact that there are no traces of worship of the monkey in the Veda, save so far as Vrishākapi (Rigveda, x. 86) may be regarded as the object of such (cf. the conflicting views of Bergaigne, *Religion védique*, ii. 270–272; Oldenberg, *Religion des Veda*, 172–174; Geldner, *Vedische Studien*, ii. 22–42; and Hillebrandt, *Vedische Mythologie*, iii. 278). But this line of proof overlooks the fact that the Veda is concerned with official religion, and that Hanuman may have been worshipped unofficially without any record of the fact being available. At the same time it is by no means improbable that the cult is to some extent based on an aboriginal predecessor, for we can hardly suppose that the Aryan-speaking invaders brought it with them from regions where the monkey is less prominent, if not non-existent. Hanuman is distinctly a species god; but we cannot discover the origin of the cult. The resemblance of the monkey to man, which has been suggested as the origin, has not produced the same effect elsewhere, and seems inadequate to account for a cult, however satisfactory it may be as an explanation of a rich monkey mythology.

6. *DELUGE, EARTH-FINDING.*—In legends of a deluge, animals figure in two capacities. In the first place, they are simple messengers, like the raven in the Book of Genesis; the crow, hare, dog, pigeon, and other animals go out to see if the waters are abated or how large the new earth is, sometimes causing it to increase magically in size by making the circuit of it. In other cases the waters show no signs of abating, and the water birds or animals are made to dive, and bring up mud, sand, or earth; from this the new earth is formed and laid on the waters; it grows to the size of the present world. This form of the *terre pêchée* is especially common in America, where it also occurs as a cosmogonic myth. Among the Mordvins and in the Altai the incident figures in a Creation myth. Among the Yorubas a hen plays a somewhat similar part in producing the earth from beneath the waters. See DELUGE.

7. *DIVINATION.*—For the purpose of divination, the entrails, the liver, and frequently the shoulder-blade of dead animals are used. Animals also serve to give indications which are more properly classifiable under 'divination' than under 'omens.' Ashes were strewn on the floor in Peru, and from the character of the tracks found on them was inferred the kind of animal into which the soul of a dead person had passed. In Mexico snuff was spilt on the altar, and inferences were drawn from the footprints of eagles, etc. (Tschudi, *Reisen*, p. 337; Bancroft, iii. 438). In Australia the ground near a corpse is carefully smoothed; if a track is found on it, they infer from it the totem of the person who caused the death of the man. In other cases a watch is kept, and the movements of an insect or its flight decide the direction in which the malevolent magician resides. Another method of using animals in divination is to make dice or other instruments of their bones; knuckle bones are especially used for this purpose.

8. *DOMESTICATION.*—The problem of the history of the domestication of animals has seldom been attacked, and up to the present no satisfactory solution has been propounded; we are in complete uncertainty as to why or how man in the first instance came to tame animals, bring them up in captivity, and induce them to perpetuate their species. In the Pacific the frigate bird is often tamed. The Indians of South America frequently keep tame animals in their huts. But in neither of these cases can we properly speak of domestication. In the New World the domestic animals known before the advent of Europeans were few; the dog is, of course, nearly universal, but with this exception domestic animals were found only in Mexico and Peru, and then only the turkey, llama, alpaca, and perhaps one or two more, of which the llama and alpaca alone were economically important. In the Old World the main centre of domestication seems to have been Asiatic; but little, however, is known as to the localities in which the domesticated species first came under the dominion of man.

Probably the dog (see below) attached itself to man, but in other cases a process of domestication seems to be a necessary assumption. Totemism by itself seems inadequate, even when we make allowance for the additional leverage of the segregation of totem kins. Probably some form of cult (see 'Cattle' below) was in many cases the determining factor.

9. *EARTH-CARRIER.*—The problem of the stability of the earth has been solved, more especially by the people of Southern Asia and the Asiatic Islands, thanks in some degree to Hindu and Muhammadan influence, by the hypothesis that some great animal supports the world; the myth is also found in other areas, but only sporadically.

Among the Iroquois the world-turtle who received Aataentsic on his back, before the world was brought into existence, is clearly a mythical animal of this description; the Winnebagoes too, according to Knortz, made the earth rest on four animals and four snakes, which were in the end unequal to their task; but since a bison has joined his forces with theirs, the safety of the earth is assured. In India we find various myths; one account gives the snake, another the elephant, as the world-bearing beast (Ward, *View*, i. 3; Pinkerton, vii. 369); another view is that eight elephants bear the world on their backs (Monier-Williams, *Indian Wisdom*[3], p. 430), and the Lushai (Soppitt, *Short Account*, p. 26) and Daphtas (Bastian, *Völker am Brahm.* p. 16) make the world rest on the same animal. Another Hindu myth makes both turtle and serpent (dragon) rest upon an elephant (*Calc. Rev.* xi. 407), while a later myth gives the boar as the supporter. In Ceylon the world-carrying giant rests on a serpent, which rests on a turtle; the turtle rests on a frog, and beneath the frog is air (*Miss. Herald*, xviii. 365). The Indian boar recurs in Celebes (*Journ. Ind. Arch.* ii. 837; *Med. Ned. Zend.* vii. 114). Another account gives the buffalo (*ib.* x. 285), which recurs in the Moluccas (De Clercq, in *Bijdr.* 1890, p. 132). In Arabia and Egypt are found the cow and bull (Andree, *Ethnog. Par.* p. 102; Lane, *1001 Nights*, i. 21), which are also said to rest on a rock, and that on a fish. Probably as a result of Muhammadan influence, the bull or ox is found in Bulgaria (Strausz, *Bulg.* p. 36); Sumatra (Hasselt, *Volksbes.* p. 71), where it rests on an egg, this on a fish, which is in the sea; and in Java (Coolsma, *Voorlez.* p. 73). The turtle in a Kalmuk myth seems to play the part of the world-carrier (Bastian, *Geog. Bilder*, p. 357); the snake in Nias (*Tijdschr. T. L. V.* xxvi. 113), Sumatra (*Allg. Misszts.* xii. 404, etc.), and Java (*Tijdschr. Ned. Ind.* 1893, i. 10); the fish in Sumatra (see above), among the Ainus (Batchelor, p. 278), and in Europe in the Middle Ages (Mone, *Anzeiger*, viii. 614). The frog recurs among the Mongol Lamas (Tylor, *Prim. Cult.* i. 365). Among the Slavs four whales are said to support the world (*Berl. Lesekabinett*, 1844, 210), and among the Temnes of West Africa a trace of Muslim influence may be seen in the undescribed animal who bears all on his back (*Ausland*, 1850, 189). In many cases the movements of the earth-carrier are alleged to be the cause of earthquakes (see below).

10. *EARTHQUAKES.*—Most of the peoples enumerated in the preceding section account for earthquakes by the movements of the animal supporting the earth. In addition we find the snake in the Moluccas (Bastian, *Indonesien*, i. 81), interchangeably with the ox, in Bali (*Globus*, lxv. 98), Roti (Müller, *Reisen*, ii. 345), Flores (Jacobsen, *Reise*, p. 51), Mindanao (*ZE* xvii. 47), and among the Dayaks of Borneo (Perelaer, *Ethn. Bes.* p. 8). In Flores a dragon myth is also found (*loc. cit.*). The earthquake fish of Japan is placed sometimes under the earth, sometimes in the sea (*Natur*, 1878, 551; Brauns, *Jap. Märchen*, p. 154; Chamberlain, *Things Jap.* p. 120). In Sumatra the crab is found as a variant to the snake, Naga-padoka, whose horns are perhaps due to Muslim influence

(v. Brenner, *Besuch*, p. 524). In Flores (Jacobsen, *loc. cit.*), and Persia (Ritter, *Asien*, vi. 563), the dragon is the cause. In Kamtchatka the earthquake is said to be due to the dog of Touila, whose name is Kozei; the snow collects on his coat and he shakes himself to get it off (Krachenninikow, *Descr.* i. 94). The movements of the other animals are put down to a bee or mosquito stinging them.

11. *ECLIPSES.*—Animals figure in some of the primitive explanations of eclipses. Among the Potawattomies they are caused by the combat of the dog with the old woman who makes the basket (*Ann. Prop. Foi*, xii. 490). The dog plays the part of a protector, as does probably the bird in a Mongol myth (*Auṣland*, 1873, 534), and possibly in the Lules myth (Lozano, *Desc. Corog.* p. 91). More commonly it is said that the moon is swallowed or attacked by an animal. In Burma the Karens say that wild goats are devouring the moon, and they make a noise to drive them away, or that frogs are eating it (*Miss. Cath.* 1877, 455). In Eastern Asia the dragon myth is common; it is found in China (Grimm, *Deut. Myth.* ii. 589), Siam (Bastian, *Reise*, p. 243), Sumatra (Marsden, *Hist.* p. 194), and Tidore (De Clercq, *op. cit.* p. 73). This form of the myth is not far removed from that which makes a giant or undescribed monster attack the moon or sun.

The dragon myth is found sporadically in Asia Minor (Naumann, *Vom Goldenen Horn*, p. 75), in Carinthia (*Zts. d. Myth*, iv. 411), and among the southern Slavs (v. Wlislocki, *Volksgl.* p. 54); among the latter a bird myth is also found (*ib.*). In Sumatra (*Globus*, lxv. 96), and Celebes (*Med. Ned. Zend.* xi. 248; *Zts. Ges. Erdk. Berlin*, xxxi. 370), it is the snake that produces an eclipse, among the Nagas the tiger (Bastian, *Völker am Brahm.* p. 30), among the Chiquitos the dog (Tylor, *Prim. Cult.* i. 328), who tears the flesh of the moon and reddens her light with the blood which flows. Among the Tupis the jaguar was the animal which was believed to attack the sun (*ib.* p. 329), and the Peruvians held it to be some monstrous beast (*ib.*). The jaguar recurs among the Manaos (Martius, *Beitr.* i. 585), and the Guaranis (Ruiz de Montoya, *Conquista*, p. 12 ff.). The Tagbanuas tell a myth of a huge crab (Worcester, *Philippine Isl.* p. 497). The old Norse (Grimm, i. 202; ii. 588, iii. 207) held that a wolf attacked the sun or moon; and the same idea is found in France (*ib.* ii. 404). In many cases the dogs are beaten or incited to attack the monster which is assailing the heavenly body.

12. *FABLES.*—Animals figure largely in the folk-tales, no less than in the myths or sagas of primitive peoples (see Bleek, *Reynard the Fox*; Dennett, *Folklore of the Fjort*; MacCulloch, *op. cit.* etc.). In these they think and act and move like human beings, so much so that a lawsuit on the Congo turns on such questions as what the hare said to the elephant, instead of on legal procedure. At a later stage the beast story is complicated with a moral (Æsop's *Fables*). Beast stories are found in most collections of *Märchen*; for India, see especially the Pañchatantra.

13. *FAMILIAR.*—All the world over the witch or wizard is associated with an animal, termed 'the familiar,' which is sometimes conceived as real, sometimes as a spirit which stands at the beck and call of the human being. Just as the injury to the *nagual*, or bush-soul, has fatal results for its possessor, so the familiar's life is bound up with that of the witch; if a witch-animal is wounded, the owner will be found to have suffered an injury at the corresponding part of the body. Sometimes magical powers are attributed to whole classes, such as the Boudas, *i.e.* blacksmiths and workers in clay of Abyssinia, who are believed to have the power of turning into leopards or hyænas, instead of simply having the animals or their spirits at their command.

In the Malay Peninsula the alliance between the *pawang* (priest) and the tiger is said to be the result of a compact entered into long ago between the species and mankind; the office is hereditary, and the son must perform certain ceremonies to prevent the familiar from being for ever lost to the tribe. In Siberia the *ye-keela* (witch-animal) is said to be sent out by a shaman to do battle with the ye-keela of a hostile shaman, and the fate of the man depends on the fate of his ye-keela, which refuses the fight if it thinks it cannot beat its adversary.

In curative magic the wizard carries figures of his familiar and imitates them; sometimes his familiar is said to appear before he meets with success.

14. *FASCINATION.*—The power of fascination actually possessed by the serpent has been attributed to many other animals, among them the lion (Aelian, *de Nat. An.* XII. vii.; cf. Maspero, *Études*, ii. 415), μάντις (*Schol. ad Theoc.* X. xviii.), basilisk (see below), toucan (Smith, *Brazil*, p. 559), and, naturally, above all the serpent (*Mélusine*, iv. 570, v. 18, 41). The power of fascination is attributed to the wer-wolf in the East Indies (*Tijdschr.* xli. 548 f.). Something similar is believed of the ordinary wolf in Norway (Liebrecht, *Zur Volkskunde*, p. 335). See EVIL EYE.

15. *FOOD TABUS.*—The use of animals as food is prohibited for many different reasons. The totem kin usually abstains from eating the totem, the *nagual* is sacrosanct to the man with whom it is associated, and certain animals, like the cow in India, or in fact cattle generally among pastoral tribes, are never or only very seldom eaten. But whereas the totem is absolutely tabu, cattle, on the other hand, supply the pastoral peoples with a large part of their subsistence. Another class of animals which is commonly tabu, at any rate for those who claim kinship with them, are soul-animals (see below).

Sometimes special persons, by virtue of their position or occupation, are forbidden the use of certain meats. In Fernando Po the king may not eat deer and porcupine, which are the ordinary food of the people. Egyptian kings were restricted to a diet of veal and goose. Certain tabus are also imposed on mourners; in Patagonia the widow may not eat horse flesh, guanaco, or cassowary. Certain foods are tabu to men but not to women; among the South African Bantus men may not eat fish, fowl, or pig. Other foods are forbidden to women but not to men; on the island of Nias, in the Dutch East Indies, the former may not eat monkey flesh. Especially in Australia there is an extensive system of food tabus in connexion with initiation; as one gets older, these are abrogated one by one; emu flesh is usually reserved for old men. Similarly girls may not eat various meats at puberty; among the Dénés their sole non-vegetable diet is dogfish. Sometimes marriage removes some of the tabus. On the Murrumbidgee, ducks are the food of married people only.

In many cases only certain parts of an animal are tabu to certain persons: a Déné girl may not eat moose nose or reindeer head; among the Ottawas blood is tabu to the unmarried; the heart, liver, etc., are tabu to a Dakota after initiation till he has killed an enemy. The female animal is frequently tabu; in sickness the female animal only might be eaten by some of the New England peoples.

During pregnancy and after the birth of a child many kinds of food are prohibited to one or both parents; in New South Wales the woman does not eat eel or kangaroo; in Martinique both parents abstain from turtle and manatee. The reason generally given is that the nature of the food influences the offspring. Thus a turtle is deaf, and eating a turtle would make the child deaf too; a manatee has small eyes, and the child would have small eyes too if the parents did not abstain from it. Just as animals are eaten to gain their qualities, so their use as food is prohibited in order to avoid incurring them; this is the explanation often given for abstinence from the flesh of deer, the hare, and other timid animals.

Especially in West Africa food tabus are imposed upon members of a certain family by a priest, and the tabu is sometimes thenceforth hereditary. Among the Andamanese some food is prohibited to every individual, generally some kind which, in the opinion of the mother, disagrees with the child; but if it is not selected in this way, each person is free to determine what food is to be tabu for himself.

Other food tabus are connected rather with seasons than with anything else. It is not uncommon in south-east Europe to find a prejudice against eating lamb before a certain day.

In connexion with food tabus may be mentioned the prohibition against cooking certain kinds of animals together. In Kamtchatka different kinds of meat may not be stewed in the same pot; the Saponas of the Eastern States of America would not cook venison and turkey together, on the ground that they would have ill success in hunting if they did. See TABU.

16. *FUTURE LIFE:* (1) CERBERUS.—It is a common belief that the soul has to traverse a river on its journey into the other world. Sometimes the bridge over which it passes is said to be an animal; the Ojibwas said that a great serpent served as a bridge, and that he threatened to devour those who were in a trance (Keating, *Expedition*, ii. 154). In New Caledonia a serpent serves as a bridge from Morou to Tum, and allows to pass only such as find grace in his eyes, in other words, those who are tatued in due form (*Ann. Prop. Foi*, xxiii. 369). In other cases an animal guards the passage; in North Borneo the belief is that a fiery dog watches at the gate of Paradise and takes possession of all virgins (Forster and Sprengel, *Beiträge*, ii. 239). The idea of a dog at the end of the soul-bridge is also found among the Iroquois (Le Beau, *Aventures*, i. 359). Sometimes the river contains fish which devour the souls which fall in (*Globus*, xlvii. 108, among the Dayaks). In other cases the function of the animal is to turn back the souls of those who are to live; the Assiniboines held that a person in a trance went as far as the river, but was driven back by a red bull (Coues, *Henry and Thompson, MS. Journ.* ii. 521). The Senels of California also made a bull obstruct the path of the soul; but it was the bad who fell victims to him (*Cont. Am. Ethn.* iii. 169). In the Dayak mythology figures a bird, who lives aside from the direct road of the soul; if the soul turns aside, however, the bird sends it back (Ling Roth, *Natives of Sarawak*, i. 210). In the Solomon Islands the function of the bird is quite different; the natives of San Cristoval say that the soul becomes a ghost (*'ataro*) when it leaves the body, but that it fails to recognize that it is dead; a kingfisher strikes it on the head after two or three days, whereupon it becomes a real spirit (Codrington, *Melanesians*, p. 257).

The soul pursues in the other world the same occupations as it followed in this life. Consequently it is commonly represented as chasing the animals on which the living man depended for his sustenance on earth. The belief is especially common among the American Indians, whose 'happy hunting grounds' are proverbial (Matthews, *Hidatsa*, p. 49; *Rev. Hist. Rel.* xxx., xlii. 9 f.).

Sagard, one of the early Jesuit missionaries in Canada, tells us: 'The Indians say that the souls of dogs and other animals follow the road of souls; . . . the souls of the dogs serve the souls of their masters in the other life; the souls of men go hunting with the souls of their tools and arms' (*Histoire du Canada*, pp. 497, 498).

To this idea of the functions of animals and the lot of the soul in the other world is due in great part the custom of burial sacrifice (for the horse see *Teutonia*, ii. 148–162). Sometimes the object of the sacrifice is only to bear witness to the importance of the deceased in this life and thus influence his future lot (Abinal and Vaissière, *Vingt ans à Madagascar*, p. 221).

17. *FUTURE LIFE:* (2) SOUL-ANIMALS.—Few beliefs are more common than that the souls of the dead pass into animals. In South Africa it is the prevailing belief, but it is found in Europe (*Folk-lore*, xi. 234), America (Tylor, ii. 6–8), and Asia (*ib.* p. 9 f.; *Mission Life*, N.S. i. 459; *T'Oung Pao*, ii. 11, etc.). Especially in the form of the doctrine of transmigration, as a punishment for evil done in this life, the belief prevails not only in India (see, *e.g.*, Manu, ii. 201, xii. 55–69), but also in Oceania and New Guinea (*Golden Bough*², iii. 432–4) and Australia (*Man*, 1905, No. 28; for a collection of references, see *Rev. Hist. Rel.* xxxvii. 385; see also below, 'Bat,' 'Crocodile,' 'Lion,' 'Lizard,' 'Tiger,' etc.).

The causes which are supposed to lead to this re-incarnation are various. Among the Mokis it is the form of the totem animal that a man assumes at death (Frazer, *Tot.* p. 36). In South Africa the different clans believe that their members pass into the animals which they venerate (*Man*, 1901, No. 111). The Zulus believe that their dead pass into snakes, called *amadhlozi* (*Golden Bough*², iii. 411); according to another account, the chiefs inhabit one kind of snake, the common people another, while the old women are re-incarnated in lizards (Callaway, *Religious System*, p. 200). According to the Masai, the souls pass into different kinds of snakes, one of which receives the souls of each clan or family (Hollis, *Masai*, p. 307). In Madagascar the body is thrown into a sacred lake, and the eel that gets the first bite at the body is the abode of the soul (v. Gennep, *Tabou*, p. 291). In China the soul of the drowned man is held to make a rush for the nearest living being; consequently they take the first crab seen in the mud to be the receptacle of the soul (*Mission Life*, *loc. cit.*). The Barotse hold that they can choose into which animal they shall pass (Bertrand, *Au Pays*, p. 300). In the Solomon Islands a man tells his family which animal will be his re-incarnation (*Golden Bough*², ii. 433). In the Argentine Republic it is the animals which are seen about the grave that come in for respect as soul-animals (*Bol. Inst. Geog. Arg.* xv. 740). In Brazil a kind of hawk is believed to inoculate with the souls of the dead the animals on which it perches to extract maggots from their flesh (Spix and Martius, p. 1084). It is a common belief in Europe, that if a cat jumps over a corpse, it becomes a vampire; in other words, the soul of the deceased passes into the cat. The Macusis believe that souls which are unable to rest come back to earth and pass into the bodies of animals (Waterton, *Wanderings*, p. 177). In Paumotu it was also believed that the wicked found refuge in the bodies of birds, which the priests accounted holy (Arbousset, *Tahiti*, p. 289).

In many cases the lodgment of the soul in an animal is held to end the matter. If the animal is killed, the soul passes into another beast of the same species (*Man*, 1904, No. 118). In Madagascar, however, the death of the animal is held to set free the soul lodged in it (*Miss. Cath.* 1880, p. 551). The Chiriguanos, on the other hand, hold that the soul enjoys a few years of liberty and then passes into the body of a fox or a jaguar (*Globus*, xlviii. 37).

Some tribes can describe in more or less detail the process of transmigration. The Amandabele of South Africa believe that the souls of chiefs pass into lions, but that the process takes place underground; for which reason the corpse does not remain long unburied. The body is put into a large wooden trough and hidden away in a cavern; some time afterwards it is found to have become a lion's whelp, which grows rapidly (Thomas, *Eleven Years*, p. 279). The Betsileos are more explicit. The *fanany* (soul-animal) is in the form of a lizard, which comes to the surface after burial; the family approach it and ask if it is really the relative they have lost; if it moves its head they make offerings to it. It then returns to the tomb and grows to a large size; it is the tutelary spirit of the family (v. Gennep, *Tabou*, p. 272). According to another account, the corpse is attached to the central pillar of the hut until decomposition sets in; whereupon a large worm develops, which becomes a boa at the end of several months (*ib.* p. 278).

In several of these accounts the soul seems to become an animal rather than to enter into an animal; this is notably the case with the Amandabele belief; the Betsileos seem to waver between two opinions, if we take account of all the data. In other cases the belief is more explicit. In the Solomon Islands the common people turn into white ants in Marapa, the island of the dead, and in this form serve as food for the spirits of the chiefs, the warriors, and the successful men, who, however, in the long run suffer the same fate as the common people (Codrington, *Melanesians*, p. 260). Sometimes the change is regarded as the result of evil-doing; the Chins believe that the bad go to dark caverns, in which are the entrails of all sorts of animals; they are hungry, and stretch out their hands to find food; but as soon as they touch the entrails they themselves are transformed into the shape of the animal whose entrails they have grasped (*Miss. Cath.* 1884, p. 468). On the other hand, among the Montagnais, of whom P. le Jeune writes, the transformation of the soul is the result of simple misfortune or carelessness; the souls go to the extremity of the earth, which is flat with a great precipice beyond, at the foot of which is water; they dance at the edge of the abyss and some fall over; these are forthwith turned into fish (*Rel. des Jés.* 1637, p. 53).

The soul-animal is usually respected, for which two reasons are assigned. The injuring of the animal is the injuring of a relative or of a friend, for it is believed that the animals into which the souls pass do not injure those with whom they were allied on earth as men. By eating the animal, men may even eat the soul of a relative, and perhaps inflict unmerited hardship on it in its non-human existence. On the other hand, the eating of the animal may be an insult rather than an injury; but it may provoke the wrath of the dead man or of his fellows, and thus recoil upon the living. As a rule, however, the objection to injuring a relative is the prevailing feeling; for we find that, though a man will not injure his own family animal, he will not hesitate to kill the family animal of another man (*Golden Bough*[2], ii. 433). In the same way a man does not injure his own totem, but will kill that of another.

18. *FUTURE LIFE:* (3) PSYCHOPOMP.—The duty of convoying souls to the other world is sometimes assigned to animals. The Araucanians believe that Tempulcague, an old woman, appears in the form of a whale and carries off the soul of the dead man (Molina, *Historia*, p. 70). On the Orinoco huge snakes are said to carry off the souls in their belly to a land where they entertain themselves by dancing and other delights (Ruiz Blanco, *Convercion del Piritu*, p. 63). In Brazil the duty was assigned to the humming-bird (Alencar, *O Guarany*, ii. 321). Among the Saponas, the soul, after an old hag had condemned it, was delivered over to a huge turkey buzzard, which flew away with it to a dark and barren country where it was always winter (Byrd, *History of the Dividing Line*, p. 96 f.).

Sometimes the animal is not a mythical one. The object of some burial sacrifices is to provide the dead man with a conductor. In Mexico the dog (see below), according to one account, fulfilled this office. Among the Yorubas of West Africa the young men who attend a funeral kill a fowl and throw its feathers in the air as they walk, subsequently cooking and eating the flesh. This fowl they call Adie-Irana, 'the fowl which purchases the road'; its function is to precede the dead man on his road (*Miss. Cath.* 1884, p. 342).

19. *IDOLS.*—It is not difficult to trace the main lines of the development of idols, so far as animals are concerned. It is a common custom, when the sacred animal is sacrificed annually, to keep its skin for the ensuing twelve months, just as the various figures made of the new corn are suspended in the house till the next harvest. From the custom of keeping the skin there arises, by a natural transition, the practice of stuffing it in order to give it a more lifelike appearance. Then it is found more convenient to have a wooden or stone image, and the skin is drawn over it, as was the ram's skin over the image of Ammon; and the idol is a *fait accompli.* There is, however, a tendency to anthropomorphize animal gods. We find, therefore, that in Egypt, India, and even Siberia, idols compounded of man and animal appear; sometimes the head only is human, as in the case of the Sphinx; sometimes it is the head which is animal, as in the case of the crocodile-god Sebek. Sometimes the head and body are human, but some minor portion is animal; the Fauns had goats' feet, and Dagon a fish's tail. With the appearance of the mixed form the course of evolution is completed, so far as the animal is concerned. It ceases to be an idol, and henceforth becomes an attribute of the god; he carries it on his shoulders, leads it, or stands in relation with it in some other way. Finally, if it is sacrificed to him, it ends by being regarded as his enemy.

20. *INSPIRATION.*—One of the methods by which inspiration may be produced is by drinking the blood of the sacrificial victim; possibly the result is in part due to physiological causes. Near Bombay, in the ceremonies of the Komatis, an old man, nearly naked, carried a kid round a car used for hook-swinging, and tore open its throat with his teeth; when he had sucked the blood of the kid, he was regarded by the populace as a god (*Miss. Reg.* 1818, p. 157). In this case no mention is made of any signs of inspiration; but in some parts of Southern India, when a devil dancer drinks the blood of a sacrificial goat, he shows evident signs of being possessed. As if he had acquired new life, he begins to brandish his staff of bells and to dance with a quick but unsteady step. Suddenly the afflatus descends. His eyes glare, and he leaps in the air and gyrates. Having by these means produced an auto-hypnotic condition, he is in a position to give oracles; he retains the power of utterance and motion, but his ordinary consciousness is in abeyance (*Golden Bough*[2], i. 134). The Sabæans explained the inspiration thus produced as due to the obsession of the blood-drinker by demons, whose food they held blood to be. They expected to gain the gift of prophecy by entering into communion with the demons (*ib.* p. 135).

21. *LIFE INDEX.*—It is a wide-spread belief that any injury done to the familiar of a witch will be shown on the corresponding portion of her body; similarly the wer-wolf is *solidaire* with the wer-man; a disaster to the bush-soul (see 'Nagual' below) of the West African spells disaster for the man himself. But it is by no means necessary that the relationship between the man and the animal should be conditioned by magical rites; it may be acquired from circumstances connected with the birth of a child (Hartland, *Legend of P.* i. *pass.*), or may be selected by the person himself

(*Golden Bough*[2], iii. 412). In the latter case the story usually takes the form that the soul of the person with whose life that of the animal is bound up has been deposited for safety in the animal. A few instances have been recorded in Australia in which the life of one of a totem kin is believed to be bound up with the life of the totem animal (Frazer, *Tot.* p. 7).

22. *MAGIC.*—The term 'magic' is vaguely used to denominate a great number of different conceptions, but these need not be distinguished in a brief survey of the part played by animals in magic. (1) Many forms of sacrifice (see below) are magical. (2) As the *nagual* (see below) or familiar, the animal gives man greater force than he would otherwise possess. (3) Just as in dying the dead animal sets free the magical power within it, so in life it may repel evil influences or attract them to itself and neutralize them. (4) By eating animals men acquire their qualities; lion's flesh gives courage, hare's meat makes a man a coward. By partaking of long-lived animals a man may overpass the ordinary span of life; by consuming wise animals he will acquire the gift of prophecy. (5) The external qualities of animals are susceptible of transference in like manner; by rubbing bear's grease on the head a plentiful growth of the hair is assured, for the bear is a hairy animal. This is called *the doctrine of signatures.* (6) Just as the familiar represents the witch and any injury done to the animal reappears in the witch, so any animal may be selected to represent a given person; a girl who wishes to compel the presence of an absent lover may, in Wales, take a frog's heart and stick it full of pins. (7) Diseases in the human being may be got rid of by transferring them to an animal. (8) Certain animals, like the frog (see below), are connected with certain departments of nature; by injuring or otherwise constraining them, these animals can be forced to produce the natural phenomena desired by the magician; thus frogs are whipped to produce rain. (9) Magical, too, from some points of view is the torture applied to the favourite animal of a god (*Golden Bough*[2], i. 108), to compel the deity to supply man with what he demands. From being used in magic the animal may come to be sacrosanct, as the crocodile (see below) among the Bantus of South Africa. See also 'Nagual,' 'Familiar,' etc. Although some animals are in greater request, it is probable there are few that are not in demand for magical purposes of some sort (v. Jühling, *Die Tiere in der Volksmedizin*; *Mélusine*, viii. 14, 32 f.). Especially important in European magic are the first animals seen in the spring, and the feathers, etc., of birds and animals carried in annual processions (see 'Wren' below, and art. MAGIC).

23. *MARRIAGE.*—Animals figure largely in European marriage customs. The custom of the 'Hahnenschlag' (*Folklore*, xi. 25) is sometimes practised, but more often the cock, or other bird or animal, is eaten by the bride and bridegroom or by the guests in general. Sometimes the bird is a mere ornament to the bridal waggon; sometimes it is killed by being burned in a bonfire, or hunted, or simply thrown into the house of the newly married, or rocked in a cradle before them; in some cases it is merely a gift from the bridegroom to the bride or her parents; or a game such as 'fox and geese' is played at weddings; or the newly married hunt the living animal. Custom sometimes requires a younger sister who marries first to give a white goat to the elder. The animals which figure in wedding ceremonies are the cat, cock or hen, crane, duck, goat, goose, owl, ox, partridge, pig, pigeon, quail, sheep, swan, and wren. The object of the ceremonies seems to be in some cases simply to avert evil by the ordinary method in use at other times of the year; sometimes the more definite object of securing fertility seems to be held in view. The tail, which is sometimes given to the bride, may perhaps have a phallic significance. The mimetic dance at weddings (*Cong. des Trad. pop.* 1900, p. 100) is perhaps intended to secure fertility. Sometimes an animal mask or dress only is worn. The bride is sometimes called 'lamb,' 'partridge,' etc., but this seems to be merely allegorical.

24. '*MEDICINE,*' *AMULET*, *TALISMAN.*—When the American Indian kills his medicine animal, he usually takes some portion of it, such as its pelt, claw, or wing, as a talisman and puts it in his medicine bag. It is held in some tribes that the medicine, once lost, cannot be replaced; it may, therefore, be conjectured that the medicine is regarded as the seat of the tutelary spirit whose aid is secured at puberty (cf. *Golden Bough*[2], iii. 432). In this connexion may be quoted a remark (Wied, *Reise*, ii. 190) that many Indians believe they have an animal, bison, tortoise, etc., in their bodies. The central idea of African 'fetishism' is that a spirit which temporarily inhabits a stone, bone, or other object, becomes for the time being the servant of the possessor of that object. The magical apparatus is sometimes composed of a bag made of the skin of some rare animal which contains various talismans, such as dried monkeys' tails, claws, etc. The same idea may be traced in the East Indies. If a Batta has a tooth as a talisman, he will, on the approach of danger, swallow it; this may perhaps be to ensure a greater measure of protection for himself; but it is more probably to ensure the safety of the talisman, which thus equals in importance the medicine of the American Indian. The uses of animal amulets are innumerable. Just as the American Indian believes that his medicine makes him invulnerable, so in Central Africa the leopard skin girdle is held to be a complete protection. In France the milk of a black cow is thought to confer the gift of invisibility. In Scotland serpent soup will make one wise like the serpent, but the serpent can also be made to assist the possessor of its skeleton. Often the particular purpose to be served is no longer remembered, and the talisman is simply carried for luck. In the Isle of Man the feathers of the wren are distributed at each house where the bearers call (see 'Wren' below).

25. *MIMETIC DANCES, MASQUERADES, ETC.*—Many primitive peoples are in the habit of imitating the movements and cries of animals, and usually in so doing assume the animal mask or dress. In some cases the object seems to be simple amusement, but this kind of dramatic representation is usually magical or religious in its purpose. (1) The initiation dance is frequently mimetic, and may perhaps have at its root the idea of transforming the man into a member of the kin by imparting to him a share of the nature of the animal. (2) Other dances, also performed at initiation, have for their primary object the conferring of magical power over the animal in the chase. (3) This magical power is also sought by mimetic dances performed immediately before a hunting expedition. (4) Mimetic dances before hunting may also be sympathetic in their purpose; the animal in human form falls a victim to the hunter, and in the same way the real animal will fall beneath his darts. (5) Sometimes mimetic dances are performed after a hunt also; their object seems to be protective (see 'Leopard' below), like so many of the other ceremonies after killing animals. (6) It may, however, be intended sometimes as productive magic, for the purpose of increasing the numbers of the animal and perhaps bringing to life again those laid low by the hunter. (7) With the object of provid-

ing for the due increase of the species, some American Indian tribes mimic the buffalo, the men taking the part of the males, the women of the females. (8) In many of the Central Australian ceremonies the movements of the totem are imitated in the ceremonies intended to provide for its due increase. (9) Conversely, imitation of the movements of animals and birds forms a part of some European marriage ceremonies, and seems to be here, too, a rite intended to promote fertility. (10) Where animals are sacred to a god, mimicry of their movements is equivalent to prayer and adoration, just in the same way as graphic representations of them. (11) The object of these prayers is often to produce rain or wind or some other natural phenomenon associated with the animals (see 'Frog' below); possibly in its origin the mimetic dance was intended by its magical power to produce these effects without the intervention of a god. (12) The wearing of animal disguises and imitation of animal movements during the chase have probably the purely rational object of deceiving the animal.

26. *MYTHS OF ANCESTORS, CHILDREN, HELPFUL ANIMALS, SWAN-MAIDEN STORIES.*—Sometimes as a totemic ætiological myth (Frazer, *Tot.* p. 3 f.), but often as a myth of tribal origin (Hearne, *Northern Ocean*, p. 342; D'Orbigny, *Voyage*, iii. 209 ff.; Liebrecht, *Gerv. Tilb.* p. 115, *Zur Volksk.* p. 17 ff., etc.), the descent from an animal ancestor is found all over the world. In the same way stories are told of animal births, which sometimes are simply ætiological myths of the origin of totem kins (Frazer, p. 6), and sometimes narratives of facts believed to occur at the present day (see 'Crocodile,' and cf. *Mélusine*, iii. 212, etc.). In another type of myth, animals are said to bring the children (*Folklore*, xi. 235, see also 'Lizard' below; *JRAS, S.B.*, 7, 146; Alencar, *O Guarany*, ii. 321). Corresponding to the animal form of the soul of the dead, we have the belief that the soul of the new-born child is in the form of an insect (*Miss. Cath.* 1894, 140) or of a bird (Skeat and Blagden, ii. 4), which the expectant mother has to eat. The helpful animal figures in many *Märchen* (Hartland, *Legend of P.*, *pass.*, see also v. Gennep, 214–292; MacCulloch, 225–253, etc.). Sometimes animals figure as guides in tribal migrations, etc. (Wackernagel, *Kl. Schriften*, iii. 203 ff.). Under this head we may perhaps class the animal nurse (Frazer, *Paus.* iii. 234, 250; Farnell, *Cults*, p. 443; *Rep. Ind. Eth. Com.* 1866–7, p. 52). Connected with the myth of the animal ancestor is the swan-maiden story (Frazer, *Paus.* iv. 106; Hartland, *Science of Folklore*, pp. 255–332, 337–352; *Romania*, xxi. 62; *Aust. Ass. Adv. Sci.* iv. 731. See also 'Seal').

27. *MYTHS (ÆTIOLOGICAL).*—A great part of the mythology of savages is simply their idea of the history of the Universe. They account for natural facts, beliefs, customs, and rites by telling what some god or hero once did, by endowing all nature with sensibility and volition, by positing the same conditions in the heavens as exist on the earth, and so on. In particular, they account for the existence and peculiarities of animals by telling stories of what happened in the early days of the world. Once men went on all-fours, and pigs walked like men; but something fell on the head of a pig, and since then they have gone on all-fours and men walk upright.

The Indians of Brazil tell how the daughter of the great serpent married a young man who had three faithful slaves. At that time there was no night upon the earth; the young wife said her father had it, and the slaves were sent for it. They received it in a nut sealed with resin, which they were on no account to open. *En route* they heard a buzzing in the nut; it was the hum of the insects at night. Curiosity overcame them; they opened the nut, and night spread over the earth. Then everything in the forest changed into animals and birds; everything in the river into fishes. A wicker basket became a jaguar; the fisherman in his canoe turned into a duck, the oars forming the feet. When the woman saw the morning star, she said, 'I am going to separate night and day.' Then she rolled a thread of cotton, and said, 'You shall be the pheasant'; she coloured it white and red. She rolled another thread and made the partridge. These two birds call, one at dawn, the other at dusk. For their disobedience the three servants were changed into monkeys (Magalhanes, *Contes indiennes*, p. 5).

The relations of animals to man, and especially their sacrosanctity, are explained by ætiological myths. In Madagascar the Vazimbas account for the respect paid to the kingfisher by the following story: 'The Vazimba sent the kingfisher to visit their relatives with a message of good-bye to the father and mother, and an injunction to send fowls and sheep; when it had fulfilled its errand it came back, and the Vazimba said that as a reward for its bravery and wisdom they would put a crown on its head and dress it in blue by day and by night. Moreover, young kingfishers should be cared for, and the penalty of death inflicted on any one who sought to kill them' (v. Gennep, *Tabou*, p. 265). More common is the explanation that the animal in some way helped an ancestor of the kin (v. Gennep, *pass.*; see also 'Owl' below). In N.W. America an adventure with the animal is a prominent motive in the myths. Descent from the totem-animal seems to be the prevailing form of the story in the remainder of North America (for ætiological myths in Africa see *Folklore*, xv. 110; Rançon, *Dans la Haute Gambie*, p. 445; Merensky, *Beiträge*, p. 133 n., etc.); see also 'Eclipse,' 'Earth-carrier,' 'Earthquakes,' etc., above).

28. *NAGUAL.*—In Africa, Australia, and America it is the custom to undergo some ceremony, usually at the age of puberty, for the purpose of procuring a tutelary deity, which is commonly an animal. This is called *tornaq* (Eskimo), *manitou* (Algonquin), *nagual* (C. America), *yunbeai* (Euahlayi of E. Australia), etc. Among the Eskimos the bear (see below) seems to be the usual animal. Among the Thlinkets a young man goes out and meets a river otter; he kills it, takes out its tongue and hangs it round his neck, and thenceforth understands the language of all animals (*JAI*, xxi. 31; Krause, *Die Tlinkit-Indianer*, p. 284). Among the Eastern Dénés each hunter selects some animal, invariably a carnivorous one (*Smiths. Rep.* 1866, p. 307). Elsewhere the initiant has to dream of his medicine animal, and sometimes kills it in order to procure some portion of its body as a talisman (Frazer, *Tot.* p. 54). In Africa it is the magician who provides the tutelary beast; in one case a blood-bond is said to be performed with the animal selected. In Australia also the medicine-man sometimes provides the *nagual*; sometimes it is acquired by a dream. The animal thus brought into relation with a man is usually sacrosanct for him; if he loses his talisman, he cannot get another medicine animal (parts of America); the death of the *nagual* entails the death of the man (Nkomis of W. Africa); in Australia the *yunbeai* is sacrosanct, though the totem is not.

Closely connected with the *nagual* is the 'bush-soul' of West Africa. Possibly only our limited knowledge disguises their identity. A man will not kill his 'bush-soul animal,' for that would entail his own death; he cannot see it, but learns what it is from a magician. A 'bush-soul' is often hereditary from father to son, and from mother to daughter; sometimes all take after one or the other parent. In Calabar many are believed to have the power of changing into their *ukpong*. Something of the same sort is known in Europe, for in Iceland each family had attached to it an *ættar-fylgja*; each individual too had his *fylgja*, which took the shape of a dog, raven, fly, etc. (*Folklore*, xi. 237; Meyer, *German. Myth.* p. 67).

The *nagual* seems to be closely related, on the

one hand, to the 'soul-animal' (see above); on the other, it stands very near to the 'familiar' (see above) of the witch, and the 'wer-wolf' (see below). It has been argued that kin totemism arises from the *nagual*, which becomes hereditary. Up to the present no trace of animistic ideas has been found in connexion with totemism, if we except some doubtful cases in Australia (*Man*, 1902, No. 85). Nor has it been explained how the totem, the descent of which is, in Australia, predominantly in the female line, has developed from a *nagual*, which is seldom, if ever, possessed by women or inherited from the maternal uncle.

Closer to the *nagual* than the kin totem is the sacred animal of secret societies (which see), the initiation ceremonies of which, it should be noted, bear a strong resemblance to those practised by totem tribes. The *nagual* is the lineal ancestor of the 'genius' of the Romans, no less than of the 'guides' of modern spiritualism.

29. *NAMES.*—Animal names are very commonly used, and not among primitive peoples only, for three per cent. of English surnames are said to be derived from animals (Jacobs, *Studies in Bibl. Arch.* p. 68; for Indo-Germanic theriophoric personal names see Fick, *Griechische Personennamen, passim*). (1) Tribes are named after animals; the name of the Aruntas in Central Australia is said to mean 'cockatoo'; the Wakelburas are the eel people. In America we have the Dog Rib Indians, who trace their descent from the dog. In India the Nagas are a serpent tribe. (2) Far more common is the practice of naming totem kins after animals; it is one of the tests of totemism. In Australia we have a long list of Arunta and other totems in the works of Spencer and Gillen (for other kins see Frazer, *Totemism*). (3) The two sections into which most Australian tribes are divided are, especially in the south, often named after animals, and in particular after the eagle, hawk, and crow. Similarly we have the raven and wolf phratry among the Thlinkets (see also Frazer, *op. cit.*). (4) The intermarrying classes in Australia are also known by animal names; on the Annan River they are called after the eagle, hawk, and bee; at Moreton Bay they are named from the kangaroo, emu, etc. (5) In America the age classes and the closely connected secret or dancing societies are named after animals; in West Africa there is the leopard society. (6) In Zululand, possibly as a relic of totemism, the regiments are named after animals; we find similar names in Welsh history. (7) Both in America and in Australia sections of tribes are named from their principal food (*Globus*, xxxi. 381; lxix. 59). (8) Local divisions of Australian tribes have animal names. These are not to be confused with local totem groups. (9) Priests and worshippers are named after animals (see art. PRIEST). (10) Totem kins in America, and rarely in Australia, name their members after some part of the totem animal. (11) In South Africa the chiefs of animal-named kins bear the name of the animal. (12) Especially in America personal names derived from animals, either for magical purposes or as indications of the characters of their bearers, are very common. In Central America a child is named after some animal, which is thenceforward his *nagual* (see 'Nagual' above; cf. *Jahrb. Geog. Ges. Bern*, xiii. 150). (13) As a mark of respect kings and nobles receive names of animals as titles of address. (14) Gods are named from animals associated with them (see 'Goat,' 'Fox,' 'Mouse'). (15) Divisions of the calendar are named after animals in East Asia, and children take their names from them. (16) The signs of the zodiac, the constellations, etc., are named after animals. (17) Animal names are sometimes applied in Europe to the bride and bridegroom. (18) The reaper of the last ears, as representative of the corn-spirit, conceived in animal form, is called the cow, etc. At Easter or Whitsuntide, St. Thomas's Day, etc., animal names are applied to the last person to get up, or to an individual selected in some other way; cf. 'gowk,' *poisson d'Avril*. (19) Various games are known by animal names, in particular 'Blind Man's Buff' (see 'Sacrifice' below). (20) Animal nicknames are common in Europe, and probably in other parts of the world (Lang, *Social Origins*, App.). (21) The last ears of corn, as embodiments of the animal corn-spirit, receive animal names.

30. *OATH, ORDEAL.*—Just as in more advanced societies it is the custom to call upon the gods to bear witness to the truth of an assertion or to ensure the fulfilment of a promise, so the savage calls upon his sacred animal (see 'Bear,' 'Dog'). In later times this is regarded as an appeal to the gods, but originally the animal itself was believed to punish the perjurer, either by persecuting him as a ghost-animal or by devouring him as a living animal. The procedure varies, sometimes the hand is laid upon the animal or on its skull, sometimes its blood is drunk, sometimes the foot is put upon its skin. The Bantus of South Africa take an oath by their *siboko*, the Hereros by the colour of their oxen. In the island of Eibo the oath is taken by the Christmas boar. Corresponding to the oath by animals is a class of ordeals, in which the person to be absolved exposes himself to dangerous beasts by swimming across a river full of crocodiles, or by similar means.

31. *OMENS.*—In many cases it is impossible to point out either the causes which determine the augural character of an animal or those which make the appearance of a given animal favourable or unfavourable. Broadly speaking, omen animals may be classified as—(1) Totem or tutelary animals whose appearance is equivalent to a promise or grant of help to the receiver of the omen; their appearance may, however, be interpreted unfavourably (Frazer, *Tot.* p. 23). (2) The messengers of evil spirits or animal forms of evil spirits, whose appearance is equivalent to the announcement that a magician is seeking to do an injury to some one (see 'Owl'). (3) The animal is divine and has foreknowledge; by the manner of its appearance it shows what the future will be (see 'Hawk'). (4) The animal is the messenger of a god, who sends it to instruct man (see 'Hawk'). (5) The animal is possessed of magical influence, which tends either to promote or to retard the enterprise to which the omen is taken to relate; consequently its appearance is favourable or the reverse.

Omen-giving animals are (1) always of evil augury; (2) always of good augury; (3) auspicious or the reverse, (*a*) according to the manner in which they behave, or (*b*) according to the number which appear, or (*c*) according to the actions of the augur, who may change a bad omen into a good one by magical or other means, *e.g.* by killing the animal, by turning round three times, by spitting, or by purificatory ceremonies.

32. *POSSESSION.*—A belief in possession by animals is not uncommon. In New Guinea it is held that the witch is possessed by spirits, which can be expelled in the form of snakes, etc., just like any other disease. In the East Indies wer-wolfism is regarded as a disease of the soul which is communicable by contagion, or perhaps as a kind of possession in which the soul may be regarded as poisoned by the evil principle in the form of animals or reptiles. In South Australia the natives believed that they were sometimes possessed by certain animals, and it is no uncommon belief in Africa and Samoa that an offence against a totem or other sacred animal will be followed by its

growth within the body of the offender, which is equivalent to a kind of possession. Among the Ainus madness is explained as possession by snakes, etc., and they hold that it is caused especially by killing some sacrosanct animal. Thus a man who kills a cat is liable to be possessed by a cat, and he can prevent this only by eating part of a cat; it is called cat punishment. There is also bear punishment, dog punishment, and punishment by all the other animals. In Japan the obsessing animal is regarded as the physical incarnation of the sins of the sufferer, and is said to leave him after a while. In particular, foxes are held to possess people who have damaged the fields, etc., of their owners; and certain families are said to own foxes which enter the bodies of offenders and cause them to blurt out their crimes. In other parts dogs are the animals used; they are held to go out in spirit form; the body may even die in the absence of the vivifying principle; if so, the spirit enters the body of the owner of the dog, who is then more powerful than ever as a magician. Belief in the possession of wizards being so widely found, it is probable that the statement of the Prince of Wied (*Reise*, ii. 190), that many American Indians believe they have an animal in their bodies, refers to possession by the medicine animal. There are, however, traces of a similar belief in Australia with regard to totems.

33. *POWER OVER ANIMALS, ETC.*—Magical powers over the totem are frequently claimed by the kin in Australia, and occasionally in other parts of the world. Mimetic dances (see above) are held to give the same control. The eating of the flesh of an animal is believed to give power to cure diseases, which are often known by the name of that animal. Wizards and others sometimes claim immunity from the bite of serpents, etc.; in some cases this is said to be the result of inoculation at initiation. See also 'Familiar,' 'Nagual.'

34. *SACRIFICE.*—An account of the origin, function, and theories, savage and civilized, of sacrifice will be found in the article on that subject. It will suffice here to enumerate the various explanations, real or assumed. (1) The commonest view is that the animal is a gift or tribute to a god, a mark of homage or of self-denial. (2) From the facts of totemism the theory has been developed (Robertson Smith) that the animal killed is really the god; the object of the sacrifice, and especially of the following ritual meal, is to re-establish or strengthen the tie between the god and his worshippers. (3) It is in fact found that a savage will kill and eat the animal god of his enemy (*Miss. Reg.* 1822, 254); this may be explained on the same principle—the bond established by the ritual meal prevents retaliation, for an alliance has been entered into, unwillingly but none the less effectively. (4) Starting from the conception of the slain god (2), it has been surmised (Frazer) that the killing of the sacred animal, no less than of the god, has for its object the preservation of the Divine life, conceived as something apart from the living animal, from the pains and penalties of old age, and from the weakness to which they would reduce the being on whose strength the preservation of the people, or the growth of the crops, or some other important fact, depends. (5) From (2) follows also the magical totem-sacrifice, found as a totem rite in full activity only in Central Australia, by which the multiplication of the animal is promoted and the species at the same time desacralized for men other than the totem kin. Desacralization seems to have been also one of the purposes of the sacrifice of the corn-spirit, although here the object may have been primarily sacralization of the participants. (6) One means of the expulsion of evils is the scapegoat (see 'Scapegoat'); the purificatory sacrifice attains the same object by killing the animal, perhaps by disseminating the *mana* of the sacred animal, and thus counteracting hurtful influences. (7) Corresponding to (6) we have the magical sacrifice intended to produce direct benefits; the animal representative of the corn-spirit is killed and its blood sprinkled, or its bones mixed with the seed as a means of increasing fertility. (8) The burial sacrifice is intended to provide the dead with means (*a*) of subsistence in the other world, (*b*) of guidance to the other world, (*c*) of proving his earthly status in the other world, etc., or to purify the living from the dangers of mourners. (9) The deificatory sacrifice provides (*a*) the individual with his *nagual* or individual tutelary spirit; (*b*) a building with a protecting spirit; (*c*) a frontier with a guardian spirit, etc. (10) We have, further, the inspirational sacrifice, where the priest drinks the blood of a victim in order to procure obsession by his god. (11) In the messenger sacrifice, an animal is killed that it may go as an envoy to the dead (see 'Bear,' 'Turtle,' etc.). The simple food sacrifice must of course be distinguished from this. (12) A common ætiological explanation among the ancients was that an animal was killed because it was the enemy of the god or had in some way injured him.

Various forms of sacrifice are found. The victim may be slaughtered, burnt, thrown over a precipice or from a height, immured or buried; to these modes may be added the setting free of the bird or animal (see 'Scapegoat'). The skin of the victim may be put on an idol, used for a sacred cloak, hung upon a tree, etc. The flesh is frequently eaten; or part may be eaten and part burnt or buried. Special care is frequently taken of the bones. The priest sometimes arrays himself in the skin or mask of the animal to be sacrificed; if the sacrifice is that of the animal-god, the priest thereby assimilates himself to his god, and by putting on the Divine character sanctifies himself for his task. In any case, the donning of the skin and mask may be regarded as a rite of sacralization, fitting the human being for contact with divine things. Not only so, but the priest is actually called by the name of an animal. The worshippers of Ephesian Artemis were 'king bees,' the priestesses of Demeter, Proserpine, and the Great Mother, and possibly those of Delphi, were 'bees'; those of Dodona were 'doves'; youths at the Ephesian festival of Poseidon were 'bulls'; the girls at the Brauronian festival were 'bears' (Frazer, *Paus.* iv. 223). In Laconia the priests of Demeter and Kore were πῶλοι (de Visser, *Götter*, p. 198).

In this connexion may be noticed some facts connected with the game of 'Blind Man's Buff.' All over Europe the game is known by the names of animals [*Folklore*, xi. 261; to the names there given add cuckoo (*Rev. des Trad. Pop.* iii. 345), hoopoe (Maspons y Labros, *Jochs*, p. 45), sheep (Rolland, *Rimes*, p. 154), wryneck (Fagot, *Folklore*, p. 84); the name 'blind fly' is also found in India]. The players in the Middle Ages wore masks, as may be seen in Strutt's *Sports and Pastimes*, and we may certainly infer that they wore the mask of the animal by whose name the game was known. The significance of these facts is seen when we discover that the procedure in the game of 'Blind Man's Buff' is precisely that of many popular customs, in which cocks, cats, etc., are killed (*Folklore*, xi. 251 ff.). It cannot, however, be assumed that the game is a mere imitation of rituals in which animals are sacrificed, for it was not by children only that it was played or performed in the Middle Ages. In this connexion it should not be overlooked that in Sierra Leone the leopard society don leopard skins when they seize a human victim for sacrifice (Kingsley, *Travels*, p. 537). In this case, however, the human victim may have taken the place of a leopard; the leopard hunters of the Gold Coast likewise dress like leopards and imitate their actions when they have killed one (see 'Leopard').

As to the priority of human or animal sacrifices, no general law can be laid down. On the one hand, we find in Central Australia the ritual eating of the totem, and this is certainly not derived from any antecedent human sacrifice. On the other hand, we find, also in Australia, a ceremony of child sacrifice in connexion with the initiation of the magician, where the priority of animal sacrifice is in the highest degree improbable. In America the ritual killing of the medicine animal (see 'Nagual'), as the central feature of the initiation rite, cannot be regarded as anything but primitive. But the human sacrifices of Mexico seem to be secondary in their nature, due, possibly, to a scarcity of domestic animals. How far the agricultural sacrifice of a girl among the Pawnees can be regarded as primitive it is difficult to say; the idea of the animal corn-spirit was certainly known to them, and the influence of cannibalism may have determined a transition from animal to human sacrifice, if indeed it did not at the outset bring about a practice of human sacrifice. Where, as in Africa and the East Indies, the sacrifice is frequently of the character of an offering to a dead man, we have no reason to argue that one form preceded the other. At the same time we cannot affirm that these sacrifices were the original form in those regions. The question is in most cases insoluble.

35. *SCAPEGOAT.*—Diseases and evil influences are commonly conceived by savage and barbarous peoples as persons, often as spirits; and as a logical consequence they hold that it is possible by suitable means to expel or otherwise render innoxious all the ills with which they are from time to time afflicted. One method of doing so is to cause them to enter the body of an animal, or sometimes, where the personal form of the evil influences is less emphasized, to load them upon the animal, and drive it from the neighbourhood of human habitations. In India the scape-animal may be a pig (as for Sītalā, the smallpox goddess), a goat or buffalo (for cholera in Berar), or a cock (for cholera among the Pataris, and, in light epidemics, in Berar); and it is noteworthy that the buffalo, goat, or cock must be black (as the vehicle of Yama, the god of death). In many cases, moreover, the scape-animal becomes an actual sacrifice, as among the Hill Bhotiyas, where once a year, in honour of the village god, a dog is intoxicated with bhang and spirits, and then beaten and stoned to death, so that no disease or misfortune may visit the village during the year (Crooke, i. 141 f., 166 f., 169–174).

When the Piaroas of the Orinoco build a new hut, they believe that it is occupied by an evil spirit who must be dislodged before it is possible for them to take possession of their new abode. They capture some bird, by preference a toucan, alive, wrap it up in banana leaves, and place it across the threshold, so as to prevent the spirit from escaping. The men of the family dance, gesticulate, and menace the evil spirit, which at last endeavours to leave the hut; it cannot pass over the body of the toucan, and is compelled to enter it. The bird, terrified by the noise and confusion, struggles within its covering of banana leaves; its movements are observed by an old woman; at the proper moment she sets it free and herself flees at full speed into the forest. The bird makes use of its recovered liberty and carries away the evil spirit (*Tour du Monde*, 1888, ii. 348; for similar customs see *GB*[2] iii. 102 ff.).

Sometimes it is held sufficient to make images of animals instead of using living animals; in Old Calabar the expulsion of ghosts or devils is called *ndok*; rude images of crocodiles, leopards, etc., called *nabikom*, are placed in the street, and guns fired to frighten the spirits into the images, which are then thrown into the river (Goldie, *Calabar*, p. 49; Hutchinson, *Impressions*, p. 162). Sometimes the scapegoat is a divine animal; the people of Malabar share the Hindu reverence for the cow, but the priests are said to have transferred the sins of the people into one or more cows, which then carried them away to whatever place was appointed by the Brāhman (*Golden Bough*[2], iii. 111).

There is a European custom of hunting the wren and other animals, usually in the winter season, and especially about Christmas, at which time the expulsion of evils among peoples of lower culture usually takes place. The wren and other animals which figure in these customs are sometimes simply set free (Rolland, *op. cit.* ii. 297; *Volkskunde*, vi. 155, etc.). It is not improbable that one of the ideas at the bottom of the practice is the expulsion of evils (*FL* xvii. 258 f.). It should be observed that a frequent feature of these popular customs is a procession in which the wren or other animal is carried round the village or town. A similar practice prevailed in Dahomey (*Miss. Cath.* 1868, 107), where every three years the serpent god Danbe was carried round in a hammock, his bearers killing dogs, pigs, and fowls on their way; this ceremony they explained as intended to rid the community of its ills and diseases. In the hunting of the wren and similar customs the striking at the animal with sticks, etc., is a prominent feature; this appears to be the method by which the sins and evils of the community are put away. In Bombay the Mhars celebrate the Dusserah festival, at which a young buffalo is set free and pursued, each of his pursuers striking him with his hand or some weapon. The effect of this ceremony is held to be to make the animal the bearer of the sins of every person who touches him (*Globus*, xvii. 24).

36. *SKULL, GABLE-HEADS.*—Reaching back to classical times, and in the present day extending far beyond European limits, is the custom of hanging up the skulls of slain animals, or sometimes their jawbones. The head is often regarded as the seat of the soul, and in the East Indies this is the reason given for preserving the jawbone; probably the Eskimo custom of preserving the heads of seals has a similar idea at its base. More commonly the head is put up in a field or a vineyard as a talisman to keep off evil influences; in the same way, after a head-hunting expedition, the head of a buceros (see below) is put up as a defence. American farmers frequently fasten the skulls of horses or cattle to barns and other outhouses, although the object is now merely decorative. Arising out of this use of the skull, which had its counterpart in Europe, we find the practice of carving horses' and other heads on the gables (*Folklore*, xi. 322, etc.), but here again their magical significance seems to have been lost. In the Middle Ages the Wends put up a skull when there was a plague among the cattle, but in modern days the practice is rather to bury it; from the stories of the revival of the disease when the skull is dug up, it is clear that the idea now is that the plague is buried; the same idea is found in India. The skull is sometimes important in ritual (see 'Bison').

37. *TABU.*—Respect for totems or other sacrosanct animals may be shown positively or negatively. The system of prohibitions by which respect is shown negatively is commonly called *tabu*. It is very generally forbidden to kill the animal (Frazer, *Tot.* p. 9; *Folklore*, xi. 239–242; and below, *pass.*). It may not be eaten, even if killed by another person; or in some cases even touched, save sometimes for the taking of an oath. In South Africa it is held to be unlucky to see the *siboko* (tabued animal), and in many cases there is an objection to using the ordinary name of an animal. Sometimes it is forbidden to imitate the voice of an animal or bird; it is often accounted unlucky to keep it in or near the house. The eggs of birds may not be taken, and there is a strong objection to the use of the feathers of certain birds in making feather beds.

The penalties for violation of these tabus, which are, of course, seldom found exemplified completely in any one area or in the case of a single animal, are varied. It is a common belief in England that the harrying of a robin's nest is punished by an accident to the offender, usually the breaking of a bone. Of other birds it is said that he who kills them is killing father or mother. Sometimes an injury done to a sacrosanct animal is believed to be followed by ill-luck or sickness in the family or among the cattle. In the Congo area it is thought that the women of the kin will miscarry or give birth to animals of the totem species, or die of some dreadful disease, if a totem animal is eaten. Leprosy, madness, death by lightning, and various diseases are among other penalties for disrespect to sacred animals. In Samoa the sacred animal was thought to take up its abode in the man who broke the tabu protecting it, and thus kill him; a 'man of the turtle' would not object to helping a friend to cut up a turtle, but would take the precaution of tying a bandage over his mouth, lest an embryo turtle should slip down his throat and cause his death.

No sharp distinction can be drawn between sacred and unclean animals. The mere fact that an animal is the subject of tabus is indecisive.

Name-tabu.—It by no means follows that all tabus are an indication of respect for the animal whose name is avoided. In the case of dangerous or destructive animals the use of their name may have the result of summoning them, just as the use of the name of a dead man calls him. Various words are forbidden among fishermen; but it may be that it is unlucky for seafaring folk to mention things connected with the land, just as the Eskimos think that land and sea animals must be kept apart in cooking. Or it may be that the naming of an animal or fish will warn it that it is being pursued. Or the words may be, for some reason, of ill omen. See TABU.

38. *TATU, PAINT, KELOIDS, DEFORMATIONS.*—In America and New Guinea totem kins frequently bear their totem tatued on their bodies (Frazer, *Tot.* p. 28). In South Africa (*ib.* p. 2) teeth are knocked out in order that a resemblance to oxen may be produced. In British Columbia the totem is painted upon the face (*Globus*, lxxiv. 194). In South America some of the tribes of Brazil tatu their faces so as to resemble birds (Spix and Martius, *Travels*, p. 1027), which they respect and mourn for when they die, and into which they believe that they pass at death (von den Steinen, *Naturvölkern*, p. 512). The Californian Indians burned their *naguals* into their flesh, just as the Indians of Canada tatued theirs (Frazer, p. 55). In Africa some of the tribal marks, probably in raised pattern, are intended to make the wearer resemble a lion or a panther (*Tour du Monde*, 1891, i. 63). Some Hindu tatu marks, which are, for the most part, restricted to women, are intended to represent animals, but they are selected merely according to the desire of the person to be tatued, and, though perhaps originally totemistic, are now regarded simply as ornamental (Crooke, ii. 30–33). The totem mark in America and the tribal mark in Africa are sometimes emblazoned on the property of the totem kin or of the tribe (Frazer, *op. cit.* p. 30; *Tour du Monde, loc. cit.*). In Australia the tribes of the Upper Darling are said to carve their totems on their shields (Frazer, p. 30). The wizard frequently has animals carved on his wand or painted on his dress.

39. *TONGUE.*—Hunters frequently cut out the tongues of slain animals, and the tongues are eaten as sacred food. In folk-tales the test of the tongues is a frequent means of deciding between two claimants. The tongue of the sacrificial victim is important, and in Bohemia fox's tongue is held to confer the gift of eloquence. In N.W. America the shamans wear otter and eagle tongues round their necks as a means of acquiring supernatural knowledge. In particular, an otter's tongue is held to confer a knowledge of the language of all inanimate objects, all birds, beasts, and living creatures (*Golden Bough*[2], ii. 421, 422; cf. Krause, *Die Tlinkit Indianer*, p. 284). The shamanistic rattles contain the tongue *motif* carved on them as a rule in this part of America, and similar figures have been found in the Pacific (*Ann. Rep. Bur. Ethn.* 1881–1882, pp. 111–112). Tongue masks are recorded in New Zealand (Parkinson, *Journal*, pp. 98, 128; see also Frobenius, *Weltansch.* p. 199).

40. *TOTEMISM.*—Under ordinary circumstances, totemism is a relation between a group of human beings and a species of animals, characterized by three main features: (1) the assumption by the totem kin of the name of the animal; (2) the prohibition of the intermarriage of persons of the same totem name; (3) respect paid by every member of the totem kin to the totem animal. Each of these features is liable to deformation; we find totem kins which respect an animal other than their eponymous one; kin exogamy becomes local exogamy or disappears altogether; the totem animal is eaten ritually or otherwise. Other features of totemism are present only occasionally, and their absence in no way invalidates the totemic character of the relation. More especially in America the connexion between the kin and the animal is explained as one of descent, the animal sometimes having united itself to a human being, sometimes having transformed itself into the ancestors of the kin by a gradual process, and so on. But it must not be supposed that totemism exists or has existed wherever we find a myth of descent from an animal (see 'Myths of Ancestors' above). More especially in Australia the totem is held to aid his kinsmen by omens or in other ways. Conversely, in Central Australia, the kin perform magical rites to promote the increase of the totem species; traces of magical influence over the totem are found elsewhere; but it does not seem legitimate to assume that all cases of magical influence of this sort are totemic in origin. Sometimes the kin indicate their totem by tatuing or other marks, sometimes by deformations, or by the mode of wearing the hair, or by their dress.

In determining the totem of a child, kinship is usually reckoned through the mother. On the other hand, the usual course at marriage is for the female to remove to the husband's house or district. The result of this is that the kins in any area are (1) intermingled, and (2) continually changing. Where the parent from whom the child takes its totem continues to reside in his or her own district, the tendency is for the totem kins to become localized. The result of this is that certain animals are respected in certain districts; in this way perhaps originated the local cults of Egypt. Tribal respect for the totem of the chief, and ancestor-worship are also paths by which totemism may have been transformed.

Totemistic tabus do not differ markedly in form from those connected with other sacred animals; they may therefore be dealt with together in this article (see 'Tabu' above).

Sex totems.—A peculiar relation exists in Australia between the two sexes and two species of animals which might better be termed 'animal brothers and sisters.' It is found from South Australia as far as Brisbane, and the animals thus related to the men and women are lizards, owls, bats, emu-wrens, superb warblers, and goatsuckers. Although the life of a man or woman is believed to be bound up with the life of one of these animals, and although they are in consequence jealously protected by the sex to which they belong, as a preliminary to marriage it is the custom among the Kurnais for one of the 'animal relatives' to be killed by the opposite sex (*Golden Bough*[2], iii. 414–416).

41. *VEGETATION.*—In the ancient world a number of minor deities, especially connected with vegetation, were believed to possess animal or semi-animal form. Not only were the bull and goat closely associated with Dionysus, but Pan, the Satyrs, and the Fauns are especially associated with goats (see below). The only explanation hitherto sug-

gested of this connexion is that the goat naturally wanders in the forest and browses off the tender shoots of trees, so that the animal which so boldly appropriates the property of the tree-spirit can be none other than that spirit in bodily form. Frazer has explained the ceremonies performed at various periods in the spring as intended in part to promote the growth of vegetation by killing the old, and therefore weak, spirit of the previous year, replacing him by a more youthful and vigorous representative. Many of these ceremonies are performed during the Carnival or at Mid-Lent; among the animals which appear at that period are the bear (in effigy), the ox, the goat, the wolf, etc. But these ceremonies seem to have had another purpose too,—that of the expulsion of evils,—so that we cannot identify all the animals that so appear with the spirit of vegetation. In the same way various animals (the squirrel, fox, cat, etc.) are thrown into the bonfires at Easter or other periods of the year, —Frazer says as sun-charms. It is hardly legitimate to regard these as so many representatives of the spirit of vegetation. In China the spirits are bull-shaped (de Groot, *Rel. Syst.* iv. 279).

42. *WATER.*—In Greece, Poseidon and river gods generally seem to have been conceived under the form of bulls (*JHS* xiv. 126, 129). The festival of Poseidon was called *Tauria*, and his priests were termed 'bulls' (de Visser, *Götter*, pp. 41, 193). In the north of Europe, on the other hand, the horse seems to have been considered a more appropriate form for the god of water (see 'Horse'; cf. *Folklore*, v. 116). In South Africa and Australia the form attributed to water-monsters is that of the serpent (see below). In India and Eastern Asia the conception of a dragon replaces that of a serpent; we find traces of the same idea in Europe in the story of Perseus and its many variants. See also 'Dragon,' 'Serpent.'

43. *WER-WOLF.*—The belief in wer-wolves is connected, on the one hand, with the pathological condition known as lycanthropy, in which the sufferer believes himself turned into an animal; on the other, with the belief in *naguals* (see above), familiars and tutelary spirits which serve the human beings who can secure their services. Corresponding to these two sources of the belief, there are two different forms of it. In the first place, the man is conceived to put off his own form and assume that of the animal—in Europe most commonly the wolf, as the last dangerous animal to be exterminated or to survive in the west and south. This transformation may be temporary or permanent, may be due to eating human flesh, to the sins of the transformee, or to some magical procedure such as the drawing on of a wolf's skin, or to contagion, such as eating food left by another wer-wolf. In the second place, it may be simply the spirit of the wer-man which undergoes the change, his body being left torpid at home; or, according to another form of the belief, the wer-animal is simply his servant, and the man himself goes on with his ordinary occupations while it is on the prowl; his life, however, depends on its security.

In Europe the wer-wolf is supposed to fall upon his victim like ordinary wolves. In the East Indies the procedure of the wer-animal is more complicated. He attacks solitary individuals, who forthwith become drowsy. Thereupon the wer-man assumes his own form, cuts up his victim, eats his liver, and puts the body together again. There are various signs by which a wer-wolf can be recognized, and ordeals are prescribed for discovering it. The wer-wolf is, as a rule, in the form of a living man; but sometimes the dead are believed to return in animal form (see 'Soul-animal' above) and practise the same arts as wer-wolves proper. A method of burial is prescribed in Celebes for preventing the revival of the dead wer-man. The wer-wolf as form of the dead is closely connected, if not identical, with the vampire in some of its forms. See also 'Nagual,' 'Totemism' above. See LYCANTHROPY.

44. *PARTICULAR ANIMALS.*—**Ant.**—We learn from Greek writers that ants were worshipped in Thessaly; the Myrmidons revered them and claimed descent from them (de Visser, *Götter*, p. 157; Lang, *Myth*, ii. 197). In Dahomey and Porto Novo, ants are regarded as the messengers of the serpent-god Danbe (*Miss. Cath.* 1884, 232). In Jabim, New Guinea, it is believed that a second death after the first is possible, in which case the soul becomes an ant (*Nachr. K. Wilhelmsland*, 1897, 92). We find in Cornwall the belief that ants are the souls of unbaptized children (*FLJ* v. 182). In France it is held that it brings ill-luck to destroy an ant's nest (Rolland, *Faune*, iv. 279). The ant is fed by Hindus and Jains on certain days, and is regarded as associated with the souls of the blessed dead (Crooke, ii. 256).

In South America and California one mode of initiation was to allow the boy or girl to be stung by ants (*Golden Bough*[2], iii. 215); it is said to make them brisk and impart strength. The Piojes submit to it in order to acquire skill with the blow-tube (*JAI* viii. 221). The Athapascan Dog-Ribs believed that the gift of prophecy was acquired by secretly putting an ant under the skin of the hand (Franklin, *Second Expedition*, p. 291). On the other hand, the Aruntas hold that a medicine man must not go near the nest of the bull-dog ant; for if he were bitten, he would lose his power for ever (Spencer and Gillen, *Nat. Tr.* p. 525). In Bulgaria and Switzerland, ants are regarded as of bad omen (Strausz, *Bulgaren*, p. 298; *Schw. Arch.* ii. 216). The Esthonians regard them as of good omen (*Gel. Ehst. Ges. Schriften*, No. 2, p. 28); and for the Huculs red ants are lucky, black unlucky (Kaindl, p. 105).

Not only the ant but also the ant-hill is the object of superstitious observances. The Juangs take an oath on an ant-hill, and the Kharrias use it as an altar (*Miss. Cath.* 1897, 369, 380). At Poona a dance round an ant-hill is part of a religious ceremony (*Bombay Gaz.* XVIII. i. 293). In West Africa, ants' nests are regarded by the Susus as the residence of demons (Winterbottom, *Sierra L.* i. 222). Elsewhere they are brought into connexion with the souls of dead chiefs (Bastian, *Bilder*, p. 181). In South Africa the bodies of children are buried in ant-hills that have been excavated by ant-eaters (*Account of Cape of Good Hope*, 143). In the Sudan it is believed that a hyæna-man assumes his animal form at an ant's nest (*Globus*, xlii. 157). For myths and folk-tales of the ant see de Gubernatis, *Zool. Myth.* ii. 44 ff.

Ass.—The Romans believed that the Jews worshipped the ass (Tac. *Ann.* v. iii. 4; Diodor. iv. 148; cf. Reinach, *Cultes*, i. 342; Krauss, in *JE* ii. 222–224). In Greece at the present day the *pagania* are believed to have asses' heads; the people believe them to be Jews who worshipped the ass (Pouqueville, *Voyage*, ii. 415; cf. Tsuntas, Ἐφ. Ἀρχ. 1887, p. 160, pl. x.). At Frickhausen in Württemberg the peasants are said to keep a wooden ass in a cellar as the tutelary deity of the village (Mannhardt, *Germ. Mythen*, p. 411). In explanation of the poverty of Silesian vineyards, it is said that the ancient Silesians ate the ass on which Silenus rode (Sinapius, *Olsnographia*, i. 342, 3). Typhon was represented with an ass's head, and the inhabitants of Coptos threw an ass down a precipice as his representative (Plut.

de Is. et Os. 30). The Armenians sacrifice an ass at the grave of the ancestors of a person against whom they have a claim, in the belief that if their claim is not satisfied, the soul of such ancestors will pass into an ass (Haxthausen, *Transkaukasia*, ii. 21). In parts of Germany, children are said to come from the ass's pond (Mannhardt, *Germ. Mythen*, p. 411). At Erfurt it is the custom to sell earthenware images in the shape of donkeys at an annual fair (*ib.* p. 414). In Moldavia, Calabria, and Portugal, an ass's head is a means of averting evil or the influence of the evil eye from the fields or orchards (Rolland, *Faune*, iv. 191; Trede, *Heidenthum*, p. 210; *Mélusine*, viii. 14). Near Meiningen the last stroke of the reaper was said to kill the oats, barley, or lentil ass, just as in other parts other animals are regarded as incarnations of the corn-spirit (Haupt's *Zeitschr. f. D. Altertum*, iii. 360 ff.).

Prominent among mediæval festivals was the *fête des ânes* or *festa asinaria* (Chambers, *Medieval Stage*, i. 282, 306, 331 ff.; *Zts. des Alpenvereins*, xxviii. 135–154), and there are traces of the performers wearing ass masks (Chambers, *op. cit.* p. 332). It seems probable that in spite of its ecclesiastical associations it was simply a popular festival of the same nature as the 'white horse' (*Rev. Hist. Rel.* xxxviii. 334) and other customs, the existence of which far back in the Middle Ages is well attested by ecclesiastical fulminations. In the present case the association of the ass with Palm Sunday made it possible for the Church to throw a veneer of religion over the pagan rite. In Augsburg in the 16th century a wooden ass was drawn through the streets; palms were thrown down before it; a priest prostrated himself and was beaten by another priest; and the first palm to be caught up was used in magical ceremonies (*Germania*, xvii. 81). Many of these celebrations are kept up unofficially at the present day at various times in the spring — Mid-Lent, Palm Sunday, Easter, Whitsuntide (*Tradition*, vi. 197, 226; *Bavaria*, II. i. 163; Reinsberg-Düringsfeld, *Festl. Jahr, pass.*; *Zts. f. Volksk.* iii. 307, iv. 33). The ass also appears in connexion with St. Nicholas on Dec. 6th, and in Zug children on this day carry round a wooden ass's head (*Schw. Archiv*, i. 64). In Grisons the ass of St. Nicholas is said to carry off the children and throw them down a precipice (*ib.* ii. 167). On the Thursday before Christmas the *Posterlijagd* is held at Entlebuch; people from other villages arrive, and one of them represents Posterli, sometimes in the shape of an ass. The image is left in a corner of the village (Stalder, *Schweizer. Idiotikon*, i. 208). For myths of the ass, its supposed phallic meaning, and folk-tales relating to it, see de Gubernatis, *Zool. Myth.* ii. 359–399. The story of Midas is also discussed by Ciszewski, *Bajka o Midasowych uszach.*

Basilisk.—Accounts of the basilisk (βασιλισκος), a king of the serpents, have come down from Pliny (XXIX. xix.) and Heliodorus (*Æthiopica*, iii. 8). It was believed to be a small serpent with a cock's head; its look was fatal. In mediæval and modern Europe the basilisk or cockatrice is supposed to be hatched from the egg of a seven-year-old cock or from the hundredth egg of a hen (*Mélusine*, v. 18–22). On the other hand, the first egg of a black hen is held in Bohemia to be the dangerous one; there is, however, another belief, according to which it produces the *šotek*, or demon of good luck (Grohmann, *Abergl.*, Nos. 77, 543, 544).

Bat.—Among the Cakchiquels the chief god, Chamalcan, took the form of a bat (Bancroft, iii. 484). A sacred bat figures in a Queensland myth; the first man and woman were told not to approach it, but the woman disobeyed and the bat flew away; after that death came into the world; the form of the myth, however, suggests Christian influence (Ballou, *Under the Southern Cross*, p. 141). Among the Bongos, bats are called by the same generic term as witches and spirits—*bitabok* (Schweinfurth, *Heart of Africa*, i. 144). In West Africa an island on the Ivory Coast is peopled with huge bats, which are regarded as the souls of the dead, and are sacrosanct for that reason (*Golden Bough*[2], ii. 431). The Bantus of Natal will not touch a bat (Fleming, *Southern Africa*, p. 265). In Tonga, bats are sacred, probably as the abode of the souls of the dead (Bässler, *Südseebilder*, p. 318). No native in Victoria will kill or eat them for this reason (Parker, *Aborigines*, p. 25), and the Adjahdurahs also respect them (*R. G. S. Aust., S. Aust. Br.* II. iii. 17). They are respected in Bosnia (*Wiss. Mitt.* iv. 471) and parts of Shropshire (Burne, *Shrop. Folkl.* p. 214), but in other places they are killed. In Kusaie, or Strong Island, bat flesh is tabu to men (Hernsheim, *Südsee*, p. 49). Among various Victorian tribes the bat is a 'sex totem,' better termed a 'man's brother' (Frazer, *Tot.* p. 52). In China the bat is the emblem of the four desirable things (*Miss. Cath.* 1899, 359). In Poland it is of good omen before sunset (*Tradition*, viii. 138). It is considered lucky in Sarajevo for one to come into the house (*Wiss. Mitt.* iv. 441). On the other hand, it is usually considered of bad omen (Wiedemann, *Ehsten*, p. 451; Strackerjan, p. 24, etc.), and in Salzburg it is believed to bring death into the house (MS note). In Sicily the bat is regarded as a form of the devil, and a verse is sung to it; when it is caught it is killed by fire or nailed up with outspread wings (de Gubernatis, *Zool. Myth.* ii. 203). For the song, compare Ledieu, *Monogr. d'un Bourg picard*, p. 41. The custom of nailing up bats is common (Sébillot, *Trad. de la H. Bret*, p. 94; Trede, *Heidenthum*, ii. 249; Böcler-Kreutzwald, p. 143). A bat's heart is believed to bring luck at cards (Köhler, *Volksbrauch*, p. 417).

Bear.—Although the bear is an object of fear and respect to most of the uncultured races who are acquainted with it, there is but little to say of it so far as mythology is concerned. In a few cases we find a myth of descent from the bear; the Modocs of California believe that they are sprung from the union of a daughter of the Great Spirit, who was blown down Mount Shasta, with a grizzly bear; before this bears were like men, but the Great Spirit then made them quadrupeds. As a mark of respect they never mention the bear by name; if an Indian is killed by a bear, he is buried on the spot, and all who pass by the spot for years afterwards cast a stone upon the place (Miller, *Life among the Modocs*, p. 242). Some of the totem kins of the Amerinds trace their origin to bears (Dwight, *Travels*, iv. 184; Schoolcraft, *Ind. Tr.* iii. 268). In Europe, as well as in Syria and in Dardistan, stories are or have been told of girls who are abducted by bears and produce sometimes human, sometimes half-human, offspring (Rolland, *Faune pop.* i. 53; Twysden, *Hist. Angl. Scr.* x. 945; Leitner, *Languages and Races of Dardistan*, iii. 12; MacCulloch, 270 f.). The Crees tell a similar story, but here the offspring are bears which are later transformed into men (Petitot, *Traditions*, p. 460). The Malays tell of the bear a story of the Gelert type (*JRAS, S.B.*, No. 7, p. 23).

As a useful and at the same time dangerous animal, the bear receives in many parts of the world a tribute of respect during its lifetime, which is often manifested by a disinclination to pronounce its name (see below, 'Name tabu'). It is, however, but seldom that it receives actual worship before it has been laid low. In Japan there is a tradition of a white bear-god which lives in an inaccessible mountain (*Mitt. d. Ges. N.V. Ostasiens*, xlix. p. 431). Among the Tatars the earth spirits take the form of bears among other animals, and on this account they are accorded increased respect (Castrén, *Vorlesungen*, p. 230), but there is nothing to show that they receive actual worship. One authority says that the Ostiaks worship the image of a bear (Ides, *Travels*, p. 29); and in India the bear is believed to scare away disease, so that ailing children are made to ride on the backs of tame animals of this species (Crooke, ii. 242).

Name-tabu.—Some animals are not called by their ordinary names for fear of summoning them, but in the case of the bear the use of special terms seems to arise from a fear of offending it and a desire to do it honour. In Sweden it is called 'grandfather,' by the Esthonians 'broadfoot'; analogous to this case, though with a difference of usage, is the Ottawa practice of terming the bear kin 'broad feet.' The Finns call the bear 'the apple of the wood,' 'beautiful honey paw,' etc. (*Golden Bough*[2], i. 455; see also *ARW* ii. 332; Kaindl, *Huzulen*, 103). The Yocuts never express enmity to the bear, lest he should hear and take vengeance (*FLJ* v. 73).

Far more marked is the respect paid to the dead bear. Indeed, more than one observer has asserted of some of the East Asiatic peoples that the bear is their chief divinity. There can, however, be no doubt that the Ainus and others kill the bear whenever they can, and that its flesh forms their staple food. The subject has been treated at length by Frazer (*Golden Bough*[2], ii. 375 ff.), whose account is here followed, and who explains the custom as an atonement offered to the species, through the medium of single individuals, for the loss it sustains in the slaughter of so many of its members for food.

In preparation for the Ainu festival, a young bear is caught about the end of winter and brought into the village; it is fed until its strength increases and it threatens to escape from its wooden cage; then, in the autumn, the festival is held. The giver of the feast invites all his friends; libations are offered to the bear and various deities; and the women dance round the cage, addressing the animal in terms of endearment. After the men have shot at it with blunt arrows, a number of men put an end to its life by kneeling on it and pressing its neck against a log, the women all the time uttering lamentations behind them. The carcass is set up before certain sacred wands and decorated in various ways. Libations are offered to it, and the women, laying aside all marks of sorrow, dance merrily before it. The animal is next skinned and cut up, and its blood is drunk, so far as is known, by men only. The liver and brain are eaten on the spot, and the remainder of the flesh is divided among those who have been present. The Gilyaks hold a similar festival; but the bear is shot with arrows in this case; at the end of the ceremonies the skull is placed on a tree (*GB*[2] ii. 380). There seems to be a practice of imputing the guilt of the slaughter of the bear to the toad, which has an evil reputation among the Gilyaks (*ib.* p. 383). Before being sacrificed the bear is led round the village, and ceremonies are performed in its honour (*ib.* p. 382).

According to a later account, which is important for our attitude towards the whole of the East Asiatic bear ceremonies, the Gilyaks celebrate a festival for any bear which they kill in hunting, as well as for those they rear; as soon as the ceremony is over, the soul of the animal, which has permitted itself to be killed, goes to the 'Lord of the Mountain,' Pal, accompanied by dogs killed in his honour, and by the souls of gifts of which it is the recipient.

The bear festival proper is instituted in honour of a recently deceased kinsman. It is prepared by the *gens* of the deceased, but forms a general feast of several *gentes*, which are a more important factor in its celebration than the *gens* which provides the festivity. When the time comes to kill the bear, the chief guests are the husbands of the women of the host's kin; they bring with them their sons-in-law, whose duty it is to kill the bear. The guests are called *narch*, and they are entertained by the 'lord of the bear.' Women are excluded from the ceremony of killing the bear, which is preceded by a trial of skill with the bow, in which the *narch* take part as well as the kin of the 'lord of the bear'; it is a point of honour for the latter to shoot badly. The *narch* then settle among themselves who is to give the fatal wound. When the guests have gone, the nearest kinsmen of the dead man proceed to cut up the bear, which is placed in a majestic pose after being killed, its head to the west. Its head is carried off by the women on a sacred sledge, on which are also tobacco, sugar, bow and arrows, etc., gifts to the dead beast, who takes their souls with him. The guests of honour alone partake of the flesh of the bear; their hosts get only bear soup. Before they depart, the *narch* leave several dogs tied near the head of the bear. These are directed to follow their master the bear, and are then killed on the same spot. The flesh of the dogs is consumed by all persons of the kin of the dead man. On the following day the head of the bear is taken to its last resting-place, and then its soul goes to the 'Lord of the Mountain' (*ARW* viii. 260–272).

If the precise meaning of these ceremonies is not apparent, it is at least clear that the cult of dead kinsmen is one of the elements at the present day; it may be noted that the 'kin gods' of the Gilyaks are human beings who have met with a violent death, but whether it is only in honour of such that the festival is held does not appear (*ib.* p. 259). A second element is possibly that of purification (*ib.* p. 273).

On the whole, we must regard the Gilyak ceremony as analogous to the Zuñi turtle-killing—a means of communication with the dead of the tribe.

The Ostiaks, on the other hand, appear to pay equal honour to every bear which they kill; they cut off its head, hang it on a tree, and, surrounding it, pay respect to it; then they run towards the body and lament over it, explaining that it is not they but the Russians who have killed it (Autermony, *Voyage*, ii. 92). As a mark of respect, Samoyeds allow no woman to eat of its flesh (Erman, *Reise*, i. 681). If the Ostiaks show respect to the bear, they also give evidence of very different feelings; its skin is stuffed with hay and spat upon to the accompaniment of songs of triumph (*ib.* 670), but they subsequently set up the figure in a corner of the court and treat it for a time as a tutelary deity (*ib.*). (For songs in honour of the bear see *Beiträge zur Kenntniss*, xxv. 79).

We find a similar custom among the Pottawatomies. The head of the bear is set up and painted with various colours, and all participants in the feast sing songs in its honour (Baumgarten, *Allg. Ges. Am.* ii. 542). Although no special ceremonies are observed by the Kamtchatkans, the killer of a bear is obliged to invite all his friends to partake of the flesh (Krachenninikow, ii. 107). Among the Lapps the bear hunt is the occasion of various ceremonies. When the animal is dead, they beat it with rods and then transport it on a sledge to a hut constructed on purpose; they then go to a hut where their wives await them; the latter chew bark to colour their saliva red, and spit in the faces of the men (probably as a purificatory ceremony).

Continence is observed for three days, and then the flesh is prepared and eaten by men and women separately; the women may not approach the place where the bear is cooked or partake of flesh from the rump (*Voyages et Av. des Emigrés français*, ii. 150). The Montagnais prohibit bear's flesh to women and children (Hind, *Explor.* i. 179); the Ojibwas will not allow dogs to touch a dead bear (*JAI* iii. 111). The Tacullies eat bear's flesh at the feast of the dead (Harmon, *Journ.* 289). The Mohawks offered bear's flesh to Agreskoui when they had met with ill-success in war (Megapolensis, *Beschrijving*, p. 48).

In East Asia an oath by a bear is not uncommon. In some cases the skin or a piece of flesh is brought (Schrenck, i. 408); or an offering of a skin is made (Ides, p. 19), and in case of perjury the animal comes to life; we may take this to mean that they believe the bear will devour the perjurer, for the Samoyeds make a man bite a bear's head, and hold that a bear will devour him if he swears falsely (Billings, i. 228; cf. Latham, *Russian Empire*, p. 124).

There is a European practice, possibly connected with agricultural rites, of dressing a man up as a bear, especially in the winter season, and going with him in procession (Mannhardt, *Ant. W. u. Feldculte*, 188 ff.; *Zts. Ver. Volks.* vi. 429). The custom is especially prevalent in the Lausitz, a Wendish area (MS notes). In Poland the 'bear' is thrown into the water (Kolberg, *Poznanskie*, i. 134, 136, 139, ii. 350).

The Central Eskimos believe that they can acquire a bear spirit as tutelary deity, or *tornaq*. The would-be *angakok* must travel to the edge of the great ice-floe and summon the bears. When they appear, he falls down at once; and if he falls upon his face, a bear steps forward and asks his will. The man recovers and goes back with the bear (*Ann. Rep. Bur. Eth.* 1884–1885, p. 591).

The bear is especially associated with Berne, the name of which means 'bear,' and the town has kept bears for centuries. The explanation given is that duke Berthold delivered them from a gigantic bear, but this is simply ætiological and probably late; for it is certain that the bear was associated with the town centuries before Berthold. In 1832 a statuette of a goddess, Artio, was discovered in the neighbourhood, which dated from Roman times. Now Artio is certainly connected with Irish *art*, Lat. *ursus*, Gr. ἄρκτος, and means the goddess of the bear or something of that sort. A bear was also discovered among the other statuettes, but was not until later brought into connexion with the goddess, before whom it was standing in the original form of the group (*Rev. Celt.* xxi. 280). See CELTIC RELIGION, § x. 8.

In Greek cult, bears were burnt in honour of Artemis Λαφρία at Patræ (Paus. VII. xviii. 8), and 'bear Artemis' was one of the names by which she was known. There is a good deal of evidence to connect Artemis with a cult of the bear (Farnell, *Cults*, ii. 435). Callisto, in an Arcadian myth, is changed into a bear, and she seems to be only another form of Artemis (Müller, *Proleg.* pp. 73–76), who is also called Καλλίστη. Moreover, at Brauron, Athens, and Munychia, Artemis Βραυρωνία was worshipped (cf. Lang, *Myth*, ii. 212–215) in ceremonies which were perhaps a survival of initiation customs. Young maidens danced in a saffron robe, and, like the priestesses, were called 'bears'; the dance was called ἀρκτεία, and the participants were of ages from five to ten; the celebrations were quinquennial, and no girl might marry before undergoing the rite. There is a trace of a bear sacrifice at Brauron (Farnell, ii. 437), but the animal usually offered was the goat or hind. For folk-tales of the bear see de Gubernatis, *Zool. Myth.* ii. 109–119. For myths see Bachofen, *Der Bär*.

Bee.—The Tchuwashes of East Russia have a bee-god, and celebrate a bee festival at which they drink beer sweetened with honey (*Globus*, lxiii. 323). The priests of Ephesian Artemis were called 'king bees'; the priestesses of Demeter, Proserpine, and the Great Mother were known as 'bees.' From the fact that the priests of the horse-goddess Demeter were called 'horses,' we may infer that the goddesses in question were bee-goddesses, or that their cult had included a local cult of the bee (Frazer, *Paus.* iv. 223). As a means of attacking or defending cities, bees figure in Quiché and European sagas (Liebrecht, *Zur Volksk.* p. 75). In North Guinea beehives are actually hung at the entrance to a village, but the intention is probably magical (Wilson, *Western Africa*, p. 158). For myths of bees proceeding from the bodies of animals, as in the story of Samson (Jg 14[8]), see *Globus*, xxxix. 222. The soul is believed in parts of Europe to take the form of a bee (*ib.* li. 316; Jecklin, *Volksthümliches*, i. 59).

In European folklore the bee is everywhere sacrosanct (*Folklore*, xi. 239), but, as often happens, the first bee may be killed for use in magic (*ib.* p. 254). As ominous animals, bees vary in their signification; in some parts of Wales a swarm entering a house is a bad omen; elsewhere the reverse is the case (*Rev. Hist. Rel.* xxxviii. 308). If they leave their hive it is a death omen (Brand, *Pop. Ant.* ii. 175, 219; Rochholz, i. 148). A swarm on a house means fire (*Globus*, xxvii. 96; Rochholz, *loc. cit.*). The European peasant attributes special intelligence to bees; they suffer no uncleanliness of any sort near them; they should not be sold; the death of a member of the family must be announced to them, and mourning put on their hives (*Globus*, xxxix. 221 f.). At certain times in the year honey should be eaten (*ib.*). For myths and folk-tales of the bee see de Gubernatis, *Zool. Myth.* ii. 215–223. For the symbolism of bees see Pauly-Wissowa (1894), p. 446 ff.; for myths, p. 448 ff. See ARYANS.

Beetle.—The cult of the scarab was general in Egypt (Budge, *Gods*, ii. 379). At the present day it is feared by the Hottentots, of whom Kolbe says that they sacrifice sheep and oxen to a beetle (Walckenaer, *Hist. Gen.* xv. 372). The beetle is tabu in various parts of Europe (*Folklore*, xi. 239, 242). Killing it is believed to cause rain (Rolland, *Faune*, iii. 324; Napier, *Folklore*, p. 116; MS notes). In East Prussia it is held to be lucky to set a beetle on its feet when it has got 'cast' (MS note; cf. Afzelius, *Sagohäfder*, i. 13). In Schleswig-Holstein its name connects it with Thor (Schiller, *Thier . . . buch*, p. 11). It is sometimes kept in a cage for luck (Napier, *Folklore*, p. 116; Böhme, *Kinderspiel*, p. 424). In Scotland the stag beetle is killed because it is the devil's imp; the black beetle is killed whenever it is found, and a story is told to explain the custom (*Gent.'s Mag.* 1876, ii. 510; cf. Rolland, *Faune*, iii. 327). In Lautenthal, boys put a stag beetle in the ground and strike blindfold at its horns; the one who hits it is the winner and takes the beetle home (Kuhn, *Nordd. Sagen*, p. 377). In the Grafschaft Mark the horns are used for divination (Wöste, p. 56).

The ladybird is often tabu (Grohmann, *Abergl.* No. 1686; Strackerjan, *Abergl.* p. 45). It is said to bring the children (Mannhardt, *Germ. Mythen*, p. 272). It is regarded as of good omen.

The cockchafer is also tabu (*Folklore*, xi. 240). It is greeted in the spring (*Bavaria*, IV. ii. 357), carried in procession (*La Fontaine*, p. 62), and sold in the spring (*Germania*, vii. 435; *FLR* iii. 138; cf. Rolland, *Faune*, iii. 340). It is considered of good omen for one to settle on the hand (*Bavaria*, IV. ii. 402). Children often repeat verses to the ladybird (Ledieu, *Monographie*, p. 40; Rolland, *Faune*, iii. 351–358). In Picardy it is the custom to kill the ladybird (Ledieu, *loc. cit.*). A beetle is carried for luck (Spiess, *Aberglauben*, p. 417), and used in magic (Heyl, *Volkssagen*, p. 787; Wuttke, *Der Aberglaube*, *passim*). In the mythology of the Sia the beetle was entrusted with a bag of stars; getting very tired, he peeped in, and they flew out and covered the heavens (*Ann. Rep. Bur. Ethn.* 1889–1890, p. 35). For the folklore of the beetle see de Gubernatis, *Zool. Myth.* ii. 209 ff.

Bison.—One of the Omaha clans traced its descent from a bison, which is said to have been originally under the surface of the water; they believed that they returned to the buffaloes at death (Frazer, *Tot.* pp. 4, 36). Both Iowa and Omaha males dress their hair in imitation of the bison when it is their totem (*ib.* p. 27). A southern tribe, probably the Kwapas, propitiated the dead bison; they adorned its head with swan and bustard down dyed red, and put tobacco in its nostrils and in the cleft of its hoofs. When they had flayed it, they cut out its tongue and replaced it by a piece of tobacco. Two wooden forks were then stuck into the ground and a crosspiece laid upon them, on which were placed pieces of flesh as an offering (*Hist. Coll. Louisiana*, i. 181). Another account says that the Louisiana Indians bewailed the bison before they set out for the chase (Hennepin, *Desc.* p. 80). Possibly the Blackfoot practice of putting a bison skull on an altar is part of a similar propitiation (*Miss. Cath.* 1869, 359).

Many tribes performed mimetic dances in order to increase the supply of bison (Frazer, *Tot.* p. 41; Battey, *A Quaker*, p. 172). The Sioux believed that they could attract the bison by imitating the bark of the coyote (*Tour du Monde*, 1864, i. 54). The Pawnees used to 'dance the bison' for their neighbours; they dressed in war costume and covered their heads with a bison skin with the horns still attached (Perrin du Lac, *Voyage*, p. 334). It does not appear whether this had anything to do with the belief in the bison form of the corn-spirit, but the Creek dance was performed at the time of their Green Corn dance; men, women, and children took an active part in the ceremony, dressing themselves in the scalp of the bison with horns and tail attached; uttering sounds in imitation of the animal, they danced in a circle, their bodies in a half bent position, their weight being supported on two sticks which represented the forelegs of the animal (Stanley, *Portraits*, p. 10). The bison is associated with corn in various ways by the Pawnees (Dorsey, *Traditions of Skidi Pawnee*, pp. 85, 344). For their corn dance preparations are made by killing a bison; this is done by a woman; the pericardium is dried and filled with various kinds of corn. For the dance itself the floor must be as clean as possible; sacred bundles of corn and bison flesh are prepared, and a bison skull and two hoes of bison bone are placed before them; the women dance, holding their hoes, and every one searches for buffalo hairs; if they see any they say, 'Now we are going to be successful in our hunt and in our corn' (Grinnell, *Pawnee Hero Stories*, p. 372). They give the name of 'mother' to the dried skull of a bison cow painted red, which they place at the bottom of the hut on a sort of altar; they think that it has the power of attracting bison. At seed-time the corn is brought to the hut, and the old men bring out little idols and bird skins, and sing all day to obtain a good harvest. Offerings of first-fruits are also made (Du Lac, *Voyage*, p. 270). Probably the same ideas prevailed among other tribes; for we find that the Osages had a myth that corn was given them by four bison bulls (*Ann. Rep. Bur. Ethn.* viii. 379; cf. Matthews, *Ethn. of Hidatsa Indians*, p. 12).

Buceros (rhinoceros-bird).—This bird is important in the East Indian area. In Borneo the gables of some of the houses have a buceros in wood; and with this may be connected the fact that when they have taken a head on a head-hunting expedition, a wooden buceros is set up with its beak pointing towards the foe; on the gable it is said to bring luck. In Celebes the priests put the head of a buceros on a magic staff, and it is also believed to attract purchasers to shops on which it is placed. Under the central post of the house it is believed to avert evil from the dwelling. The head-hunter sometimes wears a buceros head on his own, probably for the same reason that one is set up; in Borneo it has become general to wear feathers and carved bills, but the right to do so is restricted to those who have taken a head with their own hands. It figures in the death dance of the Battas; a mimetic dance in Borneo seems to have in the present day no other object than amusement. At a ceremony of peacemaking the Ibans suspend from a wooden buceros a great number of cigarettes, which are taken down and smoked ceremonially by all the men present (*REth* iv. 312 ff.; *JAI* xxxi. 180, 198; *Tijdschr. T.L.V.* xxviii. 517, xxxi. 349).

Buffalo.—Like many other pastoral peoples, the Todas show their domestic animal, the buffalo, a degree of respect which does not fall far short of adoration. As often happens, the flesh of the female is never eaten; once a year a bull calf is killed and eaten by the adult males of the village in the recesses of the wood. It is killed with a club made of a sacred wood; the fire is made of certain kinds of wood, produced by rubbing sticks together (Marshall, *Todas*, p. 129 f.; see also Rivers, *Todas*, p. 274 ff.). In other parts of India the animal serves as a scapegoat in case of cholera (*Golden Bough*², iii. 101). The Mhars of Bombay sacrifice a buffalo at the Dusserah festival; they lead it before the temple of Bhavānī, and the chief strikes it on the neck with a sword; thereupon it is hunted and struck with the hand or with a weapon; in this way it is laden with the sins of those who succeed in touching it. After being driven round the walls, its head is struck off at the gate; a single stroke must suffice if the sacrifice is to be efficacious. Then they fall upon the victim and tear it in pieces; a procession round the walls follows, in which the demons are prayed to receive the offering; pieces of flesh are thrown backwards over the wall for them (*Globus*, xvii. 24). A somewhat similar sacrifice is performed among certain hill-tribes at the festival in honour of Nanda, Krishna's foster-father, and was also celebrated formerly by the Bhumij. The buffalo is frequently sacrificed, moreover, in honour of Durga, the consort of Śiva, and in art is the vehicle of Yama, the god of death, the female being regarded as the incarnation of Savitrī, the wife of Brahmā (Crooke, i. 112, ii. 236 f.). The Zulus hold that the souls of the dead pass into the Cape buffalo (Fritsch, *Eingeborene*, p. 139). The Ewe tribes hunter observes tabus when he kills a buffalo (*Mitt. d. Schutzgeb.* v. 156). Among the Ewe tribes, when a buffalo bull has been killed, it is cut up and sold before the hut of the hunter. With an old woman as president, he and older companions partake of a meal in a hut, and the entrails of the buffalo are wound round some of the guests. The successful hunter must remain in his hut for some days, and for nineteen days wear no clothes. He is led by an older man through the villages during this period, and is permitted to capture and take home chickens. He may eat the flesh of warm-blooded animals only, and may eat no pepper, though salt is permitted. This period of tabu is concluded by a general festival, at which a mimetic representation of a hunting scene is given. At the close the hunter who killed the buffalo is carried home (*Zts. Geog. Ges. Thür.* ix. 19).

Butterfly, moth.—In a Pima myth, the Creator, Chiowotmahke, takes the form of a butterfly, and flies until he finds a place fit for man (Bancroft, iii. 78). Many of the Malagasy trace their descent from a sort of moth, and believe that it was a man who was changed into a moth at death. The Sihanakas believe that the soul has to suffer after death till the body is only a skeleton; if it cannot endure this it becomes a butterfly; the Antimerinas call the soul by the same name as the butterfly (v. Gennep, *Tabou*, p. 292). In Samoa the butterfly was one of the family gods (Frazer, *Tot.* p. 13). Butterflies are tabu in Europe (*Folklore*, xi. 239; Napier, *Folkl.* p. 115). In Bukowina they should not be taken in the hand (*Zts. Oest. Volksk.* ii. 352). In the Vosges, France (Sauvé, *Folklore*, p. 317; Noel du Fail, ed. Asseyrat, i. 112), they should be caught. In Oldenburg the first butterfly should be caught and allowed to fly through the coat sleeve (Strackerjan, *Abergl.* p. 105). In Suffolk, butterflies are 'tenderly entreated,' and white butterflies are fed in the west of Scotland (*Suffolk Folklore*, p. 9; Napier, *Folklore*, p. 115), while at Llanidloes (*Montgom. Coll.* x. 260) the coloured ones are killed; in Scotland it is unlucky to kill or to keep them. Moths are killed in Somerset and Dorset (Rolland, *Faune*, iii. 316), red butterflies in the North of England (*Denham Tr.* ii. 325), the small tortoiseshell in Pitsligo (*FLJ* vii. 43), the first butterfly in Devonshire (Hone, *Tablebook*, p. 339); while in Essex the directions are to catch the first white butterfly, bite off its head, and let it fly away (MS note). The Magyars say that it brings great luck to catch the first butterfly (Jones and Kropf, *Folktales*, xlix.). In Yglau it is put in the gun to make it impossible to miss (*Zts. Oest. Volksk.* iii. 273). Some of the customs point to a scapegoat ceremonial; in other cases there is a belief that butterflies and moths are the souls of the dead (*Arch. Rev.* iii. 226). In Scotland, Friesland, and Bosnia, moths are regarded as witches (Gregor, *Folklore*, p. 147; *Wiss. Mitt.* vii. 315; *Globus*, xxvi. 158). In Germany the butterfly is sometimes said to bring the children (Ploss, *Kind*, i. 12).

There is a curious diversity in the omens given by butterflies. In North Hants three butterflies are a bad omen (*NQ*, 8th ser. iv. 165). In Brunswick a white butterfly seen first means death, a yellow butterfly a birth, and a coloured one a marriage (Andree, *Braunschw. Volksk.* p. 289). Elsewhere a white butterfly means a rainy summer, a dark one thunderstorms, and a yellow one sunshine (*Am Urdsbrunnen*, iv. 16). The Ruthenians hold that a red butterfly in spring means health, and a white one sickness (*Globus*, lxxiii. 245); while for the Bulgarians the dark butterfly announces sickness (Strausz, *Bulgaren*, p. 286).

Cat.—The cat was generally respected in Egypt, and mummified at Thebes; but this is not enough to establish cat-worship proper. In many parts of Europe it is considered unlucky to kill a cat (*Folklore*, xi. 239), and the same belief is found in Africa; the Washambas respect the cat, and believe that if one is killed, some one in the family falls ill; a sheep is led four times round the sick person, and then slaughtered; its head is buried, a living cat is caught, and part of the sheep's heart, covered with honey and fat, is given it to eat; if it will not eat it, the illness is put down to another cause; finally, the cat has a dark neckband put on and is set free (*Mitt. von d. Schutzgebieten*, ix. 313, 325; *Zts. Geog. Ges. Thür.* xi. 108). It has been stated, but incorrectly, that in Egypt a cat is regarded as holy, and that if one is killed, vengeance will sooner or later fall on the person who committed the deed (*PEFSt*, 1901, 267). On the Gold Coast a cat which had been of good omen received offerings; it was also held that the souls of the dead passed into cats (Bosman, *Reise*, p. 444; Müller, *Fetu*, p. 97). At Aix, in Provence, on Corpus Christi the finest tom-cat in the country, wrapped like a child in swaddling clothes, was publicly exhibited in a magnificent shrine (Mills, *History of Crusades*, quoted in *Gent.'s Mag.*, 1882, i. 605).

The cat is one of the animals sacrificed in Europe at various times (*Folklore*, xi. 253; Lund, *Danmark og Norges Historie*, vii. 160, etc.), in some cases by being thrown from a tower (Coremans, *L'Année*, p. 53; *Mitt. des Ver. für Ges. der Deutschen in Boehmen*, x. 347, etc.). In other cases the cat is burnt (Rolland, *Faune*, iv. 114; *Golden Bough*², 324; Chesnel, *Dict. Hist.* etc.). The explanation of these customs seems to be that they are survivals of a custom of expelling evils; this interpretation is borne out by the fact that at Wambeck the custom took the form of throwing the cat out of the village on a day known as 'Kat-uit.' In Bohemia they kill it and bury it in the fields sometimes, in order that the evil spirit may not injure the crops (*Volkskunde*, vi. 155; Grohmann, *Aberglaube*, No. 367). Sometimes the cat is associated with marriage ceremonies. In the Eifel district the 'Katzenschlag' follows the marriage by a few weeks; in Creuse a cat is taken to the church and afterwards killed by striking people with it; it is then cooked and given to the newly married couple (Schmidt, *Sitten*, p. 47; Rolland, *Faune*, vi. 102). In Poland, if the man is a widower, a pane is broken in the window and a cat thrown in; the bride follows through the same opening (*Tradition*, v. 346). In Transylvania the farm hands bring a cat in a trough the morning after the wedding and rock it on the cradle before the bride (Haltrich, *Zur Volksk.* p. 290). Probably the idea of getting rid of evils is in part an explanation of these customs, in part a magical rite to promote fertility. In India, on the other hand, the cat, being regarded as an uncanny animal, is respected, and it is a serious offence to kill it (Crooke, ii. 241, 270 f.).

The corn-spirit is sometimes believed to appear in the form of a cat (*Golden Bough*², ii. 270). At the Carnival in Hildesheim a cat is fastened in a basket at the top of a fir tree; influence over the fruit harvest is attributed to it (Kehrein, *Volksp.* p. 142). In Sumatra and the East Indies a cat is used in rain charms (*Golden Bough*², i. 102; *Tijdschr.* vi. 83). There is a curious conflict of opinion as to the omen to be drawn from the sight of a cat. In Germany, Scotland, the Vosges, etc., a cat, especially a black one, is of bad omen (Gregor, *Folklore*, pp. 123, 125; *ZE* xv. 90; Sauvé, *Folklore*, p. 116). On the other hand, in Hildesheim and other parts of Germany the black cat is held to bring luck (*Niedersachsen*, vi. 61; *Zts. des V. f. Volksk.* x. 209; *Alemannia*, xx. 284; Schreiber, *Taschenbuch*, p. 329). In the United States it is an evil omen for a cat to cross one's path, but good luck to be followed by a black cat, while a strange cat, especially a black one, brings good fortune to the house which it chooses to make its home. For folk-tales of the cat see de Gubernatis, *Zool. Myth.* ii. 53–66, and for Jewish material Jacobs, in *JE* iii. 613 f.

Cattle.—Among the cults of domesticated animals the most important is that of cattle. The question of the origin of the cult is complicated by the problem of the origin of domestic animals; for if the pastoral peoples who in historical times have respected or worshipped their cattle obtained them from a single centre, where they were originally domesticated, possibly, in part at least, through practices connected with religion (Hahn, *Demeter* *und Baubo, pass.*), we cannot base any argument on the attitude of the cattle-keeping tribes of the present day. If, on the other hand, no sanctity attached to cattle when they came to them, the respect—and even love—which these peoples feel for their herds is important as a factor in the evolution of the more definitely religious attitude.

Pastoral peoples, of whom in pre-European days there were many representatives in Africa, commonly live on milk or game (Alberti, *De Kaffers*, p. 37; Fleming, *S. Africa*, p. 260). The Damaras cannot comprehend how any one can live upon meat from such a source; when they have any special feast, the killing of the cattle is almost a sacrificial function, and falls to the lot of the chiefs. In the same way bulls in ancient Egypt were killed only as a piaculum (Herod. ii. 41); and cows, as among the Phœnicians (Porphyry, *de Abstin.* ii. 11), were never eaten on any pretence.

In these cases there is no positive cult, though the cow is recorded to have been sacred to Hathor-Isis. With the male animal it was different. Conspicuous among Egyptian animal cults was that of the bull, and the worship of Apis (Ḥāp) goes back to the earliest times. According to Herodotus (iii. 28), it was the 'calf of a cow incapable of conceiving another offspring; and the Egyptians say that lightning descends upon the cow from heaven'; on the latter point another story was that the god descended on the cow as a ray of moonlight (Wiedemann, *Religion*, p. 188; Plut. *de Is. et Os.* xliii., *Quæst. Sympt.* viii. 1). Various accounts are given of the marks by which it was recognized; Herodotus (*loc. cit.*) says 'it is black, and has a square spot of white on its forehead; on its back a figure of an eagle; in its tail double hair; and on its tongue a beetle.' Pliny, however (viii. 72), says that a white crescent on its right side was the mark, and adds that after a certain age it was drowned in the fountain of the priests. Oxen were sacrificed to Apis, and had to be pure white (Herod. ii. 38). When the old Apis died, a new one was sought; the owner of the herd in which it was found was honoured; the discoverer was rewarded, and the dam of the bull was brought with it and confined in a second sanctuary at Memphis (Wiedemann, *loc. cit.*; Strabo, xvii. 31). Once a year a cow was presented to Apis and then killed (Pliny, viii. 186); others were regarded as concubines and permitted to live (Amm. Marc. xxii. 14. 7; Solinus, *Polyh.* c. 32). Its food consisted of cakes made of flour and honey; a special well was provided for its use. Its birthday was celebrated once a year; when it appeared in public, a crowd of boys attended it. Women were forbidden to approach it save during its four months' education at Nicopolis, when they exposed themselves before it (Diodorus, i. 85).

Oracles were obtained (1) by the behaviour of the bull, (2) by dreams which came to sleepers in the temple, and (3) by the voices of children praying before the temple. Both the living and the dead Apis were connected with Osiris, and its soul formed with Osiris a dual god Asar-Ḥapi (Serapis). The dead bull was carefully mummified and buried in a rock tomb. The cult of Apis was national. Less wide-spread was the cult of Mnevis, also consecrated to Osiris (see Budge, ii. 351 ff.).

At the present day similar observances have been noted on the Upper Nile. The Nuba (=Shilluk and Bonjack) venerate a bull, according to Petherick (*Travels*, ii. 10), usually a piebald one; it leads the cattle; its aid is invoked to avert evil. At its death it is mourned with great ceremony; at its master's death it is killed, and its horns fixed on his grave. This latter feature suggests that it may have been regarded as the abode of its master's soul, or possibly of the soul of the previous head of the family. Another account says that it is venerated under the name of Madjok (the Great God), and worshipped with music and dancing (Hassan, *Vita*, i. 58). Among the Nuers the bull is likewise honoured; it is regarded as the tutelary deity of the family, and receives the name *Nyel-edit*, which is also applied to thunder and perhaps to their Supreme Being (Marno, *Reisen*, pp. 343, 347; *Mitt. Ver. Erdk.*, Leipzig, 1873, p. 6).

Among the Angonis the spirit of a dead chief was located in a bull, which was then set apart and considered sacred. Offerings were made through it to the indwelling spirit; if it died, another was put in its place. This cult ceased as soon as the next chief died (*Folklore*, xiv. 310).

The Sakalavas of Madagascar have a black bull in a sacred enclosure in the island of Nosybe, which is guarded by two hundred priests. When it dies, another takes its place. In January the queen visits the island and a bull is sacrificed, whose blood is held to drive away evil spirits from the neighbourhood of the sacred enclosure (v. Gennep, *Tabou*, p. 248). In some parts of Madagascar myths of descent from cattle are told (*ib.* p. 239). When the sick perform the *bilo* ceremony to remove the tabu under which they lie, a bull is sometimes selected, which is thenceforth sacred until its master's death (*ib.*). Cattle played a great part in the as yet unexplained ceremony of Fandroana at the New Year (*ib.* p. 240). Cattle were kept for their milk and as sacrificial animals only (*ib.* p. 241). The sacrifice was eaten, and custom prescribed the persons to whom particular parts of the animal should fall (*ib.* p. 243). A child born on an unlucky day was usually put to death, but its life might be saved if the ordeal by cattle so determined (*ib.* p. 245). Among the most honourable terms of address were 'bull' and 'cow' (*ib.* p. 247).

The origin of the Hindu respect for the cow is an unsolved problem. Unlike Egypt, it is clear that India developed a respect for the animal in historic times. Of actual worship there is little to record; but the *pañcha-gavya*, or five products of the cow, are important factors in exorcism and magic; as a means of annulling an unlucky horoscope, re-birth from a cow is simulated; the pious Hindu touches the tail of a cow at the moment of dissolution, and believes that it will carry him across the river of death; just as, in the last re-incarnation before the assumption of the human form, the cow receives the spirit and brings it across the river Vaitaraṇi, which bounds the lower world. Cattle festivals are celebrated in Nepāl and Central India, but their object seems to be mainly magical. The nomadic Banjaras, however, devote a bullock to their god Balaji, and call upon it to cure them in sickness (Crooke, *Pop. Rel.* ii. 235–236). In Iranian mythology the moon is closely associated with the bull, and is regarded as containing the seed of the primeval bull (*Būnda-hishn*, iv. x.), whence one of the standing epithets of the moon in the Avesta is *gaočiθra*, 'having the seed of the bull.' Here the underlying idea is evidently a fertility-concept (Gray, 'Maonha Gaocithra' in *Spiegel Memorial Volume*). In Zoroastrianism, moreover, as in Brāhmanism, the urine of the bull is one of the chief modes of religious purification (*Muséon*, ix. 105–112). For the bull and cow in the Veda, see de Gubernatis, *Zool. Myth.* i. 1–41; in later India, p. 41; in Persia and North Asia, p. 90 ff.; for the Slavs, p. 171; Teutons and Celts, p. 221; Greeks and Romans, p. 261 ff. For other cases of respect for cattle, see Hahn, *Demeter*, p. 60. For the bull as form of water god, see 'Water' above; see also de Gubernatis, i. 265.

In Greek cult the bull was associated with

Artemis Ταυροπόλος and Ταυρική, which Farnell interprets as referring to the agricultural functions of the goddess; in the worship of Ταυροπόλος the bull and cow were rarely, the calf never, sacrificed; the goddess is represented with horns on her shoulders, which are usually supposed to refer to the moon; the horns certainly appear in the representations of Selene, but the bull figures in the cult or representations of many non-lunar divinities, such as Themis, Dionysus, Demeter, Hestia, Apollo, Poseidon, etc. (Farnell, *Cults*, ii. 451, 454, 456, 529). The bull was one of the chief sacrificial animals in the cult of Zeus (for βουφόνια see below); and a cow was, in one form of the myth, his nurse (*ib.* i. 37, 95). Hera is termed βοῶπις by Homer; but there is no monument showing her as cow-headed, and her eyes are often unlike those of the cow (*ib.* i. 20, 228); at Mycenæ, Schliemann found cow ἀναθήματα; but this is of no value as evidence (*ib.* i. 181). White oxen drew the priestess in the ἱερὸς γάμος (*ib.* i. 188). The bull was prominent among victims offered to Athene (*ib.* i. 290); an Athene Boarmia ('ox-yoker') was worshipped in Bœotia (*ib.* p. 291). In Crete two cults seem to have been mingled—that of a Semitic goddess whose animal was the goat and whose lover was the bull, and that of Zeus-Dionysus and Europa; the bull may originally have belonged to the latter, but it was certainly associated with Dionysus and to some extent with Zeus (*ib.* ii. 632, 645). The bull was important in the ritual of Astarte (*ib.* ii. 676). In the cult of the Syrian goddess worshippers sometimes cast their children from the Propylæa of her temple, 'calling them oxen' (*ib.* i. 92). For the bull in Celtic religion, see CELTIC RELIGION, § x. 8.

Bouphonia.—The sacrifice of an ox at the altar of Zeus Πολιεύς on the Acropolis requires to be noticed at length. The myth of origin is as follows: A certain Sopatrus, a stranger, was offering cereals, when one of his oxen devoured some of his corn; Sopatrus slew it; he was then seized with remorse and buried it; after which he fled to Crete; a dearth fell upon the land, and to remove the curse the sacrifice of the βουφόνια was instituted. The oracle directed that the murderer should be punished and the dead raised; all were to taste the flesh of the dead animal, and refrain not. The ritual was as follows: At the festival of the Diipoleia oxen were driven round the altar, and the one which tasted the cereals was the chosen victim. The axe with which the deed was done was sharpened with water brought by maidens and handed to the sacrificer; another cut the throat of the victim, and all partook of its flesh. The hide was stuffed with grass and sewn together, and the counterfeit ox was yoked to the plough. The participants in the sacrifice were charged with ox murder (βουφόνια), and each laid the blame on the other; finally, the axe was condemned and thrown into the sea (Farnell, *Cults*, i. 56–58). This sacrifice has been interpreted by Robertson Smith as totemistic, but no totem sacrifice of this kind is known elsewhere. On the other hand, Mannhardt and, following him, Frazer have regarded it as connected with agriculture; but, as Farnell points out, the sacrifice of the corn-spirit is not attended elsewhere with a sense of guilt. The admission of Sopatrus to citizenship as a result of his sacramental meal lends little or no support to the totemistic hypothesis, although there was an ox-clan (Boutadæ) at Athens.

In modern European folklore the corn-spirit is frequently understood to take the form of a bull or cow (*Golden Bough*², ii. 279 ff.). Perhaps we may look to this conception for an explanation of the custom of leading round, about Christmas, a man clad in a cowskin (*ib.* 447; Evans, *Tour in S. Wales*, p. 44; Panzer, *Beitrag*, ii. 117; *FLJ* iv. 118; *Schweiz. Archiv*, ii. 228, cf. 178; Rolland, *Faune*, vi. 91; *NQ*, 9th ser. vii. 247, etc.). The same explanation probably holds good of the Athenian sacrifice of the Bouphonia (see above), after which a mock trial took place, in which the instruments of sacrifice were condemned to be cast into the sea. Possibly we may apply the same explanation to the spring ox of the Chinese (*Zool. Garten*, 1900, p. 37). The emperor offers a hecatomb annually to heaven and earth; the animals must be black or red-brown (*ib.* p. 31).

In Egypt and India the bull or cow played the part of a scapegoat (*Golden Bough*², iii. 1). Among the Abchases a white ox, called Ogginn, was sacrificed annually, perhaps as a 'pastoral' sacrifice (see above).

The Ova-Hereros have some practices which have been interpreted as totemistic. They are divided into *eanda* and *oruzo*; membership of the *eanda* is inherited through the mother, and is inalienable; the *oruzo*, on the other hand, descends, like the chieftainship and priesthood, in the male line. The *omaanda* are named after the sun, the rock rabbit, rain, etc.; the *otuzo*, after the chameleon, etc.; they are distinguished (1) by the practice of keeping or not keeping cattle with certain marks, and (2) by practising certain abstinences with respect to cattle and other animals; the *orosembi oruzo*, for example, do not keep grey oxen or injure the chameleon. It seems clear that the *omaanda* comes nearer the totem-kin, though no totemistic practices are assigned to its members (*Zts. Vgl. Rechtsw.* xv.; *Mitt. Or. Sem.* pt. iii. v. 109; *Ausland*, 1882, p. 834). It has been recorded that certain plants are sacred to each 'caste,' but whether *eanda* or *oruzo* is meant is not clear (Andersson, *Lake Ngami*, 228). The Batokas break their upper teeth at puberty to make themselves like cattle; but here, too, there is no connexion with totemism (Livingstone, *Miss. Trav.* p. 532), for it is not confined to any special clan.

Among the Bechuanas a cow or bull that beats the ground with its tail is regarded as bewitched (Mackenzie, *Ten Years*, p. 392). In the Hebrides, oracles were given by a man wrapped in a fresh bull's hide and left all night at the bottom of a precipice near a cataract (Saussure, *New Voyages*, Lond. 1819, vol. viii. 92). The Kalmuks take an oath by the cow; the accused stands on the skin of a black cow, moistened with blood, and jumps over the threshold (*JAI* i. 415).

In opposition to the practice of the African pastoral peoples, of the Hindus, and probably of ancient Europe (Hahn, *Demeter*, pp. 60–61), the East Asiatic culture area abstains from the use of milk, regarding it as a pathological product (*ib.* p. 21). These peoples employ their cattle for draught purposes only, over a considerable area (*ib.* p. 60; *Zool. Garten*, 1900, p. 34), without using them as an article of food; they explain their abstinence on the ground that it is improper to eat an animal which labours to provide them with food. There is nothing to show that the Hindu and Chinese explanation of the sacrosanctity of cattle within their areas is incorrect; and possibly the African tabus are explicable on similar grounds. It seems clear, however, that the Chinese learned to know cattle as draught animals, possibly as sacred animals, and not as direct factors in the economic situation. *Prima facie* this leads us to suppose that cattle were domesticated for a long period before the use of milk was introduced, for otherwise the practice of abstinence in China is hard to explain. On the other hand, it seems probable that a certain sanctity attached to cattle at their introduction into the East Asiatic culture area; for there does not seem to be any difficulty in the way of breeding cattle for food and at the same time making use of their labour in agricultural operations.

Hahn has argued (*Die Haustiere*, Leipzig, 1895; *Demeter und Baubo*, Lübeck, 1896) that we must look to a religious motive as the decisive factor in the domestication of cattle. If neither the milk nor the flesh was originally used, we are left to choose between the religious and utilitarian theories of domestication. It is by no means impossible that the idea of replacing hoe culture by plough culture may have occurred to a people destitute of domestic animals; and they may have proceeded to tame and utilize cattle for this purpose. But in this case we should expect to find that man as a draught animal preceded the ox as the motive power of the plough; there is, however, no evidence of this. It seems, however, far more probable that man already had cattle in partial subjection, and that possibly on religious grounds he proceeded to employ them in agriculture, than that he took but a single stride from hoe culture to ploughing with cattle. The use of milk in early times as an offering seems to point in the same direction; for there would be no special reason for attaching sanctity to the products of an animal domesticated for utilitarian purposes. As to the grounds which led to cattle becoming associated with religion in the first instance, Hahn has put forward a theory that it was the shape of their horns which brought them into connexion with the crescent moon. The cult of the moon has undoubtedly been wide-spread, and was indisputably important in the West Asiatic area, where appearances suggest that we may locate the domestication of cattle. There is, however, no evidence that the horns of the ox were in fact brought into connexion with the sickle of the moon at an early period. On the whole, it seems more probable that cattle, like the bison among the Pawnees, were associated with agriculture, possibly as a form of the corn-spirit, before they came under man's domination. The association of the moon with vegetation would naturally result in bringing cattle into close connexion with the moon-goddess. Just as the Pawnees use the bones of the bison as hoes, it would be a natural idea to impress cattle, on this theory, into the service of agriculture on magical grounds, even if they were not employed at an earlier period as draught animals for the car of the god or goddess, and thus inured to labour. If their employment as draught animals in the sacred car was the primitive usage, it seems probable that the processions would visit the fields, and herein we may see another factor which may have suggested the use of the draught animal for the plough.

See also 'Earth-carrier,' 'Earthquakes,' 'Vegetation,' 'Water,' in present article.

Coyote.—The coyote figures largely in American mythology, especially among the tribes of California. The Gallinomeros attributed to him the creation of the sun, with the aid of the hawk, from a ball of tules (Bancroft, iii. 85). The Neeshenams made him their ancestor, and told how he rescued them later from a terrible old man (*ib.* 546). In Shuswap and Kutenay myths he is the Creator (Brinton, *Myths*, p. 161). According to the Chinooks, he was the creator of the human race, but fashioned men clumsily, so that another powerful spirit had to open their mouths and teach them how to make canoes (Bancroft, *ib.* 95). The Cahroks attributed to him the rôle of Prometheus; fire was in the possession of some old hags, and the coyote outwitting them brought a brand away in his mouth (*ib.* p. 115). They also said that he stocked the river Klamath with salmon (*ib.* p. 136). Many tribes held that they were descended from coyotes; the Potoyantes, or Coyote Indians, related how the primeval coyotes gradually assumed the shape of man (*ib.* p. 87). Many tribes worshipped the coyote (Bancroft, iii. 137; Brinton, p. 161). The Nahuas erected a temple to him and buried him at death (*ib.*). Among the Acagchemens the coyote was one of the forms under which the god Chinnigchinich was worshipped (Bancroft, iii. 166). The coyote figures in the Deluge myth of the Papagoes; he warned Montezuma, and with him escaped the Flood (*ib.* p. 75). The Pomos made him the hero of one of the widely spread myths of a water-swallower; he drank up Clear Lake and lay down to sleep off the effects; a man pierced him; the water flowed out, and with it the grasshoppers on which he had made a meal; and they became the fish that are found in the lake (*ib.* p. 86). The Shastas told a legend of how there were once ten suns and ten moons, so that man was in danger of perishing by heat and by cold alternately; the coyote slew nine of each, and saved the human race (*ib.* 547) (for other coyote myths see Bancroft, iii. 545, 549; Müller, *Geschichte*, pp. 64, 108*b*, 134). According to some of the Navahos, bad men are turned into coyotes at their death (Bancroft, iii. 528).

Crab, lobster.—The lobster was generally considered sacred among the Greeks; if the people of Seriphus found a dead lobster, they buried it, mourning over it like one of themselves; a living one caught in their nets they put back into the sea (Frazer, *Tot.* p. 15). They held that it was dear to Perseus (Hartland, *Legend of P.* i. 9). In New Caledonia a crab goddess or demon is known, who has a sacred grove, on the trees of which are hung little packets of food for her. She is in the form of an enormous land crab, and causes elephantiasis; she is the enemy of married people: the little crabs are her messengers, and are feared as such (*Miss. Cath.* 1879, p. 28). In one district of Madagascar the lobster is tabu; it is never eaten or caught (v. Gennep, *Tabou*, p. 292).

Crocodile.—The Egyptian god Sebek was believed to take crocodile shape; sometimes he was represented as wholly animal, sometimes only with a crocodile head; offerings of cake, meat, and honey wine were made to the sacred animals, which were tame with the priests; oracles were drawn from their behaviour; they were embalmed at death (Wiedemann, *Religion*, p. 191). The alligator is said to be put into a tank in India sometimes and worshipped (Crooke, ii. 253). In West Africa, Bastian saw crocodiles fed in a pond, but it does not appear whether they were regarded as sacred (*Bilder*, p. 161). The crocodile is respected in many parts of Africa and Madagascar (*Int. Arch.* xvii. 124 ff.; v. Gennep, *Tabou*, p. 279 ff.), the Malay Peninsula (*JRAS, S.B.*, No. 7, p. 24), and New Georgia (*JAI* xxvi. 386). In New Guinea and the East Indies crocodiles are frequently respected as being the abodes of souls of ancestors (Hagen, *Unter den Papuas*, p. 225; Hawkesworth, *Voyages*, iii. 759); so, too, in West Africa (Hutchinson, *Impressions*, p. 163); any one who falls a victim to a crocodile is supposed to have incurred the vengeance of some one who has taken that form; those who kill crocodiles are supposed to take that form after death. Slightly different is the Malagasy view, which makes the crocodile the ally of the magician in his lifetime (v. Gennep, *Tabou*, p. 280). The Matabele hold that killing a crocodile is a serious crime, because its liver and entrails can be used as charms (Decle, *Three Years*, p. 153); so, too, the Bechuanas (Mackenzie, *Ten Years*, p. 390). On the other hand, some of the Bantu tribes —it is not clear whether the Bakuenas alone or not (probably not; cf. Chapman, *Travels*, i. 46)—seem to regard the crocodile in another light. A man over whom a crocodile splashes water is excluded from the village, in other cases a man bitten by a crocodile (Merensky, *Beiträge*, p. 92; *ZE* i. 43); the dead crocodile is handed over to the doctors to make medicine of; if one is killed, the children cough, and a piacular sacrifice of a black sheep must be offered (Merensky, *loc. cit.*). In many places the crocodile is attacked only if it has already shown its hostility to man. The Anti-merinas trace their descent from the crocodile, which, however, formerly waged war on them, after which a treaty was made. If this is violated, notice is given in the district, and complaint is made of the offence on the shores of the lake; the crocodile tribe is called upon to hand over the offender, and to make matters more certain a baited hook is thrown into the water. On the following day the capture is hauled up, condemned to death, and executed on the spot. Thereupon the persons present begin a lamentation; and the body is wrapped up in silk and buried with the ceremonies usual at the interment of a man. On its grave a tumulus is raised (v. Gennep, *Tabou*, p. 281 ff.). The same precautions are taken and the same respect is shown in Borneo and Sumatra (*Golden Bough*[2], ii. 390 ff.). In the Philippines, offerings were made even when the islanders had no intention of attacking the animals (Marsden, *Sumatra*, p. 303). In North Arakan the ceremony of *ya*, or 'tabu,' is strictly performed when any one belonging to a village has been killed by an alligator (*JAI* ii. 240). This is perhaps explained by the belief of the Philippine Tagalogs that any one so killed becomes a deity, and is carried up by the rainbow (Marsden, *Sumatra*, p. 301). Connected possibly with the belief that the crocodile is a magician or his servant, is the Basuto belief that a crocodile can seize the shadow of a passer-by and draw him into the water; it is believed to suck the blood of the men and animals thus captured, but not to injure them otherwise—a point which still further brings it into relation with the magician (Arbousset, p. 12). Among the Jabuns and in Celebes it is believed that women sometimes give birth to crocodiles or to twins one of which is a crocodile (Hagen, *Unter den Papuas*, p. 225; Hawkesworth, iii. 756). In Celebes, families which tell of such a birth constantly put food into the river for their relatives; more especially the human twin goes constantly at stated times to fulfil this duty, neglect of which is said to cause sickness or death. In South Africa the Bawendas draw the figure of a crocodile on the ground at the girls' initiation ceremony (*ZE* xxviii. 35). In the west of Ceram boys are admitted to the Kakian association at puberty; in some parts the boys are pushed through a crocodile's jaw of wood, and it is then said that the devil has swallowed them, and taken them to the other world to regenerate and transform them (*Golden Bough*[2], iii. 442). Amours between crocodiles (or caimans) and human beings are recorded in Senegambian, Malagasy, Basuto, and Dayak folklore (MacCulloch, 260, 267).

Crow, raven.—The most important area for the worship of the crow, or, if not worship, for the pre-eminence of the crow in the pantheon, is the north-west coast of America. Among the Thlinkets the chief deity, sometimes identified with the raven (but cf. *JAI* xxviii. 144), is Yehl. In the Creation myth he plays a part similar to that attributed to the thunder-bird in the Chippewayan myth, and produces dry land by the beating of his wings; probably Chethl, the name of the thunder-bird, and Yehl, the Creator, are variants of the same word, which is also written Jeshl (Bancroft, iii. 100 ff.). The neighbouring Haidas of Queen Charlotte Islands make the raven their ancestor (Frazer, *Tot.* p. 5; *Mission Life*, iii. 32; Macfie, *Vancouver*, i. p. 452; but see Boas, *Indianische Sagen*, p. 306 f., where the chief incident is a contest between Yehl and his uncle). The crow figures as Creator in the Eskimo and Chukchi mythology (Seemann, *Voyage of Herald*, ii. 30, 67, 72; *Zts. Geog. Ges. Thür.* vi. 120). It also figures in a Javanese myth of origin (*Med. Ned. Zend.* xxxii. 131). Among the Gros Ventres it played an important part in the creation of the world (Coues, *Henry and Thompson, MS Journals*, i. 351). The crow appears occasionally in Deluge myths (*Rel. des Jés.* 1633, p. 16; *Am. Rev.* viii. 397; *Ann. Prop. Foi*, xiv. 52, etc.), and the early date of the first notice seems to establish the native character of the myth; in several cases the crow is said to have been originally white, but to have suffered a change as a punishment (*Ann. P. F.; Am. Rev.*, *loc. cit.*, Boas, p. 273), or for some other reason (Leland, *Algonquin Legends*, p. 27); a similar myth is found in Europe (Wiedemann, *Ehsten*, p. 404; *Zts. deutsches Altertum*, N.S. x. 15). In the north-west of America the crow is a culture hero, who brings the light, after tricking the power in whose possession it is, or gives fire to mankind (Bancroft, *loc. cit.*). The same trait is found in Victoria (Parker, *Aborigines*, p. 24; but cf. Dawson, *Aust. Abor.* p. 54, where the crows are represented as keeping the fire to themselves). Among the Algonquins the crow was held to have given man Indian-corn and beans (Williams, 'Key into the Language of America' in *Mass. Hist. Soc.* iii. 219). A Spanish expedition in California in 1602 reported that the Indians of Santa Catalina Island venerated two great black crows; but it seems probable that they were in reality buzzards (Bancroft, iii. 134), which are known to have been respected and worshipped in California (*Golden Bough*[2], ii. 367). As a parallel fact may be quoted the keeping of ravens at Nimeguen at public expense (Hone, *Everyday Book*, i. 44). The Ainus also keep crows, and reverence them (Frazer, *Tot.* p. 14). For Indian crow myths, etc., see Crooke, i. 166, ii. 243–245.

The *name* of the crow is sometimes tabu (Holzmaier, *Osil.* p. 41; cf. Wiedemann, *Ehsten*, p. 492, for another form of respect). It is not killed in Victoria (Morgan, *Life of Buckley*, p. 58; Parker, *Abor.* p. 25), New England (Williams, in *Mass. Hist. Soc.* iii. 219), among the Gilyaks (v. Schrenck, *Reisen*, iii. 437), parts of Europe (*Folklore*, xi. 240; *New Voy.*, London, 1819, iv. 60), and North America (Pennant, *Arctic Zoology*, p. 246), the explanation given being that it contains the souls of the dead (Morgan, Parker; cf. Crooke, ii. 243). Connected possibly with the idea of the crow as a soul-animal, is the belief that it brings the children (*Germania*, xvii. 349; Ploss, *Kind*, p. 12; *Zts. d. Altertum*, N.S. x. 11; cf. Aelian, *de An. Nat.* iii. 9; Hesychius, *Lexicon*, *s.v.* κουριζόμενος, etc.). The crow is one of the birds which figure in the annual processions so commonly found in Europe (Schütze, *Holst. Idiot.* iii. 165; *J. des V. f. Meckl. Ges.* ii. 123). Either a living crow or the nest was carried round. Frazer's suggestion (*Golden Bough*[2], ii. 446 n.) that the crow song of the ancient Greeks (Athenæus, viii. pp. 359, 360) was used in connexion with a similar ceremony may be regarded as certain. In some cases the crow is killed (*Niedersachsen*, v. 126). The ceremony is probably connected with the idea of the expulsion of evils. Offerings are made to crows at funerals in India (*Home and For. Miss. Rec.* 1839, p. 303).

As a bird of omen, the crow, raven, or rook is inauspicious (Dorman, *Prim. Sup.* p. 224; Purchas, ii. 1758; Billings, i. 231; *Zts. des V. f. Volksk.* iii. 134; Wolf, *Beiträge*, i. 232; Henderson, *Folklore of N. C.* p. 20, etc.; the Talmudic tractate *Shabbath*, 67*b*). Occasionally it is the reverse (*Autob. of Kah-ge-ga-bowh*, p. 48), especially at a funeral (Crooke, ii. 243). The crow is specially associated with sorcerers in Australia (*JAI* xx. 90), America (Schoolcraft, *Ind. Tr.* iv. 491; Adair, *Hist.* pp. 173, 194), and Europe (Clouston, *Folklore of Raven*, p. 20). The Twanas hold that when a person is very sick the spirit of some evil animal, sent by a wizard, has entered into him and is eating away his life (Eells, *Ten Years*, p. 43). Ancient diviners sought to imbue themselves with the spirit of prophecy by eating the hearts of crows (*Golden Bough*², ii. 355); and raven broth in Denmark is held to confer the powers of a wizard on the person who tastes it (Clouston, *loc. cit.*). The crow is largely used in magical recipes (*Folklore*, xi. 255). A stone found in its nest is believed to confer invisibility (*FLJ* vii. 56; Alpenburg, *Alpenmythen*, p. 385). Both in India and Greece the brains of crows were regarded as specifics against old age (Crooke, ii. 245; *Golden Bough*², ii. 355). For folk-tales of the crow see de Gubernatis, *Zool. Myth.* ii. 250–258, and Pauly-Wissowa, *s.v.* 'Aberglaube,' p. 76.

Cuckoo.—In various parts of Europe are performed ceremonies named after the cuckoo. At Pollern, near Thieux, was held, on August 21st, a cuckoo court; husbands whose wives deceived them had to appear, and at the end of the proceedings the last married man in the village was thrown into the water (Düringsfeld, *Cal. belge*, ii. 115). In other parts the ceremony was in the middle of April (Rolland, *Faune*, ii. 91). At Stembert a man called the cuckoo was placed on a waggon with the last married man of the village by his side; they were dragged through the village and the cuckoo was thrown into the water (Harou, *Contrib.* IX. ii.). With these customs we may perhaps connect a Harz custom of putting a cuckoo into the bride-chamber, probably as a fertility charm (Pröhle, *Harzbilder*, p. 87), and the cuckoo dance at North Friesland marriages (*Ausland*, lvii. 810). In S.E. Russia at Whitsuntide, a pole is put up with a cuckoo upon it; round this a dance is performed (*ib.* lix. 253). A cuckoo dance was also known in Lithuania, for which the third day after Easter was the proper season (Wurzbach, i. 216). Among the Rajputs of India the girls paint a cuckoo on a tree or board at the Dusserah festival, and lay flowers and rice on it; they then call till a cuckoo comes (*Bombay Gaz.* IX. i. 137). The scavenger caste also worship cuckoos (*ib.* p. 380). A cuckoo tabu is very common in European folklore (*Folklore*, xi. 240), and in Madagascar (v. Gennep, *Tabou*, p. 264). Like many other migrants, it should be greeted in the spring by leaping or running (*Traditions pop.* iii. 345). It is said to lay Easter eggs (*Schw. Arch.* i. 115), and 'cocu-mallard' is one of the names given to 'Blind Man's Buff' (*Trad. pop.*, *loc. cit.*). The cuckoo is a bird of bad omen (Böcler-Kreutzwald, *Ehsten*, p. 140; Russwurm, *Eibovolk*, sec. 358; *Mélusine*, i. 454). It is connected with rain (Panzer, *Beitrag*, ii. 172; de Gubernatis, *Zool. Myth.* ii. 235). It is commonly believed that it is not a migrant, but turns into a hawk (cf. de Gubernatis, ii. 231). For cuckoo myths, beliefs, etc., see *ZM* iii. 209–298, and de Gubernatis, *Zool. Myth.* ii. 226–235.

Deer.—Tame deer were kept in Guatemala, which were held sacred by the inhabitants on the ground that their greatest god had visited them in that form (Bancroft, iii. 132). The natives of Nicaragua had a god whose name was that of the deer, but the animal was not regarded as a god; they explained it by saying that this god had to be invoked by those who hunted the deer (*ib.*). Deer are tabu in Sarawak, and both there and in California they are held to be the abode of souls of deceased ancestors (*JAI* xxxi. 187, 193; Bancroft, iii. 131). In West Africa an antelope is sacrificed annually (Ellis, *Tshi-speaking Peoples*, p. 224). Especially in America, deer, moose, and elk were treated with great respect by hunters; their bones might not be given to the dogs, nor might their fat be dropped upon the fire, because the souls of the dead animals would know that they were not being properly treated and tell the others. In Honduras the Indians preserved the bones till their houses were quite encumbered, for they believed that otherwise they would not be able to take other deer. If a man were ill among the Chiquitos, the medicine-man would explain it by saying that he had thrown deer flesh away, and the soul of the deer had entered him and was killing him. The Tzentales and Kekchis offered copal to a dead deer before they ventured to skin it. Cherokee hunters ask pardon of the deer they kill, otherwise Little Deer, the chief of the deer tribe, who can never die or be wounded, would track the hunter by the blood drops and put the spirit of rheumatism into him. The Apache medicine-men resorted to certain caves, where they propitiated the animal gods whose progeny they intended to destroy. When the Thompson River Indians of British Columbia killed a deer, they thought the survivors were pleased if it was butchered cleanly and nicely; if a hunter had to leave some of the meat behind, he hung it on a tree, especially the head, so that it might not be contaminated by dogs and women. Venison was never brought in by the common door, because women used it; the head was never given to the oldest or the second son of a family, for that would make the deer wild (*Golden Bough*², ii. 406). The Eskimos of Hudson Bay believe that a white bear rules over the reindeer. They pray to him to send the deer, and assure him that they have been careful to treat the deer well (*ib.* p. 408). Deer and sea-animals may not come in contact with one another (*2nd Ann. Rep. Bur. Ethn.* p. 595).

The deer is eaten by more than one tribe in connexion with the feast of new corn. Among the Delawares, venison and corn were provided, and divided into twelve parts, according to the number of the old men who took part in the ceremony; after they were eaten, the new corn was free to all: in the evening, venison was again eaten and the remainder burnt, for it might not remain till the sun rose, nor might a bone be broken. A deer burnt-offering was made with much ceremony once a year (Beatty, *Journal*, p. 84; cf. Rupp, *History of Berks*, p. 23, quoting a letter of W. Penn). The Housatunnuks also had a deer feast, but it is not brought into connexion with agriculture (Hopkins, *Hist. Memoirs*, p. 10). Probably the deer was regarded as a form of the corn-spirit; for in Florida it was the custom to take as large a deer hide as could be procured, leave the horns on it, and at the end of February fill it with all manner of herbs and sew it together. They then proceeded to an open space and hung the skin upon a tree, turning the head to the east. A prayer was then offered to the sun, asking that these same fruits might be given. The hide was left up till the following year (*JAI* xxxi. 155; cf. the account quoted on p. 156 from Prætorius). Probably a Papago rain dance performed beneath a deer's head stuck on a pole in the month of July may be similarly interpreted (*ib.*). A small deer figures largely in Malay and other folk-tales (Skeat, *Fables*).

Dog.—It can hardly be doubted that the dog is the oldest, as it is also the most widely spread of the domestic animals. It has been maintained (*Ausland*, 1881, p. 658) that man's association with the dog was due in the first place to its being used as food. Though there is no reason to suppose that the religious factor entered into the causes which brought about its domestication, the food theory seems less probable than the view that the dog made himself the companion of man, rather than that he was brought into subjection by the acts of man (cf. Much, *Heimat der Indogermanen*, 182–185). The dog is used as an article of food by a large number of peoples of low grades of culture, and sometimes by higher grades, *e.g.* the Chinese. It was used by neolithic man in Europe for the pursuit of game, and is employed in a similar way all the world over at the present day. In some cases the breed has become in no way specialized thereby; but among the Batuas (*Int. Arch.* ix. 111), pigmies of the African forests, a great advance in this respect is found. Among the Ainus the dog is used for capturing fish (Howard, *Life*, p. 51). Mainly in Arctic and sub-Arctic regions it is used as a draught animal; occasionally as a beast of burden. It was used by the Cimbri in war; the same usage prevailed in Uganda and Usukuma. (For the uses to which the products of the dog are put, see *Int. Arch.* ix. 140 ff.).

'Dog' is found as a term of abuse among Semitic and most Muhammadan peoples; among the Romans the contempt thus expressed was less than in modern Europe.

A myth of dog ancestry is not uncommon; it is found in Alaska (Lisiansky, pp. 196–197), among the Dog-Ribs (Petitot, 311 ff.), the Ojibwas (Frazer, *Tot.* p. 4), in Madagascar (v. Gennep, p. 231), Indo-China, (*As. Q. Rev.* 3rd ser. i. 140), Kirghiz (Petermann, 1864, p. 165), New Guinea (Chalmers, p. 151), among the Kalangs of Java (Raffles, i. 328), and even in Europe (Liebrecht, p. 19; see also in general MacCulloch, 263 f.). In the Pomotu islands the first race of men are held to have been made into dogs (*Miss. Cath.* 1874, 343).

Especially in N. America the dog (coyote) figures in Creation myths (Bancroft, *pass.*), and occasionally in Deluge myths (see 'Deluge'). The Pottawatomies believe that in the moon is an old woman making a basket; the earth will be destroyed when it is finished; but a great dog ruins her work at intervals and then results an eclipse (*Ann. Prop. Foi*, xi. 490). Among the Mongols, Mbocobis (*Int. Arch. l.c.* 147), Chiquitos (Tylor, i. 329), Chinese (*Ann. Prop. Foi*, xxii. 355), etc., a similar association of the dog with eclipses is found. In Kamtchatka, earthquakes are attributed to Touila's dog, Kozei (Krachenninikow, i. 94). Classical mythology tells us of Cerberus (*q.v.*), who guards the entrance of the Infernal Regions (see Bloomfield, *Cerberus, the Dog of Hades*). In N. Borneo a fiery dog is held to watch at the gate of Paradise, and to lay claim to all virgins (Forster, ii. 239); the Massachusetts also believe that a dog watches the gate (Wood, p. 104); so, too, the Eskimos (*ZE*, 1872, 238); and the Iroquois the bridge by which souls had to pass (*Rel. des Jés.* 1636, 104).

Yama was held to have two dogs, whom he sent out to bring in wandering souls (*Rig Veda* x. xiv. 10–12; *Atharva Veda*, viii. 1, 9); and these dogs, described as four-eyed (*i.e.* with two spots above the eyes), recur in the Avestan dogs that guard the Chinvat Bridge, which leads from this world to the future life (*Vendīdād*, xiii. 9; *Sad Dar*, xxxi. 5; cf. Scherman, *Materialien zur Geschichte der indischen Visionsliteratur*, pp. 127–130, and the references there given).

The Aztecs sacrificed a red dog to carry the soul of the king across a deep stream (Bancroft, ii. 605), or announce his arrival (*ib.* iii. 538; cf. Ober, p. 320); in Louisiana they killed their sick and sent dogs on to make the announcement (Stoddart, p. 421).

The Tlaxcalans hold that a wer-man appears as a dog (*Dav. Ac.* viii. 122). In Béarn a great white wer-dog was believed to sit at cross roads (Wahlen, i. 330).

The Baschilange (*Mitt. Af. Ges.* iv. 255) and Tonkinese (*Z. allg. Erdk.* i. 108) believe that human souls take up their abode in dogs.

Actual dog-worship is uncommon. The Nosairis and others are said to worship a dog (W. R. Smith, p. 291). According to Raffles (i. 365), the Kalangs worship a red dog, and each family keeps one in the house; another authority says they have images of wood in the shape of dogs, which are worshipped, and burnt 1000 days after the death of the person (*Tijd.* xxiv. 427). In Nepāl, dogs are said to be worshipped at the festival called Khicha Puja (Wright, 39 ff.; for other Indian cases see Crooke, ii. 218 ff.). The Yorubas have a demi-god, Aroui, god of the forest, with a dog's head (*Miss. Cath.* 1884, 221). Among the Harranians dogs were sacred, and held to be the brothers of the mystæ (W. R. Smith, p. 291). In ancient Egypt, dogs were commonly respected and mummified, in particular at Cynopolis (Strabo, 812). In ancient Persia the dog was held in the highest esteem, and most rigorous penalties were exacted for killing it (*Vendīdād*, xiii. xv. 19–51; *Dēnkarṭ*, viii. 23). It was employed, moreover, in the *sagdīd*, 'dog's gaze' of the Parsi funeral ceremony, in which a 'brown four-eyed' dog or a 'white dog with yellow ears,' was made to look at the corpse three times, and was also led three times back over the road traversed by the corpse (Geiger, *Ostiranische Kultur*, 264–265; Karaka, *History of the Parsis*, i. 197; Jackson, *Persia Past and Present*, 388 f., 391 f.). The Bahnars say the dog is under the protection of Bok Glaih, god of thunder (*Miss. Cath.* 1894, 133). Sometimes only the use of dog's flesh is prohibited. The dog is found as a totem in Alaska (Lisiansky, 196) and in West Africa (Ellis, *Tshi-sp.* p. 206); a dog-kin is found in Madagascar (v. Gennep, p. 234). In German New Guinea an offering of food is made to the spirit of a dog (*Nachr. K. W. land*, 1897, 88). Among the Ot Danums the bodies of dogs are buried near the houses, rice and salt are given them in the grave, and rice is strewn on the grave to induce the gods to send the souls to the dog-heaven (Schwaner, 78). The Woguls lay the bodies of specially useful dogs in a small hut (Ides, p. 7). In Egypt a family shaved clean when the dog died (Herod. ii. 66); and so, too, the owner among the Masai (*Ausl.* 1857, 442), The Gonds purify themselves when a dog dies (Hislop, *Papers*, p. 6). The Tunguses take an oath by the dog, drinking its blood (Ides, 45). The exposure of the dead to dogs may spring from a similar idea; it is found among the Magi, Bactrians, Hyrcanians, and others (Spiegel, iii. 703), in Tibet (*JRAS, S.B.* lix. 212), Java (*Verh. Bat. Gen.* xxxix. 40), and Kamtchatka (Krachenninikow, p. 189). Omens are frequently drawn from dogs (Crooke, ii. 222 ff.; *Ausland*, 1891, 874; *Z. Ver. Volksk.* iii. 134, etc.). The Kalangs strew ashes on the floor, and if a dog's footmarks are seen, judge that the ancestors are favourable to a marriage (*Tijd. T.L.V.* xxiv. 424).

Connected with the sanctity of the dog is its use in art; in Borneo it is a frequent tatu pattern (*JAI* xxxv. 113). As might be expected, the dog is frequently sacrificed. The best known case is that of the Iroquois, who kill a white dog in January as a scapegoat; it is then burnt, and the ashes sprinkled at the door of every house; but there is some doubt as to the antiquity of the practice (*Golden Bough*², iii. 72, 109). Other authorities vary the details (*Ontario Arch. Rep.* 1898, 91; Sanborn, *Legends*, p. 7; *Miss. Her.* xxv. 91, etc.). Other dog-sacrifices are found among the Sacs and Foxes (*Miss. Her.* xxxi. 86), the Ottawas (Perrot, *Mœurs*, 19), the Mayas at New Year (Bancroft, ii.

703), and in the cacao plantations in May (*ib.* 692), in Honduras before war (*ib.* i. 723), etc. (see Bancroft, *passim*). The Fuegians offer dogs (*Voice from S. Apr.* xiii. 211). In Asia, dog-sacrifice is found in China (*Ann. Prop. Foi*, xxxvii. 217), Aracan (*Miss. Cath.* 1881, 69), Java (*Med. Ned. Zend.* xvi. 307), etc. In Luzon the firstborn of a bitch are drowned (*Globus*, xlviii. 186). In Africa a dog is sacrificed by the Baghirmis (Barth, iii. 571; see also *Int. Arch.* ix. 144, xvii. 135, for further references).

In Greece the dog was regarded as unclean, but was used for ceremonies of purification in Bœotia, probably as the animal of Hecate, to whom the Argives offered a dog. The Spartan ephebi offered a young hound to the war-god (Farnell, *Cults*, ii. 507 n.). The Romans connected dogs with the Lares (Fowler, *Rom. Fest.* 101). They were sacrificed on April 25 (*ib.* p. 90), and in the Lupercalia (*ib.* pp. 313–314).

The dog is frequently used in magic. In Dahomey a dead dog is hung up as a protection against sorcery (Robertson, *Notes on A.* 291; Ellis, *Ewe*, 93). In Greece its flesh was used as medicine (Paus. iii. 250); so, too, among the Chukchis (Sauer, *Reise*, 236). Among the Kimbundas its flesh is reserved for warriors (Magyar, *Reisen*, 309). The dog figures in more than one ceremony of uncertain import. In China a big dog is dressed like a man and carried round in a palanquin in times of drought (*Ann. Prop. Foi*, xxii. 355). The Orang Dongus whip a black dog round the kampong in the first new moon after the rice season (*Journ. Ind. Arch.* ii. 692). The resemblance of the custom to the dog-whipping of the Carnival, handed down as a popular custom here and there in England (Nicholson, *Folklore*, p. 22), suggests that it is meant as an expulsion of evils (cf. Waling Dykstra, p. 318). For Jewish beliefs concerning the dog see Kohler, *JE* iv. 631 f.

Dragon.—Although the dragon is usually associated with the peoples of East Asia, it is by no means unknown in Europe. Not only is the story of St. George and the dragon told (Hartland, *Legend of Perseus, pass.*), but we find in the Mabinogion the same legend of the fighting dragons as occurs in the Malay Peninsula (cf. Skeat, *Malay Magic*, p. 304). In European folklore the dragon is taken round in procession at many places (*Grande Encyclopédie, s.v.* 'Dragon'), and there are many local dragon legends. Part of Anglesey is said to have been ravaged by a dragon; at last a champion tackled it, but his victory brought him reproof, not reward, for he had done his deed on Sunday. In the Alps a dragon inhabits a tarn; if a stone is thrown in, rain will follow, however good the weather may be; for if it hits the dragon, its movements throw up so much spray that a mist appears from which the rain condenses (Jecklin, *Volkst.* i. 44). On Norse houses the dragon sometimes figures as a weather-vane or gable decoration. Germanic mythology abounds in stories of dragons, which inhabit air, water, and earth, bringing woe (and, more rarely, weal) on men and animals, spitting forth fire and venom, and guarding treasures (Meyer, *Germanische Mythologie*, 95–100). There is, moreover, an entire cycle of tales, exemplified in the story of Perseus and Andromeda, in which human sacrifices must be made to a dragon, who is finally slain by the hero (MacCulloch, 381–409).

The association of the dragon with water is by no means confined to the West; in China the waterspout is regarded as a dragon, which is never seen completely, for its head or its tail is always invisible. The dragon and the tiger are at enmity, and if a tiger's bones are thrown into a 'dragon's well,' rain will follow within three days, for the animals fight, and when the dragon moves, rain falls (Doolittle, *Social Life*, ii. 264, i. 275). The great dragon lives in the sky, and the emperor is the earthly dragon (Gould, *Mythical Monsters*, p. 215; see pp. 215–257, 377–404). In Japan the dragon is associated not only with water but also with a variety of other things. The dragon produces nine young at a birth, each with different qualities; hence dragons are carved on bells, musical instruments, drinking vessels, weapons, books, chairs, and tables, according to the particular tastes of the different kinds of dragon. One kind loves dangerous places; consequently it is put upon the gables of houses (*Natur*, 1878, p. 549). India, too, had its dragons; one used to lie in wait for boats or ships, hiding itself on a neighbouring mountain; a criminal obtained his life on condition of ridding the country of the pest; he had human figures made, and the bodies filled with hooks, etc.; the dragon devoured them, and perished (*Lettres édif.* xviii. 409; cf. Crooke, ii. 129–131). In the same way in the last century a dragon on the borders of Wales was said to have been induced to meet his fate by putting red flannel round a post on which sharp spikes were fixed. Tiamat is the cosmogonic dragon of Babylonia (see BAB.-ASSYR. RELIGION).

Eagle.—The eagle is frequently respected, but, except in Australia, the respect does not seem to have risen to an actual cult. In many parts of Australia the eagle-hawk is one of the names of the phratries into which many tribes are divided; in Victoria, Pundjel seems to be a deified eagle-hawk (Brough Smyth, i. 423); elsewhere it is the evil spirit, so-called, which is the eagle-hawk. Mullion is the name of the former, Malian of the latter, and their identity is established by the belief and practice of the Wellington district, where the eyrie of the eagle-hawk was formed on the ground, at initiation, in memory of his contests with an anthropomorphic god, Baiame (*Man*, 1905, 28). The Apaches think there are spirits of Divine origin in the eagle and other birds (Bancroft, iii. 132). The Ostiaks regard a tree as holy on which an eagle has nested (Latham, *Russian Empire*, p. 110). In the island of Tauri, off New Guinea, a certain kind of eagle is tabu, but there are no totemic ideas connected with it (*Zts. vgl. Rechtswiss.* xiv. 325); the osprey is *hope* ('sacred') in New Georgia (*JAI* xxvi. 386). The Osages would turn back from an expedition if an eagle were killed (Nuttall, *Travels*, p. 87). The Samoyeds account it a crime to kill an eagle, and if one is caught in a snare and drowned, they bury it in silence (Schrenck, *Reisen*, i. 168). The Bosnians regard it as unlucky to kill an eagle (*Wiss. Mitt.* iv. 442). Some of the aboriginal Peruvians asserted their descent from eagles (Frazer, *Tot.* p. 5). The Buriats hold that the good spirits sent an eagle as shaman, to counteract the evil deeds of the bad spirits; the first human shaman was the son of the eagle and a Buriat woman (*JAI* xxiv. 64). The Zuñis, Dakotas, and others keep eagles for the sake of their feathers. The Mokis fasten an eagle to the roof in spring, and kill it at the summer solstice in order to get its feathers for ritual purposes; the body is buried in a cemetery, and it is believed that the soul of the eagle goes to the other eagles and returns again as an eagle (*Globus*, lxxvi. 172). The Hopi hunter purifies himself before going after eagles, and makes an offering; one bird has a prayer-stick tied to its foot and is set free (*Am. Anth.*, new ser., iii. 701). The Blackfoot hunter practises many tabus when he is on the hunt for eagles (Grinnell, *Blackfoot Lodge Tales*, p. 237). The Pimas connected the eagle with the Deluge; a bird warned one of their chief prophets, but the warning was disregarded, and only one man was saved (*Smiths. Rep.* 1871, p. 408). In Jabin, New Guinea, a blighting influence on bananas is attributed to the eagle, and no one plants them when an osprey is in sight (*Zts. Geog. Ges. Thür.* xii. 95). Among the Ojibwas the sailing of an eagle to and fro was a good omen (*Autob. of Kahgegahbowh*, p. 48; for the eagle see also de Gubernatis, *Zool. Myth.* ii. 195–197). The eagle is likewise important in Indo-Iranian mythology. In the Rigveda (especially iv. 27) the eagle brings the sacred *sōma* (which see) to mankind (cf. Macdonell, *Vedic Mythology*, 111 f. and the references there given); while in the Avesta an eagle dwells on the 'tree hight All-Healing' (*Yasht*, xii. 17) in the midst of Lake Vouru-kasha (the Caspian), aided by his fellow (*Dīnā-ī Maīnōg-ī Khraṭ*, lxii. 37-41). From the Avesta the eagle passes into Persian literature as the *sīmūrgh*, whence is developed the *roc* of the *Arabian Nights*. The feathers of the sīmūrgh, which dwells on Mount Kaf or Mount Albarz, form talismans for the heroes Tahmuraf and Zāl (Casartelli, in *Compte rendu du congrès scientifique international des Catholiques*, 1891, sec. vi. 79–87).

In classical mythology the eagle occupied an important place; it was the first of ominous birds, and Roman legions took up their winter quarters where there was an eagle's nest. The eagle is associated with Zeus and the lightning; its right wing was buried in fields and vineyards as a protection against hail. The eagle stone (ἀετίτης) and parts of the eagle's flesh were used in magic (Pauly-Wissowa, *s.v.* 'Adler'). It was believed that the eagle was never struck by lightning. Its appearance was auspicious (*ib. s.v.* 'Aberglaube'). The eagle is the constant attribute of Zeus in the older monuments (Farnell, *Cults*, i. 128), as also of Jupiter (Preller, *Röm. Myth.*³ ii. 327).

Eel.—For many of the Malagasy the eel is a forbidden food, and various ætiological myths are told to explain the fact (v. Gennep, *Tabou*, p. 290). By the Imerinas it is regarded as a soul-animal; the Betsileos believe that the lower classes pass into eels; when the body is thrown into the sacred lake, the first eel that takes a bite becomes the domicile of the soul (*ib.*). The eel is also a soul-animal among the Igorrotes (Wilken, *Het Animisme*, p. 72) as well as in Ceram (*ib.*), and receives a daily portion of food. In the Paumotu Archipelago the eel seems to have been held sacred; when one was captured, prayers were offered at a shrine apparently devoted to a cult of female ancestors or relatives; there was an 'enmity between eels and women,' and the latter might not look on them (*Miss. Cath.* 1874, 366). In N. Siam, Muang Naung was covered with water because its inhabitants ate white eels and thus enraged Thegya, the ruler of the world (*Zts. Geog. Ges. Thür.* iv. 149). In N. Queensland a connexion between eels and a flood seems to exist (Lumholtz, *Among Cannibals*, p. 205); although the passage may also be interpreted to mean that those who eat eels have the gift of prophecy. This belief is found in Europe (Wolf, *Beiträge*, i. 232, No. 594). Sacred eels were also known to the Greeks (Pauly-Wissowa, *s.v.* 'Aal'); and the eel is a totem of the Mundari Kols of Bengal and of the Oraons (Crooke, ii. 255). Neither they nor the Nosairis eat eels (Dussaud, *Histoire et religion des Nosairis*, p. 93).

Elephant.—In Siam it is believed that a white elephant may contain the soul of a dead person, perhaps a Buddha; when one is taken, the capturer is rewarded, and the animal brought to the king to be kept ever afterwards, for it cannot be bought or sold. It is baptized and fêted, and when it dies it is mourned for like a human being (Young, *Kingdom of the Yellow Robe*, p. 390 ff.). In Cambodia a white elephant is held to bring luck to the kingdom, and its capture is attended with numerous ceremonies (Moura, *Cambodge*, i. 101). In some parts of Indo-China the reason given for the respect paid to it is that it has a soul, and may do injury after its death; the whole village therefore fêtes it (Mouhot, *Travels*, i. 252; see also Bock, *Temples and Elephants*, p. 19 ff.). The cult of the white elephant is found also at Enarea, south of Abyssinia; but in view of the frequent respect accorded to white animals it is unnecessary to see in this any proof of Indo-Chinese influence. They are regarded as the protectors of mankind, and any one who killed a white or light-coloured elephant would pay the penalty with his life (*Int. Arch.* xvii. 103). Among the Wambugwes the elephant is believed to be the abode of the souls of their ancestors (*ib.*). The elephant is regarded as a tutelary spirit in Sumatra (*Tijdschr. T.L.V.* xxvi. 456). The name is sometimes tabu (*Golden Bough*², i. 457).

The hunting of the elephant is attended with numerous ceremonial observances. The Wakamis of East Africa prepare for the chase by passing a night with their wives on a kind of ant-hill, of which they believe that the female elephant makes use to feed her young one. On the day of the hunt a dance is held, and they make certain marks on their forearms. The hunter buries the trunk and cuts off the end of the tail; the latter he rolls up in palm leaves and puts in his bag; until he next goes to the chase this bag must remain in his wife's care; she also has a right to purchase something with the proceeds of the sale of the ivory; if the hunter quarrelled with her, his next hunt would be unlucky (*Miss. Cath.* 1874, 44). The Amaxosas offer a sacrifice after killing an elephant (Shaw, *Story of my Mission*, p. 452); the hair on the end of the tail is hung at the entrance to the cattle-fold; the end of the ear and the trunk are cut off and buried, the tusks are taken out, and no use is made of the remainder (Kay, *Travels*, p. 138). According to another authority, excuses are made and the elephant is appealed to during the chase not to crush his pursuers (Lichtenstein, *Travels*, i. 254), and the tusks are sent to the king (*ib.* p. 270). The Hottentot hunter must sacrifice a sheep or some other small animal, and none but he may partake of its flesh; any one, on the other hand, may eat of the slain elephant (*Zts. Geog. Ges. Thür.* vi. 42). The Wanyamwezis seek to propitiate the dead elephant by burying his legs, and the Amaxosas inter with the end of the trunk a few of the articles which they buy with the proceeds of the ivory (*Golden Bough*², ii. 400). In India the elephant is the representative of Gaṇeśa, who is also figured with the head of this animal; and in later Hinduism the earth is supported by eight elephants. Some elephants can fly through the air, and all have in their frontal lobes magic jewels. Touching an elephant is a chastity-test, and the hairs of its tail serve as amulets (Crooke, ii. 238–241). According to one account, the world rests upon an elephant (Tylor, i. 365). In West Africa, elephants which destroy plantations are regarded as wizards, and feared (Wilson, *West Africa*, p. 164). On the Congo the end of an elephant's tail is used as a sceptre (*Int. Arch.* xvii. 103). According to the Talmud (*Berākhōth*, 57*b*), it is a bad omen to dream of an elephant. For elephant myths see de Gubernatis, *Zool. Myth.* ii. 91–94, cf. 77. See also 'Earth-carrier,' above.

Fish.—Although sacred fish are not uncommon, a fish-god seems to be a somewhat rare phenomenon. Dagon is often regarded as a fish-god (but see *EBi*, *s.v.* 'Dagon'), but it is certain that he had a human head and hands; possibly his body was scaly, or he had the tail of a fish; for that he was a fish-god seems certain from the fact that his worshippers wore fish skins (*JHS* xiv. 104, quot. Menant, *Glypt. Or.* ii. 63). A figure probably intended for, at any rate regarded as, Artemis Eurynome was depicted with a fish's tail (de Visser, *Götter*, p. 187; cf. Farnell, *Cults*, ii. 522), and there were sacred fish in the temples of Apollo and Aphrodite at Myra and Hierapolis, which raises a presumption of a fish cult (de Visser, pp. 177–178; cf. p. 163). Atargatis is said to have had sacred fish in a pool at Askelon, which were fed daily and never eaten; according to another account, they were the food of the priests. From Xenophon (*Anab.* I. iv. 9) we learn that the fish of Chalus were regarded as gods; and Hyginus tells us that the Syrians looked on fish as holy, and abstained from eating them (*EBi, s.v.* 'Fish'; for fish tabus see W. R. Smith, p. 292 ff.). In modern days fish are sometimes sacred in India, where they also play a considerable part in folklore, often serving as life-indexes. They likewise form the favourite food of *bhūts* (ghosts). Varuṇa rides on a fish, and Vishṇu had a fish-avatār (Crooke, i. 243, ii. 156, 253 f.). The 'Small People' of Cornwall hate the smell of fish (Hunt, *Popular Romances of the West*³, 109). According to the Talmud, fish eaten in the month of Nisan are conducive to leprosy (*Pesahim*, 112*b*). Iranian mythology likewise has the *kara* fish which guards the white Hōm (*Yasht*, xiv. 29, xvi. 7; *Būndahishn*, xviii. 3–6, xxiv. 13), as well as the 'ox-fish,' 'which exists in all seas,' and whose cry makes 'all fish become pregnant, and all noxious water-creatures cast their young' (*Būndahishn*, xix. 7). Fish are kept in parts of Wales to give oracles. Most of the South African Bantus will neither eat nor touch fish, giving as their reason that fish are snakes (Fritsch, *Drei Jahre*, p. 338). Other fish tabus are found in various parts of Africa (*Internat. Archiv für Ethnographie*, xvii. 128). Among the Yezidis only the lowest classes are said to eat fish (Badger, *The Nestorians and their Ritual*, p. 117). In North Aracan fish may not be eaten at harvest time (*JAI* ii. 240), and pregnant women are forbidden them in Servia (*Globus*, xxxiii. 349), thus reversing the teaching of the Talmud, which especially recommends them to women in this condition (*Kethūbim*, 61*a*).

The economic importance of fish makes it natural that fishermen often propitiate them. In Peru sardines are said to have been worshipped in one region, skate in another, dogfish in another, and so on, according to the species that was most plentiful (*Golden Bough*², ii. 410). Many tribes do not burn the bones of fish, because if they did the fish could not rise from the dead (*ib.*). The Thlinkets pay special respect to the first salmon which they take, and many other tabus are observed (*ib.* p. 411 f.; for treatment of the first fish see also Sébillot, *Folklore des Pêcheurs*, pp. 131, 254, 256). In the Ægean, sacrifices are still made to the melanurus (Walpole, *Memoirs*, p. 286; cf. Pliny, XXXII. ii.). In other cases magical ceremonies are resorted to in order to secure a good catch. In the Queen Charlotte Islands the fish are strung on a rope with feathers as charms, and put on the top of a pole stuck in the bed of the river. One of the tribe is banished to the mountains during the fishing season, and may not have a fire or communicate with the tribe, or the fish will leave the river (*Mission Life*, v. 103). In Jabim, New Guinea, the fishermen may not be mentioned, no noise may be made in the village, and women and children must remain at a distance from the fishers (*Zts. Geog. Ges. Thür.* xii. 95). In New Caledonia for one kind of fish appeal is directed to ancestral spirits in the sacred wood; offerings are made there, and when the men go into the water, the women extinguish all fires but one; then they perform a dance, and silence follows. For the sardine a stone wrapped in dried twigs is taken to the cemetery and put at the foot of a post and two sorcerers perform ceremonies (*Miss. Cath.* 1880, 239). In some countries a fish is sacrificed for success in fishing (Sébillot, *op. cit.* p. 116; Krassoff, *Peuple Zyriane*, p. 101).

The Ottawas held that the souls of the dead passed into fish (*Rel. des Jés.* 1667, p. 12; cf. 'soul-animals,' p. 493). In Japan the earthquake is explained as the result of the movements of a great fish in the sea or under the land (*Natur*, 1878, p. 551). In the Middle Ages the same explanation was given in Europe (Mone, *Anzeiger*, viii. 614). Fish are found as totems in South Africa (Fritsch, *Eingeborenen*, p. 153), Alaska (Trimmer, *Yukon Terr.* p. 109), and among the American Indians (Frazer, *Tot.* p. 4, etc.). Myths of fish descent are also found (*ib.* p. 6). For fish myths see de Gubernatis, *Zool. Myth.* ii. 331–353; for the crab, *ib.* pp. 354–359.

Fly.—In Greek mythology both Zeus and Apollo had names connecting them with flies, but it is doubtful whether either of them can properly be termed a fly-god; for the appeal to the god was that he would keep flies from interfering with a sacrifice (Farnell, *Cults*, i. 45). It is equally uncertain whether Beelzebub, whose name is commonly translated 'Lord of Flies,' had any connexion with them. In Africa, however, there seems to be a real fly-god. Flies are kept in a temple (Beecham, *Ashantee*, p. 177). The Kalmuks regard the fly as a soul-animal and never kill it (*JAI* i. 401). In North Germany it is held to be unlucky to kill the last flies, and any one who keeps one alive through the winter will receive a sum of money (Bartsch, *Sagen*, ii. 186). In Greece the 'brazen fly' was one of the names of 'Blind Man's Buff' (Pollux, *Onomastikon*, ix. 123); it is known as the 'Blind Fly' in Italy (*Folklore*, xi. 261) and North India (*Panjāb NQ*, iv. 199). In the latter country it is a lucky omen for a fly to fall into the ink-well (Crooke, ii. 257). According to the Avesta (*Vendīdād*, vii. 2, viii. 71), the demon of death assumes the shape of a fly. For Jewish legends concerning flies, see Krauss, *JE* v. 421 f.

Fowl.—The cock is one of the most important sacrificial victims (for Africa see *Int. Arch.* xvii. 145–148), and has probably replaced larger and more valuable animals in many cases. In some of the Bantu tribes the men abstain from eating domestic fowls (*JAI* xix. 279). The Araucanians do not eat the domestic fowl, because they regard it as a transformed man (*Bol. Inst. Geog. Argent.* xv. 740). Fowls are also tabu in East Africa and Abyssinia (*Globus*, xxxiii. 78). A refusal to eat eggs is more widely found, but does not necessarily point to a tabu of the fowl; abstinence from milk in the same way does not imply a tabu of cattle.

The cock figures in spring ceremonies in Europe; in Schiermonnikoog a green branch is fastened at the top of the May-pole, and on it is hung a basket containing a live cock (*NQ*, 8th ser. x. 194). In the same way at Defynog boys put the figure of a cock at the top of a rod and carried it round on the eve of the first day of May (*Montgom. Coll.* xvii. 268). The cock is one of the forms in which the corn-spirit is supposed to appear (*Golden Bough*², ii. 266). The cock is sometimes used in the expulsion of evils (*ib.* ii. 103). Modern Jews sacrifice a white cock on the eve of the Day of Atonement (*ib.* p. 109; cf. p. 25). We may probably interpret in the same sense the numerous European customs in which a cock or hen is hunted or beaten (*Folklore*, xi. 250, 251; *RHR* xxxviii. 341); connected with these customs is the name of the 'blind hen' used in parts of Europe for 'Blind Man's Buff.' These customs frequently re-appear in wedding ceremonies, perhaps with the same meaning. The eating of a cock (*Tradition*, iv. 364; *Anthropologie*,

iii. 552; *Bavaria*, i. 390; *Russische Revue*, xii. 269, etc.) may be a fertility charm; and in like manner a cock and hen were carried before a bridal couple on their wedding day among the Jews of the Talmudic period (*Giṭṭin*, 57*a*; for other Jewish beliefs concerning fowls see *JE* iv. 139, vi. 344). Occasionally a dance is performed in which fowls are imitated (*Bavaria*, I. i. 394, II. i. 317; Pröhle, *Harzbilder*, p. 8, etc.). In many of the games with fowls the successful player is termed the 'king.'

Sometimes witches are believed to take the form of cocks, and, according to the Talmud, the demons had cock's feet (*Berākhōth*, 6*a*); in Holland a cock put in a vessel over the fire is burnt to ashes to overcome the devil (*Globus*, xxvii. 195). The cock scares demons and ghosts (cf. *Hamlet*, I. i. 149–155), and witches are obliged to return from their Sabbat when the cock crows (cf. art. SATANISM). It is universally held to be a bad omen for a hen to crow like a cock; the remedy is to kill it; sometimes it is also thrown over the house top. The crowing of a red cock is held in Germany to betoken that a fire will break out in the building on which it is perched; the same belief is found in China (Matignon, *Superstition*, p. 43). The cock is used in various magical ceremonies in China. When a boy is named at the beginning of his sixth year, two priests push a cock backwards and forwards through a wooden cylinder (*Zool. Garten*, 1900, 70). On the coffin of a Chinaman whose body is being brought home is a white cock in a basket. One of the three souls is buried with the corpse, but it has to be caught; it can find no rest till the grave is covered with earth; the cock is to show the soul its way back to the body (*ib.* 71). For folk-tales and myths of fowls see de Gubernatis, *Zool. Myth.* ii. 278–291.

Fox.—Dionysus had the surname of *Bassareus*, not, probably, because his worship coalesced with that of an earlier fox-deity, but because as lord of the vine he protects the vineyards against the little foxes (*ClR* x. 21). A fox-god was also known in America (Müller, *Urrelig.* p. 320). Among the Chiriguanos it seems to be a soul-animal (*Lettres édif.* viii. 335). In Europe it is one of the forms in which the corn-spirit appears (*Golden Bough*, ii. 283); it was also burnt in some of the annual fires. A fox tabu is found at Inishkea (*Proc. R. Irish Acad.* iii. 631).

At the Cerealia at Rome foxes were set on fire and hunted about the circus, but it seems probable that they were originally driven over the fields (Fowler, *Rom. Fest.* p. 77 f.); Liebrecht draws attention to the similarity between this custom and the incident in the Samson story (*Zur Volksk.* i. 261 ff.; Frazer, *Paus.* iv. 178). In Finnic mythology the aurora is known as the light of the fox (Grimm, *Reinhart Fuchs*, p. xxxi). In China and among the Eskimos the fox is a wer-animal who appears in the shape of a beautiful woman and seduces the youths (*Arch. Anth.* v. 135; Rink, *Eskimoiske Sagen*, Nos. 16, 18). The same belief exists in Japan, where some families are noted for their ownership of foxes (see 'Possession,' above), and others refuse to intermarry with them on the ground of their magical powers (Chamberlain, *Things Jap.*, *s.v.* 'Fox'). The fox is the hero of a number of Japanese tales (*Globus*, xxi. 332). In Schleswig-Holstein a procession with a fox in a basket takes place in summer, and presents are collected (Schütze, *Idiotikon*, iii. 165). To the fox is sometimes attributed the production of Easter eggs (*Globus*, xxxiv. 59). The name of the fox is sometimes tabu (*Golden Bough*[2], i. 454). As an ominous animal the Lithuanians regard it as inauspicious (Tettau und Temme, *Volkssagen*, p. 280); but in Masuren and Siebenbürgen the opposite view is taken (Töppen, p. 77; Haltrich, viii. 4). For folk-tales and myths of the fox see de Gubernatis, *Zool. Myth.* ii. 121–142.

Frog, toad.—In more than one European country the frog and the toad are hardly, if at all, distinguished; they may therefore be treated together. That this confusion is found in the New World seems clear from the association of the toad with rain, exactly as the frog is, justifiably, associated with water in Europe. In Ceylon the frog was held to be the undermost of the supporters of the earth; on its back was a turtle, then a serpent, then a giant; and he upholds the world (*Miss. Her.* xviii. 385). In South America the Chibchas gave the frog a place among their divinities, and had an annual ceremony in connexion with the calendar, in which the frog figured (Bollaert, *Researches*, p. 49; Dorman, *Prim. Sup.* p. 256). Among the Araucanians of Chile the 'land toad' was called the lord of the waters (*ib.*). In the mythology of the Iroquois it is told how all the water was originally collected in the body of a huge frog, by piercing which Ioskeha formed rivers and lakes (*Rel. des Jés.* 1636, p. 102). A similar story is told by the Micmacs (Leland, *Algonquin Leg.* p. 114), and the Australian blacks have Deluge legends in which the Flood is caused by the bursting of a water-swallowing frog (Brough Smyth, i. 429, 477). Among the Wends the frog is believed to bring newborn children; with this may be compared the Sea Dayak belief that the goddess Salampandai takes the form of a frog; if a frog comes into a house, sacrifice is offered to it and it is released; Salampandai is held to make the children, and a frog is seen near a house when a child is born (*JRAS, S.B.* vii. 146; Schulenburg, *Wend. Volkstum*, i. 94).

In Bohemia, children are believed to hop about the meadows in the form of frogs (Ploss, *Kind*[2], i. 12); with this may be connected the Brandenburg belief that a woman who digs up a toad will soon bear a child (*Zts. Ver. Volksk.* i. 189). A Shan tribe, the Wa, believes itself to be descended from tadpoles (*Asiatic Q. Rev.*, 3rd ser. i. 140). The Bahnars of Indo-China respect the frog, holding that one of their ancestors took that form (*Miss. Cath.* 1893, 140, 143), and in this shape he is believed to guard their fields. The Karens of Burma explain eclipses by saying that a frog is devouring the moon (*ib.* 1877, 455).

We have seen that the frog is associated with water. Like the Araucanians, the Orinoco Indians held the frog to be the lord of the waters, and feared to kill it even when ordered to do so; they kept it under a pot and beat it in time of drought (*Golden Bough*[2], i. 103; Blanco, *Conversion del Piritu*, p. 63). The Newars of Nepāl worship the frog, which is associated with the demi-god Nagas in the control of rain. A sacrifice of rice, ghi, and other objects is made to it in October (*Golden Bough*[2], i. 104; cf. Latham, i. 83, who says August). Water is also poured over a frog in India, or a frog is hung with open mouth on a bamboo, to bring rain (Crooke, i. 73, ii. 256).

In Queensland, British Columbia, and Europe, frogs are also associated with the procuring of rain (*GB*[2], *loc. cit.*), and among the Bhils (*Bombay Gaz.* IX. i. 355), etc.; in the Malay Peninsula the swinging of a frog is said to have caused heavy rain and the destruction of a kampong (*JRAS, S.B.* iii. 88). The toad is sometimes regarded as a tutelary deity in Europe (de Gubernatis, *Zool. Myth.* ii. 380). The Tacullies of British Columbia are said to have no gods, but say, 'The toad hears me' (Maclean, *Twenty-five Years*, p. 265). The Caribs are recorded to have had idols in the form of toads (Sprengel, *Auswahl*, i. 43). In some parts of Germany the toad is regarded as a household genius (*Zts. Ver. Volksk.* i. 189; MS notes). With this compare the belief of the Roumanians that killing a frog or toad is an omen that the killer will murder his mother (*Zts. Oest. Volksk.* iii. 373). In accordance with this belief, the frog and toad are spared (*Folklore*, xi. 240, 241; *Brandenburgia*, viii. 418; Wiedemann, *Ehsten*, 454; Russwurm, § 356, etc.). On the other hand, they are regarded as witches (*FLJ* v. 198; Haltrich, *Zur Volksk.* vii. 4; Müllenhof, *Sagen*, i. 212; Holzmaier, *Osiliana*, p. 37). Accordingly they are often killed (*Zts. Ver. Volksk.* i. 182; Rolland, *Faune pop.* iii. 49 f.; cf. *Devonshire Assoc.* xxviii. 63). For magical purposes they were killed at certain times of the year (Wuttke, *Der Abergl.* p. 95; Rolland, *op. cit.* iii. 54). In Zoroastrianism frogs and toads are evil animals, and are to be killed (*Vendīdād*, xiv. 5); and in Armenia the frog causes warts (a belief found also in the United States) and makes the teeth fall out (Abeghian, *Armenischer Volksglaube*, 30 f.). To cure these warts, meat must be stolen, rubbed on the excrescences, and buried; as the meat decays, the wart will disappear.

In a Mexican festival one of the ceremonies consisted in a dance round the images of the Tlalocs placed in a pond alive with frogs and snakes, one of which each dancer had to eat during the dance. More definite was the belief of the Choctaws, who assigned to the king of the frogs and other aquatic animals the function of initiating the rain-makers (*Miss. Reg.* 1820, 408). We may put down to the same idea the belief of the Guaranis that if a frog enters a boat one of the occupants will die (Ruiz de Montoya, *Conquista*, § 12). The southern Slavs attribute a magical influence to the name of the frog, which may not be mentioned before a small child (Krauss, *Sitte*, 549). The precious jewel in the head of the toad is mentioned by Shakespeare (*As You Like It*, II. i. 13 f.); a similar belief is found in Germany (*Germania*, vii. 435). For myths and folk-tales of the frog and toad, see de Gubernatis, *Zool. Myth.* ii. 371–379, 379–384.

Goat.—In Greek mythology the goat was associated at Argos with the cult of Hera; youths threw spears at a she-goat, and he who struck her got her as a prize (Farnell, *Cults*, i. 189), exactly as in modern Europe many animals are shot at, struck at blindfold, or otherwise gamed for (*Folklore*, xi. 25). The custom was explained by a myth that Hera had once fled to the woods and the animal revealed her hiding-place. The goat was usually a prohibited animal in the cult of Athene, but was once a year sacrificed on the Acropolis (Farnell, *Cults*, i. 290); it has been suggested that the ægis (which see) was simply the skin of the victim. Αἰγοφάγος is found among the titles of Zeus, and there is a myth in which the animal figures as the work of Zeus; he is called αἰγίοχος, just as Dionysus is termed μελάναιγις ('wearer of the black goat-skin'); in spite of the connexion of αἰγίς, etc., with the wind, the original epithet was probably connected with the goat (*ib.* p. 100). In the worship of Brauronian Artemis, a worshipper sacrificed a goat, 'calling it his own daughter' (*ib.* ii. 436)—possibly a trace of human sacrifice. In Sparta a goat was sacrificed to Artemis before charging the enemy; at Ægina torches attached to the horns of goats are said to have scared away invaders (cf. Liebrecht, *Zur Volksk.* p. 261), and in Attica 500 she-goats were a thank-offering for Marathon (Farnell, ii. 449 f.). Aphrodite is the 'rider on the goat' (*ib.* 684), probably because it was her sacred animal.

At Rome goats were sacrificed at the Lupercalia, and youths clad themselves in the skins of the victims. After feasting they ran round the base of the Palatine, striking with thongs of goatskin the women whom they encountered, or who offered themselves to their blows (Fowler, *Rom. Fest.* p. 311). The Flamen Dialis was forbidden to touch a goat, and it was excluded from the cult of Jupiter (*ib.* p. 313). For the goat see also Pauly-Wissowa, *s.v.* 'Aberglaube,' p. 2.

Dionysus was believed to assume the form of a goat (*Golden Bough*², ii. 165), probably as a divinity of vegetation. Many minor divinities like Pan, Silenus, the Satyrs, Fauns, etc., either are in goat form or have some part of their body taken from the goat, and they are all more or less woodland deities. In similar fashion, the devil is commonly believed, in Europe, to have one foot in the form of a goat's hoof; and throughout mediæval demonology the goat is associated with Satan and with witches; while at the Sabbat the Evil One frequently was believed to assume the form of a goat. In Northern Europe, the wood-spirits Lēshi are believed to have the horns, ears, and legs of goats, and the goat is a form in which the corn-spirit is supposed to appear (*Golden Bough*², ii. 271, 291). In the 17th cent. the Circassian Tatars offered a goat on St. Elias day, a date on which the lamb is also offered in some parts. After proving the victim to be worthy, they drew its skin over its ears and hung it upon a pole; the flesh was then cooked, and consumed by men and women together; the men then prayed to the skin, and the women left them to their brandy and devotions (Strauss, *Reise*, p. 116). In Africa the Bijagos are said to have the goat as their principal divinity; on the Massa River the goat is kept as a tutelary deity. It is sometimes regarded as the resting-place of the souls of the dead (*Int. Arch.* xvii. 104). The king of San Salvador was believed to have deposited his soul in a goat during his lifetime (*Golden Bough*², iii. 407; Bastian, *Fetisch*, p. 12), and possibly this belief explains the position of the 'goat of the law' which Soyaux saw near Old Calabar (*Aus West-Africa*, i. 106).

The name of the goat is tabu in the Sunda Islands (*Golden Bough*², i. 462). The animal itself is similarly hedged round in South Africa (Galton, *Travels*, p. 84), Madagascar (v. Gennep, *Tabou*, p. 238), and in West Africa (*Int. Arch.*, *loc. cit.*). The goat is tabu to some of the Bechuanas (Mackenzie, *Daydawn*, p. 65 n.) ['Bushmen' in the text should be corrected to 'Bechuanas'], who believe that to look upon it would render them impure, as well as cause them undefined uneasiness; it does not, however, appear to be a totem. If a goat climbs on the roof of a house, it is speared at once, because it would bewitch the owner if it were not put to death (Mackenzie, *Ten Years*, p. 392). The antipathy, therefore, depends on its association with wizards. The goat is an important sacrificial animal, especially in Africa (*Int. Arch.* xvii. 136). In Athens it was excluded from the Acropolis, but once a year it was driven in for a sacrifice (*Golden Bough*², ii. 314). Frazer conjectures that the goat was originally a representative of Athene.

From the Jewish custom of sending a goat into the wilderness laden with the sins of the people (see 'Scapegoat,' above, and art. AZAZEL), has been derived the name for the whole class of animated beings so employed in the expulsion of evils (*Golden Bough*², iii. 101 ff.). The goat itself is the animal employed by the Lolos (Vial, *Les Lolos*, p. 12) in West Africa (Burdo, *Niger*, p. 182) and in Uganda (Ashe, *Two Kings*, p. 320). In Tibet a human scapegoat is dressed in a goat's skin; he is kicked and cuffed, and sent away after the people have confessed their sins (*South Am. Miss. Mag.* xiv. 112).

The Karens of Burma attribute eclipses to the fact that wild goats are eating the luminary; they make a noise to drive them away (*Miss. Cath.* 1877, 455).

In Europe the goat appears in processions and

other functions at Christmas, the Carnival, etc. (Mannhardt, *Antike Wald- u. Feldkulte*, 184 ff., 197). In Bohemia it is thrown from the church in September (Mannhardt, *Myth. Forsch.* 163 n.), but this apparent association with the harvest may be late; for in Wendish parts the date was July 25th (Kosche, *Character*, iv. 481). In Transylvania a goat dance is performed at weddings, probably as a fertility charm (Mannhardt, *Myth. Forsch.* 198). For the same reason, perhaps, the goat is given to the parents of the bride in Bulgaria, where, as in the Upper Palatinate, it forms the recognized dish (*Anthrop.* ii. 587; Schönwerth, *Aus der Oberpfalz*, i. 98; cf. 342). Among the Matabele of South Africa the husband gives the bridesmaids a goat to eat (*JAI* xxiii. 84). In the Vosges the younger sister who marries first must give her elder sister a white goat (*Mélusine*, i. 454).

'The goat' is one of the names by which the 'blind man' in Blind Man's Buff is known (*Folklore*, xi. 261). For myths and folk-tales of the goat see de Gubernatis, *Zool. Myth.* i. 401–428.

Goose.—The goose was one of the animals which were tabu to the Britons (Cæsar, *de Bello Gall.* v. xii.). The Norsemen also refused to eat it (*Life of Bede*, ch. xxxvi.). At Great Crosby it is still regarded as tabu (*Arch. Rev.* iii. 233). But, on the other hand, it is not infrequently eaten with more or less ceremony. The Michaelmas goose is certainly a very old custom. The bird is hunted or killed in various parts of Europe (*Folklore*, xi. 253; for ceremonial eating see p. 259). In China two red geese are given to the newly married; the explanation offered is that they are faithful to each other, as human beings should be (*Zool. Garten*, 1900, p. 76). The goose is also a gift to the newly married at Moscow (*Anthrop.* iv. 324); it has perhaps in some cases taken the place of the swan (see below). The Mandans and Minnetarees made their goose medicine; the dance was to remind the wild geese, which then prepared to migrate, that they had had plenty of good food all the summer, and to entreat them to return in the spring (Boller, *Indians*, p. 145). There were sacred geese in the Capitol and in Greek temples (de Visser, *Götter*, p. 175). In mediæval times, the goose, like the goat (see above), was associated with witches who frequently used these birds as vehicles to carry them to the Sabbat. For myths and folk-tales of the goose, swan, and duck, see de Gubernatis, *Zool. Myth.* ii. 307–319.

Hare.—Although the hare is one of the most important animals in the belief and practice of the uncultured, it cannot be said that it is anywhere regarded as divine, unless it be among the Kalmuks, who call it Sākyamuni (the Buddha), and say that on earth the hare allowed himself to be eaten by a starving man, and was in reward raised to the moon, where they profess to see him (Crooke, ii. 50). The connexion of the hare with the moon is also found in Mexico (Sahagun, vii. 2) and South Africa, where the Hottentots tell the story of how death came into the world, and explain it by a mistake made by the hare in taking a message from the moon (Merensky, *Beiträge*, p. 86; Bleek, *Reynard the Fox*, pp. 69–74). In North America, all the Algonquin tribes had as their chief deity a Great Hare (see 'Cult' above) to whom they went at death; he lived in the east, or, according to some accounts, in the north. In his anthropomorphized form he was known as Manibosho, Nanabojou, Michabou or Messou (Brinton, *Myths*[3], p. 193). In one aspect he is a culture hero, who teaches to the Indians the medicine dance and the arts of life; in another aspect he is a buffoon, who tries his magic art on various animals and fails ludicrously. In a New England Flood legend the survivors took a hare with them to the mountain on which they found refuge, and learnt of the assuaging of the waters by its non-return (Josselyn, *Account*, p. 134).

The name of the hare is frequently tabu (Russwurm, *Eibovolk*, § 358; Holzmaier, *Osiliana*, p. 105; *FLJ* v. 190; *Brit. Ass. Ethnog. Survey Rep.* [Toronto Meeting], 353; Grimm, *Deut. Myth.* cxxiv; *GB*[2] i. 457). It is unlucky to kill the hare (*Folklore*, xi. 240) or eat its flesh (Lyde, *Asian Mystery*, p. 191; Dussaud, *Hist. des Nosairis*, p. 93; *Globus*, xxxiii. 349; *Ausland*, lxiv, 58, etc.). There is a wide-spread belief that hare-lip is caused if a pregnant woman puts her foot in a hare's form.

Like many other animals, the hare is hunted annually at many places (*Folklore*, iii. 442, xi. 250; *Mem. Soc. Ant. France*, iv. 109; *Mélusine*, i. 143; *Ons Volksleven*, viii. 42), and sometimes eaten ritually (*Folklore*, xi. 259). Sometimes the hare is offered to the parish priest (*Ann. Soc. Em. Flandre*, 5th ser. i. 436; *Folklore*, iii. 441 f.). The hare is more especially associated with Easter (*Folklore*, iii. 442), and is said on the Continent to lay Easter eggs (*Das Kloster*, vii. 928; *Schweiz. Arch. Volksk.* i. 115). It is one of the animals in whose form cakes are made at Christmas (Bartsch, *Sagen*, ii. 227; Kolbe, *Hessische Volkssitten*, p. 7; Curtze, *Volksüberl.* p. 441). Among the Slavs hare-catching is a similar game to Blind Man's Buff (Tetzner, p. 86). In Swabia it is said that children come from the hare's nest (Mannhardt, *Germ. Mythen*, p. 410). The hare is said to change its sex every year (Liebrecht, *Zur Volkskunde*, p. 362).

The hare is almost universally regarded as an unlucky animal; when a Kalmuk sees one, he utters a cry and strikes a blow in the air (*JAI* i. 401). The Hottentots kill it, though they do not eat it (*Zts. Geog. Ges. Thür.* vi. 42). Its appearance in a village is thought to betoken fire, both in England and Germany (MS notes; Grohmann, *Abergl.* 375; *Am Urquell*, iii. 107; *Zts. Ver. f. Volksk.* x. 209). In Oesel it is sometimes of good omen (Holzmaier, p. 43). Probably the association of hares with witches is in part responsible for the hare's evil augury. In Gothland the so-called milk-hare is a bundle of rags and chips of wood; it is believed to cause cows to give bloody milk (*Globus*, xxiii. 47). On the other hand, hares' heads are found on the gables in the Tyrol, probably as a protection against witchcraft (Heyl, p. 156); a hare's foot is a counter charm against witchcraft (Hone, *Tablebook*, iii. 674). Among the American negroes, in like manner, a most lucky charm is the left hind foot of a rabbit caught jumping over a grave in the dark of the moon by a red-haired, cross-eyed negro. It is also to be noted that the rabbit is one of the chief figures in the folk-tales of the negroes of the southern United States, where he outwits 'Brer Wolf' and all other animals (Harris, *Uncle Remus, his Songs and his Sayings; Nights with Uncle Remus*, etc.). The hare is one of the forms believed to be assumed by the corn-spirit (*Golden Bough*[2], ii. 269). For myths and folk-tales of the hare see de Gubernatis, *Zool. Myth.* ii. 76–82.

Hawk.—According to the Gallinomeros of California, the hawk flew in the coyote's face in the primeval darkness; apologies ensued, and the pair together made the sun, put it in its place, and set it on fire (Bancroft, iii. 85). According to the Yocuts, the hawk, crow, and duck were alone in the world, which was covered with water; the two former created the mountains from the mud brought up by the latter (*ib.* p. 124).

The most important area for the cult of the hawk seems to be North Borneo (*JAI* xxxi. 173 ff.). The Kenyahs will neither kill nor eat it. They address it, as they do anything regarded in its spiritual aspect, by prefixing 'Balli' to its name; they always observe its movements with keen interest, and formally consult it before leaving home for distant parts. The rites are very elaborate, and, if successful, secure that the hawks which gave the omens serve as tutelary deities during absence. After a war expedition, pieces of the flesh of slain enemies are set out as a thank-offering to Balli Flaki for his guidance and protection. The hawk's aid is sought before agricultural operations are entered upon, and a wooden image of a hawk with its wings extended is put up before a new house. During the formal consultation of the hawk, women may not be present; but they keep in their sleeping-places wooden images with a few hawk's feathers in them, which serve magical purposes during illness. In this tribe the hawk seems to be regarded as a messenger of the Supreme God, Balli Penyalong; but the thanks seem to be offered to the birds exclusively. The Kayans have gone some distance in anthropomorphizing the hawk, though they still retain the idea that it is the servant of the Supreme God; they appeal to it for help, but if they get no reply, they transfer their prayer to Laki Tenangan. The hawk-god, Laki Neho, is described as living in a house at the top of a tree; but the individual hawk is still of importance. Among the Sea Dayaks the hawk-god, Singalang Burong, has become completely anthropomorphized. He is the god of war, but they say that he never leaves his house; consequently, though they take other bird omens, they do not regard the hawk as his messenger. He is the god of omens, clearly developed from a divine hawk species, and, as such, is the ruler of the omen birds; a trace of his hawk nature is found in the belief that, though he put on the form of an Iban to attend a feast, he flew away in hawk form at the end of it, when he took off his coat. It is instructive to note that in the opinion of the Ibans there are only thirty-three of each kind of ominous bird, though all are respected because of the impossibility of distinguishing ominous from non-ominous individuals of the same species.

In Madagascar (v. Gennep, *Tabou*, p. 261) various species of hawk are ominous. Some Sakalava families regard one species as sacred and bury it. In Imerina prayers are addressed to it, and portions of the wing, leg, or body serve as charms. One tribe is called by the name of a species of hawk, and the hawk is its emblem. The omens given by hawks are good or bad, according to the species.

In America the Kailtas held that when a man died his soul was carried to spirit-land by a little bird; if he had been a wicked man, the burden of his sins enabled a hawk to overtake the bird and devour the soul (Bancroft, iii. 524).

In Europe the hawk is regarded as lucky; in Baden one kind is kept or allowed to nest on the house; its presence is thought to avert a flash of lightning; in Bohemia a kind of hawk is regarded as a luck-bringing bird (Mone, *Anzeiger*, vii. 430; Grohmann, *Aberglaube*, No. 459). Like the owl and the bat, it is sometimes nailed on the doors of stables (*Mélusine*, viii. 21). For hawk myths see de Gubernatis, *Zool. Myth.* ii. 92–94.

Horse.—In Greek cult there was at Colonus a common altar to Poseidon Hippius and Athene Hippia (Farnell, *Cults*, i. 272). Artemis was also associated with the horse (*ib.* ii. 450); so, too, Aphrodite (*ib.* ii. 641), perhaps in her maritime character. Cronus is said to have taken the form of a horse, and the Illyrians sacrificed a horse to him (*ib.* i. 29). But in none of these cases does the connexion of the animal with the deity justify the supposition that we have to do with a horse-cult which has undergone development, except perhaps in the case of Poseidon. There are, however, other deities intimately associated with the horse, in a manner which makes it legitimate to suppose that they have undergone anthropomorphization or taken up earlier theozoic elements. In the cave of Phigalia, Demeter, according to popular tradition, was represented with the head and mane of a horse, probably as a legacy from an older theriomorphic non-specialized corn-spirit (*Golden Bough*², ii. 303). In Laconia her priests were called πῶλοι (de Visser, *Götter*, p. 198; cf. *JHS* xiv. 138). Not only Poseidon but also the river-gods were, as a rule, conceived as tauriform, but at Rhodes four horses were cast into the sea (Smith, *Rel. Sem.*² p. 293); though this was interpreted as a sacrifice to the sun, it may have been connected with the horse form so commonly attributed to water-gods in Gaul, Scotland, and North Europe generally (*Teutonia*, ii. 72; Black, *Orkney and Shetland Folklore*, p. 189 ff.). In Gaul we find a horse-goddess, Epona, whose name is derived from *epos*, 'horse'; there are also traces of a horse-god, Rudiobus (*Rev. Celt.* xxi. 294). Of less specialized forms of horse-worship traces are to be found in Persia, where white horses were regarded as holy (Herod. i. 189; Geiger, *Ostiran. Kult.* 350 f.), and Teutonic regions, where their use was restricted to kings, and they were kept in holy enclosures (Tacitus, *Germ.* 9, 10; Grimm, *Deut. Myth.*⁴ ii. 552; Weinhold, *Altn. Leben*, p. 47). Horses seem to have attained sanctity early in India (Crooke, ii. 204), and the cult is not unknown at the present day (*ib.* p. 208). Koda Pen, the horse-god of the Goṇḍs, is a shapeless stone, like the tiger-god of the Waralis (Hislop, *Papers*, p. 51 n.). (For the horse in mythology see Negelein in *Teutonia*, ii.; de Gubernatis, *Zool. Myth.* i. 290–296, 330–355. For superstitions see Pauly-Wissowa, *s.v.* 'Aberglaube,' p. 76).

The horse or mare is one of the forms of the corn-spirit in Europe (*Golden Bough*², ii. 281), and the sacrifice of the October horse at Rome is usually connected with this idea (but cf. Fowler, *Rom. Fest.* pp. 248–249; see also Gruppe, *Griechische Culte*, p. 839 n.). A horse race was held, and the right-hand horse of the victorious team was offered to Mars. Its head was cut off and adorned with a string of loaves, for which the inhabitants of two districts contended; its blood was caught and used to fumigate the flocks in the spring (Fowler, *Rom. Fest.* p. 241 f.; *Golden Bough*², ii. 315 f.; cf. iii. 122). The head was fixed to the palace or the Mamilian tower. The custom of fixing horses' heads to buildings is still common, though it does not follow that we can explain the old custom on the same lines; the modern explanation is usually that the skulls are intended to keep away evil influences (Trede, *Heidenthum*, iii. 210). A similar custom exists in Germany and other parts of Europe of carving animals', commonly horses', heads at the end of the gables (Petersen, *Die Pferdeköpfe*; *Folklore*, xi. 322, 437). The horse is very commonly sacrificed in the Old World (*Teutonia*, ii. 90–148), especially in burial rites (*ib.* pp. 148–162). It is also offered in South America (*S. Amer. Miss. Mag.* xxviii. 38).

Processions in which a horse figures take place, commonly at Christmas, in Germany, France, and England (*Teutonia*, *loc. cit.*; Nore, *Coutumes*, pp. 70, 72, 76, 203, 205; *RHR* xxxviii. 334). The interpretation of these customs is uncertain; the German ceremonies are often brought into connexion with Wodan in popular belief; a connexion with the corn-spirit has also been suggested; possibly they may be associated with a mid-winter festival of the expulsion of evils, of which other traces can be found (Panzer, *Beitrag*, ii. 115 f.).

At Whitsuntide it was the custom to hold a horse race (Mannhardt, *Antike Wald- und Feldkulte, pass.*), to which we find a Roman parallel in the October race; they may probably be brought into connexion with the cult of vegetation.

The horse is important as an ominous animal (*Teutonia*, ii. 15), and in modern folklore omens are drawn in particular from the white horse. It is frequently regarded as being of ill omen (*RHR* xxxviii. 298; Grohmann, *Abergl.* Nos. 336–337) or a foretoken of death; but at the same time in Bohemia the white horse brings good fortune to the house where it is stabled (*ib.*); and in Northern India it is a lucky omen for a horse and his rider to enter a field of sugar-cane while it is being sown (Crooke, ii. 207). The horse, like the bull, is a fertility animal (*ib.*). If a boy is put on a horse immediately after his birth, Mecklenburgers think that he has the power of curing various maladies from which horses suffer (Ploss, *Kind*², i. 74). Some part of the magical importance of the horse-shoe is perhaps derived from the horse itself. In Wales and Ireland are found stories of the Midas type (*Folklore*, xi. 234).

Hyæna.—One of the chief centres of the hyæna-cult is the Wanika tribe of East Africa. One of the highest ranks of their secret society is that of the Fisi or hyænas, so called from the power of administering to suspected persons the oath by the hyæna, which, before the practice of burial was introduced, devoured the bodies of the dead. It is held that a false oath by the hyæna will cause the death of the perjurer. The Fisi also protect the fields from thieves by consecrating them to the hyæna, which they do by making certain marks near the boundaries (*Report on E. African Protectorate*, 1897, p. 10 ff.). The Wanikas look upon the hyæna as one of their ancestors, or as in some way connected with their origin and destiny. The death of one is an occasion of universal mourning, and a wake is held over it by the whole people, not by one clan only. It is a great crime to kill one, and even imitation of its voice entails payment of a fine (New, *Life Wanderings*, p. 188). Hyænas are tabu in Accra (*Int. Arch.* p. 101), and the Ewe tribes hold that they are inhabited by a god or spirit. The Masai expose their dead to be eaten by hyænas; and if a corpse has to wait more than a day for burial, it is a token of ill-luck, to be countered by the sacrifice of cattle (Baumann, *Massailand*, p. 163). South African Bantus likewise expose their dead to be eaten by hyænas (*Account of Cape of G. Hope*, p. 143), which they never kill. The hyæna is a common form of the wizard (*Int. Arch., loc. cit.*), and there are various stories told of the *budas* in Abyssinia and others having transformed themselves in the sight of other people (Tylor, *Prim. Culture*³, i. 310); gold rings are said to be found in the ears of dead hyænas similar to those worn by the *budas*, who are workers in clay and iron. Among the Matabele, wizards are said to go to fresh graves and dig up corpses, to which they give medicine and transform them into hyænas (Thomas, *Eleven Years*, p. 293), which they then employ as their messengers, or upon which sometimes they ride themselves. When the voice of the hyæna is heard, the hearer must remain perfectly still. If a hyæna is wounded at night and escapes to another kraal, the place is thought to be the residence of a wizard. The sight of a hyæna at night is unlucky; and if a man discovers a dead one, he runs away and remains perfectly silent about it. A wizard or diviner, when his training is over, has to put on the skin of a hyæna, as a sign that the Amadhlozi have endowed him with the necessary powers (*ib.*). In ancient Arabia it was believed that, if a hyæna trod on a man's shadow, it deprived him of the power of speech and motion; and that, if a dog, standing on a roof in the moonlight, cast a shadow on the ground and a hyæna trod on it, the dog would be dragged from the roof as if a rope had been made fast to it (*Golden Bough*², i. 287). In Talmudic belief (*Bābā ḳammā*, 16*a*), the male hyæna goes through the stages of a bat, *'arpad*, nettle, thistle, and demon, each lasting seven years.

Leopard.—The cult of the leopard is widely distributed in West Africa. In Dahomey it is especially sacred to the royal family; it is also an Ewe totem. A man who kills a leopard is liable to be put to death; but usually he pays a fine and performs propitiatory ceremonies. No leopard skin may be exposed to view, but stuffed leopards are objects of worship. Some of the king's wives in Dahomey were known as *kpo-si* ('leopard-wives'). A man wounded by a leopard was regarded as specially fortunate (Ellis, *Ewe-speaking Peoples*, p. 74; Labarthe, *Reise*, p. 153).

The Bakwiris regard the leopard as possessed by evil spirits (*Beitr. zur Kolonialpol.* iii. 194). On the Gold Coast it is regarded as the abode of the spirits of the dead (Müller, *Fetu*, p. 97), or of evil spirits (*Mitt. Geog. Ges. Thür.* ix. 18), which may endanger the life of the hunter or make him fire at a man in mistake for an animal. The hunter, when successful, announces his triumph to those who have killed a leopard previously; then a blade of grass is put in his mouth as a sign that he may not speak; his comrades tell the leopard why it was killed—because it had killed sheep; a drum gives the signal for an assembly; and the leopard is fastened to a post, its face to the sky, and carried round the town, its slayer behind it on the shoulders of another man; on their return the leopard is fastened to a tree, and the hunter is besmeared with coloured earth, so as to look like a leopard. Thereupon they imitate a leopard's movements and voice; for nine days after the death of the leopard they have the right to kill all the hens they can catch. In the afternoon the body is cut up, and portions are sent to the chief of the village and others; the hunter retains the teeth, head, and claws (*ib.*). In Agome the hunter observes the same ritual interdictions as at the death of his wife (*Mitt. d. Schutzgeb.* v. 156). Among the Fjorts the king has a right to the body of the leopard; people loot each other's towns when one is killed; and the killer has the right to appropriate any article outside a house when he is on his way to take a leopard to the king (Dennett, *Seven Years*, p. 180). In Loango a common negro who kills a leopard, which is regarded as a prince, is tried, and must excuse himself by saying the leopard was a stranger; a prince's cap is put on the leopard's head, and dances are held in its honour. In olden times the capture of a leopard was one of the few occasions on which the king could leave his *chibila* (Bastian, *Loango-Küste*, p. 243 ff.; *Int. Arch.* xvii. 98). When a leopard is killed in Okeyou, its body is treated with great respect and brought to the hunter's village. Representatives of neighbouring villages attend, and the gall-bladder is burnt *coram populo*; each person whips his hands down his arms to disavow guilt (Kingsley, *Travels*, p. 543). In Jebel Nuba a hunter, on killing his first leopard, may not wash himself for several weeks; the skin belongs to the chief; the hunter's tabu is broken when the last novice to kill a leopard has given him a slice of meat and received from him his shoes and the animal's skin (*Miss. Cath.* 1882, 461). In South Africa a man who has killed a leopard remains in his hut three days; he practises continence and is fed to satiety (Kolbe, *Pres. State*, i. 252).

The leopard society is common in West Africa. Members wear leopard skins when they seize their victims for sacrifice (Kingsley, *Travels*, p. 537).

Among the Yaos, leopards are among the animals whose figures are drawn on the ground at the initiation of girls (Macdonald, *Africana*, i. 131).

The leopard is one of the forms assumed by wizards in West Africa (Wilson, *West Africa*, p. 398), among the Madis and Latukas (Stuhlmann, *Mit Emin Pascha*, p. 801), and the Baris (*Int. Arch.* xvii. 99). The Nubas believe that the spirit of a panther passes into the *kudjur* ('priest') when he gives an oracle; he sits upon a stool covered with panther skin and imitates the panther's cry (von Hellwald, *Naturgesch.* ii. 235). In Calabar, on the other hand, the leopard is one of the animals whose images are placed in the streets at the Ndok, or purification festival, for evil spirits to pass into (Bastian, *Fetisch*, p. 21 ff.). In South Africa the heart of the leopard was sometimes eaten to gain courage, and portions of the animal were scattered over the warriors by magicians (*JAI* xix. 282). Among the Fans a leopard-skin girdle was held to render them invisible (Du Chaillu, *Voy. et Av.* p. 502). Zulu warriors ate leopard flesh to make them brave, and a Zulu would sometimes give his children a leopard's blood to drink, or its heart to eat, in order that they might become strong and courageous (*Golden Bough*², ii. 354). The gall of a leopard is regarded as poison, and in West Africa its whiskers are believed to have magical properties (Kingsley, *op. cit.* p. 543).

Lion.—In Egyptian mythology the tunnel through which the sun passed was supposed to have a lion at each end; statues of lions were placed at the doors of palaces and tombs to ward off evil spirits. There was a lion-god at Baalbek, and songs were sung when it devoured a calf. It was associated with Ra and Horus, and possibly the Sphinx with its human head and lion's body was intended as an abode for Ra (Budge, *Gods*, ii. 360; Damascius, *Vit. Isid.* p. 203). There was a lion-headed goddess Sekhmet, and the Arabs had a lion-god Yaghuth (*EBi* iii. 2804). In modern Africa we find a lion-idol among the Balondas. It is made of grass covered with clay, and resembles a crocodile more than anything else; it is placed in the forest, and, in cases of sickness, prayers are offered and drums beaten before it (Livingstone, *South Africa*, pp. 282, 304).

In comparison with its traditional position as king of the beasts, the lion occupies, however, an undistinguished place among the animals in savage belief and custom. It is regarded as the abode of the souls of the dead on the Congo and the Zambesi, as well as among the Wambugwes, Bechuanas, and Mashonas (Bastian, *Loango-Küste*, ii. 244; Livingstone, *Zambesi*, p. 159; Baumann, *Massailand*, p. 187; Brown, *On the S. A. Frontier*, p. 217; cf. Speke, *Journ.* pp. 221, 222). As a rule, it is the chief who is thus transformed; but among the Angonis there is a universal desire to be transformed into a lion after death (*ZE* xxxii. 199). The name-tabu is not by any means uncommon; the Arabs call the lion *Abū-l-'Abbās*; the negroes of Angola call it *ngana* ('sir'); both Bushmen and Bechuanas avoid using its proper name (*Golden Bough*², i. 456); the Hottentots avoid using its name on a hunting expedition, and call it *gei gab* ('great brother'). In South Africa the same ceremonies are gone through by the slayer of a lion as of a leopard or a monkey (see below). Another account says that the hunter is secluded for four days, purified, brought back, and feasted (Lichtenstein, *Travels*, i. 257). In East Africa the dead lion is brought before the king, who does homage to it, prostrating himself on the ground and rubbing his face on its muzzle (Becker, *Vie en Afrique*, ii. 298, 305). Among the Fulahs the killer of a lioness is made prisoner, and women come out to meet the party; the lioness is carried on a bier covered with white cloth. The hunter must be released by the chiefs of the village when he pleads, in reply to the charge that he has killed a sovereign, that it was an enemy (Gray and Dochard, *Travels*, p. 143). The lion is one of the animals whose shape is said to be assumed by wizards; this belief is found on the Luapula (*Petermanns Mitt.* 1874, 188) and on the Zambesi (Livingstone, *Zambesi*, p. 159), where a certain drink is said to have the power of transforming them; among the Tumbukas, men and women wander about smeared with white clay, and are held to have the power of assuming the shape of lions (Elmslie, *Among the Wild Ngoni*, p. 74); the Bushmen say that the lion can change itself into a man (Lloyd, *Short Account*, p. 20). In Greek cult a lioness was led in a procession at Syracuse in honour of Artemis (Farnell, *Cults*, ii. 432). The lion is used in magic to give courage (*Golden Bough*², ii. 354, 356; *JAI* xix. 282). It figures in Masai fables, where it is outwitted by the mongoose (Hollis, *Masai*, p. 198), and among the Bushmen (Lloyd, *loc. cit.*). In Hottentot stories it is outwitted by the jackal (Bleek, *Reynard*, p. 5); in another story the lion thinks itself wiser than its mother, and is killed by a man (*ib.* p. 67). In like manner, in an Indian story, first found in the *Pañchatantra* (i. 8; cf. Benfey, *Pantschatantra*, i. 179 ff.), and widely borrowed, appearing even in Tibet (O'Connor, *Folk-Tales from Tibet*, pp. 51–55), the lion is outwitted by the hare. For lion myths see de Gubernatis, *Zool. Myth.* ii. 153–159.

Lizard.—Of lizard myths unconnected with any cult or tabu there are but few, the best known and most widely distributed being the Bantu account of the origin of death; according to this, the chameleon was sent to man with a message that he was to live, the lizard some time after with a contrary message; the chameleon dawdled on its way, and as a result man is subject to death (Kidd, *Essential Kafir*, p. 76). In the Sandwich Islands lizards are believed to form part of the food of the soul which goes with the body after death (*Miss. Cath.* 1880, p. 626), while in Zoroastrianism the lizard forms part of the food of the damned (*Būndahishn*, xxviii. 48). In the Malay Peninsula the Orang Laut regard the small flying lizard as the emissary of the great flying lizard, which guards each man's life-stone; they cause the souls of the newborn to enter their bodies. They can change at will into crocodiles, and cause the death of any one whose life-stone is buried (*ZE* xxxviii. 187). With this may be compared a Polynesian myth about Moko (Gill, *Myths*, p. 229). The Maoris tell a story according to which the first of their race was drawn out of the water at the Creation by a lizard (Gerland, *Südsee*, p. 237). In South Australia the lizard is believed to have divided the sexes; it is a so-called sex-totem, the men destroying the female and the women the male lizards (Frazer, *Tot.* p. 52). Stories of lizard births are told in Indonesia and New Guinea (Wilken, *Het Animisme*, p. 73; *Ber. Utrecht Zendelingsver.* 1891, p. 20). In New Zealand, Yap, and the Banks Islands, the lizard is regarded as the residence of the souls of the dead (Shortland, p. 93; cf. *JAI* x. 288, 297, xix. 120; Hernsheim, *Südseeerinn.* p. 22; Codrington, *Melanesians*, p. 180; cf. 'Future Life,' above).

The main areas of lizard-cult are Polynesia (Wilken in *Bijdragen T.L.V.* 6th ser. vol. v. p. 468 ff.) and West Africa (*Int. Arch.* xvii. 112). The evidence in the latter case is, however, unsatisfactory; Dahomey is mentioned as one of the seats of the cult, but Ellis (*Ewe-speaking Peoples*) does not notice it. In Bonney, however, there appears to have been a practice of rescuing lizards which were in danger (Bastian, *Bilder*, p. 160); and Crowther is said to have abolished the worship of the lizard-god (*Globus*, x. 285, xii. 256). An old writer describes a custom of bringing food to a lizard-god; it seems to have been the sacred animal of a secret society (Pruneau de Pommegorge in Cuhn's *Sammlungen*). On the other side of Africa the tribal god of the Shilluks is said to appear in the form of a lizard (Ratzel, ii. 43). In Polynesia respect for the lizard was wide-spread. In New Zealand, according to one account (but cf. Shortland, p. 93), it was regarded as an incarnation of Tangaloa, the heaven-god; a green lizard was more especially associated with him, perhaps from its habit of coming out and basking in the sun (Dieffenbach, *Travels*, ii. 116; Wilken, *loc. cit.*); so, too, in Samoa (*Globus*, lxxiv. 256 ff.). In the Hervey Islands, Tongaiti or Matarau (the night-heaven) was likewise identified with a spotted lizard, which comes out at night (Gill, *Myths*, p. 10). In Samoa not only family gods but general deities assumed lizard form, among them Le Sa, Pili, and Samaui (Turner, *Samoa*, pp. 44, 46, 72). An idol in lizard form, or rather a house-god, is reported from Easter Island (Geiseler, *Osterinsel*, p. 32; *Man*, 1904, No. 46). Moko, the king of the lizards, is recognized all over Polynesia (Gill, *Myths*, p. 229). In Micronesia lizard-worship was found in the shape of a cult of the dead. Lizards were kept in special enclosures, and their power over lightning and rain was held to pass into their keepers or priests, to whom offerings were made from all parts of the island (Hernsheim, *Südseeerin.* p. 22). In New Caledonia, a Melanesian area with Polynesian immigrants, the lizard was one of the animals respected and termed 'father,' probably as the abode of the soul of a dead man. Lizards were also worshipped or respected in Sumatra, Boeroe, the Mentawei Islands, Bali, etc., and seem to be identified in some cases with imported Hindu gods (Wilken, *loc. cit.*). In Madagascar the *fanany* is, according to the Betsileos, the re-incarnation of the soul of a dead man, and takes the form of a lizard; it is buried in a pot, and communication with the surface established with a bamboo; if, when it appears, it tastes the food offered, it becomes a tutelary deity of the family and the neighbourhood (v. Gennep, *Tabou*, p. 272). The lizard is commonly respected in Europe (*Folklore*, xi. 240). In Central Celebes it is killed to prevent ill-luck (*Bijd. T. L. V.* i. 88), probably as the familiar of a wizard; but this attitude is uncommon, although the Zoroastrians consider it an evil creature, the same belief surviving in Armenia (Abeghian, *Armenischer Volksglaube*, p. 31). We find the lizard in S.E. Australia as the familiar of a wizard (*JAI* xvi. 34); and the Maoris, though some lizards were respected, are recorded to have killed them as 'witch-animals' (*Aust. Ass. Adv. Sci. Reports*, vii. 774), or as the cause of sickness (Taylor, *Te Ika i Maui*, pp. 409, 44–5, etc.; cf. *JAI* xix. 120). As a messenger of the gods, or of the dead (Gill, *Myths*, p. 229; *Deutsche Geog. Bl.* x. 280), the lizard is ominous, also as the familiar of the wizard. The lizard is especially ominous in India (Pandian, *Indian Village Folk*, p. 130; *Asiatic Researches*, 1824, 421 ff.). The Musheras sacrifice a lizard (*Calcutta Rev.* lxxxviii. 286). The lizard is frequently employed in magic, sometimes as a love-charm (*Ausland*, liv. 912), or curative charm (Jones and Kropf, *Folktales*, xlix.), or for luck (Rolland, *Faune*, iii. 12). A lizard buried alive under a threshold is a protection against sorcerers (*Mélusine*, viii. 22; Müllenhof, *Sagen*, i. 212), but elsewhere it is regarded as maleficent in this position (Rochholz, *Deutscher Glaube*, ii. 167). In Madagascar the lizard is buried to cure fever (v. Gennep, *Tabou*, p. 271). In Tripoli the sight of a lizard is held to cause women to bear speckled children (*Globus*, xxxiv. 27). Connected doubtless with its magical qualities is the wide-spread use of the lizard as an art *motif* (*Publ. Kgl. Mus. Dresden*, vii. 14; *Bastian Festschrift*, p. 167). In classical antiquity the lizard was used in medicine (Pauly-Wissowa, *s.v.* 'Aberglaube'). For myths and folk-tales of the lizard see de Gubernatis, *Zool. Myth.* ii. 385–387.

Magpie.—It is held to be unlucky to kill the magpie (*Folklore*, xi. 241), but in Sweden it is the custom to rob its nest on May day and carry the eggs or young round the village (Lloyd, *Peasant Life*, p. 237). A magpie's nest betokens ill-luck (*Jahrbücher f. Schleswig-H.* viii. 92), but the omens drawn from it usually vary according to the number of birds (Napier, *Folklore*, p. 113; Gregor, *ib.* p. 137). In Norse belief the form of the magpie is assumed by witches (Meyer, *Germ. Myth.* p. 112). For magpie omens see Liebrecht, *Zur Volksk.* p. 327; *Jahrb. f. Roman. Lit.* N.S. i. 232; Socin, *Die neuaram. Dial.* p. 175; Wigstroem, *Sagor*, p. 114; Rolland, *Faune*, ii. 137, etc. The magpie is supposed to show the presence of foxes or wolves; and in Poitou it was the custom to fasten a bunch of heath and laurel to the top of a high tree in honour of the magpie (*Mem. Soc. Antiq.* viii. 451). For myths and folk-tales of the magpie see de Gubernatis, ii. 258–260.

Mantis.—A prominent figure in Bushman mythology is Ikaggen or Cagn (Bleek, *Brief Account*, p. 6; *Cape Monthly Mag.* 1874, July, pp. 1–13; Lloyd, *Short Account*, p. 5, etc.). Some doubt was thrown by Fritsch (*Eingeborenen*, p. 340) on the worship of the mantis by the Bushmen, and no very satisfactory evidence could be quoted with regard to them (*Int. Arch.* xvii. 131) until the publication of Mr. Stow's collection (*Native Races of South Africa*, pp. 531, 533), from which it seems abundantly clear that Cagn was sometimes conceived under the form of the mantis, sometimes under the form of the caterpillar, *ngo* (see 'Cult' above). It seems clear that the Hottentots regarded the insect as auspicious (Merensky, *Beiträge*, p. 86), and worshipped it on that account; the whites called it the 'Hottentots' god'; they abstain from injuring it (Schinz, *Deutsch S.W. Africa*, p. 101). Among the Tambukas, certain insects, among which is the mantis, are supposed to give residence to ancestral souls (Elmslie, *Wild Ngoni*, p. 71). In the Bismarck Archipelago there are two exogamous phratries, one of which is named after the mantis (*JAI* xxi. 28).

Monkey.—Even if it was not a common savage trait to believe in the descent of man from one of the lower animals, the resemblance between human beings and monkeys would be sufficiently strong to suggest such a tale. Consequently we find not only that man is regarded as an evolved monkey, but also that the monkey is explained as a degraded man (Tylor, *Prim. Cult.*^{3} i. 376 f.; *Miss. Cath.* 1081, 97; Spix, iii. 1107). It is seriously believed in Africa and South America that monkeys can talk, but do not do so for fear of being made to work. Another group of stories tells how the great apes carry off women to the woods; while the belief in tailed men has been held by Europeans as well as savages (cf. MacCulloch, p. 277).

The chief home of the cult of monkeys is India, with its monkey-god, Hanuman. In orthodox villages the life of the monkey is safe from harm, and its magic influence is implored against the whirlwind, while it is also invoked to avert sterility. The bones of a monkey are held to pollute the ground (Crooke, i. 87–89). Mentioning a monkey brings starvation for the rest of the day, but it is regarded as lucky to keep one in the stable (*ib.* ii. 49). As at the famous monkey-temple at Benares, monkeys are said to be worshipped in

Togo, Africa, where the inhabitants of a village daily put meals for their benefit. The Kunamas and Bareas are also said to worship them (*Int. Arch.* xvii. 93). At Porto Novo, where twins are not killed, they are believed to have as tutelary spirits a kind which animate small monkeys; such children may not eat monkey meat (*Miss. Cath.* 1884, 249). Among the Hottentots the name of the monkey is tabu to the hunter (*Zts. Geog. Ges. Thür.* vi. 41). The Nkomis do not eat gorilla meat, and give three reasons: first, that their fathers did not; second, that the gorilla has no tail; and third, that it drinks the blood of the dead (*Miss. Cath.* 1894, 601). There is an ape tabu among the Battas (*Tijdschr. T. L. V.* xxi. 209). Among the Maxurunas a young mother may eat no ape meat (Spix, iii. 1188); and this tabu is extended to all women on the island of Nias (*Tijdschr.* xxvi. 282). In many cases the respect for the monkey is based on the belief that it is the abode of a human soul (*Int. Arch.* xvii. 93; *Home and For. Miss. Rec.* 1889, 302; v. Gennep, *Tabou*, p. 221); sometimes it is believed that a man who kills a monkey is turned into one after death (Hutchinson, *Impressions*, p. 163); the sacrosanct monkey is affirmed to be so only to certain families (Bastian, *Bilder*, pp. 145, 160). In Madagascar the babakoto is bought out of captivity, and in some parts the natives will not kill it or trap it (v. Gennep, *Tabou*, p. 214); the Betsimarakas bury dead monkeys, and call the babakoto their grandfather, holding it to be the abode of the souls of the dead (*ib.* p. 216). In some cases an ætiological myth is told to account for the respect shown by the Malagasy (*ib.* pp. 217–220). Among the Basutos the monkey is a totem (Casalis, *The Basutos*, p. 221; Arbousset and Daumas, p. 92; *Folklore*, xv. 112). Among the Hottentots the killer of a baboon has to sacrifice a sheep or goat and hang the lowest vertebra round his neck, or he will suffer from lumbago (*Zts. Geog. Ges. Thür.* vi. 42). The Tucunas of Brazil wear a monkey mask in some of their ceremonies (Spix and Martius, iii. 1188). In China a monkey is regarded as lucky in a stable—to keep away sickness (*Zool. Garten*, 1898, 23). In Java a magical ceremony which includes an offering to the king of the monkeys is performed to cure sterility (*Verh. Bat. Gen.* xxxix. 48). For myths, etc., of the monkey see de Gubernatis, *Zool. Myth.* ii. 97–119.

Mouse.—The mouse was especially associated with Apollo Smintheus; in his temple at Hamaxitus a mouse was portrayed near his statue, and mice were actually kept in the temple (de Visser, *Götter*, pp. 158, 178, 181). Various stories were told to account for this association of the animal with the god, none of which is necessarily true. We need not assume that there was originally a mouse-cult at Hamaxitus; the association of Apollo and the mouse may be late. If the god was appealed to, as god of day, to drive away the mice, which come in the night, his statue might well symbolize his conquest of them by putting the figure of a mouse beneath his feet; from his power over mice might arise the belief that he was the god of mice; thence the custom of keeping mice in the temple. It does not seem necessary to regard Apollo as an anthropomorphized mouse, any more than Dionysus as a transformed fox, because he was known as Bassareus. (For a discussion of the question, and of myths of mice gnawing bow-strings, etc., see *ClR* vi. 413, etc.; Grohmann, *Apollo Smintheus*). The Dakotan explanation of the waning of the moon is that it is eaten by a multitude of mice (Riggs, *D. Grammar*, p. 165). The Chippewayans attribute a flood to the mouse having taken some of the bag in which the heat was stored, in order to mend his shoes, thus causing the snow to melt (Petitot, *Traditions*, p. 376). According to a Hucul myth, the mouse gnawed a hole in Noah's ark, and is unclean (Kaindl, p. 95). According to the Haidas, the mouse contains the soul of a dead man; in every one's stomach are numbers of mice, the souls of his deceased relatives (*JAI* xxi. 21). In Germanic belief, in like fashion, the soul assumes the form of a mouse, and in this form may come forth from a sleeper's mouth (Meyer, *German. Myth.* p. 64). In Celebes the *tanoana* soul is believed to turn into a mouse and eat the rice; the soul of a suicide is especially dangerous; if mice eat the rice, they take away its soul (*Med. Ned. Zend.* xliii. 221, 243). The name of the mouse is tabu in parts of Europe (*Golden Bough*², i. 455). The Huculs hold that it is unlucky for a girl to kill a mouse (Kaindl, p. 73); and in India it is a sin to kill rats, which, if troublesome, must be induced to cease molestations by promise of sweetmeats (Campbell, *Spirit Base of Belief and Custom*, p. 267). In Bohemia a white mouse should not be killed; it should be taken out of the trap and fed, otherwise luck will desert the house and other mice increase in numbers (Grohmann, *Abergl.* No. 405). Sometimes spells are used to keep down the number of mice (*Golden Bough*², ii. 424); sometimes the same result is aimed at by catching a mouse and burning it (*Med. Ned. Zend.* xxvi. 240). Elsewhere one or two mice are caught and worshipped, while the others are burnt; or four pairs of mice are married and set adrift, in the idea that this will cause the other mice to go away (*Golden Bough*², ii. 425). In England, shrews must be thrust alive into a tree trunk, to prevent them from paralyzing the sheep or ravaging the lands (Hone, *Tablebook*, iv. 468). The belief that a shrew dies when it reaches a path is found among the Eskimos (*11th Ann. Rep. Bur. Ethn.* p. 273), and in Greece (Pauly-Wissowa, *s.v.* 'Aberglaube,' p. 80). The 'blind mouse' is a common name for 'Blind Man's Buff.' A mouse mask is used in an Austrian ceremony (*Folklore*, xi. 261, 263). Mice are an omen of death; they leave the house at the death of the master (Rochholz, *D. Glaube*, ii. 173, i. 157). Near Flensburg a white mouse is a death omen; in Wendish districts it is a good omen (MS notes). (For a discussion of the Mouse Tower of Bingen and similar stories, see Liebrecht, *Zur Volkskunde*, p. 1 f.). Mice figure in the mythology of the Kamtchatkans, and are represented as playing many tricks on the stupid deity Kutka (Steller, *Kamtch.* p. 255). The mouse is an evil animal in Zoroastrianism, and the killing of one mouse is equal in merit to slaying four lions (*Sad Dar*, xlii. 9; cf. Plutarch, *de Invidio et Odio*). In Jewish folk-belief eating anything gnawed by a mouse causes loss of memory; whence cats, which eat mice, do not remember their masters (*Horāyoth*, 13*a*). For mouse myths and folk-tales see de Gubernatis, *Zool. Myth.* ii. 65–72.

Owl.—Although the owl is ominous in many parts of the world, it does not seem to figure largely in mythology. The Kalmuks have a saga as to the owl's having saved the life of Jingis Khan, resembling the story of Bruce's escape. From that time they are said to wear a plume of owl's feathers on their heads, and reverence the white owl. Whenever they celebrate any great festival, according to another account, they wear coloured owls' feathers. The Woguls are said to have had a wooden owl to which they fastened the legs of a natural one (Strahlenberg, *Hist. Geog. Desc.* p. 434). The owl was respected in Lithuania (*Globus*, lxiii. 66) and Mecklenburg (*Folklore*, xi. 241), and is not killed by the Macusis of British Guiana, as being the familiar of the evil spirit (Waterton, *Wanderings*, p. 223). Some of the S.E. Bantus will not even touch it, probably on account of its association with sorcerers (Fleming, *Southern Africa*, p. 265).

Among the Bechuanas it is regarded as a great calamity if an owl rests on a house, and the witch-doctor is sent for at once; he scrambles up to the place where it has perched, and purifies it with his charms (Mackenzie, *Ten Years*, p. 392). In the same way the appearance of an owl in the Capitol demanded that the place should be purified with water and sulphur (Hopf, *Orakeltiere*, p. 101). According to the Talmud, it is unlucky to dream of an owl (*JE* ix. 452); while in Germanic folk-lore witches and cruel stepmothers appear in the form of this bird (Meyer, *German. Myth.* p. 112). The owl is particularly important among the Ainus; its cry may not be imitated, because it can bewitch (Batchelor, p. 409); the eagle-owl is regarded as a mediator, and is worshipped on the chase; its head and beak are worn at feasts (*ib.* p. 413); these owls are kept in cages, like the bear, and killed (*ib.* p. 414); they are regarded as unlucky, and the barn-owl may not be eaten (*ib.* pp. 424, 428). Many American tribes associated the owl with the dead; the bridge over which the dead had to pass in the Ojibwa belief was known as the 'owl bridge' (Dorman, *Prim. Sup.* p. 262). In Australia, the owl is a so-called sex-totem (*Golden Bough*², iii. 415). The Chinese offer owl's flesh roasted in oil when they dig up the *phytolacca acinosa*, whose properties are believed to be those of the man-drake; the object of the offering is to appease the soul of the plant (*T'Oung Pao*, vi. 342). The Buriats keep an owl, or hang up the skin of one, to protect children against evil spirits (*Globus*, lii. 252). It is one of the animals hunted in Europe (*Folklore*, xi. 250). Owls are frequently associated with magicians; the Zulus believe that they are sent by wizards (*JAI* xx. 115); among the Yorubas the owl is the messenger of sorcerers, who gather at the foot of a tree and send owls out to kill people; if one gets into a house, the inmates try to catch it and break its claws and wings, believing that this injures the sorcerer (*Miss. Cath.* 1884, 249). The Ojibwas believe that within three days after the burial of a man the evil spirit comes in the form of an owl, shooting out fire from his beak, and takes out the heart of the dead man; they endeavour to drive it away before it effects its purpose (*Manitoulin*, p. 49). Among the Pawnees, on the other hand, the owl is the chief of the night, when it gives both aid and protection (*22 RBEW* ii. 21, 40). The Greek priests carried a stuffed owl as the badge of their profession (Brinton, *Myths*, p. 128), and in Brazil the appearance of an owl is accounted a proof of its connexion with supernatural beings (Martius, *Zur Ethn.* p. 78). In the Malay peninsula the owl is one of the messengers of the pontianak (Begbie, *Malay Pen.* p. 464). In Madagascar the Antimerinas give the name *lolo* ('owl') to the souls of sorcerers (v. Gennep, *Tabou*, p. 262). Slightly different is the Californian belief that the great white owl is an evil spirit, on which account they wear its feathers as a cloak, to propitiate it (*Cont. Am. Eth.* iii. 143), or, more probably, as a countercharm, just as in Garenganze the use of a whistle made of the windpipe of the horned night-owl is held to avert the ill-luck it brings (Arnot, *Garenganze*, p. 238). On the same principle, possibly, the owl is frequently seen nailed to the barn or stable door.

The owl is sometimes used in magic. If its heart and right foot are laid on a sleeping person, it is said that he must confess all he has done. If an owl's liver is hung on a tree, all the birds collect under it (Wolf, *Beiträge*, i. 232). Sometimes, in spite of its character as a bird of ill omen, it is regarded as bringing good fortune. If it flies into a dovecot, it brings luck (Wolf, *loc. cit.*). Its cry frees from fever, and its feathers bring peaceful slumber (*Globus*, iii. 271). Its appearance near a house where a pregnant woman is forecasts an easy delivery, among the Wends (Haupt, *Volkslieder*, ii. 258); or the birth of a boy, or other good fortune, in Dalmatia (*Wiss. Mitt. aus Bosnien*, vi. 593). In Athens, as the bird of Athene, it was auspicious (Pauly-Wissowa, *s.v.* 'Aberglaube,' p. 70). In India owl's flesh is an aphrodisiac, and at the same time causes loss of memory. On the other hand, eating the eyeballs of an owl gives the power of seeing in the dark, while, if an owl is fed with meat all night by a naked man, the latter acquires magic powers. Nevertheless the owl is a bird of ill-omen in India (Crooke, i. 279, ii. 50). For the mythology of the owl see de Gubernatis, *Zool. Myth.* ii. 244–250.

Peacock.—Peacock-worship has often been attributed to the Yezidis. The latest account is that given by J. W. Crowfoot (*Man*, 1901, No. 122), who got his information from an Armenian. It appears that the Malik Tā'ūs ('King Peacock') is shaped like a bird; it has a hole in the middle of its back with a lid to it. It is brought by the head of the village, wrapped in linen, and filled with water. The priest kisses the image and sips water through the beak, the others following his example. Five bronze images are sent round continually, and every Yezidi must visit the figure three times a year. An equation, Tā'ūs = Tammuz, has been proposed, which explains the rites as a survival of Tammuz worship, the peacock coming in through a piece of folk etymology, though the Yezidis themselves hold that 'Malik Tā'ūs revealed himself in the form of a handsome youth with a peacock's tail when he appeared in a vision before Sheikh Aadi, the prophet of the faith' (Jackson, *Persia, Past and Present*, p. 12). Elsewhere in Asia Minor the peacock is regarded as the embodiment of evil (*Man, loc. cit.*; *JAI* xx. 270). According to a Javanese (Muhammadan) myth, the peacock was guardian at the gate of Paradise and ate the devil, thus conveying him within the gate (*Med. Ned. Zend.* xxxii. 237 ff.). On the other hand, in Kutch the peacock may neither be caught nor annoyed (*Zts. Geog. Ges. Thür.* xv. 59). In Europe, peacocks' feathers are considered unlucky; their cry is of bad omen. In Greek religion the bird was associated with Hera and was kept in her temple (de Visser, *Götter*, p. 175). In India the peacock is the totem of the Jats and Khandhs, and in the Panjāb snake-bites are healed by smoking a peacock's feather in a pipe. The feathers of the bird are also waved over the sick to scare disease-demons, and are tied on the ankles to cure wounds (Crooke, ii. 45, 150, 233, 250). For the mythology of the peacock see de Gubernatis, *Zool. Myth.* ii. 323–329.

Pig.—The pig is the most important sacrifice animal of Oceania, and is also a frequent victim in Africa (*Int. Arch.* xvii. 145). Its flesh is tabu to Muhammadans and Jews generally, to the males of S. African Bantus (*JAI* xix. 279), etc. It is a frequent form of the corn-spirit in Europe (*Golden Bough*², ii. 285; *RHR* xxxviii. 339). There are good grounds for supposing that the cult of Demeter was in part developed from that of a porciform corn-spirit (*GB*², p. 299). It is possible to explain features of the myths and cult of Attis and Adonis in a similar way (*ib.* p. 304), and Frazer has maintained the same of Osiris (*ib.* p. 310). Pigs were tabu in Egypt, and swine-herds might not enter a temple; but once a year pigs were sacrificed to Osiris (*ib.* p. 306). The Harranians abstained from pork (Dussaud, *Hist. des Nosairis*, p. 94), but ate it once a year (Chwolson, *Die Ssabier*, ii. 42). The Jews ate it secretly as a religious rite (Is 65^3 $66^{3.17}$). Pigs were worshipped in Crete (de Visser, *Götter*, p. 161). (For Greek facts see *JHS* xiv. 152–154). There is some reason for connecting the Celtic Ceridwen with the pig; in modern Welsh folklore the pig figures as a bugbear for children, and is believed to appear at Allhallows (*RHR, loc. cit.*). Both in Madagascar and Polynesia the pig is tabu (v. Gennep, p. 224; Turner, *Samoa, pass.*; Codrington, *Melanesians*, p. 249, etc.). In European folklore we find the pig hunted at certain times (*Folklore*, xi. 252), there is a story of a pig ancestor in Wales (*ib.* 234), and the grunting of pigs is imitated during an eclipse of the moon (Panzer, *Beitr.* ii. 313). The pig is regarded as lucky in the towns of Germany, but its original augury was inauspicious. In Oesel, on the other hand, it is regarded as of good omen (Holzmaier, *Osiliana*, p. 43). In Germanic mythology the pig is associated especially with storms, and, as a fertility animal, with the harvest-time (Meyer, *Germ. Myth.* pp. 102 f., 286 f.). In Celebes the pig supports the earth, and causes an earthquake when he rests against a tree (*Journ. Ind. Arch.* ii. 837). The pig is sacrificed in India to propitiate the cholera-goddess and other disease-demons, as well as to certain sainted dead, and to ghosts to prevent them from molesting the living (Crooke, i. 126, 137, 197, 200, ii. 58). In Zoroastrianism the form of the boar is one of those assumed by Verethraghna, the god of victory (*Yasht*, xiv. 15). For the cosmogonic boar see *ARW* v. 374 f.

Pigeon.—Various species of pigeon are tabu in Madagascar (v. Gennep, *Tabou*, p. 266), India (Crooke, ii. 246), and Europe (*Folklore*, xi. 341; *Ausland*, lvi. 1016, etc.). They are somtimes kept in houses for magical purposes (Lütolf, *Sagen*, p. 357), but are elsewhere considered unlucky (*Rev. des Trad. pop.* v. 601; *Wiss. Mitt. aus Bosnien*, vii. 349). In Albania a spring is said to be blessed annually by the descent of two doves (Hobhouse, *Journey*, p. 390). At Florence a pigeon of combustible materials is run along a line in the Cathedral at Easter (*Folklore*, xvi. 182; cf. Trede, *Heidenthum*, iii. 211; de Gubernatis, *Zool. Myth.* p. 571; Düringsfeld, *Cal. Belge*, p. 351). In Swabia it is carried in procession (Panzer, *Beitrag*, ii. 90). In Hohenzollern-Hechingen a nest with a living pigeon in it is put on a post at Carnival; a mock contest takes place, and the bird is finally carried off amid the lamentations of the people that 'the summer bird' is stolen; the thief is caught and thrown into the water, and the bird is solemnly set at liberty (Mannhardt, *Myth. Forsch.* p. 134). Among the Brāhmans of Bombay two pigeons are brought to the bride and bridegroom on the second or third day after the wedding; they oil them and smooth their feathers (*Bombay Gaz.* IX. i. 62). Pigeons are also given or eaten in European marriage customs (Baumgarten, *Die komischen Mysterien*, p. 312; *Anthropologie*, ii. 423, n. 1; Schönwerth, *Aus der Oberpfalz*, i. 123; Vaugeois, *Hist. de l'Aigle*, p. 583, n. 110). The pigeon is of good omen in Königsberg (*Am Urquell*, i. 123), and Russia (Erman, *Archiv*, p. 628), but forebodes fire in Styria (*Zts. Oest. Volksk.* iii. 12), and very frequently a death (Kehrein, *Volksspr.* p. 269; Gregor, *Folklore*, p. 146, etc.). The souls of the blessed dead are sometimes held to take the form of doves (Meyer, *Germ. Myth.* p. 63; cf. the use of the dove in modern funeral-pieces).

In Greece the dove was associated with the cult of Aphrodite, and doves were kept in her temples (de Visser, p. 173). Similarly pigeons are attached to the shrines of Sakhi Sarwar in the Panjāb (Crooke, i. 209) and of Shakir Padshah in Khotan (Stein, *Sand-buried Ruins of Khotan*, pp. 179–180; for the mythology of the dove and pigeon see de Gubernatis, *Zool. Myth.* ii. 297–306). There is no proof that the priestesses of Zeus at Dodona were ever called 'doves' in the historical period; nor were dove-oracles known. Possibly Sophocles refers to some vague tradition when he speaks of the two doves through which the oak spoke to Heracles (Farnell, *Cults*, i. 38 n., 39 n.).

Quail.—The quail is one of the birds in Germany which it is unlucky to kill (Wuttke, *D. Abergl.*[3] p. 163; Strackerjan, *Abergl.* p. 45). In the Lausitz it is held to protect the house against lightning (*ib.*). It is also tabu in Madagascar (v. Gennep, *Tabou*, p. 267). In Hungary it is an accursed bird (Jones and Kropf, *Folktales*, p. lxi). It is one of the forms assigned to the corn-spirit in Silesia (Peter, *Volkstüml.* ii. 268), and is eaten by a newly married couple in Lithuania (*Russ. Rev.* xii. 268). In France the hearts of two quails are held to ensure the happiness of a married couple, if the husband carries that of the male, the wife that of the female (Rolland, *Faune*, ii. 343). Among the Greeks the quail was used in a game in which the players struck at it blindfold, exactly as the cock and other birds and mammals are used in Europe at the present day (Pollux, *Onomastikon*, IX. clviii.). The quail was sacrificed by the Phœnicians at its return in the spring, and they explained the festival as a commemoration of the resurrection of Heracles (*Athen.* ix. 47); possibly the first quail was killed—a practice to which there are many European analogues. In Greek mythology Artemis seems to have been vaguely associated with the quail (Farnell, *Cults*, ii. 433; she was called Ortygia, which is also a place name). For the quail in mythology see de Gubernatis, *Zool. Myth.* ii. 276–278.

Seal.—Among the Eskimos, women stop work when a seal is taken, until it is cut up; when a ground seal is killed, they stop work for three days (*5th Ann. Rep. Bur. Ethn.* p. 595). The heads of seals and other marine animals are kept (*ib. 8th Rep.* p. 434). In Kamtchatka they do a piece of mimetic magic before they go seal fishing. A large stone is rolled into the court to represent the sea; small stones do duty for the waves, and little packets of herbs for the seals. A kind of boat of birch bark is made and drawn along the sand; the object of the ceremony is to invite the seals to let themselves be taken (Sébillot, *Folklore*, p. 125). In the west of Ireland and the islands north of Scotland there are certain people who believe themselves to be descended from seals, and who refuse to injure them (*Folklore*, xi. 232; *Orkney and Shetland Folklore*, pp. 170–189). The same belief is found in the Faroes (*Antiquarisk Tidschrift*, 1852, p. 191). A local legend records that they are the descendants of Pharaoh's army, which was lost in the Red Sea (Annandale, *Faroes*, p. 25). In the island of Rügen it is believed that the seal is descended from drowned human beings (*Folklore*, xi. 235). Among the Kwakiutls the chief group of dancers' societies is that of the seal (*Report of United States National Museum*, 1895, p. 419).

Serpent.—(For serpent-worship proper see separate article). The serpent is respected among many peoples who do not worship it in the sense of offering prayer or sacrifice to it; this is especially the case in South Africa and Madagascar. The Malagasy regard serpents as objects of pity rather than of veneration (v. Gennep, *Tabou*, p. 273), holding them to be the abode of dead men's souls. But the Antimerinas had a serpent idol, whose worshippers carried serpents (*ib.* p. 275); in the case of the Betsileos it is difficult to say whether we have to do with serpent-worship or not; they regard the *fanany* as the re-incarnation of a deceased ancestor, make it offerings of blood, and even tend it in an enclosure (*ib.* p. 277). If these attentions are offered it without *arrière pensée* and solely because it is one of the kin, we are hardly entitled to regard them as worship, which rather implies that an offering is not strictly disinterested.

Among the Zulus the souls of the dead are said to take up their abode in serpents, termed *idhlozi* (pl. *amadhlozi*). Various forms of the belief are recorded; according to one, the serpent form is assumed only by an ancestor who wishes to approach a kraal; another version, but slightly different, says that only the serpents which frequent the neighbourhood of a kraal are *amadhlozi*; a third authority says that the soul is not bound, as in some of the Malagasy beliefs, to the single soul-animal, but is incarnate in all the species, like the animal-gods of Samoa; a fourth account, probably unreliable, makes the *idhlozi* the soul-animal of the living (*Int. Arch.* xvii. 121; *Man*, 1904, No. 115; *Golden Bough*², iii. 409, etc.). As in Madagascar, different species of snakes are the abodes of different classes of men, one for chiefs, another for the common people, another for women (*Int. Arch., loc. cit.*). Among the Masai, on the other hand, the difference of species marks a difference in the family of the deceased (Hollis, *The Masai*, p. 307). In Europe, the form of the serpent, like that of the mouse (see above), may be assumed by the soul of a sleeper (Meyer, *Germ. Myth.* p. 63 f.). The serpent is respected over a large part of East Africa, sometimes as an ancestor of the tribe, sometimes as the soul-animal of deceased ancestors (*Int. Arch., loc. cit.*). Many of the tribes in New Caledonia never eat serpents, but no reason is given for this (Patouillet, *Trois Ans.* p. 113). In North America they were respected (Brinton, *Myths*, p. 129). In South America the Airicos believe themselves to be descended from serpents (Tirado, *Estudios*, p. 31; for other stories of descent see J. F. M'Lennan, *Studies*, 2nd series, p. 526). Serpents are respected over a large part of Europe, especially those which live in or near human dwellings—probably as a survival of ancestor-worship. In like manner, harmless snakes are tutelary household divinities in the Panjāb hills (Crooke, ii. 141 f.). The name of the serpent is also frequently tabu (Böcler-Kreutzwald, p. 120; Lloyd, *Peasant Life*, p. 230; *Tradition*, v. 149; *Asiatic Observer*, 1821, p. 421, etc.).

It is only rarely that ceremonies of purification are prescribed for the killer of a serpent; the Amaxosa custom prescribed that the killer of a boa had to lie in running water for weeks together; during this time no animal could be slaughtered; finally, the body of the snake was buried close to the cattle-fold (Kay, *Travels*, p. 341). On the other hand, certain precautions are to be taken in Japan; if the head of the snake is not crushed when it is killed, more will come to take its place (*Mitt. d. Ges. Natur- u. Volkerk. Ostas.* xv. 282). In Bombay it is believed that barrenness is the penalty for killing a snake (Crooke, i. 226), while in Germanic mythology such an act causes the child of the house to waste away (Meyer, *loc. cit.*).

The snake is commonly associated with water (see above), and said to reside in water-holes, rivers, etc. (Salvado, *Memoirs*, p. 260; Merensky, *Beiträge*, p. 126; Philip, *Researches*, ii. 117; *Church Miss. Rec.* xiv. 30; Strahlenberg, *Das N. u. O. Teil*, p. 420; Brinton, *Myths*, p. 130, etc.). Snakes are likewise guardians of treasure in folklore generally (Crooke, ii. 134–136). Mythical serpent-monsters are also found as earth-carriers (see 'Earth-Carrier'), or destroyers of the human race (*Mitt. d. Schutzgeb.* xiii. 45), or Creator (see 'Creator'); in Chile one is connected with the Deluge myth (Medina, *Aborigenes*, p. 28 ff.), and the Micmacs place two on the road followed by the souls of the dead (Rand, *Legends*, p. 233); the Hurons made a monster-serpent the source of all maladies (*Rel. des. Jés.* 1678, p. 75), and for the natives of Victoria the serpent Mindi is the cause of death (Parker, *Aborigines*, p. 25); for the Aruntas the Magellanic clouds are the teeth of a gigantic serpent, and silence is to be preserved when they are visible (*R.G.S.A.*, S. Aust. Br. ii. 36). In America, according to Brinton, the serpent is often associated with the lightning (*Myths*, p. 135). Mention should also be made, in this connexion, of the 'snake-dances' of the Hopis, which are probably expressions of clan totemism, not of ophiolatry (*19 RBEW* 963 ff.). In South America, serpents are held to be the chief food of the dead (Spix and Martius, ii. 695).

A good deal of mythical lore has gathered round the serpent in Europe. A king is their ruler (*Ausland*, lxiii. 1031; *Globus*, iv. 333, etc.), and wears a crown which is coveted for its magical properties; the king is often white, and the skeleton of the white snake makes its possessor the owner of a familiar spirit (*ib.* xxvi. 203). There is a stone in the snake's nest which draws poisons out of a man's body (Jecklin, *Volkstüml.* ii. 153; cf. Crooke, ii. 141 f.). In Hindu belief serpents have in their heads jewels of marvellous properties (Crooke, ii. 143 f.). He who eats the great white snake understands the language of birds (Russwurm, *Eibovolk*, § 357), or of the raven (*ib.* § 400). If a snake is hung up head downwards, it will rain (*FLJ* v. 91; Wuttke, *Volksabergl.*³ § 153). St. Patrick banished all snakes from Ireland, and even Irish cattle have the gift of killing the snakes in the meadows where they are (*Northumb. Folklore*, F. L. S. p. 8). The snakes know a root by which they bring to life a snake that has been killed (Lepechin, *Reise*, ii. 105). The belief in the king of serpents is also found among the American Indians (Brinton, *Myths*, p. 137). Folklore likewise knows of many cases of the union of serpents with human beings (MacCulloch, 255–259, 264–267).

In the ancient world the serpent was associated with leechcraft (see DISEASE and SERPENT); the same idea is found in Madagascar (*Int. Arch.* xvii. 124), and also among the American Indians, perhaps because the snake is in America so often associated with the magician, who is also the leech (Brinton, *Myths*, pp. 132, 133). The snake is sometimes held to be unlucky (*Globus*, lxix. 72), but is more often welcomed as the 'Hausgeist.' A snake shot out of a gun is a charm against witchcraft (Liebrecht, *Zur. Volksk.* p. 332; Müllenhof, *Sagen*, p. 229); and a Huculian hunter carries a piece of snake to attract game (*Globus*, lxxvi. 274). In Sussex the first snake should be killed for luck (*FLR* i. 8). In Bulgaria and France the killing of a snake is a good work, probably because the snake is regarded as the incarnation of a witch (Strausz, *Die Bulgaren*, p. 34; Rolland, *Faune*, iii. 36). Snakes are burnt in the midsummer fire (*Athenæum*, 1869, July 24; Jones and Kropf, *Folktales*, p. lix). In North Africa the Aissaouas and other sects of fanatics eat serpents annually or at intervals during the year (Walpole, *Memoirs*, p. 396; Denon, *Travels*, i. 300; Pliny, *HN* VII. ii., VIII. xxv., XXV. x., XXVIII. iii.; Pausanias, IX. iv. etc.; cf. Bancroft, iii. 429).

The serpent is commonly of good omen; so among the South African Bantus (*Miss. Cath.* 1896, 371; Merensky, *Beiträge*, p. 126), in Arabia (Nolde, *Innerarabien*, p. 96), and in mediæval Europe (Panzer, *Beitrag*, ii. 259). In Albania it is unlucky before sunrise and after sunset (Rodd, *Customs*, p. 158). In Silesia it is held to be lucky, but its appearance is a warning that misfortune is near (Peter, *Volkstüml.* ii. 33). In Suffolk it is a death omen (*Suffolk Folklore*, F. L. S. p. 32). On the other hand, there is an elaborate table of omens drawn by the Zoroastrians from the appearance of a snake on each of the thirty days of the month (Al-Bīrūni, *Chronology of Ancient Nations*, tr. Sachau, p. 218); so, too, in Norway, when it crawls across the road (Liebrecht, *Zur Volkskunde*, p. 326). In Zoroastrianism the serpent is a most evil creature, and to be killed (*Vendīdād*, xiv. 5; Herodotus, i. 140); it was formed by Ahriman (*Būndahishn*, iii. 15). A similar horror of the serpent exists in Armenia (Abeghian, *Armenischer Volkglaube*, p. 30). For the serpent, see, further, de Gubernatis, *Zool. Mythol.* pp. 389–419, Pauly-Wissowa, *s.v.* 'Aberglaube,' p. 77, and *JE* xi. 203.

Shark.—In New Calabar the shark is regarded as a god (*Globus*, x. 285). Sharks are sometimes regarded as enchanted men (Wilson, *Western Africa*, p. 161). The shark was formerly protected by a death penalty inflicted on the killer of one, but this was subsequently abolished by a religious revolution (Bastian, *Bilder*, p. 160). Shark-worship is said to have existed in Huahine (Montgomery, *Journal*, i. 245). In the Solomon Islands the shark is addressed as 'grandfather' (*Zts. Geog. Ges. Thür.* x. 34). Sharks were worshipped in the Sandwich Islands; and if a man who adored them happened to have a child still-born, he endeavoured to lodge its soul in the body of a shark. In order to do this he flung the body into the sea, performing various ceremonies at the same time. There were temples with shark-idols; the priests rubbed their bodies night and morning with salt and water to give them a scaly appearance (*Golden Bough*[2], ii. 432). In New Georgia the shark is *hope* ('sacred'), because it eats men. It may not be touched in Rubiana, but in the eastern part it may be killed but not eaten (*JAI* xxvi. 386). Sharks are very often the form in which dying people announce their intention of re-appearing; offerings are made to them. In Saa special coconut trees are reserved for them, but men who intend to become sharks may also use the trees. Other men will join them sometimes and ask for coconuts with the voice of a shark-ghost (*Golden Bough*[2], ii. 434–435).

Sheep.—In Greek cult the ram was connected with Zeus; at Eleusis and elsewhere its fleece was used in rites of purification (Farnell, *Cults*, i. 65; Smith, *Rel. Sem.*[2] 474). As a substitute for the eldest scion of the Athamantids, a ram was offered (Farnell, i. 94). A prayer for rain was offered to Zeus on Mount Pelion by youths clad in fresh ram-skins (*ib.* p. 95). Zeus Ammon is derived from Egypt (*ib.*). In the cult of Artemis the sheep was sometimes tabued (*ib.* ii. 431). In a sheep-offering to Aphrodite in Cyprus the worshippers wore the skin (W. R. Smith, p. 474). Aphrodite is represented as riding on the ram (Farnell, ii. 675).

Although the sheep is one of the most important sacrificial animals (*Int. Arch.* xvii. 139, for Africa), it is only in Egypt that we find a sheep-god proper. Amon was the god of Thebes; his worshippers held rams to be sacred, and would not sacrifice them. At the annual festival of the god a ram was, however, slain, and the image of the god was clothed in the skin; they mourned over the body and buried it in a sacred tomb. Amon is represented as a ram-headed god (*Golden Bough*[2], ii. 368 f.). Among the Nilotic tribes the Madis practise an annual sacrifice of a lamb, possibly as a means of expelling the evils which have accumulated. They are sad before the ceremony, and show great joy when it is over. They assemble by a stone circle, and the lamb is led four times round the people, who pluck off bits of its fleece as it passes and put them in their hair; the lamb is then killed on the stones and its blood sprinkled four times over the people. It is then applied to each person individually. As each rises to go away, he or she places a leaf on the circle of stones. The ceremony is observed on a small scale at other times, particularly when trouble comes upon a family; it is also practised on joyful occasions, such as the return of a son after a long absence (*Proc. R. S. Edin.* xii. 336). The piacular sacrifice of a ram is occasionally found in European folklore; near Maubeuge a ram is killed by one of the squires of the neighbourhood, and is believed to be laden with the sins of the people (Rolland, *Faune*, v. 206). But more commonly the sacrifice is performed without any specific reason being given for the ceremony. It is a common practice in Bohemia, Hungary, and other districts for a ram to be thrown from the church tower in the autumn in order to procure a good harvest in the following year (Mannhardt, *Myth. Forsch.* 139 n.). In Finland a lamb which has not been shorn since the spring is killed in the autumn; it must be slaughtered without using a knife, and no bones must be broken. When it is served up, water, which probably has taken the place of blood, is sprinkled over the threshold, and a portion of the meal offered to the house-spirits and the trees which will serve as May-poles in the following year (Böcler-Kreutzwald, *Der Ehsten Aberg. Geb.* p. 87). In East and Central Europe a lamb is commonly sacrificed at Easter or rather later, the day chosen being usually April 24th (*Globus*, xxvi. 158, xxx. 93, xl. 71, etc.; cf. *Golden Bough*[2], ii. 438). In West Europe there are traces of such a custom at Whitsuntide; in Hamburg, lambs, real and of wood, were on sale without the gate on the Friday before Whitsuntide; children received them as presents, and they were eventually consumed by the family (Schütze, *Schleswig-Holst. Idiotikon*, iii. 7); they were also brought as presents to the schoolmasters (*Jahrb. f. Schl.-Holst.* x. 29). In Virgen, a lamb is taken in procession on the Friday after Easter to a mountain-chapel and subsequently sold (*Zts. Ver. Volksk.* v. 205). The sheep also figures at the Carnival (Mannhardt, *Antike Wald- und Feldkulte*, p. 191 n.), the Kirmess or church festival (Pfannenschmid, *Germ. Erntefeste*, *pass.*), and at Christmas (*Tradition*, vi. 285; Mannhardt, *op. cit.* p. 196). In Wales, people dressed in sheep-skins went round on All Souls' Day (*Bye-gones*, May 6, 1891). In some cases the ram or sheep was hunted with or without a subsequent sacrifice (*Folklore*, xi. 251; Ducange, *s.v.* 'Agnus Dei'). Probably all these customs are in some degree connected with the idea of the expulsion of evils.

In Madagascar the sheep is one of the animals in which are incarnated the souls of ancestors; various families are forbidden to eat its flesh (v. Gennep, *Tabou*, p. 236). In India there is reason to believe that the sheep was once a sacred animal (Crooke, i. 163 f., ii. 226). A large number of Chinese have a prejudice against mutton; the sheep is, however, regarded as a lucky animal, and its skull is hung over the door to prevent theft (*Zool. Garten*, 1900, 6). In France a lamb is blessed in the church at Christmas in Nouvion, and allowed to die of old age (Rolland, *Faune*, v. 160). In the same way rich Kalmuks consecrate a white ram under the title of 'the ram of heaven'; probably the object is, as in France, to provide the flocks with a tutelary animal (*Golden Bough*[2], ii. 438).

The sheep is auspicious as an ominous animal. It is lucky to touch it (Desrousseaux, *Mœurs*, ii. 284). The skull of a sheep wards off evil (Wiedemann, *Ehsten*, p. 482; Russwurm, *Eibovolk*, ii. 281, 283, 402; *Mélusine*, viii. 33). The sheep figures in various European ceremonies connected with marriage; probably the rites are magical and performed as ceremonies of fertilization. In Poitou the newly married had to pursue a ram (*Mem. Soc. Ant. France*, i. 437); at Chatillon-sur-Seine the bride drove the animal thrice round a tub (*ib.* iv. 119). In Bulgaria and Russia the bride receives a lamb or sheep as 'Morgengabe' (*Anthropologie*, ii. 587; Holderness, *New Russia*,

p. 236). The Gallas take an oath by the sheep (Pinkerton, *Africa*, i. 8).

Spider.—In the Creation myth of the Sias there was only one being in the lower world, the spider Sussistinnako; he caused men, animals, etc., to come into existence, and divided them into clans (*10th Ann. Rep. Bur. Ethn.* 1889–1890, p. 26 ff.) In like manner, among the Hopis the spider represents the 'medicine' power of the earth (*21 RBEW* p. 11). According to the Tetons, Ikto, the spider, was the first being in this world who attained maturity. He was the first to use human speech, and is more cunning than man. All the animals are his kindred, and he commands them. In their myths the spider is deceived by the rabbit (Dorsey, *Siouan Cults*, p. 472). The Tetons pray to grey spiders. When they are going on a journey, they kill a spider if they see one, and pray; it is unlucky to let it pass or to kill it in silence. They tell it that the Thunder-beings killed it (*11th Ann. Rep. Bur. Ethn.* p. 479). In the mythology of the Akwapim, Anansi, the spider, is a sort of demiurge; he races the cat for the privilege of marrying the daughter of the god; hence the cat and the spider are enemies (*Petermanns Mitt.*, 1856, 466; Frobenius, *Weltanschauung*, p. 294). Many of these myths are now found in the West Indies (P. C. Smith, *Anansi Stories from Jamaica*). The Adjahdurrahs believe that the islands were made by the spider *R.G.S.A.*, S. Aust. Br. II. iii. 18). In another Australian myth the spider is a monster, and injures everything which the squirrel makes (*S. Amer. Miss. Mag.* xiv. 112). The Haidas also have a story of a spider who was the mortal enemy of man; he was overcome by T'skanahl, who threw him into the fire; he shrivelled up and became a mosquito (*Smiths. Report*, 1888, p. 326; cf. Ehrenreich, *Myth. u. Legend. d. südamer. Urvölker*, p. 33 f.). In a Kayowe myth, 'Old Spider' escapes the flood and is concerned with the early history of the human race (*Ausland*, 1890, 901). For the Flatheads the residence of their grandsires, the spiders, was in the clouds. Both in Australia (Howitt, *Native Races*, p. 388) and in America the spider's web is a means of getting up to the sky (*Trs. Ethn. Soc.* iv. 306). The Cherokees told how the spider brought fire on its web, but was captured before it reached the earth (Foster, *Sequoyah*, p. 241). It is held in several parts of Europe to be unlucky to kill the spider (*Folklore*, xi. 241; *Zts. f. Oest. Volksk.* ii. 252). In Tuscany it is the custom to kill a spider seen in the morning (Andree, *Ethn. Par.* p. 8). It is also killed in Poland (*Trad.* iv. 355). The Southern Slavs use it in magic; a girl takes a spider and shuts it up, calling on it to show her the destined lover, and promising to set it free if it does so, and if not, to kill it (Krauss, *Sitte*, p. 173).

There is a curious diversity in the omens given by spiders; in Ditmarschen a small black spider is a death omen (*Am Urquell*, i. 7). A spider in the evening is lucky, in the morning unlucky (*ib.* p. 64). In Stettin the reverse is the case (*Balt. Studien*, xxxiii. 169). In Jewish folklore the spider is hated (*JE* vi. 607). For other spider omens see John of Salisbury, i. 13; Wolf, *Beitr.* ii. 457; Meier, *Sagen*, p. 221; Birlinger, p. 119, etc. For the spider in folk-tales see de Gubernatis, *Zool. Myth.* ii. 161–164.

Stork.—The stork was sacrosanct in ancient Thessaly, and a killer of one was punished as though he were a murderer (de Visser, *Götter*, p. 157). It enjoys the same respect wherever it is found in Europe. It is also respected in Egypt (*Globus*, lxix. 257), and in Morocco (Clarke, *Travels*, III. i. 34 n.), where there is said to be a hospital for sick storks and a fund for burying dead ones. The stork is commonly said to bring the children. Its presence brings luck to the house; in particular, it is a safeguard against the danger of fire; its efficacy is discounted by the stork's supposed practice of removing its nest from a house that is shortly to be burned down. Occasionally the stork, however, is thought to bring bad luck (Wiedemann, *Ehsten*, p. 454), for, where one nests, one of the family or a head of cattle dies. So, too, in Bohemia, a stork settling on the roof, or twelve storks circling over a house, means fire (Grohmann, *Abergl.* Nos. 438, 439; cf. Meyer, *Germ. Myth.* p. 110). For other omens and beliefs see *Globus*, xxiv. 23.

The stork is one of the migrants which must be greeted when they appear in the spring; the house-stork must learn all that has happened in his absence. In other countries he is a man (*Zts. deutsche Phil.* i. 345). In spite of the sacrosanctity of the stork, it is used in magic (*ib.*; Grohmann, *Abergl.* No. 434), and its gall cures a scorpion's bite in Jewish folk-belief (*JE* xi. 559). For the stork in folk-tales see de Gubernatis, *Zool. Myth.* ii. 261–262.

Swallow.—There seems to have existed a custom in ancient Greece of carrying a swallow round from house to house, singing a song (Athenæus viii. pp. 359, 360). Swallow songs sung at the appearance of the bird in spring are very common (Kuhn and Schwartz, *Nordd. Sagen*, p. 452). We find the swallow carried round in modern Greece, a wooden bird on a cylinder, and a song is sung (Rodd, *Custom and Lore*, p. 136; cf. p. 271). In Macedonia the wooden swallow is encircled with leaves. Eggs are collected and riddles are asked, the answer to which is 'swallow' (Bent, *Cyclades*, p. 434). The same practice prevails in Bulgaria and Little Russia, and the songs refer to the advent of spring (Miladinov, *Bulgarski narodni pesni*, p. 522).

The swallow is everywhere regarded as sacred; it is unlucky to kill it (Kaindl, *Huzulen*, p. 104; Strackerjan, *Abergl.* p. 45; *Globus*, xl. 325; *Brit. Ass. Ethnog. Surv. Scotl.* Nos. 379–383; Alvarez, *Folklore*, i. 224, etc.); it may not be touched (*Tradition*, v. 100), or caught (*Rev. des Trad. pop.* iv. 229; *Blätter für Landesk. N. Oest.* ii. 101; Grohmann, *Abergl.* No. 489), and its nest may not be taken (*ib.* No. 494 f.; *FLR* i. 8). In the West of Scotland, however, it is feared as having a drop of devil's blood in its veins (Napier, *Folklore*, p. 112). Its presence is regarded as lucky (*Zts. Ver. Volksk.* x. 209; Rochholz, *D. Glaube*, ii. 107). In spite of its sacred character, it is used in magic; in Bohemia the blood of the first swallow drives away freckles (Wuttke, *D. Abergl.*[3] p. 159). The first swallow is important in other respects; it has long been the custom to draw omens from it (Pliny, *HN* xxx. 25; Hoffmann's *Fundgrube f. Ges. d. Spr. u. Lit.* i. 325, and many modern instances; Bartsch, *Sagen*, ii. 172; *Germania*, xix. 319). As a rule it is of good omen, but in Thuringia it means a death in the family if a young swallow is thrown out of the nest (*Zts. Ver. Volks.* x. 209). A swallow in a room is a death omen (Erman, *Archiv*, p. 628). For other omens see Grohmann, *Abergl.* Nos. 496, 504, etc. Swallows are sold in Paris and elsewhere and set free by the purchasers (Rolland, *Faune*, ii. 321; *Rev. des Trad. Pop.* iv. 229). A similar custom exists in Japan, and is especially practised at funerals (MS note). For the swallow see also Pauly-Wissowa, *s.v.* 'Aberglaube,' p. 79.

Swan.—In the opinion of Jacob Grimm, the goose has supplanted the swan in mythology to some extent; but the opposite view seems nearer the truth. Perhaps the same applies to the duck. In European folklore the swan is most prominent in a class of *Märchen* to which it has given a name, —'swan-maiden stories' (see 'Myths' above),—but in Picardy we find the duck taking the place of the swan (*Romania*, viii. 256). It may be noted that the subjects of transformation are not necessarily female (*ib.*; cf. Mannhardt, *Germ. Mythen*, pp. 378–379).

The swan is important in the religion of N. Asia (cf. Cochrane, *Ped. Journey*, ii. 163; Georgi, *Bemerkungen*, p. 282). Among the Tatars a man who catches a swan passes it on to his next neighbour and receives in return his best horse; its new possessor passes it on, and so on, until it is no longer presentable, when it is let loose (Castrén, *Vorlesungen*, p. 230). The oath by the swan was well known in the Middle Ages. In Moscow a swan is sometimes given to the newly married, who alone, in the opinion of the common people, have a right to eat it (*Rev. des Trad. Pop.* iv. 324). In Germanic folk-lore the swan is associated with the Norns, who sometimes assume its form (Meyer, *Germ. Myth.* p. 168). Its cry foretells a thaw, and it is pre-eminently a bird of prophecy, often of coming ill (*ib.* p. 112).

Thunderbird.—Widely spread over the American continent is the belief in a great bird as the cause of thunder, which also figures in the Creation myths of some tribes, notably the Chippewayans, as the being which brought the world from beneath the waste of waters (Mackenzie, *Voyage*, p. cxviii; cf. Dunn, *Oregon*, p. 102). The Hare-skin Indians describe it as a gigantic bird which dwells in winter in the land of the dead in the West-South-West, together with migratory birds and animals. When the warm weather comes, it returns with the ghosts in its train. When it shakes its tail-feathers, it makes the thunder, and the flash of its eyes is the lightning. It causes death; it is an evil deity (Petitot, *Traditions*, p. 283). The Iroquois believed that Onditachiæ controlled rain, wind, and thunder. The thunder they conceived as a man in the form of a turkey (?); the heaven was his palace, and he retired there in good weather; when it thundered he was collecting snakes and other 'oki' objects; he caused lightning by opening his wings (*Rel. des Jés.* 1636, p. 114; for other references see Bancroft, vol. iii. *passim*; Schoolcraft, *Indian Tribes*, etc.). In Vancouver Island the Ahts call the thunderbird Tootooch; his wings make the thunder, his forked tongue the lightning. Once there were four such birds, but Quawteaht, their great deity, drowned the rest in the sea (Sproat, *Scenes*, pp. 177, 213). The Dakotas say that the old bird begins the thunder, but the young birds keep it up and do the damage; the old bird is wise and good, and kills no one (Tylor, *Prim. Cult.*[3] i. 363). In Central America we find the bird Voc associated with Hurakan, the god of the tempest (Brasseur de Bourbourg, *Popol Vuh*, p. 71). In South America the idea is found among the Brazilians (Müller, *Am. Urrel.* pp. 222, 271; but see also Ehrenreich, *Myth. und Legend. d. südamer. Urvölker*, p. 15). The same conception is found in West Africa among the Ewe-speaking peoples. Khebioso or So, the god of lightning, is conceived as a flying god, who partakes of the nature of a bird; his name means 'bird that throws out fire.' He casts the lightning from the midst of the black cloud; the thunder is caused by the flapping of his wings. Various ideas of the same order are found among the Bantus. The Zulus think a brown bird is found at the spot where the lightning strikes; the Amapondos say that the bird causes the lightning by spitting out fire; according to the Bomvanas, the bird sets its own fat on fire and causes the lightning. The thunder is the flapping of its wings; the female bird causes loud, crackling thunder, the male distant, rumbling sounds. In Natal they hold that a white bird is the cause of the lightning (Kidd, *Essential Kafir*, p. 120 f.; cf. Moffat, *South Africa*, p. 338; Casalis, *Basutos*, p. 266; Callaway, *Religion of Amazulu*, p. 119). The conception of the thunderbird is also found in the Hervey Islands (Ellis, *Researches*, ii. 417; Williams, *Enterprises*, p. 93), and the Marshall Islands (*Mitt. d. Schutzgeb.* i. 66), and the Karens have a similar idea (Mason, *Burma*, p. 217).

Tiger.—A myth of descent from a tiger ancestor is found among the Bhils and Rajputs (Crooke, ii. 211). It is associated with Śiva and Durgā, but tiger-worship proper is confined to wilder tribes; in Nepāl the tiger festival is known as Bagh Jatra, and the worshippers dance disguised as tigers (*ib.* p. 212). The tiger is likewise worshipped by the Santals (*ib.* p. 213), while in Mirzapur, Bagheswar, the tiger-god, is located in a *bira* tree, and is said to take human form at night and call people by name; those who answer fall sick (*ib.* i. 256 f., ii. 78). The Waralis worship Waghia ('lord of tigers'), a shapeless stone smeared with red lead and ghī, which is held to protect them from tigers (*Home and For. Miss. Rec.* 1839, 390; cf. *Rec. of Free Ch.* vii. 252). In Hanoi a tiger-god is worshipped; a shrine contains an image of a tiger (*XI. Cong. Orient.* ii. 294); and a tiger-god is also found in Manchuria (*Miss. Cath.* 1895, 239). The tiger is represented in Sumatra as the abode of the souls of the dead (Marsden, p. 292; Junghuhn, *Battaländer*, p. 308), and a name-tabu is practised. A like custom is found in Sunda (*Tijdschr. T.L.V.* vi. 80) and parts of India, where the souls of those he devours sit on his head (Crooke, ii. 211). For other cases of name-tabu see Frazer, *Golden Bough*², i. 457.

The hunting of the tiger is naturally attended with much ceremony. The Sumatrans attack tigers only when a friend or relative has been wounded, or in self-defence. The Menangkabauers try to catch them alive in order to beg their forgiveness before killing them; they show them other marks of respect; no one will use a path that has been untrodden for more than a year; at night they will not walk one behind another or knock the sparks off a firebrand (*Golden Bough*², ii. 393 ff.). The people of Mandeling have a tiger clan which honours the tracks of a tiger, and claims to be spared by it; when a tiger has been shot, the women of the clan offer it betel (*ib.*). When the Battas have killed a tiger they bring its corpse to the village with great ceremony; people of the tiger clan make offerings to it; a priest then explains why it has been killed, and begs the spirit to convey his message to the soul of the tiger, so that it may not be angry and do harm; after this a dance is held, and most of the body is buried, only those parts being saved which are useful in medicine; in particular, the whiskers are burnt off at an early stage, so that they may not be used as poison (*Golden Bough*², ii. 394; *Tijdschr.* xxxiv. 172). Connected with the atonement for the death of a tiger is the Indian belief that a garden where a tiger has been killed loses its fertility (Crooke, ii. 212). Not only is it dangerous to kill a tiger, but being killed by one also has its perils; the 'tiger ghost' is worshipped (Crooke, p. 213). Among the Garrows a man who has been killed by a tiger is believed to appear in a dream and tell his relatives to change their names (*Mission Life*, N. S. x. 280). In North Aracan the ceremony of 'ya,' or tabu, is strictly enforced when any one has been killed by a tiger (*JAI* ii. 240). Connected with tiger-worship is the practice of taking an oath by it. The Juangs, Hos, and Santals are all sworn on a tiger skin (*Miss. Cath.* 1897, 369; Crooke, *loc. cit.*). Among the Goṇḍs, two men, believed to be possessed by Bāgheswar, appear at marriage ceremonies and fall upon a kid with their teeth (Crooke, ii. 216).

Besides being the abode of the soul of a dead man, a tiger may be the temporary or permanent form of a living human being. In India a root is said to effect the transformation, and another root is the antidote (Crooke, ii. 216). In Central Java the power of transformation is hereditary, but the wer-tiger is held to be friendly, especially if his friends call his name; he guards the fields. For the variant of this belief which makes the tiger the soul of a dead, not a living man, see *Tijdschr.* xli. 568. The belief in the wer-tiger is also found in the Malay peninsula (Skeat, *Malay Magic*, p. 106) and China.

Closely connected with the wer-tiger is the familiar of the wizard in tiger form. A connecting link is found in the Thana belief that mediums are possessed by a tiger spirit (*Bombay Gaz.* XIII. i. 185). The Binuas of Johore believe that every pawang has a tiger subject to him, which is immortal (*Journ. Ind. Arch.* i. 276, 277). The Malays believe that the soul of the dead wizard enters the body of a tiger; the corpse is put in the forest and supplied with rice and water for seven days, during which the transmigration, which is the result of an ancient compact made by the pawang's ancestors, is effected. If the son of the pawang wishes to succeed his father, he must perform a ceremony to secure his soul (Newbold, ii. 387). The tiger is largely used in magic. In North India and Korea it is eaten in order to gain courage (*Golden Bough*², ii. 356). In India the fangs, claws, and whiskers are used in love charms and as prophylactics against possession, especially in the case of young children (Crooke, ii. 214 f.). The whiskers are regarded as poisonous in Sumatra (*Tijdschr. loc. cit.*) and in India (Crooke, *loc. cit.*). Tiger's flesh is burnt to keep blight from the crops (*ib.*). Some Dayaks keep a tiger's skull in the head-house; to move it is said to cause heavy rain, and to touch it is punished by death by lightning, while its complete removal would cause the death of all the Dayaks (*JRAS, S.B.* No. 5, p. 159).

Corresponding to lycanthropy in Europe, there is in India a pathological condition in which the sufferer believes that he is turned into a tiger (Sprengel, *Auswahl*, iii. 27). The Garrows say that the mania is connected with a certain drug, which is laid on the forehead. The wer-tiger begins by tearing the ear-rings out of his ears, and then wanders about, avoiding all human society. In about fourteen days the mania begins to subside. Although fits of this kind are not attributed to witches in India, the patients are said to be seen with 'their eyes glaring red, their hair dishevelled and bristled, while their heads are often turned round in a strange convulsive manner.' On the nights of such fits they are believed to go abroad and ride on tigers (Malcolm, *Memoir of Central India*, ii. 212). It seems, therefore, not improbable that the fit in question is of the same nature.

Tortoise, turtle.—Both in Asia (*Miss. Herald*, xviii. 385; cf. Bastian, *Bilder*, p. 356; Crooke, ii. 255) and in America the turtle is one of the mythical animals on which the world rests. In the Iroquois myth the world was at first covered with water, and when Aataentsic fell from heaven, the animals held a conference to decide how she was to be received, and the turtle caught her on his broad back; with the aid of mud or sand brought up by water-fowl the earth was formed (*21st Ann. Rep. Bur. Ethn.* p. 180, etc.). The turtle is an important Iroquois totem, and the clan traces its descent from a turtle that threw off its shell (Frazer, *Tot.* p. 3). In like manner the tortoise is a totem of the Mundari Kols, and is also worshipped and sacrificed elsewhere in India (Crooke, *loc. cit.*). In Zoroastrianism, on the other hand, the tortoise was an evil creature, and consequently was to be killed (*Vendīdād*, xiv. 5). A turtle tabu exists in Madagascar (v. Gennep, *Tabou*, p. 289), Java (*Tijdschr. T.L.V.* xxv. 573), and Pomotu (*Rovings in the Pacific*, p. 243); and the Kwapas were not allowed to lift a small water-tortoise by its tail, lest there should be a flood (*Journ. Am. Folklore*, viii. 130). The turtle was sacrificed in Pomotu (*Miss. Cath.* 1874, 378). The Zuñis have the turtle as one of their totems. Sometimes they send to fetch turtles with great ceremony, and apparently each family receives one; the day after it arrives the turtle is killed, its flesh and bones deposited in the little river, and its shell made into a dance rattle. The object of the ceremony is obscure; Frazer suggests that the dead are fetched in the form of turtles and sent back to spirit-land; it seems very probable that the turtle is killed in order that it may be a messenger; but it does not seem that the ceremony is performed only by the turtle clan; how far, therefore, the kinship terms applied to it are merely complimentary it is impossible to say (*Golden Bough*², ii. 371). Turtle-fishing is an occupation surrounded by many tabus; in Madagascar the fisher had to eat the turtle on the shore, and the shell had to be left there too; it might not be used. All the village took part in the turtle feast, and it was not allowable to eat other food with it. If these tabus are not observed, the turtles leave the shore (v. Gennep, *Tabou*, p. 287). In the islands of Torres Straits many magical ceremonies were performed to prepare a canoe for turtle-fishing. There were many tabus connected with the fishing, chiefly of a sexual character; turtle dances were also performed to ensure success in the fishing (*Camb. Univ. Exp. Reports*, vol. v. pp. 196, 207, 271, 330–336). For the myths and folk-tales of the tortoise see de Gubernatis, *Zool. Myth.* ii. 93–95, 360–370.

Whale.—The Tongans regard the whale as the abode of certain deities, and never kill it; when they chance to come near one, they offer it scented oil or kava (*Prim. Cult.*³ ii. 232). Among the Haidas the fin-backed whale is tabu, on the ground that a dead man's soul sometimes enters it (*JAI* xxi. 20). As a rule, however, the whale, like other large mammals, is feared but not exactly worshipped. In Madagascar they have a certain veneration for it, and have a special ritual for the whale fishery; before the voyage begins, both husband and wife submit to a certain number of tabus, of which chastity is one: the man remains in his hut and fasts regularly; in his absence his wife does the same. After various magical ceremonies, the boat is covered with branches by the magicians, the fishers sing supplications to the old whales, which they do not pursue, to give them their young ones. After bringing the whale to land, the canoe backs away from the shore and then returns at full speed, the harpooners in the bow; they harpoon the animal again, and are then seized and carried to their huts, where, as a part of the ceremonies, their continence at once comes to an end; the whale is then cut up, and preparations for a feast are made; the carcase is decorated with necklaces, and one of the fishers makes a long prayer or address. Thereupon the whale is divided, and each hut receives a portion (v. Gennep, *Tabou*, p. 254 ff.).

In preparation for the whale fishing the Aleutians celebrate a festival; after killing a number of dogs, they carry a wooden image of a whale into a hut with loud shouts, and cover it up so that no light can get in; then they bring it out again and shout together, 'The whale has fled into the sea' (Krachenninikow, ii. 215). The Kaniagmiuts consider whalers to be in communication with evil spirits, and fear them. They seem to have expiated the death of the whale as the Ainus do that of the bear. Whalers were initiated and lived in a special village; dead whalers were buried in caves, and were regarded as tutelary divinities; they were placed in positions resembling those which they took during the chase of the whale; offerings were made to them; it was believed that if a man put a piece of slate at the entrance to the cave the dead would prepare a spearhead (*Rev. d'Anth.* ii. 679–80). On the island of Ihack whalers were tabu during the fishing season; before it began, they searched for eagles' feathers, bears' hair, etc., as talismans; when the season was over, they hid their fishing implements in the mountain caves with the dead bodies; they stole the bodies of successful fishermen, some said as talismans, others in order to prepare poison from them (Lisiansky, *Voyage*, pp. 174, 209). In Vancouver Island whale-fishers are carefully selected; for months before the fishery they abstain from their usual food, practise continence, wash three times a day, redden their bodies, etc. Any accident during the fishery is put down to a violation of these tabus, and punishment is inflicted (Sproat, *Savage Life*, p. 227). The whole of the village shares in the proceeds of the fishing (*Rev. Sci.*, Nov. 4, 1899). A whale dance is performed at Cape Flattery (Swan, *Indians*, p. 70). In Nootka Sound a feast is held after the whale fishery, and the chief, before distributing the portions to the guests, performs a sort of pantomime, during which he imitates the blowing of a whale (de Saussure, *New Voyages*, ix.; Roquefeuil, p. 34). The great chiefs are buried in a special hut, which contains eight images of whales made of wood and placed in a line; after the bodies have been under ground some time, they dig them up, take off the heads, and place them on the backs of these images; the reason given is that it is done in memory of their skill in throwing the harpoon; but it has more probably a magical intention. When a whale is caught, the chief goes to the hut to offer some of its blubber to his ancestors and return thanks to the sun (?); after the festival mentioned above, the chief carves a wooden whale and puts it before the shed (*ib.* p. 102). The Eskimos of Greenland put on their best clothes for the whale fishery, because the whale cannot endure dirtiness; if they wore dirty clothes or some one took part in the chase who had touched a dead body, the whale would escape (Laharpe, xvi. 206; Egede, p. 18). The whale also in Norse folk-lore carries witches, and is himself a magician, being even associated with the dragon of Midgard (Meyer, *German. Myth.* p. 112 f.). Among the Yahgans the initiants are bound to abstain from certain parts of the whale (*South Am. Miss. Mag.* iii. 117). In South Africa the Yaos make images of whales on the ground, at the initiation of young men (Macdonald, *Africana*, i. 131). The Antimerinas believe that earthquakes are due to whales (v. Gennep, *Tabou*, p. 257). The belief suggests that they, like the Russians and others, hold that a whale supports the world. The Russians attribute a deluge to the death of one of the four whales (*Berl. Lesekabinett*, 1844, p. 210). On the Gold Coast the stranding of a whale is regarded as a presage of great misfortunes (Reclus, xii. 438).

A story resembling that of Jonah and the whale is a fairly wide-spread myth (Tylor, *Prim. Cult.*^{3} i. 339). For the Dog-Rib Indians the swallowing of a man, and his escape through being drawn out by his sister's shoe-lace, form the introduction to a Deluge myth; the whale in his wrath raised great waves and inundated the earth (Petitot, *Traditions*, p. 319). The same incident of the swallowing is found among the Haidas and other tribes of the North-West Coast (*Am. Ant.* xi. 298, x. 370; Swan, *N.W. Coast*, p. 68). One of the incidents of Manibosho's career is the victory over a monster who has swallowed him (Schoolcraft, *Algic Researches*, i. 138). At Eromanga a story is told of a man who fell into the water and was swallowed by a whale, but escaped because his ear-rings pricked the inside of the monster (Murray, *Missions*, p. 180; Turner, *Nineteen Years*, p. 496). The same incident is found in the Paumotu archipelago (*Miss. Cath.* 1884, 343). The Bechuanas attribute the destruction of all save one woman to a monster who swallows them (Casalis, *Langue Sechuana*, p. 97). Among the Warangis of East Africa it is a snake which comes out of the sea (*Mitt. d. Schutzgeb.* xiii. 45).

Wolf.—Outside Europe, where the wer-wolf figures prominently in the popular belief of many countries, the wolf is, from a mythological point of view, comparatively unimportant. The Thlinkets have a god, Khanukh, whose name means 'wolf'; he is the head of the wolf phratry (Bancroft, iii. 101). It has, nevertheless, been denied that Khanukh the god has anything to do with the wolf (*JAI* xxviii. p. 144). These tribes are, however, stated to have a kind of image which they preserve with great care, as a safeguard from evil; one is in the form of a wolf's head (*Miss. Herald*, 1829, p. 368). This may, on the other hand, refer to the individual's tutelary deity; for it is a common practice to carry an image of the *manitou* (Frazer, *Tot.* p. 54).

In Europe the wolf was especially associated by the Greeks with Apollo, who was called Λύκιος (Frazer, *Paus.* I. xix. 3). Probably the wolf was originally worshipped or received offerings, as was the case among the Letts (*Golden Bough*^{2}, ii. 429); in process of time the cult was associated with that of Apollo, and it was supposed that he received his title from having exterminated wolves (*ib.*). Many stories connected Apollo with the wolf, some possibly due to a misunderstanding of his epithet λυκηγενής (*Iliad*, iv. 101, 119), probably meaning 'twilight-born' (Meyer, *Handb. der griech. Etymologie*, iv. 519), but interpreted by popular etymology as 'wolf-born.' In Delphi was a bronze image of a wolf; this was explained as commemorating the finding of a treasure with the aid of a wolf. Like Romulus and Remus, many children of Apollo by human mothers were said to have been suckled by wolves (Lang, *Myth*, ii. 220; Liebrecht, *Zur Volkskunde*, p. 18). The wolf was also associated with Zeus in connexion with Mount Lycæus, where a human sacrifice took place, succeeded by a cannibalistic feast, participation in which was believed to result in transformation into wolves; according to a later legend, one portion of the human flesh was served up among the other sacrificial dishes, and the eater was believed to become a wer-wolf (Lang, *Myth*, etc., ii. 263). At Rome the wolf was associated with Mars, and the Lupercalia is sometimes interpreted as a wolf-festival; if the Luperci were wolf-priests, it is probably due to the connexion of the wolf with Mars and the wolf cave (Fowler, *Rom. Fest.* pp. 310–321).

The Kamtchatkans celebrated a wolf festival and related an ætiological myth (Krachenninikow, p. 129). When the Koriaks have killed a wolf, they dress one of their number in its skin and dance round him, as they do round the bear, saying that it was a Russian who killed him (*Golden Bough*^{2}, ii. 397); the Tunguses kill a wolf with fear (Erman, *Archiv*, xxi. 25). When the Kwakiutl Indians of British Columbia kill a wolf, they lay it on a blanket and wail over the body; each person must eat four morsels of its heart. They bury it and give away the weapon with which it was killed. They believe that killing a wolf causes scarcity of game (*Golden Bough*², ii. 396). In the same way in ancient Athens any one who killed a wolf had to bury it by subscription (*ib.*). Possibly the Cree custom of painting the faces of young wolves with vermilion or red ochre is a propitiatory ceremony (Hearne, *Northern Ocean*, p. 363), for there is a prohibition of killing wolves among them, which is not, however, universally observed (*ib.* p. 243). A neighbouring tribe, the Chippewayans, forbid women to touch a wolf skin (Dunn, *Oregon*, p. 106). It is very common to use another name for the wolf than the ordinary one (*Golden Bough*², i. 454; Rolland, *Faune*, i. 118; *FLJ* vii. 55, etc.). The Romans regarded the wolf as unclean, and purified the city with water and sulphur if a wolf got into the Capitol or the temple of Jupiter (de Gubernatis, p. 529).

The wolf is frequently found among the tutelary animals of the dancing or secret societies of North America. The Nootkas relate that wolves once took away a chief's son and tried to kill him; failing to do so, they became his friends, and ordered him on his return home to initiate the other young men into the society, the rites of which they taught him. In the ceremony a pack of wolves, *i.e.* men with wolf masks, appears and carries off the novice; next day they bring him back apparently dead, and the society has to revive him (*Golden Bough*², iii. 434 ff.). Similar associations are found among the Kwakiutls (*Report U.S. National Museum*, 1895, 477–479), and among the Dakotas, by whom parts of the animal are used in magic, though they may not kill it (except, probably, at initiation), or eat it, or even step over or on it (Frazer, *Tot.* p. 50; cf. Schurtz, *Altersklassen*, p. 164; and for these societies in general, pp. 150, 390 ff.). In connexion with these societies may be mentioned a curious confraternity that existed in Normandy till late in the last century. A prominent part in the midsummer ceremonies was taken by the Brotherhood of the Loup Vert and its chief; they ran round the fire hand in hand, and had to capture (while belaboured by) the man selected for the headship, to which was attached the title of Green Wolf, in the following year (*Golden Bough*², iii. 282).

The corn-spirit is believed to take the form of a wolf (*Golden Bough*², ii. 264 ff.), and the binder of the last sheaf is sometimes called 'the wolf.' The wolf also appears at Christmas in Poland (*ib.* 266), and at the Carnival in Nuremberg (Mannhardt, *Ant. Wald- und Feldkulte*, p. 323). In Norse mythology witches and giantesses ride on wolves yoked with serpents (Meyer, *Germ. Myth.* p. 142), while the demonic Fenrir-wolf is too well known to require more than passing mention here. In Zoroastrianism wolves rank as most evil animals (*Yasna*, ix. 18), and should be killed (*Vendīdād*, xviii. 65). A wolf must be seen by a man before it spies him, or evil results will follow (*Yasna*, ix. 21)—a belief which has its parallels in classical lore and in modern Europe (Darmesteter, *Études Iraniennes*, ii. 244). In Armenia, in like manner, wolves are even more evil than serpents, and numerous charms are used against them (Abeghian, *Armen. Volksglaube*, 114–116).

As the last dangerous animal to survive in many parts of Europe, the wolf has given its name to the group of beliefs based on the idea of the temporary or permanent transformation of living men into wolves or other animals (see LYCANTHROPY). The people of the Caucasus say that women are transformed into wolves as a punishment for sin, and retain the form for seven years. A spirit appears to them at night bearing a wolf skin, which the woman has to put on; thereupon she acquires wolfish tendencies, and devours children. At times she puts off the wolf skin, and if any one can burn it the woman vanishes in smoke (Haxthausen, *Transkaukasia*, i. 323. For wer-wolves in general see Tylor, *Prim. Cult.*³ i. 312; Hertz, *Der Werwolf*; Baring-Gould, *Book of Werwolves*). A very similar belief is found in Armenia (Abeghian, *op. cit.* 116–118). As an ominous animal the wolf is commonly auspicious. For myths and folk-tales of the wolf see de Gubernatis, *Zool. Myth.* ii. 142–149. For the wolf see also Pauly-Wissowa, *s.v.* 'Aberglaube,' p. 81.

Wren.—All over Europe the wren is called the 'king of the birds' (*Golden Bough*², ii. 442), and a German story tells how it gained the position in a contest with the eagle (de Gubernatis, ii. 208). In France and the British Isles it is accounted unlucky to kill a wren or harry its nest (*Golden Bough*², *loc. cit.*), but there was also a custom of hunting it annually (*Folklore*, xi. 250; *RHR* xxxviii. 320; *NQ*, 6th ser. x. 492, xi. 177, 297; Croker, *Researches in the S. of Ireland*, p. 233) at Christmas or somewhat later. In the Isle of Man the bird was killed on the night of Dec. 24, and fastened, with its wings extended, to a long pole. It was then carried round to every house, and finally taken in procession to the churchyard and buried. The feathers were distributed, and certain lines sung which seem to indicate that the wren was formerly boiled and eaten. In Ireland and Wales the bird was sometimes carried round alive. In France the bird was struck down, and the successful hunter received the title of 'King' (*Golden Bough*², ii. 445). In Limousin the 'roi de la Tirevessie' was named, whereupon he had to strip naked and throw himself into the water. He then took a wren upon his wrist and proceeded into the town, where he stripped the bird of its feathers and scattered them in the air; finally, the wren was handed over to the representative of a squire (*Tradition*, iv. 166). Thereupon a wooden wren was attached to a high post and shot at; if it was not hit, a fine had to be paid. In Berry the newly married took a wren on a perch to the squire; it was put on a waggon drawn by oxen (*ib.* p. 364; Rolland, *Faune*, ii. 297). At Entraigues the wren had to be set free (*ib.*). It is probable that these ceremonies are connected with a former annual expulsion of evils; in Kamtchatka a similar ceremony is performed in connexion with an annual festival (Krachenninikow, p. 147); a small bird is captured in the forest, roasted, and tasted, and the remainder thrown into the fire.

The wren is considered of good omen in Japan (Chamberlain, *Kojiki*, p. 241 n.), and among the Ainus (Batchelor, p. 439); in the Isle of Man fishermen take one to sea (Rolland, *Faune*, ii. 295), and it is used in the Tyrol folk-medicine (Heyl, p. 139). Among the Karens it is believed to be able to cause rain (*Miss. Cath.* 1888, 261). In Australia the emu wren is a 'sex totem' (*Golden Bough*², iii. 416); near Tanganyika it seems to be a totem (*Miss. Cath.* 1885, 381). Both in Europe (*Ann. Phil. Chrét.* 3rd ser. ii. 148) and in Victoria (Dawson, *Aust. Ab.* p. 52) the wren is said to have brought fire from heaven or elsewhere. The wrens of one brood are said to be re-united on Christmas night (*Ann. Phil. Chrét.* 1 f.). A song of the wren figures in the Pawnee Hako-ceremony (*22 RBEW* ii. 191 f.).

LITERATURE.—The following is a complete list in alphabetical order (with date and place of publication) of the books mentioned throughout the article, with a few additions. Anonymous books and periodicals follow, also in alphabetical order.

I. *BOOKS.*—M. Abeghian, *Armenischer Volksglaube*, Leipzig, 1899; Abinal and La Vaissière, *Vingt ans à Madagascar*, Paris, 1885; J. Adair, *History of the American Indians*, London, 1775; A. U. Afzelius, *Swenska Folkets Sagohäfder—Fäderneslandets Historia*, Stockholm, 1839; L. Alberti, *De Kaffers aan de Zuidkust van Afrika*, Amsterdam, 1810; J. de Alencar, *O Guarany*, Rio de Janeiro, 1893; von Alpenburg, *Alpenmythen*, Zurich, 1857; C. J. Andersson, *Lake Ngami*, London, 1856; R. Andree, *Braunschweiger Volkskunde*, Brunswick,

1901, and *Ethnographische Parallelen*, Stuttgart, 1878, 1889; **N. Annandale**, *The Faroes and Iceland*, Oxford, 1905; **Arbousset**, *Tahiti et les îles adjacentes*, Paris, 1867; **Arbousset and Daumas**, *Relation d'un voyage d'exploration*, Paris, 1842; **F. S. Arnot**, *Garenganze*, London, 1889; **R. P. Ashe**, *Two Kings of Uganda*, London, 1889; **Autermony**, *Voyage de St. Petersburg à Pekin*, Paris, 1756; **J. J. Bachofen**, *Der Bär in den Religionen des Altertums*, Basel, 1863; **G. P. Badger**, *The Nestorians and their Ritual*, London, 1852; **A. Bässler**, *Südseebilder*, Berlin, 1895; **M. M. Ballou**, *Under the Southern Cross*, Boston, 1888; **H. H. Bancroft**, *The Native Races of the Pacific States of North America*, San Francisco, 1875–76; **S. Baring-Gould**, *The Book of Werwolves*, London, 1865; **H. Barth**, *Reisen in Nord- u. Central-Afrika*, Gotha, 1859; **C. Bartsch**, *Sagen, Märchen, und Gebräuche aus Mecklenburg*, Vienna, 1879; **A. Bastian**, *Die deutsche Expedition an der Loangoküste*, Jena, 1874–75, *Der Fetisch an der Küste Guineas*, Berlin, 1884, *Geographische und ethnologische Bilder*, Naumburg, 1873, *Indonesien*, Berlin, 1884–94, *Reise in Siam*, Leipzig, 1866–71, *Völker am Brahmaputra*, Berlin, 1883; **J. Batchelor**, *The Ainu of Japan*, London, 1892; **T. C. Battey**, *Life and Adventures of a Quaker among the Indians*, Boston, 1876; **O. Baumann**, *Durch Massailand zur Nilquelle*, Berlin, 1894; **J. Baumgarten**, *Die komischen Mysterien des französischen Volkslebens*, Leipzig, 1873; **S. J. Baumgarten**, *Allgemeine Geschichte der Länder und Völker von Amerika*, Halle, 1752; **C. Beatty**, *Journal of a two Months' Tour with a View of Promoting Religion*, Lond. 1768; **C. le Beau**, *Avantures du Sieur le Beau*, Amsterdam, 1738; **J. Becker**, *La Vie en Afrique*, Paris, 1887; **J. Beecham**, *Ashantee and Gold Coast*, Lond. 1841; **P. J. Begbie**, *Malayan Peninsula*, Madras, 1834; **J. T. Bent**, *The Cyclades*, Lond. 1885; **A. Bergaigne**, *Religion védique*, Paris, 1878–83; **A. Bertrand**, *Au pays des Barotsi*, Paris, 1898; **J. Billings**, *Reise nach Siberien*, Berlin, 1803; **A. Birlinger**, *Volksthümliches aus Schwaben*, 2 vols., Freiburg i. B., 1861; **G. F. Black**, *Orkney and Shetland Folklore*, Lond. 1905; **W. H. K. Bleek**, *Reynard the Fox in S. Africa*, Lond. 1864, and *Brief Account of Bushman Folklore*, Cape Town, 1875; **M. Bloomfield**, *Cerberus the Dog of Hades*, Chicago, 1905; **F. Boas**, *Indianische Sagen von der Nordpacifischenküste*, Berlin, 1895; **C. Bock**, *Temples and Elephants*, London, 1884; **Böcler-Kreutzwald**, *Der Ehsten abergläubische Gebräuche*, St. Petersburg, 1854; **F. M. Böhme**, *Deutsches Kinderlied und Kinderspiel*, Leipzig, 1897; **W. Bollaert**, *Researches in New Granada, Equador, Peru, and Chile*, London, 1860; **H. A. Boller**, *Among the Indians*, Philad. 1868; **J. Bosman**, *Reise nach Guinea*, Hamburg, 1700; **J. Brand**, *Popular Antiquities of G. Britain*, Lond. 1870; **Brasseur de Bourbourg**, *Popol Vuh*, Paris, 1861; **D. Brauns**, *Japanische Märchen und Sagen*, Leipzig, 1885; **J. v. Brenner**, *Besuch bei den Cannibalen Sumatras*, Würzburg, 1893–94; **D. G. Brinton**, *Essays of an Americanist*, Philad. 1890, and *Myths of the New World*³, New York, 1896; **W. H. Brown**, *On the S. African Frontier*, Lond. 1899; **E. A. W. Budge**, *The Gods of the Egyptians*, Lond. 1904; **A. Burdo**, *Niger et Benue*, Paris, 1880; **C. S. Burne**, *Shropshire Folklore*, Lond. 1883; **W. Byrd**, *History of the Dividing Line*, Richmond, 1866; **H. Callaway**, *Religious System of the Amazulu*, Natal, 1868; **J. S. Campbell**, *The Spirit Base of Belief and Custom*, Bombay, 1885; **E. Casalis**, *The Basutos*, Lond. 1861, and *Études sur la langue Sechuana*, Paris, 1841; **M. A. Castrén**, *Vorlesungen über finnische Mythologie*, St. Petersburg, 1857; **P. du Chaillu**, *Voyages et aventures dans l'Afrique équatoriale*, Paris, 1863; **J. Chalmers**, *Pioneering in New Guinea*, Lond. 1887; **B. H. Chamberlain**, *Kojiki, or Records of Ancient Matters*, Yokohama, 1883, and *Things Japanese*, Lond. 1902; **E. K. Chambers**, *The Medieval Stage*, 2 vols., Lond. 1903; **J. Chapman**, *Travels in the Interior of S. Africa*, Lond. 1868; **A. Chesnel**, *Dictionnaire historique des institutions de la France*, Paris, 1855; **D. Chwolson**, *Die Ssabier und der Ssabismus*, 2 vols., St. Petersburg, 1856; **S. Ciszewski**, *Bajka o Midasowych uszach*, Krakow, 1899; **E. D. Clarke**, *Travels in Europe, Asia, and Africa*, Lond. 1810–19; **F. S. A. de Clercq**, *Bijdragen tot de Kennis der Residentie Ternate*, Leyden, 1890; **W. A. Clouston**, 'Folklore of the Raven,' in Saxby's *Birds of Omen*, Lond. 1893; **J. D. Cochrane**, *Pedestrian Journey through Russia and Siberian Tartary*, Lond. 1824; **R. H. Codrington**, *The Melanesians*, Oxford, 1891; **S. Coolsma**, *Twaalf Voorlazingen over West-Java*, Rotterdam, 1879; **Coremans**, *L'Année de l'ancienne Belgique*, Brussels, 1844; **E. Coues**, *MS. Journals of A. Henry and D. Thompson*, Lond. 1897; **T. C. Croker**, *Researches in the South of Ireland*, Lond. 1824; **W. Crooke**, *Popular Religion and Folklore of N. India*, Westminster, 1896; **E. W. Cuhn**, *Sammlungen merkwürdiger Reisen in das Innere von Afrika*, Leipzig, 1790–91; **L. Curtze**, *Volksüberlieferungen aus dem Fürstenthum Waldeck*, Arolsen, 1860; **J. Dawson**, *Australian Aborigines*, Melbourne, 1881; **J. Darmesteter**, *Études iraniennes*, Paris, 1883; **L. Decle**, *Three Years in Savage Africa*, Lond. 1898; **R. E. Dennett**, *Seven Years among the Fjort*, Lond. 1887, and *Folklore of the Fjort*, Lond. 1898; **D. V. Denon**, *Travels in Upper and Lower Egypt*, Lond. 1803; **A. Desrousseaux**, *Mœurs populaires de la Flandre française*, Lille, 1889; **E. Dieffenbach**, *Travels in New Zealand*, Lond. 1843; **J. Doolittle**, *Social Life of the Chinese*, N. York, 1867; **R. M. Dorman**, *Origin of Primitive Superstitions*, Philad. 1881; **G. A. Dorsey**, *Traditions of Skidi Pawnee*, Washington, 1902; **J. O. Dorsey**, 'Siouan Cults' in *11 RBEW*; **J. Dunn**, *History of the Oregon Territory*, Lond. 1844; **R. Dussaud**, *Histoire et religion des Nosairis*, Paris, 1900; **T. Dwight**, *Travels in New England*, Newhaven, 1821; **M. Eells**, *Ten Years of Missionary Work among the Indians*, Boston, 1886; **H. Egede**, *Nachrichten von Grönland*, Copenhagen, 1790 (tr. Lond. 1818); **P. Ehrenreich**, *Mythen und Legenden der südamerikanischen Urvölker*, Berlin, 1905; **A. B. Ellis**, *The Ewe-speaking Peoples of the Slave Coast*, Lond. 1890, and *The Tshi-speaking Peoples of the Gold Coast*, Lond. 1887; **W. Ellis**, *Polynesian Researches*, 4 vols., Lond. 1832; **W. A. Elmslie**, *Among the wild Ngoni*, Lond. 1899; **Erman**, *Archiv f. wissenschaftl. Kunde von Russland*, Berlin, 1841; **G. A. Erman**, *Reise um die Erde durch Nordasien und die beiden Oceane*, Berlin, 1838; **J. Evans**, *Tour in S. Wales*, Lond. 1804; **E. J. Eyre**, *Expeditions of Discovery into Central Australia*, Lond. 1845; **P. Fagot**, *Folklore du Lauragais*, Villefranche, 1891–94; **N. du Fail**, *Oeuvres facétieuses*, Paris, 1874; **L. R. Farnell**, *Cults of the Greek States*, Oxford, 1896–1907; **A. Fick**, *Griechische Personennamen*, Göttingen, 1874; **F. Fleming**, *Southern Africa*, Lond. 1856; **de la Fontaine**, *Luxemburgische Sitten*, Luxemburg, 1883; **Forster and Sprengel**, *Beiträge zur Völker- und Länderkunde*, Leipzig, 1781–90; **G. E. Foster**, *Sequoyah*, Philad. 1885; **W. W. Fowler**, *Roman Festivals*, Oxford. 1899; **J. Franklin**, *Second Expedition to the Shores of the Polar Sea*, Lond. 1828; **J. G. Frazer**, *Totemism*, Lond. 1887, *Pausanias's Description of Greece*, Lond. 1898, and *The Golden Bough*, Lond. 1901; **G. Fritsch**, *Drei Jahre in Südafrika*, Breslau, 1868, and *Die Eingeborenen Südafrikas*, Leipzig, 1872; **L. Frobenius**, *Die Weltanschauung der Naturvölker*, Berlin, 1898; **W. Geiger**, *Ostiranische Kultur im Altertum*, Erlangen, 1882; **Geiseler**, *Die Osterinsel*, Berlin, 1883; **K. Geldner**, *Vedische Studien*, Stuttgart, 1889–1901; **A. v. Gennep**, *Tabou et totémisme à Madagascar*, Paris, 1904; **J. G. Georgi**, *Bemerkungen einer Reise imrussischen Reich*, St. Petersburg, 1775; **G. Gerland**, *Südsee* (*Anth. der Naturvölker*, vol. vi.), Leipzig, 1872; **W. W. Gill**, *Myths and Songs of the S. Pacific*, Lond. 1876; **H. Goldie**, *Calabar and its Mission*, Lond. 1901; **C. Gould**, *Mythical Monsters*, Lond. 1886; **Gray and Dochard**, *Travels in W. Africa*, Lond. 1829; **W. Gregor**, *Folklore of the N.E. of Scotland*, Lond. 1881; **J. Grimm**, *Reinhart Fuchs*, Berlin, 1834; **J. and W. Grimm**, *Deutsche Mythologie*, 1875–78; **G. B. Grinnell**, *Pawnee Hero Stories*, N. York, 1889, *Blackfoot Lodge Tales*, N.Y. 1892, Lond. 1893; **J. V. Grohmann**, *Apollo Smintheus*, Prague, 1862, and *Aberglauben und Gebräuche aus Böhmen u. Mähren*, Prague, 1863; **J. J. M. de Groot**, *Religious System of China*, Leyden, 1897; **O. Gruppe**, *Die griechischen Culte*, Leipzig, 1887; **A. de Gubernatis**, *Zoological Mythology*, Lond. 1872; **B. Hagen**, *Unter den Papuas*, Wiesbaden, 1899; **E. Hahn**, *Die Haustiere*, Leipzig, 1896, and *Demeter und Baubo*, Lübeck, 1896; **J. Haltrich**, *Zur Volkskunde der Siebenbürger Sachsen*, Vienna, 1885; **D. W. Harmon**, *Journal of Voyages and Travels in the Interior of N. America*, Andover, 1820; **A. Harou**, *Contributions au Folklore de la Belgique*, Paris, 1892; **Harris**, *Uncle Remus, his Songs and his Sayings*, N. York, 1880, and *Nights with Uncle Remus*, N. York, 1884; **E. S. Hartland**, *Science of Fairytales*, Lond. 1891, and *Legend of Perseus*, 3 vols., Lond. 1894–96; **Hassan**, *Die Wahrheit über Emin Pascha*, Berlin, 1893; **A. v. Hasselt**, *Volksbeschrijving van Midden Sumatra*, Leyden, 1882; **M. Haupt**, *Französische Volkslieder*, Leipzig, 1877; **J. Hawkesworth**, *Account of the Voyages . . . in the Southern Hemisphere*, Lond. 1773; **Baron v. Haxthausen**, *Transkaukasia*, Leipzig, 1856; **S. Hearne**, *A Journey . . . to the Northern Ocean*, Lond. 1795; **F. v. Hellwald**, *Naturgeschichte*, Stuttgart, 1880–82; **W. Henderson**, *Folklore of the Northern Counties*, Lond. 1879; **L. Hennepin**, *Description de la Louisiane*, Paris, 1688; **F. Hernsheim**, *Südsee-erinnerungen*, Berlin, 1883; **W. Hertz**, *Der Werwolf*, Stuttgart, 1862; **J. A. Heyl**, *Volkssagen, Bräuche u. Meinungen in Tirol*, Brixen, 1897; **A. Hillebrandt**, *Vedische Mythologie*, Breslau, 1891–1902; **H. Y. Hind**, *Explorations in the Interior of the Labrador Peninsula*, Lond. 1863; **S. Hislop**, *Papers relating to the Aboriginal Tribes*, Nagpur, 1866; **A. H. Hoffmann**, *Fundgrube für die Geschichte der deutschen Sprache und Literatur*, Breslau, 1830; **M. Holderness**, *New Russia*, Lond. 1823; **A. C. Hollis**, *The Masai*, Oxford, 1905; **Holzmaier**, 'Osiliana,' in *Verhandlungen der gelehrten Ehstnischen Gesellschaft zu Dorpat*, vii. (1872); **W. Hone**, *Everyday Book and Tablebook*, Lond. 1831, etc.; **L. Hopf**, *Orakeltiere und Tierorakel*, Stuttgart, 1888; **S. Hopkins**, *Historical Memoirs relating to the Housatunnuk Indians*, Boston, 1753; **Howard**, *Life with Trans-Siberian Savages*, Lond. 1893; **A. W. Howitt**, *Native Races of S.E. Australia*, Lond. 1904; **T. J. Hutchinson**, *Impressions of Western Africa*, Lond. 1858; **E. Y. Ides**, *Three Years' Travels*, Lond. 1706; **A. V. W. Jackson**, *Persia Past and Present*, New York, 1906; **J. Jacobs**, *Studies in Biblical Archæology*, Lond. 1894; **J. A. Jacobsen**, *Reise an der Nordwestküste Amerikas*, Leipzig, 1884; **D. Jecklin**, *Volksthümliches aus Graubünden*, Chur, 1874; **Jones and Kropf**, *Folktales of the Magyars*, Lond. 1889; **J. Josselyn**, *Account of two Voyages to New England*, 1674; **J. Jühling**, *Die Tiere in der deutschen Volksmedizin*, Mittweida, 1900; **F. Junghuhn**, *Die Battaländer auf Sumatra*, Berlin, 1847; **R. F. Kaindl**, *Die Huzulen*, Vienna, 1894; **D. F. Karaka**, *History of the Parsis*, Lond. 1884; **S. Kay**, *Travels and Researches in Caffraria*, Lond. 1883; **W. H. Keating**, *Expedition to the Source of St. Peter's River*, Lond. 1825; **J. Kehrein**, *Volkssprache und Volkssitte im Herzogthum Nassau*, Weilbing, 1860; **D. Kidd**, *The Essential Kafir*, Lond. 1904; **M. H. Kingsley**, *Travels in W. Africa*, Lond. 1898; **J. A. E. Köhler**, *Volksbrauch in Voigtlande*, Leipzig, 1867; **W. Kolbe**, *Hessische Volkssitten u. Gebräuche*, Marburg, 1888; **P. Kolben**, *Present State of the Cape of Good Hope*, Lond. 1731; **W. Kolberg**, *Poznanskie*, Krakow, 1875, etc.; **C. T. Kosche**, *Character, Sitten, u. Religion aller bekannten Völker*, Leipzig, 1791; **S. P. Krachenninikow**, *Histoire et Description du Kamtchatka*, Amsterdam, 1770; **A. Krassoff**,

La vie du peuple zyriane, Paris, 1900; **A. Krause**, *Die Tlinkit Indianer*, Jena, 1885; **F. S. Krauss**, *Sitte u. Brauch der Südslaven*, Vienna, 1885; **A. Kuhn**, *Norddeutsche Sagen, Märchen, u. Gebräuche aus Mecklenburg*, Leipzig, 1848; **P. Labarthe**, *Reise nach der Küste von Guinea*, Vienna, 1804; **Laharpe**, *Abrégé de l'histoire générale des voyages*, Paris, 1816; **E. W. Lane**, *1001 Nights*, Lond. 1895; **A. Lang**, *Myth, Ritual and Religion*, 2 vols., Lond. 1899, and *Social Origins*, Lond. 1903; **R. G. Latham**, *Native Races of the Russian Empire*, Lond. 1854; **A. Ledieu**, *Monographie d'un bourg picard*, Paris, 1890; **G. W. Leitner**, *Languages and Races of Dardistan*, Lahore, 1877; **C. G. Leland**, *Algonquin Legends of New England*, Boston, 1884; **H. Lichtenstein**, *Travels in S. Africa*, Lond. 1812–15; **F. Liebrecht**, *Des Gervasius von Tilbury Otia Imperialia*, Hanover, 1856, and *Zur Volkskunde*, Heilbronn, 1879; **U. Lisiansky**, *A Voyage round the World*, Lond. 1814; **D. Livingstone**, *Missionary Travels and Researches in S. Africa*, Lond. 1857, and *Expedition to the Zambesi*, Lond. 1865; **L. Lloyd**, *Peasant Life in Sweden*, Lond. 1870; **L. C. Lloyd**, *Short Account of further Bushman Material*, Lond. 1889; **G. H. Loskiel**, *History of the Mission of the Evang. Breth. among the Indians of N. Amer.*, Lond. 1794; **P. Lozano**, *Description corografica del . . . Gran Chaco*, Cordova, 1733; **C. Lumholtz**, *Among Cannibals*, Lond. 1889; **T. Lund**, *Danmark og Norges Historie*, Copenhagen, 1879; **A. Lütolf**, *Sagen, Bräuche und Legenden*, Lucerne, 1865; **S. Lyde**, *The Asian Mystery*, Lond. 1860; **J. A. MacCulloch**, *The Childhood of Fiction*, Lond. 1905; **Duff Macdonald**, *Africana*, Lond. 1882; **A. A. Macdonell**, *Vedic Mythology*, Strassburg, 1897; **M. Macfie**, *Vancouver Island and British Columbia*, Lond. 1865; **Machado y Alvarez**, *Folklore, Bibliotheca de las Traditions populares*, Seville, 1883, etc.; **A. Mackenzie**, *A Voyage from Montreal*, Lond. 1801; **J. Mackenzie**, *Ten Years North of the Orange River*, Edinb. 1871, and *Day-dawn in Dark Places*, Lond. 1884; **J. Maclean**, *Twenty-five Years' Service in the Hudson's Bay Territory*, Lond. 1849; **J. F. M'Lennan**, *Studies in Ancient History*, Lond. 1886; **C. de Magalhanes**, *Contes indiennes du Brésil*, Rio de Janeiro, 1882; **L. Magyar**, *Reisen in Südafrika*, Leipzig, 1859; **J. Malcolm**, *Memoir of Central India*, Lond. 1823; **W. Mannhardt**, *Germanische Mythen*, Berlin, 1858, *Baumkultus*, Berlin, 1875, and *Antike Wald- und Feldkulte*, Berlin, 1875–7; **E. Marno**, *Reisen im Gebiete des blauen und weissen Nil*, Vienna, 1874; **W. Marsden**, *History of Sumatra*, Lond. 1811; **W. E. Marshall**, *A Phrenologist among the Todas*, Lond. 1873; **C. von Martius**, *Beiträge zur Ethnographie u. Sprachenkunde Amerikas*, Leipzig, 1867; **F. Mason**, *Burma*, Rangoon, 1860; **G. Maspero**, *Études égyptiennes*, Paris, 1879–80; **F. Maspons y Labros**, *Jochs de la Infancia*, Barcelona, 1874; **J. J. Matignon**, *Superstition, Crime et Misère en Chine*, Lyons, 1899; **W. Matthews**, *Ethnology and Philology of the Hidatsa Indians*, Washington, 1875; **J. T. Medina**, *Los Aborigenes de Chile*, Santiago, 1882; **J. Megapolensis**, *Kort Ontwerp van de Mahakuare Indianen*, Amsterdam, 1651; **E. Meier**, *Deutsche Sitten, Sagen, und Gebräuche aus Schwaben*, Stuttgart, 1852; **J. Menant**, *Glyptique orientale*, Paris, 1883; **A. Merensky**, *Erinnerungen aus dem Missionsleben in Südostafrika*, Leipzig, 1888; **E. H. Meyer**, *Germanische Mythologie*, 1891; **L. Meyer**, *Handbuch der griechischen Etymologie*, Leipzig, 1901–2; **D. Miladinov**, *Bulgarski narodni pesni*, Sophia, 1891; **J. Miller**, *Unwritten History, or Life among the Modocs*, Hartford, 1874; **R. Moffat**, *Missionary Labours and Scenes in S. Africa*, Lond. 1842; **G. I. Molina**, *Historia . . . de Chile*, Madrid, 1788; **F. J. Mone**, *Anzeiger für Kunde der deutschen Vorzeit*, Karlsruhe, 1835, etc.; **J. Montgomery**, *Journals of Voyages and Travels*, Lond. 1831; **J. Morgan**, *Life and Adventures of W. Buckley*, Hobart, 1852; **H. Mouhot**, *Travels in the Central Parts of Indo-China*, Lond. 1864; **J. Moura**, *Le Royaume de Cambodge*, Paris, 1883; **M. Much**, *Heimat der Indogermanen*, Berlin, 1902; **W. Müllenhof**, *Sagen, Märchen, und Lieder des Herzogtums Schleswig-Holsteins*, 1845; **W. J. Müller**, *Beschreibung der afrik. auf der Goldküste gelegenen Landschaft Fetu*, Hamburg, 1673; **J. G. Müller**, *Geschichte der amerikanischen Urreligionen*, Basel, 1867; **K. O. Müller**, *Prolegomena zu einer wissenschaftlichen Mythologie*, Göttingen, 1825; **S. Müller**, *Reizen en Onderzoekingen in den indischen Archipel*, Amsterdam, 1857; **A. W. Murray**, *Missions in Western Polynesia*, Lond. 1862; **J. Napier**, *Folklore in the West of Scotland*, Lond. 1879; **E. Naumann**, *Vom goldenen Horn zu den Quellen des Euphrat*, Munich, 1893; **C. New**, *Life Wanderings and Labours in E. Africa*, Lond. 1874; **Newbold**, *British Settlements in the Straits of Malacca*, Lond. 1839; **J. Nicholson**, *Folklore of E. Yorkshire*, Lond. 1890; **Nilus**, in *PL* lxxi; **E. Nolde**, *Reise nach Innerarabien*, Brunswick, 1895; **A. de Nore**, *Coutumes, mythes, et traditions des provinces de France*, Paris, 1840; **T. Nuttall**, *Travels into the Arkansas Territory*, Philad. 1821; **F. A. Ober**, *Travels in Mexico*, Edinburgh, 1880; **W. F. O'Connor**, *Folktales from Tibet*, Lond. 1906; **H. Oldenberg**, *Religion des Veda*, Berlin, 1894; **A. d'Orbigny**, *Voyage dans l'Amérique méridionale*, Paris, 1825–47; **T. B. Pandian**, *Indian Village Folk*, Lond. 1898; **F. Panzer**, *Beitrag zur deutschen Mythologie*, Munich, 1848; **E. S. Parker**, *The Aborigines of Australia*, Melbourne, 1854; **S. Parkinson**, *Journal of a Voyage to the South Seas*, Lond. 1773; **J. N. Patouillet**, *Trois ans en Nouvelle Calédonie*, Paris, 1873; **T. Pennant**, *Arctic Zoology*, Lond. 1784–87; **Perelaer**, *Ethnographische Beschrijving der Dajaks*, Zalt-Bommel, 1870; **F. M. Perrin du Lac**, *Voyage dans les deux Louisianes*, Paris, 1805; **N. Perrot**, *Les Mœurs, etc., des sauvages de l'Amérique septentrionale*, Paris, 1861; **A. Peter**, *Volkstümliches aus Oesterreichisch-Schlesien*, Troppau, 1873; **Petersen**, *Die Pferdeköpfe auf den Bauernhäusern*, Kiel, 1860; **J. Petherick**, *Travels in Central Africa*, Lond. 1869; **E. Petitot**, *Traditions indiennes du Canada nord-ouest*, Paris, 1886; **Pfannenschmid**, *Germanische Erntefeste*, Hanover, 1878; **J. Philip**, *Researches in S. Africa*, Lond. 1828; **J. Pinkerton**, *General Collection of the best and most interesting Voyages and Travels*, Lond. 1808–14; **H. H. Ploss**, *Das Kind*, Stuttgart, 1876; **F. C. Pouqueville**, *Voyage en Morée*, Paris, 1885; **L. Preller**, *Römische Mythologie*, Berlin, 1881–83; **H. Pröhle**, *Harzbilder*, Leipzig, 1855; **Purchas**, *His Pilgrimes*, Lond. 1625; **T. S. Raffles**, *History of Java*, Lond. 1830; **Rançon**, *Dans la Haute Gambie*, Paris, 1895; **F. Ratzel**, *History of Mankind*, Lond. 1896; **S. Reinach**, *Cultes, mythes, et religion*, Paris, 1905; **O. V. Reinsberg-Düringsfeld**, *Das festliche Jahr*, Leipzig, 1863, and *Calendrier belge*, Brussels, 1861; **S. R. Riggs**, 'Dakota Grammar,' in vol. ix. of *Contributions to North American Ethnology*; **H. J. Rink**, *Eskimoiske Eventyr og Sagn*, Copenhagen, 1866–71; **C. Ritter**, *Asien*, Breslau, 1832; **W. H. R. Rivers**, *The Todas*, Lond. 1906; **G. A. Robertson**, *Notes on Africa*, Lond. 1819; **Rochholz**, *Deutscher Glaube und Brauch*, Berlin, 1867; **R. Rodd**, *Customs and Lore of Modern Greece*, Lond. 1892; **E. Rolland**, *Faune populaire de la France*, Paris, 1877–83, and *Rimes et jeux de l'enfance*, Paris, 1883; **C. de Roquefeuil**, *Voyage autour du monde*, Paris, 1823; **H. Ling Roth**, *Natives of Sarawak and British North Borneo*, Lond. 1896; **Ruiz Blanco**, *Convercion del Piritu*, Madrid, 1690; **A. Ruiz de Montaya**, *Conquesta Espiritual*, Madrid, 1639; **J. D. Rupp**, *History of the County of Berks*, Lancaster, 1844; **C. Russwurm**, *Eibovolk*, 2 vols., Reval, 1855; **T. G. Sagard**, *Histoire du Canada*, Paris, 1636; **B. de Sagahun**, *Historia de la Conquista de Mexico*, Mexico, 1829; **R. Salvado**, *Mémoires historiques sur l'Australie*; **J. W. Sanborn**, *Legends, etc., of the Seneca Indians*, Gowanda, 1878; **L. A. N. de Saussure**, 'Voyage' in *New Voyages*, Lond. 1819; **L. F. Sauvé**, *Le Folklore des Hautes Vosges*, Paris, 1889; **L. Scherman**, *Materialen zur Geschichte der indischen Visionsliteratur*, Leipzig, 1892; **Schiller**, *Zum Thier und Kräuterbuch des mecklenburgischen Volkes*, Schwerin, 1861–59; **H. Schinz**, *Deutsch Südwestafrika*, Oldenburg, 1891; **F. Schmidt**, *Sitten u. Gebräuche bei Hochzeiten*, Weimar, 1863; **F. X. v. Schönwerth**, *Aus der Oberpfalz*, Augsburg, 1857–59; **H. R. Schoolcraft**, *Algic Researches*, N. York, 1829, and *The Indian Tribes of the United States*, Philad. 1857–60; **H. Schreiber**, *Taschenbuch für Geschichte und Altertum in Süddeutschland*, Freiburg, 1839–46; **L. v. Schrenck**, *Reisen und Forschungen in Amurlande*, St. Petersburg, 1858–75; **A. G. Schrenk**, *Reise nach dem Nordosten des europäischen Russlands*, Dorpat, 1848; **W. v. Schulenburg**, *Wendisches Volkstum in Sage, Brauch u. Sitte*, Berlin, 1882; **H. Schurtz**, *Altersklassen u. Männerbünde*, Berlin, 1902; **J. F. Schütze**, *Holsteinisches Idiotikon*, 4 vols., Hamburg, 1800–06; **C. A. Schwaner**, *Borneo*, Amsterdam, 1853; **G. Schweinfurth**, *Heart of Africa*, Lond. 1878; **P. Sébillot**, *Folklore des Pêcheurs*, Paris, 1901, and *Traditions et Superstitions de la Haute Bretagne*, Paris, 1882; **B. Seeman**, *Voyage of H.M.S. Herald*, London, 1853; **W. Shaw**, *Story of my Mission in S.E. Africa*, London, 1860; **E. Shortland**, *Traditions of the New Zealanders*, Lond. 1856; **Sinapius**, *Olsnographia*, Leipzig, 1706; **W. W. Skeat**, *Fables and Folktales from an Eastern Forest*, Cambridge, 1896, and *Malay Magic*, Lond. 1898; **Skeat and Blagden**, *Pagan Tribes of the Malay Peninsula*, 2 vols., Lond. 1906; **H. H. Smith**, *Brazil*, Lond. 1879; **P. C. Smith**, *Anansi Stories from Jamaica*, Lond. 1898; **W. R. Smith**, *Religion of the Semites*², Lond. 1894; **R. Brough Smyth**, *Aborigines of Victoria*, 2 vols., Melbourne, 1878; **A. Socin**, *Die neuaramäischen Dialekte*, Tübingen, 1882; **C. A. Soppitt**, *Short Account of the Kuki-Lushai Tribes*, Shillong, 1887; **H. Soyaux**, *Aus West-Africa*, Leipzig, 1879; **J. H. Speke**, *Journal of the Discovery of the Source of the Nile*, Edinb. 1863; **Spencer and Gillen**, *Native Tribes of Central Australia*, Lond. 1899; **F. Spiegel**, *Eranische Alterthumskunde*, Leipzig, 1871–78; **M. Spiess**, *Aberglauben des sächsischen Obererzgebirges*, Dresden, 1862; **Spix and Martius**, *Reise in Brazilien*, Munich, 1823–31; **M. C. Sprengel**, *Auswahl der besten Nachrichten*, Halle, 1794–1800; **G. M. Sproat**, *Scenes and Studies of Savage Life*, Lond. 1868; **F. J. Stalder**, *Versuch eines schweizerischen Idiotikon*, Basel, 1806–12; **J. M. Stanley**, *Catalogue of the Portraits*, Washington, 1852; **M. A. Stein**, *Sand-buried Ruins of Khotan*, Oxf. 1903; **K. von den Steinen**, *Unter den Naturvölkern*, Berlin, 1894; **G. W. Steller**, *Beschreibung von Kamtschatka*, Frankfurt, 1774; **A. Stoddart**, *Sketches of Louisiana*, Philad. 1812; **G. W. Stow**, *Native Races of S. Africa*, Lond. 1905; **J. Strachey**, *Historie of Travaile in Virginia*, Lond. 1849; **Strackerjan**, *Aberglaube u. Sagen aus Oldenburg*, Oldenburg, 1867; **P. I. Strahlenberg**, *Das Nord u. östliche Teil von Europa*, Stockholm, 1730, Eng. tr., Lond. 1736; **J. J. Strauss**, *Reise durch Italien*, Gotha, 1832; **A. Strausz**, *Die Bulgaren*, Leipzig, 1898; **J. Strutt**, *Sports and Pastimes*, Lond. 1801; **F. Stuhlmann**, *Mit Emin Pascha ins Herz von Africa*, Berlin, 1894; **J. G. Swan**, *North-West Coast*, N. York, 1857, and *The Indians of Cape Flattery*, Washington, 1869; **R. Taylor**, *Te Ika i Maui*, Lond. 1855; **Tettau and Temme**, *Volkssagen der Altmark*, Berlin, 1829; **F. Tetzner**, *Die Slowinzen*, Berlin, 1899; **T. M. Thomas**, *Eleven Years in S. Africa*, Lond. 1872; **E. F. im Thurn**, *Among the Indians of Guiana*, Lond. 1883; **Restrepo Tirado**, *Estudios sobre los aborigenes de Colombia*, Bogota, 1892; **M. P. Töppen**, *Aberglauben aus Masuren*, Königsberg, 1867; **T. Trede**, *Wunderglaube in Heidenthum*, Gotha, 1901; **F. M. Trimmer**, *Yukon Territory*, Lond. 1898; **J. F. v. Tschudi**, *Reisen durch Südamerika*, Leipzig, 1869; **G. Turner**, *Nineteen Years in Polynesia*, Lond. 1861, and *Samoa*, Lond. 1884; **R. Twysden**, *Historiæ Anglicanæ*, Lond. 1652; **E. B. Tylor**, *Primitive Culture*³, 2 vols., Lond. 1891; **J. F. G. Vaugeois**, *Histoire des antiquités de la* *ville de l'Aigle*, L'Aigle, 1841; P. Vial, *Les Lolos*, Shanghai, 1898; J. N. W. de Visser, *Die nicht menschengestaltigen Götter der Griechen*, Leyden, 1903; W. Wackernagel, *Kleinere Schriften*, Leipzig, 1872–74; A. Wahlen, *Mœurs, usages et coutumes de tous les peuples*, Brussels, 1843–44; C. A. Walckenaer, *Histoire générale des voyages*, Paris, 1826–31; Waling Dykstra, *Uit Frieslands Volksleven*, Leeuwarden, 1892–96; R. Walpole, *Memoirs relating to Turkey*, Lond. 1817; W. Ward, *View of the Hist. Lit. and Religion of the Hindus*, Madras, 1863; C. Waterton, *Wanderings in S. America*, Lond. 1882; C. Weinhold, *Altnordisches Leben*, Berlin, 1856; Prinz zu Wied, *Reise nach Brasilien*, Frankfurt, 1821; F. J. Wiedemann, *Aus dem innern u. äusseren Leben der Ehsten*, St. Petersburg, 1876; E. Wigstroem, *Sagor af Afventyr*, Stockholm, 1884; G. A. Wilken, *Het Animisme bij den Volken van den indischen Archipel*, Leyden, 1885; J. Williams, *Missionary Enterprises in the South Sea Islands*, Lond. 1837; Monier Williams, *Indian Wisdom*[3], Lond. 1875; J. L. Wilson, *Western Africa*, Lond. 1856; T. Winterbottom, *Native Africans in the Neighbourhood of Sierra Leone*, Lond. 1803; H. v. Wlislocki, *Volksglaube u. Volksbrauch der Siebenbürger Sachsen*, Berlin, 1893; J. F. L. Woeste, *Volksüberlieferungen in der Grafschaft Mark*, Iserlohn, 1848; J. W. Wolf, *Beiträge zur deutschen Mythologie*, Göttingen, 1852–57; W. Wood, *New England's Prospect*, Lond. 1634; D. C. Worcester, *Phillipine Islands*, N. York, 1898; D. Wright, *History of Nepāl*, Cambridge, 1877; C. F. A. Wuttke, *Deutscher Volksaberglaube der Gegenwart*[3], Berlin, 1900; E. Young, *Kingdom of the Yellow Robe*, Lond. 1898.

II. *PERIODICALS, ETC.*—*Account of the Colony of the Cape of Good Hope*, Lond. 1819; *Alemannia*, Bonn, 1872; *Allgemeine Missionszeitschrift*, Gütersloh, 1878, etc.; *American Anthropologist*, Washington, 1888, etc.; *American Review*, N. York, 1845, etc.; *Am Urdsbrunnen*, Hamburg, 1886–89; *Am Urquell*, Lunden, 1890–96; *Annales de la Propagation de la Foi*, Lyons, 1826, etc.; *Annales de la Société d'Émulation pour l'histoire et les antiquités de Flandres*, Bruges, 1839, etc.; *Annales de Philosophie chrétienne*, Paris, 1830, etc.; *Annual RBEW*, 1881, etc.; *Anthropologie*, Paris, 1890, etc.; *Antiquarisk Tijdschrift*, Copenhagen, 1843–63; *Archæological Review*, London, 1888–90; *Asiatic Observer*, Calcutta, 1823; *Asiatic Quarterly Review*, London, 1886, etc.; *Athenæum*, Lond. 1828, etc.; *Ausland*, Munich, 1828–92; *Australian Association for the Advancement of Science Reports*, 1889, etc.; *Baltische Studien*, Stettin, 1832; *Bastian Festschrift*, Berlin, 1896; *Bavaria*, Munich, 1860–67; *Beiträge zur Kenntniss des russischen Reichs*, St. Petersburg, 1839; *Beiträge zur Kolonialpolitik*, Frankfort, 1899, etc.; *Berigten van de Utrechtsche Zendelingsvereiniging*, Utrecht, 1860, etc.; *Bijdragen tot de Taal- Land- en Volkenkunde* Hague, 1853, etc.; *Blätter für Landeskunde von Nieder-Oesterreich*, Vienna, 1865; *Boletin del Instituto Geografico Argentino*, Buenos Ayres, 1895; *BG*, 1877–1904; *Brandenburgia*, Berlin, 1891, etc.; *Byegones*, Oswestry, 1871, etc.; *Cambridge University Expedition to Torres Straits Reports*, Cambridge, 1903, etc.; *Cape Monthly Magazine*, Cape Town, 1861, etc.; *Calcutta Review*, Calcutta, 1846; *Church Missionary Record*, Lond. 1830–90; *Congrès des Traditions populaires, Compte rendu*, Paris, 1903; *Congress of Orientalists (International)*, 11th Session; *Contributions to North American Ethnology*, vols. i.–vii., ix., Washington, 1848; *Davenport Academy of Sciences Proceedings*, Davenport, 1877–1893; *Denham Tracts*, Lond. 1892–95; *Deutsche geographische Blätter*, Bremen, 1877, etc.; Ἐφημερὶς Ἀρχαιολογική, Athens, 1837, etc.; *FL*, Lond. 1891, etc.; *FLJ*, Lond. 1883–90; *FLR*, Lond. 1878–82; *Gelehrte Ehstnische Gesellschaft Schriften*, Dorpat, 1863, etc.; *Gentleman's Magazine*, Lond. 1731; *Germania*, Stuttgart, 1856, etc.; *Globus*, Hildburghausen, 1867, etc.; *Historical Collections of Louisiana* (B. F. French), N. York, 1846–53; *Home and Foreign Mission Record of the Free Church*, Edinb. 1843, etc.; *Internationales Archiv für Ethnographie*, Leyden, 1888; *Jahrbuch des Vereins für Mecklenburgische Geschichte*, Schwerin, 1835; *Jahrb. f. romanische Literatur*, Berlin, 1859, etc.; *Jahrbücher f. Schleswig-Holstein und Lauenburg*, Kiel, 1858–69; *Jahresbericht der geographischen Gesellschaft*, Berne, 1879, etc.; *JAFL*, Boston, 1888; *JAI*, Lond. 1871, etc.; *JAOS*, Newhaven, 1843, etc.; *Journal of the Indian Archipelago*, Singapore, 1847–59; *JRAS, Straits Branch*, Singapore, 1878, etc.; *JRAS Be*, Calcutta, 1832, etc.; *Kahgegaghabowh: Life, History, and Travels*, Albany, 1847; *Das Kloster* (J. Scheible), Stuttgart, 1845–49; *Lettres édifiantes et curieuses des missionnaires étrangers*, Paris, 1780–83; *Man*, Lond. 1901, etc.; *Massachusetts Historical Society, Collections*, Boston, 1792, etc.; *Mededeelingen van wege het Nederlandsche Zendelinggenootschap*, Rotterdam, 1857, etc.; *M*, Paris, 1878–1901; *Mémoires de la Société des antiquaires de France*, Paris, 1807, etc.; *Missionary Herald*, Boston, 1821, etc.; *Missionary Register*, Lond. 1813–55; *Mission Field*, 1856, etc.; *Mission Life*, Lond. 1866–90; *Les Missions Catholiques*, Lyons, 1868, etc.; *Mitteilungen der afrikanischen Gesellschaft*, Berlin, 1886–89; *Mitt. d. geogr. Gesellsch. f. Thüringen*, Jena, 1882; *Mitt. d. Gesellsch. f. Natur- u. Völkerkunde Ostasiens*, Yokohama, 1873, etc.; *Mitt. des orientalischen Seminars*, Berlin, 1898, etc.; *Mitt. des Vereins f. d. Geschichte d. Deutschen in Böhmen*, Prague, 1862, etc.; *Mitt. d. Vereins f. Erdkunde*, Leipzig, 1873, etc.; *Mitt. von Forschungsreisenden aus den deutschen Schutzgebieten*, Berlin, 1888, etc.; *Montgomeryshire Collections*, Lond. 1868, etc.; *Nachrichten für u. über Kaiser-Wilhelmsland*, Berlin, 1886, etc.; *Natur*, Halle, 1852, etc.; *Niedersachsen*, Bremen, 1885; *Northumberland Folklore*, 1904; *Ons Volksleven*, Brecht, 1884; *Ontario Archeological Report*, Toronto, 1890, etc.; *PNQ*, Allahabad, 1886; *O Patriota*, Rio de Janeiro, 1813, etc.; *Petermanns Mitteilungen*, Gotha, 1855, etc.; *Proceedings of the Royal Irish Academy*, Dublin, 1837, etc.; *PRSE*, Edinb. 1840, etc.; *Publicationen des königlichen Zoologischen Museums in Dresden*, Leipzig, 1881, etc.; *Relations des Jésuites*, Quebec, 1858; *Report on E. African Protectorate*, Lond. 1897; *Rep. of Indian Ethnog. Committee*, Nagpur, 1868; *Rep. of U.S. National Museum*, Washington. 1875; *RAnth*, Paris, 1872–89; *RCel*, Paris, 1870; *RHR*, Paris, 1880, etc.; *RSI*, Washington, 1849, etc.; *Revue des traditions populaires*, Paris, 1886, etc.; *REth*, Paris, 1882–89; *RS*, Paris, 1871, etc.; *Transactions of the Royal Geog. Soc. of Australia*, Adelaide, 1886, etc.; *Romania*, Paris, 1872, etc.; *Rovings in the Pacific*, Lond. 1851; *Russische Revue*, Leipzig, 1863–64; *Schweizerisches Archiv für Volkskunde*, Zürich, 1897, etc.; *S. American Missionary Magazine*, Lond. 1867, etc.; *Suffolk Folklore*, Lond. 1897; *Teutonia*, Königsberg, 1902; *Tijdschrift voor indische Taal- Land- en Volkenkunde*, Batavia, 1853, etc.; *T' Oung Pao*, Leyden, 1890, etc.; *Tour du Monde*, Paris, 1860, etc.; *La Tradition*, Paris, 1887–1903; *Verhandelingen van het Bataviaasch Genootschap van Kunsten*, Batavia, 1779; *Voice from S. America*, Lond. 1863–66; *Volkskunde*, Ghent, 1889, etc.; *Voyages et Aventures des emigrés français*, Paris, 1799; *Wissenschaftliche Mitteilungen aus Bosnien*, Sarajevo, 1893, etc.; *Zeitschrift der Gesellschaft für Erdkunde*, Berlin, 1866, etc.; *Zeitsch. für allgemeine Erdkunde*, Berlin, 1853, etc.; *Zeitsch. des deutschen u. österreichischen Alpenvereins*, 1869, etc.; *ZDA*, Leipzig, 1841–75; *Zeitsch. f. deutsche Mythologie*, Göttingen, 1853, etc.; *Zeitschr. f. deut. Philologie*, Halle, 1869, etc.; *ZE*, Berlin, 1867; *Zeitsch. f. oesterreich. Volkskunde*, Vienna, 1895, etc.; *ZVRW*, Stuttgart, 1878, etc.; *Zeitsch. des Vereins f. Volkskunde*, Berlin, 1891, etc.; *ZVK*, Leipzig, 1889, etc.; *Zoologischer Garten*, Frankfort-a'-M. 1859–1905.

N. W. THOMAS.

ANIMISM.—*Definition and Scope.*—In the language of philosophy, Animism is the doctrine which places the source of mental and even physical life in an energy independent of or at least distinct from the body. From the point of view of the history of religions, the term is taken, in a wider sense, to denote the belief in the existence of spiritual beings, some attached to bodies of which they constitute the real personality (*souls*), others without necessary connexion with a determinate body (*spirits*). For convenience in treating the subject, it will be of advantage to study Animism separately under the following three forms:—(i.) Worship of the souls of men and animals, manifesting itself above all as worship of the dead (*Necrolatry*); (ii.) worship of spiritual beings who are not associated in a permanent way with certain bodies or objects (*Spiritism*); (iii.) worship of spiritual beings who direct the permanent or periodically recurring phenomena of nature (*Naturism*).

Animism in the sense just stated represents an attempt to explain in a rational way all the facts of the Universe. It is the religion and the philosophy of all non-civilized peoples. It predominates at the commencement of all the historical forms of worship. Finally, it still shows itself, in its complete development, among the survivals of folk-lore.

In all probability, from the moment when man began to inquire into the cause of phenomena, external or internal, he thought to find it in the only source of activity with which he was directly acquainted, namely, an act of will. Objects which moved, or which he believed capable of moving, gave him the impression either of bodies set in motion by hidden beings, or of bodies endowed, like himself, with will and personality. Our languages bear witness to a mental condition in which those who created them attributed life, personality, and sex to the forces of nature.*

The imaginary personalities that controlled the sun, the moon, the stars, the clouds, the waters, etc., were not thought of separately from their

* A similar conception is found at the present day among non-civilized peoples. 'The Ashivis or Zuñis,' writes Mr. Frank Cushing, 'suppose the sun, moon and stars, the sky, earth and sea, in all their phenomena and elements, and all inanimate objects as well as plants, animals and men, to belong to one great system of all-conscious and inter-related life, in which the degrees of relationship seem to be determined largely, if not wholly, by the degrees of resemblance' (*PBE*, Smithsonian Institution, vol. ii. [1883] p. 9). Again, Sir E. im Thurn relates that the natives of Guiana look upon men and animals, the heavenly bodies, atmospherical phenomena, and inanimate objects, all as beings of the same nature, alike composed of a soul and a body, and differing only in the extent of their powers (*JAI*, vol. xi. p. 377).

visible garb, any more than the personality of a man was conceived of apart from his body. But it cannot have been long before a new inference made its presence felt. The experience of dreams led men to the conclusion that their *ego* was different from their body, that it could separate itself from the latter—temporarily during sleep, finally at death—and yet continue to exist. Thus a native of Australia, being asked by a traveller whether he believed that his *yambo* could quit his body, replied: 'It must be so; for, when I sleep, I go to distant places, I see distant people, I even see and speak with those that are dead' (Howitt, 'On some Australian Beliefs' in *JAI*, vol. xiii. [1884] p. 189).

i. **Necrolatry.**—It will of course be understood that, in employing the terms 'soul,' 'spirit,' 'personality,' we do not mean to attribute to savages any notion of immaterial entities, such as is arrived at by making abstraction successively of all the properties of matter except force. The soul is to them simply a being of a more subtle essence, generally invisible but not always intangible, subject in a certain measure to all the limitations of human beings, but endowed at the same time with mysterious faculties.

Hitherto no people has been met with which does not believe in the existence and the survival of human souls, which does not admit the possibility of their intervention in the affairs of the living, and which does not seek to enter into relations with them by processes which are everywhere closely analogous—either by offering to them anything of which they were fond during their lifetime, or by applying to them the methods resorted to by sorcery in order to avert or to control superhuman powers. The assertions of some authors to a contrary effect are due to incomplete observation, hasty generalization, or misunderstanding of the sense of the terms employed.

The souls of living beings are generally believed to be the pale and vague image of the body itself.* It is the *double*, as it appears in dreams. Sometimes the soul is assimilated to the shadow cast by the body ('the shades' of poetical language), or to its reflexion in water. At other times we find it confounded with the breath (Lat. *anima*, Gr. ἄνεμος, Skr. *prâṇa*, Heb. *rûaḥ*= 'breath,' 'wind'), or with the beats of the heart and the pulse. Again it may have a special form attributed to it, borrowed from living beings or what are viewed as such: birds, serpents, insects, *ignes fatui*, meteors, wreaths of vapour, etc. There are peoples who imagine that man possesses a plurality of souls, each with its distinct rôle.

Souls, it is supposed, may feel the counterstroke of wounds inflicted upon the body or of diseases which attack it. Again, the same body may become successively the seat of a number of souls, and, conversely, the same soul may inhabit in turn various bodies. Hence the magical processes, not uncommon among non-civilized peoples, whereby it is sought to replace the original soul by a superior one; and the custom, observed amongst the most diverse races, of putting to death, the moment he shows the first signs of mental or physical decrepitude, the personage—sorcerer, chief, or king—whom it concerns the tribe to preserve in the full possession of his faculties. In this way his soul is thought to pass yet unimpaired into the body of his successor.

What becomes of the *double* after death? In general it is supposed to continue to haunt the corpse as long as any part of it remains, or to frequent the vicinity of the tomb. At times the notion of survival is limited to the more or less vivid recollection retained of the deceased.

'Ask the negro,' writes Du Chaillu (*TES* i. 308), 'where is the spirit of his great-grandfather, he says he does not know; it is done. Ask him about the spirits of his father or brother who died yesterday, then he is full of fear and terror.'

At the end of a certain period, or as the result of certain rites, the soul, as is sometimes held, reincarnates itself; or, more frequently, it is believed to take its departure to another world—situated under ground, beyond the sea, on the summit of a mountain, above the vault of heaven, in the stars, etc. There it leads a vague, colourless, miserable existence (this is the peculiar quality of subterranean abodes, *Sheol* or *Hades*); or, it may be, an existence moulded more or less closely upon the earthly life, each shade retaining his rank and his circumstances.

But, even upon this hypothesis of another abode, the soul is still supposed to intervene in the affairs of the living, especially when the deceased wishes to do a good turn to his descendants or to take vengeance upon his enemies. Hence the importance assumed by **Ancestor-worship,** a practice which has played so large a part, as has been shown by Herbert Spencer, in the consolidation of families and tribes. This cult has its origin at once in the fear of ghosts, in filial affection, and in the desire to preserve for the family the benefits of paternal protection. Once it is admitted that death does not interrupt the relations between men, it is logical to suppose that a father after his decease will retain a prejudice in favour of his descendants, and will seek to add to their welfare and to protect them against dangers at home or abroad. The children, for their part, in order to preserve his favour, will have to continue to show him the consideration he demanded in his lifetime; they must also maintain the organization of the family and assure the permanence of the home, so that this cult may never be interrupted.

By the side of ancestors, and at times above them, a place comes to be taken by the *manes* of illustrious personages who have profoundly impressed the popular imagination—chiefs, sorcerers, conquerors, heroes, legislators, and reputed founders of the tribe or the city.

The worship of ancestors sometimes includes the belief that all the members of a tribe are descended from some individual who is held to have possessed the form of an animal or, more rarely, of a plant. This involves certain relations of consanguinity with all the representatives of this species. See TOTEMISM.

The notion that the lot of souls in the future life is regulated by their conduct in the present life belongs to a more advanced stage in the evolution of religious ideas. Its appearance and development can be traced in the majority of historical religions. The first stage is to accept the principle that souls have awarded to them a better or worse existence according as they have or have not, during their sojourn on earth, deserved the favour of the superhuman powers. The last stage is reached when it is supposed that, upon the analogy of what happens in well ordered societies, the lot of the soul is made the subject of a formally conducted process of judgment, where good and evil actions are weighed. The favourite titles to future happiness are at first services rendered to the gods, pious actions, sacrifices; afterwards they are services rendered to the community which it is the aim of the gods to protect. Thus the theory of *retribution* finds room by the side of the theory of *continuation*, and probably succeeds to it. But

* The emperor Hadrian, when dying, gave a definition of his soul which well expresses this notion:

'Animula vagula, blandula,
Hospes comesque corporis.'

(Ælius Spartianus, 'Adrianus,' c. xv., in *Scriptores Historiæ Augustæ*).

even this method of regulating the destiny of souls after death does not exclude such an eventuality as their temporary return to earth and entrance into relations with the living.

ii. **Spiritism.**—Once a start has been made by attributing to all living beings, and even to a great many inanimate objects, a mental equipment which differs from a man's own merely in the degree of activity and power, it is a logical inference that souls may, in their turn, separate themselves temporarily from their bodies, and, if the latter be dissolved, may survive them. These souls assume, as a rule, the physiognomy of a *double*, or a form appropriate to their function, but always chosen so as to imply movement and life. Moreover, at this stage of intellectual development, man will cherish a belief in the existence, as independent agents, of a multitude of analogous souls proceeding from beings and objects which he has not known. These souls, from the very circumstance that they have lost their connexion with particular bodies, acquire a fitness for assuming all aspects and performing all offices.

Such is the origin of *spirits*, to whose agency are finally attributed all phenomena which men can neither explain by natural causes nor set down to the account of some superhuman being with functions exactly defined. The most benighted savages, even when they have no idea of the distinction between natural and supernatural, perceive quite clearly that certain events are due to causes whose connexion is self-evident. They did not need to wait till a Newton came to reveal the law of gravitation, in order to convince themselves that, if an apple detached from a tree falls to the ground, there is nothing in this phenomenon but what is natural and capable of being foreseen. But everything that strikes them as unusual and unexpected—and this category includes the great majority of phenomena—seems to them due to the action of invisible powers acting through mysterious processes. These powers bear, amongst all non-civilized peoples, a generic name which corresponds in their respective languages to our term 'spirits.'

The disembodied spirits may introduce themselves into any body whatsoever. When they invade the body of a man, they take the place of his personality, or at least introduce disorders; to them are attributed the phenomena of possession, inspiration, second sight, intoxication, disease. All non-civilized peoples without exception ascribe diseases either to the entrance of a spirit into the body, or to wounds inflicted by a spirit from outside, or to the removal of the soul by a malevolent spirit. When spirits penetrate into a material object, they make it the vehicle or the organ of their own personality, and thus transform it into a **fetish**. The fetish differs from the *amulet* (or the *talisman*) in that the latter owes its efficacy to a property transmitted from without, whereas the fetish itself always owes its virtue to the presence of a spirit lodged within.

When one begins to introduce something like order amongst the superhuman powers, spirits are grouped in classes according to the sphere which they inhabit or the function which they discharge. Thus we have spirits of the air, of the under world, of the waters, of fire, of plants, of flocks, etc. The physical form attributed to them is generally one borrowed from living animate beings, but enriched with fantastic features.

iii. **Naturism.** — The souls of natural objects endowed with the character of permanence or of periodicity (such as the sky, the earth, the heavenly bodies, the elements, vegetation, etc.) often tend to assume a special importance. They are, none the less, regarded as distinct from their visible garb, and likewise have a proper physical form assigned to them, which is ordinarily the human form or that of one of the higher animals. The genii so conceived of may temporarily leave their domain and even intervene in a number of affairs that have no connexion with their original function. They thus tend to encroach upon the sphere of the souls of ancestors and upon that of ordinary spirits. When we look at them from another side, we note that, while the majority of spirits are regarded as malevolent, and are dreaded and treated accordingly, the genii of Nature are sometimes ill-omened and at other times propitious, like the phenomena over which they preside; and hence they tend to awake in their worshippers a mingled sentiment of fear and of affection, corresponding to this double aspect of their nature. We frequently note a disposition to exaggerate their benevolent side, and, above all, their power by the use of flatteries, unconscious or deliberate, which in the end are brought forward as the expression of the truth. Certain genii tend thus to outstrip the other superhuman powers, and to become man's allies in his conflict with the hostile forces of Nature.

To the above differentiation in the conception of souls there corresponds a certain variety in the forms of cult. Propitiatory acts—sacrifice, prayer, homage—predominate in the relations with the higher rank of the Divine Powers; on the other hand, it is acts of conjuration—evocation, incantation, exorcism—that are employed by preference when spirits have to be dealt with. This explains why magic is the ordinary companion of Spiritism. Where the evolution of religion has developed neither veneration for the forces of Nature nor the worship of Ancestors, the cult consists almost exclusively—as we see in the case of the negroes, the Australians, the natives of Siberia and South America, etc.—of processes intended to avert or to subjugate the superhuman powers. Among these peoples the conception of the world as a domain abandoned to the caprices of arbitrary and malevolent wills makes of religion a reign of terror, weighing constantly upon the life of the savage, and barring all progress. On the other hand, where Animism develops into polytheism, it may be viewed as a first stage in that evolution which leads to making the Divine Power the supreme agent who seeks order in nature and the good of humanity.

[The subject will be more fully dealt with under SOUL and SPIRIT].

LITERATURE.—E. B. Tylor, *Primitive Culture*[3], London, 1891; Herbert Spencer, *Principles of Sociology*, pt. vi., London, 1885; Albert Réville, *Religions des peuples non civilisés*, 2 vols., Paris, 1883; A. W. Alger, *A Critical History of the Doctrine of Future Life*, New York, 1878; Andrew Lang, *Myth, Ritual, and Religion*, 2 vols., Edinburgh, 1887; J. G. Frazer, *The Golden Bough*[2], London, 1902; Goblet d'Alviella, *Origin and Growth of the Conception of God* (Hibbert Lectures), London, 1892; L. R. Farnell, *The Evolution of Religion*, London, 1905; cf. also *JAI* (*passim*).

GOBLET D'ALVIELLA.

ANNAM (Popular Religion).—A characteristic of the Annamese is the multiplicity and variety of their cults. Influenced more by tradition than by conviction, they are only indifferently versed in the three great religions of foreign origin that prevail in their country—Chinese Buddhism (*Phât giáo*), which is celebrated in the pagoda (*chùa*); Confucianism (*Nho giáo*), in the temples of the educated (*văn miêu, văn chi*); and Taoism (*Thờ tinh, thờ các ba*), in the palace (*phu dên*). These are official cults, practised especially by the upper classes and the learned.

So also the cult of the Sky and the Earth, which allows no other celebrant than the sovereign, and the cult of the ruling Emperor receive from the Annamese only subordinate veneration. We shall not describe these cults, which are all of Chinese importation, but refer the reader to art. CHINA.

The masses retain their preference for ancestor-worship (*thờ' ông bà ông vai*), which the head of the family offers in a reserved part of the house (*nhà tô*); for the Genii and Spirits of all kinds, which are invoked in the chapels (*miếu*); and for the numerous magical performances (*phép thuật*), which have come from China, from India, and from the other races of the Indo-Chinese Peninsula, or which are simply autochthonous. No one has yet succeeded in finally deciding what belongs to each of these various influences. They all co-operate in perpetuating the old animistic beliefs, which have remained very deep-rooted in Annam as elsewhere.

1. Animism.—To the inhabitant of Annam life is a universal phenomenon; it is the common possession not only of men and animals, but also of things—stones, plants, stars, and of the elements—earth, fire, water, wind, etc.

To all he gives a sex and a rank. The sun is male; the moon, his wife, is female; the stars send good fortune and bad from on high. Then some animals have been *anthropomorphized* or even deified, which implies fear and at the same time reverence for them; *e.g.* in Annam they always speak of 'Sir Tiger' (*Ông Cọp*). Hence that worship, which is so strange, of the whale, the dolphin, and the tiger.

The Annamese not only admits that life is common to all existing things, but conceives of that life not as isolated, but as collective; he sees it in groups, not in individuals. This difficulty in conceiving individualism is one which is not confined to the Annamese. It exists in almost all primitive races, and still continues among those of slow development, as in China, for example, where the idea of collective solidarity, the conception in groups, has legal consequences. When a crime is committed in China, not only is the guilty one punished, but his forefathers, his descendants, his parents, his friends, and even his neighbours. In the collection of taxes, the upper classes in the community are always responsible to the treasury for the general crowd.

In addition to these two ideas of universality and collectivity of life, the Annamese believes in the contiguity and permeability of beings who do not form distinct categories, but can pass from one genus or species to another under certain conditions of space and time. Hence theriomorphism and totemism.

The elephant was born from the star Giao Quang, the rabbit from the moon. A fox at the age of fifty years can change into an old woman; at a hundred years into a lovely maiden, very dangerous to her lovers; at a thousand years of age, if he happens to find in a cemetery a human skull which fits his head, he may become a spectre, or a being similar to the Hindu *preta*. Sows can go the length of changing into courtezans.

The fish after a thousand years becomes a dragon, the rat at the end of a hundred years a bat, and the bat after another hundred years a swallow. Any one who can catch it at the time of its metamorphosis and eat its flesh becomes immortal.

Tigers' hairs may give birth to worms. Even plants are capable of similar transformation: the chuối tree (a kind of banana), on reaching a thousand years of age, becomes a blue goat. The people maintain that a banyan tree (*Ficus indica*, Linnæus) which grew within the precincts of a temple near Hanoï, on being cut down, became transformed into a blue buffalo. The ngô-dông (*Elæococca vernicifera*, Linnæus) has the power of changing itself at night into a ghost with a buffalo's head. These transformations, possible to plants and animals, are still more so to supernatural beings, and even to man. The fairies (*bà tiên, nang tiên*) often take the shape of butterflies, the genii those of men and monkeys. The mother of an Annamese king of the Trân dynasty (1226–1402) appeared in the form of a red serpent on the altar on which the first sacrifice to her *manes* was being offered. Some sorcerers have a still more extensive power: certain of them create swarms of bees from grains of rice, with which they fill their mouths and which they then blow out forcibly into the air; others ride on a simple sheet of paper, which they can at will transform into a donkey and then change back to its original state.

In this reciprocal and continuous intermingling of the life of all beings, pairing cannot be determined or limited by species. The legend of the founding of Cô-loa tells of the union of a maiden with a white cock. Dinh-bô-Lãnh, at one time a drover in the Ninh-bình mountains, who founded the national Annamese dynasty in the 10th cent., is said to have been the son of a woman and an otter. These totemic legends enable us to understand such names as the Fox clan, the Dragon clan, the clan of the Red Sparrow-hawks, assumed in semi-historical times by the tribes among which Annam was divided. The Annals state that, down to the 14th cent., the kings of Annam tatued their bodies with the representation of a dragon, in allusion to their legendary origin.

For a similar reason, but with a more practical object, the inhabitants of fishing villages used to tatu themselves with the figure of a crocodile in order to establish their relationship with the numerous crocodiles of their shores, and to be spared by them. Others in the same way used to adorn their bodies with a serpent, in order to avoid being bitten by those formidable reptiles.

Union was possible not only between men and animals, but also between human beings and supernatural beings, genii, or vampires, especially as vampires often assume the appearance of men, to be better able to deceive the women they wish to possess. O-loi, a famous personage at the court of the Hanoï kings, was, the legends affirm, the son of the genius of the Ma-la pagoda and the wife of Si-Doang, Annamese ambassador to the court of China.

The phenomenon of conception, in the popular beliefs of the Annamese, not only does not always presuppose the identity of species of the two parents, but can even be accomplished without sexual intercourse between them. Nearly all the heroes of the semi-historical period in Annam, as well as China, are the result of miraculous fertilization. The mother of the assassin of king Dinh-Tiên-Hoàng, who ascended the throne in 968, became pregnant after dreaming that she was swallowing the moon. Another king was born from a fresh egg that his mother had taken from a swallow's nest and eaten. The legends abound with analogous cases in which fertilization is due to spring-water, the touch of a handkerchief, the fall of a star, etc.

Another result of this absence of limits to beings and things is that everything that resembles a certain individual, in however small a degree, may at a given moment be regarded as the individual, and undergo the treatment that was to befall him. Here we come upon the spells often practised by the Annamese sorcerers. The effigy or the sign may replace the thing signified so effectually that they sacrifice to the genii of epidemics the effigy of the person whom they wish to see dead. By analogous reasoning, they burn at the graves paper representations or even merely a list of all the objects (clothing, furniture, jewels, houses, etc.) that the dead man is supposed to take away with him.

Similarly, any particular condition is transmissible by contact, without regard to the person's own will. That is why a person who wants to avoid all misfortune has to keep constantly in the shade. A pregnant woman must be careful not to accept betel-pellets from a woman who has already had a miscarriage, under penalty of abortion. She must not eat double bananas if she does not want to give birth to twins. A person carrying straw must avoid passing a field of rice in blossom; the rice would change to straw. They believe also in the contagion of death, and several parts of the funeral ceremony aim specially at guarding them from it.

Lost in the midst of the universal life which surrounds him, haunted by the terrible and manifold forms that that life can take to destroy him, the Annamese lives constantly on the defensive. If he tries by sacrifices and offerings to gain the favour of the good spirits, he seeks still more to appease the malignant ones, under whatever form they appear, and to foresee, and consequently to avoid, all the misfortunes which may befall him. Hence the cults of the good and evil genii, of certain animals and of souls, the belief in magic and presentiments, and a whole series of prophylactic ceremonies before each important event in life, especially birth, marriage, and death.

2. Good Spirits.—In the first rank of good spirits is Dôc-Cu'ó'c, the one-footed Spirit, whose worship, the Annamese assert, was brought from Nam-quan in China to Tonkin by a Taoist priest. He flourished chiefly in Nghê-An, but he has worshippers throughout the whole of Tonkin. Dôc-Cu'ó'c assumes the form of a warrior of noble bearing, brandishing an axe in his only hand, which is always represented in profile. His body, cut in two lengthwise, rests on a single foot. A prayer taken from the ritual of the spirit praises his merits thus: 'The one-footed Spirit has only one eye and only one foot, but he is swift as lightning and sees all that happens in the world. He sees afar the evil spirits who bring plague, ruin, and misfortune. He calls to his aid the millions of celestial soldiers. He protects and avenges men. Tigers and demons dread him. He sends good or bad weather as he chooses, makes the sun to shine or the rain to fall, and cures all diseases.'

An inscription in memory of the erection of his temple in the hamlet of Ngo-ru'o'u (Tonkin) eulogizes him in these words: 'The one-footed Spirit is powerful; he protects the country. Every one fears, loves, and reveres him. Armed with a golden axe, he hovers on the clouds and scours the country, always present though invisible. By his favour the student is successful in his examinations, the farmer is assured of his crop, the buffaloes are strong and active, the farmyard is prosperous, gold and silver are amassed in the coffers, there are no longer any poor people in the village. All this is due to the influence of the one-footed Spirit, because he is pleased with our homage, and glad to see his temple erected in a propitious place.'

To obtain a favour from the one-footed Spirit they trace a formula on a white paper, and place the paper on his altar with a small sum of money (generally equal to about 1s. 6d.), where it must remain for one hundred days.

The ritual of the one-footed Spirit contains a series of formulas which, written in a certain way on paper or on shells, form precious charms for the most diverse cases: invisibility, toothache, barrenness, different diseases; they banish malicious powers, ensure the sex of a child during pregnancy, silence children who cry through the night, ward off nightmares and ghosts, prevent demons from entering the mouth of the celebrant when he is invoking the one-footed Spirit, and from replying instead of him.

Dôc Cu'ó'c can, moreover, transfer a part of his power to small figures of straw, wood, or paper made by his priests. These figures can then go to the places to which they are sent, in order to work as much harm as possible to men, animals, and objects chosen for their vengeance, who are not long in being struck down by death, disease, ruin, or destruction.

In the same way, in cases of demoniacal possession, the priest of the one-footed Spirit can, by his exorcism, constrain the demons to leave the possessed person and to take refuge in a rough wooden or straw doll, which is then burned.

Around the one-footed Spirit crowd legions of good spirits (*thần lành*), who preside over the events of life in general. The tutelary genii of the village (*thần kì*) and the patron guardians of the home and the family (*thần tù'*) are also worshipped. These spirits are infinite in number, as every action and even every object is, for the Annamese, placed in dependence upon a superior power, whose favour they must win, especially to thwart the continual temptations of the *ma*, or evil spirits.

It is for this reason that, during the first three days of a new year, when all Annam is rejoicing, each Annamese workman, after worshipping his ancestors, whose special festival it is, seeks to gain the favour of the spirit who presides over his special work. The peasant offers a sacrifice to the spirit of the buffaloes in the stable or in the fields. The offerings consist of cooked rice, a little salt, palm-sugar, incense, leaves of gilt paper, and as many large cakes as the farmer has cattle. The shape of these cakes varies according to the sex of the animal. The female buffaloes' cakes, which are square and flattened, contain other smaller cakes, intended for the young buffaloes which they are supposed to carry in the womb. The buffaloes have their horns decorated with gilt paper, and into each of their mouths is put a little of each offering, the remainder being left to the drovers. Then each buffalo is led out to trace three furrows.

Thus also the blacksmith sacrifices to his forge, or rather to the spirit of his forge, after having adorned his bellows with gilt paper. The limeburner sacrifices to his limekiln, the hunter to his nets and snares, the merchant to his hampers, and the master of the house does not forget the three hearthstones and the lime jug, which are also covered with gilt paper. The lime jug is filled to the brim so that it may have abundance, and that in return its spirit may see to the welfare of the family.

Invocation and sacrifice take place also when in a new house the head of the family installs the lime jug, whose contents will be used in the composition of the national masticatory of the natives of the Far East—betel-pellets. In it the guardian of the house (*chu nhà*) is incarnated. Its premature end would forebode the death of one of the members of the household, whom they wish to see crowned with hoary hairs, as the jar itself is with lime. When, in spite of all precautions, it breaks, a new one is bought, but great care is taken not to throw the other into the ashpit. Its spirit would dearly avenge such irreverence. They go and place it with great ceremony on the branches or trunks of certain trees near the pagodas, either to serve as an offering to the wandering souls who come to take shelter in these trees, or to be delivered there to a spirit which is powerful enough to prevent it from taking vengeance on the inmates of its former home.

When hunters catch an animal in their nets, they kill it and then pull off a part of its left ear, which they bury in the spot where the animal was caught, as an offering to the Spirit of the soil (*Thô Thần*). Then the prey is flayed and dismembered. Its heart, cut up into small pieces, is cooked on burning coals. These pieces are then laid on broad leaves on the ground; and the chief of the hunters, prostrating himself four times, informs Thô Thần that such and such a band of men from such and such a village has taken the liberty of depriving him of such and such an animal. The animal is then divided among all the hunters.

In fields of eatable or market-garden plants (cucumbers, water-melons, etc.), they often erect a miniature chapel of straw to the Lord of the earth (*Thô Chu*). In this way the field is placed under the protection of the spirit; and thieves are far more afraid to come near it, for it is Thô Chu, and not the owner, that they dread having anything to do with.

For the same purpose of protection, travellers, on leaving the river for the sea, make offerings of gilt paper at the mouth of the river, in order to secure the favour of the sea-spirits. Those who travel by land throw them at the turnings of the road to avoid accidents, especially the teeth of the tiger.

There are also female spirits (*chu' vi*), who inhabit forests, springs, thickets, and certain trees. At their head are the five great fairies:

(1) Thuy-Tinh-công-Chúa, 'Star of the Waters.'
(2) Quinh-Hoa-công-Chúa, 'Hortensia Flower.'
(3) Quê-Hoa, 'Camellia Flower.'
(4) Bach-Hoa, 'White Flower.'
(5) Hoàng-Hoa, 'Yellow Flower.'

Their goodwill is secured through the intermediaries *bà-dông*, or priestesses, who correspond to the sorcerer-priests of the evil spirits.

Then the people also render regular worship to the *Bà-Dú'c-Chúa*, or the Three Mothers, whose three images, dressed in red, are set up in a side chapel in nearly all Buddhist and Taoist temples. They represent, according to the Annamese, the Spirit of the Forests, the Spirit of the Waters, and the Spirit of the Air and Sky.

3. Evil Spirits.—Far more numerous and more dreaded are the maleficent powers, which, for the Annamese, inhabit all space. They include the whole of the *Ma* and the *Qui*, evil spirits or devils, hobgoblins, vampires, and ghosts, which are constantly adding to their number by recruiting from the millions of the wandering souls of the dead.

Physical and moral pain, epidemics, ruin, and accidents come from them. There is the Spirit of Cholera, of Small-pox, of Bad Luck, etc. It is for this reason that the Annamese seek by every means to appease them, and are far more deeply concerned about them than about the good spirits. For, whereas the good spirits harm human beings only when they are offended or slandered by them, the evil spirits are incessantly trying to work mischief. They can be disarmed only by means of sacrifices, or rendered harmless by the protection of the good spirits.

In the first rank we must place the worship rendered to the spirits of the autochthones (*chu' ngu*), the original possessors of the soil, which wander about famished, because their descendants are no longer alive and cannot offer them sacrifices, and look with a jealous eye upon others possessing their goods. Not only are they granted a share of the oblations which are made at stated times by the bonzes, sorcerers, or private individuals, but every year each landowner, in one of the first three months, offers a sacrifice to them. And if unforeseen evils befall the farmers or their cattle, if they are the victims of misfortune, it is evident that the anger of the *chu' ngu* is affecting them. They must appease him by a sacrifice (generally an expensive one), in which they buy or hire his land from him, in order to live peaceably with him. With the help of a medium they enter into communication with the spirit and make him sign the contract of this mystical sale, the amount of which they pour out to him in imitation paper money. Henceforward the landowner has nothing to fear from the *chu' ngu.*

Of a more dangerous kind are the *Ma-lai*, 'wandering demons,' who have all the signs of life, and often assume the form of a pretty girl; but at night their head, followed only by the complete alimentary canal, becomes separated from the body and goes about feeding on excrement and taking part in a kind of infernal 'witches' midnight orgy.' The prosperity of a house which has been entered by a *Ma-lai* is very soon affected by it.

It is well also to guard against the *Ma-tro'i* or *ignes fatui*, which, thin and worn, wander through the fields quite naked, with dishevelled hair, walking a foot above the ground; and also against the *Con-tinh*, or spirits of young maidens who have died prematurely—spirits which are of the most malicious kind. They hide in trees, from which they are heard laughing with a weird laugh and calling. The passer-by who is so imprudent as to answer their call feels his soul fly from his body and becomes mad. One must also beware of the *Ma-gia*, or spirits of the drowned who have not received burial. They sit in trees at night, and try either to attract passers-by or to cause boats to sink. It is the *Ma-gia* that sends the fatal cramp to the swimmer, which paralyzes him and causes him to drown. The best means of appeasing this spirit is to call back the soul in order to construct a tomb for it (*chiêu hồn dấp nếm*).

This ceremony consists in re-making a body for the person who has disappeared, and in re-uniting the soul of the drowned person to this body by means of magical ceremonies, after which the funeral is celebrated. This artificial body, whose bones are made from mulberry branches, its entrails from five threads of different colours, its flesh and viscera from earth and wax, and its skin from flour pancakes, is dressed in the most beautiful clothes of the dead person, and put into a coffin. The ceremony of fixing the soul in this new body requires the aid of a sorcerer and of a medium who is provided with three sticks of incense and a coat that had belonged to the deceased. These two men go in a boat to the real or supposed place where the person was drowned, the medium stretching out the hand in which he holds the coat. If this hand begins to tremble, they conclude that the spirit of the dead man (*viâ*) is re-instating itself in the coat. The medium then jumps into the water, and after a time comes up, saying that he has succeeded in getting possession of the spirit of the drowned man. They put the coat that was used in the ceremony into the coffin, which is then shut, and they proceed with the burial.

The *Ma-loan*, or spirits of soldiers who have died in the wars of the Empire, are recognizable by their hurried and unintelligible whisperings. The *Ma-giâu, Ma-dziua, Ma-dzem, Ma-riu*, or phantoms which mislead people in the night, form a ring and turn round about the traveller, or talk in front of him until, struck by illusion and exhausted with following the phantoms, he falls in some lonely spot to which he has been lured. A magical ceremony is necessary to bring back life or reason to the victims of these treacherous phantoms.

The *Ma trôt-trôt*, or souls of beheaded persons, are the cause of whirlwinds. The Annamese scare these demons away by calling out 'Chem! Chem!' ('I behead you').

The *Ma thân-vòng*, or souls of those who have hanged themselves, try to entice to another attempt at suicide those who have been saved when attempting to hang themselves. For these the charm is broken by cutting the string, not by undoing it. If this precaution has been omitted, the danger may still be obviated by a ceremony in which a *Ma thân-vòng* is represented with a rope in his hand. They burn this little figure, and then the rope of the hanged man is cut in pieces.

The *Con-hoa*, the souls of those who have perished in fires, glide under the roofs in the form of bluish smoke on the anniversary of the day of their death, or at fixed times, and cause spontaneous fires very difficult to extinguish.

The *Con-sắc*, or vexatious spirits, are especially fond of tormenting young children, in whom they cause frights, convulsions, head eruptions, etc. Twelve in number, they each rule an hour of the day. An offering of twelve red handkerchiefs, twelve mirrors, and twelve fans, while the mother and the child are under a bamboo frame, wards off their evil influence. Amulets, such as tigers' claws, vultures' vertebræ, or a tiger's skull, hung above the children's cradles, drive away the *Con-sắc*.

The *Môc-chân* dwell in trees, and continue to live in them even when their dwelling-place has been cut down and used as material for building houses. These demons, lying down on people when asleep, give them nightmare.

It is well to beware also of the *Ma-dun*, gigantic ghosts of buffaloes and elephants, and especially the *Cô-hồn*, or abandoned souls, who, having died a violent death, return to torment the living. They are appeased by offerings of leaves of imitation gold or silver, or counterfeit bank-notes. The wandering souls which have not had burial take shelter by 'millions and tens of millions' in the shade of shrubs and trees. At night they come in crowds to attack people passing on their way, and they send misfortune to those who forget them. So large is their number and so sad their lot, that small temples of wood or plaited bamboo are erected for them, or small stone altars, sometimes formed simply by a stone at the foot of a tree. The individual whose business is in danger tries to gain the favour of these miserable souls by oblations, which almost always consist of paper representations of bars of gold or silver,* paper shoes, and rice. The rice is scattered broadcast to the four cardinal points, while the offerer says: 'This is for the miserable souls who wander among the clouds, at the mercy of the winds, and whose bodies have rotted by the wayside or under the water. Let each single grain of rice produce one hundred. Let each hundred produce ten thousand, and let the wandering souls be satisfied.' The souls then hasten forward under the supervision of two spirits, one of which notifies them by ringing a bell, while the other, sword in hand, sees to the just division of the rice among the hungry souls.

4. Animal-worship.—From their ancient animal-cult the Annamese have retained some forms of worship, as well as a veneration born of fear, for a certain number of animals. The animal most dreaded is *Ông Cọp*, a title of respect equivalent

* The bar (*nén*) is a parallelopipedal ingot used as money. The bar of gold (*nén vàng*) weighs 390·5 gr., and is worth 1386·80 francs. The bar of silver (*nén bạc*) weighs 382 gr., and is of variable value.

to 'Sir Tiger.' This awe-inspiring feline is worshipped in many places, and has special priests or sorcerers, the *thầy-dông*. Small stone temples are erected to him, provided with two altars, the one a little back and on the top of the other. On the lower one a huge lamp burns in honour of the spirit who is the real patron of the temple. At the foot of this altar, *Ông Cop* is painted on a screen, seated, with bristling whiskers and sparkling eyes. Sometimes the temple has nothing on its altar except a stone tiger.

The *thầy-dông*, by means of a medium called *dông*, enter into communication with the spirits, and in their name exorcize, cure, give advice for the success of such and such a matter, etc.

This tiger, although so greatly respected, is nevertheless, in practical life, hunted with great keenness; and the Annamese, while eagerly pursuing it, from fear of being devoured by it, are careful to honour it and to speak of it with the most reverential fear. Among them fear or horror is often expressed by such exclamations as: '*Ma cop*,' 'Tiger's ghost!' '*Cọp lại*,' 'The tiger is coming!' etc.

To excuse the unreasonableness of this conduct, they imagine two kinds of tigers: those which feed on human flesh, are always on the outlook for slaughter, and which men should kill mercilessly; and the real tigers, creatures which are endowed with supernatural powers, have a horror of human flesh, and live in solitude at the foot of the mountains.

Being devoured by a tiger implies predestination or heredity. Predestination would come from a misdeed committed in a former existence, and thus avenged by the tiger. Heredity would be explained in another way: the soul and spirit of a man devoured by the tiger become, as it were, the tiger's servants, and even slaves. They must accompany him everywhere and beat down his prey before him. They entice prey by imitating the cry of an abandoned child, thus causing men to lose their way in the mountains, and they always attach themselves preferably to members of their own family. Hence, when the father is devoured by the tiger, there is every likelihood that the son will have the same fate. For this reason, when a person has perished by the teeth of the tiger, he is not buried in the family tomb, and his relatives cover themselves with talismans or prophylactic amulets.

The hairs of the tiger's whiskers may be used for making very dangerous poisons. So they are burned whenever the animal is caught. The tiger's claws ward off evil spirits. From his bones and teeth an efficacious cure for hiccough is derived.

They have a very great regard also for *Ông-Voi*, 'Sir Elephant,' who is considered as strong as he is modest, and for *Con trâm nư'ở'c*, 'the water buffalo,' a fabulous animal which causes the waters to divide before it. The person who holds a hair of this buffalo in his hand can cross a river dry-shod.

The dolphin (*Cá nư'ọ'c*, *Cá voi*) is very much revered, especially by the maritime population. He is believed to save shipwrecked sailors by carrying them on his back. They also give him the title of *Ông*, 'Grandfather,' 'My Lord,' 'The Venerable.' They make use of a periphrasis to announce his death, or say that he is dead and has received the official name of 'Spirit with the jade scales.'

The dead body of a dolphin encountered at sea is a presage of good fortune. It is taken ashore and buried with ceremony. The captain of the vessel that discovers it becomes the 'son of the dolphin,' conducts the obsequies, and wears the prescribed mourning. The bones of the dolphin, exhumed after three months and ten days, are laid in a sanctuary, this being a guarantee of prosperity for the whole village. Every boat, too, during its voyages, is on the outlook for the death of a dolphin. A village which possesses several dolphins' tombs may give one of them to a less fortunate village. The transference takes place with solemn rites, after the consent of the dolphin has been obtained in a ceremony with sacrifices.

Ông Tí, 'Sir Rat,' is invoked both by farmers, that he may not devour the rice which is being sown, and by sailors, that he may not gnaw their boat of woven bamboo.

Ông Tằm, 'Sir Silk-Worm,' is treated with the greatest deference during its breeding, in order to counteract the great mortality of its species. To *Ông Chà*, 'Sir Stag,' the peasants offer sacrifices, and beg of him not to devastate the fields of rice which they have planted in a newly-cleared corner of a forest, since normally the stag has every right to regard this very place as his home.

Ông Chang, 'Sir Boar' or 'Sir Wild Buffalo,' is implored in the same way to spare the harvests.

Serpents are the object of a worship equal to the fear which they inspire. They and the tigers are the great animal powers dreaded by the Annamese.

To meet a serpent is a bad omen. If they succeed in killing the serpent, they must be careful not to cut off its head with a knife, since it would escape and pursue them. So also, when holding a serpent by the tail, they must not let it wriggle about in the air, for feet would immediately grow on it. Pythons' fat (*con trăm*) makes a very good depilatory.

Certain millepeds have in their mouths a bright stone, the possession of which renders a person invulnerable to serpent bites.

The leech is the symbol of immortality, because it is indestructible. When killed it lives again; when cut in pieces it multiplies; if it has been dried, it becomes re-animated whenever it is put into water; if it is burnt, from its moistened ashes is born a crowd of young leeches. There is only one way of getting rid of it, to put it into a box along with some honey; then it disappears. There is reason to beware of the leech; for, if put into a person's ear, it creeps into the brain, multiplies in it, and devours it.

Pigeons have the gift of reading the future and foreseeing misfortune. When they abandon a house, it is a very bad omen.

The little gecko, or ceiling lizard (*Hemidactylus maculatus*, Dum. and Bib.), is dreaded because of its bite, which causes fatal suffocation. To avoid the consequences, the person must snatch a cornelian button from the first one he meets, rasp it in water, and swallow the beverage thus obtained.

The skink (*Euprepes rufescens*, Shaw) also causes a serious wound that may be cured by drinking the blood which escapes from a black cat's tail, the end of which has been cut off. When cooked, the skink is an excellent remedy for asthma and quinsy (mumps) in pigs.*

A mad dog inflicts bites which are fatal, unless some one manages to pull the three dog hairs that grow soon after on the bitten man's head; then he may recover.

Certain vegetables, material objects, and even the elements, require reverential treatment, for they may be receptacles of a mysterious power.

When a junk or a house is built, the sorcerer is sent for before it is occupied, and he exorcizes the spirits which might still be dwelling in the pieces of wood and might bring misfortune.

Before putting a new junk into the water, the sailors sacrifice to *Ông Hà Bá*, 'Lord of the River.' If, during their voyage, they notice in the middle of the water a tree-trunk which might knock against and capsize their vessel, they immediately sacrifice to *Ông Gốc*, 'Sir Tree-trunk.' They treat *Ông Thoi*, 'Sir Wind,' with equal consideration. If Annamese children, during their play, want to reach the fruit on a tree, they throw their sticks up at it and call on 'Sir Wind' to help them.

Aerolites (*tâm sét*), or 'meteoric stones,' are the objects of great reverence. They are supposed to be intimately associated with the lightning. They fall at each lightning flash followed by a thunder-peal, sink into the ground, and after three months and ten days † come out of it again.

The possession of an aerolite is a guarantee of good luck Aerolites chase away the evil spirits, which are terrified at their fall, and which at each peal of thunder run to take shelter under the hat or umbrella of the people they meet. Accordingly, at every peal of thunder the Annamese take care to raise their hats or umbrellas a little to guard against their intrusion.

Aerolite powder mixed with water keeps children safe from evil spirits. In smallpox it ensures regular and favourable suppuration.

The skull of a male (more especially of a child or a youth) who has been struck by lightning, which afterwards has had formulas recited over it, becomes a useful charm, and even a very good medium.

5. Priest-sorcery.—Beliefs so numerous and so entangled produce very complicated cults. All the various kinds of spirits have different requirements, and in order to secure their favour it is necessary to be fully aware of what they desire and of the offerings which they prefer. The common people are quite at a loss among their numerous charms, magical songs, exorcisms, and sacrifices. Hence arises a body of special priest-sorcerers among the Annamese.

The most numerous class is that of the *thầy phù thủy*, 'the masters of amulets and purificatory

* Needless to say, the virulence of the hemidactyl is a fable, and the skink seldom bites.

† The length of time of nearly all magical occurrences among the Annamese.

waters,' who have no regular temples, and who, when they go home, take their altar and the cult-objects with them. Some of them are the celebrants in temples erected by individuals. They officiate there at certain anniversaries, or when a person is imploring the intervention of the spirit of these temples.

Another class, of a higher order, the *thầy-pháp* or *thầy-dồng*, practise only in their homes. Having a very numerous clientèle, they are often able to build stone temples in which to officiate, and which are their own property. They are assisted by a *dây*, or 'suppliant,' who acts as a medium between the invoked spirit and the petitioner; for hypnotism, real or feigned, plays the chief rôle in these ceremonies. All these sorcerers derive their power from certain good or evil spirits, to which they have dedicated themselves, and which, after being raised, remain in direct communication with them, possessing them and speaking through their voices. The sorcerers can not only command the spirits, but are also able to influence the normal order of occurrences in nature. They raise the dead, cast lots, practise spells, and send telepathic suggestions to persons whom they wish to employ against others. They can instantaneously change the nature of beings and substances, transform a savoury dish into filth, or change a dog into a cock; they can send diseases, defects, or pains to whomsoever they choose.

They can also employ their power to do good. It is they who cure illnesses, exorcize people possessed and houses haunted by demons, cause rain to fall or to cease, and find out treasures. They do not all have an equal amount of power, and when any one is annoyed by the spite of a sorcerer, the only thing to do is to set a more powerful sorcerer against him.

The sorcerers still manufacture love philtres and talismans, for ensuring success in love, from the bodies (which are difficult to get) of two serpents that have died while fighting with each other, and one of which has been half swallowed by the other. To achieve the same end the ordinary people make use of less complicated charms, which consist in scorching in a pan the whole or part of a garment belonging to the person by whom they wish to be loved.

Some sorcerers are regular spell doctors, who perform their spells by the use of tubercules (*ngâm-ngai*). They themselves are called *thầy-ngai*, and have great skill in killing, causing illness, and inspiring love or hatred. They secretly cultivate the tubercules in their garden or their house, or in some isolated place, and then go and choose the one that they need at the appointed hour. While uprooting it, they recite incantations over it, informing it of the cruel design to be accomplished and of the hour at which it is to take place. Then, either directly or by means of a third person, who in most cases knows nothing about the part which they are making him play, they endeavour to bring the least particle of *ngai* into contact with the enemy whom they wish to harm. The latter is immediately struck by disease, and may die unless he happens to get the better of it, or unless the hatred of the avenger does not go the length of death. Only another sorcerer can cure him.

A popular superstition claims that these *thầy-ngai* are not the only persons who threaten the safety of the people; that there are in existence some families of professional poisoners, who, on various pretexts, slip into their houses and poison their provisions, especially the water. These persons poison from filial piety, because one of their ancestors poisoned somebody. His descendants must imitate him at least once a year, to pacify his spirit. If they did not succeed, they would have to sacrifice one of their own kin. That is the reason why, when their odious practices have achieved the slightest success, they stop them and go away, having thus performed their duty. On account of this fear, the Annamese take great care that strangers do not get near the family provisions, especially the jars where they keep the water.

6. Fortune-telling.—The Annamese have also fortune-tellers (*thầy-bói*), who are nearly always blind, and rather poorly remunerated. They cast nativities by means of copper coins, whose position, heads or tails, determines the prediction.

In the temples the divining logs and rods may be interrogated. The logs are two pieces of lacquered wood, like cotyledons, which give an affirmative answer when both fall on the same side, and a negative if the other way.

The rods, about thirty in number, have figures in Chinese characters, which, on being referred to a horoscope, give the reply of destiny. Other oracle books are read by means of wooden dice.

The Annamese practise cheiromancy, physiognomy, and phrenology. Several fortune-tellers, instead of examining the hand of the querist, obtain their prognostications from a cock's or hen's foot. Others tell fortunes from the lines of the hand, the lines of the face, and the protuberances of the head all at once.

7. Superstitions.—Is it necessary to add that the Annamese believe in signs and omens? The following is a list of the most common superstitions:

They must begin the year with a lucky transaction if they want to make sure of ending it in luck. It is for this reason that during the first days of the year shopkeepers sell cheap in order to sell much, and thus guarantee a regular sale all the year.

On the other hand, they all shut their doors until midday on the first of the year, in order to avoid seeing or being visited by people bringing bad luck.

Meeting an old woman is a sign of failure.

Meeting a pregnant woman has the same significance. If they have come out on business, it is wise, after such an omen, to go back to the house.

A tradesman who enters a house where there is an infant less than a month old, is followed by misfortune for three months and ten days, unless he wards it off by burning a handful of salt immediately on his return home.

Every son whose father has died a violent death is threatened with the same fate if he does not appease the evil spirits.

If a person who has weak eyes enters a room where a husband and wife are lying, he becomes totally blind.

The wick of a lamp burning well means work and prosperity. If it gets blackened and sputters, beware of thieves.

Numerous gossamers announce a bad crop; in the eye, coming blindness.

A singing fire means discord in the house.

To walk on paper with writing on it is in itself a serious fault. If there are Cambodian, Shan, or Arabo-Malayan characters written on it, misfortune will certainly follow; and if it is a pregnant woman that commits the fault, she will miscarry.

A lamp that goes out, a broken cup, and girls or women looking into a gambling-house without playing, are omens of loss for the banker.

When young people of either sex who have not arrived at the age of puberty touch the unformed flowers or fruits of mango or banana trees, they cause them to fall.

When trees persist in yielding no fruit, it is necessary, in order to obtain it, to threaten, on the fifth day of the fifth month, to cut them down. Every year some cuts are made with a hatchet in the mango trees to persuade them to produce fruit.

A locust flying low, a cawing crow, and a croaking frog, are all signs of rain.

A buffalo coming into a house, a bird flying round about it, and a spider at the end of a thread, are presages of misfortune.

A fish leaping into a boat signifies a bad catch, unless it is immediately cut in two and thrown back quickly into the water.

Fishing for the porpoise, the messenger of the demons, rouses their anger.

The cry of the *khách* bird (*Crypsirhina varians*), heard in the East, foretells a visit; in the West, news.

The cries of the gecko, 'Tokkê! tokkê!' an odd number of times are of good omen; an even number, of bad omen.

The cry of the musk-rat foretells a visit that evening or the following day.

The prolonged whining of dogs signifies a calamity.

The crowing of a cock at midday gives rise to fear that the daughters of the house will become ill.

The cry of night-birds announces illness or death.

The grating or cracking of inanimate objects foretells their future. If it is a coffin that cracks, it means that it is going to be bought. If it is a safe, it means that it is to receive money.

Do not open a safe during the night for fear of attracting thieves. Do not open it on the last day of the year, or the first three days of the next year. It is a sign of expense.

When a sword appears in a dream, it is a sign that one will soon have to be used. When it strikes against the wall, it means that an execution is near.

Guns that shake denote the approach of the enemy. Guns are, besides, regarded as being endowed with a sort of life. The Annamese sometimes think them ill, and give them medicine.

8. Diseases.—It is quite natural that, in a country where diseases are supposed to result from the malevolence of a spirit or the vengeance of a sorcerer, the popular medicine should consist of empirical remedies and magical performances.

The doctor and the sorcerer attend the invalid in turn, and it is not the former that is most listened to. The people try to prevent misfortune and its visitations by amulets and sacrifices to the spirits. If these precautions fail, they have recourse to the doctor (and they do not pay him unless he succeeds in curing the patient); and in grave cases they nearly always call in the sorcerer instead.

The two most terrible diseases that the Annamese have to do with are *cholera* and *smallpox.* Quite special talismans are needed against the demon of cholera, those which serve in ordinary illnesses being insufficient. The frightful rapidity of the disease does not allow of lengthy therapeutics.

Smallpox, which is even more frequent, is perhaps dreaded still more. It is never spoken of except in periphrases, and its pustules receive the reverential designation of 'Ông.' Smallpox is attributed to evil spirits, and especially to the souls of persons who have already died of smallpox (*Con ma dâu*). The latter are responsible for all the serious cases. The mild cases are due to predestination. Whenever a sick person is attacked by smallpox, he is isolated, not from fear of contagion, but from fear of the evil spirits which have taken possession of the invalid. Nevertheless, especially if a child is the victim, the family never leave him alone, and they surround him with a net to prevent the approach of the *Con ma dâu.*

When the disease takes a serious turn, many of the physicians abandon their patients, not so much, perhaps, to avoid attempting an impossible task, as to be safe from the anger of the *Con ma dâu.* In fact, one of their proverbs says: 'If you cure smallpox, it will have its revenge; if you cure phthisis, it passes over to the curer.' It is believed that the children of doctors die from the smallpox from which their father has saved others.

During times of epidemic, if a family has already lost a child from smallpox, they are afraid that he will come and take away his surviving brothers and sisters, and they sacrifice at his grave to prevent him from leaving it. Amulets and witchcraft are the only cures for smallpox.

During the course of the illness they place under the bed of the smallpox patient a *cá trê*, a fish with a smooth green skin, of the *siluridæ* genus, which is believed to become impregnated with the venom of the smallpox until it stiffens with it.

In order that the erythematous stage may pass quickly into the pustular, and to favour the further formation of crusts, the patient eats shrimps and crabs. On the other hand, when desquamation has set in, he eats fish with scales in order to help the peeling-off process. Vermicelli is expressly prohibited, for it would change into a multitude of worms in the softened liver and lungs of the patient.

So also, if the smallpox patient wishes to prevent a relapse when convalescent, he must avoid walking barefooted on hens' dung.

Lastly, when smallpox (or any other epidemic) is raging, everybody sacrifices to the crowd of maleficent spirits known by the generic name of *quan-ôn*, the primary cause of all ills. For these sacrifices, at the beginning of the hot season, when the death-rate is highest, they manufacture or buy paper figures representing the people whom they wish to be saved, and burn them in the village square. The offerings intended to appease the evil spirits are placed in little paper boats, which they send off at the edge of the water.

9. Birth.—The Annamese, who are a very prolific race, are anxious to have numerous posterity. They try above all to avoid miscarriages, still-born children, and infant mortality. In their eyes still-born or prematurely born children are special spirits in short successive incarnations, denoted by the name of *Con lôn* ('entering life'). The mother of a *Con lôn* is considered contagious. No young woman would accept a betel-pellet from her. They even avoid speaking about her.

Successive miscarriages are believed to be re-incarnations of the same spirit. In order to get rid of this evil influence, when a woman who has had one or more miscarriages is about to be confined again, a young dog is killed and cut in three pieces, which are buried under the woman's bed; and with the blood of the dog amulets are traced, which are taken to the future mother.

The evil spirit which presides at these premature deaths is called *Mẹ con ranh,* 'the mother of abortions.' It is represented in the form of a woman in white, sitting in a tree, where she rocks her children.

To drive away this demon from the body of the pregnant woman, they exorcize it. For this purpose they make two small figures representing a mother with a child in her arms, and burn them, after the sorcerer has adjured the evil spirit with threats no longer to torment the family which is performing the exorcism.

When a woman is pregnant, there is a very simple way of determining beforehand the sex of the child. Some one calls the woman, and she turns to reply. If she turns to the left, a boy will be born; if to the right, a girl.

At the time of her confinement the woman is subjected to a special diet of dry salted food, and a fire (*nám bêp*) is kept burning under the bed—a custom which is common to all the Indo-Chinese. They invoke the twelve goddesses of birth and other deities.

If the parturient woman is in danger, the father prostrates himself and entreats the child to be born. Immediately after the birth the young mother is trampled under foot by the matron who has been attending her, and then fumigations and washings take place.

The part of the umbilical cord that is close to the section is preserved. It is, according to the Annamese, a powerful febrifuge for the use of children. Then they fix the prohibition post (*cám kham*) before the door. It is a bamboo cane, on the top of which is placed a lighted coal, the burning side turned towards the inside for a boy, towards the outside for a girl. It gets its name from the fact that it prohibits from entering the house women whose confinements have been difficult or followed by accidents, and who might bring bad fortune.

Thirty days after the birth, during which the mother has been isolated, all the things belonging to her are burnt.

Various ceremonies then take place, with offerings of fowls, bananas, rice, etc., to thank the goddesses of birth, and afterwards to give fluent speech to the child. They take special care not to pronounce any words of evil omen, as, *e.g.*, speaking of illnesses, among others of thrush, for fear of giving it to the child. They also avoid frying anything in the house. That would cause blisters on the mother and the newly-born child.

As it is not quite customary to enter the room where the mother and the child are lying, each member of the family, in order that the child may make his acquaintance and not cry on seeing him, dips a part of his coat in a little water, which is given to the child to drink.

Towards the end of the first month after the birth, they sacrifice to the birth-goddesses and give the child a name. As far as possible, this name must never have belonged to any member of the father's or the mother's family. The rice that is offered on this occasion is tinted in five colours: white, black, red, blue, and yellow. Each of the invited guests presents a gift to the child.

The child that sucks the milk of a pregnant woman soon dies (of mesenteric atrophy), because that milk is supposed not to have reached its maturity.

It is supposed that, on awakening in the morning, a person's bite is venomous, though it ceases to be poisonous when the vapours which cause the venom have passed away. In order to avoid such a bite, the Annamese mother does not suckle her infant until it cries.

When a child remains sickly and difficult to bring up, to baffle the evil spirits which are tormenting it, the parents pretend to sell it either to the spirit of the hearth, or to the sorcerer, or to the Buddhist bonze. It then receives another name and is re-sold to its parents, as if it were a strange child.

When the child is one year old, a fresh sacrifice to the birth-goddesses takes place. Then they spread out playthings and tools before the child. From his choice they infer his future aptitudes.

When a child less than a year old sneezes, they call to him '*Com cá*' ('rice and fish!'). The same cry is raised when he faints, or when he starts nervously in his sleep.

When a child is subject to hiccough, they stick on his forehead the end of a betel-leaf bitten off by the teeth.

When a young child is taken away on a journey, they make a stroke or a cross on his forehead with a cinder from the hearth, so that the spirit of the hearth may protect him from the evil spirits during the journey.

When they cannot take a child under seven years of age away on a journey, they stick a little wax on his head in order that he may not regret his parents.

10. Marriage.—Marriage does not admit of so many magical rites. But when a marriage has been arranged and presents exchanged, the engaged couple consider themselves as married; and if one of them were to die, the other would wear mourning.

Misconduct of the girl before her marriage is strictly forbidden. In case of pregnancy, she is compelled to name her seducer. If he denies his guilt, he is retained until the birth of the child. An official proof by blood then takes place, which is called *thich man*. They link one of the infant's fingers with one of the suspected person's, make a slight incision in each, and catch the blood in a vessel. If the two kinds of blood form two separate clots, the accused is declared innocent; if they mix, he is guilty, and receives punishment.

11. Death.—Funerals are as complicated as they are long and expensive. That is why certain families are not able to celebrate them until five or six months after the death, and are obliged to inter their dead provisionally.

The funeral rites include the putting on of mourning garments and the beginning of the lamentations. At the head of the funeral procession which conducts the dead man to his last resting-place walks the bonze; next come men bearing white streamers, on which are inscribed the virtues and the name of the deceased; next, under the shade of a large umbrella, the hearse of the soul, a small winding-sheet which is supposed to contain the soul, sometimes replaced by the tablet of the deceased; then, in grand funerals, a puppet, dressed in beautiful clothes, representing the deceased; and last of all the hearse, followed by the family and friends. All along the road they throw gold and silver papers representing money, to attract the attention of the evil spirits and secure an uninterrupted passage. The coffin, after being lowered into the grave, is not covered with earth until the sorcerer has ascertained, by means of a compass, the best orientation for it. A lengthy and pompous sacrifice, which only the rich can afford, terminates the ceremony.

Fresh sacrifices take place after seven weeks, then after a hundred days, one year, two years, and twenty-seven months after the death. About three years after the death, the corpse is exhumed in order that its bones may be enclosed in the regular tomb, after which there is an anniversary sacrifice—a ceremony in which they burn a copy of the imperial diploma conferring a posthumous title, and a new ceremony, of Buddhist origin, called the great fast or deliverance of the souls, which will obtain for the deceased the remission of all his sins. The sacrifice concludes with offerings to the wandering and hungry souls.

LITERATURE.—A. Landes, 'Notes sur les mœurs et les superstitions populaires des Annamites' in *Cochinchine française: Excursions et Reconnaissances*, vi., 1880, 447–464, vii., 1881, 137–148, viii., 1881, 351–370, xiv., 1882, 250–269, xv., 1883, 580–593, and 'Contes et légendes annamites,' *ib.* xx., 1884, 297–314, xxi., 1885, 130–151, xxii., 1885, 359–412, xxiii., 1885, 39–90, xxv., 1886, 105–160, xxvi., 1886, 297–316; L. Cadière, 'Les pierres de foudre' in *Bulletin de l'École française d'Extrême-Orient*, ii., 1902, 284–285, 'Coutumes populaires de la vallée du Nguônso'n,' *ib.* 352–386; and 'Philosophie populaire annamite' in *Anthropos*, ii. 1907, 116 ff., iii. 1908, 248 ff., etc.; G. Dumoutier, *Les chants et les traditions populaires des Annamites*, Paris, 1888, *Les symboles, les emblèmes et les accessoires du culte chez les Annamites*, Paris, 1891, *Le rituel funéraire des Annamites*, Hanoï, 1904 (45 plates), and 'Étude d'ethnographie religieuse annamite: sorcellerie et divination' in *Actes du xiᵉ congrès international des orientalistes*, sec. 2, Paris, 1899, 275–410; E. Luro, *Le pays d'Annam*, Paris, 1897; A+B (E. Souvignet), 'Variétés tonkinoises' in *Paganisme annamite*, 241–324, Hanoï, 1903; P. Giran, *Psychologie du peuple annamite*, Paris, 1904; E. Diguet, *Les Annamites, société, coutumes, religions*, Paris, 1906; Dỗ Thân, 'Une Version annamite du conte de Cendrillon' in *Bull. de l'École franç. d'Ext.-Or.* vii. 1907, 101–107.

ANTOINE CABATON.

ANNIHILATION.—It has been a matter of dispute whether anything once brought into existence can ever be utterly annihilated; and further, that possibility being conceded, whether this fate is in store for the souls of the impenitent wicked. Of these questions the first is purely theoretic and academic, appealing only to the interest of the few; the second, like other eschatological problems, has been keenly and widely debated. It is a remarkable example of the divergence in point of view between East and West, that the destiny which in the one hemisphere has been propounded as the final reward of virtue should in the other be regarded as the extremest penalty of obstinate wickedness. Where the theory of annihilation has found favour with Christian believers, its acceptance has usually been due rather to a recoil from the thought of the eternal duration of future punishment, than to the influence of the positive philosophical and theological arguments which can be urged on its behalf. Distracted between an equal reluctance to accept the eternity of hell or to admit the universal salvation of all men, some thinkers have found a way out of their difficulty by questioning the truth of the exclusive alternative between eternal blessedness and eternal woe hereafter. Thus they have been led to examine a third possibility, viz. the complete extinction of the wicked. The discussion of the problem belongs to that region of thought where both philosophy and theology have a claim to be heard. Whether the nature of the soul is such that the cessation of its existence is conceivable, is a question which cannot be argued except upon a basis of philosophical principles; what may be the bearing of the teaching of the Bible and of the commonly received tradition of the Church upon the point can be determined only by exegesis and by study of the history of dogma.

1. The question stated.—Obviously, the controversy concerning annihilation, so understood, arises only among those who are at least agreed as to the fact of survival after death. It is legitimate, therefore, at the outset to dismiss from consideration those theories which represent death as being of necessity the end of individual being. We are not here concerned to rebut the opinions of the materialist, who holds life to be a function of matter, or of the pantheist, for whom death is the moment of the re-absorption of the individual life into the common fund of existence. Subsequent, however, to agreement as to survival after death comes a parting of the ways, according as men accept or reject the view that the life so prolonged is destined to continue for ever. That it must so continue is the opinion of believers in the natural immortality of the soul. Nor must those who hold this view be accused of making an extravagant claim on behalf of human nature, as though they maintained the soul's independent and absolute immortality. Admitting that the life of the soul, though prolonged to infinity, must always rest upon the sustaining power of God, they contend that this relation of dependence is outside the bounds of time, and everlasting. By the annihilationist, on the other hand, the opinion of the soul's natural immortality, even in this restricted and legitimate sense, is considered a dangerous error, the root out of which has grown a false eschatology. In place of the conception of an immortal life belonging essentially and inalienably to the soul, he would substitute that of an existence naturally destined to extinction, except under certain specified conditions. Upon this denial of the soul's natural immortality he bases his theory, and, though professing a positive creed and ready to give an account of it, he justly claims that, logically, the *onus probandi* as to immortality lies rather with those who affirm than with himself who denies that doctrine.

2. The natural immortality of the soul called in question.—This is not the place in which to state at any length or with any completeness the argument for the immortality of the soul. It will be sufficient if we so far indicate the grounds of belief as to render intelligible the objections which have been urged on the other side. Undoubtedly, the strongest force working in favour of a general acceptance of the belief in natural immortality has been the dominant influence of Platonism in the earlier stages of the development of Christian doctrine. 'Our creeds,' it has been said, 'are the formulæ of victorious Platonism.'* And though that statement may stand in need of some qualification, yet it is true in the main of the belief in immortality. The conclusion of the *Phœdo* has become the accepted tenet of the Church. Moreover, it is remarkable how comparatively insignificant are the additions which have been made to Plato's argument since it was first constructed by his genius. In the reasons commonly urged to-day for belief in immortality we may recognize the main features of his proof, if only due allowance be made for the translation of his thought from the modes of ancient Greece to those of the present age. His argument, it will be remembered, is threefold.

It begins with insistence on the fact that in nature there are no absolutely new beginnings, but an alternation from one state to its opposite, as from motion to rest and from rest to motion. Since, in the history of the soul, life and death are thus related to one another as alternations, the latter, he argued, cannot possibly be a state of non-existence. Secondly, the soul's capacity for the recognition of truth is compared with memory, and is brought forward as proof of her pre-existence before union with the body. Hence may be inferred her continued existence after the dissolution of that union by death. Thirdly, the kinship of the soul with the ideas of which she is cognizant, and her identification with the idea of life, render self-contradictory, and therefore inconceivable, the thought of her annihilation.

The three lines of Plato's argument supply us with a classification under which the modern pleas for immortality may be arranged. Parallel with the first division of his proof is the modern appeal to the principle of the conservation of energy. As in the physical world energy is neither created nor destroyed, but transformed, so it is inferred that psychical energy likewise must be subject to transformation rather than to annihilation. Secondly, all idealist philosophers have found their most powerful argument for the immortality of the soul in the fact that she apprehends truth by means of powers which transcend the limits of time and space. The *a priori* forms of thought are taken as proofs of the immortal nature of the soul. Thirdly, Plato's insistence on the relation of the soul to the eternal and unchanging ideas is parallel to the appeal of religion to the kinship of the soul with the eternal and unchanging Divine Being. Lastly, the practical and ethical value of the belief in immortality and in the prospect of future rewards and punishments has been keenly appreciated alike in ancient and modern times.

Is it possible along these lines to establish a certain conclusion in favour of the soul's natural immortality? In that case, the theory of annihilation would be barred at the outset. But the required certainty is not forthcoming. However firmly convinced the student may be in his own mind of the fact of human immortality, he must nevertheless admit that, technically, the philosophic proof of the doctrine is far from reaching the standard of demonstration. The history of human thought enforces the admission. Even among the immediate inheritors of the Platonic tradition there were many to whom the opinion of the master on this point carried no conviction. Still less was the tenet of individual immortality acceptable to Peripatetics, Stoics, or Epicureans. And as in ancient times the world remained unconvinced, so to-day the philosophic arguments for individual immortality, however combined and expanded, are by no means universally admitted.

If we take the arguments in the order given above, we shall find that each in turn has been subjected to damaging criticism. Energy (it is retorted) cannot indeed be destroyed, but it may be dissipated. What reason, therefore, have we for thinking that the force which underlies the individual life will be exempt from the general law of dissipation? If the premises of the idealist philosophy be conceded, there is, doubtless, a legitimate inference to the existence of an immortal element in the human spirit, but that conclusion does not decide the question of the destiny of the individual. Even the admission of the kinship of the soul with the Divine Being is consistent with the denial of individual immortality. The ethical instinct which demands that the injustices and inequalities of the present life shall be rectified in the future—certainly by far the most powerful influence in inducing the belief in immortality—might be satisfied by the conception of a survival not necessarily endless. 'In truth,' writes Lord Macaulay, 'all the philosophers, ancient and modern, who have attempted without the aid of revelation to prove the immortality of man—from Plato down to Franklin —appear to us to have failed deplorably.'* Whately is of a like opinion. 'That the natural immortality of man's soul is discoverable by reason may be denied on the ground that it has not been discovered yet.'† Were it necessary, it would be easy to multiply quotations to the same effect.

That there is a living principle in man which cannot be affected by bodily death is a proposition from which few but declared materialists would dissent. That this living principle will manifest itself in a prolongation of the individual life is a conclusion for which there is a large measure of philosophic probability, though no demonstrative proof. That the life so prolonged will continue for ever is a tenable hypothesis, but it cannot be presented as an inference from universally admitted premises. Hence, in the absence of any proof of the conviction of natural immortality, theories of annihilation must obviously be given a fair hearing. They cannot be dismissed *in limine* on the plea that they are in contradiction to one of the accepted truths of natural religion.

3. Arguments for annihilation.—The hypothesis of annihilation has in its favour the following considerations.—(*a*) *Cosmological.* If the souls of the wicked are eventually to be annihilated, then the process of creation and redemption may be represented as destined to issue in unqualified success. When all that is evil shall have been finally removed, nothing will remain but light and love; whereas every theory of everlasting punishment involves the admission that a shadow of impenetrable darkness will hang for ever over a portion of the universe.

It was maintained by some mediæval theologians that the existence of this shadow would intensify by contrast the enjoyment of the light by the saved.‡ A more humane age recoils from the suggestion of such a reason for the everlasting duration of misery, and indeed takes precisely the opposite line, holding that the happiness of the saved could not be complete while other members of their race were suffering (cf. Rothe, *Dogmatik*, iii. § 48). Even though evil be regarded as powerless and fettered, stripped of all its capacity for assault and intrigue, yet its continued existence would seem to constitute a protest against the Divine government—a melancholy proof that the perversity of free will had in some measure frustrated the Divine intention. Advocates of the theory of annihilation maintain that the improbability of the everlasting continuance of evil in any shape gives the measure of the probability of the total destruction of the wicked.

(*b*) *Psychological.* A further argument in the same direction is derived from the nature of the

* Inge, *Personal Idealism and Mysticism*, 1907, p. 67.

* *Essays*, iii. 211 (pop. ed. 1870, p. 549).

† *On the Future Life*, p. 17; cf. E. White, *Life in Christ*, p. 84.

‡ Thomas Aquinas, *Summa*, iii. sup. xciv. 1.

soul and its relation to moral evil. All evil is self-contradictory, and therefore tends to be self-destructive. The wicked soul is not only at enmity with others, but divided against itself. And if the doctrine of natural immortality be abandoned, what is there to prevent the internal discord from accomplishing the work of disintegration, and ending in the final dissolution of the individual being? That evil is in its essence negative rather than positive, has been a widely accepted theory. It would seem to suggest the conclusion that the soul which identifies itself with this principle of non-being will become less and less alive, until it passes out of existence altogether. Sin, it has been said, may be regarded as a 'poison to which the vital forces of the soul must in the end give way by passing into sheer extinction' (cf. Gladstone, *Studies subsidiary to Butler*, 1896, p. 218).

(*c*) *Practical.* So strong is the tendency towards Pragmatism at the present day, that little objection is raised when the acceptance of a theory is justified by an appeal to its supposed beneficial effects upon practice. To judgments of value, as distinct from judgments of fact, is assigned a special validity of their own. In accordance with these principles, annihilationists have pointed to the influence of their doctrine upon the moral life of man. The prospect of annihilation for the wicked, and eternal life for the righteous, provides (they tell us) a legitimate appeal alike to the hopes and to the fears of mankind. Nothing can be a greater inducement to moral effort than the hope of acquiring an immortality otherwise unattainable; nothing a greater deterrent than the threatened doom of total extinction. If capital punishment upon earth arouses in the highest degree the fears of the criminal, the thought of an execution in which soul as well as body shall be involved in a common destruction is sufficient to appal the most indifferent and the most hardened.

4. Counter arguments.—Counter considerations to the above arguments are not wanting, and have been brought forward with effect by critics of the theory. (*a*) Whatever plausibility there may be in the argument that sinners must cease to exist in order that the final state of the universe may be altogether holy, is greatly lessened by reflexion on the obvious truth of our profound ignorance with regard to the whole problem of evil. Where the mystery is so impenetrable, it is well to remember that any inference must be hazardous in the extreme. And, after all, the ultimate and inexplicable riddle of the world lies in the present fact of evil rather than in the questions concerning its origin and its end. If we cannot reach even an inkling of the solution of the mystery of evil, present though it be before our eyes and lodged in our own hearts, we are in no position to indulge in rash speculations as to the mode of its introduction into the universe, and the likelihood of its final removal therefrom. Though confession of ignorance is never a very acceptable conclusion to any argument, yet along this line we can arrive at no other result.

(*b*) Nor, again, does the argument from the nature of the soul produce conviction. Advocates of the theory of annihilation are too apt to confuse absence of proof with proof to the contrary. Right as they may be in questioning the demonstrative cogency of the commonly received arguments for the immortality of the soul, they go beyond the mark in thereupon assuming its mortality. The positive arguments which can be produced to prove that the soul is subject to decay are at best conjectural. Ultimately they depend upon the assumption that the nature of the soul is complex, and therefore capable of disintegration. And that assumption is as much an unproved hypothesis as is the contrary theory of the soul's indiscerptibility.

(*c*) Lastly, the utilitarian arguments in favour of annihilation suffer from the weakness inherent in all considerations of that type. In spite of the stress which Pragmatists lay on the will to believe and on the credit due to judgments of value, it still remains true that the claims of the pure reason in speculation cannot be disregarded with impunity. A strong sense of the beneficial effects which will follow from a given belief may properly lead the inquirer to a diligent search for arguments pointing that way; it cannot dispense him from the obligation of finding them. Hence, though it be admitted that threatenings of hell-fire and never-ending torments belong to a stage of theological thought now outgrown, and have ceased to exercise a deterrent effect upon sinners; and though it be granted that a crude presentment of the theory of universal restoration may deaden the conscience and encourage a lamentable slackness of moral effort; and though it were true that an obvious way of avoiding these opposite dangers might be found in the adoption of the doctrine of annihilation, yet such a case would still be lacking in solid support. And, indeed, whatever be thought of the first two admissions, it cannot be denied that the last of the three is dubious in the extreme. Even where temporal interests only are concerned, it is one of the hardest problems of practical government to calculate correctly the deterrent effects of different punishments. *A fortiori* must it be a hopeless task to discover the comparative deterrent effects of the fear of eternal punishment and the fear of total extinction. If the theory of annihilation fails to commend itself on the grounds of reason, it can hardly hope to win general acceptance as a judgment of value.

5. Annihilation and Biblical eschatology.—In the literature of annihilation a great deal of space is devoted to the examination of passages of Scripture supposed to bear more or less directly upon the subject. In this article no attempt will be made to deal with particular passages and texts; it will be sufficient to point out why neither in the OT nor in the NT can we expect to find an explicit negative or affirmative answer to questions as to natural immortality. The gradual emergence of the hope of a future life among the Jews has formed the subject of prolonged and minute study, leading to some generally accepted results. Belief in a future life, beginning in Prophetic times as little more than a dim and uncertain hope, developed under the stress of national suffering and disaster until it succeeded in establishing itself as an integral part of the national creed. Long as the process was, yet throughout its whole course the issue of the soul's natural immortality seems never to have been raised.

Nor is this surprising, when the conditions under which the belief grew up are recognized. Belief in immortality did not supersede a definitely formulated view to the contrary, viz. a belief in the soul's mortality. In early times the Israelites had shared the common Semitic conceptions of the destiny of man after death. They had looked forward, not to annihilation, but to a shadowy existence in Sheol. It is maintained by Dr. Charles (*Critical History of the Future Life*, p. 47 ff.) that the gradual development of their monotheistic religion actually deepened the fear of death among them. The conclusion is less paradoxical than it appears at first sight. Believing the blessing of communion with God to be confined to this life, the more highly they came to rate that blessing, the more they dreaded its termination in death, the darker and drearier became the prospect of Sheol. In contrast with the state of the living, the abode of the dead was the land of forgetfulness, of darkness, and of emptiness. This gloomy view of death was still current among the Jews in the time of Christ, and we find it pressed to its logical conclusion in the Sadducean denial of the resurrection. Yet life in Sheol, however bare of all that makes life desirable, was better than nothingness.

Except in the latest books of the OT canon, where we may already trace the influence of Greek thought at work, the possibility of complete annihilation is not contemplated in the OT. Hence, though it is true that in the OT there is no declaration of belief in the soul's natural immortality, yet it is equally true that there is no counter declaration of its possible extinction. The question whether the soul could or could not die entirely had not yet been asked. To attempt to find in the language of the writers of the OT a definite 'yes' or 'no' is to be guilty of an anachronism.

In the NT the situation is somewhat different. Contact with Greek thought and with the prevalent scepticism of the heathen world had by this time familiarized Jewish thinkers with the philosophic aspect of the problem. So far there is no reason why any NT writer should not deal with the question of the nature of the soul's life, and with the possibility of its death. In some Apocalyptic writings of earlier date than the Christian era, the annihilation of the enemies of Israel is foretold as one of the events of the last days (cf. Enoch xxxviii. 5, 6, Apoc. Bar. lxxii. 4-6 ; Charles, *op. cit.* pp. 240, 305). But in the NT the indications as to the ultimate fate of the wicked are of doubtful interpretation.

Nor is the reason far to seek. Apostles and Evangelists were concerned primarily not with the theory of human destinies, but with the practical task of propagating the faith. In their preaching, a doctrine of the last things undoubtedly occupied a prominent place; but the time for any discussion of the presuppositions of Christian eschatology had not yet arrived. It was enough for them to insist on the glorious certainty of eternal life through Jesus Christ, and on the inevitable penalty of the wrong-doer in the hereafter. The language of which they make use must not be treated as though it were deliberately chosen in view of possible differences of opinion as to the duration of the future life of the wicked.

When due allowance is made for the inexactitude of popular language, it will appear that the NT no less than the OT leaves the question of the soul's natural immortality altogether undetermined. On the one hand, the expression 'immortal soul' is notably absent, and, so far as it goes, this is evidence of the absence of the idea from the cycle of primitive Christian conceptions. On the other hand, the words 'death' and 'destruction,' freely employed in the NT to describe the fate of the wicked, cannot carry the weight of inference which the annihilationists desire to place upon them.

E. White's book, *Life in Christ*, affords an example of the attempt to discover evidence for an Apostolic doctrine of annihilation in the language of the NT. Of this work, J. Agar Beet, who himself raises an emphatic protest against the rigid enforcement of the traditional doctrine, sums up his criticism as follows: 'Thus fails, in my view, Mr. White's main argument. Throughout his interesting and able volume I find no proof of the ultimate extinction of the wicked except that contained in "the plain meaning" of two Greek words [ἀποθνήσκειν, ἀπόλλυσθαι]. And that this is their plain meaning, *i.e.* the only one they fairly admit, is disproved by their use in classical Greek and in the Greek Bible' (*The Last Things*, p. 301). Neither for nor against annihilation is the language of Scripture explicit beyond the reach of controversy.

6. Annihilation and Patristic eschatology.— The eschatological thought of the Early Fathers was influenced alike by the ideas which Christianity inherited from Judaism, and by conceptions as to the life and nature of the soul generally current in the ancient world. The difficulty which they experienced in harmonizing conceptions gathered from different sources into one consistent view, reveals itself in the occasional ambiguity of their language on this matter. They do not speak with unequivocal clearness as to the natural immortality of the soul. Christianity stimulated and encouraged that keen sense of the value of individual existence which made the Greeks turn with abhorrence from the thought of extinction.

How vehement was their antipathy is indicated in a well-known passage in Plutarch. 'I might almost say,' he writes, 'that all men and women would readily submit themselves to the teeth of Cerberus and to the punishment of carrying water in a sieve, if only they might remain in existence and escape the doom of annihilation.'*

* *Non poss. suav. vivi sec. Epicur.* 1104.

Yet, notwithstanding the force of this feeling against extinction, the denial of its possibility contained in the Platonic doctrine of the soul's natural immortality did not find general acceptance. It was rejected, for example, by Justin Martyr (*Tryph.* v.), by Tatian (*ad Græcos*, xiii.), by Theophilus of Antioch (*ad Autolyc.* II. xxvii.), by Irenæus (*adv. Hær.* II. xxxiv.), and by the *Clement. Homil.* (III. vi.). At the same time it must be remembered that many of these denials may be most naturally interpreted as repudiations of the theory that the soul is independently and inherently immortal, and must not therefore be taken to be identical with an assertion of belief in the eventual extinction of wicked souls. This explanation, however, will not hold good in every case. In Arnobius, for example, there is no possibility of misunderstanding. He is unmistakably an annihilationist.

It is remarkable how closely Arnobius anticipates many of the modern arguments, insisting on the ethical value of his theory, and maintaining that the doctrine of an ineradicable immortality, no less than the supposed prospect of immediate extinction at the moment of death, renders men careless of the rewards and punishments of a future life; whereas no more powerful influence can be brought to bear upon the character than the offered alternative between life and death (*adv. Nation.* II. xxxii.). The extinction which he foretells is to be the inevitable result of the punishments which the wicked will justly incur hereafter: 'Hæc est hominis mors vera, cum animæ nescientes Deum per longissimi temporis cruciatum consumentur igni fero, in quem illas jacient quidam crudeliter sævi, et ante Christum incogniti et ab solo sciente detecti' (c. xiv.).

But Arnobius stands alone in his development of this theory. Platonic conceptions as to the nature of the soul and its essential immortality became predominant. To this result Augustine contributed the weight of his immense influence. He is, however, careful to warn his readers against attributing any independent immortality to the soul.

Commenting on the Biblical account of the creation of man, he writes: 'Cavendum est ne anima non a Deo facta natura sed ipsius Dei substantia tamquam unigenitus filius, quod est verbum eius, aut aliqua eius particula esse credatur, tamquam illa natura atque substantia qua Deus est quidquid est commutabilis esse potest' (*Epp.* ccv. 19).

7. Annihilation and Scholastic philosophy.— In later centuries, the Schoolmen discussed the abstract question whether it is conceivable that anything should pass absolutely out of existence. Thomas Aquinas answered in the negative. His argument, briefly recapitulated, is as follows:

In theory it is possible that God should annihilate His creatures, *i.e.* there would be no self-contradiction involved in His so doing. As He brought them into existence under no compulsion, but by the free act of His will, so might He by a similar free act reduce them again to nothingness. Not, indeed, that He, the source of life, could directly cause the death of anything; but inasmuch as the creature continues in existence only through the Divine conservation, the mere withdrawal of that support would be equivalent in effect to an act of annihilation. Having thus conceded the possibility of annihilation, he denies that it takes place in fact, on the following grounds: No natural process can end in annihilation; for in the case of material things the component parts will still continue in existence after the disintegration of the composite whole; and as to immaterial beings, 'in eis non est potentia ad non esse.' Further, the idea of a miraculous act of annihilation is rejected on the ground that the object of a miracle is to manifest the Divine grace; and the Divine goodness and power are revealed rather by the maintenance of things in life than by their annihilation (*Summa*, I. civ. 3, 4).

These metaphysical considerations, abstruse as they sound, bring out the real difficulty of introducing the conception of a Divine act of annihilation into a consistent and coherent view of the universe. At the same time there were other and more direct arguments by which the Schoolmen were led to a belief in the indestructibility of the soul. To them it appeared that the truth was sufficiently indicated, if not asserted, in Scripture. Inspired writers (so they contended) would not have asserted the survival of the soul after separation from the body so unconditionally, had that survival been due not to the nature of the soul, but to some miraculous interposition (cf. Suarez, *Anima*, I. x. 9). The balance of authority inclined strongly towards the doctrine of natural immortality. At the 5th Lateran Council in 1513 A.D. Leo X. condemned in set terms the opinion of the mortality of the soul, and at the same time strictly commanded all and sundry philosophers, in their public lectures at the universities and elsewhere, to rebut and disprove that opinion.* It was not until the crisis of the Reformation had broken the fetters upon free speculation, that a theory of annihilation, not unlike that which had been expounded by Arnobius, was once again suggested and defended.

8. Annihilation in post-Reformation thought.—In this matter, as in so much else, Spinoza displays his originality and independence. His writings reveal a marked change of opinion in the course of his life. In the *Cogitat. Metaphys.* he had upheld the doctrine of the soul's immortality on the ground that the soul being a 'substantia' could not pass away. In the treatise, *de Deo*, etc., he takes up a different position, affirming that the destiny of the soul will be determined by her decision between alternative courses. She may unite herself either with the body of which she is the idea, or with God the source of her existence. In the first case she perishes at death, in the second her union with that which is unchangeable will confer upon her the privilege of immortality (*de Deo*, etc. II. xxiii., Suppl. 209, 211). 'It is obvious,' writes Dr. Martineau, 'that an immortality no longer involved in the soul as substance, but depending on the direction of its love, passes from the necessary and universal to the contingent and partial.'†

The influence of Hobbes was also making itself felt in the same direction. However little credit he deserves for sincerity, he is sufficiently explicit in his denial of the natural immortality of the soul:

'That the soul of man is in its own nature eternal and a living creature independent of the body, or that any mere man is immortal otherwise than by the resurrection in the last day, except Enoch and Elias, is a doctrine not apparent in Scripture' (*Works*, Lond. 1839, vol. iii. p. 443).

On the ground of a careful examination into the various Biblical passages bearing on the subject, he sums up in favour of a theory of the annihilation of the wicked:

'Though there be many places that affirm everlasting fire and torments into which men may be cast successively one after another as long as the world lasts, yet I find none that affirm there shall be an eternal life therein of any individual person, but to the contrary an everlasting death which is the second death. . . . Whereby it is evident that there is to be a second death of every one that shall be condemned at the day of judgment, after which he shall die no more' (*ib.* p. 451).

Locke also conceived of the soul as being, under present conditions, subject to the law of death. In the short treatise, *On the Reasonableness of Christianity*, which exercised so profound an influence on the course of religious speculation in the next generation, he begins by insisting that the consequence of the Fall of man was to reduce him to a condition of mortality, the death-penalty involving the destruction of both body and soul. Through Christ alone is the doom reversed, and man becomes capable of immortality. Those who obey His precepts and imitate His example are delivered from death, and rewarded with the gift of life; and life and death are interpreted in their plain meaning of existence and non-existence. Thus Locke, in his attempt to recover the original simplicity of Christianity and to free it from the supposed accretions of theology, substitutes a doctrine of annihilation for the traditional doctrine of inherent immortality. Moreover, he seems to feel no doubt of his success in discovering evidence of the truth of the theory in the words of Scripture. His opinion gave occasion to some controversy on the point at the beginning of the 18th century.‡

But the question of the particular fate in store for the wicked was soon lost sight of in the interest of the wider discussion between Deists and orthodox as to the essence of Christianity. It was not until the middle of the 19th cent. that the topic came again into prominence. From that time forward the conception of annihilation has formed the underlying presupposition of all theories of conditional immortality, and guesses have been hazarded as to the nature of the process which will end in this result. While some writers have imagined a bare continuance of existence together with a loss of consciousness, others have adopted the more thorough hypothesis of entire extinction. Some, again, have assumed a future interposition of the Divine power in a sudden act of annihilation, others have preferred the idea of a gradual dilapidation of the soul. And the various theories about annihilation have been put forward with very various degrees of confidence. Cautious thinkers, like W. E. Gladstone and J. Agar Beet, have not ventured beyond the assertion that the Christian revelation certifies indeed the finality of the Judgment, but makes no pronouncement as to the duration of the pains of the lost. More eager advocates have believed that they can find positive proof of their theories in reason and Scripture (see art. CONDITIONAL IMMORTALITY).

9. Impossibility of comparison with Buddhist doctrine of Nirvāṇa.—Between the theory which we have been considering and the Buddhist doctrine of Nirvāṇa there is some superficial resemblance. Both involve the conception of annihilation; both assert survival after death together with the possibility of ultimate extinction, the total loss of individual existence. But the resemblance is more apparent than real, and affords little help in the elucidation of the problem. Things which are entirely heterogeneous not only cannot be compared, but cannot even be contrasted. And the difference between Christian and Buddhist religious conceptions amounts to heterogeneity. The two systems are committed to radically opposite interpretations of the universe, the one looking for the solution of all problems in the knowledge of God, the other ignoring His existence; the one regarding life as the great boon every increase of which is to be welcomed, the other as the great evil in deliverance from which the reward of virtue will be found. When views about God, the world, and the self are thus essentially divergent, no true relation of comparison can be established by the mere fact that in East and West alike some sort of annihilation of the individual is contemplated. Comparative Religion is a fascinating study, but it is well to remember that the religious conceptions of different nations are often incommensurable; and, even when similar terms are used, the underlying ideas may be very far from coincident. This is notably the case with the respective eschatologies of Christianity and Buddhism. See NIRVĀṆA.

10. Conclusions.—Metaphysical and ontological considerations must of necessity enter into any estimate of the theory of annihilation, although it is notorious that the present age is impatient and distrustful of abstract reasoning. Arguments based upon the supposed unity and simplicity of the soul carry less weight to-day than when the methods of philosophy were in more general use and favour. This is perhaps one of the reasons why the theory of annihilation has rapidly acquired a considerable popularity. Owing to the temper of the age, the philosophic difficulties have been insufficiently recognized. It is not easy to deny the contention that the doctrine of annihilation tends

* Labbe, *Concilia*, tom. xiv. col. 187.

† *Study of Spinoza*, p. 291.

‡ Cf. H. Dodwell, *Epistolary Discourse proving that the Soul is a Principle naturally Mortal*, 1706; reply by John Norris, *Philosophical Discourse*, etc., 1708.

in some measure to lower that high conception of the value and dignity of human personality which has been the direct outcome of traditional Christian teaching as to the nature of the soul. Man destined sooner or later to eventuate in a blank nothingness, such as is commonly supposed to await the animals, is widely different from a being Divinely endowed with the supreme gift of immortality. He stands on an altogether lower level. To make immortality dependent on response to the action of the Divine grace is to leave the position of man as man vaguely indefinite in the scheme of creation. So vast a gulf divides beings endowed with immortality from those for whom final extinction is the natural end, that the difficulty of conceiving a creature 'capable of both' may well seem insuperable. And yet there are doubtless many to whom a difficulty of this kind is less than that of admitting evil to be an ineradicable and eternal element in the universe. They see no escape from the conclusion that, if evil is irreformable, its annihilation is inevitable. If pressed for an answer as to the mode in which this result will be attained, it is doubtless open to any one to fall back on the conception of the Divine omnipotence, and to believe or hope that, by some Divine act analogous to creation but opposite in its effect, evil will be utterly abolished from the final state of the universe. By taking this line certain difficulties are avoided. The act of annihilation, so conceived, is an exceptional interposition discontinuous from the rest of the Divine action upon the created world, and therefore *ex hypothesi* not admitting of explanation. But the hypothesis of Divine interpositions becomes less and less acceptable as men realize, alike in the kingdoms of nature and of grace, the presence and action of the unchanging God. Hence, for the most part, preference has been given to that theory of gradual annihilation which has been under discussion. It is a solution of the problem which has commended itself to many; it may probably secure even wider acceptance in the future; but even its advocates will admit that the difficulties involved in it deserve to be more fully faced and met than has yet been done.

LITERATURE.—W. R. Alger, *Crit. Hist. of the Doctr. of a Future Life* (1885); Arnobius, *adv. Nation.* (Vienna ed. 1875); Augustine, *de Immortalitate Animæ*; J. Baldwin Brown, *Doctr. of Annihilation* (1875); J. A. Beet, *The Last Things* (new ed. 1905); E. M. Caillard, *Individual Immortality* (1903); R. H. Charles, *Crit. Hist. of the Doctr. of a Future Life* (1899); H. Dodwell, *Epistolary Discourse proving that the Soul is a Principle naturally Mortal* (1706); L. Elbé, *Future Life in the Light of ancient Wisdom and modern Science* (1907); W. E. Gladstone, *Studies subsidiary to Butler* (1896); A. Harnack, *Hist. of Dogma*[2] (1897); T. Hobbes, *English Works* (1839); H. Keyserling, *Unsterblichkeit* (1907); J. M. E. M'Taggart, *Some Dogmas of Religion* (1906); D. Palmieri, *de Deo creante* (1878); E. Petavel, *The Problem of Immortality* (1892); E. Rohde, *Psyche*[4] (1907); R. Rothe, *Dogmatik* (1870); S. D. F. Salmond, *Christ. Doctr. of Immortality*[2] (1896); Suarez, *de Anima* (*Opera*, Lyons, 1621); Thomas Aquinas, *Summa*, I. civ.; E. White, *Life in Christ*[3] (1878).

G. C. JOYCE.

ANOINTING.

ANOINTING.—**1.** Unction,* anointing with oil, is a minor act of ritual, which possesses, however, considerable significance for the history of sacramental religion. Its forms correspond generally to the practical purposes for which, in early culture, animal and vegetable fats and oils were so largely employed, while in both principle and practice it has connexions with painting and dress, decoration and disguise, nutrition and medicine, lustration and the various uses of water and blood.

2. The application of unguents to the skin and the hair has obtained, as a daily cosmetic practice, in most, if not all, sections of the human race, from the Tasmanians to the ancient Greeks and Romans. The material varies, in both secular and sacred uses, from crude animal fat to elaborate and costly perfumed vegetable oils. Among the lower races, animal fats are employed, frequently in combination with ochre, occasionally with such substances as charcoal, soot, and ashes. Higher stages of culture prefer vegetable oils, with gums, balsams, vegetable pastes and powders, such as turmeric, sandal and mustard, sawdust and flour, or the sap and pollen of plants, some of which are occasionally used without oil. Perfumes were usually prepared in the form of ointments. Lastly, the term 'unguent' is in most languages made to include, by analogy, such substances as blood, saliva, honey, mud, pitch, and tar. (See art. BLOOD. For anointing with blood see H. C. Trumbull, *The Blood Covenant* [1887], *s.v.*)

3. Anointing usually follows washing or bathing, and completes the toilet of the skin. The action of oil is to produce a sensation of comfort and well-being. Some peoples regard it as conducive to suppleness of the muscles and joints. The Australian aborigines relieve the languor consequent on a long and tiresome journey by rubbing the limbs with grease (W. E. Roth, *Ethnological Studies among the North-West-Central Queensland Aborigines* [1897], 114, 162). Oil closes the pores of the skin, and partially represses perspiration; hence the use of unguents by the Greeks and Romans before exercise, and after the bath which followed. Similarly, the Hindu anoints himself before bathing. In extremes of heat and cold these properties have an increased value, and anointing is almost a necessary of life in very hot and very cold climates. Being a bad conductor, oil protects the skin against the sun, and also prevents the escape of body heat. It is a useful emollient for burnt or chapped skin, and a valuable food for the nerves.

4. The cosmetic use soon acquired æsthetic associations. The gloss produced by oil has itself an æsthetic value, which is heightened by the addition of coloured substances. Of the majority of early peoples it may be said that grease and ochre constitute their wardrobe. The use of unguents as the vehicles of perfumes became a luxury among the Persians, Hindus, Greeks, and Romans, while among early peoples generally it is a common practice on both ordinary and ceremonial occasions, the object being to render the person attractive. Thus the natives of West Africa grease the body, and powder it over with scented and coloured flour. On the Slave Coast, 'magical' unguents, supplied by the priests, are employed for such purposes as the borrowing of money and the obtaining of a woman's favour. Swahili women use fragrant unguents in order to render themselves attractive. Similarly, Homer describes how Hera, when desirous to obtain a favour from Zeus, cleansed her skin with ambrosia and anointed herself with fragrant oil. In the islands of Torres Straits, the boys, at the close of initiation, are rubbed with a pungent scented

* The etymological identifications, still to be met with in dictionaries, of Eng. *salve*, etc., and Lat. *salvus*, etc., and of Lat. *unguo*, etc. and Gr. ἄγος, etc. are unfounded. F. W. Culmann in his *Das Salben im Morgen- und Abendlande* (1876) has discussed the etymology of 'anointing' in Indo-European and Semitic languages.

substance, which has the property of exciting the female sex. The Ewe-speaking peoples of West Africa scent the bride with civet, and make her skin red with the bark of the *to*-tree (F. Ratzel, *The History of Mankind* [Eng. tr.], ii. 397, iii. 108; A. B. Ellis, *The Ewe-speaking Peoples*, 94, 156; Velten, *Sitten und Gebräuche der Suahili*, 212; Homer, *Il.* xiv. 170 ff.; A. C. Haddon in *JAI* xix. 412).

5. Anointing thus stands for physical refreshment, well-being, and personal attractiveness. It is, therefore, naturally regarded as being essential on festal occasions. The Australian native, we are told, is fond of rubbing himself with grease and ochre, especially at times when ceremonies are being performed. Among the ancient Egyptians, Greeks, and Romans, unguents, as representing the completion of festal attire, were offered to guests. In the Homeric age, bathing and anointing formed an indispensable part of welcome. The use of anointing as a mark of honour naturally ensues. Thus, when a Ceramese warrior has taken his first head, he is anointed with fragrant oil by the young women of his village (Spencer-Gillen [a], 38; Wilkinson, i. 425; W. R. Smith, 233; Homer, *Od.* iii. 466, viii. 454; J. G. F. Riedel, *De sluik- en kroesharige Rassen tusschen Selebes en Papua*, 118).

Parallel to the cosmetic use of fats and oils is their application to food-stuffs as a 'dressing'; to tools, utensils, weapons, furniture, and buildings, as a lubricant, preservative, or polish; and to perishable substances as a preservative (E. F. im Thurn, *The Indians of Guiana*, 314; K. Langloh Parker, *The Euahlayi Tribe* [1905], 123; Roth, *op. cit.* 102).

6. In the *magical-religious* sphere a further principle makes its appearance. In addition to their cosmetic, sanative, decorative, and other merits, unguents now develop a more potent, though not specifically distinct, virtue. The principle may be put thus: according to primitive psychology, organic matter and, to some extent, inorganic also, is instinct with a Divine force or vital essence. The chief centres of this are sacred persons, objects, and places; later, the gods and their temples, their representatives and apparatus. This essence, with its gifts of life or strength, and magical or supernatural power, is transmissible by various methods, primarily contact. Inasmuch as its most obvious and convenient source is the flesh and blood of men and animals, the most direct method of assimilation is provided by eating and drinking; but an equally certain method is external application—a method which, in the form of anointing, is peculiarly adapted to the case of fats and oils. Unction is thus based upon the same sacramental principle as the practice of eating the flesh and drinking the blood of sacred persons and animals. The Divine life is transmitted, and communion with the sacred source attained, by anointing the worshipper with the sacred essence. Fat is the most primitive unguent, and is regarded in early thought as a very important seat of life. Ideas of sacredness are perhaps implicit even in its ordinary use, inasmuch as it is animal-substance. (Ernest Crawley, *The Mystic Rose* [1902], *passim*, also *The Tree of Life, A Study of Religion* [1905], 110, 223; W. R. Smith, 383). Where the idea of the sacredness of animal life has been developed to an extreme, as amongst the Hindus, animal fat is tabued.

To take illustrations: the Arabs of East Africa anoint themselves with lions' fat, in order to acquire courage. The Andamanese pour melted pigs' fat over children to render them strong. The Namaquas wear amulets of fat. The Damaras collect the fat of certain animals, which they believe to possess great virtue. It is kept in special receptacles; 'a small portion dissolved in water is given to persons who return home safely after a lengthened absence. . . . The chief makes use of it as an unguent for his body.' The fat of the human body possesses a proportionately higher sanctity and potency. It is especially the fat of the *omentum* that is regarded as possessing this vital force (Becker, *La Vie en Afrique*, ii. 366; E. H. Man, *The Andaman Islands*, 66; C. J. Andersson, *Lake Ngami*, 330, 233; W. R. Smith, *op. cit.* 383). The Australian savage will kill a man merely to obtain his kidney-fat with which to anoint himself. It is believed that the virtues of the dead man are transfused into the person by anointing. It is a regular practice throughout Australia to use for this purpose the fat of slain enemies. These natives also employ it to make their weapons strong; sick persons are rubbed with it in order to obtain health and strength. In India a prevalent superstition relates to the supernatural virtues of *momiāi*, an unguent prepared from the fat of boys murdered for the purpose. Grease made from the fat of a corpse is a potent charm among the Aleuts (R. B. Smyth, *Aborigines of Victoria*, i. 102, ii. 289, 313; *JAI* xxiv. 178; C. Lumholtz, *Among Cannibals*, 272; J. Dawson, *The Australian Aborigines*, 68; W. Crooke, *The Popular Religion and Folk-lore of Northern India*, ii. 176; H. H. Bancroft, *Native Races of the Pacific States*, iii. 145). A piece of human kidney-fat, worn round the neck, was believed by the Tasmanians to render a man proof against magic influence. The virtues of human fat as a curative and magical ointment are well known throughout the world. By its use love may be charmed, warriors rendered invulnerable, and witches enabled to fly through the air. Transformation into animals, as related in folklore, is effected by magical ointments, originally the fat of the animals in question (J. Bonwick, *The Tasmanians*, 179; Apuleius, *Metam.* iii. 2. 1; Lucian, *Lucius*, 12).

7. There are two further considerations to be taken into account in treating of the origin of unction. Sacred fat, in the first place, may be regarded as too holy, and therefore too dangerous, to be eaten. External application is a safer method of assimilating its virtues. In the second place, neither fat nor oil is, properly, an article of food in and by itself (W. R. Smith, 232, 386), but rather a medium or vehicle. Even in its cosmetic uses, oil is frequently a vehicle only, and when used alone would be regarded as the medium of a hidden virtue. In its sacred applications, therefore, we may take it that the oil of anointing is the vehicle of a sacred or Divine life or vital-essence, which is either inherent in the material or induced thereinto. When the primitive conception of the virtues of human and animal fat decays, the Divine essence is, as it were, put in commission, and may be transmitted to any unguent by various methods of consecration. Apart from the sacredness which it carries, a holy unguent is distinguished from other vehicles chiefly by its original cosmetic, decorative, sanative, and other properties.

The sacramental principle is thus the controlling factor in the theory of anointing; but it is always possible to trace the connexion between the essence and the accidents of holy oil, between the magical force or supernatural grace and those material properties which, to quote a Catholic theologian, 'well represent the effects of this Sacrament; *oleum enim sanat, lenit, recreat, penetrat ac lucet*' (P. Dens, *Theologia Moralis et Dogmatica* [1832], vii. 3). Ceremonial unction in all religions satisfies the condition laid down by Catholic theology for the Catholic rite of unction; the *differentia* of the sacrament consists in the fact that 'the sign of the sacred thing, the visible form of invisible grace' (Augustine), should be 'such as to represent it and bring it about.'

The methods of transmitting the sacred essence to the unguent are material contact, magical and religious formulas, intention, blessing, and prayer. The results of unction develop from the decorative and sanative through the magical stage to a supernatural consecration, which imparts spiritual refreshment and strength—in Christian doctrine, grace and the gifts of the Holy Spirit.

8. In the very widely spread use of fats and oils for the treatment of the sick, physical, magical, and religious ideas shade off into one another imperceptibly. Some typical examples will illustrate the range and the working of these ideas. Thus the Australians use various fats to assist the healing of wounds and sores; but to cure a sick man it is necessary to 'sing' the grease with which his body is rubbed (K. Langloh Parker, *The Euahlayi*

Tribe, 38; Spencer-Gillen[a], 250, 464; Roth, *op. cit.* 157, 162). The *shamans* of Asiatic Russia charm the blubber, reindeer-fat, or bear's grease with which the body of a patient is anointed. So, more definitely, the Melanesian medicine-man imparts *mana*, magical or spiritual force, to the unguent. On the other hand, the most powerful unguent in the Chinese pharmacopœia owes its virtues to gold-leaf. Gold is considered to be the most perfect form of matter, and this unguent transmits life to the human body. The unguent employed by the priests of ancient Mexico, when sacrificing on the mountains or in caves, contained narcotics and poisons. It was supposed to remove the sense of fear, and certainly soothed pain. It was used in the treatment of the sick, and was known as 'the divine physic.' The holy oil of Ceram Laut may be manufactured only by a boy and a girl who are virgins. A priest superintends and repeats formulas over the oil. The Amboynese offer oil to the gods. What is left over is returned, and now possesses Divine virtues. It is used to anoint sick and sound alike, and is believed to confer all manner of blessings (V. M. Mikhailovskii in *JAI* xxiv. 98; R. H. Codrington, *The Melanesians*, 198 f.; J. J. M. de Groot, *The Religious System of China*, iv. 331 f.; Acosta, *History of the Indies* [Hakluyt Society], ii. 365–367; J. G. F. Riedel, *De sluik- en kroesharige Rassen tusschen Selebes en Papua*, 179; F. Valentijn, *Oud en nieuw Oost-Indien*, iii. 10). To return to magical ideas, variations of method are seen in the practice of anointing the weapon which dealt the wound; in the East Indian custom, whereby fruits and stones are smeared with oil, and prayer is made that the bullets may rebound from the warriors as rain rebounds from what is covered with oil; and in the Australian superstitions connected with bone-pointing. Here it is possible for the user of the magical weapon to release his victim from the wasting sickness he has brought upon him, if he rubs the apparatus or his own body with grease, in some cases giving what is left of the unguent to the sick man. On the principle of sympathy, a mother will grease her own body daily while her son is recovering from circumcision (J. G. Frazer, *GB*[2] i. 57 ff.; C. M. Pleyte in *Tijdschrift van het Nederlandsch Aardrijkskundig Genootschap* (1893), 805; Langloh Parker, *op. cit.* 32; Spencer-Gillen[b], 466, also [a], 250).

9. The *anointing of the dead* is based on the principle that, as the Chinese say, the dead man 'may depart clean and in a neat attire from this world of cares.' Africa, North America, and the Fiji and Tonga Islands supply typical examples of the custom. The corpse is washed, oiled, and dressed in fine clothes (J. J. M. de Groot, *op. cit.* i. 6, 20; F. Ratzel, *The History of Mankind*, i. 328; Williams and Calvert, *Fiji and the Fijians*, i. 188; J. Adair, *History of the North American Indians*, 181). The ancient Egyptians, Greeks, and Romans thus prepared their dead for the last rites. The Egyptians also oiled the head of the mummy; the Romans poured perfumed oils over the ashes and the tomb. At the annual commemoration of those who fell at Platæa, the Archon washed the grave-stones with water and anointed them with oil. The Greeks placed in the tomb vessels (λήκυθοι) containing unguents for the use of the dead. The Kingsmill Islanders, like many other peoples, preserved the skulls of dead relatives. These were oiled and garlanded; food was offered to them as if they were alive (Wilkinson, iii. 363; Servius on Virgil, *Æn.* v. 219, ix. 483; Lucian, *de Luctu*, 11; Schömann, *Gr. Alterthümer*, ii. 595, 600; Wilkes, *U.S. Exploring Expedition*, 556). The pious affection shown in such customs is elsewhere very commonly developed into practices which aim at a closer union with the departed. Thus in Australia we find a prevalent custom among mourners of anointing themselves with oil made from the decomposing fat of the corpse. This practice has typical examples in the Dutch East Indies, Africa, and North America. The Creek Indians anoint themselves with oil mingled with the ashes of the dead. A curious custom obtains in the Aru Islands of the Dutch East Indies. As soon as a man is dead, his widow runs round to the houses of all his friends and smears the doors with oil (Spencer-Gillen[b], 530; Fison and Howitt, *Kamilaroi and Kurnai*, 243; Riedel, *op. cit.* 308; *First Report BE*, 145, 155; Riedel, 268). The Catholic rite of Extreme Unction doubtless derives from the general principle of anointing the sick; but, apart from such customs, there would seem to be no definite case elsewhere of the practice of unction immediately before death.

10. It will be convenient at this point to draw out the connexion between *ceremonial anointing and the principles of tabu.* In the first place, grease, oil, and fat are convenient vehicles for the application of ashes, charcoal, and other marks of mourning, and of the red paint that denotes such persons as the shedder of blood and the menstruous woman. These states, being tabu, possess one form of sanctity; but it is a general rule that anointing proper, together with decent apparel, should be discarded during their continuance. Similarly, anointing, with other aids to well-being, is renounced by the ascetic. Differences of cosmetic custom produce exceptions to the rule; thus, among the ancient inhabitants of Central America it was the custom to smear the body with grease as a mark of fasting and penance. During the penitential season which preceded the New Year festival, every man was thus anointed daily; the festal use of paint was resumed as soon as the feast commenced (H. H. Bancroft, *op. cit.* ii. 690, 696). In the second place, we have to recognize the cleansing powers of unction. Anointing is positive, lustration negative; but this original distinction is not kept intact, for consecrated water not only cleanses, but imparts the Divine life of which it is the vehicle (W. R. Smith, 190); and consecrated oil, conversely, both imparts virtue and cleanses, by the action of the Divine life which it carries within it. Early peoples, it must be noted, employ fat and oil-refuse as a detergent. Anointing thus not only produces the sanctity of consecration, but also removes the sanctity of tabu. In the latter case, its result is re-admission to the normal life (which itself possesses a measure of sanctity [W. R. Smith, 426]), and to that extent it brings about a re-consecration of impaired sanctity. The following cases show how unction and lustration tend to assimilate. The *ghī* of the Hindus is held to purify by virtue of its sacred essence, while the sprinkling with sacred water which constitutes the *abhiṣeka*, or anointing of a king, possesses not only the name but the function of ordinary anointing. The Yoruba 'water of purification' is really an unguent, prepared from shea-butter and edible snails. The 'neutralizing rice-flour' of the Malays has both positive and negative virtues (A. B. Ellis, *The Yoruba-speaking Peoples*, 141; W. W. Skeat, *Malay Magic*, 77, 376, 385). Lastly, in the very widely spread ritual of blood, the material is either sprinkled like water, poured like oil, or smeared like ointment, while the results of the ceremony are both to cleanse and to confer a blessing.

11. The examples which follow illustrate the use of anointing to remove tabu, and comprise various principles of ceremonial unction. In the Ongtong-Java Islands all strangers are met by the priests immediately on landing. Sand and water are sprinkled about, and the visitors themselves are sprinkled with water, anointed with oil, and girt with pandanus-leaves. Galla warriors on returning home are 'washed' by the women with fat and butter, and their faces are painted red and white (R. Parkinson in *Internat. Archiv für Ethnographie*, x. 112; P. Paulitschke, *Ethnographie Nordost-Afrikas*, 258). Before starting on a journey the Wanjamwesi smears his face with a sort of porridge, and the ceremony is repeated on his return. The Australian who has smitten his enemy with sickness by the use of 'the bone' may release him from the curse by rinsing the magical weapon in water or by rubbing it with fat. Similarly, as noticed above, the operator may produce this result by greasing his own body. The customs connected with war and slaughter supply remarkable cases of this form of unction. In Ceram Laut, when war is decided upon, the chief anoints the feet of the aggrieved person with oil. It is a kind of consecration. The man then raises the warcry and rouses the people. The *Illapurinja*, 'female avenger,' among the Central Australians, is rubbed with grease and decorated. On her return, her husband removes the decorations and rubs her afresh with grease. The Fijians observed an elaborate ritual for the son of a chief after slaying his first man. He was anointed from head to foot with red turmeric and oil. For three days he lived in seclusion with several other youths, anointed and dressed like himself. They were forbidden to lie down, or sleep, or change their clothes, or enter a house where there was a woman (F. Stuhlmann, *Mit Emin Pascha ins Herz von Afrika*, 89; Roth, *op. cit.* 157; Riedel, *op. cit.* 158; Spencer-Gillen[a], 466–468; Williams and Calvert, *op. cit.* i. 56). In the cases cited above many principles of early thought may be discerned. It is sufficient to note that war is a holy state, and that it must be inaugurated and concluded with ceremonial observance.

12. The removal of tabu coincides with the renewal of normal life and normal sanctity, and anointing is employed here no less regularly than for the inauguration of a highly sacred state. Thus mourners are anointed, as in Africa and North America, when their period of sorrow is ended. Throughout Africa it is the custom to anoint the mother with fat and oil shortly after child-birth. The practice is common throughout the world, after sickness generally, with women after the monthly period, and with children after the ceremonial observances at puberty. The practice in the last instance often takes a peculiar form. In Australia, for instance, and the Andamans, a boy is made free of a forbidden food by the process of having fat rubbed over his face and body (J. Shooter, *The Kaffirs of Natal*, Lond. [1857], 241; *1 RBEW*, 146; Maclean, *Compendium of Kaffir Laws and Customs*, 94, 99; D. Macdonald, *Africana*, i. 129; Dennett, *Folklore of the Fjort*, 137; Spencer-Gillen[a], 386; E. H. Man in *JAI* xii. 134; Howitt, *ib.* xiii. 455, xiv. 316).

13. Passing now to cases of *consecration* proper, we find anointing used to inaugurate periodic sacredness, as in rites corresponding to baptism and confirmation, in marriage and in worship. The customs last noted tend to merge into these. (*a*) It is a custom of wide extension that the new-born child should be rubbed with oil (Roth, *op. cit.* 183; Ratzel, ii. 286; Williams and Calvert, i. 175; Caron's 'Japan' in Pinkerton's *Voyages and Travels*, vii. 635; Ellis, *Yoruba-speaking Peoples*, 141). This practice soon becomes ceremonial, and suggests baptismal analogies. The Ovaherero ceremony of naming the child combines so many principles that it may stand for a typical summary. The rite takes place in the house of the sacred fire, and is performed by the chief man of the village. He first takes a mouthful of water, and spurts this over the bodies of mother and child. Then he addresses the ancestors thus: 'To you a child is born in your village; may the village never come to an end.' He then ladles some fat out of a vessel, spits upon it, and rubs it over his hands. He next rubs more fat in his hands, spurting water upon it. Then he anoints the woman. In doing this he crosses his arms, so as to touch with his right hand her right side, and with his left hand her left side. The process is repeated with the child. Finally he gives it a name, while touching its forehead with his own (E. Dannert in *South African Folklore Journal*, ii. 67).

(*b*) The anointing of boys and girls as a preliminary to the ceremonies observed at puberty is of wide extension; it is most prominent in Australia and Africa. In Central Australia the candidate is rubbed with grease at various times during the protracted ceremonial. At the circumcision festival of the Masai the boys were allowed to gorge themselves with beef. They rubbed the fat over their bodies, much as a Dayak rubs himself with the blood of a pig, or as a carnivorous animal rolls in the flesh of his prey (Spencer-Gillen[b], 93, 135, also [a], 242; *JAI* xxiv. 418; C. J. Andersson, *Lake Ngami*, 465).

(*c*) In the ceremonial of marriage we find typical examples of anointing. The Central Australian, for a few days after receiving his wife, rubs her daily with grease and ochre. A few days before marriage the Angola bride is anointed with oil from head to foot, and until she is handed over to her husband is treated like a queen. The custom is frequent in Africa, and occurs in Fiji. The Malays anoint both bride and bridegroom. In what amounts to a ceremony of re-marriage, performed after the birth of the first child, the Basuto pair are anointed by a medicine-man with a mixture of roots and fat. In Australia we find the custom of anointing pregnant women (Spencer-Gillen[b], 135, 606; G. Tams, *The Portuguese Possessions in South-West Africa* [Eng. tr.], i. 175; Williams and Calvert, i. 169; Skeat, 385; *ZE* [1877] 78).

(*d*) As a preliminary to worship, anointing is frequently incumbent on the people, more frequently on the priest. In ancient Greece, those who consulted the oracle of Trophonius were washed and anointed with oil. When a native of the Slave Coast worships the guardian spirit who resides in his head, he rubs his head with oil; the priests anoint themselves before entering the house of the god. The priests of Mexico and Central America were anointed from head to foot with a sacred unguent, which was also applied to the images of the gods. Returning to Greece, we learn that in the feast of Dionysus the men who carried the sacred bull to the temple were anointed with oil. Similarly, the Luperci at Rome were anointed and garlanded. An interesting side-light on the theory of anointing reaches us from Fiji and the Dutch East Indies. At shamanistic ceremonies the person into whom the god is to enter is anointed with fragrant oil, by way of rendering him attractive to the deity (Pausanias, viii. 19. 2, ix. 39. 7; Ellis, *Yoruba-speaking Peoples*, 126, also *Ewe-speaking Peoples*, 76; Acosta, *History of the Indies*, ii. 364; Bancroft, *Native Races*, ii. 323, iii. 341; Lactantius, *Inst.* i. 21. 45; G. A. Wilken, *Het Shamanisme bij de Volken van den Indischen Archipel*, 479 f.; Williams and Calvert, *op. cit.* i. 224).

14. For the special *consecration of priests*, anointing is a not uncommon piece of ritual, obtaining in various parts of the world. The Slave Coast of Africa provides a typical case. The candidate's body is smeared with a decoction of herbs. Then the priests who officiate anoint his head with 'a mystical unguent,' and ask the god to accept him. If he is accepted, the deity is supposed to enter into him. A new cloth is put upon the ordained novice, and a new name conferred. Among the Buriats a *shaman* is consecrated by being anointed with the blood of a kid. In North America, among the Chikasaws, the candidate fasted for some time, and was consecrated by a bath and unction with bear's grease. The Toltecs and Totonacs of Central America consecrated their pontiffs with an unguent made of india-rubber oil and children's blood. For the anointing of their spiritual king, the Aztecs employed the unguent used at the enthronement of their temporal monarch. The priests of ancient Egypt were consecrated with holy oil poured upon the head (Ellis, *The Ewe-speaking Peoples*, 143 f., *JAI* xxiv. 89; Adair, 122; Bancroft, ii. 214, iii. 433, ii. 201; Wilkinson, iii. 360).

15. The *anointing of kings*, with which Semitic

and Christian custom has familiarized the world, is a spectacular rite of rare occurrence outside the sphere of Hebrew tradition. It is found, however, in a more or less perfect form among the ancient Egyptians, the Aztecs, and the Hindus ancient and modern. The Pharaoh was anointed after investiture with the sacred robes. The monuments give representations of the ceremony, and in the Tell el-Amarna letters the king of Cyprus sends to the king of Egypt 'a flask of good oil to pour on your head, now that you have ascended the throne of your kingdom.' The Aztec ceremony of royal unction preceded coronation. The king-elect went in procession to the temple of Huitzilopochtli. After paying homage to the god, he was anointed throughout his whole body by the high priest, and sprinkled with holy water. He was then clothed in ceremonial robes, and about his neck was hung a gourd containing powerful remedies against sorcery, disease, and treason. The unguent used was the black oil with which the priests anointed their own bodies and the images of the gods. Its name is variously given, *ulli*, or *ole*, and its chief constituent was india-rubber juice. The Quichés and Cakchiquels bathed the king at his coronation, and anointed his body with perfumes. Candidates for the order of Tecuhtli, the Garter of the Aztecs, were anointed with the same sacerdotal unguent (Wilkinson, iii. 360; W. M. Flinders Petrie, *Syria and Egypt from the Tell el-Amarna Letters*, 45; H. Winckler, *The Tell el-Amarna Letters* [Eng. tr.], 87; Bancroft, ii. 144 f., 641, 196, iii. 385).

The anointing of kings and priests combines several principles, and is not to be explained on one separate line of development. It is, in the first place, a part of the festal dress essential on such occasions (W. R. Smith, 233, 453). Secondly, we have the various ideas connected with consecration,—the transmission of sanctity, power, and new life (*ib.* 383 f.), on the one hand; and, on the other, the 'hedging' of a dedicated person with sacredness, for his protection and the performance of his office.

16. The *anointing of sacrifice and offering, the altar and the temple, and the sacred apparatus* generally, supplies many details of ritual which fall into line with the main principles of religious unction, while giving prominence to such as are more closely connected with worship. The human sacrifices of the ancient Albanians of the Caucasus, of the Aztecs, and of the people of Timor, were anointed before being slain. The last case has to do with coronation. The princes of Kupang in Timor kept sacred crocodiles, and believed themselves to be descended from this animal. On the day of coronation, a young girl was richly dressed, decorated with flowers, and anointed with fragrant oil, to be offered as a sacrifice to the sacred monsters. In the remarkable human sacrifice of the Khonds, the *Meriah* was anointed with oil, *ghī*, and turmeric, and adorned with flowers. He received 'a species of reverence which it is not easy to distinguish from adoration.' Every one who could touched the oil on the victim's body and rubbed it on his own head. The oil was regarded as possessing the same virtue as his flesh and blood conferred on the fields (Strabo, ii. 4. 7; Bancroft, iii. 333; Veth, *Het eiland Timor*, 21; S. C. Macpherson, *Memorials of Service in India*, 118; J. Campbell, *Wild Tribes of Khondistan*, 54 f., 112).

The custom of 'dressing' offerings with oil was regular in the worship of the ancient Greeks. When the natives of West Africa sacrifice an animal, they sprinkle it with palm-oil by way of attracting the spirits. At the festival of the New Fruits among the Creek Indians, the priest took some of each sort and smeared them with oil before offering them to the spirit of fire. The people of Gilgit drench with wine, oil, and blood the branch of the sacred cedar used in their agricultural ceremonies. Similarly the Malays, in their ceremony of bringing home the Soul of the Rice, and the Javanese, in the Marriage of the Rice Bride, anoint the rice with oil (Schömann, ii. 236; Pausanias, viii. 42; A. B. Ellis, *The Yoruba-speaking Peoples*, 155; Adair, 96; Biddulph, *Tribes of the Hindu Kush*, 106; Skeat, *op. cit.* 235; Veth, *Java*, i. 524).

The natives of Celebes on great occasions anoint the flag and other emblems of state. The Santals anoint their cattle when celebrating the harvest-home. The Shans of Indo-China and the natives of Celebes purify with water and anoint with oil the plough used in their ceremonial ploughing of the rice-fields (G. K. Niemann in *Bijdragen voor de Taal- Land- en Volkenkunde van Nederlandsch Indië*, xxxviii. 2. 270; W. Crooke, *op. cit.* ii. 308; E. Aymonier in *RHR* xxiv. 272; B. F. Matthes, *Bijdragen tot de Ethnologie van Zuid-Selebes*, 93).

When we pass to cases more definitely representative of worship, we find a development of two ideas: first, that the sacred life immanent in the sacred symbol or image needs periodical renewing; and, secondly, that the spirit connected therewith requires conciliation; anointing the sacred object renews its vigour and also brings the worshipper into union with the deity. When the Wawamba of Central Africa or the Australian of Queensland anoints his sacred stone with fat when asking it for rain, we may infer that the sacred object is supposed to be revived and rendered gracious by the cosmetic virtues of unction. Similarly the Central Australians rub their *churinga* with fat and ochre whenever they examine them. The *churinga* is supposed to have human feelings, and the process of anointing is said to 'soften it' (F. Stuhlmann, *op. cit.* 654; Roth, *op. cit.* 158; Spencer-Gillen[b], 255, 265, 270, also[a], 161). Here the use of grease for utensils combines with cosmetic anointing. In many cases it is natural to find these ideas merging in the notion of feeding the divine object; but it would be incorrect to derive the anointing of sacred stones from the practice of feeding the god. The custom of smearing blood upon sacred symbols and images is of wide extension, but it is not a survival from any practice of pouring the blood into the mouth of an image. The practical primitive mind does not confuse anointing with nutrition, though well aware that the two are allied. As illustrating the extension of the custom, a few examples are here brought forward. The Greeks and Romans washed, anointed, and garlanded their sacred stones. The ὀμφαλός of Delphi was periodically anointed and wrapped in wool (Schömann, ii. 236; Lucian, *Alex.* 30; Apuleius, *Flor.* i. 1; Minucius Felix, *Octav.* iii.; Pausanias, x. 24, and J. G. Frazer, *Commentary on Pausanias*, v. 354 f.). The Malagasy anoint sacred stones with fat or oil or the blood of victims. The Wakamba neat-herd anoints a rock with oil and offers fruits, in order to get his cattle through a difficult pass (J. Sibree, *History of Madagascar*, 305; *ZE* x. 384). This combination of nutrition and unction is found among the Kei islanders; every family here possesses a sacred black stone, and to obtain success in war or trade a man anoints this with oil and offers fruits to it. In Celebes, sacred images, apparatus, and buildings are smeared with oil by worshippers. The ancient Egyptians anointed the statues of the gods, applying the unguent with the little finger of the left hand. The Arval Brothers anointed the image of their goddess, *Dea Dia*, on festival days. At the ceremony of mourning for the dead god, the stone image of Attis was anointed. This was probably the unction of the dead. When the image was brought out from the tomb on the day of Resurrection, the priest anointed the throats of the worshippers. The religion of ancient Greece provides a curious instance of the meeting of the practical and the religious spheres. The old temple-statues of the gods, made of wood, were rubbed with oil to preserve them from decay, while to preserve the magnificent creations of gold and ivory, such as the image of Zeus at Olympia, oil was run in pipes throughout the statue (Riedel, *op. cit.* 223; Matthes, *op. cit.* 94; Wilkinson, *op. cit.* iii. 361; *CIL* vi. 9797; Firmicus, *de Errore*, 23; Pausanias, v. 11, and Frazer's *Com. ad loc.*).

17. The principle of communion with the deity by means of anointing the sacred symbol or the worshipper himself is more apparent in the elementary stages of worship. The Assiniboins, we are told, venerate the bear, and try to keep on good terms with him. They pray to him when they wish to be successful in a bear-hunt, and so to secure a good supply of bear's flesh to eat and of the bear's grease with which they are always anointed. The natives of Central Australia, at the *Intichiuma* ceremony for maintaining the supply of kangaroos, eat a little of the flesh of this animal and anoint their bodies with the fat. In order to obtain success in hunting euros, they rub themselves with stones supposed to be parts of that animal. Similarly, before eating snakes they rub their arms with snake fat. At a higher stage of development we find the West African negro anointing that part of his own body where his guardian spirit resides (de Smet, *Western Missions and Missionaries*, 139; Spencer-Gillen[a], 206, also[b], 182, 255; Ellis, *Yoruba-speaking Peoples*, 126 f.).

18. The oil of anointing, as we have seen, transmits the sacredness latent within it in either of two directions—to the worshipper or to the god. If we look at the controlling source of its virtue, the potentially sacred substance of the human body, and compare the earliest forms of consecration, we see that the theory of anointing leads us back to pre-theistic and even pre-fetishistic times. The elementary stages of dedication illustrate the less common direction of anointing, in which the worshipper or the priest confers sanctity instead of receiving it. The dedication, more or less informal, of sacred buildings and apparatus by anointing obtained in Egypt, Greece, and Italy; it is remarkably prominent in India, ancient and modern, but does not appear to have been general elsewhere. It is, of course, connected with the use of oil for tools, utensils, and furniture, but also has associations with fetishistic methods of making gods (Crawley, *The Tree of Life, A Study of Religion* [1905], 232). The ritual of renewing the sacred vigour of a sacred symbol has already been referred to; here we note the original induction. Thus every man on the Gold Coast makes for himself a *suhman*, or tutelary deity. When he has made it, he anoints it with butter. Among the Bataks the *guru* inducts a spirit into the fetish with various ceremonies, chief among which is the application of a vegetable-unguent (Ellis, *Tshi-speaking Peoples*, 100 f.; Hagen in *Tijds. v. Taal- Land- en Volkenk. van Ned. Indië*, xxviii. 525; Matthes, *op. cit.* 94). But the Central Australian, rubbing a newly made *churinga* with fat, is an unconscious exponent of the embryonic stage of consecration by unction.

19. In its latest developments anointing passes into a theological metaphor of *quasi*-doctrinal import. *Spiritual unction* carries with it from the sacramental to the ethical-religious plane the various gifts of consecration, leaving in its course such traces of mysticism as 'the White Ointment from the Tree of Life,' found in the baptismal formula of the Ophites, and Justin's adaptation of Plato's fancy, to the effect that the Creator impressed the Soul of the Universe upon it as an unction in the form of a χ (Justin, *Apol.* i. 60; Plato, *Timæus*, 36).

In conclusion, the history of anointing in its connexion with religion shows that of all sacramental media the sacred unguent is the most spiritual, and that from beginning to end holy unction is the least material of all purely physical modes of assimilating the Divine. Its characteristic is soul.

LITERATURE.—Esp. W. R. Smith, *The Religion of the Semites*[2] (1894). Other references—*Encyc. Brit.*[9]; J. G. Frazer, *The Golden Bough*[2] (1900), ii. 364 f.; A. E. Crawley, *The Mystic Rose* (1902), 105 ff.; F. W. Culmann, *Das Salben im Morgen- und Abendlande* (1876).

A. E. CRAWLEY.

ANOINTING (Hindu).—Unguents have been in regular use from the earliest times for every form of cosmetic, luxurious, medicinal, and ceremonial unction. Cosmetic and medicinal oils and pastes are found in greater number and variety in India than in any other country, though animal fats are there, of course, prohibited. Scented and coloured preparations are frequent; for ceremonial purposes, sandal-paste or oil, oil and turmeric, and ghī are chiefly used. Sandal-oil is popular on account of its fragrance; ghī and turmeric are extensively employed in medicine and cookery; turmeric and mustard-oil possess invigorating properties. Oil is applied to the head and body before and frequently after the bath. The practice is said to invigorate the system, and it is noted in the ancient literature that diseases do not approach the man who takes physical exercise and anoints his limbs with oil. Infants are well rubbed with mustard-oil, and are then exposed to the sun; it is asserted, on scientific authority, that the practice is a preventive of consumption. The hair is always well pomaded, coconut-oil being chiefly used. Sandal- or rose-water is offered to guests; and this custom (*mālaya-chandana*) is the ancient *arghya*. During mourning and sickness anointing is discontinued, also on fast-days, on visits to sacred places, by Brāhmans in the stage of life as student or ascetic, and by women during menstruation. At the conclusion of her period a woman is rubbed with saffron-oil; and anointing, more or less ceremonial, marks recovery from sickness and the end of mourning.*

Magical unguents, to which potency was given by *mantras*, were and still are used to inspire love, and to prevent or cure evil and disease. A still prevalent superstition is that of *momiāī*, the essential element of which is an unguent prepared from the fat of a boy murdered for the purpose. This is believed to heal wounds and to render the body invulnerable. The *amṛta* oil made men strong and women lovely; it ensured offspring, averted misfortune, promoted prosperity, and guaranteed long life. Its manufacture was preceded by purificatory rites. The Brāhman, when about to anoint himself, should think of the *Chirañjīvins* ('the long-lived'), seven half-divine persons.

At the hair-parting ceremony (*sīmantonnayana*), performed during pregnancy, the woman is bathed and fragrant oil is poured on her head. Immediately after birth the child is rubbed with warm mustard-oil. The tonsure (*chāula*) takes place at the age of three; the child is anointed with oil

* U. C. Dutt, *Materia Medica of the Hindus*, pp. 13 ff., 225; J. E. Padfield, *The Hindu at Home*, Madras, 1896, p. 90; A. F. R. Hoernle, *The Bower MS., passim*; W. Ward, *History, Literature, and Mythology of the Hindoos*, i. 92, 275, iii. 345; Bhagvat Sinh Jee, *Aryan Medical Science*, pp. 45, 62; Lāl Behāri Day, *Govinda Sāmanta*, 1874, p. 57; J. A. Dubois, *Hindu Manners, Customs, and Ceremonies*[2], tr. by H. K. Beauchamp, Oxford, 1899, pp. 188, 713; *Laws of Manu*, tr. by G. Bühler, *SBE* cxxv. Oxford, 1886, p. 62; Monier Williams, *Brāhmanism and Hinduism*[4], London, 1891, pp. 153, 307; Rājendralāla Mitra, *Indo-Aryans*, Calcutta, 1881, i. 434, 439, ii. 17 ff.; S. C. Bose, *The Hindoos as they are*, 1881, pp. 17, 23.

and washed. Girls, on arriving at puberty, are decorated and anointed with oil, or oil and turmeric (*haridrā*). Brāhman boys, on investiture with the thread, are similarly anointed with oil and *haridrā*.* The ceremony of *gātra-haridrā* is performed during the preliminary marriage-rites and on the wedding-day. Bride and bridegroom are anointed with oil and turmeric. The 'sandalwood stone,' which they have to touch with their feet, is rubbed with oil. The bride's brother smears the hands of the bride with ghī, and sprinkles parched rice upon them. At a Yānādi wedding the mothers of the contracting parties anoint them with oil, turmeric, and sandal-paste. They then bathe and put on new clothes. Among the Kannādiyans the village barber sprinkles ghī over the heads of the bridal pair, who afterwards take an oil bath. For the *sindūrdān*, sandal-paste, blood, or vermilion are chiefly used. Oil or paste is a common medium for sacred marks.

After death, the body is washed and anointed with sandal-paste, oil, and turmeric, or ghī. In some cases the chief mourner touches each aperture of the body with his lips, repeats a *mantra*, and pours ghī on each. The forehead of a dying man is, if possible, smeared with the sacred mud of the Ganges. At the burial of the urn the chief mourner anoints himself with ghī.

At the ordination of a Buddhist priest, his hair is touched with oil before being cut.† The important ceremony of *abhiṣeka* (wh. see), the royal baptism or consecration, is in principle a form of unction; the holy water, with its numerous ingredients, consecrates rather by infusion of divine force than by lustration. This rite was celebrated towards the close of the protracted ceremonies of the *rājasūya*. The proper time for its celebration was the new moon after the full moon of Phālguṇa, *i.e.* about the end of March. Eighteen ingredients were necessary, the chief being the water of the sacred river Sarasvatī. The others included ghī, milk, cow-dung, honey, sugar, sandal-water, perfumes, earths, turmeric, and rice-meal. The *adhvaryu* mixed them from eighteen pitchers in a bucket of *udumbara* wood, repeating a *mantra* at every stage, *e.g.*, 'O honeyed water, whom the Devas collected, thou mighty one, thou begotten of kings, thou enlivener; with thee Mitra and Varuṇa were consecrated, and Indra was freed from his enemies; I take thee.' 'O water, thou art naturally a giver of kingdoms, grant a kingdom to my Yajamāna' (naming the king). 'O honeyed and divine ones, mix with each other for the strength and vigour of our Yajamāna.' The king, after a preliminary sprinkling, put on a bathing-dress, the inner garment of which was steeped in ghī, and took his seat on a stool covered with a tiger-skin, facing the east, and, as the pouring commenced, raised his arms. On his head was a rose-head of gold, through which the sacred liquid was to spread in a shower. The contents of the one bucket were transferred to four; these the *adhvaryu*, the Brāhman priest, a *kṣatriya*, and a *vaiṣya* poured in turn over the head of the king from their respective positions. *Mantras* were recited, such as—

'O Yajamāna, I bathe thee with the glory of the moon; may you be king of kings among kings. . . . O ye well worshipped Devas, may you free him from all his enemies, and enable him to discharge the highest duties of the Kṣatriya. . . .'

At the close the Brāhman said, 'Know ye that he has this day become your king; of us Brāhmaṇas Soma is the king.'* Noteworthy details are the prayers to 'the divine Quickeners,' the belief that the gods consecrated the king, and that through the rite he was filled with divine force. The essence of water is vigour; this and the vitalizing essence of all the ingredients of the sacred liquid enter into him. One *mantra* states that he is sprinkled with priestly dignity.† The hair of the king was not to be cut until a year had elapsed. Three forms of *abhiṣeka* are mentioned—*abhiṣeka* for kings, *pūrṇābhiṣeka* for superior kings, and *mahābhiṣeka* for emperors. According to the Vārāha Purāṇa, a man may perform the ceremony on himself in a simplified form: 'He who pours sesamum-seed and water on his head from a right-handed *śaṅkha* destroys all the sins of his life.'

A modified form of *abhiṣeka* is still employed at the coronation of Rājahs. In Assam, for instance, the water for the ceremony is taken from nine holy places, and is mingled with the juices of plants. A similar account is given of coronation in Mysore. In Rājputāna the ceremony is unction rather than baptism. A mixture of sandal-paste and attar of roses is the unguent employed, and a little of this is placed on the forehead with the middle finger of the right hand. The royal jewels are then tied on.‡

As in Vedic times, the Brāhman washes and anoints himself with oil or ghī before performing religious duties. The institutor of a ceremony also anoints himself. On the first day of the festival *Saṅkrānti* it is the custom for every one to take a bath, in which rubbing the body with oil forms a conspicuous feature. In the *nirūdhapaśubandha* rite the tree from which the sacrificial post was to be cut was anointed, and the victim, after being rubbed with oil and turmeric and washed, was anointed with ghī just before the sacrifice. In the *Yagña* sacrifice the ram is rubbed with oil, bathed, covered with *akṣatas*, and garlanded.§ At the *Durgā-pūjā* festival a plantain tree is bathed and anointed with several kinds of scented oils.

The consecration of buildings by means of unction is a well-developed feature of Hindu ritual. There is a ceremony analogous to the laying of foundation-stones, in which a piece of wood (*śaṅku*) is decorated and anointed, being thereby animated with the spirit of the god Vāstupurusha, who becomes the tutelary deity of the house. Again, when the principal entrance is put up, the woodwork is anointed with sandal-oil and worshipped. The same ceremony is performed over the ridge-plate and the well, and for the house generally, when first entered.

The images of the gods in the temples are bathed, anointed, and dressed by the priests daily. Unguents for this purpose (*vilepana*) are one of the 'essential offerings' presented by worshippers. Sacred stones are also anointed and decorated; and the worshippers of Śiva anoint the *liṅga*.

The principle of consecration is well brought out in the Hindu ritual of anointing, while the allied principles of decoration and purification are fully recognized.‖

A. E. CRAWLEY.

ANOINTING (Semitic).—If we find traces of anointing among the Arabs in pre-Islāmic days,

* H. Oldenberg, *Die Religion des Veda*, 1894, pp. 499, 513; *The Bower MS.*, ii. 104 ff.; Dubois, pp. 23, 86, 160, 273; Monier Williams, p. 357; Ward, i. 74; S. C. Bose, *The Hindoos as they are*, p. 86; in general, Hillebrandt, *Vedische Opfer und Zauber*, 1897, pp. 43, 49, 62, 67.

† Lāl Behāri Day, p. 126 f.; Dubois, pp. 50 f., 188, 227, 336, 492; S. Mateer, *Native Life in Travancore*, p. 88; Bose, pp. 50 f., 250; *Madras Government Museum Bulletin*, iv. 3, 152, 156, 204; Ward, i. 168 f., 176, iii. 354; Monier Williams, pp. 298, 363; Rājendralāla Mitra, ii. 144.

* Rājendralāla Mitra, ii. 3, 37 ff., 46 ff.

† H. Oldenberg, pp. 428, 472; *Śatapatha Brāhmaṇa*, tr. by J. Eggeling in *SBE*, vol. xli. p. 68 ff.; A. Weber, *Über die Königsweihe, den Rājasūya*, Berlin, 1893, pp. 4, 33 f., 42–45, 110–117.

‡ Rājendralāla Mitra, ii. 46 ff., i. 286; B. Hamilton, in W. Martin, *Eastern India*, 1838, iii. 611; L. Bowring, *Eastern Experiences*, p. 393; E. G. Balfour, *Encyclopædia of India*, *s.v.* 'Anointing.'

§ H. Oldenberg, p. 398; R. Mitra, i. 369 f.; Dubois, p. 518.

‖ Bose, p. 101 f.; M. Williams, pp. 197, 221, 420, 443; B. Hodgson, *Nepal and Tibet*, p. 140; *JRAS*, 1843, p. 20; *Asiatic Researches*, vii. 394; Dubois, p. 589; *Mahānirvāṇa Tantra*, v. 91.

we must perforce assume that, though still clinging by force of habit and tradition to rites and practices that fall within the category of primitive religious customs, resting upon distinctly primitive beliefs, they had advanced beyond these beliefs sufficiently to cause the rise among them of the longing to come into direct touch—not merely through the mediation of a special body of men—with the higher powers. A custom of this kind is vouched for in the pre-Islāmic period in connexion with the visit to the old sanctuary at Mecca, known as the Ka'ba, when the worshippers, in order to acquire and take, as it were, into their own person some of the sanctity associated with the deities of the place, rubbed their hands over the images of the gods (Wellhausen, *Reste Arab. Heid.*[2] p. 105) or pressed themselves against the edifice itself. Although no unguent which we commonly associate with anointing appears to have been employed, it is significant that the verb used to express this pressing (*taḳarrub*) comes from the stem that in both Heb. and Assyr. embodies the idea of 'offering,' while the rubbing (*tamassuḥ*) is from a stem that in Hebrew becomes the generic term for anointing, and in the form *m^{e}šî'aḥ* (Messiah) becomes one of the most significant terms in the religious nomenclature of both Judaism and Christianity.

Unless the kissing of the gods or of sacred objects, as, *e.g.*, the 'black stone' at the Ka'ba, be included, the ancient Semites do not appear to have gone further than to symbolize in these rites of pressing and rubbing the desire to reach out to the sanctity associated with images or objects. The use of wine and oil belongs to a still later stage of religious custom, and, when they are met with in ancient Arabia, are probably due to external influences. On the other hand, the antiquity of the blood-rite as a ceremony, used in covenanting, being vouched for (Trumbull, *Blood Covenant*, ch. i.), some of the uses to which blood is put in the sacrificial ritual of the ancient Semites may properly be classed under the category of anointing. To be sure, the custom of pouring or rubbing the blood of a sacrificial animal over a sacred stone on which the slaughtering is done, is not looked upon as a species of anointing, for the purpose of the act is to symbolize that the deity, represented by the stone, or supposed to reside in it, has accepted the animal by receiving the blood as the vital element (Wellhausen, *l.c.* p. 113). However, in the ancient Semitic method of covenanting by dipping the hands in blood (Trumbull, *l.c.* ch. i.) a union of the contracting parties is symbolized, and if the deity is introduced into the act by rubbing the blood also over his symbol—whatever it may be—it is with the view of making the deity a party to the covenant, and in so far the thought of a direct union with the deity—a blood relationship—is present. Yet even here a direct transfer of sanctity from the deity to his worshippers does not appear to take place, as would be involved in anointing, viewed as a religious rite. It is significant, as Wellhausen (*l.c.* p. 99) points out, that the 'black stone' of the Ka'ba is not smeared with blood. This may be taken as a proof that communion with the deity had its decided limitations among the ancient Semites, so that the sprinkling of blood over the door-posts and lintels, or the threshold of a dwelling, and such other practices as are instanced by Curtiss and Doughty as survivals of primitive religion among the inhabitants of Syria and Arabia, in which the blood is rubbed or sprinkled on animals or fields or newly erected or newly occupied dwellings as a protection against demons (*jinn*), or, in more positive terms, 'for a blessing' (Curtiss, *Primitive Semitic Religion To-Day*, ch. xv.; Doughty, *Arabia Deserta*, i. pp. 136 and 499, ii. p. 100, etc.), are not to be interpreted as anything more than the placing of the objects in question under the control of the gods invoked through the sacrificial animal. The use of blood in the Hebrew ritual, such as the sprinkling over the worshippers (Ex 24), or over the altar and the sanctuary (Lv 4), for which Robertson Smith (*Rel. of Sem.*[2] p. 344) may be consulted, embodies the same general idea.

Considerations of this nature lead us to the conclusion that the prominent rôle played by anointing among the Hebrews, with the application of unguents to sacred objects or to persons invested with sanctity, as priests and kings, is an expression of considerably advanced religious beliefs, in which the symbolical transfer of qualities associated with the Divine essence enters as a prominent factor. That this use of unguents in religious rites represents the transfer to the sphere of religion of originally secular rites, marking the adornment of one's person, may be granted; but this view, so brilliantly set forth by Robertson Smith (*l.c.* p. 232 ff.), must not blind us to the fact that in the transfer something more than the mere desire to show honour to sacred objects or persons was intended. The act was meant actually to symbolize the sanctity bound up with such objects and persons, and was to be understood as the investiture with such sanctity. The use of oil and wine as unguents—both symbols of luxury accompanying a more advanced culture—seems at all times to have been bound up with anointing among the Hebrews as among the other nations of antiquity, and is practised to this day in the Roman and Greek Churches for the consecration of sacred edifices. We have in this way instances of the anointing of altars, as, *e.g.*, the stone at Bethel (Gn 28^{18} 35^{14}); and, incidentally, it may be noted that the reference to oil, which a wanderer like Jacob could hardly have carried with him, indicates the projection of a late custom into the remote past. A similar projection is to be seen in the statement that the furniture of the Tabernacle and the Tabernacle itself were anointed with oil (Ex 30^{26} 40^{10}). Similarly, the high priest was anointed with oil, sprinkled and poured on his head (Lv 8^{12}), while in the case of the ordinary priests, the oil was only sprinkled on them (Lv 8^{30}). The anointing of kings represented the formal investiture with an office that was always regarded as a sacred one among the Hebrews. We have explicit references to such anointing in the case of Saul (1 S 10^{1}), David (1 S 16^{13}, 2 S 2^{4} 5^{3}), Solomon (1 K 1^{34}), Joash (2 K 11^{12}), Jehoahaz (2 K 23^{30}), and we may therefore assume that the rite was a general one from the beginnings of kingship among the Hebrews. That the act indicated, besides the purely formal investiture, the actual transfer of Divine powers to the person anointed, may be concluded from the explicit statement in connexion with the anointing ceremony, that 'the spirit of Jahweh' rested with the anointed one; so in the case of David (1 S 16^{13}). Correspondingly, the Divine Spirit leaves Saul (v.^{14}) as an indication that he is no longer in touch with the Divine Essence, *i.e.* is deposed from his sacred office.

In the further spiritualization of the fundamental idea underlying the rite of anointing, namely, the transfer of sacred or Divine qualities to an object or individual, the prophets are naturally viewed as the 'anointed' ones (Ps 105^{15}), even though the ceremony itself was not performed, except possibly in the single instance of Elisha, and even in this case the order given to Elijah to perform it (1 K 19^{16}) may be intended only as a metaphor to indicate the transfer of the Divine Spirit to Elisha. The metaphorical application is clear in the case of Cyrus, who is called the 'anointed' of the Lord, to indicate that he acts in accordance with the Divine quality with which he is imbued. The same interpretation is to be put upon the appellation 'anointed' employed in a late Psalm (105^{15}). From this it was a natural step to designate Israel as the chosen people of Jahweh, as His 'anointed' one (Ps 84^{9} $89^{38.51}$, Hab 3^{13} etc.), in which case 'anointed' has become a synonym for holy, *i.e.* endowed with the holy Essence. The final stage is reached in the doctrine of the Messiah as the 'anointed' one to bring salvation to His people and to mankind in general. In Christianity, Jesus becomes the 'Messiah' *par excellence* (Gr. Χριστός), while Jewish theology in rejecting Jesus as the Redeemer of mankind was gradually led to abandon the doctrine of a personal Messiah, and to accept in its stead the outlook towards a Messianic age. The association of anointing with the Divine Spirit passed over into the Christian Church, which, to emphasize the descent of the Holy Spirit on all believers (2 Co 1^{21}, 1 Jn $2^{20.27}$), instituted the practice of anointing with oil in conjunction with the rites of baptism and confirmation.

As yet no traces of anointing as a religious rite have been found in Babylonia and Assyria, though this does not preclude the possibility of our yet coming across the rite in cuneiform documents, especially for those periods when kingship and Divinity were in close union, as appears to have been the case in the days of Sargon, and during the reign of the Ur dynasty (*c.* 3000 to *c.* 2400 B.C.). In later times we have the pronounced tendency towards the secularization of the office of royalty, with a concomitant centralization of Divine prerogatives in the priesthood; and it would appear that among the Phœnicians likewise the position of the king, under the influence of the late Bab.-Assyr. conception, became a distinctively secular one, connecting itself with that of a lay-judge rather than with that of a priest-king. As for anointing as a secular rite among the Semites, there is every reason to believe that its origin is bound up with the use of unguents as medicinal remedies. In the medical prescriptions preserved on the cuneiform tablets of Ašurbanipal's library, copied from originals that probably date from as early as 2000 B.C., oils of various kinds to be applied to the skin are mentioned. The frequent mention of unguents as remedial agents, both in the OT and NT (Is 1^{6}, Ezk 16^{9}, Lk 10^{34}, Mk 6^{13}, and especially Ja 5^{14}), points in the same direction, and forms the basis of the Roman Catholic sacrament of Extreme Unction, and the Greek and (previous to 1552) Anglican anointing of the sick. The cleansing qualities of unguents appear also to have been recognized at an early period in Babylonia, as well as their power in the prevention of diseases of the skin, so common in hot and moist climates. The use of unguents thus became at once a part of the toilet and an adornment of the person, like dress and ornaments. With the increase of luxury, expensive and highly scented oils were used, and, as a natural corollary to this stage of the custom, anointing became a symbol of prosperity (Ps 92^{10}), while the general tendency in mourning rites to return to the customs of an earlier age led to the view that anointing was not appropriate during the prescribed period of lament for the dead, so that it was discontinued at such times. In the Semitic Orient popular customs are apt to become hardened into ceremonial obligations, and thus the anointing of a guest takes its place as a ceremony of greeting and hospitality, and also as a means of bestowing honour. The account of Mary's anointing Jesus with precious *nard* is an illustration of the observance of the ceremony down to a late period. Anointing oneself before paying ceremonial visits falls under the same category (Ru 3^{3}).

LITERATURE.—Besides the references in this art. see the *Hebrew Archæologies* of Benzinger and Nowack, and the literature in Hastings' *DB*, *s.v.* 'Anointing.' See also *Jacob at Bethel* by A. Smythe Palmer (1899), pt. iii., 'The Anointing,' with some references to literature given there.

MORRIS JASTROW, JR.

ANSELM OF CANTERBURY.—

1. Life.—Anselm was born of noble parents at Aosta (not Gressan) in 1033. After a sheltered youth spent in study, on the death of his mother he crossed the Alps, and after three years of wandering settled in 1059 at the abbey of Bec in Normandy, newly founded (1039) by the saintly Herlwin. There Lanfranc was then at the zenith of his fame as a teacher. In 1060, on the death of his father, Anselm took the cowl, and when Lanfranc removed to Caen (1063), Anselm was elected his successor as prior. The fame of Bec as a school grew greater still. Anselm's genius as a teacher was remarkable; his gentle methods mark an epoch in pedagogics (see esp. Eadmer, *Vita*, i. cc. 10, 11, 22). On the death of Herlwin (Aug. 1078) the reluctant Anselm was appointed abbot. One result of this election was of far-reaching consequences. Bec had been endowed with vast estates in England, and Anselm's journeys in their interest brought him into touch with both the Conqueror and William II., and endeared him to the whole nation. On the death of Lanfranc (May 28, 1089) all men looked to Anselm as his successor. But Rufus, whose settled principle was the spoliation of the Church by keeping sees vacant and claiming their revenues, refused to appoint a new archbishop. In 1093 the king fell ill at Gloucester, and in one of his spasms of remorse sent for Anselm, and after some delay appointed him archbishop (March 6, 1093). To procure Anselm's acceptance violence was almost necessary, but once nominated, the 'furious bull,' already repentant of his penitence, discovered that the 'weak old sheep' (Ead. *Hist. Nov.* [*HN*] 36) was more than his match. Anselm insisted on the restitution to Canterbury of all its estates, and on the recognition of Urban II. (already recognized in Normandy) as the true pope. To this last William II., who had taken advantage of an anti-pope (Clement III.) to seize Peter's pence for himself, was driven to verbal consent by Anselm's threat of retiring to Bec. At last Anselm was enthroned (25th Sept. 1093), doing homage for his temporalities, a matter of interest in view of later disputes.

The question of the recognition of Urban was, however, not really settled, and in 1095, William, angered by Anselm's insistence on his own reformation, as well as by his omission to give bribes, once more refused to acknowledge Urban. 'No man,' he said, 'may acknowledge a pope in England without my leave. To challenge my power in this is to deprive me of my crown' (Ead. *HN* 53). All that Anselm could obtain was the reference of this to a Great Council held at Rockingham (Feb. 25, Eadmer, *Vita*, ii. 16; or March 11, Eadmer, *HN* 53). There, in spite of the defection of the bishops, who were all, with the exception of Gundulph of Rochester, 'king's men,' Anselm virtually won, chiefly through the support given him by the barons (1905).

On the outbreak of other disputes, and the impossibility of obtaining any reformation, Anselm appealed to Rome—a procedure as yet unheard of in England (Oct. 1097). His journey thither was, however, useless, and after two years he left, 'having obtained nought of judgment or of advice' (*HN* 114). Urban, in fact, had troubles enough of his own, and his prelates (Ead. *HN* iii.; cf. Will. Malm. *Gest. Pont.* 34) seem to have been won over by William's gold. But the two years were not lost, for during the summer heat Anselm finished at Schiavi (modern Liberi), in the Alban mountains, his *Cur Deus Homo*. At Urban's request he also attended the Council of Bari (Oct. 1098), and vindicated before the Greeks the Latin doctrine of the Procession of the Holy Spirit. From Rome Anselm, refused admission to England, retired to Lyons, but on the death of Rufus (Aug. 2, 1100) was summoned back to England by Henry I. To his influence, in fact, Henry owed his crown in his struggle with his brother Robert. A new dispute on the subject of lay investitures soon broke out. In England this was undoubtedly an innovation on Anselm's part on the 'customs.' In reality it was a part of the great conflict on the matter on the Continent, first started by Hildebrand, which after a struggle of 56 years, in which 60 battles were fought, was settled at last by the compromise of Worms (Sept. 23, 1122). After many attempts on the part of Henry to win over pope Paschal II., Anselm journeyed once more to Rome to defend his own views. He was forbidden by Henry to return to England (Christmas, 1103). For eighteen months he lived in banishment at Lyons, but on his preparing to excommunicate Henry, the king, influenced by his English queen, Eadgyth or Maud (whose marriage was due to Anselm), gave way, and on August 1, 1107, a compromise was agreed to, virtually a victory for Anselm (*HN* 186).

Before the peace was made, Anselm had returned to England (Aug. 1106), and was received with enthusiasm by king and people. But he had come home to die. For six months he gradually faded away, kept alive by his desire to write a treatise on the origin of the soul. On Wednesday, April 21, 1109, he fell asleep. His canonization, a suit for which was begun by Becket in 1163 (*Hist. Becket*, R.S., v. 35), was deferred, through the troubles over Becket's murder, until 1494 (Wilkins, *Conc.* iii. 641). By one of the ironies of history, it was then the work of the profligate pope Alexander VI. But Anselm had already been enrolled by a greater than Alexander among the immortals (Dante, *Par.* xii., last lines). His feast day is April 21 (*Acta Sanct.*, *s.v.*).

2. Character and place in history.—In character Anselm was a true saint, whose mingled sanctity and sagacity, gentleness and firmness, tenderness and austerity, acted as a charm on all who came under his influence, from the rudest brigands (Ead. *HN* 89), the Conqueror (*Vita*, i. 31), and Duke Roger's Apulian Saracens included (*Vita*, ii. 33), to the most obstinate novice (*Vita*, i. 10) or the pious saint. He possessed that personal magnetism invariably associated in the Middle Ages with miraculous gifts (Eadmer, *Descript. Miraculorum* (R.S.), 425 ff.). His unfeigned humility in all circumstances was the natural result of that mystical detachment which gives abiding interest to his writings.

Anselm's place in the ecclesiastical history of England cannot be exaggerated. Hitherto England had been but loosely connected with Rome, and as a Church had possessed her own customs and a considerable degree of independence. This independence the Conqueror was prepared to continue, as we see from his famous letter of 1076, in reply to Hildebrand (Freeman, *Norman Conquest*, iv. 433). The Conqueror insisted on the complete subordination of Church to State; the modern *congé d'élire* was with him the invariable rule. The powers of convocation were limited by his pleasure; papal letters could not be received unless they had first obtained his sanction (cf. Eadmer, *HN* i. 9). That William I.'s successors could not maintain his position was due to the stand taken by Anselm. This Italian of Aosta, by the force of his piety, character, and learning, succeeded in imposing upon the English Church the ideals of Hildebrand, and bringing the Church in England into close relation with the Church abroad. In many aspects the Reformation was but the rude undoing of his work and a return by the Tudors to the policy maintained by the Conqueror.

3. Writings and place as a thinker and theologian.—Anselm's writings may be classified as follows:—

(i.) Four books of *EPISTLES.*—These letters (over 400 in all) are proof of a wide correspondence, and of the singular regard in which Anselm was held as a director of souls by all sorts and classes. While of value for the details of his life, and for their revelation of his character, there is scarcely a reference in them to the stirring events of the day—another sign of his philosophic detachment of soul.

(ii.) *DEVOTIONAL AND HORTATORY.*—Of these the most important are his *Orationes* (Migne, *PL* clviii. 855 ff.) and *Meditationes* (*ib.* 710 ff.). This last has singular charm; Anselm's mystic communings with his own soul breathing throughout a passionate love for Christ (cf. *Med.* xii. and xiii., both worth reading).

(iii.) *POETICAL.*—That he wrote certain hymns for canonical hours may be reasonably accepted. Much also may be said for assigning to him the *Mariale*, a poem in honour of the Virgin sometimes attributed to St. Bernard, and commonly known as the *Prayer of St. Casimir* of Poland (Rigg, *Anselm*, 97–103; first published in full by Ragey, Lond. 1888). But neither in the *Carmen de Contemptu Mundi* (Migne, *PL* clviii. 687 ff.), with its amazing indifference to quantities, nor in several rude poems on the Virgin attributed to him (*ib.* 1055 ff.), is there any evidence of his authorship save some late and vague traditions. That he had the Italian's passion for the Virgin is, however, clear from his *Orationes* (cf. Rigg, 46–60; Migne, *PL* clviii. 942 ff.).

(iv.) *THEOLOGICAL AND PHILOSOPHICAL.*—Of these the most important are—

(*a*) *Monologion de Divinitatis Essentia.*—In this work, written about 1070, when still prior at Bec (*Epp.* iv. 103), he gives the famous so-called *a priori* proof of the existence of God which has thence found its way into most theological treatises. It is really an application of the Platonic Ideas to the demonstration of Christian doctrine by a logical ascent from the particular to the universal. In the world of experience we are confronted by transitory imperfect phenomena which inevitably lead the mind upward toward an eternal necessary perfect Being. Our recognition of goodness, for instance, in phenomena, drives us to believe in a supreme nature that is good *per se*, and which must be the final *causa causans*, the supreme objective reality in whom our 'ideas' inhere. Thus the existence of God is implicit in ordinary experience.

The criticism of this argument, which rests on certain Realistic presuppositions, would take us too far into philosophical discussions. But we may point out here a criticism that applies to all Anselm's works—his extreme anxiety to satisfy reason ('credo ut intelligam,' *Proslog.* c. 1 fin.; cf. *Cur Deus*, i. 25, last answer of Boso). Anselm in this is akin, though with a difference, to Abelard rather than Bernard (see ABELARD, p. 14, for further discussion of this). He attempts to establish on rational grounds not merely the Trinity, but also the Incarnation; but all knowledge, he holds, must rest on faith.

(*b*) *The Proslogion*, so called because it is in the form of an address to God, is an extension of the *a priori* argument to an attempt to prove the existence of God by a single deductive argument, instead of, as in the *Monologion*, by a long inductive chain. The fool's very denial of God, he argues, involves the idea of God, and of this idea existence is a necessary part. In other words, thought leads by an inherent necessity to the postulate of the Absolute, an argument substantially the same as that employed 600 years later by Descartes. To this reasoning Count Gaunilo († *c.* 1083), a monk of Marmoutier, replied in his *Liber pro Insipiente* or *Apology for a Fool* (printed in Migne, clviii. 242–8) that the idea of the fabled Isles of the Blest does not posit their existence (c. 6). Anselm replied briefly in his *Liber Apologeticus* that there is all the difference between the idea of the *Summum Cogitabile*, or eternal necessary idea, and any particular empirical idea of things which had a beginning, and will have an end (c. 9); contingent existence as such contradicts the idea of the *Summum Cogitabile*, which cannot be conceived save as existing.

The after history of those ontological arguments of Anselm belongs to the history of philosophy. They were too Platonic to be accepted by the Aristotelian schoolmen, with the exception of Duns Scotus (I. *Sent.* D. ii. 2 ii.), but have found their way in various forms into the systems of Descartes, Spinoza, Leibniz, and Hegel. Their most effective critic is Kant (*Pure Reason*, i. (2) ii. (2) iii. (4)). Anselm's obligations to Augustine are also most clear (*e.g. de Trin.* viii. c. 3).

(*c*) *de Fide Trinitatis*, an answer to Roscellin's denial of universals as 'empty words,' was composed in 1098 at Schiavi. Roscellin's denial led him practically to the choice between Sabellianism and Tritheism; for the Trinity is itself a universal in respect of its comprehension therein of a threefold personality. Anselm meets Roscellin's monism by pointing out that it is a fallacy to suppose the universal and the individual to be repugnant *inter se*. Those who care for ingenious similitudes to the doctrine of the Trinity will find, in words that remind us of the Athanasian Creed, a parallel between a 'fountain, river, and lake,' each of which may be called the Nile (c. 8).

(*d*) To one great doctrine of the modern Roman Church Anselm gave a powerful impulse in his *de Conceptu Virginali*. In this work (c. 18), as well as in the *Cur Deus* (ii. 16), he argued for the congruity of the entire sanctification of the Virgin before she conceived of the Holy Ghost. Between this and the doctrine of the Immaculate Conception there is but a step, which he himself may have taken in his last thought (see the tractate of his nephew on the matter, Migne, *PL* clix. 302 ff.). According to Mansi (xxv. 829), Anselm inaugurated in England the Feast of the Immaculate Conception (cf. Ragey, ii. 243–7). In this treatise (cc. 25–28) Anselm defends most rigorously the damnation of all unbaptized children—a logical deduction from his views on original sin.

(*e*) *de Veritate*, a short work which reminds the student of Malebranche. Truth is the accurate perception of the archetypal ideas in the mind of God.

(*f*) *de Libero Arbitrio.*—Mere freedom is not the power of choosing between alternatives, but of persevering in righteousness for its own sake (c. 13)—a doctrine afterwards more fully developed in Kant's *Metaphysic of Ethics.* It is of importance to notice that Anselm points out that original sin need not involve total depravity. Man is still left in possession of an impaired but real 'natural' freedom (c. 3) and the power of will to govern motives (cc. 5, 6).

(*g*) *Cur Deus Homo* (begun in 1094, finished in 1098).—In this most important of his works, which marks an epoch in the development of doctrines of the Atonement, Anselm destroyed once for all (i. 7) the old conception of a ransom paid to the devil. [This theory, propounded by Origen (in *Matt.* xvi. 8, ed. Lommatzsch, iv. 27) was developed by Gregory of Nyssa, Ambrose, and Augustine (*de Lib. Arbit.* iii. 10), and dominated the Church from Gregory the Great to Anselm.] In place of this he substitutes a conflict between the goodness and justice of God, familiar in all forensic ideas of the Atonement, and which reminds the student of Roman doctrines of *lèse majesté.* The defects of this theory (which may be described in brief as the interpretation of the relationship between God and man in terms of the Roman law familiar to Anselm—of Teutonic law Anselm would know nothing—), in addition to its tendency to destroy, as in much current theology, the essential ethical unity of the Godhead, lie in the essential opposition between God and the external world which it posits, leading to the idea of arbitrariness on the part of God, and the absence on the part of the individual of his own personality as an essential factor. This last, we may remark, is a common defect of scholastic Realism. The immanence of God can find no place, and the Pauline mystical conception of union with the Risen Christ (*Rom.* vi. esp. v. 5) is left out of consideration. This is the more remarkable, inasmuch as the Pauline idea would have appealed strongly to Anselm's cast of thought, if he could have freed himself from juridical bondage. But instead we have the superabundant payment by Christ, the substituted sinless God-man, of a debt due from man to the justice of God (i. 12, 23), which debt man, by reason of his original sin, cannot discharge. The keynote of the treatise is thus the paradox 'man *must*, man *cannot*' (ii. 6: 'quam satisfactionem nec potest facere nisi Deus, nec debet nisi homo; necesse est ut eam faciat Deus Homo'). Anselm's theory of the Incarnation in this treatise is far from satisfactory. In his anxiety to avoid conceptions now known as kenotic, he limits the sufferings of Christ to His human nature (i. 8: 'Divinam naturam asserimus impassibilem'). The digression on the restoration from among men of the number of the angels who have fallen (cc. 16–19) is characteristically mediæval.

(*h*) *de Processione Spiritus Sancti.*—This great work, the outlines of which were given at Bari and completed shortly before his death, moves in the main on lines traced out by St. Augustine's *de Trinitate.* The unity of God is absolute save so far as limited by His threefold Personality. The procession of the Holy Ghost from the Son ('Filioque') is more consonant with this absolute unity than the Greek doctrine, which rends the co-inhesion in the unity of the Godhead of the Three Persons (see esp. c. 29).

LITERATURE.—(1) *LIFE OF ANSELM*: We are primarily dependent on his *Letters* (in Migne, *PL*, see below) and his secretary **Eadmer's** *Historia Novorum* and *de Vita Anselmi*, two most conscientious records (best ed. by Martin Rule in Roll's Series, 1884, to which all references have been given; also in Migne, *PL*). Of other sources, **William of Malmesbury**, *de Gest. Pontif* (R.S.), and **Ordericus Vitalis**, *Hist. Eccles.* (ed. Le Prevost, Paris, 1838–55), are of most value. Of modern lives, the best by far is that of **J. M. Rigg**, *Anselm of Canterbury* (1896), especially valuable for the philosophy; **Martin Rule's** *St. Anselm* (2 vols. 1883) is a good storehouse of facts, far from judicial in tone. **Freeman** has dealt at length with Anselm in his *Norman Conquest*, and more fully in his *William Rufus*. For the general reader, who is indifferent to Anselm's position as a theologian, **Dean Church**, *St. Anselm* (1st ed. 1873, often reprinted), may be commended. Of foreign works the best perhaps is **Ch. de Remusat**, *St. Anselme* (2nd ed. 1868). **Ragey's** *Eadmer* (1892) and *S. Anselme* (1877, and abridged ed. 1891) are also of service. The Life of Anselm by **Dean Hook**, *Archbishops* (1860–76), is a valueless Erastian caricature. **Dean Stephens'** account, *English Church*, vol. 2 (1901), is judicious and sympathetic.

(2) *EDITIONS.*—The first complete edition was that of **Gerberon** (Paris, 1721), still often quoted. The earliest dated printed ed. would appear to be at Nuremberg, 1491. All editions, save for Eadmer (see above), are now superseded by that of **Migne** (1853), *PL* clviii. and clix., including Eadmer and many spurious works. There are many reprints of the *Cur Deus Homo*.

(3) *REVIEWS* of the philosophy of Anselm are many. The student should consult **Ueberweg**, etc. Attention may also be drawn to Cremer's contention that Anselm owed much to Teutonic law conceptions as distinct from Roman. See **Cremer**, *SK*, 1880, 759. On the other side Loofs, *Dogmengeschichte*, 273 n.; **Harnack**, *History of Dogma*, iii. 342, n. 2.

H. B. WORKMAN.

ANTEDILUVIANS.—The term 'antediluvian' (Lat. *ante diluvium*) was formerly applied to men or races who lived before the Flood, the latter being regarded as a Deluge universal in extent, and destroying all men excepting Noah and his family. But the term also came to be used by some ethnologists to describe certain races which were believed to have survived the Deluge, the latter being supposed by them to be concerned only with a single race of men, those descended from Adam. This pre-Adamite theory, as it was called, found many advocates during last century. Thus George Catlin referred the American Indian tribes to an antediluvian genus or family called *Anthropus Americanus* (*O-kee-pa*, London, 1866; for a later exponent of this view, see Alex. Winchell's *Pre-Adamites*, Boston, 1880). Now that the belief in a universal Deluge has been generally given up, the name 'antediluvian' has come to have a literary, or it may be a mythological, rather than an ethnological significance. The purpose, then, of this article will be to inquire into, and to some extent compare, the beliefs of various nations concerning those who lived before the great Deluge, especially where that event has come to be part of a definite traditional belief.

1. The Bible antediluvians.—(*a*) *The traditions of J* (and secondary elements [J^s]).—Man is moulded out of the dust of the ground, and becomes a living being by the inspiration of the breath of Jahweh (Gn 2^7); woman is made out of a rib taken from the first man while he slept ($2^{21.\,22}$). He lives at first on the fruit of the garden (2^{16}), in the simple innocence of childhood (2^{25}). He learns sexual knowledge as a consequence of disobedience, and his sense of shame sets him to provide a form of dress (3^7) much like what is still used by the pigmy women of the African Ituri Forest. On his expulsion from Eden this is exchanged for clothes of skin, implying the slaughter of animals (v.^{21}). Their use for sacrifice from this point is implied in the story of Cain and Abel (Gn 4 J^s), though the staple food is still vegetables and cereals, which can be obtained only through hard labour—in evident contrast to the fruit of the garden produced by Divine agency (3^{17-19}). A more important result of the Fall is that man becomes mortal (3^{19}; cf. Ro 5^{12}, 1 Co 15^{21}). On the other hand, 3^{22-24} (J^s) seems to imply that man was naturally mortal, and that immortality could be acquired; but this passage does not accord with $3^{3.\ 17}$, which speaks only of one forbidden tree, and is probably a separate tradition incorporated with J (see *Oxf. Hex., ad loc.*).

The primitive industries are tillage (3^{19}), and also pasturage ($4^{2.\ 3}$ J^s). According to J, pasturage and the nomad life were first introduced by Jabal, the son of Lamech (v.[20]). The same generation witnessed the invention of musical instruments, and the art of smelting brass and iron (vv.[21. 22]). The art of building, on the other hand, is primitive, the first to build a city being Cain (v.[17]).

The attitude of the antediluvians towards religion and morality is more difficult to determine, and here again differences between J and J^s, and even between different sections of J^s, show themselves. The statement that in the time of Enoch men began to call on the name of Jahweh (4^{26} J^s) is hardly consistent with the story of Cain and Abel (J^s). 4^{1b} is too ambiguous to help us much. The story of the origin of the Nephilim from the unnatural union of the 'sons of God' and the daughters of men ($6^{1.\ 2.\ 4}$), in its present connexion with $6^{3.\ 5-8}$, appears to be a reason for the depravity and violence which were the cause of the Deluge. But it is at least possible that this story was originally quite independent of the Deluge story, and that the latter belongs to a later cycle of traditions (J^s), inconsistent, as it obviously is, with $4^{20.\ 21}$ (see *Oxf. Hex.* and art. DELUGE). If so, the term 'antediluvian' is not strictly applicable so far as J, as distinguished from J^s, is concerned.

The names of the antediluvians according to J (+J^s) are Adam, Seth, Enosh ($4^{25.\ 26}$ J^s), Cain, (Abel), Enoch, Irad, Mehujael, Methushael, Lamech (Adah and Zillah), Jabal, Jubal, and Tubal-Cain (4^{16b-24} J). Of these Abel dies childless; Adah and Zillah are the wives of Lamech; Jabal, Jubal, and Tubal-Cain are Lamech's three sons. The rest appear in two genealogical lines, (1) Adam—Enosh, (2) Cain (the elder son of Adam)—Lamech, who is the seventh in the line.

(*b*) *The antediluvians of P.*—The first were made out of nothing by a direct fiat of God, in God's image and after His likeness, male and female simultaneously (Gn $1^{26.\ 27}$ 5^2); were appointed the lords of creation ($1^{26.\ 28}$); and were vegetarians till after the Deluge (1^{29} 9^3). The names of the antediluvians are given in one line only (Gn 5). Their relation with those of J can best be seen by the following table:

P (5)	J^s ($4^{25.\ 26}$)	J
Adam	Adam	(Adam)
Seth	Seth	
Enosh	Enosh	
		$4^{(16-18)}$
Kenan (קינן)		Cain (קין)
Mahalalel (מהללאל)		Enoch
Jared (ירד)		Irad (עירד)
Enoch		Mehujael (מחויאל, מחייאל)
Methushelah (מתושלח)		Methushael (מתושאל)
Lamech		Lamech
Noah		

A comparison of these lists makes it evident that P has combined the two lists of J (+J^s), merely transposing the names of Mahalalel and Enoch. The changes in the form of the names are no more than we find in other parallel lists, and were probably due originally to copyists' errors. P has ignored the tradition that Cain was a son of Adam. Of these antediluvians, Seth is described as begotten in Adam's likeness and his image, implying that the Divine nature of Adam is reproduced in his offspring (5^3, cf. 5^1). Of Enoch it is said that he 'walked with God: and was not; for God took him' (5^{24}), meaning probably that he was translated (for the first phrase cf. 6^9, where it is used of Noah). From this it has been inferred that there is a hint of the translation of Noah comparable to that of Sîtnapišti in the Sumerian Deluge story (see DELUGE).

There is no trace given of the progress of civilization, or any suggestion of a physical difference before and after the Deluge, except that the age of man, which, but for Enoch, had been on an average about 900 years, began to decline rapidly.

2. The Babylonian antediluvians [see Fragm. of Berossus in Eus. (Migne, 1857) *Chron.* Bk. I. ch. i. (2); Driver's *Gen. in loc.*]. Berossus agrees with P in giving (1) 10 antediluvians, and (2) these in one line. (3) Some writers, especially Hommel and Sayce, have found a further agreement in the meaning of some of the names *occupying the same place* in the two records. Thus, in their opinion, Amelon = Bab. *amîlu* = 'man' = Enosh (אנוש), and Ammenon = Bab. *ummânu* = 'artificer' = Kenan (קינן) 'smith.' A more probable identification is that of Evedoracus or Edoranchus with Enoch. Evedoracus is believed to be another form of Enmeduranki, a legendary king of Sippar, a town sacred to the sun-god. This god called Evedoracus to intercourse with himself, taught him secrets of earth and heaven, and instructed him in divination, and thus he became the mythical ancestor of diviners. This identification is confirmed by the 365 years of Enoch's life, which, though having no parallel in Berossus, appear to have some connexion with the 365 days of the solar year. (4) A further point of contact lies in the fact that the sum of the reigns of the Babylonian antediluvians amounts to 432,000 years. If a *soss* (a period of 5 years) be substituted for a week in the Bible record, the period before the Deluge in the latter, 1656 years, will agree with the Babylonian (see Oppert, art. 'Chronology' in *JE*; Driver, *Genesis*, pp. 78–81).

On the other hand, it is difficult to reconcile this probable connexion of Berossus and P with the obvious derivation of the latter from J (+J^s). The difficulty may be got over on the supposition that P indeed took his list of names from J (+J^s), and altered the position of Enoch to agree with that in the list of Bab. antediluvians; that the agreement of the number 10, if it existed in the Babylonian traditions of P's time, was a fortunate coincidence; and, further, that P derived his date of the world's history from a Babylonian tradition, dividing the time among the antediluvians according to a method of his own. It must be admitted that apart from Enoch the identifications of names are ingenious rather than convincing. It must also be borne in mind that Berossus may very probably have himself departed from ancient Babylonian tradition by substituting a *soss* for a week, and possibly even the number 10 for an earlier 7. The translation of the 7th antediluvian, Enoch, Gn 5^{24} (like that of Sîtnapišti, the Sumerian Deluge hero), suggests the possibility that according to ancient tradition there were only 7 antediluvians, the last being Enoch = Lamech = Noah = Sîtnapišti.

3. Antediluvians in the mythological systems of other races.—It is not necessary to say much concerning these. It may suffice to remark that, whereas among Semitic peoples the antediluvians are, if indeed somewhat super-normal, at least human beings, among many other races they are described as more or less abnormal, and not infrequently as monsters, and that the purpose of the Deluge was to do away with them. Thus the antediluvians of a Tibetan legend were ape-like creatures (Andree, *Die Flutsagen*, § 6). In a Fiji legend two races were destroyed by the Deluge, one consisting of women only, the other of men with dogs' tails (Andree, § 37). The Quiché Indians of Guatemala have a curious story connected with the origin of the tribe. Men were first made of clay, but they had neither speech nor intelligence, and were destroyed by a flood of water. Then the gods made another race, the men of wood and the women of resin. These could speak, but only in a senseless fashion, and were destroyed by a storm of burning resin and an earthquake, except a few who became wild asses. The third time men were made of white and yellow maize, and were so perfect that the gods themselves were afraid of them. They therefore took away some of their higher qualities, and they became normal men (Andree, § 73). See, further, DELUGE.

LITERATURE.—See the literature at DELUGE and AGES OF THE WORLD; also the Commentaries on the early chapters of Genesis, esp. S. R. Driver, *The Book of Genesis* (London, 1904), Introd. p. xxxi ff.; A. Dillmann, *Genesis* (Eng. tr., Edin. 1897); F. Delitzsch, *New Com. on Genesis* (Eng. tr., Edin. 1888–9); M. M. Kalisch, *Genesis* (new ed., London, 1879); C. J. Ball, 'The Book of Genesis' in *SBOT* (London, 1896); G. W. Wade, *The Book of Genesis* (London, 1896); T. K. Cheyne, *Traditions and Beliefs of Ancient Israel* (London, 1907); H. G. Mitchell, *The World before Abraham* (London, 1901); A. R. Gordon, *The Early Traditions of Genesis* (Edin. 1908); A. H. Sayce, 'The Antediluvian Patriarchs' in *ExpT*, vol. x. (1899) p. 352 f.

F. H. WOODS.

ANTHROPOLOGY.

[R. MUNRO].

Definition and scope.—Anthropology ('the science of man,' from ἄνθρωπος, 'man,' and λόγος, 'discourse'), in the modern acceptation of the term, treats more particularly of man's origin and place in the animal kingdom; his development as an individual (Ontogeny) and as a race (Phylogeny); the physical and mental changes he has undergone during his career on the globe; his new departure in the organic world as an implement-using animal; and finally, the development of articulate speech and the principles of religion, ethics, altruism, and sociology, which, at the present time, constitute the great landmarks of human civilization. The claims of Anthropology to be recognized as a separate science were for some time successfully opposed on the ground that the phenomena bearing on the history of mankind were already fully dealt with under the sciences of Biology, Anatomy, Physiology, Psychology, Theology, Ethics, Philology, Ethnology, etc. But the startling discoveries made in the collateral sciences of Geology, Palæontology, and pre-historic Archæology, about the beginning of the second half of last century, which culminated shortly after the publication of Darwin's *Origin of Species* (1859) in the general acceptance by scientific men of the theory of organic evolution, conclusively proved that there were ample materials in this new field of research which were by no means covered by any of these sciences. While, therefore, Anthropology may be justly regarded as comprising all the elements of a comprehensive monograph on mankind—all that they are, or have been, or have done, since their generic founder came into existence—, practically it is restricted to an investigation of the earlier stages of humanity, leaving the details of its later phases to be worked out by these other sciences, on the principle of the division of labour. But, even after this limitation of the scope of Anthropology, its remaining materials, which are rapidly increasing in number and variety, present a greater attraction to the philosophic mind than those of any other department of speculative knowledge, because they are so impregnated with human interest that it is felt as if they were data intimately affecting one's own origin and pedigree.

In order to present a brief but reasoned summary of the conclusions to be derived from a study of so fascinating a science, it becomes almost necessary to arrange its scattered materials along certain well-defined lines of investigation, which may be thus categorically stated: (1) Man's physical characteristics; (2) his fossil remains; (3) his handicraft products; (4) his mental superiority over other animals; (5) his social evolution; (6) and lastly, some concluding remarks.

I. MAN'S PHYSICAL CHARACTERISTICS.—So long as the *Hominidæ* were believed to occupy a higher platform in the organic world than other animals, in virtue of specially created endowments, no one apparently thought of looking for evidence of their origin and history in the obscure vistas of prehistoric times. The long-cherished traditions and myths which had gathered around the problem left little room for any other hypothesis than that man's appearance on the field of life, as a fully equipped human being, was the last and crowning achievement of a long series of creative fiats which brought the present world-drama into existence. But to eliminate man altogether from the processes of organic evolution is not only an unwarranted assumption, but is unsupported by any evidence that can be characterized as scientific. No fair-minded person who is conversant with the close anatomical and physiological resemblances between the structural details of man and those of the anthropoid apes—every bone, muscle, nerve, and blood-vessel being virtually the same—and the striking analogy between the complex mechanism of their organs of sense, can seriously deny their community of descent, at least from the purely physical aspect of the subject.

But even the acceptance of the so-called orthodox view, viz. that a male and female were originally specially created, from whom all the present varieties of mankind have descended, would by no means get rid of the evolution theory. For, since Huxley's time, it has generally been admitted that the gulf between civilized and savage man is wider than that between the savage and the highest ape. If, therefore, the ancestors of the white-, black-, and red-skinned people of to-day were originally one undivided stock, why should it be regarded as improbable that that primitive stock itself was a branch of an older stem which included also the ancestors of the anthropoid apes of to-day? The causes of variation which evolved the typical Negrito and Caucasian from one common ancestor were quite adequate to evolve that ancestor from the anthropoid stock in the Tertiary period.

The striking analogy between the bodily structure of man and that of the nearest of the anthropoid apes becomes still more apparent when we consider the phenomena of the fœtal life of animals. Not only does the human embryo start from an ovule similar to, and indistinguishable from, that of many other animals, but its subsequent changes follow on precisely the same lines. All the homologous organs in full grown animals, as the wing of a bird, the flipper of a seal, and the hand of man, are developed from the same fundamental parts of the embryo.

'It is,' says Professor Huxley (*Collected Essays*, vol. vii. p. 92), 'only quite in the later stages of development that the young human being presents marked differences from the young ape, while the latter departs as much from the dog in its development as the man does.

'Startling as the last assertion may appear to be, it is demonstrably true, and it alone appears to me sufficient to place beyond all doubt the structural unity of man with the rest of the animal world, and more particularly and closely with the apes.'

The illustrious von Baer, who first directed special attention to the importance of embryology, formulated a law to the effect that structural differentiation in fœtal development was from a general to a special type. Haeckel, looking at the same phenomena from a different standpoint, came to the conclusion that the development of the individual is a recapitulation of the historic evolution of the race. If this astounding generalization be true, the study of embryology should supply the anthropologist with a method of reaching the goal of his inquiry, by making the progressive stages of man's development the subject of experimental illustrations within the precincts of the laboratory. But, until greater progress is made in this special branch of morphological research, we have few data to guide us in forming precise conclusions on the subject. Meantime, it may be remarked that, if embryology is as conservative of energy as other organic processes, it would be expected that, in course of passing through a series of progressive increments, some of the minor links would ultimately drop out altogether. Nature is full of short cuts. As a parallel instance in ordinary life may be cited the instinct which leads the common honey-bee to fix always on a hexagonal cell instead of the simpler globular form used by the humble bee. Here we have an act of practical intelligence which must have been originally acquired through the ordinary processes of natural selection, but which is now directly transmitted through heredity—thus altogether skipping over its intermediate evolutionary stages.

The theory of man's descent from the lower animals is also greatly strengthened by a number of vestigial, or so-called rudimentary, organs described by anatomists as being normally present, or occasionally to be met with, in the human body. Such organs as canine teeth, the coccyx, inter- and supra-condyloid foramina of the humerus, the *cœcum* and *appendix vermiformis*, fibrous traces of various muscles, etc., are apparently useless in the human economy, while their homologues in other animals have well-defined functions assigned to them. But, indeed, the homological structure of the entire human body is utterly inexplicable on any other hypothesis.

'Thus we can understand,' writes Mr. Darwin, 'how it has come to pass that man and all other vertebrate animals have been constructed on the same general model, why they pass through the same early stages of development, and why they retain certain rudiments in common. Consequently, we ought frankly to admit their community of descent; to take any other view is to admit that our own structure, and that of all the animals around us, is a mere snare to entrap our judgment. This conclusion is greatly strengthened, if we look to the members of the whole animal series and consider the evidence derived from their affinities or classification, their geographical distribution and geological succession' (*Descent of Man*, p. 25).

But if the races of mankind are so closely related both in structure and mode of development to the anthropoid apes, what, it may be asked, are the essential characters which differentiate them from the latter? Flower and Lydekker, in *Mammals Living and Extinct* (p. 740), thus answer the question:

'The distinctions between the *Hominidæ* and *Simiidæ* are chiefly relative, being greater size of brain and of brain-case as compared with the facial portion of the skull, smaller development of the canine teeth of the males, complete adaptation of the structure of the vertebral column to the vertical position, greater length of the lower as compared with the upper extremities, and greater length of the *hallux*, or great toe, with almost complete absence of the power of bringing it in opposition to the other four toes. The last feature, together with the small size of the canine teeth, is perhaps the most marked and easily defined distinction that can be drawn between the two groups.'

Of the above distinctions it will be seen, from various passages in this article, that we have assigned the chief place to the erect attitude, because its attainment was the means of setting free the fore-limbs for the development of their higher functions as tool-making organs, which constitute the true starting-point of humanity. Throughout the animal kingdom there are many morphological changes which strike one as remarkable instances of the adaptation of special means to special ends, such, for example, as the evolution of the fore-limbs into fins and wings so as to make them suitable for locomotion in the different media of water and air. But nature's operations will be searched in vain for a series of phenomena comparable to those which ushered man on the field of life as a skilled craftsman. The preliminary step in this great event was the attainment of the erect attitude which to this day distinguishes him from all other vertebrates. This divergence from the pithecoid group of animals took place sometime in the Tertiary period, and was finally completed by the adjustment of certain muscles and bones so as to balance the upper part of the body on the spinal column, and facilitate bipedal locomotion, which henceforth became man's normal mode of progression.

The organic changes involved in the transformation from the semi-erect attitude of monkeys to that of men cannot be regarded as a very arduous piece of work; so that the assumption of bipedal locomotion, and the differentiation of the hands and feet, would have been effected in a comparatively short period. It was, however, very different with mental evolution, as the formation of brain substance in response to the progressive stimuli of the manipulative organs is a much more elaborate process—a process which has no limits, and indeed is still in operation. Hence, the time requisite to complete the former, or transition, period in the evolution of man is by no means comparable, in point of duration, to the long ages which have elapsed since he became a tool-maker. The evolutionary stages of organic life often run in grooves, and may be long or short in proportion to the facility afforded by the exciting causes in the environment and the benefits conferred by the change. Moreover, it is probable that the attainment of the erect attitude, together with its attendant morphological changes, was completed within a comparatively small area on the globe, so that the chances of finding the fossil remains of a typical specimen of the human representative of this early period are extremely small. On the other hand, the probability of discovering erect beings, with crania in all grades of development, from a slightly changed simian type up to that of civilized man, is enormously greater, not only because of the great length of time since they came into existence, but also because of their increased numbers and wide distribution on the globe. Whatever may have been the precise circumstances which induced the first anthropoid animals to resort to bipedal locomotion, the perpetuation of the habit soon became hereditary; and it has continued ever since to be one of the most distinguishing characteristics of man.

It will be observed that the angle which the axis of the spine of a vertebrate animal makes with the axes of its supporting limbs varies from 90° to zero. In man alone this angle reaches the vanishing point, because the vertebral axis has actually come to coincide with the vertical direction of the two lower limbs, which in his case exclusively support the body. The erect attitude is thus not only peculiar to men, but the ultimate goal of all improvements in the advance of vertebrate life, since the bilateral parts of the body are nicely balanced on the spinal column and the two posterior limbs. It is, therefore, the most conspicuous physiological line of demarcation that exists between man and the lower animals. Moreover, it was indirectly the means of profoundly affecting the subsequent career of mankind on the globe; for the exclusive appropriation of the fore-limbs to manipulative purposes virtually inaugurated a new phase of existence, in which intelligence and mechanical skill became henceforth the dominating factors. The co-operation of these two factors was the starting-point of the long series of inventions and ingenious methods by which mankind have gradually worked out the elements of modern civilization and acquired dominion over all other animals.

Linnæus, in his *Systema Naturæ*, described the genus *Homo* as comprising four primary varieties, viz. Negro, Mongolian, Caucasian, and American, all of which were connected by numerous intermediate forms. To these Blumenbach added the Malay, as a fifth variety. On the other hand, Cuvier reduced them to three, viz. Caucasian, Mongolian, and Ethiopian,—a classification adhered to by M. Verneau in his *Races Humaines*. The description of these various races of mankind, their relation to each other and distribution on the globe, form the special domain of Ethnology and Ethnography (wh. see). For precise details of the anatomical changes consequent on the attainment of the erect attitude, readers are also referred to special works on the subject (see *Memoirs of John Goodsir*, 1868, vol. i. pp. 207–280).

With regard to Cuvier's division of the *Primates* into *quadrumana* and *bimana*, it may be observed that he is only partially accurate; for, although anatomically the four limbs of the former are truly prehensile organs, yet the upper two are decidedly more differentiated as hands than the lower. Even in the apes the distinction between hands and feet had already begun. In man the structural difference between the upper and lower limbs has greatly widened in two opposite directions, the former becoming exclusively adapted for prehensile and manipulative purposes, and the latter as exclusively adapted for locomotion.

II. Some remains of fossil man.—With the completion of the bodily changes involved in the attainment of the erect attitude, the evolution of the present human form, with the exception of some remarkable modifications in the cranium, facial bones, and probably the larynx, was practically completed. As soon as bipedal locomotion became habitual and firmly secured on anatomical bases, there was no apparent reason why the osseous characters of the lower limbs should be sensibly affected by any subsequent increase in the quantity or quality of brain-matter. For example, the femurs, which had henceforth to support the entire weight of the body, would not be in the least degree affected by the nature of the component ingredients of that load. It would, however, be very different with the brain-case and its attachments. For, by the substitution of manufactured weapons in lieu of nature's means of self-defence, the subsequent well-being of these novel bipeds became absolutely dependent on their skill in converting the laws and forces of their environment into useful mechanical appliances. As soon as they recognized that the reasoning faculties were the true source of such inventions, no doubt a premium would be put on useful discoveries. In this way strong motives for the production of more perfect weapons, tools, and other appliances were constantly coming within the scope of their daily avocations, the result of which would be a progressive increase in intelligence and a corresponding increase in brain substance. Now, according to the well-established doctrine of the localization of brain function, the additional brain molecules and cells thus acquired had their seat of growth for the most part somewhere in the cerebral hemispheres, which lie well within the anterior portion of the brain-case. The mere mechanical effect of this increment to the physical organ of thought would be to increase the weight of the anterior half of the head, and so to upset its finely equipoised position on the top of the spinal column. But, as any interference with the free and easy rotatory movements of the head would manifestly be disadvantageous to the individual in the struggle of life, it became necessary to counteract the influence of this disturbing element by the action of some other concurrent morphological process, which would not be prejudicial to the general well-being of the human economy. This object was partly attained by a retrocession, or contraction, of the facial bones, especially the jaw-bones, towards the central axis of the spinal column, and partly by a backward shifting of the cerebrum over the cerebellum. As the gradual filling up of the cranial cavity progressed *pari passu* with those cranial alterations, we have, in the facial angle of Camper, a rough mechanical means of estimating the progress of mental development during the period of man's existence as a human being, *i.e.* since he attained the erect attitude.

One of the results of this retrocession of the facial bones was the gradual contraction of the alveolar borders of the jaws, thereby diminishing the space allotted to the teeth,—a fact which plausibly accounts for some of the peculiarities differentiating the older fossil jaws from modern specimens. Thus, in the dentition of the former, the last, or third, molar is the largest, whereas in the latter it is the smallest. Not only so, but among some European races of to-day the last four molar (wisdom) teeth make their appearance at a later date in the individual's life than in early prehistoric times (a fact which has also been noted in a few Neolithic specimens), so that the so-called wisdom teeth seem to be on the highway to become vestigial organs. It is interesting to note that this shortening of the dental portion of the human jaw attracted the attention of Darwin, who, however, attributed it to 'civilized men habitually feeding on soft, cooked food, and thus using their jaws less.'

Another peculiarity of civilized races is the greater prominence of the chin, a feature which may also be due to the contraction of the alveolar ridges, and the more upright setting of the incisor teeth in their sockets. But whatever the precise cause may have been, there can be no doubt that the gradual formation of the chin has had a striking parallelism with the progressive stages in man's intellectual development ever since he started on his human career.

The evidence on which these views are founded consists of a few fossil skulls and other portions of human skeletons (necessarily fragmentary owing to the ordinary processes of decay). A short description will now be given of one or two of the more interesting specimens.

(1) *Java skull*.—Perhaps the oldest and most controverted of such remains are a *calvaria*, two molar teeth, and a left femur, found in 1891–1892 by Dr. Eugène Dubois in Upper Pliocene strata in the island of Java. After comparing these bones with the corresponding parts of other human skeletons, both fossil and modern, and of some anthropoid apes, Dr. Dubois published, in 1894, a very complete memoir on the subject, with descriptive details and photogravures of each bone. In this memoir (*Pithecanthropus erectus: eine menschenähnliche Uebergangsform aus Java*, Batavia, 1894) he assigns these remains to an animal having an erect attitude like man, and a brain-case with mixed characters, partly simian and partly human, to which he gave the name *Pithecanthropus erectus*. Unfortunately these bones, though found in the same horizontal strata, were not close together,—the skull-cap being 15 mètres from the femur—and consequently there is room for the objection that they did not belong to the same individual. Expert opinion was greatly divided as to the conclusions to be derived from these relics. Most of the anatomists who critically examined the femur pronounced it human—the late Prof. Virchow being almost alone in maintaining that it might have belonged to one of the anthropoid apes. As to the two molar teeth, there was so much difference of opinion among specialists—some regarding them as

simian and others as human—that it is quite unnecessary to advance any further proof of their intermediate character. But the 'bone of contention,' *par excellence*, was the *calvaria*, with regard to which some twenty experts of various nationalities ranged themselves into three groups, according as they held it to be human, simian, or a transition form (see Munro, *Prehistoric Problems*, pp. 165–168).

The following is a brief description of its prominent characters:—External surface generally smooth and without any marked ridges; sutures almost entirely obliterated; frontal bone slightly keel-shaped in the line of the frontal suture; *glabella*, supra-orbital ridges, and occipital protuberance strikingly prominent; cranial vault depressed, and on section (antero-posterior) showing an arch intermediate between that of the anthropoid apes and that of an average European man. Its general dimensions may be thus abbreviated:

Antero-posterior diameter (max.)	185 mm.
Transverse diameter	130 ,,
,, ,, (behind the orbit)	90 ,,
Height in the parietal region (max.) .	62 ,,
Cephalic index	70 ,,
Estimated cranial capacity . . .	1000 c.c.

The specially interesting features of the Java *calvaria* are its estimated small cranial capacity, the great prominence of the supra-orbital ridges and the occipital protuberance, and its remarkably low and retreating forehead. In the absence of the facial bones, we can only surmise that, to be in keeping with the above simian characters, the individual who owned this skull presented a highly prognathic appearance, something approaching to that of *Hylobates*, to which Dr. Dubois compares it. But whatever views may be held as to the anthropological value of this *calvaria*, the femur found in the same stratum conclusively proves that there had then been in existence a being of the genus *Homo* which had assumed the erect attitude as its normal mode of progression, *i.e.* at a time prior to the advent of that great landmark in the physical history of the northern hemisphere known as the Glacial period.

(2) *Neanderthal skull.*—In 1857, Prof. Schaaffhausen and Dr. Fuhlrott published an account of a skeleton found, the year before, in the cave of Feldhofen, situated at the entrance to a small ravine called Neanderthal, on the right bank of the river Düssel. The cave has long been quarried away, but its dimensions are reported to have been about 16 feet in length, 11 feet in breadth, and 8 feet in height. On its uneven floor lay a mass of consolidated mud, about 5 feet in depth, without stalagmitic deposits, but sparingly mixed with rounded fragments of chert. On this deposit being removed, the human bones in question were discovered. No other animal remains, with the exception of a bear's tooth of which neither the position nor character was determined, were found in the cave.

The Neanderthal human remains, especially the skull, presented such remarkable peculiarities that, when they were first exhibited at a scientific meeting at Bonn, doubts were expressed by several naturalists as to whether they were really human. The limb-bones were characterized by great thickness, with unusual development of the elevations and depressions for the attachment of muscles, and the ribs had a singularly rounded shape and abrupt curvature—all characters indicating great muscular power. The left humerus was more slender than the right—a fact which suggested the idea that the two did not belong to the same individual; but this peculiarity was shown to have been the result of an injury during lifetime. The cranium, which was of great size and thickness, was characterized by a long elliptical shape, a low retreating forehead, excessive development of the frontal sinuses, and a great projection of the occipital region. The sutures were nearly obliterated, and the line of the frontal suture was marked by a slight ridge. Its dimensions were as follows:

Antero-posterior diameter (max.)	.	200 mm.
Transverse ,,	.	144 ,,
Frontal ,, (min.)	.	106 ,,
Frontal ,, (max.)	.	122 ,,
Cephalic index	.	72 ,,
Estimated cranial capacity (Huxley)	.	1330 c.c.

With regard to this skull, Professor Huxley, writing in 1863, says:

'There can be no doubt that, as Professor Schaaffhausen and Mr. Busk have stated, this skull is the most brutal of all known human skulls, resembling those of the apes not only in the prodigious development of the superciliary prominences and the forward extension of the orbits, but still more in the depressed form of the brain-case, in the straightness of the squamosal suture, and in the complete retreat of the occiput forward and upward, from the superior occipital ridges' (Lyell's *Antiquity of Man*, p. 84).

Here also, as was the case with the Java *calvaria*, we have no means, owing to the absence of the facial bones, of judging of the degree of prognathism of this very pronounced pithecoid specimen of humanity.

(3) *Les Hommes de Spy.*—In 1886 two human skeletons were found deeply buried in undisturbed débris at the entrance to a grotto called Belcheaux-Roches, at Spy-sur-l'Orneau, in the province of Namur, Belgium. The interior of the grotto had been examined more than once, but in front of it there was a terrace, projecting 13 yards, which had not been previously excavated. It was in this terrace that MM. Lohest and de Puydt made excavations which unearthed these skeletons. The outer skeleton was found at a distance of 26 feet from the entrance to the cave, under a mass of rubbish 12½ feet in depth and composed of four distinct strata, none of which appeared to have been hitherto broken through. It lay on the right side, across the axis of the cave, with the hand resting on the lower jaw, and the head towards the east. The other was 8 feet nearer the present entrance to the cave, but its position was not determined with so much accuracy as the former. Associated with these skeletons were worked flints of the type known as *Moustérien*, and some animal remains representing the following fauna:

Rhinoceros tichorhinus (abundant).
Equus caballus (very abundant).
Cervus elephas (rare).
Cervus tarandus (very rare).
Bos primigenius (pretty abundant).
Elephas primigenius (abundant).
Ursus spelæus (rare).
Meles taxus (rare).
Hyæna spelæa (abundant).

Immediately over the skeletons was a hardened layer composed of chippings of ivory and flint, pieces of charcoal, and some angular stones of the surrounding limestone rock. Above this there was a reddish deposit containing remains of the same fauna, but the worked objects indicated a decided advance in civilization—awls and borers of flint, together with needles, beads, and ornaments of bone and ivory. Above this was a bed of yellowish clay, in which were still found bones of the mammoth and various flint implements; and lastly, a mass of clay and fallen rocks, without relics of any kind.

The osteological characters of one of the Spy crania correspond in a remarkable degree with those of the Neanderthal skull, as may be seen from the following measurements by Professor Fraipont (*Congrès international d'Anthropologie et d'Archéologie préhistoriques*, Paris, 1889, p. 333):

	Spy.	Neanderthal.
Antero-posterior diameter (max.) .	200 mm.	200 mm.
Transverse	140 ,,	144 ,,

	Spy.	Neanderthal.
Frontal (min.)	104 mm.	106 mm.
,, (max.)	114 ,,	122 ,,
Horizontal circumference . . .	580 ,,	(571?) 590 ,,
Cephalic index	70 ,,	72 ,,

As regards the great development of the superciliary prominences, the low retreating forehead, and the depressed and elongated form of the cranium, both these skulls present a more brutal appearance than any human skull known up to the time of the Java discovery.

According to M. Fraipont, the entire anatomical characters of the Spy skeleton are in harmony with the same lowness of type shown by the skull. The jaws are deep and powerful, the chin slopes away from the teeth downwards and backwards, while the teeth and alveolar border have a striking prognathic appearance. The last molar teeth are not smaller than those immediately in front of them. The long bones are materially different from those of the normal Belgians of the present day, being generally shorter and stouter.

It is, however, only just to note that the pithecoid characters of the other Spy skull appear to be less pronounced, the cranial vault being more lofty and the cephalic index at least 74.

It has already been surmised that the individuals to whom the Java and Neanderthal skulls belonged had prognathic profiles, on the ground that this feature harmonized with their other observed simian characters. It is, therefore, particularly interesting to note that the jaws of these Spy men are highly prognathic—a fact which greatly strengthens the inference as to the two former.

(4) *Naulette jaw.*—Among isolated cranial bones occasionally discovered, the lower jaw, being merely attached to the skull by muscular and ligamentary tissues, is most frequently met with. Perhaps the most instructive of these fossil jaws is the *Naulette mâchoire*, discovered in 1885, in the *Trou de la Naulette*, by M. E. Dupont, Director of the R. N. H. Museum at Brussels. The cave known under the above name is situated on the left bank of the river Lesse, near Dinant, and contained much débris and remains of the Quaternary fauna, among them being this jaw, at a depth of 4·50 mètres beneath its final or modern floor. Though in a fragmentary condition, it presents certain peculiarities which strongly differentiate it from the corresponding bone in modern civilized man. Its characteristics, according to M. Dupont (*L'Homme pendant les Âges de la Pierre*, p. 99), may be thus stated:

(*a*) Its small height, in proportion to the thickness of the body, gives it an exceptionally stumpy appearance.

(*b*) The chin, instead of projecting forwards, slopes backwards; and the 'genial tubercules' (*apophyse géni*) on its inner surface are wanting.

(*c*) The posterior molars are larger than the others, and present the appearance of having five roots, as shown by the size of the sockets, all the teeth being absent from the mandible when discovered.

Dr. Broca came to the conclusion that the Naulette jaw, in its anatomical characters, approached the simian type more than any previously known.

'Nous serons autorisés à conclure,' he writes, 'que cette mâchoire, dont l'antiquité prodigieuse remonte au temps du mammouth, est de tous les restes humains que l'on connaît jusqu'ici celui qui se rapproche le plus du type des singes' (*Congrès International*, etc., Paris, 1867, p. 401).

With respect to the retreating slope of the chin and the character of the teeth, he considered that the individual who owned the Naulette jaw held an intermediate place between man and the anthropoid apes; and in support of this view he exhibited a sketch of a number of human mandibles showing a regular upward gradation from the extremely sloping chin of a chimpanzee up to that of a modern Parisian (*ib.* p. 399). These facts go far to establish the generalization that, as men advanced in intelligence, the prognathism which they inherited from their simian-like ancestors became gradually smaller, until the face assumed the almost straight and classic profile of modern times. This view is further strengthened by evidence derived from a comparison between the skulls of modern civilized people and those of the lower races still inhabiting the globe. This method of inquiry has yielded some striking results as regards the degrees of gnathism and frontal development which they respectively exhibit. The extent of this difference is well illustrated by Professor Owen (*Comparative Anatomy*, vol. ii. pp. 558, 560), in a comparison which he makes between the cranium of a native Australian and that of a well-formed European, from which it will at once be seen that the former has a low retreating forehead and a highly prognathic profile. The characters of the European skull, which present a very marked contrast to the former, are thus described by the Professor:

'In more intellectual races the cranial cavity is relatively larger, especially loftier and wider. The fore-parts of the upper and lower jaws, concomitantly with earlier weaning, are less produced, and the contour descends more vertically from the longer and more prominent nasals. The ascending ramus of the mandible is loftier. The malar is less protuberant, and the mastoid more so.'

(5) That other crania supposed to be of great antiquity have been recorded whose anatomical features do not, apparently, harmonize with these views so well as do those of the Java, Neanderthal, and Spy specimens, need not cause any surprise, considering the difficulty which sometimes occurs in correctly estimating their antiquity. Thus, the famous *skull of the old man of Cromagnon*, long regarded as originally belonging to one of the hunter-artists of the late Palæolithic period, shows a decided approach in all its characters to the normal type of civilized man. Its cephalic index is 73·6 and its capacity 1590 c.c. The height of its original owner was 1·82 mètres. The lower jaw has a large ascending ramus, behind which, on both sides, the third molar is partly hidden. These two teeth are also smaller than the other molars, being in this respect more allied to the dentition of Neolithic and modern races. For these reasons, as well as for the fact that the Cromagnon skeletons were found on the surface of the Palæolithic débris of the rock shelter of Cromagnon, some anthropologists maintain that this old Cromagnon man belonged to the early Neolithic period. But between the latest phase of the life of the Palæolithic artists of middle Europe and the earlier Neolithic people there was probably no great interval of time. Although the Cromagnon human remains were lying over the true culture débris of the *Moustérien* period, the amount of superincumbent talus under which the skeletons lay shows that they could not have been much later than the transition period. Moreover, there are other human remains with regard to which no such doubts have been raised, such as *the skulls of Chancelade and Laugerie Basse*, both found in the Dordogne district, which show equally advanced cranial characters.

(6) The recent discovery of two skeletons in the *Grotte des Enfants* near Mentone, which Dr. Verneau describes as belonging to a race intermediate between the Neanderthaloid and Cromagnon races, marks an important addition to fossil craniology. They belonged to a young man and an aged female of small stature, and lay on a hearth-layer at a depth of 7·75 mètres. The cephalic index of the former is 69·72 and of the latter 68·58, and both have prominent negroid jaws. But the interesting feature of the discoveries in this cave was that, a little more than 2 ft.

higher up in the débris, another skeleton of the Cromagnon type was found, measuring 6 ft. 3 in. in height and with a cephalic index of 76·26 (*L'Anthropologie*, vol. xiii. pp. 561–583). That these two distinct races should be thus brought nearly on the same chronological horizon by no means discredits Dr. Verneau's theory, as it is not improbable that, while a higher race was being developed, individuals of an older and lower race still survived in Europe. In corroboration of this we have the record of two skulls, of a distinctly negroid type, having been found among Neolithic remains in Brittany (*BSAP*, ser. v. vol. iv. p. 432). But, even accepting the Cromagnon race, whose skulls indicate a great stride in mental capacity over those of Spy and Neanderthal, as belonging to the latest phase of the Reindeer period in France, it does not appear to the present writer that they disclose a greater brain-case than would be expected of a people who displayed such artistic feeling and mechanical skill as the authors of the art gallery of the Reindeer period (see § III.).

(7) Some forty or fifty human skulls, more or less imperfect, and supposed to date back to Quaternary times, have been recorded up to this date from almost as many different localities throughout Europe, occasionally in alluvial deposits, but more frequently in the accumulated débris of caves and rock-shelters. Some years ago (*Crania Ethnica*, 1873–1879), MM. Hamy and de Quatrefages carefully examined all the fossil remains then known, and classified them under the names of the localities where the most typical specimens were found. Among dolichocephalic, or long-headed, they described two distinct races, one represented by a portion of a *calvaria* found at Canstadt and the other by the skull of the old man of Cromagnon. The brachycephalic, or broad-headed, were made to represent four races, under the generic designation of *Furfooz*, the name of a cave in the valley of the Lesse, thus:

1. The race of Canstadt,		Cephalic index,	72
2. The race of Cromagnon,		,,	73·76
3. The race of Furfooz,	1st, Furfooz,	,,	79·31
	2nd, ,,	,,	81·39
	3rd, Grenelle,	,,	83·53
	4th, La Truchère,	,,	84·32

It was subsequently ascertained that these Furfooz skulls were the osseous remains of Neolithic interments, which shows both the difficulty and the danger of making chronological classifications on imperfectly observed data.

As the outcome of this short review of fossil craniology, perhaps the most important outstanding feature is that the three skulls above described as typical examples are all dolichocephalic. The race of Cromagnon was, in all probability, separated from the Neanderthal and Spy troglodytes by an interval of time which can be only approximately measured by the duration of the larger part of the Glacial period. The appearance of brachycephalic races in Central Europe only at the beginning of the Neolithic period is an ethnological problem not yet satisfactorily explained. It has been abundantly proved, by the contents of dolmens and other sepulchral tombs, that two races, one dolichocephalic and the other brachycephalic, lived contemporary with each other in the South of France (*RAnth*, 1873; *Matériaux pour l'histoire primitive et naturelle de l'homme*, vol. xii. 1877, etc.). From the remains in the artificial caves of Petit-Morin, investigated and described by Baron de Baye (*Archéologie Préhistorique*), the two races seemed to have more or less coalesced. From the amalgamation of these varied races the highly mixed populations of modern Europe can be readily accounted for; but whether the brachycephalic were developed from the dolichocephalic people at an earlier period still remains a controverted problem. These passing glimpses of the early races of man in Europe support the hypothesis that two peoples widely separated had come into contact in Southern France, and perhaps elsewhere in Europe, at the close of the Reindeer period. Of these the dolichocephalic appear to have been long indigenous to the locality, and were probably the direct descendants of the Palæolithic men whose skeletons were found in the caves of Spy and Neanderthal.

III. MAN AS A TOOL-MAKER. — Man may be differentiated from all other animals by the fact that he is a skilled mechanic, and manufactures a great variety of objects which he largely utilizes instead of the organs of offence and defence with which nature originally endowed him. In lieu of the specially developed teeth, claws, horns, hoofs, etc., used more or less for these purposes by other animals, man has provided himself with a multiplicity of knives, axes, swords, spears, arrows, guns, etc., through the instrumentality of which his self-preservation is more efficiently maintained.

(1) Looking at the accumulated products of man's mechanical ingenuity, which have been gathered on the highways and byways of his primeval life, from an archæological standpoint, there can be no doubt that they are characterized by successive increments of improvement, both in technique and execution, from the rudest forms up to the most perfect appliances of modern times. That, during the transition period, broken pieces of wood and natural stones would be used as missiles, without being fashioned into any particular shape, may be assumed as a corollary to the theory that man passed from a state of existence in which tool-making was unknown; also that, in the course of time, such missiles would give place to stones so slightly worked as not to be readily distinguished from the accidental operations of nature. Objects which come under this category are named *eoliths* (ἠώς, 'dawn,' and λίθος, 'stone'). They are recorded as having been found among gravels on chalk plateaus in various parts of the South of England, notably on the Kent plateau. Mr. Read, who describes and figures some of these eoliths in his *Guide to the Antiquities of the Stone Age in the British Museum*, thus refers to them (p. 10):

'It is not the province of this Guide to enter into the arguments which have been brought forward against or in favour of the artificial character of Eoliths, but it may be said that, whether their claims can be substantiated or not, the existence of implements of a ruder kind than those of the drift is in itself not improbable. For no invention reaches perfection suddenly, and each stage of advance is attained by an infinitely slow progress from the simple to the more complex. The majority of the drift implements are clearly something more than the first efforts of an unpractised hand: they show, on the contrary, signs of a comparatively long development, and it may be fairly argued that their ruder prototypes must exist somewhere. It was only to be expected that they should have escaped notice for a longer time than the typical Palæoliths, if only because they must necessarily be more difficult to distinguish from naturally fractured flints.'

(2) The recognition, even among anthropological savants, that some peculiarly shaped flints, now known as palæoliths, were manufactured by man and used as implements, is scarcely half a century old. A fine pear-shaped flint of this type was found along with an elephant's tooth at Gray's Inn Lane, London, about the end of the 17th century, but, though described in the Sloane Catalogue and preserved in the British Museum, its true significance became known only when Sir W. Franks pointed out its identity with those found in the Valley of the Somme (*Ancient Stone Implements*, p. 521). Also, as early as 1797, Mr. John Frere, F.R.S., described to the Society of Antiquaries some flint 'weapons' found, associated with the bones of extinct animals, at a depth of 12 feet in

brick-earth at Hoxne, in Suffolk. He was so much struck with the situation that he gave a precise account of the circumstances, and he regarded the implements as belonging 'to a very remote period indeed, even beyond that of the present world' (*Archæologia*, vol. xiii. p. 204). Mr. Frere presented specimens of the Hoxne implements to the Museum of the Society; yet here they lay, unheeded and unsuggestive, till 1859, when Sir John Evans, on his return from Amiens and Abbeville, recognized them as similar to those in the collection of M. Boucher de Perthes.

(3) It was about the beginning of the second quarter of last century that Kent's Cavern, near Torquay, first became a subject of archæological interest, owing to the researches of the Rev. J. MacEnery, who asserted that he found in it flint implements, associated with bones and teeth of extinct animals, beneath a thick continuous sheet of stalagmite. But the legitimate inference from these facts, viz. that man was contemporary with these animals and lived before the deposition of the stalagmite, had little chance of being accepted when opposed by the teaching and authority of so famous a geologist as Dr. Buckland, author of *Reliquiæ Diluvianæ* and of the Bridgewater Treatise on Geology and Mineralogy.

The facts on which Mr. MacEnery based his conclusions were verified by fresh excavations made by Mr. Godwin-Austen, F.G.S., in 1840, and subsequently by a committee appointed by the Torquay Natural History Society in 1846. Papers embodying the results of these investigations were read at the Geological Society of London and at the meeting of the British Association in 1847. But, according to the late Mr. Pengelly, F.R.S., the reception given to these researches was not encouraging, and the inconvenient conclusions arrived at 'were given to an apathetic, unbelieving world.'

(4) Another discovery of a similar character was the Windmill-Hill Cavern at Brixham, explored in 1858, under the auspices of a committee appointed by the Royal and Geological Societies of London. The first paper on the result of this investigation was read by Mr. Pengelly in September 1858, at the meeting of the British Association, then held at Leeds, in which it was announced that 'eight flint tools had already been found in various parts of the cavern, all of them inosculating with bones of mammalia at depths varying from 9 to 42 inches in the cave-earth, on which lay a sheet of stalagmite from 3 to 8 inches thick, and having *within* it and *on* it relics of the lion, hyæna, bear, mammoth, rhinoceros, and reindeer.' This paper, to use the phraseology of Mr. Pengelly, produced a decided 'awakening,' besides indirect results of the highest importance.

(5) The discovery by M. Boucher de Perthes of rude flint implements, associated with bones of the mammoth and other extinct animals, in the ancient gravel beds of the valley of the Somme, at various levels considerably above the present highest flood-marks of the river, equally failed to attract scientific attention. An account of his researches, under the title *Antiquités Celtiques et Antédiluviennes*, was published in 1847, but for upwards of ten years it lay absolutely unheeded. Nor can there be any doubt that the ultimate recognition of the importance of his discoveries was one of the indirect results of the less sceptical tone prevalent in scientific circles in Britain in consequence of the exploration of the Brixham Cavern just referred to.

Excluding the eoliths as too controversial a subject to be discussed in this brief review, it would appear that certain flint implements found at various depths in the higher gravels of our present river systems are the oldest evidence of man's handicraft in Europe. These gravels had been left high and dry long before the rivers had excavated the winding valleys at the bottom of which they now flow. The Hoxne implement, above referred to, is a typical specimen of what French archæologists call the *coup de poing*, probably the earliest type of hand-implement known, which came to be widely imitated among the earlier races of mankind. Implements of the *coup de poing* type vary considerably both in form and in size, the degree of variability being, however, strictly compatible with their function as hand-tools. They have been discovered in widely separated localities in Europe, Asia, and Africa; and nearly all possess the peculiarity of being made by chipping a nodule so as to convert it into a suitable hand-tool—the flakes struck off being apparently of no use.

The original manufacturers of these Palæolithic tools are supposed to have entered Europe from Africa at a time when there was easy communication between the two continents by several land bridges across the basin of the Mediterranean. The climate being sub-tropical, these naked nomads appear to have inhabited the wooded banks of rivers, living on fruits and the smaller fauna, till the advent of the Glacial period forced them to take shelter in caves and to protect their bodies by skins of animals. It is difficult to realize how much the severe climate which then supervened contributed to the improvement of their physical and mental attributes. It roused their dormant energies to the pitch of being able to adapt their mode of life to the changing conditions of their environment—for the adage that necessity is the mother of invention was as applicable then as now. The natural food productions of a warm climate gradually disappeared, until finally there was little left but wild animals,—mammoth, reindeer, chamois, horse, bison, etc.—many of which came from arctic regions. To procure necessary food and clothing in these circumstances greatly taxed the skill and resources of the inhabitants. The difficulty was ultimately solved by the manufacture of special weapons of the chase, with which they successfully attacked the larger wild animals which then occupied the country. The *coup de poing*, which for a long time served all the purposes of primitive life, gradually gave place to spear- and lance-heads fixed on long handles, together with a great variety of minor weapons and tools, made of stone, bone, horn, and wood. When the Palæolithic people finally emerged from this singular contest with the forces of nature, they were physically and mentally better than ever equipped for the exigencies of life. A greater power of physical endurance, improved reasoning faculties, an assortment of tools adapted for all kinds of mechanical work, and some experience of the advantage of housing and clothing, may be mentioned among the trophies which they carried away from that long and uphill struggle.

Of the kind of life which these early people of Europe led we have remarkably precise evidence in the food-refuse, and the lost, broken, and worn-out implements, weapons, and ornaments which have been discovered by excavating the caves and rock-shelters they had from time to time inhabited. The result of these investigations has disclosed a steady progress in the manufacture of industrial implements, weapons of the chase, and personal ornaments. When it was ascertained that the larger flakes could be utilized as sharp cutting tools, attention began to be directed to the art of producing them for teleological purposes. After some experience, it was found that a skilled workman could produce a flake of any required size and shape. By subjecting these flakes to secondary chipping, implements of great variety and efficiency were in the course of time abundantly produced. This was indeed an important step of advance in flint industry, evidence of which is to be found in the fact that henceforth flakes were the useful products, while the residuary core was rejected as waste. The worked flints found in the earlier inhabited caves of France and Belgium, such as Moustier and Spy, show that secondary flaking was already in progress—thus proving that their habitation was later than the formation of the river-drift gravels containing worked flints.

From a careful inspection of the handiwork of these troglodytes, it will be seen that it is characterized by a gradual development from simple to more complete forms. Implements, tools, and weapons were slowly but surely made more efficient, thus evincing on the part of their manufacturers a progressive knowledge of mechanical principles. Art and ornament, too, had taken deep root among these primitive hunters, and before the end of their civilization they evinced a remarkable artistic taste and power of execution. Hence G. de Mortillet classified their industrial remains in chronological sequence into *Moustérien*, *Solutréen*, and *Magdalénien*, — a nomenclature which he founded upon the names of the most typical stations then explored. The earliest of the Palæolithic stations was Le Moustier, situated on the right bank of the Vezère (Dordogne). During its habitation by man the climate was cold and damp, and among the contemporary fauna were the mammoth, woolly rhinoceros, cave-bear, and musk-ox. The special features of the industrial remains of this period were the scarcity of the *coup de poing*—which was so characteristic of the older river-drift deposits—and the splitting up of flints into smaller implements, such as scrapers, trimmed flakes, etc. The next typical station in ascending order was the open-air encampment of Solutré (Saône-et-Loire).

The stage of culture here disclosed was characterized by great perfection in the art of manufacturing flint implements, especially spear- and lance-heads in the form of a laurel leaf, and by the abundance of horses and reindeer used by the inhabitants as food. The climate was mild and dry, the great glaciers were on the wane, and the rhinoceros seems to have disappeared from the scene. The third and last of the typical stations was the well-known rock-shelter of La Madelaine, characterized by the abundance of objects made of bone and horn, the development of a remarkable artistic talent, the predominance of a northern climate and fauna, and the extinction of the mammoth towards the close of the period.

The civilization thus developed represents the outcome of a system of human economy founded on the application of natural laws to mechanical purposes, but little affected by the principles of religion or ethics. The mysteries of the supernatural had not then been formulated into the concrete ideas of gods and demons. The notions of good and evil, right and wrong, were still dominated by the cosmic law that might is right. Neither gloomy forebodings nor qualms of conscience had much influence on the conduct of these people. Their philosophical and sentimental speculations, if they had any, centred exclusively on the habits of the animals they hunted, and on the strategic means by which they could be waylaid and captured. During this time they made great progress in the manufacture of mechanical appliances, as shown by the number of flint implements —saws, borers, scrapers, etc.—with which they made needles, pins, ornaments, weapons, and other objects, including the so-called *bâtons de commandement*. Upon the whole, it would appear as if their minds were engrossed with the chase and its exciting scenes and incidents, for the relics of their domestic economy indicate little more than the art of roasting or broiling the flesh of the captured animals, and of converting their skins into garments. Possibly some round pebbles, abundantly found in the débris, may have been used as 'pot-boilers,' but a few stone mortars, which occasionally turned up, would seem to have been used only for mixing colouring matter to paint their bodies. Of agriculture, the rearing of domestic animals, the arts of spinning and weaving, and the manufacture of pottery, they appear to have been absolutely ignorant. But yet, in an environment of such primitive resources and limited culture associations, these wild hunters developed a genuine taste for art, and cultivated its principles so effectually that they have bequeathed to us an art gallery of over 400 pieces of sculpture and engraving, many of them being so true to their original models that they bear a favourable comparison with analogous works of the present day. They adorned their persons with perforated teeth, shells, coloured pebbles, and pendants of various kinds. They depicted the animals with which they were familiar, especially those they hunted for food, in all their various moods and attitudes, often with startling fidelity. Harpoons, spears, and daggers of horn and bone were skilfully engraved, and sometimes their dagger handles were sculptured into the conventional form of one or other of their favourite animals. In several instances they also adorned the walls of the caverns they frequented with incised outlines of the neighbouring fauna, and made actual colour-paintings of them in black and ochre, or in one of these colours.

The other characteristic feature in the lives of these people was that they lived exclusively on the produce of the chase, for without agricultural and pastoral avocations they could do little else than organize daily hunting and fishing expeditions. During the later stages of Palæolithic civilization their principal prey consisted of reindeer and horses, which then roamed in large herds throughout Western Europe, thus rendering themselves more liable to be ambushed, trapped, or speared by their wily enemies. The weapons used by these hunters were harpoons, generally made of reindeer-horn; spear- and lance-heads of flint; and short daggers of bone or horn. It is not likely that with these weapons they would take the initiative in attacking the hyæna, lion, or cave-bear, except in self-defence. That, however, these formidable creatures were occasionally captured by them, is suggested by the fact that their canine teeth were highly prized and used as personal ornaments, or as mementoes of their prowess in the chase.

When the physical conditions which called these human accomplishments into existence passed away, and the peculiar fauna of the Glacial period disappeared from the lowlands of Central Europe, —some by extinction, and others by emigration to more northern regions or to the elevated mountains in the neighbourhood—we find the inhabitants of these old hunting grounds in possession of new and altogether different kinds of food. Finding the produce of the chase becoming so scarce and precarious that it was no longer possible to live a roaming life, now gathering fruits and seeds, now hunting wild animals, they fell somehow into the way of cultivating special plants and cereals, and rearing certain animals in a state of domestication. Whether this new departure was a direct sequence of the highly developed intelligence of the Palæolithic people of Europe, or was derived from new immigrants into the country, is a debatable question. At any rate, it was eminently successful, and may be regarded as the starting-point of Neolithic civilization. In the course of time these Neolithic people cultivated a variety of fruits, wheat, barley, and other cereals; they reared oxen, pigs, sheep, goats, horses, and dogs; they became skilled in the ceramic art, and in the manufacture of cloth by spinning and weaving wool and fibrous textures; the flint industry continued much the same as in the later stages of the Palæolithic period, but in addition to chipping they now ground stone implements so as to give them a sharp cutting edge; in hunting the forest fauna of the period they used, besides spears, lances, and daggers, the bow and arrow; they built houses, for both the living and the dead—thus showing that religion had become an active and governing power among them. But of the artistic taste and skill of their predecessors they had scarcely a vestige, and what they did by way of ornament consisted mainly of a few scratches, arranged in some simple geometrical pattern. The fundamental principles of the two civilizations are really so divergent that the Neolithic can hardly be regarded as a direct development from that of the Palæolithic period in Europe, although there are several instances on record in which their characteristic remains were chronologically superimposed, without any apparent break in continuity, as at Campigny, Reilhac, Mas-d'Azil, etc. The probability is that, while the reindeer-hunters were still in existence, people beyond this area, possibly of the same stock, were passing through the evolutionary stages which connected the two civilizations.

IV. MAN'S MENTAL ENDOWMENTS.—The great superiority of man's mental manifestations over those of all other animals is too patent to be called in question by any serious worker in the field of anthropology. Indeed, according to some eminent psychologists, the gap between them cannot be bridged over by the doctrine of organic evolution. On the other hand, evolutionists in general believe that it is explicable on the ordinary principles of physiology and psychology. If, then, it is to be held that man, like other animals, is a product of the ordinary organic forces of the Cosmos, it may well be asked why, and by what means, he has so far out-distanced all other beings in the struggle of life. The attempt to minimize this remarkable disparity between man and brute has not met with much support from any class of investigators. Anti-Darwinians have no object in discussing this question, their argument being that no speculation founded on materialism can account for it. Accordingly, various hypotheses have been formulated by way of explaining this psychological enigma, which now fall to be noticed.

That there is a physical stratum, common to man and some of the higher mammalia, which brings them both within the domain of organic evolution, has already been advocated in these pages (§ I.), and may be accepted as beyond controversy. This being so, we have to investigate the two following propositions: (1) What are the mental faculties common to both?; and (2) What psychological phenomena are peculiar to man? On these problems Mr. G. J. Romanes writes thus:

'If we have regard to Emotions as these occur in the brute, we cannot fail to be struck by the broad fact that the area of psychology which they cover is so nearly co-extensive with that which is covered by the emotional faculties of man. In my previous works I have given what I consider unquestionable evidence of all the following emotions, which I here name in the order of their appearance through the psychological scale—fear, surprise, affection, pugnacity, curiosity, jealousy, anger, play, sympathy, emulation, pride, resentment, emotion of the beautiful, grief, hate, cruelty, benevolence, revenge, rage, shame, regret, deceitfulness, emotion of the ludicrous.

'Now, this list exhausts all the human emotions, with the exception of those which refer to religion, moral sense, and perception of the sublime. Therefore I think we are fully entitled to conclude that, so far as emotions are concerned, it cannot be said that the facts of animal psychology raise any difficulties against the theory of descent. On the contrary, the emotional life of animals is so strikingly similar to the emotional life of men—and especially of young children—that I think the similarity ought fairly to be taken as direct evidence of a gentle continuity between them' (*Mental Evolution in Man*, p. 7).

Similarly, Mr. Romanes deals with Instinct, Volition, and Intellect, and strongly argues that there is only a difference of degree between their respective manifestations in man and other animals. So far these views have been more or less accepted by leading psychologists; but at this stage a serious divergence of opinion crops up among them, some holding that the principles of evolution are inadequate to account for the origin and working of the higher faculties of man. But these dissentients are seldom in agreement as to the precise nature of their objections. The eminent French anthropologist, Professor de Quatrefages, regarded man's entire organization, physical and mental, with the exception of the faculties of conscience and religion, as the work of evolution. Others extend the range of their objections so as to include the intellectual faculties. Mr. St. George Mivart, while denying that the principles of evolution are applicable to man, makes the following admissions as to the resemblance between the mental actions of men and animals:

'I have no wish to ignore the marvellous powers of animals, or the resemblance of their actions to those of men. No one can reasonably deny that many of them have feelings, emotions, and sense-perceptions similar to our own; that they exercise voluntary motion, and perform actions grouped in complex ways for definite ends; that they to a certain extent learn by experience, and combine perceptions and reminiscences so as to draw practical inferences, directly apprehending objects standing in different relations one to another, so that, in a sense, they may be said to apprehend relations. They will show hesitation, ending apparently, after a conflict of desires, with what looks like choice or volition: and such animals as the dog will not only exhibit the most marvellous fidelity and affection, but will also manifest evident signs of shame, which may seem the outcome of incipient moral perceptions. It is no great wonder, then, that so many persons little given to patient and careful introspection, should fail to perceive any radical distinction between a nature thus gifted and the intellectual nature of man' (Presidential Address at Biological Section, British Association, 1879).

Professor Huxley thus expresses his views on this phase of the subject:

'I have endeavoured to show that no absolute structural line of demarcation, wider than that between the animals which immediately succeed us in the scale, can be drawn between the animal world and ourselves; and I may add the expression of my belief that the attempt to draw a psychical distinction is equally futile, and that even the highest faculties of feeling and of intellect begin to germinate in lower forms of life. At the same time, no one is more strongly convinced than I am of the vastness of the gulf between civilized man and the brutes; or is more certain that whether *from* them or not, he is assuredly not *of* them. No one is less disposed to think lightly of the present dignity, or despairingly of the future hopes, of the only consciously intelligent denizen of this world' (*Man's Place in Nature*, p. 109).

On the other hand, Mr. Alfred Wallace, F.R.S., who holds such a distinguished position in this special field of research, has promulgated a most remarkable theory. This careful investigator, an original discoverer of the laws of natural selection, and a powerful advocate of their adequacy to bring about the evolution of the entire organic world, even including man up to a certain stage, believes that the cosmic forces are insufficient to account for the development of man in his civilized capacity.

'Natural selection,' he writes, 'could only have endowed savage man with a brain a few degrees superior to that of an ape, whereas he actually possesses one very little inferior to that of a philosopher' (*Natural Selection and Tropical Nature*, p. 202).

The present writer has elsewhere made the following comments on Mr. Wallace's position with regard to the application of the doctrine of evolution to man:

'This deficiency in the organic forces of nature he essays to supply by calling in the guiding influence of a "superior intelligence." In defending this hypothesis from hostile criticism, he explains that by "superior intelligence" he means some intelligence higher than the "modern cultivated mind," something intermediate between it and Deity. But as this is a pure supposition, unsupported by any evidence, and merely a matter of personal belief, it is unnecessary to discuss it further. I would just, *en passant*, ask Mr. Wallace why he dispenses with this "superior intelligence" in the early stages of man's evolution, and finds its assistance only requisite to give, as it were, the final touches to humanity?' (*Prehistoric Problems*, p. 103).

That mind in its higher psychical manifestations has often been looked upon as a spiritual essence, which can exist independently of its only known physical basis, need not be a matter of astonishment, when it is considered how ignorant we are of the machinery of thought—how the pleasing abstractions of the poet, the fascinating creations of the novelist, and the profound speculations of the man of genius come forth as from a hidden cavern, without exciting any suspicion of having behind them not only a physical equivalent of brain matter, but also a laboratory in which thoughts are evolved. It is this marvellous power of volitional reflexion in summoning ideas from the materials stored up in the various localized portions into which the brain is divided, and utilizing them for other and nobler purposes than mere animality, that gives a *prima facie* plausibility to this theory. From this point of view abstract reasoning, imagination, conception, idealization, moral sense, altruism, etc., may be regarded as by-products of mental operations which are due to the ordinary reasoning faculties, and which have their chief stimuli in the external environment.

Leaving, however, the field of speculation aside, and reverting to the opinions of the four eminent authorities quoted above, it is manifest that they all recognize the magnitude of the psychological gulf which separates humanity from the rest of the animal world. Nor does Professor Huxley himself give any clear ideas as to how it is to be bridged over—certainly it has never been shown that this is possible on the Darwinian principle of the 'survival of the fittest.'

Such were some of the leading opinions on this particular phase of the evolution theory, as applied to man, when the present writer ventured to refer to the subject in his Presidential address to the Anthropological Section of the British Association in 1893. In that address (*Prehistoric Problems*, ch. ii.) he advocated the hypothesis that one of the main factors in the production of the higher brain-development of man was the conversion of the upper limbs into true hands. From the first moment that the being recognized the advantage of using a club or a stone in attacking his prey, or defending himself from his enemies, the direct incentives to a higher brain-development came into existence. He would soon learn by experience that a particular form of club or stone was more suitable for his purposes; and if the desiderated object were not to be found among the natural materials around him, he would in the course of time proceed to manufacture it. Certain kinds of stone would be readily recognized as better adapted for cutting purposes than others, and he would soon learn to select his materials accordingly. If these were to be found only in a special locality, he would visit that special locality whenever the prized material was needed. Nor is it an unwarrantable stretch of imagination to suppose that circumstances would lead him to lay up a store for future use. The power to make and wield a weapon was a new departure in the career of man, and every repetition of such acts became an effective object-lesson, and an ever-accumulating training force for further progress. The occupation of these primitive tool-makers, once fairly in operation, afforded frequent opportunity of comparing the merits and demerits of their respective mechanical products—thus supplying a fruitful medium for the development of abstract reasoning. In this way the function of the hand and the function of the brain became intimately correlated, the conjoint result of their long-continued action being a larger brain, greater intelligence, and a more highly specialized manipulative organ than were ever before seen among the products of the organic world.

That there is an amount of *cortex cerebri* in the human subject, corresponding to his greater mental powers, cannot be seriously controverted, as the size of the human brain, relatively to the rest of the body, is enormously greater than in any other animal. According to Sir William Turner, the cranial capacity of an average European is about 1500 c.c., while that of the gorilla, which is a larger animal, does not exceed 590 c.c. (*Journ. Anat. and Physiology*, vol. xxix. p. 436). That the largest portion of this increase in the substance of the human brain is to be correlated with the higher mental powers of man, as cause and effect, seems therefore to be indisputable; nor, in our opinion, can there be any doubt that its chief stimulus, at least in the earlier stages of human development, was the function of the hand. That subsequently there were other powerful factors working in the same direction is not denied, as will be seen from the following remarks on articulate speech.

Next to the invention of mechanical appliances, the use of articulate speech was, undoubtedly, the most potent factor in the mental evolution of man, especially when conjoined with its later offshoot, the art of writing. By articulate speech is meant the faculty of uniformly associating certain words or sounds with definite ideas, so that these ideas can be understood by those previously instructed in the process. Of course, the members of a family or tribe would be conversant with it from birth. Spoken language is virtually an extension, or rather a concentration, of the power which many of the more intelligent animals possess, in common with the *Hominidæ*, of giving expression to emotions and simple sensations by various ejaculatory sounds, grimaces, and gestures. The acquisition of full human speech was, unquestionably, the result of slow growth; for there is no known race, however low and savage, but 'has an articulate language, carried on by a whole system of sounds and meanings, which serves the speaker as a sort of catalogue of the contents of the world he lives in, taking in every subject he thinks about, and enabling him to say what he thinks about it' (Tylor, *Anthropology*, p. 132).

Of the importance of articulate speech in the intellectual and social development of man it is unnecessary to produce detailed evidence, as its elaboration must have proceeded *pari passu* with the higher development of the brain almost since man entered on his human career. 'A complete train of thought,' writes Mr. Darwin, 'can no more be carried on without the aid of words, whether spoken or silent, than a long calculation without the use of figures or symbols.'

As to the stage in the evolution of man to which articulate speech is to be assigned, there is little agreement among anthropologists. Darwin regarded it as having an early origin in the stem line of humanity, while Romanes made it subsequent to the art of manufacturing flint implements.

'For my part,' says Professor D. J. Cunningham, in his Presidential address to the Anthropological Section of the British Association, Glasgow, 1901, 'I would say that the first word uttered expressive of an external object marked a new era in the history of our early progenitors. At this point the simian or brute-like stage in their developmental career came to an end, and the human dynasty, endowed with all its intellectual possibilities, began.'

Professor Haeckel, in describing the evolutionary stage of *Pithecanthropus erectus*, thus writes:

'The brain is considerably enlarged. Presumably it is still devoid of so-called articulate speech; this is indicated by the fact that children have to learn the language of their parents, and by the circumstance that comparative philology declares it impossible to reduce the chief human languages to anything like one common origin' (*Last Link*, Lond. 1898, p. 72).

One of the latest contributions on the subject is from the pen of Professor D. J. Cunningham (*Huxley Lecture*, 1902), who thus expresses himself:

'I have already hinted that by the study of the early conditions of the cerebral cortex in man, information may be attained regarding the evolution of function. . . . We have seen that the bulging of the arm-area in the human cerebrum occurs very early—somewhere about the middle or end of the sixth month. The portion of cortex devoted to speech assumes shape much later. Indeed, it does not appear until shortly before birth, and is not fully developed until the end of the first year of infancy. This might be considered to give some basis of support to Dr. Munro's plea that man attained the erect attitude, and that the arm was set free for the development of its higher functions, before articulate speech was elaborated.'

There are two well-attested general observations which appear to throw some light on this obscure point, viz.—(1) that none of the apes of the present day have even the rudiments of articulate speech; and (2) that language (as quoted above from Mr. Tylor) is well developed among all the *Hominidæ*. The present writer's interpretation of these facts is that the origin of articulate speech was subsequent to the separation of the genus *Homo* from the *simian* stem, but prior to the development of the races of mankind—a view which places it subsequent to the attainment of the erect posture and the development of the human hand.

V. MAN'S SOCIAL EVOLUTION.—It has now been amply shown that, from whatever standpoint we contemplate the great drama of human life, it stands forth as a unique development in the organic world. Starting, possibly as early as the Miocene period, with a progenitor whose physical and mental attainments were on a par with those of existing anthropoid apes, his successors, the *Hominidæ* of to-day, have gradually forged their way into what is virtually a new world—the world of ethics and moral responsibility. Almost from the very beginning they acquired manipulative methods, with latent capabilities which (as we can now realize) were tantamount to a new force in the organic world, viz. the art of manufacturing tools and using them for the advancement of their own welfare. Unlike the more helpless creatures around them, who were largely at the mercy of a fickle environment, these implement-using animals soon learned to accommodate themselves to all its vicissitudes. With a knowledge of the use of fire, the skill to manufacture garments, and, ultimately, the art to construct houses, they braved the rigours of frost and snow with comparative impunity. As they became more and more conversant with the laws and forces of nature and their own power over them, they laid a usurping hand on the reins of Cosmic evolution itself, by the cultivation of selected plants and animals, and the destruction of others which were found unsuitable for their own purposes.

The far-reaching consequence of securing food supplies by means of agriculture and the domestication of animals, led to more social and sedentary habits. The appearance of large communities concurrent with the development of various trades and professions was but a matter of time, the outcome of which is now a vast system of international commerce. Already the greater portion of the earth capable of being cultivated is converted into gardens and fields, whose choice productions are readily conveyed to all the chief towns of the civilized nations of the globe. Flesh diet is everywhere abundant, but it is no longer necessary to hunt the animals in their primeval haunts. Skin-coats, dug-out canoes, and the *coup de poing* are now lineally represented by woven fabrics, Atlantic liners, and Long Toms.

Concurrently with their ever-increasing inroads into the secret arcana of nature, these skilled artizans became religionists as well as legislators, and founded social institutions and laws for the guidance of a rapidly increasing population. In the course of their long sojourn on earth they had no doubt many difficulties to overcome before they succeeded in establishing the great landmarks of civilization as they now present themselves to us, not only in works of art, architecture, engineering, electricity, etc., but in constructive philology, religion, ethics, altruism, and the sense of honour, all of which may be said to be still in process of development, though their sources reach far back into pre-historic times.

Some of the lower animals have accompanied man so far on the road to reasoning intelligence as to be able to associate certain natural results with their natural causes, as crows do when they keep at a safe distance from a man with a gun. But none has ever reached the stage of being able to adjust the circumstances so as to produce the desired effect. Man not only sows the seed, but waters the field should the fickle environment refuse the seasonal showers. No other animal in a state of nature has attempted to do anything comparable to this simple act of practical ratiocination.

It is probable that religion came first to the front as a modifying influence to the stern decree of the survival of the fittest. Some grounds for this suggestion may be seen in the readiness with which the early races of mankind identified the obscure forces of nature with supernatural spirits who were believed to have control over human destinies, and were, therefore, worshipped as gods or demons; and in the prevalence among savages of magic and fetishism. But such polytheistic notions, as well as the pretended art of magicians to control the so-called supernatural agencies, are rapidly giving way to the precise methods of scientific research. Nevertheless, it must be admitted that for many ages religion has proved a weighty influence in mitigating the harsh effects of the Cosmic law that might is right, which is implied in the doctrine of the survival of the fittest. As already stated (§ III.), there is little evidence in support of the belief, advocated by some, that religion was practised by the Palæolithic people of Europe, at least to the extent of making a display of idolatry, so that the development of this governing force in the institutions of men is comparatively late. In Neolithic times its predominating influence throughout Europe is attested by a whole series of memorials of the dead—ossuaries, chambered graves, cairns, cists, urns, etc. That the Neolithic people believed in a life beyond the grave somewhat similar to the present may be inferred from the character of the grave-goods,—vessels with food and drink, implements, weapons, favourite wives and animals, often being buried along with the body.

Next to religion in point of importance, if not also in chronological sequence, comes the moral faculty, or conscience, which regulates judicial and ethical actions. Its position in psychology may be aptly compared to that of instinct in the organic world,—the point of analogy being that their sudden actions appear to be the outcome of an impulse rather than a deliberate act of ratiocination. The most rational explanation of this peculiarity, in both conscience and instinct, is that the successive increments of reasoning on which their respective injunctions were originally founded have more or less lapsed in the course of time.

But perhaps the most important formula which has hitherto emanated from the laboratory of ethics is altruism (which see), which may be described as a product of conscience and the acquired sense of equity. Its object is the relief of suffering humanity, and for this purpose it has received the support of the civilized world. Many regard the motives of all such good deeds as having been instilled into the Cosmic mind by a revelation from heaven; but this is an unnecessary assumption; for in the accumulated deliberations of wise men during long ages we have an adequate pabulum for its birth and maturation. But whether heaven-born or earth-born, altruism has become a *sine qua non* in human civilization. So long as the laws of our wisest Solons are liable to error, and the environment contains a residuum of unexplained forces, there will be a certain proportion of failures among yearly births, whose fate can be mitigated only by altruism. Under this category come the deaf, the blind, the lame, the poor, the friendless, and, in short, all who are ushered into the world without the means of successfully entering on the struggle of life. Our original interference with Cosmic methods by living in large communities under the most imperfect sanitary arrangements, has greatly increased the number of such wastrels. Hence their immediate relief, so far as that is possible, is a moral obligation on all who derive benefit from the social government under which they have inherited or acquired wealth, position, and influence, possibly without any effort on their part. On this phase of the subject there is a conflict between Cosmic methods and those of the ethical code of humanity. The influence of the one is directed to the survival of the fittest; that of the other to 'the fitting of as many as possible to survive.' The former has left man with the garb and qualities of a savage; the latter has endowed him with mental culture, the refinement of civilization, and moral responsibility for his actions towards his fellow-creatures.

VI. CONCLUDING REMARKS.—The *Hominidæ* of the present day not only possess more highly developed brains than those of their early ancestors, but also derive great advantages in their life struggle from the accumulated experiences of their predecessors in the form of all sorts of mechanical inventions, organized institutions for scientific research, altruistic laws, and other ethical enactments acquired as results of their progressive culture. Thus they at once start on a higher rung in the ladder of human life. It is by these means that they have come to hold such a predominating position in the organic world; and it is through the general diffusion of such attainments that further progress can be expected. Among the more urgent reforms by way of rectifying past mistakes and safe-guarding the future interests of the race, may be mentioned the eradication of obsolete doctrines and pernicious superstitions, the enforcement of just and equitable laws, the prevention of crime, the popularization of scientific methods, and especially strict attention to sanitary improvements. There is, however, a limit to human powers over the laws of environment, for occasionally the most learned communities find themselves helpless amidst the operations of nature. But yet it is in this direction alone that prospects of future betterment lie.

From various data advanced in the previous sections, it will be seen that there are two distinct lines on which investigations into the past history of mankind may be profitably conducted. The first relates to man as a biological entity, and comprises, in addition to his ontogenetic and phylogenetic development, a few fragments of skeletons of his predecessors which by some fortuitous circumstances have to this day resisted the disintegrating forces of nature. This department is generally known as *Physical Anthropology*. The evidential materials to be gathered along the second line of research consist of the remains of man's handicraft works, which, being simply preserved impressions of his skill in the different stages of culture through which he has passed, may be characterized as *Cultural Anthropology*. The successive modifications which these respective materials have undergone during a long series of ages, though different in kind, are found to bear a decided ratio to the progress of human intelligence. Thus, taking the human skull at the starting-point of humanity as comparable to that of one of the higher apes, we know, as a matter of fact, that during the onward march of time it has undergone some striking changes, both in form and capacity, before reaching the normal type of modern civilized races — changes which can be classified in chronological sequence. Similarly, the products of man's hands show a steady improvement in type, technique, and efficiency—commensurate with his progressive knowledge of the laws of nature and his ability in applying them to mechanical and utilitarian purposes. Indeed, the trail of humanity along its entire course is strewn with the discarded weapons and tools which, from time to time, had to give way to others of greater efficiency. Between these two departments, though separated by a strong line of demarcation, there is a striking affinity which, in the words of Mr. W. H. Holmes (*Report of United States National Museum*, 1901, p. 256), is thus stated: 'If the physical phenomena of man include all that connects him with the brute, his culture phenomena include all that distinguishes him from the brute.'

These remarks will give some idea of the interesting and profound problems embraced by the science of Anthropology. Not since the material world became an object of human study and reflexion has there been accomplished such a complete and far-reaching revolution in current philosophical opinion. From the standpoint of evolution, the entire organic world, not excluding man, reveals a unity, a harmony, and a grandeur never before disclosed under any system of speculative philosophy.

What may be the outcome and destiny of humanity on the lines of modern civilization lies within the deepest shadow of futurity. One thing alone appears certain—that since human government on the anthropo-cosmic principles of ethics and altruism became a matter of real concern among the civilized nations of the world, there is no turning back from its behests, no alternative but to strengthen the ethical fabric by every means that human ingenuity can suggest. Above all, a national *esprit de corps*, with the motto 'Honour bright,' must be fostered among the members of each community; for if the steersman once relaxes his hold on the wheel, he and his freight may again be swept into the vortex of Cosmic evolution.

LITERATURE.—Owing to the number of works more or less bearing on the natural history of man, all that can be attempted here is to make as judicious a selection as possible:—**Broca**, *Instructions générales pour les Recherches Anthropologiques*, 1865, *Caractère physique de l'Homme Préhistorique*, 1868, etc.; **Cartailhac**, *La France Préhistorique*, 1889; **Boyd-Dawkins**, *Cave Hunting*, 1874, *Early Man in Britain*, 1880; **Darwin**, *Origin of Species*, 1859, *Descent of Man*, 1871; **Duckworth**, *Morphology and Anthropology*, 1905; **Draper**, *Intellectual Development of Europe*, 1863; **Dubois**, *Pithecanthropus erectus*, 1894; **Dupont**, *L'Homme pendant les Âges de la Pierre*[2], 1872; **Sir J. Evans**, *The Ancient Stone Implements, Weapons, and Ornaments of Great Britain*, 1872; **Fergusson**, *Rude Stone Monuments in all Countries*, 1872; **Falconer**,

Palæontological Memoirs, 1868; **Frazer**, *The Golden Bough*[2], 1900; **J. Geikie**, *Prehistoric Europe*, 1880; **Haeckel**, *Anthropogenie*, 1874, *Evolution of Man*, 1904; **E. T. Hamy**, *Précis de Paléontologie Humaine*, 1870; **Hartman**, *Anthropoid Apes*, 1885; **Huxley**, *Man's Place in Nature*, 1863; **Keane**, *Man, Past and Present*, 1899; **Keller**, *The Lake Dwellings of Switzerland*, 1866; **A. Lang**, *Myth, Ritual and Religion*, 1887, *Magic and Religion*, 1901; **Lubbock** (Lord Avebury), *Prehistoric Times*[3], 1890, *Origin of Civilization*[5], 1902; **Sir Ch. Lyell**, *Antiquity of Man*, 1863; **Manouvrier**, 'On Changes consequent on the assumption of Erect Posture' (*Revue Scientifique*, 1896, p. 297), also numerous contributions to anthropological societies; **G. de Mortillet**, *Le Préhistorique*, 1883; **Munro**, *The Lake Dwellings of Europe*, 1890, *Prehistoric Problems*, 1897; **Pengelly**, *Literature of Kent's Cavern*, 1868; **Pouchet**, *Plurality of the Human Race*, 1864; **Prichard**, *The Natural History of Man*, 1848; **de Quatrefages**, *Hommes Fossiles et Hommes Sauvages*, 1884, *The Human Species*, 1879, *Crania Ethnica* (conjointly with E. T. Hamy), 1873–1879; *Reliquiæ Aquitanicæ* (Report of excavations in the Dordogne caves by Lartet and Christy), 1865; **Romanes**, *Mental Evolution in Man*, 1888, *Scientific Evidences of Organic Evolution*, 1882, etc.; **Schmerling**, *Recherches sur les Ossements fossiles découverts dans les Cavernes de la Province de Liège*, 1833; Schmidt, *The Doctrine of Descent and Darwinism*, 1881; Schrader, *Prehistoric Antiquities of the Aryan Peoples*, 1890; Spencer, *Principles of Sociology*, 1876; Topinard, *Éléments d'Anthropologie Générale*, 1885; **Tylor**, *Researches into the Early History of Mankind*, 1865, *Primitive Culture*[3], 1891, *Anthropology*, 1881; **Verneau**, *Les Races Humaines*, 1890; **Vogt**, *Lectures on Man*, 1864; **Waitz**, *Anthropologie der Naturvölker*, 1859–1864; **Wallace**, *Contributions to the Theory of Natural Selection*, 1870; **Weismann**, *The Evolution Theory*, 1905; **Sir D. Wilson**, *Prehistoric Man*, 1863; *Matériaux pour l'Histoire Primitive et Naturelle de l'Homme*, 1864 (22 vols.); *Congrès International d'Anthropologie et d'Archéologie Préhistorique* (12 vols.), 1866–1902; *Dictionnaire des Sciences Anthropologiques*, 1882.

ROBERT MUNRO.

ANTHROPOMORPHISM. — Generally, and perhaps always in the past, man has believed that there are powers other and greater than he. He has felt it not only desirable, but possible, to enter into communication with them; that is to say, he has taken it as a fact that they can understand him when he addresses himself to them; that he can more or less understand them; that he can win their sympathy and assistance, if he sets about doing so in the right way. Further, he has believed at some times that these powers possess the shape of man; at other times, that their shape is that of beasts or of plants; at others, that they are visible in and as the sun, moon, or stars, or audible in the storm, the earthquake, or the rustling of leaves. That deities have been supposed in all stages of human development, from that of the Fuegians to that of the ancient Greeks, to possess human form is a truth which needs neither demonstration nor illustration. Indeed, Xenophanes (frag. 17, ed. Bergk) even went to the length, whether in jest or earnest, of supposing that cattle, lions, and horses, were they able, would make the gods in their own likeness. It is also obvious that deities originally theriomorphic tended to become anthropomorphic: the Egyptian gods which have gained human bodies and limbs, but retained their animal heads, are an obvious instance of this tendency. And the human form given by Greek sculptors to Helios suffices to show that nature powers, if not originally conceived in human form, tend eventually to take it.

1. Physical anthropomorphism. — The belief, then, that deities have bodies and limbs like those of men is a belief which has had a beginning and an end. Religion has survived its disappearance; and though it is impossible to prove that before its appearance religion was, it is in the same way impossible to prove that religion then was not. We may therefore reasonably be influenced by the fact that though theriomorphic deities become anthropomorphic, as in Egypt, the reverse process never takes place; anthropomorphism is in some cases preceded by theriomorphism, but theriomorphism is never generated out of anthropomorphism. We may then, perhaps, assume that there was a pre-anthropomorphic stage in the history of religion. But if we make that assumption, we can do so only by limiting the term 'anthropomorphism' to the sense in which it means that deities have bodies and limbs like those of men, and by excluding from the content of the term the sense in which it implies that deities have thoughts, emotions, and wills like those of men, though transcending them. Further, it may be said that to limit the meaning of the term to the first of the two senses which may be put upon it is to break, or rather to ignore, the continuity which is characteristic of—indeed, essential to—evolution in all its forms, whether evolution of religion or of anything else; whereas, by including in the meaning of the term the second sense as well as the first, we are enabled to grasp the principle which underlies and runs through the whole evolution of the idea of God.

2. Psychical anthropomorphism. — From this point of view, then, man has always ascribed, and does now ascribe, to Deity thought, emotion, and will. He may originally have worshipped animals, or even stocks and stones, as the fetish-worshipper does; but if he did so, it was because he ascribed to those objects thought, emotion, and will; and the characteristics so ascribed were none the less human because they were ascribed to the deity in a transcendent degree. In the second stage of this evolution, not only did aniconic objects of worship become iconic, not only did pictures and statues of the gods in human form supplement, and more or less drive out, the stocks and stones which were the object of the older cult, but the very conception of the god, as it existed in the mind of the worshipper, became more and more definitely human—and did not in the process become more divine, as the example of Ares and Aphrodite in Homer will show. The third stage in the process of evolution is reached when religion comes to denounce the idea that the deity has a body or limbs like a man or an animal; but though religion in this stage becomes iconoclastic, and ceases to be anthropomorphic in the narrower of the two senses of the word, it continues to believe, in this stage as in the previous stages, in a personal deity. In this stage of evolution the same impulse that leads religious minds to deny that the deity can be conceived, or ought to be portrayed, as possessing bodily form, also leads to the conclusion that some human virtues cannot be ascribed to a deity: thus it would be degrading, if it were not unmeaning, to ascribe to deity the temperance or the courage which Ares ought to have possessed—the reason being that those qualities, and others of the same kind, imply defects which have to be overcome in the persons of whom they are predicated; and such defects are *ex hypothesi* excluded from the concept of a perfect being. This line of argument may, however, be continued, apparently in the same direction, until it brings us to a fourth stage in the evolution of the idea of God. It was, indeed, so continued in one of the arguments considered in Cicero's *de Natura Deorum* (iii. 15), where it is argued that knowledge of good and evil cannot be ascribed to a good God, 'for he who can do no evil requires no such knowledge'; and in the same way reason cannot be ascribed to Him—'shall we assign reason which makes dark things plain? But to a god nothing can be dark.' In modern times the same feeling finds expression in the doctrine that the cause of all things is the Unknowable, to which we are not warranted in ascribing thought, emotion, or will. If we seek so to ascribe them, we land ourselves in self-contradiction. In the interests of clear thinking, therefore, we must abstain from so ascribing them. Power, indeed, must be assigned to this Unknowable cause—but not personality. The anthropomorphism which has characterized religion from the beginning characterizes it to the end. In the progress of human thought, anthropomorphism tends gradually to be sloughed off; at first, indeed, the tendency is to provide the gods more and more definitely and precisely with human limbs and bodies; but that tendency is eventually defeated by its own realization—when fully realized, it becomes intolerable, as it was to Plato, and then is doomed. Next, the tendency is for religion to insist on investing the deity with the mental and moral qualities of man; and that tendency too—on this theory—eventually reveals its own inner and essential self-contradictions. When this, like the previous form of anthropomorphism, comes to be felt untenable and intolerable, religion, in any ordinary sense of the word, becomes impossible.

3. **Origin of anthropomorphism.** — Looked at from the point of view of evolution, the fate of the belief in anthropomorphism was determined from the beginning. If it is seen in the end to be logically incoherent and impossible, it is so because it has carried within itself the seed of its own destruction from the very beginning. We have only, it is argued, to consider its origin in order to see its want of validity. The tendency to personify objects is exhibited by children—and even by animals—at play. Such personification, indeed, in the case of both children and dogs, may be involuntary and a source of terror; and the terror may be removed when the object personified is shown not to be a living thing. The same tendency is shown by the African negro, who, starting out on some business, happens to have his attention arrested by some object, say a bright pebble, and, immediately associating it with the business he is engaged on, picks it up as a fetish, regarding it as a personality which has the power, if properly treated, of understanding what he wants and of giving him assistance. The same tendency to personify objects and to associate them with the fortunes of the man who discovers their personality, will account for the fact that an object thus personified by the father of a family or the most influential member of a clan comes to receive the worship of the whole family or clan, and thus becomes not a personal fetish but a family god or a tribal god; and may possibly survive and eventually become a national god. But the African negro may find out that he gets no assistance from the object he picked up; and then, though he may cast it away as not being really a fetish, still he usually keeps it, even though he pays it no worship, because it may perhaps after all turn out to be an operative fetish. In the same way, amongst the African negroes and elsewhere, we find traces of gods who, though the names and the memory of them linger on, receive no worship, because they are no longer believed to do good or evil. The belief in such gods, and in such fetishes, evidently has a lessening degree of validity; or perhaps it never was really valid at all—its want of validity has merely grown more and more patent. That is to say, the origin, as well as the history, of the belief shows that it has no validity; the tendency to personify objects — whether objects of sense or objects of thought—which is found in animals and children as well as in savages, is the origin of anthropomorphism, which is puerile therefore in character as well as in origin. The evolution of the idea of God, on this argument, is simply the process by which a childish error is developed slowly to its fullest extent, and now that its inherent inconsistencies and self-contradictions are coming to be fully recognized, is being cast off. It is a case in which the psychological 'projection of the self' into the world is made the basis of an attempt to explain all things, and is ultimately found to afford no explanation which is satisfactory, morally or intellectually, of the not-self.

4. **The method of science.**—From this point of view, the not-self, the world around us, must be accepted on its own terms, so to speak, and must be studied objectively; we must not make the mistake of assuming it to be a subject, or the expression of a subject's reason or will. We must not assume its ways to be our ways or to be explicable by them or by analogy with them. We must take them as they are and study them as they are given, without presuppositions and without assumptions. In a word, we must take as our method that of science, the objective method. So we shall escape from the error of foisting on the facts an anthropomorphic explanation which they will not tolerate.

Now, the object of science is to understand the world; and it may fairly be said that any attempt to explain the world assumes the course of the world to be explicable. It is assumed not only that the course of things is or may be to some extent intelligible to the human reason, but also that it is fundamentally rational; every problem that presents itself to science is attacked by science with the firm conviction that there is a solution. Such a problem is a challenge to science; and the challenge is never declined on the ground that the problem is insoluble. The challenge is ever presenting itself; the problems submitted are continually being solved. The course of the world is continually being exhibited by science as more and more intelligible; and science is perpetually being confirmed in its fundamental assumption of the rationality of things. The world becomes daily more and more intelligible, on the assumption that the reason of things and the reason in things is intelligible to the human reason.

5. **Objective rationality.**—Are we then to say that science also is anthropomorphic, or are we to deny it? In the one case we shall say that science, like religion, starts from the human reason, and persists in measuring everything by it and interpreting everything in conformity with it. In that case, if we hold that anthropomorphism eventually breaks down in the hands of religion, and proves in the long run to be but a puerile 'projection of the self' into the external world, then the anthropomorphism of science, its assumption or presumption to read reason—human reason—into things, may, like the anthropomorphism of religion, pass muster for a while, but eventually must be found untenable and intolerable. Indeed, it may be said, science as well as religion has already come to that pass. It is vain to deny 'the possibility that being may be rational only in a very narrow sphere, and that it might some day turn towards us another side, about which we could build no structure of connected and practical thought' (Höffding, *The Problems of Philosophy*, p. 114). Not only does the reason in things cover only a very narrow sphere, but its hold on that sphere is wanting in security. 'With the same right with which we reason from the possibility of rational knowledge to a unifying force in Being, we might, apparently, reason to an irrational power in Being, to a cosmological principle that prevented the elements of Being from standing in a rationally determinable relation to one another' (*ib.* p. 135). If Being is fundamentally irrational, science's explanation of things is purely anthropomorphic. If, on the other hand, the reason which science professes to discover in things is really found there, and not put there, by science, then the reason so found is not human reason; nor does the fact that it is intelligible to man avail to prove that it is human. It is intelligible because it is reason, not because it is human. Science, therefore, in postu-

lating that the world is intelligible to man is not guilty of anthropomorphism; it does not assume that the reason which it strives to understand is human, and it does not make the reason which it finds. But even so—granted, that is, that to some extent, so far as it has gone, science finds in things a reason which it does not put there—the possibility remains that Being may any day turn to us another side, displaying no reason, but irrationality. The possibility indeed remains, but science scouts it or systematically ignores it; or, perhaps we may rather say, faith in science forbids us to acknowledge it. No unsolved problem in science is admitted to be insoluble. In other words, if the rationality of things, so far as it has been discovered by science, is a fact and not an assumption, still it is an assumption so far as it has not yet been discovered. It is not, of course, discredited by the fact that it is an assumption, for we must begin with an assumption—by assuming either that things are or that they are not, or that they partly are and partly are not, rational. And the assumption that things will continue to reveal a reason which, though it is not man's, is intelligible to man, is at any rate harmonious with the discoveries which science has thus far made, even though it be an assumption and an act of faith.

But, granting that we make the assumption and show the faith which science demands, we have only got thus far, viz. that the power which displays itself in things is rational in the sense that it is logical. More, indeed, we could not expect to get than this, for science aims at nothing more: its position is that things are logically comprehensible; its coherence is a logical coherence which it finds in things and does not put into them. Even then, if we take it that reason and logic are possible only to a mind, and that a mind must be self-conscious, the utmost that we can get out of science, or hold to be implied by science, is that there is a self-conscious mind whose power acts logically; and even if we grant that there is nothing anthropomorphic in this,—on the ground that the reason and logic in things are found in them and not imputed to them by science—still the mind or power thus revealed as superhuman is revealed as merely logical. It is distinctly not revealed as moral, or as recking aught of man. Its laws extend to, just as its rain descends on, the unjust and the just alike; and science affords not the slightest ground for holding that the ultimate working of the laws which it discovers favours the just rather than the unjust.

If, then, man can discover and does discover in things a logic and a reason which he does not put there, if the logic and reason so found are objective, and are not created by him, are not images of his own making,—are not, in a word, pieces of anthropomorphism,—can we go further and discover in man's experience anything else which is similarly given to him and not created by him? The fact that a thing is comprehensible by man is no proof that it is the work of man's reason; if a reason, partially intelligible to man's reason, is found in things by science,—which looks only for logic and reason,—can man and does man, when he looks for more, find more than mere reason? Does science exhaust objectivity, or does the realm of objectivity include other things than reason? Is man's experience of the universe that it discloses reason alone to him? Man's experience has been that he has found something more in it than a reason partially intelligible to him; he has found in it the workings of a power which awakes in him a sense of gratitude, of duty, of awe, and of fear.

But the experience in which these workings of this power are thus disclosed or felt is distinguishable, if not distinct, from the experience, or from the aspect of experience, of which science is the interpretation or the expression. Whether we term the aspect of experience with which science has to do sense-experience or experience of the physical or the external world, it is, however defined, at any rate marked off from the rest of man's experience, as being but a part and not the whole of human experience. Or, if we go so far as to say there is nothing in human experience which may not be investigated scientifically, we still indicate by the adverb 'scientifically' that the point of view of science is only one point of view, and that the aspect of reality which science confronts is not the only aspect which human experience presents to man. One and the same set of facts, for instance, may be viewed psychologically by science, may be pronounced valid or not valid from the point of view of logic, may be estimated right or wrong from the standpoint of morality, holy or sinful in the eyes of religion. The scientific aspect is not the only aspect of our experience. The scientific is not the whole account of that experience.

6. Ethical qualities.—If, then, the reason which science finds in things is not the creation of science, is not made after the image of human reason, and is not put into things by science, but is found in them and is found to be partially intelligible to man, then the same experience, which when studied by science reveals a reason which is not man's, may, when regarded in its entirety, or even when regarded from other points of view than that of science, reveal yet other aspects of that reason in things which is studied by science. If that power when studied by science is seen more and more clearly, the more it is studied, to be rational and self-consistent, it may, when regarded from other points of view, disclose other aspects than that of logical rationality. It may disclose ethical qualities. It may disclose qualities, in the apprehension of which by the heart, and not merely by the intellect, religion consists. Whether it does, as a matter of objective fact, disclose such qualities is not the question now before us for discussion. The point is that, in thus interrogating experience, we are no more guilty of anthropomorphism than is science when it interrogates experience. The question, in the case both of religion and of science, is what experience discloses when interrogated. Science discovers in things the operations of a reason which is not human reason; religion discovers in the experience of man the operations of a power whose ways are not the ways of man. Above all, religion discovers the operations of a personal power. The personality of that power is only partially disclosed in those of its operations with which science concerns itself; and it is disclosed only partially, because science is concerned with only a partial aspect of its operations. Even when we attempt to view its operations from a more comprehensive point of view than science pretends to offer, the conception we then form of it is, doubtless, shaped to some extent by our human limitations, and may be, nay, has been, generally distorted by those limitations. Of course, every apprehension must, to whatever extent, be so shaped, but it does not follow from this that nothing is apprehended. A thing to be misapprehended, even, must be apprehended; and, to be apprehended, it must be there. Will it, then, be said: Granting heartily that it must be there, still it can be apprehended only by being anthropomorphized? The statement, then, is, first, that the power is not personal or spiritual; and next, that, owing to the infirmity of the human mind, it can only appear, or be conceived, as personal. In other words, the religious experience of God as a person is alleged to be not experience, but an interpretation of experience—a false interpretation, and an interpretation which, from the nature of the case, must be false. What, then, are the grounds on which we can say, *a priori*, that this interpretation, if it is an interpretation, must be false? They can only be that we know something which proves that it is false; that we know, to start with, that the power is not personal. But that is precisely what we do not know; that is precisely the point which is at issue. The allegation, on the one side, is that in religious experience God is known as personal. If, on the other side, that is denied, then the dispute is as to the nature of religious experience, and the dispute can be settled only by reference to that experience; it cannot be settled by assuming the point at issue, by begging the question. The question, then, becomes whether the personality of God is a fact of experience, or an inference—possibly a false inference—from experience. Now, those who have not had a given experience—for instance, a blind man who has not had experience of colour—are, obviously, on unsafe ground if they allege that other people have not had that experience, *e.g.*, of colour, but have had some other experience, *e.g.*, such as touch, which the blind man also enjoys, and from it have drawn the inference that they see. No blind man is, of course, so foolish as to argue in this way. He accepts the fact that sighted persons are blessed with an experience which he has not; he may be unable to form any idea of what the sensation of colour is, but he does not make his incapacity a reason for disbelief, or for arguing that sight is not an experience, but an inference—a false inference—from experience.

7. Testimony of experience.—We are, then, thrown back upon the necessity of interrogating experience, of asking what is found there. A person who is not accustomed to a microscope will not see what is undoubtedly to be seen through it; and we cannot accept the fact that he sees nothing as proof that nothing is to be seen. So, too, in the interrogation of religious experience we must accept what is found there, and not deny that it is objectively there because some of us fail to see it. The position that religion rests on the existence of God as a fact given in experience, and not reached by a process of inference, which may or may not be correct, is a position which this article assumes and has not to prove; here we have to consider simply in what sense, if any, religion is anthropomorphic. Now it is undeniable that the existence and the personality of God may be, and in many or most of the stages of religious development have been, anthropomorphized: He has been pictured in human form, as indeed also in animal form; and, even when this misrepresentation has been cast aside, He has been depicted as having passions which are specifically human. But though this is perfectly true, it is equally true, and philosophically more important, that this process of anthropomorphism has also been combated by the highest religious minds as incompatible with the personality of God as revealed in the religious consciousness; and its incompatibility, when thus pointed out, has been recognized by others as true to the facts of that religious consciousness. Thus, as a mere matter of historic fact, it appears that anthropomorphism has been, and is recognized to be, a limit and a hindrance to the comprehension and realization of the personality of God as revealed in the religious consciousness. That being so, the attempt to exhibit anthropomorphism as 'a producing condition of this Personality' is manifestly at variance with the facts; it is not a producing condition, but a distortion of the personality of God. That the distortion should be greatest in the least mature minds and the lowest forms of religion is a point which it is easy to recognize, and the recognition of which is compatible with—indeed assumes—the recognition that there is something there to start with which can be distorted, that is to say, anthropomorphized. That misinterpretation precedes recognition of the facts as they really are is illustrated by the history of science quite as fully as by the history of religion. But that the facts were not there, at the beginning, to be recognized is a position which neither science nor religion can take up. If it be said that science, starting from things as they appeared to the mind of primitive man, has eventually come back to pronounce them very different from what they then appeared, it is also true that some of the things are discovered to have been really facts by the science which eventually discerns their right relations. So, too, the growth of religion would have been impossible if there had not been at least one fact—the personality of God—which it not merely started from, but to which it constantly returns, and in which, properly understood, it finds its constant touchstone of truth. From this point of view, the proper understanding of the personality of God is a test of religious truth; and that personality is not properly understood so long as it is interpreted on the analogy of human personality—so long, that is, as it is interpreted anthropomorphically. So long as it is thus interpreted, or rather misinterpreted, the limitations of the finite are necessarily, and self-contradictorily, imposed on the Infinite. Escape from the self-contradiction is possible only so far as we reverse the process, and recognize, with Lotze, that 'perfect Personality is in God only; to all finite minds there is allotted but a pale copy thereof.' When that is recognized, anthropomorphism is seen for what it is—a misinterpretation of what is given in consciousness, leading necessarily, if slowly, to the assertion that God is not revealed in consciousness for what He is, but is given either for what He is not—the Unknowable—or is not given at all.

It may perhaps be said that human knowledge, to be human, must be contained in human minds, and, being so contained, it must be shaped by that which contains it; in fine, that in admitting it to be human we are asserting it to be anthropomorphic; in denying it to be anthropomorphic we are denying that it can be known to man. Thus, whatever knowledge is poured into human minds must be shaped by the mould into which it is poured, and so must be anthropomorphic. But this argument seems to assume both that the mould is shaped before anything is poured into it, and that the shape is purely human. It fails to consider the possibility that the vessel is plastic, and may be shaped in part by that which is put into it; and that consequently, even if the vessel is human, it may take a form more or less divine, if that which informs it be divine. It tacitly assumes that man makes God in his own image; or, at any rate, that man cannot possibly, under any circumstance of inspiration or aspiration, mould himself on the image of God: all he can do is to make God in his own image. But the assumption that man can shape the facts with which he comes in contact, but cannot in the least be shaped by them, is one which will scarcely bear examination. The facts cannot, of course, shape him if they are unsubstantial. But if they are unsubstantial, neither can he shape them. Scepticism at once emerges from this line of argument; it starts by crying of the facts, 'They are naught! they are naught!' And as long as it continues to do so, it is condemned to immobility.

But if we use the metaphor of the vessel,—whether it be a vessel of clay or of skin, whether it shapes or is shaped—we should remember that it is a metaphor; and if we cannot speak without metaphors, we may at least vary them. We speak of rising above ourselves, and a fact, fortunately, is expressed thereby; in morality and in religion we may rise above ourselves, even as, from the metaphysical point of view, we may 'transcend self.' These facts, or rather the metaphorical expression of them, may serve to remind us that we do not merely receive facts and shape them into our own likeness, but that we go forth into a world of reality and there encounter things which we have not made, which are not in our likeness, but on which we may model ourselves.

8. Testimony of feeling.—We have considered the question of anthropomorphism thus far, rather from the point of view of knowledge than of feeling. But no answer will afford permanent satisfaction which appeals to knowledge only and not to feeling. Practically, the question is one of feeling rather than of knowledge; it is: Are we to doubt the goodness and love of God, and to suppose that it is by the fallacy of anthropomorphism that we ascribe them to Him? To that question the only answer is that we do not doubt God's love; we know it. But the 'knowledge' is not purely or primarily or essentially intellectual; and if it be said that then His love is not a matter of knowledge but of feeling, the simple and sufficient reply is: How else is love to be known? If it were a matter of knowledge, it might be a matter of inference; and the inference would be subject to examination, and therefore to doubt. It might be represented as an inference from the love of man for God, and so as anthropomorphic, as a human quality ascribed to Him. But an essential quality of it—without which it would not be what it is—is that it is experienced as His, and not as something which remains as it is, whether ascribed to Him or not. As a fact of experience, it must be accepted on the evidence of those who experience it, that our love is a response to His, and that it is His which calls forth ours. It is so felt. Beyond that, or behind it, it does not seem possible to go. Feelings, after all, are facts.

9. Testimony of action.—Feeling and knowledge issue in action. Omniscient love must, from the religious point of view, be the source from which all God's actions flow. From the religious point of view, therefore, nothing can be ascribed to Him save that which issues from such a source. Human actions, on the other hand, have other springs; and anthropomorphism is exhibited when actions are ascribed to God, or to the gods, which cannot without self-contradiction be imputed to a love that is omniscient. Human actions proceeding from human passions are essentially characteristic of anthropomorphism — more essentially indeed than are human parts. The gods of Greece were as anthropomorphic in their passions and actions as in their forms; and only in their forms were they typical of human beings at their best. The cowardice of Ares, the incontinence of Aphrodite, the lusts of Zeus, were doubtless a bequest to Greek civilization from barbarous or savage times; and they were a *damnosa hereditas*. If the bequest was not rejected but tolerated, with more or less acquiescence, by most of those who were born to it, the reason doubtless was that the philosophy summed up in the sentence, 'Man is the measure of all things'—πάντων μέτρον ἄνθρωπος—was characteristically Greek: even the gods were made in man's image, and they did not do credit to it. Xenophanes spoke bitterly when he said that the gods of men were anthropomorphic, just as the gods of animals, if animals believed in gods, would be theriomorphic. He failed to note, apparently, that anthropomorphic gods do not always even stay anthropomorphic, but revert to theriomorphism and to bestial conduct. Where a plurality of gods is believed in, the gods are necessarily conceived as objects, as items in the world of objects, and therefore as limited and circumscribed in their action and reaction. The action of any one of them is liable to be frustrated by the action of the rest; and behind and over-topping them all there tends to rise the vague figure of destiny or fate, to which all are subject; omnipotence cannot remain in the hands of any anthropomorphic god. If anthropomorphism were a fallacy which infected religion alone, the position of those who see in religion nothing but that fallacy would be stronger than it is. On reflexion, however, it is manifest that science, as well as religion, has had that fallacy to contend with; in the animistic period of man's history, the tendency is to account for the action and behaviour of all—even inanimate—things by the assumption that their action is anthropomorphic, and to influence their behaviour by proceedings based on that assumption. Only when that assumption is discredited or ignored does it become possible to study the interaction of things scientifically—*rerum cognoscere causas*—to discover in them a reason not modelled on man's, though intelligible to it, provided that we reject the fallacy of anthropomorphizing their action. Religion, also, as well as science, has to throw off the fallacious tendency to anthropomorphize God's action. Polytheism is rendered by its very structure incapable of rejecting the fallacy. Monotheism escapes from it only by degrees; not only is vengeance the Lord's, but the worshipper may pray Him of His goodness to 'slay mine enemies.' The tendency to assume that God's ways are as our ways is the essence of anthropomorphism. To yield to the tendency and to follow it out to its logical extreme is to make God after man's own image. Science, by studying its facts objectively, succeeds in escaping from anthropomorphism. Religion succeeds in making the same escape only where it similarly renounces the *a priori* method of interpreting God's action, and further renounces the desire to utilize it as a means to making man's will be done. Religion rises for the first time clear of anthropomorphism when the prayer goes up from the heart, 'Thy will be done.' Then, and not till then, does the will of God become a fact presented to the religious consciousness, a fact which for the religious mind possesses as much objectivity as for the scientific mind do the facts studied by science, and for the non-religious mind is as meaningless as for the non-mathematical mind a mathematical formula is. The difference may be illustrated by contrasting the petition, 'Slay mine enemies,' with the command to love our enemies: the former is properly addressed to an anthropomorphic god; the latter could only proceed from a very God, and be accepted as of objective validity only by a religious mind. The fact that religion is not anthropomorphic is shown by the way in which the Christian revelation set as ideals before mankind lines of action (such as humility, love of enemies) which were paradoxical and foolish in the eyes of the world, though wise to those who had eyes to see. And the motives suggested were to do God's will, to be like unto Him, to be pure even as He. Should it be objected that validity is accorded even by non-religious minds to the precept of loving our enemies, we may use another illustration: the command to give your coat also to him who takes your cloke is one which cannot be justified on the principles of any non-religious system of ethics, and is one which is not accepted as valid by common sense: it is one which no anthropomorphic deity could self-consistently enunciate. The words in which the command is couched are, of course, intelligible to all; the value of the command is for the non-religious mind naught; only for him to whom it is revealed as God's will, as the course of action which will be followed by him so far as God's will operates through him, does it become an objective fact possessing the same objectivity for him that the facts of science have for the scientific mind. It is not that the same thing is presented to the religious and the non-religious mind and produces different effects in the two cases: it is that the will of God is accepted by the one and rejected by the other, and that for him who accepts it all things become new—God is no longer anthropomorphic. To allege that religion is necessarily belief in an anthropomorphic god is to close our eyes to the fact that the point on which the fate of practical religion turns is whether God's will shall be done or man's. In the one case God—if a God be believed in—is anthropomorphized; in the other, man is conformed to God. If he be so conformed, God's will acts in him and through him. So far as he is thus conformed, God's kingdom comes, His will is done. It is in his action, when it is directed to doing God's will, that man shows likest God.

10. In conclusion, the view that religion is anthropomorphic seems to be based on an assumption, viz. that reason and love, because they occur in man, are limited to man. If that assumption be conceded, then it necessarily follows that to find reason and love elsewhere is a piece of pure anthropomorphism; the reason and love thus projected on to the clouds are, *ex hypothesi*, merely phantasmagoric, whether they be the reason proclaimed by science or the love proclaimed by religion. The reason thus projected is human reason; the love, human love. We may have soared for a while into the clouds, but the string of anthropomorphism all the time was round our feet, and brings us back to the facts we started from,—there they are just as they were when we started. We never have got clear of human limitations, never have lost ourselves in the Divine Love. We may have lost sight of self; but we come down to earth, and recognize that it was the self who imagined that self was transcended or lost. We have simply seen ourselves, our form, our human form, projected on to the clouds. Yet, after all, it is merely an assumption—and not the only possible assumption—that reason and love, because they occur in man, are limited to man. It may equally well be that reason and love are not limited to man, but revealed to him. And the question then becomes one of fact, whether such revelation is experienced. As a question of fact and of feeling, it can be answered only by experience and with reference to the experience. Those who have not the experience must make some assumption with regard to it; those who have it need make none. Experience excludes hypothesis.

LITERATURE.—Plato, *Euthyphro*; Aristotle, *Nicomachean Ethics*, x. viii. 7; Lotze, *Microcosmus*^{4}, 1894, bk. ix. ch. 4; A. Pringle-Pattison, *Man's Place in the Cosmos*^{2}, London, 1902, p. 287 ff. (cf. pp. 61 and 206), and *Hegelianism and Personality* (1887); Cousin, *History of Philosophy* (tr. Wight, 1852), i. 34; J. Martineau, *A Study of Religion*^{2}, Oxford, 1889, i. 313; H. L. Mansel, *Limits of Religious Thought*^{5}, 1867, Lect. i.; E. Caird, *Evolution of Religion*, Glasgow, 1893, i. 239; J. Fiske, *The Idea of God as affected by Modern Knowledge*, London, 1901, p. 111; C. N. Scott, *Foregleams of Christianity*, London, 1893, p. 43; J. R. Illingworth, *Personality Human and Divine*, London, 1894, p. 219; G. A. Coe, 'Necessity and Limitations of Anthropomorphism' in *New World*, viii. (1899) p. 447.

F. B. JEVONS.

ANTICHRIST.—**1.** The name ἀντίχριστος occurs for the first time in *Christian* literature (1 Jn 2^{22} 4^{3}, 2 Jn ^{7}). The ideas which are associated with this name, in particular the conception of a God-opposing tyrant and ruler of the last times, reach back with certainty to the most flourishing period of Jewish Apocalyptic literature. It is most likely that they have their deeper roots not in definite historical phenomena and experiences, but in a mythological and speculative idea, namely, the idea of the battle of God with the devil at the end of the world.

This conception seems to have arisen in the Persian eschatology (the battle of Ahura Mazda with Angra Mainyu; cf. Bousset, *Rel. d. Judentums*^{2}, 584 ff.), and to have penetrated from this source into the Jewish Apocalyptic literature. The opposition between God and the devil, who is introduced under the names Βελίαρ, σατανᾶς, διάβολος, πνεῦμα ἀέριον, is the chief of the leading ideas of the Jewish source of the *Testaments of the Twelve Patriarchs*, which undoubtedly arose in the Maccabæan period. Even here Beliar appears as the enemy of the last times. It is said of the Messiah (Levi 18^{12}): 'And Beliar will be bound by Him, and He will give His children power to trample on the evil spirits.' In the same way, the description of the last great battle in *Assump. Mos.* (10^{1}) begins as follows: 'And then will His (God's) rule over all creatures be manifest, then will the devil be brought to naught.' The same thought is also to be found in the Gospels (Mt 12^{28}, Lk 11^{20}, Jn 12^{31} 14^{30} 16^{11}; cf. Rev $12^{8f.}$ $13^{1ff.}$ 16^{13} $20^{1\text{-}3.\ 7\text{-}10}$; Bousset, *Rel. d. Judentums*^{2}, 288 ff., 382 ff.).

It is very likely that *'Antichrist' is originally nothing else than the incarnate devil*, and that the idea of the battle of God with a human opponent, in which all devilish wickedness would become incarnate, arose under the influence of definite historical conditions.

2. In fact it is very probable that the roots of the conception of Antichrist are even more widespread. We shall have to assume that the idea of the battle of God with the devil was closely interwoven with *related mythological fancies regarding the battle of God with a dragon-like monster*.

Traces of these ideas, which probably take their rise from the Babylonian battle of Marduk with Tiamat, are already to be found in all parts of the OT (cf. Gunkel, *Schöpfung und Chaos*, 1895). In this way the figure of the devil and the dragon-like monster of chaos are combined into one (cf. Rev 12). Thus we need not be surprised if the figure of the devil incarnate, the figure of Antichrist, here and there bears distinct traces of the features of that mythical monster, and manifests a ghostly superhuman character which cannot possibly be explained from the definite historical situations of the separate predictions. Thus even in Dn 8 the figure of Antiochus IV. is depicted with the superhuman features of the monster, where we read that the little horn raised itself against the host of heaven and cast down some of them to the ground. In the same way Pompey in the song of triumph over his death (Ps. Sol. 2) is described as the dragon of Chaos, whom God destroyed because he rose up against Him. It is also a significant fact that Antichrist in a series of later passages receives the name which in the older sources (*Test. Patr.*, etc.) was applied to the devil—Beliar (acc. to Ps 18^{5} in all probability originally a god of the under world); cf. 2 Co 6^{15} (?) *Ascens. Is.* $4^{2ff.}$, *Sibyll.* iii. 63 ff., ii. 167.

3. The *idea of Antichrist itself* can be traced back to the 2nd cent. B.C., and appears first of all in the Book of Daniel, which belongs to the Maccabæan age. The historical figure whose features have in the first place been attributed to Antichrist is the *Syrian king Antiochus IV. Epiphanes*, the persecutor of the Jews. In particular, the representations of Dn $7^{8.\ 19\text{-}25}$ $8^{9\text{-}12}$ $11^{21\text{-}45}$ have been of lasting influence. That Antichrist ('the king of the North,' 11^{40}) will appear as a mighty king with great armies, that he will destroy three kings (the 'three horns,' $7^{8.\ 25}$), that Edomites, Moabites, and Ammonites are to be spared by him (11^{41}), that Libyans and Cushites will follow in his train (11^{43}), that he will persecute the saints (7^{25}), that he will reign $3\frac{1}{2}$ years (7^{25} etc.), and that he will set up in the Temple the 'abomination of desolation' (βδέλυγμα τῆς ἐρημώσεως, 8^{13} 9^{27} 12^{11})—all this belongs, from this time onward, to the standing requirements of the Antichrist legend. The end predicted by 'Daniel' did not come, but his book received a place in the canon; and thus the faithful still expected the fulfilment of his predictions in the future, and handed them on from generation to generation. In this process the figure of 'Antichrist' came to be separated from the historical figure of Antiochus IV., and became the type of the God-opposing tyrant who was discovered now in this and now in that historical character.

To the author of the *Psalms of Solomon*, it is Pompey, the captor of Jerusalem, the blasphemer of the sanctuary of God, that is the Divine adversary, the 'dragon' of the last times; and his destruction is celebrated in triumphant strains by the writer as a great act of his God ($2^{26ff.}$). In the *Assumption of Moses* (ch. 8) a remarkable prophetic picture of the cruel tyrant is outlined; and, if minutely examined, it seems to be a figure possessing the mixed features of Antiochus Epiphanes and Herod the Great.

In the Roman period the character of *the Emperor Caligula* (A.D. 37–41) influenced the history of the legend. The fearful time of anxiety, when Caligula, embittered by the revolt of the Jews at Jamnia, gave the order to the governor Petronius to erect his statue in the Temple, recalled afresh the prediction of Daniel. The prediction regarding the βδέλυγμα τῆς ἐρημώσεως seemed to receive its fulfilment. The ever-recurring expectation of later times, that Antichrist would take his place in the Temple of Jerusalem, dates in all probability from this period. The small Jewish Apocalypse, adopted to a large extent in Mk 13 and Mt 24 and interwoven with words of Christ, may date from this time. In the same way the attempt has been widely made to find in Rev 13 a source belonging to this time, chiefly for the reason that the name Γάϊος Καῖσαρ actually makes up the number 616; and several manuscripts of Rev 13^{18} preserve this number (instead of 666). Then we shall see later how the expectation of Antichrist was carried over to the *person of Nero*. Finally, in 4 Ezr 5^{6}, too, we find in quite general terms attention called to the last hostile tyrant of the last times: 'regnabit, quem non sperant' (cf. the Syrian Apoc. Bar. 40).

4. Christianity took over from Judaism this whole cycle of ideas, and we meet numerous traces of these conceptions in the NT. In the eschatological chapters (Mk 13, Mt 24) we have in all likelihood, as has already been indicated, a small apocalypse of Antichrist, interwoven with words of Jesus, if we are entitled to interpret the βδέλυγμα τῆς ἐρημώσεως (Mt 24^{15}, Mk 13^{14}), which stands in the holy place, in terms of 2 Thess 2^{4}. In particular, the predictions of the Revelation of John borrow their fundamental tone from the fancies regarding Antichrist. The eleventh chapter, with its prediction of the beast rising from the abyss (a mythical idea), who, as a hostile tyrant, surrounded by great armies, appears in Jerusalem and kills the witnesses of God, is entirely on the lines of Jewish Apocalyptic prophecy. Finally, if the beast, who is called up by the devil (Rev $13^{1ff.}$), and who rises out of the sea, is regarded as indicating the Roman empire, or more particularly a Roman ruler, we have here, too, the character of the Antichrist, the God-opposing tyrant, preserved.

5. A *strongly marked transformation* of the whole idea, from a specifically Christian standpoint, is indicated by the discussion in 2 Th 2, which the present writer, in spite of renewed and energetic opposition on the part of Wrede (*TU*, new ser. lx.[2]), prefers to ascribe to St. Paul himself. Certainly here, too, the figure which controls the Jewish Apocalyptic thought forms the fundamental conception, as is proved by the names ($2^{3f.}$) ὁ ἄνθρωπος τῆς ἀνομίας (perhaps Beliar; cf. the OT בְּנֵי־בְלִיַּעַל), ὁ ἀντικείμενος, as well as by the play upon Dn 11^{36}, which is found here. But, on the other hand, the Antichrist is *no longer the God-opposing tyrant*, but *a seductive agency*, which works by signs and wonders, and seeks to obtain Divine worship. Antichrist here is a false Messiah, a prophet who, it is assumed, will call forth the faith of those Jews who have rejected the true Messiah (2^{10-12}). At the same time the idea is raised still further into the realm of the superhuman (2^{4}, ἀποδεικνύντα ἑαυτόν, ὅτι ἔστιν θεός). Accordingly, this false Messiah is now for the first time in a real and proper sense regarded as the opponent of the true Messiah. By means of the latter his destruction shall be accomplished, and this is described in 2^{8} in the words of Is 11^{4} (καὶ ἐν πνεύματι διὰ χειλέων ἀνελεῖ ἀσεβῆ. . . . The Targum on the passage, too, interprets the 'lawless one' as Antichrist). A remarkably puzzling trait is the 'sitting' of the ἄνθρωπος τῆς ἀνομίας in the temple of God—probably, as we saw above, a reminiscence from the time of Caligula. But this trait also fits into the new comprehensive picture of the seductive personality. If, finally, the enigmatic reference to a power which still keeps the appearance of Antichrist in check (τὸ κατέχον, ὁ κατέχων) be correctly interpreted as referring to the Roman empire, then the separation of the idea of Antichrist from the political tendency, which up to this time adhered to it, comes more clearly to the front. Accordingly the significant change, which 2 Thess. has effected in the idea of Antichrist, consists in this, that here out of the God-opposing tyrant the seductive adversary of the last times has been developed, so that, while the original idea led to the proclamation of the Roman empire or of a Roman emperor as Antichrist (Revelation of John), here the figure of the ἀντικείμενος obtains a non-political, purely ideal signification. In this process of re-moulding, which has become of world-wide historical importance, the genius of St. Paul is in all probability manifested, or in any case the genius of youthful Christianity, freeing itself from Judaism and placing its foot in the world of the Roman empire.

This new conception seems to have found acceptance in wide-spread Christian circles. The author of the Fourth Gospel, too, appears to give expression to the thought that the Jews, because they have not believed on the true Christ, who was sent of God, will place their faith in the false Messiah, who will come forward in his own name (5^{43}). From this point of view we are enabled to understand how, in the *Epistles of John*, Antichrist is connected with false teaching (1 Jn $2^{18.\ 22}$ 4^{3}, 2 Jn ^{7}), and how in general the appearance of false teaching is thought of as one of the signs of the last time—as the crowning point of Satanic malice (1 Ti 4^{1}, 2 Ti 3^{1}, 2 P 3^{3}).

The Διδαχὴ τῶν ιβ' ἀποστόλων, 16^{4}, in its description of Antichrist, manifestly borrows from 2 Th. (καὶ τότε φανήσεται ὁ κοσμοπλάνος ὡς υἱὸς τοῦ θεοῦ καὶ ποιεῖ σημεῖα καὶ τέρατα). In the *Christian Sibyllines*, iii. 63 ff., probably of a late date (cf. Bousset, art. 'Sibyllen' in *PRE*[3]), in the conception of which the figure of Simon Magus has been influential, 'Beliar' is in the first place a wonder-worker endowed with Satanic powers. In fact, even the author of the *Revelation of John* has paid his tribute to the new conception! In the second beast, which comes from the land (ch. 13), he has introduced into his prediction the figure of the anti-Christian false prophet (16^{13} 19^{20}), who performs signs and wonders to seduce the world. Of course he could not give the latter any independent significance; so he made it the servant and assistant of the first beast, the anti-Christian Roman empire (Bousset, *Kom. zur Offenbar. Joh.*, *ad loc.*).

6. But this anti-Jewish conception, which corresponded better with the position of Christianity in the Roman State, was prevented from obtaining exclusive predominance in the Christian tradition. This was due to the acceptance in wide circles of a remarkable combination of the Antichrist legend with the popular expectation of the return of Nero, prevalent originally among the heathen classes. Not long after the death of Nero, the rumour arose that he was not dead, but was still alive, or that after his death he would re-appear (Sueton. *Nero*, 57; Tacitus, *Hist.* ii. 8). As Nero had stood in friendly relations to the Parthians in his lifetime (Sueton. 47, 57), the report was now circulated that he had fled to them, and would return with a Parthian army to take vengeance on Rome. Deceivers made use of the rumour to appear under the mask of Nero. Such an one came forward as early as the year A.D. 69, under Otho (Galba) (Tacitus, *Hist.* ii. 8–9; Dio Cassius, lxiv. 9; Zonaras, xi. 15), and a second appeared under Titus (Zonaras, xi. 12; probably also Sueton. 57). Even in 100 A.D. the belief that Nero was still alive was held by many (cf. Bousset, *Com.*[2 (5)], 411 ff.; Charles, *Ascension of Isaiah*, lvii ff.). This popular heathen belief was now adopted first of all by the Jewish Apocalyptic writers. While the author of the 4th (*Jewish*) *Sibylline* (79 A.D.) takes it over simply without any special tendency (iv. 137–139), the author of the (Jewish?) original basis of Rev 17 (Bousset, 414–415) expects the return of Nero with the Parthians to take vengeance on Rome, because she had shed the blood of the saints (17^{6}, destruction of Jerusalem [?]; καὶ ἐκ τοῦ αἵματος τῶν μαρτύρων Ἰησοῦ is a later addition). In the 5th *Sibylline*, which for the most part (with the exception of vv. 1–51) was written by a Jewish writer at the end of the 1st cent. (J. Geffcken, 'Komp. u. Entstehungszeit der Orac. Sibyll.,' *TU*, new ser. viii. 1, p. 22 ff.), the subject of the return of Nero is mentioned by the author no fewer than three times (137–154, 214–227, 361–385). Here the figure of Nero is already distorted into a ghostly demon; his return and the terrible war, which will then convulse the world, will be the beginning of the last end. The *Christian* as well as the Jewish Apocalyptic thought took possession of the Nero legend, and on this soil the figure of the returning Nero was quite identified with that of Antichrist. Then we have to take into account the additional circumstance that the longer the period from the death of Nero became, the less could a simple return of the *living* Nero be expected, and the more did the expectation of his return from the under world grow. In this way, too, his figure became more and more hellish and ghostly: the relation to the Parthians is lost sight of, and instead of an adversary of Rome he becomes an opponent of God and Christ.

In particular, this is the form taken by the legend of Nero in the mind of the *final redactor of the Book of Revelation*, who composed ch. 13 in comparative independence, and in ch. 17 (see above) worked over a more ancient document. Here Nero is the beast that rises out of the abyss (17^{8}), which was, is not, and again shall be, in order that it may go into perdition (17^{11}); he is 'the head as it had been slain' ($13^{3.\ 14}$), the cruel adversary of the Lamb; and so both are indicated by the same phrase *ὡς ἐσφαγμένον(η)*; he is the tyrant who receives worship over the whole earth ($13^{4.\ 8}$, etc.), and the terrible opponent of the Lamb in the last great decisive battle (17^{14} $19^{19ff.}$). Without doubt the 'number of the beast' (13^{18}) refers to him (according to the great majority of manuscripts, 666=נרון קסר; the other reading, however, leads to the Latin form: 616=נרו קסר).

In the small apocalypse in the *Ascens. Is.* 3^{13b}–4^{18}, which dates from the second, or perhaps only from the third, decade of the 2nd cent. (Harnack, *Chronol. der altchristl. Lit.* i. 573), we clearly see the final combination of two figures originally quite foreign to each other, when we read that Beliar, the king of this world, will descend from the firmament in the form of a man, who is depicted as the matricidal tyrant Nero. The beginning of the 5th *Sibylline* (vv. 1–51), too, probably a Jewish composition inserted by the redactor in the time of Marcus Aurelius, identifies Nero with the figure of Antichrist (vv. 28–34; *εἶτ' ἀνακάμψει ἰσάζων θεῷ αὐτόν*). In the 8th *Sibylline* (viii. 68 ff., 140 ff., 151 ff.), which dates from the period immediately preceding the death of Marcus Aurelius, only faint reminiscences are to be found. But Victorinus of Pettau, who wrote his *Com. on the Revelation* in the age of Diocletian, still knows the relation of the writing to the legend of Nero (Bousset, 53 ff.). The apologist Commodian, who probably did not write his *Carmen apologeticum* till the beginning of the 4th cent. (A. Harnack, *Chronol.* ii. 433–442), is acquainted with two figures of Antichrist, one of which he still identifies with *Nero redivivus*.

7. But even in the 2nd cent. the legend of Nero lost its influence on the minds of men, and in the same degree the *anti-Jewish conception*, borrowed from 2 Thess. 2, which was free from historical and political limitations, gained the upper hand. On the ground of exegetical combinations, in particular, under the influence of a renewed use of the predictions of Daniel, and by the help of other traditions—here the combination with the idea of a world-conflagration, which also in all probability arose from the Persian apocalyptic, is specially to be mentioned—the conception was filled out in detail, and continued to exhibit in all its particulars a remarkable persistency.

Antichrist is to come from the tribe of Dan (cf. Rev 7^{5}; also Bousset[2], p. 282). He shall appear in Jerusalem as a mighty ruler, subdue three rulers, assemble the armies of the world around him, perform signs and wonders, and demand Divine worship. Elijah and Enoch, who both appear as witnesses against him, shall be subdued and slain. The Jews shall believe on him, and he shall rebuild the Temple. He shall persecute those among the Jews who refuse him their faith. These, however, shall be saved by a miraculous interference of God (the angel). He will put his seal upon his faithful, so that only he who bears this seal shall be free to buy and sell (cf. Rev $13^{16f.}$). Finally, the famine of the last times shall overtake him, from which he will not be able to save his followers; then at the last he shall be subdued and destroyed by Christ, and the general conflagration follows. These are the ever recurring features of this picture of the future, which continues to persist throughout the centuries (cf., for the proofs in detail, Bousset, *Antichrist*).

The same ideas are already to be found in broad outline in the eschatological portions of Irenæus (*adv. Hæreses*, v.), and in Hippolytus (*de Antichristo* and *Com. on Daniel*). In times of political excitement during the course of the following centuries, men always turned afresh to the prophecy regarding Antichrist. The external features of the prophecy change, and special historical prophecies come to the front, but in the background the prediction of Antichrist, connected with no definite time, remains pretty much unchanged. Thus we find in the beginning of the *Testamentum Domini*, lately edited by Raḥmani, an apocalypse of the time of Decius, although it has undergone a later redaction (Harnack, *Chronol.* ii. 514 ff.). In this work the description of the external appearance of Antichrist is of interest (cf. also the Coptic and the Jewish *Apocalypse of Elijah*; see below). The time of Aurelian and Gallienus, with its embittered struggles between the Romans and the Persians as well as between the Roman emperors and pretenders, seems to have given new food to the Apocalyptic fancy. From this time, in all probability, dates the Jewish *Apocalypse of Elijah*, which is preserved to us in Hebrew, and in which, if Buttenwieser's conjectures (*Eine heb. Eliasapokalypse*, Leipzig, 1897) are correct, Odhænat of Palmyra appears as Antichrist. In the same period arose undoubtedly the prophecy of the 13th *Sibylline*, which ends in a glorification of Odhænat, but does not belong to the Antichrist predictions proper. It is also possible that the special Antichrist passages in the 3rd *Sibylline*, v. 63 ff., and at the end of the 2nd *Sibylline*, belong to these circumstances (Bousset, *PRE*[3] xviii. 273 ff.). Finally, it seems as if the puzzling Coptic *Apocalypse of Elijah*, contained in two partially preserved revisions, which shows signs of repeated corrections, had been worked over perhaps for the last time in this age (Steindorff, *TU*, new ser. ii. 3; Bousset, *Ztschr. f. Kirchengesch.* xx. 2, pp. 103–112).

Lactantius, in the *Divin. Institut.* vii. 14 ff., presents the Antichrist legend in an original and interesting form, which shows a certain amount of contact, on the one hand, with the *Apocalypse of Elijah*, which has just been mentioned, and, on the other hand, with the *Carmen apologeticum* of Commodian (belonging to the first decades of the 4th cent.).

8. A new turn in the history of the legend is represented by the so-called *Tiburtine Sibylline*. By means of the investigations, which all point to the same conclusion, undertaken by Sackur (*Sibyll. Texte und Forschungen*, p. 114 ff.), by Kampers (*Die deutsche Kaiseridee*, p. 18 f.), and by Bousset (*Antichrist*), it has been settled that the Tiburtine Sibylline, which appears in various editions and revisions of the Middle Ages, goes back to an original document which was composed in the 4th century. Since Basset published a 'Wisdom of the Sibyl' (*Les Apocryphes éthiopiennes*, x.) from Ethiopic and Arabic sources, which in itself is closely connected with the Tiburtina, but is enlarged by predictions which go down to the date of the sons of Harun al-Rashid, it has become still more easy to re-construct the original of the old Tiburtina. This Sibylline, dating from the 4th cent., and celebrating the Emperor Constans as the last ruler, is of importance, because in it occurs for the first time the *prophecy regarding the last emperor*, who, before the advent of Antichrist, shall obtain dominion over the whole world, and at the end of his reign shall march to Jerusalem and lay down his crown on Golgotha. From this time onwards *the last ruler of the world before Antichrist* becomes a standing requisite of the legend. In the treatise on Antichrist preserved in Latin under the name of Ephraim (Isidore), which probably dates from the 4th cent., and which has been published by Caspari (*Briefe und Abhandlungen*, 1890, pp. 208 ff., 429 ff.), this change in the legend is also already indicated: 'Christianorum imperium traditur Deo et patri' (ch. 5).

There are, besides, quite a number of writings on Antichrist which have been handed down to us under Ephraim's name, as, *e.g.*, a *λόγος εἰς τὴν παρουσίαν τοῦ κυρίου καὶ περὶ συντελείας τοῦ κόσμου καὶ εἰς τὴν παρουσίαν τοῦ Ἀντιχρίστου* (Assemani, ii. 222–230, iii. 134–143; related treatises are to be found among

Ephraim's works in Bousset, *Antichrist*, 23 f.); further, a Syrian homily (Th. J. Lamy, iii. 187 ff.), which—it is true—in its present redaction predicts the rising of Islām. Closely related to the Greek Ephraim are the *περὶ τῆς συντελείας τοῦ κόσμου* of pseudo-Hippolytus and a pseudo-Johannine Apocalypse (Tischendorf, *Apocalypses apocryphæ*). The fifteenth Catechesis of Cyril of Jerusalem should also be mentioned here.

9. Antichrist Apocalypses flourished again in the age of Islām. In the very beginning of it we meet with the most curious and notable of these prophetic books, viz. the *pseudo-Methodius*, which is extant in no fewer than three Greek recensions, a Latin translation, and various Greek and Latin redactions (the original Greek text is found in Istrin [see below], the Latin text in Sackur, *op. cit.*). Here the emperor of the future, who shall miraculously wake out of sleep, overcome Islām, and obtain the dominion of the world, has already become the most striking figure in the picture of the future. Then a number of *Byzantine prophecies*, which accompany the reigns of the Byzantine emperors and their fates, are influenced by pseudo-Methodius.

One prophetic composition, written in verse and adorned with pictures, which is ascribed to Leo VI. the philosopher (Migne, *Patrol. Græca*, cvii. 1121 ff.), predicts, *e.g.*, the fall of the house of the Comneni, and celebrates the emperor of the future, who, waking miraculously from the sleep of death, shall rise out of his grave. The legend of the sleeping emperor of the future is everywhere closely interwoven with the tradition of Antichrist. We possess, further, a Greek prophecy associated with the name of Daniel (alongside of a probably more ancient Armenian Daniel-apocalypse, Bousset, *Antichrist*, 41 ff.), which, in the period of the Latin empire, predicts the restoration of the Greek rule (Bousset, *Ztschr. f. Kirchengesch.* xx. 289 f.).

In the regions of the East which were ruled over by Islām, the age of Islām and the Crusades was exceedingly productive of prophecies of Antichrist. To this period belong the Apocalypses which are contained in the so-called *Liber Clementis discipuli St. Petri* (*Petri apostoli apocalypsis per Clementem*) in the Arabic, Ethiopic, and probably also the Syriac tongue (Bousset, *Antichrist*, 45 ff.), the Coptic (14th) *Vision of Daniel* (in the appendix to Woide's edition of the Codex Alexandrinus, Oxford, 1799), also the above-mentioned Ethiopic-Arabic *Wisdom of the Sibyl*, and finally the later Syriac *Apocalypse of Ezra* (Bousset, *Antichrist*, 45 ff.). In the age of Islām we have also a revival of *Jewish* Apocalyptic literature, probably to a large extent caused by the Christian prophetic writings. One of the most interesting of the writings here to be indicated is the Jewish history of Daniel which is handed down in the Persian tongue (Merx, *Archiv zur Erforsch. des AT*, i.). Alongside of this work there is a series of other writings: the *Mysteries of Simeon-ben-Jochai*, the *Midrash Vajoscha*, the *Signs of the Messiah*, the *Book of Zerubbabel*, etc. (cf. Buttenwieser, *Neo-Apocalyptic Jewish Literature*, 1901).

10. This whole type of predictions came to *the West* in the book of pseudo-Methodius, which was early translated into Latin. The Tiburtina, too, with its numerous recensions, accompanying the history of the German emperors, plays a special rôle. Finally, great influence was exerted by the letter which the monk Adso (954) wrote to the queen Gerberga: *de Ortu et Tempore Antichristi* (cf. Sackur, *Sibyll. Texte und Forschungen*, ii.). Then the legend of Antichrist passed through its classical period in the West, in which it even made history. Since the beginning of the 2nd Christian millennium a strong increase in the eschatological direction can be observed. This was intensified by the excitement which was produced in the lands of the West by the Crusades. All these fantastic eschatological tendencies found their intellectual focus in the person and activity of the abbot Joachim of Floris (end of 12th cent.); in particular, the intellectual movements which he originated found ready acceptance in the Franciscan order, and especially among those Franciscans who were inclined to form an opposition. Thus the time came when people saw Antichrist, or the forerunner of Antichrist, in every ecclesiastical, political, national, or social opponent, and the catchword 'Antichrist' sounded on all sides: in the struggle between the Emperor and the Pope, the Guelfs and Ghibellines, opposing Franciscans and the Papacy, between heretics and the Church, reformative social movements and the ruling powers opposed to them (*Reformatio Sigismundi*, *Onus Ecclesiæ* of Berthold of Chiemsee); in sculpture and painting (*e.g.* cf. Signorelli's picture in the cathedral of Orvieto), in lyric, epic, and dramatic poetry (cf. esp. the *Ludus de Antichristo*, ed. W. Meyer), the motives were supplied by the prophecy of Antichrist. In particular, the belief that the *Pope of Rome* was Antichrist, or at least his forerunner (*antichristus minor, mysticus*), became of world-wide historical importance. This view was assiduously cultivated by the Franciscans of the opposition, who had remained true to the original ideal of poverty. From them the conviction passed over to the pre-Reformation sects; the Bohemians Milič of Kremsier (*Libellus de Antichristo*) and Matthias of Janow are connected with them in a way which can quite easily be traced. Wyclif and his follower Michael Purvey (the probable author of the work edited by Luther [1528], *Com. in Apocalypsin ante centum annos editus*), as well as Huss on the other side, are firmly convinced of the anti-Christian nature of the Papacy.

In a particularly instructive monograph, H. Preuss has shown how important a rôle the idea of Antichrist played in the age of Luther among the widest classes of the people—how the idea gradually dawned on Luther's mind, and became fixed, that the Pope of Rome was the incarnate Antichrist, and how this conviction led him to more keen and daring opposition to the Papacy, and filled his soul with all the passion and remorselessness of battle. Thus in the Articles of Schmalkald, which were composed by Luther himself, the proposition that the Pope is Antichrist has been raised to an article of faith (Part ii. art. iv. 'de Papatu,' § 10 f.); while in the drawing up of the Augustana, political reasons prevented this conviction from being expressed.

In the centuries that followed the Reformation, the doctrine that the Pope was Antichrist gradually receded into the background. It was, of course, still resolutely held by Protestant scholars, particularly by commentators on the Apocalypse even in our own times. But it came to be more and more only learned pedantry, and the belief no longer possessed the power of forming history. With this last phase the interest in the legend entirely disappeared, and it is now to be found only among the lower classes of the Christian community, among sects, eccentric individuals, and fanatics.

LITERATURE.—The respective artt. in *PRE*[3], Hastings' *DB*, Smith's *DB*, the *EBi.*; Guthe's *Bibelwörterbuch*. For the legend of Antichrist in Jewish and Christian times: R. H. Charles, *Ascension of Isaiah*, 1900, Introd. li–lxxiii; W. Bousset, *Rel. d. Judentums im neutest. Zeitalter*[2], 1906, p. 291 ff., *Die Offenbar. Johannis*[5] (in Meyer), 1906, *passim*; and generally the modern comm. on Revelation and 2 Thessalonians. For the history of the Nero-legend: J. Geffcken, *GGN*, 1899, p. 446 ff.; Th. Zahn, *ZKWL*, 1886, 337 ff.; W. Bousset, *Kom. zur Offenbar. Johannis* (on ch. xvii.) and art. 'Sibyllen' in *PRE*[3] xviii. 265; Nordmeyer, 'Der Tod Neros in der Legende,' *Festschrift d. Gymnasiums z. Mörs*, 1896. On the later history of the legend: W. Bousset, *Antichrist*, 1893 [Eng. tr.; here is to be found a detailed discussion of almost all the later sources mentioned in the text]; also 'Beiträge z. Gesch. d. Eschatologie,' *Ztschr. f. Kirchengesch.* xx. 2 and specially xx. 3 (on the later Byzantine prophecies); Istrin, *Ctenija* of the Society for Russian Language and Antiquities in connexion with Moscow University, 1897 (the text of the Greek Methodius and related material); E. Sackur, *Sibyll. Texte und Forschungen*, 1898 [(1) Methodius in the Latin text, (2) *Epistola Adsonis*, (3) The Tiburtine Sibylline]; Vassiliew, *Anecdota Græco-Byzantina*, i., Moscow, 1893 (text of a number of Byzantine prophecies); F. Kampers, *Die deutsche Kaiseridee in Prophetie und Sage*, Munich, 1896, and 'Alexander der Grosse und die Idee des Weltimperiums' (*Studien und Darstellungen aus dem Gebiet d. Gesch. von H. Grauert*, i. 2–3), 1901; E. Wadstein, *Die eschatol. Ideengruppe, Weltsabbat, Weltende u. Weltgericht*. 1896; W. Meyer, 'Ludus de Antichristo' in *Sitzungsber. d. Münchener Akademie*, phil.-hist. Klasse, 1882, No. 1); Kropatschek, *Das Schriftprinzip d. luther. Kirche*, 1904, i. 247 ff.; H. Preuss, *Die Vorstellung v. Antichrist i. späteren Mittelalter b. Luther u. i. d. konfessionellen Polemik*, 1906.

W. BOUSSET.

ANTINOMIANISM.—Antinomianism (ἀντί 'against,' and *νόμος* 'law'), as a distinct theological phenomenon, originated with Johannes Agricola (1492–1566), who was an early coadjutor of Luther in the Reformation. It is the counterpart of modern political anarchism, being directed towards the destruction of the Moral Law of the OT in the interest of the new freedom of Christians and the testimony of the spirit. Antinomianism, as John Wesley defined it, is the doctrine that 'makes void the Law through faith.' Christians are free from the Law. The Law primarily referred to was the Law of Moses. Agricola denied that Christians owed subjection to any part of this law, even to the Decalogue.

In its widest sense the term is used to designate the doctrines of extreme fanatics who deny subjection to any law other than the subjective caprices of the empirical individual, though this individual is generally credited as the witness and interpreter of the Holy Spirit. It is uncertain just how far Agricola went towards this wider capriciousness of the individual. For we get from history the usual exaggerations of theological controversies, when we read the debates between Luther and Agricola on the subject. Agricola began, and intended to remain, true to the great Reformation principle of *justification* through faith alone, without works. It was the fear of *work*-righteousness that led him to argue against the Moral Law—at least that of the Decalogue. He wished to establish Luther's condemnation of the Roman Catholic doctrine of *good works*, or *work-righteousness*, on some distinctively gospel principle. After making a secret propaganda for some ten years, he maintained, in a public disputation at Wittenberg in 1537, that works are indifferent, and that a man is saved by faith alone without any regard to his moral character. He said: 'Art thou steeped in sin, an adulterer or a thief? If thou believest, thou art in salvation. All who follow Moses must go to the devil. To the gallows with Moses.'

It was then that Luther characterized the teaching as being *antinomian*, and identified it, in principle, with the anarchism of the Anabaptists. Agricola retracted and was reconciled with Luther, but the controversy was carried on by others. One of the followers of Agricola, a certain Ammsdorf, said that good works imperilled salvation. Agricola claimed that he was only expounding the teachings of Luther and Melanchthon. Indeed we find Luther (*Werke*, xx. 203) saying: 'We do not wish to see or hear Moses. For Moses was given to the Jews, not to us Gentiles and Christians. We have our Gospel and New Testament. They wish to make Jews of us through Moses, but they shall not.' And Melanchthon says (*Loci communes*, 1st ed. by Augusti, p. 127): 'It must be admitted that the Decalogue is abrogated.' But the controversy with Agricola was only the occasion for Luther to give the definite term 'antinomianism' to a view far older than the German Reformation. This view showed itself even in NT times. Luther himself characterized the Epistle of St. James as 'an epistle of straw,' because of its emphasis upon good works. Then we find the Apostles (Ro $3^{8.31}$ 6^{1}, Eph 5^{6}, 2 P $2^{18.19}$) warning Christians against perversions of their doctrines as an excuse for licentiousness, or antinomianism. The Gnostic sects, hyper-spiritual in doctrine, were sensualistic in their morals. They held that the spirit (πνεῦμα), as part of the eternal Divine energy, existed absolutely separate and apart from the soul (ψύχη) and the material body. Hence, all acts of the soul and body were things indifferent to the spirit. Hence, soul and body might wallow in licentiousness without detracting from the salvation of the spirit (πνεῦμα). Here we find with the Valentinian Gnostics the most frank and definite statement of Antinomianism in its widest and most immoral form.

A tract of Augustine (*contra adversarium legis et prophetarum*) seems to indicate the existence of Antinomianism in the 4th century. There are traces of it to be found during the Middle Ages. It comes out strongly among the Anabaptists of Germany and Holland. During the Commonwealth, it existed in England among the high Calvinists. These argued that, if a man was elected and predestined to salvation, no power in heaven or on earth could prevent it; and hence, no matter what the moral conduct of a man might be, his salvation was sure if he was one of the elect; the wicked actions of such a man were not sinful, and he had no occasion to confess his sins or to break them off by repentance. Saltmarsh, Cromwell's chaplain, was among these 'sectaries.' But they never became an independent sect. Antinomianism existed in the 18th cent. in England both in the Church of England and among the Dissenters. Again, it appeared in England among the followers of John Wesley, who made earnest protest against it. This gave occasion for John Fletcher to write a strong book, entitled *Checks to Antinomianism*.

It is not in place to carry the discussion of this term beyond its proper theological rôle. We may only add that the principle of the thing—opposition to law—is found in every sphere of the organized or institutional activities of humanity. All who advocate doctrines subversive of the Family, the State, or the Church, are antinomians. All moral sophists are antinomians. All who pervert the principle that 'the end justifies the means,' into a disregard for established moral laws, so that some personal or finite end be attained, are antinomians. And every individual who pleads special exemption from obedience to the common law of morality is an antinomian.

We may cite Epiphanes, the sensual son of the Gnostic Carpocrates, as one of the lowest types of antinomians. He died at the age of seventeen from the effects of debauchery, after having written a work on *Righteousness*, in which he advocated the generous principle—'Follow your own nature, against all established laws.'

Jacobi may be taken as the highest type of an antinomian in his fervent protest against moral rigorism: 'Nay, I am that atheist, that profane person, who, in despite of the will that wills nothing, will lie, like the dying Desdemona; prevaricate and deceive, like Pylades representing himself to be Orestes; will murder, like Timoleon; break law and oath, like Epaminondas and Johann de Witt; resolve on suicide, like Otho; commit sacrilege, like David; nay, pluck ears of corn on the Sabbath, only because I am hungry, and the law was made for man, and not man for the law.'

For a modern representative of moral antinomianism we may mention Nietzsche in his doctrine of 'Die Unwertung aller Werte'—the unvaluing of all values, the illegalizing of all laws.

J. MACBRIDE STERRETT.

ANTINOMIES.—Kant first introduced this term into philosophy, although the conception for which it stands had been used by the Eleatic Zeno, by Plato (*Phœdo*, 102; *Rep.* 523; *Parmenides*, 135) and by Aristotle. With Kant an antinomy is the unavoidable contradiction into which reason falls when it seeks to satisfy its necessary demand for the unity of the world as a whole. This is the subject-matter of Rational Cosmology. We can never perceive or conceive the world as a whole. But we are compelled to *think* it. The conflict then is—the world as we *know* it under the categories of the understanding, and the idea under which we *think* it by the Reason. Reason goes beyond the limits of a possible experience, and is met with a flat contradiction the moment it attempts to construe the unconditioned totality in terms of the conditioned, or the world of possible experience. In this knowable world, every phenomenon is determined in relation to other phenomena *ad indefinitum*, not *ad infinitum*. Hence no determination can be complete and final. But the idea of reason demands this very completeness and finality. This is the conflict between the understanding (*Verstand*) which *knows* and Reason (*Vernunft*) which *thinks*. Reason says, 'If the conditioned is given, then the whole sum of conditions, and therefore the absolutely unconditioned, must be given likewise.' But, as Kant limits knowledge to the syntheses of the understanding, he turns to it to prove the idea of reason. But it is limited to the conditioned, and therefore can never reach to knowledge of the unconditioned. An unconditioned condition is absurd. And yet this is what reason demands.

The idea of reason is too large for the capacity of the knowing understanding, and the definite knowledge of the understanding is too small for the idea of the reason. Hence the hopeless back and forth swing between the *dicta* on laws of the two faculties.

Kant gives four antinomies or pairs of theses and antitheses.

The first is the *antinomy of quantity*. Two mutually exclusive propositions can be proved with equal force in regard to the quantity of the world:

I.

THESIS.	ANTITHESIS.
The world had a beginning in time, and is limited also with regard to space.	The world had no beginning, and has no limits in space, but is infinite in respect to both time and space.

He then shows that the denial of either member of both the thesis and the antithesis involves an absurdity.

The second is the *antinomy of quality*, and relates to the divisibility of matter.

II.

THESIS.	ANTITHESIS.
Every composite substance in the world consists of simple parts, and nothing exists anywhere but the simple or what is composed of it.	No composite thing in the world consists of simple parts, and there exists nowhere in the world anything simple.

Here the same *reductio ad absurdum* is applied to both the thesis and the antithesis. These first two antinomies are styled the *mathematical*, as considering the world quantitatively and qualitatively. The next two he styles *dynamical*, as considering the world, not as a total of dead things, but as consisting of things dynamically and organically related to each other.

The first of these is the *antinomy of relation*, dealing chiefly with the relation of causality.

III.

THESIS.	ANTITHESIS.
Causality, according to the laws of nature, is not the only causality from which all the phenomena of the world can be deduced. In order to account for these phenomena, it is also necessary to admit another causality, that of freedom.	There is no freedom, but everything in the world takes place entirely according to the laws of nature.

Here, again, Kant's reasoning is to the absurdity of the opposite of both thesis and antithesis. For the *thesis* it is argued that without free causality there is no *vera causa*, but everything is merely an effect, and not even that, unless it presupposes a *vera causa* which can never be found in any member of the causal series. For the antithesis it is argued that if free causality be allowed, then it must itself be held to be uncaused, and thus contradict the law of causality—that everything must have a cause.

The next is the *antinomy of modality*, and relates to 'the unity in the existence of phenomena,' or the ultimate nature of the universe.

IV.

THESIS.	ANTITHESIS.
There exists an absolutely necessary Being belonging to the world, either as a part or as the cause of it.	There nowhere exists an absolutely necessary Being, either within or without the world, as the cause of it.

Kant claims that no *dogmatic* solution of these antinomies can be given. His own *critical* solution follows from this theory of Knowledge. Knowledge is only of phenomena. We *must think* noumena. But we cannot *know* them as phenomena. It is the attempt to do this that gives rise to these antinomies. His critical solution is that these antinomies arise (necessarily too) only from a confusion between knowable phenomena and unknowable (but real) noumena. It is this that constantly leads one's reasoning on either side to involve a μετάβασις εἰς ἄλλο γένος. Besides these four antinomies of the *Pure Reason*, we find Kant stating one antinomy of the *Practical Reason*, that is, an *ethical* antinomy. It is that between perfect virtue and perfect happiness. *Du sollst also du kannst* is Kant's bed-rock of morality. Unconditional obedience to the categorical imperative is the *summum bonum*. But the *bonum consummatum* includes perfect happiness. What bridge can there be found between perfect virtue and perfect happiness? Here comes the antinomy. Virtue denies happiness as a motive. Virtue demands happiness as the *bonum consummatum*. But virtue cannot be connected with happiness as its cause or its effect.

THESIS.	ANTITHESIS.
The endeavour after happiness produces a virtuous mind.	A virtuous mind necessarily produces happiness.

Here we find Kant saying that the *thesis* 'is absolutely false.' He really goes on to make a *thesis and an antithesis* out of the antithesis. His real antinomy, therefore, is this:

Thesis: Virtue is causal of happiness.

Antithesis: Virtue is not causal of happiness.

To take the antithesis first, it is easily shown that virtue is not causal in the world of experience. Fire burns and poison kills the virtuous as well as the vicious.

Then as to the *thesis*, it is false so far as virtue is considered as a cause in the sensible world. But it is true so far as I am a denizen of a supersensuous world. But even there it is true only because I must have an indefinitely prolonged life in which to approximate to a virtuous mind, and because, finally, there must be a God as the cause adequate to equalizing or proportioning happiness to virtue, that is, a cause adequate to effecting this union of virtue with happiness.

In Kant's Third Critique, *The Critique of Judgment*, we find two other antinomies—the *æsthetic* and the *teleological* antinomies.

First, the *antinomy of taste* (§ 56):

THESIS.	ANTITHESIS.
The judgment of taste is not based on conceptions; for otherwise *de gustibus non disputandum*.	The judgment of taste is based on conceptions; for otherwise we could not argue about it, and there would be no norm of taste.

Second, the *teleological antinomy* (§ 70):

THESIS.	ANTITHESIS.
All production of material things and their forms must be judged to be possible according to merely mechanical laws.	Some products of material nature cannot be judged to be possible according to merely mechanical laws.

Hegel (*Encyclopädie*, § 48) blames Kant for his small list of antinomies. He holds that antinomies 'appear in all objects of every kind, in all representations, conceptions, and ideas.' It is this view that is the vital element of the dialectic, forcing thought onward to ever higher and more concrete forms till it reaches the Absolute Idea in which all contradictions are forms of self-relation. 'The true and positive meaning of the antinomies is this: that every actual thing involves a coexistence of contrary elements. Consequently, to know, or in other words to *comprehend*, an object is equivalent to being conscious of it as a unified group of contrary determinations' (§ 48, Zusatz). Hegel's whole *Logic* is an exhibition of the antinomial dialectic of all finite thought, in its indwelling tendency to absolute and final thought, as 'the life and soul of scientific progress, the dynamic which alone gives an immanent connexion and necessity to the subject-matter of science' (§ 81). Of every thing and every conception we say *it is* and *it is not*, because *it is more* than what it is in its unmediated form. With mere identity, A=A, there can be no progress. But nothing in the world is mere identity:

'Nothing in the world is single;
All things by a law divine
In one another's being mingle.'

The truth of any thing or thought is always a unity of identity and difference, of *thesis* and *antithesis*. Synthesis is the truth of both. But all finite syntheses develop antinomies on the way to the ultimate synthesis of thought and reality, where antinomies are no more.

J. MACBRIDE STERRETT.

ANTIOCHENE THEOLOGY.

[J. H. SRAWLEY].

THE title 'Antiochene Fathers' is generally applied to a school of Church teachers, all connected with Antioch, whose activity covers the latter half of the 4th and the first half of the 5th century. Its most famous representatives were Diodorus, bishop of Tarsus († 394); John Chrysostom, bishop of Constantinople († 407); Theodore, bishop of Mopsuestia († 429); and Theodoret, bishop of Cyrrhus († 457). But the theology of these Fathers has its roots in an earlier period, and reproduces the traditions of a school of Christian learning at Antioch, the history and characteristics of which form a necessary introduction to a study of the later writers.

I. *THE SCHOOL OF ANTIOCH: HISTORY AND CHARACTERISTICS.*—The city of Antioch, founded by the Seleucid kings and made by them the capital of their dominions, was the metropolis of the East and the third city of the Roman Empire. It was a centre of Greek life and culture, and was noted for its pursuit of art and literature. The Church of Antioch had played an important part in the early spread of Christianity, and from early times had been the centre of important movements in the region of thought. It was the home of the early Gnostics, Menander and Saturnilus, while the writings of Theophilus, bishop of Antioch, in the latter years of Marcus Aurelius and under Commodus, attracted the notice of the West, and show that the attention of the Church had been directed to the statement and defence of Christian truth. The earliest reference to anything like an organized Christian school of instruction occurs in connexion with the condemnation of the heresy of **Paul of Samosata** in the year 269. At the council of bishops, which met at Antioch in that year and condemned Paul, the latter's teaching was exposed by Malchion, a presbyter, who was the head of a school of Greek learning at Antioch. From Eusebius' description (*HE* vii. 29) it has been argued that the Church of Antioch already possessed some institution resembling the Catechetical School of Alexandria, in which sacred learning was combined with secular studies, and the pursuit of rhetoric and dialectic found a place (*σοφιστοῦ τῶν ἐπ' Ἀντιοχείας ἑλληνικῶν παιδευτηρίων διατριβῆς προεστώς*). How far the teaching of Paul himself is representative of a distinct school of thought at Antioch it is difficult to say, but there are features in it which are reproduced by the later Antiochene theologians (*e.g.* his appeal to the historical Christ and his rejection of metaphysics. See below, II. 6).

It is, however, in the time of **Lucian** († 311–312), the presbyter and martyr, that the school of Antioch first comes clearly to light. He is said to have studied in the schools of Edessa and at Cæsarea. From the latter he probably acquired that interest in Biblical studies which was due to the influence of Origen, and for which the school of Lucian was also celebrated. In conjunction with Dorotheus, who combined knowledge of Hebrew with Greek learning (Euseb. *HE* vii. 32), he completed a revision of the LXX, and to him has also been attributed the early Syrian revision of the text of the NT (on these see Swete, *Introd. to OT in Greek*, p. 81 f.; Westcott and Hort, *Introd. to NT in Greek*, p. 138). There is also extant a fragment of his Commentary on the Book of Job (Routh, *Rel. Sacr.* iv. p. 7 f.). But equally important with the Biblical labours of Lucian was the influence exerted by him on the theology of the Eastern Church. In what way he was connected with Paul of Samosata is uncertain (see, however, Harnack, *PRE*[3] xi., art. 'Lucian der Märtyrer'); but the influence of Paul's teaching upon him is unmistakable, and between the years 270 and 299 he appears to have been outside the communion of the Church (Theodoret, *HE* i. 3). His teaching represented a compromise between the Adoptianism of Paul and the Logos Christology of Origen (see below, II. 6). At the same time he taught the idea of a created Logos, and in this respect he handed on to his disciples a tradition which found its most logical expression in Arianism. The school of Lucian was 'the nursery of the Arian doctrine' (Harnack). The Arian leaders, Arius and Eusebius of Nicomedia, were pupils of Lucian, and the title Συλλουκιανισταί was at once a recognition of their reverence for their master, and a common bond of union. Our sources of information as to the teaching of the more prominent Arians exhibit two characteristics which re-appear in the later history of the school of Antioch: (1) the use of the dialectical philosophy of Aristotle; (2) the grammatical and literal exegesis of Scripture. On the former of these see Harnack, *Hist. of Dogma* (Eng. tr. 1899), vol. iv. p. 6. The latter characteristic is illustrated in the commentaries of Eusebius of Emesa, a disciple of Lucian, and a moderate Arian in doctrine, who had studied in the schools of Edessa, Cæsarea, and Alexandria, as well as at Antioch, and who, according to Jerome, exercised an influence upon the exegesis of Diodorus (Jerome, *de Vir. Illustr.* c. 119).

Harnack has pointed out the close parallel which exists between the principles of the school of Lucian and those of the earlier Roman Adoptianists, whose chief representative was Theodotus. In both alike we find the same use of Aristotle, and the same literal and critical exegesis of the Bible. Both schools opposed the dominant mystical and allegorizing tendencies of their time by a full use of empirical and critical methods (Harnack, *Hist. of Dogma*, vol. iii. p. 23 f., vol. iv. p. 6).

But it was not the Arians alone who handed on the traditions of the school of Antioch. **Eustathius**, bishop of Antioch (exiled in 341), in his *de Engastrimytho* attacks the allegorical interpretation of Origen, and exhibits the true Antiochene exegesis. Flavian, the colleague and friend of Diodorus at Antioch (Theodoret, *HE* iv. 22), and Meletius, the patron of Chrysostom, constitute links between the earlier and the later school of Antioch.

The history of the later school of Antioch really begins with **Diodorus** (bishop of Tarsus, 378–394). A fellow-student of Basil at Athens, and later on the colleague of Flavian, he had upheld the Nicene cause at Antioch in the days of Meletius' exile. His friendship with Basil (Basil, *Ep.* 135) is important as marking the union between Cappadocian and Antiochene orthodoxy (Harnack, *PRE*[3] iv., art. 'Diodorus'). Only fragments of his voluminous writings are extant, but they appear to have included treatises on philosophy and theology, and commentaries on the Old and New Testaments. In his opposition to Apollinarism he was led to conceptions of the Person of Christ which in later times caused him to be regarded as a precursor of Nestorianism. In his exegesis of the Scriptures, the principles of which he expounded in a treatise entitled Τίς διαφορὰ θεωρίας καὶ ἀλληγορίας, he contested the Alexandrian method of interpretation, and, while affirming the need of insight into the inner spiritual meaning of Scripture, he asserted the importance of grammatical and historical methods of exegesis. Lastly, Diodorus' importance consists in the fact that he was the inspirer and teacher of the two most famous representatives of the school of Antioch—Theodore and Chrysostom.

Theodore, bishop of Mopsuestia († 429), developed on bold and original lines the teaching of his master Diodorus. As an independent thinker and systematic theologian he was the greatest of the Antiochenes. His theology contains a fully thought out system, embracing the nature and destiny of man and the Person and work of Christ. He has points of contact with the Pelagians in his teaching on sin and the Fall, free-will and grace; and in his Christology he was the immediate precursor of Nestorius. No less important were his contributions to the study of Scripture. In his subjective criticism of the Canon of Scripture, his insistence on the primary meaning of OT prophecy, and his endeavour to bring out the full historical meaning of Scripture, he represents the climax of Antiochene teaching.

Three other representatives of the school of Antioch during the period of its greatest fame call for notice, though none of them carried out so fully as Theodore its essential principles.

Polychronius, bishop of Apamea († *c.* 430), and brother of Theodore, exhibits in his commentaries on the OT the traditions of Antiochene exegesis.

John Chrysostom, bishop of Constantinople († 407), was the disciple of Diodorus and Flavian, and shows the influence of his Antiochene training alike in his doctrinal teaching and in his exposition of Scripture, though in both respects he was in closer accord than Diodorus or Theodore with the Church tradition of his time. Chrysostom was, however, the popular teacher and preacher rather than the exact theologian, and his commentaries on Scripture, which are marked by profound insight into human nature, are the work of a homilist rather than a critical student.

Theodoret, bishop of Cyrrhus († 457), was a disciple of Theodore, and played an important part in the Christological controversies of his time, in which he exercised a mediating influence between the conflicting principles of Antiochene and Alexandrian theology. He exhibits, alike in his theological and Biblical works, the Antiochene tradition. But he modified in several respects the teaching of his master. As a commentator he exhibits learning, judgment, and terseness of expression, though he is inferior in originality to Theodore and Chrysostom.

On the later history and influence of the school of Antioch, see below, III.

II. *THE TEACHING OF THE SCHOOL OF ANTIOCH.*—1. **Holy Scripture and Revelation.**—With the Antiochenes the Scriptures of the Old and New Testaments held a foremost place as the source of Christian doctrine. In their Canon of Scripture they followed the tradition of the Antiochene and Syrian Churches (which is also represented in the Peshitta or Vulgate Syriac Version), and did not include in the NT Canon the Apocalypse, 2 Peter, 2 and 3 John, or Jude. Theodore, on subjective grounds, also rejected the Epistle of St. James. In dealing with the OT books, Theodore recognized degrees of inspiration, and submitted them to a rigorous subjective criticism. The Book of Job he regarded as the production of a pagan Edomite and a work of dramatic fiction, which was lacking in higher inspiration. Similarly, he denied inspiration in the higher sense to Proverbs and Ecclesiastes. The Song of Songs was merely the marriage-song of Pharaoh's daughter, and lacked the authority both of the synagogue and of the Church. He assigned little value to Chronicles, Ezra, Nehemiah, and Esther, partly owing to doubts as to their acceptance in the Jewish Canon, and partly because they seemed to lack the prophetic insight which marked the other historical books. (Loofs, however, thinks that the only books which Theodore rejected from the OT Canon were Esther and the Apocryphal books. See *PRE*[3] xix. p. 604). He also rejected the inscriptions of the Psalms, and assigned a late date to the composition of many of the Psalms, placing some in the period of Hezekiah, others in that of Zerubbabel, and others again in Maccabæan times. These views, however, were rejected by Chrysostom and Theodoret, who adhered to the general sentiment of the Church.

The Antiochenes held the LXX in the highest reverence, and appear to have used Lucian's recension of its text. But Theodore and Chrysostom were unacquainted with Hebrew, and none of the teachers of the later school took up Lucian's textual labours or interested themselves in such studies (see, however, Chase, *Chrysostom*, p. 82 f.).

In their treatment of the inspiration of the Scriptures, while recognizing a real influence of the Holy Spirit upon the writers, the Antiochenes maintained that the individual character of the authors was imprinted on the style of the books. They recognized, too, the principle of accommodation to the time and circumstances of those who were addressed (Chase, *op. cit.* p. 42). Revelation is progressive. The OT has a preparatory character, and is the unfolding of one Divine purpose, which reaches its culmination in the Incarnation and the Christian dispensation. In their exegesis of Scripture the Antiochenes exhibit a pronounced opposition to the allegorical interpretation of the Alexandrian school. Eustathius, Diodorus, and Theodore all wrote works against the allegorists (see also Theodore on Gal 4^{24} and *procem. in Ose.*). Against Origen they maintained that the historical books contain true history, and are to be interpreted historically. But the history contains spiritual lessons, which, however, are to be deduced from it, and not arbitrarily imposed upon it. The moral difficulties of the OT histories and of the imprecatory Psalms presented obstacles to them, which they do not always satisfactorily overcome. Chrysostom often minimizes them, or occasionally resorts to allegory (Chase, *op. cit.* p. 53 f.). The typical character of the OT narratives is fully recognized. The incidents, persons, and objects mentioned are types of realities found in the NT (Theodore, *procem. in Jon.*). This harmony between type and antitype was foreseen and foreordained by the Divine purpose in order to assist men in recognizing the truth (Theodore *in Ose.* 1^1; *procem. in Am.*, Migne, lxvi. 125, 141). Hence the obscurity of the OT is due to the fact that it contains shadows and imperfect images of the truth, but is not the truth itself (Chrys. *Hom.* 61 *in Genes.*). The language of the OT is often hyperbolical and figurative, if referred to its original object, and finds its full content only in the higher realities of the gospel (Theodore, *in Joel* 2^{28}). The principles of the interpretation of prophecy were set forth in the most thoroughgoing manner by Theodore. He starts from the historical standpoint of the school, and maintains that, with the exception of a few passages which are directly Messianic, it is only by way of accommodation that the language of the Psalms and Prophets can be applied to the Christian dispensation (*in Rom.* 3^{12}, *Eph.* 4^8). He distinguishes three classes of prophecies—(1) Those which have a primary application to Christ, and no other historical reference. These were few in number;

e.g. Theodore recognized only four Psalms (2. 8. 45. 110) as directly Messianic. (2) Prophecies which have a primary reference to OT events, and refer only typically to the NT, *i.e.* such prophecies as are quoted in the NT. (3) Prophecies which have no Messianic reference, but refer only to the OT (*e.g.* Mic 4^{1-3}, Zec $11^{4ff.}$, Hag 2^{1-9}, Mal 1^{1-11} 3^{2-5}). See Kihn, *Theodor v. Mops.* p. 143 f.

Theodore has a profound realization of the significance of the idea of the Kingdom of God as set forth in the OT. The whole course of OT history was intended to prepare the way for the coming of Christ. Theodore's application of critical methods to the OT, though often arbitrary and vitiated by his ignorance of Hebrew, exhibits at times an acumen and insight which were far in advance of his age. In his subjective criticism of the OT books he found no successors, but through the later Antiochenes—Chrysostom and Theodoret, who followed in the main his methods, while modifying his conclusions—the science of exact and literal exegesis gained a foothold in the Church, and exercised a far-reaching influence both in the East and in the West. See below, III.

2. Doctrine of God and of the Trinity.—The Antiochenes exhibit little interest in metaphysical speculation upon the Being of God or the proofs of His existence. Photius, however (*Bibl. Cod.* 223, see esp. p. 209*b*; Migne, *PG* ciii. p. 833), gives an account of Diodorus' work *Against Fate*, in which the latter propounds the cosmological argument for the existence of God. The world, Diodorus maintains, is subject to change. But change itself is a condition which implies a beginning, and requires us to assume something constant behind it. Moreover, the variety of existing things and the wisdom displayed in the very process of change point to an underlying unity of origin, and suggest a Creator and a Providence. Both Chrysostom and Theodore wrote works upon the providence of God, in which they endeavoured to show that this providence extends to particulars.

Diodorus and Theodore were staunch supporters of the Nicene theology. Accepting its conclusions, Theodore set forth the doctrine of the Trinity by the help of careful exegesis of Scripture, rather than by speculative arguments. From the baptismal formula in Mt 28^{19} we may learn that Father, Son, and Holy Ghost are three self-subsistent Persons, and equally belong to the Divine and eternal Being. In the OT the distinction of Persons was not yet revealed (*in Hag.* 2^{1-5}). But when the OT speaks of the Divine nature, its language may be applied not only to the Father, but to the Son also, by reason of their community of nature (*in Heb.* 1^{12}). The Holy Spirit is a Person (ὑπόστασις) of the Trinity, and has His subsistence (ὕπαρξις) from the 'being' of the Father (*in Matt.* 1^{18}). Chrysostom's treatment is similar to that of Theodore. Careful exposition of the language of Scripture takes the place of metaphysical speculation upon the Trinity. Theodoret expounds in his *Eranistes* (*Dial.* i. p. 33 f., Migne) Basil's distinction between the terms 'being' (οὐσία) and 'person' (ὑπόστασις), but, like Theodore and Chrysostom, he contributes little to the subject.

In one respect, however, Theodore and Theodoret occupy an important place in the history of the doctrine of the Trinity. Theodore's teaching upon the Holy Spirit exhibits a clear conception of the essential Procession of the Holy Spirit from the Father. In his comment on Jn 15^{26} he affirms that the Holy Spirit's 'going forth' (ἐκπορεύεσθαι) was no mere external mission, but 'a natural procession' (φυσικὴ πρόοδος). But in the Creed put forth by him (Hahn, *Bibliothek der Symbole*³, p. 302) he denies that the Holy Spirit received His subsistence through the Son (οὔτε διὰ τοῦ υἱοῦ τὴν ὕπαρξιν εἰληφός). This position was attacked by Cyril of Alexandria in the ninth of his anathemas against Nestorius, and the Spirit was declared to be the 'very own' (ἴδιον) Spirit of Christ. Theodoret, in his reply to Cyril (*Reprehens. Anathemat.* 9), re-affirmed the contention of Theodore, and pronounced the opposite opinion to be blasphemy. Possibly the motive underlying the denial of the Procession through the Son may have been the fear of introducing the heresy of the Pneumatomachi (so Swete, *DCB*, art. 'Holy Ghost').

3. The Creation of Man.—The chief representative of Antiochene teaching, Theodore of Mopsuestia, exhibits a fully thought out conception of human nature in its constitution and development. In this respect he is superior to the Alexandrian theologians, and shows a deeper interest than they in questions affecting the origin and history of man. Theodore's treatment, as in the case of his exegesis of Scripture, is empirical, and rests upon the observed facts of human nature. (1) He starts from the conception of the universe as a living whole (ἓν σῶμα, *in Rom.* 8^{19}; so the Platonist Fathers, *e.g.* Gregory of Nyssa), which exhibits the combination of visible and invisible, or material and spiritual elements (see CAPPADOCIAN THEOLOGY, vii. (2)). Man was designed to be the bond (σύνδεσμος, συνάφεια, φιλίας ἐνέχυρον) between these two parts of creation (*ib.*; cf. the similar treatment of Gregory of Nyssa, *Or. Cat.* 6). Just as a king's statue is set up in a town which he has built and adorned, in order to remind the citizens of the builder, so man is set in creation as the image of God, in which all created beings may find their meeting-point, and be led to give God the glory which is His due (John Philop., *de Mundi Creat.* vi. 9, in Galland, *Bibl. vet. Patr.* xii. 581). Hence man was endowed with all the powers necessary to enable him to fulfil the destiny assigned to him. He possesses a body taken from the visible and material creation, while on his higher side he is akin to the spiritual creation (*in Rom.* 8^{19}; cf. Greg. Nyss. *op. cit.*). Creation was meant to serve man, and the angels appointed by God to superintend the processes of nature minister to his good (*ib.*). Through man creation has access to the Creator (Sachau, *Theodori Mops. fragm. Syr.* p. 18). In order to fulfil the purpose of his being, man was endowed with all necessary powers, including the gift of free-will. Theodore has a more profound conception of man's freedom than any of his contemporaries. Freedom is with him no mere indifference to good or evil. Nor is it, as with some other Eastern Fathers (*e.g.* Origen and the Cappadocians), the mere possibility of change or development. True freedom is rather the power of self-determination, which is exercised in harmony with the guidance of the Divine Spirit. It is 'the higher unity of liberty of choice and necessity' (Dorner). Especially important is Theodore's conception of love as the means by which man's freedom in relation to the influence of the Divine Spirit is realized (*de Incarn.*, Migne, lxvi. p. 977; see below, § 6). Hence freedom implies moral growth and development. It cannot be complete from the first. In this respect Theodore is superior to Pelagius and the Alexandrians. (See, further, below, § 6; and cf. Dorner, *Person of Christ*, II. i. 36, 38).

(2) From the first, God made man's nature liable to mortality. As a result of this mortality, man is subject to passions and liable to change. Theodore distinguishes between two stages (καταστάσεις) in the history of created beings, a present stage, in which the creature is subject to change and death, and a future stage, in which all will be brought to a condition of immutability and immortality (*in Genes.*, Migne, lxvi. 634). God exhibited the

beginning of this second stage in the Incarnation of His Son (*in Jon.*, Migne, lxvi. 317), but it was His purpose that man should first pass through the earlier stage, in which he is subject to conflict, temptation, and mortality. In thus creating man mortal, however, there was a beneficent purpose. (*a*) This mutable and mortal condition was intended to train man's will by exercising his power of choice between good and evil (*in Gal.* $2^{15.16}$). (*b*) In view of man's fall, which He foresaw, God attached the penalty of actual death (as distinguished from the liability to death) to disobedience, in order to deter men from sin. (*c*) Man's mortal condition rendered it possible for 'the body of sin' to be destroyed along with the dissolution of his body. Had man sinned, being immortal, his fall would have been irremediable (*in Genes.* 3^{17}; there is a somewhat similar treatment in Methodius and Gregory of Nyssa). Hence the purpose of the command to Adam, and later on of the Law, was to call forth the knowledge of good and evil, to provoke sin, and to show man his inability to attain perfect righteousness. It was only through the struggle and the conflict of this mutable life that man could learn his need of the Divine principle of life revealed in Christ, in order that he might attain his true end (*in Rom.* 7^{8}, *in Genes.* 3^{17}, *in Gal.* $2^{15.16}$).

4. The Fall.—Theodore taught that by man's disobedience the liability to mortality became an actual fact, for God had not said, when He threatened man with death as the penalty of disobedience, 'Ye shall be mortal,' but 'Ye shall die' (Marius Mercator, ed. Baluze, p. 340). Death came by sin, and the result of death was the separation of soul and body in man. Thus, too, the bond of the Universe, which had held together the visible and invisible parts of creation, was broken. Sin gained an entrance into the world, and in Adam's descendants the same experience was repeated. As each of them sinned in turn, he became subject, like Adam, to death (so Theodore interpreted Ro 5^{14}). A further result of the actual mortality which resulted from sin was that it increased the tendency to sin, by fixing man's thoughts upon the present order of things and by ministering to his passions (*in Rom.* $7^{14.17.18}$, *in Gal.* $2^{15.16}$).

5. Original Sin.—The summary which has been given above of Theodore's teaching shows that he allowed no place for the idea of inherited sin. Even the 'death which passed unto all men' is regarded as the result of man's own transgressions, not as the result of Adam's sin. In the fragments of Theodore's work, *Against the Defenders of Original Sin*, preserved by Marius Mercator (ed. Baluze, p. 340 f.), his attitude towards the standpoint of Jerome and Augustine is clearly shown. He affirms that Adam was created mortal, and he repudiates the idea that Noah, Abraham, David, Moses, and other righteous men should be subject to punishment for Adam's sin. Such a view he regards as inconsistent with the Apostle's words (Ro 2^{6}), that God will render to every man according to his deeds. Thus, too, in speaking of baptism, he distinguishes between the forgiveness of the sins of the individual, and the sinless state which will be fully revealed only at the general restitution of all things, and he maintains that in the case of infants the former cannot be taken into account.

Such teaching made Theodore a valuable ally to the Pelagian leaders, and in 418 Julian of Eclanum and his companions sought refuge with him after their banishment from the West. The points in which Theodore's teaching resembles that of Pelagius are: his insistence that man was created mortal, his emphasis on free-will, his denial of inherited sin, and his treatment of man's growth in knowledge and obedience through the discipline of the commandments and the law of God. On the other hand, his idea of redemption is different from that of Pelagius. For, according to Theodore's teaching, the original constitution of man as mortal and mutable rendered it impossible for him to attain the goal of his existence apart from the deliverance which came through Christ. Again, as we have seen, Theodore's conception of free-will is more profound than that of Pelagius, with whom freedom is simply the indifference of the will to good or evil (see above, § 3).

Chrysostom in his teaching on human nature exhibits the same practical bent and absence of speculative interest which appears in other directions in his writings. Scarcely any of Theodore's distinctive ideas occur in Chrysostom's treatment of man's history. His conception of the Divine image in man, which he regards as consisting in his dominion over creation, recalls Diodorus and Theodore. He regards the Fall as resulting in a privation of gifts which were not a part of man's natural constitution. He does not teach a complete loss of the Divine image. He agrees with Theodore in insisting on free-will and denying original sin. But in both cases this was probably due to his practical bent of mind, and to his association with that side of Eastern thought which, while emphasizing free-will, had not yet embraced the ideas found in Origen and Gregory of Nyssa, which approximated to Western teaching on Original Sin. As a preacher, Chrysostom saw the danger of any form of teaching which seemed to lessen the sense of responsibility or encourage the indifference and sluggishness of men's wills. To deny free-will was to take the virtue out of goodness (1 *Cor. hom.* 2). It is the bad will which is the root of evil (1 *Cor. hom.* 17). He denies that mortality is the cause of sin (*ib.*). Chrysostom, in fact, realizes far less than Theodore the weakness of man and his inability to attain to righteousness. In other respects Chrysostom's teaching exhibits points of contact with the later Pelagians. In a passage appealed to by Julian of Eclanum, he refuses to connect infant baptism with infant sin, though Augustine (*c. Julian.* i. 6) explained the passage as referring to actual sin.

Theodoret also presents few points of contact with the characteristic teaching of Theodore. Like Diodorus and Chrysostom, he maintains that the Divine image consisted in the dominion over creation, and, like all the Antiochenes, he emphasizes man's free-will. Thus he interprets the 'vessels of wrath' in Ro 9^{22} of those who have become such by their own free choice, and, like other Fathers, he misinterprets Ro 8^{28} by understanding κατὰ πρόθεσιν to refer to man's own act of choice. The words of Ro 7^{15} indicate not a necessity, but the weakness of human nature. Man embraces sin or virtue not by a natural necessity, but of his own free-will (*in Ro* 9^{21}). Theodoret again shows his connexion with Antiochene teaching in his treatment of the consequences of Adam's sin. Like Theodore, he holds that Ro 5^{12} refers to the actual sins of Adam's descendants, which involved them in the same penalty of death as Adam. The 'old man' denotes not the nature, but the evil will (*in Rom.* 6^{6}). In other respects Theodoret is more in accord with general Church teaching.

The Antiochene conception of human nature, as exhibited in its most fully developed form in Theodore, tends to a purely teleological view of man's development. Its philosophical basis, like the rest of the Antiochene theology, is Aristotelian. Mortality, rather than sin, is the great enemy of man, and it involves him in weakness and subjection to the passions. The history of man is the story of the struggle of his will towards a perfection which can come only from a new creation, and from the introduction of a higher stage (κατάστασις) of existence, when this mortal and mutable condition will be transformed into one which is immortal and immutable. In this presentation the disorder introduced by sin occupies only a secondary place. The extent of the consequences of sin is minimized, and the religious view of sin tends to disappear. Redemption comes to have a different meaning from that which it has in the teaching of St. Paul, St. Athanasius, and St. Augustine (see below, § 7). In logical consistency, Theodore's conception of human nature surpasses that of other Greek Fathers. But it fails to take account of those elements in the religious consciousness of man to which St. Augustine gave full expression (cf. Harnack, *Hist. of Dogma*, vol. iii. p. 279 f.).

6. Christology. — The Christology of the Antiochenes, which was closely connected with their doctrine of human nature, constitutes their chief importance for the history of doctrine. Their teaching has links of connexion with the teaching current in earlier periods at Antioch (cf. above, I.), and, as Harnack has observed (*Hist. of Dogma*, vol. iv. p. 166, n. 1), there is an essential unity in scientific method between Paul of Samosata, Lucian, Eusebius of Emesa, Eustathius, Diodorus, Theodore, Chrysostom, and Theodoret. The features common to this treatment are (1) the rejection of metaphysical speculation (cf. above, I.); (2) the attention paid to the historical portrait of Christ in the Gospels; (3) the ethical interest, which leads them to assert a true moral development in the humanity of Christ; (4) the Aristotelian basis of their conception of *οὐσία*, which was taken by them to denote a particular individual being (Harnack, *Hist. of Dogma*, iii. p. 46; Bethune-Baker, *Introd. to Early Hist. of Christian Doctr.* pp. 112, 235). This rendered it difficult for them to conceive of a complete nature which was not personal.

But, while there is a general resemblance in the method of treatment exhibited by all these writers, there are considerable divergences in their theological standpoint. Lucian of Antioch, starting from the teaching of Paul of Samosata, departed from him in affirming (with Origen) the personal and pre-existent character of the Logos, who was united with the man Jesus. The later Antiochene school, which began with Diodorus, was further marked off from Lucian by its acceptance of the full Nicene teaching upon the consubstantiality of the Son with the Father (in place of the subordinate created Logos of Lucian; cf. above, I.). In other respects, however, this later school, represented by Diodorus, Theodore of Mopsuestia, Chrysostom, and Theodoret, still retained the essential characteristics of the earlier Antiochenes. Diodorus and Theodore represent the more fully developed form of this teaching. Chrysostom is more practical and less scientific, though in his case, too, the underlying conceptions show the influence of his Antiochene training. Theodoret, in his criticism of Cyril's anathemas, exhibits the Antiochene standpoint, though later on he expressed himself more nearly in accord with the position of Cyril of Alexandria.

The Christological language of the Antiochenes was influenced partly by their desire to avoid the suggestion of a confusion of natures, and partly by traditional usage derived from the undeveloped theology of an earlier period. It has, however, been thought to show an 'Adoptianist' bias. Thus (1) they commonly speak of God as 'dwelling in Christ' (Eustath., Diod., Theod., Theodoret, Nestorius) rather than of God becoming man. (2) They apply to the humanity the terms *ναός, οἶκος, σκηνή*. These terms were, however, derived from Scripture (Jn 2[19], Pr 9[1], Jn 1[14]), and are occasionally found in Athanasius. (3) They use language which seems to imply a personal human subject distinct from the Divine subject in Christ (*ὁ ἄνθρωπος, ἄνθρωπος ἀναληφθείς, ὁ λαβών, ὁ ληφθείς, ὁ χρίσας, ὁ χρισθείς*; so Eustath., Diod., Theod., Nestorius, Theodoret). Such language, however, finds occasional parallels in Athanasius and the Cappadocians (see art. CAPPADOCIAN THEOLOGY, § vi. (4)). (4) Side by side with these phrases, however, they use impersonal expressions to denote the human nature (*τὸ ἀνθρώπινον ὄργανον*, forma servi, *σάρξ*, quod assumptum est, natura assumpta). (5) They approach more nearly to the language of Athanasius and Cyril when they speak of the Divine personal subject as 'assuming' (*λαμβάνειν*, assumere, *ἀναλαμβάνειν*, Eustath., Diod., Theod., Theodoret) man (or human nature), as 'bearing' (*φορεῖν*, Eustath., Nest.) man, or, lastly, as 'becoming' man (Eustath.). The expressions, 'homo deifer,' 'homo deum ferens,' quoted from Eustathius by Gelasius (Migne, *PG* xviii. 694), are probably due to a misreading of the original *θεόφορος* (for *θεοφόρος*). If *θεόφορος* were the original, the phrases would be parallel to the language quoted above (*ἄνθρωπον φορεῖν*). See Bethune-Baker, *Christian Doctrine*, p. 276 f.). On the state of Christological speculation before the rise of Apollinarism, see Athanasius, *Ep. ad Epictetum*.

Apart from the influences of their training, the Antiochenes were largely affected by the controversy with Apollinarism, which led them to affirm the reality and completeness of the human nature assumed by Christ, to emphasize especially His possession of free-will, and to guard against any idea of the confusion of the two natures or of a transformation of the human nature into the Divine nature.

Our chief sources of information about the Christology of Diodorus are the fragments of his work against Apollinaris (*πρὸς τοὺς συνουσιαστάς*), found in Marius Mercator (ed. Baluze) and in Leontius of Byzantium, *c. Nest. et Eutych.* (iii. 43). For Theodore we have the fragments of his works, *de Incarnatione* and *contra Apollinarium*, collected from various sources; the Acts of the Fifth General Council, the works of Facundus and Leontius, and the Syriac MSS translated into Latin by Sachau. See Migne, *PG* lxvi.; Swete, *Theodore of Mops. on the Epp. of St. Paul*, vol. ii., Appendix; Sachau, *Theodori Mops. fragmenta Syriaca*. Of special value is Theodore's confession of faith contained in the Acts of the Council of Ephesus, and in a Latin form in Marius Mercator (see Hahn, *Bibliothek der Symbole*[3], p. 302 f.).

The teaching of Diodorus and Theodore may be summarized as follows:—

(1) Against Apollinaris, Theodore asserted the completeness of the manhood of Christ and His possession of a reasonable soul as well as human flesh (see 'Creed' in Hahn, p. 302 f., and Sachau, p. 38). Especially important is his insistence on the freedom of the human will in Christ (on his conception of freedom, cf. above, § 3). As freedom cannot, according to his view, be ready-made, it involves a process of development in the humanity (cf. the *προκοπή*, or 'moral advance' of Paul of Samosata). Further, in accordance with Theodore's conception of two stages in the history of created intelligent beings (cf. above, § 3), it was necessary that Christ should assume humanity in its mutable state, subject to bodily weakness and the passions of the soul. Christ submitted to the assaults of the Tempter, and underwent the moral struggle between the higher and lower impulses (Migne, *PG*, lxvi. 720, 992, 995). By this struggle He mortified sin in the flesh and tamed its lusts (*ib.* 720). Theodore further admitted a real ignorance in Christ, and an advance in human knowledge (*ib.* 977, 981). Similarly, Diodorus asserts that the Godhead did not impart to the manhood of Christ all wisdom at the moment of birth, but bestowed it gradually (Marius Mercator, ed. Baluze, p. 349). Cf. CAPPADOCIAN THEOLOGY, vi. (2).

(2) But it is in their conception of the relations of the human and Divine natures that the teaching of Diodorus and Theodore exhibited a tendency which finds its extreme expression in Nestorianism. It is here, too, that the traditional 'Adoptianism' of Antiochene teaching appears. Both Diodorus and Theodore drew a sharp distinction between the human and Divine elements in Christ, and thus exposed themselves to the charge of teaching the existence of two persons in Christ. Thus Diodorus distinguished (Leontius, *c. Nest. et Eutych.* iii. 43) in Christ two sons: one by nature, God the Word; the other by grace, the man who was born of Mary. God the Word is not to be supposed the son of Mary. He may, however, be called *καταχρηστικῶς*, 'Son of David,' because of the shrine of God the Word which came from David, just as He who was of the seed of David may be called 'Son of God' by grace, not by nature. Similarly, Theodore denies that God was born of Mary (Migne, p. 997); though elsewhere he asserts that Mary may be called both *θεοτόκος* and *ἀνθρωποτόκος* ('God-bearing' and 'man-bearing'), the latter in a natural sense, the former because God was in Him who was born (Migne, p. 992; cf. Nestorius in Loofs' *Nestoriana*, pp. 167, 301). When it is said that 'the Word became flesh,' this must be understood of appearance only, for the Word was not changed into flesh (Migne, 981). The object of both writers in these statements is jealously to guard against any idea of a confusion of the two natures. But, apart from this negative aim, both Diodorus and Theodore exhibit a positive tendency to regard the human nature as possessed of an independent personality. This led them to conceive of the union of the two natures as a moral

union of grace (whereas Cyril started from the conception of One Divine Person, who has become incarnate, and maintained a hypostatic [καθ' ὑπόστασιν] union).

The nature of the union is discussed most fully by Theodore in the *de Incarnatione* (Migne, p. 972 f.). He distinguishes three possible modes of the Divine indwelling. The first is by 'essence' or 'being' (οὐσία). But in Scripture the Divine indwelling is spoken of as a special privilege of the saints (Lv 26[12], 2 Co 6[16]). This excludes therefore an 'essential' indwelling, since the οὐσία (or 'being') of God is not circumscribed by place. A second mode of indwelling is by the operation or energy (ἐνεργεία) of God. But this is common to all created things. Accordingly the only remaining mode in which the Divine indwelling is possible is by the Divine approval or complacency (εὐδοκία), the moral union by which God dwells in those who are pleasing to Him. How then did the union of God with the man Christ differ from His union with the saints? The answer is that He dwelt in Christ as in a Son (Migne, p. 976). Christ received the whole grace of the Spirit, whereas in other men the participation in the Spirit was partial (*ib.* p. 980; cf. Diodorus *ap.* Marius Mercator, ed. Baluze, p. 351; Nestorius, Loofs, p. 206). This indwelling of Christ began with His formation in the womb of the Virgin, and was a result of the Divine foreknowledge of what Christ would be (Migne, pp. 974, 980, 994). At His baptism Christ further received the grace of adoption. As a result of His supernatural birth, His inseparable union with the Word, and His unction by the Holy Spirit, Christ exhibited a hatred of evil and an irrepressible love of good (see below (3)). He was preserved by His union with the Word from the inconstancy of mutable human nature, and passed from stage to stage of virtue with the greatest ease (*ib.* 977). He thus proved Himself worthy of the union, and became our example and way, until after the Resurrection and Ascension He exhibited the union with the Word in its final completeness (*ib.* 977).

(3) In its treatment of the unity of Christ's Person, the teaching of Diodorus and Theodore exhibits a lack of precision and logical completeness. As we have seen, they tended to view the two natures apart, and to conceive of their union as a moral union of grace. Moreover, their idea of a complete human nature involved the notion of a distinct human personality (cf. above). 'When we distinguish the natures,' says Theodore, 'we maintain that the nature of God the Word is perfect, perfect too the person (πρόσωπον)—for it is not possible to speak of a distinct existence (ὑπόστασιν) which is impersonal (ἀπρόσωπον)—perfect too the nature of the man, and the person (πρόσωπον) likewise. But when we look to the conjunction of the two, then we say that there is one person (πρόσωπον)' (Migne, p. 981). The nature of the unity thus attained is in one passage compared by Theodore to that of marriage. As the Lord said of the man and the woman, 'They are no longer twain, but one flesh' (Mt 19[6]), so it may be said of the union that there are no longer two persons (πρόσωπα) but one, the natures, of course, being kept distinct (Migne, p. 981). Elsewhere he compares the unity to that of the rational soul and flesh in man (*adv. Apoll.* ap. Facund. ix. 4). Theodore employs the terms ἕνωσις ('union') and συνάφεια ('conjunction') to denote the union of the natures. In his interpretation of this union he uses phrases which imply that it consisted in the harmonious relation of the human and Divine wills in Christ (cf. the phrase ἑνώσας αὐτὸν ἑαυτῷ τῇ σχέσει τῆς γνώμης; Migne, p. 989). Theodore, however, was conscious that the charge of teaching two sons might be brought against him, and he repudiated it. 'The Son,' he says, 'is rightly confessed to be one, since the distinction ought of necessity to remain, and the unity of person (πρόσωπον) ought to be guarded without interruption' (Migne, p. 985; see the 'Creed' in Hahn, *op. cit.* p. 303; cf. Nestorius, Loofs, p. 330 f.). Similarly Diodorus refutes the charge of teaching two sons by saying that he neither affirms that there are two sons of David, nor that there are two sons of God according to substance, but that the Word of God dwelt in Him who came from the seed of David (Marius Mercator, ed. Baluze, p. 350).

For a fuller discussion of the question, see Dorner, *Person of Christ*, II. i. 47 f. Theodore has points of contact with the mystical theology when he emphasizes love as the principle which brings the humanity of Christ into harmony with the Word. 'The thought and volition of the man Jesus were, in point of *contents*, the thought and volition of the Logos.' 'The *form* in which the mind of Jesus actually expressed itself was determined by the Logos; though, in consonance with his theory of freedom, he represented this determination as a mere influence of the Logos' (Dorner, *l.c.*).

(4) Both Diodorus and Theodore assert the unique character and privileges of the sonship acquired by the man Christ. They both apply the words spoken at the baptism, 'This is my beloved Son, in whom I am well pleased,' to Christ and not to the Word (Marius Mercator, p. 350; Theodore, *in Mt* 3[17]; *de Incarn.*, Migne, p. 980). The title Son is applied both to God the Word and to the nature assumed by Him, by reason of its union with Him (Theodore, *de Incarn.* ap. Facund. ix. 3; cf. Nestorius, Loofs, p. 336). As a result of the union with the Word and His adoption as Son, the man Christ shares in the worship which is offered to the Word. 'We worship,' says Diodorus, 'the purple for the sake of Him who is clothed in it, and the temple because of Him who dwells in it; the form of the servant because of the form of God; the lamb because of the high priest; Him who was assumed, because of Him who assumed Him; Him who was formed of the Virgin, because of the Maker of all. Confessing this, offer one worship' (Marius Mercator, ed. Baluze, p. 351; cf. Theodore, *in Col* 1[13-16]; *de Incarn.*, Migne, pp. 991 f., 996; Nestorius, Loofs, p. 262).

This teaching of Diodorus and Theodore, which apparently escaped censure during their lifetime, attained public notoriety through Nestorius, the patriarch of Constantinople. Nestorius merely popularized the teaching of his master, Theodore, without exhibiting the same fundamental depth of treatment. The real parent of Nestorianism as a system of Christology is Theodore. See, further, art. NESTORIANISM.

The Christology of three other representatives of the school of Antioch calls for notice here.

Eustathius of Antioch is an important link between the earlier and later stages of the school. His works exhibit some of the characteristic Antiochene features. He ascribes to Christ a true human development, and speaks of the human nature as the temple of the Deity. The Divine nature is dissociated from the experiences of the human nature. It was the latter alone which was anointed and glorified. He further implies that Christ acquired the Divine gifts and graces gradually. Hence Dorner (*Person of Christ*, I. ii. 250) says that with him, as with the later Antiochenes, 'the deity and humanity remain separate and distinct, and do not constitute a living unity.' Yet Eustathius affirms the closeness of the union between the humanity of Christ and the Logos (Migne, xviii. p. 689, συνδιαιτωμένη κυρίως ἡ ψυχὴ τοῦ Χριστοῦ τῷ Λόγῳ καὶ θεῷ. 'He is God by nature, yet He has become man of a woman, even He who was formed in the womb of the Virgin' (Migne, lxxxiii. p. 90). See fragments collected in Galland, *Bibl. vet. Patr.* iv. 577 f.; Mai, *Script. vet. Nova Coll.* (1832) vii. 135, 203; Cavallera, *S. Eustathii in Lazarum Hom.*, App. I. *de fragmentis Eustathii* (1905).

Chrysostom approaches Christological questions from the practical rather than from the speculative side. Like all the Antiochenes, he emphasizes the completeness of the humanity of Christ. Christ shared our mortal nature, but without sin, and was subject to the physical needs, the human emotions, and the sufferings of our humanity. He exhibits the characteristic Antiochene spirit when he asserts that Christ did all that He did in a human manner, not only to teach the reality of His incarnation, but as a pattern or ideal of human virtue. But the idea of Theodore, that the human nature was gradually moulded by the influence of the Word finds no place in his teaching. Chrysostom further shows signs of Antiochene influence in dealing with the union of the two natures. He repudiates the idea that the Incarnation involved any change of place in the Deity, or that the Logos descended into the flesh of Christ. He interprets the humiliation of Christ (Ph 2[8]) as a humiliation of mind. Again, he distinguishes, after the manner of the Antiochenes, the experiences of the humanity from those of the Godhead, and, like Eustathius, he declares that it was the humanity, and not the Godhead, which was anointed and exalted. Lastly, he speaks of the humanity as the temple of the Word. On the other hand, he asserts the unity of the two natures, and explains the passages which suggest Christ's dependence on the Father as the language of accommodation (συγκατάβασις). But he nowhere clearly defines the character of the union of the two natures, and much of the language quoted above suggests a merely ethical union and a dynamical relationship rather than a full personal union. Chrysostom's Christology, in fact, exhibits an undeveloped character. He is content to put side by side the affirmation of the two natures and the assertion of their union. Though he shares to some extent the Antiochene point of view, the more fully developed conclusions of the school were, in his case, held in check by his own practical bent and the influence upon him of other forms of Church teaching. See, further, Förster, *Chrysostomus in seinem Verhältniss zur antiochenischen Schule*, p. 101 ff.

Theodoret occupies a mediating position in the Christological controversies of his time. On the appearance of Cyril's anathemas against Nestorius, he published a refutation in which he charged Cyril with Apollinarism. (The *Reprehensio Anathematismorum* is printed in Schulze's edition of Theodoret, v. p. 1 ff., and in Migne, lxxvi. p. 391 f.). In this work he exhibits the same tendency to accentuate the distinction of the two natures which characterizes Theodore and Diodorus, and the same inability to conceive of a complete nature which is not personal. He denies that God the Word was naturally (φύσει) conceived of the Virgin, and prefers to say that 'He fashioned for Himself a temple in the Virgin's womb, and was with (συνῆν) that which was formed and begotten.' Similarly, he maintains that the weaknesses of the humanity cannot be attributed to God the Word. Lastly, it was not the Christ (*i.e.* the Word) who suffered, but the man assumed by God. He maintains, however, that the 'form of the servant' may be confessed to be God on account of the 'form of God' united to it. The Formula of Concord (A.D. 433), by which the differences of Cyril and the Antiochenes were reconciled, is probably the work of Theodoret, and represents a *rapprochement* between the two points of view. In place of Cyril's phrase, 'one incarnate nature of God the Word' (μία φύσις τοῦ θεοῦ λόγου σεσαρκωμένη), it speaks of the unconfused union of two natures (δύο φύσεων ἕνωσις ἀσύγχυτος). At the same time it admits the term θεοτόκος, while carefully explaining it (Hahn, *Bibl. der Symbole*[3], p. 215). In the *Eranistes* (*Dial.* ii., Migne, lxxxiii. p. 145 f.), written in A.D. 447, he states the idea of a *communicatio idiomatum* in a way which is quite in accord with the later theology of the Church. Though we may not attribute to one nature what belongs to the other, we may attribute to the One Person what is proper to either of the natures. Theodoret nowhere goes so far as Theodore in affirming that the union of the natures was a moral union (κατ' εὐδοκίαν). He maintains that in Christ there was one undivided Person (ἓν πρόσωπον ἀδιαίρετον), though he does not anywhere acknowledge one hypostasis (ὑπόστασις), or employ Cyril's phrase, ἕνωσις καθ' ὑπόστασιν ('hypostatic union'). Finally, at the Council of Chalcedon, Theodoret made an orthodox confession.

Theodoret maintained that Christ assumed mutable (τρεπτή) human nature, which was subject to human passions, though it was kept free from sin. He experienced the temptations arising from the natural appetites, but not the sinful motions to which they commonly give rise (*Repr. Anathem.* 10; *Pental.*, Migne, lxxxiv. 68; *Hæret. Fab.* 5, Migne, lxxxiii. 497). He further acknowledged a true human ignorance in Christ, and an advance in knowledge 'as the indwelling Godhead revealed it.' So, too, in the *Repr. Anathem.* (10), he maintains that Christ attained perfection by efforts of virtue, and learnt obedience by experience, 'though before His experience He was ignorant of it.' In these statements we see the true Antiochene spirit, though Theodoret is far removed from the more extreme conclusions of Theodore. For a fuller discussion of Theodore's Christology, see Bertram, *Theodoreti Ep. Cyrensis Doctrina Christologica*; J. Mahé in *Revue d'histoire ecclésiastique*, vii. (1906), art. 'Les anathématismes de Saint Cyrille d'Alexandrie et les évêques orientaux du patriarchat d'Antioche.'

The Christology of the Antiochenes was the outcome partly of their training, and partly of their opposition to Apollinarism. The historical study of Scripture, and the high conception entertained by them (esp. Theodore) of the dignity and destiny of human nature, led them to emphasize to the fullest extent the humanity of the Lord. Their ideas of free-will and the moral development of man impelled them to oppose any teaching which impaired the reality of our Lord's human experiences, or tended (like Apollinarism) towards a docetic view of His humanity. The Alexandrian school, on the other hand, started from the Divine aspect of Christ's Person. It was the truth that God Himself was revealed in Christ which from the days of Athanasius had been emphasized in Alexandrian teaching. Hence Cyril of Alexandria was led to lay stress upon the unity of the Word Incarnate. The humanity of Christ does not belong to Himself. It is not the humanity of an individual and independent man, but of God the Word. The human element was subordinated to the Divine. The Word has taken human nature into the unity of His Divine Person, which remains one and the same after as well as before the Incarnation. The Antiochenes had not clearly faced the problem as it presented itself to Cyril. They had affirmed the integrity of the two natures, and they had asserted their ineffable union. But the nature of this union and the exact relations of the two natures had not been considered by them. Hence arise the apparently inconsistent statements of Theodore that the humanity is personal (πρόσωπον), yet Christ is one Person (πρόσωπον).

Much of the misunderstanding between Cyril and the Antiochenes arose out of the undeveloped stage of doctrine at the time, and the absence of any clear definitions of the words πρόσωπον ('person), ὑπόστασις ('hypostasis'), and φύσις ('nature'). Nor had the union of the natures been clearly defined. The terms 'mixture,' 'blending,' 'union,' 'connexion' (μίξις, κρᾶσις, ἕνωσις, συνάφεια) had been used indifferently by earlier writers to denote this union (see art. CAPPADOCIAN THEOLOGY, § vi. (3)). The Antiochenes, from traditional habit, attributed to each of the natures that which befitted it, when regarded as independent. Cyril, on the other hand, referred everything to the personal subject, who is the Word. When brought face to face, both schools of thought admitted the unity of Person, and both asserted the integrity and distinction of the two natures. The difference between them was exaggerated by misunderstanding and controversy. The unguarded language of Diodorus, Theodore, and Nestorius was, doubtless, largely responsible for this, but the Formula of Concord agreed upon by Cyril and the Antiochenes exhibits the fundamental agreement of the two Christologies. The Antiochenes accepted and explained the word θεοτόκος, the unity of the two natures was affirmed, and Cyril's misunderstood expressions, φυσικὴ ἕνωσις, ἕνωσις καθ' ὑπόστασιν, μία φύσις τοῦ θεοῦ λόγου σεσαρκωμένη ('natural union,' 'personal union,' 'one incarnate nature of God the Word'), were dropped. See, further, Mahé in *Revue d'histoire ecclésiastique*, referred to above; for Nestorius see Loofs, *Nestoriana* (1905), and Bethune-Baker, *JThSt* viii. p. 119 f.

While Cyril affirmed a truth of vital importance to Catholic theology,—the truth that He who assumed human nature was personally God, and took human nature into vital union with Himself,—we are justified in maintaining the importance of the stand made by the Antiochenes in defence of the reality and completeness of Christ's human experiences. It was a valuable protest against an almost docetic tendency which had already appeared in Apollinarism, which was latent in Alexandrian theology (even in Athanasius), and which re-appeared in Monophysitism. If the Church was finally enabled to overcome the latter, it was largely due to what it had learnt from the teaching of the Antiochenes.

7. The Work of Christ.—Theodore alone among the Antiochene Fathers developed a distinctive conception of the work of Christ. His views upon human nature and sin led him to find the central significance of Christ's work not so much in His Death as in His Resurrection. The purpose of the Incarnation was the perfection (τελείωσις) rather than the restitution of humanity. Christ is the new creation, who exhibits God's plan in its final completeness. In Him there is set forth that image of God which man was meant to attain, but which he failed to attain. The work of Christ was not only to restore the broken order of the universe and exhibit man in his true place at the head of creation, but to inaugurate that new stage (κατάστασις; cf. above, § 3) in the life of man, in which he should be free from the mutability and mortality of his present state. As a result of His struggle and victory, accomplished by the exercise of His free-will and through the union with the Word, Christ overcame the mutability of human nature, which was crucified with Him and rose with Him (*in Rom.* 6^{6}). The deliverance which He has won for men is already potentially theirs, though it is only in the future that it fully takes effect.

The omissions in this presentation are significant. The conceptions of guilt and responsibility, and the idea of Christ's death as an atonement, are absent. Death is but a necessary stage, through which Christ passes to the Resurrection and inaugurates the higher and final stage of man's development. The necessity of the Incarnation is not based upon the Fall, but upon the general conception of the Divine purpose for man, which required that he should be delivered from his present state of mortality. There are points of contact in this teaching with the teaching of Irenæus, Athanasius, and the Cappadocians, especially in the emphasis laid upon death and mortality. But we miss in Theodore the strong interest in the redemptive side of Christ's work which characterizes Athanasius, and the deeper teaching upon death which he and other Fathers exhibit. Again, Theodore's emphasis on man's free-will led him to assert, as Dorner says (*Person of Christ*, II. i. 51), not so much 'the thorough reality of the incarnation of God,' as 'the reality of the freedom of the human aspect of Christ's Person.' The purpose of Christ's work was to exhibit the development of human nature in its completeness. And in this development the thought of the forgiveness of sins and the work of grace is subordinate to that of the need of moral effort. See, further, Dorner, *l.c.*; cf. above, § 5, and below, § 8.

Chrysostom and Theodoret are much nearer to the general tradition of the Church in their teaching upon Christ's work. The conception of Christ as the 'first-fruits' (ἀπαρχή) of human nature, which is consecrated in Him, was suggested to them, as to Theodore, by their exegesis of Scripture. But it was not peculiar to the Antiochenes. More characteristic of Antiochene teaching is Chrysostom's picture of Christ as the original pattern or ideal of human virtue, to exhibit which was the purpose of His human life and experiences (*in Joh. hom.* 48). In their conception of the Atonement, Chrysostom and Theodoret echo much of the current teaching of their time (*e.g.* the deception of Satan, Christ's contest with him and overthrow of his dominion over mankind), but they exhibit nothing characteristic of the Antiochene standpoint. The same is true of the idea found in Theodoret (*de Providentia, Or.* x., Migne, lxxxiii. pp. 753, 756), that Christ paid the debt and endured the chastisement and penalty due to us for our sins. Chrysostom, though he emphasizes the importance of the Resurrection, does not, like Theodore, make it the central point of Christ's work.

8. The work of Salvation.—(1) The task of reconciling man's free-will with God's predestination was attempted by both Theodore and Chrysostom. Both reject the idea of an absolute predestination in favour of a conditional predestination. God's purpose, says Theodore, is dependent on man's free-will (*in Rom.* 8^{28}; cf. Chrys. *in Joh. hom.* 46). Both, too, regard God's eternal election of men as determined by His foreknowledge of what they would be (Chrys. *in Matt. hom.* 79; Theodore, *in Rom.* $9^{10.14}$; so, too, Theodoret, *in Rom.* 8^{30} 9^{11}). On their interpretation of Ro 9, see Chase, *Chrysostom*, p. 165 f.; Sanday-Headlam, *Romans*, p. 270.

(2) In dealing with man's appropriation of salvation, the Antiochenes, owing to their views upon human nature, fail to do justice to St. Paul's conception of justification by faith. Though Theodore denies that man can be justified by works, yet the initiative of the individual occupies so prominent a place in his conception that faith enters into it only as a secondary idea (*in Cor.* 11^{34}). Moreover, the faith of which he speaks is different in character from that of St. Paul, being directed rather to the future resurrection life, which man shares at present, through his incorporation in Christ, only in anticipation (*in Gal.* $2^{16.20}$). Chrysostom's treatment is practical. In some passages he emphasizes the act of will by which man turns from evil and inclines to good, and in others he maintains the importance of faith, and attributes all to grace. But the two ideas are not clearly brought into relation with one another (see Förster, *Chrysostomus*, p. 152 f.).

(3) From what has been said above, it will appear that the Antiochene attitude towards the question of the relations of grace and free-will resembled that of the Semi-Pelagians (on the relations of Theodore and Julian of Eclanum, cf. above, § 5). In the teaching of both Theodore and Chrysostom the initiative lies with the individual will, though both affirm the necessity of grace (Chrys. *in Joh. hom.* 17, *in Rom. hom.* 16. 19; Theodore, *in Marc.* 4^{26-29}, *in 1 Cor.* 11^{34}, *in Heb.* $4^{1.2}$).

9. The Sacraments.—There is no formal treatment of the Sacraments in the Antiochene Fathers. They accept the traditional Church teaching and practice, and assign a real value to the Sacraments in the furtherance of the spiritual life (Theodore, *in Cor.* 11^{34}, *in 1 Tim.* 3^{6}). In Baptism, according to Theodore, man receives the gift of union with Christ through the Spirit and the pledge of the immortality which he is destined to share hereafter with Christ (*in Eph.* $1^{22.23}$).

In speaking of the Eucharist, Theodore and Chrysostom use the current language of their time. Thus Theodore, in commenting on Mt 26^{26}, speaks of the words of institution in terms which recall the language of Cyril of Jerusalem, and says that Christ teaches us that we are not to regard the nature of that which lies before us, but to consider that, by the thanksgiving pronounced over it, it is changed into flesh and blood. In his comment on 1 Co 10^{5}, however, he speaks of the change as spiritual. Chrysostom uses the emotional and rhetorical language of popular devotion, and goes much further in asserting a conversion of the elements (see Batiffol, *Études d'histoire et de théologie positive*, 2ième série, p. 268 f.). But the two most characteristic contributions to the doctrine of the Eucharist from the Antiochene standpoint are to be found in the writings of Nestorius and Theodoret. Both writers approach the subject in connexion with the Christological disputes. In reply to Cyril of Alexandria, who had affirmed that the flesh of Christ given in the Eucharist is 'life-giving' (ζωοποιόν) by virtue of its union with the Word, Nestorius maintains that this view tends to an Apollinarian confusion of the two natures. He appeals to the language of St. John (6^{56}) and St. Paul (1 Co $11^{23 f.}$), and urges that it is the 'flesh,' and not the Godhead, which is spoken of as 'eaten.' Christ said, 'This is my body,' not 'This is my Godhead.' St. Paul speaks of that which is eaten as 'bread,' and, adds Nestorius, it is bread 'of which the body is the antitype.' The Eucharist is the 'memorial' of the death of the Lord, *i.e.* of the Son of Man (not the Word). See passages in Loofs, *Nestoriana*, pp. 227–30, 355–7, and in Cyril, *c. Nest.* iv. 3–6. These statements led Cyril to accuse Nestorius of denying the virtue of the Sacrament, and of confining it merely to the commemoration of the death of a man (*c. Nest.* iv. 6).

But probably the real difference between Cyril and Nestorius as to the nature and efficacy of the Sacrament was less than Cyril allows, and was due rather to the difference in their Christological statements. There is a fine recognition of the religious value of the Eucharist in Nestorius' sermon on Heb. 3^1 (Loofs, *Nestoriana*, p. 241 f.).

More important is the contribution of Theodoret. In the *Eranistes* (*Dial.* i. p. 56, Migne; *Dial.* ii. p. 165 f., *ib.*), where he is arguing with a Monophysite opponent, he introduces an analogy from the Eucharist to show that the two natures in Christ are not to be confused. From the current appellation of the elements as 'types' or 'symbols' of the body of Christ, the orthodox disputant maintains that Christ still possesses a real body. The Monophysite opponent rejoins by a counter-assertion that just as the elements after the invocation undergo a change, so the Lord's body after the union with the Divinity is changed into the Divine substance. This the orthodox speaker denies. 'Even after the consecration the mystic symbols are not deprived of their own nature; they remain in their former substance, figure, and form; they are visible and tangible as they were before. But they are regarded as what they have become, and believed so to be, and are worshipped as what they are believed to be.' And again he says (*Dial.* i. p. 56) that Christ 'honoured the visible symbols by the appellation of body and blood, not because He had changed their nature, but because He had added grace to their nature.' In this presentation (which resembles that of Pope Gelasius in the *de Duabus Naturis*) Theodoret exhibits a view of the Eucharist which has been called 'Dyophysite' (Batiffol), and which, while preserving the reality of the outward and inward parts of the Sacrament, guards against those theories of a conversion of the elements which, from the 4th cent. onwards, gained ground in the Eastern Church. The change, according to Theodoret, is in the region of grace (κατὰ χάριν), not in the natural sphere. See, further, art. EUCHARIST.

10. Eschatology.—The Antiochene conception of man's history and of the work of Christ culminates, as we have seen, in the hope of immortality. Hence the Antiochenes were profoundly interested in eschatology. From Eph 1^{10} Theodore drew the conclusion that all men and all rational creatures will finally look to Christ and attain perfect harmony. The eschatological teaching of Diodorus and Theodore is one of the few points of agreement between them and Origen (see also CAPPADOCIAN THEOLOGY, § x. (3)). Both Diodorus and Theodore express, like Origen, the hope that, though the wicked will suffer just punishment for their sins, this punishment will not be everlasting. Diodorus protests against the idea that the punishment of the wicked will be unending, on the ground that it would render useless the immortality prepared for them. God rewards the good beyond their deserts. So, too, the extent of His mercy exceeds the debt of punishment which the wicked have to pay (Assemani, *Bibl. Orient.* III. i. p. 323 f.). Similarly, Theodore asks what would be the benefit of the resurrection to the wicked, if their punishment were unending (Marius Mercator, ed. Baluze, p. 346). When the wicked have been led through punishment to see the evil of sin and to fear God, they will at length enjoy His bounty. Such texts as Mt 5^{26} and Lk $12^{47.48}$ inspire him with the hope that the full debt of punishment may be paid, and the wicked finally delivered (Assemani, *l.c.*).

III. *LATER HISTORY OF THE SCHOOL OF ANTIOCH.*—The condemnation of Nestorianism by the Church in A.D. 431 was fatal to the development of the school of Antioch and to the reputation of its great representatives. Marius Mercator about 431 maintained that Theodore was the real author of Pelagianism, and later on called attention to the Nestorian tendency of his teaching. The use made by the Nestorians of Theodore's writings further increased this animosity. Rabbulas, bishop of Edessa, and later on Cyril of Alexandria, condemned the teaching of the great Antiochene and of his predecessor Diodorus. In the 6th cent., amid the Monophysite controversy, the Emperor Justinian issued the edict of the Three Chapters (544), in which the writings of Theodore, the treatises of Theodoret against Cyril, and the letter of Ibas to Maris were condemned; and this condemnation was repeated by the Fifth General Council in 553, which by an irony of fate also condemned the works of Origen, the representative of the rival school of Alexandria. The same Council likewise condemned Theodore's methods of Biblical interpretation. But, while the proscription of Nestorianism was fatal to the school of Antioch and led to its decline, its teaching was carried on under Nestorian influence in the schools of Edessa and Nisibis. Ibas, the head of the school of Edessa († 457), translated the works of Diodorus and Theodore into Syriac, and when finally the school at Edessa was broken up in 489 through the proscription of Nestorianism by the Emperor Zeno, the refugees found a home in the school of Nisibis, which was founded by Barsumas. Here the Biblical studies to which the Antiochenes had given so great an impetus were renewed, Theodore's memory was held in the highest reverence, and he came to be regarded as 'the Interpreter' *par excellence* among East Syrian Christians. In these schools the study of Aristotle, also inherited from the school of Antioch, was carried on and transmitted by the East Syrian Church in later times to the Muhammadans, by whom it was brought back to Europe in the days of Muslim civilization. Lastly, these East Syrian Christians became a centre for a wide field of missionary activity in the far East, extending as far as India and China.

In the Greek Empire, though the fame of Diodorus and Theodore became obscured through the controversies which gathered around their memories, the exegesis of the Antiochenes continued to exercise a wide influence through the works of Chrysostom, whose orthodoxy was not exposed to the attacks which had been levelled against other members of the school. Isidore, Nilus, and Victor of Antioch took Chrysostom as their guide in the commentaries which they wrote, while a long line of Greek catenists and commentators from the 6th to the 11th cent. show the greatness of their debt to the Antiochene expositors. Even in the West their influence was not unrecognized. Jerome had points of contact with the school and was influenced by its exegesis (Kihn, *Die Bedeutung der antioch. Schule*, pp. 59, 194; Hergenröther, *Die antioch. Schule*, p. 66). Cassian, a disciple of John Chrysostom, carried on the teaching of his master in the Church of Southern Gaul. The controversies about the Three Chapters aroused interest in the writings of Theodore, and it is probably to this period that we owe the Latin translation of some at least of Theodore's commentaries on St. Paul, which, passing into currency under the name of St. Ambrose, secured a place in the works of the later Western compilers (Swete, *Theodore of Mops. on the Minor Epp. of St. Paul*, i. pp. xlv., lviii.). Two other famous works produced in the West show the influence of Theodore's teaching. The first is the *Instituta regularia* of Junilius Africanus (*c.* 550), an introduction to the study of the Scriptures, which, as the author tells us, was derived from Paul of Nisibis, and which reproduces all the essential features of Theodore's principles of Biblical interpretation as well as of his doctrinal teaching. This work of Junilius, whom later ages transformed into a bishop, was widely popular in the West. The *de Institutione divinarum literarum* of Cassiodorus a few years later shows a similar connexion with the East Syrian schools, and exhibits the influence of methods and principles which had been derived from the Antiochenes (Kihn, *Theodor v. Mops. und Junilius Africanus*, pp. 210 f., 215 f.).

Nor was the West wholly uninfluenced by the doctrinal teaching of the Antiochenes. As has been already indicated (see II. 5), Theodore was brought into contact in his later years with several of the Pelagian leaders. Julian of Eclanum, one of the most prominent of these, was an admirer of Theodore's writings, while another, the deacon Anianus, has been claimed as the translator of some of Chrysostom's homilies, his object being to uphold, by appealing to Chrysostom, the cause of man's free-will (Swete, *op. cit.* vol. i. p. lii f.). The Christological teaching of Leporius, a monk in the monastery of Marseilles, who is spoken of by Cassian as a Pelagian, shows clear points of contact with that of Theodore. In North Africa, during the 6th cent., amid the controversy upon the Three Chapters, the works of Theodore found many defenders, and the language of Facundus of Hermiane has been thought to suggest that they had already been translated into Latin. Finally, the Spanish Adoptianists exhibit a close resemblance in their Christology to Theodore, and Neander has suggested that Felix of Urgel was indebted to the writings of Theodore, possibly through a Latin translation made in Africa (Swete, *op. cit.* vol. i. p. lv f.; Neander, *Ch. Hist.* v. 219; Harnack, *Hist. of Dogma*, v. 284 f.).

IV. *GENERAL SUMMARY*.—The permanent service of the Antiochene school lies in its effort to correct a one-sided view of the factors and methods of revelation. To the emotional, mystical religion, which tended to lose the human element in the Divine, whether in inspiration, or the Person of Christ, or the relations of grace and free-will, it opposed conceptions which endeavoured to do justice to the dignity and worth of human nature. While the Alexandrian theology started from the Divine side, and deduced all its conclusions from that as its source, the Antiochenes followed the inductive and rationalistic method, which consisted in a careful examination of the facts of human nature and experience. The philosophical basis of the one was Platonist, while that of the other was Aristotelian. In Christology the school of Antioch centred attention upon the historical Christ; in its doctrine of inspiration it affirmed the immediate and historical reference of Scripture; in anthropology it insisted upon the reality of human freedom. It regarded the purpose of the Incarnation as the accomplishment of man's destiny rather than as the deliverance of him from the consequences of sin. The struggle and conflict provoked by the commandment became a means of educating man to realize his freedom of choice and his weakness, and so of raising him out of the stage of subjection to the passions and mortality into the higher life of immortality and sinlessness which has been won for him by Christ. The two standpoints, the Alexandrian and the Antiochene, represent complementary aspects of Christian theology. If the Alexandrian and mystical standpoint has found fuller expression in the later thought and teaching of Christendom, the problems of modern thought, and the evolutionary view of the Universe, have once more called attention to the point of view which underlies the teaching of the Antiochenes.

LITERATURE.—(1) *HISTORY OF THE SCHOOL OF ANTIOCH*: **H. Kihn**, *Die Bedeutung der antioch. Schule auf dem exeget, Gebiete* (1866); **P. Hergenröther**, *Die antioch. Schule und ihre Bedeutung auf exeget. Gebiete* (1866); **Harnack**, art. 'Antiochenische Schule' in *PRE*^{3}, vol. i. (1896), and *History of Dogma*. Eng. tr. vols. iii. and iv.

(2) *BIOGRAPHICAL AND LITERARY*: on Paul of Samosata see **Harnack**, *Hist. of Dogma*, vol. iii., and art. in *PRE*^{3}; on the disputation between Paul and Malchion see **Bardenhewer**, *Gesch. der altkirchl. Litteratur*, vol. ii. (1903); on Lucian of Antioch see **Harnack**, *Gesch. der altchristl. Lit.*, vol. i. (p. 526 f.), and art. in *PRE*^{3}, vol. xi. (1902); and on Lucian and Dorotheus see **Bardenhewer**, *op. cit.* On Eusebius of Emesa, Eustathius, Diodorus, Chrysostom, see artt. in *DCB* (Smith-Wace) and in *PRE*^{3}. On Theodore see **Loofs**, art. in *PRE*^{3}, vol. xix. (1907); **Swete**, art. in *DCB*, and *Theodore of Mops. on the Minor Epp. of St. Paul*, vol. i. (1880); **Kihn**, *Theodor v. Mops. und Junilius Africanus als Exegeten* (1880); on Polychronius see **Bardenhewer**, *Polychronius Bruder Theodors v. Mops. und Bischof v. Apamea* (1879); on Theodoret see artt. in *DCB* and *PRE*^{3}, vol. xix. (1907); also **N. Glubokowski**, *Der selige Theodoret, Bischof von Cyrus, sein Leben und seine Schriftstellerische Thätigkeit* (in Russian), 2 vols. (Moscow, 1890).

(3) *THE EXEGESIS OF THE ANTIOCHENES*: Kihn, Hergenröther (*opp. citt.*); **Kihn**, *Theodor v. Mops.* (cited above); **G. C. H. toe Water**, *de Theodoro Antiocheno xii Prophet. min. interprete* (1837); **Sieffert**, *Theodor. Mops. V.T. sobrie interpretandi vindex* (1827); **F. A. Specht**, *Der exeget. Standpunkt des Theodor v. Mops. und Theodoret* (1871); **Sanday**, in *Expositor*, 1st series, vols. xi., xii. (1880); **F. Baethgen**, art. 'Der Psalmencommentar des Theodor v. Mops. in syrischer Bearbeitung' in *ZATW* v. (1885); **Swete**, art. 'Theodore' in *DCB*; **F. H. Chase**, *Chrysostom: A Study in the History of Biblical Interpretation* (1887).

(4) *THE THEOLOGY OF THE ANTIOCHENES*: (*a*) General: **Neander**, *Church History*, vol. iv.; **Harnack**, *Hist. of Dogma*, vols. iii. and iv.; **Dorner**, *Doctr. of Person of Christ*, II. i.; **Bethune-Baker**, *Introd. to Early History of Christian Doctrine* (1903). (*b*) Special treatises: on Paul of Samosata see **A. Réville**, 'La Christologie de Paul de Samosata' in *Études de critique et d'histoire*, 2ième série (Bibliothèque de l'école des hautes études, Sciences religieuses, vii., 1896); on Theodore see **Swete**, art. in *DCB*, and *Minor Epp. of St. Paul*, vol. i. Introd.; **Kihn**, *Theodor v. Mops.*; art. 'Theodore of Mops. and Modern Thought' in *CQR*, i. (1875); on Chrysostom see **T. Förster**, *Chrysostomus in seinem Verhältniss zur Antioch. Schule* (1869); on Theodoret see **Bertram**, *Theodoreti doctrina Christologica* (1883); **J. Mahé**, art. 'Les anathématismes de saint Cyrille d'Alexandrie et les évêques orientaux du patriarchat d'Antioche,' in *Revue d'histoire ecclésiastique*, vii. (1906).

(5) *THE LATER HISTORY OF THE SCHOOL OF ANTIOCH*: see works of Kihn, Hergenröther, cited above; **Chase**, *Chrysostom* (cited above); **Swete**, art. 'Theodore' in *DCB*, and *Theodore of Mops. on Minor Epp. of St. Paul*, vol. i. Introd.; **Harnack**, art. 'Antiochenische Schule' in *PRE*^{3} (cited above). On Junilius Africanus see **Kihn**, *Theodor v. Mops. und Junilius* (cited above).

J. H. SRAWLEY.

ANTIPATHY.—Antipathy is a state of mind or feeling expressing some sort of dislike or hatred of an object or person. Its proper reference is to persons, and it is often a milder or more polite term for hostility. Its analogue is found in the repulsion existing between elements of matter under certain conditions, as sympathy has its analogue in attraction or affinity between them. Thus an æsthetic man may have an antipathy or aversion towards an unæsthetic or vulgar person; an unbeliever may have an antipathy towards a religious believer. Anything that excites our dislike creates antipathy. It is a state of mind quite consistent with morality, and may actually be essential to it in certain stages of development; but it does not imply anything either moral or immoral, though it may be a state of mind making certain moralities effective. Anger and hatred are closely associated with ethical implications, but antipathy has no such associations, but rather connotes the fact of mental or emotional antagonism without regard to ethical considerations.

JAMES H. HYSLOP.

ANTI-SEMITISM.—I. **Historical.**—The expression 'Anti-Semitism,' which was coined about thirty years ago, signifies not opposition to Semites in general, but a hostile or at least an unfriendly disposition on the part of Aryans towards Jews, both socially and commercially.

The expression 'Semitic languages' was used for the first time in the year 1781 (contemporaneously by the two Göttingen professors, August Ludwig von Schlözer and Johann Gottfried Eichhorn) as a comprehensive designation for those related languages which were spoken by peoples brought into connexion with Shem, in the table of peoples in Gn 10. The Bonn professor, Christian Lassen, was the first to give expression to the view that these peoples, the 'Semites,' were in many respects distinct from the Aryans and other races (cf. *Indische Alterthumskunde*, vol. i. pp. 414–417, Bonn, 1847).

Lassen ascribes to the Indo-Germanic race a 'higher and a more complete mental endowment.'

'The point of view of the Semite is subjective and egoistic. His poetry is lyrical, and therefore subjective. In his religion he is self-seeking and exclusive. The characteristic features of the Semitic spirit, the passionate disposition, the obstinate will, the firm belief in their exclusive rights, in fact the whole egoistic trend of mind, must have in the highest degree fitted their possessors for great and daring deeds. A bold spirit of enterprise, an energetic and persevering courage, great skill, and a fine discernment how to take advantage of favourable circumstances and means of help among strangers, characterize first the Phœnicians, and later the Arabs. As soldiers, sailors, and enterprising traders, not only can they place themselves on a par with Indo-Germanic peoples, but they have to some extent excelled their contemporaries of this race and been their predecessors.'

Ernest Renan has expressed himself in similar terms in *Hist. gén. des lang. sémit.*[1], Paris, 1855, and in *Études d'hist. relig.*[1], 1857. The Anti-Semites extracted from Renan many catch-words and lines of attack, although Renan's intentions did not lie in this direction. What he had said about Semites in general, they applied specially to the Jews. The influence of Renan's judgment of the Semites comes clearly to the front, *e.g.*, in an article which received much notice in its time, published anonymously, but written by the well-known ethnologist Friedrich von Hellwald, 'Zur Charakteristik des jüdischen Volkes' in *Das Ausland*, 1872 (Stuttgart), Nos. 38 and 40. We shall quote a few sentences here.

'In the case of the Jews, we have to do with an entirely different ethnic group. . . . This people, scattered and settled in Aryan Europe, is purely Semitic. From an anthropological point of view, the Jew who lives in our midst stands quite as far apart from us as the Arab; and the emphatic contrast between the two, usually indicated by the opposites, Christian and Jew, is for the most part exactly the same as the existing opposition between Aryanism and Semitism. The European feels, so to speak, instinctively in the Jew who stands over against him the foreigner who has immigrated from Asia. . . . From the time of their entrance into Canaan the Jews can boast of an almost exclusive national type, which has persisted with remarkable purity to the present day. . . . A further specific feature of Judaism is its extraordinary geographical extent and its remarkable power of adaptation. . . . All over the world, in all climates, Jews live in content and prosperity, in spite of having in some places to suffer very hard civil and social pressure. . . . In the east of Europe the Jew is sharply distinguished from the other elements of the population; he is an object of hate, but still an almost indispensable constituent of social life. Quite as rough and ignorant as the non-Jewish peasant, but in character ignoble and mean, while possessed of that cunning which is a natural endowment of the Semitic race, the Jew has understood how to make himself in economic relations master of the Christian population, which stands far below him in keenness of intellect, and whose hate he repays by plundering them in every conceivable direction. The Jews, like most of the Semites, possessed from the very beginning a cunning exceedingly valuable for all purposes of trade, a cunning which naturally tended to develop still further [owing to the oppression to which they were subjected]. . . . We cannot do otherwise than designate the Jews the very canker from which the lands of Eastern Europe suffer. No means (provided they are not violent; for everything for which personal courage is demanded is opposed in general to the Semitic, and especially to the Jewish, character) are too wicked for them to use in order to secure a material advantage. . . . In the civilized world there would be nothing to distinguish the Jew from his Aryan neighbours, were it not that nature has inscribed with indelible characters his certificate of birth on his countenance. . . . The difference of race, thanks to the free development which was possible, has been still more clearly emphasized than before.'

F. v. Hellwald speaks of the frugality of the Jews, of their love to their parents and children, of their system of mutual assistance, and of their extraordinary fertility.

'The great influence which the Jews, especially amid the Teutonic nations, have acquired in political, literary, and economic conditions, comes, too, from their excessive zeal for learning. Dark spots in the Jewish racial character are a consciousness of their own merits, often ridiculously exaggerated, and a boundless egoism. . . . Self-sacrifice, devotion, and love of country are conceptions foreign to the Jewish mind. The Jew everywhere feels himself a cosmopolitan. . . . The entire tendency of Jewish effort can be summed up in one word, "exploitation." Thanks to this method, instinctively and systematically employed, the Jews have actually reached a stage which enables them to control the rest of the population. . . . They have succeeded in concentrating in their hands enormous wealth. . . . Recognizing the power of the printed page on the masses, they have especially exerted themselves to obtain control over the daily press. . . . In many places journalist and Jew are identical conceptions. Equipped with a superficial and imperfect knowledge, they come forward as teachers of the people, accessible to every influence which suggests possibilities of gain. They form a focus of corruption more devastating than can well be imagined.'

These extracts from F. v. Hellwald, although they contain many false along with some correct opinions, are given here because many 'Anti-Semites' of the present day express themselves in exactly similar terms. He was one of the first to bring to clear expression what many at that time felt only in a vague way, and consequently his writing made so deep an impression and exerted so great an influence.

The expression 'Anti-Semite,' as will be clear from what has been said, is, so far as the present writer is aware, scarcely three decades old. In the year 1880, W. Marr published, at Chemnitz, under the general title *Antisemitische Hefte*, three short essays, 'Der Judenkrieg,' 'Oeffnet die Augen, ihr deutschen Zeitungsleser,' and 'Goldene Ratten und rothe Mäuse.'

Anti-Semitism, however, is more than two thousand years old. Cf. Est 3[8] 'And Haman said unto king Ahasuerus, There is a certain people scattered abroad and dispersed among the people in all the provinces of thy kingdom; and their laws are diverse from all people; neither keep they the king's laws: therefore it is not for the king's profit to suffer them.'

But, leaving this passage out of account, we may regard Egypt, and especially Alexandria, as the seat of Anti-Semitism.

Cf. Felix Stähelin, *Der Antisemitismus des Altertums in seiner Entstehung und Entwicklung*, Basel, 1905; E. Schürer, *GJV*[3] iii. pp. 102–107, 397–420 (1898); Th. Reinach, *Textes d'auteurs grecs et romains relatifs au Judaïsme*, Paris, 1895.

As early as the times of the first Ptolemys many Jews resided in Alexandria. Their number increased especially during the time of the persecution of the Jewish religion by Antiochus Epiphanes. This persecution resulted in the Jews becoming more exclusive than ever in relation to adherents of other religions. Hateful accusations and bitter taunts, both to a large extent resting on ignorance, formed the answer of the heathen. Unfortunately the work of Flavius Josephus, *Against Apion*, is almost the only source of information we have. The earliest 'Anti-Semitic' author was the Egyptian priest Manetho (B.C. 270–250). Apion the grammarian (a contemporary of Christ) is best known to us from the still extant work of Josephus just referred to. Among the Romans we may mention Tacitus (*Hist.* v. 2 ff.) and the poets Horace, Juvenal, and Martial. The mockery of these writers was directed against circumcision, against abstinence from swine's flesh, and against the celebration of the Sabbath. The chief accusations brought against the Jews (apart from the assertion that the Jewish race was of late origin and had done nothing for culture) were: firstly, ἀθεότης, *i.e.* that the Jews rejected all Divine worship but their own, and consequently every image; secondly, ἀμιξία, *i.e.* the social exclusiveness connected with the laws of food and the Levitical laws of purity, which was interpreted for the Jews as 'adversus omnes alios hostile odium' (Tacitus, *Hist.* v. 5).

After Christianity obtained the supremacy over

heathenism in the Roman Empire, the Emperors (at a later date the Churches) of the separate lands, and many rulers regarded it as their duty to oppose Jewish influence, in order that the heathen, who had been newly won to Christianity, should remain Christians, and that the number of adherents might be more easily increased (cf. *e.g.* Fried. Wiegand, *Agobard von Lyon und die Judenfrage*, Erlangen and Leipzig, 1901). At a later date the wealth of many of the Jews, acquired for the most part by money-lending, attracted the cupidity of Christians. This was the case, *e.g.*, at the first Crusade (1096), and at the expulsion of the Jews from France by Philip IV. the Fair (1306). Religious motives were operative in the Jewish persecutions in the beginning of the second Crusade (1146; Abbot Peter of Clugny in France, the monk Rudolph of Mainz in Germany), as well as in the exclusion of the Jews from Spain in 1492 and from Portugal in 1497. In England, as early as the 12th cent. the maxim 'ipsi Judæi et omnia sua regis sunt' held as law (Hovedon, *Annales*, ed. Stubbs, ii. 231). The Jews were regarded as the milk cow of kings; and as enormous sums of money were repeatedly demanded from them, they were almost compelled to procure these by means of usury. In this way the Jews called down the hate of the people upon themselves. Stories, some true, many fabricated, of acts of vengeance on the part of the Jews (murder or crucifixion of Christian children at the time of the Easter festival) were fitted, and were actually used, to rouse this hatred to uncontrolled passion. It was in the 13th cent. that the 'blood accusation' first came to the front in its latest and most objectionable form, viz. that the Jews required Christian blood for ritual purposes (cf. H. Strack, *Das Blut*[8], pp. 126, 194). In the same century attacks on the Talmud became very violent (cf. H. Strack, *Einleit. in den Talmud*[3], p. 68). The charge that Jews poisoned wells occurs probably for the first time in the 12th cent., in Bohemia; often in the 14th cent., in Switzerland and France, but especially in Germany. In the whole history of the Jews we find all too frequent proofs of hostile disposition and outbreaks of hatred, oppression, persecution, expulsion, and tyranny.

The French Revolution forms an important epoch in the history of the Jews. On the 27th of September 1791, the National Assembly declared the repeal of all exclusive measures directed against the Jews; the constitution of the year iii. (1795) recognized the Jews as possessing equal rights. The following legislation, as well as the Restoration, brought the Jews some restrictions, but these were set aside by the Revolution of July 1830. The Jews of Alsace, however, obtained this emancipation later, by means of the exertions of Adolphe Crémieux.

The course of events in France was not without influence in Germany. From 1799 onwards a great number of publications, some in favour of the Jews, and some against them, made their appearance.

Cf. J. de le Roi, *Gesch. der evang. Judenmission*[2], Leipzig, 1899, i. pp. 109–118. Several works against the granting of equal rights to the Jews may be mentioned here: C. W. F. Grattenauer, *Wider die Juden*, Berlin, 1803; O. G. Tychsen, *Gutachten über die Erweiterung der staatsbürgerl. Rechte der Juden in Mecklenburg-Schwerin* 1812 (see A. Th. Hartmann, *Oluf Gerhard Tychsen*, i., Bremen, 1818, pp. 227–259, cf. pp. 202–208); Fried. Rühs, *Über die Ansprüche der Juden an das deutsche Bürgerrecht*, Berlin, 1816, and *Das Recht des Christenthums und des deutschen Reiches vertheidigt gegen die Ansprüche der Juden und ihre Verfechter*, Berlin, 1816.

In the year 1830, H. E. G. Paulus, the well-known representative of rationalism, demanded that the Jews should give up their ritual law as the condition of obtaining equal political rights (*Jüdische Nationalabsonderung*); a similar view was maintained by Carl Streckfuss in his *Über das Verhältniss der Juden zu den christlichen Staaten*, Halle, 1833 (a second pamphlet with the same title appeared in Berlin, 1843). The Rostock Orientalist, Anton Theodor Hartmann, who was well read in the Jewish literature, demanded that the Jews should expressly renounce the principles of injustice to be found in the Talmud and the *Shulḥān 'Arūkh* (i.e. those principles which, in the view of Hartmann and many others, allowed injustice against non-Jews or were otherwise opposed to morality). He demanded, further, that they should restrain themselves from all disparaging statements with regard to Jesus and those who were not Jews.

His writings on this subject are the following: *Joh. Andr. Eisenmenger*, Parchim, 1834; 'Darf eine völlige Gleichstellung in staatsbürgerlichen Rechten sämmtlichen Juden schon jetzt bewilligt werden?' in the *Archiv für die neueste Gesetzgebung aller deutschen Staaten*, ed. Alex. Müller, vols. v., vi. 1834–35; *Grundsätze des orthodoxen Judenthums*, Rostock, 1835 [a reply to Salomon's first letter]. Hartmann's views were keenly and in many respects cleverly attacked in two pamphlets by the Jewish preacher of Hamburg, Gotthold Salomon: *Briefe an Herrn Anton Theodor Hartmann*, Altona, 1835, and *Anton Theodor Hartmann's neueste Schrift 'Grundsätze des orthodoxen Judenthums' in ihrem wahren Lichte dargestellt*, Altona, 1835.

The commencement of the reign of the Prussian king Frederick William IV., who cherished the ideal of a 'Christian State,' gave a fresh stimulus to writings on the Jewish question. Among those who opposed the granting of equal civil rights to the Jews we have the following writers: H. E. Marcard, *Über die Möglichkeit der Juden-Emancipation im christlich-germanischen Staat*, Minden, 1843; and the well-known radical theologian, Bruno Bauer (died 1882), *Die Judenfrage*, Brunswick, 1843.

By the law of 3rd July 1869, absolute religious equality was granted within the North German Confederation, and soon after the same law was extended to the whole of the German Empire.

Modern Anti-Semitism arose in Germany in the eighth decade of last century (cf. J. de le Roi, *Geschichte*, i. pp. 258–272; A. Leroy-Beaulieu, *Israël chez les nations*[2], Paris, 1893). An important external cause was the daring attack made by many newspapers, possessed or edited by Jews, and appearing for the most part in Berlin, on many Christian topics (faith, constitution, recent events, ecclesiastical parties, and prominent persons connected with these); cf., *e.g.*, Franz Delitzsch, *Christentum und jüdische Presse*, Erlangen, 1882. As reasons for the rise and speedy spread of the Anti-Semitic movement, we may further mention, *secondly*, the great influence which the Jews had obtained in public affairs—to a large extent, of course, owing to the carelessness of the Christians. *Thirdly*, in newspaper writings, in the theatre, in some branches of art (music, *e.g.*, cf. Rich. Wagner, *Das Judenthum in der Musik*, Leipzig, 1869), in trade, and in several branches of industry (*e.g.* manufacture of ready-made articles of dress), the influence of the Jews appeared to many unreasonably great. *Fourthly*, the proud and ostentatious demeanour of many *nouveaux riches* Jews, who had acquired sudden wealth by speculation on the Stock Exchange, excited hatred. The same effect was produced, *fifthly*, by the economic dependence on the Jews into which many districts and occupations had fallen: *e.g.* a portion of the peasant population of Hesse had become dependent on cattle- and grain-merchants, while dress-makers and needlewomen were in the power of Jewish merchants; *sixthly*, by the support given to the Social Democratic party by Jewish leaders and Jewish money; *seventhly*, by the union among Jews of the whole world, *e.g. Alliance Israëlite Universelle*; and *eighthly*, by the exaggerated sensibility to every criticism and exposure of weaknesses on the part of Jews. *Ninthly*, there was a wide-spread feeling that the Jews were foreigners among the Germans: the stricter Jews not only rejected intermarriage with Christians, but they also kept themselves socially separate from them, *e.g.* on account of the laws of food. Many Jews, particularly the Zionists, openly avow Palestine as their real fatherland, although for the time being it is beyond their reach.

We cannot here inquire more exactly how far these reasons, taken individually, justify opposition to the Jews, seeing that the conditions are widely different in the many lands where the Jews are numerous. An unprejudiced mind, examining the matter carefully, will, in our opinion, be compelled to recognize on the one hand that there are reasons for opposition, and on the other hand that jealousy of the wealth amassed by some Jews has enormous influence with great numbers.

We may mention here the following works from among the important pamphlets designed to spread and deepen the Anti-Semitic movement: C. Wilmans, *Die goldene Internationale und die Nothwendigkeit einer socialen Reformpartei*, Berlin, 1876 [3rd ed. 1876]; W. Marr, *Der Sieg des Judenthums über das Germanenthum vom nichtconfessionellen Standpunkt aus betrachtet*, Bern, 1879 [11th ed. 1879], *Wählet keinen Juden! Der Weg zum Siege des Germanenthums über das Judenthum*, Berlin, 1880 [4th ed. 1880]; Adolf Stöcker, *Das moderne Judentum in Deutschland, besonders in Berlin*, Berlin, 1879 [5th ed. 1880]; *Christlich-Social. Reden und Aufsätze*, Bielefeld, 1885 [2nd ed. 1890]; Heinrich von Treitschke, *Ein Wort über unser Judenthum*, Berlin, 1880 [4th ed. 1881]. Further papers and pamphlets are mentioned by Joseph Jacobs: *The Jewish Question, 1875–1884, Biographical Handlist*, London, 1885; Joh. de le Roi, *Nathanael* (ed. by H. Strack), 1887, pp. 65–89, *Geschichte*, i. pp. 258–271; and Deutsch, art. 'Anti-Semitism' in *JE* i. 641.

A very great influence was exerted by two speeches delivered before the Christian Social Labour party by Adolf Stöcker in Berlin in Sept. 1879: 'What do we demand from modern Judaism?' and 'Defence against modern Judaism' (both are printed together in the above-mentioned pamphlet on modern Judaism). In them Stöcker demands three things: 'a little more modesty, a little more tolerance, and a little more equality.' Hein. von Treitschke is the author of the phrases, frequently used since then, 'trousers-peddling young Poles' (*hosenverkaufende polnische Jünglinge*), and 'the Jews are our misfortune,' as well as the sentences: 'We do not wish that on the thousands of years of Teutonic civilization there should follow an age of a mixed German-Jewish culture,' and: 'We Germans are a Christian people, and the Jewish question in Germany will not be settled till our fellow-citizens of the Jewish race are persuaded that we are and will remain a Christian people.' An equally decided attitude has been taken, as is well-known, by Catholics in Germany, Austria, France, and Italy (cf. Deutsch in *JE* i. 643).

The irritation increased, and the conditions were made worse owing to the enormous emigration of Jews from the lands of Eastern Europe to the West, especially, since 1881, from Russia and Roumania, at first to Germany and then to America and England. The preventives used on the part of the German Government were: *firstly*, restriction, and later almost entire refusal, of nationalization to Jews coming from the East; *secondly*, regulations by means of which a rapid passage of the migrating Jews through Germany was assured, *e.g.* the appointment of special localities for the temporary sojourn of emigrants at the great centres of commerce on the route (Ruhleben near Berlin, Hamburg, Bremen, etc.); *thirdly*, turning out by the police authorities of persons without means or occupation, especially where there was any suspicion that those in question belonged to the Nihilists or Anarchists. The first measure of prevention adopted in England was the Aliens Bill. In the United States every immigrant is now required to show a small sum of money, in order to prevent the immigration of persons entirely destitute of means of support.

Only a few years later than in Germany, the flame of Anti-Semitism was kindled in Austria and in Hungary, by Istóczi in the Hungarian Parliament, and by Georg von Schönerer in the Austrian Imperial Assembly in Vienna (1882). In France a loud and successful agitator was found in the person of Ed. Drumont, whose book, *La France juive* (1st ed., Paris, 1886), has seen more than 100 editions. Since 1892 he has edited the Anti-Semitic journal *La libre Parole.* The case of Albert Dreyfus was long used, from 1894 onwards, as a means of rousing the passion of the Anti-Semites, especially in France. The matter ended in the year 1906 with the rehabilitation of Dreyfus and with his reappointment as Major in the French army. At the Berlin Congress of 1878 a resolution was passed that in Roumania all citizens, without distinction of religious belief, should enjoy equal rights. The Roumanian Government, however, supported by the Anti-Semitic majority in Parliament, devised a means of rendering this provision worthless. The Constitution declared that no one should be prevented by his religion from possessing civil and political rights, but it was immediately declared that the Jews were foreigners, and not Roumanians—a breach of trust unworthy of a government and a people professing to be Christian. Besides, good school education and admission to public hospitals were made almost impossible for Jews, and the authorities have sought, by means of a series of new laws, regulations, and police restrictions, to make it unbearable for Jews to remain in Roumania.

For the Jews of the Russian Empire, the death of Alexander II. in 1881 was fraught with grave significance. Soon after the accession of Alexander III., fearful persecutions of the Jews (*pogrom*, pl. *pogromy*) were begun, and by the laws passed in May, 1882, the freedom of movement of the Jews in the 15 provinces of the territory for settlement, already small enough, was still further limited. The chief attacks on the Jews took place in the years 1903 (at Easter in Kishenev; see H. Strack's remarks in his periodical *Nathanael*, 1903, pp. 78–93, and 1904, pp. 62–64; L. Errera, *Les Massacres de Kishinev*, Brussels, 1903; I. Singer, *Russia at the Bar of the American People*, New York, 1904; C. Adler, *The Voice of America on Kishineff*, Philadelphia, 1904), 1905 (in October at Odessa and many other towns), and 1906 (at Bialystok and other places). In view of the events of the year 1905, the Seventh International Jewish Missionary Conference, held at Amsterdam, April 25th, 1906, carried unanimously the following motion, brought forward by the present writer and the Rev. Louis Meyer of Chicago (now of Cincinnati):

'The Seventh International Jewish Missionary Conference hereby records its deepest sympathy with the poor sufferers from the latest persecutions of the Jews in Russia. One hundred and fifty villages, towns, and cities of Russia where Jews dwelt have been devastated, many hundreds of Hebrews have been slaughtered, and many thousand Jewish families have been deprived of all their possessions, and even of the possibility of gaining a livelihood. Though there may have been faults upon the Jewish side, no human or Divine right permitted Russian officials of Government and Police to incite the lower classes against the Jewish people, which as such are innocent, that in the persecution of the Jews these lower classes should forget their own sufferings, caused by bureaucratic maladministration and by refusal of liberty of thought and religion. Such action we condemn, because it necessarily must close the hearts of the Jews to the gospel call still more than heretofore.'

Those chiefly responsible for the anti-Jewish attacks in Kishenev were the Minister of the Interior, von Plehwe, and the vice-governor, Ustrugow. The latter had refused to grant protection from plundering and murderous bands to defenceless Jews who implored his help, because he himself was an Anti-Semite, and because he was certain that his inactivity would not be censured by the Minister. The former used the Jews as a lightning-conductor, by means of which the dissatisfaction of the population with regard to the arbitrariness of the police and the organs of Government might be directed into another channel. He could do this all the more easily that the Jews were in any case largely regarded with unfriendly eyes by the lower classes of the people, who had grown up in ignorance and superstition. The statement is often made that the Jews, as proprietors of dram-shops, have contributed much to the impoverishment of the Russian peasants, and have thereby aroused hatred. It is true that in Jewish persecutions, and, in general, in every disturbance, the Jewish drink-shops are often the first to be plundered. That, however, is easily understood without ascribing any special guilt to the possessors of these shops.

Unfortunately, it is by no means improbable that the extension of Anti-Semitism will still continue. The repetition of such outbreaks as have taken place in Russia in recent years will, indeed, be more difficult if a Government binding itself, or bound to, a constitution actually comes into existence. It is, however, quite possible that at no distant date serious Jewish persecutions will arise in the United States, in Hungary, or in France. And in Prussia there has at least been no lack of sinister attempts to incite the population to acts of violence, since for years Count Pückler (of Klein-Tschirne, Silesia) has dared in public assemblies in Berlin and elsewhere to summon the masses to a 'fresh joyous war' against the 'cursed Jewish band.'

2. Arguments of the Anti-Semites, and attempts to refute them.—The means made use of by almost all Anti-Semitic agitators have very materially contributed to the fact that Anti-Semitism has not only extended to the widest circles, but has also been turned into a slanderous malignity and a wild passion for persecution (cf. M. C. Peters, *Justice to the Jew*, New York, 1899).

(*a*) The most dangerous of these means since the 13th cent. has been the 'blood accusation' mentioned above (p. 595[a]). The most influential propagator of this accusation was the canon August Rohling in Prague in the years 1883–1892 (see Strack, *Das Blut*[8], pp. 109–120). Only the most important instances of modern times can be mentioned here.

On April 1st, 1882, a maid-servant, Esther Solymosi, fourteen years of age, in Tisza-Eszlár, disappeared. The evidence of the Crown witness Moritz Scharf, who had asserted that he saw the murder of the girl through the keyhole, was shown by the judicial investigation to be impossible; the suspected Jews obtained a verdict of not guilty (see P. Nathan, *Der Prozess von Tisza-Eszlár*, Berlin, 1892; S. Mannheimer in *JE* xii. 148–150). The eight-year-old girl murdered in Korfu in the night between 12th and 13th April 1891 was not a Christian, Maria Desylla (there was no such person there at the time), but a Jewess, Rubina Sarda. The Jewish butcher Adolf Buschhoff, in Xanten, in the Rhine province, was accused of murdering, on June 29th, 1891, the 5½-year-old boy Johann Hegmann. The public prosecutor, however, stated: 'In my long experience of criminal cases I have never seen a clearer case, where so convincing and connected a proof was brought forward, that the accused did not commit the crime in question.' Every suspicion that the murder was committed with a view to obtaining the blood of the victim was removed by the *post-mortem* examination (cf. *Der Xantener Knabenmord vor dem Schwurgericht zu Cleve, 4–14 Juli 1892, Vollständiger stenographischer Bericht*, Berlin, 1893; Deutsch in *JE* xii. 574). The Jewish shoemaker Leopold Hilsner was pronounced guilty of murdering Agnes Hruza on March 29th, 1899, in Polna, Bohemia. However, Arthur Nussbaum (*Der Polnaer Ritualmordprozess: Eine kriminalpsychologische Untersuchung auf aktenmässiger Grundlage, mit einem Vorwort von Franz von Liszt*, Berlin, 1906) has convincingly proved: (1) that the throat wound in Agnes was no slaughter-cut, and that the amount of blood which could reasonably be expected in the circumstances was present; (2) that the reasons produced for the guilt of Hilsner were utterly worthless, that the statements of the accusing witnesses attained to definiteness only in the course of time; (3) that they were contradictory of each other or incredible in themselves; and (4) that there was no motive adduced why Hilsner should murder Agnes which had even a shade of probability. Very great interest was aroused by the murder of the 18½-year-old High School boy Ernst Winter in Konitz, West Prussia, in March 1900. The highest medical authorities in Prussia came unanimously to the conclusion that the cut on the neck of Winter's dismembered body was not made till after his death, nor was his death caused by loss of blood (cf. *Die Gutachten der Sachverständigen über den Konitzer Mord*, Berlin, 1903; Deutsch in *JE* vii. 552–555).

More detailed information on the history of the Blood-accusation is given by the present writer in *Das Blut im Glauben und Aberglauben der Menschheit, mit besonderer Berücksichtigung der 'Volksmedizin' und des 'jüdischen Blutritus'*[8], Munich, 1900; see also the work of the Roman Catholic priest Fr. Frank, *Der Ritualmord vor den Gerichtshöfen der Wahrheit und der Gerechtigkeit*, Regensburg, 1901; Chwolson, *Die Blutanklage und sonstige mittelalterliche Beschuldigungen der Juden (aus dem Russischen übersetzt)*, Frankfurt-a'-M., 1901; *JE* iii. 260–267.

(*b*) Another important means of attack used by the Anti-Semites is the agitation against the killing of animals according to the Jewish rites. If the Jews are refused the exercise of the form of slaughter appointed by their religious laws in any town, permanent residence in that place is made very difficult for them. If the prohibition is extended over a whole country, life there is made almost impossible for Jews. Accordingly, the Anti-Semites of Germany have entered Societies for the Prevention of Cruelty to Animals, and since 1883 have addressed petition after petition to the authorities and to Parliament against Jewish slaughter of animals. On 18th May 1887, the German Imperial Parliament rejected a proposal petitioning for legislation against the practice throughout the Empire. In 1892, however, Jewish slaughter was declared illegal in the Kingdom of Saxony by the Home Minister, and in the same year the prohibition of this form of slaughter was declared in Switzerland to be an essential element of the constitution of the union. In recent times, Anti-Semitic town councils in Prussian towns have attempted to make the custom impossible by means of slaughter-house regulations; and a new and very energetic agitation has begun in the Societies for the Prevention of Cruelty to Animals.

Cf. the works of the physician and Russian Jew, J. A. Dembo, *Das Schächten im Vergleich mit anderen Schlachtmethoden*, Leipzig, 1894; *Gutachten über das jüdischrituelle Schlachtverfahren*, Berlin, 1894; F. Weichmann, *Das Schächten (Das rituelle Schlachten bei den Juden), mit einem Vorwort von H. L. Strack*, Leipzig, 1899. In these writings conclusive proof is given that the Jewish method of slaughter does not constitute cruelty to animals.

Among other objects of attack on the part of the Anti-Semites we may mention here (cf. above, p. 595):—

(*c*) The Talmud. There is no truth whatever in the assertions that the Jews seek by every conceivable means to keep the Talmud secret, that they fear lest its contents may become known, and that they declare it a crime worthy of death for a Jew to reveal its contents. The writings on the Talmud (explanations, monographs, translations of whole treatises, etc.) by Jews themselves are very numerous in all European languages. As a practical proof that Christians are not dependent for a scientific judgment regarding the Talmud on what a Jew may think fit to communicate, it may be mentioned that the present writer in 1887 wrote an introduction to the Talmud without having asked or received the slightest detail of information from Jews or Jewish Christians. The Talmud contains no report or statement which the expert Christian scholar cannot discover.

(*d*) The *Shulḥān 'Arūkh* (Ezk 23[41] 'table prepared'), the ritual code of Joseph Karo († 1575 in Safed, Palestine), was printed for the first time in Venice in 1564–5. A fanatical and slanderous attack was made by the proselyte, 'Dr. Justus' (pseudonym = Aaron Brimann), in *Judenspiegel oder 100 neuenthüllte, heutzutage noch geltende, den Verkehr der Juden mit den Christen betreffende*

Gesetze der Juden, Paderborn, 1883. A learned and suggestive treatise, but coloured somewhat in favour of the Jews, was published by D. Hoffmann, *Der Schulchan-Aruch und die Rabbinen über das Verhältniss der Juden zu Andersgläubigen*, Berlin, 1884 [2nd ed. 1894]. For a thorough examination of both sides of the question we are indebted to G. Marx (=G. Dalman), *Jüdisches Fremdenrecht, antisemitische Polemik und jüdische Apologetik*, Leipzig, 1886.

(*e*) The alleged existence of Jewish secret writings and secret sects. As early as 1900 the present writer publicly and solemnly declared that there are no secret Jewish writings. Of course, to those who do not understand Latin, Cæsar's *Gallic War* is a secret writing, especially if they are not acquainted with any of the numerous translations in English, German, etc. Judaism has always been tolerant of the faith and practice of the individual, but it has always persecuted sects, recognizing quite correctly that sects would be very dangerous to the existence of Judaism itself. The most important sect in Judaism is that of the Karaites, which arose in the 8th cent. A.D., and of which small remnants, even at the present day, are to be found living in the Crimea, in Poland, and in Cairo, with a few in Jerusalem. Karaites and Talmudists have been always most bitterly opposed, and even at the present day hate each other. If the Talmudist Jews, either as a whole or in sections, had a 'blood-rite' or other ordinance, which Christians would regard as abominable or destructive of the common good, the Karaites would not have failed to point expressly to it; and it is just as little likely that the Talmudist Jews would have kept silent if it had been possible for them to accuse the Karaites of observing a 'blood-rite' or other repulsive laws.

(*f*) The formula *kol nidre*, 'all vows,' by means of which the Jews on the eve of the Great Day of Atonement in the synagogue declare all vows which they may make in the next year to be non-binding, does not refer to oaths which are made to others, but only to obligations which one lays upon oneself. It is not admissible to use this custom to cast doubt on the good faith of the Jews in taking oaths in general (cf. the present writer's art. 'Kol Nidre' in *PRE*³ x. 649–653; M. Schloessinger in *JE* vii. 539–542).

(*g*) A very foolish but, in Western Germany and Bavaria, widely credited accusation is that the Jews, before selling meat to non-Jews, must defile it (Lat. *mingere*) in the most loathsome manner (see the present writer's *Sind die Juden Verbrecher von Religionswegen?* Leipzig, 1900).

(*h*) The assertion is often made that a comparatively large percentage of Jews are punished as criminals (see, *e.g.*, W. Giese, *Die Juden und die deutsche Kriminalstatistik*, Leipzig, 1893). On the other hand, the Berlin Committee for answering Anti-Semitic attacks has published *Die Kriminalität der Juden in Deutschland*, Berlin, 1896. For a criticism of both writings by F. Nonnemann cf. *Nathanael*, 1896, pp. 44–78 (cf. also H. Lux, *Die Juden als Verbrecher*, Munich, 1894; Deutsch in *JE* iv. 362 f.).

(*i*) A publication by the same Committee, *Die Juden als Soldaten*, Berlin, 1896, with copious statistical tables, has in a thoroughgoing manner sought to meet the assertion which is frequently made, that the Jews are cowards (cf. also S. Wolf, *The American Jew as Patriot, Soldier, and Citizen*, Washington, 1894; M. C. Peters, *The Jew as a Patriot*, New York, 1901).

3. Conclusion.—The Jews have undoubtedly suffered great and bitter wrongs. On the other hand, justice must recognize that Jewish apologists have frequently failed to observe due moderation. Evil motives have often without proof been ascribed to opponents, who have been covered with hateful calumny. They have been scoffed at in an exaggerated way on account of single mistakes, as if thereby all other accusations and reasons were demonstrated to be false. Jewish apologists have often sought to put a favourable construction on something done by a Jew simply because a Jew did it, although the act could not be seriously defended. The non-Jewish majority has more than once been irritated by stupid aspersions (cf., to name only a single instance, P. P. G[rünfeld]'s *Ben Sirah Militans, Abgebrochene Sätze für A-B-C-Kinder*, Stuttgart, 1880).

The most important literature from the Jewish side has been mentioned above at various points. A very useful collection of materials is supplied by Josef Bloch, *Acten und Gutachten in dem Prozesse Rohling contra Bloch*, Vienna, 1890; cf. also *Antisemiten-Spiegel: Die Antisemiten im Lichte des Christenthums, des Rechtes und der Wissenschaft*², Dantzig, 1900. The most largely circulated book on the side of the Anti-Semites is the *Antisemiten-Katechismus*, Leipzig, which, from 1887 to 1893, went through 25 editions, and is now published under the title: Theodor Fritsch, *Handbuch der Judenfrage: eine Zusammenstellung des wichtigsten Materials zur Beurteilung des jüdischen Volkes*, Hamburg, 1907.

In conclusion a word may be said on *the duty of Christians* with regard to Anti-Semitism. We have in the first place to maintain in all circumstances veracity and justice. We must thus not only refrain from slander and false accusations, but contradict these in cases where Jews have difficulty in defending themselves. The question, *e.g.*, as to the criminality of Jews can, with the help of statistics available to every inquirer, be discussed quite as well by the Jew as by the Christian. If, however, Jews were to write on the 'blood accusation' or the Talmud, even the most upright Jew might easily fall under the suspicion of concealing or colouring the facts in favour of his nation and his religion. On this account, Franz Delitzsch (born Feb. 23rd, 1813, died Mar. 4th, 1890), the present writer, and others have regarded it as their duty again and again to show that many attacks directed by the Anti-Semites against the Jewish religion, and thus against the Jews generally, are based on falsehood, and are in fact slanderous.

Franz Delitzsch, *Rohlings Talmudjude*, Leipzig, 1881, 7th ed. 1881; *Was Dr. Aug. Rohling beschworen hat und beschwören will*, Leipzig, 1883; *Schachmatt den Blutlügnern Rohling und Justus*, Erlangen, 1883; *Neueste Traumgesichte des antisemitischen Propheten*, Erlangen, 1883. Hermann L. Strack wrote first against the 'blood-accusation' on the occasion of the case of Tisza-Eszlár in Zöckler's *Evangelische Kirchen-Zeitung*, 12th August 1882, No. 32. The murder in Korfu occasioned the publication *Der Blutaberglaube bei Christen und Juden*, Munich, 1891, 4th ed. *Der Blutaberglaube in der Menschheit, Blutmorde und Blutritus*, 1892, 5th to 8th ed. *Das Blut im Glauben und Aberglauben der Menschheit*, 1900; *Einleitung in den Talmud*, Leipzig, 1887 [4th ed. 1908]. See also the papers mentioned above, 2 (*f*) and (*g*).

It is, secondly, our duty to show in word and deed neighbourly love to the Jews. We dare not allow our love to be confined to those who share our religious beliefs (cf. Gal 6[10]), but we must always remember the lesson taught in the parable of the Good Samaritan (Lk 10). Thirdly, we are bound to furnish proof that the Christian religion rightly claims to be the universal religion. For this end we have to show the influence which Christianity has exercised and still exercises (*a*) on humanity as a whole; (*b*) on the individual; and (*c*) specially on Judaism (preaching in the language of the country, the work of the so-called Home Mission, *e.g.* spiritual care for prisoners, etc.).

Great complaints are made about the relatively excessive and still increasing influence exerted by the Jews in public life, not only in trade, but also in the press, in municipal councils, etc. We cannot here inquire where and how far such complaints are justified. One thing is certain:

violence and exclusive legislation will not lead to the removal of such evil conditions, but will simply replace them by still greater evils. But every non-Jew who is convinced that the Jews in any place exert too great an influence on their non-Jewish surroundings, must with double faithfulness perform his duties as a subject of his State (*e.g.* as Briton or as German) and as citizen (*e.g.* in London or in Berlin), and stimulate other non-Jews to a like faithful fulfilment of their duty. Here also the maxim holds: if we are dissatisfied with our environment, we must first ask what *our* fault is. Let us become better ourselves, and the state of affairs will improve. HERMANN L. STRACK.

ANURĀDHAPURA.—Anurādhapura was the capital of Ceylon for nearly 1500 years. It was founded, according to the tradition handed down in the earliest sources,* by a chieftain named Anurādha (so called after the constellation Anurādhā) in the 6th cent. B.C. on the bank of the Kadamba River. Nearly a century afterwards king Paṇḍukābhaya removed the capital, which had been at Upatissa, to Anurādhapura; and there it remained down to the reign of Aggabodhi IV. in the 8th cent. A.D. It was again the capital in the 11th cent., and was then finally deserted.

The name Anurādha as the name of a man fell out of use; and we find in a work of the 10th cent. (*Mahābodhivaṁsa*, p. 112) the name of the place explained as 'the city of the happy people' from *Anurādha*, 'satisfaction.' The Sinhalese peasantry of the present day habitually pronounce the name Anurāja-pura, and explain it as 'the city of the ninety kings,' *anu* meaning 'ninety,' and *rāja* meaning 'king.' The ancient interpretation of the name—Anurādha's city—is the only correct one. The second is little more than a play upon words, and the third is a *Volksetymologie* founded on a mistake. English writers on Ceylon often spell the name Anarajapoora, or Anoorajapura.

The exact site of Anurādha's original settlement has not been re-discovered. Paṇḍukābhaya constructed the beautiful artificial lake, the Victoria Lake, Jaya Vāpi, more usually called, after the king's own name (*Abhaya*, '*sans peur*'), the Abhaya Vāpi. It still exists, but in a half-ruined state, about two miles in circuit. Its southern shore is rather less than a mile north of the Bodhi Tree. It was on the shores of this lake that the king laid out his city, with its four suburbs, its cemetery, its special villages for huntsmen and scavengers, its temples to various pagan deities then worshipped, and residences for Jotiya (the engineer) and the other officials. There were also abodes for devotees of various sects—Jains, Ājīvikas, and others. North of all lay another artificial lake, the Gāmini Lake, also still existing, and now called the Vilān Lake. Apart from the two lakes, nothing has been discovered of the remains of what must have been even then, to judge from the description in the 10th chapter of the Great Chronicle, a considerable city.

But the foundations of the fame and beauty of the place were laid by king Tissa (so called after the constellation Tissā), who flourished in the middle of the 3rd cent. B.C., and was therefore contemporary with the Buddhist emperor of India, Aśoka the Great. The friendship of these two monarchs, who never met, had momentous consequences. Tissa, with his nobles and people, embraced the Buddhist faith; and, no doubt in imitation of Aśoka, erected many beautiful buildings in support of his new religion. Those at Anurādhapura numbered ten,† the most famous of them being the Thūpārāma, still, even in ruins, a beautiful and striking object. It is a solid dome, 70 feet high, rising from a decorated plinth in the centre of a square terrace, and surrounded by a number of beautiful granite pillars in two rows. It is not known what these pillars were intended to support. It would seem to appear from *Mahāvaṁsa*, ch. xxxvi. (p. 232, ed. Turnour), that they supported a canopy over the tope; but it is difficult to see how that can have been done. Perhaps each of them had, as its capital, some symbol of the faith. Such pillars, surmounted by symbols, put up by Aśoka in various parts of India, still survive. But in that case they are always solitary pillars. Bold flights of steps led up to the terrace from the park-like enclosure in which it stood; and the dome was supposed to contain relics of the Buddha. It was, in fact, a magnificent, highly decorated, and finely placed burial mound.

* *Dīpavaṁsa*, ix. 35; and *Mahāvaṁsa*, pp. 50, 56, 65.

† Enumerated in the *Mahāvaṁsa*, ch. xx. p. 123 (ed. Turnour).

Another still existing building of this time is the Issara Muni Vihāra, a hermitage constructed by king Tissa on the side of a granite hill, for those of his nobles (*issara*) who entered the Buddhist Order. Naturally only the stonework has survived; but this includes caves cut in the solid rock, bas-reliefs on the face of the granite, two terraces (one half-way up, one on the top of the rock), a small but beautiful artificial tank, and a small *dāgaba*. It is a beautiful spot, and must have been a charming residence in the days of its glory.

Of the rest of the ten buildings no remains have been found; and it is very doubtful whether any of Tissa's enclosure round the Bodhi Tree has survived. The tree itself, now nearly 2200 years old, still survives. The soil has been heaped up round its base whenever it showed any signs of decay. Planted originally on a terrace raised but little above the level of the ground, it now springs up in three detached branches from the summit of a mound that has reached to the dimensions of a small hill. The tree planted by Tissa, a branch of the original Bodhi Tree at Gayā in India, was sent as a present by the Emperor Aśoka. The auspicious event was celebrated in two bas-reliefs on the eastern gateway of the Sānchi Tope,* probably put up by Aśoka himself.†

The capital was taken by the Tamils not long after Tissa's death, and was re-captured, about a century afterwards, by Dushṭa Gāmini Abhaya, the hero of the Great Chronicle. He occupies in Ceylon tradition very much the place occupied in English history and legend by king Arthur. We have information about the buildings he erected in his capital. Undoubtedly the most splendid was the so-called Bronze Palace. This was built on a square platform supported by a thousand granite pillars, which still remain *in situ*. Each side of the square was 150 feet long. On the platform were erected nine storeys, each square in form and less than the one beneath it, and the total height from the platform was 150 feet. The general effect was therefore pyramidal, the greatest possible contrast to the dome-shaped *dāgabas* in the vicinity, just as the bronze tiles which covered it contrasted with the dazzling white of the polished *chunam* which formed the covering of the domes. The building was almost certainly made of wood throughout, and its cost is given in the Chronicle‡ as 30 *koṭis*, equivalent in our money to about £300,000.

The other great work of this king was the Dāgaba of the Golden Sand; but this he did not live to complete. According to the Chronicle (ed. Turnour, p. 195), it cost one thousand *koṭis*, equivalent to a million sterling. It is still one of the monuments most revered by all Buddhists; and even in ruin it stood, in 1830, 189 feet above the platform on which it rests. Its Pāli name is

* Reproduced in Rhys Davids's *Buddhist India*, pp. 301–303.

† For fuller details see BODHI, where the question of the evolution and meaning of the Wisdom-Tree conception will be more appropriately treated.

‡ *Mahāvaṁsa*, ch. xxvii.

usually simply *Mahā Thūpa*, 'Great Tope,' the name given above being a rendering of its distinctive title *Hemavali* in Pāli, *Ruwan Wæli Dāgaba* in Sinhalese. Five chapters in the Great Chronicle (ch. xxviii.–xxxii.) are devoted to a detailed account of the construction and dedication of this *stūpa*, and of the artistic embellishment of its central chamber, the relic chamber. This has never, it is believed, been disturbed; and as the exterior has, quite recently, been restored, there is now little chance of the historical secrets there buried being revealed.

For some generations after these great events the city enjoyed peace. But in B.C. 109 the Tamils, with their vastly superior numbers, again broke in, and took Anurādhapura. It was not till B.C. 89 that the Sinhalese were able to issue from their fastnesses in the mountains, and drive the Tamils out. Their victorious leader, Waṭṭa Gāmini, celebrated the recovery of the capital by the erection of a still greater tope than all the former ones—the Abhaya Giri Dāgaba. This immense dome-shaped pile was 405 feet high from ground to summit, and built, except the relic chamber, of solid brick. Its ruin is still one of the landmarks of all the country round. The Vihāra attached to this tope, and built on the site of the garden residences given by Paṇḍukābhaya to the Jains, obtained notoriety from a curious circumstance. The principal of the college, though appointed by, and a great favourite of, the king, incurred censure at an ecclesiastical court composed mainly of residents at the older Vihāra, the Great Minster, close to the Bodhi Tree. There ensued a long-continued rivalry between the two establishments, usually confined to personal questions, but occasionally branching off into matters of doctrine. For five centuries and more this rivalry had an important influence on the civil and religious history of the island.

With the completion of these buildings, the city assumed very much the appearance which it preserved throughout its long history. The Chronicle records how subsequent kings repaired, added to, and beautified the existing monuments. It tells us also how they and their nobles built palaces for themselves and residences for the clergy. These have all completely vanished. The only new building of importance that still survives is the Jetavan Ārāma, another huge dome-shaped pile, built about two miles due north of the Bodhi Tree at the beginning of the 4th cent. A.D.

It is at the beginning of the next century that we have the earliest mention of Anurādhapura from outside sources. Fa Hian, the Buddhist pilgrim from China, stayed there for the two years A.D. 411–412. He gives a glowing account of its beauty, the grandeur of the public buildings and private residences, the magnificence of the processions, the culture of the Bhikshus, and the piety of the king and people. The reason for Fa Hian's long stay in the city was his desire to study and to obtain copies, on palm leaf, of the books studied. For Anurādhapura was at that time the seat of a great university rivalling in the South the fame, in the North of India, of the University of Nālandā on the banks of the Ganges. Among the laity, law, medicine, astrology, irrigation, poetry, and literature were the main subjects. The Bhikshus handed down from teacher to pupil the words of the sacred books preserved in Pāli, to them a dead language, and the substance of the commentaries upon them, exegetical, historical, and philological, preserved in their own tongue. They had handbooks and classes for the study of the grammar and lexicography of Pāli; of the ethics, psychology, and philosophy of their sacred books; and of the problems in canon law arising out of the interpretation of the Rules of the Order. And they found time to take a considerable interest in folklore and popular and ballad literature, much of which has been preserved to us by their indefatigable and self-denying industry. All this involved not only method, but much intellectual effort. Students flocked to the great centre of learning, not only from all parts of the island, but from South India, and occasionally from the far North. Of the latter the most famous was the great commentator, Buddhaghoṣa (*q.v.*), who came from Gayā, in Behar, to get the information he could not obtain in the North.

'For there, in that beautiful land, the most fruitful of any in India or its confines in continuous and successful literary work and effort, there have never been wanting, from Asoka's time to our own, the requisite number of earnest and devoted teachers and students to keep alive, and to hand down to their successors and to us, that invaluable literature which has taught us so much of the history of religion, not only in Ceylon, but also in India itself.' *

The Chroniclers were not, therefore, very far wrong in emphasizing this side of the life of Anurādhapura. To it the city owed the most magnificent and the most abiding of its monuments, surpassed in historical value only by its intellectual achievements.

When Buddhaghoṣa was in Ceylon, the water supply of the city was being re-organized. The artificial lakes in the vicinity, which added so much to its beauty, were found insufficient; and king Dhātu Sena, in A.D. 450, constructed, 50 miles away, the great reservoir called the Black Lake (*Kāla Vāpi*). The giant arms of its embankment still stretch for 14 miles through the forest. It was 50 miles in circumference; and the canals for irrigation on the route, and for conducting the water to the capital, are still in fair preservation. A breach in the bank has lately been restored at great expense. This reservoir was, no doubt, at the time of its construction, the most stupendous irrigation scheme in the world.

This was the last great work undertaken at Anurādhapura. There ensued a series of dynastic intrigues and civil wars of a character similar to the Wars of the Roses in England. Each party fell into the habit of appealing for help to the Tamils on the mainland, whither the defeated were wont to flee for refuge. The northern part of the island, in which Anurādhapura lay, became more and more overrun with Tamil freebooters and free lances, more and more difficult to defend. Finally, in A.D. 750, it was abandoned as the seat of government, which was established at Pulastipura, under the shelter of the Southern hills. Anurādhapura fell into the hands now of one party, now of another. For a brief interval in the 11th cent. it claimed, under a Sinhalese pretender, supported by Tamil forces, to be again the capital. But the pretender was driven out, and the city reverted to the Pulastipura government. Finally, at what date is not exactly known, but probably about A.D. 1300, the whole district, stretching across the island, from 50 miles north to 50 miles south of Anurādhupura, became a kind of no man's land, and relapsed rapidly into jungle. Neither the Tamil kings of Jaffna in the north, nor the Sinhalese kings in the south, were able to exercise any real sovereignty over it. The once beautiful and populous city dwindled away to a few huts round the Bodhi Tree, now left in the charge of two or three solitary monks. The earliest notice of the ruins received in Europe was in Knox's *Historical Relation of the Island of Ceylon* (1681), iv. 10. Held a captive for twenty years in the mountains, Knox escaped in 1679 through the jungle round Anurādhapura, and his naïve words vividly portray the utter desolation of the place.

* *Buddhist India*, pp. 303, 304.

'Here is a world of hewn stone pillars, standing upright, and other hewn stones, which I suppose formerly were buildings. In three or four places are ruins of bridges built of stone, some remains of them yet standing on stone pillars. In many places are points built out into the water, like wharfs, which I suppose have been built for kings to sit upon for pleasure.'

The English Government has now made good roads, and a railway has been opened through to Jaffna. Several officials are resident at the station, and a settlement is growing up. For some distance round this settlement the undergrowth has been cut away, and there is now grass growing under spreading trees. The ruins are being cleared, and some of them preserved from further injury; and some excavation has been carried out.

LITERATURE.—*Mahāvaṁsa*, ed. George Turnour, Colombo, 1837; *Dīpavaṁsa*, ed. Hermann Oldenberg, London, 1879; Sir J. E. Tennant, *Ceylon*², London, 1859; W. Knighton, *History of Ceylon*, Colombo, 1845; *Mahā-bodhivaṁsa*, ed. S. A. Strong, Pāli Text Society, 1891; *Fa Hian*, translated by J. Legge, Oxford, 1886; T. W. Rhys Davids, *Buddhist India*, London, 1903; *Ceylon Archæological Reports*, Colombo, 1868–1907; H. W. Cave, *Ruined Cities of Ceylon*, new ed., London, 1900; Don M. de Zilva Wickramasinghe, *Epigraphia Zeylanica*, pts. i.–iii., London, 1904–1907; Robert Knox, *Historical Relation of the Island of Ceylon* (1681), 2nd ed., London, 1817.

T. W. RHYS DAVIDS.

APACHES.—The Apaches are the southernmost group of the Athapascan stock of American Indians, who originally covered the territory from the Arctic Coast to New Mexico, and from the Pacific to Hudson Bay, their kinship being plainly traceable through their language. However, the name 'Apache' is a misnomer, apparently from the Zuñi *ápachu*, 'enemy,' and not found in their vocabulary, as they are known among themselves, not as 'Apaches,' but as 'Inde' (N'de, Dĭnë, Tinde), or 'People.' Mentioned by Juan de Oñate as early as 1598 (*Doc. inéditos de Indias*, xvi. 114) in the 'Snowy Mountains' of New Mexico, they were not found as far west as Arizona, their present home, until the middle of the 16th cent., when they were a large and warlike tribe, whose numbers were increased by captives from their more peaceful neighbours, and whose customs, habits, and beliefs they assimilated to a certain extent.

Prior to their reservation life, the Apaches were a nomadic people, practising agriculture only to a limited extent, living mainly by foraging and by the hunt. They were and are now divided into tribal groups, designated by the locality to which they belong (see the list in Hodge, *Handbook of American Indians*, i. 66), but have always lacked the organization for which so many of the other tribes are noted, and to-day they are found living in bands and villages along the cañons and waterways, or in the rich valleys, tilling small farms and caring for their stock during the summer, and in the winter moving their camps to the heavily timbered sections, both for protection and more accessible fuel. Naturally their homes are of the most temporary character—usually willow poles thrust into the ground, fastened together at the top, oval in form, and of sufficient height to allow a person to stand erect, with an opening at the centre through which the smoke passes from the fire-place directly underneath. The sides are interwoven and thatched with bear grass, over which canvas is sometimes drawn, with a single opening for a door. Among the San Carlos Apaches these *khúvas* are excavated between one and two feet. The Jicarilla Apaches live in brush *wikiups* or in tents, the latter habitation being preferred also by the Lipan and many Mescarillo Apaches. There seems to be no ceremony or symbolism attached to the house, though Hrdlička observed one San Carlos family pray on entering a new *khúva*, while another house had two eagle-feathers tied as fetishes to one of the poles. The Apaches use smoke signals, columns of smoke being passed from camp to camp. One smoke column denotes attention; two, establishment of a camp, quiet, safety; and three, alarm; a greater number urging a correspondingly greater need of haste (Mallery, *1 RBEW* p. 538 f.). The Apaches have always been known as the cultivators of grain, particularly corn, from which *tis win*, their favourite drink, is made. Their additional food-stuffs consist of seeds, berries, nuts, melons, and small game, while fish and every species of fish-eating birds are tabued.

In appearance there is no uniform Apache type, this being due to their nomadic habits, and to their assimilation with neighbouring peoples. As a rule, they are sinewy and strongly built, with good lung power, and well-developed lower limbs. In early times the men's dress consisted of a breech cloth and moccasins, with long uppers extending to the knee, and often to the thigh, with rawhide soles, turned upward at the toe and decorated with painted designs. In winter a *poncho*, or buckskin shirt, made of two skins with an opening for the head, and fastened with thongs beneath the arm, was worn. A band round the head kept the hair back from the face; the hair was generally worn long or trimmed square on a level with the chin. The women wore a buckskin over one shoulder, which was fastened beneath the opposite arm, a short skirt of buckskin, coming just below the knee, with fringes of the same, and pendants of metal or shell. Girls and unmarried women wore their hair drawn back on the nape of the neck, and rolled in a club shape; while attached to the roll was a hair ornament made of leather in the shape of the figure eight, studded with brass-headed tacks; they also wore wristlets of brass and copper, and ear-rings and necklets of shell or seeds. Only of late years have they tatued, but now it is quite common to see various geometric designs on their foreheads and chins, and sometimes on the cheeks. On reaching puberty, girls have their eyebrows and eyelashes pulled out.

Polygamy is practised by the Apaches, a man generally marrying his wife's sisters as they mature, since they believe less friction will exist in the family. A widow cannot marry within a year of her husband's death, but his brother can take her to wife any time within the period of mourning; if he does not, however, she is free to marry any one she pleases. Marriage is generally arranged by the parents or near relatives, and is generally by purchase. If a man has more than one wife, they usually live in separate camps, the children belonging to the mother. The morality of the girls is always good before marriage. When a man marries, he avoids meeting or speaking to his mother-in-law. If they should meet by accident, the first to see the other hides or looks in the opposite direction. A girl is of marriageable age when she reaches the age of puberty, her parents making the announcement by a feast and dance, at which she is forbidden to be present, and which lasts through the night; afterwards she is open to proposal.

Women do all the household work, the planting and tending of the crops, and the carrying of the burdens. To-day their principal income is derived from the sale of hay, grain, and wood to the agency, military posts, ranches, and towns adjacent to the reservations. At home the Apache is fond of talking and entertaining his friends. Both men and women are inveterate gamblers.

Among Apache games are tossing arrows or darts at an arrow or dart already on the ground, so that they cross: the hoop and pole game (the principal gambling game), in which the pole is hurled through the rolling hoop; 'hide the button' (Jicarilla); 'cat's cradle' (White Mountain); foot races; and dice, the women's game (Culin, *24 RBEW* pp. 385, 449–457, 345, 762, 803 f., 86–91). The hoop and pole game, in which, amongst the White Mountain Apaches, the red pole is female and the yellow is male, has an esoteric religious meaning, which is jealously guarded by the *dēē-yin* ('medicine-men'). It is said to have been taught first by one of the minor deities called Ghons; but the Jicarilla cosmogony describes it 'as having been made by Yolkaiistsun, the White-bead woman, for her two sons, children by her of the Sun and the Moon. She told them not to roll the wheel toward the north. They played for three days, when the Sun's son rolled the wheel toward the east, south, and west. His brother then persuaded him to roll it toward the north. An adventure with an owl followed, and the two boys were set to perform a succession of dangerous feats, which accomplished, they went to live in the western ocean' (Culin, *op. cit.* p. 449).

The principal Apache handicraft is basket-weaving, of which there are several forms, the conical shape for carrying burdens, the bowl shape, and the *toose*, or water-bottle. All the baskets are built on coils, and sewn with willow and other splints woven in geometric or figured designs of black, and made from the pod of a species of Martynia.

A close study and intimate knowledge of the various Apache tribes reveal no religious organization, but there are many forms of worship, not as the white man recognizes worship, but in the form of sacrifice, prayers, fasts, and physical penance to appease the wrath of the evil spirits. Perhaps the nearest approach to one of the classified forms of worship of the Apaches is the elemental, or nature-worship, though there are traces of animism as well as of animal-worship in their reverence for the bear, jack rabbit, snake, etc., to which they offer the sacrifice of *hoddentin* (see below). The number four is sacred, as among the American Indians generally; and so is eight, though to a minor degree. As far back as the 16th and 17th cents., the Jesuits and Franciscans formed missions, and worked with their accustomed zeal, but with little success. After years of toil and sacrifice, the field was wholly abandoned, and, apart from the various signs of the cross and sacred cords that might be traced to the rosary, no influence seems to have remained of these early teachings. And as these symbols were so common among the aborigines, it is doubtful whether even these are relics of former Christian influence. The belief in spirits both good and bad, and in the necessity of sacrifice, is prominent in their worship, as will be seen by their offering of *hoddentin* to appease every known spirit on every occasion.

To be properly understood, however, the beliefs and superstitions of the Apaches must be studied through their medicine-men and women, who wield a marvellous influence in fastening on them their belief in the occult, an influence little understood or appreciated by the civil authorities. Through this lack of understanding, the Apache Indians have been much maligned, and a great deal of the trouble with Government representatives in the past has arisen through not taking into consideration their superstitions and methods of reasoning. Great freedom exists as to the selection of the *shaman* or medicine-man. Any man, woman, or child who seems to be endowed with spiritual or occult powers and able to interpret omens, is free to follow his own inclinations and invent his own symbols. It is customary, however, for them to place themselves as assistants to some medicine-man who has gained power and influence, paying him liberally for his tuition, a year or more being the usual length of time given to study.

The Apache believes that all ills of the body are caused by evil spirits, which must be expelled or subdued. When any one is sick, he sends for his favourite medicine-man. If the patient is wealthy, the medicine-man will have the assistance of several others, often bringing his family along with him, and camping near the patient. The family and friends of the sick supply the medicine-man and his family with food and help. Before the medicine-man's arrival, the sick one's family generally prepares as many cans of *tis win* as they can afford; and when he arrives, a corner of the camp is reserved for his use, the best blankets are given for him to rest on, and the choicest food is placed before him. When he has finished his repast, large cans of *tis win* are placed before him, and he drinks and calls from among his friends those whom he wishes to drink with him.

While the feast is going on, the medicine-man begins to bargain his service; and if everything is satisfactory, he proceeds to arrange a programme for his patient's care. If there is but one person sick in the camp, the exercises consist of singing, chanting, and drumming; but if there are more sick, or an epidemic is raging in the settlement, dancing takes place, prayers are recited, the women and children joining in the weird and monotonous cadence. *Hoddentin* is sprinkled round the couch of the sick, and applied to his forehead, tongue, and, in the form of a cross, to his breast, the medicine-men placing this same powder on their own tongues to give strength and divination. The singing and dancing are often continued until the leaders are completely exhausted. All the while they mumble a sort of gibberish that they claim to be understood only by themselves, and to possess the magic that is a part of their individual power. The Apache materia medica consists mainly of a few roots, leaves, and vegetable matter, always with the application of *hoddentin*. *Hoddentin* is the pollen of the *tule*, a species of cat-tail rush, and is gathered without any special ceremony. A small bag of it is carried by every man, woman, and child, even the infant in its cradle having a small bag attached to it. No undertaking, compact, or agreement is entered into without the sacrifice of some of this powder; a small portion of it is blown into the air at dawn and darkness; it is blown toward the sun to appease its heat and bring rain for the crops. Every phase of the life of the Apaches is surrounded by superstition and subject to necromancy, over which the medicine-men have control. Like the fraternity of physicians of more scientific learning, they specialize, one being consulted for rain, another to recover stolen property, another for sickness, etc.

In addition to this sacrificial powder, there are many other sacred emblems that are much relied on by the Apaches. The *izze-kloth*, or sacred cord, which is worn by leaders as well as by medicine-men, the bull-roarer, the medicine-hat, and the medicine-shirt are all firmly believed to possess certain special properties. The bull-roarer is an oblong piece of wood, about 1¼ in. wide and 7 or 8 in. long, made with a round head through which a cord is passed, while on the main body are irregular furrows. It is usually of pine or fir, and if obtained from the mountain heights, and previously struck by lightning, it possesses special qualities in controlling the elements. This bull-roarer the medicine-men twirl rapidly. It then gives the sound of a sudden rush of wind, and exerts a compelling influence on the bringing of rain to the crops. The *izze-kloth*, used by leaders and laity alike, is the most sacred emblem the Apache possesses, so much so that it must be hidden from sight and protected from profane touch, both the *izze-kloth* and the medicine-hat losing their efficacy when in any way handled by an unbeliever.

The Apaches worship and sacrifice to the sun, moon, and other planets, as well as to the lightning, wind, etc.; and hold various dances, such as spirit-, ghost-, sun-, and snake-dances, though the snake-dances are not so common or so regular as among the Hopis and other neighbouring tribes.

Regarding the success of the medicine-men, it is well with them in cases of sickness if they do not lose too many patients; but when unsuccessful, they generally claim that there is some other influence at work overcoming or counteracting their own. The present writer has seen several incidents where the medicine-man managed to shift the responsibility to another, knowing that the relatives of the deceased were dissatisfied with his work. While the body was still warm, the medicine-man drew from his medicine-bag a flake of flint, with which he made an incision in the side of the deceased where he had suffered most, put his lips to the incision and began to moan, and in a short time turned around and spat on the ground a mouthful of blood, and with it a small stone, which he claimed had been fired into the deceased by an old woman living forty miles away. That night a party went to the old woman's camp and killed her as a witch. The individual interpretation given to each one's beliefs and imaginations precludes any set form of worship; but in a general way they all centre round those symbolic influences and superstitions that debar progress and hold them effectually to the faith of their fathers.

The characteristic Apache burial is in natural rock shelters in cliffs and crevices, either on the rocky sides of mountains or in the earth and talus at the base of the hills. Nooks in small unfrequented cañons are also utilized. After the removal of the earth and talus, the body is laid on the resulting platform and covered with a frame of poles and brush, over which rocks are heaped, the mound being from 4 to 10 ft. broad, 6 to 15 ft. long, and 2½ to 4 ft. high. No coffin is used, but the corpse is clothed and well wrapped up. A shovel (and sometimes an axe, or, in the case of a woman, a carrying basket), is frequently left on the grave, of which no subsequent care is taken. Among the White Mountain Apaches tree-burial occurs.

LITERATURE.—Hodge, *Handbook of American Indians north of Mexico* (*Bull.* 30 *BE*), Washington, 1907, i. 63–67 (with excellent summary of the history of the tribe), 335, 369, 394, 453, 492, 496, 512, 604 f., 642, 711, 768 f., 825, 863 f.; Drake, *Indian Tribes of the United States*, Philadelphia, 1884, i. 416–424; Bourke, 'Medicine-Men of the Apache,' in *9 RBEW* pp. 451–603; Russell, 'Myths of the Jicarilla Apache' in *Journal of American Folklore*, 1898; Mooney, 'Jicarilla Genesis' in *American Anthropologist*, old series, xi. (1898); Hodge, 'The Early Navajo and Apache,' *ib.* viii. (1895); Hrdlička, 'Notes on the San Carlos Apache,' *ib.*, new series, vii. (1905); Cremony, *Life among the Apaches*², San Francisco, 1877; Buschmann, 'Das Apache als eine athapaskische Sprache erwiesen' in *ABAW*, 1860–1863; Pilling, *Bibliography of the Athapascan Languages*, Washington, 1892.

ANTONIO APACHE.

APADĀNA.—The name of one of the books in the Pāli Canon. It contains 550 biographies of male members and 40 biographies of female members of the Buddhist Order in the time of the Buddha. The book is therefore a Buddhist *Vitæ Sanctorum*. It has not yet been edited, but copious extracts from the 40 biographies are given in Eduard Müller's edition of the commentary on the Therī Gāthā (*PTS*, 1893). One of those extracts (p. 135) mentions the Kathā Vatthu, and apparently refers to the book so named, which was composed by Tissa about the middle of the 3rd century B.C. If this be so, the Apadāna must be one of the very latest books in the Canon. Other considerations point to a similar conclusion. Thus the number of Buddhas previous to the historical Buddha is given in the Dīgha Nikāya as six; in later books, such as the Buddha Vaṁsa, it has increased to 24. But the Apadāna (see Ed. Müller's article, 'Les Apadānas du Sud' in *The Proceedings of the Oriental Congress at Geneva*, 1894, p. 167) mentions eleven more, bringing the number up to thirty-five. It is very probable that the different legends contained in this collection are of different dates; but the above facts tend to show that they were brought together as we now have them after the date of the composition of most of the other books in the Canon.

There exists a commentary on the Apadāna called the Visuddha-jana-vilāsinī. In two passages of the Gandha Vaṁsa (*JPTS*, 1886), pp. 59, 69, the authorship of this commentary is ascribed to Buddhaghoṣa.

According to the Sumaṅgala Vilāsinī, p. 15 (cf. p. 23), the repeaters of the Dīgha maintained that the Apadāna had been included in the Abhidhamma Piṭaka, while the repeaters of the Majjhima said it was included in the Suttanta Piṭaka. This doubt as to its position in the Canon is another reason for placing the work at a comparatively late date.

The word Apadāna means 'pure action,' 'heroic action'; and each of the Apadānas gives us first the life of its hero or heroine in one or more previous births, with especial reference to the good actions that were the cause of his or her distinguished position among the early Buddhists. There then follows the account of his or her life now. An Apadāna therefore, like a Jātaka, has both a 'story of the past' and a 'story of the present'; but it differs from a Jātaka in that the latter refers always to the past life of a Buddha, whereas an Apadāna deals usually, not always, with that of an Arhat (*q.v.*).

When the Buddhists, in the first century of our era, began to write in Sanskrit, these stories lost none of their popularity. The name was Sanskritized into Avadāna; and several collections of Avadānas are extant in Sanskrit, or in Tibetan or Chinese translations. Of these the best known are the Avadāna-Śataka, or 'The Century of Avadānas,' edited (in part only as yet) by J. S. Speyer, and translated by Léon Feer; and the Divyāvadāna, edited by Cowell and Neil, not yet translated. As a general rule, these later books do not reproduce the stories in the older Apadāna. They write new ones, more in accordance, in spirit and implication, with the later doctrines then prevalent. Most of these Avadānas are on the lives of Arhats. But the main subject of the longest of all the Avadāna books, the Mahā-vastu-avadāna, is a series of the previous lives of the Buddha, though it also includes a few of the old Apadānas in new versions.

LITERATURE.—H. Oldenberg, *Catalogue of Pāli MSS in the India Office Library* (*JPTS*, 1882, p. 61); V. Fausböll, *The Mandalay MSS in the India Office Library* (*JPTS*, 1896, p. 27); Ed. Müller-Hess, *Les Apadānas du Sud* (Extrait des Actes du Xe Congrès des Orientalistes, Leyden, 1895); *Sumaṅgala Vilāsinī*, ed. Rhys Davids and Carpenter (*PTS*, 1886), vol. i. pp. 15, 23; *Avadāna-śataka, a Century of edifying Tales*, ed. J. S. Speyer (St. Petersburg, parts 1–3, 1902–4), translated by Léon Feer in the *Annales du Musée Guimet*, Paris, 1891; *Divyāvadāna*, ed. Cowell and Neil (Cambridge University Press, 1886); *Mahāvastu*, ed. E. Senart (3 vols., Paris, 1882–1897).

T. W. RHYS DAVIDS.

APATHY.—The Greek doctrine of apathy (ἀπάθεια) is usually regarded as a leading characteristic of the Stoic School, but it undoubtedly belongs to an earlier date. This is the view of the anonymous commentator on Aristotle's Ethics (*Comment. in Aristot. gr.* xx. p. 128, 5 : ἰστέον δὲ ὅτι καὶ πρὸ τῶν στωικῶν ἦν ἡ δόξα αὕτη). There are certainly marked tendencies towards it in the Cynic School, with its complete renunciation of all pleasure and its glorification of work. If it is the case that Aristotle's *Nic. Eth.* ii. 2, 1104b, 24 (διὸ καὶ ὁρίζονται τὰς ἀρετὰς ἀπαθείας τινὰς καὶ ἠρεμίας) alludes to the Cynics, the latter must already have made use of the expression ἀπάθεια. In any case, it had influenced Stilpo the Megarian, who found happiness in the *animus impatiens* (Seneca, *Epist.* I. ix.), and seems to have used the word ἀοχλησία (Alex. *de Anim.* 150, 34, Bruns). Zeno, the founder of the Stoa, however, was influenced by the Megarian as well as by the Cynic philosophy.

On the other hand, Democritus described εὐθυμίη, the human happiness consisting in μετριότητι τέρψιος καὶ βίου ξυμμετρίῃ (*Frag.* 191, Diels), in the same way as apathy is described later. For apathy he is said to have used the term ἀταραξία, which appears again among later Sceptics. His doctrine, through the medium of Anaxarchus of Abdera (Diog. Laert. ix. 60), surnamed εὐδαιμονικός and celebrated especially on account of his ἀπάθεια, had an influence on Pyrrho, the founder of Scepticism, who taught ἀπάθεια probably even under this name (Cic. *Acad.* ii. 130; Plut. *de Prof. in Virt.* ii. p. 82 f.). His disciple Timon praises his constant cheerfulness (γαλήνη, *Frag.* 63, Diels) and his freedom from πάθη (*Frag.* 9); other passages mention his ἀδιαφορία and ἀταραξία (Diog. Laert. ix. 66, 68), which result from the withholding of judgment (ἐποχή) on all the events incident to human life: he who ventures no opinion about the worth of a thing may regard it as either good or evil, and so his tranquillity of mind cannot be disturbed thereby. It is true that Epicurus did not advocate the extermination of the emotions (πάθη), yet he occasionally depicts the imperturbable tranquillity of mind of the wise man in such colours that he approaches the Stoic standpoint.

Cf. the statement from the third epistle (*Epicurea*, ed. Usener, p. 62): τούτου γὰρ χάριν πάντα πράττομεν, ὅπως μήτε ἀλγῶμεν μήτε ταρβῶμεν. ὅταν δὲ ἅπαξ τοῦτο περὶ ἡμᾶς γένηται, λύεται πᾶς ὁ τῆς ψυχῆς χειμών; also *Frag.* 457: ἔρωτι φιλοσοφίας ἀληθινῆς πᾶσα ταραχώδης καὶ ἐπίπονος ἐπιθυμία ἐκλύεται; and the well-known statement (Cic. *Tusc.* ii. 17): 'In Phalaridis tauro si erit, dicet, "Quam suave est, quam hoc non curo."'

Such ideas are in accordance with the general feeling of the Hellenistic period, which was quite willing to recognize the happiness of the individual in a kind of *quietism*.

Entire freedom from the emotions was now demanded of the Stoic sage (*Frag.* 207, Arnim) by Zeno, who, however, made to the healthy human intellect the concession that even the sage, although unaware of the emotions themselves, is nevertheless conscious of a shadow of them (*Frag.* 215). This doctrine was more clearly expounded by his pupil Dionysius in his separate treatise περὶ ἀπαθείας (Diog. Laert. vii. 166), but more especially by Chrysippus (*e.g.* in περὶ δικαιοσύνης and περὶ ὁρμῆς), whose fragments on this subject are collected in Arnim, *Stoic. vet. Fragm.* iii. 443–455. The emotions belong to the irrational and immoderate (πλεονάζουσαι) class of impulses (ὁρμαί), which bring unrest into the mind of man. They arise from false judgments on the worth of things, or rather from the thoughtless assent (συγκατάθεσις) to such judgments (Dyroff, *Ethik der alten Stoa*, p. 152 ff.; Epict. iii. 19. 3: οὐδὲν ἄλλο ταραχῆς ἢ ἀκαταστασίας αἴτιόν ἐστιν ἢ τὸ δόγμα). The philosopher, as the physician of the soul, has to combat the passions, the chief of which are: desire, fear, pleasure, and grief,—pity is also included in them,—by demonstrating the falseness of the judgment and cultivating the virtues of moderation and courage. As virtue is perfected reason (λόγος), the irrational impulses are incompatible with it, and thus in the soul of the wise man there is left no trace of passion (*Frag.* 447); the ὁρμαί are completely blended with the λόγος; the wise man is ἀπαθής, and therein consists his happiness (Diog. Laert. vii. 117; Cic. *Tusc.* iv. 37).

It was inevitable that against this extreme doctrine lively opposition should arise. Plato had already deliberately opposed apathy (cf. *Philebus*, pp. 21 D, 60 E, 63 E: ἀλλ' ἃς γε ἡδονὰς ἀληθεῖς καὶ καθαρὰς εἶπες, σχεδὸν οἰκείας ἡμῖν νόμιζε, καὶ πρὸς ταύταις τὰς μεθ' ὑγιείας καὶ τοῦ σωφρονεῖν), and his disciples had, therefore, taken up their position almost on the standpoint of Aristotle and the Peripatetics, who strove after μεσότητες ἐν τοῖς πάθεσι (*Nicom. Eth.* ii. 1108a, 30; the later writers call it μετριοπάθεια), and could not approve of apathy. No more could Epicurus, whose ἡδονή was actually regarded by the Stoics as one of the chief passions (Stobæus, ii. 90. 16). Carneades summed up this contradiction in his successful attack upon the Stoic exaggerations. He started from the fact that man is not only soul, but also body; that, consequently, certain bodily impulses are inevitable, among which pleasure assumes the first place; since it cannot be an evil, apathy is impossible (Gell. xii. 5, 7). This opposition resulted in the yielding of the Middle Stoa (Schmekel, *Philos. d. mittl. Stoa*, p. 364); Panætius after the fashion of the Peripatetics perceives virtue in the avoidance of extremes, and allows the ὁρμαί as legitimate in themselves. For him bodily pleasure is something natural, and therefore not to be exterminated; grief, on the other hand, is contrary to human nature, and therefore human nature is justified in avoiding it. Posidonius laid stress on the contrast between body and soul, and held that only the soul, so far as it remains pure, can be ἀπαθής, but not the body; he admitted, besides, a παθητικὸν μέρος τῆς ψυχῆς (Plut. *de Virt. Mor.* 3, p. 411*d*; Galen. *de Hipp. et Plat. plac.* p. 408 M). He thus abandoned the old Stoic attitude on principle, although in some single statements he approached very near it (*e.g.* Cic. *Tusc.* ii. 61). The later philosophers are strongly influenced by this more moderate attitude. Epictetus is the only one who returns to the old rigorism; his wise man must again be ἀπαθής and ἀτάραχος, δίχα ὀρέξεως καὶ ἐκκλίσεως, and he fought expressly against μετριοπάθεια (iv. 1, 175; cf. Bonhöffer, *Ethik des Epiktet*, p. 46). Seneca also opposes it in one of his writings (*Epist.* 85), but otherwise he assumes Posidonius' point of view. This view occasionally persists in the later philosophy, and Neo-Platonism, with its withdrawal from this world and its mortification of the flesh, is decidedly in its favour. Thus Philo resolutely demands apathy (Zeller, v. 4, p. 449), and so also with Porphyry it appears as the highest stage of virtue, while metriopathy receives a lower place (*op. cit.* p. 717).

LITERATURE.—Dyroff, *Ethik der alten Stoa* (1897), p. 152; Schmekel, *Philos. d. mittl. Stoa* (1892), p. 364; Zeller, *Stoics, Epicureans, and Sceptics* (Eng. tr. 1870), pp. 243–254 and 290–292; Bonhöffer, *Ethik des Stoikers Epiktet* (1894), p. 46; Sidgwick, *History of Ethics*³ (1892), p. 73; Ueberweg, *Hist. of Philosophy* (Eng. tr. 1871), i. 198; Davidson, *The Stoic Creed* (1907), pp. 149, 189.

W. KROLL.

APHRODISIA (Ἀφροδίσια).—The general name of festivals in honour of Aphrodite. The cult of Aphrodite may be regarded as having been universal in one form or another in the Mediterranean lands. In all the great centres of Hellenic life it occupied an important place, prevailing from Naucratis in Egypt to Phanagoria in the Black Sea, and from the Troad to Italy and Sicily (see the long list, with the evidence, in Pauly-Wissowa, art. 'Aphrodite'). The Ægean islands were among its most famous centres, notably Cythera, Crete, and Cyprus. There is, however, no real ground for regarding the cult, in its later specialized form as the cult of a goddess of physical beauty,* as having been aboriginal in Greek lands. Probably Aphrodite was originally an Oriental nature-divinity, and she retained many Oriental traits in her local cult as a specialized divinity in Greece.† The more refined cult of the goddess as the patroness of married life is probably a genuinely Hellenic development, for this aspect of her is either altogether lacking or at least is not prominent in its Eastern forms. Contrary to a very general but erroneous conception, originating in Plato's well-known distinction between Ourania Aphrodite who personifies the intellectual love of the soul, and Aphrodite Pandemos who personifies the sensual love of the body (Plat. *Sympos.* 180 D), it is precisely this title of Οὐρανία, 'Heavenly,' that is the clearest sign of her Eastern origin; the Platonic distinction was not recognized in the State religion, and the moral and spiritual meaning of the title is of late growth (Farnell, *op. cit.* 629 ff., 659 ff.). In the same way, that aspect of Aphrodite under which she was worshipped at Athens and elsewhere as Pandemos, 'Guardian of the body politic,' was not an independent Hellenic development, but a survival and development of an Oriental conception (Farnell, p. 663).

With regard to the nature of the cult, ethically considered, it is to be observed that much of the modern conception is based upon a radically false notion, and the unguarded application to Hellenic practice of ill-understood Oriental phenomena.

* As a 'departmental goddess, having for her sphere one human passion' (J. E. Harrison, *Prolegomena to the Study of Greek Religion*, p. 309) she is depicted in the Homeric Hymn.

† For an examination of this question of origin, consult Farnell's *Cults of the Greek States*, Oxford, 1896, ii. 619 ff.

Until the decline of Greek civilization, the cult of Aphrodite, so far as we know it from our literary or monumental sources, was indistinguishable in point of purity and austerity from that of Zeus or Athene, and was in this respect, in fact, on a higher plane than that of Artemis. Rules of chastity, for example, were in some cases imposed upon her priestesses (Paus. ii. 10. 4). It was at Corinth alone in Greece, and there in connexion with the worship of the 'Heavenly' Aphrodite, that impure practices were found established as part and parcel of the ritual of worship. The fact is that a careful distinction must be drawn between Greek religion and ritual, which is upon the whole pure, and the mythological stories, which are often the reverse, and are, moreover, conveyed to us largely through the impure medium of degenerate poetry. Degeneracy did indeed exhibit itself in the cultus, as in other domains of Greek life and practice—a symptom of the loosening of the moral bonds in the Hellenistic period,—and later in the erection of altars and temples, and the establishment of festivals under the name of Aphrodite to the mistresses of the successors of Alexander and others (Athenæus, 253, 595).

Probably the festival of Paphos was the most celebrated of those held in honour of the goddess; and there also in all probability many features that had no parallel in Greece, save perhaps at Corinth, were to be seen. Great crowds assembled at the temple from all parts (Strabo, 683: καὶ πανηγυρίζουσι διὰ τῆς ὁδοῦ ταύτης κατ' ἔτος ἐπὶ τὴν Παλαίπαφον ἄνδρες ὁμοῦ γυναιξὶν συνιόντες καὶ ἐκ τῶν ἄλλων πόλεων). The title Ἀγήτωρ borne by the high priest at Paphos would probably indicate his conduct of the vast procession. Sacrifices of blood were not offered, though victims seem to have been slain for purposes of divination: or there may have been two altars, one for incense, the other for sacrifice (cf. Tac. *Hist.* ii. 3: 'Hostiæ, ut quisque vovit, sed mares deliguntur: certissima fides hædorum fibris. Sanguinem aræ obfundere vetitum: precibus et igne puro altaria adolentur'). A ritual bath and mimic dance probably formed part of certain mysteries which were celebrated (Harrison, *op. cit.* pp. 283, 312; cf. Farnell, *op. cit.* p. 651: 'in Cyprus, in some religious ceremony, some scenic representation of the Adonia perhaps, the image of the dead goddess was exposed, and then after due performance of certain rites she was supposed to be restored to life'). Those who desired to be initiated ἐν τῇ τέχνῃ μοιχικῇ received on entering the temple a *phallus* and a lump of salt, and gave a piece of money to the temple treasury.*

Most Oriental in character of all the Greek cities was Corinth. Euripides celebrates Acrocorinthos as the holy hill of Aphrodite (*Frg.* in Strabo, 379: ἥκω περίκλυστον προλιποῦσ' Ἀκροκόρινθον, ἱερὸν ὄχθον, πόλιν Ἀφροδίτας; cf. Alciphr. iii. 60). The most un-Hellenic of the elements of the Aphrodite cult was the practice of religious prostitution (Strabo, 378), alluded to by Pindar when he celebrates the 'hospitable young women, the ministrants of Persuasion in rich Corinth, whose thoughts often flit towards Ourania Aphrodite' (Pind. *Frg.* 87, ed. Boeckh). At Corinth, apparently alone in Greece, these *hetæræ* took part in the State ritual; for whenever public prayers were addressed to Aphrodite on matters of moment, as large a number as possible of the *hetæræ* were taken to aid in the ceremony; and individuals privately often vowed to consecrate a certain number of these women to the goddess (such would be in general bought slaves of Greek or foreign origin). We hear of them as putting up public petitions on behalf of the Greek cause in the Persian Wars (Athen. 573 C). Naturally, therefore, the *hetæræ* took a conspicuous part in the festivals of Aphrodite, one day being given up to them, and another to the respectable women. Doubtless much of Eastern licence was seen on these festival days at Corinth; the city was notoriously dangerous in this respect to visitors (cf. Strabo, 378: οὐ παντὸς ἀνδρὸς ἐς Κόρινθόν ἐσθ' ὁ πλοῦς).

At Argos the chief festival of Aphrodite was called Hysteria (ὑστήρια), because swine were sacrificed to her—probably an indication of the cult of Aphrodite in conjunction with Adonis, for ordinarily the Greeks, as we learn from Aristophanes (*Ach.* 793), did not sacrifice swine to Aphrodite. Probably, wherever the pig was sacrificed to Aphrodite, it was a mystery, the pig representing Adonis himself (see Frazer's note in Paus. ii. 10. 5; Farnell, *op. cit.* p. 756). Connected with the same form of the cultus was the strange hermaphroditic festival of the goddess at Argos, which bore the special name of the Feast of Wantonness (ὑβριστικά), at which women dressed as men, and men as women, the men even wearing veils (Plut. *de Virt. Mul.* 245 E). The festival was popularly explained as commemorative of the brave defence of Argos by the poetess Telesilla in 510 B.C.; but such interchange of garments as a religious rite is not uncommon elsewhere (cf. Macrob. *Sat.* iii. 8; and references in Farnell, p. 755), so that probably the story of Telesilla is merely ætiological (see Frazer on Paus. ii. 20. 8; Nilsson, *Griechische Feste*, p. 371).

In Ægina the festival of Aphrodite seems to have been combined with one to Poseidon (Plut. *Quæst. Gr.* 44), the details suggesting that the cult was one of Aphrodite as a divinity of death (about which see Farnell, *op. cit.* p. 652). In Thessaly, women alone appear to have taken part in the festival; it was at one such celebration that the courtezan Lais was murdered (schol. in Aristoph. *Plut.* 179: αἱ Θετταλαὶ γυναῖκες ἐφόνευσαν αὐτὴν ξυλίναις χελώναις τυπτοῦσαι ἐν τῷ ἱερῷ τῆς Ἀφροδίτης, πανηγύρεως οὔσης, ἐν ᾗ ἄνδρες οὐ παρεγίνοντο). In Zacynthos, athletic contests, especially racing, were part of the festival (Dion. Hal. *Ant. Rom.* i. 50). Some details connected with the festival of Aphrodite as Pandemos are furnished by an inscription found at Athens, in which the Senate recommends to the Assembly that the police officials (ἀστυνόμοι) on the occasion of the public procession (πομπή) in honour of the goddess, prepare for the cleansing of the temple a dove, cleanse and whitewash the altars, wash the images, etc. (Dittenberger, *Sylloge*², 556=*BCH*, 1889, p. 162; Nilsson, p. 374).

Finally should be noticed a usage of the word Ἀφροδίσια in a more general sense of 'festival gathering,' without religious significance. It is so found in Xen. *Hell.* v. 4. 4: ὡς Ἀφροδίσια ἄγουσιν ἐπ' ἐξόδῳ τῆς ἀρχῆς (of the Polemarchs of Thebes. Cf. Plut. *Cim. and Luc. comp.* 1: ἤδη λοιπὸν Ἀφροδίσια τῶν πολέμων καὶ στρατηγιῶν ἄγοντα παίζειν; Athen. 4, p. 128 B, Ἀντιγόνου τοῦ βασιλέως δεῖπνον Ἀφροδίσια ἐπιτελοῦντος. Such celebrations might naturally be annual; cf. Alciph. *Ep.* 2. 1, τὰ Ἀφροδίσια ποιῶ ταῦτα κατ' ἔτος).

W. J. Woodhouse.

APHRODITE.—See preceding art. and Greek Religion.

APOCALYPTIC LITERATURE, APOCRYPHA.—See Bible.

* Clem. Alex. *Protr.* 14: ἐν ταῖς τελεταῖς ταύτης τῆς πελαγίας ἡδονῆς τεκμήριον τῆς γονῆς ἁλῶν χόνδρος καὶ φαλλὸς τοῖς μυουμένοις τὴν τέχνην τὴν μοιχικὴν ἐπιδίδοται· νόμισμα δὲ εἰσφέρουσιν αὐτῇ οἱ μυούμενοι, ὡς ἑταίρᾳ ἐρασταί; Arnob. *adv. Gent.* 5. 169; Justin, xviii. 5. 4: 'mos erat Cypriis virgines ante nuptias statutis diebus dotalem pecuniam quæsituras in quæstum ad litus maris mittere, pro reliqua pudicitia libamenta Veneri soluturas.' For this sacred prostitution, an Oriental practice, see Herod. i. 199, speaking of the cult of the Babylonian Mylitta (=Ištar, Astarte), cf. Strabo, 532; Ramsay, *Cities and Bishoprics of Phrygia*, Oxford, 1895, i. 94; J. G. Frazer, *Adonis, Attis, Osiris*, Lond. 1906, p. 21. For similar institution in connexion with the Cappadocian goddess Ma, cf. Strabo, 535. See also Nilsson, *Griech. Feste*, p. 365 ff.

APOLLINARISM.—Apollinaris, the younger, of Laodicea († *c.* 390), was the founder of a heresy which forms the connecting link between Arianism in the 4th and Nestorianism and Monophysitism in the 5th century.

1. Life of Apollinaris.—Of the events of his life not very much is known. His father, who was also named Apollinaris, was a grammarian from Alexandria who came to Berytus (*Beirut*) and then went on to Laodicea (*Ladikiye*) in Syria. Here he married and had a son, Apollinaris the younger, the future heretic (Socrates, *HE* ii. 46). Socrates says that the father was 'joined in the closest bond of friendship' with a Sophist named Epiphanius, and that Theodotus, the Bishop of Laodicea, forbade him this acquaintance, as being dangerous to his faith. Eventually Theodotus, or perhaps his successor George, excommunicated Apollinaris, together with his son, either because they would not give up their intimacy with Epiphanius, or because they kept the faith of Nicæa and Athanasius, whereas the bishop was a semi-Arian (*ib.*).

Apollinaris the father, who had been ordained presbyter at Laodicea, tried to supply his fellow-Christians with a substitute for the Greek classics which Julian had forbidden them to teach. He appears to have arranged nearly the whole Bible in the form of poems of various metres. 'He expounded the books of Moses in heroic verse, and edited the other historical books of the Old Testament, partly as elegiac poems, partly as tragedies with different metres' (Socr. iii. 16). The son, having learnt this art from his father, wrote out the Gospels as Platonic dialogues (*ib.*). But there is some confusion between the father and son about these paraphrases of the Bible. Sozomen attributes them all to the son (Sozomen, *HE* v. 18).

Apollinaris the younger must have been born not very long after the year 300. Epiphanius speaks of him in 376 as a 'venerable old man' (*Hær.* III. ii. 2), and if he was excommunicated together with his father by Theodotus, he must have been more than a child before that bishop died (335). Socrates says that he was ordained Reader (ἀναγνώστης) and became a teacher of rhetoric (*HE* ii. 46). All his contemporaries speak of his great learning. After his separation from the Orthodox Fathers, they still write of him with much more respect than they usually give to heretics, and even with a certain affection. He was 'learned in science' (Socr. iii. 16); 'skilled in all knowledge and learning, a man of manifold erudition and accomplishments' (Soz. v. 18). Epiphanius says that he himself, as well as St. Athanasius and 'all Catholics,' loved the 'illustrious and venerable old man, Apollinaris of Laodicea,' and that when they first heard of his heresy they could not believe that so great a man had fallen into such an error (*Hær.* III. ii. 2).

In this first period, before he had proclaimed his heresy, while he was still known only as a scholar, a poet, and a zealous defender of the faith of Nicæa, he came into friendly relations with a number of Fathers. In 346, when St. Athanasius was on his way back to Alexandria after one of his numerous exiles, he passed through Laodicea in Syria, and there became 'a companion and particular friend' of Apollinaris (Soz. *HE* vi. 25). St. Jerome had learnt from Apollinaris as from so many other teachers, and he says that he had never embraced his heretical doctrines (*Ep.* lxxxiv. 3). To Epiphanius he is 'always most dear' (*Hær.* III. ii. 2). St. Basil says that he had once corresponded freely with him (*Ep.* cxxxi.); years afterwards, when he had broken off all relations with the heretic, he still writes with regard of the man 'whom we had expected always to find our ally in the defence of truth' (*Ep.* cclxv.), and he still doubts whether all the harm that is told of his old friend can be true (*Ep.* ccxxiii. 5). Apollinaris at first distinguished himself as a defender of the Nicene creed against Arians and semi-Arians. It was possibly for this cause that he had been excommunicated by his bishop. And then, according to Sozomen, he, having asked in vain to be received back into communion, 'being conquered by his grief, began to disturb the Church with his new doctrine' (*HE* vi. 25). It seems true that he first conceived his theory as a defence of Homoousianism.

We hear of him next as bishop, apparently of Laodicea. It is true that neither St. Basil, Gregory of Nazianzus, Epiphanius, Socrates, nor Sozomen mentions him as a bishop, and that Leontius of Byzantium speaks of him only as 'Apollinaris the presbyter' (*de Sectis*, Act. iv., *PG* lxxxvi. 1217). And Photius doubted whether he had been bishop (in *ep. Philost.* viii. 15). On the other hand, St. Athanasius speaks of certain monks who had been sent to Alexandria by 'Apollinaris the bishop' (*Tom. ad Antioch.* ix.), Philostorgius relates the fact as having been 'told by some people' (*HE* viii. 14), Theodoret says that he generally lived at Laodicea (*HE* v. 4), and St. Jerome, who had known him well, calls him 'Bishop of Laodicea in Syria' (*de Vir. Ill.* 104). But Pelagius had succeeded George as bishop of the same city about the year 363 (Lequien, *Or. Christ.* ii. 794), so it seems that Apollinaris had been set up as Homoousian bishop in opposition to the semi-Arian line. It must have been about 360 that he began to be commonly known as the teacher of a new doctrine. The Synod of Alexandria in 362 seems to know and reject his ideas. It 'confessed that the Saviour did not assume an inanimate or insensible body. . . . Not only the body but also the soul receives salvation from the Word' (Athan. *Tom. ad Ant.* 7). But it does not mention his name. By the year 370 all the Orthodox Fathers speak of him as a heretic. St. Basil says, 'We have no communion with Apollinaris' (*Ep.* cxxxi. 2, etc.). He denounces him to 'the Westerns' (*Ep.* cclxiii. 4), and rejoices later that they have condemned him (*Ep.* cclxv. 2). This condemnation is that of the Roman Synod in 374 (Mansi, iii. 479). Apollinaris is not mentioned in any of its ten canons, but they are plainly drawn up as condemnations of his theory. The Synod of Antioch, held in 378 under Meletius, anathematizes those who 'say that the Word of God dwelled in human flesh in the place of a reasonable and intelligent soul' (Mansi, iii. 486). The first canon of the Synod of Constantinople in 381 condemns a number of heretics, of whom the last are the 'Apollinarists'; its seventh canon ordains that the Apollinarists shall be received back into communion if they retract their heresy and present a written declaration (λίβελλος) of the true faith (Mansi, iii. 558–563).

As soon as he had formulated his particular doctrine and had begun to be opposed by other bishops, Apollinaris gathered his following into a definitely organized sect. At Antioch he set up a certain Vitalis as anti-bishop, 'a man distinguished by his honourable life and educated in the teaching of the Apostles, but corrupted by this poison' (Theodoret, *HE* v. 4). Sozomen says that this Vitalis had joined Apollinaris because of a quarrel with Flavian of Antioch (*HE* vi. 25). And there were other Apollinarist bishops throughout Syria. St. Basil writes ironically of this heretical hierarchy: 'a great mystery of godliness, bishops bearing empty titles without either clergy or people' (*Ep.* cclxv. 2).

Meanwhile St. Athanasius (or the other author of the two books against Apollinaris that bear his name) and St. Gregory of Nyssa had written their treatises against the heresy (see below). Apollinaris died, leaving behind him an organized Apollinarist Church, about the year 390 (Jerome, *de Vir. Ill.* 104).

2. The Apollinarist heresy.—Apollinaris began as a zealous defender of Homoousianism against the Arians. Sooner or later the question was bound to arise: How could the Logos be joined to a human nature? It was around this question that the later Nestorian and Monophysite disputes turned. Apollinaris' solution, in which his heresy consisted, was an attempt to save the unity of Christ's Person at the expense of His human nature. In this way he was a sort of forerunner of Eutyches. He is certain that God Himself became man in Christ. He is also certain that the whole Divine nature cannot be joined to the whole nature of a man. He maintains this by the same arguments as were afterwards used by the Monophysites. Two perfect natures always remain two separate persons; 'two perfect beings cannot become one.' This axiom, quoted by Athanasius as one of his 'sophisms' (*contra Apoll.* i. 2), was the starting-point of his system. He illustrates it by various examples. We may not adore a man, we must adore God. So it would follow that Christ must be both adored and not adored. Moreover, a perfect man is necessarily sinful, 'where there is a perfect man, there is sin' (*ib.*); but Christ could not become sinful. And He would be neither really God nor really man, but a man-god (ἀνθρωπόθεος), a monstrous and impossible hybrid of two incompatible species, like the Minotaur, the centaurs, dragons, and other mythological absurdities (Greg. Nyss. *Antir.* 49). He goes on to argue that he would certainly not be a man, for all men consist essentially of three parts, body, soul, and spirit, whereas He would have four parts, adding to these His Divinity. In short, 'a person, being one, cannot be combined of two' (*ib.*). He finds the solution of the difficulty in the application of a general principle of philosophy. The Neo-Platonic school taught that human nature is the composition of these three elements—a *body*, a *soul* that actuates and *informs* the body (to use the later mediæval term), thus making us living beings, and the *mind*, or *spirit*, that makes us reasonable beings, which spirit is the special characteristic of man.

Apollinaris thinks that the doctrine of the three elements of man, body, soul, and spirit (σῶμα, ψυχή, πνεῦμα or νοῦς), is confirmed by Scripture. He quotes the text: 'Bless the Lord, O ye spirits and souls of the just' (Dn 3^{86} [=Three ^{64}]; cf. Greg. Nyss. *Antir.* 46). We are told to serve God in spirit and to adore Him in spirit and truth (Ro 1^{9}; *Antir.* 49); St. Paul prays that the Thessalonians may be sanctified in spirit, soul, and body (1 Th 5^{23}); and he distinguishes the carnal (ψυχικός) from the spiritual (πνευματικός) man (1 Co $2^{13.\,14}$, cf. 3^{1} $15^{45f.}$;

Antir. 49). Of these three elements the body and the soul make up the 'natural' (φυσικός) being (the machine, Plato would have said), which is ruled and guided by the mind.

But the guiding principle in man is changeable, fallible, sinful. It cannot be so in Christ. Therefore in Christ the Divinity, the Logos, takes the place of a human mind. He is a natural man (*i.e.* body and soul) guided and ruled by the Logos. He too, like us, consists of three parts only, and He is therefore really a man and not an impossible being of four parts. Only one part, the most important, is not human but Divine. That is at any rate the eventual and fully developed form of Apollinarism. It has been suggested (Lietzmann), and some answers of his opponents seem to suppose, that its author did not at first trouble about a subtle distinction between soul and spirit, but simply said that the Logos instead of a human soul was joined to Christ's body. However, the stress of controversy soon made him adopt the Neo-Platonic theory as the basis of his theology, and he and his school then made so much of it that all through the Middle Ages the psychology of the three elements was associated with one name only, that of Apollinaris. He thinks that he has found texts to prove his explanation of the hypostatic union by the absence of a human soul, or, later, of a spirit in Christ. St. Paul, for instance, says that the first Adam was made a living soul, the second a life-giving (therefore Divine, not human) spirit; the first was carnal (ψυχικός), the second spiritual (πνευματικός, 1 Co 15[45-49]; *Antir.* 11–12). The Incarnation is described as the assumption by the Logos, not of a whole man but of a physical body only. It is the 'mystery that appeared in the flesh' (1 Ti 3[16]; *Antir.* 2), the Word was made, not man, but flesh (Jn 1[14]; *Antir.* 16, etc.), Christ assumed the *form* of a servant (*i.e.* the body), and was found in the (outward) *habit* of a man (Ph 2[7f.]; *Antir.* 20, 21).

So in this way the Logos and the man Jesus are really one being. Christ was not two separate persons, but Divinity and manhood joined inseparably in one person. And we adore this person without making distinctions, because in Him even the human nature is actuated, and so made Divine, by the Logos that guides it.

The contemporary orthodox Fathers who reject this theory are not much concerned about the truth or falsehood of the statement that human nature consists of three elements. That question was raised again much later by the mediæval schoolmen when 'Apollinarist' became a favourite name of abuse given by Thomists to the Scotists who denied that the reasonable soul is the form (*forma substantialis*) of the body. But the first opponents of Apollinarism are offended chiefly by the assertion that Christ lacked an element of complete human nature. They quote against it the texts in which He is said to be like us in everything except only sin (He 4[15]), to be really and completely man (Jn 8[40]; *Antir.* 45), and to have not only a soul but also a spirit (Lk 23[46]; *Antir.* 17, Jn 11[33]; Athan. *contra Apoll.* i. 15, Jn 19[30], ii. 16). They also undertake to refute Apollinaris' arguments. If the quotation 1 Co 15[45] proved anything in this question, it would follow that Adam had no spirit at all (*Antir.* 12), and that the word 'flesh' in Jn 1[14], as elsewhere, stands for the whole human nature (*Antir.* 27); and they insist on the conclusion which Apollinaris himself would not admit, namely, that if the Logos had become one of the elements of Christ's human nature, the Logos too would have suffered and died (*Antir.* 30, etc.).

3. The Apollinarist sect.—In spite of the opposition of a long list of Fathers (Athanasius, Basil, the two Gregorys, and many others), Apollinarism outlived its author for many years. He had set up a hierarchy all over Syria, and his sect existed and carried on his teaching till it seems to have been gradually absorbed by the far more important Monophysite movement. Vitalis was Apollinarist Bishop of Antioch. We hear of one Timothy of Beirut, who wrote a history of the Church, and who 'had no other object in so great a work but to commend Apollinaris, inasmuch as from him and to him an endless number of letters were written and written back' (Leontius Byz. *c. Nestor. et Eutych.* iii. 40, *PG* lxxxvi., who proceeds to point out that a man's greatness is not to be measured by the size of his correspondence). A certain Valentinus wrote a defence of Apollinarism, called 'Against those who accuse us of saying that the body is of the same substance as God' (*adv. Fraudes Apollinaristarum*, among the works of Leontius Byz. *PG* LXXXVI. ii. 1947–1976; some passages from both Timothy and Valentinus are quoted in this treatise). It seems that the unknown interpolator of St. Ignatius' letters (a Syrian in the beginning of the 5th cent.) was an Apollinarist. He twice (*Philipp.* v. 2 and *Philad.* vi. 6) expressly denies that Christ had a human mind.

Although the movement gradually disappears as its place is taken by Syrian Monophysitism, one still occasionally hears of Apollinarism in the ever-growing list of heresies; and as late as 691 the *Quinisextum* Synod in its first canon does not forget to condemn 'Apollinaris, leader of wickedness, who impiously declared that the Lord did not assume a body endowed with both soul and mind' (Mansi, *Collectio*, 1759–1798, xi. 936).

4. Writings of Apollinaris.—There is the most complete agreement among his contemporaries that Apollinaris was a learned as well as a very prolific writer. St. Jerome says that he had written 'countless volumes about Holy Scripture,' and that his thirty books against Porphyrius were greatly esteemed (*de Vir. Ill.* 104). Philostorgius tells us that his arguments against Porphyrius were superior to those of Eusebius (*HE* viii. 14). St. Basil says that 'as he had great facility in writing on any subject, he filled the world with his books' (*Ep.* ccliii. 4). Sozomen gives a long list of his poems, and mentions a work 'Concerning Truth' (Ὑπὲρ ἀληθείας), an apology against Julian and the Greek philosophers, in which 'he shewed their errors concerning God without using texts from Scripture' (*HE* v. 18). We hear also of a refutation of Eunomius (*de Vir. Ill.* 120; Philost. *HE* viii. 12) and of a book against Marcellus of Ancyra (*de Vir. Ill.* 86). Epiphanius, too, writes with great appreciation of his learning and talents (*Hær.* III. ii. 24).

Of all these works scarcely anything is left. Of the poetic versions of the Bible written either by him or by his father, one volume remains, the *Paraphrase of the Psalms* (*PG* xxxiii. 1313–1538; it includes the 151st Psalm). It cannot be described as a success. A version of the OT in hexameters, into which the author has crowded every possible reminiscence, allusion, and idiom from the pagan classics, must obviously lose all the feeling and quality of the Bible without becoming more than a very feeble imitation of the real classics. So it is not wonderful that after Julian's death, as soon as Christians were allowed to return to the real thing, Apollinaris' substitutes were soon forgotten. Socrates says that in his time these Biblical poems had 'disappeared as completely as if they had never been written' (*HE* iii. 16).

There is, however, a constant tradition that after the death of Apollinaris his followers published their master's works under the names of orthodox Fathers. Leontius of Byzantium (or whoever the real author of the treatise 'Against the Frauds of the Apollinarists' was) begins his work by saying: 'Some of the followers of Apollinaris, or Eutyches, or Dioscor, in order to confirm their heresy, have ascribed (ἐπέγραψεν) certain works of Apollinaris to Gregory Thaumaturgus, or Athanasius, or Julius, in order to deceive the simple'; and the whole of this little work is a compilation of texts which the author thinks to be cases in point. Its full title is, 'Against those who offer us certain works of Apollinaris, having falsely inscribed them with the names of holy Fathers.'

So one of the chief problems concerning Apollinaris has always been the discovery of any of his writings which may be hidden under other names. In the case of some such works the matter may be said to be now definitely settled. Leontius (*l.c.*) had already declared that the little treatise called *The Partial Faith* (ἡ κατὰ μέρος πίστις) among the works of Gregory Thaumaturgus (the text is published by Dräseke and Lietzmann; see below) was written by Apollinaris; this is now admitted by every one. Other works also commonly acknowledged to be by him are: pseudo-Athanasius, *Of the Incarnation of the Word of God* (Περὶ τῆς σαρκώσεως τοῦ θεοῦ λόγου, Dräseke, pp. 341–343); pseudo-Julius of Rome's *Letters to Dionysius of Alexandria* (*ib.* 348–351), and, very probably at least, the tract, *Of the union in Christ of the body to the Divinity* (Περὶ τῆς ἐν Χριστῷ ἑνότητος τοῦ σώματος πρὸς τὴν θεότητα, *ib.* 343–347), also under the name of Julius. Lastly, there are fragments of Apollinaris' writings in various Greek Catenæ (cf. Krumbacher, *Byzant. Litteratur*, Munich, 1897, pp. 206, 211) and in the quotations from him made by his adversaries (Athanasius, Gregory Naz. and Gregory Nyss.). Dräseke (*Apoll. v. Laod.*) proposes to attribute to him a large number of other writings, all pseudo-Justin, including the *Cohortatio ad gentes*, which he thinks to be Apollinaris' book 'Concerning Truth'; the third and fourth books of St. Basil *against Eunomius* (which would then be his work against Eunomius mentioned by Jerome and Philostorgius); the first three dialogues of Theodoret of Cyrrhus *on the Trinity*; some sermons of Gregory Thaumaturgus; pseudo-Athanasius' *Dialogues on the Holy Trinity*; as well as almost any more or less contemporary anonymous works, including even the poem *Christ Suffering* (Χριστὸς πάσχων, cf. *JPTh*, 1884, pp. 657–704), which is really a mystery play of the 11th or 12th cent. (Krumbacher, *Byzant. Litt.* pp. 746–749). These identifications are now generally considered to have been premature and mistaken (Bardenhewer, *Patrologie*, 1894, pp. 224–225; Krüger in *PRE*³, art. 'Apoll. v. Laod.'; Harnack, *Lehrb. der Dogmengesch.*, 1895, pp. 309–321). Lietzmann (*Apoll. Laod.*) suggests a more reasonable list.

LITERATURE.—The first sources for a knowledge of Apollinaris' life and ideas are, after the fragments of his own works, those of his earliest opponents. These are: **Athanasius** (but there is some doubt about the authorship), *Two books concerning the Incarnation of our Lord Jesus Christ against Apollinaris* (Περὶ σαρκώσεως τοῦ κυρίου ἡμῶν Ἰησοῦ Χριστοῦ κατὰ Ἀπολλιναρίου, *PG* xxvi. 1091–1165); **Gregory of Nyssa**, *A Denier of the things said by Apollinaris* (Ἀντιρρητικὸς πρὸς τὰ τοῦ Ἀπολλιναρίου, *PG* xlv. 1123–1269) and his *Letter to Theophilus of Alexandria* (*ib.* 1269–1277). **Theodore of Mopsuestia** wrote a work against Apollinaris, of which fragments remain (*PG* lx. 993–1004). All these contain quotations from his own works. **Gregory of Nazianzus** speaks of him and of his heresy in several letters (ci. and cii., *to Cledonius*, *PG* xxxvii. 176–201, and ccii., *to Nectarius of Constantinople*, *ib.* 329–333). **St. Basil's** letters (*PG* xxxii.) also contain many references, and **Leontius of Byzantium** in the beginning of the 7th cent. (or another writer of that time; the authorship is doubtful) wrote the treatise, *Against the Frauds of the Apollinarists* (*PG* lxxxvi. 1947–1976).

MODERN LITERATURE: **C. P. Caspari**, *Alte und neue Quellen*, etc. (Christiania, 1879, pp. 65–146); **A. Ludwich**, *Apollinarii metaphrasis psalmorum*, 1–111 (Königsberg, 1880); **J. Dräseke**, *Apollinarios von Laodicea, sein Leben und seine Schriften*, Appendix: *Apollinarii Laod. quæ supersunt dogmatica* (Leipzig, 1892, in Gebhardt and Harnack's *Texte u. Untersuchungen*); 'Des Apoll. v. Laod. Schrift wider Eunomios' (*Ztschr. für Kirchengesch.*, 1889, 22–61); 'Apoll. v. Laod.: Dialoge über die h. Dreieinigkeit' (*SK*, 1890, 137–171); **G. Voisin**, *L'Apollinarisme* (Louvain, 1901); **H. Lietzmann**, 'Apollinaris von Laodicea und seine Schule,' *TU* i. (Tübingen, 1904, part ii. is not yet [1908] published); **J. F. Bethune-Baker**, *Introd. to Early Hist. of Christ. Doctrine* (London, 1903), p. 239 ff.

ADRIAN FORTESCUE.

APOLLO.—See next art. and GREEK RELIGION.

APOLLONIA (Ἀπολλώνια).—In the case of Aphrodite it was only by rare exception that her festivals bore a special name (see art. APHRODISIA), but festivals in honour of Apollo were, as a rule, known by special appellations. 'Apollonia,' as the actual title of such festivals, seems, in fact, to be confined to the following instances:—(1) At Delos, where the inscriptions speak of τὰ Δήλια καὶ Ἀπολλώνια, and often Ἀπολλώνια alone.* This was probably a double name for a complex festival, the famous Delian festival spoken of by Thucydides, iii. 104 (see Farnell, *Cults*, iv. 290). (2) At Myndus (Dittenberger, *Sylloge Inscriptionum græcarum*², 677). (3) At Miletus (*ib.* 627). (4) At Epidaurus (*ib.* 690). (5) At Hierapolis in Asia Minor (Gr. Inscr. in Brit. Mus. 615; see Nilsson, *Griechische Feste*, p. 179 n.). The use of the word Ἀπολλώνια by Dio Cass. of the festival of Apollo in Rome does not fall to be considered here.†

Apart from the above examples, festivals in honour of Apollo bore special names, all of which seem to have had originally no connexion with him, but to have reference to primitive, and perhaps to some extent pre-Hellenic, usages which only later were brought into relation with Apollo, who came into Hellas with the Hellenic tribes from the North (cf. J. E. Harrison, *Proleg. to Gr. Religion*, p. 30; Farnell, *op. cit.* 99 ff.). The cult and ritual of Apollo is throughout a blend of primitive and advanced ideas and practice; 'being certainly the brightest creation of polytheism, he is also the most complex; so many aspects of the people's life and progress being reflected in his cult . . . and in reviewing his cults one is surveying the career of a people in its transition from the lower barbarism into the highest social and intellectual life' (Farnell, *op. cit.* 98). It is not intended here to go into the details of the various festivals of Apollo, but to point out the features of significance.

Festivals in honour of Apollo belonged to the spring, summer, or autumn season; none is known to have fallen actually in the winter season. Certain days of the month were sacred to him—the first, seventh, fourteenth, and twentieth; especially sacred was the seventh, which was regarded as his birthday, and on that date most of his great festivals began.‡ The Epiphany, or the day of Apollo's coming, was celebrated by certain States, usually in the spring, or early summer, *e.g.* in the *Daphnephoria*, a spring-festival in Bœotia (Paus. ix. 10. 4, with Frazer's note) celebrated every eighth year, or, as the Greeks expressed it,

* *BCH*, 1879, p. 379: Λαοδάμειαν κανηφορήσασαν Δήλια καὶ Ἀπολλώνια Ἀπόλλωνι Ἀρτέμιδι Λητοῖ (date, 2nd cent. B.C.); *ib.* 1883, pp. 105–121, lists of οἱ χορηγοῦντες εἰς Ἀπολλώνια from 286 to 171 B.C. Dittenb. *Syll.*² 209: ἀναγορεῦσαι τὸν ἱεροκήρυκα ἐν τῷ θεάτρῳ τοῖς Ἀπολλωνίοις—to which formula the inscr. *BCH*, 1878, p. 332, adds the words: ὅταν οἱ χοροὶ τῶν παίδων ἀγωνίζωνται.

† Dio Cass. xlvii. 18: καὶ συνέβαινε γὰρ ἐν τῇ αὐτῇ ἡμέρᾳ καὶ τὰ Ἀπολλώνεια γίγνεσθαι; *ib.* xlviii. 33: ἐν τῇ τῶν Ἀπολλωνείων ἱπποδρομίᾳ.

‡ Aesch. *Sept.* 800: τὰς δ' ἑβδόμας ὁ σεμνὸς Ἑβδομαγέτης | Ἄναξ Ἀπόλλων εἵλετ'. Hesiod, *Op.* 770: πρῶτον ἕνη τετράς τε καὶ ἑβδόμη, ἱερὸν ἦμαρ, | τῇ γὰρ Ἀπόλλωνα χρυσάορα γείνατο Λητώ. Cf. Herod. vi. 57 (at Sparta). At Delphi, the 7th of Busios, his birthday. At Delos and Athens, the 7th of Thargelion. At Mykonos, a sacrifice on the 7th of Hekatombaion. Attic Pyanopsia on the 7th of Pyanepsion. Seven a sacred number in connexion with a festival of Apollo at Sicyon (Paus. ii. 7. 7). 'No satisfactory explanation, astronomical or other, has been suggested for these facts' (Farnell, *op. cit.* 259).

every ninth year. At Delphi there was a feast on his birthday on the 7th of Busios, the first spring-month, and this seems to have been identical with the *Theophania* (Herod. i. 51; Plut. *Quæst. Græc.* 9, p. 292 F; *BCH*, 1895, p. 11).

The more purely agrarian festivals may be distinguished from those in which the artistic character is more prominent. The former are festivals of first-fruits, or harvest-festivals, presenting many analogies to the peasant festivals of other lands. Examples of this type are the *Karneia* of Laconia, falling on the 7th of the month Karneios =Attic Metageitnion (Aug.), and the *Hyakinthia* celebrated in May–June at Sparta (Paus. iii. 19. 3; Wide, *Lakonische Kulte* [Leipzig, 1893], 289 ff.; Xen. *Hell.* iv. 5. 11).* Above all, the *Thargelia* of Athens, falling in the latter end of May, is a harvest-festival, for at that date in Greece the first cereals and fruits are ripe.† The *Thargelia* is a combination of a primitive harvest-festival with a rite of purification (the curious ceremony of the Pharmakos) which may have belonged originally to the Earth-goddesses and was afterwards appropriated to Apollo. The Attic *Pyanopsia* or *Pyanepsia*, the only recorded Apolline festival that fell in late autumn, was also an agrarian festival —a thanksgiving service for the later cereals and fruits (Farnell, *op. cit.* 286).

The festivals held at Delos belong to a higher order, being closely connected with art and poetry, although here also the agrarian or primitive element enters (Paus. i. 31. 2). So also the great Pythian festival held at Delphi on the 7th of the month Bukatios, the second summer month of the Delphian calendar (*CIA* ii. 545), may have been originally a harvest-festival; but if so, in historical times it is entirely identified with the higher aspects of Greek culture, and, moreover, the athletic side of that culture did not predominate at the Pythia, as it did at the Olympian festival, over the artistic and intellectual.

'The earliest competitions were musical and poetical, tragic recitations being subsequently added. . . . Prizes were awarded not only to the poets and musicians, but even to painters; and, in fact, the Pythia may be regarded as the prototype of the art-exhibitions of modern Europe, for in this festival alone we hear of the famous artists exhibiting their works and competing. The great Delphic celebration then was pre-eminently the consecration of the highest life of Hellas to Apollo; a detailed account of it would form a special chapter in the history of Greek music' (Farnell, *op. cit.* 292).

Other festivals of Apollo held at Delphi, though less brilliant, are of great importance to the student of Apolline ritual. The festival of the god's Epiphany in early spring has already been mentioned. To this should be added the *Theoxenia*, in which the newly-arrived god extended his hospitality to the other deities, especially to Dionysos, as appears from one of the lately discovered Delphic hymns, in which Dionysos is invoked 'in these holy hours of spring,' and entreated to show this hymn to the brother-god in the yearly *Theoxenia*.‡ This festivity, therefore, included poetic competitions; it included also a sort of vegetable show, for a prize was given to him who exhibited the finest leek (Athen. 372 A: *ὃς ἂν κομίσῃ γηθυλλίδα μεγίστην τῇ Λητοῖ, λαμβάνειν μοῖραν ἀπὸ τῆς τραπέζης*). Finally, we must notice the festival called the *Stepteria*, a feast of purification which is described by Plutarch (293 C, 418 A, 1136 B; cf. Ælian, *Var. Hist.* iii. 1), as in part a holy drama enacting the death of Python and the subsequent flight of Apollo to Tempe, where he is purified, and whence he returns in triumph with the sacred laurel. The following is the outline of the ritual ('no recorded religious service is so characteristically Hellenic, and perhaps none so fascinating,' Farnell, *op. cit.* 293):—On a certain day in spring, a noble Delphian boy went with a band of boys of the best family, under the escort of sacred women with torches, in complete silence to a cabin built near the Pythian temple in the form of a royal palace, in which the Python was supposed to be lurking. They set fire to the cabin, overturned the table, and fled without looking backwards through the temple-doors. Then the boy feigned to go into exile; afterwards they all went together to Tempe, where they were purified at an altar, and, having plucked the sacred laurel and crowned themselves with its leaves, returned home along the sacred Pythian way, and in a village near Larissa, called Deipnias, the boy-leader partook of a solemn meal of a sacramental nature. They then returned in triumph to Delphi, to the music of flutes, and the sacred laurel they brought served to fashion the crowns for the Pythian victors (see Farnell, *op. cit.* 293 ff.). This festival is closely connected with the cathartic or purificatory function of Apollo, a function which nowhere received fuller public recognition than at Athens, especially in connexion with homicide. Such cathartic ceremonies were, however, probably a late development of Apolline ritual.

W. J. WOODHOUSE.

* For details of these festivals, consult Farnell, *op. cit.* 259 ff., or the handbooks of Antiquities. In the *Hyakinthia* we have a combination of an older and a more recent religious rite (Farn. *op. cit.* 127).

† For the *Thargelia* see Farnell, *op. cit.* 267 ('the most complex and the most important for the study of Greek religion'). Treated at length by Miss Harrison, *Proleg. to Gr. Rel.* 77; the Pharmakos element, on p. 96 ff. (See art. SCAPEGOAT).

‡ Plut. 557 F. Pæan to Dionysos discovered at Delphi, *BCH*, 1895, p. 406, ll. 110–112: *δεῖξαι δ' ἐγ ξενίοις ἐτείοις θεῶν ἱερῷ γένει συναίμῳ τόνδ' ὕμνον.* Cf. Paus. vii. 27. 4.

APOLLONIUS OF TYANA in Cappadocia is in several respects a notable figure in the history of religion. Apart from the fact that he was a religious reformer of no little fame, he gave rise, as early as the time of Eusebius of Cæsarea, to a controversy which has continued almost down to the present day. The details of his life are to be found in a work by Philostratus the elder (3rd cent.), which was written at the request of Julia Domna († 217), 'the patroness of every art, and the friend of every man of genius' (Gibbon). Septimius Severus was a passionate student of magic and divination, and had chosen Julia Domna as his second wife on account of her 'royal nativity.'* Philostratus' patroness, who was also a collector of books, had been made acquainted with some memoirs by Apollonius' disciple, Damis the Assyrian.† These were not well written, and Philostratus was requested to copy them, improve the style, and in fact to compile as complete a biography as possible. He tells us himself that several 'Lives' of Apollonius were in existence, and that to some of them—those of Maximus of Ægæ and Mæragenes—he had access. He also used letters of Apollonius.‡ Moreover, he himself travelled into most parts of the known world, and everywhere heard the 'inspired sayings' of Apollonius. The biography, however, which Philostratus composed is of a romantic character.§ It is clear that the story of Apollonius, though much of it may be regarded as more or less true, has been greatly embellished. Many of the embellishments are of

* Gibbon, *Decline and Fall of the Roman Empire*, Bury's ed. vol. i. p. 126.

† Philostr. i. 3. 'Damis the Assyrian' has been regarded as purely a literary device; so F. C. Baur and Ed. Zeller. But although his character seems to have been intentionally drawn in such a way as to illustrate the moral and intellectual superiority of his master, there is no reason to doubt his existence. Boswell, with whom he has been compared, has made his own character appear somewhat unnatural. Apollonius and Damis have also been compared with Don Quixote and Sancho Panza. See A. Réville, p. 52; G. R. S. Mead, p. 112.

‡ The so-called 'Letters of Apollonius' which have come down to us are generally regarded as spurious. See Hercher, in *Epistolographi Græci*, Paris, 1873.

§ It has been described as a 'Tendenzroman' or 'Märchenbuch.' F. Ueberweg (*Hist. of Philos.*, London, 1875, vol. i. p. 233) speaks of it as a 'philosophico-religious romance.' Julius Jessen thinks the work was composed with the help of a Greek romance. See also Rohde, pp. 438–442.

such a nature as to suggest that they were made to suit the taste of Julia Domna, which was, of course, well known to Philostratus. Besides this, the compiler of the biography, in the manner of ancient writers, has added in the text many notes or glosses of his own without distinguishing them from the information derived from his original sources. Like Thucydides, too, he has composed a number of speeches and put them in the mouth of his hero; and it has been noted by F. C. Baur and others that the Babylon of Apollonius is identical with that of Herodotus.*

Apollonius, whose parents seem to have been wealthy, was born about B.C. 4. The country people said he was a son of Zeus,† but he called himself ‡ the son of Apollonius. At an early age he displayed a wonderful memory and great power of application. He was also very beautiful. When he was 14, his father took him to Tarsus to study rhetoric with Euthydemus. But the boy thought the people of Tarsus frivolous, and soon afterwards retired to Ægæ, where he conversed with the disciples of the great philosophers in the temple of Asklepios. At 16 he became an enthusiastic disciple of Pythagoras, and determined to follow his strictest teaching (i. 7). He gave up eating meat, regarding only productions of the earth as pure, refused to touch wine, went barefoot, let his hair grow long, and wore only linen.§ At this period he spent much of his time in the temple of Asklepios, and was allowed to see the cures which were wrought there (i. 8). We are told that through him the temple became a Lyceum and Academy. When of age, he returned to Tyana. Here, his father having died, he gave his brother, who was a spendthrift, half his own inheritance, and set to work to reform him. He then distributed the rest of his inheritance among those of his relatives who needed money,‖ and for his own part determined never to marry (i. 13). As a disciple of Pythagoras, he then observed the five years' silence, spending the time partly in Pamphylia and partly in Cilicia, and making himself understood by signs or, when necessary, by writing. These years were devoted to study and observation (i. 14 f.). Afterwards he went to Antioch, where he visited various temples and suggested reforms in religious practices (i. 16).

Apollonius now decided to go to the East, particularly to India. When he reached Nineveh, he met Damis, who thenceforward became his devoted disciple and companion. Damis told him that he knew the languages of the countries in which they proposed to travel, but Apollonius replied that he knew all tongues, because he could read men's thoughts (i. 18).¶ In Babylon he seems to have met the Magi. He also met, and was entertained by, the king, Bardanes, but refused to take part with him in a sacrifice involving the shedding of blood, or to go to the chase with him, regarding the sport as cruel to animals (i. 25–38). After visiting the surrounding cities (i. 39), they made for the Indian frontier, and seem to have entered India by the Khyber Pass (ii. 6). A guide having conducted them to Taxila (Attock, ii. 20), Apollonius was entertained by king Phraotes, who afterwards gave him a letter to Iarchas, the eldest of the wise men (ii. 40). Crossing the tributaries of the Indus (ii. 43) to the valley of the Ganges (iii. 5), they at length reached the goal of their journey, the castle or monastery of the wise men (iii. 10). Apollonius was conducted alone by a messenger to the castle (iii. 10). Here he was allowed to ask any questions he pleased.** A messenger was then sent to invite Damis to attend as well (iii. 34), Apollonius, during his stay, besides learning many secrets from these Brāhmans or Buddhists,†† was allowed to witness certain cures. Iarchas touched a cripple and healed him; he also restored sight to a blind man, and the use of his hand to a paralytic (iii. 39).* They made the homeward journey partly by ship, going from the Indus to the mouth of the Euphrates (iii. 52–58). Then, by way of Babylon, Nineveh, Antioch, Seleucia, and Cyprus, they came to Ionia (iii. 58). Visiting Ephesus, Apollonius warned the inhabitants of an approaching plague. They disregarded his warning, and he retired to Smyrna (iv. 1–5). When the plague came, ambassadors were sent to him to implore his help. He returned to Ephesus and calmed the inhabitants.† They next visited Pergamus, where Apollonius cured diseases (iv. 11), Troy, Lesbos (iv. 13), and eventually sailed for Athens.‡ We next find them in Corinth (iv. 25).§ When at length they came to Rome, all Apollonius' companions but eight fled. In Rome the reformer was very outspoken. Moreover, a distemper broke out to which Nero became a victim. The people prayed for his recovery, and Apollonius is reported to have said that 'the gods were to be forgiven if they took pleasure in the company of buffoons and jesters' (iv. 44). Tigellinus had him arrested on a charge of high treason. But he was impressed by his conversation, and, taking him for a god, released him. While Apollonius was at Rome, a girl of consular family, who had 'seemingly died,' was carried out to burial. Apollonius touched her, and 'wakened her from that death with which she seemed to be overcome' (iv. 45).‖ He left the city when Nero published an edict excluding philosophers from Rome (iv. 47). He now went to Spain, landing at Gades (Cadiz). After staying here a short time (iv. 47), he went to Africa, and thence by sea to Sicily, where he visited the principal cities and temples (v. 11–14). Returning to Greece (v. 18), he sailed from Piræus for Chios (v. 21), and then went by way of Rhodes to Alexandria, where the people looked upon him as a god (v. 24).¶ Going up the Nile as far as Ethiopia, he visited certain gymnosophists or ascetics (vi. 1–27). He next returned to Alexandria (vi. 28), and Titus, having been declared emperor, requested him to confer with and advise him at Tarsus (vi. 29–34). After this he seems to have returned to Egypt. We then find him crossing from Egypt to Greece, taking ship at Corinth, and sailing by way of Sicily to Puteoli. Thence he journeyed to Rome, foreknowing that the Emperor Domitian had decided to have him arrested (vii. 10–16). The Prætorian prefect Ælian interviewed him privately, and warned him of the charges that would be made against him (vii. 13), one of which was that he had allowed the people to call him a god. He was put in prison (vii. 22), and later the Emperor ordered his hair to be cut off (vii. 34).** Before he went to make his defence before the Emperor, Apollonius sent Damis to Puteoli: there, after he had made the defence, he was to come to him and another friend Demetrius (vii. 41). The Emperor, after hearing Apollonius' replies to his questions, acquitted him, but bade him remain to converse with him privately.†† Later he returned to Greece (vii. 15), where

* Again, several gaps have been detected in his story (the first after Bk. i. ch. 15; another of about twenty years from A.D. 72).

† We are also told that before his birth, Proteus, the Egyptian god, announced to his mother that the child she would bear would be an incarnation of himself. It is said that he was born in a meadow, and that a chorus of swans sang in unison to celebrate the event (i. 4 f.).

‡ We are told later (viii. 24) that in Greece Apollonius' disciples called themselves Apollonians.

§ He refused, that is to say, to wear clothes made from living creatures.

‖ So Philostratus tells us here. Whenever Apollonius visited a temple, he was no doubt treated as a guest. But he must have required money for his travels, and there are indications elsewhere in Philostratus' story that Apollonius must have kept back part of his inheritance; so Tredwell, p. 49.

¶ This is clearly what Apollonius means. When we are told (i. 20) that he knew the language of animals, the idea is the same. We are told elsewhere that he sometimes made use of an interpreter. See Max Wundt, p. 320 f.; G. R. S. Mead, p. 112.

** In reply to the question, what the wise men thought of themselves, Iarchas said 'gods,' and explained, 'because we are good men' (iii. 18).

†† When Apollonius said that they were 'on the earth, and yet not on it,' it is clear that the words are to be interpreted spiritually (so Max Wundt, p. 313; G. R. S. Mead, p. 86). But, on the strength of this, Damis explains that they were able to float at a height of two cubits above the ground; and A. P. Sinnett thinks they were able to 'elevate' themselves in a modern spiritualistic sense. For parallels of such levitation see Rohde, p. 180, n. 1; Gray, in *AJTh*, vii. 309.

* In a letter of farewell to Iarchas, Apollonius says: 'I will continue to enjoy your conversation as if still with you, if I have not drunk of the cup of Tantalus in vain.' A. P. Sinnett (p. 18) thinks of telepathy; G. R. S. Mead (p. 88) says it is evident that the 'cup of Tantalus' is identical with the 'wisdom' which has been imparted to Apollonius, and is once more to be brought back by him to the memory of the Greeks.

† Philostr. iv. 10. We are told that Apollonius transported himself thither at once, and that he told the people to stone an old man with a bad squint who was begging. When they had done this, they found in place of the old beggar a large dog.

‡ Here, we are told, Apollonius cast a demon out of a young man, and as it went forth it overthrew a statue (iv. 20).

§ Here, we are told, Apollonius exorcized a demon, an *empusa* or a *lamia*, who in the form of a fair maiden had captivated one of his pupils, Menippus. Cf. Keats, 'Lamia'; and Burton, *Anatomy of Melancholy*.

‖ Philostratus evidently thinks that she was not dead. Apollonius seems to have awakened her out of a catalepsy or hypnotic sleep. On this see Joseph Lapponi, *Hypnotism and Spiritism*, London, 1907. J. M. Robertson (*Christianity and Mythology*, London, 1900) derives the story of the awakening of the daughter of Jairus in Mt 9[18ff.] from this episode in Philostratus. But, in spite of the resemblance, there is no reason to see any direct connexion between the two events (so Erwin Rohde, p. 368, n. 5). F. C. Baur and Albert Réville think that the story in Philostratus was modelled on that of the raising of the young man at Nain or of the daughter of Jairus. If, however, the story was borrowed, the model, as Julius Jessen suggests (p. 18 f.), is no doubt to be found in Asclepiades (Pliny, *HN* xxvi. 3, 8).

¶ Here he met Vespasian (v. 27), and is said to have hinted to him that the temple of Jupiter Capitolinus had been burned down at Rome. That is to say, he saw the fire as a clairvoyant. Swedenborg is said, when in Gottenburg, to have seen clairvoyantly a fire in Stockholm by which his own home was threatened (see Joseph Lapponi, *Hypnotism and Spiritism*, p. 142 f.). Psychologically, Swedenborg's vision is more intelligible.

** F. C. Baur fancifully compares the sufferings of Apollonius with the Passion of Jesus, and the conduct of his rival Euphrates with that of Judas Iscariot.

†† We are told that he did not stay, but shortly afterwards disappeared suddenly. This was before noon; in the afternoon he appeared to Damis and Demetrius at Puteoli (viii. 10). Pythagoras also is said to have had the power of suddenly disappearing (see Iamblichus, *Vit. Pyth.* ch. 217; Max Wundt, p. 321). It has been claimed that the same kind of phenomenon has been noted in modern times (as recently as in 1901). See

he stayed two years (viii. 24). Here he insisted on visiting the cave of Trophonius * at Lebadea in Bœotia, forcing his way in (viii. 19). Having returned to Ephesus, while he was in the middle of a discourse there, he saw and announced the death of Domitian.† He disappeared altogether at the end of the reign of Nerva, having purposely sent Damis away to Rome (viii. 28).‡ At what age he died is uncertain. It has been put at 80, 90, or 100.

There is no valid reason for questioning the historical existence of Apollonius. His character on the whole is quite intelligible; his teaching is clear and consistent. He was a Neo-Pythagorean religious reformer, a vegetarian, an ascetic, and a student of medicine; and in his creed, a worshipper of Helios, a universalist and humanitarian. § We need not doubt that he was able to cure certain diseases; and it is possible that, consciously or unconsciously, he made use of telepathy; ‖ but whether he travelled quite as much as Philostratus represents him to have done is open to question. Nor is there any reason to doubt that he was an author. The works attributed to him, besides Letters, are *Initiations and Sacrifices*, a *Testament*, *Oracles*, a *Life of Pythagoras*, a *Hymn to Memory*, and *Divination by the Stars*.

The pupil of a disciple of Apollonius is satirized by Lucian; and Apollonius himself is ranked by Apuleius with Moses and Zoroaster. Dio Cassius, who was also patronized by Julia Domna, tells us in his *History* (lxxvii. 18) that Caracalla (211–216) erected a chapel or monument to his memory; and Lampridius (*Life of Alexander Severus*, xxix.) says that Alexander Severus included Apollonius, with Christ, Abraham, and Orpheus, amongst his household gods. We learn from Vopiscus (*Life of Aurelian*, xxiv.) that, when Aurelian (270–275) was besieging Tyana, Apollonius appeared to him, whereupon the Emperor vowed him a temple. Porphyry and Iamblichus mention him as one of their authorities for the 'Life' of Pythagoras. A more famous reference to him is that of Hierocles (*Discursus Philalethes*, c. 305), proconsul of Bithynia under Diocletian; in criticizing the claims of the Christians, he cited the wonders of Apollonius in order to show that 'miracles' were not the peculiar property of Christianity. Eusebius of Cæsarea replied to him in a treatise, *contra Hieroclem*. Lactantius also (*c.* 315) attacked Hierocles. Later, however, Jerome and Augustine speak highly of Apollonius' character at least, and Sidonius Apollinaris says that 'perchance no historian will find in ancient times a philosopher whose life is equal to that of Apollonius.' Ammianus Marcellinus and Eunapius also eulogize him.

Hierocles contrasted the miracles of Apollonius with those of Jesus. Later writers have contended that Apollonius was invented as a pagan rival of Christ.¶ This is the view of F. C. Baur and Albert

Joseph Lapponi, *Hypnotism and Spiritism*, p. 131f. A. P. Sinnett thinks it not impossible for Apollonius to have made himself invisible. He would then have been able 'immediately afterwards to levitate himself and pass out, over the heads of the people assembled, from such a building as a Roman court, open to the air, no doubt, in many directions' (p. 26, cf. p. 18). The truth is, no doubt, that this is one of the touches introduced to suit the taste of Julia Domna.

* F. C. Baur compares this with the descent of Christ to Hell.

† The story is also told by Dio Cassius (lxvii. 18). Joseph Lapponi (*Hypnotism and Spiritism*, p. 138) refers to this as one of the early instances of clairvoyance or telepathy.

‡ We are told that subsequently he appeared in a vision to a young man, and convinced him of the truth of immortality.

§ He protested against gladiatorial shows, and against every form of cruelty to animals. The slaves of his companions he regarded as part of his philosophic community (iv. 34). Cf. Jean Réville, p. 212 f.

‖ There seems to be sufficient evidence for cures of a like nature in modern times (see Albert B. Olston, *Mind Power*, London, 1906, p. 108).

¶ In the 15th cent. Apollonius was denounced as a detestable magician. In 1680, Charles Blount published, with a polemical purpose, a translation of part of Philostratus' work, with notes which have been attributed to Lord Herbert of Cherbury. Voltaire and others made a similar use of Apollonius.

Réville, who find a number of more or less fanciful parallels between the story of the Gospels * and that of Philostratus; only they think that the latter was written not, as earlier critics supposed, in a hostile sense, but in the spirit of the religious syncretism of the age. More recent critics, however, have rightly maintained that there is no trace of any direct connexion between the two stories. In Philostratus the whole narrative bears a Greek stamp; † and his model for the life of Apollonius, if he had one, was Pythagoras.‡ As Julius Jessen further points out (p. 12), if Philostratus' work had had a polemical purpose, certain important miracles of healing would have been ascribed to Apollonius rather than to the Indians. Nor is it remarkable that two religious reformers should have lived about the same time and have had somewhat similar experiences (cf. Ed. Baltzer, p. 388). It should be mentioned, in conclusion, that the newest view about Apollonius is that he was a kind of spiritualist. § It is held by A. P. Sinnett, and to some extent by G. R. S. Mead. Mr. Sinnett, writing in 1898, says that 'until the occult revival of the last twenty years, no modern students of philosophy were in possession of any clue by which it would have been possible for them to have understood Apollonius' (p. 4; cf. G. R. S. Mead, p. 116).

Literature.—(i.) Text : A. Westermann, Paris, 1848 ; C. L. Kayser, Leipzig, 1870. (ii.) Translations : Edward Berwick, *The Life of Apollonius of Tyana*, London, 1809 ; A. Chassang, *Le Merveilleux dans L'Antiquité*, Paris, 1862 ; Ed. Baltzer, *Apollonius von Tyana*, Rudolstadt i/Th., 1883. (iii.) Other works : F. C. Baur, *Apollonius von Tyana und Christus*, Tübingen, 1832 [reprinted by Eduard Zeller, *Drei Abhandlungen zur Gesch. d. alten Philosophie*, Leipzig, 1876] ; J. H. Newman, 'Apollonius Tyanæus' in Smedley's *Encyc. Metropol.*, London, 1845, x. pp. 619–644 ; Ed. Müller, *War Apollonius von Tyana ein Weiser oder ein Betrüger oder ein Schwärmer und Fanatiker?* Breslau, 1861 ; Albert Réville, *Apollonius of Tyana, the Pagan Christ of the Third Century*, [Eng. tr.], London, 1866 ; C. L. Nielsen, *Apollonios fra Tyana*, Copenhagen, 1879 ; C. H. Pettersch, *Apollonius von Tyana der Heidenapostel*, Reichenberg, 1879 ; Julius Jessen, *Apollonius von Tyana und sein Biograph Philostratos*, Hamburg, 1885 ; Jean Réville, *La Religion à Rome sous les Sévères*, Paris, 1886 ; D. M. Tredwell, *A Sketch of the Life of Apollonius of Tyana*, New York, 1886 ; G. Wotherspoon, *Apollonius of Tyana, Sage, Prophet, and Magician*, London, 1890 [a Lecture] ; Eduard Zeller, *Philos. der Griechen* [5], Leipzig, 1892 ; A. P. Sinnett, 'Apollonius of Tyana' in *Transactions of the London Lodge of the Theosophical Society*, No. 32, 1898 ; Erwin Rohde, *Der Griech. Roman* [2], Leipzig, 1900 ; G. R. S. Mead, *Apollonius of Tyana : The Philosopher-Reformer of the First Century A.D.*, London, 1901 ; J. M. Robertson, *Pagan Christs*, London, 1903 ; Thomas Whittaker, *Apollonius of Tyana*, London, 1906 ; Max Wundt, 'Apollonius von Tyana : Prophetie und Mythenbildung' in the *ZWT*, 1906, p. 309 ff.; cf. Froude's *Short Studies*, vol. iv.

MAURICE A. CANNEY.

APOLOGETICS.—

A. *Historical Introduction*.
B. *Apologetics of To-day*.
  I. Outline of a progressive Apology.
  II. Methods of Apology and modern needs.
  III. Arguments arranged according to the sphere in which they lie.
    (i.) The physical realm.
      1. *The evidence of nature*.
        (a) *The argument from matter, life, and mind*.
        (b) *The argument from design in nature*.
      2. *The problems of nature*.
        (a) *Miracles*.
        (b) *Evolution*.
        (c) *Monism, true and false*.
        (d) *Suffering*.

* Baur and Réville (p. 64) also contend that Apollonius 'combines in his own person many of the characteristics of the Apostles.'

† So Pettersch, p. 22 ; Max Wundt, p. 321. Baur's most important point is that the Greek and Roman literatures of the time are not familiar with the idea of the casting out of demons as found in the story of Apollonius. But, as J. M. Robertson says (p. 285), this is 'to make the arbitrary assumption that the superstitions of Syria could enter the West only by Judaic or Christian channels.'

‡ So Julius Jessen, p. 30 f.; and J. M. Robertson, p. 285.

§ Baltzer, writing in 1883, wondered that modern spiritualists had not claimed him.

(ii.) THE PSYCHICAL REALM.
1. *Historical arguments.*
   (a) *The Jews and OT prophecy.*
   (b) *The historical Christ.*
   (c) *The Resurrection of Christ.*
   (d) *The history of Christianity and of the Church.*
2. *Psychological arguments.*
   (a) *The changed life of the disciples, and the conversion of St. Paul.*
   (b) *The witness of Christian customs and institutions.*
   (c) *The success of Christianity.*
   (d) *The abiding unity of faith.*
   (e) *The argument from the psychological nature of religion.*
   EXCURSUS:—The general superiority of Christianity to other religions.
3. *Metaphysical arguments.*
   (a) *The argument from intelligence, will, and conscience.*
   (b) *The argument from consciousness.*
   (c) *The argument from the idea of God.*
   (d) *The Cosmological or Ætiological argument.*
   EXCURSUS:—The anthropological attack.

(iii.) THE MORAL REALM.
1. *Arguments for theistic belief from the moral realm of thought.*
   (a) *The universal idea of God and cultivation of religion.*
   (b) *The moral sense in man, the conscience and the sense of sin.*
   (c) *The moral course of the world's history.*
2. *Arguments for Christianity from the moral realm of fact.*
   (a) *The Christian Scriptures.*
   (b) *The morality of Christianity.*
   (c) *The Person of Christ, the moral ideal.*

(iv.) THE SPIRITUAL REALM.
   (a) *The testimony of the spiritual faculty.*
   (b) *The testimony to Christianity of the spiritual yearnings of men.*
   (c) *The testimony of holy lives.*
   (d) *The personal experience of the Christian.*

A. *HISTORICAL INTRODUCTION.*—We define the term 'Apologetics' as the Christian defence against attack by non-Christians. Facing outwards as it does, it therefore need not include reference to the doctrine and theology which lie behind it. We may further limit this wide subject, in order to reduce it to the compass of an article, by omitting its history altogether. As different ages have had to face different attacks, this would be altogether impossible, were it not that the results of centuries of assault and defence have in our own age been collected in an academic form, so as to be the basis of a scientific system of *Apologetics*, as a regular branch of Christian literature and activity.

The need and use of Christian apologetics have existed from the beginning. All early Christian literature is in a sense an *apologia*, as is shown even in the NT from the first words of the first sermon onwards (Ac 2^{14-16}). With regard to the recognized 'Apologists' of the succeeding age, we shall note only two features. On the one hand, they found themselves called on to defend not so much the beliefs of Christianity as the behaviour of Christians; and, on the other hand, they developed the offensive as well as the defensive method of answer. Among the chief names are those of Justin Martyr, Aristides, Melito of Sardis, Minucius Felix, Tatian, and Tertullian.

From the 3rd cent. attacks became less personal and more doctrinal, and in the hands of such enemies as Celsus, the more hostile Neo-Platonists, and Julian, the Scriptures had become an object of ridicule. The later apologists are therefore of a somewhat different stamp, and we can only refer to such varied writers as Origen (*against Celsus*), Arnobius, Lactantius, Cyril of Alexandria (*against Julian*), Macarius Magnes, and Augustine (*de Civitate Dei*). Gradually the need for such works ceased, and, as we pass to the later centuries, we find that apologists deal no longer with the faith generally, but with special problems in connexion with it. It is the philosophic aspect that the Middle Ages give us, and the works of chief importance are the *Monologion* and *Proslogion* of Anselm, the *Dialogus inter Philosophum Judæum et Christianum* of Abelard, and the *Summa Theologiæ contra Gentiles* of Thomas Aquinas. The work of Anselm is of the most abiding interest, for it was he who first formulated the famous *a priori* proof of the being of God known as the Ontological argument. A new era began with the rise of Deism in the 18th cent., when the effort was made to set up a 'religion of nature' in place of Christianity. In England the chief answer came from Bishop Butler, who saw that the deistical admissions as to the existence and supremacy of God, the sins of men, and the reality of judgment, were valuable premises on which to base an argument for the acceptance of the whole of the faith. Starting with natural religion, he showed in his *Analogy*, by an argument which will always remain a famous Christian apologetic, that revealed religion follows from it, as neither more difficult nor more incredible.

The next attack, as represented by David Hume, was upon the credibility of miracles, and Paley's *Evidences of Christianity*, in answer, remains a classic in the history of English apologetics. The 19th cent. saw a more determined assault on the supernatural, and the growth of Positivism, Agnosticism, and Scepticism has been such that it must still be reckoned with in discussing the apologetics of the present day, and count has still to be taken of Huxley and Herbert Spencer, as well as of Haeckel, in setting forth, as we now proceed to do, the present state of the problem.

See **J. Donaldson**, 'The Apologists' (vols. ii. and iii. of *Hist. of Chr. Lit.*), 1864; **J. Patrick**, *The Apology of Origen in reply to Celsus*, 1892, pp. 121–262; **J. M. Rigg**, *St. Anselm of Canterbury*, 1896; **J. Cairns**, *Unbelief in the 18th Century*, 1880; **W. A. Spooner**, *Bishop Butler*, 1901.

B. *APOLOGETICS OF TO-DAY.*—Instead of giving the outline of any one present-day apologetic work, an attempt is made below to state in general terms the chief arguments that are being used to-day to defend the Christian faith. Naturally they will be given by way of statement and not by way of argument, and will be placed in an order which is meant to be scientific, rather than such as will make the most forcible appeal to readers.

For the subject generally, see **A. B. Bruce**, *Apologetics: or, Christianity defensively stated*, 1892; **C. A. Row**, *Christian Evidences in relation to Modern Thought* (Bampton Lectures, 1877); **W. L. Robbins**, *A Christian Apologetic*, 1902; **Lonsdale Ragg**, *Evidences of Christianity* (Oxford Ch. Text Bks., 1905); **F. Ballard**, *Miracles of Unbelief*, pop. ed. 1904; *Christian Apologetics*, ed. W. W. Seton, 1903; **G. P. Fisher**, *Manual of Christian Evidences*, 1892; **W. H. Turton**, *The Truth of Christianity*, 1900; **A. J. Harrison**, *Problems of Christianity and Scepticism*, 1891; **J. R. Illingworth**, *Reason and Revelation: an Essay in Christian Apology*, 1906.

First, it will be well to indicate the limitations in his arguments which the wise apologist is ready to concede. He does not claim that they afford irrefragable proof of his beliefs. To assert that Christianity can be conclusively demonstrated by merely intellectual proof is to stultify the nature of a true revelation. If an essential of true religion be the exercise of *faith*, and if God has revealed Himself by appealing to a faculty in men which is *not* their reason, it will be impossible to make a man a Christian by mere argument. The final appeal is to the heart; the appeal to the mind must content itself with proving without a shadow of doubt that Christianity is rational, credible, and probable. This is specially true of the arguments for the being of God. None of them amounts to positive proof, and yet it must not be forgotten that there are many of them, and that their cumulative force adds enormously to their weight.

I. Outline of a progressive Apology.—We now proceed to give an outline of the successive stages by which the argument leads up from simple Theism to the Christian creed.

(a) NATURAL RELIGION.—God exists, and may be known apart from revelation. This is proved by — (1) *The argument from General Consent.* That which is merely subjective when applied to the spiritual experience of the individual, and is therefore viewed with suspicion by opponents, becomes objective when it shows a 'consensus gentium' to belief in a God. (2) *The Cosmological or Ætiological argument,* which suggests the universe as an effect which must have a cause. (3) *The Teleological or Design argument,* which suggests that the order of nature implies a First Cause who is intelligent and free. (4) *The Ontological argument,* which points to God as the highest imaginable object of thought, and the ground of thought itself. (5) *The Moral argument,* which takes man's conscience as implying a lawgiver who inspires him without being identified with him. (6) *The Historical argument,* which points to the sense of purpose and design running through human history.

(*b*) REVEALED RELIGION.—(1) Natural religion leads us to expect something further, and suggests a Deity who would be sure to make Himself known. (2) This further step necessarily involves the supernatural. The objections to a supernatural revelation must be faced, viz. (*α*) such inadequate theistic theories as Pantheism, Deism, and Modern Theism; (*β*) such anti-theistic theories as Atheism, Agnosticism, and Materialism. Miracle must be discussed in its relation to natural law and to the purpose of revelation. (3) The Christian revelation must be shown to be intrinsically superior to other religions—Polytheism, Buddhism, and Muhammadanism—and to be the successor and higher fulfilment of Judaism. (4) The argument is led to that around which all centres—the Person of Christ. The Christ of the Gospels and Epistles is shown to be historic, the Resurrection makes all other miracles possible, and Christ remains the moral miracle of the world. (5) This is naturally followed by the history and influence of Christianity, as educating and regenerating the world, and showing a superhuman power of recuperation and continued existence. (6) This leads to the dispensation of the Holy Spirit and the work of the Church. Christian institutions, such as the ministry, the Sacraments, and the Christian year, are seen to be witnesses both to Christ and Christianity.

II. **Methods of Apology and modern needs.**— The bitter attack upon miracles in the 19th cent. has caused recent apologists to seek some line of proof that should be independent of this confident assault. It is on the *moral* aspects of Christianity that the chief stress is now laid. And the subject is no longer divided according to the old divisions of Natural and Revealed Religion. In the attempt to use every line of defence, it is preferable to marshal the evidences in accordance with the successive spheres in which they lie.

(1) Lowest stands the *physical* realm, but it is the arguments of science with which it is filled. The development of physical science during last century, as shown in new theories of which we connect the beginnings with the name of Darwin, and the attacks of Huxley and of Herbert Spencer, and yet more recently of Haeckel, make this an important part of modern Apologetics. The question of miracles lies only partly within it, for the Christian still adopts the attitude of Paley towards Hume, and refuses to admit that any Christian miracle is a merely physical occurrence. But the arguments in favour of a theistic religion, which, in the face of modern Materialism and Agnosticism, must still form the basis of a defence of Christianity, are many of them physical and physiological in form. Besides actual arguments found in the physical sphere, there are many problems connected with nature which need discussion. These are best placed under the same head, and include not only such questions as that of suffering, and the theory of Evolution in the forms which the last fifty years have made familiar, but that latest battleground of faith and unbelief which is represented by the word 'Monism.' At the present moment it seems likely that the honest and well-equipped apologist will have to re-consider each of his theistic positions in the light of the monistic tendency of the latest results of science, and indeed this has already been done in recent works to which reference will be made. But it will be impossible in this article to do more than show that, if a naturalistic Monism is invoked on one side, an even stronger weapon may be found in spiritual Monism on the other. The main features of this latter and its bearing on the faith can only be mentioned, and its authorities referred to.

(2) The next sphere of evidences is the *psychical*, when we have passed from nature generally to human nature, from physics and matter to metaphysics and mind. Properly speaking, the realm of psychology belongs only to the present, but it need not exclude those other spheres of mental activity which we speak of in the past and the future. The consideration of the past must necessarily embrace a large part of Apologetics, for Christianity is essentially a historical religion, and takes its stand upon the facts of long ago. Under this head we prefer to place the Christian defence of miracles, focussing attention on the supreme miracle of the Resurrection, which is supreme not only in the sense that, if its difficulty is overcome, the other miracles follow naturally, but also in the sense that with its truth as a fact of history Christianity stands or falls. And every century the lengthening history of the faith affords a further means of building argument upon the past. In the sphere of more direct psychology which concerns the individual mind, we are led to such questions as the conversion of Paul, and the position of the writers of the NT.

Some would postulate a separate sphere as the *metaphysical*—the sphere in which mental phenomena are in a special sense marshalled by reason. Others are content to give a metaphysical tinge to the stages which reach higher than the physical realm.

(3) The next sphere is the *moral*, raised as far above the mental as the mental is above the physical. Under this head come such theistic arguments as the universal idea of God, the conscience of man, the individual consciousness, and the sense of sin. But the supreme moral argument centres in the Person of Christ. He Himself and His earthly life and moral teaching are now made the chief argument for the truth of the religion that He founded. He is at the same time the moral miracle which cannot be explained by 'natural' causes, and the answer to the moral instincts of humanity, the key to unlock not only the unique monotheistic morality of Judaism, but such problems as those of sin and suffering, and of the purpose and the goal of human existence. Our generation is coming to realize more than those gone by that 'Christianity is Christ.' And the result, for the apologist, has been stated thus (W. L. Robbins, *A Christian Apologetic*, 1902, p. 25 f.): 'The fundamental ground of Apologetics must be shifted from miracles to the moral character of Jesus Christ, and verifiable facts of present religious experience. . . . This would seem to be the most wide-reaching modification required in modern Apologetics—a shifting of the accent from the past to the present, from the miraculous to the moral.'

(4) Highest and last is the *spiritual* realm. Here we reach without doubt the final argument, and

yet it is of but little use in Apologetics. For a spiritual religion must be spiritually understood, and it is only to the spiritual that it can make its final appeal.

It may therefore be said that the moral argument from the Person of Christ forms the chief line of defence, and the separation of these higher realms of evidence from the physical is in itself a reply to those opponents who try to confine the entire issue to the latter.

III. Arguments arranged according to the sphere in which they lie.—(i.) THE PHYSICAL REALM.—**1.** *The evidence of nature.*—(*a*) *The argument from matter, life, and mind.*—We begin with the mystery of 'Being,' and a study of the objects of sense reveals that *matter* is the basis of them. But material substances are of different kinds, and some of them are marked off from the rest as self-acting, or *living*. These are compound substances, capable of reduction to the same elementary substances as the rest, but possessed of the faculties of feeding, growing, and reproducing. But the *life* which they possess is far more than the sum-total of the material substances of which they are composed; it is a mystery, with no explanation of its origin. And there is a further mystery, for connected with some of these living material beings is *mind*, which is not demonstrably derivable from life, any more than life is from matter; for thought, which is the expression of mind, appears to be far more than simply a movement of matter. But there is an attribute of all being, known as *force*, which is an important factor throughout. As mental force, and as vital force, it must necessarily be conceived of as inherent in mind and life. But as physical force, in the lowest of the three stages, it has to be regarded, as Newton insisted, as exterior to matter, and acting upon it. Thus far, physical science can speak plainly. But what answer is to be given when the question is pushed a stage further back? How did these things come to be thus? How did matter originate? How is the gulf to be bridged that separates life from matter and mind from life? And whence comes the force that acts upon them all?

Materialism and Agnosticism have their answer; but are they as reasonable as is the following Christian explanation? Force is derived from an eternal force. Matter has not always existed, but was created at the fiat of His will. This implies a personal Creator, a First Cause who is both single, as shown by the unity of nature, and supernatural, because all the laws and forces of nature do not contain Him, but show His work. This by no means denies the Atomic Theory, but explains how the 'favourable circumstances' for the new formations of atoms came about; and the theory of Evolution is seen to be the method of His working, while there is no need of lame attempts to bridge the chasm between matter, life, and thought. Such an answer is no mere *a priori* argument to make certain preconceived ideas about religion fit in with science; rather is it the most reasonable induction from the facts of the physical realm. It lays no blame on science for getting no further back than matter and force; for it holds a true agnosticism which denies that it is the province of science to go further. Merely weighed by probabilities, it can claim to be the most rational and the least difficult explanation of the problem of being.

See **Aubrey Moore**, *Science and the Faith*, 1889; **G. Sexton**, *Baseless Fabric of Scientific Scepticism*, 1879; **W. F. Wilkinson**, *Modern Materialism* (Pres. Day Tracts); **A. B. Bruce**, *Apologetics*, 1892, ch. iv.; **F. R. Tennant**, *The Being of God in the Light of Physical Science* (Camb. Theol. Essays), 1905; **J. Ward**, *Naturalism and Agnosticism*[2], 1903; **P. N. Waggett**, *Religion and Science*, 1904; **J. Fiske**, *Through Nature to God*, 1899; **H. Wace**, *Christianity and Agnosticism*, 1895; **W. R. Inge**, *Christian Mysticism*, 1899; **J. R. Illingworth**, *Divine Immanence*, 1898; **H. M. Gwatkin**, *The Knowledge of God*, 1907; **J. Watson**, *The Philosophical Basis of Religion*, 1907.

(*b*) *The argument from design in nature.*—This evidence, so keen a weapon in the days of Paley's *Natural Theology*, is said by opponents to have become blunted by the theories of modern science. Romanes claimed that the place of supernatural design has been taken by natural selection, basing his claim upon the fact that all species of plants and animals were slowly evolved, and not separately and suddenly created. But creation by God need not be sudden, and we welcome all the processes of evolution as so many examples of His method of working. Perhaps it is sufficient to insist that evolution is a process, not a cause. It serves only to push the evidence of design further back, and therefore to increase our admiration for the Designer. And it is to be noted that if the evidence of nature suggests the *existence* of a personal Creator, the evidence of design does more, for it suggests His *foreknowledge*.

To imagine that such exquisite mechanism as that of the human eye, or such wonderfully suitable material in all its properties as a man's bones, was due to the inanimate and fortuitous working of matter and force, makes a far greater demand than any Christian miracle.

The popular objection to the evidence of design lies in pointing to 'nature red in tooth and claw.' This opens the question of the problem of pain, which, as far as it relates to man, requires separate treatment. With regard to the sufferings of the animal world, some exaggeration of them seems to be made in these days, by attributing to lower creatures our own standard of sensibility. This is a department in which the apologist must be careful not to ignore the discoveries of modern Biology. See BIOLOGY, SUFFERING.

See **F. Ballard**, *The Miracles of Unbelief*, pop. ed. (1904), p. 65, etc.; **G. P. Fisher**, *The Grounds of Theistic and Christian Belief* (rev. ed. 1903), pp. 42–67; **J. T. Tigert**, *Theism, a Survey of the Paths that lead to God*, 1900. See also, for the kindred argument from the sublime and the beautiful in nature, **R. St. J. Tyrwhitt**, *Natural Theology of Natural Beauty*, 1882; **J. B. Mozley**, *University Sermons*, Sermon on 'Nature,' 1876; **G. Rawlinson**, *The religious Teachings of the Sublime and Beautiful in Nature* (Pres. Day Tracts).

2. *The problems of nature.*—(*a*) *Miracles.*—The apologist refuses to limit the discussion of miracles to the physical realm, claiming their explanation through the historical and the moral aspect of them. But it is on the material side that the attack has come. The modern instinct revolts from miracles, and echoes Hume's assertion that no amount of testimony can render them credible. In our defence of them we must be careful where to begin. To one who does not believe in a God they are indeed incredible. He exalts certain so-called 'natural laws' into the supreme place, and rules out all that does not seem to agree with them. But if it be assumed that the world had a Creator (according to the foregoing arguments from nature, and those suggested by other lines of thought), miracles at once become possible. For a miracle may be defined as 'an act of God which visibly deviates from the ordinary working of His power, designed, while capable of serving other uses, to authenticate a Divine message.' If we begin with this assumption, we may still argue, as Paley did, that miracles have the same degree of probability as God's revelation of Himself to men.

Therefore, if we begin with the objection 'Miracles are impossible,' we must take the objector a stage further back, and discuss with him the belief in a God. But miracles are not always discredited by such reference to the main issue. The following are some of the objections levelled against them:—

(*a*) Miracles are inconsistent with the order of

nature. This argument not only ignores the working of a God who still has control over His creation, but also gives a rigid uniformity to certain so-called 'natural laws,' which after all are based only on the imperfect induction and limited experience of the human mind. If modern science has arrived at these laws by induction from a study of the universe, and not by the arbitrary assumption that these laws *are* uniform, all evidence must be taken into account. And as miracles lay claim to evidence, science must needs take them into consideration, or it will be stultifying its own methods. Such evidence, however, lifts the question out of the physical realm.

(β) It is further objected that the admission of miracles implies a lax or unscientific conception of the course of nature. And it is, indeed, true that Christians sometimes speak as if *only* miracles were the signs of God's working, and as if they interfered with the course of nature by subverting its laws. But we must insist that in speaking of miracles as 'supernatural,' we do not refer them to any other agency than that of so-called 'natural' events. We claim only that, if both historical and moral reasons demand it, it is both credible and reasonable that God should occasionally do what is outside man's ordinary experience of the working of created things. If man himself can interrupt the ordinary course of nature, he must certainly expect that God will do the same.

(γ) Perhaps the favourite attack on miracles today is the rationalizing of Biblical miracles one by one. It is claimed that such miracles may after all be brought into harmony with nature, for they are really to be referred to 'natural' causes. To have exalted them into more is the result of mistake or fraud. We reply that the only answer is in the weighing of the evidence. We are taken at once out of the physical realm into that of psychology and history.

(δ) Attempts are continually made to discredit all miracles by pointing to those that Christians themselves do not accept. But we may confine the issue to those Biblical miracles which have their climax in the Resurrection. We are not called on to explain the work of Pharaoh's magicians, the many marvels of the Middle Ages, or the achievements of occultism to-day. It is enough to prove that certain miracles actually happened, as an attestation of a Divine revelation.

See **Mozley**, *Miracles* (Bampton Lectures for 1865); **Lord Grimthorpe**, *Review of Hume and Huxley on Miracles*, 1883; **A. T. Lyttleton**, *The Place of Miracles in Religion*, 1899; **A. B. Bruce**, *The Miraculous Element in the Gospels*, 1886.

(*b*) *Evolution.*—The modern theory of Evolution touches the faith at many points. The sceptic uses it to discredit the design argument (see above), and to show that there is no room for the existence or working of a God; to explain the life of the one Perfect Man as due simply to natural causes in the evolutionary progress of the race; and to point to the origin and development of Christianity as an evolution from natural causes and previous sources. The apologist refuses to hand over Evolution to be a mere weapon in the enemy's hand. He claims that it is also his own. He sees in it the visible processes (or rather, the theories about them which the human mind has tried to express) whereby God works. The evolution of Christ and Christianity he refuses to discuss merely in the physical realm, but applies the historical method to both, and finds that they can be shown to be evolved from natural causes only by arguments which ignore the first principles of Evolution itself. But the Christian apologist is not content merely to apply the theory of Evolution in the same sphere as his opponent. He claims that the principle may be extended more widely to embrace the moral world in the present as well as the physical world in the past, to strengthen the conviction and hope of the Christian with regard to the future. The following words will illustrate such a position (J. M. Wilson, *Evolution and the Holy Scriptures* [1903], p. 18): 'Evolution is showing us in very plain ways some of those truths that we have grasped only in words, the Unity of Nature, the Divine Plan, the Omnipotence and Omnipresence of God. . . . It is, moreover, a marvellous help to faith and patient work to believe that as there has been an evolution in nature in the past, so there is such a process in man and in the moral world now going on.'

See **J. Iverach**, *Evolution and Christianity*, 1894; **E. Griffith-Jones**, *The Ascent through Christ*, 1899; **J. Cairns**, *Is the Evolution of Christianity from mere natural Causes credible?* (Pres. Day Tracts); **J. M. Wilson**, *Problems of Religion and Science*, 1900; **F. B. Jevons**, *Evolution*, 1900, and *Religion in Evolution*, 1906; **J. Ward**, *Naturalism and Agnosticism*², 1903; **H. Calderwood**, *Evolution and Man's Place in Nature*², 1896; **J. M. Baldwin**, *Development and Evolution*, 1902; **G. H. Howison**, *The Limits of Evolution*², 1905.

(*c*) *Monism, true and false.*—The tendency of modern science has been to discover a closer unity in all things than had been imagined. Upon this the opponents of Christianity have not been slow to seize. They have never been able satisfactorily to bridge the gulf between matter and spirit. Now they have the word of science that such dualism has been discredited by recent research, and that all phenomena, whether material or spiritual, must be explained as essentially one, and that therefore the only rational theory of the universe is some form of *Monism*. The wise apologist does not meet this with a denial. He is ready to listen to science as long as science retains its proper sphere; and if monistic belief seems the most rational, he does not reject it because it has been said to controvert Theism, but first examines the matter, and then re-considers his theistic position in the light of his conclusion. Therefore, the first question to be asked is what is meant by Monism, and the second is what is its bearing on Christian belief.

(*a*) Monism is a word which is growing in popularity, but it certainly does not always mean the same thing. There is a naturalistic, or scientific, and there is a spiritual Monism. The case is like that of Evolution: one aspect of the theory is said to overthrow Christianity, but another side is claimed as supporting it. There is no doubt that the Monism which makes itself most heard is that of the naturalistic kind, such as is identified with the name of Haeckel. It does, indeed, claim not to be materialistic, and recognizes Spirit as well as Matter; but it refuses to allow a dualistic distinction between God and the world, and regards Force and Matter as only two sides of one reality or Substance, which does everything and is everything. There is an invariable 'Law of Substance' whereby this Substance is in a process of evolution which causes eternal motion throughout the Universe. Such evolution is succeeded in turn by dissolution, and thus new worlds are continually being born and re-born. There is no place left for God, freedom, or immortality. The one single Substance operates of necessity and without ceasing, through all things, so that everything is determined by what has gone before; and when each individual has served his turn, he gives way to another, and disappears. But there are modifications of such Monism which are not necessarily anti-theistic. Some allow that there is an underlying Source of all things, of which Force and Matter represent 'only two different sides or phenomenal aspects,' and even the name of God may be admitted if 'stripped of its theological and anthropomorphic associations, and not opposed to or set above the principle of the unity of nature.'

But there is quite a different kind of Monism which the Christian may fearlessly accept and assert, and that is *Spiritual* Monism. The term has been explained (W. L. Walker, *Christian Theism and a Spiritual Monism*, 1906, p. 202) as 'adopted in order to set forth both *agreement* with Science in acceptance of its facts, and *difference* from the interpretation which some in the name of Science give to these facts. It acknowledges the two-sidedness that is everywhere manifested, and sees everything and every being in the world to be the result of the working or unfolding, or development in its conditioned form, of a single Power manifested as both material and spiritual. But, instead of giving the predominance to the material side, or equal value merely to the two sides, or leaving them both unexplained, it regards the spiritual side as that which is logically first and deepest—that which the material side only expresses and serves—that which manifests its supremacy in our own consciousness.' And the claim that this form of Monism makes is this: 'So far as we are able at all to understand ourselves, and to look out upon the immeasurable vastness beyond, no monistic scheme can be tolerated which does not both do us justice and transcend us. And certainly a monism which treats the world of phenomena as real, whilst regarding as illusory, or as ultimately mechanical, the world of noumena, sufficiently discredits itself. Spiritualistic monism is not guilty of the latter, nor can it be denied that it fairly fulfils the former' (F. Ballard, *Theomonism True*, 1906, p. 378).

Before passing to our other question, we note the impossibility of trying to confine the issue to the merely physical realm.

(*β*) The bearing of Monism upon Christian belief can only be briefly indicated, and may perhaps be best expressed in the outline of the argument as given in the last-named work (pp. 380–400). (i.) There is no contradiction, or even collision, between Spiritual Monism and Theism. (ii.) It causes no weakening of preceding reasons for Theism. (iii.) It leads up to Divine Personality. (iv.) It refuses, with Theism, to treat man as an automaton. (v.) It demands, however, the purification and enlargement of theistic phraseology. (vi.) A twofold development is involved, namely, a fuller recognition of Divine Immanence, and a blending of this with Divine Transcendence. It is in such directions as this that the greatest change is coming over Apologetics at the present moment.

See W. L. Walker, *Christian Theism and a Spiritual Monism*, 1906; F. Ballard, *Haeckel's Monism False*, 1905, and *Theomonism True*, 1906; J. Morris, *A New Natural Theology*², 1905; F. R. Tennant, *Cambridge Theological Essays*, 1905; J. F. Tristram, *Haeckel and his Riddles*, 1907.

(*d*) *Suffering.*—This is a problem which has perplexed mankind in every age. It has to be faced in relation to every system, and it has often been used in the attempt to discredit Christianity. The unmerited sufferings of men are adduced as showing that there is not a God who looks after the world as a Father, and the sufferings of the rest of creation are said to point to a 'nature red in tooth and claw' such as no beneficent Creator would allow. We have to admit that the problem still remains for us a perplexing one, but at the same time we claim that Christianity is the only system under which it may be viewed in a satisfactory and hopeful light. Taking physical pain as the simplest form of suffering, we may see in it a useful and beneficent purpose, as forming a 'danger signal,' without which far more harm would follow. And then we may apply this to suffering of a more complex kind. In arguing with any but the mere hedonist, we may assume that the purpose of life is something other than enjoyment. If it be 'the growing development of our faculties through the discipline of life,' then it is easy to see how it is helped by suffering. And we may recognize in it a twofold use, partly for the education of the individual, and partly for the well-being of the race even at the cost of the suffering of the individual.

But what is the bearing of Christianity on the problem? (*a*) The belief in a re-adjustment hereafter explains the inequalities of suffering in the present world. (*β*) The Fatherhood of God teaches that He is in sympathy with the sufferings of His creation, and the realization of such a sympathy has already proved 'the secret of endurance in the sufferings of the world.' (*γ*) The Cross of Christ, as not merely an isolated act of vicarious suffering, but the manifestation of the abiding union of the Divine in suffering, proves that the Divine sympathy is real. The deeds of Christ are inseparably linked with His words, His example with His precept, and the sufferer sees the problem wrapt in a new glory in the light of such echoes as 'Not my will but thine be done,' and 'He that loseth his life shall find it.' (*δ*) Not only does Christianity throw light on the problem in the case of the Founder, but the Christian is bidden to take up his cross and follow Christ; the facing of it in His Master's spirit and strength is a necessary and a joyful part of his creed. The belief in his own redemption through suffering makes him ready to 'fill up that which is behind of the afflictions of Christ,' and voluntarily seek suffering in the service of his brethren, as well as patiently accept that involuntary suffering which he realizes will be for his eternal good, and make him more like the Master who was 'made perfect through suffering.' No other religion explains and glorifies suffering thus, and therefore we claim that it attracts men to the Christian faith, instead of repelling them and discrediting it in their eyes.

See Masterman, 'The Problem of Suffering' in *Topics of the Times* (S.P.C.K.), 1906; Illingworth in *Lux Mundi*, 1889; J. Martineau, *A Study of Religion*², ii., 1889; and art. SUFFERING.

(ii.) THE PSYCHICAL REALM.—1. *Historical arguments.*—(*a*) *The Jews and OT prophecy.*—While Christianity is not bound to answer the objections that are levelled against Judaism, it accepts Judaism as its parent. And the Jews and their sacred literature form a strong apologetic argument for our faith. Their *external history* is in itself a marvel from first to last, while their spiritual *theology* and *worship* amid the debased beliefs of the ancient world, as embodied in their ideas of God and man and in the Messianic hope, and above all their *prophetic instinct*, which has its only explanation in the facts of the founding of Christianity, offer an argument the value of which is coming to be once more appreciated in our own day.

See E. A. Edghill, *The Evidential Value of Prophecy*, 1906; W. Sanday, *Bampton Lectures*, 1903, ch. viii.; H. A. Redpath, *Christ the Fulfilment of Prophecy*, 1907.

(*b*) *The historical Christ.*—The Person of Christ makes a higher appeal than that of mere history. But, viewed from the historical side, we claim (*a*) that the birth, work, death, and resurrection of Christ are among the best attested facts of human history. (*β*) That their historicity would never have been called in question were it not for the miraculous element inseparably bound up with them. (*γ*) That we have already shown that the only scientific treatment of miracles is to regard them as capable of verification, and to weigh the evidence for them accordingly. (*δ*) That when all the evidence for the miraculous element in Christianity, both psychical and moral, has been sifted, the whole history of its founding remains as true as any other fact of ancient history.

But the sifting of historical evidence implied under the last head involves a study of topics which will be dealt with under their own titles. We must, therefore, be content to mention them, and to refer to books where they are discussed.

(1) The authenticity of the four Gospels; the claim that either they record facts, or else nothing whatever can be said about Jesus of Nazareth; the arbitrary and unscientific nature of the attempt to offer any other history than that of the Gospels; the mutual relation of the Synoptic Gospels; the strengthening of the evidence through their various lines of testimony; the witness of the Fourth Gospel in relation to them.

See **B. Weiss**, *Introd. to the NT* (tr. Davidson, 1887-8); **Gore**, *The Incarnation* (Bampton Lectures, 1891); **Westcott**, *St. John's Gospel* (Introd.), 1892; **Burkitt**, *The Gospel History and its Transmission*, 1906; **Sanday**, *The Life of Christ in recent Research*, 1907; **J. Orr**, *The Incarnation and recent Criticism*, 1907.

(2) The historical accuracy of Acts; the impossibility that it is a sequel to anything but the history of the Gospels; its witness to the historical Person of Christ.

See **Ramsay**, *St. Paul the Traveller* (1895); **Harnack**, *Luke the Physician* (tr. Wilkinson, 1907), etc.

(3) The Epistles; the earliest witness to the life of Christ; the value of their incidental allusions; the basis afforded by the four uncontroverted Epistles of St. Paul.

See **R. J. Knowling**, *The Witness of the Epistles*, 1892, *Literary Criticism and the NT*, 1907; **Howson**, *Evidential Conclusions from the Four greater Epistles of St. Paul* (Pres. Day Tracts).

(4) The arguments for a historical Christ deducible from Jewish and heathen literature; Josephus, and the Talmudic account of Jeschu; Suetonius, Pliny, Tacitus, and, indirectly, the *True Account* of Celsus.

See **E. Crawley**, *The Tree of Life*, 1905, ch. v.; **Paley**, *Evidences of Christianity*, 1794.

(*c*) *The Resurrection of Christ.*—This, of course, is included in the proof of His historical Person on the lines indicated above. But from the beginning it formed the central evidence of Christianity, and, at the same time, as the supreme miracle of revelation, it has been the centre of attack. It must, therefore, receive separate treatment, owing to its profound importance; for it is the very centre of the Christian position. With it there stand or fall both the claim of Christ to be Divine and the Christian's hope in his own resurrection. At the same time, as the supreme miracle of the Christian revelation, it will bear the weight of all the other Gospel miracles. To have proved it to be historic is to have routed the attack on miracles, while isolated assaults on minor wonders must be brought to face this main issue. The evidence for the Resurrection has been summed up under the following heads:—

(*α*) The evidence of St. Paul. Not only is the risen Christ the mainspring of his changed life, but he asserts that he, as well as certain others whom he specifies, has seen Him with his own eyes. This is the earliest written testimony we have.

(*β*) The evidence of the other Apostles and NT writers. Not only is this found all through their writings, but it forms the text and centre of the sermons recorded in Acts.

(*γ*) The indirect evidence contained in the records, which establishes the fact that the appearances were under varied circumstances, to those in different frames of mind, in the same country and generation as they are said to have happened, and the cause of a changed life to believers and of bitter opposition from their enemies. The sudden change from sorrow to joy in the first disciples is incapable of any other explanation.*

(*δ*) The evidence of the empty grave. Had Christ's enemies possessed the corpse, they would have produced it; had His followers possessed it, Christianity would have been consciously founded on a gigantic fraud. This view is now held by no one.

(*ε*) The evidence of Christ's life before the Crucifixion. The records show that He fully expected this sequel, though His disciples were quite unable to grasp it or to realize it when it had actually happened.

(*ζ*) The evidence of the Church. Not only has the Resurrection been the central belief of the Church from those days until these, but such institutions as Sunday and the Eucharist, and the joy that is contained in them, cannot be explained by any other means.

Such evidence is far stronger than that which supports most of the accepted history of the ancient world. Such objections as the absence of eyewitnesses and the inconsistency of the accounts would never have been raised, but for the stupendous issue depending on the historic truth of the Resurrection.

Opponents are powerless to deny that the evidence was sufficient from the earliest days to enable every Christian absolutely to accept the fact, and make it the centre of his belief and conduct. All that they can do is to try to account for this belief in such a way as to deny the actual fact.

Bruce reduces such non-Christian hypotheses to five.

1. *The thief theory.*—The disciples stole Christ's body, as perhaps He had told them to, in order to make men believe in a resurrection. Such a theory as this of Reimarus is now universally discredited.

2. *The swoon theory.*—Christ did not really die, but revived, escaped, and pretended to have risen. This view of Paulus and Schleiermacher has been refuted even by Strauss as inconsistent with the character of such a moral reformer, while its practical difficulties are insuperable.

3. *The vision theory.*—Renan and Strauss assert that the belief arose from the hallucination of several disciples, the first to suggest it being Mary Magdalene, an excitable woman who had once been possessed. But this directly contradicts every word of the only existing records, which show that excited expectancy was entirely absent. Nor is it possible to think, if the Resurrection was only subjective, that these visions suddenly gave place after six weeks to the calm strength of the early Church.

4. *The theory of objective visions, or telegram hypothesis.*—This is Keim's attempted compromise. The appearances were not purely subjective, but the objective cause was not a risen body of Christ, but His glorified Spirit comforting them by 'sending telegrams from heaven.' But such a theory, without avoiding the supernatural, does not free the disciples from hallucination, for they certainly thought their Master was there in the flesh, and not in heaven.*

5. *The mythical theory.*—There were no appearances at all, but the strong way the disciples spoke of the continued life of their crucified Master was misunderstood by the Apostolic Church. Hence arose the myth of the Resurrection, which was later embodied in the legendary accounts contained in the Gospels. Thus Weizsäcker and Martineau would say that all is accounted for as an evolution from the conviction that flashed upon the disciples in their sorrow that 'Heroes die not,' and after all their Master was not dead. The craving for something more objective led to the invention of legendary Christophanies. We can only answer here, that there is no time for the growth of a myth that would change the human Jesus into the Divine Christ of our Gospels, that it even demands that such a change of belief should have taken place before Pentecost, and that such an explanation of the experience of the first disciples cannot be made to fit with the only records we have of their words and conduct. We thus turn back to the Christian theory as the only rational and historical explanation of the facts. Any further discussion of the nature of the glorified body belongs to the province of theology. It is enough to have assurance that the supreme miracle on which Christianity is based is a historic fact.

See **Bruce**, *Baur*, pp. 383-398; **W. Milligan**, *The Resurrection of our Lord*, 1881; **H. Latham**, *The Risen Master*, 1901; **Sparrow Simpson**, *Our Lord's Resurrection*, 1905, and art. 'Resurrection' in *DCG*.

(*d*) *The history of Christianity and of the Church.*—Here, again, is involved, in the first place, a study of Acts and the Epistles. Their early date must be proved. Christianity is not the creation of St. Paul. The early Church did not develop as Baur suggested, but as indicated by the early Fathers. The primitive existence of Church order witnesses to the same effect.

* **See below, under Psychological arguments, (*a*) concerning their changed life.**

* However, the theory must not be entirely discounted which accepts the evidence of *α*, *β*, and *γ* above, while it rejects that of *δ*. See **K. Lake**, *The Historical Evidence for the Resurrection*, 1907.

See L. Pullan, *The Books of the NT*, 1901; Gore, *The Church and the Ministry*[4], 1900; Neander, *History of the Planting and Training of the Christian Church* (tr. Ryland, 1851); A. B. Bruce, *Ferdinand Christian Baur* (Pres. Day Tracts); Salmon, *Introd. to the NT*, 1885.

2. *Psychological arguments.*—We must explain that this term is used for convenience to denote that class of argument which is not strictly historical, but which deals either with the feelings of individuals, or with the inferences which may be drawn from Christian practices, or the relation of Christianity to other systems. The following are given as examples of such arguments:—

(*a*) *The changed life of the disciples, and the conversion of St. Paul.*—Up to the death of Christ the disciples had shown themselves timid in their behaviour and earthly in their expectations. They suddenly became full of boldness and joy and a new spiritual force which nothing could resist. The psychological difficulty of such a change is enormous. It is overcome only by the explanation that their Master rose again, spiritualized their ideas, and gave them an abiding gift of the Holy Spirit. And even if these unlettered Galilæans had been deceived, it is impossible that they could have in their turn deceived a cultured and expert Jewish Rabbi. The conversion and apostleship of St. Paul alone, duly considered, was of itself a demonstration sufficient to prove Christianity to be a Divine revelation.

See G. Lyttleton, *Conversion and Apostleship of St. Paul*, 1869; R. J. Knowling, *Testimony of St. Paul to Christ*, 1905.

(*b*) *The witness of Christian customs and institutions.*—Allusion has already been made to these in their special relation to the Resurrection. But there are other evidential uses to which may be put such recognized parts of Christianity as the Ministry, the Sacraments, and the Christian Year. They satisfy the cravings of human nature, its needs, tendencies, and aspirations, in a way that no other religion does. The *ministry* is founded on the theory that man is social, and needs organization, continuity, and authority in the guidance of life. The *sacramental system* takes into account the composite nature of man, using and welding into one both the material and the spiritual elements, and at the same time conveying in a definite form that communication of Divine grace which we should naturally expect to be the climax of any revelation which God makes of Himself to the individual. The *Christian Year* links us with the first centuries. Easter and the Lord's Day were already observed in NT times, the observance of Friday as the day of the Crucifixion is of early origin; and so the list might be continued. Not only do these things witness to the historicity of the facts which they commemorate, but, viewed from the sphere which is psychical rather than historical, they bring the whole question of Apologetics out of the past into the present, and enable us to postulate the real life of those roots of Christianity which are hidden in the past, when we examine carefully those living and growing branches which are visible in the present.

See Lonsdale Ragg, *Evidences of Christianity*, 1905, 102–121.

(*c*) *The success of Christianity.*—Apart from the moral aspect of the question, an estimate of facts and their relation to mere human possibilities of explanation, suggests an evidence of the Divine origin of Christianity, and of the work of the Holy Spirit in the history of the Church. At the same time it has to be remembered that other religions may make a counter-claim, so that the claim of Christianity must be shown to be unique. The following are the chief points in the argument:—

(*α*) The early, wide, and, within certain limits, irresistible diffusion of Christianity. It required an enormous power to kill polytheism for ever, and to leave not a shrine of a heathen god behind; but this was what Christianity did.

(*β*) Its power of revival and restoration after every declension and decay. This may be traced throughout history, through the Middle Ages, the Reformation, and more modern revivals, and Christianity may be shown to possess elements which Muhammadanism cannot claim.

(*γ*) The resistance which it has been able to offer to successive assaults. From the days of the earliest martyrs persecution has been powerless to crush it. All the forces of the ancient world were arrayed against it, but the only result was the decay and fall of Rome itself. And it has faced all objections of later days, and can point to a confusion among its opponents which makes one school of anti-Christian thought contradict another.

(*δ*) It is specially armed with means and motives for self-propagation. Its work of proselytizing, founded on the pure motives of the missionary spirit, is on a different plane from Buddhism and Muhammadanism. The rule of faith expressed in its creeds, the universal application of its sacred writings, the organization of the Church, her ministry, her sacraments, her worship, and her government, are fitted in a unique way for passing on the faith whole and unimpaired from age to age and from land to land.

(*ε*) Its success is in harmony with its own predictions and anticipations. It is here that the argument from prophecy has its fullest force. For it begins with the earliest literature, in the promise that the seed of the woman should bruise the serpent's head, and continues through centuries. And when it reaches the NT, it shows such unlikely features as the anticipation of the corruptions of Christianity, from the parable of the Tares at the beginning to the expectation of Antichrist at the end.

Various natural causes have been adduced to account for such a success, but one by one they may be proved insufficient, and we fall back on the conclusion that the origin and growth of the faith must be attributed to a Divine agency.

See J. Cairns, *The Success of Christianity and modern Explanations of it* (Pres. Day Tr.).

(*d*) *The abiding unity of faith.*—In the face of the divisions of Christendom, and the misunderstandings which separate branches of the Catholic Church, it may seem bold to found an argument on the unity of Christendom in its belief. But when a broader view is taken, and Christianity is compared with other religions, a strong argument for the Divine origin and preservation of the Faith is found to lie in its continued acceptance. The Creeds themselves, handed on intact from age to age, present a remarkable phenomenon. Their silence on non-essentials combines with their insistence on fundamentals to prevent their ever being out of date. No other religion can point to so broad a unity. The unity of Muhammadanism or Buddhism is either local or at least Oriental, and can make no such appeal to the whole world. And the fundamentals upon which Christian belief has been based, *quod semper, ubique, et ab omnibus*, are just those truths which are not shared by any people outside Christendom. Such are the spirituality and Fatherhood of God, the moral condition of man and the blackness of his sin, the possibilities of universal salvation by redemption through One Person, in whom a human and a Divine nature are combined, the Personality and Divinity of the Holy Spirit, and His work in and among men, with the visible Body of Christ as His sphere of working, the approach through the sacraments, the authority of the Scriptures and of the Church, the necessity of faith, and the importance of an eschatology such that the thought of the future resurrection of the body influences men in the present.

And this unity of faith is also manifested in a unity of aspiration. The biographies of different Christians in all ages reveal a kinship in spiritual life and belief, and the same is shown by a study of hymnology throughout the centuries.

It is a profound marvel that the Churches in different localities in the first days did not soon begin to show some cleavage of faith and the practices that result from it. It is a still greater marvel that in recent generations the multiplication of sects, the revolt against authority, and the rise of free speculation within the Church, have not made more impression on the fundamental unity of the Faith. The least difficult explanation of such phenomena lies in the Divine origin and preservation of Christianity.

See **J. Stoughton**, *Unity of Faith* (Pres. Day Tracts).

(*e*) *The argument from the psychological nature of religion.*—This is the result of a study of religion which is of comparatively recent growth. Kant began the investigation of religion not merely by reflexion on what was positive and objective, but by taking it as an internal and mental fact. Consciousness proves the existence of religion as a subjective or mental state ; but consciousness itself must be analyzed, in order to analyze religion. In this way a threefold division of mental phenomena has been established—into cognitions, emotions, and volitions. Religion must be a state of intellect, sensibility, or will, or some combination of two or all of these factors. Hegel identified religion and thought. Yet no mere intellectual act constitutes religion, though the exercise of reason is an essential part of religion. If religion has no rational foundation, it has no real foundation. Others resolve religion into feeling or sentiment. But every feeling requires an explanation, which can be found only in an exercise of *intellect*. Hume traces religion to fear, Feuerbach to desire, Schleiermacher to a feeling of dependence, to which Mansel adds the conviction of moral obligation. Strauss combines all these. Kant identifies religion with morality. But it is *not* simply these things, though it includes them. Rather is the religious process at once rational, emotional, and volitional, and is to be connected with all three—knowing, feeling, and doing—in its threefold aspect of knowledge, affection, and self-surrender. If one general notion can be made to embrace the universal instinct of men as regards a definition of religion, it is this, that it belongs to the whole man, in accordance with the psychology sketched above. The question remains, which religion answers best to this description? It is only theistic religions that can claim to do it ; polytheism, pantheism, deism, and rationalism are ruled out. 'Of the three great theistic religions, Judaism, Christianity, and Muhammadanism, the last is far inferior to the other two, and the first is a transition to and preparation for the second' (Flint, *Theism*[3], p. 44). Christianity is left, as alone giving a perfect representation of God.

EXCURSUS:—*The general superiority of Christianity to other religions.*—

(1) *Polytheism.*—Polytheistic beliefs are the characteristic of the whole ancient world, with the single exception of the Jews. Such beliefs continually broke down with the advance of culture, and it is perhaps sufficient to say of them that they have abundantly been proved to be ethically degrading, as not linked with morality, and philosophically unsatisfying, as offering no final revelation. Some of the religions of India are pantheistic as much as polytheistic, and admit of the fatal objection that they ignore the transcendence of the Deity. See artt. POLYTHEISM, PANTHEISM.

(2) *Buddhism.*—This deserves a word of separate treatment, as its moral code is profoundly attractive, and it counts almost as many adherents as Christianity. But really it is not so much a religion as a philosophy, an inherently atheistic system which does not offer a real Deity for worship, and suggests no hope for a future life. The very fact that its followers have instinctively demanded an object for worship, has caused it to become corrupted and obscured by the introduction of pure polytheism.

See **C. F. Aiken**, *The Dhamma of Gotama the Buddha and the Gospel of Jesus the Christ*, 1900.

(3) *Muhammadanism.*—Here it is its success which forms the chief recommendation of the religion ; but this has been largely discounted by the forcible means of propagation which have been required. Its pure monotheism brings it into relation with Judaism and Christianity, but its God is as distant as He is sublime, and 'its theological outcome is simply awe and submission, not loving intercourse.' The lowness of its moral standard prevents it from having a civilizing influence, and the moral state of society under it may be judged by the painfully degraded position of woman. The fact that it is founded, not on a life but on a book, checks its power of expansion and adaptation, and has reduced it to a code which is the enemy of all real progress.

(4) *Judaism.*—This is the one pure religion of the ancient world, and might be a formidable rival of Christianity if the latter were obliged to treat it as false. But, on the contrary, it claims for itself all that is best and purest and most permanent in Judaism. Historically, the one religion grew out of the other ; theologically, the germ of Christian doctrine is to be found in the OT doctrines of God and man, its progressive revelation, and its Messianic hope. There is no desire to belittle the one pure religion of the ancient world, but there is much in it that is incomplete. Christianity simply claims to fulfil it, to answer its problems, and to carry it forward to finality. The question of the position of the OT is here involved.

See **R. L. Ottley**, *Aspects of the OT*, 1897 ; **J. Orr**, *The Problem of the OT*, 1906.

It must be noted that the general superiority of Christianity to these religions includes the fact that it sums up all that is best in them. We do not stigmatize them as utterly false, but we recognize them as a feeling after that truth of which Christianity claims to be the final expression (see *Excursus* at the end of the 'Psychical Realm,' p. 620[b]).

For the whole subject, see **Flint**, *Theism*, Lect. ii. (Baird Lectures, 1876) ; **A. B. Bruce**, *Apologetics*[3], 1904, chs. iii.–vii. ; **Jevons**, *Introd. to Hist. of Religion*, 1896 ; **Lefroy**, *Mahomedanism: its Strength and Weakness* ; **Liddon**, *Essays and Addresses*, 1892, pp. 1–60 ; **Eliot Howard**, *Non-Christian Religious Systems*, 1906 ; **Westcott**, *The Gospel of Life*, 1892, esp. ch. v. ; **Marcus Dods**, *Mohammed, Buddha, and Christ*, 1877 ; *Pan-Anglican Papers*, i. 1908 ; *JE*, *passim* ; **G. Matheson**, *The Distinctive Messages of the Old Religions*, 1892.

3. *Metaphysical arguments.*—(*a*) *The argument from intelligence, will, and conscience, commonly called the Ontological argument.*—In nature, because we are thinkers ourselves, we realize that what is before us is the result of thought. We grasp by our intelligence that intelligence is exhibited in all work in which there are parts which bear an ordered relation to each other, and in which the whole is something more than the mere sum of the individual parts. Therefore we infer that what the mind detects, mind has produced, and that a creative intelligence underlies order. In *morality*, the sense of a moral law, and the demand for ethical perfection, in the voluntary fulfilment of such non-natural requirements as the dictates of duty, imply a standard, a superhuman will, a Holy One, such as has been revealed to the world in Christ. In the realm of *conscience*, there lies in the human mind an instinct which expresses itself in the conviction of a survival after death and of future retribution and reward. In the face of all ills and miseries, man desires to continue to exist, and anticipates a re-adjusting of the balance which will not terminate until the full demands of that moral law, of which conscience is the representative and ambassador, have been met in full. The intelligence, the will, and the conscience thus combine in a threefold suggestion of an Intelligence which creates, of a Lawgiver who imposes a superhuman will, and a Judge who re-adjusts the balance. But in view of the unity of nature, and the unity with it of our human nature, that which lies behind all nature, and which the various parts of our human nature suggest, will in itself be *One*. We therefore arrive at a Personal God, as He has been revealed in Christ.

See J. A. Fleming, *The Evidence of Things not Seen*, 1904.

(*b*) *The argument from consciousness.*—We cannot stay to discuss that part of Herbert Spencer's philosophy which deals with the consciousness (see J. Iverach, *The Philosophy of Mr. Herbert Spencer examined* [Rel. Tract Soc.]). But human consciousness or personality affords an argument which is indeed kindred to the foregoing, but has been put in a form of which the following is an outline.

1. 'Through direct consciousness of himself man discovers that he is possessed of a Permanent Personality, endowed with will, intelligence, moral and spiritual affections. 2. Through consciousness further developed by reflexion on himself and the universe, he attains the conviction that over all is a Supreme Personality, endowed with omnipotent Will, infinite Intelligence, perfect Righteousness, and Love. It is contended that these results of consciousness rest on the same basis, and stand or fall together. If the primary consciousness of a human self is denied, all the rest vanish with it. On the other hand, if it is accepted, it carries all the rest in its train. Thus it is from the knowledge of himself that man rises to the knowledge of God. Theism is the fruit of belief in man's real humanity; agnosticism, of a virtual denial of his humanity.'

See Brownlow Maitland, *Theism or Agnosticism*, 1878.

(*c*) *The argument from the idea of God.*—Whence does the idea of God come to us? It is not originated by any of the arguments we use, whether ontological, cosmological, or teleological. They help to verify it, but they postulate it as already existent in the mind. It cannot be traced to man's conscience, heart, or reason, though these faculties may verify and develop it. There is no place where the idea of God has not existed. Therefore God exists. Kant overthrew the original ontological argument by asserting that any cognition of things is impossible where there is no empirical matter to work upon. But we refuse to allow that God cannot be empirically known. Agnosticism really asserts not only that man cannot know God, but that God cannot make Himself known. And to say this is to deny His existence. But a flat denial of God's existence is possible only for the man who has passed through every sphere in his search for Him. In short, in order to be able to assert authoritatively that no God exists, a man must be omniscient and omnipresent, *i.e.* he must himself be God, and himself give the lie to himself.

(*d*) *The Cosmological or Ætiological argument.*—We have the idea of causality inherent in us. We attribute everything to some cause, but even though we feel ourselves on a higher level of causality than ordinary nature, we do not feel self-caused. Our notions fall back to a First Cause, which is the final cause of all, and itself uncaused. The study of the universe suggests that this cause must be, not mechanical, but full of order and intelligence, and the study of our own personality leads us further to think of this *Causa causans* as a personal God.

See, for the metaphysical and philosophic aspect, Caldecott, *The Being of God in the Light of Philosophy* (Camb. Theol. Essays, 1905); J. R. Illingworth, *Personality Human and Divine*, 1894, and *Reason and Revelation*, 1906; and, for the influence of modern knowledge on the main theistic arguments, Ballard, *Theomonism True*, 1906, pp. 68-346.

EXCURSUS:—The anthropological attack.—The analogies between Christian beliefs and practices and those of some of the other great religions of the world, have long formed the basis of an attack upon the faith. In recent years the study of more primitive religions, and of anthropology generally, has suggested further analogies, and given rise to a fresh attack. The attempt is being made to explain away Christian history and ideas as merely the survivals of what has now been found to exist in primitive cults all over the world. Various modes of defence have already been employed, but the apologist must not ignore the parallels afforded by recent discoveries. The facts collected in such books as Frazer's *Golden Bough* or Crawley's *Mystic Rose* or Robertson's *Pagan Christs* must rather be claimed and used for the Christian argument. As illustrations of the hostile use of them we may mention the theory that Christ is to be connected with Eastern Sun-worship, the twelve Apostles being the signs of the zodiac, and that the Sacrament of Communion is merely an adaptation of the wide-spread primitive belief, with its degrading accompaniments, that to partake of a life means to inherit its virtues. And strange elaborations have followed, such as Frazer's theory of the Crucifixion, which suggests that the Jews had transferred to the feast of Purim the customs of a strange kind of Saturnalia, wherein a mock king was first pampered and then killed, and that Christ only met 'the fate that annually befell the malefactor who played Haman' (see J. G. Frazer, *The Golden Bough*², iii. 190 ff.).

The Christian answer to which we would briefly point is that all religion is one, and that its 'primary function is to affirm and consecrate *life*' (Ernest Crawley, *The Tree of Life*, 1905, p. 270). If Christianity is God's final answer to human needs, we shall expect to see those needs manifesting themselves elsewhere. 'We can see a deeper meaning in the parallelism which forms so remarkable a bond between Christianity and the lower religions. These analogies from savage culture show that religion, everywhere and always, is a direct outcome of elemental human nature, and that this elemental human nature remains practically unchanged. This it must continue to be so long as we are built up of flesh and blood. For instance, if a savage eats the flesh of a strong man or divine person, and a modern Christian partakes sacramentally of Christ's body and blood under the forms of bread and wine, there is evidently a human need behind both acts which prompts them and is satisfied by them, and is responsible for their similarity. . . . Christianity is no survival from primitive religion, but a higher development from the same permanent sources' (E. Crawley, *The Tree of Life*, 1905, p. 261 f. See also J. R. Illingworth, *Divine Immanence*, 1898, ch. iv.).

(iii.) THE MORAL REALM.—It has been said that the moral element in our nature is as much higher than the mental as the mental is above the physical. The weight of moral arguments is therefore greater, and perhaps for this reason this sphere has been chosen by recent apologists for their main line of defence. It has already been mentioned that Christ Himself in His moral aspect is the supreme apologetic of to-day; but there are other lines of moral argument which are placed first, owing to their priority in the sequence of thought.

1. *Arguments for theistic belief from the moral realm of thought.*—(*a*) *The universal idea of God and cultivation of religion.*—This argument is sometimes called 'the evidence of general consent.' Cicero witnessed long ago: 'There was never any nation so barbarous, or any people in the world so savage, as to be without some notion of

gods.' The belief in some form, and the expression of it in worship, are found in every system, ancient and modern. To ascribe this instinct to accident is to raise a moral difficulty which cannot easily be surmounted.

(*b*) *The moral sense in man, the conscience and the sense of sin.*—Kant, while rejecting other arguments, placed the whole weight of proof on this one. There is in our nature a sense of moral responsibility, a feeling of what we *ought* to do, regardless of our present wishes and immediate advantage. This sense, commonly called conscience, cannot come either from our own liking or the will of the community, against the opinion of which it sometimes acts. The only explanation of its working is in the existence of a perfect moral Being, independent of ourselves, a perfect Lawgiver and Judge, to whom conscience feels itself responsible. It is here that we are brought closest to the vast problem of evil and of sin. A discussion of it belongs to theology rather than to apologetics. But we may quote the saying of Leibniz, that 'metaphysical evil consists in imperfection, physical in suffering, moral in sin.' As we trace the upward development of the race, we find that just where the sense of individual personality comes to the front, a conflict begins to be realized between the claims of others and those of self. Man is unique as placed in a position from which he may either rise higher or fall lower. He has a consciousness of something higher; if he wilfully chooses that which is lower, it is *sin*. But since his moral nature does realize the choice, struggling upward to the higher, in spite of the certainty that he will never fully reach it, and filled with humiliation when he has failed in the struggle and acquiesced in the sin, we are pointed to a perfect moral Being who is averse to sin, and to whom the moral sense in man knows itself to be responsible.

See Liddon, *Some Elements of Religion*, 1872, pp. 66–71; Inge, 'Sin and Modern Thought' (in *Topics of the Times*, 1906, pp. 142–167); Coe, *The Religion of a Mature Mind*, 1902, p. 361.

(*c*) *The moral course of the world's history.*—The tangled skein of human history is found, when unravelled, to exhibit a continual progress towards a more and more perfect exhibition of righteousness and goodness. There is a purpose running through history, indicating a moral governance. This may be studied in the development of the various sides of human institutions, as the life of nations, social life, crime, law, and religion. But such a moral government of the world, and such an education of the human race, imply a moral Governor and Educator; for it is impossible that such tendencies should be unconscious and impersonal.

See Fisher, *Grounds of Belief*[2], 1902, p. 69; Flint, *Theism*, 1902, pp. 227–261; Liddon, *Some Elements of Religion*, 1872, pp. 142–148.

2. *Arguments for Christianity from the moral realm of fact.*—(*a*) *The Christian Scriptures.*—As the study of nature suggests an intelligence behind, and a study of history suggests a moral Governor, so the study of the Bible suggests a power higher than that of the men who contributed to this great literature which contains so many varied elements. Stress must be laid on (1) its organic unity, manifested in an OT and a NT fitting into each other exactly in spite of the changes of time and thought, in the wonderful symmetry that is presented by the two, and in the advancing morality which may be traced in their pages; (2) its authority, the moral force and power of conviction that its writers possess in an absolutely unique degree, its tone of certainty and genuine ring as the authoritative message of God; and (3) its exact correspondence with the deepest instincts of human nature, so that conscience welcomes its words as the highest expression of morality and religion.

See J. A. Fleming, *The Evidence of Things not Seen*, 1904, p. 40 ff.; J. Orr, *The Bible under Trial*, 1907.

(*b*) *The morality of Christianity.*—The success of Christianity has already been dealt with. But nothing has been said about the inward and radical transformation which it has effected. Its elevation, from the first days until these, of those who embrace it, is a moral miracle absolutely without parallel. The early apologists were already able to point to the effects of Christianity, as seen in a complete moral change in Christians. The argument has been increasing in force ever since. For the inevitable introduction of half-hearted members into a growing community, which soon extended as widely as civilization itself, is more than compensated by the contrast between the civilization which has been leavened by Christianity, and any other civilization in the history of the world. It is true that Christian morality is founded on the morality of Christ, and can be explained as a perpetual endeavour to fulfil His precepts and imitate His example. But this only takes the argument one stage further back, as we shall see shortly. And the very fact that the sustained endeavour has been made gives an additional proof that the morality of Christ was not a human and natural product. Two points in Christian morality must be insisted on. (1) It presents an ideal which no one except its Founder has ever fulfilled or expected to fulfil. And yet men have gone on trying. They have none of the satisfaction which belongs to those who fulfil a lower standard, such as that of Muhammadanism. And their reason for trying is not personal advantage, for the ideal has to be sought through self-sacrifice; in Christianity it is the losing of one's own soul that is to save it. (2) And not only is Christian morality different from what the natural man would wish for himself, but it is different from anything that he would invent. Its code is of the most unexpected kind, and has no real parallel or preparation elsewhere, in whatever setting we view it. And perhaps least of all was it likely to arise at such a place and time as Palestine in the 1st cent. of our era. If we reject the explanation of it which lies in the person of the Founder Himself, the alternative conclusions are difficult indeed of acceptance.

See F. Ballard, *Miracles of Unbelief*, esp. pop. ed. 1904, p. 242.

(*c*) *The Person of Christ the moral ideal.*—The morality of Christ's teaching is universally accepted as the highest the world has ever seen. The point need not be laboured here. But it is not merely a matter of His teaching; it is His example that stands highest. And in this too there is agreement among all. Even a writer like Lecky can say (*History of European Morals*[8], vol. ii. p. 9): 'The simple record of three short years of active life has done more to regenerate and to soften mankind than all the disquisitions of philosophers, and all the exhortations of moralists. This has indeed been the well-spring of whatever is best and purest in the Christian life.'

It is upon the moral ideal presented by the Person of Christ that modern apologetic takes its stand. It boldly asks, 'Whence hath this man these things?' and demands a rational answer.

(*a*) Is it replied that this is simply derived from our records, and need have no place in the history of actual fact? But this is no answer; for we ask, Whence then came the Gospel portrait of Christ? Whatever view be taken of the composition of the Gospels, it involves in *some one* an exquisite conception of the ideal which has no parallel in the world. It is impossible to believe that various men, whether few or many, whether actual disciples or only compilers working up traditions in later years, succeeded in forming a unity, a harmonious picture, such as is found in the Gospel portrait. The only explanation of their work lies in there having been an original to be painted.

(β) May we, then, retain the moral part of the portrait, and take it out of its miraculous surroundings? It will be found that the two are so interwoven that separation is impossible. Take away the supernatural, and nothing but a shadow is left. For the miracles are not interspersed amid the various indications of the character; they are the outward manifestation of it. They are not wrought, except on rare occasions, with an evidential purpose, but simply as the natural acts of so exalted a character.

(γ) And what of the Divine claim of Christ? Is it possible to regard it either as interwoven in the tale by His mistaken followers, or as an individual mistake owing to a wrong estimate of His own Person? Both alternatives seem incredible, in view of the fact that this claim is the only key to His life, His words, and His work. Take such a public declaration as 'I am the light of the world; he that followeth me shall not walk in darkness, but shall have the light of life' (Jn 8^{12}). If anything in the record is true, surely that solemn utterance, in the presence of His enemies and before the multitudes who had thronged to the feast, is not a figment of after years. And if He made the claim Himself, more presumptuous than could have come, not only from a Galilæan carpenter, but from the holiest of men, what must we say if it were not true? That He was either an impostor or a deluded enthusiast. No one nowadays dare assert the former, and to do so would only make it a greater miracle how the highest moral ideals of humanity have for eighteen centuries been linked with such a man. And if the latter alternative be chosen, it is absolutely impossible to reconcile the self-sacrificing devotion and utter humility of His whole life and work with a distorted moral obliquity and infatuated self-assertion which could make so preposterous a claim. The familiar dilemma, 'Aut Deus aut homo non bonus,' has not yet been avoided by those who would hold such views. If the moral ideal which His Person presents forbids the latter, the former is the only rational explanation which remains.

(δ) But is not Evolution to be allowed to enter and explain? Is it not simply that in Christ the upward movement reached its climax, and in Him we see the moral sense of the human race reaching its perfection? But it is the reverse of true that such a character can be explained by its antecedents and environment. The arguments of Paley are still true of 'the originality of Christ's character.' He assumed a part which was in many ways the direct opposite of the Messiah of popular expectation. And the one catholic Man, whose teaching is adapted to all nations and all ages, sprang from the narrowest and most bigoted nation of antiquity. And those who deny His Divinity change the virgin birth into an illegitimate one. They rob themselves of the argument that He was only evolved as the purer son of a pure virgin. They assert in effect that 'the most marked and mighty impulse of the past towards all that is purest, worthiest, loftiest, in the evolution of human nature, emanated spontaneously from the untutored, peasant-bred son of an adulteress' (Ballard, *Miracles of Unbelief*, p. 275). Such things are a denial of the first principles of evolution, and constitute a moral miracle far more difficult to accept than that a pure virgin 'was found with child of the Holy Ghost.' This line of defence is thus seen to lead to a direct attack on the enemy's position.

See Liddon, *The Divinity of our Lord*, 1867; Gore, *The Incarnation of the Son of God*, 1891; Ballard, *Miracles of Unbelief*, pop. ed. 1904, ch. viii.; Row, *Manual of Christian Evidences*, 1886, pp. 27–122; Robbins, *A Christian Apologetic*, 1902.

(iv.) THE SPIRITUAL REALM.—We here reach the highest form of Christian evidences, and the most convincing, for the proofs are brought within the range of personal experience. But, at the same time, they are useless in arguing with an opponent. We can do no more than point out to him that it is wholly rational that spiritual things should be spiritually discerned, and that in a spiritual religion like Christianity the final proof must be a spiritual one, while the cumulative arguments that lead up to it do not in themselves amount to absolute proof, but are as high as an outsider is capable of rising. It is true that God leaves not Himself without witness in the physical sphere, and that there is abundant testimony in the mental and ethical realms; but man approaches Him most closely in that which is least material, and therefore the spiritual faculty of faith is not to be mocked as contrary to reason, but accepted as transcending it. We must therefore take into account—

(*a*) *The testimony of the spiritual faculty.*—The spiritual faculty mentioned above may be simply spoken of as 'faith,' and we claim that it is distinct from the other organs of knowledge, so that it must be added to the senses and reason in order to complete our cognitive being. Often the testimony of the senses is contradicted by reason, and in the case of such a word as 'finite' it is positive and real to reason, though wholly imperceptible to the senses. And in the same way faith may sometimes contradict the conclusions which have been arrived at by the reason. To reason the word 'Infinite' is purely negative, but to faith it is entirely real and positive. So we claim that faith is that faculty or organ of knowledge whereby we apprehend the Infinite. Other religions may contain the knowledge of the presence of the Infinite, but Christianity is unique in not only telling men that their duty is to know God, but in giving them the successive steps whereby they may do so. Though he has arrived at his conclusion neither by the senses nor by the reason, the Christian has arrived at a real and legitimate form of human knowledge when he can say, 'I know whom I have believed.'

See Miller, 'The Idea of God,' in *Topics of the Times* (S.P.C.K., 1906).

(*b*) *The testimony to Christianity of the spiritual yearnings of men.*—Perhaps the two plainest of these yearnings are shown in the instinct to worship, and the hope of immortality, both of which are practically universal. The former opens the whole question of prayer, and the latter the wide subject of eschatology. Neither can be discussed here, but the argument must lead on to the fact that both are satisfied in a unique degree by the practice and belief of Christianity.

See F. Ballard, *Miracles of Unbelief*, pp. 280–310.

(*c*) *The testimony of holy lives.*—It has always been realized, from the days of the early Apologists, that one of the most telling of evidences lies in the spiritual life of Christians. Few men are argued into a belief in Christianity. They may verify their acceptance of it by its appeal to reason and the senses, but the real motive power consists in a touching of their heart. And this is done not by the words, but by the life of Christians. Apologetics may be exalted into a science, but the work of turning men is but little due to the professed apologist. Every Christ-like life is in itself a powerful apology, and often succeeds where all else fails.

(*d*) *The personal experience of the Christian.*—This can be the only final proof. The Christian can test all he has been told, in the sphere of his own spirit, and its relation to God as revealed in Christ. And this experience has been multiplying in the lives of millions for nearly 2000 years. If we are charged with undue bias, it can be answered that 'initial unbelief is a prepossession as much as faith.' Thus do we pass upwards out of the region of Apologetics. We must be content to add the various arguments together, and claim that their sum-total raises so great a probability in favour of the Christian religion that there are far greater difficulties about any other explanation of the facts of the case. And the nature of our faith is such that the rest must be done in the region of the Spirit, wherein alone the probability can pass upward into certainty. T. W. CRAFER.

APOSTASY (Jewish and Christian).—The deliberate abandonment of one religion for another, *e.g.* Judaism for Christianity or *vice versa*, made voluntarily or under compulsion. The word is usually employed in a bad sense, and consequently from the standpoint of the religion deserted. Heretics, *i.e.* those who embrace one form of a religion in place of another, are not here reckoned as apostates. In Christian jurisprudence, apostasy is regarded as a far more serious offence than even heresy.

The word *ἀπόστασις* is used in classical Greek of a revolt or defection from an alliance. *ἀποστασία* is a later form, found in the LXX, Plutarch, and Dionysius of Halicarnassus. In the LXX these words, with their kindred forms, *ἀποστατέω*, *ἀποστάτης*, fem. *ἀποστάτις*, are used in the sense of rebellion against Jahweh (Jos 22[22]) or an earthly monarch. Thus the 'rebellious children' of Is 30[1] are called *τέκνα ἀπόστατα*; the idolatry of Ahaz is his *ἀποστασία* (2 Ch 29[19]); and in 1 K 21[13] 'men of Belial' is rendered *ἄνδρες τῆς ἀποστασίας*. In 1 Mac. the word *ἀποστασία* is used in its modern sense (2[15] *ἦλθον οἱ καταναγκάζοντες τὴν ἀποστασίαν*). In the NT, St. Paul is accused of teaching 'an apostasy from Moses' (Ac 21[21]), and he speaks in 2 Th 2[3] of the great *ἀποστασία* at the end of all things, before the revelation of the 'Man of Sin' (see below). Augustine calls the 'Fall of Man' the *apostasia primi hominis* (*c. Jul.* lib. iii.), and he uses this term because the absolute freedom of our first parents, unhampered by original sin, to choose between obeying and disobeying God, made there a voluntary defection (see Shedd, ii. 148 ff.). St. Thomas Aquinas (Qu. 12, Art. 1) says of disobedience: 'apostasia videtur omnis peccati principium.'

1. Although we have many examples of **national apostasy in the OT,** instances of individual desertion of the religion of Israel are rare; but in the Deuteronomic law the provisions against those who try to persuade the people to 'serve other gods' are naturally severe (Dt 13[6-11]). In Ezekiel we have examples of secret worship of heathen deities practised in the very temple of Jahweh (Ezk 8[5ff.]). On the whole, however, it may be said that, with the exception of the great apostasy in the days of Ahab and Elijah, the infidelity of Israel towards Jahweh was, as a rule, shown in attempts either to combine this worship with that of the local divinities, or to serve Him with rites similar to those practised in the worship of the gods of Canaan.

We first meet with distinct acts of apostasy from Judaism during the fierce persecution under Antiochus Epiphanes, when Jews either voluntarily or under compulsion renounced the worship of God for that of the deities of Greece. The degree of apostasy varied between a total abandonment of all pretence of Judaism, and the adoption of certain Greek customs like the practice of athletics and the wearing of the *petasos*, or broad-brimmed Greek hat, which the more rigid Jews regarded as an act of disloyalty to Jahweh.

Antiochus Epiphanes (B.C. 175–164) did not cause the tendencies of the Jews to Hellenize which manifested themselves early in his reign. The inhabitants of Jerusalem, especially the priests, had already conformed to the Greek dress and frequented the *palæstra* (2 Mac 4[13-15]). Jason the high priest even sent presents for the sacrifices to Hercules at Tyre, though his messengers refused to employ the money for such an object, and handed it over to the royal navy (2 Mac 4[18. 19]). When the persecution began in B.C. 168, and the Jews were compelled to sacrifice and to eat swine's flesh, many of them apostatized (1 Mac 1[43]); and it was the slaying of one of these by Mattathias, the father of the famous Maccabees, that gave the signal for the revolt (1 Mac 2[24]). The Hellenizing Jews held the citadel of Acra in Jerusalem with the Syrians (1 Mac 1[34]), and were not dispossessed till B.C. 142.

Apostasy of a different kind is mentioned in the Book of Wisdom. The Alexandrian Jews adopted in some cases the philosophy of Greece, especially Epicureanism (Wis 2[1-11]). In the Talmud the term *Epiqūrōsin* is applied to apostates (see below).

2. Examples of **apostasy among Christians** are to be found in the NT; but in many cases the falling away of the converts was not strictly apostasy, but a relapse into Judaic Christianity or even heresy. Still Jesus Christ foretold that in the days of trial many would fall away; and in the Epistle to the Hebrews (if we may still believe this Epistle to be addressed to Jewish Christians) there are indications that many Jews who had embraced Christianity were forsaking the Church for the synagogue, when the choice between the one and the other became imperative. We have only hints of newly converted Christians becoming idolaters.

Mt 24[10] (*σκανδαλισθήσονται πολλοὶ . . . καὶ μισήσουσιν ἀλλήλους*) is possibly a prediction of the bitterness of the apostates towards their former friends; also (v.[12]) the *ἀνομία* will cause the love of the many to wax cold. The 'antichrists' spoken of in 1 Jn 2[18f.] may be classed as apostates, but see Westcott, *ad loc.* The important passage in He 6[4ff.], which speaks of the impossibility of renewing unto repentance those who fall away (*παραπεσόντας*) after enlightenment, and crucify (*ἀνασταυροῦντας*) to themselves the Son of God, seems to allude to apostates to Judaism. The warnings against apostasy in this Epistle are frequent (cf. esp. ch. 10). Though in the Epistle to the Galatians the abandonment of the Apostle's teaching was not a complete surrender of Christianity, yet he himself evidently regards it as a practical apostasy (Gal 5[4]). Indications that apostasy was not unknown may be found in the letters to the Churches in the Apocalypse and in the Pastoral Epistles.

In conformity with our Lord's warnings, the early Christians looked for a great falling away before His Second Coming. In 2 Th 2[3] St. Paul tells his converts not to be perturbed because they know that there can be no *Parousia* *ἐὰν μὴ ἔλθῃ ἡ ἀποστασία πρῶτον*. Whatever the exact nature of the apostasy in the present connexion is, it must be at least a religious apostasy, and one, moreover, as the use of the definite article proves, regarding which the Apostle's readers were already fully informed. From the Biblical use of the word *ἀποστασία* it would appear that there is an allusion to a falling away from God; but it has been maintained that the coming revolt of the Jews against the Imperial power of Rome was in the mind of St. Paul.

See art. 'Man of Sin' in Hastings' *DB*; Lightfoot, *Notes on the Epistles of St. Paul.* G. Milligan, *Thessalonians* (1908), Note J, p. 169 ff., gives a catena of the explanations of this passage.

In the primitive Church there were many cases of Christians forsaking the communion of the Church and relapsing into idolatry. Some of those accused of Christianity before Pliny admitted that they had left the Church for many years, and had no hesitation in complying with the proconsul's requests: 'Hi quoque omnes et imaginem tuam deorumque simulacra venerati sunt et Christo male dixerunt' (Pliny, *Ep.* x. 96). Ammonius Saccas, the founder of the Neo-Platonic school, is said to have been a Christian originally, and to have apostatized (Euseb. *HE* vi. 19); and there is a tradition that Aquila, the translator of the Heb. Scriptures, was an apostate to Judaism. Apostasy to heathenism was considered the gravest crime of which a Christian could be guilty, and even if it was due to fear of torture or imprisonment, no pardon or hope of reconciliation could be extended to the guilty person. It was not till the time of St. Cyprian (A.D. 252) that the idea of restoring an apostate to communion was even so much as entertained, and then only owing to the immense popular reverence for those who confessed the faith during the persecution of Decius.

Wilful apostasy was, of course, an inexpiable offence, and ranked with murder and adultery; but it appears that up to the time of Cyprian even involuntary apostasy excluded a person for ever from the visible Church. Hermas has been taught that there is no forgiveness for sin after baptism; and it is only by special revelation that he learns from the Angel of Repentance that one post-baptismal penitence is accepted (Hermas, *Mand.* iv. 3). Tertullian, in his earliest work, *ad Martyras* (ch. 1), says that those who could not find peace with the Church sought it from confessors awaiting martyrdom;

but it does not appear from the context that this means that they could restore an apostate to communion. In his treatise *de Pudicitia*, written in his Montanist days, the same writer, whilst denouncing Zephyrinus (?), Bishop of Rome, for allowing penitence to those guilty of carnal sins, enforces his argument by showing that these offences are in the same category as idolatry and murder—unpardonable in a Christian. It seems fairly certain that the re-admission of the *lapsi* was a novelty in the days of Cyprian. 'Evidently,' says Abp. Benson, 'the question which to some was presenting itself was not when, or upon what terms, the lapsed should be re-admitted, but whether it was possible for the Church to remit such guilt' (*Cyprian*, 1897, p. 108).

The law of the early Church in regard to apostasy was very severe. The offence consisted not merely in deliberate desertion of the Church, but in any compliance with paganism, *i.e.* a man was not permitted to continue a member of the Church who was engaged in any trade ministering to idolatry, superstition, or licentiousness; nor was he allowed to conform to custom by offering sacrifice in an official capacity.

When the days of persecution ceased, the severity of the canons was considerably modified, and apostates were re-admitted to communion after due penitence. The strictness of primitive Christianity is seen in the enactments of the Council of Elvira (Illiberis) in Spain, held during the persecution of Diocletian (A.D. 303). Apostasy to Judaism was much feared, especially in Spain and Gaul, and Christians were forbidden to attend Jewish banquets or to have any intimate dealing with Israelites. After the conversion of Constantine, apostasy became a civil offence punishable by law. Apostates to Judaism were liable to confiscation of property, and lost the right of making wills. Repentance was of no avail as regards the civil penalties incurred by apostasy, which included dismissal from all posts of dignity. 'Perditis, hoc est sacrum Baptismus profanantibus, nullo remedio pœnitentiæ (quæ solet aliis criminibus prodesse) succurritur' (Codex Theod. xvi. 7. 4–5).

In the time of Cyprian (A.D. 252) no hope whatever was extended to apostates. Even if they are slain for the name, they cannot be admitted to the peace of the Church (Cyp. *Ep.* lv.). This is confirmed by the legislation of the Council of Elvira, which refuses deathbed communion to adults who have deliberately sacrificed (*can.* 1), to Christians holding hereditary priesthoods who have performed the duties (ii.), and to informers who have caused the death of a Christian (lxxiii.). At the Council of Ancyra, held a year after, the edict of Milan allows the worst class of apostates to be received back to the Church after a due penitence extending over ten years (*can.* 9); and the Œcumenical Council of Nicæa (A.D. 325) allows such to be admitted to communion after twelve years in the ranks of the penitents (*can.* 11). In 397 the Council of Carthage actually forbids apostates to be excluded for ever from the Church: 'Apostaticis conversis vel reversis ad Dominum gratia vel reconciliatio non negetur.'

See Bingham, *Antiq.* xvi.; Smith, *DCA*, art. 'Apostasy'; Dale, *Synod of Elvira*; Hefele, *Conciliengeschichte*, vol. i.

The name 'Apostate' has been specially applied to the Emperor Julian, whose defection from Christianity threatened to undo the work of the conversion of Constantine. There is no absolute proof that Julian was ever baptized, though, as he held the office of a *reader* in his youth, it is, to say the least, highly probable. The Christianity he professed, moreover, must have been of an Arian type. The religion which he embraced after his 'apostasy' was a description of Neo-Platonism, which endeavoured to give a spiritual interpretation to the myths of antiquity. He depressed the Church by every means in his power short of actual persecution; but nothing caused so much consternation or gave such serious offence as his edict forbidding Christians to teach the classics in the schools and universities of the Empire (*Ep.* 42).

The main events of his life are as follows: Born in A.D. 331, the son of Julius Constantius, brother of the great Constantine, he was saved in the massacre of the Imperial family in 337, and educated by his cousin Constantius. In 351 he began to show a disposition towards heathenism, but fear of Constantius compelled him to dissemble. He was Cæsar in Gaul from A.D. 355 to 360, when the army of the province declared him Augustus. He was sole emperor from the death of Constantius, Nov. 3, 361. He was killed in a battle with the Persians, whose territory he had invaded on June 26, 363, and a Christian was immediately elected imperator by the army in the person of Jovian. An interesting study of the character of Julian is to be found in Ibsen's *Emperor and Galilæan*.

3. In the Talmud much is naturally said about apostates from Judaism. Four different kinds are mentioned: *Minim*, *Meshummadin*, *Masōrōth*, and *Epiqūrōsin*. The *Meshummadin* are those who wilfully transgress part of the ceremonial law; the *Masōrōth* are delators or political betrayers; the *Epiqūrōsin* freethinkers.

The *Minim* demand more special attention. It is an open question whether they were Jewish Christians or a Gnostic sect in Judaism. At any rate they were heretics desiring to keep their place in the community of Israel, who had to be detected and cast out. Thus the famous R. Eliezer was arrested on a charge of *Minuth*, but acquitted. In his sorrow for having been suspected he was consoled by the great R. ʿAqiba. The *Minim* are also spoken of in the Talmud as a separate sect, but at the same time they regarded themselves as being so little different from Jews that they could ask for, and obtain, a Jewish Rabbi of unimpeachable orthodoxy to be their teacher. A Gentile is never called a *Min*. The most famous of the *Minim* was Elisha ben-Abuyah, known also as Aḥer, 'the changed one.'

See R. T. Herford, *Christianity in Talmud and Midrash*, 1903, who devotes the greater part of his valuable work to the discussions between the Rabbis and the *Minim*. Friedländer in his *Der vorchristliche jüdische Gnosticismus* maintains that the *Minim* were Gnostics of the Ophite sect. The passage mentioned as enumerating the different classes of apostates destined for Gehinnom is *Sanh.* xiii. 45: 'The *Minim* and the apostates and the betrayers and *Epiqūrōsin*, and those who have lied concerning the Torah, and those who depart from the ways of the congregation, and those who have lied concerning the Resurrection of the dead, and every one who has sinned and caused the multitude to sin,' etc.; see also Deutsch in *JE* i. 665 f.; Kohler and Gottheil, *ib.* ii. 12–18; Broydé, *ib.* viii. 594 f.

4. In the Middle Ages apostasy and heresy were punished with the utmost severity, but it is scarcely possible to conceive of the open abandonment of Christianity where the jurisdiction of the Church was all-powerful. We have, however, a curious example of a deacon in England embracing Judaism in order to marry a Jewess, and being burned at Oxford on 17th April 1222, of course after degradation from his clerical office. This is one of the few cases of the execution of a heretic in England before A.D. 1401; and it seems that the Sheriff of Oxfordshire was blamed for his undue severity in so speedily executing this criminous clerk. In Spain also, under Alfonso X. (the Wise), A.D. 1250, conversion of a Christian to Judaism was made a capital crime; the influence of the Jewish race in that country being especially feared from the earliest times.

For the execution of the deacon see Maitland, *Canon Law in the Church of England*, ch. vi., 'The Deacon and the Jewess.'

The destruction of the Order of the Knights Templar by Philip the Fair and his accomplice Pope Clement V. may be mentioned as an example of the charge of apostasy being used by the Inquisition for a political purpose. The Order, which in 1119 consisted of nine knights devoted to the pious task of keeping the roads to Jerusalem clear of robbers, in the 13th cent. became one of the wealthiest monastic bodies in Christendom, and a military force of the most formidable description. With the fall of Acre in A.D. 1291 the Templars had ceased their activity in the Holy Land, and in 1307 Philip the Fair conceived the idea of embroiling them with the Church, in order to procure the abolition of the Order and the confiscation of their immense wealth. The profound secrecy which enveloped the meetings and even the religious services of the Order gave their enemies the requisite handle to bring charges of the foulest immorality and apostasy against them. The

Templars were accused of making every candidate for admission to their body apostatize by thrice renouncing Christ and spitting upon the crucifix. Torture was freely employed to extort confessions, but upon the whole the evidence obtained was of the most absurd and contradictory character, and the majority of those examined persisted in the innocency of the Order; and though the processes went on simultaneously throughout Europe and the Levant, no seriously incriminating evidence seems to have been obtained except in France. The cruelties which accompanied the suppression culminated in the burning of the Grand Master Du Molay and his companion on the Ile des Juifs on the Seine, 19th March 1314.

Lea, *History of the Inquisition*, vol. iii. pp. 239–334; Milman, *Latin Christianity*, bk. xii. ch. 1. Hallam, *Middle Ages*, vol. i. p. 137, is inclined to credit the charges against the Templars on account of the publication of Count Hammer Purgstall's essay, *Mines de l'Orient exploitées* (1818), charging the Templars with apostasy to a sort of Ophite Gnosticism. The subject is discussed by Castle in the *Transactions of the Quatuor Coronati Lodge*, vol. xix. pt. 3.

The Spanish Inquisition originated for the purpose of suppressing not heresy, but apostasy. The *maranos*, or Jewish converts, were suspected of practising their ancestral religion in secret, though outwardly conforming to Catholicism. It was to root out this crypto-Judaism that the tremendous machinery of the Holy Office in Spain was devised, and the sufferers under Torquemada were those who had relapsed to Judaism.

5. There have been many examples of Christians among the Turks and Moors abandoning their faith in order to enjoy the privileges reserved for Muhammadans; and the renegado often enjoyed high official positions in Turkey. Naturally such persons abandoned their nationality with their religion. Apostasy from Christianity to Judaism is extremely rare, as the Jews themselves do not encourage the reception of proselytes. One notable example of such apostasy is that of the fanatical and unfortunate Lord George Gordon, who was the cause of the famous No Popery riots in 1780. In 1788, after he had been found guilty of a libel on Marie Antoinette, he fled to Amsterdam, whence he was expelled, and on his return to England he made a public profession of Judaism. He was imprisoned in Newgate in the following year, and died in 1793, conforming in all respects to the ceremonies of his new religion.

In recent times there have been cases of Europeans and Americans of Christian parentage embracing Muhammadanism and Buddhism, and conforming to the practices of these religions. In France it has been asserted that *Diabolisme* is practised as a religion, of course involving a distinct apostasy; but the evidence of such persons as Leo Taxil, who declared that a church existed in France for the worship of Satan, seems to have been discredited by his subsequent disavowals, and Satanism (*q.v.*) seems to be little more than the revival of some of the follies of the Black Art of the Middle Ages. F. J. FOAKES-JACKSON.

APOSTASY (Muhammadan).—'He that adopts any other religion shall be put to death.' Such, according to the sacred Muslim tradition, was the command of the Prophet; and on this basis all Muslim jurists are unanimous in deciding that apostasy from Islām (Arab. *irtidād*) must be punished by death. The Ẓāhirites, who, as is well known, adhere as far as possible to the outward meaning (Arab. *ẓāhir*) of the sacred texts, are even of opinion that the apostate (Arab. *murtadd*) must be put to death immediately, that is to say, without initiating any inquiry as to whether he might possibly be converted to Islām again, because the words of the Prophet present no indication of any delay. This was also the view held by Mu'ādh ibn Jabal, Muhammad's governor of Yaman. According to a well-known tradition, this official came to Abū Mūsā, whom he found engaged in questioning a prisoner. On hearing that this man had apostatized from Islām, Mu'ādh refused to take a seat until the apostate had been put to death, saying: 'Such was the decision of Allāh and his Apostle.'

But, according to the opinion of the majority of jurists, it is desirable (according to others, even a duty) before proceeding to carry out the punishment by death, to make an effort to bring the apostate to repentance (Arab. *tawba*). If such a one declares that he turns again to Islām, then the inquisitors are to be satisfied with the response and let him go away in peace. If, on the contrary, he refuses to return to Islām, they are bound, according to many, to allow him a delay of three days (according to others, even longer) as a period for reflexion. He is still retained in prison and may within this interval go back upon his error. In support of this practice, reference is made to the example of the Khalīf 'Omar. When he learned that a man of the troops of Abū Mūsā during the siege of Tustar, in the year 17, had been put to death on account of apostasy from Islām, he was extremely indignant at the deed. 'Why,' he inquired, 'did you not keep him in prison for three days and deal with him in order to bring him to repentance?' And all the companions of the Prophet who were present showed by their silence that they agreed with him.

The Ḥanafites are inclined to think that the punishment of death on account of apostasy is applicable only to men. According to them, women are only to be kept in prison until they repent, because the Prophet has forbidden the putting to death of unbelieving women. According to others, this prohibition has reference only to the killing of the wives of unbelievers in the Holy War. A similar difference of opinion exists with regard to the punishment of apostates while yet in their minority. These, according to some lawyers, may be put to death immediately, according to others only after attaining their majority.

The punishment by death is to be carried into execution only by the sword. From the sacred sources of tradition, it is known that the Khalīf 'Alī caused the adherents of Abd Allāh ibn Sabā to be burnt to death because they proclaimed heretical doctrines and held that 'Alī himself was God. 'Alī regarded this conduct as tantamount to apostasy from Islām. But when Ibn 'Abbās learned the occurrence, he said: 'I should indeed have put them to death, but certainly not burned them, for the Prophet has forbidden that any one shall be punished by fire, because this mode of punishment belongs exclusively to Allāh.' On this account, the opinion prevails that the infliction of death by the stake is prohibited in Islām. But other modes of torturing to death are also expressly repudiated by Muhammadan jurists.

Various other legal consequences of apostasy from Islām are mentioned in detail in the Muslim law-books. For example, the marriage of the apostate is thereby legally annulled. So also he loses the reward of all good works which he may previously have performed, and must make everlasting atonement for his sin in hell. His corpse is not to be interred among the graves of other Muslims, etc.

Apostasy does not necessarily consist only in an express declaration that one is no longer a Muslim, but may also at times be deduced from various other circumstances. If, for example, a Muslim declares to be lawful what the canonical law forbids to him, or, on the contrary, unlawful what the law permits to him, then such conduct is a clear token of unbelief. In like manner this is so, if, at any time, a Muslim worships the sun or the stars or idols, or declares the Prophet to be a liar, or makes the existence of Allāh a matter of doubt.

According to the view of the Shāfi'ites, it is not only apostasy from Islām that is to be punished with death, but also apostasy from other religions, whenever this is not accompanied by conversion to Islām. A Jew who becomes a Christian will thus have to be put to death, according to the Shāfi'ites, because the Prophet has commanded in general that every one shall be put to death 'who adopts any other religion.'

LITERATURE.—A. N. Matthews, *Mishcāt-ul-Masābīh* (Calcutta, 1810), ii. 177 f., and other collections of traditions; Ch. Hamilton, *The Hedaya or Guide* (London, 1791), ii. 225–246; E. Sachau, *Muhamm. Recht nach schafiitischer Lehre* (Berlin, 1897), pp. 843–846; Dimishki, *Rahmat al-ummah fi'Khtilāfi'l-a'immah* (Bulaq, 1300), p. 138, and other Muslim law-books; J. Krcsmárik, 'Beiträge zur Beleuchtung des Islamitischen Strafrechts mit Rücksicht auf Theorie und Praxis in der Türkei' in *ZDMG* lviii. 92 f.; C. Snouck Hurgronje in *De Indische Gids* (1884), i. 794.

TH. W. JUYNBOLL.

APOSTLES' CREED.—See Creeds.

APOSTOLIC AGE.—1. Chronological limits.

—The phrase is commonly used for the period in the history of the Church extending from the death of Christ to the end of the 1st cent., when, according to ancient tradition, John, the last of the twelve Apostles, passed away.

If the term 'apostle' were taken in the broader sense in which it was commonly used in the earliest days, the Apostolic age might be regarded as extending well on into the 2nd cent., when there were still many travelling missionaries bearing the name 'apostles' (see *Didache*, 11). But the term soon came to be applied exclusively to the Twelve and Paul, and has been used in this sense ever since. It is true that no sharp line of demarcation can be drawn between the late 1st and early 2nd centuries; and even assuming that John lived to the time of Trajan, which is by no means certain, his death had no special significance for the history of the Church. As a consequence, some historians have made the Apostolic age end with the destruction of Jerusalem in A.D. 70, or with the death of Paul. But to give such an emphasis to the former event is to overestimate its significance for the history of the Christian Church; and to make Paul's death the close of the Apostolic age is to imply that he was the only Apostle, when as a matter of fact there were others before he came upon the scene, and after he had passed away; for Peter himself, to say nothing of John, very likely outlived him by half a dozen years (see McGiffert, *Apostolic Age*, p. 592). If the designation is to be retained at all, it is better, then, to use it in the traditional sense for the period from *c.* 30 to *c.* 100 A.D.

2. Sources.—Our sources for a knowledge of the Apostolic age are meagre, and yet on the whole more satisfactory than for the generation immediately succeeding. Most important of all are the Epistles of Paul, which are very rich in historical material. The Book of Acts is also indispensable, based as it is in considerable part upon older sources, and containing a great deal of information not to be found elsewhere. But, like any other historical work written by one not himself an eye-witness of the events recorded, it has to be used with caution.

Into the question of the authorship and sources of the Book of Acts it is impossible to enter here (see the special studies by Sorof, *Die Entstehung der Apostelgeschichte*, 1890; Feine, *Eine vorkanonische Ueberlieferung des Lukas in Evang. und Apostelgesch.* 1891; Spitta, *Die Apostelgesch. ihre Quellen und deren gesch. Werth*, 1891; Clemen, *Die Chron. der Paul. Briefe*, 1893, p. 97 ff., and in *Th. Stud. und Krit.* 1895; J. Weiss in *Th. Stud. und Krit.* 1893, 1895; Jüngst, *Die Quellen der Apostelgesch.* 1895; Hilgenfeld in *Zeitsch. für Wiss. Theol.* 1895, 1896; and the summary in Moffatt, *The Historical New Testament*, 1901, p. 655 ff.). In a recent work entitled *Lukas der Arzt* (1906), Harnack maintains, in opposition to the prevalent critical opinion, that Luke, 'the beloved physician,' mentioned by Paul in Col 4^{14} (2 Ti 4^{11}, Philem ^{24}), was the author of the book, including the famous 'We' passages (16^{10-17} 20^{5-15} 21^{1-18} 27^{1}–28^{16}). Harnack has made out a strong, though, in the present writer's opinion, not a conclusive case for the traditional view; but even if his contention were accepted, it would not particularly affect the historical value of the Book of Acts, for those who deny the identity of the author of the 'We' passages with the author of the book as a whole recognize the general trustworthiness of the 'We' passages; and, as Harnack himself admits, the author was probably an eye-witness only as far as they extend, and was dependent upon others for his information in other parts of his book, where his acquaintance with Paul by no means guarantees his historic accuracy (see Schürer's review of Harnack's book in *Theol. Lit. Zeitung*, 1906, p. 406 ff., and Harnack's reply, p. 466 ff.). In any case, whoever the author may have been, his book must be controlled, and at many points corrected, by the Epistles of Paul.

In addition, we have the Gospels, which reflect in part the conditions of the age when they were written, the Epistle to the Hebrews, First Peter, the Pastorals, the Apocalypse, Clement's Epistle to the Corinthians, the three Johannine Epistles, and James and Jude. Other writings, such as the Didache, Barnabas, and the Epistles of Ignatius, throw light back upon the late first century; fragments of Papias and Hegesippus give us some information; and passing references occur in certain non-Christian writers, *e.g.* Tacitus and Suetonius.

3. Outline of the history.—The age falls into three periods: pre-Pauline, Pauline, and post-Pauline.

(*a*) *Pre-Pauline period.*—Of this period we have an idealized picture in the early chapters of the Book of Acts; but those chapters contain also some trustworthy information drawn from older documents, and perhaps in part from current tradition; and the Epistles of Paul, though chiefly reflecting later conditions, throw some light back upon earlier days. We are thus enabled to control the account in Acts, and to trace the course of events, at least in a general way.

The centre of interest during the period was Jerusalem. Here the disciples who had been scattered at the time of Jesus' death gathered again, when convinced of His resurrection and glorification, to carry on the work which they believed He had entrusted to them, and to prepare their countrymen for the establishment of the Kingdom which was to take place upon His return. They continued to live as Jews, and apparently had no thought of breaking with the traditions or customs of their people. Christianity meant simply the belief that Jesus was the promised Messiah, who was soon to return to inaugurate the Messianic Kingdom. The benefits of this Kingdom they believed, as devoutly as any of their contemporaries, were to be enjoyed by Jews alone, native or proselyte. That the Jewish law was to be abrogated, and Christianity to become a new and independent religion, apparently occurred to none of them. They were devout Jews, and their Christian faith did not in any way interfere with the practice of the religion of their fathers. But they were distinguished from their neighbours by their belief that Jesus was the Messiah and would soon return to do Messiah's work; and this conviction dominated their lives. They were Messianic believers in a sense true of none of their fellow-countrymen, and were thus bound very closely together. At the same time, they did not at first form an organized sect, and they had apparently no synagogue of their own. Their Christian life found expression rather in familiar domestic intercourse, and did not interfere with or become a substitute for their accustomed religious life in temple and synagogue. In the strict sense, we cannot speak of a Christian Church at this time in Jerusalem. The Christians all belonged to the one Jewish Church, and knew no other.

The early disciples felt themselves to be citizens of the future Messianic Kingdom, and their interest centred there rather than in the present. As a consequence, they were not in any sense social reformers. The community of goods, of which we have an account in Ac $2^{44ff.}$ $4^{32ff.}$, represented no new social ideal, but was simply an expression of the feeling of brotherhood which prevailed within the little Messianic circle, and of an indifference to the goods of the present world entirely natural in men who expected its speedy displacement by a new and more glorious order of things. There was nothing in Christianity as understood by them to necessitate a break with existing Judaism. In their zeal for the new faith, and in their efforts to win others to it, they created disturbances, and so came into conflict with the authorities (Ac 4 and 5). Such conflicts were of little significance; but the attack upon Stephen, and the persecution which followed, were a different matter, being due to the fear that the new faith threatened the stability of Jewish institutions,—a fear which the Christians themselves did not at all share (see McGiffert, p. 84 ff.). The trouble which arose at this time seems to have been only temporary. But it was impossible for non-Christian Judaism to regard the growing Christian sect with friendly eyes. The Christians, in fact, had to endure the steadily increasing hatred of their countrymen; and their flight from Jerusalem shortly before the siege of 70 A.D., and their refusal to take part in the Bar Cochba rebellion in 132 ff., only served to make the break complete and permanent. Though hated and repudiated by their countrymen, they still clung to their ancestral law and custom, and lived for the most part in isolation from the rest of the Christian Church, being known commonly as Ebionites or Nazarenes. Finally, after some centuries, Jewish Christianity entirely disappeared. The future was not with it, but with another form of Christianity altogether, of which the Apostle Paul was the greatest champion.

(*b*) *Pauline period.*—For this period our sources are Paul's own Epistles and the Book of Acts. The account in the latter is fuller and more trustworthy than for the earlier period. The author's information, however, was not always accurate and adequate even here, and his account has to be used with caution, and corrected or supplemented at many points by the Epistles, which are a primary source of the first rank.*

The second period is distinguished from the first by a change of leaders, of scene, and of principles. In place of personal disciples of Jesus, a new figure came to the front who had never known Him; in place of Palestine, the Roman empire at large was now the scene of activity; and instead of a mere form of Judaism, Christianity became a new and independent religion.

The conversion of Paul has always been recognized as an epochal event in the history of the Church. To him it was chiefly due that Christianity became a factor of importance in the life of the great Roman empire, and ultimately a world-wide religion. It is true that even before his Christian activity began, the new faith had been carried beyond Palestine and had made converts among the Gentiles,—he was not the first and not the only Apostle to the heathen,—but it was he who gave permanence and stability to the work, and thus became the real founder of the world-Church. Under his leadership Jewish propagandism became Christian propagandism, and the influence of Judaism in the world at large was made to promote the spread of a faith which became its worst foe. No wonder that Paul the Christian was hated by so many of his countrymen both within and without the Christian circle. It was he who made Jewish propagandism ineffective, by substituting for it a propagandism which conserved all its attractive features with none of its limitations. Paul was himself a strict Jew, zealous for the traditions of the fathers; but he was also a citizen of the Roman empire, born and bred in the midst of a Greek civilization to which Judaism meant little or nothing. It was inevitable that he should be interested in the spread of Judaism in the world at large, and that, when he became a Christian, the relation of the new faith to the life of the Roman empire should occupy his thought. But it was out of his religious experience before and after his conversion that there was born the principle which revolutionized Christianity and made it an independent religion. His conversion to Christianity was not the mere result of the conviction that Jesus was the Messiah, making of him simply another Messianic believer. It was the fruit rather of a moral struggle of peculiar intensity, out of which he emerged victorious only because he discovered in Christ a liberator from the bondage of law, and the creator of a new life of moral liberty. His moral struggle was not the effect of his conversion, but an antecedent of it, and his Christianity was simply the answer to his moral need. In it, therefore, there was a universality quite foreign to the Christianity of the early Jewish disciples. To them it had meaning only as a Jewish thing; it was the realization of their national Messianic hope. But to Paul it was the solution of a universal moral problem and the answer to a universal moral need. Wherever there was the desire for righteousness and the consciousness of failure in its pursuit, Christianity had place, and so it was just as much for Gentiles as for Jews. Messianic hopes and ideals had little to do with it; it was simply a new moral principle needed by all; for all, Paul believed, were under the bondage of sin. Thinking thus, it was impossible for him to limit Christian propagandism in the way the earlier disciples did. To them Christianity was exclusively Jewish; and if, under the pressure of events, they were constrained to admit that a Gentile might conceivably become a Christian without first becoming a Jew (witness, for instance, the case of Cornelius), they believed that this was provisional only, and would lead ultimately to the full acceptance of Judaism. If Christianity, then, reached the Gentiles at all through them, it could do so only under narrow limitations and burdensome restrictions. But the gospel of Paul, proclaiming, as it did, freedom from sin through the possession of a new moral power—the spirit of Christ—could be preached on equal terms and with equal effectiveness to men of all races. Paul's attitude towards the Jewish law was but an incident of his general position; but inasmuch as that Law constituted the chief distinction between Jews and Gentiles, and in its observance strict Jews saw the sum and substance of all righteousness, his attitude toward it was of immense significance. The Jewish law, he believed, like all law, was given by God in consequence of sin. Where the spirit of holiness has control no law is needed, any more than God Himself needs law to keep Him holy. Law is for the purpose of controlling a person and preventing him from living out his natural character, and therefore is needed only where the character is bad. When a man is freed from the dominion of sin by the possession of the spirit of Christ, he is freed also from the dominion of law; his character is holy and needs no law. Filled with the spirit of Christ, he cannot do otherwise than live in that spirit, which is the spirit of love, of purity, and of peace. Paul himself might continue to observe the precepts of the fathers, and on occasion he might even urge his converts to do the same; but on his own principles he could not insist on such observance, and the moment it was insisted on by others as essential, he must resist them and stand for his fundamental principle of Christian liberty. This might not have affected practical conduct in the least had Christianity been confined to the Jews, whose holiness expressed itself naturally in the observance of the Law, and

* The contention of van Manen and others of the Dutch school, that the Book of Acts is more trustworthy than the Epistles, is not sound, and has commended itself to few scholars.

to whom its ceremonial precepts were as sacred as its moral. But when Gentiles became Christians, it was another matter. To them much of the Jewish law seemed unnecessary and quite without relation to holy living. The result was a serious crisis, much more serious than had been precipitated by the case of Cornelius. The matter was considered at the conference in Jerusalem described in Ac 15 and Gal 2, and a compromise was reached which provided for the recognition of two forms of Christianity, a Jewish and a Gentile. The latter was free from the obligation to observe the Jewish law, the former was still bound by it. The compromise might have answered as a practical expedient had the two forms remained entirely isolated, but it was not long feasible in communities where there were both Jewish and Gentile Christians. Unless there was to be schism within the Christian brotherhood itself, all must live as Jews, or all the Jews must modify, at least in part, the strictness of Jewish practice which prevented familiar intercourse with the Gentiles. Where Paul's principles prevailed, only the latter course could be adopted. The former would have meant the subjection of his Gentile converts to the bondage of a law from which on his own principles they were completely free, while the latter meant only a liberty for Jewish Christians which on the same principles was equally theirs. Ultimately, as the Gentile wing of the Church grew, the principle of liberty thus asserted resulted in complete emancipation from Jewish ceremonial—an emancipation resisted by many stricter spirits in the Church, whom Paul calls Judaizers, but promoted by his powerful influence, and also by the wide-spread existence in the Roman world of a liberalized Judaism already largely indifferent to ceremonial and interested only in the more spiritual and ethical features of the ancient faith (cf. Schürer, *GJV*[3] iii.). Into the heritage of the older Jewish propagandism the new Pauline Christianity entered, offering the world all that and more than Judaism had offered it, in a form stripped of all its offensive features, and claiming to be not merely a modified Gentile phase of the Jewish faith, but a religion as truly Gentile as Jewish. It is no wonder that it speedily became a formidable rival of Judaism, and ultimately completely outstripped the latter in the race.

It is not necessary to trace here the Christian activity of Paul, which covered a period of nearly 25 years, from the beginning of his work in Antioch until his execution in Rome. He was the greatest Christian missionary of the period, and the only one about whose activity we have any extended knowledge. The fact that some of his Epistles have been preserved to us, and that the second half of the Book of Acts is devoted exclusively to his work, enables us to follow his career with considerable accuracy. But our meagre knowledge about others is no reason to suppose that there were no others doing similar work in different parts of the world, and even in those parts where he himself was active. Considerable districts of western Asia Minor, Cyprus, Macedonia, and Achaia seem to have owed their Christianity chiefly or in the first instance to him, but Rome was evangelized independently. At his death Christianity had already entered every province bordering upon the Mediterranean from Syria to Italy, with the exception of Thrace, and had penetrated into the interior of Asia Minor as far as Galatia.

His death at the close of his two years' imprisonment in Rome was due not so much to the fact that he was a Christian, as to his implication in successive disturbances in the East, leading the authorities to regard him as a dangerous character. It was this that caused his imprisonment in Cæsarea, and his execution followed his conviction before the Emperor upon the same charge (see McGiffert, p. 419 ff.). His conviction and execution therefore did not mean an attack upon Christianity by the Imperial government, and, so far as we can learn, did not in any way affect the status of Christianity in the Empire. With the death of Paul passed away the greatest of the Apostles, and the one who did most for the spread of Christianity in the Roman world. To him the Christian Church of history is chiefly due.

(*c*) *Post-Pauline period.*—For this our information is less abundant than for the previous period. The Book of Acts does not carry us beyond the Roman imprisonment of Paul, though, like the Gospels, it reflects in some degree the ideas of the age when it was produced. The Epistle to the Hebrews, First Peter, the Johannine Epistles, the Apocalypse, First Clement, and probably the Pastorals and the Epistles of James and Jude, also belong to this time, and throw some light on conditions in Rome, Asia Minor, and Corinth. We get glimpses of persecution here and there, and discover traces of the development of organization, of the diminishing spontaneity of religious life, and of the stereotyping of moral principle and practice. But the picture is vague and the details very few. No great figure dominates the history, as was the case while Paul was on the scene. It is a period of rapid growth and consolidation, and yet the actors in the history and the course of events are almost unknown to us. The persecution of Nero, to which Peter probably fell a victim, was caused apparently by the accident that the Christians were brought to his notice as convenient scapegoats upon whom to throw the blame for the conflagration of Rome (Tac. *Ann.* xv. 44). While confined to the capital, this persecution brought the Christians into unpleasant notoriety, and gave them the reputation of being dangerous characters, hostile to the public weal. Under the morose and suspicious Domitian both Christians and Jews suffered, because of the Emperor's doubts as to their loyalty. The First Epistle of Peter and the Apocalypse testify to conditions during this reign; and the Epistle to the Hebrews, and the Book of Acts with its apologetic interest, are best read in the light of these conditions. The Christians were evidently coming increasingly into conflict with the authorities, at any rate in certain quarters; and the letter of Pliny to Trajan, dating from 112, shows that already before he became governor of Bithynia the mere profession of Christianity had come to be generally regarded as a crime, though there is no evidence that any law had been passed upon the subject.

The most notable phenomenon of the period is the Johannine literature, and the existence of a Johannine school in Ephesus to which it testifies. That John the son of Zebedee was not its author is regarded by us as certain. We think it even doubtful whether he was ever in Ephesus (see Harnack's *Chronologie der altchristlichen Litteratur*, p. 673 ff.), but the presence there of an important personality of the name of John is beyond question, and the school which gathered about him bears a very pronounced type of its own, Pauline in its basal principles but highly developed in an original way. The Epistle to the Hebrews, with its large infusion of Philonism, is also an interesting and instructive document, illustrating, in our ignorance of its author, the paucity of our information touching the leading characters of the day. So far as our evidence goes, Christianity during this period spread no further than it had before the death of Paul, except toward the east and north in Asia Minor, where it reached Cappadocia, Pontus, and Bithynia (1 P 1[1]). The Apocalypse gives us the names of some churches in Asia Minor (Smyrna, Pergamum, Sardis, Philadelphia, and Thyatira) not mentioned in Paul's letters or the Book of Acts, and the Epistle to Titus shows that Christianity had already reached Crete. For Alexandria we have no direct evidence, but Christianity must have gone there early, in all probability long before the end of the 1st century. In general the scene of the history in this, as in the Pauline period, was the lands lying along the eastern and northern shores of the Mediterranean from Palestine to Italy. The close of the Apostolic age saw Christianity firmly established at least in Asia Minor, Greece, and Italy, and already well started on the conquest of the Roman world. The Christians were an object of suspicion to the State, and were widely disliked by the populace, because of their lack of patriotism, their clannishness and exclusiveness, their hostility to prevailing religious beliefs and practices, their fanatical disregard of common worldly interests, and their puritanic denunciation of popular amusements and pastimes. They came chiefly from the lower grades of society, particularly the class of slaves and freedmen (another ground of offence against them in the opinion of many); but there were some among them of wealth and social standing (cf. Ph 4^{22}, Ja 2^2 4^{13}; Eusebius, *HE* iii. 18). The movement was not ostensibly a social one, and yet it had social consequences because of its recognition of the moral and religious possibilities of the lowest, and its emphasis upon Christian brotherhood and equality. The Christians were still expecting the speedy return of Christ, involving the downfall of the great Roman empire and the end of the present age; and they had a profound belief in the elect character of the Church and its ultimate enjoyment of the blessings promised to believing Israel. They therefore found their life largely in the future. Their religious services had taken on a more or less stereotyped character, and their local societies or churches were already somewhat definitely organized. They were conscious of belonging to one great Church of Christ, and the feeling of unity between the most widely separated communities found constant expression. Their hopes and ideals were everywhere much the same, and they were in possession of many of the beliefs and principles which still control Christendom. The Church at large was not yet an organized institution, but Christianity was already well started upon its historic career.

4. **Development of theology.**—The first disciples were not theologians, and did not concern themselves particularly with theological questions; but their conviction that Jesus was the Messiah led to a considerable modification of traditional beliefs, and became the starting-point in the development of a specifically Christian theology. Believing Jesus to be the Messiah, they were thrown into consternation by His untimely death, coming as it seemed while Messiah's work was still undone and the Kingdom not yet inaugurated. Their belief in His Messiahship could not have survived had it not been for the conviction that He was alive again, which speedily took possession of them. That conviction meant the rehabilitation of their old hopes. Jesus had risen in order to do Messiah's work, and if He did not at once 'restore the kingdom to Israel' (Ac 1^6),—if He were absent for a time,—it was only that Israel might be prepared by repentance and righteousness for the enjoyment of the blessings of the Kingdom which He would speedily return to establish. The supreme duty of His followers, then, was to proclaim His coming, and to prepare their countrymen for it. But their proclamation must seem absurd to those who did not believe Him to be the Messiah; and so the imperative need of the hour must be to convince their fellows of His Messiahship.

Proof was found in His wonderful works, and particularly in His resurrection (Ac $2^{22ff.}$ 3^{15} etc.), the disciples' testimony to the latter fact being confirmed by an appeal to OT prophecy ($2^{25ff.}$). To the seemingly fatal objection that He had, after all, done nothing that the Messiah was expected to do, and that His life and death were entirely unworthy of the Messianic dignity, it was replied that He would return to do Messiah's work when Israel was prepared, and that the Scripture foretold a twofold Messianic coming—the one in humility, involving suffering and death, and the other in glory, for the setting up of the Kingdom ($3^{18ff.}$). Here lay the nerve of the first disciples' preaching. In this novel assumption of a Second Coming is to be found the distinctive feature of primitive Christian theology. Their apologetic did not consist in showing that Jesus had already done Messiah's work; it did not involve any great modification or spiritualization of traditional ideas as to the character of that work and as to the nature of the Messianic Kingdom. It aimed only at proving that Jesus was really the Messiah, and that He might therefore be trusted yet to do all that had been expected. In their emphasis upon the second coming they lost the full significance of the first, and failed to understand Jesus' complete transformation of traditional values. Why, contrary to common expectation, should there be a twofold coming? Why had Jesus, being the Messiah, lived a life of humility and died upon the cross? That they found the situation foretold in the Scriptures seems to have satisfied them, though they very likely believed, as was not unnatural, and as Paul's words in 1 Co 15^4 perhaps suggest, that the first coming had its place in the promotion of repentance and righteousness, and so in the preparation of the people for the Kingdom, which could not appear until they had repented (Ac $3^{19ff.}$). But this was a subordinate matter.

The question of Jesus' origin, nature, and relation to God, which later became so important, was not raised among these early disciples. The common traditional idea of the Messiah as a man called and supernaturally endowed by God seems to have been accepted without question (Ac $2^{22.\,36}$ 3^{13} etc.). Nothing in Jesus' words or deeds or in the events of His life led them to modify the existing view. The one controlling belief was in the future coming, and the one imperative duty was preparation for the enjoyment of the blessings of the Kingdom then to be established.

With the conversion of Paul a new period opened in the history of Christian theology. The central truth to him was not the second coming of Christ, but the transformation of man's nature here and now by the indwelling of the Divine. His theology was rooted in his religious experience. Out of that experience, interpreted in the light of contemporary Greek thought, was born a theory of redemption entirely unlike anything known to the early disciples. The theory involved the transformation of man's evil fleshly nature by the power of the Divine Spirit, Christ, with whom he is mystically united through faith. Thus united to Christ, a man dies with Him unto the flesh and rises with Him unto a new life in the Spirit, a life of holiness and freedom. Salvation is thus a present, not merely a future, reality; and the true spiritual resurrection of the Christian takes place now and here. The future resurrection will mean only the substitution for the present fleshly body, in which the Christian is compelled to dwell while on earth, of a new spiritual body fitted to the spiritual life which has already begun. Paul's theory involved also the Deity of Christ, through mystical union with whom a man's nature is transformed. It was in his doctrine of redemption that the historic belief in the Deity of Christ found its basis.

Into the details of Paul's thought we cannot enter further here. His system is found in all its essential features in the earliest of his extant writings—the Epistle to the Galatians—as well as in the latest (see McGiffert, ch. iii., also pp. 221 ff. and 378 ff.).

The peculiar type of thought of which Paul is the earliest representative appears also in a fragmentary way in the First Epistle of Peter; and the Fourth Gospel and First Epistle of John are dominated by it (so also the Epistles of Ignatius of the early 2nd century). Though Jesus is represented as speaking so extensively in the Fourth Gospel, it is the thought of the author rather than of Jesus Himself that appears both in Gospel and Epistle. In both we find the conception of the need of the transformation of man's nature by the indwelling of the Divine, and the belief in the Deity of Christ, through union with whom the transformation is effected. In spite of many divergencies between John and Paul, the general type of thought is the same, and the agreements far outweigh the differences.

In the other writings of the NT and in Clement's Epistle to the Corinthians an altogether different type of theology appears, more nearly akin to that of the early Jewish disciples. The influence of

Paul is hardly seen except in the common belief that the Jewish law has been abrogated, and that Christianity is open on equal terms to men of every race. To all these writers the gospel is the promise of salvation for those who keep the law of God. Salvation is a future thing, involving, in the thought of some, who retained the conception of the early Jewish disciples, a share in an earthly kingdom to be set up by Christ at His return and to endure for a season (Rev 20[4ff.]), and in the thought of all, the enjoyment of a blessed immortality in heaven. The principal condition of salvation is the keeping of God's commandments as revealed by Jesus Christ. This must be preceded by repentance, and repentance by faith,—which means, primarily, the conviction that God will reward those who keep, and punish those who break, His law,—without which faith no one will repent and obey God's commandments. The work of Jesus Christ was to bring to men a knowledge of God's law and its sanctions, and by Him they would be judged. He was thus at once Mediator of salvation and Judge of the world, and the titles 'Saviour' and 'Lord' were both commonly applied to Him. The exalted position which He occupied led Christians to think of Him as standing in a relation of peculiar intimacy with God, and in course of time to speculate about the origin aud nature of that relationship. By some it was thought that His supernatural endowment began at the time of His baptism, when He was called by God and equipped for His work by the gift of the Spirit (cf. the accounts of the baptism in the Gospels, esp. the text given in Justin Martyr's *Dialogue with Trypho*, 103, and also the testimony of Justin, *ib.* 48, and Eusebius, *HE* v. 28. 3). By others He was given a supernatural origin, being represented as the child of the Holy Spirit (as in the Gospels of Matthew and Luke); while still others pushed His origin even further back, and thought of Him as a pre-existent Being who had come down from heaven (thus, *e.g.*, the Pastoral Epistles, Hebrews, Apocalypse, and Clement). Where this general type of thought prevailed, an adequate motive for assuming the Deity of Christ, such as actuated Paul and those who felt the influence of his theory of redemption, was lacking. Endowment with the Spirit at baptism, supernatural birth, pre-existence —none of them involved Deity in the strict sense. It was not due to these Christians, but to Paul and his school, that the doctrine of the Deity of Christ finally became a part of historic Christian theology.

The two types of thought that have been described developed for the most part independently of one another for some generations; but even in writings representing controllingly one or the other type, traces of the opposite tendency sometimes appear, and towards the close of the 2nd cent. the two were combined by Irenæus, bishop of Lyons, who made both man's obedience to the Divine law and the transformation of his nature through the infusion of Divine grace necessary to salvation, and so laid the foundations of historic Catholic theology. In the combination much of Paul's thought was lost; but the essential feature of it—that human nature is evil and must be transformed by union with the Divine—was permanently conserved, and became the basis of the sacramental system, which we find, as a matter of fact, already foreshadowed in 1 Co 10 and in Jn 3 and 6.

5. Ethical ideals. — To the primitive Jewish disciples, Christianity was primarily not an ethical but a Messianic movement. It is true that they believed, with John the Baptist and with Jesus, that righteousness was a condition of sharing in the blessings of the coming Kingdom (cf. Ac 2[38]). It was because of the unrighteousness of the people that Jesus had not established it during His earthly life, and not until there was general repentance would He return (Ac 3[19f.]). But they interpreted righteousness in the ordinary Jewish way as the keeping of the revealed Law of God in all its parts, and introduced little change in current ethical ideals. They saw in Christianity the promise of the speedy realization of the Messianic Kingdom and their own participation in its blessings, but apparently they did not feel the need of new ethical ideals and new moral power, and they did not think of looking to Christianity for them.

To Paul, as has already been seen, Christianity was an altogether different thing. He had experienced a serious moral crisis, and had passed through a severe moral struggle such as the earlier disciples had not known, and he found in Christianity, above all else, the satisfaction of his moral needs. Christianity, as he conceived it, was a religion offering to him and to every man a new moral power sufficient to transform him from an evil to a good being, from a sinner to a saint. His theory of redemption did not find general acceptance,—in fact it was commonly quite misunderstood,—but his conviction that Christianity has to do fundamentally with release from sin and with the promotion of holiness speedily became wide-spread. From him, too, came the sharp contrast between 'flesh' and 'spirit' which has dominated Christian thought ever since. Those who came after him were not, as a rule, so thoroughgoing as he at this point, but the idea of the Christian life as a moral conflict—the warring of two opposing principles, a fleshly and a spiritual—was common at an early date. Holiness thus came to be regarded as the principal mark of the Christian life, and sins of the flesh were esteemed the worst of all sins. Primitive Christian literature is full of exhortations to purity, and of denunciations of unchastity and lust. The lenient view taken of sexual immorality by the contemporary heathen world, and the close connexion between it and some of the religious cults of the day, doubtless had much to do with the frequent references to the subject in early Christian documents; but behind it all, even though seldom coming to expression, lay the Pauline contrast between flesh and spirit, and the conviction that impurity of the flesh drives away the Holy Spirit and makes His continued presence with the individual and with the Church impossible (cf., in addition to the many passages in Paul's own Epistles, He 10[29], Jude [19], and esp. the 2nd cent. writings—Hermas, *Mand.* v. and x., and 2 Clement 14). Paul himself was not an ascetic in any strict sense; he even opposed asceticism in matters of food and drink, when it appeared in Rome and Colossæ (Ro 14 and Col 2); but hints of an ascetic tendency appear in his Epistles (Ro 8[13], 1 Co 5[5] 9[27]), particularly in connexion with the relation of the sexes (cf. 1 Co 7). In fact, the subsequent development of Catholic asceticism was already foreshadowed, though the process was still in its incipiency, in the Apostolic age (see the protest against it in 1 Ti 4[1ff.]). See ASCETICISM (Chr.).

Another controlling contrast in primitive Christian ethics, due in part to the same cause, in part to the prevailing expectation of the speedy return of Christ, was that between this world and the next—promoting a spirit of unworldliness, or other-worldliness, which has remained a permanent feature of the Christian view of life. The disciples early came to regard themselves as a people called out of the midst of a corrupt generation and set apart as God's own; and to live as citizens of another world, to fix one's affections upon higher than earthly things, to be separate from this world and superior to its interests and concerns—this was regarded as the truly Christian attitude (cf., *e.g.*, 2 Co 6^{17}, Gal 6^{14}, Ph 3^{20}, Col 3^{2}, Ja 4^{4}, 1 Jn 2^{15}; and also the striking passage in the 2nd cent. *Epistle to Diognetus*, 5 ff.). Not harmony with one's environment, as in classic Greek ethics, but revolt against it, and the carrying on of a life entirely detached from it—this was the Christian ideal already in the Apostolic age. And this spirit worked together with the controlling emphasis upon fleshly purity to promote asceticism, and ultimately, though not yet in the Apostolic age, its natural fruit—monasticism (cf. the prophetic remark of Paul in 1 Co 5^{10}).

The sharp contrast between the two worlds, and the recognition of the present world as evil, did not result in a desire to change existing conditions; no social revolution was contemplated. The division of society into rich and poor, master and slave, was treated as normal. The effort was made to introduce Christian principles into all the relations of life, but the desire to escape from the class to which one happened to belong was not encouraged (cf. 1 Co $7^{20\text{ff.}}$). There is frequent emphasis in the writings of the age upon one's common duties as father, husband, wife, child, servant (Eph 5, Col 3, 1 P 2, 1 Ti 6, Tit 2), and even occasionally as citizen (Ro $13^{1.7}$, 1 P $2^{13.17}$, Tit 3^{1}, 1 Clement 60. 61). However evil the present world may be, the Christian is to walk in such a way as to give no just ground of offence to outsiders, is to show proper respect to all men, and to live honourably, quietly, peaceably, and blamelessly with every one (Ro $12^{17\text{ff.}}$ 13^{7}, Ph 2^{15}, 1 P 2^{17} etc.).

The ideal of social service and the desire to promote the spirit of brotherhood in the world at large had little place among the early Christians. Rather to gather out of the world a company of holy men, heirs of the promised Kingdom—this was their great aim (cf. the Eucharistic prayers in the early 2nd cent. *Didache*, 9. 10). It is true that love is frequently insisted upon in the writings of the Apostolic age, but it commonly takes the form of love for the Christian brethren, which is to be manifested in charity, hospitality, sympathy, concord, forbearance, tender-heartedness, forgiveness, humility, etc. And even when it is not so limited, it usually appears as only one of a number of virtues (cf. 1 Ti 2^{15}, 4^{12}, 6^{11}, 2 Ti 2^{22}, 3^{10}, Ja 1^{27}, 2^{8}). The place of supremacy given to it by Christ and after Him by Paul is accorded to it by no other writers of the age. (The striking passage in 1 Clement 49 ff. is hardly sufficient to justify us in making an exception of the author). But the influence of Jesus is seen nevertheless in the general emphasis—common to most of our sources—upon the virtues of gentleness, peaceableness, forbearance, and humility. Nothing is said of the duty of insisting upon one's rights and demanding proper recognition from others. Self-abnegation in one's relations with one's fellows, rather than self-assertion, is the recognized ideal.

But the contrast with the prevailing ethical sentiment of the Roman world was not confined to a difference in ideals. The Christians recognized the moral law, which it was their duty to obey, as given directly by revelation from God, the revelation involving also an announcement of the future sanctions attending obedience and disobedience. There was thus a definiteness and compulsion about Christian ethics not commonly found elsewhere. Emphasis upon the hope of reward and the fear of punishment, as grounds of moral conduct, is very common in our sources (*e.g.* 1 Co 6^{9} 9^{25} 15^{32}, 2 Co 9^{6}, Gal 5^{21} 6^{9}, Col 1^{5}, 1 P 3^{9}, He 2^{2} 10^{25}, 1 Ti 6^{19}). But higher motives are also frequently urged: to walk worthily of one's calling as God's elect, to please and glorify God, to be like Christ, to be true to one's opportunities and responsibilities, to help, not harm, one's brethren, to promote the good name of Christianity in the world at large (cf. 1 Co 6^{20}, Ph 2^{15}, Col 3^{3}, 1 Th 2^{12} 4^{1}, 1 P 1^{15} $2^{9.12}$ 4^{1}, 1 Clement 30). It meant much also that the early Christians believed that Christianity was for all men, low as well as high, and that they recognized the moral possibilities even of the meanest. Christianity, indeed, supplied a new and mighty moral enthusiasm for the masses of the people, and that in spite of the fact that already the ominous distinction between two grades of morality, one for the common man and the other for the spiritual *élite*, was beginning to appear (cf. 1 Co 7 and *Didache*, 6).

So far as moral performance was concerned, it evidently left much to be desired. Of this the repeated exhortations and warnings in the Christian literature of the period are sufficient evidence, and we have direct record of some striking examples of immorality (*e.g.* Ac 5, 1 Co 5. 11, Jude $^{4\text{ff.}}$). It is worthy of notice, too, that the Christians bore a bad moral reputation among their pagan neighbours, due largely, no doubt, to prejudice, but also in part well founded (cf. 1 Th 4^{11}, 2 Th 3^{11}, 1 P 2^{12}). But in spite of all this, it is clear that Christianity was a controllingly moral movement, and that it involved a real moral improvement on the part of many of its adherents. The very insistence upon the matter in our sources shows that there was a strenuous ethical ideal, and that the Christians themselves recognized its binding character; and we have abundant testimony to the effects of Christianity upon the lives of its converts (see not only the writings of the Christians themselves, but also the tacit witness of Pliny's letter to Trajan). In general, it may be said that the common notion of the Christians was that the aim of Christianity is to make men purer and better here, in order to a blessed immortality hereafter.

6. Development of organization.—In primitive Jewish Christianity no organization was needed in the beginning, for the disciples regarded themselves simply as heralds of the coming Kingdom. It might perhaps have been expected that they would form in Jerusalem a separate synagogue, but this they apparently did not do, and the failure to do it shows how little they regarded themselves as a distinct sect. Their desire was to convince their fellow-countrymen of Jesus' Messiahship, and so win Him disciples, rather than to form a religious cult or society of their own. Certain Christians, particularly James the brother of Jesus, and others who had stood in relations of intimacy with Him, such as the Twelve, naturally had large influence in the Jerusalem circle, but there is no sign that this involved any official position or appointment. Some sort of an organization, however, the disciples had at an early date. As a brotherhood they felt it their duty to care for the necessities of the needy among them, and so a committee was appointed for the distribution of aid (Ac 6). Beyond this we do not know that the early Jerusalem Christians went; but ultimately, after the final break with their unbelieving countrymen, the Jewish Churches were organized as independent institutions, though the exact form which the organization took is unknown to us.

In the non-Jewish world conditions were different. Here, too, the expectation of the speedy consummation made any careful organization seem unnecessary, and the conviction of the presence of the Spirit made human officials seem superfluous. But the founding of churches began at an early date; and in them, although for some time leadership devolved naturally upon men specially endowed by the Spirit, such as apostles, prophets, and teachers, gradually the necessities of the case led to a more formal organization, substitutes being required for the inspired men who might not always be present. Two classes of officials—bishops and their assistants, the deacons—existed in some churches before the end of the Apostolic age; but the development of the threefold ministry —bishop, presbyter, and deacon—belongs to the 2nd century.

7. Religious services.—The early Jerusalem disciples were devout Jews, and continued to observe the religious practices and to attend the religious services of their people. Their common religious life as Christians expressed itself not so much in formal services as in informal gatherings from house to house, where their community of feeling as disciples of Jesus and heirs of the approaching Kingdom found natural and familiar expression. Concerning the subsequent development within the Jewish Christian Churches we have no information.

In the Gentile world all seems at first to have been equally informal; but the attitude of hostility towards the religious practices and principles of the heathen world, taken by Paul and other early missionaries, made it necessary for converts to Christianity to repudiate, as a rule, their old cults, and to find their religious life wholly within the Christian circle. Thus it was inevitable that a Christian cult should early develop, to meet the need of those who were cut off from the religious exercises to which they had been accustomed. Christian worship became ultimately very elaborate and ornate, and took on many of the features of the cults which it displaced, but in the Apostolic age we discover only the beginnings of the development. Our information on the subject is almost wholly confined to the Church of Corinth, and there all was very simple and informal. The Christians met frequently for religious worship and mutual edification, and also at other times to partake of a common meal. The former occasions are referred to by Paul in 1 Co 14. At these meetings the Christians engaged in various religious exercises,—prayer, praise, prophecy, teaching, speaking with tongues,—the whole service being controlled by the Pauline idea of the presence of the Holy Spirit, by whose influence the disciples were inspired to pray or prophesy or engage in other religious exercises. Perfect freedom of expression was granted to all, but it was assumed that only those who were prompted thereto by the Spirit would take active part in the services. The freedom was not for the individual as an individual, but as a mouthpiece of the Spirit. At the time when Paul wrote, this liberty had already resulted in serious disorder, and the meetings had degenerated into scenes of confusion and discord. In dealing with the difficulties, he laid down two principles of far-reaching importance. The first was that the services are solely for the edification of those present, and all the exercises must be conducted with that end in view. Only such gifts must be employed, and only under such conditions, as will promote the good of all. But how can one refuse to utter what the Spirit imparts, even though it be unintelligible or untimely? In reply to this question, Paul stated a second general principle of equal importance with the first: 'The spirits of the prophets are subject to the prophets,' that is, an inspired man has the right and duty to exercise judgment in the use of his spiritual gifts, and to employ them only in such a way as to promote edification. The utterance of these two principles foreshadows the passing of the original freedom. If an individual fails to exercise discretion in the use of his gifts, he must be controlled by his brethren, and thus the way is prepared for a regular order of service, and for the appointment of certain persons to take charge of the meetings, and to see that all is done decently and in order. There is no sign that Paul himself contemplated such a result, but the stereotyping process ensued in course of time. In Rome, before the end of the 1st cent., it was already well under way, and regularly appointed officials were in control of the services (cf. 1 Clement, 40 ff., 44); and before long the early freedom had given way almost everywhere to liturgical rules (cf. *Didache*, 9 f.; Justin, *Apol.* 67; Ignatius, *Magn.* 7, *Trall.* 7, *Smyrn.* 8).

In addition to the meetings already described, the Christians at Corinth were in the habit of gathering from time to time to share in a common meal. At this meal they not only partook of food and drink for the ordinary purpose of satisfying hunger and thirst, but it was their custom, as was apparently the case among the early Jerusalem disciples, to eat bread and drink wine in commemoration of Jesus. At the time when Paul wrote, the meals had degenerated into scenes of discord and debauchery. Under these circumstances he informed the Corinthians that the commemoration of Christ's death was the chief purpose of the meal, and not eating and drinking for their own sake; and he commanded them to satisfy their hunger at home, that they might be able to commemorate Christ in the right spirit, and make the meal wholly a religious service (1 Co 11[22. 34]). The immediate effect of Paul's attitude in this matter we do not know. The common meals continued in some quarters for generations, but ultimately they were everywhere given up, and the religious ceremony known as the Eucharist or Lord's Supper alone remained. In subsequent centuries it became the central feature of the Christian cult. A very elaborate ceremonial grew up in connexion with it, and it was regarded as the most sacred and mysterious of all religious rites (see artt. AGAPE and EUCHARIST).

In the *Didache*, 9, it is commanded that none except baptized persons be allowed to partake of the Lord's Supper. This is the earliest explicit statement of a general rule which, it may fairly be supposed, was commonly operative from the beginning; for the sacred meals of the early Christians can hardly have been shared by any not belonging to the Christian circle, and admission to it was commonly, if not invariably, marked by the ceremony of baptism (see art. BAPTISM).

8. Significance of the Apostolic age. — The Apostolic age is the period of Christian origins, and as such has a significance attaching to no other in the history of the Church. It was during this period that the Church as an organization came into existence, and the foundations were laid upon which all subsequent ages built. Most of the tendencies that appear in Christian history are to be found at least in germ in the Church of the 1st century.

It is through the Apostolic age also that we get our knowledge of Jesus Christ. To it we owe not simply the written accounts of His life, but also the impression of His personality which constitutes an integral part of our picture of Him. It is true that the very change of emphasis from Christ's message about God to His personality as Messiah involved a changed interpretation of His controlling purposes, which has coloured Christian thought ever since. Nevertheless, it is through the Apostolic age that we approach Him, and from it that we get the information which enables us to understand Him in some respects better than His own disciples did. His person dominated the age, and the memory of His presence was a vivid and compelling reality. The days in which men who knew

Him face to face were still alive and influential must always stand apart from other days in the regard of His followers.

On other accounts, too, the Apostolic age will always have peculiar religious value. As the period of beginnings, there is an incomparable freshness about it. Its vivid sense of the approaching consummation gives it an inspirational quality not found elsewhere; and in it were produced the classic documents of Christianity from which all Christians since have drawn religious sustenance. This fact alone is enough to mark it off from all other ages in the history of the Church.

But another significance has been ascribed by Christian tradition to the Apostolic age. During the 2nd cent. there grew up a conception of Apostolic authority which has prevailed ever since, and has given the 1st cent. a worth and dignity to which the fact that it is the period of Christian origins and nearest in time to Jesus Christ would not of itself entitle it. In the effort to repudiate the errors of the Marcionites and Gnostics, which were spreading rapidly in the 2nd cent., certain leaders of the Church began to insist upon the teaching of the Apostles, that is, the Twelve and Paul, as the sole standard and norm of Christian faith, on the ground that they had been chosen by Christ to be the founders of His Church, and had been endowed with the Spirit in such measure as to render them infallible witnesses to the will and truth of God. In the effort to define the teaching of the Apostles, and to show that they gave no support to the vagaries of Marcion and the Gnostics, it was claimed that they had left certain writings together constituting an authoritative Scripture canon, and had framed a creed containing the fundamental tenets of the Christian faith. Whoever would be a member of the true Church, and so an heir of salvation, must unfeignedly accept all that was taught both by canon and by creed. A sharp line of demarcation was thus drawn between the age of the Apostles and all subsequent generations. In the Apostolic age was found the standard for all time to come. The Apostles themselves came to be regarded as figures supernaturally endowed for the unique work of establishing the Church, and raised above the ordinary frailties and limitations of humanity. Their official character was so emphasized that all sense of their individuality was lost. The differences between them were forgotten, in the conviction that as men divinely inspired they must all have been completely one. Apart from Paul, history knows practically nothing of their several careers, of the regions where they laboured, and the work they did; and not until the 3rd cent., long after all authentic sources of information had disappeared, did tradition begin to busy itself with them as individuals—a striking illustration of the indifference to historic reality to which the 2nd cent. theory of Apostolicity gave rise. As a result of that theory, all that the Apostles were supposed to have taught, whether by precept or example, acquired infallible authority; and nothing in doctrine, in polity, in ritual, or in practice could be regarded as Christian unless directly or indirectly of Apostolic origin. Development on all these lines was made possible by the belief that the Apostles had also instituted a perpetual Apostolic office for the government and guidance of the Church, the incumbents of which were endowed with the power to interpret infallibly the will and truth of God. Bible and creed were thus supplemented by the living voice of the Catholic episcopate, and the Church was enabled to conform to new conditions and to meet new needs as they arose, without ostensibly breaking away from its Apostolic foundations or giving up its theory of Apostolic authority. The Protestant reformers of the 16th cent. rejected the Catholic doctrine of an infallible episcopate, but the Catholic belief in Apostolic authority was retained, and the Bible was regarded as the complete and final expression of Apostolic teaching on all conceivable subjects. Revelation and inspiration were supposed to have ceased with the age of the Apostles, and the development that had taken place under the ægis of episcopal authority was repudiated. The effort was made to return to the conditions of the Apostolic age, and to bring the Church into complete conformity to its principles and practices in all respects, nothing being regarded as truly Christian unless it enjoyed the authority of Apostolic precept or example. Cf. next article.

This belief still prevails widely in connexion with doctrine, but in the matter of ritual and polity it has been generally abandoned. Moreover, the whole conception of Apostolic authority has been given up by many in modern times, and it has come to be widely held that the age of the Apostles was essentially like any other in the history of the Church, that it was confronted with its own problems and difficulties, and that the men who met and solved them were of like passions and limitations with Christians of all ages.

This change of attitude has been of immense historical and religious value. A reality attaches to the Apostolic age and to the figures of the early leaders of the Church which they never possessed before. For the first time an understanding of the period and a genuinely historical treatment of it have become possible, and from the religious experiences of the Apostles and their companions, now more clearly understood and appreciated, modern Christians are gaining new inspiration and instruction.

LITERATURE.—Of older books on the Apostolic age should be mentioned: **Neander**, *Geschichte der Pflanzung und Leitung der christlichen Kirche durch die Apostel*, 1832 (Eng. tr. 1842); **Baur**, *Paulus der Apostel Jesu Christi*, 1845 (Eng. tr. 1873 ff.) [an epoch-making work setting forth the conception of early Christian history which was adopted by the Tübingen school in general], followed in 1853 by *Das Christenthum und die christliche Kirche der drei ersten Jahrhunderte* (Eng. tr. 1878 ff.); **Ritschl**, *Entstehung der altkatholischen Kirche*, 1850 (2nd ed. 1857, entirely worked over) [in its second edition another epoch-making book, which did more than any other to break the dominance of the Tübingen interpretation of early Church history]; **Renan**, *Histoire des Origines du Christianisme*, 7 vols., 1863 ff.; of more recent works, **Weizsäcker**, *Das apostol. Zeitalter der christl. Kirche*, 1886 (3rd ed. 1902; Eng. tr. 1895) [the most influential of modern histories of the Apostolic age]; **Pfleiderer**, *Das Urchristenthum*, 1887 (2nd ed. 1902), also *Die Entstehung des Christenthums*, 1905 (Eng. tr. 1905); **McGiffert**, *Hist. of Christianity in the Apostolic Age*, 1897 (rev. ed. 1899); **Bartlet**, *The Apostolic Age*, 1899; **Wernle**, *Die Anfänge unserer Religion*, 1901 (2nd ed. 1904; Eng. tr. 1903 ff.); **Dobschütz**, *Die urchristl. Gemeinden*, 1902 (Eng. tr. 1904), and his brief sketch, *Das apostolische Zeitalter*, 1906 (in the *Religionsgeschichtliche Volksbücher*); **Knopf**, *Das nachapostol. Zeitalter*, 1905; **Ropes**, *The Apostolic Age in the Light of Modern Criticism*, 1906. The various standard lives of Paul, works on NT literature and theology, Church histories, and histories of doctrine, which deal more or less fully with our subject, it is not necessary to specify.

A. C. McGIFFERT.

APOSTOLIC SUCCESSION.—I. The principle of ministry in the NT.—That from the Apostles' time there has existed in the Christian Church a ministry exercising official functions by regular devolution of authority is a fact which few historians would have disputed, if no claim had been made on its behalf to be a necessary part of the institution of Christ. But as this claim is put forward on behalf of Churches retaining the canonical orders, and also by Presbyterians, Apostolic succession becomes a significant fact, and therefore a doctrine. Consequently it demands a closer and more vigorous scrutiny than would otherwise attend an investigation into the origin of the Christian Ministry. The theory is that Christ, having established a society primarily visible and historical, gave to that society a recognizable unity and cohesion, not only by instituting in Baptism a sacrament of initiation, and in the Eucharist a sacrament of corporate life, but also by perpetuating its collective witness in a continuous and authoritative ministry.

This principle has often, and not unnaturally, been expressed in crude and unhistorical forms. It has, for example, been common to confuse the question of a true principle of ministry with that of the manner in which this principle has been realized in history. This has led to discussions on the Divine right of bishops as an exclusive form of Church government; and caused stress to be laid on an all but mechanical system of devolving episcopal authority which the facts of early Church history, so far as known, do not justify, and which is too formal to be consistent with an organically developing society. Hooker was right when, in opposing the Presbyterian theory, he contented himself with affirming that episcopacy 'best agreed with the sacred Scripture' (*Eccl. Pol.* iii. 16, but cf. vii. 11).

Or, again, the sacerdotalism of the third cent. has been unwarrantably intruded into the first, and the whole matter treated as though it were a question whether Christ had set up a priestly caste, to which the mysteries of religion were entrusted, and without which spiritual life was not only hindered but impossible. These methods of thought have led to narrow and technical inquiries into the sacramental character of holy orders, the form and matter of the rite by which they were conferred, and the precise conception of the various powers which from time to time it has been intended to convey. Such, for example, is the papal Bull *Apostolicæ Curæ*, condemning Anglican orders on the ground that the Ordinal of Edward VI. departed from the intention of its mediæval predecessors in denying sacrificial power to presbyters.

But the crudest form of the argument, in spite of Macaulay's ridicule (Essay on *Gladstone on Church and State*), witnesses to certain facts of the Church's development which may not be ignored. The Nicene canons, A.D. 325 (No. 4), make careful arrangements, on the basis of universal custom, for the due perpetuation of the ministry in all parts of the Church. In the 3rd cent. Cyprian can speak of the united episcopate as retaining the authority entrusted by Christ Himself to the Twelve (see below). The end of the 2nd cent. witnessed a universal episcopate, the descent of which from Apostles was not questioned, but used in argument by writers like Irenæus (*adv. Hær.* iii. 2, 3, iv. 40, 42, 53, v. 20) and Tertullian (*de Præscript.* 32, *adv. Marc.* iv. 5, *Apol.* 47; cf. Hegesippus, in Euseb. iv. 22). In the early days of the 2nd cent. Ignatius wrote that, apart from the threefold ministry, 'there is not even the name of church' (*Trall.* 3). It is not, therefore, scientific to dismiss the doctrine of Apostolic succession because the statement of it has been inadequate or extravagant. This is true of most, if not all, Christian doctrines.

The object of the present article is to show what reasons there are, in view of the facts and principles of the NT, for believing that the great institution of the Christian ministry belongs to the substance of Christianity. Whatever variations may have attended its transmission (as, *e.g.*, in the case of the supposed right of the Alexandrian presbyters until the time of Bishop Heraclas, A.D. 233, to consecrate their own chief pastor [Jerome, Ep. 146 *ad Evangelum*; see Bigg, *BL* p. 40; Gore, *Ch. and Min.*, Note B; J. Wordsworth, *Ministry of Grace*, pp. 135, 136]), the Ministry preserved an unbroken continuity in all churches till the 16th century. The theory built upon this fact does not stand or fall with a sacerdotal conception of orders, but arises out of the facts of the Gospel narrative. 'We find the Church,' says Archbishop Temple, 'from the very beginning flowing out of the ministry' (*Sermon at Consecration of Truro Cathedral*). Whatever may be the function of the Church, whether it be the teacher of truth or the dispenser of sacraments, the inquiry is not vitally affected. Where, as in the Western Church of the Middle Ages, great stress is laid upon the due celebration of the Eucharist, Apostolic succession will appear mainly as a sacerdotal theory. Where, on the other hand, as in the age of the Gnostics, resistance to doctrinal error is the foremost consideration, the ministry will appear rather as the Divinely appointed guardian of the Apostolic witness to evangelical truth. The two questions that are fundamentally important are: (*a*) Is the Church of Christ as the object of salvation prior to the individual Christian? (*b*) Does the Church as established by Christ present any of the features of a historical institution? It is only as these questions are answered that we can proceed to discover from history how the organic life of the society has been in fact developed.

Apostolic succession being accepted as a principle of the Church's life, we do not commit ourselves to any one theory of the reasons which led, in the evolution of the Christian society, to the establishment of the various orders of ministers. If the Seven of Ac 6 be, as is frequently supposed, the original deacons, then we know that, whatever functions may from time to time have been engrafted on the office in the course of history, the neglect of the Hellenistic widows was the occasion of their first election and ordination. Whether a similar need for the due administration of the common purse (Hatch, *BL* 2), or the requirement of a foreign correspondent to represent each community in its relations with the rest (Ramsay, *Church in the Roman Empire*, xv. 3, xvii.), or the demand for a vicar apostolic to guard the evangelical deposit from the attacks of heresy, be the cause of the establishment of bishops; or whether, as is more probable, a complexity of causes, some more influential in one region than in another, produced the universal episcopate, the Church still remains a differentiated and structural body, not a promiscuous gathering of persons professing Christian discipleship and organizing themselves for the promotion of common ends. On the other hand, unless it be held that the Apostles exercised an absolute authority in the primitive Church, and that the clergy, or any one order amongst them, succeeded to all the functions of the Apostolate—and neither view agrees with the facts of the NT—it is manifest that a ministry regularly ordered from Apostolic times may adapt itself to democratic institutions as readily as, for example, that of Congregationalism, which, as Dr. Dale has shown, is in theory no more dependent on the popular will than any other (*History of English Congregationalism*). The question at issue, therefore, really resolves itself into this—whether Christ is merely the source of a spirit which has found for itself a body, or whether the body also has Christ for its direct author.

A. *IN THE GOSPELS*.—The Gospel of Mark registers the stages by which the Christian community, with its characteristic message of forgiveness and endowment of the Holy Spirit, was established through the public work of Jesus Christ (F. C. Burkitt, *St. Mark's Account of the Birth of the Church*, pp. 3–5, cf. his *Gospel History and its Transmission*, ch. 3). It is important to observe, as revealed in this Gospel, the principles which appear as impressed upon it from the first. The headline of Mark's narrative is, '*The beginning of the gospel* of Jesus Christ, the Son of God' (1^1). That the gospel is virtually identical with the Kingdom, of which it is the proclamation, is apparent from vv.$^{14.\,15}$ in which Jesus is described as taking up the work of the Baptist and announcing as His message the approach of the Kingdom (cf. Mt 4^{23}, Lk $4^{16\text{-}21}$). The identification of the forerunner with the voice, which, according to the evangelical prophet (Is 40^3), was to herald the return of God's people to the sacred city (Mk 1^2), and the recognition of Jesus in His baptism as uniting the attributes of the expected Messiah with those of the Servant who is to be Jahweh's agent in the process of restoration (1^{11}; cf. Ps 2^7, Is 42^1), mark out the 'coming of Jesus' from Nazareth to Jordan and the descent of the Spirit (vv.$^{9.\,10}$) as the first stage in the development of the Kingdom.

The second stage is its proclamation by Jesus Himself on His return from the wilderness to Galilee (vv.$^{14.\,15}$). This is immediately followed by the call of Simon, Andrew, James, and John (vv.$^{16\text{-}19}$), whose designation to a future Apostolate seems to be indicated in the words, 'I will make you to become fishers of men' (v.^{17}). To these is subsequently added Levi or Matthew (2^{14}). The method of the earlier ministry, as a scheme of selection from the multitude of those prepared to follow Him, is clearly seen in the avoidance of popularity and the frequent retirement by which it is marked ($1^{35\text{-}38.\,44.\,45}$ 3^7).

Then follows the first great crisis out of which the incipient community issues with the impress of a definite form, never to be lost through all subsequent developments. Christ retires with His adherents to the Sea of Galilee (3^7). He ascends 'the mountain' (v.^{13}). He calls 'whom he himself would' (v.^{13}), thus constituting the outer ring of His 'disciples,' who become a society resting upon the Lord's choice, no longer a promiscuous following united only by the uncertain bond of a common, though variable, devotion to one Master. Within this circle Jesus constitutes twelve (v.^{14}); Luke adds 'whom also he named apostles' (6^{13}). But the importance of this appointment is clearly seen by what in a narrative so concise as that of Mark cannot be without significance. He includes the list (3^{16-19}) repeated by each of the other Synoptists (Mt 10^{2-4}, Lk 6^{14-16}), and also in Acts (1^{13}). The words 'He made twelve' (ἐποίησε δώδεκα) are noticeable. Christ created an office, the purpose of which was to extend His own mission by proclaiming the Kingdom and exercising authority in casting out the rival kingdom of Beelzebub (Mk 3^{22-27} 6^{7-13}). To this end those who now in a narrower sense become 'the disciples' are first to be 'with him' (3^{14}, cf. Lk 22^{28}), so that from this point the narrative acquires a different character, being a record, on the one hand, of growing opposition on the part of the Jews to a movement now definitely embodied in an organized society, and, on the other, of the training of the Twelve for thrones in the Kingdom which Christ has appointed to them (Lk $22^{29.30}$). The call to the Twelve is renewed, and further defined, by the preliminary mission on which they are sent throughout the villages of Galilee. Their commission corresponds to the stage which Christ's work has already reached. They preach repentance, cast out demons, and heal the sick. The exact words of the Evangelist (Mk 6^{7}) are worthy of attention: 'He began to send them forth' (ἀποστέλλειν). Just as the whole narrative is the beginning of that Gospel the history of which is still in process of development, so here we have *the beginning of the Apostolate*, ultimately to become universal in its scope.

Two further preparatory stages are, however, necessary, before the Church can be built upon the Apostles (Mt 16^{18}; cf. Eph 2^{20}, Rev 21^{14})—the confession of Jesus' Messiahship, and the disclosure of suffering and death as the channel through which the gospel of the Kingdom was to become the witness to a crucified and risen Saviour.

The critical conversation at Cæsarea Philippi is narrated with greater detail by Mt. (16^{13-20}; cf. Mk 8^{27-29}, Lk 9^{18-20}). Mt. connects with the Apostolic confession the grant of the keys, and reveals the occasion as a further stage in the building of the Church, against which the gates of Hades are not to prevail. The authority to bind and loose here committed to St. Peter was, according to Cyprian (*de Unitate*, 4), extended to the Twelve on the occasion recorded in Mt 18^{15-20}. It is, however, difficult to suppose that the *Ecclesia* in v.^{17} does not primarily refer to the local Jewish synagogue (see Hort, *Christian Ecclesia*, p. 9), especially in view of the words 'Gentile and publican'; and it is quite in accord with Mt.'s manner to string together utterances not originally related. When, therefore, ἐκκλησία came to be interpreted of the Christian society, it would be quite natural to add, not only the promise of vv.$^{19.20}$, but the charter of authority given in v.^{18}, which is at least evidence that it was not regarded as applying to St. Peter only. And it is probable that the authority in question was extended to the Twelve, and that v.^{18}, even if not originally spoken in that connexion, accurately expresses the fact. The Fourth Gospel, in recording one of the appearances of the risen Lord, represents Him as imparting the Holy Spirit by breathing on the disciples, and renewing the authority, not now in the old Hebraic form, but in language connecting the Apostolic ministry with the atoning work: 'Whosesoever sins ye forgive,' etc. (Jn 20^{19-23}). The suggestion that Jesus here addressed not the Eleven, but a promiscuous gathering of disciples (see Westcott, *Gospel acc. to St. John* 20^{23} n.) seems to be negatived by the whole course of the Johannine narrative. It is true that John notes the absence of Thomas (v.^{24}). But he is specially mentioned as 'one of the Twelve,' and it is difficult to suppose that an Evangelist who gives at great length the last discourses addressed to the Eleven only does not intend to convey the same impression to the end. Nor can the renewed commission to St. Peter recorded in 21^{15-17} be regarded, in the light of the Denial, otherwise than as a specific restoration to a position that might else have seemed to be forfeited.

We find, then, in the Gospels a Christian society already in existence, within which the Apostles are an inner circle of more immediate disciples, recapitulating and intensifying the characteristics of the general body. This becomes apparent from the moment of the choice recorded in Mk 3^{14}, and is emphasized in the conversation at Cæsarea Philippi. Hort favours the view that the words 'whom also he named apostles' (RVm, cf. Lk 6^{13}) belong to the genuine text (*Christian Ecclesia*, p. 22). But it is clear that during the Lord's own ministry discipleship is the prominent feature. They are called 'the Twelve' (Mk 14^{20}), 'the twelve disciples' (Mt 20^{17}), and simply 'the disciples' (Mt 26^{26}). But the name 'apostles' is also given to them, and the second reason for their selection as recorded by Mark, viz. 'that he might send them forth' (ἀποστέλλῃ, 3^{14}), points to the ultimate purpose of their closer companionship. There is nothing to indicate a more permanent commission than that of ch. 6, in relation to which alone the term ἀπόστολος is subsequently used (6^{30}, but see above). Luke, however, clearly employs the word in the light of its subsequent use in Acts (Lk 6^{13} 17^{5} 22^{14} 24^{10}). Matthew uses it only in connexion with the Galilæan mission (10^{2}), but it is in giving the list of names—a fact in itself significant of the wider purpose lying behind the immediate commission.

When we reach the last Passover, the importance of the narrative attains its height. From the confession at Cæsarea, the training of the Twelve takes a course clearly differentiating it from that of all others. The acknowledgment of Messiahship is not to be the complete witness of the disciples. It prepares the way for a fuller disclosure. From that time '*he began to teach them*' (Mk 8^{31} ἤρξατο, cf. 1^{1} 6^{7}) concerning his suffering. The Transfiguration anticipated a more spiritual glory than that of the Jewish Messiah, to be attained through the ἔξοδος about to be fulfilled at Jerusalem (Lk 9^{31}). The experience of the Last Journey had its appropriate sequel in that of the Upper Room. Mark says that 'when it was evening, he cometh with the twelve' (14^{17}); Mt., that 'he was sitting at meat with the twelve disciples' (26^{20}); Lk. significantly styles them 'apostles' (22^{14}); while St. John introduces his more intimate narrative by calling this select company 'his own,' whom Jesus 'loved unto the end' (13^{1}). Bearing in mind the general purpose of Mk. (see above), we shall naturally regard his account of the Supper from the point of view of the establishment of the Christian community. It must be remembered that the Eucharist was everywhere celebrated in the Christian congregations as the characteristic act of Church fellowship. Regarding the events of the Upper Room, Mark confines himself, with the single exception of the indication of Judas as traitor, to the shortest possible account of the institution of this rite, as the act by which the Christian community is formally incorporated (14^{22-25}). The representative character of the Twelve is indicated by the dependence in which the Church is thus made to stand upon them. The Eucharist became theirs in virtue of the conditions under which it was first celebrated; and only through them, and as they transmitted it, does it pass to the community. This is in accordance with the relations brought out by John. Those who are hereafter to believe are to do so 'through their word' (17^{20}). The High-Priestly Prayer reaches out through the disciples, who are to bear the primary witness, to those who are mediately chosen by Christ out of the world.

The post-Resurrection narratives do but confirm the impression of the special separation of the Twelve which culminates in the seclusion of the Upper Room. The narrative of Mark is cut short; but the command given to the women, themselves Jesus' disciples, to 'tell his disciples and Peter' (16^{7}) of the empty tomb, shows the Eleven as a distinct body. Mt. gives the commission to make disciples and to baptize as entrusted to the 'eleven disciples' (28^{16}). Lk. shows other disciples gathered at Jerusalem when the risen Christ appeared to them (24^{33}). But the Eleven are distinguished from them (*ib.*), the rest being expressly spoken of as they 'that were with them.' Even if, therefore, the appearance recorded in Jn 20^{19-23} refer to the same occasion, the words 'Receive ye the Holy Spirit,' etc., must also certainly have a special bearing on the Apostolic office.

B. *IN THE ACTS.*—With the Acts we reach a further and a final stage in the foundation of the Christian society. The gospel of the Kingdom now becomes the organized *witness to the Resurrection.* The ministry of reconciliation finds its full expression in the proclamation of forgiveness through the Cross. This we find specially committed to the Apostolate ($1^{2. 8. 22. 25}$ 10^{41})—a term which gains a correspondingly determinate meaning. The list of the Eleven is again given in connexion with this developed function (1^{13}), and the choice of Matthias is based upon the necessity of completing the number of the official witnesses (vv.$^{21. 22}$). The phenomena of the early chapters are precisely what a study of the Gospels would suggest. The Church enters upon its career as an organized body, the Apostles being differentiated from the brethren. From the first the brotherhood continues in 'the apostles' teaching,' and in 'the fellowship' thus established (2^{42}). That this relation did not involve submission to an Apostolic despotism appears in the choice of Matthias and of the Seven. In the former case, two were 'put forward' (1^{23}), apparently by the whole assembly, the final decision being reserved for the unseen though present Master (v.^{24}). In the latter, the brethren were expressly charged by the Apostles to 'look out' from among themselves seven men (6^{3}), who, after prayer, were set apart with the laying-on of Apostolic hands (v.^{6}). All the elements of ordination are here. At the outset of ministerial appointment it would seem as though the Apostles disclaimed any lordship over God's heritage. They do not even exercise a veto. The responsibility of supplying the need of ministrations, as the circumstances of the Christian community disclose themselves, belongs to the society itself. The Apostolic imposition of hands is, like the sacraments, a form of covenanted prayer (Calvin, *Instit.* iv. 19, § 31: 'I admit it to be a sacrament in true and legitimate ordination'). Those set apart represent, not the Apostles, but Christ. The Seven have been traditionally regarded as the first deacons. If this be so, it is obvious that what subsequently became the third order of the ministry was not explicitly appointed by Christ. The general impression conveyed by Acts is that of a society extending and organizing itself as opportunity offered or circumstances suggested. But the laying-on of hands in this instance represents a principle conspicuous throughout the book, viz. the requirement of mission from Christ Himself, of which Apostolic recognition was the pledge. But there is no evidence even that 'the ministry of the word,' which, in directing the appointment of the Seven, the Apostles expressly reserved (v.^{4}), demanded absolute submission. No doubt, the actual gospel itself was inviolate and unchangeable. But not even an Apostle, according to St. Paul, was to be believed if he deviated from that standard (Gal 1^{8}). As primary witnesses to the Resurrection the Apostles have no successors. The gospel is an Apostolic report of incommunicable experience, once for all delivered to the whole body of the saints (Jude ^{3}). The formation of the NT canon was based upon the test of Apostolicity, and consequently the appeal to Scripture has become the permanent form in which, as regards matters of faith, the Church of every age sits at the Apostles' feet. But, even apart from the gospel, the Acts suggests that a recognition of Apostolic authority was not inconsistent with the freedom of prophecy (19^{6} $21^{9. 10}$) and with the participation of the community as a whole in spiritual decisions (15^{22}). What is constant is the maintenance of a Christian society, rendered coherent by dependence on a stewardship of the word mediated through the Apostles from Christ Himself (Lk $12^{41. 42}$). Philip, for example, though he evangelizes Samaria, cannot complete his work without the intervention of the Apostles at Jerusalem (Ac 8^{14}). As local Churches are founded, presbyters are 'appointed' for them (14^{23}; χειροτονήσαντες, being used of Paul and Barnabas, cannot here bear the meaning of 'elect,' which it has already lost in Hellenistic Greek [see Hatch, art. 'Ordination' in *DCA*]; it equals καταστήσαντες [cf. Tit 1^{5}, Clem. Rom. xliv. 2, *Didache* 15]; but it is equally far from connoting a particular mode of appointment).

With two exceptions, the existence of an extended Apostolate beyond the circle of the Twelve is scarcely apparent. Prophets are mentioned five times (Ac 11^{27} 13^{1} 15^{32} 19^{6} $21^{9. 10}$), the gift in one case (19^{6}) attesting the presence of the Spirit in the baptized after the imposition of hands. The suggestion in each case is that the prophets have as yet no structural relation to the *ecclesia*, but are persons of either sex, directly endowed with a gift of declaring the Spirit's mind, and thus indicating courses of action, as when Barnabas and Saul are to be sent forth by the Church at Antioch. Teachers are coupled with prophets in Ac 13^{1}, as though representing a similar gift, and Barnabas is placed in this combined class. When in Ac 21^{8} Philip is called 'the evangelist,' it seems likely that this function was not conferred upon him as one of the Seven, but discharged, like the office of prophet, in virtue of a special gift or χάρισμα. It is, however, clear that men exercising what has been called a charismatic ministry in relation to the whole *ecclesia* held a recognized place in the Apostolic Church (1 Co $12^{5. 6}$, Eph 2^{20} 4^{11}, cf. Ro 16^{7}). But these do not constitute any infringement of the Apostolic authority. Whether Barnabas was an Apostle in the full sense of the word is doubtful, because the name is applied to him only in relation to his missionary labours (Ac 14^{14}). That by imposition of hands in the Church at Antioch he was entrusted with a mission rather than ordained to an office is the probable interpretation of Ac 13^{1-13} (see Hort, *Christian Ecclesia*, pp. 63, 64), though he was apparently associated with Paul in the appointment of presbyters (14^{23}). But the same cannot be said of James 'the Lord's brother' and St. Paul himself. The former, who is ranked among the pillar Apostles in Gal 2^{9} (cf. 1 Co 15^{7}), and who extends the right hand of fellowship to St. Paul, is almost certainly not one of the Twelve (see Lightfoot, *Galatians*, 1^{19} n.; also dissertation on 'The Brethren of the Lord'). Yet he is evidently the chief authority in Jerusalem (Ac 15^{13}, Gal 2^{12}). The plan of Acts, which, after describing the beginnings of the Church in Palestine under the Twelve, passes into a narrative of its extension in the Empire under the preaching of St. Paul, witnesses to the permanent character of his commission as an Apostle. This is repeatedly claimed by St. Paul himself as depending on the direct choice of Christ (Ro 1^{1}, 1 Co 1^{1} $9^{1. 2}$ 15^{8-10} etc.). He lays hands on the baptized, as did Peter and John (Ac 19^{6}). The presbyterate in Churches of his foundation depends on his appointment (14^{23}, cf. $20^{17. 28}$).

The picture, therefore, with which Acts leaves us is that of a federation of Christian communities under the immediate guidance of presbyters, who themselves owe their appointment to Apostles—a body of direct witnesses of the Resurrection, discharging a sort of general episcopate and including the Twelve, whose precise relation to the wider Apostolate is not clearly defined. Within these communities are exercised certain spiritual gifts, among the possessors of which the prophets seem to approach most nearly to a regular order, but are nevertheless not, like presbyters, Apostolic delegates. There is nothing to indicate any method by which the organic structure was to be maintained after the decease of the Apostles. The scope of the book carries us no further than what we now see to have been but a preliminary stage in the accomplishment of Christ's purpose and command—that the Apostles should be His witnesses to the uttermost parts of the earth. When the writer had brought St. Paul to Rome, the task, as his contemporaries would view it, was in a sense fulfilled. A delay of centuries in the return of Christ visibly to reign in the midst of His people was not contemplated. That is the true answer to the suggestion that the method of continuing a Christian ministry was among the things pertaining to the Kingdom, of which the risen Christ spoke to the disciples during the Forty Days. This could not well have been without a revelation as to the postponement of 'the restoration of the kingdom to Israel,' which it is clear the primitive community did not possess. The continuance of the Apostolic office itself beyond the lifetime of the original witnesses was, in the nature of the case, impossible. The terms of their appointment involved personal testimony to the facts of our Lord's life. The question, therefore, of ministerial succession could not arise until it became probable that the Apostles were not to tarry until Christ came.

C. *IN THE EPISTLES.*—The Epistles confirm, and in some points render more explicit, the testimony of the Acts. Here we are mainly concerned with the Pauline group, where the corporate aspect of Christianity is always prominent. But the Epistle to the Hebrews enjoins obedience to 'them that have the rule,' clearly implying accountability, not to the congregation, but to that 'great shepherd of the sheep' to whom reference is immediately made (He $13^{7.\,17.\,20.\,24}$). And as the general tendency of the Epistle is to isolate the eternal priesthood of Christ in contrast with the transitory and therefore successive priesthood of the OT, it is well to remember not only that the body of Christian believers is here represented as a flock with many under-shepherds, but that the same idea is definitely presented under the figure of the house, in a passage distinctly anticipating a later and more developed view of the ministry (3^{1-6}). St. James apparently witnesses to a part of the Apostolic commission, viz. the healing of the sick, as vested in the presbyterate (5^{14}); and St. Peter develops the conception of the Christian congregation as a flock entrusted to the presbyters under the Chief Shepherd (1 P 5^{1-4}; cf. Mt 26^{31}, Lk 12^{32}, Jn 21^{15-17}, Jude ^{12}, Ps 80^{1} etc.). And it is noticeable that, calling himself a 'co-presbyter' (5^{1}), he regards the presbyterate as inherent in his own office, and yet again in that of Christ Himself as the 'Shepherd and Bishop' of souls (2^{25}). The Apocalypse, being mystical, has little to the purpose beyond the clear fact that the twelve Apostles of the Lamb are indicated as the foundation-stones of the heavenly city (21^{14}). The angels of the Seven Churches are almost certainly their mystical representatives, not their earthly presidents (see Swete, *Apocalypse*, p. 21 f.). But the conception of an ordered life and organic unity, inseparable from the idea of a city, is here, as elsewhere in the NT, prominent.

St. Paul in his earliest Epistles recognizes the two lines of authority, which subsequent ages have never succeeded altogether in adjusting, and which respectively represent the historical and the evangelical elements in the Church. On the one hand, there must be no quenching of the Spirit through contempt of the free ministry of prophecy (1 Th $5^{19.\,20}$); on the other, Christians are to know and esteem those that are over them in the Lord (vv.$^{12.\,13}$). The importance of the latter becomes clearer in 2 Thessalonians, which shows the forces of disintegration in the community, already operating through the disorders consequent upon the expectation of an immediate Parousia (3^{6-15}). That the function of government and discipline is in its origin an 'apostolic' gift, exercised by those entrusted with it in virtue of a Divine commission, is witnessed by St. Paul's treatment of the Corinthian offender (1 Co 5^{3-5}) and his vindication of his office (1 Co 15^{10}, 2 Co 4^{1} etc., Ro 11^{13} 15^{16}). The Pastoral Epistles show Timothy and Titus, in Ephesus and Crete, entrusted with a larger measure of government than the presbyters, as delegates of an absent Apostle (1 Ti 1^{3} $4^{11.\,12}$ $5^{1.\,17}$, Tit 1^{5} $3^{1.\,10}$, 2 Ti 2^{2} 4^{5}), who, in the case of Timothy at any rate, appears to contemplate a continuance of authority beyond his own lifetime (2 Ti 4^{6}). Both have that supreme authority which arises out of the commission to ordain others to the presbyterate. In them we see provision made for the reproduction of the local pastorate. In them the principle of Apostolic delegation is transmuted into a principle of succession. There is nothing to show that the same method was adopted in the case of other Churches, or that, in making this provision, the writer was doing more than developing, in relation to the immediate needs of the Churches concerned, an authority capable of many applications. But none insists more strongly than St. Paul on the structural character of the Body of Christ (Ro $12^{4.\,5}$, 1 Co 12^{12-14}, Eph $4^{4.\,16}$), on the definite relation of ministry to this structure (Eph $4^{11.\,12}$), on the primary character of the Apostolate (1 Co 12^{28}, Eph 4^{11}), or on the due subordination of spiritual gifts to the development of a society (1 Co 12^{4-29} 14^{12} etc.), a building of which Christ is the cornerstone (Eph 2^{20}). The foundation is twofold (*ib.*), the Apostles and prophets—the latter representing in principle the ministry of the word, the former, in so far as the office is disciplinary, that of sacraments. Both would seem to have been united in the ordination of Timothy (1 Ti 4^{14}), as though the historic, external call and the free activity of the Spirit were both apparent in the determinations of the primitive community. It was the separation, which inevitably arose in days of decaying fervour, between the outward links of continuity in the historic body and the manifestation of the Spirit, that raised the question of the seat of Apostolic authority in the Christian society.

Note on priesthood in the NT.—One other point remains to be discussed before leaving the NT. We have already seen that the problem of the ministry is capable of consideration, and ought to be considered, apart from any sacerdotal theory. In the hieratic sense of a caste which, by interposing between the worshippers and God, denies, while it appears to guarantee, the priestly character of the people for whom it acts, sacerdotalism is an idea foreign to the NT. On the other hand, the theory that every individual is in his own right a priest is equally inconsistent with the Christian idea. It is primarily the society that is a royal priesthood (1 P 2^{9}, Rev 1^{6} 5^{10}), having boldness of access to the throne of grace in Christ (He 10^{19}, Eph 2^{18}). It is the people of God, the holy nation (1 P $2^{9.\,10}$), the commonwealth of the spiritual Israel (Eph 2^{12}), that answers to Israel after the flesh, differing from it only in those points wherein the priestliness of the latter was imperfect. It does not imply an absence of differentiation, which is essential to the life of the body. And the Epistle to the Hebrews, in designating Christ the great Shepherd of the sheep in His priestly character as 'brought again from the dead with the blood of the eternal covenant' (He 13^{20}), attaches a derived priesthood to the under-shepherds, who have just been spoken of as having rule in the Christian community, and watching for souls 'as they that shall give account' (v.^{17}). But while, in the light of the NT, priesthood is an aspect under which the Christian ministry may be legitimately regarded, it becomes from the 3rd cent. onwards its technical and essential character (see Lightfoot's dissertation on 'The Christian Ministry' in *Philippians*, pp. 255–264), with the consequent reversion to Jewish, if not pagan, ideas. 'The ministry of reconciliation' (2 Co 5[18]) never in the NT loses its ethical character. There is nothing to suggest that the performance of any particular rite is in principle restricted to an order, or that a ceremonial investiture must precede the exercise of functions precisely defined and limited. On the other hand, it is something more than a merely moral authority, dependent for its sanction upon results, with which the ministry of the NT is seen to be clothed. It is a principle of organic life.

2. The principle as preserved in the facts of Church history.—Passing from the NT to ecclesiastical history, we have to ask, not what were the opinions of ancient authors on the subject of the ministry, but how as a matter of fact the principles embodied in the Gospels, continued in the Acts, and attested by the Epistles, were retained in the succeeding life of the Church. How was what is seen to be a structural unity preserved from degenerating into a concourse of unrelated units? The Apostolic teaching is preserved in the canon of Scripture, in the formation of which Apostolicity was the invariable test. Where is the corresponding mark of Apostolicity in the structure of the Christian society?

A. *WRITINGS OF THE SUB-APOSTOLIC AGE.*—(1) *The Epistle of Clement* (*c.* 97 A.D.), in which, as in the *Didache*, there is no trace of diocesan episcopacy (the word ἐπίσκοπος being still, as in the NT, apparently synonymous with πρεσβύτερος), definitely asserts the Apostolic character of the ministry as succeeding to a pastoral authority.

The passage is xliv. 1-3: 'And our Apostles knew through our Lord Jesus Christ that there would be strife over the name of the bishop's office. For this cause, therefore, having received complete foreknowledge, they appointed the aforesaid persons, and afterwards *they provided a continuance*, that if these should fall asleep, *other approved men should succeed* to their ministration.' [The translation and readings are those of Lightfoot in *The Apostolic Fathers*]. A variant, which Gore adopts, and which makes the passage more distinctly 'episcopal' in complexion, will be found in that author's *Church and the Ministry* (ch. vi. 4). In either case, the writer seems to have believed that the ministry was propagated on a plan directly sanctioned by Christ. His words show that in the West, where the method of 'continuance' is less distinctly traceable than in the communities of Asia Minor, the principle of Apostolic order was unquestioned. The facts of the Church's life are stated in terms of succession. The Apostles 'appointed their firstfruits to be bishops and deacons' (xlii. 4). 'Christ is from God, and the Apostles are from Christ' (*ib.* 2). What is thus handed on is a ministry of the gospel and a priesthood of offering (xxxvi. 1, xl. 2-5, xlii. 1-4). The latter phrase, as also the comparison between the resistance of the Corinthians to their presbyters and the rebellion of Korah against the Levitical priests (xliii., xliv. 4), lends itself in a hierarchical atmosphere to a sacerdotal interpretation, but for Clement himself the point of the analogy is limited to the due observance of order in worship. The 'sceptre of God . . . came not in the pomp of arrogance or of pride' (xvi.). Clement sees the law of service in the adjustments of an organic universe (xx.), and Christ embodies the will and mind of the Creator (xxxvi.). As in St. Paul, nature is the true analogy of the Christian society. It is active in all its parts, laic as well as presbyterial (xxxvii. etc.). The consent of the whole Church is as much an expression of the Spirit as Apostolic appointment (xliv. 3). Not passive obedience, but observance of the limits which his 'ordinances' impose upon him, is the duty of every member (xl. 3-5). The relations of the several ranks are moral rather than technical.

The Epistle does not suggest a rigid system by which the performance of sacred rites is the exclusive function of a mediatorial class. But it is conspicuously plain that for Clement the Christian society is prior to the individual, and that the continuity of its vital relation to Christ depends on the persistence of facts of Church life not dependent on the choice of the several members.

(2) The testimony of *Ignatius* is not altogether easy to appreciate, because words and phrases are apt to be understood in the light of later developments. Unlike Clement, he nowhere explicitly states the principle of succession, but within the sphere of his experience a ministry of three orders is the type of Church government, and is apparently regarded as universal. The argument from silence, based upon the absence of references to ministerial orders in the epistle to the *Romans* similar to those which abound elsewhere, is of doubtful force in view of the statement in *Trall.* 3, that 'apart from these there is not even the name of a church.' Though there is little reason to doubt that monepiscopacy was established in the Churches of Asia by St. John, as Tertullian and others assert, and though the frequent association in Ignatius between obedience to the constituted ministry and observance of the Divine commands (*Magn.* 4, *Philad.* 1, *Smyr.* 8) suggests the inference that he regards this action of the Apostle as resting upon the explicit injunction of our Lord with respect to the permanent organization of His body, we are not justified in concluding, apart from direct evidence, that any such injunction was in fact given. Irenæus seems to say the same about the work of the four Evangelists; but his conviction of the mystical necessity of a fourfold Gospel (*adv. Hær.* 11) is parallel to the declaration of Ignatius, that Christ is the mind of the Father, even as the 'bishops that are settled in the farthest parts of the earth are in the mind of Jesus Christ' (*Eph.* 3),—a mystical inference from the facts of Church life which has no certain value for history. This vein of mysticism in Ignatius must never be forgotten in estimating the evidence of his letters. Nor in his most emphatic assertions of episcopal authority does Ignatius appeal only to the word of Apostles, or even of Christ Himself, but to the moral and spiritual results of schismatic action already apparent in the current experience of the Church.

The main idea of Ignatius is unity (ἑνότης, ἕνωσις—*Eph.* 4, *Magn.* 7. 13, *Philad.* 5). All things are from God and unto Him (*Eph.* 14, *Philad.* 9). This is realized primarily in the relation of the Father and the Son (*Eph.* 3. 5, *Magn.* 7, etc.). It is the purpose of Christ to unite men to God through Himself (*Eph.* 5. 9, etc.). This result Ignatius in his own case feels to be not yet fully attained. He only begins to be a disciple (*Eph.* 3). Martyrdom he believes to be necessary that this union may be consummated, and that he may 'attain unto God' (*Rom.* 2). This relation is thus no mere technical association through external bonds, but involves the moral elements of faith which is the body, and love which is the blood of Christ (*Trall.* 8). It is checked by spiritual experience. The Divine method by which the union with Christ is achieved is the Incarnation, expressed in the four facts of the Virgin-birth, Baptism, Passion, and Resurrection of Jesus (*Smyr.* 1)—those limitations of hard fact which alone give reality and assurance to Christ's work (*Magn.* 11: πραχθέντα ἀληθῶς καὶ βεβαίως ὑπὸ Ἰησοῦ X.), without which it is mere appearance (*Smyr.* 2: τὸ δοκεῖν). Without this acknowledgment there is no 'assurance' (*Magn.* 13) in Christian life. It is they who refuse to receive these cardinal facts that are a mere 'appearance' (*Trall.* 10: αὐτοὶ ὄντες τὸ δοκεῖν). Here is the second appeal to experience. The teaching which St. Paul combats in the Epistle to the Colossians, which appears in a yet more virulent form in the Pastorals, and which provoked the uncompromising hostility of the disciple who saw the blood and water flow from Jesus' side, had spread like a moral pestilence throughout Asia in the form of Docetism. As in the first age the retention of the pure gospel had been guaranteed by continuance in 'the apostles' doctrine and fellowship,' so now a faithful adherence to Apostolic commandments and submission to the bishop (*Eph.* 6, *Trall.* 2, *Philad.* 7, *Smyr.* 8), with the presbyters (*Eph.* 4 and *passim*) and deacons (*Magn.* 6, etc.) established everywhere in the communities as constituted by the Apostles themselves, give the only pledge of that union with Christ through the Incarnation by which the believer attains to God (e.g. *Trall.* 7).

We must observe: (*a*) That acceptance of the limitations imposed by loyalty to a duly constituted Christian society follows, in the thought of Ignatius, the principle of the Incarnation (*e.g. Eph.* 3). (*b*) Obedience to episcopal authority is represented as a moral obligation rather than as a technical condition of salvation. To follow one who makes a schism (*Philad.* 3), or to live without episcopal ministrations, is condemned. 'Do nothing without the bishop' is an injunction expressed in terms so general as to include more than the celebration of sacred rites, and thus indicates a spirit rather than a rule. (*c*) Baptism and the Eucharist are dependent for their 'validity' not upon the official character of the ministrants (a question not raised), but upon episcopal sanction (*Symr.* 8: οὐκ ἐξὸν ἐστιν χωρὶς τοῦ ἐπισκόπου κ.τ.λ.), the spiritual importance of which is apparent in the case of the latter—a sacrament of unity—, the neglect of the principle resulting in decline of faith and love. (*d*) 'Validity,' *i.e.* assured spiritual efficiency, admits of degrees. Disregard of the ministry is the beginning of that spiritual declension which is perfected in the denial of the Son. 'Invalid' does not mean null and void. There is nothing to show that persons baptized 'apart from the bishop' would have been treated as unbaptized. βέβαιος as applied to sacraments must be interpreted in view of the wider use of the word and its cognates in these epistles (*Magn.* 4. 7. 13). The best translation will, perhaps, be 'regular' or 'standard.' (*e*) While we must refrain from fixing upon Ignatius a conception of the Church which reduces it to a nicely adjusted hierarchical machine, the principle of his thought warrants us in claiming him as an undeniable witness for the continuance into the sub-Apostolic age of a society duly subordinated, in the facts of its exterior order no less than of its spiritual life, to that presbytery which the Father's incarnate Representative gathered around Himself in the persons of the Apostles. Promiscuous powers of association, the alternative to structural continuity, are foreign to his whole conception. In that sense Ignatius is an unimpeachable witness to Apostolical succession in the early 2nd century.

(3) *Polycarp*, whom his friend and pupil Irenæus declares to have been appointed bishop of Smyrna by Apostles (*Iren.* iii. 4), writes to the Philippians, like Clement to the Corinthians, and Ignatius to Ephesians or Trallians, a letter addressed officially to the whole Church, not only in his own name, but in that of his presbyters. The evidence is equivocal as to the existence of a bishop at Philippi; for, though mention is made only of presbyters and deacons, the former are not called ἐπίσκοποι as in the Pauline Epistle to the same Church (*Polyc.* 5. 6. 11). But it does show that ministerial authority is a particular determination of that which attaches to the whole community acting constitutionally. It is the principle of obedience that Polycarp emphasizes—'Be ye all subject one to another' (10). God is the Father, Jesus Christ His Son the eternal High Priest (*pontifex*) (12). His coming and those commandments which are its issue, *i.e.* not moral precepts merely or chiefly, but the witness of the Cross, the Passion and Resurrection, which form the subject of the gospel, involve obedience on the part of Christians to the voices of the prophets who foretold, and the Apostles who proclaimed the gospel (6). The perversion of this truth, its accommodation to human lusts, by a Docetic teaching which denies bodily resurrection and eternal judgment, is still the fact of experience that constitutes the chief danger to faith (7). Though milder in form, Polycarp's teaching evidently tallies with that of Ignatius, whose letters comprise 'every kind of edification which pertaineth unto our Lord' (13). The Philippians are to submit themselves to the presbyters and deacons as to God and Christ (5).

(4) The importance of the *Didache* depends upon its character as a Hebrew-Christian document of a date not later than the early 2nd century. Internal evidence suggests that it represents a condition of affairs such as would exist among a community of Jewish disciples in Syria, whose members had been baptized on acceptance of the Pentecostal message that Jesus was the Messiah, had adopted the primary Christian practices of the breaking of bread and prayer, and were subject to the influence and teaching, if not of the Twelve directly, yet of original prophets and teachers like Philip, but were strangers to the developed theology of the Epistles (see J. Wordsworth, *Ministry of Grace*, pp. 16, 17). In observing the life of this community, we look not so much for settled principles as for indications of the way in which organization was taking shape in an inchoate and rudimentary stage. We notice: (*a*) That the community acts and may be addressed as a whole, resembling in this particular both the societies to which Clement and Ignatius write and the Churches of the NT. (*b*) Prophecy, which at a later date was emphasized in opposition not only to Gnosticism but to an official ministry, occupies a prominent place, not, however, as a promiscuous gift, but as realized in a more or less well defined order (*Did.* 10. 11. 13). Here again there is correspondence with the Acts and NT generally, where προφητεία is already tending to give rise to a class of προφῆται. In the *Didache* they possess a λειτουργία or right of service (15), which, while it evidently includes leadership in worship, is not precisely defined, does not apparently depend on ordination, and is moral rather than technical in type. As in the NT, so here ἀπόστολος is not confined to the Twelve, but seems to be applied to the προφῆται as a class (11: 'if [the apostle] ask money, he is a false prophet'), together with another name, διδάσκαλος (15). They are described by such vague phrases as οἱ τετιμημένοι (15), which devolves also upon the presbyters and deacons as admitted to a share in the same λειτουργία. Clement speaks of other ἐλλόγιμοι ἄνδρες as equally with Apostles appointing presbyters to a λειτουργία (Clem. Rom. xliv.). Taking this passage along with the *Didache*, there is some ground for the suggestion that the prophets, in addition to the Twelve, St. Paul, and possibly other 'apostles,' were an original source of the succession, which would therefore be Apostolic rather as possessing the sanction of the Twelve than as flowing by direct delegation from them (see Gore, *Ch. and Min.* ch. 6). It is at any rate clear that this must have been the case with appointments made by St. Paul. Whether prophecy might re-appear from age to age as a constantly renewed and immediate source of authority, is a question not contemplated by the *Didache*, which, especially in view of the expected Parousia, is not concerned with a remoter future. But the community is to exercise its right of testing the prophet's claim by the standard of disinterested sincerity and conformity with a rule of faith (11. 12). If, however, he satisfies this test, he is to be admitted either temporarily or permanently to an authority described as that of a high priest (13)—the type, if not the source, of all other ministries. The community are to appoint for themselves bishops (*i.e.* presbyters) and deacons, who are to 'perform the service of the prophets and teachers' (15). Though χειροτονήσατε does not necessarily mean 'elect' (see above), yet the word clearly involves action similar to that required of the Church in the selection of the Seven (Ac 6^3)—a choice which was not an alternative to the imposition of hands. The presumption would rather be, as noted above, that the prophets, whose ministry they were to share, would repeat the action of the Apostles at Jerusalem.

B. *DISCIPLINARY CONTROVERSIES OF THE THIRD, FOURTH, AND FIFTH CENTURIES.*—The limitations of the principle of historic succession are defined in the course of the discussions concerning discipline (A.D. 200–450), which gather round the controversies involved in Montanism, Novatianism, and Donatism. The question in all these disputes was in reality not, What did the Apostles ordain, but What do the facts of the continuous history of the Church involve? The problem is parallel to that which centred round the Person of Christ, and issued in the dogmatic definitions of the 4th and 5th centuries. It may be admitted in either case that the matter is not merely one of terminology, but that a certain inadequacy of thought was often consistent with loyal acceptance of the facts, leading not unnaturally, under stress of new conditions, to positions ultimately found to be departures from primitive Christianity.

(1) To describe *Montanism* as an innovation, in the sense of a conscious rejection of an authoritative system, is to misconceive the situation. Hitherto the inroads of Gnosticism had been met by insistence on submission to the principle of unity expressed in the organization of the Christian society. The appeal of Ignatius was developed by Irenæus (iii. 2, 3, 4, 40) and Tertullian (*de Præscript.* 30–32), who pointed to the episcopal succession as a guarantee for the preservation of Apostolic teaching. Nor were these alone in their contention. Hippolytus speaks of bishops as 'successors of the Apostles' and guardians of the word (*Hær.* prooem. p. 3). Hegesippus, again, after speaking of the Corinthian Church as continuing 'in the right word' till the episcopate of Primus, says that he had made a list of the succession (διαδοχή) up to Anicetus (*ap.* Euseb. iv. 22). Such evidence, together with that of the 'Church Orders,' which belong to the same period and in which we find careful regulations for ordination (*e.g.* the Roman Church Order, commonly called the *Canons of Hippolytus*), points to the importance attached to the structural unity of the Church by men who, inheriting the spirit of the Fourth Gospel and the Pastorals, regarded Christianity as a life manifested in facts (1 Jn 1[1]), not a system of knowledge. Montanism was not in intention a denial of this position. Writers like Tertullian fell back upon what seemed to them a more sure defence of orthodoxy in the spirit of prophecy. As with Novatian in the next age, who was careful to obtain a regular consecration to the episcopate, there was no separation from the external form of the Church. It was the Church itself that condemned them. Nor was the opposition to Montanism based on the illegitimacy of prophecy when unconnected with any outward delegation of authority, but simply on the nature and circumstances of the utterances themselves, which were pronounced on their merits to be not of God. In the continuance of prophecy there was nothing inconsistent with the authority of the ministry, and, though doubtless the claim of Montanus might in its issues become fatal not only to a canon of Scripture, but also to the historic fabric of the Christian society, it was only the authority to absolve sinners and repress prophecy that was actually assailed. The 'Church of the Spirit' was not a rival to the historic body, but rather the source of authority within it. And the immediate expectation of the Parousia, characteristic of the Montanists, absolved them from the necessity of thinking out the problem of continuity. There is no evidence of the creation of a fresh local ministry, as with the Irvingites, by the voice of the Spirit. There were Montanist bishops and presbyters, as subsequently there were Arian or Nestorian clergy. But though the question was brought to a final issue, the problem was essentially the same as had been involved in Gnosticism, and it was met by the Church in the same manner. Just as there is a 'form of doctrine,' an Apostolic gospel, a written word, so there is a historic structure, 'the witness and keeper of Holy Writ,' 'the pillar and ground of the truth.' This was involved in the claim to 'try the spirits' made on behalf of the Church acting through its organization.

(2) *Novatianism* produced a definite theory of the facts of organized Church life in Cyprian's *de Unitate*. To discuss the historical value of the distinctive claims of the episcopate put forth in that treatise does not fall within the scope of this article. It represents the facts as they were in the 3rd cent., and as in the mind of the writer they had been from Apostolic times. As a vindication of the Apostolic authority of the Church acting in a corporate capacity, it is in general agreement with Ignatius, Irenæus, and the opponents of Montanism. Its weakness lies in the impetus given to a ministerial sacerdotalism binding the activity of the Spirit to official channels (see Lightfoot, *Philippians*, p. 258). So far as Novatianism, following in the wake of Montanus, was resistance to growing officialism, it stood for the freedom of the gospel. The movement involved: (*a*) deference to the confessors, who, as manifesting the Spirit, were in deed what the prophets had been in word; (*b*) supersession of such bishops and other ministers as did not manifestly fulfil certain spiritual conditions. The Roman Cornelius was accounted no bishop, because, like Callistus, he was held to be deficient in a genuinely spiritual rigour. This was in effect to make the voice of the Spirit, not Apostolic succession, the decisive Church principle. Against it Cyprian elaborated his famous doctrine of the episcopate as the true centre of unity. The Apostolic authority, first entrusted to St. Peter, but immediately extended to the other eleven Apostles (*de Unit.* 4), was transmitted by succession from them to the bishops (5). Each bishop, representing the particular Church which he ruled, possessed an undivided authority, though in practice limited by a similar jurisdiction conferred upon his neighbours, the episcopate being regarded as exercised jointly and severally ('Episcopatus unus est cujus a singulis in solidum pars tenetur,' 5).

It is not easy to see precisely how Cyprian expected this principle to work out, and difficulties arose within his own lifetime in the controversy with Stephen of Rome concerning rebaptism. But there is no uncertainty whatever as to his theory. Christ founded a society, which from the first He entrusted to the college of Apostles, which reproduces itself from age to age in the universal college of bishops. Though, however, the days of exact constitutional limitations had not yet arrived, Cyprian does not appear to have contemplated an episcopal absolutism, for in practice he allows, and even insists upon, something in the nature of an organic exercise of authority on the part of the several dioceses, giving due recognition to presbyters, deacons, and even the laity, in synodical decisions (*Ep.* xvii. 1, xxxviii. 1, lxiv. 1, xix. 2). The right of the laity to withdraw from the communion of a sinful bishop is recognized (*Ep.* lxvii. 3). To the voice of the Plebes the bishop himself owed his position. But the tendency of this explicit theory and the character of an age which needed a disciplinary system were undoubtedly towards the identification of the Spirit's work with official acts assigned to the various grades of an accredited hierarchy. If Novatian applied a narrow human criterion to the work of the Spirit, by refusing to recognize His presence, when such manifestations as the members of a Church, itself imperfectly spiritualized, could discern, were found to be absent; so imperfectly did Cyprian understand the limits of the principle, by which he opposed the schism, that his hard-shell conception of the Church gave rise to a new Novatianism, in that bureaucratic idea of Christian society which led him to refuse recognition to the baptism of schismatics, which denies spiritual validity outside its own borders, and which finds its latest development in what Cyprian would have vehemently resisted—Ultramontanism and papal infallibility.

(3) The earliest form in which this exclusiveness organized itself was *Donatism*, appealing to the authority of Cyprian for the re-baptizing of all who had been 'sprinkled in the schism.' They differed, however, in one important respect, for whereas the latter inconsistently declined to break communion with bishops who, unlike himself, received Novatianists without a fresh baptism, the Donatists refused to recognize as Christians any who held the validity of what, as they viewed it, was a schismatical sacrament. It was claimed that, inasmuch as the Holy Spirit belonged to the Church, schismatics did not possess the gift, and therefore could not convey it. Against this narrow sacerdotalism Augustine, while not invalidating the principle of authority as expressed in the historic ministry, affirmed a conception of the Christian society wide as the universal purpose of Christ. The Church is catholic; no good thing can fall outside its unity. If there is no salvation outside

the Church, the Church for this purpose cannot be interpreted in a merely constitutional sense. The 'validity' of baptism depends, not on the authority of him who administers, but upon Christ's intention. How far-reaching this principle is does not at once appear.

That 'valid' here means, as with Ignatius, not 'genuine' but 'regular,' is clear from the fact that Augustine did not regard baptism as spiritually operative so long as the recipient adhered to Donatism. But while in Ignatius there is nothing to show whether baptism administered without episcopal sanction would have been treated as void, Augustine asserts that it may not be repeated. But the hindrance to grace is the absence of charity, which in experience is found to be in opposition to the spirit of unity and love, not the formal exclusion from covenanted channels of those who create division. What Augustine failed adequately to realize, probably owing to the historical fact that on the whole the 'fruits of the Spirit' were conspicuously lacking among the Donatists, was that responsibility for separation is usually divided, and that it is difficult to determine which of two contending parties is schismatic. It is this fact that makes apparent historical parallels seriously defective when applied to later controversies. What is of permanent value is the recognition that schism is a moral fault, not an ecclesiastical situation; that it is to be recognized in spiritual experience and healed by the appeal to conscience, not refuted by technical argument. A third point to observe is that apparently the validity of a sacrament is not dependent on the order of the minister who dispenses it. If it be argued that, as baptism, of which a layman may be the minister (see Bingham, *Hist. of Lay-baptism*; but cf. Waterland, *Letters on Lay-baptism*) is alone in question, the ordained ministry is not involved, the answer must be that the whole matter is argued on the basis of want of jurisdiction, which applies equally to the case of the Eucharist. For Cyprian had maintained his attitude towards re-baptizing on the ground of separation from the Catholic Church, which equally nullified schismatic ordinations. The time had not yet arrived for the distinction between character and jurisdiction in the matter of orders (see Bingham, *Ant.* xvii. 2. §§ 5, 6). A deposed cleric became a layman. Whether, therefore, a schismatic priest could create the Real Presence in virtue of a mystic power inherent in his ordination, would have been an unmeaning inquiry. The problem was simply whether a sacrament administered without authority was *ab initio* null and void. The reply was in the negative. In the ante-Nicene period the clerical order was simply the normal repository of authority. Clement of Rome indeed says that the layman is bound by the layman's ordinances (xl. 5), but this means no more than due subordination to 'them that had the rule' in the common discharge of the universal priesthood. Ignatius' 'Do nothing without the bishop' (*Philad.* 7. 2), applying as it does equally to Baptism and the Eucharist together with general Church discipline, does not exclude delegation by the bishop, in particular instances, of any priestly function to those who had no general authority in the matter, whatever may have been, and indeed were, the normal channels.

There are many indications that respect for the ministry as the seat of Apostolic authority did not at first involve the idea that the celebration of sacraments by laymen was essentially sacrilegious. The acknowledgment of lay baptism, for example, already mentioned, which, though not universal, is nevertheless general, rests upon no commission granted to laymen by council or canon, but simply upon practice; and there is no reason in the nature of things why, if occasion had arisen, a similar recognition should not have been extended to the other sacrament so ministered. It seems clear that, though in the NT presbyters tended to labour in the word and teaching (1 Ti 5^{17} etc.), and though in the succeeding age the function of the prophet tended to devolve upon the bishop, yet the primary function of the local ministry was ruling (1 P 5^{1-3}, 1 Ti 3^{5}, He 13^{17}), and other offices might be discharged by the gifted. Tertullian distinctly affirms that 'where there is no bench of clergy, you offer, baptize, and are priest alone for yourself' (*de Exh. Cast.* 7). It is usual to discount this statement on the ground that it appears in a Montanist treatise, and is contradicted, for example, by his own earlier opinion that 'offering' is a distinctive 'munus' of the clergy. In the *de Præscriptione* he charges the Gnostics with carelessness in the matter of ordination and of granting even to the laity sacerdotal functions ('nam et laicis sacerdotalia munera iniungunt,' 41). Not only in the later work does he seem totally unaware that his statement is controversial and contradictory of his former views, but there is really no opposition between them. That both the Eucharist and Baptism are rightly celebrated by the ordained ministry he expressly declares, even when he affirms that 'where three are, there is a church, although they be laics' (*ib.*). 'The difference,' he says, 'between the order and the people' rests on 'the authority of the Church' (*ib.*). And it was precisely that authority as Apostolic, and therefore derived from Christ, which he emphasized against the Gnostics. There can be no question that from the time of Clement and Ignatius, or rather from the days of the Apostles (Ac 2^{42}), it was perceived that unity of worship was as vital to the continuity of the Church as stability of doctrine, and that an Apostolic ministry was the guarantee of both. But it is also true, as the present condition of Eastern Christendom testifies, that the territorial conception of 'one bishop one area,' though it may have been the ideal (see *Nic. Can.* 8; Bingham, *Ant.* ii. 13), is a development that belongs rather to the West. The point, however, is that, although normally and naturally officers were duly appointed by 'Apostolic' authority to fulfil the various functions of both discipline and worship, the dominant conception of priesthood asserted by one early writer after another (as, *e.g.*, by Justin, *Dial. c. Tryph.* 116), and never lost even in the most narrowly hierarchical age, attached this character, inherited from the OT, to the whole community. Within the society the ministry, belonging as it did to its structure, was the permanent guarantee of its continuity as a vertebrate institution both in faith and in life. When this ministry is likened to the Aaronic priesthood, the shifting manner in which the analogy is applied by various writers shows that this aspect is not essential.

It is the merit of Augustine, in his handling of the Donatist controversy, to have pointed out the lines along which alone Apostolic succession can be given its true place in the Christian economy. Machinery cannot be exalted at the expense of spiritual experience. Had the Eucharist, like Baptism, been a sacrament incapable of repetition in the life of the individual, it cannot be doubted that the 'validity' of 'schismatic' Eucharists would have been decided in the same sense as that of Baptism. Both sacraments, as so administered, were equally regular or irregular according to the point of view. What may be called the 'channel theory' of sacraments, which regards Christian ordinances as vehicles of grace down which spiritual energy may be led, has operated disastrously, to produce a technical view of a succession equipped with the power of working the 'miracle of the altar.' It is not affirmed that this theory is purely mediæval, and that it was not present in germinant form in the first five centuries, and possibly even in the Apostolic Church. But it is the view of succession as preserving the fulness of Apostolic authority, and as the guarantee of a gospel which is 'not of men neither by man,' *i.e.* as realizing the principles upon which Christ established His society, that is alike primitive and permanent.

While any theory of the ministry, which involves a denial of the personal consciousness of the Spirit in the experience of individuals or the manifestations of His presence in the corporate life of any Christian communities in any age, is inconsistent with plain facts and the Christian conscience, it is yet, in the opinion of the present writer, probable that the present tendency towards reunion among Christians, with the instinct of social and corporate witness which it manifests, will inevitably, as it progresses towards yet wider amalgamations, reveal Apostolic succession as a subject of more than sentimental or antiquarian interest, and quicken inquiry into the conditions which shall be necessary to make the fabric of universal Church life in the future structurally one with the Church of a continuous, though not undivided, past.

LITERATURE.—Aquinas, *Summa*, pt. ii. 2, 184, 6, 1; 185, 5, sc.; pt. iii. 67, 2, 1; 72, 11, c.; Calvin, *Institutes*, bk. iv. chs. 3 and 4; Hooker, *Ecclesiastical Polity*, bk. v. chs. 76–78, bk. vii. 1–14; Bilson, *The Perpetual Government of Christ's Church*, 1593, and *Jus Divinum Ministerii Evangelici*, pub. by the Provincial Assembly of London, 1654; Bingham, *Antiquities of the Christian Church*, 1708–22, bk. ii. chs. 1–3, 5, 6, 17, 20, bk. iv. 1–7; Latham, *Pastor Pastorum* (1890); A. W. Haddan, *Apostolical Succession in the Church of England* (1869); Lightfoot, Dissertation on 'The Christian Ministry' in *Com. on Philippians*[8] (1888); E. Hatch, *Organization of the Early Christian Churches* (1882); C. Gore, *Church and the Ministry* (1900); R. C. Moberly, *Ministerial Priesthood* (1907); E. W. Benson, *Cyprian* (1897); J. Wordsworth, *The Ministry of Grace* (1901), chs. 1, 2; G. W. Sprott and T. Leishman in *Scottish Church Society's Conferences*, 1st series (1894); J. Cooper, J. Ramsay Sibbald, G. W. Sprott, and T. Leishman in *The Pentecostal Gift* (1903). For a general criticism of 'institutional Christianity' the reader may be referred to A. M. Fairbairn's *Catholicism Roman and Anglican*[3] (1899).

J. G. SIMPSON.

APOTHEOSIS.—See DEIFICATION.

APPERCEPTION.—The term 'apperception' was introduced into philosophy by Leibniz, being derived from the French *s'apercevoir*, 'to be aware of' or 'conscious of.' Its use is not wholly free from obscurity even in its inventor, while it has been applied by his successors in at least two widely different senses. With Leibniz it indicates: (1) a higher degree of perception—a perception which is distinct, vivid, relatively persistent, in contrast with perceptions which, lacking these qualities, affect the soul only in the mass, and which, as they do not emerge into individual consciousness, may be called *unconscious*.

'There is at any moment an infinite number of perceptions in us, but without apperception and reflexion, *i.e.* changes in the soul of which we are not conscious, because the impressions are either too slight, or too great in number, or too even (*unies*), so that they have nothing sufficiently distinguishing them from each other; but, joined to others, they do not fail to produce their effect and to make themselves felt at least confusedly in the mass' (*Nouveaux Essais*, Pref. [Langley's tr.] p. 47).

Leibniz's favourite example—the noise or roar of the sea as made up of the insensible noises of the separate wavelets—does not really hold; but a modern instance may be given from Helmholtz: the *over-tones* which give the peculiar quality or colour to the tones of different instruments cannot be separately noticed or 'apperceived' by the untrained ear, although in their mass they have a quite distinct and recognizable effect (Helmholtz, *Tonempfindungen*, p. 107 [Ellis' tr.[2] p. 62]). In Leibniz also apperception becomes: (2) the basis of a distinction in kind between beings or 'monads.' The lowest monads, which have *perception* alone, are merely passive mirrors of external events, while the highest monads or 'spirits' rise to *apperception*, 'which is consciousness, or the reflective knowledge of this inner state (perception), and which is not given to all souls nor to the same soul at all times' (*Principles of Nature and of Grace*, § 4 [Latta, p. 410]). In perception proper the soul is passive; in apperception it is active, self-conscious. 'There is not only an order of distinct perceptions which constitutes the *empire* of the soul, but also a mass of confused perceptions, or passions, which constitutes her *slavery*' (*Théodicée* [Janet's ed.], p. 143).

Although not incompatible, these two uses of the term in Leibniz are at least distinct. The second meaning, in which it suggests an internal sense, or reflexion, and self-activity, is that in which Wolff, and after him Kant, understood the term; but it was applied by the latter in a quite distinctive way (see KANT).

With Herbart, the theory of apperception enters on a new phase. It now means a process taking place between one presentation or idea and another idea or group of ideas (*Psychol. als Wissen.* ii. § i. ch. 5 [Hartenstein's ed. vol. vi. p. 190]). When a new sensation, perception, or memory enters the mind, it awakes or reproduces a number of older presentations or ideas referring to the same object. So far as these contain similar elements, it coalesces with them, and assimilates or is assimilated by them (*Verschmelzung*); so far as they contain opposite elements, there is mutual competition and conflict (*Hemmung*), each restricting the normal development of the other in the mind. The same process takes place also between those more complex series, masses, or systems, of ideas and thoughts, which result from combinations of all kinds at lower levels. The appropriation or absorption of an idea, from whatever source, by a more complex idea or system already present in the mind, is what Herbart calls 'apperception.' It is *external* or *internal*, according as the idea to be appropriated is a sense-perception or a representation of any kind; but this distinction, really inconsistent with Herbart's psychology, was afterwards rejected by Steinthal. The characteristics of the *apperceiving* mass are, (1) that it succeeds the *apperceived* idea in time, and (2) that it is stronger, more powerful, from some cause, and therefore compels the other to modify in accordance with it, while it itself continues to develop according to its nature (*ib.* p. 194; cf. *Lehrbuch zur Psych.* § 41). Thus it is relatively the active, the other relatively the passive element. An instance is the way in which our habitual modes of thought and action influence our apprehension of new ideas, our criticism of the conduct of others, etc. Not only *how* we see things, but *what* we shall actually see, is determined for each of us by our past experience and the use we have made of it. Psychologically, such experience is active only as a *present* system of ideas, according to Herbart. Apperception does not take place in the child or in the savage, because such systems are as yet unformed; it fails also under intoxication, fatigue, passion, etc., because the existing systems are disorganized. Education, intellectual and moral alike, is the gradual formation and strengthening of the due apperceptive masses. The slow and painful beginnings, the final rapid mastery and assimilation of a science, give further illustration. The modification is not wholly on one side, however; ideas 'act, as it were, chemically upon one another, decomposing one another and entering into new connexions.' Apperception is also the basis of *memory*; nothing can be recalled unless it has been built into a series or system of ideas, forming links by which the mind may reach it and drag it forth (*Psych. Untersuch.* iii. [Hartmann, vii. p. 591]). A further feature is the suppression, by the *apperceiving* mass, of whatever in perception or recollection conflicts with itself: in this, with the correlative raising up and isolating of the *apperceived* element, apperception is identical with attention (*Briefe*, p. 497). See ATTENTION.

In Volkmann also 'apperception' is defined as the coalescence of a new and isolated mass of ideas with an older mass which exceeds it in the number of its constituents, and in internal adjustment or systematization (*Lehrbuch der Psych.*[4] ii. 190). With both Lazarus and Steinthal the range of apperception is greatly extended; it becomes, indeed, coextensive with mental life. It is the *creative* process in mind; in it one content does not merely 'become aware of' another, but both are transformed, 'melted into a higher and richer third.' An idea becomes a centre of apperception through its *Macht*, or force, which does not imply either intensity or clear consciousness, but depends on the number of connexions which the idea has with other ideas, and on the closeness of the ties by which its constituents are bound together. Steinthal recognizes four chief forms of apperception, which are derived from those of Logical Judgment: Identifying, Subsuming, Harmonizing (with its negative, Disharmonizing), and Creative Apperception (*Kleine Schriften*, i. p. 60; *Einleitung in die Psychol.* p. 207).

With Wundt there is a return to the theory of Leibniz and Kant. A presentation or idea may be in consciousness simply, or also in the *focus* of consciousness, which, however, is not strictly a point, but rather a limited field. There are thus two *thresholds*,—the outer—that of consciousness or intensity; and the inner—that of apperception or clearness. The entrance of an idea into the focus of consciousness is its apperception, which may be either passive or active. Thus it is simply one side or aspect of the process of attention. Apperception is also identified by Wundt with will, and in this connexion acquires a strongly metaphysical colouring. This conception of apperception as a pure activity, which is yet directed or stimulated by presentations, has been criticized from different points of view by Volkmann, Hartmann, and the Associationist Psychologists, such as Ziehen, etc. In English Psychology the theory of apperception has been developed, mainly along Herbartian lines, by Dr. Stout. The following indicates his standpoint:—In all apperception 'a presentation acquires a certain significance for thought, by connecting itself with some mental preformation as this has been organized in the course of previous experience' (*Anal. Psy.* p. 110).

LITERATURE.—Leibniz, *Monadology*, *Principles of Nature and of Grace*, *New Essays*, *Theodicy*, etc.; Herbart, *Psychologie als Wissenschaft* (1824-25), *Lehrbuch zur Psych.*[3] (1887) *Psychol. Untersuchungen* (1839-40), iii., *Briefe über die Anwendung der Psychol. auf die Pädagogik*, *Umriss pädagog. Vorlesungen*, p. 74 ff.; Lazarus, *Leben der Seele*[3], 1883-97; Steinthal, *Zur Sprachphilosophie*, *Kl. Schr.* i. p. 45 ff., *Einleit. in die Psych.*[2] (1881) pp. 166-263; Volkmann, *Lehrbuch der Psychol.*[4] (1894) ii. 189 ff.; V. Hartmann, *Moderne Psychologie* (1901), p. 138, etc.; Ziegler, *Das Gefühl*, p. 47; Wundt, *Physiol. Psychol.*[5] (1903) iii. p. 331 ff., *Logik*, ii. p. 508 ff. etc.; K. Lange, *Ueber Apperception*[6], 1899 [tr. Boston, 1893]; O. Staude in *Philosophische Studien*, i. (1882) pp. 149-212 (Historical); Stout, *Analytic Psychology*, i. (1896).

J. LEWIS M'INTYRE.

APPETITE.—**I.** *Psychological.*—Appetite may be defined as a recurring sense or consciousness of want in the bodily organism, accompanied with a craving or desire for satisfaction, leading to efforts at fulfilment, under the impulse of uneasiness, which may become, under certain circumstances, more or less pronounced pain. It belongs to the animal side of our being, and is primordial to the human constitution. Most of the appetites—hunger, thirst, sleep, repose, rest—are connected with the conservation and welfare of the individual; sex has reference to the propagation and continuance of the species.

The characteristics of these natural physical wants (over and above uneasiness and efforts to remove it) are:—(1) They are not permanent, but intermittent: they disappear on being satisfied, but recur at stated times or periods. (2) If pressed beyond the natural limits of satisfaction, they breed satiety, and injury is done to the system. (3) They constitute our lower wants, in contradistinction to the higher or ideal wants of our nature, such as knowledge and friendship: we do not identify them with our inner self—they are *mine*, but they are not *me*.

The uneasiness in an appetite leads to action, mainly reflex and instinctive, not deliberately purposive, for the removal of it, and the gratification of the appetite brings pleasure. Hence, the original propensity to act under uneasiness may come to assume the form of desire for pleasure (as we see in the gourmand or the epicure), and what would be quite sufficient to remove the bare appetite (as in hunger) may be superseded by elaborate and refined modes of ministering to the desire, as shown in the art of cookery. It is thus that appetite may be specially effective on the will: it prompts to the acquisition and continuance of pleasure, not only to the getting rid of uneasiness or disquiet. These two things—*the pleasure that accompanies (say) eating, and the conscious and deliberate pursuit of the pleasure of eating*—are by no means identical. On the contrary, if desire of the pleasure become the predominant fact, the original normal and healthy craving in appetite may be supplanted by an abnormal craving, such as we see in gluttony; or an artificial craving, 'an acquired appetite,' may be produced, such as we see in the craving for tobacco or for alcohol. There is here, obviously, no appetite proper, but an induced desire, under the prompting of anticipated pleasure, which, in turn, is the product of individual pleasurable experience.

Hence, we must discriminate between appetite and desire for pleasure. Appetite simply craves for its object (the means for the attainment of the object being included in the conception of the object itself), and, given the object (food, for instance, for hunger), the appetite is satisfied—satisfied, no doubt, gradually, as the object is gradually realized, but fully in the realization of it. On the other hand, desire of pleasure is a consciously representative process, ideational in its nature, dependent on experience of pleasure (therefore, involving memory), and craving for that pleasure and, in the case of 'acquired appetites,' for the increase, as well as for the repetition, of it.

Appetite, like instinct, is native to the human being; but it differs from instinct in the following respects:—(1) It is an organic craving, whereas instinct acts under external stimulus. (2) In instinct, while there are an end to be effected and means to be used for the purpose, the individual is born with ability to employ the means without requiring to be taught how (as seen, for instance, in the sucking of the child)—in other words, the individual can unhesitatingly employ the means from the beginning, without, however, any consciousness of the end or deliberate purpose to achieve it. (3) In instinct there is also an untaught propensity, as well as an untaught ability, to act—'a propensity prior to experience, and independent of instruction.'

The pleasure that the satisfaction of an appetite gives is in general proportional to the craving. But there are cases where the strength of the craving is far greater than the pleasure of the gratification. Such a case we find in the glutton or the drunkard, whose passion, being persistent and whetted by successive gratifications, craves an indulgence which the object of it is incapable of adequately meeting. Here, excess has created a situation where pain has got the mastery—the craving does not disappear in its own fulfilment and periodically return, but persists and thrusts itself unseasonably upon attention: in other words, the object of desire when reached fails to appease completely, and the craving for satisfaction continues.

Although, therefore, in appetite proper, there is not involved the deliberate control of reason, nor is there any need for such, this control comes to be required when appetite would transgress its bounds. Such transgression is easy because of the pleasure associated with appetite, and because of the readiness with which abnormal conditions of the bodily system may be induced through excess. Hence, the appetites come to have a distinct and an important bearing on Ethics. Although in their normal action and in their rightful sphere they guide us in a way that calm reason could not —prompting us effectively, for instance, to eat for the support of life at the time and to the degree that the body requires, and not leaving the 'when' and the 'how much' to be settled by rational calculation—their pleasure-giving or 'felicific' property has to be watched, lest it make voluptuaries or debauchees of us; and thus reason has its function in relation to them. This would seem to mark the distinction between man and the lower animals: in man, the appetites are rationalized; in the brutes, not so.

2. *Ethical.*—The appetites in themselves are neither selfish nor unselfish, neither virtuous nor vicious; they are simply a part of human nature, indispensable to the being and welfare of the whole. But inasmuch as they are intimately associated with pleasure, they may be abused, and thus become ethically significant. Not that there is anything selfish or morally wrong in accepting the pleasure that they bring—such pleasure is a sign of physical health (as pain is of disease) and is to be welcomed and cherished (as the other is to be avoided or got rid of); but it may be sought for and estimated beyond its value—it may be pursued immoderately or at wrong times or in a perverted manner, to the detriment of the system and to the exclusion of higher good. If it is characteristic of the appetites that they have a tendency to overstep just limit, it is characteristic of them also that they grow imperious in their demands. Eating may degenerate into gluttony, repose into sloth, love (appetitive) into lust; and when degeneracy sets in, each becomes as a daughter of the horse-leech, crying, 'Give, give!' Hence the appetites need to be regulated and controlled: they need to be placed under rational government. If left to themselves unbridled, they would ruin the higher nature. Hence asceticism is but the exaggeration of a deep spiritual truth; and self-mortification, or 'keeping under' the body, has a real justification in psychical fact. But this means that, in a rational being, the appetites become transformed: they cannot be in him what they are in a non-rational creature. A clear conception of their place and function inevitably changes their nature, and entails responsibility as to our use of them. As Spinoza puts it (*Ethics*, v. prop. 3), 'An affection which is a passion ceases to be a passion as soon as we form a clear and distinct idea of it.' This is a very important truth, explaining to us many things in Ethics,—as, for example, how it is that the instinctive love of a mother for her offspring assumes quite a different aspect when we are dealing with human mothers from what it does when we are considering simply the lower animals. In both cases, there is instinct or natural affection; but, in the one case, it is rationalized (duly located in a system of thought or a scheme of values, and so lifted out of the sphere of mere instinct), in the other, not.

The situation as between the appetites and reason, or between the lower and the higher nature, or, still again (in Scripture language), between the flesh and the spirit, was put strikingly from the ethicist's point of view by Plato in the fable of the Charioteer and his Steeds. In *Phædrus*, the soul is aptly represented as a charioteer, riding in his car, drawn by two winged horses of different colour, nature, and temperament, requiring different management. On the one side, there is the black and vicious horse, 'ignoble and of ignoble breed,' ever refractory and plunging through unruly desire, 'the mate of insolence and pride,' and needing to be kept back by bit and bridle, yet 'hardly yielding to whip and spur.' On the other side, there is the white decorous horse, 'noble and of noble breed,' ever responsive 'to word and admonition,' on which bit and bridle sit lightly, and for which no whip is required. Here is a significant allegory. The charioteer is reason (τὸ ἡγεμονικόν); the white steed orderly and always harmonious with reason, represents 'the moral and spiritual element in man'; and the gross and sensual tendencies of human nature find their symbol in the dark and untractable steed. But the task of the charioteer is far from easy—not every one can successfully drive a team; the taming of the refractory steed costs him many an effort, and hard work and skill. Obedience is the result of a strong hand and a determined will, and of sore punishment repeated; only 'when this has happened several times and the villain has ceased from his wanton way, is he tamed and humbled, and follows the will of the charioteer.'

The right by which reason rules the appetites, or the rational basis of the distinction between higher and lower in our nature, is found here:—The appetites are non-ideal, and, consequently, individualistic. We cannot share them with any one else, neither is an appetite in itself susceptible of indefinite gratification. On the other hand, all the natural wants that we regard as higher—knowledge, friendship, virtue, religion—are distinguished by this, that (*a*) we share them with others, and yet we ourselves are none the poorer but all the richer—they are essentially altruistic and social; and (*b*) they do not cease with their immediate satisfaction—on the contrary, the desire increases with its gratification, as we see pre-eminently in knowledge, where the more we know the more we desire to know. They aim at an ideal; and it is the ideality with which they are bound up that produces their insatiableness: no limit is placed by nature to their culture, and so satiety cannot ensue; the capacity increases with what it feeds on.

It is needless to say, further, that both human happiness and human progress depend on the rational control of the lower nature; and this control is effective only when it becomes self-control, only when the individual acts as his own 'plagosus Orbilius,' gains the mastery over himself and exercises it spontaneously. How this self-control is acquired, through strengthening and directing the will, may be read in any good treatise on Psychology (*e.g.* Höffding's). Anyhow, if the individual's soul becomes, as Plato puts it, a well-ordered State—where there are gradation of functions, harmony, and order everywhere, mutual subservience of the parts to the interests of the whole and for the realization of its highest good—then the appetites and their pleasures count for much and have their own part to play in the economy of the human being: neither will they be ignored and starved (as Stoicism would fain effect), nor will they be made supreme and cultivated without stint (as some forms of Hedonism would appear to countenance).

But while there is thus a ground for the rationalizing of appetite, and for the subordination of the lower to the higher, in the nature of the different natural wants themselves, there is a further ground in the ethical dangers connected with the appetites. These are mainly as follows:—(1) In the first place, an appetite, strictly speaking, is neither selfish nor unselfish; but a depraved or unrestrained appetite is essentially selfish—thus turning a neutral thing into a positive evil. Vile appetites minister to the individual's cravings, but they may be made the means of corrupting others. (2) Depraved or unrestrained appetites lower the character, and stunt and check moral progress—they bring 'leanness' into the soul; for it is a law of the human mind that we cannot indulge intemperately without lessening our moral force, just as we cannot harbour base desires without thereby shutting out noble ones, or choose falsehood without rejecting truth. Consequently, while they vitiate the taste, they enfeeble the will—*i.e.* they deprive us of the power of resisting temptation and of initiating reformation; which, otherwise expressed, means that they leave us the prey to impulse, and so the end thereof, in Scripture language, 'is death.' (3) Perverted appetites are a bondage: they drag us at their heels, and through them we lose our moral freedom—we are enslaved. The peculiarity is that, while we yield to them, we *protest*: the will is overborne, but we still retain our perception of the right and our appreciation of it,—'I see the better *and approve*, I pursue the worse' (Ovid, *Met.* vii. 21). In other words, our moral energy is felt not to be adequate to our moral insight; we are conscious of being coerced. This fact of the bondage of the appetites and passions is the theme of all great ethicists, from Plato downwards: it was kept before the mediæval world by the *Consolation of Philosophy* of Boëthius, and it is a heritage to modern philosophy from Spinoza, the fourth part of whose *Ethics* deals with this very subject of 'Human Bondage,' and the fifth part with 'Human Liberty.' It is also a leading theme of the Christian religion, and lies at the basis of the scheme of salvation. (4) Appetite unduly set on pleasure leaves a sting behind. 'But what shall I say of the pleasures of the body? This —that the lust thereof is indeed full of uneasiness (*anxietas*), but the sating, of repentance' (Boëthius, *Consol. Phil.* Lib. iii. prosa 7).

3. *Religious.*—The distinction thus drawn between the appetites and reason, the estimation put upon it, and the conception of the soul as a well-ordered, self-governed State, were taken over by Christianity; only, it is to be observed, Christianity has its own way of explaining the conflict between the lower and the higher in man, and it has its own means of ending the conflict. *That* is its peculiarity, marking it off from mere Ethics. On the one hand (using St. Paul as our guide—more especially, as he expresses himself in Ro 7 and Gal 5), the lower and concupiscent element in man is identified with 'the flesh' (σάρξ). This unruly principle—the black horse of Plato—rebels against the human reason and overpowers the human will ('mind' or νοῦς in Pauline phraseology), and causes the individual to exclaim in agony, 'O wretched man that I am! who shall deliver me out of the body of this death?' The deliverance comes not from the man himself, not even from his active reason, although the natural function of active reason is to control; but from without—'I thank God through Jesus Christ our Lord.' For man's impotence of will, according to Scripture, arises from a religious cause and needs a religious remedy: it arises from the fact that man is 'fallen,' is 'sold under sin,' has deliberately rebelled against God, and so has forfeited his rightful power of self-mastery; and the rectifying and conquering force must come to him from above—it must be a gift from heaven. This Divine gift, in accordance with the whole Christian doctrine of regeneration and re-creation, is 'the Spirit.' And so, in order to be delivered from the hard bondage of the lower self, which is the bondage of sin, man must be raised from the 'natural' or 'psychical' plane into the 'spiritual' realm—he must himself become a temple of the Holy Ghost, and through the indwelling Spirit he will conquer. 'But, I say, walk by the Spirit, and ye shall not fulfil the lust of the flesh. For the flesh lusteth against the Spirit and the Spirit against the flesh; for these are contrary the one to the other; that ye may not do the things that ye would. . . . And they that are of Christ Jesus have crucified the flesh with the passions and the lusts thereof' (Gal 5[16. 17. 24]). Thus the Christian faith incorporates Ethics, but transcends it. It is, consequently, effective on human life and practice in a way that Ethics, standing alone, cannot be.

LITERATURE.—I. *PSYCHOLOGICAL*: Thomas Reid, *Active Powers*, pp. 543–545 (Hamilton's ed.); Bain, *The Senses and the Intellect*[4], pp. 260–264 (1894); Höffding, *Outlines of Psychology*, vii. (Eng. tr. 1st ed. 1891); James Ward, art. 'Psychology' in *Ency. Brit.*[9]; W. James, *The Principles of Psychology*, ch. xxvi. (1891); G. F. Stout, *A Manual of Psychology* (1899), and *Groundwork of Psychology* (1903); W. L. Davidson, *Theism and Human Nature*, Lect. v. (1893).

II. *ETHICAL*: Spinoza, *Ethics*, Parts iii.–v. (Eng. tr. by White and Stirling, 1899); Dugald Stewart, *The Philosophy of the Active and Moral Powers of Man*, Bk. I. ch. i.; T. H. Green, *Prolegomena to Ethics*[2], Bk. II. (1884); James Seth, *A Study of Ethical Principles*[3] (1898); J. H. Muirhead, *Chapters from Aristotle's Ethics* (1900); J. S. Mackenzie, *A Manual of Ethics*[4] (1901); W. L. Davidson, *The Logic of Definition*, p. 223 (1885).

III. *RELIGIOUS*: The Bible—particularly the New Testament, with any of the standard Commentaries (*e.g.* Lightfoot's on *Galatians, Philippians, Colossians*); T. B. Strong, *Christian Ethics* (1896); W. L. Davidson, *Christian Ethics*[3] (1907); W. S. Bruce, *The Formation of Christian Character*[2] (1908); Newman Smyth, *Christian Ethics* (1892); T. B. Kilpatrick, *Christian Character* (1899); H. H. Scullard, *Early Christian Ethics in the West* (1907).

WILLIAM L. DAVIDSON.

A PRIORI.—*A Priori* is one of those terms, by no means rare in philosophy, the meaning of which has in the course of centuries undergone divers changes. Originally an unobjectionable expression, denoting an ordinary mental act about which there can be no controversy, it has eventually become the index of one of the most stubborn problems which set the minds of men at variance. According to Prantl,* the earliest occurrence of the phrase is in the writings of **Albert of Saxony** (14th cent.), who draws a contrast between *demonstratio a priori*, the proof from what is before, *i.e.* from the cause, and *demonstratio a posteriori*, the proof which retrocedes from the effect. The usage can be traced to Aristotle, who in the *Second Analytics* states that that upon which proof is based must be prior to, and better known than, that which is to be proved, and continues thus: 'The earlier and better known has a twofold meaning. That which is prior by nature is not identical with what is prior for us; nor again is that which is in itself better known the same as what is better known to us. "The prior and better-known in relation to us" is the name I give to what lies nearer to our sense perception; what lies farther from that I call "the prior and better known in itself." The most remote of all is the universal; the nearest is the individual object.' The connexion of the term A Priori with Aristotle is thus quite evident. But while he differentiates the meaning of 'prior' according as the starting-point is the thing perceived or the process of perception, Albert of Saxony does not take this difference into account: with him *demonstratio a priori* signifies the proof from causes. It merely denotes a special mode of mental operation; in other words, *a priori* is a term of formal logic. The knowledge which proceeds from cause to effect, or knowledge a priori, rightly claims a higher degree of certainty than knowledge a posteriori, or from effect to cause, so long as the terms keep rigidly to the meanings assigned, and so long as the limits of formal logic are not transgressed. But the problem of knowledge goes beyond the scope of formal logic. The moment any shifting takes place in the meaning of A Priori and A Posteriori, and they show a tendency to coalesce respectively with knowledge based upon conceptions and knowledge based upon experience, and when, further, the province of logic is relinquished for that of psychology, it is no longer possible to maintain the higher certainty of a priori knowledge. For, with such change, perception appears as the earlier and more certain, while the general conception is the later, and thus A Priori and

* *Geschichte der Logik*, iv. 78.

A Posteriori have simply exchanged meanings. Hence Gassendi, in his polemic against the Aristotelians, impugns the dictum that the *demonstratio a priori* is more certain and conclusive than that *a posteriori*, and demands its warrant. Since on his view the *demonstratio a priori* becomes the proof from causes *and general conceptions*, and since the *demonstratio a posteriori* becomes the proof from effects and less general conceptions, he shows that he has abandoned the strictly logical usage of the terms. But in that case it is clear that there is but one answer to his question whether effects are not better known than causes; and the inevitable inference is that a priori knowledge depends upon a posteriori.* Gassendi's criticism shows that the term A Priori had become ambiguous; it was so far free to assume a new meaning.

Its new content was supplied by **Leibniz.** It is indeed true that Leibniz did not always use the term in one and the same sense. Thus, in connexion with the ontological proof of the existence of God, he argues that existence does not follow from conception, but that the possibility of the fact signified by the conception must first of all be established. This possibility, however, may be cognized either a priori or a posteriori: the former, if the various characteristics of the concept are mutually consistent; the latter, when the thing itself is an object of perception.† A similar usage appears in the passage where the criterion of a clear and distinct idea is said to be its capacity of yielding the knowledge of a number of truths by a priori proof.‡ Here A Priori is really concerned with the elucidation and explanation of conceptions, and with knowledge won from conceptions by correct reasoning. It is employed in a somewhat different sense in the passage where the knowledge which proceeds from God to created things and that which recedes from created things to God are respectively designated a priori and a posteriori.§ Still another usage is observable in the statement that in regard to the mysteries of the Christian faith, such as the Trinity and the Incarnation, a priori proofs on rational grounds are neither possible nor requisite, and that in this case the knowledge of the fact is sufficient, though the *why* remains unknown. A priori proof is here equivalent to the intuition of rational cause.‖ In discussing the relationship subsisting between the human and the animal soul, Leibniz comes to the conclusion that the faculty of simple empirical association is common to both. A dog being trained to perform a trick gets a tit-bit; a Dutchman travelling towards Asia will ask for his beer, perhaps even in a Turkish inn. The connexion between trick and tit-bit, between inn and beer, is in each case casual, not necessary; but the man differs from the animal in that he seeks for a *necessary* connexion. The mere data of experience are not sufficient for him, nor does he rely on experiments alone; he goes beyond them a priori, by means of first principles. A Priori thus acquires an implication of necessary relation.¶ According to Leibniz, then, knowledge a priori is found in the following contingencies:—(1) when the possibility of a fact is established by showing the self-consistency of its conception; (2) when from a clear and distinct idea further cognitions are deduced; (3) when thought proceeds from God to created things; (4) when the rational grounds of an actual truth are investigated; (5) when an essential relation is established. Thus A Priori has various shades of meaning; but it may be asserted that, as used by Leibniz, the expression tends generally to become identified with knowledge gained from pure reason. This is its meaning when he contrasts knowledge *par la pure raison ou a priori* with *philosophie expérimentale qui procède a posteriori*;* and when, in the *Nouveaux Essais*, the reason which is the basis not only of our judgment, but also of the truth itself, is made to rank as reason in the distinctive sense, or reason a priori.† A Priori is thus an attribute of that species of knowledge of which every constituent is furnished by reason alone.

Lambert also is of opinion that 'without qualification and in the strictest sense the term a priori can be applied only to that in regard to which we owe nothing whatever to experience.'‡ **Wolff,** on the other hand, reverts to the more general sense of the term, applying it to any kind of knowledge arrived at by reasoning, even when the conceptions employed in the premises are derived from experience.

The view of **Kant** demands a somewhat fuller treatment, since in this as in other respects he marks the consummation of the previous development, and the starting-point of the new. Besides, the problem indicated by the phrase *a priori*, according to him, stands at the very centre of thought, as it does with no philosopher before him. His entire system, indeed, may be regarded as an answer to the great question, How are synthetic judgments a priori possible? Alike in his theoretical and his practical philosophy, in his treatment of æsthetics and of religion, his aim was to discover and establish synthetic judgments a priori. He is at one with his predecessors in assuming the existence of a priori cognition, and in believing that it cannot be regarded as originating in experience. But he felt that justice had not been done to the problem involved.

If such a priori knowledge really exists, he argues, then it must be expressible in judgments which are a priori, and, indeed, synthetic. Merely analytical judgments, *i.e.* those which do no more than analyze and elucidate a given concept, while they render our knowledge explicit, do not augment it; only synthetic judgments, *i.e.* those which link a new predicate to the subject, furnish a genuine addition to knowledge. Hence the judgments a priori which are of any use at all are precisely those the predicate of which goes beyond the subject, adding something that was not contained therein. Such a synthetic judgment is exemplified in the dictum, 'Every event has a cause.' It is synthetic, since the concept 'event' does not involve the idea of a cause; the predicate, therefore, adds something new; it is a priori, since, while mere experience, or perception, certainly shows that events follow one another, it does not show that they are causally connected, still less that they are *always* so connected. Clearly we have a problem here. It is easy to understand how there should be synthetic judgments a posteriori, since perception itself supplies the predicate and its connexion with the subject. When I say, *e.g.*, that light-rays are refrangible, I am merely telling what I have learned by a simple experiment. But how can I say that every event has a cause, seeing that experience cannot be my warrant? How then are synthetic judgments a priori possible? Clearly because reason itself must contain a priori elements; and one great desideratum will be a complete inventory of these elements. But the mere fact of their existence does not warrant their embodiment in judgments having a real value for knowledge; hence their applicability must be vindicated, their relevancy made good. But even this demonstration does not complete our task. For there is an illegitimate as well as a legitimate use of them, and we must endeavour to fix the limits of their efficiency. It was Kant's conviction that all previous investigations of the problem had been inadequate in three ways: he felt the lack of (1) care in securing the full number of a priori elements; (2) proof of their applicability, and (3) precise definition of the limits of their efficiency. Only in the proper discharge of these three tasks do we obtain a truly exhaustive investigation, a Critique of Pure Reason.

1. If the a priori elements are discoverable at all, they must carry marks of recognition. And such marks they certainly have, for we actually find ourselves in possession of cognitions which are distinguished from all others by their universality and their necessity. Now these cannot originate in experience, for experience can tell us only that something is, not that it *always* is; can say only that it *is* this or that, never that it *must* be such. The marks of the A Priori are therefore true universality and strict necessity. But these do not forthwith provide us with rules for the discovery of the a priori elements

* *Exercitationes paradoxicæ adversus Aristoteleos*, lib. ii. exerc. 5.
† Leibniz, *Werke*, ed. Erdmann, p. 80. ‡ *Ib.* 272*b*.
§ *Ib.* 451*b*. ‖ *Ib.* 494*b*. ¶ *Ib.* 464*b* f.

* Leibniz, *Werke*, ed. Erdmann, 778*b*. † *Ib.* 393*a*.
‡ *Neues Organon, Dianoiologie*, § 639.

of reason. Such rules, however, will be suggested by the following reflexions. In trying to discover what belongs to pure reason, we must isolate it by eliminating all alien material. Now, since the faculty of knowledge has two aspects, namely, the receptivity of perception and the activity of thought, these will necessarily meet us again in pure reason. But as the material element, that which is given in sensation, obviously lies outside the territory of pure reason, we may perhaps delimit this territory, if only we can disengage what sensation supplies. What then remains, when we make this elimination? Obviously, the universal *forms* of perception, namely, Space and Time. And what remains when we similarly separate all material elements from the products of active thought, *i.e.* our judgments? Clearly the pure *form* of the judgment itself. This pure form of the judgment, however, points to a function of the understanding, and the sum of such forms will give us the complete list of these functions, *i.e.* the categories. Now formal logic has already distinguished all the possible forms of the judgment, and has tabulated them under four heads, each having three momenta, and consequently the functions of the understanding, or categories, can be arranged in the same way. Thus the *quantity* of judgments as universal, particular, or singular, gives the categories of quantity: Unity, Plurality, Totality; the *quality* of judgments as affirmative, negative, or infinite, yields the categories of quality: Reality, Negation, Limitation; the *relation* of judgments as categorical, hypothetical, or disjunctive, provides the categories of relation: Substance and Accident, Cause and Effect, Community or Reciprocity; while, finally, the *modality* of judgments as problematic, assertoric, or apodictic, gives us the categories of modality: Possibility—Impossibility, Existence—Non-Existence, Necessity—Contingency. Thus the a priori elements are the pure forms of conception—Space and Time—and the twelve Categories. They are a priori, because they are truly universal and strictly necessary; and their number is complete, since they alone remain after our exhaustive process of elimination. Our first problem is therefore solved.

2. We turn next to the task of determining the function of these a priori elements, and the vindication of their applicability to the objects of knowledge. So far as space and time are concerned, the task is an easy one. They are forms of perception, since every object of perception is presented to us in one or both of them. Moreover, we have two sciences whose validity and truth are beyond question, viz., geometry and kinematics. Neither comes from experience, for geometry, not finding its figures to hand in nature, constructs them arbitrarily; and in the same way kinematics enunciates its propositions without the slightest reference to experience: both exhibit an unconditional necessity, which perception can never do. How then are these sciences possible? Clearly because, on the one hand, geometry rests upon the fact that there is an a priori perception of Space, while, on the other, kinematics rests upon the fact that there is an a priori perception of Time. The existence of these two sciences, then, vouches for the efficiency and validity of the a priori forms of perception. It is more difficult to demonstrate the function and competency of the categories, which are not forms of perception. What significance must we assign to them? Is it not enough that all objects of perception should manifest themselves in Space and Time, and are the categories not therefore superfluous? What can they add to spatial and temporal perception? But we must recollect that bare perception, *i.e.* perception conditioned by Space and Time, is not knowledge, and does not deserve the name of experience properly so called. Perception alone could yield nothing but a chaos of phenomena, without order among its parts, without rule in its changes, without coherence. True knowledge, true experience, is in fact impossible without the unity of consciousness, without an orderly synthesis; and it is at this point that the function of the categories reveals itself, and their validity is established. They exhibit the various ways in which the unity of consciousness effectuates the orderly synthesis of phenomena. Knowledge, genuine experience, becomes ours only when, by means of the categories of Quantity and Quality, we come to understand, arrange, and organize phenomena as extensive and intensive magnitudes; when in virtue of the categories of relation we are able to posit something permanent (Substance) amidst the flux of phenomena, to introduce a causal order into the stream of their succession, and to reduce their mere collocation to a vast system of perfectly interrelated parts; and when, finally, by the categories of modality, we are in a position to determine the gradations of things in respect to possibility, actuality, and necessity. Perception in itself can furnish nothing of this, as is best seen in regard to the categories of relation. It gives us only a constant flux, never anything permanent; only succession, never regular connexion; only collocation, never reciprocity; and accordingly it cannot give knowledge. But no less in the case of the other categories it may be shown that they superimpose something upon bare perception, and are a necessary condition of knowledge or experience in the strict sense of these terms. It is true, of course, that perception as such gives us extensive magnitudes, but it is only by means of the category of Quantity that we can formulate a universal law, thus bringing all phenomena under a common measure, without which they could not be grasped by thought. It is also true that perception yields intensive magnitudes, but again it is the category of Quality alone which sets forth the universal law that *every* phenomenon must have some degree of intensity; it alone renders possible an absolutely uniform and progressive scale of intensity, by which phenomena are actually compared and comprehended. Perception, finally, places everything upon a level; it yields no gradations. But where all things coalesce, knowledge is out of the question. Only the categories of modality afford the requisite gradation, enabling us to take into consideration questions regarding Possibility and Impossibility, Actuality and Non-Actuality, Necessity and Contingency. Thus, to sum up, it is by means of the categories alone that we can attain to knowledge, to experience in the proper sense; and contrariwise, the actual existence of knowledge and experience witnesses to the validity of the categories. Our second problem is thus solved.

3. The answer to the question involved in our third problem, viz., To what extent is the a priori element valid? is given in what has already been said. Our conclusion so far is that true experience is made possible by the A Priori. We must now say: Experience *alone*, nothing beyond it. It is mere illusion to suppose that by means of the categories we can attain to a knowledge entirely beyond experience. Rational Psychology, which undertakes to prove the existence of the soul as immaterial and indestructible, is naught but a mass of illegitimate inferences. Rational Cosmology, which presumes to decide regarding the beginning or non-beginning of the world in time, and its limitation or infinity in space, the simplicity and indivisibility of atoms, or their infinite divisibility and the consequent impossibility of indivisible atoms, the universality of natural causation and the denial of freedom, or the assertion of it, the existence or non-existence of an absolutely necessary being—simply lands us in antinomies, of which both the thesis and the antithesis may be shown to be equally valid. Rational Theology, again, achieves its aim of proving the existence of God only by the manœuvre of making the conclusion contain more than the premises, as, for instance, in the ontological proof, according to which the *existence* of God follows from the *conception* of Him, existence in the premises being but a *conceptual* predicate, while in the conclusion it has become a *real* one.

Rational Psychology, Cosmology, and Theology are in point of fact concerned with *Ideas*, for which experience provides no corresponding reality. But however forcibly we must deny that the Ideas guarantee the existence of their correlative objects, still as Ideas they possess a real value. They are an expression of that striving after unity and totality which reason itself makes, and so point to a work which is at once necessary and ever incomplete. However incoherent and mutually independent the facts of perception may seem, reason demands unity and totality, and seeks to realize both by the endless process of linking together all the phenomena and preventing any of them from assuming an absolute independence. That is the true element in Rational Psychology. Again, reason endeavours to bring the aggregate of things which we call the universe into line with its own requirements of unity and totality. But since these requirements cannot be satisfied empirically, the process is one which can never stop. Carry the causal series as far as we may, we never reach an ultimate or unconditioned cause. Thus reason progresses ever from more to more; its object is not a universe rounded and complete, but one which it builds up with ceaseless travail. That is the truth of Rational Cosmology. Finally, Rational Theology seeks the unity and totality of all existence whatsoever—the first cause and the final purpose of the whole—and this search constitutes *its* element of truth. But all this is presented to reason not as a fact, but as a task—a labour forced upon it, yet never finished. In other words, the Ideas of Soul, World, God, are regulative, not constitutive principles, and indicate and direct the endeavour of reason after unity and totality. Our conclusion then is, that the sole purpose of the A Priori is to make experience possible; its function is an immanent, not a transcendental one.

So far, then, our result is this: the forms of perception and thought are a priori; their function is to make experience possible, and they do not avail beyond experience. But with a view to a complete explanation it remains to establish the two following theses: (1) the A Priori is not to be interpreted *psychologically*; and (2) the A Priori is not equivalent to innate.

(1) A psychological interpretation was given by Schopenhauer, who writes: 'The philosophy of Locke was a criticism of the functions of sense; Kant furnishes a criticism of the functions of brain.'* Helmholtz agrees with this, as does also F. A. Lange, who states that 'the psychological equipment which constrains us to condition objects by space and time, is certainly anterior to all experience.'† But so to understand Kant is to misunderstand him. Such an interpretation of the A Priori places it on a level with the other psychical functions. For we likewise see colours and hear tones in virtue of our psycho-physical constitution, and we should thus have to recognize an a priori element in these also. Kant, however, would altogether repudiate this. To understand anything psychologically is to apprehend it as the property or state of a subject, a soul, a psycho-physical organism. Psychology never goes beyond

* *World as Will and Idea*, I. i.

† *Hist. of Materialism*, ii. 36.

the psychological subject and its relations to the surrounding world, whether that world be looked at from the standpoint of Realism or of Idealism in the Berkeleyan sense. The true A Priori compasses both the psychological Ego and the world. A variation in our psychological organization would never involve more than the alteration of a part of our knowledge. If, for instance, the faculty of colour-perception were to become more sensitive or less so, were it even to disappear altogether, then, with the solitary exception of colour, everything would be as before; and, in fact, were the senses as a whole to suffer any drastic change, some being lost, some displaced by others, it would signify no more than the donning of a new garment; the intrinsic constitution of the mind would remain inviolate. But an alteration in the A Priori would be nothing less than a revolution. Take away space and time, and the world itself falls to pieces. We must accordingly guard against a psychological reading of the A Priori.

The difference between the A Priori and the psychological may be further illustrated as follows. The a priori space-perception of Kant and psychological space-perception are by no means identical. It may be the case that Kant ignored the distinction, but that is irrelevant meanwhile. It is a mistake to suppose that we refute Kant by showing that the faculty of space-perception is not congenital, but is acquired gradually, that our perception of a surface is prior to that of tridimensional space, and that we localize accurately only after having learned to do so. All that is true, but it does not conflict with the theory of Kant. The development of the psychological space-perception presupposes the a priori. Psychological space is limited, and we can in a manner discern its limits; a priori space knows no limit. Hence we may assert that what is a priori is not psychological, and *vice versa*. Once a psychological interpretation was put upon A Priori, it was quite proper to proceed to its analysis, as was done by the evolutionists. They maintained that what is now an A Priori for the individual was at first an A Posteriori for the race; that in the course of thousands or even millions of years mankind at length acquired what is now the congenital endowment of the individual person (so Spencer, Haeckel, etc.). Such a theory, however, though valid as against what we may call the psychological A Priori, cannot infringe the true A Priori.

(2) The proof of the second thesis, viz., that a priori is not equivalent to innate, is contained in what has just been said, and for its elucidation a few words will suffice. We may rightly apply the term 'innate' to anything which belongs to the natural endowment of the psychological subject, but precisely on that account it is not a priori. The innate is what is given, but, from Kant's point of view, the given and the A Priori are antithetical. What is given must needs be capable of being set forth as a quality or as something passive; but this is impossible in the case of the A Priori, which is from first to last an *activity* of the mind. We do not discover it as we discover an external object of perception; it forms the presupposition of all our thinking. We cannot seek for it as for other things, for in our very search that which we are looking for is already *in operation*. If, on the other hand, we wish to elicit the innate, the object of our search is not a factor in the process. Kant also insists that the A Priori must not be taken as applying to supposed inborn, ready-made ideas. He writes: 'Criticism admits the existence of no such ideas at all, but regards all ideas, whether belonging to perception or conception, as acquired. There is, however, also an *acquisitio originaria* (as writers on Natural Law were wont to say), and therefore also of something which did not previously exist, nor belonged to anything before the act.'* Hence, if criticism has to do with the A Priori, it has, for that very reason, nothing to do with the innate.

Having thus explained the A Priori in Kant's theoretical philosophy, we proceed to deal with his assumption of a similar element in the practical activity of reason or mind. In respect of morality and religion, no less than logical thought, reason possesses something all its own, and not derived from experience, which can be expressed in synthetic judgments a priori. This consists, in a word, of Ideas, by which the empirically real must needs be controlled. The demands of the moral law and of the Kingdom of God must be realized in the external world. It has, indeed, been recently questioned whether we can justifiably speak of a practical A Priori. Thus Stange, in his *Einleitung in die Ethik*, holds that there is hardly any resemblance between the A Priori of the *Critique of Pure Reason* and that of the *Critique of Practical Reason*, and points out the following contrasts: (1) The *Critique of Pure Reason* treats of an A Priori both of sense and understanding, viz. the pure perceptions, Space and Time, and the pure forms of judgment, viz. the Categories; the *Critique of Practical Reason* treats only of an A Priori of Reason. (2) According to the first *Critique*, the A Priori and the empirical must collaborate; according to the second *Critique*, the A Priori alone must determine the will. (3) In the former work, universality and necessity are given as the characteristics of the A Priori; in the latter, those tests are not applied, since they do not suffice to determine the A Priori. Thus the desire for happiness is also universal and subjectively necessary, but it is not a priori. These strictures are canvassed by Hägerström in his comprehensive exposition of *Kants Ethik*.†

Admitting, however, as we must, the differences between the two *Critiques*, we must likewise admit the propriety of applying the term A Priori in the practical sphere. There, too, we discover an endowment peculiar to the mind, and not derived from experience—a fact which is evinced by the Categorical Imperative, which reveals itself as a synthetic judgment a priori. This Imperative imposes unconditional commands upon the will, declaring that this or that ought to be done, and paying no regard whatever to human desire or pleasure, to natural disposition or circumstances—hence it is a priori; and further, since the obligation to obey an unconditional command cannot be deduced from the concept 'will' by simple analysis, the Categorical Imperative is a synthetic judgment. In the *Grundlegung zur Metaphysik der Sitten*, Kant decomposes the Imperative into the following three principles: (1) Act as if the maxim of thy action were to become by thy will a universal law of nature; (2) so act as to treat humanity, both in thine own person and in that of every other, always as an end, never as a means only; (3) act according to the idea that the will of every rational being is a universally legislative will. The constituent elements of these three principles we may denominate Ideas, by which human conduct must be ordered if it is to be morally good, and thus we discover the Ideas of a motive, an end, and a law, each of which is universally valid. They are not the resultants of experience, but are severally ideal creations of the practical reason, and as such are a priori. Just as we saw, however, in the case of the categories, that a material element was also necessary to the existence of actual knowledge, so must the practical A Priori be referred to empirical reality as the material for its elaboration. In other words, the practical A Priori, on Kant's view, is, equally with the theoretical, of a formal, not a substantial, character. But even as the theoretical A Priori is the necessary condition of experience in the true sense, so is the practical A Priori the pre-requisite of moral action, since it alone brings human conduct under the control of inviolable law. Without it, our active life were the sport of chance, incapable of a determinate aim, and morality were impossible.

Religion, too, has its synthetic judgments a priori; necessarily so, since neither God nor eternal life is an object of perception. But how are the synthetic judgments possible which assert the existence of God and the fact of immortality? We have found morality to be something actually existent; but we have likewise found it to be perfectly adequate to its own ends, needing to seek no sanction in the concept 'God.' We must bear in mind, however, that Reason cannot disregard the *results* of moral

* Hartenstein's ed., vi. 37. Cf. Caird, *Crit. Phil. of Kant*, i. 480.

† Pp. 346–349.

action; on the contrary, it is necessarily concerned, not merely with the individual practice of morality, but with the *genesis of a moral world*. The proposition, 'There ought to be a moral world,' is itself a synthetic judgment a priori—a priori, because a moral world is not an object of experience; and synthetic, because the proposition, not being involved in the conception of morality, is not discovered analytically, but reveals itself only when to the conception of morality there is added that of an end of moral action. How, then, is the moral world possible? Manifestly not in virtue of human action only, since we cannot conceive how the moral action of mankind should evoke a moral world from a world subject to entirely different laws. If our proposition, therefore, is not to be a mere futility, we must inevitably proceed to affirm the existence of an omnipotent Being who will secure the result aimed at in human morality. We can accordingly assert that there is a God—a proposition shown to be an a priori synthetic judgment, by the manner of its deduction. We must finally note that, as the realization of the moral ideal is an endless task, it postulates the endless existence of man. Thus we arrive at the a priori synthetic judgment that man is immortal. Religion also, then, has an A Priori, and is indeed based upon it. The religion that we actually find in the world is often but a sorry mixture, but in the process of development its a priori element is able to realize itself and to produce ever purer forms. For it does not subsist in severance from empirical reality, any more than does the A Priori of the theoretical or the practical sphere.

It was Kant's belief that every genuine form of human experience was a combination of a priori and a posteriori factors. The absence of either was a sure sign of sophistry; no knowledge was possible save by the corporate union of both. Without the A Priori, our perceptions were formless and lawless, and therefore fitful and evanescent; without the A Posteriori, we should have but the blind play of concepts. No less in the sphere of religion and morality must the empirical data be controlled and moulded by the A Priori. In the absence of the latter, we should have no morality, no religion, only the lawless flux of desires, only the figments and fabrications of superstition, while, if the empirical factor were absent, the a priori ideas, having no material to organize, would resemble the shades of the under world in the *Odyssey*, which must first have blood in their veins ere they can come to life.

It was Kant's design in these conclusions to arbitrate between Rationalism and Empiricism. He had striven to do justice to both the contending schools, and at the same time to confine each to its proper province. To rationalism in its fancied independence of the A Posteriori, as to empiricism in its repudiation of the A Priori, he rejoined that genuine knowledge resulted only from the interaction of the two elements. But the dispute was by no means at an end. Kant's solution was felt, after all, to be dualism, which it was necessary to transcend; Fichte, Schelling, and Hegel were sensible of the impossibility of regarding the A Priori and the A Posteriori as two distinct *sources* of knowledge, of which only one sprang from reason. They held that *everything* belongs to reason, since even the material element of knowledge has no other origin. So far, therefore, all is a priori. It was not, of course, the empirical consciousness of the individual, with its slow development and its gradually multiplying contents, to which they attributed this creative power; it was rather, to use meanwhile a non-committal phrase, a hyper-individual spiritual something, which at once produces and comprises all that is real. From the standpoint of the merely individual consciousness, everything is a posteriori. Thus, according to **Fichte**, 'the science of knowledge, quite irrespective of perception a priori, traces out that which, in accordance with the same, must be present in perception a posteriori. For that science, therefore, these terms apply, not to different objects, but to different aspects of one and the same object; very much as a clock is used a priori as pointing the hour, but a posteriori in our actual reading thereof.' * **Schelling's** view is set forth in his *System des transcendentalen Idealismus*. He regards not merely

* *Sämtliche Werke*, ed. I. H. Fichte, ii. 355.

the a priori conceptions, but also the objective world, as beyond the empirical consciousness, adding only: 'As the Ego generates everything from itself, so everything—not merely this or that conception, or, as has been supposed, only the form of thought—all knowledge whatever, indeed, as one and indivisible, is a priori. But as we are not conscious of this generative process, there is nothing a priori for us: everything is a posteriori.' * **Hegel,** too, draws a distinction: a posteriori knowledge is the concern of the empirical sciences. Their function is important, but subordinate to that of philosophy, since they can only discover facts without being able to demonstrate the necessity thereof, whereas philosophy deduces all reality from one supreme principle, thus giving to the contents of the empirical sciences the form of the freedom of thought and the warrant of necessity.† Thus, while for Kant every real cognition is a product of both a priori and a posteriori elements, his successors recognize not only a *pure* a priori, but also a *pure* a posteriori knowledge. Either kind has its own truth, but only the a priori is perfect, and forms the special method of philosophy. We must, however, incidentally remark that these philosophers are not perfectly at one regarding the A Priori: according to Fichte, the vital element of mind is moral action; according to Schelling, it is artistic creation; according to Hegel, logical thought.

Vast as was the influence of these systems, and of the Hegelian in particular, yet their solution of the problem could not long prove satisfactory. Of necessity it came to be felt more and more that the attempt to resolve all existence into Pure Reason was one which, though made with signal courage and amazing ability, had in the event come to nought. The mind of man was obviously inadequate to such a task. True, as indicated above, it was no purely human faculty to which was assigned the work of generating and sustaining the universe; nevertheless, the human spirit was credited with the power of penetrating directly into the creative activity of the absolute spirit, and of beholding it at work. A reaction was inevitable. Philosophy was thrown aside, and the empirical sciences, notably exact physical science, made vigorous advance. With the question of an A Priori, science had no concern; it looked for direction to experience, to perception alone. But, as might be expected, it was not possible for any length of time to ignore the fact that experience itself involves a problem. Of necessity it came to be recognized that perception as such does not make experience; that the mind, far from being merely passive, is very largely active, and that this activity is the truly constituent element in experience. What then are the resources which the mind brings to its work? With this question we are again face to face with the problem of the A Priori. The influence of Kant entered upon a new lease of life, the turning-point being signalized by **Liebmann's** *Kant und die Epigonen* (1865), with its *ceterum censeo*, 'Back to Kant.' Once more knowledge came to be viewed as the joint product of the A Priori and the A Posteriori. From this point the theories regarding the nature of, and the shades of meaning therein assigned to, the A Priori became so numerous and varied that it is quite impossible even to distinguish them all by name.

The A Priori is frequently regarded as equivalent to consciousness in general, on the ground that all we know lies within consciousness, which must therefore form the logical prius to any particular constituent thereof. Just as objects in space are subject to the universal laws of space, so must the facts of consciousness accord with *its* universal laws. It is impossible to abstract from consciousness. Thus Ferrier points out that in everything the ego knows, it always recognizes

* *Sämtliche Werke*, iii. 527 ff.

† Cf. *Encyklopädie*, ed. 2 (1843), i. § 12 [Wallace, *Logic of Hegel*, 19 ff.].

something of its own. **Green**, again, sets forth the real universe as an all-embracing system of relations, the presupposition of which, however, is a unifying principle, a combining agency, such as we find in our individual consciousness. To these must be added **Shadworth H. Hodgson**, who, though he rejects a priori forms, holds that existence in the philosophical sense means that which exists in consciousness. By A Priori, again, has been understood the peculiar uniformity which belongs to the operations of thought. Thus **Wundt**: 'There exist within us only the universal functions of logical thought, *i.e.* those activities of relational comparison which are embodied in the primary laws of logic, and which in turn presuppose the facts of perception as the requisite material for them to work upon.'* Similarly, **H. Cornelius** regards thought as introducing necessity and uniformity into the flux of phenomena.† According to **Renouvier**, all ideas are subject to the categories, which are logically prior to them, and of which he enumerates nine, very different from those of Kant, namely, relation, number, position, succession, quality, becoming, causality, purpose, personality. Still another interpretation is given by **Sigwart**, who in his *Logic* maintains that our thinking is an endeavour to comprehend the world. The ideal of a world completely known looms before us in all we think, an ideal which possesses perfectly definite characteristics, namely, a vision of the world as complete in space and time, an exhaustive classification of all existence in a rounded system of conceptions, and, finally, intuition of the necessity of the given, in the form of an all-pervading causal nexus. Our whole mental life proceeds upon the feasibility of this ideal. Without the conviction that our thought is not aimless, all our striving after knowledge would be futile. Since, however, the possibility of attaining the ideal is manifestly not a datum of experience, the presupposition of it is a priori, not, indeed, as a self-evident truth, but as a postulate. We postulate, in the exercise of thought, the attainability of an ideal knowledge of the world, and therefore the characteristics of this ideal, as given above, namely, the vision of things as a complete whole, exhaustive classification, and intuition of necessity, are themselves postulates. These exhibit a certain affinity with ethical principles. Finding it impossible to surrender them, we brace ourselves, in spite of every failure, again and again to the task of realizing them, convinced that we are acting under the imperative of a moral idea. And in the sphere of practice, too, there hovers before our thought an ideal, which springs from the longing after perfect unity and harmony in our acts of will—the ideal of the highest good. Thus, on Sigwart's view, the essential A Priori, whether in the realm of reason or in that of practice, consists of postulates concerning the possibility of realizing lofty ideals. They can be realized, however, only by the effort of our conative faculty; we can reach the goal, even in the intellectual realm, only by exercise of will. It is significant that Sigwart thus makes out a connexion between the theoretical and the practical, and that in his opinion the A Priori has a meaning which transcends the former, being based ultimately, in fact, upon volition, *i.e.* the practical determination of the mind.‡ Sigwart also contends for an A Priori that may be taken as expressing the uniformity and activity peculiar to thought. The formation of number, in particular, rests upon an act of thought. Number cannot originate in sensible impressions, but only in the activity of thought, which in its combination of impressions, posits unity. No mere process of abstraction can possibly yield number. From a variety of red objects we can abstract the colour red as a property of all; but how, from a heterogeneous group of things, say, sun, moon, stars, trees, chimes, shall we isolate the idea of number as common to all? In virtue of our ability to delimit any particular portion of our experience, we can spontaneously posit such portion as a unity; we may, for instance, take a tree, or, if we please, its trunk, its root, a branch, a leaf, and think of each as *one*. By repeated acts of thus positing unity we obtain a numerical series, and at the same time the law of its formation. In this connexion Sigwart gives a full discussion of the views of **J. S. Mill**, who maintained that even in this field we owe everything to experience. Mill held that it is the evidence of the senses alone which convinces us that when, for instance, ten balls are variously distributed into two groups, as 1 and 9, 2 and 8, 3 and 7, etc., their sum is always 10. To this Sigwart rejoins that, if this be so, Mill must still accept the evidence of sense when an expert conjurer operates with three pebbles in such a way as apparently to produce two groups of 2 each, and to finish by showing that there are but 3 after all. Now, even if, in consequence of any miraculous change, two pairs of things were to produce 5 in all, we would indeed say that two *things* added to two *things* made five *things*, but we should still maintain that $2+2=4$. Hence numeration is based upon acts of thought, and is therefore of an a priori character.§ Moreover, space and time are a priori, though in a more limited degree than Kant supposed; likewise the axiom that two different objects cannot occupy the same portion of space at the same time, an axiom which regulates the very idea of an object,‖ etc.

Consistent empiricists, such as Czolbe and Mill, repudiate the A Priori altogether, as does also R. Avenarius with his empiriocriticism. On such a theory there is no difference in principle between psychical and physical, subject and object, consciousness and existence. According to **Avenarius**, *pure* experience is the starting-point, and again, as freed from every perversion and error, it is the goal. The individual discovers in pure experience both himself and the constituents of his environment. Every experience consists of two elements, the facts of the environment and the judgments of the mind, distinguished by Avenarius as R-values and E-values respectively. Both are equally present: there is no essential difference between them: they inhere in the *one* experience. An A Priori is therefore out of the question.*

In the question as to the recognition of an A Priori in *Consciousness*, the point at issue is really whether the mind is like an empty vessel, filled only from without, or whether it manipulates its own materials. When we state the question thus, we necessarily imply that we have to deal with something more than a problem in Epistemology. The matter cannot be settled in reference to knowledge alone; it also involves morality, art, religion, culture, and these perhaps in a more marked degree. The utterly misleading character of the empty-vessel metaphor appears from the fact that knowledge never simply comes to us, but is won only by effort. Such a passive acquisition as the metaphor would imply is a sheer impossibility. Even natural science, the experiential science *par excellence*, depends upon and advances by mental activity. Consciousness, therefore, is not anything quiescent, or merely receptive; it is something operative and constructive. We must further ask, however, whether the mind works simply as a machine, elaborating raw material into definite shape, and is thus of a merely formal character, or whether it does more. According to Kant, as to most of the present-day thinkers whose views have been touched upon in the foregoing survey, the mind's contribution is entirely restricted to the formal, the material quota being furnished in full by experience. Now it must certainly be admitted that natural science—to refer to it once more—is grounded in experience; it must begin with experience, and keep in constant touch with it. But it is none the less certain that natural science is continually begetting ideal entities, without which it could make no headway; such are, for instance, the conceptions of 'atom,' 'law' even 'matter' itself, not one of which is yielded by the senses. Thus the mind interweaves the data of sense with its own products. Nor is this discredited by the fact that such ideas as 'atom' and 'matter' are vigorously assailed at the present day, and may eventually be abandoned, since any conceivable surrogate thereof must come, not from bare experience, but from the mind itself, as is illustrated, for example, in Ostwald's *Vorlesungen über Naturphilosophie*, where the conception of matter gives place to that of energy. Everywhere, in short, does natural science set up a scaffolding of ideal construction, without which it would fall to pieces. Thus the mind exhibits even in this sphere a real productivity, which is certainly called into operation, but is in nowise created, by experience.

When we come to *Art*, the case is clearer still. To think of art as having no other function than to reproduce the external world as accurately as possible is totally to misconceive it. In its transition stages such extrinsic work may be of importance—*e.g.* in painting, the representation of light, atmosphere, and colour, and in the drama, the imitation of vernacular dialect and idiom; these things make for a more flexible technique. Nevertheless, they are but preparatory. Genuine art begins in the bodying forth of spiritual entities. It must express the best that men feel and think, that to which language in itself would be inadequate. The highest art, in fact, has often a prophetic cast; it is the herald of what ought to be; or, again, it wrestles with the deepest problems of life, being intimately connected with one's philosophy of things. In all this, however, it does not draw upon external reality, but manifests

* *System der Philosophie*, ed. 1, 218.
† *Einleitung in die Philosophie*, 329 f.
‡ *Logik*, ed. 2, ii. § 62. § *Ib.* ii. § 66. ‖ *Ib.* ii. § 72.

* *Kritik der reinen Erfahrung; Der menschliche Weltbegriff.*

creative power, and is thus an additional witness to the fact that the mind has something all its own.

In *Morality*, again, everything depends upon the inner life. Morality cannot conceivably be a product of experience. For in this province the mind furnishes its own laws, and frames the ideas to which the outer world must conform, *e.g.* the idea of justice, of brotherly love. The man who sees in morality nothing more than the rules of conduct indispensable to human intercourse, is simply blind to its essential character. It is not designed to institute some commonplace relationship amongst men, being primarily directed towards the realization of truth and purity in the individual; indeed, it may even be the most uncompromising enemy of a given social state, and, should unveracity, luxury, or baseness have become dominant therein, it must threaten the fabric with destruction, whatsoever outward grandeur may perish in its fall. It was thus, for instance, that early Christianity sapped the foundations of a civilization which had become a sham.

Now, it forms no reasonable objection to this theory of a productive energy in mind to say that, since these Ideas are, like all else, facts of consciousness, as is maintained by the thinkers who would identify philosophy with psychology, they are therefore evolved from mere experience. If consciousness is to cover everything, then all its various 'facts' would be co-ordinate and of equal value, and any gradation amongst them out of the question. Arbitrary changes of consciousness, or even changes determined by mechanical causality, would simply follow upon one another, and no arrangement or grouping thereof would mean more than any other. Amid such conditions we could not even so much as ask for the truth. Now, in point of fact, all distinctively mental creations claim to have judicial authority; judgments purport to be more than collocations of psychical products; æsthetic and ethical Ideas involve more than feelings and desires. They claim, in short, to be authoritative, to be the standard of truth and law for what is given in experience. We must distinguish between the *quæstio facti* and the *quæstio juris*; it is one thing to ask what *is*, quite another to ask what *ought to be*. In dealing with the distinctively mental, we discover something beyond the fact of determination by natural law, namely, *regulative* law. The laws of logic, of æsthetics, and of morality, unlike the laws of nature, formulate that which ought to take place, not that which actually and invariably does take place. Thus we cannot deny the fact of the mind's peculiar heritage, as evinced by this unique claim to regulative authority. We must allow, nevertheless, that the objection indicated above, namely, that even these peculiar intellectual products must manifest themselves in consciousness, is something more than a truism; it expresses the fact that the real cannot be evolved by purely logical processes from abstract conceptions alone. Speculation at large is mere sophistry; typical examples of the method are Hegel in philosophy, and in theology Rothe, who, in speaking of thought, says: 'While engaged in speculation, it shuts its eyes for the time to all that is external, and looks only within, contemplating the dialectic movement amid which it has placed itself. Without a single side-glance, it pursues only the dialectic necessity with which each conception as it comes to birth in turn begets new conceptions in virtue of its inherent fertility.'* But it is manifest that this speculative method cannot evolve reality, even spiritual reality, from conception. It is therefore quite legitimate, in opposition to a mode of thought which arrogates to itself creative omnipotence, to emphasize the experiential character of our knowledge. But, on the other hand, empiricism is in error when it narrows down experience to experience of what is external; the mind has also an experience of itself. The real nature of mind can be manifested only in consciousness—and upon this fact depends the experiential character of our mental life; but what concerns us here is the mind's experience of its own peculiar endowment, which, as we have seen, claims to possess regulative authority, and thus carries us beyond the bare experience of empiricism.

This doctrine is not only in conflict with the purely speculative method, but is also at variance with the view of Kant. Kant believed that he could completely and finally determine that which belonged to mind or reason; but his conclusions were of a purely formal kind. The view advocated here involves not only a much greater amplitude in our mental life, but also a capacity for producing even *real* elements. What the mind really is cannot be determined once for all; an avenue must ever be left open for further developments. In other words, there is a historical element in consciousness, or at least in human consciousness. We are not for ever tied down to the same unvarying forms, into which all kinds of material must be pressed; the truth is, rather, that we possess creative Ideas which are ever proposing fresh problems to experience, and setting it new tasks. We must insist upon the fact of development and movement in our intellectual life, and decline to identify its essential principle with the invariability of its formal determinations. In giving birth to Ideas, the mind puts definite questions to the empirically real, and assimilates the answers thereof, thus winning for its Ideas a structure increasingly delicate, and an organization increasingly rich.

The answer given by empirical reality varies according to the kind of question put to it. It is obvious that, on the one hand, Aristotle's investigation of nature by means of the conception of entelechy, *i.e.* a form realizing its own Idea in matter, and, on the other, that of modern science, with its conception of a causal uniformity reducible to mathematical formulæ, must result in wholly diverse views of the world. Neither entelechy nor causality is as such a product of experience; both are concepts of the mind, both purport to be questions regarding the materials of sense, to which appropriate answers can be given by empirical reality, and thus to be capable of bringing the world under the domain of mind. That the Aristotelian conception has been supplanted by the modern does not imply that the former was an illusion pure and simple, or that it was inferior to the latter; as a matter of fact, each is a hypothesis; but the modern conception of causal uniformity has shown itself better adapted to certain purposes than the ancient entelechy. Even the belief that the world can be interpreted on mathematical and mechanico-causal principles was at first an Idea, regarding which it could not be ascertained beforehand whether experience would ratify or confute it. But the Idea has proved fruitful, and has accordingly become increasingly rich in content. From the first it signified more than the purely formal, involving indeed a conviction regarding the actual constitution of the world.

Similarly the manifold æsthetic and ethical Ideas, which are certainly more than mere forms, find their function in organizing the real. We need not go further into that matter here. Suffice it to say that the human mind has brought a great variety of Ideas to bear upon the real, and that it did not begin its task with the same inherent

* *Theologische Ethik*, ed. 2, i. 19.

equipment with which it pursues it. In fine, the mind also has a history.

Now the question arises whether these Ideas should be called a priori. If they are related to history, they must also be related to experience. Nothing save the tedious discipline of facts could have compelled man to form a fresh Idea. We may say with absolute certainty that the mind is not something ready-made, anterior to all experience; it is in reality built up by intercourse with the facts of experience and history. But for that very reason it is not the product of these. What they supply to the mind is but the stimulus to its own creative activity. Accordingly the fresh element generated by this spontaneous activity is an A Priori in reference to the whole province of empirical reality, which thus becomes the mind's *palæstra*, that which is to be organized by means of the Idea. Just as, according to Kant, the a priori forms of reason are the necessary condition of experience in the higher sense, so also are the Ideas generated by the mind. We must likewise note that these Ideas exist only in virtue of the mind's own activity, and that, were this to cease, they would forthwith pass away—another link of affinity with the A Priori of Kant. We must accordingly assign to them the efficiency which marks the A Priori. The fact that they undergo changes and transformations, or that they supplant one another, need not perplex any one who does not postulate the original perfection of the mind. We must grant, of course, that we can win a truth only by much effort, and that our approach to the ultimate and supreme end is asymptotic, never issuing in complete realization. Nevertheless in all our effort and travail we assume the reality of absolute truth; we must, in fact, make this assumption, else were all our striving fruitless, and even partial truth beyond our grasp. Just as the various parts of space lie within one and the same Space, so partial truths are constituents of the one absolute Truth. That this eternal, absolute truth is no *ignis fatuus* appears from the fact that there exists in us a mighty unrest, ever urging us beyond the position we have won. Whence this unrest? Certainly not from without. Were our mind sufficient to itself, no external force could move it onwards. There must exist, therefore, something *in* itself, which ever and anon provokes it to dissatisfaction with what it has achieved, and exposes the errors and imperfections thereof. Hence it is no arbitrary assumption that the human consciousness is interpenetrated by an Absolute Consciousness. The actual existence of this Absolute Mind would thus be the ultimate and supreme A Priori, and we recognize it as such even though we must refrain from analyzing it more particularly. We cannot once for all expiscate its constituent elements by logical operations or by introspection; but it gradually reveals itself in the process of our intellectual life.

To sum up: The A Priori has a threefold significance. It embraces (1) the formal laws of mind, of which logic furnishes the best example; (2) the Ideas generated by the mind; and (3) the contents of the absolute mind. This view, or one all but identical, is championed by the new Idealism, whose principal representative is Prof. **R. Eucken**, of Jena.

It remains to deal shortly with the significance of the A Priori for *Religion*. It was Kant's conviction that an A Priori is necessary to the very existence of religion; that genuine religion has its source in pure reason. All externals, according to him, such as rubrics and creeds, are incidental, and to look for the procreative forces of religion anywhere else than in pure reason leads to sheer error. Here we have a truth of paramount importance. For if religion is possible only in virtue of an original, inherent resource of the mind, it is clear that every effort to trace the origin of religion to something which is not religion is foredoomed to failure. Research into the most primitive cults never discovers the spot where religion issues from a non-religious soil; it can never get behind some primordial element of the mind. Still less convincing are the hypotheses —ingenious as they often are—which profess to *explain* the origin of religion. A vast prestige is enjoyed by the theory that it arises from the antinomy between our feeling of dependence upon the environment and our consciousness of freedom. Man sees himself conditioned at every point, and in thrall to non-spiritual forces, yet at the same time he is cognizant of his freedom and of his superior dignity in comparison with all that is merely natural; and so, in order to preserve his spiritual personality, he seeks to attach himself to the Absolute Spirit, the result being religion. But it is simply inconceivable how religion should originate in this way—to say nothing of the unproved assumption that such ideas as dependence upon environment and personal freedom prevailed among primitive mankind. Religion as we now have it may perhaps have some connexion with the antinomy in question; its natural growth may even be accelerated thereby; but it cannot possibly arise therefrom. We must carefully distinguish between what can and what cannot be done by historical and psychological research in this sphere. Historical investigation may disclose a continuous regress from highly developed religions to forms ever more simple, till at length the ostensibly lowest is reached; indeed, circumspect reasoning may warrant us in postulating an even more primitive stage, but what is thus elicited is still of the nature of religion. Again, by psychological study we may try to ascertain the particular modes of thought, feeling, and volition with which religion is specially connected—to determine, for instance, whether it is mainly concerned with the conservation and furtherance of the physical or of the moral life; but religion is presupposed in the very inquiry. Kant is therefore quite justified in recognizing an A Priori in religion. His characteristic error lay in the attempt to fix its limits once for all. Here also, however, we must insist upon the fact that fresh formations emerge in the process of development, as, for instance, in the prophets of Israel, or in Jesus. That religion has a link with history is beyond controversy; only in the fulness of time—to use the very language of religion—does the New Revelation come. Nevertheless the fact remains that what is essential, new, and great in such revelation is never an outcome of the actual historical situation, but always a creation of the spirit itself. No scrutiny of nature or history, however assiduous, can of itself bring us into touch with the God of holy love acknowledged by Christianity. We conclude, therefore, that there is an A Priori in religion also, and that its contents are of such a character as cannot be definitely ascertained, but are revealed in what they create.

Kant's results require modification in still another respect. He approached religion from the side of morality. He regarded the A Priori of the former, in contrast with that of the latter, as in some degree derivative. In point of fact, he was not resolute enough in regard to the independent position of religion, and it is **Schleiermacher** who makes good the deficiency. The latter vindicated the distinctive character of religion as something independent of thought or moral action. True, his own definition of religion as 'the feeling of absolute dependence' is most defective. It may be, and has often been, misunderstood, since 'feeling' has a psychological reference which tends to obscure its a priori signification. Hence the protest of Hegel: 'It is matter of experience that the ingredients of feeling are of the most fortuitous character; they may be of the purest, or of the basest. If God lives in feeling, He is in no way superior to the worst, for on this soil the kingliest flower may shoot up beside the rankest weeds.'* Schleiermacher's real meaning, however, is not affected by this criticism. His 'feeling of absolute dependence' has nothing in common with the emotions aroused by sensuous phenomena, and distinguished as pleasant or painful. Within the limits of the purely empirical we can never have the feeling of *absolute*, but only of partial, dependence. Schleiermacher's definition has thus a metaphysical reference, and lies beyond the scope of ordinary psychology. But the misinterpretation is in part due to himself; he fails to give adequate and unambiguous expression to the non-experiential side of religion, *i.e.* its A Priori. He does justice, however, to its independence of thought and morality. We may now, in fact, take for granted that neither thought (as it was applied, *e.g.*, in the so-called proofs of God's existence) nor morality (as, *e.g.*, it was put into requisition by Kant) can of itself create religion or the elements thereof. Religion, with all that belongs to it, is something *sui generis*. It must, therefore, carry its own authority. Its independence implies its inherent certainty.

We have thus been brought to the question regarding the truth of religion, and at the same time have given an answer in part, viz., that a truly logical demonstration is yielded neither by history nor experience, neither by scientific thought nor morality. The truth of religion lies ultimately in itself alone. It is based neither upon experience, nor science, nor art, nor morality, nor culture; on the contrary, all these are ultimately based upon religion. All of them purport to be more than merely subjective activities, and this larger significance is valid only if the spiritual life of man is encompassed and sustained by a superhuman, cosmical spiritual Life. But no other proof of the presence of the Absolute Spirit in the human is so convincing and incisive as that afforded by religion. It is possible, indeed, that our religious certitude may be shattered; but when that happens, we only need to show, in order to restore it, that science, art, morality, and culture must likewise go by the board, and that accordingly the assured position of these indirectly endorses the truth of religion. Such an indirect proof cannot, of course, finally override every doubt; only a more intense experience of the religious facts themselves can do that. All this goes to show the importance of the A Priori for the truth of religion. In the A Priori the independent and self-evidencing character of religion finds its clearest manifestation; in it likewise is revealed the operation of a Power superior to the human. In the religious sphere, as everywhere else, the A Priori claims to have the authority of law. Not man's present condition, but the Imperative of the a priori Idea, is that which must prevail; and the emergence of such Ideas in human life is inexplicable save on the view that the spiritual life of man is interpenetrated by an Absolute Spirit. The ultimate and supreme A Priori subsists in God, and without His self-manifestation, without revelation, there could be no religion.

LITERATURE.—Special treatises on the subject are few; particular mention must be made of **Eucken**, *Gesch. und Kritik der Grundbegriffe der Gegenwart*, 1st ed. 1878, 2nd 1893, 3rd (under the title *Geistige Strömungen der Gegenwart*) 1904 [the three editions differ thus: the 1st is mainly historical, the 3rd mainly analytical, the 2nd combines both aspects]. To these may be added: **Eucken**, *Gesch. der philos. Terminologie*, 1879; **Eisler**, *Wörterbuch der philos. Begriffe*, 1904; **Scheler**, *Die transzendentale und die psychologische Methode*, 1900; **Prantl**, *Gesch. der Logik*, 1855 ff.; **Tröltsch**, *Psychologie u. Erkenntnistheorie in der Religionswissenschaft*, 1905; **Cassirer**, *Das Erkenntnisproblem in der Philosophie u. Wissenschaft der neuern Zeit*, 1906–7. The works of the philosophers themselves must be studied; above all, **Kant's** *Kritik der reinen Vernunft*, to be read along with **Vaihinger's** *Kommentar zu Kants K. der r. V.* i. 1881, ii. 1892. The A Priori in Kant's ethics is dealt with by **Stange**, *Einleitung in die Ethik*, 1900; *contra* Stange's view, **Hägerström**, *Kants Ethik*, 1904; the A Priori in Kant's philosophy of religion, by **Kalweit**, *Kants Stellung zur Kirche*, 1904; cf. also **Caird**, *Crit. Phil. of Kant*, 1889, *passim*, see Index.

PAUL KALWEIT.

* *Religionsphilosophie*, i. 73.

AQUINAS.—In the church of St. Catarina at Pisa, at the third altar on the left, is a picture by Francesco Traini, the most gifted pupil of Orcagna, representing St. Thomas of Aquino. The figure of the saint is of colossal size. Upon his knees are four books, representing the four parts of his *Summa contra Gentiles*. In his hands is a larger volume, the Sacred Scriptures, displaying Pr 8^7 'Veritatem meditabitur guttur meum, et labia mea detestabuntur impium.' Above is Christ enthroned in a mandorla, surrounded by cherubim. From His mouth proceed rays of light, one to each of the six Biblical teachers, prostrate at His feet—to His left Moses, St. John, and St. Mark; to His right St. Paul, St. Matthew, and St. Luke. Three rays pass down to the head of St. Thomas, which also receives one ray from each of the Biblical teachers. To the right of the saint stands Aristotle, holding up his *Ethics*; to the left Plato, with the *Timæus*. From these proceed rays reaching the ears of the saint. From his own books proceed rays illuminating the faithful, grouped to right and left. In the middle lies Averroës, struck down by the light—the impious, whom the lips of the great teacher abhor. By his side lies his Great Commentary, transfixed by a ray proceeding from the books on St. Thomas' knees.

This picture faithfully represents the position of the greatest teacher of the mediæval Church, her greatest philosopher, who was also her greatest theologian, absorbing into himself all the sources of wisdom, human and Divine. In his teaching he brought Scholasticism to its highest development, harmonizing the Peripatetic philosophy with the doctrine of the Church.*

1. Life.—Aquinas was born in 1225 or 1227 (the date is uncertain), most probably at the castle of Rocca Secca, 5 km. from Aquino. His father was Count of Aquino, a rich fief in the kingdom of Naples. His mother, Theodora, was of the line of the old Norman kings of Sicily. His family was therefore connected with the Hohenstaufen, and so the great doctor of the Church was related to Frederick II., its scourge. At the age of 5 he was placed under the charge of his uncle, the Abbot of Monte Cassino, and he there received his first instruction. This he completed at the University of Naples, recently restored by Frederick II. (1224), and specially favoured by him in opposition to Bologna, which had incurred his wrath by joining the Lombard League. The mendicant orders were then at the zenith of their fame. Thomas was drawn towards them, and in the year 1243 joined the Dominicans without the knowledge of his family. His pious mother was at first not at all dissatisfied with the decision. She only wanted to be allowed to see her son. This the friars were not disposed to permit, fearing lest the claims of family ties might make them lose their promising convert. The mother made known her grief to her other sons, who held high rank in the Emperor's

* Sandys, *Hist. of Classical Scholarship* 2, p. 582, gives a copy of this picture from Rosini, *Pittura Italiana*. (See also Renan, *Averroes* 3, p. 305; Gsell-Fels, *Mittel-Italien*, p. 561). For a similar picture in the Cappella degli Spagnuoli at Florence (Taddeo Gaddi?), *ib.* p. 385.

army, and besought them to get their brother back again. They succeeded in recovering him from the Dominicans, but no pressure could induce him to lay aside the habit of the order, and even two years' imprisonment in the castle of Rocca Secca could not break his purpose. He employed this time of solitude in studying the Bible and the Sentences. When his mother was convinced that it was impossible to change his will, she herself helped him to escape. He let himself down by a rope from the window, and rejoined the Dominicans. Towards the end of 1244 he accompanied Johannes Teutonicus, the head of the order, to Cologne, to study under Albertus Magnus. They travelled on foot, and reached their destination in 1245, after a journey of three months.

The many stories told of his youth, *e.g.* the well-known one of the *Bos mutus Siciliæ*, show that, as is the case with many great intellects, his development was slow, but before the age of 20 Albertus had discovered his powers, and made him his *alter ego*. On the 4th of June, 1245, at a general chapter of the order held at Cologne, it was decided to send them both to Paris. In 1248 they returned to Cologne. In 1252 Thomas was sent back to Paris to receive his degrees, and to establish an independent school there. This residence was interrupted by the contest of the mendicant orders with the university authorities headed by William of St. Amour. Thomas was sent to Rome to plead the cause of his order before Alexander IV. This he did with success. On his return to Paris he received in 1256 the degree of Magister which had been refused him before on account of his habit. The University bore him no ill-will, and shortly afterwards referred to the young doctor the much agitated question whether the accidents in the Eucharist really exist, or are only appearances.

In 1261 he was summoned to Italy by Urban IV., who tried in vain to persuade him to accept high ecclesiastical preferment. He taught at Ostia, Viterbo, Anagni, Perugia, Bologna, and Rome. In 1269 he returned to Paris, and taught there for three years.* He was then sent by the Order to Naples at the request of the king of Sicily, brother of St. Louis, to give the authority of his name to the school where he had himself received his first important instruction. In 1273 he was summoned by Gregory X. to the Council of Lyons, which was convoked to promote the Crusade and the re-union of the Greek and Latin Churches. Though in bad health, he started, accompanied by brother Reginald, his ever faithful assistant. At the Castle of Magenza—the possession of one of his nieces, the Countess of Ceccano—he fell into a long ecstasy, which much enfeebled him, and after which he felt his end to be near. As he wished to die in a house of his own order, he continued his journey, but was obliged to stop at the Cistercian Abbey of Fossa Nuova near Terracina. There he died, 7th March, 1274. At the time of his death, he was, at the request of his hosts, dictating for them an exposition of the Song of Solomon. He had got as far as 'Filiæ Jerusalem dicite dilecto meo, quia præ amore morior,' when his strength gave way. The report was current that he had been poisoned by Charles of Anjou.†

For nearly a century the Dominicans and Cistercians disputed the honour of possessing his remains. The quarrel was not yet settled when, 49 years after his death, he was canonized by John XXII. It was finally decided in 1368, by a bull of Urban V., that the body should be surrendered to the Dominicans of Toulouse, the mother church of the order. An arm was given to the Convent of St. Jacques at Paris, where St. Thomas and B. Albertus had taught. In 1286 he was raised by the Dominicans to the rank of *Doctor Ordinis*. In 1567 he was made by Pius V. the fifth 'Doctor of the Church,' and thus placed on an equality with St. Jerome, St. Ambrose, St. Augustine, and St. Gregory the Great.*

His works fill 17 folio volumes in the edition of Pius V. (Rome, 1570). Their exact chronological order is not yet completely decided, and the genuineness of some is disputed. He began his literary work at Cologne with the *de Ente et Essentia* (No. 30 of the *Opuscula* in the Roman edition). The most important are the *Summa contra Gentiles*, the materials for which he began to gather at Paris, during his first period of teaching there, at the request of Raymond de Pennaforte; the *Summa Theologica*, begun in 1265 in Italy and left incomplete at his death; the *Quæstiones disputatæ* (1261–1264); the *Quodlibeta*, of which the first five were composed at Paris, the last six at Rome; and the Aristotelian commentaries, begun at the instance of Urban IV.† Besides these, there are commentaries on books of Sacred Scripture, of which the best known is the *Catena Aurea*, properly called *Expositio continua*, and the commentary on the Sentences, which was the first extensive work composed by him.

This enormous literary output is all the more remarkable, when it is remembered that it was far from being the only occupation of these strenuous twenty years. During the whole time Aquinas was busily engaged in teaching. The attraction of his lectures was so great that it was difficult to find a hall large enough to contain the audience. At times he employed three or four secretaries at once, and dictated to them about different subjects without confusion. It is a mistake to speak of him as 'pure embodied intellect perfectly passionless.'‡ This is not the meaning of the primacy of the intellect over the will as taught by him. His hymns are proof enough of this—'the famous sequence, "Lauda Sion Salvatorem," "Pange lingua gloriosi corporis mysterium," "Verbum superne prodiens" (there is a hymn of St. Ambrose beginning with the same line), "Sacris solemniis juncta sint gaudia," and "Adoro te devote latens Deitas."' They were written for the festival of Corpus Christi, the observance of which was decreed by Urban IV. at his instance (1264). They are 'powerful in thought, feeling, and expression,' and probably exercised important influence on the general acceptance of the dogma of transubstantiation, the doctrine of which is set forth in them with a wonderful degree of scholastic precision.§ Every day he had a portion of a book of edification read aloud to him (*Rufini collationes Patrum*); and when asked why he withdrew this time from speculative thought, he answered that he considered the rousing of the spirit of devotion to be the due preparation for the sublimity of speculation. When the feeling of devotion was roused, the spirit rose all the more easily to the contemplation of the highest truth. He never began to study, to lecture, or to write, without first giving himself to prayer to obtain Divine illumination. When doubts intruded upon his investigations, he interrupted them to seek en-

* On the disputed point of the length of this stay at Paris see Mandonnet, *Siger de Brabant*, etc., p. 99.

† See Dante, *Purg.* xx. 67 ff., and Scartazzini's note.

* For a complete account of the tributes of respect paid to St. Thomas by the Popes, from Alexander IV. onwards, see Kleutgen, *Die Theologie der Vorzeit vertheidigt*, iv. p. 106. To his list must now be added the Encyclical of Leo XIII., 'Æterni Patris,' 1879.

† On the Aristotelian question and the prohibition of Paris see de Rubeis, xxx. c. 7.

‡ Milman, *Latin Christianity*, ix. 132.

§ Lord Selborne, *EBr* xii. 584; cf. also on the hymns of St. Thomas, Julian, *Dict. of Hymnology*, pp. 22, 662–664, 878–880, 986, 1217–1219.

lightenment in prayer. The fact that the *Summa Theologica* was left incomplete was not due entirely to want of time. In the *Acta* we read: 'The witness—Bartholomew of Capua—declared that brother Reginald, seeing that the holy doctor did not continue the third part of the *Summa*, after the questions dealing with the sacrament of penance, asked him why he had stopped this great work, which he had begun for the glory of God, and which would enlighten the world. St. Thomas, filled with the thought of having soon to appear before the Supreme Judge, replied that he *could* not continue: that all he had written so far appeared to him to be nothing in comparison with the wonderful things that God had been pleased to reveal to him recently.' St. Thomas had a sane mysticism of his own, not the spurious kind that would banish reason from religion altogether, and drown itself in the wild fancies of the *Evangelium æternum*, but that which recognizes, with St. Augustine, that no real progress in the religious life can be made without corresponding progress in knowledge, and for which the supreme communion with God has no other content than that of the *Visio Dei*, i.e. essential knowledge.*

2. Sources.—(1) *The Sacred Scriptures.*—St. Thomas has, of course, a profound knowledge of Scripture according to all the four methods of interpretation (*Sum. Theol.* I. i. art. 10). He insists very strongly on the importance of not sacrificing the historical. For instance (*ib.* I. cii. 1), in discussing the question *Utrum Paradisus sit locus corporeus*, he says: 'Ea, quæ de Paradiso in Scriptura dicuntur, per modum narrationis historicæ proponuntur. In omnibus autem, quæ sic Scriptura tradit, est pro fundamento tenenda veritas, et de super spirituales expositiones fabricandæ.' It is to be noted that in his exposition of Isaiah 8 he has so faithfully presented the *sensus litteralis*, that Cornelius a Lapide and others declare it 'judaica expositio, Divi Thomæ ingenio prorsus indigna.' The three other senses are explained (*ib.* I. i. 10): 'Secundum ergo quod ea quæ sunt veteris legis significant ea quæ sunt novæ legis: est *sensus allegoricus.* Secundum vero quod ea quæ in Christo sunt facta vel in iis quæ Christum significant sunt signa eorum quæ nos agere debemus: est *sensus moralis.* Prout vero significant ea quæ sunt in æterna gloria: est *sensus analogicus.*'

The testimony of Erasmus to St. Thomas' merits as an interpreter of Scripture is amply justified: 'Nam meo quidem animo nullus est recentiorum theologorum, cui par sit diligentia, cui sanius ingenium, cui solidior eruditio: planeque dignus erat, cui linguarum quoque peritia, reliquaque bonarum litterarum supellex contingeret, qui iis quæ per eam tempestatem dabantur tam dextre sit usus' (Rom. i. 5, le Clerc, vol. vi. p. 554).

He had at hand some who were not unacquainted with Hebrew (*e.g.* he knows that רוח is feminine), but this does not prevent him from falling into pitfalls of translation, *e.g.* the use of *verbum* in Lk 1[37] (*Sum. Theol.* I. xxv. 3).†

(2) *The Fathers.*—De Rubeis has counted 56 Greek and 22 Latin Fathers as used by Aquinas. The greater part are taken at first hand. He informs us himself: 'Quasdam expositiones doctorum Græcorum in Latinum feci transferri' (Preface to *Catena aurea*). He makes special use of Dionysius. The charge of Monophysitism made against this author, which has recently been revived, has been amply examined and refuted by de Rubeis in his ninth Dissertation.

(3) *Secular authors.*—Dr. Sandys has noted that the *Summa Theologica* is an embodiment of the scientific spirit of the 13th cent., which stands in sharp contrast with the literary and classical spirit of the 12th.*

(*a*) Aristotle is, of course, the chief. How far his Aristotelianism is pure, and how far coloured by Neo-Platonism, is still *sub judice.* It must be remembered that this process of Platonizing Aristotle had begun by the time of Alexander of Aphrodisias. When Prantl † says that St. Thomas corrupted Aristotelianism and Platonism by the mysticism of the book *de Causis*, this statement needs a good deal of qualification. Aquinas was well aware that Proclus was the author of this book, and he gives the correct title to it, '*elementatio* [not *elevatio*] *theologica.*' ‡ It is to be noted that in the crucial question of the νοῦς ποιητικός he is quite free from Neo-Platonic influences. Brentano says: 'He gives an explanation, which is most notably, in all the points above mentioned, in agreement with the fragment of Theophrastus which is preserved in the paraphrase of Themistius.' And again: 'If we ask which of the earlier interpreters has come nearest to the truth, it is undeniable that we must give this honour to St. Thomas. I do not know whether I ought not to say that he has grasped correctly the whole teaching of Aristotle.' § This question of the νοῦς ποιητικός was the central point of the discussion with Averroism (see *Opusc.* 16, 'de Unitate intellectus'). The charge brought against St. Thomas and Scholasticism in general of following Aristotle blindly has been too often refuted to need any notice.

(*b*) Of Plato he knows only the *Timæus* in Chalcidius' version. He says expressly that the *Republic* was not accessible.

(*c*) Of the Latin philosophers he uses mainly Boethius, Cicero, Macrobius, and Seneca. He is familiar with the *Digest*. De Rubeis (xxx Dissertatio, c. iv.) notes that in the *Summa Theologica* there are quoted 46 Greek, Latin, and Arabic philosophers, besides orators and poets.

(*d*) *The Arabic and Jewish philosophers.*—The indebtedness of Aquinas to these sources has been the subject of much controversy. Some have gone so far as to say that had there been no Maimonides there would have been no Aquinas. This is an exaggeration, but Aquinas had certainly learnt much from the *Moreh Nebuchim.* Compare the arguments about the creation of the world in *Sum. Theol.* I. xlvi. 1 with *Mor. Neb.* ii. c. 15 [ed. Munk, vol. ii. p. 121]. His attitude to Ibn Gebirol is very hostile. 'In opposition to the Franciscans, who carefully preserved and circulated certain opinions of Avencebrol, St. Thomas, like his teacher Albert, rejects his opinions.' ‖ He is the bitter enemy of the Andalusian school of Arabic philosophers, and is as well acquainted with Avempace, who is very often referred to in the *Summa contra Gentiles*, as with Averroës.

Of equal importance with his own contributions to the interpretation of Aristotle is the fact that Aquinas secured the making of new translations from the Greek, which displaced the earlier ones which were made from the Arabic. It was at his instance that William of Brabant—William de Moerbeka—is said to have produced in 1273—doubtless with the help of others—a literal translation of the Greek text of all the works of Aristotle.¶

In connexion with this work, the question has

* For a full account of the mysticism of St. Thomas, see Harnack, *Dogmengesch.* iii. 383. He notes that Denifle has shown that Meister Eckhart owed everything to St. Thomas.

† See de Wulf, *Hist. de la philos. médiévale*, p. 330, note 2, from Asin y Palacios.

* *History of Scholarship*[2], p. 583, after Abbot Gasquet. See also Mandonnet, *Siger de Brabant*, p. 20.

† *Gesch. der Logik*, iii. 114.

‡ See Bardenhewer, *de Causis*, p. 256 ff.

§ Brentano, *Psychol. des Aristoteles*, pp. 24 and 226; see also, for the whole question, Schneid, *Aristoteles in der Scholastik*, p. 72 f. For his general attitude to Aristotle see Talamo, *L'Aristotelismo della Scolastica*, ch. 1; and Mandonnet, *l.c.*, p. 175.

‖ Wittmann, *Die Stellung des hl. Thomas von Aquin zu Avencebrol*, p. 76.

¶ See de Rubeis, xxiii. ch. 2, on the custom of sending Dominicans to Greece for study.

been raised as to St. Thomas' own knowledge of Greek. This question cannot be answered decisively until all his works have been critically edited. De Rubeis has shown that he was certainly not a complete stranger to the Greek language. 'In his commentary on the *Ethics*, the presentation of the right reading misspelt, and of a ludicrous etymology side by side with one that is very nearly right, seems to show that, while Aquinas had about him people who knew Greek, he had himself no substantial knowledge of it.' *

3. Main points of system.—The age of St. Thomas was also that of Frederick II. of Hohenstaufen and of St. Louis, and these names are representative of the conflicting tendencies of the period. The 12th cent. had witnessed a revival of learning, which was less important than that of the Renaissance, only in point of literary form. It had two sources—Arabian and Byzantine. The former has been fairly well investigated. There is a great deal about the latter that is still obscure. The result was seen at first in the rapid growth of speculative heresy, popular pantheism (David of Dinant), and the more serious, and therefore more dangerous, tendency of thought which afterwards crystallized into Averroism. Hence the prohibition of 1210, and the letter of Gregory IX. to the Parisian masters of theology, 1228.† The question at issue was whether the Church would be able to assimilate the new learning, or whether its doctrines would be gradually corroded away by it. That the former was the case is due to the work of Albertus as completed by St. Thomas. That work was therefore twofold—to harmonize the new scientific teaching with the doctrine of the Church, and to refute heresy.

The distinctive characteristics of the system of philosophy which Thomism displaced in the Western Church are well summed up by de Wulf as follows: 'Absence of any formal distinction between the domain of philosophy and that of theology, *i.e.* between the order of rational and of revealed truth; primacy of the notion of the good over that of the true, and in consequence primacy of the will over the intellect both in God and man; the necessity of an immediate illuminative action of God in accomplishing certain intellectual acts; actuality, in a low degree, but still some positive actuality in primitive matter independent of any substantial form; the presence in matter of *rationes seminales*; ‡ even spiritual substances are composed of matter and form; plurality of forms in natural things; individuality of the soul independently of its union with the body, especially in man; the identity of the soul with its faculties' (*Gilles de Lessines*, p. 15). The philosophical element incorporated in this school was essentially Platonic.

For this Thomism substitutes Aristotelianism: not blindly, for 'locus ab auctoritate est infirmissimus' (*Sum. Theol.* I. i. 8, ad. 2), but critically, 'si audierit omnes quasi adversariorum dubitantium' (*Metaph.* iii., Lect. 1), though respectfully. The novelty of the teaching of St. Thomas is universally dwelt upon—novelty not only in method, but in matter. The main novelties were: strict distinction between Natural and Revealed Theology; unity of the substantial principle, as opposed to the plurality of forms; passive evolution of matter, as opposed to the theory of *rationes seminales*; the doctrine of subsistent forms, as opposed to the notion of spiritual substances being composed of matter and of form; the real distinction of the substance of the soul and its faculties,

* Sandys, *l.c.* p. 583 f.; de Rubeis, xxx. c. 3; Mandonnet, *l.c.* p. 55.

† This letter is given in Denzinger's *Enchiridion*, § 379.

‡ On *rationes seminales*—an idea derived from St. Augustine—see Kleutgen, *Philos. der Vorzeit*, i. 125.

as opposed to the Augustinian doctrine of their identity; the primacy of the intellect over the will.* The new system was, of course, not received without a struggle, which continued long after the death of St. Thomas. The articles of 1277 were directed not merely against Averroism, but against Peripateticism in general.†

Notwithstanding the vast extent of St. Thomas' writings, a sufficient knowledge of his whole system may be obtained from the two *Summæ*. The *Opuscula* are useful for giving a more elaborate treatment of special subjects, but the whole is to be found in the two great works. There is little sign of gradual development in his writings, because he early reached his complete system. In the *Acta*, p. 670, we have the evidence of Ægidius of Rome (afterwards bishop of Bourges): 'In this marvellous and memorable doctor, it was a manifest token of the subtlety of his genius and the accuracy of his judgment, that as a master neither in teaching nor in writing did he change the new opinions and arguments which he upheld as a bachelor, with very few exceptions.' ‡ The fact is that Albertus had laid the foundations, St. Thomas completed and elaborated in detail. But both the *Summæ* must be employed. The better known *Summa Theologica* handles many philosophical problems very briefly, which are dealt with at length in the other, which is in consequence often called 'Summa Philosophica.' In the short preface to the *Sum. Theol.* the author says that it is intended to be a compendium for beginners, and that he will deal with the questions 'breviter et dilucide.' These questions are dealt with in the Commentaries on Aristotle at even greater length; but it is a mistake to expect to find in these invariably St. Thomas' own opinions. Those of Albertus are modelled after Avicenna, and are therefore dissertations on the principal points dealt with by the Greek philosopher. St. Thomas proceeded 'quodam singulari et novo modo' (*Acta*, p. 661). This new method was that of Averroës, not following the text servilely, but expressing its meaning as faithfully as possible. They therefore are intended to give Aristotle's own meaning, which may or may not be that of the writer. They ought not, therefore, to be quoted as always giving St. Thomas' views; there may even be found in them some traces of the influence of the great commentator whose system it was the object of St. Thomas to overthrow.

SUMMA PHILOSOPHICA.—*Summa de veritate catholicæ fidei contra gentiles* is the title as given by Uccelli from the autograph MS, though the work is not addressed to Gentiles in the proper sense, but to Muhammadans, Jews, heretics, and unbelievers of all sorts, *i.e.* all outside the Church. Since the opponents either do not recognize the authority of sacred Scripture at all or only imperfectly, and do not recognize that of the Church, it is necessary in their case 'to have recourse to natural reason, although in things Divine this is insufficient.' The work is divided into four books. In the *First*, Aquinas deals with the existence and attributes of God. In the *Second*, he shows how all things proceed from God as regards their being and their distinctive characteristics. The development of this subject leads him to speak of the different kinds of substances, and especially of the *substantiæ intellectuales*, regarded in them-

* On this matter Mandonnet, *l.c.* p. 66; de Wulf, *La Philos. médiévale* 2, p. 369, and *Gilles de Lessines*, p. 15.

† One of the strongest opponents of Thomism was John Peckham, Abp. of Canterbury. See the two letters in the Rolls edition of his register (vol. iii. p. 864), to the Chancellor and University of Oxford, and (p. 870), to certain cardinals. See *Acta Sanct.*, March 7, p. 710.

‡ These exceptions are to be found mainly in his commentary on the sentences. For them see Mandonnet, *l.c.* pp. 63 and 259; de Wulf, *Philos. médiév.* p. 370; de Rubeis, xiii. cap. 5, xxvii. cap. 2.

selves, in their relations to body, and in their operations. He dwells specially, of course, upon the human soul, demonstrates its spiritual nature and its personality, and develops his theory of knowledge. The *Third* shows that all things are ordered towards one end, which is God, and that the supreme and final blessedness of man consists in the contemplation of God; that Providence embraces the whole universe, that it extends to intelligent creatures, without destroying their liberty, and prescribes to them laws, which are the norm of all their duties. The *Fourth* gives an exposition of revealed truth. This is above the powers of unassisted human intellect. All that can be done, therefore, is to show that these truths are beyond, not contrary to, human reason.

SUMMA THEOLOGICA.—This is divided into three parts. The *First* deals, in 119 *Quæstiones*, with God, and the procession of all things from God. The *Second* is divided into two sections, the first of which deals with Ethics in general, in 114 *Quæstiones*; the second with Ethics *in speciali*, in 189 *Quæstiones*. The *Third* deals with Christ and the sacraments, but breaks off in the middle of the sacrament of penance. In the short preface to this part the scheme is laid down to deal first with the Saviour Himself; then with the sacraments by which we attain salvation; thirdly, with immortal life, which we reach through Him by the Resurrection. To complete the work, therefore, the rest of the sacraments and the eschatology have been added from the commentary on the Sentences.* Each *Quæstio* is divided into a number of *Articuli*, and each article consists of three parts. (1) The difficulties are alleged, which seem to negative the *Quæstio*; (2) the authorities are quoted, sacred and secular; (3) then follows the philosophical discussion based on first principles, and the resolution of the difficulties. The whole is one of the most magnificent monuments of the human intellect, dwarfing all other bodies of theology into insignificance. Apart from its importance as the authoritative code of Latin Christianity, it is great as a work of art. At the Council of Trent it was placed on the desk, side by side with the sacred Scriptures, as normative of the discussions.

The Præambula Fidei.—The principal novelty in theology is the strict separation of natural from revealed. It had not so been laid down by any of the Fathers, or by any of the preceding Schoolmen; but it has remained in force, not only in Catholic but in Protestant countries.† The principles of the division are laid down as follows: It is the object of wisdom, taken absolutely, to discover the truth, and therefore, incidentally, to unmask falsehood. By truth is here meant, not any special truth, such as is the object of a special science, but the ultimate absolute truth, which is the foundation of all special truths (*Sum. c. Gent.* i. 1). The way of attaining to this truth is double. There are some things which are true about God, which transcend entirely the powers of human reason, such as the doctrine of the Trinity in unity, and all the distinctively Christian dogmas. There are others to which natural reason can attain, such as those of the existence and the unity of God. These things the philosophers have demonstrated exactly, under the guidance of the light of human reason (*ib.* i. 3).

When we speak of this double nature of truth, this must be understood relatively to ourselves, not as concerning the nature of truth absolutely. When we speak of a double truth in things divine, this is not to be understood in reference to God Himself, who is the one and simple truth, but in reference to our own knowledge, which has different ways of reaching this Divine truth (*ib.* i. 9).

(1) The first way is *ratio naturalis*. It is not the intention of St. Thomas in any way to vilipend reason, and so to drive it outside the sphere of religion altogether. It is *deficiens*, *i.e.* insufficient for ascertaining the truth completely, but not deceptive. It is 'the impression of the Divine light in us.' The light of natural reason by which we discern between good and evil, in that which appertains to the natural law, is nothing else than the impression of the Divine light in us (*Sum. Theol.* II.a. xci. 2). Human reason is perfected by God in two ways: first, by a natural perfection, according to the light of reason; secondly, by a supernatural perfection, by means of the theological virtues. Although this second perfection is greater than the first, the first perfection is possessed by man in a more perfect way; for the first is held by man, as it were, in full possession. The second is held only imperfectly, because such is our knowledge and love of God (*ib.* II.a. lxviii. 2).

(2) The second way is *faith*. The knowledge of God by faith comes to us by Divine revelation (*Sum. c. Gent.* iv. i.). Since the knowledge of God to which man can attain by reason is deficient, He has, out of His superabundant mercy, to make it more perfect, revealed to us certain things about Himself which transcend human knowledge. In this revelation a certain order is observed, such as is suited to man, so that he may proceed by degrees from the imperfect to the perfect. At first they are so revealed as not to be understood, but only to be believed, as it were, on hearsay, because the intellect of man, when in that state in which it is bound to things of sense, cannot raise itself at all to behold those things which exceed all the analogies of sense; but when it is freed from the bondage of sensible things, then it can rise to contemplate the things that are revealed (*ib.*). There is therefore in one sense a *triple* division of man's knowledge of Divine things, on account of this division of faith into two degrees (*ib.*).

This second means of reaching truth is needed: (*a*) On account of the imperfection of natural reason. The human intellect cannot succeed by its natural powers in grasping the substance of God, because the knowledge of our intellect according to the mode of this present life begins with the objects of sense. We see that there are various grades of intelligence. The simple rustic cannot understand what is intelligible to the philosopher, nor can the philosopher understand that which is intelligible to the angel (*ib.* i. 3). (*b*) Out of mercy it extends even to those things which natural reason could discover, because few could thus attain to them. The process of investigation takes a long time, and is not certain to be successful, because falsehood creeps in on account of the weakness of the intellect and the disturbing element of the fancy (*ib.* i. 4). Faith, therefore, supersedes but does not destroy reason. The lesser light is not darkened by the greater, but is rather increased, as the light of the air is by that of the sun; and in this way the light of science is not darkened, but rather grows brighter, in the soul of Christ by means of the light of Divine knowledge (*Sum. Theol.* III. ix. 1 ad 2). Still less is it contrary to it. Because it transcends reason, it is thought by some to be contrary to it; but this is impossible (*Sum. c. Gent.* i. 7). The relation, therefore, between philosophy and theology is clear.—(i.) Each has its proper province. In the teaching of philosophy, which considers the creatures in themselves, and leads us from them to the knowledge of God, it is the creatures who are considered first, and finally God. But in the teaching of Faith, which considers the

* On this supplementum see de Rubeis, xiii. cap. 6.

† In 1271 a decree was made at Paris that no teacher of the philosophical faculty should deal with any of the specifically theological questions. See Thurot, *De l'organisation de l'Enseignement dans l'Université de Paris*, p. 105.

creature only in its relation to God, it is God who is the first object of consideration and the creatures afterwards (*Sum. c. Gent.* ii. 4). (ii.) Natural reason must keep to its own department. Only those things can be known about God by natural reason which belong to the unity of His essence, but not those which belong to the division of the Persons. Therefore the attempt to prove the doctrine of the Trinity by human reason injures faith in two ways: (α) as concerns the dignity of faith itself, *i.e.* that it is concerned with things invisible, which, therefore, transcend human reason; (β) as regards the benefit of bringing others to the faith. For when a man brings reasons that are not cogent to demonstrate the faith, he only provokes the scorn of the unbelieving (*Sum. Theol.* I. xxxii. 1).* But natural reason can defend the Articles of the Faith, by showing that they are not repugnant to reason (*Sum. c. Gent.* iv. 1). (iii.) Those truths that can be discovered by natural reason, though they form part of revelation, are not *articuli fidei*, but only *præambula ad articulos* (*Sum. Theol.* I. ii. 2).†

Ethics.—To Ethics is devoted the third part of the *Sum. c. Gent.* and the second part (in two divisions) of the *Sum. Theol.* The numerous sources of St. Thomas' learning have led to much complexity in his ethical system. It is based on that of Aristotle, but the fourfold division of Plotinus is also introduced (II.a. lxi. 5 from Macrobius). In the development of the idea of virtue, and the division of virtues into moral and intellectual, he follows Aristotle. The intellectual take precedence, because the contemplative life, if the contemplation be theological, stands higher than the practical: 'Ultima et perfecta beatitudo non potest esse nisi in visione divinæ essentiæ' (II.a. iii. 8), and 'beatitudo est præmium virtuosarum operationum' (II.a. v. 7). The moral value of actions is determined by three elements: (1) *ex objecto*; (2) *ex circumstantia*; (3) *ex fine* (II.a. xviii.), and 'bonum virtutis moralis consistit in adæquatione ad mensuram rationis' (II.a. lxiv. 1). There are three intellectual virtues: (1) *sapientia* ('quæ considerat altissimas causas'); (2) *scientia* (*conclusionum*); (3) *intellectus* ('habitus primorum principiorum,' II.a. lvii.). The moral virtues differ according to their objects. Some regulate actions, some passions. The first are comprised under the general name of *justitia* ('omnis virtus quæ facit bonum debiti et recti in operationibus est justitia,' II.a. lx. 3). The other ten Aristotelian virtues are brought under the heads of (1) *prudentia* ('omnis virtus quæ facit bonum in consideratione rationis'); (2) *temperantia* ('quæ cohibet passiones et deprimit'); (3) *fortitudo* ('quæ facit firmitatem animi contra quascunque passiones,' II.a. lxi. 3). These are the *virtutes acquisitæ*, and are subordinate to the theological virtues ('virtutes infusæ'), viz. *Faith*, which completes our knowledge by the truths, which can only be known by revelation; *Hope*, which renders accessible the Divine end, which passes the forces of nature; and *Charity*, by which the will unites itself to that end, and so to speak transforms itself into it. *Fides* without *caritas* is *informis*.

The question of the will and its freedom is discussed at length (I. lxxxii. and lxxxiii.): 'voluntas media est inter rationem et concupiscibilem et potest ab utroque moveri' (II.b. clv. 3). It corresponds to the understanding, just as the natural appetite does to the senses (II.a. cix. 2). The question is discussed 'utrum homo possit velle et facere bonum absque gratia.' The answer given is carefully qualified.

It is a characteristic of Thomism that it maintains that good is *per se*, not *ex institutione* ('perseitas boni'). This is based upon Aquinas' view of the will, which in God as well as in man has knowledge for its presupposition and basis.

One of the most remarkable sections of the *Prima Secundæ* is the discussion on law (xc.–cviii.)—the first scientific discussion of the subject in post-classical times, and, says Jourdain, the best introduction to the study of law which has ever been written.* In the operation of the moral law on the mind, Aquinas distinguishes between the *synderesis* and *conscientia*, the former being the general moral consciousness—the latter applying this to particular cases (I. lxxix. 13 ad 3): 'Habitus autem ex quibus conscientia informatur etsi multi sunt, omnes tamen efficaciam habent ab uno primo principio, scilicet ab habitu primorum principiorum, qui dicitur synderesis.' Aquinas is decidedly anti-Socialistic (II.b. lxvi. 1), and, of course, no advocate of toleration (II.b. xi. 3).

The influence of Aquinas has been all-powerful over those who have come after him, not merely within the limits of Scientific Theology; *e.g.* in Dante's *Paradiso*, x. 8. 2, it is St. Thomas who speaks in heaven;† his writings had a mysterious influence over Savonarola;‡ and Baillet tells us that St. Thomas was the favourite author of Descartes, and the only theologian he ever wished to study.§ How much Hooker was his debtor any one may see who compares the first book of the *Ecclesiastical Polity* with St. Thomas' section upon 'law.'

Is Thomism a system still valid for our times, or are we to regard it as an overpassed standpoint? This is the question that lies at the root of the debates about the Encyclical *Pascendi*. One thing is clear, that Thomism is absolutely incompatible with the conception of Evolution—Transformism—that dominates modern thought. 'Nulla forma substantialis suscipit magis et minus' (*de Potentia*, III. ix. ad 9; de Wulf, *Gilles de Lessines*, p. 59). But is Transformism compatible with the theology of the Catholic Church?

LITERATURE.—An elaborate Bibliography of works bearing on St. Thomas is given in Ueberweg-Heinze's *Gesch. der Philos.*[8] ii. p. 272 ff. Since then have appeared (among many others): **Wittmann**, *Die Stellung des hl. Thomas von Aquin zu Avencebrol*, 1900; **Grünwald**, *Gesch. der Gottesbeweise im Mittelalter*, 1907 [both in Baeumker's *Beiträge*]; **Luquet**, 'Aristôte et l'Université de Paris pendant le xiiie Siècle,' 1904 (*Bibliothèque de l'École des hautes études*); **Eucken**, *Thomas von Aquino und Kant, ein Kampf zweier Welten*, 1901; **Picavet**, *Hist. générale et comparée des Philosophies Médiévales*[2], 1907, where ch. ix. gives a useful survey of Neo-Thomism.

The authorities for the life are in the Bollandist *Acta Sanctorum*, March 7. The principal one is William de Tocco. Mandonnet (*l.c.* p. 81) considers him weak in chronology.

The fullest account of Thomism (philosophical) is **Kleutgen**, *Die Philos. der Vorzeit vertheidigt*[2], 1878; (theological) do., *Die Theol. der Vorzeit vertheidigt*[2], 1867, 6 vols. The system is well summed up from the Catholic side in **Schwane**, *Dogmengesch.* 1882, vol. iii.; and **Willmann**, *Gesch. des Idealismus*, 1896, ii. pp. 442–541; and from the Protestant in **Harnack**, *Dogmengesch.* iii. p. 424 ff. **De Wulf**, *Hist. de la Philos. médiévale*[2], is specially to be recommended; as also, for the conflict with Averroism, **Mandonnet**, *Siger de Brabant*, etc., 1899.

H. Sidgwick gives a good summing up of the Ethics of St. Thomas in *EBr* viii. p. 594 (to which the present writer owes obligation). **R. L. Poole**, *Illust. of Hist. of Mediæval Thought*, 1884, p. 240, gives a good review of his political theories.

Of the edition of the complete works (Leo XIII.), 12 vols. have now appeared, the last completing the *Summa Theologica*. In the first are the invaluable dissertations of de Rubeis. There is a convenient edition of the *Sum. Theol.* published at Rome in 6 vols. 1894 (Editio aureo numismate donata a S. P. Leone XIII.). See also **Uccelli**, *Sum. c. Gent.* from the autograph MS, 1878;

* This point is elaborated in his *contra Græcos, Armenos et Saracenos*, cap. 2, No. 3 of *Opuscula* in Roman edition.

† Therefore, of course, philosophy is *ancilla Theologiæ* (*Sum. c. Gent.* ii. 4: 'Unde et theologia maxima sapientia dici debet, utpote semper altissimam causam considerans, et propter hoc ipsi, quasi principali, philosophia humana deservit.'

* Rashdall speaks of the result of the study of Civil Law at Bologna as the most brilliant achievement of the intellect of modern Europe (from Sandys, *l.c.* p. 583).

† See Ozanam, *Dante et la Philos. Cathol.*, p. 317 f.

‡ Villari, *Savonarola*, vol. i. p. 5: 'Le opere di San Tommaso lo attiravano con una forza quasi misteriosa'; p. 329: 'Aveva poi, sin da fanciullo, preso nel leggere e studire San Tommaso una strana passione.'

§ Baillet, *La vie de M. Descartes*, 1691, p. 286 (from Jourdain).

De Maria, *Opus. Philos. et Theol. et Quodlibeta*, Città di Castello, 3 vols., 1886.

The principal works on St. Thomas are:

Jourdain, *La Philos. de St. Thomas d'Aquin*, 2 vols., 1858; **Werner**, *Thomas von Aquino*, 3 vols., 1858 (new ed. 1889); **Frohschammer**, *Die Philos. d. T. v. Aquino kritisch gewürdigt*, 1889; **Guttmann**, *Das Verhältniss des Thomas von Aquino zum Judenthum*, etc., 1891.

For the translations of St. Thomas' works into other languages, see de Rubeis, xiii. c. 8; and **Steinschneider**, *Heb. Uebersetz. des Mittelalters*, pp. 483–489; also **Jellinek**, *Thomas von Aquino in der jüd. Literatur*, 1853.

For St. Thomas' psychology, cf. **Siebeck**, *Gesch. der Psychol.* vol. ii. pp. 448–472; **Schütz**, *Thomas Lexicon* 2, 1895.

[By this bibliography the writer desires to express a general sense of indebtedness, especially to Werner, Jourdain, and de Rubeis, in addition to what is expressed in direct reference].

J. M. HEALD.

ARABS (ANCIENT).

[TH. NÖLDEKE].

THE term 'ancient Arabs' is used in this article to denote the pre-Muhammadan population of the greater part of the Arabian Peninsula and of the neighbouring districts to the North, which were inhabited by Arabs (*i.e.* the Syrian Desert, etc.). But the ancient civilized population of Southern Arabia, the Sabæans or Ḥimyarites, is not included, since their religion demands a separate treatment. See SABÆANS.

The evidence which we possess does not enable us to form anything like a complete and vivid picture of the religion of the ancient Arabs. Wellhausen was therefore quite justified in entitling his treatise *Reste Arabischen Heidentums* ('Remains of Arabian Heathenism')*—a work which throws into the shade all previous books on the subject, and sets forth very many of the results embodied in the present article. As regards the older period, we are dependent mainly upon isolated statements of Greek writers, and upon Greek or Semitic inscriptions,† which mention various deities, either expressly or implicitly, as one of the elements in compound proper names of human beings, but supply us with scarcely any detailed information. These authorities relate exclusively to the Arabs of the northern regions. Somewhat fuller evidence, respecting the religion of the tribes who inhabited the Peninsula in the latest heathen period, is furnished by Arabic literature. Occasional references to the heathen religion are found in the ancient poets,‡ and some information may be gathered from the polemical allusions in the Qur'ān. Moreover, the ancient narratives which deal with the manners and customs of the heathen Arabs contain some passages bearing on the religion of those times. Much credit is due to a few of the early Muhammadan scholars, who laboriously collected, and handed down to posterity in a systematic form, whatever it was possible to ascertain about the heathen mythology and ritual. Among these scholars a specially prominent place must be assigned to Hishām b. Muhammad al-Kalbī, usually known as Ibn al-Kalbī († 819–820 A.D.), the author of the 'Book of Idols' (*Kitāb al-aṣnām*), the substance of which is known to us in the form of quotations, though the work itself is no longer extant.* Finally, we have to take into consideration the fact that Muhammad incorporated in his religion a number of heathen practices and beliefs, with little or no modification, and also that various relics of heathenism, which are alien to orthodox Islām, have been retained by the Arabs down to the present day. That the adoption of a new faith does not completely transform popular beliefs, and that the old conceptions, disguised under somewhat different names, frequently persist, with or without the sanction of the religious authorities, is a matter of common observation.†

But, scanty as the evidence is, it suffices to show that Muhammad's contemporaries and the generations immediately preceding them were, as a rule, little influenced by their religion. They followed the religious customs of their ancestors out of mere respect for tradition, the genuine Arab being essentially conservative; but no great significance was attached to such things. Nowhere do we find an instance of real devotion to a heathen deity. The hardships of nomadic life—and it must be remembered that the great majority of the Arabs were nomads—are, in general, unfavourable to the development of religious feeling, as we may perceive even at the present day. Moreover, the leading spirits, without being clearly conscious of the fact, had to some extent outgrown the old religion, which, taken as a whole, was of a very low type; and, in addition to this, Jewish and Christian influences had begun to make themselves felt. Such influences are particularly evident in the case of some of the most famous poets, Nābigha and A'shā, for example, who had much intercourse with Arabian Christians, chiefly at the courts of princes on the northern frontier, where a more or less superficial Christianity prevailed. Hence the vehement opposition which Muhammad encountered is to be explained as due, partly to the dislike of a personal ruler and of any firm government whatsoever, partly to the desire of retaining certain material advantages which were inseparably connected with the local sanctuaries; but to suppose that the Arabs fought against the Prophet *on behalf of their religion* would be a mistake. Among his opponents no trace of heathen fanaticism appears. A marked tendency to religious fervour, and even to fanaticism, is generally characteristic of the Semites; among the Arabs of the period these capabilities existed in a latent condition, and were manifested on a great scale as soon as they had imbibed the new religion. Similarly, at the present time, Bedawîn, who are lukewarm about religion, no sooner adopt a settled mode of life than they become transformed into bigoted Muhammadans.

Of the deities who were worshipped in Arabia a long list might be drawn up. They are known to us chiefly through so-called 'theophorous' proper names, that is, names which describe the bearer as 'servant,' 'gift,' 'favour,' etc., of this or that deity. But as to the nature of the gods, these names do not tell us much. How little should we know of the more important Greek deities, if our information about them were derived, to a great extent, from such names as Ζηνόδοτος, Ποσειδώνιος,

* 1st ed. Berlin, 1887; 2nd ed. 1897. See the review in the *ZDMG* xli. 707 ff., by the author of the present article.

† In the first few centuries after the Christian era the Nabatæans and the other Arabs of the North-West wrote their inscriptions in Aramaic, but their Arabian nationality is proved, beyond doubt, by the names which they bore and by other indications. The Palmyrene inscriptions likewise contain many Arabic names; a large proportion of the Palmyrenes were unquestionably of Arabian origin, though they had probably in all cases become assimilated to the Aramæans. We possess very many Greek inscriptions set up by Arabs or Aramæans, at that period or later still. The inscriptions in the district of Ṣafā, to the south-east of Damascus, are in Arabic. Of these latter the author of the present article has not made an independent investigation, and he has accordingly followed the decipherments of Enno Littmann—see his 'Semitic Inscriptions' (New York, 1904), p. 102 ff., in Part iv. of the publication of an American Archæological Expedition to Syria in 1899 and 1900.

‡ Some references of this kind have been obscured by alterations of the text on the part of Muhammadans; in a few rare cases a verse has been transmitted to us both in its original and in its altered form. Fortunately this process of tampering with heathen passages was never carried out systematically. In dealing with the ancient poems, early Muhammadan philologists display an amount of historical and linguistic criticism which is worthy of great praise. This is shown, in particular, by the fact that they have handed down to us poems which contain virulent personal attacks upon the Prophet.

* See especially the *Geographical Dictionary* of Yāqūt († 1229 A.D.). The 'Book of Idols' was still extant in the time of the author of the *Ḫizānat al-adab* († 1682 A.D.), who quotes it independently.

† See, for example, Lucius, *Die Anfänge des Heiligenkults in der christlichen Kirche* (Tübingen, 1904), where the survival of ancient hero-worship, in the form of the veneration of martyrs, is elaborately proved.

'Απολλόδωρος, 'Αθηναγόρας, Θεοφάνης, etc.! It would therefore be futile to reproduce all this 'rubbish-heap of divine names,' as Wellhausen calls it. For the present we must confine our attention to those gods who are prominent in some respect or other, particularly by reason of the diffusion of their cult over a wide area. But of Arabian *mythology* there is very little to relate. The luxuriant imagination which gave birth to the mythologies of the Indo-European race was denied to the Arabs, nor had they anything at all resembling the highly artificial and somewhat prosaic theology and cosmology of ancient Babylonia.

This is not, of course, the place to discuss the origin of the religious sentiment among the Arabs, for if we attempted any such thing it would be necessary to inquire into the origin of religion itself. To deal with these obscure questions is a task which we must leave to others. But it may be not inappropriate to observe that the saying *Primus in orbe deos fecit timor* is, with some qualification, to be accepted as true.* At all events we cannot fail to notice that, even in later times, the dread inspired by the more mysterious phenomena of nature leads man to personify the powers that produce them, and such powers he timidly endeavours to conciliate. The *fear* of God afterwards assumes a nobler character, but nevertheless retains traces of its origin.† The Arabic terms *ittaqā* 'to be pious,' *taqwā* or *tuqā* 'piety,' *taqī* 'pious,' properly denote the idea of 'being on one's guard against' something; thus they presuppose that man must take pains to protect himself against the injury which would be inflicted upon him by the higher powers, if he did not continually strive to pacify them.‡ In primitive ages the relation between man and the deity was not regarded from a moral standpoint. It is true that in historical times the original meaning of *ittaqā*, *taqwā*, etc., as religious terms, was no longer clearly present to the minds of the Arabs. But the weird beings who were supposed to haunt the desert and the darkness had not ceased to inspire terror, and are still dreaded by the Bedawîn of to-day (see below, p. 670).

I. INDIVIDUAL GODS AND GODDESSES.

1. *THE HEAVENLY BODIES AND OTHER POWERS OF NATURE.*—It has often been supposed that the religion of the Arabs, or even of the Semites in general, is entirely based upon the worship of the heavenly bodies. This theory, however, is scarcely in accordance with the facts. That the Arabs, at a comparatively late period, worshipped the sun and other heavenly bodies, is unquestionable, but they had various other deities also who cannot be explained as astral powers. The Sun (*Shams*, construed as feminine) was honoured by several Arabian tribes with a sanctuary and an idol. The name *'Abd Shams*, 'servant of the Sun,' is found in many parts of the country.§ In the North we meet with the name *Amrishams* ('Αμρίσαμσος), 'man of the Sun.' According to Strabo, *Helios* was the chief god of Petra; but there he seems to have borne a different name (see below, p. 663).

For the worship of the rising Sun we have the evidence of the name *'Abd ash-Shāriq*, 'servant of the Rising One,' which, it is true, occurs only once. In the extreme South there was a god called *Dharīḥ* or *Dhirrīḥ*, which appears likewise to denote the rising Sun. In both of these cases the Sun is treated as masculine, contrary to the general usage. Once we meet with the name *'Abd Muḥarriq*; here *Muḥarriq*, 'the Burner,' may perhaps be another title of the Sun-god. The *Muḥarriq* who is mentioned as the ancestor of certain royal houses admits of a similar explanation.

The constellation of the Pleiades (*ath-Thuraiyā*), which was supposed to bestow rain, appears as a deity in the name *'Abd ath-Thuraiyā*; the name *'Abd Najm* probably refers also to the Pleiades, for the latter are often called simply *an-Najm*, 'the constellation.'

* For the contrary view see Robertson Smith, *Rel. Sem.*[2] p. 54 ff.

† The Greek σέβεσθαι likewise expresses primarily the notion of fright; see *Iliad*, iv. 242, xviii. 78, and esp. the Hymn to Demeter, 190, αἰδώς τε σέβας τε ἰδὲ χλωρὸν δέος.

‡ See a paper by the author of the present article in *ARW* i. (1898) p. 361 ff.; and cf. ἡ πρὸς (or περὶ) τὸ θεῖον εὐλάβεια, Plut. *Camillus*, 21, *Numa*, 22; also the μετὰ εὐλαβείας καὶ δέους of He 12[28].

§ This name is more widely diffused than would appear from the statements of Wellhausen, *Reste*[2], p. 10.

The evidence for the worship of Sirius (*ash-Shi'rā*) is not altogether above suspicion. Possibly the statements on the subject are mere inferences drawn from the Qur'ān, *Sūra* liii. 50, where God is called 'the Lord of Sirius'; this may have been interpreted as a condemnation of the belief that Sirius itself is a divine power.

Far more important, at least in historical times, was the cult of the planet Venus, revered as a great goddess under the name of **al-'Uzzā**, which may be rendered 'the Most Mighty.' The Syriac poet Isaac of Antioch, who lived in the first half of the 5th cent., bears witness to the worship of 'Uzzā by the Arabs of that period; in another passage he identifies 'Uzzā with the planet Venus. In the first half of the 6th cent., Mundhir, the Arab king of Ḥīra, sacrificed to 'Uzzā a large number of captive nuns, as we learn from a contemporary Syriac author. Procopius, also a contemporary, tells us that this same Mundhir slaughtered in honour of Aphrodite (*i.e.* 'Uzzā, the planet Venus) the captive son of his Christian rival, king Arethas (Ḥārith). The Arabian cult of the planet Venus is mentioned likewise by Ephraim Syrus (who died in A.D. 373), by Jerome, Theodoret, and later still by Evagrius. Nilus, about A.D. 410, gives us an account of a wild Arab tribe who offered sacrifices of a singularly barbarous kind to the morning star, doubtless under the name of 'Uzzā (see below). As early as the 2nd cent., or thereabouts, references to a priest of this goddess occur in two Sinaitic inscriptions, found not far from the district in which the scenes described by Nilus took place. Another Sinaitic inscription mentions the name *'Abd al-'Uzzā*, which at a later time, just before the rise of Islām, was extremely common among the Arabs.* The phrase 'by the two 'Uzzās,' used in swearing, presumably refers to Venus as the morning and as the evening star. In the same manner we may explain the two pillars or obelisks, called *al-Gharīyān*, 'the two objects smeared (with blood),' which appear in connexion with human sacrifices offered by a king of Ḥīra, the very place to which reference has been made above. 'Uzzā figures in the Qur'ān (*Sūra* liii. 19) as one of the three great goddesses of Mecca, who were supposed to be daughters of Allāh. That Muhammad himself offered sacrifices to her in his younger days is expressly stated by tradition. At Naḥla, near Mecca, this goddess had a sanctuary, which is said to have consisted only of three trees. Whether the Meccans and the other inhabitants of central Arabia at all realized the astral character of 'Uzzā is very doubtful. A deity is, in the eyes of its worshippers, an actual person, and does not necessarily represent anything else. We are not to suppose that the pious men who sacrificed to Apollo or Athene thought of inquiring what was the original significance of these deities as personifications of natural phenomena.

The expression 'by the Lord † of the blessed (*sa'īda*) 'Uzzā and by the god before whose house (*i.e.* the Ka'ba) Sarif ‡ lies' is once used by a poet as a form of oath. Hence Wellhausen very plausibly argues that the term *as-Sa'īda* 'the Blessed,' which occurs elsewhere as the name of a deity at Medina and of a sanctuary on the lower Euphrates, whither the Arabs made pilgrimages, is nothing more than an epithet of 'Uzzā which had come to be regarded as a proper name.

Kuthrā, which probably means 'the Most Rich,' the name of an idol destroyed by order of Muhammad, is perhaps only another title of 'Uzzā. We also read of a man called *'Abd Kuthrā*, belonging to the tribe of Ṭai, in the very centre of Arabia. Here the absence of the definite article proves that the name Kuthrā is ancient.

Qozaḥ was possibly at one time a god of storms.

* Finally, 'Uzzā has been found to be a goddess of the Sabæans too.

† This is probably a Muḥammadan correction for 'by the life.'

‡ Sarif is a place about 5½ miles from Mecca.

This we may infer from the fact that the rainbow is called in Arabic 'the bow of Qozaḥ,' and also from the use of Qozaḥ as the name of a certain spot, within the sacred territory of Mecca, where pilgrims were accustomed to kindle a fire. This god had once been worshipped by the Edomites, as we learn from Josephus (*Ant.* xv. 253 [Niese], where the name is spelt Κοζέ); but among the later Arabs he had lost all significance, and his cult does not seem to have survived anywhere.*

The Sun-god who, according to Strabo (784), was held in especial honour by the Nabatæans, is very probably to be identified with **Allāt**, as Wellhausen has pointed out. We have already seen that the sun is properly feminine in Arabic and in most other Semitic languages; hence the name *Allāt*, which, so far as we can judge, means simply 'the Goddess,' is particularly suitable in this case. The same goddess appears in Herod. i. 131, iii. 8, as Ἀλιλάτ, the older form of Allāt (cf. *Al'ilāh*, the older form of Allāh). In both passages Herodotus identifies her with Οὐρανίη. But from this we can infer no more than that she was a great celestial goddess; to regard it as a definite interpretation would be illegitimate. Similarly we find that in later times her worshippers identified her with Athene.† In the second passage Herodotus goes so far as to assert that Ἀλιλάτ and Ὀροτάλτ are the sole deities of Arabia; the latter name, which he describes as the equivalent of Dionysus, unfortunately does not admit of any plausible explanation. Thus Alilat must have occupied a very prominent place in the religion of those Arabs to whom Herodotus alludes, namely, the inhabitants of the Sinaitic Peninsula and of the immediate neighbourhood. That Ἀλιλάτ is identical with Allāt, a goddess frequently mentioned, has long been an acknowledged fact. References to Allāt are found in several Nabatæan inscriptions; in one of them she is called 'the Mother of the gods.' Moreover, proper names compounded with Allāt appear both among the Nabatæans and the Palmyrenes. In the inscriptions of Safā her name is spelt 'LT and perhaps HLT, which apparently should be pronounced *Hallāt*. Among the later Arabs this goddess was no less venerated. In the Qur'ān (*Sūra* liii. 19) she is one of the three daughters of Allāh. She is also mentioned occasionally in poetry. Thus one poet says: 'I swore to him, in the presence of the throng, by the salt, by the fire, and by Allāt, who is the greatest of all.' Of the names compounded with Allāt, which were widely diffused, some at least must be of considerable antiquity, since the first of the two component parts is an obsolete word.‡ The cult of the goddess flourished, in particular, at the sanctuary of Ṭā'if, a town to the east of Mecca; the tribe of Thaqif, who dwelt in that district, spoke of her as their 'mistress.' The tradition that she once was worshipped there has survived among the inhabitants down to the present day.

2. *ABSTRACT DEITIES.*—Some Arabian deities were originally personifications of abstract ideas, but they appear to have been conceived in a thoroughly concrete fashion. In particular, it is to be noticed that the Arabs, from a very early period, recognized the existence of certain powers on which human prosperity and adversity were supposed to depend. It is true that most of these beings are mere poetical, not real, personifications. Thus, for instance, Time in the abstract was popularly imagined to be the cause of all earthly happiness and especially of all earthly misery. Muhammad in the Qur'ān (*Sūra* xlv. 23) blames the unbelievers for saying, 'It is Time that destroys us.' The poets are continually alluding to the action of Time (*dahr*, *zamān*), for which they often substitute 'the days,' or 'the nights.' Time is represented as bringing misfortune, causing perpetual change, as biting, wearing down, shooting arrows that never miss the mark, hurling stones, and so forth.* In such cases we are often obliged to render 'time' by 'fate,' which is not quite correct, since time is here conceived as the determining factor, not as being itself determined by some other power, least of all by a conscious agent. But it must be admitted that the Arabs themselves do not always clearly distinguish the power of Time from that of Destiny pure and simple. Occasionally we come across such passages as the following: 'Time has brought woe upon him, for the days and the (allotted) measure (*qadar*) have caused him to perish.'† Or again: 'I submit not to the injustice of Time, and I behave as though unaware that the measure (allotted to me) hindered me from attaining aught.' Various other expressions are used by the poets in speaking of the 'portion' allotted to them, or of the goal that is set before them. The notion of a personified Μοῖρα is here vaguely present, but she has not yet become a living deity. The fatalism of the poets, as we might expect, is neither clearly formulated nor consistently carried out. Rigid dogmas on the subject of determinism and free-will were quite out of the question. Once we meet with the phrase 'till it be seen what the Apportioner shall apportion to thee' (*mā yamnī laka 'lmānī*), which apparently refers to a god; but this is an altogether exceptional case. The word here translated 'apportion' originally means 'to count,' hence 'to reckon' a thing to some one. From this root is derived *Manīya*, 'doom of death,' 'destruction,' a favourite expression with the poets; the plural *Manāyā* is used in the same sense. Manīya appears in poetry as driving man into the grave, piercing him with an arrow, handing to him the cup of death, lying in ambush for him, receiving him as a guest (when he is about to die), and so forth. Not unfrequently the possessive suffix is added, 'when my Manīya overtakes me,' 'his Manīya has come upon him,' and the like. We also find, but rarely, the synonymous forms *Manā* and *Manūn*, the latter derived from the cognate root MNN. These personifications, as we have seen, are merely poetical. But the same etymological group includes the ancient *Mĕnī* (Is 65^{11}), perhaps a Canaanite deity, and also the great goddess *Manāt*, who figures in the Qur'ān (*Sūra* liii. 20), by the side of 'Uzzā and Allāt, as one of the three 'daughters of Allāh' revered at Mecca. Since she had been raised long before to the dignity of a real goddess, we may assume that her worshippers were no longer conscious of her original character. Curiously enough, the two oldest documents which mention her, namely, a Nabatæan and a Latin inscription,‡ use the plural form *Manawāt* (spelt *Manavat* in Latin), just as the plural *Manāyā* is used for *Manīya*. Among the Arabs, Manāt had a sanctuary in the territory of the tribe Hudhail, not very far from Mecca. She was especially venerated by the inhabitants of Yathrib (afterwards called Medīna).

* The opinion of some native scholars that Qozaḥ was 'a Satan' is merely a deduction drawn from the name of the rainbow.

† The son and co-regent of Zenobia, *Wahballāt* (Οὐαβάλλαθος, Vabalathus), *i.e.* 'Gift of Allāt,' also calls himself Ἀθηνόδωρος.

‡ Among these names we must reckon *Taim Allāt*. *Taim* is not, as has been commonly supposed, a synonym of *'abd*, 'servant'; perhaps it should be rendered 'distraught,' 'frenzied,' so that *Taim Allāt* would mean 'frenzied by (or for the sake of) Allāt.'

* Many examples are given by W. L. Schrameier in his work, *Ueber den Fatalismus der vorislamischen Araber*, Einleitung (Bonn, 1881). But the list is very far from being exhaustive.

† With this it agrees that from the word *ḥīn*, 'moment of time,' 'brief period,' is formed the verb *ḥāna*, 'to be handed over to one's time,' 'to be doomed to death,' and also the substantive *ḥain*, 'death.'

‡ Referring to a soldier in Hungary who was of Palmyrene extraction (*CIL* iii. 7954).

Moreover, a number of proper names compounded with Manāt prove that her cult extended over a great part of Arabia.

There exists in Arabic a rare word for 'time,' namely, *'auḍ.** A poet, who belonged to the tribe of Bakr b. Wā'il, in the North East of Arabia, says in describing his old age: 'The arrows of 'Auḍ have pierced my limbs and joints.' This does not differ at all from those poetical personifications which have been enumerated above; the same poem, it may be observed in passing, alludes to 'the changes wrought by time' (*ṣurūf ad-dahr*). But an isolated verse, not unfrequently quoted, contains the phrase, 'I swear by the blood (of the sacrifices) that flows round 'Auḍ'; here 'Auḍ, 'time,' 'fate,' appears as a real deity, with a regular cult, and Ibn al-Kalbī expressly states that 'Auḍ was an idol worshipped by the Banū Bakr b. Wā'il, the very tribe of which the aforesaid poet was a member.

Gad, equivalent in meaning to τύχη but construed as masculine, is the name of a deity who was venerated by various Semitic peoples (see Is 65[11]). That the Israelite tribe of Gad derived its name from this cult is not improbable. The form *Gaddā*, which occurs in Nabatæan inscriptions, might appear to have been borrowed, at a comparatively late period, from the neighbouring Aramæans. But since we meet with the proper name *'Abd al-Jadd* in a few cases (which, it is true, are confined to the coast of Yemen), and since the noun *jadd*, 'luck,' remained in current use among the Arabs, it is more natural to regard the Nabatæan *Gaddā* as an Aramaized form of the native Arabic word *al-Gadd* (*al-Jadd*).

To this category belongs **Sa'd**, 'fortune' (used in a good sense only). According to a certain verse and the statements of the commentator, Sa'd was the name given to a rock not far from Jidda, to which divine honours were paid. Moreover, we meet with the name *'Abd Sa'd* in quite a different part of Arabia, to the north-east. At an earlier period a man's name which seems to be compounded with Sa'd occurs in the inscriptions of Ṣafā.

Another deity who appears to have been designated by an abstract term is **Ruḍā**, 'good-will,' 'favour.' The commentary on a verse in which the name is mentioned informs us that Ruḍā was worshipped, in the shape of an idol, by the great tribe of Tamīm. The proper name *'Abd Ruḍā* is found among several Arabian tribes. To the nature of the deity in question the name supplies no clue. It might even be supposed that it was originally a euphemistic title given to some malignant power. The remarkable fact that in the above-mentioned verse *Ruḍā* is construed as feminine (whereas this grammatical form would be normally masculine), naturally suggests that at that period, about the time of Muhammad, people still realized that *Ruḍā* was merely an epithet applied to a goddess who properly bore some other name. But against this hypothesis it may be urged that the name is of considerable antiquity, as is proved by the Palmyrene inscriptions, where it occurs separately in the form 'RṢU, and in theophorous proper names as RṢU; the pronunciation is fixed approximately by the Latin transcription *Themarsa*.† The RḌU of the Ṣafā inscriptions seems to denote the same deity.

Wadd, also pronounced *Wudd* or *Udd*, *i.e.* 'friendship,' 'affection,'‡ was, according to the Qur'ān (*Sūra* lxxi. 22), a god worshipped by the contemporaries of Noah. But it would be a mistake to conclude that his cult was obsolete in Muhammad's time, for we have sufficient evidence to the contrary. The poet Nābigha says once, 'Wadd greet thee!' There was a statue of this god at Dūma, a great oasis in the extreme north of Arabia. The name *'Abd Wadd* occurs in a number of wholly distinct tribes. But Wadd is another instance of a deity whose character remains altogether obscure. As we are told that his statue had a bow and arrows attached to it, we might be tempted to imagine that he was a kind of Eros, and this would imply a foreign origin. But though the root WDD means 'to love,' 'to feel affection' for an object, it is never used in a sexual sense.* Moreover, the statue in question bore not only a bow and arrows, but likewise a sword and a lance from which hung a flag; the god was also fully clad, and therefore does not look like a copy of the Greek Eros. Finally, it should be remembered that there were other Arabian idols which had weapons suspended to them.

* It is used chiefly as an adverb, meaning 'at any time.'

† *CIL* viii. 2511, 2512. A similar form is given by Syriac authorities.

‡ That we should take the word as an adjective, meaning 'friendly,' is a less probable view.

The name **Manāf**, 'height,' 'high place,' is also a kind of abstract noun. That Manāf was worshipped as a god is proved by the testimony of a verse, and is confirmed by the occurrence of the name *'Abd Manāf*, which was especially common at Mecca and among the neighbouring tribe of Hudhail. Furthermore, J. H. Mordtmann has pointed out that the word Μάναφις, in an inscription from the Ḥaurān, is derived from the name of this god (=Μανάφιος); he also makes the very plausible suggestion that, in an inscription set up in Hungary by an Oriental soldier, the sentence *diis patriis* MN · PHO† *et Theandrio votum solvit* is to be understood as a reference to the same deity.‡

3. *DEITIES BEARING NAMES OF ANIMALS.*—The Arabian deities who bear animal names are few in number, and it is naturally impossible for us to ascertain their true significance. That they were originally totems is scarcely probable, for of totemism no clear traces are to be found among the Arabs, and the hypothesis that these names date from a very primitive age does not rest on sufficient evidence.§ In the case of the Lion-god, whose existence is proved only by the mention of a man named *'Abd al-Asad*, 'servant of the Lion,' belonging to the tribe of Quraish, such a supposition would be especially hazardous, since *asad* is a comparatively modern word for 'lion,' not the old word common to the various Semitic languages.‖

One of the gods worshipped by the contemporaries of Noah, according to the Qur'ān (*Sūra* lxxi. 23), was **Nasr**, 'the vulture.'¶ The Talmud (*'Abodah zara*, 11*b*) and the Syriac *Doctrine of Addai* (of the 4th cent.), p. 24, mention *Neshrā*, the Aramaic form of Nasr, as an Arabian god. These statements, taken by themselves, might be explained as referring to some cult practised among the Aramæans in the Roman province of

* For the idea of sexual affection the Arabic language has plenty of other expressions.

† This is the reading now adopted, see *CIL* iii. 3668; *Ephem. Epigr.* ii. 390, No. 22. We may assume that the original spelling, or at least the spelling originally intended, was MANAPHO. Mordtmann had before him the incorrect form MANALPHO, which rendered the identification all the more difficult.

‡ *ZDMG* xxix. 106. The god Theandrios (with some variations of form) occurs repeatedly in inscriptions from the Ḥaurān. What Oriental name lurks under this Greek disguise we cannot say.

§ This point has been discussed by the author of the present article in the *ZDMG* xl. 156 ff., and in his *Beiträge zur semit. Sprachwissenschaft* (Strassburg, 1904), p. 74.

‖ Viz. *laith*.

¶ This is the meaning which the word always has in Arabic. In the North-Semitic languages the corresponding form (with *sh*) is applied to the eagle, but, in the case of large birds of prey, popular usage does not sharply discriminate between the various species. Even in the NT (Mt 24[28], Lk 17[37]) carrion vultures are called ἀετοί.

Arabia, since elsewhere we undoubtedly meet with an Aramæan god Neshrā, for instance, in the Syriac proper name *Neshryabh*, 'Neshr has given.' But it is to be noticed that the Sabæans likewise had a god called Nasr. Thus the worship of the Vulture-god was once widely diffused over the Semitic lands; in Arabia, however, it became nearly obsolete. Ibn al-Kalbī was unable to find any personal name compounded with Nasr; nevertheless it is not impossible that the Νεσραῖος mentioned in the ancient inscription of Memphis * was an Arab.

'Auf, in the fairly common name *'Abd 'Auf*, means 'the great bird (of prey).' This signification, it is true, does not actually occur in Arabic, but there are certain phrases in which a trace of it remains.† *'Auf* has, in particular, the sense of *augurium*, and it may be that the name of the god did not refer to the bird but to the omen drawn from it; in this case, 'Auf would be a synonym of *Sa'd* (see above).

4. *DEITIES NAMED AFTER PLACES.*—The god **Dhu 'sh-Sharā**, 'pertaining to ash-Sharā,' seems to have derived his name from a place. But there were several places called *ash-Sharā*, and the difficulty of determining with which of them the god was originally connected is increased by the fact that his cult goes back to very early times. The localities which bore this name appear to have been moist and rich in vegetation; such a spot, in the midst of a sterile country like Arabia, easily became a centre of worship. The inscriptions of the Nabatæans and of the neighbouring peoples not infrequently mention a deity whose name is spelt Δουσάρης in Greek; there is a corresponding Semitic form, and the theophorous names *'Abd Dhū Sharā*, *Taim Dhū Sharā* (Sinaitic), Δουσάριος also occur. Greek authors ‡ supply us with some information respecting him. The most important of these statements is that at Petra, the Nabatæan capital, he was worshipped in the form of a four-cornered block of unhewn black stone, 4 feet in height and 2 in width. The blood of sacrificial victims was poured upon it, or in front of it; underneath it stood a golden pedestal, and the whole sanctuary blazed with gold and with votive offerings. According to Epiphanius, the festival of Dusares was celebrated at Petra and the neighbouring town of Elusa on the 25th of December, that is to say, about the time of the winter solstice. This we may accept as true; it indicates, no doubt, a connexion with Sun-worship.§ In the district which formed the centre of his cult, Dusares was identified with Dionysus; hence it is natural to regard him as the patron of luxuriant vegetation, which agrees with the fact that his home was at ash-Sharā. Nor does this view at all conflict with his character as a Sun-god. The interpretation which Greek authors obtain by changing Δουσάρης into Θευσάρης, and treating the latter form as equivalent to Θεὸς Ἄρης, has, of course, no value. Among the later Arabs *Dhu 'sh-Sharā* did not occupy a prominent position. He was represented by an idol in the territory inhabited by the tribe of Daus, not far from Mecca, and among them the proper name *'Abd dhi 'sh-Sharā* still survived.

Another god who appears to have been named after a place is **Dhu 'l-Ḥalaṣa** or *Dhu 'l-Ḥulaṣa*. He was greatly venerated at a place in the north of Yemen, apparently the district now called 'Asīr. Between his sanctuary and the sanctuary at Mecca there existed a certain amount of rivalry.

5. *DEITIES NAMED AFTER LIMBS OF THE BODY.*—From a grammatical point of view, the gods **Dhu 'l-kaffain**, 'He who has two hands,' and **Dhu 'r-rijl**, 'He who has a foot,' must be classed with the two foregoing ones. Perhaps these names may have been originally applied to sacred stones or fetishes, which by means of rude carving were made to bear a partial resemblance to the human form.

6. *ANCESTRAL AND TRIBAL DEITIES.*—Sometimes Arabian deities are designated by titles fashioned after the manner of 'the God of Abraham,' 'the God of Nahor' (Gn 31[53]). Thus among the Nabatæans we meet with 'the god of Rab'ēl,' 'the god of Qaṣīū,' and the phrase Θεῷ Μαλειχάθου occurs in an inscription which mentions also a man named Μαλείχαθος (Malīkat), not to quote other instances. Similarly, Muhalhil b. Rabī'a swears by 'the god of Rabī'a'; perhaps *Rabī'a* here refers not to the father of Muhalhil, but to the great group of tribes called Rabī'a, to which he belonged. This would be after the analogy of the formula 'by the god of the Quraish,' which occurs elsewhere.

Here we may mention a god who bore the curious title **Shai' al-qaum** (apparently 'the Companion of the people'), as we learn from a Palmyrene and a Nabatæan inscription. In the former he is called 'the kind god who rewards (or, who is grateful), and who drinks no wine,' *i.e.* to whom no libations of wine are offered. In the Ṣafā inscriptions he appears as Sh'HQM, which should probably be read *Shē' haqōm*.

7. *OTHER DEITIES OF THE TIME OF NOAH.*—The god **Yaghūth**, whose name evidently means 'Helper,' was, according to the Qur'ān (*Sūra* lxxi. 23), another of the deities worshipped in the time of Noah. Unless we are willing to adopt the very hazardous conjecture of Robertson Smith, who identifies Yaghūth with Yĕ'ūsh,* an ancestor of the Edomites mentioned more than once in Gn 36 and elsewhere in the OT, we find no trace of this god in early times, for his namesake Ἰεγοῦθος, a man who figures in the above-mentioned inscription of Memphis, cannot be cited as a proof. But at a later period we hear of a god Yaghūth, whose idol was an object of contention among the tribes of northern Yemen, and the name *'Abd Yaghūth* occurs in various parts of Arabia, even in the tribe of Taghlib on the north-eastern frontier.

The name of the god **Ya'ūq**, who is mentioned in the Qur'ān together with Yaghūth, probably means 'the Preserver'; his cult seems to have been confined to Yemen. **Suwā'**, who is also included among the gods worshipped by Noah's contemporaries (*Sūra* lxxi. 20), was apparently of no great importance. He had a sanctuary at a place in the territory of the Hudhail, but none, so far as we know, elsewhere. The meaning of his name is altogether obscure. Neither Suwā' nor Ya'ūq seems to occur in theophorous proper names. It is hardly necessary to remark that the transferring of all these Arabian deities to the age of Noah was a fantastic anachronism due to Muhammad himself.

8. *HUBAL.*—**Hubal** was worshipped at Mecca; his idol stood in the Ka'ba, and he appears to have been, in reality, the god of that sanctuary. It is therefore particularly unfortunate that we have so little information respecting him. Wellhausen has plausibly suggested that Hubal is no other than *Allāh*, 'the god' of the Meccans. It would be unsafe to trust the descriptions of the idol in question which are given by writers of a later

* This inscription dates from the 2nd cent. B.C.; see the *RA* for Feb. 1870, p. 109 ff., and *Cat. gén. des. Ant. Ég. du Musée de Caire* (Gr. inscr.), Oxford, 1905. It is a curious coincidence that among the names here enumerated we find the Greek Ἀετός.

† Thus the verb *'āfa*, which is derived from it, means 'to wheel in the air,' as birds of prey are wont to do.

‡ See the excellent paper by J. H. Mordtmann in the *ZDMG* xxix. 99 ff.

§ Cf. Wellhausen in *GGN*, 1905, p. 131.

* The correct pronunciation is, perhaps, *Yā'ish* or *Yā'is* (with *sīn*); we may assume that originally the name was always spelt Y'Sh, without any vowel-letter after the '.

period; there is reason, however, to believe that the god had a human form. We may likewise accept as historical the statement that near him were kept divining-arrows, used for the purpose of ascertaining his will or forecasting future events. It is related that the idol was brought by ʿAmr b. Luḥai from Maʾāb (Moab), a tradition which may contain some element of truth, for we have independent evidence indicating that this god was known in the North. He seems to be mentioned in a Nabatæan inscription at Ḥejr; and the tribe of Kalb, who dwelt in the Syrian Desert, used *Hubal* as the name of a person or clan; the same tribe, it may be noticed in passing, used in like manner the names of Isāf and Nāʾila, two other deities peculiar to Mecca. Moreover, ʿAmr b. Luḥai is the representative of the Ḥuzāʿa, a tribe who, according to tradition, occupied the sacred territory of Mecca before it passed into the hands of the Quraish. The assertion that ʿAmr introduced the worship of idols into Mecca for the first time is, of course, utterly incredible. But the hypothesis that Hubal was a late importation from a foreign country is further supported by the fact that we hear nothing of him in other parts of Arabia, and that even at Mecca personal names compounded with *Hubal* were unknown. When the Meccans had gained a victory over the Prophet in the immediate neighbourhood of Medīna, their leader shouted, 'Hurrah for Hubal!' Thus they regarded him as the natural enemy of the God preached by Muhammad.

9. 'LORD' AND 'GOD.'—Here we may notice certain deities whose titles in themselves seem to designate them as occupying a position of supreme importance in the eyes of their worshippers. Among these is **al-Malik**, 'the King,' a name which corresponds to the North-Semitic *Malek* (not to mention other forms)* as applied to a god; in Arabia, however, al-Malik is represented only by the rare personal name ʿ*Abd al-Malik*.†

The divine title **Baʿl** or **Baʿal**, 'the Lord,' which was very common among the Northern Semites, survived among the Arabs of the Sinai Peninsula in the form *al-Baʿlū*, which occurs in their inscriptions together with the proper names ʿ*Abd al-Baʿlī*, *Aus al-Baʿlī* 'gift of the Lord,' and *Garm al-Baʿlī*, probably 'act of the Lord.' A trace of the worship of this god may be found in *Sharaf al-Baʿl*, the name of a place which lay somewhere on the route between Medīna and Syria. The Arabs of later times were not aware that any such deity had existed, but certain phrases in their language clearly prove that he had once been known. Thus the term 'soil of *Baʿl*,' or simply '*Baʿl*,' is applied to land which does not require rain or artificial irrigation, but has an underground water supply, and therefore yields fruit of the best quality.‡ In this case the god seems to be regarded as the lord of the cultivated land. That here the word *Baʿl* really refers to him is shown by the synonymous, or nearly synonymous, expression ʿ*aththarī*, derived from ʿ*Aththar*, a deity whose name had likewise sunk into oblivion among the Arabs of that period, whereas it appears in all the older Semitic languages with the usual variations of form (ʿ*Ashtart*, ʿ*Athtar*, and so forth). Again, the verb *baʿila* and other derivatives of *Baʿl* mean 'to be bewildered,' properly 'to be seized by the god *Baʿl*.'

Among the Northern Arabs of early times, particularly in the region of Ṣafā, the word **Ēl**, 'God,' was still very commonly used as a separate name

of the Deity. It is true that it does not actually occur except in compound proper names of persons, Οὐάδδηλος, *Wahb Ēl*, and many others. Some of these, such as *Wahbīl*, 'gift of Ēl,' ʿ*Abdīl*, 'servant of Ēl,' appear also among the Arabs of a later age, but at least in certain cases they must have been borrowed from the Sabæan language,* while in other cases they are restricted to the extreme north of Arabia. It may be added that the divine name *Iyāl*, which occurs once in an ancient verse, is possibly a plural of majesty formed from *Ēl*; *Uwāl* is a variation of the same name.

Allāh, in the Ṣafā inscriptions *Hallāh*, 'the god,' enters into the composition of numerous personal names among the Nabatæans and other Northern Arabs of an early period, e.g. *Zaid Allāhī*, 'increase of God' (that is, increase of the family through the son given by God), ʿ*Abd Allāhī*, and so forth. In the Nabatæan inscriptions *Allāh* does not seem to occur separately as the name of a god, but in the inscriptions of Ṣafā the separate use is found. Among the heathen Arabs of later times *Allāh* is extremely common, both by itself and in theophorous names. Wellhausen cites a large number of passages in which pre-Islāmic Arabs mention Allāh as a great deity; and even if we strike out some passages (for instance, on the ground that the text has been altered by Muhammadan scribes), so many still remain over, and so many more which are quite above suspicion can without difficulty be found, that the fact is clearly established. Moreover, *Allāh* forms an integral part of various idiomatic phrases which were in constant use among the heathen Arabs. Of special importance is the testimony of the Qurʾān, which proves, beyond all doubt, that the heathen themselves regarded Allāh as the Supreme Being. Thus, men turn to Allāh when they are in distress (*Sūra* x. 23, xxix. 65, xxxi. 31). Solemn oaths are sworn in his name (vi. 109, xvi. 40, xxxv. 40). He is recognized by mankind as the Creator and the Giver of rain (xxix. 61 ff.). Their crime consists only in the fact that they worship other gods beside him; the three goddesses, Manāt, Allāt, and ʿUzzā are believed to be his daughters (xvi. 59 ff.).

In the Nabatæan inscriptions we repeatedly find the name of a deity accompanied by the title *Alāhā*, 'the god.' Hence Wellhausen argues that the Arabs of a later age may also have applied the epithet *Allāh*, 'the god,' to a number of different deities, and that in this manner Allāh, from being a mere appendage to the name of a great god, may gradually have become the proper name of the Supreme God. In any case it is an extremely important fact that Muhammad did not find it necessary to introduce an altogether novel deity, but contented himself with ridding the heathen Allāh of his 'companions,' subjecting him to a kind of dogmatic purification, and defining him in a somewhat clearer manner. Had he not been accustomed from his youth to the idea of Allāh as the Supreme God, in particular of Mecca, it may well be doubted whether he would ever have come forward as the preacher of Monotheism.

II. THE NATURE OF THE GODS.

As to the manner in which the Arabs conceived of their gods, the theophorous proper names give us some information, though it does not go very far. We have, of course, to remember not only that the persons who coined these names naturally wished to be on the best possible terms with the deities in question, and to approach them in the most conciliatory fashion, but also that later generations, who made use of ancient names, did not pay much attention

---

* *Amlăk*, the plural of majesty, formed from this noun, is used in Ethiopic as the ordinary word for 'God.'

† In the days of Islām, *al-Malik* became one of the epithets of Allāh, and hence the name ʿ*Abd al-Malik* re-appears among Muhammadans.

‡ This applies primarily to the date-palm, which requires much moisture at its root but none above.

* Names commonly used in dynasties, or distinguished families, who originally came from districts where Sabæan or some other peculiar dialect of southern Arabic was spoken, naturally had a tendency to spread among the Arabs in general.

to the original meaning;* hence it may be concluded that, when Muhammad first proclaimed his mission, popular ideas as to the relation between gods and men had already begun to grow dim. It is also to be noticed that, in consequence of the abbreviations which names of persons are liable to undergo in daily life, compound proper names were often deprived of their divine element; thus *Aus Manāt*, 'gift of Manāt'; *Zaid Allāt*, 'increase (bestowed) by Allāt'; *'Abd Allāh*, 'servant of God,' became *Aus*, 'gift'; *Zaid*, 'increase'; *'Abd*, 'servant,' respectively. In theophorous proper names the deity sometimes appears as a lord, while the human individual is his servant, his handmaid, his obedient subject (*ṭau'*); sometimes, again, the deity is described as gracious, while the human individual is his gift, his reward, his act of favour, the aid which he supplies, his *protégé* who seeks refuge with him, etc. At other times the deity is represented as increasing the family, as sending a good omen and good fortune. The human individual is also said to be the 'man' of the deity, his 'companion,' and so forth. Some of these compounds are of doubtful meaning. With the exception of a very small number of uncertain cases found in inscriptions, there are absolutely no names which designate a human being as the kinsman or descendant of a deity, like those which we find among the Hebrews and other Semites.†

III. THE CULT.

1. *IDOLS, ALTARS, AND SACRIFICES.*—It has already been remarked that the scantiness of our knowledge respecting the Arabian gods is largely due to the fact that our information dates, for the most part, from the close of the heathen period, that is to say, from a time when the Arabs themselves had no very clear ideas on this subject. The traditional cult was duly practised; but mythology, not to mention religious dogma, could scarcely be said to exist. Even as to the fundamental question of the relation in which the Deity stood to the *sacred stones, idols, and other objects of worship*, no definite belief seems to have prevailed. If the heathen Arabs reflected about such matters at all, they probably imagined that the block of stone which served as a fetish (after the primeval Semitic fashion so clearly portrayed in the OT) was pervaded by a divine power, and, in its turn, exercised a divine influence. We have already had occasion to mention the black stone of Dusares at Petra; to this, it would appear, Clement of Alexandria alludes when he says that 'the Arabs worship stone' (*Protr.* iv. § 46). The veneration of the black stone in the wall of the Ka'ba has been adopted even by Islām; and, as Snouck Hurgronje has shown,‡ there exist in Mecca and the immediate neighbourhood various other sacred stones, which were originally fetishes, but have acquired a superficially Muhammadan character by being brought into connexion with certain holy persons. Stones of this kind served at the same time as *altars*; the blood of the victims was poured over them or smeared upon them,§ an act whereby the worshipper entered into communion with the god to whom the drink-offering of blood was presented. Upright blocks or slabs of stone (στῆλαι) formed an essential part of the cult; the Arabic equivalent of στήλη is *nuṣub* (pl. *anṣāb*), also *manṣib* (Heb. *maṣṣēbāh*). As early as the time of Herodotus, our oldest authority, the Arabs were accustomed to establish a blood-brotherhood by smearing sacred stones with their own blood, while they invoked the god and the goddess (iii. 8). Examples of a similar use of blood, in the solemn ratification of a treaty or in the swearing of an oath, occur at a much later period.* The blood is licked, or the hands are dipped in it; sometimes water or a perfumed liquid is employed as a substitute.†

A detailed account of a kind of sacrifice, performed about A.D. 410, is given by Nilus (Migne, lxxi. 612 ff.). The wild 'Saracens' of Arabia Petræa, he tells us, had no image of a god, but only an altar rudely built of stones,‡ on which they sacrificed, in great haste, a human being or a white camel to the morning-star (*i.e.* Venus, or 'Uzzā; see above, p. 660) before sunrise, evidently in order that the star might be visibly present during the whole ceremony. Thrice they marched round the sacred spot, chanting a hymn; then the chieftain, or an aged priest, struck the first blow at the victim, and drank some of the blood, whereupon the crowd, rushing forward, devoured the animal, raw and only half-flayed, together with the bones and entrails, before the sun appeared.§ One of the most peculiar features in this description is the drinking of the blood; in other cases, the Arabs, like the ancient Hebrews, allowed the blood of the victim to flow away, giving back the element of life to the deity, or else they applied it directly to the idol.

As is stated above, the Arabs of Petræa sacrificed not only animals, but also *human beings*; the son of Nilus was on the point of being slaughtered in honour of the morning-star, and escaped by a mere accident. Testimony of a somewhat earlier date is supplied by Porphyry, who tells us (*de Abstin.* ii. 56) that 'the people of Duma,‖ in Arabia,' annually sacrificed a boy and buried him under the altar, which served also as an idol (ξόανον); here we have another instance of the same object being used for both purposes. The vast human sacrifices offered, at a later period, by king Mundhir of Ḥīra to the planet Venus, the goddess to whom Nilus also refers, have already been mentioned.¶ But in Arabia proper we have no clear trace of human sacrifice.** Possibly among the Arabs of the extreme North, the continuance, or it may be the revival, of the ghastly ancient rite was due to the influence of the neighbouring peoples, whose religion had remained barbarous in spite of their advanced material civilization.

At the period to which our principal authorities relate, the Arabs sacrificed *camels, sheep, goats, and apparently less often kine.*†† We frequently

* These remarks, and many of those which follow, apply to other peoples also, both Semitic and non-Semitic.

† On all these questions see the art. 'Names' in *EBi*, p. 3271 ff. (by the author of the present article); and Littmann, *Oriental Inscriptions*, p. 121 ff.

‡ *Mekka*, i. (Hague, 1888) p. 21.

§ Very similar rites exist among other nations, *e.g.* in Bengal—see the *JRAS of Bengal* for 1903, Anthropol. Series, p. 82 ff. For blood ritual in Syria and Arabia, from heathen times to the present day, see Curtiss, *Prim. Sem. Rel. To-day* (London, 1902). Cf. also Musil, *Arabia Petræa*, iii. (Vienna, 1908); and Tauzzen, *Coutumes des Arabes au pays du Moab* (Paris, 1908).

* Count Landberg, *La Langue arabe et ses dialectes* (Leyden, 1905), p. 74, mentions a remarkable specimen of blood-ritual which is still practised in a certain district of South Arabia at the conclusion of a contract of service.

† The anointing of fetishes, as we find it in Gn 28^{18}, and as it appears elsewhere, both among the Northern Semites and other peoples, is likewise to be considered a secondary form of homage.

‡ Similarly, at an earlier period, the altar in the sacred palm-grove, probably near the southern extremity of the Sinaitic Peninsula, was ἐκ στερεοῦ λίθου, according to Agatharchides, cited by Diodorus, iii. 42.

§ In like manner the 'Aisāwa, a Muhammadan confraternity existing at the present day in the district of Tlemsen, Algeria, perform a religious rite in the course of which they devour a he-goat raw, with the skin and hair—see Doutté, *Les Aïssâoua à Tlemçen* (Châlons-sur-Marne, 1900), p. 13. This must be a piece of primitive African savagery; it was certainly not imported from Arabia. But there is reason to believe that similar things took place in the paroxysms of excitement which accompanied the Dionysiac cult. The *Bacchæ* of Euripides contains no very precise evidence on the subject.

‖ Probably not the oasis Dūmat al-jandal, where Wadd was worshipped (see above, p. 662), but Dūma in the Ḥaurān, which was included in the province of Arabia.

¶ These sacrifices may be compared with the savage custom of 'devoting' vanquished enemies, which was in vogue among the ancient Hebrews (see, for instance, Nu 21^3, Dt 2^{34}, Jos 2^{10}, 1 S 15^8).

** The word *hadī*, 'conducted,' cannot be cited as an argument. When applied to a single individual, it denotes a prisoner, a person who is under the protection of another, or a bride who is brought to her husband. When applied to sacrificial victims, it is always a collective, the singular being then *hadīya*. Thus it would not be correct to say that a prisoner is called a 'victim.'

†† The most usual words for animals offered in sacrifice are *'itr* and *'atīra*; hence we may conclude that the Heb. *ha'tīr*, 'to entreat,' *ne'tar*, 'to be moved by entreaty,' originally referred to sacrifice, accompanied by prayer, and to the effect which it produces on the deity.

read of the blood of the victims being applied to the sacred stone or pillar. The number of the animals slaughtered must sometimes have been very large, since the poets hyperbolically compare warriors slain in battle to a multitude of sacrificial victims. Offerings of other kinds are rarely mentioned. On one occasion we hear of a *milk-offering*, presented to the god Wadd (see above, p. 662), and another passage refers to an oblation consisting of barley and wheat over which milk was poured. Most of the Arabs being very poor, these less pretentious kinds of offering may perhaps in ordinary life have played a larger part than we should at first be inclined to suppose. But the words *nusuk*, *manāsik*, 'outpouring,' which are applied to religious ceremonies in general, and have become part of the terminology of Islām, certainly do not refer, in the first instance, to drink-offerings of this sort (as is the case with the Hebrew *nesekh*), but to the outpouring of blood. The flesh of the sacrifice was usually eaten by the worshippers, the god contenting himself with the blood. Sometimes, however, sacrifices were left to be devoured by vultures; hence a certain idol which stood in the neighbourhood of the Ka'ba was called *muṭ'im aṭ-ṭair*, 'the feeder of the birds (of prey).' In this case the god was probably imagined to be—through human instrumentality, it is true—an example of those virtues which the Arabs place above all others, namely, hospitality and munificence. But originally every sacrifice, properly so called, was regarded as food consumed by the god, or at least as a means of gratifying his sensations.* Thus the sacrificial meal brought the worshipper into close connexion with the Deity.

The Arabs, like the Hebrews, were in the habit of sacrificing *the firstlings of their flocks and herds*. But how far the custom extended it is impossible to say.† Soon after the birth of an infant, his head was shaven, and a sheep was sacrificed on his behalf; perhaps this was originally a ransom, offered as a substitute for the sacrifice of the child.

We may here mention a totally different kind of offering, namely, the practice of *setting an animal at liberty*, either in fulfilment of a vow or as an expression of gratitude to the deity for the increase of the flock; thenceforth the animal in question was not to be used for any purpose, except perhaps by needy travellers who might be allowed to milk it. Of these consecrated animals there were various sorts, each denoted by a distinct term. But as to the precise meaning of the terms, no trustworthy information was possessed by later scholars, since the Qur'ān had abolished these customs, together with the religion of which they formed a part. It is probable that the animals to which we have referred pastured in districts sacred to the deity, and generally were held inviolable.

The practice of *marching round the sanctuary* on the occasion of a sacrifice, as the Saracens described by Nilus were wont to do, prevailed in many parts of Arabia. Sometimes, at least in Mecca, this marching took place also when no sacrifice was being offered. It would seem that among the Arabs of later times *the solemn shout* (*tahlīl*) corresponded, in some measure, to the 'hymn' of the early Saracens. We may be sure that what the Qur'ān contemptuously calls 'whistling and clapping' (*Sūra* viii. 35) was not confined to the Meccan sanctuary.* The act of standing (*'ukūf*) in a devout posture before the sacred stone or image likewise formed an essential part of the ritual.

In addition to these traditional forms, there were other means of influencing the gods, namely, extemporized prayers, requests for special favours, benedictions, and, above all, imprecations. The effect of an imprecation was heightened by its being uttered in a sacred month and at a sacred spot, for instance, in the month of Dhu 'l-qa'da at 'Okāẓ.

We have already seen that the gods were represented not only by rude blocks of stone, but also by *statues* executed with more or less skill. The most usual word for a divine statue, whether of stone or wood, is *ṣanam*, derived from the Aramaic *ṣĕlĕm*, and perhaps introduced into Arabia together with the object itself. The other word, *wathan*, is certainly indigenous, and seems primarily to mean nothing more than 'stone.'†

Examples of *tree-worship* are likewise to be found among the Arabs. The tree known as *Dhāt Anwāṭ*, 'that on which things are hung,' received divine honours; weapons and other objects were suspended from it. We also hear of a sacred palm-tree which was decked with apparel. At Naḥla, as has been mentioned above (p. 660), the goddess 'Uzzā is said to have been worshipped in the form of three trees. We may assume that the deity was supposed to stand in the same relation to the tree as to the fetishes of stone. The garments, rags, and other things which were placed upon it are to be regarded as a substitute for sacrifice.‡

The *kindling of a fire* in honour of a god was quite exceptional among the Arabs. It took place in connexion with the great festival of the pilgrimage, at the spot called Qozaḥ; moreover, the term *as-Sa'īr*, which occurs in an ancient verse of poetry referring to some particular cult, may not improbably be explained as meaning 'fire,' 'blaze,' in accordance with the ordinary use of the word, rather than as the name of a god, although the latter interpretation might seem, at first sight, to suit the context.

2. *PLACES OF WORSHIP*.—Temples, properly so called, were certainly very rare, unless we include buildings in the Græco-Roman style erected by the Arabs of the extreme North. The primitive simplicity of the Ka'ba, which was held in such especial honour, proves that the sanctuaries of Arabia are by no means to be imagined as imposing edifices. The three temples which stood, according to Agatharchides (Diod. iii. 45), on a hill near the Arabian seacoast, may have been somewhat handsomer specimens of architecture, but it would seem that they were built by a foreign prince, probably a Sabæan. Yet in spite of their humble appearance, the houses of the gods were regarded with extreme veneration, as is shown by the proper names *'Abd ad-dār*, 'servant of the (holy) dwelling' (the ancestor of the family who were actually in charge of the temple at Mecca); *'Abd al-bait*, 'servant of the (holy) house'; and *'Abd al-Ka'ba*, 'servant of the Ka'ba.'§ The word *masjid*, 'mosque,' 'temple,' which has become part of the terminology of Islām, was originally derived from the

* Hence, wherever human sacrifices are offered—and this can be proved to have been the case among almost all peoples—we may assume that in the very earliest times cannibalism also existed. The idea that sacrifices are consumed by the gods appears, for instance, in Dt 32^{38}, but it is entirely rejected in Ps 50^{9-13}.

† The remarkable, but well attested, statement that the Arabs considered it unlucky if the firstborn of a woman was a boy, may perhaps be explained as a survival from a time when they, like the Hebrews, offered to the deity their own firstborn, as well as the firstborn of animals. That the father should have been specially unwilling to sacrifice a boy is natural.

* Robertson Smith very justly remarks (*Rel. Sem.*^{2} p. 340, note 2): 'The festal song of praise (חלל, *tahlīl*) properly goes with the dance round the altar (Ps $26^{6ff.}$), for in primitive times song and dance are inseparable.'

† As to the distinction in meaning between these two expressions the native authorities supply no trustworthy information.

‡ Sacred trees, to which rags are attached, exist in Arabia at the present day, and still more frequently in Syria. They are found in other countries also, but the rites connected with them present many difficulties of interpretation. On tree-worship in general see Frazer, *Golden Bough*^{2}, i. 166 ff.

§ Among the Syrians we find the name *'Ebedh haiklā*, 'servant of the temple.'

Aramaic, as is shown by the occurrence of *masgĕdhā*, 'place of worship,' in the Nabatæan inscriptions. The sanctuary in which an idol stood was usually not enclosed with walls, but marked off by means of boundary-stones, after the fashion described by Nilus.

3. *PRIESTS.*—That all the details of the cult could not be mastered without special training is sufficiently obvious. In connexion with several of the sanctuaries and idols we read of ministrants, who bore the title of *sādin* (pl. *sadana*); this term originally meant 'one who holds the curtain,' that is, one who admits to the shrine. But it is improbable that in the times with which we are mainly concerned there were men who had no other function than that of priest. At an earlier period, it is true, such persons existed. We learn from Agatharchides (Diod. iii. 42; Strabo, 776) that a man and a woman acted as priests, during their whole lifetime, in the sacred palm-grove, and wore the costume of primitive ages, consisting entirely of skins. In the Sinaitic inscriptions several individuals are expressly designated as 'priests,' which implies that they occupied posts of some dignity. This conclusion is supported by the fact that some of the persons in question appear from the inscriptions to have belonged to the same family.[*] Furthermore, Ibn al-Kalbī, in his account of the various gods, sometimes mentions the name of the priestly family by whom this or that god was served, and in the case of the Ka'ba we possess a considerable amount of detailed information as to the division of the several departments of the cult among a number of families closely related to one another. Wellhausen points out that in some cases the ministrants of a sanctuary belonged to a tribe other than that which owned the surrounding country. Usually this is to be explained by the supposition that the priestly family remained attached to the spot after their fellow-tribesmen had emigrated or been driven out. Occasionally it may have happened that a strange clan acquired control of a sanctuary by force or fraud; that this was the case at Mecca itself is not impossible.[†] In the inscriptions the word for 'priest' is *kāhin*, which seems to have been borrowed from the Aramaic; these persons, it is evident, were priests in the full sense of the term, as appears from the fact that one of them is called a '*kāhin* of 'Uzzā.'

IV. MECCA.

THE 'OMRA AND THE ḤAJJ.—The Ka'ba at Mecca was an unpretending edifice, erected, in the second half of the 6th cent. after Christ, on the site of an older sanctuary which had been destroyed by fire. The new building was constructed by a native of the Roman Empire, partly out of timber obtained from a stranded ship, wood suitable for architectural purposes being a rare article in most parts of Arabia. To the heathen Arabs the Ka'ba was an important centre of worship, and it afterwards acquired, through Muhammad and Islām, a world-wide fame, surpassing even that of the Church of the Holy Sepulchre or of St. Peter's at Rome. At what period a Ka'ba, that is, a durable building with rectangular walls,[‡] was set

up for the first time in that altogether sterile valley, we have absolutely no means of determining. It has been plausibly conjectured that the selection of the spot was due to the existence of the well called **Zamzam**, which has a tolerably abundant supply of water, and might naturally be regarded as a gift of the gods by the caravans which passed to and fro between Yemen and Syria, though the water of Zamzam, it must be admitted, is of an inferior quality, judged even by Arabian standards, and as compared with some other springs which are to be found no great way off. But, however this may be, the primitive structure in question, which was little more than a box containing, it is true, a repository for treasures, first appears in history as a sanctuary in the hands of the Quraish, surrounded by a stretch of sacred territory (*ḥaram*), and visited by strangers who performed a pilgrimage ('*omra*) to the place. The traditions which relate to the early history of Mecca are extremely untrustworthy, and many of them have been perverted in the interest of various parties; but there is no reason to doubt the statement that this territory, unattractive as it is in itself, had once, if not oftener, been overrun and seized by violence.[*] The ceremony of marching round the Ka'ba, and the accompanying rites, such as the procession between the two great stones, called Ṣafā and Marwā, which stood in the immediate vicinity, were rigidly fixed. The greater part of this ritual was incorporated into Islām by Muhammad, who from the first recognized the Ka'ba as the temple of Allāh (*Sūra* cvi. 3); only a few modifications were introduced, but there is reason to suspect that the changes made by the Prophet chiefly affected those very details which, if they were known to us, would have supplied the surest clue to the original meaning of the whole. In particular, he abolished all the idols[†] after the capture of his native city, whereas he retained a sample of the most primitive fetishism, the Black Stone, connecting it, as he connected the Ka'ba itself, with Abraham. According to one tradition, which has all the appearance of trustworthiness, the Prophet forbade his followers to march round the sacred spot naked; the practice in question must therefore have existed previously. The idea seems to have been that those who took part in the festival ought not to appear before the Deity in their ordinary garb; hence, if any one had not the means of borrowing a suit of clothes at Mecca, he was obliged to perform the ceremony in a state of nudity. The custom of worshipping at a shrine in garments lent by the priest occurs also elsewhere in Arabia. In one case, we are told, a Bedawî, who belonged to the neighbouring tribe of Hudhail, marched round the Ka'ba with his buttocks uncovered, apparently imagining that this was a

---

[*] A man named '*Amĕū* calls himself 'a priest of '*Uzzā*' (Euting, 550), and a certain *Ḥarīshū*, son of '*Amĕū*, is also a priest (Euting, 249). A second Ḥarīshū is likewise so described (Euting, 348). In another inscription, which is unfortunately not quite clear, we find an allusion to a priestess; and the name '*Amĕū* appears again (Euting, 228). Although these names occur elsewhere, the fact that they are both contained in the only inscriptions which refer to priests plainly indicates some relationship between the persons in question.

[†] The native tradition itself supplies tolerably clear evidence that Qusai, the ancestor of those families who had charge of the Ka'ba and the pilgrims, belonged to the tribe of 'Odhra, whose territory lay far to the north of Mecca.

[‡] The word *Ka'ba* occurs thus, as an appellative, in the *Mufaḍḍalīyāt*, xxv. 72. 'The castle of Sindād with the Ka'bas'

(*Ibn Hishām*, 57. 3, and elsewhere), was doubtless a group of buildings, or at least a structure composed of separate parts. The theory that there was ever a sacred *tent* in the valley of Mecca is sufficiently refuted by the consideration that dwellers in tents, *i.e.* nomads, could never have found pasture there. Robertson Smith's statement that 'almost every holy place at the time of Muhammad was a little centre of settled agricultural life' (*Rel. Sem.*[2] p. 113), is wholly inapplicable to Mecca.

[*] Compare the account by Agatharchides (Diod. iii. 43; Strabo, 777) describing the subjugation of the tribe which was in possession of the sacred palm-grove by another tribe.

[†] It is expressly stated that traces of the paintings which had been effaced were still visible on the inner walls of the Ka'ba when the building was wrecked in the days of Ibn Zubair (A.D. 683). We have no reason to doubt this assertion, though it is naturally impossible for us to say what objects were there represented—a matter about which scarcely any information could be obtained at the period in question. But it seems by no means improbable that the tradition according to which the Ka'ba contained portraits of Jesus and the Virgin Mary is actually correct, for it might easily have occurred to the artist (whose name is said to have been Bāqūm, *i.e.* presumably Pachomios, showing that he was an Egyptian Christian) to paint such figures in a temple owned by ignorant and inoffensive heathens.

peculiarly effective means of appealing to the god. It is said that the Meccans and certain tribes known as *Ḥums*, who were nearly akin to them, used to wear sandals when they went through the ceremony—a rule which may be explained by the supposition that they regarded the place as their home; members of other tribes, on the contrary, always entered the sacred precincts barefoot.

Wellhausen has had the merit of discovering and carefully pointing out that the solemn procession from the hill called 'Arafāt to the valley of Minā, the real pilgrimage (*ḥajj*) κατ' ἐξοχήν, originally had nothing whatever to do with Mecca and the Ka'ba.* It is true that the route followed by the procession lay, for the most part, within the limits of the *ḥaram*, which was generally acknowledged to be the sacred territory of the Meccans; but the fact that the opening ceremonies, the halt on the hill of 'Arafāt † and the kindling of lights on the hill of Ilāl, took place outside the *ḥaram*—for which reason the Meccans and the Ḥums as a whole had no share in them—is quite sufficient to prove that the festival was not really connected with the city. Moreover, it should be observed that even at the present day, in spite of the changes introduced by the Prophet, who endeavoured to assimilate the ritual as far as possible to the theory of Islām, the festival, properly so called, comes to an end when the sacrificial victims have been slaughtered at Minā; the subsequent visit to the Ka'ba is not an integral part of the *ḥajj*. Nevertheless, we cannot deny that by the time of Muhammad the pilgrimage had come to be closely associated with Mecca. The Quraish were sufficiently astute to appreciate the advantage which they derived from the sacrosanct character of their domain, and from the annual assemblage of pilgrims out of all parts of the country; these two circumstances together formed the basis of their trade, which rendered them intellectually far superior to other Arabs. The hospitality which they extended to the starving Bedawîn at the time of the festival was amply repaid by the security guaranteed to the Meccan caravans.

Ḥagg or *ḥajj* is a very ancient Semitic expression; whatever its original meaning may have been,‡ it corresponds for practical purposes to our word 'festival' (see, for instance, 1 S 30[16]). In Arabic the verbal form of this root is used also transitively, signifying 'to visit' a shrine. How familiar the idea of pilgrimage was to the ancient Arabs is shown by the fact that *Ḥaggāgū*, *al-Ḥajjāj*, 'he who is wont to go on pilgrimage,' appears not unfrequently as a proper name; furthermore, *maḥajja*, which originally meant a 'pilgrim-route,' is used for a 'route' in general, and *ḥijja*, 'annual festival,' has become a synonym for 'year.' That the festivals attended by pilgrims could take place only at fixed seasons is obvious; thus the pilgrimages were intimately connected with the remarkable institution known as the *sacred months*, that is to say, months during which *a universal peace* prevailed, no vengeance could be executed, and even the murderer enjoyed security. How such an institution can have established itself among uncivilized nomads remains a profound mystery; § in any case it was generally accepted among the Arabs. Its existence is attested by Procopius (*Pers.* ii. 16), though, of course, we cannot be quite sure that the months to which he refers are precisely the same as those with which the concourse at Mecca was associated. The question is closely connected with the theory of the ancient Arabian calendar, about which some doubt still prevails. It appears tolerably certain, however, that Rajab, the sacred month which stood by itself, which was the favourite season for sacrifices, and seems to have been the proper time for the pilgrimage (*'omra*) to the Ka'ba, normally fell in the spring, whereas the three consecutive sacred months, in the second of which the great *ḥajj* took place, coincided with the autumn.* Similarly, we learn from Nonnosus, who lived during the first half of the 6th cent., that two annual festivals were celebrated in the sacred palm-grove, which is probably to be identified with the grove described by Agatharchides (see above, p. 666), but is nowhere mentioned in Arabic literature.† At the beginning of the *ḥajj*, a man who belonged to a certain family renowned for skill in such matters solemnly informed the assembly whether the ensuing year was to contain an intercalary month or not; in this manner the calendar was fixed annually. But the methods employed by the Arabs were of a crudely empirical kind, and hence, as we might have expected, their year gradually shifted to a considerable extent. ‡ The pilgrims, who came to the festival from far and near, all wore a peculiar but very simple costume, known as the *iḥrām*, and abstained from shaving their heads until the ceremonies were over. It would seem that washing also was forbidden—a privation which most of the Arabs probably did not feel very keenly. Among certain tribes it was the rule that no one might enter a house by the door so long as he wore the garb of a pilgrim; in other words, during the time of the pilgrimage they dispensed with every sort of shelter; if, however, a man found it necessary to enter his house, he was allowed to creep in at the back (see *Sūra* ii. 185). § The animals brought by the pilgrims had sandals, strips of plaited bark, and other objects attached to them, in order to show that they were intended for sacrifice. The festival began at 'Arafāt on the 9th day of the month of Dhu'l-ḥijja (*i.e.* the month of the feast); here the assembled pilgrims made merry with lighted torches and probably with other adjuncts which are not known to us. From the first day to the last—and this applies to the institution even in its Muhammadan form—the proceedings were conducted with much noise and, from a European point of view, without solemnity. On every side were heard cries of '*Labbaika!*', 'At thy service!' ‖; but whether this invocation was addressed by every one to the same deity is uncertain. A little before sunset the whole of the vast throng, on foot or on camels, began to race towards Muzdalifa, a journey of some two hours; here they were joined by the

* On the whole of this subject see the excellent inaugural dissertation of Snouck Hurgronje, *Het Mekkaansche Feest* (Leyden, 1880), which errs only in being somewhat too sceptical on certain points; and also his great classical work, *Mekka* (Hague, 1888, 1889).

† We also meet with the sing. form *'Arafa*; perhaps this refers properly to some particular summit, whereas the pl. *'Arafāt* may be used to include the whole ridge.

‡ The theory that it primarily refers to 'dancing' rests on no evidence.

§ It is less difficult to understand how sacred spots and districts came to be regarded as inviolable, for in early times it was natural to suppose that the god of the place would punish those who profaned it, and this reverence would acquire the force of a tradition. But how a widely dispersed and altogether lawless people, who had no conception of the heinousness of bloodshed in itself, can have been induced to suspend their feuds for the space of whole months, it seems quite impossible to imagine.

* In the Arabian calendar as given by Epiphanius (*Hær.* li. § 24), the month called *ḥaggat albait*, *i.e.* 'pilgrimage to the (holy) house,' likewise falls in the autumn. This name probably refers, not to the Meccan sanctuary, but to some other.

† According to Agatharchides, a great festival, at which hecatombs of camels were slaughtered, took place every fifth year—a very remarkable statement.

‡ If the adjustment of the lunar months to the solar year had been carried out at all rationally, Muhammad would hardly have conceived the unfortunate idea of imposing upon his followers a purely lunar year without any intercalation whatsoever.

§ Similar naïve attempts to deceive the Deity occur among other peoples.

‖ The grammatical derivation of this term is altogether obscure. Perhaps Professor Bevan is right in suggesting that it may be the Aramaic *lappaik*, 'towards thee (O God)!'

Quraish and their associates the Ḥums (see p. 668). At Qozaḥ, in the immediate neighbourhood, a fire was kindled. During the night spent at Muzdalifa every one remained awake, and as soon as the sun rose, the assembly started for the valley of Minā, about two hours farther on. On the way thither, at three different places, every individual threw some pebbles upon a heap of stones. At Minā the sacrificial animals were slaughtered; part of the flesh was consumed by the owners on the spot, and distributed among those who had nothing to offer, while part of it was cut into strips and dried in the sun for subsequent use. Thereupon the pilgrims shaved their heads, and the festival came to an end.

The practice of kindling lights on the hill of Ilāl, the fire at Qozaḥ, combined with the observation of the setting and rising sun as temporal limits, seem to indicate that the festival was held primarily in honour of the Sun-god. Just as the Saracens described by Nilus were careful to offer their sacrifice to the morning star before it vanished in the brightness of the dawn, so the pilgrims at ʻArafāt regulated their proceedings by the sun.* But whether the whole march from ʻArafāt to Minā was determined by a single plan, having a consistent mythological signification, whether, in other words, each individual rite is to be regarded as an integral part of a mythological drama and is capable of being so interpreted by us, appears extremely doubtful, notwithstanding the ingenious theory which Houtsma has propounded.† The custom of throwing stones is particularly hard to explain. We have to take into account the fact that ceremonies of the same kind were performed by the Arabs in at least two other places, and occur in every part of the world.‡

The great festival which we have described had gradually thrown all others into the shade. At several places not very far from Mecca, feasts, which originally had a religious character, were celebrated on fixed days in the course of the sacred months; but these assemblies became in process of time little more than fairs, where men came together for purposes of business or pleasure. This applies, in particular, to the fair held at ʻOkāẓ. It must, of course, be understood that the great *ḥajj* itself was also utilized for commerce and other secular objects. The influence of these gatherings extended over a vast area. Thus at the fair of Dhu'l-majāz, a place some four miles from ʻArafāt, peace was concluded about the beginning of the 6th cent., through the intervention of Mundhir, king of Ḥīra, between the two kindred tribes of Bekr and Taghlib, who had long been deadly enemies, although the town of Ḥīra and the territory of the tribes in question lay far to the north-east of Dhu'l-majāz.

It is necessary to add that there were certain tribes, not very distant from Mecca, who did not recognize the sanctity of the festivals associated with that city, and even went so far as to plunder the pilgrims. The case of the brigand-poet Shanfarā, who boasts that he slew a pilgrim at Minā in the midst of the festive throng, thus violating at once the holiness of the place and of the occasion, belongs to a somewhat different category, since this was merely an example of individual impiety on the part of a man who in more than one respect showed a contempt for established usages.

* Muhammad deliberately modified the connexion of the festival with the sun, for he ordered that the departure from ʻArafāt should take place soon after sunset, and the departure from Muzdalifa shortly before sunrise.

† 'Het Skopelisme en het steenwerpen te Mina,' p. 22 ff. (= *Verslagen en Mededeelingen der Kon. Akad. van Wetenschappen*, Letterkunde, 4th ser., vi. 206 ff.).

‡ See, especially, Frazer, *Golden Bough*², iii. pp. 3–13, where the rite is explained as an attempt to transfer an evil. Cf. also Doutté, *Les Tas de pierres sacrés en Maroc* (Algiers, 1903). The practice of pelting with stones the graves of unpopular persons probably has a different origin, although the belief of Muhammadans, that the stones which they throw in the valley of Minā are directed against Satan, suggests this explanation.

V. VARIOUS PRACTICES AND BELIEFS.

1. *CIRCUMCISION.*—The practice of circumcision (*q.v.*) was universal among the Arabs.* Obscure as its origin is, it seems highly probable that the rite in the oldest times was connected with religion. In historical times the Arabs regarded circumcision as obligatory, not offering any reason for it except that it had always been their custom; hence, without any formal sanction, it was adopted into Islām.

2. *THE SACRIFICE OF INFANTS.*—It is possible that the habit of burying female infants alive, which prevailed very widely, was likewise associated with some crude religious belief. The child may have been originally offered as a sacrifice to subterranean deities. In any case it is important to observe that the victim was slain without shedding of blood. But the real motive for the act was doubtless that which is assigned in the Qur'ān (*Sūra* vi. 152, xvii. 33), namely, poverty. It is well known that the same cause has led to infanticide in other countries.

3. *DEMONS.* — In addition to the gods who were publicly recognized, though sometimes half-forgotten, we meet with a great mass of shadowy beings, everywhere present yet nowhere distinctly perceived, the demons or, as the Arabs call them, the Jinn. The meaning of the name is probably 'covert' or 'darkness'; another form is *Jānn* (pl. *Jinnān*), to which the Ethiopic *Gānēn*, 'demon,' approximately corresponds.† The demons are always, in the main, objects of fear, crafty, mischievous, or even destructive beings. The notion that the Jinn were regarded by the heathen Arabs as partly benevolent seems to have arisen under the influence of Islām, which teaches that at least some of the Jinn are true believers, though it cannot be denied that, even in the pre-Islāmic age, certain friendly acts may occasionally have been ascribed to them: the Devil himself has moments of good temper, and strict consistency is not to be expected in a world of phantoms. The Jinn are usually invisible, but are capable of assuming various forms, especially those of snakes, lizards, scorpions, and other creeping things; hence the word *jānn* may be used to denote a snake. In this case also two separate ideas have been confounded; on the one hand, that of repulsive animal forms, particularly of the snake, which in every country has given rise to weird fancies; on the other hand, the invisible terrors of the desert.‡ It is related that the Meccan clan of Sahm once suffered injuries at the hands of the Jinn, and accordingly marched out to a certain spot, where they proceeded to kill so many snakes, beetles, etc., that the Jinn were forced to sue for peace; here the creatures slain are evidently regarded as being themselves Jinn. It was natural to suppose that these demons haunted particular places, remarkable either for their loneliness or for their unhealthy climate. When Ḥarb, the grandfather of the Khalīf Muʻāwiya, together with another man, was engaged in clearing a marsh for purposes of culti-

* This might be inferred from the account of the circumcision of Ishmael in Genesis. The Jewish treatise *Mekhiltā*, composed in the 2nd cent., expressly states that all Arabs were circumcised.

† The word is possibly connected with other religious terms used in the Semitic languages, but on this point nothing can be affirmed with certainty.

‡ Jāḥiẓ, an author of the 9th cent., gives a very rational explanation of the belief in demons (see van Vloten's remarks in the *WZKM* vii. 241); the passage is cited by Masʻūdī, (*Prairies d'or*, iii. 323 ff.). The articles by van Vloten, 'Dämonen, Geister und Zauber bei den alten Arabern,' in the above-mentioned periodical (vols. vii. and viii.), are peculiarly instructive.

vation, white serpents were seen to fly out of the burning weeds; and when both persons died forthwith, every one perceived that the Jinn had slain them. Perhaps we may hazard the rationalistic conjecture that their death was due to the poisonous air which they had been breathing. There are many other stories in which the Jinn kill or carry off human beings; their spiteful nature also leads them sometimes to prevent cattle from drinking. They utter a peculiar sound.* Their limbs are often very powerful; hence a strong man is said to resemble them. Occasionally they ride upon ostriches, as befits inhabitants of the pure desert. A brave warrior is described as alarming even 'the dogs of the Jinn,' so that they growl. These are merely samples of the fantastic notions connected with them; as we might have expected, there were equally fantastic devices for the purpose of warding off their influence.

Frequently a Jinnī (*i.e.* one of the Jinn) enters into a human being, rendering him possessed or mad.† But this belief, familiar as it was to the Arabs in historical times, seems to have been originally a foreign importation, or at least to have been greatly intensified through contact with foreigners. In the OT scarcely a trace of such a conception appears, whereas in the NT it is extremely common, phrases like δαιμονιζόμενος, δαιμόνιον ἔχειν occurring repeatedly. The idea was introduced into Palestine from Irān. The Persian word for 'madman' is *dēvāna*, literally 'demoniac' (from *dēv*, originally *daiva*, 'demon'), whence comes the Aramaic *daiwān*; on the other hand, the Aramaic *shēdhān* (from *shēdh*, which was used as the equivalent of the Persian *dēv*) passed into Persian in the form *shēdhā*. In pre-Islāmic times the Arabs borrowed from their northern neighbours not only many of the elements of civilization, but also much that was fanciful and superstitious; the latter class includes the belief in demoniacal possession. Even heathen Arabian poets speak of Palmyra as having been built for king Solomon by the Jinn;‡ in this case the foreign origin of the legend is quite obvious.

The Arabs almost invariably use a collective noun in referring to demons; an individual demon has no distinct character, and consequently bears no personal name. To regard *Shaiṭān* as a proper name is scarcely permissible. It seems tolerably certain that this word was known to the Arabs before the days of Muhammad, and it actually occurs as the name of human individuals; but its form agrees so closely with that of the Ethiopic *Shaiṭān*, which is derived from the Heb. *Sāṭān*,§ that we are forced to consider it a loan-word.‖ The occasional use of *shaiṭān* for 'serpent' is even less primitive than the use of *jānn* in the same sense.

Though the Jinn have no individuality, they fall into various classes, and certain of these are sometimes mentioned as particularly harmful. The most dangerous kind of all is the **Ghūl** (a feminine noun), of which the plural is *Ghīlān* or *Aghwāl*; this word comes from a root signifying 'to destroy,' perhaps originally 'to assault.' The Ghūl is supposed to lie in wait at some place where men are destined to perish; she also entices them thither, especially by night. 'The Ghūl has carried him off' is sometimes merely a poetical expression meaning 'he has perished.' She has the power of changing her shape, that is to say, of beguiling men in order to destroy them. But usually she is described as a hideous monster. A poet relates how the Ghūl, 'the daughter of the Jinn,' came one night to the fire which he had kindled, and how he cut off her head. It was a frightful object, like the head of a cat, but with a forked tongue; moreover, she had the legs of an infant prematurely born, limp and fleshless, and a hairy skin, resembling that of a dog or a rough and crumpled garment. In another poet we meet with the phrase 'arrows sharp as the canine teeth of Ghūls.'

The poets also mention a kind of female demon called **Siʻlāt**, of which the plural is *Saʻālī*; this term scarcely ever occurs except as a simile, for the purpose of describing swift horses or camels, formidable warriors, and frightful women. A certain Arabian clan was supposed to have sprung from a marriage between a man and a Siʻlāt. Whether this ancestry was originally regarded as an honour or the reverse is doubtful; in any case no great importance can be attached to the story which was related on the subject.

In passages referring to the Jinn we occasionally meet with the expression *Ḥabal*, *Ḥābil*, or some other derivative of the root ḤBL, which primarily means 'to destroy,' and is applied, in particular, to the destruction of the reason, or, in other words, to madness. Usually the term is employed in an abstract sense and as a mere figure of speech, but sometimes the beings so designated are conceived as personal; thus, for instance, a poet says to his wife, 'Leave me in peace, even though I should give away my substance to the Jinn and the Ḥabal!'

The mysterious tribe called *Banū Uqaish* seem likewise to be a class of demons. In order to scare them away, it was the custom to rattle a number of dry skin-bottles one against another.*

The demons were never the objects of a cult, in the strict sense of the word; but on certain occasions, as, for example, at the building of a house, it was thought prudent to conciliate them with some offering, lest they should frustrate the work.† The curious proper name *ʻAbd al-Jinn*, 'servant of the Jinn,' may here be mentioned. Whether it was actually in use does not seem quite certain; in any case it cannot have been common.

The belief in this motley assemblage of inferior spirits was, on the whole, maintained by Islām; in fact, the Prophet went so far as to recognize the existence of the heathen gods, classing them among the demons (see *Sūra* xxxvii. 158). Hence these primitive superstitions not only held their ground in Muhammadan Arabia, but were further developed, spread over the rest of the Muhammadan world, and often combined with similar, in some cases much more elaborate, conceptions which prevailed among foreign peoples. Thus later narratives which refer to such subjects may, if examined with due caution, be used to illustrate the ideas of the ancient Arabs; but we must beware of accepting too readily the statements of those Muhammadan scholars who endeavoured to reduce demonology to a system.

4. *SOOTHSAYERS AND MAGICIANS.*—The notion that certain persons are under the immediate influence of the gods, and so possess the power of foretelling events or of performing other superhuman feats, prevailed generally in the ancient

* The word applied to it is *ʻazf*, apparently a harsh, dull sound. It is also used to denote the clanging of a bowstring.

† 'To be possessed' is *junna*, and the participle *majnūn* means 'possessed.'

‡ The idea that Solomon was concerned in the building of Palmyra (*Tadmor*) is due to an ancient textual corruption in 2 Ch 8[4], where *Tadhmōr* stands for *Tāmār* (see 1 K 9[18]). The demons were brought into the story because the edifices of the city seemed too marvellous to be the work of men.

§ From the Hebrew and the Aramaic several religious expressions passed into the Ethiopic language at an early period, through the influence of Jewish or Christian missionaries.

‖ This is by no means the only Arabic word which was borrowed from the Ethiopic.

* Some words which are often understood as referring to demons really have a different sense. Thus *zaubaʻa* is not a personal being, but simply 'whirlwind.' *ʻIfrit* in the Qur'ān (*Sūra* xxvii. 39) is an epithet of somewhat doubtful meaning, applied to a demon, but it is not the name of a particular class of demons. The belief current in later times, that the *ʻIfrīts* or *ʻAfrīts* are demons of a specially dangerous kind, is due to a misunderstanding of this passage.

† Here we have an instance of the so-called 'foundation sacrifice' which is practised in many parts of the world; see, in particular, *ZE*, vol. xxx.

world. It is certainly significant that the term *kāhin*, which, as we have seen (p. 667), retained among the Sinai-Arabs its original meaning of 'priest,' was used by the later Arabs in the sense of 'soothsayer.' In early times the Deity had been wont to make revelations to His priests; the divining arrows of Hubal and of other gods—things which, we may be sure, only the ministers of the sanctuary ventured to use—survived as relics of a more primitive age.* In the various stories which refer to soothsayers, we find no other traces of their connexion with the gods properly so called. We are sometimes told, it is true, that a soothsayer or a magician had a 'follower' (*tābi'*); in other words, a familiar spirit† who occasionally revealed secrets to him, but was not always at his disposal. This spirit seems also to have been called a *ra'ī*, 'one who is seen,' or perhaps we should translate 'seer,' assuming that the term was originally applied to the soothsayer himself, like the Heb. *rō'e*, the ancient word for 'prophet.' The Hebrew synonym *ḥōze* has an exact equivalent in the Arabic *ḥāzī*, 'seer,' 'presager,' 'diviner,' which is often used, as well as the verb corresponding to it.‡ In the same category we may include the '*arrāf*, 'sage,' who is acquainted with hidden things, to some extent the *ṭabīb*, 'physician,' literally 'skilful, well-informed,' who in many cases is an enchanter (*rāqī*), and even the man whose wisdom qualifies him to act as arbitrator (*ḥakam*). The word *shā'ir*, 'one who knows,' must in early times have denoted a man who uttered sayings inspired by some higher power; afterwards it gradually became the technical term for a 'poet.'§ In general, any one who possesses secret powers is called a *sāḥir*, 'magician.' Among the Arabs, as among other nations, it was particularly in this sphere that the mysterious depth of the feminine soul made itself felt; we read both of female soothsayers and female enchanters. A female familiar spirit (*ra'īya*) is likewise mentioned.

Arabic literature contains many stories about *kāhins* and many utterances which were attributed to them; but of all these only a very small proportion can be considered trustworthy, and a great deal is pure invention due to later writers. Nevertheless the passages in question enable us at least to form an idea of the style in which the soothsayers expressed themselves; the same style re-appears in the oldest chapters of the Qur'ān. The fact is that the conceptions which the soothsayers embodied were raised by Muhammad to a far higher level. He felt in himself an inspiration which proceeded from the one true God. But if he had not had before him the example of the heathen *kāhins*, it is hard to believe that any such idea would have entered his mind; on the other hand, we cannot wonder that his prosaic fellow-citizens called him a soothsayer, a magician, and a 'possessed poet.' Nor is it impossible that his most formidable rival, Maslama‖ ibn Ḥabīb of the tribe of Ḥanīfa, was likewise sincerely convinced of his own divine inspiration.¶

* Cf. 1 S 30⁷ etc.

† Hence any man noted for his intelligence is supposed to have a *tābi'*, who reveals all manner of things to him.

‡ The root was no longer employed by the Arabs in the simple sense of 'beholding'; even in Hebrew this usage is confined to the poetical or rhetorical style.

§ The connexion between poetical inspiration and the unseen world was not entirely forgotten even in later times, though the allusions which a poet makes to his 'demon' or 'Satan' are little more than jests. A very primitive stage in the development of this idea is represented by the story of Balaam in Nu 22–24; cf. Goldziher, *Abhandlungen zur arab. Philologie*, i. (Leyden, 1896) pp. 1–205.

‖ By the Muhammadans he was contemptuously called *Musailima*, *i.e.* 'little Maslama.'

¶ This would partly account for the fact that his adherents were the only Arabs who displayed real courage and stubbornness in contending against Islām.

5. *OMENS.*—The belief in signs as betokening future events was, of course, no less common among the Arabs than among other nations. Some birds were regarded as lucky, some as unlucky. The animals that crossed a man's path and the direction in which they moved alike conveyed a meaning. Many of these signs were such as every one could understand; others were intelligible only to persons specially trained. One peculiar art consisted in scaring birds and drawing omens from their flight; this operation was known as *zajr*. Various other superstitions of the same order might be enumerated, but such beliefs and practices do not properly belong to the domain of religion, and it is therefore sufficient to notice them in passing.

6. *THE SOUL.*—The Arabs, like all other Semites, identified the breath (*nafs*) with the principle of life, or the soul.* So completely did *nafs* convey, from the earliest times onward, the idea of human personality, that the word is used, with the addition of the possessive suffix, as an ordinary reflexive pronoun: *nafsī*, 'my soul,' means 'myself'; *nafsaka*, 'thyself'; *linafsihī*, 'for himself,' etc.† When the *nafs* permanently quits a man, death is the result; but the words of the Qur'ān (*Sūra* xxxix. 43), 'Allāh takes the souls to Himself when they die, and those who have not died (He takes) in their sleep,' presuppose the belief that during sleep also the soul is absent from the body.‡ It is true that the conception of the 'breath' as the principle of life does not harmonize very well with the theory that the life resides in the blood (see above, p. 665). But this latter view is much less popular among the Arabs than it was among the Israelites, and when the *nafs* of a man dying from wounds is said to 'flow away,' we need not assume, with the native Arabic commentators, that *nafs* here means simply 'the blood.' Even the Heb. *nephesh* (the equivalent of the Arabic *nafs*) is identified with the blood only in so far as the shedding of the blood causes death. It would appear that the life-giving soul (*nafs*) was supposed to have its seat in the heart; when the soul moves upwards, it is about to depart; in other words, death is imminent. The 'breath' escapes through its natural passage, the mouth or the nostrils.§ Thus, in passages referring to deadly peril, we read, 'when your soul had reached your throat,' 'before the soul rises above the ribs,' 'he just escaped with his soul in the corner of his mouth,' etc. In phrases of this kind *nafs* is sometimes omitted as being the implied subject of the sentence; for instance, in the words of the Qur'ān, 'when it (*i.e.* the soul, which is unexpressed) reaches the throat' (*Sūra* lvi. 82, lxxv. 26), meaning, 'when a man is at the last gasp.'‖ A view which at first sight seems to differ from the foregoing appears in a story told of a certain aged Arab who fell into the hands of a hostile clan. Seeing that they were determined to shed his blood, he presented a sword to them, saying, 'Cut off my head, for the soul (*nafs*) is in it,' which they accordingly proceeded to do.¶

* The Ethiopic *nafest*, 'that which contains the *nafs* (breath, life)' means the living human body (cf. *animus*, *anima*, etc.). The Arabic *rūḥ* properly denotes the 'breath' only; its use in the sense of 'spirit' was unknown to the heathen, and when so employed it is to be regarded as one of the foreign religious terms which were introduced by Islām.

† The corresponding forms are similarly used in Hebrew and Aramaic.

‡ This conception prevails very widely. It is due to the belief that dreams are real experiences through which men pass while they are apparently lifeless. See Frazer, *Golden Bough*², i. 255 ff.

§ See Frazer, *op. cit.* i. 251.

‖ The common phrase *māta ḥatfa anfihī*, 'he died a natural death,' similarly refers, it would appear, to the cessation of the breath, since the 'nose' (*anf*) is here associated with the idea of 'dying' (*māta*); but the special meaning which *ḥatfa* has in this connexion remains obscure.

¶ See the Commentary on the *Naqā'iḍ* of Jarīr and al-Farazdaq,

These words, however, are probably to be taken as nothing more than a statement, based on ordinary experience, that the severing of the head puts an end to life, not as the expression of an idea opposed to the deeply-rooted popular belief which has been described above (see also footnote ‖, p. 671[b]).

In reading the Qur'ān we might be tempted to conclude that the heathen Arabs regarded the departure of the *nafs* as equivalent to annihilation; but in reality all that Muhammad's opponents denied was the novel, and to their minds absurd, doctrine of the resurrection and the other world.* Their notions as to the state of departed souls were, of course, vaguer, if anything, than the notions of Homer's fellow-countrymen as to the ψυχή. Nevertheless, the usual invocation addressed to the dead, 'Be not far away!' does not admit of any satisfactory interpretation, unless we presuppose the belief that the dead had a dwelling-place, and might be induced by entreaty to remain in the neighbourhood of his people.† It is true that the formula in question dates from a period when such things were more vividly conceived. Sometimes we meet with sober reflexions of the following kind: 'They will say, when they bury me, "Be not far away!" but what place can then be far away, if mine is not?'

Nothing seems to the Arabs more obvious than that blood must be expiated by blood.‡ Hence one who has been slain longs for vengeance, and thirsts for the blood of the murderer. These phrases must originally have been understood in quite a literal fashion,§ whence we may conclude with certainty that some sort of life was ascribed to the departed. On this subject strange fancies prevailed. The soul of the murdered man was represented as appearing in the form of an owl, and as continually crying out, 'Give me to drink!' until vengeance had been executed. It must be remembered that the scene of the murder was, in most cases, a lonely spot where the weird cry of the feathered anchorite would not be out of place. The term applied to the departed is *hāma*, properly 'skull,' the skull being the most characteristic part of the dead body; ‖ the voice of the departed is called *ṣadā*, 'echo.' Hence 'skull' and 'echo' come to be used as designations of the ghostly bird, or owl, that cries for vengeance.* Moreover, the rites of burial, simple as they were, presuppose some kind of future existence. In order to show honour to the dead, it was the practice to tether a camel, which had previously been lamed, near the grave,† and to let it die of starvation. This usage can be explained only on the hypothesis that the soul of the camel was supposed to be ridden by the dead man. The custom of slaughtering sacrifices at a grave has maintained itself in various parts of Arabia down to the present day.‡ It is particularly interesting to note that about the year 1100 after Christ certain Arabs of Northern Yemen (apparently near the mountain-range of 'Asīr) showed their respect for a dead man, in accordance with their traditional practice, by breaking 1000 swords and 300 bows, and by laming 70 horses; § this was undoubtedly a survival of an ancient heathen rite. That the objects destined for the service of the departed must be rendered useless to the living is an idea which might easily occur to the fancy of primitive man.‖ We likewise find traces of hair-offerings presented to the dead, but scarcely any traces of drink-offerings. Poets, it is true, often express the wish that the graves of those whom they love may be refreshed with abundant rain; ¶ but whether this implies a belief that the dead themselves are capable of being refreshed is extremely doubtful; such passages may be mere figures of speech, referring to the verdure with which the grave is to be covered. In like manner, the greetings which poets sometimes address to the dead are purely rhetorical, and do not presuppose any notion of real intercourse with the departed.

The practice of refusing sepulture to an enemy, and of casting forth his corpse to be devoured by beasts and birds, prevailed no less among the Arabs than among the Homeric warriors or the peoples of Palestine (1 S 17[44], cf. Ezk 29[5]). There can be no doubt that this was originally regarded as a positive injury to the dead, as depriving them of rest in the grave, or the like. But in historical times such conceptions had begun to become obsolete; ** the poet Shanfarā (see above, p. 669), who was outlawed by his tribe, disclaims all wish for burial, and invites the hyæna to rend his dead body on the battlefield.†† In general, however, the Arabs paid great attention to proper interment, and special care was taken to construct the grave so that it could not be violated by the hyænas. That all this may be done without any notion of bene-

Bodleian MS (Pococke, 390, fol. 53[b]): the passage in question has been communicated by Professor Bevan to the author of the present article.

* Primitive man must have been quite unable to grasp the idea of his personality being completely annihilated at death. Even to us such a thing is, strictly speaking, unimaginable.

† Poets modify the expression in various ways; thus, when one poet says, 'May Allāh not suffer thee to be far away!' we must beware of taking the words to imply a definite religious idea. Moreover, the poets use the same formula with reference to other things, *e.g.* 'May God not suffer youth to be far away!' One poet, whose hand had been cut off, actually says to it, 'Be not far away!' The primitive sense of the phrase is completely lost in the verse of the poetess Ḥansā, alluding to her departed brother, 'May the grave that contains his body not be far away!' The invocation 'Be not far away' is even at the present day addressed to the dead by certain Bedawîn.

‡ The substitution of a blood-wit (*diya*) for blood-revenge is a later modification. But in historical times the blood-wit had become very common; well-disposed persons eagerly furthered this device for maintaining peace, often at great sacrifice to themselves. Nevertheless it was not considered quite honourable to accept 'milk' (*i.e.* camels or other animals that could be milked) instead of 'blood.'

§ In reality, of course, the thirst for blood is felt by the surviving relatives. The daughter of the aged hero Duraid ibn Ṣimma, who was miserably slain by a Muslim just after the battle of Ḥunain (A.D. 630), says in a poem, 'When we march against them, may He (*i.e.* Allāh) give us to drink of the blood of their noblest ones on the day of battle!' This is evidently metaphorical; but we can scarcely doubt that the phrase was coined at a time when men actually drank the blood of their slain enemies, partly in order to quench the burning thirst for vengeance, partly, it would seem, in order to absorb the strength of the vanquished. It must not be forgotten that, after the battle of Uḥud, Hind bint 'Otba, a woman of remarkable intelligence, bit the liver of her fallen enemy Ḥamza, who in a previous battle, at Bedr, had with the aid of two companions killed her father, her son, and her uncle.

‖ Perhaps this use of *hāma* may be partly due to the notion that in the head, as the poet says, is the 'greater part' of the man,—an expression which refers, not to the brain, but to the external organs of sensation.

* As Professor Goldziher has observed, the saying ascribed to Muhammad, that the souls of believers slain in fighting for the faith are deposited in the stomachs of green birds, which drink of the rivers of Paradise, eat of its fruits, and perch upon the lamps suspended in the shadow of God's throne, obviously stands in contrast to the gloomy beliefs of the heathen. The beatified martyrs do not thirst for blood, and the birds that contain them are clad in the colour of vegetation, which to the inhabitants of the desert is synonymous with life.

† The Arabs practised burial only; the burning of corpses was unknown to them. It should be observed that the root QBR, which properly expresses the idea of 'burying,' is common to all the Semitic languages, and that the synonymous root DFN is not confined to Arabic.

‡ See Goldziher, *Muhamm. Studien*, i. (Halle, 1888) 239 ff.; Landberg, *Arabica*, iii. (Leyden, 1895) 103, and *Dialectes de l'Arabie mérid.* i. (*ib.* 1901) 434, by the same author.

§ *'Oumâra du Yemen*, ed. H. Derenbourg (Paris, 1897–1903), i. 18.

‖ Some similar cases have been pointed out to the writer of the present article by Professor Schwally, who is specially versed in these subjects.

¶ On the other hand, a curse sometimes takes the form of a prayer that no rain may fall upon the grave of the individual in question.

** The substitution of a crudely material Paradise and Hell for the vague or wholly negative beliefs of the heathen respecting a future existence, was doubtless one of the most important factors in the conversion of the Arabs to Muhammad's teaching.

†† Nevertheless in an elegy composed upon his death the ancient formula occurs, 'May Shanfarā be not far away!'

fiting the departed is sufficiently obvious from the usages of modern Europe.*

The belief which exists among many primitive races, that the dead are malevolent, and seek to injure the living, is one of which no traces are to be found among the Arabs.

VI. MORALS.

It is almost superfluous to say that the Arabs had a generally recognized code of morals, which, we must admit, did not always reach a very high ethical standard. Some element of religion is contained in the maxim, which the poets repeat in various forms, that the misuse of strength leads to calamity;† there are likewise narratives which inculcate the same doctrine. Moreover, the poets sometimes bring the Deity into immediate connexion with the fulfilment of duties, for instance, as vindicating the sanctity of compacts. But in general it may be said that the maintenance of morality was due much more to respect for traditional usages and public opinion than to fear of Divine wrath.

LITERATURE.—L. Krehl, *Die Religion der vorislam. Araber*, Leipzig, 1863 [antiquated]. The great work on the subject is Wellhausen's *Reste arab. Heidentums* (=*Skizzen u. Vorarbeiten*, drittes Heft), Berlin, 1887 [2nd ed. 1897]. Much of value will be found in W. Robertson Smith's *Religion of the Semites*, Edinburgh, 1889 [2nd ed. 1894], and in the works of Ignatius Goldziher, esp. his *Abhandlungen zur arab. Philologie*, erster Theil, Leyden, 1896. See also the works cited in the body of this article. The present writer cannot recommend D. Nielsen's *Die altarab. Mondreligion*, Strassburg, 1904.

TH. NÖLDEKE.

ARAKH.—A tribe of cultivators and field-labourers in Northern India, of Dravidian origin, which at the Census of 1901 numbered 76,436, practically all of whom are found in the United Provinces. They claim to be Hindus, but their religion is really an advanced form of animism, and they are never initiated into any of the orthodox sects. Their tribal goddess is Devī, whom they propitiate by a sacrifice of goats, the service being done by a class of Brāhmans of low rank. They observe the usual Hindu feasts, and at that of the Karvā Chauth in October–November their women worship the moon by pouring water on the ground from an earthen pot with a spout (*karvā*). In Central India, as in the United Provinces, they are not assisted in their domestic worship by Brāhmans, and their worship is chiefly devoted to a snake god whom they call Kartal Deo.

LITERATURE.—Crooke, *Tribes and Castes of the North-Western Provinces and Oudh*, 1896, i. 83 f.; Luard, *Census Report, Central India*, 1901, i. 202.

W. CROOKE.

ARAMÆANS.—See SYRIANS.

ĀRAṆYAKAS.—The *Āraṇyaka* literature of the Hindus holds a position intermediate between the Brāhmaṇas and the Upaniṣads; in a formal and technical sense supplementary to the Brāhmaṇas, but sharing generally the themes and subject-matter of the Upaniṣads, which in their turn are appended to or form a part of the Āraṇyakas (see art. UPANIṢADS). These treatises are therefore *śruti*, revealed and inspired Scripture. The name indicates either that they were composed in the forest (*araṇye*) by the hermits who devoted themselves there to a life of seclusion and meditation, or that they were intended to be there read and studied. The latter is the Indian view.‡ Perhaps both are correct. Strictly speaking, also, each Brāhmaṇa had its own Āraṇyaka, just as each *śākhā*, or school of Vedic teaching, had its Brāhmaṇa; and the Āraṇyaka was completed and supplemented by a corresponding Upaniṣad.

This accepted classification of the Sanskrit sacred literature is not unconnected with the theory of the four *āśramas* (see art. ĀŚRAMA). The Brāhmaṇas were the text-books of the Brāhman householder, upon which he relied for the due performance of his obligations as *gṛhastha*. Later in life, during the third period, after his retirement into the forest as *vānaprastha*, he devoted himself to the study of the Āraṇyaka, as sanctioned and adopted in the *śākhā* to which he belonged.*

It has been shown that the Āraṇyaka literature in general is chronologically of more recent date than the *saṁhitās* of the Veda, which are known to it essentially in the form in which they have come down to us; and that it is later also than the Brāhmaṇas. On the other hand, the greater part at least is anterior to the period of the *sūtra* compositions, to the character and style of which the more recent portions of the Āraṇyakas approximate. Pāṇini† is said to be unacquainted with them; but in this instance the supposed ignorance may be only a matter of name.

The extant Āraṇyakas belong to the Rigveda and the Yajurveda. There are no known Āraṇyakas of the Sāmaveda or the Atharvaveda.

The *Aitareya Āraṇyaka* of the Rigveda is described as a distinct and separate treatise, not forming a part of the Ait. Brāhmaṇa. It consists of five divisions, or *āraṇyakas*, of which the last two are ascribed to the authors Āśvalāyana and Śaunaka, and are written in a later style, suggesting the peculiar features of the sūtra literature. Chapters 4–6 of the second āraṇyaka form the Upaniṣad proper. The first āraṇyaka details the rules for the morning, mid-day, and evening offerings on the *mahāvrata*, or great vow day, the last day but one of the *gavām-ayana*, the 'procession of cows.' The first three chapters of the second āraṇyaka treat of the allegorical significance of the *uktham*, the spoken word;‡ while in the third part is discussed, quite after the upaniṣad manner, the meaning of the letters of the alphabet and their combinations.§

The *Kauṣītaki Āraṇyaka* also belongs to the Rigveda, but is attached to a different *śākhā*, or school, that of the Kauṣītakins. It contains fifteen *adhyāyas*, or chapters, some of which coincide with chapters of the Aitareya Āraṇyaka. Adhyāyas 3–6, according to the usual numbering, form the Upaniṣad; but their position is said to vary in the different manuscripts, as though the four chapters of the Upaniṣad had originally existed, and been in circulation apart from the Āraṇyaka.‖

Of the Yajurveda two Āraṇyakas are known, the *Bṛhad-āraṇyaka* and the *Taittirīya Āraṇyaka*, belonging respectively to the White and Black Yajurveda. The former is part of the Śatapatha Brāhmaṇa, of which it forms the last six *adhyāyas* or five *prapāṭhakas* of the fourteenth or last book according to the Mādhyandina school; but in the *śākhā* of the Kāṇvas it is reckoned separately as the seventeenth book. Thus the Upaniṣad and the Āraṇyaka coincide; but the whole of the last book in the Mādhy. recension also is sometimes considered as the Āraṇyaka.¶ The *Taittirīya Ār.* consists of 10 books or *prapāṭhakas*, of which the first six are the Āraṇyaka proper. These books discuss the *mantras* for various ceremonies, the training and Vedic studies of a Brāhman, and the offerings to the Fathers. Books vii. to ix. are the Taitt. Up.; and book x. is supplementary, the so-called Mahānārāyaṇa Upaniṣad. The style and contents seem to betray a comparatively late date.**

* The outburst of popular indignation which proved fatal to the victorious commanders after the battle of Arginusæ shows that, near the end of the 5th cent. B.C., the bulk of the Athenians, notwithstanding the rationalistic doctrines of the Sophists, still adhered to the belief that funeral rites were of great importance to the dead. From the same standpoint we must regard the conduct of Antigone; it is not merely a *formal* expression of piety.

† For example, one poet says, 'Those who graze on the pasture of iniquity are smitten with pestilence.'

‡ Sāyaṇa on the Taittirīya Āraṇyaka: 'The rule is that this āraṇyakam is for forest-study; it should be studied, therefore, in the forest,' etc. (Max Müller, *Ancient Sanskr. Lit.*[2] p. 313).

* Āruṇeya Upaniṣad, 2: the sannyāsin (*kuṭīchara*) is to live without the mantras of the Veda, but to observe the three daily ablutions, to meditate on the ātman, and 'of all the Vedas to recite the Āraṇyaka and the Upaniṣad' (Deussen, *Sechzig Upan.* p. 693). Cf. Yājñavalkya, *Dharmaśāstra*, 3. 110: 'He who wishes to attain Yoga should know the Āraṇyaka'; *Mahābh.* 1.258: 'this body of the Mahābhārata is truth and immortality; it is . . . like the Āraṇyaka from the Vedas.' The last two quotations are in Max Müller, pp. 330 n. 2, 315 n. 1. See also E. W. Hopkins, *Great Epic of India*, New York, 1901, p. 9.

† About the latter half of the 4th cent. B.C. (B.C. 350 acc. to O. Böhtlingk). Others assign to him an earlier date. See C. M. Duff, *Chronology of India*, London, 1899, p. 7; Macdonell, *Sanskrit Literature*, p. 430 f.

‡ 'The beginning of the Ait. Ār. is in fact a commentary on the Rigveda' (Max Müller, p. 153 f., cf. p. 341).

§ P. Deussen, *Sechzig Upan. d. Veda*, p. 10 ff.; Max Müller, *l.c.*

‖ Deussen, p. 21 f.; Max Müller, p. 337 f.; A. B. Keith in *JRAS*, 1908, p. 363 ff., who prefers the name Sāṅkhāyana.

¶ Max Müller, p. 329 f.; *SBE*, vol. xliv., Introd. p. xlix f.

** Max Müller, p. 334 f.; Deussen, p. 213 f.

LITERATURE.—The Aitareya and Taittirīya Āraṇyakas have been edited in the *Bibliotheca Indica*, Calcutta, 1876 and 1872; the Bṛhadāraṇyaka, by O. Böhtlingk, Leipzig, 1889, and elsewhere; the first two *adhyāyas* of the Kauṣītaki Āraṇyaka have been published by W. Friedländer, Berlin, 1900, adh. iii.–vi. by E. B. Cowell, Calcutta, 1901, and the remainder is being edited by A. B. Keith (see *JRAS*, 1908, p. 363 ff.). See **Max Müller**, *Hist. of Anc. Sanskr. Lit.*[2], London, 1860, pp. 147, 153 f., 313–318, 334–341; **A. Barth**, *Religions of India*[2], London, 1889, p. 3 f.; **P. Deussen**, *Sechzig Upanishad's des Veda*, Leipzig, 1897, pp. 3 f., 10 ff., 21 f., 213 f., 373 ff.; **A. A. Macdonell**, *Sanskrit Literature*, London, 1890, pp. 34, 50, 204 f., 208 f., 211 ff.

A. S. GEDEN.

ARBITRARINESS is, according to the popular use of the term, that quality which is ascribed to an act of will (*arbitrium*), and whatsoever follows from it, not merely in so far as it is free, but in so far as the choice of the individual who wills is not influenced by consideration for others or respect for any law which is not self-imposed. Hence arbitrariness tends to imply capriciousness, irrationality, and an incalculable character generally. It must be in this wider sense that the word is employed by critics of the indeterminist theory of the Freedom of the Will (wh. see), when they say that that doctrine implies total arbitrariness of the will.

The theory of the arbitrariness of good, advanced by the Scotists, Occam and Descartes, is the doctrine that good is good because it proceeds from the undetermined will of God, who has chosen and commanded it; a moral act is not intrinsically good. Cf. Windelband, *Hist. of Philos.* (Eng. tr.) 332, 394.

G. R. T. ROSS.

ARBITRATION is an arrangement by which two persons, having a difference, agree to submit it to the decision of a third, and to abide by that decision when it has been given. Such an agreement precludes either party from instituting a suit in the ordinary Courts of law on the matter in question; and indeed those Courts are so favourable to arbitration that they will make the submission to arbitration a rule of Court, so that the decision of the third person, called the arbiter or arbitrator, may be enforced at law by either party against the other.

The reasons which induce persons who would otherwise become litigants to prefer a reference to arbitration to a suit at law are: (1) that it does not involve the personal hostility caused by legal proceedings; (2) that it is more economical in its cost; (3) that the arbitrator is at liberty to consider the whole circumstances of the matter in dispute, and to arrive at what in his opinion is an equitable solution of it; (4) that the arbitrator is a person selected by themselves upon the ground of his special fitness to deal with that matter.

It does not often happen, however, that the two parties at variance are able to agree upon a third who possesses equally the confidence of both. The ordinary form of arbitration is, therefore, the appointment by each party of a different arbitrator, and the appointment by the two arbitrators of a third person as oversman or umpire, by whom any difference between the two arbitrators shall be decided. In England the proceedings in arbitration are regulated by statute, and are, therefore, only a degree less formal than those of a suit at law. They begin with a submission to the arbitrators of the question in dispute; then there is the acceptance by the arbitrators of the burden of the reference, and the fixing by them of a time for hearing the parties. At that time each party may be heard in person or by solicitor or counsel; the evidence of witnesses and of documents may be tendered, and the arbitrators may administer an oath to each witness, or take his affirmation, which will render him liable to the penalties of perjury if his evidence be false in any material particular.

The decision of the arbitrator or umpire, when duly arrived at, is binding upon both parties, and the Courts will not enter upon any inquiry whether it is right or wrong. He draws it up in the form of an award, and, speaking generally, the Courts accept that award as conclusive. There are cases, however, where it may appear to the Court that the arbitrator has neglected the elementary principles of justice, as by refusing to hear evidence, or has not brought his mind to the consideration of the subject, or has not disposed of the question really at issue, or has in some other way failed in the due exercise of his functions; and the Court will in such case either refer the matter back to him, or hold that it is not ousted of its own inherent jurisdiction to determine that matter. For these reasons the parties in their choice of an arbitrator, and the arbitrators in their choice of an umpire, should be careful to select a person who, whether a practising lawyer or not, has a mind imbued with the principles of law, and has had some experience in their practical application, as well as an expert knowledge of the definite questions at issue.

In certain cases, in order to avoid the cost of litigation, a recourse to arbitration has been prescribed or authorized by statute. The Savings Banks Acts, the Friendly Societies Acts, the Building Societies Acts, and the Industrial and Provident Societies Acts contain provisions to this effect. In the case of the Savings Banks, including the Post Office Savings Banks, all disputes between a depositor or other claimant and the Bank are to be settled by the Registrar of Friendly Societies, and the jurisdiction of the Courts of law is ousted. As, however, the depositor has no choice in the matter, this is in effect only the creation of another Court having final jurisdiction, and using cheaper and more speedy methods than those of the ordinary Courts. In the other cases the statutes enable a society to provide by its rules that all disputes shall be referred to arbitration, and to define in those rules the manner in which the arbitrators shall be chosen. Where the rules contain such a provision, the jurisdiction of the Courts of law is equally ousted, and the member or other claimant has no other remedy than to avail himself of the arbitration thus provided.

In regard to the trade disputes between employer and employed, which frequently lead to much suffering and loss when pursued by the ordinary methods of trade warfare—strikes and lockouts—much may be done by means of arbitration and conciliation. Thus among the ironworkers of the country a permanent Board of Conciliation has been established, consisting of a given number of workmen and of representatives of the employers, who meet periodically to adjudicate on any questions of dispute that may have arisen in the course of the employment, and to prescribe any change in the current rate of wages that may be necessary. Their decisions are accepted by both parties, and the establishment of the Board has procured a long industrial peace in that particular trade. By the Conciliation Act of 1896 the parties to any trade dispute may apply to the Board of Trade to appoint a conciliator, and this method has been adopted with success in many important trade disputes. Lord Rosebery, Lord James of Hereford, Mr. Asquith, and other eminent statesmen have accepted the office of conciliator, and the results have been in general satisfactory—not only in saving the workmen and their families from much distress and the employers from heavy loss, but in re-establishing friendly and kindly relations between them. In like manner, arbitration has frequently been invoked in the United States in cases of conflict between capital and labour, as when, in the great miners' strike of 1902, President

Roosevelt appointed a Board of Arbitration which satisfactorily settled the disputes in question. Some States, as New Jersey, have regularly appointed State Boards of Arbitration.

Another still more important development of the principle of arbitration, rich in its promise for the peace of the world, has been its application to disputes between nations. Such disputes, even more than those between individuals, are apt to be coloured with local prejudice, *amour propre*, and all the elements that go to make up the sentiment of patriotism. Nothing is more difficult than for the people of one country, party to such a dispute, to appreciate the strength of the case of the other party. The nation's honour and prestige are thought to be at issue on the result of the dispute; and nothing is easier than to create an unreasoning popular clamour for war. To substitute for the appeal to arms—with all its consequences to both countries in bloodshed, suffering, waste, and demoralization—an appeal to argument and to calm reason is a triumph of civilization. The superstition of the ancients led them to think that the gods would defend the right, and even in Christian times we have seen two hostile armies each appealing to the god of battles for success upon that ground; but, in fact, the recourse to war is nothing but a resort to brute force.

An instance in point is afforded by the dispute between Great Britain and Venezuela. A question arose between those two States as to their rights in certain portions of the territory called British Guiana. In 1890 the Venezuelan Government proposed a reference to arbitration on this question, which Great Britain refused. Thereupon the Government of the United States of America interposed, upon the ground that any hostile action taken by Great Britain against Venezuela would be an infringement of the Monroe doctrine, and President Cleveland took upon himself to appoint a Commission to ascertain the rights of the matter. The British Government having refused to recognize this Commission, a wave of warlike enthusiasm swept over the United States, and if popular excitement had had its way, a war between those two great and kindred nations would have resulted, with all its horrible consequences, arising out of a matter of no real importance to either. Fortunately, better counsels prevailed, and Great Britain and Venezuela agreed to a reference to arbitration. The result of that arbitration was a concession to Venezuela of territory which Great Britain had more than once offered to that State, and the confirmation in other respects of the contentions of the British Government.

A still more famous instance is that known as the 'Alabama' arbitration. During the Civil War in the United States, resulting from the secession of the Southern or Confederate States, a vessel was built at Birkenhead, which was allowed to leave English waters, and was armed and commissioned by the Confederate Government. The United States ambassador had complained to the British Government of the breach of neutrality involved in the building and equipment of this vessel, and orders were given to stop it; but by an accident those orders were delayed till after the ship had actually sailed. In the course of the following two years this ship, named the 'Alabama,' destroyed much property belonging to citizens of the United States, and at the close of the war the Governments of those States claimed the value of that property from the British Government as damages for which Great Britain was liable through its unintentional breach of neutrality. The British Government accepted the responsibility, and agreed to refer the settlement of the amount payable to arbitration. The amount awarded was 15½ million dollars.

E. W. BRABROOK.

ARCANI DISCIPLINA.—The name given by Dallæus to the custom in the Early Catholic Church of keeping the administration of Baptism and the Holy Supper, with related doctrines and rites, a secret from all except the baptized. Various reasons for this practice have been suggested by scholars. It was not due to any teaching of the NT, and the openness with which Justin Martyr describes the worship of the Church, and the fact that the followers of Marcion had not the practice, show that it was not usual before the third quarter of the 2nd century.

There is every reason to suppose that the celebration of the Holy Supper by the congregations in Apostolic times was virtually private. Danger of persecution led to concealment of the Christian assemblies and rites. The measures of the Roman government prevented the celebration of the Supper and the Agapæ at night, and compelled the observance of the former in connexion with the open preaching of the word in the daytime, and perhaps the gradual abandonment of the latter. The catechumens were then dismissed before the communicants entered upon the Holy Supper itself. The catechumenate afforded a period of probation. In the first part of it the candidates were instructed in the general principles of religion. It was just before their baptism that they were instructed in the mysteries of the faith. The Creed, and perhaps the doctrine of the Trinity which explained the formula of Baptism, were not imparted to them until just before their baptism; and the Lord's Prayer not until afterwards. The example of the heathen Mysteries was felt. Those who had been admitted to the Communion, having gone through the grades of the catechumenate, and having transacted successive renunciations and exorcisms, were spoken of as 'The Initiated.' Finally, it became usual to regard those rites from which all but the full members of the Church were excluded as 'Mysteries,' and to transfer to them the awe that belonged to ethnic Mysteries. As Th. Harnack says, 'The mystical became mysterious, and the liturgical became theurgic.' He traces the great change to the gradual concentration of all the authority of the Church in the episcopate, due to the necessity of opposing its authority to Gnostic sects and their teachings. The rites of the Church were thought to have no validity apart from the bishops; and those performed by them were invested with mysterious awfulness. To this conception of Divine worship, Roman Catholic writers have joined the notion of a secret tradition of doctrine from the Apostles, in addition to the teaching of the NT. To this tradition they ascribe, for instance, the doctrine of Transubstantiation, and also the reverence for images and for the saints.

This *Secret Discipline*, beginning about A.D. 175, was in vogue until the end of the 5th century. Its features may, perhaps, be best set forth by the following quotations from Fathers and teachers of the 3rd and 4th centuries.

Tert. (*Prescrip. Hær.* xli.): 'To begin with, it is doubtful who is a catechumen and who a believer; they have all access alike, they hear alike, they pray alike—even heathens, if any such happen to come among them. That which is holy they will cast to the dogs; and their pearls, although (to be sure) they are not real ones, they will fling to the swine. Simplicity they will have to consist in the overthrow of discipline, attention to which on our part they call pandering.'

Basil (*de Sp.* 27): 'Of the beliefs and practices whether generally accepted or publicly enjoined which are preserved in the Church, some we possess derived from written teaching; others we have received delivered to us "in a mystery" by the tradition of the Apostles; and both of these in relation to true religion have the same force.'

(In a note in the *Nicene Fathers*, vol. viii. p. 41, Photius is quoted: 'In this work Eulogius [Patriarch of Alexandria 579–607] says that of the doctrines (διδαγμάτων) handed down in the church by the ministers of the word, some are δόγματα, and others κηρύγματα. The distinction is that δόγματα are announced with concealment and prudence, and are often designedly compassed with obscurity, in order that holy things may not be exposed to profane persons or pearls cast before swine. Κηρύγματα, on the other hand, are announced without any concealment').

'For we are not, as is well known, content with what the Apostle or the Gospel has recorded, but both in preface and conclusion we add other words as being of great importance to the validity of the ministry, and these we derive from unwritten teaching. Moreover, we bless the water of baptism and the oil of the chrism, and besides this the catechumen who is being baptized. On what written authority do we do this? Is not our authority silent and mystical tradition? . . . Does not this come from that unpublished and secret teaching which our fathers guarded in a silence out of the reach of curious meddling and inquisitive investigation? Well had they learnt the lesson that the awful dignity of the mysteries is best preserved by silence. What the uninitiated are not even allowed to look at was hardly likely to be publicly paraded about in written documents. . . . . Moses was wise enough to know that contempt attaches to the trite and to the obvious, while a keen interest is naturally associated with the unusual and the unfamiliar. In the same manner the Apostles and Fathers who laid down laws for the Church from the beginning thus guarded the awful dignity of the mysteries in secrecy and silence, for what is bruited abroad at random among the common folk is no mystery at all. This is the reason for our traditions of unwritten precepts and practices, that the knowledge of our dogmas may not become neglected and contemned by the multitude through familiarity. "Dogma" and "Kerygma" are two distinct things: the former is observed in silence; the latter is proclaimed to all the world.'

Cyril Jer. (*Catech.* vi. 29): 'These Mysteries, which the Church now explains to thee who art passing out of the class of Catechumens, it is not the custom to explain to heathen. For to a heathen we do not explain the mysteries concerning Father, Son, and Holy Ghost, nor before Catechumens do we speak plainly of the Mysteries; but many things we often speak in a veiled way, that the believers who know may understand, and they who know not may get no hurt.'

Ambrose (*c. Myster.* i.): 'The season now warns us to speak of the Mysteries, and to set forth the purport of the sacraments, which if we had thought it well to teach before baptism to those who were not yet initiated, we should be considered rather to have betrayed than to have portrayed the Mysteries. And then, too, another reason is that the light itself of the Mysteries will shed itself with more effect upon those who are expecting they know not what, than if any discourse had come beforehand.'

Origen (*c. Cels.* i. 7): 'Crucifixion, Resurrection, Incarnation are well known. But that there should be certain doctrines, not made known to the multitude, which are (revealed) after the exoteric ones have been taught, is not a peculiarity of Christianity, but also of philosophic systems, in which some truths are exoteric and some esoteric.'

When, in consequence of the conversion of the Empire and the prevalence of Infant Baptism, the old catechumenate of adults fell away, the *Disciplina Arcani* ceased to be, although in the Greek Liturgy the distinction between a *Missa Catechumenorum* and a *Missa Fidelium* is still marked by the deacon's warning to all the catechumens to go out of the church.

LITERATURE.—Art. on 'Arkandisciplin' in *PRE*[2] (v. Zezschwitz) and *PRE*[3] (Bonwetsch); 'Disciplina Arcani' in the *Dict. Christ. Ant.*; also Th. Harnack, *Der christ. Gemeindegottesdienst im apostol. u. altkathol. Zeitalter* (1854), esp. pp. 3–60; Edwin Hatch, *The Influence of Greek Ideas and Usages upon the Christian Church* (1888), pp. 283–309; John Dallæus, *De Scriptis quæ sub Dionysii Areopagitæ nomine circumferuntur* (1666); Meier, *De recondita veteris ecclesiæ theologia* (1670); Schelstrate, *Antiquitas illustrata circa concilia generalia et provincialia* (1678); Bingham, *Antiquities of the Christian Church*, x. xiv. xv. (1708–1722, Engl. 1875); Fromman, *De Disciplina Arcani* (1833); Richd. Rothe, *De Disciplinæ Arcani Origine* (1841); Th. Zahn, *Glaubensregel u. Taufbekenntnis in d. alten Kirche*; Anrich, *Das antike Mysterienwesen in seinem Einfluss auf das Christentum* (1894); Horn, *Outlines of Liturgics on the basis of Harnack* (1890).

EDWARD T. HORN.

ARCHÆOLOGY.—1. Archæology is a descriptive science, dealing with the interpretation of the remains of past phases of human civilization. Etymologically, the name denotes the study of *origins* generally (from Gr. ἀρχή, 'origin'; ἀρχαῖος, 'original'), and strictly it implies that the remains which it studies are interpreted as members of an originative or developmental series, irrespective of their nearness to the present time. Popularly, however, archæology is restricted to mean the 'study of antiquity,' and is understood to mean the interpretation, *either*, generally, of all the available evidence for past phases of civilization (in which sense it includes formal 'history' among its subdivisions); *or*, more particularly, of such evidence as is furnished by the material remains of human handiwork. In the latter and commoner sense, archæology stands alongside formal history, which is concerned with the interpretation of documents; and it is to be regarded essentially as the 'past tense' of technology, and of the æsthetic criticism of manufactured objects. Archæology, like palæontology and geology, which are the analogous 'past tenses' or 'historical' aspects of biology and geography, is a science of observation solely. Experiment is contemplated only in so far as it may be possible to test interpretation (*e.g.* of the evidence for an obsolete mode of manipulation) by re-constituting now the presumed conditions of the ancient process, so as to attain an analogous result.

It is only in its wider signification that archæology comes into contact with the study of religion or ethics. Ancient technology and ancient æsthetic, considered specially, occupy their own domain apart. But there are few, if any, religions which have not prompted the production of monuments, ornaments, utensils, and other ritual accessories; or affected the form and decoration of the instruments of daily life. And as these material expressions of religious ideas, once produced, are capable of preservation independently of their makers, they may be, and often are, the only evidence which has been preserved of the religion of an extinct people, whose beliefs and traditions have perished with it.

2. Archæological evidence may establish the occurrence of an act or a custom within assignable limits either of (*a*) space or of (*b*) time.

(*a*) To prove the distribution of an occurrence in *space*, the method of archæology is geographical. The instances which have been observed are tabulated in their geographical context, and in the absence of evidence to the contrary may be presumed provisionally to indicate a continuous distribution over the intervening areas. Such evidence to the contrary would be supplied *inter alia* by diversity of physical circumstance, exempting humanity locally from the need, or the inducement, to act in the manner presumed; or by evidence of the presence locally of other human observances inconsistent with the act or custom in question. The quality, as well as the quantity, of evidence requisite to give archæological proof varies almost indefinitely. But in general, quality is incomparably more cogent than quantity, and positive evidence than negative: a single really well-authenticated occurrence (*e.g.* of an object of human manufacture or of recognized style in a given area), not only supplies the contradictory instance to all negative generalities, but gives a positive though indefinite presumption that further instances exist. This characteristic, archæology shares with all branches of knowledge which are concerned with discontinuous series; the area actually open to inspection is at the same time so arbitrarily assigned, and so small a proportion of the whole, that the probable value of every positive instance is in any case somewhat greater, and of every negative instance somewhat less, than it would be in a region of which the larger part has been already explored. This theoretical consideration is in the main confirmed by a retrospect of the archæological work of the last century. As in geology, a very small number of well-selected data from small areas isolated from each other, and indicated by accidental circumstances, have permitted a hypothetical re-construction of the human culture of wide regions, which subsequent evidence, more copious, continuous, and cogent logically, has done little if anything to modify, or even to confirm.

Archæology, being concerned with evidence which has already been exposed for a while to the accidents of time, is confronted with discontinuous evidence in another sense also. Some classes of objects, no less characteristic and instructive than the rest, are composed of materials which decay readily, and leave little or no trace even when deposited in closed chambers. Consequently, archæology is concerned in most cases with evidence which has already undergone a process of quite arbitrary selection, and is compelled to qualify its conclusions accordingly. And even where the remains themselves are durable, the ravages of man or animals—the latter often far more elusive and perplexing than the former—have restricted the evidence again, objects of intrinsic value, or distasteful significance (such as the monuments of a hated ruler or an alien creed) disappearing most readily, and causing the most serious breaks in the record.

(*b*) To prove the distribution of similar occurrences in *time*, or the sequence of dissimilar occurrences, archæology depends, again, like geology, on the comparison of simultaneities. Sequence of manufacture, among a series of relics of antiquity, may be determined either directly on the evidence of sequence of deposition (as in a stratified rubbish-heap, where the under layers must be older than those which overlie them); or indirectly, by comparison of style. The latter method, however, gives, strictly speaking, a series which is only morphological, not historical; it is evidence of change, not of development; and in many cases such a series is capable of being read in either direction, since no precise criterion exists to distinguish immaturity from decadence. When doubt arises from this cause as to which is the initial end of a series, recourse must be had in the long run to the evidence of stratification; but an *approximate* proof can frequently be constructed if it is possible to correlate a number of concurrent series.

For example, on a given site, a large number of tombs may be found, each containing examples of pottery, metal-work, stone-work, and other manufactures, of varying design. There is a probability that the tombs represent burials of a considerable number of successive generations. The pottery, weapons, and so forth, form morphological series, independent but approximately concurrent; *i.e.* phase *D* of the pottery is always found with phases *c d* or *e* of the metal-work; phase *Q* always with phases *p q* or *r*, never with *o* or *s*. In these circumstances, clear evidence as to the direction in which any one series is to be read biologically is conclusive for the remainder, and for the culture as a whole; and such evidence would be supplied if any one kind of object began to appear suddenly and copiously as a useful implement at *k*, for example, and was replaced in adjacent phases by substitutes of less appropriate forms or materials, or otherwise clearly imitative. If these after-types occur at *l*, *m*, and after, the historical order of the whole series is from *a* to *z*; if at *j* and before, the order is from *z* to *a*.

It is, of course, often the case that a purely morphological series is concurrent at one or more points with another series which belongs to a 'historic' civilization, that is, to one in which the relative antiquity of each phase can be represented by an 'absolute' or chronological date. In these circumstances alone is it possible to determine the actual rate of technological progress, and thereby of other elements of a civilization.

Such cases of contact between concurrent series representing the civilizations of different areas or régimes can only show valid contemporaneity when the proof is bilateral.

In locality A, for example, a group of objects of diverse styles are found together as the result of a single act of deposition, such as a burial, or the laying of a foundation-stone. In such a case, obviously, none of the objects which compose the group can be of a later date of manufacture than the date of its deposition in that group. On the other hand, any of them may have been of any imaginable age already, at the moment of deposition. External evidence (of custom, workmanship, and the like) alone can decide in each case whether the indigenous objects *aaa* included in the find-group fairly represent the phase of culture α, at which it has been ascertained that the group was deposited in the place where it was found. Now, if this find-group at A contains, not only indigenous objects *aaa* of relative date α in the series characteristic of this locality A, but also an object of exotic origin *b*, the circumstance (otherwise demonstrated) that the object *b* is of the relative date β in the series B does not prove that the phase α, to which the group as a whole belongs, is contemporary with phase β, but only that it is not of any *later* date; for the object *b* may have been of any age already at the moment of its deposit at A. If, however, even a single object of origin *a* and date α is found at B with objects of origin *b* and date β in the B-series, then by the same reasoning α is not of later date than the objects *bbb* with which it has been found. And if so, the proof is complete, that α and *b* are contemporary; for it was already known that an object *b* could not be of later date than *aaa*.

It is merely a matter of accurate observation to determine whether in any given case it is certain that the exotic object was really deposited simultaneously with the rest of the find-group, and not intruded into it at some later time.

3. The combination of evidence derived from *distributions* in space and *sequences* in time gives archæological proof of the *transmission* of new characters from one centre of civilization to another.

A character *x* which has already appeared at phase γ in series (or region) A does not appear in series B until phase ϵ (which has been shown otherwise to be contemporary with *e* in series A); it is absent, moreover, from series C until phase *k*. Here alternative interpretations are offered. The character may have been introduced from A to B, or it may have arisen spontaneously also at B. At C, moreover, it may have arisen spontaneously, or have been introduced directly from A; or in addition, it may have been introduced directly from B and only indirectly from A, and so forth, the number of alternatives increasing directly with that of the series or regions in question. The conclusive proof of direct transmission is given only when, in addition to objects of *similar* style to the archetype at A, but of demonstrably local origin, B yields an object which demonstrably originated at A. Such proof is furnished most clearly by unpremeditated evidence supplied by the physical composition of the object; *e.g.* knives of an unusual style but made of bronze occur on an island B which yields copper and tin but not iron; there is no adequate proof that these are not due to indigenous invention. But if there occurs also at B a knife of the same style but made of iron, and iron knives of exactly this exotic style are also found in an accessible iron-yielding area A, the probability becomes very strong that the knife found at B is exotic, and the prototype of the bronze examples, which differ from it only in being of indigenous material. The proof, however, becomes conclusive only when it is shown that bronze, or this particular variety of bronze, was not in use at A. Otherwise there is still the possibility that the bronze knives at B may also be imports either from A or from some other region C which culturally is dependent on A.

JOHN L. MYRES.

ARCHITECTURE.

ARCHITECTURE (Ægean).—Of the architecture in Greek lands before the true Hellenic architecture appeared upon the scene we know comparatively little, but even that little is great compared with our almost entire ignorance of the subject a generation ago. The account of the great discoveries of Schliemann at Tiryns, Mycenæ,* and Troy, restoring to us the Homeric world, of whose

* The author of this art. and artt. on Christian, Greek, and Roman Architecture always uses the Greek spelling of Greek names, but in the case of familiar words he has submitted to the spelling elsewhere adopted in the Encyclopædia.

very existence the greatest scholars were sceptical, reads like a fairy story. Since then a long series of excavations, carried out with greater and greater scientific precision throughout the whole Ægean area, has provided for us a mass of material which it will probably require the scholarship of many years to analyze and reduce to anything like systematic order. As yet no conclusions can be more than tentative.

This pre-Hellenic architecture can hardly be considered the parent of Greek architecture: its influence was on the whole smaller than might have been expected; indeed, the difference between them serves to emphasize the originality and independence of the Hellenic style that came after. It is convenient to term this architecture and the civilizations to which it belonged 'Ægean,' as it flourished not only in Greece itself but throughout all the coasts and islands of the Ægean Sea. But, at the same time, although there is a certain continuity of development with no decided break, such as exists between itself and the architecture of the Hellenes, it is nevertheless marked by changes and new departures that seem to imply influences from without, if not political and racial upheavals. These are at present exceedingly obscure and open to controversy, and it is difficult to do more than glance at the main trend of development.

(1) During the neolithic age in the Ægean, at some time which may be put approximately 6000 years before the Christian era, there was a primitive but flourishing civilization, implying a highly developed commerce, extending as far as Egypt, with some powers of navigation. Its centre apparently was in Crete, and is marked by the exploitation of the obsidian in the island of Melos, which, some considerable time afterwards, developed its own resources during the flourishing epoch of the town, now known to archæologists, from the name of the neighbouring village, as Phylakopi. In this very remote era the neolithic remains at Knossos contain obsidian, and Melos is the only known source of obsidian anywhere near the Eastern end of the Mediterranean. Obsidian beads are found in Egypt in remains to which a rough date of the seventh millennium may be assigned, and obsidian flakes occur there some 600 years or so later. By the time of the foundation of the first city at Phylakopi the trade was very considerable. The architectural achievement of this age must have been of an exceedingly simple nature, probably merely wattle and daub huts, as the marked clay strata testify wherever there have been settlements. Wooden or half-timber houses may conceivably have succeeded them, but they have left no remains, and we have nothing but an inference from a later mode of construction to point in this direction. Something, however, of the working of quarried stone is seen, at any rate towards the close of the neolithic period, in the cist graves found principally at Amorgos and at Pelos in Melos. It is therefore quite possible that a few of the more important buildings may have been of stone, but of these there is practically no evidence. At the very close of the neolithic period we seem to have stone-walled houses appearing at Purgos in Paros and also in S.W. Naxos, and these may represent an older tradition. It is also conceivable that sun-dried bricks may occasionally have been used, which, under certain conditions, can disappear, leaving practically no trace of their form.

(2) A definite style of stone building begins to appear about the commencement of the fourth millennium. The settlements are marked by their unwalled and unfortified nature, and, as far as the slight evidence goes, seem to have been laid out almost as scattered groups of buildings, yet in the main preserving a certain parallelism of plan, although they do not seem to be arranged along definite street lines. The building is rough rubble work of comparatively small stones built with clay and mud, and plastered over with the same; lime mortar is not yet used. So far there are no signs of any religious buildings as such, and indeed throughout the whole of the Ægean development there seems to have been hardly anything of the nature of religious architecture. This is one of the essential contrasts between these peoples and the Greeks, whose religious buildings were of such marvellous excellence and occupied so prominent a place in their style. The nature of the architecture, however, is of importance for the purposes of this article, as it is necessary to grasp both the resemblances and the differences between the architectural principles of the two styles, in order fully to understand the position of Greek religious architecture in the history of the art.

(3) A third architectural stage is reached roughly about B.C. 3000, when a closer system of town building, generally although not necessarily fortified, is adopted. It is marked by an elaborate system of street planning, with a distinct preference for rectangular rather than convergent systems. There is a very considerable advance in the art of building, with a regular drainage system beneath the streets. We find lime beginning to be used. There are great walls and fortifications, and the towns in the generality of cases are no longer open. The probable cause seems to have been pressure from the north, which rendered these fortifications necessary. They apparently first made their appearance upon the mainland, and worked their way southward, the cities of the maritime power of Crete remaining unwalled, probably on account of that very sea power. The great brick city of Troy, the second in the series, already shows this type completely developed, and its final destruction must have been at least as early as B.C. 2000. The second city at Phylakopi is of this type, and it was probably founded somewhere about B.C. 3000, reaching its prime about B.C. 2500.

Of the general character of building, it may be said that it passes from a comparatively rude to a highly developed style, and indeed might be divided into periods. But the variations of type are far greater in their local than in their chronological aspect, which latter is much more visible in the paintings and the minor arts of pottery. Architecturally, the second city of Troy is more akin to the great sixth city than either is to any period of Knossian architecture. The architecture seems to reach its zenith somewhat earlier than the other arts, and begins to show signs of decadence while they are still in some ways advancing.

It may seem strange to sum up a period, running into many hundreds of years, as though there were a single style throughout. But in the present state of our knowledge, particularly in the extreme uncertainty of the chronology, some such simplification is necessary if lengthy controversial matter is to be excluded. Very approximately it may be said that the architecture was at its finest at a time ranging round the 17th century B.C. But certain broad general characteristics may be noticed. The materials and construction used seem to have differed very considerably locally, such intractable material as basalt appearing at Phylakopi, and limestone, gypsum, brick, schist, etc., in other places; and varying from the roughest blocks, hardly shaped at all, to the finest jointed masonry, such as we see at Phaistos or in the walls of the great megaron at Knossos. Even early in the period there is good sound work with headers and stretchers roughly shaped, as at Phylakopi. On the whole, work on the Greek mainland is rougher and less carefully finished, the so-called cyclopean masonry at Tiryns and elsewhere being typical. This would point to the civilizing influence proceeding from the south northward. Troy seems to be somewhat outside the main stream. Its architecture, particularly its fortifications, is very advanced, although in other particulars its civilization seems to be behind the rest of the Ægean.

There is a great tendency from the first to use rubble for interior walls and for less important structures. This is faced with plaster and frequently elaborately painted, as in the fresco of the Flower Gatherer at Knossos, or the absolutely delightful example of the Flying Fish at Phylakopi. Another method is to build one or two courses with great blocks of ashlar masonry and raise the rubble walls upon the top. In outside work some such foundation is almost

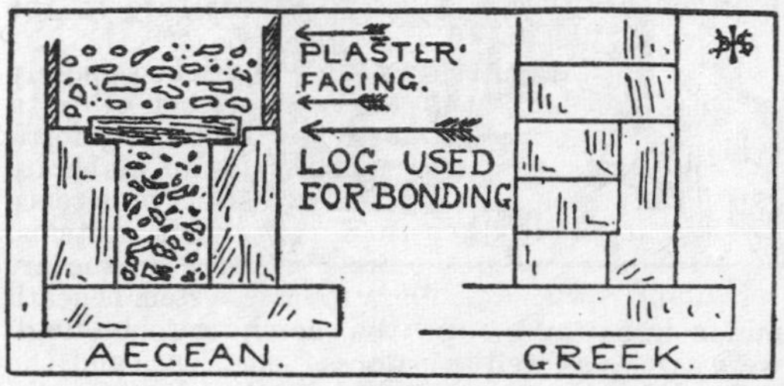

FIG. 1.

necessary. In the early second city of Troy, built mainly of sun-dried brick, there is a substructure of stone to protect the brick from the wet. Rubble tends to become more common in later work, and sometimes later rubble walls are found built upon older stone foundations. The system may be the origin of the orthostatai of later Greek architecture (*q.v.*). Sometimes there is also a projecting plinth, as in the case of the limestone blocks below the gypsum in the West Court at Knossos, or the reverse arrangement, with the gypsum blocks below, on the southern terrace (fig. 1). This is quite possibly the origin of another Greek feature, the stylobate [see ARCHITECTURE (Greek)]. Another method, which on account of its material was not likely to survive to our day, seems to have been something of the nature of a half timber construction, in which courses of short lengths of timber set transversely in plaster across the wall were used at intervals in the ashlar, or plastered rubble, as the case might be (fig. 2). There are grounds for supposing that we have the remains of such a course in the megaron at Knossos. In interiors the ends of these were masked by rosettes or medallions. In the last phase of Ægean architecture, the

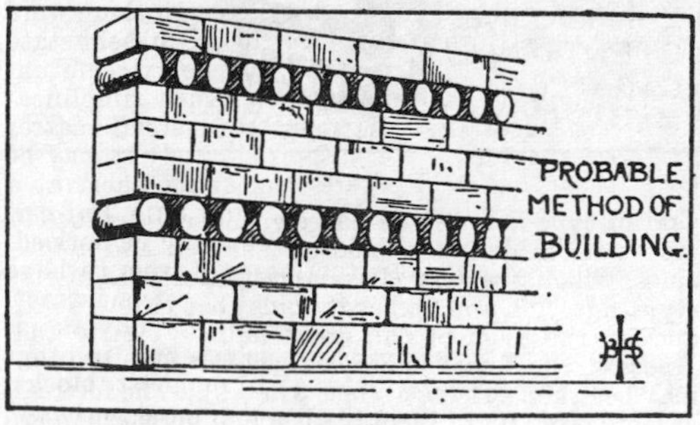

FIG. 2.

Mycenæan, there seems to have been an interesting survival of this technique executed in stone over the doorway of the so-called Treasury of Atreus [see p. 683 and figs. 3 and 17].

On the whole it may be said that there is a distinct architectural decadence which in Crete becomes obviously marked about the 14th century B.C. But in the north it seems to be otherwise, and the masonry continues to improve until a later date, as, for instance, in the very fine beehive tombs at Mycenæ, which may be not much earlier than the 13th century. This may be accounted for by the fact that the artistic impulse spread from the south. Hence the north would be longer in developing; and, on the other hand, a northern subjugation of Crete, which seems to be probable, would have greatly arrested progress there.

The spanning of openings seems in most instances to have been with timber lintels, and in early work the stones are not even gathered over above. Stone lintels, however, were sometimes used. The jambs of doors were very commonly of stone, and in later work certainly an inward inclination was usual, which is very possibly the origin of the same feature in Greek doorways (fig. 3 below and fig. 8, ARCHITECTURE [Greek]). Windows, as contrasted with Greek architecture, seem to have been of frequent occurrence. They appear to have had timber lintels, jambs, and sills, and we may notice a remarkable anticipation of the modern window in the division into 'panes' of which we have clear evidence in tablets found at Knossos (fig. 3). The nature of the filling is unknown; it may

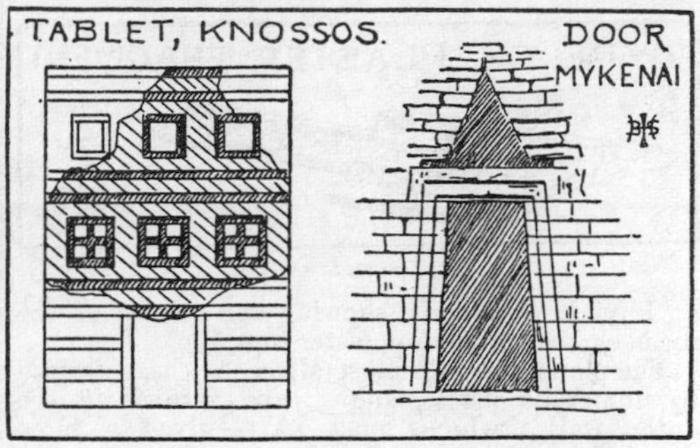

FIG. 3.

have been oiled cloth or parchment, and is indicated in red colour on the tablets.

Timber seems to have played a large part in the construction, especially in the columns, which were commonly of wood, although with bases of stone. The columns, and generally the bases, were circular in form, and it is noticeable that the columns tapered towards the lower end (figs. 4 and 12), the exact contrary of columns in Greek architecture. The taper, however, is generally exaggerated in drawings. The charred remains of actual columns

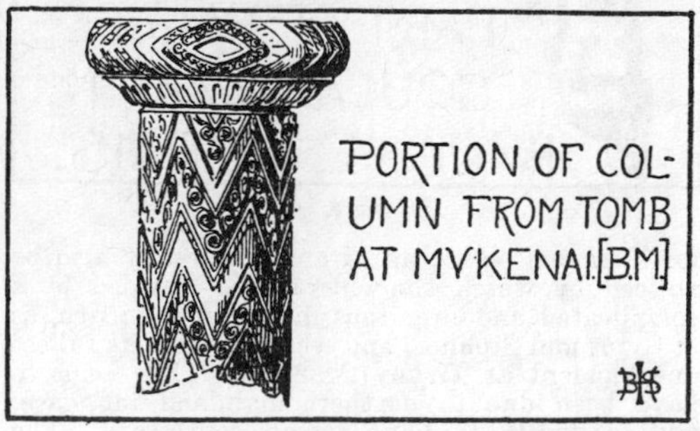

FIG. 4.

were found both at Knossos and at Phaistos. Stone examples of similar shape but of much later date occur at Eleusis and Mycenæ. They were treated with different kinds of fluting as ornaments, sometimes vertical, sometimes diagonal (fig. 4), and this may even have suggested the Doric flute. The anta was used both in stone and in wood, and is possibly the prototype of that feature in Greek architecture. It is interesting to notice that when stone columns were used they were almost always square in section, especially in early work, as in the case of the Northern Portico at Knossos, the so-called 'pillar rooms' at Phylakopi, and at Knossos both in the palace and in houses outside. They are also of rectangular shape in the court at Phaistos, and by the N. entrance at Knossos, and even in the megaron itself, although there they are recessed. This is important in view of the discussion regarding the origin of the Greek column [see ARCHITECTURE (Greek)]. The inter-columniations were wide, and the architrave apparently was a wooden beam upon which the upper masonry rested.

In spite, however, of the use of wood, it does not seem to have been used for floors. The floor joists were of circular logs of wood, and above these was laid clay, and upon that a fine hard cement or a pavement. On the ground floor cement seems to have been the favourite material for exterior work, and is often laid over paving; but in interiors fine gypsum slabs are not uncommon. The ceilings, where there was no floor above, were in all probability of thick reeds covered with plaster. Remains of plaster have been found

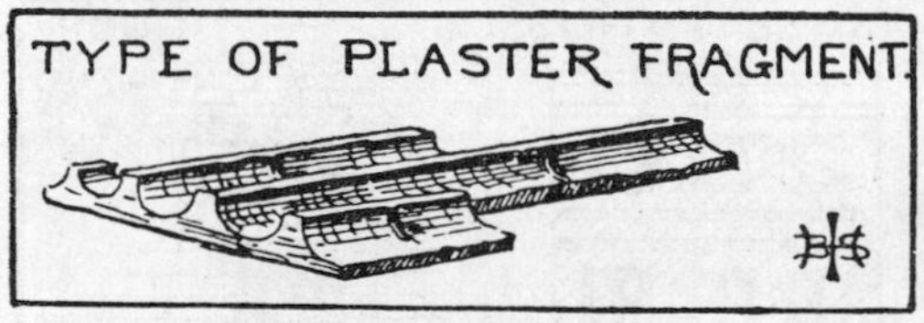

FIG. 5.

at Phylakopi, clearly showing the shapes of the reeds embedded in the plaster (fig. 5).

The plans are in almost all cases characterized by numerous offsets, angles, and returns in the outer walls, which must have given a most delightful effect of light and shade to the complete elevation, and which are carried out with a lofty indifference to the extra work that they must have entailed (figs. 6, 8, and 9). Where

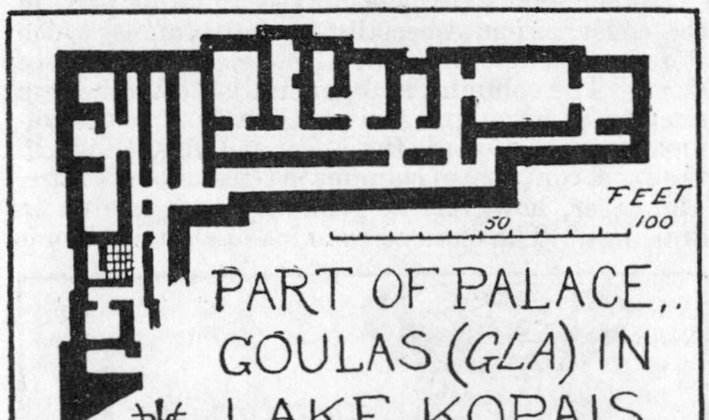

FIG. 6.

fortifications occur, an arrangement may also be noticed by which the entrance is guarded by a complicated and circuitous means of approach, as at Syros and Siphnos, and which attains its fullest development at Tiryns (fig. 8, E). This seems to have been due to northern mainland influence, and gradually to have spread southward. The buildings of greatest importance were the palaces of the kings, which show in almost all cases a remarkable complexity of plan; but there are certain marked variations. Both in the north and in the south there is a distinct parallelism in the arrangement, but the Cretan plan is more regular and conceived more definitely as an artistic whole. The equal balancing of the main masses about a central court is also a southern feature. In the north this is less obvious, and the court partakes more of the nature of a fore-court, and is surrounded by a colonnade. The greater regularity is doubtless mainly because in the islands the question of fortification was of

FIG. 7.

minor importance. In the north the buildings were castles as well as palaces.

But there is also a difference in the artistic *motif* that cannot thus be explained. The northern plan tends to rooms comparatively square in shape; the

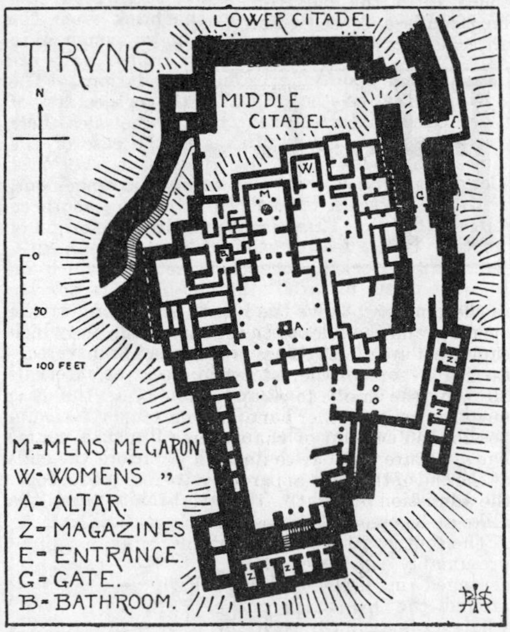

FIG. 8.

Cretan type is long and narrow. The difference is most noticeable in the smaller chambers and magazines, which are very characteristic features of the style (figs. 7, 8, and 9), but it holds good throughout, and is true even of the great halls. Tiryns and Knossos, the finest examples and the best known, may be taken as typical (figs. 8 and 9). The fortress of Goulas or Gla in Bœotia, although northern in its main features, is to some extent an exception, and shows affinities with the southern type. Propylæa are common throughout, but here a northern type can be distinguished which is almost the exact counterpart of the later Greek examples (fig. 10).

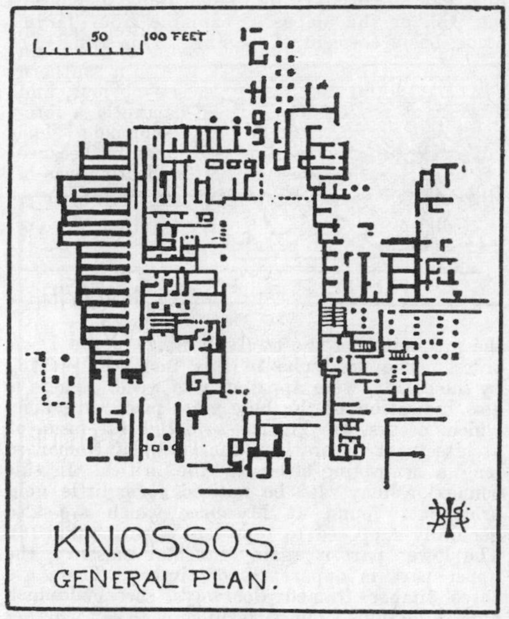

FIG. 9.

(The magazines are the narrow chambers on the left.)

But the most marked difference between north and south is in the megaron itself. The northern megaron is a broad rectangular chamber with an antechamber and a portico, and contains the hearth

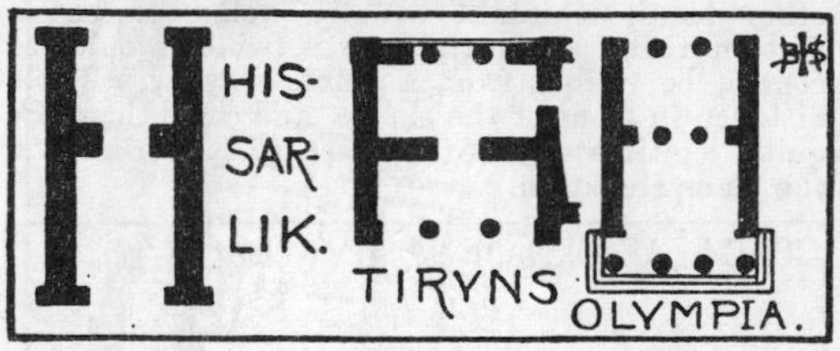

FIG. 10.

in the centre. Above the hearth was probably an opening, and the sides of the opening were normally supported upon four columns which in all likelihood carried a sort of clerestory admitting light and allowing the smoke to escape. The typical Cretan megaron, on the other hand, has no central hearth, possibly on account of the warmer climate; but it has a feature peculiar to itself in the open chamber at the end of the hall, apparently open to the sky for the admission of light. This 'light-well' is found alike at Knossos, Phaistos, and Hagia Triada.

The southern type also contains columns which presumably supported the roof; but they are arranged in lines, as the square arrangement around the hearth is unnecessary. Moreover, whatever may have been the case in the north, there is no doubt that in Crete there were halls upon different storeys one above the other.

The northern type, although belonging to the ruder style, eventually supersedes the other, and we find it appearing in the south in the late third city at Phylakopi (compare the examples in fig. 11). In this northern type we see a plan closely resembling that of the classical Greek temple; and if it is really the origin of the temple form, it may be considered the most important of the Ægean influences upon later Hellenic architecture.

It is, of course, natural that we should know a great deal more about the plans than the elevations, but we have a certain amount of valuable

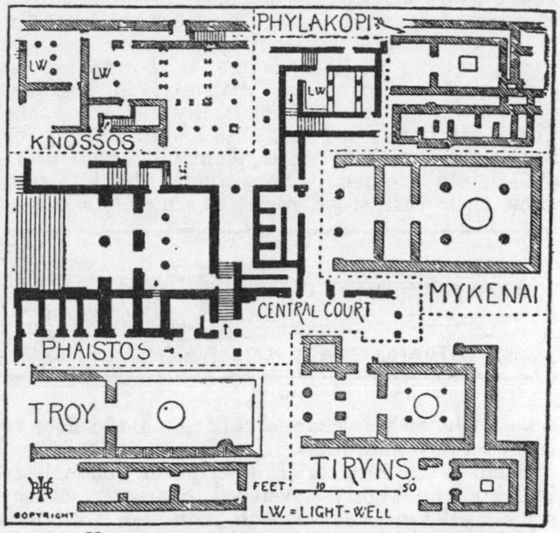

FIG. 11.—MEGARA, DRAWN TO COMMON SCALE, SHOWING N. AND S. TYPES.

evidence about the latter. In the south there is no doubt that there were several storeys, and in each storey the column played an important part. As in Spanish architecture, the main architectural features were in the interior, but the deep wells, with their tiers of columns and great staircases, must have produced a fine effect (fig. 12). There is some evidence that columns played a part in the external façade also. In

FIG. 12.—RESTORATION OF GENERAL EFFECT; HALL OF COLONNADES, KNOSSOS.

the north, upper storeys, above the megaron, were unlikely because of the hearth.

On the whole, it may be said that the northern influence is much more marked in the temple architecture of Greece than any influence we can trace to the southern types.

The columned storeys rising magnificently one above another are startling indeed, occurring at a date some 18 centuries before Christ, in a European civilization of which we had never previously heard; but the elaborate drainage system is almost equally surprising, finding its parallels only in the beautiful systems of the best work of the Middle Ages, and in those of modern times. Street drains were generally built of stone with large flat slabs above and below, but an open terra-cotta channel sometimes occurs. In small underground drains terra-cotta pipes with a collar were used (fig. 13), whereas in the great palace systems the main drains were well built passages large enough to allow of a man entering them for cleaning purposes. Sanitary conveniences were supplied; and if there was not the extensive accommodation that was demanded in the Middle Ages, where in many instances every room has its own separate arrangements, at least there is no reason to suppose that it was less than satisfied the last generation, or than is commonly found on the Continent to-day. The same remarks apply to bath-rooms, which were plentiful, and often elaborately treated. Sometimes there was a sunk bath with steps, sometimes merely a move-

FIG. 13.

able bath with a channel all round the floor to carry off any splashings.

Such is a very brief description, enough to indicate the highly developed character of the style. When we turn to consider religious architecture, it is obvious that there was little or none, and the main importance from that point of view is the influence exerted upon succeeding styles. Yet there are just a few points that may be noted. We have in the 'pillar rooms' at Knossos and Phylakopi something of obvious religious significance. It does not seem to be necessary to suppose that the pillar was not purely structural in its function,—even a sacred sign upon the top does not preclude the possibility of its supporting other blocks. Many of the blocks of the palaces in Crete are marked with sacred signs, which may be paralleled by the numerous masons' marks upon our own mediæval buildings. But there does seem to have been a special sacredness attaching to the pillar form, and in the case of a 'pillar room' in a house at Knossos, a great number, some 200, of little inverted cups were discovered, beneath which were found the charred remains of small vegetable offerings (fig. 14). If we cannot

FIG. 14.

say that these rooms are examples of religious architecture, it can at least be said that some religious significance was attached to their architecture.

We have also a fresco, mentioned above, which in the light of the secular architectural discoveries of the palaces, admits of interpretation, and seems to represent a temple or shrine (fig. 16). Below we have the great gypsum blocks that we have seen in the palace, and above half timber work with its frescoes on the plaster. The pillars, presumably of wood, are of the usual inverted form of Ægean architecture, and their sacredness is thought to be indicated by the horned cult object set before them. An interesting frieze, resembling that of porphyry-like stone found at Knossos (fig. 15), or the alabaster example from Tiryns, occurs below the central opening. This seems to be

FIG. 15.

the progenitor of the triglyph frieze of the Doric order. The triglyphs in this instance, judging by the colour, were apparently of wood. There is also indication of the blue glass paste or enamel which occurs at Tiryns—a delightful form of architectural decoration—the κύανος of Homer, so long a stumbling-block to the critics. In this connexion may also be noticed some little gold ornaments found at Mycenæ, which are also generally supposed to represent a shrine (fig. 16). The lower part is again of ashlar masonry, the upper part is apparently of timber. There are three timber-framed doorways through which appear columns; but it is difficult to say whether they are meant to be within the building or form part of the façade. In front of them are the same sacred horns. The most interesting point is that the central part is higher than the sides, and it certainly does suggest a nave and aisle construction with clerestory lighting. On the other hand, it might equally well represent a lantern rising above the hearth, which would, of course, be visible from a point of view a little distance in front of the shrine, and could therefore quite legitimately be represented pictorially in the plane elevation.

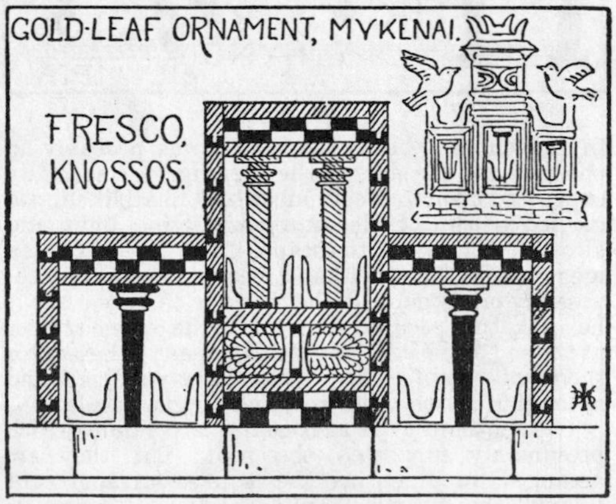

FIG. 16.

Lastly, there remain to be considered the tombs, which were of a sacred and in some instances definitely religious character. The famous shaft graves of Mycenæ—deep shafts sunk vertically in the rock—represent for us a stage of burial that can hardly be considered architectural. So also with the larnax burials of Crete, where the corpse was first skeletonized in the earth and afterwards deposited in an earthenware sarcophagus or larnax and buried. But in the chambered tombs and the still more elaborate domed structures we have something very different.

They are found widely distributed over the Greek mainland, where the best specimens occur, but have been found at Phaistos, Palaikastro, Praisos, in Crete, and also in Melos.

The chambered form is that of a square chamber cut in the rock, with a gabled roof and approached by a dromos, or passage. It seems probable that it is merely a development of the shaft grave, and the dromos is simply a means of closer and more ready approach to the tomb itself for the worshippers of the shade of the deceased. This finally develops into the great domed chamber out of which in some cases the tomb itself opens, and which can hardly have served any other purpose than one connected with religious ceremonies in relation to the deceased. This development is borne out by the shaft-construction of the grave at Orchomenos, in some respects the finest example of these beehive tombs. It is, however, not in as perfect a condition as the so-called Treasury of Atreus at Mycenæ, which was a trifle larger than this example (fig. 17).

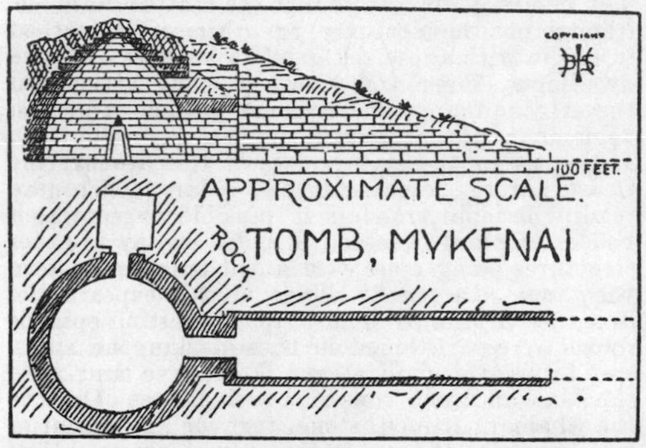

FIG. 17.

In both cases a large domed chamber, of beehive shape, about 47 feet in diameter, is cut out in the hill-side and lined with masonry of large blocks

FIG. 18.

built on the corbelled system (fig. 17). Opening out of the central chamber is a smaller side chamber, which in the case of the Orchomenos example was, like the shaft graves, clearly excavated by a shaft sunk from the top. The bottom was first lined with small stone masonry and then covered with marble slabs. This was roofed over with great slabs of green schist elaborately decorated with a typical Mycenæan pattern (fig. 18), and the marble walls were decorated in the same way. Above was another chamber to relieve the ceiling of weight, and above that again the shaft was filled up with débris.

The vault part is marked with numerous holes, some still containing bronze nails, and, as was also the case with the Mycenæan example, it was covered with bronze rosettes.

The fine doorway to the latter tomb can be restored with some degree of accuracy. A great door, narrower at the top than at the bottom, is flanked by two half columns, which taper downwards and are adorned with zigzag flutings. Above is an enormous lintel, the pressure upon which is relieved by a great triangular space originally filled with a light triangular slab. The architrave was ornamented with a pattern, clearly recalling the short log construction mentioned above, and below this was probably a series of lions' heads.

LITERATURE.—There is no work on Ægean Architecture as such, but some of the most useful sources of information are: T. J. Dörpfeld, *Troja und Ilion*, Athens, 1902; C. Schuchhardt, *Schliemann's Excavations*, tr. Eugénie Sellers, London, 1891; *Excavations at Phylakopi in Melos, conducted by the British School at Athens*, London, 1904; C. Tsountas and J. I. Manatt, *The Mycenæan Age*, London, 1897; see also *The Annual of the British School at Athens*, esp. vol. vi. f., London, and *Monumenti Antichi dei Lincei*, Rome.

J. B. STOUGHTON HOLBORN.

ARCHITECTURE (American).—Both in character and in material the dwellings and temples of the American Indians present the widest variety, ranging from the brush *wikiups* of the Pai Utes, and the snow *igloos* of the Eskimos, to the elaborate stone palaces of the Mayas of Yucatan. This diversity, however, must not be construed as racial in origin, since closely related neighbouring tribes frequently have dwellings of different types; nor is the cause any essential intellectual limitation. The divergency is climatic and economic in source. The snow-covered wastes of the extreme north, the forests of the Atlantic coast, the prairies which once abounded in herds of bison, the arid regions of the south-west, and the tropical luxuriance of Central America, each produced a distinct type of architecture. The dwellings of the American Indians admit of a triple classification: temporary, portable, and permanent, the first being exemplified by the Pai Ute *wikiup*, the second by the Dakota *tipi*, and the third by the stone *pueblo*.

1. The temporary dwelling is represented in its simplest form by the *wikiup* of Arizona. This is constructed by placing branches about 10 feet in length so as to form half or three-quarters of a circle. The tops are then brought together and smaller branches are thrown over them. The entire structure is, therefore, little more than a wind-break, and may be a development of the *kisi* of the Hopis, which is a rough shelter set up in the fields to protect those who watch the flocks. This general type of temporary dwelling is especially characteristic of the less developed tribes of the western desert, where the arid soil furnishes little building material beyond brush and mud. Closely akin to the *wikiup* is the Navaho *hogan*, a hut built either of branches covered with smaller boughs or of poles plastered with mud; and the same statement holds true of the Pimas and Mohaves. Such dwellings are frequently abandoned, since the materials of which they are composed are not portable, and the region affords no other kind. Religion also enters into the migrations of these tribes, since they do not occupy a dwelling which has been entered by death. Here too may be mentioned the grass houses still built by the Wichitas, but formerly characteristic of the Cadoans (except the Pawnees and Arikaras, who built, instead, the 'earth lodges' noted below).

2. A higher grade of American architecture is found, under more favourable economic circumstances, among the prairie tribes. Here the *wikiup* yields place to the *tipi*. The typical form of this structure is found among the Omahas, and is constructed by tying twenty or thirty long poles together at the top, and spreading out the bottom so as to form a circle. This frame is covered with skin or canvas, and an opening is left at the top for the escape of the smoke. Yet these tribes were by no means restricted to the *tipi*, since in the summer they sometimes built lodges covered with bark or earth, the former suggesting the Algonquin *wigwam*, and the latter what may be supposed to have been an earlier stage of *pueblo* construction. At all events, both represent a transition to the permanent dwelling. While the *wikiup* is naturally devoid of any ornamentation, the *tipi* often received somewhat elaborate adornment, this decoration being frequently totemistic, and sometimes the result of a vision or other omen. Here the form of the dwelling is conditioned by the material at hand, since trees are comparatively rare, while the herds of buffalo, which formerly ranged the plains, furnished an abundance of skins to form the covering of the poles. According to Dakota tradition, the tribes formerly dwelt in houses of bark in the present State of Minnesota, and were first forced by the invasions of the whites to adopt a nomadic life, and, in consequence, portable houses.

3. The *tipi* thus forms the transition from the temporary dwelling to the permanent. The latter form of house is characteristic of a settled people, and is, therefore, found among the most highly civilized American Indians. In its simplest form it may be exemplified by the *wigwam* of the Algonquins, which is constructed of a framework of poles, as are the *tipi* and the *wikiup*, but is covered with bark instead of brush, mud, or skins. This type is possible only in a wooded country, where the abundance of game and other necessities of life renders a certain degree of permanence possible. At the same time, the dwelling is capable of enlargement, and thus secures an advance in social life. The permanent type of dwelling was common throughout the continent at the time of its discovery, being found not only among the Algonquins and Iroquois, but in the Mississippi valley, Florida, the North-West Coast, and Arizona, and, in its highest form of development, among the Aztecs and Mayas. From the permanent house was evolved, moreover, the permanent village, in contrast to the temporary encampments found, for example, among the Pai Utes and the Dakotas. These villages were frequently defended by palisades, as among the Algonquian Lenni-Lenape, the Virginians, and the Cadoan stocks of the Mississippi valley. A remarkable feature of many of these permanent dwellings was their elevation on mounds of earth, which were frequently formed artificially. The original motive was, in the main, sanitary, dampness being thus avoided. This practice was also common among the natives of Florida, where these artificial elevations are described as being 'a kind of platform two or three pikes in height, the summit of which is large enough to give room for twelve, fifteen, or twenty houses, to lodge the cacique and his attendants. At the foot of this elevation they mark out a square place, according to the size of the village, around which the leading men have their houses. . . . To ascend the elevation they have a straight passage-way from bottom to top, fifteen or twenty feet wide. Here steps are made by massive beams, and others are planted firmly in the ground to serve as walls. On all other sides of the platform the sides are cut steep' (quoted from Garcilasso by Thomas, *Mound Explorations*, p. 647). The temples naturally stood at a still higher elevation than the houses of the people. Even dwellings of the permanent type here described, however, were liable to speedy decay if long abandoned for any reason, and the ruins of such houses no longer exist. Yet in them probably lies the secret of many of the mysterious mounds so common in the Ohio valley, which were formerly supposed to be the work of a race differing widely from the American Indians. Excavations of these structures have shown that their builders were simply American Indians, differing in no respect from their congeners elsewhere in the continent. The great majority of mounds are doubtless mortuary in origin, and thus do not properly come within the scope of architecture (cf. Yarrow, *Introduction to the Study of Mortuary Customs among the North American Indians*, Washington, 1880, pp. 17–29). Others, such as the Serpent Mound of the Ohio valley or the pyramid of Cholula in Mexico, were structures designed for purposes of religion, the latter, at least, serving as the base of a temple. Yet it is not impossible that the religious mounds (though not the mortuary) are ultimately identical in origin with those designed to support ordinary dwellings. The *hodenosotes*, or 'long houses,' of the Algonquian and Iroquoian stocks—mere developments of the *wigwam* noted above—find their analogues in the slab houses of the North-West Coast. Here the abundance of cedars, which may readily be split, renders it possible to construct houses of planks instead of poles and bark, these structures being more permanent than the eastern wigwams. In the dwellings of this type, moreover, as in the Iroquois 'long house,' separate rooms were partitioned off, thus marking a distinct step forward in civilization. Farther to the north, the Alaskan Aleuts construct their houses of ribs of the whale, driftwood, stone, turf, or any material which may be at hand in that barren region. The dwellings are not infrequently built entirely of turf cut in slabs. The most curious form of American Indian architecture, in some respects, is the Eskimo *igloo* (properly *iglugeak*, 'house-snow'). This is made by cutting compact blocks of snow, which are so laid on a circular base as gradually to slant towards the centre, thus forming the only case of a true arch among the North American aborigines. A house designed for occupancy throughout the winter is some 12 feet in height and 15 in diameter. It is heated with stone lamps filled with seal oil, while additional light is admitted by a window of ice or the intestine of a seal. Whenever his supply of material renders it possible, however, the Innuit constructs a still more durable dwelling of whale-ribs, driftwood, and the like, thus approximating to the Aleut house. In this same region, moreover, were semi-subterranean dwellings, especially among the Aleuts, Eskimos, coast Salishans, and kindred tribes. Their affinity with the subterranean houses of the Gilyaks, Kamtchatkans, Koryaks, Chukchees, and Yukaghirs of North-Eastern Asia is too striking and too close not to be due to borrowing on the part of the American Indians (Jochelson, in *XVe Congrès international des Américanistes*, Quebec, 1907, ii. 115–128). Among the Pawnees, as among the Arikaras, Osages, Omahas, Poncas, and other tribes, are found 'earth lodges,' also semi-subterranean and somewhat analogous to the Navaho *hogans* mentioned above.

Of these dwellings Miss Fletcher writes as follows (in Hodge, *Handbook of American Indians*, i. 411): 'These tribes are said to have abandoned the grass house of their kindred at some distant period and, under the teaching of aquatic animals, to have learned to construct the earth lodge. According to their ceremonies and legends, not only the animals were concerned with its construction — the badger digging the holes, the beaver sawing the logs, the bears carrying them, and all obeying the directions of the whale—

but the stars also exercised authority. The earlier star cult of the people is recognized in the significance attached to the four central posts. Each stood for a star—the Morning and Evening stars, symbols of the male and female cosmic forces, and the North and South stars, the direction of chiefs and the abode of perpetual life. The posts were painted in the symbolic colours of these stars—red, white, black, yellow. During certain ceremonies corn of one of these colours was offered at the foot of the post of that colour. In the rituals of the Pawnee the earth lodge is made typical of man's abode on the earth; the floor is the plain, the wall the distant horizon, the dome the arching sky, the central opening the zenith, dwelling-place of Tirawa, the invisible power which gives life to all created beings.'

The room, found in the permanent dwellings of the Iroquois and on the North-West Coast, reaches a high stage of development among the 'cliff-dwellers' and the Pueblo tribes. In the deserts of the south-western United States the country is arid and treeless, although verdure at once springs up if irrigation be successfully practised. Cañons and cliffs abound, and the caves in the sides of these precipices, often modified artificially, are utilized as dwellings, especially since trees of any considerable size are extremely rare. A cliff-dwelling, moreover, is usually comparatively difficult of access and easy to defend, an important consideration when hostile Apaches stand ready to attack less warlike tribes. The houses in the cliffs are generally at a considerable elevation, and have the crevice on the face of the rock carefully walled up, both for shelter and for protection. An excellent example of this kind of dwelling is found in the Mesa Verde, where in a large crevice in the cliff is constructed a regular *pueblo* building, forming a marked contrast to the simple wall on the edge of the rock. The crevice is frequently modified to suit the requirements of its inhabitants, and the cliff-dwelling is divided into rooms. These apartments, which are of various shapes, average 7 feet in height and 10 by 17 feet in area. The only communication with the outer world is by a door, which is usually approached by steps cut in the face of the cliff. The floor was levelled off, and an effort was evidently made to avoid dampness by constructing low *adobe* ridges, across which poles covered with skins may have been laid. The chief districts of the cliff-dwellers were the Northern Rio Grande valley, the valley of the San Juan river, the San Francisco mountain region, and the valley of the Rio Verde.

4. Where cliffs were not available, and, perhaps, where a higher grade of civilization had been attained, the American Indians of the South-west constructed the so-called *pueblos*, the most remarkable type of communal dwelling on the American continent. The settlements of this type now in existence number about thirty, and are found chiefly in New Mexico and Arizona, although the area formerly extended from the Pecos to the middle Gila, and from central Colorado and Utah to Mexico. Many of the *pueblos* were constructed upon plateaux or mesas—an evident reminiscence of the cliff-dwellings—while all are obviously designed for defence, especially against the Navahos and Apaches. The *pueblo* consists of a number of square rooms of *adobe* or stone, which are constructed either side by side or one upon the other, the latter type being either pyramidal or in a series of steps, with the back of the entire structure dropping perpendicularly. The roof of each room is flat, and has a trap-door which forms the only entrance, the approach being a temporary ladder placed against the side of the building. As occasion requires, the *pueblo* is enlarged. The roof of one tier, which forms the floor of another, has as its basis a number of small logs, across which poles are laid at short intervals and covered with grass or twigs, serving to support the visible floor of *adobe* and earth.

The *pueblos* are also important as forming the transition to stone structures. The Pecos ruins in North-western New Mexico have walls of sandstone slabs; and round stone towers, frequently with two or three concentric walls, are not infrequent in the South-west. Some of these latter structures seem to have been like the modern Moki *kivas*, or places of general assembly for the men of the *pueblo*. The method of construction of the walls of the *pueblos* varies considerably. In the *pueblo* of Pewa they consist of stone slabs laid in mortar of *adobe* (mud mixed with straw), while the Rio Grande *pueblos* are built of *adobe* bricks. The famous Casa Grande, near Florence, Arizona, was built by the *cajon* method, in which *adobe* mud is rammed into large wicker frames and left to dry, after which the mould is removed and used for the next portion of the wall. This mode of building was modified in some of the buildings in the Salt River valley, by ramming earth between two rows of posts wattled with weeds and plastered on the outside with *adobe* mortar. These frames, unlike those on the *cajon* method, were permitted to remain. This system of construction is termed *pisé*, while a third system of plastering a single row of wattled posts on both sides with *adobe* mud so as to form a thin wall is called *jacal*. In Mexico the *pueblo* type of construction seems to have been common at the time of the Spanish conquest. Although these dwellings have long since disappeared, except in the remains of the Casas Grandes in Chihuahua, their modern representatives, as well as the accounts of the Spanish conquerors, show that the habitations of the common people differed little from those of their New Mexican congeners, except that they were usually but one storey in height, or at most two. They covered a large area in many instances, and may sometimes have been communal dwellings. In the valley of the Lake of Mexico many houses were built on piles over the water, finding an analogue on the one hand among the American Indians of the North-West Coast, and on the other among the South Americans of Lake Maracaibo. The *adobe* dwellings were frequently constructed on foundations of stone, while the temples, as already noted, were elevated on high platforms of earth or stone, the Toltec pyramid of the sun at Teotihuacan having measured 680 ft. at the base by 180 in height. The so-called pyramid is, in fact, one of the chief characteristics of Aztec, Toltec, and Maya architecture. It differs essentially from the Egyptian pyramid in its object, since it is designed simply and solely as a foundation for a building, while the African structure is a gigantic tomb. The Great Mound of Cholula is almost 1000 ft. square at the base, and reaches an altitude of 200 feet. The pyramid of Huitzilopochtli and Tlaloc in Mexico itself had five terraces, the lowest 360 ft. square and the highest 70, and was ascended by a flight of 113 steps, the processions to the chapels on the summit winding round each terrace before mounting to the next. Not only temples but palaces were constructed on platforms, so that the Maya palace of Palenque stands on an oblong mound 310 ft. in length by 260 in width, and 40 ft. in height.

5. North and Central American architecture reached its zenith among the Mayas of Yucatan, Honduras, and Guatemala. Over all this territory are scattered ruins of ancient cities, and many more, hidden in the tropical vegetation, doubtless still await discovery. The final history of the art and architecture of this region cannot, therefore, be written for many years, for it is by no means unlikely that even more extensive and important remains may yet be found than are thus far known. The sites hitherto best described are as follows: in Yucatan, Uxmal, Kabah, Zayi, and Labná in what may be termed the central group; Chichen-

Itza and Tuloom in the east; Izamal, Ticul, Mayapan, Mérida, and Aké in the north; Labphak in the south; in Honduras there are Tenampua, Calamulla, and, above all, Copan; and in Guatemala mention must be made of Quiriguá, Cinaca-Mecallo, Patinamit, Utatlan, and Tikal. Here, too, must be classed the ruins of Palenque, in the Mexican State of Chiapas, which are akin to those of Yucatan, but with western Honduras the line of architectural remains in Central America seems to be drawn.

Of the sites here noted—the list does not pretend to be complete—the most important for a knowledge of Central American architecture are Palenque, Uxmal, and Chichen-Itza. From these three centres a general idea may perhaps be gained of the main outlines of a Maya city, supplementary information being obtainable from a study of other sites. It becomes, therefore, advisable to give a brief summary of the principal structures still preserved at each of these three cities. At Palenque the chief ruins are those of the Palace and the Temples of the Three Tablets, the Cross, and the Sun. By far the most elaborate of these is the first-named, though there is, of course, no evidence that it was actually intended to be a palace. This structure is erected on a quadrangular pyramid some 40 ft. high, measuring about 260 by 310 ft. at the bottom, originally faced with stone (perhaps once painted or plastered) and ascended by broad central stairways on the east and north. The palace itself, which nearly covers the upper surface of the pyramid, measures about 180 by 228 ft. and has a height of 30 ft. In the outer wall were some 40 doorways, 8½ ft. high and 9 ft. wide, while above them runs a cornice pierced with small holes which may have held poles for the support of an awning. 'The main building is found to consist of two corridors, formed by three parallel walls and covered by one roof, which extend entirely round the circumference of the platform, and enclose a quadrangular court measuring about 150 by 200 ft. This court also contains five or six buildings, some of them connected with the main edifice, others separate, which divide the court into four smaller ones' (Bancroft, *Native Races*, iv. 308). The walls of the corridors vary between 2 and 3 ft. in thickness, and the corridors themselves have a width of 9 ft. and a height of 20 ft., the latter half of which is formed by corbel vaulting. In the main doorway through the central wall is found a trefoil arch, and niches of similar form occur frequently on either side of it. The pavement of the interior courts is 8 or 10 ft. below that of the corridors, and is approached by stairways. Of the buildings which divide this court into four parts, the most remarkable is a tower of solid masonry about 50 ft. high, in its present state, resting on a base about 30 ft. square, and with three storeys, each receding slightly and each having a door in the centre of each side. The pyramid itself contains 'apartments, or galleries, with walls of stone plastered, but without ornament, of the same form and construction as the corridors above. . . . The southernmost gallery receives a dim light by three holes or windows leading out to the surface of the pyramid; the other galleries are dark and damp. . . . These rooms are variously regarded as sleeping-rooms, dungeons, or sepulchres, according to the temperament of the observer' (Bancroft, *op. cit.* p. 320 f.). The restoration of the palace, given, for example, by Bancroft (p. 323), well illustrates the high architectural abilities of the Mayas. Mention should also be made, in this connexion, of a bridge in the vicinity of Palenque, built of hewn stone, with a convex conduit 9 ft. wide. The bridge itself is 56 ft. long, 42 ft. wide, and 11 ft. high.

At Uxmal the ruins are still more extensive than at Palenque, the principal remains being the Casa del Gobernador, Casa de Tortugas, Casa de Palomas, Casa de Monjas, and Casa del Adivino, as well as a number of pyramids. The most remarkable of these is the Casa de Monjas, or 'Nunnery.'

'This is perhaps the most wonderful edifice, or collection of edifices, in Yucatan, if not the finest specimen of aboriginal architecture and sculpture in America. The supporting mound . . . is in general terms 350 ft. square, and 19 ft. high, its sides very nearly facing the cardinal points. The southern, or front, slope of the mound, about 70 ft. wide, rises in three grades, or terraces, 3, 12, and 4 ft. high, and 20, 45, and 5 ft. wide, respectively, from the base. There are some traces of a wide central stairway leading up to the second terrace on this side, but none of the steps remain in place. On this platform stand four of the typical Yucatan edifices built round a courtyard, with unequal intervals between them at the corners. The southern building is 279 ft. long, 28 ft. wide, and 18 ft. high; the northern building, 264 ft. long, 28 ft. wide, and 25 ft. high; the eastern, 158 by 35 ft., and 22 ft. high; the western, 173 by 35 ft., and 20 ft. high. The northern building stands on a terrace of its own which rises about 20 ft. above the level of the main platform on which the others stand. The court formed by the four edifices measures 258 by 214 ft. It is 2¼ ft. lower than the foundations of the eastern, western, and southern buildings, and traces of low steps may yet be seen running the whole length of the sides. Its area is paved with stone, much worn by long usage. . . . Each of the four buildings is divided longitudinally into two parallel ranges of apartments . . . with doorways opening on the interior court. The only exterior doorways are on the front of the southern building and on the ends of the northern; these, however, afford access only to the outer range of rooms, which do not communicate with the interior. In only one instance do more than two rooms communicate with each other, and that is in the centre of the eastern building, where are two communicating apartments, the largest in the "Nunnery," each 13 by 33 ft., with an ante-room at each end measuring 9 by 13 ft. . . . The rooms of the Casa de Monjas, 88 in number, . . . are plastered with a thin coat of hard white material like plaster of Paris. Those of the southern building average 24 ft. long, 10 ft. wide, and 17 ft. high. They all present the same general features of construction—angular-arched ceilings, wooden lintels, stone rings, or hinges, on the inside of the doorways, holes in the sloping ceilings for hammock-timbers, entire absence of any openings except the doors. . . . The platform on which the buildings stand forms a narrow promenade, only 5 or 6 ft. in width, round each, both on the exterior and on the court. The entrance to the court is by a gateway . . . in the centre of the southern building. It is 10 ft. 8 in. wide and about 14 ft. high, the top being formed by the usual triangular arch. . . . Opposite this gateway . . . a stairway 95 ft. wide leads up to the upper terrace which supports the northern building. On each side of this stairway, . . . on the slope of the terrace, is a ruin of the usual construction, in which six small apartments may be traced. . . . The sides and ends of each building are . . . plain and unplastered below the cornice, which extends round the whole circumference just above the doorways. Above this cornice the whole surface, over 24,000 sq. ft. for the four buildings, is covered with elegant and elaborate sculptured decorations. The four interior façades fronting on the court are pronounced by all beholders the *chefs-d'œuvre* of aboriginal decorative art in America, being more chaste and artistic, and at the same time less complicated and grotesque, than any other fronts in Yucatan. . . . The northern building, standing on a terrace 20 ft. above the platform which supports the other structures, and consequently overlooking them all, was very probably intended by the builders as the crowning feature of the Casa de Monjas. Its court façade was crowded with sculptured designs. . . . Apparently from no other motive than to obtain more space on which to exercise their talent for decorative art, and thus to render this front more striking, the builders extended the front wall at regular intervals above the upper cornice, forming 13 turrets 17 ft. high and 10 ft. wide, placed generally above the doorways' (Bancroft, *op. cit.* pp. 173–179, 187 f.)

The chief remains at Chichen-Itza are the Nunnery, Akab-Tzib (Maya, 'Writing in the Dark,' from the hieroglyphics upon its walls) originally level with the plain instead of on a mound, but with the ground surrounding it excavated, the Castle (or Pyramid), the Gymnasium (also called the Temple, and by the natives the Iglesia), the Chichanchob ('Red House,' also called the Prison), a series of 380 pillars from 3 to 6 ft. high recalling the 'Hall of Columns' (on a miniature scale) at Mitla, and the Caracol. The last is the most curious structure and is unique of its type. It is a circular, domed building, 22 ft. in diameter and some 24 ft. high, with two narrow corridors surrounding its apparently solid core. It rests on a pyramid of two rectangular terraces, the lower 150 by 223 ft., and the upper 55 by 80 ft.

As already noted, many other ruins of Central America are of deep interest. Here mention may be made of the Casa de Justicia at Kabah; the Casa Grande at Zayi with its three storeys built around (instead of upon) a mound, the first storey being 120 by 265 ft., the second 60 by 220 ft., and the third (on the summit of the mound) 18 by 150 ft.; a room with an acute-angled roof at Nohcabab; the Castle at Tuloom; and the great fort of El Resguardo at Utatlan.

It is thus clear that among the Mayas, as among the Aztecs, and even the Cadoans, Floridians, and at least some of the 'Mound Builders,' the mound is almost universally the substructure, and though only the palaces and temples remain, the dwellings of the people having long since disappeared through the destructive climate, enough has survived to give some idea of the civilization adopted by the ruder Aztecs when they invaded Mexico. The walls of the Maya structures are of oblong dressed stones, usually laid without mortar, and richly carved. The walls were very thick, and the buildings were only one storey in height. The rooms were long and narrow, since the Mayas possessed little skill in roofing. Thus at Uxmal the main rooms of the 'Governor's Palace' are 60 ft. long and only 11 or 13 wide. The roof was frequently constructed by a sort of corbel arch, each course of masonry being gradually advanced towards the other until the opening could be covered with a single slab. On the roof was a roof comb—one of the most distinguishing features of Maya architecture. The comb on the 'Temple of the Cross' at Palenque was a latticed superstructure of stone and stucco in two storeys, one 7 ft. in height and the other 8, the main building being 40 ft. high. Closely similar was the architecture of the Zapotecs, of which the best remains are preserved at Mitla in the Mexican State of Oaxaca. Here, as among the Mayas, the rooms were long and narrow, one of them being 121 ft. long by 12 wide, while the architecture again resembles that of the Mayas in having no windows. The roof comb was lacking, however, and the structure of the roof was essentially different, the corbel arch being abandoned in favour of wooden beams covered with earth and slabs of stone. The most remarkable feature of Zapotec architecture is found in the 'Hall of Columns,' a part of the palace of Mitla. This hall contains six monoliths about 12 ft. in height and 9 in circumference, set at intervals of some 15 feet. These are the only monolith columns thus far discovered in American Indian architecture, although built up piers are found in *pueblos*, and wooden columns are frequent in the slab houses of the North-West Coast.

6. In South America the types of architecture are as varied as in North and Central America. The early Brazilian houses, according to Lafitau (*Mœurs des sauvages amériquains*, ed. Paris, 1727, iii. 8), were 'faites en forme de berceau. . . . Elles sont fort longues; cinq ou six cabanes composent un gros village. Il est vrai que dans chaque cabane il y a jusqu'à soixante et quatre-vingt personnes partagées en différents ménages.' In Guiana pile-dwellings are common, those of the Warraus being 7 or 8 ft. long, and built on piles 5 or 6 ft. high. Similar structures are found even on the savannahs. The walls are of leaf or bark plastered with mud, although thatches are also common. In the forests the Arawaks, Ackawais, and Caribs build open unwalled houses, whereas in the open savannahs the Macusis, Arecunas, and Wapianas construct dwellings with thick mud wattled walls, often 2 ft. in thickness. The Ackawai houses, moreover, are generally communal, frequently having eighteen hammocks in a structure 20 by 30 ft., while the Arawak dwellings often have partitions of palm-leaf or bark. The development of the Guiana house is shown by the temporary dwelling, or *benaboo*, a rough affair, triangular in base and covered with palm-leaves, the triangle being later replaced by a square, the usual form of the houses of this region (Im Thurn, *Among the Indians of Guiana*, London, 1883, pp. 202-210). The Chiriguanos of Bolivia had quadrangular thatched houses with frameworks of reeds or posts, arranged in circular villages, having an open space in the centre. Those of the Guatos of the Amazon are about 4 metres square and thatched on the sides with leaves (Schmidt, *Indianerstudien in Zentralbrasilien*, Berlin, 1905, pp. 177-178), while the Laguas of the Paraguayan Chaco construct dwellings of long, low, rough booths, either of papyrus reed or of sticks thatched with grass, although for stormy weather they place poles in a circle, and then bring them together to be covered with rushes, leaves, and similar material (Grubb, *Among the Indians of the Paraguayan Chaco*, London, 1904, pp. 72-73). On the Pampas tents were used, consisting of a framework of poles covered with horse-hide, and in Patagonia likewise tents of skin were used. The framework of these latter structures was frequently between 10 and 12 ft. in length, 10 in width, and 7 in height, and the interior was divided into a number of rooms, thus forming a sort of small communal dwelling. In Tierra del Fuego, on the other hand, with its far inferior civilization, wretched huts are built of sticks wattled with grass or rammed with mud, marking one of the lowest types of architecture to be found on the American continent.

7. Midway between North and South America stands the architecture of the Antilles. The majority of houses on these islands were round, pointed huts, with leaf roofs and wattled sides, often of perfumed reeds and elaborately adorned. The villages were small. There were, however, large houses, especially in Cuba, where some lodged between 100 and 200 men, and the residences of the caciques naturally received special adornment. The larger dwellings frequently had covered porches, and were divided into a number of rooms. While it is not impossible that in the most archaic period the inhabitants of Porto Rico, Haiti, Cuba, and other West India islands were, at least in part, troglodytic, by the time of the first discoveries they were largely village-dwellers, their groups of houses being palisaded as in Florida, Virginia, etc. The Haitian (and probably the Porto Rican) houses, called *buhios*, *caneyes*, and *eracras*, were of two types: circular, with upright sides supporting a sloping roof converging at the apex and thatched with leaves or stalks of cane, the door forming the only opening; and rectangular, constructed of similar material, but with windows and a small porch. No remains of stone or *adobe* houses are known on any of these islands; but since the accounts of the early discoverers and such analogues as may be traced in the modern cabins (which resemble the second rather than the first type) agree in general with the domiciles along the Orinoco and its tributaries, 'this resemblance is one of the many which can be advanced to indicate kinship of the people of South America with those of Porto Rico' (Fewkes, 'The Aborigines of Porto Rico and Neighbouring Islands,' in *25 RBEW* p. 46).

8. Architecture reached its zenith in South America among the Chibchas of Colombia and the Quichuas of Peru. The ordinary houses of the former people were built of straw and earth, and were frequently 100 ft. long and 20 wide; and even in Cuzco the common houses were of wood and thatched with straw (Botero, *Relationi universali*, Venice, 1600, i. 234). Stone structures, however, were unknown, even in the case of the temples. This is the more remarkable since sculpture was known to the Chibchas, who were also acquainted with the column. The architecture of the Peruvians forms the South American counterpart to that of the Aztecs and the Mayas, although its spirit is entirely different. The Peruvian buildings which have survived are mostly of stone, and many of them, unlike those of Mexico and Central America, are true examples of cyclopean construction. A monolithic gateway at Tiahuanaco measures 13 ft. 5 in. in length, 7 ft. 2 in. in height above the ground, and 18 in. in thickness, with a door 4 ft. 6 in. high and 2 ft. 9 in. wide. At this same site are a large number of monoliths bounding a rectangle 445 ft. in length by 388 in width. These pillars vary from 14 ft. to 2½ ft. in height. Elaborate sun-circles, bounded by monoliths, also occur, as at Sillustani; and the latter site and its vicinity are also of importance for the *chulpas*, or funeral towers. These are plain towers, usually round, with corbelled cupolas, and ranging from 16 to 40 ft. in height, containing, within walls of extreme thickness, a very small funerary chamber (cf., further, art. DEATH AND DISPOSAL OF THE DEAD [Peruvian]).

The chief sites of ancient Peruvian (and Bolivian) remains are Pachacamac, Gran Chimu, Marca Huamachuco, Huanuco Viejo, Vilcas Huaman, Cuzco, Ollantaïtambo, Pisacc, Sillustani, Tiahuanaco, and the islands of Lake Titicaca. At Pachacamac are found the ruins of the Temple of the Sun and the House of the Virgins of the Sun, the former covering an area 600 by 450 ft., and the latter one of 350 by 200 ft. Over the four hills which form the site of the ancient city are scattered the remains of other large structures, including communal dwellings which recall the *pueblos* of New Mexico. But Pachacamac, like Ancon, is more noteworthy for its necropolis than for its architecture; nor are the coast sites of Peru, generally speaking, as important in their contributions to a knowledge of the ancient architecture of the country as the more inland remains. Nevertheless, mention should be made of the elaborate fortress at Paramonga. Here a hill about 825 ft. high, surrounded by an *adobe* wall, sustains a fortress of three terraces with a detached *quasi*-bastion of similar construction facing the sea. A similar, but far more extensive, wall is found at Marca Huamachuco; and the presence of such structures in Peru is the more noteworthy when it is remembered that in the corresponding culture-regions of Mexico and Central America the sole clear example is found in the Maya site of Tuloom. This wall at Marca Huamachuco is nearly 10 ft. high, and it encloses the still imposing ruins of two oblong rectangular buildings, originally of three storeys, surrounding central courts. The exact purpose of these buildings, known locally as the Church and the Castle, is uncertain; but close by are the undoubted remains of extensive llama-stables. On a third hill—the Cerro de la Monja—surrounded by a triple wall, is the Convent, an appellation which may not be without reason. The entire group of structures at Marca Huamachuco is dominated by the Cerro del Castillo, where the rulers evidently dwelt; and the entire community was, accordingly, thus divided, running from north to south: Cerro Amara (residences of the warriors and citizens), Cerro del Castillo, Cerro de la Falda (llama-stables), Cerro de la Monja (nunnery), and Cerro Viejo (purpose unknown).

Huanuco Viejo, which, according to the *conquistador* historian Xerez, covered an area three leagues in circumference, still has a perimeter of nearly a league, even when the dwellings of the people have disappeared, and only the palace, baths, temples, and wall surrounding the principal buildings remain. The building material is hard grey stone, and a noteworthy feature is the baths 'se composant de onze piscines murées en pierre et surmontées de parois d'un appareil admirable, pourvu de niches au fond desquelles sont fixés des bancs en pierre' (Wiener, *Pérou et Bolivie*, p. 211). Mention should likewise be made of the elaborate system of courts and of an avenue with four large pylonic gates. Vilcas Huaman is noteworthy chiefly for a truncated rectangular pyramid in three stages, ascended by a flight of steps, and surrounded by a wall with doors whose sloping sides resemble those of Huanuco Viejo. The structure is strikingly suggestive of the Aztec and Maya pyramids.

At Ollantaïtambo, some 12 leagues from Cuzco, are the remains of vast palaces, with their terraces, pylons, stairs, aqueducts, and cisterns, and distinct traces of the ancient city, as well as of the so-called Tribunal and Prisons; while about 2 miles away are enormous fortifications. Pisacc also has an interesting group of ruins, comprising a fort, a temple of the sun (*intihuanatana*), and traces of the ancient city. There is, in this series of elaborate fortifications throughout Peru, a marked divergency from the architectural remains elsewhere in America (unless an exception may be made in certain structures of the 'Mound-builders'). And it is also noteworthy that not only does the building material change from *adobe* to stone as one proceeds from the coast, but that the construction becomes, *pari passu*, more and more cyclopean.

Peruvian architecture reached its height of grandeur in the structures at Tiahuanaco and the islands of Lake Titicaca. At the former site are the remains of the Fortress, Temple, Palace, Hall of Justice, and Sanctuary. The Temple measures 388 by 455 ft., with a sunken court 280 by 190 ft.; while the Hall of Justice is a cyclopean platform 131 by 23 ft. with a group of seats at each end and in the centre, these groups being separated by monolithic doorways. Copper clamps were used to hold the stones together. (On the entire site cf. Strübel and Uhle, *Die Ruinenstätte von Tiahuanaco*, Breslau, 1882). On the islands of Titicaca and Coati are buildings dedicated respectively to the sun and the moon. The former island contains the Palace of the Incas (also called the Temple of the Sun), the Storehouse of the Sun, and the Bath of the Incas. The Palace, or Temple, 51 by 44 ft., is in two storeys, and originally had painted and stuccoed walls; while the Bath is 40 by 100 ft. and 5 ft. in depth. The island of Coati is especially famous for its Palace of the Virgins of the Sun, which, also in two storeys, is 183 by 80 ft. It contains numerous apartments, but, rather curiously, none of the structures on these two islands is cyclopean in type, nor is there any approach to such monuments as the monolithic gateways at Tiahuanaco, mentioned above.

Although less ornamental than the Maya structures, Peruvian architecture is of a higher type. The arch is occasionally found, especially at Pachacamac and Vilcas Huaman, and windows were not unknown in the interior, though they do not seem to have been constructed on the coast. The most important advance over the architecture of Mexico and Central America, however, was the roof, which obviated the necessity of the excessively narrow room which forms so marked a characteristic of the more northern style. The smaller structures seem to have been covered with a hip roof, at least in some cases, while in the larger buildings it has been suggested that the interior was lined with wooden columns supporting a sort of verandah which did not cover the entire floor space. Although there is, naturally, no trace of columns in the present condition of the Peruvian ruins, this hypothesis is confirmed by the small footpaths which border the interior of the walls. Such a form of roof, moreover, would admit the necessary light to the dwellings, and the entire structure would thus present an analogue to the Roman *atrium*. Rooms were formed in the Peruvian houses by curtains. The doors varied remarkably in form, some of them being trapezoids, while others were truncated ovals, and still others resembled the reversed spade of the conventional playing card. A noteworthy feature of Peruvian architecture was the niche in the wall, usually either a rectangle or a trapezoid, sometimes perhaps serving for a closet and again for ornament. Stairs of considerable elaboration were frequent. Again, deviating from Maya and Aztec architecture, many of the larger structures, especially the palaces, contained many rooms, presenting ground-plans of much complexity, as in the palaces at Chimu. Structures of several storeys were erected, as in the case of the palace at Marca Huamachuco and the palace of the Inca on the island of Titicaca, the ground-plan of the second storey of the latter structure being entirely different from that of the first floor. Some buildings, notably the fortress of Paramonga, almost suggest the *pueblo* type of North America in their pyramidal construction, although neither motive nor type of building was at all analogous. A decided analogy of form also exists between the Aztec *teocallis* and the Peruvian *huacas*, although the latter were used, not as pyramids to support the temples, but as places of interment. Finally, it may be noted that the Incas—altogether the most civilized race of South America, and the rivals even of the Mayas of Yucatan—were able to construct bridges of stone and elaborate aqueducts, as well as admirable roads and cyclopean terraces.

LITERATURE.—Dellenbaugh, *North Americans of Yesterday* (New York, 1901); Thomas, *Introduction to the Study of North American Archæology* (Cincinnati, 1898); Hodge, *Handbook of American Indians* (Washington, 1907), i. 77–82, 515–519; Brasseur de Bourbourg, *Monuments anciens du Mexique* (Paris, 1866); Charnay, *Ancient Cities of the New World* (New York, 1887); Bancroft, *Native Races of the Pacific States*, iv. (San Francisco, 1883); Squier, *Peru* (*ib.* 1877); Wiener, *Pérou et Bolivie* (Paris, 1880); Waitz, *Anthropologie der Naturvölker*, iii. (2 parts, Leipzig, 1862–1864); T. M. Prudden, *The Great American Plateau* (New York, 1907); and many monographs in the reports of the American *BE*, the United States National Museum, the Field Columbian Museum, the Peabody Museum, and the American Museum of Natural History.

LOUIS H. GRAY.

ARCHITECTURE (Assyro-Babylonian).—In the absence of clear statements as to the history of the architectural forms found in the sacred buildings of the Babylonians and Assyrians, much doubt as to their origin naturally exists. The two principal forms are the temple on its earthen foundation, without any upper storeys, and the temple-tower, or *ziqqurat*, in stages. It is probable that the former preceded the latter in date.

As elsewhere, the temple in Babylonia has been regarded as originating from the tomb—a very natural development, in view of the probability that certain of the gods of the Babylonians were nothing more than venerated heroes of remote ages who had become deified. So far, however, no sepulchre which may be called an edifice in the true sense of the word has been found, either in Babylonia or Assyria.

Most of the temples probably originated from small beginnings, as is suggested by a document of about 2000 B.C. in the British Museum. In this Nûr-ili-šu founds a temple to Nûr-ili (or Lugala) and Šullat (probably Merodach and his spouse Zēr-panîtu^{m}), and dedicates it for the preservation of his life.* One priest only is named, so the building was probably a very simple structure—an oblong hall with a recess at one end for the statues or emblems of the deities to whom it was dedicated, and one or two rooms for sacred utensils and robes. In this case the motive for the foundation seems to have been to provide a temple for the gods of Babylon in a district where the sun-god was the patron deity, and it seems not improbable that other temples and shrines may have been founded in the same way.†

One of the most interesting temple-plans is that of the goddess Nin-maḫ, as excavated at Babylon by the Deutsche Orient-Gesellschaft (Delitzsch, *Im Lande des einstigen Paradieses*, p. 39). The ruin lies on the eastern side of the Ištar-gate, and, as is usual in the sacred buildings of Babylonia and Assyria, has its corners towards the cardinal points. It is of sun-dried brick, and its remains have even now traces of white decoration. The entrance on the N.W. led into a large vestibule communicating with a room on the left, and giving access to a court-yard with six other doorways serving the remaining chambers, eleven in number. Four of these had smaller rooms, probably the sanctuaries where were kept the statues or the shrines of the deities worshipped there (for the temple Ê-maḫ probably resembled others in Babylonia in associating certain companions with the principal divinity). The first hall was entered from the court-yard by a doorway nearly facing that giving access to the court-yard from the vestibule, and this, in its turn, led to the inner hall—the holy place. There seems to have been no rule for the position of the small rooms which probably contained the statues or shrines, some of them being at the S.W. end (when the halls to which they were appended ran N.E. and S.W.), and at the N.E. end (when the room ran N.W. to S.E.). The court-yard was not in the centre of the building, but set more towards the S.W. side, so that there was space on that side for only one row of two narrow rooms, whilst on the N.E. side there are two rows of rooms, narrower and longer, with sanctuaries for statues or shrines. Behind the 'holy place' are two narrow rooms only.

To all appearance the temples of Babylonia and Assyria were built upon the same general plan. From the outside the visitor gained access to a vestibule, which, in its turn, admitted him to the court-yard, or to a hall around which were the doorways leading to the remaining halls and chambers.

More ornate, to all appearance, than the temple of Nin-maḫ at Babylon was that built by Sargon of Assyria at Khorsabad. This edifice lay in the 'temple-court' of the palace, on the S.E. side of which were the 'priests' rooms,' the temple itself being on the S.W. side of the court, facing the state-apartments. A flight of stone steps gave access to a platform of crude brick (faced by a retaining wall of black basalt with a cornice of grey limestone). Two chambers were traced, floored with a mixture of stone and chalk. The fragments of black basalt bas-reliefs found here showed that the ornamentation was the same as that in the palace, but the subjects were religious.‡

A better example, however, is the Assyrian temple excavated by Sir H. Layard in the mound of Nimrûd (Calah). This lay at the S.E. angle of the great temple-tower, but was apparently unconnected with it. Here also we have an outer court, an entrance leading into a vestibule, a side-chamber (with two entrances), and a hall with a

* *JRAS*, Jan. 1899, p. 103 ff.

† A temple of these modest dimensions may have been simply an enlargement of the popular household sanctuary.

‡ Rawlinson's *Monarchies*, vol. i. pp. 369–371.

recess at the end. It differs from the Babylonian temple of Nin-maḫ, however, in having no interior court-yard. Its importance for Assyrian art, on the other hand, was considerable, many slabs of a religious nature having been found; and its pavement-slabs give the history of the reign of Aššur-naṣir-âpli (B.C. 885–860), its builder. Its main entrance was adorned with winged man-headed lions, and the entrance leading into the side-room had reliefs showing the deity expelling an evil spirit, represented as a winged dragon, from the place.* At the side of this doorway was the arch-headed monolith with the representation of the king (Aššur-naṣir-âpli) in his divine character, with an altar before it, implying that sacrifices of some kind were made to him.† The smaller temple apparently had no vestibule, and the visitor entered at once into the holy place, which had a recess for the statue or shrine at the left-hand end. Chambers supplying the place of the vestibule were constructed at each end. Altars for libations were placed in angles made to receive them on each side of the main entrance. These objects were hollow, and were decorated with gradines, similar to those of the walls already described.

On one of the sculptures found at Khorsabad is a small building which has been regarded as a fishing-pavilion,‡ because built on the banks of a stream, and also, by some, as a small temple. It is one storey high only, and is built, as usual, upon a platform. The roof is supported by two columns resembling the Doric of the Greeks. Above the columns the entablature broadens out into a deep cornice, which is surmounted by gradines like those above the walls of the temples and temple-towers, but rather smaller. No doorway is shown, so that the building looks like a mere shelter from the rain.§ That it is really a temple is also implied by the similar structure sculptured on a slab from the palace of Aššur-bani-âpli in the British Museum. It shows a temple on rising ground beside a terrace on arches (possibly the 'hanging gardens' of Babylon).‖ It is flanked by thickish columns, and has two slender ones in the centre, but no entrance is shown. The entablature above the columns has gradines, but its cornice is provided with a more elaborate moulding. On the left is an outbuilding surmounted by a shallow moulding and gradines, but otherwise, to all appearance, plain. The arch-headed stele in front was evidently detached from it. It has the figure of a Babylonian king in the usual conventional attitude, and an altar like those found by Layard at the smaller temple, at Nimrûd, already described.

Though there may be doubt as to the origin of the Babylonian temple—whether it was a development of the tomb or of the simple household shrine—the testimony in favour of the temple-towers of Babylonia being tombs is exceedingly strong, and is rendered still more so by the analogy of the pyramids of Egypt, which they resembled in their general appearance. Ctesias says (Diodorus, II. vii. 1) that the great sepulchral mound built by Semiramis at Nineveh on the Tigris was erected over the body of her husband Ninus; and Ovid (*Metam.* IV. 98) speaks of the 'tomb of Ninus,' under whose shadow the tragedy of Thisbe and Pyramus took place. On the other hand, this tomb-theory of the origin of the Babylonian temple-towers is quite unsupported by the older writings (Gn 11[4ff.]; Berossus, *ap.* Euseb. *Chronicon*, 13, *Præp. Evangel.* IX.; Jos. *Ant.* I. iv.; Syncellus, *Chron.* 44), which state that the tower at Babylon was for the purpose of reaching heaven. As far as the Babylonian records are known, this statement is likewise unconfirmed, though the use of the Bab. term (*ziqquratu*), applied to them to indicate the 'peak' of the mountain on which the Babylonian Noah sacrificed on coming out of the ark, would seem to support the idea that these erections were for the purpose of getting nearer to the deity when sacrificing, and likewise, probably, when offering prayers. It has also been suggested that the original inhabitants of the plain of Shinar, having come from a mountainous country, desired to break the monotony of their new home, and therefore built these mountain-like structures, which they turned to pious uses.

Apart from the descriptions given by explorers, perhaps the best account of a Babylonian temple-tower is that of Herodotus when describing the temple of Belus at Babylon (i. 181–183)—the building called by Nebuchadrezzar 'the Tower of Babylon.' Herodotus describes it as a massive tower 200 yards square at the base, within an enclosure 400 yards each way, and provided with gates of bronze. The stages, or 'towers,' as Herodotus calls them, amounted to eight in number, and, like the temple-tower found by the French explorers at Khorsabad, were provided with an inclined pathway on all four sides of each, enabling the visitor to reach the top. About the middle of the ascent (apparently the fourth stage) was a stopping-place, with seats to rest upon. On the topmost stage was a large cell, with a couch and a golden table, but no image, as the god himself was said to descend thither when he visited the woman chosen by him to pass the night there. The image of the god was in a cell below, with a table, probably for offerings, and an altar outside. Image, table, and altar are all said to have been of gold, and the last-named was for sucklings only. An altar for full-grown animals, and one for frankincense on the occasion of the god's festival, were also there. See ALTAR (Sem.), p. 353.

A detailed description of this famous temple is much needed, that given by Nebuchadrezzar being altogether inadequate. The late G. Smith was once fortunate enough to have in his hands a Babylonian tablet in which the building was described, and this is probably the most trustworthy account of it in existence.* Adopting his estimate of the metric system used, the 'grand court' of the temple measured 1156 ft. by 900 ft., and the next, 'the court of Ištar and Zagaga,' 1056 ft. by 450 ft., with six gates admitting to the temples.

The next division is described as a space or platform, apparently walled, called, in Sumero-Akkadian, *kigalla* or *zur*, and in Semitic Babylonian *kigallu* or *birûtu*—words apparently meaning an enclosed and levelled space. It was described as square, 2 *ku* each way (this is possibly the portion described by Herodotus as 'the temple' or sacred precinct, which measured 2 stadii—1213 ft. 6 in.—each way, and was furnished with bronze gates). In accordance with the usual Babylonian custom, the angles indicated the cardinal points, and each side had an entrance. Inside the enclosure, at the time the tablet was written, stood some kind of erection 200 ft. square, connected with the *ziqqurat*, or tower, and having round its

* Nimrûd Gallery, British Museum; Layard's *Monuments of Nineveh*, plate 5.

† Assyrian Transept, W., British Museum; Layard's *Nineveh and Babylon*, plate, p. 351.

‡ Botta, *Monuments de Ninive*, plate 114; Rawlinson, *Monarchies*, vol. i. p. 387.

§ An altar upon a hill to the right of this building suggests that it may have been merely for worship, the sacrifices being made on this 'high place' outside. Similar chapels or small temples are also found in Phœnician architecture (see p. 765).

‖ Assyrian Saloon, British Museum, No. 92; Rawlinson, *Monarchies*, vol. i. p. 388.

* *The Athenæum*, Feb. 12, 1876; repeated by Prof. Sayce in his *Hibbert Lectures*, 1887, p. 437 ff.

base the chapels or temples of the various gods, on all four sides, and facing the cardinal points.

On the E. side was a building 70 or 80 cubits long and 40 broad, containing sixteen shrines, the chief ones being dedicated to Nebo and Tašmêt, his consort. On the N. were temples to Êa or Aa and Nusku, and on the S. a single temple dedicated to Anu and Bel.

It was on the W. side, however, that the principal buildings were to be found—a 'double house' or temple with a court between two wings of differing dimensions. The building at the back was 125 cubits by 30. Mr. Smith was unable to make out with certainty the disposition of all the erections, but in the W. chambers stood the couch of the god, and the throne of gold mentioned by Herodotus, besides other furniture of great value.

The main building was the *ziqqurat*, or temple-tower, square, and with its corners towards the cardinal points. The lowest stage was also the largest, being 300 ft. square by 110 ft. high. It had the usual recessed or panelled ornamentation of Babylonian architecture. The second stage was 260 ft. square by 60 ft. high. An obscure term was applied to it, which G. Smith suggested might mean that it had sloping sides; probably they were hollowed out. This change in form would break the monotony of the structure.

The third stage commenced a regular series all equal in height, namely, 1 *gar* or 20 ft., but decreasing in size. The third was 200 ft. square, the fourth 170 ft., the fifth 140 ft., the sixth (the dimensions of which were omitted) apparently 110 ft. On this was the topmost stage, the seventh, which was the upper temple or sanctuary of the god Bel-Merodach. Its dimensions G. Smith makes to be 80 ft. long, 70 ft. broad, and 50 ft. high, the total height of the tower being 300 ft., exactly equal to the dimensions of the base. The raising of the base above the level of the ground would naturally make the height above the plain greater than this.

Weissbach's estimate of the measures does not differ greatly from that of G. Smith; he makes the base to have been about 100 metres, or 328 ft.*

The differing heights of the stages of the great 'Tower of Babylon' are in contrast with the regularity of Sargon of Assyria's well-proportioned structure at Khorsabad. At present this latter shows portions of four stages on a low platform; and those who visited it gained the summit by means of the gently sloping exterior passage leading to the topmost portion, which was about 140 ft. above the platform. Though in their restorations Perrot and Chipiez † do not place any chambers in the structure, it is not improbable that such existed, if not at some intermediate point, at any rate on the topmost platform.

Exceedingly noteworthy, however, are the excavations made by Layard in the ruins of the temple-tower at Nimrûd (Calah). Wishing to find out what authority there might be for supposing that Ctesias and Ovid were right in indicating that these towers were of the nature of tombs, he cut through the masonry in certain places, and was at last rewarded by finding a vault on the platform-level 100 ft. long, 12 ft. high, and 6 ft. broad. There is no doubt that this discovery justified him in regarding these temple-towers as being originally tombs, as stated, but that it is 'the tomb of Sardanapalus which, according to the Greek geographers, stood at the entrance of the city of Nineveh,' must be left doubtful, notwithstanding that Calah (Nimrûd) may have been regarded as part of Nineveh, at least in later times. Layard's statement that it had been entered at some unknown period by people who must have known exactly where to make the opening, is also in favour of his supposition: they had apparently entered for the purpose of rifling the tomb. The vaulted gallery found by Layard runs east and west. Details concerning the upper part of the monument are unfortunately wanting. Layard regarded it as having been a tower in five stages, which is probable enough, but the dimensions of all but the lowest are unknown. This last was built massively with a thick facing of stone, exactly 20 ft. high, and finished at the top with a line of gradines. The stones were carefully fitted together, without any mortar, though mud may have been used instead, as at the present time. As far as preserved, the upper part is of brick.*

As has been pointed out by Canon Rawlinson, the Babylonians and Assyrians made their temples insignificant in comparison with the dwellings of their kings, thus apparently not imitating the Egyptians. As the Babylonians and Assyrians, like all the Semitic nations, were exceedingly religious, this shortcoming was probably due to some extent to climatic conditions and the want of suitable building-stone; perhaps, too, more of the temple-revenues may have been appropriated by the priests. The want of stone was more especially felt in Babylonia; the Assyrians made use of it largely, though not to the same extent as brick. The possession of stone enabled the Assyrians to adorn their temples with many fine bas-reliefs.

As an accessory of a temple, and therefore belonging to religious architecture, may be mentioned the Ištar-gate at Babylon. This is situated near the ruins of the temple Ê-maḫ, and consists of massive walls—the sides of the gate—decorated with bulls and the fabulous creatures called *ṣir-ḫuššû*—strange and impossible serpent-dragons. These alternate vertically from top to bottom, and are exceedingly well preserved. The beauty of the workmanship and the excellence of the enamel were not surpassed even by the artizans of the Persian period. From the Ištar-gate a 'festival-street' led northward to 'the place of Fate,'† where the oracles were declared yearly in Nisan. This is an excellently-paved causeway, apparently decorated with tiles imitating valuable stones.

In the temple of the Sun at Abu-habbah (Sippar, identified, though doubtfully, with the Biblical Sepharvaim), bitumen seems to have been used for the pavement; and beneath this, in a corner of one of the rooms, was found an earthenware coffer containing the celebrated 'sun-god stone'‡ (see ART [Assyr.-Bab.]). Receptacles for sacred objects were probably made in all temples in Babylonia. It seems likely that there were but few erections of the kind which had not closed recesses, at each corner, for the reception of the cylinders recording the building, re-building, or repairing of the edifice.

Naturally there are a number of religious erections whose real use is at present difficult to discover or to prove. At Babylon, on the site which the German explorers regard as being that

* *Das Stadtbild von Babylon* (1904), p. 23. The site of this temple-tower is the rectangular depression now called *Sahan*, which is of the dimensions stated.

† *Hist. de l'Art dans l'Antiquité*, 'Chaldée,' pp. 404-405.

* Layard's *Nineveh and Babylon*, plan 2, and p. 123 ff. The stones 'were bevelled with a slanting bevel, and in the face of the wall were eight recesses or false windows, four on each side of a square projecting block between gradines' (Layard, p. 125). The northern side had a semicircular hollow projecting in the centre, flanked by three pilasters on the E. and five on the W. The western side had no projection, but the pilasters were eleven in number. The eastern and southern sides were perfectly plain.

† The inner walls of this building, Nebuchadrezzar states, had been overlaid with silver; but this he took away, substituting pure gold.

‡ See H. Rassam's 'Recent Discoveries of Ancient Babylonian Cities' in *TSBA*, vol. viii. pp. 175-176.

of 'the place of Fate,' several chambers were found, which may have formed part of that edifice. This seems to point to the probability that the oracles of the Babylonians and Assyrians were declared in special buildings, though such things may, from time to time, have been delivered in the temples, such as are described above. At present we know nothing of the lives of the declarers of their oracles, or of the rites which accompanied their declarations of events, so that the nature of the building they needed receives no illustration from the ruins which have come down to us.

At Lagaš were discovered a number of cells whose uses seemed to be religious, though in what way was not clear. Some of them contained a bronze figure of a kneeling bull upon a shank or tang, others had a figure of what has been described as 'the god with the firestick.' They were accompanied by inscriptions on stone dedicating them to a deity. The figures are thought to have been for the protection of the buildings in which they were found. Here and there tanks and cisterns occurred, suggesting some connexion with libation-ceremonies. Two tombs were discovered, containing skeletons, a lamp of glazed ware, and vases with short handles. Notwithstanding the early objects found in the tombs, it is regarded as certain that they are of late date.

In the inscriptions referring to offerings, at least one reference to a *bît-ili* or *bethel*, 'house of god,' is found,* but in what these differed from other religious buildings is unknown. The large temples seem always to have been dedicated to some special deity, notwithstanding that several deities may have been worshipped within them. These *bethels*, however, had no special designation: any deity, it may be supposed, could be worshipped there. Perhaps, as they were regarded as the abode of the god without specifying his attributes, any worshipper could enter, and perform his religious duties there. That it was simply an emblem of divinity, or of the presence of the divinity, without any walls to shield it from the gaze of the careless passer-by, seems, from the inscriptions, to be unlikely. The places where oracles were declared must have contained chambers where the animals were killed when it was intended to examine their entrails or other parts.

The bricks used by the Babylonians and Assyrians vary in size from 11¼ in. square and 2½ in. thick to 13 in. square by 3 in. thick and 16 in. square by 7 in. thick. Sometimes crude and burnt brick are used in alternate layers each several feet in thickness, but more commonly the unbaked brick was used for the internal parts of a building or for the core of a temple-tower, and the baked brick for the parts exposed to the weather. The layers of reed-matting which are found seem to have been used for buildings of unbaked brick. The use of this is exemplified by the ruins of the temple-tower at Warka (Erech), dedicated to Ištar, which is now called *Bowariah*, 'reed-mats.' The mass of the structure is of unbaked brick, the lower part buttressed with baked brick. That these buildings have resisted so long is remarkable, but they must always have been unsatisfactory. As a contrast to the temple of Ištar at Erech may be mentioned that of Nebo at Borsippa (the traditional Tower of Babel), where there are masses of brickwork of extraordinary hardness. This ruin still awaits complete excavation.

Besides brick in Babylonia, and brick and stone in Assyria, the building-materials mentioned in the inscriptions are cedar, terebinth (?), oak (?), palm-wood, cypress, pistachio-wood, etc. Nebuchadrezzar speaks of the cedar-beams from Lebanon which were used for the roofing of the temples of Babylon, which, he adds, were overlaid with shining gold. Besides this, silver, bronze, copper, rare stones, and ivory were used for their adornment. As before mentioned, baked and unbaked brick took the place, with the Babylonians, of the building-stone used by the Assyrians, bitumen being generally used for mortar, as stated in Gn 11^3.

Concerning the ornamentation, the inscriptions give but little information. The principal architectural decoration of the upper terminations of the walls were the gradines already referred to. The panellings of the walls, which were also a speciality of Assyro-Babylonian architecture, are an application of the gradine pattern to form recesses in the brick or stone walls in a vertical direction, and, when well carried out, had a sufficiently decorative effect.

Failing stone, certain of the buildings of Babylonia were decorated with reliefs of enamelled brick; and though this cannot be proved for the temples, it is extremely probable that some of them at least had ornaments of this nature, more especially as some of the fragments found seemed to have been parts of fabulous or mythological beings (see ART [Assyr.-Bab.]). In these there was an attempt at reproduction in natural colours, and there were inscriptions in white characters on a blue ground, the whole showing considerable knowledge and skill.

The Babylonians seem often to have employed, however, the same method of decoration as the Assyrians, namely, fresco, traces of which have been found. In the case of the temple Ê-maḫ at Babylon, the distemper, as far as preserved, is white, probably chosen as the groundwork for decorations in colours, similar to the more or less geometrical flower-forms of the painted tiles and other decorations of the temple called *Kidimuri* at Calah. The centres of the tiles, which were circular or lozenge-shaped, are generally provided with a knob pierced with a hole, probably for the purpose of hanging a lamp, though no remains of lamps are stated to have been found. Other Assyrian ornamentation consists of rosettes between two coloured borders, and red, blue, and black rosettes above a similar border supported by a kind of arcade-ornament—perhaps the original suggestion for the true arcades of architecture. The colours in Assyrian distemper-ornamentation were exceedingly bright.*

The principal portals of the temples of Assyria were guarded by colossal bulls and lions, with the usual sacred figures, which, in the case of the smaller temple at Nimrûd, were generally covered with inscriptions. The bas-reliefs always represent religious subjects. The exterior walls of this building seem to have been faced with enamelled bricks, some of which were found. Whether the temples at Babylon had their entrances flanked by colossal winged bulls or not is doubtful, but this seems probable, at least in some cases, as they are to all appearance referred to by Aššur-banî-âpli, king of Assyria, in his account of the destruction wrought by his grandfather Sennacherib at Babylon on the occasion of his final conquest of the city (see Aššur-banî-âpli's great cylinder, col. iv. line 70). T. G. PINCHES.

ARCHITECTURE (Celtic).†—We have no definite information about the religious architecture of the Gauls. In the case of the Celts, ancient writers never describe places devoted to worship by the word ναός or *ædes*; they make use of vaguer

* See *The Babylonian and Oriental Record*, vol. ii. pp. 142–145. See also Hastings' *DB*, vol. ii. p. 301b, where the *bethel* of cedar at Haran is referred to.

* See Layard's *Monuments of Nineveh*, 1st series, pl. 86, 87.

† This art. deals with pre-Christian Celtic Architecture; for Christian Celtic Architecture see ARCHITECTURE (Christian).

terms, such as *locus consecratus* (Cæsar, *de Bell. Gall.* vi. 13. 17), ἱερόν (Diod. v. 27. 4; Strabo, iv. 4. 5; Plut. *Cæsar*, 26; Dio Cass. lxii. 7; cf. xxvii. 90), *templum* (Livy, xxiii. 24. 11; Suet. *Cæsar*, 54), τέμενος (Strabo, xii. 5. 2; Diod. v. 27. 4), and σηκός (Strabo, iv. 1. 13).

The sacred places of the ancient Celts, therefore, resembled neither the sanctuary of the Greek temples nor the great buildings which constituted the temples of the Romans. There is no doubt that they were enclosures frequently situated in the woods. Lucan (iii. 399–425) describes a sacred wood near Marseilles where sacrifices were offered to the gods with barbaric ceremonies, and where there were altars on which cruel rites were performed; all the trees in the wood were purified with human blood; the miserable effigies of the gods were devoid of art—shapeless masses of tree-trunk. Pomponius Mela (iii. 2. 17) remarks that the large sacred woods of Gaul lent a pleasing appearance to the country. Cæsar mentions the sacred place in the territory of the Carnutes where year by year the Druids assembled to administer justice (*de Bell. Gall.* vi. 13), and states that in the sacred places of many races were to be seen pieces of spoil taken from enemies, and that a Gaul would never dare to keep a part of the booty in his house, or carry off anything from these stores (vi. 17). The Arverni had hung up in front of a temple (πρὸς ἱερῷ) the little sword that Cæsar had left with them during a battle. Plutarch (*Cæsar*, 26), who reports this fact, seems to have been influenced by the Greek and Roman custom, and we cannot conclude from this statement that a building was referred to. At Toulouse the sacred places included lakes, where great treasures were eventually accumulated under the water (Strabo, iv. 1. 13; Justin, xxxii. 3, 10).

There were temples among the Cisalpines; and it was to one of them that the Boii brought their booty and the head of the consul Postumius. There they made this head into a cup hooped with gold, and it was this sacred vessel that was used by the priests of the temple on their feast-days (Livy, xxiii. 24). Polybius mentions a temple (ἱερόν) of Athene among the Insubrians where the ensigns of war were kept (ii. 32). There is nothing to show that these temples were anything else than uncovered enclosures.

The Britons in the time of Queen Boadicea had sacred places, and they offered human sacrifices in the sacred wood (ἄλσος) of the goddess Adrastia (Dio Cass. lxii. 7). In B.C. 61, Suetonius Paulinus ordered the sacred woods of Mona, which were devoted to savage superstitions, to be cut down (Tac. *Ann.* xiv. 30).

The council of the Galatians of Asia Minor met to judge cases of murder in a place called Δρυνέμετον. The second part of this word means, in Celtic, 'sacred wood.' Probably it refers to a place consecrated to worship (Strabo, xii. 5. 1).

It must further be added that the Druids were regarded as the inhabitants of the forests. According to Pomponius Mela (iii. 2. 19) they taught, and according to Lucan (i. 493) they lived, in caves or secret glades. Pliny states that it was in oak-forests that they gathered mistletoe. The oldest etymology of the name 'Druids' made them 'the men of the oaks,' from the Gr. δρῦς (Pliny, xvi. 95, 249).

If we may calculate the shape of the sacred enclosures from the ruins of Gallo-Roman temples, they were almost perfectly square. But nothing more can be determined concerning the Gallic period from the numerous stone temples of which ruins have been found in Gaul, and which date from the Roman epoch. If there were small buildings sacred to the gods in Celtic countries in ancient times, these buildings, like the Gallic houses, were made of wood and wicker-work (Strabo, iv. 4. 3; Cæsar, v. 43; Vitruvius, ii. 1. 5). The Gauls did not use stone except for building the walls of their *oppida*, and even then it was unhewn stone, adjusted by means of wooden cross-pieces and iron bolts (Cæsar, vii. 23). They seem to have been ignorant of the art of hewing stones and joining them with mortar.

They probably found it as ridiculous to enclose the gods in any kind of house as to represent them in human form. Diodorus tells that Brennus laughed very much on seeing wooden and stone statues of anthropomorphic gods in a Greek temple (xxii. 9. 4). Lucan, when describing the sacred wood near Marseilles, and Cæsar, when speaking of the Gallic Mercury (vi. 17), use the word *simulacra* to denote the representations of the gods. Does this refer to more or less rough wooden statues similar to the ξόανα of primitive Greece, or to shapeless stone statues like some of the extant menhirs? It is possible that the Gallic races employed now the one method of representing their deities and now the other, according to the nature of the soil. The deities of the Gallo-Roman period—the Bull, the Woodman, the god with the mallet, the god with the wheel—undoubtedly arose from a new religious conception due to the influence of the Romans. No text gives evidence of the Druids having forbidden idolatry, and no text states clearly that there were real statues of gods among the Celts; therefore we cannot affirm that their sacred enclosures contained anything but very rudimentary symbols similar to those of savage tribes. The huge bronze statue of Zeus which the Galatians had at Tavium was probably of Greek origin, like the cult of the god whom it represented (Strabo, xii. 5. 2).

There do not seem to have been any buildings devoted to worship in pagan Ireland. Idols were apparently erected in the open air, as, *e.g.*, the large stone idol called 'Cromm Cruach,' which was surrounded by twelve smaller idols covered with brass and bronze ornaments. There were similar idols in various parts of Ireland, and some of them were believed to deliver oracles, *e.g.* the famous 'Lia Fail' at Tara. The idol Bel, in honour of which bonfires (through which cattle were made to pass) were kindled on the 1st of May, does not seem to have been enclosed in a temple any more than the other idols.

As regards the civil architecture of ancient Ireland, it is practically the same as that of races at the same stage of civilization. The houses were usually round in shape, built of wood and wicker-work, and covered with thatch. They were very small. The chief room served as kitchen, dining-room, drawing-room, and bed-room. Among the higher classes of society, small recesses were fitted in along the walls, each containing one or more beds. But the common people undoubtedly slept on beds arranged along the wall, as was the custom in Gaul and in Scotland during the same period. The fire was in the middle of the house, and the smoke escaped through an opening in the roof. The beds were placed in such a way that the sleepers had their feet towards the fire. Each bed contained often two and sometimes three persons. It was only in the houses of chiefs that arrangements were made to avoid too complete promiscuity, and that beds were surrounded with curtains.

LITERATURE.—Bulliot and Roidot, *La cité gauloise selon l'histoire et les traditions*, Autun, 1879; Jullian, *Histoire de la Gaule*, Paris, 1907, ii. 155–157; Dottin, *Manuel pour servir à l'étude de l'antiquité celtique*, Paris, 1906, pp. 120 f., 123, 250–254; Joyce, *A Social History of Ancient Ireland*, London, 1903, ii. 20–103.

G. DOTTIN.

ARCHITECTURE (Chinese).—As the world is still in the dark with regard to the whole problem of China and the Chinese, so is it with

Chinese architecture. From an architectural point of view, this is a very novel and interesting subject. A style never dreamed of by Europeans is adopted quite freely, and a design which they call irrational and unnatural is executed with success. Little wonder, therefore, that we find few students of Chinese architecture, and those few touching on the subject but superficially.

The style of the architecture is a combination of the trabeated and arcuated systems, the materials consisting of wood, brick, and stone. The curved roof, with the skyward-projecting eaves, forms the principal feature of the building. This feature is especially noticeable in Southern China. Generally speaking, however, both the plan and the elevation are monotonous, and the complete structure is rigidly symmetrical. The mode of decoration is strikingly peculiar. The exterior is usually coloured bright red; and temples and palaces are sometimes decorated with ornamental sculptures and paintings. Gorgeous colours are applied to the interior, and the whole appearance of rooms and furniture is very picturesque. Red is the predominant colour, and then blue, green, and yellow (gold). Northern China is destitute of trees, as rain falls only once a year. Hence the building materials are principally brick and stone. Consequently a trabeated system of wood and an arcuated of stone have developed simultaneously. On the other hand, the abundance of trees in the South has given an impulse to a considerable development of wooden buildings, with deeply curved and boldly projecting eaves. As to the origin of the concave outline of the roof, there is diversity of opinion. The present writer considers it but a natural result of the necessity of making a gradual change in the slope of the roof as it approaches the eaves, and of the maintenance of harmony with their curves. The fact is that the bold curve of the eaves always follows the bold concave of the roofs. It is rather strange that the plan of Chinese architecture is always an arrangement of rectangular blocks; not a single example of roofing on irregular plans is known. This is due to the direct transmission of the ideas of primitive times, and is a good illustration of the stagnant mind of the people.

Chinese architecture may be called the architecture of colouring. Without colours it is a bare, rugged skeleton. Both without and within colours are profusely adopted. The fondness for red betrays the primitive mind. But this primitive colouring is in harmony and uniformity with the taste of the primitive plans and elevations. The simplicity and coarseness of the construction and the carelessness of workmanship are beyond expression, especially in the productions of recent date. The exaltation of art and the execution of details have been entirely ignored by modern architects.

Historically, Chinese architecture may be arranged as follows: (1) Chinese architecture proper (B.C. 2200–A.D. 68, *i.e.* from the earliest historical age to the introduction of Buddhism: Hsia, Shang, Chou, Ch'in, and the earlier Han Dynasties); (2) the rise of Buddhist architecture (A.D. 68–A.D. 618, *i.e.* from the introduction of Buddhism to the Six Dynasties: the later Han, both Chins, Sung, Ch'i, Lian, Chên, and Sui Dynasties, and also Wei, Ch'i, Chou of the North Dynasties); (3) Buddhist architecture in full splendour (A.D. 618–A.D. 1260, *i.e.* T'ang, Wutai, and Sung Dynasties); and (4) the introduction of Lāmaism (A.D. 1260–present day, *i.e.* Yuen, Ming, and Ch'ing Dynasties).

(1) The first was the period of palace building. Unfortunately, no ruins are in existence for our investigation. From a study of the time, however, we find that there existed during this period magnificent palaces and towers, great in design and majestic in style, such as A-Fang of the Ch'in emperor Shih-Whuan-Ti, and Chang-Lê, and Wei-Yang of the Han. The relics which show most clearly the structural aspect and treatment of details of that time are the reliefs of Wu-Lian-Tzu, though the monument itself belongs to the later Han Dynasty. From them we can trace long projected wooden eaves, balustraded towers, various kinds of caryatids, richly decorated roofs, etc.

(2) The second period may be divided into the later Han and the North and South Dynasties. During the North and South Dynasties the influence of Buddhist architecture began to be felt. The style of Buddhist architecture remained without much alteration, any change being confined to the inner arrangement and decorations. But for pagodas and those particular buildings required by the new religion, an entirely new system was imported from Central Asia. Scarcely any architectural relics of the Six Dynasties have been discovered, but the style is fairly well represented in the treatment of cave temples and reliefs. Specimens of the later Wei are found at Shih-fou-szu in Yün-gan, near Ta-T'ung, Shan-si; at Kung-hsien, Ho-nan; at Lung-men, near Lê-yang, etc.

(3) The third period may be divided into the earlier T'ang, the later T'ang, and Sung. In the earlier T'ang, Buddhist architecture and all other branches of art had reached the height of their grandeur, and from the later T'ang to Sung they began to decline continuously. During that time elaborate Taoistic temples were also built. The pagodas of Tz'u-wen-szu and of Chien-fou-szu, at Si-an, Shen-si, are specimens of the earlier T'ang. The two pillars and the two stone pagodas of Ling-yin-szu at Hang-chow, Che-kiang, are most probably remains of the Five Dynasties. Besides, dilapidated temples and pagodas belonging to the Five Dynasties and Sung are found in various parts of Southern China.

(4) The fourth period is divided as follows: (*a*) The Yuen. With the introduction of Lāmaism changes were brought about in art. A fine specimen of this time is the arch of Chü-yüng-kwan, near Pe-king. There are also the rock-cut sculptures at Feh-lei-fung, at the front of Ling-yin-szu, Hang-chow. (*b*) The Ming. Remains of this period are abundant everywhere. The old palaces at Nan-king and several of the Pe-king palaces are examples, and there is also an innumerable number of pagodas. (*c*) The Ch'ing. Somewhat noteworthy relics belonging to the reigns of the emperors Kung-hsi and Ch'ien-lung are in abundance, but the productions of later date are valueless.

Thus Chinese architecture developed rapidly with the introduction of Buddhism, and reached its golden age under the T'ang Dynasty. From the Sung it gradually degenerated down to the present day, when its ancient splendour has entirely vanished.

For convenience' sake, we may classify Chinese architecture according to the religions which have influenced the thoughts and arts of the people: Confucianism, Buddhism, Taoism, and Muhammadanism. Others, such as Zoroastrianism, Manichæism, Nestorianism, and Judaism, were of a temporary nature, and have left no architectural remains. Then we have a group of secular architecture: castles, palaces, dwelling-houses, etc., which will be treated below.

1. Confucian Architecture.—The religion which has spread all over China, and is held in reverence by all the people, is Confucianism. Temples, known as *Hsin-shih-miao* or *Wên-miao* (the latter different from *Wu-miao* [see § 3]), are dedicated everywhere in cities and towns. The most celebrated one is in Ch'ü-fou-hsien, Shantung, the birthplace of the sage. The temples of Pe-king and of Nan-king are well known, the former on account of the stone drums in the *Ta-ch'êng-mên*, and the latter on account of its immense size. But from an architectural point of view they show very little variety of plan and elevation.

The main edifice of the temple is the *Ta-ch'êng-tien*, built on a high platform, two-storeyed, and mostly hip-roofed. In the centre of the interior the tablet of Chi-sheng-k'ung-tzu ('the most sacred Confucius') is enshrined. To its left, the tablets of Tsung-sheng-ts'êng-tzu and Ya-sheng-mêng-tzu, and to the right, those of Fu-sheng-yuen-tzu and Shu-sheng-tzu-szu-tzu, are arranged. As a rule, there are also the tablets of the twelve disciples. In front of the *Ta-ch'êng-tien* is the *Ta-ch'êng-mên*, and in front of the *mên* is a pond, and still farther forward is a *pai-lou* (popularly known as the *Ling-hsing-mên*). On the sides of those buildings there are the East and the West corridors. Occasionally behind the *Ta-ch'êng-tien* there is a building which is sometimes called *Chung-sheng-tzu*. Within the

Ta-ch'êng-mên there are sometimes a bell-tower and a drum-tower facing each other. The general arrangement of these buildings resembles that of the Buddhist temple: e.g. *Ta-ch'êng-tien* stands for *Fou-tien*, *Ta-ch'êng-mên* for *T'ien-wang-tien*, etc. As a rule, the *Wên-miao* is combined with the institution of learning. One of the most famous institutions is Pai-lu-shu-yüan, at the foot of Wu-lao-fêng, a south-east peak of Lu-shan in Nan-kung-fu, Kiangsi. This was established by Chu-tzu. The largest among numerous buildings in the compound is *Hsien-hsien-shu-yüan*. Within the gate there is a court-yard, with fifteen cells on either side. Then comes the *Wên-hui-t'ang* ('meeting-hall'), and behind it another court, with five cells on either side. Last of all, the two-storeyed *chün-fêng-lou* is reached. The architectural system of educational buildings is more or less similar to the above. The *Kung-yüan* is an examination hall for the degree of *chü-jên*, and is noted for its extensive scale. One in Nan-king is said to be ample enough to accommodate over ten thousand students. In fact, learning in China means Confucian teaching; hence the relation of schools to the *Wên-miao* is similar to that of monasteries to the Buddhist temple.

2. **Buddhist Architecture.**—The most important factor in the development of Chinese architecture is Buddhism. History says that in the reign of Ming-ti of the later Han the new religion was first introduced into China (65 A.D.), and Pai-ma-szu was built at Lê-yang. Henceforward it spread and flourished continuously, until the meridian was reached under the Six Dynasties and the T'ang. The North Dynasty felt its influence more than the South, the earlier Si-an and Lê-yang and the later Lu-shan and Chien-yeh (now Nan-king) being the centres. The highest pagoda ever recorded was built in Yung-ning-szu by the Empress Dowager Hu of the North Wei. It is said to have been 900 ft. high, with a finial of 100 ft. But Buddhism suffered from the corruptions and disorders that were prevalent from the later T'ang to the Five Dynasties, and no temples of any importance were built. A temporary revival began under the earlier Sung, resulting in elaborate temple-building in Southern China during the South Sung Dynasty. T'ien-tai-shan, Lin-gan (now Hang-chow), Ching-ling (now Nan-king), and their neighbourhoods were the centres. Under the Yüan Dynasty, Lāmaism was made the State religion. The architectural style of Lāma temples does not differ from that of Buddhist, except in the occasional application of Tibetan styles to details, and the importation of new images and ritual articles. One new feature is the introduction of a pagoda which is a direct copy of a Tibetan model. Since the Ming Dynasty, Buddhism has been in a dormant state, greatly influenced by Lāmaism. In earlier days, Buddhism was divided into thirteen sects, but under the later T'ang only three prevailed: Vinaya sect, Dhyāna sect, and Sukhāvatī sect. Dhyāna was subdivided into five sects. At present this is the ruling sect, other shades of belief being indistinguishable. We may say that the architectural features are practically common to all sects. Among the temples now existing are Yung-wo-kun in Pe-king and several other temples on the Western hills outside of the city. Wu-tai-shan in Shan-si, T'ientai-shan, Pu-t'o-shan, T'ien-t'ung-shan, T'ien-omu-shan in Chê-kig, Lu-shanan in Kiang-si, Womei-shan in Szu-chwan, etc., are widely known, but they are almost in ruins and deserted, without a trace of their former splendour.

The commonest arrangement of Buddhist architecture is as follows:—In the main front there is the first gateway (*shan-mên*), wherein usually two guardian figures (*er-tien*) are kept. Then comes the *t'ien-wang-tien* ('temple'). In the centre of this temple an image of Maitreya with the features of Pu-tai is enshrined; behind Maitreya, and back to back, is a standing figure of Vedadeva. In the four corners are the *su-tien-wang* ('four heavenly kings'): in the North-east is Virûpâksha with a harp, in the South-east Dhrita-râshtra with a sword, in the North-west Vaisravana with an umbrella, and in the South-west Virûdhaka grasping a serpent. Behind the *t'ien-wang-tien* is the *ta-tien*, known by various names, such as *Ta-hsiung-pao-tien* or *Fou-tien*. Here the Buddha and eighteen Arhats are enshrined.

Still further behind the *ta-tien* are sometimes the *fa-t'ang* ('preaching hall'), *tsang-ching-kê* ('library'), and *fan-chang* ('cloister for head priest'). To the right and left of the above buildings are corridors, divided into sections, used for various purposes. Generally there are the *ke-t'ang* ('reception hall'), *ch'ieh-lan-tien* ('shrine for the guardian god'), *tsu-shih-tien* ('shrine for the founder of the sect'), *shan-t'ang* ('meditation hall'), *ch'i-t'ang* ('eating hall'), *yün-shui-t'ang* ('cloister for mendicant priests'), etc. To the right and left of the *t'ien-wang-tien* a bell-tower and a drum-tower stand facing each other, sometimes with the addition of a pagoda.

The pagoda is the most interesting and tasteful of Buddhist buildings, there being numerous varieties of form. Its origin is the *stūpa* of India, obviously transported from Central Asia and India. The process of the modification of form is not yet plain, as even the pagodas of a very remote period seen on reliefs and carvings are many-storeyed, already losing the shape of the original *stūpa*. The pagoda of Tzu-en-szu, Si-an, is the oldest now in existence, and is said to be a copy of a model from Central Asia. It is seven-storeyed, and square in plan. Others are mostly seven- to thirteen-storeyed, octagonal, and built of brick. One in T'ien-ning-szu, Pe-king, is an example of the kind. In the Southern China and Yanze valleys seven-storeyed and hexagonal pagodas are also seen. The Lāma pagoda is merely a copy of a Tibetan model, the origin of which is an Indian *stūpa*. They are abundantly seen in Northern China, and a beautiful example is that of Pai-ta-szu of Pe-king.

3. **Taoist Architecture.**—There is no special style of architecture in Taoism, as it is practically borrowed from Buddhism. With a slight modification of the images and ritual articles, a Buddhist temple gives a good idea of the Taoist temple, such as is represented in Pai-yun-kuan at Pe-king. Behind the entrance *pai-lou* there is a *shan-mên*; and then comes a *ling-kuan-tien*, where at the centre and in the four corners the images of Lin-kuan are enshrined, corresponding to the *t'ien-wang-tien* of a Buddhist temple. Then there is the *yü-huang-tien*, where Yü-huan is worshipped; the *lao-lü-tien* for the seven sages of Taoism; the *ch'iu-tsu-tien*, and the *su-yü-tien* successively follow. In the last hall even the 'Eight Treasures' of Lāmaism are contained.

Temples for Chinese gods owe their origin to Taoism. The architectural style is Buddhist, with the following exceptions: at the front they have a stage for theatrical purposes, and before the stage there is an extensive court-yard; the architectural details are more minute, and the decorations more elaborate. The *Kuan-ti-miao*, or *Wu-miao*, is seen everywhere in China. Here Kuan-yü is worshipped, always attended by his two followers, Ch'ou-ts'ang and Kuan-ping. The *cheng-huang-miao* is a guardian temple of town and village. Numerous temples, such as *Wên-chang-miao* ('Temple of the Star-god'), *Ts'ai-shen-miao* ('Temple of the god of Wealth'), *Huo-shen-miao* ('Temple of the god of Fire'), *Fêng-shen-miao*

('Temple of the god of Wind'), *Shui-shen-kun* ('Temple of the god of Water'), *Niang-niang-miao* ('Temple of the god of Love'), and many others for 'profane' gods, and occasionally many-storeyed temples such as *Yün-huang-kê* and *K'uei-hsing-lou*, are abundant all over China.

4. **Muhammadan Architecture.**—Since the first mosque was built at Canton in the 7th cent. A.D., Muhammadanism has seen many ebbs and flows during the course of time, but it is flourishing far and wide. Ardent adherents are numerous, especially in the provinces of Kan-su and Shen-si. All the architectural relics of old days have been lost; according to investigations made by the writer, there is none older than the early part of the present dynasty. The temple is known by the one name *Ch'ing-chên-szu*, or popularly, *Li-pai-szu*. In style it resembles an ordinary Chinese temple; but the plan and the interior arrangement show the characteristic traits of the faith of foreign origin. The building consists of porch, hall, and sanctuary. The roofs are also divided into three distinct sections. The sanctuary is either square or hexagonal in plan, two- or three-storeyed, and pagoda-shaped, instead of domed like the mosques in other countries; the inner wall is niched, with a *miḥrāb*, and decorated with arabesque and Arabic characters. The hall is usually divided into front and back portions, with an arcade between. The *minbar* is placed at the right-hand corner of the back hall, where decorations of arabesque and Arabic characters are again executed here and there. Near the hall there is sometimes a fountain, and sometimes a hall for purification. Occasionally halls for the head priest, for receptions, etc., are arranged as in a Buddhist temple. Often even the interior of the hall is of a Chinese style, entirely losing all signs of Muhammadanism. Thus in a Chinese mosque there is neither dome nor minaret; it is but a slight modification of an ordinary Chinese temple.

5. **Tombs.**—The ancient Chinese tombs were simply low artificial mounds where coffins were kept. Later on, monuments were erected, accompanied by stone figures of men and animals. This custom was prevalent as early as the later Han Dynasty, and still exists at the present day. Massively designed mausoleums of the T'ang Dynasty may be seen in the neighbourhood of Si-an. Earth is raised in a mound, and human and animal figures of stone are erected on the site. Hsiao-ling in Nan-king and Shih-san-ling in the north of Pe-king are the mausoleums of the Ming Dynasty. They are of the same design: *pai-lou*, *ta-hung-mên*, *pei-lou*, stone-men, stone-animals, and then again gates and archways leading to the last mound. The mausoleums of Tai-tsu and Tai-tsung of the present dynasty are near Mukden. They are simply copies of the Ming mausoleum. In the tomb of an ordinary person there are no stone-figures. It is a little cone-shaped mound, often enclosed by earth heaped up in the shape of a horse-shoe. Sometimes the coffin is placed in a cave made on a hill-side and covered with stone slabs. Sometimes a stone chamber is built to contain the coffin. The tombs of priests are pagodas of either brick or stone, or pagoda-shaped monuments of some architectural design. There are, of course, many varieties.

6. **Secular Architecture.**—Castles, palaces, meeting-halls, dwelling-houses, and the like, are distinguished from ecclesiastical architecture. The castle is surrounded by high strong walls of brick. Battlements, with embrasures, are erected on the walls. The entrances consist of double gates (*yüeh-chêng*): beyond the first the path turns sharply and leads to another. The upper part of the gate is a two-storeyed tower, and beneath is a vaulted passage, which can be closed at will by huge doors strengthened by bands of iron. On a large building in the main street of the city there stand bell- and drum-towers for reporting the time, the upper part being the tower and the lower the passage. The present mode of palace architecture in general is the same as that of the past. The Pe-king palace is similar to the old Ming palace of Nan-king. It is called *Chiu-chung-tien-mên* ('Nine-fold system'). The front part, which is used for public audiences, is called *chao*, and the back, for private audiences, is *t'ing*. The architectural mode of the *tien* and the *mên* does not differ from that of the temples already described. Here the T'an, or platform for nature- and ancestor-worship, may be included, for which the T'ien-t'an at Pe-king is so famous.

A building called *hui-kuan* is an assembly-hall for colonial clans and commercial guilds. The club-system is wonderfully developed in China, and there are magnificent buildings for the purpose. In front they have a theatrical stage facing an extensive court-yard, which is surrounded by corridors.

Dwelling-houses in Northern China vary in some respects from those of the South. In general, the premises are enclosed by high walls. At the entrance is a gate with a cell, and then a court-yard. A second gate with corridors, a second court-yard, a third gate with corridors, a third court-yard, etc., are repeated in the same manner, the number of gates and yards indicating the wealth and rank of the occupant. The house itself is a simple repetition of rectangular blocks and corridors. The unsuitable materials, the heavy mode of construction, the defectiveness of lighting and ventilation, etc., detract from its architectural value; but, on the whole, with its fantastic features, it presents a picturesque appearance.

C. ITO.

ARCHITECTURE (Christian).—Although it is possible to discuss the different edifices erected by Christians in divers times and places, it is most important, at the outset, to dispel any of those misconceptions which would suppose that there ever was any Christian style as such. The Gothic architecture of the Middle Ages has often been spoken of as Christian architecture *par excellence*, and undoubtedly it is the most important of the styles in which Christians have erected their buildings, and being the style of our own country, it naturally demands the largest share of our attention. But Christianity, as such, never has created, and never could create, a style of architecture, any more than it could create a style of mathematics, or science, although it may make use of all of them. It has used buildings of the Latin, Byzantine, Moorish, Gothic, and Renaissance, and even the Greek styles, which differ from each other as much as one style of architecture can differ from another; and the differences are due to differences in the æsthetic expression of the people. These may be associated with other differences of character which may affect the forms of Christianity itself, but they are both the outcome of causes behind; the one is not the cause of the other. A certain type of man will produce a certain type of art and a certain type of Christianity, but the type of Christianity does not make the type of art, any more than the type of art makes the type of Christianity. Even schools of science or philosophy may be coloured in the same way. The failure to grasp this very simple fundamental principle has led to much absurd criticism and a complete misunderstanding of art and architecture. Doubtless the cause is to be sought in the fact that to be a Christian it is not necessary to be an artist, and many a good Christian, quite innocent of any knowledge of art, has endeavoured, in the light of what he did understand, to interpret things which he did not understand.

All this does not alter the fact that a church is a definitely Christian building erected for Christian purposes, and as such it will in many ways reveal this fact; but, at the same time, its principal architectural qualities are æsthetic rather than religious, and a building such as St. Paul's is architecturally more akin to Castle Howard than to Westminster Abbey, which, in its turn, claims a closer kinship with Westminster Hall or the town halls of Belgium. The architecture of the Middle Ages was as much an architecture of castle and hall as of cathedral and church, and is as closely related to the spirit of chivalry and romance as to Christianity. Mediæval Christianity, chivalry, romance, and architecture are alike the outcome of the mediæval man; one is not the cause of the other, even although there is a certain amount of interaction. To speak of Christian architecture, then, as a parallel term with Greek architecture, is entirely illogical. In this article, therefore, we can examine Christian buildings in various styles of architecture, although we cannot strictly speak of Christian architecture as such. It may also be possible to show how Christian building doubtless left some impress upon the several styles of which it made use.

I. Latin Architecture.—The earliest form of church with which we have any intimate acquaintance is the so-called Christian **basilica**, and its origin is exceedingly difficult to trace. One thing at least is clear; it is not directly derived from the Roman basilica, as was absurdly suggested in an uncritical and unhistorical age. The Christian church naturally developed from humble beginnings, where two or three might gather together; and such a lordly prototype is impossible. It used even to be suggested that the actual basilicas were the first Christian churches. But, as Christianity was some 300 years old before the conversion of Constantine, the Christians could not have had the remotest chance of using these buildings. Moreover, even after A.D. 312 (the date of Constantine's conversion), the basilicas were still required for their original purpose, and could not have been handed over to what, even at that time, was but a minority of the people. During all these three hundred years the Christians had required places of worship, and undoubtedly a more or less definite arrangement of their buildings by that time had become crystallized.

As an instance of the feebleness of the argument, not to say the gross perversion of the contexts, we may note the following—one of the main passages quoted in favour of this theory. In a laudatory piece of writing by Ausonius addressed to the Emperor Gratian thanking him for the consulship, we find the following passage: 'Quis, inquam, locus est, qui non beneficiis tuis agitet, inflammet? Nullus, inquam, Imperator Auguste, quin admirandum speciem tuæ venerationis incutiat: non palatium, quod tu, cum terribile acceperis, amabile præstitisti: non forum, et basilica olim negotiis plena, nunc votis, votisque pro tua salute susceptis.' The passage is given by Professor Baldwin Brown in his admirably suggestive work, *From Schola to Cathedral* (1886), and, as he points out, vows for an Emperor's welfare in palace, forum, basilica, or senate house (mentioned later), are scant evidence that any one of these places was turned into a church, and why the basilica should be singled out from the others with which it is coupled remains a mystery.

Leaving such puerilities, it remains perfectly true that the Christian basilica in the 4th cent. A.D. bore *some* resemblance to the Roman basilica, although it has never been proved that the Roman basilica was even roofed in; but one might as well argue from a modern fleet as to the appearance of the Spanish Armada, the interval of time being the same, and the development of Christianity as rapid as that of our fleets. What was the case in A.D. 350 is of little value as evidence for what was the case at the beginning of the Christian era, in architecture just as in anything else.

The earliest Christian services were held in the Jewish synagogues, and in private houses; and in comparatively early times we find the Christians legally occupying the position of the *sodalicia*, which correspond to our Friendly and Burial Societies. These Societies often possessed a *scuola*, or lodge-room, where they held their banquets in honour of the deceased.

These three forms of building may all have influenced the early form of the Christian church, although it should be noted that the *scuola*, with its apse, was probably itself derived from the large private hall, which often had an apsidal termination.

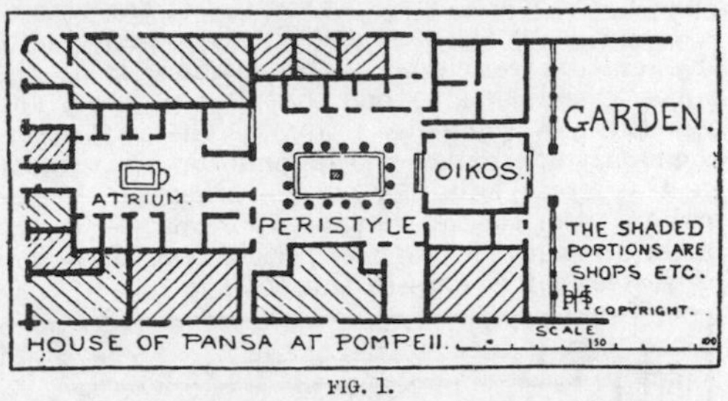

FIG. 1.

On the whole, the largest influence may be assigned to the private house (fig. 1). Certainly such houses were made over to the Christians for their use, and it may be even more than a coincidence that we find in the atrium of the early church the atrium of the Græco-Roman house, in the cloisters the peristyle of the house, and in the church itself the hall, *œcus*, or principal chamber, as at St. Ambrogio, Milan (fig. 2), or the Church of the Nativity at Bethlehem, where the atrium is reduced to a simple narthex.

The narthex, which gradually disappears from the Christian church, was the outer vestibule into which catechumens and penitents were permitted to enter, who were not admitted into the church

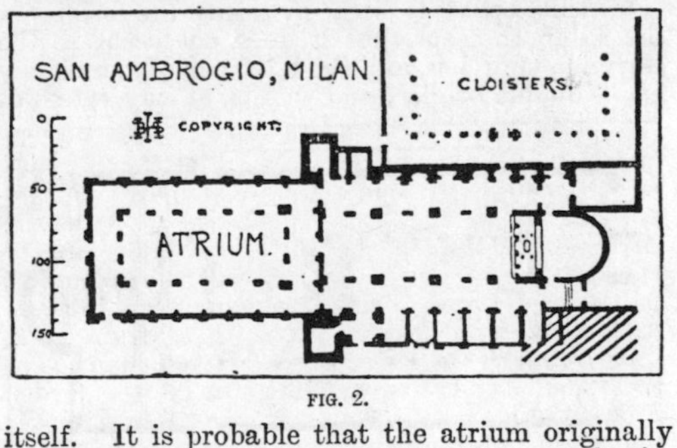

FIG. 2.

itself. It is probable that the atrium originally served a similar purpose, and the idea may be derived from the Court of the Gentiles in the Jewish Temple.

Some of the earliest actual places of meeting that still exist are the little chapels such as that in the catacomb of St. Agnese (fig. 3); but their value as evidence is slight, as the conditions were peculiar, and the form caused by throwing two or three cells together was the result of ne-

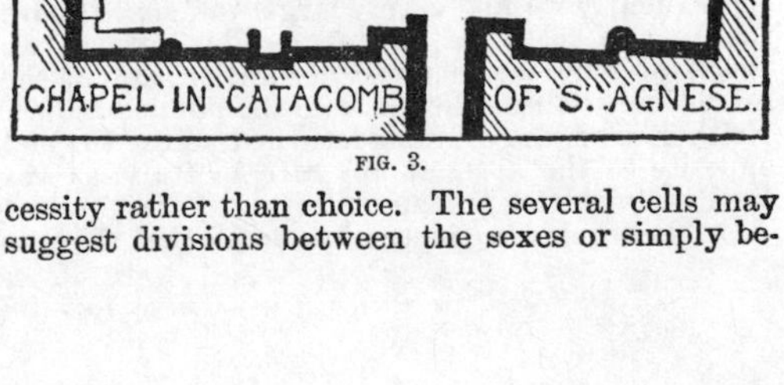

FIG. 3.

cessity rather than choice. The several cells may suggest divisions between the sexes or simply between clergy and laity, the clergy fairly obviously occupying the end cell and the bishop the seat at the end. The altar must have been somewhere in the body of the chapel, and as there is no trace of it, it was presumably in the form of a wooden table. But even this cannot be dated earlier than A.D. 250, and there is room for much change in a couple of hundred years.

What, then, are the characteristics of the early Christian basilica when first it emerges into the light of history? It is a three- or five-aisled hall, with the central aisle rising higher than the others and lit by a clerestory. At the end of the central aisle, generally the west end, is an apse containing the seats of the clergy. The entrance is at the opposite end, and beyond that is a narthex, and sometimes a complete atrium. The baptistery, commonly of circular or octagonal form, is usually in a separate building, on the other side of the atrium, or of the narthex, as at Parenzo. In the latter arrangement we may possibly see the origin of the German two-apsed church.

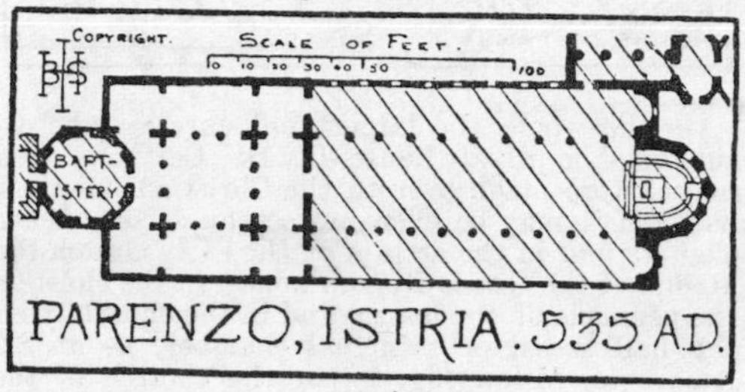

FIG. 4.

Occasionally, particularly in Rome, there is a space in front of the apse, and a great arch is thrown across the last pair of columns, known as the triumphal arch, as in Santa Maria in Trastevere (figs. 5, 7, and 10).

In this space is seen by some the origin of the later transept, but it does not occur in the Ravenna churches, and the later transept probably has a double origin; and this is, at any rate, not

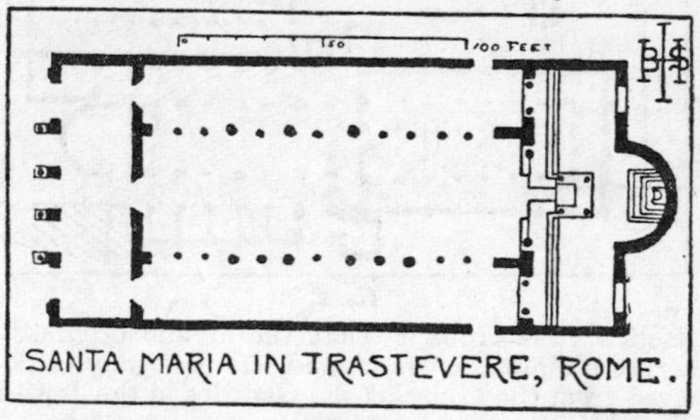

FIG. 5.

the only factor. The building was apparently roofed with a simple open timber roof. The flat ceilings that occur in some Roman examples are late Renaissance, although they may possibly represent something older. They are rarely found elsewhere, but are supposed by some to have been a feature of the Roman public basilica (fig. 6). The walls were generally of brick, and comparatively thin, as there was only the wooden roof to support. Unlike the Roman basilica, it had no galleries, and consequently we find a very large wall space above the line of columns (fig. 7). This formed an excellent field for pictorial decoration, and at the same time distinguished it from the public basilica. Neither were the columns returned across the end opposite to the apse, at any rate in Italy, as was the case with the Roman building.

On the whole also, it seems probable that the apse was not a usual feature of the public basilica, and, when it did occur, it was practically in a separate part of the building. The columns in the Christian basilicas, particularly in the case of Rome, were stolen from earlier buildings, and it is very usual to

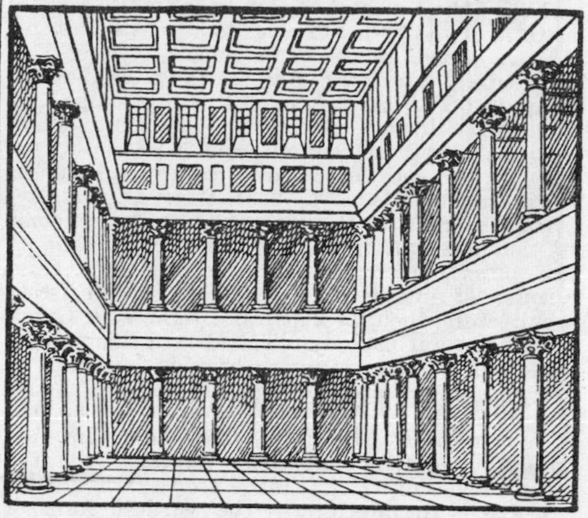

FIG. 6.—PAGAN BASILICA.

find that they do not match. This also accounts for the poor proportions of the earlier Christian buildings in Rome, as compared with those in Ravenna, where there was no such available spoil to hand, and the builders had to fall back upon their own resources. At first the horizontal entablature is more common, but it is gradually superseded by an arcade of arches, which gives an appearance of

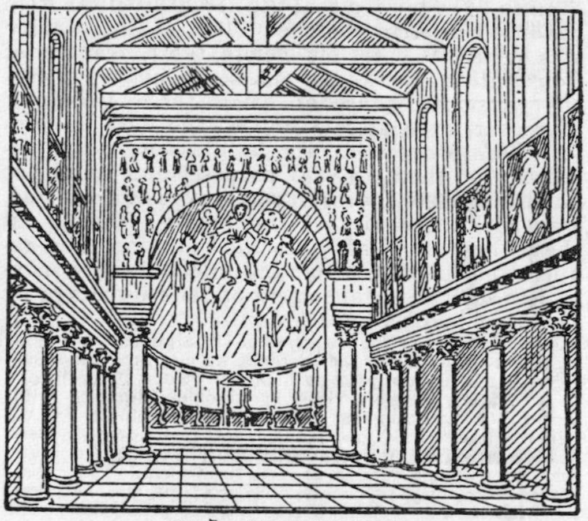

FIG. 7.—CHRISTIAN BASILICA.

greater height to the building, although the necessarily wider intercolumniations detract somewhat from the effect of length. The principal entrance was perhaps more often at the east end, following the arrangement of the temples of Greece. But the question of orientation was of little moment, and churches faced in any direction. After the custom of having the entrance at the west, and the altar at the east, came into vogue, as in England to-day, it was hardly ever more than a Northern fashion. Moreover, the first fashion was exactly the reverse way, with the altar at the west. The first church that we know to have had an altar at the east end was built in A.D. 470 (St. Agatha, Ravenna). Of the early churches in Rome 40 out of 50 have not their altars at the east.

The altar or table in the 5th cent. was at the opposite end from the main entrance, but in the body of the church in front of the apse, so arranged that the faithful sat round it, the clergy on one side and the laity on the other. Of course, this arrangement in most instances has been altered, but

FIG. 8.

the following churches in Italy show the old plan more or less undisturbed:—Torcello Cathedral, St. Apollinare in Classe, Ravenna, and Parenzo Cathedral (figs. 8, 11, and 4). (The bishop presided in a raised seat in the centre of the apse, very much as did the president at the table in the early *scuolæ*.) Outside Italy, in the East, where there has been less change and alteration, such churches are quite numerous, but the following instances will suffice: —Ezra, Pitzounda, Mochwi, Bedochwinta, Abu Sargah (fig. 14), Dair-as-Suriani. Bedochwinta has the seats at the back and down both sides, advancing even beyond the altar (fig. 9).

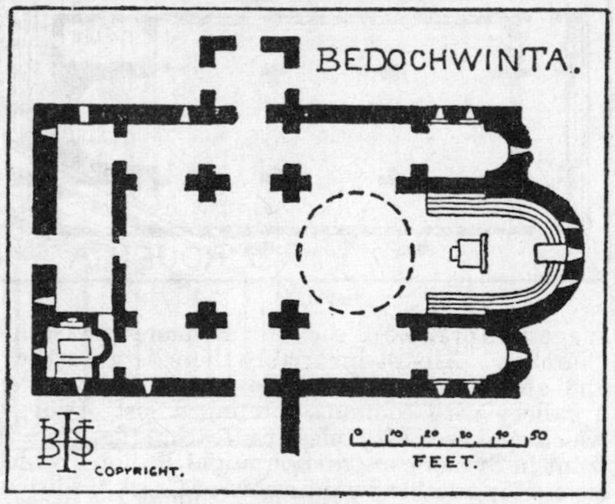

FIG. 9.

Churches with the altar in the body of the church, and the bishop's seat behind, but without the other seats, are familiar in Italy. There seems also to have been an arrangement, at any rate sometimes, for the lesser clergy and choir, whereby they occupied all the space immediately in front of the altar and were separated from the laity by a low screen. In the old church of St. Clemente in Rome, this screen, part of which is built from the actual pre-existing screen, may be taken to represent the original arrangement.

The floors of the churches were of ordinary marble mosaic, but this has often been altered in later times, and we see the so-called Cosmati work made with large pieces of coloured marble, surrounded by small mosaic, and this, again, by bands of white marble.

A good example of the basilican church is S. Paolo fuori le mura, Rome (fig. 10). This, although almost entirely a modern restoration after the fire of 1823, is still the best representative of a

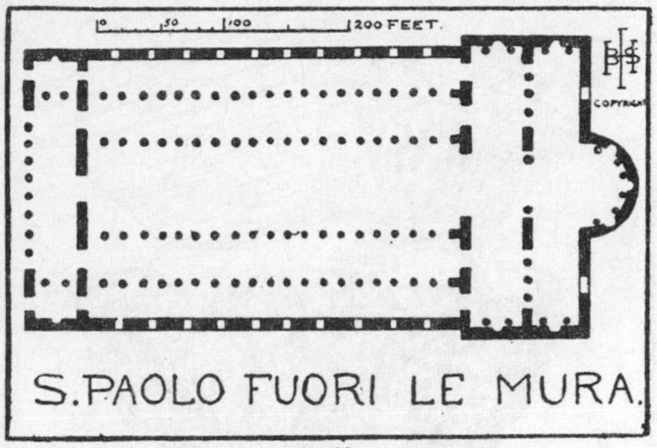

FIG. 10.

great five-aisled basilica that has come down to us. It is 400 ft. long and 200 ft. wide, with a central aisle of 78 ft. The complete atrium of Old St. Peter's is here represented only by a narthex. The bema hardly projects beyond the aisle walls, and is peculiar in being double. It is in area among the largest churches in Christendom; but it is quite a simple thing to build these comparatively low buildings, with their light wooden roofs. There are 19 columns with pseudo-Corinthian capitals and a sort of Attic base. They are without flutings, and carry a series of simple, round arches. Above is a cornice, and where there would be the gallery in a Roman basilica, or the triforium in a Gothic church, is a series of medallions. The triumphal arch is carried upon a pair of columns on plinths. These columns have Ionic capitals, and the whole arch forms a very imposing feature, although not comparable with the great arches of the crossing in a Gothic cathedral. The general vista is fine, although, partly from excessive breadth, and still more from an inadequate marking of the bay divisions, which is so well managed in a Gothic cathedral, the length here is not felt. The church at present has a rich coffered ceiling, but it is doubtful whether this would have been the case with the original church of the 4th century.

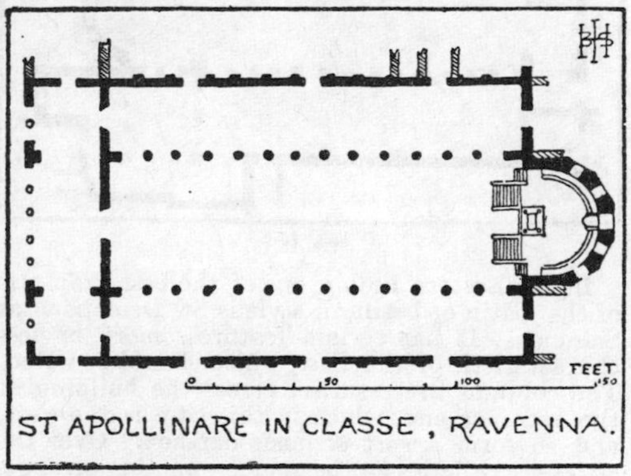

FIG. 11.

In Ravenna perhaps the noblest example is St. Apollinare in Classe. It illustrates the characteristics of the place, which on the whole shows the indebtedness to Greek work even more than to Rome. As a result, the work forms a far more complete artistic unity. Everything is designed for the position that it occupies, and is not the spoil from other days. The church is a three-aisled basilica and has no transeptal space before the apse, this, as already stated, being what we should expect in Ravenna. In the dosseret above the capitals, as at S. Vitale (fig. 12), and the polygonal exterior to the apse, we see Byzantine features.

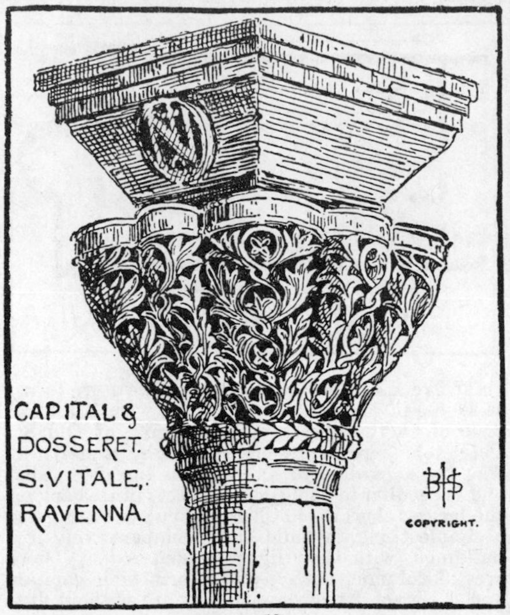

FIG. 12.

The capitals are carved for their place. Above the nave arcade is a series of medallions, as in S. Paolo fuori le mura. The apse is raised, with a small crypt below it, and it retains the seats round the altar on the side opposite the entrance. The brick exterior is bald to hideousness.

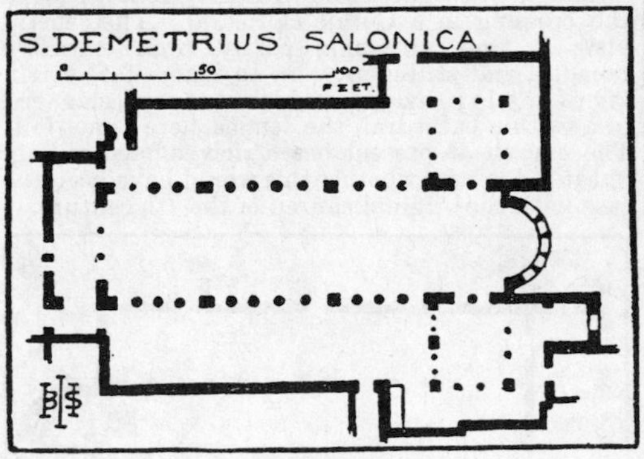

FIG. 13.

In the Eastern Empire one of the best examples of the Latin or basilican style is St. Demetrius at Salonica. It has certain features, more or less characteristic of the East, which should be noted. The columns are returned across the building at the entrance end, which in this case is the west, and so form a sort of inner narthex. Over the aisles are galleries for the women—another arrangement common in the East. The capitals are finely carved, as we have here the still living Greek influence. This, as already indicated, was felt in the West. It was long before the Italians could carve capitals or lay mosaics for themselves, and either they made use of the old work, as we have seen, or else the new work was executed by Greek workmen. Even in the 8th and 9th centuries, when the Italians began to copy the old work, theirs is very inferior and rude in comparison. In St. Demetrius there are fairly clearly defined projections which perhaps may be termed transeptal, but they are at the extreme end of the church, even projecting beyond the apse, and they are cut across by the main arcade of the church which makes them more or less invisible, and, in short, they are side chambers rather than a transept. Consequently there is no triumphal arch.

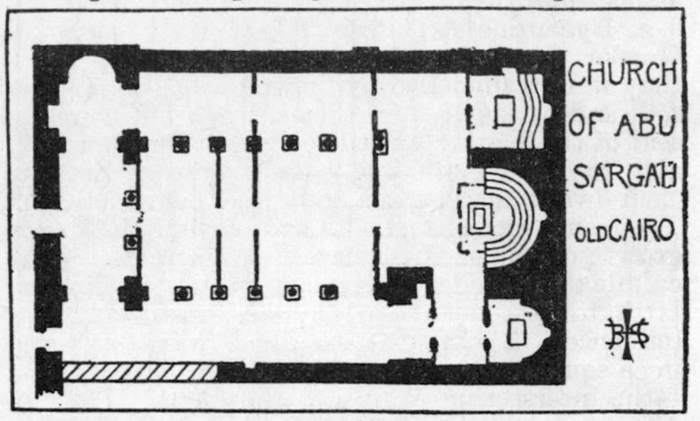

FIG. 14.

Other modified forms of the basilican church are found in Egypt and in Syria. In both cases there seems to be a tendency to keep the form of the apse only on the inside and to make the outside of the building square. The Coptic churches in Egypt are generally triapsidal with three altars, an apse occurring at the end of each of the side aisles—a form we shall meet again later (fig. 14). Syrian churches generally show a marked reminiscence of the style of Ancient Greece, and are finer in their work than those of the West. Not only were there many remains of ancient Greek work, but doubtless after the conquests of Alexander there was a certain admixture of actual Greek blood in the population. In many cases piers, and not columns, are used, and the church is divided into a few great square bays. The result is curiously

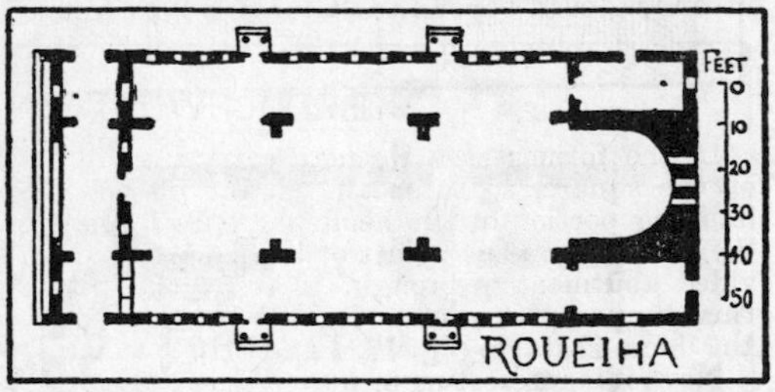

FIG. 15.

suggestive of some of the later Romanesque Gothic churches. Almost invariably there is a narthex, and above this, and outside the building, often a gallery with columns, forming a sort of loggia which makes a very pleasing feature (fig. 15). A point in Syrian construction might be noted which is possibly another reminiscence of Greek tradition. There is a distinct aversion to the arch construction, and often an arch is merely an arch in form, or is reduced by corbelling to the smallest possible limits (fig. 16). Note also another common form shown in the figure.

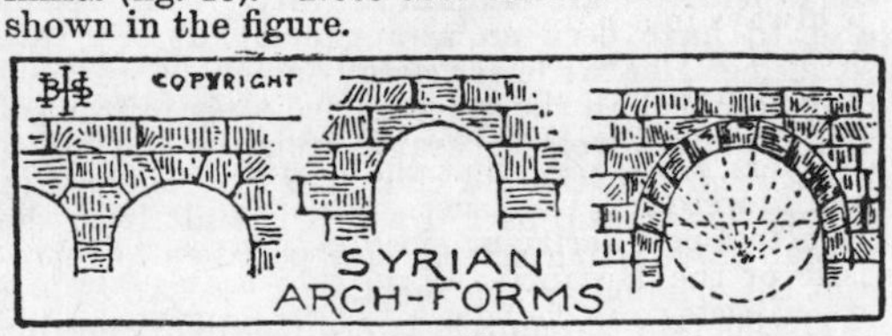

FIG. 16.

The Christian basilica, then, may be considered as a type of building, but hardly a style of architecture; and although we have seen that it was erected in various styles, they are all more or less a continuation of the later Roman manner, affected nevertheless by different influences, as in Ravenna or Syria. It is perhaps convenient to group the whole together as the Latin style, and remember that other buildings than churches were built in it, but, as is natural from the lack of sacred association, they have very largely perished.

2. Byzantine Architecture.—In Italy, although Greeks to a great extent executed the work, they were trammelled by the traditions on an alien soil, and by the masters they served; but when the seat of the Empire passed to Byzantium they were able to build more freely on their own lines, in their own country, and among their own traditions. The result was marvellous, and we find the speedy growth of one of the greatest styles of the world, culminating under Justinian, which itself gave birth to descendent styles, and is still a living influence. There are two great ways of covering a square space so as to leave all the sides open —the intersecting vault and the dome. The first was used by the Romans, yet the full comprehension of its principles and possibilities was not grasped until the Gothic architects invented the true rib. The dome was used by the Byzantines, and although they cannot exactly be said to be the inventors, they perfected the system, and herein lies the great achievement of the style. The problem involved is the fitting of a hemisphere upon a square. Now, the circle may be made to touch either at the corners or at the centres of the sides. In the one case it is too big; in the other it is too small (fig. 17, I and II).

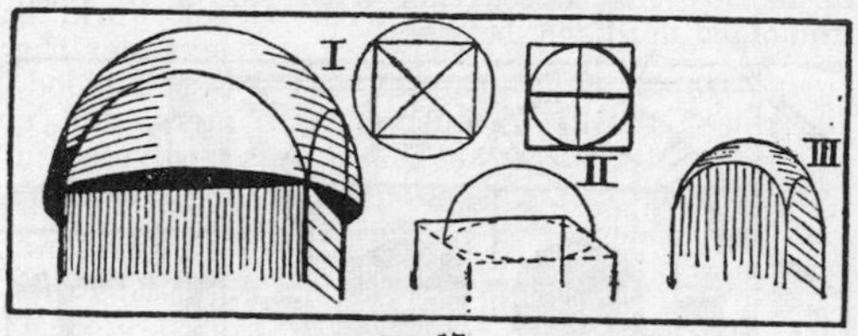

FIG. 17.

In the former case we may carry up the sides of the square, so to speak, cutting off the overhanging portion of the hemisphere, and the dome then rests upon the points of the square, and, provided abutment is brought to resist the outward thrust upon the arches formed by this process, the dome is stable (fig. 17, I and III).

Now, it is interesting to notice that these arches, formed by the intersection of the planes of the sides of the cube below the dome, are semicircular, and, further, the intersection of a sphere by a plane always gives a circle, and therefore it is always possible to raise such a dome upon semicircular arches; moreover, it is always possible to place one such dome up against another, and *it is not necessary for the two domes to be of the same size.* It is only necessary that the chords upon which the arches rest should be of the same length; the arches themselves will always be semicircles. It may also be put conversely that the intersection of two spheres is always in a *plane* circle, and therefore the intersection of two domes always allows of the building of a plane arch; and thereby the Byzantine architect escaped the greatest difficulty of the Gothic builders, who found that the intersections of their vaults were not in planes. This was perhaps the principal peculiarity or most individual characteristic of the Byzantine style, which, in certain of its aspects, can be described as a congeries of globular forms growing out of one another, as in the case of a mass of soap bubbles, which perfectly illustrates the system (fig. 18, St. Sophia).

But although such a dome, in its simple form as thus described, occurs in Byzantine architecture, it is open to certain objections. The apparent height is given only by the part above the arches, and the

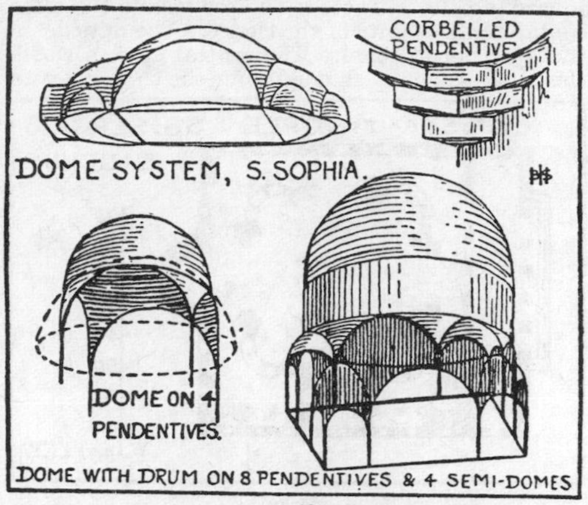

FIG. 18.

resulting effect is comparatively low and flat. In order to remedy this, the dome is raised in one of two ways. The first is another instance of the intersecting spheres. A dome (as in fig. 17, II) with diameter equal to the diameter of the square, intersects, and rests upon, a dome (as in fig. 17, I) with diameter equal to the diagonal of the square. Of the lower, nothing is left, save the ring upon which the upper hemisphere rests, and the four triangular portions that remain after the four sides of the square have been raised in the manner indicated above. These triangular portions are termed pendentives (fig. 18).

This is the characteristic method of the first great period of Byzantine architecture. But the dome may be even further raised by the introduction of a cylindrical drum between the dome itself and the pendentives. This is, on the whole, the characteristic arrangement of the second period of Byzantine architecture, although it is not universal. The same pendentive method may be employed above an octagon as above a square, and it is not uncommon to find such an octagon set within a square, and the lower dome, resting on the octagon and forming the pendentives, itself intersected by little domes that form semi-domes in the corner of the square (fig. 18). Another method, and one frequently used in the case of a dome upon an octagon, is a system of corbelling, wherein squared stones are set horizontally, instead of radiating to the required curve of the dome. It is really the same system as the domed chambers of the Mycenæan civilization, but in this case the surface of the stones is not rounded off to the curved surface of the vault (fig. 18, Corbelled Pendentive).

The first great period of Byzantine architecture may be said to be from A.D. 500 to 600, but its principal achievements were all accomplished in the first 50 years. Its crowning glory is St. Sophia, completed in A.D. 537. Then follows a blank interval during the Persian and Saracenic wars, until we come to the second great period which lasted from the middle of the 9th cent. to the end of the 12th. In this period the great masterpiece is St. Mark's at Venice. After this follows a long period of decline, lasting till about the end of the 16th century.

(*a*) In the first period the plan generally approximates to a square, and there is almost invariably a narthex, and often an exo-narthex beyond that. The church is commonly entered by three doors, and a great dome covers the central area of the church, which contains the principal available open space. The dome rests upon piers, generally eight in number, between which are columns forming, in the alternate intervals, semicircular niches which extend the central area toward the corners of the square (fig. 19). There is an apse behind the altar containing the seats of the clergy. The outside of the apse is polygonal. The central apse in which the altar stands is shut off from the church by an

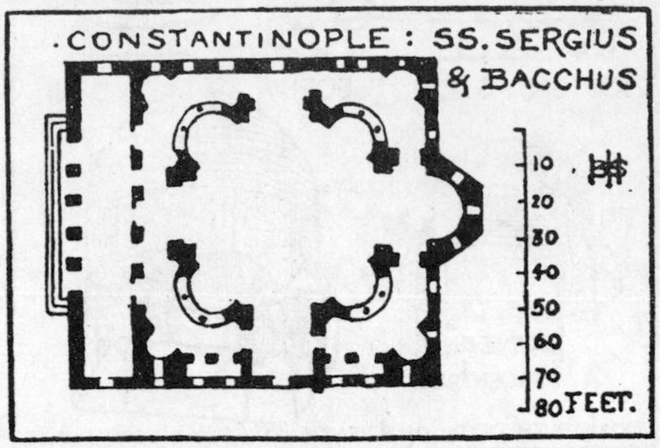

FIG. 19.

iconostasis, and where there are two side apses there are generally two more of these screens. The side apses, except in the rarest instances, do not contain altars.

The whole style is much lighter and more skilful than that of the Romans, and the Byzantine builders made their domes generally of brick, using no concrete. Consequently the supporting piers were much less massive. Columns were used, as we have seen, not as an essential feature of construction, but rather as screens, and to break up the building. Thus, by this slight use of the principle of multiplicity, they produce an effect of scale that the open, undivided building would lack. The columns have bases with a few simple moldings,* and a capital, generally most elaborate in execution. Above the capital is the dosseret—one of the sign marks of Byzantine architecture. It is sometimes said that its use is to enable the column to support the very thick wall above it. It may be so, but the upper section of the dosseret is generally about the same area as that of the capital itself, and, in any case, there is no advantage in diminishing to the bottom of the dosseret, and then starting with a large top to the capital, so as to diminish again. The very function of a capital is to do this work, and there is no reason why, if necessary, its sides should not slope inwards more sharply. A capital that cannot do its work is a solecism. It seems, perhaps, more likely that the dosseret is a curious survival of the entablature (fig. 20). In any case it is not a pleasing feature. When it is so reduced as to make merely a sort of double abacus, there is not the same objection, as the diminution in the upper one, or dosseret, makes it a mere molding, emphasizing the horizontal nature of the abacus, as in some examples in St. Sophia (fig. 21) The shafts are commonly monoliths of coloured marble, generally with an entasis but no flutes, and the whole style depends for its effect upon colour rather than upon solid forms. The forms that are used depend for their value upon pattern, not upon mass, doubtless as the result of the same æsthetic preferences where surface rather than solidity is used as the medium of expression. Hence we find no great cornices, as in classic architecture, and no subdivided columns or ribs upon the vaults, as in Gothic architecture. The wall surfaces are flat and the decorations are flat. There are practically no moldings, and the arches have plain soffits. Plinths or basemolds to the wall, and string courses, are insignificant or altogether absent. The very corners, even, are rounded off to allow of mosaics being carried round them. Hence the carving is all surface carving,

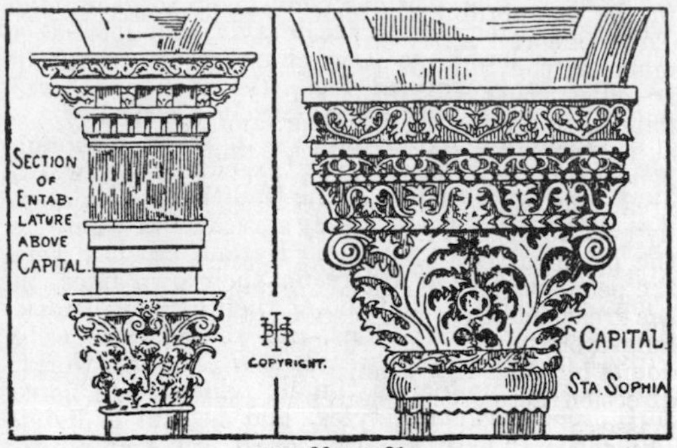

FIGS. 20 AND 21.

and does not stand out from the background. The drill plays an important part, and there is but little modelling; the effects are those of patterns with a dark background formed by deep drilling, which is sometimes undercut, so that the pattern is detached from the stone behind. Even the capitals have the same character; projecting masses are rarely found. As wholes they are comparatively formless, although covered with the most intricate surface work. Doors are square-headed, although usually with an arch and tympanum above. Windows are generally simple semicircular-headed openings, but sometimes two or three lights, with semicircular heads, are placed together with shafts, or plain unmolded mullions, between.

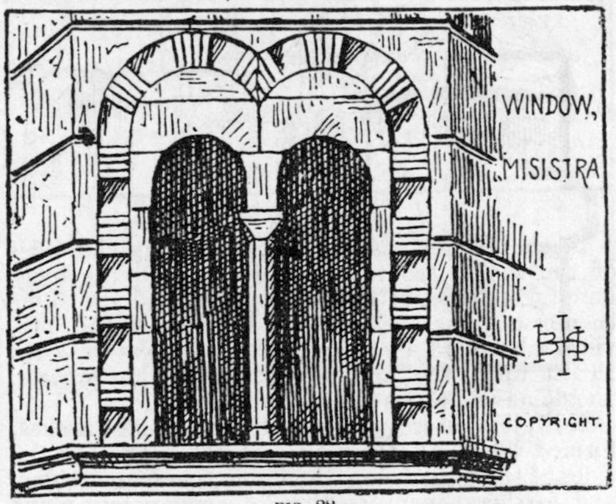

FIG. 22.

Large semicircular windows are occasionally divided up by shafts, and even by a sort of transom bar, as at St. Sophia. The result is not beautiful. A more beautiful device is the thin slab of marble, often carved with the most exquisite patterns, which frequently fills the smaller windows. These patterns are cut deeply into the marble, which is sufficiently translucent to allow the light to come through. It is conceivable that this represents a Greek tradition.

The total result is a style easily grasped as far as its main architectural features are concerned. The variety which actually exists is perhaps surprising, considering that it is achieved within such comparatively narrow limits. Of course it cannot amount to the variety found in the Gothic style, which depends for its æsthetic expression largely upon complexity, whereas the Byzantine style, in its purely architectural character, is wholly simple. Complexity, with a touch of Eastern barbarism, makes its appearance only in the surface ornament.

The glory of Byzantine architecture of the first

* This is the correct mediæval spelling now generally adopted.

period—indeed of the whole style—is St. Sophia. This church was begun in A.D. 532 and completed in the extraordinarily short period of six years. This time can apply only to the architecture, and much of the interior decoration must have been added afterwards. In the centre is a great dome, a trifle over 100 feet in diameter, and nearly as large as the dome of St. Paul's, London. It rests on pendentives raised upon four immense piers. The great feature is the extension of this central space by two huge semi-domes of the same diameter as the principal dome, abutting against the arches of the pendentives. These semi-domes, together with the great masses of the piers in the direction of the length of the church, resist the thrust of the great dome in that direction. But the thrust in the direction across the church is met by enormous masses of masonry carried by arches over the aisles, and forming a bold, if somewhat extraordinary, feature upon the outside of the building. The

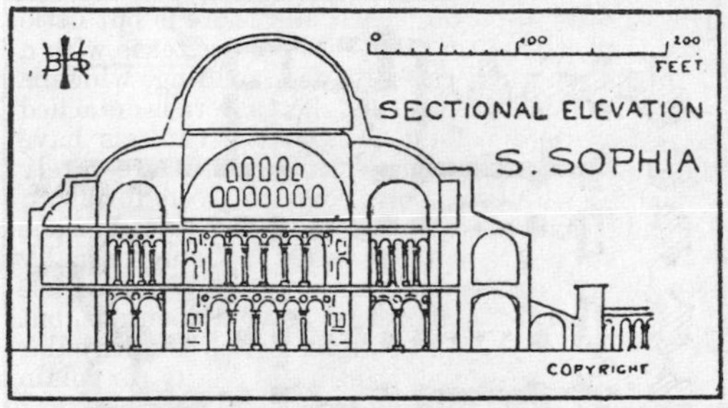

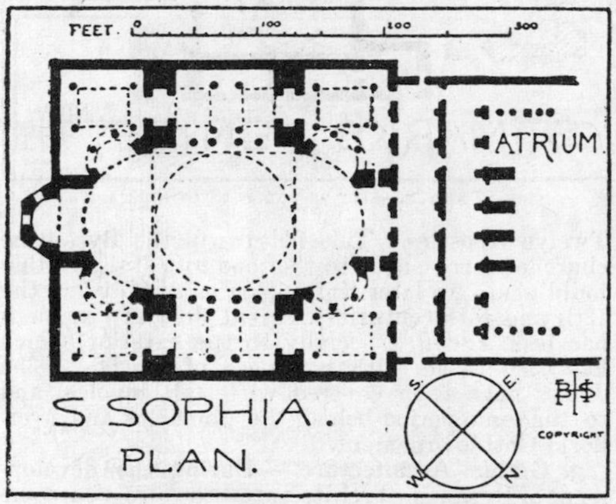

FIGS. 23 AND 24.—SECTION AND PLAN OF ST. SOPHIA.

result is the most spacious interior in the world. In order, however, to preserve the apparent as well as the actual size, there is a skilful arrangement of columns, in two storeys, in the great arches at the S.E. and N.W. sides, and in the semicircular niches that we have already seen as characteristic of the first period of Byzantine architecture. These columns give something of the principle of multiplicity, and provide a unity of measurement, without destroying the majestic simplicity of the whole.

The central area is surrounded by aisles covered with intersecting groined vaults, after the Roman manner, and at the lowest end is a fine narthex 205 ft. long. Over it is a gallery for the women, which is continued on either side over the aisles. A gallery for the women is the usual arrangement in Byzantine churches, and may be contrasted with the curious arrangement in the Basque provinces, where there are two or three galleries, one above the other, for the men and the boys. The lighting is effected by forty windows round the central dome and five in each of the semi-domes and the minor domes. Above the two tiers of columns on the sides are two tiers of windows (fig. 23). There are also large windows in the aisles. But in no case is the window arrangement satisfactory, and this is the weakest feature in the church.

St. Sophia was by far the most important church in Christendom built in this epoch, and it is interesting to notice that there is no attempt made to orientate it: the axis is one degree south of S.W.

The majesty and simplicity of the interior of St. Sophia, with the richness of its colouring, make it by far the finest interior of its kind in the world. It is difficult to compare things that are so utterly unlike as a Gothic cathedral and this building; each is wonderful in its own way; but certainly there is nothing in St. Sophia that warrants us in ranking it after any interior whatever. The exterior is different. One may work up a qualified admiration for it; but, in spite of a certain dignity of mass which it shares with all great engineering works, it is hardly architectural, and finds its compeers rather in the pyramids or in a modern railway station.

St. Vitale at Ravenna is generally classed as one of the great churches of the first Byzantine period; but, as Fergusson points out, it shows affinities with the so-called temple of Minerva Medica at Rome, quite as marked as any resemblances between it and SS. Sergius and Bacchus at Constantinople. There is, however, Greek influence in the Roman building, so there is something to be said for this view.

(*b*) The churches of the second period are smaller than those of the first, and have several characteristics of their own, although in the main they follow the earlier work. The lighting of the dome had always been a difficulty. Windows in a dome are, of course, not vertical, and the effect is always unpleasant. The difficulty can be met on the exterior by raising a vertical wall, which at the same time is helpful in resisting the thrust, acting as a pinnacle would in Gothic architecture. The outside of the dome is then generally treated with a double curve (fig. 25).

FIG. 25.

Viewed from the exterior, this naturally suggests the drum, which we find as the characteristic feature of the second period, even if it made its first appearance earlier. It is, however, not invariable. The effect of the drum is on the whole pleasing, forming an effective lantern in the interior, and giving altitude and architectural character to the exterior (fig. 26), which latter is so much needed at St. Sophia. The central dome is still the leading feature of the design, but subsidiary domes are frequently grouped round it. In St. Mark's, Venice, there are five domes. The dome is almost invariably, in this period, placed upon four supports only, instead of the eight common in the earlier period; and the semicircles (as in fig. 19) do not occur. The general proportions of the building show more variety than the practically square outline of the previous period. Sometimes we find an elongated rectangle or an approximation to the cruciform plan. The triple apse is almost universal in this period, with the altar in the bema before the central apse. In other features the two great Byzantine periods are not markedly different.

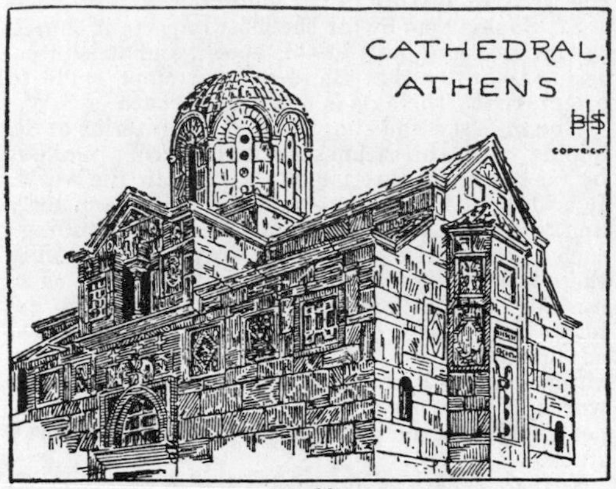

FIG. 26.

Of this period the greatest church is undoubtedly St. Mark's at Venice, which, in spite of numerous later alterations, still preserves in its interior its principal Byzantine features. The Byzantine parts of the church of St. Mark's, as we now see it, are the result of extensive alterations, amounting nearly to a re-building, in the middle of the 11th cent., of an earlier basilican church of A.D. 976, itself containing parts of a still earlier building. The western narthex, the walls and arcade of the nave, and portions of the east end, are practically all that remains of the basilican church. The columns in the eastern part of the church were removed, and six great piers were introduced—two at the west end and four in the centre of the building. These are themselves pierced by arches of the same height as the nave arcade. Two transepts were added, the east end was lengthened, and the narthex was continued round the two sides of the building. Above the nave and the crossing were erected two large domes and three somewhat smaller domes over the bema and the transepts, which are made slightly smaller than the crossing by the width of the pilaster shafts that support the arches leading into the three arms. By this skilful device a perspective effect of greater size is obtained. Great arches, which are practically barrel vaults, cross from pier to pier, and upon these the domes rest. Above the nave arcade is a narrow gallery, some 3 ft. wide, which represents the women's galleries of the Eastern Byzantine churches. It is, however, valuable as providing a unit of measurement, and thus giving size to the church, rather than for any utilitarian purpose. The capitals are not very characteristically Byzantine, being of a sort of pseudo-Corinthian type. They probably belonged to the original basilican church, and are of very excellent workmanship. Above them is a double abacus, or abacus and reduced dosseret. The church is not nearly so well lit as St. Sophia, the principal light coming from sixteen windows in each dome, placed just above the springing.

The colour effect is the main feature of the building: the marble columns, and the famous floor with the wonderful Byzantine mosaics on their golden ground, and even the pictorial mosaics of a later age, all give a richness unsurpassed elsewhere. Hence we find the usual flat Byzantine treatment with few moldings of any kind, although St. Mark's, figs. 27 and 28, has an unusual amount of carving of a bolder type than one associates with Byzantine work, most of it, however, not belonging to the Byzantine design of the building. St. Mark's retains a magnificent example of an iconostasis with figures of the Virgin, St. Mark, and the

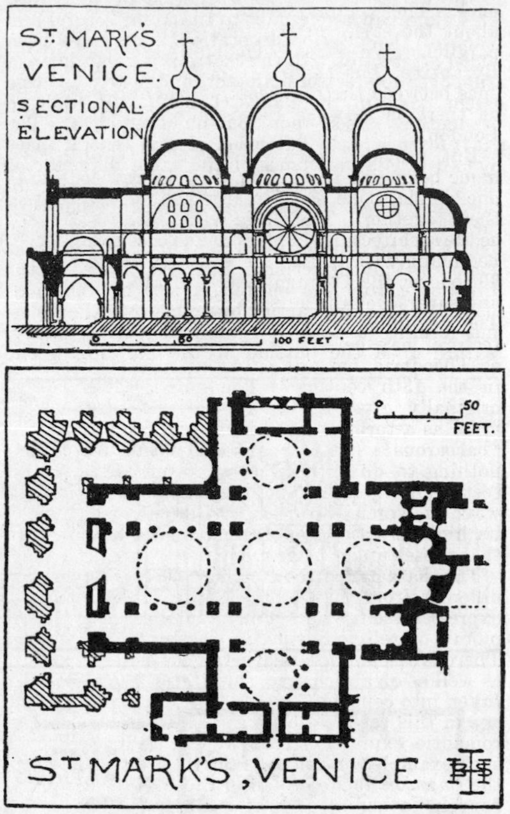

FIGS. 27 AND 28.—SECTION AND PLAN OF ST. MARK'S.

Twelve Apostles. This feature in the Byzantine churches corresponds to the rood loft of the Gothic buildings. In later times, particularly during the 13th and 14th centuries, a great deal of ornament has been added, especially to the exterior, which has been cased with a veneer of marble. The domes have been covered with tall cupolas, and to the same period belong the pinnacles and over-florid Gothic ornament.

3. Gothic Architecture.—During the development of Byzantine architecture—the direct outcome of the æsthetic character of the people of the regions where it occurs—we have another style developing in the West, a little later in reaching its maturity, but roughly the contemporary of the Byzantine. This style, to which the name 'Gothic' is not altogether inappropriately given, if we extend the term a little beyond its usual and somewhat arbitrary limits, was the style principally used by the Christians of the North. Those of the East made use chiefly of the Byzantine, and Italy of the Latin style—one, as we have seen, much more closely related to the Roman. Of course other styles have been used by Christians in different countries, as, for instance, in Norway or in Russia. Even in N.W. Europe, although it is convenient to group the styles of several countries under the one heading, there are in reality several styles; and the more one studies, say, the Gothic architecture of England and France, the more one realizes how little they have in common. It is true that to some extent the great wave of Romanticism marks the æsthetic character of the whole area, so that a church in England is, of course, more like a church in France than a church in Russia, Constantinople, Italy, or Norway; but it is only a very inartistic or superficial observer that fails to see the enormous difference. The comparatively little that is known about the styles of the East offers an interesting parallel. We class Armenian architecture as Byzantine, but there is almost as much difference between the cathedral at Ani and St. Sophia as there is between St. Sophia and St. Paul's, London.

But, provided we remember that 'Gothic' is a name belonging to a group of styles rather than to one single style, it is really helpful to consider them together. The Gothic, then, may be defined as the architectural expression of those races which, beginning with Alaric the Goth (d. 410 A.D.), and Theodoric the Ostrogoth (d. 526 A.D.), overthrew and superseded the power and civilization of Rome. The beginnings of the Gothic tendency in architecture may perhaps even be taken as far back as Theodoric, but the culmination of the style is in the 13th century. The name 'Gothic' was originally given at the time of the classical revival as a term of contempt, practically meaning 'barbarous'; but although the actual Goths had nothing to do with what we term Gothic architecture, nevertheless they were the pioneers in that wave of North European civilization which finds its highest artistic expression in the architecture that passes under their name.

The character of the Northern races is essentially different from that of the South of Europe, and expresses itself, whether on its intellectual, artistic, moral, or religious side, in a manner of its own. There is also, undoubtedly, the character of an age as well as of a race, and this factor has also to be taken into consideration. As a result of race and age in this case, we have in the artistic world the romantic expression that we see at its height in such examples of art as Malory's *Morte d'Arthur*, the *Chanson de Roland*, the Cloth Hall at Ypres, Lincoln Cathedral, or Bodiam Castle. Chivalry on the social side, as Romanticism on the æsthetic, is the outcome of the same root characteristic; the one is not the result of the other; they are cognate characteristics proceeding from a fundamental trait at the back. It is important to notice this, as it is a safeguard against some of the common errors of those who, perhaps learned in their own departments, have no practical artistic knowledge. All artists are familiar with the attempts of laymen to explain perfectly natural artistic forms that arise inevitably from artistic causes by reasons based upon moral or religious grounds. It is perfectly true that there may be close parallels in the moral or religious world, but these artistic forms are not derived from them any more than they from the art forms, although both they and the artistic forms may proceed from something behind them both. The Gothic form of art seeks to express itself by the principle of multiplicity rather than by simplicity, and by suggestion rather than completion. [For a further examination of this ques tion, see the article ART (Christian).]

The beginnings of Gothic architecture are to be found in what is perhaps best termed Romanesque Gothic—a style commonly known as Romanesque, and largely dependent upon Roman architecture. The term by which it is known is hardly a matter of much importance; the chief interest in the style is in the points wherein it showed its living force in developing from Roman architecture, and in pointing the way towards the later Gothic, rather than in its dependence upon the former. The style, moreover, is largely influenced by other elements that have nothing to do with Rome: the Celto-Saxon influences of our own country, for instance, or even the influence of Byzantium.

After the downfall of the Western Roman Empire, while Europe was in the melting-pot, architecture seems to have been somewhat stationary. It is, however, difficult to make certain, as later re-building has practically destroyed all evidence. Even if the conquerors were desirous of building, there was much less opportunity for it than in times of peace. About the beginning of the 9th cent. we find men's thoughts turning towards an architectural expression that rapidly blossomed into great things. In Burgundy and Provence, along the Rhine valley, in Lombardy, in Normandy, and in our own country, arose architectural schools, all of great interest, with their own individual characteristics, which endeavoured to express this artistic principle of romantic, suggestive, complex unity. In spite of its many parts, there is in the developed Gothic more homogeneity than in any other style save the Greek. The stone vault upon the stone walls, stone columns and arches, though doubtless to some extent a practical precaution against fire, is still more the expression of this æsthetic principle. The effect of organic growth, rather than of aggregation, marked by an extraordinary æsthetic appropriateness in every member to the function which it has to perform, all helps towards the final scheme. Above all, the suggestiveness of a certain intricacy of plan and elevation, of structural features and of ornament, marks out the æsthetic character of the Northern peoples and the age during which these buildings were erected.

It has been suggested that the Latin style had in itself a power of development that would have given us the future forms quite independently of the North; but, without entering into the argument, it is practically sufficient to point out that Central Italy itself never produced anything of the kind, even when the North had invented the style and carried the art to perfection. The different schools were not equally successful. Burgundy and Provence, with their barrel vaults, exercised comparatively little influence; and although the Rhine churches at first were in the van, they dropped behind and left it for England and Normandy, and the slightly later school of the Île de France, to perfect the art. The influence of the Île de France school ultimately became the greatest of all, although the Durham dates have now been settled beyond dispute, and prove that the Durham, or at any rate the English, school was first in the field, with perhaps the two greatest inventions of the Gothic architects—the shell vault on ribs and the flying buttress. But English architecture, uninfluenced, pursued its own line of development to the last, ignoring the French work alike at Canterbury and at Westminster.

In a short article such as this, a sketch of the development of our own school, and a brief comparison with that of the Île de France, will perhaps be the best way of illustrating the leading features of the age.

(*a*) *Celto-Saxon work.*—Putting aside for the present all architecture save that of church building, —although the influence of domestic and civil work upon churches is enormous and commonly overlooked—we find that we have in this country a Celto-Saxon type of church, resulting from the composition of divers elements, of which the more important are as follows:—

In the first place we have a purely Celtic element in the architecture, partly surviving through the Celtic or British population, partly resulting from the architecture introduced by the Celtic missionaries of St. Columba from the North. This spread over the whole country save the South-Eastern portion. St. Columba himself died in 597, but his missionaries continued to further his work. In the year in which St. Columba died, St. Augustine came over to Canterbury, with the powers of a bishop, to convert the English, and he introduced a Latin element. But this influence was small, and affected the style but little.

Later we have an influence of Northern monasticism, which must be distinguished from the great Norman influence of the Conquest, but which also represents the Romanesque Gothic of Northern Europe. East Anglia was converted by a Lombard priest, Felix, afterwards bishop, and even until quite a late date we find a distinctly un-English influence at work in the great Benedictine foundations of East Anglia. Sussex was converted by Birinus, an Italian or Lombard monk, early in the 7th cent., and to some extent East Anglia, Kent, and Sussex remained the stronghold of Continental influence until the last. Monastic builders from Normandy were employed at Romsey Abbey in 967, and upon Bishop Ethelwold's cathedral, Winchester, during the reign of Edgar, who with Dunstan as his administrator largely reformed the monastic system.

The *first element* is by far the most important in the formation of the Celto-Saxon type of church. It is characterized by a narrow rectangular plan, commonly of two or more chambers, of which Trinity Church, Glendalough, Ireland; Egilsay, Orkney; St. Regulus, St. Andrews, Scotland; Escomb, Durham, and Bradford-on-Avon, Wilts, England, may be taken as typical. The different characteristics to be noted are—(1) the general length as compared with the breadth; (2) separate rectangular chambers; (3) large porches, or side chambers, as at Bradford, Repton, Deerhurst, etc.; (4) a western tower of defence, round or square, usually entered from within the church; this is a

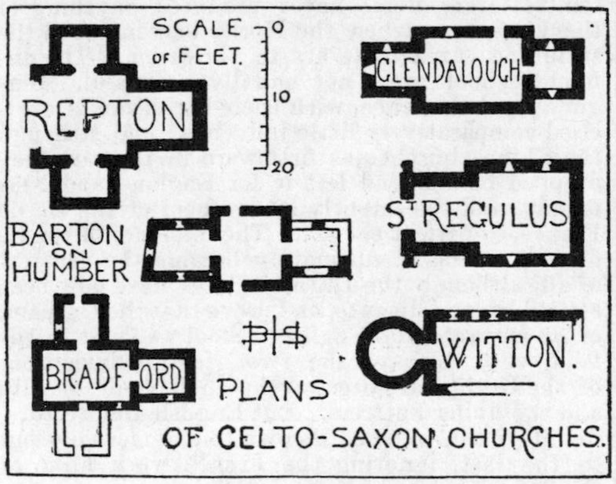

FIG. 29.

common feature; occasionally, as at Brechin, it is separate from the church; (5) a type that occurs as at Studland, Dorset, Barton on Humber, or Basing, Hants, where the tower actually forms the body of the church (fig. 29).

All these features continue to play a prominent part in English architecture, and help to distinguish it from that of the Continent. In the first place, the extreme length of the English churches is one of their most important characteristics; they are the longest in the world. Secondly, the rectangular, instead of apsidal, endings to English churches are too familiar to need comment. Although the apse was introduced, it speedily disappeared, and never made way at all in the West of England. Thirdly, we may notice the English tendency to a series of more or less separate chambers—the separate closed-in choir, the nave being often, as at Canterbury or Windsor, completely shut off, and the separate extensions at the east end, as at St. Albans, Wells, Gloucester, Hereford, Winchester, and indeed most of our cathedrals. Fourthly, the large porches or side chambers have a double influence. As entrance porches they are exceedingly common, *e.g.* Worcester, Gloucester, Canterbury, etc., and in hundreds of small parish churches. It is said that our inclement Western weather is the original cause of the western entrances being rarely used or altogether absent in this country. We also see these side projections in the very marked English transepts, as compared with those of the Continent (see figs. 55 and 56). Frequently there is a second transept; many of our English cathedrals have three, while Lincoln has four, pairs of such projections. Fifthly, the single western tower, so familiar a feature in the English parish church, can be traced back to this source, and it hardly ever occurs in France. With regard to the last feature—when the tower forms the centre of the church—we reach by the addition of the characteristic side chamber a cruciform central towered type (*e.g.* Braemore, Hants, and the Priory, Dover Castle). There are doubtless other influences that give us this type, but it is probably the double influence that preserves it as the typical English great church, right through the Middle Ages.

The *second element* in the Celto-Saxon style is the Latin style introduced direct from Rome by St. Augustine, *i.e.* the basilican type of church; but the Augustine influence seems to have been local and of little moment. The original church at Canterbury was quasi-basilican with an eastern as well as a western apse, the altar presumably being in the western at so early a date. There are one or two basilican examples up and down the country, but they are very rare. It is, indeed, not at all certain whether the type as found at Wing in the vale of Aylesbury has anything to do with St. Augustine, and may not rather be a survival of the old Romano-British type of far earlier date, such as, presumably, we see in the plan at Silchester.

Latin influence, however, does make itself felt, but through an indirect channel, and the division into nave and aisle is introduced through *the third great element*—the Northern monastic church. The aisle, however, never becomes quite the popular feature in this country that it is on the Continent. Five aisles, so common abroad, practically do not occur in English cathedrals. It is also largely to this influence that we owe the great central towered cross-church plan. But even this would probably have disappeared along with other importations had it not practically coincided with a type of more native origin. To this composite influence we may be said to owe the unequalled pyramidal composition of Salisbury, or the dominance of the central tower in such magnificent tower groups as Durham, Lincoln (fig. 57), or Lichfield, quite unapproached by the Continental architects.

The details of the Celto-Saxon style are very largely of Celtic and Teuto-Scandinavian origin, although decadent Roman work is also a factor to be considered. There are certainly affinities with early German work, particularly noticeable in the method of wall building, which is solid, and not built with a rubble core after the Roman method found in France. A brief résumé of the principal details is as follows:—

(1) Long and short work, or massive corner quoins. (2) Absence of buttresses. (3) Pilaster strips, stone carpentry, or strap work—a feature whose origin is obscure, but a far-away derivation from the Roman pilaster is perhaps the most probable. (4) The arches are semicircular, and often cut out of a single stone, or else they are straight-sided—a peculiarity not found in other styles. (5) The windows are often divided by baluster shafts, which are set in the centre of the wall, with a long stone forming a sort of abacus that runs from front to back

through the whole thickness of the wall. (6) The windows are widely splayed, both internally *and externally*. (7) There is a great fondness for parallel lines as ornament, foreshadowing the later characteristic English parallel moldings of many bands, which contrast with the simpler flatter treatment of the Continent. (8) The interlacing bands and characteristic Celtic curves seem also to foreshadow the English ornamental work of the 13th century. There is a vast difference in the character of English and French ornament, which is generally overlooked. It is probably connected with a difference in origin.

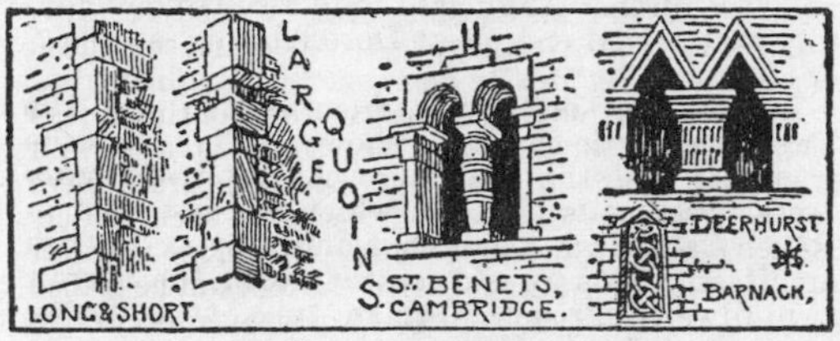

FIG. 30.—CELTO-SAXON DETAILS.

Such are some of the principal points in connexion with the Celto-Saxon work—a style much more important than is commonly supposed, which tends to be ignored on account of the greatness of the next style of architecture that made its appearance in these islands, and was in its turn made use of for Christian purposes.

(*b*) *The Rise of English Gothic.*—The Norman Conquest produced in Britain a massive style of architecture, of towers, fortresses, and strongholds. The churches, which naturally are always built in the style of the country, partake of the same character, so that a change comes over the church building in these lands. Contrasted with the comparatively light buildings of Celto-Saxon work, we find heaviness almost the leading feature of the new work. But the English soon made their own influence felt, and for a time English church architecture undoubtedly led the way in Europe.

In the first place, the number of churches built is entirely without parallel. During the hundred years that followed, when the country had settled down after the disturbance of the Conquest, there were built between three and four hundred great cathedrals and monasteries, churches of first-class rank, besides numberless smaller buildings. In the last hundred years, with a population nearly twenty times as large, and enormously improved methods of transit and mechanical appliances, we have built only one great church, nearly completed a second, and laid the foundations of a third. Not only, however, was the number of churches remarkable, but the scale of the English churches very greatly exceeded all other churches in the world that were built about that time. In all the rest of Europe there were built only two churches of over 50,000 sq. ft. area. In England there were four churches that exceeded even 60,000 sq. ft.

AREAS OF GREAT MEDIÆVAL CHURCHES
built or in course of construction in A.D. 1100.

THE CONTINENT.		ENGLAND.	
Mayence	*c.* 36,000 sq. ft.	Gloucester	*c.* 38,000 sq. ft.
Worms	40,000 „	Norwich	*c.* 40,000 „
Tournai	44,000 „	The Confessor's, Westminster	40,000 „
St. Sernan, Toulouse	46,000 „	York	42,000 „
Spiers	53,000 „	Lanfranc's, Canterbury, with Conrad's Choir	46,000 „
		Durham	49,000 „
		St. Albans over	60,000 „
		St. Swithin's, Winchester	66,000 „
		St. Paul's, London	66,000 „
		St. Edmund's, Bury	68,000 „

Cluny half a century later contained 54,000 sq. ft.

In many respects the very fact that England led the way was against her, because her great churches were already built when advancing art would have allowed her to build greater. Still more was she hampered in re-building and enlargement by the sizes already fixed. A new choir built on to an old nave cannot be made altogether out of scale with it.

That England led the way in number and size shows an activity, a resource, and an initiative that, even taken by themselves, would be strong presumptive evidence in favour of her being a leader in style; and this we shall afterwards see to be the case.

The Romanesque Gothic is marked by the cruciform plan, and the Norman form has the central lantern tower. The origin of both these features is far from clear. The transept is generally considered to be the development of the space in front of the altar in the Latin style. This, however, is not found at Ravenna, for instance, and is not common outside Rome, and the intermediate steps in any case can hardly be said to be traceable. The central lantern is still more doubtful in origin. Some have suggested a Byzantine origin for the whole North European Cross church as explaining both the cross and the central lantern; but although it may explain the cross better than the basilican church, and there is at least the lantern dome, while the basilica has no such thing, it is still a far cry from a Byzantine dome of the first period to a Norman lantern tower. The few dated examples are merely enough to make us beware of drawing hasty conclusions. There seems no particular reason for not supposing that the central tower was invented in the North, except that it is the fashion just now to believe that no one ever invented anything—which is true only within certain limits. The object of the lantern tower was twofold. In the first place, it threw light into the centre of the building, where the high altar was put; and, in the second place, it formed a unifying central feature, both within and without. The removal of the high altar from its proper position to the east end leaves the lantern tower to throw its light upon an empty space.

In any case, we find two distinct types of Cross church making their appearance in this country, both of which the national genius modified to suit its own æsthetic conceptions. First, we have the multapsidal type, and, secondly, the chevet type. The origin of the multapsidal type is possibly to be sought in the Byzantine or Egyptian types already noted, or it may be directly derived from the basilica, but it certainly becomes quite a common variety. The Normans in Normandy treated it in their own way, squaring the end two bays beyond the crossing, in a manner perhaps foreshadowed at St. Apollinare Nuovo at Ravenna, and then adding

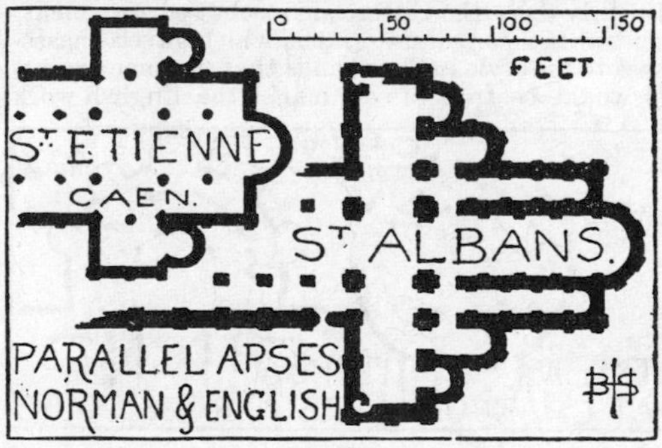

FIG. 31.

the apse (fig. 31). The Anglo-Normans took this plan, and it at once began to assume the first English characteristic of greater length. We find a typical example at St. Albans, with its long parallel apsed chambers (fig. 31). This becomes one of the great types of Benedictine orthodoxy in the East of England.

But it is to the West and the North that we have to turn to find the truly English manner. Here we find Hereford with a square end as early as 1079–1095, and Llandaff and Romsey early in the next century. It has been said that the square end was introduced into this country by the Cistercians. This is impossible, as it was in use before the Cistercian order was founded. But it is interesting to observe that from this very Western district came Stephen Harding, one of the original founders, and head of the order, and abbot of Citeaux in 1109. It seems most probable that the Cistercians owe their square East ends to him. Hence, when we find the Cistercians at a later date building their square East ends in England, they are merely bringing back an English feature that naturally falls in with, and helps to strengthen, the native tradition.

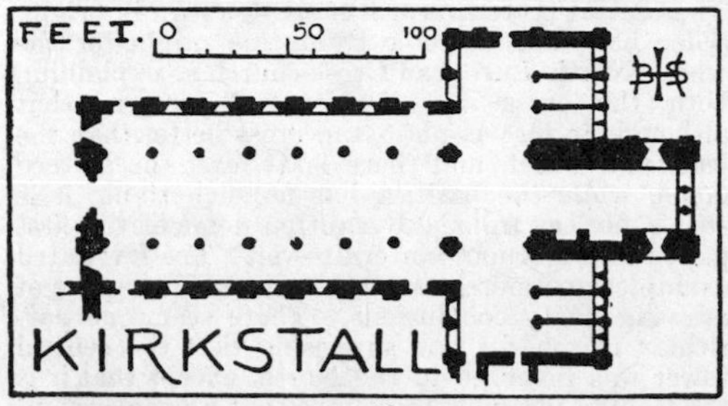

FIG. 32.

So we find that in English hands the multapsidal type develops a squared form, such as we see in Kirkstall Abbey, Yorkshire.

The Reformed orders, Cistercians and Augustinians, mainly in the West and North, worked out the English manner, and although the great Benedictine abbeys of the East have had the fortune to survive, it is rather to the ruined abbeys of Yorkshire and the Welsh Border that we must turn if we wish to see the English style in the making. Hence, while the conservative Benedictine abbeys were still using the round arch and the apsidal termination, we find the pointed arch and the square end in the North and the West. The change of style is, as in France, partly due to an Episcopal influence that furthered advance and reform. In the latter country the bishops joined hands with the laity against the old Monastic orders, and we get the great laic cathedrals of France. In this country they joined hands with the Reformed orders, and to this is due the strongly marked Monastic character of English building. In early days the Cistercians eschewed ornament, central towers and triforiums, which gave a chasteness to the style in their hands that, to some extent, it would be true to say, marks the English work

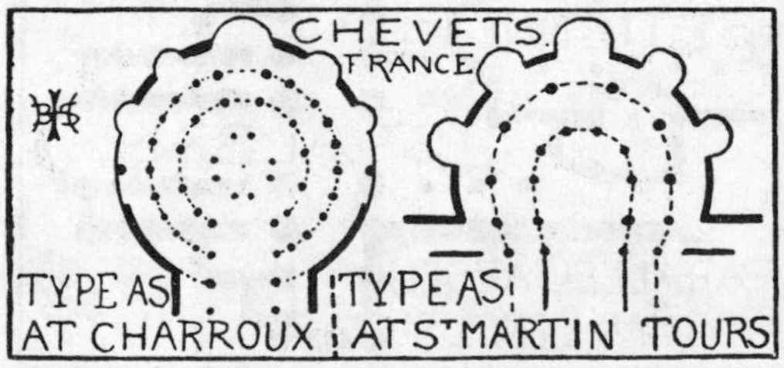

FIG. 33.

until well into the 14th cent., even after such luxuries as towers and triforiums had become common again.

The other great type is the chevet type, which, as Fergusson points out, is very probably a development from the circular church by the addition of a nave, the circular part becoming the choir. The development is apparently French (fig. 33). In England the circular churches have had choirs built on to them, and the circular part becomes the nave. The chevet type, with or without its circumscribing chapels, is found at Bury St. Edmunds, Norwich, Edward the Confessor's, Westminster Abbey, etc., and is always lengthened in the English manner (fig. 34). This we also find still further Anglicized with a square ambulatory at the east end, as at Dore Abbey, Salisbury, or Glasgow.

Besides the lengthening from east to west, the English æsthetic character shows itself in the wide transepts and the still more characteristic transeptal west ends (fig. 55), which we find even in Rouen Cathedral, a church planned by an English architect. This we can contrast with the narrow twin-towered French Norman type, such as we see at St. Etienne, Caen.

FIG. 34.

The Anglo-Norman church of Bury St. Edmunds had a wide-spreading front of 260 feet. Ely was planned for a west front of 200 ft., although it is doubtful whether this front was ever completed. These two are about three times as wide as the nave.

WIDTH OF WEST FRONTS, NAVES, AND MAIN TRANSEPTS OF ENGLISH CHURCHES.

	West Fronts. Feet.	Naves. Feet.	Main Transepts. Feet.
Peterborough	170	82	190
Rouen (English design)	185	120	195
St. Albans	150 (?)	77	190
Ely	200	77	180
Bury St. Edmunds	260	80	240
Lincoln, 13th cent.	180	100	245
Wells ,, ,, (a small church)	150	80	150
Pre-Conquest Westminster	..	..	155
Reading	..	..	c. 190
Glastonbury	..	..	c. 190
Winchester	..	85	215
York, 13th century	..	140	245
Old St. Paul's, 13th cent. (probably nearly the original Anglo-Norman plan)	170	110	250
Compare these with			
Notre Dame	155	155	170
Rheims, 13th century	155	135	200
Amiens ,, ,,	150	160	220

The best way to obtain a general survey of each period is to work from the ground plan upwards. It has already been pointed out that Romanesque Gothic in England, perhaps best termed Anglo-Norman, is massive in its treatment, and this naturally shows on the ground plan. A single pier of Durham contains as much material as the whole set of piers of some of the later churches. The walls are always immensely thick, even when they support only a wooden roof, which on the

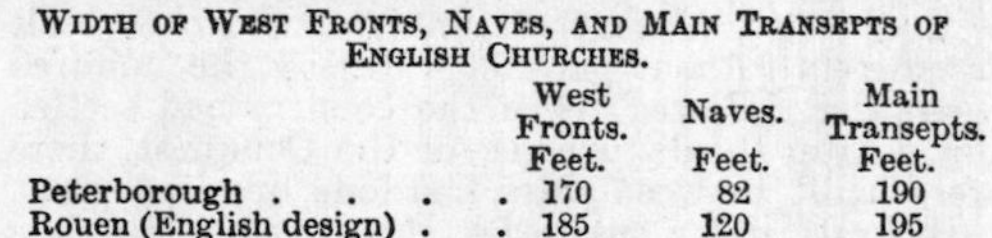

FIG. 35.—WALL DIAGRAM AND SECTION OF CHURCH.

whole is the commoner arrangement; but when they have to resist the thrust of a stone vault, this is even more the case. Buttresses are as yet quite rudimentary, and the history of Gothic architecture might be described as a progression from a heavy wall with a wooden roof to a glass wall and a stone roof. The projection of the buttresses becomes greater and the wall thinner, and the progress might be diagrammatically represented as in fig. 35. So what practically happens is that the wall is turned round in sections upon itself, whereby, with the same or even less material, a greater resisting power is obtained (fig. 35).

Before passing upward to details, the general treatment of the elevation should be noted. The Anglo-Norman great church is a three-aisled building of three storeys (fig. 35). The nave-arcade is the principal series of arches in the church, and divides the central aisle, or nave, from the side aisles. In order to light the central aisle it is raised above the roof of the side aisles, whereby we obtain a clerestory, through which the light passes, and which is contrasted with the blind storey or triforium that occupies the space of the aisle roof. Sometimes the triforium is transparent, as it is termed; that is, it is treated as a gallery

FIG. 36.—JEDBURGH.

with windows over the side aisles. This treatment is more common in France than in England.

There is more variety in the bay treatment in this country than in France, arising in part from a different initial standpoint. The French architects were more interested in the logic of construction, and the tendency for their buildings is to become, as it were, skeleton constructions, and for the wall as such to disappear. The English, however, continued to regard the wall as a feature in itself, giving an æsthetic sense of horizontal continuity, as distinct from the vertical skeleton expression of French architecture. The wall, therefore, continues to some extent to be regarded as a field for decorative treatment on its own account. A single instance must suffice, and is seen in the interesting bay treatment, favoured mainly by the Augustinians, in which the triforium is treated as a hanging gallery, depending from the main arcade. Examples may be seen at Jedburgh, Romsey Abbey, Oxford Cathedral, Glastonbury, and Dunstable. It gives a sense of height greater than either the simple two-storey or the simple three-storey treatment.

Anglo-Norman piers are of two main types. In the first, which is more or less columnar, we probably see a far-off descendant of the columns of Greece. There are two distinct varieties, of which one, although generally built up in courses, and not in single drums, still, in general proportion of capital, and base, preserves the characteristics of a true column. The other is a huge mass of masonry with a few moldings round the top in lieu of a capital. This partakes more of the nature of a pier, and is peculiar to this country. Examples may be seen in Gloucester, Durham, Tewkesbury,

FIG. 37.—NORMAN PIERS.

etc. The second type is the pier proper, developed from a section of wall left between the arches.

Both these types develop in two ways which mutually influence each other; first, the struc-

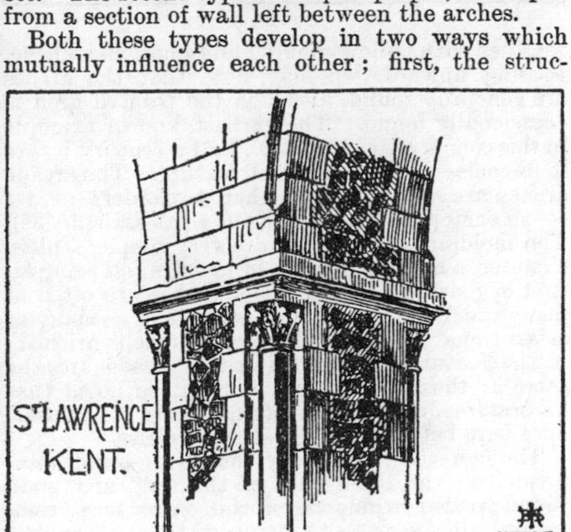

FIG. 38.

tural, which is more particularly characteristic of France; secondly, the decorative, which is more particularly characteristic of this country. In the first system additions are made to the pier, in order to support sub-arches and vaulting shafts; thus we get a composite type of pier where each part is assigned to the performance of some definite function. In the decorative system the pier also becomes composite, but in a different manner. The corners of the pier, for instance, may be chamfered off so as to form an octagon, or cut out as at St. Lawrence, Kent, and ornamental shafts inserted (fig. 38), thus giving a sense of lightness to the whole. Later we find these ornamental shafts arranged round the octagon formed by cutting off the corners. The octagon may become a circle. In the decorative system the change begins with the shaft, and the abacus remains square, and, in any case, the detached shafts have no direct connexion with the load above. When both load and support become very complex, the eye is sufficiently satisfied with the complex support for the complex load, without logically following out each subordinate part. The carpal and metacarpal bones in the beauty of the human anatomy may be taken as a parallel. The bases are generally set on a square plinth, often with an ornament to fill up the angles. The commonest form of molding is a hollow above a round (fig. 39).

There are three types of capital: (1) a pseudo-classic, a sort of debased Corinthian or Ionic, much commoner on the Continent than here; (2) a cushion-shaped capital which seems an original invention; and (3) the scalloped capital, a type derived from the cushion variety, which in its turn has important influences upon the next period. The abacus is always square, first with plain cham-

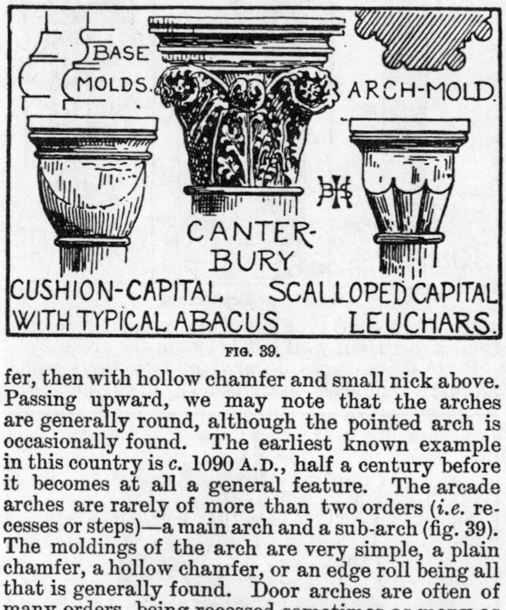

FIG. 39.

fer, then with hollow chamfer and small nick above. Passing upward, we may note that the arches are generally round, although the pointed arch is occasionally found. The earliest known example in this country is *c.* 1090 A.D., half a century before it becomes at all a general feature. The arcade arches are rarely of more than two orders (*i.e.* recesses or steps)—a main arch and a sub-arch (fig. 39). The moldings of the arch are very simple, a plain chamfer, a hollow chamfer, or an edge roll being all that is generally found. Door arches are often of many orders, being recessed sometimes as many as seven times. They are frequently much enriched.

The features of the triforium arcade are the same as those below, but it might be noted that decorative development often makes its appearance here before it is seen anywhere else.

The clerestory generally shows an ornamental arcade on the inner face of the wall, and plain round-headed windows on the outer face, commonly with a passage between the two in the thickness of the wall. The Anglo-Norman window is generally widely splayed within, and set near the outer face of the wall, in which respect it may be contrasted with the Celto-Saxon window. It is not treated with the elaboration of the door. Some later Anglo-Norman windows show rich decoration on the outside, but it is interesting to notice that, whereas the door becomes a less important member as Gothic architecture advances, the window gradually becomes the most important of all.

In the roof we reach the most complex and most interesting feature in Gothic architecture. It has even been said by some that Gothic architecture is nothing more than the art of building stone vaults. This, of course, is ridiculous; the early writers, such as Rickman, whose work still remains one of the most interesting on the subject, wrote of Gothic architecture with hardly any reference to the vault at all. There is certainly enough that is distinctive, and shows the whole spirit of the thing, without taking notice of the vault. Gothic architecture is not the mechanical treatment of any one feature, neither the vault nor the buttress, nor even the window, which probably, after all, is both more influential and more characteristic than any other single feature. It is not even a question of mechanics; Gothic architecture is architecture—a truism, one would have supposed; it is neither engineering nor building, as some writers would have us believe. Hence it depends fundamentally upon æsthetic principles, which, so to speak, set the mechanical problems for the mechanicians to solve, and the latter are essential, it is true, but only means to an end.

Of course any one is at liberty to define 'Gothic' as he pleases; but to deny the title to such a building as Eltham Palace or St. Peter Mancroft, Norwich, is so to circumscribe the sphere of inquiry as to make it of comparatively little importance. It is a primary and more fundamental question to find what is the root principle common alike to Crosby Hall, Exeter Cathedral, and Notre Dame, and differentiating these buildings from St. Sophia and St. Stephen's, Walbrook, than to find what differentiates them from each other—not that this latter inquiry has not great importance within the larger sphere.

A full discussion of the vault would be impossible within the limits of this article, but it may be thus briefly summed up. In early days it was more common to find an open-timber roof, but a desire to give organic unity to the whole conception, coupled doubtless with the advantages of greater security against fire, led to the gradual substitution of the roof of stone. This we find first in the aisles, and then over the wider spans, such as the great English Chapter Houses, some of them 40 ft. wide, or the high vaults over the naves of the great

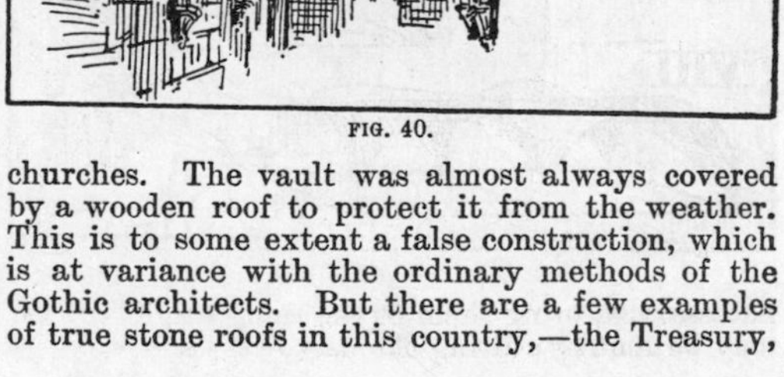

FIG. 40.

churches. The vault was almost always covered by a wooden roof to protect it from the weather. This is to some extent a false construction, which is at variance with the ordinary methods of the Gothic architects. But there are a few examples of true stone roofs in this country,—the Treasury,

Merton College, Oxford; Willingham, Cambridge; Minchinhampton; Rosslyn; and Bothwell.

The simplest form of vault is the plain barrel or waggon vault, which gives a great continuous thrust throughout its length, and therefore requires a very thick continuous wall. The effect is gloomy, because the lighting problem is difficult of solution. Large windows are impossible in a wall bearing a continuous thrust, and sloping windows in the vault are both weak and ugly. If a window is put in the vault, it is a natural step to carry up the vertical surface of the wall below, as we saw in Byzantine architecture (fig. 25). This at once suggests the treatment of intersecting barrel vaults, which is eminently suitable for the vaulting of a square space, A, O, C, being the square of intersection of two half cylinders of hemispherical section, corresponding to A′, O′, C′ (fig. 41, I and II). This form of vault was used by the Romans, and the tradition never completely died out; and this vault, the ribless quadripartite vault, as well as the simple barrel vault, is used by the early Romanesque builders, as in the castle at Oxford.

The intersection of two cylinders is not a circle, as in the case of intersecting spheres (see p. 701), but an ellipse. This elliptical line of intersection is termed the groin of the vault. Directly the space to be vaulted is not square, difficulties arise, and as long as semicircular vaults are used they will not intersect at the crown at all, as the vaults are of different height (fig. 41, III). It is therefore

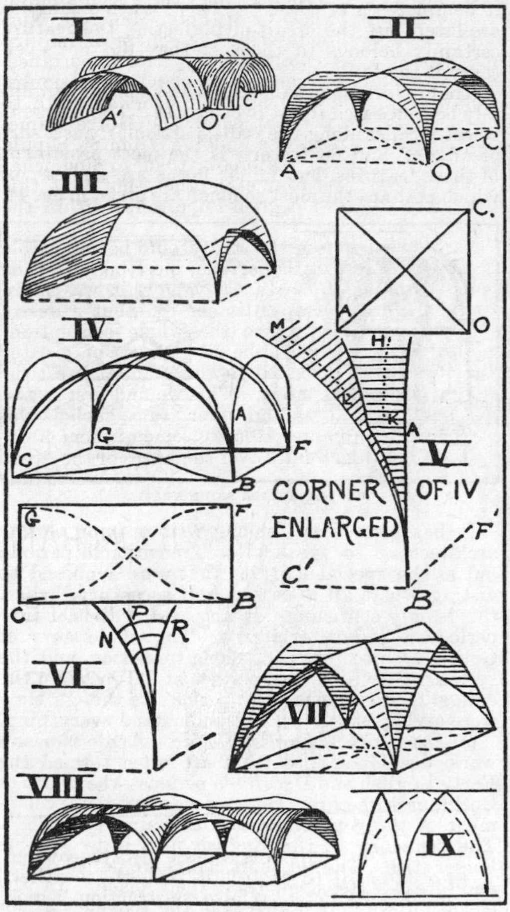

FIG. 41.

necessary to bring them to the same height, which may be done by stilting the narrower vault, that is, raising it on two vertical walls that serve the purpose of stilts. This may also be helped by using less than a semicircle for the larger vault. But, in any case, the groins will become twisted in plan, as may be seen in fig. 41, IV and V. In the narrow vault it is obvious that any point in that vault, up to the height of the stilt, must be vertically above the line CB. Any point, therefore, being on the line of intersection of both vaults, must be vertically above the line CB. The groin also must keep close above the side CB, until a height above A is reached. On the other hand, in the bigger vault, there is no vertical portion, and it curves gradually away from the side BF at the outset; the groin, therefore, will tend away from above BF, but keep close above CB. When the top of the stilt is reached, however, the narrow vault curves rapidly over to the other side, but the larger vault continues its gradual curve, so that the groin now crosses rapidly over to the other side, and then keeps similarly close above GF until it reaches G. In actual building the curve is generally coaxed a little, so as slightly to reduce the violent break in the line, as seen in the plan above, but in any case it is excessively ugly and weak, as the weight of the vault rests upon the groins. By making the vaults enormously thick and filling in the back with concrete, until the whole becomes one solid mass for some way up the vault, the weakness is counteracted, but it means an undue weight upon the walls and supports.

Now the great invention of the Gothic architects was the substitution of another principle. So far the vault has been regarded as the intersection of two continuous cylindrical tunnels, and the groin is merely the line of intersection. At any point along the vault we have, say at ML or HK (fig. 41, V) a section of a perfect cylinder; the line of the groin, however, we saw was not in a plane, but twisted. The invention is to build the groin regular (*i.e.* in a plane), and then accommodate the vaults to fit the groin, which is made in the form of a strong rib to support the whole. The vault is built by first erecting a series of arches of regular shape (*i.e.* in planes), not twisted, to form the ribs. The short ends may be stilted, the diagonals segmental, and the broad ends semicircular, so as all to be of equal height. The vault itself is then built, as a light shell, resting on these ribs. This shell is built in courses, as NP, PR (VI), which are practically straight, but very slightly arched to the ribs upon which they rest. The consequence is that, as now the shell must follow the curve of the groin ribs, it cannot itself be part of a regular cylinder; and as before the diagonals were twisted to suit the vault surface, now the vault surface is twisted to suit the diagonals. The result is a curved surface very much resembling that of a ploughshare.

The ribbed vault—and by ribbed vault is meant a ribbed shell vault upon the above principle, *i.e.* one which is structurally based upon the rib curvature—is perhaps the most distinctive invention made by the Gothic architects. Ribs may occasionally have been used in earlier days to strengthen the groins of vaults, based upon the curvature of the vault surface, but that is not the Gothic vault. There is no doubt that the earliest vaults of this type of which we have any knowledge are those of Durham Cathedral. Such were the high vaults of the choir begun in A.D. 1093. The earliest properly attested date in France is, at the very least, more than thirty years later.*

* The whole discussion of these dates, with regard to England and France, is given in J. Bilson's able little book, *Beginnings of Gothic Architecture* (1899). No other writer approaches Bilson in his thorough grip of his subject. A short résumé of the subject is given in the present writer's book now in the press (Fairbairns & Co.).

As to the cause of the compartments assuming the rectangular form instead of the square, it can hardly be questioned that the primary reason was æsthetic and non-mechanical, as the great English Chapter Houses, with spans of 40 ft., where there were no structural considerations, are so built. The immense improvement to the vista, and the beauty of the apparent length thereby gained, quite apart from any principle of unified complexity, are sufficient to account for it (fig. 42). The French continued to use the square vault for a long time, taking two compartments of the aisle to one of the nave, even inventing the sexpartite vault (fig. 41, VIII) to get over the difficulty before finally following the English lead. The introduction of the pointed arch into the vault followed not long after. It offers an æsthetically more pleasing solution of the problem of vaulting over a rectangle, at the same time preserving the level crown, than does the stilted arch (fig. 41, VII). The pointed arch in every rib gives a far more satisfactory sense of æsthetic unity than the mixture of segmental and stilted arches, and it also reduces the ploughshare twist.

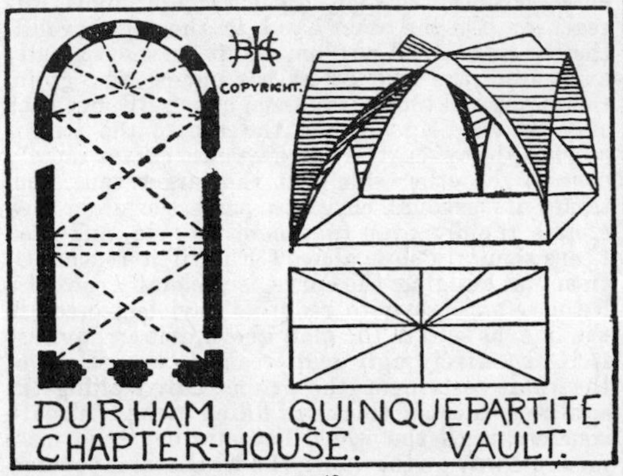

FIG. 42.

The pointed arch was used by no means solely in order to keep the level crown over the different spans, because in France the domical vaults, used when the ribbed system was introduced, continue even after the introduction of the pointed arch in the vault, and there is no attempt to make the crown level. Nevertheless, the fact that pointed arches of the same height can be erected over varying widths (fig. 41, IX) is one of their many advantages, as we may see in numbers of transept crossings, *e.g.* St. Bartholemew's, Smithfield.

An interesting variant of the sexpartite vault, which we might term quinquepartite, occurs in the aisle vaults of Lincoln, which is an ingenious and more justifiable use of the principle, as there are two windows on one side and only one opening on the other (fig. 42).

The origin of the pointed arch is another of those unsolved problems, but it occurs in the East long before it is found in Northern Europe. It is even found in Roman work—in the bridge of Severus in the Levant. It was certainly in common use in France earlier than here, although an example is found at Gloucester (*c.* 1090), of which Bilson gives an illustration. The pointed arch cannot be considered a specially Gothic feature, being found in various Eastern styles; and, moreover, many buildings where it does not occur are obviously completely Gothic in feeling.

In connexion with the ribbed vault appears the other great invention of the Gothic architects, namely, the flying or oblique buttress, where the buttress, instead of descending vertically to the ground, is carried obliquely upon an arch over an intervening space. This enables the abutment of the high vault to be carried across the aisles. The beginnings of this are seen in the demi-berceau or half-barrel vault of Gloucester (*c.* 1090), strengthened at intervals with buttresses or ribs. But the perfect system brings the abutment to bear, not continuously, but only so as to meet the resultant thrust of the vault ribs that support the vault. This we find in Durham choir (commenced A.D. 1093), where the buttress is carried over a semicircular arch. It occurs also at Chichester (commenced 1091), whereas the later development, namely, where the buttress is carried over a quadrant, was probably actually built at Norwich in 1096. It was certainly planned and half executed at that date, as that which remains after later alterations attests. The nave of Durham shows it complete (A.D. 1125).* The French examples are later, but the credit of perfecting the feature certainly belongs to them, if they did not even carry it too far.

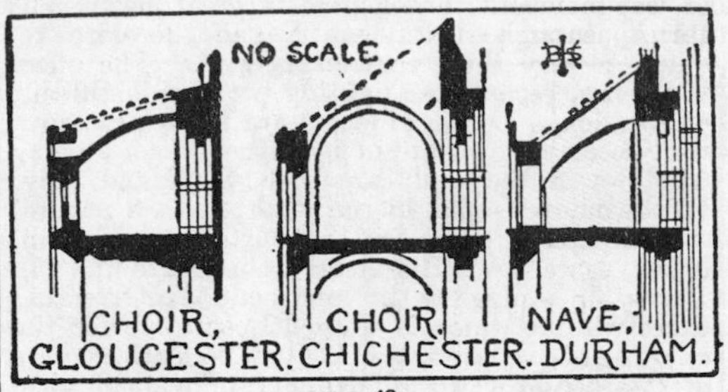

FIG. 43.

Anglo-Norman ornament, at first sparing, gradually becomes rich if not over-ornate. The frequent use of arcades along the walls, particularly as a sort of 'dado,' and on towers, is the most prominent of these features, but minor forms are endless, of which perhaps the most common are given in fig. 44.

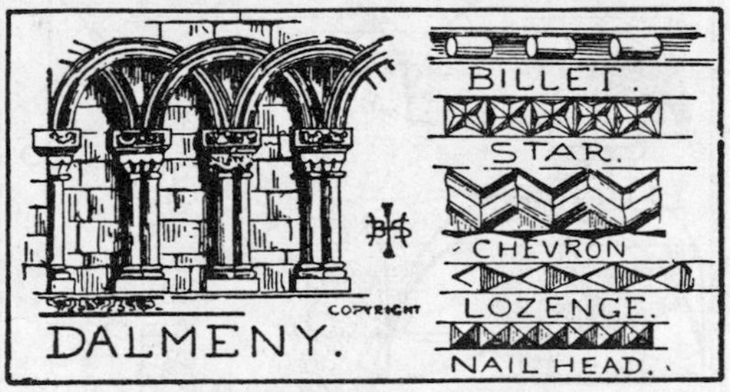

FIG. 44.—ARCADE AND MOLDINGS.

It has been usual among writers upon Gothic architecture to speak of a Transitional period; but as the special features that were supposed to distinguish it all appeared half a century earlier, this is only confusing. In any case, a division into periods is purely arbitrary. The whole story of Gothic architecture is one long transition, and the system of division into periods at all opens up the danger of considering the periods as though they were styles, which is to misunderstand everything.

(*c*) *The zenith of English Gothic.*—Anglo-Norman work developed into what are often termed the Early English and Decorated periods—the zenith of Gothic architecture. Here we see a further development of those principles we have already noticed. The tendency of the English plan is to become longer still. The old short choirs are pulled down, and great extensions take their place. In the elevation we may notice that the tendency is for the bay divisions to become wider in proportion to their height, and for the triforium to diminish.

* See references quoted above *re* the vault.

On the exterior the lofty spires of these two periods are the most distinguishing features.

The decorative sense develops and shows itself in every member. Three great types of pier make their appearance—the South-Western, the South-

FIG. 45.—PIER TYPES.

Eastern, and the Northern. The South-Western is formed by triplets of shafts attached to a central core and ranged regularly round it (Pershore, fig. 45). It is probably directly derived from the Anglo-Norman composite pier. But it makes little

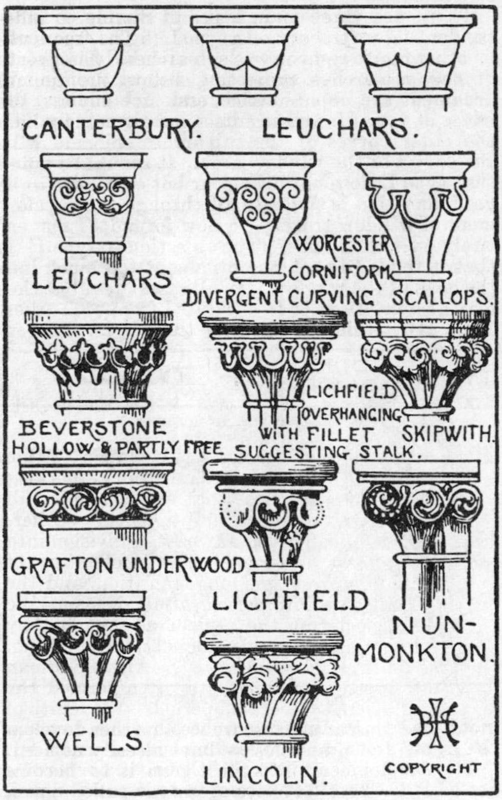

FIG. 46.—THE DEVELOPMENT OF THE 13TH CENT. CAPITAL.

headway beyond its own district, and gradually dies out. Not so the South-Eastern and Northern varieties. The South-Eastern type is formed by a central core with detached shafts round it, generally, although not invariably, of purbeck marble or some local variety (fig. 45). The central core is built up, and the shafts are monoliths, or in two or three long sections with annular bands. The Northern type, *e.g.* Roche and Sweetheart abbeys (fig. 45), is a composite pier of several shafts all united in one, without a central core, and seems to have originated from such forms as we see in Bishop-Auckland Castle, York crypt, Durham galilee, or Selby triforium. In these cases there are a number of separate shafts not grouped round a central mass. In the Northern type the composite pier is built up in horizontal courses, and the shafts composing it are therefore not continuous.

For a time the South-Eastern type carries everything before it and drives back the Northern, so that during the 13th cent. (Early English period) it practically becomes the type of the period, and is found, for instance, as far north as Durham. In the 14th cent. (Decorated period) the Northern re-asserts itself, and the South-Eastern type is driven back and disappears. The Northern type remains supreme, as long as Gothic architecture lasts, and is found all over the kingdom. A very beautiful example occurs at Grantham, with the fillets particularly common to this type. In the same church is an early example of the South-Eastern type (fig. 45).

The commonest base in the 13th cent. is characterized by the water-holding molding (fig. 47), developed from the so-called Attic base (fig. 2, ARCHITECTURE (Greek)). In the 14th cent. the hollow is filled by a round, the lowest member often overlapping the plinth. The English capitals are distinguished from those of the Continent by the characteristic abacus, which in English work is almost always round, and in the thirteenth century consists of a roll and fillet deeply undercut, and in the 14th of a scroll molding. The neck-molding is generally a plain astragal in the 13th cent. and a scroll molding in the 14th. Those capitals that have foliage are marked in the 13th cent., by a beautiful type, apparently derived from the scallop capital (see fig. 46), and very different from the French type derived from the classical capitals. The English variety, which we may term stiff stem foliage, is generally said to have the same origin as the French capitals, being derived from the classical volutes; but a careful examination of the capitals of the West Country and the North, where the national style has its origin, has led the present writer to the above conclusion. Doubtless the Continental variety was not without its influence; but not only does the other derivation explain the general form more satisfactorily, with its stiff stem and without the lower band of foliage found in French work, but it also explains another peculiarity of the English capital. The English foliage

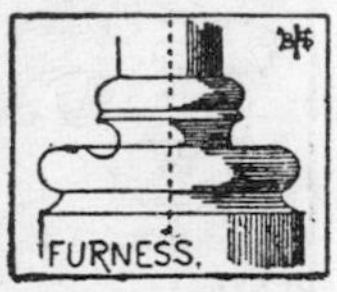

FIG. 47.

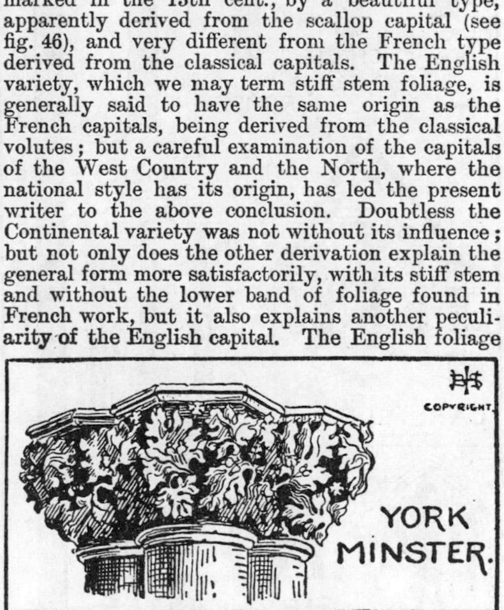

FIG. 48.

tends to twirl round the capital instead of standing out from the centre as in Continental work.

In the 14th cent., although the forms are sometimes exceedingly beautiful, there is a distinct artistic decadence. An attempt to be true to nature results in being untrue to the stone material in which the artist is working—a much more serious fault. The forms are ill adapted to stone, and, moreover, instead of growing up from the neck, are twined round like a harvest festival decoration, and have no part in the organic unity of the whole.

The arches are pointed and with numerous moldings, of which those in fig. 49 are typical. The Early English moldings are marked by freehand drawing and numerous independent members, separated by deep hollows, *e.g.* Peterborough. Characteristic members are the roll and fillet and the pointed bowtell. Decorated moldings are set out by the compass instead of being drawn freehand. The fillets on the triple roll and fillet are set differently. The ogee curve makes its appearance, and a three-quarter hollow often marks off the orders of the arches (fig. 49). Up to the end of the 14th cent. the orders of the arch are generally clearly distinguished.

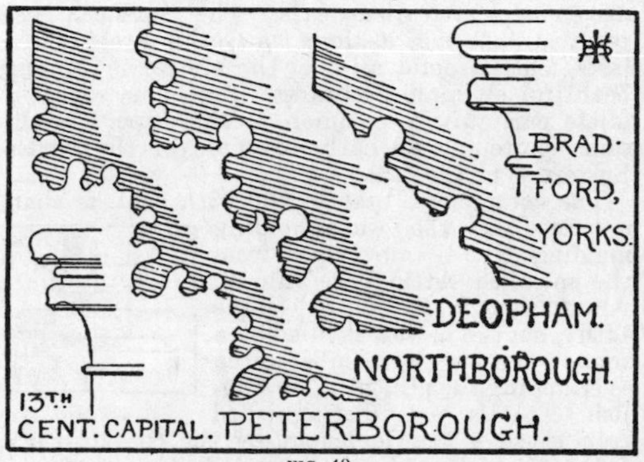

FIG. 49.

The development of the window is a long story, whose course can only be briefly indicated. The

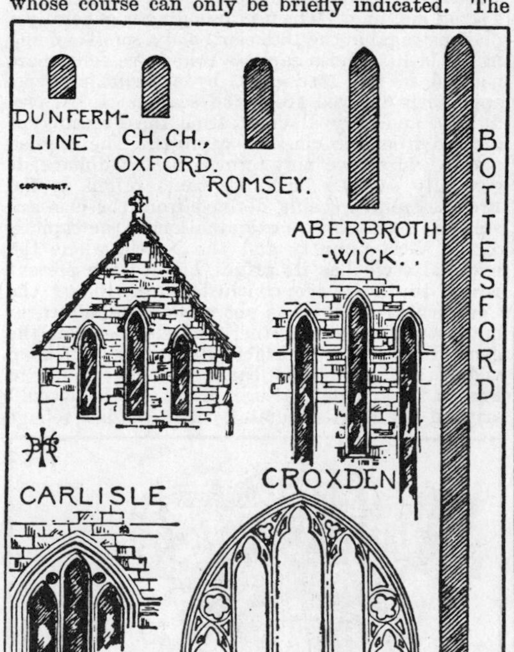

FIG. 50.

normal early Anglo-Norman window is a square with a semicircle over it. This tends to become longer in its proportions, and the process continues after the introduction of the pointed arch, producing the so-called lancet window, until such extreme examples are reached as at Bottesford, which is 8 in. wide and 15 ft. 6 in. high. The natural result is to group windows together, one being insufficient for lighting purposes (fig. 50).

In the gable end the normal arrangement in the first half of the 13th cent. is three windows, the central one raised to fill the gable. At first the windows are quite distinct; then a common hood mold gradually draws them together, and finally includes them under one arch. The small spandrels are first pierced with various shapes and finally cut out altogether, and then cusped as at Cirencester or Peterborough Cathedral. But this pushes all the ornament up into the extreme head; and it is perhaps the two-light window in the aisle, which follows suit, that tends to the filling with tracery of the whole head of the window above the springing (see examples in fig. 50).

We thus pass from the lancet period to the first traceried period, which has been called the Geometrical period. This is a most misleading name, as it implies that the curves of the next period are not set out with a compass. Although at first glance they may not appear to be parts of circles, they invariably are. The real distinction is between curves of single and double curvature; or the first period may be described as composed of independent figures—circles, curvilinear triangles, and squares (not spherical, of course), quatrefoils, trefoils, etc., filling the head of the window. The terms Simple and Compound would be short and self-explanatory.

There are three main types of Simple or independent-figure tracery. In type I. (fig. 51) the circle or other figure rests on two sub-arches. The points of the sub-arches projecting below the central ornament are objectionable, and probably are the cause of type II. making its appearance, in which the outer curves of the sub-arches coincide with the curves of the window arch. It should be noted that type I. does not disappear but continues to be used, and this is the case all through the development of window tracery; a new form does not entirely oust an old one. The objection to type II. is that it tends to push the ornament too much into the head of the window. In all cases the sub-arches may also intersect or be separated from each other. **Type III.**, which is really a three-light develop-

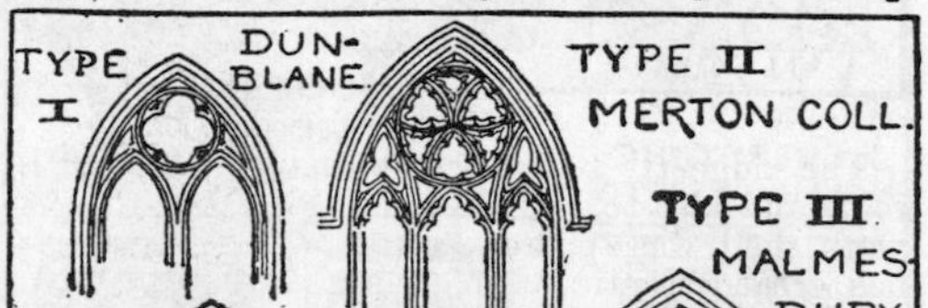

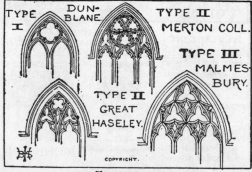

FIG. 51.—SIMPLE TRACERY.

ment, has no leading sub-arches, but the arches of the lights alone, and no leading central ornament.

The development into the Compound or flowing period is the result of attempts to improve type I. Divers devices had been tried to get rid of the objectionable points, the best being the disguising of them by a pointed trefoil. It occurred, however, to some unknown English genius that an exceedingly simple and obvious device—as is the case with most great discoveries—was to omit the points, and continue the curve of the sub-arch into the curve of the circle. Thus is obtained a curve of double curvature or an ogee curve. The other side of the sub-arch is made to correspond, and we have a circle supported on ogee arches (fig. 52, A). The bottom and top of the circle then disappear, leaving us the completed type I. of the Compound period. This develops on lines similar to the independent-figure period with a second and third type (fig. 52).

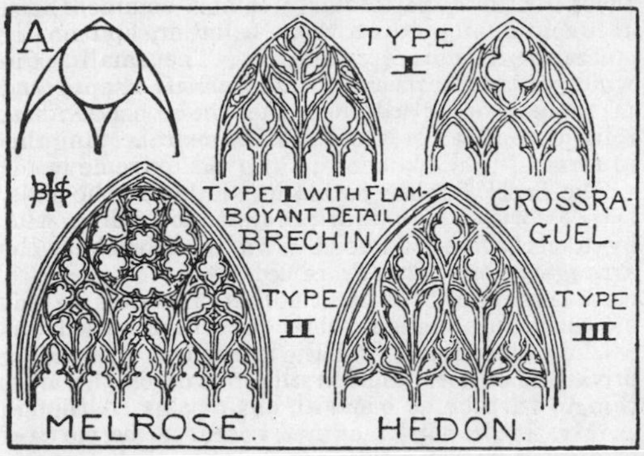

FIG. 52.—COMPOUND TRACERY.

The vaulting continues to develop. First, in order to reduce the ploughshare curvature, resort is had to elliptical ribs, involving a most difficult and complex problem in the setting out and erection of every vault. This is superseded by pseudo-elliptical vaulting, where, instead of a true ellipse, an approximation to the ellipse is made by parts of circles, which join at points where the tangent is common to both circles, so as to avoid breaks in the curve (fig. 53). The line of the pier or shaft from which the vault springs is also tangential to the arch curve.

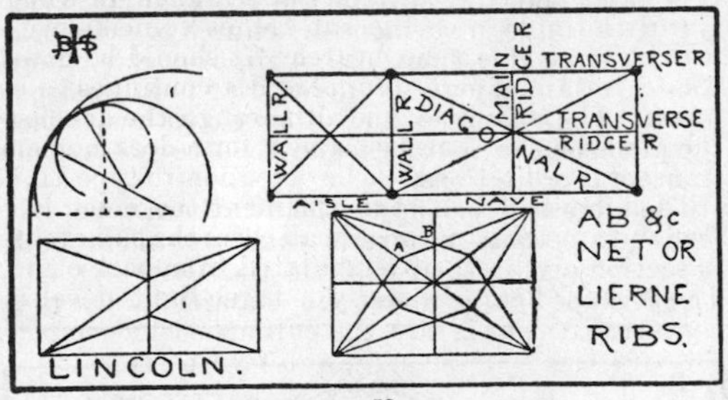

FIG. 53.

The ridge rib to mark the leading line of the roof, and also to provide a line of fitting for the vault shell, was apparently first used at Ripon. It has great æsthetic value, giving continuity to the whole and a line of emphasis to the vista. It is, in fact, the dominant æsthetic line of the building, corresponding to the keel of a boat. The French architects could not use it with any effect, on account of their broken ridge lines caused by the domical vault. Where they have used it the result is unpleasantly suggestive of the sea.

In order to reduce the space between the ribs, and to make the filling easier, subsidiary ribs are introduced, called *tiercerons* by the French architects. They were invented by the builders of Lincoln Cathedral and used first in a peculiar way (fig. 53). In the 14th cent. lierne or net ribs make their appearance, and give great complexity to the vaults (fig. 53).

The buttresses in the 13th and 14th centuries become more prominent, and the pinnacle, giving additional resisting power to the buttress, soon appears in the Early English period. Angle buttresses in the 14th cent. are commonly set diagonally, instead of in pairs at right angles (fig. 54).

FIG. 54.—BUTTRESSES.

It is difficult, and indeed inadvisable, to try to assign any particular date or period for the summit of Gothic architecture. In many points it continued to advance down to a very late date, more particularly in the development of towers and of the vault, but the decorative foliage certainly declines after the 13th century. For beauty of lighting nothing equals the so-called lantern churches of the 15th cent., but the window itself is perhaps at its best in the 14th. It is so with all arts; decadence does not come suddenly throughout the whole, but shows itself here and there, while the main trend is still forward. It would be much easier to assign a definite summit to French than to English architecture. In France there is a more or less definite single effort culminating in the 13th century. In England there are continuous new impulses: vault, wall, pier, foliage, window, and vault again; each in turn seems to play the leading part.

As said at the outset, the French and English styles are entirely different. A summing up at this point of a few of the differences between the plan of a great English and a great French church may show that it is surprising, not that they are now seen to be different, but that any one ever thought they were the same.

The English church is long and narrow with three aisles. The French is short and broad with five aisles.

The English West Front is broad. The French West Front is narrow, in Notre Dame narrower even than the nave.

The English transepts project enormously beyond the main lines, and often the English church has two or three of these

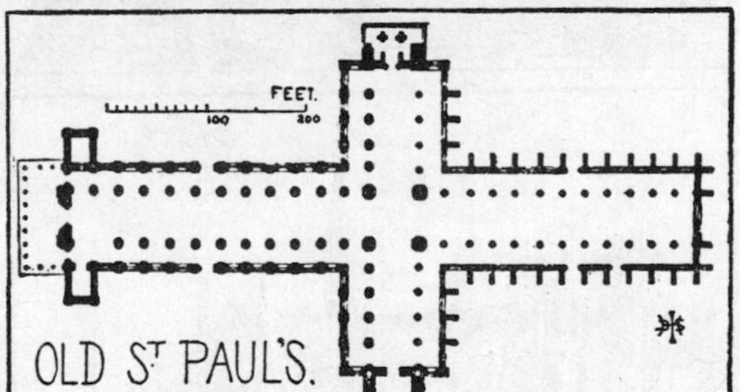

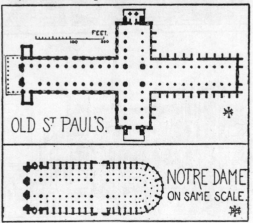

FIGS. 55 AND 56.—METROPOLITAN CHURCHES OF ENGLAND AND FRANCE.

projections. The French transepts hardly project at all, and one only is attempted.

The English church has a square East end. The French church has a semicircular chevet.

The English church has a long choir, generally more or less

shut off from the nave, being largely the result of monastic influence. It has no side chapels. The French church is broad and open throughout, with a short choir, largely the result of lay influence, and has numerous side chapels dear to the laity.

The four enormous central piers in the English church show the central tower that dominates the whole. The French church has great Western towers, but nothing, or merely a 'flèche,' at the crossing.

The English church is cut up by screens and divisions. The French church is open (figs. 55–58).

The interior of a French church is hard to surpass. It is exceedingly lofty, which gives it a most impressive character. The internal effect of the chevet is often exquisitely lovely, and the grace of the proportions as a whole, width of bays, and width to height, is in every way admirable.

The English church in its interior depends for its impressiveness upon length rather than height, except where modern folly, as at Norwich, has planted an enormous organ that entirely destroys the whole *raison d'être* of the building, completely (not partially) blocking the vista which would be, in its way, perhaps the finest in the world. Both English and French effects are delightful, but perhaps the French is the finer. Yet there is no reason why they should not be combined.

But with regard to the exteriors there is no comparison. The English here loses something by want of height. (Visit Chartres, Amiens, and then Lincoln within two days of each other, and the result will be startling.) But the dominant central tower, the wonderful skyline, together with the tower-groups, the grand projecting transepts and fronts, with their fine shadow effects, make the French examples look in comparison a shapeless mass. Where there is a narrow tall twin-towered front, there is an unpleasant effect of an overweighted end suggestive of a giraffe. The Franco-

FIGS. 57 AND 58.—LINCOLN AND AMIENS.

German church of Cologne is perhaps the worst example of this effect. The differences extend to every molding and every detail, and to the spirit in which everything is carried out: the French is more logical, the English more picturesque.

(*d*) *The Decline of English Gothic.*—The last period of English architecture is marked by rectangular forms and horizontal lines, and is generally called 'Perpendicular.' This word in most minds is so closely associated with vertical, that 'Rectangular' is a more satisfactory name.

Roofs become nearly horizontal, tops of doors and windows and all the arches follow the same tendency. There is often an actual straight horizontal line, strongly emphasized, above these features, particularly in the case of doors. Horizontal topped towers take the place of spires, horizontal transom bars appear in the windows, and horizontal topped panellings, instead of niches, occur all over the walls. Even the foliage and other ornaments become rectangular in form.

The Early English period was an age of Ecclesiastic reform, and the work of that period is marked by a certain ecclesiasticism in its planning and arrangements. The Traceried period of the 14th cent. is the age of the great nobles; the very ecclesiastics themselves aped the pride and pomp of worldly splendour; and the churches, with their private chantries and heraldic ornament and such things, partake to some extent of this character, as Mr. Prior points out (*History of Gothic Art in England*, 1900). The people, too, are beginning to assert themselves. The worship of Our Lady being particularly the cult of the people in England, we find the Lady chapels being built all over the country, in most instances actually at the east end, and approached from behind the high altar. The ecclesiastic privacy of the monastic choir perforce disappears. During the Wars of the Roses, the great barons gradually vanished, and the trading classes made their influence felt. This is the age of the guild chantries, and above all of the parish churches of the people. The large proportion of our parish churches belong to this date, and are built in the rectangular style. Hardly a single great monastic church or cathedral was built at this time, although, of course, there was a certain amount of re-building and enlargement. The chantries and other extensions affect the plans of the churches, and tend to obscure all transeptal projections.

The piers still belong to the Northern type, but incline to become meagre in their treatment both in section and in their capitals and bases (fig. 59). The S-shaped curve under the chamfered abacus is characteristic, as is also the curious cushion mold-

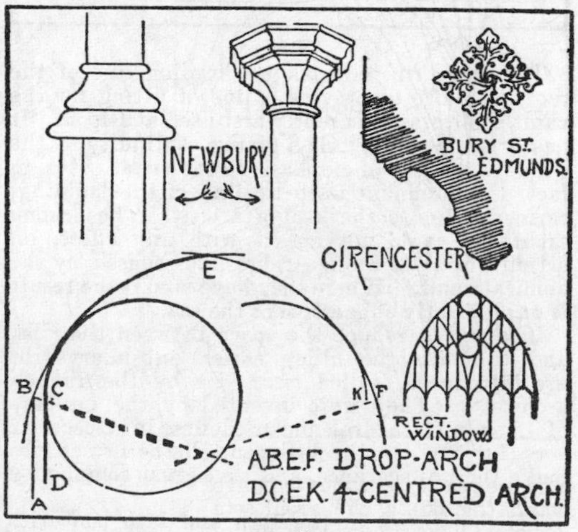

FIG. 59.

ing in the base and the bell shape above it. Capitals sometimes disappear altogether, and the moldings run right round the arch without a stop. Foliage when found is rectangular in treatment (fig. 59).

The arches above show the same attenuation in the treatment of their moldings, and the distinction between the orders of the arch is often quite lost. The most characteristic feature is the cavetto, a deep hollow in the middle of the group (fig. 59). The arch, both in the main arcades and in the window, is often of the four-centred variety. Most arches are struck from two centres, but a four-centred arch, while rising without a break from the springing, allows the crown to be comparatively flat (DCEK, fig. 59). A drop arch, as it is called, gives the flat crown, but produces a broken effect where it springs from the shafts (B, fig. 59).

The triforium, owing to the horizontal tendency in the roofs, practically disappears and becomes a mere band of ornament.

The window gradually becomes a series of rectangular panels, partly as offering increased strength for the vast windows that become common, partly to further the easy arrangement in the glass of rows of saints standing in niches. The vertical lines at first appear timidly in the head of the window, then ascend from sill to crown, and finally even cut across the tracery sub-arches (fig. 59).

The vault still continues its development until we reach the wonderful fan tracery characteristic of this country. The multiplication of tiercerons seems to have suggested a polygonal form for the vault conoid, and from this to a circle is easy,

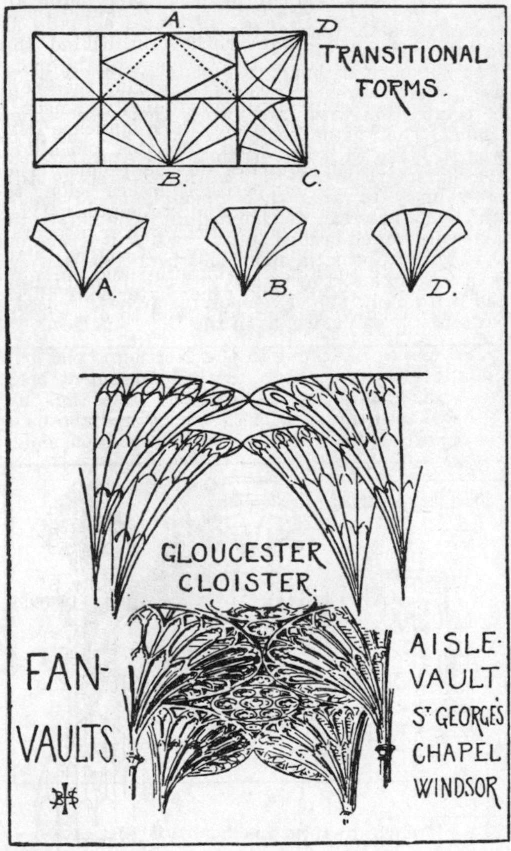

FIG. 60.

and we reach the concavo-convex conoid of the fan vault (fig. 60). The architects of the Gloucester cloisters have produced a delightful piece of work on this principle. But there is one objection, namely, that the flat central space makes an abrupt break with the lines of the ribs. It is probably this that led to the introduction of the four-centred arch, which allows the line of the ribs to pass imperceptibly into the central space (fig. 60, Windsor).

This is very satisfactory for a vault over a square, but the problems of satisfactorily vaulting a rectangular space begin again. The most complete solution is by the Oxford architects in the Divinity schools and the Cathedral, which are not true fan vaults (fig. 61); and the same principle, somewhat meretriciously carried out in a true fan vault, appears in Henry VII.'s Chapel, Westminster. The principle is practically that of dividing up the rectangular space to be vaulted into a new nave and aisles, as it were. The springings of the vaults are then supported upon great transverse arches thrown across the whole space. In this way a square compartment is obtained in the middle, which is easy to vault, and the small minor compartments can be treated by some other method. In the case of the Cathedral at Oxford they are very effectively treated as barrel vaults.

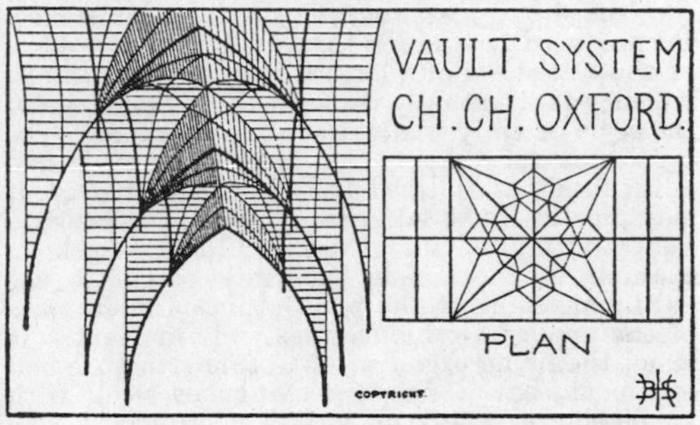

FIG. 61.

The influence of domestic architecture upon that of the church is a subject of great interest which has hardly yet received the study that it deserves. In early days many of the problems were first worked out in the Norman castles. Later, the domestic window with its transom bars and the beautiful open timber-roofs of the great halls had considerable effect upon church architecture. Of course, the plans and arrangements are different, but the spirit of the two is the same. Sometimes, as, for instance, in Belgium, the greatest achievements are in civil architecture; and although the bulk of these buildings in our own country have perished, such examples as the small Town Hall at Cirencester have a charm quite equal to that of the churches. But in any case, whether the building is for the Church, the State, the Borough, or the private individual, the artistic qualities triumph over the special difficulties involved in the particular instance, and the series of buildings—castles, cathedrals, halls, palaces, and churches—is as noble as that in any style.

Renaissance Architecture.

When, at the time of the Renaissance, men's minds began to turn back to the glories of the classical epoch, the result was naturally seen in architecture as in everything else. It was also natural that the beginning of the architectural change should be in Italy, as was the case in other departments of the movement, particularly in view of the large number of actually existing remains upon Italian soil. The development, however, was considerably stimulated by the discovery of the manuscript of Vitruvius Pollio, the architect of Augustus, who wrote the *de Architectura*. This famous treatise, in ten books, upon the architecture of the Augustan epoch, was translated into Italian in A.D. 1531. In spite of the impetus thus given to the study, it would appear to have been by no means entirely beneficial in its results. Vitruvius seems to some extent to have been the Palladio of his day, viewing the art in a cut and dried and somewhat lifeless manner, which was not without its effect upon his followers of a later generation. It is true that Vitruvius' work was drawn chiefly from Greek sources, although these were probably very late; but it must always be remembered that, in the main, Renaissance architecture was founded not upon the Greek but upon the Roman style—a style itself a hybrid and full of solecisms. Many of the criticisms that are brought against Renaissance work apply equally to that of Rome, in such instances as the profuse use of meaningless decoration, and the unintelligent application of features imperfectly understood, *e.g.* the architrave that supports no ceiling, the incomplete drums, flutings, or drafted stones copied from unfinished Greek work, and chopped off sections of entablature, as in the church of St. Spirito, Florence.

It may be said that Bruneleschi, the Florentine, was the first great architect of the Renaissance. He produced a plan for the building of the dome of the Cathedral of Florence soon after A.D. 1407, which was eventually carried out. The spread of the style in Italy was extraordinarily rapid. The cause was very largely that the Gothic style had never firmly established itself in Italy: indeed, it may practically be said that it never penetrated to Central Italy at all. Even in Florence such an example as the famous campanile of Giotto has hardly anything of the real Gothic spirit, in spite of the applied Gothic features and ornament. It is not the living organism of Gothic structure and ornament, but a simple rectangular block with an elaborate veneer of surface adornment. The Italian mediæval churches were mainly 'Latin' in motive, and it was natural that the Italian mind should turn whole-heartedly toward a style which it had never in essence entirely abandoned.

From Italy the movement spread throughout Western Europe with varying degrees of rapidity, and was strenuously fought by the architectural traditions of the lands into which it made its way. The Renaissance style made no headway in the East, because the Greeks, who for centuries had been the most cultured people of Europe, were at this time overwhelmed by the Turks. In fact, the sack of Constantinople in A.D. 1453, although it was the final blow to Greek civilization in the East, scattered the Greeks over Europe, and very largely made the Renaissance what it was.

In the case of any revival or Renaissance style, it is always more difficult to make a division into periods than in the case of a style of true growth; because, in the first place, the individual factor is stronger, depending upon study and research, and also at any moment fortuitous circumstances may combine to make a particular building a more complete representation of the old style. But it may be said that Renaissance architecture was by no means wholly a 're-naissance'; it was in many respects a living style. And it may be noticed that it did pass through three more or less clearly marked stages, although these vary considerably both in manner and in date in different countries.

The first period is marked by a distinctly Gothic tendency, besides showing a comparatively limited knowledge of the nature of ancient work.

The second period, the period of maturity, shows a much greater knowledge of classical detail and arrangement, and is marked by a much more definitely classical spirit. The picturesque irregularity of Gothic planning and elevation gives way to a precise and calculated symmetry. The style reaches its zenith and exhibits itself in many of the world's noblest buildings, although the lover of Gothic architecture will always feel a certain coldness about them, and the lover of Greek architecture will be repelled still more by their lack of spontaneity, subtlety, and delicate restraint. In the work of the second Spanish period there is a certain restraint, it is true, but it is rather a formal coldness, and does not resemble the reserved but intense passion of Greek work. The nearest approach to the true Greek restraint is in the best work of Florence. It is to this second period that we have to look for the true work of the Renaissance. It is here that we learn what are really its characteristics. The first period is but one of transitional preparation, and the last of over-ripeness and decay.

The third period, sometimes known as the 'Rococo,' is marked by exaggeration, ostentation, and a still more mechanical application of rule, which proceeds side by side with a tendency towards slavish reproduction of ancient work. The latter tendency resulted in what is sometimes called the 'neo-Classic revival,' doubtless hastened as an antidote to the extravagances of the Rococo.

1. In the **first period**, then, the new style was fighting its way. Even in Italy, although the architects themselves were probably completely unconscious of the fact, the influence of Gothic work was quite marked, whereas in other countries the Gothic influence for a long time remained paramount, and the period of transition was enormously prolonged. In France, even in late Renaissance days, when Wren was building in England in a severely classical style, the high roofs and other features betray a Gothic origin.

In Florence, although the classical orders were used, they were very much subordinated, and in comparison with later work their use seems timid. Their actual scale was small, and this also was the case with the ornamental features which are characteristic of Gothic work. There was still a tendency towards that multiplicity of parts which characterizes Gothic feeling. Windows are generally round-headed, often with sub-arches in the typical Gothic manner, and occasionally they even contain a sort of tracery, especially in France and Britain (fig. 62). Even pointed arches are used, particularly in Venice, as in the Doge's palace.

FIG. 62.

In Florence great use is made of rustication—one of the typical affectations of the Renaissance, which seems to have had its origin in ancient Roman work, where unfinished Greek work was copied in which only the outer borders of the stones had been dressed. Ugly and meaningless as it frequently is, particularly in its aggressively finished forms, it is not so hideous or so foolish as the leaving of occasional square blocks in a round column—a device that even the most extreme admirer of Renaissance work does not attempt to defend. This, however, does not appear until the style is more or less advanced. It becomes common in France during the reign of Charles IX. (A.D. 1560–1574). Rustication was never popular in Venice, where there had always been a certain true Gothic feeling, mingled with Byzantine, which was distinctly opposed to anything Roman. Indeed, it was doubtless partly a survival of this feeling that caused the Renaissance style to be reluctantly adopted in Venice only when the 16th cent. was well advanced. A rather charming device common in Venice at this period may at this point be noted, namely, the so-called shell ornament (fig. 62).

Another objectionable feature, apparently first used by Alberti in St. Maria Novella at Florence, in A.D. 1470, is the inverted console placed above the aisles. Presumably it may be regarded as the successor of the flying buttress of Gothic work, but it is utterly unfitted to perform any function structurally or æsthetically. A curve suited for a small decorative bracket becomes ridiculous when applied to a feature of the main composition over a score of feet in length (fig. 63).

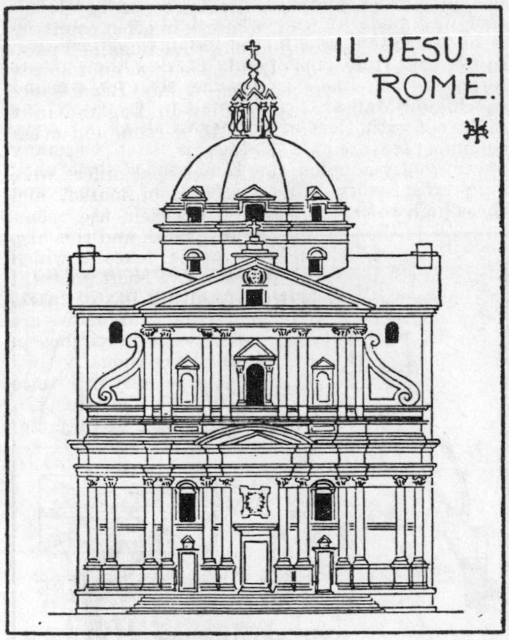

FIG. 63.

On the whole, it may be said that, although many churches were built in Italy during the Renaissance, partly as a result of the counter-Reformation of the Jesuits, in the North the Gothic epoch had more than supplied all the churches that were required. Hence, religious buildings in the North, particularly during the first period, are comparatively rare, and it is only in such instances as the churches of London built after the Great Fire that there is anything very extensive in the way of ecclesiastical work. It was rather a palace-building epoch, such as is shown in the great *châteaux* on the Loire, of which the Château Chambord may be taken as typical. In the North, Renaissance architecture made its way very slowly, at first appearing only in minor accessories such as altars, tombs, pulpits, doorways, and occasional enlargements, as the apse of St. Pierre at Caen. When the main fabric itself is attempted, the result is a building entirely Gothic in planning, arrangement, and construction, and the surface ornament merely is of the classical type. Pilasters take the place of buttresses, and cornices the place of corbel tables, and so on, as, for example, in St. Eustache, Paris—an excellent specimen of the first period of Renaissance work in France. In Britain, although Inigo Jones and Wren introduced a pure classical style earlier than anything of the kind in France, this transitional feeling continued in certain districts very much longer, particularly in Oxford. As late as 1648–1652 the charming little church of Berwick-on-Tweed affords a most pleasing instance of the fusion of the two styles.

In the South of France much of the work was done by bands of travelling Italians, who have left a considerable impress upon the minor features of the period in that district. In the main it is true to say that French work of the time of Francis I. (1515–1547) is marked by a special elegance which is peculiar to itself. It is doubtless the outcome of the elegant French-Gothic acting upon the Renaissance style, and applies especially to domestic examples. In England the Early period, which may be said to cover the reigns from Henry VIII. to James I., may be divided into two. The earlier part, from the close of Henry VII.'s reign to the death of Edward VI., is marked by Italian influence, as in the case of Torrigiano's tomb made for Henry VII., and the later part is marked by Flemish and German influence; but throughout the whole period everything is tentative and experimental.

2. In the **second period** we have the matured Renaissance style, when buildings were classical not only in detail, but in spirit. This may be said to have been inaugurated in Italy when in A.D. 1506 Bramante commenced the church of St. Peter's in Rome, a date which was about contemporaneous with the very first beginnings of Renaissance influence in Britain.

In this second period the picturesqueness of Gothic planning almost entirely disappears. It is,

FIG. 64.

however, to be noticed that the great cross plan of the large churches, although carried out in a severely symmetrical manner, is the indelible impress of the Gothic hand upon the succeeding age. Even St. Peter's itself is so planned. Not only so, but, in the case of both St. Peter's, Rome, and of St. Paul's, London (figs. 64, 68)—the two greatest buildings of the style—the more severely symmetrical plan of the Greek cross, as designed by the architects, was altered to the long-naved Latin cross in deference to Gothic tradition. Both churches suffered by this arrangement, St. Peter's very seriously.

The orders in this period are no longer used in an unobtrusive manner, but become, except perhaps in Florence, the main feature of the style, although, as in ancient Roman work, they are generally little more than mere ornament unrelated to the anatomy of the building. They are generally treated on Roman lines; but there was considerable latitude, the shafts occasionally being even fluted spirally, or wreathed with bands of foliage and fruit, or, worst of all, broken by square blocks. The Tuscan order becomes clearly defined in Renaissance work as a separate order. In Spain a new kind of capital appears, termed the 'bracket capital,' in which two or more brackets spring from the head of the column. It has the advantage of reducing the strain on the architrave.

FIG. 65.

In the best designed work one order is used for each storey; and in France this arrangement was practically universally observed. This was owing to the supreme influence in that country of Barozzi da Vignola, author of *The Five Orders of Architecture*, who had been brought back to France by Francis I. But in Venice Palladio introduced a system wherein one order ran through two or more storeys, minor orders being introduced in the storeys themselves. This unsatisfactory arrangement, which still further degraded the orders as mere applied ornament, unfortunately became popular in Britain, owing to the influence of Palladio, who was the inspirer of Inigo Jones.

One might even make a division of Renaissance architecture according as the orders or the windows formed the main element of the wall design. The latter is distinctly more Gothic in feeling, and is found more particularly at the beginning and end, before the Gothic art had quite disappeared, and after the Renaissance had spent its force. To some extent the division would be one of locality. In Florentine work the order is always less dominant than in either the school of Rome or that of Venice, and this distinction may also be noticed in those countries respectively influenced by these schools.

The column itself frequently bears the arch, particularly in early work, although the more usual arrangement is a massive pier with attached pilasters. Occasionally the unpleasant device is used of a section of entablature above the columns from which the arch is made to spring.

The moldings of the orders and other parts were the simple circular sections of Roman work. The great series of receding moldings on the arches of Gothic architecture were replaced by square soffits; and string courses and moldings generally become comparatively scarce. Effect is given by strongly marked entablatures dividing off the storeys of the building, and altogether horizontal features become very pronounced. In Italian and particularly Florentine work, a great cornice of very large proportions is often used on the top storey, suited in its size to the whole height of the building and not merely to the storey in which it occurs. This on the whole gives a pleasing effect with its marked shadow line.

The ornament is founded upon classical Roman work; but in the best Renaissance examples, especially in Florence, it is more refined. It should be noticed that Renaissance carving was almost invariably executed after the building was set up. In Gothic buildings every stone was completed before it was put into its place. The result is that the jointings often cut unpleasantly across Renaissance work, whereas Gothic jointing and the carving-design are thought out together. It is simply one aspect of the principle that the Gothic pile was always essentially a building; the Renaissance pile was rather a monument, treated somewhat after the manner of a picture.

The old Roman ribless vault was revived, at least in form, but a considerable geometrical improvement was made. In the plain barrel form it remained semicircular, but in the case of intersecting vaults over a rectangular space the curve of the vault was made elliptical, so that the diagonal groins might be projected as straight lines upon the plan (fig. 66). It should, however, be observed that in an enormous number of cases the vault was a mere plaster sham, and not part of the construction, as in Roman or Gothic work. All roofs in Italy were hidden within by ceilings, but in France and Germany the open timber-roof was made an important feature. The roof is of low pitch, and in the majority of instances so low that from most points of view the parapet forms the sky-line. In France, however, we find the high 'Mansard' roof; and in Germany the high roof with tiers of dormer windows is a very common feature. The fact is that Germany never wholly adopted the Renaissance style until long after every other country in Europe, and these high roofs are mediæval in character.

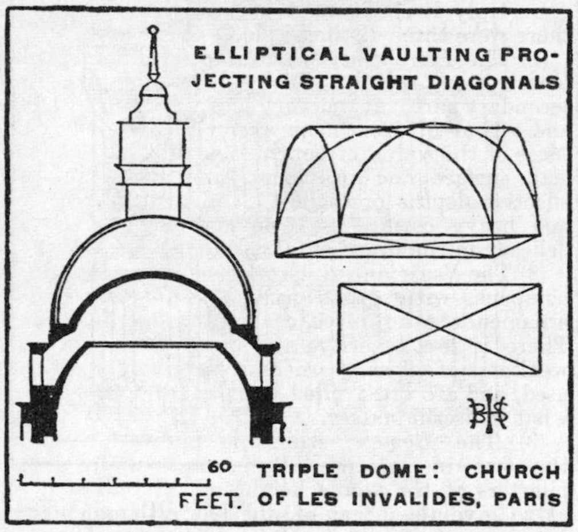

FIG. 66.

The glory of the style is the dome, which in its general treatment follows the Byzantine method. There is almost universally a drum, as in the second Byzantine period; but it is made an even more important feature, and very commonly is enriched by a colonnade. It was usual to build these domes with an outer and an inner shell of different curvature and a space between. The outer dome is frequently a mere timber-framed erection, resting upon the other, as in Sansovino's S. Giorgeo dei Greci at Venice, or the outer dome of the Église des Invalides, Paris, which consists of three domes (fig. 66). In this connexion may be noticed the very great use of carpentry all through Renaissance work, which has been compared by some writers to the modern use of iron. St. Paul's, London, has an outer and an inner dome, with a brick cone between. St. Peter's, Rome, has two brick domes.

Renaissance spires were not of common occurrence save in England and Spain. They seem to have been invented first by Sir Christopher Wren, but the Spanish use is possibly independent.

In the second period round-headed windows were less frequent, and square-headed windows, often with small pediments over them, were the rule. The rustication, so common in Florence in the early period, was now generally confined to the quoins, as in the Pandolfini Palace designed by Raphael, and more or less freely copied in The Travellers' Club, London. At the same time there was a tendency for all wall space to disappear, and for the whole surface to be covered with an exuberance of applied architectural features. The detail and moldings became more vigorous and elaborate, but lacked the earlier refinement.

The Roman method of building had been largely one of veneers. The inner part of the wall was of inferior material, but the outside was cased with fine stone or more often marble. The Romanesque Gothic had made use of a double wall with a rubble core, derived from Roman use; but this system was gradually abandoned, and in the best Gothic work the wall was built solid, or at least all the face stones were bonded into and formed an integral part of the wall. The Renaissance architects realized that this was a better system, and endeavoured to follow it out in their work. At the same time veneer was not infrequently used, and plaster facing was by no means uncommon. This was particularly so in the last period, when panels, cornices, and ornaments even upon the exterior were of plaster—a most unsatisfactory arrangement.

In Italy itself it may certainly be said that there were three distinct schools of the art:

(1) The *Florentine*, which depended largely on fenestration, and in which the orders played a secondary part. It was very severe, with a breadth and vigour of treatment exemplified in the due sense of the value of contrast as applied to plain wall surface and ornament, and again in the effective depths of shadow given by deep recesses and heavy cornices. It is marked by extreme delicacy in the ornamental carving.

(2) The *Venetian*, which was shallower and more pompous, with great ornaments introduced for ornament's sake, often coarse and over-insistent. There is less severity, and many curves give a weakness of effect. Orders of varying heights are used, and are often piled upon other orders somewhat indiscriminately.

(3) The *Roman*, which is midway between the two in severity. It is marked by great pilasters of the whole height of the building, so as to give the effect of one storey, and in consequence of this it has had a greater influence upon church architecture. The pilaster and not the column is used, as the inter-columniations upon so huge a scale would make the span of the architrave impossible.

3. In the **third period** there was a distinct decline, and a great deal of extravagance and affectation, such as broken entablatures, and pediments, and curved and irregular cornices. In Italy there is a peculiar lack of inspiration, and the work of Maderno and Bernini may be taken as typical. One of the most pleasing examples is that of St. Maria della Salute, by Longhena, in Venice (A.D. 1632). Its proportions and general mass are excellent, although the details leave something to be desired. Doubtless it owes a great deal to its situation. St. Genevieve (The Pantheon), Paris (A.D. 1755), although greatly superior to most work of the time, belongs to this period. It was built from Soufflot's designs, and is interesting as having the smallest amount of area of supports of any Renaissance church, comparing even with Gothic work in this respect. Compare its plan (fig. 67) with that of St. Peter's or St. Paul's (fig. 68). It has not been successful, however, for it has been necessary to prop and support it several times.

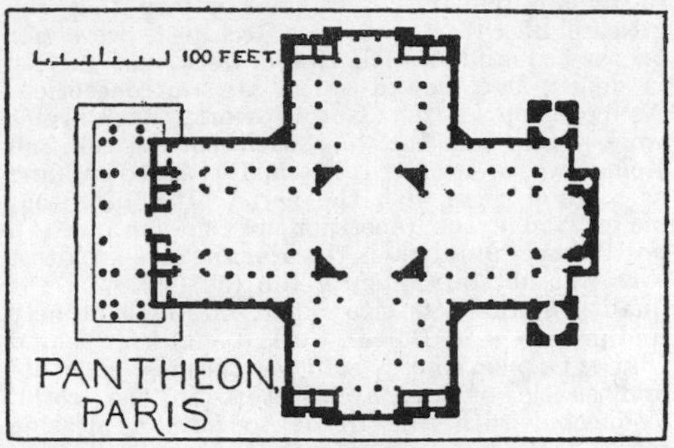

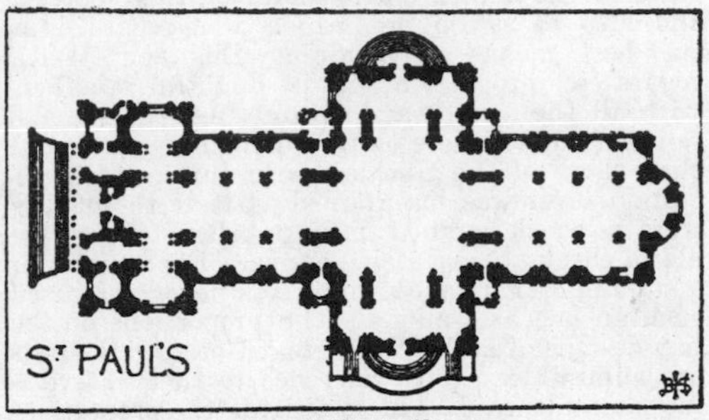

FIGS. 67 AND 68.

The extravagances of the 'Rococo' in France are even surpassed by the work in Spain generally known as 'Churriguerresque,' after the architect Churriguerra, doubtless partly caused by a revulsion from the over-bald mechanical style of such men as Herrera in the previous period.

In considering the Renaissance style as a whole, certain broad characteristics should be noticed. In the first place, there was a very distinct tendency, particularly in the case of its Italian inventors, to view the whole composition as a matter of line and proportion rather than as a building. There is often very little relation between the uses of the building and its form. Architecture is an applied art, and therefore, unless it be well adapted to the function that it has to perform, it cannot be a success. But, further, it is not only upon these grounds that so much Renaissance work must be condemned. Even upon æsthetic grounds, in the erection of a monument as distinct from a building, it is necessary that the thing should form an organic whole; and a column which is the outcome of the æsthetic endeavour of many ages to express the beauty of support, is clearly out of place when it supports nothing. The concealment of construction and arrangement is a similar but different question. An enormously heavy lantern, rising above what is apparently a dome of light construction, may, it is true, be defended upon the grounds that it is obvious that there must be some further support within. The eye would, however, probably be æsthetically more satisfied if there were some indication of this support, as otherwise there is considerable though not absolutely certain danger of the artistic unity being marred. To treat the matter as a moral question is, of course, absurd, and simply shows entire ignorance of the nature of all æsthetic philosophy. One might as well argue that a portrait was false because it was not flesh and blood but paint and canvas. But there is no doubt that Renaissance architects were in the habit of sailing very near the wind, and there is frequently a distinct want of harmony in their work. Some of the faults are directly traceable to Roman influence, and it is a pity that the greatest of the Renaissance architects were not better acquainted with Greek work, not merely in detail, but viewed as an artistic conception. As contrasted with Gothic work, Renaissance work—as is also the case with both Greek and Roman work—is more concerned with the building as a whole than with the parts. It is this that makes the exact repetition of similar parts a possibility. But when the Renaissance architect —as was not infrequently the case—allowed the quality of the detail to suffer, although he may find precedent in Roman work, he falls far behind that of Greece, whose detail was the most exquisite and subtle of any architecture in the world. Connected with the desire to form a pleasing whole, is the immense attention paid to proportion and also to symmetry, which was regarded as the best means of attaining this end. With regard to proportion, it is doubtful whether, with all their rules and formularies, the Renaissance architects were on the whole more successful than those of the Gothic era in this respect. A certain level was maintained; but if these laws were a check against falling below, they were also a check against rising above. For an interior vista the Renaissance architects never surpassed such an one as Amiens. The proportions of the bay designs of most of the great Gothic cathedrals are admirable. With reference to their exteriors more may be said; but as regards the proportionate disposition of its masses, it would be hard to find any Renaissance building to rival Durham: certainly not St. Peter's, Rome, whose façade and minor cupolas are entirely out of proportion with the rest. It is true it is a work of many architects, but so is Durham. St. Paul's, London, is perhaps the one rival; and St. Paul's, taking all things into consideration, is the finest of all Renaissance buildings. As for façades, the simple inevitableness of such an one as York Minster has deprived it of the praise it deserves. A façade such as that at Certosa will not stand comparison for a moment, neither will that of the Invalides at Paris nor the Pantheon, good as far as it goes, and certainly not Bernini's façade to St. Peter's. Again St. Paul's is the only possible rival.

A great deal of nonsense has been talked about Renaissance proportions. One of the most characteristic qualities of Renaissance work is its treatment of scale. The parts themselves are few in number, but of great size. The result is to give the impression of the building as a whole being very much smaller than it actually is. St. Peter's, Rome, is the largest church in the world, but in effect of size it is surpassed by many a Gothic cathedral not approaching it in area. It is probable that the contrary result was expected, but such is the fact. It is true that there is a certain calm and even dignity about the system, but this should rather be set against the loss of mystery and suggestiveness.

Renaissance architecture is largely the product of scholarship, and as such it challenges criticism in a way that is not the case with less 'studied' styles. It is therefore easy to form an erroneous notion of its value as a style in the architecture of the world, and to fail in giving it the place that it deserves.

LITERATURE.—J. Fergusson, *Illustrated Handbook of Architecture*, vol. ii. (Christian), Lond., 1855; G. Baldwin Brown, *From Schola to Cathedral*, Edin., 1886, and *The Arts in Early England* (vol. ii.), 1903; T. Rickman, *Architecture in England*[6], Oxf., 1862; J. H. Parker, *Introduction to the Study of Gothic Architecture*[3], Oxf., 1867, and *Glossary of Architecture*[5], Oxf., 1850; Edward S. Prior, *A History of Gothic Art in England*, 1900; Sir G. G. Scott, *Lectures on Mediæval Architecture*, Lond., 1879; R. Willis, *Remarks on the Architecture of the Middle Ages*, Camb., 1835; Francis Bond, *Gothic Architecture in England*, Lond., 1905; John Bilson, *The Beginnings of Gothic Architecture*, Lond., 1899; M. H. Bloxam, *The Principles of Gothic Ecclesiastical Architecture*[11], Lond., 1882; E. Corroyer, *Gothic Architecture*, Lond., 1893; G. E. Street, *Gothic Architecture in Spain*[2], Lond., 1869, and *Brick and Marble in the Middle Ages (Notes of Tours in the N. of Italy)*[2], 1874; W. R. Lethaby, *Mediæval Art*, Lond., 1904; D. MacGibbon and T. Ross, *Ecclesiastical Architecture of Scotland*, Edinb., 1896; E. E. Viollet le Duc, *Dictionnaire raisonné de l'Architecture française* (10 vols.), Paris, 1859; R. W. Billings, *Baronial and Ecclesiastical Antiquities of Scotland*, Edinb., 1848; J. Britton, *Cathedral Antiquities* (13 vols.), 1814–35, and *Architectural Antiquities* (5 vols), 1807–26; E. Sharpe, *Seven Periods of English Architecture*[2], 1871, and *Rise and Progress of Window Tracery in England* (2 vols.), 1849; F. A. Paley, *Gothic Moldings*[4], 1877; C. Texier and R. Pullan, *Byzantine Architecture*, Lond., 1864; R. Blomfield, *A History of Renaissance Architecture in England*, Lond., 1897; Banister F. Fletcher, *Andrea Palladio: His Life and Work*, Lond., 1902; Banister Fletcher and Banister F. Fletcher, *A History of Architecture*, Lond., 1905; F. M. Simpson, *A History of Architectural Development*, vol. i., Lond., 1905; J. B. Stoughton Holborn, *The Gothic Era* (in the Press)

J. B. STOUGHTON HOLBORN.

ARCHITECTURE (EGYPTIAN).—We shall here deal only with the religious architecture; but as that is by far the greater part of what exists, the discussion will involve most of the known facts. The divisions of the subject are (1) Materials and conditions, (2) Plans, (3) Elevations, (4) Decoration, (5) Furniture, (6) Popular shrines.

1. The materials.—The materials necessarily condition the style and decoration of all architecture. In Egypt the commonest materials used by the peasantry are maize stalks, mud, mud brick, palm sticks, and palm logs. The simplest huts are made by lashing maize stalks (stems of the *durrah*, called *bûs*) together by means of palm-fibre; the flat screens thus formed are set upright at right angles, and lashed together down the corners. If the weather is cold and the wind strong, they are plastered over with mud. In this form the temporary dwellings in the fields are set up for two or three months of the pasture season. Where a column is required, a bundle of maize stalks is bound together, from 4 to 10 in. in diameter, and plastered with mud, thus forming an extremely stiff and unbreakable mass. Two such columns are even used to support the *shaduf*, or water-lift, which weighs two or three hundredweight, and is kept continually in swinging motion. In ancient times the papyrus stem was also commonly used, as well as the maize stalk. Mud brick was the principal building material in Egypt in all ages; even in the rainy climates of Syria and Babylonia it was universal, and in the general drought of Egypt it is an excellent material. The mud requires to be mixed with so much sand that the grains shall be almost in contact, and then rain has but a slow effect upon it. Another way of making it durable was to mix it with chopped straw, or even grass roots, which bind it together. The brick down to the VIth dynasty was generally pure mud; the sandy and gravelly bricks are of later age. Another form of brick is thin and wide like a tile, and ribbed on the face, in order to build it up by adhesion of mud on the faces, in forming arches. The palm-stick is used for fences, the tops being left with side leaves to form a barrier to men and animals. The logs of the palm tree are used for roofing-beams, but never for columns.

The nature of these materials has led to the general features of the architecture. The constant use of a portico or verandah in front of house, temple, or tomb, results from the common use of bundles of maize stalk. The palm capital results from strengthening the column with a coat of the harder palm branches, whose thin tops were left loose around the capital. The sloping walls of the pylon result from tilting the courses of bricks inward, so as to prevent them from being easily dislodged. In order to save the corners of reed huts or brickwork from being broken away, bundles of stalks were lashed on down the edge; these were the origin of the torus molding marked by diagonal winding bands along the angles of the buildings. The fence, formed of palm-sticks with loose heads, lashed together near the top to a line of cross sticks, is the source of the cavetto molding with torus roll below it. The palm-log roof is copied in stone in tombs at Gizeh and Abydos. Thus the forms adopted for the stone architecture belong to the earlier materials, as in Greece.

2. The plans.—The plans of the temples vary considerably in different ages. The earlier temples are scarcely known except from the plans of the Osiris temples at Abydos, and the views of primitive shrines. The hieroglyph for a shrine in early times retained the appearance of a plain square hut, with a fence in front of it, and two tall poles at the sides of the entrance. Another form is a hut with a domed top, and a low enclosed court before it, having two tall poles at the entrance, and the standard of the deity placed in the middle of the court. The oldest plan of a temple at Abydos is a wall about 16 in. thick, enclosing a space at least 25 ft. wide and 42 ft. long; the entrance is a passage between walls 4 ft. apart and 35 ft. long, facing south. This is probably of the age before the first dynasty. Of the first dynasty is a much larger and more solid building, 42 ft. E.-W. and 21 ft. N.-S., with the entrance probably on the north; the wall is about 8 ft. thick. A great temenos wall was built round the site, and a block of store chambers placed at the side of the temple. The same form continued through the IInd and IIIrd dynasties. Khufu of the IVth dynasty changed the whole worship, and made a great hearth of burnt-offering, where clay models only were sacrificed. This hearth was about 12 ft. N.-S. by 8 ft. E.-W.; it was in a chamber about 15 ft. wide, probably entered from the north. Round this was subsequently added a stone wall reaching about 6 ft. farther out.

In the VIth dynasty, under Pepy I., a great re-construction took place at Abydos. The new temple had the principal door to the north, and a lesser one to the south. The building was of mud brick, with stone doorways; it was 49 ft. N.-S. and 23 ft. E.-W. in the middle hall, or with side chambers 58 ft. wide inside. The walls were 5 ft. thick. From the position of the doorways this seems to have been a processional temple, open front and back, for the processions to enter, deposit the sacred bark, and pass out by the other door. The surroundings were also altered. The old temenos wall had a stone gateway inserted, and outside of it, 40 ft. in advance, was built the outer temenos wall, with another stone gateway. A colonnade led from the outer to the inner gate. To this temple Mentuhotep added a colonnade on the eastern side.

Another entire re-modelling took place in the XIth dynasty under Sankh-ka-ra. A square of brickwork 47 ft. E.-W., 48 ft. N.-S., held the foundation of a stone temple, probably 44 ft. square. As this mainly overlies the Pepy temple, it was probably entered from the north, like that. The temple of Sankh-ka-ra was, however, not grand enough for Senusert I., who pulled it all down, and laid foundations over the pavement of his predecessor. This temple seems to have faced the East, as the outside length of it was 133 ft. E.-W., while only 75 ft. N.-S. The limits of it are shown by the corner deposits of the foundation. A great temenos was built around it, 192 ft. distant to the eastward, with a wall 23 ft. thick. To this temple Sebekhotep III. added a chapel and doorway on the south.

The XVIIIth dynasty saw all this re-built still larger. The temenos was 264 ft. long, E.-W.; in it lay the stone temple facing east, 215 ft. long, and 129 ft. wide; the temenos wall was nearly 30 ft. thick, with gateways of red granite. Lastly, in the XXVIth dynasty, there was an entirely new stone temple, facing east, 132 ft. square. It seems not improbable that this also was of the processional type, open back and front. We have detailed these successive temples as they are the only examples that have yet been observed and recorded, showing the growth and alterations throughout Egyptian history on one site. Many secondary details, and the outlying store-rooms, are not noticed here, nor buildings of the XIXth and XXth dynasties which were in adjacent positions, but are too much ruined to be traced. The total result is that there were seven entirely different plans on one site, beside alterations to these. The direction of facing was successively S., N., N.?, N., N.?, E., E., E.

Another early temple plan is that of Hierakonpolis. This was entirely of brick, but can hardly be earlier than the XIIth dynasty. Its shrines consisted of five chambers in a row, each 8 ft. wide and 20 ft. long. The whole block was 92 ft. wide over all. The shrines were each a closed cell with one door, and not of the processiona type.

Coming now to the temples which can still be examined in a more or less perfect state, the oldest is that of Medum, built by Seneferu of the IIIrd dynasty. This is merely an enclosed courtyard (nearly 20 ft. by 8) against the side of the pyramid, containing an altar between two tall stelæ. The approach to it is through two chambers placed with their length across the whole breadth of the building. Next is the granite temple of Khafra of the IVth dynasty, near the sphinx; the entrance to it is still buried, so that its nature is unknown. The first hall is 12 ft. by 60 ft. wide; the second hall is 22 ft. from back to front, divided by a row of six pillars, and 81 ft. wide; and from this branches another hall 33 ft. wide, divided by two rows of five pillars, and 55 ft. long. The whole is built of red granite. Neither of these was a temple in the usual sense, but a place for religious services for the benefit of the deceased king.

The oldest temple of which we have full plans is of Tahutmes III. at Medinet Habu. It is solely a processional resting-place for a sacred bark, open at both ends, with a colonnade round it for the procession to pass, and six store chambers behind. Of the same type were the subsequent temples of Amenhotep III. at Elephantine, of Ramessu III. at Karnak, of Alexander at Luqsor, of Philip Arrhidæus at Karnak, and of the Ptolemaic age at Kom Ombo and Dakkeh.

The other type of temple was not adapted for processions, nor, perhaps, for barks of gods, but had a small cell as the sanctuary, probably to contain a single large statue too heavy to be moved. Of this type there seem to be two of Amenhotep III., at Luqsor and at el-Kab; but all the others are Ptolemaic, as at Dendereh, Deir el-Medineh, Edfu, Philæ (Isis, Harendotes, Arhesnofer), and Kalabsheh. Probably also of this type were all the late temples with monolith shrines, which were mostly set up in the Delta (Saft el-Henneh, Nebeshah, Tmey el-Amdid, Sebennytos, Bubastis, Baqlieh) and less often in Upper Egypt, as at Abydos and Edfu.

The third type of temple was funerary, for ceremonies of offering to the deceased king, and neither for processions with a bark, nor for holding a statue in a naos. Such are those of Deir el-Bahri,

EGYPTIAN TEMPLE PLANS.

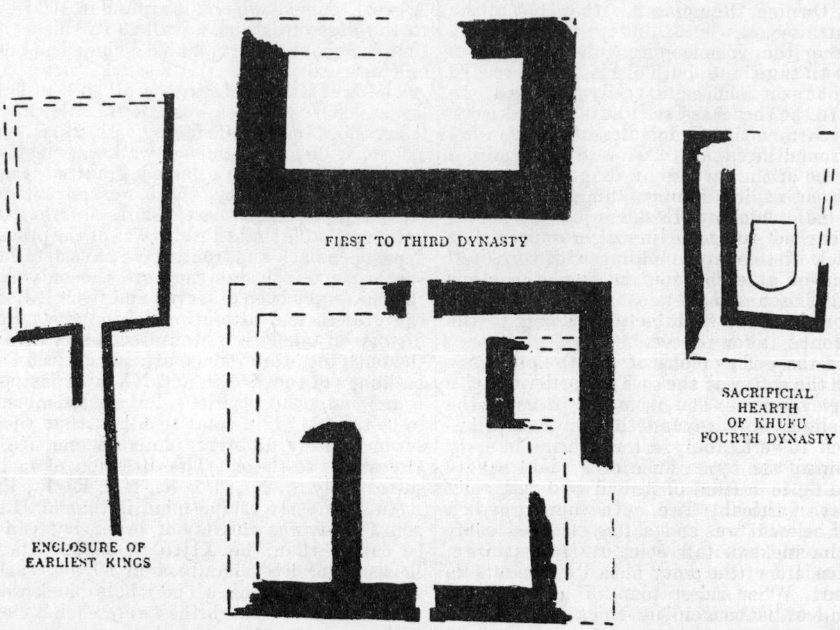

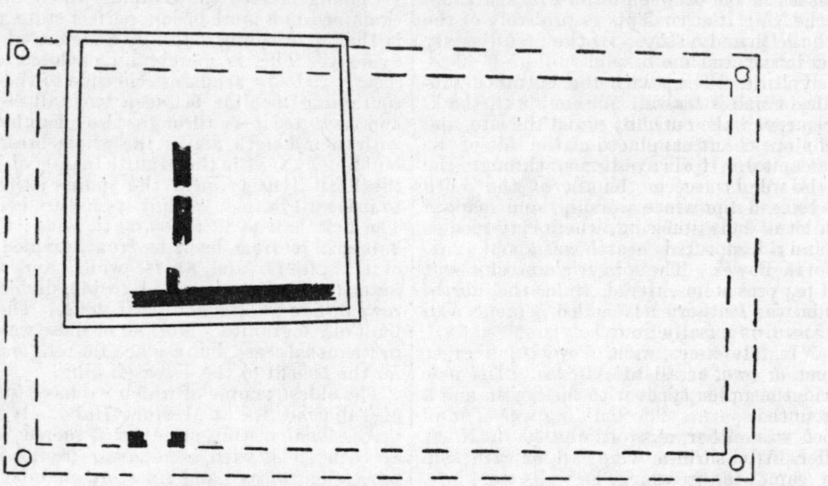

SMALL SQUARE (ELEVENTH) AND OBLONG (TWELFTH DYNASTY) TEMPLES OF OSIRIS, ABYDOS

[All above, 1 : 400]

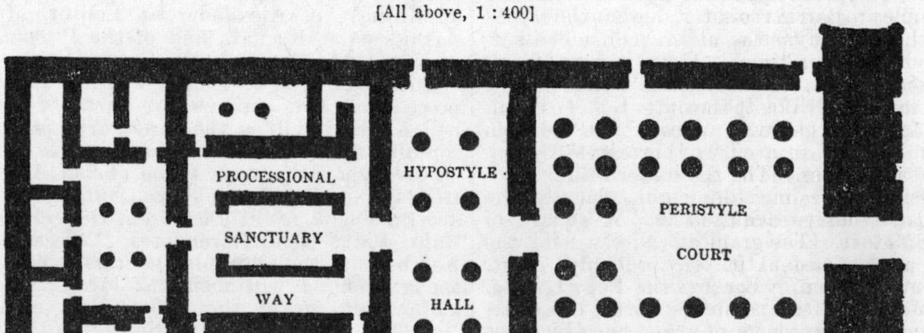

COMPLETE TEMPLE OF TWENTIETH DYNASTY, OF KHONSU, KARNAK

[1 : 750]

Sety I. at Qurneh, Ramessu II., Merenptah, and Ramessu III.

For noting the various divisions of a temple it is best to take one built in a single reign, such as that of Khonsu at Karnak built by Ramessu III. The massive pylon leads to the peristyle court, with a single or a double row of columns around three sides. This is the expansion of the portico of the dwelling-house, with a court-yard in front of it. Behind this is the closed hypostyle hall, which originated in the hall of the house which had sometimes a single column in it. At the back of this is the actual sanctuary, with store chambers at each side, and sometimes also behind it. The sanctuary was either a long chamber, with wide doors front and back, and a wide passage around it for processions to pass bearing the bark of the god; or else it was a closed naos containing the statue of the god.

3. The elevations.—The elevations show almost always a slight slope inwards of the face of the wall, which is vertical inside, and thus becomes thinner toward the top. This form was inherited from building in brick. The doorways are, however, always vertical. The overhanging cornice with a roll below it was copied from the loose ends of the palm-sticks left free at the top, the roll being taken from the cross stick to which they were lashed. When elaborated, the cornice always has a palm leaf pattern on it. The columns are of various orders. The square pillar without any capital is seen in the temple of Khafra, and in the courts of the XVIIIth dynasty. Octagonal columns occur in the XIth and XIIth dynasties. The further truncation to sixteen sides belongs to the XIIth and XVIIIth dynasties. The palm column is apparently the bundle of maize stalks stiffened by a coat of palm-sticks round the outside, with the leafy ends of the palm-sticks left hanging free around the top, forming a capital. It always had a square abacus to carry the weight free of the projecting leaves. The lotus column represents a similar bundle decorated with lotus buds stuck into the hollows of the binding, and a sculptured capital imitating a half-opened lotus flower. The papyrus column is a bundle of papyrus stems, with a sculptured capital copied from the feathery head of the plant. The Hathor capital is usually on a polygonal column, or circular in late times, with a head of the goddess on one, or two, or all four sides. In Roman times various complex types with foreign elements were introduced.

The roof was either of wood, brick, or stone. The earlier little shrines were evidently roofed with the same stems which formed the sides. Brick roofing was certainly used largely for houses and tombs, and probably, therefore, for the smaller brick temples. Barrel roofs 6 ft. across were common in the VIth dynasty, and larger ones up to 15 ft. wide in later times. For stone buildings, roofs of stone were naturally used, either of limestone or sandstone like the walls. But so strong was the influence of brick arching that the roofs are often cut out in a curve beneath, while flat above, as at Abydos. The earlier stone roofs are very massive. The limestone slabs on the tombs of the IIIrd dynasty reach the size of $20 \times 8 \times 3\frac{1}{2}$ ft., weighing 33 tons. The granite beams in the great pyramid are at least 21 ft. long, 4 to 5 ft. wide, and about as deep. For greater security, the early roofs were often pointed, and on the cantilever principle; the centre of gravity of the block was over the wall, and it would not tend to fall even if the opposing block were absent. Such blocks sloped from 30° to 40°; and with their great depth, as much as 7 ft., their resistance as beams was enormous. In the pyramids there are generally three layers of such beams, one over the other. The roofing of temples was on a similar scale. Deep stone architraves rested on the columns, and large slabs stretched across the passage and chambers; those which roof the axial passage at Karnak are 28 ft. long.

4. The decoration.—The decoration was the life of an Egyptian temple. At first the walls are severely plain; at Medum there is not a single figure or hieroglyph, even on the funeral stelæ. At the granite temple of Khafra nothing is seen but perfectly smooth granite and alabaster, without even a molding. But in the Vth dynasty the Ra temple of Ra-enuser is as richly sculptured as the tombs of that age. The temple walls of the XIIth dynasty were very finely sculptured, and sometimes richly coloured (see *Koptos* and *Kahun*). In the XVIIIth dynasty the more complete temples enable us to follow the scheme of design. But it is in a quite perfect temple, such as that of Dendereh, that we can see the connexions of the scenes with the use of each part. On the outer screens between the columns is shown the king leaving his palace, followed by his *ka*, and preceded by an incense offerer. Then Horus and Thoth purify him, and the goddesses of south and north bless him. Mentu and Atmu—of Thebes and Heliopolis—bring him before Hathor, the goddess of Dendereh. On entering the hypostyle hall the king is shown sacrificing to the gods of Dendereh; and along the lowest line of the wall are the scenes of the founding of the temple by the king, hoeing the foundation, and presenting the bricks for the building. In the next chamber the king proceeds to worship the gods. And on reaching the sanctuary itself, the king is shown ascending the steps to the shrine, removing the band from the door, breaking the seals on the doors, opening the door, gazing on the goddess, praying to her, censing the sacred barks, and worshipping before the barks. Finally, he presents the image of truth to the goddess. Thus the decoration all has its purpose as an outline of the ceremonies proper to each part of the temple; it is a kind of ritual and rubrics in stone, like the scenes and figures of the early tombs, so that eternally the king should be considered to be performing the divine service in his spiritual person.

Apart from the ritual decoration, there were many details of customary ornament. The palm-leaf cornice we have already noticed. On the screens of stone between the columns, and on the tops of shrines, a cornice of uræi was often placed. Such was originally proper to the judgment-hall, the deadly uræus serpent being the emblem of the right of capital punishment. A favourite combination was the disc of the sun, the uræus in front of it, a vulture's wings at the sides, and ram's horns above it. This represents Ra, in three aspects, as Creator—the ram's horns belonging to Khnumu, the creative rain god; as Preserver—the vulture's wings spread out being the emblem of maternal care; and as Judge or Destroyer—the serpent being the sign of judicial right. Where the disc is shown over a king's head, it is often seen without the serpent, and with the wings drooping to embrace the king, as he is protected but not judged by Ra. Similarly on the roofs of tombs, especially the kings' tombs, there is a painting of vultures, with outspread wings across the passage, along the whole distance, showing the protection given to the soul.

A favourite structural decoration was a dado of papyrus plants along the lower part of walls. This seems to have been used in the Ist dynasty, to judge by the ribbed green tiles; it often appears in later times, and was usual in Ptolemaic and Roman temples. Similarly the ceilings are covered with a dark blue ground, spangled with golden stars. The stars are always five-rayed; and the representation of stars with rays suggests that the ancient Egyptians were short-sighted like the modern, for stars appear only as points of light to long-sighted eyes.

Of minor decoration there is a very ancient form in the figure of a door surrounded by panelling, which became the emblem of the tomb entrance, and is often shown painted below the sacred hawk. The *ka* name of the king is always written above such a doorway. The very elaborate coloured patterns of the panelling on examples in the Old and Middle Kingdoms should be noticed. The small square panels are probably an imitation of a woodwork screen built up of small pieces. Such construction was requisite in so dry a climate, where wood warped and shrank so much, and only small pieces could be trusted to keep their form. The mediæval Arab woodwork met this difficulty in the same way. Another decorative use of wood was in the open-work carving of a pair of lotus leaves tied together, or a group of *dad* signs, which formed a fretwork over the ventilating holes in the screens. Similarly stiff bracing of woodwork was inserted to steady the framing of chairs and tables by fretwork groups of hieroglyphs, as the girdle tie of Isis, the *dad*, the *ankh*, and other signs. Such furniture work passed on into stone decoration of wall surfaces. Vegetable decoration had a great part in Egyptian life. Every festivity, every sociality, was a field for floral ornament with wreaths, garlands, and streamers of convolvulus; every water-jar had flowers over it and round it, and every group of offerings on an altar was heaped with flowers. Hence wreaths became a customary decoration on surface carvings and paintings. Also a favourite ceiling design was a vine trellis; and along the beams purple bunches of grapes hung down, made in glazed pottery.

5. The furniture.—The furniture of the temples is frequently represented. The central object of devotion was the sacred bark. This was a boat about 8 ft. in length (*Koptos*, xix.), fastened down to a framework of poles by rope ties (*Temple of Kings*, vi.). This framework was put upon the shoulders of the priests for carrying it in procession; as many as twelve to twenty priests are represented, each probably carrying a burden of half a hundredweight. To set down this bark a high stand was needed. This was sometimes of wood, a sort of square box with decorated panels (*Temple of Kings*, iii.-vi.), or a block of granite, like one in the British Museum with figures of six gods around it (see illustration in ART [Egyptian]). Upon the bark there stood a canopy or catafalque of slender wooden pillars and a springy top of board; and from this was suspended the square shrine of the god, hung by ropes, and kept from swaying by guide ties at the bottom. The detail of the structure is shown in a working drawing on papyrus. This shrine was elaborately carved and decorated, and was almost always half-swathed in a linen wrapper. Fore and aft of the shrine were statuettes of the king and of various gods, adoring the divinity. At each end of the bark was a figure-head, and a great engraved collar of metal hanging below it. Some shrines had a winged figure of Maat, the goddess of truth, at each end, embracing the shrine with her wings. Such seems to be the prototype of the winged cherubs on the Jewish ark. Of other furniture there were the standards of the gods upon long poles, which were carried in procession, as well as the stands for holding the libation jars and other vases used in the ceremonies; the framed wooden stands for water-jars hung round with garlands; and the tall trumpet-shaped stands of pottery or metal for holding jars. In the papyrus of Ramessu III. are named the tables of gold, silver, and bronze, the collars and ornaments for decorating the statues on the festivals, and a great balance plated with electrum. The buildings and chambers which now seem so bare and blank were radiant with plated tables and stands, glittering with precious vases of gold and silver, and bright with garlands of flowers.

6. The popular shrines.—These shrines were scattered all over the country by the waysides, doubtless like the modern Muhammadan *wely*. Such local worship is directly contrary to Islām, and must, therefore, have persisted from earlier times, like so many other customs. There still exist models of these shrines of Roman ages, which were used for domestic worship in the house. They are shown as small chambers crowned with a pediment, supported by six columns—three on each side—which were connected by lattice screens; or as an arched roof carried on four columns, with a dwarf wall joining them; or as a small domed chamber with a doorway, exactly like a modern *wely*. The shrine in the house was a framed wooden cupboard surmounted by a pillared recess, covered with a cornice of uræi; inside this recess a lamp burned before the figure of the god.

W. M. FLINDERS PETRIE.

ARCHITECTURE (Greek).—The subject of Greek architecture is one that has been curiously neglected in this country, and the student finds himself beset by an insufficiency of data and an atmosphere of uncertainty immediately he enters upon the study. This accounts for the vagueness and incompleteness of what little has been written upon the question. It is therefore especially necessary in dealing with the subject of origins to be upon one's guard against certain popular fallacies, particularly when those origins are lost in the obscurity of a remote antiquity. A mere resemblance between two forms is absolutely no evidence that one is derived from the other, and nothing is more harmful to true knowledge than the shallow kind of art criticism that makes such an assumption without a very careful weighing of the evidence. Art is in its essence creative, and, in a great art, even when it does borrow, the important element is always not what it takes, but what it gives of itself. At the same time, the higher the art the more subtle it is, and consequently by the inartistic observer the primitive borrowed element is absurdly over-emphasized.

A familiar parallel is seen in the case of faces. The shallow observer is always noticing 'likenesses'; the artist notes differences. The stranger notices the 'likeness' among members of a family; those who really know the faces note the differences. Twins at first sight are often almost indistinguishable; later, as knowledge grows, we wonder that we ever noted any marked resemblance. (An excellent instance of this is seen on p. 715b.)

The architecture of Greece, the most refined, the most subtle, and in some respects the most artistic, that the world has seen, is pre-eminently the natural architectural expression of the gifted race that produced it. The Hellenic peoples were marked by extraordinary individuality and independence in a most unusual degree, and therefore, except where there is real evidence, it is not unreasonable to give them credit for invention, when the forms are such as might be developed from the simplest elements by any people of intelligence; and it is unnecessary to seek for far-fetched resemblances to bolster up improbable theories. At the same time, of course, due weight must be given to the conditions of previous and contemporary art, whose influences doubtless made themselves felt.

Of these influences three possible sources may be briefly noted—Egypt, Assyria, and the Ægean civilizations. In each case the most striking fact is the extreme difference in purpose, sentiment, treatment, and detail that distinguishes them from Greek architecture.

(1) The earlier periods of architecture in *Egypt*—of pyramids and tombs—hardly need be considered; partly because they belong to a time that had long since ceased to exercise any influence in Egypt itself, partly because they are entirely foreign in intention to anything built by the Greeks, who were never a race of tomb builders at all. Of the later Egyptian architecture, of the Theban period, it may be said that it was erected with more definitely religious intent than was that of Greece. The artists were, to some extent at least, under the thumb of a priestly caste, and although art itself is in essence free, the purposes of the buildings naturally influence to a certain degree the channels in which it moves. The effects after which the Egyptian artist strove were mainly internal rather than external. Throughout, the artistic motive is immensity and suggestion, as contrasted with the special grandeur of Greek art, which expresses itself in reserve, refinement, and grace. Like the Greek style, it is trabeated, but as this is the first and most obvious method that occurs to every builder, it certainly does not necessarily constitute an 'influence.' The stone construction is also a little too obvious an expedient to be interpreted as a sign of influence, and there remains the frequent use of columns as the only resemblance. But these are of so essentially different a character, and their gradual development in Greece is so easily explained, that there is no need to make reference to Egyptian practice at all.

(2) *Assyrian* architecture offers even less resemblance. It was of brick construction, a non-trabeated style, characterized by the arch or the vault. It was primarily secular, and neither tombs nor temples played any important part, but, as far as remains attest, the architectural spirit expressed itself in palaces. The ornamental detail in some ways resembles that of Egypt, and it is here that Greek work seems to have certain affinities, although probably not more than can be accounted for by a perfectly natural process of development or suggestion from pre-historic work in Greek lands.

It may, however, be noted that the influence of minor ornament is always more wide-spread than that of major forms, from the fact of its occurring upon more portable objects. But it is a *petitio principii* to assume that the influence passed from Assyria to the Ægean any more than *vice versa*. The probabilities are rather that there was a certain amount of interaction between the early Ægean, Assyria, and Egypt.

In the case of *Persian* architecture, which may at earliest be said to date from B.C. 558, although again entirely different in general intention from Greek architecture, there are certain minor features of detail which offer slight resemblances, particularly in the columns. But as the styles are contemporary—a fact invariably overlooked—it seems at least conceivable that we should assume a certain amount of interaction rather than definitely assert that the less original and less artistic race alone exerted influence. The great hall at Persepolis may be dated *c.* 485 B.C. Therefore, to suppose that it can have had any influence upon Greek Ionic architecture is absurd. The temple of Ephesus, for instance, whose perfect Ionic capitals can be seen in the British Museum, dates from the time of Crœsus, whose empire *ended* B.C. 546. The influence is almost certainly that of Greece upon Persia, and not the other way.

(3) In the third place, there are the great *Ægean civilizations*, of which little or nothing was known a generation ago, and of which our knowledge increases daily. Here on Greek soil most probably may be sought those influences which earlier writers have endeavoured to find in the afore-mentioned countries. Original as the Ægean work undoubtedly is, it is not to be understood that it was entirely untouched by the neighbouring art of Egypt. The most original art may adapt to its own purposes ingredients borrowed from its contemporaries, or even from the past, although this latter is a sign of a fully developed art—one, if it may so be phrased, that has become distinctly self-conscious. But the point to be noticed is that any Egyptian influence coming through such a channel to Greek art can, in any case, be only indirect.

Here again, in the case of Ægean architecture, the entire spirit of the styles, which are those of palaces and tombs, and not the work of temple-building peoples at all, allows at most of a limited range of influence. The wholly different art character of the two peoples, if we may group the Ægean peoples as one and the Greeks as another, is, however, a far more fundamental line of cleavage. The earlier art is more luxurious and less restrained. It is less structural in its character, depending more for its effect upon applied surface ornament. Further, the earlier art seems to have been less definitely intellectual, and expressed itself largely by an arbitrary symbolism, whereas the Greek, even when rudimentary, is marked by an attempt at a rational and self-explanatory embodiment of its content—a characteristic that grows more obvious as Greek art reaches its prime.

There may, however, be a real though limited amount of influence in the case of Ægean art, even though such influence be denied to Egypt and the East. A point of architectural significance may be found in a method of building which inclines to the use of stone for the lower part of the work and of lighter sun-dried brick or rubble above, faced either with stucco or a veneer of ornamental stone. This method is characteristic of certain Ægean work, and seems actually to have been used by the Hellenes in early work, as, for instance, in the temple of Hera at Olympia. This, therefore, does point to an early dependence; but it is soon thrown off. The *orthostatai*, or facing-blocks, at the foot of the wall in later Greek work may point to this origin (p. 679, fig. 1). It has been suggested that the very plan of the Greek temple itself is derived from the megaron in a chief's house, as at Tiryns (p. 680, fig. 8). The plan of the Hera temple shows a very great advance upon this, which must have taken a considerable time to effect, implying several earlier stages. The temple has been dated as early as B.C. 1100, in which case it becomes doubtful whether it should be considered as originally an early Greek temple, or a late Ægean building, adopted and gradually altered to the Doric style. The remains certainly show gradual and continual alterations, whatever may be the explanation of them.

There are, however, questions of great import in this connexion. The Greek races as a whole, and the greatest of them all in particular, namely the Athenians, were in all probability a mixed race, descended partly from an Ægean stock (probably non-Aryan) and an Aryan-speaking people coming from the North. Therefore, although we cannot point to distinct borrowings and definite features, directly inherited from the indigenous stock, which for convenience is here called 'Ægean,' nevertheless it was the spirit of the Ægean peoples, combined with that of the Northern incomer, that produced the true Hellenic architecture. It may even be hazarded as a suggestion that the ultimate decadence of Greek work was due to the gradual re-assertion of the indigenous stock over that of the incomer, and that the glories of what we might term the crossed fruit ultimately succumbed to the characteristics of the original wild crab. In that case the decadence is not a simple decadence, such as we may trace in the history of the art of coinage in Northern Europe, from the stater of Philip of Macedon to the BODVOC coins of Britain, but the re-assertion of an older, more ornate, and less restrained style. If, as seems most likely, we are to regard Byzantine Greek work as the true descendant of Greek art, this view receives a certain amount of additional confirmation. [An account of Ægean architecture will be found elsewhere (see p. 677 ff.)].

Of Hellenic architecture it may be remarked that it was a stone-built trabeated columnar style. It would be incorrect to say that its buildings were predominantly religious, although religious architecture played an important, perhaps the leading, part. It must always be remembered that a religious building is the most likely to survive, partly from the natural conservatism of religion and religious veneration, partly as belonging to a corporate body in contrast to all private property. We should always, therefore, expect, even in the case of an age where the building activity was evenly distributed, that remains of religious buildings would be the most numerous, of other public corporations next, and of domestic buildings last. The greater resources of a corporation, whether religious or otherwise, tend to a greater scale and possibility of survival; and, comparing religious and other public buildings, there is always the greater need for alteration and change in the case of the latter. Even the change from one religion to another, as in the case of St. Sophia, the Pantheon, or the Parthenon, is of itself only a partially destructive tendency, and indeed to this we owe the preservation of many buildings that would otherwise have been destroyed. An interesting case in point is the small temple of the Ilissus, which survived changes of religion for 2000 years; yet directly the ægis of religion was withdrawn the temple disappeared.

The same is true of Gothic architecture, and it is a mistake for the student to assume, as is frequently done, that the predominating character of an architecture is religious, or that it owes its features and style to religious influences, simply because such remains are the most numerous. The greatness of scale in so many religious buildings doubtless had its results in influencing other buildings, but this is only one factor among many. In the case of Athens itself the Stoa Basileios, the Stoa Eleutherios, the Stoa Poikile, the Bouleuterion, and the Prytaneum (see footnote, p. 677) must have ranked with the greatest religious buildings, and the greatest conception of all that has come down to us, judged from the purely architectural standpoint, is the Propylæa, which can hardly be classed as a religious building, actually having come into direct conflict with the religion of the day.

Greek architecture is generally considered as divided into three 'orders'—the Doric, the Ionic, and the Corinthian—which are variations in the arrangement or order of the essential constituents. These constituent parts, the stylobate, the column, and the entablature, are found in all three orders.

With regard to the temples, at any rate, it may be said that every building rested upon a platform or stylobate, generally of three steps. In this it may be distinguished from all other styles, where, although a base-mold or plinth may be found, nothing of this nature occurs. Upon this, as its name implies, stood the columns, and these in their turn supported the entablature or stone lintel which is the main characteristic of the style. This lintel, or trabeated, construction was used, not because the Greeks were unacquainted with the arch: apparently they deliberately rejected it upon æsthetic grounds. They knew of the arch in the East, and quite early made use of it occasionally for purely structural purposes, as in the case of a water-drain at Athens, a barrel-vault at Sicyon, the passage to the stadion at Olympia, an arch in Acarnania, and in the lower storey of a stoa at Alinda. It is not altogether improbable that the Tholos at Athens was covered by a small dome. The arches of the Ægean period are not, as a rule, built with radiating voussoirs, although an example occurs in Arcadia. The arch principle is really involved at Tiryns, perhaps unconsciously, but it is not truly the corbelled system. One may suggest that the reason is to be sought in the Greek type of mind, as it expresses itself both in religion and art, partly in its sense of reserve, the *μηδὲν ἄγαν* of the temple at Delphi, partly in its tendency to seek the highest in a completed and finished perfection that does not lead out beyond itself. Hence it is more readily satisfied in the rectangular self-contained composition of Greek architecture than in a style involving the distribution of thrusts and the æsthetic incompleteness of the line of the arch. This became one of the most expressive features of the essentially suggestive, rather than perfected or finished, mediæval style.

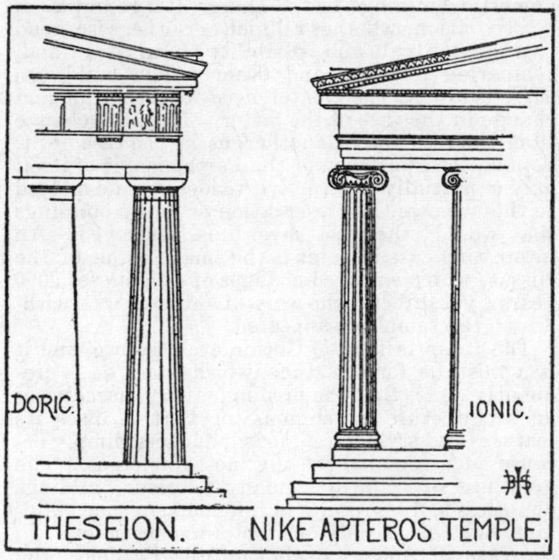

FIG. 1.

The further major divisions of the order may be tabulated as follows :—

- Order
  - Entablature
    - Cornice
      - Cymatium
      - Corona
      - Bed-mold
    - Frieze . . . .
    - Architrave . . . .
  - Column
    - Capital
      - Abacus
      - Ovolo
      - Neck
    - Shaft (including apophyges)
    - Base
      - Base moldings
      - (Plinth)
  - Stylobate or Crepis (the former is strictly applicable only to the top step).

1. The **Doric order** has generally been considered the oldest; but there is no adequate reason for supposing so, although it is not unlikely. The pre-Persic remains from the Acropolis of Athens and the temples at Ephesus and Samos, Neandria and Naucratis, show Ionic work of very remote date. Indeed, one might even suppose that they are cognate developments from a common beginning, rather than that the one is derived from the other or is a later invention. The Doric order is marked by somewhat massive proportions; for instance, the columns of the temple at Corinth are 4·47 diameters, and those of the Parthenon, 34 ft. high, are 6·025 diameters. The entablature is similarly heavy in proportion to the whole.

The Doric column consists of a shaft and capital only; there is no base. It is conceivable that there was originally a plain square base, and that a series of these have coalesced to form the top step of the stylobate. The early columns at Corinth (*c.* 650 B.C.) are monoliths, but in other cases the columns are built up in drums, fitted together with the most marvellous accuracy. The shafts are invariably fluted, with a sharp arris between the flutes (fig. 2). These flutes are generally 20 in number, but other numbers are not so rare as is commonly supposed. Thus :—

8 Flutes,	Trœzen.
8 ,,	Bolumnos.
12 ,,	Assos.
16 ,,	Sounion.
16 ,,	Ægina.
16 ,,	Shaft found at Olympia, probably Young Geloans' Porch.
16 ,,	A shaft of the Heræum.
18 ,,	Pronaos of Assos Temple.
20 ,,	Megarian's treasury at Olympia, but only 11 facets fluted: the remainder at the back are flat.
24 Flutes,	Temple of Poseidon at Pæstum.
25 ,,	Isolated column *in situ* at Assos.
28 ,,	Fallen fragment at Ephesus.
32 ,,	Two drums from Samos.
32 ,,	Epidaurian's house at Olympia (every alternate corner has a bead instead of a sharp arris).
44	Naxian's treasury at Delphi.

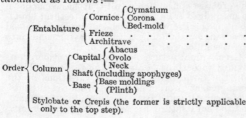

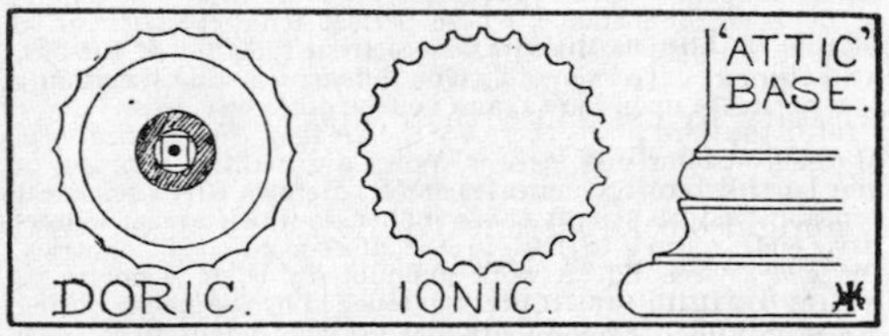

FIG. 2.

The flutes are probably a perfectly natural development from the square pillar—a form not unknown in Ægean art—and, moreover, the anta in Greek work is square in section to the last. At first the corners would be cut, giving an octagon, as at Trœzen, then these would again be cut, giving sixteen sides. This would be done, doubtless partly for utilitarian reasons, so as to admit more light and give easy ingress and egress. But that the main reason was æsthetic is shown, in the first place, by the fact that the columns never became plain circles, and, in the second place, by the fluting or hollowing out of the sides of the polygon. These greatly accentuate the effect, and thereby give æsthetic emphasis to the verticality of the column, emphasizing the outline of the column, and making it tell, whether against a very dark or a very light background. The suggestion that it was derived from Egypt may be dismissed as fanciful, as the supposed prototypes at Beni Hassan belong to an age too remote to have had any influence. The primitive artist is not an eclectic archæologist. In the second place, the Beni Hassan columns are not fluted, but flat-sided. The flute, on the whole, points to a stone rather than a wooden origin, as it seems pretty clearly to be derived from a square, and not from the round posts of a primitive wooden style. Other Egyptian polygonal types are even less likely.

The capital is composed of three parts. The abacus is a square flat block that takes the bearing of the architrave. Below this is the echinos or capital itself—a bold molded member eminently suggestive of powerful support. Below this are three fillets to emphasize the neck. This gently curves into the shaft by means of the apophyges, and at the top of the shaft, immediately below the apophyges, are three sinkings which prepare the eye, as it ascends, for the change from the vertical lines of the shaft to the horizontal lines of the capital.

The entablature is divided into three portions—the architrave or lintel proper, the frieze and the

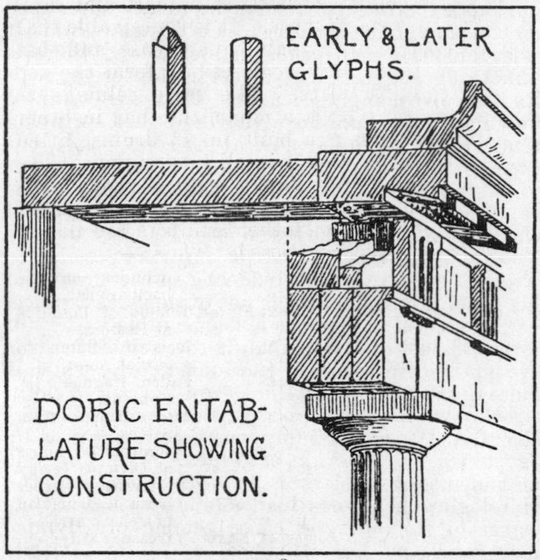

FIG. 3.

cornice. The architrave is quite plain—a single solid block. In very large examples it may be necessary to use more than one block, but they are placed on their edges so as to present a single face to the front. The frieze is divided into spaces by upright blocks of stone (triglyphs) which support the real weight—a fact æsthetically emphasized by the upright channelling that gives them their name. These three glyphs, or channels, are arranged with two complete in the middle and one half on either side. The early form of the glyph seems to have been nearly round-headed (fig. 3).

The spaces between are filled with slabs which do not support anything. These are termed metopes. The metŏpē (*i.e.* the thing behind, or after, or at the back of the ope; cf. *μετάφρενον*) is the slab that goes behind the ope, hole or opening, in the frieze (fig. 3). This does perhaps imply that the interval was originally open. In a cella wall this would give light to the building (*ὀπή* in later writers means a window). In a peristyle it would become useless; and the introduction of the peristyle may have done away with the custom.

It does not throw much light on the beam-end theory, as the opening would be there in any case; but the method of fitting invariably used—which is to put the slab at the back of the hole—and the name—which does not mean 'between the triglyphs' but 'behind the opening'—if they point any way at all, suggest that the metope was always fitted as we find it, at the back of or behind the opening (fig. 3), which would not be possible if there were beam-ends. In rich examples the metopes are sculptured, particularly at the end of the building.

The cornice moldings need not be enumerated, but it might be observed that the uppermost member, the cymatium, is generally very similar to the ovolo molding of the echinos of the capital. This molding is carried up over the pediment at the ends of the building, and the corona or flat member beneath it is repeated, occurring once over the triglyph frieze, and once, with slight modifications, under the cymatium of the pediment.

The Doric order is the most severe and refined of the Greek orders, and this characteristic enables it the better to act as the frame of the glorious sculpture with which it was adorned. The tympanum, or triangular space in the pediment or gable, was generally filled with free sculpture, and some or all of the metopes were occupied by sculpture in very high relief. In rich examples, as, for instance, in the Parthenon, it would seem to have been permissible to introduce sculpture elsewhere.

In that example the famous Panathenaïc frieze runs round the upper part of the cella, within the outer range of columns.

It is generally said that sculpture is a speciality of the Doric order, and is not found in Ionic, but for absolutely no reason. The Erechtheum, the temple of Athene Nike Apteros, the temple of the Ilissus, the great temples of Artemis at Ephesus, the temple of Aphrodite at Aphrodisias, the Mausoleum, and the Ionic order in the interior of Phigalia, were all richly decorated with sculpture.

2. The Ionic order is marked by several important characteristics. In the first place, it is a lighter style; its columns are of more slender proportions and more widely spaced. At the same time it should be noted that, in proportion to the weight that they carry in the lighter entablature, they are no lighter than the Doric. It is less severe, and in any hands but those of the Greeks might have become over-ornate. The columns have bases which show very considerable variety in their moldings. The so-called Attic base is not a widespread form, occurring only in a single instance in the north porch of the Erechtheum and not elsewhere even in that building (fig. 2). The Corinthian example of the monument of Lysicrates is, however, but slightly different. The influence of this base upon the architecture of the world was extraordinary, but not more than its extreme simplicity and great beauty justify (p. 713, fig. 47, and context). The original form of Ionic base seems to have been a torus molding above a sort of plinth with several astragals. The scotia below the torus was first introduced, and then the second torus below.

The flutings are generally 24 in number, and much deeper than the Doric. They are separated by a fillet in place of the sharp arris, which gives a very different effect to the column (fig. 2). In early examples the flutings were more numerous—40 at Naucratis, 40 at Ephesus, 44 on a votive column at Delphi. The sharp arris is also found in these early instances. The capital is lighter and the most distinctive feature of the order. It may be described as resembling a scroll upon two rollers, which form the well-known Ionic volutes. There is a very small circular abacus which has ornamental carving. The head of the capital, the echinos, immediately below and between the volutes, is also carved, and sometimes, as in the Erechtheum, the neck also is richly decorated.

There seem to have been two early forms of the Ionic capital, that which may perhaps be termed Æolic and the Ionic form proper (Neandria and Heræum, fig. 4). It may also be noted that the egg and dart of the small echinos of the Ionic capital tend to diminish and become pushed up into the volute part of the capital. It is quite possible that this part is really the descendant of free overhanging leaves in an earlier form (fig. 4, Delphi). The architrave is not simple but divided into three facias, each slightly projecting over the one below (fig. 1). The frieze is a continuous band unbroken by triglyphs and frequently sculptured. The cornice is more elaborate than the Doric, and the lowermost mem-

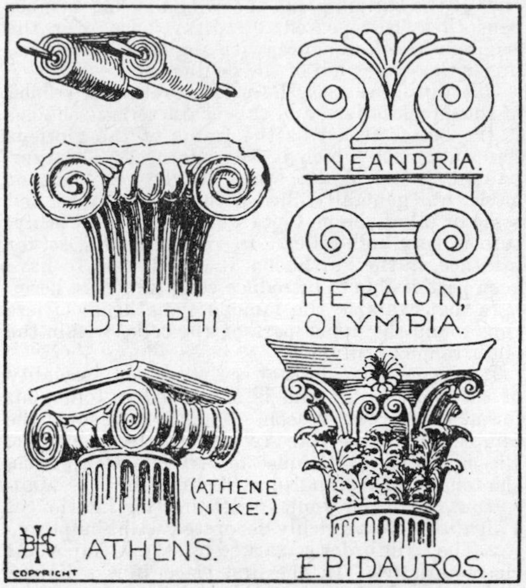

FIG. 4.

ber, as found in Asiatic examples, and afterwards borrowed in the Corinthian order, is very distinctive. This is the dentil band, which may be described as a series of small blocks set below the cornice, giving the appearance of a square serration. The uppermost member of the cornice is almost invariably the molding known as the cyma recta (fig. 9). On the whole it may be said that the Ionic style is less robust than the Doric, and depends more upon architectural ornament.

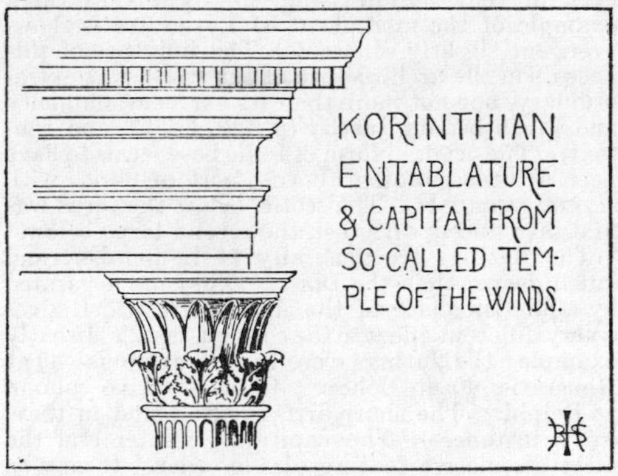

FIG. 5.

3. The **Corinthian order** is practically only the Ionic with a different capital. We are told by Vitruvius that Callimachus saw an acanthus plant at Bassæ near Phigalia, which had twined itself about a basket of sepulchral offerings, and that this suggested the idea of the Corinthian capital. A single capital of this type occurred at the S. end of the main chamber of the temple of Apollo at Phigalia, all the other capitals being of a peculiar Ionic type. This temple was built as a thank-offering for immunity during a great plague in either B.C. 430 or 420. It might even be hazarded as a suggestion that Callimachus was associated with the architect Ictinus in this case, just as Phidias was in the case of the Parthenon. The ultra-restlessness of the design of the frieze, and an almost over-elaborate treatment of the drapery, carried out though it may have been by Peloponnesian workmen, would point to the influence of an extreme Attic tendency, such as we would associate with Callimachus rather than with Phidias and his school. That Ictinus, the most famous Athenian architect, built the temple, and Phidias himself made the temple image, suggests some famous Athenian designing the sculptural decorations.

It is fairly clear that the Corinthian capital was an individual invention, as it suddenly appears complete, late in the history of Greek architecture. What more likely then than that in this single central capital, among a set of another kind, we have the original itself? This is strengthened by the fact that at Phigalia we also get the first departure from the true Ionic capital, showing obvious experimental tendencies in new directions on the part of the architect. Callimachus himself was famous as a worker in metal, and there is something suggestive of metal in the design, with its free overhanging leaves. That the inventor may have been familiar with the upward springing tendency of Egyptian capitals is conceivable, but to suggest an Egyptian origin is merely to go out of one's way to find things utterly unlike. The capitals of the Horologium, or so-called 'Temple of the Winds' (fig. 5), have the lotus leaf, but so have those at Persepolis. Vitruvius may very possibly be wrong, but to reject his evidence on the ground of his general unreliability is not of much assistance.

The capital is found in a considerable variety of forms, almost always including some small tendrils or spirals, totally unlike the Ionic volute, which is more of the nature of a thick scroll, or roll of cloth. Greek examples are not very common. Besides Phigalia, Pausanias informs us that it was used by Scopas in the interior of Tegea. The Choragic monument of Lysicrates is Corinthian, and the Horologium has Corinthian columns with acanthus leaves of Roman type. The temple of Olympic Zeus and the Corinthian Stoa, all in Athens, are other instances. A beautiful and somewhat peculiar example exists from the lesser Propylæa at Eleusis. The temple of Apollo Didymæus at Miletus shows fine examples, and there is an archaic Corinthian capital of uncertain date also found at Branchidæ near Miletus. But the loveliest of all Corinthian capitals are those of the Tholos at Epidaurus, obviously fairly early in date, and, with all their richness, marked by the chasteness and refinement of Greek work. The Corinthian order became the favourite of the Romans, and these subtle restrained delicacies were lost. It may be noted that in Greek work the acanthus leaf is worked with a crisp sharp edge, which becomes blunt and rounded in Roman hands (fig. 6).

This slight survey of the general characteristics of the orders prepares the way for the consideration of the commonly accepted theory of the wooden origin of Greek architecture. It is generally said that the Doric order is of unmistakably wooden origin, although it may be more doubtful in the case of Ionic. The grounds for suggesting this are the triglyphs, which are supposed to represent the beam ends, and the upward slope of the mutules, which represent the ends of the rafters. These features do not occur in the Ionic order.

In the first place, the general similarity in the main essentials of the two orders is far too marked for the principal source of origin and inspiration not to be the same. At the same time there are probably different contributory influences.

The stylobate can hardly be claimed as anything but a stone feature, even though the upper part were timber. In Doric architecture, as contrasted with Ionic, the columns have no base, and the base is one of the supposed signs of a wooden origin, either representing a metal shoe to prevent splitting—a feature hardly consonant with a primitive style—or a flat stone laid on the ground to distribute the weight. However, it might be remarked that the distribution of weight is æsthetically demanded in any case by the slender Ionic column. The massive Doric column requires no base, and if it ever had one, it was early seen to be unnecessary. Its proportions are obviously those of stone, as are the narrow intercolumniations. The more slender Ionic with its considerably longer lintel has a closer resemblance to wooden proportions. It should further be noticed that the oldest Doric columns are the most massive, and most obviously the outcome of their stone material. The tendency of development from a wooden origin would naturally be in the reverse direction. Pausanias says that one of the columns of the Heræum at Olympia was of oak. It has been suggested that this was the last of the original wooden set, which were gradually replaced. There are, however, difficulties with regard to the entablature, which would not fit equally well upon a set of stone Doric columns of more or less normal proportions and upon wooden ones. Nevertheless it is conceivable, and the intercolumniations are certainly wider than usual.

The heavy Doric abacus projecting on all four sides is also obviously of stone; a wooden one would split off. To some extent the same might be said of the echinos, but its whole shape is essentially non-wooden.

In the Ionic capital, however, we find proportions that are not square and that would be eminently adapted to wood. The grain of the wood would run parallel with the line of the architrave. The spreading support is obtained, and at the same time the capital does not overhang at the front or the back, so there would be no danger of splitting off. Again, the spirals are a natural primitive incised ornament, equally applicable to stone and wood, although their final form is more suited to stone. Early incised and painted capitals have been found on the Acropolis of Athens. The Doric echinos, however, though subtle in its curvature, is a natural primitive stone form, claiming kinship with such a form as the rude primitive cushion capital of the Normans (fig. 37, p. 710).

It is just possible that the different fluting points the same way. A polygon when fluted can give only a sharp arris. It is a natural and simple expedient, in borrowing the idea of fluting from the stone Doric form and applying it to the circular form, to leave the plain fillet which we find in Ionic work. The surfaces of the fillets are on the circumference of a circle and are not flat. The circular form is the natural shape of the tree-trunk; the polygonal form is the natural development from the square block of quarried stone.

But it is in the Doric entablature that the wooden origin is supposed to be most conspicuous. The general proportions, which may be contrasted with the light entablature of the Ionic, are certainly true stone proportions as we find them. The massive architrave in a single block certainly does not suggest anything but the stone block which it is, whatever may be said for the three facias of Ionic work.

The triglyph frieze is generally said to represent the ends of the beams, and it is suggested that the guttæ represent the heads of the pins. What the regulæ are, from which the guttæ depend, is gracefully omitted from the theory. Now, in the first place, the actual position of the guttæ suggesting a vertical pin is quite impossible as at δ (fig. 6); but even if we try a diagonal position such as at γ (fig. 6), the pin would be absolutely useless, as it would draw, and this is really equally impossible. A pin might be placed at α or a huge pin directly underneath at β, but in neither place are the guttæ found. A true artist may have had the guttæ suggested to his mind by pin-heads, and then created a genuine stone feature, but that has nothing to

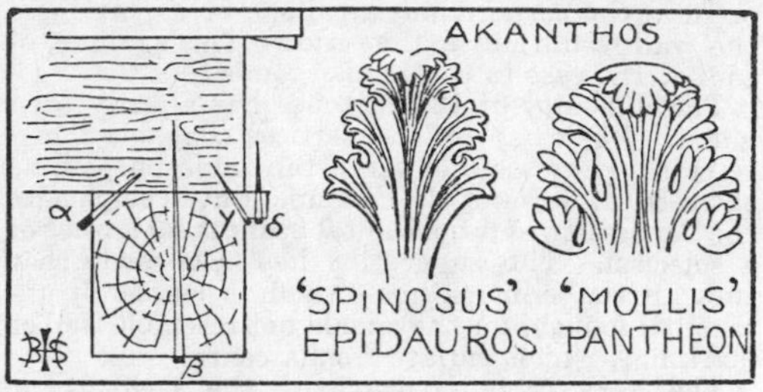

FIG. 6.

do with a wooden origin for architecture, any more than the acanthus leaf implies a haystack as an architectural prototype. The raindrops may equally well have suggested the idea and have spontaneously suggested rain-drops to children, who did not know the meaning of the word *gutta*.

But the most serious objection to the pin theory is that *guttæ* are not found in early work. They do not occur in the Bouleuterion at Olympia or the Selinuntine treasury, or in the newer, but still early, porch of the Geloans. They are not found at Assos or in the early Athenian fragments, or in the temple of Demeter at Pæstum.

With regard to the triglyphs, they are in the first place needlessly enormous for any ceiling joists. They might be the right scale for tie beams, but they are then placed at impossibly close intervals. The dentils of the Ionic order would in many examples, although most of them late, approximate more nearly to a reasonable scantling. But the most pertinent question to ask is how one could have beam ends all round the building at the same level—which is a hopeless impossibility. Now, in the case of the Lycian tombs at Xanthos (fig. 7), where we have actual copies of timber work in stone, we see, of course, where ends and sides of the building are visible, that the ends of the beams show only at the sides of the building. We also get a feature resembling purlin ends under the gable roof. It should be noticed that where we find timber construction reproduced in stone, as at

FIG. 7.

Xanthos, Beni Hassan (Egypt), or Naksh-i-Rustam (Persia), it is in no case a building, but simply a representation carved out of the solid, and is entirely non-structural. It is, in short, merely a pictorial representation. Every material demands its own methods of construction, and this is perhaps particularly necessary in days of early development. Further, if they were beam ends, they would not occur at the corners, but a metope or a portion of the wall would finish the series. This again is, of course, the case in the Lycian tombs.

The difficulty of the metopes has already been noted. But what are the vertical channels themselves? They seem to serve the same purpose as the vertical flutes of the column. But to emphasize the verticality of a horizontal beam is somewhat of a solecism. The suggestion has been made that they are timber markings—which is not merely untrue but foolish, for they could not resemble timber markings, which radiate from a centre.

The very early treasury of the Geloans at Olympia is so early that it is not even Doric in character, but it is undoubtedly stone; and if its influence may be considered at all, it points in this direction. Although probably of the 7th or 6th cent., it may be set against the supposed original wooden Heræum. In several features, particularly its stylobate, its columns,* and its characteristic waterspouts, it anticipates Greek work of a later date. It might further be noted that the dentil band in Ionic work, which may possibly represent beam ends, is above the frieze, whereas the beams of the coffered ceilings in Doric work are above the frieze, making triglyphs as beam ends impossible.

The construction of the triglyph frieze, with rebated uprights and slabs behind, is found in the dado or frieze discovered at Knossos (fig. 15, p. 682). There it was obviously a stone construction from the outset, and was applied to the face of the wall. This is quite a conceivable origin for the triglyphs.

In early examples the triglyph and metope are frequently worked in one piece, as in several of the treasuries at Olympia. This is also found in many of the stones of Libon's temple of Zeus (also at Olympia), and was the case on the sides of the Athenian Hekatompedon. This of itself is enough to constitute a fatal objection to the whole theory.

The slope of the under side of the mutules would not coincide with the slope of rafters, and (like that of the under slope of the cornice itself) is sufficiently explained as a slope to throw off the rain and pre-

FIG. 8.

vent its running under and down the face of the frieze. This device is common in stone architecture of all styles. It occurs even in string courses of Gothic moldings. The mutules above and the regulæ below the triglyphs are a delightful way of softening the effect of these members and also of providing for the eye an æsthetic support or introduction to the frieze and cornice respectively. They correspond to the corbel tables of Gothic architecture, which are more æsthetic than structural.

It should be noticed that Greek doors are narrower at the top than at the bottom (fig. 8). This is obviously to reduce the interspace for the stone lintel, and would be quite pointless in a wooden construction. Even as it is the lintels have often cracked. The exquisitely beautiful doorway of the Erechtheum had to be repaired in classical times.

Perhaps then it may be said that we have in Greek architecture the work of a stone-building people, modified in the East by a wooden type of work resulting in the Ionic style, and perhaps slightly affected in Greece itself by a mixed style of stone and wood. To some extent the two materials have always been used together: doors, ceilings, and roofs tend to be of wood in a stone building, and door-sills and hearths of stone in a wooden one. In any case it is the remarkable adaptability of every detail to the stone material in the perfected style, and the inevitableness of Greek architecture, that give it its charm.

Greek architectural ornament consisted in the first place of sculpture, either free, as in the case of the pedimental sculptures in the tympana, and the *akroteria* (figures placed on the summit of the pediment, and on little platforms at the lower extremities and standing out against the sky), or in reliefs, as in the case of the metopes and friezes. Sculpture also occurs upon the lowest drum of the column, as in both the archaic and later temples at Ephesus. Figures in the round are used as supports, as in the Telemones at Agrigentum or the Caryatids of the Erechtheum or at Delphi. In the second place, there are the exquisite moldings, which seem to be entirely original, and in any case the actual refinement in the forms used has no parallel in any other architecture in the world. The most important are the ovolo, *e.g.* in Doric capitals; the cyma recta, *e.g.* in the capital of the Doric anta; the cyma reversa, or ogee, used in string moldings; the torus, *e.g.* in the Ionic base; the scotia, a large hollow of double curvature, also found as a base molding; the fillet, a small projecting square-edged mold; and the astragal, a small projecting round molding; this when sunk is termed a bead (fig. 9).

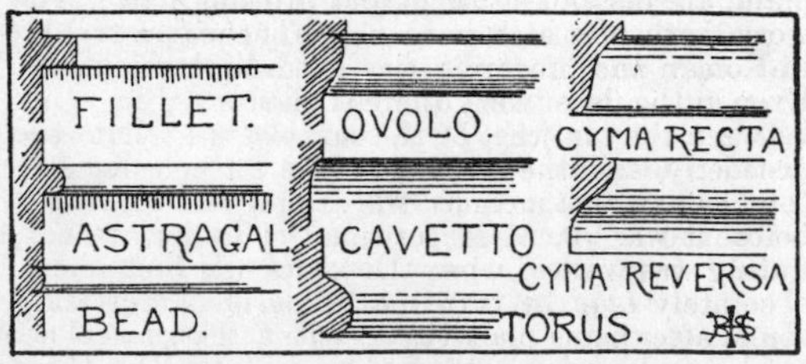

FIG. 9.

A remarkable quality of Greek ornament is the adaptation of the surface decoration to the molding which it enriches. The outline of the ornament tends to be the same as the section of the molding; thus the egg ornament is found on the ovolo, the honeysuckle ornament on the cyma recta, the water leaf on the cyma reversa, and the guilloche on the torus (fig. 10).

In the third place, the Greek architects made use of colour, as for instance on the echinos molding of the Doric capital, and traces of it are not infrequent in many places. It is possible that more

* There is some doubt about the assignment to this building of a column found at Olympia.

was used than would be pleasing to a modern eye, particularly in cases where marble stucco was

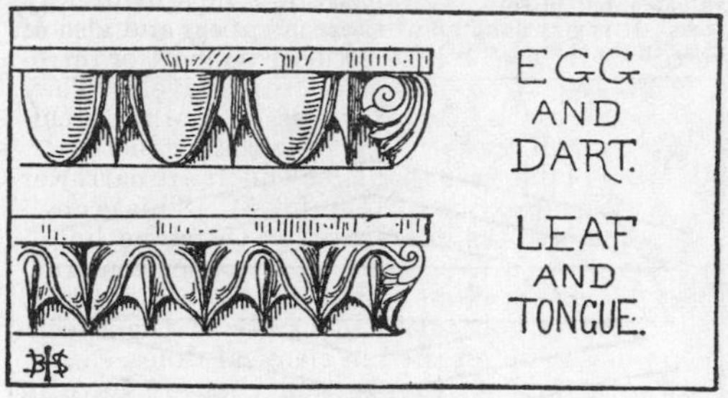

FIG. 10.

applied to some inferior quality of stone such as poros. But we are not to imagine that the Greeks were not keenly alive to the beauty of their exquisite Parian, Pentelic, and other marbles, and the major portions of the surface of the buildings remained without colour. A very small amount of colour judiciously applied certainly enhances the effect of the marble, which looks almost staringly white without it, when new; and the comparison between buildings with and without colour may profitably be made in modern Athens to-day.

The workmanship of Greek architecture has never been approached, although some of their methods of construction are not above criticism, particularly in early work, as for instance in the blocks placed on edge on the face of the foot of the wall, forming a course much higher than the other courses (*orthostatai*) (fig. 1 in ARCHITECTURE [Ægean]). Very little bond is used in Greek work, but the size of the blocks makes these things a matter of small moment. Mortar was never used, yet so accurately are the stones fitted that in some instances they have actually grown together, and survived the accident of a fall without coming apart. Dowels are very frequently used, however, and their different shapes are useful for the determination of dates.

The methods employed can largely be gathered from internal evidence, particularly in the case of unfinished buildings. The building was apparently completed before the final dressing of the stone, which was done from the top downwards as the scaffolding was removed. The fine dressings on the faces of the stones, worked only for a short distance from the joint, and the short flutings of an inch or two at the top and bottom of columns, otherwise plain, are instances that may be cited of unfinished work, both of which have been ignorantly copied in Roman and modern times as though complete. Even in the finest work there is always a difference between the top joint of the column, which shows distinctly, and the others; as the flutings on the top block, which included the capital, were worked before it was placed in position. The rest of the fluting was worked when the joints had been made absolutely true by turning the blocks round and round after being placed in position. This seems to be the explanation both of their finer joints and of the wooden plugs and pins that have been found in the centre of the Parthenon drums (fig. 2, p. 679). The pin would be just strong enough to stand the turning of the drum but could not add any real strength to the building. The ankones, or projecting pieces found on unfinished drums and on other blocks, must have been used for this turning process. Doubtless they would also have been convenient for hoisting, but a quite unnecessary luxury, whereas the turning of a round drum would have been impossible without some such thing. The uppermost block could not be turned for fear of chipping the finished edge, hence the difference between that and the joints that were finished afterwards, which is always noticeable. The joints in the walls were probably made accurate by a similar process of pushing the blocks backwards and forwards, so as to grind the contiguous surfaces absolutely true, with the result that the finest knife blade could not be inserted anywhere between these mortarless joints. For this again the ankones would be useful. Every piece of carving, as for instance in the moldings of the Erechtheum, is executed with a minuteness of finish that one would naturally associate with ivory carving rather than with work in stone.

It is, however, the subtle curvatures in Greek architecture that are its most remarkable refinement, and the whole problem connected with them offers in itself a wide field for study. The following points may, however, be noted here. In the first place, it may be broadly stated that there are no straight lines in a Greek building of the finest class—a rather startling discovery to those who are accustomed to think of a Greek building as composed of nothing else.

Taking the principal lines of a building, the stylobate and the architrave, we find in each case a slight curve amounting to a rise of about $3\frac{1}{2}$ in. in the case of the long sides of the Parthenon, 228 ft. in length, and about 2 in. in the short sides, 101 ft. in breadth. These curves occur in the temple of Hephæstus and the Propylæa, but apparently not in the colonies or at Bassæ or Ægina. The next most important curve is the entasis of the columns, which is a convex departure from the straight amounting in the Parthenon to $\frac{2}{3}$ of an inch at a point about $\frac{2}{5}$ of the height from the ground, the columns being 34 ft. in height. The entasis of the Erechtheum shafts is even more subtle, $\frac{1}{1080}$ of the length of the shaft and $\frac{1}{134}$ of the lower diameter, against $\frac{1}{552}$ and $\frac{1}{110}$ in the Parthenon. It should be noticed that these curves are not segments of circles but parabolic, or in some cases hyperbolic; but whether they were laid out mathematically or by eye seems to be uncertain. We may assume that the eye which would be sufficiently accurate to appreciate such a subtle distinction of curvature would probably be equal to the task of drawing the curve with a sufficient degree of precision. In the case of the

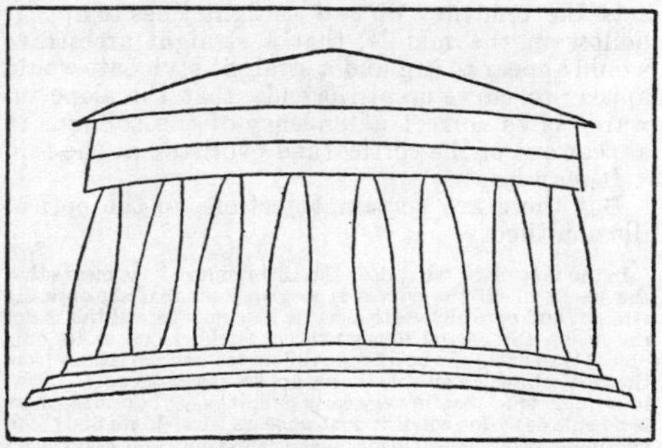

FIG. 11.—SUBTLE CURVES, ETC., OF PARTHENON EXAGGERATED.

echinos of the Parthenon, what appears at first glance to be a straight line rounded off at the end is found to be a subtle curve throughout, but the application of a 'straight-edge' to it reveals how minute this curvature is.

In addition to these refinements of curvature, others may be noticed. The columns that appear to the modern eye to be vertical really incline inwards towards the centre, so that the lines of the side columns in the Parthenon would meet at a point a mile and a quarter above the earth (fig. 11). The inclination of front to back is similar, and of course all the intermediate columns incline proportionately. It is also preserved in the faces of the entablature and the pediment and the steps of the stylobate. But here a counter subtlety is introduced, and the faces of the higher moldings are slightly inclined the reverse way, so as to counteract undue foreshortening, occasioned by the other process and by their actual height above the ground.

It might also be observed that the angle columns are an inch or so wider than the others. The intercolumniations are slightly smaller, so as to bring the angle column under the triglyph. There is an exception in the temple of Demeter at Pæstum, where the last metope is made larger so as to attain the same result.

The extraordinary skill and refinement required may perhaps best be realized, as Professor E. Gardner suggests, by considering the case of the bottom corner drum. Here then what do we find? In the first place, the base of the drum has to be cut so as to allow for the curve of $3\frac{1}{2}$ in. in 228 ft. But the mason has also to consider the curve, running at right angles to this, of 2 in. in 101 ft. This would be sufficiently puzzling if the axis of the column were vertical; but it is not. It has to be so inclined that it shall meet the axis of the corresponding column at the other end of the front, at a point $1\frac{1}{2}$ miles above the earth, and a similar inclination has to be made in the other direction along the side. Added to this, the edge of the step from which he works is not vertical; and, further, he has to allow for the beginning of the entasis a curve of $\frac{2}{3}$ in. in 34 ft. Those who are familiar with the extreme difficulty of cutting a voussoir for an arch in a curved wall—a comparatively simple process—will appreciate the work of the Greek mason. For not only did he conform to these requirements, but he executed it all with a nicety that would not admit of a sheet of paper being put into the joint. The voussoirs of the arches in such a building as the circular nave of the Temple Church, London, are well cut, but it is mere child's play in comparison.

It may well be asked for what purpose all these things were done, and in any case the answer seems to throw light upon the character of the Greek mind, confirming what might have been otherwise deduced.

It has generally been said that these are optical corrections, that the entasis of the column counteracts the tendency of two straight lines to appear hollow in the middle, that a straight architrave would appear to sag and a straight stylobate would appear to curve up at the ends, that the slope inwards is to correct a tendency of the columns to appear out of the vertical and overhang at the top.

It may be so.

But there are certain objections to the optical illusion theory.

In the first place, what does this theory mean? It means that the result of all the curves is to give lines that are optically straight and optically vertical as the case may be. If this is not the result, the optical illusion theory is ridiculous, as its only object is to avoid the appearance of curves and deviations from the vertical, which on this theory are *ex hypothesi* ugly. Now, it is quite true that in very early buildings, *e.g.* Corinth, there is no entasis. But when it first appears what do we find? An enormous swelling visible for miles, that no optical illusion could ever make look straight. The curve can be there for no conceivable object but that it should be seen. But, further, the parabolic curve with its maximum deviation at $\frac{2}{5}$ from the base would not be correct for the correction of an optical illusion, whatever the amount of the curvature. In the case of the echinos there is no possible suggestion of such a theory, but we find a similar curve; and what is most important is that, in the early examples, it is coarse, just as in the case of the entasis, and ultimately becomes refined. These curves, then, were obviously delighted in for their own sake, and, as the eye became more trained, it naturally demanded that they should become more subtle. There remain, then, the curves of the entablature and the stylobate. Now, if the side of the building be viewed from some little distance, the optical illusion caused by these lines would be the same as that caused by the lines of the column; in other words, the architrave would drop in the middle and the stylobate rise, in which case the correction for the stylobate should be the reverse of what it is. To one standing upon the stylobate or very near it and above it, this correction might be valuable, but in that case the architrave would be wrong in its turn. It is very doubtful whether there is any optical illusion at all in the case of straight-sided columns. If there were concave curves (or lines at an angle near them, as in the pediment and architrave) this might be the case. The line of the architrave is a legitimate instance because of the triangular pediment, but the line of the stylobate is not, and would appear to curve down at the ends even though there is no curve or angle below it (see diagram and test with ruler).

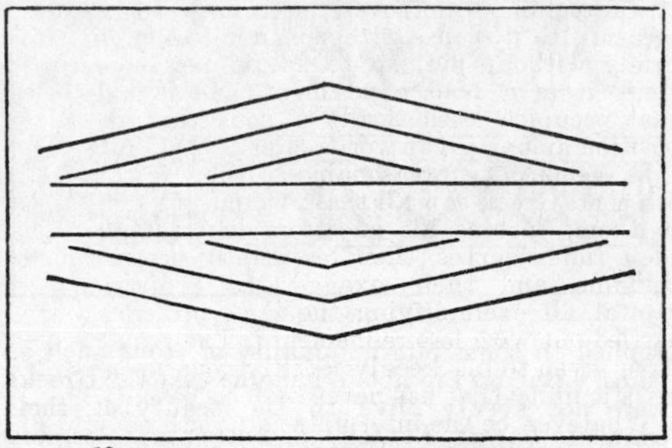

FIG. 12.—DIAGRAM SHOWING OPTICAL ILLUSION CAUSED BY ANGULAR LINES IN PROXIMITY TO PARALLEL LINES.

As to the inclination inwards of the columns, the upholders of this theory urge in the same breath that it is a correction of an illusion of the column not looking vertical, and that it gives a beautiful pyramidal appearance. If it does one, it cannot do the other.

That optical illusions were also considered, seems, however, certainly to be the case; the thickness of the angle columns and several other such subtleties appear to show it. Moreover, at Priene is an interesting diagram on the faces of the antæ of a temple, showing the correction of proportions as they appear to the eye in perspective.

Although, then, the optical illusion may have some influence, it seems more rational to fall back upon principles of æsthetic for the main reasons. It is clear in the case of the entasis and the echinos curve that it is pure delight in the curve. Doubtless this is associated with what we might term a mechanico-æsthetic reason. These curves are undoubtedly suggestive of strength and of organic growth, and may be paralleled by the exceedingly subtle curves in a human arm. The shape, indeed, would actually be stronger, although of course there is no practical need for it, as the margin of material to work done, allowed by the Greek, was very large, something like 3 to 2. In the case of the architrave and the stylobate there is the possibility of actual sagging in the centre upon soft ground, and therefore an appearance of greater strength is certainly given by the upward curve in the centre. In the case of the architrave the optical illusion would exaggerate the suggestion of weakness, and may have been taken into account. Earthquakes and weather, and the great powder explosion in the Parthenon, have made it more difficult to determine the original nature of the architrave curve than of the stylobate.

But all these things are an interesting illustration of one of the most elementary of art principles carried out with exceptional subtlety. A thing must not only be right, but must look right. In this case, therefore, it must not only be strong, but look strong. A plate-glass shop front, however excellently built, could never be æsthetically beautiful unless the eye were in some way satisfied as to the support of the walls above. In the echinos we have not only this principle exemplified, but also the still more fundamental principle of organic unity of design; and the vertical lines of the columns and horizontal lines of the architrave become one whole by the intervention of the echinos. It is curious that the eye does not demand a base to the Doric column for the same reason. Indeed, some people have felt the want. But the side lines are diverging at the base, whereas they are converging at the top; the foot of the column, moreover, is so large as in some measure to dispense with such a necessity; it sits firmly without aid, so to speak. At the same time, it is a bold experiment, and is a feature that occupies æsthetically a somewhat peculiar position among great works of art.

It seems not unreasonable to suppose that the 5th cent. Greek saw all these things and delighted in them, just as his ancestors had delighted in their ruder curves, their less subtly proportioned columns, and their exaggerated projection of capital, all exemplifying the same principles, but carried out with less refinement. The result must have given to his keenly sensitive eye an organic artistic unity that has never been surpassed.

Whatever be the interpretation of these subtleties, one inference at least is certain, namely, the accuracy and refinement of the Greek eye, coupled with an æsthetic demand for a completeness and thoroughness in even the minutest particulars that go to make up perfection in a work of art. The immense importance that these must have had for the Greek, to make him expend such extreme care upon them, can be paralleled in modern times only outside the field of art, as in the making of a modern rifle barrel or an observatory telescope. Even optical illusions we are practically content to leave alone. But alongside this minuteness is a breadth and majesty equally astonishing. The composition as a whole is simple in the extreme, and the dignity of its proportions is unsurpassable.

In these things we find the key to the interpretation of Greek art, and there are certain distinct advantages in approaching that art through its architecture. Much can here be demonstrated by rule and line which only the highly-trained eye can see in the sculpture. The whole artistic feeling, too, which inspired every detail of Greek architecture and art, has its corresponding parallels in the Greek conception of religion and in Greek intellectual investigations. Naturally it is necessary to beware of the error of the superficial inquirer, who would make one the mere result of the other, rather than go deep enough to find their common basis. This does not mean that the one had no influence upon the others, but that each, as it were, remained master in its own house with its own fundamental principles. In the case, however, of the plan and general arrangement of the Greek temple the æsthetic and religious factors are somewhat closely connected. The general design of the building is naturally largely determined by religious requirements. It is hardly necessary to point out that the Greek temple was not a place of worship: the act of worship took place in the open air, generally in the temenos, or enclosure surrounding the temple; and here the altar was placed. The image within the temple was not the object of worship; the altar architecturally is therefore entirely unrelated to it. The temenos itself and the altar in it are supposed by some to represent the forecourt with its altar in the Mycenæan house. Small subordinate altars there seem to have been within the building; and doubtless there were always two tendencies at work—that which is essentially Greek, and culminates in the highest flights of Greek philosophy and art, and the grosser and more superstitious side which was shared with others. It is not always easy to disentangle these elements, but the essential Greek characteristic, that which distinguishes them, rather than that which they share with all mankind, is, of course, the main question. Doubtless it is easier to discern it in the time of its full growth, but the tendency is there from the outset; and it is this tendency that made the Greeks what they were, and that was their contribution to the world of humanity. Whatever may have been the origin of the temple image, which it would be out of place to discuss here, it may briefly be said that in the golden age of Athens it was certainly not a fetish or an idol, in the sense of a spirit or spiritual quality embodied in a material object. Nor can it even be regarded as a symbol; it is rather the rational self-explanatory expression of a concept, viewed, it is true, from the æsthetic side, in which we may say Greek art preceded Greek philosophy. It was not an idol, for it was not regarded as possessing any power *per se*. It was not a symbol, for it rationally explained itself without interpretation. Least of all was it a portrait or likeness; it represented no traditional appearance, and pretended to no inspired vision on the part of the artist. But it did express the outward beauty of certain inward qualities mentally conceived, and these qualities were the qualities of deity. It would perhaps seem a little strained to describe the temple image as the formulated creed of the Greek religion æsthetically expressed, yet it is hardly possible to look upon the later images of Phidias and Scopas in any other light. The natural superstition and conservatism of humanity among the masses were counteracting tendencies, but at the same time declining ones, and the essential Greek characteristic tends away from these. The *intellectual* expression in *art* of a *religious* and *ethical* position is an instance of the complete balance of the æsthetic, intellectual, and moral nature, tersely embodied in their motto, *γνῶθι σεαυτόν*, and its concomitant *μηδὲν ἄγαν*, implying a complete knowledge and development of all that makes man man, and yet excess in nothing. It is this that makes the Greeks unique among the peoples of the world.

The temple may be considered as the casket containing the image, and it is on this account that it is the outside, rather than the inside, which on the whole receives the first consideration. At the same time it is æsthetically the embodiment of the same general principles as are contained in the image itself. The idealism of Greek religion in its highest aspect had not to wait for Plato for its exposition, in the case of those who could understand. It is already æsthetically complete at the time of Phidias, and beginning to advance to what perhaps may best be termed a transcendentalism, culminating, as far as extant work can be taken as evidence, in Scopas. Probably it was closely approached by Praxiteles, whom we are apt to misjudge from the weakness of the copies of his work, read in conjunction with certain minor traits in the Hermes. It would be hard to say whether Greek philosophy ever reached the parallel to this second position; and even architecture shows only the beginnings of it in buildings such as the Propylæa and the Erechtheum; although in sculpture it is already making its appearance in the work on the Parthenon, particularly in the frieze.

It is therefore natural that the plan of the temple should be simple and remarkable for its perfection rather than its size—an appropriate casket for its treasure. This is all in marked contrast to the Egyptian temple, which is extensive and of many courts and chambers. The decoration of the Egyptian temple is almost entirely within, and it is dark, vast, and mysterious. The Greek temple is comparatively small, and the open-air worship in the temenos surrounding the temple is characteristic of the Greek nature, frank, free, and outspoken, fearless in inquiry, and anxious to bring the light to bear upon all things. The priestly caste and the artificial mystery of the Egyptian were entirely alien to the Greek mind. There was no priestly caste, and hardly anything that could be called a priestly order; and we find this reflected in the popular character of their ceremonies and the open simplicity of their religious architecture. To say that the extraordinary progress of thought in the 5th and 4th centuries, the most rapid and far-reaching that the world has seen, was either the result of these things or their cause, would perhaps be an error, but the interrelation is unmistakable, and they are alike the product of the Greek mind. It should be said that one important religious building which survives, at least in plan, is to some extent an exception to the general rule—the Telesterion (so-called temple of Demeter) at Eleusis (fig. 14).

FIG. 13.

To the simple primitive rectangular cella a second rectangular chamber is apparently an early addition; but throughout Greek history there is hardly a departure from the general rectangular plan, although circular religious buildings do occur, such as the Thymele at Epidaurus.

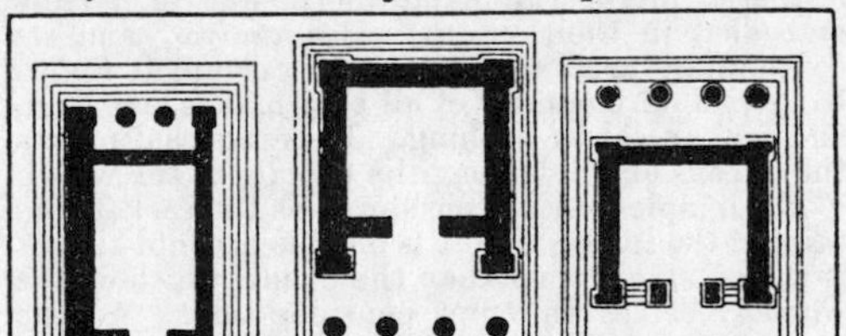

FIG. 14.

The simplest form is a three-walled building with an open end divided by two columns 'distyle in antis' (fig. 13). The trabs or architrave, resting upon a column, required a support at the other end that would satisfy the eye as well as merely subserve its utilitarian end. It was not sufficient, therefore, that it should rest upon the wall, but a special feature was built for its support, a flat column of rectangular section attached to the wall, called an anta. Hence, wherever we have an architrave passing from a column to a wall, there is invariably an anta to receive it with its own capital and base. This capital and base mark the double character of the member, and are not the same as those of the column, but are in some respects more closely related to the flat wall (fig. 13). The anta with its clearly defined function degenerates into the Roman pilaster of later date. It has been suggested that the origin of the anta is an end-facing to a rubble wall. This does not explain the capital and base, or its frequent position not at the end of a wall. On the other hand, the anta is never found where it does not support an architrave.

The 'distyle in antis' arrangement may be at one or both ends, as at Rhamnus or Eleusis (figs. 13, 14). There is, however, no entrance to the temple at the back, the temple image being placed at that end of the temple with its back to the wall—an arrangement occasionally modified in the larger examples. The next development that may be noticed is a portico in front, 'prostyle'; or one in front and one behind, which is by far the more common arrangement, 'amphiprostyle,' as in the charming little temple of Athene Nike Apteros at Athens and the one by the Ilissus, both destroyed in comparatively modern times, although the former has been re-built. In the largest examples a range of columns is carried right round the building, 'peristyle'; and sometimes there is a double row of columns, 'dipteral,' as in the temple of Olympic Zeus in Athens. A single line of

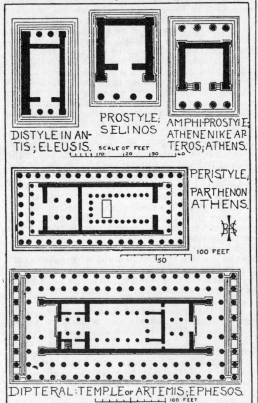

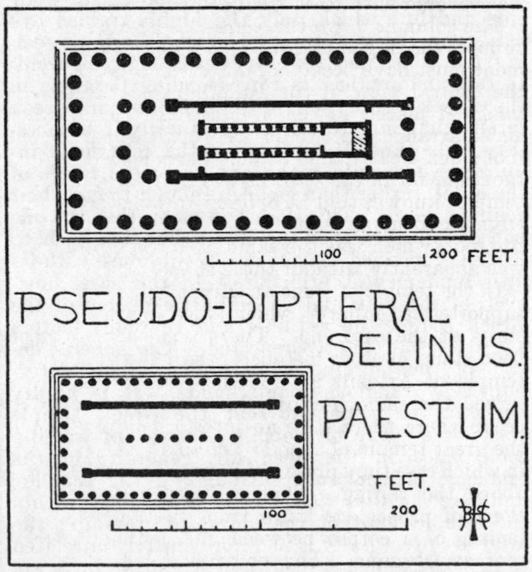

FIG. 15.

columns at a considerable distance from the central building, or naos, is termed 'pseudo-dipteral,' as at Selinus (fig. 15). A temple is also sometimes described according to the number of columns at the ends—hexastyle, octostyle, and so on.

In the smaller temples the roof was apparently of a single span, leaving the floor space perfectly free. But in larger temples we find columns inside. They may be down the centre, as in the Doric temple at Pæstum (fig. 15), or the Ionic temple at Locri. The temple of Apollo at Thermum in Ætolia shows the same arrangement. More commonly we find two ranges of columns, forming three aisles, as

FIG. 16.

in the temple of Poseidon at Pæstum or the Parthenon. These were apparently in two tiers, one above the other, as those remaining *in situ* attest (fig. 16). The roof, presumably, was of timber, and was covered with tiles, frequently of marble.

The columns down the centre seem obviously to support the ridge piece of the roof; but the arrangement must have been very unsatisfactory, blocking the central view of the building, and the temple image if placed in the middle line. The three-aisled arrangement would also lend support to the roof; but clearly that cannot have been the only function, for in the case of the two largest Doric temples known, that at Selinus and the temple of Olympic Zeus at Athens, a considerable part of the roof, which was the same breadth throughout, was apparently without these supports.

In the temple of Zeus at Olympia the lower tier supported a gallery, which was approached by stairs at the east end. There seem also to have been stairs in other instances, as in the great Ionic temple of Artemis at Ephesus, which may have served the same purpose (fig. 14). But they also occur where there were no interior columns, as in the great temple of Apollo Didymæus at Miletus, in which case they presumably only led to the space above the ceiling. That ceilings existed below the roof proper, we know from the record of the finding of a corpse between the ceiling and the roof at Olympia. The columns seem partly to have served a *quasi*-ritual purpose, for we find that a low screen often existed between them, as in the Parthenon or the Zeus-temple at Olympia. In the case of the Parthenon and the temple of Artemis at Ephesus the columns are returned at the west end (fig. 14). Only the priests would be allowed within the screens, and possibly only favoured persons would be admitted to walk round the gallery or aisles, and so obtain varying views of the statue.

It is also possible that the two-aisled arrangement may have had something to do with the lighting of the cella, which has always been a difficult problem. There are several possibilities. (1) It is suggested that all the light was admitted through the great temple doors, and when the great brilliancy of the light in Greece is considered, it does become just conceivable. But let any one who holds this theory seriously examine such plans as those of the great temple at Selinus, the temple of Artemis at Ephesus, or the temple of Olympic Zeus at Athens. A distance of 115 ft. through two doors and five sets of columns will bedim almost any light. After all, it is hard enough to see the part of the Parthenon frieze *in situ*; and this is outside. The interior frieze at Phigalia would be absolutely invisible.

(2) A second suggestion is that of artificial light, which doubtless would produce a certain richness of effect with a statue made of such materials as gold and ivory. Of course one cannot disprove such a theory, but it is a strange and unsatisfactory arrangement.

(3) It is suggested that the light was largely given by what filtered through the marble tiles. This almost precludes the possi-

FIG. 17.

bility of a ceiling, as, even if spaces were left in it, such a comparatively dim light would by this additional screen be still further reduced. In this connexion, however, it seems worth noticing that in Byzantine architecture, which may even represent a Greek tradition, thin slabs of marble, deeply carved, so as to become still more translucent, were actually used as windows.

(4) Some sort of opening in the roof is suggested, which may be of two kinds. There might be one or more comparatively small openings in the tiles, or one single great hypæthral opening. The former receives some support from tiles found by Professor Cockerell at Bassæ (fig. 17), and the latter from sarcophagi found in the form of little model temples (fig. 17). We are told that the temple at Miletus was open, and had shrubs growing inside — the temple image being in a small shrine within the temple. Strabo, however, mentions it as peculiar and not intentional, but due to the fact that it was found to be too big to roof. Vitruvius says that the temple of Olympic Zeus at Athens was hypæthral, but the temple was not completed until long after Vitruvius' death, so that this statement is valueless. We may therefore assume, first, that these temples were exceptional, and secondly, that they were merely unfinished buildings. A hypæthral opening would certainly sadly mar the line of the roof, and would admit rain and moisture that would have been very destructive. However, it is generally

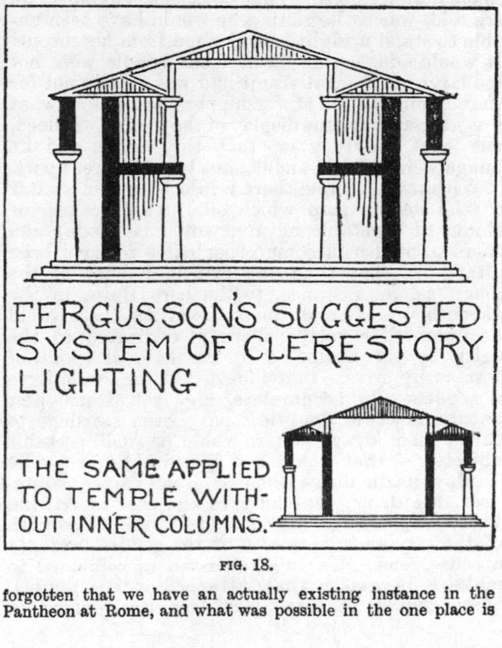

FIG. 18.

forgotten that we have an actually existing instance in the Pantheon at Rome, and what was possible in the one place is conceivable in the other. There seems, in some cases at least, to have been a *parapetasma*, or curtain, before the image, which may have been to protect it from the weather. It has to be admitted that this theory, although in some ways the least pleasing, has a certain amount of real evidence in its support.

(5) The fact that the covers of the coffers in the ceiling of the peristyle of the Theseum are movable, and marked with letters, has been used as evidence that light was obtained thus by reflexion from the pavement below, and then presumably reflected a second time from the roof. The amount of light thus obtained would be exceedingly small, and to reduce it under any circumstances by putting the covers on would seem to be quite unnecessary. The markings were probably simply for the convenience of the builders, just as a mediæval or modern mason marks a stone cut for a special position.

(6) The presence of the internal columns, as pointed out above, suggests the most ingenious and beautiful theory of all, if not the most probable. It is the theory of Fergusson, who suggested a kind of clerestory somewhat after the Egyptian manner. It is a tempting theory, but there is nothing to support it, save the bare fact that Fergusson anticipated so many of the so-called discoveries of other people, more particularly upon Gothic architecture, and has shown the keenest insight of the writers that have ever written upon the subject. It may be noted that the system is possible without interior columns, although the windows can be made much larger when they are present. The theory receives some measure of support from the fact that the columns certainly were not used solely to decrease the span, as shown above, nor were there generally galleries (fig. 18).

Unless new evidence be found the problem is likely to remain unsolved.

In size the Greek temples corresponded to our parish churches rather than to our cathedrals, making up, however, for the lack of size in the extreme refinement of workmanship. Moreover, the mass of material was considerable, and the actual size of blocks enormous, many of them weighing as much as 20 or 30 tons. The largest stone at Baalbec, very likely of Greek workmanship, weighs approximately 1100 tons. The cella almost invariably faced the east in the case of temples of the gods, although there were slight variations, probably in order that the image might catch the first rays of the morning sun on the day sacred to the god. This may even be trusted to give us the dates of their erection, calculated astronomically. In the case of heroes, the general rule seems to have been the reverse, and the temple to have faced west. In this matter of orientation the Greek usage may be contrasted with the Roman, which paid no attention to such things.

Within the temple, the temple statue held the place of honour, facing the entrance, and from the 5th cent. B.C., at any rate, this statue was of colossal dimensions. That of Zeus at Olympia, we are told, was so large that he would have been unable to stand upright had he risen from his throne. It would add to this effect if the temple were not too large; and what size it had was clearly not for the accommodation of worshippers, but simply what was necessary for the display of the statue. Indeed, one must clearly grasp that the temple and its image were a unity, and cannot be considered apart.

Within the temple there would be a minor altar to the deity, upon which offerings of cakes, or things of vegetable nature, would be made; and there seem also in some other cases to have been altars to other than the principal deity of the place, as, for instance, to the hero Butes in the Erechtheum. In addition to the altars, there would be numberless votive offerings dedicated to the deity by the State, as in the case of spoils of war, or by private individuals. These would have a tendency to accumulate, and yet, from their nature, it would doubtless have been sacrilege to throw them away. There would be small portable objects too, that would not be suitable for public display, particularly when of great value. Moreover, the deity, especially in the case of Athene Polias, represented the city herself, and the wealth of the city and the wealth of the goddess were, in a sense, one. These circumstances combined to make it necessary that, attached to the temple, there should be some place for the storing of treasure. Hence, in the larger temples we frequently find at the back of the cella (ναός, or temple proper) another chamber prolonging the rectangular plan, and used for the above purposes. Indeed, the treasure chambers of the temples may in some senses be regarded as the State banks. The porticoes themselves were not infrequently closed in by railings between the columns.

In considering the plans of the larger Greek temples, we must not suppose that they were built upon any one pattern. Quite the contrary is the case, and it would be truer to say that there are almost as many different arrangements as temples. Perhaps the two most irregular plans are those of the Erechtheum (fig. 19) and the temple of Apollo at Bassæ. [The building at Eleusis is not a temple.] The irregularity of the first of these

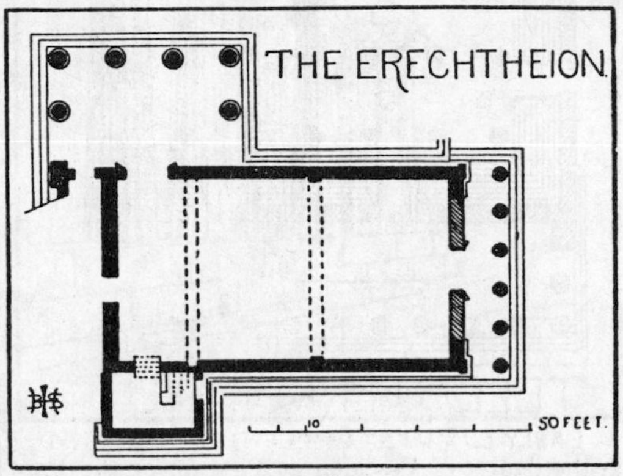

FIG. 19.

is well known, occasioned partly by the irregularity of the site, partly by its having to house the image of more than one deity, and possibly in order that it might include certain sacred objects, such as the marks of Poseidon's trident and the salt spring.

The temple at Phigalia is interesting partly because of the curious arrangement of attached Ionic columns running round the interior of the building with the beautiful frieze above, which form a series of small recesses the whole way round, but even more as showing the importance attached to the correct orientation of the statue. It was more convenient to build the temple with its longer axis from north to south; the cella, therefore, had a door in the east side of the temple through which the statue looked eastward (fig. 20). The effect of lighting, to one entering the temple from the north during the morning light, must have been most impressive, and the æsthetic value of such an arrangement would doubtless influence the architect. It is possible that the actual cella occupied the site of a smaller sanctuary of normal orientation. The temple in some respects bears a curious resemblance to the Heræum at Olympia.

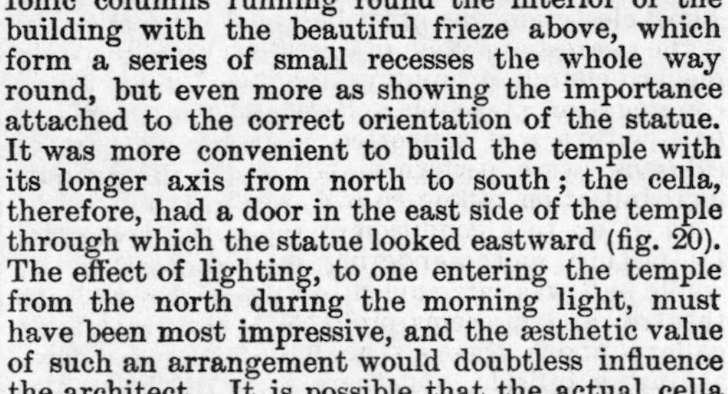

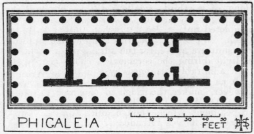

FIG. 20.

It is a hexastyle building, and its long proportions with 15 columns down the sides are those of an early temple, the tendency being for the later temples to be wider. The Ionic half columns attached to the short side walls also recall the

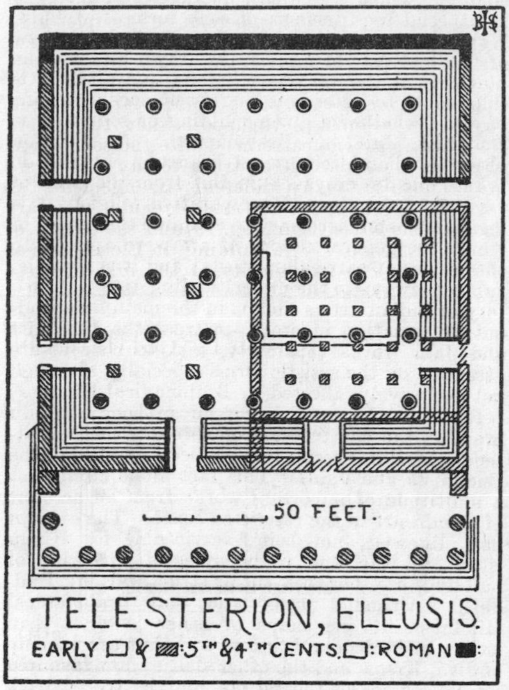

FIG. 21.

earlier building. Richter figures an Ionic capital from the Heræum, presumably from the interior, which, in the proportions of its volutes and the arrangement of the continuation of the volute-bead, strikingly anticipates the later capitals at Bassæ.*

The plans of one or two religious buildings other than temples may be briefly noted in conclusion. The Telesterion, the great hall at Eleusis (fig. 21), is the nearest approach in Greek architecture to the modern church, a building designed for holding a congregation of people. Here, in a large square hall, with a roof supported by seven rows of six columns, were performed the sacred drama and final initiation of the *mustai*, after they had been worked up to a condition of religious excitement by fasting and wandering in the dark. The whole hall was surrounded by tiers of seats as in a theatre, and it seems probable that there was a gallery above these. The building was erected against a hillside, and there were six entrances, two on each of the free sides. The plan is traditional, and takes the place of a much earlier and smaller building of similar design, whose foundations can be traced. Below this are the foundations of a third, smaller still. This building was begun by Ictinus, *c.* 425 B.C., and was not completed until *c.* 315 B.C., when Philon built the porch. We know that the temple had windows and shutters above, for the admission or exclusion of light during the ceremonies. This could have been admirably arranged by a clerestory system such as Fergusson suggests (fig. 18). Fergusson, however, makes the ridge of the roof run from N.E. to S.W., so that Philon's portico would have no pediment, which, though quite possible, particularly as it was intended to carry the portico round as a sort of stoa, may not have been the case. But the roof might have been as in fig. 22. In his restoration, all but the end column of the central row are omitted; but although this would

FIG. 22.

provide a wider open space and better lighting, and account for the curious disposition of the columns, six on the sides and seven on the end, nevertheless it is not necessary. If most of Philo's interior columns were Doric, as those of his portico undoubtedly were, there might have been a single

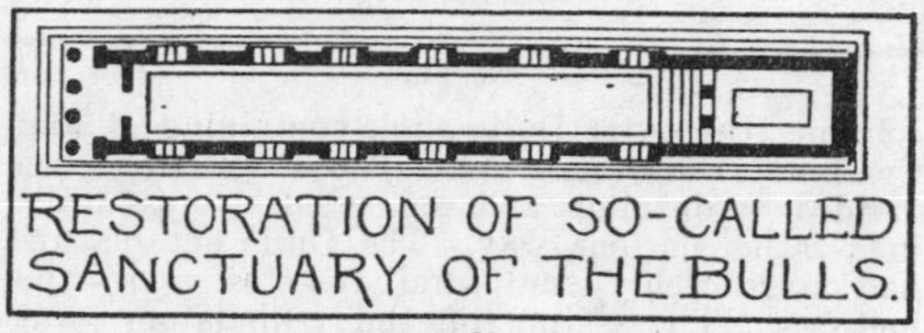

FIG. 23.

range of the more slender Ionic columns down the centre instead of the two-storey arrangement, a device used where columns of two heights were required. Those in the so-called Parthenon-chamber of the Parthenon were possibly Ionic columns of the height of the two tiers of Doric columns in the cella. Unfortunately, little exists but the ground plan, and there are practically no architectural remains from which to deduce the character of the building. The existing remains are mainly of Roman date, with Ionic columns.

In the island of Delos are the remains of the so-called 'sanctuary of the bulls,' the building containing the horned altar of Apollo, reckoned among the seven wonders of the world. In this building is said to have taken place the celebrated dance of the Delian maidens. It was extraordinarily long and very narrow, 219 ft. by 19 ft. (fig. 23). It was built upon a granite base with marble steps. The building was divided into three parts, a long central hall, with a sunken area, in which presumably the dances took place, and at the southern end a Doric portico, possibly tetrastyle, possibly 'distyle in antis.' At the north end of the long hall was the chamber containing the altar. It was entered between two composite piers, formed by a half Doric column on the one side, and an anta with two recumbent bulls as a capital on the other side. Above was a frieze with bulls' heads upon the triglyphs. It is these bulls that give the name to the building.

The Thymele (*i.e.* 'place of sacrifice'), the so-called Tholos, at Epidaurus (fig. 24) is one of the few round buildings, used for religious purposes, that have come down to us. Others were the Arsinoeion at Samothrace sacred to the Great Gods, the very small building, if so it may be called, whose circular foundations may be found in the Asklepieion at Athens, and the *quasi*-religious Philippeion at Olympia, which may be regarded as a sort of Heroon of Philip. It seems to have been one of the loveliest buildings of antiquity. The foundations are probably of older date, but the principal remains date from the end of the 4th cent. B.C., when it was built by the architect Polyclitus (possibly a grandson of the famous sculptor). It was 107 ft.

* The present writer has not been able to see this capital, and does not know where Richter saw it (fig. 4).

in diameter, and stood upon ring walls 4 in number. Upon the outermost and widest were two circles of

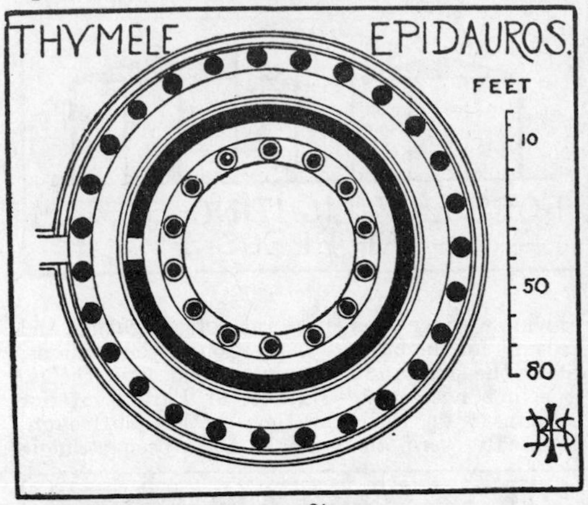

FIG. 24.

columns, the outer Doric circle containing 26, and the inner Corinthian, 14. The inner rings are divided by openings and connected by cross walls in a rather curious way. The Doric entablature had large richly sculptural rosettes upon the metopes. The ceiling of the ambulatory was executed with beautiful marble coffers. The capitals of the Corinthian order, as has already been noted, are in their way the acme of Greek art. The use of the building has been much discussed, but its name, and its correspondence to its miniature prototype or copy in the temenos of the same god at Athens, point on the whole to the building covering a sacrificial pit. That sacred serpents may have been kept in the spaces between the ring walls is also conceivable, without interfering with the first theory.

In its own way Greek architecture has never been surpassed, and probably never will be. It has said the last word upon such problems as nicety of construction and proportion, and has carried the delicacy of ornamental treatment to the furthest limits that are visible to the most highly trained human eye. The Greeks may be said to have set out to achieve perfection, and they have achieved it. Their style was original and practically entirely self-created. It is not until we reach the architecture of the Gothic architects that we again find an entirely original creation. The Gothic architects, however, did not aim at perfection, but at something different, and they, too, in their way were unsurpassed. In order fully to comprehend even the general spirit of Greek architecture, it would be necessary to have some knowledge of other than religious buildings, which alone come properly within the scope of this article. But in the main it is an extension of the same principles, showing, however, more variety and power of practical adaptation than is perhaps evident in the sacred buildings here considered.

LITERATURE.—V. Laloux, *L'Architecture Grecque*, Paris; I. Durm, *Die Baukunst der Griechen*, Darmstadt, 1892; W. J. Anderson and R. Phené Spiers, *The Architecture of Greece and Rome*, London, 1902; R. Sturgis, *A History of Architecture*, vol. i., London, 1907; James Fergusson, *Illustrated Handbook of Architecture*, vol. i., London, 1855; F. C. Penrose, *An Investigation of the Principles of Athenian Architecture*, London, 1888; J. T. Clarke, *Investigations at Assos*, Boston, 1902; C. R. Cockerell, *The Temples of Ægina and Bassæ*, 1860; A. Defrasse and H. Lechat, *Epidaure; restauration et description des principaux monuments du Sanctuaire d'Asclepios*, 1895; E. A. Gardner, *Ancient Athens*, 1903; J. H. Middleton, *Plans and Drawings of Athenian Buildings*, 1902; E. Pontremoli and M. Collignon, *Pergame; restauration et description des monuments de l'Acropole*, Paris, 1900; C. Waldstein, *The Argive Heræum*, London, 1902.

J. B. STOUGHTON HOLBORN.

ARCHITECTURE AND ART (Hindu).—The adherents of all the Indian sects and religions used for their several purposes the art of each age and country, which was applied, as occasion arose, to the special requirements of each form of worship. No fundamental distinction, from the point of view of the historian of art, can be drawn between the buildings of the various religions, and often it is impossible to determine merely by considerations of style whether a given building or sculpture is Buddhist, Jain, or Brāhmanical. As Le Bon observes, 'l'architecture est beaucoup plus fille de la race que des croyances.' But from the point of view of the student of comparative religion, it is legitimate and necessary to examine the modes in which the general canons of art were applied to the service of particular creeds; and it is possible, subject always to the understanding that the history of Indian art as such is in the main independent of variation in creed, to treat the Buddhist and Jain works separately, and to concentrate attention on the artistic forms especially, although not exclusively, affected by Brāhmanical Hindus.

Relic-worship not being an orthodox Hindu practice, the construction of *stūpas* with their attendant railings seems to have been confined to the Buddhists and Jains. This fact alone eliminates a multitude of important works from an account of Hindu art in the restricted sense. The *chaitya* hall, likewise, not being serviceable for Hindu ritual, all the known examples of this kind of building, whether rock-cut or structural, are Buddhist. Although it is true that Brāhmanical Hinduism in one shape or other is older than either Buddhism or Jainism, and that the worship of Śiva, Kṛṣṇa, and the other deities now favoured by the masses of the people, may be traced back to a distant antiquity, the material remains of ancient Hinduism are extremely rare, and nearly all the really old monuments are either Buddhist or Jain. Whatever may be the correct explanation of this, the fact is certain, and affords a further practical justification for the separate treatment, for certain purposes, of specifically Hindu works as distinguished from those of Buddhist or Jain origin.

Architecture is the dominant art of India, and almost all other modes of art have been developed as accessories to it. No Hindu ever spontaneously set to work to produce a statue or picture for its own sake, as a thing of beauty by itself, without reference to an architectural composition. The few detached images which exist were usually intended to be worshipped, and were designed primarily for religious not artistic purposes. It is hardly necessary to observe that Indian life in all its aspects—art included—is governed by religious motives, and the consequence necessarily follows that all notable works of art in India are associated with buildings dedicated to the service of religion. The examples of architectural skill applied to purely secular purposes are rare and comparatively unimportant, while the minor decorative arts as applied to articles of ordinary use or special luxury are largely dependent upon mythological motives. Practically, therefore, a discussion of Hindu architecture and art must deal almost exclusively with the architecture and decoration of temples appropriated to Brāhmanical worship. The decoration is nearly all the work of the sculptor, the few examples of Indian painting deserving the name of works of art being all, probably without exception, either Buddhist or Muhammadan.

For a discussion of Hindu architecture generally, the reader is referred to Fergusson's standard work. Here it will suffice to observe that the essential part of every temple is the shrine, containing the image or symbol of the deity. That shrine very often is not the principal element in the composition, being overshadowed by the subsidiary parts added for the purpose of giving the desired impression of dignity and mass—not for congregational uses, which Hindu ritual excludes. The leading styles of Brāhmanical temple architecture are six in number, namely, four northern and two southern. The northern styles are (1) the 'Indo-Aryan' of Fergusson; (2) the Gupta; (3) the Kaśmīrī; and (4) the Nepālese. The southern styles are (5) the Dravidian, and (6) the 'Chālukyan' of Fergusson, better designated as that of the Deccan. We proceed to indicate briefly the geographical distribution, chronology, characteristics, and principal examples of each of these six styles. The reader who desires to pursue the subject will find a great mass of information recorded in the selected works named at the end of this article, and in the unnamed multitude of other books dealing with Indian archæology.

1. The 'Indo-Aryan' style is characterized by the bulging steeple with curvilinear outlines which surmounts the shrine or sanctuary containing the image, and frequently is repeated in other parts of the design. In Orissa an early temple sometimes consists of nothing more than the steepled shrine with a low-roofed porch, devoid, or almost devoid, of pillars; but larger examples have additional pillared chambers. The great temples at Khajurāho, in Bundelkhand, dating from the time of the Chandel dynasty, are built on a cruciform plan, with naves and transepts, which results in buildings of imposing dignity. The style in one variety or another is found all over northern India, between the Himālayan and the Vindhyan mountains. The most elegant examples may be assigned to the period between A.D. 950 and 1200, but some of the Orissan temples are supposed by Fergusson to date from A.D. 600. As a rule the material is stone, but a few brick temples in this style are known. The best preserved specimen built of brick is that at Konch in Bihār, to the north-west of Gayā, which is assigned to the 8th cent. A.D. (Cunningham, *Archæol. S. Rep.* vol. xvi. p. 58). Certain brick temples in the Cawnpore district, rather earlier in date, probably had steeples of the standard form, but are too much ruined to admit of certainty. The most ancient known Brāhmanical temple is one built of decorated moulded bricks, discovered by Dr. Führer in 1891–92 at Ahichhattrā in Rohilkhand, and assigned for good reason to the first century B.C. (*Archæol. S. for N.W.P. and Oudh*, Progress Report, 1891–92). Unfortunately no description of the building has been published. It is probable that the style was developed originally in brick, but it is not known how it originated. Nor is the genesis of the curvilinear steeple easy to explain. The most plausible suggestion is that the design was modelled on the form of a frame of bamboos fastened together at the top. In modern buildings the tendency is to diminish greatly or dispense with the curvature of the outline, and many temples of recent date have slender straight-line spires, closely resembling European church forms.

2. The Gupta style, with which Fergusson was not acquainted, is so named because it was favoured by architects in the 4th and 5th centuries A.D., when the imperial Gupta dynasty ruled northern India (see art. CHANDRAGUPTA, 2, 3). The recorded examples, about thirteen in number, including a good one at Sānchi, are found in the southern parts of the United Provinces and the neighbouring territories. Cunningham, who first distinguished the style, enumerates its seven characteristic features as follows:

(1) Flat roofs, without spires of any kind, as in the cave temples; (2) prolongation of the head of the doorway beyond the jambs, as in Egyptian temples; (3) statues of the rivers Ganges and Jumna guarding the entrance door; (4) pillars with massive square capitals, ornamented with two lions back to back, with a tree between them; (5) bosses on the capitals, and friezes of a very peculiar form, like Buddhist *stūpas*, or beehives, with projecting horns; (6) continuation of the architrave of the portico as a moulding all round the building; (7) deviation of plan from the cardinal points (Cunningham, *Archæol. S. Rep.* vol. ix. p. 42, and *ib.* vols. i. v. x. xi. xiv. xvi. xx. xxi.).

3. The Kaśmīrī style is restricted to the valley of Kaśmīr and the Salt Range country in the Panjāb, between the Indus and the Jhelum. Its peculiarities are distinctly marked, and include pyramidal roofs, fluted pillars closely resembling those of the Doric order, arches with trefoil-shaped openings, and dentils as ornaments. The temples are usually small, but in some cases are surrounded by cloistered enclosures of considerable magnitude. The notion that such enclosures were intended to contain water is erroneous. The oldest example to which a date can be assigned is the well-known temple of the Sun, under the name of Mārtāṇḍa, which was built by order of king Lalitāditya, about A.D. 750 (Stein, trans. of *Rājataraṅgiṇī*). All known specimens of the style may be dated between A.D. 600 or 700 and 1200. The obviously Greek character of the pillars has attracted much attention from European writers; but it is not easy to ascertain how *quasi*-Doric pillars became the fashion in Kaśmīr and the Salt Range, and nowhere else. Perhaps, as Le Bon conjectures, the style was introduced from Persia during the rule of the Arsacids.

4. The Nepālese style in its characteristic form is mainly Chinese, being merely a local modification of the Chinese style described as follows by Dr. Bushell (*Chinese Art*, vol. i. p. 49, London, 1904):

> 'The most general model of Chinese buildings is the *t'ing*. This consists essentially of a massive roof with recurved edges resting upon short columns. . . . The roof is the principal feature of the building, and gives to it, when finished, its qualities of grandeur or simplicity, of strength or grace. To vary its aspect the architect is induced occasionally to double, or even to triple it. . . . The great weight of the roof necessitates the multiple employment of the column, which is assigned a function of the first importance. The columns are made of wood. . . . The stability of the structure depends upon the wooden framework; the walls, which are filled in afterwards with blocks of stone or brickwork, are not intended to figure as supports.'

Most of the Nepālese temples are constructed on the same principles, but the curvature of the roof is much less marked than in China. The small valley of Nepāl proper, measuring about 20 miles by 15, in which the three towns Kāthmāṇḍū, Pātan, and Bhātgāon, are situated, probably contains more temples than any other equal area in the world. The total number is believed to exceed 2000, of which the great majority are in the towns above named. In modern Nepāl the practices of Brāhmanical Hinduism and Buddhism are so inextricably mingled that the symbols of both religions are found indifferently in the shrines. Le Bon has rightly laid stress upon the proposition that the existing state of things in Nepāl goes a long way towards explaining the process by which, in India, Buddhism gradually melted away into Hinduism. The oldest monuments in Nepāl are Buddhist *stūpas*, which may go back to the time of Aśoka (wh. see); but the Indo-Chinese structures described above are all comparatively modern, none probably being older than A.D. 1500. The Nepālese temples built entirely of stone vary much in form, and do not admit of summary classification as regards style. Examples of some of the most notable varieties are given in Le Bon's plates.

5. The Dravidian style is so named because it is that prevalent in the countries occupied by peoples speaking Dravidian languages. These countries correspond closely with peninsular India to the south of the Krishna (Kistna) river, and are nearly equivalent to the Madras Presidency. The Brāhmanical temples in this style may be devoted to the worship of either Śiva or Viṣṇu. Whichever god is specially honoured, the style is the same. Mr. Fergusson defined its characteristics as follows (p. 325):

The temples consist almost invariably of the four following parts, arranged in various manners, as afterwards to be explained, but differing in themselves only according to the age in which they were executed:

1. The principal part, the actual temple itself, which is called the *vimāna*. It is always square in plan, and surmounted by a pyramidal roof of one or more storeys; it contains the cell in which the image of the god or his emblem is placed.

2. The porches, or *maṇḍapas* (*mantapa*), which always cover and precede the door leading to the cell.

3. Gate pyramids, *gopuras*, which are the principal features in the quadrangular enclosures which always surround the *vimānas*.

4. Pillared halls, or *choultries*, which are used for various purposes, and are the invariable accompaniment of these temples.

Besides these, a temple always contains tanks or wells for water, to be used either for sacred purposes or the convenience of the priests; dwellings for all the various grades of the priesthood attached to it; and numerous other buildings designed for state or convenience.

Except in the earliest rock-cut examples, the roofs and almost all parts are bounded by right lines. The bulging curvilinear steeple of the 'Indo-Aryan' style is unknown in the south. The celebrated Seven Pagodas at Māmallapuram (Mahābalipur) near Madras, executed under the orders of Pallava kings in the 6th and 7th cents. A.D., and certain other rock-hewn temples in the North Arcot and Trichinopoly districts, mark the earliest known stages in the development of the style, which then showed distinct traces of specially Buddhist forms. At Ellora, in the Nizam's dominions, we possess in the magnificent rock-cut Kailās a perfect Dravidian temple, as complete in all its parts as any later example of the style. This edifice is made to simulate a structural temple by the complete cutting away of the superfluous rock, both externally and internally, so that the temple stands out freely. It was excavated in the reign of Kṛṣṇa I. Rāṣṭrakūṭa, about 760 A.D.

The great structural temples of Southern India are much later in date. They are extremely numerous, and remarkable for their vast size. Fergusson was personally acquainted with 'upwards of thirty great Dravidian temples, or groups of temples, any one of which must have cost as much to build as an English cathedral, some a great deal more.' One of the most notable is the temple erected at Tanjore by the victorious Chola king, Rājarāja, between A.D. 985 and 1011, which has the great merit of having been 'commenced on a well-defined and stately plan, which was persevered in till its completion.' The numerous inscriptions on this temple have been edited by Dr. Hultzsch (*South Indian Inscr.* vol. ii.). Other huge similar structures, less laudable in plan but still magnificent, are to be seen at Srīraṅgam, Chillambaram, Rāmeśvaram, Madura, and many other places. The adequate description of any one of these would fill a large volume. The central corridor of the *choultrie* at Rāmeśvaram has an uninterrupted length of 700 feet, that is to say 100 feet longer than the nave of St. Peter's; and these figures may suffice to give some notion of the large scale on which the southern temples are designed. Fergusson expressed the opinion that the Dravidian temples 'certainly do form as extensive, and in some respects as remarkable, a group of buildings as is to be found in provinces of similar extent in any part of the world—Egypt, perhaps, alone excepted; but they equal even the Egyptian in extent' (*op. cit.* p. 379).

6. The so-called Chālukyan style, which may be designated more fittingly by a territorial name as that of the Deccan, is, as Le Bon correctly observes, a transitional one connecting the forms characteristic respectively of the North and South. If we exclude the purely local and isolated styles of Kaśmīr and Nepāl, the two extremes of Indian architecture are formed by the Indo-Aryan and the Dravidian styles. The Gupta and Chālukyan both possess an intermediate character, and are to some extent related to each other. The latter has two well-marked varieties, that of Mysore, described by Fergusson, and that of Bellary, described by Rea.

The Chālukya empire, which comprised at its greatest extent most of Mysore, parts of the Nizam's territories, and some districts now British, was founded about A.D. 550, and lasted under the first dynasty for about two centuries. The second dynasty was established in A.D. 973, and came to an end, as a power of importance, about A.D 1190. But early in the 12th cent. the Chālukya kings lost the Mysore country, which passed under the government of a Hoysala dynasty, and the splendid temples at Halebīd (Dorasamudra) and Bēlūr, which excited the enthusiastic admiration of Fergusson, who gave the inappropriate name Chālukyan to their style, really were built under the orders of the Hoysala kings. The Bēlūr temple was erected by king Viṣṇu when he was converted from Jainism to Hinduism in A.D. 1117, and the Halebīd temple belongs to the same reign, a few years later (*Epigr. Carnatica*, vol. v. p. 36).

The Mysore style, as described by Fergusson, is characterized by a richly carved base on which the whole temple stands, polygonal star-shaped in plan, with a stepped conical roof, not rising high enough to become a steeple, and a peculiar vase-like ornament crowning the summit. The Bellary variety, to which Rea has devoted a monograph, has a rectangular plan, and the buildings would be classed more properly as Dravidian than as a subdivision of the Deccan style. Rea, while using the name Chālukyan, admits that the temples discussed by him 'might best be described as an embodiment of Chālukyan details engrafted on a Dravidian building.' These works seem to belong wholly to the 12th century. The decorative sculpture is remarkable for its marvellous intricacy and artistic finish even in the minutest details, the ornament generally being completely undercut, and sometimes attached to the solid masonry by the most slender of stalks. The effect is described as being that of the incrustation of foliage placed upon the wall. The beautiful style of Western India, sometimes described as the Jain style, may be regarded as a variety of the Chālukyan.

Space will not permit of lengthy discussion of the manner in which the art of sculpture has been applied in countless temples to the service of Brāhmanical religion. The flat bas-reliefs, so much esteemed by the early Jains and Buddhists, have been rarely, if ever, used by the more orthodox sects, but the change of practice seems to have been due to modifications of taste rather than to religious motives. Regarded from the artistic point of view, no sound distinction can be drawn between the sculpture of the Brāhmanical Hindus and that of the rival religions. As a matter of fact, however, the early bas-reliefs are all Buddhist or Jain, while the later figure sculpture in high relief is predominantly Hindu. Each figure, individually, is rarely of much account as a work of art, but the mass of sculpture exhibited on a temple of the best age, when regarded, in the manner intended by the artist, as an essential part of the architectural design, produces on the mind an impression of extraordinary magnificence, and extorts from the most unwilling critic expressions of fervid admiration. The exuberance of fancy, and the patience in execution displayed by the Hindu sculptors, are almost incredible, and cannot be appreciated without study of either the original works or large-scale photographs.

Hindu mythology supplies the subjects for the decoration of a multitude of minor articles of art manufacture in metal, wood, ivory, and stone, made in many parts of the empire. Numerous examples exist which display rich fancy in design, and unsurpassed delicacy in execution. The magnificent manuscript of the Razm Nāmah—a Persian abstract of the Mahābhārata—preserved in the Royal Library at Jaipur, exhibits the myths of Rāma, Kṛṣṇa, and other Hindu deities as represented in colour by artists of Akbar's time (A.D. 1588), trained in the Persian style. The illustrations cost four lakhs of rupees, or more than £40,000.

The existence of extant fragmentary and corrupt copies proves that a considerable body of Sanskrit treatises dealing with the rules of Indian architecture, both religious and civil, existed at one time. The dates of the composition of these treatises have not been ascertained, and the little that is known about their contents is to be found almost exclusively in the essay by Rām Rāz, who collected the remains of the architectural literature procurable in southern India, and published the results of his inquiry in 1834. The works examined by him are certainly ancient, because they lay down rules for the provision of sites for Jain and Buddhist temples, as well as for those of orthodox sects; but the materials for a more exact determination of their dates do not seem to exist. The following abstract of the contents of the treatise named *Māyāmata* will suffice to give a notion of the nature of these scriptures, known as the *Śilpaśāstras.*

The work 'opens with the mystical rites performed in honour of the *Vāstu*, or the spirit presiding over the ground on which buildings are erected, and proceeds to give rules for the examination of the soil, the preparation of it for buildings in general, the construction of a gnomon for the purpose of determining the cardinal points, the division of the ground-plan into several parts for religious as well as domestic purposes, and the performance of sacrifices previous to the commencement of the work; after which it describes the several sorts of villages, cities, and fortresses, *upapīṭhas* or pedestals, the *adhiṣṭhānas* or bases, the *pādas* or pillars, the *prastaras* or entablatures, the ornaments used in cavettos under the cupola, the seats raised for the reception of idols, the *śikharas* or the domes [*sic*, 'towers'] of temples, the ceremonies observed in laying the first and the last stone of an edifice, the several sorts of temples, the courts by which they are surrounded, the pyramidal gateways, the *mantapas* [*maṇḍapas*] or porticoes, the altars to be raised in the front of temples; and concludes with instructions for the carving of images,' etc. (Rām Rāz, p. 6). If an editor, skilled alike in Sanskrit and the technicalities of architecture, could be found, it is clear that an adequate edition of one of these treatises would throw much light upon the ideas of the Dravidian architects.

LITERATURE.—The only book dealing with Indian art generally is Maindron, *L'Art indien*, Paris, 1898, a small, popular work. For the architecture the standard authority is Fergusson, *Hist. of Indian and Eastern Architecture*, London, 1876, reprinted 1899; but a revised edition is needed and promised. Le Bon, *Les Monuments de l'Inde*, is valuable, with fine plates, and gives the best account of Nepālese architecture. Special monographs are, Rea, *Chālukyan Architecture*, Arch. Surv. of India, New Series, vol. xxi., Madras, 1896; and Fergusson and Meadows Taylor, *Architecture in Dharwar and Mysore*, London, 1866. Cunningham's *Archæological Survey Reports*, 24 volumes, and numerous other publications of the Survey by Burgess and various writers give copious unsystematic information on architecture and sculpture. For the minor arts generally the best authority is Birdwood, *The Industrial Arts of India*, London, 1880. The most magnificent publication on the subject is Hendley, *Memorials of the Jeypore Exhibition, 1883*, in four large quarto volumes. The *Journal of Indian Art and Industry*, 16 vols., may also be consulted with advantage. Rām Rāz, *Essay on the Architecture of the Hindus*, London, 1834, is the sole authority for the ancient Indian literary tradition of architectural laws, as practised in the south. Burgess explains the nature of the architectural *śāstras* of Gujrāt in ch. ii. of vol. ix., *Archæol. Survey of Western India*. An important work, E. B. Havell, *Indian Sculpture and Painting* (Murray), is announced as in the press.

VINCENT A. SMITH.

ARCHITECTURE (Jewish).—Materials for a history of ancient Hebrew architecture are accumulating to an extent that must upset some conventional theories. The new Elephantine papyri reveal the existence in Egypt, at the end of the 5th cent. B.C., of a Jewish temple, with five portals of sculptured stone, copper-hinged doors, cedarwood roofing, and gold and silver chalices. Flinders Petrie, again, has been able to identify the Onias Temple, which was also built in Egypt more than two centuries later. Here we have a tower-like structure, with massive walls of drafted stone, a substantial brick retaining wall, and Corinthian ornamentation. Half a century later Jewish architecture is represented by such buildings as the palace of Simon the Maccabee unearthed by R. A. S. Macalister at Gezer. The remains of Herodian buildings in Jerusalem, and the ruins of synagogues in Galilee, dating from the 1st cent. A.D., carry on the story. These stone synagogues seem to have had on the façade three doors,—one in the centre, large, the others at the sides, smaller. The Galilæan synagogues were built south and north, with entrance in the south. The interior (as at Tell Ḥum, Meiron, and Kefr Birim) was divided into three by two rows of pillars. The central space of the Tell Hum synagogue was surrounded by a gallery on three sides, and traces of similar galleries have been found elsewhere (Schürer[4], ii. p. 521). If these structures were meant for women, then the women's gallery, which became a distinctive feature of synagogues only after the Middle Ages, is traceable to an older date.

Though there was no legal prescription on the subject, the favourite shape for synagogues was the basilica, and square or oblong buildings are still the prevalent form everywhere. The Temple courts, where prayer-meetings were held, were rectangular, and the famous synagogue of Alexandria (destroyed in the time of Trajan) was a basilica. In modern times a number of octagonal synagogues have been built, but the basilica form remained constant despite the changes due to local style and taste. In Italy the Renaissance, in Spain the Moorish, influence, modified the decorations and columns; but there were certain essential requirements which kept the synagogue to one general plan. There was first the ark to contain the scrolls of the Law, secondly the Reading Desk or Almemar, thirdly the Entrance. The ark was by preference placed in the east, though this rule was frequently neglected. The Almemar (properly *al-minbar*, Arabic for 'pulpit') was mostly a rectangular structure occupying the centre of the building. It was used primarily for reading the Scriptures, but in Spanish synagogues it was also the place whence the prayers were read. In many parts, especially in the East, the prayers are still read from a depressed part of the floor near the ark, to comply with the text, 'Out of the depths have I cried unto thee' (Ps 130^1). One of the greatest changes in synagogue architecture in modern times is due to the alteration in the position of the Almemar. This is now placed on the east side in many synagogues, forming with the ark one ornate structure containing the receptacle for the scrolls and the platform for precentor and preacher. Many of the older synagogues made no provision for a pulpit; for sermons were not regularly delivered in the synagogue until the 19th century. The place for the sermon was the school, or Beth Hammidrash. This modification of the position of the Almemar has also affected the seating arrangements. In former times (and also at present in the majority of cases) the benches for men ran lengthwise on two sides of the building, the centre being empty with the exception of the Almemar. Nowadays the seats tend rather to face the ark, so that the worshippers are always turned to the east, the posture required during certain parts of the service. In the older mediæval synagogues there were no galleries for women. Women had a separate prayer-room, which opened into the synagogue by a small window. When the synagogue proper became used by large numbers of women (as began to be habitual from the 14th cent.), the gallery became a prominent feature of synagogue structure. The gallery ran round three sides of the building, and was protected by a lattice sufficiently thick to render the occupants of the gallery invisible from below. This grille has, however, been abandoned in modern times.

A somewhat unreasonable preference for a pseudo-Moorish style of decoration has prevented synagogue architects from adopting classical styles, which are really more suited to the purpose. This, however, is now changing, and there are some fine specimens of classical types in various parts of the world. The contrast between the exterior and the interior of the synagogue has often been noted. The Talmud preferred an elevated site for the synagogue, but it became impolitic for the Jews to draw upon themselves the attention of the world by making their places of worship too prominent. Hence there grew up a tendency towards mean exteriors with low elevations. Compensation was sought by deepening the floor. In the case of the old Karaite synagogue in Jerusalem the building is practically under ground. In Persia it was long forbidden for the synagogue to rise higher than any neighbouring mosque. It should, in passing, be remarked that in the East a good many synagogues resemble mosques, and the domes of Moorish buildings in Spain have found wide imitation among the synagogues of Europe and America. Though the exteriors of synagogues were often poor, this was compensated for by the beauty of the interiors. In many cases, indeed, sobriety and even severity of taste prevailed, and no ornament at all was admitted. But the general tendency was towards ornate decoration: the lion, flowers, fruits, interlaced triangles, and other geometrical patterns (on Arab models), elaborate gilding, and arabesques, fine ornamentation of lamps, and such utensils of worship as are described in the article on ART (Jewish)—in these directions much was possible. There were, by preference, twelve windows in the synagogue, but this number was not general. There were painted windows in the Cologne synagogue in the 12th cent., but it is only in recent times that such ornament has become at all common. Much more often the floor was richly covered with marble mosaics. A feature which added effect to the synagogue was the open space round it. This was sometimes laid out as a garden; but, even when merely a court-yard, it lent itself to the marriage and other processions in which the Jews were adept.

LITERATURE.—See under ART (Jewish).

I. ABRAHAMS.

ARCHITECTURE (Mithraic).—According to Porphyry (*de Antro Nymph.* 6), Zoroaster had consecrated to Mithra in the mountains of Persia 'a cave adorned with flowers and watered by springs,' and from that fact the adherents of the sect had derived and kept the custom of performing their initiatory rites in natural or artificial caverns. Modern investigation has confirmed the correctness of at least this latter statement. The worshippers of the Persian god, in order to carry on their worship, often took up their abode in rock-caves, and chose by preference for their sanctuaries places where a spring rose, or, at any rate, where water was in the neighbourhood. The origin of this custom is more doubtful. Does it go back, as Porphyry states, to ancient Zoroastrianism? We know that in the time of Herodotus the Persians offered their sacrifices on the tops of the mountains (Herod. i. 131). Caverns may have been the first places where they put their gods under shelter (cf. Strabo, xi. 7, 5, p. 510 C). On the other hand, caverns have served as temples in such different religions and among so many various races (Bötticher, *Tektonik der Hellenen*, ii.[2] 414 ff.; W. R. Smith, *Rel. Sem.*[2] p. 197 ff.) that it is difficult to ascertain what influences may have enforced the universally obeyed law that Mithra must be worshipped in subterranean *spelæa*.

Sometimes the followers of the sect chose their abode in a spacious cavern, whose mouth then marked the threshold of the sanctuary which was entirely contained within it. Sometimes, on the other hand, the narrower caverns served simply as a shrine to the temple which extended before their entrance. When a subterranean cavern was unobtainable, they sometimes chose a circular group of rocks which could be roofed in, or they hollowed out the side of a hill, so that at least two of the four sides of the building might be formed by the solid rock. Often they were even content to carve the image of the bull-slaying Mithra on a vertical rock, which served as a support for a structure of which it formed the back wall.

Thus we see the sanctuary gradually becoming separate from the mountain which at first enclosed it completely, and we can accordingly follow the successive stages of a development which little by little rendered the temple independent of the rock, from which it was originally inseparable.

A last step was taken when in the towns or the plains, far from any rock-cave or natural spring, there arose 'mithræums' without a natural support on any side. But they were always built in imitation of the caverns which they superseded, and continued to bear the technical name of *spelæum* (Justin Martyr, *Dial. cum Tryph.* 8; Porphyry, *de Antro Nymph.* 6; Tertull. *de Corona*, 15; for inscriptions, cf. Cumont, *Mon. Myst. Mithra*, ii. 536), although sometimes they received the more general name of *templum*. These two terms, like *specus, spelunca, antrum* (or *ædes*) and *sacrarium* (which on rare occasions are substituted for them), are used to denote one and the same kind of structure, as has been definitely shown by M. Wolff (*Das Mithrasheiligtum*).

We possess at present the exact plans of a score of these subterranean temples which have been drawn in Italy, in Pannonia, in Dacia, in Brittany, and especially in Germany. Their likeness to each other proves that an almost uniform type was everywhere adhered to. In these temples, the orientation of which is very variable and not settled by any liturgical rule, different portions may be distinguished. They are enumerated in an inscription of Apulum (*CIL* iii. 1096) which mentions 'cryptam cum porticibus et apparatorio et exedra.'

A portico (*porticus, CIL* iii. 1096, 3960) faced the street. It was doubtless composed of a colonnade surmounted by a pediment. Thence one entered into a large hall, the *pronaos*, situated on the level or above the level of the ground (*CIL* xiv. 61). Through the wall at the back a door led as a rule into a smaller hall, the *apparatorium* (*CIL* iii. 1096, 3960), that is to say, doubtless, the sacristy, where preparation was made for the celebration of the mysteries. From this sacristy, or, when it was absent, immediately under the portico, there was a flight of steps by which descent was made into the sanctuary proper, the *crypta*. This crypt imitated the appearance of the gloomy caves which it represented; occasionally even the walls were made to look like rock, and the crypt was always roofed with a vault, in which the worshippers saw an image of the sky. This was sometimes constructed in masonry, *e.g.* at St. Clement in Rome (Cumont, *op. cit.* ii. No. 19, fig. 30); sometimes the effect was produced by an arched and plastered ceiling. This ceiling was then attached to a gable roof covered with tiles, as is shown by the recent excavations at Carnuntum (*ib.* No. 228*bis*; cf. i. 60, n. 1). The crypt consisted first of all of a kind of platform which occupied the whole width of the hall; the remainder of the hall was divided into three parts—in the middle a passage of an average width of 2½ metres, and on the two sides massive ledges of masonry stretching along the side-walls of the temple. The average height of these was about 80 centimetres, and the width about 1½ metres.

Modern archæologists have applied to the passage the name *cella*, and to the ledges that of *podia*, but these terms do not appear in the inscriptions, like the Latin names previously cited. Attempts have been made to compare this arrangement of the 'mithræums' with the division of churches into three aisles, but the likeness is purely superficial. The *podia*, whose upper surfaces are slanting and whose width is not great, were occupied by the worshippers, who knelt there, while the *cella* was reserved for the officiating priests. Here it was that the victims were sacrificed, and that the ceremonies of initiation took place. In a 'mithræum' of Ostia (*ib.* 84*d*), 7 semicircles marked in the pavement undoubtedly indicated the places where the priest paused to invoke the planets represented on the sides of the lateral ledges. In other parts certain receptacles appear to have held the water employed in purifications.

At the end of the sanctuary facing the entrance there always rose a great piece of sculpture, the venerated image of Mithra sacrificing the bull (cf. art. ART [Mithraic]), and before that were generally placed two altars, one of which seems to have been especially dedicated to the sun and the other to the moon. The extremity of the *spelæum* where the great bas-relief was placed had no absolute fixity in its arrangement. Sometimes it occupied an apse (*absidata, CIL* iii. 968; *exedra*, iii. 1096), making a projection in the exterior wall at the back; sometimes, on the other hand, two walls sloping inwards formed a niche where the sculpture was placed. Occasionally the bas-relief, revolving on itself in this niche or apse, could, during the services, present successively its two sculptured sides to the worshippers. There were also cases when the architect dispensed with these additions. The wall at the back was plain and the sculpture was made to fit into a recess in its thickness, or to rest upon a base. The part of the temple, generally raised above the rest, where this sacred image was displayed, formed a kind of inner shrine accessible apparently only to the priests, and sometimes screened off by wooden railings.

It is difficult to settle the origin of the arrangement in the 'mithræums' which we find in vogue under the Empire. We have no exact information regarding the sanctuaries of Mithra in the East, and we do not know if the plan adopted in Europe was already followed there. We are, however, in a position to state that the portico and the pediment were imitated from the Greek temples, which transmitted their Greek name, *pronaos*, to this fore-part of the building. We may surmise that the apse, which, moreover, is often wanting, is borrowed from the Roman basilicas, but the interior arrangement of the crypt remains as yet inexplicable. The division of this hall into three parts of unequal height does not offer, so far as the present writer knows, any likeness to any other kind of ancient architecture, and its resemblance to the early Christian basilicas is purely superficial. We must not conceive of these 'mithræums' as structures of vast proportions. Covered as they were by a single roof, they could not easily be enlarged. The most considerable of them are 20 metres in length by 6 to 8 in width, and not more than a hundred persons could find room on the stone ledges. Thus there are often several temples collected in the same place, even in very small towns (five at Ostia, four at Aquincum and Apulum, three at Heddernheim and Friedberg, etc.).

These small buildings were brilliantly ornamented. In the richest sanctuaries, marbles and mosaics covered the ground, the walls, and even the roof; in the poorest, stucco-work and plaster-coatings decorated with brilliant colours sufficed. When the lamps were lit, this gorgeous ornamentation was intended to harmonize with the various colours of the bas-reliefs and the statues in order to produce a more vivid effect.

Often, instead of building a temple for a body of worshippers, wealthy Romans used to place a cellar at their disposal. The traditional plan of the 'mithræums' had then to be modified in accordance with local peculiarities. The division of the crypt into three parts was always preserved, but the accessory constructions, the *pronaos* and the apse, disappeared. The *apparatorium* was removed to a contiguous hall, which was used as a sacristy. It is thus often difficult, in examining ruins, to ascertain where the owner's oratory ended and where his kitchen commenced.

LITERATURE.—Wolff, 'Ueber die architektonische Beschaffenheit der Mithrasheiligtümer' in *Das Mithrasheiligtum von Gross Krotzenburg*, Cassel, 1882, pp. 85, 101; Cumont, *Textes et monuments figurés relatifs aux mystères de Mithra*, Brussels, 1894–99, i. 54–67, of which we have given a résumé here. Nothing of importance has been found since the publication of this book. The principal discoveries are those of the 'mithræum' of Housesteads [Borcovicus] on the Roman Wall (Bosanquet, *Archæologia Æliana*, 1904, xxv. 258 ff.), and of Saalburg (near Frankfort), which has been re-constructed by the skill of the architect Jacobi, and can be visited.

FRANZ CUMONT.

ARCHITECTURE (Muhammadan).—*Introduction.*—Muhammadan architecture deserving of the name is that style of architecture which has sprung up alongside of the Islāmic civilization, and which borrows from the very characteristics of the social conditions in the midst of which it has been developed a distinctly peculiar and well-defined impress. As a matter of fact, it should be remarked that, although architecture is an art whose productions originate in the fulfilling of an actual need and the accomplishing of a useful purpose, and consequently are primarily utilitarian, yet, among all the arts, it is that one which expresses itself in the least realistic way, which demands for its comprehension the greatest power of abstract thought, and whose monuments are able to produce on the mind the most refined impressions. One might almost say that architecture, with music, is one of the most striking creations of the human mind, since, like music, it borrows its means of expression not from concrete things, as sculpture and painting do, but from successions of abstractions, of relations, of emotions and associations which affect the least material portions of our being. Architecture is an art whose origins lie far back in the past, and yet even at the earliest period the fundamental characteristics of architectural composition were clearly defined. This remarkable fact is due to the simplicity of the component parts, the regularity of the plans, the grandeur of the façades, and the mystery inseparable from sanctuaries dedicated to the Deity. As a matter of fact, it is in the construction of temples that the first architects worthy of the name produced their first works. The temple is thus the first building on which the newly-developed human spirit desired to impress a more lofty character than that required to satisfy the material needs of the utilitarian. Men aimed at giving to the building intended for the worship of Deity a character superior not only to that given to ordinary human dwellings, but to that of royal palaces.

When Islām came on the scene, the human race had already travelled far from its origins, and the religious idea had already found diverse expression in the monuments of Chaldæa, Assyria, Babylonia,

Egypt, Persia, India, Greece, Etruria, Rome, and Byzantium. Thus the first Muhammadan temples, the first mosques during the early centuries of the Hijra, assumed no other forms than those derived from imitation of monuments already existing where the new religion was established by right of conquest. The first architects and artificers of Islām, therefore, had no other means of expression than the procedure or tradition of the art of the Byzantines, Copts, Sasanians, or Indians. But these pre-existing elements were applied to new purposes: the new religion had neither mysteries, nor sacraments, nor priesthood properly so called. None of its temples was to enshrine the wonder-working image of a Deity, or of a saint, or the Divinity itself contained in consecrated elements. The mosque was only a place of prayer, of preaching, and, up to a certain point, of instruction. It was, properly speaking, a place of meeting in the general sense of that word (the *jāmi'*, *jama*, *gama*). The first mosque at Medīna, where the Prophet collected his earliest disciples, was an enclosure open to the sky, having one part sheltered by a flat roof supported by wooden pillars covered with plaster, and the Prophet ascended some steps in order to preach.

Here, then, we have in their simplest form the elements of the mosque—a court, porches to shelter the worshippers, the pulpit for the preacher to stand in, and the recess, or *miḥrāb*, the situation of which indicates the *qibla*, or the direction in which one ought to turn in order to have one's face directed towards the central shrine, the Ka'ba of Mecca.

This Ka'ba, the real sanctuary of Islām, and the only one which has a supernatural significance, is not a mosque. It is the 'House of God' built by Abraham, and there is set in the side of it a miraculous and Divine stone. It is the Egyptian 'naos,' or rather the Jewish 'ark,' where the invisible and indivisible God is present. But it is not the prototype of the mosque. The form specially typical of the mosque is the pillared hall, like the 'Amr mosque at Cairo, the mosque of Sidi Okba at Kairwan, the primitive al-Aqṣā mosque at Jerusalem, the mosque of Cordova, the great mosque of Samarra, etc. The origin of this form is easily explained when we remember that in order to recite their prayers the Musalmāns are arranged in ranks parallel to the wall at the end of the mosque where the *miḥrāb* is, which indicates the direction of Mecca. This is the original and specially Islāmic plan of a place for worship.

The Muhammadans, whose energetic advance had, so to speak, extended the limits of the ancient world, had continued their progress from the Pillars of Hercules to Java; and from the early centuries of the Hijra the empire of Islām united under one faith the most widely differing nations. The very diversity of the races conquered by Islām was destined to give rise to variety in Muhammadan architecture, for wherever the new religion was planted, it found itself face to face with fully formed civilizations possessing a well-defined architecture, and often very skilful workmen. The result was that the architecture of the early Muhammadan buildings was the native architecture, more or less strongly affected by new ideas, and without the representations of living creatures. We ought then to divide the study of Muhammadan architecture into as many sections as these distinct nationalities. But it is possible to bring them under more simple divisions. All Muhammadan buildings, or rather all the schools of Muhammadan architecture, may be arranged in five great subdivisions. (By this term 'school' is meant the division or distinction of styles in the same way that, with regard to painting, we use the expressions 'school of Bologna,' 'school of Florence,' 'school of Venice,' etc.) Under these headings, we may enter all hitherto existing monuments without consideration of the periods in which they occur. This method of subdivision seems sufficiently justified, firstly by geographical, secondly by historical considerations. These great subdivisions will then take the following titles:—(1) The Syro-Egyptian school (comprising monuments of Egypt, Syria, and Arabia). (2) The Moorish or Maghrib school (monuments of Algeria, Morocco, Tunis, Spain, and Sicily). (3) The Persian school (monuments of Persia, Mesopotamia, Armenia, Caucasus, Turkestan, Afghanistan, and Baluchistan). (4) The Turkish or Ottoman school (monuments of Constantinople, Anatolia, and Turkey in Europe). (5) The Indian school (monuments of Hindustan). We shall not here speak of the mosques of China, which have nothing of special interest for us, since they are built in the pure Chinese style, and are not distinguished by any characteristic from the architecture used in the public or religious buildings of China (see ARCHITECTURE [Chinese]).

General characteristics of Muhammadan architecture.—Muhammadan architecture, as stated above, is derived, generally speaking, from local architectures modified by Muhammadan ideas. What are these ideas, and in what did they differ from former ones? This is the principal question to settle; for architecture may be considered in a general way as the art of carrying out given ideas by methods which allow the materials at one's disposal to be employed to the best practical and æsthetic advantage.

These ideas in the department with which we are now more particularly engaged, that is to say, religious architecture, are, as we already said when treating of the mosque, entirely different from those governing Christian churches or ancient temples. Other Muhammadan buildings are also inspired by a religious purpose; these are the schools, the *madrasas*—colleges or academies—the *zāwiyas*, or places of meeting, and the shrines to which are attached religious endowments, such as schools, fountains, and alms-houses.

Another condition to be fulfilled was the exclusion of representations of living creatures from the ornamentation used. Although it may be proved that this restriction hardly applied except to religious buildings, and that the texts, as well as the monuments, show us that representations of living creatures were not systematically excluded from the ornamentation of private or public buildings, palaces, houses, etc., it is none the less true that, in general, the architectural decoration of Muhammadan buildings has conformed to this principle. Consequently all the subjects of decoration in Muhammadan art have been found in ornamentation borrowed from the vegetable kingdom and from geometry.

The first architects, whether Muhammadans or Christians, who raised the mosques of Islām drew from sources which differed according to their country. But these influences, whether Byzantine, Coptic, Sasanian, Indian, Africo- or Ibero-Latin, have been in a fashion mingled, and as it were interpenetrated, often because of circumstances quite peculiar to Islām. These will be indicated presently. Finally, nomadic art, if we may use such an expression, had a profound influence on the art of Islām. The art of nomads, which includes the ornamentation of tents, the decoration of saddlery, of carpets, of hangings—an art which may still be studied in the productions of the nomadic tribes from the extreme west of Morocco to the centre of Turkestan—which is based upon tradition, and sometimes reaches a high pitch of refinement, has not existed without exercising a remarkable and important influence on the internal and external ornamentation of buildings. Of this we shall find numerous examples throughout the course of this article.

The Arab, a nomad in a special degree, developed, among all the nations where he planted his new religion, a taste for distant journeys, and the prescribed ritual of the Meccan pilgrimage has been the most striking token of this. Arabic literature, so rich in stories of travel, also witnesses to it. This pilgrimage, binding on every Musalmān, has brought into contact the most widely differing peoples; and it has been, so to speak, by a kind of reciprocal interfusion that the most heterogeneous civilizations have seen certain of their elements mix with foreign ones to form Muhammadan civilization.

From the point of view of the arts these reciprocal influences were not less remarkable. The artificers who made the pilgrimage to Mecca, having arrived in the Holy City, and being impelled thereto by an instinct of affinity, certainly did not fail to enter into relations with their fellow-tradesmen who were also there on pilgrimage. From this there undoubtedly arose an interchange of ideas and of skill; and all the more because, this journey being excessively laborious, the less wealthy of these workmen, either in going or in returning, were obliged to halt on their way in order to work at their trade to provide the means necessary for accomplishing the next stage of the journey. It is, on a much larger scale, a similar experience to that of the travelling journeymen of France in the Middle Ages.

Finally, the enormous extent of Islām from China to Morocco facilitated commercial interchange in a very remarkable way. Ships by sea and caravans by land brought the silks, perfumes, and precious things of the East to the West in a very short time. It is therefore quite natural that Chinese art should have in many cases influenced that of Turkestan and Persia, and that Indian art should have been able to exercise on the artistic products of Mesopotamia, Syria, Egypt, Persia, and even of Spain, an influence which certain passages of the historians explain to us, and of which we obtain a good idea from the observations to be made on many of the decorative details.

In bringing this preliminary survey to a close, we must dwell on one very remarkable aspect of Muhammadan art. It is a common, indeed hackneyed, remark, that Oriental *luxury* is the standing example of a degree of wealth and extravagance which has rarely been reached in other civilizations. This is, in fact, a special characteristic of Islām, and is explained partly by the peculiarity of the Muhammadan mind and partly by the events of history.

The chief characteristic of the Muhammadan mind, although not the absolute fatalism so often charged against it, is entire submission to the will of God. This submission accordingly implies the possibility of reverses of fortune which can in a short time destroy the greatest prosperity. The natural result of the mutability of fortune is to incite men to enjoy as rapidly and as intensely as possible the transitory possessions which fortune places at their disposal. The precariousness of absolute power and the enormous resources which despotism placed in the hands of the Khalīfs both had the same result. Despots, like common folk, were obliged to enjoy rapidly the means of luxury which they had within their reach. To this may be traced the extremely luxurious character of Muhammadan architecture, and also, unfortunately, the want of solidity in most of the private dwellings, palaces, mansions, or country-seats. The buildings dedicated to worship, or built upon plans inspired by religious ideas, were, as a rule, more durably constructed.

1. The Syro-Egyptian school.—This division is treated in a separate article—ARCHITECTURE (Muhammadan in Syria and Egypt)—and will not be discussed here.

2. The Moorish or Maghrib school.—The term 'Maghrib' indicates the whole of Northern Africa lying, of course, west of Egypt. Two elements have contributed to form the Muhammadan art of the Maghrib: on the one side the local traditions, Roman, Romano-Berber, and Byzantine in Africa, Roman, Romano-Iberian, and Visigothic in Spain; and, on the other, the introduction of Oriental architecture which appears to have been in the first place the Byzantine architecture of Syria, for certain Syrian forms seem to have been introduced directly into Africa. To be convinced of this, one has only to compare the Aghlabid gates of the great mosque of Tunis and the eastern façade of the great mosque of Sfax with the lateral façades of the great church of Qal'at Sim'ān (de Vogüé, *Architecture civile et religieuse dans la Syrie centrale et le Haouran du ier au viie siècle*). Another source of inspiration borrowed from the East, but this time from the Muhammadan East, is the plan of the mosques. The present writer has shown in his manual of Muhammadan architecture (*Manuel d'art musulmane*, Paris, 1907, i. [*History of Architecture*]) the likeness existing between the plan of the Zituna mosque at Tunis and that of the great mosque of Damascus, which itself is suggested by the plan of the great church of St. Simon at Qal'at Sim'ān (de Vogüé, *op. cit.* ii. pl. 139), two of the great aisles of which were joined at the ends by a transept running at right angles to them. This comparison has never been made so far as the present writer knows; it is, however, very remarkable. G. Marçais has mentioned in the *Revue Africaine* the numerous ideas borrowed, according to the Arab historians of Spain, from the Arab monuments of Syria by the architects of the Khalīfs of Cordova. This process of borrowing was quite natural because of the Syrian origin of the Umayyads of Spain. But the prototype of the great mosque of Cordova cannot be looked for at Damascus; its plan presents no resemblance to that of the great mosque of that city. We must find it at Jerusalem in the plan of the chief mosque al-Aqṣā. Guy le Strange, in his work, *Palestine under the Moslems* (London, 1890), has given a restored plan of it according to the description of Muqqadasī, which shows its arrangement in A.D. 985.* The ancient mosque of Jerusalem was 15 aisles in breadth and 21 in length; that of Cordova 11 aisles in breadth and 21 in length (at least originally); both have side-gates on the eastern façade. Idrīsī, quoted by le Strange (*op. cit.* p. 108), seems to have noticed this likeness, which le Strange has perfectly understood (p. 103). As to the decoration of the mosque at Cordova, it is borrowed partly from Byzantine art, and partly from Arab or Syrian or Mesopotamian ornamentation. This is certainly no longer doubtful, so that we can ascertain the origin of the serrated arches used systematically in the great mosque at Cordova, and recurring in the palace of Harūn al-Rashīd at Racca (Saladin, *op. cit.* p. 323, fig. 291), the al-Ashik palace at Samarra (*ib.* p. 325), of which General de Beylié † was the first to publish a very correct view (de Beylié, *Prome et Samarra*, Paris, 1907, pl. xiii.), and in the interior archivolts of the southern windows of the great mosque of Samarra (*ib.* p. 81). The horse-shoe arch is also of Oriental origin—Mesopotamian or Sasanian (exemplified in the secondary gate of the Palace of

* It was the mosque re-built by 'Abd al-Malik towards 691 of our era, and restored in 746 by al-Manṣūr.

† Cf. also the work of Herzfeld published since that of General de Beylié.

Ctesiphon ; see Herzfeld, *Samarra*), for it is found in Persia at Firuzabad and at Ṭāq-i-Girra. This mosque-plan of which we have just been speaking is, to a certain extent (except in the proportion between the breadth and the length of the building), that of the mosques with aisles, like the 'Amr mosque at Cairo, and those of Samarra which de Beylié and Herzfeld have described, and that of Abū-Dilif which de Beylié was the first to portray, but these are later than the mosque of Cordova. They are mentioned here as giving the characteristics of the typical plan of the mosque, and comprising in themselves all that we know at present regarding the most ancient Muhammadan monuments of Mesopotamia ; for the monuments of Samarra and of Abū-Dilif owe absolutely nothing to Syrian architectural traditions, which are based upon the use of dressed stone. These, on the other hand, are constructions of brick, and consequently connected with the pure Mesopotamian tradition, though strongly influenced by Sasanian art.

Thus, then, Spain appears to have been more directly influenced by Syria and Mesopotamia than was the case with Northern Africa. The great mosque of Kairwan in Tunis, for example, borrows an ancient or Byzantine character from all the ancient and Byzantine fragments which have been employed for its construction in columns, bases, and capitals. Arab historians, however, attribute to a Syrian architect the dome covered with green enamelled tiles which Ibrāhīm ibn al-Aghlab caused to be constructed above the porch of the celebrated mosque.

On the other hand, it is indisputable that the horse-shoe arch, the employment of which may be considered one of the characteristic principles of Moorish art, is borrowed from Sasanian architecture, for it is found in Persia in the Ṭāq-i-Girra, the palace of Sarvistan, and in Mesopotamia in the celebrated palace of Chosroës at Ctesiphon—in the gates on the ground floor. It appears to have been employed there in a systematic fashion, while in the Christian monuments of central Syria and in certain buildings of Armenia it appears to have been used only in an intermittent way. The most ancient examples of the use of this arch may be seen in Tunis in the inner window of the *maqṣūra* of the mosque of Sidi Okba at Kairwan, in the central motive of the interior façade of the Zituna mosque at Tunis, and in the eastern side façade of the great mosque at Sfax. This arch, which has been justly compared in shape to a horse-shoe, has been systematically used in the celebrated mosque of Cordova. It is found in the windows, the gates, and the interior arches, whether they are many-lobed or not.

Finally, local Christian art, whether African or Spanish, also had much influence on the architecture of the Maghrib. Byzantine art did not operate in the same way. Although some very important buildings were erected by the Byzantines in Carthage, it is not possible to assert, from what we at present know of them, the Byzantine character of the gates built or of the binding stones used at Tunis or at Sfax. At both Tunis and Sfax they are connected with the forms of Byzantine art belonging to central Syria. Such are the drums which support the domes of the Zituna mosque at Tunis, the Aghlabid gates of this mosque, and the gates of the eastern façade of the great mosque of Sfax. Moorish Spain, on the contrary, received, by means of artists summoned from Constantinople to Cordova, a genuine influx of decorative Byzantine art, recognizable in the first instance in certain parts of the sculpture of the *miḥrāb*, but above all in the admirable enamelled mosaics executed on the spot by the Byzantine artists who came for the purpose from Constantinople.

We may here recapitulate the chronology of these early monuments of the Maghrib :

Hijra.	Christian Era.	
50	670	Founding of the great mosque at Kairwan by Okba ibn Nāfi.
114	732	Founding of the Zituna mosque at Tunis by Ubaid Allāh ibn al-Habhab.
153	770	Founding of the great mosque of Cordova.

As early as the 8th cent. the new style in Spain assumed quite a distinct character ; for the great mosque of Cordova is obviously a building of a style absolutely and clearly defined. On the contrary, we do not find in Northern Africa, whether in Tunis, or Algeria, or Morocco, such a homogeneity of style in the first Arab buildings. The successive restorations of the mosque of Sidi Okba at Kairwan, the traces of which are still sufficiently visible on the building itself, the Aghlabid portions of the Zituna mosque at Tunis, of the great mosque of Beja, and of that of Sfax in Tunis, no longer give us the impression of a well-defined style. The reason for this must very probably be found in the fact that the commencement of the Umayyad Khalīfate of Cordova constituted a political and social régime on a sufficiently firm basis to give to the country such prosperity that the magnificence of the buildings far surpassed those of Africa, which was then a much poorer country. On the other hand, the continual relations of Cordova with Syria, and the arrival in Spain of a great number of followers of the Umayyads, made Arabized Andalusia at this time, so to speak, a second Arabized Syria. The proofs of this are abundant in the Arab historians and even in the buildings.

In the 11th cent. the influence of Middle Asia, that is to say, of Mesopotamia and perhaps even of Persia, was making itself felt in Africa in the style of the buildings of Qal'a of the Beni Hammād, and probably in those of Bougie, which are unfortunately thus far not known to us except from descriptions of Arab writers. It made itself felt also in Sicily, which had passed from the yoke of the Aghlabids under that of the Fāṭimids, and in which we recognize the Arab style only by the traces which Arab arts have left in the buildings of the 12th cent., erected there by the Norman kings.

At the end of the 11th cent., from the time when Yūsuf ibn Tāshfīn united Spain and the Maghrib under his authority, a modification seems to be introduced into the Arab architecture of Spain ; and it appears that this modification is due to Moroccan artists ; this cannot, however, be positively established by examples of an authentic date. The magnificence of Fez and of Marrakesh under the Almoravids completely explains how the architects who contributed to the adornment of these two towns were consequently able to exercise influence, either directly or by means of their pupils, on the tendencies of the school of Andalusia. This change of style is apparent at Toledo in the Puerta del Sol, and later under the Almohads in the great mosque of Tlemsen, and in certain portions of the mosque of Tinmel, which has recently been discovered and described by Doutté.

It was not till the 12th cent. of our era that the new style really spread in a wonderful manner, by this time freed from antique or Byzantine imitations, and clearly marked by qualities of taste, of sobriety, of elegance and restrained luxuriance, which render the monuments bequeathed to us true masterpieces.

A short enumeration will give the chronological sequence of these.

Hijra.	Christian Era.	
398	1007	Founding of the mosque of Qal'a of the Beni Hammād (Algeria, in the present province of Constantine).
459	1068	Founding of the mosque of Bougie by an-Nāṣir.
460	1069	The Almoravids found Marrakesh and beautify Fez.
478	1085	Conquest of Spain by Yūsuf ibn Tāshfīn.
481	1088	Puerta del Sol at Toledo.
524	1131	Tlemsen restored by Abd-al-Mu'min.
530	1136	The cupola of the great mosque of Tlemsen built.
570	1174	Construction of the great mosque of Seville.

From 574 A.H. (A.D. 1178) to 590 A.H. (A.D. 1194) Ya'qūb al-Manṣūr covered Morocco and Andalusia with numerous buildings. In Morocco, Chella, Rabat, Marrakesh, Ceuta, Alcazar-Kabir, Manṣūra, mosques, fortifications, and buildings of every kind are ascribed to him. In Spain, and especially at Seville, he built mosques, *qasbas*, fortifications, quays, and aqueducts, and he completed the great mosque whose minaret is still standing almost entirely intact. The Kutubīya of Marrakesh, the tower of Ḥasan at Rabat, the minaret of Chella, and its fortified enclosure may be considered the most perfect types of this fine architecture. In A.H. 596 (A.D. 1199) the Alcazar of Seville was founded, but the 13th cent. was destined to inaugurate for the Moorish style a period of luxuriance and florid abundance quite different from the preceding one.

The tomb of Sidi bū Madina at Tlemsen gives an idea of this new development. In 1230 the Alhambra of Granada was commenced, in 1231 the mosque of the Qasba at Tunis was founded by Abū Zakarīya, a work of Andalusian architecture in which nothing any longer recalls the first Arab monuments of Tunis. For a large number of emigrants from Andalusia had a hand in it, not only because of the fall of the Almohads, but especially because, owing to the want of native artists, the Ḥafṣids, as Ibn Sa'īd tells us, imported their architects, their workers in enamel, and even their gardeners from Andalusia. Enamelled earthenware, in fact, had been used in the Maghrib from a considerably remote period; we cannot precisely fix the introduction of it previous to the buildings of Qal'a of the Beni Hammād which date from the commencement of the 11th cent. of our era, and in the ruins of which Paul Blanchet discovered a considerable quantity of fragments of enamelled facings, bricks, pieces of binding masonry and mosaic, etc. From that period this manufacture, which must have been introduced by Asiatic workmen, spread in the Maghrib. Their origin is Asiatic, since the only architectural enamelled earthenware work we know in the Maghrib, previous to this period, consists of the famous squares with metallic reflexions with which Ibrāhīm ibn al-Aghlab adorned the *minbar* of the mosque of Sidi Okba at Kairwan, and which he caused to be brought from Baghdad. By successive improvements this art rapidly attained to that delicacy of execution which we admire in the monuments of Tlemsen, Seville, Granada, and Morocco. Enamelled earthenware is at first used in mosaic, consisting of pieces cut out by hand and placed together, either in hollows cut in slabs of marble or of hard stone, as in the Qal'a buildings of the Beni Hammād, or on a coating of mortar as at Tlemsen and at Chella; in those cases its use is combined with that of enamelled brick. It is very probable that at first faience was used in this way in order to imitate the mosaics of marble which the Arab artists, following the example of the Romans and the Byzantines, had constructed in Syria, in Egypt, and in Sicily. They had even found in Africa some ancient specimens to copy, for the present writer once sketched a fragment of white marble inlaid with coloured marbles found at Lixus (Morocco) by H. de la Martinière. This fragment dates from the 5th cent. of our era, and evidently belongs to that series of works in marble mosaic which served as models to the Arab workmen. This work in faience mosaic, or rather in marquetry, was afterwards succeeded by square tiles, on which pieces of enamel in slight relief showed the usual ornamentation. Later they contented themselves with tracing in black lines on the white enamel a polygonal design with tracery worked in different colours. At a still later date the purely geometrical ornamentation was replaced by a floral decoration or one of some conventional pattern. In Persia and in Turkestan we shall be able to trace a similar development in ceramic decoration. There is no doubt that this art was of Asiatic origin. The similarity between the Spanish enamelled decorations and those in the famous frieze of archers in the *apadāna* of Susa is obvious. On the other hand, the likeness of the enamelling of the most ancient enamelled vases found at Racca (Mesopotamia) to the enamel-work of the Maghrib at once leads us to connect the latter with an Asiatic origin, since we may confidently assign the most ancient enamel-work of Racca to the period of the Abbāsids. But the intermediary link which would enable us to connect the enamel ornamentation of the Achæmenians with that of the Abbāsids is still wanting. We do not know what sort of fictile art was used in the architecture of the Arsacids and the Sasanians, although from a passage in the *Life of Apollonius of Tyana* by Philostratus we may conclude that, at the time when the latter wrote, enamelled earthenware still formed one of the most characteristic components of the architectural decoration of the monuments and palaces of Babylon.

This digression, though somewhat long, on the use and origin of enamel-work in Moorish architecture, is, however, indispensable in order to show by how slight a link Moorish art is connected with that of the Mesopotamian East. We have seen above that Racca and al-Ashik show us in their Abbāsid monuments the many-lobed arches to the use of which Moorish architecture owes one of its most elegant characteristics. The plan of the Moorish mosque was originally the plan with aisles, as in the 'Amr mosque at Cairo. This plan, which recurs in Tunis, in Algeria, and in Morocco, slightly modified by the broadening of the central nave and the aisle which runs along the *miḥrāb*-wall, undergoes a gradual alteration. Already in the Qal'a buildings of the Beni Hammād an enclosed chancel was outlined before the *miḥrāb*. This is only slightly indicated in the great mosque of Tlemsen (530 A.H. = A.D. 1136), but is clearly defined two centuries later in the mosque of Manṣūra at Tlemsen (737–744 A.H. = A.D. 1337–1344). It comprises the following: a fore-court, a minaret commanding the entrance, side porticoes in the court, a large hall with parallel aisles, and at the end the *maqṣūra*, or chancel, in front of the *miḥrāb*, marked by a cupola crowning a square hall. This is the same arrangement as exists in principle in the great mosque of Cordova, but at Tlemsen it is differently emphasized. This *maqṣūra*, instead of seeming to be a mere adjunct of the building as at Cordova, is at Tlemsen an integral portion of it, and forms, so to speak, the main feature, thus indicating in a formal way the real sanctuary of the mosque.

As this article is limited chiefly to the study of the religious monuments, we shall dwell on civil architecture only very briefly. The buildings, however, which the Moors have left in Spain—the palaces of Tunis, of Algiers, of Morocco, of Fez, and of Mequinez, cannot be passed over.

The architecture of the houses of the Maghrib contains at the same time suggestions from Roman and Byzantine houses, and very probably also from houses of Mesopotamia and Persia. We do not know any very ancient Arab houses in the North of Africa, but the persistence with which the plan of these houses is reproduced, with very few variations, leads us to believe that the prototype has never lacked the features with which we are familiar: an interior court, the division of the house into the *selamlik*, or open portion, used for receptions, and the *harīm*, or private part, unentered by visitors, and reserved exclusively for women and domestic life. It is accordingly a variation of the Roman house. This is understood more easily when we remember that the early Arab conquerors of Northern Africa took up their abode at first in the Roman or Byzantine houses, which still existed in great numbers, just as the French took up their abode, at the commencement of their occupation of the country, in the Arab houses of Tunis and Algeria.

From the earliest period the palaces have been buildings of great magnificence, and the descriptions of the Arab historians give us full information regarding the luxurious style in which they were decorated and furnished. Of these we may mention, by way of example, the famous palace of Medinet-az-Zahra near Cordova, the palace of Mustanṣir in Tunis (described by Ibn Ḥaldūn, *History of the Berbers*), which possessed elevated pavilions, cupolas, kiosks, aqueducts, fountains, and large basins, forming, as it were, liquid mirrors. These were also to be found in the Sasanian palace of Qaṣr-i Shīrīn, and have remained from that time a traditional ornament in Persia. Mustanṣir's palace also contained pavilions with marble columns and wainscottings of marble and faience mosaics. The palace of the Sultan Hamadites of Bougie, and those of Fez, Morocco, and Mequinez, were not less magnificent. We can have, so to speak, an ocular demonstration of the splendour to which Moorish architecture had attained in the Alhambra of Granada, of which the greater part is still standing, although by an unaccountable whim Charles V. caused the south wing to be destroyed in order to build in its place a palace of lamentable mediocrity.

Part of the plan of the Alhambra is an extension of the plan of the Arab house. There are always numerous structures surrounding courts bordered by porticoes, with fountains or large uncovered basins. There is no need to enlarge, in addition, on the lavishness and taste with which a great wealth of constantly varied decoration has been expended on every portion of this delightful palace, which is the glory of Granada and of Arabized Spain (see ART [Muh.]).

After the final expulsion of the Arabs from Spain, Morocco, Algeria, and Tunis received the exiles, who carried thither their artistic traditions. These underwent profound changes in Algeria and Tunis; but in Morocco they were preserved, not entirely in their pristine purity, yet in a way so nearly complete as to give to the Moroccan buildings, down to the latest times, an artistic character very superior to that of the buildings of Algeria and Tunis.

Chronology of the Buildings of the Maghrib.

Hijra.	Christian Era.	
50	670	Okba ibn Nāfi founds Kairwan and its great mosque.
84	703	Ḥasan ibn Nū'mān re-builds the great mosque of Kairwan, and builds the al-Ksar mosque at Tunis.
114	732	Ubaid Allāh ibn al-Habhab founds the Zituna mosque at Tunis.
153	770	Founding of the great mosque of Cordova.
222	837	Ziyadet Allāh restores the great mosque of Kairwan.
248	859	Founding of the Kairuīn mosque at Fez.
325	936	'Abd ar-Rahman III. founds the palace Medinet-az-Zahra near Cordova.
398	1007	Hammad ibn Bulukkīun ibn Zayri founds the Qal'a mosque of the Beni Hammād.
459	1068	An-Nāṣir founds the mosque of Bougie.
460	1069	The Almoravids found the mosques of Morocco (Marrakesh).
530	1136	Cupola of the great mosque at Tlemsen.
548	1153	'Abd al-Mu'min enlarges the Tinmel mosque at Morocco.
570	1174	The architect 'Abd Allāh ibn Amr commences to build the great mosque of Seville.
590	1194	Buildings of Ya'qūb al-Manṣūr at Rabat, Chella, Morocco, Seville.
596	1199	Tomb of Sidi bū Madina at Tlemsen. Building of the Alcazar of Seville.
608	1211	Completion of the great mosque of Bougie.
629	1231	Mosque of Qasba at Tunis.
698	1299	Abū-Ya'qūb an-Nāṣir builds in three years the town of Manṣūra near Tlemsen.
718	1318	Mosque of Sidi Ibrāhim at Tlemsen.
721	1321	Restoration of the Andalusian mosque at Fez.
754	1353	Mosque of Sidi al-Halwi at Tlemsen.
755	1354	Completion of the Alhambra of Granada, founded in 628 A.H. (A.D. 1230).
865	1460	Zāwiya of Sidi ibn Aruz at Tunis.
985	1577	Al-Manṣūr-az-Zahihi builds the famous palace al-Bedi' at Morocco, and a kiosk in the Kairuīn mosque at Fez.
1041	1631	Mosque Hamūda Pasha at Tunis.
1112	1700	Completion of the mosque of Sidi Mahrez at Tunis.

3. The Persian School (Persia, Mesopotamia, Turkestan, etc.).—We have already spoken of the mosques of Mesopotamia, Samarra, and Abū-Dilif. In Persia the style is quite different. Yet the most ancient Persian mosques whose plans are known to us are built with aisles like the primitive mosques. The arrangement of these is still recognizable in the plan of the Juma mosque at Iṣfahān built in 142–153 A.H. under the Khalīfate of the Abbāsid al-Manṣūr; but in this plan there is a peculiar arrangement: in the court there is an isolated structure on a square plan. Dieulafoy describes a similar square pavilion in the centre of the old mosque of Shiraz built in A.D. 875 by Amr ibn Laith. This pavilion is evidently a reminiscence of the Ka'ba of Mecca, for it is known at Shiraz by the name of *Khuda Khan*, or 'House of God.' We should mention also the Juma mosque of Kazvin, re-built by Harūn al-Rashīd in A.D. 790 on the plan of the ancient mosque erected in the early years of the Hijra by Muhammad ibn al-Ḥajjāj.

At a period which it is as yet impossible to define, a remarkable development affects the arrangement of the Persian mosques: on the four sides of the court of the mosque there open enormous porches of great height and in the form of an immense arcade. These *līwāns*, as they are called, are certainly a reminiscence of the *līwān* of Chosroës, the Tāj-i-Kisrā of Ctesiphon, the magnificence of which had astonished the first Arab conquerors, and the recollection of which was always present in the minds of Oriental monarchs when they were erecting great buildings. Muhammadan historians, in fact, when they wish to emphasize the splendour of a building raised by one of their monarchs, always compare it to the *līwān* of Chosroës, to the buildings of Mada'in, etc. In the plan of all the Persian mosques this detail (the *līwāns*) always re-appears, and we find the same architectural feature in certain mosques of Turkestan and especially of Samarcand—mosques which also serve the purpose of *madrasas*, *i.e.* schools or academies, or rather universities. When we closely examine the plan of the Juma mosque of Iṣfahān, we easily see how Malik Shah, Shah Tamasp, and Shah Abbās, in their successive enlargements of the building, changed its original appearance in order finally to give it that definite character which has been, so to speak, the type to which the Persian mosques have conformed, and which is so admirably condensed in the plan of the imperial mosque of Iṣfahān erected under Shah Abbas. This latter may be considered as the *chef d'œuvre* of religious architecture in Persia, where we find no other mosques with aisles, but only the four great *līwāns*, one of which serves as a porch of entry, and the other three as distinct places for prayer, each possessing its own *miḥrāb*.

We see, accordingly, that just as the Persians sharply divided themselves from the majority of the Muhammadans (who are Sunnites, forming a sort of heretical sect by themselves), since they are Shī'ites and therefore abandon the purely Muhammadan tradition,* they gave to their religious architecture quite a different character from that of the buildings to be seen in Syria, Egypt, and in the Maghrib. When the mosques are deprived of a central court, as was the case with the blue mosque of Tabris,† the praying place is always square-shaped, and is led up to by a large square hall surrounded by very broad galleries. Then we have nothing left to recall the primitive mosque, which is really derived from the shelter built along the wall of the *miḥrāb*, which allows the crowd of the faithful to line out along this wall and in files parallel to it, but with faces always turned in the same direction. The tendency in Persia would rather appear to be that of uniting the worshippers in a closed sanctuary in order to secure for them the isolation which favours collectedness of thought and prayer.

We see, therefore, that by a kind of natural development the changes through which the Persian mosque passed, while tending more and more towards a closed sanctuary, would produce successive forms approaching gradually those of certain Christian churches—those of Armenia, for instance.

The earliest Muhammadan architecture in Persia has also quite a special character. The leading elements in Persian architecture are, in fact, almost entirely borrowed from local traditions, that is to say, from the architecture of the ancient Persians and from that of the Sasanian period :

(1) The tapered column, accompanied by flat ceilings and terraces, which seems to be derived principally from Assyrian and Median art.

(2) The arch carried on drums or on columns standing in sets of four. (This arrangement was soon changed into a tetragonal pillar strengthened by four joined columns.) Since the arch and the pillar are constructed of rubble-stone or more frequently of bricks, we cannot doubt that the origin of this system of architecture must be sought in Chaldæa, whence it passed into Persia. As to the arch of dressed and cut stone and structures with binding masonry, they seem to be of Armenian origin, and to have passed from Armenia into the North-west provinces of Persia, where alone they are found.

The arch constructed of bricks was a matter of choice for the Persians ; and this system seems to have been chosen because of the scarcity of timber in the greater part of the country. In this kind of structure they attained to a degree of artistic skill, ingenuity, and cleverness which has never been excelled anywhere. The use of unbaked and baked brick and of enamelled brick came to them both from Chaldæa and from Susiana. It is probably from the early Persian buildings adorned with enamelled bricks or faience mosaic that this process, so fertile in graceful applications, reached the West by way of Tunis and Algiers as far as Morocco and Spain, where the Moorish artists were able to elaborate it to a pitch of perfection as high as that reached in Persia by the Persians.

It was very probably from the use of bricks, whether by corbellings or by projecting stones, that stalactites came into use, which have always been one of the most interesting features of Persian and Syro-Egyptian brick architecture ; but it is possible that stone and wood stalactites have not the same origin although very often similar in appearance. Finally, just as Roman architectural traditions have influenced the development of decoration in the Maghrib alongside of geometrical ornamentation, the origin of which is not yet clearly established, it seems that in Persian art the style of ornamentation has been influenced by Sasanian, Hindu, and, later, by Chinese traditions. Parallel with this also has proceeded a development of geometrical decoration which appears to be an element common to all the countries of Islām, and the origin of which, perhaps because of its Muhammadan character, should be sought in Arabia, not in the buildings of Yemen before Muhammad's time, but possibly in the ornamentation employed by the nomad Arabs in their embroideries, carpets, etc.

The origin of the lancet-arch, which was used in the ancient buildings of Egypt along with the catenary arch, and which has been found also in Assyria, appears thus to be settled, but its use seems to be reserved for the hidden parts of buildings, and those where solidity and economy in construction were both required. The palace of Chosroës at Ctesiphon in its visible portions has only semicircular arches, whether of horse-shoe shape or not, except its great arch, which is catenary ; but the groovings disposed at the top of the tympanum of the arch, which were not seen because they were in the interior of the building and above the arches, had pointed groinings. This pointed arch was a feature as frequently employed by the Persians as the horse-shoe arch was by the Moors, but the Persians very soon recognized that the pointed arch formed by two skew arches involved a complication in construction easy to avoid by closing the curve by two straight lines ; it is for this reason that their arches are of such an original and distinct character. We find in the West this predilection for closing brick arches by rectilineal portions in France, in the Roman architecture of Toulouse and its neighbourhood, and in England in numerous brick buildings, from which it passed into buildings of stone under the name of the Tudor arch.

The other religious buildings of the Persians are the *madrasas*, or religious schools, and the tombs. These *madrasas* assumed in Persia a still more important development than they did in Egypt or in the Maghrib. One of the most ancient which have been described is the *madrasa* of Mustanṣir, built at Baghdad in A.H. 630 (A.D. 1232), of which a summary plan is given by General de Beylié (*Prome et Samarra*, fig. 18). It consists of a suite of buildings arranged round a rectangular court, with a *līwān* in the centre of each of its four sides. These buildings, pierced by numerous arcades, contained the cells of the students. The likeness of the plan on which they

* The Sunnite mosque seems to be derived from the mosque of Medina, which originally consisted only of a wall with a *miḥrāb* approached by very rude porticoes. The Shī'ite mosque, on the other hand, seems to be derived from the mosque of Mecca. In the centre of the court (*haram*) is the *Khuda Khan*, or 'House of God,' an imitation of the Ka'ba, and places for prayer are arranged on the four sides of the court.

† This mosque was certainly erected by a Sunnite monarch, but the architect who constructed it has drawn his inspiration solely from the architectural traditions of Persia. Compare this plan with that of the mosque of Mir Buzurg Kawām-ad-din, built at Amul in A.D. 1379.

are built to that of the caravanserais with which Persia is covered will not escape any one, any more than its similarity to the plans of the great Persian mosques. If we could ascertain the most ancient types of these buildings, for example the Persian or Sasanian caravanserais, we should perhaps have the origin of that cruciform plan which the Persian architects have been able to turn to such excellent account.

One of the most remarkable *madrasas* which have been built in Persia is the Madrasa-i-Shah Sultan Husain at Iṣfahān (A.D. 1693). As a caravanserai was built close beside it at the same time, by merely examining the two plans in juxtaposition we understand what a striking likeness exists between them.

This arrangement has been reproduced in the great mosque-*madrasas* of Samarcand and Bokhara, and indeed in those of all the large towns of Turkestan, whence it is certain that the first architects of these buildings were Persians. In the case of some of them the proof is ready to hand. The *madrasa* Shir-Dar near Samarcand is the reduction to a comparatively small scale of the Persian *madrasa*; the mosque, *madrasa*, and tomb of Bibi Hanum at Samarcand is the expansion of it on a colossal scale (the plans are given by Schubert von Soldern, *Baudenkmale von Samarkand*, 1898).

The tombs and sepulchral monuments in the Persian school of architecture have also quite a special character. In the Maghrib they generally consist merely of a square structure surmounted by a cupola, which seems simply a detached portion of what ordinarily constitutes a mosque, for we have seen that generally the entrance is crowned by a cupola and the *miḥrāb* of the mosque by another; this is, at any rate, the arrangement which exists in the most ancient mosques of Tunis (Kairwan, Tunis, Gafsa, Beja, Sfax) and of Morocco (as in the Kairuīn mosque at Fez).

In Persia these buildings are of an entirely different character. They consist of square, polygonal, or cylindrical towers covered with conical or pyramidal roofs, or crowned by a bulb-shaped cupola, *e.g.* at Maragha, Nakshevan, Demavend. At Sultanīya, at Merv, in the tomb of the Sultan Sanjar, the plan is even more complicated, and sometimes, as in Persian Mesopotamia, these tombs of polygonal construction are crowned by cupolas composed of a series of stalactites superimposed on each other, and the outline they present is striking. Such are the tomb of Zubaida at Baghdad, and the tomb of Daniel at Susa.

Around these tombs of various styles are grouped different buildings, as, for example, at the tomb of the Sheikh Sufi at Ardabil; but the finest of all these sepulchral monuments is certainly the tomb of Timur or Gur Emir at Samarcand, built in 808 A.H. (A.D. 1405) by Muhammad, son of Mahmud of Iṣfahān. The whole effect of this impressive monument is very beautiful. The tomb, properly speaking, consists of a great square hall, the sides of which are grooved with large square niches, and which is crowned with a bulb-shaped cupola set on a drum decorated with enamelled bricks, the cupola being also adorned in the same way. The porch of the tomb opens on a square court surrounded with cells, at the four corners of which formerly rose four great cylindrical minarets of which only one now remains; two others flanked the entrance porch of the court. Other very striking tombs are still to be found near Samarcand adjoining the mosque of Shah-Zindah, and we can trace in them with a singular variety of detail the whole development through which the use of baked enamelled earthenware for the construction and decoration of these buildings had passed at this time. Besides the Persian artists engaged in the construction of the buildings of Samarcand, Chinese artists in pottery, summoned by Bibi Hanum (who was a Chinese princess), the wife of Timur, have exercised an indisputable influence both on the technique of enamelled earthenware-work and on the style of this decoration.

It is also certain that in these great specimens of enamelled decoration the Persian architects drew their inspiration from suggestions afforded by the decoration of tapestry, embroidery, cloths, and especially carpets. As the present writer has described in his manual of the history of Muhammadan architecture, the perfection of this enamelled decoration—a perfection attained at the commencement from an æsthetic point of view—can be explained only by the fact that they applied to decoration rules established by the long practice of manufacturers of carpets and painted cloths—rules which, by a process of continual selection, had eliminated imperfect elements from decorative compositions in order to preserve only such as were satisfactory.

Secular architecture in Persia has, perhaps more than religious, remained impregnated with the ancient traditions of the country. The Persian palaces have been compared above to the Sasanian palaces of Qaṣr-i Shīrīn; they might also be compared to the ancient Achæmenian palaces of Susa and of Persepolis. It is doubtless to this uninterrupted tradition that we should assign the use of terraces supported on long wooden columns, which are found in the palaces of Iṣfahān, of Shiraz, and of Teherān. The authentication of this tradition is all the more remarkable because wood is a comparatively rare and costly substance in nearly all the provinces of Persia.

In the royal palaces of Iṣfahān these columns were covered with little squares of looking-glass not only on the front of their shafts, but on their capitals; the stalactites of the ceilings and arches were also covered with them, and the flashing of these thousands of mirrors, the brilliance of the paintings, and the facings of faience, made these lofty halls, with glittering ceilings, marvels of taste and luxuriance, more remarkable even than we have seen in the Moorish palaces of Andalusia.

The Persian house, like all Muhammadan houses, is divided into an *anderun*, or part reserved for the women and the family, and a *birun*, or part reserved for the reception of guests. But its arrangement no longer presents any likeness to that of the ancient house. The building is no longer arranged round the front court. This court in Persia is replaced by a garden. If the house is a simple one, the *anderun* is on the first floor; if it belongs to a richer class, the *birun* opens on the garden and on the street, and at the bottom of the garden is the *anderun*. The Persians also built enormous bazaars, streets roofed in and lined with shops; and all their large towns still possess them, the finest certainly being those of Iṣfahān. These bazaars contain not only roofed streets and shops, but baths, or *ḥammāms*, mosques, schools, tombs, and city caravanserais, in which merchants with their wares put up. Other caravanserais are disposed at different stages along the roads; these are resting-places for travellers and caravans. Herodotus mentions that Cyrus had had them placed all along the roads of his empire. Here we have again in Persia a tradition dating from before the time of Islām.

The Sasanian kings had built a number of remarkable bridges. The Muhammadan sovereigns of Persia followed their example. Without counting the numerous bridges constructed in Persia since the Muhammadan conquest, we ought not to forget to mention the two very striking bridges of Iṣfahān, that of Allāh-Verdi-

Khan and that of Baba Rukn-ad-din, which are real masterpieces.

In a country as barren as Persia, the discovery, securing, and conveyance of water were naturally questions of vital importance. Subterranean aqueducts, or *qanāts*, made possible the search for water, often at great distances, for the purposes of supply and irrigation. These aqueducts supplied either large subterranean reservoirs (called *ābambār*) in the towns and villages, or vaulted cisterns, placed along the roads near the caravanserais. At other times the river-water was held back by dams to be conducted into irrigation canals. M. Dieulafoy has described two of them, the dam of Saveh and the Band-amir.

We shall not enter in this section, any more than in the preceding one, on the examination of military architecture. That of the Maghrib is known to us by a large number of drawn or photographed buildings; that of Persia, on the contrary, is as yet almost unknown to us.

The Persian school of architecture spread its influence as far as Baghdad and even Armenia, and exercised an indisputable effect on the Seljuk architecture of Asia Minor and on the Ottoman architecture derived from it. It has directly influenced the architecture of Turkestan, and we shall see that, as regards India, it is absolutely certain that the finest buildings of the Mughal period were immediately inspired by the finest architectural and decorative traditions of Muhammadan Persia.

But, since among Muhammadan arts architecture is absolutely supreme and all the other arts are based more or less on the principles which govern architectural construction, we ought not to be surprised at the immense importance of the influence of Persian decorative art on all the arts of other Muhammadan countries.

Chronology of the Buildings of Persia and of Turkestan.

Hijra.	Christian Era.	
137	755	Tombs at Rai.
142	760	Founding of the Juma Mosque at Iṣfahān.
174	790	Juma Mosque at Kazvin.
261	875	Juma Mosque at Shiraz.
408	1017	Founding of the great mosque of Ardabil.
552	1157	Tomb of Sultan Sanjar at Merv.
583	1187	Mausoleum of Mumin-i-Hatum at Nakshevan.
630	1232	Mausoleums of the Saids at Amul.
659	1261	Tomb of the daughter of Hūlāgū at Maragha.
704	1304	Mosque of Uljaitu Shah-Khodabandah at Sultaniya.
722	1322	Mosque of Veramine.
781	1379	Mosque of Mir Buzurg Kawām-ad-din.
791	1389	Mosque of Bibi Hanum at Samarcand.
805	1403	Great or blue mosque at Tabris.
901	1496	Darwāza-i-Kieuchk at Iṣfahān.
942	1535	The town of Iṣfahān embellished with magnificent buildings.
1021	1612	Masjid-i-Shah at Iṣfahān.
1104	1693	Madrasa and caravanserai Madrasa-i-Shah Sultan Husain at Iṣfahān.
1206	1791	Buildings of Teherān.
1223	1808	Embellishment of Iṣfahān by Fath-Ali-Shah.

4. The Ottoman School (Turkey in Europe and Asia Minor).—The first real entrance of the Osmanli Turks on the stage of history is at the time when the last Seljuk ruler of Konia, Ala-ud-din III., conquered by the Mongols, yielded his empire to Othman, that is to say, in the 14th cent. of our era.

The Seljuk kingdom was therefore the germ of the future Ottoman empire. We also find that the buildings erected by the Seljuks of Rūm (*i.e.* the kingdom of Konia) are the first which exhibit the union of Persian and Syro-Egyptian influences still distinct and even widely differing in these buildings. These are the influences the fusion of which with the constructive traditions of Byzantine architecture produced the striking art of the Turkish buildings of Brūsa, Adrianople, and Constantinople. For this reason we should study them first. We find, in fact, in the buildings of Konia, Syrian features in the porches, the small columns joined together, the niches, the stalactites, and those long girths ornamented with eight-rayed half-stars which we see so frequently in buildings of the 13th cent. in Syria, and especially at Damascus. However (what we do not find in Syria, while the buildings of Konia and its neighbourhood show us numerous examples of it), there are various applications of enamelled earthenware and brick to the interior decoration of the buildings, and even to some interior elevations of them, such as that of the inner court of the Sircheli Madrasa at Konia. This, with its enamelled facings, seems to be a Persian building transplanted bodily to Konia, although the porch of its exterior façade is entirely of stone, and of a very decided Syrian style.

When the Turkoman tribes arrived in Asia Minor after a long sojourn and long wanderings in Persia, they imported thither the industries necessary to the life of nomad communities: saddlery and the manufacture of cloths, of carpets, and of embroideries. This art of the nomads has influenced in a very high degree not only the extremely original decoration of the mosque of Inje-Minareli at Konia, but still more the striking north gate of the great mosque of Divrigi, the complicated ornamentation of which is distributed over the whole façade in an arbitrary and unsymmetrical way (cf. Saladin, *Manuel*, fig. 335). Some of these mosques, like that of Ala-ud-din at Konia, or that of Echrif-Rūm-Jami at Beishehr, or, again, that of Houen at Kaisarīya, are arranged on plans with aisles like the ancient mosques of Egypt or of the Maghrib. Others are *madrasas* with their *līwāns* arranged crosswise, *e.g.* the Sircheli Madrasa at Konia, the Ibrāhīm Bey Madrasa at Akserai, the *madrasas* of Sivas and of Erzerum, etc. We find caravanserais also as in Persia, but with an entirely different plan. These caravanserais rather recall the plan of the Roman or Byzantine *castellum*, comprising, as they do, storehouses, dwelling-rooms, and stables. One of the most imposing of these buildings is the Sultan Khan, north-east of Konia, all the details of which have been carried out with remarkable skill. Its enclosure is strengthened by enormous buttresses, which reveal more decidedly than usual its defensive character, but a magnificent porch which adorns the entry prevents it from presenting too forbidding an appearance. This doorway is still quite Syrian in character; nevertheless we can already trace in it the chief tendencies which, modified and brought to perfection by the architects of the Green Mosque at Brūsa and of the Bayazidīya of Constantinople, evolved those splendid porches of the most ancient Turkish mosques. In the middle of the court a small square building serves as a mosque, representing the *Khuda Khane* of the Persian mosques. The interior decoration of this caravanserai is reduced to its most simple expression, as befits a building erected for public use. But these caravanserais no longer follow the Persian plan at all, while on the other hand the *madrasas* or mosque-*madrasas* still draw their inspiration from it. But at Erzerum, for example, the plan of the madrasa is doubled by a long nave, at the end of which is a tomb (Imaret Ulu Jāmi' or Chifte Minaret; cf. Texier, *Arménie, Perse, et Mésopotamie*), and assumes almost the appearance of a church-nave preceded by a hall surrounded with dwelling-rooms. In this case we must trace in it a Byzantine tradition.

As to the mausoleums, or tombs, they share as much in the Persian as in the Armenian tradition (cf. the tombs of Akhlat; see Lynch, *Travels in*

Armenia, ii. 181 f.). It is certain that Armenia also exercised a very strong influence on Seljuk architecture. The chief reasons for this will be found in the present writer's *Manuel*. We might, therefore, sum up the character of Seljuk art by describing it as a mixture of Persian, Syrian, and Armenian art. The fact is completely explained by the geographical position of Konia (Iconium). We may remark, moreover, that as we travel northwards the Seljuk buildings assume an uncouth and heavy style of decoration which seems to be strictly due to the predominance of Armenian influence; on the other hand, the more we approach the south, the more Syrian influence reveals itself by its refinement, distinction, and exactitude. The harmonious collocation of forms of stone architecture and of enamelled decoration did not at once reach complete perfection. It is easy to understand that brick architecture and stone architecture, which proceed from entirely different starting points, and consequently have quite distinct characters, could be harmonized only after many bungling attempts and trials. One of the most interesting of these is that made by the architects of the Ottoman sultans at Brūsa. The Yeshil Jāmi', or 'Green Mosque,' presents, in fact, a very homogeneous exterior harmony of marble architecture: a great porch opens on a façade pierced with windows and grooved with niches; the porch is still the Seljuk porch, but simplified, corrected, and admirably crowned by a kind of half-dome in stalactites; the latter is encircled by very fine arabesques, which are themselves set, as is the entire porch, in a majestic door-frame decorated with sculptures and inscriptions in magnificent characters. The interior is completely decorated with faience mosaics of the greatest beauty. The *miḥrāb*, entirely of enamelware, is very lofty, and the general impression made by it recalls a little that of a great Seljuk doorway; the walls are decorated with a ceramic panelling surmounted by a magnificent frieze, and the inner wall of the mosque opposite the *miḥrāb*, which is generally bare of decoration, here assumes a singular importance by reason of two great *līwāns* on the ground floor, and a fine alcove on the first floor, all entirely executed in very beautiful enamel-work. The plan of this mosque at Brūsa, although rendered totally different from those which we have already studied by a very skilful use of large cupolas, recalls, although in an imperfect manner, the cruciform plans of the *madrasas*, because of these two lateral *līwāns* which flank the chief cupola. This enamel decoration is still Persian in its workmanship and suggestion, and even the first secular buildings of Constantinople, such as the Chinli Kiosk, built at the Seraglio in 1466, in their plan and appearance are still altogether Persian.

At the time of the occupation of Constantinople by the Turks, however, the influence of the Byzantine buildings immediately made itself felt on the productions of the Sultans' architects who built for them their first mosques. Thus the mosque of Sultan Bayazid, commenced in 1497, reproduces on a small scale the plan of St. Sophia at Constantinople, *i.e.* its main characteristic is a great cupola resting on pendentives, supported in front and behind by two large demi-cupolas of equal radius. But this mosque is already distinguished from the mosques of Brūsa by a correction in the plan, and in the general arrangement of the outer and inner parts, a correction which shows an art already completely master of its methods. This art, now that it has been able to borrow from Byzantine art the chief element of structural arrangement, may be regarded as complete, for till the conquest of Byzantium the mosques did not possess that character of boldness, exactness, and definiteness which an architectural work must possess in order to rank among works of art. As long as the plan is undetermined, the work of architecture cannot be considered as complete.

The Turkish mosque consists, then, of a praying place properly so called—a large rectangular hall covered by an enormous cupola supported by two large demi-cupolas. The *miḥrāb* of marble or of enamel-work faces the entrance. Coloured panes set in plaster traceries light the mosque. The Turkish mosques are much the best lit of all, even when nearly all their glass panes are preserved, which is not often. In front of the mosque is a court surrounded by porticoes; in the centre a fountain, the φιάλη of the Byzantine churches, and commanding the four corners of the court, gigantic minarets like monolithic pillars crowned by a pointed roof. Such is the type of the Ottoman mosque from Bosna-Serai to Cairo.

From this time Ottoman art made giant strides, and the wonderful great mosques, the outlines of which still in our day adorn the capital of Turkey, are erected one after another. Such are the mosque of Muhammad II.; that of Sultan Selim; the Sulaimanīya, or mosque of Sulaimān the Magnificent, with its court surrounded with porticoes, its four minarets, its colossal dome supported by four enormous pillars, its great antique columns of porphyry and syenite seized from the Imperial palaces, its coloured panes and its enamel-work; the mosque of Shahzada; that of Sultan Ahmad, the largest of all; and the Jāmi' of Yeni Valideh, one of the finest.

Sulaimān's architect, the celebrated Sinan, is the builder of the finest mosques raised during the reign of the great legislator, but his masterpiece is perhaps not at Constantinople; it is possibly his last work, the Selimīya of Adrianople, which is the most perfect of all, with the extreme simplicity of its plan, the harmony of its proportions, and the perfection of its outline. Unfortunately the decadence of this fine art was rapid; contact with Western art was fatal to it. Already in the mosque Nur-i-Osmanīya (1748–55) we see the introduction of European elements into Ottoman architecture. That intermixture, which perhaps in skilful hands might have been able to bring about a happy modification of Turkish art, was left in the hands of second-rate French or Italian architects. These, by their unskilfulness, rapidly brought about the decay of that art which had produced such great masterpieces.

A few words remain to be said on other architectural works. The Ottomans built numerous schools, madrasas, and monasteries, or *takīyas*. These are generally occupied by dervishes of the Mevlevi order, who played such an important part at the commencement of the history of the Ottoman empire, and do so still in a quiet way, since it is their Grand Master who at the consecration of each Sultan girds the new sovereign with the Prophet's sabre in the old mosque of Ayyūb. Frequently the architecture of these buildings is affected by local traditions, and their case differs from that of the mosques which from the commencement of Sulaimān's reign were all erected on plans derived more or less directly from the types invented by Sinan.

The tombs of sovereigns and of great personages are influenced more or less, as regards their plan, by the use of the cupola. To give a list of them here would be tedious. We shall mention especially those which are near St. Sophia, those of the sultans Selim, Murad, and Muhammad IV., that of Sultan Ahmad, and, above all, those of Sulaimān and Roxalana, near the Sulaimanīya. Turkish tombs are often simplified to mere stelæ, but it also happens that these stelæ, passing through stages of increasing richness of decoration, are evolved into monuments luxuriantly gilded and carved, which are sheltered under kiosks or cupola-crowned pavilions.

From their ancient nomad life the Turks have preserved a love of nature and of gardens; they regard the houses or palaces they erect only as transitory dwellings. Except the palaces of the sultans, it is rare to see in Turkey houses other than those of wood, or with wooden frameworks; such is, at any rate, generally the character of the Turkish house. Even when rich or luxurious, it is only a transient decoration; and this feeling seems to be essentially Muhammadan, for we find it in all the countries of Islām, where men build only for themselves, not for their children. At the zenith of their splendour the Ottomans were great constructors of buildings for public use—fountains, caravanserais, bridges, aqueducts, reservoirs, roads, *imārets*, or kitchens for the poor, and hospitals and shelters for the sick or for pilgrims. The sultans, their ministers, and persons of position vied in strenuous rivalry in erecting during their lifetime such buildings as might perpetuate their memory. The study of Ottoman art has been, so far, merely superficial; but it cannot fail to afford great interest from the parallel suggested between the magnificence and wide scope of the conceptions of the Ottoman architects and the splendour and energy which characterize the history of the Ottoman sultans. We might say that the characteristic of Persia is elegance, that of Syria and Egypt wealth, that of Moorish art abundance, and even redundance, and that of Turkey force—characteristics which are found both in the history and in the art of these nations.

This study of the Turkish buildings would be incomplete if unaccompanied by a chronology, which is accordingly appended (including the Seljuk buildings from which, without a doubt, Ottoman art is derived).

Hijra.	Christian Era.	
555	1160	Palaces of the Seljuks at Konia.
613	1216	Tash madrasa at Ak-shahir.
614	1217	Shifaiah madrasa at Sivas.
617	1220	Mosque of Ala-ud-din at Konia.
627	1229	Caravanserai of Sultan Khan.
640	1242	Sircheli madrasa at Konia.
700	1300	Mosque of Houen at Kaisarīya.
758	1357	Ulu Jāmi' at Brūsa.
818	1415	Yeshil Jāmi' at Brūsa.
856–81	1452–76	Muhammad II. builds the mosque of Ayyūb, the palace of the Old Seraglio, the mosque named after him at Constantinople.
902	1497	Mosque of Sultan Bayazid at Constantinople.
919	1513	Built at Constantinople, during the reign of Sulaimān: the mosques of Shahzada, Selimīya, Mihrimah, Sulaimanīya, Rustam Pasha, etc.
		Built at Scutari: Inkelessi, Buyuk, Ayasma, Jahangir, etc.
978	1570	Selimīya at Adrianople.
1018	1609	Mosque Ahmadīya at Constantinople.
1044	1634	Kiosk of Baghdad at the Old Seraglio.
1060	1650	Founding of Yeni Valideh Jāmi' at Constantinople.
1072	1662	Kiosks, gardens, and fountains at the Seraglio of Adrianople.
1141	1728	Fountains of Bāb-i-Humayūn, Azab Kapū, Top Hane at Constantinople.
1161	1748	Mosque of Nur-i-Osmanīya at Constantinople.

5. The Indian School.—Islām, as it spread westward, had transformed everything in its passage. We have seen that in converting Persia it had not been able to effect a thorough conversion to the new doctrine, since the Muhammadans of Persia differ so strongly from those of Turkey, Arabia, and the Maghrib, that the former and the latter form, so to speak, two distinct sects, Shī'ites and Sunnites, each of which considers itself the only orthodox party. Similarly the Muhammadan art of Persia differs more fundamentally from the arts of other Muslim countries than the latter differ among themselves. We shall see that in India Islām had difficulty in taking artistic shape, and in creating devices and forms whose Islāmic character might differentiate them from those consecrated to other religions. We shall also see subsequently that in the far East, in China, Muhammadan art tends to disappear entirely under the effect of the strong originality of the Chinese character. In that country there is an 'influence of the mass,' as chemists would say. In India and in China the Muhammadan is only in a minority; he disappears in the crowd, and despite his stubbornness of principle he submits to circumstances without being able to defend himself against them or to escape them.

The first Muhammadan conquest of India dates from A.D. 712. The first Indo-Muhammadan kingdom was in the 10th cent. A.D., that of Ghazni, which united under one sway the Panjāb, Multān, Gujrāt, and Kaśmīr up to the Ganges. Delhi became the capital of the Afghan House of Ghor after the destruction of Ghaznī (A.D. 1152). It was sacked in 1398 by Timur. Bābar (1494–1530), his great-grandson, founded a stable empire on the ruins of the ancient Muhammadan kingdoms of India. It was then that, under the dynasty of the Great Mughals, was set up one of the most remarkable régimes and civilizations of Muhammadan history. Up to the time of the Great Mughals the reaction of the native element against Islām had been so powerful that the art devoted to Muhammadan buildings had, in spite of all, preserved a marked local character. Bābar and his successors, by admirable general organization, unity of policy, and remarkable administrative ability, bestowed on their Empire a transient homogeneity, which forms its most striking characteristic, and which is reflected even in the buildings that they have left.

Accordingly, previous to the time of the Great Mughals, the Muhammadan buildings of India exhibit, in proportion as we approach the early times of the Hijra, features of increasing importance, borrowed from local traditions and from native art. From these the Muhammadans eliminated all representations of men and animals. Among them we find traditions of the Jain style of construction, the piling up of materials, corbellings, methods borrowed from timber-work, ceilings with simple or superimposed panels.

With the Great Mughals, on the contrary, we see the distinct impress of Persian influence which, commencing under Bābar, continued under Akbar, to become dominant under his successors.

Fergusson, the best historian of the Muhammadan architecture of India, proposes the following classification of the Muhammadan styles of that country:

(1) Style of the Ghaznavids.

(2) Pathan style (Northern India, 1193–1554).

(3) Style of Jaunpur (1394–1476).

(4) Style of Gujrāt (1396–1578), derived almost exclusively from the architecture of the Jain buildings.

(5) Style of the buildings of Malwa (from 1401 to the Mughal conquest), allied to that of Delhi.

(6) Style of Bengal (1203–1576).

(7) Style of Kalburga (1347–1525).

(8) Style of Bijapur (1489–1660), which exhibits an almost exclusively Persian character.

(9) Style of Golconda (1512–1572), in which decadence already appears.

(10) Mughal buildings, on which nearly all these different schools are based, especially those which have undergone the influence of Persian art. The chief monuments are at Fatḥpur, Agra, and Delhi.

(11) Buildings in Sindh, of a Persian character.

(12) Buildings of Oudh (1756–1847).
(13) Buildings of Mysore (1760–1799).

In all these different countries, as elsewhere, the Muhammadans have left mosques, *madrasas*, and tombs. It is naturally in these buildings that we ought to look for Muhammadan characteristics, and yet in the early Indian mosques like that of Ajmīr (A.D. 1200) and the Mosque of Kutab at Delhi, though the façade overlooking the large court is furnished with pointed window-bays, more or less recalling Western Muhammadan art, the interior of the building possesses an exclusively Hindu character. As Fergusson says with so much accuracy, it is a screen in the pointed style before a Jain temple. Historians agree in saying that these two mosques and many others were built of fragments which were taken from pagan temples. Cunningham discovered in the mosque of Kutab at Delhi an inscription stating that twenty-seven pagan temples were despoiled in order to provide materials for them. Thus, to quote Fergusson again (on the plan of the mosque of Ajmīr, *Indian and Eastern Architecture*, 1899, p. 129), 'If we refer to the plan of Vimala-Sah at Mount Ābū, and remove in our thought the principal cell and its porch in the centre of the court and the constructions in front of it from the side of the entrance, keeping only the portico which surrounds the court and that at the back with the cupolas, we have the type of the plan of the mosque, provided the back-wall be turned towards Mecca.' Later on the mosque becomes gradually free from Hindu forms, and under the Mughals all its features are Persian, a little softened, however, by the tendency of the Hindu genius to curve the lines. The public buildings, caravanserais, and bungalows, dams, bridges, and reservoirs also reveal the magnificence of the Muhammadan rulers of India. Historians have depicted for us the splendour of their State ceremonials, with a lavish expenditure of details which makes an indelible impression.

We have already spoken of the early mosques of India, that of Ajmīr and that of Delhi. We speak of the buildings of Ghazni only by way of making the record complete, for they have an almost exclusively Persian character. By the side of the mosque of Kutab at Delhi rises the tomb of the Sultan Altamsh (1235), the pointed arches of which are still dressed with horizontal joinings, while the overhanging stones at the corners are roofed with courses of corbelling. Consequently the local tradition still persists behind this pointed decoration. The doorway of Ala-ud-din at the same mosque already contains a much greater number of Western elements, and the arches are dressed with *voussoirs*. But the small columns of the principal porch and a thousand details exhibit the tenacious life of the local traditions.

After the reign of Ala-ud-din the style of building becomes more severe (tomb of Tughlaq at Delhi, and the tomb of Shīr-Shah at Sasseram in Shahabad). At Jaunpur the mosques are great vaulted halls, but the porticoes preserve a Jain appearance. The mosques of Gujrāt, while retaining the features of the local style, display a remarkable spaciousness of conception. In Bengal, brick architecture assumes a majestic type, which is extremely striking, as in the mosque of Khedimar-Rassul at Gur. The Adina mosque at Malda has an almost Western plan; it is the same at Kalburga, where vaulted construction almost entirely replaces that by corbellings. At Bijapur the Persian style dominates, but possibly the first sultan of Bijapur, who was a son of Sultan Murad II., contributed to this artistic revolution by summoning experienced architects from Turkey and Persia; such is the opinion of Fergusson—a correct one in the present writer's judgment. The masterpiece of the architects of Bijapur is the tomb of Mahmud, with its enormous cupola of 40 metres in interior diameter, and 55 metres in height under the crown.

The buildings of Sindh are also in the Persian style, but of brick, with bulbous domes. In the 16th cent. appear the buildings of the Great Mughals, and it is in them that we may say that Persia played in relation to the Muhammadan art of India, the same part which the Italy of the quattrocento and of the Renaissance played in relation to France and Spain. The buildings under the reign of Bābar (d. 1530) are few, but in a chaste and graceful style. Under Akbar architectural style assumes a remarkable force and magnificence, keeping all the while its great originality. Here Persian grace and elegance, destined to preponderate under Akbar's successors in the buildings of Agra and Delhi, mingle with the strength of the Pathan and Jain styles. This is noticeable in the wonderful buildings of the Fatḥpur-Sīkrī palace, tomb, and mosque. This last, which possesses a triumphal gate in the grand style and of an almost exclusively Persian aspect, is situated in the background of a rectangular court, surrounded with porticoes. This mosque is of triple formation. In the centre is a praying-place under a cupola like that of the Juma mosque at Iṣfahān; on each side is a porticoed mosque, possessing a kind of closed *maqṣūra* as a *miḥrāb*. Do not these three sanctuaries placed side by side suggest a trinitarian idea, that of the old Hindu Trinity? The great mosque of Agra, also built by Akbar, already shows an increased tendency towards the Persian style; similarly the tomb of Akbar at Sikandra, with its Persian porches. If the tomb of Itmād-ud-daula at Agra, possibly a little Jainesque in appearance, has purely Persian details (arches, windows, ornaments), the Tāj Mahal, erected by Shāh-Jahān at Agra in memory of his wife, the Empress Mumtāz-i-Mahal, is itself purely Persian as a whole and in details (built between 1630 and 1647). Twenty thousand artizans worked on it for seventeen years. But what interests us more than the particulars of its cost in time and money, is to see in what a masterly fashion the architect of this imposing building has been able, while preserving Persian devices and details invented, arranged, and reduced to rules for the use of brick and enamelled earthenware, and while transferring these forms to marble architecture, to deduce from them effects so novel and so striking that the Tāj Mahal rightly passes for one of the most wonderful buildings in the world. On a large platform measuring 95 metres each way rises the Tāj, the pointed and slightly bulbous dome of which is about 210 ft. in exterior height. This cupola crowns the hall containing the tomb, supported by four accessory halls and four great pointed porches on the four sides. The whole building is of marble, inlaid with the rarest kinds of hard stones, black or coloured marbles, with parts gilded. In the interior the hall of the tomb, which holds only an imitation of the sarcophagus, is decorated even more luxuriantly than the exterior of the building.

The Tāj forms the centre of a plan in which gardens, terraces rising one above another, porches, pavilions, basin-shaped reservoirs, and marble aqueducts combine into a whole of wonderful beauty and harmony.

The decorations of the palace of the early Mughals were in a style befitting their power and splendour, and the remains of their palace at Delhi still exhibit portions admirable from an architectural point of view. Unfortunately, this wonderful efflorescence of art was only temporary;

the mausoleums of Golconda already seem heavy, badly put together, incoherent. After the power of the Mughals was shattered in consequence of the death of Aurangzīb, several kingdoms rose on its ruins, and this confusion was immediately reflected in the most thorough disorder of architectural tendencies. Decadence had set in beyond hope of cure.

It is not necessary to mention any Chinese mosques here. Nothing in their decorations presents any feature whatever which differs in character from the purely Chinese style. We shall conclude this account with a short chronological list of the buildings of India.

Hijra.	Christian Era.	
	10th cent.,	Buildings of Ghazni.
	11th cent.,	Mosque of Kutab at Delhi.
606	1209	Mausoleum of Alamuk at Delhi.
723	1323	Mausoleum of Tughlaq at Delhi.
748	1347	Mosque of Kalburga.
760	1358	Mosque of Khedim ar-Rassul at Gur.
829	1426	Great mosque of Ahmedabad.
929	1522	Tomb of Shīr-Shah at Shahabad.
952	1545	Bābar summons pupils of the celebrated Turkish architect Sinan to India.
962	1554	Tomb of Humayun at Delhi.
964	1556	Akbar makes Agra one of the most beautiful cities of India.
968	1560	Akbar founds Fatḥpur-Sīkrī and its mosque.
1036	1626	Tomb of Mahmud at Bijapur.
1040	1630	As the result of a conference, the architect Isa Muhammad is commissioned to build the Tāj Mahal at Agra.
1138	1725	Buildings of Jaipur.

LITERATURE.—I. *GENERAL.*—**A. Choisy**, *Histoire de l'Architecture*, Paris, 1899; **J. Fergusson**, *Hist. of Architecture*, Lond. 1865–7; **Franz Pascha**, *Die Baukunst des Islam*, Darmstadt, 1896; **J. de Goeje**, *Bibliotheca geographicorum Arabicorum*, Leyden, 1870–89; *Manuel d'art musalman*, (i) **H. Saladin**, *L'Architecture*, (ii) **G. Migeon**, *Les Arts plastiques et industriels*, Paris, 1907.

II. *SPECIAL.*—**Abulfeda**, *Description du pays du Mogreb* (tr. Ch. Solvet), Algiers, 1839; **Caveda**, *Gesch. der Baukunst in Spanien*, Stuttgart, 1858; **Doutté**, *Merrakesh*, 1906; **Owen Jones**, *Plans . . . of the Alhambra*, Lond. 1842–7; **Girault de Prangey**, *Essai sur l'Architecture des Arabes et des Maures en Espagne, en Sicile et en Barbarie*, Paris, 1841; **W. and G. Marçais**, *Les Mon. arabes de Tlemçen*, Paris, 1903; **Ravoisie**, *Architecture . . . de l'Algerie*, Paris, 1907; **H. Saladin**, *La mosquée de Sidi Okba à Kairouan*, Paris, 1903; **Max van Berchem**, 'L'art musal. au musée de Tlemçen' in *Journ. des Savants*, Aug. 1906; **F. Sarre**, *Denkmäler persischer Baukunst*, Berlin, 1901–4; *L'archit. ottomane*, Constantinople, 1873; **Parvillée**, *Architecture et décoration turques au xv*e *siècle*, Paris, 1874; **F. Sarre**, *Reise in Kleinasien*, Berlin, 1896; **J. Fergusson**, *Hist. of Indian and E. Archit.*, Lond. 1890; **J. Griffiths**, *The Paintings in the Buddhist Cave-Temples of Ajanta*, Lond. 1896–7.

H. SALADIN.

ARCHITECTURE (Muhammadan in Syria and Egypt).—**1. Mosques.**—The mosque dates from the beginnings of Islām. The simplicity of Muslim worship demanded a simple plan, which was settled as early as the first centuries of the Hijra. It consisted of a large square court (*ṣaḥn*), surrounded with porticoes (*riwāq*), which were covered with a flat roof (*saqf*) supported by arches (*ṭāq*), with stone (*ḥajar*) columns (*'āmūd*) or brick (*libn*) pillars (*rukn*). The elements of this plan seem to be borrowed, on the one hand, from the Persian palaces of the Achæmenian type, perhaps, but indirectly, from the Egyptian palaces, and, on the other hand, from the Christian churches of Egypt and Syria.

Like the church, the mosque is oriented, but in the direction of Mecca (*qibla*), towards which, in accordance with a rule in the Qur'ān (*Sur.* ii. 139), Muslims turn for prayer. The real orientation therefore depends on the latitude. In Syria it is to the S., in Cairo to the E. or rather E.S.E. In order to accommodate the crowd of worshippers, the portico on the *qibla* side is extended, and admits of a larger number of aisles than the other three. It is called *al-īwān al-qiblī*, 'the oriented hall,' in popular language *līwān qiblī* or simply *līwān*. This prayer-hall is often divided into two parts by a railing of carved wood, the *maqṣūra*. On the side facing the court it contains the platform (*dikka*) for the clerics (*muballigh*) who repeat the words of the *imām*. At the back of the prayer-hall opens the niche (*miḥrāb*), indicating the direction of Mecca (*qibla*), with the pulpit (*minbar*) at the side, from which the high priest (*imām*) and the preacher (*ḥaṭīb*) preside at prayer and divine service.

This arrangement presents clear analogies to that of primitive churches. The court surrounded by porticoes, the centre of which is occupied by the basin for ablutions (*mīḍā'*), recalls the *atrium*, which was also surrounded by porticoes, and adorned with a centre-basin for ablutions. The prayer-hall corresponds to the body of the church, the railing is a sort of rood-screen, and the *miḥrāb* a miniature apse. Lastly, the minaret (*manāra, ma'dhana*), perhaps derived from the steeple, and provided with galleries for the call to prayer (*'adhān*), became the visible outward sign of the mosque. Like the primitive steeple, it has no fixed position, and is built sometimes in a corner and sometimes against a face of the building. These analogies are easily explained. The conquering Muslims, finding a more advanced art among the conquered peoples, took possession of it, and began by transforming a large number of churches into mosques. We may mention two famous buildings of this kind: the great Mosque at Damascus and the al-Aqṣā Mosque at Jerusalem, which at the first glance betray their Christian origin.

The style and methods of construction were modified during the course of time, particularly as to choice of materials, gateways, façades, and minarets, profile outline of the interior arches and decoration; but the general plan of the mosque remained the same until the Ottoman conquest.

The classical and primitive name of the mosque was *masjid*, 'place of prayer.' The Qur'ān does not contain any other expression, and the ancient writers designate by that name every mosque, large or small. But towards the 4th cent. of the Hijra, on account of the progress of culture and of architecture, the mosque divided in a fashion into two. The *great Mosque*, in which the congregation of worshippers (*jamā'a*) attended the Friday service (*jum'a*), took the name of *masjid al-jamā'a*, or *m. lil-jum'a*, or *m. jāmi'*. Very soon it was called simply *al-jāmi'*, 'the great Mosque.' Since that time the word *masjid* has been reserved for mosques of the second rank, the number of which is constantly diminishing. No great Mosques continue to be called *masjid* except those of Mecca, Medīna, and Jerusalem (al-Aqṣā). Tradition, following the Qur'ān, calls them by this name, and it has thus remained popular.

This evolution of terms traceable in literature is reflected in the inscriptions, which furnish definite, official, and dated evidence. The great Mosque of Aḥmad ibn Ṭūlūn, built in Cairo in 265 (879), still bears the name of *masjid* in its dedicatory inscription. But two centuries later the Mosque of the Nilometre, built in Cairo in 485 (1092), is called *jāmi'* in its three foundation inscriptions.

2. Madrasas.—When diffusing the Shī'ite heresy in Egypt and Syria, the Fāṭimid khalīfs did not modify the general mosque-plan; we meet with it again especially in those which they built in Cairo. But soon after their time the movement of religious ideas and the political situation created by the Mongol invasions and by the dismemberment of the khalīfate of Baghdad called forth in the Muslim East an orthodox or *Sunnite* reaction, directed specially against 'Alid or Shī'ite sects and dynasties. This religious (Ash'arite) and political (Sunnite) reaction caused a series of reforms in all domains of civilization. One of the most important was the extension of the *madrasa*. Originating in Khorasan about the beginning of the 4th cent. A.H., the madrasa was at first simply a private school of religious sciences, *i.e.* of tradition, exegesis, and law, according to the Sunnite rites. But in the 5th cent. A.H. the Seljuk sultans of Baghdad, having become powerful vassals of the Abbāsid khalīfate, and the official protectors of Sunnism and Ash'arism, transformed the madrasa into a State institution, intended to produce a select body of officials for all branches of administration. From that time the madrasa became a powerful centre of religious and political propaganda, the school of official Sunnism, and almost a government institution. It was in this form that it was introduced into Syria in the 6th cent. A.H. by the Sunnite Atābeks, particularly Nūr-ad-dīn; then into Egypt by Saladin.

If the madrasa differs from the mosque in its character and purpose, its origin and history, it is also distinguished from it by its plan. When Saladin introduced it into Egypt, this plan was already settled: a small square court with open top (*ṣaḥn* or *qā'a*), enclosed by four high walls, with four halls (*līwāns*) in the form of a Greek cross, opening on to the court by a high arch (*'aqd*), and, in the outer corners of the building, offices for the attendants and the work of the establishment. This symmetrical plan with four branches was admirably suited for the *quadruple madrasa*, i.e. the school devoted to the four chief Sunnite sects (*Ḥanafite, Shāfi'ite, Mālikite*, and *Ḥanbalite*). Each sect was installed in one of the four *līwāns*, as is testified by the inscriptions in the large madrasa of the Sultan Ḥasan, built in Cairo in 764 (1363). This plan seems to have originated in Syria. It is found in a curious Syrian monument, of a far earlier date than the Syro-Egyptian madrasas, the *Qaṣr* of 'Ammān. Like the plan of the mosque, it combines elements of various origin: the *līwāns* are arched in the Persian style (Sasanian palaces), but their arrangement in a cross around a central court recalls the symmetrical plan with two axes of certain Byzantine and Syrian churches, which the Qaṣr resembles in many other architectural details.

Like the mosque, the madrasa became in time modified in its style and methods of construction. Thus, until the end of the 14th cent. A.D., its *līwāns* were covered with barrel-vaults (*qabu* or *'aqd*) of brick (*libn*), following the Persian and Byzantine methods (without centrings). The last large vaulted madrasa is that of the Sultan Barqūq, built in 788 (1386). Then the vaults were replaced by a flat wooden (*ḥashab*) roof (*saqf*) and ceilings whose rich polychrome decoration merely disguises a serious decadence in the art of building. The only vault that remained was that of the front arch of the four *līwāns* opening on the court, built with arch-stones. But, in spite of these modifications, the plan and general arrangement of the madrasa subsisted until the Ottoman conquest.

The Sunnite reaction gave rise to some institutions analogous to the madrasa, particularly the *dār al-ḥadīth*, the 'school of tradition' (Sunnite). But these establishments, not having the same political standing, remained in the background and created no type of architecture; or rather, being simply varieties of the madrasa, they adopted its general plan.

Under the Ayyūbids, who may have feared a troublesome return of the Shī'ite doctrines, the madrasa retained its character as a State institution with political tendencies. Its first result was to destroy the Fāṭimid school, the *dār al-'ilm*, a kind of academy with eclectic tendencies, where, along with Shī'ite doctrines, were taught the sciences inherited from Persia and ancient Greece. But Sunnism did not encounter the Shī'ite sects only. The Crusades had stirred up another opponent, the Latin kingdom of Jerusalem. Saladin and his successors, impeded by feudal administration and political decentralization, had weakened but not destroyed these foes, who finally fell before Baibars. On the ruins of Ayyūbid feudalism he founded the kingdom of the Mamlūks, a centralized State, defended by a regular army, and governed, from high to low, by a hierarchy of officials. With this powerful lever he overturned at once the Latin kingdom and the fortresses of the Assassins, the last bulwark of Shī'ite heresy in Syria. He afterwards established his prestige in the eyes of the Muslim masses by welcoming to Cairo the wreck of the khalīfate of Baghdad, which had been overturned by Hūlāgū (1258). In re-establishing, for his own benefit, the duality of the spiritual and temporal powers, he re-tied the thread broken by the Mongol invasion, and completed the work begun by the great Sunnites of the preceding century.

Then the struggle ended, and the militant spirit of Sunnism, inspired by the Holy War (*jihād*), became softened and turned towards pious works and contemplative study. The madrasa, having carried out its fighting rôle, had to lose for ever its original character and assume that of the mosque. All the large madrasas were then fitted up for the Friday service. The *līwān qiblī*, which was larger than the other three, served as prayer-hall and sheltered the pulpit and the *miḥrāb*. Last of all the minaret came to give to the madrasa the complete appearance of a mosque. But it had acquired such prestige that, instead of merging in the mosque, it threatened rather to supplant it. While the number of the great Mosques of classical plan continued to diminish, that of the madrasas of cruciform plan increased until the Ottoman conquest.

This evolution is reflected in linguistic usage also. The madrasas set apart for religious worship took the name of *madrasa lil-jum'a*; then they were called simply *jāmi'* like the great Mosques. Maqrīzī, who drew up his *Topography of Cairo* in the first quarter of the 15th cent. A.D., gives this name to the majority of the large madrasas of the Mamlūks. Finally, epigraphy officially established this use from the year 830 (1427). From that time the word *madrasa* fell into the background as the old word *masjid* had done. At the present day in Egypt it is applied exclusively to a civil and lay school; every great religious building is a *jāmi'*.

Thus the original mosque, the masjid, became subdivided into great Mosque (*jāmi'*) and small mosque (*masjid*). The madrasa, in its turn, subdivided into jāmi' and lay school. These two classes of jāmi' became blended in their purpose but not in their plans. They remained distinct until the Ottoman conquest, which caused the madrasa-plan to disappear. In Egypt and Syria the Ottomans continued to build jāmi's on the plan of the great Mosques, but modified under the influence of the Turkish school, whose mosques are built on the St. Sophia plan (the dome type).

3. Monasteries.—The Sunnite reaction, which brought the madrasa from Persia to Egypt, mingled during its course with tributaries of ancient origin, quite foreign to primitive Islām. One of the most important was *Ṣūfiism*, i.e. Eastern monasticism with mystic tendencies of Persian origin. The public building of Ṣūfiism is the Ṣūfī monastery, the *ḥānaqāh*, a Persian word which penetrated with the building first into Syria and then into Egypt, through Saladin, the founder of the first Egyptian ḥānaqāh. About that time it became confused with the *ribāṭ*, an Arabic word denoting an ancient military settlement, which had also become, by a profound change of the original idea, a Ṣūfī monastery.

The ribāṭ and the ḫānaqāh flourished under the Ayyūbids, and then under the Mamlūks, but without creating any real type of architecture. These monasteries sometimes assume the plan of the great Mosque (monastery of the Emir Shaiḫū in Cairo, 756 [1355]), and sometimes that of the madrasa (monastery of the Sultan Baibars II. in Cairo, 709 [1310]). Like these two types, they possessed all the visible appliances for worship: minaret, prayer-hall, pulpit, and *miḥrāb*. But their dependencies, fitted up for cenobitic life, and arranged in long lines of cells, give a peculiar appearance to their plan. Several curious traces of them still survive, especially in Cairo, where the monastery of the Sultan Ināl (858 [1454]) affords the most complete specimen.

At the Ottoman conquest the ribāṭ and the ḫānaqāh gave way to the *takiyya*, the monastery of Turkish dervishes, the plan of which also came under the influence of the Constantinople school (porticoes with domes). We may mention, lastly, the *zāwiya*, a word which means, in the Muslim West, a cell, a hermitage, and then a real monastery, but which in Egypt is applied only to a very small mosque, an oratory, or a chapel.

4. Fountains and Schools.—Connected with these three great types—the mosque, the madrasa, and the monastery—are two secondary types, the *sabīl* and the *kuttāb*. *Sabīl* means 'road'; *fī sabīl allāh*, 'in the way of Allāh,' 'for the sake of God,' is said of every pious work, of the Holy War as well as of almsgiving, and especially of foundations for the free use of the public. Now, in the East water is a treasure; according to a saying attributed to Muhammad, to give a drink of water is one of the most meritorious charities. Every free foundation is a sabīl, but the sabīl *par excellence* is the *public fountain*.

In Syro-Egyptian architecture, the sabīl is rarely isolated. It is placed at the corner of a mosque, a madrasa, or a monastery, on the ground-floor, and can be recognized by its two large square windows at right angles, closed with beautiful bronze railings and decorated with charming carvings. Above the sabīl is situated the *primary school* (*kuttāb* or *maktab*), which is rendered conspicuous at a distance by its elegant loggia, open on both sides, in rows of arches on small pillars. This graceful *motif* of the *sabīl-kuttāb* subsisted until the Ottoman invasion. At that time the sabīl became separated, first along with the kuttāb, and then quite alone. Its style has degenerated down to our time, when the fountain displays all the false taste of the modern Turkish school.

5. Mausoleums.—For the obscure dead a grave is sufficient. The illustrious dead, not content with a tomb, require a mausoleum. As far back as it is possible to go, the Syro-Egyptian mausoleum possessed its own peculiar architectural form: a cubical hall, square in plan, covered with a dome. Is this type a distant recollection of the ancient Egyptian *mastaba*? It seems to be more directly connected with a Christian type, the *kalybe* (καλύβη), some traces of which still survive in Syria. The problem of building the dome on a square plan, outlined in these old Syrian kalybes, receives in Muslim architecture the most varied solutions, which reflect the successive efforts and inventions of the Persians, Romans, and Byzantines. The transition between the square and the circle is built of bricks dressed or arranged in corbels, of beams covered with stucco, of hanging arches in semi-cupolas, or of beautiful stone pendants like stalactites. The materials, proportions, outline of the square, of the drum, and of the dome, the decoration—all, in a word, that constitutes the style—changed from age to age, but the general plan remained the same until the Ottoman conquest.

The classical name of the mausoleum is *turba*. But as the dome was its most conspicuous feature, the name of the latter (*qubba*) was extended to the whole building. In literature and the Syro-Egyptian inscriptions these two words are indifferently applied to the mausoleum as a whole, *i.e.* the architectural envelope of the tomb, which itself is called *qabr* or *madfan* or *marqad* or *ḍarīḥ*, the last an Arabic word of Aramaic origin.

The mausoleum is often built by itself, isolated in a cemetery. Sometimes there are several together in a single enclosure (*ḥōsh*), but not forming an organic whole. Frequently the mausoleum of a great person is placed in the corner of a religious building which he has founded. Like the great Italian *condottieri* of the Renaissance, the Sultans and Emirs, former slaves who had risen to fortune, and who were always uncertain of the future, took care to provide for their own tombs beforehand.

This association creates three chief combined types: the *mosque-mausoleum*, the *madrasa-mausoleum*, and the *monastery-mausoleum*. We may mention in Cairo: the mosque of the Sultan Shaiḫ (823 [1420]), the madrasa of the Sultan Qāyt-Bāy (879 [1474]), and the monastery of the Sultan Faraj (813 [1411]), popularly called the tomb of Barqūq.

We find also more complicated types, *e.g.* the *monastery-madrasa-mausoleum*. We may cite those of the Sultans Barqūq (788 [1386]) and Ināl (858 [1454]). All these combined types contain the sabīl-kuttāb *motif*, and unite one or several minarets to one or several domes. They do not have special names. The inscriptions of these huge buildings, agreeing with the literary texts, refer to them sometimes under one name and sometimes under another, according to the part of the whole that they wish to emphasize.

Like all the types of Syro-Egyptian architecture, the turba disappeared after the Ottoman conquest. The name continued in use, but it refers to tombs of any kind. Since the 16th cent. A.D., Egypt and Syria have not had any mausoleums worthy of their past.

6. Holy places and pilgrimages.—In spite of the express intention of its founder, Islām at an early date adopted the worship of saints, and the belief in miracles accomplished by their intervention. This cult was too deeply rooted in the Oriental religions for Muhammad to make it disappear. In Syria, especially, the old pagan cults connected with local gods, which had resisted Christianity, lay hidden under Islām, which had to tolerate while apparently assimilating them. The tenacity of these local traditions explains the manifold origin of Muslim saints. Some of them are pagan gods, transformed by an association of ideas, beliefs, or mere words into Muslim saints; others are the great personages in the Qur'ān, Muhammad, Jesus, and the Jewish prophets; others again are heroes of history, conquerors, or famous sovereigns; and others, ascetics, monks, or scholars, celebrated during their life and canonized by the common people with their irresistible inclination towards the supernatural. All these saints have their sanctuaries (*mashhad*). The belief in miracles wrought by their intervention makes these sanctuaries places of pilgrimage (*mazār*).

The mashhad has not created any special type of architecture. As it is almost invariably erected at the grave of the saint, it takes the plan of the mausoleum. From the architectonic point of view it is simply a variety of the turba, perhaps the oldest. It is found in all sizes, from the small chapel with a little dome, whitened with lime (*marabut*, *shaiḫ*, *walī*, *nabī*, *maqām*), to the large classical mausoleum; all have the dome on the square plan. The only one of these buildings that departs from the traditional plan is the famous Dome of the Rock, the Qubbat aṣ-Ṣaḫra in Jerusalem, built by the Khalīf ʿAbd al-Malik, in 72 (691), and many times restored since then. Its huge dome, on a circular plan, surrounded by a double octagonal enclosure, harbours, along with the famous rock, a whole cycle of Jewish and Christian legends. This circular-octagonal plan, which undoubtedly proceeded from that of the Christian building prior to the Qubba, is found again in a group of pre-Muslim Syrian churches (Bosra, Ezra, Qalʿat Simʿān, etc.). But apart from the Dome of the Rock and a few secondary buildings derived from it (Dome of the Chain in Jerusalem, mausoleum of the Sultan Qalāwūn in Cairo, etc.), it has not been adopted in Syro-Egyptian architecture.

Apart from the turba and the mashhad, the dome is used in only one instance in Syro-Egyptian architecture: a small dome, also called *qubba*, is erected in large mosques, at the back of the prayer-hall, in front of the *miḥrāb*. This ancient feature may probably again be a relic of the church, namely, the dome which certain basilicas erect at the crossing of the transept in front of the choir. This was the only place used for the dome in the great Mosques until the Ottoman conquest, which systematically introduced domes over the porticoes and the prayer-halls of the great Mosques, after the style of the Constantinople school.

MAX VAN BERCHEM.

ARCHITECTURE (Persian).—The account of the development of the architecture of Persia is almost synonymous with the land's own history. From the crude beginnings in early Median or pre-Median times, before the 7th cent. B.C., we may trace the evolution of the builder's art down to the Achæmenian period (B.C. 550–330), thence through the Seljuk and Parthian eras (B.C. 330–A.D. 224) and the following centuries of the Sasanian empire (A.D. 224–661). At the close of that period, in the 7th cent. A.D., Iran was completely changed by the Arab conquest and subsequent Muslim sway, from which epoch to the present time the history of Persian architecture forms a special branch of the study of the development of Muhammadan art.

1. Early Iranian and Median period (before B.C. 550).—Our knowledge of the architectural conditions during the early Iranian and Median periods is limited in extent, both because of the absence of historic remains surviving from that remote date, and because of the lack of definite descriptions in ancient texts that might serve to elucidate the subject. Nevertheless, from incidental allusions in the Avesta, from references in the Greek historians, and from chance statements in later writings from which deductions may be drawn, we are able to form some sort of a picture of the architectural status in ancient Media, or Western Iran, and in early Bactria, or Eastern Iran. Herodotus (i. 96–99) affirms that, down to the time of Deioces, the founder of the Median empire, the Medes used to live in villages, and that they were first gathered into cities by Deioces when he made Ecbatana his capital, and fortified it as his royal residence. From the conditions portrayed in the Avesta, so far as that work may be regarded as reflecting the age in question, and from the sight to-day of village after village of flat-roofed mud huts spread over much of the territory which once was ancient Media, we may infer that the primitive condition of architecture in that region of Iran was really represented by Herodotus' statement, and that the same was true of ancient Bactria. But this judgment must not be pressed too far; for, while the Avesta refers to habitations of so crude a sort that they might be removed or destroyed if a man died in them (*Vendīdād*, viii. 1–13), it also alludes to houses that were 'strong, well-built, lofty, handsome, shining and conspicuous, constructed with a special chamber, balcony, verandah, and enclosing wall, or erected with high columns, or with a thousand columns,' as we know from a number of passages from which the adjectives here given are drawn (cf. *Vend.* ii. 26; *Yasna*, lvii. 21; *Yasht*, v. 101). The columnar architecture referred to in the last two attributes anticipates by many years the pillared halls of the Persian kings at Persepolis.

The chief old Iranian terms for 'house,' apart from the Avesta *vaēsma*, 'abode' (*Yasht*, x. 86), and the old Persian *hadiš*, 'palace' (cf. the curious, though probably merely accidental, use of the linguistically cognate ἕδρανον to denote the palace of the Persian kings in Æschylus, *Persæ*, 4), are *nmāna* (Gāthic *demānā*) and *kata*, the latter, however, being the 'room' rather than the 'house' (the view that *kata* denotes 'underground house,' expressed, *e.g.*, by Geiger, is scarcely correct).

The houses, doubtless simple in construction, were built of wood (cf. *dāuru-upadarana*, *Vend.* viii. 1) or were sometimes mere felt-covered tents (cf. *nematō-aiwivarana*,' *ib.*), although the use of bricks and mortar, being mentioned in connexion with non-architectural construction (cf. *Vend.* vi. 51, viii. 8, 10), was doubtless common also in building houses. Besides the 'columns' (or 'pillars'), 'verandahs,' etc., already mentioned, the Iranian houses had both doors and windows (*Vend.* vii. 15, iii. 29, etc.), though how they were closed, we know no more than how the entire house was roofed. It may readily be supposed, nevertheless, that the roofs were of reeds or turf laid on beams, or even of simple sun-dried bricks, such as are still utilized in Iranian regions (cf. Geiger, *Ostiran. Kultur*, p. 219).

Turning from the Avesta to the description given by Herodotus (i. 98) of the fortified abode of Deioces at Ecbatana, we find a citadel that must have resembled an Assyrian or Babylonian *ziḳḳurat*. Its massive walls rose tier above tier in seven circles, and were crowned by battlements of various colours, white, black, red, blue, and orange (probably coloured gypsum and glazed tiles), while the ramparts of the topmost fortifications, where the palace stood, were decorated respectively with silver and gold. This description is probably not overdrawn if we may judge from the account which Polybius (x. 27) gives of the magnificence and gorgeous decorations of the temple of Aena or Anaias at Ecbatana (the goddess Anāhita in the Avesta) in the 2nd cent. B.C.; and the fact that we have no remains of such splendour is due not alone to the vandalism of Alexander, Antigonus, Seleucus Nicator, and Antiochus the Great, as described by Polybius, but also to the circumstance that the Medes probably constructed their buildings largely of wood, sun-dried bricks, and clay, even though they were lavish in adornment.

As to the architectural style of their palaces, it is probable that the Medes, like the Persians after them, were largely influenced by Assyrian, Babylonian, and Chaldæan models. Regarding their religious architecture, we know practically nothing beyond the description by Polybius, just referred to; it is a fact, moreover, that Zoroastrianism does not appear to have been favourable to temple-building, for the Persians had no temples in the Greek sense, as Herodotus (i. 130) expressly states; yet it is equally certain that they must have had some sort of a sanctuary to protect the holiest of their sacred fires, and such shrines are presumed by the Pahlavi writers of a later date to have existed in those early times (cf. *Pahlavi Bahman Yasht*, iii. 30, 37, 40; *Zāṭ-sparam*, vi. 22, xi. 8–10; *Būndahishn*, xii. 18, 34, xvii. 7, etc.), so that it is possible that the temple at Ecbatana, as described by Polybius, may have preserved some architectural features from ancient days. In the mortuary customs enjoined by their religion, moreover, the early Iranians, whether Medians or Bactrians, made use of temporary structures, called *dakhmas* (wh. see) in the Avesta (*Vend.* iii. 9, 13, vii. 54, vi. 44–51, etc.), on which to expose the dead, just as their modern representatives, the Parsis (wh. see) and Gabars (wh. see) still follow the custom in their 'Towers of Silence'; but what the shape of these receptacles may have been in ancient times is only a matter of inference.

2. Achæmenian period (B.C. 550–330).—With the victory of Cyrus of Persia over the Median king Astyages, the supremacy of N. Iran passed to S. Iran, and a new dominion, the sovereignty of the Achæmenians, or the combined rule of the Medes and Persians, came into being. The architectural remains, both religious and civil, which belong to this period are abundant, and they show the art of the builder in early Persia at its zenith. Terraced platforms of massive masonry and palaces of stone graced by halls with tall fluted columns, crowned by bull-headed capitals, were typical of the age.

Ecbatana, Pasargadæ, Persepolis, and Susa were the capitals of the Medo-Persian empire, and the chief seats, therefore, of architectural relics. The site of Ecbatana is now occupied by Hamadan; and there, or in its vicinity, are to be found portions of broken columns, and a few carved stones, remnants of walls that belonged to ruined structures, and may date back even to Median times. But as yet no systematic excavations have been carried on to determine their age, or tell whether extensive finds of a similar character may yet be made. If we leave Ecbatana out of account, the earliest remains of Achæmenian architecture are to be seen at Pasargadæ, the capital of Cyrus the Great, in the plain of the modern Murghab, between Iṣfahān and Shiraz. As we approach it from the north, we first pass the remains of a ruined platform on the crest of a range of low hills overlooking the plain. It was apparently designed to support an audience-hall of Cyrus, but was never completed. Spread over the surface of the plain itself traces of the royal city are to be seen. Nearest to the ridge is a single shattered wall of a massive stone building which must have been 40 ft. high by 10 ft. square, and which may have served as a shrine for the sacred fire, although some authorities (on less good grounds, it seems) believe that it was a princely tomb. A second group of ruins lies not far distant to the south, and comprises a high round column (not fluted), some angle-piers of an edifice that once surrounded a royal court, and a stone shaft consisting of three blocks, on the uppermost of which is inscribed in cuneiform characters, 'I Cyrus, the King, the Achæmenian.' A huge slab stands somewhat to the east of this group, and on its face is carved in low relief a winged representation of the Great King, above whose head was similarly inscribed the device of Cyrus just quoted, although the part of the stone containing it has been sawn off and lost within the last century. Still another collection of ruins lies somewhat to the south-east, and shows vestiges of pillars and stone door-sills grouped around a paved court that belonged to some edifice of Cyrus.

Most important of all the ruins is the tomb of Cyrus, which lies about a mile beyond in a south-westerly direction. It is known to be his mausoleum from descriptions in the classics. The structure resembles a small house, with a slightly pointed roof, and is made of a handsome white sandstone resembling marble. It stands high upon a sub-basement, built of the same material and consisting of a large foundation plinth, nearly 50 ft. long, 40 ft. wide, and 2 ft. high, surmounted by a series of six stone layers that form a pyramidal series of high steps approaching the mausoleum from every side. The mammoth blocks that make up the tomb itself were originally fastened together by iron clamps, but without the use of mortar; and so perfectly were they set that the structure still forms a compact whole, even though falling more and more into ruin. The sepulchre, measured from the outside, is about 20 ft. long, by 17 broad, and 18 high. A very low door in the western side serves as an entrance. The mortuary chamber measures 10½ ft. long, by 7½ ft. wide, and 8 ft. high (the exact measurements in metres may be found in Jackson, *Persia*, p. 288). It is needless to add that the chamber is now empty. In architectural style the tomb of Cyrus is thought to show Lycian influence, since somewhat similar burial edifices have been found in Asia Minor, the land first conquered by Cyrus after Media; but it may also be possible that the idea of such a vault for the dead may have owed something to the Avestan *kata*, 'house,' a temporary structure for the body before it was carried to the *dakhma*. Around the tomb, moreover, there once stood a decorative colonnade, as is clear from the fragments of columns still upright, and a few hundred yards beyond it are the vestiges of a platform on which was once erected a habitation for the Magian priests who were custodians of the tomb, as we know from Arrian (*Anabasis*, vi. 29. 7).

A single other vestige of Achæmenian architecture, religious in its character, is found at some distance to the N.W. in the same plain; it is in the form of the bases of two altars, used by the Magi in celebrating their sacrificial rites, as they did, in the open air.

Illustrations and descriptions of all the architectural monuments in the Murghab Plain are to be found in the works of Texier, Flandin and Coste, Ker Porter, Stolze and Andreas, Dieulafoy, Perrot and Chipiez, Curzon, and Jackson; and they convey a good idea of the architecture of Cyrus's capital.

Far grander than the ruined monuments of Pasargadæ are those of Persepolis, the capital of Darius, and Xerxes, and their successors. These tokens of a vanished empire are spread over a considerable area in the Plain of Murghab, some forty miles to the south of Cyrus's capital. The first vestiges of this important series are the traces of the lost city of Stakhra, indicated by some broken columns, remains of portals, and scattered fragments of building blocks at the site now called Stakhr or Istakhr. The southernmost point of this city is now marked by a small granite staging, some 40 ft. square and 7 ft. high, which the natives call *Takht-i Tā'ūs*, 'Peacock Throne,' or *Takht-i Rustam*, 'Throne of (the hero) Rustam.' A mile or so farther south rises the Platform of Persepolis itself, with its magnificent stairways and palace-crowned terraces, which the Persians call *Takht-i Jamshīd*, 'Throne of Jamshīd,' after the legendary king of that name, or *Chihil Minār*, 'Forty Pillars,' from the columns that remain standing. Although the site as a royal residence may date back to legendary times (cf. possibly *Būndahishn*, xxix. 14), we know from an inscription on the southern wall that it owed its origin as a stronghold to Darius I., apparently about B.C. 516–513, and it is generally believed that Greek designers were employed in its construction (see Justi, 'Gesch. Irans' in Geiger and Kuhn's *Grundriss*, ii. 448–449). Even when considered apart from the edifices that stood upon it, the platform is a remarkable piece of constructive art. It measures over 1500 ft. from north to south, varying from 20 to 50 ft. in height, according to the elevation of the three main terraces, and it has an expanse running back eastward for nearly 1000 ft. until it merges into a low range of hills, called *Kuh-i Raḥmat*, 'Mountain of Mercy,' the spurs of which have been partly cut away to furnish material for its construction. By the aid of inscriptions, and judging from the position of the different ruins, the columns that remain standing, and the arrangement of the bases of those that have fallen, as well as from the outlines of the walls, portals, stairway approaches, and sculptured pediments, we are able to identify each of the buildings that once occupied this site. Opposite the Grand Staircase of approach at the northern end, is the Porch of Xerxes; 50 yards to the south stand the relics of the Audience Hall of Xerxes; still farther southward, and near a mound, are the better preserved remains of the Palace of Darius; while a short distance southward again, across a ruined courtyard, are some traces of a Palace of Artaxerxes III. Ochus, identified by an inscription on the stylobate. Directly behind this is the Palace of Xerxes himself, with a minor edifice still farther back, while at some distance northward is the great Hall of a Hundred Columns, erected by Darius, with a portico near its south-western corner, showing in stone the king seated on his throne of state. The destruction of these gorgeous buildings is attributed to the drunken act of Alexander the Great, when he burnt the citadel after his victory over the last Darius; but though the hand of the conqueror destroyed the beauty of the edifices and left them a ruin for all time, it could not obliterate those traces that still in after ages bear witness to their ancient glory.

Some further remains of royal architecture are to be seen at Persepolis and in its vicinity; they are the rock-hewn tombs of the Achæmenian kings. Three of these sepulchres are cut in the hills, behind the great platform already described. They are believed to be the mortuary chambers of Artaxerxes II. Mnemon (B.C. 404–358), of Artaxerxes III. Ochus (B.C. 358–337), and of Darius III. Codomannus (B.C. 335–330), if we are justified in regarding the unfinished grave as that of the last of the Achæmenians. More imposing in their situation and older in point of time are the four tombs carved in the rocky front of the necropolis cliff of Naksh-i Rustam, on the other side of the plain, about 6 miles north-west of the platform. These sepulchres, which were the model for the three later ones, are each hewn in the shape of an immense Greek cross, and sunk deep in the face of the rock. They are elaborately carved in architectural style to represent a façade decorated with bull-capped pillars, two on either side of the doorway, and surmounted in each case by an entablature richly sculptured with a bas-relief of the king, his subjects, and Ormazd. An inscription shows that one of these tombs was the sepulchre of Darius the Great; the other vaults, it is believed, belonged to Xerxes, Artaxerxes I., and Darius II. A few yards distant from the tomb last named there is a square stone edifice which closely resembles the rectangular structure at Pasargadæ, already mentioned, but well preserved, and, like the latter, probably a fire-shrine rather than a tomb. Near the base of the necropolis hill, but hidden from the shrine by a spur of the cliff, are the remains of two altars, hewn out of the living rock and serving as fine examples of the stonecutter's work for religious purposes in Achæmenian times. To the same age may likewise belong some rude cuttings in the rocks on the crest of the cliff, apparently designed as repositories for exposing the bodies of the dead in accordance with the ancient Zoroastrian custom, but the date is not certain. To a later age, however, we must assign the seven sculptures cut in the rock beneath the tombs themselves, since their subjects prove them to be of Sasanian origin. The list of Achæmenian tombs is to be supplemented by several other sepulchres, somewhat resembling those of Naksh-i Rustam, but probably dating from an earlier period than they or the Persepolitan tombs, and without inscriptions or ornamentation, excepting one which has a crude bas-relief. These are found near the village of Sahnah, between Hamadan and Kermanshah, at Holvan in Western Persia, and Takhrikah in Azarbaijan, as well as elsewhere (see de Morgan, *Mission scientifique en Perse*, iv. 292–302, and Justi, *op. cit.* ii. 455, 456).

The fourth and last of the great Achæmenian capitals was Susa, whose remains were first made known by Loftus in 1852, and were excavated with very important results by Dieulafoy in 1884, 1885, 1886, followed by de Morgan in 1897, 1898, 1899. The site which they occupy was the winter residence of the Achæmenian kings and the old seat of government of Elam. The ruins extend over several *tells*, or hillocks, between the river Chaur, or Jaur, and the Kerkhah, in the vicinity of the modern Dizful and Shuster. Four principal groups of remains are distinguishable, according to the results of the explorations that have been mentioned: They are, first, the *tell*, called the Citadel; second, the Royal City, where stood the palaces of the successors of Darius; third, the traces of the city itself; and, fourth, the vestiges of the inhabited town along the river's edge. If we may judge from the elaborate finds made by Dieulafoy, the Citadel and the Royal City must have made an imposing spectacle in the days of their pristine glory (see the plates in Dieulafoy, *L'Acropole de Suse*); and the same investigator's researches have revealed, among other ruins, the remains of the *apadāna*, or throne-room, of Artaxerxes II. Mnemon, which was erected on a site earlier occupied by a palace of Darius I. which had been destroyed by fire. It was here that the archæological expedition, led by Dieulafoy and his wife, discovered the frieze of archers and a lion-frieze, together with the remains of an enamelled staircase and various other objects that enrich our knowledge of early Persian architecture and art. In point of style the Susian remains are quite like those of Persepolis, even as regards the character of the so-called 'Persepolitan column,' and, like the latter, they are thought to show traces of Greek influence combined with Assyro-Babylonian elements and other features already mentioned, although they are so thoroughly Persianized as to possess an individuality of their own.

The ruins of one other edifice in Persia may be referred to here as belonging possibly to the latter part of the Achæmenian period; it is the remains of the great temple of Anaitis (see ANĀHITA) at Kangavar, between Hamadan and Kermanshah. A portion of the N.W. wall of the stylobate on which the temple stood is still intact, and is crowned with the remains of a colonnade of pillars, while on the south-eastern side of the temple precinct there is a disordered mass of large granite blocks and columns, whose size conveys an idea of the vanished magnificence of the sanctuary which is now a mass of ruins. Owing to the presence of certain characteristics in the columns, which seem to show later Greek or Syro-Roman affinities, Dieulafoy and some others propose to assign this temple to the Parthian period; but, to the present writer, the evidence seems stronger in favour of attributing its erection to Artaxerxes Mnemon or some other of the later Achæmenians. For the sake of completeness it should be added that Dieulafoy, on the contrary, assigns to the Achæmenian period some of the ruins at Firuzabad and Sarvistan in S.W. Persia; but other authorities, like Perrot and Chipiez, de Morgan, and Gayet, are better justified in assigning them to the Sasanian epoch.

3. Seljuk and Parthian periods (B.C. 330–A.D. 224).—The interregnum of seventy years occupied by the sway of Alexander's direct successors and the Seljuk rule exercised no appreciable effect on Persian architecture, unless it was to extend the sphere of possibility for Greek influence. The Parthians were Philhellenes, as is shown by their employing the Greek language and Greek devices on their coins; but they were not great architects, as is clear from the Parthian ruins—practically the only ones surviving—at Hatra and at Warka, although these are built with crude solidity, if not with beauty of design. The structure at Hatra, the modern *al-Ḥadhr*, in Mesopotamia, was either a palace or a temple, or possibly both combined in a single precinct, for which reason it is commonly spoken of as a palace-temple. The ruins show a brownish-grey limestone edifice, 366 ft. long, 210 ft. broad, and with thick walls proportionately high. The building consists of a series of seven large chambers arranged side by side, with several smaller rooms leading into them, and a large square hall—apparently a throne-room—added in the rear near the left-hand corner of the edifice. The front of the building was, for the most part, open, so that the light was good, and it was probably shaded by awnings. The walls of the greater apartments were strengthened by pilasters, and decorated by bas-relief sculptures and ornamental friezes, which added to the effect of the general architectural design. As to its date, the palace-temple at Hatra may be assigned with reasonable probability to the latter half of the Parthian period, or between the 1st and 3rd cent. of the Christian era, since the city was in a flourishing condition, and able to resist the siege of Trajan in A.D. 116, and of Severus in A.D. 198, but was a deserted ruin in the 4th century.

The second of the Parthian architectural remains is found at *Warka*, the ancient Erech, on the Euphrates, a city mentioned in Gn 10[10]. This ruin consists of a sepulchral chamber built over a tomb in which was found a coffin of the Parthian period. The description which Loftus gives of this structure, with its bases of columns, capitals, cornices, friezes, and bits of painted plaster, shows that the Parthians in later times were not averse to decoration and artistic touches in their buildings, even if they had affected a rude simplicity in earlier times. This fact is further borne out by the account of the palace at Ctesiphon, as given in Philostratus' *Life of Apollonius* (ed. Olearius, i. 25). According to de Morgan (*Mission scientifique en Perse*, ii. 137 and plate lix.), there is a ruin of a Parthian palace or temple at Velazjord, near Kangavar, and mention has already been made of the view which would associate the ruined temple at Kangavar with the Parthian era. The scarcity of Parthian remains is probably to be accounted for, as in other cases, by the fact that brick was more largely used than stone in the construction of their buildings. As to originality in architectural art, it may be added that the Parthians are credited with the development of the arch- and tunnel-shaped roof, in contrast to the flat ceiling and square lintel of the Achæmenian period.

4. Sasanian period (A.D. 224–661).—The Sasanian monarchs, unlike their Parthian forerunners, were great builders, and distant architectural rivals of the Achæmenians. An enumeration of the places where monuments that date from their reign are found would take in a large part of Persia, as is clear from such a list as that given by Justi (*op. cit.* ii. 540–541). These remains show advances in constructive art over the Parthian period, more especially in the development of the dome, an outgrowth of the arched vault, and in the elaboration of the façade of such a palace as that at Ctesiphon, whose high recessed entrance, with galleried panels on either side, anticipates the sweeping curve of the grand portal and the panelled front which is typical of the mosque and madrasa architecture in Muhammadan times. The standard of royal magnificence under the Sasanians is shown in the ruins of Qaṣr-i Shīrīn, the castle built by Khusru II. Parvīz (A.D. 600), for his favourite, on the road between Baghdad and Kermanshah, and is evident in the sculptured grotto at Ṭāq-i Būstān, near the latter city. To about the same epoch belong the ruins at Mashito and at Ammān (the 'Rabbah of the children of Ammon' of Dt 3[11]), as well as the palace called Aivan-i Khusru, not far from Susa. The religious architecture of the period is represented by the remains of numerous fire-temples, like the *ātash-Kadah*, near Iṣfahān, and that at Abarguh or at Jaur, in the district south of Shiraz; or, again, by a portion of the crumbling sanctuary of brick at Ṭāq-i Sulaimān, south-east of Lake Urumiah. The style of construction of a Sasanian caravanserai may be judged by the stone ruins, said to be the work of Khusru I., 'Anūshirvān the Just' (A.D. 531–579), at Aghuan, between Teherān and Meshed. Sasanian architectural engineering is illustrated by several bridges and dams, as at Dizful and Shuster, or the stone aqueducts, descriptions of which may be seen in the standard works mentioned at the end of this article.

5. Muhammadan period (from A.D. 661).—As already stated, the history of the Muhammadan period of Persian architecture forms a special branch of Muslim art, and the best examples of its development are found in the mosques, the religious edifices which supplanted the old fire-temples after Persia adopted Islām as its national faith, and which are characterized by towering domes (sometimes bulbous in shape), high façades with immense recessed arches, graceful minarets that give balance on either side, and ornamental exteriors decorated with glazed tiles and scroll-like arabesques. The architectural remains of the first period of the Khalīfate, the Umayyads and Abbāsids (A.D. 661–847), have mostly been destroyed by the long series of wars that have devastated Persia from time to time; but the foundation of the mosque of Harūn al-Rashīd at Kazvin (A.D. 786) belongs to that epoch, and a mosque at Shiraz, built in the latter part of the 9th cent. by the Safarid Amr ibn Laith, is numbered among the older remains. To the early Ghaznavid age (10th cent. A.D.) may possibly belong the tower-like tombs at Rai and Hamadan, but it is more probable that they come from the later Seljuk era (roughly, 1030–1150) or from the Mongol age (1160–1260). The same is true of a crumbling mausoleum at Tus, near Meshed, as it is said to be the tomb of the poet Firdausi, who died in the year A.D. 1020; but although the poet's grave is actually near by, it is more likely that the structure is of Seljuk origin, since it closely resembles the mausoleum built by Sultan Sanjar at Merv about 1150. Good examples of the earlier Mongol period are to be seen in the tower-tombs of Jenghiz Khan's grandson Hūlāgū (d. 1265) and his queen at Maragha, the royal seat of the

Mongols in north-western Persia; while the mausoleum of Uljaitu Khodabandah (d. 1316) is of the later Mongol period. The best illustration of the architecture which flourished during the rule of the Tartars, after Timur's invasion, is the beautiful Masjid-i Kabud, or 'Blue Mosque,' erected in 1403 by Shah Jahan at Tabriz. Muhammadan architecture in Persia reached its height in the reign of Shah Abbās the Great (1585–1628), and is well illustrated by the Masjid-i Shah, or 'Royal Mosque,' erected in 1612 at Iṣfahān, and by the other imperial edifices of the same ruler. The architectural activity of Shah Abbās was not confined to his capital, however, or to palaces and places of worship, but was exercised in the construction of caravanserais, bridges, and other useful structures in many parts of Persia, so that his name is widely known throughout the land as the patron of the builder's art.

The cities which best show the different styles of Muhammadan architecture are those which had the honour at one time or another to be the royal capital, like Iṣfahān, Kazvin, Tabriz, Sultanīya, and Shiraz; but hardly of lesser fame are Kum, Kashan, Meshed, Būstān, and Ardabil. Modern architectural tendencies are best observed in the present capital, Teherān, where it is possible to see even European elements combined with the most conservative features of the past. When viewed as a whole, it may be said that Persia's contribution to the history of architecture, if not distinctly original, is, nevertheless, considerable, and deserves the attention of the student of religious art as well as the architectural specialist.

LITERATURE.—For a general description consult Perrot-Chipiez, *Hist. de l'art dans l'antiquité*, v., Paris, 1890; Gayet, *L'Art persan*, Paris, 1895; Geiger, *Ostiran. Kultur im Alterthum*, Erlangen, 1882, pp. 216–222; Saladin, *Manuel d'art musulman*, i. ch. iv. ('École Persane'), Paris, 1907. For special discussions, illustrative drawings, and photographic reproductions, see Flandin-Coste, *Voyage en Perse*, 8 vols., Paris, 1843–54; Texier, *Description de l'Arménie, la Perse, et le Mésopotamie*, 2 vols., Paris, 1842–45; Dieulafoy, *L'Art antique de la Perse*, 5 vols., Paris, 1884–86, and *L'Acropole de Suse*, Paris, 1890–92; Mme. Jane Dieulafoy, *À Suse: journal de fouilles, 1884–86*, Paris, 1888; de Morgan, *Mission scientifique en Perse*, iv., Paris, 1896; Rawlinson, *The Five Great Monarchies of the Ancient Eastern World*, 4 vols., London, 1862–67, *The Sixth Great Oriental Monarchy*, London, 1873, *The Seventh Great Oriental Monarchy*, London, 1876, and *The Story of Parthia*, New York, 1893, pp. 372–385; Justi, 'Geschichte Irans' in Geiger and Kuhn's *Grundriss der iran. Philologie*, ii. 447–457, Strassburg, 1896–1904; Sarre, *Denkmäler persischer Baukunst*, Berlin, 1901.

A. V. WILLIAMS JACKSON.

ARCHITECTURE (Phœnician).—Worshippers of the powers of nature, it is not surprising that the Phœnicians, in the earlier stages of their national existence, should have discarded the work of the architect and builder, and taken to worshipping in the 'high places' so often referred to in the Old Testament. That these were natural eminences, and not artificial erections, like those of the Babylonians and Assyrians, is quite clear from the statements concerning them. They were within easy access from the cities, and thither the people resorted when assembling for worship. How common they were may be gathered from the fact that they were the customary places for worship among the Israelites until the 7th cent. B.C.* The oracle on Carmel, which, according to Tacitus and Suetonius,† Vespasian consulted, was possibly a sacred place of this kind. The god consulted had neither statue nor temple, but only an altar which was much revered. This altar was probably of unhewn stones, like the one dedicated to Jahweh upon that same mount Carmel which Elijah re-built and consecrated anew on the day when he confounded the prophets of Baal.*

* Hastings' *DB* ii. 381b.

† Tac. *Hist.* ii. 78; Suet. *Vespasian*, 5.

In all probability the Phœnicians would have continued worshipping in the same way, without temple and image, had it not been for foreign influence. The close relations, however, which the Phœnicians had with Egypt, brought them under the influence of that nationality, with its splendid temples and elaborate ritual, and the result was that they sought to imitate them, though they did so only to a certain extent, as far as our present knowledge goes.

The most perfect of the small imitations of Egyptian temples is that now called *al-Ma'bed*, 'the temple,' at Amrît near Tartûs. This erection is built in a court, 52 yds. by 60, hewn in the rock and levelled, the S. wall being about 16 ft. high. If there ever was any wall on the N. or front side, as is probable, it has now disappeared, and is replaced by a hedge. Remains of columns near the corners of the court suggest that the walls were flanked by cloisters. The 'temple' is in reality a cella,† and stands on a square mass of rock more than 10 ft. high and about 18 square, being composed of three enormous blocks of stone covered with a monolithic roof. The blocks having been superimposed, the structure was apparently carved out in the form it now presents. The opening is towards the N.; and the plain cornice with which it is decorated is the usual Egyptian one, advancing in front over the anterior face of the rock. It is thought probable that the entablature was supported by columns of metal. The ceiling is vaulted. The flooring within is slightly sunken, and is flanked by narrow platforms or benches, graded and sloping upwards towards the back, possibly to render those taking part in the ceremonies more visible to the people outside.‡ Slots for a rod at the opening suggest that a curtain hid the interior from the passers-by when there was no public ceremony, and square sunken holes near the entrance seem to mark the positions of candelabra or, perhaps, sacred columns. Renan has suggested that the rock-hewn court may anciently have been covered with water from a spring near, when the wall on the N. was in existence; and the appearance of the surface confirms this. If that be the case, it resembled two other similar sanctuaries near *'Ain al-Ḥaiyât*, 'the Serpent-Spring.' The more complete of these is a little monolithic chapel, now in ruins. It was rectangular in form, with a square opening in front, where it has an Egyptian cornice surmounted by uræus-serpents. It rested upon a rectangular block of stone about three metres thick by five wide, carried by a plinth of much smaller dimensions. On each side of the great rectangular stone are traces of a little stairway, which gave access to the platform formed by its upper surface.§ This shrine was about 5·50 metres high, and its slightly-vaulted ceiling was sculptured in relief with two great pairs of wings, one pair springing from the globe flanked by two uræi, and the other seemingly having as its centre an eagle's head.

Facing the chapel just described, and about 10 metres to the E., are the base and lower part of another chapel, nearly like it, but seemingly rather larger. There is hardly any doubt that they both formed part of the same architectural scheme, and it is possible that one was dedicated to a god and the other to a goddess, his spouse. They rise out of the water of a small lake or pond

* 1 K 18[30-32]. There was also a 'high place' at Gezer, without a temple, and marked off by monoliths or 'pillars' such as are often mentioned in the OT.

† Renan, *Mission de Phénicie*, pl. 10; Perrot-Chipiez, *Phénicie*, fig. 40.

‡ Renan, *ib.* pl. 10; Perrot, *ib* figs. 185, 187.

§ Renan, *ib.* pl. 9; Perrot, *ib.* fig. 188.

supplied by the spring, and it is possible that this was also the case in ancient times. Backed by verdure, it must have been a secluded and sufficiently picturesque spot, and the difficulty of access to the shrines would naturally prevent their desecration.*

It is improbable, however, that these remains show the common religious architecture of their time, and the fanes of Astarte at Sidon and Melqart at Tyre were undoubtedly much more important and imposing structures, though Herodotus' description of the latter (ii. 44) does not enable any idea of its form to be gathered; to all appearance he was most struck by its two pillars (στῆλαι), 'one of pure gold and the other of an emerald stone of such size as to shine by night.' Another important shrine was that of Eshmûn on the left bank of the Nahr Auli, about an hour N. of Sidon. This was a rectangular erection built apparently on the side of the slope, remains of the walls and masonry of the terraces being still in existence. The slope looks towards the N., and it is possible that the sanctuary to Eshmûn was a shrine like that at Amrît, which has the same orientation. Large numbers of votive statuettes were found on the site. The stones of the shrine, however, seem to have been long ago carried away by the inhabitants of the country to build their houses with, and some, with holes, are used in olive-pressing.†

Of greater importance, perhaps, are the indications available for the architecture of the temple at Gebal, made known by coins of the Roman period.‡ On the left is shown a chapel, the front surmounted by a pediment. The whole front was open, flanked by pilasters supporting the pediment. At the top of the steps giving access to the interior was a tripod table, perhaps for offerings, and a strange emblem surmounted the point of the roof, which seems to have been decorated on each side with three rows of sunken panels.

Naturally the architecture of this building suggests Greek influence, and to all appearance it is a simple reproduction of the Egyptian shrine, but it may be noted that Babylonian architecture had something analogous (see p. 682), and may have been the true origin of the structure. What would seem to be due to Greek influence is the pointed roof.

The real ancient part, however, was probably the structure on the right, which shows a colonnade to which access was gained by a flight of steps, and a large court-yard, with columns—a kind of arcade—behind. The representation of this building was evidently altogether too much for the die-sinker, whose ideas of perspective were on a level with those of the Assyrians. Above the cornice of the colonnade is an erection of open work, behind which one sees a conical object towering high in the open—the emblem of the god of the place, corresponding with the sacred stones in which the divinity was supposed to reside.§

And here we again have the 'high place,' not formed out of the solid rock by the laborious quarrying of all the mass which was not needed, but by an enclosure of hewn stone, ornamented with a colonnade all round. This was naturally much more elaborate than the simple clearings in the open, and also more æsthetic than the hill-enclosures marked off by simple rows of tall stones.

* Renan, *Mission*, pl. 9; Perrot-Chipiez, *Phénicie*, fig. 189.

† Von Landau, *Vorläufige Nachrichten über die im Eshmuntempel bei Sidon gefundenen phönizischen Altertümer*, with plans, etc., by Makridy Bey from *RB*, 1902.

‡ Donaldson, *Architectura Numismatica*, No. 30; Perrot, *Phénicie*, fig. 19.

§ Upon these objects see p. 884.

But it will be asked: Were these two forms—the 'high place' and the chapel or mountain-shrine—the only architectural creations of the Phœnicians for the purpose of worship? All that can be said is that they are the principal forms found. It seems not improbable, however, that they had others, and, as is well known, the temple of Solomon at Jerusalem was built by workmen and material supplied to that king by Hiram of Tyre. If not in that king's structure, there is at least in the temple as described by Ezekiel (40^{1}–43^{27} etc.), according to Chipiez's restorations,* a certain likeness to the Phœnician temples as shown on the coins of Cyprus, which seem to have been erections of imposing architectural appearance.

In Cyprus the most famous temples were those of Paphos, Amathus, Idalium, and Golgos, in which places were Phœnician settlements, as also, probably, at Citium (now Larnaca), Salamis, and other sites. From Cypriote coins,† an idea may be gained of the celebrated temple at Paphos, dedicated to Venus or Astarte. It consisted of a central erection—a kind of pylon—in the form of two narrow towers connected, in the upper part, by a chamber or chambers furnished with three windows. Below this was the entrance, in which the spectator could see the sacred figure adored there—a conical stone surmounted by a naïve indication of a head, and two rudimentary arms. Perrot suggests that the size of the opening has been purposely exaggerated by the engraver in order to exhibit the divine image, which was, in reality, not at the entrance, but at the far end of the sanctuary. On each side of the pylon were porticoes or colonnades, flat-roofed, hardly more than half the height of the central portion, surmounted by images of the doves sacred to the goddess. Under these arcades objects like candelabra are shown, the upper part arranged either for the purpose of giving light or for the burning of incense. Above the upper structure, and between the two towers, are shown a star and the crescent moon—emblems of the goddess. The space in front of the building seems to be represented paved, and enclosed by a semicircular railing, provided with a double gate. Within this enclosure is a dove, apparently seeking food. The details vary somewhat in the different coins,‡ and it is to be supposed that the engraver had no intention of giving more than a general idea of the building, so that numerous accessories have been omitted. According to Di Cesnola, the body of the edifice was rectangular, 67 metres by 50, surrounded by a court-yard 210 by 164, more or less. As it is based upon actual exploration, it is to be preferred to the plan given by Gerhard after the indications of travellers who visited the site in the early years of the 19th cent.;§ but how the latter could have obtained the exceedingly probable details of the interior which he gives is difficult to understand. According to his plan, there were two enclosures, the first provided with four entrances, and surrounded by a colonnade. A doorway admitted to the second enclosure, in which was the temple. There we see the semicircular railing, the paved forecourt, the sites of the towers, the central portion of the building, divided into a vestibule, a large hall, and a sanctuary wherein was the sacred image; likewise the lateral structures, each with four chambers, to which admission was gained only

* Perrot-Chipiez, vol. iv. pp. 263, 275, 289, and pl. v.

† Guigniant, *Religions de l'antiquité*, pl. liv., p. 206; Perrot-Chipiez, *Phénicie*, fig. 199.

‡ Cf. Perrot-Chipiez, *Phénicie*, fig. 58 (reproduced from Donaldson's *Architectura Numismatica*) with fig. 199.

§ Perrot-Chipiez, *ib.* fig. 200 (from Gerhard's *Akademische Abhandlungen*, pl. 41).

from the large central hall, and one (that at the end) which could be entered only from the sanctuary. The two plans are so different that one asks whether they could have been taken from the same remains. According to Tacitus,* the stone emblematic of the goddess was in the open air, indicating that the place where it stood had no roof; notwithstanding this, it is said never to have been wet with rain. This rather favours Di Cesnola's plan, which, however, does not agree with the picture on the coins. Probably further exploration is needed.

In the neighbourhood, but nearer to the sea, Di Cesnola† found two conical stones still in position, which, it is suggested, are all that remain of some sacred spot—perhaps the traditional landing-place of the goddess when she first visited the island. If this be correct, the site was the spot where the pilgrims to the sacred places on the island commenced their pious visits. Perrot suggests that this site is represented on another Cypriote coin,‡ in which two sharply-pointed cones are shown, one on each side of two columns, resembling the side-posts of a doorway, standing on bases, and connected at a distance of about three-quarters of their height by joists, intended, to all appearance, to hold them in position. The whole seems to have been provided with some protective covering of the nature of an awning. Under this seeming doorway is a conical object on a plinth, surmounted by a flat top, on which stands a dove, the emblem of the goddess. In front is a semicircular enclosure with a single central gate. The whole shows a simple form of the temple at Paphos, without the lateral structures or aisles.

At Golgos the temple was a parallelogram,§ the roof supported by five rows of three columns each. There were two doors, one S., the other E. A large cone of grey stone found on the site implies that the building was dedicated to the goddess of Paphos. It resembles in form, but on a large scale, the terra-cotta cones found in such numbers at Telloh in S. Babylonia. Many figures of women holding or suckling their children, and cows suckling their calves, were discovered at many points on the site. Numerous pedestals, each of which anciently bore a statue, and some of them two, were found. Ceccaldi, who studied the objects disinterred there, has given a very vivid picture of the appearance of the temple when it was still standing. Its four walls were of sun-baked brick covered with white or coloured cement, and the pillars were of wood, with stone capitals, the two sides of the roof which they supported having only a very slight slope, forming a terrace, like the present Cypriote roofs. The roof was of wood covered with reeds and mats, upon which was spread a thick layer of earth beaten down hard. The exterior was therefore of a very simple appearance. The interior was lighted only by means of the large doorways, wherein one saw a motionless and silent crowd of stone-carved figures, their features and robes tinted with the colour of nature, surrounding the mystic cone as perpetual worshippers. Shrine-like stone lamps illuminated the grinning ex-votos hanging in recesses on the walls, which last were adorned with curious pictures. Strange sculptures adorned the circuit of the building, where the slanting rays of light were reflected on the white and polished tiling of the floors.

* *Hist.* ii. 3.

† Di Cesnola, *Cyprus*, p. 214; Perrot-Chipiez, *Phénicie*, fig. 203.

‡ Gerhard, *Akademische Abhandlungen*, xliii. 17; Perrot-Chipiez, *ib.* fig. 202.

§ Di Cesnola, *Cyprus*, p. 139; Perrot-Chipiez, *Phénicie*, fig. 204.

This is a vivid and probable picture, of which, however, some of the details require verification. Perrot suggests that this building was simply a treasury or museum belonging to the real temple.

A few underground buildings exist, the most noteworthy being the crypt at Curium,* in which were found many objects of value. Having descended the steps and passed along a short passage, one finds three successive bayed rooms, and at right angles with these, a fourth, with a further length of the passage. This interesting and well-built structure seems to have been used as a treasure-chamber, but whether it was originally intended for such is uncertain. That at Larnaca is known as the *Panaghia Phaneromini.* Enormous blocks, as well as small stones, have been used in this construction, which consists of a vestibule with a door leading to a small chamber, within which was found an old spring, probably some sacred source. The roof was formed of two large blocks of stone considerably arched on the under side. It has been thought to be a tomb; but in view of the existence of the spring, this is unlikely. It was probably a sacred well, much resorted to by the inhabitants and the people of the neighbouring port.

Far behind the perfection of the temples of Phœnicia and Cyprus are those of Malta and Gaulos (now Gozzo). Artistically and architecturally, a wide gap separates them from the structures of the Phœnicians, but the conical (sacred) stones found therein have caused them to be regarded as certainly Phœnician. Evans and others, however, are of opinion that these buildings are really Libyan. At Gozzo there are two temples,† side by side, and joined together by a wall, which forms a kind of rough façade. Passing through a narrow entrance, one reaches, in the case of the larger building, first a small and afterwards, continuing along the passage, a larger hall arranged at right angles thereto. The rear termination of the building is an apse in the form of a semicircle, and the whole suggests the arrangement of a church choir with deep bays. In consequence of its nearness, the smaller building has the first hall larger than the second, and the semicircular apse at the end is decidedly smaller; otherwise the arrangement is in both cases the same. In the various apses of which the building consists, the ground is made to mount by means of steps and sloping pavement. Barriers possibly railed off these raised bays, which then resembled the chapels in Catholic churches. It was in the right-hand bay, in the first hall, that the cone was found which gave the clue to the nature of these structures. Though symmetrically planned, the individual bays are not by any means regular in shape, and the stone supports for the furniture or sacred objects of the shrines seem to be placed without any attempt at orderly arrangement.

Still more irregular in shape and careless in arrangement is the temple of Hagiar Kim,‡ Malta, in which, moreover, the want of care and regularity extends also to the arrangement of the stones that form the walls, which are in some cases of enormous size.§ There are two entrances, giving access to two bays or apses on the E. and

* Di Cesnola, *Cyprus*, p. 304, reproduced in Perrot-Chipiez, *Phénicie*, fig. 216.

† They are called the *Gigantiga*, the enormous stones used in their construction having led to the tradition that they were the work of giant builders. Plans and views, from La Marmora, *Nouvelles Annales de l'institut de correspondance archéologique, publiées par la section française*, i., Paris, 1832, pp. 1–32 and pl. i.–ii., are published in Perrot-Chipiez, *Phénicie*, figs. 221–224.

‡ Caruana, *Report on the Phœnician and Roman Antiquities in the group of the Islands of Malta*, Malta, 1882, reproduced in Perrot-Chipiez, *ib.* fig. 225.

§ *Ib.* figs. 219, 220.

four on the W., but the southernmost of each seems to have been separated from the rest, and partitions in the case of two others are shown on the plan. Stones decorated with spiral ornaments show that attempts at decoration were made; the ground upon which the spirals are carved is covered with a number of minute holes, emblematic, it is supposed, of the starry vault of heaven.* A striking altar,† with flutings, decorated with a representation of a growing tree, has the same ground-work, which covers also many of the great blocks of stone used in the building. Another altar, like a small table‡ with a thick central support—a type met with often in Syria—was found in one of the large bays.

Sculptures show that similar temples to those in Syria existed, in Punic times, in Sicily and Carthage. One of these was known under the name of *Erek Ḥayim*, 'Length of Lives,' and was dedicated to Astarte as goddess of longevity, whence the name of Eryx, given by the Greeks to the city where it was. It arose on the peak of a mountain, within that mighty wall which protected the summit. Judging from a stele found at Lilybæum (Marsala), a temple to Hammon existed there. The upper part of this monument§ shows a priest adoring before a candelabrum, or fire altar, behind which is the sacred cone with 'arms and head,' similar to the symbols found on the votive stelæ at Carthage. Inscriptions dedicated to *Ba'al Samaim*, 'the lord of the heavens,' *Astarte Erek Ḥayim*, 'Astarte length of lives,' *Eshmûn*, *Ba'al Ḥammôn*, and *Elat*, make it probable that Phœnician temples to these deities existed in Sardinia, where they were found. A shrine‖ in the Egyptian style, found at Sulcis (height 28 in.), has on the cornice a disc, and a row of uræi above. In another example from the same place,¶ carved with a goddess in Greek costume, we have a mixture of styles, Doric columns being introduced as supports of an entablature showing the Egyptian winged disc surmounted by a row of uræi.

Carthage and its dependencies have but little to offer in the way of religious architecture in the Phœnician style. At Ebba a lintel of a doorway** carved with two lotus-flowers, the sun with rays above them, and two crescent moons on each side, and at Jezza a capital of a column†† in modified Ionic, suggesting Cypriote influence, testify to buildings erected there. At Carthage itself the great temple of Eshmûn, demolished by the Romans, was re-built as the temple of Æsculapius; but nothing now exists of it, as the church of St. Louis and its dependencies at present cover the site.

The ornamentation of the Phœnician temples has been referred to from time to time in the preceding pages, but a few additional words thereon are necessary. The cornices are often plain, but when a row of uræi-serpents was added,‡‡ the effect was decidedly decorative. Exceedingly effective was the mixed style of the entablature of the temple at Gebal,§§ with its Græco-Roman decoration, including scrolls and flowers flanking a conventional Egyptian winged disc-emblem with uræi. The doorway at Umal-Awamid,‖‖ being much more Egyptian in style, forms a striking piece for comparison. Egyptian influence is again manifest in the relief showing a sphinx, beautifully carved, found at Arad.¶¶

* Perrot-Chipiez, *Phénicie*, fig. 227.
† *Ib.* fig. 228. ‡ *Ib.* fig. 229, also 226.
§ *CIS*, pl. 29, reproduced in Perrot-Chipiez, *Phénicie*, fig. 232.
‖ Perrot-Chipiez, *Phénicie*, fig. 233.
¶ *Ib.* fig. 193. ** *Ib.* fig. 234. †† *Ib.* fig. 235.
‡‡ Renan, *Mission*, pl. 9; Perrot-Chipiez, *Phénicie*, fig. 61.
§§ Perrot-Chipiez, *ib.* fig. 48. ‖‖ *Ib.* fig. 68.
¶¶ *Ib.* fig. 73.

Apparently it was a favourite decoration with the Phœnicians, for it occurs also as the support of a throne in the decorative panel-relief showing a seated personage in the presence of the sacred fire (see below, p. 885 f.). Gradine ornaments,* such as are found in Assyro-Babylonian reliefs showing fortifications, occur on alabaster slabs from Gebal, now in the Louvre. They suggest the Assyro-Babylonian temple-tower, surmounting a decoration of flowers in squares over a band of laurel. This gradine-ornament is also applied to altars,† even of the Roman epoch. As in the case of the round tower-like monument of the tomb of Amrît,‡ however, the idea that it was really a battlement is lost by the material between the gradines being left; there are no openings. The great disadvantage to the modern student of their decoration, however, is that the remains are so scanty.

There is hardly any doubt that the architecture of the Phœnicians has had an influence on that of the nations around. Perrot and Chipiez cite the old mosques of Cairo, Amru, and Ṭûlûn, with their great rectangular courts surrounded on all four sides by rows of columns, the idol alone being absent. 'If one wish to have the type complete, one must go as far as Mecca, and enter into the Ka'ba, where even the triumph of the Qur'ān has not succeeded in ousting the primitive bethel, the black stone, which, set up in the sanctuary, has received the homage of the Arab tribes throughout many centuries' (*Phénicie*, p. 315 f.).

But perhaps these temples are not derived directly from Phœnician architecture. We have always to take into consideration the possibility of their having come down to the nations which produced them by some collateral line, and the likeness between them and the fanes of Phœnicia may be due to action and reaction. Whatever reservations may be made, however, the evidence of history and the monuments seems to show that the influence of Phœnicia preponderated.

T. G. PINCHES.

ARCHITECTURE (Roman).—GENERAL CHARACTERISTICS.—If it be necessary in the case of Greece to point out that religious buildings were but a part of the architectural activity of the people, it is still more necessary in the case of Rome. Roman religious architecture plays a very small and comparatively unimportant rôle. Her baths, her palaces, her amphitheatres, and other public buildings were all upon a grander scale than her temples.

When Rome became mistress of the world, although she had at that time no architecture of her own, she made use of artists from all nations, and thus arose a composite style of the architectures of the world, in which Greece played by far the largest part. The origin of the Roman temples seems to have been partly Etruscan, partly Greek; but whatever part Etruscan architecture played in other branches of Roman architecture, the Roman temple in its final form was almost wholly Greek. The fact was that the great development of Roman architecture was almost entirely in the hands of Greek artists, and it is by no means easy to determine how much can really be considered Roman at all.

The true Greek style was trabeated, the arch, as has been shown, being only occasionally used. The style of the Romans, however, was a hybrid, partly arcuated and partly trabeated, and in their hands the fusion of the two elements never became complete. It is generally said that the arch in Roman architecture is the arch of the Etruscans: it is, however, doubtful whether it was not an introduction of the Greek artists of the East

* Perrot-Chipiez, *Phénicie*, fig. 77.
† *Ib.* fig. 78. ‡ *Ib.* fig. 95.

and Alexandria. In any case both the arch and the barrel vault date back to remote ages in the East, and the later Greek architects were more likely to be influenced by these traditions than by the comparatively obscure work of Etruria. At the same time, fine arches with large voussoirs were built by the Etruscans, as in the canal on the Marta at Graviscæ, supposed to date from the beginning of the 7th cent. B.C., or the Cloaca Maxima at Rome of the 6th. If, however, the Romans themselves had continued the tradition and built in a fine stone arched style, it at least seems probable that some remains, however scanty, would have come down to us. Indeed, we know that early Roman architecture was of brick, and brick vaulting with voussoirs occurs in Egypt as far back as B.C. 3500. Even the intersecting vault is found in a Greek example at Pergamos dating from the 2nd cent. B.C. The earliest surviving Roman building that had arches is the Tabularium, and it dates only from B.C. 78, long after the sack of Corinth, when Rome passed under the rule of Greece intellectually and artistically. Arches were in common everyday use in Greece, at any rate for structural purposes, as early as the time of Eumenes I. (B.C. 263–241), so there is no reason to suppose that Greek architects working for Rome were in any way necessarily indebted to the Etruscans for their conceptions. Even the triumphal arch—that ornamental form which we are wont to consider typically Roman—was built in Athens in B.C. 318. The earliest instance of such an arch in Rome is that of Scipio Africanus (B.C. 190), of which we have the record, but no remains. The most that can be said, then, is that it is not impossible that the Romans may have had a developed arcuated style derived from the Etruscans before they fell under the dominion of Greece; but there is no evidence of any kind, and, as far as existing remains are concerned, there are no new developments that precede Greek work. The attached column, for instance, sometimes spoken of as a Roman invention, occurs in the Arsinoeion in but slightly modified form, in the monument of Lysicrates in Athens, and at Phigalia, even if those of the Erechtheum were of Roman date.

With regard to their brick and concrete construction it is otherwise. The Romans were certainly great engineers. There is, however, not the same intellectual nicety about Roman work that there is in Greek work, and this was never acquired. When the Roman Empire was finally divided, the Greek or Byzantine portion at once began to develop a more scientific style in marked contrast with the ruder work of the West. Roman work was practical, rough and ready, often grandiose, but lacking in the finer artistic sense.

It is likely that we shall never be able to say what elements are Roman and what are Hellenistic, but it is possibly in the general planning that the Roman influence is strongest.

The Romans borrowed the Greek orders; or perhaps a more correct way of putting it is to say that the Greek architects working for Rome used their own orders, and by slow degrees trained a native school. **The Doric order** became very debased, and is found in a great variety of forms. The simpler of these forms are commonly grouped together as Tuscan, but they differ very much among themselves, and there is no historical evidence for any Tuscan origin. Vitruvius uses the term, but it is impossible to draw any clear dividing line between Tuscan and the debased Doric. The cause of the common error is that the Renaissance architects did make such a hard and fast division. The term as applied to Renaissance work has a definite meaning, but has no relation to anything in Rome. There was a Roman tendency to dispense with the fluting of Greek work both in Doric and Ionic, and occasionally in the Corinthian order, which greatly detracts from the strong refined vertical character of the shaft. Flutings were expensive to work, and were not showy enough to please Roman taste, which preferred monolithic shafts in hard brightly-coloured marbles in which flutings would have little effect. The column loses the sturdy proportions of Greek Doric, and tends to assimilate itself to the proportions of the other orders. In most of the existing examples of Roman Doric there is a base, but this is absent in early examples such as those at Pompeii, which are much more Greek in feeling. It has been suggested that the origin of the base is Etruscan, but its absence in early work is against this theory; and the part that Vitruvius would assign to Etruscan influence in architecture is not much more of a reality than the part assigned by Virgil to Æneas in Roman history. The contours gradually deteriorate, and the echinos of the Doric column speedily becomes a simple quarter round. In the almost unique early example of the Temple of Hercules at Cora the hyperbolic curve is found, and is obviously executed by Greeks. The architrave shrinks in importance, and the whole entablature is much shallower. There is a marked tendency for the intercolumniations to become wider. This is mainly the result of the fact that the order as such is not an essential part of the construction in Roman work. It does not govern the building, but is merely something applied afterwards, and has to suit its proportions to the available space. It is to this that we owe the introduction of the pedestal as a regular feature, which occurs only occasionally in Greek work. The architrave is set farther back than in Greek architecture, and the line of its face tends to fall within the base (fig. 1). The beautiful sculpture

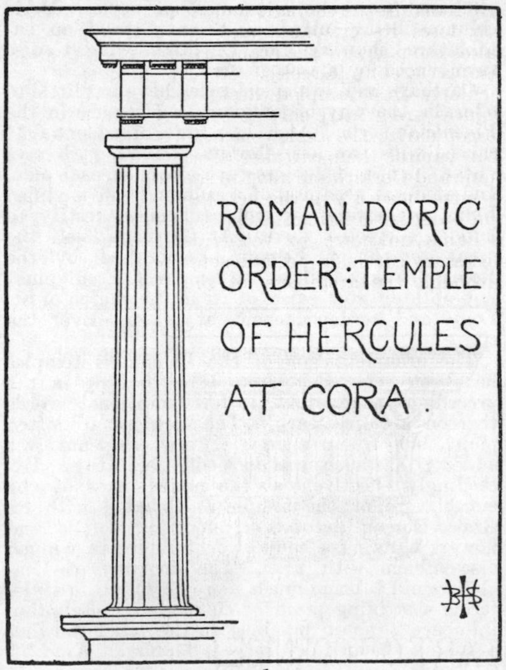

FIG. 1.

which was the glory of Greek buildings, and particularly of the Doric order, is absent, and its place is often taken by trivial conventionalities, such as wreathed skulls. The origin of this feature is probably to be found in the actual skulls of victims hung upon the altars. **The Ionic order** remains the same in its principal features, but the

FIG. 2.

capital is not infrequently found with the volutes set anglewise (fig. 2). They are, however, comparatively rare, although the text-books speak of them as almost universal. This arrangement in Greek work at Phigalia has already been noted, and its first known occurrence in Italy is at Pompeii, where the refined carving marks it as the work of Greek hands. The volute in Roman Ionic projects very much less than in Greek examples, and the proportions are not at all satisfactory. There is generally a dentil course beneath the cornice as in Asiatic Greek examples: this occurs even in Roman Doric in the Theatre of Marcellus. The Roman dentils, however, are set much closer together and are shallower than in Greek work, generally with a fillet underneath.

The tendency throughout is towards greater enrichment, clearly seen in the choice of **the Corinthian** as the favourite Roman order. In Greek hands, as at Epidaurus, or the choragic monument of Lysicrates, this order, in spite of its richness, is yet restrained and most delicate in its refinement. In Roman work this is lost, and mere carving takes the place of the sculpture which is still found in the choragic monument. The foliage, too, loses its crispness, and the acanthus mollis takes the place of the acanthus spinosus (fig. 6 in ARCHITECTURE [Greek]). In some instances, particularly in triumphal arches, the small angle volutes are greatly enlarged, and may have helped to popularize the angle treatment of Roman Ionic. The capital then partakes of the nature of both Ionic and Corinthian, and the egg and dart molding is introduced above the acanthus. Thus treated, the order is sometimes called the Composite order, a name unknown to Vitruvius, and not at all necessary: it is in no true sense a distinct order, although the architects of the Renaissance en-

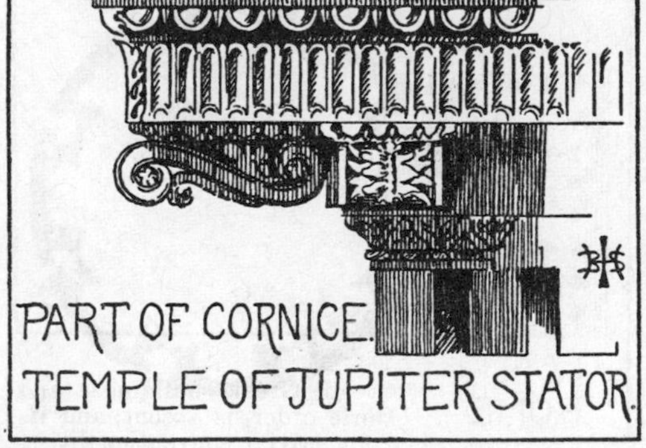

FIG. 3.

deavoured to make it so. The origin of the arrangement is as usual Greek, and in the temple

of Apollo at Naucratis, the Erechtheum itself, and a capital in the forum of Trajan, we see it in its undeveloped form.

The entablature in Roman Corinthian work is very ornate. The architrave is divided by several moldings more or less enriched. The frieze is often decorated with continuous scroll work founded on the acanthus leaf, which is beautiful in itself although giving a restless effect as the result of over-ornamentation. Below the corona a new feature is introduced in the modillions—ornamental brackets which give an æsthetic sense of support (fig. 3).

RELIGIOUS BUILDINGS.—Of course in most of the great secular work the arch plays an important part, and the orders are placed as ornaments in front of the real arched construction; but except in the case of the propylæa in the East before the sacred temenos, the arch practically plays no part in religious work. The vault, however, does occur (see below). The religious buildings of the Romans were of comparatively small importance, and the great *thermæ* are far more typical of Roman work than the temples. The temples, too, were used for many other besides religious purposes, just as was the case with the great mediæval cathedrals. The temple of Concord was not only an art museum of the spoils of the world, but was often used for meetings of the senate, as also was the temple of Mars Ultor. The public weights and measures office was in the temple of Castor. But the Roman temples, although in their main features simply modifications of the Greek, have certain distinctive marks of their own. It seems probable that the early Etruscan temples were often of three cellæ placed side by side, and, moreover, that it was the custom to erect them upon a lofty base, or podium.

The Etruscan architecture apparently was largely of wood, and terra-cotta ornaments played a very important part, noticeably in a peculiar fringe of ornamented terra-cotta tiles hanging from under the eaves and apparently also from the main beam of the portico. These features can be traced in Roman work—the lofty podium with a great flight of steps approaching the main portico, the wide intercolumniations, and the use of terra-cotta ornaments—and even the three-celled temple may have had its influence in the great breadth of the Roman temple, or in the case of a triple temple such as occurs at Sbeitla in N. Africa. [See ART AND ARCHITECTURE (Etruscan and Early Italic), p. 863].

The ruins of the temple of Mars Ultor and three columns of the temple of Castor and Pollux (completed A.D. 6) are probably the earliest extant remains. There may, however, have been earlier examples, as Greece can be said to have begun its dominion over Rome in B.C. 146. The temple of Jupiter Capitolinus was possibly largely Etruscan. Generally speaking, the earlier the date the purer the work and the more marked the Greek influence. It has been observed that the Greek temple was orientated; but this was not the case with Roman temples, and we find them facing in all directions, generally planned in relation to their architectural surroundings. We find them all round the Forum Romanum, for instance, each facing into the forum. As in the case of Greece, the altar was not in the temple but outside, and the exact *raison d'être* of the temple itself is by no means so clearly defined.

The typical Roman temple, then, is a rectangular building with a cella very much wider than was usual in Greece. In the temple of Concord the width was greater than the depth. This may possibly have been the result of the earlier three-celled temple or of the many uses to which the

Roman temple was put. The architectural effect was always concentrated upon the front, and the back of the temple was often absolutely plain. As part of the same tendency we may notice that the temples were generally only *pseudo*-peripteral, with attached columns round three sides of the cella and an abnormally large front portico. The temple of Fortuna Virilis is a good early example; there is a very fine later temple known as the Maison Carrée at Nîmes (fig. 4).

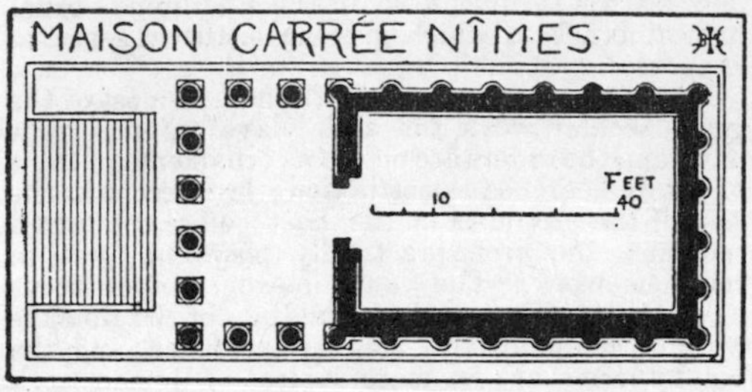

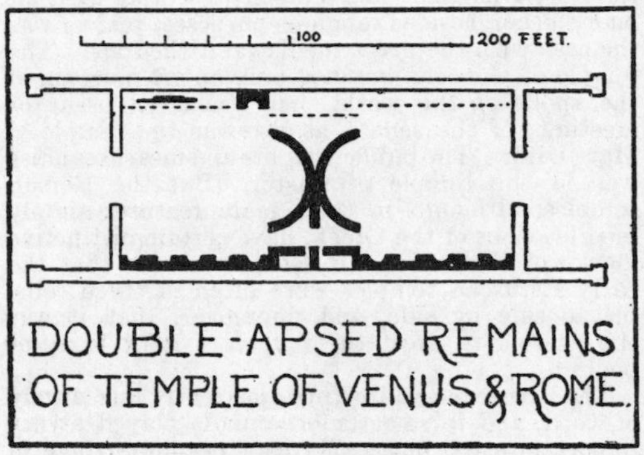

FIGS. 4 AND 5.

The Roman temples within were apparently rarely divided into nave and aisles, so that a greater floor space was obtained, but the span was sometimes reduced by internal columns close against the wall, after the manner of the Greek temple at Phigalia. Occasionally there was an apse, as in the temple of Mars Ultor; and in the temple of Venus and Rome there was an interesting arrangement of a double temple with two cellæ and apses back to back (fig. 5). The whole in this case was surrounded by a court and stoa.

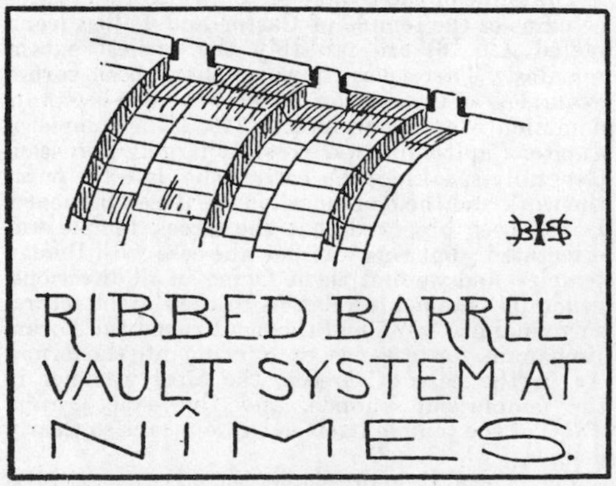

FIG. 6.

The roof appears to have been normally of wood, but certainly in a few instances a concrete or stone vault was employed, as in the above-mentioned temple of Venus and Rome, the temple of Neptune, the temple of Ceres and Proserpine, and the temple at Nîmes known as the Nymphæum or the Baths of Diana, which has a stone barrel-vault supported on stone arches which rested upon attached columns (fig. 6).

In front of the temple was a great flight of steps generally flanked by two projecting portions of the podium, the steps not extending the entire width of the building. In the temple of Minerva at Assisi the steps are carried between the columns which are raised on pedestals. This was probably from want of space.

A favourite form of temple with the Romans was the circular building which had become popular in Greece during the 4th and 3rd centuries B.C. It has been suggested that the Roman circular temple had an independent Etruscan origin. Even if this be the case with regard to the mere fact of the plan being circular, it has certainly nothing whatever to do with the actual form, which is simply a copy of Greek work. The lofty podium is generally found in Roman examples; but this, too, occurs in Greek examples of much earlier date. The picturesquely situate temple of Vesta at Tivoli is a fine example, of which the cella itself may even date back to the close of the 1st cent. B.C., although the Corinthian peristyle is later (fig. 7).

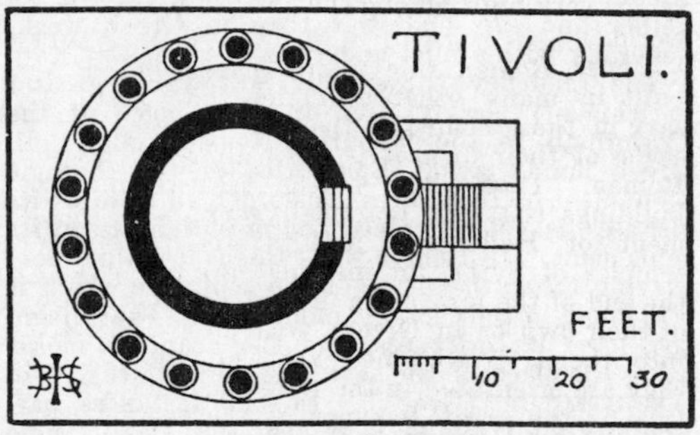

FIG. 7.

By far the most remarkable of the circular temples, and indeed of all the Roman temples, is the celebrated Pantheon (fig. 8)—a great building 142 ft. 6 in. in diameter, 2 ft. in excess of the domed reading-room of the British Museum. The exterior is plain, not to say ugly; but originally the brick was faced with marble up to the first string course, and above this with stucco, which may possibly have somewhat improved the general appearance although not actually affecting the building architecturally. It is approached by a great portico built from the spoils of Agrippa's temple, which

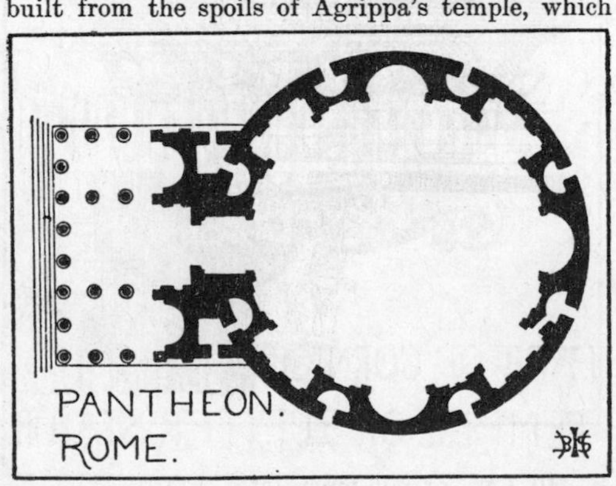

FIG. 8.

was taken down for that purpose. This fact was discovered in 1892, and is some consolation to those who have always maintained that the portico is hopelessly out of place, and ruins the severe dignity that the plain circular building might otherwise have possessed. The date of the main building also has conclusively been proved to be A.D. 120–124, from the stamps upon the bricks of which it is constructed. This is a most important fact, as the assignment of the building to Agrippa has led to many wrong inferences with regard to the history of dome construction.

The building occupies the site of what was once an open circular piazza, the pavement of which has been found some 7 or 8 ft. below the floor of the present building. The walls are 20 ft. in thickness, containing eight great recesses three of which are apses: the highest faces the entrance on the main axis, and the other two are at the extremities of the diameter, at right angles to the main axis. The entrance itself is a great rectangular recess covered by a barrel-vault, and between these four recesses are four others, all of rectangular form. Except in the case of the entrance and the main apse opposite to it, all the recesses have two columns *in antis* in front. The dome is divided in its lower part by vertical and horizontal ribs into five ranges of thirty-two coffers. Above this it is plain, and the whole building is lit by a huge circular hypæthral opening 30 ft. across. Altogether the interior effect ranks very high among the great buildings of the world.

Under Roman rule many great temples were built in many other countries than Italy, but, save in those countries that had no architectural styles of their own, it is misleading to call them Roman. Particularly in the East we find many buildings that are practically simply a development of Hellenistic architecture. The great temples of Syria, for instance, are not placed at the end of the fora as in Rome, but in a temenos of their own as in Greece, with propylæa leading into them. With one exception too (Baalbek) they are orientated in the Greek manner. Of this type is the great temenos of the temple of the Sun at Palmyra. In most instances, just as at Athens, the propylæa have a wider intercolumniation in the centre, but it was spanned by an arch, round which the entablature is carried. The propylæa of Damascus (fig. 9), which may be dated

FIG. 9.

c. 110 A.D., or not much later, are probably the first instance, and a similar dated example occurs in the temple of Atil (A.D. 151). Baalbek (A.D. 160) and probably Palmyra were the same. The invention—if so it may be termed—appears to be that of Apollodoros, a Greek of Damascus, and seems a natural development of the arches of later Greek tradition already noted. It afterwards appears in Diocletian's Palace at Spalato, on the north-east coast of the Adriatic (*c.* 305 A.D.). It marks an important step, because hitherto the arch had always been carried by portions of walls or piers. On the other hand, the columns had never before carried anything but a horizontal entablature; and the piers and arches behind, with the columns and entablature in front, always remained two distinct and irreconcilable elements. Indeed, it was left for the Byzantine and Gothic architects to work out truly homogeneous styles of column and arch.

Of these Syrian examples the finest is that at Baalbek, which is built upon a great platform forming an acropolis. The general setting out is probably not Roman, and some of the substructure is pre-Roman in date. It was approached by great propylæa of Roman times, the restoration of which is largely conjectural. An interesting feature is the hexagonal court, surrounded by a double peristyle upon which the propylæa opened. The hexagonal court leads in its turn to a great square court, at the end of which, somewhat in the Roman manner, is the larger of the two temples. Apparently it was never completed. The other temple to the south, the temple of Jupiter, is a very fine piece of work. In some ways the building was a compound of Greek and Roman feeling. It was peripteral with two ranges of columns in the front, but the portico was very deep, and the central intercolumniation was wider than the rest. The interior had attached columns after the manner of the temple at Phigalia, except that the entablature was broken and carried round and back between the columns. It probably had a flat roof, except at the far end, where there was a small vaulted recess, about half the total width, approached by a flight of steps. A curious feature is a two-storey division into shallow niches between the columns, which has a very unpleasing effect. The lower one is arched, with a horizontal cornice, and the upper has only the cornice, but is surmounted by a pediment. The carving is bold and good, and shows the influence of Greek tradition.

Construction.—The Roman method of construc-

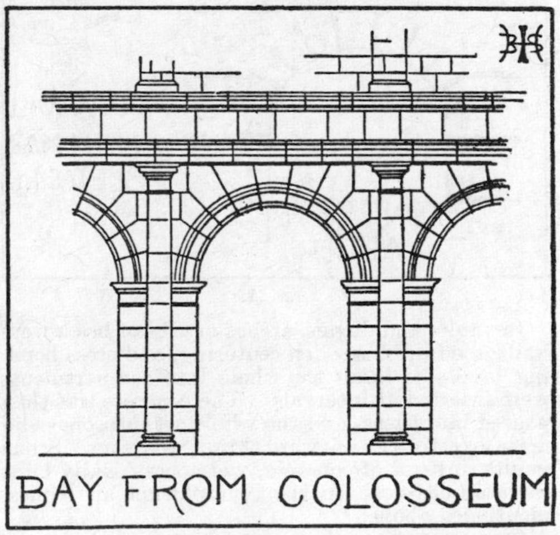

FIG. 10.

tion was very different from that of Greece. Whereas the Greeks generally built in large stone blocks bonding right through the wall, the

Romans built mainly in brick and concrete, and the finer materials were used only for facing. In Rome itself even brick was never used throughout, although in the provinces brick walls or courses of stone and brick alternately are not uncommon. Whether brick or stone was used in the core of the wall or not, the outer face was invariably covered with stucco or some finer material. When brick or stone occurs, its use is not easy to determine, as it would neither add to the strength of the wall, nor admit of its being built without planking to keep the concrete in position while setting. Bricks were of flat triangular shape, and stones pyramidal. 'Opus incertum' was work where the stones were more or less irregular in shape, and 'opus reticulatum' where they were dressed to a true square, and set diagonal-wise in the wall (fig. 11). In either case occasional courses of large flat bricks, 1 ft. 11 in. long, bonding through the wall, were used. A similar method was adopted with arches to prevent the concrete from spreading and settling down before it had set (fig. 11). The marble or other facings were secured to the wall by iron or bronze cramps running into the body of the wall (fig. 11).

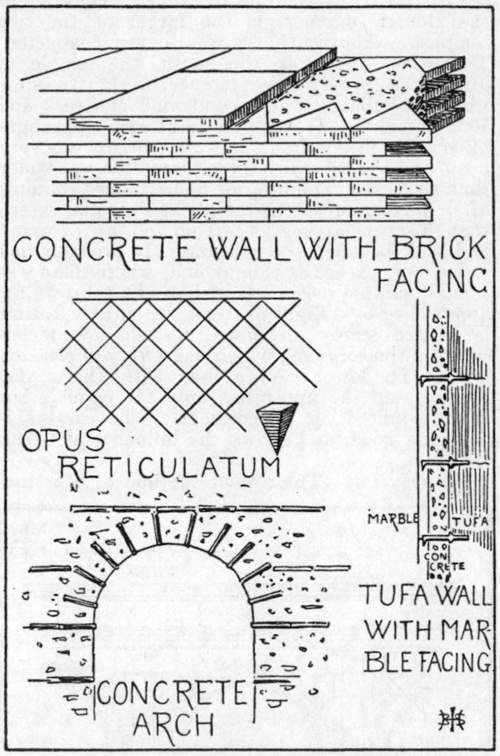

FIG. 11.

In vaults and domes, arches or ribs of brick were built upon light wooden centering, and cross bonding bricks dividing the whole into compartments were inserted at intervals. The concrete was then poured into these, and the whole set into one solid mass, exerting no outward thrust whatever. Stone vaults, instead of concrete, were occasionally built in later days, as in the Nymphæum at Nîmes, mentioned above.

Ornamentation.—The ornamental work of the Romans was not nearly so good as their construction, which was sound and workmanlike, and of great durability. One even regrets that they ever attempted ornament at all, as the bold and simple majesty of their great work is only spoilt by the applied ornament. After all there is very little Roman work, if any, more pleasing than the Pont du Gard at Nîmes; and it has no ornament at all. One of the most delightful of their more purely architectural works is the gateway at Trèves, which is practically devoid of ornament. The ornament used by the Romans was all derived from Greek sources, but there is a roughness and want of delicacy that shows an entire ignorance of the subtlety and refinement of Greek work. The profiles of the moldings are nearly always segments of circles, instead of the subtle parabolic and hyperbolic curves of Greek art. Moreover, the molding, as a rule, does not depend for its effect upon the subtle gradations of light and shade produced by its own contour, but upon the elaboration of the carving cut upon it. Somewhat similarly we find a preference among the Roman architects for the acanthus mollis with its rounded and less precise form, whereas the Greeks preferred the acanthus spinosus with its more crisp refined lines (fig. 6, ARCHITECTURE [Greek]). It is true that the acanthus spinosus badly drawn is less satisfactory even than the other, but this kind of thing is well known—the greater the height, the worse the fall. The carving, too, although vigorous in its way, is rougher and much more mechanical than that of Greece. Instead of the fine sculpture that adorned the temples of Greece, we frequently find endless repetitions of ox-skulls and hanging festoons of fruit and flowers between. There was a great tendency to use the ornament in such profusion that it stultified itself. Such an example, for instance, as the arch at Beneventum is so overloaded that there are practically no plain surfaces at all, and the whole effect is worried and unsatisfying.

Colour was used in their buildings by the Romans as by the Greeks, and the great fondness of the Romans for marbles of many colours gave their buildings an opulence in effect that was one of their most marked characteristics.

One of the most important adjuncts of Roman ornament was the mosaic, which, however difficult to work satisfactorily, is undoubtedly more in consonance with architectonic feeling than any mere surface pigment.

Adequately to appreciate Roman work, it would be necessary to study much more than the religious architecture. Rome's finest achievements were in the *thermæ*—the great baths, which were the centres of Roman life, where literature was read and discussed, and politics debated. In these magnificent buildings it was the interior that was the greatest achievement. It was in interior effects that the Roman architects made the real architectural advance, giving to them a magnificence hitherto undreamed of. Magnificence was the aim and end of Roman art; subtlety and refinement were beyond its comprehension. However, of existing remains, it is a religious building—the Pantheon—that gives us the clearest conception of what this interior magnificence was; and for us the Pantheon, with its fine interior and poor exterior, is the great typical example of Roman achievement, as the Parthenon, with its delicate subtleties and sculpture of unsurpassable loveliness, is of Greek.

LITERATURE.—A. Choisy, *L'Art de bâtir chez les Romains*, Paris, 1873; W. J. Anderson and R. Phené Spiers, *The Architecture of Greece and Rome*, London, 1902; J. H. Middleton, *The Remains of Ancient Rome*, London, 1892; J. Gwilt's translation of Vitruvius, 1826; R. Lanciani, *Ancient Rome in the Light of Recent Discoveries*, London, 1888; F. M. Simpson, *A History of Architectural Development*, vol. i., London, 1905; R. Sturgis, *A History of Architecture*, vol. i., London, 1907; James Fergusson, *Illustrated Handbook of Architecture*, vol. i., London, 1855.

J. B. STOUGHTON HOLBORN.

ARCHITECTURE (Shinto).—There are indications that the original Shinto place of worship was, like the Roman *templum*, not a building, but simply a plot of ground consecrated for the purpose. It was probably enclosed by a row of twigs of the sacred evergreen *sakaki* tree stuck in the ground. 'Spirit terraces' for Shinto worship are mentioned in the old records, and the common word for a Shinto shrine, viz. *yashiro*, means 'house-equivalent,' *i.e.* a make-believe house for the god—no doubt a plot of ground of this kind. Another word for a shrine is *miya*, which means 'august house,' and is applied alike to a palace and a shrine. Sir Ernest Satow says (*TASJ*, 1874):

'The architecture of the Shinto temples is derived from the primeval hut, with more or less modification in proportion to the influence of Buddhism in each particular case. Those of the purest style retain the thatched roof, others are covered with thick shingling, while others have tiled, and even coppered, roofs. The projecting ends of the rafters (called *chigi*) have been somewhat lengthened, and carved more or less elaborately.'

It appears from a passage in the *Nihongi* that the *chigi* were restricted to Imperial residences and to Shinto shrines. Another distinctive feature of the shrine is a row of cigar-shaped pieces of timber laid cross-wise on the roof-tree. The walls consist of planks: the pillars supporting the roof are round, and without bases. The shrine has a wooden floor, raised some feet above the ground. There is a sort of balcony all round, with a flight of steps up to the entrance. A certain amount of brass ornament and wood-carving is used in some shrines, but, generally speaking, they are characterized by great simplicity. The wood-carving and metal ornamentation of some of them are traceable to Buddhist influences, and were removed when the shrines were 'purified' after the restoration of the Imperial power in 1868. They are always of wood, without paint or lacquer, which, of course, limits their duration. The shrines of Ise are renewed every twenty years. Nor are they of great size. In the 8th cent. a 'greater shrine' had only fourteen feet frontage. At the present day the outer shrine of Ise—that in honour of the Goddess of Food—measures 34 feet by 19 feet. The great majority of Shinto shrines are very tiny edifices.

The more important Shinto shrines are surrounded by a cluster of subsidiary buildings, which serve various purposes. There is a small oratory, where the Mikado's envoy performs his devotions. No provision is made for the shelter of the ordinary worshipper. He remains outside in front of the shrine whilst he utters a brief invocation. The joint worship of a congregation of believers is a rare phenomenon in Shinto. Within the precinct there are usually a number of smaller shrines (*massha*) to other deities than the one worshipped in the main building. At Ise there were formerly more than a hundred of these. Sometimes there is an *emadō*, or picture-gallery, for the reception of *ex voto* offerings of this kind. A characteristic feature of Shinto architecture is the *torii*, or honorary gateway, which adorns the approaches to the shrine, sometimes in great numbers. These arches consist of two upright pillars leaning slightly towards one another. Near the top they are connected by a cross-beam or tie. Another beam rests on the upright columns, projecting a little on each side. It is often made to curve upwards slightly at each end. The *torii* is usually constructed of wood painted red, but may also be of stone, bronze, or even occasionally iron. The whole has a simple but graceful effect. Mr S. Tuke has shown that the *torii* is identical with the Indian *turan*, the Chinese *pailou*, and the Korean *hongsalmun*, which are similar in form and purpose. The name is probably Japanese. It means literally 'bird-rest,' *i.e.* hen-roost; and the gateways were so called from their resemblance to this familiar object.

LITERATURE.—B. H. Chamberlain, *Things Japanese*[3] (Lond. 1898); B. H. Chamberlain and W. B. Mason, *Handbook for Travellers in Japan*[7] (Lond. 1903). W. G. ASTON.

ARCHITECTURE AND ART (of the pagan Slavs).—The pagan Slavs seem to have had only the most rudimentary ideas on the subject of art. The few monuments which are ascribed to them are very crude, and it cannot yet be asserted with absolute certainty that they are the work of Slav artists. There is no connexion between these monuments and the more or less grotesque descriptions given in some of the Chronicles of the Middle Ages. These chronicles we owe to the Germans, Adam of Bremen of the 11th cent. (*Gesta Hammenburgensis ecclesiæ pontificum*), Helmold of the 12th cent. (*Chronicon Slavorum*), Thietmar, Bishop of Merseburg (976–1011), Saxo Grammaticus the Dane (12th cent.) in his *Gesta Danorum*, and the biographers of Bishop Otto of Bamberg (12th century).

The majority of the Slavs seem to have worshipped only idols and in the open air, and to have been quite unacquainted with temples. The existence of temples among the Slavs of the Russian Empire is very questionable. Hilarion, a monk of the 10th cent., writes: 'We are no longer building *kapishta*, but churches of Christ,' from which we may infer that the *kapishta* (from *kap*, 'idol') were pagan temples. But the oldest Russian chronicles speak only of idols, and the word *kapishta* may mean simply idols. Among the Baltic Slavs we find the existence of temples attested by German writings, in which the descriptions are not always very plausible. According to the statements of Helmold, the temple of Svantovit in the Island of Rügen was the great sanctuary of the Baltic Slavs. It was built in the town of Arkona. Saxo Grammaticus gives a glowing description of it. 'It was,' he says, 'a very beautiful wooden temple. The exterior or inclosing wall of the building was ornamented with thin roughly painted sculptures representing various objects. It was entered only by a single door. The temple was surrounded by a double wall. Inside the building stood a huge idol.' He adds that the temple was decorated with purple cloth and wild animals' horns.

According to one of Otto of Bamberg's biographers, the god Triglav had at Stettin four temples called *continæ* (from a Slav word meaning 'building'). The most important of these *continæ* was marvellously decorated and ornamented with sculptures representing men, birds, and animals, so cleverly reproduced that one could have believed them living, and so ingeniously coloured that neither rain nor snow could injure them.

At Gostkov, according to one of Otto of Bamberg's historians, there stood sumptuous temples adorned with colossal idols. In the town of Riedgost (perhaps Rhetra [?]) Thietmar describes a temple built of wood and resting on animals' horns (though the statement seems rather curious). The outside walls were covered with wonderful carved representations of gods and goddesses. In the interior stood gods made by hand, with their names engraved, arrayed in armour and helmets.

It is not our duty to discuss here the question as to the characters in which the gods' names might have been inscribed. This point, upon which much has been written, is probably purely imaginary. 'As many districts as there are in these parts' (*i.e.* among the Baltic Slavs or Slavs of the Elba), says Thietmar, 'so many temples are there, and the images of demons are worshipped by the infidels. It is to the temple that they come when on the point of making war; to it they bring gifts after a successful expedition.'

Did the Slavs themselves build those temples, which were probably very small? Did they call in foreign architects? We do not know. The Arab geographer Mas'ūdī (10th cent.) had heard of their temples, but he gives an absolutely imaginary description of them, which cannot be believed, and he places the people whom he is describing in districts no less fanciful (*Les prairies d'or*, ch. lxvi.).

We have practically no specimen of the architecture of the pagan Slavs; and no ruined temple is in existence. We know the names of a number of idols worshipped in ancient Russia and among the Baltic Slavs—Svantovit, Perunŭ, Triglav. The present writer has reproduced in his *Mythologie slave* (1901) illustrations of some of the idols which have been discovered in Germany and in Galicia (Austria). They are believed to be of Slav origin; but we are not absolutely sure, as we have no trustworthy information. German and Ancient Russian writings alone bear witness to the existence of these idols. When Christianity reached the Slavs, they adopted the architectural style of the neighbouring races, from whom the gospel had come to them—the Roman style prevailing among the Western Slavs, and the Byzantine among the Slavs of Russia, Bulgaria, and Servia.

LOUIS LEGER.

ARDASHIR I. (Artashīr, Artakhshathr, Artaxerxes).—Ardashir I. (A.D. 226–241), the founder of the Sasanian dynasty, was the son of Pāpāk, 'king' of Khir (Chir), south-east of Persepolis. Having made himself master of Persia and some neighbouring kingdoms, Ardashir killed the Parthian 'king of kings,' Artaban, in 224, and seems to have conquered the capital, Ctesiphon, two years later.

From the beginning Ardashir identified his political aims with the restoration of the Mazdayasnian faith, which, notwithstanding the superficial sway of Hellenism, had never lost its hold on the people. He thus secured a mighty ally—the Zarathushtrian priesthood, the 'race of the Magians'—and continued and accomplished a work already begun by Parthian monarchs. In his zeal for the national religion, he seems to have kept to familiar traditions—his grandfather Sāsān having been attached to the temple of the goddess Anāhita in Istakhr (Persepolis)—as well as to his personal feelings. 'He was devoted to the Magian rites, and he himself celebrated the mysteries' (Agathias, *Hist.* ii. 36). The Avesta texts, destroyed and scattered in the time of Alexander and the following centuries, were collected by Ardashir, and completed by his high priest Tansar (according to a tradition reported in *Dīnkarṭ*, iii.), who thus gave 'a faithful image of the original light.' Another passage, in *Dinkarṭ*, iv., which corroborates the king's having called Tansar to his capital in order to gather the scattered texts, adds the important fact that canonical authority was attributed only to the collection of Tansar, all doctrines that did not originate from him being considered as heretical. The collection was not completed until the reign of Ardashir's successor Shāhpūhr I. (241–272). A different tradition, reported in the introduction to the Persian translation of *Arṭā Vīrāf Nāmak*, makes Ardashir collect the Avestan texts and the Zend commentaries from the memories of the priests summoned to the capital (Haug and West, *Book of Arda Viraf*, Bombay, 1872, pp. xv–xviii). The custom of reciting a chapter, called *isnād* (*Yasna*), dates, according to Mas'ūdī, from Ardashir's time. Hence we may perhaps conclude with Darmesteter (*Zend-Av.* iii. p. xxxii) that Ardashir and his Hērbad of Hērbads regulated the liturgy. The two chief facts of the restoration, viz. the collection of texts, legends, traditions, laws, and doctrines, and the monopolizing of true worship and of true faith by the king, are expressed in the letter from Tansar to Gushnasp, king of Tabaristān (south of the Caspian), preserved, with additions and alterations, in a Persian translation of an Arabic version of the Pahlavi original (Darmesteter, *op. cit.* xxv–xxx).

The pretended letter of Tansar is discussed in a most thorough way by L. H. Mills ('Tansar's alleged Letter' in *Zoroaster, Philo and Israel*, 21–76), who, in pointing out the peculiar elements of this document, especially a certain ascetic tendency evidently contrasting with the Zarathushtrian law, considers it 'as being in its present form a subtle political fiction.' He goes much further than Darmesteter in eliminating spurious parts and in reducing the remainder, but he expressly recognizes a historical nucleus.

Ardashir has immortalized his political and religious restoration by his theory of the mutual aid of the two powers, the State and the Church, if Mas'ūdī (*Les prairies d'or*, text and tr. by C. Barbier de Meynard and Pavet de Courteille, ii. 162) has correctly rendered his testament to his son Shāhpūhr: 'Religion and kingship are two sisters that cannot exist the one without the other, because religion is the foundation of kingship, and kingship is the protectress of religion.'

LITERATURE.—For the Dīnkarṭ passages see Haug, *Zand-Pahlavi Glossary*, Bombay, 1867, pp. xxxi–xxxviii; West, *SBE* v. 199, xxxvii. 414, xlvii. 85, 127; Darmesteter, *Le Zend-Avesta*, Paris, 1892–3, iii. pp. xxv–xxx; Geldner in *Grundriss der iran. Philologie*, ii. 33 f. In general, Justi in *Grundriss d. ir. Ph.* ii. 512 ff.; *Kār-nāmak-i Artakhshir Pāpakān*, ed. with transliteration, translations, etc., by Edalji Keresāspji Āntiā, Bombay, 1900; Browne, *Literary Hist. of Persia*, Lond. 1902–6, i. 136–150; Nöldeke, 'Gesch. des Artachšīr' in *Bezzenberger's Beiträge*, iv. 1879, 22–69.

N. SÖDERBLOM.

ARHAT (lit. 'fit,' 'worthy').—In its Pāli form, *arahat*, it is met with in the earliest Buddhist texts, and is used there in two senses, according as it is applied to the Buddhist *arahats*, or to those belonging to other communities. In the latter sense, which is exceedingly rare (*Vinaya*, i. 30–32; *Saṁyutta*, ii. 220), it means a man who has attained to the ideal of that particular community, to what was regarded in it as the fit state for a religious man. This sense is not found in pre-Buddhistic literature; but the usage by the early Buddhists makes it almost certain that the term was employed, before Buddhism arose, among the religious communities then being formed in N.E. India. In the more usual, the Buddhist sense, the technical term *arahat* is applied to those who have reached the end of the Eightfold Path, and are enjoying the fruits of it, the *maggaphalaṭṭhā*. They had perfected themselves in each of the eight stages of the Path—right views, aspirations, speech, conduct, mode of livelihood, effort, mindfulness, and rapture (*Saṁyutta*, iv. 51; *Puggala*, 73). They had conquered the three so-called 'intoxications' (*āsavas*) of sensuality, re-births, and ignorance (*Dīgha*, i. 84). In a list of punning derivations in *Majjhima*, i. 280, the *arahat* is said to be one from whom evil dispositions are far (*ārakā*). The first five disciples attained *arahat*-ship on perceiving that there was no sign of a soul in any one of the five groups of bodily and mental qualities constituting a sentient being (*Vinaya*, i. 14). Rāhula, the Buddha's son, claims to be an *arahat* because he has overcome the 'intoxications,' and will incur no re-birth (*Thera Gāthā*, 296; cf. 336). Every *arahat* has the *sambodhi*, the higher insight, divided into seven parts—self-possession, investigation, energy, calm, joy, concentration, and magnanimity.* There is extant in the Canon a collection of hymns, 264 of which are by men, and 73 by women, who had become *arahats* in the time of the Buddha. Fifteen of these claim also to have

* The question of *sambodhi* has been discussed at length in the present writer's *Dialogues of the Buddha*, Oxford, 1899, pp. 190–192.

gained the three *vijjas*, or 'sorts of knowledge': the knowledge of their own and other people's previous births, and of other people's thoughts. Laymen could become *arahats*. A list of twenty who had done so in the time of the Buddha is given in *Aṅguttara*, iii. 451. Every Buddha was an *arahat*. The word occurs in the standing description applied to each of the seven Buddhas known in the earliest documents (*Dīgha*, ii. 2). The *Jātaka* commentator says that the Buddha made *arahat*-ship the climax of his discourse (*Jātaka*, i. 114, 275, 393, 401). That is so far the case that either *arahat*-ship, under one or other of its numerous epithets, or the details of the mental and moral qualities and experiences associated with it, forms the climax of the great majority of the Dialogues. Thus the first Dialogue in the *Dīgha* deals with the first stage in the Path. The second is started with the question, by a layman, as to what is the use of the religious life. After a lengthy enumeration of various advantages, each nearer than the previous one to *arahat*-ship, the discussion of the question ends with *arahat*-ship. The third is on social rank, and ends with the conclusion that *arahat*-ship is the best. In the fourth the climax is that the *arahat* is the true Brāhman. The fifth discusses the question of sacrifice, with the result that *arahat*-ship is the best sacrifice. The sixth is on the aim of the members of the Buddhist Order, and ends with *arahat*-ship; and so on through the remaining seven Dialogues in that volume. Ten out of thirteen chapters, if we may so call them, lead up to this subject, the other three being concerned with it only incidentally. The proportion in the rest of the *Dīgha* is less, in the *Majjhima* it is probably about the same.

The last discourse of the Buddha to his disciples is summarized in *Dīgha*, ii. 120, as follows:—

'Brethren, ye to whom the truths I have perceived have been made known by me, when you have made yourselves masters of them, practise them, think them over, spread them abroad in order that pure religion may last long for the good and happiness of the great multitudes. . . . Which are these truths? They are these: the four modes of mindfulness, the fourfold struggle against evil, the four footsteps to majesty, the five moral powers, the five organs of spiritual sense, the seven kinds of insight, the noble eightfold path. These are they.'

In *Vinaya*, ii. 240, these seven groups are called the jewels of the *Dhamma-vinaya*, the doctrine and discipline, in whose ocean the *arahats* dwell. The total of the numbers in the seven groups amounts to thirty-seven. These are identified in the commentaries with the *Sambodha-pakkhiyā dhammā*, the qualities which are the 'sides,' that is, constituent parts, of the insight of *arahat*-ship. These are mentioned already in the canonical books (*Aṅguttara*, iii. 70, 71, iv. 351; *Saṁyutta*, v. 227, 239). But it would seem from the discussions on the use of this term by E. Hardy in his Introduction to the *Netti* (p. xxx ff.), and by Mrs. Rhys Davids in her Introduction to the *Vibhaṅga* (p. xiv ff.), that the commentators' interpretation of its meaning is later, and that it originally referred simply to the *sambodhi*, the seven divisions of which, already given above, form only the seventh division of the thirty-seven qualities. The term is so used in the *Vibhaṅga*, p. 249.

It would follow from this that in the later Pāli writers the conception of *arahat* was extended to include all the thirty-seven of these characteristics. So also the *Milinda* distinctly adds to the conception of *arahat*-ship the possession of the four *Paṭisambhidās*.*

As the meaning of the term was extended, so the reverence for the *arahat* increased. In the old texts we are informed of a custom by which, when a *bhikkhu* thought he had attained, he could 'announce his knowledge,' as the phrase ran. The 112th Dialogue in the *Majjhima* gives the six questions which should then be put to the new aspirant. If he answered these correctly, his claim should be admitted. By the time of the commentators this was obsolete. They speak of no *arahats* in their own day; and we hear of none mentioned, in any source, as having lived later than the 3rd cent. of our era. The associations with the word became so high that only the heroes of old were esteemed capable of having attained to it.

The Sanskrit form *arhat* has had a precisely contrary history. First used some centuries after the rise of Buddhism by those Buddhists who then began to write in Sanskrit, its use was confined to those who tended more and more to put the conception of *bodhisattva* in place of that of *arahat*, as the ideal to be aimed at. In the literature of this period *arahat*-ship has ceased to be the climax; it is not even the subject of the discourses put into the mouth of the Buddha. Neither in the *Lalita Vistara* nor in the *Mahāvastu* can the present writer trace the word at all, except when used as an epithet of the Buddha, or of the early disciples. In the *Divyāvadāna* (a collection of stories of different dates, put together probably some time after the Christian era), whenever the legend refers to personages who lived in the Buddha's time (pp. 404, 464) the term *arhat* is used very much in the old sense. So also in the story of Vītāśoka, the brother of Aśoka, we find at pp. 423 f. and 428 f. the term used in a manner that shows it was familiar to those who recorded this particular legend, in the sense of one who had reached emancipation in this life. It is used incidentally, in the midst of the narrative; and throughout the volume attention is directed to the edifying legend rather than to the discussion of this or any other point in Buddhist ethics. The word had survived; the interest in the doctrine had waned.

In the *Saddharma-puṇḍarīka* ('Lotus of the True Law'), *arhat* is used a score of times of a Buddha, and is, in fact, a standing epithet of each of the numerous Buddhas invented in that work. It is also used as an epithet of the early disciples, but with distinct depreciation. Thus at p. 43 of Kern's translation * *arhats* are called conceited if they do not accept the new doctrine. At p. 189 the stage of *arhat* is declared to be a lower stage. At p. 330 ff. the merit of one who hears a single word of the new doctrine is said to be greater than that of one who leads a vast number of men to become *arhats*. There is a similar argument beginning on p. 387. We find, then, in these works that *arhat*-ship is first passed over, or put on one side, and finally is openly attacked.

T. W. RHYS DAVIDS.

ARIANISM.

1. Christianity recognizes Unity of God and Divinity of Christ.
2. Arius charges Bishop Alexander with Sabellianism. System of Arius.
3. Constantine intervenes. The Council of Nicæa.
4. State of parties after the Council.
5. From the death of Constantine to the Council of the Dedication.
6. State of affairs till A.D. 346.
7. The ten years' truce, A.D. 346–356.
8. Expulsion of Athanasius from Alexandria. The Creeds of Sirmium.
9. Reaction against *Anomœan* Arianism.
10. The Council of Alexandria, A.D. 362.
11. Arianism under Valens, and down to the Council of Constantinople, A.D. 381.
12. Character of Arianism.
13. The Arian controversy inevitable.
14. Controversies arising out of Arianism.
15. Arianism among the Teutons. Ulfilas.
16. Arianism supreme among the conquerors of the Western forms. Conversion of Clovis.
17. National strength of Teutonic Arianism.
18. The barbarian kingdoms abandon Arianism.
19. Spain returns to orthodoxy.

* ed. Trenckner, London, 1880, p. 104 [tr. by Rhys Davids in *SBE*, vol. xxxv. p. 157].

* *SBE*, vol. xxi., Oxford, 1884. The text has not yet been edited.

20. The Lombards and Arianism.
21. Revival of the Trinitarian controversy at the Reformation.
22. Re-appearance of Arianism in the 17th century.
23. Arianism in England in the 18th century.
24. Concluding remarks.

The promulgation of the heresy of Arius, which followed the close of the contest between the Christian Church and the Roman Government by only a few years, may justly be regarded as the culmination of all the various controversies in the early Church concerning the relation of the 'Persons' of the Holy Trinity to one another.

1. The Christian consciousness recognized from the first the supreme necessity of maintaining the absolute Unity of God. According to one of the earliest apologists, Aristides, the worship of the Christians was more purely monotheistic even than that of the Jews (*Apol.* xiv., xv.). But, whilst acknowledging Unity to be the essential of Divinity, Christians of every description perceived the momentous consequences of the Incarnation. Whether Judaic, Pauline, or Gnostic, all who professed to follow Christ saw in Him the one means by which God the Father had been made known to man. 'Thus the Lord's divinity was from the first as fixed an axiom of Christianity as the unity of God' (Gwatkin, *Studies of Arianism*[2], 1900, p. 5). The earliest controversies about our Lord bore on the question of the reality of His sufferings and His humanity; and it was not till the old Docetic heresies had become comparatively insignificant that the nature of the Divinity of the Son and His relation to the Father occupied an important place in Christian speculation.

By the close of the 2nd cent. the conditions under which a theological question could be debated were practically the same as those which have prevailed down to the dawn of modern criticism. It was no longer a question of rival Scriptures, the majority of the books of the NT being already acknowledged as authoritative; the orthodox tradition of the Church had practically prevailed over all opposition; the question as to the recognition of the OT by the Church had been decided. There were already definite methods of exposition, and collections of Scripture proofs for use in controversy with Jews and pagans had been formed from a very early date. None of the facts of the Gospel story was disputed; Christian philosophy identified Jesus Christ with the Divine Logos; faith acknowledged His pre-existence, His miracles, His Resurrection and His Ascension as unquestionable facts. No doubts were raised as to the authorship or authority of those passages in the OT and NT which were accepted as the basis of the Christology of the age. The utterances of the Prophets, the words of David and Solomon in Psalm and Proverb, the doctrine of St. Paul and St. John, were all admitted to be the source and basis of Christian doctrine. It is of great importance to bear in mind the fact that the premises from which orthodox and heretic alike drew their conclusions in the 3rd and 4th centuries were different from what would now be accepted; and it is not always by the arguments used in this controversy that we must form our judgment in regard to the decision finally reached.

The problem was, of course, the reconciliation of the two apparently conflicting beliefs in the Unity of the Godhead and in the real distinction of Personality in the Trinity. The controversy naturally turned first on the meaning of the characteristic Christian doctrine of the Divinity of Jesus Christ. In attempting to maintain the Unity of the Godhead, the Christian teacher ran the risk of sacrificing either the Personality or the Divinity of our Lord. On the one hand, Praxeas, Sabellius, and their followers represented the appearance of our Lord as hardly more than a temporary means whereby God had been dramatically manifested to the world, making the Trinity an economy by which the Divine is revealed in different aspects. But the Christian conscience could not thus allow a personality of the Divine Master without real permanence. 'It is clearly impossible, on any Christian theory of the world and of the Divine economy, that God should exist even for a moment only in a single mode, or that the Incarnation should be only a temporary and transient manifestation' (Bethune-Baker, *Christian Doctrine*, 1903, p. 106). Equally impossible was it for the Church to assent to a practical reversion to the old Ebionite doctrine that Jesus was simply an ordinary human being deified by reason of His eminent virtue. Theodotus, Paul of Samosata, and others who held this view were not unnaturally ranked among the heretics. But the question was too difficult to be settled by the rejection of these alternatives, and it was further complicated by misunderstandings as to the significance of the terms employed to expound the mystery of the Trinity, as the correspondence between Dionysius of Rome and his namesake Dionysius of Alexandria abundantly testifies (Feltoe, *Letters and other remains of Dionysius of Alexandria*, 1904). These interesting letters reveal two opposite tendencies—that of the West, which so emphasized the eternal unity as to obscure the distinction of the Persons in the Trinity, and the teaching of the Easterns, who, under the influence of Origen, insisted on the theory that subordination explained the existence of the threefold Personality. Dread of the Sabellian Christology was especially potent in influencing the course of theological speculation throughout the East.

At the beginning of the 4th cent. the most famous Christian scholar was **Lucian**, who, after the deposition of Paul of Samosata, founded a theological academy at Antioch. He seems to have been looked upon at least with suspicion by three successive bishops—Domnus, Timæus, and Cyril; but his exemplary conduct, ascetic practices, and, above all, the fact that he was one of the last martyrs in the Diocletian persecution, caused him to be regarded with particular reverence by his disciples, who felt especially bound to one another by the memory of their common master. The school of Lucian numbered among its adherents the bishops Eusebius of Nicomedia, Menophantus of Ephesus, Theognis of Nicæa, Maris of Chalcedon, Leontius of Antioch, and Athanasius of Anazarbus, the sophist Asterius, and the presbyter Arius (Harnack, *Hist. of Dogma*, vol. iv. p. 3, Eng. tr.).

It is a matter of considerable doubt whether Arianism is to be traced to Antioch or to Alexandria, and also how far it is due to the teaching of Origen. Newman is of opinion that Arianism is the outcome of the grammatical literalism of Antioch as opposed to the more spiritual method of interpreting Scripture current in Alexandria (*Arians*, ch. i. sec. i.). Professor Gwatkin, on the other hand, points out (*Studies of Arianism*[2], p. 19) that though Antioch was undoubtedly Arian in the later days of the controversy, when Alexandria, owing to the influence of Athanasius, had become orthodox, it was not so at the beginning. The language of Arianism was borrowed from Origen, and especially from Dionysius, who speaks of the Second Person as ποίημα τοῦ θεοῦ, ξένον κατ' οὐσίαν, and says οὐκ ἦν πρὶν γένηται—phrases which were adopted into the terminology of Arianism. Arius, moreover, had a very strong party in Alexandria when he promulgated his heresy. Harnack (*op. cit.* vol. iv. p. 3) considers that Lucian continued the work of Paul of Samosata at Antioch, and gives credit to the statement of Alexander (Theodoret, i. 4), which Gwatkin rejects, that Lucian remained a long time outside the Church of Antioch. Lucian is called 'the Arius before Arius.' The high honour, however, in which his memory was held, as the Synod of Antioch in A.D. 341 testified by accepting one of its confessions of faith as 'the creed of Lucian the martyr' (Sozomen, iii. 5), makes it difficult to believe that he was ever considered as a teacher of heresy. The question of Origen's responsibility for Arianism is an extremely vexed one, and is admirably discussed by Bishop Robertson (*Prolegomena to Athanasius*, p. xxv f.). As Athanasius showed in his *de Sententia Dionysii*, the language of two theologians may be almost identical, whilst the spirit in which they employ it is quite different.

2. The years A.D. 318 and 319 found the Church of Alexandria in great confusion, distracted by the obscure Meletian schism and by a controversy between the bishop **Alexander** and the presbyter **Arius** (Ἄρειος) of the district of Baucalis. Alexander, in a charge to his clergy, impressed upon them the unity in the Trinity of the Godhead. According to the historian Socrates (i. 5), Alexander in this discourse somewhat exceeded the limits of discretion (*φιλοτιμότερον . . . ἐθεολόγει*) in insisting on what is, after all, a single aspect of the truth in the mystery of the Trinity. Arius forthwith accused his bishop of teaching Sabellianism, and proceeded to formulate his own scheme of doctrine.

Alexander's doctrine is summed up in the following words in the letter of Arius to Eusebius of Nicomedia: *Ἀεὶ θεός, ἀεὶ υἱός, ἅμα πατὴρ ἅμα υἱός, συνυπάρχει ὁ υἱὸς ἀγεννήτως τῷ θεῷ, ἀειγενής, ἀγενητογενής, οὔτ ἐπινοίᾳ οὔτ' ἀτόμῳ τινὶ προάγει ὁ θεὸς τοῦ υἱοῦ, ἀεὶ θεός, ἀεὶ υἱός, ἐξ αὐτοῦ τοῦ θεοῦ ὁ υἱός* (Arius' letter to Eusebius *ap*. Theodoret, *HE* i. 4). Arius, considering that this definition detracted from the unique majesty of the Father and introduced confusion, maintained the complete distinction between the Father and the Son, and the subordination of the latter. Harnack (*op. cit.* vol. iv. p. 15) enumerates eight points of the view advanced by Arius—

(1) The characteristic of the One and Only God is solitude and eternity. He can put nothing forth from His own essence. He was not always Father, but only after He begat (*i.e.* created) the Son.

(2) Wisdom and the Word (λόγος) dwell within this God, but they are powers, not persons.

(3) To create the universe, God brought into being an independent substance (*οὐσία* or *ὑπόστασις*) as the instrument by which all things were created. This Being is termed, in Scripture, Wisdom, Son, Image, Word, etc.

(4) As regards His substance, the Son is a separate being from the Father, different from Him in substance and nature. Like all rational creatures, the Son is endowed with free will, and consequently capable of change.

(5) The Son is not truly God, but is only the so-called Word and Wisdom. He has no absolute, but only a relative, knowledge of the Father.

(6) The Son is not, however, a creature like other creatures. He is the perfect creature (*κτίσμα τέλειον*), and has become God, so that we may term Him 'the only-begotten God,' etc.

(7) Christ took a real body, but it was a *σῶμα ἄψυχον*, the Logos taking the place of the soul. From the Gospel record we see that this Logos is not an absolutely perfect being, but is capable of suffering.

(8) Amongst other created beings the Holy Ghost is to be placed beside the Son as a second, independent substance. According to Arius, apparently, the Spirit is the creation of the Son.

Such, then, was Arianism—a theory of the mutual relations of the Persons in the Trinity based nominally on the words of Scripture, but arrived at really by the methods of the heathen philosophers. It led either to polytheism by allowing the existence of the Logos as a secondary God, or to Judaic Unitarianism by denying His proper Divinity.

The Arian system never really commended itself to the general conscience of Christians, and, as was usually the case in the early days of Christianity, the heresy found its support among the clergy, whilst the less instructed laity remained orthodox. Its tendencies were essentially pagan. As Harnack points out, Arianism was a new doctrine in the Church, and was really Hellenism tempered by the constant use of Holy Scripture (*op. cit.* iv. p. 41). From a very early time the conception of the God of the OT and the Heavenly Father of the NT had tended to give ground before the Hellenic idea of an abstract unknowable Deity. Clement of Alexandria had paved the way for Arianism by his doctrine of God: 'Stripping from concrete existence all physical attributes, taking away from it in the next place the three dimensions of space, we arrive at the conception of a point having position.' 'There is yet a further step,' says Bigg, 'for perfect simplicity has not yet been gained. Reject the idea of position, and we have reached the last attainable abstraction, the pure Monad.' This, as he observes, is essentially a heathen conception, and can be developed consistently only on heathen principles. Clement has gone astray from the first by his mode of approaching the subject. He has propounded as his question, not What is Spirit? or What is Good? but What is the simplest thing conceivable? This he assumes to be the cause of all that exists. Nothing that is part of the effect can belong to the cause. . . . The result is a chimera, a cause divided by an impassable gulf from all its effects (*Christian Platonists of Alexandria*, pp. 63–65). This is really the Arian conception of the Father, the unknown and unknowable Cause, of whom the Son is a creature as incapable of knowing or revealing Him as any other creature. Arius deliberately severs all possible connexion between the created and the uncreated, the human and the Divine. Christ is no mediator, no saviour. As Dr. Harnack forcibly remarks (*op. cit.* iv. p. 42), Arius and his friends are nowhere in their theology concerned with communion with God. Rightly, therefore, does Schultz (*Gottheit Christi*, p. 65) say that 'the Arian Christology is inwardly the most unstable, and dogmatically the most worthless, of all the Christologies to be met with in the history of dogma.' But if unsatisfactory in its conclusions, and leading to the ultimate subversion of Christianity, Arianism was most difficult to refute, owing to the confusion of thought prevalent at the time of its appearance.

In the controversy which ensued, Alexander seems to have acted with some moderation, and even to have allowed his hesitation to proceed to such extremes as to be made an excuse for a schism. Arius had no scruples in forming a party of his own. He enlisted the support of two bishops, Secundus of Ptolemais in the Pentapolis, and Theonas of Marmarica, and also that of several presbyters and virgins. To secure popular favour, he put his opinions into doggerel verse, adopting the metre of the licentious poet Sotades, in order that the sailors and dock-labourers of Alexandria might sing at their work of 'How the Father was not always Father,' etc. His *Thalia*, as this strange collection of songs was called, popularized his system among the formidable proletariat of the capital of Egypt. But Arius' strongest support was his 'fellow-Lucianist,' Eusebius of Nicomedia, the most influential prelate in the East. In A.D. 321, Alexander held a Council at Alexandria; Arius was excommunicated and left the city (see the *Depositio Arii*, included in the Benedictine Edition of *Athanasius*, and claimed as his by Newman. It is translated in the *Nicene and post Nicene Fathers*, 'Athanasius').

3. Two years later, Constantine defeated Licinius (A.D. 323) and became sole master of the Roman world. Affairs in Alexandria had become very serious, and indeed the whole Eastern Church was in the utmost confusion. The question as to the keeping of Easter distracted the Christians as a matter of practice as seriously as Arianism was doing as one of doctrine. Accordingly the Emperor sent his episcopal adviser Hosius, bishop of Cordova in Spain, to Alexandria with a very remarkable letter to Alexander and Arius, begging them to lay aside their logomachies and co-operate with him in restoring peace to the distracted world. But an Imperial letter, 'though marvellous and full of wisdom,' as Socrates describes it, could not allay so embittered a strife, and Constantine decided to submit all matters in dispute to a **Council** of the whole Church, to assemble in the year A.D. 325 at **Nicæa**, on Lake Ascanius, in the north of Asia Minor. The first act of the Council as regards Arius was with practical unanimity to pronounce his doctrine heretical. That the Son had been created out of things that were not (*ἐξ οὐκ ὄντων*), that He was of another essence than the Father, that, even before time was, the Father was without the Logos, were on all sides regarded as blasphemous assertions. It was not till the question arose as to how the error should be refuted that there was any serious difference of opinion. The Fathers had met to affirm the ancient faith of the Church against novelty; but when they wished to express what they meant in words, they found that none to which they had been hitherto accustomed were capable of escaping the evasions of such masters as the Arians in the art of making Scripture phrases assume a meaning contrary to the teaching of Scripture. In consequence of this, the Council, probably at the suggestion of Hosius, was induced to adopt the expression ἐκ τῆς οὐσίας τοῦ Πατρός and the word ὁμοούσιος, neither of which is to be found in the Bible.

ὁμοούσιος (*ejusdem substantiæ*) was a word which presented no difficulty to the Latins who followed the teaching of Tertullian, *adv. Praxeam*, and Novatian, *de Trinitate*. Dionysius of Rome in his correspondence with his namesake of Alexandria had protested against any undue separation (μεμερισμέναι ὑποστάσεις) of the Father and the Son, thus virtually insisting on the ὁμοούσιον. Tertullian had also, in his *de Anima* (c. 32), carefully distinguished *substantia* (οὐσία) from *natura*. The Latins and the anti-Origenists at the Council desired to press the unity rather than the equality of the Son with the Father; and to them the word was eminently acceptable. But the majority of the Greek-speaking bishops had a strong objection to both expressions, ἐκ τῆς οὐσίας and ὁμοούσιος, on the following grounds: (1) They had no Scripture warranty. (2) The Council against Paul of Samosata (A.D. 269) had condemned the use of ὁμοούσιος. (3) The idea of an οὐσία common to the Trinity might countenance Sabellianism. (4) The words might either imply an οὐσία prior to the Father and the Son, or countenance materialism (οὐσία being conceived as an equivalent to εἶδος or ὕλη) (Bethune-Baker, *Chrstian Doctrine*, p. 171 n.).

On this rock the Council nearly split; and Eusebius of Cæsarea, the trusted adviser of the Emperor, and by far the most learned man of his age, was especially mistrustful. Ultimately, however, Eusebius and the Origenist party accepted a creed containing the expressions in dispute, and Arianism was explicitly condemned.

Eusebius first offered the Council the baptismal creed of his own Church, perhaps a little amplified. In this the Lord Jesus Christ was declared to be the λόγος and God from God (θεὸς ἐκ θεοῦ), and also firstborn of all creation (πρωτότοκος πάσης κτίσεως, Col 1[15]) and only-begotten Son (υἱὸς μονογενής). Constantine himself, prompted no doubt by Hosius, suggested the ὁμοούσιον. The creed differs from our 'Nicene Creed' in its definition of the doctrine of the Son in several important points (see Hort, *Two Dissertations*, p. 61; Bethune-Baker, *Chr. Doct.* p. 168). After a bare profession of belief in the Holy Spirit, the creed concludes with anathemas of all the distinctive teachings of Arianism, (1) that there was a time when the Son was not, (2) that He was not before He was begotten, (3) that He came into being out of nothing, (4) that He is of a different essence (ὑπόστασις) or being (οὐσία) from the Father, or (5) that He is created or capable of change or alteration. It is generally agreed that at Nicæa οὐσία and ὑπόστασις, which afterwards were carefully distinguished, were practically synonymous.

4. Into the intrigues which culminated with the banishment of **Athanasius**, who became bishop of Alexandria on 8th June, 328, it is needless to enter, it being sufficient for us to inquire into the causes which prevented the Creed of Nicæa from being the immediate conclusion of the controversy. Few of the bishops, whilst abhorring the heresy of Arius, understood the exact merits of the question. They feared the error of Sabellius, and to this the *Homoousion* seemed to have committed them. Moreover, with the natural conservatism of men pledged to hold fast to the faith 'once delivered to the saints,' they distrusted words unsupported either by Scripture or by tradition. The Emperor himself, who to the end of his life believed himself faithful to the Creed of Nicæa, when he saw that its promulgation had failed to give peace to the Church, was less enthusiastic in its favour, and showed so much readiness to welcome back its opponents that he received Eusebius of Nicomedia not long after the Council; and, but for the sudden death of the heresiarch, Arius would, at his command, have been reconciled to the Church.

How new the phrases introduced into the Creed were as formulæ of belief is shown by Athanasius' defence of them in his *de Decretis* (sec. 25 ff.). He refers to similar language of Theognostus, Dionysius of Rome, and Dionysius of Alexandria. 'This anxious appeal to theological writers,' says Hort (*Two Dissertations*, p. 55), 'sets in strong relief the absence of authority derived from public creeds.' Eusebius's objections and his reasons for ultimately accepting the word ὁμοούσιος are set forth in his letter to his Church at Cæsarea. In this letter he discusses three expressions in the Creed, ἐκ τῆς οὐσίας τοῦ πατρός, γεννηθέντα οὐ ποιηθέντα, and ὁμοούσιος. He accepted the first on being assured that it meant that the Son was of the Father, but was not a part of Him. 'Begotten, not made,' passed, because 'made' was an appellative common to the other creatures which came to be through the Son, though the Son bore no likeness to them. As for ὁμοούσιος, Eusebius received it as implying 'that the Son bears no resemblance to the originated creatures, but that to His Father alone who begat Him He is in every way assimilated.' It is easy enough to see that Eusebius did not assent to the definitions of the Creed *ex animo*; and he is still more ready to explain away the anathemas. The letter is preserved in Athanasius, *de Decretis*, as an appendix, secs. 9, 10, being omitted by Socrates, *HE* i. 8.

5. On the death of Constantine (A.D. 337), his Eastern dominions passed to his son Constantius, who encouraged his bishops to draw up a creed to supersede that of Nicæa, to which all the Asiatic and Syrian Churches seemed opposed. The result of their labours is apparent in the five creeds of Antioch, which exhibit the tendencies of the different factions, whose only point of union seems to have been antagonism to Athanasius and the Nicene formula. These confessions of faith, together with the creeds drawn up at **Sirmium** and elsewhere, served only to show that there was no possible compromise between avowed Arianism and the *Homoousian* doctrine. The orthodox opponents of the language of the Creed of Nicæa, whom Professor Gwatkin terms 'the Conservatives'—men like Eusebius of Cæsarea, whom dread of Sabellianism and hatred of innovation drove into opposition to Athanasius—were being made use of by those who were at heart Arians to force an Arianizing creed upon the unwilling Church. The weak and unstable Constantius was always in the hands of those whom he believed capable of pacifying the Church by a new creed. He was in reality aiming at a comprehensive State-religion acceptable to all parties, and thought that a sort of modified Arianism would supply this want in the provinces over which he at this time bore rule. In A.D. 339, Athanasius was driven out of Alexandria, and in A.D. 341 the formal reaction against the Nicene doctrine began with the famous council assembled for the dedication of the Golden Church at **Antioch**.

Athanasius and Marcellus of Ancyra went to Rome to lay their cause before Julius, to whom the bishops assembled at Antioch wrote in A.D. 339. The Pope's answer is described by Professor Gwatkin (*Arianism*², p. 117) as 'one of the ablest documents of the entire controversy' (Athanasius, *Apol. contra Ar.* secs. 21–35; Socr. *HE* ii. 17; Soz. iii. 10).

In all probability, Dianius, bishop of Cæsarea in Cappadocia, presided at this synod, and there were also present Eusebius of Nicomedia, now bishop of Constantinople, who gave the name by which the opponents of Athanasius were at this time known, and Acacius, the successor of Eusebius Pamphilus in the see of Cæsarea.

The opponents of Athanasius were called οἱ περὶ Εὐσέβιον, or the *Eusebians*, as the words have been somewhat inexactly rendered. The term is used in two senses: (1) literally denoting the personal entourage of Eusebius, *i.e.* the court party, crypto-Arians all of them; (2) more generally the majority of the Asiatic bishops who were discontented with the Nicene Council. These latter ultimately became the Semi-Arian party.

Four creeds were put forward by this Council—all attempts to dispense with the objectionable word ὁμοούσιον. The most celebrated was the so-called second Creed of Antioch, to which the name of Lucian the martyr was attached. In this the Persons of the Trinity were said to be One by reason of the harmony existing between them—τῇ μὲν ὑποστάσει τρία, τῇ δὲ συμφωνίᾳ ἕν.

The honour in which the Council of Antioch was held in after days—St. Hilary of Poitiers speaks of it with great respect (*de Syn.* c. 32), and the canons were quoted by the popes themselves as authoritative (see Hefele, *Councils*, sec. 56)—is sufficient proof that the Church did not regard the bishops there as heretics. Yet they undoubtedly, by their endeavours to find some more acceptable substitute for the creed of Nicæa, played into the hands of the Arian party. The four creeds of Antioch were: (1) The first creed, which begins with a repudiation of

Arius: 'We have never become followers of Arius, for how shall we who are bishops follow a presbyter?' This creed was suspiciously like the confession which Arius himself had made before his restoration was ordered by Constantine. (2) The second creed, which became the watchword of the anti-Athanasian party. It declared the Son to be the unchangeable image (*ἀπαράλλακτον εἰκόνα*) of the Godhead, essence (*οὐσία*), counsel, power, and glory of the Father. It laid special stress on the reality of the Fatherhood and Sonship and on the office of the Holy Spirit—*τῶν ὀνομάτων οὐδὲ ἁπλῶς οὐδὲ ἀργῶς κειμένων ἀλλὰ σημαινόντων ἀκριβῶς τὴν οἰκείαν ἑκάστου τῶν ὀνομαζομένων ὑπόστασιν καὶ τάξιν καὶ δόξαν*. The anathemas were worded in such a way that an Arian could easily subscribe them. (3) A profession of faith by Theophronius of Tyana. At the conclusion the doctrines of Marcellus of Ancyra, as representing the Sabellianizing tendency of the Nicenes, as well as those of Sabellius and Paul of Samosata, are anathematized. (4) A decidedly Arian creed drawn up a few months later than the actual Council by certain bishops who met *δῆθεν περὶ πίστεως*, as Athanasius bitterly remarks (*de Synodis*, sec. 25). These creeds are to be found in Athanasius' *de Syn.* secs. 22–25. See Hahn, *Bibliothek der Symbole*, pp. 153–156.

By A.D. 341 the parties at strife can be described almost in geographical terms. The Western Church, under the guidance of Rome, had ranged itself under the banner of Nicæa, whilst the Orientals rallied to the cry of 'No un-Scriptural terms in the Creed.' The leaders of the Arians, too prudent to show their hand openly, were content to allow the 'conservative' opponents of Athanasius to prepare the ground for them. As long as Athanasius was in exile, the Nicene theology had no foothold in the East. Circumstances, however, were preparing for a temporary triumph of the Athanasian party. After his death and the massacre of the collateral members of his family, Constantine's dominions were divided between his three sons—Constantine II. at Trèves, Constans in Italy, and Constantius in the East. The two former supported Athanasius.

6. When Constantine II. was killed in A.D. 340, his dominions seem to have passed under the sway of Constans, who was thus ruler over the greater part of the Roman world. As he supported Athanasius, Julius, and the party of the Nicene council, the *ὁμοούσιον* was upheld by the more powerful of the two remaining Emperors. The result of this state of affairs was that Constans, the patron of Athanasius, was able to insist in A.D. 343 on a joint meeting of the Eastern and Western bishops to re-try the case. The place selected was **Sardica**, the modern Sophia in Bulgaria, near the frontier of the dominions of Constans and Constantius; but when the bishops arrived, it was evident that no mutual understanding was possible. The Westerns insisted upon Athanasius and Marcellus of Ancyra taking their seats in the Council, and confirmed the Creed of Nicæa. The Orientals withdrew to Philippopolis, where they subscribed the Arianizing fourth creed of Antioch, and specially condemned Marcellus of Ancyra. Envoys were sent from Constans to his brother at Antioch, and a truly diabolical plot was hatched by Stephen the bishop to discredit them. The Eastern bishops had enough sense of rectitude to depose Stephen at a Council held at Antioch in A.D. 344, where a creed was drawn up called from its prolixity the Macrostich (*μακρόστιχος ἔκθεσις*), or fifth creed of Antioch. In it Marcellus and his disciple Photinus were expressly condemned. Constantius now seemed disgusted with the failure of the anti-Nicene party, and in the autumn of 346 Athanasius was allowed to return to Alexandria.

The Council of Sardica revealed the fundamental difference between the Western and Eastern Churches at this time. It is noticeable that up to this time the Eusebians had not directly attacked the Creed of Nicæa or even the doctrine of Athanasius (Harnack, *op. cit.* iv. 64), the accusations against the bishop being purely personal. The object of the Eusebians was to get the *Homoousion* set aside and to substitute a less controversial creed for that of Nicæa, and also to attack Athanasius through his friend Marcellus of Ancyra (Harnack, p. 67; see also Zahn's *Marcellus von Ancyra* and Eusebius of Cæsarea's two books against him). Hosius took the lead at Sardica, and, according to Athanasius (*ad Antiochenos*, 5), a fruitless attempt was made to supplement the Creed of Nicæa. A creed, however, was drawn up by Hosius and Protogenes of Sardica, which, though it did not emanate from the Council (Hefele, § 63), expressed the theological teaching of the West. It is found in Theodoret, ii. 8, and a Latin translation has been discovered. It declares there is but one substance in the Trinity (*μίαν ὑπόστασιν* [Lat. *substantiam*], *ἣν αὐτοὶ οἱ αἱρετικοὶ οὐσίαν προσαγορεύουσιν*), and its doctrine of the Son is such that we can well understand how the Westerns refused to condemn Marcellus (Harnack, *op. cit.* iv. 60). Athanasius, when he was asked his views on the orthodoxy of Marcellus by St. Epiphanius, would only smile, showing that he had an equally poor opinion of his friend as a theologian and of his inquirer as a man of sense (Epiph. 72. 11). The tendencies of the West inclined to Sabellianism, and those of the East to Arianism, and before orthodoxy could be satisfied each had to be checked. The infamous plot of Stephen of Antioch against the two Western delegates Vincentius of Capua and Euphrates of Cologne is related by Athanasius (*Hist. Arian.* c. 20).

7. During the next ten years (A.D. 346–356) the two parties were outwardly at peace, but yet busily arming for the conflict. At Alexandria, Athanasius, who had been welcomed back with surprising enthusiasm, maintained his influence undiminished, and set a seal upon the loyalty of his church to the Creed of Nicæa. The monastic movement was in all the vigour of its first enthusiasm, and the ascetics, recognizing the earnestness of the bishop, became his firmest supporters. At Antioch, Leontius, whose early indiscretion was similar to that of Origen (*Hist. Arian.* 28), though an Arian at heart, had managed to maintain the peace by his cautious policy. This wise old prelate, however, knew well that the tranquillity his discretion had secured was only temporary, and in allusion to his death he would pathetically touch his grey hairs and say: 'When this snow melts, there will be much mud.' At Rome, Photinus of Sirmium, whose indiscretion outran even that of Marcellus, had been sacrificed for his Sabellian teaching; but the death of the wise and politic pope Julius in A.D. 352 was a serious loss to the cause of orthodoxy. His successor Liberius lacked both his firmness and his wisdom. Political events were also precipitating the crisis. Athanasius' faithful friend, the Emperor Constans, was killed by the usurper Magnentius. From the end of A.D. 350, when he was at or near Sardica on Dec. 25, to the close of A.D. 359, Constantius spent his time in his Western dominions, being most frequently to be found at Sirmium or Milan (Gwatkin, *Studies of Arianism*², App. ii. 'Movements of the Eastern Emperors'). Sirmium, not Antioch, was destined henceforward to be the scene of creed-making.

8. Many of the original disputants in the controversy had already passed away, and a new generation had arisen. Parties were becoming more and more defined. As their system was developed, stern logic forced the Arians to become more Arian than their founder. Some of the old conservatives were drifting towards Arianism, whilst others shrank back in dismay at its encroachments. The general tendency favoured the obliteration of the old party landmarks and the rise of new factions. The place of Eusebius of Nicomedia as Imperial adviser had been taken by Valens, bishop of Mursa in Pannonia, the province bordering on Illyricum, to which Arius had been exiled after the Council of Nicæa. Valens, with his friend Ursacius, bishop of Singidunum, was a most uncompromising Arian, and his policy was not, like the old Eusebians, to fight Athanasius by means of conservative prejudice, but to force an Arian creed on the Church in place of that of Nicæa (Robertson, *Athanasius*, p. liv). Valens had won great influence over Constantius, who believed that the bishop had received from an angel the news of the victory of Mursa (A.D. 351), and from this time an organized campaign was conducted against Athanasius, which culminated in the *coup d'état* at Alexandria, when the bishop was expelled by military violence (A.D. 356). Valens' ablest assistants in the East were Acacius, the successor of Eusebius Pamphilus in the see of Cæsarea, and Eudoxius, bishop of Antioch and Constantinople successively. In A.D. 357 there appeared from **Sirmium** the first really Arian creed, called by Hilary of Poitiers 'the blasphemy of Sirmium.' Other formulæ of belief were promulgated from the same place, notably the 'dated creed' in which the consuls of the year are mentioned, a fact of which Athanasius is not slow to take advantage in his *de Synodis*. The Arians, supported by the Emperor, did not hesitate to push their claims; and finally, at the great assemblies of Westerns at **Ariminum** and Orientals at **Seleucia**, an Arian creed was accepted as the official doctrine of the Empire. Thus in A.D. 359 it seemed as though the Nicene profession of faith was repealed and Arianism was triumphant.

The creeds of Sirmium are as follows. The 1st was drawn up against Photinus in A.D. 347. The 2nd (A.D. 351)—but commonly known as the 1st—is identical with the fourth creed of Antioch (δῆθεν περὶ πίστεως). The 3rd (A.D. 357), called the 'blasphemy,' (*a*) distinctly denies the true Divinity of the Son; (*b*) forbids the use of the terms οὐσία, ὁμοούσιον, ὁμοιούσιον as un-Scriptural, maintaining that it is impossible to declare the Nativity of the Son, because it is written *generationem eius quis enarrabit*; (*c*) in opposition to the teaching of the creed proposed but not accepted at Sardica (see above), makes the Divine nature of the Son as contrasted with that of the Father passible (see Bethune-Baker, *Introd.* p. 181 n.). This extreme teaching startled the bishops of Asia Minor, and under the presidency of Basil of Ancyra a synod was held at that place in A.D. 358. At this synod the extreme Arians, Eudoxius, Aëtius, and others, were excommunicated with anathemas condemning all who will not acknowledge the complete likeness (ὁμοιότης) of the Son to the Father, as well as the terms ὁμοούσιον and ταὐτοούσιον (Anathema xix. [Hahn, p. 201]). The result of the stand made by Basil and his friends was an attempt to compromise, *i.e.* to allow that the Son was *like* the Father. The 4th, or 'dated creed' (A.D. 359), composed by Mark, bishop of Arethusa, declared the Son to be ὅμοιον τῷ γεννήσαντι αὐτὸν πατρί with the addition 'according to the Scriptures,' which allowed the Arians to put their own sense on the words. It was this *Homœan* Arianism that was accepted under Imperial pressure at Ariminum Seleucia.

9. Already, however, a reaction had begun. In the first place, the Arianizers were divided among themselves. Logical and consistent Arians, like Aëtius and his disciple Eunomius of Cyzicus, were prepared to push the teaching of Arius to its ultimate conclusion. If the Son was not God in the same sense as the Father, He could not be like Him, for there can be nothing like God. Their argument, different as was the inference drawn from it, was the same as that used by Athanasius himself. 'Like is not predicated of essence, but of habits and qualities; for in the case of essences we speak not of likeness, but of identity' (*de Synodis*, 53). From their denial of the likeness of the Son to the Father this class of Arians were called *Anomœans*. But the majority of Arians were men of compromise and evasion, having no other idea than to insinuate their opinions under the guise of apparently innocuous phraseology. These, led by the dexterous Acacius of Cæsarea, allowed that the Son might be acknowledged to be *like* the Father, and were consequently called *Homœans*. Lastly, there was the party headed by Basil of Ancyra, the successors of those conservatives who had opposed Athanasius. These men, who constituted the strength of the episcopate of Asia Minor, were as hostile to Arianism as Athanasius himself, and were ready to accept the term οὐσία in their definition of the Godhead. Fearing that Sabellianism underlay the use of ὁμοούσιον, they rejected the Nicene test word, but were ready to admit that our Lord was like in substance (ὁμοιούσιος) to the Father. This formidable combination was known as the party of the Semi-Arians (*q.v.*). At heart most of them were orthodox, and this the two great champions of the Nicene faith, Athanasius and Hilary, bishop of Poitiers (who had been exiled by Constantius to Asia Minor), had the wisdom to perceive. After their triumph at Seleucia and Ariminum, the Arians and Homœans had the folly to attempt to crush these Semi-Arians at the Synod of Constantinople (A.D. 360), and thereby drove them in self-defence into the arms of the Nicenes. It needed only the rise of the great Cappadocian Fathers, Basil of Neo-Cæsarea, Gregory of Nyssa, and Gregory of Nazianzus, to complete the triumph of the Nicene Christology.

The Semi-Arians and the Cappadocian Fathers are subjects of separate treatment in this work; and it is unnecessary to do more here than allude to the important dispute as to the final settlement of the Arian controversy. The question at issue is whether the *Homoousion* was ultimately accepted in the sense of *Homoiousion*. This Dr. Harnack maintains to have been the case. His contention is very ably disputed by Mr. Bethune-Baker in *The Cambridge Texts and Studies* ('The meaning of Homoousios'). Attention should be paid to Professor Gwatkin's most instructive survey of the importance of Asia Minor to the Eastern Empire, which 'as long as that was unsubdued, remained upon the whole the strongest power on earth' (*Studies of Arianism*[2], p. 94). With true historic insight Gwatkin points out that in the Arian controversy Asia really played the part of the deciding factor. Disliking the *Homoousion* because it was an innovation, the steady conservatism of Asia accepted it when it was proved to be the only means of averting worse evils. 'Even the later Cappadocian orthodoxy,' he adds, 'rested on a conservative rather than a Nicene basis.' One of the chief representatives of Semi-Arianism is Cyril of Jerusalem (see Hort, *Two Dissertations*, p. 84).

10. The Arian party in A.D. 360 'was in a position too plainly artificial to be permanent' (Bright, *DCB* i. 197[a]), and the death of Constantius on 3rd Nov., 361, revealed its inherent weakness. Rome and the West at once returned to adherence to the Nicene faith, as though the Council of Ariminum had never assembled. Just before the Emperor's death, Meletius was, at the instigation of Acacius, elected bishop of Antioch, and his dramatic declaration of his faith at his installation showed the strength of popular feeling against Homœan Arianism. Constantius demanded that the new bishop should preach on the text κύριος ἔκτισέ με, 'The Lord created me,' *i.e.* wisdom; for so Pr 8[22] is translated by the LXX, and on this the Arians based their doctrine that the Son was a κτίσμα. To the delight of the people, always at this time more orthodox than the bishops, Meletius declared that the word ἔκτισε was a mistranslation of the Hebrew קנה, 'possessed,' and gave a decidedly Nicene interpretation to the text (the sermon is preserved by Epiph. *Hær.* 73. 29–33). 'This bold confession,' says Professor Gwatkin, 'proved to be the first effective blow at the Homœan supremacy' (*op. cit.* p. 187 f.). But perhaps the most crucial point was the return of Athanasius to Alexandria under Julian, when he held a small but very important Council at **Alexandria,** the great work of which was to clear up the misunderstanding due to the employment of such words as οὐσία and ὑπόστασις. It was agreed that there might be a fundamental agreement between those who employed these terms in different senses, but that the language of the Nicene Council was the safest which could be made use of. This paved the way for a reconciliation between the conservatives, with their dread of Sabellianism, and the Athanasian and Western Christians, who clung to the importance of the Unity of the Divine essence. As Bethune-Baker says, 'By the 4th cent. it was becoming clear that the only solution of the problem was to be found in a distinction inside the divine unity . . . it was necessary to revise the idea of divine personality and to acknowledge not three individuals but three eternal aspects of the Divine' (*Chr. Doct.* p. 157 n.). This was done when the distinction in meaning between οὐσία and ὑπόστασις was agreed upon, and the ambiguity of the Latin and Greek terminology removed.

In the early days of the controversy the terms οὐσία and ὑπόστασις were used interchangeably. The confusion caused great misunderstanding, because, whilst one part of Christendom spoke of τρεῖς ὑποστάσεις in the Trinity, the other acknowledged only one. By distinguishing between οὐσία and ὑπόστασις, and explaining the mystery of the Trinity as μία οὐσία τρεῖς ὑποστάσεις, the ambiguity was removed. This was the work of the Cappadocian Fathers, but it really began with the Council of Alexandria. In Latin legal language *substantia* means property, and *persona* a being with legal rights, a 'party' in an action at law. Thus a *persona* might own several *substantiæ*, and a *substantia* might belong to more than one *persona*. Tertullian uses *substantia* in the sense of essence, or 'substance,' of which Father, Son, and Holy Ghost partake; but he seems to hesitate to use *persona* if he can avoid it. He takes the word from the Old Latin Bible *quotidie oblectabar in persona eius* (Pr 8[30]), and *Spiritus personæ eius Christus dominus* (see Bethune-Baker, *op. cit.* pp. 139, 235, 'Meaning of Homoousios,' p. 21; Bigg, *op. cit.* pp. 163, 164; Harnack, *op. cit.* iv. 83; Gwatkin, p. 209 ff.). The Council of Alexandria forecasts the future development of doctrine by implicitly condemning Apollinarism (*q.v.*) and the denial of the Divinity of the Holy Ghost which subsequently became characteristic of Semi-Arianism.

11. But though Arianism may justly be described as collapsing with the death of Constantius, it remained, in its *Homœan* form, the official religion of the eastern half of the Roman Empire down to A.D. 378. On the death of Jovian (A.D. 364), Valentinian was chosen as emperor by the army on Feb. 26, and associated his brother Valens with him on the 29th of March, taking upon himself the government of the Western provinces, and assigning the Eastern to Valens. The stern but just Valentinian pursued a rigidly impartial policy in matters of religion, and though Milan, the governmental capital of Italy, remained under an Arian bishop, orthodoxy generally prevailed in Italy, Gaul, Spain, and Africa. **Valens**, on the other hand, supported the Homœans, thereby forcing the Semi-Arian party to open negotiations with Liberius, bishop of Rome, and his successor Damasus. The Homœan supremacy lasted down to the defeat and death of Valens at Adrianople (Aug. 9th, 378). Valentinian had died three years earlier, and his son Gratian had the magnanimity to appoint Theodosius, son of a distinguished official who had been put to death under Valentinian and Valens, as his colleague in the Eastern provinces. Theodosius, an orthodox Spaniard, cleared the Roman territory of victorious Goths, and, being afflicted with sickness in the year following his accession (A.D. 380), accepted baptism at the hands of Ascolius, bishop of Thessalonica. Theodosius took the faith of Rome and Alexandria as the norm of Christian belief in a law commanding all to follow the faith 'committed by the Apostle Peter to the Romans, and now professed by Damasus of Rome and Peter of Alexandria' (Cod. Theod. xvi. 1, 2). He allowed Gregory of Nazianzus to establish himself in Constantinople and to preach the doctrine upheld so strenuously by his friend Basil, bishop of Neo-Cæsarea (d. 379), in the evil days of Valens. The room in which Gregory delivered his discourses against the Arians became the Church of the Anastasia, the Resurrection of the Faith. In 381 the comparatively insignificant assembly, afterwards known as the **Second General Council**, met at **Constantinople** to confirm the faith of Nicæa. Further overtures were made to the Arians in the ensuing years; but in A.D. 383, Arianism was finally proscribed, and ceased to be legal for Roman citizens to profess.

Of the interval between the Councils of Alexandria (A.D. 362) and Constantinople (A.D. 381), though extremely important in the history of dogma, it is not necessary to treat at length in an account of Arianism, whose very triumph in the last days of Constantius made its ultimate downfall only a matter of time. In the present article it is only requisite to mention a few landmarks, referring the reader to the articles CAPPADOCIAN THEOLOGY and SEMI-ARIANISM. The Semi-Arians were at first favoured by Valens and allowed to assemble at Lampsacus, where they declared the Son to be ὅμοιος κατ' οὐσίαν to the Father, and cast out the Homœan Eudoxius and Acacius. Eudoxius, however, gained the Emperor's ear, and Valens expelled the Semi-Arians from their sees for refusing to communicate with the Homœans. One of their most distinguished leaders, Eleusius of Cyzicus, complied with the Imperial demands and acknowledged Eudoxius, but he repented bitterly of his action. Then came the negotiations with Rome, culminating in the Synod of Tyana (A.D. 367). The Semi-Arians were not really disposed to accept the Nicene faith in its entirety; and under the name of Macedonians many refused to acknowledge the proper Divinity of the Holy Spirit (Hefele, *Hist. of Councils*, § 88). The work of Basil and his friends, hampered as it was by the unfortunate schism at Antioch, was directed to a real reconciliation of those who were at heart orthodox to the Homoousian doctrine. For the question as to which creed was accepted by the Council of Constantinople in A.D. 381 see Gwatkin, *The Arian Controversy*; Burn, *Introduction to the Creeds*; and, above all, Hort, *Two Dissertations*.

12. Arianism may be defined as an attempt to determine the relations of the Persons of the Trinity on a basis of distinction and subordination. Despite all the efforts of Arius to popularize his opinions, they never found favour with the people. The movement was clerical rather than lay; the difficulties it sought to overcome were those of Origenist theologians perplexed by philosophical doubts and seeking an explanation where none was possible. Nor did Arianism pure and simple ever fail to arouse a strong feeling of indignation: the creed of Arius at Nicæa, the Sirmian 'blasphemy,' the opinions of Aëtius and Eunomius, all caused a storm. It was only by insinuating itself in the plausible guise of Scriptural phraseology that Arianism ever obtained a hearing. Nor could it be otherwise. An Arian Christ, a created Logos unable to reveal an unknown God, could never be the Christ acknowledged by Christians as the Incarnate Word, the sole Mediator between God and man, the supreme Sacrifice for the sin of the world. All who acknowledged this adhered at heart to the Nicene doctrine, however they might object to the language in which it was expressed. The great merit of Athanasius was his ability to recognize this truth; and he and Hilary were ready to make any concessions to those who shared the spirit, though they might not adopt the phraseology, of Nicæa. The test word *Homoousios* hardly appears in the works of Athanasius.

Arianism does not seem to have sprung from any strong ethical impulse. Its philosophy was pagan, and the object of its leaders was political rather than religious. 'Arius tried to interpret the Christian revelation in such a way as to render it acceptable to men whose whole conception of God and of life was heathen' (Bethune-Baker, *op. cit.* p. 156). His heresy was, in short, a symptom of the disease of the Church in the 4th cent. induced by the desire of ingratiating itself with the civil power. What the Roman government required when it invited the Christian Church to enter into alliance with it was that the Faith should cause as little disturbance as possible to the existing order of society. Arianism promised to provide this, in the form of a creed offering an easy and almost imperceptible transition from paganism to Christianity. By the edict of Milan, Christianity, the religion of the minority, had been virtually accepted by the Roman government, which thereby had committed itself to the policy of making it the religion of the majority. Arianism, by surrendering the chief characteristic of Christianity, the proper Divinity of Christ, made the new faith less hard to accept; and for this reason the Emperors, though from time to time encouraging the Nicene theology, were naturally disposed, especially in the Eastern provinces, towards Arianism. But, as the long controversy showed, the Arian doctrine led not merely to an accommodation to pagan theology, but also to an approach to pagan morality. For though some, especially of the extreme Arians, were faithful to their opinions, the majority of the party were dexterous politicians ready to serve the interests of the corrupt court of Constantius. Bishop Robertson sums up the character of many of the Arian intriguers when he says of Acacius of Cæsarea: 'The real opinions of a man with such a record are naturally not easy to determine, but we may be sure that he was in thorough sympathy with the policy of Constantius, namely, the union of all parties in the Church on the basis of subserviency to the State' (*Athanasius*, p. liv). The men most opposed to the rapid secularization of the Church which characterized the 4th cent. were almost uniformly opposed to Arian teaching.

13. None the less, the Arian controversy was not wholly unreasonable; indeed, it was the inevitable outcome of the tendencies of the age. A Sabellian Christology would have been as fatal to Christianity as that of Arius, since it would have robbed the Incarnation of its reality, making it little more than a phase in the revelation of God, and depriving the Church of an ever-present Divine Master. Eusebius of Cæsarea was only reasonable when he demanded at Nicæa that the creed should not be perverted to encourage this error; and the views propounded by Marcellus of Ancyra and Photinus served to justify his action and that of the conservative and Origenist bishops of the East. It was not indeed till the Creed secured the adherence of Asiatic Origenists like the Cappadocians, Basil, Gregory of Nyssa, and Gregory of Nazianzus, that it was really accepted. The episcopate of Basil, the eloquence of Gregory of Nazianzus, and the philosophy of Gregory of Nyssa were alike instrumental in inducing the bishops of Asia and Syria to accept the *Homoousion* as the one and only safeguard of the Divinity of the Son against the specious teaching of the Arians.

14. But though the Arian controversy virtually ended with the Council of Constantinople in A.D. 381, it was fruitful in new disputes destined to distract and divide Christendom. As early as the time of his banishment to Phrygia (A.D. 356), Hilary of Poitiers was able to foretell the approach of a heresy concerning the Divinity of the Holy Spirit (*de Trin.* lib. ii. and viii.; Swete, *Hist. of the Doct. of the Procession of the Holy Spirit*, p. 112). In 358 the rise of the Tropici caused St. Athanasius to enter, in the *Letters to Serapion*, upon the subject of the Divinity and Procession of the Spirit (Swete, *op. cit.* p. 91; see also pp. 47–49). The subject was also considered at the Council of Alexandria (A.D. 362); and about the same time Macedonius, the Semi-Arian bishop of Constantinople, deposed by the Homœan Synod in A.D. 360, was elaborating the theory (which was afterwards known by his name) that the Son was like, and the Holy Spirit unlike the Father. Though the controversies caused by this question never roused the world like those on the Divinity of the Son, the consequences were even more serious, the question of the Procession of the Holy Ghost being the pretext of the schism between Eastern and Western Christendom. Even more fruitful in divisions was the problem raised by Apollinaris of Laodicæa, one of the chief opponents of Arianism, concerning the relations of the Manhood to the Godhead of Christ. See APOLLINARISM.

The principle for which Athanasius contended so nobly, and which he asserted in early youth before the appearance of Arianism, was the union between God and man brought about by the Incarnation (*de Incarnatione*). But the zeal with which the Divinity of the Son was asserted tended, as Harnack truly says, to obscure the historical Jesus (*op. cit.* iv.); and theology occupied itself with the dogmatic aspect of the Divine rather than with the practical example of the human Christ.

15. It is a remarkable fact that one of the results of the great dogmatic controversies in the early Church was that the defeated party displayed conspicuous zeal in missionary effort; and, without sparing condemnation of the self-seeking and unscrupulous spirit of the political Arians, we have also to remember that some later Arians, like the heresiarch himself, were ready to condescend to instruct the simple. Possibly Arius believed that by re-stating the theology of the Church in terms suited to his age he was doing good service in rendering the faith acceptable to the heathen; and his followers found ready converts among the Teutonic invaders of the empire. The exile of Arius to Illyricum resulted not only in the appearance of those two champions of his heresy in the West, the bishops Ursacius and Valens, but also, if we are to judge from results, in the conversion of the neighbouring Goths, and through them of the Teutonic nations, to Christianity of an Arian type. For long years the dividing line between the Roman and the Teutonic invader of his territory was that of religion rather than that of race. It is our misfortune that we have little or no information concerning the labours of the unknown Arian apostles of the Goths, Vandals, Lombards, and Burgundians. The fact that Cyrila, the Vandal bishop or pope of Carthage, knew Latin very imperfectly (Victor Vitensis, lib. ii.), and the appearance of the famous Gothic version of the Scriptures, would seem to indicate that the barbarians were taught the doctrines of Christianity in their own languages, in which case their Arianism must have differed much from the refined subtlety which distinguished that of the schools of the Empire, and is perhaps expressed in the blunt refusal of the Burgundian Gundobald to worship three Gods (Avitus, *Ep.* xli.). But there seems little doubt that the transforming effects of the Christianity which the barbarians adopted were genuine. Both Salvian and Orosius praise the virtues of the Arian conquerors of Roman territory, and Augustine (*de Civitate Dei*, i.) relates how moderately the Visigothic Arians who captured Rome under Alaric treated the inhabitants of the city, and what respect they showed for the sanctity of the Christian Churches. The long reign, moreover, of the Arian Theodoric in Italy, and his impartial government, extort, as Milman remarks, 'the praise of the most zealous Catholic' (*Latin Christianity*, bk. iii. ch. iii.).

Ulfilas is mentioned by Socrates (ii. 41, iv. 33), Sozomen (vi. 37), Theodoret (iv. 33), Philostorgius (*HE* ii. 5), and Jordanes (ch. 51), but the most important document is the fragment of his pupil Auxentius, Arian bishop of Dorostorus (now Silistria), discovered by Waitz (*Ueber das Leben und die Lehre des Ulfilas*, 1840). Auxentius made remarks in the margin of a copy of the Acts of the Council of Aquileia (A.D. 381), at which the Catholics were led by St. Ambrose against the Western Arians under Palladius and Secundianus. In the course of his criticisms of the *Acta*, Auxentius makes mention of his master Ulfilas, who brought him up both physically and spiritually as his son in the faith. The facts of the life of Ulfilas seem to be that he was born of noble Gothic parentage, or, according to Philostorgius, he was the descendant of Cappadocians who had been carried captive. According to Socrates, he was a Christian from childhood, a pupil of Theophilus, the Gothic bishop present at Nicæa. He was ordained a reader, and about A.D. 340 he was sent on an embassy to Constantinople. In the following year he was made a bishop at the Council of the Dedication by Eusebius of Nicomedia. He laboured among his people in Dacia, but owing to a persecution he led the Christian Goths into Mœsia, at the foot of Mount Hæmus, where they were allowed by the Emperor Constantius to settle. These *Gothi minores* are described by Jordanes. Both Philostorgius and Auxentius compare Ulfilas to Moses; and if a more modern instance is permissible, we may recall the work of John Eliot, the Puritan of Jesus College, Cambridge, among the Algonquin Indians in the 17th century. Like Ulfilas, Eliot gave his converts the Bible in their vernacular. Ulfilas on his deathbed declared his belief, which is given by Auxentius, who comments in a decidedly Arian fashion on it. In this creed the Divinity of the Holy Spirit is expressly denied. Harnack (*op. cit.* vol. iv. p. 44, Eng. tr.) says it is the only Arian creed which is not polemical. It is found in Hahn, § 198. Theodoret says that Ulfilas was persuaded by Eudoxius that the controversy was unimportant; but from the statement of Auxentius he seems to have been a convinced Homœan Arian (see C. A. Scott, *Ulfilas*, 1885).

16. In the Western provinces of the Empire during the 5th and part of the 6th cent., Arianism was the religion of the conquerors, and orthodoxy that of the conquered. Nor did the Catholic faith triumph by force or worldly power so much as by persuasion, since at one time there was not a single orthodox ruler in the Empire or among the barbarians. It was then that the belief of Rome, and the Churches in communion with her, won its most signal triumph in the conversion of Clovis and the Salian Franks (A.D. 496). The strength of the organization of the Church of the fallen Empire stands in remarkable contrast to the weakness of the less disciplined national churches of its Arian invaders. As Dr. Hodgkin remarks, 'The Arian bishops took their fill of court favour and influence while it lasted, but made no provision for the future. They stood apart from one another in stupid and ignorant isolation. Untouched apparently by the great Augustinian thought of the world-encompassing city of God, they tended more and more to form local tribal churches, one for the Visigoths, another for the Vandals, another for the Burgundians. And thus in the end the fable of the loosened faggot and the broken sticks proved true of all the Arian monarchies' (*Italy and Her Invaders*, vol. iii. p. 345; see also Gwatkin, *op. cit.* p. 272).

The events which followed the conversion of Clovis showed the immense political power of the Catholic-Nicene Church of the West. The important Visigothic kingdom of Toulouse, which lasted for nearly a hundred years, and reached the acme of its power under Euric (A.D. 466–484), fell before the Frankish arms at the decisive battle of Vouglé (A.D. 508). The war of Euric against Auvergne, in defence of which Ecdicius and the bishop Sidonius Apollinaris played so valiant a part, was one of Arian against Catholic; and the triumph of the former was followed by severe measures of repression, which have been termed a persecution. (For a discussion of these measures see C. A. Scott, *Ulfilas*, p. 185; and *DCB*, art. 'Euric,' by Mrs. Humphry Ward, who quotes the letter of Sidonius [*Ep.* vii. 6]). Mrs. Ward suggests that Gregory of Tours has misunderstood Sidonius' allusion to the natural death of bishops, to whose vacant sees Euric refused to permit a successor to be chosen, and imagined that they were slain by Euric. After the conversion of Clovis the Catholics had their revenge; that astute prince realized the value of their assistance, and made the expedition against Alaric, the son of Euric, a holy war. 'Valde moleste fero' were his pious words, 'quod *hi Ariani* partem teneant Galliarum, eamus cum Dei adjutorio, et, superatis eis, redigamus terram in ditionem nostram' (Greg. Tours, ii. 37). In the case of the Burgundian Gundobald, the Catholic spokesman Avitus, bishop of Vienne, held out, as an inducement to him to embrace orthodoxy, that he would be protected against Clovis (Avitus, *Ep.* v. 17, quoted by Hodgkin, *Italy and Her Invaders*, vol. iii. p. 347). The fall of the Visigothic kingdom in Italy is an even stronger proof of the political strength of orthodoxy. The admirable rule of Theodoric, his fairness and toleration, were of no avail to save his dynasty; directly an orthodox Emperor was on the throne at Constantinople, the Church intrigued against him and his family. 'Totila,' says Professor Gwatkin, 'was a model of barbarian justice; yet even Totila could never venture to arm the provincials against the orthodox oppressor' (*op. cit.* p. 272).

Mr. C. A. Scott, in his useful monograph on Ulfilas, gives the secret of the broad distinction between the Arianism within and without the Empire. He explains the fact that the Christian Romans who adopted the opinions of Arius showed from the first a tendency to moral deterioration, whereas the barbarians improved in every respect under the influence of a creed which relegated the Son to a lower position than the Father, by reminding us that, whereas in the case of the Arianizing clergy in the days of Constantius, there was a fall from a higher to a lower conception of Christianity, the Teutons were making a distinct advance in substituting an Arian Christianity for heathenism (*Ulfilas*, ch. viii.).

In the same chapter (p. 172 ff.) Mr. Scott gives some useful hints about the few traces of Arian Church organization among the barbarians—a subject on which we are almost entirely in the dark.

17. It may be that the northern invaders found in Arianism an easy transition from polytheism to Christianity (Hodgkin, *op. cit.* p. 88); and their firm adherence to the doctrines which they had been taught, though they can have understood only imperfectly the subtle distinctions between *Homœan* and *Homoousian* Christianity, is very remarkable. But, despite Professor Gwatkin's assertion that the victory of Clovis over the Visigoths was an evidence of the inferiority of the Arian theology of the barbarians to the Nicene doctrine accepted by the Franks (*op. cit.* p. 273)—a view which the present writer himself formerly held (*Cambridge Theological Essays*, p. 500)—we are convinced that the Arianism of the Visigoths, Lombards, Vandals, etc., was no more than a phase in the ecclesiastical struggle between the Teutonic and the Roman conception of Christianity. The barbarians desired to have their own national Church, and when they found a form of Christianity which kept them separate from the despised provincial and independent of the clergy of the Empire, they held to it with the proud firmness of a conquering race. Their natural reverence for Roman civilization made them as a rule nobly tolerant of the religion it sanctioned; and when they are said to have been persecutors, the motive must have been mainly political. Euric's 'persecution' in Toulouse has been compared with the *Kulturkampf* in Germany, and it bears an even stronger resemblance to the more bitter struggle between Church and State in France, where the reason given for depressing the former is the determination not to submit to any external interference.

The inherent weakness of the barbarian occupants of the Roman territory was their incapacity for organization, whilst the strength of the Romans in both their civil and their ecclesiastical polity lay in a system tested by the experience of centuries. The Arian churches were as little able to maintain themselves as the short-lived Teutonic kingdoms, and their clergy had ultimately to surrender at discretion to the better disciplined church of the Roman provincials. The destruction of Arianism as a rival system is one of the most important factors in the genesis of modern European civilization; for, had the barbarian conquerors professed one form of Christianity and the weaker race another, no progress would have been possible. Oppressive as the unregulated feudalism of the dark ages was, it would have been intolerable if the conquerors had not had the claim of a common Christianity to encourage consideration for their vanquished subjects.

The chief authorities for the history of Arianism among the Teutons, besides those already cited, are St. Gregory of Tours (especially vi. 48, the story of the interview between Gregory and Opila, the Spanish ambassador to Chilperic. When examined as to his creed, Opila said, 'Credo patrem et filium et spiritum sanctum unius esse virtutis.' 'In that case,' answered Gregory, 'why will you not receive the communion with us'? 'Quia, inquit, gloriam non recte respondetis, nam iuxta Paulum apostolum nos dicimus Gloria deo patri per filium; vos autem dicitis, Gloria patri et filio et spiritui sancto,' etc.). See Sidonius Apollinaris, *Epistles*, bk. vii. The ninety-one letters of Avitus, bp. of Vienne, should be consulted; see also Gibbon, *Decline and Fall*, ch. xxvii.; Revillout, *Arianisme chez les peuples germaniques*; Maimbourg, *Hist. of Arianism*, bk. x.; Hodgkin, *Italy and Her Invaders*.

18. Every barbarian kingdom ultimately abandoned Arianism, or else, as in the case of the Ostrogoths in Italy and the Vandals in Africa, Arianism proved one of the causes of national ruin. The principal Arian nations were the Burgundians, the Visigoths, and the Lombards; and each in turn, after a severe struggle, abandoned the form of Christianity in which they had been instructed for the Niceno-Roman faith. As the chief reasons for their conversion were political, the reader is referred to the history of the period; all that is possible in this article is to give the main features of the struggle with the orthodox prelates, in which each of the three nations mentioned eventually succumbed. The Burgundians do not seem to have been originally Arians; indeed, if we are to believe Socrates, who wrote in the reign of Theodosius II. (*c.* A.D. 430), they were originally Catholics (*HE* vii. 30); see also *DCB*, artt. 'Gundicarius,' and 'Orosius.' It would seem that the Burgundians were never entirely Arian, though the majority of the nation at the time of Clovis were

of that persuasion. It is an open question whether Gundobald, the contemporary of Clovis, was Arian or orthodox (Greg. Tours, *Hist. Franc.* ii. 34, iii. prologue; Avitus, *Ep.*). His son, the unfortunate Sigismund, was certainly orthodox, whilst the next king Godomar (also a son of Gundobald) was an Arian. In A.D. 534 the Franks subdued Burgundy; but Arianism seems to have continued to drag out an obscure existence till the end of the century (Revillout, *op. cit.* p. 218).

19. After their defeat by Clovis, the Visigoths were gradually driven out of all Gaul except Septimania, the coast from the Pyrenees to the Rhone, being otherwise confined to the Spanish peninsula. In their dominions as elsewhere the Roman provincials remained orthodox, and in the seaport towns the influence of Constantinople was still considerable. **Spain**, however, was the great stronghold of Arianism, which made a long and obstinate struggle before it gave way to the orthodox belief of the Empire. In A.D. 569 the able Leovigild became king of the Visigoths; and, after a series of successful campaigns, reduced his people to almost complete submission to his authority. His son Hermenigild was married to Ingunthis, daughter of Sigibert and Brunichildis of Austrasia. The bride (she was only thirteen years of age) was expected to become an easy convert from Frankish orthodoxy to Visigothic Arianism. She proved, however, very firm in her faith, and absolutely refused to be re-baptized by the Arians, though her grandmother Goiswintha, the wife of Leovigild, treated her with great brutality. To prevent further trouble in his family, Leovigild made his son king, and gave him a separate establishment at Seville. There, it is said, by the influence of his uncle, the famous bishop Leander, and that of his wife, Hermenigild became a Catholic. The young prince soon rebelled against his father, and with the assistance of the Catholic provincials and the Byzantines his party became very formidable. To conciliate his subjects, Leovigild visited the churches, and professed that his belief was Catholic save for his denial of the Divinity of the Holy Spirit, for which he was able to find no Scriptural warrant. He also made a remarkable concession to the prejudices of his subjects, by allowing them to go from the *Roman* to the *Catholic Church*, for so the Arians denominated their body (*de Romana religione ad nostram catholicam fidem*), without any repetition of the baptismal rite, but merely by imposition of hands and saying the *Gloria* in the Arian form, 'Patri per Filium in Spiritu Sancto.' The rebellion of Hermenigild was suppressed, and Leovigild is said to have persecuted the orthodox faith with severity. The unfortunate Hermenigild was put to death, and received, on somewhat doubtful authority, the honours of canonization at the hands of Pope Urban VIII. (1623–1644). Leovigild died in A.D. 586, and was succeeded by his son Reccared. One of the first acts of Reccared was to declare himself in favour of the Catholics, and, according to Gregory of Tours (ix. 15), he arranged a disputation in A.D. 587 between the adherents of the two creeds, after which he embraced the Nicene faith; but this Synod is passed over in all collections of Councils save Mansi's (Hefele, *Councils*, sec. 286). Two years later, Reccared held the famous third **Council of Toledo**, at which 67 bishops and only 5 nobles were present. The leading bishops were St. Leander of Seville, uncle to the king, and Massona of Emerita. Twenty-three anathemas were pronounced against Arianism, the most interesting of which are *the third*, which declares the procession of the Holy Ghost from the Father *and the Son*; *the seventh*, against those who maintain that the Son is ignorant of anything; *the ninth*, against declaring that the Son in His Godhead was ever visible; *the fourteenth*, prescribing the correct form of the *Gloria*; *the sixteenth*, condemning the 'abominable treatise which we composed' to seduce the provincials into the Arian heresy, *i.e.* at the Arian Synod at Toledo (581); and *the seventeenth*, against those who refuse to condemn the Synod of Ariminum (A.D. 359). 'The holy creed' (the Niceno-Constantinopolitan) was ordered to be recited before communion after the manner of the Greek Fathers; and, as is well known, the creed to which Reccared and his queen Badda, together with the bishops including eight Arians, subscribed, contained the fateful addition of the *Filioque*. Arianism, however, was not suppressed by Reccared without force, as many of the Gothic nobles held out for some years.

For fuller particulars concerning this Council see Gams, *Kirchengesch. von Spanien*, vol. ii. pt. i. secs. 6–16; also Dahn, *Urgeschichte der german. und roman. Völker*, p. 515. The native chronicler is Johannes Biclarensis (Migne, *Patrol. Lat.* vol. lxxii.). It is noteworthy that from Spain proceeded the one important Western heresy concerning the person of the Son—the Adoptian (see ADOPTIANISM), promulgated by Elipandus, metropolitan of Toledo, and condemned at the Council of Frankfort (A.D. 794).

20. The **Lombard** conquerors of Italy were Arians down to the close of the 6th cent., and, even in the days of St. Gregory the Great, Autharis, their king, forbade any of his Lombards to give their children Catholic baptism. But shortly before his death Autharis married the Bavarian princess Theodelinda, who had been brought up in the Catholic faith. So great an impression did her wisdom and beauty make on her people, that, when she became a widow, the dukes of the Lombards begged her to select her own husband and continue to reign over them. She chose Agilulf, and by her persuasions the new king was gradually reconciled to the Catholic faith. It was to Theodelinda that Gregory addressed that most interesting revelation of the credulity of his age, the *Dialogues*. Traces of Arianism remained among the Lombards down to the middle of the next century, and it is not at all certain by what means the whole nation was induced to abandon the heresy. The Roman pontiffs regarded them always with the greatest apprehension and abhorrence. For the correspondence between Gregory and Theodelinda see Hodgkin, *Italy and Her Invaders* (1899), vols. v., vi., and Homes Dudden, *Gregory the Great* (1905).

The whole subject of the transition of the Teutons from Arianism to Catholicism is one of great obscurity, and deserves careful investigation. Of the Churches nothing seems to have survived, and, except Ulfilas' translation, there is no literature which has come down to us. The three important factors in the destruction of Arianism were the power of the Franks enlisted on the side of orthodoxy, the weight of influence which the subject Roman provincials were able to throw on the side they favoured in any struggle between rival barbarians, and the part taken by the wives of the kings and chieftains in bringing their people over to the religion of the Romans. Teutonic Arianism was at best a semi-barbarous Christianity; and it is interesting to observe that a form of Christianity, which began with the highly educated bishops of the East as a speculative creed, ended in the West as the national religion of ignorant barbarian warriors. But the struggle between Catholicism and Arianism in Western Europe was no less critical and far more protracted than in the eastern provinces.

21. During **the Middle Ages** there seems to have been little if any revival of Arian opinions properly so called, the tendency being perhaps in the direction of Sabellianism rather than otherwise, though the drift of Christian thought led men to speculate more on the nature of the Church, and eventually on the position of the Virgin Mary in the hierarchy of heaven, than on Christ (Dorner, *Doct. of the Person of Christ*, Div. II. vol. i. [Third Section]).

'Subordinationism, on the contrary,' says Dorner, 'durst no longer raise its head in the form of naked Arianism within the bosom of the Church; it was, however, permitted to conceal itself beneath a species of Tritheism, as in the case of Roscellin; or to unite itself with Sabellianism, as in the case of the Abbot Joachim of Floris, whose view is suggestive of Tertullian's trinity of the three ages of the world. But they touched Christology merely at a few points.'

It was not till more freedom in theological speculation became possible and theology was subjected to criticism in a rationalistic spirit that anything resembling Arianism made its appearance, and then in a shape different from the opinions of Arius and his adherents. After the Reformation the term 'Arian' was frequently misapplied to those who really held Unitarian views; and before discussing the later developments of those opinions which derogated from the supreme Godhead of the Son, it may be well to explain the difference between the position assumed by the Arians of the 4th cent. and their more modern followers. The Arian controversy proper concerned the Nature of the Divine Logos rather than the historic Christ of the Gospels. Arius and all his disciples acknowledged the pre-existence of our Lord, and concerned themselves but little with His Humanity. Indeed, Arius practically denied the manhood of our Lord, by teaching that His human body was animated by the Logos. But this Logos, though the creative principle by which all things were made, was, according to his teaching, not really of God, but a demi-god called into being to create the world, and, in the Incarnate Christ, to save mankind. No serious attempt was made to renew this heresy at the time of the Reformation.

Unitarianism started, on the other hand, with the denial of the pre-existence of Christ, who was declared to be no more than man, though miraculously born of the Virgin Mary and actually raised from the dead. The first Unitarians were Italians, and the majority took refuge in Poland, where the laxity of the laws and the independence of the nobility secured for them a toleration which would have been denied to their views in other countries. They were divided into two main parties: those who declared that worship ought to be paid to Christ, and those who held that to adore Him, a creature, was idolatry. The leader of the former party was **Faustus Socinus** (Sozzini), and those who followed him are often termed Arians to distinguish them from genuine Unitarians like Blandrata and Francis Davidi. These opinions, however, must be considered apart from Arianism proper, which is the subject of the present article.

See Toulmin's *Memoirs of Faustus Socinus.* In his introduction this author says that some of the Unitarians adopted Arian notions, and he distinguishes these from the followers of Socinus (see Liddon's *Bampton Lectures*, Lect. vii.). In mentioning Legate, the unfortunate heretic who was burned at Smithfield in the reign of James I., we observe that most Church historians style him 'an Arian.' According to Fuller (*Church History*, x. iv. 9), Legate held that Christ had no existence before His conception by the Virgin. Milton has been charged with Arianism on account of his representation of the sending of the Son by the Father to pronounce sentence on Adam and Eve (*Paradise Lost*, x. 55):

'But whom send I to judge them? whom but thee,
Vicegerent Son? To thee I have transferr'd
All judgement . . .'

But even if it is fair to judge a poet for words evidently dramatic, this subordinationism is not Arianism in its strict sense. Compare the expressions in the fragment, *In illud omnia*, attributed to Athanasius by Bp. Robertson, *Athanasius*, p. 87. In the tract *de Doctrina Christiana*, published by the Camden Society and in Bohn's *Prose Works of Milton*, the theological views of the poet are put forward. He opposes the teaching of the Calvinists on Free Will, and works out from the Bible a Christology of a Semi-Arian character. He does not appear to have been deeply read in the Fathers (*Dict. Nat. Biog.*, art. 'Milton'). For Sir Isaac Newton's views of Athanasius, which were decidedly hostile to the bishop and favourable to Constantius, see Sir David Brewster's *Life of Newton*, vol. ii. p. 342; Hallam's *Literature of Europe*, vol. iv. p. 36.

22. In the 17th cent. there was a tendency towards Arian opinions, due partly to the arguments advanced by the learned Jesuit **Petavius** in justification of the claim of the Roman Church to prescribe fresh articles of belief; for, though Sandius, a Unitarian, accuses Petavius of secretly holding Arian opinions, Bull was charitable and acute enough to see that the drift of his thesis, that the Anti-Nicene Fathers did not hold the doctrine of the Council, was completely different, and that he had the cause of the Papacy rather than that of Arius in his mind ('pontificiæ potius quam Arianæ causæ consultum voluisse,' *Def. Fidei Nic.* Proem. § 8). Bull's famous treatise in defence of the faith of Nicæa appeared in 1684; and ten years later he wrote his *Judicium Ecclesiæ Catholicæ* in answer to views similar to those of Petavius advanced by the Remonstrant Episcopius, an amiable and learned man, whose object was not so much to attack the Trinitarian position as to maintain its comparative insignificance as an essential of Christianity ('frigidum nimis tantæ veritatis vindicem se ostendit,' *Introd.*; see also Nelson, *Life of Bull*, ch. lxvi.). The *Judicium*, as is well known, was highly commended by the great Bossuet, bishop of Meaux, and the clergy of the Gallican Church (*Life*, ch. lxvii.). The opponents of Bishop Bull were not, as a rule, Englishmen, anti-Trinitarian opinions in Britain having as yet no prominent advocates, but rather, as Bp. Van Mildert styles them in his *Life of Waterland* (p. 37), 'importers of foreign novelties.' Perhaps the best known English work advocating Arianism in the 17th cent. was the *Naked Gospel*, by Dr. Bury, rector of Exeter College (Oxford, 1690). In the same year, Dr. Sherlock, dean of St. Paul's, published his *Vindication of the Doctrine of the Holy and Ever-blessed Trinity*, in which, following some suggestions made by Cudworth, he maintained views which were denounced by South with his customary vehemence as countenancing Tritheism. Sherlock's opinions were condemned by the Vice-Chancellor and heads of houses at Oxford, who declared that it is 'false, impious, and heretical, contrary to the doctrine of the Catholic Church, and especially of the Church of England, to say "that there are three infinite, distinct minds and substances in the Trinity, or that the three Persons are three distinct infinite minds or spirits"' (Appendix to Dorner, by Patrick Fairbairn).

23. Professor Gwatkin in his *Gifford Lectures* ('Knowledge of God,' ch. xvii.) says incisively: 'Arianism is one of the most modern of the old heresies strangely English in its impatient common sense.' And it was in the **England of the 18th cent.** that the controversy revived.

'A variety of circumstances combined to give this turn to religious thought in England. The reaction from Puritanism, now that the tide of fortune had set in so powerfully against it and scope no longer existed for mental energy in that direction, was alone sufficient to account for it. . . . Partly springing, too, from the same reaction, and inspired by other influences, a philosophy came into vogue, heralded by Cudworth but properly founded by Locke, which in its bearings on morals and religion was peculiarly cold and rational. . . . Reason with this school of philosophical divines was placed in a sort of antagonism to faith; as the one element rose the other fell. . . . With those who still maintained a certain belief in Christianity, the prevailing spirit chiefly operated in disposing them to rob it of its more distinctive features, and, as regards the specific subject of our Lord's Person, led them either to reject altogether the doctrine of His divinity, or, with the Arians, to hold it but a quasi-divinity—something of an essentially subordinate nature to that of the Father' (Appendix to Dorner, *Person of Christ*, p. 350 ff.).

The two English divines properly deserving of the name of Arians were William Whiston, who succeeded Sir Isaac Newton in the chair of Mathematics at Cambridge, and his friend Dr. Samuel Clarke. **Whiston** was a man of high attainments, marred by many eccentricities. His study of Christian documents led him to place the *Apostolical Constitutions* on a par with the Gospels, and to choose Eusebius of Nicomedia as the exponent of the true tradition of Christian doctrine. He repudiated the name of Arian, but his outspoken utterances caused him to be deprived of his professorship. His more cautious friends, among them Benjamin Hoadly, rose to the highest and most lucrative positions in the Church of England (Abbey and Overton, *The English Church in the Eighteenth Century*, vol. i. p. 490 ff.). **Dr. Samuel Clarke**, Rector of St. James's, Piccadilly, London, in 1712 published his *Scripture Doctrine of the Trinity*, in which no fewer than 1257 texts were cited and examined, with the result that the Father was declared to be alone Supreme, the Son Divine only so far as Divinity is communicable by the Supreme God, and the Holy Spirit inferior to the Father and the Son, not in order only, but also in dominion and authority. This avowed Arianism (for it was pointed out that of the fifty-five propositions advanced by Dr. Clarke there was only one to which an ancient Arian could not have subscribed) was the signal for an important controversy in England. The chief supporters of the new Arianism were Dr. Whitby and Mr. John Jackson, rector of Rossington and vicar of Doncaster. Clarke's work was condemned by Convocation in 1714; but the dispute was not thereby silenced, and in 1719, **Dr. Waterland**, archdeacon of St. Albans, published an answer to Jackson in his *Vindication of Christ's Divinity*. In the long war of pamphlets which followed, Waterland was conspicuous alike for basing his doctrine on Scripture alone and for the respect he showed for the Fathers. The Arian dispute in England marks, indeed, the close of the age when the Fathers were confidently appealed to in theological disputes. Nor was the Church of England alone disturbed by the question, since from the time of Emlyn's condemnation in Dublin (1702) and his expulsion from his church, the Nonconformists were disturbed by the presence of Arianism, which culminated in the Salters Hall Conference in 1718 between Presbyterians, Baptists, and Congregationalists. The Arianism of the early 18th cent. was succeeded by anti-Trinitarianism; and the subordinationist theories of the first decades gave way to more distinctly Unitarian doctrines, the discussion of which is scarcely within the scope of the present article.

For English Arianism see Nelson, *Life of Bull*, 1713; Van Mildert, *Life of Waterland*; Whiston, *Memoirs*, 1749–50; the Appendix to Dorner's *Person of Christ* (Eng. tr. 1865–68); Abbey and Overton, *English Church in the Eighteenth Century*, 1878, ch. viii.; Sykes, *Anti-Trinitarian Biography*; Dale, *History of Eng. Congregationalism*[2], 1907.

24. As a philosophy of religion, Arianism struck a blow not only at the root of the Creed, but at the whole principle of Scriptural revelation. 'Is,' asks Harnack at the beginning of his chapter on the subject (*op. cit.* vol. iv. Eng. tr.), 'the Divine, which appeared on the earth and has made its presence actively felt, identical with the supremely Divine that rules heaven and earth? Did the Divine which appeared on earth enter into a close and permanent union with human nature, so that it has actually transfigured it and raised it to the plane of the eternal?' The OT teaches that the One True God revealed Himself, in part at any rate, to Israel; and the NT supplements this by showing that humanity is made one in the Christ (ὁ Χριστός), and by this is brought into complete harmony with the God and Father of All. Arianism declared God to be unknowable, and the Son completely detached from Him. Humanity can therefore never be brought by Christ to the truly Divine, but only to a sort of pseudo-divinity created in the Son by the Father. Such an evacuation of the purpose of the Christian revelation has always been repudiated whenever the doctrine is presented in its crude form. But we must carefully distinguish between the logical results of such a system as Arius propounded and the opinions of those who have upheld it. Arius himself, in his dread of Sabellianism, may have advanced a theory of the Trinity without consideration of all that it involved. As a matter of fact, he was ready in later life to subscribe to a creed approximating to that of Nicæa. Of his opinions the famous Unitarian Dr. Priestley rightly says in his *Church History* (vol. ii. p. 189): 'Nay, the proper opinions of Arius, viz., that the Son was made out of nothing, and that there was a time when He did not exist, were really adopted by very few. So that what we call Arianism arose much later and spread much less rapidly than has been generally imagined.' The Arian Controversy resulted, however, in bringing forward two conclusions of which Christians had to choose one. If Jesus Christ existed from eternity, and is Head of a Kingdom which shall have no end, if He is indeed to be worshipped and received as God, then the Nicene doctrine is true, and He is of one substance with the Father. Otherwise, Christians have been mistaken from the first in their conception of Him, and He is not Divine, but a creature; not eternal, but belonging to time: either, as Arius suggested, a second God, using the term 'God' in its looser polytheistic sense, or, as the Unitarians maintain, a mere man eminent for goodness, but subject to human limitations, and unable to bring those who trust in Him to peace and communion with the Father. It is not without significance that Socinus expressly denied the doctrine of atonement through Christ.

F. J. Foakes-Jackson.

ARISTOTLE, ARISTOTELIANISM.

—**I. Life.**—Aristoteles—son of Nicomachus, friend and physician of Amyntas, king of Macedonia—was born B.C. 384 at Stagira or Stagirus, a city of Chalcidice. In his eighteenth year (367) he came to Athens and joined the Academy, of which he continued to be a member, learning and teaching, during twenty years. Tradition relates that he taught rhetoric in opposition to Isocrates. That is to say, whereas at this time the school of the politico-rhetorical sophist Isocrates and the Academy, the school of Plato, were rival colleges, Isocrates was professor of rhetoric in the one, Aristotle in the other. In 347, when Plato died and his nephew Speusippus succeeded him as scholarch, Aristotle and Xenocrates, on the invitation of Hermias, lord of Atarneus and Assos, who was himself an Academic, betook themselves to his court. After a three years' residence there, Aristotle removed to Mitylene; and about this time, after the death of Hermias, he married Pythias, a near relative of his friend. In 343 Aristotle received and accepted a call to the Macedonian court to undertake the education of Alexander, then thirteen years old. This task occupied him during three years (343–340). A stay at Stagira followed; and it was not till Alexander had ascended the throne, and was about to start on his Asiatic expedition, that Aristotle finally left Macedonia. Meanwhile, in 339, Speusippus had died, and Xenocrates, after a contest with Heraclides Ponticus and Menedemus, had succeeded him as head of the Academy.

In 335 Aristotle returned to Athens and founded a school of his own in the gymnasium known as the Lyceum. There he spent twelve busy years, teaching in the morning a select class of advanced students, and in the afternoon a larger audience. From his habit of walking to and fro as he discoursed, the members of the school were called **Peripatetics** (Περιπατητικοί). Towards the end of this period of twelve years he lost the favour of Alexander, whose jealousy of Antipater and suspicion of Callisthenes prejudiced him against their friend and correspondent. Nevertheless, when Alexander died in 323, the anti-Macedonian party at Athens vented their spite against Aristotle in a charge of 'impiety.' The accusation, based upon a hymn to virtue, in which he was alleged to have represented Hermias as a god, was plainly frivolous; but Aristotle prudently left Athens and retired to his house near Chalcis in Eubœa. There he died in the summer of the following year (322). The story that he committed suicide by drinking hemlock or by drowning himself in the Euripus appears to have no foundation. Dr. Waldstein in 1891 opened a tomb near Eretria which he supposes to be that of the great philosopher.

2. Writings.—Cicero extols 'the golden stream of Aristotle's discourse'; Quintilian, its 'grace and fertility'; and Dionysius of Halicarnassus, its 'force, clearness, and grace.' These praises must needs refer to Aristotle's published writings, and, in particular, to his *Dialogues*, of which only fragments have come down to us. The philosophical writings, upon which his fame rests, are wholly deficient in literary quality. The style is curt, abrupt, jejune. The language is careless and conversational. The exposition is sometimes incomplete, sometimes redundant, sometimes inconsistent. There are reminders, recapitulations, revisions. Arguments are sometimes indicated without being worked out; inquiries which are promised are sometimes tacitly dropped. In a word, these writings, which have so profoundly impressed the thought of many centuries, would seem to be neither completed and published works nor text-books for use in the school, but informal records of oral teaching addressed to a few advanced pupils. In this way, and perhaps in this way only, are explicable the rough and ready terminology, the diagrams and examples, the references to the furniture and the decorations of the lecture-room and to members of the class, the occasional sentences which have no beginning, and, in one instance, the peroration addressed to an audience. But if these are records of oral teaching, some of them more completely finished than others, by whom were they prepared? Are they Aristotle's notes made with a view to his lectures? Are they notes of his teaching made by his hearers? Are they compilations made by an editor who had before him both Aristotle's notes for lectures and his hearers' notes of them? In the opinion of the present writer the treatises which have come down to us are in the main the notes of Aristotle himself. If they were the notes of pupils, and, *a fortiori*, if they were compilations, much of the roughness and the obscurity would have disappeared.

For example, in *Metaphysics*, Λ iii. 1069ᵇ 35 and 1070ᵃ 5 the words μετὰ ταῦτα ὅτι would not have survived, and in A ix. 990ᵇ 11-15 we should not find indications of three Platonic arguments and Aristotle's objections to them packed into four lines. It would seem that Aristotle's notes, made for his own use and supplemented and corrected by himself, but never revised for publication, were treasured in the school; so that we possess, not indeed always his last thoughts, but at any rate his thoughts; and the inconsistencies which trouble us prove only that his thinking was progressive.

The chief of the so-called 'acroamatic' treatises attributed to Aristotle may be classified under their mediæval titles as follows:—

i. LOGIC: the *Organon*, including *Categoriæ, de Interpretatione, Analytica Priora, Analytica Posteriora, Topica, de Sophisticis Elenchis.*
ii. PHYSICS: *Physica* or *Physicæ Auscultationes, de Cœlo, de Generatione et Corruptione, Meteorologica.*
iii. BIOLOGY: *Historiæ Animalium, de Partibus Animalium, de Incessu Animalium, de Generatione Animalium, de Anima, Parva Naturalia.*
iv. PHILOSOPHY: *Metaphysica.*
v. ETHICS AND POLITICS: *Ethica Nicomachea, Ethica Eudemia, Magna Moralia, Politica, Œconomica.*
vi. LITERATURE: *Rhetorica, Poetica.*

It is not possible to speak with any certainty about the chronology of these writings; for there can be no assurance that references from one to another are Aristotle's and not the additions of editors. But we know that the collection of treatises from which we gather Aristotle's ontology was early placed after the treatises on Natural History: for this, and no more, is implied in the title τὰ μετὰ τὰ φυσικά, whence we derive our convenient misnomer 'metaphysics.'

Besides the 'published works' (ἐκδεδομένοι λόγοι), and the 'lectures' (ἀκροαματικά), there were also 'memoranda' (ὑπομνήματα). Under this last head may perhaps be placed certain summaries of the teaching of philosophers, the προβλήματα, and the πολιτεῖαι, *i.e.* notices of the constitutions of 158 political communities. The recently discovered Ἀθηναίων πολιτεία appears to have contained (1) a brief constitutional history of Athens and (2) a citizen's handbook; but the want of proportion obvious in the former of these two sections suggests that it was a compilation, made by some member of the school, from extracts and documents which Aristotle had casually collected.

Strabo and Plutarch relate that Aristotle's library, including his own writings, became the possession of Theophrastus, and after his death passed into the hands of Neleus of Scepsis in the Troad; that his heirs, for fear of the lords of Pergamos, hid them in a cellar; that about B.C. 100 Apellikon bought them and brought them to Athens; and that in 86 they came into the hands of Sulla, and so became known to the grammarian Tyrannion, whose copies were the basis of an edition prepared about 70 by Andronicus of Rhodus, the eleventh scholarch. This curious story is probably true; but it must not be taken for granted either that the school had no philosophical library or that its library did not contain copies of Aristotle's principal writings.

3. Philosophical system.—We have seen that Aristotle entered the Academy and continued to be an active member of it during twenty years. In later life he still regarded himself as an Academic; for even when he is criticizing certain of Plato's tenets, he speaks of them as doctrines which *we* hold. Indeed, it would appear that, had he been at Athens in 339, he might have succeeded Speusippus as head of the School; for in the list of scholarchs, it is expressly noted that when Xenocrates was elected, 'Aristotle was in foreign parts.' But though an Academic, Aristotle cannot be regarded as a Platonist. The master and the pupil differed fundamentally in their attitude towards inquiry, Plato taking his departure from that which is eternal, Aristotle from that which is actual in time and space. Yet, in spite of this disagreement, they were at one in resting their schemes of scientific research upon the assumption that there are in Nature determinate kinds of species, which may be studied in their resemblances and their differences. After all, Aristotle had more sympathy with Plato than Speusippus, a biologist who assumed the existence of natural kinds without attempting a metaphysical explanation of them; and more appreciation of Plato than Xenocrates, a moralist, who, when he ventured into Platonic metaphysics, was soon out of his depth; and whereas Speusippus dropped the theory of Ideas, and Xenocrates blended it with Pythagorean fancies, Aristotle was, at any rate, careful to formulate his dissent. In a word, Plato propounded an idealist ontology and rested upon it a theory of natural kinds, which should be the basis for the study of cosmic existences; Aristotle, rejecting the idealist ontology, proceeded to restate the theory of natural kinds, resting it upon an ontology of his own. The criticism of his master's idealism is indeed Aristotle's starting-point, and for this reason it will be convenient, in the present account of Aristotle's system and encyclopædia, to give precedence to 'First Philosophy' (πρώτη φιλοσοφία) or 'Theology' (θεολογική).

(1) *FIRST PHILOSOPHY.*—There are, thought Aristotle, four principal lines of inquiry, having for their ends the discovery of four causes (αἰτίαι) or principles (ἀρχαί). These causes or principles are the *material* cause (ὕλη), the *essential* cause (οὐσία, τὸ τί ἦν εἶναι), the *moving* cause (ἀρχὴ τῆς κινήσεως), and the *final* cause (τὸ οὗ ἕνεκα, τέλος). Apart from

accidents or attributes which are not common to all the members of a natural kind, each of its members is, in thought though not in fact, resolvable into a specific soul or life, which is its form, and an appropriate body, which is its proximate matter. But again, the body is resolvable, in thought though not in fact, into organs and constituents. Further, these constituents are compounds of the four elements—fire, air, water, and earth. Finally, fire, air, water, and earth have for their ultimate matter a purely indeterminate potentiality which is the recipient of four primary qualities—hot and cold, wet and dry: fire is the combination of hot and dry; air, that of hot and wet; water, that of cold and wet; earth, that of cold and dry. The ultimate matter of the member of a natural kind is then a potentiality, in virtue of which that member exists in time and space: its form is the sum of its specific characteristics, in virtue of which it is what it is. What we can know of the member of a natural kind is its specific characteristics. Anything which is peculiar to an individual member or to individuals is not known but perceived.

Such is Aristotle's analysis of the particular member of the natural kind. It may serve as a statement of the aims which he has in view in his classificatory researches; but it leaves the adaptation of body to soul, the organization of body, and the differentiation of species wholly unexplained; and when he tells us vaguely that 'Nature' works always to an end and 'does nothing at random' (οὐδὲν ἀτελὲς [or μάτην] ποιεῖ ἡ φύσις), it is plain that 'Nature' is no more than a *deus ex machina*.

For the proximate moving cause, by which the particular member of a natural kind is brought into existence, Aristotle looks, not to any transcendental cause eternally operant, but to a previous member of the species which in its maturity transmits the specific characteristics to its offspring. This principle is expressed in the formula 'man generates man' (ἄνθρωπος ἄνθρωπον γεννᾷ). The final cause, the end sought, is the maintenance of the species. For though, under the influence of the sun as it approaches and recedes in its apparent progress through the signs, the life of the particular animal or vegetable waxes and wanes and ultimately ceases, Nature is 'careful of the type.'

It is necessary, however, to account not only for the existence of the animal and vegetable kinds, but also for that of the earth and the heavenly bodies, and for their motions, especially if, as the use made of the sun suggests, animal and vegetable life is to be dependent upon them. For this purpose Aristotle postulates (*a*) a prime unmoved movent (πρῶτον κινοῦν ἀκίνητον), eternal, existent, essentially operant, exempt from matter, and (*b*) other unmoved movents (κινοῦντα ἀκίνητα). The prime unmoved movent, with the other unmoved movents, attracts (κινεῖ ὡς ἐρώμενον) the material universe, and so causes to rotate the spheres which are necessary to account for the motions of the earth and the heavenly bodies. Of such spheres Eudoxus had postulated 26, Callippus 33; Aristotle finds 55, or at any rate 47, necessary. The prime unmoved movent is mind (νοῦς), which, with itself for object, thinks continually (ἐνεργεῖ ἔχων), and is conscious of its thinking (ἡ νόησις νοήσεως νόησις). The other unmoved movents, though Aristotle does not say it, must needs be the thoughts of the prime unmoved movent. For, at the end of Metaphysics Λ, criticizing Speusippus on the ground that his system makes the universe 'episodical,' Aristotle adds epigrammatically: 'Real existences refuse to submit to a bad constitution: as Homer says, a plurality of kings is bad; let us have one king.' Plainly Aristotle supposes himself to escape this condemnation: and so he does, if the other unmoved movents are the thoughts of the prime unmoved movent; for 'mind and its thoughts are one and the same' (1072^b 21, 1075^a 3).

Such is the substance of Aristotle's *First Philosophy*. But *First Philosophy* is also a 'Theology.' The mind, the prime unmoved movent, which, with its thoughts, the unmoved movents, originates and maintains the orderly motions of the earth and the heavenly bodies, is emphatically described as God; and, simple as his language is, Aristotle seems to be moved beyond his wont when he writes: 'It is wonderful that God should have always an excellence which we have sometimes: that he should have a greater excellence is still more wonderful. But so it is.' 'God is perfect: he has life, continuity of existence, eternity of existence; that is what God is.' 'He is one; and therefore the firmament which he sets in motion is one.' 'The belief in a Divinity which invests the whole of Nature goes back,' Aristotle adds, 'to remote antiquity; but, for the persuasion of the many and in the service of the law, an anthropomorphic mythology has been built upon it. Strip away the accretions, and then "first existences are gods" is a divine word.'

The lacunæ in the system here described are obvious. In particular, we desiderate an explanation of the part played by 'Nature'; and the omission is the more startling because we find Aristotle endeavouring to bring his scheme of unmoved movents into relation with the contemporary astronomy. His chief care was perhaps to show the possibility of resting the theory of natural kinds on a metaphysical system other than that of Plato. According to Plato, everything is directly or indirectly the thought of universal mind. Fire, air, earth, and water are its geometrical conceptions of space. The stars are modes of life implanted by it in fiery spheres. Animals and vegetables are modes of life, conceived by universal mind, but combined by the stars with bodies appropriately fashioned out of the elements. The particular member of an animal or vegetable species is a phenomenal copy or reflexion, in appropriately corporealized space, of the transcendental idea. Aristotle's immanent form received from the previous member of the species corresponds to Plato's phenomenal copy or reflexion of the Idea; Aristotle's Nature's design corresponds to Plato's Idea. The truth is that there is little difference between the two analyses when once it is understood that Plato emphasizes the transcendental idea at the expense of the immanent reflexion, and that Aristotle emphasizes the immanent form at the expense of Nature's design. But the fact always remains that, whereas Plato regarded matter also—that is to say, space—as the creature of universal mind, and so was a monist, Aristotle distinguished matter—that is to say, potentiality—from supreme mind, and was therefore a dualist.

In the *Metaphysics*, Aristotle's answer to the question, What is the primarily existent (τὸ πρώτως ὄν)?, is to the following effect. It is not the receptive substratum called 'matter,' because, being purely potential, matter is not actually anything. It is not a mere universal (καθόλου), for the common characteristic or characteristics by which species are artificially combined in a genus, and particulars within a species are artificially combined in a group, *make* the genus or the group, and are not resemblances and differences discovered by comparison of species made by Nature. It is not the particular in which form and matter are combined, for with matter come in accidental attributes peculiar to individuals. It is the form and nothing but the form; that is to say, it is the sum of the characteristics of the species to which the particular belongs. Such is the doctrine of *Metaphysics* Z. Nevertheless, in the *Categories*, primary existence is ascribed to the particular or composite of form and matter. The inconsistency is one of terminology and not of thought. For the specific form which is the primary existence of the *Metaphysics* exists only in the members of the species; and the primarily existent particular of the *Categories* is known only in so far as it represents the species to which it belongs. Aristotle coined many technical terms; but he allowed himself a large licence in the use of them, and he was not always careful to harmonize the terminology of one treatise with that of another. In this case, the terminological discrepancy is unfortunate; but, in the opinion of the present writer, it is a mistake to infer from it either confusion or vacillation.

(2) *PSYCHOLOGY.*—The conception of mind, exempt from matter, reappears in the *Psychology* (περὶ ψυχῆς). In this treatise Aristotle begins with a review of previous and existing opinion, from which it appears that some had regarded soul exclusively as the organ of motion, others exclusively as that of sensation and cognition. For himself, he proposes to include under this name all activity, which, whether manifested or not, is implicit in living body, and distinguishes living body from body which is lifeless. (Perhaps this is all that Aristotle meant in the first instance by defining soul as 'the first actuality of a natural organized body' [ἡ πρώτη ἐντελέχεια σώματος φυσικοῦ ὀργανικοῦ]; but when he adds that, while soul is actuality of body, body is not actuality of soul, the definition becomes a declaration of soul's supremacy.) Having thus widened the scope of psychology, Aristotle proceeds to enumerate the faculties of soul. Nutrition (together with generation), sensation, appetition, locomotion, intellection, follow one another in this order; and the possession of a higher faculty implies that of all the faculties below it. The soul of plants is nutritive only. The soul of animals is not only nutritive, but also sensitive, appetitive, motive. The soul of man has all the faculties of animals, and is intellective also. In sensation the form of the sensible, without its matter, reaches the sense through an intervening medium; and the sense perceives the sensible in virtue of the change which the advent of the sensible brings about in it. Hence, when subject and object are in the like condition, there is no sensation; and when the sensible is in excess, the organ may be deranged or disabled. Touch is the primary sense. Besides the five special senses, Aristotle recognizes a common or central sense, which (*a*) is conscious of sensation, and (*b*) distinguishes and co-ordinates the impressions received by the special senses. Its organ is the heart. So far we have been dealing with faculties which man shares with the animals. Passing next to reason—the faculty which belongs distinctively to man—Aristotle distinguishes a passive reason (παθητικὸς νοῦς), which receives from the senses their impressions, and an active, constitutive reason (ποιητικὸς νοῦς), which provides forms of thought for the interpretation of the impressions received from the senses. Such is the function of the active reason in the individual; but it and it alone of the psychical faculties may exist apart from soul and from body. When it exists apart, 'independent of external objects, having no inessential attributes, essentially operant,' and 'only when it so exists,' it is immortal and eternal. Now the active reason, as thus conceived, is the prime unmoved movent, the God, of the *Metaphysics*. In so far as man possesses this reason, it comes to him from without. Plainly the passive reason is interposed in order to bring the recepta of sense into relation with the divine faculty.

(3) *LOGIC.*—Of all Aristotle's achievements the greatest was perhaps the invention of *logic*. The group of treatises known as the *Organon* includes a formal logic, a theory of scientific research, a treatise on disputation, and a classification of fallacies. The formal logic comprises an enumeration of categories or heads of predication; a study of the quality, quantity, and conversion of propositions; a detailed investigation of the syllogism and its figures; and a careful discrimination between *adduction* (ἐπαγωγή), or generalization from known particulars in regard to those particulars, and *example* (παράδειγμα), or inference from known particulars in regard to unknown particulars, effected by ascent to an imperfectly certified *general* and subsequent descent from it. Within the limits of the *Organon*, Aristotle takes account at once of *dialectical debate*, by which the premises of demonstration are provisionally justified, of *demonstration*, by which the consequences of given premises are ascertained, and of *sophistry* or *eristic*, pursued irrespectively of truth with a view to argumentative success.

(4) *SCIENCE.*—While the formal logic still holds its ground, Aristotle's scientific writings were no more than stepping-stones. His physical speculations occupied the field for eighteen centuries; but they were never more than stop-gaps; and the time came when, by reason of his great name, they were positive hindrances to progress. His biological works are still praised for the observation, the insight, and the knowledge, of which they afford conclusive evidence.

(5) *ETHICS AND POLITICS.*—In the *Nicomachean Ethics* and the *Politics*, Aristotle raises and discusses anew the old question, What is man's chiefest good (τὸ ἀνθρώπινον ἀγαθόν)?, regarding it in the one, as the end sought by the individual, and in the other, inasmuch as man is a social animal and cannot realize himself except as a citizen, as the end sought by the city-State (πόλις). Thus the two treatises are contributions to the architectonic science of Politics (πολιτική); but the one (ἠθικά) is concerned with the 'character' of the individual, the other (πολιτικά) with the 'constitution' of the State.

All are agreed that man's good or end is well-being (εὐδαιμονία), that is to say, well-living (εὖ ζῆν) or well-faring (εὖ πράττειν); and man's well-being —the term 'happiness' should be avoided—is the satisfactory performance of those functions which are distinctively human. In a word, 'man's chief good or end is a psychical activity characteristic of an excellence (ἀρετή), or, if there are more excellences than one, characteristic of the best and completest of them, such activity being continued during a complete period of existence.' Setting aside nutrition and growth which man shares with plants, and sensation which he shares with animals, we find that man's distinctive functions are reason, reasoning, and the rational control of appetition, under which head are included desires and passions. What, then, are the excellences of these functions? And which of the excellences is the best and the completest? There are two sorts of excellence—moral excellence, the excellence which the appetitive part of soul displays when it is duly obedient to the rational part, and intellectual excellence, the excellence of the rational part. Moral excellence (or virtue) is 'a deliberate habit which enables the individual, with the help of his reasoning faculty—subject to an appeal to the man of practical wisdom —to attain what is for him the mean between vicious extravagances.' The principal moral virtues are courage, temperance, liberality, munificence, magnanimity or self-respect, gentleness, justice. The intellectual excellences are practical wisdom or prudence (φρονησις), the excellence of that subdivision of the rational part of soul which controls the appetitive part, and speculative wisdom (σοφία) the excellence of that purely intellectual part which is called reason (νοῦς). Practical wisdom and the moral virtues must be developed *pari passu*. Now, reason is obviously the best part of the soul, and therefore its excellence, speculative wisdom, is the best of excellences. This best of excellences has for its activity (ἐνέργεια) study (θεωρία). Consequently, the completest well-being of the individual is to be found in the life of the student (θεωρητικὸς βίος), who, however, must loyally do his duty as a member of the city and the family. This completest well-being brings with it the highest of pleasures. Next to the life of the student ranks the practical life of moral virtue. For the production of excellence, three things are requisite: first, natural aptitude; secondly, instruction, for its guidance; thirdly, habituation, to establish the habit. Inasmuch as well-being implies not merely the possession of a habit, but also its exercise, we require for the realization of well-being those external goods upon which the exercise of the habit depends. The doctrine that well-being implies the exercise of a habit and not merely the possession of it, and the corollary that external goods are indispensable conditions, distinguish Peripatetic from Academic ethics.

As in the *Ethics* Aristotle is concerned with the well-being of the individual, so in the *Politics* he is concerned with the well-being of the community. The city (πόλις) is a complex organism, developed out of the village (κώμη), which again has its origin in the patriarchal family (οἰκία). Right polities (ὀρθαὶ πολιτεῖαι) are those in which the sovereign (κύριος)—whether one, few, or many—rules for the benefit of the community; perversions (παρεκβάσεις) are those in which the sovereign—whether one, few, or many—uses power for personal advantage. The right polities are aristocracy, monarchy, polity proper; the perversions are democracy, oligarchy, and tyranny. The best of cities would be one in which absolute power was exercised for the benefit of all the citizens by one person, or more persons than one, superior to the rest in mind and in body. But we cannot hope to find rulers thus exceptionally qualified, and accordingly monarchy and aristocracy must be regarded as unattainable ideals. Thus of the three right polities one alone remains, namely, polity proper, in which all free men are admitted to a share in the administration and at the same time submit themselves to the 'passionless intelligence' of law. Of all polities this is, in Aristotle's estimation, the most stable; for inasmuch as all in turn rule and are ruled, the middle class has a preponderant influence. For the maintenance of polity proper, Aristotle would rely, as Athens did and as the United States do, upon supreme or constitutional laws (νόμοι), alterable only by special formalities, to which supreme or constitutional laws, upheld by courts of justice, all ordinary enactments (ψηφίσματα) must conform. Of the three perversions—democracy, oligarchy, tyranny—democracy, which has the smallest power for evil, is the least bad; tyranny, in which such power is greatest, is the worst. Tradition places at the end of the treatise a fragmentary scheme for a perfect State; but, unlike Plato, Aristotle had no hope of its realization. In the intervening books, on the strength of a careful study of known constitutions, Aristotle inquires what sorts of constitution are suitable to given sorts of people; how a constitution may be established and maintained in accordance with given assumptions or conditions; what is the best constitution for the generality of States; what circumstances tend to change, to overthrow, and to maintain the several constitutions. The reader of the *Politics* must not forget that, on the one part, the citizen population of a Greek State was very small, so that Aristotle knew nothing of representative government; and that, on the other part, the number of slaves was, in comparison with the number of free men, very great, so that what he calls a democracy was in some sort an aristocracy.

In these two treatises, the *Nicomachean Ethics* and the *Politics*, Aristotle is an acute and judicious student of human nature. They have a Shakespearean quality which makes them perennially interesting. But it must be clearly understood that they do not pretend to offer a theory of morality. Aristotle says nothing about the Good, about Duty, about the distinction between Right and Wrong; and very little about the faculty which discriminates them. Moreover, inasmuch as he concentrates his attention in the *Ethics* upon the well-being of the individual, and in the *Politics* upon the well-being of the State, the relations of man to man and of citizen to citizen are insufficiently handled. Indeed, they find a place, and that a subordinate place, only in so far as the particular virtues of justice and friendship are concerned with them. In a word, Aristotle works upon the lines of Plato's *Republic*.

In the *Eudemian Ethics*, which is now generally regarded as a summary prepared, *mutatis mutandis*, by Aristotle's disciple Eudemus, the line of argument is similar to that of the *Nicomacheans*. But (*a*) Eudemus chafes under the limitations of the inquiry, and would fain seek an explanation of moral differences; (*b*) regarding pleasure, not as the concomitant of an energy, but as identical with it, he sees in εὐδαιμονία the best of pleasures; and (*c*) abandoning the distinction drawn in the *Nicomacheans* between the activity of the student and the activity of the man of the world, he finds man's well-being in a life of culture (καλοκαγαθία) which combines both. It would appear that Aristotle himself, when he was writing the *Politics* (see IV. [VII.] iii. 1325^b 14), had learnt to regard statesmanship as a proper subject for scientific study. In the opinion of the present writer, Books v. vi. vii. of the *Nicomacheans*, which appear also as Books iv. v. vi. of the *Eudemians*, belong to the *Eudemians*, which they resemble both in their doctrine and in their style.

(6) *RHETORIC, ETC.*—In the *Rhetoric*—a treatise on oratory and style, apparently framed on lines marked out by Plato in the *Phædrus*—and in the fragmentary *Poetics*, Aristotle shows himself a literary critic of a high order. In particular, his appreciations of the tragedians have a permanent value. Perhaps no literary judgment has given rise to more controversy than the remark that tragedy, 'by raising pity and fear, purges the mind of those passions.' This theory of the 'homœopathic purgation' effected by tragedy (see Milton's Preface to *Samson Agonistes*) is Aristotle's answer to Plato, who in the *Republic* condemns tragedy as an incentive and stimulus to mischievous emotions.

The greatness of Aristotle was not fully understood until the Middle Ages, when the Church borrowed from him the framework of its theology, when the whole of civilized Europe saw in his encyclopædic writings the summary of the sciences, and when Dante hailed him as 'the master of those who know.' In the present article no more has been attempted than to describe in outline the philosophy upon which the schoolmen built, and to indicate the scope of Aristotle's labours. See, further, SCHOLASTICISM.

LITERATURE.—The following editions of Aristotle's writings deserve special mention: **Bekker**, *Opera Omnia*, 5 vols., Berlin, 1831–70; **Pacius**, *Organon*, Frankfort, 1592; **Waitz**, *Organon*, 2 vols., Leipzig, 1844–6; **Aubert and Wimmer**, *Historia animalium*, 2 vols., Leipzig, 1868; **Hicks**, *de Anima*, Cambridge, 1907; **Bonitz**, *Metaphysica*, Bonn, 1848–9; **Bywater**,

Ethica Nicomachea (text), Oxf. 1890; Stewart *Ethica Nicomachea* (commentary), Oxf. 1892; Newman, *Politica*, 2 vols., Lond. 1887; Spengel, *Rhetorica*, 3 vols., Leipz. 1853–6; Cope, *Rhetorica*, 3 vols., Camb. 1877; Butcher, *Poetica*², Lond. 1898; Bywater, *Poetica*, Lond. 1898. For Aristotle's philosophy see Zeller, *Die Philosophie der Griechen*, Eng. tr., Costelloe and Muirhead, 2 vols., Lond. 1897; Gomperz, *Griechische Denker* [Eng. tr., *Greek Thinkers*, Lond. 1901]; Ueberweg's *Grundriss der Geschichte der Philosophie* (Eng. tr., Smith and Schaff), contains, together with a useful summary of Aristotle's system, a very valuable bibliography. The Clarendon Press is now bringing out a series of English translations of Aristotle's writings.

The writer of the present article has occasionally used in it sentences and phrases borrowed from a sketch of the history of Greek philosophy down to Aristotle, which he contributed to the Cambridge *Companion to Greek Studies*.

HENRY JACKSON.

ARK.—In an inquiry into the nature and use of sacred arks, our interest centres chiefly in that which is familiar to us from the OT, the so-called Ark of the Covenant.

This name, which occurs in the Deuteronomistic literature, is not, however, the earliest one, older designations being apparently 'Ark of Jahweh,' 'Ark of God,' and 'Ark of our God.'* But the word 'God' (*'ĕlōhîm*), when used in the genitive, may have two meanings; *i.e.* it may be either possessive or adjectival, in the latter case denoting connexion not so much with the one true God as with the class or order of supernatural beings, the supernatural world. Accordingly the expression 'ark of God' may mean either 'God's ark' or 'ark connected with the supernatural world,' *i.e.* 'sacred ark.' In order to decide which of these two renderings is the correct one, we must inquire what name the writer uses to denote the Deity. If, like the author of Gn 1, he habitually uses the word *'ĕlōhîm*, then the phrase *'ărôn hā-'ĕlōhîm* may mean 'God's ark.' If, however, he habitually uses the name *Jahweh*, the only possible translation of the phrase is 'the sacred ark'; for a Hebrew, unlike an English writer, does not attempt to vary his style by the use of synonyms. In the case of an ark associated with the worship of Jahweh, the mere mention of the name of Jahweh would be sufficient to show the sacred character of the ark, and the simple phrase *'ărôn Jahweh, i.e.* 'Jahweh's ark,' would naturally be used.

To this theory the objection may be made that in two passages (1 S 3^{3} and 4^{11}) *'ĕlōhîm* seems to be used as a *possessive* genitive, for an indefinite expression is not to be thought of in 4^{11}, and would scarcely be natural in 3^{3}. But the interchange of *'ĕlōhîm* and *Jahweh* as synonymous names of the Deity is so un-Hebraic that it is scarcely possible to imagine that the text has in these instances come down to us as it left the hands of the original writer. It is noteworthy that the messenger who in 1 S 4^{17} tells Eli the events previously recorded in 4^{11}, says *'ărôn hā-'ĕlōhîm*; it is therefore not impossible that 4^{11} is a late addition by a writer to whom *'ĕlōhîm* and *Jahweh* were interchangeable synonyms. Ch. 3 has undergone considerable editorial modification, for neither the dimness of Eli's eyes nor the fact that the lamp had not yet gone out has anything to do with the theophany to Samuel. In any case we are certainly not justified in setting aside a well-marked rule on the strength of these two passages.

What purpose would such an Ark or chest serve? Strange to say, there is no explicit statement on the subject in any very early passage of the OT, the assertion that the Ark was the receptacle of the Tables of Stone being first found in Dt 10. On the one hand, the oldest documents of the Pentateuch, J and E, in describing the Tables of Stone, make no mention of any receptacle for them; and, on the other, the oldest passages outside the Pentateuch which mention the Ark give no hint that it was regarded as a receptacle for a sacred Law, but imply rather that it was regarded as containing the symbol of Jahweh Himself. Thus, to quote Cheyne, 'the Ark was not a symbol of the revealed Law, but the focus of Divine powers.' The formula given in Nu $10^{35.36}$, and similarly the account of the capture of Jericho, imply that the Ark was regarded as the visible symbol of Jahweh's presence. Still more striking is the narrative of the capture of the Ark by the Philistines. On hearing of its arrival in the camp of Israel, the Philistines exclaim (1 S 4^{8}), 'Who shall deliver us out of the hand of these mighty gods?' and the natural interpretation of 1 S 6^{3} implies the virtual identification of the ark with Jahweh (cf. 6^{14}). Similarly, the language of 2 S 7^{2}, where David's dwelling in a house of cedar is contrasted with the dwelling of the Ark within curtains, appears more natural if the Ark was regarded as localizing the Deity* than if it merely contained the tables of His Law. It is noteworthy also that David's dance before the Ark is described as performed 'before Jahweh' (2 S 6^{14}).

* See Cheyne's art. 'Ark of the Covenant' in *EBi* i. 300.

Professor Cheyne (*EBi* i. 302) considers it probable that in the earlier form of the story of the Tables of the Law, as originally given in JE, the shattered tables were not renewed but whether this be so or not, the uncertainty which prevailed as to the code inscribed on the tables (cf. Ex 34 with Dt 5 and Ex 20), coupled with the absence of any mention in JE that the tables were placed in the Ark, or in any other book that they were ever taken out of it, makes it extremely probable that the statement in Dt 10 is merely an inference drawn by the Deuteronomic writer, who supposed, reasonably enough, that, an empty box being meaningless, the sacredness of the Ark must have been due to the sacred character of its contents. In this connexion, since his religion forbade him to think of any idol, the objects which would naturally occur to his mind would be the sacred Stone Tables.

It has been suggested that the Tables of Stone were originally *bætyls*, possibly meteorites, or, according to Professor G. F. Moore (*EBi* col. 2155), more probably 'a stone from the "mount of God," by taking which with them the Israelites were assured of the presence and protection of Jahweh when they wandered away from His holy mountain.' But of such *portable* stones we have no other example in Israel. Moreover, the difference between *tables*—*i.e.* hewn stones—engraved with a code of laws and *fetish stones* is so great that it is difficult to suppose that the latter could be the only basis for the story of the former. A discussion of the original form of the 'Ten Words' would be out of place in the present article; but it is by no means improbable that in early times the Law of Israel was summed up in ten sayings, and that these sayings were inscribed on two tables. The *form* of the sayings varied from time to time, the Decalogue of Ex 34 being superseded by that of Dt 5, and again by that of Ex 20; but the traditional number, ten, was retained. Since even the Decalogue of Ex 34, with its prohibition of idols, cannot be the earliest code, it is at least possible that subsequently to the reforms of Hezekiah, when the tables containing the earliest code were broken up by the iconoclastic zeal of 'Moses,' two fresh tables were hewn like unto the first, whereon was engraved a Decalogue (viz. that which forms the basis of the Law in Ex 34), similar to that which was on the first tables, but amended in harmony with the growing hatred of images.

But since there is nothing in any early document to connect the Ark with the stone tables, and since, when the first passage which does so connect it (Dt 10) was written, the Ark itself had long disappeared, we may safely disregard this comparatively late tradition, and seek in the earlier writings of the OT some indication of the purpose of the Ark.

There is no mention of the Ark in the inventory of Temple furniture carried off by Nebuchadrezzar—an omission which cannot be due to lack of interest in the Ark, as is evident from Jer 3^{16}; it seems, therefore, necessary to suppose that it had disappeared before the destruction of the Temple. But, such being the case, we cannot but inquire the cause of its disappearance. It may, indeed, have been carried off in one of the invasions of Jerusalem, such as that of Shishak (1 K $14^{25f.}$), or of Hazael (2 K $12^{17f.}$), or of Sennacherib. But, great as are the gaps in the historical records of the OT, it is difficult to account for such an omission. The omission of the account of the destruction of the Temple at Shiloh is not quite parallel; for the editor who incorporated in his book an account of the capture of the Ark may have deemed it unnecessary to describe what, in his eyes, must assuredly have been of less importance, viz. the destruction of the sanctuary which had contained the Ark. At any rate, considering the fairly consistent tradition concerning the Ark in the books of Samuel and Kings down to the time of its deposition in the Temple of Solomon, and the utter absence of any mention of it thereafter till the 7th cent. references in J and E, which seem to imply that the exact nature, at all events, of its contents had been forgotten, we may fairly argue that it had disappeared in the interval, for it is surely unnecessary to assume a 'pious fiction' on the part of the Deuteronomic writer.

The precise description of the Ark given in the Priestly Code is not a proof that any of the sons of Zadok who were carried captive to Babylon had actually seen it. At the same time, there is no difficulty in believing that tradition had preserved a general description of its form, which was eventually idealized in the same manner as the Tabernacle itself and its furniture.

Attention has already been drawn to the fact that the early references to the Ark imply that it contained some symbol of Jahweh, and it is now

* The phrase יֹשֵׁב הַכְּרוּבִים (*e.g.* 1 S 4^{4}) suggests that the Ark was regarded as being in some way the abode or throne of God.

freely admitted that idol images of Jahweh were formerly common in Israel. It is natural, therefore, to regard the Ark as the portable shrine or receptacle of some such image, which upon this supposition must have been deposited by Solomon in the Temple of Jerusalem.* Have we any indication of the existence of such an image? The golden calves are not to be thought of, for there is no evidence that Jahweh was ever worshipped under this form among the Leah tribes; since it must be remembered that the original image at Dan, if it really was in the form of a calf—which is doubtful—was made not by Jonathan the Levite, but by Micah the Ephraimite.

But at Jerusalem there was an image of Jahweh to which sacrifice was offered, viz. the bronze seraph, or, to call it by the name by which it is generally known, the brazen serpent, which in the age of Hezekiah was believed to have been made by Moses (2 K 18^{4}; cf. Nu $21^{8.9}$), and may therefore be supposed to have been as old as the Ark. It is therefore a not unlikely inference that it was for this image that the Ark was made. It is noteworthy that these are the only two objects, traditionally connected with the worship of Israel in the wilderness, of the existence of which there is any evidence in the period of the Kings.† The traditions which assigned the making of the first golden calf and the brazen serpent to Aaron and Moses respectively are of the utmost importance; for the fact that the essential part of these traditions—viz. that images were made—survived even the iconoclastic commandments shows how deeply rooted must have been the traditions themselves. And if, as will be generally admitted nowadays, the narrative of Nu $21^{8.9}$ is the attempt of a later age to explain the origin of an object which seemed inconsistent with its iconoclastic law, and if the brazen serpent really was an image coming down from the time of Moses, or at least from the days of the Israelite conquest of Palestine, it is reasonable to suppose that the history of the brazen serpent was identical with the history of the Ark. But if the brazen serpent really existed in such an early period of Israelitish history (and both Nu $21^{8.9}$ and 2 K 18^{4} agree in this respect), it must either have been carried off by the Philistines with the Ark or have been preserved by the priests who fled from Shiloh to Nob.‡ Of the latter alternative there is not the slightest hint; and it would have been strange if David had celebrated so joyfully the recovery of the Ark, and had disregarded an image which to subsequent ages, and presumably to David's own age, was an object of adoration.

If, as seems probable, we are right in concluding that the Ark and the brazen serpent shared the same vicissitudes, or, in other words, that the Ark *contained* the brazen serpent, we are at once able to explain both the existence of the latter in the days of Hezekiah, and the veneration shown to the former in the narratives of Joshua, Samuel, and Kings. And if the iconoclastic zeal of the reforming party in the days of Hezekiah destroyed the brazen serpent, the Ark, if this was the shrine of the serpent, would have shared the same fate.

Objection may perhaps be made to this theory, on the ground, first, that the narrative of Nu 21 implies an image which could not have been contained in the Ark; and, secondly, that it is the Ark itself which is always spoken of as sacred, no reference being made to its contents.

In answer to the first objection, it is sufficient to say that the conventional representation of the brazen serpent as twined about a pole is not necessitated by the language of Nu $21^{8.9}$, which merely states that, in order that the serpent might be visible, it was placed upon a standard (*nēs*, which is not necessarily a 'pole'; in Ex 17^{15} it is used of an altar).

The second objection appears more serious; but when we remember the awe with which serpents in general, and the brazen serpent in particular, were regarded, it is by no means unlikely that men spoke of the Ark because they shrank from mentioning the sacred object within it.

But the question may still be asked, Why should a box have been necessary at all, since there existed a tent in which to keep the idol? In the case of a large image (and the writer of 1 S $19^{13\text{ff.}}$ evidently thought of the *teraphim* as being the size of a man), a box would perhaps not have been necessary, though it might have been convenient for carrying the image about in time of war; moreover, the size of the Ark, of which the later tradition gives the dimensions as $2\frac{1}{2} \times 1\frac{1}{2} \times 1\frac{1}{2}$ cubits, would have been unsuitable to such an image. A comparatively small object, however, such as we must suppose the brazen serpent to have been, would certainly have needed some sort of case to preserve it when being carried about. But it is not improbable that the origin of the Ark may be due to another cause. The worship of a brazen serpent doubtless had its origin in the worship of a living serpent, for which some sort of receptacle would, of course, have been necessary. The conservatism of religious ritual would preserve this, even after the substitution of a metal serpent for a live one.

It is not necessary to suppose that a live serpent was reverenced in the time of Moses. The substitution of the metal image for so primitive a god may have taken place long before the age of Moses. There are, however, parallels which seem to point in this direction. Thus, on an amphora in the British Museum (*B. M. Cat.* E 418) there is a representation of the story of Erichthonios, which is reproduced by J. E. Harrison (*Prolegomena to the Study of Greek Religion*, 1903, p. 133): 'The sacred chest stands on rude piled stones that represent the rock of the Acropolis, the child rises up with outstretched hand, Athene looks on in dismay and anger, and the bad sisters hurry away. Erichthonios is here a human child with two great snakes for guardians, but what the sisters really found, what the maidens really carried, was a snake and symbols like a snake.' Additional evidence for the same practice of carrying snakes in sacred chests is to be found in the class of coins known as *cistophoroi*, of which a representation is given by J. E. Harrison (*Prolegomena*, p. 400).

For the existence of snake-worship in Palestine, there was, until recently, no evidence apart from the OT. But in 1903 Mr. R. A. Stewart Macalister, in the course of his excavations at the Canaanite 'High Place' of Gezer, came across a circular structure '13 feet 8 inches in diameter at the floor level . . . surrounded by a rude wall now standing to a maximum height of 6 feet.' Within this structure, among a number of broken pieces of pottery, there 'was found a small bronze model of a cobra, rudely but unmistakably portrayed' (see 'Report on the Excavation of Gezer,' *PEFSt*, July 1903, p. 222). Although the discovery at Gezer did not include anything of the nature of an ark, it is not impossible that it may throw light on the *raison d'être* of the *prototype* of the Ark. Mr. Macalister's discussion of the place of the discovery is so suggestive that it may be quoted *in extenso*. 'The structure in which the serpent was found completely puzzled me, but an ingenious suggestion was made by Mr. J. Stogdon, of Harrow, when on a visit to the excavations—namely, that it was possibly a pit for keeping live serpents. The building is as suitable for such a purpose as the pits in which bears and other animals are kept in a modern zoological garden. In such a case the fine broken pottery and the bronze model might be in the nature of votive offerings. We are reminded of the practice of keeping live snakes at certain Greek shrines, notably at the temple of Æsculapius at Epidaurus, where they were in some way instrumental in effecting the miracles of healing there wrought (see Rouse, *Greek Votive Offerings*, pp. 193–205; see also p. 209). It is not inconceivable that among the orgies or rites which were celebrated in the high places of Palestine some form of snake-charming was included, and that the snakes required for the purpose were kept in this enclosure—perhaps specially prepared poisonous serpents with the fangs extracted. The tricks of modern holy men with serpents, which, if I be not mistaken, were described by Mr. Baldensperger in the *Quarterly Statement* some years ago, may be a survival of such rites' (*PEFSt*, July 1903, p. 223).

It is possible, however, that objection may be made to the view here put forth, that the Ark contained the bronze serpent, on the ground that the method of carrying the Ark is at variance

* On the other hand, it is urged by Schwally (*Semit. Kriegsaltertümer*, p. 10) that it is not necessary to suppose that the Ark contained anything.

† The mention of the holy vessels and the tables of stone in 1 K $8^{4.9}$ is due to the Deuteronomic editor.

‡ The only other alternative is to regard the brazen serpent as a distinctively Judæan idol, which existed in Judah long before David gained possession of the Ark. It is, however, to be noted that the story of the making of the brazen serpent is plausibly assigned to the Ephraimite writer E (see Carpenter and Battersby, *Hexateuch*, vol. ii. p. 222), while the reference to the Ark in Nu 14^{44} appears in its original form to belong to J.

with any such supposition. It is a safe inference from 1 S $6^{7ff.}$, 2 S $6^{3ff.}$ that the recognized method of carrying the Ark in early times was in a sacred cart (*i.e.* a cart that had been used for no other purpose) drawn by cows or bulls.* The use of horned cattle might possibly denote that the Ark was in some way connected with lunar worship; in any case, however, they probably imply that the god contained in the Ark was regarded as the god of fertility (see Frazer, *Adonis, Attis, Osiris*, pp. 46, 80).† At first sight it is difficult to suppose that a serpent could ever be regarded as a god of fertility, but whatever the origin of serpent-worship may be—and we need not assume that it has been everywhere identical—there can be little doubt that in some cases, at all events, it is celebrated with a view of ensuring fertility thereby. On this point the statement of the scholiast on the *Hetairæ* of Lucian, quoted by J. E. Harrison (*Prolegomena to the Study of Greek Religion*, pp. 121, 122), is very suggestive: *ἀναφέρονται δὲ κἀνταῦθα ἄρρητα ἱερὰ ἐκ στέατος τοῦ σίτου κατεσκευασμένα, μιμήματα δρακόντων καὶ ἀνδρῶν σχημάτων.*

But whether the view here advocated that the Ark of Israel originally contained the brazen serpent be correct or not, it is at any rate certain that the Ark was the shrine or feretory of some object which symbolized Jahweh to His worshippers. On this point the evidence which we possess concerning similar arks among other peoples is conclusive (cf. Schwally, *Semit. Kriegsaltertümer*, p. 10). And as the sacred object was certainly not in every case a live serpent, we naturally inquire why it should be placed in a box, and not rather set on a pedestal or throne in a temple. The answer to this question is to be found in the conception of the god which prevails among primitive peoples, in whose minds the fetish or image is so identified with the spirit which is supposed to animate it that the two are indistinguishable. In times of need or danger man requires a god that is near, and not a god that is far off. It is by no means a primitive conception which we find in the dedicatory prayer put into the mouth of Solomon (1 K $8^{44f.}$), that, if people go out to battle against their enemy, and they pray to their God towards the house which is built to His name, He will make their prayer and supplication heard to the heaven in which He really dwells.* Primitive warriors wanted to have their gods in their midst. Of what use was the Divine Father (see Nu 21^{29}) at home, when his sons were in danger in the field? It was but natural, therefore, that the gods should be carried out wherever their help was needed (2 S 5^{21}; cf. Polyb., VII. ix. 2; Schwally, *op. cit.* p. 9).

Man is slow to give up idolatry. In the course of the ages, indeed, he modifies his primitive conceptions of God; the inanimate fetish gives place to the bestial form, and this again to an anthropomorphic representation, tending more and more towards the spiritual. But the truly spiritual conception of God, enunciated alike by the prophet Jeremiah ($23^{23.\,24}$) and by our Lord (Jn $4^{21.\,24}$), which is incompatible with local presence, seems ever to have been beyond the comprehension of the majority of mankind. Jeremiah's warning (3^{16}) has been disregarded even by those who have called themselves Christians. At any rate, in the minds of many ignorant folk, the place of the gods of heathenism has been taken by the Saints, and the shrines containing relics of these have been venerated as being virtually dwelling-places of divinity. Between the mediæval reliance on the protection afforded by holy relics and the primitive Israelite trust in the Ark, there is but little real difference. In theory the mediæval Christian denied that his shrine contained a god, but his practice too often gave the lie to his theory.

R. H. KENNETT.

* The idea that the Ark could legitimately be carried only by hand may have arisen from the fact that it was so carried into Zion (2 S $6^{13ff.}$). There is no mention on that occasion of any priest other than the king himself. The account of the carrying of the Ark in the Book of Joshua belongs to a later development of the religion of Israel.

† A moon god and a god of fertility are not, however, incompatible conceptions (see Frazer, *Adonis, Attis, Osiris*, p. 297 ff. and cf. Dt 33^{14}).

* The phrase וְשָׁמַעְתָּ הַשָּׁמַיִם אֶת־תְּפִלָּתָם וגו׳ has long been a crux to grammarians. We venture to emend the passage by pointing וְשִׁמַּעְתָּ (as *Pi'el*), and understand הַשָּׁמַיִם as the accusative of direction (cf. v. 30). The writer believes, like the prophet of Is 66^{1}, that 'heaven is God's throne,' but trusts that the prayers offered at the earthly sanctuary will be, as it were, made audible by the Lord at His heavenly throne. The quaintness of the expression is due to the writer's attempt to combine the phraseology of more primitive religion with his own spiritual faith.

ARMENIA.

ARMENIA (Vannic).—The present article deals with Proto-Armenian religion as revealed in the Vannic or 'Khaldian' cuneiform inscriptions. The Indo-European Armenians, who are described by Herodotus (vii. 73) and Eudoxus (*ap.* Steph. Byz. *s.v.* Ἀρμενία) as immigrants from Phrygia, did not become masters of the Armenian highlands till the close of the 7th cent. B.C. Kretschmer (*Einleit. in die Gesch. der griech. Sprache,* pp. 209–11) brings them from Ormenion in Thessaly by way of Armenê, near Sinôpê (cf. Hirt, *Die Indogermanen*, 136; Prášek, *Gesch. der Meder und Perser*, i. 147). The name Armenia (Old Pers. *Armina*, New Sus. *Arminiya*) is first met with in the Bab. and Pers. cuneiform inscriptions of the Achæmenian age, and may be connected with the Vannic *armani*, 'written tablet.' The country had been previously known to its southern neighbours as *Urarṭu* (Heb. *Ararat*), which the Babylonian scribes explained as a compound of *Ura-Urṭu* or 'Highlands.' *Urṭu* is the name of the district near Lake Erivan in a Vannic inscription of Sarduris II. (Sayce, lxxxii. 6), though in the bilingual inscription of Topzawa *Urarṭu* is the Assyr. representative of the Vannic *Lulus*. The usual title assumed by the Vannic princes was 'king of Biainas' or 'Bianas,' the district in which their capital Ṭuspas (Tosp), the modern Van, was situated. Biainas is the Buana of Ptolemy (v. 13), now Van.

The Vannic inscriptions, which extend from about B.C. 840 to 640, are written in the cuneiform characters of Nineveh, but in a language which is neither Indo-European nor Semitic, and is believed by some scholars to be related to Georgian. It seems to have been spoken over the larger part of the later Armenia, and to have been connected with that of Mitanni in Northern Mesopotamia. Like the language, the religion of the Vannic population was peculiar, and is difficult to correlate with that of any other people.

At the head of the pantheon was Khaldis, whose children the Vannic kings and people regarded themselves as being in a special sense. Hence they called themselves 'the Khaldians,' a name also applied to the numerous local deities who were 'children of Khaldis.' But though Khaldis was the national god, he could be localized like the Semitic Baal, and we hear of a 'Khaldis of the north (?)' and a 'Khaldis of the south (?),' while a dedication is sometimes addressed to 'all the Khaldis-gods.' Along with two other divinities, Teisbas the Air-god (Assyr. Hadad-Ramman) and Ardinis the Sun-god, Khaldis was the member of a triad which occupied the supreme place in the

Vannic divine hierarchy, and the conception of which may have been borrowed from Babylonia. Below the triad came the multitudinous deities of inferior rank, including even the 'Khaldis-gods,' or local forms of Khaldis. A long list of these, with the offerings to be made to them, is engraved on a rock called Meher Kapussi, two miles east of Van (Sayce, v.). Among them is Selardis the Moon-god, as well as the gods of various cities and countries incorporated into the Vannic kingdom by conquest or otherwise. Most of these deities were merely deified States, and consequently had no individual names of their own; it was only when they were within the limits of the district originally inhabited by the tribe whose supreme god was Khaldis that they properly became forms of the national god, and could be called 'Khaldians.' As the Vannic kingdom extended, however, and the idea of a common nationality grew stronger, the deified State, even if originally outside 'the land of Khaldis,' tended to pass into a Khaldis; thus the deity called at Meher Kapussi 'the god of the city of Ardinis' (the Muzazir of the Assyrians), became, a century later, in the time of Sargon, himself a 'Khaldis.' Only one goddess is mentioned in the inscriptions, and since her name, Saris, seems to have been borrowed from the Assyrian Ištar, it is possible that she was of foreign origin. The later (Armenian) legends which bring Semiramis into the plain of Van are possibly an echo of the fact.

How far Vannic religion, as it comes before us in the inscriptions, may have been influenced by Assyria or Babylonia it is impossible to say. Teisbas, however, who was afterwards united into a triad with Khaldis and the Sun-god, appears originally to have been the god of a tribe or nationality which was distinct from that of the Vannic 'Khaldians,' while among the neighbouring Hittites each city had its Sun-god, who was identified with the deified State. The conception of gods in the Assyro-Babylonian sense may have been due primarily to contact with the cultured lands of the south, like the titles 'lord of multitudes' and 'faithful shepherd of mankind' given to Khaldis. At all events, underneath the divine hierarchy of the official cult we find clear traces of an earlier phase of belief, in which the material fetish takes the place of the god. Sacrifices were made not only to Khaldis and his brother deities, but also to 'the gate of the land of Khaldis,' 'the gate of Teisbas in the city of Eridias,' 'the gate of the Sun-god in the city of Uisis'—all of which are carefully distinguished from 'the Khaldis-gods of the door' or 'the Khaldis-gods of the chapel'—as well as to 'the shields of the land of Khaldis,' and even to 'the foot-soldiers of the land of Khaldis' and 'the foot-soldiers of Teisbas' (Sayce, v. 13). These foot-soldiers were the temple-guards, armed priests, and attendants, who were called Seluians, Urbikans, etc. A prominent object of veneration was the vine, the sacred tree of the Vannic people, which was sometimes planted by the side of the temple of Khaldis (*ib.* v. 30, 31, lxxxvi. 10), sometimes in a sacred enclosure of its own. Sar-duris II., in one of his inscriptions (*ib.* li.), describes his endowment of one of these vines, which he had consecrated and named after himself on the north shore of the lake of Van. The vine was often planted in the middle of a garden which was attached to the temple. Spears and shields, specimens of which from Toprak Kaleh are now in the British Museum, were hung up on either side of the entrance to the temple, large basins of bronze or terra-cotta, on stands, being placed in front of the shrine for the purpose of ablution.

The endowments made to the temples usually took the form of provision for the sacrifices and offerings, which were numerous and plentiful. The great inscription of Meher Kapussi gives a long list of the sacrifices to be offered to each deity and sacred object recognized in the vicinity, on every day of the month. Thus 6 lambs were to be offered to the Vannic triad, 17 oxen and 34 sheep to Khaldis, 6 oxen and 12 sheep to Teisbas, 4 oxen and 8 sheep to the Sun-god, 1 ox and 2 sheep to the gate of the land of Khaldis, 2 oxen and 4 sheep to the foot-soldiers of the land of Khaldis. Libations of wine were also to be poured out, the wine being made, it would seem, from the fruit of the consecrated vines. Comparatively few, however, of the vast herds of oxen and sheep presented to the gods could actually have been offered in sacrifice; according to the inscription of Kelishin (Sayce, lvi.), when 'the gate of the land of Khaldis' was dedicated to Khaldis, 112 oxen, 9020 sucklings and lambs, and 12,490 sheep were presented to the god. Most of these must have been intended to serve as a source of income. Similarly the prisoners who were devoted to Khaldis would have been given as temple slaves. In the case of victory, the share of the god, we are told, was a sixtieth of the spoil (*ib.* xliii. 16). The temples, of which there were several varieties, probably possessed festival halls, since we hear of sacred feasts in honour of the gods.

LITERATURE.—Sayce, 'The Cuneiform Inscriptions of Van Deciphered and Translated,' in *JRAS*, 1882, 1888, 1893, 1894, 1901, 1906; C. F. Lehmann, *SBAW* xxix., 1900; Belck and Messerschmidt, *Anatole*, i., 1904. For the history of the kingdom of Ararat and the Khaldi see Prášek, *Gesch. der Meder und Perser* (Gotha, 1906), 54.

A. H. SAYCE.

ARMENIA (Zoroastrian).—The sources of our information for the earlier epoch of Armenia's religious history are the Urartic or Vannic inscriptions (see preceding art.). For the Indo-Germanic period down to Christian times the most important native sources are Agathangelos (5th cent., ed. Venice, 1862), Moses of Chorene's *History and Geography of Armenia* (5th cent., ed. Venice, 1865), Faustus of Byzantium (5th cent., ed. Venice, 1889), Eznik (5th cent., ed. Venice, 1826), Anania Shiragaçi, (7th cent., ed. Patkanean, St. Petersburg, 1877), and (for names) the ancient Armenian version of the OT. We also gather short but valuable notices from Xenophon's *Anabasis*, Strabo's *Geography*, and the works of Dio Cassius, Pliny, and Tacitus. Considerable as the material is, it is but incidental to the main purpose of these ancient authors, and is, therefore, very fragmentary. We may, however, hope for important additions to our knowledge of Zoroastrianism in early Armenia from the critical study of Armenian folk-lore and popular superstitions, when enough shall have been collected for the purpose.

Originally there was nothing in common between the Iranian races and the ancient inhabitants of Armenia, who were probably connected with the Hittites in the West and the Caucasic races of the North (Jensen, *Hittiter und Armenier*, Strassburg, 1898; Messerschmidt, *Die Hittiter*², Leipzig, 1902, p. 10; Winckler, 'Westasien' in Helmolt's *Weltgeschichte*, Leipzig, 1901, iii. 125 ff.; Hommel, *Grundriss der Geog. und Gesch. des alten Orients*, Munich, 1904, pp. 37 ff.; Prášek, *Gesch. der Meder und Perser*, Gotha, 1906, i. 57, 65). But Armenia, owing to its geographical position, was destined to come into contact with Iranian politics and civilization when the Medes began their political career. Towards the end of the 7th cent. B.C. the Vannic, or Khaldian, kingdom (see preceding art.) fell before the invading hordes of Cimmerians and Scythians, and during this period of anarchy the Armenians seem also to have entered the country which was henceforth to bear their name (Hirt, *Die Indogermanen*, Strassburg, 1905–07, p. 138). Meanwhile the Medes had begun their national career not long before 935 B.C. (Justi, 'Gesch. Irans' in Geiger-Kuhn's *Grundriss der iran. Philologie*, Strassburg, 1904, ii. 404–406), and the Median empire had been founded, probably in 678–677 B.C. (Prášek, *op. cit.* i. 108). From that time Iranian influence was strongly felt in the politics, language, and social organization of Armenia, and the Iranian religion, with its terminology, names of divinities, and many folk-beliefs, permeated Armenian paganism. How far the resultant religion may be treated as Zoroastrianism will become clear from a more detailed study of the material available, which may most conveniently be arranged under the main rubrics of Zoroastrian theology.

I. *CELESTIAL HOSTS.*—**1. Ahura Mazda.**—The chief deity of ancient Armenia was Aramazd, the Zoroastrian Ahura Mazda (see ORMAZD). In Agathangelos, the historian of the conversion of Armenia, King Tiridates calls him 'the maker of heaven and earth; father of all the gods, especially of Anahit, Mihr, and Nanē; giver of abundance and fatness' (Agathangelos, pp. 58, 61, 106, 590, 591, 593); while Moses of Chorene incidentally remarks: 'There is no such thing as Aramazd; but among those who would be Aramazd, there are four who bear the name, and one of them is Kund Aramazd' (*Hist. of Armenia*, i. 31). It is uncertain whether this refers to the Greek Zeus or to the Iranian Ahura Mazda. In the first case it might mean 'the bald (φαλακρός) Zeus'; in the second, *kund* might be translated 'brave,' 'strong' (Stepané's modern Armenian translation of Moses of Chorene, p. 395). In fact, 'great' and 'brave,' or 'strong,' are frequent epithets of the Armenian Ahura Mazda (Agathangelos, pp. 52, 61, 106).* The name *Aramazd* reminds us of the *Auramazdā* of the Old Pers. inscriptions, rather than of the Avesta or Pahlavi forms *Ahura Mazda* or *Aūharmazd*, *Ohrmazd* (cf. Armen. *Ormizd*). There is another important passage in Agathangelos (p. 623) about Aramazd, which may be tentatively translated thus: 'In the season of the god of the New Year, (who is) the bringer of new fruits, of the festivities of the hospitable god.'

The later Greek translation reads: *καὶ τὰ μνημόσυνα τῶν ἐνεχθέντων ἔταξεν εἰς τὴν μεγάλην πανήγυριν τῆς λεγομένης Διαπομπῆς, τῆς ματαίως εἰς τιμὴν τῶν παλαιῶν σεβασμάτων γενομένης ἀπὸ τῶν καιρῶν τῶν νέων εἰς τὰς ἀπαρχὰς τῶν καρπῶν, ξενοδέκτων θεῶν λεγομένης τῆς πανηγύρεως, ἣν ἐπιτελοῦσιν ἐν τῷ τόπῳ ἐκείνῳ εὐφραντικῶς ἀπὸ τῶν ἀρχαίων καιρῶν ἐν ἡμέρᾳ τῆς πληρώσεως τοῦ ἐνιαυτοῦ*, 'And he ordered the commemoration of the (saints) brought in on the great feast of the so-called Diapompe, which was vainly held in honour of the ancient gods from the new seasons unto the first fruits, this being the festival called that of the hospitable gods [mistranslation of *dik'*, 'god'], which they joyfully celebrate in that place from olden times, on the last day of the year.'

This translation shows that the Gr. supposes a different, but none the less obscure, Armen. recension. The text must have become corrupt in early times, and yet St. Clair-Tisdall (*Conversion of Armenia to the Christian Faith*, London, 1896, p. 50) sees in it a new deity Amenabeλ, who had for a title Amanor ('New Year'). Others recognized Vanatur, 'hospitable,' as a separate deity, and explained it as 'deus hospitalis' (Gelzer, *Zur Armen. Götterlehre*,† pp. 133, 146) or 'Lord of Van' (Hommel, *op. cit.* p. 39). Moses of Chorene, however, in his allusion to this festival (ii. 66), treats *Amanor* simply as a common noun; nor does anything in the text of Agathangelos as it stands, either here or elsewhere, make it necessary to take either Amanor or Amenabeλ as the name of a deity. As for Vanatur, the only other time we find it mentioned (Armen. tr. of 2 Mac 6^2 LXX, Διὸς Ξενίου, Vulg. *Iovis hospitalis*), it is used as an adjective qualifying Aramazd. We can, therefore, fairly infer that it is simply the Greek Ζεὺς Ξένιος (see also Alishan, *Ancient Faith of the Armenians*, Venice, 1895, p. 256), whose functions were transferred to Aramazd under the Hellenizing influence of the Seljuks, or of Tigranes the Great and his successors. Very probably the festival of Amanor or Navasard, which is poetically described as a *fête champêtre* (Grigor Magistros), was celebrated in honour of Aramazd, who was the lord of the New Year, quite as the six days' celebration of the Zoroastrian New Year began on the day Aūharmazd of the month Fravaṛtīn in honour of the creation of the world in six days by Ahura Mazda (Mar. 15; cf. al-Bīrūnī, *op. cit.* pp. 199–204). Navasard fell, according to the later calendar of pagan Armenia, in August, when the new fruits began to be gathered; and the Armenians still perpetuate the memory of this early autumn celebration by distributing and eating fruits on New Year's day.

The most prominent sanctuaries of Aramazd were in the ancient city of Ani in Daranali, the burial-place of the Armenian kings (Agathangelos, p. 590), as well as in the village of Bagavan in Bagravand (*ib.* p. 612), and on Mount Paλat or Pashat ('The coming of the Rhipsimean Virgins' in Alishan's *Hayapatum*, Venice, 1901–02, p. 79).

It is not easy to determine what the Armenians understood by the fatherhood of Aramazd, as no goddess is mentioned as his consort, not even Spandaramet. It is through sheer ignorance that a late martyrology (quoted by Alishan, *Ancient Faith*, p. 260) calls Anahit the wife of Aramazd, she being rather his daughter (see below). The fatherhood of Ahura Mazda, however, is not altogether foreign even to the Avesta, which represents him as both the father and the husband of Spenta Armaiti (*Yasna* xlv. 4, xxxiv. 10; *Yasht* xvii. 16), as well as the husband of other female divinities (according to the Pahlavi commentary on *Vendīdād* xi. 5, of the Fravashis; cf. also *Yasna* xxxviii. 1; *Visparad* iii. 4), and the parent of Asha Vahishta (*Yasna* xlvii. 2), Sraosha, Rashnu, Mithra Ashi (*Yasht* xvii. 16), Atarsh (*Yasna* xxxvi. 3, etc.), Haoma (*Yasna* xi. 2), and, indeed, of all the Amesha Spentas (*Yasht* xvii. 2). On the whole, one may affirm that the Armenian Aramazd agrees quite well, in the little that we know about him, with the Avesta Ahura Mazda. In the Armenian of the 5th cent. *Ormizd*, the variant form of Aramazd, generally refers to the later form of the Zoroastrian Ahura Mazda; but the adjective *Ormzdakan*, 'Ormazdian,' may also have been used in reference to the Armenian Aramazd and the Greek Zeus.

2. Amesha Spentas.—Of these Zoroastrian archangels (see art. AMESHA SPENTAS), only Spenta Armaiti is unmistakably present in the Armenian pantheon. Her name appears in two forms, *Spandaramet* and *Sandaramet*, with a difference of meaning, the latter term denoting 'abyss,' 'Hades' (cf. Hübschmann, *Armen. Gram.*, Strassburg, 1897, i. 73–74); but *Spandaramet* never occurs in the abstract theological meaning that the Avesta attached to the Indo-Iranian spirit of the earth and the keeper of vineyards (cf. the Pahlavi *Shāyast-lā-Shāyast*, xv. 5; Gray, *ARW* vii. 364–371). It is owing to this latter function of Spenta Armaiti, however, that the Armenian Christian writers of the 5th cent. used her name to translate Διόνυσος in 2 Mac 6^7, although, by a strange inconsistency, they translated the same name by *Ormzdakan gad*, 'Ormazdian,' in 2 Mac 14^{33} and 3 Mac 2^{29}. *Spandaramet* in the form of *Sandaramet*, as already noted, came to be a synonym of Hades, and was very frequently referred to in theological books and in the Church

* Cf. such common Avesta epithets of Ahura Mazda as *mazišta* ('most great'), '*sevišta* ('most mighty'); *e.g.* *Yasna* xvi. 1.

† *Berichte der. könig. sächs. gesellsch. der Wissensch. phil.-hist. Classe*, 1896, pp. 99–148.

hymnary. This sense is not altogether foreign to the Avesta itself, where, from being the genius of the earth, Spenta Armaiti gradually becomes the earth itself, with the dark, woeful under world. 'The darkness of Spenta Armaiti' (*Vendīdād* iii. 35) is a well-known expression of the Avesta, which has this in common with the Bab. cosmology, that the earth is also identical with the Hades which it contains, and that the powers of Hades have something to do with the fertility of the ground and with agriculture (Jeremias, *Hölle und Paradies bei den Babyloniern*, Leipzig, 1900, p. 19; for references to Spandaramet see Lagarde's *Purim*, Göttingen, 1887, p. 42).

Besides Spandaramet, we probably see the traces of the Amesha Spentas Haurvatāt and Ameretāt ('health' and 'immortality') in the Armenian *haurotmaurot*, the name of a flower (*hyacinthus racemosus Dodonei*), first mentioned by Agathangelos, p. 480 (cf. Abeghian, *Armen. Volksglaube*, pp. 62–63).

In the Qur'ān, ii. 96, Hārūt and Mārūt are mentioned as the names of two angels in Babel, who, according to Muslim tradition, having shown themselves impatient with human sinfulness, were sent down to earth by God to assume human flesh and to live in human circumstances. They could not, however, resist the temptations of lust, and were condemned to stay on earth, where they thereafter taught witchcraft. In the Arabic story of Bulūqyā, incorporated with the story of Ḥasīb Karīm-ad-Dīn in the *Arabian Nights* (tr. Payne, v. 72–73; cf. Horovitz in *ZDMG* lv. 523), Ḫillīt and Millīt, or, in Tha'labi's *Qiṣāṣ al-Anbiyā*, Jiblīt and Timlīt, are mentioned as the first inhabitants of hell. Burton and Eb. Nestle (*ZDMG* lv. 692) identify these with Hārūt and Mārūt, which have long been recognized as the Pahlavi Horvadaṯ (or Khūrdāṯ) and Amerōdaṯ (or Amūrdaṯ), or the Avesta Haurvatāt and Ameretāt. The Muhammadan legend in regard to these fallen angels has many parallels in Rabbinical literature, and the whole is, ultimately, a Rabbinical elaboration of the intermarriage of the sons of God and the daughters of men (Gn 6[4]; cf. Geiger, *Was hat Mohammed aus dem Judenthume aufgenommen?* Bonn, 1834, pp. 105–106; Hirsch in *JE* v. 333). How the Zoroastrian archangels were drawn into this Rabbinical legend of the Qur'ān, and by what curious accident, instead of the later Pahlavi forms, we have *Hārūt* and *Mārūt*, which find their parallel only in the Armenian name of a flower, is very problematical. Either *Hārūt* and *Mārūt* are Parthian, or even Syrian, corruptions of the archangels' names, and found their way both to Armenia and Arabia, or they are purely Armenian forms, and reached Muhammad from the north. At all events, Hārūt and Mārūt were not remembered in Armenia as angels. We know, on the other hand, that the two Zoroastrian archangels in question were protectors of the vegetable world (Darmesteter, *Haurvatât et Ameretât*, Paris, 1875, *passim*), and two flowers were respectively consecrated to them—the lily and the *camba* (*Bundahishn*, xxvii. 24; perhaps the *Michelia Champaca*, or Champak); so that Haurvatāt and Ameretāt may once have been known in Armenia as tutelary deities of plants.

According to Strabo (p. 512), Omanos (Vohu Manah) and Anadatus (Ameretāt), with Anaïtis (Anāhita) as a chief deity, formed a triad in Zela—a cult which has not yet entirely disappeared (Gelzer, *ZÄ*, 1875, 14 ff.). This peculiar cult, however, had probably spread northward from Cappadocia, where there was a purer type of Mazdaism than in Armenia (Cumont, *Les mystères de Mithra*[2], Brussels, 1902, ch. i.).

3. Yazatas.—The Zoroastrian *yazatas*, or angels, are better represented in the Armenian religion than the Amesha Spentas. We shall discuss them in the order adopted by Jackson in *Grundriss der iran. Philologie*, ii. 640–645.

(1) *Atar, or fire.*—We cannot tell whether fire-worship was a part of the ancient cult of the Urarṭian period, or was first introduced in Iranian times. Moses of Chorene (ii. 77) mentions a fire-altar in Bagavan, upon which Ardashir, after the conquest of Armenia,* commanded that the fire of Ormazd be kept unquenched. Anania Shiragaçi, in his discourse on the Cross, speaks of a *hurbak* in Armenia, which Hübschmann (*Armen. Gram.* i. 181) rightly interprets as a loan-word from the Pahlavi *frōbāg* (Avesta **hvarenō-baγa*, '[fire of] divine glory'), a fire established, according to Iranian tradition, in Chorasmia, and later removed to Kabul (*Bundahishn*, xvii. 5–6). In the hagiography called the 'Coming of the Rhipsimean Virgins' (Alishan, *Hayapatum*, p. 79), wrongly ascribed to Moses of Chorene, we read that on the top of Mount Paλat (?) there was a house of Aramazd and Astλik (Venus), and on a lower peak, to the south-east, there was 'a house of fire, of insatiable fire, the god of incessant combustion.' At the foot of the mountain, moreover, there was a mighty spring. The place was called Buth. 'They burnt the Sister Fire and the Brother Spring.* In the caves of the rocks dwelt two dragons, devilish and black, to which young men and young virgins were sacrificed. And the devils, gladdened by this bloodshed, produced, by means of the altars of the fire and the spring (?), terrible sights, lights, and rolling thunder; and the deep valley was full of snakes and scorpions.' Elsewhere we read: 'Because they called the fire sister, and the spring brother, they did not throw the ashes away, but they wiped them with the tears of the brother' ('Story of the Picture of the Holy Virgin' in Moses of Chorene, *Works*, ed. Venice, 1865).

This form of fire-worship in a volcanic region has hardly anything in common with Zoroastrianism, though we have a true remnant of fire-worship, even in modern times, in the annual bonfire kindled everywhere by Armenians on the festival of Candlemas, or the Purification of the Blessed Virgin Mary (Feb. 13 = 2), when the fire is kindled from a candle on the altar. It is an occasion of rejoicing and good augury. The festival is called in popular language *Tērntaz*, and in the Church calendar the commemoration is called *Tearnedaraǰ*, 'Presentation of the Lord' (Abeghian, *op. cit.* p. 72).

It seems that the ashes of the sacred fire were also honoured, and the Christian writers love to remind their readers of the times when their ancestors were ash-worshippers (Agathangelos, p. 77; Anania Shiragaçi, *Praise of the Cross*, quoted by Alishan, *op. cit.* p. 45 ff.); while Thomas Artsruni applies this name to the Zoroastrians (*Hist.* i. 9–10). Nevertheless, vestiges of ancient fire-worship are still to be found among the Armenians of the interior (Abeghian, *op. cit.* pp. 66–74).

It is quite possible that two types of fire-worship existed among the Armenians—one, older and more primitive, in which fire was a feminine principle, and stood in close association with water, as a masculine principle; the other type similar to the Zoroastrian.

(2) *Water.*—Water was honoured in Armenia as a masculine principle. Many rivers and springs were sacred, and endowed with beneficent virtues. According to Tacitus (*Annals*, vi. 37), the Armenians offered horses as sacrifices to the Euphrates, and divined by its waves and foam. Sacred cities were built around the river Araxes and its tributaries. Even now there are many sacred springs with healing power, and the people always feel a certain veneration towards water in motion.

Transfiguration Sunday in the Armenian Church was amalgamated with an unmistakably pagan water-festival, during which the people amused themselves, as they still do, with throwing water at each other. A similar custom connected with New Year's Day is reported of the Persians (Alishan, *op. cit.* p. 305; al-Bīrūnī, *Chronology*, pp. 199, 203). The Armenian water-day, or feast of the Transfiguration, is called *vardavaṙ*, or 'rose-festival' (from *vard*, 'rose'). It falls in the last days of the year, according to the ancient Armenian calendar (Alishan, *op. cit.* pp. 283, 305).

* Shapur, not Ardashir, actually took possession of Armenia about A.D. 250.

* On water and fire as brother and sister see Abeghian, *op. cit.* p. 67. Lazar of Pharpe says (ed. Venice, p. 203): 'They took the (sacred) brazier and dashed it into the water, as into the bosom of its brother, according to the saying of the false teachers of the Persians.'

The great Zoroastrian water-*yazatas*, however, do not seem to be connected with water-worship in Armenia, even when they have a place in the Armenian pantheon. Of these *yazatas* we perhaps recognize Āpām Napāt in the name of *Npat*, the Νιφάτης of Strabo, a sacred mountain of Bagravand, Npat being also the designation of the 26th day of the Armenian month, which was consecrated to the mountain.

(3) *Anahit.*—This goddess, doubtless an importation from Persia, was the most popular deity of Armenia. In Agathangelos she is called 'the great lady [queen] Anahit, the glory and life-giver of our nation' (p. 51) 'through whom the country of the Armenians exists and has life' (p. 61), and she is 'the mother of sobriety, the benefactress of all mankind, and a daughter of Aramazd' (p. 52). She is invoked, in an edict of Tiridates, to protect and watch over the country (p. 106). She was also called the golden mother (p. 607), and statues of massive gold were consecrated to her (pp. 591, 607), one of which (at Erēz?) was captured by the soldiers of Antony (Pliny, *HN* xxx. 24). With this may be compared the description of Ardvī Sūra Anāhita in the Avesta (especially *Yasht* v. 64, 78, 101–102, 123, 126–129), 'who purifyeth the seed of all males; who purifyeth the wombs of all females for birth; who maketh all females bear with ease; who giveth all females meet (and) timely milk' (*Yasna* lxv. 2 = *Yasht* v. 2), besides multiplying herds and lands (*Yasht* v. i.). Although the Iranian texts nowhere consider her the daughter of Ahura Mazda, she is 'his only water' (*Yasht* v. 5); and the epithet 'golden' of Agathangelos is paralleled by her Avesta attributes, 'laced with gold' (*Yasht* v. 64), 'wearing a golden kerchief' (*ib.* 123), 'with square golden earrings' (*ib.* 127), and 'with a golden diadem' (*ib.* 128; for further details, cf. Windischmann, *Die pers. Anâhita oder Anaïtis*, Munich, 1856). While the sacrifices offered to Anāhita as described in the Avesta (*e.g. Yasht* v. 15, 21) are quite conventional, the Armenians offered her green branches and white heifers (Agathangelos, p. 49). Lucullus (Plutarch, *Lives*) saw in Yashtishat (?) herds of these heifers, which were used only for sacrifices, at all other times 'wandering up and down undisturbed, with the mark of the goddess, a torch, branded on them.' Anahit was sought also in cases of great sickness (Moses of Chorene, ii. 60).

Three elements are to be distinguished in the Avesta Anāhita. She is a planet (Venus), a goddess of the fertilizing waters, and a female deity presiding over the birth and nursing of children, and the increase and maintenance of all things. The Armenian Anahit is pre-eminently a goddess, with no reference to a planet or water. The fact that in Erēz this goddess admitted of obscene forms of worship, such as are generally associated with the orgiastic nature-cults of Asia Minor, must be explained by the proximity of Akilisene to Asia Minor, as well as by the part which the Avesta Anāhita plays in human conception. Strabo says of this special cult (p. 532):

> 'Both the Medes and the Armenians honour all the sacred matters of the Persians; but above everything the Armenians honour Anahit, to whom they erect temples in other places, and specially in Akilisene [Ἐκελεαç]. There they consecrate to her servants, male and female,* and this is not surprising; but the most illustrious men of the nation give to her their virgin daughters, who, according to custom, give themselves up to fornication for a long time near the goddess, after which they are given in marriage, and none thinks it unworthy to live with them.'

We have absolutely no proof, however, that this sacred prostitution was characteristic of the Armenian Anahit throughout the country, especially as native Christian writers do not mention it, although they might have used it to great advantage in their attacks upon the old religion.

* Cf. the male and female temple-prostitutes of the ancient Semites, adopted by the Cappadocians as well as by the Armenians.

Besides the great sanctuary in Akilisene, which was also called the Anahitian district (Dio Cassius, xxxvi. 88), Anahit had temples in Artashat (Artaxata) (Agathangelos, p. 584) and in Yashtishat (p. 606); while a mountain, now difficult to identify, was called the throne of Nahat (Faustus of Byzantium, v. 25), probably owing to the presence of a great sanctuary of the goddess there.

An image of Anahit is said to have existed in the district of the Anzavatzis near the 'Stone of the Blacksmiths,' where, as in Buth, there was a mixed worship of fire and water, along with magical practices (Alishan, *Hayapatum*, p. 50).

The great festival of Anahit was celebrated, according to Alishan (*Ancient Faith*, p. 269), on the 15th of Navasard with processions and rejoicings. The 19th day of every month was also consecrated to her (Tcherpet, 1820, quoted by Alishan, *Ancient Faith*, p. 143).

(4) *Sun and moon.*—Moses of Chorene makes repeated allusions to the worship of the sun and moon in Armenia. In oaths the name of the sun was almost invariably invoked (ii. 19), and there were also altars and images of the sun and moon (ii. 77). Of what type these images were, and how far they were influenced by Syrian sun-worship, we cannot tell. Agathangelos, in the alleged letter of Diocletian to Tiridates, unconsciously bears witness to the Armenian veneration for the sun, moon, and stars (p. 125). But the oldest witness is Xenophon, who notes that the Armenians sacrificed horses to the sun (*Anabasis*, iv. 5. 35; Weber in his *Die kathol. Kirche in Armenien*, Freiburg, 1903, p. 28, understands this ἥλιος as Mithra). The eighth month of the Armenian year and, what is more significant, the first day of every month, were consecrated to the sun and bore its name, while the first day of the Persian month was assigned to Ahuramazda, the eleventh day being given to the sun in the Zoroastrian calendar. The twenty-fourth day of the Armenian month was consecrated to the moon, as was the twelfth in the Avesta system. The Armenians, like the Persians and most of the sun-worshipping peoples of the East, prayed towards the rising sun, a custom which the early Church unconsciously adopted, so that to this day the Armenian churches are built and the Armenian dead are buried toward the east, the west being the abode of the devil (see below). As to the moon, Anania Shiragaçi says in his *Demonstrations* (ed. Patkanean, p. 66): 'The first fathers called her the nurse of the plants,' an idea which has its parallel, and probably its source, in the short *Māh-yasht* of the Avesta, particularly in that vegetation grows best in the time of the waxing moon (*Yasht* vii. 4; al-Bīrūnī, *Chronology*, p. 219). Ohan Mantaguni (5th cent.) combats the general belief that the moon prospers or mars the plants (*Discourses*, Venice, 1860, pp. 198–199). The Armenians also shared the superstitions about the eclipse of the sun and moon current among the Persians, who held that these phenomena were caused by two dark bodies,* offspring of the primeval ox, revolving below the sun and moon, and occasionally passing between them and the earth (*Dāṭistān-ī-Dēnīg*, lxix. 2; *Shikand gūmānīg Vijār*, iv. 46). It was, moreover, a popular belief that a sorcerer could bring the sun or moon down from heaven by witchcraft (Eznik, *Refutation of Sects*, p. 217), though this does not find a parallel in the extant Zoroastrian writings.

No doubt the Persian worship of the sun and moon found a similar worship of long standing in Armenia, that of the Urarṭians (see preceding

* The modern Armenians still speak of an 'evil star' which causes the eclipses.

art.), and could do little more than influence it to a certain extent.

It has been suggested, with some plausibility, that the famous hymn to Vahagn, quoted by Moses of Chorene (i. 31), sounds like a sun-hymn:

'The heavens travailed; the earth travailed;
Also the purple sea travailed;
And in the sea
The red reed travailed.
From the stem of the reed there arose a smoke;
From the stem of the reed there arose a flame;
From the flame ran forth a young man.
He had fiery hair;
He had a beard of flame;
And his eyes were suns.'

Both sun- and moon-worship have left deep traces in the popular beliefs of the present Armenians (see Abeghian, *op. cit.* pp. 41–49; Tchéraz, 'Notes sur la mythologie Arménienne,' in *Transact. of 9th Internat. Congress of Orientalists*, London, 1893, ii. 823 ff.).

In the Armen. writers from the 11th to the 14th cent. we meet with a sect or tribe called 'the Sons of the Sun,' first mentioned by Grigor Magistros (11th cent.), who says, placing them between the Armenian Paulicians and Thondracians: 'Behold, some of the Persian Magi of the Mage Zoroaster and the sun-worshippers envenomed of them, called Sons of the Sun, many of whom live in Mesopotamia, call themselves Christians, but we know how viciously and abominably they conduct themselves.' When, however, David, son of Alauk, says, a little later: 'The Paulicians or Euchites are the tribe of the Sons of the Sun,' he is evidently confusing three distinct things. From the letter of Nerses Shnorhali (12th cent.) about the 'Sons of the Sun' we learn that they wished to be received into the flock of Christ, so that, in his opinion, they were Armenians both in language and in nationality, who had remained unconverted in the times of Gregory the Illuminator, but now abjured their errors and their evil ways. Nerses gives special instruction about their reception into the Christian Church, about their moral life, and about giving up their magical practices, especially among women. 'Teach them to abstain,' he writes, 'from mixing impure things in the food and drink of the Christians for the purposes of their own diabolical love.' Nerses also mentions their worship of the sun and their reverence for the poplar. Later the Catholicos Mkhit'ar, in a letter to the pope, says: 'At that time (middle of the 14th cent.) there were Sons of the Sun in Manazkert'; and in the same century, Mkhit'ar Apareneçi writes: 'There are some Armenians by birth and language who worship the sun, and are called Sons of the Sun. They have neither writing nor literature. Fathers teach children by tradition what they have learned from the Mage Zoroaster, the chief of the fire-temple. Whithersoever the sun goes, they worship him in that direction, and they reverence the poplar, the lily, the cotton plant, and the other plants which turn towards the sun. They make themselves like those flowers in faith and action, high and fragrant. They offer sacrifices for the dead, and they pay taxes to the Armenian priests. Their chief is called Hazrbed, and twice or oftener every year all of them, men and women, sons and daughters, gather in a very dark pit.' In another place we read:

'A woman feels no disgust towards
A Son of the Sun;
Nor towards a Turk or an Armenian;
Whomsoever she loves, he is her faith.'

In the 14th cent. Thomas Mejop'eçi tells us that Timurlang came to Mardin (Mesopotamia) and destroyed four villages of the Sons of the Sun—Shol, Shemeλač, Safari, and Maraλ; 'but by the machinations of the devil they multiplied in Mardin and Amid.'

These quotations are drawn from Alishan's *Ancient Faith of the Armenians*, and from Grigor Vantzian's art. in *Handēs Amsoria*, 1896, p. 13 ff. Some of them are evidently of little value. Vantzian tries to prove that the Sons of the Sun were not Armenians, because (1) they had no literature, (2) they were not persecuted fanatically by the Christian Armenians. Moreover, he finds it difficult to identify them with the ancient Zoroastrians, because they had no magi or fire-worship. These conclusions disregard the best contemporaneous authorities on the subject. Even Grigor Magistros interposes them, in his allusion to them, between the Armenian Paulicians and the Thondracians. They spoke Armenian and called themselves Armenians. If they were not persecuted, this may well be due to the fact that the Christian Church has always shown more animosity against its own heresies than against heathenism, even within the boundaries of the national Church. There is, of course, no evidence of an organized Zoroastrianism or of a sacred fire among the 'Sons of the Sun'; but they might very well have been the remnants of a scattered community which had lost its magi and sacred fire. They may possibly have belonged originally to some district of Eastern Armenia, or they may have been descendants of Armenian converts during the strong Zoroastrian propaganda of the 5th cent. in Armenia. This, however, must still remain an open question, although it should be noted that they have lately been found to have some points of contact with the Yezidis (*q.v.*).

(5) *Tishtrya.* — Another important *yazata* of Zoroastrianism is Tishtrya (Sirius), the 'bright and glorious star' (*Yasna* i. 11, xxvii. 2, etc.), who assumes the form of a bull with golden horns (*Vendīdād* xix. 37), and again, as a white horse with yellow ears and golden bridle, fights against the demon Apaosha (drought) and pours upon the earth the fertilizing rain and the seeds of all plants (*Yasht* viii. 18–33; *Bundahishn* vii. 4–13). He is the chief of all the stars (*Yasht* viii. 44; Plutarch, *de Iside et Osiride*, 47), or at least of the stars of the East (*Bundahishn* ii. 7); and the eighth *Yasht* is devoted to his praise. Besides Tishtrya there was also Tīr, the genius of the planet Mercury, to whom, according to the *Bundahishn* (v. 1), Tishtrya was opposed.

In Armenian mythology also we find a Tir or Tiur, who has often been wrongly identified with Tishtrya, but who is, in reality, another divinity altogether. The Armen. Tiur (which Jensen, *Hittiter und Armenier*, pp. 186–187, endeavours to derive from Armen. *dpir*, 'writer,' 'scribe,' which would be a title of the Bab.-Assyr. Nabu, who was both the scribe of the gods and the planet Mercury [Orelli, *Allgem. Religionsgesch.*, Bonn, 1899, pp. 185–186]) is undoubtedly identical with Tīr, whose name is so often used in such theophorous compounds as Tiridates and Tiribazus (cf. Nöldeke, *SWAW*, *phil.-hist. Classe*, cxvi. 417–420; Justi, *Iranisches Namenbuch*, Marburg, 1895, p. 325 ff.), and who was widely known and honoured as an independent deity, being probably identified with the planet Mercury, although Tīr is not found in Armenian with this meaning.

Both in Cappadocia and in Armenia the fourth month was consecrated to this Tīr; and this was also true of the Parsi calendar, although, for theological reasons, the Parsis later made Tīr the equivalent of Tishtar (cf. *Bundahishn* xxv. 3, with *Āfrīngan* iii. 8).* The Armenian Tīr was famous as 'the interpreter of dreams,' as the tutelary deity of arts and learning, and as the scribe of Ormizd (Agathangelos, p. 584). Among the Armenians of modern times 'the writer' (very probably Tīr) has much to do with human fate and death. 'The writer take him!' is a common imprecation.† Tīr is, therefore, the Armenian Nabu, and there can be little doubt that the description given of him by Agathangelos whose Greek translator equates Tīr with Apollo (Lagarde, *Gesammelte Abhandlungen*, Leipzig, 1866, p. 294), agrees, in the main, with the general belief among other Oriental nations about Tīr.‡ In fact, the planet Mercury also is known among the Persian poets as 'the writer' (Stackelberg). The expression 'Scribe of Ormizd' applied to Tīr in Agathangelos has a Persian tinge, for the Armenians very seldom used the name Ormizd for their own Aramazd.

(6) *Mithra.* — Last, but by no means least, among the Zoroastrian *yazatas* is Mithra, the genius of the light of the heavens, and the god

* The Zoroastrian calendar also devotes the thirteenth day of each month to Tishtrya (Avesta) or Tīr (Pahlavi) (cf. *Sīrōza*, i. 13, ii. 13; *Yasna* xvi. 4, with *Bundahishn* xxvii. 24). That Tīr here refers primarily to the planet Mercury, and not to Tishtrya (Sirius), is confirmed by al-Bīrūnī's statement, in his account of the Tīragān, celebrated on the day Tīr of the month Tīr (*Chronology*, pp. 205–206): 'The name of this day is Tīr or Mercury, who is the star of the scribes.' The difficult problem of the replacing of Tīr by his opponent Tishtrya (cf. Spiegel, *Avesta Uebersetzt*, Leipzig, 1852–1863, iii. Introd. 21–22; Nöldeke, *loc. cit.*) is perhaps best explained by Justi, *op. cit.* p. 325: 'Da die Planeten später als feindliche Wesen galten, ward Tīr als Schutzgenius des 4. Monats und des 13. Monatstages durch den Tištrya (seinen Gegner) ersetzt; im Alterthum galt Tīr als guter Genius, wie die Eigennamen, deren ersten Theil sein Name bildet, beweisen.' The derivation of Tīr, 'Mercury,' is uncertain.—[Louis H. Gray].

† Cf. also Abeghian on the Groλs, or the 'writers,' as spirits of disease (*op. cit.* pp. 122–123). The words *Tir* and *Ti* were also used as exclamations: '*Tir*, forward!' Their relation to the deity's name, however, is not quite certain.

‡ In Egypt this god had his parallel in Thot, the moon-god of Chemun (de la Saussaye, i. 207).

of truth and faithfulness, whose praises are especially celebrated in the tenth *yasht*. Derzana was the centre of Armenian Mithra-worship, and he also had a famous temple in the sacred village of Bagayaṙinj (Agathangelos, p. 515), although we have no proof whatever that Mithraism had obtained any foothold in Armenia proper. Mihr, the Armenian Mithra, was specially called the son of Aramazd (Agathangelos, p. 593; cf. *Yasht* xvii. 16); but, owing to the strong worship of the sun and Vahagn among the Armenians, he does not seem to have become as prominent in Armenia as in Persia, his place seeming, indeed, to be usurped by Vahagn (see below). Nevertheless, his name occurs frequently as a component part of many proper names of persons, such as *Mihran*, *Mihrdat* (Mithridates), and *Mehružan* (Hübschmann, *Armen. Grammatik*, i. 52–54), while the Armenian *mehean*, 'pagan temple, idol, altar,' has also been traced to the same source (cf. Hübschmann, *op. cit.* i. 194). The seventh month of the year and the eighth day of each month were his; and in the Zoroastrian calendar the seventh month and the sixteenth day were consecrated to him. We know nothing, however, of the functions or other duties of the Armenian Mithra.

(7) *Fravashis.* — Chief among the Zoroastrian *fravashis* (lower angels), is Verethraghna, the genius of victory, to whom the Avesta consecrates the fourteenth *yasht*. Like Mithra, he is of Indo-Iranian origin. In Pahlavi times his name was thinned down to *Bahrām*, often used by Persian kings, and in Armenian to *Vāhrām* and *Vṙam.* It is also very possible that Vrt'anēs, the name of the second son of Gregory the Illuminator, reflects the Parthian form for *Verethraghna*. Since Lagarde, there has been a strong tendency to identify the Armenian Vahagn, probably the god of war and victory (Agathangelos, p. 106), with Verethraghna. According to Armenian phonetic laws, this is quite possible, although the termination *-agn* and the complete disappearance of both *r*'s constitute a difficulty. There was, moreover, a noble family called the *Vahevunis* (Elisæus, pp. 70, 127, 160, 173); while the list of the Armenian nobles in Mesrop's *Life of St. Nerses* gives *Vohevuni* (p. 33), but further below it adds the *Vahuni* (p. 34) as a different family. Moses of Chorene (i. 31, ii. 8, 12, 88) knows a priestly family of the name of *Vahnuni*, whom he makes descendants of Vahagn. Probably in all these cases Vahagn was the tutelary god, and the first syllable of his name was treated as independent.

Although in the ancient Armenian triad of Aramazd, Anahit, and Vahagn (Agathangelos, p. 106), Vahagn has the place of Mithra in the Old Persian triad (Art. Sus. a, 5; Ham. 6), he must be interpreted, despite the minor phonetic difficulties already mentioned, from the Avesta Verethraghna. Essentially a deity of victory, the latter fittingly declares: 'I will conquer the malignancies of all the malignant: the malignancies of demons and men, of wizards and witches, of oppressors, *kavis*, and *karaps*' (*Yasht*, xiv. 4), while the very form of his name recalls its Sanskrit equivalent *vṛtrahan*, the Vedic epithet of Indra as the slayer of the cloud-demon Vṛtra. The reflexion of his career in the Avesta is seen in the statement that 'Vāhrām the victorious is the stimulator of the warlike' (*Shāyast-lā-Shāyast*, xxii. 20), although the Iranian texts preserve no tradition of his conquests over dragons in the strict sense of the term. On the other hand, in Hellenic times Vahagn was compared with Herakles, and called the dragon-killer (Agathangelos, p. 606), while the Greek Agathangelos translates *Vahagn* as Ἡρακλῆς, and, reversing the process, the Armen. version of 2 Mac 4^{19} renders Ἡρακλῆς by *Vahagn*. Ancient Armenians told, moreover, of Vahagn's stealing straw from Barsham (the Syrian god Ba'al-Shemīn, 'Lord of Heaven'), which he let drop on the way, thus forming the Milky Way (Anania Shiragaçi, p. 48; cf. Abeghian, *Armenischer Volksglaube*, pp. 49–50). The Vahagn-song, the parallelism of Vahagn with Herakles, and his relations to Mithra and Barsham, tend to create the presumption that he was also a sun-god. The most famous temple of Vahagn was in Yashtishat in Taraun* (Faustus of Byzantium, iii. 14; Agathangelos, pp. 606–607), where he was also known as the lover of Astλik, the Syrian Aphrodite (Agathangelos, p. 607; Moses of Chorene, p. 88).

II. *INFERNAL HOSTS.*—**1. Ahriman.**—Ahriman (Armen. *Arhmn*) is never referred to in connexion with ancient Armenian paganism; but the absence of his name may be easily understood when we remember that, while Christian writers had a reason for arguing against the ancient deities, Ahriman (*q.v.*) and his retinue naturally coincided with Christian demonology. Other Zoroastrian evil spirits were known among the Armenians, however; and Ahriman could hardly fail to be known as their chief. Alishan (*Ancient Faith*, p. 210) suggests, with some plausibility, that he was known under the name of Çar, 'the evil one,' a word which is frequently found in that sense in Armen. theological writings and old popular spells. Besides *Arhmn*, the forms *Haraman(i)* and *Kharaman(i)* were also current in Armenia, *Haraman* being apparently the older (Arsacid) and *Arhmn* the younger (Sasanian) form (Hübschmann, *op. cit.* i. 26–27); so that the pagan Armenians possibly used *Haraman* to denote the Ahriman of their religion. Haramani is used as an epithet of snakes by Abraham of Zenag, a 5th cent. writer.

2. Demons.—Of the six Zoroastrian archdemons there is no mention. The *Asmodæus* of the Book of Tobit (3^8 etc.) was transliterated by the Armenians as *Azmod*, which plainly shows that the name suggested nothing familiar to them.† The word *dev* (Avesta *dæva*), 'demon,' was current among the Armenians, although they had also native words like *ais*. The *devs* preferred stony places (Moses of Chorene, iii. 55) and ruins (Eznik, p. 98). They appeared as serpents (Faustus of Byzantium, v. 2) and in many other monstrous forms (Eznik, p. 98); some of them were corporeal, others incorporeal (*ib.* p. 97).

The *družes* were lying, perjuring, harmful spirits, probably believed to be feminine, like their Avesta counterparts, the *drujes*. What the Avesta says in regard to their third mode of self-propagation—by the semen emitted in the *pollutio nocturna* (*Vendīdād* xviii. 45–52)—seems to have been a current belief among the Armenians (Eznik, p. 178; Abeghian, *Armen. Volksglaube*, pp. 35–36). The *yātus*, 'sorcerers' of the Avesta, who were able even to slay men (*Vendīdād* vii. 3), are well known and much feared among the modern Armenians as *jatuks*. The *pairikās* (Armen. *parik*), destructive female demons (cf. *Yasna* xvi. 8; *Yasht* viii. 54, xiii. 104; *Vendīdād* i. 9, xi. 9), were also believed in, but Eznik (p. 97) classes them with such chimeras as the *yuškapariks* and *hambarus* (see below).

3. Monsters and chimeras.—Aždahak (Avesta *Aži Dahāka*) and Višap, especially the latter, occupied a large place in ancient Armen. superstition; and Moses of Chorene (i. 30) states that

* This temple was called the 'eighth sanctuary' (Agathangelos, p. 606), possibly because Vahagn-worship, and specially this temple, rose to importance long after the seven main sanctuaries (Agathangelos, p. 34) had established themselves.

† It should be noted that the divergences between the Jewish אשמדאי and the Avesta *aēšma*, '(demon of) wrath,' are so grave that the usual view that the two are identical is not free from suspicion (cf. Ginzberg in *JE* ii. 219).—[Louis H. Gray].

Aždahak is, in Armenian, the same as Višap. The latter word is, it should be noted, a loan-word from the Avesta ἅπαξ λεγόμενον *višāpa*, 'whose saliva is poison,' used as an epithet of *aži*, 'serpent,' in *Nīrangastān* 48. The story of the war between Aždahak of Media and Tigranes I. (i. 24–30) probably contains traces of an old dragon-legend. In a later chapter Moses states that Aždahak was fettered and imprisoned in Mount Dembavend by Hruden, escaping only to be re-captured and guarded by his conqueror in a cave of the same mountain; just as, in Zoroastrian legend, Aži Dahāka, after a reign of 1000 years, was enchained by Thraētaona (Armenian, Hruden; Pahlavi, Frēṯūn) under Dimāvand, whence he is to arise at the Last Day and be slain by Sāma Keresaspa (*Bundahishn* xxix. 9; *Dāṯistān-ī Dēnīg* xxxvii. 97; *Dīnā-i Maīnōg-i Khraṯ* xxii. 38 - 39; *Dīnkarṯ* vii. 1, 26). Moses likewise records that Aždahak was kissed on the shoulders, and that from this kiss sprang serpents, which were fed on human flesh.* Though the extant Avesta does not note this, Aži Dahāka there being 'three-mouthed and three-pated' (*Yasna* ix. 8), the *Dāṯistān-ī Dēnīg* (*loc. cit.*) alludes to it in describing Dahāk, 'on whom most powerful demons and fiends in the shape of serpents are winged.' The legend is further elaborated by Firdausi in the *Shāh-Nāmah* (ed. Vullers-Landauer, 28, 99–30, 144; 35, 12–14), according to whom the kiss was bestowed by Iblīs. The legend of Aži Dahāka was also treated at length in the twentieth section of the lost *Sūṯkar Nask* of the Avesta (*Dīnkarṯ* ix. 21).

The *višaps* (Eznik, pp. 102–107) were corporeal beings which could appear both as men and as serpents, and could soar in the air by the help of oxen (?). They were fond of carrying the grain away from the threshing-floor, either by assuming the shape of mules and camels, or by real mules and camels of their own. In such cases, the Armenians called '*Kal! kal!*' 'Stop! stop' (Eznik, p. 103). They also sucked the milk from cows (Vahram Vartabed [13th cent.], quoted by Alishan, *Ancient Faith*, p. 172). The *višaps* went hunting on horseback; they had houses (Eznik, pp. 104, 107; cf. also *Yasht* xv. 19, and Darmesteter's note, *ad loc.*, on the palace of Aži Dahāka). They kept royal princes and heroes captive (Eznik, p. 104), among whom were Alexander the Great and Artavazd, king of Armenia (p. 105). They sometimes appeared enormous, and compelled men to worship them (p. 105). They entered into human beings; their breath was poisonous (p. 107). There was a whole colony of them at the foot of Masis (Moses of Chorene, i. 30), with whom Vahagn fought (*ib.* i. 31; Agathangelos, p. 607), and who later stole the child Artavazd and left a *dev* in his stead (Moses of Chorene, ii. 61; cf., further, on the *višap*, Abeghian, *op. cit.* pp. 78–83).

Closely connected with the *višaps* were the *nhangs* (Eznik, pp. 102–107)—a term borrowed from the Pers. *nihang* 'alligator, crocodile.' They lived chiefly in the rivers (Eznik, p. 106). According to Eznik, both *višaps* and *nhangs* appeared in deceptive forms, but the former were 'personal' (spirit-like), while the latter were not so (p. 102), so that he specifically declares: 'There is no personal *nhang*' (pp. 103, 107). Although they could assume different forms, they had no body (p. 102). Preferably they appeared as women (mermaids?) in the water (p. 106); but at other times they became seals, and, catching the swimmer by the feet, dragged him to the bottom (*ib.*). An unpublished manuscript of the *Geography* ascribed to Moses of Chorene in like manner reports the general belief that there were *nhangs* in the Araçani, a tributary of the Euphrates, as well as in the Euphrates itself. They used their victims for their lust, and then sucked their blood and left them dead. The Armen. translators use the word *nhang* for 'hippopotamus' and 'crocodile.'

The *šahapets*, or 'protectors' (cf. Avesta **šōiθrapaiti*, 'protector of the homestead,' Skr. *kṣetrapati*, 'lord of a field'), are mentioned in Agathangelos as the protecting genii of graves (p. 56). They appeared in the shape of men or serpents, like the *višaps* (Eznik, p. 106), and kept the vineyards and olive trees, according to the ancient Armen. tr. of St. John Chrysostom on Isaiah.

Another class of fabulous monsters which seem to have a Persian origin is that of the *hambarus*. According to von Stackelberg, *hambaruna* in Persian means 'genius of houses,' but we know little as to how the *hambarus* were imagined. In the Armen. tr. of the LXX Is 34^{13} the word is used to render σιρήνων (Vulg. *draconum*). They were female beings, had a body, and were probably thought to live on land. 'They were born and they died,' says Eznik (p. 97), who mentions them along with *yuškapariks* and *pariks*. The *yuškapariks*, or 'ass-*pariks*' (cf. Pers. *vušk*, 'ass'), used to render ὀνοκένταυροι in LXX Is 13^{22} $34^{11.14}$, lived chiefly in ruined places (Eznik, pp. 97–98), while the *pariks*, to whom allusion has been made above, were seductive female demons, living not only in the water, but also in forests and meadows, as well as on the banks of streams. They are, primarily, water-deities, and correspond closely to the European mermaids, whom they also resemble in their frequent intrigues with mortal lovers. This erotic trait is an evident reminiscence in Armenia of the seductive *pairikās* of Zoroastrianism (see above; cf. also Abeghian, *op. cit.* pp. 103–104). Eznik (p. 99) likewise mentions the *covaçuls*, or 'sea-bulls,' which lived in lakes, propagating through kine, they themselves being born of cows. He also alludes to *pays*, which were born of men (pp. 98–99), and must doubtless be distinguished from the *pariks*. All these beings, as well as the *aṙlēz*, were held to be generally invisible, though occasionally they were seen of men (Eznik, p. 99). There are, moreover, other classes of demons in Armenian faith, such as the *yaveržaharsunks*, *k'ajk's* (husbands of the *pariks*), *mardagails* ('werwolves'), *als* (corresponding roughly to Lilith), the 'evil eye,' and disease-demons of various sorts (cf. Abeghian, *op. cit.* pp. 102–110, 116–127). Another clear survival of Armen. Zoroastrianism is the horror felt towards snakes, frogs, and ants (Abeghian, *op. cit.* pp. 30–31; cf. *Vendīdād* xiv. 5, and Darmesteter's note, *ad loc.*; Herodotus, i. 140), while the cat is an uncanny object, as in Parsi belief (Darmesteter, *loc. cit.*; *SBE* xviii. 419, where a demoniac father is attributed to it).*

III. *DEATH AND THE FUTURE LIFE.*—The abode of evil spirits and of the wicked dead was called *Džokhk'* (Pers. *Dūzakh*), and perhaps also *Sandaramet* (see above). We have absolutely no description of the Armen. Hades or Paradise; and the Avesta *garō-nmāna*, 'house of song, paradise,' appears in Armenian in the loan-word *gerezman*, 'grave.' After death, the soul lingered around the body until the corpse was buried, after which it remained in the vicinity of the grave or of its former dwelling for a year, though in later Armenian belief it passes to the future world within a day after burial (Abeghian, *op. cit.* p. 18). On its way, as in Iranian eschatology, the soul had to

* Faustus of Byzantium also (v. 22) tells a similar legend of King Pap.

* On the other hand, the Armenians lack the extreme veneration for the dog which is so characteristic of the Avesta (cf. *Vendīdād* xiii., xv. 5–6, 19–51; *Dīnkarṯ* viii. 23), so that *šun*, 'dog,' is also used in the sense of 'adulterer.'

cross a hair-bridge; if righteous, it reached the opposite shore in safety; if sinful, it dropped down into the stream of hell-fire. There was a middle place for those that were neither good nor bad (Abeghian, p. 20).*

We find absolutely no trace, however, of *dakhmas*, or 'towers of silence,' or of the custom of exposing bodies. On the contrary, there were great mausoleums for kings in the ancient city of Ani, and graveyards outside the cities. We also know that the Achæmenian kings did not obey the Avesta injunction concerning the exposure of dead bodies; while, according to Herodotus (i. 140), the Persians covered the corpse with wax and then buried it.

The Armenian burial-customs seem to have been more akin to the ancient Babylonian (Jeremias, *Hölle und Paradies bei den Babyloniern*, p. 10 ff.). The friends and relatives of the deceased came to the ceremony of wailing (Faustus of Byzantium, iv. 15); and at the funerals of the rich, professional mourners were employed (Moses of Chorene, ii. 60), led by the 'mother of the dirge,' who sang the story of the life and death of the deceased, while the nearest relatives tore their garments, plucked their hair and screamed (Faustus of Byzantium, *loc. cit.*). They cut their arms (?) and faces (*ib.* v. 31). During the funeral they had music, produced by horns, violins, and harps. Men and women danced facing each other, and clapped their hands (*ib.*). Johannes Garneçi (quoted by Alishan, *op. cit.* p. 413) says: 'Forbid wailing (over the dead) . . . cutting of the hair, and (other) evil things.' When the deceased was a king or a great personage, servants and slaves committed suicide over his grave (Moses of Chorene, ii. 60). Ancient gravestones are found in the shape of horses and lambs, perhaps symbolic of sacrifices for the dead. The modern custom of distributing bread and raisins and strong drink after the burial, moreover, is probably a survival of an ancient sacrificial meal (cf. Abeghian, *op. cit.* pp. 20–23). To this day it is quite customary to make two holes on the gravestones.

Death was a decree of fate (Eznik, p. 153), inevitable (p. 161), and foreordained (p. 162). In fact, the whole life of man was thought to be led by Fate (Ohan Mantaguni, quoted by Alishan, *op. cit.* p. 411). Later Armenians also spoke of Hogeaṙ, the 'soul-taking' angel, who is frequently identified with Gabriel (Abeghian, *op. cit.* p. 17).

There is little to be said about the eschatology of the Armenians, although they certainly believed in resurrection and immortality.

There is an ancient Armenian legend about the end of the world. Artavazd, son of king Artashes, seeing that many people committed suicide over his father's grave, said, 'Thou didst depart, and tookest with thee the whole country. Shall I rule over ruins?' Thereupon his father cursed him, saying:

'When thou goest a-hunting
up the venerable Masis,
May the *K'ajk's* seize thee and
take thee up the venerable Masis!
There mayest thou remain and see no light!'

Artavazd is said to have perished, while on a hunting party, by falling with his horse from a high precipice. One Armenian legend says that he is chained in a cave of Masis, and two dogs, gnawing at his chains, try to set him free in order that he may bring the world to an end. The chains become very thin about the season of Navasard (New Year's festivities in August). Therefore, on those days the blacksmiths used to strike a few blows with their hammers on their anvils in order to strengthen Artavazd's chains and save the world, a custom which was continued even into Christian times (Moses of Chorene, ii. 61; Eznik, p. 105). This legend seems to have some affinity with that of Biurasp Aždahak, which Moses of Chorene gives at the end of the first book of his *History of Armenia* (see above).

IV. *Worship and Ceremonial.*—There were probably temple-books which Christianity systematically destroyed. The temples were numerous, both in the country and in the cities; and there were also special temple-towns, such as Bagavan and Yashtishat, containing several important sanctuaries. Christian churches and monasteries succeeded both to the wealth and to the veneration belonging to the ancient sacred sites. Of ancient open-air worship we hear nothing, but there were sacred places on mountain tops, like the throne of Nahata (Faustus of Byzantium, v. 25). Besides the ordinary temples, the Armenians boasted, like other neighbouring and distant nations, seven main sanctuaries (Agathangelos, p. 34), which were often the scenes of great concourses of people gathered there for worship and religious festivities. Treasure-houses were connected with the great sanctuaries (*ib.* pp. 586, 591, 594; Moses of Chorene, ii. 48; Thoma Artsruni, i. 7), as they now are associated with the churches. Tiridates and Gregory plundered many of these on behalf of the poor and of the Church, during their campaign against the pagan sanctuaries of Armenia; and images and statues of deities were common, at least in later pagan times (Agathangelos, *locc. citt.*; Moses of Chorene, ii. 14).

Agathangelos (p. 34) describes the sacrifices of Chosroës after his return from victorious incursions.

'He commanded to seek the seven great altars of Armenia, and he honoured the sanctuaries of his ancestors, the Arsacids, with white bullocks, white rams, white horses and mules, with gold and silver ornaments and gold embroidered and fringed silken coverings, with golden wreaths, silver sacrificial basins, desirable vases set with precious stones, splendid garments, and beautiful ornaments. Also he gave a fifth of his booty and great presents to the priests.'*

In Bayazid (the ancient Bagravand) an old Armenian relief was found with an altar upon which a strange animal stands, and on each side a man clothed in a long tunic. One is beardless, and carries a heavy club. The other has a beard. Their head-gears, Phrygian in character, differ in details. Both of them raise their hands in the attitude of worship (Alishan, *op. cit.* p. 161).

The prevalent word for a pagan priest in Armenian, *k'urm*, is a loan-word from the Syriac *kūmrā*, 'priest,' although *mog*, 'magian,' may also have been used. The place of sacrifice was perhaps called *spandaran* (connected with Avesta *spenta*, 'holy'), a word which is now current only in the sense of 'slaughter-house.' This makes it possible that originally slaughtering had a sacrificial character. Christianity did away with all impure rites and human sacrifices which were of a local character, but animal sacrifices survived the fall of paganism (Conybeare in *AJTh* vii., 1903, p. 63).

In many of the sanctuaries, which, like the modern monasteries, were also places of religious hospitality, particularly in the country, sacrifices were distributed to strangers (Moses of Chorene, ii. 66). Besides animals, flower-wreaths and green twigs (the *barsom* of the Avesta?) were offered (Agathangelos, p. 49), and probably also fruit and money.

The priesthood must have been hereditary in a well-organized caste. There was a high priest, sometimes of royal blood (Moses of Chorene, ii. 53, 55), and the *Vahunis* are mentioned as a priestly family by Moses of Chorene (ii. 8), while another priestly family was perhaps that of the *Spandunis*. The priests were probably very numerous in temple-towns, and they certainly possessed great wealth and extensive lands and villages, which were later confiscated for the benefit of the Christian Church (Agathangelos, pp. 586 ff., 590, 594, 610). Of native Armenian magi as a caste

* The belief that the soul remains on earth for a year seems to be Muhammadan (Wolff, *Muhammed. Eschatol.*, Leipzig, 1872, pp. 78–79; cf. Rühling, *Beiträge zur Eschatol. des Islam*, Leipzig, 1895, p. 43); while the Iranians held that it journeyed to the place of first judgment at dawn of the fourth day after death (*Yasht* xxii. 7, 25; *Dāṯistān-ī-Dēnīg* xx. 2–3; *Dīnā-ī Maīnōg-ī Khraṯ* ii. 114–115, 161; *Arṯā-ī Vīrāf* iv. 9–15). The bridge in Armenian belief is obviously the *činvat*-bridge of the Avesta—which is fully described in *Dāṯistān-ī-Dēnīg*, xxi. 3–7, and which occurs not only in Iran but in India, mediæval Europe, and elsewhere (Scherman, *Materialien zur Gesch. der ind. Visionsliteratur*, Leipzig, 1892, pp. 102–110, 117–119; Becker, *Contribut. to Compar. Study of the Mediæval Visions of Heaven and Hell*, Baltimore, 1899, pp. 18, 44, 76, 83, 90, 97), as well as in Muhammadanism (Rühling, *op. cit.* pp. 62–63). The 'middle place,' moreover, finds its Iranian source in *Hamēstagān*, 'ever-stationary' (*Arṯā-ī-Vīrāf* vi.; *Shāyast-lā-Shāyasṯ* vi. 2; *Dīnā-ī Maīnōg-ī Khraṯ* vii. 18–19, xii. 14; *Dāṯistān-ī-Dēnīg*, xxiv. 6, xxxiii. 2), where dwell the souls of those whose good and evil deeds exactly balance each other.

* Sacrifices were occasions of great rejoicing, and it would seem that not only the flesh of the animals, but also their blood, was consumed (Agathangelos, pp. 73–74; Faustus of Byzantium, iv. 4).

we have no record, although we read of magians (Moses of Chorene, ii. 48). The existence of priestesses in ancient Armenia is not absolutely certain, although we have the old compound *krmanuish* meaning 'priestess.'

A critical study of the Armenian Church calendar and ceremonies would probably reveal much that could be referred to the pre-Christian ritual. During Lent, for example, the morning service is opened with an abjuration of the devil and all his works—an elaborate formula, which is recited while the whole congregation turn their backs to the altar and look towards the west, with arms hanging rigidly at the sides. Although the abjuration is usual in the baptism of all ritualistic churches, this particular form may well have been derived from the ancient cult of the country. Evidently the Armenians considered the west as the abode of the devils, for Eznik says in his aphorisms (p. 313): 'Honey is sweet, but it harms a diseased body. Good counsel and rebuke are useful, but they do not benefit those who have set their faces westward.'*

The old Armenian calendar also bears traces of ancient Persian influence. *Trē* (Tīr), *Mehekan* (Mithra), *Ahekan* (Atarš), and *Hrotiç* (Pahlavi *Fravarṭīgān*) are common also to the Persian year (cf. art. CALENDAR [Persian]). The other months of the ancient Armenian calendar have names of Armenian and perhaps also two of Caucasic (Georgian) origin (Hagopian, 'Armenian Months,' in *Banssēr*, 1900; Gray, 'On certain Persian and Armenian Month-Names as influenced by the Avestan Calendar,' in *JAOS* xxviii.). The names of the days of the month, as given by Shah Tchrped (Alishan, *op. cit.* p. 143), have but few points of contact with the Zoroastrian (*Yasna* xvi. 3-6; *Sīrōza* i.–ii.; *Bundahishn* xxvii. 24; *Shāyast-lā-Shāyast* xxii.–xxiii.; al-Bīrūnī, *Chronology*, p. 53).

The Armenians shared with the Persians some of the characteristic superstitions and usages of the Avesta. One of them is the evil eye (*Vendīdād* xx. 3, 7, xxii. 2; *Bundahishn* xxviii. 33, 36). In Moses of Chorene, ii. 47, we read that king Ervand had so powerful an evil eye that he could break stones asunder by looking fixedly at them. The general belief is that people upon whom the evil eye is cast pine away without knowing the cause of their ailment, and nothing is safe from it. There are special prayers and ceremonies to break the spell of the evil eye (Alishan, *op. cit.* p. 385; Abeghian, *op. cit.* pp. 123-127). The modern Armenians have the same abhorrence for parings of nails and hair as the Avesta (cf. *Vendīdād*, xvii.); nor may fire and water be defiled (Abeghian, *op. cit.* pp. 57-58, 66). These superstitions of the later Armenians, like many other beliefs noted above, were probably imported in ancient times. Among the greatest requirements of the Avesta we find next-of-kin marriages (cf. Justi in *Grundriss der iran. Philologie*, ii. 434-437; Jackson, *ib.* 682, and the references there given). The only well-known instance of this in Armenia is the marriage of Tigranes III. with his sister Erato, a few years before the Christian era, although it seems to have been frequent among the nobles (Moses of Chorene, iii. 20; Faustus of Byzantium, iv. 4).

V. *CONCLUSIONS.*—Our study suggests the following reflexions:—(1) Great as is the mass of Zoroastrian material in Armenian paganism, it has also serious gaps. Was it ever complete? (2) We find the existing material in a quite uncertain shape. The substantial deviations from Zoroastrianism are considerable, as in the case of Anahit and in the worship of fire and water. The Zoroastrian angels are full-fledged deities in Armenian paganism; but primitive traits are not lacking, as in the case of Spenta Armaiti. (3) There is no trace of a highly developed system of theology, ritual and legalistic observance, as in Zoroastrianism. Abstract beings, the personifications of ideas, virtues, and vices, are quite absent. We find no theological systematization of the heavenly army, no developed dualism, no caste of magi, and no widely spread fire-altars. (4) There is no record of any Zoroastrian propaganda in Armenia, or of any religious fellowship between Persia and Armenia. When the Sasanians persecuted Christian Armenia, about A.D. 450, they said nothing about a return to the ancient faith, nor did the Armenians ever call their paganism Zoroastrian. (5) It is probable that Zoroastrianism gradually penetrated Armenia under the Achæmenian kings and under the Arsacids, but we have no exact knowledge as to when or how. (6) The study here presented must not be regarded as a complete picture of Armenian paganism. Both the pantheon and the world of minor spirits contained other non-Zoroastrian names and beliefs which have been omitted; but the old religion of Armenia was mainly Iranian, and may be described as Zoroastrianism of a corrupt type.

It is probable that the ancient Armenians themselves conceived their pantheon as containing the following deities: Aramazd, as chief god; Anahit, as chief and favourite goddess; Vahagn, as the national god of war and heroism; the sun and the moon; Mihr; and Tīr as the god of human destiny, whose relation to learning and eloquence has a Greek flavour. Deities of a lower magnitude of importance disappeared more easily from the popular memory. Along with these Persian deities, there were also an Elamitic goddess Nanē (the Babylonian Nanâ, cf. also the 'Persian' goddess Nanæa of 2 Mac 1[13]), the Syrian Astλik (Venus), and the Syrian Barsham (Ba'al-Shemīn). These three must have migrated into Armenia during post-Alexandrian times, perhaps *Doppelgänger* of some of the native deities, though whether they formed a group, Barsham-Astλik-Nanē, corresponding to Aramazd-Anahit-Vahagn, as Jensen (*Hittiter und Armenier*, p. 181 ff.) suggests, is a less plausible hypothesis. At all events they soon asserted themselves as independent and separate deities, so that Astλik could become the paramour of Vahagn and have a temple in the sacred town of Yashtishat, where Anahit also had a sanctuary. After Alexander, and especially in Roman times, the Armenians came under strongly Hellenistic influences, and began to seek parallels between the Greek and their own deities. It would also seem that during this period the worship of the sun and the moon became somewhat neglected. Otherwise, we cannot understand why Agathangelos makes so little of them. The ancient Armenians were also very much given to divination and witchcraft (Moses of Chorene, i. 30, ii. 66; Ohan Mantaguni, *op. cit.* xxvi.; Alishan, *op. cit.* pp. 360-409).

LITERATURE.—Windischmann, 'Die persische Anâhita oder Anaitis' in *Abhandlungen der könig. bayr. Akad. der Wissensch.* I Cl. viii. pt. 1, Munich, 1856; **Emin**, 'Recherche sur le paganisme arménien' in *Revue de l'orient*, N.S. v. 18; **Lagarde**, *Armen. Studien*, Göttingen, 1877, and *Purim*, Göttingen, 1887; **Johannissiany**, *Armen. Bibliothek* iv., 'Märchen und Sagen,' Leipzig, 1887; **Sarkissian**, *Agathangelos and his many-centuried Mystery* (Arm.), Venice, 1892; **Mkrttschian**, *Die Paulikianer*, Leipzig, 1893; **von Gutschmid**, *Kleine Schriften*, iii., Leipzig, 1892; **Tchéraz**, 'Notes sur la mythol. armén.' in *Transact. of the 9th Internat. Congress of Orientalists*, ii., London, 1893; **Nazarethian**, 'Armenians and Armenian Mythology' in *Bazmawēp* (Arm.), 1893-94; **Karakashian**, *Crit. Hist. of Armenia* (Arm.), pt. i. ch. 8, Tiflis, 1895; **Balassanian**, *Hist. of Armenia*[2] (Arm.), Tiflis, 1895, p. 74 ff.; **Cumont**, *Textes et mon. figurés relat. aux mystères de Mithra*, Brussels, 1895-99, and *Die Mysterien des Mithra*, Leipzig, 1903; **Gelzer**, 'Zur armen. Götterlehre' in *Berichte der könig. sächs. Gesellsch. der Wissensch.*, phil.-hist. Classe, 1896, pp. 99-148; **Alishan**, *Ancient Faith of the Armenians* (Arm.), Venice, 1895; **St. Clair-Tisdall**, *Conversion of Armenia to the Christian Faith*, Oxford, 1897, p. 43 ff.; **Hübschmann**, *Armen. Gram.* i., Leipzig, 1897; **Jensen**, *Hittiter und Armenier*, Strassburg; 1898, p. 177 ff.; **Abeghian**, *Armen. Volksglaube*, Leipzig, 1899; **Carrière**, *Les huit sanctuaires de l'Arménie payenne*, Paris, 1899; **Stackelberg**, 'Iranian Influence on the Religious Beliefs of the Ancient Armenians' in *Report of Imperial Archæolog. Soc. of Moscow, Oriental Comm.* ii. pt. 2 (Russian), Moscow, 1901; **Daghavarian**, 'Ancient Religions of the Armenians' in *Banssēr* (Arm.), 1903; **Weber**, *Die kathol. Kirche in Armenien*, Freiburg, 1903, p. 25 ff.; **Hommel**, *Grundriss der Geog. und Gesch. des alten Orients*, i., Munich, 1904; **Geiger-Kuhn**, *Grundriss der iran. Philologie*, ii., Strassburg, 1904; **Arakélian**, 'La Relig. anc. des Arméniens' in *Verhandl. des zweiten internat. Kongresses für allgem. Religionsgesch.*, Basel, 1905, pp. 291-292; also numerous articles in *Handēs Amsōreay*, Vienna, 1887 ff., and in Pauly-Wissowa.

M. H. ANANIKIAN.

ARMENIA (Christian).—I. *THE BEGINNINGS OF CHRISTIANITY.*—The national legends and traditions of Armenia are rich in information regarding the introduction of Christianity into the country.

* In the Avesta the north is the dwelling-place of evil spirits (*Vendīdād* vii. 2, xix. 1; *Arṭā-ī-Vīrāf* xvii. 11).

In particular, it is said to have been preached by Apostles or disciples of Apostles, such as St. Bartholomew and St. Thaddæus. But it has been proved that these legends did not appear till late in the literature of Armenia, and that they were borrowed largely from the literature of Greece. Christianity certainly penetrated to Armenia, as elsewhere, by means of the living voice. The Apostles and their successors had early formed the habit of visiting the Churches founded by them; and the teaching of the gospel was continued and propagated in the Christian communities long before written documents came into use; but the names of these first preachers have not come down to us with any certainty. Yet, however meagre the information furnished by history may be, we are quite entitled to maintain that Christianity reached Armenia through Antioch, before the time of Gregory the Illuminator. The first Christian documents that the Armenians made use of were written in Syriac, and this language was used in the Armenian liturgy till the reform of Gregory the Illuminator. After Antioch we might mention Edessa and Nisibis as centres from which Christianity spread into the different provinces of the kingdom of Armenia.

LITERATURE.—The works, in Armenian and in translation, of Armenian writers: Koriun, Elisæus the Teacher (*Vartabed*), Eznik, Agathangelos, Lazarus of Pharpe, Sebeos, Zenobius of Klag, Faustus of Byzantium, Moses of Chorene. A. Lipsius, *Die apokr. Apostelgesch. und Apostellegenden* (Brunswick, 1883–1890); A. Carrière, *La Légende d'Abgar dans l'histoire d'Arménie de Moïse de Khoren* (Paris, 1895); H. Gelzer, 'Die Anfänge der armen. Kirche' in *Berichte der königl. Sächs. Gesellschaft der Wissenschaften*, phil.-hist. Classe (1895); Petit,* fasc. vii. col. 1892–1893.

II. *EXTENSION OF CHRISTIANITY IN ARMENIA.* —**St. Gregory the Illuminator.**—Gregory the Illuminator belonged to the royal race of the Arsacids. When quite young he escaped the massacre of his family (A.D. 238), and took refuge in Roman territory. He studied at Cæsarea, and returned to Armenia when the kingdom was re-established under Tiridates II. (A.D. 261). After being persecuted for his faith, he attained to honour, and baptized the king and a large number of his subjects. He went again to Cæsarea, where he was consecrated bishop by Bishop Leontius, thus forming the link of spiritual connexion between the Cappadocian metropolis and the young Armenian Churches. When he was made bishop, Gregory fixed his residence at Yashtishat, and had a church and an episcopal palace built there. He substituted Armenian for Greek as the language of the liturgy, in order to have easier access to the masses of the people, and created twelve episcopal sees, at the head of which he placed, as titulars, converted pagan priests. He instituted ecclesiastical offices, making them hereditary in the sacerdotal families, and he created in his own family the supreme office of *Catholicos*. At first this title designated only the principal bishop of the country; later it came to mean an independent patriarch. The Gregorian and national Armenian Church, founded afterwards, lived its own autonomous life, while recognizing for some years a sort of supremacy in the mother Church of Cæsarea.

LITERATURE.—Mgr. Ormanian, *Le Vatican et les Arméniens* (Rome, 1873); von Gutschmid, *Kleine Schriften* (Leipzig, 1892); H. Gelzer, 'Die Anfänge der armen. Kirche' in *Berichte der königl. Sächs. Gesellsch. der Wissensch.*, phil.-hist. Classe (1895); Petit,* fasc. vii. col. 1893; S. Weber, *Die katholische Kirche in Armenien* (Freiburg, 1903); Malan, *Life and Times of St. Gregory* (Eng. tr. 1868).

III. *THE GREGORIAN ARMENIAN CHURCH.*—**1. Doctrine.**—The creed of the Armenian Church is identical with the pseudo-Athanasian Creed which was introduced into Armenia by the Syrians, and in the 6th cent. took the place of the Nicene Creed. In the 14th cent. another creed was much in use in the Armenian Church. It was a compilation of formulas borrowed from various creeds, and was current until the middle of the 19th century. The religious heads of the Armenian Church several times formulated *professions of faith* intended to complete, explain, and fix the meaning of the Armenian Creed. We must mention the profession of faith addressed in 1166 by Nerses Shnorhali to Manuel Comnenus; that presented to pope Pius IV. by Abgar, the Ambassador of the Catholicos Michael of Etchmiadzin (1562–1563); that of the Catholicos Azarias of Sis (1585); that addressed in 1671 by David, the Armenian archbishop of Iṣfahān, to Louis XIV.; those addressed to the same king by Stephen and James, the Armenian archbishops at Constantinople (1671), and by Gaspar, the Armenian bishop of Cairo. On the other hand, the Roman Curia imposed on the Armenian Church two professions of faith: (1) the constitution of Eugenius IV., *Exultate Deo*; (2) the creed of Urban VIII., intended for all the Christians of the East.

LITERATURE.—Le chevalier Ricaut, *The Present State of the Greek and Armenian Churches, A.D. 1678* (London, 1679); E. Dulaurier, *Histoire, dogmes, traditions et liturgie de l'église armén. orientale*[2] (Paris, 1857); A. Balgy, *Historia doctrinæ catholicæ inter Armenos* (Vienna, 1878); Aršak Ter-Mikelian, *Die armen. Kirche* (Leipzig, 1892); J. Catergian, *De fidei symbolo, quo Armenii utuntur observationes* (Vienna, 1893); F. Kattenbusch, *Das apost. Symbol* (Leipzig, 1894); Hahn, *Bibliothek der Symbole und Glaubensregeln der alten Kirche*[3] (Breslau, 1897); Macler, Nos. 141, 145.

The following are the chief points of doctrine on which the creed of the Armenian Church differs from that of other Christian communities. As regards the Procession of the Holy Spirit, after much hesitation and even much indifference, the Gregorian Armenians profess that the Holy Spirit proceeds from the Father, and reject the *Filioque*. The Armenians reject the decisions of the Chalcedon Council relative to the Incarnation; they call themselves Monophysites, admitting only one nature in Christ. The Gregorians, in reciting the *Trisagion*, retain the addition *qui crucifixus es pro nobis*, while some Catholic Armenians have rejected it. The Gregorians deny *purgatory*, but they pray for the dead like the Catholics, consecrating to this devotion the day after Epiphany, Easter, the Transfiguration, the Assumption, the Exaltation of the Cross, and the day of the holy Vardanians.

There is diversity of opinion among the Armenian doctors regarding the primacy of the Pope. The patriarchs, being equal in power, are *co-ordinate* the one with the other, and not *subordinate* to a superior patriarch. The Churches were founded by the Apostles and their disciples. These were sent by Jesus Christ, not by Peter; thus nothing enjoins the primacy of the Pope as a fundamental dogma of the Christian Church. The Armenians *baptize* by immersion, repeated at the name of each of the Divine Persons; hence a triple immersion. The anointing is with holy oil, and the person baptized receives the name of the saint whose festival is celebrated on the day of the baptism. Only the priest can baptize, and baptism may be administered even to a child already dead. *Confirmation* follows very soon after baptism. The anointing is done on the forehead, the eyes, the nostrils, the ears, the mouth, the shoulders, the breast, the hands, and the feet. Each anointing is accompanied by a special formula. The Armenians make use of unleavened bread and of wine unmixed with water as elements for the Eucharist. They make confession principally on the occasion of the great festivals, preferably at Epiphany or at Easter. They admit in theory the sacrament of *Extreme Unction*, but they never

* In this art. the foll. abbrevv. are used:—Petit=L. Petit, 'Arménie' in *Dict. de théol. catholique* (Paris, 1902); Macler=F. Macler, *Catalogue des manuscrits arméniens et géorgiens de la Bibliothèque Nationale* (Paris, 1908).

administer it. The Gregorians have a hierarchy of orders very carefully organized, including the office of precentor and reader; then the inferior orders of porter, reader, exorcist, and candle-lighter; and the superior orders of sub-deacon, deacon, and priest. The consecration of bishops is reserved for the Catholicos. Marriage is permitted to the inferior clergy, rigorous celibacy being enjoined only on the vartabeds and the bishops. Women are not excluded from the functions of the deacon. In Anatolia the Catholic Armenian priests are generally married; elsewhere they observe more freely the law of celibacy, which is not obligatory on them. When a priest has to say Mass, he passes the preceding night in the church. When a priest who is already married has to receive ordination, he spends forty days in the church; then there is a social repast, during which the wife of the priest sits on a stool, and keeps her mouth, her eyes, and her ears shut, as a sign of the reserve which she exercises with regard to the functions of her husband.

LITERATURE.—Galano, *Conciliatio Ecclesiæ Armenæ cum Romana* (Rome, 1690); de Moni, *Histoire critique de la créance et des coutumes des nations du Levant* (Frankfort, 1693); G. Avedichian, *Dissertazione sopra la processione dello Spirito Santo dal Padre e dal Figliuolo* (Venice, 1824), and *Sulle correzioni fatte ai libri ecclesiastici armeni nell' anno 1677* (Venice, 1868); J. B. Asgian, 'La chiesa armena e l'Eutichianismo' in *Bessarione*, vii.; E. Azarian, *Ecclesiæ armenæ traditio de romani pontificis primatu, jurisdictione et inerrabili magisterio* (Rome, 1870); A. Balgy, *Historia doctrinæ catholicæ inter Armenos unionisque eorum cum Ecclesia romana in concilio Florentino* (Vienna, 1878); J. Issaverdenz, *Rites et cérémonies de l'église arménienne* (Venice, 1876); Petit, fasc. vii. col. 1950–1958.

2. Councils.—Besides the councils common to Christianity, the Armenian Church has national councils, of which the following are the most important. Setting aside the traditional accounts relative to the first councils, the authenticity of which is more than doubtful, we must mention the Council of Yashtishat (*c.* 365 A.D.), held under Nerses the Great. Regulations were laid down regarding the laws of marriage, fasting, hospitals, and the schools where the young were taught Greek and Syriac. The laws for the monastic orders were there determined. Later, Sahak is said to have promulgated in A.D. 426, at a Council of Valarshapat, a certain number of rules intended to regulate the observance of festivals, funeral feasts, and the conduct of the clergy and priests. The canons of the Council of Shahapivan (A.D. 447) have for their special aim the refutation of the heresies which invaded Armenian Christianity and threatened to extinguish it. This was also the aim of the Council of Yashtishat (A.D. 449). At the Council of Valarshapat (A.D. 491) the Armenians made common cause with the Georgians and the Albanians in condemning the Council of Chalcedon; and this decision was maintained and affirmed still more definitely at the Council of Tvin (A.D. 525), where the two festivals of Christmas and Epiphany were fixed for the 6th of January. In A.D. 596 another Council of Tvin condemned the Chalcedon decrees. At the Council of Karin (*c.* 633 A.D.), Heraclius summoned the Greeks and Armenians, and had the union between these two nations proclaimed; the festivals of Christmas and Epiphany were fixed for different days, and the formula *qui crucifixus es pro nobis* was removed from the Trisagion. Another Council of Tvin (A.D. 645), condemned once more the Council of Chalcedon. John of Odzun, who is said to have summoned the Council of Manazkert about A.D. 719, gathered into a volume the canons of the Fathers and of the councils previous to the 8th century. About A.D. 770 the Synod of Partav fixed the books of the Old Testament which the Armenians regarded as authentic, and made rules relating to certain details of ecclesiastical discipline. At the Council of Shirakavan, held in A.D. 862, the Armenians accepted the decrees of the Chalcedon Council, anathematized the Councils of Manazkert, settled the articles of their faith in fifteen canons, and made peace with the Greeks. In the reign of Manuel Comnenus, several attempts were made to bring about a union between the Greeks and the Armenians. They resulted in the Council of Rom-Kla (A.D. 1179), at which Nerses of Lambron delivered a discourse on conciliation which is still famous. At the Council of Tarsus (A.D. 1196), Nerses of Lambron delivered another discourse with a view to the union. The Council of Sis (A.D. 1243) laid down rules regarding the election and nomination of priests, bishops, etc.; the Councils of A.D. 1307 and 1316 ratified the preceding ones, and furnish a complete profession of faith of the Armenian Church at this time. In A.D. 1439 the Armenians took part in the Council of Florence.

Along with these principal councils there were a number of special councils and synods, for the decrees of which we refer our readers to the works which deal specially with them.

LITERATURE.—Cl. Galano, *Conciliatio Ecclesiæ armenæ cum Romana* (Rome, 1690); H. Gelzer in *Berichte d. kgl. Sächs. Ges. d. Wiss.* (Leipzig, 1895); J. B. Asgian, 'La Chiesa armena e l'Arianismo' in *Bessarione*, vi.; J. Issaverdens, *Hist. of the Armenian Church* (Venice, 1875); F. C. Conybeare, 'The Armenian Canons of St. Sahak, Catholicos of Armenia' in *AJTh*, vol. ii. (1898), p. 828; Karapet Ter-Mkrttschian, *Die Paulikianer im byzantinischen Kaiserreiche* (Leipzig, 1893); Hefele, *Hist. of the Church Councils* (Eng. tr., Edin., 5 vols., 1896); E. Dulaurier, *Recherches sur la chronologie arménienne* (Paris, 1859), *Historiens arméniens des Croisades* (Paris, 1869), t. i.; *Domini Joannis Ozniensis opera*, ed. by J. B. Aucher (Venice, 1834); E. Azarian, *Ecclesiæ armenæ traditio de romani pontificis primatu* (Rome, 1870); Mgr. Ormanian, *Le Vatican et les Arméniens* (Rome, 1873); P. Hunanian, *Hist. of the Œcumenical Councils of the East* (in Armenian) (Vienna, 1847); Mgr. Abel Mikitariantz, *Hist. of the Councils of the Armenian Church* (in Armenian) (Valarshapat, 1874); the works, in Armenian and in translation, of Koriun, Agathangelos, Elisæus, Eznik, Sebeos, Moses of Chorene; Petit, fasc. vii. col. 1925–1933; J. Dashian, *Catalog der armen. Handschriften . . . zu Wien* (Vienna, 1895); Macler, *s.vv.* 'Conciles,' 'Canons,' and the names of places where the councils were held.

3. Festivals.—The Armenian Church celebrates five principal festivals: Christmas, Easter, Transfiguration, Assumption, and Exaltation of the Holy Cross. The day before these festivals is devoted to the Church, the day after to the commemoration of the dead.

The day before Christmas the poor boys of a village or town go from door to door, or from terrace to terrace, holding in their hands lanterns made from gourds, sing a Christmas carol, and receive fruit and cakes as a reward.

The festival of the Transfiguration (*Vardavaṙ*) is called the Festival of Roses, after an old heathen festival which was celebrated on the same day. On the day preceding this festival, the commemoration of the Tabernacle of the Jews is held. On that day people sprinkle each other with water when they meet in the streets; and in certain provinces of Armenia pigeons are set free, either in recollection of the Deluge, or as a symbol of Astlik, the Armenian Venus.

On the day before the Assumption, the vision of Gregory the Illuminator is commemorated.

According to the canons of the Armenian Church, the priests are allowed to receive as offerings the skin and the right shoulder of the animals sacrificed in the churches on the days of the great festivals, in commemoration of the souls of the dead, or in honour of some great saint.

Other festivals play an important part in the religious life of Armenia. The day before *Candlemas* (Presentation in the Temple), fires are lit in the courts of the churches, and the people dance round them, jump over them, and so on.

The festival of *Vičak* (Fate) is one of the principal Armenian festivals, and one of those which seem to be relics of pagan times. It begins on the day before Ascension Thursday, and lasts till the

Sunday of Pentecost. The day before Ascension the young girls of the village meet together and choose several of their number to organize the festival. The members of this committee take a pitcher made of baked clay, fill it with water drawn from seven fountains or seven wells, and close the mouth of the pitcher with flowers gathered from seven fields; then each of the girls throws some object into it (bracelet, ring, button, bead from a rosary, etc.), wishing at the same time some good wish for her father, brother, or sweetheart. They have to shut their eyes while throwing the object into the pitcher and meditate deeply on their wish. On the Wednesday or Thursday night they hide the pitcher in the corner of a garden in the open air, to expose it to the influence of the stars, and they watch that it is not taken by the boys, who prowl about there all night, and try to discover it and carry it off. If the young men succeed in taking it, they give it back to the girls only in exchange for a large quantity of eggs and olive oil, which they have to offer. If, on the other hand, the young men do not succeed in getting possession of the pitcher, the girls sing songs in which they are made fun of (A. Tchobanian, *Chants populaires arméniens*, pp. 57–59; M. Abeghian, *Armenischer Volksglaube*, Leipzig, 1899, pp. 62–66.

Marriage, baptism, and burial are family festivals which are the occasion of special ceremonies and customs in Armenia.

(*a*) *Marriage.*—'Among the Armenians, children are betrothed from their earliest youth, sometimes when only three years old, sometimes as soon as born. When the mothers on both sides have agreed to marry their son and daughter, they propose the union to their husbands, who always sanction the choice of the wives. The mother of the boy then goes to the friends of the girl, with two old women and a priest, and presents to the infant maiden a ring from the future bridegroom. The boy is then brought, and the priest reads a portion of the Scripture, and blesses the parties. The parents of the girl make the priest a present, in accordance with their means, refreshments are partaken of by the company, and this constitutes the ceremonies of the betrothals. Should the betrothals take place during the infancy of the contracting parties, and even should twenty years elapse before the boy can claim his bride, he must every year, from the day he gives the ring, send his mistress at Easter a new dress,' etc. (Jones, *Finger-ring Lore, historical, legendary, anecdotal*, Lond. 1877, p. 312 f.).

It frequently happens that the bridegroom-elect does not see his betrothed during the engagement. On the marriage day a priest and a sub-deacon go to the house of the bride. The bridegroom arrives there with great pomp, and receives for that day the title of *king*, while the bride is called *queen*. The latter is then veiled, the priest says some prayers and blesses the young husband and wife, and then they set out for the church, where the nuptial blessing is pronounced and Mass is celebrated. The priest places on the head of each a crown, which they retain from three days to a week. The company sing wedding hymns on the way to and from the church. After a few days the priest goes and receives back the crowns, and then the young people's married life begins. Marriage cannot be celebrated during fasts or the dominical festivals, of which there are about 260 in the year.

(*b*) *Baptism.*—A short time after the birth of a child, the parents and the god-father carry him to church. They stop at the entrance, and the priest recites some prayers, after which they go into the church, making as many genuflexions as the number of days of the child's life, and the god-father makes confession. Then the infant's clothes are taken off, and he is immersed three times, his head turned towards the west, his feet towards the east, and his face towards the sky. After the baptismal water the priest anoints the child's head several times with holy oil, and clothes him in a linen robe. The child is then made to adore the Cross, and is taken home in state.

(*c*) *Burial.*—The day before that on which the body is to be carried to the church, the relatives, neighbours, and friends of the deceased meet in the house, each bringing a lamp with three or seven wicks, which they arrange, all lighted, round the coffin, and then they begin to sing in turn some funeral hymns. On All Souls' days (Christmas, Easter, Assumption, Transfiguration, Invention of the Cross) the families invite a popular poet to sing over the grave at the cemetery the praises of the person who has just died (A. Tchobanian, *op. cit.* p. 119). For some days after the funeral ceremony the priest goes to visit the relatives of the deceased; then on the Saturday of this week of mourning the relatives and friends meet and take part in a social repast, the remains of which are distributed among the poor.

LITERATURE.—E. Boré, *Arménie* (Paris, 1838); J. Issaverdenz, *Rites et cérémonies de l'église arménienne* (Venice, 1876); Petit, fasc. vii.; A. Tchobanian, *Chants populaires arméniens* (Paris, 1903), *Les Trouvères arméniens* (Paris, 1906), p. 130; F. C. Conybeare, *Rituale Armenorum* (Oxford, 1905).

4. Saints of the Armenian Church.—A glance at the Armenian Menology will suffice to show that the Armenian Church has adopted a large number of the saints of the Greek and Latin Churches. It has, besides, its national saints, for whom it has naturally great veneration. The principal of these are St. Rhipsime and St. Gaiana, who fled from Rome to avoid the carnal desires of the Emperor, and took refuge in Armenia, where their blood was shed for the cause of the gospel; the saintly translators, Moses of Chorene, David the Philosopher, Eznik of Kolb, Elisæus the Vartabed, St. Mesrop; and St. Sahak, St. Leo, St. Nerses Shnorhali, St. Nerses of Lambron, St. Gregory the Illuminator, and St. Nerses I. the Great. St. Vardan is the national saint and patriot *par excellence*. When Armenia was struggling in the 5th cent. against Persia and the introduction of Mazdaism, Vardan Mamikonian became the moving spirit in a general insurrection and in the struggle of Armenian Christianity against the Zoroastrian religion. He perished at the battle of Avarair; but the agitation for independence started by him continued for many years. St. Sarkis (Sargis or Sergius) is the saint invoked by prisoners, captives, those with difficulties to face, and especially by young girls in order to obtain a handsome sweetheart. If it snows at the festival of St. Jacob or St. James, it is said that the beard of the saint is falling on the earth. St. Karapet (John the Baptist) is regarded in Armenia as the most influential of the saints. His seat is at Mush, where his relics are found in the church named after him, which is one of the principal places of pilgrimage of the Armenians. Women are forbidden to enter the enclosure within which is the tomb of the saint, because it was women, Herodias and Salome, who caused John the Baptist to be beheaded. Young girls give a needle to friends going to kiss the tomb, begging them to rub it against the tombstone, so that they may be able with this sanctified needle to produce marvellous embroidery. Young women cannot go and kiss the tomb unless they make a vow never to marry. Those who have made this vow are allowed to sing with the choir during Mass (A. Tchobanian, *Chants populaires arméniens*, p. 149, n. 1). According to John Mamikonian, a very pious Armenian princess who was determined to enter the sanctuary was almost immediately smitten by Heaven as a punishment for her presumption (V. Langlois, *Collection des historiens anc. et mod. de l'Arménie*, i. 348, 362 f.). St. Karapet is the patron of the bards (*trouvères*), who go on pilgrimage to ask him to heighten their poetic imagination.

LITERATURE. — H. F. B. Lynch, *Armenia, Travels and Studies* (London, 1901); A. Tchobanian, *Les Trouvères arméniens* (Paris, 1906); 'Zenob de Klag' and 'Jean Mamikonian' in V. Langlois, *Collection des historiens anc. et. mod. de l'Arménie* (Paris, 1867), t. i.

5. **Sects.**—Armenian Christianity, in the course of the centuries, has had to struggle against the assaults of different sects and heresies in order to preserve its homogeneity. Gnosticism penetrated into Armenia in the 2nd cent.; Marcionism also crept into the Armenian Church and was refuted by Eznik (*Des Wardapet Eznik von Kolb, wider die Sekten*, tr. by Joh. Michael Schmid, Vienna, 1900, p. 172). About the same time are found traces of the Borboriani and the Messalians, of which sects the Paulicians seem to be a continuation through the Middle Ages. Mention is made also of the existence of Adoptianist churches as early as the 3rd century. The most important sect of the Middle Ages was that of the Paulicians, famous for their struggle against the worship of images. It has been established by Conybeare that they were Adoptianists. They believed that Jesus was born a man, and that He became Christ at the moment of His baptism; but they did not regard Him as equal to God the Father. The Paulicians practised adult baptism. The Thondracians, a sect founded about A.D. 820 by Smbat, rejected infant baptism, the worship of the saints, of the Virgin and of images, purgatory and the hierarchy. There still exist in the Caucasus some adherents of this sect. The Arevordians ('Sons of the Sun') are met with in the 12th cent.; their doctrine recalls the old ideas of Armenian paganism.

LITERATURE.—*Nersetis Clajensis opera omnia*, ed. J. Cappelletti (Venice, 1833); *Domini Joannis Ozniensis philosophi Armeniorum catholici opera*, ed. J. B. Aucher (Venice, 1834); Karapet Ter-Mkrttschian, *Die Paulikianer im byzantinischen Kaiserreiche und verwandte ketzerische Erscheinungen in Armenien* (Leipzig, 1893); 'Die Thondrakier in unsern Tagen' in *Zeitschr. für Kirchengeschichte* (1893); F. C. Conybeare, *The Key of Truth, a Manual of the Paulician Church of Armenia* (Oxford, 1898); Petit, fasc. vii. col. 1900; S. Weber, *Die katholische Kirche in Armenien* (Freiburg, 1903).

6. **Superstitions and Peculiarities.** — The Armenians, although Christians, have, like other Christian peoples, popular beliefs and superstitions which have passed down through the ages. The peasant women believe that there exist three *spirits of childbirth*—the spirits of the evenings of Tuesday, Thursday, and Saturday. The first two are virgins and sisters, and the third is their young brother. If the wives have not spent the evenings of Tuesday, Thursday, and Saturday with their husbands, these spirits aid them in childbirth. The Sunday spirit remains near the door of the birth-chamber and fulfils all his sisters' orders; he carries water and eggs, makes the fire, etc. The two sisters take the child, bathe it and prepare the omelet for the mother; and sometimes they present a gift to the newly-born child. But these spirits are also vindictive; and when a woman does not respect them, they avenge themselves by tormenting her, and sometimes by killing the baby (*Revue des traditions populaires*, x. [1895] 2). Each child has from its birth a guardian angel who protects him against evil spirits. This angel's duty is to cut the child's nails and amuse him with the golden apple which he holds in his hand. When the child is old enough, the guardian angel goes back to heaven. The child smiles to him and stretches out his little arms (*ib.* x. 4). The Armenian peasants believe also that *spirits of disease* exist. They are small in stature and wear triangular hats; and they hold in their hands a white, a red, and a black branch. If they strike any one with the white branch, he will fall ill, but will soon recover; if it is with the red, he will have to stay in bed for a long time; but if it is with the black, then it is all over with him, and nothing will cure him. The spirits have books in which are written the names of the men who must die or fall ill, and the appointed days; and the spirits act according to these books. The people believe also that there is a spirit called the 'Writer' (*Grol*), who writes men's names and the date of their death in a book called the 'book of the non-existent.'

The *devs* are tyrants possessing seven heads. They can throw the largest rocks a great distance. Their wrestling is like the shock of mountains, which causes lava to pour forth. The female *dev* is about the size of a hill; she throws back her left breast over her right shoulder, and her right breast over her left shoulder. The *devs* prefer to dwell in very thick forests or deep caverns. They are very rich in gold and silver, and possess horses of fire which enable them to cover great distances in the twinkling of an eye. *Devs* covet the company of young women of the human race, to whom they grant everything they ask. The young men are continually at war with the *devs* in order to get back the women, who show the men how to carry out ruses by which they may become the masters of the *devs*, who are ignorant, cowardly, boastful, and narrow-minded (*RTP* x. 193–196; Grikor Chalatianz, *Märchen und Sagen*, Leipzig, 1887, pp. xiv–xx). The witches are old women who have a tail which is not visible during infancy, but which develops with age. They can become invisible when they wish, enter anywhere, and cross the world in a few minutes. They mount on earthen jars, take in their hands a serpent which serves as a whip, and, flying to the seventh heaven, pass over all the universe. They act chiefly in love intrigues. Their ordinary business is to enchant the heart of a young man or woman, carry off a young girl in spite of her parents, and kill the irreconcilable rival or make him fall asleep (*RTP* x. 196). There are also good sorcerers, who are quite disposed, with the aid of supernatural powers, to render service to human beings (G. Chalatianz, *Märchen und Sagen*, p. xxxi ff.; F. Macler, *Contes arméniens*, Paris, 1905). The Armenians believe also in the existence of dragons, and possess numerous tales and legends which refer to these supernatural beings. The Armenians, especially those of Eastern Armenia, make great use of *rolls of prayers* containing magical or talismanic formulas, intended to protect them against the evil eye, slander, the anger of enemies, against sorcerers and enchanters, false love, and the bite of serpents, to conciliate lords, kings, generals, and the great, and to exorcize demons and other impure beings. These rolls of prayers are called *kiprianos*, or rather *girpaharan*, because they include prayers attributed to St. Cyprian. They are generally ornamented with vignettes, which belong to somewhat rudimentary art, but are very much used by the people (see 'Amulette' and 'Cyprianus-Buch' in P. Jacobus Dashian, *Catalog der armenischen Handschriften in der Mechitharistenbibliothek zu Wien*, Vienna, 1895; Macler, Nos. 97–102).

LITERATURE. — M. Abeghian, *Armenischer Volksglaube* (Leipzig, 1899); G. Chalatianz, *Märchen und Sagen* (Leipzig, 1887); H. von Wlislocki, *Märchen und Sagen der Bukowinaer und Siebenbürger Armenier* (Hamburg, 1892); A. G. Seklemian, *The Golden Maiden, and other Folk-Tales and Fairy Stories told in Armenia* (Cleveland, Ohio, 1898).

IV. *ARMENIAN CATHOLIC CHURCH OR ARMENIAN CATHOLICS.*—There have been in almost all times Armenians who recognized more or less the supremacy of Rome. But it was recognized only in a sporadic and casual way until the time of the Crusades, when the Armenians of the kingdom of Cilicia, or Lesser Armenia, were in constant contact with the Crusaders, and consequently with the Roman Curia. Later, in the 14th cent., Dominican missionaries founded influential communities of disciples in Armenia. These were the class of native missionaries known as 'Uniters' (*unitores*), and had as their first superior John of Kerni (or of Khrna). He had a translation made of the works of Bartholomew of Bologne, who was sent to Armenia by Pope John XXII. in 1318 (Macler, No. 149). Subsequently, especially in the 17th cent., other orders established missions among the Armenians, particularly among the Armenians of Persia: the Augustinians at Iṣfahān, the Jesuits at Iṣfahān, Julfa, Erivan, etc. The French Lazarists settled at Tauris and at Iṣfahān. Soon all the communities extended their ramifications into all the principal Armenian centres of the East—Iṣfahān, Ormuz, Shiraz, Banderabbas, Hamadan, Shamakia, Erzerum, Trebizond, etc.

Until the middle of the 18th cent., Catholic Armenians did not form an autonomous community; now they have a hierarchy of their own, a recognized religious autonomy, and a patriarch who resides at Constantinople. These results have sprung from the dissensions which occurred between 1737 and 1740 in connexion with the catholicate of Sis in Cilicia. The Catholicos of Sis was deposed, and he retired to Lebanon, where he founded the convent of Bzommar and a new religious order. This new state of things caused intestine quarrels between the Catholic and the Gregorian Armenians. We may note especially the quarrel of the Hassunists and the publication of the Bull *Reversurus*.

LITERATURE.—Galano, *Conciliatio Ecclesiæ armenæ cum romana* (Rome, 1690); E. Scrosoppi, *L'Empire ottoman au point de vue politique vers le milieu de la seconde moitié du xixe siècle* (Florence, 1875); A. Balgy, *Historia doctrinæ catholicæ inter Armenos* (Vienna, 1878); A. Boré, *L'Arménie* (Paris, 1838); L. Alishan, *Sisacan, contrée de l'Arménie* (Venice, 1893), an art. devoted to the 'United Brethren' in the cantons of Erinjak; de Damas, *Coup d'œil sur l'Arménie* (Paris, 1888); J. B. Piolet, *Les Missions catholiques au xixe siècle* (Paris, 1900); H. F. B. Lynch, *Armenia, Travels and Studies* (London, 1901); Petit, fasc. vii.; S. Weber, *Die katholische Kirche in Armenien* (Freiburg, 1903). For the disputes which have arisen over the subject of Avedik and Aghtamar see *Bibliographie analytique des ouvrages de M. Marie-Felicité Brosset* (St. Petersburg, 1887); Dashian, *Catal. der arm. Handschr. in der Mechitharistenbibl. zu Wien* (Vienna, 1895); F. Macler, *Catal. des manuscrits armén. et géorg. de la Bibliothèque Nationale* (Paris, 1908).

V. *PROTESTANT ARMENIANS.*—The work of the Protestant missions among the Armenians dates from the beginning of the 19th century. It was specially prosperous from the day on which the Sublime Porte granted independence to the Protestant community. The Protestant missions in Armenia belong, on the one hand, to the Missionary Societies of England and America, and, on the other, to those of Basel. They have stations in the most important centres of Turkey in Asia, and some in Persia (Tauris, Teherān, Iṣfahān), and in Russia (Shusha, Tiflis). There are nearly 200 pupils in the Robert College at Constantinople; the college at Scutari is reserved for girls.

LITERATURE.—E. Scrosoppi, *L'Empire ottoman au point de vue politique vers le milieu de la seconde moitié du xixe siècle* (Florence, 1875), pp. 78–81; H. F. B. Lynch, *Armenia, Travels and Studies* (London, 1901); Petit, fasc. vii. col. 1920.

VI. *MUSALMĀN ARMENIANS.*—The attachment of the Armenians to Christianity is well known, and when they are abroad their religion stands to them in the place of nationality. In spite of this love of their religion, some Armenians, persecuted by the Musalmāns, have adopted Muhammadanism. Thus, two or three centuries ago, the Armenians of Hamshen, to the east of Trebizond, after some bloody massacres, accepted in thousands the law of Islām. They are therefore Turks, but they speak a dialect which betrays their Armenian origin. The Kurds, it is said, are ancient Armenians who have passed under the law of Islām.

About 1751, a certain Chalabi, who was very fanatical, associated himself with the Persian Musalmāns, and conceived the plan of massacring the Armenians if they would not be converted to Muhammadanism. He tortured them first, cutting off their ears so that they might not hear the singing in church, cutting out their tongues so that they might not speak their mother language, and putting out their eyes to strike fear into the other Christians. Chalabi inflicted these tortures on the poor, and granted honours and titles to the rich to impose silence on them. By this means thousands of Armenian families became Musalmāns, especially in the province of Oudi. In this province above all, the Muhammadans destroyed the churches and Christian sanctuaries, so that the Christians might the more quickly forget their original religion. In the province of Oudi many names recall their Armenian origin; at Gis is found a much venerated sanctuary of St. Elisæus. The Musalmāns as well as the Christians make pilgrimages to it, light candles, and address very fervent prayers to the saint; and in several villages in the neighbourhood of this sanctuary the Musalmān Armenians swear by St. Elisæus. They have preserved some old Christian customs. For example, when a mother is putting her child to sleep, she makes the sign of the cross over it, and murmurs the name of Jesus. When the paste is prepared, a young Armeno-Musalmān wife makes a cross on it with her fore-arm before putting it into the oven. The Armeno-Musalmān villagers of the province of Oudi are very bigoted and very suspicious; they distrust all foreigners, and never speak of matters of religion.

In Lasistan, also, several Armenian villages have become converted to Islām, from fear of tortures and massacres. There are found among them the same traces of Christianity as among their brothers of Oudi and elsewhere.

LITERATURE.—*Aghouanits erkir iev dratsikh* (Tiflis, 1893); *Loys*, Calendar for 1905 (Tiflis, 1904), pp. 191–196 (both in Armenian).

VII. *ARMENIAN COLONIES.*—There are Armenian colonies spread over all parts of the world; for example, in Europe: Poland, Sweden, Denmark, Holland, Russia, Turkey, Bulgaria, Transylvania, Roumania, Lower Danube, Macedonia, Greece, Dalmatia, France, Italy, Spain, Portugal, etc.; in Asia: Persia, Afghanistan, India, Japan, Palestine, China, etc.; in Africa: Egypt, Ethiopia; in America: United States; the English and Dutch Indies, Batavia, etc. These colonists generally lose their nationality, and adopt that of the country in which they are living; but they remain faithful to their religion, which is now the bond of the Armenian nation, since they no longer have a political autonomy.

LITERATURE.—L. Alishan, *Sisacan* (Venice, 1893).

FRÉDÉRIC MACLER.

ARMINIANISM.—I. Occasion of Arminianism.—Arminianism was a revolt against certain aspects of Calvinism, of far-reaching importance in the history of the Reformed Theology. It took place in the dawn of the 17th century. Against the Catholic absolutism of the external Church, Calvinism had set the absolutism of the eternal decrees. The situation was rigid with a new dogmatism. A recoil was inevitable. Many symptoms of dissent were manifest before Arminianism arose as a definite reaction. After Calvin's death, the more rigorous Calvinistic divines, including Beza, asserted that the Divine decree to salvation, being antecedent to the Fall, required for its accomplishment the decree to sin. Sin was ordained not as an end, but as a means; it is here because there was something that God could not accomplish without it. What is first in the Divine intention is last in the Divine execution.* The primal purpose was the decree to save. But if man is to be saved, he must first be lost. Hence the Fall was decreed as a consequence of a decreed salvation. Those who held this position were **Supralapsarians.** It is doubtful whether Calvin himself held it. More moderate exponents of Calvinism connected the Fall with the permission of God, instead of with His foreordination. The Divine decree takes the existence of sin for granted, deals with man as fallen, and elects or rejects him for reasons profoundly indifferent to human judgment. This was the **Infralapsarian** position. An unequal rivalry between the exponents of these two schools was the immediate occasion of the rise of Arminianism. In Holland, which, in the 17th cent., owing largely to the immigration from France of Protestant theologians of distinction, had become, more than Switzerland, the centre of theological activity, the extreme views of the Supralapsarians found much favour. An acute and effective criticism was directed against them by James Arminius (Jacobus Arminius or Jakob Harmensen or Van Herman; also known as Veteraquinas, from *Veteres Aquæ* or Oudewater, the name of his birthplace). Arminius, who was born in 1560 and died in 1609, was a scholar of considerable reputation. He had studied at Leyden, resided at Geneva, and travelled in Italy; he was a learned and popular preacher at Amsterdam, with a pastoral career marked by fidelity and heroism; eventually he became, in 1603, professor of theology at Leyden. Even his enemies testified to his blameless and noble character. He was a consummate controversialist and a lucid expositor, with a remarkable gift of method. Trusted by the Supralapsarian leaders, he was requested in 1589 to answer Theodore Koornhert, of Amsterdam, who had attacked the high Calvinistic doctrine of Beza and the Genevan school, of which Arminius had been a distinguished disciple. Others had already replied to Koornhert, who were disposed to surrender Beza's extreme position in favour of one equivalent to Infralapsarianism. In preparing his reply, a process of doubt culminated in Arminius embracing the tenets he had undertaken to refute. He clearly perceived that the doctrine of the absolute decrees involved God as the author of sin; that it unworthily restrained His grace; and, leaving myriads without hope, condemned them for believing that for them there was no salvation either intended or provided in Christ. He saw, moreover, that it gave to those who believed themselves to be the elect a false security based upon no sufficient ethical principle. Arminius' conversion was succeeded by cogent criticism; and criticism by prolonged controversies, during which he was led by successive and careful stages to a luminous and impressive constructive exposition of those theological positions antagonistic to Calvinism which have since been associated with his name. Though it is probable that Arminius himself was less Arminian than his followers, yet the most distinguished of these, Episcopius (his successor at Leyden), Uyttenbogaert (his close friend), Limborch and Grotius, who most ably elaborated his positions—all men of great talents—only carried his conclusions to issues which the early death of Arminius probably prevented him from reaching. Arminianism spread amongst the clergy. Political differences and difficulties confused the purely doctrinal issue. Great statesmen, like Olden Barneveld, advocated Arminianism and Republicanism, as Calvinists preferred Supralapsarianism and Maurice, Prince of Orange. The martyrs for Arminianism probably suffered for political rather than for doctrinal heresy. From the beginning the Arminians were greatly outnumbered by their opponents. Their main strength lay in the genius and learning of their leaders. Dialectically they were victors; ecclesiastically and politically they were vanquished. With their defeat came many disabilities and some temporary persecution.

* *Cambr. Mod. Hist.* ii. 717.

2. **Doctrinal positions.**—The creed of the Arminians was set forth in the Five Articles of the Remonstrance addressed in 1610 to the States-General of Holland and West Friesland, from which fact its adherents received the name of **Remonstrants.** The articles were drawn up by Uyttenbogaert and signed by forty-six ministers. The Remonstrance is first negative, stating the five Calvinistic articles in order to reject them, and then positive, stating the five points of the Arminian position. Briefly summarized, the following are their positions. The first asserts conditional election, or election dependent on the foreknowledge by God of faith in the elect and of unbelief in those who are left in sin and under condemnation. The second asserts universal atonement in the sense that it is intended, although it is not actually efficient, for all. The third asserts the inability of man to exercise saving faith, or to accomplish anything really good without regeneration by the Holy Spirit. The fourth declares that the grace of God is indispensable in every step of the spiritual life, but that it is not irresistible. The fifth asserts that the grace of the Holy Spirit is sufficient for continual victory over temptation and sin; but the necessity of the final Perseverance of all believers is left doubtful. This last article was afterwards so modified by the followers of Arminius as to assert the possibility of falling from grace.

Gomarus, the university colleague of Arminius, but his chief antagonist in personal controversy, now engineered a counter-Remonstrance drawn up in less moderate terms. Negotiations for peace failed. An embittered controversy became involved with political intrigue. The famous **Synod of Dort** was assembled (1618–9) more to exercise ecclesiastical discipline than to reconcile the disputants. The Arminian theologians were excluded, and the Synod constituted itself accuser and judge. The Arminian articles were condemned, their preachers deposed, and recalcitrants banished. The Synod promulgated five heads of doctrine of its own, which present Calvinism in its unadulterated but not in its extreme form. Within the Arminian system processes of development set in, all moving in the direction of liberalism and comprehension. These will be noted in their place. Our present interest is with the leading principles of Arminianism. These are: (*a*) the universality of the benefit of the Atonement; (*b*) a restored freedom of the human will as an element in the Divine decrees and in opposition to the assertion of the absolute sovereignty of God. Apart from these and kindred questions involved in the problem of predestination, Arminianism has no definite theological distinctness. It attempts no fresh statement of the doctrines of God and man. These were accepted as they stood in the recognized creeds and confessions of Christendom; its general theological system was that of the orthodox Protestant Churches. But its specific contribution was of sufficient importance to rank it amongst the few really outstanding and permanent developments in theological thought. The three fundamental terms of theological definition and discussion—God, Man, and the essential relations between them—are represented in the three great controversies of historical theology by the names of Athanasius, Augustine, and Arminius. Athanasius represents the movement which gave specific definition to the Church's doctrine of the Divine nature. Augustine stands as the great exponent of the inner moral significance of human nature and of the relation of the individual to the race. Arminius found his place as the interpreter of the ethical relations between God and man. His system recognized and expounded the developed doctrine of God and of man, which the Church had long accepted as established positions, but which her theologians had never satisfactorily related. Calvin had revived Augustinianism, and had pushed it to further logical issues. He made much of God, as Pelagius had made too much of man. Both gave isolation and distance to terms that could be completed only in mutual relations. Neither provided a scheme of reconcilation. The aim of Arminius was to express with dialectic vigour the only doctrinal position consistent with the necessary relations between God and man. This relation within the sphere of the provision and administration of redemption provided the points of controversy between his system and that of Calvin. The mission of Arminianism was to show how God could be what the Church taught He was, and man what the Church declared him to be, at one and the same time. The mode of re-adjustment of the disturbed and abnormal relations of man to God by justification was the central point of Protestant theology generally; the announcement and the ethical interpretation of the significance of the mutual relations between God and man in that adjustment was the contribution to theology offered by Arminianism. Its system is a *via media*; it strove to avoid sources of inevitable and historical error arising from the tendency to magnify either of the related terms by the virtual or formal suppression of the other. The exaltation of the Divine agency to the complete suppression of the human in that adjustment issued in simple Determinism; the exaltation of the human in complete suppression of the Divine in the same sphere led to the extreme positions of Pelagianism. Arminianism claimed to have stated, for the first time, with scientific care a balanced judgment on those relations of God and man in which their harmony and mutual recognition could be stated as a working principle, verifiable and verified by experience.*

To appreciate the *theological* value of Arminianism, it is important to review and interpret the points which differentiate it from Calvinism. To estimate its influence philosophically, it is needful to state and illustrate its two great principles—its ethical recognition of justice, and the emphasis it lays upon the human in the redemptive relations between God and man.

3. Criticism of Calvinism.—Arminianism regarded the Calvinistic position as open to attack on two sides—the side of God and the side of man. Its treatment of these was considered to be disproportioned and ethically unfair. The sphere in which God exercised His will was the soul of man. That will, therefore, concerned man and his acts. If such acts were performed solely because God had so determined, two consequences followed:—the acts would reveal the quality of the will, and man would not be consciously free; he would know himself as an instrument rather than as an agent. The criticism was urged therefore as much in the interest of man and of morality as of theology. In fact, Arminianism was at the bottom an attempt to formulate a protest against Calvinism from an ethical standpoint. It used much circumspection in the attempt. It carefully rejected, with Calvinism itself, the pagan leaven, which had lingered in the old Church, in the form of reliance placed upon human nature alone. But it renewed the sense of reality to human responsibility, and emphasized the moral conditions of reward and penalty. At the same time it sought to give psychological consistency, especially by its great doctrine of prevenient grace, to the common Protestant principle that man is entirely dependent, in all that concerns his salvation, upon the grace of the Spirit of God. The task undertaken by Arminianism was to re-state what was regarded as the primitive and Scriptural view, held by the Church before Augustine, concerning the relation between God and man in the work of salvation; and in this view the sole responsibility of man for his own damnation was evident. The criticism of Calvinism, therefore, found centres of attack in the following five points:—

* *Amer. Meth. Qtly. Rev.* (1857) 346.

(1) *Predestination.*—This the Calvinist held to be absolute and unconditioned. The decree to elect was without foresight of faith or of good works. In its operation the Divine will was unmotived from without, moved only from within, either by the grace or by the necessity of the Divine nature. The decree to reprobation was conditioned by no specific demerit of the reprobate. He was not distinguished in or by his personal sin. His reprobation was simply because of sinfulness of nature or habit, which, being common to all men, involved all men in equal guilt and penalty. No ethical difference was discernible between elect and reprobate. The Arminian criticism insisted on the ethical incompleteness of this view. The principle of the election of grace is maintained. The Divine will is absolutely supreme. But its supremacy is moral. God is not more bound to punish than to forgive. The Divine decree, whether elective or reprobatory, is conditional throughout. God elected to salvation or to reprobation only those whose faith or final disbelief He foresaw. The Divine foreknowledge logically precedes the Divine volitions; it is not an inference from them; it is intuitive, but not necessitative. What God knows, though its issue is absolutely certain, is not necessitated by that cognition.

(2) *Atonement.*—The Calvinist held the Atonement to be strictly limited. Its relation to the non-elect was incidental; its intention was for the elect alone. For them its efficacy was absolute. It so satisfied Divine justice on their behalf that they could not fail to be saved. For were any lost, the penalty of sin would be twice inflicted—once upon Christ and again on the sinner for whom He had died. This was a thing impossible to Divine justice. The Arminian held that the Atonement was universal. It was of infinite value, designed for all, accomplished for all. It made the salvation of no man actual, but rendered the salvation of all men possible, the result being in every case conditioned by faith. Christ died for all, but only believers receive the benefit.

The character of Arminian theology is illustrated in one of its most important writings, the treatise of Grotius on the *Satisfaction of Christ*, written in opposition to Socinianism. He develops the doctrine towards an issue not strictly in harmony with the position of Arminius, by stating what is known as the **Governmental Theory.** Both aimed at mediating between the rigorous Anselmic view of a satisfaction which is the substitution of a strict equivalent for the penalty due to sin and the Socinian rejection of all vicarious intervention. They agree that the atoning reparation satisfied not the rigorous exaction of Divine justice, but chiefly the just and compassionate will of God, emphasizing the love rather than the justice of God as honoured in the Atonement. The death of Christ is not the payment of a debt to a creditor, but a substitution counted sufficient by God the Father for a judicial penalty. Grotius emphasized the relation of God to man as a Ruler, and carried out the Arminian conception of 'the wrath of God' as His goodness regulated by wisdom. He regarded the motive of the Divine government as the desire and provision for the happiness of the governed. In this rectoral relation the ruler has a right to remit a penalty, provided the end for which the penalty was appointed is otherwise attained. This end is the preservation of order and the prevention of future transgressions. The death of Christ as a 'penal example' secures this end, showing impressively what sin deserves and what the penalty would be were it actually inflicted on the transgressor. It is a manifestation of the Lawgiver's hatred of sin. It is not actual punishment, but rather the symbol of it. As it is not the literal penalty, God may freely determine what other conditions for bestowing pardon are suitable. In the light of the Calvinistic view of the absolute sovereignty, this rectoral theory was a surrender of the theory of satisfaction. But the Arminianism of Arminius laid much stress on the inflexibility of God's righteousness, which consists, according to Episcopius, in maintaining His truthfulness in attaching a penalty to His commandments. Episcopius himself, however, still held to a modified Anselmic position by regarding the sacrifice of Christ as a price; because God is willing so to regard it. Limborch is a closer representative of Arminianism. He asserted that Christ suffered as a Divinely appointed sacrifice, and reconciled God to man as if the sinner had suffered himself. Arminianism generally renounces the commutative theory of exact and mutual compensation, since some perish for whom Christ died.*

(3) *Depravity.*—The Calvinist held this to be total, involving bondage of the will and inability to any spiritual good. By the Fall the nature of man was poisoned at its inmost core, and original holiness and righteousness changed into absolute depravity. No distinction was made between imputed guilt and inherent depravity. Arminianism held that depravity was a bias, which left the will free and man responsible for his own destiny through the choice of faith or unbelief. The Adamic unity of the race was preserved, but its inherited tendencies to evil were met and neutralized by the free and universal grace communicated to the race in Christ—the second Adam. Absolute reprobation cannot therefore be based upon the doctrine of original sin. Arminianism denied that the sin of Adam is imputed to his posterity in the sense of their being guilty of, and chargeable with, the sin Adam had committed. A clear distinction is made between actual and original sin. The free gift of grace to the whole race in Christ is the foundation of the entire Arminian system. Its great contribution to the discussion of sin was the decisive assertion of the doctrine of prevenient grace, due to the universal diffusion of the influences of the Holy Spirit, and consequently the acceptance in every age of those who strove after natural uprightness. Grace, therefore, though not the solitary, is yet the primary cause of salvation. To this primary cause is due the co-operation of freewill; for upon its stimulus by grace prevenient depends the co-operation of the will with grace efficient.

Later Arminianism declined in some degree from this position. Less exalted views of the original state of man were current. To preserve intact the original freedom of the will, the conception of a primitive state of perfect holiness was discounted. A state of primitive innocence must have been allied with primitive ignorance. It was also doubted whether immortality originally belonged to the nature of man. With milder views of original sin greater stress was laid on the physical impurity of human nature; it was also denied that its corruption had in it the true characteristics of sin. The inclinations to evil inherited from Adam are not in themselves blameworthy; they are only different in degree from the same appetites in Adam. It is only consent to them that becomes real guilt. The 'innate liberty of the human will' was regarded as able to co-operate of itself with the Divine law. The Arminianism of Methodism reverted to the earlier position, holding that whatever power there is in the human will—in its ability or its choice—is the issue of redemption. No ability remains in man to return to God. The co-operation of grace is of grace. The Augustinian idea of 'common grace' is rejected in favour of the co-ordinating of the universality of grace with the universality of redemption. No man is found in a state of mere nature; nor, unless he has finally quenched the Spirit, is he wholly devoid of the grace of God. The virtues of unregenerate man are not *splendida vitia*, but works of the Spirit. Such virtues are a universal experience of the race. If Adam brought a universal condemnation and seed of death upon all infants, so Christ brings upon all a general justification and a universal seed of life.

(4) *Conversion.*—Both Calvinist and Arminian regard this as the work of the Holy Spirit. But Calvinism maintained the grace of God to be irresistible. The calling of God was both effectual and efficacious, and due to the immediate operation of the Spirit of God upon the soul. The Arminian asserted that the Divine action was mediate, through the truth, and thus moral and persuasive, as distinguished from physical and necessitating. Moreover, the grace which is effective to the processes of repentance and renewal may be finally resisted. The firm maintenance of universal redemption by Arminianism naturally affected its theory of justification at many points. Whilst holding, in common with the Reformed standards generally, that Christ's obedience is the only meritorious cause of justification, and faith its sole instrumental cause, and that good works have no kind of merit, Arminianism did not distinguish between the active and passive obedience of Christ. Gradually also it denied the direct imputation of Christ's righteousness. Faith came to be regarded as justifying, not as an instrument uniting the soul to Christ, but as an imperfect righteousness, which is mercifully accepted by God as if it were perfect. Whilst repudiating the view that works merit salvation, the Arminians asserted that the faith which justifies is regarded by God as a faith which includes obedience. This is the position both of Arminius himself and of his followers. It is allied with a tendency, distinctly marked, to define faith in terms of intellectual assent rather than as trust. It became a simple reception of the doctrines and laws of revealed religion. The influence of grace was by no means merely of a moral nature. It wrought in and accompanied the word of God. Its influence therefore, whilst supernatural in its character, was in its mode of operation analogous to the natural power of all truth. This tendency to invest faith with merit as a means of justification was suspected of approaching ultimately the Roman doctrine of merit by works on the one side, and of favouring the antinomian tendencies which had been condemned as inherent in Calvinism, on the other. A fair criticism of its attitude applied to it the term *Neonomianism*, because of its supposed introduction of a new law—the law of grace—according to which the legal righteousness for ever impossible to man finds a human substitute in an evangelical righteousness accepted of God, though imperfect, for Christ's sake. The title detected the perilous tendency, which the later history of Arminianism did not escape, of the notion that Christ has lowered the demands and standard of the moral law.

Methodist Arminianism met these tendencies in two ways:—(1) It declared that, though God requires faith, it is also His gift. He does in Christ pardon the imperfection of the good work wrought by faith, but He does not repute it as perfect so far as concerns our justification. This would be the imputation of righteousness to the believer himself. It is the faith of the ungodly which is reckoned for righteousness, even before it can produce its first act towards good works. (2) There was the definite insistence in Methodist theology upon the necessity as well as the possibility of entire sanctification. This teaching formulates and urges the demand that faith must be justified by works. It protests against the distinct imputation of the active obedience to man, whilst it clings to the imputation of Christ's righteousness generally. The Methodist teaching on entire sanctification was quite in harmony with the main contentions for which Arminianism stands, and ought to be regarded as a supplement to the views of the early Arminians, who wrote much on the question of Christian perfection. They left its principles and processes, however, largely indefinite. Compelled by their theological convictions, they maintained that such holiness as God reputes perfect may be attained in this life. If grace is free, it will be full. They distinguished between a first perfection of the beginning of Christianity, a second of the unimpeded progress of regeneration, and a third of established maturity of grace. Of the means, assurance, and limitations of the last stage they made no positive declaration. Perfection is proportionate and progressive. It is not sinlessness, but the 'expulsive power of a new affection,' excluding the habit of sin. Arminianism exhibits its doctrine more in opposition to the Roman works of supererogation or Calvinistic antinomianism than in its profound relation to sin and

* Pope, *Comp. Christ. Theol.* ii. 312.

love, and to evangelical perfection. Arminius writes: 'While I never asserted that a believer could perfectly keep the precepts of Christ in this life, I never denied it; but always left it as a matter to be decided' (*Works*, i. 608). The vital question of the abolition of sin was never, either by Arminius or his successors, decided upon. His protest against ultra-Calvinism was taken up by the German Pietists, and, in purer form, by the English Platonists, who prepared the way for the Methodist modification of doctrine on this subject, which was both mystical and ethical. Its chief contribution was the emphasis laid upon entire sanctification of the believer, as a provision of the covenant of grace, directly administered by the Holy Spirit, in response to faith—a faith working by love, and retained by constant union through faith with the living Christ (see METHODISM).

(5) *Final Perseverance.*—The Calvinist held the indefectibility of the saints. Men unconditionally elected, absolutely purchased by the death of Christ, and irresistibly called out of their depraved and lost estate by the direct operation of the Holy Spirit, could not possibly fall from grace. The Arminian criticism hesitated at first to meet this position by a direct negative. But such a position was speedily seen to be inevitable. And, as a result of its other doctrinal positions, the possibility of a true believer falling from grace was declared. This found warrant also and verification in examples and personal experiences that could not easily be mistaken. Moreover, as the Arminian method revealed a growing distrust of the authority of the Symbolical documents, it was easy to assert that the Calvinistic position professed not so much to be based upon direct Scripture support as to rest upon the necessary principles of the so-called Covenant of Redemption. The provisions of this imaginary covenant between the Father and the Son, before time began, in respect of the certain number to be redeemed and given to the Redeemer, as the reward of His atoning submission, had produced the idea of a fixed and unalterable division of mankind. To this canon every Scripture must be made to conform. It was easily shown that no Scripture evidence of such an unconditional covenant existed. It was less difficult still to urge against it the criticism that its ethical issues provided reasons against its provisions.

Theologically, Arminianism is a mediating system throughout. Its most characteristic feature is conditionalism. Absolutism is its persistent opposite; moderation, the mark of its method. The failure to appreciate this position accounts for the frequent and grave misunderstanding of Arminianism, and for the natural ease with which its delicately balanced judgment has declined, in the hands of some of its exponents, towards theological positions with which it had no true affinity. These have been chiefly Socinianism and Pelagianism — systems due to an over-emphasis upon the human. Much that in certain periods passed for Arminianism was really a modification of one or other of these systems, which a true Arminianism justly repudiates. In Holland, Arminianism, gliding by almost imperceptible degrees, ultimately reached a position with little to distinguish it from Socinianism. In England, where there was a presage of Arminian thought long before the time of Arminius and his system, its principles found an interesting development, and their profession an unusual environment. The influence was seen in the ambiguity or comprehensiveness of the Articles of the English Church. Latimer and Hooper, Andrewes and Hooker might with propriety have been called Arminians, if Arminianism as a system had been in vogue when they wrote. Arminian teaching by Baro, Professor of Divinity at Cambridge, gave rise to the Lambeth Articles also. But Arminianism became a political question, with the singular result that, through the influence of Laud and Juxon, it became allied with the side of the King, whilst it was the Calvinists, with the distinguished exception of John Goodwin, one of the ablest defenders of Arminianism, who stood by the Parliament. But the Arminianism of Laud was not the Dutch Arminianism. Arminius would have denounced its sacramentarianism as superstition. With the issues of the Civil War, Arminianism suffered eclipse, but it returned with prelacy at the Restoration; and for more than half a century its influence was supreme in the Anglican Church. But the later divines of this school depreciated the doctrines of grace, dwelling more upon the example of Christ than upon His atoning work, and the Arminian principle persisted mainly as a negation of Calvinism. Cudworth, Jeremy Taylor, Tillotson, Chillingworth, Stillingfleet, Burnet, Pearson, Whitby, and others, down to Copleston and Whately, were Arminian theologians of eminence in the Church of England. The positive temper of Arminianism, however, suffered under their treatment of the system. Its fine balance between Calvinism and Pelagianism was lost. It was blended with tendencies to Latitudinarianism and Rationalism; and became a negative rather than a constructive or mediating system. It was from this setting, however, of Arminianism in its non-juror environment and atmosphere, that the restored Arminianism of Arminius, with its emphasis on the grace of God, emerged into strength in England in the Evangelical Revival of the 18th century. The Wesleys came of a sturdy Arminian stock of this type. And probably the ablest expositions in English of the Arminian system are to be found in the writings of John Wesley, John Fletcher, Richard Watson, and William Burt Pope, the Wesleyan theologians. Methodists throughout the world, with the exception of the Calvinistic Methodists in Wales, who represent the Calvinistic attitude of Whitefield, who withdrew from co-operation with the Wesleys on this ground, are convinced Arminians, who profess to adhere to the original Arminianism of Arminius and his followers of the earlier type before it approximated to the rationalistic temper of Socinians or Latitudinarians, or was merged in the prevailing tendencies of Restoration theology or American Unitarianism. The Wesleyan type of Arminianism, with its Evangelical note, is at present the most influential. It has spread widely throughout the British Empire and America, and is based upon the conviction that the Calvinistic positions are incompatible with Divine equity and human freedom, whilst its loyalty to the doctrines of grace is the best vindication of Arminianism from the common charge of Pelagianism and Socinianism. Lacking the doctrinal loyalty and the Evangelical vitality of the Arminianism of Methodism, Dutch Arminianism is a dwindling force. The inclination towards freedom of speculation, the rejection of all creeds and confessions, a preference of moral to doctrinal teaching, Arian views respecting the Trinity, the virtual rejection of the doctrines of Original Sin and imputed righteousness, and the depreciation of the spiritual value of the Sacraments, have resulted in the gradual reduction of Arminianism in Holland to a negligible theological quantity, and to the dimensions of an insignificant sect, numbering only some twenty congregations.

4. Underlying principles.—The supreme principle of Arminianism is conditionalism. It provides a philosophical *via media* between Naturalism and Fatalism. As an active criticism of Calvinism it is based upon two positions—the restless and dominant demand for equity in the Divine procedure, on the one hand, and such a reference to the constitution of man's nature as will harmonize with the obvious facts of his history and experience, on the other. It sought to construct a system which should be dominantly ethical and human throughout. It contended, therefore, that moral principles and laws consistently condition the manward activities of the Divine will, and set human limits to the Divine action. The Calvinistic conception of justice was based altogether on the supremacy or rights of God; Arminianism so construed justice as to place over against these the rights of man. Sin, it declared, had not so transformed human nature that man had become a mere vessel of wrath or of mercy, a creature who was reprobate because of guilt he had inherited, or saved by a grace which operated without rational distinctions and without regard to foreseen faith or good works. In equity the worst criminal had his rights. A fair trial before a fair tribunal was one which sin did not invalidate. The consideration of these rights did not cease because the judge was God, and the accused, or even the condemned, was man. The Creator owed something to the creature He had fashioned, because of the manner of His fashioning; and these obligations did not cease because the first man had sinned. In a perfectly real sense sin had only increased the obligation of God to be just. If original sin was what Augustine had stated it to be, and what Calvinism had maintained it was, then it would be truer to the facts it involved to speak of it as a radical wrong from which man unjustly suffered. The race had not been consulted by the first man; in no true sense was he the representative of the individual members of the race; for they had no voice in his appointment, and no veto upon his acts. By every law of justice, therefore, they were to be regarded as objects of commiseration rather than persons to be blamed for what they had suffered, since they suffered as the consequence of the first man's sin, altogether apart from their own voluntary acts of kindred disobedience. And although Arminianism retained the federal principle, and held that the federal relationship had resulted in a weakened will for the individual, and had afflicted him with a bias towards evil, it urged that it was difficult to conceive anything more nearly approaching infinite injustice than allowing such a relation, of itself, to involve millions of men of every age and in every age in eternal death. If all had sinned, all had an equal right to be considered in the provision and administration of any redemptive processes that might be operative. The introduction into these relations of the Arminian principles resulted in a criticism that seemed irresistible; for the moment the idea of equity was admitted to a place in the consideration of the relations of man and God, the old absolute unconditionalism became untenable. If justice reigned, and its principles were common to God and man, it meant that God must be just to man, even though man was disobedient to God; and justice could not tolerate the condemnation of man for a sin which was committed without his personal knowledge or responsibility, any more than it could approve of a salvation which had no regard for the personal will or choice of its recipient.

Arminianism was always most successful when its argument proceeded upon principles supplied by the moral consciousness of man. This recognition of the value of the testimony and of the entire contents of human consciousness was the correlate in Arminianism to the idea of equity; its exposition of the idea of man provided the second of its two main principles. It regarded man as free and rational; sin had not destroyed either his reason or his freedom. By the one he had the ability to believe, by the other the ability to choose. Even if the racial connexion had weakened or perverted these faculties in the individual, the result was not incapacity to act, because the racial connexion with the second Head was intact and operative in the communication of the energy of prevenient grace. In justice, therefore, God must deal with man as possessed of such abilities. On their co-operation with the Divine activity the results in salvation or reprobation depended. Thus the free will of man was regarded as conditioning the absolute will of God. In the realm of nature His physical attributes ruled; His omnipotence was unconditioned. In the realm of mind and will His love and moral attributes governed, and their rule was conditioned. Man was not a part of physical nature merely, or a mechanism involved in the impersonal or unmotived motion of non-moral creatures. His destiny could not therefore be deduced by logical processes from the premise that God is the Sovereign Will, which can do as it chooses; for He has chosen to create man free and responsible; and His attitude and conduct towards man will consequently be conditioned by the nature He has made. If it has been His good pleasure to create man moral, it will not be His will to deal with him as if he were merely physical. If Creator and creature are alike moral in character, it follows that necessitating action on the one side, and necessitated action on the other, are both excluded. By His own voluntary act God has limited the range and exercise of His physical attributes, and so the terms which express His relations to man must be those of reason and freedom, not those of will and necessity. Arminianism offers no disparagement to grace in general, and deepens the emphasis on prevenient grace in particular. But whilst the peculiarity of Calvinism is found in holding fast to the absolute idea of God in opposition to all 'idolatry of the creature,' the centre of gravity of the Arminian system is found in the sphere of anthropology. Its doctrine of man probably differentiates it more definitely from Calvinism than its doctrine of God.*

5. Theological and philosophical influences.—The twofold emphasis of Arminianism on the ethical and human elements in its system declares the sphere and defines the source of the modifying influences it exerted on subsequent theological and philosophical thought. These influences were essentially mediating; and they were mostly indirect. They reached the sphere of philosophical speculation chiefly through theology. But the leading principles of Arminianism were potential in both spheres, in the succeeding periods of intellectual revival. It is well to keep in mind the fact that, in the history of European thought, the 16th cent. was great in theology rather than in philosophy, and that the 17th was great in philosophy rather than in theology. But without the religious thought of the earlier century, the later would have been without its problems, and therefore without its thinkers. The pre-eminence of the one in religion involved the pre-eminence of the other in philosophy. In this influence of theology upon philosophy, and, later still, upon more distinctly ethical thinking, Arminianism had a considerable share. Although questions directly upon ultimate philosophical principles were, on the whole, not in the spirit and thought of the age of Arminianism, yet Arminianism, as more generally true to the whole of the facts of existing problems, was distinctly more open to the access and authority of the modern spirit than Calvinism. By its underlying principles of equity and freedom it was more perfectly fitted than its rival system for a period of intellectual transition. It became the form of Re-

* Fairbairn, *Christ in Mod. Theol.* p. 170.

formation theology which most easily allied itself with the advance of knowledge and with the humanism of the new learning. The Cartesian philosophy, which was bringing about a gradual transformation of theological views, especially in the Netherlands, where already a liberal spirit was showing itself in general uneasiness under the yoke of the Symbolical documents, found especial favour with the Arminians. They had also within their ranks many eminent men, who were progressive thinkers and leaders of thought outside a distinctly theological circle, who exerted a beneficial reaction upon Protestant theology by their thorough scientific attainments and the mildness and toleration of their views. Arminianism stood generally for the strengthening of the scientific temper and for the principle of moderation, which represented dawning methods of far-reaching importance in the intellectual life of the modern nations. On the other hand, this attitude favoured the growing tendency towards Rationalism and Latitudinarianism into which Arminian theology frequently drifted. But that this drift represented any necessary effect of the Arminian movement is disproved by the fact that it was the Arminian system of thought which lay at the theological sources of the great Methodist revival in the United Kingdom and America during the 18th cent., whose leaders re-stated Arminianism in modern theology in its purest form, and vitalized it with the warmth of religious emotion and the joyous assurance of the Evangelical spirit. Arminianism in the glow of the spiritual enthusiasm of the early Methodist evangelists has been truly described as 'Arminianism on fire.'

The Arminians were the fathers of toleration. Amongst its earliest representatives are found stalwart advocates of religious freedom, who were willing to suffer for their views. Within the sphere of opinion Calvinism did not spontaneously incline to toleration; it was inflexibly dogmatic; its instincts and ideals were aristocratic rather than democratic in relation to ethical authority. It is curious to note, however, in spheres more purely political, that an interesting reversal of the natural order of the two systems occurs. As in England the Laudians were Arminian, and the Parliamentarians Calvinistic, so in France the Jansenists were Calvinistic, and the Jesuits Arminian. The natural tendencies of Arminianism to toleration may be instructively traced in the Latitudinarian teaching of the Cambridge Platonists, who were greatly influenced by the writings of Arminian scholars, particularly by those of Episcopius. They pleaded for liberty of conscience, and studied to assert and examine the principles of religion and morality in a philosophical method; they declaimed equally against superstition on the one hand and enthusiasm on the other. Moderation was the first law. They were conspicuous for their advocacy of freedom of inquiry, their toleration of diversities of opinion in non-essentials, their genial temper in controversy, their effort to bring about a reconciliation between theology and philosophy, their recognition of religion as less a doctrine or a ritual than an inward life, and their strong purpose to establish a rational theology, which should avail as a reply to the atheistic polemic. Arminianism, however, made common cause with all religious parties in resisting the dogmatism of the philosophy of common sense, which was declaring open war against the belief in the positive authority of Revelation. And the association of Arminianism with Deism and Naturalism, because of a supposed common fundamental ground in the appeal to reason, may be regarded as an unwarranted exaggeration of the Arminian emphasis on the human. Arminianism could be under no necessity to deny or depreciate the supernatural. By the time the age of speculative criticism and of the antagonism between faith and knowledge was reached, Arminianism as a distinctive doctrinal position had been established and its peculiar contribution made to Systematic Theology. Its influence on such later controversies is only indirect. That the influence was real cannot well be doubted, because of the emphasis on moderation and the more genuine welcome afforded to the products of modern speculation by Arminianism. Whether its influence, through its demand for the recognition of the authority of reason in the theological sphere, affected the philosophical thinking which resulted in the rationalism of Kant, or in its reaction in the subjective theories of Herder, or in the theology of Jacobi or Schleiermacher, it is difficult to say. Certainly Kant's doctrine of the Practical Reason, with its claim for the recognition of the ethical constitution of human nature, was developed in obvious harmony with the Arminian emphasis upon the authority of the moral consciousness as a factor in the interpretation of the relation of God to man. Schleiermacher's doctrine of absolute dependence had definite relation to Calvinism. Only in the place he gives to religious feeling is affinity with the Arminian principles likely to show itself.

With the distinct problems of modern speculative thought—'creation,' 'immanence,' 'mind and matter'—Arminianism, like the other Protestant theologies, had comparatively little concern. The theistic position of the creative act, with its implications, was generally accepted; there was no sufficient evidence, from the scientific study of nature, to suggest irreconcilable differences from the traditional view. In one point, however, Arminianism was peculiar. It laid special stress on creation being the work of the Father as distinct from the equal creative activity of the three Persons in the Trinity. The movement of Arminian thought was set in a framework of political, social, and economic changes which cannot be dissociated from its influences without missing their complete significance; but these are obviously beyond the scope of this article. One fact of importance ought, however, to be noticed. When the problems of 'natural rights' and the distinction between *jus naturale* and *jus gentium*, which had been raised by the philosophers and jurists of antiquity, passed, as a result of the Renaissance, from the region of academic speculation into that of practical politics, the transition was accomplished through an Arminian channel. Grotius was the first to start the question of the distinction between natural and conventional rights, and was thus the father of the modern exponents of the 'Philosophy of Law.' How profound was the influence of this transition upon the course and character of modern systems of Ethics will be obvious. It is here that we come into the presence of one of the less appreciated, but influential services rendered by the Arminian definition and advocacy of its fundamental principles—equity and human freedom. These principles represent the prevailing tendency of the leading ethical theories of the present. Without them the advance beyond the ethics of Scholasticism would have been impossible. Calvinism missed them, and, in doing so, missed the opportunity and the possibility of becoming the basis of an intellectual statement of ethical obligation satisfactory to the modern mind. Although the Calvinistic conception of the Church, as being based upon the individual rather than upon the institutional principle, was essentially different from that of Rome, the Calvinistic ethics is, nevertheless, based upon outward authority—

the authority of a truly organized Church and of the Scriptures truly interpreted by such a Church. This position was not accidental; it was of set purpose. Calvin deliberately subordinated ethics to dogmatics. From the Protestant point of view this was fundamentally reactionary; it was Scholastic in method and aim. The true ethics, and the only ethics consistent with the essential Protestant principle, must be based upon the inward compulsion of conscience, not upon any external authority. External authority could result only in casuistry. This was the Roman method and practice. The ethics of Thomas Aquinas and of Ignatius Loyola expounds a closed system given in the teachings of the Church; the ethics of Calvinism expounds a closed system given in the written Word. 'For true ethical development there is no more room in logical Calvinism than in logical Romanism.' * Ethically, Calvinism and Jesuitism have a common foundation in that they depend upon external standards and sanctions. On this account Calvinism has not, as a matter of history, contributed to the development of ethical theory in any degree commensurate with its magnitude as a religious force. It is beyond question that, as an inspiration to high ethical endeavour, Calvinism has produced types of sacrificial devotion to right conduct which have frequently touched a lofty heroism in the lives both of individuals and of communities in which its doctrinal system has been dominant. Yet it must be acknowledged that the influence of Calvinism, as a system, in the philosophical re-construction of modern ethics has been reactionary. The expansion, on the other hand, of the fundamental principles of Arminianism has wrought harmoniously with the processes of ethical development, which are based upon the manifold ideals and constraints of the moral consciousness of the individual. It was the plaint of the aggrieved moral nature, quite as much as the philosophic intellect, that was articulate in the Arminian protest. The deterministic depreciation of the rights of human nature to the value of a mechanical movement in the presence of the Divine will was the ethical weakness of Calvinism in which Arminianism found its advantage. This stress on the place and functions of human nature in the interpretation of, and co-operation with, the Divine mind was the distinction consistently maintained between the rival systems.

Arminianism was the medium by which the humanistic spirit of the Renaissance was translated into the theological and exegetical sphere. Its great men — Grotius, Episcopius, Limborch, Brandt, Le Clerc—are all men of literary faculty and humanistic temper. In Calvinism the spirit is more distinctly speculative and scholastic, and the intellect deductive and constructive. Its great men—Calvin, Zanchius, Gomarus, Twisse, Rutherford—are all men of speculative genius. It thus easily happened that the tendencies of Arminianism were often—and sometimes rightly—suspected of affinity with Pelagian and Socinian views. These affinities were strengthened by the mingling with the Arminians of Socinian scholars returning from exile; and in many cases Arminianism merged its identity in these phases of thought. It is well known that the exaggeration of Subordinationism by the Remonstrant divines, especially by those of the later age of Arminianism, glided by subtle degrees into the Socinian position. They denied the aseity of the Son, which Calvin had taught. His subordination to the Father, as the Spirit is subordinated both to the Son and the Father, was urged. It was held that, though the Divine nature belongs to the Son and the Spirit, the Father is first in dignity and power. Arminian leaders also favoured the Nestorian conception of the Person of Christ. The agency of the Logos was regarded as a 'special influx' or 'operation' of the Divine nature. It is an assistance of God, involving a communication of Divine powers so far as a creature can receive them. Much more recently the influential Unitarianism of America has succeeded the lingering Arminianism of the New England States, as a one-sided development of prevailing ethical principles respecting the responsibility of man and the enthusiasm for his prerogatives.

* *Hibbert Journ.*, Oct. 1907, p. 180.

Arminianism arose historically in the great age of Protestant Symbolism, which succeeded the period of the earlier expositions of the Reformation theologians, who had based their authority more simply upon the appeal to spiritual experience and its warrant and confirmation in the Scriptures. It was the age of Protestant dogmatics, of which the characteristic was the substitution of creeds and the compulsion of confessions in place of the personal contact of the individual mind with the immediate sources of truth accessible in the writings of inspiration. Arminianism strove to emancipate exegesis from the thraldom of dogmatics. It resisted the tendency to erect everywhere a formulated creed into the position of a supreme arbiter of truth. The formal principle of authority was denied the first place. Ecclesiastical theology had tended to become dominant over Biblical. The Bible was looked upon as an authoritative text-book from which doctrines and proofs of doctrine were to be drawn with little or no discrimination as to the use to be made of the different sacred books. The Word of God and the Bible were identical. No critical distinctions were tolerated. Divines had not to reason their systems, but to unfold them from certain fixed and unquestioned postulates. In the Reformed Church predestination was accepted as the initial principle for the systematic exposition of the Christian religion. Dissent upon any point was treated as heresy. There was no antagonism in Arminianism to the formal principle of Protestantism—the immediate relation of the religious consciousness to Christ—or to the ultimate authority of Scripture. What Arminianism suspected and resisted was the prevailing tendency, which was far from the intention of the original authors of the Symbols, to assign to the Symbolical books of the Protestant Churches the same authority over faith which had been ascribed to tradition in the Roman Church. The Arminians sought to preserve a moderate and less dogmatic orthodoxy, and to introduce generally milder features into the prevailing hard cast of doctrinal systems. At the same time Arminianism, although apparently less intensely antagonistic than Calvinism to Rome, because of the emphasis it laid upon the value of the human in religion, was more truly Protestant in rejecting the Roman principle of the authority of tradition in its Protestant guise of authoritative Symbols. For similar reasons Arminianism was a protest against the mystical principle of interpretation which insisted upon the supremacy of the internal word as a sufficient exponent and infallible judge of the external. Constantly discounting dogma and mysticism alike, the Arminian divines appealed to the analogy of faith, to experience, to reason, to the aid of the Holy Spirit, as essential elements in the interpretation of Scripture. Authority was composite, and involved the whole contents of consciousness. A statement is not true because it is found in the Bible, but it is found in the Bible because it is true of itself. This position—that the Scriptures contain the truth, but are not of themselves the truth—gave considerable impulse to the speculative treatment of theology, and, through the writings of Grotius and Episcopius, issued in methods of theological discussion which gradually extended to the whole Evangelical Church.

The Arminian effort to meet 'the idolatry of Scripture' by the exaltation of the authority of the moral consciousness occasioned the charge against Arminians of laxity in views of inspiration. Their position was confused with the Socinian method of subordinating the authority of Scripture to that of reason, and of making its interpretation depend upon the so-called truths of reason. Here again, however, pure Arminianism is the mediating position. Whilst disagreeing with Luther's position that reason is blind in spiritual things, it resisted the Socinian extreme, as it resisted the rigid and narrow adherence to the letter of Scripture which marked later Protestant theologies. Some of the later Arminians added the canon that Scripture cannot contradict reason. The general position, however, was that reason must be followed in interpretation; that the foundation of religion, on its intellectual side, should be in personal thought and investigation; that neither antiquity nor universality was a proper or sufficient ground of belief; and that every passage of Scripture must be considered separately and in its historical setting and limits. This appeal of Arminianism from the Symbolic methods to the critical treatment of the text and substance of Scripture was a precursor of the methods of careful exegetical study now current, and of their issue in the restoration to authority of Biblical as distinguished from Systematic and Dogmatic Theology.

The reaction from the hardening processes of the Lutheran and Calvinistic divines upon the views, generous for their time, of Luther and Calvin, respecting the human and fallible element in Scripture, which were illustrated in the terms of the Helvetic Formularies and in the Buxtorfs' irrational contention for the inspiration of the Hebrew vowel-points, was inevitable. It was initiated by the Arminian writers, who reserved the direct action of the Holy Spirit for matters of faith, and left historical research and the memory of human writers to their fallible functions. Arminianism thus asserted positions in Biblical interpretation which have proved a basis and authority for the methods now known as the Higher Criticism. Sanctions were also provided for the science and practice of Textual Criticism through the access afforded by Arminian principles to an atmosphere of freer inquiry into the preservation and historical growth of the received texts of the OT and NT.

The Arminian principles of human freedom and personal responsibility, with the humanitarian spirit they tended to evoke, gave a new impulse to the awakening movement towards Foreign Missions, which succeeded the era of rationalistic influence in the Protestant Churches. If the Atonement was universal, and the salvation of the whole race possible, then the sense of responsibility for making known the conditions of salvation to the race was deepened, and a note of urgency was added to the claim for the expansion of Christianity. Moreover, the weak place in the great Protestant confessions had been the anthropological. One of the many effects of this deficiency was seen in the judgment of the Church in respect to the heathen races, which was obviously prejudicial to aggressive enterprise. Calvinistic thought had strengthened this judgment. The application of Arminian principles was amongst the earlier signs of the dawn of the new light upon the nature and history of the races of mankind, and upon their religious possibilities, which has since broken in the ethnic results of the kindred sciences of Anthropology and Comparative Religion. And the system, amongst the Protestant theologies, least discredited by the new light, is Arminianism.

Reference must be made finally to a great service Arminianism has rendered to theological thought generally. This is discovered in the subtle influence it has exerted in the gradual softening and humanizing of the harsher forms of theological definition. As a separate and separable system, either ecclesiastically or theologically, its reign was brief; as a genial and vitalizing influence, suffusing itself through all the discussions of the relation of God to man, its authority is ageless. It has wrought, often secretly and unacknowledged, towards the approximation of the position of modern theology respecting Predestination to that which was held by Catholic Christendom before the age and teaching of Augustine. Substantially the Churches of East and West were united, before his time, in holding the primitive and Scriptural view of the relations between God and man in the work of salvation, and of the sole responsibility of man for his own damnation, which it was the effort of Arminianism to restore. How far the disturbance of the thought of the Church on these relations, brought about by the revived and intensified Augustinianism of Calvin, has been redressed by the influence of Arminianism, is at present only partially discernible. It is, however, certain that it has greatly modified the specific views which were the objects of its original contention, as they are now held by Calvinistic theologians; it has also become a dominant factor in the current re-statement, to the present generation, of the doctrines of grace. The reduction of the area of Calvinistic influence, and its partial disintegration in communities where it had long been established, are facts that cannot fail to challenge attention. When Arminianism arose, very early in the 17th cent., the Calvinistic creed prevailed largely in Bohemia and Hungary; it was supreme in Switzerland, Holland, the Palatinate, and in the Protestant Churches of France, Scotland, and England, where, until the close of Elizabeth's reign, it was the prevalent theological influence; and shortly afterwards it grew to strength in the Puritan settlements of America. Over all these areas a steady disintegration of its force may be traced. Many factors have co-operated in this result. But of those which may be regarded as theological and ethical, the active principles upon which Arminianism insisted have been prime causes.

In France an early and interesting illustration of the modifying influence of Arminianism occurred in the theology of the school of Saumur, associated particularly with the name of Amyraut (see AMYRALDISM), and later with that of Pajon. Amyraut endeavoured to mitigate the harsh repugnance of the Calvinistic doctrine of election by his theory of hypothetic universal grace, which was substantially equivalent to a doctrine of universal atonement. God, in some proper sense, wills or desires that all men should repent and be saved. In case all should repent, no purpose of God would stand in the way of their salvation. But the indispensable means of repentance—regenerating grace, following election—is not bestowed upon them. In the order of nature the decree of election follows the decree providing the atonement. The main peculiarity of Pajon's attempt to blunt the edge of Calvinistic particularism was his conception of regenerating grace. The Spirit uses the truth of the Gospel as its instrument in effecting the antecedent intellectual change; but He also uses all the circumstances and providential environment of the individual. To this aggregate of objective influence, which is not the same in different individuals, regeneration, where it takes place, is due. It is the act of God because the antecedent circumstances are the effect of God's ordering, and are adapted by Him to produce the result. Pajonism aroused wide-spread interest in the French Church.

In Germany the strength of Lutheran influence was already in sympathy with the Arminian movement. Its influence was also strong, though silent, in the bosom of the Reformed Church itself; and by the time of the Wolfian movement, the Reformed dogmatics were moving from the doctrine of the absolute decrees. Amongst the English-speaking peoples, in addition to the influences, already referred to, which strongly modified the theology of the great school of Anglican divines, the influence of Butler became a powerful ally of Arminianism. His doctrine of probation was not the Calvinistic doctrine of the probation of the race, but the Arminian insistence on the probation of the individual in his unshared and unshareable responsibility.

In the Methodist revival Arminianism became aggressive. Associated with the renewed vitalities of personal godliness, the Arminian theology, carried by singers and preachers, passed swiftly across the Atlantic, and accompanied the earliest settlers as they moved, from east to west, across the continent. In the newer British Colonies at the Antipodes a similar influence has wrought, until, at the present day, Arminianism, as understood and taught by Methodist preachers, dominates what is probably the largest Protestant Church in the world, reckoning some thirty millions of adherents. In America the matchless intellectual gifts of Jonathan Edwards were consecrated to the task of checking and devitalizing the forces of Arminian doctrine. But the ultimate results were disappointing to Calvinistic theologians. The New England theology, where it has not passed under Unitarian influences, has revealed a persistent modification of the Calvinistic position. The distinctively Calvinistic formularies of faith in Great Britain and America have undergone revision, mostly at those precise points which were the objective of the Arminian attack.

Modern theology in general has tended to forsake the harshness and absolutism of doctrinal statement, without surrendering the deeper significance of the ultimate supremacy of the Divine will. And this position was the original idea and ideal of Arminianism. There is a deep and almost universal dissatisfaction with the declaration and issues of a limited Atonement, which was a main element in the Arminian objection to Calvinism; and a strong conviction prevails that the salvation of the non-elect is an object of sincere desire to the mind of God. Yet it will be obvious that it is not the doctrine of Predestination *per se*, in which Calvinism has enclosed the realms of nature and providence in a network of teleology, that excites the strongest repugnance to the system against which Arminianism rose to protest.* For Determinism in philosophy and Selection in biological science are still acceptable and popular equivalents for Election in the realm of grace. Differentiation is a basal principle in each of these spheres; but differentiation involves inequality; and inequality involves preference; for it is admitted that the differences are original, so far as individuals are concerned. Biology posits differences in the single cell. Psychological ethics starts the career of individual character with differences *ab initio*. Popular inferences assume that the difference between Cain and Abel, or between Esau and Jacob, is an illustration of the same principle that differentiates the hawk from the dove or the hart from the swine. It is rather towards the Calvinistic eschatology that the antagonism is most keenly felt. The aspect of injustice and cruelty which this element in the Calvinistic system wore to the early Arminians, it wears to the modern mind. The humanity of God has become an element in the standard of judgment applied to the Divine activity. Fatherhood has dispossessed Sovereignty. Immanence has modified transcendence. When to such tendencies is added the momentum of the critical and exegetical methods which prevail in the modern interpretation of Scripture, to which Arminianism gave countenance and impetus at their origin, it may be possible to show some justification for the claim, made by the advocates of Arminian principles, that they possess the requisite possibilities of adaptation for the re-statement of the doctrines of grace demanded by the appeal to the conditions of modern thought. Moreover, the persistence and prevalence of Arminian principles presage a place of prominence for them among the contributory forces which appear to be making for an inter-confessional and international theology, based upon critical exegesis and upon a philosophy which includes the whole facts of human nature, whilst yielding reverent allegiance to the mystery and reality of the Divine Sovereignty.

* Fisher, *Hist. Christian Doctr.* p. 550.

LITERATURE.—(1) *FOR LIFE AND TIMES OF ARMINIUS*:—His funeral oration by his friend, **Petrus Bertius**, *de Vita et Obitu J. Arminii Oratio*; **Caspar Brandt**, *Historia Vitæ J. Arminii* (Amsterdam, 1724) [republished and annotated by Mosheim (Brunswick, 1725), and translated into English by John Guthrie, 1854]; **Bangs**, *Life of Arminius* (New York, 1843).

(2) *FOR EARLY PERIOD OF CONTROVERSY*:—*Writings of Arminius* (mostly occasional treatises drawn from him by controversial emergencies) collected and published at Leyden in one quarto vol. 1631 [Eng. tr. by Nichols, vol. i. in 1825 and ii. in 1829 by J. Nichols; and vol. iii. in 1875 by Wm. Nichols; later edition, with vol. iii. by W. R. Bagnall, in 1853]; *Acta synodi nationalis Dordrechti* (Dort, 1620); *Acta et scripta synodalia Dordracena* (Harderwyck, 1620); **Schaff**, *Creeds of Christendom* (New York, 1877), vol. iii. 550–597; **Uyttenbogaert**, *Kerckelijcke Historie* (Rotterdam, 1647); **Gerhard Brandt**, *Historie der Reformatie* (Amsterdam, 1663 [Eng. tr. by Chamberlayne, 4 vols. 1720]; **Limborch**, *Historia Vitæ Sim. Episcopii* (Amsterdam, 1701), and *Relatio Historica de Origine et Progressu Controversiarum*, etc., appended to later edition of his *Theologia Christiana*, 1714; **Episcopius**, *Institut. Theol.* 1650. For valuable list of other writers see **Cattenburgh**, *Bibliotheca Scriptorum Remonstrantium* (Amsterdam, 1728).

(3) *FOR PERIOD OF DEVELOPMENT*:—**Burnet**, *Exposition of Thirty-nine Articles*; **Browne**, *On Thirty-nine Articles* (1864); **Laurence**, Bampton Lecture, 1804; **Whitby**, *Discourse on Five Points* (London, 1817); **Nichols**, *Calvinism and Arminianism Compared* (2 vols., London, 1824); **Playfere**, *Appeal to Gospel for true Doctrine of Predestination* (pub. in Cambridge Tracts, 1717); **Hoard**, *God's Love to Mankind*, etc. (London, 1633); **Neander**, *Hist. of Chr. Doctr.*, vol. ii. 678 ff.; **Gess**, *Gesch. d. prot. Dogmatik*, vol. i. 379 ff.; **Ebrard**, *Christl. Dogmatik*, §§ 24–43; **G. S. Francke**, *Hist. Dogm. Armin.* (Kiel, 1814); **Shedd**, *Hist. of Doctr.*, Bk. iv. ch. viii., Bk. v. ch. vi.; **Hagenbach**, *Hist. Doctr.* (Eng. tr., Edin. 1880), vol. iii. 22–225; **Fisher**, *Hist. Christn. Doctr.* (Edin. 1902), 337 ff.; **A. M. Fairbairn**, *Christ in Mod. Theol.* (1894) 169 ff., 431 ff.; *Cambridge Mod. Hist.* (1903), vol. ii. 717 f.; **Stuart**, 'Creed of Arminius' (*Bib. Repos.*, Andover, vol. i. 1832); **Orr**, *Progress of Dogma*, 295 ff.; **Cunningham**, *Essays on Theol. of Reformation* (1865); **Girardeau**, *Calvinism and Evangelical Arminianism Compared* (Columbia, 1890); **Curtiss**, *Arminianism in History* (Cincinnati, 1894).

(4) *FOR THE METHODIST TYPE OF ARMINIANISM*:—*Works of John Wesley* (14 vols., London, 1840); **John Fletcher**, *Five Checks to Antinomianism* (in Complete Works, 8 vols., London, 1836); **Richard Watson**, *Theol. Institutes* (3 vols., London, 1823); **William Burt Pope**, *Compendium of Christian Theology* (3 vols., London, 1879); **W. F. Warren**, *Amer. Meth. Quart. Rev.*, July 1857.

FREDERIC PLATT.

ARNAULD, ARNAULDISM. — See PORT ROYAL.

ART.

THE religious art of savage and barbarian races constitutes a field of inquiry the limits of which are exceedingly difficult to trace with any accuracy. There seems to be no doubt that among some tribes religion dominates almost the whole of individual as well as of social life. The Pueblo Indians in Arizona and New Mexico may be quoted as an example of such thoroughly religious peoples. The better the customs of these Indians have become known, the more evident it has become that even the apparently most trivial actions are to them associated with religious feelings and ideas. From birth to death the Pueblo Indian is, passively or actively, partaking in an almost continuous act of religious worship. In the art production of such tribes the religious purposes are naturally apt to become almost exclusively predominant.

It is true that the Pueblo tribes appear to be quite exceptional in their inclination towards pious practices. But if the word 'religion' be taken in its widest sense, as including magical ideas and superstitious beliefs, there might easily be found many other tribes among whom religion exercises an all-predominating influence on art production. And the field of religious art becomes further widened if, as has been done by several authors, traditionalism is included under the head of religion. Among almost all uncivilized nations, everything that has been transmitted from ancestors to descendants is treated with a respect which closely resembles religious feeling. And in art, even if the products we meet with be of recent origin, the methods employed in production have almost everywhere been transmitted from earlier generations.

It is only natural, therefore, that several authors should have been led to consider all ethnic art as essentially religious. This opinion is represented by some of the most eminent German ethnologists. According to Dr. Gerland, the distinguished continuator of Waitz's *Anthropologie der Naturvölker*, dances, pantomimes, and dramas, however meaningless they may now appear, have always originally been connected with religious ceremonies. The articles of dress and ornament with which primitive man decorates his body are, by ethnologists of this school, interpreted by preference as magic signs or religious symbols. And in works of art, such as rock paintings and engravings, the sacred and serious meaning has been taken for granted.

Against this line of thought, however, a reaction has set in among other German ethnologists. In his remarkable essay on petroglyphs (*Ethnographische Parallelen*) Andree has branded as a learned bias the general tendency to look for some sacred meaning in all ancient drawings, many of which may have had their origin simply in the impulse of the idle hand to scratch lines and figures on inviting surfaces. Other ethnologists have pointed out how easily the simplest dances and songs are to be explained as outbursts of an emotional pressure, which in itself has nothing to do with religious feeling. And it has been urged that the religious sanction, which traditionalism confers upon all ancient customs, does not in itself give us any information as to the real origin of these customs.

However sound in its principle, the reaction against the religious interpretation may, nevertheless, easily lead to a too radical scepticism. The case of the carved ornaments of the Hervey Islanders is most instructive in this respect. Notwithstanding the deriding strictures originally passed, in the name of common sense, on the symbolic interpretations of Stolpe and Read, an unbiassed examination can lead only to the conclusion, that in these apparently meaningless figures we really meet with a symbolic art which is full of religious significance (Stolpe in *Trans. of the Rochdale Lit. and Scientif. Soc.* 1891).

By such examples it is proved beyond question how impossible it is to uphold any *a priori* assertions as to the religious or non-religious character of primitive works of art. In order to estimate with exactness the influence exercised by religion on the earlier stages of æsthetic development, it would be necessary to examine in detail and from a philosophical point of view the artistic productions of all tribes of mankind. Such an examination has as yet been undertaken with regard to only a few tribes: the Hervey Islanders, the inhabitants of the Torres Strait regions, the Dayaks of Borneo, the Pueblo Indians, and some others. In an article for an Encyclopædia, there could in no case be any question of endeavouring to supplement these gaps in our knowledge. The only thing therefore that can safely be done is to interpret, at the risk of incompleteness, such works and manifestations alone as display their religious character on the surface. And it will be necessary, in order to keep the survey within reasonable limits, to exclude all works the origin of which is to be found in an exclusively magical purpose. Thus the various kinds of dramatic rain-making rituals, and the magically-medical cures, although generally executed by the religious profession, will not be treated of in this connexion (see MAGIC).

1. Dramatic art.—The simplest of all forms of religious art, from a theoretical point of view, are those dances and songs which are resorted to in order to bring about exaltation. The ceremonies of the Muhammadan dancing and howling dervishes and of many other well-known sects, might be quoted in proof of the fact that, among civilized as well as among barbarous peoples, a highly strung emotional state, even if produced by purely physical agency, is considered as a religious feeling. And it is significant that the only form of artistic manifestation that has been observed among the lowest of all savages—the wood Veddahs of Ceylon—consists of an exalted dance, which has justly been compared with the antics of the Siberian shamans and with the performances of the howling dervishes. As to the exact purpose of this ceremony, travellers do not all agree. Some take it to be intended as a kind of propitiation, addressed to the divinity of the arrow—an arrow being always stuck in the earth in the centre of the dancers. According to others, the dance might be explained as a kind of thanksgiving; others again see in it a rite, aiming at the expulsion of demons. But however much these interpretations may differ, the religious character of the ceremony has been taken for granted by almost all the different authorities. And their descriptions of the 'arrow dance' coincide at all important points (P. and F. Sarasin, *Naturwiss. Forsch. auf Ceylon*, iii.; Emerson Tennent, *Ceylon*; Hoffmeister, *Travels*; Deschamps, *Au Pays des Veddas*; Schmidt, *Ceylon*).

The participants in the dance are all men. At the outset, they advance slowly around the arrow without touching each other. Every dancer turns round on one foot, whilst performing some spasmodic movements with the free leg. The arms describe circles in the air, and the head is thrown backwards and forwards, to make the long, entangled hair stand out like a brush from the crown. The music is a simple melody, which is sung, or rather howled out, by the dancers. The time is marked by strokes of the hand on the nude belly. All this is begun in relative tranquillity. But gradually the time grows quicker, the movements become more violent, and the howling louder. Thus the dancers work themselves up to the utmost frenzy, and finally, one after another, fall to the ground in exhaustion. Some of them lie on their backs 'as stiff as a fallen tree,' whilst others, continuing the howling, tremble in convulsive vibrations.

This 'arrow-dance' is typical of a large class of dance-performances, examples of which are met with amongst most of the lower races, sometimes as mere amusements, but more often as religious rites. The means employed in order to bring about the exaltation and the convulsions may, indeed, be more complicated than those resorted to by the Veddahs. Thus, among some North American Indian tribes (cf. Schoolcraft, *Indian Tribes*, v.) the dancers prepare themselves for their performance by some days of fasting, and increase their state of exaltation during the dance by partaking of drugs or inhaling poisonous smoke. The clappings on the nude belly are, at higher stages of culture, replaced by the sound of some instruments capable of a greater suggestive power. But the spirit of the performance is none the less the same all over the world. Whether the dancers belong to the Ainus, to some of the aboriginal tribes of India (Aquis, Kurs, Santals), or to some South- or West-African race (Basutos, Tshi-speaking peoples on the Gold Coast), their chief endeavour is always to throw themselves, by violent movements and sounds, into a state of exaltation, which borders upon, or really passes over into, insensibility and unconsciousness; and it is the same endeavour which characterizes the celebrated shamanistic performances of the tribes of Northern Asia (cf. *e.g.* Radloff, *Sibirien*; Mikhailovski in *Journ. Anth. Inst.* xxiv. 62, 126).

In the shamanistic rites, however, we meet with one important feature that is not represented in the Veddah dance. In this example, the frantic scenes seem to be over at the moment unconsciousness is attained. In the higher developments of the arrow-dance type, however, it is from this moment that the real performance begins. And what follows, far more than the dance itself, is apt to give a religious character to the rite.

It is well known that on the lower stages of culture lunatics are generally considered as possessed by some divinity, and are consistently treated with a kind of religious respect. It is only natural that the same attitude should be upheld in those cases where the mental disorder is acute instead of chronic. And the shamanistic psychosis is the more liable to be interpreted in a supernatural way, since the shamans, in accordance with the traditionally-fixed programme of their performances, invariably astonish the bystanders by jugglery and feats of insensibility, such as eating fire, lacerating themselves with knives and needles, etc., made possible by their exalted and anæsthetic state (see SHAMANISM). The sudden change in the voice and behaviour of the convulsive dancer, together with the apparently supernatural power he exhibits, must necessarily lead the primitive spectators to the inference that a divine personality has taken hold of the shaman, while he himself is endeavouring by all means in his power to confirm the spectators in this belief. He delivers oracular utterances in a mystic voice, which is taken to be the voice of the god, or he keeps up long dialogues with the divinity, who is supposed to be visible to him, but is audible only to the bystanders. We have not in this connexion to decide whether these representations are wholly fraudulent, or whether they may have their origin in some visual and auditory hallucinations of the shamans. The important fact, from our point of view, is that in either case the orgiastic and, so to say, lyrical dance, which forms the beginning of the shaman performance, has passed over into something which, in its effect, if not in its intention, is to be considered as a work of dramatic art.

2. Pictorial art.—In these dramatic representations we meet with an expression of the belief—which may partially have been prompted by the facts of shamanistic possession—that the priests are, or may for a time become, inhabited by the divinity. If, as primitive peoples seem to believe all over the world, the priest really is a kind of 'god-box' (to use the picturesque expression of the Polynesians), then it is evident that the actions he is representing must impress his pious spectators as an eminently religious drama. But even if there had been no belief in a particular class of 'god-boxes,' dramatic representation would still have acquired a religious importance, on the ground of the belief in the magical effects which imitations of things and movements are supposed to exercise upon the things and movements that have been imitated. According to this belief, the god may be conjured to take up his abode in the body of the performer, who imitates what are believed to be his appearance, movements, and behaviour. And the artistic production, which has been called into existence by this principle of sympathetic magic, does not restrict itself to the department of dramatic art. It has attained a great importance within the domain of pictorial imitation.

The transition from dramatic to pictorial art is marked by those masks which, in many tribes, such as the Bellacoolas, the Melanesians, etc., are worn by the dancers in religious dances (cf. Boas, Dall, Woldt, on the Bellacoolas; Haddon and Codrington on the Melanesians). The effect produced on the spectators by these painted faces is partially dependent upon the dramatic acting—the singing and the movements—of the performers. But the masks themselves are, no doubt, apt to awaken feelings of terror and awe. And among all primitive tribes they are regarded as sacred things, scarcely less holy than the religious paintings and statues venerated by more developed nations.

Among the most primitive tribes, however, one scarcely meets with any pictorial representations of the deity. This, probably, has less to do with the technical inability of the lowest savages than with the deficient anthropomorphism in their notions of the deity. Where a god is imagined as some vague and formless being, certain rude and shapeless fetishes may be considered as satisfactory representations or vehicles of the Divine power. But as soon as a god has taken the form of animal or man, pictorial art will be resorted to as a means of facilitating—by virtue of sympathetic magic—communications between man and the divinity.

The images and statues of primitive man must not, however, be interpreted as in any way similar to those pictorial representations of which barbarous—or sometimes even civilized—men avail themselves in order to bring about some effects of magic or illusion. It seems, on the contrary, as if similarity and lifelikeness had not even been aimed at in the idols and ancestral statues of the lowest savages. And what we know about the way in which these statues are made gives us reason to believe that their supposed efficacy rests only partially upon the principle of a magical connexion between similar things. A most instructive example has been quoted by Ellis in his description of West African fetishism. When the Negroes wish to transplant the wood deity from his original home to their towns and villages, they construct a wooden doll of branches taken from the tree in which he is supposed to live. The god is, no doubt, believed to feel a special temptation to take up his abode in the idol made in his own likeness; but it is evident that the material link established by the choice of the wood is thought of as being of no less, perhaps even of greater, importance than the resemblance (cf. Ellis, *Yoruba Peoples*, p. 278; *Tshi Peoples*, p. 81).

When the personality to be represented is not a nature-god but an ancestor, it is still easier to bring about a material connexion between him and the image. Thus the Melanesian religious masks often consist of a part of a human skull which has been painted in glaring colours. And among Melanesian, Malay, and West African tribes the skull of the dead is often inserted in the head of the statues which are made in their likeness (De Clercq in Schmeltz, *New Guinea*; Brenner, *Kannibalen Sumatras*). When the cannibals of Sumatra prepare their celebrated richly-sculptured magical staffs, they always enclose in the head of the uppermost figure of the staff the brain of a young boy, who has been killed for the purpose (Brenner, *l.c.*, cf. also the author's *Origins of Art*, p. 291). It is probable that whatever power such images are believed to possess is given to them chiefly by their material contents. The worship and respect shown to the statues are developed out of a worship of skulls, and the statues themselves have originally been considered, not as images of the body, but as receptacles for some part of the body itself. The more, however, the form of these receptacles has been elaborated, the more there must also arise a subjective illusion, which to the primitive spectators brings the image into connexion with the imitated reality. The crude character of savage statuary is no obstacle to such an illusion, as in primitive peoples the want of technical ability is counterbalanced by a naïve suggestibility. And as soon, on the other hand, as the image itself—as image—has acquired a magical or religious efficacy, there will also appear an endeavour to heighten the suggestive effect by increasing the lifelikeness and the resemblance of the statues. Thus superstitious and religious motives will tend gradually to increase the artistic value of the religious images. The religious statues of the Melanesians and the idols of the West African Negroes, for instance, undoubtedly owe something of their wild and fantastic lifelikeness to an attempt to awaken as intense an impression as possible of the divine powers which they are intended to represent. At somewhat higher stages of evolution, on the other hand, as, for instance, among the Pueblo Indians, religious motives tend to restrain the impressiveness of pictorial representation within some traditionally-fixed limits.

However crude and simple an idol may be, it will none the less, by virtue of its mere existence, bring about some important changes in man's attitude towards his god. By the idol a divinity, who has originally been considered as distant or vaguely localized, becomes concentrated in an approachable vehicle. The pious adorers thus acquire a fixed object for their worship. And the holiness of this object makes it necessary to shelter it from the environment. Thus, around the idol, there naturally arises a temple.

Among the lowest savage tribes these temples have no qualities entitling them to be enumerated among works of art. But at a somewhat higher stage of development, the house of the god is often decorated in a most gorgeous way. The ancestral houses—which are temples in the literal sense of the word—display, especially among some Malaysian and Melanesian tribes, a wealth of ornamental art (see TEMPLES). [See, further, 'Note on the Use of Painting in Primitive Religion,' following this article].

3. **Propitiation in art.**—In order completely to explain the motives which have led to these architectural constructions and decorations, it is not sufficient to appeal to those philosophical and superstitious ideas which have hitherto been mentioned. In the foregoing we have devoted our attention exclusively to man's endeavour to create, by dramatic or pictorial art, a representation of the god—a receptacle, so to say, of the divine spirit—by means of which he may enter into relations with the divinity. Alongside of this endeavour, however, there can always be observed another tendency, which has been of scarcely less importance for the history of art—the effort to flatter and propitiate the divinity. This effort has naturally become more and more marked the more the idea of God has become localized, fixed, and vivified through artistic representation. Thus the ornamental art which is lavished on the decoration of primitive temples may in most cases be interpreted as homage to the god who is believed to inhabit the temple or to visit it. But the tendency to flatter and propitiate is by no means dependent upon the degree of development reached by the idea of God. It manifests itself among tribes who conceive their divinity as a vague, unlocalized, and impersonal being, as well as among tribes who have adopted anthropomorphic or zoomorphic religions. Those of its manifestations, however, that are most important from a general point of view cannot possibly be treated of in this connexion. For there is nothing artistic in the various forms of *material* sacrifice—with the exception, perhaps, of the sacrificial vessels, which, in virtue of their religious purpose, may be elaborated and decorated with a

greater care than ordinary vessels. On the other hand, the *dramatic* and *poetic* forms of sacrifice—prayer and homage—afford us an ample store of examples which exactly fall within the scope of the present article.

A kind of sacrificial purpose may indeed be discovered even in those shamanistic dances which to the superficial observer appear to have their only motive in the desire to bring about a state of exaltation. As every effort is taken to be agreeable to the divinity, the dancers may in many cases nourish a hope of softening the hard heart of their god by their violent exertions. And this seems the more probable since the dances are often connected with self-tortures, *e.g.* scarifications, devouring of disgusting things, etc. But, on the other hand, these feats of endurance may as well be explained either as a means of imposing upon the spectators, or as immediate results—analagous to the self-woundings of hysterical and hystero-epileptic patients—of the pathological insensibility which has been brought about by the exaltation.

It is easier by far to interpret those less exalted dances, songs, and dramatic performances which tend only to provoke, or to express, a state of mild, pleasurable feeling. For the purposes of explanation it is advantageous to make a distinction between those artistic manifestations through which man aims intentionally at flattering or amusing the divine spectator, and those manifestations in which the expression of man's own feelings of thankfulness or happiness appears to be the chief motive. It is to be remembered that these two classes of religious art, which are to be differently analyzed and interpreted, may in reality often be blended together.

The most instructive examples of the first class are to be found among the melodramatic representations given at the tomb of the deceased. As the spirit of the dead man is considered to be a divinity, these performances are undeniably of a religious character. But as, on the other hand, the deceased are believed to preserve all the tastes and likings of the living, the means employed in order to amuse or flatter their spirits will closely resemble the various forms of secular art. As a matter of fact, there is no difference between, *e.g.*, the dances performed before a living king or chief, and the dances performed before the invisible spectator in the tomb. Yet the motives may in some cases give a peculiar character to the manifestations of funeral art. While the performances before a living spectator tend chiefly to produce in his mind an æsthetic pleasure, the funeral dramas and dances may often fulfil a magical purpose. In some cases the dances and songs aim at a stimulation of the spirit, which certainly needs an increase of force in order to surmount all the hardships and the weary wanderings of its transitional life. In other cases, funeral art is evidently intended to produce some terrifying effects upon the invisible enemies of the dead, who are believed to endeavour to possess themselves of his body. Sometimes one may even believe that the survivors try to frighten the spirit itself away from their homes by terrifying dances and pantomimes. Lastly, it is probably in the endeavour to exert a sympathetic influence upon the combats which the deceased has to undergo before he can attain his peace and rest, that survivors hold magic war-dramas (*e.g.* sham-fights and tugs of war) over his grave.

When—as has probably been the case in some tribes—the cult of some individual ancestor is transformed into a cult of a general divinity, and, in consequence thereof, the small spirit-house above the grave is replaced by a temple, some of the ancient funeral performances may still be kept up as religious observances. Although their original purpose is forgotten, their character will scarcely become changed. When magical ideas have died out, magical ceremonies will still survive as a means of religious homage. And when, at a later stage of development, the notion of a divine spectator has been forgotten, the same ceremonies may still be performed as mere amusements, for which the religious tradition offers a welcome justification. Thus it is more than difficult to decide in individual cases whether the artistic manifestations fulfil a religious, a magical, or a purely æsthetic purpose.

The same difficulty meets us when we have to do with purely lyrical dances and songs, through which the performers express their gratitude and devotion to the god. Psychologically there is an easy transition from the feeling of joy—when it is pure and complete—to the feeling of loving thankfulness. The fulness of the emotion seeks expression, and the expression seeks some one to whom it may address itself. Thus in happiness we experience a desire to imagine a god who may receive our gratitude. And among peoples who consider every happy occurrence as a benefit which has been especially accorded to them by the divinity, pleasure will easily cause some manifestations which embrace both emotions in one common expression. As the most typical and best known example of this kind of religious art, we may quote the song and dance of the Israelites after having passed the Red Sea (Ex 15). It is true that in this case the poetic and orchestic hymns were called forth by an exceptional and unique occurrence. But there are always some regular events of happy importance in the life of primitive man which will tend to make thanksgiving ceremonies a fixed institution. Thus the return of the spring will be saluted with dance and song among the nations that have been suffering from long and hard winters, *e.g.* the Eskimos, the Chukchis, etc. Among agricultural nations the occasion of a bountiful harvest will give rise to some joyful festivals, in which the participants amuse themselves at the same time as they pay homage to their divinity. Such festivals seem to be especially frequent among the North American Indians.

The dances performed at these ceremonies, as has already been mentioned, closely resemble the manifestations of pure and simple joy. But there are some gestures which, although originally connected immediately with the expression of this simple feeling, may gradually become peculiar to the honorific ritual. Thus hand-clappings (which, as is well known, accompany states of great joy both among savages and among children) have, among Polynesians as well as among the ancient Egyptians, acquired the sense of a pious and reverential gesture, by which the adorers manifest their love and thankfulness towards the god.

4. Ethical instruction in art.—The facts hitherto quoted have referred almost exclusively to an art which, while it addresses itself chiefly to the divine spectator, aims at bringing about an immediate relation between him and his adorers. This indeed appears to be the prominent purpose of religious practices among the most primitive tribes. But it must not be thought that savage and barbarous religions were entirely devoid of a didactic and moralizing side. Even the shamanistic dances may, as has already been pointed out, pass over into small pantomimes, by which the spectators are initiated into the transactions between the shaman and the god. And however much magical ideas may have to do with these dramatic and pictorial representations of the divinity, the theurgic purposes will soon combine themselves with the intention of explaining and illustrating the facts of religious history. In such dramatic representations as, for instance, the great Kachina dance of the Zuñi Indians, this didactic tendency seems to be especially prominent. In masquerades of the type represented by the Mumbo Jumbo dance in Central Africa and the 'Kinas' of the Fuegians, we meet with the moral, or pseudo-moral, motive of terrorizing women and children into subjection by showing them the awful aspects of the gods. Finally, in the dramas, songs, and dances at the initiation of boys and girls into maturity, magical, didactic, and moralizing purposes have all combined to create the most marvellous manifestations which are to be met with in the department of primitive art. It is true that the instruction conferred at these ceremonies refers chiefly to practical utility. But even among peoples at so low a degree of development as the Australian aborigines, religious and, one might say, philosophical doctrines are expounded to the young men. Thus in a kind of miracle play, to which some curious analogies have been found among the Fijians and the East Africans, the old men enact before the boys a representation of death and resurrection. Although less elaborate in dramatic detail and stage-management, the fragmentary dramas in which the American Indian shaman-novitiates are supposed to be killed and recalled to life present to us a scarcely less interesting illustration of the same great thought. There are indeed, especially in this last example, good reasons for assuming that the simulated death and resurrection are supposed to effect, in a magical way, some kind of spiritual regeneration in the novices on whose behalf the drama is performed. But while admitting this, we may nevertheless take it for granted that an endeavour to elucidate the doctrines of the priesthood may be combined with the magical rite in question. And similarly with regard to analogous ceremonies in other tribes, we feel justified in assuming the presence of a didactic purpose. The more the dogmatic system becomes fixed and elaborated, the greater need will there ensue of affording these doctrines a clear expression in the objective forms of art.

It is evident that poetry more than any other art is fitted to serve such a purpose. And, in fact, among several tribes at the stage of higher savagery and barbarism there have been found some more or less complete mythical poems. These songs, however, will be more properly treated of under the headings MYTHOLOGY, CHARMS, and HYMNS.

LITERATURE.—In addition to the works mentioned above, the following books may be consulted with advantage:

On DECORATION and ORNAMENT in connexion with religion: Henry Balfour, *The Evolution of Decorative Art*, London, 1893; A. C. Haddon, *Evolution in Art, as illustrated by the Life Histories of Designs*, London, 1895; A. Hamilton, *The Art-Workmanship of the Maori Race*, Dunedin, 1896 f.; A. R. Hein, *Die bildenden Künste bei den Dayaks auf Borneo*, Vienna, 1890.

On MUSIC, DRAMA, and POETRY in connexion with religion: C. Letourneau, *L'évolution littéraire dans les diverses races humaines*, Paris, 1894; Posnett, *Comparative Literature*, London, 1886; R. Wallaschek, *Primitive Music*, London, 1893.

On the general ÆSTHETICS of primitive man: E. Grosse, *Die Anfänge der Kunst*, Freiburg i. B. 1894; Yrjö Hirn, *The Origins of Art*, London, 1900.

YRJÖ HIRN.

NOTE ON THE USE OF PAINTING IN PRIMITIVE RELIGION.—Besides the realistic and symbolic representation of his divinities or of his religious conceptions and aspirations by means of various art methods—images or statues, carvings, sacred dances, sacred hymns and chants—painting has occasionally been brought into the service of religion by primitive or savage man, as well as by his more civilized successor. The purpose of this note will be sufficiently fulfilled by reference to such painting in the Stone Age, among the rudest savages, and with a semi-barbaric people. In all alike the ends aimed at are precisely the same as those intended by the image or carving—the obtaining of power over or from the being represented, the vivid depicting of the worshipful object or person so that the worshipper, by means of the picture or symbol, may have his religious sense re-awakened, or may also be brought into contact and communion with the divinity. In the first example to be referred to—that of the Palæolithic cave-artists—the paintings are not those of divinities but of animals. Even if these had no totemistic significance, the pictures played a highly important part in the magico-religious ceremonies which, *ex hypothesi*, were performed before them.

Within recent years, French archæologists have discovered the existence of engravings and paintings of animals on the walls of caverns in Périgord and the Pyrenees. Similar paintings were, almost simultaneously, found in grottoes at Altamira in Spain. They are executed on rocks in the darkest part of the caves, far from the entrance. Artificial light must therefore have been employed in designing them, as is proved by the discovery of a stone lamp ornamented with an incised figure of a reindeer, and thus dating from the Reindeer age of the Palæolithic epoch—the age of simple engravings with which the great Glyptic period of Quaternary times terminated. Probably these wall engravings and paintings belong to this closing period also. The animals represented are mammoths, reindeer, bison, oxen, horses, goats, saigas, etc. Some of these are engraved; others, besides being engraved, have the outlines filled in with reddish-brown colour, or, in some cases, bluish-black, exactly as totemic grave-posts used by the American Indians have incised figures painted over with vermilion; in others the engraving lines are accentuated by a thin band of colour. Frequently a design is outlined in black, and the surface covered with red ochre. We are yet ignorant how the colour was applied; it may have been daubed on by means of some primitive brush, or blown from the mouth, as is the case with some Australian rock-paintings. The interest of these paintings, for us, consists in the theory regarding their purpose enunciated by a French *savant*, M. Salomon Reinach. He notes regarding these paintings as well as Quaternary art in general, that *motifs* borrowed from the animal world are the most numerous, and that the animals represented are those which form the food supply of a nation of hunters and fishers. They are *desirable* animals; others, not represented, *e.g.* the lion, tiger, jackal, etc., are undesirable, and this, he believes, is not the result of chance. Among modern savages it is not uncommon to find that the image of a creature or object is held to give its author a *prise* over the object or creature through a process of mimetic magic. Hence many savages object to be drawn or painted. In the same way pantomimic and dramatic exhibitions have for their purpose the actual result of what is thus imitated symbolically (rain-making, animal-dances). Among the Central Australians, in order to cause a multiplication of such a totem-animal as the witchetty-grub, the members of this totem clan assemble before a rocky wall on which are painted great representations of the grub, and there they sing in chorus, invoking the insect to multiply and be fruitful (Spencer-Gillen, *Native Tribes of Central Australia*, 170). Similar ceremonies, including the depicting, more or less symbolically, of the desired animal, are employed by other clans, *e.g.* the emu clan. The blood of some members of the clan is shed on the ground, and on the reddened surface is painted with coloured earth and charcoal an emu, along with yellow and black circles representing its eggs. Many other totemic designs, mainly of a symbolic character, are painted on rocks, and are tabu to women and children.

M. Reinach notes the fact that the Quaternary paintings are executed on the walls of caves far from the entrance and at the end of corridors difficult of access, as if with a view to secrecy. Not only so, but the caves are in total darkness, and, as has been said, the paintings must have been executed and looked at by means of artificial light. Hence the impossibility of assuming that they were executed for mere pleasure. They must have had a religio-magical character, and their purpose was to secure, 'by magical practices, the multiplication of the game on which depended the existence of the clan or tribe. Ceremonies, in which adults alone took part, were performed with that end in the darkest part of the cavern, entrance to which was forbidden to the profane.' These paintings formed the object of the cult, addressed not to the individuals represented, but to the species, over which the worshippers had influence by reason of the individual being thus depicted. The animals, as a result of these ceremonies, would multiply and would frequent the neighbourhood. The various sculptures and engravings of the Reindeer age may have had such a purpose also, while the so-called *bâtons de commandement* doubtless played their part in magical and totemistic ceremonies, as M. Bernardin had already suggested in 1876 (*Revue Savoisienne*, Feb. 1876). Thus the art of the period was neither a luxury nor an amusement, but the expression of a rude yet intense religion, based upon magico-religious practices having for their object the attainment of the food supply. While we cannot admit that Palæolithic man's artistic powers were used only for magico-religious purposes—the beauty of some of his designs, and the care in reproducing exactly what he saw, suggesting the artist pure and simple—it could not fail that they should be frequently employed in such ways as M. Reinach has suggested. Everywhere else this has occurred, and art has been freely enlisted in the service of both religion and magic.

In the times of transition to the Neolithic age, though the brilliant art production of the earlier period is unknown, art was again used in the cult. This, already shown by the symbolic engravings and markings on rocks, megalithic monuments, etc., is further suggested by the painted pebbles found by M. Piette at Mas d'Azil. Some of the designs represent numbers, others are alphabetiform signs corresponding to the letters of the later Ægean and Cypriote syllabaries; others are pictographs, with or without a symbolic meaning. It is in these last that we may find the use of painting as an accessory to the cult. Among them are the cross by itself or within a circle, a circle with a central dot (solar symbols, some of which occur as engravings on the megalithic monuments of the Neolithic age), the serpent, tree, etc. All are painted with peroxide of iron upon white pebbles. Later, the carved symbols of the Neolithic period, *e.g.* the symbolic axes and female figures (divinities) on the walls of the grottoes of La Marne, etc., show traces of having been covered with colour, like the carved images of later ages.

For the cave paintings see *L'Anthropologie*, 1902; *Revue mensuelle de l'école d'anthrop.* 1902. M. Reinach's paper will be found in *L'Anth.* 1903, p. 257. See also his *Story of Art throughout the Ages*, ch. i. M. Piette's discoveries are described in *L'Anth.* vi. 385, xiv. 643 f. For the symbolic carvings of La Marne, see Cartailhac, *La France préhistorique*, 240 ff.; Baron de Baye, *L'Archéologie préhistorique.*

Some Australian instances of the use of painting for magico-religious purposes have already been referred to. Among the Northern tribes of Central Australia similar paintings are used in the totemic ceremonies. The men of the Thalaualla or Black Snake totem, when they perform the Intichiuma rites for the purpose of increasing the numbers of this snake species, paint partly symbolic and partly imitative designs on the ground with red ochre and other coloured earths and charcoal. These depict the mythic history of the ancestral snake, which is also dramatically represented (Spencer-Gillen, *Northern Tribes of C. A.* 302, 737). Similar ground paintings are used in the Wollunqua snake totem ceremonies. Each one represents, 'or rather was associated with, the various spots at which the animal stood up, performed ceremonies, and left spirit children behind him' (*op. cit.* p. 239). In this case the paintings are entirely symbolic, and consist of concentric circles and curved lines outlined in white dots on a ground of red or yellow ochre, painted on the surface of the earth previously prepared for the purpose. Spencer and Gillen describe at some length the sacred rock-drawings of the Central Australian tribes. These, which are usually executed in red ochre, are mainly conventional geometrical designs, all of which, however, have a definite meaning to the natives who use them. They are seen only by the men who have been initiated, and are painted on the rocks near the place where the sacred *churinga* of the clan are deposited. Among other Australian tribes, drawings and paintings on the ground or on trees are also found in connexion with the *bora*, or sacred initiatory ceremonies, and are shown only to the initiated. Sometimes gigantic figures of divine beings—Baiamai, Gunnanbuly, etc.—are outlined in the turf or formed out of a heap of earth; in other cases sacred figures are cut in the bark of trees. Similar figures are also painted with red ochre and pipe-clay on trees, or on sheets of bark, which are then hung up on or rested against the trees. The rock-paintings, which may or may not have a religious or mythic significance, are either stencilled by the object to be depicted being placed against the rock, which is moistened and upon which the colour is blown or applied with a kind of brush; or painted in outline, the inner space being sometimes filled in with the same colour, or shaded by strokes of some different colour.

With the symbolism of the painted pebbles of Mas d'Azil may be compared the designs painted or incised on Australian *churinga*. The *churinga* is a piece of wood or stone of long oval shape supposed to have been dropped by a spirit ancestor as he, for the purpose of re-incarnation, entered the body of a woman. The child thus born becomes the owner of the *churinga*, which is deposited, along with those of the other members of his totem clan, in a sacred place. The design has in each case a distinctive meaning, connected with the totem-beliefs of the people, and generally illustrating some incident of the mythic history of the totem ancestor. Among the designs are concentric curves and circles, parallel lines, etc. These exactly resemble designs painted on the pebbles, which also resemble the *churinga* in shape, as well as those incised on the megalithic monuments of the Neolithic age. It has been suggested that the Azilian pebbles may have been the *churinga* of a pre-historic totemistic people (A. B. Cook, *L'Anthropologie*, xiv. 655). In any case, the analogy of Australian sacred art shows that they had a religious value.

For Australian art see Spencer-Gillen, *Northern Tribes of Central Australia*, p. 696 ff., and *Native Tribes*, p. 614 ff.; Stirling in *Report of Horn Scientific Expedition*, 'Anthropology,' pt. iv.; R. H. Mathews, *JAI* xxv. 146 ff., 299 ff.

Among the more cultured tribes of the North American continent—Zuñis, Tusayans, South Californians, and Navahos—a curious kind of painting is used as an adjunct to certain religious ceremonials whose purpose is usually the healing of disease, and which are characterized by great elaborateness and length. As practised among the Navaho Indians, the ceremony continues for nine days, and is conducted by a theurgist and several assistants. Every part of the ritual has a special significance, and must be performed with the strictest attention to traditional detail, lest fatal consequences should ensue from the least infringement of it. Several men personate the gods and goddesses and take part in the ceremonies; each day's proceedings include pantomimic action, symbolism, offerings to the gods, singing of sacred chants, and prayers, and the whole ends with an elaborate dance. The whole ceremony is known as *yebitchai*, a word meaning 'giant's uncle,' and, as in several Australian mysteries, it is used to awe children, who, on the eighth day, are initiated into the ceremony, and discover that the men personating the gods are their fellow-tribesmen. The paintings are made with dry sand and pigments of various colours sprinkled on a ground of yellow sand with the thumb and forefinger of the operator. The colours used are yellow, red, white, black, and a blue prepared from a mixture of charcoal with white, red, and yellow sands. These colours, as well as the pictures themselves, are made according to instructions given by the gods, as the Navaho myth of 'The Floating Logs' relates. All the paintings represent gods and goddesses, usually about three feet in length, and depicted in a somewhat conventional manner. Face, arms, and legs are carefully done; the body is long and narrow; each divinity is usually depicted with various emblems; a god is denoted by a round head, a goddess by a rectangular head. Considering the method in which the colours are employed, the resulting picture is a marvellous piece of art work, full of minute details, while many of the colour lines in the dress and sash decorations of the divinities are like threads. The first sand-painting is made on the fifth day of the ceremony, and represents three divinities; in the painting of the sixth day, there are four pairs of divinities, male and female, each sitting on the limb of a cross, with their appropriate emblems; outside the painting are four gods, one on each side, and the whole is surrounded by the rainbow goddess. The seventh day's painting represents fourteen divinities in two rows, again surrounded by the rainbow goddess, 25 ft. in length. Twelve divinities are shown in the eighth day's painting; in their midst is a huge picture of a corn-stalk, the main subsistence of life; a square base and triangle represent clouds, and three white lines the roots of the corn. The rainbow goddess again surrounds this picture. A detailed account of this last picture will show its symbolic nature. The divinities are the Zenichi, who live in a rock, represented by a long black parallelogram. Those parts of their bodies and faces which are painted red, denote red corn; black signifies black clouds. Zigzag lines on the bodies mean lightning; certain black lines round the head, zigzagged with white, are cloud baskets holding red corn.

All these paintings are arranged on the floor of a medicine-lodge in which are assembled the invalid, the theurgist and his assistants, and certain privileged spectators. In each case the sick man is seated on the central figure of each painting, having previously sprinkled the design with sacred meal. Several ceremonies, chants, and prayers follow, during which one of the representatives of the gods touches the feet, heart, and head of each figure respectively with his right hand, each time touching the corresponding parts of the invalid's body. This appears to be the vital part of the ceremony, bringing the sick man into relation with the gods through their pictures and by their representative, thus transferring their power to him so that his disease may be overcome. This seems to be certain, as, before the pictures are obliterated at the end of the day's proceedings, the people crowd round to touch them, and then, having inhaled a breath over their hands, rub their bodies so that they may be cured of any malady, moral or physical, by the divine effluence. The sacred pictures thus exercise the *quasi*-sacramental power of the idol, fetish, or symbolic image, wherever found. Being like the gods, and made, as is believed, according to divine directions, they have all the power of the gods themselves. So the colours used in other American Indian ceremonies are believed to have been originally given by the divine *manitous* (see *BE*, Fourteenth Annual Report, p. 91).

James Stevenson, *Ceremonial of Hasjelti Dailjis and Mythical Sand Paintings of the Navajo Indians*, with illustrations of the paintings, in *BE*, Eighth Annual Report, 1891.

Reference may also be briefly made to: (1) Zuñi religious paintings on vessels, representing the Creation and other myths current among the people. The colours themselves are symbolic (see **Cushing**, *Study of Pueblo Pottery*, 1886; **J. W. Fewkes**, *Journ. of Amer. Ethnol. and Archæol.* ii. 1892).—(2) Painting or tatuing the body (*a*) for magical purposes, as among the Aracan hill tribes and Burmese (**St. John**, *JAI* ii. 235; **Symes**, *Embassy to Ava*, p. 312, and others); (*b*) with totem designs, *e.g.* the tribes of Malacca (**Haddon**, *Evol. in Art*, p. 252 f.); (*c*) on certain ceremonial occasions, as with the Australians (**Spencer-Gillen**, *op. cit.*); (*d*) for mourning.—(3) Painting the bodies or skeletons of the dead, usually with red, but occasionally (Andaman Islanders) with yellow—a custom which, beginning apparently in late Palæolithic times (grottoes of Baoussés-Rousses, Mentone), occurred frequently in the Neolithic period, and is found among various savages—Australians, American Indians, etc. (**Cartailhac**, *La France préhistorique*, 105, 292, 302; *L'Anthropologie*, vi. 4; *BE*, First Report, p. 107; **Grosse**, *Anfänge der Kunst*, p. 42).—(4) Painting totem-designs on weapons, furniture, houses, totem-posts, and grave-posts (**Frazer**, *Totemism*).—(5) The use of pictographs to illustrate chants used in religious mysteries and as mnemonic symbols among the American Indians (*BE*, Fourteenth Report, p. 107); see also TATUING, TOTEMISM.

These various examples show that, like every other branch of art, painting, realistic or symbolic, has been used by man to set forth his religious beliefs, to represent or symbolize his divinities, or, in accordance with his religio-magical theory of the universe, to gratify his wishes, to act as a protection, or to transfer the power of the person or object depicted to himself. 'Art for art's sake' was not unknown to primitive and savage man, but on the whole he made it subserve a useful purpose, *e.g.* in bringing it under the sway of religion. It is thus scarcely correct to say, as Grosse does (*Anfänge der Kunst*), that the art of primitive peoples is not connected with religion. Whatever be its origin, whether arising from some instinctive impulse to imitate the things man saw around him, or from some other cause, art soon lent itself to enhance and satisfy man's needs. At the same time, the purely æsthetic pleasure on the part of the artist in making an artistic object or design which was to be used for religious or other purposes must not be overlooked.

LITERATURE.—In addition to works cited throughout this article, see **Andree**, *Ethnologische Parallelen*, 1889; **Hirn**, *Origins of Art*, 1899.

J. A. MACCULLOCH.

ART (Primitive and Savage). — Before the acquisition of the art of writing by any people, the only method of recording facts or ideas, except by word of mouth, is by means of some kind of graphic representation. The carving or drawing may be intended to be realistic, though, even so, the realism may be imperfect; but one frequently finds that a suggestion of an object answers all the purpose of a representation of the whole object. Thus, an animal may be indicated by a limb, a zigzag may stand for the wings of an insect, bird, or bat; in other words, a convention may thoroughly satisfy the need of expression. When an object is decorated with conventional designs, these may be so remote in form from their original that they are usually described as 'geometric,' and consequently they stand the chance of no further interest being taken in them; whereas, if information be obtained from the designers, it is nearly always found that they have a significance that cannot be discovered by inspection alone. Experience has proved that designs which have frequently been regarded as merely decorative have an import that could not otherwise have been predicated for them. Hence, the futility of an endeavour to elucidate the significance of designs without an adequate investigation in the field.

At the outset it must be acknowledged that all the designs of a 'primitive' people are not necessarily significant. The æsthetic sense which manifests itself in symmetry, balance, and decoration seems to have been present, to a greater or less degree, from the earliest times of which we have any record; and it is often quite marked among the less advanced peoples of the present day. It is useless to try to read a meaning into simple patterns unless we are sure of the key, as they may very well be nothing more than an expression of the artist's feeling for beauty as he experiences it, or as limited by his skill or by the materials at his disposal. For example, it appears useless to attempt to extract significance from the patterns engraved on bones by Palæolithic man, or from most of the designs of other pre-historic folk. The same applies to the decorative art of other peoples; indeed, the greater part of the decorative art of present-day civilization is meaningless; but it may for all that satisfy an artistic craving, or at all events it is an acknowledgment of an æsthetic need. The particular designs, however, may be suggested to the artist by what he sees around him, and he may apply them without relevancy, merely to please himself. It seems fairly certain that it is only among the culture-folk that inventive fancy has full play. The nature-folk may produce intricate or complicated designs, but these are nearly always found to be modifications or groupings of simple motives, and these latter are generally those which lie ready to hand. For example, mat-making and basketry are of universal occurrence where the materials exist for their manufacture; the plaits of the former and the weaves of the latter are limited in number, but the various sequences give rise to patterns. By means of differently coloured strips in the original foundation or applied thereto, or by pigments or other devices, these patterns can be emphasized, or new ones produced; but these are practically confined to straight and angled lines, chequers, and the like. These patterns are always before the native eye, and it is no wonder that they are transferred to clubs, wooden bowls, or pottery. The designs are incidental to the technique of plait-work, but are inappropriate to most of the other objects to which they are applied, although they satisfy the artistic craving. The same applies to lashings and various kinds of string- and thong-work; sometimes carved representations of string or braid may be expressions of an antecedent fastening together of separate parts, but more often they are merely decorative.

Artistic representation may be solely for the purpose of *depicting objects*, or for *recording events*, or for *giving information*, as in the case of much of the interesting graphic art of the Eskimos, or of the ruder attempts of certain Siberian tribes. Probably to this category belongs the pictorial art of the ancient cave-dwellers of Western Europe, who painted in caves or engraved on bone the animals that were daily before their eyes, as did the Bushmen of recent times; but the latter frequently depicted hunting scenes, and even fights with Zulus. The pictographs on the buffalo robes of the Dakotas, the most famous of the 'winter counts,' as they are termed, indicate the most salient incident of the previous year, and thus a pictorial history is painted which in this case extended for about seventy years (Mallery, *Fourth* and *Tenth Ann. Rep. Bureau Eth.*). The pictorial blazings or notice boards of the Alaskans gave definite information to friends and travellers (Mallery, *l.c.*).

Apart from the foregoing and the utilization of decorative art as an exhibition of wealth or for social distinction, we find that *magic* and religion have exercised a preponderating effect on the artistic impulse; nor is this surprising, considering the vast importance they play in the life, thought, and feeling of mankind. From the nature of the case that aspect of sympathetic magic known as 'homœopathic' lends itself to artistic treatment rather than does the 'contagious.' The representation of an object is as effectual as the object itself; and as there is virtue in words and power in a name, so there is efficacy in a pictograph, which, after all, is a graphic as opposed to an oral or written expression. According to von den Steinen (*Unter den Naturvölkern Zentral-Brasiliens*, 1894), certain designs on a Bakaïri paddle represent various kinds of fish, some of which are drawn within the meshes of a net; and the author believes that the object of this decoration is simply to bring fish close to the paddle so that they may be caught in the fisherman's net. Many other examples of simple magical pictography might be cited, but the most elaborate examples are those recorded by Vaughan-Stevens from the Semang and Sakai of the Malay Peninsula. These are hunting jungle-folk who undoubtedly come under the unsatisfactory designation of savages. The English reader will find the fullest account of their extraordinary designs in Skeat and Blagden's *Wild Tribes of the Malay Peninsula*. There has been a good deal of uncertainty concerning the *bona fides* of Vaughan-Stevens, but these authors are inclined to credit in the main the explanations given by him of the engravings on combs and bamboos which he undoubtedly collected from the natives. Some of the Sakai bamboo designs represent diseases, and the whole design on a bamboo is intended as a prophylactic against a specific disease. One bamboo design represents the swellings caused by the stings of scorpions and the pricks of centipedes; these creatures also are engraved together with an Argus pheasant. The significance of this bamboo is that, as the Argus pheasant feeds on centipedes and scorpions, its help is invoked against them by striking the bamboo against the ground. The decoration of one bamboo is a charm for rain; one is a pictographic formula to enable a man who wishes to build a house to find easily the necessary materials; one is supposed to protect the harvest and the plantations round the house from injurious animals; another helps women to catch fish, and also protects them from poisonous ones. The Semang women possess numerous combs, which are decorated with various designs, each of which is a prophylactic against a particular disease. When a woman goes into the jungle, she inserts at least eight of the combs horizontally in her hair, so that the disease-bearing wind-demon, who is the emissary of Kari, the thunder-god, on meeting the protecting pattern may fall to the ground; but should the woman not wear a comb with the appropriate pattern, the disease is deposited on her forehead, whence it spreads over the body. In a recent paper, Dr. Westermarck (*JAI* xxxiv. 211) has demonstrated the use of designs in averting the malign influences of the evil eye in Morocco. Silver amulets and numerous objects of everyday use are decorated with crosses, and groups of five knobs or two intersecting squares; all these indicate the five fingers or finger-tips, which are employed in a gesture to throw back the harmful gaze of those who possess an evil eye. Similar designs and representations of eyes, often as triangles, decorate saddle-cloths, pottery, money-boxes, leather pouches, etc., and are embroidered upon or woven into the garments of the people, so that at all times and from all points they, their animals, and their personal effects may be protected from premeditated or casual harm.

Professor Maspero says of the decorative art of Ancient Egypt: 'The object of decoration was not merely to delight the eye. Applied to a piece of furniture, a coffin, a house, a temple, decoration possessed a certain magical property, of which the power or nature was determined by each word inscribed or spoken at the moment of consecration. Every object, therefore, was an amulet as well as an ornament' (quoted by Goodyear, *The Architectural Record*, iii.). The lotus is the parent, writes Hamlin (*Architect. Rec.* viii.), of a greater number and variety of ornament-forms than any other *motif* known. It was the most conspicuous and beautiful flower known to the Egyptians, and its intrinsic decorative value, as well as its importance in their mythological symbolism, gave it an extraordinary vogue as an ornament. Associated as it was with Horus and Osiris, with the idea of Nature's reproductive power, with the life-giving Nile, and with all the solar elements of Egyptian mythology, it was in constant and universal use as a symbol and amulet, both in its natural or concrete form, and in decorative representations of the flower. Whether or not its symbolic use as an amulet preceded or accompanied from the outset its decorative use as an ornament, it underwent the operation of that universal law by which ornament forms lose in time their original significance and receive new and diverse applications. Hamlin also states that symbolism alone does not sufficiently account for the fact that four-fifths, perhaps nine-tenths, of the ornamental patterns of Egyptian art are based upon the lotus; the real reason for the extraordinary vogue of this single *motif* is to be found in the decorative possibilities of the type itself. The lotus seems to have been symbolic of the sun. It was also largely employed in funeral rites, and also symbolized the resurrection; but this latter idea was associated in the Egyptian mind with reproductive power. As the intensely religious mind of the ancient Egyptians was permeated with the problems of death and elevated by the prospect of immortality, it is not surprising that the flower which symbolized the resurrection should be depicted in such profusion in their tombs and elsewhere. How the Grecian artists borrowed this motive and transfigured it, how it was still further modified by the Romans, and how it spread to the British Islands through Celtic and Scandinavian channels, has been described by Goodyear (*Architectural Record*, ii. iv., 'The Grammar of the Lotus'), Hamlin (*loc. cit.*), Coffey (*Journ. Roy. Soc. Ant. Ireland*, 1894–1895), and Haddon (*Evolution in Art*).

Whereas, for our present purpose, magic may be regarded as a direct action by means of which man endeavours to accomplish his desire, *religion* is the recognition of some outside power or entity who can give aid directly or indirectly, or with whom an emotional relationship has been established; though it is not always easy to distinguish between magic and religion. In a paper on the decorative art and symbolism of the Arapahos, who are typical Plains Indians of the W. Algonquin linguistic stock, Kroeber informs us (*Bull. Am. Mus. Nat. Hist.* xviii. pt. 1 [1902]) that the closeness of the connexion between the symbolism and the religious life of the Indians cannot well be overestimated by a white man. Apart from the decorative symbolism on ceremonial objects, the making of what have been called tribal ornaments is regularly accompanied by religious ceremonies. Some styles of patterns found on tent-ornaments and *parfleches* ('rawhide bags') are very old and sacred, because originating from mythic beings. A considerable number of objects are decorated according to dreams or visions. Finally, 'all symbolism, even when decorative and unconnected with any ceremony, tends to be to the Indian a matter of a serious and religious nature' (Kroeber, *loc. cit.* p. 150).

While totemism is largely a social factor, it has a religious aspect which is often not far removed from magic. When a people is in the totemic stage, the human members of the kin or clan are prone not only to carry about with them portions or emblems of their totem, but to mark their body by paint, scarification, or tatu with realistic or conventional representations of their totem. Not only so, but they may decorate their personal belongings with their totem (cf. Spencer and Gillen's *Native Tribes*, and *Northern Tribes*, and the *Reports of the Camb. Anth. Exped. to Torres Straits*, vols. iv. v. vi.). The Western Torres Straits Islanders frequently engrave on bamboo, tobacco pipes, drums, and other objects, representations of their respective totems; almost without exception the latter are animals. Not only the totem animals are pictured, but in a few instances others as well, of which there is no evidence that they ever were totemic. In this case it would seem that the habit of animal-drawing has been extended from totems to a few other forms. On the adjacent mainland of New Guinea we find plant totems associated with animal totems, and they too appear in the decorative art. At the mouth of the Fly River, plant totems greatly preponderate, and certain pipes and drums brought from some little distance up that river are decorated solely with plant motives. It is only when we come to the opposite extremity of British New Guinea—the Milne Bay district—and the neighbouring archipelagoes, that we again meet with animal forms, more especially birds, frequent in decoration, carved realistically and conventionally, and modified into a wealth of scrolls, curves, and circles; and once more we find totemism as a living cult (cf. Haddon, 'Dec. Art of Brit. New Guinea' in *Roy. Irish Acad.* 1894). Also in parts of Melanesia, where there is totemism, frequent representation of animals occurs (Stephan, *Südseekunst*, 1907). It would be safe to say that where totemism exists there is usually an expression of the cult in decorative art; but it would be very rash to assume totemism wherever we find representation of animals or plants.

Throughout the greater part of America the belief in guardian spirits has led to representations of the *manitou*, *wahubi*, *okki*, *sulia*, *nagual*, or by whatever name it may be termed. More especially is this the case along the North-West Coast, where blankets, boxes, hats, spoons, pipes, as well as the so-called 'totem posts,' are decorated or carved with representations of the guardian spirit of the owner or those of his ancestors. These highly esteemed and jealously guarded crests and emblems originated among the Salish, according to Hill-Tout (*Trans. Roy. Soc. Canada*, sect. ii. 1901), from two sources. The crest springs from pictographic or plastic realization of the *sulia* [or 'dream-totem']. The totemic (*sic*) emblems and insignia are symbolic records of some event or adventure more or less mythic in the life of the owner or of his ancestors from whom he inherited them. In neither case do they regard themselves as descendants of their 'totems.' Speaking of the more northern of the North Pacific group of peoples, Boas says (*Rep. U.S. Nat. Mus.* 1895–1897) that each man acquires a guardian spirit, but he can acquire only such as belongs to his clan; thus a person may have the general crest of his clan, and besides use as his personal crest such guardian spirits as he has acquired. This partly accounts for the great multiplicity of combinations of crests on the carvings of these people.

Totemism frequently gives way also before an ancestor- or a hero-cult, and thus the human form makes its appearance in religious art. In the Papuan Gulf district the great bulk of decorated objects are ornamented with representations, sometimes highly conventionalized or degraded, of the human face (cf. *Dec. Art Brit. New Guinea*). In this district, at the initiation ceremonies, masks are worn to simulate the ancestral gods, and bull-roarers are whirled; these and other ceremonial objects, as well as the carved wooden belts that only warriors may wear, are decorated with faces or figures of the same apotheosized ancestors. It is highly significant that this is the only region of British New Guinea where 'gods' have been evolved (Holmes, *JAI* xxxii. 426 ff.); and at the same time it is the only district where the human form or face enters at all prominently into the decorative art of the natives, but here the human face is the dominant motive. It is worthy of note that, while animal forms are common in art in the extreme west and east of British New Guinea where totemism is rife, and the human face in the Gulf district where there are 'gods,' in the central district, where, so far as is known, there is no religion as defined above, the decorative art is devoid of animal or human representations, and is characterized by 'geometric' designs. While an ancestor-cult may develop into the worship of gods, the same result may be arrived at by other roads. In Torres Straits a hero-cult, presumably introduced from New Guinea, had invaded the original totemism, and we can trace the amalgamation of the old cult with the new, and its final disappearance and replacement by the higher religion. In the intermediate stage we have a strange confusion of the totem animal with the human hero. In the ritual this was symbolized by the wearing of masks of animal form, or of part animal and part human form. The same occurs also in the Papuan Gulf district, and occasionally these masks are represented pictorially. There does not appear to be any record of a totem animal actually becoming metamorphosed into human form. It may have occurred, but, judging from the Papuan evidence, it is more probable that a substitution took place owing to contact with an ancestor- or hero-cult, and during the transition the demi-god would partake of his double ancestry. In this way we can explain the beast-headed divinities of ancient Egypt. That a part of the religion of ancient Greece had its origin in totemism may be admitted. The ox, the mouse, wild beasts and birds, and similar associates of the Olympian hierarchy, whatever they were to the enlightened pagans who endeavoured to rationalize and even to spiritualize them, are to us milestones which mark the road traversed by Hellenic religion; the Egyptian had been petrified at an earlier phase. When gods had been evolved, it was very important for men to retain the remembrance of those family ties between them and mankind which were in danger of being snapped through the length to which they were drawn and the degree of attenuation which consequently ensued. The statements of tradition as to the descent of mortals from gods are re-inforced by the representations of artists of the unlettered races, just as they are enshrined in the written cosmogonies of more cultured folk, the main difference being that anybody may understand the one if he knows the written characters, whereas the other is practically a pictograph, and requires the interpretation of the natives who have the traditional knowledge of the symbols. We are probably justified in assuming that very early in time the custom existed (still widely spread among backward peoples) of carving or painting the pedigree of the man from the god, of the human from the divine, as at a still earlier time the reverse process had taken place. Gill states that significance is 'invariably attached to ancient Polynesian carving' (*Jottings from the Pacific*, 223). Several investigators have studied the peculiar wood-carving of the Hervey Islanders (Haddon, *Evolution in Art*), and many of the designs can be shown to be modifications of the human figure. Stolpe says: 'Ancestor-worship is a characteristic feature of Polynesian religion. The souls of the departed become the guardian spirits of the survivors. Their worship demanded a visible form . . . it appears to me that the peculiarly hafted stone adzes of the Hervey Islands have a religious signification, that they are especially connected with ancestor-worship, and that they were probably the very symbols under which this worship was performed' (*Ymer*, 1890, 232, 234). Colley March first suggested that the carved shafts of the sacred paddles and adzes were pedigree-sticks, the patterns being 'the multitudinous human links between the divine ancestor and the chief of the living tribe' (*JAI* xxii. 324). This seems to be a probable explanation of these beautiful carvings, which thus illustrate the origin of man from his god, and his continued connexion with and dependence upon him. What more can religious art teach?

Symbolism is a universal method of religious expression, and most of the decoration in connexion with shrines and altars has this significance. Primitively this was entirely the case, as may be seen from the researches of Cushing, Fewkes, Voth, Stevenson, and others on the religion and ceremonies of the Pueblo Indians of New Mexico and Arizona (*2, 15, 21,* and *23 RBEW*; *Field Columb. Mus.*, Anth. Ser. iii.; *Journ. Am. Eth. and Arch.* i.–iv.; *Am. Anthropologist*, and *JAFL*, various vols.). The sand-paintings, decorated tablets, and other ornamented ceremonial objects appear to be not merely representations of the desires of the worshippers, or pictures of the gods and their attributes, but many may be regarded as actual pictorial prayers. The Huichol of Mexico also spends a great part of his life at ceremonies and feasts, many of which are for making rain. Very important in the religious life of the Huichols is the use of the *hikuli*, a small cactus known in the south-western United States as 'mescal buttons.' The plant is considered as the votive bowl of the god of fire, who is the principal god of the Huichols, and it has to be procured every year, or there will be no rain. Hence conventional representations of this stimulating, colour-vision-producing plant are placed on ceremonial objects or painted on the face. There are numerous other gods. Religious feeling pervades the thoughts of the Huichol so completely that every bit of decoration he puts on the most trivial of his everyday garments or utensils is a request for some benefit, a prayer for protection against evil, or an expression of adoration of some deity. As Lumholtz says (*Unknown Mexico*, 1903, ii. 204 ff.), the people always carry their prayers and devotional sentiments with them in visible form. Girdles and ribbons, inasmuch as they are considered as rain-serpents, are in themselves prayers for rain and for the results of rain, namely, good crops, health, and life; also the designs on these objects may imitate the markings on the backs of the real reptiles. Of similar significance are patterns composed of representations of conventionalized or vestigial double water-gourds, or of the fire-steel which represents the great god, or of the toto flower which grows during the wet, corn-producing season, and therefore becomes a prayer as well as a symbol for corn. The eye is the symbol of the power of seeing and understanding unknown things, and 'god's eyes' are commonly combined with other designs in woven patterns, in order that the eye of the god may rest on the wearer (Lumholtz, *Memoirs Am. Mus. Nat. Hist.* iii.). Thus these people are literally clothed in prayers.

LITERATURE.—General subject: H. Balfour, *The Evolution of Decorative Art*, Lond. 1893; A. C. Haddon, *Evolution in Art*, Lond. 1895 (with numerous references); F. Boas, 'The Dec. Art of N. Am. Indians' in *Pop. Sci. Monthly*, Oct. 1903; *Bull. Am. Mus. Nat. Hist.* ix.; 'Prim. Art' in *Am. Mus. Journ.* iv.; Flinders Petrie, *Egyptian Decorative Art*, Lond. 1895. Few of these deal with the relation of religion to art.

A. C. HADDON.

ART (American). — The art of the American Indians, like their architecture, is of many varieties and many grades. The chief forms are weaving, basketry, pottery, carving and sculpture, painting, metallurgy and jewellery, and mosaics, which may be taken up in the order named.

1. **Weaving.** — The art of weaving is found among many North American Indian tribes, particularly in the south and west, although some, such as the Apaches, are unacquainted with it. The material for the loom is very divergent in character. The Menomonis, an Algonquian stock, form their thread from the inner bark of young basswood sprouts, while the southern and south-western tribes use cotton, and the Kwakiutls of the north-west coast employ wool, hair, and even birds' feathers. The fabrics produced by the looms of the Western American Indians are woven with extreme closeness, and the colours are very gaudy, although the blankets for ordinary use are dark blue and white, or black and white, or are even left the natural colour of the wool. The figures, both in the Navaho blankets and in the closely related Hopi work, are frequently elaborate, and the effect is pleasing. It is among these two tribes, indeed, that weaving is best developed in North America. The native colours of the Navahos, who are able to make blankets that are impervious to rain, are red, yellow, and black, but here, as in the Orient, chemical dyes have largely impaired the excellence of native workmanship. Most of the weaving is done by the squaws, who make up their designs, which are largely in angles and straight lines, as they go along, occasionally tracing model patterns in the sand. Considerable symbolism attaches to the designs. The square with four knit corners represents the four quarters of heaven and the four winds, thus corresponding to the use of the *swastika* in America; while the *tau*-cross is a symbol of protection and a prayer to the Great Spirit. A spiral is said to typify the purified soul and a double spiral the struggles of the soul. The colours, in like manner, have a religious significance; so that black is the symbol of water (also indicated by wavy lines), or the female principle, and red the sign of fire, the male element. The Chilkat blankets of the Alaskan coast, woven in elaborate and artistic figures, with a warp of cedar-bark twine and a woof of mountain-goat wool, are also important in this connexion. The designs on these blankets, as might be expected, are very like those on the totem-poles and other carvings of the north-west coast. The natives of the Antilles were also acquainted with weaving, and even made cotton puppets in which the bones of the dead were placed. Among the Aztecs weaving was highly developed, a conspicuous part of the adornment of the warriors being mantles of woven feathers, decorated with the art which was a national characteristic of this marvellous people. The most striking remains of ancient American Indian weaving, however, which even include lace and drawn work, are those preserved in the great Peruvian necropolis of Ancon, near Lima, where the elaboration of the designs and the richness of the colouring surpass all other examples of American textile art (see W. Reiss and A. Strübel, *The Necropolis of Ancon in Peru*, tr. by A. H. Keane, 3 vols., Berlin, 1880–1887).

The general course of development of weaving designs among the Peruvians is thus summarized by Wiener (*Pérou et Bolivie*, p. 636 f.): 'Les étoffes les plus simples ont pour ornements de simples lignes droites parallèles, d'autres des lignes croisées. . . . Cependant ces dessins se développent, le méandre remplace d'abord les lignes croisées, et puis petit à petit nous trouvons la reproduction de fruits, de poissons et d'animaux, pour nous élever finalement à la représentation de l'homme. Cependant les difficultés techniques empêchaient le libre développement de la ligne. La courbe est toujours remplacée par une ligne cent fois brisée et se mouvant suivant des angles droits. C'est ainsi que le crâne devient une pyramide à gradins, que l'œil devient un rhomboïde, le nez un triangle, la bouche un quadrilatère.' Yet, despite the restrictions necessarily imposed on the Peruvian artists, their figures of men, animals, and other objects have a distinct charm, and frequently suggest in many respects the products of the Orient.

Mention should also be made, in connexion with weaving, of the bead-work of the American Indians. The primitive basis of this form of art may well have been pebbles, seeds, nuts, claws, teeth, and similar objects of adornment, which continued to be employed side by side with the more artistic beads. 'Beads of marine or fresh-water shells were made by grinding off the apex, as in the case of dentalium, or the unchanged shells of bivalves were merely perforated near the hinge. Pearls were bored through the middle, and shells were cut into disks, cylinders, spheres, spindles, etc. In places the columellæ of large conchs were removed and pierced through the long diameter for stringing. Bone beads were usually cylinders produced by cutting sections of various lengths from the thigh or other parts of vertebrate skeletons' (Mason, in Hodge, *Handbook of American Indians*, i. 138). Ivory and amber beads were used by the Eskimos, while turquoise was carved into ornaments in the south-west, in Arizona, and in New Mexico. The principal uses of beads were personal adornment, the decoration of vessels and of articles of dress, as insignia of office, as records of intertribal treaties and other important events, and as money. In the last two uses the strings of beads are known as *wampum*. The value of beads naturally varied considerably. Pink shells were especially prized, while in New England dark purple wampum was made from the small round spot in the inside of the quahoy shell. The northern Pacific tribes affected dentalium shells. But here, as in blanket weaving, the invasion of the whites brought modifications, and glass beads and silver coins (the latter particularly among the Navahos) are now extensively worked up into ornaments. Woven beadwork is found among the Sioux, Winnebagoes, Apaches, and other tribes, the Sioux preferring geometric designs, while the Winnebagoes and others are noted for their designs of flowers and animals. Closely akin to beadwork is quillwork, especially among the Plains Indians (now done in its purity by few except the Eskimos, the tribes of the north-west coast, and the northern Athapascans), which, in its turn, is supplemented by featherwork, the latter carried, as already noted, to its highest perfection among the Aztecs.

2. **Basketry.**—Like weaving, basketry is largely the work of women among the American Indians. Its forms are classified by Mason ('Aboriginal American Basketry,' in *Report of the United States National Museum for 1902*, pp. 222–258) into

woven and coiled. The former is subdivided into checker-work, twilled, and wicker-work, wrapped, and twined, the latter further occurring as plain twined, twilled twined, crossed or divided warp with twined work, bird-cage weaving, and various forms of three-strand twining. Coiled basketry included the following: coiled work without foundation, simple interlocking coils with foundation, single-rod foundation, two-rod foundation, rod-and-splint foundation, three-rod foundation, splint foundation, grass-coil foundation, and Fuegian stitches (the buttonhole stitch). The forms of American baskets are equally various, ranging from flat trays, as among the Tulares of Central California or the Hopi food trays, which are little more than woven mats, to the elaborate water jugs of the same Hopis. The baskets are richly adorned with shells, beads, feathers, and the like, as well as coloured with dyes and painting, and interwoven with materials of different colours.

Basketry is used in America for the most varied purposes, as for transportation, cradles (especially on the Pacific coast), armour (as among the Massawomekes of Chesapeake Bay), clothing (particularly the basket hats of the Thlinkets, Haidas, and Hupas of the west coast), preparing and serving food, building (as among the Pomos of northwestern California), furniture, trapping, general receptacles, and in burial. Baskets likewise play an important part in the ceremonial of the Hopis, as in the 'basket-dances,' the same tribe also including among its masks some made of basketry. The decoration on North American basketry is reduced by Mason (*op. cit.* p. 295) to the following *motifs*: lines in ornament, squares or rectangles, rhomboidal figures, triangles, polygonal elements, and complex patterns. Here the type of weaving adopted necessarily conditions the general style of decoration, the simplest being that obtained from checker-work, and perhaps the highest being such coiled basketry as that of the Salishans and Tulares. The decoration thus obtained may be heightened by the use of colours and by the addition of feather-work, bead-work, shell-work, and the like. But to convey an idea of the vast variety of design and colour of American Indian basketry without several hundred illustrations would be impossible, and reference can therefore only be made to the monograph of Mason already cited and to the bibliography given by him (*op. cit.* pp. 545–548), as well as to his *Indian Basketry* (2 vols., London, 1905)

Allusion has been made to the fact that basketry is employed in ritual, particularly in the Hopi women's festivals, celebrated in September and October respectively, of Lalakoñti and Owakülti (Fewkes, in *21 RBEW* pp. 22 f., 58). Symbolism in American Indian basketry is now confined to the western part of the continent; yet, even among those tribes and stocks which now show merely decorative designs in their basketry, symbolism still exists, 'for with Algonquian, Siouan, Kiowan, the substitutes for basketry, rawhide receptacles, as well as moccasins, cradles, and objects in three dimensions, are covered with idealism in painting and embroidery' (Mason, *op. cit.* p. 318). The chief modern symbolic basket-makers are the Hopis, the Thlinkets (cf. the similar designs on the Chilkat blankets), the Salishans, and the tribes of northern California and southern Oregon. It must be borne in mind, however, that the same design may represent totally different concepts among different tribes, and that the conventionalization is carried to such an extreme that only the makers themselves can truly interpret them, for 'to appreciate symbolism fully one must know the sign, hear the story, and then study the skies, the landscape, and the social environment. To attempt to discover an alphabet in this primitive art would be useless, for each tribe adapts old and new standard forms to its own concept myths' (Mason, p. 315). From the wealth of symbolic baskets allusion may be made to representations of the Corn Maiden (*Palahiko mana*) on Hopi basketry, and to the four birds of the cardinal points on trays of the same marvellous people, as well as to Navaho baskets with four crosses which give a double symbolism of the four cardinal points. Here the colours also are symbolic, and it is interesting to note, in this connexion, that the Pomos of north-western California have, according to J. W. Hudson (quoted from MS. by Mason, *op. cit.* p. 328), the following colour symbolism: red, bravery, pride (personified by the woodpecker); yellow, amatory success, gaiety, fidelity (lark); blue, demoniac cunning, perfidy (jay); green, astuteness, discretion, watchfulness (duck); black, conjugal love, beauty (quail); and white, riches, generosity (wampum). The *swastika* and labyrinth *motifs* are also found.

The relative perishability of basketry is obvious; and it is equally evident that its use was far more wide-spread in America than the extant remains would imply. It existed, for example, among the Pequots of Connecticut and the tribes of Virginia; fragments are found in the mounds of Ohio; and the means of re-constructing its designs in the Mississippi valley will be noted in the following section. Baskets were likewise known, according to the early explorers, among the Antilleans, some of them so interwoven with leaves as to be waterproof. Not only were baskets used in many religious ceremonies, but, like the Orinoco tribes, the Antilleans often preserved the skulls of the dead in baskets made specially for the purpose.

Throughout South America basketry is found. Thus, the Indians of Guiana make excellent baskets, which they adorn, as in North America, with geometrical figures. Along the Amazon the baskets receive their ornamentation primarily from the rectangles formed in weaving—another interesting proof of the influence of the older on the younger art. These designs, it should be noted, are extended to painting and drawing, and are apparent even in the drawings of men, fish, and birds made by the Indians of this region (Schmidt, *Indianerstudien in Zentralbrasilien*, Berlin, 1905, pp. 330–418), while some of the wooden masks of the Amazonian Indians have in their ornamentation obvious analogues with the more primitive woven masks. Of Peruvian basketry many specimens are known, particularly from the great necropolises, but they present scarcely any features not already known from North America.

3. Pottery.—The first utensil for holding water, grains, etc., at least in some cases, was the gourd, which was often slung in basketry for convenience, or reinforced with reeds or grasses, later still with earth or clay. It is not impossible that when these clay-covered gourds were left in the sun, the gourds were found to crack, while the clay became hardened. For a time pottery was accordingly made by covering gourds and basketry with clay, the former being destroyed by heat, and the latter retaining, in its hardened form, its original shape and the markings of its former mould. Still later, the mould was no longer used, since clay containing sand or particles of shell could easily be formed into the familiar shapes, and then be baked to the requisite firmness. It is significant, in this connexion, that the Navahos still term earthenware pots *kle-it-tsa*, or 'mud baskets,' thus recognizing the fact that American pottery is a direct development of basketry. In the further course of development, resinous gums were put on the clay vessels while still hot, thus forming a glaze which enabled the otherwise porous receptacles to hold liquids. As pottery gradually evolved, moulds were dug in the ground, and clay ovens were constructed in the hill-sides. The coiled basketry, noted above, also finds its application in pottery, as among the Hopis, who both coil ropes of damp clay around a wicker nucleus and construct similar vessels by freehand modelling. It has already been stated that basketry was more wide-spread in America than the extant remains would indicate, and proof of this is afforded by many specimens of the pottery of the Mississippi valley, where casts taken of the clay vessels reveal the pattern of the basket shell on which they were constructed. There is, however, no decisive evidence that the potter's wheel was known in aboriginal America.

Pottery was primarily used for storing, cooking, and transporting food and water, later being used in religious ceremonial, and formed into various fancy figures, as masks, gaming implements, and even toys. Burial urns are also found in the Mississippi valley, and clay pipes are common, particularly among the Iroquois. In general, it may be said that the pottery of North America decreases steadily, in both quality and quantity, as one goes toward the north, until among the Eskimos it is represented only by lamps of the rudest description. The farther south one proceeds, on the other hand, the more abundant and excellent the pottery becomes, thus further exemplifying the fact that the peoples of Mexico, Yucatan, and Peru stood at the acme of all pre-Columbian American civilization. Pottery is a characteristic, moreover, of a sedentary people, and would thus find less use among the comparatively nomadic stocks and tribes of the northern parts of the American continent.

The shapes of the pottery of North America are numerous and, in many cases, artistic. Vases, dishes, and cups occur with especial frequency, either plain or with handles, the vases being both completely open and partially covered at the top. Bottles have also been found, as in Arkansas, and early writers on America relate that they saw earthenware drums in use, these being now represented in part by the earthenware rattles used in the ritual, as by the Pueblo tribes. At least one case of earthenware burial-caskets is known from Tennessee, and funeral jars with obvious death-masks are not uncommon in the Mississippi valley. The anthropological value of the latter form of pottery needs no comment. Frequent and most interesting forms of pottery are the figurines of fish, turtles, birds, and animals. It is noteworthy that these figurines are restricted to Pueblo Indians, who, indeed, represent the zenith of American pottery north of Mexico. It would be impossible within reasonable limits to give any detailed account of the forms of either construction or decoration of American pottery, whether in the northern or the southern continent. In the most primitive specimens of North American pottery there were merely the marks of the wicker mould. The early ornament of the coiled clay vessels was, as might be expected from their form and model of construction (see above), a direct imitation of the patterns of the basketwork vessels. With further progress the impress made by the fingers of the designer gradually came to have regular modifications, which resulted in producing artistic patterns of more or less regularity. The rope coils, at first pinched involuntarily, were later purposely thus modified into regular designs, a Pueblo pot, for example, having the pinch marks so obliterated as to leave rows of triangles attached to each other at the corners. Various tools were likewise employed, pointed ones for incising and gouges for scraping, as well as many varieties of stamps for impressing designs upon the clay before baking. Examples of fictile ware have been found, especially in Arkansas, engraved, after being burned first, with designs of true artistic merit.

The most common mode of decorating pottery, however, was to give the vessel a wash of fine clay, which was painted in various colours and designs, as well as polished, before the pottery was finally burnt. This was particularly the case among the Pueblo and Arkansas Indians. There is a wide range of colour, especially white, black, red, brown, yellow, and green. The designs are so numerous as scarcely to admit of classification; but as the material of baskets led most easily to the production of right-angled decoration, so in the pottery circles and curves form a prominent feature. At the same time, angular designs are not uncommon, doubtless derived from basket patterns; and both angular and curved decorations appear with great frequency on one and the same specimen. While many of the patterns are purely ornamental, and while representations of birds and animals seem, at least in many cases, to be simply decorative, other figures on Pueblo pottery possessed religious symbolism. The three 'lines of life' occur, for instance, on a food bowl from Chevlon, which site also shows raincloud symbols on another bowl. The raincloud symbol, indeed, is well-nigh as important on Pueblo pottery as in the ritual of the Hopis and kindred tribes. The chief raincloud symbols in the modern Hopi ritual are the rectangle (usually appearing as a stepped triad), the semicircle (also usually in triads), and the triangle. These and similar symbols occur frequently in ancient Pueblo pottery, as on a food bowl from Four-mile Ruin; and on another bowl from Homolobi the *swastika* (typifying the four cardinal points), on a red ground, is surrounded by a slate-coloured margin, each arm of the *swastika* pointing to straight red lines representing rain, and the intervening sub-quarters being occupied by three wavy red lines each. These few examples may serve to indicate the wealth of symbolism which may be traced on Pueblo pottery. Nor must it be forgotten that many designs which at first blush seem merely decorative are in reality fraught with deep religious symbolism. Here, in connexion with the pictures of birds and other living creatures, the investigator will do well to bear in mind the words of Fewkes: 'In all these representations of mythical animals the imagination had full sway. It was not the bird with which the artist was familiar through observation, but a monstrous creation of fancy, distorted by imaginations — real only in legends — that the potter painted on the vessels. Hence, we cannot hope to identify them, unless we are familiar with the mythology of the painters, much of which has perished. The comparatively large number of birds on the ancient pottery indicates a rich pantheon of bird gods, and it is instructive to note, in passing, that personations of birds play important parts in the modern ceremonies which have been introduced into Tusayan from the south' (*22 RBEW*, pt. 1, p. 146 f.).

Numerous specimens of pottery have also been found in Porto Rico, Santo Domingo, St. Kitts, Grenada, Trinidad, etc. This is, in general, coarse, unpainted, and rude. The most usual decorations are incised lines or relief figures, the former being preferably lines (especially parallels), triangles, spirals (rare), and circles. There are no traces of either painting or slip. The pottery of Porto Rico and Santo Domingo is distinctly characterized by an indentation of the extremity of each line in rectilinear decoration by 'a shallow pit that was apparently made with the same instrument as the line itself; or it was sometimes slightly separated from the end of the line' (Fewkes, in *25 RBEW* p. 180). Pottery from St. Kitts, on the other hand, shows red ware with a fine superficial polish and incised lines filled with white pigment.

The art of painting pottery is also known among the South American Indians of the central Amazon and Guiana, the latter tribes adorning their pottery with juices extracted from the bark of various trees, thus making crude designs of animals or geometric figures in red, brown, black, and other colours.

North of the Isthmus of Panama pottery was carried to its highest development among the Aztecs, Zapotecs, Mayas, and kindred peoples. There not only vessels of various exquisite shapes and of a noteworthy degree of finish were made, but also elaborate funeral jars and water-pipes, and life-size figures of terra-cotta. Some of the Zapotec funeral urns are 20 inches in height, and are fashioned in the conventional forms of the sculpture of this region—a feat all the more difficult when the material used for the modelling is borne in mind. In South America the most elaborate fictile ware is found in Peru. Dishes and vases of all shapes, some of them of great intricacy of design and decoration, are found in large numbers. The forms of various fruits, animals, birds, reptiles, and fishes are represented with much fidelity, and clay vessels in human shape abound. The most important of the latter class are those which represent the head only; and while many are evidently conventional, others are plainly intended for portraits, and are thus valuable for a study of ancient Peruvian physiognomy. Groups were also represented; and fidelity to nature, which was the aim of the ancient potters of Peru, was increased by making some of their vessels a kind of mechanical toy, which could give a sound imitating the cry of the animal or bird represented, similar figurines also being found in Central, and even in North, America. A noteworthy form of Peruvian pottery was the water-jar, an article of prime importance in so arid a country. One of the chief forms is the twin bottle; and it has been suggested that one reason for the intricate shape of many Peruvian jars was the desire to prevent insects, etc., from finding their way into the interior. The pottery was often painted or engraved just as it was drying, after the clay itself had first been mixed with powdered ashes, carbon, or graphite, while in more common ware chopped straw was also employed. The decoration was, for the most part, purely conventional, although important exceptions are not lacking. The symbolism, which may well have existed, is not as yet worked out.

4. Carving and sculpture.—The carving and sculpture of the American Indians are still more limited than pottery in territory. This is but natural, in consideration of the fact that wood and stone are far less tractable substances than the clay of the potters. Excepting on the north-west coast, sculptured figures are rare, although a few rough heads have been found as far east as New Jersey. Among the so-called 'mound-builders' the tobacco-pipe attains a considerable degree of artistic development, and among the Eskimos rude carvings on ivory, copied in the scrimshaws of the whalers, frequently represent the forms of animals and other objects with remarkable fidelity. In the Mississippi valley carved shell gorgets have been discovered, which, in some cases, are curiously similar to Aztec work. Rude shell masks are also found, some as far east as Virginia. The most important specimens of North American Indian carving, however, are found among the tribes of the north-west coast, such as the Haidas, Thlinkets, and Kwakiutls, who are also skilful engravers on slate and metal. The totem-poles of these tribes are most elaborate, and are sometimes covered almost to their full height, which frequently reaches 50 feet, with representations of totemistic animals, birds, or fish. In addition to the totem-poles, the posts of the houses on the north-west coast are also elaborately carved, and both they and the totem-poles are gaudily painted in red, yellow, black, and other primary colours. Here, too, belong the wooden masks of the same tribes, which, like the totem-poles and the carved posts supporting the main rafter of the house, have religious significance, and suggest in design the basketry of the region and the Chilkat blankets. The Haida canoes are also elaborated, carved, and decorated with totemistic and other religious designs. The Pueblo Indians, so advanced in other respects, were singularly deficient in carving and sculpture, and there is a wide extent of territory from the Haidas to the Aztecs (except for a few stone whale-killer figurines among the Santa Barbara Indians of the southern California coast) before any real examples of these arts are found. It is only among the Aztecs, Toltecs, Zapotecs, and Mayas, moreover, that any carving or sculpture is found actually to be artistic. The elaboration of the Aztec calendar stone and of the sculptures of Palenque, Chiriqui, and Copan are unsurpassed in any part of the American continent, being far superior even to Peruvian art. Individualistic statues, likewise, occur in these regions, and the walls of temples are elaborately sculptured. The close connexion between sculpture and painting is exemplified in the resemblance of the carved figures to the pictures in Aztec and Maya manuscripts. Carving in wood was known in ancient Mexico, but naturally few examples of it have survived. Large stone figures are found from Mexico to Nicaragua, terminating, towards the south, in the idols of Zapatero and Pensacola and elsewhere, some of them 12 ft. high. They are, however, rude in structure, and far inferior to the polished productions of the Mayas. The archæological remains of Porto Rico and the neighbouring islands, which have become known from the researches of Jesse W. Fewkes in 1902–1904 (contained in his 'The Aborigines of Porto Rico and Neighboring Islands,' in *25 RBEW* pp. 3–220), give some striking contributions to American art from a region hitherto imperfectly explored. The remains are rude artistically, yet they serve to supplement our knowledge of the Orinoco tribes, with which he justly holds Antillean civilization to be connected. Here mention may first be made of stone pestles, chiefly from Santo Domingo, adorned with rude heads and figures of animals, birds, and men, the type being unlike any found in any other part of America. Besides objects more or less familiar elsewhere, such as beads, pendants, stone balls (perhaps used as roof-weights or fetishes), small stone heads and discs with human faces, stools (recalling the forms in South America), pillar stones (generally with rough and grotesque attempts to represent the human form), and rude wooden idols (some possibly imported by the Spaniards from Africa for the negro slaves), there are three classes of sculpture which are apparently peculiar to this region. These are three-pointed stones (either plain or with faces of birds, beasts, reptiles, or men, restricted thus far to Porto Rico and the eastern end of Santo Domingo), stone 'collars,' and 'elbow stones.' The first are regarded by Fewkes (*op. cit.* p. 131) 'as clan idols or images of tutelary totems,' fastened to some unknown object; and the third class may have been connected with the 'collars' (*op. cit.* pp. 172–174). There thus remain the 'collars,' which are either massive ovals or slender ovates, and either partially decorated or plain.

Their use is entirely problematical (cf. Fewkes, *op. cit.* pp. 167–172); but similar objects have been found in Totonac ruins in eastern Mexico. They are accordingly held by Fewkes (*25 RBEW* pp. 251–261) to be connected with the Aztec 'sacrificial yokes,' which he seems inclined to regard as fertility symbols (cf. the more conventional view advanced, perhaps incorrectly, by the present writer in art. ALTAR [American], above, p. 336). At all events, the problem of the real meaning of these 'collars,' which measure as high as 19 by 17 in., can as yet scarcely be said to be solved.

Turning to South America, one finds rough carvings on trees among the Indians of Central Brazil, while their chairs are made in the shape of birds, and they have vessels in the form of various birds, bats, fishes, and tortoises. On the Chaco, on the other hand, art consists only in scratching natural objects roughly on gourds and making rude topographical scenes (Grubb, *Among the Indians of the Paraguayan Chaco*, London, 1904, p. 98). Among the most remarkable sculptures, if such they may be called, of the South American Indians are those of the natives of Guiana. One of the most typical of these is on Temehri Rock in the Corentyn river, and measures 13 feet in length by 5 feet 7 inches in width. The carving represents a number of figures of men, monkeys, snakes, and the like, and also has simple combinations of two or three curved lines. The figures are in all cases extremely rude, and those of less importance are sometimes painted instead of carved. Some of these carvings are of comparatively recent date, for one at Ihla de Pedra in the Rio Negro represents a Spanish galley (cf. Im Thurn, *Among the Indians of Guiana*, London, 1883, pp. 391–410). The sculptures of the ancient Peruvians, although naturally superior to any others of the South American continent, were, as already noted, far inferior to the work of the Aztecs and their neighbours. Expert cyclopean architects though they were, they were but indifferent sculptors, and even the few specimens of wood carving which are still extant are but rough work. Like the Central Brazilian Indians, the Peruvians paid considerable attention to their chairs, and specimens have been preserved which are supported by figures of some artistic merit. Chairs of similar form are also found in Nicaragua and Porto Rico. A few admirable granite heads have been found, as at Pashash; and the fountain of Quonnacha is, at least at first sight, a remarkable work of art. Nevertheless, the rudeness of the head of a porphyry idol, now at Collo-Collo, and the shapelessness of the granite statues of Tiahuanaco, when contrasted with the Maya sculptures of Copan, bespeak most clearly the inferiority of the Peruvians in this form of art. The elaborate sculptures on the buildings, moreover, are far less frequent than among the Aztecs and their congeners.

5. Painting.—This art, at least in its crude forms, doubtless prevailed through most of the North American continent; but the best modern examples are to be found among the Indians of the West. The tribes of the north-west coast, where, as just noted, carving in wood is relatively highly developed, paint their totem-poles, canoes, chests, batons, and other objects in gaudy colours, while the Hopis and other Pueblo peoples are also acquainted with this art, as is shown by the masks, often of leather or basketry, and garments used in the personations of the gods in the great winter festivals. In like manner, much of the pottery discovered in the 'cliff-dwellings' is painted, frequently in conventional designs of pleasing effect and with the general systems of symbolism noted above (p. 829b). Among the Aztecs and related peoples the manuscripts still extant are painted with considerable skill, but with the high colouring characteristic of so much of early art. As if to atone for their somewhat curious deficiency in painting, however, the inhabitants of ancient Mexico were noteworthy for their skill in making pictures of trees and flowers, and even copies of European paintings, in mosaics of feathers, with a degree of excellence which aroused the admiration of the Spanish invaders (see above, § 1; and cf. Mason, in Hodge, *Handbook of American Indians*, i. 455 f., and the bibliography there given). The Peruvians also possessed the art of painting; but among them, as among the Aztecs, it was undeveloped as compared with their achievements in other departments of art. Their representations of the human form, however, as is clear from their vase-paintings, were far superior to those of the Aztecs, and the same statement holds true in general with regard to all ancient Peruvian painting. The problem of symbolism here, as elsewhere throughout America, must be solved together with the interpretation of the pottery, basketry, and kindred arts. Outside the empire of the Incas painting seems scarcely to occur in South America. It must be borne in mind, however, that painting is pre-eminently a sessile art, and one which requires a considerable degree of civilization before it can be acquired with any measure of real merit. It is less utilitarian even than carving and sculpture, and arises at a later period, while it is still more tardy in development as compared with weaving, basketry, and pottery, and for a like reason.

Certain special forms of painting among the American Indians call for notice in this connexion. Of these the first is 'dry-painting,' which is practised especially by the Navahos, Apaches, and the Pueblo tribes of Arizona and New Mexico, and in ruder form by the Cheyennes, Arapahos, and Siksikas. These paintings are used exclusively in religious ceremonies, as in the Hopi altars (see ALTAR [American], p. 336), and seem to be most highly developed among the Navahos. Here the paintings are sometimes 10 or 12 ft. in diameter, and are, of course, filled with symbolism representing deities, natural phenomena, and living beings of sacred import. The sand is laid to a depth of 2 or 3 in., and the colours are white, yellow, red (these made of powdered sandstone), blue (really grey, being a mixture of black and white sand), and black (pulverized charcoal). Working generally from the centre and according to the plan prescribed by the ritual (except in a few definite cases), the artist, in applying the pigments, 'picks up a small quantity between his first and second fingers and his opposed thumb and allows it to flow slowly as he moves his hand. . . . When he makes a mistake he does not brush away the coloured powder, but obliterates it by pouring sand on it, then draws the correct design on the new surface. . . . When it is finished, ceremonies are performed over it, and then with song and ceremony it is obliterated. When no semblance of it remains, the sand of which it was made is gathered in blankets and thrown away at a distance from the lodge. In the ceremonies of the Pueblo Indians a picture is allowed to remain several days' (Matthews, in Hodge, *Handbook of American Indians*, i. 403 f.). The Hopis, unlike the Navahos, begin their dry-paintings at the periphery, commencing with the north; and when the painting is effaced, pinches of the sand used in its composition are deposited in certain spots prescribed by the ritual.

A sort of heraldry was perpetuated by means of painting, particularly among the Plains Indians. This applied especially to the *tipis* and shields, and involved certain tabus, while the basis of the design was drawn from the visions obtained by the young braves (cf. COMMUNION WITH DEITY [American Indian]). As in many other lands, the painting of the face and body was and is common among the American Indians. This may be purely decorative in intent, or it may have symbolism relating to religion, war, or social status. Thus, the Mandans often painted their bodies reddish brown and drew red or black figures on their arms, while their faces were coloured vermilion or yellow. These designs, being merely ornamental, might be varied at pleasure; but the transition from the ornamental is shown by the practice of the same tribe of painting the entire face jet black after performing an exploit (Maximilian von Wied-Neuwied, *Travels in the Interior of North America*, London, 1843, pp. 340–386). Hearndon (*Exploration of the Valley of the Amazon*, Washington, 1853, i. 201) describes a Conibo dandy as 'painted with a broad stripe of red under each eye; three narrow stripes of blue were carried from one ear, across the upper lip to the other—the two lower stripes plain, and the upper one bordered with figures. The whole of the lower jaw and chin were painted with a blue chain-work of figures.' Ritualistic face-painting is exemplified among the White Earth Ojibwas of Minnesota, the first degree of their Ghost Society being indicated, according to Hoffmann (*American Anthropologist*, 1888, pp. 209–229), by a red stripe across the face from near the ears over the tip of the nose; the second by a similar stripe plus another across the eyes, temples, and root of the nose; the third by painting the upper half of the face green and the lower half red; and the fourth by painting the forehead and the left cheek green and impressing four vermilion spots on the brow and four on the cheek. The 'war paint' of the American Indians is, in general, either red or black, or a combination of both; and the same colours are frequently used for mourning (cf., in general, on American Indian face-painting, Mallery, in *10 RBEW* pp. 619–634).

Allusion should also be made to the pictographs which are scattered over North, Central, and South America. Since these are in great part mnemonic, chronological, or historical in purpose, or are intended to convey messages, notices, and the like, they will more properly be discussed under the head of WRITING (American Indian). Here, however, it may be noted that the artistic powers evinced in these pictographs (which are mainly petroglyphs) are decidedly primitive. Their interpretation, when they are not mere ornaments or idle *graffiti*, is often problematical, and requires, in many cases, a knowledge of traditions, local surroundings, and the like. An important class of pictographs is given in the representations of tribal designations (cf. the list in Mallery, *10 RBEW* pp. 377–388; and see in general on the subject his 'Pictographs of the North American Indians' in *4 RBEW* pp. 13–256, and 'Picture-Writing of the American Indians,' in *10 RBEW* pp. 25–822; supplemented for Porto Rico by Fewkes, in *25 RBEW* pp. 148–159). They likewise symbolize personal names (Mallery, in *10 RBEW* pp. 442–460), and religious symbolism is also prominent, being found not only in the Micmac pictographs from Kejimkoojik Lake, Nova Scotia, but also among the Ojibwas, Menomonis, Dakotas, and Haidas (Mallery, pp. 461–512). More than this, there are well defined pictographic signs for the *swastika*, the sky, the heavenly bodies, day and night, lightning, eclipses, and meteors, and representations of *tipis* and even *pueblos* are also found (Mallery, pp. 694–735). The older American pictographs are naturally on stone and uncoloured; but bone, skin, gourds, copper, wood, and textiles also bear like figures, frequently in colours.

6. Metallurgy and jewellery.—The Indians of North and Central America were acquainted with copper, silver, gold, iron, galena, lead, and tin, knowledge of the last two being restricted to the Aztecs, Toltecs, and Mayas. Nevertheless, the use of metal in personal adornment was comparatively rare in North America, shells, beads, and the like being used instead, although bracelets of copper were frequently worn and were highly valued, in view of the difficulty of mining the metal in pre-Columbian days. The metals were worked chiefly by cold-hammering and grinding, but there is no evidence of a knowledge of casting. Silver is now worked with considerable elaboration among the Navahos, and bells of copper have been found in Tennessee, while elaborate sheet copper *repoussé* figures occur in the Etowah mounds, Georgia, and the Hopewell mounds, Ohio; and the copper 'tokens' of the north-west coast are famous in many ceremonies. The Aztecs and other Mexican peoples were expert metallurgists, and their gold vessels and adornments were the marvel of their conquerors.* They imitated the forms of animals and birds, and manufactured personal jewellery, often enhanced in beauty by gems. They likewise possessed the art of making an amalgam of copper and tin, thus forming a bronze of considerable hardness, while specimens of copper plating are known from the mounds of Florida, Alabama, and Ohio. Gold ornaments are also known from Florida and the West Indies. The metallurgical remains of the Peruvians include silver bracelets and collars; gold, silver, copper, and bronze vases; and animals and birds, such as jaguars, deer, monkeys, and parrots, in copper, bronze, and silver, as well as human figures. Apart from this, however, South America falls behind the northern continent in the amount and excellence of metallurgical products and jewellery, as it does in nearly all other requisites and tokens of human progress in civilization.

7. Mosaics and minor arts.—The art of making mosaics was known especially in the Pueblo regions of Arizona and New Mexico and among the Aztecs. The modern products of the former region are much inferior to the ancient specimens, 'which consist of gorgets, ear pendants, and other objects. . . . Turquoise was the favourite material, but bits of shell and various bright-coloured stones were also employed. The foundation form was of shell, wood, bone, and jet and other stone, and the matrix of gum or asphaltum. Although the work is neatly executed, the forms are simple and the designs not elaborate' (Holmes, in Hodge, *Handbook of American Indians*, i. 947). Rude mosaics have been found in graves in southern California. One of the most interesting mosaic objects north of Mexico is a shell used as a pendant and found by Fewkes at Chaves Pass, Arizona, in 1896. This is a frog formed by imbedding turquoises in pitch on the shell of a *Petunculus giganteus*, with a small rectangle of red jasper set in the centre of the back (cf. Fewkes, in *22 RBEW*, pt. 1, p. 86 f.). Mosaics from Mexico have long been known, particularly a knife with a blade of semi-translucent chalcedony, the handle being a crouching man, clothed in an eagle's skin, his head issuing from the beak (cf. Bancroft, *Native Races*, iv. 557–559). Of these mosaics some twenty-three are thus far known; and for comparison with the Chaves Pass frog, allusion may be made to a

* The gold was an alloy of copper, varying from almost pure gold to almost pure copper. When the baser metal was used, it was frequently coated (plated?) with pure gold. The technical processes used were exceedingly skilful, but what they were is uncertain.

double jaguar now in the Berlin Museum für Völkerkunde. This is described by Lehmann (in *XVe Congrès international des Américanistes*, Quebec, 1907, ii. 340–344) as follows:—The figure is carved of tough reddish brown wood, 32 cm. long and 10 cm. high at the head at each end, one of which is turned towards the spectator and the other averted. The belly, which has no mosaic work, is painted with black and bluish green. The bed for the mosaics is a dark brown resin 3 or 4 mm. deep, and the stones themselves are chiefly green or greenish-yellow turquoise and blue malachite, their shapes varying between polyhedrous, rectangular, and round, and all carefully polished. The neck and the extremities are almost covered with turquoises, and rosettes of the same material are evidently intended to represent the jaguar's spots. Rows of turquoise alternate with rows of obsidian on the body, and the ornamentation is enhanced by mother-of-pearl and bits of white, yellow, red, and violet mussel-shells. It would also seem that the eyes and nose were originally covered in part with gold-leaf (see in general on Mexican mosaics, *Globus*, 1906, pp. 318–322).

The account thus given of American Indian art, like that of the architecture of the same peoples, cannot pretend to be exhaustive. Besides the large categories here outlined, there were other arts, such as bark-work. This was used for cord, mats, receptacles of all kinds, dishes, canoes, and houses; for cradles and for burial; for clothing and for writing-tablets; and for religious dance regalia and masks (cf. Mason, in Hodge, *Handbook of American Indians*, i. 130–132, and the literature there cited). Among the more northern tribes and along the Pacific coast bone is almost as important as bark, being used not only for personal adornment and as household utensils, toys, and fetishes, but even for weapons and in the construction of dwellings, canoes, and the like. Bones were elaborately carved, and were also inlaid by the ancient Pueblo Indians, while even a copper-plated bone has been found in a Florida mound (cf. the summary of Holmes, in Hodge, i. 159 f.). Horn was likewise sometimes employed, as for dishes among the Salishan tribes.

LITERATURE.—Dellenbaugh, *North Americans of Yesterday* (New York, 1900); Thomas, *Introduction to the Study of North American Archæology* (Cincinnati, 1898); Hodge, *Handbook of American Indians*, i. (Washington, 1907); Bancroft, *Native Races of the Pacific States*, iv. (San Francisco, 1883); Kingsborough, *Antiquities of Mexico* (9 vols., London, 1830–1848); Maudsley, 'Archæology' in *Biologia Centrali-Americana* (London, 1899–1901); Wiener, *Pérou et Bolivie* (Paris, 1880); Baessler, *Ancient Peruvian Art* (Eng. tr. by Keane, 4 vols., Berlin, 1902–1903); von den Steinen, *Unter den Naturvölkern Zentral-Brasiliens* (Berlin, 1894); Waitz, *Anthropologie der Naturvölker*, iii. (2 parts, Leipzig, 1862–1864); and many monographs in the reports of the American *BE*, the United States National Museum, the Field Columbian Museum, the Peabody Museum, and the American Museum of Natural History. The present writer's thanks are also due Mr. F. D. Van Arsdale of Newark, N.J., for private information, especially concerning pottery.

LOUIS H. GRAY.

ART (Assyro-Babylonian).—The religion of the Babylonians and Assyrians, which, according to the received opinion, was animistic in its origin, may be regarded as going back to between 4000 and 5000 years B.C. This long period, added to the nature of their faith, has supplied us with an enormous amount of material illustrating their religious art, which the student can trace, in all its variant styles, through the ages of its existence, noting the changes in religious thought which it reflects, and the reaction of its influence on the people themselves.

Before B.C. 4500 (as far as is at present known) no monuments exist, so that there is practically no record of that animistic period in which the religion of the Babylonians had its origin. A wide gulf must therefore exist between the religious conceptions of the simple-minded savages of early Sumerian and Semitic times and those of the men of even the remotest civilization of Babylonia when works of art are found.

Babylonian religious art therefore comes before us only when it had attained a certain measure of perfection. It is true that a number of comparatively rude examples have come down to us, but such are a speciality of no particular age, and at all periods excellent examples, principally in stone, exist, among them being numerous engraved seals, mostly cylindrical. Many good bronzes, too, have been found, some of them being as early as the 3rd millennium B.C.

In all probability the art of Babylonia is best divided into periods, though the schools of the various States (Ur, Erech, Akkad, Babylon, Lagaš, etc.) could also be taken into account if we had sufficient material. With our present knowledge, however, it is often difficult to place the examples, and even the question of date is not without its difficulties, as the chronology does not admit of a clear line of demarcation in the matter. The divisions, therefore, can be only roughly determined, somewhat as follows:

1. Babylonia.
(1) From the earliest period until the time of the Dynasty of Babylon (*c.* 2000 B.C.—Lagaš, Niffer).
(2) Until the end of the dynasty of the Land of the Sea (*c.* 1700 B.C.—Babylon, Sippar, Erech).
(3) The Kassite period (*c.* 1700 B.C.—*c.* 1100 B.C.).
(4) From *c.* 1100 B.C. until the downfall of the Babylonian empire (B.C. 538).

2. Assyria.
The artistic period may be regarded as extending from the 9th cent. or earlier (we await the results of the German excavations at Aššur) until about B.C. 606.

Though, like the art of Egypt, that of Babylonia comes before us only when it had attained a certain amount of perfection, it is, in a way, more interesting than that of Egypt, in that it shows a much greater variety of styles; and the Assyrian school, when it comes into existence, has a distinct stamp of its own. We have also to distinguish, besides the perfect and artistic, the amateurish (which is sufficiently rare) and the rough and unfinished—generally cylinder-seals 'dashed off' by the hand of one accustomed to do such work, and probably to be regarded as cheap productions for the poorer classes, who naturally needed things similar to those required by the well-to-do, though they could not pay the price. At all times these classes of religious artistic productions had existed, and among the perfect and artistic are now and then to be found things of noteworthy beauty of workmanship, due, doubtless, to the presence of artist-workmen of wonderful talent.

1. Babylonia.—(1) Among the best of *the earliest examples* of Babylonian religious art are the very interesting cylinder-seals impressed upon tablets found at Tel-loh (Lagaš) in S. Babylonia. They show a man and a woman, nude, the former struggling with a stag, and the latter with a bull, whilst two lions, whose bodies cross each other symmetrically (a common device of Assyro-Babylonian engravers) attack the two animals at the same time. Various mystic emblems appear—a bat or bat-headed bird, an animal's fetlock and hoof in outline, and a young bull—whilst beneath the name of the owner are two bull-men whose bodies cross each other, as in the case of the lions. The wide-open mouth of the man, and the closed mouth and the large ear of the woman, suggest that we may have here primitive representations of the deities Nebo, 'the proclaimer,' and Tašmêtu, his spouse, 'the hearer'; but the crown with points which the woman wears is rather against this identification, on account of analogies elsewhere. Concerning the art here revealed, a few words may be said. The animal-forms, especially the heads, are good, and the manes of the lions are well treated, but the human forms are less satisfactory, the body of the man being thick, and the arms in both cases abnormally thin. The head of the man regards the spectator, and, though too large, is more successful than that of the woman, which has the same defect, to which must be added the fronting eye in the profile face, fitting, as it were, into the somewhat pointed nose, which makes the figure grotesque. The close-shut mouth (the line of the lips is invisible in the impression) and the abnormally large ear, taken in conjunction with the wide-open mouth of the man, shows that the design has a deeper meaning than appears at first sight. This seal belonged to En-gal-gala, the superintendent of the women's house during the reigns of Lugalanda and Uru-ka-gina, about B.C. 4500.*

Scenes similar to this are common, though no woman is shown as one of those struggling with the animals. From the same site, Tel-loh, the de Sarzec expedition † obtained a very fine seal showing a bearded man struggling with a bull, and a bearded and crowned personage struggling with a lion. These animals cross each other like the lions in the other design, and the bull-men beneath the inscription of En-gal-gala's cylinder are replaced by two human-headed bulls, one of which is held by a nude bearded man, a bird, probably intended for an eagle, occupying the space between them. If the short inscription *Nin-in* or *Ni-in*, close to the crowned personage, refers to him, it probably represents the ancient deified king Ninus, who, with Semiramis, is said by Diodorus (ii. 8, 6) to have been represented on the walls of Babylon in enamelled brick, hunting the leopard and the lion.‡ The objects here described suggest that there was not only a legend referring to the goddess Nina, patron of Nina on the Euphrates and of Nineveh in Assyria, but also a male deity of similar name. Semitic influence, with its veneration for the male, is probably the cause of the substitution of the male deity for the hearing but silent female.

The occurrence of these early designs on cylinder-seals reminds us of an important fact in connexion with Babylonian art, namely, that in Babylonia there is neither building-stone nor even blocks in any number suitable for sculpture either in relief or in the round. It is therefore not impossible that the earliest works of art were primitive attempts at engraving, first as charms, and afterwards as charms and seals combined, on the cylindrical beads which were for many centuries the favourite form of seal in Babylonia and Assyria, and which afterwards travelled to the extreme west of Asia and Egypt.

Presenting a large surface in a small space, these cylinder-seals became suitable for all kinds of pictures, and we find engraved thereon the Babylonian idea of several of the legends with which we have become familiar from the tablets. Thus it happens that, in a scene showing a nude bearded figure struggling with a bull which is being also attacked by a lion, we see a representation of a boat and a personage within rowing,§ which is generally supposed to show the Babylonian Noah in the ark. Several copies exist also of that exceedingly interesting scene which shows Etanna riding in the air upon an eagle, whilst people on the earth below interrupt their daily work to gaze upon them.* Another noteworthy example is well known as a possible Babylonian picture of the Fall. It shows two personages seated one on each side of a palm-tree bearing fruit, and stretching forth their hands as if about to grasp it, whilst behind the figure apparently representing the woman a wavy serpent raises himself. The work is rough, but implies some technical skill.†

Noteworthy are the early engravers' attempts to cope with the scene representing the overthrow of the dragon Tiamat by Merodach. The best is one figured by Hayes Ward, in which the head of the Babylonian pantheon is seen striding or running along Tiamat's wavy body, and thrusting his weapon into her mouth as she turns her horned head towards him. Two of Merodach's helpers seem to follow behind. Another picture of the same, which is apparently of late date and Assyrian workmanship, shows the dragon with a long and straight, but apparently scaly, body, erecting herself at an angle where the feet spring forth. She does not turn her head towards him, and the god attacks her with thunderbolts, striding along on her body behind, followed by two of his helpers.‡ Other scenes, possibly from legends, occur, but have not as yet been identified. Thus a cylinder-seal in two divisions shows, on the right, a deity (the sun-god) dividing food, of which the owner of the seal, standing before him, seems to partake; and on the left another deity bending down a tall thin tree apparently to conceal a goddess and a (? child-) deity coming forth from its trunk (cf. the classical story of Adonis [Ovid, *Metam.* x.]). All the figures on this cylinder-seal (except that of the owner) wear the horned hat indicating divinity.§

The design in the right-hand division, which shows the owner of the cylinder before the god whom he worshipped, is probably, in its various forms, the commonest found, especially in the period preceding 2000 B.C. The deity is generally seated, and often holds a cup in his right hand. Before him is sometimes a vase, and the worshipper (the owner of the seal) is led into his presence by a divine personage.‖ A divine attendant sometimes brings up the rear.¶ The worshipper is generally bare-headed and clean-shaven, the latter peculiarity probably indicating his priestly office.** Variants of this oft-repeated design are found; one, which is regarded as exceedingly ancient, is a fragment of a bas-relief †† showing a seated deity holding a cup in his right hand, and wearing on his head a hat with two horns, one at the front and the other at the back, instead of one or more on each side, as in the later designs. The work is rough and primitive, the artist having apparently found his material not altogether satisfactory (it is a calcareous limestone, probably of sufficient hardness to make its working difficult).

* See the *Amherst Tablets*, vol. i. p. 2. The woman's crown appears in the reproduction published by M. N. de Likhatscheff, St. Petersburg, 1907.

† E. de Sarzec, *Découvertes en Chaldée*, pl. 30, 5*b*.

‡ Fragments of enamelled brick with portions of what appeared to be fabulous animals, and white inscriptions on a blue ground, were found at Babylon by Rassam. See also Delitzsch, *Im Lande des einstigen Paradieses*, pp. 34–38.

§ Smith, *Chaldean Genesis*.

* E. de Sarzec, *Découvertes en Chaldée*, pl. 30 *bis*, No. 13; *Cylinder-Seals in the Possession of Sir Henry Peck*, 1890 (plate, No. 18).

† Smith, *Chaldean Genesis*.

‡ L. W. King, *Babylonian Religion*, p. 102.

§ *Découvertes en Chaldée*, pl. 30 *bis*, 17*b*. It is not exactly known why the Babylonians and Assyrians represented their deities wearing horned hats. In the primitive design described above (p. 833), the demons or bull-men have horns placed directly upon their heads. Perhaps this is an artist's device to show who, among the figures in the picture, are gods and who are men, just as the star placed before the names of deities in the inscriptions is not an indication that all the deities are stars (though some of them were so regarded), but simply means that the gods belonged to the place where the stars are, namely, the heavens.

‖ Numerous representations of this kind will be found in the *Amherst Tablets*, vol. i. pp. 40, 63, 83, 141, 158, 196, etc.

¶ *Ib.* pp. 80, 170.

** A very fine but fragmentary relief, showing Gudea (*c.* 2500 B.C.) brought before his god by two introducers, is given in Meyer's *Sumerien und Semiten in Babylonien* (Königliche Preuss. Akad. der Wissenschaften, 1906), pl. vii.

†† *Découvertes en Chaldée*, pl. 1, No. 1.

The deities at this period are represented wearing mantles which recall, in a measure, the Roman cloak wound round the body, and thrown over the left shoulder, leaving the right shoulder and arm bare. These garments seem sometimes to be represented as made of the skin of some animal, such as the goat (which seems to have been a sacred animal), sewn together in long strips giving the appearance of flounces. This costume distinguishes divine personages, or those who claimed divine kinship. A squat little figure in alabaster, standing with folded arms, and wearing a dress of this kind, the head bound round with a fillet crossing behind the long carefully-arranged hair,* may be a divinity, or the priest of a god.

It is noteworthy that though, in the archaic fragment above described † and on the cylinder-seals, the deities are represented in profile, in bas-reliefs of somewhat later date they are often shown front-face. Whether front- or side-face, however, the horns on their hats, which vary from two to eight in number, are shown as if the front of the head-dress were towards the spectator.‡ Goddesses are shown dressed similarly to the gods, in horned hat and robe of skin, but the right shoulder is covered as well as the left. One small fragment § shows a goddess wearing a hat with a single horn on each side. Her hair descends in graceful curves upon her shoulders, necklaces adorn her neck, upon which is also a triple row of beaded work which disappears beneath the low-cut neck of her goat-skin robe, over which, from each shoulder, descends a beaded stole. She holds in her hands a vase from which flows a twofold stream of living water. Here we have something really good and artistic—almost æsthetic. The work is so dignified, the idea intended to be conveyed (that of a beneficent goddess bearing the water of life) so well expressed, that the spectator realizes that he has before him the work of a people who knew what they wished to express, and had skill to express it.

After that, the picture of a god,‖ apparently of the same period, is disappointing, though even this has its excellences. Its shortcomings are probably due mainly to the damage which the stone has received. A deity, front-face, bearded, and holding what seems to be a staff or symbol, is seated on a low-armed chair with a high and slightly bent back. He wears the usual robe of skin, and hair falling upon his shoulders. In spite of the damage to the stone, the dignity of the face is striking. Reliefs in terra-cotta, apparently produced from moulds, also occur. A very good example ¶ shows a male figure nearly nude, wearing a horned hat, and plaited hair descending to each side of his longish beard, where it ends in two tightly-arranged curls.

The bronzes, though not numerous, are excellent of their kind. They represent *canephoroi* (priestly rulers as bearers of gifts to the temple), human figures and seated bulls, on a kind of tang for insertion in a socket, and the well-known kneeling figures in horned hats holding inscribed cones (regarded by some as the god with the fire-stick). They are of the nature of votive statuettes,** and were used as the bearers of stone inscriptions detailing the building of temples.

(2) *With the advent of Semitic influence* (*c.* 2100 B.C.) there is a change in the representation of certain of the deities. The horned hats and the skin robes are found, but, in the case of what may be regarded as the warrior-gods, short tunics and thick-brimmed hats appear, and the deity grasps in his right hand a short weapon, held close against the body. The beard also spreads over the breast. Sometimes the thick-brimmed hat is combined with the long flounced robe of skin. The cylinder-seals of this period are often very finely engraved, especially those of hæmatite. The bas-reliefs follow the style of the cylinder-seals, but seem to keep more to the old costumes. A very good specimen of the lapidary art of this period is the representation of Ḫammurabi before the sun-god Šamaš, at the top of that king's Code of Laws.* Ḫammurabi has flowing robes reaching to his feet, and a thick-brimmed hat. His right shoulder is bare, and his hand is raised as if addressing the deity. The sun-god, heavily bearded, wears a flounced robe without any indication whatever of a hairy surface. Upon his head is a pointed hat, with four horns curving upwards in front—eight in all. Wavy rays proceed from his shoulders. His seat has four superimposed recesses, such as are often found both in bas-reliefs and in designs on cylinder-seals. His right shoulder is bare, and in his hand he holds a staff and a ring, emblematic of his endless course and his authority as judge of the world. The work is good and well finished, but wanting in lightness and detail. The bronzes of this period seem to have maintained the excellence which those of the preceding period show. One, probably now in private hands, is a good reproduction, in the round, of one of those divine attendants so often shown in the cylinder-seals as a graceful female figure in a horned hat and wearing a robe of skin, holding up her hands with the palms facing each other. When the deity and the owner of the seal are absent, these attendants are sometimes shown in the same attitude of adoration before the divine name contained in the inscription.

(3) *In the Kassite period* we meet with another style for the cylinder-seals, the work being exceedingly plain and flat, and wanting detail. The designs are, moreover, confined to single figures, either sitting or standing, and accompanied by some emblem—a cross, one or more birds, etc.; and in one case even a fly, suggesting that the deity may have been the Babylonian Beelzebub. These designs probably form the transition to the later Babylonian style of art, in which the robes are likewise very plain; but the work, which seems to fall off somewhat during the Kassite period, later assumes remarkable accuracy and finish.

It is to the Kassite period mainly, however, that the boundary-stones which have come down to us belong. These objects (generally inscribed with grants of land) are sculptured with 'the signs of the gods' as a protection against the wrongful alteration of the boundary or changing the conditions of the deed, etc. Those found by the de Morgan expedition at Susa † are of special value, as they have sometimes short inscriptions which enable the signs upon them to be identified. The sun is represented by a disc having a flaming star within; the moon by a crescent; Venus by a star; Nusku ('the light of fire') by a lamp; Gula, goddess of healing, by a female figure in horned hat and robe of skin, etc. We see on them also the fish-goat, the scorpion, and the bull emblematic of Addu (Hadad). The signs vary on each stone, and the work is seldom really well finished, that of Nebuchadrezzar I. in the British Museum being in all probability the finest specimen.‡

(4) Comparatively early in *the latest period* (*c.* 900 B.C.) comes that magnificent specimen of Babylonian art, the sun-god stone, found beneath the

* *Découvertes*, pl. 1 *ter*, No. 3.
† *Ib.* pl. 1, No. 1.
‡ *Ib.* pl. 25, No. 5, is an interesting example of this.
§ *Ib.* pl. 8 *bis*.
‖ *Ib.* pl. 22, No. 5.
¶ *Ib.* pl. 39, No. 3.
** *Ib.* pl. 5 *bis*, 1*a*, 1*b*, 1*c*; and pl. 28.

* *Délégation en Perse, Mémoires*, vol. iv. pl. 3.
† *Ib.* vols. i. and vii.
‡ *Cuneiform Inscriptions of Western Asia*, vol. v. pl. 57; *British Museum Guide to the Bab. and Assyr. Antiqs.* pl. xi.

pavement of the temple of the sun at Abu-habbah by Mr. H. Rassam. It shows a design derived from the early cylinder-seals. The sun-god sits in his shrine, wearing horned hat, robes of skin, and long beard. In his right hand he grasps his staff of justice and the circlet of his everlasting course. At the top of the shrine two little figures, personifying righteousness and justice, guide with cords the great disc of the sun erected on the table below. A divine personage leads Nabû-âbla-iddina, the king who had the stone sculptured, into the presence of the god, and a divine attendant in the usual attitude of veneration follows behind. The ground consists of wavy lines (the waters above the firmament) with stars below, pointing to the probability that the scene is laid in heaven. The figures are a little too broad, but the work is excellent, and may be regarded as maintaining all the traditions of Babylonian art.*

Figures of deities during this late period are rare, but there is evidence in the antiquities found that they did exist. On the cylinder-seals emblems similar to those found on the boundary-stones of the preceding period often take their place, such as the sun's disc and the moon's crescent mounted on a tall object set on square corniced and panelled plinths. A burly clean-shaven priest stands before the emblems in an attitude of adoration. The fish-goat and other deities copied from the boundary-stones also appear.

2. Assyria.—But it is Assyria, from about B.C. 885, that furnishes us with the greatest wealth of material for the study of Assyro-Babylonian religious art. In the sculptures of that date (time of Aššur-naṣir-âpli) the king is represented as the great high priest. Assyria being a country possessing stone, the sculptors were not dependent on such chance fragments as they could get, and magnificent bas-reliefs indicate what her artists were capable of. The examples from Nimrûd (Calah) show us the king, clothed in garments splendidly embroidered with representations of all kinds of mystic emblems and ceremonies,† himself engaged in ceremonial acts, surrounded by his eunuchs and drinking from the sacred cup, while winged genii offer him the divine pine-cone, or something of similar shape. In other sculptures we see him worshipping before the sacred tree, above which hovers the winged disc representing Aššur, the chief god of the Assyrians.‡ Familiar to all are the reliefs showing the adoration of the sacred tree,§ and the winged figures carrying offerings of flowers and young animals.‖ An admirable example of religious art is the sculpture from the entrance of the temple of Ninip, representing the expulsion of the dragon of evil from the building, which was repeated on the other side of the doorway.¶ As a testimony to the divine status of the king we have the image of Aššur-naṣir-âpli on an arch-headed monolith, and the sacrificial altar which stood before it at the entrance to the temple.** Though the figures are too thick-set, the work is excellently finished, and the details carefully indicated. This applies also to the winged bulls and lions of this reign, though they are wanting in vigour.†† The effect is somewhat marred by the long inscriptions which are carved across the sculptured work of this reign.

* *Cuneiform Inscriptions of Western Asia*, vol. v. pl. 60; *TSBA*, vol. viii. plate between pp. 164–165.

† Layard's *Monuments of Nineveh*, 1st series, pl. 6, 8, 9, 43 ff.

‡ For various forms of this see G. Rawlinson's *Ancient Monarchies*, vol. ii. pp. 232–233.

§ Layard's *Monuments*, 1st series, pl. 7, 7*a*, 25 (king adoring).

‖ *Ib.* pl. 34, 35, 37, 38, 39.

¶ *Ib.*, 2nd series, pl. 5, and *Nineveh and Babylon*, plate, p. 351.

** See Layard's *Nineveh and Babylon*, plate, p. 351.

†† Layard's *Monuments*, 1st series, pl. 3, 4, 42 (with human arms).

Based upon these or similar models are also the religious sculptures of Tiglath-pileser III., Sargon, Sennacherib, Esarhaddon, and Aššur-banî-âpli; but though they belong to the same school, the improvement in style can easily be traced, until we reach the delicate perfection of many of the sculptures of the last-named. Whilst the sculptures of Aššur-naṣir-âpli give us the Assyrian idea of the sea-god Ea (Syncel. *Chron.* 28; Euseb. *Chron.* 5, 8), who was clothed with a fish's skin,* Dagon, according to a sculpture of Sargon from Khorsabad, was shown as a deity with a horned hat, carefully-curled hair and beard, and a close garment reaching to his waist, where the scaly lower part, ending in a fish's tail, begins † (cf. 1 S 5⁴ [' the stump of] Dagon,' AVm ' the fishy part'). Noteworthy, though clumsy, are the statues of Nebo standing in what is regarded as an attitude of meditation.‡ On a cylinder-seal, apparently of the time of Aššur-banî-âpli, and bearing a dedication to Nebo, is shown a divine figure holding two winged bulls by one foreleg, whilst they incline their heads gracefully towards him. If this be Nebo, and the design have a symbolical meaning, it may typify the power of the wise to overcome the strong.§ Turning to the bas-reliefs of Aššur-banî-âpli, we may note the scene where, to the sound of zithers, the lions which the king has killed in the chase are brought home, and before a sacred emblem and a table with viands he pours out an offering of wine over the beasts lying on the ground.‖ This is in the best Assyrian style; the figures of Aššur-banî-âpli ¶ and his brother of Babylon as basket-bearer at the restoration of the temple Ê-zida there, though good, fall somewhat short of the sacrificial scene.

Whether it is votaries or ministering spirits in the form of Ištar or of Maḫ (Merodach's spouse as she who presided over births) who are represented by Aššur-naṣir-âpli as making offerings before the sacred tree,** is uncertain—probably the latter. Ištar is apparently represented on a cylinder of the British Museum as a goddess in warlike guise, armed with bow and arrows, and standing upon a lion, which turns its head to lick her feet. A eunuch-priest stands before her, and the design is completed with the palm-tree and rearing goats whose bodies cross symmetrically. It is a gem of Assyrian religious art.††

The sculptors of that time likewise give us an idea of the spirits, evil and otherwise, in whom the Assyrians believed. Besides the four-winged genii, demons with snarling lion-heads, ass's ears, and eagle's claws, are shown. Sometimes they threaten each other with dagger and mace,‡‡ at other times they raise their weapon menacingly against a person unseen. But they are powerless in consequence of the protecting spirit in the form of a man in front, who with mystic sign casts an unseen spell. In some cases there is also a bearded and ringleted spear-bearer behind, similar to the nude figures on the Babylonia cylinder-seals of B.C. 2500, showing how long these things persisted.

No artistic remains from Assyria later than the reign of Aššur-banî-âpli are known.

There is hardly any doubt that the high level of Assyro-Babylonian art is due to the deep religious feeling of the two nations. Their sincerity is re-

* Rawlinson's *Monarchies*, vol. i. p. 167; *British Museum Guide*, pl. iv.

† Botta, *Monuments de Ninive*, pl. 32–34.

‡ *Bible Readers' Manual* (W. Collins Sons & Co.), pl. 6.

§ Perrot and Chipiez, *Histoire de l'art dans l'antiquité*, 'Chaldée,' p. 673.

‖ Rawlinson's *Monarchies*, vol. ii. p. 134.

¶ *British Museum Guide to the Babylonian and Assyrian Antiquities*, pl. xiii.

** Layard's *Monuments*, 1st series, pl. 7.

†† *The OT in the Light of the Records of Assyria and Babylonia* (S.P.C.K.), pl. iii. No. 2.

‡‡ Rawlinson's *Monarchies*, vol. ii. p. 266.

flected in their work, which, if the nations producing it had continued to exist, might have attained a perfection which would have rivalled even the art of Greece and Rome. How far the influence of their art extended, it is difficult to say. Connexion with that of Phœnicia may be traced, the most striking instance being Esarhaddon's clay seal (referred to on p. 884).

LITERATURE.—Perrot and Chipiez, *Histoire de l'Art dans l'Antiquité*, '*Chaldée et Assyrie*,' Paris, 1884 (Eng. ed., Chapman and Hall, 1884). See also Layard, *Nineveh and Babylon*, 1853; G. Rawlinson, *Five Great Monarchies*, Lond., 1878, vols. i. and ii., and other works mentioned in the footnotes.

[A number of the pictures from Botta and Layard are given by Bonomi, *Nineveh and its Palaces* (Bohn's Illustrated Library), London].

T. G. PINCHES.

ART (Buddhist).—See artt. on BURMA, CENTRAL ASIA, CEYLON, CHINA, INDIA, JAPAN, JAVA, SIAM, TIBET, and art. TEMPLES (Buddhist).

ART (Celtic).—The article 'ART (Christian)' is designed to bring into view the various forms in which art in the modern era has been made the expression of religious feeling. Special attention is there given to that phase of Christian art in which there is little or nothing of the representative element, but on the other hand a lavish display of taste and skill and care, all consecrated to the production of a worthy offering of beauty for the service of religion. Celtic art represents this form of artistic expression perhaps more perfectly than the art of any other time or people, and this is one of the reasons why it here receives a special treatment. The spirit of monastic craftsmanship, in all its single-minded devotedness, is nowhere seen in such purity as in the ornamentation of Celtic manuscripts, or the exquisite ecclesiastical metal-work that had its home in the Ireland of the early Middle Ages.

Definition and scope.—By Celtic art is meant, of course, Celtic ecclesiastical art,* and this is related to Christian art in general just as Celtic Christianity is related to the whole religious system of the West. In each case we have to deal with a distinct province, the characteristic features of which are the outcome of special historical and geographical conditions. The Celtic religious area was practically un-Romanized, and it differs in this from all the other regions of Western Christendom. Part of the area lay entirely outside the Roman Empire, and other parts were only dubiously within it, while, on the other hand, after the area had received Christianity, it developed its church life and institutions in complete independence of the Roman ecclesiastical system. In like manner, the art of this same area differs from Christian art in general in that it is far less dependent on Roman tradition and models. Some of the forms of ornament which the Celtic Christians employed in the service of the Church were drawn, not from the familiar *répertoire* of classical motives developed and used by the Mediterranean peoples, but from a stock of forms of hoary antiquity that existed in Central and Northern Europe from a time before the beginning of distinctive classical culture in Greece and Italy. In connexion, therefore, with Celtic art, we are brought into contact with fresh and interesting artistic motives that we hardly meet with elsewhere in the wide domain of Christian art in general.

A word may be said on the local setting of Celtic church life, and of the art which was its outcome and its adornment. At the time of the introduction of Christianity the Celtic peoples in Eastern and Central Europe had yielded place to tribes of Teutonic descent, but they were still in possession in Gaul and in the British Isles, where they had developed, on Central European traditions, some elaborate and beautiful forms of decorative art. The conquest of Gaul and of Britain up to the Forth and Clyde Romanized to a considerable extent these Celtic lands. Christianity was probably introduced into Gaul, not from Rome or from Italy, but from Greek-speaking lands in the wake of Massiliote or Narbonnese commerce, and spread thence into the isles of Britain at a time and by agencies that cannot now be clearly determined. That the Gallic Church was the mother Church of those in Great Britain and Ireland is sufficiently established; and, so far as all these lands were included in the Empire, the Roman municipal and provincial system furnished the Church with a ready-made framework for its organization—an organization which we know existed in Britain on Gallic lines as early as the beginning of the 4th century. This Gallo-British Church, however, pushed its missionary activity into regions entirely outside or only nominally within the limits of the Empire, and here there were no effective Roman institutions to provide this framework. Church organization here, so far as it existed, was quite different from what it was in Romanized lands. It was not territorial or civic, but tribal and personal; that is to say, the bishop, the chief ecclesiastical functionary, was not bishop of a Roman *civitas*, i.e. a town with its surrounding district, but of a tribe, and was largely dependent on the personal support of the tribal chieftain. In other respects also the differences were equally marked.

Representatives of this missionary activity were Ninian, who looked to St. Martin of Tours as his exemplar, and soon after A.D. 400 evangelized the Southern Picts of Scotland; later on, Kentigern, who laboured in Strathclyde and Wales; and, most important of all, Patrick, who, a little later than Ninian and a century before Kentigern, stamped the impress of his personality so deeply on Ireland that he has remained ever since the patron saint of the island. We can gather from Patrick's own writings that Gaul, where he had received instruction and orders, bounded his ecclesiastical horizon, and he was clearly a missioner of the same type as the others just mentioned, who was working independently on the lines laid down by the social conditions of non-Romanized Celtic lands. Under the guidance of these single-minded evangelists, Celtic Christianity in these lands was free to evolve and maintain its own special ecclesiastical character, and this was especially the case in Ireland.

This exceptional character which attaches to the outward apparatus of Christianity in Ireland was further emphasized by the fact that after the island had received the new religion it was cut off from the rest of Christendom for a century and a half by the Saxon conquest of England, which interposed a barrier of paganism between the Christian West generally and this outlying province. Direct intercourse between Gaul or Spain and Ireland, which had existed from early times, was also checked owing to the political convulsions due to the Gothic and Frankish invasions. Hence it came about in certain ecclesiastical matters that, while changes were worked out in Western Christendom generally, Ireland, in this way isolated, preserved her more primitive forms, some of which had once been common to all provinces of the Church alike.

One of these forms, which had once been common but afterwards became conspicuous for its singularity, was the monastic settlement consisting in a number of separate cells and of small churches or oratories. This was everywhere in Christendom the earliest form of the monastery, because the hermit's cell answered to the primal impulse in the votary's mind of retirement from the world. The reputation for sanctity of the first recluse drew others about him, and so a community of considerable size might be formed, numbering possibly, as Bede tells us of the British monastery at Bangor near Chester on the Dee, as many as two thousand souls. The members of such a community, whether few or many, lived beside each other but not together. The arrangements for life in common, which English and Continental ruined monasteries have made so familiar to us—the cloistered court, the common refectory and sleeping-room—were all absent. These were Benedictine features, and did not come into use till the 6th or 7th cent., from which time onwards they were gradually introduced all over the Romanized West. Eastern Christendom, which Benedictinism hardly affected, and the Celtic regions outside the Empire, or on its north-western border, remained faithful to the older system.

Monastery the home of ecclesiastical art.—Celtic monasteries of the kind indicated existed not only in Ireland but in Scotland, in Wales, and in other parts; but it is in the first-named country that they have left the clearest monumental evidence of their character. Even as early as the time of Patrick—the first half of the 5th cent.—Irish men and women were devoting themselves with ardour to the religious life, and the sites of ancient settlements are almost innumerable. Those in the remoter and less accessible regions, such as the islands and rocky headlands of the indented western coast, are, as a rule, the best preserved, and we may take as an example the settlement on the most retired spot of all, the rock of Skellig Michael, an isolated peak about 10 miles out in the Atlantic, off the coast of Kerry. Here, at the height of some six hundred feet above the sea, we find on a terrace, sustained by a magnificent retaining wall of dry, *i.e.* uncemented, stone-work,

* For pre-Christian Celtic art see CELTIC RELIGION.

half a dozen or so of hermits' cells and two or three tiny oratories used for service and private prayer. The cells, and all other structures except one of the oratories, are constructed of the same dry stone-work, and according to methods that carry us back directly to pagan times. The terrace wall is of precisely the same construction as the vast ramparts that form the successive *enceintes* round the stone forts of unknown date and origin on the headlands and islands of Galway or Kerry. The cells are round or oval in plan, and are of a bee-hive form, the layers of flat stones of which they are composed gradually narrowing their circles till a dome-like finish terminates the whole, an opening being left at the summit for the egress of smoke. This method of construction also is pagan, and may be found in the central stone chambers of the great pre-historic burial tumuli at Newgrange, Dowth, and other places beside the Boyne. That the cells on Skellig Michael are Christian is proved by the fact that over one of the doorways white quartz stones have been set in the form of a cross. The smallest of the little oratories is one of the most interesting of early Christian structures. Its interior length is only about eight feet, and it has a door at one end and a window over the altar at the other end, which is turned towards the east. The construction is similar to that of the cells, but the plan is rectangular, and the walls are made to converge till they meet in a ridge at the top. The little oratory stands apart from the rest of the structures of the settlement, on a jutting corner of the terraced platform, and we may well fancy it a place where the worshipper might tarry awhile and meditate, in this almost inaccessible eyrie between sea and sky.

Such meditations availed much for Christendom at large, for these Irish hermit monks were at the same time the most indefatigable of missionaries. That passion for solitude which drew the Celtic Christians away from the world was only one of the tendencies in their emotional piety, and is balanced by quite the opposite passion for wandering and evangelistic enterprise. To carry on this work effectively they seem to have needed to submit themselves from time to time to certain spiritual influences, which should act on their inner nature and charge them as it were with an electric force that radiated with irresistible potency when they journeyed forth as missioners. It was in places of solitude and retirement, like Skellig Michael, that the fire was kindled and fanned till it burst into the proselytizing fervour of a Columba, an Aidan, a Columbanus. We are here at the source of a stream of Christian influence that flowed with beneficent effect over all the land of Britain and far across the Continent of Europe. Ireland gave Columba to Scotland, Scotland Aidan to Northumbria, and from Northumbrian Lindisfarne proceeded the effective conversion of the Angles, while some of the greater Continental centres of the religious life looked to Celtic missionary saints as their founders.

The foregoing details are germane to the purpose of this article, for we have to note that the arrangement and the life of the Celtic monastery had great influence on the forms and æsthetic character of Celtic ecclesiastical art. It is not pretended here that all the artistic activity of the early mediæval period was centred in the monastery. The monastic craftsman plays a predominant part in the artistic history of the time, but he had no monopoly. Among the northern peoples in the pagan period, the fabrication and adornment of weapons, implements, and objects of personal wear, gave employment to artistic workmen whose skill and taste are in their way unsurpassed, and there is no reason to believe that the introduction of Christianity broke this tradition. In Ireland the Tara brooch, in Scotland the Hunterston brooch, dating about the 8th cent., are pieces of secular art, and we need not credit them to the monks. On the other hand, as the mediæval period advanced, sacred art undoubtedly preponderated over secular, and sacred art was specially cultivated in the cloister. In time, as Mr. Romilly Allen has remarked (*Celtic Art in Pagan and Christian Times*, 1904, p. 171), 'The priest took the place of the warrior as the patron of the fine arts, and monopolized all the available time of the metal-worker and enameller in making beautiful vessels for the service of the Church.' In periods of political unrest, such as on the Continent followed the breaking up of the Roman provincial administration, the convent offered conditions more favourable to artistic activity than were to be found outside, while certain forms of art in great demand at the time, such as the writing and adornment of books, were practically in the hands of the religious. The Celtic monastery may accordingly be regarded as the home of almost all the artistic production of the time that had an ecclesiastical purpose, and it will lend force to this statement to quote the nearly contemporary record as to the making and putting forth of one striking monument of Celtic art, the so-called *Gospels of Lindisfarne* or *of St. Cuthbert*, a manuscript dating from the end of the 7th or beginning of the 8th cent., and now one of the treasures of the British Museum. In an Anglo-Saxon colophon of the 10th cent. appended to St. John's Gospel, we are told that 'Eadfrith, bishop over the church of Lindisfarne, wrote this book in honour of God and St. Cuthbert, and all the company of saints in the Island; and Ethelwald, bishop of Lindisfarne, made an outer case and adorned it, as he was well able, and Billfrith the anchorite, he wrought the metal-work of the ornaments on the outside thereof, and decked it with gold and with gems.' The fact that Billfrith is called the anchorite ('se oncra') shows that fine metal-work with the setting of gems was carried on by the solitary recluse in his cell. The extreme minuteness and elaboration of this is, in fact, just what we should expect in work executed under these conditions; and this applies with even greater force to the manuscripts, wherein ingenious planning of ornamental schemes and faultless execution of multitudinous convoluted detail must have made the lonely hours pass lightly away.

Celtic ecclesiastical art in general was of a kind that could be carried out single-handed and in small interiors. Work that needed the co-operation of many hands and large spaces was little in vogue. In the Benedictine monasteries of the Continent the dominant art was architecture, and vast buildings for the accommodation of communities were devised, planned, and sometimes actually achieved by the inmates in person. Romanesque architecture is in the main monastic, and the great abbey church is its crowning achievement. In Ireland and other Celtic areas early conventual buildings were, as has been seen, smaller and simpler; and though they may possess great constructive interest, little pains have been taken with their ornamentation. From the traditional dry-stone building, illustrated on Skellig Michael, there were evolved on the one hand certain striking features in the framing of openings, etc., and on the other some interesting forms of vault construction. The single-celled oratory was enlarged by the addition of a second cell, also rectangular, forming when smaller than the first a presbytery or chancel, and when larger a nave: and this type of church plan, differing from the type with apsidal termination which belonged to the Roman tradition, appears in England after its conversion by the Celtic evangelists, who may thus have contributed towards the establishment of our insular preference for square-ended churches. The most striking peculiarity of Celtic church architecture in early mediæval times is the detached round tower, abundant in Erin, though represented by only a few stray examples in other parts of these islands. These towers are always connected with religious establishments, and it is now acknowledged that they were primarily designed as towers of refuge, though also employed as belfries. The dangers against which they furnished temporary security were the Viking inroads with which from the beginning of the 9th cent. onwards the country was scourged. It is stated by Miss Stokes in her *Early Christian Art in Ireland* (ii. 57), that, in the entries in the Irish annals,

'regarding the attacks of the Northmen from 789 to 845, it is recorded that the clergy fled for safety into the woods . . . but in the year 950, and for two centuries later, we read of the "cloiccthech," house of a bell, as a special object of attack to the Northmen.' A record relating to Brittany (quoted *ib.* p. 56) speaks of the erection near a church in that Celtic region of a 'little round tower . . . wherein to deposit the silver-plate and treasure of the same church, and protect them against the sacrilegious hands of the barbarians, should they wish to pillage it.'

The construction of the extant round towers bears out this evidence of their origin and intention, for in almost every instance the doorway of access to them is at a substantial height above the ground, and was accessible only by means of a ladder, which could be drawn up when the temporary garrison was housed within it. The interiors had wooden floors at different stages reached by ladders, and in the uppermost was the place for the bell.

The features here described are specially but not exclusively Irish. In other Celtic regions which were practically outside the Empire, and to which the influence of the ecclesiastical Rome did not penetrate till a later date, we find specimens, or at any rate relics and traces of them. Scotland, especially in the north and west, is well supplied; for example, the 'Isle of the Saints,' *Eilean na Naoimh*, not far from Mull, has a group somewhat similar to that on Skellig Michael; but Wales and Cornwall have very little to show in the way of structures that are prior to the Norman Conquest. In Ireland such structures are at once more numerous, more clearly marked, and better preserved than they are elsewhere. The plainness of these early Irish structures has already been noticed, and is remarkable in a country where the arts of ornament were flourishing in the Pagan period, and were destined to develop for Christian service into forms so elaborate and beautiful. The rude stone building gave place to cut stone-work, and to the use of the arch and of lime mortar; but the same character of plainness prevailed till about the year 1100, when a rich and somewhat fantastic style of architectural embellishment came into vogue, with which was soon mingled the undoubtedly Norman element of the chevron, or zigzag. With the development of this so-called Irish Romanesque, Celtic architecture loses that special character it had derived from the primitive methods of dry-stone construction, and comes into line with the other local styles of Western Romanesque. The subject need not therefore be further pursued.

i. STONE-SLABS, CROSSES, etc.—If the earlier Celtic masons did not carve ornament on the stones of their religious buildings, they made up for this by considerable activity in sculpture of another kind. The reference is to the incised or carved stone-slabs and crosses, a monumental form of Celtic art represented by abundant examples in all the Celtic and also in the Teutonized parts of the British isles. No complete comparative survey has yet been made of the whole body of monuments, but there exist monographs on the various groups, the most complete and elaborate of which is the ponderous volume issued in 1903 by the Society of Antiquaries of Scotland under the title, *The Early Christian Monuments of Scotland*. The subject is a very large one, for the monuments in question in the Scottish area alone number about five hundred, and it can, of course, only be touched on here.

In the matter of distribution, we may distinguish the following provinces in which the monuments occur in groups large or small. (1) Southern, eastern, and midland England. The monuments here are sporadic, and some regions are bare of examples, though in other parts, such as Derbyshire, they are well represented. (2) North-eastern England and the same side of Scotland up to the Forth, the region forming the ancient kingdom of Northumbria. Here the monuments are very numerous and of great artistic merit. In point of art they show a combination of Celtic elements with those derived from classical sources, and exhibit inscriptions partly in Roman letters and partly in runic characters derived from Scandinavia. (3) Galloway or south-western Scotland, the scene of the ministrations of Ninian to the southern Picts, represented by some interesting early monuments of a Gallo-Roman type. (4) Cumberland and the Isle of Man, and in part Lancashire, where the art of the stones betrays a Scandinavian influence. (5) Eastern Scotland north of the Forth and south of the Moray Firth, known to historians as the ancient 'Kingdom of the (northern) Picts.' The stones here exhibit certain devices peculiar to this region that are for the most part unexplained, though probably Christian in significance, but in the main their art is of the Celtic type. (6) Central, northern, and western Scotland, where Celtic art prevails with a certain Scandinavian admixture. (7) Wales, a region specially well represented by monuments of this class, in which the art is Celtic, the epigraphy partly Roman, and partly in *ogham* characters, that is, in a native Celtic style of writing answering to the Teutonic runes. (8) Cornwall and Devon, the monuments of which on the whole resemble those of Wales. (9) Ireland. This region, with parts of northern and western Scotland, was, as we have seen, entirely un-Romanized; and here the art, with the language, and to some extent also the epigraphic character, of the inscriptions, is almost wholly Celtic.

Of these provinces all but the first and second are entirely, or, to a preponderating extent, Celtic, for the 'Pictish' element in (5), though very remarkable, does not affect the general character of the monuments. The ancient Northumbria, (2), was Teutonic in government and (with of course the admixture of older races) in population, though its art was preponderatingly Celtic. That this region was effectively Christianized by Celtic missionaries from Lindisfarne has already been noticed, and it is highly significant that one of the most important of all monuments in the recognized Celtic style of manuscript illumination was produced and ornamented there by Anglian hands at a time when the Celtic monks had already retired from the island. The existence of this datable monument, noticed in this article on p. 838[b] (the *Gospels of Lindisfarne* or *of St. Cuthbert*), shows that we might expect the same Celtic style in other monuments of the region; and this we accordingly find, mingled with other elements, in the early sculptured stones now under consideration. This may be fairly held to show great vitality in Celtic art, as well as an attractiveness for the Teutonic population. In view of it, it will not be surprising to find that the monuments scattered over the rest of England, (1), exhibit also a prevailing Celtic character, which reminds us that it was influenced in almost every part by Celtic missionary activity. We are therefore justified in regarding the whole body of these monuments as so far Celtic that they cannot be excluded from any general survey of Celtic art.

It is with the art of the stones, not their epigraphy, that we are here concerned; but the inscriptions cannot be entirely disregarded, for they often afford valuable evidence of the nature and provenance of the monuments. The questions that have to be considered concern (1) the character, (2) the form, (3) the ornamentation of the stones.

1. Character.—The inscriptions show that the majority of them are sepulchral, and as such they represent a form of monument that has been in use since Neolithic times. At the single site of Clonmacnoise in Ireland, there are nearly two hundred of these tombstones, all inscribed, and many ornamented. This religious establishment beside the Shannon, a place of surpassing interest, was founded by St. Ciaran in the middle of the 6th cent., and an Irish poem thus celebrates 'the peaceful clear-streamed place':

> 'Ciaran's city is Cluain-mic-Nois,
>
> . . . .
>
> Nobles of the children of Conn
> Are under the flaggy, brown-sloped cemetery;
> A knot, or ogham, over each body,
> And a fair, just, ogham name.'

Of ogham inscriptions on these stones only one has been known in modern times, and the rest are in Roman minuscules. Among the names that can be read upon them is that of Suibine, son of Maelhumai, of the latter part of the 9th cent., celebrated as one of the most learned Churchmen of his time. Inscriptions, however, also show that many sculptured stones were not sepulchral but commemorative, or devised for other purposes. Thus at Kells in Co. Meath there is a cross with the inscription, 'The cross of Patrick and Columba,' which was erected centuries after the death of the saints whose names it celebrated. Most of the so-called 'High Crosses' of Ireland—elaborately sculptured stone monuments of the 10th cent.—were apparently of this commemorative character. In Northumbria we know, from Simeon of Durham (*Hist. Reg.* § 36), that two sepulchral crosses stood at Hexham at the extremities of the grave of Bishop Acca, who died in 740, but the Ruthwell Cross is shown by its inscription to have been a memorial of the sacrifice of Christ. We are told in the *Life of Kentigern*, by Joceline of Furness (late, but based on older materials), that the saint was accustomed to erect 'the triumphant standard of the cross' to commemorate any marked successes in conversion; and in Wessex we have evidence (*Acta Sanctorum*, Jul. 11, p. 502) that 'the sign of the Holy Cross' was set up to mark a place of Christian assembly before the building of a church. Again, some crosses were terminal, that is, they defined a boundary by a landmark which religion made inviolable. An Irish pillar stone at Killnasaggart, Co. Armagh, proclaims that the place which it marked was under the protection of St. Peter, while one of the interesting early stones at Whithorn in Galloway, Ninian's missionary centre, is inscribed 'The Place of St. Peter,' and was evidently a boundary mark.

2. Form.—In the matter of form, the earliest class of stone monuments are pillars unshaped by the tool, after the fashion of the pre-historic menhirs, and correspond to the rude stone building of the early Celtic Christians inherited from their pagan forefathers. These pillars have on them inscriptions in one or other of the languages and characters noted in the enumeration of the provinces, and sometimes incised crosses or sacred monograms. These last, though in themselves, from the æsthetic standpoint, negligible, become of importance as the origin of the form of the shaped free-standing crosses of later times. In Galloway there are upright pillar-stones with Latin inscriptions, and the Chi-Rho (☧) monogram in different forms which are early, but probably not so early as the time of Ninian himself. This monogram appears within a circle, in which we may see a reminiscence of the wreath that enclosed it on the original *labarum*, or standard of Constantine, described by Eusebius; and this wreath, or circle, becomes later the stone ring, which in the well-known 'Celtic' form of the monumental cross is seen connecting the arms. The Chi-Rho monogram changes into the form of a cross by the addition of a horizontal bar across the upright stem of the original Rho (P), and the arms of the cross, though originally enclosed within the circle, come afterwards to protrude beyond its circumference. This transformation can be seen in progress in a half-developed cross at Penmon Priory in Anglesey.

The untooled pillar-stone does not of course itself change directly into the free-standing cross, though the incised monogram it bears has influenced the development. The actual process was as follows: The pillar-stone corresponds, as we have seen, to the rude stone building. When this gives place to the construction with cut stone and cement, the former is similarly changed to a dressed monument, which may be recumbent, in the shape either of a flat slab, which is *par excellence* the Irish type as represented at Clonmacnoise, or of a 'coped' or 'hog-backed' stone, such as occurs chiefly in the north of England, and is more probably of Anglian or Scandinavian than of Celtic origin; or else may be upright, in the form of a smoothed slab like a modern tombstone. The flat recumbent Irish slabs are adorned with incised crosses, the upright slabs with crosses in relief. From these latter were developed the free-standing crosses by the following stages. When a cross head contained within a circle is carved in relief on a slab, the upper part of this may be rounded off to follow the curve of the circle, as on a stone from Papil by Shetland, in the Edinburgh Museum of Antiquities. Next, the part of the slab below the head of the cross is cut in a little to correspond with the form of the comparatively slender shaft, and we obtain the shape known as the 'wheel cross'—a shape confined to the Isle of Man, Wales, and Cornwall. The background may now shrink in still further towards the outline of the shaft, while, by a contrary process, the arms of the cross are allowed to protrude beyond the circle which has enclosed them, and the final step is taken when, as it has been said (Romilly Allen, *Celtic Art*, p. 186), 'the portions of the background of the cross between the quadrants of the ring and the arms are pierced right through the slab, thus giving us the "four hole" cross of Cornwall and the typical High Cross of Ireland,' in which the outline of the stone corresponds with the outline of the Cross.

3. Ornamentation.—The subject of the ornamentation of the slabs and crosses cannot be discussed without reference to Celtic decorative art in general. The forms in which this expresses itself, apart from the carving on the stones, are practically confined to fine *metal-work* and the *illumination of manuscripts*, for in extant specimens of the Celtic Christian period, productions in other materials, such as wood, ivory, or textiles, are so rare as to be in the meantime negligible. On stone, metal, and the parchment of books, Celtic artistic feeling externalized itself in elaborate and varied ornamental patterns, the design and technical execution of which have excited the wonder of all subsequent ages, from the time of Giraldus Cambrensis in the 12th cent. downwards. The same patterns and methods of application appear in all three forms of art, and some of the best authorities treat the stone carving as later in date than the similar work in the other materials. It is a curious fact that certain details of the Irish High Crosses have no meaning in stone-work, while there is a technical reason for them in work in metal, and this would indicate the priority of the latter. Again, the similarity between richly decorated cross-slabs, of which Scotland is the home, and the emblazoned pages of ornament in Celtic manuscripts, cannot fail to strike the observer. Hence it is maintained that the styles of artistic treatment which are in question here were first evolved on the pages of books or in metal, and then transferred to stone; and Mr. Romilly Allen believes (*Celtic Art*, p. 171) that the book-work was prior alike to that on metal and on stone. At first sight this seems contrary to natural likelihood, for there is much elaborate and beautiful Celtic metal-work of pagan date and also a certain amount of decorative carving in stone, whereas manuscript writing and illumination came in as a totally new form of craftsmanship with the introduction of Christianity. Irish experts converted to the new faith could continue for Christian service their metal-work or stone-carving, while it would take them a long time to learn the new art of caligraphy and illumination. The first books used in Christian worship would be imported, and would only very gradually be supplanted by those of native production. Hence we should expect to find Christian metal-work and stone-carving earlier than the same art applied to books.

Here, however, we are met by rather a curious fact. Christianity at its first introduction did not seem to inspire the Celtic artist, but rather to repress his activity, so that, as Romilly Allen states, 'before about A.D. 650 there was no distinctively Christian art existing in this country' (*op. cit.* p. 165). He accounts for this on the theory that the introduction into the British Isles of Christianity itself was much later than is generally supposed, and suggests A.D. 450 as the date of this. The negative evidence of the dearth of really early Christian monuments in this country had so impressed him that he has called the significant and quite unquestioned notice of the presence of three bishops of Roman towns in Britain at the Council of Arles in A.D. 314 one of 'the vague and unsatisfactory statements of the mythical period' (*op. cit.* p. 164). Archæological evidence, however, must be weighed along with literary, and not allowed to supersede it. To take an instructive parallel, if we were left only to literary evidence for the condition of the earliest Christianity at Rome, we should probably believe that art was at that time tabued. Monumental evidence, however, as shown in the article 'ART (Christian),' is conclusive that the earliest Christian Church at Rome not only accepted art as part of its external dress, but soon began to use it for definitely Christian purposes. Conversely, if we were left to monumental evidence alone for Christianity in early Britain, we should believe that it hardly existed, for Romano-British Christian monuments are extremely rare, and those belonging to the 5th or 6th centuries are few and artistically simple and even rude; yet the Romano-British Church had progressed so far by the early part of the 5th cent. as to have established the flourishing Pelagian heresy, and after the Saxon conquest it is clear that the large and active Christian community in Wales was this Romano-British Church, and not a new foundation in the 5th cent. from Gaul. Why it was that the earliest Celtic Christianity did not at once employ the native artistic resources available is a question which cannot be entered on here; it is a fact, however, that the Celtic ecclesiastical art on stones and in metal and books, which flourished from the middle of the 7th cent. onwards, used motives that were not all originally Celtic, but are found also in 'Merovingian' work in Gaul and in that of the period of the Teutonic migrations in general, and hence it is reasonable to refer the great unfolding of Celtic artistic activity in this period to the impulse which came in from England and the Continent as soon as the conversion of the pagan Saxons opened the door once more to intercourse between Celtic lands and Western Christendom.

The following are the ornamental motives that occur in the decoration of the carved stones, the objects in metal, and the manuscripts: (1) the human figure, (2) leaf-ornament, (3) animals, (4) geometrical ornament, consisting in: (*a*) step- and key-patterns, (*b*) interlacing- or knot-work, and (*c*) spirals.

(1) Celtic art proper has no place for the *human figure*; and where this is treated in native fashion, as in some of the Irish manuscripts, it is reduced to a decorative pattern with no more resemblance to nature than have the figures on court-cards. Wherever the figure is reasonably well drawn or modelled, there influence from the side of classical tradition is at work. The best figures on monuments of at any rate partly Celtic character are those on the Ruthwell and Bewcastle Crosses, and they are accompanied here by vine-foliage enclosing animals which is of distinctly classical type. The High Crosses of Ireland, which date from the 10th cent., exhibit a remarkable display of figure-work which is all due to Continental inspiration, and need not here be described.

(2) *Leaf-ornament* is also foreign to the Celtic style proper. There is hardly a trace of it in the manuscripts, but it occurs very occasionally on the stones in the purely Celtic areas of Ireland, Wales, and northern Scotland. In the ancient Northumbria, on the other hand, it is abundant, and is clearly of classical origin, for the vine is almost always the motive employed. The vine scrolls on some so-called 'Anglian' crosses, such as that of Acca, now at Durham, and the one at Bewcastle, are as charming as any decorative foliage in existence.

(3) *Animals.*—Like the human figure, animals, such as the horse, the deer, the dog, occur, naturalistically treated in some abundance; and it is of course a well-established fact that the unsophisticated artist is always better at animals than at men. There are hunting and battle scenes on some of the crosses or their sculptured bases, and on a certain class of sculptured stones in Scotland animals are represented truthfully in a very telling and artistic fashion. There is nothing here, however, that is specially Celtic. On the other hand, the conventional treatment of animal forms for ornamental purposes is a very important element not only in Celtic, but in all northern decoration. There is no attempt in this to give the animal its specific character, or even to preserve elementary truth in anatomy and proportion. The creatures barely preserve so much zoological character as resides in the possession of a head and limbs, and their bodies are elongated and flattened till they are nothing but bands. All parts that can be extended, such as a limb, a tail, an ear, a tongue, a lip, are drawn out and twisted into elaborate convolutions, and are intertwined as if the artist wished only to produce the effect of complex knot-work. Though birds are sometimes introduced, the beast is generally intended to be a quadruped; but it is drawn out to such a length and tenuity as to justify the epithet 'lacertine,' or lizard-like, which is generally applied to it. There is no question which has been more discussed than that of the origin and history of this form of ornament among the Teutonic and Celtic peoples. The latest and most elaborate work on the subject, Bernhard Salin's *Altgermanische Thierornamentik* (Stockholm, 1904), favours the view that the animals in northern art are ultimately derived from classical models, but that the northern

peoples generally made the motive their own, and worked it out with extraordinary ingenuity and patience. A close comparison of the animal ornament in Irish manuscripts and metal-work and that on objects of Teutonic provenance indicates that Celtic zoömorphic forms are of Germanic origin. These forms are very rare in the Celtic decoration of the pagan period, and do not occur in Ireland, so that a foreign origin is in accordance with likelihood.

(4) In the *geometrical ornament*, in all its forms save the spirals, the same derivation seems now accepted.

(*a*) 'Step' patterns occur in the *cloisonné* settings of Teutonic jewels. Moreover, these patterns in the manuscripts, such as the *Book of Durrow*, are shown in white lines on a dark ground, and the background has been laboriously filled in so as to leave the lines the colour of the light vellum. There may be in this somewhat artificial process an attempt to imitate the damascening in lines of silver on iron, common on buckles and similar objects found in Germanic graves. 'Key' patterns, that is, patterns of a kind of which the Greek fret is typical, are very abundant both on the sculptured stones and in the manuscripts, but are not much used on metal. They are unknown in pagan Celtic work, and their prevalence in that of Christian date is probably due to Continental influence. The Celtic artist, however, showed his originality in that he turned these patterns obliquely, so that their lines are sloping instead of vertical or horizontal.

(*b*) The interlacing- or knot-work is so characteristic of Celtic decoration in Christian times, and is developed therein to such an incredible variety of forms, that it has been popularly regarded as a Celtic speciality. The work in question does not, however, occur in the decoration of the pagan period (or only in one or two doubtful examples), and in the Christian it is so far from being a Celtic speciality that it is the most widely diffused of all the forms of geometric ornament in the early Christian and early mediæval centuries. As Salin remarks,

'in the 7th and 8th centuries the general taste seems to have turned in this direction, for we find the work everywhere from Constantinople to Ireland, and find it, moreover, represented in the most diverse forms of art, in architecture, painting, the industrial arts. It even flourished in Asiatic and African lands wherever European culture had found admittance' (*op.cit.* p. 340).

The origin of the style is still a matter of controversy, and some derive it from basket-work, while others see in it the offspring of the plait or guilloche ornament, which is very common on the Roman mosaic pavements that were to be seen in all parts of the Empire. It is also a moot point whether the style of ornament, whatever its ultimate origin, was developed independently in different centres, or spread from one centre where its capabilities had at first been discerned. In any case the Christian Celtic peoples showed that they had a special affinity for the work, which they carried much further in artistic development than was the case elsewhere. It is especially abundant on the carved stones and in the manuscripts, as the motive is not so suitable for metal, especially when treated by the *repoussé* process.

(*c*) In the *spirals* we come to a form of ornament that is in a special sense Celtic, and is inherited by Christian Celtic art from that of the later pagan times. It is not classical save in ultimate derivation, nor is it Germanic in the broad sense, though it is very finely developed among the northernmost representatives of the Teutonic stock in Scandinavia. On the pagan metal-work of late Celtic times, in Britain, in Gaul, and in Ireland, it was treated with much artistic feeling for beauty of sweeping lines and for composition, and retains these same qualities when adopted for Christian use. Spiral ornament, however, as used in late pagan and early Christian Celtic art, is not quite a simple matter. On one side it is of immemorial antiquity. Spirals occur in Egyptian decorative art from about B.C. 2700 (if not much earlier), and were adopted from this source into the art of Mycenæan Greece, where we find them in Crete and at Orchomenus, Mycenæ, and other places in the second millennium B.C. At least as early as this they appear in southern Central Europe, as at Butmir in Bosnia, and thence the motive journeyed up the valley of the Danube and down those of the Oder and Elbe to Scandinavia, where we find it developed in the Bronze Age to the utmost possible perfection. From Scandinavia it is thought to have passed over North Britain to Ireland, where it appears carved on a great stone at the mouth of the pre-historic royal burial-place at Newgrange by the Boyne. In all these cases we have to deal with regular closely-coiled spirals, which look as if they were derived from the coiling of metal strips or wire, though there is evidence that they were first developed on stone. Now, in the later or Iron Age of Celtic art, spirals of a different and more elaborate kind become the predominant ornamental form, and produce what are sometimes called 'trumpet' patterns. These are formed by double lines which are coiled round each other and then diverge, so as to produce a shape like the mouth of a trumpet. These coils and expanded offsets are ingeniously connected together, so that they can be made in combination to fill with ornament any given space. It has been argued very forcibly by Dr. Arthur Evans that these late Celtic scrolls, which are sometimes called 'flamboyant,' are in fact derived, by a process of conventionalizing, from the 'honeysuckle' patterns or acanthus scrolls of Græco-Roman classical foliage. As used in Ireland and Scotland in early Christian times, the spirals are partly closely coiled and partly flamboyant, and we may regard them as representing a combination of these classical derivatives with the far older and more severe forms of the Bronze Age spirals, the origin of which can be traced to Mycenæan Greece and to Egypt. The use of this primeval motive for the purposes of Christian decoration is a fact of much interest, to which attention was called in a previous part of this article.

We are not concerned with archæological questions of origin so much as with those of the æsthetic use made of these various motives, and of the place of this artistic activity in the life of the Celtic Church as a whole. It has been well said by Dr. Joseph Anderson:

'From whatever source or sources the different elements of the composite style of decoration of the Celtic Christian period may have been derived, the style itself belongs specially to the period of the early Celtic Church in Scotland, Ireland, and Wales, with distinctively characteristic developments in each of these separate areas, and a modified extension into the area of the early Saxon Church, especially in Northumbria. In each of these areas it produced a remarkable development of monumental sculpture; and whether we regard the whole series of their manuscripts, metal-work, and monuments collectively as one great comprehensive manifestation of Celtic ornamentation of the early Christian period, or take them separately as national developments of a common style, it is equally true that, considering the work and the time, it presents a manifestation of artistic culture altogether unparalleled in Europe' (*The Early Christian Monuments of Scotland*, ci.).

The first point to notice about the artistic use of this decoration is the method of its distribution over the surfaces to be adorned. The ornament does not meander at will, but is confined to strictly defined spaces; and these spaces, which may be termed panels, are themselves arranged in a carefully thought-out scheme of composition. The finest examples of this are the pages devoted to ornament in the Irish manuscripts, and the large cross-slabs which are best represented in Scotland.

ii. MANUSCRIPTS.—Of the Irish manuscripts now extant, the earliest is probably the *Book of Durrow*, and the most elaborate is the *Book of Kells*, both in the Library of Trinity College, Dublin; while the *Gospels of Corpus Christi College*, Cambridge, comes next in age to the former, and the *Gospels of Lindisfarne*, in the British Museum, is only second in beauty to the latter. This book, moreover, possesses the unique element of value that it is dated, and it supplies in this way a fixed point round which other examples not only in illumination but in metal-work and carving can be grouped. It was written within a few years of the date A.D. 700, and is earlier in style than the *Book of Kells* though not so early as the other two. Hence the *Book of Durrow* may be assigned to a date in the 7th, the *Book of Kells* to one in the 8th cent.; and it is satisfactory to know that Bernhard Salin endorses these dates as a result of his elaborate and detailed comparative study of the ornaments which occur in them. The decoration in these books is not more sumptuous and minute in its execution than it is clear and bold in its distribution. Leaving out of sight the figure-work, such as the representations of the Evangelists in front of their Gospels, in which classical models have been, however distantly, followed, and taking only the ornament, we find that the first word or two of each Gospel occupies a page, the initial letter spreading from top to bottom of it, and the rest of the letters of the first word filling up a good part of the folio. A border is designed to combine with the initial in framing the whole composition. If this page be a *recto*, the *verso* of the previous folio, which faces it as the book lies open, is treated as a sheet of pure ornament, the object being that the book shall present a sumptuous and beautiful appearance when placed open at the beginning of a Gospel on a reading-stand upon the altar. The scheme of design for such a page is generally based upon the form of a cross, which appears as the centre and support of a composition of variously-shaped panels filling the rest of the sheet. These panels, as has already been explained, are themselves filled in with patterns of the kinds above enumerated, while a border encloses the whole. As has been well shown by Mr. Johan Bruun, the general arrangement of these show-pages of initials or pure ornament provides spaces or panels varying in shape. Those which decorate or serve as complementary fillings for the big initial letters are often of curved outlines, while those connected with the cross opposite are commonly rectangular, or at any rate symmetrical in contour. In the decorative enrichment of these different fields, patterns of various kinds are selected.

'Spirals' (and we may add zoömorphic patterns) 'were chiefly used to fill in the irregular sections of the body of the letter and its curvilinear enclosed spaces, where, owing to a certain freedom in fixing the centres and making volutes of varying size, they were easily adapted and in keeping with the flowing outline of the margin. Interlacements were less easily adapted, but could be made to suit an irregular space, for instance, by forming a chain of knots of varying size and intricacy; whereas fret patterns were even more rarely used outside of the square or oblong panels, for which they were naturally suited. Thus the disposal of the various designs was ruled by taste, and effected the combination of contrasting elements in a graceful scheme' (*An Enquiry*, etc. p. 29).

We may connect this decision and self-control, in the matter of planning out and distributing enrichment, with the severity of the monastic discipline that prevailed in the Celtic monasteries, where this work had its home. The spirit of order and obedience to rule was as strong in the Celtic establishments as in those organized on the Benedictine plan, and the Irish regulars were not only among the most learned, but among the best-living in Christendom. And if we discern their mental rectitude and respect for law in these well considered and justly balanced schemes, in the actual execution of the ornament we are brought into contact with their intensity of devotion to the allotted task, and the infinite patience to which they were schooled by the seclusion and monotony of their daily existence. The little cells where once they sat at work are places as holy to the pilgrim of art as to the religious devotee, and we can realize there how this element of dainty loveliness in line and hue, this ingenious scheming, this minute accuracy in measurement, must have humanized and brightened spirits that might otherwise have become numbed in ascetic rigour, while an education of conscience must certainly have resulted from their scrupulous logic and exactness in pattern making. Prof. Westwood and other experts have examined Irish manuscripts with a glass 'for hours together, without ever detecting a false line or an irregular interlacement.' In the interlaced work, Mr. Romilly Allen reports that

'every cord laps under and over with unfailing regularity . . . and all the cords are joined up so as not to leave any loose ends. All the details of the spiral-work are executed with the minutest care, and there is never a broken line or pseudo-spiral. In the zoömorphic designs the beasts are all provided with the proper number of limbs and are complete in every respect down to the smallest detail' (*Celtic Art*, p. 256).

No mere description can give any idea of the variety, minuteness, and unfailing consistency of this decoration, which can now be judged of in accessible photographic reproductions, such as those in Stanford Robinson's *Celtic Illuminative Art*. As regards colour a word may be said, because it is noteworthy that the Irish scribe produced the effect of sumptuous splendour on his enriched folios without any use of gold, on which the Continental miniaturist so largely depended. This is at first sight surprising, for Ireland produced a good deal of gold; and this was not only used in her native metal-work, but, it is believed, exported to other lands such as Scandinavia. Trinity College, Dublin, possesses a magnificent and weighty gold fibula of native metal and workmanship, but the manuscripts in the library are destitute of gilding. The colours employed are not numerous, but yellow is largely used, and might have suggested to the scribe the substitution of gold. The reds, greens, blues, and purples are bright, clear, and harmoniously blended, but the best effect is gained by the free use of black, of which the scribe fully realized the artistic value. We may conclude on this subject with some words of Dr. Anderson, in which he speaks of the 'profusion of spiral, linear, and zoömorphic patterns arranged in symmetric and rhythmic designs shown up by contrasts of colour, and all carried to an extent of elaboration so bewildering, and yet so charming in the perfect balance and finish of its parts, that the more the result is studied, the deeper becomes the impression of its inimitable originality, grace, precision, and skill.'

iii. METAL-WORK.—The fine Celtic metal-work was, as we learn from some special cases, also a monastic craft in the hands of ecclesiastics. It was applied to the enhancement of the value of the manuscripts either at once in the form of covers, such as that adorned by Billfrith at Lindisfarne, or later on in that of the shrine or box, called in Ireland *cumdach*, made to contain and preserve the precious volume (p. 838[b]). These cumdachs are peculiar to Ireland. Shrines of a similar kind, also of a later date than the objects they were to protect, were made for the early hand-bells connected with the names of famous saints, which are in themselves objects of the highest interest, and may in some cases really have belonged to the saints with whom they are traditionally associated.

Their simplicity and even rudeness agree with an early date. The most primitive are four-sided, and made of plates of iron riveted at the corners. The later ones are of the same shape but of cast bronze, and these are sometimes ornamented. There are early bells of the kind in Scotland and Wales as well as Ireland, and Scotland has two bell-shrines, the rest being Irish. Celtic metal-work of early Christian date is perhaps most largely represented by the enriched penannular or annular brooches, of which the Tara brooch in Ireland and the Hunterston brooch in Scotland are the finest examples. As this article is concerned rather with things ecclesiastical, it may be sufficient to refer to four fine examples in this class, the Ardagh Chalice and the Cross of Cong in Ireland, and the Monymusk reliquary and crozier of St. Fillan in Scotland. They are all works of great interest either from the historical or the artistic side, and the first named is one of the most beautiful and elaborate examples of fine metal-work extant anywhere in the world.

The Monymusk reliquary is described by Anderson as 'a small wooden box' (it is about four inches long), 'hollowed out of the solid, and plated with plates of pale bronze and with plates of silver. . . . Its ornamentation is that peculiarly Celtic form of interlacing zoömorphic decoration, united with coloured designs of diverging spirals and trumpet scrolls, which are the principal varieties of the decorative art of the Celtic manuscripts and memorial stones of the early Christian time. It is jewelled and enamelled, and its engraved and chased designs are characterized by such excellence of execution that it must be early in date' (*Scotland in Early Christian Times*, p. 249). The special historical interest connected with the reliquary resides in the fact that there is some reason to believe it a relic of St. Columba, and a *vexillum*, or battle charm, which, like the Ark in ancient Israel, was borne out to battle with the Scottish host. It is preserved at Monymusk House, Aberdeenshire. The crozier of St. Fillan is an example of a specially Celtic form of ecclesiastical object. It is really a shrine of fine metal-work, made in the shape of, and enclosing, the head of the pastoral staff of wood traditionally belonging to an early saint. The form of the crozier is exclusively Celtic, and differs from the form that such objects take on the Continent, and in the case of that of St. Fillan authentic history shows that it was employed as a relic on which oaths of a peculiarly solemn kind could be taken, while it is surmised that it was borne as a *vexillum* into battle at Bannockburn. It is preserved in a damaged condition in the Museum of Antiquities at Edinburgh.

The Cross of Cong, at Dublin, is the one surviving example of a processional cross of the early Celtic Church. It measures 2 ft. 8 in. in height by 1 ft. 6¾ in. across the arms, and is 1¾ in. thick. It is constructed of oak, and was supposed to contain at its centre, under a boss of rock crystal, a portion of the true cross. On the exterior it is all covered with metal plates of copper which are adorned with silver mouldings and plaques, with panels of fine gold work and gilded bronze, and with bosses of coloured enamel. The panels are ornamented with gold filigree work and zoömorphic patterns, and the effect of the whole is rich and artistically pleasing. It can be dated in the first half of the 12th cent., and is a striking proof of the long survival of fine artistic taste in characteristically Celtic work in Ireland. As a rule the later objects, such as the cumdachs and the bell-shrines, though the style of the enrichment remains the same, are comparatively coarse in execution, but the Cross of Cong has fine technical qualities.

Lastly, in the Ardagh Chalice we come back to the period of the most perfect design and workmanship, of about the 8th cent., and to a masterpiece of unique value. It is a large two-handled bowl on a low stem, and will hold as much as three pints of liquid. In its construction and ornament are employed no fewer than 354 distinct pieces, and the materials are gold, silver, bronze, lead, enamel, glass, amber, and mica; and the ornamental patterns include interlaced-work, step-patterns, key-patterns, spirals, zoömorphs, and scrolls, arranged in panels after the fashion represented in the manuscripts, and of the finest period of the style. What is chiefly remarkable about the chalice is not the elaboration or variety of its detail, but the almost classic nobility of its general design. As a rule, in all barbaric enrichment, whether Celtic or Teutonic in origin, the tendency is for the ornament to cover practically the whole surface of the object under treatment, while it is only very rarely that we find that contrast between plain and richly adorned passages on which so much of the effect of classical decoration depends. The chalice, like some other objects of the pagan period in the collection of the Royal Irish Academy, has an imposing largeness of style, due to the simple contours of the plain polished silver bowl, in contrast with the bands and medallions filled in with panels of delicate ornament and studded with bosses of variegated enamel. Not the least beautiful part is the flat plate on the under side of the base, which would be visible when the chalice was raised to the lips of a communicant.

Conclusion.—It has been seen that in the manuscripts all the kinds of ornament already enumerated are used freely in conjunction, while in the metal-work zoömorphs are conspicuous, and interlacing patterns are less used than the others. Turning now to the sculptured stones, we find interlacing patterns most prominent of all, so that they sometimes form the sole decoration of a monument. As the forms of the slabs or crosses differ in the various Celtic or Celticized districts, so do the kinds of ornament with which they are adorned. Decoration in tastefully distributed panels is everywhere the rule, and in Kells churchyard, Ireland, there is an unfinished cross, on which the panels are marked out and carefully squared, though there is no carving on them. The panels, however, are differently filled according to the localities. In Ireland, where the erect crosses are comparatively late, these show figure subjects greatly preponderating over ornament; and the same may be said of the free-standing Scottish crosses of the same type, though the subjects in Ireland are more generally Scriptural than in Scotland, where hunting scenes and the like are more common. In Wales and Cornwall, on the other hand, figure sculpture of all kinds is subordinate to ornament. In the matter of ornament, spirals of good design and zoömorphs are frequent in Ireland and Scotland, but are very rare in Wales and Cornwall, and, as far as spirals are concerned, in the Isle of Man. The Irish and Scottish stones have also as a speciality that kind of knot work where curved lines are most in evidence.

The varieties of interlacing patterns in Scotland and Wales are astonishing, and these have all been analyzed with extreme ingenuity and care by Romilly Allen in *The Early Christian Monuments of Scotland*, where the subject occupies 150 quarto pages. Since these slabs and crosses were, as we have seen, not so strictly ecclesiastical in character as the manuscripts and much of the metal-work, it is not necessary to postulate the monastic craftsman as in their case the sole executant. Yet the loving care and the single-minded devotion to a laborious task of which they give evidence are just the qualities which the monastic life developed in its votaries; and though the designer of some of the elaborate cross-slabs of Scotland may have helped himself by appropriating compositions and motives from the manuscripts, yet he could never have carried out the work with such perfect execution had not his whole nature been brought into accord with the spirit that inspires it. Celtic art, as the expression on the æsthetic side of the fervour and intensity of a wonderful religious life, without which the Christian Church would have been greatly poorer, was a possession of the people at large, and is a democratic art practised alike by the unlettered mason and by the most learned scholars in Christendom.

LITERATURE.—For the whole subject, J. Romilly Allen, *Celtic Art in Pagan and Christian Times*, London, 1904, *Early Christian Symbolism in Great Britain and Ireland*, London, 1887, and *The Monumental History of the Early British Church*, London, 1889: for Ireland, Petrie, *The Ecclesiastical Architecture of Ireland*, Dublin, 1845; M. Stokes, *Early Christian Art in Ireland*, London, 1887: for Scotland, Joseph Anderson, *Scotland in Early Christian Times*, Edinburgh, 1881, and 2nd ser., Edinburgh, 1881. The art of the manuscripts can be studied in Westwood, *Facsimiles of the Miniatures and Ornaments of Anglo-Saxon and Irish Manuscripts*, London, 1868; Stanford Robinson, *Celtic Illuminative Art*, Dublin, 1908; and Johan Adolf Bruun, *An Enquiry into the Art of the Illuminated Manuscripts of the Middle Ages*, pt. i., Edinburgh, 1897. The best works on the carved stones of the various localities are, for England generally, *Journal of the British Archæological Association*, vol. xli.: for Northumbria, Greenwell, *A Catalogue of the Sculptured and Inscribed Stones in the Cathedral Library, Durham*, Durham, 1899: for North Riding of Yorkshire, *Yorkshire Archæological Journal*, vol. xix.: for Cumberland, Calverley, *Notes on the Early Sculptured Crosses, etc., in the Present Diocese of Carlisle*, Kendal, 1899: for Lancashire, Taylor, *Ancient Crosses of Lancashire*, Manchester, 1902: for the Isle of Man, Cumming, *Runic Remains of the Isle of Man*, London, 1857; Kermode, *Manx Crosses*, London, 1907, and *Catalogue of Manx Crosses*, Ramsey, 1892: for all parts of Scotland, Romilly Allen and Anderson, *The Early Christian Monuments of Scotland*, Edinburgh, 1903; Stuart, *Sculptured Stones of Scotland*, Aberdeen, 1856: for Wales, Westwood, *Lapidarium Walliæ*, London, 1876: for Cornwall and Devon, Blight, *Crosses of Cornwall*, London, 1858; Langdon, *Old Cornish Crosses*, Truro, 1896: for Ireland, O'Neill, *Sculptured Crosses of Ancient Ireland*, London, 1857; Petrie, *Christian Inscriptions in the Irish Language*, Dublin, 1872. G. BALDWIN BROWN.

ART (Christian).—**Introduction.**—The limits of this article permit of the treatment of the subject only in one or two selected aspects. There can be no attempt to enumerate the various forms of Christian art, still less to trace out their history. For several of these, provision is made elsewhere in the Encyclopædia. The noblest and most important form of Christian art, architecture, furnishes the subject of a distinct article. Illuminated manuscripts are dealt with in next article. For an account of minor forms of Christian art, such as ivories, or ecclesiastical metal-work, information will be found in Dictionaries of Christian Antiquities, or in compendia like Dom Leclercq's recent *Manuel d'Archéologie Chrétienne*.

(*a*) *Scope*.—The scope of the present article must necessarily be a narrow one, and the main object of it is to take the most characteristic forms of Christian art as we meet with them in successive ages, and consider how far each of them expressed the religious ideal. In connexion with these historical phases we shall keep in view the two main questions: (1) that of the relation of art and the element of beauty generally to the religious life, and (2) that of the actual attitude of the Church at large, and of sections of it, towards art and beauty.

(*b*) *Definition.*—It is necessary to understand at the outset what is meant by 'Art.' To the majority of people a work of art means a picture or a piece of sculpture, and such works are generally regarded from the points of view of their resemblance to nature, and of the intrinsic character of the person or scene or object delineated. Art is, however, something far wider, and it is taken here to embrace the element of beauty wherever this appears in the works of man. The tasteful embellishment of buildings and of objects of utility is just as much art as the painting of a picture, and such decoration can be in the highest degree artistic even though the representation of nature plays little or no part in it. Where the representation of nature does form an important element in the effect of a piece, this may be a very beautiful and precious work of art, though the aspect of nature it presents is comparatively trivial, whereas a markedly inferior work of art, like some modern religious pictures of the 'Doré' type, may have for its theme a subject of the highest import. In this article the subject and the religious intention of a work are not reckoned as in themselves competent to give it its rank, and only those works are regarded as illustrating the subject of Christian art that express Christian ideas in an adequate and beautiful artistic form.

(*c*) *Misconceptions concerning Christian art.*—These considerations may help us to get rid at the outset of certain popular misconceptions, such as the notions that in early Christian days pagan art was deeply tainted with impurity; that the Christians were in consequence opposed to art, and that the earliest manifestations of Christian art assumed a symbolic or didactic character as a sort of apology or disguise. We must remember that there was an immense amount of art in the pagan world of a decorative kind that filled life with beauty, but did not obtrude upon notice any special representations of mythological personages. In cases where these personages were actually in evidence, there was, as a rule, nothing in the way they were displayed that would necessarily offend the eye. As a fact, the works of the Greek and Roman chisel and brush are so far from being tainted with impurity that it would be difficult to pick out from existing galleries of antique sculpture more than one or two works that are in any way suggestive or ignoble. Antique works compare quite favourably in this respect with those that figure yearly in European exhibitions of contemporary art. It is true we are told of some great painters of antiquity that they exercised their skill occasionally on licentious themes, but this is a fact also about certain prominent Italian painters of the Renaissance. As regards extant works of painting, apart from a few examples that were never meant for public view, we find nothing displayed on the plaster of Pompeiian walls that is not perfectly innocent. There is a class of Greek vase paintings that are marked by lubricity, but they were specially executed to suit the taste of the Athenian *jeunesse dorée*, and any one can see that thousands upon thousands of painted vases on view in the museums of Europe are as chaste as a child's picture book. A false impression arose when the Christian Fathers applied somewhat uncritically the OT category of 'idol' to the classical gods and goddesses, and were prompt to note the scandalous appearances these made in pagan literature. As the early Greek philosopher complained, the poets made the gods commit all the disgraceful acts repudiated among men, but the artists steadily refused to lend themselves to any such degradation of the religious ideal. In sculpture and painting the behaviour of these mythological beings is in almost every case exemplary. In their persons and conversation the artists exhibit nothing but what is ethically noble. Hence the spirit of pagan art, liberally interpreted, was not anti-Christian; and its forms might be adapted to Christian purposes without any marked incongruity.

Again, the existence of a vast number of works of art, often of an elaborate kind, dating from all the Christian centuries, is enough to show that there has been no general opposition to art in the minds of Christians. There are, it is true, statements in the Fathers which have been interpreted as implying a condemnation of all forms of art. The statements are, however, primarily concerned with the making, embellishing, and setting forth of images connected with the pagan religion. This sort of work was naturally forbidden to the Christian, and Tertullian goes so far as to cavil at the making of the similitude of any natural object, on the plea that it might conceivably become an object of adoration. On the other hand, he points out (*de Idolatria*, ch. viii.) that the Christian artificer could properly exercise his craft on work which had no connexion with the pagan religion; and the 11th Canon of St. Hippolytus allows the craftsman to supply ordinary social demands for artistic work. Hence there is no reason to doubt that Christian houses were as pleasingly adorned, to the measure of the means and the taste of their owners, as pagan ones; but the art thus applied was of a light and decorative kind, not depending on formal pictures or statues, which probably would not make their appearance at all.

I. *EARLY TIMES*. — 1. **Before Constantine.**— The earliest existing examples of Christian art are applied not to houses but to burial-places, wherein the classical fashion is followed of giving them the same sort of adornment as the abodes of the living. The earliest known of these are decorated in much the same fashion as contemporary Roman tombs, such as the well-known ones on the Via Latina. The style is bright and cheerful. Pure landscapes are not unknown. Wreaths of fruit and flowers play a considerable part, and there occur also figure motives of a classical kind, in the form of winged genii, often engaged in vintage operations, personifications of the seasons, Cupids and Psyches, and the like, wherein the innocent classical convention of the nude is not wholly repudiated. To these purely decorative shapes there were added from the first certain others of a religious significance. The simplest of these is the Orant, a female figure with arms raised in an attitude of adoration. In the case of more distinctive personages, as the Canon of the NT was at the time only in process of formation, the representations are drawn mostly from the OT. Jonah is the favourite, and is evidently accepted, in the spirit of Mt 12^{40}, as the type of Christ. Moses striking the rock, Noah, Daniel, the youths in the fiery furnace, and Susanna, also occur, and the choice seems determined by lists of typical worthies of the Old Dispensation such as those in the Epistle of Clement of Rome to the Corinthians, or in liturgical documents such as the *Commendatio Animæ quando Infirmus est in Extremis*.

The figure of Christ appears early, but in a disguised form as the Good Shepherd, or as Orpheus who exercised a controlling charm over all living creatures. Occasionally He is presented in His own person, and the artist for preference chooses those scenes in which He appears as worker of wonders. The 'Raising of Lazarus' is specially favoured. Save in one exceptional scene of the 'mocking,' the suffering Christ does not appear, and still less the Christ crucified. Such are the characteristic subjects in the 1st and 2nd centuries, while occasionally in the 2nd, and more often in the 3rd, we meet with representations of a more or less doctrinal kind, such as the faithful round the table of the Lord, on which is placed for food the mystic fish, the symbol of Christ. It is remarkable, however, that historical representations from the actual life of the Church, especially scenes of persecution and martyrdom, are wholly absent.

About all this work we have from the present point of view to note: (1) that it is in the main decorative, the artist being more concerned to cover bare spaces and to dispose symmetrically his representations than to inculcate by them any doctrinal lesson; and (2) that classical influence remains strong, even when we have passed from the earliest period of almost exact correspondence between pagan and Christian decorative schemes. As Dom Leclercq has recently shown, many of the OT and NT figures are modelled on pagan types, while the earliest and best plastic representations of Christ as the Good Shepherd not only reproduce the familiar classical motive, but show a grace and elasticity in form and pose not unworthy of a fairly good period of classical art. Moreover, when Christ appears in His own person, He is represented as youthful and beardless, with something of the attractive comeliness of an Apollo. It is impossible in face of these facts to believe that there was any general sympathy among the early Christians with the extreme view expressed by Tertullian when he objected to any representation of figures or natural objects; or that there was any reason why Christians should turn with repugnance from the classical art that was all about them.

The OT and NT scenes that begin to appear in the catacomb frescoes of the 3rd cent. are repeated on the carved sarcophagi of the 4th and 5th. On some of these we find the same idyllic scenes of genii vintaging, the vine being, of course, in this case the True Vine, and the same semi-classic decorative motives which we meet with in the earliest frescoes; but the OT and NT scenes form the staple subjects of sarcophagus art, and Jonah, Abraham, Moses, and Daniel are seen side by side with Christ raising Lazarus, healing the blind, or touching with a magic wand of power the water-pots of Cana. If the crowning scenes of His life are touched at all, there is no attempt to deal with the deeper Christian mysteries of suffering and sacrifice. The march to Calvary becomes a triumphal procession, with the Cross borne forward as a banner; the crowning with thorns is envisaged as a royal honour.

2. **After Constantine.**—The next epoch of Christian art, after the time of Constantine, introduces us into quite a different atmosphere. Christianity has become the religion of the State, and confronts the world as a regularly constituted power. The artist needs no longer to hint but can assert, and there is demanded from him a certain amplitude and majesty in his work.

(*a*) *Mosaic art*. — The characteristic form of artistic expression for this period is the monumental mosaic. The artist's operations are no longer confined to the narrow limits of a burial chamber or the side of a sarcophagus. He has to cover with decoration the vast interior wall surfaces of the great basilican churches and the stately though much smaller baptisteries. His style changes with his task. If the bright unpretending catacomb pictures seem to have a literary counterpart in the personal expression of the lyric song, the severe and imposing mosaics possess a certain epic grandeur. The subjects of the mosaics are not, as a rule, historical or directly doctrinal, and there is the same reticence in the avoidance of those Passion scenes in the life of Christ in which He is represented as suffering or in humiliation. The aim of the mosaic artist is to present in majestic and simple forms the heroes of Christianity. It is not the adventures of the saints that attract him so much as the dignity of their presence as they stand forth triumphant after suffering—lords in heaven and earth. It is the Presence of Christ, rather than His mortal deeds and sufferings, that he strives to bring before the spectator.

The early Christian mosaics from the 4th to the 6th cent. at Rome and Ravenna are as great in their illustration of the principles of design as in their technical excellence and their artistic beauty. They adopt in the main the principle of the world-famous frieze of the Parthenon at Athens, and offer an ideal presentation of actual scenes of which the building they adorn was the theatre. One of the earliest and quite the finest of the mosaics, that in St. Pudentiana at Rome, is in respect of its main scheme canonical. In the apse of that church the stately form of Christ enthroned as teacher occupies the central position, while on a lower level and on both sides of Him sit the twelve Apostles. The arrangement transfers to the heavenly sphere the appearance of the apse of the church at service time, when the presiding official occupied the throne in the centre behind the altar, with the attendant priests on the stone bench round the curve of the apse on either side of him. Christ, behind whom in the mosaic rises a jewelled cross on a hill in the midst of a city, Jerusalem, is the invisible ideal president of the daily assembly; the spirit of the Apostles is ready to inspire the clergy. The work, which may date within the 4th cent., is notable for the classical feeling in the characterization of the Apostles, reminding us of the heads in some of Raphael's cartoons. Equally dignified, equally well chosen, is the scheme for the decoration of the Baptistery at Ravenna of about A.D. 450. Here in the centre of the dome is a noble picture of the ideal consecration to ministry, the Baptism of Our Lord, at whose feet the gaunt but imposing forms of the twelve Apostles are preparing to lay down their crowns. More extensive is the display in St. Apollinare Nuovo at Ravenna, where the worshipper on entering sees represented in mosaic, on the side walls of the nave above the arcades, on the one side a portion of Ravenna itself, and on the other the suburb Classis, the port of the Imperial city. From each there issues a procession of saints, male on the right, female on the left, who are represented advancing towards the altar end of the church, bearing crowns which they will lay at the feet of an enthroned Christ and an enthroned Mary with the Child, at the end of the nave. Here again is idealized the bodily movement of the actual worshippers from the door of the church to its altar, or from their city homes to the heavenly mansions prepared for them afar, as well as the spiritual movement of the heart from earthly to celestial preoccupations. Above these processions, between the clerestory windows, stand single figures of white-robed saints, which carry out better than any others that could be named the idea before noticed of the monumental presentation of heroic forms of epic simplicity and grandeur. Highest of all comes on each side a series of historical pictures in mosaic from the life of Christ —the first example of such representations that Christian art has to show. On the one side there are scenes from the miracles and discourses, very simply but effectively designed, and showing the protagonist of the youthful Apollo-like type met with in catacomb art and on the sarcophagi. On the other side is what would be called in later mediæval times a Passion series, but the actual scenes of the final tragedy are as a fact selected on early Christian principles, with a truly classical avoidance of anything painful, or of any situation in which the Lord would be shown as suffering humiliation.

Thus there is no scourging, no crowning with thorns, no crucifixion, no taking down from the cross or burial, and the scene in which Christ, a heroic figure, is making a sort of triumphal progress towards Calvary, is followed immediately by that of the Marys at the empty sepulchre. In the pictures of this second series Christ is represented as older and is bearded, and the marked difference in His personality in the two closely related sets of pictures is enough to show that there can have been no authentic tradition of His actual physiognomy.

(*b*) *Historical or symbolic representation.*—From this same period of the 5th and 6th centuries we can date the beginning of the most conspicuous but not always the most artistic form of Christian art —the historical or symbolic representation, of an edifying and often a didactic character. There is an often quoted saying based on Quintilian, which occurs in many early Christian writings, to the effect that pictures are the books of those who cannot read. To the ecclesiastical mind this gave a religious justification for the pictorial embellishment of the walls of public buildings, which had previously been a matter of tradition inherited from classical practice. In the middle of the 5th cent. we find St. Nilus laying down the principle that the inner walls of a church should be covered with scenes from the Old and New Testaments from the hand of a first-rate artist, in order that those who are unable to read may be reminded of the Christian virtues of those who have served aright the true God, and be inspired to emulate them. In the 6th cent. Gregory the Great recommended the use of paintings in churches in order that the illiterate might behold upon the walls what they were not able to read in books. On this idea was based a scheme of decoration which remained in use throughout the mediæval period. At the altar end of the church was displayed the figure of Christ glorified, as teacher or judge, and the faithful were to be inspired by the sight to strive for the joys of Paradise. Along the side walls were exposed historical pictures from OT or NT or from the lives of saints, in which instruction as well as edification was provided for the unlettered convert. The subjects would be chosen, and the figures, actions, and details as a rule settled not by the artist himself, but by the ecclesiastical authorities. Gregory of Tours gives us a charming picture of the wife of a bishop of Clermont in the 5th cent. sitting with her Bible in her lap in the church, and directing the operations of a company of painters who are frescoing the walls. The western or entrance wall was not at first included in the scheme, but from about the 10th cent. onwards it was utilized for a display complementary to that of the glories of Paradise over the altar. This was the Last Judgment, often with the connected scenes of the separation and after-disposition of the souls of the just and of the unjust. In the later mediæval period the Inferno was made especially prominent, with the avowed intention of affecting the souls of the worshippers by salutary terror as well as by hope. Of the subject of Christ in glory the finest examples by far are in the early Christian mosaics, but the historical scenes were not displayed in adequate artistic form till the development of the Italian schools of mural painting in the 15th century. The most impressive rendering of the scene of the Last Judgment is in the 14th cent. fresco of the subject in the Campo Santo at Pisa, which used to be ascribed erroneously to Orcagna. The treatment here is truly dramatic and moving, and is marked by a fine reticence. Later representations of the theme, such as the famous ones by Luca Signorelli at Orvieto, offend through their over-insistence on the terror of the scene, and especially on the physical torments inflicted by the demons on the lost spirits who fall into their clutches. The ecclesiastical authorities may have thought it well thus to daunt the sinner and to harry the feelings of the impressionable, but the artistic result is nothing less than deplorable. Both in these scenes, and in the representation which became very popular of Christ suspended in suffering on the Cross, the painters of the 12th and 13th centuries, especially in Italy, offend against all laws of good taste and of beauty, and prostitute art to the service of a gloomy religiosity.

From these false ideals representative art in the West was saved by certain religious revivals, embodied in Italy in the person of St. Francis of Assisi, and in Germany in the mystics of the school of Cologne. In both cases pictorial art showed itself responsive to the religious impulse, and the artistic revivals connected with the names of **Giotto** of Florence and **Meister Wilhelm** of Cologne have a distinct basis in the changed religious thought of the times. Before discussing the effect of these revivals of the 13th and 14th cents. on Christian art and on the life of the Church, we must turn back more nearly to early Christian times.

II. *MIDDLE AGES*.—The mediæval period had no sooner opened than the controversy on images (A.D. 726–842) divided the East and the West.

1. Controversy between East and West.—The opposition to all graphic and plastic representations of sacred personages on walls, panels, or portable objects, with which some of the Byzantine emperors identified themselves, was partly, no doubt, inspired by Islāmite examples, and was carried to such fanatical lengths as to involve the destruction of numberless treasures of early Byzantine art. The controversy ended in a compromise, according to which representations in colour or relief of Christ, the Virgin, angels, and saints were once more permitted on walls and on portable objects, though religious sculpture of a monumental kind never afterwards flourished in the Byzantine empire. For these representations, schemes were drawn up, and these were crystallized into books of artistic recipes, which have governed the practice of Christian art in the lands of the Greek Church all through their later history. The best known of these handbooks is that brought by the French archæologist, Didron, from the cloisters of Mount Athos, and published by him in 1845. It is known as the *Hermeneia* or *Book of Mount Athos*, and gives an impression of that fixity, not to say lifelessness, which characterizes representative religious art in Eastern Christendom, in such striking contrast to the mobility and variety of the forms of Christian art in the West.

It would be a mistake, however, to suppose that the Byzantine iconoclasts were opposed to the use of art in connexion with religion. What they revolted against was the religious reverence paid to sacred effigies, which became in a sense idols. As Woltmann has remarked, 'images had been introduced into churches first for ornament, teaching, and edification; but image-worship soon crept in unawares. The reverence for the Divine and spiritual being was transferred to the image, which was honoured with incense and obeisance' (*Hist. of Painting*, p. 195). Now, this reverence or idolatry was only a further extension, to the limit of an abuse, of the didactic idea, which the Church as a whole began in the 5th and 6th centuries to attach to representative art. Some of the Byzantine emperors most inimical to image-worship, such as Constantine V. and Theophilus, embellished the churches with decorative art in sumptuous materials, and in the simple conventional forms of the earlier catacomb period. In the West, moreover, it must not be supposed that the use of subject pictures with a view to edification was the only fact of importance concerning Christian art in the early mediæval epoch. No doubt the Fathers and bishops, who patronized pictures as the books of the illiterate, thought they had accomplished a good work in moralizing art and in setting it to ecclesiastical service. They believed that they had avoided by these means the danger latent in art in respect to those who might be tempted by the lust of the eyes, and they were at the same time apparently unconscious of the danger on the other side of reverence for these sacred effigies passing into the idolatry of which the iconoclasts accused the Christians of the West. These Fathers and bishops, in the view they thus adopted about works of art, were not regarding the matter from an æsthetic, but rather from a doctrinal standpoint; but we are fortunate in possessing mediæval productions that do not depend for their artistic value on anything that they represent, and also expressions of mediæval opinion that are more satisfying to those æsthetically minded.

2. Theophilus on Art.—Among the most interesting documents that have come down to us from the Middle Ages is a certain technical treatise on artistic processes, written about the year A.D. 1100, by a German Benedictine monk whose name in religion was Theophilus. The author, a practical expert in fine metal-work and other artistic processes and materials, has prefixed to the three books into which his treatise, called *Schedula Diversarum Artium*, is divided, Introductions in which he discourses at large on the whole question of art and the cultivation of the beautiful as a part of the religious life. The view Theophilus advances is almost startling in its breadth and sanity, and gives the modern reader a very pleasing impression of monastic culture, which he will probably have been taught to believe was slavishly narrow and ascetic.

Theophilus bases his apologia for the practice of the arts on the part of those vowed to the religious life on a view of human nature that can be thus paraphrased:

Man was made in the image of God, that is, as Theophilus implies, in the similitude of the Divine Artist who fashioned the world, and he is bound to make his resemblance to the Divine as real and effective as he can. It is true that by the machinations of the evil one this Divine image in man was obscured at the Fall, but it was not so far effaced that man cannot through care and thought win back something of the ancient heritage of art and of learning. 'Wherefore,' he writes, 'the pious devotion of the faithful should not neglect the knowledge which the prudent foresight of our predecessors has handed down to us, but should embrace it as an inheritance from the Almighty.' As such it is not the private possession of any one individual, but is a trust from God, which the skilled person holds for the benefit of his fellows. For which reason, Theophilus declares, he is ready to offer to all who desire humbly to learn, as freely as he has himself freely received it, all the gift of the Divine grace—this gift being the knowledge of the technical processes of the arts which he then goes on to unfold. In another place he discourses in the same strain, and urges the artist to 'believe that the spirit of God has filled his heart, and will direct him by the seven gifts of the Holy Ghost.' He then explains that these seven gifts embrace the special qualities of skill and taste and industry which are requisite for the practice of the arts. The spirit of Wisdom teaches that God is the creator of all things, and without Him there is nothing—this is the primal lesson. Next, the spirit of Understanding gives to the mind the capacity for discerning the right order, measure, and distribution of parts which should be applied to the work in hand. The spirit of Counsel teaches us not to hide the talent which has been given us by God, but to display it openly, with all humility, in word and act before those who are desiring to learn. Through the spirit of Might the craftsman will throw off all the torpor of idleness, and will begin his work with vigour and carry it through with all his energy and power to the end. The spirit of Knowledge, which has been granted to him, has filled his mind with abundant stores, over which he presides, and which he must produce with all boldness before his fellows. By the spirit of Piety he will rightly judge upon what object, for whom, and when, and how much, and in what manner he shall spend his labour, and will guard against the insidious inroads of avarice and greed by a most scrupulous moderation in estimating the value of what has been done. Finally, as the great lesson of the whole, the spirit of the Fear of the Lord will remind him that he can do nothing of himself, that all he possesses or desires comes from God, and that he must ascribe to the bountifulness of the Divine mercy all that he knows, or is, or hopes to be.

3. Art in the monasteries.—The existence of artistic practice as an institution of the cloister may in itself surprise, for it seems to us moderns to belong to a side of life from which the ascetic recluse would turn rigidly away. We may, however, repeat here what was intimated in connexion with the fact, to some almost equally surprising, that artistic practice existed among the earliest Christians. Art, regarded as an element of beauty attaching itself naturally to the works of men, and touching life at every point, the modern cannot readily understand, because with us this element of beauty is something artificial and extra, for which we have to make a special effort. This was not the case in old time, when it would have needed a special effort, not to *procure*, but to *exclude* this element. The earliest Christians decorated their tombs, the Christians after Constantine their churches, because not to do so would have been a forced act, for which, as we have already seen, there was no real reason. The artistic tradition, thus maintained from the first by the Church at large, was in Eastern Christendom never broken, and the Greek Church, while stereotyping the forms of its expression, has held it continuously in honour. In the West the Teutonic inroads broke up the fabric of antique culture; but though the classical tradition in art was thus in a measure severed, the barbarians were in their own way just as artistic as the Greeks or Romans, and the mediæval civilization of the West, partly classical and partly barbaric, derived its art from both these sources. Hence, when communities of monks and nuns were formed, alike in the Celtic and the once-Romanized parts of the West, the arts quietly made their appearance within the hallowed enclosures. A monastery, it must be remembered, was in theory self-supporting, and all sorts of operations in husbandry and in the mechanical crafts had perforce to be carried on by the inmates, whose bodily and mental health was greatly improved by the exercise. Of the Celtic monastery at Bangor, near Chester, Bede tells us that the two thousand inmates all lived by the labour of their hands. The rule of St. Benedict, in the 6th cent., provided that when artizans entered the Order they were to be allowed to continue working at their crafts, though they were not to take any personal pride in their productions. The quiet and order of a monastery must have been congenial to the artist, and Ordericus Vitalis tells us that, when the founder of a certain monastery in the 12th cent. invited all who joined it to continue the practice of the arts to which they were accustomed, 'there gathered about him freely craftsmen both in wood and iron, carvers and goldsmiths, painters and stonemasons, and others skilled in all manner of cunning work' (*HE* viii. 27).

The mere practice of the various crafts, artistic as well as utilitarian, in the mediæval convent is, however, one thing, and the religious enthusiasm with which Theophilus seems to regard artistic pursuits is quite another. It is this that constitutes for us the interest of the *Schedula*. The religion of the writer was evidently sincere and fervent, and it seems to him to find a natural, even a Divinely ordained, outcome in art. Though Ruskin and other eloquent modern writers have descanted on the praises of art from the moral and religious standpoint, there is a breadth and dignity about the thought of the 11th cent. monk that puts him above them all. There is, indeed, no more effective apology for the cultivation of art than this simple reminder that the love of what is beautiful is a part of human nature, or, if we take still higher ground, the more august assertion that the creation of what is beautiful is part of the law of the universe at large.

'Look around you,' we can hear Theophilus saying in effect to his hearers, 'and survey the fabric of creation. It is the work of an artist, of the Supreme Artist who has made all things beautiful in their season. He has gifted you too with a portion of His own nature and has formed you an artist, and you are bound in service to Him to exercise your creative power and make the most of your affinity with what is beautiful. In the name of religion take up the brush and tongs and mallet, and spare not cost or labour till the House of God that you build shall shine like the very fields of Paradise.'

These last words are used by Theophilus in a passage in which he foreshadows the concrete realization of the creative effort in the microcosm of an Abbey church, which is an image of the vast macrocosm of the universe. The church, he says, is to be so decorated on ceiling and walls as to present the appearance of the Heavenly Garden. It will seem to be blooming with all kinds of flowers, and green with leaves and grass, like the celestial fields where the blessed ones receive their crowns. The ceiling will be flowered like an embroidered robe, the wall resemble a garden, the windows send in a flood of variously coloured light. After the decoration of the fabric will come the provision of fittings and apparatus, including all the vessels for the service of the sanctuary, the construction and varied embellishment of which he describes in the technical chapters in the body of his treatise. There, in the workshop and among the appliances and tools which the monkish craftsman has to build and fashion for himself, we are invited to see the gold and silver and bronze, the coloured earths, the glass stained with metallic oxides, all taking shape in dainty and beautiful forms, till the mere matter, the raw material, has become spiritualized through its consecration, in a shape of beauty, to the service of the Most High. For with Theophilus the preoccupation always is with the technical manipulation of the material so as to compass an effect of beauty. From end to end of his treatise there is comparatively little about art as representative. The art he contemplates is decorative. It is not the kind of art that corresponds to the more prosaic vision of the Fathers and bishops, to whom the lessons to be drawn from the presentation of holy persons and scenes make up the chief value of art. He is, of course, aware that the beautiful forms he conjures into life under the hammer or by the glass-kiln represent something in nature, or have, at any rate, some symbolical import; but these considerations trouble him little, and, after describing some technical process, he often tells the worker to make with it 'what you will.'

The representative element in mediæval art must not, however, be ignored. Theophilus decks the walls and ceiling and windows of his church with the gaiety and colour of a garden, but he has in his mind the regular scheme of figure design for a church interior. On the walls will be displayed, he suggests, the Passion of the Lord, touching the heart of the worshipper, or the suffering of the saints will be movingly depicted. If the joys of heaven are displayed at one end of the building, and at the other the torments of the regions of the lost, the spectator will take hope from the thought of his good actions, and be terrified at the remembrance of his sins.

Though Theophilus troubles himself little about symbolism, there was no doubt a symbolical intent in many of the decorative forms employed in mediæval art. On this subject a word must be said, because it is one that is often misunderstood. There is no mystery about Christian symbolism, because it is almost entirely based upon Scripture. We are familiar in the OT and NT with figures in which animals and plants stand for personages and qualities, and know that there is little consistency in the use of these. Thus the lion is at times a type of Christ, as the 'lion of the tribe of Judah'; but at other times he may represent the evil one, who, 'as a roaring lion, walketh about, seeking whom he may devour.' In plastic or graphic art the lion may conceivably stand either for the ideal of good or the ideal of evil; but there is commonly, too, a third alternative, that the creature is purely ornamental, and may have been copied as a mere decorative motive from some indifferent source, such as an Oriental figured stuff. The whole subject of SYMBOLISM is dealt with in another article, and it is mentioned here only for the sake of warning the reader against imagining that it played any but a secondary part in mediæval design. The fact is that in every age the artist, as artist, has little care for these intellectual refinements, and it is because Theophilus is so true an artist that he troubles his reader but little with this subject. The artist's instinct is to make his work tell out at once with directness and force, and he does not desire to give the spectator the trouble of spelling out obscure allusions. The artist, however, as we have seen, often worked under the orders of theologians or of those who took a religious and literary interest, rather than a purely artistic interest, in the works produced. Such patrons might prescribe schemes of symbolism which the artist was quite willing to carry out.

The difference was that, while the theologian saw, in the shape, say, of a dragon, a reference to some allusion in the Apocalypse, the artist took a disinterested pleasure in the creature because its wings and tail were so effective for filling awkward spaces in the field of his design. Again, the persons here in view, in studying works of art already done, would find out all sorts of recondite suggestions in details which, in their origin, had probably a purely artistic purpose. In this way there came into existence in the 13th cent. the extensive work of Durandus, bishop of Mende, called *Rationale Divinorum Officiorum*, in which an elaborate symbolical interpretation was given of all the parts and fittings of the church and the apparatus of the altar. In this way, too, beast forms in art were credited with moral and religious meanings that were interpreted according to schemes of beast symbolism embodied in the so-called *bestiaria*. That beast forms in mediæval art were commonly symbolical is, however, rendered extremely unlikely by the fact that reforming churchmen of puritanical tendencies are found inveighing against such motives as barbarian and frivolous. The *locus classicus* occurs in the writings of St. Bernard, in the 12th cent., who protests against the foolish and wasteful display of these monsters on carved capitals and friezes, without any suggestion of their supposed religious significance. A later writer draws a distinction between pictures of the sufferings of Christ and the martyrs, which he praises as 'books of the laity,' and animal representations, for 'what have lions to do in a church, or dragons, or all the rest of these beasts?' (Schnaase, *Geschichte der bildenden Künste*, iv. 272).

These passages draw attention to the fact, which must not be passed over, that within the monastic system itself there was not perfect unanimity in regard to this lavish display of art in connexion with religion. There was a puritan vein in monasticism that led to protests against what was regarded as over-exuberance in the use of the element of beauty in the furnishing forth of sacred structures. The so-called reformed Benedictine Orders, beginning with the Cluniacs of the 10th cent., took, as a rule, this view, and a striking illustration of its working is to be found in the attitude of the Cistercians towards stained glass. The magnificent display of colour and imagery in the noble French storied windows of the 12th and 13th centuries, such as those at Chartres, they considered too sumptuous for the House of God, and substituted geometrical patterns in grey and yellow. Figure sculpture on the façades of their churches they also repudiated. It is, however, significant of the hold that art had obtained over the religious community in this advanced mediæval period, to note that there was no real opposition to art even among the severest of the reformed Orders, for Cistercian architecture, as the ruined abbeys of England sufficiently prove, though sparingly adorned, is of extreme beauty, and its ornamentation, with conventional foliage, of the utmost delicacy and grace.

4. **Gothic Architecture.**—We find, then, in the *Schedula* of Theophilus the conception of Christian art as a display of beautiful things carefully and cunningly wrought, that were offered as the homage of the mortal artificer to the great Artist of creation. This conception was actually realized, with a completeness and splendour of which a monk of the 11th cent. could have no idea, in the fabric and fittings of the French Gothic cathedral of the age of St. Louis. This is the most perfect embodiment of Christian art that the world has seen, because the representative element, though present and recognized as it was by Theophilus, was subordinate to direct artistic expression, first in the forms of the architecture, and next in the sumptuous display of detail and colour in the stone and wood carvings, the gilt and enamelled shrines, and, above all, in the 'storied windows richly dight' that are the glory of the Gothic fane. The subject of Christian architecture receives separate treatment, and it is necessary here only to emphasize the natural and obvious symbolism of the forms of Gothic architecture, which raises the soul in aspiration, while the sense of mystery, of the beyond, is instilled by its multitudinous elusive details, its perspectives, its magic of light and shade. Of the general artistic effect of these vast structures at the time of their glory, when the interiors, often now so cold and bare, were glancing with gold and colour, and were hung with gorgeous Eastern stuffs, we can form but an imperfect idea; but it is probable that nothing more artistically beautiful has ever been seen. The spirit of the work was still the spirit of the earlier religious decorative art of which we read in Theophilus; that is to say, it was impersonal work, unmarred by any touch of personal display so common in Italian art, simple and sincere in intent and in execution, and offered in an act of devotion for the service of the sanctuary. The representative element was at the same time present in the art, but it kept its place as on the whole subordinate to the general decorative effect. For that very reason we find in it a charm which more advanced representative work has often lost. It is the charm of *naïveté* and freshness due to the artist's unsophisticated delight in nature, and at the same time to the clearness of his mental vision, which gives him ease and assurance.

The decorative figure sculpture on the great French cathedrals, such as Chartres, Amiens, and Rheims, is really one of the most perfectly satisfactory forms of Christian art. It is a direct expression of the thought and feeling of the Gothic epoch, as they were embodied in the character and work of St. Louis, the typical man of his age. In St. Louis mediæval religion took on a new character, for his was no cloistered sainthood, of what may be termed a professional type, but the sainthood of a man versed in secular affairs though viewing them always from the standpoint of a childlike but cheerful piety. The forms of Christ and of Mary, of the Apostles and prophets, of saints and of angels, that cluster about the spreading portals, or take their stand in niches and on pinnacles on the upper stages of the buildings, are so fresh in their naturalness, so graceful and elastic in pose, so full of brightness and tenderness in expression, so pure and holy of aspect, that we feel that we never met with a company that seemed to realize better what is meant by 'the body of Christian fellowship.' On the intellectual side we trace in the figures and reliefs the working of ideas beyond the mental horizon of the carvers who actually achieved the work. At Amiens, for example, the subjects in the reliefs on the pedestals that support the noble figures of the Jewish prophets, on the western front, are drawn from the prophetic writings, and evince a knowledge of the Vulgate text that betokens the trained theologian; but if we take the sculpture as a whole, we cannot doubt that the minds of the carvers were just as alert as their hands, and that the qualities in the work which we most admire are due not to the ecclesiastical directors of the undertaking, but to the devotional feeling, the sense of beauty, and the freshly kindled love of nature, that in the France of that favoured epoch were so widely diffused throughout the community of artificers. It needs hardly to be said that the same qualities mark Gothic sculpture in other lands, and they are very apparent in the beautiful recumbent effigies in stone or bronze in which English craftsmen of the 14th cent. achieved so much success. The 'Queen Eleanor' of Westminster Abbey and the 'Edward II.' at Gloucester are among the best of these. English and German churches of the period are adorned with beautiful decorative sculpture, but the display is on a far smaller scale than is the case in central France.

We turned away from representative art in the West at a time when it was dominated by a somewhat gloomy view of religion, and exercised itself largely on subjects which, like the crucified Saviour, laid stress on physical suffering. This applies chiefly to Italy, where in the early part of the 13th cent., while French and English Gothic art had unfolded itself in forms so varied and beautiful, little was being produced but unattractive and coarsely executed pictures, on which the historians of Italian painting lavish all the terms of depreciation they can muster. The Gothic spirit is one of humanity and brightness, and it was the spread of this from central France to Italy that led to the revival of art in the Peninsula. This Gothic spirit became incorporated in St. Francis of Assisi. As Sabatier puts it:

'St. Francis is the friend of nature; he is the man who sees in all creation the work of the Divine goodness, the effluence of the eternal beauty . . . hence at the voice of the Umbrian reformer Italy began to recover herself; she found again her sound sense and her good humour: she put away those ideas of pessimism and of death as a healthy organism gets rid of the principles of disease. . . . Lifting himself as by the stroke of the wing to the religious life, Francis caused suddenly to shine forth before the eyes of his contemporaries a new ideal, in presence of which there disappeared all those strange and perverted sects, as the birds of night fly before the first rays of the sun' (*Life of St. Francis*, London, 1907, p. 45).

The beneficent influence of the genial creed of St. Francis on the revival of Italian painting is well understood, and in **Giotto** and **Simone Martini**, who at Florence and Siena respectively represent the coming in of the Gothic spirit of humanity and tenderness, we find this influence at work. It is worth noting also that a similar influence at a rather later date was exercised upon painting in Germany, and led to the beautiful art of the early school of Cologne. German representative art has often shown a tendency towards what is grotesque and terrible, and the popular early Dances of Death, or of the dead, are proof of this. In marked contrast to this tendency we find at Cologne in the last part of the 14th and beginning of the 15th cent. a school of painting marked by the most delicate idyllic grace and tenderness, and by a pure devotional feeling that few Italian pictures can match. The art is really inspired by the so-called German mystics or 'Gottesfreunde,' a body of men who without forming any sect or order felt themselves impelled to a religious life of more intense zeal than was shared by their fellows. Still remaining, like the early Franciscans in Italy, true sons of the Church, they sought to make religion consist in a more intimate personal relation between the soul and God. When this relation was established, the soul became entirely filled with an ecstatic love that was not only the love of God but also the love of one's neighbour, so that the perfectly holy man, it was said, might desire the Kingdom of heaven for his fellow-man even before himself. In this mood the mystics were visited by visions, but visions that presented only forms of beauty. The fantastic and the grim, which have exercised such fascination over the Northern imagination, seldom appeared before the eyes of **Heinrich Suso** or his fellow-seers, but their dreams were of lovely sights, of flowers, and even of celestial maidens to whom they were fain to offer adoration. Schnaase was perfectly right in connecting with this religious revival of the 'Gottesfreunde' the Cologne school of idyllic religious painting associated with the names of **Meister Wilhelm, Hermann Wynrich,** and **Stephen Lochner**, the painter of the famous 'Dombild.'

5. Development of Christian art from the 13th to the 16th century.—We thus see in Italy and in Germany alike that the artistic revivals of the late 13th and 14th cents. were preceded by and based upon certain religious movements that set in in the direction of humane and tender feeling. The influence was essentially the same as that which formed the inspiration of Gothic art in France in the century before; but whereas Gothic art is mainly decorative, we begin at the end of the 13th cent. to watch the development of painting and sculpture on their representative sides till they become capable of expressing the deeper emotions with dramatic force and verity. Up to this period the artist had never disposed of adequate means for the representation of nature. However pure in feeling, however devotional, had been the art of the catacombs, or of the monastery, or of the Gothic church, however noble the single forms, however lively in action the groups, in the mosaics or in the historical pictures from the lives of Christ or of the Saints, the delineation was always summary, the rendering of light and shade and perspective crude or faulty. From the time of Giotto onwards two centuries are occupied with the development of painting and sculpture on the technical side, till they become in a true sense mirrors of nature and clear expressions of artistic thought. This is the epoch of what would be called *par excellence* Christian art, and lies between the end of the 13th and the close of the 16th cent. in Italy, between the end of the 14th and the middle of the 16th in Germany and Flanders. From Giotto to Tintoretto in the one case, from the early Cologne masters to Quinten Massys of Antwerp in the other, painting and sculpture are Christian, in the sense that religious themes are preponderant, and that spiritual ideas are conveyed in a more or less distinct and convincing form. It would be a mistake, however, to use the term 'Christian' of this art in too absolute a sense, for the power which the artist gradually obtained over his materials he exercised on a realistic rendering of nature that resulted in a progressive secularizing of the spirit of the art, while the influence of the classical Renaissance of the 15th cent. acted potently in the same direction. All through the periods indicated, however, art that was in a strict sense Christian was being produced, though not by every artist, nor, with certain exceptions, by any artist at every time.

The lives and works of the leading representatives of art in the periods indicated are so familiarly known that it will be sufficient for the purpose of this article to indicate in a few sentences the most prominent instances in which these artists embodied distinctly Christian ideas in their productions.

(*a*) *Italian Schools.*—The artists of the school of Florence, with the exception of one or two of pronounced devotional feeling, such as Fra Angelico and Luca della Robbia, with others like Lorenzo di Credi and Fra Bartolommeo who were directly influenced by the revivalism of Savonarola, took their subjects as a rule from the human side, and are noted for characterization and for the dramatic presentation of scenes of interest rather than for pious preoccupations. These scenes are of a sacred character, but they are generally envisaged in their human aspects, as is notably the case with the greatest of the early Florentines, Giotto and Masaccio. Some of Giotto's scenes from the Passion of Christ at Padua, and **Masaccio's** magnificent designs in the Carmine at Florence, are in the truest sense spiritually elevating; but the effect is that of the sublime in art generally, and they are comparable with fine scenes in Shakespeare or Æschylus rather than with religious discourses. The same applies to some of the technically perfect achievements in religious art of the masters of the 16th cent., who bowed before Masaccio's genius in creation though they disposed of far more advanced technical science in execution than he could pretend to. The most notable of these works from this ethical standpoint are **Leonardo da Vinci's** 'Last Supper' at Milan, **Michelangelo's** frescoes on the roof of the Sistine Chapel at Rome, some of **Raphael's** less academic compositions, numerous religious pieces by **Titian** and by **Giovanni Bellini**, and the largest part of the work of **Tintoretto**. The single figures by these masters have the epic grandeur of those in the finest Christian mosaics, though we see them no longer in monumental repose, but alert and mobile and actuated by noble passion. The sacred scenes in which they figure are re-constructed on an intelligible scheme, though the deliberate intention of all the actions and details is often so much in evidence that we are chilled by a certain made-up look in the composition. The Venetians are more successful than the Florentines or Raphael in giving to these scenes a convincing air of reality, because they see them from the first as a whole instead of building them up piece by piece in conscious fashion. Perhaps the best of all these masterpieces for its direct religious impression is Titian's comparatively unpretending picture at Dresden known as the 'Tribute Money.' Christ, tempted with the insidious query about the lawfulness of paying tribute to Cæsar, has asked to see the penny, which is brought to Him by His interlocutor, and the painter has emphasized the contrast between the noble, and at the same time tender and sympathetic, lineaments of the Lord and the screwed-up cynical features of the weather-beaten Pharisee who peers cunningly into His countenance. The hand of Christ, one of the most beautiful in art, contrasts effectively with the gnarled paw that is holding out the penny at which He points. The realization of the Christ of the Gospels and the creation of the adequate and beautiful type represent one of the triumphs of pictorial art. The imaginative power shown in some of Tintoretto's vast sketches in oil, from religious themes, in the Scuola di San Rocco at Venice, has never been equalled, and Raphael's cartoons are in comparison cold and academic. The great 'Crucifixion' of the former artist at San Rocco, and the 'Christ before Pilate' opposite to it, are sublime creations.

The Italian painters of the first rank may be said to transcend the limits of an art that may technically be termed 'Christian,' and to present the sublime of human nature in such a way as insensibly to raise the mind of the spectator to Divine things. There were, however, many artists of the second order whose devout feelings found a more direct expression in works to which the adjective just used may with strictness be applied. The typical artist of this order was **Fra Angelico**, but the same spirit that animates his holy and beautiful paintings runs through the productions of the early Siennese and early Umbrian schools as a whole. Angelico's religious frescoes in the cells of the dormitory at San Marco, Florence, afford us the most perfect example of an art wholly devoted to the purpose of lifting the soul of the beholder on the wings of aspiration. Every figure, every composition, was a warning to leave the scenes of earth, and to join the celestial company around the Risen Christ, whose visionary form he constantly portrays. There is more power, more intensity, in his work than in that of the Sienese and early Umbrian painters, who in purity of soul and in simple piety are his counterparts. To match the religious design of Angelico, we must pass over a generation of artistic advance in technique, when we find in the fully accomplished painting of **Francia** and of **Luini** a devoutness equal to his own, joined with powers of execution to which he could lay no claim. The well-known 'Pietà' by Francia, in the London National Gallery, is a perfect piece of religious art, while the fragments of Luini's frescoes have filled the corridor of the Brera with some of the loveliest shapes of virgin and saint and angel that Christian art has to show.

(*b*) *German and Flemish Schools.*—Turning now from the religious art of Italy to the work of the early German and Flemish schools of the 15th cent., we find the fresh and innocent idyllic design of the early school of Cologne soon beset and overcome by the realism and the ugliness to which northern art has all along been ready to surrender itself. Out of this at the beginning of the 16th cent. **Albrecht Dürer** with difficulty fought his way, and created an art in which deep feeling and philosophical thought triumphed over the characteristic defects of Teutonic design. Many of Dürer's religious pieces, especially those representing the suffering Christ, are profoundly impressive, and were recognized by the Italians of his day as possessing qualities in design superior to those of their own productions. Dürer's finest works, however, such as the picture of the four Apostles at Munich, and the world-famed engravings 'Melancolia' and 'The Knight and Death,' are, like Michelangelo's 'Prophets' in the Sistine chapel, ethically great but not inspired by any sentiment that is distinctly Christian. It is worth notice that though Dürer remained all his life a mediævalist and a faithful son of the old Church, he held strong views about Papal abuses, and expressed the greatest admiration for Luther and some others of the Reforming party. We find proof of this in his writings as well as in some of his paintings. Once he addresses Erasmus as the 'Knight of Christ,' and bids him 'ride on by the side of the Lord Jesus.' There is a reference here, no doubt, to the figure in his own 'Knight and Death.' We find it hard to imagine Erasmus in mail and on a war-horse, and Luther's would have been a better name to invoke! The 'Four Apostles,' in the exaltation of Paul and John over Peter, betrays Lutheran prepossessions. In much of Dürer's work the German infatuation with the weird and terrible interferes with our æsthetic pleasure in its contemplation, but his woodcuts from the Apocalypse, where these qualities were in place, are charged with imaginative power. The pictures of the early Flemish religious painters, on the other hand, though in artistic rank they do not equal the masterpieces of Dürer, perpetuate in some degree the idyllic charm and tenderness of the early Cologne masters, while in the work of **Rogier van der Weyden** and some others there is distinct devotional intent. With regard to the founders of the school, the brothers **van Eyck**, we are in this difficulty: the known pictures of the younger, Jan, are on the whole realistic and secular, but there is a deeper note struck in the great altar-piece in which both brothers collaborated, the 'Adoration of the Lamb' at Ghent; and whether or not this is due to the profounder nature of the elder brother, Hubert, is one of the unsolved problems of modern painting. This school culminates and ends with the work of **Quinten Massys** of Antwerp, who died in 1530, and whose two fine triptychs, in the Museums of Brussels and Antwerp, exhibit the one a charming idyllic feeling, and the other, in the representation of the subject of the 'Pietà,' a dramatic power and pathos that make it a worthy last word of the early religious schools of painting north of the Alps.

Before passing on to the subject of Christian art under Protestantism, a few words may be said as to the later developments of religious painting on the older or pre-Reformation lines. We have seen that such painting in the Italy of the culminating period of the art tended to assume the form known as 'Academic,' in which sacred scenes and personages are represented in a somewhat 'made-up' fashion, and fail to impress us with any sense of reality and power. This form of religious art maintained itself through the 17th and 18th cents., especially, of course, in Catholic countries, but not in these alone. In Spain, though the greatest master of the age, **Velazquez**, rarely exercised his genius on religious themes, painting of an ecclesiastical kind was necessarily much in evidence, and **Murillo** (1618–1682) is a very prolific and, on the whole, sympathetic representative of this form of art, on a somewhat popular plane. In the Catholic Netherlands, **Vandyke**, who is more refined in his characterization than his master **Rubens**, painted some very good religious pictures of the conventional type, while his contemporary **Eustache le Sueur** in France (1617–1655) is one of the best of many artists of the second rank who exercised their talents on the familiar themes. Even in England religious pictures of the kind were painted, in the 17th cent. by **Isaac Fuller**, and in the 18th by **Hogarth**, who covered some very large canvases with religious compositions, the best of which is the 'Pool of Bethesda' on the staircase at St. Bartholomew's Hospital, London.

A somewhat remarkable development of art of a decorative kind was indirectly the result of the Reformation. This is the art of the so-called counter-Reformation largely engineered by the Jesuits. In the Jesuit churches, the most famous of which is the Gesù in Rome, built by Vignola in 1568, there was displayed decoration of the most sumptuous possible kind, embodying a protest against the Puritanism which had obtained a footing in the Church of the Reformation; and this same style in decoration spread to other church interiors of the 17th cent., with a result which visitors to Rome, Ravenna, and other places never cease to deplore.

Anton Springer has well characterized the style as one that 'robbed architecture of its fitting repose, and by the introduction of figures posed in startling attitudes, aroused or convulsed by agency unseen, of curves instead of straight lines, of pillar piled upon pillar, substituted a turbulent unrest. Not,' he says, 'that the style' (called generally 'Baroque') 'was without striking and artistic effect. An undoubted vigour in the disposition of detail, a feeling for vastness and pomp, together with an internal decoration which spared neither colour nor costly material to secure an effect of dazzling splendour: such are the distinguishing attributes of the Baroque style as in Rome it is to be seen on every hand.'

It is interesting to compare the spirit of ecclesiastical decorative art of this artificial kind with that of the sincere, unpretending, though in its way equally elaborate art offered by the mediæval monkish craftsman for the embellishment of his beloved fane. On a superficial view the motives may be held to be the same, but how immeasurable the difference! It is this substratum of ethical interest belonging to the history of the arts that gives this subject its importance to the student of the successive phases of human culture. It is noteworthy how much more is made of the evidence of art in historical and sociological studies on the Continent than among ourselves. The British mind is unfortunately prepossessed with the idea that the arts are merely separable accidents, detachable ornaments of human life, and not, as was really the case in the past, modes of intimate expression in which the ideas of an age or a community found embodiment.

III. *POST-REFORMATION PERIOD.*—It was inevitable that the Reformation should bring about a considerable change in the forms and the character of Christian art. Assuming the least possible alteration, let us see what would necessarily follow from the rejection of the Roman ecclesiastical system. We will suppose that the Protestant continued to recognize, as he recognizes to-day, the value of the element of beauty in human life, and the suitability of art as a form for the expression of religious ideas. The Saints would none the less all but disappear from view, and with them would go their altars and altarpieces, as well as the picturesque and varied stories which had supplied artists for centuries past with unnumbered themes. In some respects the situation of the iconoclastic period would be repeated, and representations, such as that of the crucified Saviour, or the enthroned Madonna, which had attracted something like worship, would be banished at once from the churches. The cessation of any demand for the large scenic paintings of the Last Things may at first sight seem surprising, because in some of the reformed churches the doctrine of heaven or hell became of paramount importance. Wall paintings in churches, however, had become so closely associated with doctrines and rites now repudiated that they were generally abandoned, and with them went the pictures of the Inferno that might otherwise have proved dear to Calvinistic hearts. This limitation of the artist's range of possible subjects would, however, cause the subjects that remained to stand out in greater prominence. The person and life of Christ became of far greater relative importance under Protestantism, which refused to recognize the competing claims of Mary and the Saints. As the Bible was freely perused, the literary treasures of the Old Testament became more familiar possessions, and the prospective artist would in this way find ready for him in the bosom of the Reformed Churches a range of noble subjects of an absorbing religious interest. It must be noticed at the same time that, though sacred altar pieces and mural pictures went out of fashion, a new form of religious art grew up in the Germany of the Reformation period and spread to other lands, in the shape of the engraved plates which were abundant in the earliest printed Protestant Bibles and Testaments and in pious books of other kinds. **Lucas Cranach** illustrated Luther's Bible; and **Holbein**, who in this aspect of his art was a child of the Reformation, has left us classical examples in the 'Icones Historiarum Veteris Testamenti'—a series of Bible illustrations—and plates such as the 'Christ the True Light,' of 1527. This was a very cheap and popular form of art, and made up to some extent for the loss of the monumental works. In all these Protestant designs it would be natural, though not inevitable, for the subjects to be approached from the human side. So much had been made of the mystical element in religion in the older system, that the Reformers, though untouched by rationalism, might be disposed to keep the miraculous in the background.

It follows that under an enlightened Protestant régime there might be as much expenditure in architecture and on decoration as before, and the meeting-house of the Reformed congregation would have just as much right to 'shine like the fields of Paradise' as the monastic fane of four centuries earlier, while representative art possessed in the life of Christ upon earth, and in the doings of the Old Testament worthies, a range of subjects the value of which has just been indicated. The words of Luther are in this connexion very significant, when he said that he wished to see all arts, especially music, in the service of Him who had created and had granted them to men, and repeated the old arguments in favour of pictures as more suitable for the instruction of simple folks than discourses. As a fact, however, the alteration brought about at the Reformation was far greater than we have just assumed. In Switzerland, for instance, in Luther's time pictures were condemned and banished as idolatrous; while in Great Britain, to take another example, the reaction of the Reformation period went so far that under the title 'monuments of superstition' artistic treasures of indescribable beauty and perfect innocence were ruthlessly destroyed. Between the first onslaught upon ecclesiastical property on the part of Henry VIII. and the edicts of Elizabeth that tried to put a stop to further vandalism, the loss to art was incalculable, and from this point of view those years of desolation and waste are among the darkest in our national annals. So richly equipped, however, were our English churches, and so well established had been the pre-Reformation tradition of beauty in the apparatus of worship, that, as in doctrine so here, a compromise was arrived at, and Christian art still recognized the Episcopal churches and cathedrals as its home, where, at any rate, it could dwell in peace till the Gothic revival of the early part of the 19th cent. fostered in it a new growth.

It was among the non-Episcopal sects in England, and especially in Scotland, that religious art fared worst. Like everything else in these churches, it was brought to the test of the letter of Scripture, and those parts of Scripture that were held at the time in special honour had little to say for it. A Biblical justification for art had always existed in the accounts of the Jewish temple and its ritual, and to these the lovers of art in mediæval days had appealed. Now, to the Presbyterian and the Independent, descriptions of temples and altars and priestly vestments and all the apparatus of ritual did not appeal, for all these things they could not away with, while of specially Christian or NT justification of art there was but small trace to be found in the Gospels. Their teaching, however broad it may be, ignores almost completely this side of life, which indeed would not naturally appeal to the Founder of Christianity in the temporal conditions under which His life was passed. His justification of the use made of the 'alabaster cruse of ointment of spikenard very costly' (Mk 14³) is in this respect notable, as it can be worked into the service of artistic theory. Some of the recorded sayings of Christ encourage a feeling for the beauty of natural objects, but the only one in the Synoptic Gospels bearing definitely on art is of rather the opposite character. 'And as he went forth out of the temple, one of his disciples saith unto him, Master, behold, what manner of stones and what manner of buildings! And Jesus said unto him, Seest thou these great buildings? there shall not be left here one stone upon another, which shall not be thrown down' (Mk 13¹). The going forth from the Temple, if the tradition is a genuine one, was past the immense and splendid Hellenistic triple portico of Herod—the finest, Josephus says, in the world—and out under the vast substructures of the Temple area; so that the pride of the disciple in these glorious structures must have been not a little disconcerted at the response. It was thus possible at the Reformation to find Scriptural justification of a negative kind for a starved and narrow view of art and beauty, as well as for one comparatively broad and liberal, and it is interesting to note that the following out of the first view led to the extremes of rigid Puritanism, best to be studied in the Scotland of the 17th and 18th centuries; while on the second was based, as we shall see, in Holland, a phase of religious art that is one of the glories of Protestantism.

1. Narrow view of art.—Edicts for the destruction of works, which the early Reformers, like the Byzantine iconoclasts, stigmatized as 'idolatrous,' were not confined to Great Britain, but were necessary consequences everywhere of the revolt from Rome. How far they were in each land actually carried out in practice depended on many causes. The destruction has been comparatively thorough in Scotland, but it must be remembered that south of the Forth, at any rate, this pulling down and breaking was due quite as much to the constant English ravages as to Scottish iconoclasm. The views of the first Scottish Reformers may be gathered from the so-called *Buke of Discipline* of 1560, where under 'The Thrid Head, tuiching the Abolissing of Idolatrie,' we read as follows:

'As we require Christ Jesus to be trewlie preached, and his holie Sacramentis to be rychtlie ministerit; so can we not cease to requyre Idolatrie, with all monumentis and places of the same, as Abbayis, monkeries, freireis, nunreis, chapellis, chantreis, cathedrall kirkis, channounreis, colledges, uthers then presentlie are paroche Kirkis or Sculis, to be utterlie suppressed in all boundis and places of this Realme. . . . As also that Idolatrie may be removed from the presence of all personis of quhat estait or conditioun that ever thai be, within this Realme. . . .

'By Idolatrie we understand, the Messe, Invocatioun of Sanctis, Adoratioun of Ymagis, and the keping and retenying of the same: and finallie all honoring of God, not conteaned in his holie Word' (*The Works of John Knox*, ed. David Laing, Edinburgh, 1848, ii. 188).

In accordance with the principles thus laid down, we find that, on July 25, 1567, the Lords of the Council, after receiving the abdication of Queen Mary, affirmed certain articles of the Kirk, amongst which was their intention 'to rute out, distroy, and allutirlie subvert all monumentis of ydolatre, and namelie the odious and blasphemous mess' (*Register of the Privy Council of Scotland*, i. 536). That this intention was not at the time fully carried out we may judge from the 'Acts of the General Assembly' under date July 29, 1640, where at a meeting in Aberdeen there was passed an 'Act anent the demolishing of Idolatrous monuments' that is worded as follows:

'Forasmuch as the Assembly is informed that in divers places of this kingdome, and specially in the North parts of the same, many idolatrous monuments, erected and made for religious worship, are yet extant, such as crucifixes, images of Christ, Mary, and saints departed, ordaines the said monuments to be taken down, demolished, and destroyed, and that with all convenient diligence' (*Acts of the General Assembly*, Edinburgh, 1643, p. 44).

It is to be remembered that in Scotland it was not a question merely of the Reformation, but of a long continued and embittered contest against everything that savoured of Popery, and in the course of this a good deal that might well have been saved was suffered to perish. Thus, the Ruthwell Cross was thrown down and broken in 1642.

2. Broad view of art.—It was noticed above that on a broad and liberal Protestantism was based a phase of religious art that is among the glories of Reformed Christianity. The reference is to the Scriptural pictures produced in the Holland of the first half of the 17th cent., especially by Rembrandt and some of his scholars. Holland is the one country that developed a national art as an immediate sequel to its adoption of the principles of the Reformation. Protestant Germany might have done the same, but, owing to wars and the impoverishment of the country, art after the time of Dürer ceased almost to be cultivated, and Dürer's younger contemporary, **Holbein**, left his native country for England, which on her part, by her contented utilization of his services, showed her own indifference to the work she was paying him to do. In Holland, a country both wealthy and energetic, art was national and at the same time Protestant, and in the latter aspect it was incorporate in **Rembrandt.**

A very large number of the drawings, etchings, and pictures by this master are on religious themes, drawn from both the Old and the New Testaments. Many of these, such as the 'Passion' series at Munich, are treated in a cold, almost academic fashion, though by no means on the conventional Italian lines; but, on the other hand, there exists a body of his work on these subjects that is as fresh, as warm, as dramatic in feeling as it is rich and masterly in execution. Rembrandt, whose work in this kind, it must be confessed, stands almost alone, has shown us here how it is possible to treat the person and the acts of Christ in a spirit as far removed from mysticism on the one side as from rationalism on the other, so that His Divine majesty is as convincingly apparent as His homely aspect, His friendliness, His intimate sympathy with human joys and sorrows. The writer may be allowed here to quote a sentence or two from a work of his own on the master.

'It is instructive to take the central figure of the Christian story, and to note the different situations, idyllic, epic, and dramatic, in which Rembrandt has portrayed the figure of Christ. We see with what warmth of human feeling he has invested those scenes in which the Saviour, an infant or a growing youth, makes holy by His presence the simple incidents of family life; how he rises to the height of epic dignity when Christ moves, a mature and heroic form through the acts of His earthly ministry; with how intimate a sympathy he withdraws the veil from the scars of agony, and displays the Man of Sorrows a sublime though pathetically human figure in the tragedy of His Passion; and finally, how he invests the Risen Form with a power and grace that have been made perfect through weakness and suffering, and completes the picture by embodying the eternal love that Christ revealed, in the father of the Prodigal' (*Rembrandt*, London, 1907, p. 279).

There is no need for any extended description of these masterpieces by Rembrandt, which we must remember are as fine in colour or light and shade and in technical execution as they are in the intellectual and ethical qualities of their design. A word may be said on one of the less known pieces, the 'Christ and Mary Magdalen' at Brunswick. We all know the 'Noli me Tangere' by Titian in the London National Gallery. It is a fine picture, but how unconvincing! There is no mystery, no appeal to the imagination. The figures, while sympathetically rendered, are posed for purposes of composition; the scene is full of daylight, and there is a village close by on the hill. In the 'Christ and Mary Magdalen' at Brunswick, in the mysterious garden where the Risen Lord meets with Mary amidst the gloom of rocks and trees, a touch of light on the clouds above heralds the coming morn, but the shadows of night cling about the form of Christ, whose body emits a faint ghostly radiance. His hand plucks away the robe to which the adoring Magdalen would cling; but the tender though reserved inclination of the head towards the woman, and the sympathetic gesture of the other hand, are loving-kindness embodied. We are there in the garden with the pair, and they both live before us. This, we feel, is how they looked and acted. In the Louvre picture of 'Christ at Emmaus,' where He is known in the breaking of bread, an equally imaginative treatment invests the figure with an unearthly charm, that drew from the great French critic Fromentin some of the most eloquent sentences he ever penned:

'Has any one ever yet imagined Him thus, as He sits facing us there and breaks the bread as He broke it on the night of the Last Supper, so pale and so thin, in His pilgrim's robe, with those darkened lips on which suffering has left its traces: with the large soft brown eyes whose full gaze He has directed upwards . . . a living, breathing being, but yet one who has assuredly passed through the gates of death? The attitude of this divine visitant with that intense ardour in a face whose features are hardly to be discerned, and expression is all in the movement of the lips and in the eyes—these traits inspired from what source one knows not, and produced one cannot tell how, are all of value inestimable. No other art has produced the like; no one before Rembrandt, no one after him, has made us understand these things' (*Maîtres d'Autrefois*, Paris, 1890, p. 381).

The homely warmth of feeling in Rembrandt's 'Holy Families,' and in OT or Apocryphal pieces, such as those from the story of Tobit, of which he was especially fond, is just as satisfying in its way as the imaginative power just illustrated. There is also an intellectual side to his religious art, and we have the sense in looking at some of his pieces that he has thought out the subject and consciously arranged it, though this never results in that academic coldness which is the fault of so many accomplished Italian designs. The chief example is the famous etching called the '100 Florin Plate' or 'Christ Healing the Sick.' This is one of Rembrandt's greatest masterpieces, and is well known though not always rightly interpreted. Sick persons, it is true, figure in the plate, but Christ is not healing them. The truth is that there is a great deal more in the piece than the descriptive title suggests. It is really an illustration of Mt 19, and brings together a number of distinct persons and incidents, a unity being secured for the whole by the commanding dignity and beauty of the central figure. The words at the beginning of the chapter, 'and great multitudes followed him; and he healed them there,' are the motive for the introduction on the right of the etching of that wonderful throng of the maimed and feeble and sickly that Rembrandt has rendered with such pathos and intimacy. The next verse, 'and there came unto him Pharisees, tempting him,' accounts for the company of the well-to-do on the left, whose shrewd and cynical faces and expressions of inquiry suggest the insidious queries with which they have come prepared. Christ, however, in the centre is attending to neither group, but is holding out His hand in encouragement to a woman before Him who clasps a child in her arms, while Peter, by His side, is seeking to thrust her away. This is, of course, the 'Suffer the little children, and forbid them not,' of the middle of the chapter; while in the richly clad figure of a youth, who sits musing with his face partly hidden by his hand, we recognize the young man 'that had great possessions.' The justice of the characterization throughout the piece makes it a real commentary on the passages illustrated, and the actual situation is brought before us in the lifelike impressive groups.

It may cause surprise to find that Rembrandt's treatment of these sacred themes is so broad and genial, because the Holland of his day was strongly Calvinistic, and religion wore generally a garb of austerity. Now, we possess a contemporary notice, according to which Rembrandt was a member of the religious sect called Mennonites; and as the best of these Mennonites were on the whole Broad Churchmen of the Arminian persuasion, Rembrandt's upbringing may have given him liberal views on theology which will account for the comprehensive charity which breathes from all his scriptural pieces. His very last picture, a large and solemn canvas at St. Petersburg, represents the 'Return of the Prodigal Son,' and in this moving presentment of the tattered and weary wanderer as he buried his shame-stricken face in the bosom of the father whose compassion fails not, we read the artist's belief in an all-embracing Divine love. The effacement of the personality of the hapless truant has concentrated all the interest of the scene on the father, who presses him to his heart and gazes down on him with infinite pity and tenderness. He is not only the father of the parable, but the Eternal Love incorporate; and Rembrandt's art becomes in the best sense an embodiment of the higher Christian thought.

We may accordingly regard Rembrandt's design as more satisfying to the religious sense of the liberal Protestant than that of any other artist, and with this as our standard may pass on to a brief critical survey of religious art as it has been revived in various experimental but interesting forms nearer our own time.

IV. *MODERN TIMES.* — The last part of the 17th and the whole of the 18th cent. produced practically nothing in this style that was not a mere bloodless simulacrum of the academic art of the Florentine and Roman schools. An exception may be found at the close of the 18th cent. in the work of **William Blake,** who had genius enough in art and literature to have achieved true greatness, had that genius been trained and directed aright. Blake was exceptional, in his art a romanticist before his time, and belonging to the century of Coleridge rather than of Pope. Earlier in the same century, it is worth notice that even Hogarth in his religious pieces did not attempt the homely intimate style in which he might have succeeded, but adopted the conventional types of the Italianizing figure painters of the time. The revived religious art of the 19th cent. is the child of the romantic movement. This was a reaction against the predominant classicism of the latter half of the 18th cent., and took the form partly of a return to nature in which Rousseau and Robert Burns were pioneers, and partly in a revived interest in what was mediæval, which began in Germany and spread to Great Britain and to France. In Germany mediævalism was a natural product, for her traditions of past greatness were rooted in the Middle Ages, and even a classicist like Goethe paid homage to these romantic bygone glories. A curious result in the sphere of religious art of this return to the Middle Ages has made itself seen in our own time in the pictures from the life of Christ by **Eduard von Gebhardt,** in which the costumes and the *mise en scène* are taken from the Germany of the 15th century. What we know in our own country by the name of the 'Gothic Revival'—a movement that led to the restoration of mediæval features in innumerable English churches and to the establishment of something like a cultus of the romantic in art—was at the basis of the very interesting artistic experiment known as pre-Raphaelitism, while the earlier religious painting of the German so-styled 'Nazarenes' was founded rather on the national self-consciousness of the German people firmly braced by the struggle against Napoleon; mediævalism, at any rate, played no part in it, for the Nazarenes lived and worked in Rome. Both these artistic movements, the German and the English, were sincere and earnest, even to the extreme of fanaticism, but the æsthetic result was in neither case wholly satisfactory.

1. Nazarenes. — The name 'Nazarenes' was applied in good-humoured banter to a company of young German painters who in the early years of the 19th cent. settled in Rome in an abandoned monastery, where they sought to re-constitute the life and work of the painters of the earlier religious schools. They were romanticists of the type that surrenders itself to idealism but recognizes no attraction in nature and the things of the real world. Hence their art draws its motives not directly from nature, but at second hand from the works of the older masters. This secured a certain look of style in the compositions; but, on the other hand, the figures lacked individual character, and the colouring was pale, flat, and conventional. One good piece of work the Nazarenes accomplished early in their career, which has laid modern art under an obligation. In 1815 they re-introduced the technique of fresco painting, which had been abandoned since the death of Raphael Mengs in 1779, and with the aid of one of Mengs's old journeymen executed successfully in the true process a series of paintings in a room of the Casa Bartholdi on the Pincian at Rome. These paintings are from the story of Joseph, and have been removed to the National Gallery at Berlin, where they are in a good state of preservation. Cornelius, Overbeck, Schadow, and Veit collaborated, and the works are among the best from an artistic point of view produced by the school. Modern German monumental wall-painting, which has flourished through the century, had here its origin.

Of the Nazarenes, **Friedrich Overbeck** (1789–1869) was the most characteristic figure. A devoted adherent of the Catholic Church, like most of his associates, he was intensely devotional, and his pictures breathe the same spirit of quiet and retiring devoutness that we have come to know in the early schools of Sienna and of Cologne. 'Art is to me,' he wrote once, 'a harp on which I would fain hear always sounding hymns to the praise of the Lord.' The comparative absence from his works of the qualities of colour, light and shade, and handling, which are essential to the beauty of a modern picture, makes it unnecessary from the point of view of this article to consider them further. **Cornelius** (1783–1867) was a far stronger artist than Overbeck, and covered vast wall spaces in Munich and elsewhere with compositions marked by learning and vigour, but lacking in warmth of feeling or æsthetic charm. His great fresco of the mediæval subject of the 'Last Judgment' in the Ludwigskirche at Munich, painted in 1840, may count as his masterpiece.

On the same plane of art as the Nazarenes are a once esteemed painter of religious themes, the Netherlander **Ary Scheffer,** and the accomplished Frenchman **Hippolyte Flandrin,** a pupil of Ingres, who executed beautifully drawn figure compositions on religious themes on the walls of Parisian churches, which are, however, tame in effect and wanting in charm of colour. Of all this set of artists no one had in him so many elements of true greatness as the Aberdeen painter, **William Dyce.** Had he been born in a time and in surroundings favourable to the development of monumental figure painting, he would have been a great artist, for there is in his design an originality and an intimacy of feeling, in his execution a firmness, that strike us at once as exceptional in this phase of art. Born in 1806, he met and was influenced by Overbeck in Italy, and Richard Muther in his *Modern Painting* reckons him 'with the Flandrin-Overbeck family,' though he notes that 'where the Nazarenes produce a pallid, corpse-like effect, a deep and luminous quality of colour delights one in Dyce's pictures. He is finished in grace, and with this grace he combines the pure and quiet simplicity of the Umbrian masters. . . . There is something touching in his madonnas. . . . A dreamy loveliness brings the heavenly figures nearer to us' (iii. 5). The 'St. John leading the Madonna to his Home,' in the Tate Gallery in London, is a good specimen of his art.

2. Pre-Raphaelites. — The religious art of the 19th cent. received a contribution of some value from the English pre-Raphaelites. Shortly before 1850 three or four young artists in London found themselves drawn together by something of the same feeling in art that had actuated the Nazarenes. They revolted against the academic conventions with which the name of Raphael was specially connected, and discerned salvation for art only in a return to the sincerity and simplicity of the 15th century. Unlike the Nazarenes, however, they had a strong feeling for nature, and it was from the first one of their principles that every part of a picture should be painted with the most scrupulous care directly from the living person or the natural object. The title 'Pre-Raphaelite Brotherhood' and the mystic initials 'P.R.B.' which appeared after their signatures on their paintings, were the outward signs of a union which ultimately included seven members, and the fact that two or three were writers explains the fact that the movement was from the first as much literary as purely artistic. The three original members, **Dante Gabriel Rossetti, Holman Hunt,** and **John Everett Millais,** are the only ones who need be mentioned here. Their intense earnestness, combined with their study of the early Italian masters, led them to religious themes, though these were not exclusively their objective. Indeed, they were before all things romanticists, and may be claimed by the Gothic Revival as its spiritual offspring. They were devoted to the poets, and some of the best things they accomplished in art are the illustrations to Tennyson's *Poems* published by Moxon in 1857. In Rossetti this tendency was particularly marked, and he ultimately confined himself as a painter to the romantic field, in the cultivation of which he was followed by **Edward Burne Jones.** This romantic and poetic vein kept their devotion to the facts of nature from falling into mere realism, so that in their pictures we discern a curiously matter-of-fact rendering of accessories, while the whole scene may be a fairyland of a poet's creation.

Of the distinctly religious pictures of the school, the best were some of the earliest. In 1849 and 1850 Rossetti exhibited the quaint but fascinating 'Girlhood of the Virgin Mary,' where the figures are portraits of the painter's nearest relatives, and the 'Ecce Ancilla Domini' which has now happily found a home in the national collection. For *naïveté* of feeling and poetic charm it is one of the loveliest pictures ever painted, and in its transparent sincerity it might have shamed into nothingness the commonplace conventional painting in vogue in the England of the time. The early Millais of 1850, 'The Child Christ in the Workshop of Joseph,' a far more ambitious piece, is perhaps, artistically speaking, the best religious production of the school; for Millais, as his after career showed, was far more highly endowed as a practician than any of his associates. Holman Hunt's universally known 'Light of the World' appeared in 1854, and this artist has maintained throughout his long and honourable artistic career the same religious earnestness, combined with the pre-Raphaelite faithfulness in details. 'In the whole history of art there are no religious pictures in which uncompromising naturalism has made so remarkable an alliance with a pietistic depth of ideas' (Muther, *Modern Painting*, iii. 12).

From the artistic point of view it should perhaps be pointed out that the plan of copying nature in a picture detail by detail does not really secure the truth aimed at, and with the pre-Raphaelites its adoption was due to intellectual rather than to purely artistic considerations. The experiment was of value in its time as a protest against the vague conventional rendering of nature with no true knowledge behind it, which was then the fashion in the English school, and to the non-artistic the principle will always seem attractive because of its ethical sound, but, as Horace says in the *Ars Poetica* (line 31):

'In vitium ducit culpæ fuga, si caret arte,'

and the way to represent nature truthfully in the artistic sense is not to copy bit by bit, but to render the general aspect of things in their true relations of tone and colour. This is the real difficulty of painting, and an impressionist study that secures absolute truth in these relations is at once far more difficult, and far better as art, than the most elaborate rendering of individual details with meticulous exactness. An English painter, possessed of a shrewd wit, tried the pre-Raphaelite method about 1850, but gave it up, saying, 'This cannot be right, it is too easy!' Hence it has come about that many a pre-Raphaelite painter who has carried out this principle of work has been, as Horace goes on to say:

'Infelix operis summa, quia ponere totum | Nesciet.'

Moreover, exact piece-by-piece rendering leads too often to a hardness in delineation that is destructive of pictorial effect, and when this is combined with crude and inharmonious colouring, the result from an æsthetic point of view may be disastrous. At the same time, though pre-Raphaelite pictures vary greatly in their artistic value, they are always to be respected for their earnestness and sincerity, and some of those on Biblical themes will ever remain prominent and justly-honoured representations of an interesting modern phase of Christian art.

3. **Modern experiments.** — One last phase of Christian art remains to be noticed, bringing us quite to our own day. The reference is to certain endeavours to secure convincing verisimilitude in the pictorial representation of Biblical scenes by the abandonment of all the time-worn conventions of academic design, and by the use of local types, costumes, accessories, and setting. This experiment has been tried in various forms, and always with sincerity and devout feeling. So far as these qualities are concerned, the works already noticed of the German **von Gebhardt,** whose 'Last Supper,' painted in 1870, is well known in this country through reproductions, are equal to the best; but his curious convention of a 15th cent. *mise en scène* gives them a position apart. One form which this work has taken is to place the events of the life of Christ in an Oriental setting, carefully elaborated from a study of the Palestine of to-day. The idea was first started earlier in the 19th cent., when the attention of artists was turned for the first time to Oriental subjects. **Horace Vernet,** on his Eastern tour in 1840, had noticed that the scenes of the Bible stories were laid in the East, and should be represented in Oriental settings. This was actually attempted by **Holman Hunt,** who painted religious pictures in Jerusalem and by the shore of the Dead Sea. Some German artists sought the same end by the adoption for the NT characters of the types of modern scions of the Hebrew race; but it has been reserved for a French and a Scottish painter of our own time to work the idea out with completeness. Both **James Tissot,** a French artist known first for his pictures of modern fashionable life, and **William Hole,** of the Royal Scottish Academy, conceived the idea of portraying the various incidents of the earthly ministry of Christ as they might happen in the Palestine of to-day. The lighting and colour of the landscapes, the forms of nature and of buildings, the attitudes of the figures and their costumes, the furniture, the accessories, are all drawn from actual life, as it can be studied to-day on the Mount of Olives, by the Sea of Tiberias, or at Bethany. The resulting pictures, made accessible by popular reproductions, are full of interest, and at every turn furnish some new suggestion that makes us realize and interpret better the familiar scenes. They are, however, in both cases comparatively small water colours and do not aim at greatness of effect. Indeed, the elaboration of the interesting detail often interferes with the general impression of a scene in its ethical or religious aspects. They are, nevertheless, valuable contributions to the religious art of our day.

An experiment in quite another direction has been made, also in our own day, by one or two German artists, of whom the most important is **Fritz von Uhde.** Von Uhde is probably the best painter of all those who have given themselves in this latest epoch to Scriptural themes, and his work has more of the quality we have learned to admire in Rembrandt than that of any of the other moderns. There is no attempt here at archæological correctness, and the idea of an Oriental setting never crosses the artist's mind. On the contrary, he takes the actual scenes in town or village or country of the Germany of his own day, and imagines Christ introduced into them, and dealing with those He meets as He dealt with His fellow-countrymen in Palestine. In 'The Sermon on the Mount' Christ is seated on a modern wooden bench in the fields, and is discoursing to a group of German peasant women and children, on the outskirts of which hang the men who are going home from their work, with their tools over their shoulders. 'Suffer little children to come unto me,' at Leipzig, shows us the interior of a modern schoolroom in a small town, where the master stands in the background, while a group of children of all ages are gathered somewhat timidly near the chair on which a stranger, who has just entered, has taken his seat. This stranger is Christ, and we are made to see that He is gradually drawing the little ones to Himself by the magnetism of His personality. In other pieces we see Christ entering a peasant home, or sitting at meat with His friends, as at the Last Supper; or, again, with a frank acceptance of the mystical, the artist has given us the scenes of the Annunciation or the Nativity. The pictures are always serious, devout, and at the same time warm with human feeling, and often touched with idyllic charm. Their quality as works of art gives them an equally high place with that which they claim as achievements in religious design.

The name of Rembrandt was mentioned above in connexion with these homely renderings of sacred scenes. Rembrandt, like von Uhde, in the best of his pictures took the setting from his own surroundings, though he indulges not seldom in Oriental vestments and in Jewish types. These surroundings are, however, in the first place, very much generalized, so that they might almost do for any age and country; and, in the second place, they are as unfamiliar in the eyes of 20th cent. Britons as if they were genuine Oriental transcripts. Hence the setting of Rembrandt's pieces takes them to that distance from us which is necessary in order to let the imagination have free play. In the paintings of our own time, on the other hand, both the Oriental backgrounds and the modern ones are too real and too familiar, and the appearance against them of Christ and the Apostles seems forced and almost theatrical. If we recognize who the sacred personages are, they do not appear to live in these surroundings, but to have come in in a disguise, and we half expect their interlocutors to be finding them out. On the other hand, if we accept them as modern Orientals or modern Europeans, we cannot readily realize their unique character and greatness. They have been brought down too effectively from the ideal to the actual sphere.

Summary.—In the foregoing an attempt has been made to describe and to analyze, from the points of view indicated at the beginning of this article, the chief phases of religious art as they have manifested themselves through the Christian centuries. There have been two sides to the activity of Christian artists, each of which may here suitably receive a final word.

(1) On the one hand, their activity has been essentially *decorative*, and their spirit has been that of the monkish craftsman of the 11th, the Gothic mason and carver of the 13th centuries; all they could make or do they were zealous to offer on the altar of Christian service. Theirs was the gift of beauty to the Creator of all beauty—a grateful rendering back of the boon so lavishly bestowed, the gift of skill and care to the Lord of the inventive brain and cunning hand. How far, we may ask, can we in these modern days enter into the spirit of those mediæval craftsmen, and turn any artistic gifts we may possess to this high service? Unlike the men of old, we have in these days almost to justify the bare existence of the cult of beauty and of art, for these are not a natural and necessary part of our lives. We have seen how the practice of the arts in early Christian and monastic surroundings followed inevitably from the fact that life without this element of art was in those days impossible. With us it is something extra, and is as a consequence challenged to give an account of itself. That idea of an opposition between the life of art and the practical life of service to one's fellows, which underlies Tennyson's 'Palace of Art,' is not justified by the facts of the world. It is perfectly possible, as we can learn by looking around us, to combine the practical with the contemplative life, and to exercise the æsthetic faculties without any withdrawal from the sphere of the actual. It is true that there are those who do so withdraw themselves, but it does not follow that they are tempted away by the allurements of the imagination. It may very well be that they are morbid and self-absorbed, and if a field of activity did not offer itself in the æsthetic sphere, their life might decline to a much lower level. The pleasures of art are, at any rate, innocent, and if they do not necessarily ennoble the character, they at least refine the taste.

We saw that the mediæval artist-monk exalted the practice of the crafts that produce beautiful things as not only a function of human nature but a law of the universe at large. There is a narrow religiosity that is afraid of a human nature so amply endowed, and would confine its activity within much closer limits. In the churches of to-day, however, this timid creed is already an anachronism, and most of those which have Puritan traditions at their back accept to-day the broader view to which, at any rate, the student of the history of Christian art must feel himself forced. And if this energy of art is not only wholesome, but even in a sense enjoined, in what can it be more fittingly expended than in that service to which we have seen it devoted through the centuries? The time is now past when the square barn-like meeting-house, the bare walls, the homely fittings, could satisfy the cultured worshipper.

It is true, and must never be forgotten, that the outward show is as a mere nothing to the 'truth in the inward parts,' which is demanded as much from churches and congregations as from individuals; and if worship were less sincere in a beautiful and richly adorned fane than in a simple room, it is the art that would have to be sacrificed. It is true also that in parts of our own country a sacred tradition of unselfish piety, of heroic endurance, clings to these whitewashed walls that for generations past have looked down on the defenders of a creed for which they were ready at any moment to give up their possessions or their lives. The Church at large could ill spare the Puritan spirit, and must strive to retain what is best in this, while contesting some of its negations. The introduction of instrumental music into the act of worship, and of the element of art and beauty into its material apparatus and its home, is in principle conceded almost everywhere in Christendom, and there is every reason why the mediæval tradition should be revived, and these things not merely accepted as a fashion, but embraced with the godly joy and pride of the older days.

(2) On the other hand, the activity of Christian artists has been exercised not merely on the

creation of what is beautiful, but on representations of sacred scenes and personages, or symbolic shows that had a *didactic* purpose. This work, as we have seen, has taken several different forms. We may distinguish here: (*a*) the liturgical, doctrinal, or allusive composition, which began, as we saw, in the catacombs, and flourished greatly, in the form especially of the pictures of the Last Things, in the later mediæval period; (*b*) the devotional picture, represented centrally in the work of Fra Angelico, in which the specially Christian virtues of humility, devotedness, self-abandonment, are brought to view and their practice inculcated; (*c*) the historical representation from the life of Christ or of OT or NT worthies—a form of art that we have come across in many shapes, and in which at one time the mystical, at another the human, element is most apparent; and (*d*) the great work of art in which a supreme master like Michelangelo has created types that are profoundly ethical, though not in the distinctive sense Christian.

How is each of these forms of religious art related to the Christian thought of enlightened Protestantism?

(*a*) The first kind of picture has ceased for Protestants to have any didactic or specially religious significance, and is regarded rather from the intellectual point of view as an embodiment of poetic thought. The designs of William Blake are of this kind, and a good modern instance may be found in the allusive symbolical designs which, with charming decorative feeling, Mrs. Traquair has executed in the 'Song School' of St. Mary's Episcopal Cathedral and the Catholic Apostolic Church in Edinburgh, as well as in other buildings. Such works belong more to the domain of poetry and mysticism than to that of religion in the strict sense of the term. They answer to a special phase of artistic feeling both in the creator of them and in the spectator, and, in fact, they repel some sincere lovers of art just as strongly as they attract others. So long as there are artists and lovers of art, the temperament of some of these will turn them in the direction of works of the kind. This phase of religious art is illustrated also by some of the productions of G. F. Watts, an artist of genius who was meant to be a great painter, but was drawn aside from the direct course by the copiousness and insistence of his intellectual ideas.

(*b*) The time will never come when we shall cease to take delight in the purity and devoutness of the devotional pictures of the early schools of religious art in Germany and in Italy. In so far as they express the specially Christian temper of humility and dependence, and reveal to us innocence and love and the spirit of service embodied in the Virgin mother, in saint, and in angel, they will always have a message for those religiously susceptible. The harsh theological words 'Hagiology,' 'Mariolatry,' and the like need not disturb our contemplative enjoyment of these simple and sincere expressions of a faith which in the great essentials was the same as our own. The works are, at the same time, removed into the historical region by the fact that the whole religious *milieu* which conditioned them at their forthcoming is so different from ours. We regard them with interest and affection, but recognize them as not belonging to our own time or our own range of religious ideas.

(*c*) The historical treatment of the life of Christ or of the scenes of the OT is a matter that concerns us in these days and in Protestant surroundings far more nearly. It corresponds with the modern interest in the facts of the past, and with the (partly rationalistic) tendency to emphasize the human side of Christianity. Notice has been taken in what has gone before of the many attempts which have been made in art, throughout post-Reformation times, to bring home with convincing force to the spectator the personality, and the significance of the acts, of Christ. The difficulty has always been, on the one hand, to avoid what is mystical, with all the other conventions of the professed religious schools; and, on the other, to prevent such a modernizing of the *mise en scène* as may destroy the air of remoteness from the ordinary world and of ethical supremacy, which should belong to the person of the protagonist. Rembrandt, as we have seen, has succeeded here where many have failed; and when, the whole body of his work on religious themes is placed in accessible form before the public, as has been proposed, he will probably be recognized by all as the greatest religious artist of whom the history of painting bears record.

(*d*) The impression of the Sublime, when conveyed either by the appearances of nature or by those of art, is always in one sense a religious impression, for it implies a chastening, and, in the Aristotelian sense, a purifying, of the individual emotions by the recognition of what is transcendently great. This greatness is not hostile or terrifying, for the æsthetic impression of the Sublime is destroyed when the being is shaken or cowed through fear, but it represents, as it were, a challenge, to which we respond by bracing up the powers, and by measuring ourselves with it in the strength of free intelligence and in a certain confidence that does not preclude humility. So the human spirit, in the contemplation of the Divine, is not crushed, but raised and strengthened. Now, of all the functions that the arts of form can exercise for the higher service of man, none is greater than that of presenting human nature before us in aspects of such grandeur that we feel in a measure brought into contact with the Divine. The ordinary levels of human greatness are transcended by these exceptional creations of art, and our spirit is uplifted in response. The impression thus produced is religious, but it is quite apart from any particular creed. It takes us into a region where all creeds are merged in the one all-embracing conception of the Godhead, supreme in goodness as in power. It follows from this that all art which rises to this ethical level is religious art, whatever the creed of its creator; and from this point of view the masterworks of the Hellenic sculptor may claim a position by the side of the designs of a Michelangelo, or of any other creative artist of the Christian period. The impressiveness of a great work of art depends largely on the simplicity as well as the force of its message, and it is not by inculcating any special doctrines of religion but by raising the whole being into communion with the highest that art may best serve the spiritual needs of mankind.

LITERATURE.—For the whole subject up to the end of the mediæval period, the standard work is Schnaase, *Geschichte der bildenden Künste*[2], Düsseldorf, 1866, etc. See also Woltmann, *History of Painting*, Eng. tr., London, 1880, vol. i. Baum-Geyer, *Kirchengeschichte für das evangelische Haus*[3], Munich, 1902 (illustrated), gives a very good view of the bearing of the phenomena of art on the life of the Church at different periods. The following are more special works: for Early Christian Art, H. Leclercq, *Manuel d'archéologie chrétienne*, Paris, 1907; for monastic, Theophilus, *Schedula Diversarum Artium*, ed. Ilg, Vienna, 1874; for Gothic, Gonse, *L'Art gothique*, Paris, 1891; Mâle, *L'Art religieux du xiiie siècle en France*, Paris, 1902; for Italian, Venturi, *Storia dell' arte italiana*, Milan, 1901, etc.; for Flemish, Crowe and Cavalcaselle, *Early Flemish Painters*, London, 1872; for the engraved work of the Reformation period, Woltmann, *Holbein und seine Zeit*[2], Leipzig, 1874; for Rembrandt, Baldwin Brown, *Rembrandt: a Study of his Life and Work*, London, 1907; for modern developments generally, Muther, *History of Modern Painting*, Eng. tr., 2nd ed., 4 vols., London, 1907, with full bibliographies of the various artists and schools.

G. BALDWIN BROWN.

ART IN MANUSCRIPTS (Christian).* — There is no form of Christian pictorial art that has come down to us from the Middle Ages in such abundance, in such variety, and in such a genuine and unaltered condition, as the art of miniature-painting for the illustration and decoration of manuscripts. Isolated examples dating from the 4th cent. to the 8th may be found scattered through the great libraries of Europe, while others from the 9th cent. onwards exist in considerable numbers, not only in public libraries but in many private collections—and this in spite of the enormous destruction that has taken place through their being little cared for, or liturgically out of date, or the objects of fanatical hatred. There is no doubt that the manuscripts thus destroyed must be numbered by hundreds of thousands. At the same time, it must not be concluded that the majority of these, or even a large percentage, were as attractively written and illustrated as the precious volumes exposed in our museums. A glance at the contents of any considerable mediæval library, like those of Hereford Cathedral and some of the Colleges of Oxford and Cambridge, shows us how commonplace and dull and full of tiresome contractions was the everyday scholar's book, and that in nine cases out of ten the loss of them would not be a matter for artistic regret. The richly painted manuscripts on the whitest vellum were done either as furniture for lectern and altar, in keeping with the other splendours and adornments of a great church, or for the use of wealthy laymen and ecclesiastics, who sometimes read them as little as a modern student reads the *éditions de luxe* that he buys of poems that he has learned to love in a homely setting. St. Jerome, in his preface to Job, makes light of such possessions. 'Let those who care for them,' he says, 'own books that are old, or written with gold and silver on purple skins. All I need is a good text.' This sentence shows that the spirit of the fastidious book-lover was already abroad in the 4th century. It is perhaps a matter for congratulation that not every one had so austere a taste as St. Jerome.

The earliest examples of painted books that have survived in Europe are two Vergils of the 3rd or 4th cent. in the Vatican Library; but these do not come within the scope of the present article, which deals only with this branch of art in relation to Christianity. As might be expected, nearly all the earliest Christian manuscripts that exist are either Bibles or portions of Bibles, beginning with the Vienna Genesis of the 5th cent., which contains eighty-eight miniatures, and leading to the Ashburnham Pentateuch, written at Tours in the 7th cent. and adorned with nineteen large pictures. This is now in the Bibliothèque Nationale at Paris. Of the same century is the famous copy of the Gospels known as the *Book of Kells* at Trinity College, Dublin. This book, which is at once the earliest and the finest of the Celtic manuscripts, was written by a scribe or scribes of the utmost accomplishment, and ornamented with initials and other larger decorations of miraculously interwoven lines. The Irish decorators, however, while gifted with a sureness of hand that is almost beyond belief, were totally lacking in the higher qualities of imagination, and when confronted with a subject like the Crucifixion, showed as lamentable an inability as the veriest savage to draw and compose the human figure. Next after the Book of Kells the best-known example of this style is the *Lindisfarne Gospels* at the British Museum (fig. 1, p. 890), which, though not executed in Ireland, belongs to the same Celtic tradition and to approximately the same date. All subsequent examples, which do not owe a new development to external influences, show a falling off from this high standard. There was, in fact, in the system of the Celtic draughtsmen no human element or element of growth, and when once they had achieved the mathematically perfect, only decadence and repetition lay before them. Nevertheless, their consummate skill in ornamental design gives them a unique place in the history of book decoration, and was not without some effect on later schools in other countries, though always in subordination to the more emotional impulses derived from Rome and Constantinople.

Pictorially the Roman school, best exhibited in the paintings of the Catacombs, bequeathed but little that we can admire to the book-decorators of the Middle Ages, though as late as the 10th cent. books were illustrated with pictures, usually dead both in colour and expression, that differed scarcely at all from their classical prototypes. The Byzantine pictures in copies of the Greek Gospels and Lives of Saints written at Constantinople, full of Oriental blendings of gold and brilliant colour, and with a seriousness of intention quite absent from most of the classical figure-work, had a far wider and more vivifying influence on the art of the West. Under Roman and Byzantine influences, either separate or combined, a series of sumptuous books, usually copies of the Latin Gospels, and some of them written entirely in letters of gold, were produced on the Continent between the 8th and 12th centuries. By the latter century, Byzantine art, having reached an academical stage which allowed of no further evolution, was, as it were, frozen and crystallized into forms which in Russia survive unaltered to the present day.

Meanwhile, in England, and especially at Winchester, a notable school of book-decoration had arisen. The most famous example of this school is a *Benedictional* belonging to the Duke of Devonshire, which was written at Winchester for Bishop Æthelwold between the years 963 and 984. A similar *Benedictional*, written a few years later for Archbishop Robert of Jumièges, is now in the public library at Rouen. The British Museum is rich in productions of this school, beginning with *King Edgar's Charter of Hyde Abbey* (fig. 2, p. 890), written entirely in gold in 966 and enriched with a beautiful frontispiece, in which the figures are drawn with much animation and clad in the fluttering draperies characteristic of the English miniaturists of the 10th and 11th centuries.

During these centuries and for some time longer, it is not too much to say that English book-illustration was the finest in Europe. Until the end of the 13th cent. Italian pictorial art was much less inventive and energetic than that of England and France, while Germany was likewise under a weight of enervative Byzantine tradition, which seems to have prevented its producing more than a trifling number of books of notable merit between the 12th cent. and the time of the invention of printing. In the monasteries of Flanders, Hainault, and Artois, many stately books were written and illuminated, but in the reign of St. Louis the fame of the University of Paris attracted scholars and artists from all Christendom, who thenceforth made Paris the intellectual centre of Europe. In their train came a body of writers and illuminators, independent of the monasteries, who shook off the Byzantine fetters before Giotto and Cimabue were born, and produced work of an extraordinary and almost feminine refinement of execution, which is no less attractive than the manly vigour which is more especially English (fig. 3, p. 891). For a while the two countries ran an even race, but by the middle of the 14th cent. the French illuminators had gone far beyond their English rivals, and in the second half of the 15th

* ART IN MSS (Jew.) see p. 872ª.

cent. English patrons were so ill-served by their countrymen that they had to send to Bruges and Paris for their painted prayer-books and romances.

To the Italian scribes of the 15th cent. belongs the distinction of having discarded the Gothic or black letter, which by that time had reached a cramped and ugly stage, in favour of the more rounded and legible forms of the 11th and 12th cents., *littera antiqua* as it was called when re-introduced, 'Roman letter' as we now call it (figs. 4, 5, pp. 891, 892). This revival was soon seen to be a reasonable one, and was adopted in all literary countries except Germany, which is only now coming into line with her Western neighbours. It was under the influence of the Renaissance that the finest illuminated books were produced in Italy. These were largely copies of the Latin classics; but many exquisite prayer-books were written, especially in Florence, Naples, Ferrara, and Venice, for members of the great families. Of Spanish illuminated books not many have survived, and these usually owe nearly everything to artistic influences from Naples or Bruges. In the latter city enormous quantities of dainty prayer-books were manufactured towards the end of the 15th century. The chief features of these books are the use of sprays of natural flowers and foliage in the borders, and the delicacy of the landscape backgrounds to the pictures. Dutch books are remarkable at once for great dexterity of execution and for a bluntness of conception which prevents their ever being in the first rank as works of art.

And now as to the types of manuscripts that were most frequently illustrated. With few and mostly fragmentary exceptions, all liturgical books earlier than the 13th cent. have perished, having been worn out, or cast aside on account of changes of fashion and of textual arrangement. It is certain that none of them were habitually so richly decorated as the early copies of the Gospels already referred to. These were always adorned with four frontispieces, usually representing the Evangelists in the act of writing, opposite the four opening pages of the Gospels, on which the text was written in large ornamental letters within an elaborate border. The principal liturgical books of a later date, of which there are many illuminated examples, are Pontificals, Missals, Breviaries, Graduals, and Antiphoners. The great choir-books, such as are shown in the Convent of St. Mark at Florence and in the Duomo of Siena, have survived in quantities in Italy and Spain, where they may still be seen in use. These often contain initials painted by artists of note, but they are for the most part not earlier than the 15th century. Choir-books of Northern origin, especially those of the fine period, are exceedingly rare. The best that exists is an Antiphoner in three volumes written in 1290 for the nuns of the Cistercian Abbey of Beaupré near Grammont (fig. 6, p. 892). This formerly belonged to John Ruskin, and is now (1908) in the collection of Mr. Yates Thompson.

The Vulgate Bibles that have survived from the 12th cent. are usually large folios in two or three volumes, with historiated initials at the beginning of each book, and decorative initials to the numerous prologues. One of the finest examples, a book of surpassing beauty, is in the library of Winchester Cathedral. In the 13th cent. the size of Bibles was reduced, and they were written in enormous numbers and with astonishing skill in France, England, and Italy (fig. 7, p. 893). The entire Bible, including the Apocrypha and perhaps a hundred and fifty painted initials, was often on so small a scale and on vellum of such astonishing thinness as to fit comfortably into the pouch or pocket of the Dominican and other itinerant preachers of the day. So great was the output at this time, that it seems almost to have sufficed until the invention of printing, as Bibles written in the 14th and 15th cents. are comparatively rare. Besides plain texts, portions of the Bible with extensive marginal commentaries were often finely written and illuminated for purposes of monastic study; and in England especially there were produced in the 13th cent. a number of splendidly illustrated copies of the Apocalypse, either in Latin or in French, and usually with an Exposition taken from the writings of Berengaudus. It is easy to see how the strange visions of St. John kindled the imaginations of the creative artists of this time, and with what zest they sought to interpret them (fig. 8, p. 893). In France, at the same period, a type of sumptuous picture-book was evolved, known as the *Bible moralisée*, in which the text is altogether subordinate to the almost countless illustrations. Two copies are in the Imperial Library at Vienna, while a third is divided between the Bodleian Library, the Bibliothèque Nationale, and the British Museum (fig. 9, p. 894).

From an early period the chief book of private devotion was the Psalter. In the 12th and 13th cents. every rich and devout layman seems to have possessed his own copy of the Psalms, to which were invariably added certain Canticles, the Athanasian Creed, the Litany, and a small number of Collects, sometimes followed by the Office of the Dead. It was on these books that the miniaturists, in what was certainly the culminating period of their art, lavished their utmost skill. To the more elaborate copies it was usual to prefix a series of illustrations of the Old Testament, from the creation of the world to the coronation of Solomon, and of the New Testament from the Annunciation to the Last Judgment, which series varied in length according to the wishes and purse of the individual who gave the commission; while the initials of certain Psalms—in early Psalters only Psalms 1, 51, and 101, marking the three divisions into fifty Psalms, and in later Psalters also Psalms 26, 38, 52, 68, 80, and 97, being (with Psalm 1) the first Psalms of the Office of Matins on the seven days of the week, and Psalm 109, being the first of Sunday Vespers—are invariably larger than the rest, and usually historiated with a more or less fixed sequence of subjects. Early in the 14th cent. Psalters of great size and magnificence were written in East Anglia. Among these must be named the Psalter of Robert of Ormesby, monk of Norwich (fig. 10, p. 895), now in the Bodleian Library, and two superb Psalters, both connected with Gorleston, near Yarmouth, one in the Public Library at Douai, and one in the library of Mr. Dyson Perrins.

As early as the 11th cent. certain private offices, the most important being the Hours of the Virgin, the Hours of the Trinity, and the Hours of the Passion, were added to a few Psalters. Later, these accretions came to be written separately, probably in the first instance for the use of women. Their portability and general convenience in this detached form led to their being adopted in place of the Psalter as the devotional book of the literate layfolk; and although there are but few separate Books of Hours of the 13th cent., and not many of the 14th cent., they were produced in enormous numbers in the 15th cent., and copiously illustrated with pictures which in the main illustrate the text (fig. 11, p. 894), but not seldom seem to have been calculated to withdraw the thoughts of the owner from the contemplation of heavenly things. The popularity of these painted prayer-books, of which the greatest number were written in Bruges, Paris, and Florence, was so great that they continued to be produced until long after the invention of printing.

SYDNEY C. COCKERELL.

ART (Egyptian).—The religious aspect of art in Egypt includes almost all that is known of it. The earliest sculptures are tombstones and tables of offerings for the benefit of a deceased person; the earliest statuary is of figures in which the soul of the deceased might reside, made as lifelike as possible, in order to give him satisfaction; the figures of servants with offerings, or of serfs to cultivate the ground, were for service in the next world; the whole of the tomb sculptures, paintings, and furniture—carved coffins, canopic jars, tablets, and all else—resulted from the religious theories of the future life. The buildings that remain to us are nearly all temples; the colossi which stand in them were habitations for the many *ka*-souls of the king; and even the battle scenes on the walls are all part of the display of religious fervour, and culminate in the triumphal processions of captives dedicated to the god, or led by the god as his appanage to be entrusted to the king's administration. The civil life of the lay Egyptian has almost vanished, the palaces and towns are nearly all below the plain of Nile mud; and it is only the sepulchral and religious remains that—being placed on the desert—have thus been preserved to us. Here we must notice only the main principles and examples of religious ceremonies. The page of examples given (p. 896) will illustrate the more important points.

1. Symbolism.—This begins with the rise of the art, as seen on the slate palettes. The various tribes engaged in the conquest of the country are designated by their emblems, the hawk, lion, scorpion, jackal, or pelican. The actions of the tribe are represented by the animal holding a pick and digging through the walls of a town, or by a human arm projecting from the standard on which the animal is, and clutching a cord or grasping a bound captive. The king is represented as a strong bull—as he is called in later times—trampling down his enemies; or the figure of a fish, used to write the name of a king, has two arms grasping a stick to smite his enemies; or the royal hawk has a hand which holds a cord put through the lip of the captive. In these instances it is seen how early symbolism was established as an elaborate means of historic expression. It is not surprising that in the subsequent times it should be commonly used. The kings are shown as being conducted by the gods, who also 'teach their hands to war and their fingers to fight,' standing behind the king and holding his arm in drawing the arrow; the gods place the crown on the king's head, and pour purifying water or blessings over him (see figure of Ramessu IV.); the goddess Hat-hor, as a woman or as a cow, is shown suckling the young king; and Setkhet-abui, the goddess of literature, writes the king's name on the leaves of the Persea tree. The limits between symbolism and dogma pass the critical stage altogether in the Tombs of the Kings, and a state is reached in the other world in which there is no distinction possible.

Special emblems of ideas became so common that they were used almost mechanically, like the cross in Europe. The sun and wings are noticed under ARCHITECTURE (Egyptian), 'Decoration.' And groups of hieroglyphs, such as the *ankh* for life, the *uas* for power, the *zad* for stability, the girdle tie of Isis, and other emblems, were carved as fretworks to stiffen furniture or form a trellis to windows.

2. Divine forms.—The compound theology of sacred animals and deities resulted in a variety of strange combinations. The animal element is always the head, placed upon a human body for a deity; a human head upon an animal body is used only for a sphinx, emblem of a king, and for the *ba*-bird, emblem of a soul. The combination of animal heads on human bodies is found in the second dynasty (Set, on seals of Perabsen) and the fourth dynasty (Thoth, on scene of Khufu); and it became very usual in later times. The combination is skilfully arranged, so that it scarcely seems monstrous; see the scene given (p. 896) of Horus and Thoth, where the short neck of the hawk fits directly on to the human shoulders, while the long neck of the ibis is backed by an immense wig, which after all has no possible support. Yet the effect is far better than could have been expected from such a difficult combination. The forms best known are the ram-headed Khnumu and Hershefi, lion-headed Sekhmet, cat-headed Bastet, jackal-headed Anubis, crocodile-headed Sebek, ibis-headed Thoth, and hawk-headed Horus and Mentu. Besides these, there were many compounded divinities in Ptolemaic and Roman times, formed of a deity and three or four animal parts; usually it is Ptah-Sokar who is thus elaborated. These combinations have none of the convincing dignity of the early animal-headed gods.

3. Dress.—The gods are usually clad in the oldest form of close-fitting waist-cloth; it is always older forms of dress that are thought appropriate for religious or artistic purposes, and in Babylonia the oldest figures of worshippers are entirely nude. The gods never wear the projecting peaked waistcloth common in the Old and Middle Kingdoms. Another primitive piece of costume was the animal's tail, hung at the back from the belt. This is shown as a bushy tail, like a fox's, on the archaic hunters, carved on a slate palette. It appears on all kings from the first dynasty onward (see the figure of Ramessu IV. [fig. 2, p. 896], and the kneeling Hatshepsut, where it is brought forward). And it gradually becomes almost universal for gods after the early ages. Here it can be seen on the figures of Horus and Thoth, in the long form, and thinner than usual.

The principal religious dress was the leopard skin, as on the priest in the scene of sacrifice (fig. 1, p. 896). It was worn from before the first dynasty (Narmer), and is seen not only on scenes, but also on statues in the eighteenth dynasty. It is shown on the priests when seated, or standing giving directions, or making offerings; it might be worn over a short kilt or over a long muslin dress.

4. Ceremonies.—The four chief ceremonies selected for illustration (p. 896) are Sacrifice, Offering, Laying on of Hands, and Purification.

(*a*) *Sacrifice*, as among the Semites, was the ceremonial killing of an animal for food; but there is no trace of the burning of the fat, or of the other form of whole burnt-sacrifice. In the early sculptured tombs the sons of the deceased are shown as trapping the birds, and sacrificing the ox, for the festival in their father's honour. It is rare to find representations of sacrifice later, such as this example of the nineteenth dynasty. Burnt-sacrifice was a foreign importation, and is only known in picture at Tell el-Amarna (eighteenth dynasty), and in description at the Ramesseum (twentieth dynasty).

(*b*) *Offering* is the most usual religious subject. The offerings are heaped together on a mat, a slab on the ground, or a pillar-table; in this case a mat is represented, bound with thread at the middle and the two ends, a form which originates in the third dynasty or earlier. Upon the mat is a layer of round thin cakes, much like the modern flap bread, with two circles of seeds stuck in each. A layer of joints of meat (?) follows; then three wild ducks; above, a row of gazelle haunches, upon which are three plucked geese. The whole is covered with a bundle of lotus flowers and a bunch of grapes. The queen is pouring out a drink-offering from a small spouted vase in the right hand. Such drink-offerings were of a great variety of wines and beers, as also milk, and water. In her left hand she holds an incense-burner. The Egyptian never burnt incense on an altar, but always in a metal censer held in the hand. It was a long metal rod, with a hand holding a cup for the burning incense at one end, and a hawk's head at the other end; in the middle of the length was a pan or box in which the pellets of incense were kept ready for burning. The heat requisite to light it was obtained by using a hot saucer of pottery placed in the cup, on which the resin fused. When the incense was burnt, the saucer was removed and thrown away, and thus no cleaning was required for the metal cup.

(*c*) *Laying on of hands* was represented as being done by the gods, in order to impart the *Sa*. This was a divine essence which the gods drank from the heavenly 'lake of the Sa,' and which the earthly images of the gods could impart to beings and to priests who knelt before them. The benefit was not ceaseless, but required renewal from time to time. The same form of laying on of hands was used, as in our illustration, for conferring the kingship; the inscription reads, 'giving of the kingship of both banks of the river, the complete office, to his daughter, Maat-ka-ra' (Hatshepsut).

(*d*) *Purification* was a very important idea to the Egyptian. A whole class of priests were devoted to the purification of places and things; and it was always represented by a stream poured out. Personal cleanliness was strictly observed by the priests; and the purifying of the king was performed symbolically by the gods, as shown on p. 896. Each god holds a vase from which he pours out a stream over the king. It is stated that Ramessu 'is purified with life and power.'

5. **Furniture.**—The main object in a temple was the sacred boat of the god, one of the best examples of which is shown on p. 896. The boat was a model intended to be carried on the shoulders of the priests; it rested, therefore, on two long poles, and when stationary was placed upon a square stand, so as to allow of the priests taking their station beneath the poles (see ARCHITECTURE [Egyptian], § 5, where the boat and shrine are described). This boat was probably made of wood, plated over with sheets of electrum or gold. The extent to which gold was used is hardly credible to us, who see only an excessively thin film used for gilding. Even in the 11th cent. the Countess of Sicily had the mast of her ship covered with pure gold; and the Egyptian often describes large objects as covered with gold, which was usually of considerable thickness. The reliefs were usually worked in hard stucco and then thickly gilded and burnished. The art of high burnishing upon a stucco base was kept up till Roman times. The sets of vases for the purification ceremonies and further libations of wine were kept on wooden stands, as shown below the boat. At the side of them is a stand with water jars, covered with lotus flowers, and with bunches of grapes placed below it. On another stand at the extreme left is a figure of the king kneeling, offering a large *ankh*, or sign of life; this is crowned with flowers, and has convolvulus and vine growing up beneath it. Another stand at the extreme right has a figure of the king offering a large bouquet of flowers. A main part of the religious art was spent on these statuettes of the king making a great variety of offerings. Unhappily all this wealth of figures has perished, and only a few fragments remain to give reality to the innumerable pictures of the temple riches shown upon the walls.

W. M. FLINDERS PETRIE.

ART AND ARCHITECTURE (Etruscan and Early Italic).—One can hardly speak of Italic art in connexion with the rude products of the Stone Age, even though some of the Neolithic weapons and implements in polished stone show a high degree of perfection in their way; the beginnings of a higher civilization appear more or less simultaneously in the whole country, varying in type according to the different races that inhabited the peninsula. The chief types are as follows:

1. *The 'terramare' of northern Italy.*—These are villages built upon platforms supported by wooden poles sunk into the muddy earth, a type of dwelling created for marshy districts, and frequent upon the shores of the lakes of Central Europe. From there the type spread not only down the marshy valley of the Po and its tributary rivers, but also farther south to the confines of the Emilia, and even, if we may judge by an isolated example, as far as Tarentum. What had originally been a method of building called for by the conditions of the soil was preserved and followed with religious care even in dry and mountainous regions. An invariable rule, evidently sanctioned by the religion of these 'terramaricoli,' in whom we may see the first Italic race on Italian soil, regulated the shape of these villages—a trapezoid space enclosed by a rampart of earth and by a moat, carefully orientated, accessible by a single bridge; the round huts inside were disposed in blocks, intersected by two main paths running at right angles to each other and to the ramparts, while, on the eastern side of the village, a rectangular space was reserved, evidently for the dwelling of the chief and the sanctuary or altar of the gods. The close resemblance of these arrangements to the shape and disposition of the Roman military camps is evident, and speaks for community of race; but the 'terramare' are many centuries older. The refuse accumulated under the huts contains rude pottery, numerous stone and bone implements, but only a few rare objects of bronze, which was evidently far from common at that time. The bronze fibulæ, found occasionally, allow us to assign to these primitive villages, roughly speaking, a date between 1500 and 1000 B.C. The cemeteries are simply reduced imitations of the living tribe's dwelling—miniature villages guarded by moat and rampart—rude earthen jars filled with the ashes of the dead taking the place of the huts. We find abundant traces of agriculture, a little commerce, and, if the 'terramare' of Taranto is really akin to the northern settlements, evidence of relations with the Ægean, in the shape of Mycenæan sherds and clay idols. No trace of writing has been discovered.

2. At about the same time, a more highly developed civilization was spreading through *Sicily and southern Italy.* We know these tribes, the Sikels, chiefly through their tombs, which are usually small chambers cut into the living rock. They often reproduce the shape of the living man's dwelling, either round or oval huts or square houses of wood or bricks and stone. Remains of some stone houses and even of a large building, evidently the seat of some powerful chief (at Pantalica west of Syracuse), have been discovered; and as the tombs were abundantly furnished with the necessaries of life—clay vases often delicately painted, weapons and implements of stone and bronze, and even some ornaments and jewellery of bronze, silver, gold, and ivory—we are able to re-construct, to a certain extent, this Sikelian civilization through several periods of its development. The presence of Mycenæan vases in some of the tombs fixes their date approximately. But the Sikels have no connexion with the contemporary, very much ruder, civilization of the 'terramare.' The

advent of the Greek colonists, after the decline of the Mycenæan sway, early in the first millennium B.C., almost stifled the local art of southern Italy and Sicily, which may be considered, after the 8th cent., simply as a province of Greek civilization.

3. An analogous development of local handiwork appears in *the rock-cut tombs of Sardinia.* Only here it is Phœnicia, not Greece, whose colonies modify the old order, at about the same period. But Sardinia always retains one distinctive feature of architecture, the 'nuraghe,' curious buildings of bee-hive shape, made of roughly hewn stones, sometimes well fortified and of considerable size, with internal rooms and winding passages in several storeys. The date of these buildings has never been sufficiently cleared up, nor is it decided whether they served as dwellings or tombs, or perhaps for both uses. It is, however, undoubted that the older 'nuraghe' must be placed rather early in the first millennium B.C.

4. In northern and central Italy the 'terramare' disappear towards the beginning of the first millennium B.C., and are replaced by *villages of rude huts without poles or ramparts.* We know the civilization of this period merely by its cemeteries, the first of which was excavated at Villanova near Bologna, and has given its name to this civilization. The ashes are buried in clay vases, as in the 'terramare'; but not only are these ossuaries, with their incised geometric ornaments, far more elaborate than the rude pots of the 'terramare'; they also contain, besides smaller vases, a number of weapons, implements, and ornaments far in advance of anything yet known in those parts of the country. Stone implements disappear; iron is used besides bronze—an immense step forward on the path of technical development; amber and ivory ornaments proclaim commercial relations with the north and east. Instead of the usual ossuaries, we often find the ashes of the dead buried in small clay imitations of the living men's huts, which appear to be considerably larger and better built than the primitive dwellings of the 'terramare.' But, in the older Villanova period, there is not yet any trace of writing, or of stone buildings, or of Greek vases. These appear among the natives a few generations later, with the advent of the first really developed civilization in Italy, the Etruscan.

5. The origin of *the Etruscans* is shrouded in mystery. Following the tradition almost universally accepted by ancient authors and corroborated by the archæological evidence, we assume them to have reached Italy by sea, about the 9th cent. B.C., subduing the native races of central Italy, especially the Umbrians, and founding a number of fortified towns, whose confederacy formed a powerful State. An entirely new era begins with them. The villages of rude huts are superseded by strongholds on the hills, protected by strong walls of polygonal or isodomic masonry, which are still standing on many Etruscan sites. These mighty walls of Cære, Cosa, Vetulonia, Volterra, Perugia, and other towns, belong to different periods, the oldest dating back as far as the 8th–7th cent. B.C. They have been constantly repaired in the course of the ages, and at a later date have occasionally, as at Volterra and Perugia, been provided with vaulted gates adorned with sculptured heads or the figures of tutelary divinities in relief. Within the walls, the houses were built mostly of wood, and have therefore perished. But the tombs give us a faithful representation of them. During the first century or two of Etruscan sway in central Italy, the ancient shape of the round hut still forms one prototype of the tombs. But, like the Mycenæan 'bee-hive' tombs, whose influence they seem to show, these Etruscan sepulchres are spacious cupolas of stone, provided, not for the ashes of a peasant, like the rude Villanova (Umbrian) ossuaries, but for families of wealthy warriors and merchants, whose corpses were buried in state, unburnt and surrounded by all they needed in the under world. The finest of these cupolas are found at Vetulonia, south of Pisa—one of the oldest and richest Etruscan cities—at Volterra, and one specially good specimen at Quinto Fiorentino. Other tombs of the same period, instead of the cupola, consist of rectangular vaulted chambers, either built of huge stones or cut out of the living rock, The most famous of the former is the Tomba Regulini Galassi near Cære, whose astonishing wealth of gold jewellery, precious vases and implements, is in the Vatican Museum. A fine example of the rock-hewn tomb was discovered near Veii; it is adorned with the oldest frescoes we know in Italy. These graves are doubly important. They are the earliest monuments that we can *prove* by their inscriptions to be undoubtedly Etruscan; by the Egyptian and Phœnician and Greek objects found in them, their date is fixed in the 8th–7th cent. B.C. The rectangular chambers give us an idea of the Etruscan house of wood or sun-baked brick, and a slightly younger type (7th–6th cent.) introduces us to roomy mansions. These latter tombs are always cut into the rock, and their central hall and side-chambers, with their beamed roofs and carved doorways, with couches and chairs hewn out of the rock, give a vivid conception of what an elegant Etruscan dwelling of the time looked like. Nay, in some cases, at Cære, for instance, we find two storeys above each other. The tombs built of stone blocks are simpler in design, consisting of one, rarely of two rooms, and occasionally, as at Orvieto, grouped in streets and blocks, just like real towns. The architectural forms and mouldings are of the simplest, and betray the imitation of wooden houses in stone. One detail—the doorways narrowing towards the top and surrounded by a rectangular moulding — seems to denote Egyptian influence.

These tombs are without sculptured decoration inside, except for occasional low reliefs upon the doors or the ceiling (chiefly at Corneto, the reliefs showing animals, fabulous creatures and hunters; and some funeral statues in a tomb at Vetulonia); but the mound or tumulus which covers the grave usually bears either a sculptured ornament or a stone stele with the image of the deceased in relief (standing upright in armour or reclining at a banquet), mostly accompanied by an inscription. Lions carved in stone often guard the entrance to the tomb. The walls of the sepulchral chambers are often gaily painted, and these frescoes demonstrate the development of Etruscan art, from the 6th to the 2nd cent. B.C. They and the sculptured sarcophagi also show the preponderant influence of Greek art over Etruscan; for the commercial relations between the two nations were continuous, and the Etruscans, who do not seem to have possessed a strong individual artistic genius, not only bought Greek vases and bronzes by the thousand, so that no tomb, however poor, is without its Greek objects, but also copied these imported works, more or less freely and successfully. Thus, the frescoes of the oldest painted tomb of Veii, mentioned above, show the meaningless medley of animals, fabulous creatures, and human beings which the Greek vase-painters of the 7th cent., especially in Corinth, had borrowed from the contemporary carpets and tapestries. The 6th cent. frescoes of Cære and Corneto show banqueting and hunting scenes, with an occasional marine monster and once a mythological scene, conceived in the style of Ionic art. The same art, debased by provincial Etruscan painters, appears upon some terra-cotta slabs with paintings of sacrificial and funeral rites, which adorned the walls of a tomb at Cære. Occasionally, towards the end of the 6th cent., the banquets (they are the Elysian banquets of the happy dead) are replaced by frescoes showing funeral rites, dances, mourners, games, and fights, in which local Etruscan customs are rendered in a debased Greek style. These frescoes, especially those of a tomb at Chiusi, are full of interesting details—wrestlers and acrobats, dwarfs and tame animals. Early in the 5th cent. Attic models take the place of the Ionic or Corinthian ones; Attic vases of the red-figured style illustrate this new fashion in Etruscan painting. Banqueting and funeral scenes continue to be in vogue. In the 4th cent., still under Attic influence, the frescoes take more to religious subjects. A tomb of Corneto shows us the trembling soul in Hades, amid the terrific images of the famous sinners of Greek mythology, bearing their eternal torments. The kinder artist of a tomb of Orvieto lets the dead partake of a sumptuous banquet in the very palace of Hades, who presides with Persephone, before a sideboard laden with golden vessels. The gods and heroes are Greek, even to their names, which can easily be recognized in their Etruscan travesty; the style is wholly Greek, and it is only in certain ritual details, in the winged Fates (Lasa) who call the dead to Hades, in the curious monstrosity of Charun (=Charon), the infernal boatman, that the Etruscan artists have abandoned their slavish imitation of Hellenic imagery.

The same dependence is apparent in the sarcophagi which contain the corpses, where these are not simply stretched upon rock-hewn benches. In the 6th cent., some terra-cotta sarcophagi from Cære bear the figures of the dead man and his wife reclining together on their couch at dinner, according to Ionic custom, and in a style copying the Ionic. A century later, upon a stone sarcophagus from the Chiusi district (in the Florentine Museum), we see the same couple, Attic in style, the wife sitting at the feet of her reclining husband, as was the custom for a proper Attic lady. The old Umbrian custom of burning the dead, which had been in abeyance, though it never disappeared entirely, during the first five centuries of Etruscan sway, again became nearly universal with the end of the 4th cent.; the long sarcophagi for the outstretched corpse are replaced by short square urns sufficiently large for a handful of ashes. And while the figures reclining upon these urns are merely hideously deformed pieces of provincial work, the reliefs which adorn the front copy Attic paintings, of which little sketches must have been brought to Etruria in great numbers; this explains the contrast between the fine composition and the rough execution, so noticeable in the reliefs of these urns, and also the preference for Greek mythological scenes, some of them local Attic myths, which neither the Etruscan 'artist' nor his clients can have understood. The painted tombs grow very rare in this late period, but the shape and disposition of the chambers remain almost unchanged, as is proved by two excellent examples—the Tomb of the Volumnii near Perugia, with its fine architectural moldings and good stone urns, and the Tomba dei Rilievi at Cære, decorated with brightly painted reliefs of various implements and weapons. Both these tombs have Roman inscriptions combined with Etruscan ones, and belong to the last period of Etruscan art—the 2nd–1st cent. B.C. After this period, the Etruscan civilization was entirely flooded by the Roman.

The tombs have helped us to re-construct the Etruscan temple; the sites of several have been found, but as they were built of wood, it would have been impossible to divine their shape without the architectural analogies of the rock-hewn tombs, of which some, at Castel d'Asso and Norchia near Viterbo, show fine façades, with columns crowned by sculptured pediments. A couple of cinerary urns in the shape of small temples or chapels are equally important witnesses; but the most precious are the numerous terra-cotta figures and reliefs which decorated these wooden temples. The oldest, from Cære, Falerii, and Conca [the two latter places are in the lower valley of the Tiber outside Etruria proper; but Latium at this period was artistically under the sway of the higher Etruscan civilization], date back as far as the 6th century. They are antefixes (outer roof-tiles) decorated with reliefs, heads of nymphs and satyrs, of Herakles and the cow-horned Io, groups of dancing mænads and satyrs—all in the same Ionic style which we noted in the frescoes. And the same fashion is apparent in the terra-cotta slabs with friezes of warriors and chariots, of animals and hunters, of banquets, or merely of fine palmetto and lotus chains; these slabs protected the wooden rafters, the upper line of the wooden wall, against the rain. The decorative terra-cottas follow the development of the frescoes, in their style, from the 6th to the 3rd century. In the latter half of this period, pediment sculptures in terra-cotta are added to the antefixes and friezes. Some very fine 4th cent. figures of youths and maidens came from the Faliscan region (now in the Villa di Papa Giulio in Rome). The death of Amphiaraos and the flight of Adrastos before Thebes are given in a pediment from Telamone near Pisa, with very numerous small figures (3rd cent., now in Florence); and the pediments from Luni, also in Florence, appear to render the myth of the Niobids, in their large, admirably modelled figures. Altogether, these terra-cottas are the finest works of art that Etruria has produced, again following in the tracks of Greece. We cannot make sure of the appearance of the Etruscan temples in all their details; but we may safely say that they were mostly of modest size and simple decoration, consisting of a wooden house, oblong, with one or two rooms, and an open porch supported by wooden columns, the whole resembling the Greek 'templum in antis,' yet different in style. We may imagine the walls painted; and the terra-cottas, also brightly coloured, must have produced a rather gaudy effect. The description of the Etruscan temple by Vitruvius helps us also. But our materials for actually re-constructing these buildings in their original shape are too scanty as yet.

In the minor arts, as in painting, the influence of Greece was predominant. Among the very numerous bronze statuettes found in Etruscan tombs it is often difficult to distinguish between imported Greek originals and local imitations. The same doubt obtains concerning bronze statues like the Capitoline wolf. But it would be going too far to attribute only the inferior work to Etruscan artists; they seem to have been largely dependent upon Greece for inspiration, but their skill was nevertheless recognized in Athens itself, where Etruscan bronzes adorned the houses of the richest patrons of art (Pherekrates *ap.* Athenæus, xv. 700*c*; Kritias, *ib.* i. 28*b*). Etruscan bronzes were famous in Greece, and, we may say, justly famous, judging by a number of really fine works of a greater realism than is usual in Greece. Here again the Ionic style is paramount in the older work—the statuettes, vases, and implements of the 7th–6th centuries. The first merchants who traded with Etruria hailed from the Ionic colonies of Asia Minor, and their intimate connexion with the Phœnicians explains the presence of numerous Syrian and Phœnician objects—vases, ornaments, and scarabs—in the oldest Etruscan tombs, since no direct connexion between Phœnicia and Etruria has been proved. In the later period, Attic influence again predominates, and is especially noticeable in the very numerous engraved mirrors and circular cists (toilet boxes) of bronze, some of them very beautiful, which are most nearly akin, in their style, to the reliefs of the later cinerary urns, though superior to these. Etruscan jewellery, at least in its older stages, is a great deal more independent. In fact, Greece offers nothing comparable, in technical skill and delicacy, to the wonderful gold ornaments, the gossamer filigree work, the microscopic granulations, of the bracelets, necklaces, ear-rings, and fibulæ of the oldest Etruscan tombs. The more recent ornaments show a stronger Hellenic influence, and a less perfect workmanship. Ceramic art is always more or less subservient to the more valuable metal vases. Thus, the shapes of Etruscan clay vessels reproduce bronze models, and as these models are more or less copied from Greek originals, the same imitation is apparent in the cheaper terra-cotta ware. But the technique of these vases is more independent; they are fashioned in black clay, called *bucchero*, adorned with incised or relief ornaments or figures; and though this technique is not infrequent in Greece, and again more especially in the Ionic colonies of Asia Minor, yet its predominance in Etruria is so great that only a slight Greek influence upon a strong local industry may here be granted. Painted vases are rare in Etruria, and are no more than poor copies of Ionic, Corinthian, or Attic originals; but *bucchero* may be claimed as mainly a native achievement.

Very little can be said of decorative work in ivory, or of engraved gems. Here again foreign, and chiefly Oriental, influence predominates, and the Etruscan artists have added little of their own. Even the types of their coins are merely derivatives from the superior Hellenic art.

Etruscan art and science were paramount during the earlier centuries of Roman history, throughout the whole of Latium, and even as far south as Campania. When the Greek colonies of Magna Græcia grew strong enough to hold their own, and the Etruscans were driven from Campania, towards the end of the 5th cent. B.C., their intellectual sway over Rome diminished steadily as the Greek influence increased. After the league of the Etruscan cities had been subjected to Rome, their peculiar civilization dwindled and disappeared rapidly, and it would be difficult to find a characteristically Etruscan work of art later than the 1st cent. B.C.

LITERATURE.—I. *GENERAL*: **H. Nissen**, *Ital. Landeskunde*, 3 vols. 1883–1902; **O. Montelius**, *La Civilisation primitive en Italie*, 4 vols., Stockholm, 1895–1904; several articles in the *Atti del Congresso di Storia*, vol. v. 'Archeologia,' Rome, 1904.

II. *TERRAMARE*: **W. Helbig**, *Die Italiker in der Poebene*, Leipzig, 1879; a series of articles in the *Bollettino di Paletnologia italiana*, by **L. Pigorini** and his pupils; **L. Pigorini**, in *Monumenti antichi dei Lincei*, i. (1892).

III. *SICILY, SIKEL CIVILIZATION*: **F. v. Andrian**, *Prähistor. Studien aus Sicilien*, Berlin, 1878; a number of exhaustive articles by **P. Orsi** in the *Bollett. di Paletnol. ital.* and the *Monum. ant. d. Lincei* (vol. ii. [1893], vi. [1896], ix. [1899]); 'Un villaggio siculo presso Mattera nell' antica Apulia,' by **G. Patroni** in *Monum. ant. d. Lincei*, viii. [1898].

IV. *SARDINIA*: **E. Pais**, *La Sardegna prima del dominio romano*, Rome, 1888; **G. Perrot** and **C. Chipiez**, *Hist. de l'Art dans l'Antiquité*, iv. [Paris, 1887]; **G. Pinza**, 'Monumenti primitivi della Sardegna' in *Monum. ant. d. Lincei*, xi., 1901; **G. Patroni**, *ib.* xiv. [1904].

V. '*VILLANOVA' OR UMBRIAN CIVILIZATION*: a series of articles by local archæologists, chiefly **Gozzadini**, the discoverer of Villanova; the results collected by **Montelius**, *op. cit.*; **J. Martha**, *Art étrusque*, Paris, 1889, p. 31 ff., where this civilization is claimed for the Etruscans (erroneously, in the opinion of the present writer).

VI. *ETRURIA*: **L. Canina**, *L'antica Etruria marittima*, 4 vols., Rome, 1846–1851; **G. Dennis**, *Cities and Cemeteries of Etruria*[3], 2 vols., London, 1883; **Martha**, *op. cit.*; **G. Koerte**, 'Etrusker' in Pauly-Wissowa, 1906; **T. Durm**, *Die Baukunst der Etrusker*, Stuttgart, 1905. The local art of the ancient Veneti is treated exhaustively by **G. Ghirardini** in *Monum. ant. d. Lincei*, ii. [1893], vii. [1897], x. [1901]; *Atti d. Congresso di Storia*, v. 277. For Faliscan art, see **F. Barnabei** in *Mon. ant. d. Lincei*, iv. [1894]. For Romagna and Picenum, see **Brizio**, *ib.* v. [1895]; **Mariani**, *ib.* x. [1901]. For Latium, see **Pinza**, *ib.* xv. [1905].

G. KARO.

ART (Greek and Roman).—The history of Greek art, in relation to religion, passes through three phases which correspond more or less to its three periods of rise, perfection, and decadence. During the first period, art is subjected to religious influences, and frequently trammelled by religious conservatism; during the second, the two act in co-operation, art drawing its highest inspiration from religion, and itself contributing to the dignity of religious ideals, so that it was said of the Olympian Zeus of Phidias, 'cuius pulcritudo adiecisse aliquid etiam receptæ religioni videtur'; during the third, religion supplies numerous themes to the artist; but these often tend to be regarded, mainly or in part, as affording an opportunity for his skill in characterization or execution; and even when this is not the case, he often repeats the conventions of earlier artists rather than creates a new embodiment of a religious idea. It follows that the history of art in Greece is, throughout the course of its development, closely bound up with the history of religious thought—more so, perhaps, than in the case of any other nation, but the relations of the two vary considerably at different periods.

1. Pre-Hellenic Art.—Before dealing with Hellenic art, it is necessary to say something of the art which preceded it in Greek lands, and which is conveniently named Ægean, so as to include Crete and the Archipelago, as well as the mainland of Greece. Our knowledge of the Ægean religion (*q.v.*) is gained almost entirely from the remains of early art in these regions. The chief branches of this art consist of gem-cutting, the art of the gold- and silver-smith; painting on terra-cotta coffins and vases, and in fresco on the walls of houses and palaces; and sculpture, or rather modelling in terra-cotta and other materials, including life-sized coloured reliefs in *gesso duro*. Early Ægean art in all these branches shows a strong and characteristic native development, though it owes something also to foreign influences, notably to that of Egypt. It is marked by much naturalism in detail, especially in plant and animal forms, together with a curious conventionalism, especially in the treatment of the human figure, which has an unnaturally slim waist and elongated limbs. The article ÆGEAN RELIGION shows what subjects are treated in the art of the time. We find representations of shrines and altars, and of aniconic symbols of worship, such as the double axe and the horns of consecration, and an almost realistic rendering of landscape in the representations of sacred mountains and trees. Grotesque animal forms and monstrous combinations are a favourite subject, especially on gems. We also find figures which are probably to be regarded as representations of divinities, though the skill of the artist is not sufficient to indicate any difference between these and human figures, except by signs or attributes. Rudely-fashioned images of terra-cotta, which are almost certainly to be regarded as figures of deities, are found in Crete, and are also common at Mycenæ and elsewhere in Greece.

2. The 'Dark Ages.' Art in Homer.—Between this early Ægean art and the rise of the art which may properly be called Hellenic there is a long interval of time; nor is it possible, except in a limited degree, to trace any direct connexion between the two. The two chief qualities of the earlier work are beauty of decorative design and a close observation of nature, within certain limits. In both these respects its facile and even decadent quality, in its later examples, offers the strongest contrast to the uncouth but promising beginnings of Hellenic art. Without discussing the complicated question of the racial changes that had taken place in the interval, we may admit that the innate artistic genius, of which we see the products in early Ægean art, may, after lying dormant for a time, have contributed its part to the later development, but in conjunction with new elements which entirely transformed its character. In this connexion it must be remembered that the rise and earlier stages of the development of early art in Crete and the Ægean islands go back to at least the third millennium before our era, and that the flourishing period of Cretan art ends with the destruction of the palace at Knossos about B.C. 1400, though at Mycenæ and elsewhere on the mainland of Greece a kindred art survived for two more centuries in vigorous condition, and considerably longer in a decadent stage. The rise of a strong and independent Hellenic art cannot be dated earlier than about the 7th cent. B.C. The five centuries or so which intervened are sometimes called the 'dark ages' of Greece—a time of invasions and migrations, when the old civilizations were overwhelmed, and the country relapsed for a time into comparative barbarism, so far as the external surroundings of life were concerned. It was during this time that the Homeric poems were composed; and in them there is no certain reference to any work of sculpture in the round, whether representing human personages or gods, with the exception of a doubtful passage in *Iliad*, vi. 92 and 303, where the Trojan matrons place a robe 'upon the knees of Athene.' Some authorities regard this as implying the existence of a seated statue; if the expression be not a purely metaphorical one, it is the only example of any such thing in the Homeric poems. Though temples are often mentioned, no images of the gods are referred to. Art in Homer is purely decorative, and is not distinctively Hellenic; many of the objects of finest workmanship are attributed to the Phœnicians. When scenes of an elaborate nature are described, as on the shield of Achilles, there are none of religious significance among them, though Ares and Athene are spoken of as appearing in a battle scene. Here, however, it is the gods themselves that are thought of, rather than artistic representations of them.

3. **Beginnings of sculpture.**—Many primitive images of the gods were attributed to the Heroic age; an example is the Palladium stolen by Odysseus and Diomed from Troy—a tale told in the 'Little Iliad,' of about the 7th cent. B.C. Some of these may have been survivals from pre-Hellenic times; others were probably wrongly assigned to so early a date. Some of them were attributed to Dædalus, an artist whose historical existence is doubtful, but whose reputed attainments summarize the sudden advance in the art of sculpture which seems to have taken place about B.C. 600. Shortly after this date we find several sculptors, or groups of sculptors, employed to make images of the gods, sometimes, apparently, as a new departure, sometimes to replace a primitive or aniconic object of worship. Such families of artists existed in Chios (Melas, Micciades, Archermus) as workers of marble, and in Samos (Rhœcus, Theodorus) as workers in bronze. In the Peloponnese, many statues of the gods were made by Dipœnus and Scyllis, Cretan 'Dædalids,' and by their pupils; the 'unshaped plank' which had served as the symbol of the goddess Hera at Samos was replaced by an image made by Smilis of Ægina; the Apollo of Delos was made by Tectæus and Angelion, said to be pupils of Dipœnus and Scyllis; and probably most of the other early images of the gods in human form were made in this period. From this time on we hear of numerous statues of the gods, made by almost all the chief sculptors; some of these were intended to replace more primitive images as objects of worship, others merely for dedication. In the former case the artist would in most cases be bound by religious conservatism not to depart too far from the accepted type. An example is the Black Demeter of Phigalia, whose primitive image, with a horse's head, had been destroyed; the sculptor Onatas of Ægina is said to have replaced it with remarkable fidelity, with the help of copies, and even of a vision. This is an extreme instance, but in many other cases the artists had to satisfy the religious scruples of priests and others, as well as the growing desire for a more artistic representation of the deity. In the case of dedicated statues he would naturally have a freer hand. Here the limitations would be imposed by his art. We have many statues of early Greek workmanship preserved, and these show that sculpture was confined to a small number of clearly marked types, which served for representations alike of deities and of human beings. The commonest of these types represented a fully draped seated figure, a nude standing male figure, or a draped standing female figure. All of these were used alike for figures of the dead set up over graves, for figures of worshippers dedicated in sacred places, and for images of the gods. The artist devoted his skill to perfecting these types, to getting more approach to a natural expression in the face, to improving the shape of limbs and hands and feet, to observing and recording correctly the position of bones and muscles in the body. He was too much taken up with these matters to give much attention to the representation of character or individuality, much less of a worthy ideal of the gods, though it was by his work that the tradition was being built up which enabled the masters of the 5th cent. to progress in this direction. Some other early types, however, offered an opportunity for a more direct and simple expression of divine energy. Sometimes swiftness was shown by wings, usually borrowed from decorative Oriental models, and by a position which looks like kneeling, but is meant to represent rapid running or flight; sometimes the god or goddess was shown striding forward rapidly, with an attribute of power—if Zeus, a thunderbolt; if Poseidon, a trident; if Athene, a spear—in the raised right hand. Such purely external expressions of divine activity seem often to have been derived from primitive images, which were incapable of expressing it in any subtler manner; and although some examples of this type were made, usually to carry on a religious tradition, even in the 5th cent., it gradually became obsolete as the artist acquired facility in expressing the character and power of the god under an intellectual and moral rather than a merely physical aspect. When this change had come about, the relations of art and religion were revolutionized. The sculptor no longer occupied himself with the technical problem of providing a statue suitable in age, sex, and attributes to the requirements prescribed by religion, but was himself able to contribute something to the ideal conception of the deity.

4. **Decorative and minor arts.**—So far we have considered only sculpture in the round, having as its province the making of independent statues. Minor works in bronze and terra-cotta, which were abundant on all Greek sites, naturally followed the development of sculpture, or to some extent, perhaps, even anticipated it; but what is said of sculpture applies to them also. It is otherwise with reliefs and other decorative works, whether in wood, stone, marble, terra-cotta, bronze, or other metals. So far as their religious signifi-

cance is concerned, this group of objects goes with painting, especially vase-painting; it deals with the same kind of subjects, and treats them in the same manner. This decorative art affords a link, such as is missing in the case of sculpture, with the earlier periods; for it continued to be practised to some extent during the dark ages between Mycenæan and Hellenic art; it transmitted some inherited types, and it borrowed many others from Oriental or other foreign sources. It is also of considerable importance for the study of religion and mythology, since the means at its disposal enables it not merely to represent figures of the gods and heroes, but to record or to illustrate stories about them, or scenes connected with their ritual. It is to be observed that descriptions of decorative reliefs in the Homeric poems—notably that of the shield of Achilles, which, even if later than the rest of the *Iliad*, is earlier in date than the rise of Hellenic art—do not refer to mythological scenes, but to incidents of daily life. On the other hand, the Hesiodic 'shield of Hercules' has a whole series of illustrations of mythical tales, such as the battle of Lapiths and Centaurs and the flight of Perseus from the Gorgons. In this respect it resembles actual works of decorative art that are recorded for us by ancient writers, such as the throne made by Bathycles of Magnesia for the Apollo at Amyclæ, or the chest of the Corinthian tyrant Cypselus, dedicated in the Heræum at Olympia. And the subjects recorded both on the imaginary and on the actual reliefs are just the same as we constantly find upon extant early works of decorative art—both reliefs in marble or stone or bronze or terra-cotta, and paintings upon vases. It appears, therefore, that, while the art referred to in the Homeric poems has nothing Hellenic about it except the poet's imagination, the references to works of art in Hesiodic poems and in later literature are closely in touch with the actual development of art in Greece.

The relation of art to popular belief and to literature, in its treatment of religious or rather of mythological subjects, is somewhat complicated. The decorative artist was extremely conservative and imitative in the use of his available répertoire of groups and figures. Free invention was hardly ever resorted to, except in cases where no already familiar type could be borrowed or adapted. For example, the judgment of Paris seems to offer a theme for imagination, and we find it so treated on later vases; but in early art it always takes the form of a procession, with the figures more or less differentiated; and this form is borrowed almost without modification from the procession of dancing women, headed by a musician, which is a common subject on the most primitive vases. Such mechanical repetitions may appear at first sight to preclude any strong influence of art on mythology; but in some ways their cumulative effect was greater than any that could have been due to originality of treatment, for it became almost impossible for people to figure these scenes or events to themselves in any other way than that conventionally accepted. And, moreover, the same conditions tended towards the assimilation and even identification of legends originally distinct, and so facilitated the systematization of Greek mythology. Again, the tendency of early Greek art to adopt rather than to invent led to many almost fortuitous identifications that have had great influence, not only on later art, but even on later belief. Thus the gorgon, the sirens, the sphinx, and other such monsters probably had no distinctive form in the eyes of those who first told tales about them; certainly no such form is indicated in the Homeric poems. But the early decorative artists borrowed from the East many monstrous forms of winged and human-headed beasts and birds which had probably no particular significance to those who first adopted them as decorative elements; and these forms came to be identified with the creatures of Greek myth so completely and so finally that we at the present day cannot think of Sphinx or Siren under any other form. The fact that both these fantastic figures appear as symbols of death upon tombs in Greece, in Lycia, and possibly elsewhere also, has further complicated the influence of the borrowed type, so that, in these cases and in others like them, it is now almost impossible to disentangle the contributions of art and of myth to the common conception.

5. Vase-painting.—The more technical side of the early development of decorative art in Greece concerns us here mainly as it affects the gradual acquisition of greater power of expression. In this matter sculpture in relief has much the same history as sculpture in the round, so far as the execution of individual figures is concerned. Vase-painting, on the other hand, has an independent development. It is impossible here even to sketch the development of early vase-painting in Greece; it is possible only to mention those classes of vases which are of most importance for the representation of mythological scenes. (1) The *geometrical* class, which succeeds the Mycenæan in Greece, frequently depicts scenes from actual life; this is particularly the case with the Dipylon vases of Athens, on which we see elaborate funeral processions, scenes of seafaring and combat, and classic dances; but few, if any, of these can be given any mythological significance. (2) The geometric period is succeeded by that of *Oriental* influence in various parts of the Greek world. On the coasts and islands of Asia Minor, especially in Ionia, Samos, and Rhodes, we find various classes of vases, which have certain characteristics in common, as well as clearly-marked local variations; and about the same time we find a similar development in some of the chief manufacturing centres in continental Greece, mainly at Corinth and Chalcis; and colonies such as Daphnæ and Naucratis in Egypt, and Cyrene in Libya, have each their characteristic ware. Athens also has its own pottery at this time, in succession to the Dipylon ware. The technical development varies considerably, but in all alike the tendency is towards an improvement both in the colour of the ground and of the pigment in which the figures are drawn. As a rule, in earlier examples the ground is of a buff or brownish colour, sometimes almost white, and the pigment is of a dark brown colour, varying from red to dull black. In late examples, and, above all, in Attic pottery, the ground tends to assume the beautiful reddish terra-cotta colour which is characteristic of Greek vases of the best period, and the pigment to take the form of lustrous black varnish. The monstrous forms, many of them winged, and the other beasts borrowed from Oriental fabrics, tend gradually to be replaced by scenes of some mythological meaning, or, if retained, to acquire a mythological significance; and the human figure, at first introduced as a decorative type like the rest, gradually asserts its supremacy in interest. The treatment of myths upon early vases becomes, so to speak, stereotyped along certain lines, the same figures or compositions being repeated again and again with slight variations to illustrate the same myth, or adapted to the rendering of another myth that lent itself to a similar treatment. In this way the vase-painter contributed in no small degree to the uniformity and systematization of mythology. (3) About the middle of the 6th cent. B.C. the Attic potters, assisted by the excellent clay of the Attic ceramicus, surpassed all rivals. This is the age of what is called *black-figured* ware, the figures being drawn in black silhouette, and details added in incised lines, with touches of purple or white. We have many vases signed by potters of this period, as well as of the next, which begins in the latter part of the 6th cent., and continues until the date of the Persian wars and a little later. (4) This next period, which overlaps the preceding, is known as the *early red-figured* style, the same pigments being used, but the figures being reserved in the terra-cotta colour of the clay, and the background filled in with the black varnish. In this age we find greater imagination and freedom of drawing; but the old traditions are still closely adhered to, and the advance is in the details rather than in the general conception. We find at this time the most perfect decorative treatment, and the utmost precision of line drawing. As we approach the middle of the 5th cent., we find greater dignity and severity of treatment, probably owing to the influence of the great fresco painters, above all of **Polygnotus**, who came to Athens and decorated the 'Painted Stoa' and other buildings about this time.

In Athens the work of Polygnotus consisted partly of historical paintings, such as the battle of Marathon; at Delphi his most famous works were the 'Fall of Troy' and the 'Land of the Dead,' and by these he probably exercised great influence on his contemporaries and successors. He was specially noted for the ethical character of his subjects. His paintings have not been preserved, but from imitations of them on vases and from descriptions of ancient writers, we can infer that they consisted of simply-grouped figures, arranged without perspective, and probably conventional in colouring. But the grandeur and nobility of his conception probably contributed in no small degree to the ideals of Greek art in the 5th century.

6. Sculpture of the 5th century.—The development of sculpture was at this time very rapid. The great struggle between Greece and Persia led to a new consciousness of Hellenic unity and a new pride in the superiority of Greek over barbarian; and at the same time, the spoils of victory and the offerings to the gods in thanksgiving for the great deliverance afforded both opportunities and themes for the highest energies of the artists. The full effect of these influences was hardly felt at once, and they were combined, in their most splendid manifestations, with the glory of Athens, which, taking the lead at the time of the Persian wars, became under Cimon and Pericles the example and summary of all that was best in Greece. The immediate predecessors of Phidias, though they produced works which were admired by posterity, seem still to have been mainly occupied with the study of the type and the perfection of technique and mastery over material. A statue like the 'Discobolus' of **Myron** is characteristic of this age; and however great the skill of the artist in dealing with a difficult subject, it is to be noted that he does not go beyond the expression of physical life to that of character or emotion. Even a masterpiece such as the 'Charioteer of Delphi' shows the same restriction of aim. **Pythagoras**, to whom it is probably to be attributed, was noted also for the expression of pain in his limping Philoctetes; but here, as in the wounded warriors of Ægina, it was probably the physical rather than the mental or spiritual aspect of the subject that was rendered. To **Calamis**, with his nameless grace, we might perhaps look for something more; but we have no certain work of his left, and we are not justified in assuming that he went beyond his contemporaries.

It was reserved for **Phidias** to fill the forms that had already reached so high a degree of perfection, with an inner life and meaning. His colossal gold and ivory statues have not survived, but we have some copies of them, and probably of others of his statues, and the descriptions of ancient writers; and we can also see the reflexion of his influence in all contemporary and later work. From all this evidence we can infer that his statues of the gods did not merely represent the perfection of the human form in face and figure, but embodied all that was noblest in the Hellenic conception of the gods. He is even said to have gone beyond this, and to have added somewhat to the received religion in his statue of Zeus, which was so worthy of the subject represented that 'he who is heavy-laden in soul, who has experienced many misfortunes and sorrows in his life, and from whom sweet sleep has fled, even he, I think, if he stood before this image, would forget all the calamities and troubles that befall in human life' (Dio Chrys. *Or.* xii. 51, tr. Adam). The Zeus at Olympia was the father of gods and men, full of power and benignity, the common god of the Hellenes. The Athene Parthenos at Athens represented the more intellectual conception of the goddess of Athens, the embodiment of the artistic and literary genius of the people. Statues like these doubtless transcended the ordinary notions of the gods; but they were no mere allegories or personifications; they represented the religious ideals of the whole people, and contributed in no small degree to purify and ennoble these ideals. This new influence of art upon religion came just at the time when the accepted views about the gods and the tales that were told about them were being questioned, and Phidias and Pericles were in sympathy with the most enlightened views; it can hardly be doubted that both artist and statesman had it as their aim to represent the gods to the people as they should be worshipped. From the sculpture that decorated the temples of this period, above all from the sculpture of the Parthenon, we can learn the beauty and nobility of type and the unrivalled skill in execution that supplied the means whereby such an artist as Phidias could express his ideas.

In the latter part of the 5th cent. B.C. there were several other sculptors who followed more or less closely the tradition of Phidias, and made statues of the gods, which, like his work, had a great influence on current religious conceptions. **Alcamenes**, who, after the exile or death of Phidias, was the sculptor most employed upon official commissions in Athens, made famous statues of Hephæstus and Dionysus, of Hera and Athene; **Agoracritus** made the Nemesis at Rhamnus. **Polyclitus**, the head of the Argive school, followed the Argive tradition in his study of the athletic type, and his system of proportions or 'canon' was embodied in a statue, 'The Doryphorus' or spear-bearer, as well as in a theoretical treatise. He also made a great gold and ivory statue of Hera for the Argive Heræum, which embodied the Greek ideal of the goddess, and was placed, by some who had seen it, beside the Zeus and Athene of Phidias. **Cresilas**, a Cretan sculptor who probably came under the influence of both Phidias and Polyclitus, was famous for a statue of a wounded man, and also of a wounded Amazon; he also made the portrait of Pericles, of which copies survive, and which is a typical example of the early portraiture which treats its subject as the ideal statesman rather than as an individual. In all these works we can see the character of the art of the 5th cent., which expressed, as ancient critics tell us, ἦθος rather than πάθος, fixed type of character rather than varying passions and emotions.

7. The 4th century.—The art of the 4th cent. was less abstract and dignified, more human and individual. If Phidias did something to counteract the growing scepticism about the gods by presenting them in a form which could not be rejected as unworthy, the works of **Praxiteles** and **Scopas**

may in some cases have brought the character of the gods home to men by an intense and vivid realization of their personality; but in making them so human these sculptors may have made them less divine, and have opened the way for successors who regarded even statues of the gods as a mere theme for the exhibition of their artistic skill. Early in the 4th cent. we find a conspicuous example of a tendency of which traces may be seen earlier—that to personification. A group by Cephisodotus represented Peace nursing the infant Wealth; and later on allegorical figures such as this, which appealed to the popular imagination, usurped much of the worship that formerly belonged to the Olympian gods. But the statues of Scopas and Praxiteles were for the most part taken from accepted mythology, though the subjects selected were no less characteristic of the time than the manner in which they were treated. The most famous works of Praxiteles represented Aphrodite and Eros; and he set the goddess before mortals with her beauty entirely unveiled; her nudity is not natural and unconscious like that of male figures in Greek art, but a motive for it is supplied in her preparation for the bath. He was also famous for his representation of Dionysus and his attendant satyrs; and from extant copies we can estimate the skill with which he characterized these soulless, half-human creatures of the woods. In the Hermes with the infant Dionysus, of which the original is happily preserved, we can see the mythological conception of Hermes as the protector of youth made to live in a genial and individual embodiment. In other works, such as 'Apollo the lizard-slayer,' we have what was once a religious type treated as a piece of playful *genre*. The work of Scopas is throughout more earnest and impassioned. Extant works that can be associated with him represent heroes rather than gods, but in these we can see a passionate nature and intensity of expression; his treatment of creatures of the sea, with the restless yearning of their nature, is notable; and in his 'Mænad' the enthusiasm of divine inspiration was expressed with wonderful power. Of his treatment of more dignified subjects we can judge from such a work as the 'Demeter' of Cnidus, which, if not from his hand, is certainly to be associated with him; its expression shows maternal grief and the chastened melancholy in a passionate nature. The work of Scopas and his associates may also be seen in the Mausoleum.

Great as was the influence of Scopas and Praxiteles upon their successors, that of the third great sculptor of the 4th cent., **Lysippus**, was, if not greater, at least more direct. As the head of the school of Sicyon, he represented the Peloponnesian tradition of athletic sculpture; and he established a new canon of proportions, slimmer and less massive than that of Polyclitus. He made many statues of the gods, some of colossal size; and in his portrait of Alexander he is said to have satisfied the king by his representation of his ambitious and fiery temperament. Portraits of Alexander, and other extant works that may be associated with Lysippus, show that he was not, as has sometimes been supposed, an academic master, but full of fresh observation, while in expression he seems to have fallen under the influence of Scopas. Partly owing to his association with Alexander, his pupils are most conspicuous in the next generation, and are the founders of the schools that carried the traditions of Hellenic art to the East. We have records of many other sculptors of the 4th cent. who cannot all be enumerated; among them are **Euphranor**, who was also a painter and a writer on art, and was noted for his expression of the characters of gods and heroes; and **Leochares**, who made not only statues of the gods but also a set of portraits of the family of Philip and Alexander in gold and ivory for the Philippeum at Olympia—works which exemplify the tendency to represent men in a manner hitherto reserved for the gods.

The great painters of the 4th cent. are known to us only by literary records; and in this case we cannot, as in the earlier age of Polygnotus, expect any assistance from vases. From the descriptions we learn that the painters of this age often chose dramatic or sensational subjects, and their power of rendering individual character and passion was probably comparable with that of contemporary sculptors. The greatest of all Greek painters, **Apelles** was, like Lysippus, noted for his portrait of Alexander; and he was also fond of allegorical subjects, such as his group of Calumny, of which a detailed description is left us.

8. Hellenistic art.—In the Hellenistic age Greek art followed the conquests of Alexander to new centres in the East; it is no longer to Athens or Argos or Sicyon, but to Alexandria and Antioch and Pergamos that we look for its most characteristic products. The beginning of the Hellenistic age is dominated by the personality of Alexander. He had changed the relations of East and West, and Greek civilization was henceforth the prevalent influence in western Asia. His career, which might well seem more than human, induced the Greeks to accept the Oriental custom of the deification of kings; and his features came to be repeated even in the types of the gods. His head, too, was placed upon coins—an honour hitherto reserved for the gods alone. And his successors, with a less justifiable arrogance, claimed even higher privileges. Beside such present deities—to use the phrase of contemporary flattery—the ancient gods became mere abstractions. Images of them were still made, distinguished for their size—as the 'Colossus' of Rhodes—or for their artistic excellence. But the old types and conventions were mostly repeated either in mere repetition or in eclectic imitation. Certain schools, inspired by the dramatic power of Scopas, infused some new life into the old forms, notably the school of Pergamos. On the great altar in that city was a frieze with a representation of the gods and giants, in which all the learning of the mythologists and all the technical skill of the sculptors were devoted to a complete representation of the Greek Pantheon in action against their wild adversaries. But the extraordinary dramatic vigour of this work does not hide the fact that it is more or less an artificial creation, not a spontaneous embodiment of the people's belief. While philosophers turned to a more or less abstract and monotheistic conception of the deity, which was out of touch with art, the people often turned to a more direct and intelligible worship, such as that accorded to the 'Fortune' of Antioch, embodied in a graceful representation of the city, seated on a rock with a river-god at her feet, which was made by **Eutychides**, a pupil of Lysippus. The representation of children or of rustic subjects showed a reaction against the artificiality of city life, parallel to the literary development of the pastoral. Statues of the gods were still made, but were mostly mere repetitions of established types, though occasionally we find examples of great dignity and beauty, such as the Aphrodite of Melos or the colossal works made by Damophon in Messene and Arcadia. In the inadequacy of contemporary art, we find, as often in an age of decadence, a return to the character and even to the mannerisms of early art; in extreme cases this leads to an affected archaistic work which is easily distinguished from that of the early sculptors whom it imitates. At the same time, dramatic vigour and scientific study were still kept up in some schools; and in Rhodes, in the middle of the

1st cent. B.C., there were still sculptors capable of producing such a masterpiece as the 'Laocoon.'

9. Græco-Roman art.—Græco-Roman art—that is to say, the work produced for the Roman market by Greek artists—belongs for the most part to the more conventional and less powerful survivals of the art of Greece. There was an immense demand in Rome for the decoration of public buildings and of private houses, gardens, and libraries with the products of Greek art; and this was met partly by the spoliation of Greek shrines, partly by the production of new work resembling the old nearly enough to please the taste of the patron. Even the statue of 'Venus Genetrix,' set up by Julius Cæsar in his forum and made by Arcesilaus, the most famous sculptor of the day, was a mere repetition of a type which goes back to one of the masters of the 5th century. Under such conditions there was not much scope for originality or for a fruitful relation between religion and art.

10. Roman art.—Roman art had more originality, and made some technical advances even on its Greek models; but, from the religious point of view, these do not much concern us. They are best seen in portraiture, historical reliefs, and decorative work. The old Italian gods did not as a rule lend themselves readily to artistic treatment. There were, indeed, old terra-cotta images of the gods, made in Rome under Etruscan influence, which Cato and other conservatives regarded with veneration, and preferred to the imported products of Greek workmanship. These may have had a certain vigour of individuality and realism which affected later art in Rome, and more especially portraiture. But in the art of Rome, as known to us in Imperial times, there presentations of the gods follow for the most part the types and conventions borrowed from Greece. There were indeed certain figures, above all that of Rome herself, which were new creations; but these followed the lines of impersonation common in Hellenistic art. The art of the Augustan age, though characterized by an austere beauty, was academic and classical in character. Perhaps the finest extant figures of the gods in Roman art are those on the arch of Trajan at Beneventum, which are beautiful and dignified in type, yet so animated with an interest in the action portrayed as to seem full of life. In the deification of the Emperors we also find an incentive to ideal portraiture which did something to counteract the realistic tendencies of Roman art.

Two classes of monuments are of great importance to the general history of art, and even to the transmission of religious ideas. In historical reliefs on columns and arches—above all, in the Trajan and Antonine columns—we find a continuous method of narration which lent itself admirably to the records of chronicle or story; and this method was continued, for didactic purposes, into early Christian and mediæval art. In the sarcophagi also we find a great wealth and variety of resource in the renderings of mythology, often coupled with indifferent execution; and these likewise served as models, and handed on the classical traditions to later art. Types, such as that of Orpheus, also acquired a new significance in Christian art. The Greek traditions, in varying form, survived both in Rome and in Asia Minor, and through them were transmitted to the modern world. The relation and the spheres of influence of the Eastern and Western branches constitute one of the most difficult and disputed problems of modern archæology.

LITERATURE.—I. *GENERAL*: G. Carotti, *A History of Art*, vol. i., Lond. 1908; M. Collignon, *Manuel d'archéologie grecque*, Paris (n.d.); A. S. Murray, *Handb. of Greek Archæology*, Lond. 1892; Perrot and Chipiez, *Hist. de l'art dans l'antiquité*, vols. vi., viii., 1898, 1903; S. Reinach, *The Story of Art through the Ages*, Lond. 1904, chapters iv.-x.; Springer-Michaelis, *Handb. der Kunstgesch.*[8], Munich, 1907; P. Gardner, *A Grammar of Greek Art*, London, 1905.

II. *PRE-HELLENIC*: R. M. Burrows, *The Discoveries in Crete*[2], London, 1907; artt. in *BSA* and *JHS*, 1900–1905; *Excavations at Phylapoki in Melos*, Lond. 1904; C. Schuchhardt, *Schliemann's Excavations*, tr. by Sellers, Lond. 1891; C. Tsountas and J. I. Manatt, *The Mycenæan Age*, Lond. 1897.

III. *GREEK SCULPTURE*: M. Collignon, *Hist. de la Sculpture grecque*, Paris, 1892–1907; L. R. Farnell, *Cults of the Greek States*, i., ii. (1896), iii., iv. (1907); A. Furtwangler, *Masterpieces of Greek Sculpture*, tr. by Sellers, London, 1895; E. A. Gardner, *Handbook of Greek Sculpture*[2], London, 1907.

IV. *GREEK VASES, COINS, ETC.*: A. Furtwangler, *Antike Gemmen*, 3 vols., Berlin, 1900; A. Furtwangler and K. Reichhold, *Griechische Vasenmalerei*, Munich, 1900; P. Gardner, *Types of Greek Coins*, London, 1883; B. V. Head, *Historia Numorum*, London, 1887; G. F. Hill, *Greek and Roman Coins*, Lond. 1899; H. B. Walters, *History of Ancient Pottery*, London, 1905.

V. *ROMAN ART*: R. Lanciani, *The Destruction of Ancient Rome*[2], Lond. 1901; W. M. Ramsay, *Studies in the History and Art of the E. Rom. Provinces*, Aberdeen, 1906; E. Strong, *Roman Sculpture*, Lond. 1907; F. Wickhoff, *Roman Art*, tr. by E. Strong, London, 1900.

E. A. GARDNER.

ART (Jewish).—**1.** The arts in which the ancient Hebrews excelled were poetry and music. There are no remains, whether in literary sources or in the actual results of excavation, to warrant the belief that there was in any real sense a native Hebrew painting or sculpture. There are extensive stores of Jewish pottery, but the shapes and styles are derived from Phœnician and Egyptian types, and show some Babylonian influence. In glyptic art, again, the same imitativeness appears. Phœnician and Hebrew seals are much alike 'in shape, script, and ornamentation' (Benzinger). The Phœnicians, too, excelled in metal-working; and the Hebrews, while they do not seem to have early acquired the art of metal-casting, were skilful adepts in the process of overlaying wood with metal plates. This skill presupposes some aptitude for wood-carving, but sculpture as such was not one of the attainments of the Hebrews. It is remarkable how few inscribed stones of Hebrew provenance have thus far been discovered. Religion, which is usually the most powerful aid and stimulant of art, had the very opposite effect in Judaism. The prophetic attack on idolatry carried with it an objection to images, and the representation of any form of animal life was forbidden in the Decalogue. Thus, on the one hand artistic incapacity, and on the other pietistic asceticism, combined to prevent the growth of a Jewish plastic art. And when to these causes is added what Delitzsch terms a defective sense of colour (*Iris*, p. 43 ff.), we can understand that only a rude form of painting was possible. These subjects are treated by Flinders Petrie in Hastings' *DB* i. 157.

2. Art was held in high esteem in later Jewish opinion. In the Talmud (*Rosh Hashana*, 29*b*), art is a branch of wisdom (חכמה) as distinct from mere handicraft (מלאכה). But the old dislike of animal representations continued. The Jewish coins contain no heads of rulers; here, again, the cause was partly religious. And the same phenomenon of imitativeness recurs. If the Temple of Solomon shows Phœnician influence, that of Herod was inspired by Roman models. Most of the Talmudic terms for articles of art are foreign—Greek and Latin. Custom and law are not always identical in these matters. The law forbade only the carving of projecting images (*'Abōdā Zārā*, 43*b*), and Dr. Kohler (*JE* ii. 142) rightly asserts that 'portrait painting was never forbidden by the law.' But many Jews long continued to object to portrait painting. On the other hand, though as a rule the mediæval synagogues were destitute of mural paintings, there are instances of carved lions (as at Ascoli). The lion was a frequently used Jewish emblem. In recent times there has been an increase of ornateness in synagogue decoration, and stained glass windows are becoming common, though there is still a reluctance to admit animal or human forms.

3. But in some directions a specific Jewish art was developed. In mediæval times the Jews acquired great repute as silk-dyers, as embroiderers, and as masters of the gold- and silver-smith's art. The worship of the synagogue and the home required the use of many objects in which artistic taste could be displayed. The Ark, or receptacle of the scrolls of the Law, the mantles in which the scrolls were wrapped, the crowns and bells with which they were adorned, the lamps for Sabbath and *Ḥanukah*, the cups for the sanctification over the wine, the spice-boxes (mostly of a castellated shape) used at the *Habdala*, or separation service, at the close of the Sabbath, the Seder-dishes which were used in the home on the Passover Eve—these are among the most important of the articles which the Jews loved to ornament. Beautiful embroideries were also required as curtains for the Ark. Many fine specimens of all these were exhibited at the Anglo-Jewish Historical Exhibition in 1887, and the Catalogue of that Exhibition remains a valuable source of information on all these matters. An *édition de luxe* of the same Catalogue contains some splendid photographs by Mr. Frank Hars. Throughout the volumes of the *JE* will also be found many pictures of the objects briefly described here, as well as of another branch of art in which Jews excelled.

4. This branch is the illumination of manuscripts. Artistic writing was an art in which Jews were highly skilled, and in the illumination of initial letters and the painting of marginal ornament and grotesques, they acquired considerable proficiency. Though there is no specific Jewish art in manuscript illumination, there are original Jewish elements; as Mr. G. Margoliouth well puts it, the Jewish spirit makes itself perceptible to the eye. In classifying the Jewish illuminated MSS, Mr. Margoliouth takes first the Bible, with two kinds of illumination, (*a*) the Massorah in the form of designs, and (*b*) pictorial and marginal illuminations. Of course all these ornaments are confined to codices or Bibles in the form of books; in the form of the scroll (except in the case of the Roll of Esther) the Bible was never illuminated. The Synagogue does not permit the use, in public reading, of punctuated or ornamented scrolls. The illuminated Esther rolls were hardly meant for use in Divine worship. The most usual Hebrew book for illumination was the Passover Service, or *Haggadah*. This is often profusely supplied with miniatures, initials, and full-page pictures. Less common are illuminated Prayer-Books. But all Hebrew books might be illuminated. The Code of Maimonides exists in many beautiful specimens. A very common object for illumination was the *Kethubah*, or Marriage Contract.

It must be added that in recent times many Jewish artists have attained to fame.

LITERATURE.—Besides the works referred to in the course of the preceding article, see: the publications of the *Gesellschaft für Sammlung von Kunstdenkmäler des Judenthums* (Vienna, 1897 ff.); the *Mittheilungen der Gesellschaft zur Erforschung jüdischer Kunstdenkmäler* (Frankfort, 1900 ff.); *Die Haggadah von Sarajevo*, ed. Müller and Schlosser (Vienna, 1898); Günzburg and Stassof, *L'Ornement Hébreu* (Berlin, 1905); S. J. Solomon, 'Art and Judaism' in *JQR* xiii. 553; G. Margoliouth, 'Hebrew Illuminated MSS' in *JQR* xx. 118; and D. Kaufmann, *Gesammelte Schriften*, vol. i., 1908.

I. ABRAHAMS.

ART (Mithraic).—Oriental monuments of the worship of Mithra are as yet almost entirely wanting. The beautiful sculptures discovered at Sidon (De Ridder, *Collection De Clercq*, iv. 'Marbres,' 1906, No. 46 ff.) date from the 3rd cent. of our era, and cannot throw any light on the first productions of the devotees of the Persian god. We must, accordingly, confine ourselves to studying Mithraic art in the Latin-speaking provinces of the Roman Empire, where a very considerable number of its remains have been discovered. In time they range over about two and a half centuries. The most ancient monument, which is now in the British Museum, dates from A.D. 104 (Cumont, *Mon. myst. Mithra*, No. 65; cf. vol. ii. 546; *CIL* vi. 30728), and the last of them belong to the middle of the 4th century. They therefore constitute a group whose limits in space and time are small, and whose character can be accurately described.

It must be admitted that their artistic merit is much less than their archæological interest, and that their chief value is not æsthetic but religious. The late epoch in which these works were produced destroys all hope of finding in them the expression of real creative power or of tracing the stages of an original development. It would, however, be unfair, acting under the impulse of a narrow Atticism, to confound them all in a common depreciation. Some of the groups in high and low relief (for the mosaics and the paintings which have been preserved are so few and so mediocre that they may be disregarded) hold a very honourable rank in the multitude of sculptures which the age of the Emperors has bequeathed to us.

The bull-slaying Mithra.—The group most frequently reproduced is the image of the bull-slaying Mithra, which invariably stood at the background of the temples (see art. ARCHITECTURE [Mithraic]), and specimens of which are to be found in nearly all the museums. The sacrifice of the bull recalled to the initiated the history of the creation and the promise of a future resurrection. It can be proved (Cumont, *op. cit.* ii. 180 ff.) that these representations of Mithra, whose sacred type was fixed before the spread of the Persian mysteries into the Latin-speaking world, are replicas of an original created by a sculptor of the school of Pergamos, in imitation of the sacrificing goddess Victory which adorned the balustrade of the temple of Athene Nike on the Acropolis (Kekule, *Die Reliefs des Tempels der Athena Nike*, 1881, pl. vi.). The Asiatic adapter has merely clothed the Persian god in the half-conventional Phrygian costume which was associated with a number of Oriental personages (*e.g.* Paris, Attis, Pelops, etc.), and has given the face an expression of suffering which makes it resemble that of the celebrated 'dying Alexander.' 'The emotion that pervades the features of Mithras is rendered with almost Skopasian power' (Strong, *Rom. Sculp.* p. 311).

Certain sculptures discovered at Rome and at Ostia, dating from the beginning of the 2nd cent., still reflect the splendour of that powerful work of Hellenistic art. After an eager pursuit, the god, whose mantle flutters in the wind, has just reached the sinking bull. Placing one knee on its crupper and one foot on one of its hoofs, he leans on it to keep it down, and, grasping it by the nostrils with one hand, with the other he plunges a knife into its side. The vigour of this animated scene shows to advantage the agility and strength of the invincible hero. On the other hand, the suffering of the victim breathing its last gasps, with its limbs contracted in a dying paroxysm, and the strange mixture of exultation and remorse depicted in the countenance of its slayer, throw into relief the pathetic side of this sacred drama, and even to-day arouse in the spectator an emotion which must have been keenly felt by the worshippers.

This work of the Alexandrian period has, moreover, been affected by the Roman schools of art. In some of them is shown in a more or less felicitous manner the care for details which is characteristic of the works of the Antonine period, *e.g.* in a group from Ostia (Cumont, *op. cit.* p. 79, fig. 67) which dates from the reign of Commodus, and a bas-relief from the Villa Albani (*ib.* p. 38, fig. 45). The artist has taken delight in multiplying the folds of the garments and in rendering more intricate the curls of the hair, merely to show his skill in overcoming the difficulties which he himself had created. A small piece of sculpture discovered at Aquileia (*ib.* p. 116, pl. iii.) is distinguished in this respect by a 'bewildering cleverness of technique.' The delicately carved figures are almost completely detached from their massive block base, to which they are connected only by very slender supports. It is a piece of bravura in which the sculptor displays his skill in producing in a brittle substance the same effects as the chaser obtains in metal. But these comparatively perfect works are rare even in Italy, and it must be acknowledged that the great majority of these remains are of discouraging mediocrity, which becomes more and more wide-spread towards the 4th century.

The Dadophori.—The group of the bull-slaying Mithra is almost always flanked by two torch-bearers, or *dadophori*, who were called *Cauti* and *Cautopati*. Dressed in the same Oriental garb as Mithra, one of them holds an uplifted, and the other an inverted, torch; they doubtless personify the sun at the equinoxes. The original of these two youths can be traced back, like that of the bull-slaying god, to an unknown sculptor of the Hellenistic age, who had drawn his inspiration from still more ancient models (Cumont, *op. cit.* i. 203 ff.); but this hieratic work, which did not afford scope for the expression of keen emotions, is of much less artistic worth. Yet, in the better specimens at any rate, one may notice the artistic advantage which the artist has been able to derive from the Phrygian dress, and the way in which he has been able to emphasize the different emotions of hope and sadness depicted on the faces of the two youths who are mutually contrasted. The most remarkable reproduction which we possess of this divine pair consists of two statues found near the Tiber, one of which has been taken to the British Museum, while the other is in the Vatican. They certainly date from the time of Hadrian (*ib.* 27 and pl. ii.).

The Mithraic Kronos.—The origin of the subjects just mentioned is to be found in ancient Greek art, but there is another Mithraic work which is certainly derived from an Oriental archetype. It is the lion-headed god, whose body is embraced by a serpent, and who personifies Eternity—the *Zrvān Akarana* of the Persians (see art. MITHRAISM), to whom the adherents of the sect used to give the Greek name Kronos, or the Latin Saturnus. The most celebrated specimen of this type is in the Vatican (Cumont, *op. cit.* 80, fig. 68). Like the majority of his compeers, this animal-headed monster is an exotic creation. His genealogy would carry us back to Assyrian sculpture (*ib.* i. 74 ff.). But the artists of the West, having to represent a deity entirely strange to the Greek pantheon, and being untrammelled by the traditions of any school, gave free course to their imagination. The various transformations which this figure has undergone at their hands were actuated, on the one hand, by religious considerations, which tended to complicate the symbolism of this deified abstraction and to multiply his attributes; and, on the other hand, by an æsthetic solicitude which tended to modify as much as possible the grotesqueness of this barbarous figure, and gradually to humanize it. Ultimately they did away with the lion's head, and contented themselves with representing the animal at the feet of the god, or with placing the head of the beast on his breast. This lion-headed god of Eternity is the most original creation of Mithraic art; and if it is entirely destitute of charm, the grotesqueness of its appearance and the suggestive accumulation of its attributes arouse curiosity and provoke reflexion.

We have, so far, confined our attention to the remains found in Rome and Italy, the artistic finish of which surpasses the average of the Mithraic ex-votos. But when we pass to the provinces of the Empire, we find there elaborate works of a very different kind. It is generally agreed that, during the Empire, a great number of the sculptures intended for the provincial cities were made at Rome, or by artists who had come from Rome (Friedländer, *Sittengeschichte*[3], iii. 280 f.) This is probably the case with certain of the sculptures we are considering; they come from distant studios, either those of the capital or even of Asia Minor or some other province. There is no doubt that certain tablets discovered in Germany were brought from quarries in Pannonia (Cumont, *op. cit.* i. 216). Nevertheless, the great majority of Mithraic remains were undoubtedly executed on the spot. This is obvious in the case of those which were sculptured on the surface of rocks, which had been smoothed for the purpose; but with regard to many, local workmanship is proved from the nature of the stone employed. Moreover, the style of these fragments clearly reveals their local origin. The discovery of so many Mithraic works has thus great importance for the study of provincial art under the Empire. The most remarkable of these works have been brought to light in the North of Gaul, or, more precisely, on the Rhine frontier. It seems that the whole of this group of monuments must be ascribed to that interesting school of sculpture which flourished in Belgium in the 2nd and 3rd cents. of our era, and whose productions are clearly distinguishable from those of Southern studios. Similarly, the less important bas-reliefs brought to light in the Danube provinces are certainly independent of Roman influence; they may be directly connected with certain Asia Minor models. The distinguishing feature of the most important works of these artists from the banks of the Rhine and the Danube is that the central group of the bull-slaying Mithra with his two companions is surrounded by a series of accessory scenes which represent the whole cosmogony of the mysteries and the mission of Mithra, from his birth out of a rock to his assumption up to heaven (*ib.* i. 153 ff.). Then there are added astronomical images or cosmic emblems (planets, signs of the zodiac, winds, etc.).

If we subject all these scenes and symbols to an analysis in detail, we can show that the majority of them are modifications or adaptations of old Greek subjects. Thus, Ahura Mazda destroying the monsters which have arisen against him is a Hellenic Zeus hurling his thunderbolt at the giants (*ib.* i. 157). The poverty of the new conceptions which Mithraic iconography introduces is in startling contrast to the importance of the religious movement that inspired them. At the period when the Persian mysteries overspread the West, the art of sculpture was too decayed to be revived. Whereas, during the Hellenistic period, sculptors were able to conceive novel forms for the Egyptian divinities (Isis, Serapis, etc.), happily harmonizing with their characters, the majority of the Mazdean gods, in spite of their strongly-marked nature, were obliged to assume, whether appropriate or not, the form and dress of the Olympian deities to which they were assimilated.

Art, accustomed to live by plagiarism, had become incapable of original invention. But if, without analyzing each scene and personage in detail, we contemplate the total effect of the work, we receive an impression of something entirely novel. The attempt to represent in stone, not only all the deities of the Mithraic pantheon, but the history of the world and of Mithra as creator and saviour, was a truly sublime idea. Even before this time, especially on the sarcophagi, we find a method employed which consists in representing the successive moments of an action by pictures superimposed on one another or drawn on parallel surfaces; but we cannot mention any pagan monument which can be compared in this respect with the great Mithraic bas-reliefs, especially those of Neuenheim, Heddernheim, and, above all, Osterburken (*ib.* 245, 246, 251). To find a similar attempt we have to come down to the long series of subjects with which Christian artists in mosaic adorned the walls of churches.

If we wished to criticize the details of these sculptures, it would be easy to censure in them the disproportion of certain figures, the clumsiness of some movements, the stiffness of some attitudes, and, above all, the confused impression arising from the superabundance of personages and groups. This last fault of overloaded composition is one which the Mithraic monuments share with the contemporaneous sarcophagi. But in criticizing these remains, it must not be forgotten that painting came to the aid of sculpture. The strong contrast of colours emphasized the principal outlines, and threw accessory parts into prominence. Often certain details were indicated only by the brush; and gilding also was used to set off some subsidiary parts. Without such a brilliant combination of colours the piece of statuary would have been almost invisible in the deep shadow of the subterranean crypts. Such a device, moreover, was one of the traditions of Oriental art, and Lucian (*Jup. trag.* 8) had already contrasted the simple and graceful forms of the Greek deities with the startling gorgeousness of those imported from Asia.

In spite of the numerous suggestions which it has borrowed from the treasury of types created by Greek sculpture, Mithraic art, like the mysteries of which it is the expression, remains essentially Asiatic. The idea with which it is mainly concerned is not to produce an æsthetic impression; it aims principally at arousing religious emotion, not through the perception of beauty, but rather by recalling to the mind sacred legends and teachings. Faithful in this point to the traditions of the ancient East, it confines itself to relating and instructing. The medley of personages and groups with which some bas-reliefs are thronged, the host of attributes with which the figure of Eternity (see above) is overloaded, show us that a new ideal was born with the new religion. These ungraceful or tasteless symbols, the lavish use of which is attested by the monuments, did not charm by their elegance or their dignity; they fascinated the mind by the disturbing attraction of the Unknown, and aroused in the neophyte a reverential fear in face of a tremendous mystery. They were, as St. Jerome says (*Epist.* 107 ad Lætam), 'portentosa simulacra.'

Here, above all, is to be found the explanation why this art, extremely refined as it was, in spite of all its imperfections, has exercised a permanent influence. It was linked to Christian art by a natural affinity, and the symbolism which it had helped to make popular in the West did not perish with it. Even the allegorical figures of the cosmic cycle, which the devotees of the Persian god had reproduced in such abundance (for they regarded the whole of nature as divine), were adopted by Christianity, although really opposed to its spirit. Such were the images of the earth, the sky, and the ocean; the sun, the moon, the planets, and the signs of the zodiac; the winds, the seasons, and the elements; which occur so frequently on the sarcophagi, the mosaics, and the miniatures. Even the mediocre compositions which the artists had conceived to represent the incidents of the Mithra-legend were able to inspire Christian artists. Thus the figure of the sun raising Mithra out of the ocean served to express the ascension of Elijah in the chariot of fire; and, down to the Middle Ages, the figure of the bull-slaying Mithra was perpetuated in the representations of Samson rending the lion.

LITERATURE. — F. Cumont, *Textes et Monuments figurés relatifs aux mystères de Mithra*, Brussels, 1899, i. 213–220 and *passim*; E. Strong, *Roman Sculpture from Augustus to Constantine*, 1907, p. 309 ff.

F. CUMONT.

ART (Muhammadan). — **1. Introduction.** — Our researches into Muhammadan art are as yet entirely in their infancy. So far, the historical inscriptions are only being collected, and this undertaking, upon which M. van Berchem is still engaged, is a necessary condition of all historical study in this field. It is much to be desired that, by way of supplementing this, some one would group together the literary sources which bear upon graphic art in Islām. The bibliography at the end will show that, although we possess several comprehensive writings in this department, we have very few such treatises upon Muhammadan works of art as are serviceable for scientific investigation. The present position of our researches is conditioned by the fact that no Arabic scholar has made himself proficient in the department of graphic art, while the three or four historians of art who deal with Islām at all, have only the most meagre acquaintance with the language and culture of its adherents. In the circumstances it is not to be expected that the present article should do more than acquaint the reader with the outstanding facts of the subject in their relation to religion and ethics. The writer, indeed, feels more inclined to point out the *lacunæ* than able to fill them up. His purpose is not so much to supply adequate information upon the subject proposed, as to provide the reader with a general conspectus of Muslim art.

2. Pre-Muhammadan data.—The most important of these is the action which forms the inevitable adjunct of the Muslim's every prayer, viz., the turning towards Mecca. It does not fall to the historian of art to establish the origin of this custom of turning in a certain direction, or to decide whether it was not simply a transference of the practice of orientation by the sun, as was observed also by the Christians, to the new religious centre. So long as Muhammad had regard to Jews and Christians, it was towards Jerusalem that he turned; it was only at a later stage that he made Mecca the cynosure. We speak of Mecca therefore as pre-Muhammadan only in virtue of its having been a religious centre, and not because the Muslim turns his face towards it during prayer.

Mecca can hardly be said to have any further significance in regard to graphic art. As the Ka'ba lies in the centre of the temple-enclosure, and has not, like the mosque, a definite direction at one side, it naturally dropped aside as a pattern for the mosque. On the other hand, we may surmise that in this most important focus of pilgrimage in Arabia, some kind of monumental relic must have existed from the earliest times, even before Muhammad's day. We may imagine it to have been something analogous to the Qubbat aṣ-Ṣaḥra in Jerusalem, *i.e.* a centrally situated cupola-shaped building. At the present day the temple appears as a quadrangular open court, in the middle of which stands the 'Cube' with the Black Stone. Around this there has been laid out a circular area in the court, which may indicate the form of the earlier cupola-shaped structure. The Qubbat aṣ-Ṣaḥra is surrounded by a corresponding quadrangle.

3. Muhammad. — Had Muhammad not been forced to flee from his native city, it is probable that the mosque would have taken a form somewhat different from that which prevailed before the emergence of the *madrasa*, and apart from the influence of Christian architecture as applied to churches. As Muhammad, however, established his place of prayer in Medīna, and was also buried there, this most unpretentious beginning gave the initiative to the architecture not only of places of worship, but also to some extent of tombs. Samhūdī, in his *History of the City of Medina* (ed. Wüstenfeld, in *Abhandl. d. Ges. d. Wissensch. zu Göttingen*, ix. [1860] 60), tells first of all how Muhammad obtained the site for his mosque, and proceeds as follows: 'Upon this the edifice of bricks was built, palms were used as columns, and a wooden roof was fixed above.' This mosque had three entrances—one at the back, which was built up when Muhammad began the practice of turning to Mecca instead of Jerusalem, the others being the Gate of Mercy and the prophet's private door. After the conquest of Khaibar the mosque was entirely re-built, being enlarged to twice its former size. Some idea of the interior is given by the position of the column beside which Muhammad prayed: 'It was the central column of the mosque, the third forward from the *minbar*, the third from Muhammad's tomb, the third from the south side, the third from the main road before (as Ibn Zabāla states) this was widened by the space of two pillars' (Wüstenfeld, 65). The columns fell into a state of decay during the Khalifate of Abu Bakr, and he had them replaced by fresh palm trunks. The most notable restoration—or re-construction—was that made by Walīd I., who was supplied by the Emperor of Greece with Greek and Coptic artizans, as well as with mussel shells and money. Walls and columns were built with hewn stones of equal size, and cemented with gypsum; decorations of shell-work and marble were introduced, while the roof was constructed of palm and coated with gold-colour. When Walīd inspected the completed work in 93 A.H., he exclaimed, 'What a contrast between our style of building (*i.e.* in Damascus) and yours!' to which the reply was, 'We build in the style of the mosques, you in that of the churches.' Beyond this single reference we have nothing from which to form an idea of the mosque of Muhammad as a whole, or of its imitations. We shall presently return to this.

Of the sacred accessories belonging to the interior of a mosque, such as the niche for prayer (*miḥrāb*), the platform (*dikka*), etc., the only one which we can trace to Muhammad himself is the *minbar*, or pulpit (Becker, in *Orientalische Studien Nöldeke gewidm.* 331 f.). In ancient Arabia the *minbar* was the judge's chair, but as Muhammad advanced from the position of judge to that of ruler, this originally very simple piece of furniture with its two steps became more and more of a throne. A fresco on the inner front wall of Quṣair 'Amra represents one of the first Khalīfs, or perhaps Muhammad himself, seated on a throne. As this, in view of the command against images, may well give rise to fruitful discussion, we give a reproduction of it (fig. 1, p. 897). Over the enthroned figure is a baldachin with a Kufic inscription, which is unfortunately so much abraded that only the closing words are now legible: 'May God grant him his reward, and have compassion upon him!' The personage thus pictured—with red beard, and the saint's *nimbus* about his head—must accordingly have been dead, and cannot have been, as one might naturally think, the Khalīf then reigning. The figure beside the throne holds the lance—a recognized emblem in Islām to the present day; a woman with the *nimbus* is represented on the right, applauding. The design of the enthroned figure may be traced to the *Christus-Pantokrator*; in this case it will then be the Qur'ān, not the Gospels, upon which the left hand is placed. Beneath the great throne is seen the barge of the dead. At the time when this fresco was introduced, *i.e.* subsequent to 100 A.H., the *minbar* can scarcely have had the same appearance as that shown in the illustration. As a matter of fact, the pattern furnished by Muhammad for the mosque and the *minbar* alike was framed with a view to mere utility, and the artistic elaboration thereof belongs entirely to a later period; for Muhammad had even less interest than Jesus in the graphic arts. His attitude towards figure-painting was one of avowed hostility; thus he once remained standing before the house of 'A'isha until a curtain ornamented with figures was removed, and he threatened those who made images with the direst penalties in the world to come. It was therefore impossible that art in Islām should develop the same didactic tendency as it did in early Christianity, in which the representation of figures was expressly utilized as a means of instructing those who could not read.

4. The Umayyads.—It was under these rulers that foreign culture began to stream in upon Islām. Even the mosque did not escape the general transformation, and its original design of simple convenience was left behind. The incentive to the desire for something more was first given by contact with Christianity. At the conquest of Damascus, the principal church of the city, that of St. John, was divided. Apparently it had then the same form as now: a dome in the middle, contiguous basilicas to east and west, and a pillared court to the north fronting the whole. At first the Muslims laid claim only to one of the basilicas; it was Walīd I. (A.D. 705–715) who first transformed the entire edifice into a mosque. Of this 'church-design' of mosque, except in Damascus, only two examples are now known, viz., the great mosque of Diarbekr, dating from the 12th cent., and that of Ephesus, from the 14th. Its nucleus was a Christian *martyrium* built over a pagan sanctuary, around which in time several churches were grouped, as was the case with the Holy Sepulchre in Jerusalem, the church at Nola, the church at the tomb of Menas, and the twin-churches at Ephesus.

The 'mosque-design' has no connexion with church architecture. It is certainly believed by some to be traceable to the plan of the forecourt attached to the Church of the Sepulchre in Jerusalem, of which the Muslims made a mosque for themselves; but in reality the *atrium*, or forecourt of the Christian church, still corresponds most nearly to the 'court-design' with the well in the centre. It is probably the case, however, that between the Christian *atrium* and the Muhammadan mosque there is an intermediate form—some primitive Asiatic type, such as a court with hall adjoining. The mosque exhibits this type in purer form than the church; the columnated halls, for instance, which enclose the court, grow more numerous in the direction of Mecca. Muhammad's mosque in Medīna was most probably of this form; as it stands to-day it is quite in accordance with this supposition, though, of course, it has been several times re-constructed.

The Umayyads, in building such mosques, had probably to avail themselves of columns taken from ancient or Christian ruins. Muhammad himself had used palm-trunks, and had thus left no established precedent. The oldest mosques, or at least those which survive in their rudimentary form, such as the ruins of Baalbek and Bosra, the 'Amr mosque in Old Cairo, and the great mosques of Kairwan and Cordova, are virtual column-museums, something like the façades of St. Mark's in Venice. Such embellishments have only a negative bearing upon the characteristic quality of Muslim art. As an example of an interior constructed of columns from ancient and Christian buildings, we give a view of the mosque at Kairwan (fig. 2, p. 898). Here we see a forest of columns in front; behind, to the right of this, extends the entrance wall, beside which large chandeliers are suspended between the columns, the mid-passage running thence to the *qibla*. The arches run parallel to the line of this passage; in this instance they are rounded, though as a general rule they are pointed, and disproportionately high. The variously moulded capitals are linked together by anchors, while a wooden roof is placed over the whole. Such was the prevalent type of the Muslim place of worship in early times.

From the 1st cent. A.H. come other two buildings. One of these, situated in Jerusalem, has long been known; the other has been recently discovered by an Austrian research-party. The first, the Qubbat aṣ-Ṣaḥra upon the Temple hill, is not a mosque, but a memorial edifice. Above the rock with its caves rises a dome supported by four pillars, between every two of which stand three columns. Two circular passages with eight pillars, and two columns between each pair of these, lead over to the octagonal surrounding wall. Of the original fabric erected by ʿAbd al-Malik in A.H. 72 (A.D. 691) very little remains: the columns still retain vestiges of the Cross upon the capitals, and must therefore have been taken from some Christian building, while the exceedingly valuable mosaics of the passage are of Persian origin.

On the other hand, the second monument referred to, a secular structure known as Quṣair ʿAmra, and situated in the desert adjoining Moab, is pure Syrian in character. Attached to a small bath is a hall roofed with three parallel tunnel-vaults, and showing on the south two apsidal chambers, the niche between them having a straight front-wall directly opposite the entrance. The structure as a whole recalls the type of tunnel-vaulted churches indigenous to the interior of Asia Minor. The paintings are most instructive, as has already been shown in the case of the fresco of the enthroned figure illustrated in fig. 1 (p. 897). They exhibit Umayyad art in the full current of the Hellenistic style; the frescoes of the bath-chambers might well be counted as ancient. The pictures in the hall are of far-reaching significance, furnishing the best exemplification of the tendency which, while opposed to all worship of images, was again adopted by the image-breakers in Constantinople, and which, after the example of the Assyrian relief, became associated rather with the portrayal of landscape, and of hunting and fishing scenes, instances of these being found likewise in the early Christian art of Syria and its offshoots.

We must now call attention to the fact that in ʿAmra, among scenes of hunting, fishing, and bathing, there have been introduced two pictures which, from the standpoint of religion and ethics, may well evoke much controversy in the future. Upon the front wall of the niche, opposite the entrance, appears the figure of the man seated on a throne. But it is the other picture which calls for explanation from the Muhammadan point of view; its subject is the princes overthrown by Islām, viz., the Emperor of Byzantium, Chosroës of Persia, the Negus of Abyssinia, and Roderick of Spain. How are these pictures to be brought into accordance with the interdict against graphic representation, and in what sense are we to interpret them? The picture of the Khalīf upon the throne undoubtedly gives the impression of its being a devotional piece, but that of the conquered princes can scarcely be explained in a similar way.

The Umayyads have also in recent times been spoken of as the builders of a number of large and beautiful castles in the desert, situated in the neighbourhood of ʿAmra, but more towards the inhabited country. These have been made known chiefly by the large Meshītā façade which the Emperor of Germany received as a gift from the Sultan and placed in the Berlin Museum. In these castles the present writer discerns structures so unmistakably of a Persian character as to suggest conditions which would allow of a closer connexion with Hira or North Mesopotamia. Both Meshītā and Qaṣr-aṭ-Ṭūba are immense fortified royal seats, surrounded by groups of plots, and resembling those found in the Sasanian fabrics of Mesopotamia. Both are unfinished, and their respective porticoes bear the same kind of decorations, amongst which the Persian wing-palmette amid vine-tendrils characteristically recurs.

5. The Abbāsids.—The shifting of the centre of the Muslim world from Damascus to Baghdad had very important consequences for the development of graphic art, as the Syrian, *i.e.* the Hellenistic-Christian, factor now fell into the background, while the Oriental came to the front. In the latter, it is true, there is always a double strain: on the one hand the Assyro-Sasanian tradition, and on the other a drift in part still older, which may possibly have come in with the Parthians, and certainly found a channel in the immigration of sporadic parties, or even of whole tribes, of Turks from Central Asia to Persia and Baghdad. For the remote part of Western Asia this drift has all the significance of a barbarian invasion of a long established civilization, such as was experienced by Rome at the hands of the Germans. The Turks and the Germans were in fact the emissaries of an inchoate 'Hinterland' culture, which had been quite overshadowed by the hothouse growth of Egyptian, Babylonian, and Greek art, but which, when the representatives of the older refinement began to flag, came once more into the foreground. We must likewise bear in mind the gradually weakening influence of early Christian art, as also the growing potencies of the Chinese factor.

(*a*) *Persian elements.*—A wholly unique type of mosque is found in Mesopotamia. Here again, indeed, we have the arcaded court, with the open hall lying towards Mecca, but, in keeping with the nature of the country, the supports are formed not of columns but of brick pillars. In consequence of this, and because walls, pillars, and arches are now uniformly ornamented with stucco-work, the mosque assumes a most characteristic appearance, known to us until recently only from a mosque in Cairo erected in *c.* 870 A.D. by the Ṭūlūnids, who came from Baghdad to Egypt. It has lately been shown, however, that the mosque of Ibn Ṭūlūn was built upon the model of the mosque of Samarra, as had been stated by early Arabic writers. Moreover, in Abū-Dilif, 15 km. to the north of Samarra, there still stands a mosque which agrees with that of Ibn Ṭūlūn even in the number of its supports. Of this example of the unique character of Mesopotamian mosques we give an illustration from the survey of General de Beylié, which shows the entrance-wall opposite the *miḥrāb* (fig. 3, p. 898). Here we see pillars composed of brick, with hewn-out ornamental niches, and united by arches, the springers of which still remain. The side arches leave the view open towards the surrounding wall of the mosque, and through the central arch appears the spindle-like minaret.

Even this peculiar and fantastic minaret at Samarra has been copied in the mosque of Ibn Ṭūlūn at Cairo by the erection of a winding staircase on the outside. Elsewhere the stair is for the most part on the inside, and the minaret, which is used for calling to prayer, is outwardly smooth, whether rounded or quadrate. In the period of the Fāṭimids, buildings were constructed not only in the older style prevalent along the Mediterranean seaboard, *i.e.* with columns (*al-*

azhār), but also according to the Mesopotamian mode, *i.e.* with pillars (*al-hakam*). In both styles, however, the ornamentation was of the same kind. We shall return to this, but meanwhile we must speak of the accessories of worship.

There is first of all the *qibla*, or the direction towards Mecca, which is determined by a niche (*miḥrāb*) in the wall, very small in comparison with the great apse of Christian churches, and aligned with one or two columns. Of the origin of the *miḥrāb* we have no certain knowledge. It appears to have been originally made of wood. In Cairo three ancient wooden niches with beautiful ornamentation are still to be found. The typical form was already in use in the Khalīfate epoch of Baghdad; that period, at all events, exhibits the niche let into the wall, with bounding columns at the corners—a design which emerged in the East in Hellenistic times, and which had great vogue in the later period of ancient art, especially in Syria and Asia Minor. The graduated columnar porches of Western architecture likewise find their origin here.

The *minbar* has always been constructed of wood, essays in marble or other substance being of the rarest occurrence. By 132 A.H., when all the provincial mosques received their *minbars*, it can hardly have retained its primitive form, and was certainly of a different shape from that represented in the 'Amra fresco. Its model was not the throne, but rather the Christian *ambo*, an approximation to which had gradually been developed. Numerous steps led up to the platform, and parapet and steps were richly endowed with ornaments. The oldest surviving *minbar*, that of the great mosque at Kairwan, is of plane-tree, brought from Baghdad by Ibrāhīm ibn al-Aghlab in 242 A.H. (fig. 4, p. 899).

In order to convey a distinct impression of what the art of decoration as practised by the Abbāsids in Mesopotamia could achieve, we give an illustration of the façade of the al-Aqmar mosque in Cairo, as discovered in recent years and restored (fig. 5, p. 900). According to the inscriptions, it dates from A.D. 1125. Here we already see the arrangement which also prevailed among the Seljuks of Asia Minor—a central *risalit* which stands in front of the two wings, and derives its principal embellishment from a lofty gate. We do not as yet know the source of this design. It is all the more striking as we have before us only a false façade, which has no inner apartment corresponding to it, but which is simply a high wall standing before an open court. Of still greater interest is the ornamentation upon the wall-surface. This contains designs which in all probability were originally naturalized in the Orient as stucco-work, but which are here, in Egypt, transferred to the stone in common use. The portal-niche is connected with two smaller niches on a level with the ground-floor; all three display in their arches shell-like *tori* of luxuriant outline. Here too appears, fully developed, one of the main elements of Muslim decoration, viz. the *stalactite*. We find stalactites upon the side portals, taking the place of mussel-panelling, and also as a surface-decoration above the little niches beside the main porch, while they appear in their proper and original function on the corners of the building, where in two rows of niches one above the other they form a beak. The design of the niche with inserted columns is often applied to the upper wall; the little columns on the central *risalit* already show the bell-form which came with the Ṭūlūnids or the Fāṭimids from Persia to Egypt. Along the upper extremity of the façade, which is filled out with ornaments of rosettes and lozenges, runs an inscription-frieze.

The present writer regards these stalactites as a characteristic deposit of Muslim ethics in the field of graphic art. In them constructive restraint, *i.e.* the best and obligatory design, is surrendered in favour of a freakishness capable of endless variation, which becomes all the more interesting by reason of the limitations laid down by the spatial form. The stalactite, rightly regarded, is of purely constructional origin. It served originally, as a single niche, the same purpose for which the Byzantines used the so-called pendentive, *i.e.* the filling-out of the corner which remains open when a round cupola is placed upon a square substructure. For this, later Hellenistic architecture had a definite, mathematically accurate, solution in the sector of the vault of the circumscribed circle; in Persia, on the other hand, the custom was to place a niche in the angle. Instead of the single niche, however, we occasionally find three, combined as already noticed in the case of the al-Aqmar mosque, or, more frequently, in the inverse position, one below and two above. Next a further row, of three, came to be added, thus making a group of six; then a row of four, making ten, and so on. This embellishment of the cupola-wedge was transferred to portal-niches, then to surfaces, and in this way was obtained an ornamentation which always indicates a terminal line or a transition (cf. on this point the works of Bourgoin).

This delight in the spinning out of fortuitous conceits likewise brought to maturity the second style of ornament typical of Muslim art, viz., the *arabesque*. In this also the distinctive feature is that from a theme originally given—some natural object in the present case—certain elements are grouped by the imagination to imitate nature, and for this end new themes are introduced, with which, as with conventional numbers, endless combinations may be made. As the present writer has shown in the *Jahrb. d. preuss. Kunstsammlung*, xxv. (1904), p. 327 f., the arabesque takes its inception from the Hellenistic vine-branch. In the later period of ancient art this became the most popular pattern for striated or superficial decoration. The development towards the arabesque begins when the artist divests the vine-leaf of its natural form by superimposing other leaves, or a triad of globules, upon the diverging point of the ribs, or when, further, he makes the leaf tri-lobed instead of five-lobed. But the actual transformation consists in the application to the vine-leaf of the lobate form which may really be described as the artificial flower of West-Asiatic art, *i.e.* the palmette. The vine-tendril moulded after the palmette—this is arabesque. The development proceeds in virtue of the fact that the palmette can be split up either into halves or into single lobes; while each of these lobes again may be expanded, and give rise to new ramifications. The façade of A.D. 1125, in its details, furnishes illustrations of the initial stage of this whole development: here the branch shows more of the Persian than of the Arabian form. On the other hand, fig. 6 (p. 900), representing a wooden tablet in the K. Friedrich Museum in Berlin supposed to date from A.D. 1125, exhibits all the stages side by side—the five-lobed vine-leaf with and without the grape-cluster, the trifolium, all kinds of ramifying palmettes, and also the palmette itself with ornamental branching.

In this tablet the divided palmette in the centre is surrounded by a ten-angled star which obtrudes itself into the marginal bands both above and beneath. This brings us to the third class of specifically Muhammadan ornament, viz., *polygonal lace-work*. It is already to be seen on a closer scrutiny of the Cairo façade of A.D. 1125—appearing as striated decorations in the lozenges of the surface-niches, above to the left; but here they show rather the older double-stripe design which was common also in ancient and Christian art. The distinctively Muslim variety, as we think, shows in its origin the influence of the Turkish-Mongolian nomadic races, who eventually brought the Khalīfate to an end (A.D. 1258).

Before dealing further with this subject we may draw attention to the influence exerted upon the development of Muslim art by religion and ethics —an influence revealing itself in the fact that the ornamentation of sacred buildings embraces no representation of living objects. The wonted Mesopotamian type of decoration consists in overlaying the walls, pillars, and arches with stucco ornaments. We are cognizant of no instance whatever in which this architectural decoration contains the figure of man, animal, or bird. The mosque of Ibn Ṭūlūn in Cairo; the Church of Abbot Moses of Nisibis in the Syrian monastery of the Nitrian desert, which was stuccoed by Mesopotamian artists; Maqām ʽAlī itself, on the Euphrates; Samarra—in none of these have we a trace of a living creature figured as an ornament. In this period, therefore, the commandment against the use of figures in sacred buildings would seem to have been stringently enforced. The ornaments are composed of half or whole palmettes, which are connected with one another by spiral designs, and thrown out by indentations so as to form independent configurations. To these again are added designs which are traceable in the main to the stucco-technique in its capacity to suggest the dark effects of depth. Symbolical figures, such as were favoured by Sasanian and Christian art—the crescent, the star, the wing, etc.—are entirely absent so far as religious art is concerned. If we would adequately appreciate the authority thus attaching to the precepts of religion in the sphere of graphic art, we must keep before us the delight which the Orient has always found in the mystical and symbolical use of animal forms, as is in fact exemplified by the extreme frequency with which such figures are employed in the secular art of Islām itself.

(*b*) *Turkish elements.*—One of the most singular notions still current, and one to be explained only on the ground that our vision has been deranged by our immemorial habit of seeing everything in the light of Græco-Roman institutions, is that the migratory races, whether Germans or Turks, were destitute of all art. This is to forget that the Goths brought with them into Italy a highly-developed culture, acquired upon the Greek coast of the Black Sea; and the like holds good of the peoples who forced their way from Central Asia into Persia, and who had thus passed through, or temporarily settled in, the long-civilized region beyond the Caspian Sea. Think of the discoveries in Hungary, telling of the time when the Magyars took possession of the country. This equestrian people came from the territories lying between the Altai and the Ural without coming into contact with Transoxiana; nevertheless their taste in decoration was well developed. How much more are we entitled to look for æsthetic proficiency amongst the peoples who had not only lived at close quarters with the Samanids or the Ghaznavids, but who, as, *e.g.*, the Seljuks, had made themselves masters of their lands before they conquered Persia and Asia Minor. In Egypt the new conditions were ushered in under Saladin, and continued during the period of the Turkoman and Circassian Mamlūks, until, in 1517, the Turks proper gained the upper hand.

It is worthy of remark that with the advent of the Turkish tribes are conjoined two types of building of which there are no surviving examples from Umayyad or early Abbāsid times: the large cupola-domed *mausoleum* and a new type of mosque-school, the *madrasa*. As regards the mausoleum, there is no doubt that it had already been roofed —by Constantine or even before his day—with cupolas. But a gigantic fabric of brick, such as the tomb of the Sultan Sanjar in Merv, dating from 552 A.H. (A.D. 1157), is, of course, hardly to be compared with the finely articulated edifices of Christian times. We must never forget, however, that the tombs of the Umayyads were violated by the fanaticism of the Abbāsids, or that the only tomb known to exist in the neighbourhood of Baghdad, that of Zubaida, the favourite wife of Harūn al-Rashīd, bears a curious niche-pyramid, which hardly permits of comparison with the later buildings. It is true that pyramids are found also upon the mausoleums erected in A.D. 1162 and 1186 by Seljuk Atabeks in Nakshevan, on the Perso-Armenian frontier, but these are supported by a dome-shaped vault, the walls of which are embellished with polygonal ornaments of mosaic work in stucco bricks. One of the far-famed sights of Cairo is the Necropolis, the so-called Tombs of the Khalīfs and Mamlūks (fig. 7, p. 901), which in their picturesque construction invite comparison with the massive forms of the pyramids on the opposite bank of the Nile. The mausoleums of Islām are so arranged as to permit of being dwelt in by the family of the deceased at certain seasons of the year. An even more magnificent effect, however, than that of the Necropolis of Cairo is made by the sepulchral mound of Shah Zindah, near Samarcand. The huge mausoleum of Timur (†A.D. 1405), which the terror-inspiring Mongol leader had built in his lifetime, and which is now known as the Gur Emir, lends signal distinction to the whole district. As a work of art, however, it is surpassed by the sepulchral mosque of Khudābandakhān in Sultanīya (A.D. 1304–1316), which, like the mausoleum at Merv, presents on the outside an imposing arcade style of architecture. It can hardly be a mere matter of chance that these three most important sepulchral edifices should be found in the Caspian or Trans-Caspian area.

The second architectural form which first came into general use subsequently to the incursion of the Turkish tribes, viz. the *madrasa*, likewise evolved a capacity of being applied to great monumental structures. An example of this type may be seen in the illustration (fig. 8, p. 901) of the mosque of Sultan Ḥasan in Cairo, erected in A.D. 1356–1359. It was the Ayyūbids who instituted such college houses in Egypt. The *madrasa* expresses the idea that, in order to correspond with the four sects of Islām, four separate wings are required, viz. *Madrasat al-Hanīfīya, al-Shāfiʽīya, al-Hanbalīya*, and *al-Mālikīya*. This plan of associating four schools in one building was carried out in a very ingenious way, namely, by planting them respectively in the four angles of a cross, which was formed by four tunnel-vaulted arms converging upon the open central court. Were the tunnels of this cross all of equal length, and were a cupola placed over the small court, we might fail to discriminate between this form of building, in its general plan at least, and the cruciform church with a dome. As, however, the central square is open to the sky, and the four aisles are often of very different lengths, such an identification is out of the question. We incline to believe that the plan of the *madrasa* is in its essentials of very remote origin. It is resorted to in the construction of a gateway for the citadel of ʽAmmān in Moab, and was no doubt often used in Sasanian palaces. It is accordingly a Muslim construction only in so far as it has been transferred to the institution of the four sects, and elaborated in accordance with the requirements thereof (see ARCHITECTURE [Muh. in Syria and Egypt], p. 757).

This remarkable construction impresses the native of the West as being more decidedly Oriental than even the mosque. Picture these huge tunnels, vaulted mostly in the pointed style, and strengthened by the schools built into the corners like immense supports, and yet without anything to sustain; it is the spirit of the stalactite without architectonic motive, and of the vine-branch without the link with nature. Further, in Egypt at all events, there is something which must cause the utmost amazement, viz. the 'High Gate,' or portal-niche. The niche of the mosque of Sultan Ḥasan in Cairo, built in A.D. 1356–1359, *c.* 26 metres in height, has been cut out of a wall which rises 37·70 metres above the level of the street, and is not accommodated to the main feature of the edifice as a whole, *i.e.* it does not correspond with the *qibla*, but has a relation to the line of the street, being placed in a corner obliquely to the longitudinal wall, so that any one entering the vestibule can reach the central court only by way of various narrow passages. We might all the more expect to find an axial design in the main ornament, viz. that of the porch, as the immense dome of the builder of the mausoleum towers aloft exactly in the axis behind the *miḥrāb*. This ignoring of systematic design is peculiar to Egypt, and is not found, so far as the present writer knows, in other Muslim lands, while, especially in Asia Minor, the *madrasa* is always arranged symmetrically about the central axis.

Meanwhile we must say something regarding other innovations, which make their appearance subsequently to the ascendancy of the Central Asiatic element in the Muslim world. The astonishing growth in the popular use of polygonal ornamentation already touched upon may possibly be attributed to the preference for geometrical decoration which is characteristic of nomads. Even upon the *minbar* of Kairwan, constructed probably in Baghdad in 242 A.H. (fig 4, p. 899), the double-striped lace-work in straight or curved lines so largely predominates that we can scarcely reconcile its vogue with our wonted conceptions of Sasanian and early Muslim art, in which it is rather the palmette that prevails. But, by the time when the Oriental element re-emerged from the obscurity in which it had been embedded for centuries, Hellenistic art must already have returned, more decisively than ever, to the style of the geometrical lace-work. This reversion to the primitive, then, finds ample scope for development among the nomads from Central Asia, whose taste was still in thrall to the lace-work, as to the material generally, and to caprice.

Since, in the art ancillary to the cultus, *lace-work* takes the place of animal ornament, it demands some notice at this point. As an illustrative example, we reproduce a detail of the *minbar* (A.D. 1168–1169) of the al-Aqṣā Mosque in Jerusalem (fig. 9, p. 902). Here we have a piece of work in wood and ivory, by an artizan from Aleppo, so complicated in its construction as to be hardly intelligible to Europeans. We perceive arabesques of ivory in the middle of both the vertical moldings. On either side are polygonal decorations, composed of purfled moldings in wood and fillings of ivory. From the corners which form the foci of the main lines we may be able to infer the class of polygon upon which any particular play of lines is designed—whether it is the hexagon, the one mainly resorted to, or some other fundamental figure. The discovery of this, however, merely gives us the key; the endlessly varied ways in which the purfled fillets intertwine and intersect, leaving, in ordered repetition, free spaces, which in turn are filled up with relief arabesques or coloured inlaid work, can scarcely be resolved. All this is an expression of the same exultation in elaborating designs obtained mathematically or fortuitously as was to be seen in the case of the stalactite. The fly-leaves of the Qur'ān exhibit first-rate examples of such artifices. There, indeed, they are in their right place, as in them and in the caligraphic amplification of the writing a compensation had to be found for the absence of the human form.

(*c*) *Chinese elements.*—We are not accustomed to regard China as the source of a contribution to Muslim art. Chinese elements, nevertheless, may already have found admission in Syria, as they certainly did, more powerfully, in Persia, and finally, in all probability, through the influence of the on-coming Turks. From early notices of silk as a Chinese product, and of silk materials in Egypt and in mediæval Europe, it is easy to show that in the later ancient and the Christian period there was commercial intercourse between Syria and China. In Persia during the Abbāsid dynasty the influence of China begins to be felt even in architecture, and unmistakable evidences of this influence are seen in the Talisman Gate of Baghdad, completed in 618 A.H., as well as in two reliefs of winged figures dating from about the same time. These works become intelligible only in the light of facts which were afterwards made plain by the Oriental carpet. Thus both the examples just cited as bearing upon the field of architecture find their immediate explanation in the enormous carpet now in the possession of the Emperor of Austria and known as the 'Vienna Hunting Carpet.' The illustration of this (fig. 10, p. 902) shows, in the borders, winged genii, and, in the angles of the inner field, the Chinese dragon struggling with the phœnix. The manner in which the plant-designs and the Chinese cloud-design are wrought out leave us in no dubiety regarding their origin. Yet the carpet was manufactured in Persia, as is evinced, to say nothing of the workmanship, by the hunting scenes in the inner field, where Persians with turbans and heron-feathers are shown on horseback engaged in the chase. Chinese traits are visible also in the drawing of the figures.

This brings us to the most interesting fact of all in the development of Perso-Muslim art, viz. the resuscitation of figure-representation as a result of Chinese influence. Reference has already been made to the illumination of Qur'ān manuscripts, from which figures are entirely absent. This does not entitle us, of course, to assume their absence from other classes of literature. There exist, however, a few miniature manuscripts which are decorated in the style usual in Armenian and Coptic writings. But the great majority of Persian illuminated manuscripts, and precisely those which are most valuable in an artistic sense, display alike in landscape and in figure the identical type of representation which, judging from the earliest Japanese and Chinese works of art of the class that imitates nature, we recognize as belonging specifically to the Far East. Moreover, as recent researches make it credible that the cavalier and love poetry of the earlier mediæval period in Europe caught fresh stimulus from the Perso-Muslim world with which it came into touch on Spanish ground, it cannot but amaze us to encounter, in Persian manuscripts, illustrated with designs developed in China, the very spirit known to us directly in our own literary history. In one province of Muslim art, therefore, viz. the secular, a sphere is found for a creative impulse which works freely in the expression of all human feeling, thus forming a vivid contrast to the sacred art which was fettered to the interdict against 'graven images.'

The case is somewhat different in regard to the portrayal of animals and animal fights, hunting and drinking scenes, planets, Alexander upon the dragon-chariot, and the like, as seen upon the so-called Mossul-bronzes, from the middle of the 12th cent. and onwards. It is possible that the technique seen in those vessels derived its inspiration from Central Asia, while Chinese designs likewise occur sporadically; but in the main the impulse towards the representation of figures must be traced to Persian Christians. On this hypothesis alone can we explain the adoption of the late Hellenistic picture-cycle, and, in particular, the introduction of scenes from the life of Christ, which were designed for the apartments of Muslim princes. Consequently, the figures portrayed must be interpreted, not in the ethical spirit of Hellenic-Christian symbolism, but as purely decorative. The primitive Oriental interpretation of the animal fight, as symbolical of the conflict between good and evil, is simply lost.

6. Later developments.—The great mass of the Muslim memorials of art emanates from the period after the Turkish tribes gained the absolute lordship of the civilized regions originally permeated by the Syro-Persian spirit. Art was now devoted more than ever to purposes of representation and embellishment. It is therefore very remarkable that what have come down to us from this relatively late epoch are mainly mosques and mausoleums, not palaces, the Alhambra being the only one of its class. It would appear that at this time places of worship alone were built 'for eternity,' *i.e.* of durable material. In the Seljuk kingdom of Iconium (Konia) in Asia Minor this material was principally stone. The mosques and *madrasas* of Konia and Sivas have magnificent façades of the same, or of an incomparably richer, style than the façade of the al-Aqmar mosque given in fig. 5 (p. 900). The *madrasa* approximates more to the type of the arcaded court. In Persia the predominant building material was brick. The result was that every variety of the art of facing was resorted to, the walls being veneered with stucco or many-coloured bricks, or covered with faience mosaics. The native soil of such things was not Mesopotamia or Iran alone, but, as in the case of so many other features of Muslim art, Transoxiana. There, in Samarcand and Bokhara, the most marvellous erections of the Mongols are found standing to this day.

An altogether peculiar position in Muslim art was taken by the Osmanlis, from the time that they obtained possession of Constantinople. It was the Church of St. Sophia that roused them to rivalry, so that in Stamboul we meet for the second time with mosques of Christian design, as Damascus furnished us with the earliest examples. The Osmanlis, in fact, bring to completion what had been aspired to by the great architects of Asia Minor in the inception of antique art at Constantinople, viz. the construction of edifices on a scale of amplitude hitherto unknown. We feel unable to decide whether it was intensity of religious emotion that gave the incentive to the stupendous domes in Stamboul, rising above enclosures that yield a total impression of such magnificence as is unparalleled in the Renaissance and Barocco structures of the West. We may assert without misgiving that the mosques associated with the Church of St. Sophia exhibit that ideal form which, since Bramante's time, has been sought in the all-round effect of stately interiors. Thus Islām at length achieved what lay originally far beyond its range: it gave the crowning touch to the development of the art of architecture which had evolved its designs from a Hellenistic foundation.

A second triumph was won for Islām by the too little known memorials of art in India. Here again Muslim art accommodated itself to the indigenous forms—a process rendered all the more easy as the ground-plan and elevation of the mosque, and even the fantastic play of ornamentation, had already been fully evolved in pre-Muhammadan India, though, naturally, in a style different from that of Western Asia. The magnificence of the plan of arrangement in the Indian mosque constructions is almost without parallel. It is also in India that we find palaces of vast configuration dating from Muhammadan times, and thus furnishing the necessary supplement to the secular art so slenderly represented in the Mediterranean region.

The Alhambra.—To Europeans the Alhambra represents the sum and substance of Muslim art, and, in point of fact, it is really such, so far as the province of secular art is concerned. There is one thing, however, which we must not forget—a fact of decisive import for the ethical value of the whole structure, viz. that the Alhambra must be regarded, not as an independent work of architecture, but as a component part of the natural environment, which is always taken into account in the secular art of Islām, and which, in the case before us, is a park encircling the whole rising ground about the main hill. We may gain an idea of the wide expanse sometimes given to such enclosures from the Conca d'oro beside Palermo, where the palace-grounds embrace the chateaux of Zisa, Cuba, Favara, and Monreale; note, however, that a different style was adopted by the Normans in the construction of their dwelling-place, that, namely, of the fortified stronghold. But in the citadel of Granada we meet with open courts, enclosed by lath-and-plaster work, which has been preserved as if by a miracle. The first court, called the Court of the Myrtles, still retains its garden-like character; while in the second, the Court of the Lions (fig. 11, p. 903), the fountain in the centre sends out babbling streams which flow into the halls.

Then the glittering wealth of ornaments, with their lustrous colours and their puzzling variety of form! The principal designs, the stalactite, the arabesque, and the polygon, make their appearance here once more, though employed with a more uniform ornateness than in the earlier style of art. The kind of workmanship, however, to which all this exuberance of beauty has been applied, explains why it is the Alhambra alone that has survived: the arches which are finished in such a splendid style of architecture have nothing at all to sustain; they consist simply of wood and plaster, like an ornamental sign-board. The structures which lie behind this embellishment are of a very simple kind, and characteristic of the race which produced them.

The inscriptions of the Alhambra reveal a surprisingly intimate relation between spectator and ornament. Just as the Turks had the faculty of giving individuality to each one of a long series of fountains, so the Moors must have had a fine sense of the language of ornamentation. The inscriptions pertaining to the various portions of the great fabric, as well as to the various ornaments, furnish suggestive introductions to these. Thus, for example, upon a niche at the entrance to the Hall of the Ambassadors appear the words which Schack has translated thus:

'Mich hat des Künstlers Hand gestickt, wie ein Gewand von Seide,
Und mir das Diadem besetzt mit blitzendem Geschmeide;
So wie der Thron der jungen Braut strahl ich in hellem Schimmer,
Doch bringe höh'res Glück als er, es weicht und wechselt nimmer.'

Such facts of observation prompt the inquiry whether the ethical significance of Muhammadan decorative art is not of a higher order than we commonly suppose. It is our hope that the scientific research which is only now being vigorously applied to the field of Muslim art in general, may in course of time yield fuller information on the subject than we have been able to give here.

LITERATURE.—i. *COMPREHENSIVE WORKS*: *Manuel d'art musulman*, (i.) H. Saladin, *L'Architecture*; (ii.) G. Migeon, *Les Arts plastiques et industriels*, Paris (1907).

ii. *ARCHITECTURE*: Franz Pascha, *Die Baukunst des Islam* (Darmstadt, 1896); Saladin, *La mosquée de Sidi Okba à Kairouan* (Paris, 1899); Herz Bey, *La mosquée du Sultan Hassan* (Cairo, 1899); Sarre, *Persische Baukunst* (appearing); the Russian work upon Gur Emir in Samarcand; A. F. Calvert, *The Alhambra* (London, 1907); and the recognized older literature.

iii. *DECORATION AND ORNAMENT*: Strzygowski, 'Mschatta' in *Jahrb. d. preuss. Kunstsammlung* (1904): the various works of H. Wallis, Martin, Schmoranz, and others, which are found well arranged in Migeon's *Manuel*. Inostranzeff and Smirnov have published a collection of materials for a bibliography of Muslim archæology, St. Petersburg (1906).

J. STRZYGOWSKI.

ART (Persian).—Persian art has developed more on the utilitarian side in connexion with the manufacture of rugs, draperies, embroideries, pottery, brass-work, and decorative tiles, than along the more purely æsthetic lines of sculpture and painting. Sculpture, in fact, had no chance to develop further in Persia after the Muhammadan conquest, for the teachings of the Prophet, even as modified by the Shīʻite views, to which the Iranians adhere, are adverse to representing objects that have animate life, and the Qur'ān expressly forbids the making of graven images (cf., however, preceding art, esp. p. 875 f.). In respect to sculpture, therefore, the Arab invasion marks a sharp line of division between the old régime and the new; but in other respects the history of Persian art may be traced with a fair degree of continuity for nearly twenty-five centuries.

The chief eras in the national history of the country, which it is found convenient to follow in a study of its art, have already been characterized in the article ARCHITECTURE (Persian) as: Early Iranian and Median period (before B.C. 550), Achæmenian (B.C. 550–330), Seljuk and Parthian (B.C. 330–A.D. 224), Sasanian (A.D. 224–661), and Muhammadan (A.D. 661 to the present day). As sculpture practically died out with the Muslim conquest, it may be appropriate to treat its history first, and then take up metal-work, the fictile or ceramic arts, art in textile fabrics, decorative designs, and pictorial representation.

1. Sculpture and carving.—(*a*) We know nothing definite in regard to sculpture or the state of the plastic art during the *Early Iranian period*, that is to say, prior to the 7th cent. B.C. Even if we consider that the Avesta in a manner represents that era of antiquity, we nevertheless can find in it no specific allusions to sculpture, unless we are to accept the theory, which has been advanced by some scholars, that images of the divine beings Vohu Manah (the Zoroastrian archangel of Good Thought) and Ardvī Sūrā Anāhitā, or Anaïtis (goddess of the heavenly waters), may possibly be referred to in *Vendīdād*, xix. 20–25, descriptive of cleansing, and *Yasht*, v. 126–129, describing the appearance of the divinity. Such an interpretation of the text, however (especially in the former of the two passages), is more than doubtful, even if we concede that images of these divinities were known in Strabo's time (*Geog.* xv. 114). It is indeed possible that some of the bronze figurines and small terra-cotta images that are now and then found in primitive burial-places, or unearthed in such excavations as those by Dieulafoy and de Morgan at Susa (J. de Morgan, *Mémoires—Recherches archéologiques*, i., viii., Paris, 1900, 1905), may go back to a remote Iranian age, but no truly archaic sculpture of any size has yet been found.

(*b*) A similar uncertainty prevails with regard to kindred objects attributed to the *Median age*, and also with regard to the huge stone lion at Hamadan. This statue is executed in the round, like the bull at Babylon and the taurocephalic capitals at Babylon (Dieulafoy, *L'Art antique de la Perse*, Paris, 1884–85, vol. iii. p. 13). Its age is a matter of debate. A thousand years ago Masʻūdī (d. 951 A.D.) ascribed its origin to Alexander the Great, while Yāqūt (*c.* 1220 A.D.) placed it much earlier; and a number of modern scholars are inclined to assign the statue to the Median period (Jackson, *Persia Past and Present*, New York, 1906, pp. 151–162).

(*c*) The oldest identified sculpture of the *Achæmenian period* is the bas-relief figure of Cyrus the Great at Murghab, the ancient Pasargadæ. This image (which Weissbach claims to be a representation of Cyrus the Younger) must certainly have been prior to B.C. 525, when Darius succeeded Cambyses, the son of Cyrus, and transferred the royal capital to Persepolis. The figure is carved in low relief upon a large monolith slab, and is conspicuous both by reason of the curious crown, with Egyptian affinities, that surmounts the monarch's head, and because of the four magnificent wings that rise and droop from the king's shoulders—a feature borrowed from Assyro-Babylonian art. The image of Darius sculptured above his own inscription at Bisitun, or Behistan, may be dated some time before B.C. 500, and the panel on which it is carved likewise represents figures of the king's two chief retainers, together with portraits of Gomates, or the pseudo-Smerdis, and the other eight pretenders to the throne. Above the head of Darius floats an image of the god Auramazda (Ormazd) presenting him with the circle of sovereignty, or the guardian spirit of the king, as the modern Parsis prefer to interpret the image. The god is represented as a bearded figure, wearing a cylindrical head-dress, with horns, surmounted by the disc of the sun, and as swinging in a huge circle from which proceed rays of light (King and Thompson, *The Sculptures and Inscriptions of Behistūn*, London, 1907, pp. xxii–xxiii). The whole device shows the influence of Babylonia and Assyria. Of similar character are the carvings around the tomb of Darius at Naksh-i-Rustam, and upon the palace walls at Persepolis and Susa. In several of these the king is represented in the attitude of adoring Auramazda, or with his throne supported by subject nations; but the most spirited of the bas-reliefs are those which portray Darius in combat with real or mythical monsters—a *motif* borrowed, in like manner, from Assyro-Babylonian art. The same is true of the statues of Xerxes, Artaxerxes I., II., III., and Darius II., III. (so far as we can identify them); but the finest of all the specimens of the sculptor's art under the Achæmenians is the frieze of the stylobate of Xerxes' audience-hall at Persepolis, representing the vassal nations bearing tribute to the Great King. Of imposing grandeur, likewise, are the gigantic winged bulls with human faces, in Assyrian style, guarding the Portal of Xerxes through which his audience-hall was approached (see art. ARCHITECTURE [Persian]). The influence that was exercised in general upon Persian art by Assyria and Babylonia during the Achæmenian period may be seen at a glance by looking over the illustrations in the standard works on Persepolis and Susa mentioned at the end of this article.

(*d*) In the *interregnum*, or Seljuk period, that followed after Alexander's invasion (B.C. 330–250) and during the *Parthian period*, little progress was made in sculpture, save that the Greek impress supplanted the Assyro-Babylonian influence, as is evident from the Græcizing tendency seen in the bas-relief heads on the pilasters of the palace-temple at Hatra, and in certain characteristics of the carved bases of the columns at Kangavar, if that temple be ascribed to the Parthian age—a matter that is doubtful. The principal piece of Parthian sculpture, however, belongs to the middle of the period, and is that chiselled on the panel of king Gotarzes (A.D. 46–51) at the base of the Behistan Rock. Its mutilated condition, due to the fact that at some time in the first half of the 19th cent. a tablet was incised into its very middle, renders it difficult to judge of the workmanship, but the style and execution appear to show distinct traces of Roman art.

(*e*) *Under the Sasanian dynasty* (A.D. 224–661), Persian sculpture received further inspiration from Roman art through the hands of Byzantine craftsmen, and gave no mean promise of higher development; but this was abruptly cut short by the iconoclastic Arabs when they swept over the land with their Muslim hosts. In style, Sasanian art is bold, though rather heavy, like that of its predecessors, and is marked by a superabundance of decorative *motifs*, especially in the form of crimped streamers floating from the shoulders of some of the figures, or hanging from chaplets held in the hand. The examples of Sasanian sculpture are comparatively numerous, and may best be seen in the series of seven massive bas-reliefs carved below the Achæmenian tombs at Naksh-i-Rustam, or again at Naksh-i-Rajab near Persepolis, at Shapur in the south of Persia, at Susa in the south-west, Ṭāq-i-Bustan in the west, and near the plain of Salmas in the north-west. The finest among them are the carvings in the grottos at Ṭāq-i-Bustan, near Kermanshah. They represent scenes from the life of Khusru Parviz, or Chosroës II. (A.D. 590–628), and are ascribed by popular tradition to the chisel of Farhād, the royal sculptor, whose love for Shīrīn, the king's beautiful favourite, brought ruin upon the gifted artist. At Ṭāq-i-Bustan and in two of the Persepolitan Sasanian sculptures, it is thought that the figure of the god Ormazd, or possibly of the female divinity Anaïtis, is represented.

(*f*) From the middle of the 7th cent., when the Sasanian power fell before Islām, Persia produced no more sculpture, although there was an attempt at a revival of it in the beginning of the 19th cent., when Fath Ali Shah (1798–1835) caused himself to be immortalized in stone at Rai (near Teherān) and elsewhere. His sculptures show certain survivals of the style of Sasanian times, but are combined with thoroughly modern traits. One of the two panels at Rai portrays the king in the act of spearing a lion, and is spirited in execution. Unfortunately, it was carved over the space occupied by an old Sasanian sculpture, which was destroyed to make room for it.

2. Seals, gems, and coins.—Closely connected with the glyptic art in its larger application is the more minute skill shown in the cutting of seals and gems or the sinking of dies for coins. The use of seals and cylinders from the earliest times is well known, and is sufficiently illustrated by the archaic finds made at Susa by de Morgan (*op. cit.* viii. 1–27); but if we are insufficiently supplied with evidence for the Early Iranian and Median eras, there are enough Achæmenian seals and carved gems to show the height to which artistic execution in small carvings was carried in ancient days. The art has never been lost, for we can trace its development all the way through the Parthian and Sasanian ages, and no Persian to-day is without his signature handsomely engraved on a seal for ordinary use. A similar form of skill was needed in the cutting of dies for coins, as illustrated in the Achæmenian period by the *darics* from the mint of Darius. The coins that were current under the Parthian rulers indicate to what an extent Greek influence affected Iranian art, and from that time onward the various changes may be traced by the issues from the mint of each successive ruler down to the present day, when the nickel *shāhī* (worth less than a halfpenny), inscribed on one side with the Lion and the Sun, as the national emblem of Persia, and on the other with a device in Perso-Arabic script giving its denomination, is as modern in appearance as if it had been made in a European mint.

3. Metal-work.—Owing to the mineral resources of the kingdom, the art of the metal-worker may be regarded as one of the oldest in Persia (cf. Geiger, *Ostiranische Kultur im Altertum*, Erlangen, 1882, pp. 146–148, 388–390). Specimens have been preserved in sufficient number to show the development of this phase of art from Achæmenian times, illustrated, for example, by the discoveries at Susa and the finds on the Oxus, down to the present day, when the brass-beaters of Iṣfahān and the coppersmiths of Kashan turn out some of the finest examples of artistic workmanship in the form of lamps, trays, dishes, bowls, pitchers, or damascened armour, that can be found anywhere. The various pieces of Achæmenian jewellery to be seen in the museums of Europe—the nail-studded Parthian helmet in the British Museum, two beautiful cups of the Sasanian king Chosroës II. in the Cabinet des Médailles in Paris, one of them embossed in silver, the other enamelled with gold—together with many beautiful examples of Iranian metal-work of various ages to be found in the Hermitage at St. Petersburg, may be cited as typical of the range and scope which Persia had in this branch of artistic production.

4. Fictile arts, porcelain, earthenware, and ceramics. — The artistic sense which Persia developed from the earliest times in fashioning and decorating earthenware objects, and in the making of beautiful tiles for practical and ornamental purposes, is worthy of high praise. In fact, it would be impossible to cite any rival for the wonderful frieze of archers, and the lion-frieze discovered by Dieulafoy at Susa, which show the height to which art in the making and colouring of tiles had been developed even in earlier Achæmenian times. If kindred specimens of Parthian and Sasanian tiles be missing, it is only because they have not been preserved; for the art was not lost, as is proved by the beautiful turquoise tiles on the domes of the mosques from the beginning of the Muhammadan era down to the present time. On the other hand, the remarkable skill which the Persians possessed in imparting to their tiles and plaques a metallic glint or lustrous sheen, known as the *reflet métallique*, has unfortunately been lost, since it died out some time during the 18th cent., and attempts to restore it have thus far met with the poorest success. For that reason good old tiles and plaques that display the metallic lustre are rare, even though broken fragments are still being dug up in the ruins of Rai, the city which seems most of all to have developed this peculiar product.

With reference to the early development of the ceramic art in pottery and earthenware, it may be said that some of the crude jars and bowls exhumed from the ash-hills at Urumiah (see Jackson, *Persia*, pp. 90–98), like those found by Henri de Morgan in archaic burying-grounds in Gilan and Talish (see J. de Morgan, *Mém.* viii. 251–342), may date from the Early Iranian or Median period, or even earlier. The potter's art, moreover, is mentioned in the Avesta (*Vend.* ii. 32, viii. 84), and fragments of jugs and earthenware vases, with coloured traceries as a decorative design, have been found in abundance as specimens of fictile art in the Achæmenian period. The same is true of the Parthian remains discovered at Warka; and noteworthy among these are the Parthian so-called 'slipper-coffins,' made of a beautiful green glazed ware, and decorated with a somewhat stiff small human figure, repeated a number of times. The Sasanian fondness for elaborate decoration, as evidenced in the intricate designs and flower patterns on capitals of columns and in the ornamentations at Ṭāq-i-Bustan, was shown also in their ceramic work; for it is still possible to pick up among ruins like those of the Sasanian fire-temple, or *ātash-Kadah*, near Iṣfahān, pieces of jars and bricks with decorative markings that show an artistic sense; and the potter's art, well known to all through Omar Khayyam, is actively practised to-day.

During the earlier centuries after the Muhammadan occupation, Persia's art in faience (for, strictly speaking, there is no true Persian porcelain) is believed to have received considerable impetus through importations brought from China and through Chinese artizans settling in Iran. But, whatever may have been the extent of that influence—and the influence was not without reciprocity—Persian faience never lost its marked national characteristics in shape, colour, and design. In regard to glass, we know that the glass-worker's trade is referred to in the Avesta (*Vend.* viii. 85, *yāmō-pacika*), and specimens of glass, dating back to a comparatively early period, are extant. Glass vials, thought by some to have been lachrymatories, were found among the Parthian ruins at Warka, and the glass portions of the gold-enamelled cup of Chosroës II. show that the artistic uses of glass were well known under the Sasanians; while the employment of tiny facets of mirror glass in the interior decorations of sumptuous houses has long been a favourite means of ornamentation in Persia. Glass bottles, vases, jars, and urns, generally of a bluish colour, are found in almost every age down to the present, although the glass that is used in Persia to-day is almost wholly imported from Europe.

5. Textile fabrics: rugs, draperies, and embroideries.—The art by which Persia is best known in modern times is the manufacture of beautiful textile fabrics—rugs, carpets, draperies, and embroideries. We may presume that the art of rug-making was fully developed in Achæmenian times, since Themistocles, according to Plutarch (*Themist.* xxix. 3), when first presented before Xerxes or Artaxerxes, illustrated his meaning by a simile drawn from the intricate patterns of a Persian carpet; and there is little reason to doubt that rugs were used both on the floors and for ornamental hangings in the royal palaces at Persepolis and Susa. The employment, moreover, of archaic designs, handed down by tradition in the rug-maker's conservative art (for example, conventionalized forms of the tree of life), points back to the greatest antiquity. The carpet industry is to-day widely spread throughout Persia, and among the places that are thought to produce the best rugs, both in quality and style, are the districts of Kurdistan, Khorasan, and Kerman. Aniline dyes from Europe and Occidental patterns and designs are unfortunately finding their way in to corrupt the purity of this Oriental art, but a strong endeavour is being made to preserve its native integrity and ancient prestige—a prestige recognized in all the numerous works published in the West on the subject of Oriental rugs. Among Persia's textile arts is the weaving by hand of soft white and brown felts (Mod. Pers. *namad*) for mats, cloaks, and saddle-cloths. The art is as old as the time of the Avesta (cf. Av. *nemata-*, *Vend.* viii. 1, ix. 46), and it is still carried on in many parts of the country, more especially at Hamadan, Iṣfahān, and Yazd. Mention should also be made of richly embroidered Persian shawls, delicate fabrics with elaborate designs in needlework, heavily embossed brocades, ornamental draperies and hangings, and silks of various colours and fineness of texture. Among the oldest specimens of such fabrics are the examples of Sasanian textile work in the Archepiscopal Museum in Cologne, Germany, and in the temple of Horiugi, near Kioto, Japan (cf. Münsterberg, *Japanische Kunstgeschichte*, Brunswick, 1907, p. 118, pl. 14). The introduction and development of the textile arts as well as other arts of Persia were ascribed by Firdausi (A.D. 1000) to the legendary king Jamshīd, who lived in the golden age of Iran (see Firdausi, ed. Vullers and Landauer, Leyden, 1877, i. 23, 24 [tr. Mohl, Paris, 1876, i. 34–36; tr. Warner, London, 1906, i. 32–33]).

6. Painting, decorating, designing, and the art of penmanship.—Although painting cannot be called one of Persia's special arts, the wonderful effects in colour and decorative design that were obtained by the Achæmenian artists, as shown by the tile-work discovered in ancient Susa, prove conclusively how highly developed in early times were their æsthetic sense and their productive skill. Allusion has already been made several times to the artistic manner in which they still know how to employ colour and ornamental patterns even in connexion with objects of ordinary everyday use. How far the painter's art had advanced in Sasanian times among the Manichæans (for Mani was a painter as well as the founder of a great religious sect) has recently been illustrated by the remarkable finds made in Turkestan by the expedition sent out from Berlin by the German Emperor William II. As a rule, the Persians do their best work when painting portraits and flowers, while their landscape work and perspective composition are but mediocre. Their best pictures, in fact, are those on a small scale, like the miniature portraits on papier mâché writing-cases and lacquered boxes, or on the enamelled porcelain tops of tobacco pipes; or, again, in decorative designs of roses on book-covers, for the making of which they are especially noted.

One art, however, is carried to perfection in Persia; it is caligraphy, or the art of beautiful handwriting. Originally this accomplishment as an art may owe much to Muhammadanism, but nowhere else are to be found such beautiful specimens of chirography, whether minute or large, as in Persia; and no other people are so skilled in using their alphabet for decorative purposes, as may be seen from the graceful arabesques twined about the domes and minarets of the mosques, or interlaced into monograms of wonderful intricacy. To write a good hand is an essential part of culture among the Persians, and a number of well-known authors were masters of caligraphy. Not only so, but skilled scribes have devoted infinite time to copying in luxurious style the compositions of famous Persian poets, and their manuscripts are in themselves works of art.

7. Influence of Persian art.—The influence of Assyria and Babylon, of Greece and the Roman Empire, upon Persian art and architecture during the early and mediæval periods has already been referred to more than once. The fact has also been pointed out that Persia made these borrowings and importations thoroughly her own. In mediæval and later times Persia was influenced by (and influenced) China in ceramic art, and in the non-Muhammadan representation of living beings in paintings and the like (cf. above, p. 879). If the Arabs conquered Persia, they received more in art from her than they gave, and it is probable that the arts which the Moors developed in Spain and elsewhere were largely derived from the Persians. The Mongol invaders had little if anything artistic to offer Persia, but she imparted to them in Central Asia much from her artistic taste, in the same manner as her art penetrated deep into Northern India. In the Europe of Chaucer's time Persian blue in textile fabrics was sufficiently well known to be referred to as 'pers,' and the West to-day acknowledges Persia's supremacy in the weaving of artistic rugs and carpets. In minor matters Persian art still exercises an influence on the Occident, but not without receiving some influence in return, and this gradual infusion of Western elements will doubtless tend to grow greater as time goes on.

LITERATURE.—See the bibliographical list given under ARCHITECTURE (Persian), and refer especially to Perrot-Chipiez, *Hist. de l'art dans l'antiquité*, tome v. 'Perse,' Paris, 1890; Gayet, *L'Art persan*, Paris, 1895; Murdoch Smith, *Persian Art* (Kensington Museum Handbook), Lond., 1880; Saladin, *Manuel d'art musulman*, Paris, 1907; Benjamin, *Persia and the Persians* (chap. xi. 'A Glance at the Arts of Persia'), London, 1887; Dalton, *The Treasure of the Oxus, with Antiquities of Ancient Persia and India*, London, 1905. A. V. WILLIAMS JACKSON.

ART (Phœnician).—To express the deity with the emblems of his majesty, as conceived by the worshippers, is the highest aim of religious art, and it was apparently this that animated the Babylonians, Assyrians, Egyptians, Greeks, and Romans, all of whom have produced specimens of their skill worthy of the highest admiration. The Phœnicians, on the other hand, worshipping Baalim and Baalat, did not possess any deities sufficiently distinctive in their nature to lend themselves to representation in sculpture and painting. El, Adon, and Melek were in the same case with Baal and Baalat—terms of much too general a nature. The Babylonian Tammuz, a sun-god, who became with the Greeks a simple hunter in Syria, and Ashtoreth, the Ištar of the Babylonians, spouse of Tammuz, and goddess of the moon and of the planet Venus, form exceptions, and had their influence, though they were not the chief divinities of the Phœnicians. When, therefore, they wished to represent the divinity, the emblem which they chose was in the form of a cone, of which numerous examples exist, not only in Phœnicia, but also in the countries which fell under its influence. The two Phœnicians of Malta, Abdosir and Osirsamar, did not attempt a beautiful statue of their great national god Melqart, but contented themselves with a cone-crowned plinth which the first stone-cutter they met with was able to make.*

Whether the Phœnicians felt that something better was expected, and even needed, than the commonplace, though mystic, emblem which they had adopted, is uncertain. Knowing, however, the art of Babylonia from old time, they turned to the Egyptians for their artistic education. And here it is worthy of note that they did not borrow from them, as they might have done, the gods with the heads of all kinds of beasts, in which the Egyptians delighted, but divine types taken from the human form. From every point of view this was an improvement, for they made their deities as frankly manlike as those of the Greeks.

The cone representative of the divinity is seen in the picture of the temple of Byblos (Gebal), towering high above the entrance of the great courtyard.† This cone, though found in Carthage more often than in Phœnicia itself, must have been at one time very common as a symbol in that country. Probably some would regard it as of phallic origin, but that seems to be doubtful. It is not impossible that it had some connexion with the small *cippi* with an ovoid top found at Sidon.‡ These also recall the objects with pyramidal or hemispherical

* Perrot-Chipiez, *Phénicie*, p. 78 and fig. 28.

† Donaldson, *Architectura Numismatica*, No. 10, reproduced in Perrot-Chipiez, *Phénicie*, fig. 19.

‡ Perrot-Chipiez, *ib.* fig. 121.

tops* found at Tharros, one of which,† adorned with the sun and the crescent moon reversed above it, is flanked by two truncated cones with mouldings at the top. In connexion with these cones, it is noteworthy that Esarhaddon possessed a large clay seal,‡ formed like half an egg, upon the flat face of which is a cone surmounted by a bird, recalling the similar objects set up in the temples of Aphrodite at Cyprus.§ This, whilst showing a connexion between the cone and the hemisphere, at the same time suggests that they are of different origin.

Esarhaddon's half-egg seal, besides giving the cone with the dove on it, has, on one side of that emblem, the sun as an eight-rayed star, and, on the other, the moon and seven globular objects, emblematic of the seven planetary bodies, which, in all probability, corresponded with the seven deities whom the Assyro-Babylonians called the *Igigi*. As the sun and the moon are often represented on the votive inscriptions of Carthage,‖ it is probable that these emblems also occurred very frequently in the art of the Phœnicians in their own country. Other emblems, however, accompany them—the triangle emblematic of the cone, the top finished with arms (bent at the elbow and directed upwards), and a circle at the top of the cone representing a head; ¶ the raised right hand, palm outwards; ** the candelabrum surmounted by a pyramid; †† the staff with a globe at the top surmounted by the broken ring emblematic of the crescent moon when a mere broken circlet of light; †† the plinth with the three truncated cones †† (apparently simplified forms of the two with cornices, flanking one with a pyramid on the top, already described). Such are the simple representations of the divine which the Phœnicians, apparently when uninfluenced by the nations around, produced. It is possibly an augmentation of the feeling of powerlessness in representing the deity which made their relatives and near neighbours, the Jews, go a step further, and seek to discard every image which might seem to recall idol-worship. Even a symbol derived from a living creature was a thing to be avoided.

As a type of a male divinity more or less Phœnician in character may be mentioned Baal Hammon, who, in a terra-cotta figure belonging to the Barre collection,‡‡ appears as a man in the flower of his age, with ram's horns on either side of his head, his hands resting on the heads of the rams which form the supports of the arms of his throne. A terra-cotta figure seated on a throne seems to show Tanit, his consort, the Astarte of Carthage, holding a dove in her left hand.§§ This is very roughly formed, and was apparently one of the little statuettes made in great numbers for exportation. A strange creation on the part of the Phœnicians was the pigmy-god—a little man with exceedingly short body and legs and a very large head, holding in his left hand a shield of curious shape.‖‖ These are said to be the dwarf-gods which became the pigmies of the Greeks.

* Perrot-Chipiez, *Phénicie*, figs. 172 and 173. † *Ib.* fig. 174.

‡ Now in the possession of Mr. W. Harding Smith.

§ Gerhard, *Akademische Abhandlungen*, reproduced in Perrot-Chipiez, *Phénicie*, fig. 202.

‖ *CIS*, Pars i. tom. ii. tab. ii. 450, 468, iv. 536, 545, etc.; Perrot-Chipiez, *ib.* fig. 30.

¶ *CIS*, Pars i. *passim*; Perrot-Chipiez, *ib.* figs. 14, 29, 192.

** *CIS*, Pars i. *passim*; Perrot-Chipiez, *ib.* figs. 14, 192. On Babylonian cylinder-seals of *c.* 2000 B.C. the hand has as many as seven fingers, including the thumb (Peek, *Tablets*, pp. 64, 66).

†† Perrot-Chipiez, *ib.* fig. 232 (from Lilybæum).

‡‡ *Ib.* fig. 25.

§§ *Ib.* fig. 20. Sometimes she is represented standing, wearing a pointed head-dress with thick plaits of hair descending to her shoulders, holding her robe with her right hand and the dove in her left (*ib.* fig. 142).

‖‖ *Ib.* fig. 22.

The inventive powers of the Phœnicians therefore tended towards the grotesque rather than the dignified and serious, and they were at their best as copyists. The upper part of the stele of Yehaw-melek, notwithstanding its weathered state, is a noteworthy specimen of their skill.* It shows Yehaw-melek, clothed in a Persian costume, standing before Baalat Gebal, the 'Lady of Gebal,' offering a dish probably containing the precious things which he presented to her. The 'Lady of Gebal,' however, is in Egyptian form and dress, seated and holding a lotus-staff. In her attributes she closely resembles the Egyptian Isis, and the style of the carving (relief within a sunken outline) shows Egyptian influence. At the top of the stele a mortice-hole indicates where the Egyptian disc with uræus-serpents was placed (probably carved in metal), and from this point curved wings sweep down on each side, like a canopy over the god and the king. A very fine specimen of Phœnician bronze-work reproduced by Perrot and Chipiez† seems to show the same goddess, the style differing somewhat from that of true Egyptian work. There is the disc, with the horns of the moon strangely shaped, surmounting her head, and the uræus rises upon her forehead. Perrot points out that, just as the type of the infant Ptaḥ was appropriated by the Phœnicians to represent their Kabires and pigmies, so they borrowed Isis-Hathor to represent Astarte.

The pigmy-god already referred to‡ seems to be simply an exaggerated type of the Egyptian Bes, which the Phœnicians had also adopted.§ A very fine piece of glazed earthenware is that figured by Perrot and Chipiez in their monumental work (p. 408); ‖ and if it really be Phœnician (it was found in Cyprus), it shows an imitative skill such as the cleverest forger might envy. Bes, with feathered head-dress, precisely as found in Egypt, is sitting astride upon a woman's shoulders. The latter, who holds him by the feet, stands upon a little lotus-pedestal, suggesting that the whole formed the top of a staff in the Egyptian style. In the opinion of Perrot, it is the woman's figure—naked, short, and broad—that stamps this work of art as being Phœnician rather than Egyptian.

But in all probability one of the finest efforts on the part of a Phœnician sculptor to produce the type of a divinity is preserved on the Stele of Amrit, in the de Clercq collection.¶ The owner called it the 'Phenico-Hittite Stele of Amrit,' on account of the group's likeness to certain rock-sculptures at Pterium, where a goddess is shown traversing the mountains whilst standing on the back of a lion. In this case it is a god wearing the crown of Upper Egypt with the ostrich feathers, and a close-fitting tunic in the Egyptian style, with a knotted girdle. In his left hand he holds by its hind legs a lion-cub, and in his right he raises a curved weapon like the so-called 'boomerang,' which the Assyrian hero of the sculptures of Khorsabad, who grasps in his arm a lion, likewise carries. His legs are thick and muscular, as in the Assyrian sculptures, and one foot is placed upon the head, and the other upon the curved tail, of the lion upon which he stands. The animal in question is represented walking over rocky ground, also indicated much in the Assyrian manner. Immediately above the deity's head is the crescent moon with the sun within; and forming an arch above his head, conforming to the shape of the stele, are the drooping plumes of the Egyptian winged disc. Except for the thickness of the legs and the shortness of the arms, the human form is well-proportioned, and the lion also is fairly good. It is therefore a good piece of work, and, whilst illustrating the art of the Phœnicians, is at the same time a symbol of their religion—a Phœnician idea on an Assyro-Babylonian foundation, and a Hittite design in an Egyptian dress.* There is nothing Greek in it—perhaps it was before contact with that nation, as the early style of the Phœnician inscription which it bears seems to imply. According to Philippe Berger, the deity mentioned in the dedication is probably Shôrbêl—a reading which Clermont Ganneau admits as possible, although he himself is rather inclined to read Shadrapha (Satrape).

* *CIS*, Pars i. tom. i. tab. i.; Perrot-Chipiez, *Phénicie*, fig. 23.
† Perrot-Chipiez, *ib.* fig. 26.
‡ *Ib.* fig. 22, described above.
§ *Ib.* fig. 21.
‖ Fig. 279.
¶ *Catalogue méthodique et raisonné, publié par M. de Clercq*, tom. ii. pl. xxxvi.; Perrot-Chipiez, *ib.* fig. 283.

There is naturally some doubt as to how far the Phœnicians, when they came into contact with the Greeks, imitated their art. That there are objects in the Greek style which are due to Phœnicians is undoubted, but they may have been merely ordered from Greek sculptors. This is well illustrated by the coin figured by Donaldson in *Architectura Numismatica* (No. 20),† where, in a Greek temple with a strangely un-Greek fan-shaped pediment, a winged Victory in purely Greek style, mounted on a pedestal, crowns with laurel a princely conqueror, equally Greek, holding a crozier. In fact, the whole coin may have been by a Greek engraver. A votive stele representing a shrine,‡ which was found at Carthage, and is now in the museum at Turin, is regarded as being purely Greek work. The goddess is Persephone Cora, veiling herself as a bride, and holding in her left hand a basket of pomegranates. In the pediment above is the panther of Dionysus. Though dedicated by Melekiathon the Suffete, not only the art, but also the subject, is Greek. In Cyprus the story of Hercules was probably a favourite subject, as certain objects illustrating his tenth labour, the carrying away of the flocks of Geryon, show. In the bas-relief,§ Hercules is represented with considerable artistic skill, but the statues ‖ are inferior, though some are not without merit.

The statuettes representing the worship of the power of reproduction are, as usual in the East, not in the best style of art. The mother goddess, as Perrot calls her, whether holding an infant or not,¶ is represented as thick and heavy; and the women pressing their breasts **—reproductions, perhaps, of votaries of Astarte—are far from being equal to some of the figures of a similar nature found in Babylonia. Certain figures thought to be Phœnician prototypes of the Venus de Medici are regarded as later than the Greek period, and therefore due to Greek influence. They show a female pressing one breast and hiding with the other hand the part which, in real Phœnician work, the artist intended to show openly. The best specimen †† is from Livadia, near Larnaca, and wears an Egyptian head-dress. In the purely Semitic figures, there is a direct and naïvely brutal allusion, as Perrot says, to the mysteries of fecundation and generation, but the thought which the Greek artist wished to awaken was quite different; it was Venus ashamed—the representative of woman.

Religious ceremonies are rare. One—that representing Yehaw-melek before the 'Lady of Gebal'—has already been referred to. Another—a mere fragment—seems to be simply a mural decoration.‡‡

* A similar design (a deity standing on the back of a lion) appears on a silver coin of Tarsus (de Luynes, *Numismatique des satrapies*, pl. vii. fig. 8; Perrot-Chipiez, *Phénicie*, fig. 285).
† Reproduced in Perrot-Chipiez, *ib.* fig. 67.
‡ *Gazette archéologique*, t. vii. pl. xvii.; *Phénicie*, fig. 326.
§ Perrot-Chipiez, *ib.* fig. 387.
‖ *Ib.* figs. 389–391.
¶ *Ib.* figs. 377 and 143.
** *Ib.* figs. 375, 379, 380. A better specimen, however, is that in the British Museum, from Tharros (Perrot-Chipiez, fig. 291).
†† *Ib.* fig. 382.
‡‡ *Ib.* fig. 81.

It was found in the neighbourhood of Tyre, not far from Adlun, and represents a personage, seated on a throne, holding in the left hand an object which cannot now be determined. Before him is a candelabrum or stand surmounted by a pan in which a flame is seen, whilst beside the throne or seat is a head with Egyptian head-dress, evidently part of a sphinx as supporter. The border-ornament recalls some of the designs of Assyria. This piece is extremely good, and shows what the true Phœnicians were capable of. Of an entirely different style is the statue of the Sacrificer, in the Metropolitan Museum, New York.* This shows a beardless man, with plump cheeks (perhaps a eunuch, as the Babylonian priests seem sometimes to have been), carrying a ram for sacrifice upon his shoulders, the feet, which come down in front, being held tightly and determinedly with both his hands. The style is that of the artists of Cyprus.

Greatly affected by the religion of the nations around, the Phœnicians absorbed from them ideas which they carried beyond the limits of their own domain. Strangely susceptible, they in like manner were strongly influenced by the religious art of their neighbours, which, when they migrated, they carried to other lands and modified. A series of different styles was the result, and the task of studying and understanding these is a long and difficult one. Nevertheless, it is a branch of archæology of considerable importance, though it must be admitted that the material from the various spheres of Phœnician influence is generally insufficient for a complete picture to be gained. The destruction of their temples and divine emblems and statues in Western Asia adds to the difficulty of the study; but the remains, such as they are, have a value quite their own, and reflect the religious feelings of a strong people who accomplished important work in their time. T. G. PINCHES.

ART (Shinto).—The genius of Shinto, like that of Islām, is adverse to the development of the arts of painting and sculpture. With few exceptions, no idols or paintings of the gods are to be seen in Shinto shrines. The deity is represented by a mirror, sword, stone, or other object, which is shut up in a box, and is never seen by the worshipper. In many cases the priest himself does not know what the box contains. In pre-historic times there was a practice of setting up a row of terra-cotta figures of men and animals round the tombs of Mikados, in substitution for an older custom of burying the servants of the deceased and other victims up to the neck, and leaving them to die and be devoured by dogs and crows. Several of these figures have been preserved in the Imperial Museum at Tokyo, and there is one in the Gowland Collection of the British Museum. They are of an extremely rude and primitive workmanship. This practice, however, does not appear to have given rise to a school of glyptic art, and in any case it is not directly associated with Shinto, which abhorred all connexion with death. In more modern times there is a custom of expressing gratitude to the Kami for answered prayer by making *ex voto* offerings to the shrine of pictures representing miraculous escapes from shipwreck, etc. Several of the more important shrines have galleries for the reception of such mementoes. They have no great importance in the history of Japanese art. Such galleries are called *emado*, or 'picture-horse hall,' one of the most common pictures being that of a horse—in substitution for the real living horse, which is a favourite Shinto offering. The 'seven gods of good fortune' are a common subject for the Japanese artist, but here we are dealing with quite a modern development. Nearly all of these deities, though called *Kami*, are of Buddhist origin, and in their portraiture foreign influence is easily traceable. At the present day Shinto myth is not infrequently resorted to for subjects by the Japanese artist, more especially by the book-illustrator; and wood engravings, of no great artistic value, representing the gods are sold to the pilgrims to Shinto shrines as mementoes.

* Perrot-Chipiez, *Phénicie*, fig. 402.

LITERATURE.—W. Anderson, *Catalogue of Japanese and Chinese Pictures in the British Museum*, London, 1886; Henri Joly, *Legend in Japanese Art*, London, 1907.

W. G. ASTON.

ART AND ARCHITECTURE (Teutonic).—The antiquities from Northern Europe give evidence of a high artistic development from the Stone Age downwards, but few finds of earlier date than the Iron Age can with any certainty be connected with the religious life of their owners. Of the heathen period there are no architectural remains except the graves, and the structural forms of these do not appear to have had any definite relation to the religious beliefs of the different periods to which they belong. Sacred buildings of any kind came late into use among the Teutonic races, and the scanty knowledge we possess of their temples is derived entirely from literary sources, and refers only to the last few centuries of heathendom.

1. In the Stone Age the antiquities as a whole show a remarkably high development of art. The elaborate finish of the finest examples in both pottery and weapons may imply that they were not intended for ordinary purposes, but were reserved for religious ceremonies.

Many of the axes found are obviously not made for use. Some are too thin, others too small, others have shaft holes only large enough to admit a cord, and miniature axes of amber are also common. All these are doubtless votive offerings of some sort, in all probability dedicated to the god of thunder.

2. The Bronze Age in the North is also distinguished by the artistic skill of its productions, but foreign influences may now be recognized. At first the types resemble those found in the Ægean area, and the spirals and zigzag lines so common in Mycenæan art are a frequent form of ornamentation. The most notable relic of this period is the 'disc and horse of the sun' from Nordseeland, Denmark, usually dated about B.C. 1000.

It consists of a round bronze plate mounted on wheels and drawn by a horse also on wheels, and is, no doubt, intended to symbolize the sun's passage across the heavens. The face of the disc is overlaid with gold and ornamented with spirals, and the figure of the horse strongly recalls the animals of the Dipylon style of Greece.

At a later period of the Bronze Age there are evidences of Etruscan influences in the art, and many objects have been found that are clearly imported from Etruria. Among those of native workmanship are a number of beautiful gold vessels which seem too precious for private purposes, and were probably dedicated to religious uses. Such are the eleven gold vessels with long handles that were found at Rōmminge, carefully placed inside a large bronze vase, and the two gold bowls with similar long handles, terminating in horses' heads, found with a couple of smaller gold bowls in Seeland. Other objects certainly connected with the worship of the gods are the little bronze cars on four wheels, apparently made to carry large sacrificial vessels, from Sweden, Denmark, and North Germany.

Religious symbols were frequently used in the ornamentation of the Bronze Age. The wheel cross, the symbol of the sun, occurs first in the Stone Age, and is found on many of the earlier objects of bronze. It is later replaced by the *swastika*,* and the *triskele* also appears, both of which symbols are common to all the Aryan races, and are universally agreed to have a religious signification. These same sacred signs are seen on the rock carvings from Behistan and elsewhere, which belong to this period. The purpose of these carvings is not clear; they consist of geometrical figures, ships, weapons, and other objects, animals and persons, and it seems probable that at least some of these represent the gods and their attributes.

3. In the first centuries after the introduction of iron the grave finds are scanty, and there is a scarcity of gold objects. This is partly due, no doubt, to the fact that the tribes of the North were at this time subjected to a strong Celtic influence, and it was the universal custom among the Celts to bury little else with the dead than their mere personal equipment. This Celtic influence introduced foreign elements into the style of the art, but was soon almost entirely supplanted by the spread of the classical culture due to the Roman conquests in Central Europe. Many of the finest antiquities from the graves and the bog deposits belonging to the first four centuries of the Christian era are unmistakably of Roman workmanship.

The most important of the native works of this earlier Iron Age appear to be connected with religion. Of these the earliest are the two four-wheeled chariots with long shafts, found in a bog at Deibjerg in Jutland. They are made of ash-wood, and the sides, shaft, and frame are richly adorned with bronze-work. The *swastika* is among the ornaments used. These cars are supposed to have been employed in religious ceremonies, and possibly to have been sacred carriages for images of the gods, such as are mentioned later in the sagas. Fragments of a similar one, however, which had evidently been burnt, were found inside a large bronze vessel in a grave at Fynen, so that, in this case at least, the car seems to have been given not to the gods, but to the dead man for his use in a future life. Cars have been found under similar circumstances in Celtic graves in France and the Rhine country, so that the peculiar disposal of the Fynen car may be due to imitation of a foreign custom.

Somewhat later in date, and showing a mixture of Celtic and Roman influences, is the beautiful silver bowl from Gundestrupp in Jutland. This was, no doubt, a sacred vessel, like the gold bowls of the Bronze Age already referred to; and we may compare in this connexion the statement of Strabo (p. 293), that the Cimbri sent their 'holiest bowl' to Augustus. Other bowls of similar shape to the Gundestrupp bowl have been found, but although it was in all probability made in the North, it is quite un-Northern in both style and subject. The subjects are drawn partly from classical art (there is, for example, an obvious imitation of Hercules and the Nemean lion), and partly from Celtic sources, as the representation of the Gallic god Cernunnos, with his stag-horns, ring, and serpent.

4. To the close of the Roman period, *i.e.* to the 4th cent. A.D., belong what are perhaps the finest of all the Northern antiquities—the two magnificent gold horns from Gallehus in Jutland. It is supposed that they were used as trumpets in religious services, and parallel instances can be quoted from many peoples of antiquity. Both the horns are of solid gold, and decorated with bands of carved figures; one has runes around the top, but these give only the maker's name. Both were incomplete when found. The significance of the figures upon them is not certain; various explanations have been given, and it seems probable that they have a mythological meaning, and refer to legends of the gods.

5. The later centuries of heathendom in the North may be divided into two periods: (*a*) a time very rich in gold ornaments of every kind, owing to the vast quantities of gold obtained from Byzantium; (*b*) the age of the Vikings, to which belongs the splendid profusion of silver ornaments to be seen in the museums of Copenhagen and Stockholm.

(*a*) In the first of these periods, *i.e.* from the 4th to the 8th cents. A.D., the only objects that appear to have any close connexion with religion are the gold bracteates. These were worn as pendants and necklaces, and were originally copies of Roman coins of the 4th cent., although the types soon became greatly altered, and the later bracteates appear to have a religious signification. The sacred symbols of the *swastika* and *triskele* appear on many of them, and when placed beside a human head may imply that a god is represented. The most common device is a head above a four-footed animal, and in some cases the latter seems to have a pointed beard and to be intended for a goat, an animal sacred to Thor. On others Odin is possibly to be identified, surrounded by snakes, or riding on his horse Sleipnir, with a sword in his right hand and a spear in his left, and fighting against the Midgaard serpent. Other bracteates have interlacing designs ending in animal forms—which shows that the beautiful animal ornamentation, which was elaborately developed later, already existed. This peculiar style of decoration, so characteristic of the later Northern art, seems not to have arisen from a desire to represent the animals sacred to the gods, but to be derived from creatures unfamiliar to the North, namely, the lions and griffins of classical art.

(*b*) When we reach the second, or Viking, period of the later Iron Age, we have evidence from literature, as well as from antiquities, of religion in art. Of the antiquities, the most important are the runic stones that were set up over the graves. On some of these are figures which appear to depict the gods; for example, a stone from Tjängvilde shows a figure riding on a horse with eight legs, probably intended for Odin on Sleipnir; and on the Sanda stone there are three figures in a special panel, which have been interpreted as the three chief gods, Thor, Odin, and Frey. On many of these stones Thor is invoked in the runes, and his hammer is carved to consecrate and protect the grave. Little silver pendants in the form of hammers have been found, and were doubtless worn as amulets, but these do not appear until the 10th cent., and were probably due to the influence of the cross-wearing Christians.

Under the head of amulets may be reckoned the figure of a boar, which was frequently placed on the crest of the helmet for protection in battle. This custom is referred to by Tacitus (*Germania*, 45), and there are several allusions to it in *Beowulf* (*e.g.* 303, 1113). It should presumably be connected with the golden boars of Frey and Freya mentioned in the sagas.

Two warriors wearing helmets surmounted by figures of boars are represented on one of four small iron plates from a cairn in Öland. That these plates were used to adorn helmets is evident from the similar bronze plates on the helmets from Vendel. The examples from Öland, as well as the majority of those from Vendel, are supposed to portray scenes of Scandinavian mythology. Thus

* The *swastika*, or cross with bent arms, in its simplest form appears thus , but is often elaborated into . Similarly the *triskele*, the three-armed figure, from , becomes .

one of the Vendel plates shows a cavalier armed with shield and spear, preceded and followed by a bird, and attacking a serpent; this is interpreted as Odin with his ravens Huginn and Muninn, and may be compared with the gold bracteate described above.

Regarding actual idols our only information is derived from literary sources. From the sagas we gather that the figures of gods set up in the temples were life-size, made of wood, and richly adorned with gold and silver. Thus in Olaf Tryggvason's saga, when Gunnar fought with the image of Frey and drove out the fiend inhabiting the idol, 'nothing remained but the mere stock of a tree,' and Gunnar, dressing himself in Frey's apparel, was accepted by the people as the god. Again, in the saga of Olaf the Saint a figure of Thor is described as 'a huge man's image gleaming with gold and silver . . . he bore the likeness of Thor, and had a hammer in his hand . . . he was hollow within, and had a great stand on which he stood when he came out.'

Other images are described as wearing bracelets, necklaces, and similar ornaments. The different gods seem usually to have been invested with their own peculiar attributes—Thor with his hammer or with sceptre as chief god, and Odin armed with sword and spear.

We also hear of smaller figures of the gods, such as the image of Frey which Ingimund carried in his pocket, and the ivory image of Thor which Halfred was accused of secretly carrying in his purse.

6. Turning to the heathen architecture, what knowledge we possess of the temples is gleaned from the literature of the North. Until the last few centuries of heathendom, the Teutonic races appear to have worshipped in the open air, Tacitus (*op. cit.* 9) saying: 'The Germans deem it inconsistent with the majesty of their gods to confine them within walls.' The temples that we hear of in the sagas apparently consisted of two parts: an oblong hall, the *langhús*, with an apse-shaped building, the *afhús*, at one end. It is possible that these two parts were originally separate, and that the round form of the *afhús* is due to its having taken the place of the sacred tree that was, in earlier times, the centre of worship. In this case the *langhús* would represent the dwelling of the chief (who officiated as priest) beside the tree. This *langhús* appears to have been copied directly from the simplest form of dwelling-house, and was used for the sacrificial feasts, but possessed no great sanctity. The *afhús* was the sanctuary proper, and contained the images of the gods, among whom Thor always occupied the chief place. Here also were the altar with the oath ring, the blood kettle, and the perpetual fire.

The temples were almost always constructed of wood, but the exterior as well as the interior was doubtless often ornamented. Adam of Bremen describes the chief temple of Sweden, that at Upsala, as a magnificent gilded structure. When Christianity finally drove out the old superstitions from the North, the temples were in most cases pulled down and destroyed; but the sanctity of the sites remained, and many Christian churches still mark the spots where the heathen gods were originally worshipped.

LITERATURE.—In addition to frequent references throughout the sagas, special mention may be made of S. Müller, *Nordische Altertumskunde*, 2 vols., Strassburg, 1897–98, and *Urgesch. Europas*, Strassburg, 1905; O. Montelius, *Die Kultur Schwedens in vorchristlicher Zeit*, Berlin, 1885; J. Worsaæ, *Primeval Antiquities of Denmark*, London, 1849; G. Vigfusson and F. Y. Powell, *Corpus Poeticum Boreale*, Oxford, 1883.

C. J. GASKELL.

ILLUSTRATIONS

FIG. 2. FROM THE CHARTER OF KING EDGAR TO NEW MINSTER, WINCHESTER, A.D. 966.

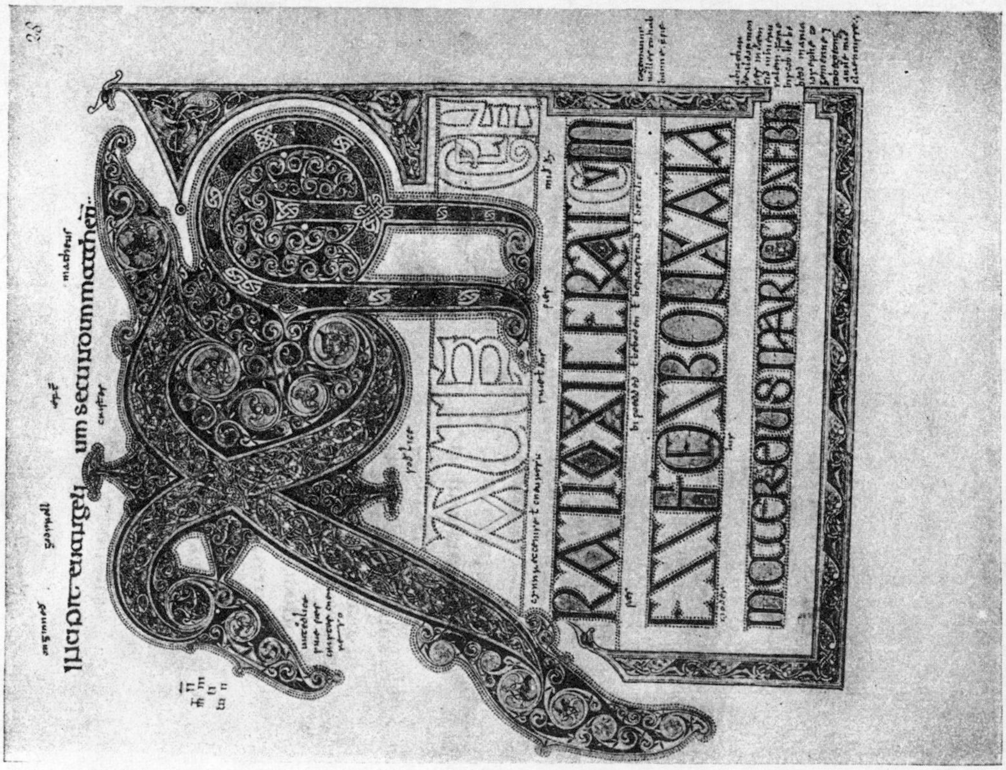

FIG. 1. FROM THE LINDISFARNE GOSPELS. ANGLO-IRISH, CIR. 700 A.D.

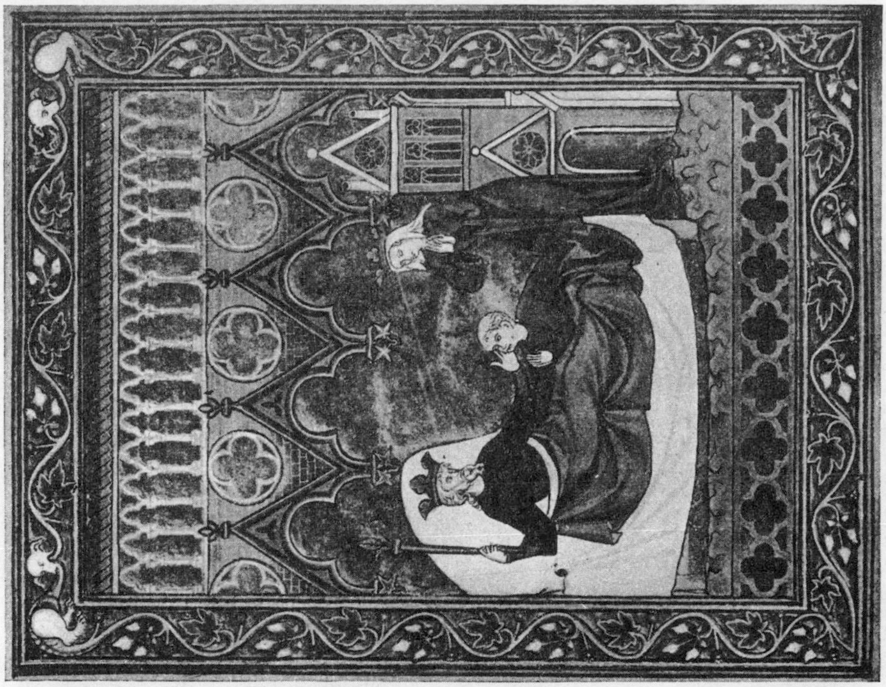

FIG. 3. FROM THE PSALTER OF ISABELLA OF FRANCE, SISTER OF ST. LOUIS. PARISIAN, CIR. 1260–70 A.D.

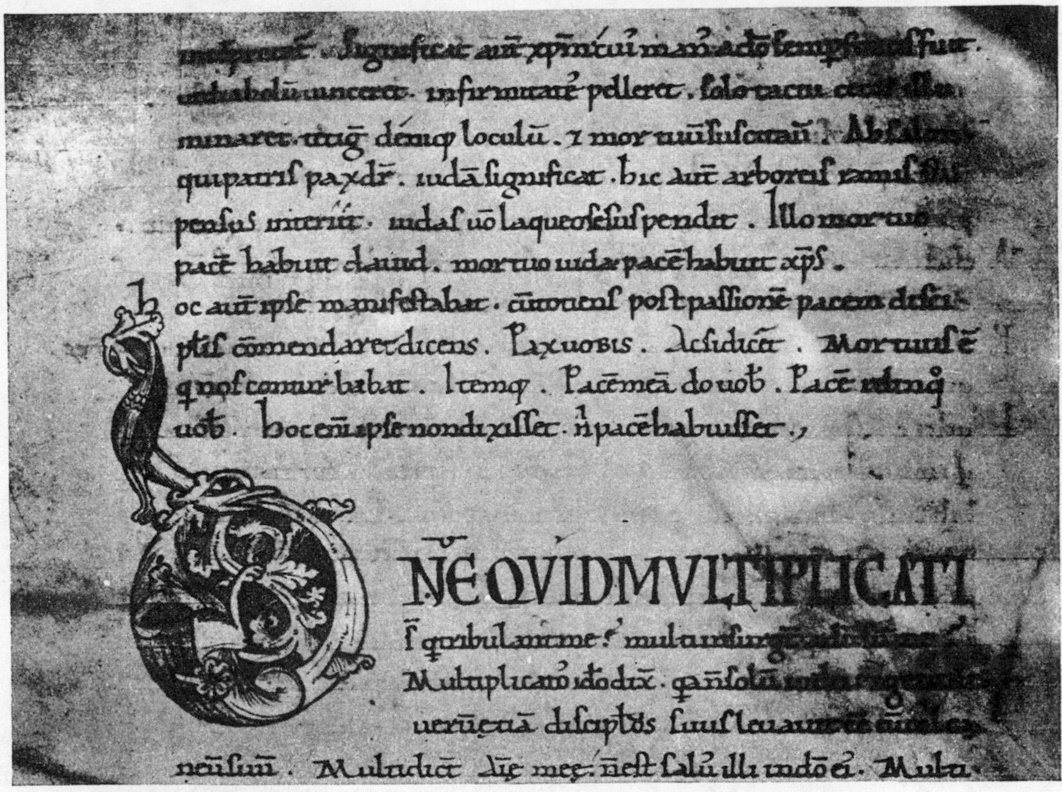

FIG. 4. FROM ODO OF ASTI'S COMMENTARY ON THE PSALMS. ITALIAN, CIR. 1125 A.D.

FIG. 5. FROM A 'PSALTER OF ST. JEROME' AND PRAYERS, WRITTEN AT NAPLES IN 1481 FOR POPE SIXTUS IV.

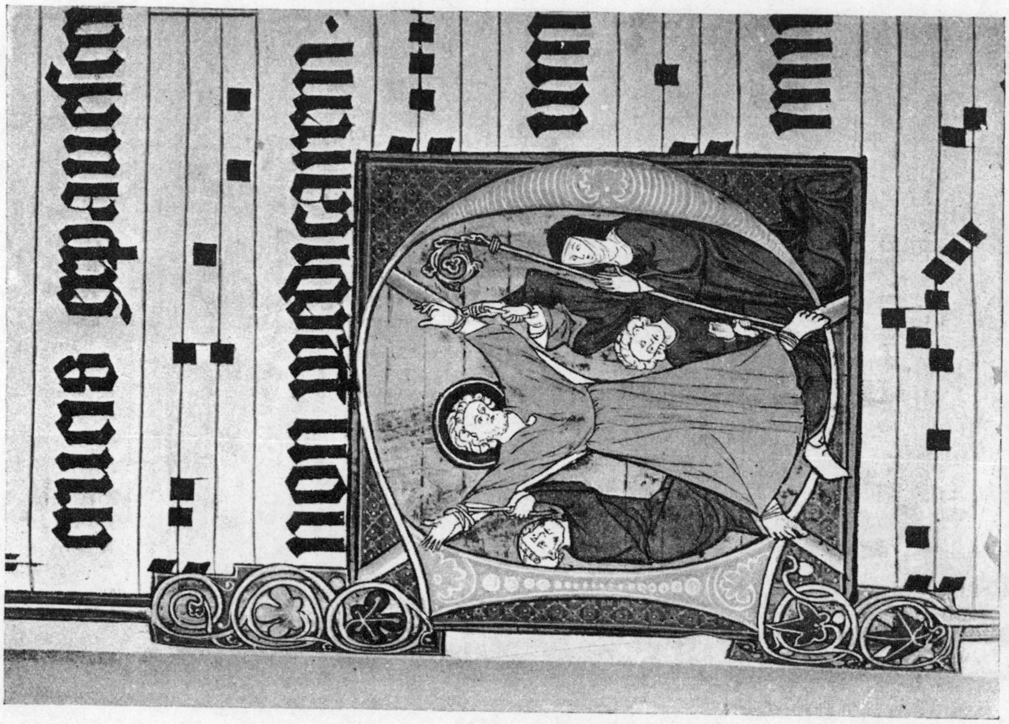

FIG. 6. FROM THE ANTIPHONER OF THE CISTERCIAN NUNS OF BEAUPRÉ, NEAR GRAMMONT. A.D. 1290.

FIG. 8. FROM AN APOCALYPSE AT THE BODLEIAN LIBRARY, WRITTEN IN ENGLAND FOR EDWARD I. TOWARDS THE END OF THE 13TH CENTURY.

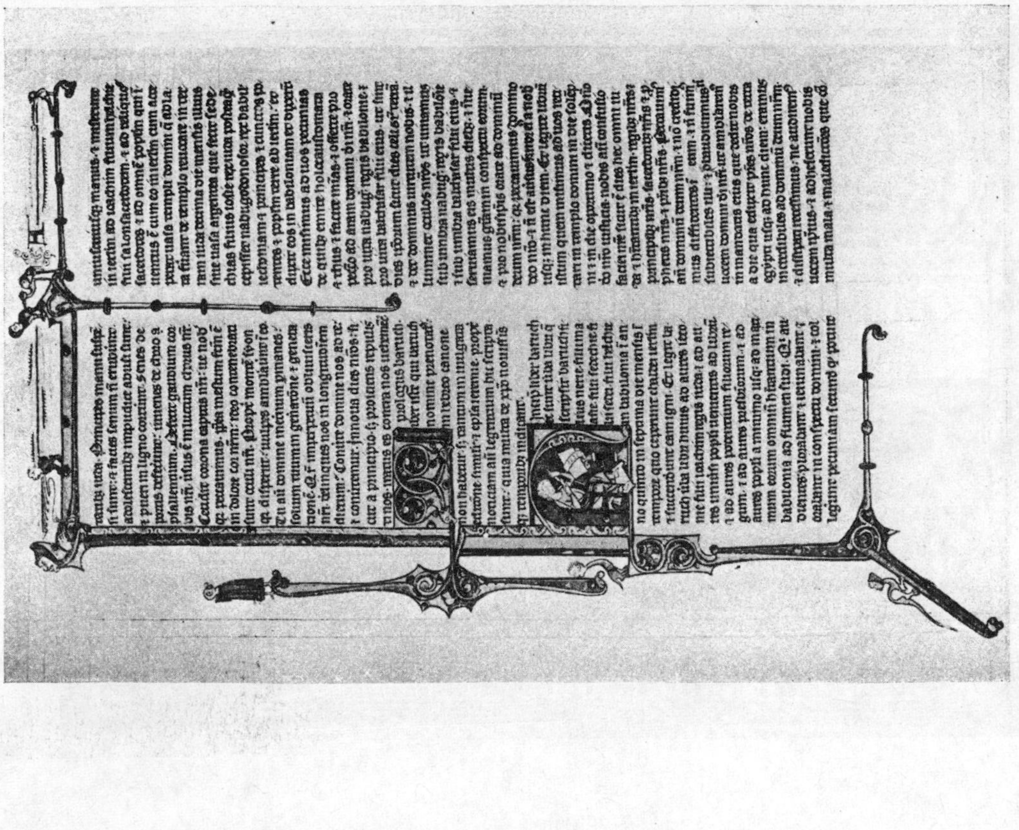

FIG. 7. FROM A VULGATE BIBLE IN THE BRITISH MUSEUM (I.D.I.) WRITTEN IN ENGLAND IN THE SECOND HALF OF THE 13TH CENTURY.

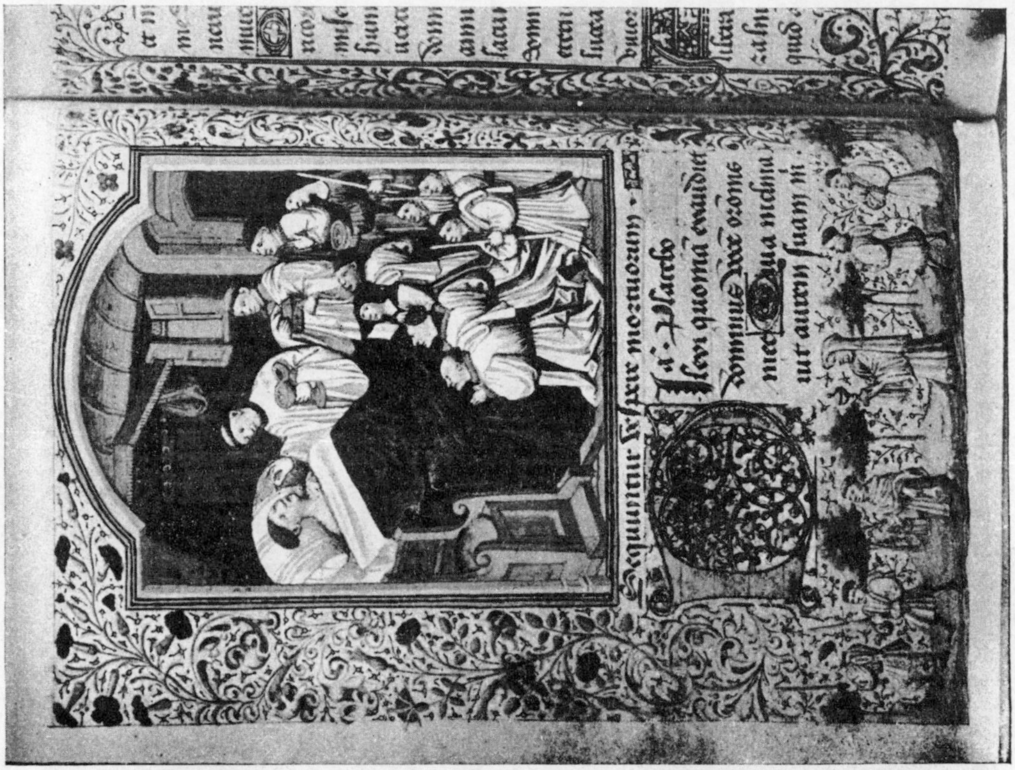

FIG. 11. FROM THE BOOK OF HOURS OF ADMIRAL PRIGENT DE COËTIVY. PARISIAN, CIR. 1440 A.D.

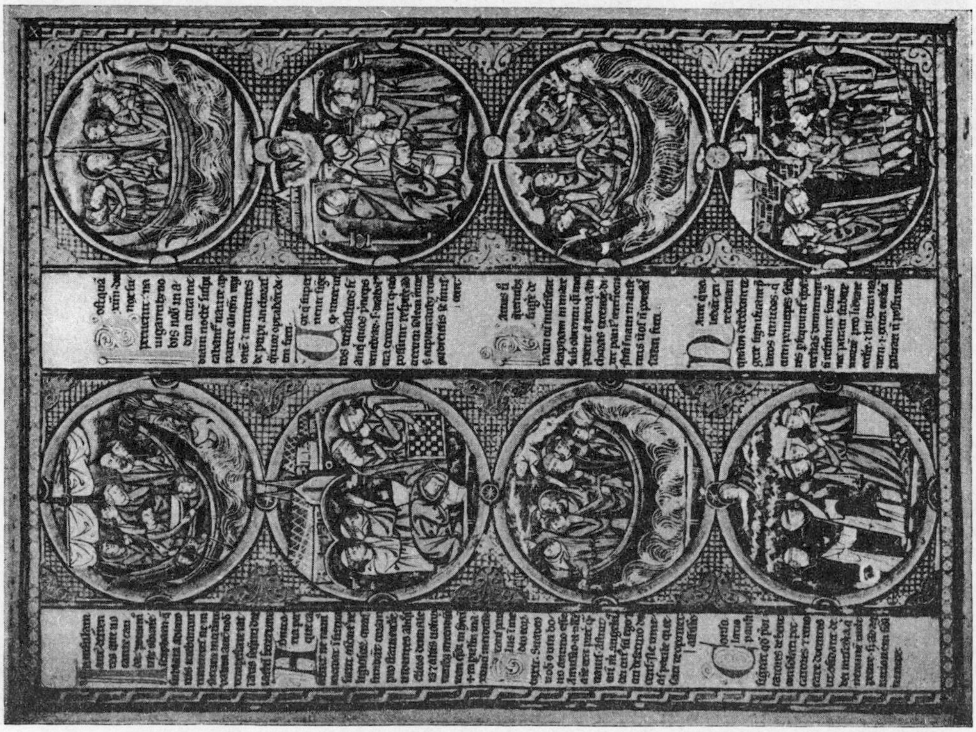

FIG. 9. FROM A *BIBLE MORALISÉE* AT THE BRITISH MUSEUM (HARLEY MS. 1527). FRENCH, MIDDLE OF THE 13TH CENTURY.

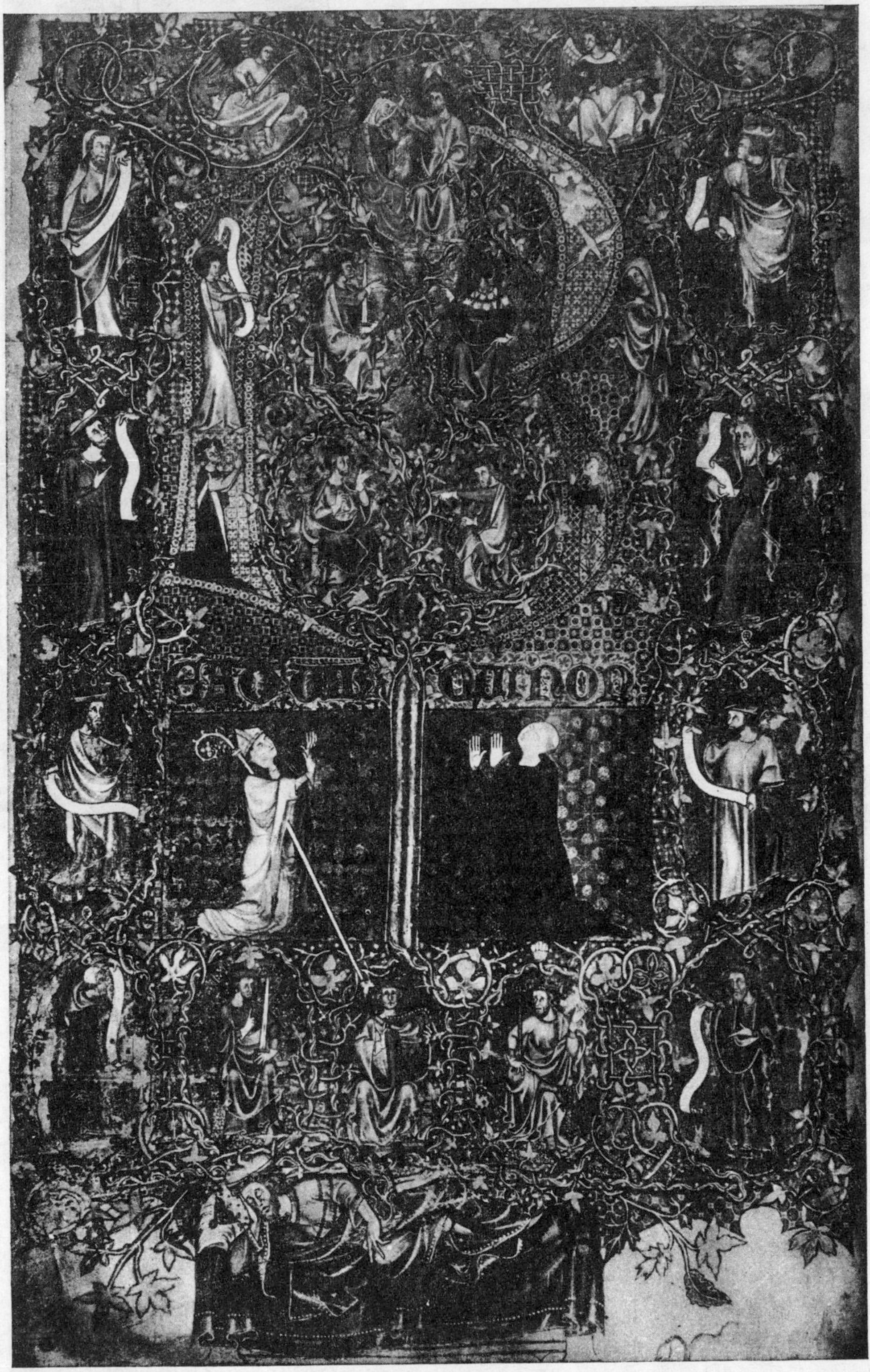

FIG. 10. FROM THE ORMESBY PSALTER AT THE BODLEIAN LIBRARY (MS. DOUCE 366).
EAST ANGLIAN, CIR. 1300 A.D.

FIG. 1. SACRIFICE.

FIG. 3. LAYING ON OF HANDS.

FIG. 2. OFFERING.

HORUS RAMESES IV. THOTH.
FIG. 4. PURIFICATION.

FIG. 5. SACRED BOAT OF A GOD UPON ITS STAND.

FIG. 1. FRESCO ON THE INNER FRONT WALL OF QUṢAIR 'AMRA.

FIG. 2. KAIRWAN. INTERIOR OF THE MOSQUE.

FIG. 3. ABŪ-DILIF (MESOPOTAMIA). ARCHES AND MINARET OF AN OLD MOSQUE.

FIG. 4. KAIRWAN. MINBAR OF THE GREAT MOSQUE.

FIG. 5. CAIRO. FAÇADE OF THE AL-AQMAR MOSQUE.

FIG. 6. BERLIN: KAISER FRIEDRICH MUSEUM. WOODEN TABLET, 1125 A.D.

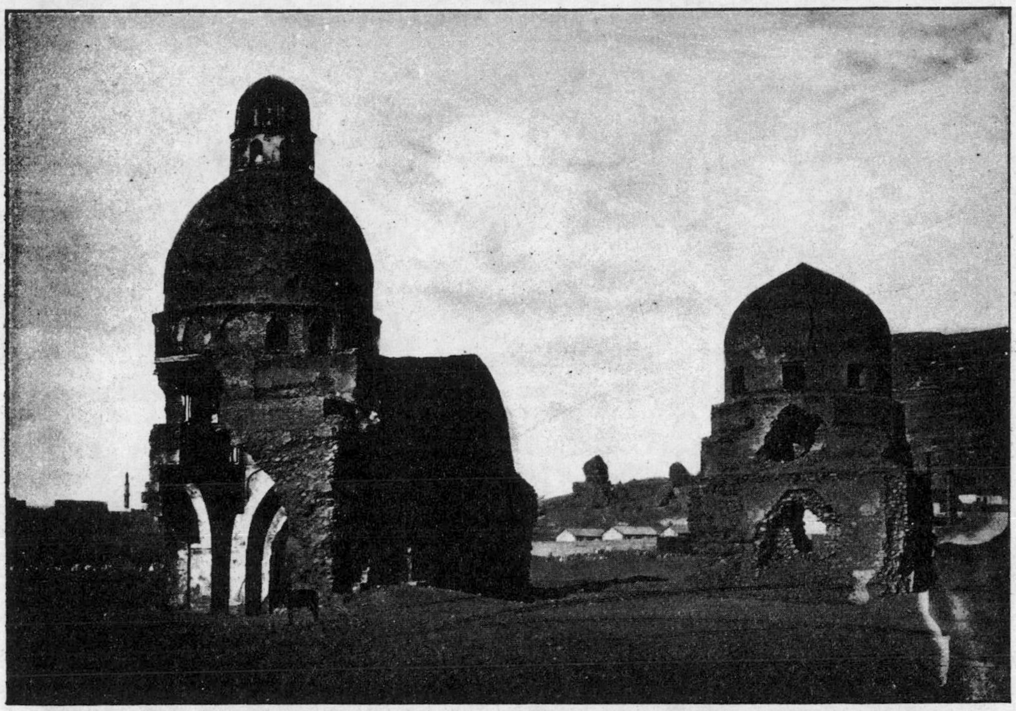

FIG. 7. CAIRO. TOMBS OF THE MAMLŪKS.

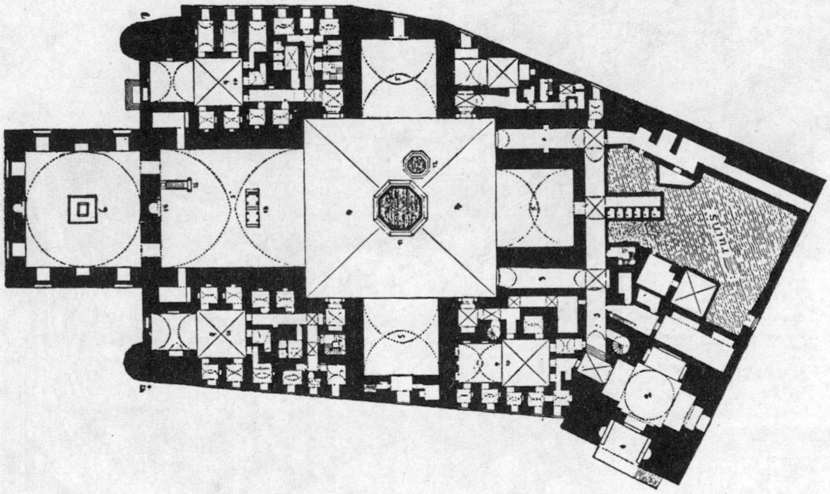

FIG. 8. CAIRO. MOSQUE OF SULTAN ḤASAN, 1356–1359 A.D.

FIG. 9. JERUSALEM. AL-AQṢĀ MOSQUE. MINBAR, 1168–69 A.D.

FIG. 10. VIENNA. HUNTING CARPET IN THE POSSESSION OF THE EMPEROR OF AUSTRIA.

FIG. 11. GRANADA. ALHAMBRA. COURT OF THE LIONS.

THE END OF VOL. I.